American
WORDPOWER
Dictionary

edited by Ruth Urbom

Oxford University Press

OXFORD
UNIVERSITY PRESS

Great Clarendon Street, Oxford OX2 6DP

Oxford University Press is a department of the University of Oxford.
It furthers the University's objective of excellence in research, scholarship,
and education by publishing worldwide in

Oxford New York

Athens Auckland Bangkok Bogotá Buenos Aires Cape Town Chennai
Dar es Salaam Delhi Florence Hong Kong Istanbul Karachi Kolkata
Kuala Lumpur Madrid Melbourne Mexico City Mumbai Nairobi
Paris São Paulo Singapore Taipei Tokyo Toronto Warsaw

with associated companies in Berlin Ibadan

Oxford and Oxford English are registered trade marks of Oxford University Press
in the UK and in certain other countries

The British National Corpus is a collaborative project involving Oxford University Press,
Longman, Chambers, the Universities of Oxford and Lancaster, and the British Library

ISBN 0 19 431319 0

Library of Congress Cataloging-in-Publication Data
American Wordpower Dictionary / edited by Ruth Urbom.
 p. cm.
 ISBN 0-19-431319-0 (pb)
 1. English Language --Dictionaries. 2. Vocabulary. I. Urbom, Ruth. 1970- .
 II. Title: Wordpower.
 PE1628.A67 1998
 423--DC21 98-22115
 CIP

Illustrations by Kevin Baverstock; Anna Brookes; Andy Cooke; Martin Cox; Angelika Elsebach;
Gay Galsworthy; Margaret Jones; Richard Lewington; Martin Lonsdale/Hardlines; Vanessa Luff;
Coral Mura; Martin Shovel; Technical Graphics Dept, Oxford University Press;
Lorna Turpin; Harry Venning; Graham White; Michael Woods.

Maps © Oxford University Press

Typesetting by Tradespools Ltd, Frome, Somerset
Printed in China

Contents

Preface

This dictionary has been written specifically for the use of learners of American English at the intermediate to upper-intermediate level. Everyone who has worked on the text of this dictionary is a current or former teacher of English to speakers of other languages. The editorial team's experience in the classroom has enabled us to produce a practical reference tool with many features which will help students develop their ability to understand and use English with confidence. The clear, easy-to-understand definitions are written in simple language using core English vocabulary. The realistic examples, which show how words are really used in today's English, are based on our analysis of a multi-million-word corpus of American English. Many useful notes help learners avoid common mistakes, recognize word families, and distinguish between commonly-confused words.

I am extremely grateful to Margaret Deuter, Miranda Steel, and Jane Taylor for their contributions to this project, and to Michael Ashby and Sharon Goldstein for the treatment of phonetics. Thanks also go to Lisa Isenman, Bob Karper, Ed McCorduck, and Diane Elisabeth Pecorari for their hard work over a long period of time. Finally, I would like to acknowledge the work of the large team that made the production of this book possible.

Ruth Urbom
March 1998

The information in this dictionary

FINDING AND SPELLING WORDS

☆ **pow·er¹** /ˈpaʊər/ *noun* **1** [C,U] the ability to do sth: *The ambassador promised to do everything in her power to make sure the hostages were not harmed.* ○ *He has great powers of observation.*

star showing **important words**

☆ **cat·a·log¹** (*also* **catalogue**) /ˈkætl·ɔg; -lɑg/ *noun* [C] **1** a book that contains information

another possible spelling given in parentheses

glim·mer¹ /ˈglɪmər/ *noun* [C] **1** a weak unsteady light **2** a weak sign of sth: *a glimmer of hope*
glim·mer² /ˈglɪmər/ *verb* [I] to give out a weak unsteady light

Words with the **same spelling** have different numbers.

la·dy·bug /ˈleɪdibʌg/ *noun* [C] a small insect that is red or orange with black spots

Dots show how to divide words into syllables.

WORDS AND PHRASES RELATED TO THE MAIN WORD

IDM **a breath of fresh air** ⇨ BREATH
in the air probably going to happen soon: *A feeling of change was in the air.*
in the open air ⇨ OPEN¹

idioms
(The arrow ⇨ shows that the meaning of the idiom is explained at the word following the arrow.)

PHRV **take after sb** to look or behave like an older member of your family
take sth apart to separate sth into the different parts it is made of
take sth away to cause a feeling, etc. to disap-

phrasal verbs
(Look at page A14 for an explanation of how to use them.)

☆ **ea·ger** /ˈigər/ *adj.* full of desire or interest: *He is eager to meet you.* ○ *eager for success* —**ea·ger·ly** *adv.* —**ea·ger·ness** *noun* [U]

derivatives of the main word (words with the same spelling but a different part of speech; or the main word plus an ending such as *-ly*, *-ness*, etc.)

MEANING

swarm¹ /swɔrm/ *noun* [C] **1** a large group of insects, especially bees, moving around together **2** a large number of people together

The **meaning** of words and phrases is given in simple English using words that are easy to understand. If there is more than one meaning, all the meanings are listed after numbers.

be·low¹ /bɪˈloʊ/ prep. at or to a lower position or level than sb/sth: *Do not write below this line.* ○ *It hurts here – just below my knee.* ○ *The temperature fell below freezing .* ○ *Her test score was below average.* ○ *He drives way below the*

The **example sentences** help you to understand the word and show how it is used in English.

glass·es /ˈglæsəz/ (*also* **eyeglasses**) *noun* [plural] two pieces of glass in a frame that a

a word which has the **same meaning**

chunk /tʃʌŋk/ *noun* [C] a large or thick piece of sth: *chunks of ice floating in the lake* ○ (*figurative*) *A big chunk of my income goes toward paying bills.*

a **figurative** use of the word (= not using a word in its true sense, but in an imaginative way in order to give a special effect)

GRAMMAR

slurp /slərp/ *verb* [I,T] (*informal*) to drink noisily: *I hate the way he slurps when he drinks coffee.* —**slurp** *noun* [C]
slush /slʌʃ/ *noun* **1** [U] snow that has partly

the **part of speech** of a word (whether it is a noun, verb, etc.)

e·mo·tion /ɪˈmoʊʃn/ *noun* **1** [C] a strong feeling such as love, anger, fear, jealousy, etc. **2** [U] strength of feeling: *His voice was filled with emotion.*

countable and uncountable nouns
These letter tell you whether the noun can be counted [C] or not [U].

ruck·us /ˈrʌkəs/ *noun* [sing.] (*informal*) a noisy argument or disturbance

a **singular noun**

pre·mis·es /ˈprɛməsəz/ *noun* [plural] (*formal*) a building and the land that surrounds it:

a **plural noun**

to·ma·to /təˈmeɪṭoʊ/ *noun* [C] (*pl.* **to·ma·toes**) a soft red fruit that is often eaten raw in

irregular plural form

hide¹ /haɪd/ *verb* (*p.t.* **hid** /hɪd/; *p.p.* **hid·den** /ˈhɪdn/) **1** [T] to put or keep sb/sth in a place where he/she/it cannot be seen: *Where should I hide the money?* ○ *The scar is partially hidden by hair.* ○ *The trees hid the house from view.* **2** [I] to be or get in a place where you cannot be seen or found: *Quick, run and hide!* ○ *Tammy was hiding under the bed.* **3** [T] **hide**

transitive and intransitive verbs
These letters tell you whether a verb is transitive [T] (= followed by an object) or intransitive [I] (= never followed by an object).

take /teɪk/ *verb* [T] (*p.t.* **took** /tʊk/; *p.p.* **tak·en** /ˈteɪkən/) **1** to carry sb/sth or to go with sb

irregular forms of verbs

hum¹ /hʌm/ verb (hum·ming; hummed) 1 [I] to make a continuous low noise like the noise

The **last letter** of the word **is doubled** before you add -*ing* or -*ed*.

☆**good¹** /gʊd/ adj. (**bet·ter** /ˈbetər/, **best** /best/) **1** of a high quality or standard: *a good book,*

the **comparative** and **superlative forms** (regular forms are not given)

☆**hap·py** /ˈhæpi/ adj. (**hap·pi·er; hap·pi·est**) **1** feeling, showing or giving pleasure or satis-

☆**scis·sors** /ˈsɪzərz/ noun [plural] a tool for cut-ting things that consists of two flat sharp blades that are joined together
☛ **Scissors** is a plural noun: *These scissors are blunt.* We CANNOT say "a scissors"; we must use the word **pair**: *I need a new pair of scissors.*

a note giving **grammatical information**

USING WORDS

☆**blame¹** /bleɪm/ verb [T] **1 blame sb (for sth); blame sth on sb** to think or say that a certain

how a word is used in a sentence (**sb** = somebody; **sth** = something)

de·pend·ent² /dɪˈpendənt/ adj. **dependent (on sb/sth)** needing sb/sth to support you:

the particular **preposition** that is used after a word

☆**a·wake¹** /əˈweɪk/ adj. (not before a noun) not sleeping: *I was awake most of the night, worry-ing.* ○ *The kids are always wide* (= completely) *awake at 6 o'clock in the morning.* ○ *They were so tired that they couldn't stay awake.* ☛ The opposite is **asleep**.

The adjective cannot be used before a noun; it must always follow a verb like *be, seem,* etc.

lone /loʊn/ adj. (only *before* a noun) without any other people; alone: *a lone swimmer*

The adjective can only be used before a noun.

beast /bist/ noun [C] **1** (*formal*) an animal, especially a large one: *a wild beast* **2** (*infor-mal*) an unpleasant or cruel person

words used in particular situations
Words may be labeled *formal* (used in formal, written English), *informal* (used in informal conversation and not usually written in essays, etc.) or *slang* (very informal and often used especially by younger people).

CHOOSING THE RIGHT WORD/VOCABULARY BUILDING

build² /bɪld/ *noun* [C,U] the shape and size of sb's body: *She has a very athletic build.* ○ *Police are looking for a young man of slim build.*
☞ Compare **build** and **figure**. **Build** usually describes size in connection with strength and muscle and is used for both men and women. **Figure** usually describes shape, especially whether it is attractive or not, and is usually used only for women.

a note explaining the **difference between words** that might be confused

☆**a·part·ment** /ə'pɑrtmənt/ *noun* [C] (*abbr.* **apt.**) a set of rooms that is used as a home (usually on one floor in a larger building).
☞ You **rent** an apartment from a **landlord** or from a company that owns the apartment. The landlord **rents** the apartment **out** to you, the **tenant**. The money you have to pay is called **rent**. Look also at **condominium**.

a note giving **related vocabulary**

sane /seɪn/ *adj.* **1** (used about a person) mentally normal; not crazy: *With a job like mine, it's incredible that I'm still sane!* **2** (used about a person or an idea, etc.) sensible; showing good judgment. ☞ The opposite is **insane**. The noun is **sanity**.

members of a **word family**

PRONUNCIATION

☆**en·gi·neer¹** /ˌɛndʒə'nɪr/ *noun* [C] **1** a person whose job is to use science and mathematics

the **pronunciation** of each word

ˌ**mass** ˈ**media** *noun* [plural] the means of communicating with large numbers of people, i.e. newspapers, television and radio

where the **stress** falls on a word with two or more parts

BRITISH ENGLISH

pet·rol /'pɛtrəl/ *noun* [U] (*BrE*) = GASOLINE

Look at the American word after the = (equals) sign to find the meaning of a **British word**.

This dictionary does not show British spellings for words which look different in British English. Here are some common types of spelling differences in British English:

American	center	color	defense	traveled
British	centre	colour	defence	travelled

Aa

A, a¹ /eɪ/ *noun* [C] (*pl.* **A's; a's** /eɪz/) **1** the first letter of the English alphabet: *"Andy" begins with (an) "A."* **2** the highest grade given for a test or piece of work: *I got an "A" on my essay.*
IDM earn/get straight A's ⇨ STRAIGHT¹

☆**a²** /ə/; *strong form* /eɪ/ (*also* **an** /ən/; *strong form* /æn/) *indefinite article* ☞ The form **an** is used before a vowel sound. **1** one: *I'll have a cup of coffee.* ○ *an apple and a pear* **2** (used when you are talking about sth in general, not one particular example of it): *A lion is a dangerous animal.* **3** (used with sb's name to show that the speaker does not know the person): *There's a Ms. Mills here to see you.* **4** (used for showing that sb/sth is a member of a group, class or profession): *She's a Muslim.* ○ *Their car's a Volvo.* ○ *She's a senator.* **5** (used with some expressions of quantity): *a lot of money* ○ *a few cars* **6** (used with prices, rates, measurements) each: *They cost 50¢ a pound.* ○ *He was traveling at about 80 miles an hour.*

a·back /əˈbæk/ *adv.*
IDM be taken aback to be surprised or shocked: *I was completely taken aback when I saw the bill from the auto mechanic.*

☆**a·ban·don** /əˈbændən/ *verb* [T] **1** to leave sb/sth that you are responsible for, usually permanently: *an abandoned car* **2** to stop doing sth without finishing it or without achieving what you wanted to do: *The search for the missing sailors was abandoned after two days.* —**a·ban·don·ment** *noun* [U]

a·bashed /əˈbæʃt/ *adj.* ashamed and embarrassed because of having done sth bad

ab·bey /ˈæbi/ *noun* [C] a building where monks or nuns live or used to live

abbr. (*also* **abbrev.**) = ABBREVIATION

ab·bre·vi·ate /əˈbrivieɪt/ *verb* [T] **1** to make a word or phrase shorter by leaving out some letters **2** to make a story, a piece of writing or speech shorter: *the abbreviated version of the story*

ab·bre·vi·a·tion /əˌbriviˈeɪʃn/ *noun* [C] a short form of a word or phrase: *In this dictionary, "sth" is the abbreviation for "something."*

ab·di·cate /ˈæbdɪkeɪt/ *verb* **1** [I] to give up being king or queen: *The queen abdicated and her son became king.* **2** [T] to give sth up, especially power or a position: *to abdicate responsibility* (= to refuse to be responsible for sth) —**ab·di·ca·tion** /ˌæbdɪˈkeɪʃn/ *noun* [C,U]

ab·do·men /ˈæbdəmən/ *noun* [C] a part of the body between the chest and the legs, in which the stomach is contained —**ab·dom·i·nal** /æbˈdɑmɪnl; əb-/ *adj.*

ab·duct /əbˈdʌkt; æb-/ *verb* [T] to take hold of sb and take him/her away illegally: *He has been abducted by a terrorist group.* —**ab·duc·tion** /-ˈdʌkʃn/ *noun* [C,U]

a·bet /əˈbɛt/ *verb* [T] **a·bet·ting; a·bet·ted**
IDM aid and abet ⇨ AID²

ab·hor /əbˈhɔr; æb-/ *verb* [T] (**ab·hor·ring; ab·horred**) (*formal*) to hate sth very much: *All civilized people abhor the use of torture.* —**ab·hor·rence** /-ˈhɔrəns; -ˈhɑrəns/ *noun* [U] —**ab·hor·rent** /-ˈhɔrənt; -ˈhɑrənt/ *adj.*

a·bide /əˈbaɪd/ *verb* (*formal*)
IDM can't/couldn't abide sb/sth/doing sth to dislike sth very much: *I can't abide getting up early.*
PHRV abide by sth to obey a law, etc.; to do what you have agreed or decided: *You must abide by the rules of the game.*

☆**a·bil·i·ty** /əˈbɪləti/ *noun* [C,U] (*pl.* **a·bil·i·ties**) the mental or physical power or skill that makes it possible to do sth: *A person of his ability will have no difficulty getting a job.*

a·blaze /əˈbleɪz/ *adj.* (not before a noun) burning strongly; completely on fire: *Within ten minutes, the whole house was ablaze.*

☆**a·ble** /ˈeɪbl/ *adj.* **1 be able to do sth** (used as a modal verb) to have the ability, power, opportunity, time, etc. to do sth: *Will you be able to come to a meeting next week?* ○ *I was able to solve the problem quickly.*

☞ In the passive **can/could** are used, not **be able**: *The arrangement can't be changed.*

2 (*formal*) intelligent; doing your job well: *an able politician* —**a·bly** /ˈeɪbli/ *adv.*

able-bodied /ˌeɪblˈbadid/ *adj.* strong and healthy: *All the able-bodied young men from our town were drafted into the army.*

ab·nor·mal /æbˈnɔrml/ *adj.* different from what is normal or usual, in a way that worries you or that is unpleasant: *I don't want to have any children. Is that abnormal?* ○ *abnormal weather conditions* —**ab·nor·mal·i·ty** /ˌæbnɔrˈmæləti; ˌæbnər-/ *noun* [C,U] (*pl.* **ab·nor·mal·i·ties**) —**ab·nor·mal·ly** *adv.*

a·board /əˈbɔrd/ *adv., prep.* on or into a train, ship or aircraft: *We went aboard the ship.* ○ *Welcome aboard Flight 397 to Caracas.*

a·bol·ish /əˈbɑlɪʃ/ *verb* [T] to put an end to or stop a law or system officially: *When was capital punishment abolished here?* —**ab·o·li·tion** /ˌæbəˈlɪʃn/ *noun* [U]: *the abolition of slavery in the U.S.*

a·bom·i·na·ble /əˈbamənəbl/ *adj.* (*formal*) very bad; very unpleasant: *abominable behavior*

ab·o·rig·i·nal /ˌæbəˈrɪdʒənl/ *adj.* **1** of or belonging to the original inhabitants of a place:

tʃ	dʒ	v	θ	ð	s	z	ʃ
chin	June	van	thin	then	so	zoo	she

A

aboriginal tribes **2 Aboriginal** of or belonging to the race of people who were the original inhabitants of Australia

Ab·o·rig·i·ne /ˌæbəˈrɪdʒəni/ *noun* [C] a member of the race of people who were the original inhabitants of Australia

a·bort /əˈbɔrt/ *verb* [I,T] **1** to end a pregnancy intentionally and cause the baby (**fetus**) inside to die **2** to end sth before it is complete: *to abort a bombing mission*

a·bor·tion /əˈbɔrʃn/ *noun* [C,U] an operation to end a pregnancy intentionally, causing the baby (**fetus**) inside to die: *to have an abortion* ○ *Abortion is illegal in that country.*

a·bor·tive /əˈbɔrtɪv/ *adj.* not completed successfully: *an abortive attempt*

a·bound /əˈbaʊnd/ *verb* [I] **1** to exist in large numbers: *Restaurants abound in this part of the city.* **2 abound with sth** to contain large numbers of sth

☆ **a·bout¹** /əˈbaʊt/ *adv.* **1** (*also* **around**) a little more or less than; approximately: *It's about three miles from here to the center of town.* ○ *I got home at about 7:30.* **2** (*informal*) almost; nearly: *Dinner's just about ready.*

IDM be about to do sth to be going to do sth very soon: *The show's about to start.*

be not about to do sth not to be willing to do sth: *I'm not about to let a little rain spoil our picnic!*

☆ **a·bout²** /əˈbaʊt/ *prep.* **1** on the subject of: *a book about Spain* ○ *I don't like it, but there's nothing I can do about it.* **2** in the character of sb: *There's something about him that I don't quite trust.*

IDM how/what about ...? **1** (used when asking for information about sb/sth or for sb's opinion or wish): *I'm going to have chicken. How about you?* ○ *What about Ruth? Have you heard from her lately?* **2** (used when making a suggestion): *How about going to a movie tonight?*

a'bout-face *noun* [C] a turn in the opposite direction; a change of opinion

☆ **a·bove¹** /əˈbʌv/ *adv., prep.* **1** in a higher place: *The people in the apartment above make a lot of noise.* ○ *I live in the hills above the city.* ☛ picture at **over**. **2** (*formal*) in an earlier part (of sth written): *the items mentioned above* **3** more than a number, amount, price, etc.: *children age 11 and above* ○ *A score of 70 and above will get you a B on the test.* ○ *You have to get above 50% to pass.* ○ *above-average temperatures* **4** too good, etc. to do sth: *She's not above telling a few lies if it makes life easier.* **5** with a higher rank: *The person above me is the department manager.*

IDM above all most importantly: *Above all, stay calm!*

a·bove² /əˈbʌv/ *adj.* mentioned before in a piece of writing: *If you answered "yes" to the above questions, go on to number 6.* **—the**

above *noun* [U, plural]: *Which of the above best describes your personality?*

ab·ra·sive /əˈbreɪsɪv/ *adj.* **1** rough and likely to scratch: *Do not use abrasive cleaning products on the bathtub.* **2** (used about a person) rude and fairly aggressive

a·breast /əˈbrɛst/ *adv.* (used after a number) next to or level with each other and going in the same direction: *The soldiers marched two abreast.*

IDM be/keep abreast of sth to have all the most recent information about sth

a·bridge /əˈbrɪdʒ/ *verb* [T] to make sth (usually a book) shorter by removing parts of it: *an abridged version of a novel* **—a·bridg·ment** (*also* **abridgement**) *noun* [C,U]

☆ **a·broad** /əˈbrɔd/ *adv.* in or to another country or countries: *My mother has never been abroad.* ○ *They found it difficult to get used to living abroad.*

a·brupt /əˈbrʌpt/ *adj.* **1** sudden and unexpected: *an abrupt change of plan* **2** (used about a person's behavior) fairly rude and unfriendly **—a·brupt·ly** *adv.* **—a·brupt·ness** *noun* [U]

ab·scess /ˈæbsɛs/ *noun* [C] a swelling on or in the body, containing a poisonous liquid (**pus**)

ab·scond /əbˈskɑnd; æb-/ *verb* [I] (*formal*) to run away from a place where you should stay, sometimes with sth that you should not take: *She absconded with all the company's money.*

☆ **ab·sence** /ˈæbsəns/ *noun* **1** [C,U] a time when sb is away from somewhere; the fact of being away from somewhere: *frequent absences due to illness* ○ *His absence from the team will greatly weaken it.* **2** [U] the fact of sth not being there; lack: *The first thing I noticed about the place was the absence of noise.*

☆ **ab·sent** /ˈæbsənt/ *adj.* **1** not present somewhere: *He was absent from work.* **2** thinking about sth else, and so not paying attention: *an absent stare* **—ab·sent·ly** *adv.*

ab·sen·tee /ˌæbsənˈti/ *noun* [C] a person who should be present but is not

ab·sent-'mind·ed *adj.* often forgetting or not noticing things, because you are thinking about sth else **—ab·sent-'mindedly** *adv.* **—ab·sent-'mindedness** *noun* [U]

☆ **ab·so·lute** /ˈæbsəlut; ˌæbsəˈlut/ *adj.* **1** complete; total: *We are aiming at absolute perfection!* ○ *The whole trip was an absolute disaster.* **2** certain; definite: *We have no absolute proof that this suspect committed the robbery.* **3** not measured in comparison with sth else: *Food prices have increased in absolute terms.*

☆ **ab·so·lute·ly** *adv.* **1** /ˈæbsəlutli/ completely; totally: *What you're saying is absolutely wrong.* ○ *I absolutely refuse to believe that.* ○ *He made absolutely no effort* (= no effort at all) *to help me.* **2** /ˌæbsəˈlutli/ (used when you are agreeing with sb) yes; certainly: *"It's a good idea, isn't it?" "Oh, absolutely!"*

i	ɪ	ɛ	æ	ɑ	ɔ	ʌ	ʊ	u
see	sit	ten	cat	hot	saw	cup	put	too

ab·solve /əb'zɑlv/ verb [T] **absolve sb (from/ of sth)** to state formally that sb is free from guilt or blame: *The driver was absolved from any responsibility for the train crash.*

ab·sorb /əb'sɔrb; -'zɔrb/ verb [T] **1** to take in and hold sth (a liquid, heat, etc.): *a drug that is quickly absorbed into the bloodstream* **2** to take sth into the mind and understand it: *I found it impossible to absorb so much information so quickly.* **3** to take sth into sth larger, so that it becomes part of it: *Over the years many towns have been absorbed into the metropolitan area.* **4** to hold sb's attention completely or interest sb greatly: *History is a subject that absorbs her.* —**ab·sorp·tion** /əb'sɔrpʃn; -'zɔrp-/ noun [U]

ab·sorbed /əb'sɔrbd; -'zɔrbd/ adj. with sb's attention completely held: *He was absorbed in his work and didn't hear me come in.*

ab·sorb·ent /əb'sɔrbənt; -'zɔr-/ adj. able to take in and hold liquid: *an absorbent cloth*

ab·sorb·ing /əb'sɔrbɪŋ; -'zɔr-/ adj. so interesting that it holds the attention completely: *an absorbing story*

ab·stain /əb'steɪn/ verb [I] **abstain (from sth) 1** to stop yourself from doing sth that you enjoy: *to abstain from eating fattening food* ☞ The noun is **abstinence**. **2** (in a vote) to say that you are not voting either for or against sth: *Two people voted in favor, two voted against and one abstained.* ☞ The noun is **abstention**.

ab·sten·tion /əb'stɛnʃn/ noun [C,U] the act of not voting either for or against sth

ab·sti·nence /'æbstənəns/ noun [U] stopping yourself from having or doing sth that you enjoy: *The doctor advised total abstinence from alcohol.*

ab·stract¹ /əb'strækt; æb-; 'æbstrækt/ adj. **1** existing only as an idea, not as a physical or real thing: *I find it hard to think about abstract ideas like the meaning of life.* **2** (used about art) not showing things as they really look: *an abstract painting*

ab·stract² /'æbstrækt/ noun [C] **1** an example of abstract ¹(2) art: *an exhibit of abstracts* **2** a much shorter version of an article, a book, etc. giving the main points or ideas from it; a summary

IDM in the abstract without mentioning particular people, objects, etc.: *I find it hard to think about a problem in the abstract.*

ab·surd /əb'sərd/ adj. that should be laughed at; ridiculous; not seeming sensible: *That's totally absurd! I can't possibly do all this work in one day.* —**ab·surd·i·ty** /əb'sərdəti/ noun [C,U] (pl. **ab·surd·i·ties**) —**ab·surd·ly** adv.: *The rules of the game are absurdly complicated.*

a·bun·dance /ə'bʌndəns/ noun [U, sing.] a very large quantity of sth

a·bun·dant /ə'bʌndənt/ adj. existing in very large quantities; more than enough: *abundant supplies of food* —**a·bun·dant·ly** adv.

a·buse¹ /ə'byuz/ verb [T] **1** to use sth in the wrong way, e.g. dishonestly: *He was accused of abusing his position for personal gain.* **2** to treat sb badly, often violently: *The girl had been sexually abused by her father.* **3** to say rude things to sb

a·buse² /ə'byus/ noun **1** [C,U] using sth in the wrong way: *an abuse of power* ○ *the dangers of drug abuse* **2** [U] bad, usually violent treatment of sb: *child abuse* **3** [U] rude words, used to insult another person: *The other driver leaned out of the car and hurled abuse at me.*

a·bu·sive /ə'byusɪv; -zɪv/ adj. **1** treating sb badly, often violently: *an abusive husband* **2** using rude language to insult sb: *an abusive remark*

a·bys·mal /ə'bɪzməl/ adj. very bad; of very poor quality —**a·bys·mal·ly** adv.

☆ **ac·a·dem·ic¹** /ˌækə'dɛmɪk/ adj. **1** connected with the educational activities of schools, colleges and universities: *The academic year begins in September.* **2** connected with subjects of interest to the mind rather than technical or practical subjects: *academic subjects such as history* —**ac·a·dem·i·cal·ly** /-kli/ adv.

ac·a·dem·ic² /ˌækə'dɛmɪk/ noun [C] a person who teaches and/or does research at a university or college

a·cad·e·my /ə'kædəmi/ noun [C] (pl. **a·cad·e·mies**) **1** a private school, or a school for special training: *a military academy* **2** (also **Academy**) a society of people who are important in art, science or literature: *the National Academy of Sciences*

☆ **ac·cel·er·ate** /ək'sɛlərɪt/ verb [I,T] to go faster; to make sth go faster or happen more quickly: *I accelerated and left the other cars behind.* —**ac·cel·er·a·tion** /əkˌsɛlə'reɪʃn/ noun [U]

ac·cel·er·a·tor /ək'sɛləreɪtər/(also *informal* **gas pedal**) noun [C] the pedal in a car, etc. that you press in order to increase speed

☆ **ac·cent** /'æksɛnt/ noun **1** [C,U] a particular way of pronouncing words that is connected with the country, area or social class that you come from: *a strong Southern accent* **2** [C] the act of emphasizing a word or part of a word by pronouncing it with greater force: *In the word "because," the accent is on the second syllable.* **3** [C] (in writing) a mark, usually above a letter, that shows that it has to be pronounced in a certain way **4** [C, usually sing.] the particular importance that is given to sth: *In all our products the accent is on quality.*

ac·cen·tu·ate /ək'sɛntʃueɪt/ verb [T] to make sth easier to notice

☆ **ac·cept** /ək'sɛpt/ verb **1** [I,T] to take sth willingly that sb offers you: *Do I have to pay cash or will you accept a check?* ○ *Why won't you accept my advice?* **2** [I,T] to say yes to sth or to

ə	y	w	t̬	eɪ	aɪ	ɔɪ	aʊ	oʊ
about	yes	woman	butter	say	five	boy	now	go

A

agree to sth: *Thank you for your invitation. I am happy to accept.* ○ *I'd be pleased to accept your offer.* **3** [T] to admit or recognize that sth bad is true: *They refused to accept responsibility for the accident.* **4** [T] to recognize that sth cannot be changed: *It is hard to accept the death of a child.* **5** [T] to believe sth: *I just don't accept that – it simply isn't true.* ○ *She didn't accept that I was telling the truth.* **6** [T] to take sth because it is suitable; to decide that sb/sth is suitable: *The vending machine won't accept my dollar bill.* ○ *I had a letter saying that I had been accepted for the fall semester.* ☞ Look at **refuse¹** and **reject**.

☆ **ac·cept·a·ble** /əkˈsɛptəbl/ *adj.* **1** allowed, often by people in general: *One or two mistakes are acceptable but no more than that.* **2** satisfactory; good enough: *We hope that you will consider our offer acceptable.* ☞ The opposite is **unacceptable**. —**ac·cept·a·bil·i·ty** /əkˌsɛptəˈbɪləti/ *noun* [U] —**ac·cept·a·bly** /əkˈsɛptəbli/ *adv.*

ac·cep·tance /əkˈsɛptəns/ *noun* [C,U] the act of accepting or being accepted: *a letter of acceptance from the university* ○ *the acceptance of a difficult situation* (= seeing that it cannot be changed) ○ *He quickly gained acceptance in the group* (= the other people thought of him as equal to them).

☆ **ac·cess¹** /ˈæksɛs/ *noun* [U] **1 access (to sth)** a way of entering or reaching a place: *Access to the attic is through this door.* **2 access (to sth)** the chance or right to use or have sth: *Do you have access to a fax machine?* **3 access (to sb)** permission, especially legal or official, to see sb: *They are divorced, but he has regular access to the kids.*

☆ **ac·cess²** /ˈæksɛs/ *verb* [T] to get or use sth, especially with a computer: *This software makes it easy to access information in the database.*

ac·ces·si·ble /əkˈsɛsəbl/ *adj.* **1** possible to be reached or entered: *Because of the snow, the farm was not accessible by car.* **2** easy to get, use or understand ☞ The opposite is **inaccessible**. —**ac·ces·si·bil·i·ty** /əkˌsɛsəˈbɪləti/ *noun* [U]

ac·ces·so·ry /əkˈsɛsəri/ *noun* [C] (*pl.* **ac·ces·so·ries**) **1** an extra item that is added to sth and is useful or attractive but not essential: *The car has accessories such as an electronic alarm.* **2** [usually pl.] a small item that is worn or carried with the main items of clothing (e.g. shoes, jewelry, a bag, etc.) **3 accessory (to sth)** (in law) a person who helps sb to do sth illegal

☆ **ac·ci·dent** /ˈæksədənt; -dɛnt/ *noun* [C] an unpleasant event that happens unexpectedly and causes damage, injury or death: *I hope they haven't had an accident.* ○ *a car accident* ○ *a fatal accident* (= when sb is killed) ○ *I didn't mean to kick you – it was an accident.*

IDM **by accident** by chance; without being planned: *We met each other again completely by accident.*

ac·ci·den·tal /ˌæksəˈdɛntl/ *adj.* happening by chance; not having been planned —**ac·ci·den·tal·ly** /ˌæksəˈdɛntəli/ *adv.*

accident-prone *adj.* frequently having accidents, and therefore more likely to have them than other people

ac·claim /əˈkleɪm/ *verb* [T] to praise sb/sth greatly: *The novel has been acclaimed as a modern classic.* —**ac·claim** *noun* [U]: *The movie received widespread critical acclaim.*

ac·cli·mate /ˈækləmeɪt/ *verb* [I,T] **acclimate (yourself/sb/sth) (to sth)** to get used to a new climate, a new situation, etc. so that it is not a problem anymore: *It took me a long time to get acclimated to the heat when I went to live in Africa.* —**ac·cli·ma·tion** /ˌækləˈmeɪʃn/ *noun* [U]

ac·com·mo·date /əˈkɑmədeɪt/ *verb* [T] **1** to have enough space for sb/sth (especially a certain number of people): *The van can accommodate up to eight people.* **2** to provide sb with a place to stay, live or work: *During the conference, you will be accommodated in a nearby hotel.* **3** to do or provide what sb wants or needs: *Should you have any special requirements, our staff will do their best to accommodate you.*

ac·com·mo·dat·ing /əˈkɑməˌdeɪtɪŋ/ *adj.* (used about a person) willing to do or provide what sb wants

☆ **ac·com·mo·da·tion** /əˌkɑməˈdeɪʃn/ *noun* **1** [U] (*also* **accommodations**) a place where people can stay for a short time, e.g. in a hotel, and the services they can receive there: *first-class hotel accommodations* **2** [U] (*formal*) the process of changing to suit sb else's needs: *This government will not make any accommodation to terrorists.* **3** [C] (*formal*) an agreement which tries to satisfy both sides in an argument: *We managed to reach an accommodation with the other party.*

ac·com·pa·ni·ment /əˈkʌmpənimənt/ *noun* **1** [C] something that naturally or pleasantly goes with sth else (especially food or drinks): *This sauce is the perfect accompaniment to grilled meat.* **2** [C,U] music that is played with singing or the main instrument: *a violin piece with a piano accompaniment*

☆ **ac·com·pa·ny** /əˈkʌmpəni/ *verb* [T] (*pres. part.* **ac·com·pa·ny·ing**; *3rd pers. sing. pres.* **ac·com·pa·nies**; *p.t., p.p.* **ac·com·pa·nied**) **1** to go with sb to a place: *Children must be accompanied by an adult.* **2** to happen or exist at the same time as, or because of, sth: *A huge ad campaign accompanied the movie's release.* **3** to give or send sth together with sth else, in addition to it: *The letter was accompanied by a check for $50.* **4** to play music for a singer or

another instrument: *She accompanied him on the guitar.*

ac·com·plice /əˈkɑmplɪs/ *noun* [C] a person who helps sb to do sth bad, especially a crime

☆ **ac·com·plish** /əˈkɑmplɪʃ/ *verb* [T] to succeed in doing sth requiring effort and/or skill; to achieve: *Very little was accomplished at the meeting.*

ac·com·plished /əˈkɑmplɪʃt/ *adj.* skilled: *an accomplished pianist*

ac·com·plish·ment /əˈkɑmplɪʃmənt/ *noun* **1** [U] the act of completing sth successfully **2** [C] something impressive that sb has achieved; a skill that sb has

ac·cord¹ /əˈkɔrd/ *noun* [C] (*formal*) an agreement, e.g. between countries: *the Helsinki accords on human rights*

IDM in accord in agreement about sth

of/on your own accord without being forced or asked: *He wasn't fired from his job; he left of his own accord.*

ac·cord² /əˈkɔrd/ *verb* [T] (*formal*) to give sth to sb: *The diplomats were accorded every courtesy during their visit.*

ac·cor·dance /əˈkɔrdns/ *noun*

IDM in accordance with sth in a way that follows or obeys sth: *to act in accordance with instructions*

ac·cord·ing·ly /əˈkɔrdɪŋli/ *adv.* **1** in a way that is suitable after what has happened: *I realized that I was in danger and acted accordingly.* **2** (*formal*) therefore; for that reason: *We accept full responsibility for the error. Accordingly, we are refunding your money.*

☆ **according to** /əˈkɔrdɪŋ tə/ *prep.* **1** as stated by sb; as shown by sth: *According to Mick, it's a great movie.* ○ *More people now have a high standard of living, according to the statistics.* **2** in a way that matches, follows or depends on sth: *Everything went according to plan* (= as we had planned it). ○ *The salary will be determined according to education and experience.*

ac·cor·di·on /əˈkɔrdiən/ *noun* [C] a musical instrument with keys like those on a piano. You hold an accordion in both hands and play it by pulling the two sides apart and then pushing them together, while pressing the keys with your fingers

ac·cost /əˈkɔst; -ˈkɑst/ *verb* [T] to approach and talk to a stranger in a way that is considered bad or frightening

☆ **ac·count¹** /əˈkaʊnt/ *noun* [C] **1** a report or description of sth that has happened: *She gave the police a full account of the robbery.* **2** the arrangement by which a bank holds your money for you: *a bank account* ○ *to open/close an account* ○ *I'd like to deposit this check into my account.*

☞ We use a **checking account** to pay for things with a **check**. We can save money in a **savings account**.

3 an arrangement with a store, company, etc. that allows you to pay for goods or services at a later date: *Please mention your account number if you have a question about your bill.* **4** [usually pl.] a record of all the money that a person or business has received or paid out: *He manages the store and his wife takes care of the accounts.*

IDM by all accounts according to what everyone says: *By all accounts, she's a very good doctor.*

on account of because of: *Our flight was delayed on account of bad weather.*

on no account; not on any account (*formal*) not for any reason: *On no account should prisoners be left without supervision.*

take sth into account; take account of sth to consider sth, especially when deciding or judging sth: *We'll take your comments into account.*

ac·count² /əˈkaʊnt/ *verb*

PHRV account for sth 1 to explain or give a reason for sth: *How can we account for these changes?* ○ *My boss asked me to account for all the money I had spent* (= to say what I had spent it on). **2** to supply the amount that is mentioned: *Sales to Europe accounted for 80% of our total sales last year.*

ac·count·a·ble /əˈkaʊntəbl/ *adj.* expected to give an explanation of your actions, etc.; responsible: *She is too young to be held accountable for what she did.* —**ac·count·a·bil·i·ty** /ə,kaʊntəˈbɪləti/ *noun* [U]: *The new law requires greater accountability from the police.*

ac·count·ant /əˈkaʊntnt/ *noun* [C] a person whose job is to keep or examine the financial records of a business, etc.

ac·count·ing /əˈkaʊntɪŋ/ *noun* [U] the profession of an accountant: *a career in accounting*

ac·cred·i·ta·tion /ə,krɛdəˈteɪʃn/ *noun* [C,U] the official approval that says a school, etc. meets certain requirements: *The school must show that it has adequate library resources to receive accreditation.*

ac·cred·it·ed /əˈkrɛdɪtəd/ *adj.* (used about a course, school, etc.) having official approval that says it meets certain requirements: *an accredited language course*

ac·cu·mu·late /əˈkyumyəleɪt/ *verb* **1** [T] to collect a number or quantity of sth over a period of time: *Over the years, I've accumulated hundreds of records.* **2** [I] to increase over a period of time: *Dust soon accumulates if you don't clean for a week or so.* —**ac·cu·mu·la·tion** /ə,kyumyəˈleɪʃn/ *noun* [C,U]

ac·cu·ra·cy /ˈækyərəsi/ *noun* [U] the quality of being exact and correct ☞ The opposite is **inaccuracy**.

☆ **ac·cu·rate** /ˈækyərət/ *adj.* careful and exact; without mistakes: *an accurate description of the house* ○ *That clock isn't very accurate.*

tʃ	dʒ	v	θ	ð	s	z	ʃ
chin	June	van	thin	then	so	zoo	she

A

☞ The opposite is **inaccurate**. —**ac·cu·rate·ly** *adv.*

ac·cu·sa·tion /ˌækyəˈzeɪʃn/ *noun* [C,U] a statement that says that sb has done sth wrong: *He said that false accusations had been made against him.*

☆ **ac·cuse** /əˈkyuz/ *verb* [T] **accuse sb (of sth)** to say that sb has done sth wrong or broken the law: *I accused her of cheating.* ○ *He was accused of murder.*

ac·cus·ing /əˈkyuzɪŋ/ *adj.* that shows that you think sb has done sth wrong: *He gave me an accusing look.* —**ac·cus·ing·ly** *adv.*

ac·cus·tomed /əˈkʌstəmd/ *adj.* **1 accustomed to sth** if you are accustomed to sth, you are used to it and it is not strange for you: *She's accustomed to traveling a lot in her job.* ○ *They had grown accustomed to life in the country.* **2** (*formal*) usual; regular: *He was sitting in his accustomed seat.*

ace¹ /eɪs/ *noun* [C] **1** a playing card which has a single shape on it. An ace has either the lowest or the highest value in a game of cards: *the ace of spades* ☞ Look at the note at **card**. **2** (*informal*) a person who is very good at a particular activity **3** (in tennis) the first stroke of a game (**serve**) that the person playing against you cannot hit back

ace² /eɪs/ *adj.* (only *before* a noun) very good: *an ace newspaper reporter*

☆ **ache¹** /eɪk/ *noun* [C, usually sing.] (usually in compounds) a pain that lasts for a long time: *to have a headache, a toothache, an earache, a stomachache, etc.* ○ *Old people suffer from a lot of aches and pains.*

ache² /eɪk/ *verb* [I] to feel a continuous pain: *His legs ached after playing soccer for two hours.*

☆ **a·chieve** /əˈtʃiv/ *verb* [T] **1** to gain sth, usually by effort or skill: *You have achieved the success you deserve.* **2** to get sth done; to complete: *They have achieved a lot in a short time.*

☆ **a·chieve·ment** /əˈtʃivmənt/ *noun* **1** [C] something that is done successfully, especially through hard work or skill: *She considered the book her greatest achievement.* **2** [U] the act of finishing sth successfully; the feeling that you get when you have finished sth successfully: *Climbing the mountain gave him a sense of achievement.*

☆ **ac·id¹** /ˈæsɪd/ *noun* [C,U] (in chemistry) a liquid substance that can dissolve metal and may burn your skin or clothes: *sulfuric acid* ☞ Look at **alkali** and **base¹**.

ac·id² /ˈæsɪd/ *adj.* **1** (used about a fruit, etc.) with a sharp, sour taste **2** (*also* **a·cid·ic**) containing an acid: *an acid solution* ☞ Look at **alkaline** and **base¹**(7).

a·cid·i·ty /əˈsɪdəti/ *noun* [U] the quality of being acid

acid ˈrain *noun* [U] rain that is polluted by acid substances from the chimneys of factor-

ies and that causes damage to trees, buildings and rivers

☆ **ac·knowl·edge** /əkˈnɑlɪdʒ/ *verb* [T] **1** to accept or admit that sth is true or exists: *He acknowledged the fact that he had been wrong.* ○ *They wouldn't acknowledge defeat.* ○ *It is acknowledged that he is the country's greatest writer.* ○ *He is acknowledged to be the country's greatest writer.* **2** to show that you have seen sb by raising your hand, smiling, etc.: *She refused to acknowledge him and walked straight past.* **3** to say that you have received a letter, etc.: *I would appreciate it if you could acknowledge my letter.* **4** to show or say that you are grateful for sth: *I would like to acknowledge all the help I have received from my family.*

ac·knowl·edg·ment (*also* **acknowledgement**) /əkˈnɑlɪdʒmənt/ *noun* **1** [U] the act of acknowledging: *I have received no acknowledgment for all the work I did.* **2** [C] a letter, etc. stating that sth has been received **3** [C] a few words of thanks that an author writes at the beginning or end of a book to the people who have helped him/her

ac·ne /ˈækni/ *noun* [U] a type of skin disease, usually affecting young people, that causes a lot of red spots (**pimples**) on the face and neck

a·corn /ˈeɪkɔrn/ *noun* [C] a small nut that is the fruit of the oak tree

a·cous·tic /əˈkustɪk/ *adj.* **1** connected with sound or the sense of hearing **2** (of a musical instrument) not electric: *an acoustic guitar*

a·cous·tics /əˈkustɪks/ *noun* [plural] **1** the qualities of a room, etc. that make it good or bad for you to hear music, etc.: *The theater has excellent acoustics.* **2** [with sing. verb] the scientific study of sound

ac·quaint /əˈkweɪnt/ *verb* [T] (*formal*) **acquaint sb/yourself with sth** to make sb/ yourself familiar with or aware of sth: *She took a few minutes to acquaint herself with the layout of the house.*

ac·quain·tance /əˈkweɪntns/ *noun* **1** [C] a person that you know but who is not a close friend **2** [U] **acquaintance with sb/sth** a slight knowledge of sb/sth: *I made his acquaintance* (= got to know him) *at a party.*

ac·quaint·ed /əˈkweɪntəd/ *adj.* (not before a noun) **1 acquainted (with sb)** knowing sb, but usually not very closely: *We had a chance to get acquainted with our new neighbors at the party.* **2 acquainted with sth** (*formal*) knowing sth: *Are you acquainted with the facts of this case?*

ac·qui·esce /ˌækwiˈɛs/ *verb* [I] (*formal*) **acquiesce (in/to sth)** to accept sth without argument, although you may not agree with it —**ac·qui·es·cence** /-ˈɛsns/ *noun* [U]

☆ **ac·quire** /əˈkwaɪər/ *verb* [T] to get or obtain sth: *The company has acquired shares in a rival business.* ○ *She acquired a southern accent*

while living in New Orleans. ○ He's acquired a reputation for being difficult to work with.

ac·qui·si·tion /ˌækwəˈzɪʃn/ noun **1** [C] something that you have obtained or bought, especially sth you are pleased with: This painting is my latest acquisition. **2** [U] the act of obtaining sth: the acquisition of wealth

ac·quit /əˈkwɪt/ verb [T] (**ac·quit·ting**; **ac·quit·ted**) **1 acquit sb (of sth)** to declare formally that a person is not guilty of a crime: The jury acquitted her of murder. ☞ The opposite is **convict**. **2 acquit yourself...** (formal) to behave in the way that is mentioned: He acquitted himself extremely well in his first game as a professional. —**ac·quit·tal** /əˈkwɪtl/ noun [C,U]

☆ **a·cre** /ˈeɪkər/ noun [C] a measure of land; 0.405 of a hectare : a farm of 200 acres/a 200-acre farm ☞ For more information on measurements, look at Appendix 2.

ac·ro·bat /ˈækrəbæt/ noun [C] a person who performs difficult movements of the body or difficult balancing acts (e.g. walking on a wire), especially in a circus —**ac·ro·bat·ic** /ˌækrəˈbætɪk/ adj.

ac·ro·bat·ics /ˌækrəˈbætɪks/ noun [U] (the art of performing) acrobatic acts

ac·ro·nym /ˈækrənɪm/ noun [C] a short word that is made from the first letters of a group of words: TOEFL is an acronym for Test of English as a Foreign Language.

☆ **a·cross** /əˈkrɔs/ adv., prep. **1** from one side of sth to the other: The stream was too wide to jump across. ○ I drew a line across the page. ○ A smile spread across his face. **2** on the other side of sth: There's a bank across the street. ☞ We can use **across** or **over** to mean "on or to the other side": I ran across/over the field. But when we talk about crossing something high, we usually use **over**: I can't climb over that wall. With "room" we usually use **across**: I walked across the room to the door. **3** measuring from side to side: The river was about 20 meters across.

IDM across the board involving or affecting all groups, members, cases, etc.: a 10% pay increase across the board

☆ **aˈcross from** prep. directly on the other side of a space between sth and sth else; facing sb/sth: Our house is right across from the high school. ○ He sat across from me at the table. ○ We sat across from each other. ☞ picture at **front**.

a·cryl·ic /əˈkrɪlɪk/ noun [U] a material that is made artificially by a chemical process and used in making sweaters and other clothes, paints, and some types of plastics —**a·cryl·ic** adj.: an acrylic sweater

☆ **act¹** /ækt/ verb **1** [I] to do sth; to take action: There's no time to lose – you must act now. ○ The government was slow to act on the problem. ○ The man we met on the plane to Tokyo

was kind enough to act as our guide (= to perform the function of guide). **2** [I] to behave in the manner stated: Don't act like a fool. **3** [I,T] to perform or have a part in a play or movie: I've never acted before. ○ He has always wanted to act the part of Hamlet.

PHRV act sth out to perform a story, ceremony, etc.: Each group can act out their scene in front of the class.

☆ **act²** /ækt/ noun [C] **1** a thing that you do: In a typical act of generosity they refused to accept any money.

☞ **Act** and **action** can have the same meaning: It was a brave act/action. **Act**, not **action**, can be followed by **of**: It was an act of bravery. **Activity** is used for something that is done regularly: I like outdoor activities such as walking and bike riding. **Deed** is a formal and old-fashioned word and often refers to very important acts: Robin Hood was famous for his brave deeds. It is the word usually used with **good**: I wanted to pay back the good deed he had done.

2 often **Act** one of the main divisions of a play or an opera: How many scenes are there in Act 4? **3** a short piece of entertainment that is usually part of a show or circus: Ladies and gentlemen, please welcome our next act, the Roncalli brothers. **4** often **Act** a decision made by Congress or by the state legislature: an act of Congress **5** (informal) a piece of behavior that hides your true feelings: She seems very happy, but she's just putting on an act.

IDM get your act together (informal) to get organized so that you can do sth

in the act (of doing sth) while doing sth, especially sth wrong. She caught him in the act of looking through her papers.

ACT /ˌeɪ si ˈti/ abbr. American College Test; an exam that some high school students take before they go to college: to take the ACT ☞ Look at **SAT**.

act·ing¹ /ˈæktɪŋ/ noun [U] the art or profession of performing in plays or movies

act·ing² /ˈæktɪŋ/ adj. doing the job mentioned for a short time: Mr. Wong will be the acting principal while Mrs. Richards is away.

☆ **ac·tion** /ˈækʃn/ noun **1** [U] doing things, often for a particular purpose: Now is the time for action. ○ I didn't like the movie – there wasn't much action in it. **2** [C] something that you do: The doctor's quick action saved the child's life. They should be judged by their actions, not by what they say. ☞ Look at the note at **act²**. **3** [sing.] the most important events that are happening, especially in a story or play: The action is set in Germany. ○ This is where the action is on a Saturday night. **4** [sing.] the effect that one substance has on another: the harmful action of acid rain on buildings **5** [U] the fighting that takes place in battle: Their

ə	y	w	t̬	eɪ	aɪ	ɔɪ	aʊ	oʊ
about	yes	woman	butter	say	five	boy	now	go

A

son was killed in action. **6** [C,U] the process of settling an argument in a court of law: *They decided not to take legal action against the newspaper.*

IDM course of action ⇨ COURSE

in action in operation; while working or doing sth: *We will have a chance to see their new team in action next week.*

into action into operation: *We'll put the plan into action immediately.*

take action to do sth, in order to solve a problem, etc.: *The government must take action to reduce unemployment.*

ac·ti·vate /ˈæktəveɪt/ *verb* [T] to make sth start working: *A slight movement can activate the car alarm.*

☆ **ac·tive** /ˈæktɪv/ *adj.* **1** able and willing to do things; energetic: *My grandfather is very active for his age.* ○ *Students should take an active part in college life.* ○ *He was on active duty for five years during the war* (= he served in the armed forces). **2** that produces an effect; that is in operation: *What is the active ingredient in this medicine?* ○ *an active volcano* (= one that can still erupt) **3** (used about the form of a verb or a sentence when the subject of the sentence performs the action of the verb): *In the sentence "The dog bit him," the verb is active.* ☞ You can also say: "The verb is in the active." Look at **passive.**

☆ **ac·tiv·i·ty** /ækˈtɪvəti/ *noun* (*pl.* **ac·tiv·i·ties**) **1** [U] a situation in which there is a lot of action or movement: *The house was full of activity on the morning of the wedding.* ☞ The opposite is **inactivity. 2** [C] something that you do, usually regularly and for enjoyment: *outdoor activities.* ☞ Look at the note at **act².**

☆ **ac·tor** /ˈæktər/ *noun* [C] a person whose job is to act in a play, movie or television program

☆ **ac·tress** /ˈæktrəs/ *noun* [C] a woman whose job is to act in a play, movie or television program

☆ **ac·tu·al** /ˈæktʃuəl/ *adj.* real; that happened, etc. in fact: *The actual damage to the car was not as great as we had feared.* ○ *Our goal for last year was $3 million, but our actual sales were much higher.*

☆ **ac·tu·al·ly** /ˈæktʃuəli; ˈækʃəli/ *adv.* **1** really; in fact: *You don't actually believe her, do you?* ○ *I can't believe that I'm actually going to England!* **2** although it may seem strange or surprising: *He actually expected me to cook his dinner for him!* ○ *Well, actually, I know a lot about computers – my dad's a programmer.*

☞ In English **actual** and **actually** do **not** mean "(existing) at the present time." We use **currently** or **right now** instead: *He's currently working for the government.* ○ *I'm studying for my final exams right now.*

ac·u·punc·ture /ˈækyəˌpʌŋktʃər/ *noun* [U] a

way of treating an illness or stopping pain by putting thin needles into parts of the body

a·cute /əˈkyut/ *adj.* **1** severe; very great: *an acute shortage of food* ○ *acute pain* **2** (used about an illness) reaching a dangerous stage quickly: *acute appendicitis* ☞ The opposite is **chronic. 3** (used about feelings or the senses) very strong: *Dogs have an acute sense of smell.* **4** showing that you are able to understand things quickly and clearly: *The report contains some acute observations on the situation.* —**a·cute·ly** *adv.*: *They are acutely aware of the problem.*

a·cute ˈangle *noun* [C] an angle of less than 90°

A.D. *abbr.* anno domini; used in dates for showing the number of years after the time when Christians believe Jesus Christ was born: *A.D. 44*

ad /æd/ *noun* (*informal*) = ADVERTISEMENT: *I saw your ad in the local paper.*

ad·a·mant /ˈædəmənt/ *adj.* (*formal*) (used about a person) very sure; not willing to change your mind: *He was adamant that he had not made a mistake.* —**ad·a·mant·ly** *adv.*

☆ **a·dapt** /əˈdæpt/ *verb* **1** [I] **adapt (to sth)** to change your behavior because the situation you are in has changed: *He was quick to adapt to the new system.* **2** [T] to change a book, etc: so that it can be shown as a movie, etc.: *a play that has been adapted for television* **3** [T] **adapt sth (for sth)** to change sth so that you can use it in a different situation: *The van was adapted for use by a person in a wheelchair.*

a·dapt·a·ble /əˈdæptəbl/ *adj.* able and willing to change to suit new conditions: *You have to be adaptable if you want to live in a foreign country.*

ad·ap·ta·tion /ˌædəpˈteɪʃn; ˌædæp-/ *noun* **1** [C] a play or movie that is based on a novel, etc.: *a television adaptation of one of Shakespeare's plays* **2** [C,U] the state or process of adapting: *a period of adaptation*

a·dapt·er /əˈdæptər/ *noun* [C] **1** a device for connecting pieces of equipment that were not originally designed to be connected: *You'll need an adapter if you want to you want to use your hair dryer in Europe.* **2** a device that allows more than one plug to be connected to the electricity supply at one point (**socket**)

☆ **add** /æd/ *verb* **1** [I,T] **add (sth) (to sth)** to put sth together with sth else, so that you increase the size, number, value, etc.: *Next, add some milk to the mixture.* ○ *They invited a magician to the party, just to add to the fun.* **2** [T] to put numbers or amounts together so that you get a total: *If you add 3 and 3 together, you get 6.* ○ *Add $8 to the total, to cover postage and handling.* ☞ The opposite is **subtract.** We often use the word **plus** when we add two numbers: *2 plus 2 is 4.* **3** [T] to say sth more: *"Don't forget to write to us," she added.*

PHRV **add sth on (to sth)** to include: *10% will be added on to your bill as a penalty for late payment.*
add up to seem as if it could be true: *I'm sorry, but your story just doesn't add up.*
add (sth) up to find the total of several numbers: *The waiter hadn't added up the bill correctly.*
add up to sth to have as a total: *The bill should add up to about $40.*

ad·dict /ˈædɪkt/ *noun* [C] a person who cannot stop taking or doing sth harmful: *a drug addict*

ad·dict·ed /əˈdɪktəd/ *adj.* addicted (to sth) unable to stop taking or doing sth, especially sth harmful: *He is addicted to heroin.* ○ *He's addicted to football.*

ad·dic·tion /əˈdɪkʃn/ *noun* [C,U] the condition of being unable to stop taking or doing sth harmful: *the problem of teenage drug addiction*

ad·dic·tive /əˈdɪktɪv/ *adj.* (used about a drug, etc.) causing sb to be unable to stop taking or doing it

☆ **ad·di·tion** /əˈdɪʃn/ *noun* **1** [U] the process of adding sth, especially of adding up two or more numbers ☞ Look at **subtraction**. **2** [C] **addition (to sth)** a person or thing that is added to sth: *They have a new addition to the family* (= another child).
IDM **In addition (to sth)** as well as: *She speaks five foreign languages in addition to English.*

☆ **ad·di·tion·al** /əˈdɪʃənl/ *adj.* added; extra: *a small additional charge for the use of the swimming pool* —**ad·di·tion·al·ly** /əˈdɪʃənəli/ *adv.*

ad·di·tive /ˈædətɪv/ *noun* [C] a substance that is added in small amounts for a special purpose: *food additives* (= to add color or flavor)

☆ **ad·dress¹** /əˈdrɛs; ˈædrɛs/ *noun* [C] **1** the number of the house and the name of the street and town, where you live or work: *Let me give you my home/business address.* ○ *She no longer lives at this address.* ○ *Please inform the office of any change of address.* ○ *an address book* (= a small book that you keep the addresses of people you know in) ○ *an e-mail address* (= a combination of letters, numbers and symbols that sb can use to send you messages by computer) **2** a formal speech that is given to an audience ☞ Look also at **public address system.**

ad·dress² /əˈdrɛs; ˈædrɛs/ *verb* [T] **1 address sth (to sb/sth)** to write (on a letter, etc.) the name and address of the person you are sending it to: *The package was returned because it had been wrongly addressed.* **2** to make an important or formal speech to a crowd or audience: *The President will address the nation tonight.* **3** to consider sth (especially a problem) and try to deal with it: *We will address the isssue at the next meeting.* **4** to talk or write to sb using a particular name or title: *She prefers to be addressed as "Ms."* **5 address**

sth to sb *(formal)* make a remark, etc. to sb: *He addressed his criticisms mainly to the new members.*

a·dept /əˈdɛpt/ *adj.* **adept (at sth)** very good or skillful at sth

☆ **ad·e·quate** /ˈædɪkwət/ *adj.* **1** enough for what you need: *The food they eat is barely adequate to keep them alive.* **2** good enough; acceptable: *Your work is adequate, but I'm sure you could do better.* ☞ The opposite is **inadequate**. —**ad·e·qua·cy** /ˈædɪkwəsi/ *noun* [U] —**ad·e·quate·ly** *adv.*: *The work was done adequately but not well.* ○ *The mystery has never been adequately explained.*

ad·here /ədˈhɪr/ *verb* [I] *(formal)* **1 adhere (to sth)** to stick firmly: *Make sure that the paper adheres firmly to the wall.* **2 adhere to sth** to continue to support an idea, etc.; to follow a rule: *This rule has never been strictly adhered to.* —**ad·her·ence** /ədˈhɪrəns/ *noun* [U]: *His adherence to his principles cost him his job.*

ad·he·sive¹ /ədˈhisɪv; -zɪv/ *noun* [C] a substance that makes things stick together: *a fast-drying adhesive*

ad·he·sive² /ədˈhisɪv; -zɪv/ *adj.* that can stick, or can cause two things to stick together: *He sealed the package with adhesive tape.*

ad·ja·cent /əˈdʒeɪsnt/ *adj.* situated next to or close to sth: *There was a fire in the adjacent building.* ○ *She works in the office adjacent to mine.*

ad·jec·ti·val /ˌædʒɛkˈtaɪvl/ *adj.* that contains or is used like an adjective: *an adjectival phrase*

☆ **ad·jec·tive** /ˈædʒɪktɪv/ *noun* [C] *(grammar)* a word used with a noun that tells you more about it: *The adjective "hot" can come either before or after a noun, i.e. you can say "that is hot soup" or "that soup is hot."*

ad·join·ing /əˈdʒɔmɪŋ/ *adj.* joining sth or situated next or nearest to sth: *A scream came from the adjoining room.*

ad·journ /əˈdʒərn/ *verb* [I,T] *(formal)* to stop sth (a meeting, a trial, etc.) for a short period of time and start it again later: *This court will adjourn until tomorrow.* ○ *The meeting was adjourned until the following week.* —**ad·journ·ment** *noun* [C,U]: *The lawyers asked for an adjournment.*

ad·ju·di·cate /əˈdʒudəkeɪt/ *verb* [I,T] *(formal)* to act as an official judge in a competition or to decide who is right when two sides disagree about sth

ad·ju·di·ca·tor /əˈdʒudəˌkeɪtər/ *noun* [C] *(formal)* a person who acts as a judge, especially in a competition

☆ **ad·just** /əˈdʒʌst/ *verb* **1** [T] to change sth slightly, especially because it is not in the right position: *The brakes on the car need to be adjusted.* ○ *The figures have been adjusted to take inflation into account.* **2** [I] **adjust (to sth)**

tʃ	dʒ	v	θ	ð	s	z	ʃ
chin	June	van	thin	then	so	zoo	she

to get used to new conditions or a new situation: *She found it hard to adjust to working at night.* —**ad·just·ment** *noun* [C,U]

ad·just·a·ble /əˈdʒʌstəbl/ *adj.* that can be adjusted: *an adjustable mirror*

ad lib /ˌæd ˈlɪb/ *adj., adv.* done or spoken without preparation: *She had to speak ad lib because she couldn't find her notes.* —**ad-lib** *verb* [I,T] (**ad·lib·bing; ad-libbed**)

ad·min·is·ter /ədˈmɪnəstər/ *verb* [T] **1** to control or manage sth: *The system is very complicated and difficult to administer.* **2** (*formal*) to give sb sth (especially medicine): *The doctor administered a pain-killing drug.*

ad·min·is·tra·tion /ədˌmɪnəˈstreɪʃn/ *noun* **1** [U] the control or management of sth (e.g. a system, an organization or a business): *The administration of a large project like this is very complicated.* **2** [sing.] the group of people who organize or control sth: *the hospital administration* **3** often **the Administration** [C] the government of a country, especially the United States: *the Kennedy Administration*

ad·min·is·tra·tive /ədˈmɪnəstreɪtɪv/ *adj.* connected with the organization and management of a country or business, etc.: *Washington is the country's administrative center.* ○ *an administrative assistant*

ad·min·is·tra·tor /ədˈmɪnəstreɪtər/ *noun* [C] a person whose job is to organize or manage a system, a business, etc.

ad·mi·ra·ble /ˈædmərəbl/ *adj.* deserving admiration or praise: *an admirable example of good planning* —**ad·mi·ra·bly** /ˈædmərəbli/ *adv.*: *She dealt with the problem admirably.*

ad·mi·ral /ˈædmərəl/ *noun* [C] an officer of very high rank in the navy who commands a group (**fleet**) of ships

☆ **ad·mi·ra·tion** /ˌædməˈreɪʃn/ *noun* [U] a feeling that you have when you like and respect sb/sth very much: *I have great admiration for his work.*

☆ **ad·mire** /ədˈmaɪər/ *verb* [T] to respect or like sb/sth very much; to look at sb/sth with pleasure: *Everyone admired the way he dealt with the problem.* ○ *I've always admired her.* ○ *We walked around the house, admiring the furniture and decorations.* —**ad·mir·er** *noun* [C]

ad·mir·ing /ədˈmaɪrɪŋ/ *adj.* feeling or expressing admiration: *an admiring look* —**ad·mir·ing·ly** *adv.*

☆ **ad·mis·sion** /ədˈmɪʃn/ *noun* **1** [C,U] permission to enter a school, club, public place, etc.: *All those who were not wearing a necktie were refused admission to the club.* ○ *Admissions to U.S. universities have increased by 15% this year.* **2** [U] the amount of money that you pay to enter a place: *The museum charges $3 admission.* **3** [C] a statement that something, usually bad, is true: *I viewed her silence as an admission of guilt.*

☆ **ad·mit** /ədˈmɪt/ *verb* (**ad·mit·ting; ad·mit·ted**) **1** [I,T] **admit to sth/doing sth; admit (that ...)** to agree, often without wanting to, that sth is true: *He refused to admit to the theft.* ○ *You should admit your mistake.* ○ *I have to admit that I was wrong.* ○ *"I was wrong," he admitted.* ○ *She admitted having broken the lamp.* ☞ The opposite is **deny**. **2** [T] **admit sb/sth (into/to sth)** to allow sb/sth to enter; to take sb into a place: *a ticket that admits a member plus one guest to the gallery* ○ *He was admitted to the hospital.*

ad·mit·tance /ədˈmɪtns/ *noun* [U] being allowed to enter a place (especially a private one); the right to enter: *The journalist tried to gain admittance to the senator's office.*

ad·mit·ted·ly /ədˈmɪtədli/ *adv.* it must be admitted (that): *The work is very interesting. Admittedly, I do get awfully tired.*

ad·o·les·cence /ˌædəˈlɛsns/ *noun* [U] the period of a person's life between being a child and becoming an adult, i.e. between the ages of about 13 and 17

ad·o·les·cent /ˌædəˈlɛsnt/ *noun* [C] a young person who is no longer a child and not yet an adult: *the problems of adolescents* ○ *an adolescent daughter* ☞ Look at **teenager**.

☆ **a·dopt** /əˈdɑpt/ *verb* **1** [I,T] to take a child into your family and treat him/her as your own child by law **2** [T] to take and use sth: *She decided not to adopt her husband's name when she got married.* ○ *All his suggestions have been adopted.* —**a·dopt·ed** *adj.*: *an adopted child* —**a·dop·tion** *noun* [C,U]: *the adoption of a new foreign trade policy* [U]: *How many teen mothers put their babies up for adoption* (= let other people adopt their babies)? [C]: *The number of adoptions has risen in the past year* (= the number of children being adopted).

a·dor·a·ble /əˈdɔrəbl/ *adj.* (used for expressing affection for a child or animal) very attractive

a·dore /əˈdɔr/ *verb* [T] **1** to love and admire sb/sth very much: *Kim adores her older sister.* **2** to like sth very much: *I adore strawberries.* —**a·do·ra·tion** /ˌædəˈreɪʃn/ *noun* [U]

a·dorn /əˈdɔrn/ *verb* [T] to add sth in order to make a thing or person more attractive or beautiful: *a building adorned with flags*

a·dren·a·line /əˈdrɛnl·m/ *noun* [U] a substance that your body produces when you are very angry, frightened or excited and that makes your heart beat faster

a·drift /əˈdrɪft/ *adj.* (not before a noun) not tied to anything or controlled by anybody (used about a boat)

☆ **a·dult** /əˈdʌlt; ˈædʌlt/ *noun* [C] a person or animal that is fully grown: *This movie is suitable for both adults and children.* —**a·dult** *adj.*: *She was born here but has spent her adult life in Chile.*

a·dul·ter·y /əˈdʌltəri/ *noun* [U] sexual rela-

i	ɪ	ɛ	æ	ɑ	ɔ	ʌ	ʊ	u
see	sit	ten	cat	hot	saw	cup	put	too

tions between a person who is married and sb who is not that person's wife/husband: *to commit adultery*

☆ **ad·vance¹** /əd'væns/ *verb* **1** [I] to move forward: *The army advanced toward the city.* ☞ Look at **retreat**. **2** [I,T] to make progress or help sth make progress: *Our research has not advanced much recently.*

☆ **ad·vance²** /əd'væns/ *noun* **1** [C, usually sing.] forward movement: *the army's advance toward the border* **2** [C,U] progress in sth: *advances in computer technology* **3** [C] an amount of money that is paid to sb before the time when it is usually paid

IDM **in advance (of sth)** before a particular time or event: *You should buy your tickets for the concert well in advance.*

☆ **ad·vanced** /əd'vænst/ *adj.* **1** of a high level: *an advanced English class* **2** highly developed: *a country that is not very advanced industrially*

☆ **ad·van·tage** /əd'væntɪdʒ/ *noun* **1** [C] **an advantage (over sb)** something that may help you to do better than other people: *Her secretarial experience gave her an advantage over the other people applying for the job.* ○ *Our team had the advantage of playing on our home field.* **2** [C,U] something that helps you or that will bring you a good result: *the advantages and disadvantages of a plan* ○ *There's no advantage in driving into Boston. There won't be any place to park.* ☞ The opposite is **disadvantage**.

IDM **take advantage of sth 1** to make good or full use of sth: *Take advantage of these discount prices while they last.* **2** to make unfair use of sb or of sb's kindness, etc. in order to get what you want: *You shouldn't let him take advantage of you like this.*

ad·van·ta·geous /ˌædvæn'teɪdʒəs; -vən-/ *adj.* that will help you or bring you a good result

ad·vent /'ædvɛnt/ *noun* [sing.] **1** (*formal*) the arrival or coming of sb/sth: *Before the advent of the computer, a project like this would have been impossible.* **2** (*also* **Advent**) (in the Christian year) the four weeks before Christmas

☆ **ad·ven·ture** /əd'vɛntʃər/ *noun* [C,U] an experience or event that is very unusual, exciting or dangerous: *She left home to travel, hoping for excitement and adventure.* ○ *an adventure story*

ad·ven·tur·ous /əd'vɛntʃərəs/ *adj.* **1** (used about a person) liking to try new things or have adventures **2** involving adventure: *For a more adventurous vacation, try mountain climbing.*

☆ **ad·verb** /'ædvərb/ *noun* [C] a word that adds information to a verb, adjective, phrase or another adverb: *In the sentence "Please speak slowly," "slowly" is an adverb.* ○ *"Happily," "well," "always," "very" and "too" are all adverbs.*

ad·ver·bi·al /əd'vərbiəl/ *adj.* used like an ad-

verb: *an adverbial phrase* (e.g. "in the afternoon")

ad·ver·sar·y /'ædvərˌsɛri/ *noun* [C] (*pl.* **ad·ver·sar·ies**) (*formal*) an enemy, or an opponent in a competition

ad·verse /əd'vərs; 'ædvərs/ *adj.* (*formal*) making sth difficult for sb; not favorable: *Our flight was canceled because of adverse weather conditions.* —**ad·verse·ly** *adv.*

ad·ver·si·ty /əd'vərsəti; æd-/ *noun* [C,U] (*pl.* **ad·ver·si·ties**) (*formal*) difficulties or problems: *to show strength in the face of adversity*

☆ **ad·ver·tise** /'ædvərtaɪz/ *verb* **1** [I,T] to put information in a newspaper, on television, on a poster, etc. in order to persuade people to buy sth, apply for a job, etc.: *a billboard advertising a new brand of soda* ○ *It's very expensive to advertise on television.* **2** [I] **advertise for sb/sth** to say publicly in a newspaper, on a sign, etc. that you need sb to do a particular job, want to buy sth, etc.: *The office is advertising for a part-time assistant.* —**ad·ver·tis·ing** *noun* [U]: *The magazine gets a lot of money from advertising.* ○ *an advertising campaign*

☆ **ad·ver·tise·ment** /ˌædvər'taɪzmənt/ *noun* [C](also *informal* **ad**) a piece of information in a newspaper, on a poster, etc. that tries to persuade people to buy sth, apply for a job, etc.: *to put an ad in the paper* ☞ An advertisement on TV or on the radio is called a **commercial**.

☆ **ad·vice** /əd'vaɪs/ *noun* [U] an opinion that you give sb about what he/she should do or how he/she should behave: *She took her doctor's advice and quit smoking.* ○ *You should get some legal advice* (= ask a lawyer to tell you what to do). ○ *Let me give you some advice…*

☞ **Advice** is an uncountable noun, so we cannot say "an advice" or "some advices." We can say: *a piece of advice* and: *a lot of advice.*

ad·vis·a·ble /əd'vaɪzəbl/ *adj.* (*formal*) that sb would recommend that you do; sensible: *It is advisable to reserve a seat.*

☆ **ad·vise** /əd'vaɪz/ *verb* **1** [I,T] **advise (sb) (to do sth); advise (sb) (against sth/against doing sth)** to tell sb what you think he/she should do: *I would strongly advise you to take the job.* ○ *The newspaper article advised against buying a house in that area.* ○ *He did what the doctor advised.* ○ *She advises the President on economic affairs.* **2** [T] (*formal*) to inform sb: *Passengers are advised that flight 365 to Dallas is now ready for boarding.*

☆ **ad·vis·er** (*also* **advisor**) /əd'vaɪzər/ *noun* [C] a person who gives advice to a student, company, government, etc.: *an adviser on economic affairs* ○ *My advisor says I need to take another math class in order to graduate.*

ad·vi·so·ry¹ /əd'vaɪzəri/ *adj.* giving advice

A

only; not having the power to make decisions: *an advisory committee*

ad·vi·so·ry[2] /ədˈvaɪzəri/ *noun* [C] (*pl.* **ad·vi·so·ries**) a report or warning that gives information about a dangerous situation: *a weather advisory*

ad·vo·cate[1] /ˈædvəkeɪt/ *verb* [T] (*formal*) to recommend or say that you support a particular plan or action: *The senator advocated a reform of the tax system.*

ad·vo·cate[2] /ˈædvəkət/ *noun* [C] **advocate (of sth)** a person who supports a particular plan, action, or group of people: *an advocate of nuclear disarmament* ○ *civil rights advocates*

aer·i·al /ˈɛriəl/ *adj.* **1** from or in the air: *an aerial attack on the city* ○ *aerial warfare* **2** taken from an aircraft: *aerial photograph of the town*

aer·o·bics /əˈroʊbɪks/ *noun* [U] energetic physical exercises that increase the amount of oxygen in your blood. People often do aerobics to music: *to do aerobics* ○ *an aerobics class*

aer·o·dy·nam·ic /ˌɛroʊdaɪˈnæmɪk/ *adj.* having smooth, curved edges that help sth to move fast and use less fuel: *the car's sleek, aerodynamic shape*

aer·o·dy·nam·ics /ˌɛroʊdaɪˈnæmɪks/ *noun* [U] the scientific study of the way that things move through the air

aer·o·plane /ˈɛrəpleɪn/ *noun* [C] (*BrE*) = AIRPLANE

aer·o·sol /ˈɛrəsɔl/ *noun* [C] a liquid substance which is kept under pressure in a container. When you press a button the liquid comes out in a fine spray: *an aerosol deodorant*

aer·o·space /ˈɛroʊspeɪs/ *noun* [U] the science that deals with the earth's atmosphere and outer space and the technology used in building planes, spacecraft, etc.

aes·thet·ic (*also* **esthetic**) /ɛsˈθɛtɪk/ *adj.* involving people's sense of beauty: *The columns are there for purely aesthetic reasons* (= only to look beautiful). —**aes·thet·i·cal·ly** (*also* **esthetically**) /-kli/ *adv.*: *to be aesthetically pleasing*

a·far /əˈfɑr/ *adv.* (*formal*)
from afar from a long distance away: *The lights of the city were visible from afar.*

☆ **af·fair** /əˈfɛr/ *noun* **1** [C] an event or situation, often an unpleasant one: *The whole affair has been extremely depressing.* ○ *The family reunion was a three-day-long affair.* **2 affairs** [plural] important personal, business, national, etc. matters: *The organization should have control of its own financial affairs.* ○ *current affairs* (= the political and social events that are happening at the present time) **3** [sing.] something private that you do not want other people to know about: *What happened between us is my affair. I don't want to discuss it.* **4** [C] a sexual relationship between two people who

are not married to each other: *He's having an affair with his boss.*

IDM **state of affairs** ⇨ STATE[1]

☆ **af·fect** /əˈfɛkt/ *verb* [T] **1** to influence or cause sb/sth to change in a particular way: *Her personal problems seem to be affecting her work.* ○ *Loud music can affect your hearing.* ☞ Look at the note at **influence**. **2** to cause sb to feel very sad, angry, etc.: *The whole community was affected by the terrible tragedy.*

☞ Notice that **affect** is a verb and **effect** is a noun: *Smoking can affect your health.* ○ *Smoking can have a bad effect on your health.*

af·fect·ed /əˈfɛktəd/ *adj.* (used about a person or a person's behavior) not natural or sincere: *an affected laugh* —**af·fec·ta·tion** /ˌæfɛkˈteɪʃn/ *noun* [C,U]

☆ **af·fec·tion** /əˈfɛkʃn/ *noun* [U] **affection (for/ toward sb/sth)** a feeling of loving or liking sb/sth: *Mark felt great affection for his sister.*

af·fec·tion·ate /əˈfɛkʃənət/ *adj.* showing that you love or like sb very much: *a very affectionate child* —**af·fec·tion·ate·ly** *adv.*: *He looked at her affectionately.*

af·fil·i·ate /əˈfɪliət/ *noun* [C] a company, organization, etc. that is connected to a larger organization: *local affiliates of the major TV networks*

af·fil·i·at·ed /əˈfɪlieɪṭəd/ *adj.* **affiliated (with sth)** (used about an organization) connected with a larger organization: *the AFL-CIO and its affiliated unions*

af·fil·i·a·tion /əˌfɪliˈeɪʃn/ *noun* [C,U] a connection made by affiliating: *The group has affiliations with the Democratic Party.*

af·fin·i·ty /əˈfɪnəṭi/ *noun* [C,U] (*pl.* **af·fin·i·ties**) **1** **affinity (for/with sb/sth)** a strong feeling that you like and understand sb/sth, usually because you feel similar to him/her in some way: *Many Americans have a real affinity for Great Britain.* **2** **affinity (with sb/sth); affinity (between A and B)** a similar quality in two or more people or things: *His music has certain affinities with Brahms.*

af·firm /əˈfɜrm/ *verb* [T] (*formal*) **1** to say clearly that you hold a particular belief: *The people affirmed their country's right to independence.* **2** to say that sth is a fact: *She affirmed that he would resign.* —**af·fir·ma·tion** /ˌæfərˈmeɪʃn/ *noun* [C,U]

af·fir·ma·tive /əˈfɜrməṭɪv/ *adj.* (*formal*) meaning "yes": *an affirmative answer* ☞ We can also say "an answer in the affirmative." The opposite is **negative**.

af·firmative ˈaction *noun* [U] a policy or program that helps to give members of different races, people with disabilities, women, etc. a better chance of getting jobs, going to college, etc. than they had in the past: *the university's affirmative action policy*

af·flict /əˈflɪkt/ *verb* [T] (usually passive) (*for-*

ər	ɪr	ɛr	ɑr	ɔr	ʊr	ʒ	h	ŋ
bird	near	hair	car	north	tour	vision	hat	sing

mal) to cause sb/sth to suffer pain, sadness, etc.: *He had been afflicted with a serious illness since childhood.*

af·flic·tion /əˈflɪkʃn/ *noun* [C,U] a thing that causes suffering: *Poor sight and hearing are common afflictions of old age.*

af·flu·ent /ˈæfluənt/ *adj.* having a lot of money: *an affluent neighbourhood* —**af·flu·ence** *noun* [U] /ˈæfluəns/

☆ **af·ford** /əˈfɔrd/ *verb* [T] **1** (usually after *can, could* or *be able to*) to have enough money or time to be able to do sth: *We couldn't afford a TV in those days.* **2 can't/couldn't afford** to not be able to do sth or let sth happen because it would have a bad result for you: *We can't afford to lose this contract. The future of the company depends on it.* —**af·ford·a·ble** /əˈfɔrdəbl/ *adj.*: *the need for more affordable housing in cities*

af·front /əˈfrʌnt/ *noun* [C] something that you say or do that is insulting to another person or thing

a·field /əˈfild/ *adv.*

far afield ⇨ FAR²

a·float /əˈfloʊt/ *adj.* (not before a noun) **1** on the surface of the water; not sinking **2** (used about a business, an economy, etc.) having enough money to survive: *We will need to borrow ten million dollars to keep the company afloat.*

☆ **a·fraid** /əˈfreɪd/ *adj.* (not before a noun) **1 afraid (of sb/sth); afraid (of doing sth/to do sth)** having or showing fear; frightened: *Why are some people afraid of spiders?* ○ *Sue is afraid of going out after dark.* ○ *I was too afraid to answer the door.* **2 afraid (that...); afraid (of doing sth)** worried about sth: *We were afraid that you would be upset.* ○ *to be afraid of offending sb*

I'm afraid (that...) (used for saying politely that you are sorry to say sth): *I'm afraid I can't come on Sunday.*

☞ Compare **afraid** and **frightened**. You can only use **afraid** after a noun, but you can use **frightened** before or after a noun: *a frightened animal* ○ *The animal was afraid/frightened.*

a·fresh /əˈfrɛʃ/ *adv.* (*formal*) again, in a new way: *to start afresh*

☆ **African-A·merican** *noun* [C] an American citizen whose family was originally from Africa —**African-American** *adj.*

☞ Some Americans whose ancestors originally came from Africa do not like to be called **Black**. They prefer to be called **African-Americans**. **Afro-American** is a similar term, but it is considered old-fashioned nowadays.

☆ **af·ter¹** /ˈæftər/ *prep.* **1** later than sth: *Shelley called just after six o'clock.* ○ *the week, month,*

year, etc. after next ○ *After finishing my homework, I went out for a walk.* **2 ...after...** repeated many times or continuing for a long time: *day after day of hot weather* ○ *I've told the kids time after time not to do that.* **3** following or behind sb/sth: *Shut the door after you.* ○ *The dog ran after its owner.* **4** following in order: *C comes after B in the alphabet.* **5** because of sth: *After the way he behaved, I won't invite him here again.* **6** (used when telling the time) later than: *We left at a quarter after five.* **7** looking for or trying to catch or get sb/sth: *The police were after him.* ○ *The company is going after younger consumers.* **8** (used when sb/sth is given the name of another person or thing): *The street is called Washington Street, after the first President.*

after all 1 (used when sth happens that you did not expect to happen, or when you discover that sth that you thought was not true is, in fact, true): *So you decided to come after all!* (= I thought you weren't going to come) **2** (used for reminding sb of a certain fact): *She can't understand. After all, she's only two.*

☆ **af·ter²** /ˈæftər/ *conj.* at a time later than sth: *They arrived at the station after the train had left.* ○ *After we had finished our dinner, we sat outside on the patio.*

☆ **af·ter³** /ˈæftər/ *adv.* at a later time: *That was in 1986. Soon after, I heard that he had cancer.* ○ *They lived happily ever after* (= forever). ☞ It is more common to use **afterward** or **afterwards** at the end of a sentence: *We played tennis and then went to Angela's house afterward.*

af·ter·ef·fect /ˈæftərɪˌfɛkt/ *noun* [C] an unpleasant result of sth that comes some time after it has happened: *the aftereffects of a serious illness*

af·ter·math /ˈæftərmæθ/ *noun* [sing.] a situation that is the result of an important or unpleasant event: *the aftermath of a war*

☆ **af·ter·noon** /ˌæftərˈnun/ *noun* [C,U] the part of a day between noon and about six o'clock: *I'll see you tomorrow afternoon.* ○ *She arrived at four o'clock in the afternoon.* ○ *Tom works two afternoons a week.* ○ *Are you busy on Friday afternoon?* ○ *an afternoon snack* ○ *Where were you on the afternoon of February 26th?*

good afternoon (*formal*) (used when you see sb for the first time in the afternoon) ☞ Look at the note at **morning**.

af·ter·shave /ˈæftərʃeɪv/ *noun* [C,U] a liquid with a pleasant smell that men put on their faces after shaving

af·ter·shock /ˈæftərʃɑk/ *noun* [C] a sudden movement of the earth's surface which follows another, more violent movement like this (**an earthquake**): *a series of moderate aftershocks*

af·ter·thought /ˈæftərθɔt/ *noun* [C, usually sing.] something that you think of or add to

sth else at a later time: *He did the grocery shopping and then bought some flowers on the way home as an afterthought.*

☆ **af·ter·ward** /'æftərwərd/ (*also* **afterwards** /'æftərwərdz/*) adv.* at a later time: *I met her at a party and saw her again soon afterward.* ○ *Afterward, Nick said he hadn't enjoyed the movie.*

☆ **a·gain** /ə'gɛn/ *adv.* **1** once more; another time: *Could you say that again, please?* ○ *Don't ever do that again!* **2** in the place or condition that sb/sth was in before: *It's great to be home again.* ○ *I hope you'll soon feel well again.* **3** (used for expressing that sth you have just said may not happen or be true): *She might pass her test, but then again she might not.* **4** in addition: *"Is that enough?" "No, I'd like half again as much, please"* (= one-and-a-half times the original amount).

IDM again and again many times: *He said he was sorry again and again.*

(but) then again ⇨ THEN

(every) now and again/then ⇨ NOW[1]

yet again ⇨ YET[1]

☆ **a·gainst** /ə'gɛnst/ *prep.* **1** touching or leaning on sb/sth for support: *Put the broom over there against the wall.* **2** in the opposite direction from sth: *We had to pedal against the wind.* **3** opposing sb/sth in a game, competition, war, etc.: *We're playing against the Cardinals on Saturday.* **4** not agreeing with or supporting sb/sth: *Are you for or against the plan?* ○ *I felt like everybody was against me.* **5** what a law, rule, etc. says you must not do: *It's against the law to buy cigarettes before you are sixteen.* **6** to protect yourself from sb/sth: *Take these pills as a precaution against malaria.*

☆ **age**[1] /eɪdʒ/ *noun* **1** [C,U] the length of time that sb has lived or that sth has existed: *She learned to drive at the age of sixteen.* ○ *Children of all ages will enjoy this game.* ○ *He needs some friends his own age.* ○ (*formal*) *Most students here are between eighteen and twenty-two years of age.*

☞ When you want to ask about somebody's age, you usually say: *How old are you?* and the answer can be: *I'm sixteen* or: *I'm sixteen years old* but NOT: *I'm sixteen years* and NOT: *I have sixteen years.* Here are some examples of other ways of talking about age: *I'm almost seventeen.* ○ *a girl of sixteen* ○ *a sixteen-year-old girl*

2 [U] one of the periods of sb's life: *a problem that often develops in middle age* ○ *the 20-30 age group* (= the group of people who are between 20 and 30 years old) **3** [U] the state of being old: *a face lined with age* ☞ Look at **youth**. **4** [C] a particular period of history: *We are now living in the computer age.* ○ *the history of art through the ages*

IDM under age not old enough by law to do sth

☆ **age**[2] /eɪdʒ/ *verb* [I,T] (*pres. part.* **ag·ing**; *p.t., p.p.* **ag·ed** /eɪdʒd/) to become or look old; to cause sb to look old: *My father seems to have aged a lot recently.*

ag·ed /eɪdʒd/ *adj.* **1** (not before a noun) of a particular age (1): *The woman had three children, aged 3, 5 and 10.* **2 the aged** /'eɪdʒəd/ *noun* [plural] old people

☆ **a·gen·cy** /'eɪdʒənsi/ *noun* [C] (*pl.* **agencies**) **1** a business that provides a particular service: *an advertising agency* **2** a government department : *the Central Intelligence Agency*

a·gen·da /ə'dʒɛndə/ *noun* [C] a list of all the subjects that are to be discussed at a meeting: *What's the next item on the agenda?*

☆ **a·gent** /'eɪdʒənt/ *noun* [C] **1** a person whose job is to do business for a company or for another person: *Our company's agent in Rio will meet you at the airport.* ○ *Most actors and musicians have their own agents.* ○ *a travel agent* ○ *a real estate agent* **2** an officer in certain government departments: *an FBI agent* ○ *Customs agents seized a shipment of drugs at the airport.* **3** a person who tries to find out secret information especially about the government of another country: *an undercover agent* ☞ Look at **spy**.

ag·gra·vate /'ægrəveɪt/ *verb* [T] **1** to make sth worse or more serious: *The country's food problems were aggravated by the hot dry summer.* **2** (*informal*) to make sb angry or annoyed —**ag·gra·va·tion** /,ægrə'veɪʃn/ *noun* [C,U]

ag·gres·sion /ə'grɛʃn/ *noun* [U] **1** the act of starting a fight or war without reasonable cause: *This is an intolerable act of aggression against my country.* **2** angry feelings or behavior that make you want to attack other people: *People often react to this kind of situation with fear or aggression.*

☆ **ag·gres·sive** /ə'grɛsɪv/ *adj.* **1** ready or likely to fight or argue: *an aggressive dog* ○ *Some people get aggressive after drinking alcohol.* **2** using or showing force or pressure in order to succeed: *an aggressive salesman* —**ag·gres·sive·ly** *adv.*

ag·gres·sor /ə'grɛsər/ *noun* [C] a person or country that attacks sb/sth or starts fighting first

ag·ile /'ædʒl; -dʒaɪl/ *adj.* able to move quickly and easily —**a·gil·i·ty** /ə'dʒɪləti/ *noun* [U]

ag·i·tate /'ædʒəteɪt/ *verb* [I] **agitate (for/against sth)** to make other people feel very strongly about sth so that they want to do sth to help you achieve it: *to agitate for reform* —**ag·i·ta·tion** /,ædʒə'teɪʃn/ *noun* [U]

ag·i·tat·ed /'ædʒə,teɪtəd/ *adj.* worried or excited: *She became more and more agitated when her son did not appear.*

ag·nos·tic /æg'nɑstɪk; əg-/ *noun* [C] a person who believes that you cannot know whether or not God exists

☆ **a·go** /əˈgoʊ/ *adv.* in the past; back in time from now: *Patrick left ten minutes ago* (= if it is twelve o'clock now, he left at 11:50). ○ *That was a long time ago.* ○ *How long ago did this happen?*

☞ **Ago** is used with the simple past tense and not the present perfect tense: *I arrived in the United States three months ago.* Compare **ago** and **before**. **Ago** means "before now" and **before** means "before then" (i.e. before a particular time in the past): *Anne married Evan two years ago.* ○ *She had left her first husband six years before* (= six years before she married Evan).

ag·o·nize /ˈægənaɪz/ *verb* [I] to worry or think about sth for a long time: *to agonize over a difficult decision*

ag·o·nized /ˈægənaɪzd/ *adj.* showing extreme pain or worry: *an agonized cry*

ag·o·niz·ing /ˈægənaɪzɪŋ/ *adj.* causing extreme worry or pain: *an agonizing choice* ○ *an agonizing headache*

ag·o·ny /ˈægəni/ *noun* [C,U] (*pl.* **ag·o·nies**) great pain or suffering: *to scream in agony*

☆ **a·gree** /əˈgri/ *verb* **1** [I,T] **agree (with sb/sth)**; **agree (that…)** to have the same opinion as sb/sth: *"I think we should talk to the manager about this." "Yes, I agree."* ○ *I agree with Paul.* ○ *Do you agree that we should go by train?* ○ *No, I don't agree.* ☞ Look at **disagree**. **2** [I] **agree (to sth)** to say yes to sth: *I asked if I could go home early and she agreed.* ○ *Andy has agreed to loan me his car for the weekend.* ☞ Look at **refuse**[1]. **3** [I] **agree (to do sth)**; **agree (on sth)** to make an arrangement or agreement with sb: *They agreed to meet again the following day.* ○ *Can we agree on a price?* ○ *We agreed that Leah would contact us if she needed help.* **4** [I] **agree with sth** to think that sth is right: *I don't agree with experiments on animals.* **5** [I] to be the same as sth: *The two accounts of the accident do not agree.* ○ *In French the adjective must agree with the noun in number and gender.*

PHR V **agree with sb** to be pleasant for sb or good for sb's health: *No, thanks. Onions don't agree with me.*

a·gree·a·ble /əˈgriəbl/ *adj.* (*formal*) **1** pleasant; nice ☞ The opposite is **disagreeable**. **2** ready to agree: *Would you be agreeable to our suggestion?* **3** acceptable; that can be agreed on: *a proposal that is agreeable to both sides in a dispute*

☆ **a·gree·ment** /əˈgrimənt/ *noun* **1** [C] a contract or decision that two or more people have made together: *Please sign the rental agreement and return it to us.* ○ *The leaders reached an agreement after five days of talks.* **2** [U] the state of agreeing with sb/sth: *She nodded her head in agreement.* ☞ The opposite is **disagreement**. **3** [U] (*grammar*) the fact that two

or more words have the same form, e.g. if the subject of a verb is plural, the verb must also be plural: *subject-verb agreement*

☆ **ag·ri·cul·ture** /ˈægrəkʌltʃər/ *noun* [U] keeping animals and growing crops for food; farming: *the U.S. Department of Agriculture* —**ag·ri·cul·tur·al** /ˌægrəˈkʌltʃərəl/ *adj.*: *agricultural land*

ah /ɑ/ *interj.* (used for expressing surprise, pleasure, etc.): *Ah yes. I see it now.* ○ *Ah, what a beautiful day!*

a·ha /ɑˈhɑ/ *interj.* (used when you suddenly find or understand sth): *Aha! Now I understand.*

☆ **a·head** /əˈhɛd/ *adv., adj.* **ahead (of sb/sth)** **1** in front of sb/sth: *I could see the other car about half a mile ahead of us.* ○ *Look straight ahead and don't turn around!* **2** before or in advance of sb/sth: *Jane and Nicole arrived a few minutes ahead of us.* ○ *New York is three hours ahead of Los Angeles.* **3** into the future: *He's got a difficult time ahead of him.* ○ *We must think ahead and make a plan.* **4** doing better than another person or team in a game, competition, etc.: *The third goal put Toronto ahead.* **5** more advanced than sb/sth else: *The Japanese are way ahead of us in their research.*

aid[1] /eɪd/ *noun* **1** [U] help: *to walk with the aid of a cane* ○ *to go to sb's aid* (= to go and help sb) ☞ Look at **first aid**. **2** [C] a person or thing that helps you: *a hearing aid* **3** [U] money, food, etc. that is sent to a country or people in order to help them: *aid to developing countries* ○ *the Red Cross and other international aid agencies*

IDM **in aid of sb/sth** in order to raise money for sb/sth: *a concert in aid of refugee families*

aid[2] /eɪd/ *verb* [T] (*formal*) to help sb

IDM **aid and abet** to help sb to do sth that is against the law: *to be accused of aiding and abetting a robbery*

aide /eɪd/ *noun* [C] a person who is an assistant to sb important in the government, etc.: *the President's top aides*

AIDS /eɪdz/ *noun* [U] an illness which destroys the body's ability to fight infection: *an AIDS victim* ○ *Thousands of people have died of AIDS.* ☞ "AIDS" is short for **Acquired Immune Deficiency Syndrome**.

ail·ing /ˈeɪlɪŋ/ *adj.* not in good health; weak: (*figurative*) *an ailing economy*

ail·ment /ˈeɪlmənt/ *noun* [C] (*formal*) an illness (that is not very serious)

☆ **aim**[1] /eɪm/ *noun* **1** [C] something that you intend to do or achieve: *Our aim is to open offices in Knoxville and Memphis before the end of the year.* ○ *His only aim in life is to make money.* **2** [U] the act of pointing sth at sb/sth before trying to hit him/her/it with it: *The hunter took aim at a deer nearby.* ○ *Her aim was good and she hit the target.*

aim

☆ **aim²** /eɪm/ *verb* **1** [I] **aim to do sth; aim at/for sth** to intend to do or achieve sth: *We aim to leave after breakfast.* ○ *The company is aiming at a 25% increase in profit.* ○ *You should always aim for perfection in your work.* **2** [T] **aim sth at sb/sth** to direct sth at a particular person or group: *The advertising campaign is aimed at young people.* **3** [I,T] **aim (sth) (at sb/sth)** to point sth at sb/sth before trying to hit him/her/it with it: *She picked up the gun, aimed, and fired.*
IDM **be aimed at sth** to be intended to achieve sth: *The new laws are aimed at reducing pollution in cities.*

aim·less /'eɪmləs/ *adj.* having no purpose: *an aimless discussion* —**aim·less·ly** *adv.*

ain't /eɪnt/ (*informal*) *short for* AM NOT, IS NOT, ARE NOT, HAS NOT, HAVE NOT ☞ Ain't is not considered correct English.

☆ **air¹** /ɛr/ *noun* **1** [U] the mixture of gases that surrounds the earth and that people, animals and plants breathe: *the pure mountain air* ○ *The air was polluted by smoke from the factory.* **2** [U] the space around and above things: *to throw a ball high into the air* ○ *in the open air* (= outside) **3** [U] travel or transportation in an aircraft: *to travel by air* ○ *an air ticket* **4** [C] **an air (of sth)** the impression that sb gives or the impression you get of a place, event, etc.: *a confident air* ○ *There was a general air of confusion outside the President's office.* **5** [U] = AIR CONDITIONING: *a house with central air*
IDM **a breath of fresh air** ⇨ BREATH
in the air probably going to happen soon: *A feeling of change was in the air.*
in the open air ⇨ OPEN¹
on (the) air broadcasting on the radio or television: *This radio station is on the air 24 hours a day.*
vanish, etc. into thin air ⇨ THIN¹

air² /ɛr/ *verb* **1** [I,T] **air (sth) (out)** to put clothes, etc. in a warm place or outside in the fresh air to make sure they are completely dry; to be put in this place: *Put the sleeping bag on the clothesline to air.* **2** [I,T] **air (sth) (out)** to make a room, etc. fresh by letting air into it; to become fresh in this way: *Open the window to air the room out.* **3** [T] to tell people what you think about sth: *The discussion gave people a chance to air their views.* **4** [I,T] to broadcast sth or to be broadcast on television or on the radio: *The interview is scheduled to air Monday evening.* ○ *The next episode will be aired in two weeks.*

'air bag (*also* **air·bag**) *noun* [C] a bag in a car that suddenly fills with air during an accident in order to protect the driver or a passenger

'air base *noun* [C] a military center from which an air force operates

air·borne /'ɛrbɔrn/ *adj.* flying or floating in the air: *airborne missiles* ○ *airborne dust particles*

'air-con·di·tioned *adj.* having air conditioning: *air-conditioned offices*

☆ **'air con·di·tioner** *noun* [C] a piece of equipment that keeps the air in a room, building, etc. cool and dry

☆ **'air con·di·tioning** *noun* [U] the system that keeps the air in a room, building, etc. cool and dry: *Close the window – the air conditioning is on.*

☆ **air·craft** /'ɛrkræft/ *noun* [C] (*pl.* **air·craft**) any vehicle that can fly in the air, e.g. an airplane, a helicopter, etc.

'aircraft carrier *noun* [C] a ship that carries military aircraft and that has a long flat area where they can take off and land

air·fare /'ɛrfɛr/ *noun* [C,U] the amount of money that you pay to travel by plane

air·field /'ɛrfild/ *noun* [C] an area of land where airplanes can land or take off. An airfield is smaller than an airport

'air force *noun* [C] the part of a country's military organization that fights in the air ☞ Look at **army, Marine Corps** and **navy.**

air·less /'ɛrləs/ *adj.* not having enough fresh air: *The room was hot and airless.*

☆ **air·line** /'ɛrlaɪn/ *noun* [C] a company that provides regular flights for people or goods in airplanes: *an airline pilot*

air·lin·er /'ɛrlaɪnər/ *noun* [C] a large airplane that carries passengers

air·mail /'ɛrmeɪl/ *noun* [U] the system of sending letters, packages, etc. to other countries by airplane

☆ **air·plane** /'ɛrpleɪn/ (*also* **plane**) *noun* [C] a vehicle with wings and one or more engines that can fly through the air: *the noise of an airplane flying overhead* ○ *I went to to Denver by plane.*

☆ **air·port** /'ɛrpɔrt/ *noun* [C] a place where aircraft can land and take off and that has buildings for passengers to wait in: *Jill went to meet her friend at the airport.* ○ *Los Angeles International Airport*

'air raid *noun* [C] an attack by military airplanes

air·space /'ɛrspeɪs/ *noun* [U] the part of the sky that is above a country and that belongs to that country by law

air·tight /'ɛrtaɪt/ *adj.* that air cannot get into or out of: *Keep the cookies in an airtight container.*

air traffic con'troller *noun* [C] a person whose job is to organize routes for airplanes, and to tell pilots by radio when they can land and take off

air·y /'ɛri/ *adj.* (**air·i·er; air·i·est**) having a lot of fresh air: *a light and airy room*

aisle /aɪl/ *noun* [C] a passage between the rows of seats in a church, a theater, an airplane, etc.: *Would you like a window seat or an aisle seat?*

ər	ɪr	ɛr	ɑr	ɔr	ʊr	ʒ	h	ŋ
bird	near	hair	car	north	tour	vision	hat	sing

a·jar /əˈdʒɑr/ adj. (not before a noun) slightly open (used about a door)

a·kin /əˈkɪn/ adj. **akin to sth** similar to or like sth

☆ **a·larm¹** /əˈlɑrm/ noun **1** [C] a machine that warns you of danger, e.g. by ringing a loud bell: *a burglar alarm* ○ *a fire alarm* **2** [C] = ALARM CLOCK **3** [U] a sudden feeling of fear or worry: *There's no cause for alarm.*
IDM **a false alarm** ⇨ FALSE
raise/sound the alarm to warn people about sth dangerous: *Scientists have sounded the alarm about the effects of air pollution.*

a·larm² /əˈlɑrm/ verb [T] to make sb/sth feel suddenly frightened or worried: *The news of the escaped prisoner alarmed the local people.*

aˈlarm clock (*also* **alarm**) noun [C] a clock that you can set to make a noise at a particular time to wake you up: *My alarm clock goes off at seven o'clock.* ○ *She set the alarm for six-thirty.* ☞ picture at **clock**.

a·larmed /əˈlɑrmd/ adj. **alarmed (at/by sth)** frightened or worried: *Government officials are alarmed at the recent rise in unemployment.*

a·larm·ing /əˈlɑrmɪŋ/ adj. that makes you frightened or worried: *The population of the world is increasing at an alarming rate.* —a·larm·ing·ly adv.

a·las /əˈlæs/ interj. (formal) (used for expressing sadness about sth)

al·bi·no /ælˈbaɪnoʊ/ noun [C] (pl. **al·bi·nos**) a person or animal with very white skin, white hair and pink eyes

☆ **al·bum** /ˈælbəm/ noun [C] **1** = RECORD¹(2) ☞ Look at **compact disc** and **single**. **2** a book in which you can keep stamps, photographs, etc. that you have collected

☆ **al·co·hol** /ˈælkəhɔl; -hɑl/ noun [U] **1** the colorless liquid in drinks such as beer, whiskey and wine that can make you drunk **2** the drinks (e.g. beer, whiskey, wine) that contain alcohol

al·co·hol·ic¹ /ˌælkəˈhɔlɪk; -ˈhɑlɪk/ adj. containing alcohol: *alcoholic drinks* ☞ The opposite is **non-alcoholic**. Drinks without alcohol are also called **soft drinks**.

al·co·hol·ic² /ˌælkəˈhɔlɪk; -ˈhɑlɪk/ noun [C] a person who is dependent on alcohol and drinks a large amount of it every day ☞ A person who does not drink alcohol at all is a **teetotaler**.

al·co·hol·ism /ˈælkəhɔlɪzəm; -hɑl-/ noun [U] the medical condition that is caused by regularly drinking a large amount of alcohol

al·cove /ˈælkoʊv/ noun [C] a small area in a room where one part of the wall is farther back than the rest of the wall

al·der·man /ˈɔldərmən/ noun [C] (pl. **al·der·men**) a member of the city council in some U.S. cities

ale /eɪl/ noun [U] a type of beer

a·lert¹ /əˈlərt/ adj. **alert (to sth)** watching, listening, etc. for sth with full attention: *Security guards must be alert at all times.* ○ *to be alert to possible changes*

a·lert² /əˈlərt/ noun [C] a warning of possible danger: *a bomb alert*
IDM **on the alert (for sth)** ready or prepared for danger or an attack: *The public was warned to be on the alert for possible tornadoes.*

a·lert³ /əˈlərt/ verb [T] **alert sb (to sth)** to warn sb of danger or a problem

al·fal·fa /ælˈfælfə/ noun [U] a plant that is used for feeding farm animals. People sometimes eat the young plants (**sprouts**) as a vegetable, especially in salads

al·gae /ˈældʒi/ noun [plural, with sing. or pl. verb] very simple plants that grow mainly in water: *If you don't clean your swimming pool, algae will grow in it.*

al·ge·bra /ˈældʒəbrə/ noun [U] a type of mathematics in which letters and symbols are used to represent numbers

a·li·as¹ /ˈeɪliəs/ noun [C] a false name, e.g. one that is used by a criminal

a·li·as² /ˈeɪliəs/ adv. (used for giving sb's false name): *Mrs. Phillips, alias Maria Jones*

al·i·bi /ˈæləbaɪ/ noun [C] (pl. **al·i·bis**) a statement by sb that says you were in a different place at the time of a crime and so cannot be guilty of the crime: *He had a good alibi for the night of the robbery.*

a·li·en¹ /ˈeɪliən/ noun [C] **1** (formal) a person who comes from another country: *an illegal alien* **2** a creature that comes from another planet

a·li·en² /ˈeɪliən/ adj. **1** of another country; foreign: *an alien land* **2** very strange and completely different from your normal experience: *The idea of eating meat was alien to her.*

al·ien·ate /ˈeɪliəneɪt; ˈeɪliə-/ verb [T] **1** to make people feel that they cannot share your opinions anymore: *The President's new policies on welfare have alienated many of his supporters.* **2 alienate sb (from sb/sth)** to make sb feel that he/she does not belong somewhere or is not part of sth: *Many young people feel alienated from the rest of society.* —al·ien·a·tion /ˌeɪlyəˈneɪʃn; ˈeɪliə-/ noun [U]

a·light¹ /əˈlaɪt/ adj. on fire; burning: *The kerosene had been set alight* (= made to start burning) *by a cigarette.*
☞ **Alight** cannot be used before a noun, but you can use **burning** before a noun: *The whole building was alight.* ○ *a burning building.*

a·light² /əˈlaɪt/ verb [I] (formal) **alight (from sth)** to get off a bus, train, etc.

a·lign /əˈlaɪn/ verb [T] **1 align sth (with sth)** to arrange things in a straight line or so that they are parallel to sth else: *to align the wheels*

tʃ	dʒ	v	θ	ð	s	z	ʃ
chin	June	van	thin	then	so	zoo	she

of a car **2 align yourself with sb** to say that you support the opinions of a particular group, country, etc.: *Canada has aligned itself with the United States over this issue.* ☞ Look at **non-aligned**.

a·lign·ment /əˈlaɪnmənt/ *noun* **1** [U] arrangement in a straight line or parallel to sth else **2** [C,U] an agreement between political parties, countries, etc. to support the same thing: *the alignment of Japan with the West*

☆ **a·like¹** /əˈlaɪk/ *adj.* (not before a noun) like one another; the same: *The two children are very alike.*

☆ **a·like²** /əˈlaɪk/ *adv.* in the same way: *We try to treat women and men alike in this company.* ○ *The musical has been a success with adults and children alike.*

al·i·mo·ny /ˈæləmoʊni/ *noun* [U] money that you have to pay by law to your former wife or husband after a divorce

☆ **a·live** /əˈlaɪv/ *adj.* **1** not dead; living: *The young woman was still alive when the ambulance reached the hospital.*

☞ **Alive** can only be used after a noun, but you can use **living** before a noun: *Are her parents still alive?* ○ *Does she have any living relatives?*

2 full of life: *In the evening the town really comes alive.* **3** continuing to exist: *Many old traditions are very much alive in this area of New England.*

al·ka·li /ˈælkəlaɪ/ *noun* [C,U] any of the chemical substances which have a pH value of more than 7 ☞ Look at **acid** and **base¹**. —**al·ka·line** /ˈælkəlɪn; -laɪn/ *adj.*

☆ **all¹** /ɔl/ *det., pron.* **1** the whole of a thing: *All (of) the food is gone.* ○ *They ate all of it.* ○ *They ate it all.* ○ *This money is all yours.* ○ *All of it is yours.* **2** the whole of the period of time: *It rained all day.* ○ *He worked hard all his life.* **3** every one of a group: *All (of) my kids can swim.* ○ *My kids can all swim.* ○ *She's read all (of) these books.* ○ *She's read them all.* ☞ Look at **y'all**. **4** everything that; the only thing that: *I wrote down all I could remember.* ○ *All I've eaten today is a slice of toast.*

IDM **above all** ⇨ ABOVE¹
after all ⇨ AFTER¹
in all in total: *There were ten of us in all.*
(not) at all in any way: *I didn't enjoy it at all.*
on all fours with your hands and knees on the ground; crawling: *The kids went through the tunnel on all fours.*
you all ⇨ YOU

☆ **all²** /ɔl/ *adv.* **1** completely; very: *He has lived all alone since his wife died.* ○ *I didn't watch that program – I forgot all about it.* **2** (in sports) for each side: *The score was two all.*

IDM **all along** from the beginning: *I knew you were joking all along.*
all but 1 almost; very nearly: *With this delay,*

it'll be all but impossible to meet our deadline. **2** everybody or everything except sb/sth: *All but $500 of the stolen money has been found.*
all over; all over the place everywhere: *We looked all over for Monica's watch.*
all right 1 good or good enough: *Is everything all right?* **2** safe; not hurt; well: *The kids are all right. Don't worry.* ○ *Do you feel all right?* **3** (showing you agree): *"You go first." "Oh, all right."*

☞ Some people write this expression as **alright**, but this is considered incorrect.

all the better, harder, etc. better, harder, etc. than before: *It will be all the more difficult with two people missing.*
not all that... (*informal*) not very: *The movie wasn't all that good.*

Al·lah /ˈɑlə; ˈælə/ *noun* the Muslim name for God

all-A·mer·i·can *adj.* **1** having qualities that people think are typically American: *Todd is a real all-American boy: he's bright, works hard and is good at sports.* **2** having members who were chosen as the best in the United States in a particular sport, etc.: *the all-American girls' high school basketball team*

all-a·round *adj.* (only *before* a noun) **1** able to do many different things well: *an excellent all-around musician* **2** including many different things; general: *The college provides a good all-around education.*

al·lay /əˈleɪ/ *verb* [T] (*formal*) to make sth less strong: *to allay sb's fears*

the all clear *noun* [sing.] a signal telling you that danger is over

al·lege /əˈlɛdʒ/ *verb* [T] (*formal*) to say that sb has done sth wrong, but without proving that this is true: *The woman alleged that Williams had attacked her with a knife.* —**al·le·ga·tion** /ˌæləˈɡeɪʃn/ *noun* [C]: *to make allegations of police corruption* —**al·leged** /əˈlɛdʒd/ *adj.*: *the alleged murderer* (= people say this person is a murderer but nobody has proved that this is true) —**al·leg·ed·ly** /əˈlɛdʒədli/ *adv.*: *The former manager allegedly stole thousands of dollars from the company.*

al·le·giance /əˈlidʒəns/ *noun* [U] (*formal*) support for or loyalty toward a leader, government, belief, etc.: *to pledge your allegiance to the American flag*

al·ler·gic /əˈlɜrdʒɪk/ *adj.* **1 allergic (to sth)** having an allergy: *I can't drink cow's milk. I'm allergic to it.* **2** caused by an allergy: *an allergic reaction to house dust*

al·ler·gy /ˈælərdʒi/ *noun* [C] (*pl.* **al·ler·gies**) **an allergy (to sth)** a medical condition that makes you sick when you eat, touch or breathe sth that does not normally make other people sick: *an allergy to cats, shellfish, pollen, etc.*

al·le·vi·ate /əˈlivieɪt/ *verb* [T] to make sth less

strong or bad: *The doctor gave me a shot to alleviate the pain.* —**al·le·vi·a·tion** /əˌliviˈeɪʃn/ *noun* [U]

al·ley /ˈæli/ *noun* [C] a narrow passage between or behind buildings

al·li·ance /əˈlaɪəns/ *noun* [C] an agreement between people, groups, countries, etc. to work together and support each other: *the country's military alliance with France* ☞ Look at **ally**.

al·lied /ˈælaɪd; əˈlaɪd/ *adj.* **1** (used about organizations, countries, etc.) having an agreement to work together and support each other: *allied forces* **2 allied (to sth)** connected with; similar: *nursing and allied health professions*

al·li·ga·tor /ˈæləɡeɪtər/ *noun* [C] a large animal with a long body and sharp teeth that lives in the lakes and rivers of the southern United States and China. An alligator is similar to a crocodile.

al·lo·cate /ˈæləkeɪt/ *verb* [T] **allocate sth (to sb/sth); allocate sth (for sth)** to give sth to sb as his/her share or to decide to use sth for a particular purpose: *Federal funding is allocated to each state.* ○ *We need to allocate some extra time for the final stage of the project.*

al·lo·ca·tion /ˌæləˈkeɪʃn/ *noun* [C] giving sth for a particular purpose; the amount that is given: *the allocation of resources for cancer research*

al·lot /əˈlɑt/ *verb* [T] (**al·lot·ting; al·lot·ted**) **allot sth (to sb/sth)** to give sb money, a piece of work, etc. as his/her share or to decide to allow a certain amount of time for sth: *Different tasks were allotted to each member of the class.* ○ *We all finished the exam in the allotted time.*

ₗ**all ˈout** *adj., adv.* using all your strength, etc.: *We're going all out for the championship.* ○ *an all-out effort*

☆ **al·low** /əˈlaʊ/ *verb* [T] **1 allow sb/sth to do sth; allow sth** to give permission for sb/sth to do sth or for sth to happen: *Children under sixteen are not allowed to buy cigarettes.* ○ *Photography is not allowed inside the museum.*

☞ Compare **allow, permit** and **let**. Allow can be used in both formal and informal English. The passive form **be allowed to** is especially common. **Permit** is a formal word and is usually used only in written English. **Let** is an informal word, and very common in spoken English. You **allow sb to do sth** but **let sb do sth** (no "to"). Let cannot be used in the passive: *Visitors are not allowed/permitted to smoke in this area.* ○ *Smoking is not allowed/permitted.* ○ *I'm not allowed to smoke in my bedroom.* ○ *My dad won't let me smoke in my bedroom.*

2 to give permission for sb/sth to be or go somewhere: *I'm only allowed out on Friday and Saturday nights.* **3 allow sb sth** to let sb

have sth: *We're only allowed half an hour for our lunch break.* **4 allow sb/sth to do sth** to make it possible for sb/sth to do sth: *Working part-time would allow me to spend more time with my family.* **5 allow sth (for sb/sth)** to provide money, time, etc. for sb/sth: *You should allow about 30 minutes for each question on the test.*

PHRV **allow for sb/sth** to think about possible problems when you are planning sth and include extra time, money, etc. for them: *The trip should take about two hours, allowing for heavy traffic.*

al·low·ance /əˈlaʊəns/ *noun* [C] **1** an amount of sth that you are allowed: *Most flights have a 70 pound baggage allowance.* **2** an amount of money that you receive for a particular purpose: *Laura gets a weekly allowance of $5 from her parents.* ○ *a travel allowance*

IDM **make allowances for sb/sth** to think about possible problems when you are planning sth and include extra time, money, etc. for them: *The design of the new school should make allowances for future increases in the student population.*

ₗ**all-star** *adj.* (only *before* a noun) including many famous actors, players, etc.: *a movie with an all-star cast*

al·lude /əˈlud/ *verb* [I] **allude to sb/sth** (*formal*) to speak about sb/sth in an indirect way: *When he mentioned "certain problems," what was he alluding to?*

al·lu·sion /əˈluʒn/ *noun* [C,U] an act of speaking about sth indirectly: *The play is full of allusions to classical mythology.*

al·ly /ˈælaɪ; əˈlaɪ/ *noun* [C] (*pl.* **al·lies**) **1** a country that has an agreement to support another country, especially in a war: *France and its European allies* ☞ Look at **alliance**. **2** a person who helps and supports you, especially when other people are against you: *the President's political allies*

al·might·y /ɔlˈmaɪti/ *adj.* **1** having the power to do anything: *Almighty God* **2** (only *before* a noun) (*informal*) very great: *Suddenly we heard the most almighty crash.*

al·mond /ˈɑmənd/ *noun* [C] an oval nut that is often used in cooking: *almond cookies* ☞ picture at **nut**.

☆ **al·most** /ˈɔlmoʊst/ *adv.* not quite; very nearly: *By nine o'clock almost everybody had arrived.* ○ *Careful! You almost spilled my drink!* ○ *The show is almost over.*

a·lo·ha /əˈloʊhɑ/ *interj.* (used in Hawaii as a way of saying "hello" or "goodbye")

☆ **a·lone** /əˈloʊn/ *adj., adv.* **1** without any other person: *The old man lives alone.* ○ *Are you alone? Can I talk to you for a minute?* ○ *I don't like walking home alone after dark.*

☞ **Alone, lonely** and **lonesome** all mean that you are not with other people. **Lonely** and **lonesome** mean that you are unhappy

A

about this, but **alone** does not usually suggest either happiness or unhappiness. **Alone** cannot be used before a noun. You can also use **on your own** and **by yourself** to mean "alone." These expressions are more informal and very common in spoken English.

2 (after a noun or pronoun) only: *You alone can help us.* ○ *The food alone cost $40. The wine was extra.*
IDM **leave sb/sth alone** ⇨ LEAVE¹
let alone ⇨ LET
☆ **a·long¹** /ə'lɔŋ/ *prep.* **1** from one end to or toward the other end of sth: *I walked slowly along the beach.* **2** in a line that follows the side of sth long: *Wild flowers grew along both sides of the river.* **3** at a particular point on or beside sth long: *Our house is about halfway along Hope Street.*

☆ **a·long²** /ə'lɔŋ/ *adv.* **1** forward: *We moved along slowly with the crowd.* **2** with sb: *We're going out for lunch. Why don't you come along?*
IDM **all along** ⇨ ALL²
along with sb/sth together with sb/sth: *Along with hundreds of others, she lost her job when the factory closed.*

a·long·side /ə,lɔŋ'saɪd/ *adv., prep.* **1** next to or along the side of sth: *a field with a small creek running alongside* ○ *We parked alongside Ben's car.* **2** together with sb/sth: *the opportunity to work alongside experienced musicians*

a·loof /ə'luf/ *adj.* **1** not friendly or open to other people; distant **2** not involved in sth; apart: *The President can no longer remain aloof from the problem.*

☆ **a·loud** /ə'laʊd/ *adv.* in a normal speaking voice that other people can hear; not silently: *to read aloud from a book* ☞ Look at **out loud**.

☆ **al·pha·bet** /'ælfəbɛt/ *noun* [C] the set of letters that you use when you are writing a particular language, especially when they are arranged in a fixed order: *There are 26 letters in the English alphabet.*

al·pha·bet·i·cal /,ælfə'bɛtɪkl/ *adj.* arranged in the same order as the letters of the alphabet: *The poems are listed in alphabetical order.* —**al·pha·bet·i·cal·ly** /-kli/ *adv.*

☆ **al·read·y** /ɔl'rɛdi/ *adv.* **1** (used for talking about sth that has happened before now or before a particular time in the past, especially if it happened earlier than you expected): *"Would you like some lunch?" "No thanks, I've already eaten."* ○ *We got there at 6:30, but Martin had already left.* ○ *Sarah was already awake when I went into her room.* **2** (used in negative sentences and questions for expressing surprise) so early; as soon as this: *Have you finished already?* ○ *You can't be leaving already!*

al·right /ɔl'raɪt/ *adv.* (*informal*) = ALL RIGHT
☆ **al·so** /'ɔlsoʊ/ *adv.* (not with negative verbs) in addition; too: *Mark Wilson paints in his spare*

time. *He also speaks Chinese.* ○ *The food is wonderful, and also very cheap.*

☞ **Too** is less formal than **also** and is very common in spoken English. **Also** usually goes before a main verb or after "is," "are," "were," etc.: *She also enjoys reading.* ○ *He has also been to Australia.* ○ *She is also intelligent.* **As well** is more formal than **also**. **Too** and **as well** usually go at the end of a phrase or sentence: *We're flying to Brazil, and we hope to visit Argentina too/as well.* Do not confuse **also** with **even**: *Even (NOT also) in the middle of summer, the nights can be cold.*

IDM **not only ... but also** ⇨ ONLY²
al·tar /'ɔltər/ *noun* [C] the holy table in a church or temple
☆ **al·ter** /'ɔltər/ *verb* [I,T] to make sth different in some way, but without changing it completely; to become different: *They've altered the plans for the new building.* ○ *This does not alter the fact that the company is having serious financial difficulties.* ○ *This skirt is too big; I'll have to alter it* (= make it smaller by sewing it). ○ *The town seems to have altered very little in the last twenty years.*

al·ter·a·tion /,ɔltə'reɪʃn/ *noun* [C,U] a small change in sb/sth: *We've made a few alterations to the design of the brochure.* ○ *The airline will inform you of any alteration in the time of departure.*

al·ter·nate¹ /'ɔltərnət/ *adj.* **1** one of every two: *He works alternate weeks* (= he works the first week he doesn't work the second week, he works again the third week, etc.). **2** (used about two types of events, things, etc.) happening or following regularly one after the other: *There will be alternate periods of sun and showers tomorrow.* **3** that you can use, do, etc. instead of sth else: *an alternate entrance to a building* —**al·ter·nate·ly** *adv.*

al·ter·nate² /'ɔltərneɪt/ *verb* **1** [I] **alternate with sth; alternate between A and B** (used about two types of events, things, etc.) to happen or follow regularly one after the other: *It's exciting music. Quiet passages alternate with sudden bursts of sound.* ○ *She seemed to alternate between hating him and loving him.* **2** [T] **alternate A with B** to cause two types of events or things to happen or follow regularly one after the other: *He alternated periods of work with periods of rest.* —**al·ter·na·tion** /,ɔltər'neɪʃn/ *noun* [C,U]

☆ **al·ter·na·tive¹** /ɔl'tərnətɪv/ *adj.* **1** (only *before* a noun) that you can use, do, etc. instead of sth else: *an alternative site for a new building* **2** not traditional; not following or accepting the usual options, styles, etc.: *alternative music* ○ *alternative lifestyles*
—**al·ter·na·tive·ly** *adv.*: *You can pay in full now or, alternatively, in five monthly installments.*
al·ter·na·tive² /ɔl'tərnətɪv/ *noun* [C] one of

ər	ɪr	ɛr	ɑr	ɔr	ʊr	ʒ	h	ŋ
bird	near	hair	car	north	tour	vision	hat	sing

two things that you can choose between: *The senator suggested community service as an alternative to imprisonment.*

☞ **Alternative** is often used for talking about more than two things: *There are several alternatives available to us right now.*

☆ **al·though** /ɔlˈðoʊ/ *conj.* **1** (used for introducing a statement that makes the main statement in a sentence seem surprising): *Although she was tired, she stayed up to watch the late night movie on TV.* **2** (used for introducing a statement that modifies the main statement) and yet; but: *There will be heavy rain in many parts of the state tonight, although it is unlikely to reach the metro area until morning.*

☞ You can also use **though**, but it is less formal than **although**. **Even** can be used with **though** for emphasis, but not with **although**: *She didn't want to go to the party, although/though/even though she knew all her friends would be there.* **Though**, but not **although**, can be used at the end of a sentence: *She knew all her friends would be there. She didn't want to go, though.*

al·ti·tude /ˈæltətud/ *noun* **1** [sing.] the height of sth above sea level: *The plane climbed to an altitude of 30,000 feet.* **2** [usually pl.] a place that is high above sea level: *You need to carry oxygen when you are climbing at high altitudes.*

al·to /ˈæltoʊ/ *noun* [C] (*pl.* **al·tos**) the lowest normal singing voice for a woman, the highest for a man; a woman or man with this voice

al·to·geth·er /ˌɔltəˈɡɛðər/ *adv.* **1** completely: *That's an altogether different situation.* ◦ *At the age of 55, he stopped working altogether.* **2** including everything: *We've got about $65 altogether.* **3** when you consider everything; generally: *Altogether, I would call the project a success.* ☞ **Altogether** is not the same as **all together**. **All together** means "everything or everybody together": *Put your books all together on the table.* ◦ *Let's sing. All together now!*

a·lu·mi·num /əˈlumənəm/ (*symbol* **Al**) *noun* [U] a light silver-colored metal that is used for making cooking equipment, etc.: *aluminum foil*

a·lum·na /əˈlʌmnə/ *noun* [C] (*pl.* **a·lum·nae** /əˈlʌmni/) (*formal*) a woman former student of a school, college or university

a·lum·ni /əˈlʌmnaɪ/ *noun* [plural] former students of a school, college or university

a·lum·nus /əˈlʌmnəs/ *noun* [C] (*pl.* **a·lum·ni** /əˈlʌmnaɪ/) (*formal*) a male former student of a school, college or university

☆ **al·ways** /ˈɔlweɪz/ *adv.* **1** at all times; regularly: *Why is the bus always late when I'm in a hurry?* **2** all through the past until now: *I've always liked music.* **3** forever: *I will always remember this moment.* **4** (with continuous

tenses) again and again, usually in an annoying way: *She's always complaining about something.* **5** (used with "can" or "could" for suggesting sth that sb could do, especially if nothing else is possible): *If you don't have enough money, I could always loan you some.*

☞ **Always** does not usually go at the beginning of a sentence. It usually goes before the main verb or after "is," "are," "were," etc.: *He always wears those shoes.* ◦ *I have always wanted to visit Egypt.* ◦ *Tammy is always late.* However, **always** can go at the beginning of a sentence when you are telling somebody to do something: *Always stop and look before you cross the street.*

am ⇨ BE[1,2]

A.M. (*also* **a.m.**) /ˌeɪ ˈɛm/ *abbr.* before noon: *10 A.M.* (=10 o'clock in the morning)

a·mass /əˈmæs/ *verb* [T] to gather together a large quantity of sth: *We've amassed a lot of information on the subject.*

am·a·teur¹ /ˈæmətʃər/ *noun* [C] **1** a person who takes part in a sport or an activity for pleasure, not for money or as a job: *Only amateurs can take part in the tournament; no professionals will be allowed.* **2** (usually used when being critical) a person who does not have skill or experience when doing sth: *The repair work on this house was obviously done by a bunch of amateurs.*

am·a·teur² /ˈæmətʃər/ *adj.* **1** done, or doing sth, for pleasure (not for money or as a job): *an amateur photographer* **2** (*also* **amateurish**) done without skill or experience

a·maze /əˈmeɪz/ *verb* [T] to surprise sb very much; to seem incredible to sb: *Sometimes your behavior amazes me!* ◦ *It amazes me that anybody could be so stupid!* —**a·maze·ment** *noun* [U]: *He looked at me in amazement.* ◦ *To my amazement, I got an A on the test.*

a·mazed /əˈmeɪzd/ *adj.* extremely surprised; feeling that you cannot believe sth: *She was amazed to discover the truth about her husband.* ◦ *I was amazed by the change in his attitude.*

☆ **a·maz·ing** /əˈmeɪzɪŋ/ *adj.* causing you to be very surprised: *She has shown amazing courage.* ◦ *I have an amazing story to tell you.* —**a·maz·ing·ly** *adv.*: *It's an amazingly expensive country to visit.*

am·bas·sa·dor /æmˈbæsədər; əm-/ *noun* [C] a diplomat of high rank who represents his/her country in a foreign country: *the United States Ambassador to Britain*

☞ The ambassador lives and works in an **embassy**.

am·ber /ˈæmbər/ *noun* [U] **1** a hard clear yellow-brown substance used for making jewelry or ornaments **2** a yellow-brown color —**am·ber** *adj.*

tʃ	dʒ	v	θ	ð	s	z	ʃ
chin	June	van	thin	then	so	zoo	she

am·bi·gu·i·ty /ˌæmbəˈgyuəti/ noun [C,U] (pl. **am·bi·gu·i·ties**) the possibility of being understood in more than one way; sth that can be understood in more than one way

am·big·u·ous /æmˈbɪgyuəs/ adj. having more than one possible meaning: *That's an awfully ambiguous statement – what exactly do you mean?* —**am·big·u·ous·ly** adv.

☆ **am·bi·tion** /æmˈbɪʃn/ noun **1 ambition (to be/do sth)** [U] strong desire to be successful, to have power, etc.: *One problem with young people today is their lack of ambition.* **2** [C] something that you very much want to have or do: *It's always been her ambition to travel around the world.*

☆ **am·bi·tious** /æmˈbɪʃəs/ adj. **1 ambitious (to be/do sth)** having a strong desire to be successful, to have power, etc.: *I'm not particularly ambitious – I'm content with my life the way it is.* **2** difficult to achieve or do because it takes a lot of work or effort: *The company has announced ambitious plans for expansion.*

am·biv·a·lent /æmˈbɪvələnt/ adj. having or showing a mixture of feelings or opinions about sth or sb: *I've always felt somewhat ambivalent about having children.* —**am·biv·a·lence** noun [U]

☆ **am·bu·lance** /ˈæmbyələns/ noun [C] a special vehicle for taking sick or injured people to the hospital

am·bush /ˈæmbʊʃ/ noun [C] a surprise attack from a hidden position —**am·bush** verb [T]

a·men /eɪˈmɛn; ɑˈmɛn/ interj. (used at the end of a prayer by Christians and Jews) let this be so: *In the name of the Father, the Son and the Holy Ghost. Amen.*

a·me·na·ble /əˈminəbl; əˈmɛn-/ adj. willing to accept sth; willing to be guided: *I'm amenable to any suggestions you might have.*

a·mend /əˈmɛnd/ verb [T] to change sth slightly, often in order to make it better: *The law needs to be amended.*

a·mend·ment /əˈmɛndmənt/ noun **1** [C] a part that is added or a small change that is made to a piece of writing, especially to a law: *The First Amendment to the U.S. Constitution guarantees citizens the right to free speech.* **2** [U] an act of amending: *The bill was passed without amendment.*

a·mends /əˈmɛndz/ noun [plural] **make amends (for sth)** to do sth for sb, that shows that you are sorry for sth bad that you have done before: *I bought her a present to make amends for the horrible things I had said to her.*

a·men·i·ty /əˈmɛnəti/ noun [C] (pl. **a·men·i·ties**) something in a place that helps to make being there pleasant or easy: *The health club offers a sauna, beauty salon, cafeteria and many other amenities.*

☆ **A·mer·i·can¹** /əˈmɛrɪkən/ adj. from or connected with the United States: *Have you met*

Bob? He's American. ○ American history ☞ Look also at **Latin American**.

☆ **A·mer·i·can²** /əˈmɛrɪkən/ noun [C] a person who comes from the United States: *His wife is an American.* ☞ Look also at **African-American** and **Asian-American**.

A·merican Indian adj., noun [C] = NATIVE AMERICAN

a·mi·a·ble /ˈeɪmiəbl/ adj. friendly and pleasant —**a·mi·a·bly** adv.

am·i·ca·ble /ˈæmɪkəbl/ adj. made or done in a friendly way, without argument: *I'm sure we can find an amicable way of settling the dispute.* —**am·i·ca·bly** adv.

a·mid /əˈmɪd/ (also **a·midst** /əˈmɪdst/) prep. (formal) in the middle of; among: *Amid all the confusion, the thieves got away.*

a·miss /əˈmɪs/ adj., adv. (not before a noun) wrong; not as it should be: *When I walked into the room, I could sense that something was amiss.*

am·mu·ni·tion /ˌæmyəˈnɪʃn/ noun [U] **1** the supply of bullets, etc. that you need to fire from a weapon: *The troops surrendered because they had run out of ammunition.* **2** (figurative) facts or information that can be used against sb/sth

am·nes·ty /ˈæmnəsti/ noun [C] (pl. **am·nes·ties**) **1** a time when a government forgives crimes, especially political crimes **2** a time when people can admit that they have done sth illegal or wrong, without fear of punishment: *The library has announced an amnesty on overdue books.*

☆ **a·mong** /əˈmʌŋ/ (also **a·mongst** /əˈmʌŋst/) prep. **1** surrounded by; in the middle of: *I often feel nervous when I'm among strangers.* ○ *The modern skyscraper looks out of place among all the old buildings.* ○ *I found the missing letter among a heap of old newspapers.* ☞ picture at **between**. **2** in the group or number of: *She is among the town's wealthiest residents.* ○ *Among the city's attractions are its museums and art galleries.* **3** to each one (of a group): *On his death, his money will be divided among his children.* **4** inside (a group): *Discuss it among yourselves and let me know your decision.* ☞ Look at the note at **between**.

☆ **a·mount¹** /əˈmaʊnt/ noun [C] **1** the amount of sth is how much of it there is; quantity: *I spent a huge amount of time preparing for the exam.* ○ *I have a certain amount of sympathy for her.* **2** total or sum of money: *You are requested to pay the full amount within seven days.*

a·mount² /əˈmaʊnt/ verb [I] **amount to sth 1** to add up to; to total: *The cost of the repairs amounted to $5,000.* **2** to be the same as: *No matter whether I tell her today or tomorrow, it amounts to the same thing.*

amp /æmp/ noun [C] **1**(also formal **ampere** /ˈæmpɪr/) (symbol **A**) a unit for measuring

i	ɪ	ɛ	æ	ɑ	ɔ	ʌ	ʊ	u
see	sit	ten	cat	hot	saw	cup	put	too

electric current **2** (*informal*) = AMPLIFIER: *a guitar amp*

am·phet·a·mine /æmˈfɛtəmin/ *noun* [C,U] a type of drug that makes your heart beat faster and that makes you feel excited. Amphetamines are sometimes taken illegally.

am·ple /ˈæmpl/ *adj.* **1** enough or more than enough: *We have ample time to make a decision.* ○ *I'm not sure how much the trip will cost, but I should think $500 will be ample.* **2** large; having a great deal of space —**am·ply** /ˈæmpli/ *adv.*: *The report amply demonstrates whose fault it was.*

am·pli·fi·er /ˈæmpləˌfaɪər/(also *informal* **amp**) *noun* [C] a piece of electrical equipment for making sounds louder or signals stronger

am·pli·fy /ˈæmpləfaɪ/ *verb* [T] (*pres. part.* **am·pli·fy·ing**; *3rd pers. sing. pres.* **am·pli·fies**; *p.t., p.p.* **am·pli·fied**) **1** to increase the strength of a sound, using electrical equipment **2** to add details to sth in order to explain it more fully —**am·pli·fi·ca·tion** /ˌæmpləfəˈkeɪʃn/ *noun* [U]

am·pu·tate /ˈæmpyəteɪt/ *verb* [I,T] to cut off a person's arm or leg (or part of it) for medical reasons: *His leg was so badly injured that it had to be amputated.* —**am·pu·ta·tion** /ˌæmpyəˈteɪʃn/ *noun* [C,U]

☆ **a·muse** /əˈmyuz/ *verb* [T] **1** to make sb laugh or smile; to seem funny to sb: *His jokes always amused her.* **2** to make time pass pleasantly for sb; to stop sb from getting bored: *I did some crossword puzzles to amuse myself on the trip.* ○ *I brought a few toys to amuse the kids.*

a·mused /əˈmyuzd/ *adj.* if you are amused you think that sth is funny and it makes you want to laugh or smile: *You might think it's funny, but I'm not amused.* ○ *I was amused to hear his account of what happened.*

IDM **keep sb amused** to make sb pass the time pleasantly, without getting bored: *These magazines should keep you amused while you're waiting for me to finish in the kitchen.*

a·muse·ment /əˈmyuzmənt/ *noun* **1** [U] the feeling caused by sth that makes you laugh or smile, or by sth that entertains you and that stops you from being bored: *There was a look of amusement on his face.* ○ *Much to the students' amusement, the teacher fell off his chair.* **2** [C] a machine, game, etc. that you can play on for enjoyment

aˈmusement park *noun* [C] an open area with games for people to play and machines for them to ride on (**rides**): *The "Wild West Train" was my favorite ride at the amusement park.*

a·mus·ing /əˈmyuzɪŋ/ *adj.* causing you to laugh or smile: *an amusing story*

an ⇨ A²

an·aes·thet·ic = ANESTHETIC

an·aes·the·tize = ANESTHETIZE

an·a·gram /ˈænəgræm/ *noun* [C] a word or

phrase that is made by arranging the letters of another word or phrase in a different order: *"Worth" is an anagram of "throw."*

a·nal·o·gy /əˈnælədʒi/ *noun* [C] (*pl.* **a·nal·o·gies**) **an analogy (between sth and sth)** a comparison between two things that shows a way in which they are similar: *You could make an analogy between the human body and a car engine.*

IDM **by analogy** If you explain sth by analogy to sth else, you compare it to the other thing and show how it is similar.

☆ **a·nal·y·sis** /əˈnæləsɪs/ *noun* (*pl.* **a·nal·y·ses** /-siz/) **1** [C,U] the careful examination of the different parts or details of sth: *Some samples of the water were sent to a laboratory for analysis.* ○ *They carried out an analysis of the causes of the problem.* **2** [C] the result of such an examination: *Your analysis of the situation is different from mine.*

an·a·lyst /ˈænəlɪst/ *noun* [C] a person whose job is to analyze things as an expert: *a political analyst*

an·a·lyt·ic /ˌænəˈlɪtɪk/ (also **an·a·lyt·i·cal** /-kl/) *adj.* looking carefully at the different parts of sth in order to understand or explain it: *analytic techniques*

☆ **an·a·lyze** /ˈænəlaɪz/ *verb* [T] to look at or think about the different parts or details of sth carefully in order to understand or explain it: *The water samples are now being analyzed in a laboratory.* ○ *to analyze statistics* ○ *She analyzed the situation and then decided what to do.*

an·ar·chist /ˈænərkɪst/ *noun* [C] a person who believes that there should be no government or laws in a country, especially one who takes action to achieve this

an·ar·chy /ˈænərki/ *noun* [U] a situation in which people do not obey rules and laws; a situation in which there is no government in a country

a·nat·o·my /əˈnætəmi/ *noun* (*pl.* **a·nat·o·mies**) **1** [U] the scientific study of the structure of human or animal bodies **2** [C] the structure of a living thing: *the anatomy of the frog* —**an·a·tom·i·cal** /ˌænəˈtɑmɪkl/ *adj.*

an·ces·tor /ˈænsɛstər/ *noun* [C] a person in your family who lived a long time before you, from whom you are descended: *My ancestors settled in this country two hundred years ago.*

an·ces·try /ˈænsɛstri/ *noun* [C,U] (*pl.* **an·ces·tries**) all of a person's ancestors, when you think of them as a group: *He was of Irish ancestry.*

an·chor¹ /ˈæŋkər/ *noun* [C] **1** a heavy metal object at the end of a chain or rope that you drop into the water from a boat in order to keep the boat in one place **2** (*also* **an·chor·man**; **an·chor·wom·an**) (*pl.* **an·chor·men**; **an·chor·wom·en**) a person whose job is to read the news on TV and to introduce news reports from other people: *a network news anchor*

ə	y	w	t̬	eɪ	aɪ	ɔɪ	aʊ	oʊ
about	yes	woman	butter	say	five	boy	now	go

A

an·chor² /ˈæŋkər/ *verb* **1** [I,T] to drop an anchor ¹; to stop a boat from moving by using an anchor ¹: *We anchored the boat in the harbor and went ashore.* **2** [T] to fasten sth firmly so that it is held in place and cannot move: *They anchored the tent with strong ropes.* **3** [T] to read the news on TV and introduce news reports from other people: *She anchors the 11 o'clock news broadcast.*

☆ **an·cient** /ˈeɪnʃənt/ *adj.* **1** belonging to or connected with the distant past: *ancient civilizations* **2** having existed for a long time: *This ceremony is an ancient Native American tradition.* **3** (*informal*) very old: *I can't believe he's only 30 – he looks ancient!*

☆ **and** /ənd; ən; *also* n; *especially after* t; d; *strong form* ænd/ *conj.* **1** (used to connect words or parts of sentences) also; in addition to: *bread and butter* ∘ *one woman, two men and three children* ∘ *a boy and a girl* ∘ *an apple and a pear* ∘ *Do it slowly and carefully.* ∘ *We sang and danced all night.*

☞ When the two things are closely linked, you do not need to repeat the "a," etc.: *a knife and fork* ∘ *my mother and father*

2 (used when you are saying numbers) plus: *Twelve and six is eighteen.* ∘ *It cost me a hundred and sixty dollars.*

☞ When you are saying large numbers, *and* is often used after the word "hundred": *We say 2,264 as two thousand, two hundred (and) sixty-four.*

3 then; following this or that: *Come in and sit down.* **4** as a result of this or that; because of this or that: *It was a terrible shock and he was very upset.* ∘ *Say that again and I'll lose my temper.* **5** (used between repeated words to show that sth is increasing or continuing): *The situation is getting worse and worse.* ∘ *I shouted and shouted, but nobody answered.* **6** (used instead of "to" after certain verbs, e.g. "go," "come," "try"): *Go and answer the door for me, will you?* ∘ *I'll try and find out what's going on.* ∘ *Why don't you come and stay with us for the weekend?*

an·ec·dote /ˈænɪkdoʊt/ *noun* [C] a short interesting story about a real person or event

a·ne·mi·a /əˈnimiə/ *noun* [U] a medical condition in which there are not enough red cells in the blood —**a·ne·mic** /əˈnimɪk/ *adj.*

an·es·the·si·ol·o·gist /ˌænəsˌθiziˈɑlədʒɪst/ *noun* [C] a doctor who gives anesthetics to patients

an·es·thet·ic (*also* **anaesthetic**) /ˌænəsˈθɛtɪk/ *noun* [C,U] a substance that stops you from feeling pain, e.g. when a doctor is performing an operation on you: *You'll be under anesthetic during the operation.* ∘ *a local anesthetic* (= one that only affects part of the body and does not make you unconscious) ∘ *a general anesthetic* (= one that makes you unconscious)

a·nes·the·tize (*also* **anaesthetize**) /əˈnɛsθətaɪz/ *verb* [T] to give an anesthetic to sb

a·new /əˈnu/ *adv.* (*formal*) again; in a new or different way

an·gel /ˈeɪndʒl/ *noun* [C] **1** (in the Christian religion) a spirit that lives with God in Heaven. In pictures, angels are often dressed in white, with wings **2** a person who is very kind or easy to love: *Be an angel and wash these clothes for me, will you?* ∘ *The baby was a perfect little angel – she slept all afternoon.*

an·gel·ic /ænˈdʒɛlɪk/ *adj.* looking or acting like an angel —**an·gel·i·cal·ly** *adv.* /-kli/

☆ **an·ger¹** /ˈæŋgər/ *noun* [U] the strong feeling that you have when sth has happened or sb has done sth that you do not like: *He could not hide his anger at the news.* ∘ *She was shaking with anger.* ☞ The adjective is **angry**.

an·ger² /ˈæŋgər/ *verb* [T] to cause sb to become angry: *It angers me that such things can be allowed to happen.*

angles

a right angle an angle of 40°

☆ **an·gle¹** /ˈæŋgl/ *noun* [C] **1** the space between two lines or surfaces that meet, measured in degrees: *a right angle* (= an angle of 90°) ∘ *at an angle of 40°* ∘ *The three angles of a triangle add up to 180°.* **2** the direction from which you look at sth: *Viewed from this angle, the building looks bigger than it really is.* ∘ *If we look at the problem from another angle, it might be easier to solve it.*

IDM at an angle not straight: *This hat is meant to be worn at an angle.*

an·gle² /ˈæŋgl/ *verb* [I] to try and make sb give you sth, without asking for it directly: *She was angling for a free ticket to the game.*

an·gler /ˈæŋglər/ *noun* [C] (*formal*) a person who catches fish as a hobby

An·gli·can /ˈæŋglɪkən/ *noun* [C] a member of the official church of England, or of a related church in another English-speaking country

An·glo /ˈæŋgloʊ/ *noun* [C] (*pl.* **An·glos**) a white person whose family originally came from Europe, especially northern Europe: *relations between Hispanic and Anglo students*

Anglo- /ˈæŋgloʊ/ (in compounds) English or British; connected with England or Britain (and another country or countries): *Anglo-American relations*

☆ **an·gry** /ˈæŋgri/ *adj.* (**an·gri·er**; **an·gri·est**) **angry (with sb) (at/about sth)**; **angry (at sb) (about sth)** feeling or showing anger: *Calm*

ər	ɪr	ɛr	ɑr	ɔr	ʊr	ʒ	h	ŋ
bird	near	hair	car	north	tour	vision	hat	sing

down – there's no need to get angry. ○ My parents will be really angry if I get home late. ○ I'm angry at them for letting me down at the last minute. **—an·gri·ly** /-əli/ adv.

an·guish /'æŋgwɪʃ/ noun [U] great pain or suffering, especially of a mental kind: The newspaper reported on the mother's anguish at the death of her son. **—an·guished** adj.: There was an anguished expression in his eyes.

an·gu·lar /'æŋgyələr/ adj. with sharp points or corners: an angular face (= one where you can see the bones clearly)

☆ **an·i·mal** /'ænəml/ noun [C] **1** a living creature that is not a plant: the animal kingdom ○ Human beings are social animals. **2** a living creature of this kind, but not including humans: She thinks that zoos are cruel to animals. ○ They raise cows, chickens and other animals on their farm. **3** a living creature that is not a human, bird, fish, insect or reptile: He studied the animals and birds of southern Africa. ○ domestic animals such as cats and dogs

an·i·mat·ed /'ænəmeɪtəd/ adj. **1** lively and interesting: an animated discussion **2** (used about movies) using a technique by which drawings appear to move: an animated cartoon

an·i·ma·tion /,ænə'meɪʃn/ noun [U] **1** the state of being lively: She spoke with great animation on the subject. **2** the technique of making movies, videos and computer games with drawings that appear to move

☆ **an·kle** /'æŋkl/ noun [C] the part of the body where the foot joins the leg: I tripped and sprained my ankle ☞ picture on page A24.

an·nex¹ /ə'nɛks; 'ænɛks/ verb [T] to take possession and control of another country or region: Many people think that the dictator plans to annex the two neighboring countries. **—an·nex·a·tion** /,ænɪk'seɪʃn; ,ænɛk-/ noun [C,U]: the annexation of Austria by Nazi Germany

an·nex² /'ænɛks/ noun [C] a building that is joined to or near a larger one

an·ni·hi·late /ə'naɪəleɪt/ verb [T] to destroy or defeat sb/sth completely: The army was annihilated in the battle. **—an·ni·hi·la·tion** /ə,naɪə'leɪʃn/ noun [U]: Modern weapons have placed mankind in danger of annihilation.

an·ni·ver·sa·ry /,ænɪ'vərsəri/ noun [C] (pl. **an·ni·ver·sa·ries**) a day that is exactly a year or a number of years after a special or important event: the hundredth anniversary of the country's independence ○ a twenty-fifth wedding anniversary ☞ Look at birthday.

an·no·tat·ed /'ænəteɪtəd/ adj. (used about a book, etc.) with notes added to it that explain and give extra information about the contents: an annotated bibliography

☆ **an·nounce** /ə'naʊns/ verb [T] **1** to make sth known publicly, in an official way: We are pleased to announce the opening of our new

store. ○ The winners will be announced in next week's paper. **2** to say sth in a loud voice or in an aggressive way: She stormed into my office and announced that she was quitting.

☆ **an·nounce·ment** /ə'naʊnsmənt/ noun **1** [C] a statement that tells people about sth: I have an important announcement to make. **2** [U] the act of telling people about sth: The announcement of the award winners will be broadcast live on TV.

☆ **an·nounc·er** /ə'naʊnsər/ noun [C] a person who introduces or gives information about programs on radio or television

☆ **an·noy** /ə'nɔɪ/ verb [T] to make sb fairly angry: It really annoys me when you act like that.

an·noy·ance /ə'nɔɪəns/ noun **1** [U] the feeling of being annoyed: Much to the annoyance of local residents, the police refused to take action against the noisy dog's owners. **2** [C] something that annoys sb: Low-flying planes are an annoyance in this area.

an·noyed /ə'nɔɪd/ adj. angry or fairly angry: She's annoyed at herself for making such a stupid mistake. ○ He's annoyed that nobody believes him. ○ I was annoyed to see that they had left the door open.

an·noy·ing /ə'nɔɪɪŋ/ adj. making you feel fairly angry: That constant hammering noise is really annoying.

☆ **an·nu·al** /'ænyuəl/ adj. **1** happening or done once a year or every year: the company's annual report ○ an annual event **2** for the period of one year: Her annual income is $30,000. **—an·nu·al·ly** adv.: China produces about 60 tons of gold annually.

an·o·nym·i·ty /,ænə'nɪməti/ noun [U] the situation where a person's name is not known

a·non·y·mous /ə'nɑnəməs/ adj. **1** (used about a person) with a name that is not known or made public: An anonymous caller told the police that the robbery was going to take place. **2** done, written, given, etc. by sb whose name is not known or made public: He received an anonymous letter. **—a·non·y·mous·ly** adv.

an·o·rex·i·a /,ænə'rɛksiə/(also formal **anorexia nervosa** /-nər'voʊsə/) noun [U] an illness that makes sb believe he/she is fat and so stop eating, which can cause a dangerous loss of weight **—an·o·rex·ic** /,ænə'rɛksɪk/ adj., noun [C]

☆ **an·oth·er** /ə'nʌðər/ det., pron. **1** one more; an additional thing or person: Would you like another drink? ○ They have three kids already and now they're going to have another. ○ Is this another one of your stupid jokes? **2** a different thing or person: I'm sorry, but I can't see you tomorrow. Could we arrange to meet another day? ○ They spent hours at the exhibit, walking from one display to another.

IDM **one after another/the other** ⇨ ONE¹

tʃ	dʒ	v	θ	ð	s	z	ʃ
chin	June	van	thin	then	so	zoo	she

one another ⇨ ONE²

A ☆**an·swer¹** /ˈænsər/ *verb* [I,T] **1** to say or write sth back to sb who has asked you sth: *I asked her what the matter was, but she didn't answer.* ◦ *I asked you a question; now please answer me.* ◦ *Answer all the questions on the form.* ◦ *When I asked him how much he earned, he answered that it was none of my business.*

☞ **Answer** and **reply** are the most common verbs used for speaking or writing in reaction to questions, letters, etc.: *I asked him a question, but he didn't answer.* ◦ *I sent my application, but they haven't replied yet.* Note that you **answer** a person, a question or a letter (no "to") but you **reply** to a letter. **Respond** is less common and more formal with this meaning: *Applicants must respond within seven days.* It is more commonly used with the meaning of "reacting in a way that is desired": *Despite all the doctor's efforts, the patient did not respond to treatment.*

2 to do sth as a reply: *I rang their doorbell, but nobody answered.* ◦ *He hasn't answered my letter yet* (= written a letter back to me).
PHRV **answer for sb/sth** to accept responsibility or blame for: *Somebody will have to answer for all the damage that has been caused.*

☆**an·swer²** /ˈænsər/ *noun* [C] **answer (to sb/sth) 1** something that you say, write or do as a reply : *The answer to your question is that I don't know.* ◦ *I wrote to them two weeks ago, and I'm still waiting for an answer.* ◦ *I knocked on the door and waited, but there was no answer.* **2** a solution to a problem: *I didn't have any money, so the only answer was to borrow some.* **3** something that is written or said, trying to give the correct information asked for on a test or exam: *What was the answer to the last question?* ◦ *to choose the right/wrong answer*

an·swer·a·ble /ˈænsərəbl/ *adj.* **answerable to sb (for sth)** having to explain and give good reasons for your actions to sb; responsible to sb

ˈan·swer·ing ma‚chine *noun* [C] a machine that answers the telephone and records messages from callers: *I called his house and left a message on his answering machine.*

ant /ænt/ *noun* [C] a very small insect with no wings that lives in large groups and works very hard ☞ picture at **insect**.

an·tag·o·nism /ænˈtægənɪzəm/ *noun* [C,U] **antagonism (toward sb/sth); antagonism (between A and B)** a feeling of hate and of being opposed to sb/sth

an·tag·o·nist /ænˈtægənɪst/ *noun* [C] a person who opposes sb and tries to make them angry or annoy them

an·tag·o·nis·tic /ænˌtægəˈnɪstɪk/ *adj.* antag-

onistic (toward sb/sth) unfriendly; showing that you disagree with sb/sth

an·tag·o·nize /ænˈtægənaɪz/ *verb* [T] to make sb angry or to annoy sb: *She tends to antagonize people with her outspoken remarks.*

Ant·arc·tic /æntˈɑrktɪk; -ˈɑrtɪk/ *adj.* connected with the coldest, most southern parts of the world (**Antarctica**): *an Antarctic expedition* ☞ Look at **Arctic**.

an·te·bel·lum /ˌæntiˈbɛləm/ *adj.* connected with the period of time before the beginning of the Civil War in the United States, in 1861: *one of the finest antebellum mansions in the South*

an·te·lope /ˈæntəloʊp/ *noun* [C] (*pl.* **antelope** or **an·te·lopes**) an animal with horns that has long, thin legs, looks like a deer and can run very fast. It is found especially in Africa.

an·ten·na /ænˈtɛnə/ *noun* [C] **1** (*pl.* **an·ten·nas**) a long metal stick on a building, car, etc. that receives radio or television signals ☞ picture on page A28. **2** (*pl.* **an·ten·nae** /-ni/) one of the two long thin parts on the heads of insects and some animals that live in shells. It is used for feeling things.

an·them /ˈænθəm/ *noun* [C] a serious song, especially one that is sung on special occasions: *the national anthem* (= the special song of a country)

an·thol·o·gy /ænˈθɑlədʒi/ *noun* [C] (*pl.* **an·thol·o·gies**) a book that contains pieces of written work or poems, often on the same subject, by different authors: *an anthology of love poetry*

an·thro·pol·o·gy /ˌænθrəˈpɑlədʒi/ *noun* [U] the study of human beings, especially of their origin, development, customs and beliefs

an·ti·bi·ot·ic /ˌæntɪbaɪˈɑtɪk/ *noun* [C] a medicine which is used for destroying bacteria and curing infections: *The doctor gave me some antibiotics for a chest infection.*

an·tic·i·pate /ænˈtɪsəpeɪt/ *verb* [T] to expect sth to happen (and to prepare for it): *to anticipate a problem* ◦ *Strong winds are anticipated in the northern part of the state this weekend.* ◦ *I anticipate that the situation will get worse.*

an·tic·i·pa·tion /ænˌtɪsəˈpeɪʃn/ *noun* [U] **1** the state of expecting sth to happen (and preparing for it): *We bought a lot of groceries in anticipation of the blizzard.* **2** the state of feeling excited about sth that is going to happen: *An air of anticipation filled the town before the President's visit.*

an·ti·cli·max /ˌæntiˈklaɪmæks/ *noun* [C,U] an event, etc. that is less exciting than you had expected or than what has already happened: *The ending of the movie was a big anticlimax.*

an·tics /ˈæntɪks/ *noun* [plural] funny, strange or silly ways of behaving: *The audience roared with laughter at the clown's antics.*

an·ti·dote /ˈæntɪdoʊt/ *noun* [C] **1** a medical substance that is used to prevent a poison or a

i	ɪ	ɛ	æ	ɑ	ɔ	ʌ	ʊ	u
see	sit	ten	cat	hot	saw	cup	put	too

disease from having an effect: *an antidote to snake bites* **2** anything that helps you to deal with sth unpleasant: *Many people find music a marvelous antidote to stress.*

an·ti·freeze /'æntɪfriz/ *noun* [U] a liquid that you add to the water in the cooling system of a car, etc. to prevent it from freezing

an·tip·a·thy /æn'tɪpəθi/ *noun* [U] **antipathy (to/toward sb/sth)** (a strong feeling of) dislike: *I experienced a feeling of antipathy toward the speaker.*

an·ti·per·spi·rant /ˌæntɪ'pərspərənt/ *noun* [C,U] a liquid, cream, etc. that you use to reduce the amount of sweat your body produces, especially under the arms ☞ Look at **deodorant**.

an·tique¹ /æn'tik/ *adj.* very old and therefore unusual and valuable: *an antique vase, table, etc.*

an·tique² /æn'tik/ *noun* [C] an old and valuable object, e.g. a piece of furniture: *He collects antiques.* ◦ *an antique shop* (= one that sells antiques) ◦ *That vase is an antique.*

an·tiq·ui·ty /æn'tɪkwəti/ *noun* (pl. **an·tiq·ui·ties**) **1** [U] a time hundreds of years ago, especially the time of the Egyptians, Greeks or Romans: *myths and legends from antiquity* **2** [C, usually pl.] a building, work of art or other object that remains from ancient times: *Greek, Roman, etc. antiquities* **3** [U] great age: *priceless objects of great antiquity*

an·ti-Se·mit·ic /ˌæntisə'mɪtɪk/ *adj.* connected with hatred of Jewish people: *anti-Semitic remarks, incidents, etc.*

an·ti-Se·mi·tism /ˌænti'sɛmətɪzəm/ *noun* [U] hatred or unfair treatment of Jewish people

an·tl·sep·tic /ˌæntə'sɛptɪk/ *noun* [C,U] a liquid or cream that prevents a cut, etc. from becoming infected: *Put some antiseptic on that scratch.* —**an·ti·sep·tic** *adj.*: *antiseptic cream*

an·ti·so·cial /ˌænti'souʃl/ *adj.* **1** not considered acceptable by other people or the rest of society: *antisocial behavior/activities* ◦ *Some people regard smoking as antisocial.* **2** not willing to be with other people; unfriendly: *We don't go out much. I guess we're pretty antisocial.*

ant·ler /'æntlər/ *noun* [C, usually pl.] a horn on the head of a male deer: *a pair of antlers* ☞ picture at **deer**.

an·to·nym /'æntənɪm/ *noun* [C] a word that is opposite in meaning to another word: *"Old" has two possible antonyms: "young" and "new."* ☞ Look at **synonym**.

a·nus /'eɪnəs/ *noun* [C] (pl. **a·nus·es**) (formal) the hole through which solid waste substances leave the body

☆ **anx·i·e·ty** /æŋ'zaɪəti/ *noun* [C,U] (pl. **anx·i·e·ties**) a feeling of worry or fear, especially about the future: *a feeling/a state of anxiety* ◦ *There are anxieties over the effects of unemployment.*

☆ **anx·ious** /'æŋkʃəs/ *adj.* **1 anxious (about/for sb/sth)** worried and afraid: *I started to get anxious when they still hadn't arrived at 9 o'clock.* ◦ *an anxious look, expression, etc.* **2** causing worry and fear: *For a few anxious moments, we thought we'd missed the plane.* **3 anxious about/for sth; anxious to do sth** wanting sth very much; eager for sth: *Police are anxious to find the owner of the white car.* ◦ *The Democratic candidate is anxious for a victory in next week's election.* —**anx·ious·ly** *adv.*

☆ **an·y¹** /'ɛni/ *det., pron.* **1** (used in negative sentences and in questions, also after *if/whether*) some: *We didn't have any lunch.* ◦ *I don't know any Canadians.* ◦ *He asked if we had any questions.* ◦ *I wanted some cookies, but there aren't any.* ◦ *I don't like any of his books.* ☞ Look at the note at **some**. **2** (used for saying that it does not matter which thing or person you choose): *Take any book you want.* ◦ *Any teacher would say the same.* ◦ *Come around any time – I'm usually in.* ◦ *I'll take any that you don't want.*

☆ **an·y²** /'ɛni/ *adv.* (used in negative sentences and questions) at all; to any degree: *I can't run any faster.* ◦ *Is there any more milk in the fridge?* ☞ Look at **anymore**.

☆ **an·y·bod·y** /'ɛni,bʌdi; -,badi/ (also **anyone**) *pron.* **1** (usually in questions or negative statements) any person: *I didn't know anybody at the party.* ◦ *Is there anybody here who can speak Japanese?* ☞ The difference between **somebody** and **anybody** is the same as the difference between **some** and **any**. Look at the notes at **some** and **somebody**. **2** any person, it does not matter who: *Anybody (= all people) can learn to swim.* ◦ *Can anybody come? Or are there special invitations?*

an·y·how /'ɛnihaʊ/ *adv.* (informal) = ANYWAY

☆ **an·y·more** /ˌɛni'mɔr/ *adv.* (used in negative sentences and in questions) **1** now; any longer: *She doesn't live here anymore.* **2** again or any longer, starting from now: *I've decided I'm not going to smoke anymore.*

☆ **an·y·one** /'ɛniwʌn/ *pron.* = ANYBODY

an·y·place /'ɛnipleɪs/ *adv.* (informal) = ANYWHERE

☆ **an·y·thing** /'ɛniθɪŋ/ *pron.* **1** (usually in questions or negative statements) one thing (of any kind): *The fog was so thick that I couldn't see anything at all.* ◦ *Did you buy anything?* ◦ *That's amazing – I've never seen anything like it!* ◦ *"I'd like a cheeseburger." "Anything else?"* (= any other thing?) ☞ The difference between **something** and **anything** is the same as the difference between **some** and **any**. Look at the note at **some**. **2** any thing or things: it does not matter what: *I'm starving! I'll eat anything.* ◦ *I'll do anything you say.*

IDM anything but definitely not: *What a surprise – the meeting was anything but dull.*

or anything (informal) or sth else of a similar

A

type: *If you ever want to go to the movies or anything, give me a call.*

an·y·time /ˈɛnitaɪm/ *adv.* at any time or times; it does not matter when: *Feel free to call us anytime.* ○ *We can go anytime you want.*

☆ **an·y·way** /ˈɛniweɪ/ (also *informal* **anyhow**) *adv.* **1** (used to add an extra point or reason) in any case: *Mexico will be very hot in August, and anyway we can't afford a vacation this summer.* **2** (used when saying or writing sth which contrasts in some way with what has gone before) however: *Sorry I can't come to your party, but thanks anyway.* **3** (used for correcting sth you have just said and making it more accurate) at least: *Everybody wants to be rich – well, most people anyway.* **4** (used after a pause in order to change the subject or go back to a subject being discussed before): *Anyway, that's enough about my problems. How are you doing?*

☆ **an·y·where** /ˈɛniwɛr/ (also *informal* **anyplace**) *adv.* **1** (usually in questions or negative statements) in, at or to any place: *I can't find my keys anywhere.* ○ *Is there a post office anywhere near here?* ○ *You can't buy the book anywhere else* (= in another place). ☛ The difference between **somewhere** and **anywhere** is the same as the difference between **some** and **any**. Look at the note at **some**. **2** any place; it does not matter where: *"Where should we go to eat?" "Oh, anywhere is fine."*

☆ **a·part** /əˈpɑrt/ *adv.* **1** away from sb/sth or each other; not together: *They always argue, so it's best to keep them apart.* **2** away from each other by the distance mentioned: *Plant the potatoes two feet apart.* **3** into pieces: *The material was so old that it just fell/came apart in my hands.* ○ *Their relationship was clearly falling apart* (= about to end).

IDM **take sth apart** to separate sth into pieces: *He took the whole bicycle apart.*

tell A and B apart to see the difference between A and B: *It's very difficult to tell the twins apart.*

a·part from *prep.* **1** (*also* **aside from**) except for: *I'm done with my homework, apart from some reading we have to do.* ○ *There's nobody here apart from me.* **2** as well as; in addition to: *Apart from their penthouse in New York City, they have a house in Florida.*

a·part·heid /əˈpɑrtaɪt; -teɪt/ *noun* [U] the former official government policy in South Africa of separating people of different races and making them live apart

☆ **a·part·ment** /əˈpɑrtmənt/ *noun* [C] (*abbr.* **apt.**) a set of rooms that is used as a home (usually on one floor in a larger building): *a three-bedroom apartment.*

☛ You **rent** an apartment from a **landlord** or from a company that owns the apartment. The landlord **rents** the apartment **out** to you,

the **tenant.** The money you have to pay is called **rent.** Look also at **condominium.**

☆ **a·partment building**, **building** (*also* **a·partment house**) *noun* [C] a large building that contains many separate apartments

ap·a·thet·ic /ˌæpəˈθɛtɪk/ *adj.* lacking interest or a desire to act: *Don't be so apathetic!*

ap·a·thy /ˈæpəθi/ *noun* [U] a lack of interest in things or of a desire to do anything

ape /eɪp/ *noun* [C] a type of animal like a large monkey with no tail or only a very short tail: *Chimpanzees and gorillas are apes.*

a·piece /əˈpis/ *adv.* each: *He gave the children $1 apiece.*

a·pol·o·get·ic /əˌpɑləˈdʒɛtɪk/ *adj.* feeling or showing that you are sorry for sth you have done: *He was very apologetic about his son's bad behavior.* ○ *I wrote him an apologetic letter.* —**a·pol·o·get·i·cal·ly** /-kli/ *adv.*

☆ **a·pol·o·gize** /əˈpɑlədʒaɪz/ *verb* [I] **apologize (to sb) (for sth)** to say that you are sorry for sth you have done: *I sincerely apologize for taking so long to reply to your letter.* ○ *You'll have to apologize to your teacher for forgetting to do your homework.*

☛ When you apologize, the actual words you use are usually **"I'm sorry."**

☆ **a·pol·o·gy** /əˈpɑlədʒi/ *noun* [C,U] (*pl.* **a·pol·o·gies**) **apology (to sb) (for sth)** a spoken or written statement that you are sorry for sth you have done, etc.: *The senator demanded a public apology from her colleague for making false statements.* ○ *a letter/note of apology*

A·pos·tle /əˈpɑsl/ *noun* [C] one of the twelve men chosen by Christ to spread his teaching

a·pos·tro·phe /əˈpɑstrəfi/ *noun* [C] **1** the sign (') used for showing that you have left a letter out of a word (as in "I'm," "can't," "we'll," etc.) **2** the sign (') used for showing who or what belongs or relates to as in "John's chair," "the boy's room" or "the car's rear window."

ap·pall /əˈpɔl/ *verb* [T] (**ap·pall·ing; ap·palled**) (usually passive) to shock sb deeply: *We were appalled by the poverty and starvation we saw everywhere.*

ap·pall·ing /əˈpɔlɪŋ/ *adj.* shocking or terrible: *appalling cruelty* ○ *Conditions in the prison are appalling.*

☆ **ap·pa·ra·tus** /ˌæpəˈrætəs/ *noun* (*pl.* **ap·pa·ra·tus** or **ap·pa·ra·tus·es**) **1** [C,U, usually sing.] a set of tools, instruments or equipment used for doing a job or an activity: *the scientific apparatus necessary for carrying out experiments* **2** [sing.] the complex structure of an organization: *the nation's military and political apparatus*

ap·par·el /əˈpærəl/ *noun* [U] (*formal*) clothing: *manufacturers of women's apparel*

☆ **ap·par·ent** /əˈpærənt; -ˈpɛr-/ *adj.* **1** (only before a noun) perhaps not true or real although

seeming to be so: *His apparent interest in the proposal didn't last very long.* **2 apparent (to sb)** clear; easy to see: *It was apparent to everyone that the man could not be trusted.* ○ *For no apparent reason, she suddenly burst into tears.*

☆ **ap·par·ent·ly** /əˈpærəntli; -ˈpɛr-/ *adv.* **1** according to what people say (but perhaps not true): *Apparently, he's already been married twice.* **2** according to how sth seems or appears (but perhaps not true): *She was apparently undisturbed by the news.*

☆ **ap·peal**¹ /əˈpil/ *verb* **1** [I] **appeal to sb (for sth/to do sth); appeal for sth** to make a serious request for sth you need or want very much: *Relief workers in the disaster area are appealing for more help and supplies.* ○ *She appeared on television to appeal to the kidnappers for her child's safe return.* **2** [I] **appeal (to sb)** to be attractive or interesting (to sb): *The idea of living in the country doesn't appeal to me at all.* **3** [I] **appeal to sth** to influence sb's feelings or thoughts so that he/she will do sth you want: *to appeal to sb's honor, sense of justice, etc.* ○ *We aim to appeal to people's generosity.* **4** [I,T] **appeal sth; appeal (to sb) (against sth)** to ask sb in authority to change a decision: *He decided to appeal his conviction.* ○ *They plan to appeal to the Supreme Court against the lower court's decision.*

☆ **ap·peal**² /əˈpil/ *noun* **1** [C] a serious request for sth you need or want very much: *The police have made an urgent appeal for witnesses to come forward.* ○ *a television, radio, etc. appeal* (= a television or radio program asking for help or money for a particular cause) **2** [C] **appeal to sth** a written or spoken statement that tries to influence sb's feelings or thoughts so that he/she will do what you want: *a powerful appeal to our sense of national pride* **3** [C] a formal request to sb in authority to change a decision: *The judge turned down the defendant's appeal.* **4** [U] attraction or interest: *I can't understand the appeal of stamp collecting.*

ap·peal·ing /əˈpilŋ/ *adj.* attractive or interesting: *The thought of a vacation in Hawaii is very appealing!*

☆ **ap·pear** /əˈpɪr/ *verb* [I] **1** to be seen; to come into sight: *The bus appeared around the corner.* **2** to begin to exist: *The disease is thought to have appeared in Africa.* **3** to be published or printed: *The article appeared in the paper on Friday.* **4** to present yourself in public to speak, perform, act, etc.: *I've been asked to appear in court.* ○ *She is currently appearing in a Broadway musical.* **5** to seem: *She appears to be very happy in her job.* ○ *It appears that you were given the wrong information.* ○ *"Do you think he will resign?" "It appears so."* ☞ The adjective is **apparent.**

☆ **ap·pear·ance** /əˈpɪrəns/ *noun* **1** [U] the way that sb/sth looks: *A different hairstyle can* completely change your appearance. ○ *He gives the appearance of being extremely confident.* **2** [C] an act of appearing in public, especially on stage, television, etc.: *The program will feature appearances by a number of top stars.* **3** [sing.] the arrival of sb/sth: *I was surprised by her unexpected appearance at the party.* **4** [sing.] the beginning (of sth never seen or used before): *the appearance of television in many homes in the 1950s*

ap·pen·di·ci·tis /əˌpɛndəˈsaɪtəs/ *noun* [U] an illness in which the appendix (1) becomes extremely painful and usually has to be removed

ap·pen·dix /əˈpɛndɪks/ *noun* [C] **1** (*pl.* **appen·dix·es**) a small tube inside your body which is attached to the intestine **2** (*pl.* **appen·di·ces** /-dəsiz/) a section at the end of a book, etc. that gives extra information

ap·pe·tite /ˈæpətaɪt/ *noun* **1** [C,U] the desire for food: *a good/healthy appetite* ○ *My two teenage sons have enormous appetites!* ○ *Some fresh air and exercise should give you an appetite* (= make you hungry). ○ *Symptoms of this illness include headache, fever and loss of appetite.* **2** [C,U] a strong desire: *Americans' insatiable appetite for new electronic gadgets*
IDM **whet sb's appetite** ⇨ WHET

ap·pe·tiz·er /ˈæpətaɪzər/ *noun* [C] a small amount of food that you eat as the first part of a meal

ap·pe·tiz·ing /ˈæpətaɪzŋ/ *adj.* (used about food, etc.) attractive and tempting: *an appetizing smell*

ap·plaud /əˈplɔd/ *verb* **1** [I,T] to clap your hands in order to show that you like sb/sth: *The audience applauded loudly.* ○ *The team was applauded as it left the field.* **2** [T] to praise sb/sth: *Many citizens applauded the decision to lower taxes.*

☆ **ap·plause** /əˈplɔz/ *noun* [U] the pleasure and approval of a group of people, shown by them clapping their hands: *The performance received enthusiastic applause from the audience.*
IDM **a round of applause** ⇨ ROUND²

☆ **ap·ple** /ˈæpl/ *noun* [C] a hard, round fruit with smooth green, red or yellow skin: *an apple tree* ○ *apple juice* ☞ Look also at **Big Apple.**

ˌ**apple ˈcider** *noun* [U] = CIDER

ap·pli·ance /əˈplaɪəns/ *noun* [C] a piece of equipment for a particular purpose in the house: *electrical appliances*

ap·pli·ca·ble /ˈæplɪkəbl; əˈplɪkəbl/ *adj.* (not before a noun) **applicable (to sb/sth)** that concerns or relates to: *This part of the form is only applicable to married women.*

☆ **ap·pli·cant** /ˈæplɪkənt/ *noun* [C] a person who applies for sth, especially a job

☆ **ap·pli·ca·tion** /ˌæpləˈkeɪʃn/ *noun* **1** [C,U] **application (to sb) (for sth)** a formal written request, especially for a job or a place in a school, club, etc.: *We are accepting applications for the position of assistant manager.* ○ *an*

A

application form (= a special form that you use to apply for a job, etc.) **2** [C,U] a/the practical use (of sth): *the application of educational theory to the classroom.* **3** [U] **application (of sth)** the action of putting or spreading sth onto a surface: *This cream is for external application only.* **4** [C] (*computing*) a computer program that you use to perform a specific function or several functions: *a word-processing application*

ap·plied /ə'plaɪd/ *adj.* (used about a subject) having a practical use: *applied mathematics* (e.g. as used in engineering)

☆ **ap·ply** /ə'plaɪ/ *verb* (*pres. part.* **ap·ply·ing**; *3rd pers. sing. pres.* **ap·plies**; *p.t., p.p.* **ap·plied**) **1** [I] **apply (to sb) (for sth)** to ask for sth in writing: *I'm going to apply for that job they advertised.* **2** [T] **apply yourself/sth (to sth/to doing sth)** to make yourself concentrate on sth: *to apply your mind to sth* ∘ *He really applied himself to his studies.* **3** [I] **apply (to sb/sth)** to concern (sb/sth) or relate (to sb/sth): *This information applies to all children born after 1990.* **4** [T] **apply sth (to sth)** to make practical use of sth: *new technology which can be applied to solving problems in industry* **5** [T] (usually passive) to use a word, a name, etc. to refer to sb/sth: *I don't think the word "antique" can be applied to this old table, do you?* **6** [T] **apply sth (to sth)** to put or spread sth (onto sth): *Apply the cream to the infected area twice a day.*

☆ **ap·point** /ə'pɔɪnt/ *verb* [T] **1 appoint sb (sth/ as sth/to sth)** to choose sb for a job, etc.: *The committee has appointed a new chairperson.* ∘ *He's been appointed (as) the new school superintendent.* **2 appoint sth (for sth)** (*formal*) to arrange or decide on sth: *the date appointed for the next meeting*

☆ **ap·point·ment** /ə'pɔɪntmənt/ *noun* **1** [C,U] **appointment (with sb)** an arrangement to see sb at a particular time: *a doctor's, dentist's, etc. appointment* ∘ *I'd like to make an appointment to see the manager.* ∘ *to keep/cancel an appointment* ∘ *visits are by appointment only* (= at a time that has been arranged in advance). **2** [U] **appointment (to sth)** the act of choosing sb for a job: *Many people criticized the appointment of such a young man to the post.* **3** [C] a job or position of responsibility

ap·prais·al /ə'preɪzl/ *noun* [C,U] an opinion about the value or quality of sb/sth; a judgment

ap·praise /ə'preɪz/ *verb* [T] to form an opinion about the value or quality of sb/sth

ap·pre·cia·ble /ə'priʃəbl/ *adj.* noticeable or important: *There has been an appreciable drop in the rate of inflation.*

☆ **ap·pre·ci·ate** /ə'priʃieɪt/ *verb* **1** [T] to enjoy sth or to understand the value of sth: *The art of Van Gogh was not appreciated during his own lifetime.* **2** [T] to understand sth (a prob-

lem, situation, etc.): *I don't think you appreciate how serious this situation is.* **3** [T] to be grateful for sth: *Thanks for your help. We really appreciate it.* **4** [I] to increase in value over a period of time: *Houses in this area have appreciated faster than elsewhere.*

ap·pre·ci·a·tion /əˌpriʃi'eɪʃn/ *noun* **1** [U] understanding and enjoyment (of the value of sth): *I'm taking an introductory course in music appreciation.* **2** [U] the feeling of being grateful for sth: *Please accept these flowers as a token* (= a sign) *of my appreciation.* **3** [U, sing.] understanding of what sth involves: *The President's visit gave him a new appreciation of the problems facing poor people.* **4** [U] increase in value: *the yen's appreciation against the dollar*

ap·pre·cia·tive /ə'priʃətɪv/ *adj.* **1** feeling or showing pleasure or admiration: *"You look nice tonight," he said, with an appreciative smile.* **2 appreciative (of sth)** grateful for sth: *He was very appreciative of our efforts to help.*

ap·pre·hend /ˌæprɪ'hɛnd/ *verb* [T] (used about the police) to catch and arrest sb: *The suspects were apprehended as they tried to board a plane to Las Vegas.*

ap·pre·hen·sion /ˌæprɪ'hɛnʃn/ *noun* [C,U] (*formal*) worry or fear about sth in the future: *feelings of apprehension*

ap·pre·hen·sive /ˌæprɪ'hɛnsɪv/ *adj.* worried or afraid: *to be/feel apprehensive* ∘ *The students were apprehensive about their upcoming exams.*

ap·pren·tice /ə'prɛntɪs/ *noun* [C] a person who works for sb for low wages, in order to learn an occupation or skill: *an apprentice electrician*

ap·pren·tice·ship /ə'prɛntəʃɪp/ *noun* [C,U] the state or time of being an apprentice

☆ **ap·proach¹** /ə'proʊtʃ/ *verb* **1** [I,T] to come near or nearer to sb/sth: *The date of her wedding was approaching.* ∘ *When you approach the town, you will see a service station on your left.* **2** [T] to speak to sb usually in order to ask for sth: *I'm going to approach my boss about a raise.* **3** [T] to begin to deal with sth (a problem, a situation, etc.): *What is the best way to approach this problem?* **4** [T] to almost reach sth (a certain standard, level, etc.): *at a depth approaching 50 feet under water*

☆ **ap·proach²** /ə'proʊtʃ/ *noun* **1** [C] a way of dealing with sb/sth: *Parents don't always know what approach to take with teenagers.* **2** [sing.] the act of coming nearer (to sb/sth): *The plane's engine stalled during its approach to the runway.* **3** [C] a road or path, etc. leading to sth: *the approach to the town*

ap·proach·a·ble /ə'proʊtʃəbl/ *adj.* friendly and easy to talk to: *She's nice, but her husband's not very approachable.* ☞ The opposite is **unapproachable.**

i	ɪ	ɛ	æ	ɑ	ɔ	ʌ	ʊ	u
see	sit	ten	cat	hot	saw	cup	put	too

☆**ap·pro·pri·ate¹** /əˈproʊpriət/ *adj.* **appropriate (for/to sth)** suitable or right: *This card is very appropriate for the occasion, isn't it?* ○ *Take whatever action you think is appropriate.* ☞ The opposite is **inappropriate**. —**ap·pro·pri·ate·ly** *adv.*

ap·pro·pri·ate² /əˈproʊprieɪt/ *verb* [T] (*formal*) **1 appropriate sth (for/to sth)** to decide to use sth, especially money, for a particular purpose: *Congress has appropriated over $150 million for cancer research.* **2** to take or use sth for your own purposes, usually without permission or illegally: *He admitted that he had appropriated some facts from another writer's article.*

ap·pro·pri·a·tion /əˌproʊpriˈeɪʃn/ *noun* [C] a thing, especially a sum of money, that is appropriated: *The proposal includes an appropriation of $72 million for loans to small businesses.*

☆**ap·prov·al** /əˈpruvl/ *noun* [U] feeling, showing or saying that you think sth is good; agreement: *Everybody gave their approval to the proposal.* ○ *She was always anxious to win her mother's approval.*

☆**ap·prove** /əˈpruv/ *verb* **1** [I] **approve (of sb/sth)** to be pleased about sth; to like sb/sth: *Her parents don't approve of her friends.* ☞ The opposite is **disapprove**. **2** [T] to agree to sth or to accept sth as correct: *We need to get an accountant to approve these figures.*

ap·prov·ing /əˈpruvɪŋ/ *adj.* showing support or admiration for sth: *"Good job," he said with an approving smile.* —**ap·prov·ing·ly** *adv.*

☆**ap·prox·i·mate** /əˈprɑksəmət/ *adj.* (*abbr.* **approx.**) almost correct but not completely accurate: *The approximate time of arrival is 3 o'clock.* ○ *I can only give you an approximate idea of the cost.*

ap·prox·i·mate·ly /əˈprɑksəmətli/ *adv.* (*abbr.* **approx.**) about: *It's approximately fifty miles from here.*

ap·prox·i·ma·tion /əˌprɑksəˈmeɪʃn/ *noun* [C] a number, answer, etc. which is nearly, but not exactly, right

a·pri·cot /ˈeɪprɪkɑt; ˈæp-/ *noun* [C] a small, round, yellow or orange fruit with soft flesh and a large hard part (**pit**) inside

☆**A·pril** /ˈeɪprəl/ *noun* [C,U] (*abbr.* **Apr.**) the fourth month of the year, coming before May ☞ For examples of the use of the months in sentences, look at **January**.

ˌ**April ˈFool's Day** *noun* [sing.] April 1
☞ On this day it is traditional for people to play tricks on each other, especially by inventing silly stories and trying to persuade other people that they are true.

a·pron /ˈeɪprən/ *noun* [C] a piece of clothing that you wear over the front of your usual clothes in order to keep them clean, especially when cooking ☞ picture at **overalls**.

apt /æpt/ *adj.* **1** suitable: *a very apt description* **2 apt to do sth** having a tendency to do sth; likely: *You'd better remind me. I'm apt to forget.*

apt. *abbr.* = APARTMENT

ap·ti·tude /ˈæptətud/ *noun* [C,U] **aptitude (for sth/for doing sth)** (a) natural ability: *She has an aptitude for learning languages.*

apt·ly /ˈæptli/ *adv.* suitably: *The hotel was aptly named "Ocean View"* (= because it had a view of the ocean).

a·quar·i·um /əˈkwɛriəm/ *noun* [C] (*pl.* **a·quar·i·ums** or **a·quar·i·a** /-riə/) **1** a glass container filled with water, in which fish and water animals are kept **2** a building, often in a zoo, where fish and water animals are kept

A·quar·i·us /əˈkwɛriəs/ *noun* [C,U] the eleventh sign of the zodiac, the Water Carrier; a person who was born under this sign ☞ picture at **zodiac**.

a·quat·ic /əˈkwætɪk; əˈkwɑtɪk/ *adj.* **1** (used about an animal or a plant) living in water **2** (used about a sport) performed on or in water

☆**Ar·ab** /ˈærəb/ *noun* [C] a member of a people who now live in many parts of the Middle East and North Africa —**Ar·ab** *adj.*: *Arab countries*

Ar·a·bic /ˈærəbɪk/ *noun* [sing.] **1** the language that is spoken by Arab people **2** the religious language of Islam

ar·a·ble /ˈærəbl/ *adj.* (used about land) suitable for growing crops

ar·bi·trar·y /ˈɑrbətrɛri/ *adj.* not based on any principle or reason; not thinking about the wishes of the other people involved: *The choice he made seemed completely arbitrary.* —**ar·bi·trar·i·ly** *adv.* /ˌɑrbəˈtrɛrəli/

ar·bi·trate /ˈɑrbətreɪt/ *verb* [I,T] to settle an argument between two people or groups by finding a solution that both can accept

ar·bi·tra·tion /ˌɑrbəˈtreɪʃn/ *noun* [U] the process of settling an argument between two people or groups by a third person (who has been chosen by them): *The baseball players and the team owners decided to go to arbitration.*

ar·bi·tra·tor /ˈɑrbətreɪtər/ *noun* [C] a person who is chosen to settle an argument between two people or groups, in formal discussions

arc /ɑrk/ *noun* [C] a curved line, part of a circle

ar·cade /ɑrˈkeɪd/ *noun* [C] **1** a large room with machines and games that you put coins into to play: *a video game arcade* **2** a large covered passage or area with stores along one or both sides; a passage with arches: *a shopping arcade*

ə	y	w	t̬	eɪ	aɪ	ɔɪ	aʊ	oʊ
about	yes	woman	butter	say	five	boy	now	go

A

arch¹ /ɑrtʃ/ *noun* [C]
1 a structure made with two columns joined over the top in a curve. An arch may support a bridge or the roof of a large building or it may be above a door or a window. **2** a monument in the shape of an arch: *the Gateway Arch in St. Louis* **3** the middle part of the inside of your foot

arch

arch² /ɑrtʃ/ *verb* [I,T] to make a curve: *The cat arched its back and hissed.*

ar·chae·o·log·i·cal (*also* **archeological**) /ˌɑrkiəˈlɑdʒɪkl/ *adj.* connected with archaeology

ar·chae·ol·o·gist (*also* **archeologist**) /ˌɑrki-ˈɑlədʒɪst/ *noun* [C] an expert in archaeology

ar·chae·ol·o·gy (*also* **archeology**) /ˌɑrki-ˈɑlədʒi/ *noun* [U] the study of ancient civilizations, based on objects or parts of buildings that are found in the ground

ar·cha·ic /ɑrˈkeɪɪk/ *adj.* old-fashioned; no longer in common use

arch·bish·op /ˌɑrtʃˈbɪʃəp/ *noun* [C] a priest in some branches of the Christian church who is in charge of all the priests and churches in a large area of a country: *the Archbishop of Philadelphia*

arch·er·y /ˈɑrtʃəri/ *noun* [U] the sport of shooting arrows using a curved piece of wood (**bow**) that is held together by a string

☆ **ar·chi·tect** /ˈɑrkətɛkt/ *noun* [C] a person whose job is to design buildings

ar·chi·tec·tur·al /ˌɑrkəˈtɛktʃərəl/ *adj.* connected with the design of buildings

ar·chi·tec·ture /ˈɑrkəˌtɛktʃər/ *noun* [U] **1** the study of how buildings are planned and built **2** the style or design of a building or buildings: *the architecture of the fifteenth century* ○ *modern architecture*

ar·chives /ˈɑrkaɪvz/ *noun* [plural] (*also* **archive** /ˈɑkaɪv/ *noun* [C]) a collection of historical documents, etc. that record the history of a place or an organization; the place where they are kept: *In the city archives, they found letters written by George Washington.* ○ *archive material on the First World War*

Arc·tic /ˈɑrktɪk; ˈɑrtɪk/ *adj.* **1** connected with the region around the North Pole (the most northern point of the world) **2 arctic** very cold: *A blast of arctic air swept across the Midwest today.*

the Arctic *noun* [sing.] the area around the North Pole

the ˌArctic ˈCircle *noun* [sing.] the line of latitude 66° 30′N ☞ picture at **earth**. Look at **Antarctic**.

ar·dent /ˈɑrdnt/ *adj.* showing strong feelings, especially a strong liking for sb/sth: *He was an ardent supporter of the President.* —**ar·dent·ly** *adv.*

ar·du·ous /ˈɑrdʒuəs/ *adj.* full of difficulties; needing a lot of effort over a period of time: *an arduous journey*

are, aren't ⇨ BE¹,²

☆ **ar·e·a** /ˈɛriə/ *noun* **1** [C] a part of a town, country or the world: *Housing is very expensive in the San Francisco area.* ○ *The wettest areas are in the south of the country.* ○ *The high winds scattered debris over a wide area.* ☞ Look at the note at **district. 2** [C,U] the size of a surface, that you can calculate by multiplying the length by the width: *The area of the office is 150 square feet.* ○ *The office is 150 square feet in area.* **3** [C] a space used for a particular activity: *I'd rather sit in the non-smoking area.* **4** [C] a particular part of a subject or activity: *Training is one area of the business that we could improve.*

ˈarea code *noun* [C] a set of three numbers at the beginning of telephone numbers in the United States and Canada, that you must use when you are calling from outside the area: *The area code for Chicago is 312.*

a·re·na /əˈrinə/ *noun* [C] **1** an area with seats around it where public events (sports, games, concerts, etc.) are held **2** where a particular activity happens: *She was well respected in the international political arena.*

ar·gu·a·ble /ˈɑrgyuəbl/ *adj.* **1** that can be argued; probably true: *It is arguable that no one should have to go without health insurance.* **2** not certain; that you do not accept without question: *Whether it is a good idea to invest so much money is highly arguable.*

ar·gu·a·bly /ˈɑrgyuəbli/ *adv.* probably; you can argue that: *She is arguably the nation's greatest living actress.*

☆ **ar·gue** /ˈɑrgyu/ *verb* **1** [I] **argue (with sb) (about/over sth)** to say things (often angrily) that show that you do not agree with sb about sth: *The people next door are always arguing.* ○ *I never argue with my husband about money.* **2** [I,T] **argue that...; argue (for/against sth)** to give reasons that support your opinion about sth: *John argued that buying a new computer was a waste of money.* ○ *He argued against buying a new computer.*

☆ **ar·gu·ment** /ˈɑrgyumənt/ *noun* **1** [C,U] **argument (with sb) (about/over sth)** an angry discussion between two or more people who disagree with each other: *Sue had an argument with her father about politics.* ○ *He accepted the decision without argument.* **2** [C] the reason(s) that you give to support your opinion about sth: *His argument was that if they bought a smaller car, they would save money.* ○ *The defense attorney began her closing arguments yesterday.*

ər	ɪr	ɛr	ɑr	ɔr	ʊr	ʒ	h	ŋ
bird	near	hair	car	north	tour	vision	hat	sing

ar·gu·men·ta·tive /ˌɑrgyuˈmɛntəṭɪv/ *adj.* often involved in or enjoying arguments

ar·id /ˈærɪd/ *adj.* (used about land or climate) very dry; with little or no rain

Ar·ies /ˈɛriz/ *noun* [C,U] the first sign of the zodiac, the Ram; a person who was born under this sign ☞ picture at **zodiac.**

☆ **a·rise** /əˈraɪz/ *verb* [I] (*p.t.* **a·rose** /əˈroʊz/; *p.p.* **a·ris·en** /əˈrɪzn/) to begin to exist; to appear: *If any problems arise, let me know.*

ar·is·toc·ra·cy /ˌærəˈstɑkrəsi/ *noun* [C] (*pl.* **ar·is·toc·ra·cies**) the people of the highest social class in some countries, who often have special titles

a·ris·to·crat /əˈrɪstəkræt/ *noun* [C] a member of the highest social class in some countries, often with a special title —**a·ris·to·crat·ic** /əˌrɪstəˈkræṭɪk/ *adj.*

a·rith·me·tic /əˈrɪθmətɪk/ *noun* [U] the branch of mathematics that involves counting with numbers (adding, subtracting, multiplying, and dividing) ☞ Look at **algebra** and **math.**

arm in arm arms folded

☆ **arm¹** /ɑrm/ *noun* [C] **1** the limb at each side of the human body from the shoulder to the hand: *He was carrying a newspaper under his arm.* ○ *They waved their arms in the air and shouted at us.* ○ *I put my arm around her.* **2** the part of a piece of clothing that covers your arm; a sleeve: *He had a hole in the arm of his sweater.* **3** something shaped like an arm: *the arm of a chair* (= where you rest your arm) ☞ Look also at **arms.**

IDM arm in arm with your arm linked together with sb else's arm: *The two friends walked arm in arm.*

cost/pay an arm and a leg (*informal*) to cost/pay a large amount of money: *I had to pay an arm and a leg for these plane tickets.*

cross/fold your arms to cross your arms in front of your chest: *She folded her arms and waited.* ○ *James was sitting with his arms crossed.*

twist sb's arm ⇨ TWIST¹

with open arms ⇨ OPEN¹

arm² /ɑrm/ *verb* [I,T] to prepare sb/yourself to fight by supplying weapons: *The country is beginning to arm itself for war.* ☞ Look at **armed** and **arms.**

ar·ma·dil·lo /ˌɑrməˈdɪloʊ/ *noun* [C] (*pl.* **ar·ma·dil·los**) a small animal that lives in the southern U.S. and Central and South America. Its body is covered in a shell of hard plates for protection.

armadillo

ar·ma·ments /ˈɑrməmənts/ *noun* [plural] weapons and military equipment

arm·band /ˈɑrmbænd/ *noun* [C] a piece of material that you wear around your sleeve: *People often used to wear black armbands at funerals.*

arm·chair /ˈɑrmtʃɛr/ *noun* [C] a soft comfortable chair with sides that support your arms

armchair

☆ **armed** /ɑrmd/ *adj.* carrying a gun or other weapon; involving weapons: *The escaped prisoners are considered armed and dangerous.* ○ *armed robbery* ○ *the armed forces* (= the Army, Navy, Air Force and Marine Corps) ○ (*figurative*) *They came to the meeting armed with all the latest information.*

arm·ful /ˈɑrmfʊl/ *noun* [C] the amount that you can carry in your arms: *She was carrying an armful of books.*

arm·hole /ˈɑrmhoʊl/ *noun* [C] the opening in a piece of clothing that your arm goes through

ar·mi·stice /ˈɑrməstɪs/ *noun* [C] an agreement between two countries who are at war that they will stop fighting

ar·mor /ˈɑrmər/ *noun* [U] clothing, often made of metal, that soldiers wore in earlier times to protect themselves: *a suit of armor*

ar·mored /ˈɑrmərd/ *adj.* (used about a vehicle) covered with metal to protect it in an attack

ar·mor·y /ˈɑrməri/ *noun* [C] a building that is used for storing weapons and as an office for a branch of the armed forces that uses people who are not professional soldiers (**the National Guard**). It is often also used for other purposes, especially in emergencies: *An emergency shelter was set up in the armory for motorists who were trapped by the blizzard.*

arm·pit /ˈɑrmpɪt/ *noun* [C] the part of the body under the arm at the point where it joins the shoulder ☞ picture on page A24.

☆ **arms** /ɑrmz/ *noun* [plural] weapons, especially those that are used in war: *a reduction in nuclear arms*

IDM be up in arms to be very angry; to be protesting about sth: *The workers were up in arms over the news of possible layoffs.*

☆ **ar·my** /ˈɑrmi/ *noun* [C, with sing. or pl. verb] (*pl.* **ar·mies**) the military forces of a country

A

that are trained to fight on land; a large group of soldiers: *the United States Army* ○ *She joined the army at the age of eighteen.* ○ *an army officer* ☞ Look at **air force** and **navy**.

a·ro·ma /əˈroʊmə/ *noun* [C] a smell (usually one that is pleasant)

a·rose *p.t.* of ARISE

☆ **a·round¹** /əˈraʊnd/ *adv.* **1** in or to various places or directions: *I don't plan to buy anything – I'm just looking around.* ○ *This is our office – David will show you around* (= show you the different parts of it). **2** moving so as to face in the opposite direction: *Turn around and go back the way you came.* **3** on all sides; forming a circle: *The back yard is very large with a hedge all around.* ○ *Gather around so that you can all see.* **4** measured on all sides: *That old tree must be at least 10 feet around.* **5** present or available: *I went to the house, but there was nobody around.* ○ *That isn't a new book. It's been around for ages.* **6** (used for activities with no real purpose): *"What are you doing?" "Nothing, just puttering around."* ○ *John likes messing around with cars.* **7** here and there, in different positions: *clothes lying around all over the floor* **8** (*also* **about**) (at) approximately: *It's around three hours' drive from here.* ○ *I'll see you around seven* (= at about 7 o'clock).

☆ **a·round²** /əˈraʊnd/ *prep.* **1** in various directions inside an area; in different places in a particular area: *They wandered around the town, looking in some of the stores.* **2** in a circle or following a curving path: *The athlete ran around the track ten times.* ○ *Go around the corner and it's the first house on the left.* ○ *She had a bandage around her leg.* ○ (*figurative*) *There doesn't seem to be any way around the problem.* **3** near a place: *Is there a bank around here?*

a·rouse /əˈraʊz/ *verb* [T] to cause a particular reaction in people: *His actions have aroused a lot of criticism.* —**a·rous·al** *noun* [U] /əˈraʊzl/

ar·raign /əˈreɪn/ *verb* [T] (usu passive) to bring an accused person into court and formally announce the crime or crimes that he/she is accused of: *Both suspects in the case will be arraigned on murder charges tomorrow.* —**ar·raign·ment** *noun* [C,U]

☆ **ar·range** /əˈreɪndʒ/ *verb* **1** [T] to put sth in order or in a particular pattern: *The books were arranged in alphabetical order.* ○ *She arranged the flowers in a vase.* **2** [I,T] to make plans and preparations so that sth can happen in the future: *Isabel's parents arranged a big party for her birthday.* ○ *He arranged for Peter to stay with friends in France.* ○ *She arranged to meet Stuart after work.*

☆ **ar·range·ment** /əˈreɪndʒmənt/ *noun* **1** [C, usually pl.] plans or preparations for sth that will happen in the future: *We're just making the final arrangements for the concert.* **2** [C,U]

something that you have agreed or settled with sb else; the act of doing this: *They made an arrangement to share the cost of the food.* ○ *Use of the swimming pool will be by prior arrangement only.* **3** [C] a group of things that have been placed in a particular pattern: *a flower arrangement*

ar·ray /əˈreɪ/ *noun* [C] a large collection of things, especially one that is impressive and is seen by other people: *The store offers a wide array of imported foods.*

ar·rears /əˈrɪrz/ *noun* [plural] money that should have been paid by an earlier date: *property tax arrears*
IDM **in arrears** owing money: *The company is $2 million in arrears on its taxes.*

☆ **ar·rest¹** /əˈrɛst/ *verb* [T] (used about the police) to take sb prisoner in order to question him/her about a crime

☆ **ar·rest²** /əˈrɛst/ *noun* **1** [C] the act of arresting sb: *The police made ten arrests after the riot.* **2** [C,U] (*medical*) the action or an act of sth stopping: *He died of cardiac arrest* (= his heart stopped beating). ○ *respiratory arrest* (= when a person stops breathing)
IDM **be under arrest** to have been arrested by the police: *He was under arrest for murder.*

☆ **ar·ri·val** /əˈraɪvl/ *noun* **1** [U] the act of reaching the place to which you were traveling: *On our arrival we were told that our rooms had not been reserved.* ○ *Amtrak apologizes for the late arrival of this train.* **2** [C] people or things that have arrived: *We brought in extra chairs for the late arrivals.* ○ *Residents near the airport have complained about the number of late-night arrivals and departures.*

☆ **ar·rive** /əˈraɪv/ *verb* [I] **1** to reach the place to which you were traveling: *We arrived home at about midnight.* ○ *What time does the flight arrive in Chicago?* ○ *They arrived at the airport ten minutes late.* ○ *Has my letter arrived yet?* **2** to come or happen: *The day of the wedding had finally arrived.* ○ *Paula's baby arrived* (= was born) *two weeks late.*
PHRV **arrive at** to reach sth: *After months of discussions, they finally arrived at a decision.*

ar·ro·gant /ˈærəgənt/ *adj.* thinking that you are better and more important than other people and not caring about their feelings; too proud —**ar·ro·gance** /ˈærəgəns/ *noun* [U] —**ar·ro·gant·ly** *adv.*

ar·row /ˈæroʊ/ *noun* [C] **1** a thin piece of wood or metal, with one pointed end and feathers at the other end, that is shot from a curved piece of wood that is held in shape by a string (**a bow**): *Native Americans traditionally hunted with bows and arrows.* **2** the sign (→) which is used to show direction: *The arrow is pointing left.*

ar·se·nal /ˈɑrsənl/ *noun* [C] a collection of weapons; a place where weapons are made or stored: *the nation's nuclear arsenal* ○ (*figura-*

i	ɪ	ɛ	æ	ɑ	ɔ	ʌ	ʊ	u
see	sit	ten	cat	hot	saw	cup	put	too

tive) The police had a whole arsenal of evidence against the suspect.

ar·son /'ɑrsn/ *noun* [U] the crime of setting fire to a building on purpose

☆ **art** /ɑrt/ *noun* **1** [U] the producing of beautiful things such as paintings, drawings, etc.; the objects that are produced: *an art class* ○ *the art of the Italian Renaissance* ○ *modern art* ○ *an art gallery* ☞ Look at **state-of-the-art** and **work of art**. **2** [C, usually sing.] a skill or sth that requires skill: *There's an art to writing a good letter.* **3 the arts** [plural] activities such as painting, writing literature or writing and performing music: *The government is threatening to cut funding for the arts.* **4 arts** [plural] subjects such as history or languages that you study at a school, college or university: *a Bachelor of Arts degree in anthropology* ○ *the university's College of Arts and Sciences.* ☞ It is more common to call these subjects the **humanities**. Look also at **fine arts** and **liberal arts**.

ar·ter·y /'ɑrtəri/ *noun* [C] (*pl.* **ar·ter·ies**) one of the tubes which take blood from the heart to other parts of the body ☞ Look at **vein**.

ar·thri·tis /ɑr'θraɪtəs/ *noun* [U] a disease which causes swelling and pain in the joints of your body (where you bend your arms, fingers, etc.)

ar·ti·choke /'ɑrtɪtʃoʊk/ *noun* [C] a plant whose flower looks like pointed leaves. The bottoms of the leaves and the center (**heart**) of the flower can be eaten as a vegetable.

☆ **ar·ti·cle** /'ɑrtɪkl/ *noun* [C] **1** a thing or object, especially one of a set: *Articles of clothing were lying all over the room.* **2** a piece of writing in a newspaper or magazine: *I read an interesting article in today's paper.* **3** a part of a legal document: *Article One of the United States Constitution* **4** (*grammar*) the words "a/an" (the indefinite article) or "the" (the definite article)

ar·tic·u·late¹ /ɑr'tɪkyələt/ *adj.* good at expressing your ideas clearly

ar·tic·u·late² /ɑr'tɪkyəleɪt/ *verb* [I,T] to say sth clearly or to express your ideas or feelings

☆ **ar·ti·fi·cial** /ˌɑrtə'fɪʃl/ *adj.* not genuine or natural but made by people: *artificial flowers* —**ar·ti·fi·cial·ly** *adv.*: *This drug cannot be produced artificially.*

ˌartificial inˌsemiˈnation *noun* [U] a scientific technique to introduce male seeds (**sperm**) into a female so that babies or young can be produced without sex

ˌartificial inˈtelligence *noun* [U] (the study of) the way in which computers can be made to imitate human thought

ar·til·ler·y /ɑr'tɪləri/ *noun* [U] a number of large guns on wheels; the part of the army which uses them

☆ **art·ist** /'ɑrtɪst/ *noun* [C] somebody who produces art, especially paintings or drawings: *I like that picture – who is the artist?* ○ *an exhib-*

ition of paintings by the American artist, Andrew Wyeth

ar·tis·tic /ɑr'tɪstɪk/ *adj.* **1** connected with art: *the artistic director of the theater* **2** showing a skill in art: *Helen is very artistic – her drawings are excellent.* —**ar·tis·ti·cal·ly** /-kli/ *adv.*

art·ist·ry /'ɑrtəstri/ *noun* [U] the skill of an artist

☆ **as** /əz; *strong form* æz/ *conj., prep., adv.* **1** while sth else is happening: *The phone rang just as I was leaving the house.* ○ *As she walked along the street, she thought about her father.* **2 as…as** (used for comparing people or things): *Tom's almost as tall as I am.* ○ *It's not as cold as it was yesterday.* **3 as…as** (used with "much" or "many" for comparing people or things): *She earns twice as much as her husband.* ○ *I don't have as many books as you do.* **4** (used for talking about sb's job): *He works as a bus driver for the school district.* **5** (used for describing sb/sth's role): *Think of me as your friend, not as your boss.* **6** (used for describing sb/sth in an unusual role or function): *I went to the party dressed as a police officer.* ○ *You could use this white sheet as a tablecloth.* **7** in a particular way, state, etc.: *Please do as I tell you.* ○ *Leave the room as it is. Don't move anything.* **8** (used at the beginning of a comment about what you are saying): *As you know, I've decided to leave at the end of the month.* **9** because: *I didn't buy the dress, as I decided it was too expensive.*

IDM as for (used when you are starting to talk about a different person or thing): *Jane's in Paris right now. As for Andrew, I have no idea where he is.*

as if; as though (used for saying how sb/sth appears): *She looks as if she's just gotten out of bed.* ○ *He behaved as though nothing had happened.*

as it were (*formal*) (used for saying that sth is only true in a certain way): *She felt, as it were, a stranger in her own house.*

as of starting from a particular time: *As of next week, Tim Shaw will be managing this department.*

as to about a particular thing: *I was given no instructions as to how to begin.*

ASAP (*also* **asap**) /ˌeɪ ɛs eɪ 'pi/ *abbr.* as soon as possible

as·bes·tos /æs'bɛstəs; æz-/ *noun* [U] a soft gray material which does not burn and which was often used in the past to protect against heat. It can cause serious diseases if you breathe it in.

as·cend /ə'sɛnd/ *verb* [I,T] (*formal*) to go or come up —**as·cend·ing** *adj.: The questions are arranged in ascending order of difficulty* (= the most difficult ones are at the end). ☞ Look at **descend**.

as·cent /ə'sɛnt/ *noun* [C] **1** the act of climbing or going up: *Their aim was the ascent of the*

A

highest mountains in the Himalayas. **2** a path or slope leading upwards: *There was a steep ascent before the path became flat again.* ☞ Look at **descent**.

as·cer·tain /ˌæsərˈteɪn/ verb [T] (formal) to find out: *It was difficult to ascertain who was telling the truth.*

as·cribe /əˈskraɪb/ verb [T] (formal) **ascribe sth to sb/sth** to say that sth was written by or belonged to sb, or that sth was caused by sth: *This piece of music was ascribed to Bach, although we now believe it was written by another composer.* ○ *The company ascribed the price increases to a shortage of raw materials.*

☆ **ash** /æʃ/ noun **1** [C,U] (also **ashes** [plural]) the gray or black powder which is left after sth has burned: *They found the ring in the ashes of the fire.* ○ *The volcano produced huge clouds of ash.* **2 ashes** [plural] what remains after a human body has been burned **3** [C] a type of tree that is found in North America and Europe

☆ **a·shamed** /əˈʃeɪmd/ adj. **ashamed (of sth/sb/ yourself); ashamed (that...); ashamed (to...)** (not before a noun) feeling sorry or embarrassed about sb/sth or about yourself or sth you have done: *She was ashamed of her old clothes.* ○ *He was ashamed of himself for having made such an unkind remark.* ○ *She felt ashamed that she hadn't visited her aunt more often.* ○ *He knew that it was his fault, but he was ashamed to admit his mistake.*

a·shore /əˈʃɔr/ adv. onto the land: *The passengers went ashore for an hour while the ship was in port.*

ash·tray /ˈæʃtreɪ/ noun [C] a small dish for cigarette ashes

☆ **A·sian** /ˈeɪʒn/ noun [C] a person from Asia, especially the eastern part of Asia —**A·sian** adj.: *Asian cuisine*

☆ **Asian A'merican** noun [C] an American person whose family was originally from Asia, especially the eastern part —**Asian-American** adj.

☆ **a·side** /əˈsaɪd/ adv. **1** on or to one side; out of the way: *She took Richard aside to tell him her secret.* **2** to be kept separately, for a special purpose: *They are setting aside $100 a month for their summer vacation.*

a'side from prep. = APART FROM(1)

☆ **ask** /æsk/ verb **1** [I,T] **ask (sb) (about sb/sth)** to put a question to sb in order to find out some information: *We need to ask about the price.* ○ *Do you mind if I ask a dumb question?* ○ *I'll ask the salesman how much the jacket is.* ○ *Did you ask Sarah about the bike?* ○ *She asked whether I wanted tea or coffee.* ○ *"What time is it?" he asked.* ○ *He asked what time it was.* ○ *He asked me the time.* ○ *I got lost coming here and I had to ask somebody the way.* ○ *I saw Mrs. Vasquez today.* *She asked about you* (= asked about your health, etc.). **2** [I,T] **ask (sb) for**

sth; **ask sth (of sb); ask sb to do sth; ask (sb) that...** to request sb to give you sth or do sth for you: *She asked for a cup of coffee.* ○ *Don't ask John for money – he doesn't have any.* ○ *You are asking too much of him – he can't possibly do all that!* ○ *Call this number and ask for Mrs. Smith* (= ask to speak to Mrs. Smith). ○ *I asked him if he would drive me home.* ○ *I asked him to drive me home.* ○ *We ask that everyone remain seated.* ☞ Look at the note at **recommend** (2). **3** [T] to say the price that you want for sth: *They're asking $2,000 for their car.* **4** [I,T] to ask permission to do sth: *I'm sure she'll let you go if you ask.* ○ *He asked to use our phone.* ○ *We asked permission to go early.* ○ *We asked if we could go home early.* **5** [T] **ask sb (to sth)** to invite sb: *They asked six friends to dinner.* ○ *He asked Eileen out* (= asked her to go out with him) *this Saturday.*

IDM ask for trouble/it to behave in a way that will almost certainly cause trouble: *Not wearing a seat belt is just asking for trouble.*

if you ask me if you want my opinion: *If you ask me, she's too young to travel alone.*

a·skew /əˈskyu/ adv., adj. (not before a noun) not in a straight or level position

☆ **a·sleep** /əˈslip/ adj. (not before a noun) not awake; sleeping: *The baby is asleep.* ○ *She was fast/sound asleep and I couldn't wake her up.* ○ *to fall asleep*

☞ Notice that you can only use **asleep** after the noun. **Sleeping** can be used before or after the noun: *a sleeping child.* Look at the note at **sleep²**.

as·par·a·gus /əˈspærəgəs/ noun [U] a plant with long green stems that you can cook and eat as a vegetable

☆ **as·pect** /ˈæspɛkt/ noun [C] one of the qualities or parts of a situation, idea, problem, etc.: *information on many aspects of American life*

as·phalt /ˈæsfɔlt/ noun [U] a thick black substance that is used for making the surface of roads, etc.

as·phyx·i·ate /əsˈfɪksieɪt/ verb **1** [T] (usually passive) (used about gas, smoke, etc.) to cause sb to die or become very sick by making them unable to breathe: *He was asphyxiated by the smoke while he was asleep.* **2** [I] to die or become very sick because you are unable to breathe: *She asphyxiated on the fumes from the car's exhaust.* —**as·phyx·i·a·tion** /əsˌfɪksiˈeɪʃn/ noun [U]

as·pi·ra·tion /ˌæspəˈreɪʃn/ noun [C,U] (often plural) a strong desire to have or do sth: *She has aspirations to become an opera singer.*

as·pire /əˈspaɪr/ verb [I] **aspire to sth/to do sth** (formal) to have a strong desire to have or do sth: *She aspired to become president of the company.*

as·pi·rin /ˈæsprən/ (pl. **as·pi·rins** or **as·pi·rin**)

ər	ɪr	ɛr	ɑr	ɔr	ʊr	ʒ	h	ŋ
bird	near	hair	car	north	tour	vision	hat	sing

A

noun [C,U] a type of medicine that reduces pain and fever: *I took two aspirin(s)* (= two aspirin pills).

as·pir·ing /əsˈpaɪrɪŋ/ *adj.* (only *before* a noun) having a strong desire to become sth: *an aspiring ballet dancer*

as·sail·ant /əˈseɪlənt/ *noun* [C] (*formal*) a person who attacks sb

as·sas·sin /əˈsæsn/ *noun* [C] a person who kills a famous or important person for money or for political reasons

as·sas·si·nate /əˈsæsəneɪt/ *verb* [T] to kill a famous or important person for money or for political reasons ☞ Look at the note at **kill**. —**as·sas·si·na·tion** /ə͵sæsəˈneɪʃn/ *noun* [C,U]: *an assassination attempt*

as·sault /əˈsɔlt/ *noun* [C,U] **assault (on sb/sth)** a sudden attack on sb/sth: *Assaults on the police are becoming more common.* —**assault** *verb* [T]: *a prison sentence for assaulting a police officer*

as·sem·ble /əˈsɛmbl/ *verb* **1** [I,T] to come together in a group; to gather or collect: *The leaders assembled in Washington for the summit meeting.* ○ *I've assembled all the information I need for my essay.* **2** [T] to fit the parts of sth together: *We spent all day trying to assemble our new bookcase.*

as·sem·bly /əˈsɛmbli/ *noun* (*pl.* **as·sem·blies**) **1** [C,U] a large group of people who come together for a particular purpose: *There will be an assembly* (= a meeting for all the students and teachers of a school) *in the auditorium this afternoon.* ○ *the United Nations General Assembly* **2** [U] the act of fitting the parts of sth together: *the assembly of cars by robots*

asˈsembly line *noun* [C] a line of people and machines in a factory that fit the parts of sth together in a fixed order: *the assembly line workers at the Toyota car plant*

as·sent /əˈsɛnt/ *noun* [U] (*formal*) agreement: *The committee gave its assent to the proposed changes.*

as·sert /əˈsərt/ *verb* [T] **1** to say sth clearly and firmly: *He asserted that the allegations were untrue.* **2** to behave in a way that makes other people listen to you and take notice of you: *You ought to assert yourself more.* ○ *to assert your authority*

as·ser·tion /əˈsərʃn/ *noun* **1** [U] the act of asserting sth/yourself: *the assertion of power* **2** [C] something that you say firmly and clearly, but that you do not prove is true: *his confident assertion that he would win*

as·ser·tive /əˈsərtɪv/ *adj.* expressing your opinion clearly and firmly so that people listen to you and take notice of you: *to speak in an assertive manner* —**as·ser·tive·ly** *adv.* **as·ser·tive·ness** *noun* [U]

as·sess /əˈsɛs/ *verb* [T] **1** to judge or form an opinion about sth: *It's too early to assess the*

effects of the price increases. **2** to estimate or decide the amount or value of sth: *The value of the house was assessed at $75,000.* ○ *to assess the cost of repairs* **3** to decide the amount of money that sb should pay as a punishment: *to assess a fine*

as·sess·ment /əˈsɛsmənt/ *noun* [C,U] the act of judging or forming an opinion about sb/sth: *to make a careful assessment of a situation*

as·set /ˈæsɛt/ *noun* [C] **1 an asset (to sb/sth)** a person or thing that is useful to sb/sth: *She's a great asset to the organization.* ○ *It's an asset to be able to speak a foreign language.* **2** [usually pl.] something of value that a person, company, etc. owns: *The court ordered the company to sell off its remaining assets.*

as·sign /əˈsaɪn/ *verb* [T] **1 assign sth to sb** to give sth to sb for him/her to use or do **2 assign sb to sth** to give sb a particular job or type of work to do: *She was assigned to the accounting department.* ○ *A detective was assigned to the case.*

☆ **as·sign·ment** /əˈsaɪnmənt/ *noun* [C,U] a job or type of work that you are given to do: *to give students a homework assignment* ○ *a reporter on assignment in Moscow*

as·sim·i·late /əˈsɪmleɪt/ *verb* **1** [I,T] to become, or to allow sb/sth to become, part of a larger thing or group: *Many immigrants have difficulty in assimilating into their new culture.* ○ *to assimilate people from other cultures* **2** [T] to learn and understand sth: *to assimilate new information/ideas* —**as·sim·i·la·tion** /ə͵sɪməˈleɪʃn/ *noun* [U]

☆ **as·sist** /əˈsɪst/ *verb* [I,T] **assist (sb) (in/with sth); assist (sb) (in doing sth)** (*formal*) to help: *Dozens of police officers assisted in the search for the missing girl.*

☆ **as·sis·tance** /əˈsɪstəns/ *noun* [U] (*formal*) **1** help: *Our center provides assistance to recent immigrants in finding housing and employment.* **2** money that is given, especially by the government, to help sb: *financial assistance for college students* ○ *people living on public assistance* (= money that the government gives to poor people)

☆ **as·sis·tant** /əˈsɪstənt/ *noun* [C] (*abbr.* **asst.**) a person who helps sb of higher rank: *The director is away today. Would you like to speak with her assistant?* ○ *the assistant manager*

as͵sistant proˈfessor *noun* [C] a teacher at a college or university who is lower in rank than a professor and an associate professor

assn. *abbr.* = ASSOCIATION(2)

as·so·ci·ate¹ /əˈsoʊʃiət; -siət/ *adj.* (*abbr.* **assoc.**) (only *before* a noun) of a slightly lower rank or status: *associate members of the organization*

as·so·ci·ate² /əˈsoʊʃiət; -siət/ *noun* [C] a person that you meet and get to know through your work: *a business associate*

tʃ	dʒ	v	θ	ð	s	z	ʃ
chin	June	van	thin	then	so	zoo	she

A

☆ **as·so·ci·ate³** /əˈsəʊʃiˌeɪt; -siˌeɪt/ verb 1 [T] as-sociate sb/sth (with sb/sth) to connect sb/sth with sb/sth else (in your mind): illnesses associated with smoking ○ Somehow, I don't associate Iowa with skiing. 2 [I] associate with sb to spend time with sb: I prefer not to associate with colleagues outside work. 3 [T] associate yourself with sth to say that you support sth or agree with sth: I do not want to associate myself with any organization that promotes violence.

as¡sociate proˈfessor noun [C] a teacher at a college or university who is higher in rank than an assistant professor, but lower than a professor

asˈsociate's degree (also asˈsociate degree) noun [C] a degree that you get after studying for two years at a college or university

☆ **as·so·ci·a·tion** /əˌsəʊsiˈeɪʃn; -ʃiˈeɪʃn/ noun 1 [U] the act of joining or working with another person or group: We work in association with our London office. 2 (abbr. assn.; assoc.) [C] a group of people or organizations who join or work together for a particular purpose: a trade association ○ the American Medical Association 3 [C,U] the act of connecting sb/sth to sb/sth else in your mind

as·sort·ed /əˈsɔːtəd/ adj. of different types; mixed: a box of assorted chocolates

as·sort·ment /əˈsɔːtmənt/ noun [C] a group of different things or of different types of the same thing; a mixture: You'll find a wide assortment of souvenirs in our gift shop.

asst. abbr. = ASSISTANT

☆ **as·sume** /əˈsuːm/ verb [T] 1 to accept or believe that sth is true even though you have no proof; to expect sth to be true: I assume that you have the necessary documents. ○ You'll be going to the meeting, I assume? ○ In your calculations, assume x is a number greater than zero. 2 to falsely pretend to have or be sb/sth: to assume a false name 3 to begin to use power or to have a powerful position: to assume control of sth ○ to assume a position of responsibility

as·sump·tion /əˈsʌmpʃn/ noun 1 [C] something that you accept is true even though you have no proof: Our figures are based on the assumption that the rate of inflation will be 5%. ○ a reasonable, false, etc. assumption 2 [U] assumption of sth the act of taking power or of starting an important job: the assumption of power by the army

as·sur·ance /əˈʃʊərəns/ noun [C,U] (formal) a promise that sth will certainly happen or be true: News reporters gave assurances that the hurricane would move away from the coast. ○ a company's quality assurance procedures

as·sure /əˈʃʊər/ verb [T] 1 assure sb (of sth/that...) to promise sb that sth will certainly happen or be true, especially if he/she is wor-

ried : I assure you that it is perfectly safe. ○ Let me assure you of my full support. 2 to make sth sure or certain: The new road will assure adequate supplies of food to the region.

as·ter·isk /ˈæstərɪsk/ noun [C] the sign (*) that you use to call attention to sth in a piece of writing

asth·ma /ˈæzmə/ noun [U] a medical condition that causes difficulty in breathing: a new medication for asthma sufferers

asth·mat·ic /æzˈmætɪk/ noun [C] a person who suffers from asthma —**asth·mat·ic** adj.

☆ **a·ston·ish** /əˈstɒnɪʃ/ verb [T] to cause sb to be very surprised: She astonished everybody by announcing her engagement. —**a·ston·ished** adj.: The President was said to be astonished by the decision.

a·ston·ish·ing /əˈstɒnɪʃɪŋ/ adj. very surprising: astonishing news —**a·ston·ish·ing·ly** adv.: an astonishingly high price

a·ston·ish·ment /əˈstɒnɪʃmənt/ noun [U] very great surprise: To my absolute astonishment, the plan was a huge success. ○ A look of astonishment crossed her face. ○ He dropped his book in astonishment.

a·stound /əˈstaʊnd/ verb [T] (usually passive) to cause sb to be very surprised: We were astounded at how well he performed.

a·stound·ing /əˈstaʊndɪŋ/ adj. very surprising: an astounding success

a·stray /əˈstreɪ/ adv. away from the right way: Teenagers are easily led astray (= persuaded to do bad things by other people).

a·stride /əˈstraɪd/ adv., prep. with one leg on each side of sth: to sit astride a horse

as·trol·o·ger /əˈstrɒlədʒər/ noun [C] a person who is an expert in astrology

as·trol·o·gy /əˈstrɒlədʒi/ noun [U] the study of the positions and movements of the stars and planets and the way that they are supposed to affect people and events ☞ Look at **astronomy** and also at **horoscope** and **zodiac**.

as·tro·naut /ˈæstrənɔːt; -nɑːt/ noun [C] a person who travels in a spaceship

as·tron·o·mer /əˈstrɒnəmər/ noun [C] a person who is an expert in astronomy

as·tro·nom·i·cal /ˌæstrəˈnɒmɪkl/ adj. 1 connected with astronomy 2 very large, often too large (describing a price, number, amount, etc.): the astronomical prices of housing

as·tron·o·my /əˈstrɒnəmi/ noun [U] the scientific study of the sun, moon, stars, etc. ☞ Look at **astrology**.

as·tute /əˈstuːt/ adj. very intelligent; good at judging people or situations

a·sy·lum /əˈsaɪləm/ noun 1 [U] protection that a government gives to people who have left their own country for political reasons: political asylum 2 [C] (old-fashioned) a hospital for people who are mentally ill

i	ɪ	ε	æ	ɑ	ɔ	ʌ	ʊ	u
see	sit	ten	cat	hot	saw	cup	put	too

☆**at** /ət; *strong form* æt/ *prep.* **1** (showing the position of sth or where sth happens): *at the bottom/top of the page* ○ *He was standing at the door.* ○ *Turn left at the next intersection.* ○ *We were at home all weekend.* ○ *Are the kids still at school?* ○ *at the theater* ○ *"Where's Peter?" "He's at Sue's."* (= at Sue's house) ○ *You can reach me at 637-2335, extension 354* (= using this telephone number). **2** (showing when sth happens): *I start work at 9 o'clock.* ○ *at night* ○ *at Easter* ○ *She got married at 18* (= when she was 18). **3** in the direction of sb/sth: *What are you looking at?* ○ *He pointed a gun at the police officer.* ○ *Don't shout at me!* **4** because of: *I was surprised at her behavior.* ○ *We laughed at his jokes.* **5** (showing what sb is doing or what is happening): *They were hard at work.* ○ *The two countries were at war.* **6** (showing the amount, price, rate, speed, etc. of sth): *Bake at 350° for 25 minutes.* ○ *We were traveling at about 50 miles per hour.* **7** (used with adjectives that show how well sb/sth does sth): *She's not very good at French.* ○ *I'm terrible at baseball.*
IDM at any rate ⇨ RATE¹

ate *p.t.* of EAT

a·the·ism /ˈeɪθiɪzəm/ *noun* [U] the belief that there is no God

a·the·ist /ˈeɪθiɪst/ *noun* [C] a person who believes that there is no God

ath·lete /ˈæθlit/ *noun* [C] a person who is a member of a sports team or who regularly plays a sport or sports

☆**ath·let·ic** /æθˈlɛtɪk/ *adj.* **1** connected with athletes or athletics **2** (used about a person) having a strong, healthy body and able to play many sports well

ath·let·ics /æθˈlɛtɪks/ *noun* [plural] sports in which people or teams compete against each other

at·las /ˈætləs/ *noun* [C] (*pl.* **at·las·es**) a book of maps

ATM /ˌeɪ ti ˈɛm/ (*also* **cash machine**) *noun* [C] automated teller machine; a machine inside or outside a bank, in a shopping center, etc. from which you can get money at any time of day by putting in a special card

☆**at·mos·phere** /ˈætməsfɪr/ *noun* **1** [C, usually sing.] the atmosphere the mixture of gases that surrounds the earth or any other star, planet, etc.: *the earth's atmosphere* **2** [C, U] the mood or feeling of a place or situation: *There was a tense atmosphere during the final minutes of the game.*

at·mos·pher·ic /ˌætməsˈfɪrɪk/ *adj.* connected with the atmosphere (1)

☆**at·om** /ˈæṭəm/ *noun* [C] the smallest part into which an element can be divided ☞ Look at **molecule** and **nucleus**.

a·tom·ic /əˈtɑmɪk/ *adj.* of or concerning an atom or atoms: *atomic physics* ☞ Look at **nuclear**.

a·tomic ¹bomb (*also* **¹atom bomb**) *noun* [C] a bomb that explodes using the energy that is produced when an atom or atoms are split

a·tomic ¹energy *noun* [U] the energy that is produced when an atom or atoms are split. Atomic energy can be used to produce electricity. ☞ Look also at **nuclear**.

a·tro·cious /əˈtroʊʃəs/ *adj.* very bad or cruel: *atrocious crimes*

a·troc·i·ty /əˈtrɑsəṭi/ *noun* [C,U] (*pl.* **a·troc·i·ties**) (an act of) great cruelty: *Both sides were accused of committing atrocities during the war.*

☆**at·tach** /əˈtætʃ/ *verb* [T] **1 attach sth (to sth)** to fasten or connect sth to sth: *A note was attached to the document with a paper clip.* **2 attach sb to sb/sth** (*formal*) to make sb join another person or group: *Tom was attached to the embassy in Beijing for three years.* **3 attach sth to sb/sth** to think that sth has a particular quality: *Don't attach too much importance to what they say.* ○ *No blame was attached to him.*
IDM (with) no strings attached ⇨ STRING¹

at·tached /əˈtætʃt/ *adj.* attached to sb/sth liking sb/sth very much: *He's become very attached to you.*

at·tach·ment /əˈtætʃmənt/ *noun* **1** [C] something that can be fastened to sth else: *a camera with a flash attachment* **2** [C,U] **attachment (to/for sb/sth)** the feeling of liking sb/sth very much: *an emotional attachment* ○ *I feel a strong attachment to this house.*

☆**at·tack¹** /əˈtæk/ *noun* **1** [C,U] **an attack (on sb/sth)** an act of trying to hurt or defeat sb/sth by using force: *The rebel forces launched an attack on the capital.* ○ *to be under attack* (= to be attacked by sb/sth) **2** [C,U] **attack (on sb/sth)** an act of saying strongly that you do not like or agree with sb/sth: *an outspoken attack on the President's policy* **3** [C] a short period when you suffer badly from a disease, medical condition, etc.: *an attack of asthma, bronchitis, etc.* ☞ Look also at **heart attack**. **4** [C] an act of trying to score a point, goal, etc. in a sports game: *The Giants made several strong attacks but failed to score a touchdown.* ○ *The home team went on the attack again.*

☆**at·tack²** /əˈtæk/ *verb* **1** [I,T] to try to hurt or defeat sb/sth by using force: *The enemy attacked at night.* ○ *to be attacked by a wild animal* **2** [T] to say strongly that you do not like or agree with sb/sth: *The senator attacked the press for misleading the public.* **3** [T] to damage or harm sb/sth: *a virus that attacks the nervous system* **4** [I,T] to try to score a point in a sports game

at·tack·er /əˈtækər/ *noun* [C] a person who attacks sb/sth

at·tain /əˈteɪn/ *verb* [T] to succeed in getting or achieving sth, especially after great effort: *to attain your objectives*

ə	y	w	ṭ	eɪ	aɪ	ɔɪ	aʊ	oʊ
about	yes	woman	butter	say	five	boy	now	go

attainable

at·tain·a·ble /əˈteinəbl/ *adj.* that can be attained

at·tain·ment /əˈteinmənt/ *noun* **1** [U] the act of achieving sth: *the attainment of the teacher's goals* **2** [C,U] a level of skill or achievement: *to measure students' educational attainment*

☆ **at·tempt¹** /əˈtɛmpt/ *verb* [T] to try to do sth that is difficult: *The prisoner was shot while attempting to escape.* ○ *She was accused of attempted murder* (= she didn't succeed). ○ *Don't attempt to argue with him.*

☆ **at·tempt²** /əˈtɛmpt/ *noun* [C] **1 attempt (to do sth/at doing sth)** an act of trying to do sth: *He managed to hit the target on the first attempt.* ○ *They failed in their attempt to reach the North Pole.* **2 attempt (on sb/sth)** an act of trying to attack or beat sb/sth: *an attempt on sb's life* (= to kill sb)

☆ **at·tend** /əˈtɛnd/ *verb* **1** [T] to go to or be present at a place: *Do you attend church regularly?* ○ *I won't be able to attend tonight's meeting.* ○ *Our kids attend the local high school.* **2** [I] **attend to sb/sth** (*formal*) to give your care, thought or attention to sb/sth: *Please attend to this matter immediately.*

☆ **at·ten·dance** /əˈtɛndəns/ *noun* [U] **1** being present somewhere: *Attendance at lectures is not mandatory.* **2** the number of people who go to or are present at a place: *Attendance at the club's meetings has decreased in recent months.*
IDM **take attendance** to check who is present and who is absent at a place, and to mark this information on a list of names

at·ten·dant¹ /əˈtɛndənt/ *noun* [C] a person who takes care of a public place or a business: *a gas station attendant* ☞ Look also at **flight attendant**.

at·ten·dant² /əˈtɛndənt/ *adj.* (only *before* a noun) (*formal*) that goes with or results from sth: *unemployment and all its attendant social problems*

☆ **at·ten·tion¹** /əˈtɛnʃn/ *noun* [U] **1** the act of watching, listening to or thinking about sb/sth carefully: *The bride is always the center of attention* (= the person that everybody is watching). ○ *I shouted in order to attract her attention.* ○ *to hold sb's attention* (= to keep them interested in sth) **2** special care or action: *The hole in the roof needs urgent attention.* ○ *to require medical attention* **3** a position in which a soldier stands up straight and still: *to stand at attention*
IDM **bring sth to sb's attention; call/draw sb's attention to sth** to make sb aware of sth
catch sb's attention/eye; get sb's attention to make sb notice sth: *I tried to get the waiter's attention.*
come to sb's attention (*formal*) to be seen or heard by sb: *It has come to my attention that you have missed a lot of classes.*
pay attention ⇨ PAY²

at·ten·tion² /əˈtɛnʃn/ *interj.* (used for asking

people to listen to sth carefully): *Attention, please! The boat will be leaving in five minutes.*

at·ten·tive /əˈtɛntɪv/ *adj.* watching, listening to or thinking about sb/sth carefully: *The waiters in that restaurant were very attentive.* ○ *an attentive audience* —**at·ten·tive·ly** *adv.*: *listen attentively to sth*

☆ **at·tic** /ˈætɪk/ *noun* [C] the space or room under the roof of a house

☆ **at·ti·tude** /ˈætətud/ *noun* [C] **attitude (to/ toward sb/sth)** the way that you think, feel or behave: *social attitudes and beliefs* ○ *She has a very positive attitude toward her work.*

at·tor·ney /əˈtərni/ (*also* **attorney at law**) *noun* [C] (*pl.* **at·tor·neys**) a lawyer ☞ Look also at **district attorney**.

at·torney ˈgeneral *noun* [C] (*pl.* **attorneys general** *or* **attorney generals**) the chief lawyer for the United States or for a particular state, appointed by the government

☆ **at·tract** /əˈtrækt/ *verb* [T] **1** to cause sb/sth to go to or give attention to sth: *to attract sb's attention* ○ *Moths are attracted to light.* ○ *The new movie has attracted a lot of publicity.* **2** to cause sb to like sb/sth: *She's attracted to older men.*

at·trac·tion /əˈtrækʃn/ *noun* **1** [U] attracting or being attracted: *I can't understand the attraction of fishing.* ○ *sexual attraction* **2** [C] something that attracts sb/sth: *Washington, D.C., offers all kinds of tourist attractions.* ○ *One of the attractions of the job is having a company car.*

☆ **at·trac·tive** /əˈtræktɪv/ *adj.* **1** that pleases or interests you; that you like: *an attractive idea* **2** pretty, beautiful or handsome: *an attractive room* ○ *an attractive man/woman* —**at·trac·tive·ly** *adv.* —**at·trac·tive·ness** *noun* [U]

at·trib·ute¹ /əˈtrɪbyut/ *verb* [T] **attribute sth to sb/sth** to believe that sth was caused or done by sb/sth: *Jamal attributes his success to hard work.* ○ *a poem attributed to Shakespeare*

at·trib·ute² /ˈætrəbyut/ *noun* [C] a quality or feature of sb/sth: *physical attributes*

atty. *abbr.* = ATTORNEY

au·burn /ˈɔbərn/ *adj.* (usually used about hair) reddish-brown

auc·tion¹ /ˈɔkʃn/ *noun* [C,U] a public sale at which items are sold to the person who offers to pay the most money: *The house will be sold by auction.*

auc·tion² /ˈɔkʃn/ *verb* [T] **auction sth (off)** to sell sth at an auction ¹

auc·tion·eer /ˌɔkʃəˈnɪr/ *noun* [C] a person who organizes the selling at an auction ¹

au·di·ble /ˈɔdəbl/ *adj.* that can be heard: *Her speech was barely audible.* ☞ Look at **inaudible**. —**au·di·bly** /-əbli/ *adv.*: *to sigh audibly*

☆ **au·di·ence** /ˈɔdiəns/ *noun* [C] **1** the group of people who are watching or listening to a play, concert, speech, the television, etc.: *The audience was wild with excitement.* ○ *Television*

ər	ɪr	ɛr	ɑr	ɔr	ʊr	ʒ	h	ŋ
bird	near	hair	car	north	tour	vision	hat	sing

can reach an audience of millions. **2** a formal meeting with a very important person: *an audience with the Pope*

au·di·o /ˈɔdioʊ/ *adj.* connected with the recording of sound: *audio equipment* ○ *audio tape*

au·di·o·vis·u·al /ˌɔdioʊˈvɪʒuəl/ *adj.* (*abbr.* AV) using both sound and pictures: *A VCR is an excellent audiovisual aid in the classroom.*

au·dit[1] /ˈɔdət/ *noun* [C] an official examination of the accounts and tax records of a person, company, etc. to see that they are correct: *a tax audit*

au·dit[2] /ˈɔdət/ *verb* [T] **1** to examine the accounts and tax records of a person, company, etc., in an official way to see that they are correct **2** to attend a course, lecture, etc. at a college or university without having to take any tests and without receiving credit for the course —**au·di·tor** /ˈɔdətər/ *noun* [C]

au·di·tion /ɔˈdɪʃn/ *noun* [C] a short performance by a singer, actor, musician, etc. to find out if he/she is good enough to be in a play, show, concert, etc.

☆ **au·di·to·ri·um** /ˌɔdəˈtɔriəm/ *noun* [C] (*pl.* **au·di·to·ri·ums** or (*formal*)**au·di·to·ri·a**) a large room like a theater where people sit and watch a performance, etc.: *The principal will be giving a speech in the school auditorium.*

☆ **Au·gust** /ˈɔgəst/ *noun* [C,U] (*abbr.* **Aug.**) the eighth month of the year, coming before September ☞ For examples of the use of the months in sentences, look at **January**.

☆ **aunt** /ænt; ɑnt/ *noun* [C] the sister of your father or mother; or, the wife of your uncle: *Aunt Ann*

au·ra /ˈɔrə/ *noun* [C] (*formal*) the quality that sb/sth seems to have: *The small town had an aura of peace and tranquility.*

au·ral /ˈɔrəl/ *adj.* of or concerning the ear or hearing: *an aural comprehension test* ☞ Look at **oral**.

aus·pi·ces /ˈɔspəsəz; -sɪz/ *noun* [plural] **under the auspices of sb/sth** with the help and support of sb/sth: *The visit was arranged under the auspices of the local church.*

aus·pi·cious /ɔˈspɪʃəs/ *adj.* (*formal*) that seems likely to lead to success: *an auspicious occasion*

aus·tere /ɔˈstɪr/ *adj.* **1** not having pleasures or luxuries: *The nuns lead simple and austere lives.* **2** very plain and simple; without decoration —**aus·ter·i·ty** /ɔˈstɛrəti/ *noun* [U]

au·then·tic /ɔˈθɛntɪk/ *adj.* that you know is true or genuine: *an authentic Van Gogh painting* —**au·then·tic·i·ty** /ˌɔθɛnˈtɪsəti/ *noun* [U]: *to check the authenticity of a document*

☆ **au·thor**[1] /ˈɔθər/ *noun* [C] a person who writes a book, play, etc.: *a well-known author of detective novels* —**au·thor·ship** *noun* [U]: *The authorship of the play is unknown.*

au·thor[2] /ˈɔθər/ *verb* [T] to be responsible for

writing a document, book, law, etc.: *The senator authored a new bill on traffic safety.*

au·thor·i·tar·i·an /əˌθɔrəˈtɛriən; əˌθɑr-/ *adj.* not allowing people the freedom to decide things for themselves: *The authoritarian government crushed all signs of opposition.* ○ *authoritarian parents*

au·thor·i·ta·tive /əˈθɔrəˌteɪtɪv; əˌθɑr-/ *adj.* **1** having authority; demanding or expecting that people obey you: *an authoritative tone of voice* **2** that you can trust because it/he/she has a lot of knowledge and information: *They will be able to give you authoritative advice on the problem.*

☆ **au·thor·i·ty** /əˈθɔrəti; əˈθɑr-/ *noun* (*pl.* **au·thor·i·ties**) **1** [C] (often plural) a person, group or government department that has the power to give orders, make official decisions, etc.: *the city housing authority* ○ *The Canadian authorities refused permission for the hijacked plane to land.* **2** [U] the power and right to give orders and make others obey: *Children often begin to question their parents' authority at a very early age.* ○ *You need to get this signed by a person in authority* (= who has a position of power). **3** [U] **authority (to do sth)** the right to act in a particular way: *Do the police have the authority to question anybody they want?* **4** [U] a quality that sb has which makes it possible to influence and control other people: *He spoke with authority and everybody listened.* **5** [C] a person with special knowledge: *She's an authority on ancient Egypt.*

au·thor·i·za·tion /ˌɔθərəˈzeɪʃn/ *noun* [U] official permission for sth: *I can't give you that information without authorization.*

au·thor·ize /ˈɔθəraɪz/ *verb* [T] to give official permission for sth or for sb to do sth: *Any new buildings have to be authorized by the city council.* ○ *He authorized his secretary to sign letters in his absence.*

au·tis·tic /ɔˈtɪstɪk/ *adj.* having a serious mental illness which makes it very difficult to form relationships with other people

au·to /ˈɔtoʊ/ *noun* [C] (*pl.* **au·tos**) (*formal*) a car: *auto insurance* ☞ It is more common to say **car**.

au·to·bi·og·ra·phy /ˌɔtəbaɪˈɑgrəfi/ *noun* [C,U] (*pl.* **au·to·bi·og·ra·phies**) the story of a person's life written by that person ☞ Look at **biography**. —**au·to·bi·o·graph·i·cal** /ˌɔtəˌbaɪəˈgræfɪkl/ *adj.*: *an autobiographical novel*

au·to·graph[1] /ˈɔtəgræf/ *noun* [C] the signature of a famous person: *We waited at the stage door to get the dancer's autograph.*

au·to·graph[2] /ˈɔtəgræf/ *verb* [T] to put your signature on or in sth: *a painting autographed by the artist*

au·to·mate /ˈɔtəmeɪt/ *verb* [T] (usually passive) to make sth operate by machine, without

A

needing people: *The system in the factory has been fully automated.*

☆**au·to·mat·ic¹** /ˌɔtəˈmætɪk/ *adj.* **1** (used about a machine) that can work by itself without direct human control: *an automatic garage door opener* ○ *a car with automatic transmission* ☞ Look at **manual**. **2** (used about actions) done without thinking or like a machine; unconscious: *Practice this exercise until it becomes automatic.* **3** certain to happen because it is part of a normal process: *Cheating will result in your automatic failure of this course.* —**au·to·mat·i·cal·ly** /-kli/ *adv.*: *The lights come on automatically when it gets dark.*

au·to·mat·ic² /ˌɔtəˈmætɪk/ *noun* [C] an automatic machine or gun: *The weapon used in the robbery was a .357 automatic.*

au·to·ma·tion /ˌɔtəˈmeɪʃn/ *noun* [U] the use of machines, instead of people, to do work

au·to·mo·bile /ˌɔtəməˈbil; ˈɔtəməbil/ *noun* [C] (*formal*) a car: *the automobile industry*

au·to·mo·tive /ˌɔtəˈmoʊṭɪv/ *adj.* connected with cars, trucks, etc.: *automotive parts and accessories*

au·ton·o·mous /ɔˈtɑnəməs/ *adj.* having the right to govern or control its own affairs: *The people in this region want to be completely autonomous.*

au·ton·o·my /ɔˈtɑnəmi/ *noun* [U] the right of an organization, region, etc. to govern or control its own affairs

au·top·sy /ˈɔtɑpsi/ *noun* [C] (*pl.* **au·top·sies**) an examination of a dead body to find out the cause of death: *to perform an autopsy*

au·tumn /ˈɔtəm/ *noun* [C,U] (*formal*) fall; the season between summer and winter

aux·il·ia·ry¹ /ɔgˈzɪləri; -ˈzɪlyəri/ *adj.* (only before a noun) giving extra help: *auxiliary personnel, troops, etc.* ○ *auxiliary equipment*

aux·il·ia·ry² /ɔgˈzɪləri; -ˈzɪlyəri/ (*also* **auxiliary verb**; **helping verb**) *noun* [C] (*pl.* **aux·il·ia·ries**) (*grammar*) a verb (e.g. *be, do* or *have*) that is used with a main verb to show tense, etc. or to form questions

AV /ˌeɪ ˈvi/ *abbr.* = AUDIOVISUAL: *AV equipment*

Av. *abbr.* = AVENUE

a·vail /əˈveɪl/ *noun* [U]

to little/no avail without success: *They searched everywhere, but to no avail.*

a·vail·a·bil·i·ty /əˌveɪləˈbɪləṭi/ *noun* [U] the state of being available: *the availability of health care in rural areas*

☆**a·vail·a·ble** /əˈveɪləbl/ *adj.* **1** (used about things) that you can get, buy, use, etc.: *Are there still tickets available for the concert?* ○ *Her latest novel is now available in bookstores everywhere.* ○ *The available evidence was not sufficient to prove that he was guilty.* **2** (used about people) free to be seen, talked to, etc.: *The senator was not available for an interview.*

av·a·lanche /ˈævəlæntʃ/ *noun* [C] a very large amount of snow that slides quickly down

the side of a mountain: *Two skiers are still missing after yesterday's avalanche.* ○ (*figurative*) *The company received an avalanche of complaints.*

a·vant-garde /ˌævɑŋ ˈgɑrd; ˌavɑŋ-/ *adj.* (used especially about art and literature) extremely new and modern

Ave. *abbr.* = AVENUE

a·venge /əˈvɛndʒ/ *verb* [T] to punish sb for hurting you, your family, etc. in some way: *He wanted to avenge his father's murder.* ☞ Look at **revenge**.

☆**av·e·nue** /ˈævənu/ *noun* [C] **1** (*abbr.* **Av.**; **Ave.**) (used in the names of some streets in towns and cities): *I live at 12 Tennyson Avenue.* ○ *at the corner of Sixth Avenue and 72nd Street*

☞ The central parts of many American cities were designed with straight **streets** and **avenues** that cross each other at right angles to form square or rectangular **blocks**. **Streets** usually run from east to west, and **avenues** usually run from north to south. Look also at the note at **road**.

2 a way of doing or getting sth: *We must explore every avenue open to us* (= try every possibility).

☆**av·er·age¹** /ˈævrɪdʒ/ *noun* **1** [C] the number you get when you add two or more figures together and then divide the total by the number of figures you added: *The average of 14, 3 and 1 is 6* (= 18 divided by 3 is 6). **2** [C] the average (1) of grades that a student receives on tests, written work, etc.: *If I get an A on the next quiz, that will bring my average up to a B+.* ☞ Look also at **grade point average**. **3** [sing., U] the normal standard, amount or quality: *Temperatures this week have been well below the average for this time of year.* ○ *On average, Americans consume more fat than people from Asian countries do.*

☆**av·er·age²** /ˈævrɪdʒ/ *adj.* **1** (only before a noun) (used about a number) found by calculating the average¹(1): *What's the average age of your students?* **2** normal or typical: *an average income* ○ *children of above/below average intelligence* **3** not very good: *I was just an average student in math.*

av·er·age³ /ˈævrɪdʒ/ *verb* [T] to do, get, etc. a certain amount as an average: *If we average 50 miles an hour, we should get there at about 4 o'clock.*

PHRV **average out (to sth)** to result in an average (of sth): *The meal averaged out to about $20 each.*

a·verse /əˈvərs/ *adj.* **averse to sth** (*formal*) (often with a negative) against or opposed to sth: *She is not averse to trying out new ideas.*

a·ver·sion /əˈvərʒn/ *noun* [C] **1** [usually sing.] **an aversion (to sb/sth)** a feeling of great dislike: *Many children have an aversion to*

vegetables. **2** a thing that you greatly dislike: *Math was always an aversion of mine.*

a·vert /ə'vərt/ *verb* [T] to prevent sth unpleasant; to avoid: *The accident could have been averted.*

a·vi·a·tion /ˌeɪvi'eɪʃn/ *noun* [U] the flying or building of aircraft: *the aviation industry*

av·id /'ævəd/ *adj.* (only *before* a noun) enthusiastic and eager: *an avid golfer* —**av·id·ly** *adv.*: *He read avidly as a child.*

av·o·ca·do /ˌɑvə'kɑdoʊ; ˌævə-/ *noun* [C] (*pl.* **av·o·ca·dos**) a fruit shaped like a pear with tough dark green skin and a large hard part (**pit**) inside

☆ **a·void** /ə'vɔɪd/ *verb* [T] **1 avoid (doing sth)** to prevent sth from happening: *He always tried to avoid an argument if possible.* ○ *She has to avoid eating fatty food* (= she must make an effort not to eat it). **2** to keep away from (sb/sth): *I leave home at 7 o'clock to avoid the rush hour.* ○ *She's been trying to avoid her boyfriend recently.* —**a·void·ance** /ə'vɔɪdns/ *noun* [U]

a·void·a·ble /ə'vɔɪdəbl/ *adj.* that can be prevented; unnecessary: *Smoking is considered the chief avoidable cause of death in the U.S.* ☞ The opposite is **unavoidable.**

aw /ɔ/ *interj.* (used for expressing affection, sympathy, disappointment, etc.): *Aw, what a cute baby!* ○ *Aw, that's too bad.* ☞ Look at **ah.**

a·wait /ə'weɪt/ *verb* [T] (*formal*) **1** (used about people) to wait for sb/sth: *Please await further instructions.* **2** (used about things or events) to be ready or waiting for sb/sth: *We were unaware of the danger that awaited us.*

☆ **a·wake¹** /ə'weɪk/ *adj.* (not before a noun) not sleeping: *I was awake most of the night, worrying.* ○ *The kids are always wide* (= completely) *awake at 6 o'clock in the morning.* ○ *They were so tired that they couldn't stay awake.* ☞ The opposite is **asleep.**

a·wake² /ə'weɪk/ *verb* (*p.t.* **a·woke** /ə'woʊk/; *p.p.* **a·wok·en** /ə'woʊkən/) **1** [I,T] to wake up; to make sb/sth wake up: *I awoke to find that it was already 9 o'clock.* ○ *A sudden loud noise awoke us all.* ☞ **Wake up** is more common than **awake. 2** [T] to make sb have a particular feeling, attitude, etc.: *His words awoke fear and hatred in the boy.*

a·wak·en /ə'weɪkən/ *verb* **1** [I,T] (*formal*) to wake up; to make sb/sth wake up: *I awakened to find the others already up.* ○ *We were awakened by a knock at the door.* ☞ **Wake up** is much more common than **awaken. 2** [T] (*formal*) to produce a particular feeling, attitude, etc. in sb: *The movie awakened memories of her childhood.*

PHRV **awaken sb to sth** to make sb become aware of sth: *The letter awakened me to the seriousness of the situation.*

a·wak·en·ing /ə'weɪkənɪŋ/ *noun* [sing.] **1** the start (of a feeling, etc.): *the awakening of an* interest in environmental issues **2** an act of realizing: *It was a rude* (= unpleasant) *awakening when I suddenly found myself unemployed.*

☆ **a·ward¹** /ə'wɔrd/ *verb* [T] **award sth (to sb)** to give sth to sb as a prize, payment, etc.: *She was awarded first prize in the music competition.* ○ *The court awarded $100,000 each to the workers injured in the accident.*

☆ **a·ward²** /ə'wɔrd/ *noun* [C] **1** a prize, etc. that sb gets for doing sth well: *This year, the awards for best actor and actress went to two newcomers to Hollywood.* **2** an amount of money given to sb as the result of a court decision: *She received an award of $5,000 for damages.*

☆ **a·ware** /ə'wɛr/ *adj.* **1 aware (of sb/sth); aware (that)** knowing about or realizing sth; conscious of sb/sth: *I am aware of the difficulties you face.* ○ *I am aware that you will face difficulties.* ○ *She suddenly felt aware of somebody watching her.* ○ *There is no other entrance, as far as I am aware.* ☞ The opposite is **unaware. 2** interested and informed: *to be politically aware*

a·ware·ness /ə'wɛrnəs/ *noun* [U] knowledge, consciousness or interest: *People's awareness of healthy eating has increased in recent years.*

a·wash /ə'wɑʃ; ə'wɔʃ/ *adj.* **awash in/with sth** having too much of sth: *The city was awash with rumors.*

☆ **a·way** /ə'weɪ/ *adv.* ☞ Look also at phrasal verbs, e.g. **give away, take away. 1 away (from sb/sth)** to a different place or in a different direction: *Go away! I'm busy!* ○ *I asked him a question, but he just looked away.* **2** at a distance from a place: *My parents live five miles away.* ○ *The town is two miles away from the ocean.* **3 away (from sth)** (used about people) not present; absent: *My neighbors are away on vacation right now.* ○ *Tom was away from school for two weeks with the measles.* **4 away (from sth)** in the future: *Our summer vacation is only three weeks away.* **5** into a safe place: *Put your books away now.* ○ *They cleared away the dishes* (= off the table). ☞ Contrast **throw that away** (= put it in the garbage can). **6** (used about a football, etc. team) at the other team's field, stadium, etc.: *Our team's playing away on Saturday.* **7** until it disappears completely: *The noise slowly died away.* ○ *The picture has almost faded away.* **8** continuously, without stopping: *They chatted away for hours.*

IDM **right away** ⇨ RIGHT²

awe /ɔ/ *noun* [U] a feeling of respect and either fear or admiration: *We watched in awe as the rocket took off into space.* ○ *As a boy he was very much in awe of his uncle.*

'awe-in,spiring *adj.* causing a feeling of respect and fear or admiration

awe·some /'ɔsəm/ *adj.* **1** (*formal*) impressive

B

and sometimes frightening: *an awesome task* **2** (*slang*) very good; excellent: *We went to an awesome party at Dave's house.* ○ *Wow! That's totally awesome!*

☆ **aw·ful** /ˈɔfl/ *adj.* **1** very bad or unpleasant: *We had an awful vacation. It rained every day.* ○ *What an awful thing to say!* **2** terrible; very serious: *I have some awful news for you.* **3** (only *before* a noun) (*informal*) very great or large: *I'm in an awful hurry. See you later.* ○ *We've got an awful lot of work to do.*

aw·ful·ly /ˈɔfli/ *adv.* (*informal*) very; very much: *I'm awfully sorry.*

awk·ward /ˈɔkwərd/ *adj.* **1** not convenient, difficult: *My mother always calls at an awkward time.* ○ *an awkward question* **2** embarrassed; not relaxed: *an awkward silence* **3** without grace or skill: *an awkward gesture* ○ *an awkward teenage boy* —**awk·ward·ly** *adv.* **awk·ward·ness** *noun* [U]

a·woke *p.t.* of AWAKE[1]

a·wok·en *p.p.* of AWAKE[1]

a·wry /əˈraɪ/ *adv.* wrong, not in the way that was planned: *Our plans went awry.*

ax[1] (*also* **axe**) /æks/ *noun* [C] a tool with a wooden handle and a metal blade used for cutting wood, etc.: *He chopped the tree down with an ax.*

ax[2] (*also* **axe**) /æks/ *verb* [T] **1** to remove or end sth: *Hundreds of jobs have been axed.* **2** to reduce sth greatly: *School budgets are to be axed.*

ax·is /ˈæksəs/ *noun* [C] (*pl.* **ax·es** /ˈæksiz/) **1** an imaginary line through the middle of an object that turns: *The earth rotates on its axis.* ☛ picture at **earth**. **2** a fixed line used for marking measurements on a graph: *the horizontal/vertical axis*

ax·le /ˈæksl/ *noun* [C] a bar that connects a pair of wheels on a vehicle

Bb

B, b /bi/ *noun* [C] (*pl.* **B's**; **b's** /biz/) **1** the second letter of the English alphabet: *"Bill" begins with (a) "B."* **2** the second-highest grade given for a test or a piece of work, lower than an "A": *I got a "B" on my essay.*

B.A. /ˌbi ˈeɪ/ *abbr.* Bachelor of Arts; a degree that you receive when you complete a program of study at a college or university

baa /bɑ; bæ/ *noun* [C] the sound that a sheep or lamb makes

bab·ble[1] /ˈbæbl/ *verb* [I] **1** to talk quickly, especially about unimportant things, or in a way that is difficult to understand: *What are you babbling about?* **2** to make the sound of water running over stones: *a babbling brook*

bab·ble[2] /ˈbæbl/ *noun* [U] **1** the sound of many voices talking at the same time: *I could hear a babble of voices coming from downstairs.* **2** the sound of water running over stones

babe /beɪb/ *noun* [C] **1** (*old-fashioned*) a baby **2** (*slang*) (used when talking to sb, especially a girl or young woman): *Hey babe, how's it going?* ☛ Many women dislike the use of this word.

☆ **ba·by** /ˈbeɪbi/ *noun* [C] (*pl.* **ba·bies**) **1** a very young child: *I've got some great news. I'm going to have a baby!* ○ *She's expecting a baby early next year .* ○ *When's the baby due?* (= when will it be born?) ○ *a baby boy/girl* **2** a very young animal or bird: *a baby rabbit* **3** (*slang*) (used when talking to sb, especially

sb that you love) ☛ Many women dislike the use of this word.

baby boom *noun* [C, usually sing.] a period of time when a lot of babies are born. In the U.S., this usually means the time between the end of World War II and about 1964: *the baby boom generation*

baby boomer *noun* [C] a person who was born during a baby boom ☛ Look at **yuppie**.

baby carriage *noun* [C] a small vehicle for a baby to go out in. A baby carriage has four wheels, a hood and a handle to push it with. ☛ picture at **stroller**.

ba·by·sit /ˈbeɪbisɪt/ *verb* [I,T] (**ba·by·sit·ting**; *p.t., p.p.* **ba·by·sat**) to take care of a child for a short time while the parents are out: *We have friends who babysit for us if we go out in the evening.* —**ba·by·sit·ter** /ˈbeɪbisɪtər/ (*also* **sit·ter**) *noun* [C]: *We can't come tonight. We couldn't find a babysitter.* ☛ Look at **daycare**.

bach·e·lor /ˈbætʃlər; ˈbætʃələr/ *noun* [C] **1** (*old-fashioned*) a man who is not yet married ☛ Nowadays it is more common to say "a single man" or "He's single."

2 (used in the name of a college or university degree that you get after studying for four years): *a Bachelor of Arts/Science* ○ *I have a bachelor's degree in biology.* ☛ Look at the note at **degree**.

☆ **back[1]** /bæk/ *noun* [C] **1** the part of a person's or animal's body between the neck and the

ər	ɪr	ɛr	ɑr	ɔr	ʊr	ʒ	h	ŋ
bird	near	hair	car	north	tour	vision	hat	sing

hips: *Do you sleep on your back or on your side?* ○ *She was standing with her back to me, so I couldn't see her face.* ○ *He swung himself up onto the horse's back.* **2** the part or side of sth that is farthest from the front: *Dan couldn't see the blackboard because he was sitting at the back of the class.* ○ *Jane sat next to the driver, and I sat in the back of the car.* ○ *The back of the house looks much nicer than the front.* ○ *There's some information about the author at the back of the book.* ○ *You need to sign the back of the check in order to cash it.* **3** the part of a chair that you lean against when you sit down: *Don't climb on the back of the couch!* **IDM behind sb's back** without sb's knowledge or agreement: *They criticized her behind her back.*
get off sb's back (*informal*) to stop bothering or annoying sb: *I wish she'd get off my back!*
in back of = BEHIND¹(1)
in the back of your mind in your thoughts, but not the main thing that you are thinking about: *Even when I'm at work, that problem is in the back of my mind.*
know sth inside out/like the back of your hand ⇨ KNOW
a pat on the back ⇨ PAT²

☆**back²** /bæk/ *adj.* **1** (only *before* a noun) farthest from the front: *Did you lock the back door?* ○ *the back row of the theater* ○ *back teeth* **2** owed for a time in the past: *back taxes* **IDM on the back burner** (*informal*) (used about an idea, a plan, etc.) left to be done or considered later: *We'll have to put that project on the back burner until our financial situation improves.*

☆**back³** /bæk/ *adv.* **1** in or to a place or state that sb/sth was in before: *'Bye! I'll be back around 6 o'clock* (= back home again). ○ *When is Joe coming back from Australia?* ○ *Go back to sleep.* ○ *Can I have my pen back, please?* **2** away from the direction you are facing or moving in: *She walked away without looking back.* ○ *Could everyone move back a little, please?* **3** away from sth; under control: *The police were unable to keep the crowds back.* ○ *She tried to hold back her tears.* **4** in return or in reply: *He said he'd call me back in an hour.* **5** in or into the past; ago: *I met him a few years back, in Seattle.* ○ *Think back to your first day in school.* **IDM back and forth** from one place to another and back again, all the time: *Traveling back and forth to work takes up a lot of time.* ○ *The dog ran back and forth, barking* .

☆**back⁴** /bæk/ *verb* **1** [I,T] to move backward or to make sth move backward: *I'll have to back into that parking space.* ○ *She backed the car into the parking space.* **2** [T] to give help or support to sb/sth: *We can go ahead with the project if the bank will agree to back us.* **3** [T]

to bet money that a particular horse, team, etc. will win in a race or game
PHRV back away (from sb/sth) to move backward because you are afraid, shocked, etc.: *He began to back slowly away from the snake.*
back down to stop insisting that you are right: *I think you are right to demand an apology. Don't back down now.*
back out (of sth) to decide not to do sth that you had promised to do: *You promised you would come with me. You can't back out of it now!*
back up to move backward, especially in a car, etc.: *Back up slowly – there might be another car coming.*
back sb/sth up to support sb; to say or show that sth is true: *I'm going to say exactly what I think at the meeting. Will you back me up?* ○ *All the evidence backed up what the man had said.*
back sth up 1 (*computing*) to make a copy of a computer program, etc. in case the original one is lost or damaged: *If you don't back up your files, you risk losing data.* **2** to move a car, etc. backward: *Back the truck up a little so that other people can get past.*

back·bone /ˈbækboʊn/ *noun* **1** [C] the line of bones down the back of your body ☞ Look at **spine.** **2** [sing.] the main strength or support: *Volunteer workers are the backbone of the organization.*

back·er /ˈbækər/ *noun* [C] a person who gives support or money to another person, a project, etc.

back·fire /ˌbækˈfaɪər/ *verb* [I] to have an unexpected and unwanted result, often the opposite of what was intended: *This decision could easily backfire on us.*

☆**back·ground** /ˈbækgraʊnd/ *noun* **1** [C] the type of family and social class you come from and the education and experience you have: *We get along really well together in spite of our different backgrounds.* ○ *a middle-class background* **2** [sing., U] the facts or events that are connected with a situation: *The talks are taking place against a background of increasing tension.* ○ *I need some background information.* **3** [sing.] the part of a view, scene, picture, etc. which is farthest away from the person looking at it: *You can see the mountains in the background of the picture.* ☞ Look at **foreground.** **4** [sing.] a position where sb/sth can be seen/heard, etc. but is not the center of attention: *The senator's husband prefers to stay in the background.* ○ *I could hear a baby crying in the background.* ○ *The restaurant kept playing the same background music again and again.*

back·hand /ˈbækhænd/ *noun* [sing.] a stroke in tennis, etc. that is made with the back of your hand facing forward ☞ Look at **forehand.**

back·ing /ˈbækɪŋ/ *noun* [U] help or support to

tʃ	dʒ	v	θ	ð	s	z	ʃ
chin	June	van	thin	then	so	zoo	she

do sth, often in the form of money: *financial backing*

back·lash /ˈbæklæʃ/ *noun* [sing.] a strong re-action against a political or social event or development

back·log /ˈbæklɔg; -lɑg/ *noun* [C, usually sing.] an amount of work, etc. that has not yet been done and needs to be done: *I have a huge backlog of mail to answer.*

back·pack¹ /ˈbækpæk/ *noun* [C] a bag that you use for carrying things on your back. You often use a backpack when you are walking, camping, going to school, etc. ☞ picture at **luggage.**

back·pack² /ˈbækpæk/ *verb* [I] to go walking, traveling, etc. with a backpack: *Before I start college, I'm going to spend a year backpacking around the world.* —**back·pack·er** /ˈbækpækər/ *noun* [C]: *We met a lot of other back-packers at the youth hostel.*

back·side /ˈbæksaɪd/ *noun* [C] the part of the body that you sit on; your buttocks

back·stage /ˌbækˈsteɪdʒ/ *adv.* behind the stage in a theater, where the actors get dressed, etc.

back·stroke /ˈbækstroʊk/ *noun* [U] a style of swimming that you do on your back: *Can you do the backstroke?*

back·up /ˈbækʌp/ *noun* **1** [U] extra help or support: *Her success is partly due to the backup she gets from her team.* **2** [C] an extra thing or a copy of sth that you can use if the original one is lost or damaged: *Always make a backup of your computer files.* ○ *We have a generator to use as a backup when the lights goes out.*

☆ **back·ward¹** /ˈbæk-wərd/ *adj.* **1** (only *be-fore* a noun) directed toward the back: *a backward step, glance, etc.* **2** not modern; not aware of other cul-tures, etc.: *Transpor-tation is very difficult in the more backward areas of the country.*

backwards

☆ **back·ward²** /ˈbæk-wərd/ (*also* **back-wards** /ˈbækwərdz/) *adv.* **1** away from the front; toward the back: *Could everybody take a step backward?* ○ *He fell backwards and hit the back of his head.* ○ *We seem to be going backwards, not forwards.* **2** in a way that is opposite to usual; with the end first: *"Dog" written backwards spells "god."* **3** with the back where the front should be: *You've got your sweater on backwards!* **4** to-ward an earlier time: *The movie was about some people who traveled backward in time.*

back ˈyard (*also* **backyard**) *noun* [C] an area behind a house with grass, plants, etc.: *You*

kids can go and play in the back yard. ○ (figura-tive) *I won't let them build a prison in my back yard!* (= near my home)

☆ **ba·con** /ˈbeɪkən/ *noun* [U] thin pieces of salted or smoked meat from the back or sides of a pig: *a hearty breakfast of pancakes, bacon and eggs.* ☞ Look at the note at **meat.**

bac·te·ri·a /bækˈtɪriə/ *noun* [plural] very small living things that can only be seen with a microscope. Bacteria exist in large numbers in air, water, soil, plants and the bodies of people and animals. Some bacteria cause dis-ease. ☞ Look at **virus.**

☆ **bad¹** /bæd/ *adj.* (**worse** /wərs/, **worst** /wərst/) **1** not good or pleasant: *The weather forecast for tomorrow is bad.* ○ *I'm in a bad mood today.* ○ *I felt really bad about leaving her standing in the rain.* **2** severe or serious: *The traffic was really bad on the way to work.* ○ *She went home with a bad headache.* ○ *a bad mis-take* **3** of poor quality; of a low standard: *Many accidents are caused by bad driving.* ○ *The company's problems are the result of bad man-agement.* **4 bad (at sth/at doing sth)** not able to do sth well or easily; not skillful or reliable: *a bad teacher, driver, cook, etc.* ○ *I've always been bad at sports.* ○ *He's really bad at keeping us informed* (= we can't rely on him to give us information). **5** (used about food) not fresh or suitable to eat; rotten: *Smell this meat – I think it's gone bad.* **6** (used about parts of the body) not healthy; painful: *He has a bad heart.* **7** (used about a person or behavior) not good; morally wrong: *Wayne isn't a bad kid – he just needs a lot of supervision.* ○ *In cowboy movies, the bad guys always wear black hats.* **8** (not before a noun) **bad for sb/sth** likely to dam-age or hurt sb/sth: *Smoking's bad for you.* **9 bad (for sth/to do sth)** difficult or unsuit-able: *This is a bad time to call – everybody's in a meeting.*

☞ Some young people like to use the word **bad** to mean "very good": *Man! That is one bad car!* When it is used as a slang word in this way, **bad** has the comparative and super-lative forms **badder** and **baddest.**

IDM **not bad**; **not too bad** (*informal*) fairly good: *"How was your vacation?" "Not bad."* ○ *He earned $100 – not too bad for four hours' work!*

too bad (*informal*) ⇨ TOO

bad² /bæd/ *adv.* (*informal*) badly: *Are you hurt bad?* ○ *I need a drink bad!* ☞ Many people consider this use of the word **bad** incorrect.

badge /bædʒ/ *noun* [C] a small piece of metal with a design or words on it which you pin onto your clothing. A badge can show pos-ition, rank, membership in a club, etc.: *a po-lice officer's badge*

badg·er /ˈbædʒər/ *noun* [C] an animal with

black and white stripes on its head that lives in holes in the ground and comes out at night

‚bad ‖language *noun* [U] words that are used for swearing: *You'll get into trouble if you use bad* ‖**language.**

☆ **bad·ly** /ˈbædli/ *adv.* (**worse; worst**) **1** in a way that is not satisfactory; not well: *"Can you speak French?" "Well, only very badly."* ○ *Some apartment houses are very badly built.* ○ *She did pretty badly on the test.* **2** greatly or severely: *He was badly hurt in the accident.* **3** very much: *He badly needed a vacation.*

bad·min·ton /ˈbædmɪntn/ *noun* [U] a game for two or four people in which players hit a type of light ball with feathers over a high net, using rackets: *to play badminton*

baf·fle /ˈbæfl/ *verb* [T] to be impossible for sb to understand; to confuse greatly: *His illness baffled the doctors.* ○ *We were completely baffled by Jerry's strange remarks.* —**baf·fling** *adj.*: *English is a baffling language.*

☆ **bag¹** /bæg/ *noun* [C] **1** a container made of paper, plastic, cloth or leather that is open at the top, often with handles, in which you can carry things: *Would you like me to put these in a bag for you?* ○ *I'll store the leftovers in a plastic bag.* ○ *Do you need help carrying your grocery bags to the car?* ○ *a brown paper bag* ○ *a shopping bag* ○ *a garbage bag* ☞ Look also at **sack. 2** a container made of paper or plastic that is closed at the top; a package: *a bag of candy, potato chips, sugar, etc.* ☞ picture at **container. 3** a suitcase or other piece of luggage: *Each passenger is allowed to check in two bags on this flight.* ○ *Let me carry the bags up to your room.* **4** a thing that looks like a bag (1): *bags under the eyes* (= folds of skin under the eyes, often caused by lack of sleep) **5** (*slang*) an unpleasant woman: *an old bag*

bag² /bæg/ *verb* [T] (**bag·ging; bagged**) to put sth into a bag: *to bag groceries*

ba·gel /ˈbeɪgl/ *noun* [C] a bread roll that is shaped like a ring. Bagels are boiled in water and then baked in an oven. ☞ picture at **bread.**

☆ **bag·gage** /ˈbægɪdʒ/ *noun* [U] bags and suitcases that you carry your clothes, etc. in when you travel: *We loaded our baggage into the car.* ○ *Baggage should be checked in* (= given to an airline employee at a counter) *at least an hour before the flight.* ☞ Look also at **luggage.**

bag·gy /ˈbægi/ *adj.* (used about a piece of clothing) hanging loosely on the body: *baggy jeans*

bag·pipes /ˈbæg-paɪps/ *noun* [plural] a musical instrument, popular in Scotland, that is played by

bagpipes
kilt

blowing air through a pipe into a bag and then pressing the bag so that the air comes out of other pipes

bail¹ /beɪl/ *noun* [U] **1** money that is handed over to a court so that a person accused of a crime can be free until the trial: *She was released on $2,000 bail.* ○ *The judge set bail at $10,000.* **2** permission for sb who is accused of a crime to be free until the trial if a sum of money is handed over to the court: *The judge felt that he was a dangerous man and ordered him to be held without bail.*

bail² /beɪl/ *verb*

PHRV **bail sb out 1** to obtain sb's freedom by paying his/her bail¹(1) : *After she had been charged, her parents bailed her out.* **2** to rescue sb or sth from a difficult situation (especially by providing money)

bail·iff /ˈbeɪlɪf/ *noun* [C] a guard in a court of law

bait /beɪt/ *noun* [U] **1** food or sth that looks like food that is put onto a hook to catch fish, or placed in a trap to catch animals or birds **2** something that is used for tempting or attracting sb: *Free offers are often used as bait to attract customers.*

☆ **bake** /beɪk/ *verb* [I,T] **1** to cook in an oven in dry heat: *I could smell bread baking in the oven.* ○ *On his birthday, she baked him a cake.* ○ *Would you like baked potatoes or French fries?* ☞ Look at the note at **cook. 2** to become or to make sth hard by heating it: *The hot sun baked the earth.*

bak·er /ˈbeɪkər/ *noun* [C] a person who bakes and sells bread, cake, etc.

☆ **bak·er·y** /ˈbeɪkəri/ *noun* [C] (*pl.* **bak·er·ies**) a place where bread, cakes, etc. are baked to be sold

☆ **bal·ance¹** /ˈbæləns/ *verb* **1** [I,T] to be or to put sb/sth in a steady position in which weight is evenly spread: *I had to balance on the top step of the ladder to paint the ceiling.* ○ *Carefully, she balanced a glass on top of the pile of plates.* **2** [I,T] to have equal totals of money spent and money received: *I must have made a mistake – the accounts don't balance.* **3** [T] to add up the amounts of money spent and received in an account and to make sure that the totals are correct: *to balance a checkbook* **4** [T] **balance sth (out) (with sth)** to have or give sth equal value, importance, etc. in relation to other parts: *It's difficult to balance the demands of a career with caring for an elderly relative.* ○ *The loss in the first half of the year was balanced out by the profit in the second half.* **5** [T] **balance sth against sth** to consider one matter in relation to another: *In planning the new freeway, we have to balance the benefit to motorists against the damage to the nearby neighborhoods.*

☆ **bal·ance²** /ˈbæləns/ *noun* **1** [U] the state of being in a steady position in which weight is

evenly spread: *You need a good sense of balance to ride a motorcycle.* **2** [sing.] **(a) balance (between A and B)** a situation in which different or opposite things are of equal importance, size, etc. or are in the correct proportions: *The course provides a good balance between oral and written work.* ∘ *Humans have upset the environmental balance of the world.* **3** [C] (*technical*) an instrument used for weighing things ☞ Look at **scale**. **4** [C] the amount of money in sb's bank account: *I asked the bank teller for my balance.* **5 the balance** [sing.] the amount that still has to be paid: *You can pay a 10% deposit now, with the balance due in one month.*

IDM in the balance uncertain: *Following poor profits, the company's future is hanging in the balance.*

keep/lose your balance to remain/not to remain steady and upright: *It's difficult to keep your balance on this icy sidewalk.* ∘ *She tripped, lost her balance and fell down.*

(catch/throw sb) off balance (to find or put sb) in an unsteady position from which it is easy to fall: *A strong gust of wind caught me off balance and I almost fell down.*

strike a balance ⇨ STRIKE²

☆ **bal·anced** /'bælənst/ *adj.* **1** including all different sides, opinions, etc. equally; fair: *a balanced report* **2** having equal totals of money spent and money received: *Do you think Congress will be able to propose a balanced budget this year?* **3** consisting of parts that are in the correct or pleasing proportions: *A balanced diet plays an important part in good health.*

‚**balance of** '**power** *noun* [sing.] a situation in which power is evenly divided among the various sides, parties, groups, etc. involved

'**balance sheet** *noun* [C] a written record of money received and money paid out, showing the difference between the totals of each

☆ **bal·co·ny** /'bælkəni/ *noun* [C] (*pl.* **bal·co·nies**) **1** a platform built on an upstairs outside wall of a building, with a wall or rail around it: *Our hotel room had a balcony where we could sit and look at the lake.* **2** an area of seats upstairs and near the back of a theater

balcony

☆ **bald** /bɔld/ *adj.* (used about people) having little or no hair on the head: *He went bald when he was only 30.* ∘ *He has a bald patch on the top of his head.* ☞ picture at **hair**.

‚**bald** '**eagle** *noun* [C] a type of large bird with brown feathers on its body and white feathers on its head. It is an official symbol of the United States.

bald·ing /'bɔldɪŋ/ *adj.* becoming bald: *a balding man in his fifties*

bald eagle

bale /beɪl/ *noun* [C] a large quantity of sth (hay, cloth, etc.) tied together in a bundle so that it can be transported

balk /bɔk/ *verb* [I] **balk (at sth)** to be unwilling to do or agree to sth because it seems difficult, dangerous or unpleasant: *Several people were interested in buying my car, but they all balked at the price.*

☆ **ball** /bɔl/ *noun* [C] **1** a round or egg-shaped object that you hit, kick, throw, etc. in games and sports: *a tennis ball* ∘ *a golf ball* ∘ *a football* ∘ *The kids were playing with a ball in the back yard.* ∘ *The ball bounced over the fence.* **2** any object that has this shape or has been formed into this shape: *a ball of yarn* ∘ *The cat curled up into a ball and went to sleep.* ∘ *The kids threw snowballs at each other.* ∘ *We had spaghetti and meatballs for dinner.* **3** large formal party at which people dance

IDM (be) on the ball (*informal*) (to be) aware of what is happening and able to react to or deal with it quickly: *With so many new developments, you really have to be on the ball.*

get/start the ball rolling to start sth (an activity, conversation, etc.) that involves or is done by a group: *I made the first comments in our discussion to get the ball rolling.*

have a ball (*informal*) to enjoy yourself very much: *We had a ball on vacation last month.*

play ball ⇨ PLAY¹

bal·lad /'bæləd/ *noun* [C] a long song or poem in simple language, telling a story

bal·le·ri·na /,bælə'rinə/ *noun* [C] a woman who dances in ballets

bal·let /bæ'leɪ/ *noun* **1** [U] a style of dancing that tells a story with music but without words: *I like opera, but I'm not very fond of ballet.* ∘ *a ballet dancer* **2** [C] a performance or work that consists of this type of dancing

'**ball game** (*also* **ball·game**) *noun* **1** [C] a baseball game **2** [sing.] (*informal*) a situation, a set of circumstances: *After living in a small town for so long, living in the big city is a whole new ball game for me.*

bal·loon /bə'lun/ *noun* [C] **1** a small colored rubber bag that you blow air or a gas into and use as a toy or for decoration: *We hung balloons around the room for the party.* ∘ *The boy cried when his balloon popped.* **2** (*also* ‚**hot·**'**air balloon**) a large bag that is filled with gas or

ər	ɪr	ɛr	ɑr	ɔr	ʊr	ʒ	h	ŋ
bird	near	hair	car	north	tour	vision	hat	sing

hot air so that it can rise into and fly through the air, carrying people in a basket attached below it: *They crossed the Atlantic in a balloon.*

☆ **bal·lot** /ˈbælət/ *noun* **1** [C] a piece of paper that is used in voting: *She put an "X" next to the candidate's name on the ballot.* **2** [C,U] the system of voting with ballots (1); an occasion when people vote in this way: *to vote by secret ballot* ○ *No candidate received an absolute majority of the votes in the first ballot.*

ball·park /ˈbɔlpɑrk/ *noun* [C] a field or sports center where baseball is played: *We spent the afternoon at the ballpark.*

IDM **in the ballpark** approximately correct: *The cost of the repairs was in the ballpark of 2 million dollars.*

a ballpark figure, estimate, etc. a number, etc. that is approximately correct

ball·point pen /ˌbɔlpɔɪnt ˈpɛn/ (*also* **ballpoint** /ˈbɔlpɔɪnt/) *noun* [C] a pen with a very small metal ball at the end that rolls ink onto paper

ball·room /ˈbɔlrum/ *noun* [C] a large room used for formal dancing

ba·lo·ney /bəˈloʊni/ *noun* [U] **1** (*informal*) nonsense: *What a bunch of baloney!* **2** = BOLOGNA

bam·boo /ˌbæmˈbu/ *noun* [C,U] a tall tropical plant of the grass family. Young bamboo shoots can be eaten; the hard, hollow stems are used for making furniture, etc.: *a bamboo chair*

☆ **ban¹** /bæn/ *verb* (**ban·ning**; **banned**) [T] **1** to forbid officially, often by law: *The government has banned the import of products containing ivory.* **2 ban sb from sth/from doing sth** to officially forbid sb to do sth, often by law: *Prisoners are banned from voting in elections.*

ban² /bæn/ *noun* [C] **a ban (on sth/sb)** an official order that forbids sb from doing sth: *There is a ban on smoking in this office.*

ba·nal /bəˈnæl; ˈbeɪnl/ *adj.* (*formal*) not original or interesting: *a banal comment*

☆ **ba·nan·a** /bəˈnænə/ *noun* [C] a long curved fruit that has yellow skin and that can be eaten: *a bunch of bananas*

☆ **band** /bænd/ *noun* [C] **1** a thin, flat, narrow piece of material used for fastening sth, or put around sth, often to hold it together: *The cards were held together by a rubber band.* ○ *He was wearing a white hat with a black band around it.* **2** a line of a color or design that is different from the one on either side of it: *She wore a red sweater with a green band across the middle.* **3** a group of people who have joined together with a common purpose: *The attack was made by a small band of rebels.* **4** a group of musicians: *a brass band* ○ *a jazz band* ○ *a rock band*

band·age¹ /ˈbændɪdʒ/ *noun* [C] a long piece of soft material that is wrapped around a wound or an injury

band·age² /ˈbændɪdʒ/ *verb* [T] to put a bandage (1) on a wound or around a part of the body: *She played the game with a bandaged knee.*

bandage

Band-Aids

Her leg is in a **cast**. His arm is in a **sling**.

☆ **Band-Aid** /ˈbændeɪd/ *noun* [C] (*trademark*) **1** a small piece of sticky material that is used to cover a cut, etc. on the body **2** an effort to improve a bad situation that does not do anything about the real source of the problem: *The loan was just a temporary Band-Aid – we needed more help than that to keep our business running.*

ban·dit /ˈbændət/ *noun* [C] an armed robber, usually in a wild place

band·wag·on /ˈbændwægən/ *noun*

IDM **jump on the bandwagon** ➪ JUMP¹

☆ **bang¹** /bæŋ/ *verb* [I,T] **1** to make a loud noise by hitting sth hard, closing sth, or putting sth down: *The man downstairs banged on his ceiling to complain about the noise.* ○ *Somewhere in the house, I heard a door bang.* ○ *She stormed out of the room, banging the door behind her.* ○ *He banged his fist on the table and started shouting.* **2** to knock against sth by accident: *As I was crossing the room in the dark, I banged into a table.* ○ *Be careful not to bang your head on the ceiling. It's pretty low.*

PHRV **bang sth up** (*informal*) to damage sth by knocking it against sth else: *I banged up my knee when I fell off my bike.*

☆ **bang²** /bæŋ/ *noun* [C] **1** a sudden, short, very loud noise: *Witnesses heard three loud bangs and saw the gunman run down an alley.* **2** a short, strong knock or blow: *Give the nail a couple of bangs with the hammer.* **3 a bang**

(informal) a feeling of great pleasure and enjoyment: *I get a real bang out of Larry's jokes!*

bang³ /bæŋ/ *interj.* (used to sound like the noise of a gun, etc.): *The kids ran around with toy guns, shouting, "Bang! Bang!"*

ban·gle /'bæŋgl/ *noun* [C] a large bracelet or metal band that is worn around the arm for decoration ☞ picture at **jewelry**.

bangs /bæŋz/ *noun* [plural] the part of your hair that hangs, usually in a straight line, over your forehead

ban·ish /'bænɪʃ/ *verb* [T] *(formal)* **1** to send sb away (especially out of the country), usually as a punishment: *They were banished from the country for demonstrating against the government.* ○ *The kids were banished to their rooms for making too much noise.* **2** to remove sth completely; to force out: *She banished all hope of winning from her mind.*

ban·is·ter /'bænəstər/ *noun* [C] (often plural) a rail supported by vertical bars at the side of a staircase, that you hold on to when you are going upstairs or downstairs

ban·jo /'bændʒoʊ/ *noun* [C] *(pl.* **ban·jos**) a musical instrument with a long thin neck, a round body and four or more strings, played with the fingers

☆ **bank¹** /bæŋk/ *noun* [C] **1** an organization that keeps money safely for its customers; the office or building of such an organization. You can take money out, save, borrow or exchange money at a bank: *Is there a bank near here where I can cash some traveler's checks?* ○ *He went to the bank and withdrew some money from his account.* ○ *She got a loan from the bank to buy a new car.* **2** a supply of things that you keep to use later: *a data bank* ○ *a blood bank* **3** the ground along the side of a river or canal: *People were fishing along the banks of the river.* ○ *We rowed to the bank and got out of the boat.* **4** any area of sloping ground: *There were grassy banks on either side of the freeway.* **5** (used about certain features of weather) a mass of sth: *a bank of clouds*

bank² /bæŋk/ *verb* [I] to keep your money at a particular bank: *I bank at the First National Bank.*

PHRV bank on sb/sth to expect and trust sb to do sth, or sth to happen: *I suppose you might get a ticket, but I wouldn't bank on it.*

bank·er /'bæŋkər/ *noun* [C] a person who owns or has an important job in a bank

bank·ing /'bæŋkɪŋ/ *noun* [U] the type of business done by banks: *She decided on a career in banking.*

☆ **bank·rupt¹** /'bæŋkrʌpt/ *adj.* not having enough money to pay your debts: *The company went bankrupt last year.*

bank·rupt² /'bæŋkrʌpt/ *verb* [T] to cause sb/sth to become bankrupt¹

bank·rupt·cy /'bæŋkrʌpsi; -rəptsi/ *noun* [C,U] *(pl.* **bank·rupt·cies**) the state when a person

or an organization is bankrupt¹: *During this period of economic difficulty, bankruptcies are becoming more common.* ○ *to file for bankruptcy* ○ *to declare bankruptcy*

ban·ner /'bænər/ *noun* [C] a long piece of cloth with words or signs on it, that can be hung up or carried through the streets on poles: *The demonstrators carried banners saying "Stop the War."*

ban·quet /'bæŋkwət/ *noun* [C] a formal dinner for a large number of people, usually as a special event at which speeches are made

bap·tism /'bæptɪzəm/ *noun* [C,U] a ceremony in which a person becomes a member of the Christian church by being placed briefly under water or having drops of water put onto his/her head. Often he/she is also formally given a name.

Bap·tist /'bæptɪst/ *noun* [C, *adj.* (a member) of a Protestant church that believes that baptism should only be for people who are old enough to understand the meaning of the ceremony and should be done by placing the person fully under water

bap·tize /'bæptaɪz/ *verb* [T] to perform the ceremony of baptism: *Were you baptized as a child?* ○ *He was baptized "George David."*

☆ **bar¹** /bɑr/ *noun* [C] **1** a place where you can buy and drink (especially alcoholic) drinks: *We had a drink in the bar before our meal.* **2** a small restaurant that serves drinks or light meals: *a snack bar* **3** a long, narrow, high table or counter where drinks are served: *She went to the bar and ordered a drink* ○ *We sat on stools at the bar.* **4** a long, thin, straight piece of metal, often placed across a window or door, etc. to make it strong or to prevent people from passing through it: *the bars of a prison cell* **5** a small block of solid material, longer than it is wide: *a bar of soap* ☞ Look also at **candy bar. 6** a thing that prevents you from doing sth: *Lack of education is not always a bar to success in business.*

IDM behind bars *(informal)* in prison

bar² /bɑr/ *verb* [T] **(bar·ring; barred) 1** to fasten with a bar¹(4) or bars: *The heavy door was barred and bolted.* **2** to stop sb from going through or into a place: *A policeman barred the entrance to the embassy.* **3 bar sb from sth/from doing sth** to forbid sb officially to do, use or enter sth: *He was barred from the club for fighting.*

bar·bar·i·an /bɑr'bɛriən/ *noun* [C] a wild, uncivilized person

bar·bar·ic /bɑr'bærɪk; -'bɛrɪk/ *adj.* very cruel and violent: *barbaric punishments* ○ *barbaric treatment of prisoners* —**bar·ba·rism** /'bɑrbərɪzəm/ *noun* [U]: *acts of barbarism*

bar·be·cue¹ /'bɑrbɪkyu/ *noun* [C] *(abbr.* **BBQ**) an outdoor party at which food is cooked on a metal frame **(a grill)** over an open fire: *Let's have a barbecue.*

bar·be·cue² /ˈbɑrbɪkyu/ *verb* [T] to cook food outdoors on a metal frame (**a grill**) over an open fire, often with a special sauce: *barbecued ribs*

barbed wire /ˌbɑrbd ˈwaɪər/ *noun* [U] strong wire with sharp points on it: *a barbed wire fence*

bar·ber /ˈbɑrbər/ *noun* [C] a man who cuts men's hair: *My hair's too long. It's time I went to the barber.* ○ *a barbershop* (= where a barber works)

ˈbar code *noun* [C] a pattern of thick and thin parallel lines on a book, product in a store, etc. It contains information that a computer can read.

☆ **bare** /bɛr/ *adj.* **1** (used about part of the body) not covered by clothing: *bare arms* ○ *a bare chest* ○ *She killed him with her bare hands* (= without a weapon). ☞ Look at **naked** and **nude. 2** without anything covering it: *They had taken the painting down, so the walls were all bare.* **3** empty; without its usual contents: *bare bookshelves* **4** minimum, basic and no more: *We were so poor that we didn't even have the bare necessities of life.* ○ *Just give me the bare facts as quickly as you can.*

bare·foot /ˈbɛrfʊt/ *adj., adv.* with nothing (e.g. shoes, socks, etc.) on the feet: *I was barefoot because my shoes and socks had gotten wet.* ○ *We walked barefoot along the beach.*

bare·ly /ˈbɛrli/ *adv.* just; hardly; almost not: *We barely had enough money to pay for our tickets.* ○ *She's barely older than you.*

barf /bɑrf/ [I] (*slang*) to bring food up from the stomach and out of the mouth **barf** *noun* [U] ☞ A more formal word is **vomit.**

bar·gain¹ /ˈbɑrgən/ *noun* [C] **1** something that is cheaper or at a lower price than usual: *At that price, it's a real bargain!* ○ *I found some good bargains at the garage sale.* **2** an agreement between people or groups about what each of them will do for the other or others: *I hope he keeps his side of the bargain.* ☞ Look also at **plea bargain.**

bar·gain² /ˈbɑrgən/ *verb* [I] **bargain (with sb) (about/over/for sth)** to discuss the form of an agreement, a price, etc.: *I'm sure that if you bargain with him, he'll drop the price.* ○ *bargain over the price*

PHRV **bargain for sth** to expect sth or to be prepared for sth: *When I agreed to take care of Al's dog, I got more than I'd bargained for.*

barge¹ /bɑrdʒ/ *noun* [C] a long narrow boat with a flat bottom that is used for transporting goods or people on a canal, river, etc.

barge² /bɑrdʒ/ *verb* [I] to move in a rough way, pushing people or things out of the way: *Don't just barge into my room without knocking!*

bar·i·tone /ˈbærətoʊn/ *noun* [C] a singing voice that is fairly low, between tenor and bass

bark¹ /bɑrk/ *noun* [U] the hard outer covering of a tree

☆ **bark²** /bɑrk/ *verb* **1** [I] **bark (at sb/sth)** (used about dogs) to make a loud, short noise or noises: *Their dog always barks at strangers.* **2** [I,T] **bark (sth) (out) (at sb)** to speak to sb in a loud voice with an angry or aggressive tone: *The boss came in, barked some orders and left again.* —**bark** *noun* [C]: *The dog next door has a very loud bark.*

bar·ley /ˈbɑrli/ *noun* [U] **1** a plant similar to grass that produces grain that is used for food or for making beer and other drinks **2** the grain produced by this plant

bar mitz·vah /ˌbɑr ˈmɪtsvə/ *noun* [C] a ceremony in the Jewish religion for a boy who is about 13 years old, after which he is considered an adult ☞ Look at **bat mitzvah.**

barn /bɑrn/ *noun* [C] a large building on a farm in which crops or animals are kept

silo **barn**

barn·yard /ˈbɑrnyɑrd/ *noun* [C] an area of land with a fence around it near a barn, in which animals are kept

ba·rom·e·ter /bəˈrɑmətər/ *noun* [C] **1** an instrument that measures air pressure and indicates changes in weather **2** something that indicates the state of sth (a situation, a feeling, etc.): *The stock market is a barometer of the nation's economy.*

bar·on /ˈbærən/ *noun* [C] a person who controls a large part of a particular industry or type of business: *an oil baron*

bar·racks /ˈbærəks/ *noun* [C] (*pl.* **bar·racks**) a building or group of buildings in which soldiers live

bar·rage /bəˈrɑʒ/ *noun* [C] **1** a continuous attack with a large number of guns in a particular direction **2** a large number of questions, remarks, etc., aimed at a person very quickly: *The mayor faced a barrage of questions from reporters.*

bar·rel /ˈbærəl/ *noun* [C] **1** a large, round container for liquids, that has a flat top and bottom and is often wider in the middle: *a barrel of wine* ○ *How much is oil per barrel?* **2** the long metal tube of a gun, through which the bullet passes when it is fired

barrel

bar·ren /ˈbærən/ *adj.* **1** (used about land) not good enough to grow crops on **2** (used about trees or plants) not producing fruit or seeds

bar·ri·cade¹ /ˈbærəkeɪd/ *noun* [C] an object or a line of objects that is placed (usually

quickly) across a road, entrance, etc. to stop people from getting through: *The demonstrators put up barricades to keep the police away.*

bar·ri·cade² /ˈbærəkeɪd/ *verb* [T] to block sth with a barricade ¹: *Rioters barricaded the road with cars.*

☆ **bar·ri·er** /ˈbæriər/ *noun* [C] **1** an object that keeps people or things apart or prevents them from moving from one place to another: *The police put up barriers to stop the crowd from getting on to the road.* **2** something that causes problems or makes it impossible for sth to happen: *Old-fashioned attitudes are a barrier to progress.* ○ *When you live in a foreign country, the language barrier is often the most difficult problem to overcome.* ○ *trade barriers*

bar·ring /ˈbɑrɪŋ/ *prep.* (*formal*) **1** except for: *Barring one or two small problems, everything's fine right now.* **2** if there is/are not: *Barring any unforeseen problems, we'll be moving to Phoenix in a month.*

bar·ris·ter /ˈbærəstər/ *noun* [C] (*BrE*) a lawyer who is qualified to speak in the higher courts in England and Wales

bar·tend·er /ˈbɑrtɛndər/ *noun* [C] a person who serves drinks from behind a bar

bar·ter /ˈbɑrtər/ *verb* [I,T] **barter sth (for sth)** to exchange goods or services for other goods or services, not for money: *In remote parts of the country, people bartered vegetables for tools.* —**bar·ter** *noun* [U]: *a barter system*

☆ **base¹** /beɪs/ *noun* [C] **1** the lowest part of sth, especially the part on which it stands or at which it is attached to sth: *the base of a statue* ○ *I felt a terrible pain at the base of my spine.* **2** a starting point from which sth develops or is made: *The car's base price is $16,800, but that doesn't include taxes or optional equipment.* **3** a strong foundation on which sth is built or maintained: *The country needs a strong economic base.* ○ *More affluent residents will increase the city's tax base.* **4** a place used as a center from which activities are done or

controlled: *Detectives are using the local school as a base for their investigation.* **5** a military center from which forces operate: *an army/an air/a naval base* **6** (in baseball) one of the four points that a runner must touch ☞ picture at **baseball**. Look also at **database**. **7** a chemical substance with a pH value of more than 7 ☞ Look at **acid**.

IDM **off base** not correct or accurate: *Your estimate of the cost of the project was way off base.*

touch base (with sb) ⇨ TOUCH¹

☆ **base²** /beɪs/ *verb* [T] **1 base sth on sth** to form or develop sth from a particular starting point or source: *This movie is based on a true story.* **2** (usually passive) **base sb/sth in...** to make one place the center from which sb/sth can work or move around: *I'm based in New York, although my job involves a lot of travel.*

☆ **base·ball** /ˈbeɪsbɔl/ *noun* **1** [U] a team game that is popular in the United States and Canada in which players hit the ball with a bat and run around four points (**bases**) on a field. They have to touch all four bases in order to score a point (**run**). **2** [C] the hard round ball that is used in this game

☞ There are nine players on a baseball team. The **pitcher pitches** (=throws) the ball to a **batter** from the other team. If the batter tries to hit the ball but misses it, this is called a **strike**. After three strikes the batter is **out** and the next batter comes to bat. If a batter manages to hit the ball so far that it goes out of the field, this is a **home run** and the batter is allowed to touch all four bases.

☆ **base·ment** /ˈbeɪsbəl/ *noun* [C] the lowest room or rooms of a building which are partly or completely below ground level: *The toy department is in the basement of the store.* ○ *a basement apartment*

ba·ses *pl.* of BASIS

baseball

second base · first base · cap · mitt · pitcher · uniform · mound · bat · home plate · third base · batter · catcher

bash¹ /bæʃ/ verb [T] (informal) **1** to hit sb/sth very hard **2** to criticize sb/sth strongly: *The candidate continued to bash her opponent's policies.*

bash² /bæʃ/ noun [C] **1** a hard blow or an act of hitting **2** (informal) a party: *The Johnsons invited us to a big bash.*

bash·ful /ˈbæʃfl/ adj. shy and embarrassed

☆ **ba·sic** /ˈbeɪsɪk/ adj. **1** forming a starting point or basis on which other ideas rest: *The basic question is, can we afford it?* **2** simplest or most elementary; including only what is most necessary: *This course teaches basic skills in first aid.* ∘ *The basic pay is $200 a week – with extra for overtime.* ∘ *The rooms in the hotel are very basic – they have no showers or televisions.* **3** (technical) (used about chemical substances) having a pH value of more than 7 ☞ Look at acid²(2) and alkaline.

☆ **ba·si·cal·ly** /ˈbeɪsɪkli/ adv. looking at what is most important or basic in a person or an object or in a particular situation: *She seems to me to be basically a very nice person.* ∘ *The design of the new car is basically the same as the old one.* ∘ *Basically, all I want is to be left alone.*

ba·sics /ˈbeɪsɪks/ noun [plural] the things that you need most or that are the most important: *You can get all the basics at the local store.*

ba·sin /ˈbeɪsn/ noun [C] **1** a large round open container that is used for holding liquids **2** an area of land from which water flows into a river: *the Congo Basin*

☆ **ba·sis** /ˈbeɪsəs/ noun [C] (pl. **ba·ses** /ˈbeɪsiz/) **1** the way sth is done or organized: *They meet on a regular basis.* ∘ *The changes have been introduced on a voluntary basis.* **2** the principle or reason which lies behind sth: *We made our decision on the basis of your reports.* **3** a starting point, from which sth can develop: *Her diaries formed the basis of her autobiography.*

bask /bæsk/ verb [I] to sit or lie in a place where you can enjoy the warmth: *bask in the sunshine* ∘ (figurative) *He basked in the admiration of his fans.*

☆ **bas·ket** /ˈbæskət/ noun [C] **1** a container for carrying or holding things, made of strips of light material such as wire or thin wood that are woven together: *a picnic basket* ∘ *a wastebasket* **2** a net that hangs from a metal ring high up at each end of a basketball court **3** a point that is scored in basketball by throwing the ball through one of the nets: *to make/shoot a basket*

handle — basket

IDM put all your eggs in one basket ⇨ EGG¹

hoop — basketball
basket

☆ **bas·ket·ball** /ˈbæskətbɔl/ noun **1** [U] a game for two teams of five players. There is a net (**basket**) hanging from a metal ring high up at each end of the court and the players try to throw a ball through the other team's net in order to score points (**baskets**). **2** [C] the large round ball that is used in this game

bass¹ /beɪs/ noun **1** [C] the lowest male singing voice; a singer with this kind of voice **2** [U] the lowest part in music **3** [C] = DOUBLE BASS **4** [C] (also **bass guitar**) an electric guitar which plays very low notes ☞ picture at **rock band**.

bass² /beɪs/ adj. producing a deep sound; connected with the lowest part in music: *a bass drum* ∘ *Can you sing the bass part in this song?*

bass³ /bæs/ noun [C] (pl. **bass** or **bass·es**) a type of fish that is caught for food or for sport. Some types of bass live in the ocean, and other types live in lakes and rivers.

bas·soon /bəˈsun/ noun [C] a musical instrument of the woodwind family which makes a very deep sound

bas·tard /ˈbæstərd/ noun [C] **1** (old-fashioned) a child whose parents were not married to each other when he/she was born ☞ You may offend people by using this word. A more neutral expression is "an illegitimate child." **2** (slang) (used as an insult) an unpleasant or cruel person

bat¹ /bæt/ noun [C] **1** a small animal, like a mouse with wings, that comes out and flies around at night **2** a piece of wood for hitting the ball in sports such as baseball or softball: *a baseball bat* ☞ picture at **baseball**. Look at **club²**(2), **paddle¹**(2), **racket¹** and **stick¹**(3).
IDM right off the bat ⇨ RIGHT²

bat² /bæt/ verb (**bat·ting; bat·ted**) [I] (used about one player or a whole team) to take a turn hitting the ball in sports such as baseball
IDM not bat an eye to show no reaction

batch /bætʃ/ noun [C] a number of things or people that belong together as a group: *to bake a batch of cookies* ∘ *The guide waited for the next batch of tourists.*

tʃ	dʒ	v	θ	ð	s	z	ʃ
chin	June	van	thin	then	so	zoo	she

bat·ed /ˈbeɪtəd/ *adj.*
IDM with bated breath excited or afraid, because you are waiting for sth to happen

☆**bath** /bæθ/ *noun* (*pl.* **baths** /bæðz; bæθz/)
1 [sing.] an act of washing your whole body when you sit or lie in a bathtub filled with water: *to take a bath* ○ *Would you rather take a bath or a shower?* **2** [C] = BATHROOM(1): *a house with three bedrooms and two baths*

bathe /beɪð/ *verb* **1** [I] to take a bath: *I prefer to bathe in the mornings.* **2** [T] to give sb a bath: *to bathe a baby* **3** [T] to wash or put part of the body in water, often for medical reasons: *She bathed the wound with antiseptic.* **4** [T] (usually passive) to cover or surround sth: *The room was bathed in sunlight.*

bathing suit *noun* [C] = SWIMSUIT

bath·robe /ˈbæθroʊb/ (*also* **robe**) *noun* [C] a piece of clothing like a loose coat that you wear before or after a bath or over pajamas, etc. ☞ picture on page A27.

☆**bath·room** /ˈbæθrum/ *noun* [C] **1** a room where there is a bathtub or a shower, and usually a sink and a toilet **2** a room with a toilet ☞ Look at the note at **toilet**.
IDM go to the bathroom (used about people or animals) to pass liquid or solid waste material from your body: *Oh, no! The dog went to the bathroom on the carpet!*
☞ This is a polite way of talking about what you do on the toilet.

☆**bath·tub** /ˈbæθtʌb/ (also *informal* **tub**) *noun* [C] a large container for water in which you sit to wash your body: *Can you answer the phone? I'm in the bathtub!*

bat mitz·vah /ˌbat ˈmɪtsvə; ˌbas-/ *noun* [C] a ceremony in the Jewish religion for a girl who is about 13 years old, after which she is considered an adult ☞ Look at **bar mitzvah**.

ba·ton /bəˈtɑn/ *noun* [C] **1** a short thin stick used by the person who directs an orchestra **2** a stick that a runner in some races passes to the next person in the team **3** a metal stick that a person who marches in front of a band holds and sometimes throws into the air and catches

bat·tal·ion /bəˈtælyən/ *noun* [C] a large unit of soldiers that forms part of another larger unit in the army

bat·ter¹ /ˈbætər/ *verb* [I,T] to hit sb/sth hard, many times: *The wind battered against the window.* ○ *High winds battered the coast again yesterday.* ○ *The parents were accused of battering the child.*

bat·ter² /ˈbætər/ *noun* **1** [U] a thin mixture of flour, eggs, milk and usually oil, used to make pancakes, etc. or to cover food such as fish before frying: *cake batter* ☞ Look at **dough**. **2** [C] a person who hits the ball in baseball

bat·tered /ˈbætərd/ *adj.* **1** no longer looking new; damaged or out of shape: *a battered old*

hat **2** having been hit many times, usually over a period of time: *a shelter for battered women*

☆**bat·ter·y** /ˈbætəri/ *noun* [C] (*pl.* **bat·ter·ies**) a device that provides electricity for a radio, car, etc.: *I need some new batteries for my Walkman.* ○ *He couldn't start the car because the battery was dead.* ☞ picture at **light**.

☆**bat·tle¹** /ˈbætl/ *noun* **1** [C,U] a fight, especially between armies in a war: *the Battle of Gettysburg* ○ *They won the first battle, but still they lost the war.* ○ *to die/be killed in battle* **2** [C] a struggle of any kind: *After three years, she lost her battle against cancer.*
IDM a losing battle ⇨ LOSE

bat·tle² /ˈbætl/ *verb* [I,T] **battle (sb/sth) (for sth); battle (with/against sb/sth) (for sth)** to fight hard; to struggle: *The rebels battled (with) police for control of the region.* ○ *These programs are aimed at battling poverty in the inner city.* ○ *The two brothers were battling for leadership of the family business.*

bat·tle·field /ˈbætlfild/ (*also* **bat·tle·ground** /ˈbætlgraʊnd/) *noun* [C] the place where a battle is fought

bat·tle·ship /ˈbætlʃɪp/ *noun* [C] the largest type of ship used in war

bawl /bɔl/ *verb* [I,T] to shout or cry loudly

☆**bay** /beɪ/ *noun* [C] **1** a part of the coast where the land forms a curve inward: *Hudson Bay* ○ *The harbor was in a sheltered bay.* **2** a part of a building, aircraft or area that has a particular purpose: *the loading bay of the factory*
IDM hold/keep sb at bay to stop sb who is chasing you from coming near; to stop sb/sth from reaching you

bay·o·net /ˌbeɪəˈnɛt; ˈbeɪənət/ *noun* [C] a knife that can be attached to the end of a gun

bay·ou /ˈbaɪu; ˈbaɪoʊ/ *noun* [C] a small river with many curves that flows slowly through an area of wet land with a lot of plants in the southern United States

bay window *noun* [C] a window in a part of a room that sticks out from the wall of a house ☞ picture on page A28.

ba·zaar /bəˈzɑr/ *noun* [C] **1** (in countries in the Middle East) a market **2** a sale where the money that is made usually goes to charity: *a church bazaar*

BBQ /ˈbɑrbɪkyu/ *abbr.* = BARBECUE¹

B.C. /ˌbi ˈsi/ *abbr.* before Christ; used in dates to show the number of years before the time when Christians believe Jesus Christ was born: *300 B.C.*

☆**be¹** /bi/ *auxiliary verb* **1** (used to form the continuous tense of verbs): *You're sitting on my book.* ○ *We were listening to the radio.* ○ *Is he coming?* ○ *How long have we been waiting?* **2** (used to form the passive): *This cheese is made in Wisconsin.* ○ *We were taken to the police station.* ○ *The car has been repaired.* **3** (used to show that sth must happen or that

i	ɪ	ɛ	æ	ɑ	ɔ	ʌ	ʊ	u
see	sit	ten	cat	hot	saw	cup	put	too

B

present tense	past tense
I **am** (I**'m**)	I **was**
you **are** (you**'re**)	you **were**
he/she/it **is**	he/she/it **was**
(he**'s**/she**'s**/it**'s**)	
we **are** (we**'re**)	we **were**
you **are** (you**'re**)	you **were**
they **are** (they**'re**)	they **were**
past participle	**been**
present participle	**being**
negative short forms	**aren't**, **isn't**, **wasn't**, **weren't**

sth has been arranged): *You are to leave here at 10 o'clock at the latest.* ∘ *They are to be married in June.* **4** (used to show that sth is possible but not very likely): *If they were to offer me the job, I'd probably take it.*

☆ **be²** /bi/ *verb* **1** (used with *there* to say that sb/sth exists or is in a particular place): *Is there life after death?* ∘ *I tried calling them, but there was no answer.* ∘ *There are some people outside.* ∘ *There are a lot of trees in our yard.* **2** (used when you are naming people or things, describing them or giving more information about them): *That's Jane over there.* ∘ *I'm Alan.* ∘ *Sue is 18.* *She's in college.* ∘ *He's a doctor.* ∘ *What's that?* ∘ *Where are the scissors?* ∘ *"What color is your car?" "It's green."* ∘ *It's 6 o'clock.* ∘ *How much was your ticket?* ∘ *The show was excellent.* **3** (only used in the perfect tenses) to go to a place (and return): *Have you ever been to Japan?*

IDM **be yourself** to act naturally: *Don't be nervous; just be yourself and the interview will be fine.*

-to-be (in compounds) future: *his wife-to-be*

beach

cliff

sand dunes

waves

beach

☆ **beach** /bitʃ/ *noun* [C] the piece of sandy or rocky land next to the ocean: *a nice sandy beach* ∘ *to lie on the beach*

bea·con /'bikən/ *noun* [C] a fire or light on a hill, a tower or near the coast, that is used as a signal

bead /bid/ *noun* [C] **1** a small ball of wood, glass or plastic with a hole in the middle for threading a string through **2** a drop of liquid: *There were beads of sweat on his forehead.*

☆ **beak** /bik/ *noun* [C] the hard pointed part of a bird's mouth ☞ picture at **bird**.

beak·er /'bikər/ *noun* [C] a glass container with a flat bottom, used by scientists for pouring liquids

beam¹ /bim/ *noun* [C] **1** a long piece of wood, metal, concrete, etc. that is used to support weight, e.g. in the floor or ceiling of a building **2** a line of light: *the beam of a car's headlights* ∘ *a laser beam*

beam² /bim/ *verb* **1** [I] to send out light and warmth : *The sun beamed down on them.* **2** [I] to smile happily: *Beaming with pleasure, she stepped forward to receive her prize.* **3** [T] to broadcast a signal: *The program was beamed live by satellite to many different countries.*

☆ **bean** /bin/ *noun* [C] **1** the seeds or seed containers (**pods**) from a plant that are eaten as vegetables: *green beans* ∘ *a can of baked beans* (= beans in a brown sauce) **2** similar seeds from other plants: *coffee beans*

☆ **bear¹** /bɛr/ *noun* [C] a large, heavy wild animal with thick fur: *a black bear* ∘ *a polar bear* ☞ Look at **grizzly bear** and **teddy bear**.

☆ **bear²** /bɛr/ *verb* (*p.t.* **bore** /bɔr/; *p.p.* **borne** /bɔrn/) **1** [T] to support: *Twelve pillars bear the weight of the roof.* **2** [T] (*formal*) to carry sth: *The waiters came in bearing trays of food.* ∘ (*figurative*) *In her position as governor, she bears a great deal of responsibility.* ∘ (*figurative*) *Customers will bear the full cost of the improvements.* **3** [T] to suffer sth without complaining or giving in: *She bore her illness bravely.* ∘ *The heat is too much to bear.* ∘ *These figures won't bear close examination* (= when you look closely, you will find mistakes). **4** [T] (with *can/could* in negative sentences or in questions) to dislike strongly; to hate: *Joanne can't bear people who are late.* ∘ *She can't bear waiting for people.* ∘ *How can you bear to listen to that music?* **5** [T] (*formal*) to give birth to children: *She bore four children, all sons.*

☞ A more common expression is "She has had four children." When you talk about a person's own birth, you use "to be born": *Robert was born in 1986.* ∘ *The baby will be born next spring.*

6 [T] to produce flowers or fruit: *The tree in our yard bears more apples than we can eat.* ∘ (*figurative*) *Our plan is beginning to bear fruit – these are the first signs of success.* **7** [T] to show the mark of sth: *The coins bear a buffalo's head on them.* ∘ *He still bears the scars of his accident.* ∘ *She bears a strong resemblance to her mother* (= she looks very much like

her). **8** [T] (*formal*) to have a feeling: *I offended him once and he bore a grudge against me for years.* **9** [I] **bear left/right** to turn or go in the direction that is mentioned: *At the fork in the road, bear left.*

IDM **bear/take the brunt of sth** ⇨ BRUNT

bear in mind (that) to remember that: *Bear in mind that the weather here can change very quickly.*

PHRV **bear sb/sth out** to show that sb is right or that sth is true: *The figures bear him out.* ○ *The figures bear out what he says.*

bear with sb/sth to be patient with: *Please bear with us while we sort out these technical problems.*

☆ **beard** /bɪrd/ *noun* [C] the hair which grows on a man's cheeks and chin: *He has a beard.* ○ *He's growing a beard.* ○ *He shaved his beard off.* ☞ picture at **moustache**.

beard·ed /ˈbɪrdəd/ *adj.* with a beard

bear·ing /ˈbɛrɪŋ/ *noun* **1** [U] **bearing on sth** relation or connection to the subject being discussed: *Her comments had no bearing on our decision.* **2** [C] a direction measured by a compass

IDM **get your bearings** to find out where you are by becoming familiar with your surroundings

lose your bearings ⇨ LOSE

beast /bist/ *noun* [C] **1** (*formal*) an animal, especially a large one: *a wild beast* **2** (*informal*) an unpleasant or cruel person

☆ **beat¹** /bit/ *verb* (*p.t.* **beat**; *p.p.* **beat·en** /ˈbitn/) **1** [I,T] to hit many times, usually very hard: *The man was beating a dog with a stick.* ○ *The rain was beating down on the roof of the car.* **2** [T] to mix quickly with a fork, etc.: *Beat the eggs and sugar together.* **3** [I,T] to make a regular sound or movement: *Her heart beat faster as she ran .* ○ *We could hear drums beating.* ○ *The bird beat its wings and tried to fly away.* **4** [T] to defeat sb; to be better than sth: *He always beats me at tennis.* ○ *We're hoping to beat the world record.* ○ *You can't beat a hot cup of coffee.*

IDM **beat around the bush** to talk about sth without mentioning the main point

beat it! (*informal*) go away immediately: *We don't want you guys around here, so beat it!*

(it) beats me (*informal*) I don't know: *"Where's Andy?" "Beats me – I haven't seen him all day."*

beat time (to sth) to move sth (a stick, your foot or your hand) following the rhythm of a piece of music

off the beaten path/track in a place where people do not often go

PHRV **beat sb/sth off** to fight until sb/sth goes away: *The muggers tried to take his wallet, but he managed to beat them off.*

beat sb to sth to get somewhere or do sth before sb else: *She beat me back to the house.* ○

I wanted to call him first, but Christopher beat me to it.

beat sb up to attack sb by hitting or kicking

beat² /bit/ *noun* **1** [C] a single stroke or hit that comes at regular intervals in a series; the sound it makes: *a heartbeat* ○ *the beat of the drum* **2** [sing.] the strong rhythm that a piece of (especially pop or rock) music has **3** [sing.] the route along which a police officer regularly walks: *Having more police on the beat helps reduce crime.*

beat·ing /ˈbitɪŋ/ *noun* [C] **1** a punishment that you give to sb by hitting him/her: *He got a beating from his dad when he was caught stealing.* **2** a defeat: *The team took a real beating at the tournament.*

beau·ti·cian /byuˈtɪʃn/ *noun* [C] (*old-fashioned*) a person whose job is to improve the way people look, e.g. by cutting and arranging their hair and giving them beauty treatments ☞ **Hairstylist** is more common nowadays.

☆ **beau·ti·ful** /ˈbyuṭəfl/ *adj.* attractive; giving pleasure to the senses: *The view from the top of the hill was really beautiful.* ○ *What a beautiful day – the weather's perfect!* ○ *He has a beautiful voice.* ○ *A beautiful perfume filled the air.* ○ *a beautiful woman*

☞ **Beautiful** is usually used for women and girls. It is stronger than **pretty**, which is also used for women and girls only. Men are described as **handsome** or **good-looking**.

—**beau·ti·ful·ly** /-fli/ *adv.*: *He plays the piano beautifully.* ○ *She was beautifully dressed.*

☆ **beau·ty** /ˈbyuṭi/ *noun* (*pl.* **beau·ties**) **1** [U] the quality that gives pleasure to the senses; the state of being beautiful: *the beauty of California's coast* ○ *Brahms wrote music of great beauty.* **2** [C] (*old-fashioned*) a beautiful woman: *She grew up to be a beauty.* **3** [C] an especially good example of sth: *Look at this tomato – it's a beauty!*

beauty shop *noun* [C] (*old-fashioned*) a business where women can have their hair cut, have beauty treatments, etc.

bea·ver /ˈbivər/ *noun* [C] an animal with brown fur, a long, broad tail and sharp teeth, which it uses to cut branches from trees to make barriers (**dams**) across rivers

beaver

be·came *p.t.* of BECOME

☆ **be·cause** /bɪˈkɔz; -ˈkʌz/ *conj.* for the reason that: *They didn't go for a walk because it was raining.*

☆ **be'cause of** *prep.* by reason of, as a result of: *They didn't go for a walk because of the rain.*

beck·on /ˈbɛkən/ *verb* [I,T] to show sb (often with a movement of your finger or hand) that you want him/her to come closer: *She*

beckoned me over to speak to her. ○ (figurative) When Doug retired, the sunny beaches of California beckoned.

☆ **be·come** /bɪˈkʌm/ verb [I] (p.t. **be·came** /bɪˈkeɪm/; p.p. **be·come**) to begin to be sth: She became president of the company in 1993. ○ Jo wants to become a pilot. ○ They became friends. ○ It became clear that they wanted to stay. ○ He is becoming stronger every day. ○ This neighborhood has become more dangerous in the last few years.

☞ **Get** is also used with adjectives in this sense: He's getting stronger every day. ○ This neighborhood has gotten more dangerous in the last few years. **Get** is very common in conversation and is less formal than **become**.

PHRV **become of sb/sth** to happen to sb/sth: What became of Eileen? – I haven't seen her for years!

twin bed **beds**

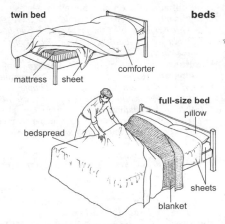

comforter
mattress sheet

full-size bed
pillow
bedspread
sheets
blanket

☆ **bed¹** /bɛd/ noun **1** [C,U] a piece of furniture that you lie on when you sleep: The kids sleep in bunk beds. ○ What time do you usually go to bed? ○ I was already in bed when he called. ○ It's time for bed. ○ to get into/out of bed

☞ There are four standard sizes of beds in the United States: **twin** (wide enough for one person), **full**, **queen** and **king** (the widest).

2 [C] the ground at the bottom of a river or the ocean ☞ Look also at **flower bed**.
IDM **go to bed with sb** (informal) to have sex with sb
make the/your bed to arrange the sheets, etc. so that they are smooth and the bed is ready for sb to sleep in

bed² /bɛd/ verb
PHRV **bed down** to make yourself comfortable and sleep somewhere: We bedded down for the night in the back of the van.

bed·ding /ˈbɛdɪŋ/ noun [U] the sheets, blankets, etc. that are used on a bed

☆ **bed·room** /ˈbɛdrum/ noun [C] a room that is used for sleeping: You can sleep in the spare bedroom. ○ a two-bedroom apartment

bed·side /ˈbɛdsaɪd/ noun [sing.] the area that is next to a bed: She sat at his bedside all night long. ○ a bedside table

bed·spread /ˈbɛdsprɛd/ noun [C] an attractive cover for a bed that you put on top of the sheets and blankets ☞ picture at **bed**.

bed·time /ˈbɛdtaɪm/ noun [C,U] the time that you normally go to bed

☆ **bee** /bi/ noun [C] a black and yellow striped insect that lives in large groups and makes a sweet yellow substance (**honey**) which people can eat

☞ picture at **insect**. A large number of bees together is a **swarm**. Bees **buzz** when they make a noise. They may **sting** if they are angry. Look also at **spelling bee**.

beech /bitʃ/ (also **'beech tree**) noun [C,U] a large tree with a smooth trunk that has small three-sided nuts

☆ **beef¹** /bif/ noun [U] the meat of a cow: a slice of roast beef ○ ground beef ☞ Look at the note at **meat**.

beef² /bif/ verb
PHRV **beef sth up** to add force or weight to sth: There are plans to beef up security around the governor's mansion.

bee·hive /ˈbihaɪv/ (also **hive**) noun [C] a type of box that people keep bees in, or a round structure that bees build and live in

been /bɪn/ p.p. of BE, GO

☞ **Been** is used as the past participle of both **be** and **go**: I've never been seriously ill. ○ I've never been to Mexico.

beep¹ /bip/ noun [C] a short high noise, e.g. made by a piece of electronic equipment

beep² /bip/ verb [I] to make a beep¹: Why is the computer beeping?

beep·er /ˈbipər/ noun [C] = PAGER

☆ **beer** /bɪr/ noun **1** [U] a type of alcoholic drink that is made from grain **2** [C] a type or glass of beer: This bar serves a wide range of beers. ○ We stopped for a couple of beers on the way home. ☞ Look also at **root beer**.

beet /bit/ noun [C] a plant with a dark red root that is cooked and eaten as a vegetable

bee·tle /ˈbitl/ noun [C] an insect that has hard coverings for its wings and often a black shiny body. There are many different types of beetles. ☞ picture at **insect**.

be·fall /bɪˈfɔl/ verb [I,T] (p.t. **be·fell** /bɪˈfɛl/; p.p. **be·fall·en** /bɪˈfɔlən/) (formal) (used about sth bad) to happen to sb

☆ **be·fore¹** /bɪˈfɔr/ prep. **1** earlier than sb/sth: You can call me anytime before 10 o'clock. ○ the week before last ○ Ellen worked in San Francisco before moving here. ○ They should be here before long (= soon). **2** in front/ahead of sb/sth

tʃ	dʒ	v	θ	ð	s	z	ʃ
chin	June	van	thin	then	so	zoo	she

(in an order): *"M" comes before "N" in the alphabet.* ○ (*figurative*) *A very difficult task lies before us.* ○ (*figurative*) *a company that puts profit before safety* **3** when sb is present: *You will appear before the court in the morning.* **4** (*formal*) in a position in front of sb/sth: *They knelt before the throne.*

☆ **be·fore²** /bɪˈfɔr/ *conj.* **1** earlier than the time that: *Turn the lights off before you leave.* **2** rather than; so that sth bad does not happen: *I'd die before I apologized to him!* ○ *Pick up your toys before somebody steps on them.*

☆ **be·fore³** /bɪˈfɔr/ *adv.* at an earlier time: *I think we've met somewhere before.* ○ *It was nice yesterday, but it rained the day before.*

be·fore·hand /bɪˈfɔrhænd/ *adv.* at an earlier time than sth: *We prepared most of the food for the party beforehand.*

be·friend /bɪˈfrɛnd/ *verb* [T] (*formal*) to act as a friend to sb; to be kind to sb

beg /bɛg/ *verb* (**beg·ging; begged**) **1** [I] **beg for sth (from/of sb)** to ask sb for food, money, etc., e.g. because you are very poor: *There are people begging for food on the streets of New York.* **2** [I,T] **beg (sb) for sth** to ask sb for sth strongly, or with great emotion: *He begged for forgiveness.* ○ *We begged him to let the kids go.*
IDM **I beg your pardon** (*formal*) **1** I'm sorry: *I beg your pardon. I picked up your bag by mistake.* **2** (used for asking sb to repeat sth because you did not hear it correctly): *"Hi, I'm Bob." "I beg your pardon?" "Bob."*

be·gan *p.t.* of BEGIN

beg·gar /ˈbɛgər/ *noun* [C] a person who lives by asking people for money, food, etc. on the streets

☆ **be·gin** /bɪˈgɪn/ *verb* (*pres. part.* **be·gin·ning;** *p.t.* **be·gan** /bɪˈgæn/; *p.p.* **be·gun** /bɪˈgʌn/) **1** [I] to take place from a particular time; to start: *What time does the concert begin?*

> ☞ **Begin** and **start** are very similar in meaning, but **start** is more often used in informal speech. They can be followed by *to* or by the *-ing* form of a verb: *The baby began/started to cry/crying.* When **begin** or **start** are themselves in the *-ing* form, they must be followed by *to*: *The baby was just beginning/starting to cry.* In some meanings, only **start** can be used: *I couldn't start the car.* ○ *We'll have to start* (= leave) *early if we want to be there by 8 o'clock.* **Commence** is much more formal than **begin** or **start** and is not usually used in conversation.

2 [I,T] to do or make a start on the first part of sth; to start: *Should I begin or do you want to?* ○ *Please begin at page 10.* ○ *I began* (= started reading) *this book last month and I still haven't finished it.* ○ *He sat down and began to cry.* ○ *Children usually begin school at age 5.* ○ *We began writing to each other in 1990.* ○ *I would like to begin by thanking everybody for*

coming. **3** [I] to form the first part of sth: *My name begins with "W," not "V."* ○ *This is where the neighbors' yard begins.*
IDM **to begin with 1** (used for giving your first reason for sth): *There's no way we can go. To begin with, it's too far, and we can't afford it either.* **2** at first: *To begin with, they were very happy.*

☆ **be·gin·ner** /bɪˈgɪnər/ *noun* [C] a person who has just begun learning sth

☆ **be·gin·ning** /bɪˈgɪnɪŋ/ *noun* [C,U] the first part of sth; the time when or place where sth starts: *The movie gets boring toward the end.* ○ *I read the article from beginning to end.* ○ *We're going away at the beginning of next month.*

be·gun *p.p.* of BEGIN

be·half /bɪˈhæf/ *noun*
IDM **in behalf of sb; in sb's behalf** (*informal*) in order to help sb: *Mrs. Rubin received an award for her work in behalf of refugees.*
on behalf of sb; on sb's behalf for sb; as the representative of sb: *Mary couldn't be there, so her husband accepted the prize on her behalf.* ○ *I would like to thank you all on behalf of the whole class.*

☆ **be·have** /bɪˈheɪv/ *verb* **1** [I] **behave well, badly, etc. (toward sb)** to act in a particular way: *Liz has been behaving very strangely recently.* ○ *He behaved very badly toward his father.* ○ *He behaves as if he were the boss.* **2** [I,T] **behave (yourself)** to act in the correct or proper way: *Now, you kids behave yourselves while we're away!*

-be·haved /bɪˈheɪvd/ (in compounds) behaving in a particular way: *a well-behaved child*

☆ **be·hav·ior** /bɪˈheɪvyər/ *noun* [U] the way that you act or behave: *Her behavior has been very strange recently.* ○ *"I will not tolerate this kind of behavior," said the teacher.*

☆ **be·hind¹** /bɪˈhaɪnd/ *prep.* **1**(also *informal* **in back of**) in, at or to the back of sb/sth: *There's a small shed behind the house.* ○ *The sun went behind a cloud.* ○ *Look behind you before you drive away.* ○ (*figurative*) *It's time you put your problems behind you* (= forgot about them). **2** later or less good than sb/sth: *The flight is twenty minutes behind schedule.* ○ *Jane is behind the rest of the class in math.* **3** supporting or agreeing with sb/sth: *Most people are behind the President's policies.* **4** causing or starting sth: *What is the reason behind his sudden change of opinion?*

☆ **be·hind²** /bɪˈhaɪnd/ *adv.* **1** in, at or to the back of sb/sth: *You go ahead. I'll follow behind in a few minutes.* ○ *Try not to look behind.* ○ *He ran off, but the police were close behind.* **2** in the place where sb/sth is or was: *Oh, no! I left the tickets behind* (= at home). **3** **behind (in/with sth)** later or less good than sb/sth: *We are a month behind with the rent.* ○ *The Bears were behind at halftime.* ☞ Look at **ahead.**

be·hind³ /bɪˈhaɪnd/ *noun* [C] (*informal*) the

part of your body that you sit on ☞ Look at **bottom** (5) and **butt**.

beige /beɪʒ/ *adj.*, *noun* [U] (of) a light brown color

be·ing /'biɪŋ/ *noun* **1** [U] the state of existing: *The organization came into being* (= started) *two years ago* **2** [C] a living person or thing: *a human being* ○ *a strange being from another planet*

be·lat·ed /bɪ'leɪtəd/ *adj.* coming late: *a belated apology* —**be·lat·ed·ly** *adv.*: *They realized, somewhat belatedly, that they made a big mistake.*

belch /beltʃ/ *verb* **1** [I] to let air out from your stomach through your mouth with a sudden noise, e.g. because you have eaten a lot ☞ Look also at **burp**. **2** [T] to send out smoke, etc.: *The volcano belched smoke and ashes.* —**belch** *noun* [C]: *Julia gave a loud belch.*

be·lie /bɪ'laɪ/ *verb* [T] (*pres. part.* **be·ly·ing**; *3rd pers. sing. pres.* **be·lies**; *p.t.*, *p.p.* **be·lied**) to give a false or untrue idea of sth: *His smiling face belied his true feelings.*

☆**be·lief** /bɪ'lif/ *noun* (*pl.* **be·liefs**) **1** [sing., U] **belief (in sb/sth)** a feeling that sb/sth is true, good or right, or that sb/sth really exists: *She has lost her belief in God.* ○ *Her salary has increased beyond belief* (= very much). ☞ Look at **disbelief**. **2** [sing., U] **belief (that...)** something you accept as true; what you believe: *It's my belief that people are basically good.* ○ *There is a general belief that things will soon get better.* ○ *Contrary to popular belief* (= unlike what many people think), *snakes do not really have slimy skin.* **3** [C] an idea that sb has about religion, politics, etc.: *Divorce is against their religious beliefs.*

be·liev·a·ble /bɪ'livəbl/ *adj.* that can be believed ☞ Look at **unbelievable**.

☆**be·lieve** /bɪ'liv/ *verb* (not in the continuous forms) **1** [T] to feel sure that sth is true or that sb is telling the truth: *He says he didn't take the money, but I don't believe him.* ○ *Nobody believes a word she says.* ○ *When she said she was leaving, I just couldn't believe it.* **2** [T] **believe (that)...** to think or suppose: *I believe they moved to Arizona.* ○ *This is yours, I believe.* ○ *The escaped prisoner is believed to be in this area.* **3** [I] to have religious faith **IDM** **believe it or not** it may be surprising but it is true: *Believe it or not, he's a dancer.* **PHRV** **believe in sb/sth** to be sure that sb/sth exists: *Do you believe in God?* **believe in sb/sth; believe in doing sth** to think that sb/sth is good or right: *I believe in the value of education.* ○ *He doesn't believe in eating meat.*

be·liev·er /bɪ'livər/ *noun* [C] a person who has religious faith **IDM** **be a (great/firm) believer in sth** to think that sth is good or right: *She is a great believer in exercise.*

be·lit·tle /bɪ'lɪtl/ *verb* [T] to make sb/sth seem unimportant or not very good

☆**bell** /bɛl/ *noun* [C] **1** a hollow metal object, usually shaped like a cup, that makes a ringing sound when it is hit: *the sound of church bells* **2** an object that makes a ringing sound, or the sound that it makes, often used as a signal: *a doorbell* ○ *Ring the bell and see if they're home.* ○ *There's the bell for the end of class.* **IDM** **ring a bell** ➪ RING²

bel·low /'bɛloʊ/ *verb* **1** [I] to make a deep low sound, like a bull **2** [I,T] to shout in a loud deep voice —**bel·low** *noun* [C]

bell 'pep·per *noun* [C] = PEPPER¹(2)

bel·ly /'bɛli/ *noun* [C] (*pl.* **bel·lies**) (*informal*) the stomach, or the part of the body between the chest and the legs: *a full/empty belly*

bel·ly·but·ton /'bɛlibʌtn/ *noun* [C] (*informal*) = NAVEL

☆**be·long** /bɪ'lɔŋ/ *verb* [I] **1 belong to sb** to be owned by sb: *Who does this pen belong to?* *Don't take anything that doesn't belong to you.* **2 belong to sth** to be a member of a group or organization: *Do you belong to any political party?* **3** to have a correct or usual place: *The plates belong in the cupboard.* ○ *I don't think this paragraph really belongs here.* ○ *It took quite a long time before we felt we belonged in the neighborhood* (= until we felt at home).

be·long·ings /bɪ'lɔŋɪŋz/ *noun* [plural] the things that you own that can be moved, i.e. not land and buildings: *The tourists lost all their belongings in the fire.*

be·lov·ed /bɪ'lʌvd/ *adj.* (*formal*) much loved: *He was a man who was beloved by all who knew him.* ○ *They sang about their beloved homeland.* ☞ When "beloved" comes before a noun, the pronunciation is /bɪ'lʌvəd/.

☆**be·low¹** /bɪ'loʊ/ *prep.* at or to a lower position or level than sb/sth: *Do not write below this line.* ○ *It hurts here – just below my knee.* ○ *The temperature fell below freezing.* ○ *Her test score was below average.* ○ *He drives way below the speed limit.* ☞ Look at the picture and note at **under**.

☆**be·low²** /bɪ'loʊ/ *adv.* at or to a lower position or level: *For further explanation of this point, please see below* (= a later part of the book, etc.). ○ *winter temperatures of 30° and below*

☆**belt¹** /bɛlt/ *noun* [C] **1** a thin piece of cloth, leather, etc. that you wear around your waist: *I need a belt to keep these pants up.* ○ *He was wearing a belt with a huge silver buckle.* ☞ picture on page A27. Look also at **seat belt**. **2** a long strip of rubber, etc. in a circle, that is used for carrying things or for making parts of a machine move: *The suitcases were carried along on a conveyor belt.* ○ *the fan belt of a car* **3** an area of land that has a particular quality: *the Sun Belt states of the Southwest*

ə	y	w	t̪	eɪ	aɪ	ɔɪ	aʊ	oʊ
about	yes	woman	butter	say	five	boy	now	go

IDM below the belt (*informal*) in a way that is unkind or not fair: *That remark really hit below the belt.*

tighten your belt ⇨ TIGHTEN

under your belt (*informal*) that you have already done or achieved: *Woods has four tournament wins under his belt.*

belt² /bɛlt/ *verb* [T] (*informal*) to hit sb hard

PHRV belt sth out (*informal*) to sing sth very loudly and with a lot of force: *She can really belt out a song.*

belt·way /'bɛltweɪ/ *noun* [C] a wide road that goes all around the edge of a city so that traffic does not have to go through the center of the city

be·mused /bɪ'myuzd/ *adj.* not knowing what to think or do; confused

☆ **bench** /bɛntʃ/ *noun* [C] **1** a long wooden or metal seat for two or more people, often outdoors: *a park bench* **2** a long narrow table that people work at, e.g. in a factory, court of law or laboratory: *a carpenter's bench*

bend

bending down bending a spoon
(*also* bending over)

☆ **bend¹** /bɛnd/ *verb* (*p.t., p.p.* **bent** /bɛnt/) **1** [T] to make sth that was straight into a curved shape, or to make sth that was upright lean forward: *Bend your knees when you pick up something heavy.* ○ *to bend a piece of wire into an S shape* ○ *She sat with her head bent forward.* **2** [I] to be or become curved: *The road bends to the left here.* **3** [I] to move your body forward and downward: *He bent down to tie his shoelaces.* ○ *She bent forward to hear what I was saying.*

IDM bend the rules to change the rules a little in order to allow sth for a particular reason

☆ **bend²** /bɛnd/ *noun* [C] a curve or turn, e.g. in a road: *a sharp bend in the road*

☆ **be·neath¹** /bɪ'niθ/ *prep.* **1** in, at or to a lower position than sb/sth; under: *It's wonderful to feel the grass beneath my feet.* ○ *He seemed like a nice person, but there was a lot of anger beneath the surface.* ☞ Look at the note at **under.** **2** not good enough for sb: *She felt that washing dishes for other people was beneath her.*

be·neath² /bɪ'niθ/ *adv.* (*formal*) in, at or to a lower position: *From the top of the tower, we gazed down on the city beneath.*

ben·e·fac·tor /'bɛnəfæktər/ *noun* [C] a person who helps or gives money to a person or an organization

ben·e·fi·cial /ˌbɛnə'fɪʃl/ *adj.* **beneficial (to**

sb/sth) having a good or useful effect: *a beneficial influence on the economy*

☆ **ben·e·fit¹** /'bɛnəfɪt/ *noun* **1** [U] the advantage or good or useful effect of sth: *Most parents want to give their children the benefit of a good education.* ○ *A change in the law would be to everyone's benefit.* ○ *I can't see the benefit of doing things this way.* **2** [C] a thing that has a good or useful effect: *the benefits of modern technology* **3** [C,U] money that the government gives to people who are sick for a long time, injured at work, unemployed, etc.: *unemployment benefit payments* **4** [C] (*also* **fringe benefit**) an extra payment or service that is given to an employee in addition to his/her salary: *Our generous employee benefits package includes health insurance and three weeks' paid vacation.* **5** [C] a concert, party, show, etc. that is held in order to raise money to help a charity, an organization, etc.: *a benefit concert to raise money for victims of the earthquake*

IDM for sb's benefit especially to help, please, etc. sb: *For the benefit of newcomers, I will explain the plan again.*

give sb the benefit of the doubt to believe that what sb says is true because there is no clear proof that it is not

☆ **ben·e·fit²** /'bɛnəfɪt/ *verb* (**ben·e·fit·ing; ben·e·fit·ed** *or* **ben·e·fit·ting; ben·e·fit·ted**) **1** [T] to have a good or useful effect: *The new tax laws will benefit people on low wages.* **2** [I] **benefit (from sth)** to receive an advantage from sth: *We've certainly benefited from the changes in the law.*

be·nev·o·lent /bə'nɛvələnt/ *adj.* (*formal*) kind, friendly and helpful to others —**be·nev·o·lence** /-ləns/ *noun* [U]

be·nign /bə'nam/ *adj.* **1** (used about people) kind or gentle **2** (used about a disease, etc.) not causing death: *a benign tumor* ☞ Look at **malignant.**

bent¹ *p.t., p.p.* of BEND¹

bent² /bɛnt/ *adj.* **bent on sth/on doing sth** wanting to do sth very much, so that you cannot accept not doing it: *She seems bent on becoming an actress, no matter how hard it is.*

IDM be/get bent out of shape (*slang*) to become very angry or upset: *The boss got totally bent out of shape about my mistake.*

be·queath /bɪ'kwiθ; -'kwið/ *verb* [T] (*formal*) **bequeath sth (to sb)** to arrange for sth to be given to sb after you die: *He bequeathed $1,000 to his church.* ☞ **Leave** is a more common word.

be·quest /bɪ'kwɛst/ *noun* [C] (*formal*) something that you arrange to be given to sb after you have died: *He left a bequest to each of his grandchildren.*

be·reaved /bɪ'rivd/ *adj.* **1** having had a relative or close friend die **2** **the bereaved** *noun* [C] a person whose relative or close friend has

died recently ☞ The plural is also **the be-reaved**.

be·ret /bəˈreɪ/ noun [C] a soft flat round hat

☆ **ber·ry** /ˈbɛri/ noun [C] (pl. **ber·ries**) a small soft fruit with seeds: *Those berries are poisonous.*

ber·serk /bərˈzərk; -ˈsərk/ adj.
IDM **go berserk** (informal) to become extremely angry and violent and unable to control yourself: *Then this guy just went berserk and started screaming.*

berth /bərθ/ noun [C] a place where a ship can be tied up in a harbor

☆ **be·side** /bɪˈsaɪd/ prep. at the side of, or next to sb/sth: *Come and sit beside me.* ○ *He kept his bag close beside him at all times.*
IDM **beside yourself (with sth)** not able to control yourself because of a very strong emotion: *Jennifer was almost beside herself with grief.*

☆ **be·sides¹** /bɪˈsaɪdz/ prep. in addition to or as well as sb/sth: *There will be six people coming, besides you and Uli.*

be·sides² /bɪˈsaɪdz/ adv. in addition; also: *I thought the hotel was too expensive. Besides, it was very close to the freeway.*

be·siege /bɪˈsidʒ/ verb [T] to surround a place with an army: (figurative) *The actor was besieged by fans and reporters.*

☆ **best¹** /bɛst/ adj. (the superlative of good) of the highest quality or level; most suitable: *Who's your best friend?* ○ *His latest book is by far his best.* ○ *It's best to call early.* ○ *Who in the class is best at math?* ○ *What's the best way to get to the airport from here?* ○ *The best thing to do is to forget all about it.*
IDM **your best bet** (informal) the best thing for you to do in a particular situation: *There's nowhere to park downtown. Your best bet is to take the bus.*
the best/better part of sth ⇨ PART¹

☆ **best²** /bɛst/ adv. (the superlative of well) 1 in the most excellent way: *She works best in the morning.* 2 to the greatest degree; most: *Which of these dresses do you like best?* ○ *one of America's best-loved TV stars* ○ *Ask Peter. He'll know best what to do.*
IDM **as best you can** as well as you can, even if it is not perfectly

☆ **best³** /bɛst/ noun [sing.] 1 something that is of the highest quality or level: *When you pay that much for a meal, you expect the best.* ○ *I'm not in the best of health.* ○ *The best we can hope for is that the situation doesn't get any worse.* ☞ Look at **second-best**. 2 **the best** [with sing. or pl. verb] a person that is best: *Even the best of us make mistakes sometimes.*
IDM **all the best** (informal) (used when you are saying goodbye to sb and wishing him/her success): *All the best! Keep in touch, OK?*
at best if everything is as favorable as pos-

sible; taking the most hopeful view: *At best, it'll be ready by the end of March.*
at its/your best in its/your best state or condition: *This is an example of Beckett's work at its best.* ○ *No one is at their best first thing in the morning.*
bring out the best/worst in sb to show sb's best/worst qualities: *The crisis really brought out the best in Tony.*
do/try your best to do all or the most that you can: *It doesn't matter whether you win or not. Just do your best.*
look your best to look as beautiful or attractive as possible
make the best of sth to accept a difficult situation and try to be as happy as possible

,**best ¹man** noun [C] a man who helps and supports the man who is getting married (**groom**) at his wedding ☞ Look at the note at **wedding**.

best·sell·er /ˌbɛstˈsɛlər/ noun [C] a book or other product that has been bought by large numbers of people

,**best-ˈselling** adj. very popular: *a best-selling novel*

☆ **bet¹** /bɛt/ verb [I,T] (pres. part. **bet·ting**; p.t., p.p. **bet**) **bet (sth) (on sth)** to risk some money on the result of sth (e.g. a horse race). If you are wrong about the result, you have to pay some money: *Which horse did you bet on?* ○ *I bet him $10 he couldn't stop smoking for a week.*
IDM **I bet (that)...** (informal) I'm sure that...: *I bet he feels stupid.*
you bet (informal) (a way of saying, "Yes, of course!"): *"Are you coming too?" "You bet!"*

bet² /bɛt/ noun [C] an act of betting: *Did you have a bet on that race?* ○ *to win/lose a bet*
IDM **your best bet** ⇨ BEST¹

be·tray /bɪˈtreɪ/ verb [T] **1** to be disloyal to a person or thing; to harm a person or organization that trusts you: *When parents get divorced, the children often feel betrayed.* ○ *to betray your country* **2** to make facts about sb/sth known to an enemy; to make a secret known: *She betrayed them to the secret police.* ○ *He refused to betray the information.* **3** to show a feeling or quality that you would like to keep hidden: *Her steady voice did not betray the emotion she was feeling.* —**be·tray·al** /bɪˈtreɪəl/ noun [C,U]

☆ **bet·ter¹** /ˈbɛtər/ adj. **1** (the comparative of good) **better (than sth)** of a higher quality or level or more suitable: *I think her second novel was much better than her first.* ○ *He's better at chemistry than physics.* ○ *It's a long way to drive. It would be better to fly.* **2** less sick or fully recovered from an illness: *I feel a little better today.* ○ *You can't go swimming until you're better.*

☆ **bet·ter²** /ˈbɛtər/ adv. (the comparative of well) **better (than sb/sth)** to a greater or higher

tʃ	dʒ	v	θ	ð	s	z	ʃ
chin	June	van	thin	then	so	zoo	she

B

degree: *I think you could have done this better.* ○ *Sylvie speaks English better than I do.* ○ *She is much better known than her sister.* ○ *I like the red one better than the blue one.*

IDM the best/better part of sth ⇨ PART¹

(be) better off 1 to be in a more pleasant or suitable situation: *You look terrible. You'd be better off at home in bed.* **2** with more money: *We're much better off now that both of us work.*

you, etc. had better you should; you would be wise to: *I think we'd better go soon.*

know better ⇨ KNOW

think better of (doing) sth ⇨ THINK

☆ **bet·ter³** /ˈbɛt̬ər/ *noun* [sing.] something that is of higher quality: *The hotel wasn't too bad, but I've certainly seen better.*

IDM get the better of sb/sth to defeat or be stronger than sb/sth: *When we have an argument, she always gets the better of me.*

between/among

a small house **between** two large ones

a house **among** some trees

☆ **be·tween¹** /bɪˈtwin/ *prep.* **1** in the space that separates two things, people, etc.; somewhere in the middle: *I was sitting between Anne and Derek.* ○ *a town between Los Angeles and San Diego* **2** from one place to another and back again: *There aren't any direct flights between here and Toronto.* ○ *the trip between home and the office* **3** involving or linking two people, groups or things: *There's some sort of disagreement between them.* ○ *There may be a connection between the two crimes.* **4** (used about two amounts, distances, ages, times, etc.) at a point that is greater or later than the first and smaller or earlier than the second; somewhere in the middle: *She must be between about thirty and thirty-five.* ○ *They said they would arrive between 4 and 5 o'clock.* ○ *a cost of between $200 and $300* **5** choosing one and not the other (of two things): *to choose between two jobs* ○ *What's the difference between "some" and "any"?* **6** by putting together the actions, efforts, etc. of two or more people: *We've got over a thousand dollars saved up between us.* **7** giving each person a share: *The money was divided equally between the two children.* ○ *We ate all the candy between us.*

☞ **Between** is usually used of two people or things: *sitting between her mother and father* ○ *between the ages of 12 and 14.* **Among** is always used for more than two people or things considered as a group, rather than as individuals: *You're among friends here.*

be·tween² /bɪˈtwin/ (*also* **in between**) *adv.* in the space or period of time that separates two things, points, people, times, etc.: *We can't get to the beach this way. There's a highway in between.* ○ *I have a meeting at 10:00 and one at 11:00, but I should manage to see you in between.*

bev·er·age /ˈbɛvrɪdʒ; ˈbɛvərɪdʒ/ *noun* [C] (*formal*) (used especially on menus) a drink

be·ware /bɪˈwɛr/ *verb* [I] (only in the imperative or infinitive) **beware (of sb/sth)** (used for giving a warning) to be careful: *Beware of the dog!* (written on a sign) ○ *We were told to beware of pickpockets in the city.*

be·wil·dered /bɪˈwɪldərd/ *adj.* confused: *He seemed bewildered by all the activity around him.*

be·wil·der·ing /bɪˈwɪldərɪŋ/ *adj.* making you feel confused and unable to decide what to do: *a bewildering array of choices*

☆ **be·yond¹** /bɪˈyɑnd/ *prep.* **1** on the other side of: *beyond the distant mountains* **2** farther than; later than: *Does the expressway continue beyond Miami?* ○ *Most people don't work beyond the age of 65.* **3** out of the range or reach of sth (so that sth is not possible): *The house was beyond what I could afford.* ○ *The car was completely beyond repair.* ○ *His success was beyond all our expectations* (= more than we expected). ○ *The fact that she is guilty is beyond doubt* (= there is no doubt about it). **4** except for or apart from: *I haven't heard anything beyond a few rumors.*

IDM be beyond sb (*informal*) to be impossible for sb to understand or imagine: *Why she wants to go and live there is beyond me.*

be·yond² /bɪˈyɑnd/ *adv.* on the other side or farther along: *We could see the mountains and the ocean beyond.*

bi·as¹ /ˈbaɪəs/ *noun* [C,U, usually sing.] (*pl.* **bi·as·es**) **1** [C] an opinion, feeling or attitude that is not fair and not based on facts: *a bias against recent immigrants* **2** [C,U] giving one side in an argument an advantage over the other; not being neutral: *The organization has been accused of political bias.*

bi·as² /ˈbaɪəs/ *verb* [T] to influence sb/sth, especially unfairly; to give an advantage to one group, etc.: *The jury members must not let these news reports bias them against the defendant.*

bi·ased /ˈbaɪəst/ *adj.* giving advantage to one group, etc.: *Good newspapers should not be biased toward a particular point of view.* ○ *Is our legal system biased in favor of the rich and powerful?* ○ *a biased* (= unfair) *report*

bib /bɪb/ *noun* [C] a piece of cloth or plastic that a baby or small child wears under the chin to protect its clothes while it is eating

☆ **bi·ble** /ˈbaɪbl/ *noun* [C] **1 the Bible** the holy book of the Christian people, made up of the

i	ɪ	ɛ	æ	ɑ	ɔ	ʌ	ʊ	u
see	sit	ten	cat	hot	saw	cup	put	too

Old and New Testaments **2 the Bible** the holy book of the Jewish people **3** a very useful and important book about a particular topic: *This is the amateur chef's bible.* —**bib·li·cal** (*also* **Biblical**) /'bɪblɪkl/ *adj.*

bib·li·og·ra·phy /ˌbɪbli'ɑgrəfi/ *noun* [C] (*pl.* **bib·li·og·ra·phies**) **1** a list of the books and articles that a writer used when he/she was writing a particular book **2** a list of books on a particular subject

bib 'overalls *noun* [plural] = OVERALLS

bi·cen·ten·ni·al /ˌbaɪsɛn'tɛniəl/ *noun* [C] the day or year two hundred years after sth happened or began: *The bicentennial of the American Revolution was celebrated on July 4, 1976.*

bi·ceps /'baɪsɛps/ *noun* [C] (*pl.* **bi·ceps**) the large muscle at the front of the top part of your arms

bick·er /'bɪkər/ *verb* [I] to argue about unimportant things: *The boys were bickering about whose turn it was to use the computer.*

bicycle: handlebars, seat, brake, pump, spokes, pedal, tire, chain

☆ **bi·cy·cle** /'baɪsɪkl/ (*also informal* **bike**) *noun* [C] a vehicle with two wheels that you sit on and ride by moving your legs: *to ride a bicycle* ○ *to go somewhere on your bicycle*

☆ **bid¹** /bɪd/ *verb* (**bid·ding**; *p.t., p.p.* **bid** or, in the idiom "bid sb farewell" *p.t.* **bid** or **bade** /beɪd; bæd/; *p.p.* **bid** or **bid·den** /'bɪdn/) [I,T] **bid (sth) (for/on sth)** to offer a sum of money in order to buy sth: *to bid for/on sth at an auction* ○ *Somebody bid $5,000 for the painting.*
IDM **bid sb farewell** (*formal*) to say goodbye to sb: *It has been a pleasure to visit your great city, but now I must bid you a fond farewell.*

bid² /bɪd/ *noun* [C] **1** an offer to pay a sum of money in order to buy sth: *We made a bid of $500 for the painting at the auction.* ○ *a higher/lower bid* **2** a formal offer to supply goods or do work at a certain price: *to submit a bid for a project* **3** an attempt to do, obtain, etc. sth: *her bid to win the championship* ○ *His bid for power had failed.*

bid·der /'bɪdər/ *noun* [C] a person who offers a sum of money in order to buy sth: *The house was sold to the highest bidder* (= the person who offered the most money).

☆ **big¹** /bɪg/ *adj.* (**big·ger**; **big·gest**) **1** large; not small: *a big house, town, salary, etc.* ○ *This dress is too big for me.* ○ *a big eater/spender*

(= sb who eats/spends a lot) **2** great or important: *They had a big argument yesterday.* ○ *That was the biggest decision I've ever had to make.* ○ *some of the big names in Hollywood* **3** (*only before* a noun) (*informal*) older: *my big sister*

☞ **Big** and **large** can both be used when talking about size or number. **Large** is more formal and is not usually used for describing people: *a big/large house* ○ *a big boy.* **Great** is mostly used when talking about the importance, quality, etc. of a person or thing. It can also be used with uncountable nouns to mean "a lot of": *a great occasion* ○ *a great musician* ○ *great happiness, care, etc.*

4 (*informal*) popular with the public: *Video games are big again this year.* **5 big on sb/sth** (*informal*) enthusiastic about sb/sth: *I've never been really big on sports.*
IDM **Big deal!** (*informal*) (used to say that you think sth is not important or interesting): *"Look at my new bike!" "Big deal! It's not as nice as mine."*
a big deal/no big deal (*informal*) something that is/is not very important or exciting: *The Fourth of July parade is a very big deal in our town.* ○ *Don't worry about it – it's no big deal.*
give sb/get a big hand to clap for sb/to be clapped for loudly: *The audience gave the little girl a big hand when she finished her song.*

☆ **big²** /bɪg/ *adv.* (*informal*) in a grand or ambitious way: *You have to think big if you want to be successful.*

big·a·my /'bɪgəmi/ *noun* [U] the crime of being married to two people at the same time

the ˌBig 'Apple *noun* [sing.] (*informal*) New York City: *I've lived in the Big Apple for 20 years.* ☞ Look at the note at **White House.**

ˌbig 'cheese *noun* [C] (*informal*) an important or powerful person: *If you want to take the afternoon off, you'll have to ask the big cheese* (= the boss).

the 'big league *noun* [C] **1** the most important division(s) of a sport, especially baseball, with the best professional teams **2** [usually pl.] the highest level of an activity, a business, etc. that you reach when you are very successful: *The company has already joined the big leagues with its popular computer games.* — **big-league** *adj.* (*only before* a noun): *a big-league baseball player* ○ *big-league politics*

big·ot /'bɪgət/ *noun* [C] a person who has very strong and unreasonable opinions and who refuses to change them or listen to other people —**big·ot·ed** *adj.*

ˈbig shot *noun* [C] (*informal*) a person who thinks he/she is more important or powerful than he/she really is: *He acts like a big shot, but nobody listens to him.*

the 'big time *noun* [sing.] the highest level of an activity, especially entertainment, that you reach when you are very successful: *This is*

ə	y	w	t̬	eɪ	aɪ	ɔɪ	aʊ	oʊ
about	yes	woman	butter	say	five	boy	now	go

the role that could help her make it to the big
time in Hollywood.

'big time adv. (slang) very much: You screwed
up big time, Wayne!

'big-time adj. (only before a noun) important
or famous: big-time drug dealing ○ big-time
politicians

☆ **bike** /baɪk/ noun [C] (informal) a bicycle or a
motorcycle: Mary has just learned to ride a
bike. ○ Bike riders should stay off the sidewalk.
○ Let's go for a bike ride.

bi·ki·ni /bɪˈkini/ noun [C] a piece of clothing,
in two pieces, that women wear for swimming

bi·lin·gual /ˌbaɪˈlɪŋgwəl/ adj. **1** able to speak
two languages equally well: Our kids are bilin-
gual in English and Spanish. **2** having or
using two languages: a bilingual dictionary

☆ **bill¹** /bɪl/ noun **1** [C] a piece of paper that
shows how much money you owe for goods or
services: to pay a bill ○ a telephone bill

☞ In restaurants we call the bill a **check**:
Could I have the check, please?

2 [C] a piece of paper money: a ten-dollar bill
3 [C] a plan for a possible new law: The bill
was discussed in Congress. ○ The bill was
passed/defeated. **4** [sing.] the program of en-
tertainment offered in a show, concert, etc.:
Diana Ross headed the bill. ○ There's a double
bill (= two different movies) of horror movies
at the theater tonight. **5** [C] the hard part of a
bird's mouth **6** [C] the pointed front part of a
hat that is above your eyes: He wears his
baseball cap with the bill facing backwards.
☞ picture at **cap**.

IDM **foot the bill** ⇨ FOOT²

bill² /bɪl/ verb [T] **1 bill sb (for sth)** to send sb
a bill¹(1) for sth: I've been billed for several
items that I didn't order. **2** to announce to the
public with an advertisement, etc.: The show
is billed as a musical comedy.

bill·board /ˈbɪlbɔrd/ noun [C] a large board
near a street or road where advertisements
are put

bill·fold /ˈbɪlfoʊld/ noun [C] = WALLET

☆ **bil·lion** /ˈbɪlyən/ number 1,000,000,000: billions
of dollars

☞ Notice that when you are counting, you
use billion without "s": nine billion dollars.

bil·lion·aire /ˌbɪlyəˈnɛr/ noun [C] a person
who has a billion dollars; an extremely rich
person

the ˌBill of ˈRights noun [sing.] the first ten
additions (**amendments**) to the basic law of
the United States (**the Constitution**), which
guarantee certain basic rights to citizens,
such as freedom of speech and freedom of
religion

bil·low /ˈbɪloʊ/ verb [I] to rise or move slowly
in the wind, like waves: curtains billowing in
the breeze

bin /bɪn/ noun [C] a large container that is

used for storing or holding things: Put those
empty cans in the recycling bin.

bind¹ /baɪnd/ verb [T] (p.t., p.p. **bound**
/baʊnd/) **1 bind A (to B)**; **bind A and B (to-
gether)** to tie or fasten with string or rope:
They bound the prisoner's hands behind his
back. ○ (figurative) The two men were bound
together by the strength of their beliefs. **2 bind
sb (to sth)** to cause or force sb to do sth: to be
bound by a law, an agreement, etc. ○ The con-
tract binds you to completion of the work with-
in two years. **3** (usually passive) to fasten
sheets of paper into a cover to form a book:
The book was bound in leather.

bind² /baɪnd/ noun [sing.]
in a bind (informal) in a difficult situation
that you do not know how to get out of: I was
in a real bind when I couldn't find my house
key.

bind·er /ˈbaɪndər/ noun [C] a hard cover for
holding loose sheets of paper together

bind·ing¹ /ˈbaɪndɪŋ/ noun [C] the part of a
cover that holds the pages of a book together

bind·ing² /ˈbaɪndɪŋ/ adj. [C] making it neces-
sary for sb to do sth they have promised or to
obey a law, etc.: This contract is legally bind-
ing.

binge¹ /bɪndʒ/ noun [C] (informal) a period of
eating or drinking too much: to go on a drink-
ing binge

binge² /bɪndʒ/ verb [I] (**binge·ing** or **bing·ing**;
binged) **binge (on sth)** to eat or drink too
much, especially without being able to control
yourself: to binge on junk food

bin·go /ˈbɪŋgoʊ/ noun [U] a game in which
each player has a different card with twenty-
five numbers on it. The person in charge of
the game calls numbers out, and the winner is
the first player to have five of his/her num-
bers in a row called out.

telescope binoculars strap

bin·oc·u·lars /bɪˈnɑkyələrz/ noun [plural] an
instrument with two tubes which you look
through in order to make objects that are far
away seem nearer: a pair of binoculars
☞ Look at **telescope**.

bi·o·chem·is·try /ˌbaɪoʊˈkɛməstri/ noun [U]
the study of the chemistry of living things

bi·o·de·grad·a·ble /ˌbaɪoʊdɪˈgreɪdəbl/ adj.
that can decay naturally: biodegradable pack-
aging

bi·og·ra·pher /baɪˈɑgrəfər/ noun [C] a person
who writes a story of sb else's life

bi·o·graph·i·cal /ˌbaɪəˈgræfɪkl/ adj. contain-
ing information about sb's life

ər	ɪr	ɛr	ɑr	ɔr	ʊr	ʒ	h	ŋ
bird	near	hair	car	north	tour	vision	hat	sing

bi·og·ra·phy /baɪˈɑgrəfi/ *noun* [C,U] (*pl.* **bi·og·ra·phies**) the story of a person's life written by sb else: *a biography of Lincoln* ☞ Look at **autobiography**.

bi·o·log·i·cal /ˌbaɪəˈlɑdʒɪkl/ *adj.* **1** connected with the scientific study of animals, plants and other living things: *biological research* **2** involving the use of living things to destroy or damage other living things: *biological weapons*

bi·ol·o·gist /baɪˈɑlədʒɪst/ *noun* [C] a person who is an expert in biology

☆ **bi·ol·o·gy** /baɪˈɑlədʒi/ *noun* [U] the scientific study of living things

birch /bərtʃ/ *noun* [C,U] a type of tree with a smooth trunk and thin branches

bird

egg

beak

nest

wing

☆ **bird** /bərd/ *noun* [C] a creature with feathers and wings that can (usually) fly

☞ Birds **fly** and **sing**. They build **nests** and lay **eggs**.

IDM **kill two birds with one stone** ⇨ KILL¹

☆ **birth** /bərθ/ *noun* **1** [C,U] being born; coming out of a mother's body: *a difficult birth* ○ *The baby weighed six pounds at birth* (= when it was born). ○ *She's been deaf since birth.* ○ *What's your date of birth?* (= the date on which you were born) **2** [U] your nationality or your place of birth: *She lives in the U.S., but she's German by birth.* **3** [sing.] the beginning of sth: *the birth of an idea*

IDM **give birth (to sb/sth)** to produce a baby: *She gave birth to her second child at home.*

birth certificate *noun* [C] an official piece of paper that states the date and place of a person's birth

birth control *noun* [U] ways of controlling or limiting the number of children you have ☞ Look at **contraception**.

birth date *noun* [C] the date on which sb was born

☆ **birth·day** /ˈbərθdeɪ/ *noun* [C] the day in each year that is the same date as the one when you were born: *My birthday's (on) November 15.* ○ *my eighteenth birthday* ○ *a birthday present* ○ *a birthday card*

☞ An **anniversary** is not the same as a **birthday**. An anniversary is the day in each year that is the same date as an important

past event: *our wedding anniversary* ○ *the fiftieth anniversary of the sinking of the Titanic* (= exactly fifty years after it happened) . When it is a person's birthday we say **Happy Birthday!** If we know the person well, we send a special card to him/her or give him/her a present. Your eighteenth birthday is an important occasion when you legally become an adult.

birth·mark /ˈbərθmɑrk/ *noun* [C] a permanent mark on your body, that you are born with

birth·place /ˈbərθpleɪs/ *noun* **1** [C] the house or area where a person was born **2** [sing.] the place where sth began: *in Greece, the birthplace of the Olympic Games*

birth·rate /ˈbərθreɪt/ *noun* [C] the number of babies born in a particular group of people during a particular period of time: *The birthrate is falling/rising.*

bis·cuit /ˈbɪskət/ *noun* [C] **1** a small plain cake that is usually not sweet. Biscuits are often eaten warm, with butter. **2** (*BrE*) = COOKIE

bi·sex·u·al /ˌbaɪˈsɛkʃuəl/ *adj.* sexually attracted to both men and women

bish·op /ˈbɪʃəp/ *noun* [C] **1** a senior person in the Christian church, who is in charge of the churches in a city or a district: *the Bishop of Joliet, Illinois* ☞ Look at **archbishop**. **2** one of the pieces used in the game of chess ☞ picture at **chess**.

bi·son /ˈbaɪsn; -zn/ *noun* [C] (*pl.* **bi·son**) a large wild animal that looks like a cow with a very large head, curved horns and thick fur on its head and neck: *a herd of bison* ☞ This type of animal is often called a **buffalo**.

☆ **bit¹** /bɪt/ *noun* [C] **1** a small piece or amount of sth: *There were bits of broken glass all over the floor.* ○ *I think these strawberries need a little bit more sugar.* ○ *Could you give me a bit of advice?* **2** (*technical*) the smallest unit of information that is stored in a computer's memory, represented by the numbers 0 or 1

IDM **a bit 1** slightly: *I'll be a bit late tonight.* **2** a short time or distance: *Could you move forward a bit?* ☞ It is more common to say **a little** or **a little bit**.

bit by bit slowly or a little at a time

a bit of a (used to say that sth is really larger, worse, etc. than you want to say it is): *I have a little bit of a problem…* ○ *It was a bit of a surprise to see him standing in the doorway!*

quite a bit ⇨ QUITE

to bits into small pieces: *Two cars were blown to bits by the explosion.*

bit² *p.t.* of BITE¹

bitch¹ /bɪtʃ/ *noun* [C] **1** (*slang*) a very unpleasant woman: *She's a real bitch.* ○ *You bitch!* (= used to insult a woman) **2** (*formal* or *old-fashioned*) a female dog

bitch² /bɪtʃ/ *verb* [I] (*slang*) **bitch (about sth)**

to complain in a very critical way: *You're always bitching about the other people at work.*

bitch·y /'bɪtʃi/ *adj.* (usually used about women or their behavior) tending to talk about other people in an unkind way: *a bitchy remark*

☆ **bite¹** /baɪt/ *verb* (*p.t.* **bit** /bɪt/; *p.p.* **bit·ten** /'bɪtn/) **1** [I,T] **bite (sb/sth); bite into sth** to cut or attack with the teeth: *Does your dog bite?* ○ *The dog bit me.* ○ *He bit into the burger hungrily.* ☞ picture at **lick**. **2** [T] (used about insects or snakes) to make a small hole in your skin and cause pain: *He was bitten by a snake.* ☞ Wasps and bees do not **bite** you. They **sting** you.

☆ **bite²** /baɪt/ *noun* **1** [C] a piece of food that you can put into your mouth: *to take a big bite of an apple* **2** [C] a painful place on the skin made by an insect, snake, dog, etc.: *a mosquito bite* **3** [sing.] (*informal*) some food: *Would you like a bite to eat before you go?*

bit·ing /'baɪtɪŋ/ *adj.* (used about sth you say) unkind and critical: *a biting comment*

bit·ten *p.t.* of BITE¹

☆ **bit·ter** /'bɪtər/ *adj.* **1** (used about a person) very unhappy or angry about sth that has happened; disappointed: *She was very bitter about the divorce.* **2** causing unhappiness or anger for a long time; difficult to accept: *His son has been a bitter disappointment to him.* **3** caused by anger or hatred: *a bitter argument* **4** (used about cold weather) extreme: *Because of the bitter cold, we stayed indoors.* **5** having a sharp, unpleasant taste; not sweet: *bitter coffee*

bit·ter·ly /'bɪtərli/ *adv.* **1** (used for describing strong negative feelings or cold weather) extremely: *bitterly disappointed* ○ *a bitterly cold winter* **2** in a bitter (1) way: *"I've lost everything," he said bitterly.*

bit·ter·ness /'bɪtərnəs/ *noun* [U] anger and unhappiness as a result of sth bad happening

bi·zarre /bɪ'zɑr/ *adj.* very strange: *The story had a bizarre ending.*

☆ **black¹** /blæk/ *adj.* **1** of the darkest color possible, the color of the night sky **2** often **Black** belonging to a race of people with dark skin, originally from Africa: *the Black population of America* ○ *Black culture* ☞ Look at **African-American**. **3** (used about coffee) without milk or cream: *black coffee with sugar* **4** (used about a situation) without hope; depressing: *The economic outlook is awfully black.* **5** funny in a cruel or unkind way: *The movie is a black comedy.* **6** very angry: *a black mood* ○ *to give sb a black look*

IDM **black and blue** covered with dark marks on the skin that were caused by hitting: *Her whole face was black and blue.*

black and white (used about television, photographs, etc.) showing no colors except black, white and gray —**black·ness** *noun* [U]

☆ **black²** /blæk/ *noun* **1** [U] the darkest color, like the night sky: *People usually wear black* (= black clothes) *at funerals.* **2** often **Black** [C] a person who belongs to a race of people with dark skin, originally from Africa: *South African Blacks*

☞ This is often considered offensive when used in the U.S. Look at **African-American**.

IDM **(be) in the black** having some money in the bank ☞ Look at **in the red** at **red²**.

in black and white in writing or in print: *I won't believe the news until I see it in black and white.*

black³ /blæk/ *verb*

PHRV **black out** to lose consciousness for a short time: *I remember losing control of the car and then I blacked out.*

black·ber·ry /'blæk,bɛri/ *noun* [C] (*pl.* **black·ber·ries**) a small black or dark purple fruit that grows on bushes

black·bird /'blækbərd/ *noun* [C] a common bird. The male is black and the female is usually brown.

☆ **black·board** /'blækbɔrd/ (*also* **board; chalkboard**) *noun* [C] a piece of dark board that you write or draw on with chalk, especially in a classroom

black·en /'blækən/ *verb* [T] **1** to make sth black: *wood blackened by fire* **2** to make sth seem bad, by saying unkind things about it: *to blacken sb's name*

black 'eye *noun* [C] an eye with dark-colored skin around it as the result of a blow: *He got a black eye in the fight.*

black·head /'blækhɛd/ *noun* [C] a small spot on the skin with a black center

black·jack /'blækdʒæk/ *noun* [U] a card game that is usually played for money, in which players try to get cards with a total value of 21

black·list /'blæklɪst/ *noun* [C] a list of people who are considered bad or dangerous: *to be on sb's blacklist* —**black·list** *verb* [T]

black 'magic *noun* [U] a type of magic that is used for evil purposes

black·mail /'blækmeɪl/ *noun* [U] the crime of forcing a person to give you money or do sth for you, usually by threatening to make known sth that they want to keep secret —**black·mail** *verb* [T]: *He was blackmailed into paying an enormous amount of money.* —**black·mail·er** *noun* [C]

black 'market *noun* [C] the buying and selling of goods or foreign money in a way that is not legal: *to buy/sell sth on the black market*

black·out /'blækaʊt/ *noun* [C] **1** a time when the electricity supply to an area is cut off **2** a period when you lose consciousness for a short time: *to have a blackout*

black·smith /'blæksmɪθ/ *noun* [C] (*old-fashioned*) a person whose job is to make and

repair things made of metal, especially horses' shoes

blad·der /'blædər/ noun [C] the part of the body where waste liquid (**urine**) collects before leaving the body

☆ **blade** /bleɪd/ noun [C] **1** the flat, sharp part of a knife, a pair of scissors, etc. ☞ picture at **pocket knife. 2** one of the flat, wide parts that spin around on an airplane, etc.: *a propeller blade* **3** a long, thin leaf of grass: *a blade of grass*

☆ **blame¹** /bleɪm/ verb [T] **1 blame sb (for sth); blame sth on sb** to think or say that a certain person or thing is responsible for sth bad that has happened: *The teacher blamed me for the accident.* ○ *Some people blame the changes in the climate on pollution.* **2 not blame sb (for sth)** to think that sb is not wrong to do sth: *"I'd like to quit this job and start my own company." "I don't blame you."* (= I can understand why). ○ *I don't blame you for feeling angry.*

IDM be to blame (for sth) to be responsible for sth bad: *The police say that careless driving was to blame for the accident.*

☆ **blame²** /bleɪm/ noun [U] **blame (for sth)** responsibility for sth bad: *to take the blame for sth* ○ *The report puts the blame on inflation.*

bland /blænd/ adj. **1** (used about food) mild or lacking in taste **2** ordinary or uninteresting: *a fairly bland style of writing* **3** showing no strong feelings or interest: *a bland smile* —**blandly** adv.

☆ **blank¹** /blæŋk/ adj. **1** without writing or anything else on it: *a blank cassette* ○ *a blank piece of paper* ○ *a blank diskette* **2** without feelings, understanding or interest: *a blank expression on his face* ○ *My mind went blank when I saw the test questions* (= I couldn't think or remember anything).

blank² /blæŋk/ noun [C] an empty space: *Fill in the blanks in the following exercise.* ○ *(figurative) I couldn't remember his name – my mind was a complete blank.*

IDM draw a blank ⇨ DRAW²

blank ¹check noun [C] a check that has been signed but that has an empty space so that the amount to be paid can be filled in later

☆ **blan·ket¹** /'blæŋkət/ noun [C] a cover made of wool, etc. that is put on beds to keep people warm: *(figurative) A fresh blanket of snow covered the fields.* ☞ picture at **bed.**

IDM a wet blanket ⇨ WET¹

blan·ket² /'blæŋkət/ adj. (only *before* a noun) affecting everybody or everything: *a blanket ban on journalists reporting the case*

blan·ket³ /'blæŋkət/ verb [T] to cover sth completely: *The countryside was blanketed in snow.*

blank·ly /'blæŋkli/ adv. with a blank ¹(2) expression

blare /blɛr/ verb [I,T] **blare (sth) (out)** to make a loud, unpleasant noise: *The radio was blaring in the room next to ours.* ○ *The loudspeaker blared out a warning.* —**blare** noun [sing.]: *the blare of a siren*

blas·phe·my /'blæsfəmi/ noun [U] writing or speaking about God in a way that shows a lack of respect —**blas·phe·mous** /'blæsfəməs/ adj.

blast¹ /blæst/ noun **1** [C] an explosion, especially one caused by a bomb: *The windows of the nearby stores were shattered in the blast.* **2** [C] a sudden strong rush of air: *a blast of cold air* **3** [C] a loud sound made by a musical instrument such as a horn: *a few blasts on his trumpet* **4** [sing.] (*informal*) a time when you enjoy yourself very much: *Why don't you come along to the party? It'll be a blast!*

blast² /blæst/ verb [T] **1** to make a hole, a tunnel, etc. in sth with an explosion: *They had to blast their way through the mountainside.* **2** to criticize or attack sb very strongly: *The governor blasted journalists for publishing secret information.*

PHR V blast off (used about a spacecraft) to leave the ground; to take off

'blast ˌfurnace noun [C] a large enclosed fire that is used for melting metal, glass, etc.

blast·off /'blæstɔf/ noun [U] the time when a spacecraft leaves the ground

bla·tant /'bleɪtnt/ adj. very clear or obvious: *their blatant dislike for each other* ○ *a blatant lie* ☞ This word is used in a critical way. —**bla·tant·ly** adv.

blaze¹ /bleɪz/ noun **1** [C] a large and often dangerous fire: *It took firefighters four hours to put out the blaze.* **2** [sing.] **a blaze of sth** a very bright display of light or color: *She suddenly appeared on stage in a blaze of light.* ○ *(figurative) The new theater opened in a blaze of publicity* (= the newspapers, television, etc. gave it a lot of attention).

blaze² /bleɪz/ verb [I] to burn with bright strong flames: *a blazing log fire*

blaz·er /'bleɪzər/ noun [C] a jacket, especially one that you wear indoors over a shirt, etc.: *Members of the school band wear special blazers with the school's emblem on them.*

bleach¹ /blitʃ/ verb [T] to make sth white or lighter in color (by using a chemical or by leaving it in the sun)

bleach² /blitʃ/ noun [C,U] a strong chemical substance used for making clothes, etc. whiter or for cleaning things

bleach·ers /'blitʃərz/ noun [plural] an area with wide seats (**benches**), usually without backs, where people sit to watch a sports game, etc.: *We sat in the bleachers.*

bleak /blik/ adj. **1** (used about a situation) bad; not encouraging or hopeful: *a bleak future for the next generation* **2** (used about a place) cold, bare and gray: *the bleak Midwestern prairies in the winter* **3** (used about the

B

ə	y	w	t̬	eɪ	aɪ	ɔɪ	aʊ	oʊ
about	yes	woman	butter	say	five	boy	now	go

weather) cold and gray: *a bleak winter day*
—**bleak·ly** *adv.*

☆ **bleed** /blid/ *verb* [I] (*p.t., p.p.* **bled** /blɛd/) to lose blood: *He was bleeding badly from a cut on his head.* ○ *Is your finger bleeding?*

bleed·ing /ˈblidɪŋ/ *noun* [U] blood flowing from a cut, etc.: *She wrapped a scarf around her arm to try to stop the bleeding.*

blem·ish[1] /ˈblɛmɪʃ/ *noun* [C] a mark that spoils the way sth looks: *makeup to hide pimples and other blemishes*

blem·ish[2] /ˈblɛmɪʃ/ *verb* [T] (*formal*) to spoil sth

blend[1] /blɛnd/ *verb* **1** [T] **blend A with B; blend A and B (together)** to mix: *First blend the flour and the melted butter together.* **2** [I] **blend (into sth)** to be difficult to tell apart from sth else: *These animals' ability to blend into their surroundings provides a natural form of defense.*

PHRV **blend in (with sth)** to look or sound good with sth else because the two things are similar: *new buildings that don't blend in with their surroundings*

blend[2] /blɛnd/ *noun* [C] a mixture: *a blend of wool and cotton* ○ *He had the right blend of enthusiasm and experience.*

blend·er /ˈblɛndər/ *noun* [C] an electric machine that is used for blending foods, especially liquids, or for cutting food into very small pieces ☛ picture at **mixer**. Look at **food processor** and **mixer**.

bless /blɛs/ *verb* [T] (*p.t., p.p.* **blessed** /blɛst/) to ask for God's help and protection for sb/sth: *At the end of the marriage service, the minister will bless the young couple.*

IDM **be blessed with sth/sb** to be lucky enough to have sth/sb: *We've been blessed with three wonderful children.*

bless you! (what you say to a person who has just sneezed)

bless·ed /ˈblɛsəd/ *adj.* **1** (in religious language) holy: *the Blessed Virgin Mary* **2** (in religious language) lucky; fortunate: *Blessed are the pure in heart.* **3** giving great pleasure: *The cool breeze brought blessed relief from the heat.*

bless·ing /ˈblɛsɪŋ/ *noun* [C] **1** a thing that you are grateful for or that brings happiness: *It's a great blessing that we have two healthy children.* ○ *a blessing in disguise* (= something which seems unlucky but turns out to be a good thing) ○ *to count your blessings* **2** [usually sing.] approval or support: *They got married without their parents' blessing.* **3** [usually sing.] (a prayer asking for) God's help and protection: *to ask for God's blessing* ○ *The priest gave a blessing.*

blew *p.t.* of BLOW[1]

☆ **blind**[1] /blaɪnd/ *adj.* **1** unable to see: *a blind person* ○ *to be completely/partially blind*

☛ We often describe a person as **visually impaired** rather than **blind**. If a person is not completely blind, but cannot see well even if he/she wears glasses, we can say that he/she is **legally blind**.

2 blind (to sth) not willing to notice or understand sth: *He was completely blind to her faults.* **3** without reason or thought: *her blind acceptance of fate* ○ *He drove down the freeway in a blind panic.* **4** impossible to see around or impossible to see from a certain position: *The accident happened at a blind intersection.* **5 the blind** *noun* [plural] people who cannot see: *ways of making buildings accessible to the blind*

IDM **turn a blind eye (to sth)** to pretend not to notice sth —**blind·ly** *adv.* —**blind·ness** *noun* [U]

blind[2] /blaɪnd/ *verb* [T] **1** to make sb unable to see: *Her grandfather had been blinded in an accident* (= permanently). ○ *For a minute I was blinded by the lights of the oncoming car* (= for a short time). **2 blind sb (to sth)** to prevent sb from being aware of sth

blind[3] /blaɪnd/ *noun* [C, usually pl.] a covering for a window which is made of many long, narrow strips of metal, plastic, or other material: *to open/close the blinds* ○ *vertical blinds* ☛ Look also at **Venetian blind**.

blind date *noun* [C] an arranged meeting between two people who have never met before to see if they like each other enough to begin a romantic relationship

blind·fold[1] /ˈblaɪndfoʊld/ *verb* [T] to cover a person's eyes with a piece of cloth, etc. so that he/she cannot see

blind·fold[2] /ˈblaɪndfoʊld/ *noun* [C] a piece of cloth, etc. that is used for covering sb's eyes

blind spot *noun* [C] **1** if you have a blind spot about sth, you cannot understand or accept it **2** the part of the road that you cannot see when driving a car, i.e. the part which is just behind you

blink /blɪŋk/ *verb* **1** [I,T] to shut your eyes and open them again very quickly: *Oh no! You blinked just as I took the picture!* ☛ Look at **wink**. **2** [I] (used about a light) to come on and go off again quickly —**blink** *noun* [C]

blip /blɪp/ *noun* [C] **1** a small point of light on a screen: *a radar blip* **2** a small problem that does not last for long: *We hope that this price increase is just a temporary blip.*

bliss /blɪs/ *noun* [U] perfect happiness: *fifteen years of domestic bliss with his wife, Mary* —**bliss·ful** /-fl/ *adj.* —**bliss·ful·ly** *adv.*

blis·ter[1] /ˈblɪstər/ *noun* [C] a small painful area of skin that looks like a bubble and contains clear liquid. Blisters are usually caused by rubbing or burning: *These shoes give me blisters.*

blis·ter[2] /ˈblɪstər/ *verb* [I,T] to get or cause blisters[1]

ər	ɪr	ɛr	ɑr	ɔr	ʊr	ʒ	h	ŋ
bird	near	hair	car	north	tour	vision	hat	sing

blis·ter·ing /ˈblɪstərɪŋ/ adj. **1** very great or severe: *the blistering summer heat* **2** showing great anger: *a blistering attack on her political enemies*

blitz /blɪts/ noun [C] a sudden great effort or attack, especially a military attack from the air: *The company launched a $30 million TV advertising blitz.*

bliz·zard /ˈblɪzərd/ noun [C] a very bad storm with a lot of snow and strong winds ☞ Look at the note at **storm**.

bloat·ed /ˈbloʊṭəd/ adj. unusually large and full because of liquid, food or gas inside: *I felt really bloated after all that food.*

blob /blɑb/ noun [C] a small piece of a thick liquid: *a blob of paint, cream, etc.*

bloc /blɑk/ noun [C, with sing. or pl. verb] a group of countries, political parties, people, etc. who have similar political ideas and who act together: *former Communist bloc countries* ○ *the importance of the Hispanic voting bloc*

☆ **block¹** /blɑk/ noun [C] **1** a large, heavy piece of sth, usually with flat sides: *a block of wood* ○ *huge concrete blocks* **2** an area of land in a town which has streets on four sides: *I went for a walk around the block.* ○ *My best friend lives three blocks away from us.* ☞ Look at the note at **avenue**. **3** [usually sing.] a thing that makes movement or progress difficult or impossible: *a block to further progress in the talks*

IDM **to have a block (about sth)** to be unable to think or understand sth well: *I had a complete mental block. I just couldn't remember his name.*

☆ **block²** /blɑk/ verb [T] **1 block sth (up)** to make it difficult or impossible for anything or anybody to go through, to see, etc.: *Many roads are completely blocked by snow.* ○ *The sink's blocked up – call a plumber!* **2** to prevent sth from being done: *The management tried to block the deal.* ○ *Get out of the way – you're blocking the view!*

PHRV **block sth off** to separate one area from another with sth solid: *This section of the highway has been blocked off by the police.*

block sth out to try not to think about sth unpleasant: *She tried to block out the memory of the crash.*

block·ade /blɑˈkeɪd/ noun [C] a situation in which a place is surrounded by soldiers or ships in order to prevent goods or people from reaching it —**block·ade** verb [T]

block·age /ˈblɑkɪdʒ/ noun [C] a thing that is blocking sth; the state of being blocked: *a blockage in the drain* ○ *blockages on some major roads*

block·bust·er /ˈblɑkˌbʌstər/ noun [C] a book or movie with an exciting story that is very successful and popular: *He's directed a string of Hollywood blockbusters.*

,**block** ¹**capital** (also ,**block** ¹**letter**) noun [C,

usually pl.] a capital letter: *Please write your name in block capitals.*

blond (also **blonde**) /blɑnd/ noun [C, adj. (a person) with light-colored or yellow hair: *Most people in our family have blond hair.*

☞ When describing women the spelling **blonde** is used: *She's tall, slim and blonde.* The noun is usually only used for women and is spelled **blonde**: *She's a blonde.*

☆ **blood** /blʌd/ noun [U] the red liquid that flows through the body: *Blood was pouring from a cut on his knee.* ○ *The heart pumps blood around the body.* ○ *red and white blood cells* ☞ Look at **bleed**.

IDM **in your blood** a strong part of your character: *A love of the wilderness was in his blood.*

in cold blood ⇨ COLD¹

blood·bath /ˈblʌdbæθ/ noun [C] an act of violently killing many people

¹**blood** ,**donor** noun [C] a person who gives his/her blood for use in medical operations

blood·less /ˈblʌdləs/ adj. without killing or violence: *a bloodless coup*

¹**blood** ,**pressure** noun [U] the force with which the blood travels around the body: *to have high/low blood pressure*

blood·shed /ˈblʌdʃɛd/ noun [U] the killing or wounding of people: *Both sides in the war want to avoid any more bloodshed.*

blood·shot /ˈblʌdʃɑt/ adj. (used about the white part of the eyes) full of red lines, e.g. when sb is tired

blood·stained /ˈblʌdsteɪnd/ adj. having marks of blood on it

blood·stream /ˈblʌdstrim/ noun [sing.] the blood as it flows through the body: *drugs injected directly into the bloodstream*

¹**blood type** noun [C] any of several different types of human blood: *Do you know which blood type you have?*

¹**blood** ,**vessel** noun [C] one of the tubes in the body that blood flows through

blood·y /ˈblʌdi/ adj. (**blood·i·er; blood·i·est**) **1** involving a lot of violence and killing: *a bloody war* **2** covered with blood: *a bloody knife*

bloom¹ /blum/ noun [C] (formal) a flower

IDM **in bloom** with its flowers open: *All the wild plants are in bloom.*

bloom² /blum/ verb [I] to produce flowers: *This shrub blooms in May.*

blos·som¹ /ˈblɑsəm/ noun [C] a flower or a mass of flowers, especially on a fruit tree: *The apple tree is covered in blossoms.*

blos·som² /ˈblɑsəm/ verb [I] **1** (used especially about trees) to produce flowers **2 blossom (into sth)** to develop well: *Their romance blossomed soon after they had met.*

blot¹ /blɑt/ noun [C] **1** a spot or stain, especially one made by ink on paper **2 a blot on**

sth a thing that spoils sb's reputation, character, future, etc.

blot² /blɑt/ *verb* [T] (**blot·ting; blot·ted**) **1** to make a spot or stain on sth, especially one of ink on paper **2** to dry spots of liquid on sth by pressing it with soft paper or cloth

PHRV **blot sth out** to cover or hide: *Heavy fog blotted out the view completely.* ◦ *She kept herself busy, hoping to blot out her unhappy memories* (= trying not to think of them).

blotch /blɑtʃ/ *noun* [C] a mark or an area of different color, especially on sb's skin: *The blotches on her face showed that she had been crying.*

blotch·y /'blɑtʃi/ *adj.* covered in blotches

☆ **blouse** /blaʊs/ *noun* [C] a piece of clothing like a shirt, that women wear ☛ picture on page A26.

blow/suck

blowing sucking

☆ **blow¹** /bloʊ/ *verb* (*p.t.* **blew** /blu/; *p.p.* **blown** /bloʊn/) **1** [I] (used about wind, air, etc.) to move: *A gentle breeze was blowing through the curtains.* **2** [I] to send air out of the mouth: *Take a deep breath and then blow.* **3** [T] to make or shape sth by blowing air out of your mouth: *to blow bubbles* **4** [I,T] to produce sound from a musical instrument, whistle, etc. by means of air: *The referee's whistle blew at the end of the game.* ◦ *He blew a few notes on the trumpet.* ◦ *All the drivers were blowing their horns.* **5** [T] (*informal*) to waste an opportunity to succeed in sth: *I think I've blown my chances of a promotion.* ◦ *You really blew it this time, Tim!* **6** [T] **blow sth (on sth)** (*informal*) to spend or waste a lot of money on sth: *She blew all her savings on a trip to China.* **7** [I,T] (used about an electric fuse) to stop working suddenly because the electric current is too strong; to make sth do this: *A fuse just blew.* ◦ *Don't turn on everything at once or you'll blow a fuse.*

IDM **blow your mind** (*slang*) to be very surprising, often in a pleasant way: *Wow! That concert totally blew my mind!*

blow your nose to clear your nose by blowing strongly through it into a piece of cloth, etc.

PHRV **blow (sb/sth) down, off, over, etc.** to move or make sth move through the air in the direction mentioned, because of the wind, etc.: *My papers blew all over the sidewalk.* ◦ *The balloons blew away into the sky.* ◦ *The wind suddenly blew my hat off.*

blow sth out to make sth stop burning by

blowing air at it: *to blow out the candles on a birthday cake*

blow over to go away; to end: *I hope those dark clouds will blow over soon.* ◦ *Our arguments usually blow over fairly quickly.*

blow up 1 to explode or to be destroyed in an explosion: *The car blew up when the door was opened.* **2** to start suddenly and strongly: *A storm blew up in the night.* ◦ *An argument blew up about money.*

blow sth up 1 to make sth explode or to destroy sth in an explosion: *The terrorists tried to blow up the plane.* **2** to fill sth with air or gas: *to blow up a balloon* **3** to make a larger copy of sth: *to blow up a picture*

☆ **blow²** /bloʊ/ *noun* [C] **1** a hard knock from your hand, a weapon, etc. that hits or is intended to hit sb/sth: *He felt a blow on the back of his head.* ◦ *She aimed a blow at me.* **2** a blow **(to sb/sth)** a sudden shock or disappointment: *It was a major blow when I heard that I hadn't gotten the job.* **3** an act of blowing: *Give your nose a blow!*

IDM **a blow-by-blow account, description, etc. (of sth)** an account, etc. of an event that gives all the exact details of it

deal sb/sth a blow; deal a blow to sb/sth ⇨ DEAL¹

¹blow-dry *verb* [T] (*p.t., p.p.* **blow-dried**) to dry and shape sb's hair using a piece of electrical equipment (**a blow dryer**) that you hold and a brush

blown *p.p.* of BLOW¹

☆ **blue¹** /blu/ *adj.* **1** having the color of a clear sky on a sunny day: *bright blue eyes* ◦ *light/dark blue* **2** (*informal*) (often used in popular songs) sad

IDM **black and blue** ⇨ BLACK¹

☆ **blue²** /blu/ *noun* **1** [C,U] the color of a clear sky on a sunny day: *I'd like some curtains with some blue in them.* ◦ *dressed in blue* (= blue clothes) **2 the blues** [plural, with sing. or pl. verb] a type of slow sad music: *a blues singer* **3 the blues** [plural] (*informal*) the state of feeling sad or depressed: *to have the blues*

IDM **once in a blue moon** ⇨ ONCE¹

out of the blue suddenly; without being expected: *The news of his death came right out of the blue.*

blue·ber·ry /'blu,bɛri/ *noun* [C] (*pl.* **blue·ber·ries**) a small, round, soft, dark blue fruit that grows on a bush: *blueberry muffins*

‚blue-'collar *adj.* doing or involving physical work with the hands rather than office work: *a blue-collar job* ◦ *blue-collar workers* ◦ *a blue-collar neighborhood* (= where many blue-collar workers live) ☛ Look at **white-collar**.

blue·grass /'blugræs/ *noun* [U] a type of traditional country music that developed among poor people in the southern U.S., and that is usually played on guitars or banjos: *bluegrass music*

blue·print /ˈbluprɪnt/ noun [C] a plan or description of how to make, build or achieve sth

bluff¹ /blʌf/ verb [I,T] to try to convince people of sth that is not really true, usually by appearing very confident: *Don't pay any attention to him – he's just bluffing.* ○ *They tried to bluff their parents into believing there was no school that day.*

bluff² /blʌf/ noun [C] **1** a steep cliff **2** an act of trying to convince people of sth that is not really true: *John keeps threatening to leave home, but I'm sure it's only a bluff!*

blu·ish /ˈbluɪʃ/ adj. (*informal*) slightly blue: *bluish green*

blun·der /ˈblʌndər/ noun [C] a stupid mistake: *We haven't made any major blunders yet.*

blunt¹ /blʌnt/ adj. **1** (used about a person, remark, etc.) saying exactly what you think in a very direct way: *I'm sorry to be so blunt, but you're just not good enough.* **2** (used about a knife, pencil, tool, etc.) not sharp: *blunt scissors* —**blunt·ly** adv. —**blunt·ness** noun [U]

blunt² /blʌnt/ verb [T] to make sth less sharp or less strong

blur /blər/ noun [C, usually sing.] something that you cannot see or remember clearly: *Last night's party is just a blur now.*

blur·ry /ˈbləri/ adj. unclear: *a blurry picture/photograph*

blurt /blərt/ verb
PHRV **blurt sth out** to say sth suddenly or without thinking: *We didn't want to tell Mom, but Ann blurted the whole thing out.*

blush¹ /blʌʃ/ verb [I] to become red in the face, especially because of shame or embarrassment: *He blushed with embarrassment.*

blush² /blʌʃ/ noun **1** [C] an act of blushing: *She admitted, with a blush, that she had been lying.* **2** [U] = BLUSHER

blush·er /ˈblʌʃər/ (*also* **blush**, *old-fashioned* **rouge**) noun [U] a red powder or cream that is used for giving more color to the cheeks

Blvd. abbr. = BOULEVARD

B.O. /ˌbi ˈoʊ/ abbr. (*informal*) = BODY ODOR

boa constrictor /ˈboʊə kənˌstrɪktər/ (*also* **boa** /ˈboʊə/) noun [C] a large snake that kills animals by squeezing them

boar /bɔr/ noun [C] **1** a male pig **2** a wild pig ☛ Look at the note at **pig**.

☆ **board¹** /bɔrd/ noun **1** [C] a long, thin, flat piece of wood used for making floors, walls, etc.: *floorboards.* **2** [C] a thin flat piece of wood, etc. used for a particular purpose: *an ironing board* ○ *a diving board* ○ *a surfboard* **3** [C] a flat and usually square piece of wood, cardboard, etc. that you play certain games on: *a chessboard* ○ *board games* (= games you play on a board) ☛ picture at **chess**. **4** [C] = BLACKBOARD: *Can everybody see the board all right?* **5** [C] a group of people who control an organization, a company, etc.: *the board of directors* ○ *She was elected to the local school*

board. **6** [U] the meals that are provided when you live at a college or university, etc.: *The price of tuition does not include room and board.*
IDM **across the board** ⇨ ACROSS
on board on a ship or airplane: *All the passengers were safely on board.*

board² /bɔrd/ verb [T] to get on a plane, ship, bus, etc.: *We said goodbye and boarded the train.* ○ *Flight 143 to Los Angeles is now boarding* (= ready to take passengers) *at Gate 27.*
PHRV **board sth up** to cover with boards ¹(1) : *Nobody lives there now – it's all boarded up.*

boarding house noun [C] a private house where you can pay to stay and have meals for a period of time

boarding pass noun [C] a card that you must show in order to get on a plane or ship: *Could passengers please have their boarding passes ready for inspection?*

boarding school noun [C] a school that students live at during the school year

board·room /ˈbɔrdrum/ noun [C] the room where a company's board of directors meets

board·walk /ˈbɔrdwɔk/ noun [C] a raised path that is made of boards, usually along a beach

boast /boʊst/ verb **1** [I,T] to talk with too much pride about sth that you have or can do: *I wish she wouldn't boast about her family so much.* ○ *He's always boasting that he's the fastest runner in school.* ☛ Look at **brag**. It is more common in informal speech. **2** [T] (used about a place) to have sth that it can be proud of: *The town boasts over a dozen restaurants.*

boast·ful /ˈboʊstfl/ adj. (used about a person or the things that he/she says) showing too much pride

boats

ship

motorboat

mast — sails

sailboat

☆ **boat** /boʊt/ noun [C] a small vehicle that is used for traveling across water: *The cave can*

only be reached by boat/in a boat. ○ *a rowboat* ○ *a fishing boat* ○ *a motorboat* ○ *a sailboat* ☛ Usually **boat** means a small vessel, but it can also be used for a large ship, especially one that carries passengers

IDM **be in the same boat** ⇨ SAME[1]

boat ˌpeople *noun* [plural] people who have left their own country in boats, usually because of a dangerous political situation: *Vietnamese boat people* ☛ Look at **refugee**.

bob /bɑb/ *verb* (**bob·bing; bobbed**) [I,T] to move quickly up and down; to make sth do this: *The boats were bobbing up and down in the water.*

bode /boʊd/ *verb*

IDM **bode well/ill (for sb/sth)** to be a good/bad sign for sb/sth

bod·i·ly /ˈbɑdl·i/ *adj.* of the human body; physical: *The AIDS virus is carried in the blood and other bodily fluids.* ○ *bodily injury*

☆ **bod·y** /ˈbɑdi/ *noun* (*pl.* **bod·ies**) **1** [C] the whole physical form of a person or animal: *the human body* **2** [C] the body (1) apart from the legs, arms and head: *She had injuries to her head and body.* **3** [C] a dead human body (1): *The police have found a body in the canal.* **4** [sing.] the main part of sth: *The main body of my work involves research in the lab.* ○ *There's some rust on the car's body panels.* **5** [C] a group of people who work or act together, especially in an official way: *Tanisha has been elected president of the student body.* **6** [C] an object: *remove a foreign body* (= something that should not be there) *from a wound*

bod·y·build·ing /ˈbɑdiˌbɪldɪŋ/ *noun* [U] making the muscles of the body stronger and larger through exercise

bod·y·guard /ˈbɑdigɑrd/ *noun* [C] a person whose job is to protect sb: *an armed bodyguard*

body ˌlanguage *noun* [U] showing how you feel by the way you move, stand, sit, etc., rather than by what you say

body ˌodor(also *informal* **B.O.**) *noun* [U] the unpleasant smell of a person's body when it is sweating

bog /bɔg/ *noun* [C,U] an area of ground that is very soft and wet: [C]

bogged down /ˌbɑgd ˈdaʊn; ˌbɔgd-/ *adj.* **1** if a vehicle is bogged down, it has sunk into mud, etc. and cannot move **2** if a person is bogged down in sth, he/she cannot make any progress: *We got bogged down in a long discussion and didn't have time to make any decisions.*

bo·gus /ˈboʊgəs/ *adj.* pretending to be sth that it is not; not genuine: *He tried to cash a bogus check.*

☆ **boil**[1] /bɔɪl/ *verb* **1** [I] (used about a liquid) to reach a high temperature where bubbles rise to the surface and the liquid changes to a gas: *Water boils at 212°F, or 100°C.* ○ *The pot's boiling* (= the water inside the pot). **2** [T] to

heat a liquid until it boils and let it keep boiling: *Boil all drinking water for five minutes.* **3** [I,T] to cook in boiling water: *Put the potatoes on to boil.* ○ *boil an egg* **4** [I] (used about a person) to feel very angry: *She was boiling with rage.*

PHRV **boil down to sth** to have sth as the most important point: *What it all boils down to is that you don't want to spend too much money.*

boil over 1 (used about a liquid) to boil and flow over the sides of a pan: *Don't let the soup boil over.* **2** (used about an argument or sb's feelings) to become more serious or angry

boil[2] /bɔɪl/ *noun* [sing.] an act or period of boiling

IDM **bring sth to a boil** to heat sth until it boils

come to a boil to begin to boil

boil·er /ˈbɔɪlər/ *noun* [C] **1** a metal container used for providing hot water and heat in a building: *the boiler room* **2** a large metal container used for producing steam in an engine

boil·ing /ˈbɔɪlɪŋ/ (*also* **boiling ˈhot**) *adj.* (*informal*) very hot: *Open a window – it's boiling hot in here.*

boiling point *noun* [C] the temperature at which a liquid starts to boil

bois·ter·ous /ˈbɔɪstərəs/ *adj.* (used about a person or his/her behavior) noisy and full of energy: *Their kids are very nice, but they can get a little too boisterous.*

☆ **bold** /boʊld/ *adj.* **1** (used about a person or his/her behavior) brave and confident; not afraid: *Not many people are bold enough to say exactly what they think.* ○ *We need somebody with bold new ideas.* **2** that you can see clearly: *bold colors* **3** (used about printed words) in thick, dark letters: *The title is written in bold type.* —**bold·ly** *adv.* —**bold·ness** *noun* [U]

bo·lo·gna (*also* **baloney**) /bəˈloʊni/ *noun* [U] a food that is made of different types of cooked meats that have been chopped into tiny pieces and formed into a large roll (**a sausage**): *a bologna sandwich*

bol·ster /ˈboʊlstər/ *verb* [T] to support or encourage sb/sth; to make sth stronger: *His remarks did nothing to bolster my confidence.*

bolt[1] /boʊlt/ *noun* [C] **1** a small piece of metal (shaped like a screw without a point) that is used with another piece of metal (**a nut**) for fastening things together. The nut screws onto the bolt. **2** a bar of metal that you can slide across the inside of the door in order to fasten it **3** a sudden flash of light in the sky during a storm: *a bolt of lightning* ○ *a lightning bolt*

bolt[2] /boʊlt/ *verb* **1** [T] to fasten one thing to another using a bolt: *All the tables have been bolted to the floor so that nobody can steal them.* **2** [T] to fasten a door, etc. with a bolt[1](2): *Make sure that the door is locked and bolted.* **3** [I] to run away very suddenly, usually in

ər	ɪr	ɛr	ɑr	ɔr	ʊr	ʒ	h	ŋ
bird	near	hair	car	north	tour	vision	hat	sing

fear or in order to escape: *The horse suddenly bolted when it heard the gunfire.*

☆ **bomb¹** /bɑm/ *noun* **1** [C] a container that is filled with material that will explode when it is thrown or dropped, or when a device inside it sets it off: *The bomb went off without warning.* ◦ *The terrorists planted the bomb in a garbage can.* ◦ *Several tons of bombs were dropped on the city.* **2 the bomb** [sing.] nuclear weapons: *How many countries have the bomb now?* **3** [C] (*informal*) a complete failure: *The movie was a bomb at the box office.*

☆ **bomb²** /bɑm/ *verb* **1** [T] to attack a city, etc. with bombs **2** [I,T] (*informal*) to fail: *The play bombed on Broadway.* ◦ *I really bombed the final exam.*

bom·bard /bɑm'bɑrd/ *verb* [T] to attack a place with bombs or guns: *They bombarded the city until the enemy surrendered.* ◦ (*figurative*) *The reporters bombarded the senator with questions.* —**bom·bard·ment** /-mənt/ *noun* [C,U]: *come under enemy bombardment*

bomb dis·posal *noun* [U] the removing or exploding of bombs in order to make an area safe: *a bomb disposal expert*

bomb·er /'bɑmər/ *noun* [C] **1** a type of airplane that drops bombs **2** a person who throws bombs or leaves them to explode in a public place

bomb·shell /'bɑmʃɛl/ *noun* [C, usually sing.] an unexpected piece of news, usually about sth unpleasant

bo·na fide /'boʊnə faɪd; 'bɑnə-/ *adj., adv.* (*formal*) real or genuine

bond /bɑnd/ *noun* [C] **1** something that links two or more people or groups of people together, such as a feeling of friendship: *Our two countries are united by bonds of friendship.* **2** a certificate that you can buy from a government or company that promises to pay you interest on the money you have lent: *Treasury bonds*

☆ **bone¹** /boʊn/ *noun* **1** [C] one of the hard parts inside the body of a person or animal that are covered with flesh and skin: *He broke a bone in his hand.* ◦ *The dog is chewing on a bone.* ◦ *This fish has a lot of bones in it.* **2** [U] the substance that bones are made of

IDM make no bones about (doing) sth to do sth without hesitating or feeling worried about it: *She made no bones about telling him exactly what she thought about him.*

bone² /boʊn/ *verb* [T] to take the bones ¹(1) out of sth: *to bone a fish, chicken, etc.*

bone mar·row (*also* **marrow**) *noun* [U] the soft substance that is inside the bones of a person or an animal

bon·fire /'bɑnfaɪər/ *noun* [C] a large fire that you build outside to burn garbage, etc.

bon·kers /'bɑŋkərz; 'bɔŋ-/ *adj.* (*slang*) (not before a noun) crazy

bon·net /'bɑnət/ *noun* [C] **1** a type of hat for babies that covers the sides of the face and is fastened with strings under the chin **2** (*BrE*) = HOOD(2)

bo·nus /'boʊnəs/ *noun* [C] (*pl.* **bo·nu·ses**) **1** a payment that is added to what is usual: *to receive an annual bonus* **2** something good that you get in addition to what you expect: *If you answer this extra question correctly, you'll get two bonus points on your test score.*

bon·y /'boʊni/ *adj.* (**bon·i·er; bon·i·est**) so thin that you can see the shape of the bones: *long bony fingers*

boo /bu/ *interj., noun* [C] (*pl.* **boos**) **1** a sound you make to show that you do not like sb/sth: *The candidate's speech was met with boos from the audience.* **2** a sound you make to frighten or surprise sb: *He jumped out from behind the door and shouted, "Boo!"* —**boo** *verb* [I,T]: *The crowd booed when they sang.*

boo-boo /'bubu/ *noun* [C] (*pl.* **boo-boos**) (*informal*) a silly mistake: *to make a boo-boo*

boo·by trap /'bubi træp/ *noun* [C] something dangerous, like a bomb, which is hidden inside sth that seems harmless —**booby-trap** *verb* [T]: *The car had been booby-trapped.*

☆ **book¹** /bʊk/ *noun* **1** [C] a number of sheets of paper, fastened together inside a cover, with words printed on them for people to read: *I'm reading a book on astrology.* ◦ *She's writing a book about her childhood experiences.* ◦ *Do you have any books by Toni Morrison?* ◦ *Open your books, please.* ◦ *to publish a book* ◦ *a library book* ◦ *a cookbook* ◦ *This book is also available on CD-ROM.* ◦ *a book report* **2** [C] a number of pieces of paper, fastened together inside a cover, for people to write on: *an address book* ☞ Look at **notebook**. **3** [C] a small number of things fastened together in the form of a book: *a book of stamps* **4** [C] any of the main divisions of a large written work: *the books of the Bible* **5 books** [plural] the records that a company, etc. keeps of the amount of money it spends or receives: *We employ an accountant to keep the books.* ◦ *to balance the books*

IDM by the book exactly according to the rules: *He always does things by the book.*

☆ **book²** /bʊk/ *verb* **1** [I,T] to arrange to have or do sth at a particular time: *It's wise to book well in advance.* ◦ *Have you booked a table, sir?* ◦ *to book a seat on a plane/train* ◦ *I'm sorry, but this evening's performance is fully booked* (= there are no seats left). ◦ *All the hotels in town are booked up* (= completely full). **2** [T] to make an official record, e.g. at a police station, of sb's name and sth that they have done wrong: *The police booked her for drunk driving* (= charged her with drunk driving).

book·case /'bʊkkeɪs/ *noun* [C] a piece of furniture with shelves to keep books on

book·keep·er /'bʊk,kipər/ *noun* [C] a person who keeps the accounts of the money that a

tʃ	dʒ	v	θ	ð	s	z	ʃ
chin	June	van	thin	then	so	zoo	she

B

company, etc., spends or receives —**book-keep·ing** *noun* [U]: *to do the bookkeeping*

book·let /ˈbʊklət/ *noun* [C] a small thin book, usually with a soft cover, that gives information about sth

book·mark /ˈbʊkmɑrk/ *noun* [C] a narrow card, etc. that you put between the pages of a book so that you can find the same place again easily

☆ **book·store** /ˈbʊkstɔr/ *noun* [C] a store that sells books ☞ Look at **library**.

book·worm /ˈbʊkwɜrm/ *noun* [C] a person who likes reading books very much

boom¹ /bum/ *noun* [C] **1** a period in which sth increases or develops very quickly: *There was a boom in car sales in the 1980s.* ○ *a boom year for exports* ☞ Look also at **baby boom**. **2** a loud, deep, hollow sound: *We heard a huge boom followed by silence.*

boom² /bum/ *verb* **1** [I] to grow very quickly in size or value: *Business is booming .* **2** [I,T] **boom (sth) (out)** to make a loud, deep, hollow sound: *guns booming in the distance* ○ *The loudspeaker boomed out instructions to the crowd.*

'**boom box** *noun* [C] (*informal*) a large radio with a cassette or CD player that can be carried around and that can be played very loudly

boo·mer·ang /ˈbuməræŋ/ *noun* [C] a curved piece of wood that returns to you when you throw it in the right way, used for hunting by the first people who lived in Australia

boon /bun/ *noun* [C] a thing that is very helpful and that you are grateful for

boost¹ /bust/ *verb* [T] **1** to increase sth in number, value or strength: *If we lower the price, that should boost sales.* ○ *The good grade on her essay boosted her confidence.* **2** to push or lift sb up from behind below: *Boost me up to the window so I can see inside.*

boost² /bust/ *noun* [C] **1** an increase; sth that encourages people: *The fall in the value of the dollar has led to a boost in exports.* ○ *The President's visit gave a boost to the soldiers' morale.* **2** an act of lifting sb up and forward: *Give me a boost over the fence.*

☆ **boot¹** /but/ *noun* [C] **1** a type of shoe that covers your foot and ankle and sometimes part of your leg: *a pair of old boots* ○ *ski boots* ○ *hiking boots* ○ *winter boots* ☞ picture at **shoe**. **2** (*BrE*) = TRUNK(3)

boot² /but/ *verb* [T] to kick sth/sb hard: *He booted the ball over the fence.*

PHRV boot sb out (of sth) (*informal*) to force sb to leave a place: *He got booted out of the club.*

booth /buθ/ *noun* [C] (*pl.* **booths** /buθs; buðz/) **1** a small enclosed place with thin walls that divide it from the rest of the room or area: *She called from a phone booth at the airport.* ○ *a ticket booth* ○ *a voting booth* **2** a

place to sit in a restaurant with a table between two long seats that are attached to the floor

boo·ty /ˈbuti/ *noun* [U] things that are taken by thieves or captured by soldiers in war

booze /buz/ *noun* [U] (*informal*) alcohol

☆ **bor·der¹** /ˈbɔrdər/ *noun* [C] **1** a line that divides two countries, etc.; the land close to this line: *The refugees escaped across/over the border.* ○ *We crossed the border into Mexico.* ○ *the Canadian border* ○ *the border between France and Italy* ○ *Italy's border with France*

> ☞ We use **border** to talk about the line that divides two countries or states: *The river forms the border between the two countries.* **Line** can also be used for the line that divides states, countries, or smaller areas: *the state/county line.* **Boundary** is also used for the line that divides smaller areas: *This fence marks the boundaries of our property.* **Frontier** is used for areas where people are just beginning to live: *frontier towns of the Wild West.*

2 a band or strip around the edge of sth, often for decoration: *a white tablecloth with a blue border*

bor·der² /ˈbɔrdər/ *verb* [T] to be a border¹(1) to; to be on the border of: *The road was bordered with trees.* ○ *Which states border Canada?*

PHRV border on sth 1 to be next to sth: *Our back yard borders on the school grounds.* **2** to be almost the same as sth: *His ideas bordered on madness.*

bor·der·line /ˈbɔrdərlaɪn/ *noun* [sing.] the line that marks a division between two different cases, conditions, etc.: *The novel is on the borderline between fiction and nonfiction.* ○ *He's a borderline case – he may pass the exam or he may fail.*

☆ **bore¹** /bɔr/ *verb* **1** [T] to make sb tired and uninterested: *I hope I'm not boring you.* ○ *Those old jokes bore me.* **2** [I,T] to make a round hole or passage through sth: *The drill can bore through solid rock.* ○ *They are boring a tunnel through the mountain.*

bore² /bɔr/ *noun* **1** [C] a person who talks or behaves in an uninteresting way: *He's a real bore.* **2** [sing.] (*informal*) something that you have to do that you find uninteresting: *It's such a bore having to study every day.*

bore³ /bɔr/ *p.t.* of BEAR²

☆ **bored** /bɔrd/ *adj.* feeling uninterested and tired because sth is not exciting or because you do not have anything to do: *I'm bored. There's nothing to do at home.* ○ *The kids get bored on long car trips.* ○ *The play was terrible. We were bored stiff* (= extremely bored).

bore·dom /ˈbɔrdəm/ *noun* [U] the state of being bored: *People say that many young people turn to crime out of boredom.*

☆**bor·ing** /ˈbɔrɪŋ/ *adj.* uninteresting; dull: *a boring movie* ○ *boring work*

☆**born¹** /bɔrn/ *verb* **be born** to come into the world by birth; to start existing: *Where were you born?* ○ *My parents were born in Korea, but they grew up in the U.S.* ○ *I'm going to give up work after the baby is born.* ○ *Their baby was born deaf.* ○ *The idea of free education for all was born in the eighteenth century.* ○ *His unhappiness was born out of a feeling of frustration.*

born² /bɔrn/ *adj.* having a natural ability to do the task mentioned: *She's a born leader.*

-born /bɔrn/ (in compounds) born in the place or state mentioned: *Samuel Beckett, the Irish-born writer, lived in Paris for most of his life.*

ˌ**born-aˈgain** *adj.* having found new, strong faith in a religion: *a born-again Christian*

borne /bɔrn/ *p.p.* of BEAR²

bor·ough /ˈbərou/ *noun* [C] a town, or an area within a large city, especially New York City, that has some form of local government: *the borough of Queens in New York City*

borrow/lend/loan

She's **lending/ loaning** her son some money.

He's **borrowing** some money from his mother.

☆**bor·row** /ˈbarou; ˈbɔr-/ *verb* [I,T] **borrow (sth) (from/off sb/sth)** **1** to take or receive sth from sb/sth that you intend to give back, usually after a short time: *I had to borrow from the bank to pay for my car.* ○ *They borrowed $10,000 to buy a new car.* ○ *Could I borrow your pen for a minute?* ○ *Can I borrow $10? I'll pay you back next week.* ○ *He's always borrowing off his mother.* ○ *I borrowed a book from the library.*

☞ Be careful not to confuse **borrow** with its opposites **lend** and **loan**.

2 to take sth and use it as your own; to copy: *That idea is borrowed from another book.*

bor·row·er /ˈbarouər; ˈbɔr-/ *noun* [C] a person who borrows

bos·om /ˈbʊzəm/ *noun* (*formal*) [C] (usually singular) a person's chest, especially a woman's breasts: *She clutched the child to her bosom.*

☆**boss¹** /bɔs/ *noun* [C] a person whose job is to give orders to others at work; an employer; a manager: *I'm going to ask the boss for a day off*

work. ○ *OK. You're the boss* (= you make the decisions).

boss² /bɔs/ *verb* [T] **boss sb (around)** to give orders to sb, especially in an annoying way: *I wish you'd quit bossing me around.*

boss·y /ˈbɔsi/ *adj.* (**boss·i·er**; **boss·i·est**) liking to give orders to other people, often in an annoying way —**boss·i·ly** *adv.* —**boss·i·ness** *noun* [U]

bo·tan·i·cal /bəˈtænɪkl/ *adj.* connected with the scientific study of plants: *a botanical garden* (= a type of park where plants are grown for scientific study)

bot·a·nist /ˈbatnɪst/ *noun* [C] a person who studies plants

bot·a·ny /ˈbatn·i/ *noun* [U] the scientific study of plants

botch /batʃ/ *verb* [T] **botch sth (up)** (*informal*) to do sth badly or to ruin sth because you are not very skillful: *a botched* (= unsuccessful) *robbery attempt*

☆**both¹** /bouθ/ *det., pron.* the two; the one as well as the other: *Both women/Both the women/Both of the women were French.* ○ *I talked to the women. Both of them were French/They were both French.* ○ *I liked them both.* ○ *We were both very tired.* ○ *Both of us were tired.* ○ *They have both seen the movie.* ○ *I have two sisters. They both live in Florida/ Both of them live in Florida.* ○ *Both of my sisters live in Florida.*

☞ Note that we CANNOT say: *the both women* or: *my both sisters.*

☆**both²** /bouθ/ *adv.* **both …and …** not only …but also …: *I like both him and his wife.* ○ *I was both hungry and thirsty.*

☆**both·er** /ˈbaðər/ *verb* **1** [T] to disturb or annoy sb: *I'm sorry to bother you, but could I speak with you for a moment?* ○ *Don't bother Sue with that now – she's busy.* **2** [T] to worry sb: *You don't look very happy. Is something bothering you?* **3** [I,T] **bother (to do sth); bother with sth** (usually negative) to make the effort to do sth: *"Should I make you something to eat?" "No, don't bother – I'm not hungry."* ○ *He didn't even bother to say thank you.* ○ *Don't bother with the dishes. I'll do them later.* ○ *Don't bother waiting for me – I'll catch up with you later.*

☆**bot·tle¹** /ˈbatl/ *noun* [C] **1** a glass or plastic container with a narrow neck for keeping liquids in: *a beer bottle* ○ *an empty bottle* **2** the amount of liquid in a bottle: *a bottle of beer*

bot·tle² /ˈbatl/ *verb* [T] to put sth into bottles: *After three or four months, the wine is bottled.*

bot·tled /ˈbatld/ *adj.* that you can buy in bottles: *bottled water*

bot·tle·neck /ˈbatlnɛk/ *noun* [C] something that slows down progress

☆**bot·tom¹** /ˈbatəm/ *noun* **1** [C, usually sing.] the lowest part of sth: *The house is at the*

ə	y	w	t̮	eɪ	aɪ	ɔɪ	aʊ	oʊ
about	yes	woman	butter	say	five	boy	now	go

bottom of a hill. ○ Look at the picture at the bottom of page 23. ○ I think I have a pen in the bottom of my bag. **2** [C] the flat surface on the outside of an object, on which it stands: *There's a label on the bottom of the box.* **3** [sing.] the least important position in relation to other people: *She started at the bottom and now she's president of the company.* **4** [sing.] the ground under the ocean, a river, a swimming pool, etc.: *The water was so clear that we could see the bottom.* **5** [C] the part of your body that you sit on: *I fell down and landed on my bottom.* ☞ Look also at **butt**. **6 bottoms** [plural] the lower part of a piece of clothing that is in two parts: *pajama bottoms* ○ *bikini bottoms*

IDM **be at the bottom of sth** to be the real cause of sth: *I'm sure Kate Mills is at the bottom of all this.*

get to the bottom of sth to find out the real cause of sth

☆ **bot·tom²** /ˈbɑṭəm/ *adj.* in the lowest position: *the bottom shelf*

IDM **the bottom line 1** the amount of money that a company earns or loses: *Our boss doesn't care about employee safety – he's only interested in the bottom line.* **2** the most important or final point in an argument, etc.: *The bottom line is that the company will go bankrupt if we don't give our customers what they want.*

bought *p.t., p.p.* of BUY¹

boul·der /ˈboʊldər/ *noun* [C] a very large rock

boul·e·vard /ˈbʊləvɑrd/ *noun* **1** [C] a wide street in a town or city **2 Boulevard** (*abbr.* **Blvd.**) [sing.] (used in the names of some streets in towns and cities): *1270 Sunset Blvd., Los Angeles*

hop/jump/bounce

jumping

hopping

bouncing

bounce¹ /baʊns/ *verb* **1** [I,T] (used about a ball, etc.) to move away quickly after it has hit a hard surface; to make a ball do this: *In tennis, the ball can only bounce once before you hit it back.* ○ *The stone bounced off the wall and hit her.* ○ *A small boy came down the street, bouncing a ball.* **2** [I] to jump up and down continuously: *The kids were bouncing on their beds.* **3** [I] (used about a check) to be returned by a bank without payment because there is not enough money in the account **4** [T] to

write a check without having enough money in the bank account: *to bounce a check*

PHRV **bounce back** to recover from a failure, disappointment, etc. and return quickly to your normal life with the same energy as before

bounce² /baʊns/ *noun* [C,U] an act of bouncing

bound¹ /baʊnd/ *adj.* **1 bound to do sth** certain to do sth: *You've done so much studying that you're bound to get an "A" on the test.* ○ *There are bound to be problems in a situation like this.* **2** (not before a noun) having a legal or moral duty to do sth: *She was not legally bound to pay for the damage.* ○ *Agents are bound by an oath of secrecy.* **3 bound (for...)** traveling or leading to a particular place: *a ship bound for Australia* ○ *the southbound lanes of the freeway*

IDM **bound up with sth** very closely connected with sth

bound² /baʊnd/ *verb* [I] to run quickly with jumping movements: *The big dog bounded up to us.*

bound³ *p.t., p.p.* of BIND¹

☆ **bound·a·ry** /ˈbaʊndri; -dəri/ *noun* [C] (*pl.* **bound·a·ries**) **1** a line that marks the limits of a place and divides it from other places: *The highway is the boundary between the two counties.* **2** the furthest limit of sth: *Scientists continue to push back the boundaries of human knowledge.* ☞ Look at the note at **border**.

bound·less /ˈbaʊndləs/ *adj.* having no limit: *boundless energy*

bounds /baʊndz/ *noun* [plural] limits that cannot or should not be passed: *Price increases must be kept within reasonable bounds.*

IDM **out of bounds** (*sports*) outside the area of play

bou·quet /boʊˈkeɪ; bu-/ *noun* [C] a bunch of flowers that is arranged in an attractive way: *a bouquet of roses*

bour·bon /ˈbɜrbən/ *noun* [C,U] a type of whiskey that is made mainly in the U.S.

bour·geois /ˌbʊrˈʒwɑ; ˈbʊrʒwɑ/ *adj.* typical of fairly rich people : *bourgeois attitudes, ideas, values, etc.* ☞ This word is used in a critical way.

bour·geoi·sie /ˌbʊrʒwɑˈzi/ *noun* [sing.] the social class that includes fairly rich people ☞ This word is used in a critical way.

bout /baʊt/ *noun* [C] **1** a short period of great activity: *a bout of hard work* **2** a period of illness: *I'm just recovering from a bout of the flu.*

bou·tique /buˈtik/ *noun* [C] a small store that sells expensive clothes, etc.

☆ **bow¹** /baʊ/ *verb* **1** [I,T] to bend your head or the upper part of your body forward and down, as a sign of respect: *All the actors came onto the stage and bowed.* ○ *He bowed his head respectfully.* **2 bow to sb/sth** [I] to accept or

ər	ɪr	ɛr	ɑr	ɔr	ʊr	ʒ	h	ŋ
bird	near	hair	car	north	tour	vision	hat	sing

obey sb/sth: *I do not think the government should bow to pressure from big corporations.* **PHR V** **bow out (of sth)** to leave an important position or stop taking part in sth: *After 12 years on the committee, she decided to bow out.*

bow² /baʊ/ *noun* [C] **1** an act of bowing¹(1) : *The actors came back to take another bow.* **2** the front part of a ship ☞ Look at **stern²**.

bow³ /boʊ/ *noun* [C] **1** a knot with two loops and two loose ends that you use when you are tying shoes, wrapping presents, etc.: *He tied the ribbon into a bow.* ○ *She had a bow in her hair.* ☞ picture at **knot**. **2** a weapon for shooting arrows. A bow is a curved piece of wood or similar material that is held in shape by a tight string. **3** a long thin piece of wood with horse hair stretched along it that you use to play a violin, etc. ☞ picture at **violin**.

bow·el /ˈbaʊəl/ *noun* [C, usually pl.] one of the tubes that takes waste food from the stomach so that it can pass out of the body

☆ **bowl** /boʊl/ *noun* [C] **1** a deep round dish without a lid that is used for holding food or liquid: *a sugar bowl* ○ *a mixing bowl* ☞ picture at **plate**. **2** the amount of sth that is in a bowl: *a bowl of cereal*

bowl·ing /ˈboʊlɪŋ/ *noun* [U] a game in which you roll a heavy ball along a special track (**lane**) toward a group of wooden objects (**pins**) and try to knock down as many of them as you can: *Let's go bowling.* ○ *a bowling alley* (= a building with many lanes for bowling)

bow tie /ˈboʊ taɪ/ *noun* [C] a tie in the shape of a bow³(1) , that is worn by men, especially on formal occasions

☆ **box¹** /baks/ *noun* [C] **1** a square or rectangular container for solid objects. A box often has a lid: *I opened the lid and looked inside the box.* **2** a box (1) and the things inside it: *a box of candy, cereal, tissues, etc.* ☞ picture at **container**. **3** an empty square or rectangle on a form in which you have to write sth: *Write your full name in the box below.* **4** a place in a post office or in an office where letters, packages, etc. are kept until they are picked up by the person that they were sent to ☞ Look also at **post office box**. **5** an enclosed area that is used for a particular purpose: *the penalty box next to a hockey rink* **6** an enclosed area in a theater, sports center, etc. in which a small group of people can sit and watch the event: *box seats in the stadium*

☆ **box²** /baks/ *verb* **1** [I,T] to fight in the sport of boxing: *He used to box at school.* **2** [T] to put into a box¹(1) : *a boxed set of CDs*

☆ **box·er** /ˈbaksər/ *noun* **1** [C] a person who boxes (1) as a sport, often professionally **2 boxers** (*also* **ˈboxer shorts**) [plural] men's underpants that are loose and cover the body from the waist to the top of the legs ☞ picture on page A26.

☆ **box·ing** /ˈbaksɪŋ/ *noun* [U] a sport in which two people fight by hitting each other with their hands inside large gloves: *the world heavyweight boxing champion* ○ *boxing gloves*

ˈbox ˌoffice *noun* [C] the place in a theater, etc. where the tickets are sold

☆ **boy¹** /bɔɪ/ *noun* **1** [C] a male child: *They have three children – two boys and a girl.* **2 the boys** [plural] (*informal*) a group of male friends

boy² /bɔɪ/ *interj.* (*informal*) (used for expressing a strong feeling): *Boy, it's hot today!* ○ *Oh boy! I can't wait to open my presents!*

boy·cott /ˈbɔɪkat/ *verb* [T] to refuse to buy things from a particular company, take part in an event, etc. because you strongly disapprove of it: *Several countries boycotted the Olympic Games in protest.* —**boy·cott** *noun* [C]

☆ **boy·friend** /ˈbɔɪfrɛnd/ *noun* [C] a man or boy with whom a person has a romantic and/or sexual relationship

boy·hood /ˈbɔɪhʊd/ *noun* [U] the time of being a boy: *his boyhood friends* (= from when he was a boy)

boy·ish /ˈbɔɪʃ/ *adj.* like a boy: *a boyish smile*

ˈBoy Scout *noun* [C] a member of an organization that teaches boys to be responsible and to help other people. Boy Scouts do sports, learn useful skills, go camping, etc. ☞ Look at **Girl Scout**.

☆ **bra** /brɑ/ (*also formal* or *old-fashioned* **brassiere**) *noun* [C] a piece of clothing that women wear under their other clothes to support their breasts ☞ picture on page A26.

brace¹ /breɪs/ *noun* **1** [C] an apparatus that is often made of metal, that is used to support weak or injured legs: *a leg brace* **2 braces** [plural] wires that are attached to sb's teeth in order to make them straight

brace² /breɪs/ *verb* **1** [T] **brace sth/yourself** to make your body stiff or press it against sth in order to prepare yourself, e.g. if sth is going to hit you, or to stop yourself from falling: *He braced himself as he began to slip on the ice.* **2** [I,T] **brace (yourself) (for sth)** to prepare yourself for sth difficult or unpleasant: *You'd better brace yourself for some bad news.*

☆ **brace·let** /ˈbreɪslət/ *noun* [C] a piece of jewelry (e.g. a metal chain or band) that you wear around your wrist or arm ☞ picture at **jewelry**.

brack·et /ˈbrækət/ *noun* [C] **1** [usually pl.] one of two marks, [], that you put around extra information in a piece of writing ☞ Look at **parentheses**. **2** a piece of metal or wood that is attached to a wall and used as a support for a shelf, lamp, etc. **3** a group of people whose ages, incomes, etc. are between two limits: *to be in a high income bracket* ○ *a magazine for people in the 30-40 age bracket*

brag /bræg/ *verb* [I,T] (**brag·ging**; **bragged**) to

tʃ	dʒ	v	θ	ð	s	z	ʃ
chin	June	van	thin	then	so	zoo	she

talk too proudly about sth: *She's always brag-*
ging about how much she earns.

pigtails

part

braid

ponytail

braid¹ /breɪd/ *verb* [T] to twist three or more
long thin pieces of hair, rope, etc. over and
under each other to make one thick piece

braid² /breɪd/ *noun* **1** [C] a long piece of hair
that has been braided: *You look nice with your*
hair in braids. **2** [U] a narrow piece of mate-
rial that is used to decorate clothes, curtains,
etc.: *a uniform with gold braid on it*

Braille /breɪl/ *noun* [U] a way of printing for
blind people, using raised dots that they touch
with their fingers to read

☆ **brain** /breɪn/ *noun* **1** [C] the part of the body
inside the head that controls your thoughts,
feelings and movements: *suffer serious brain*
damage ∘ *a brain surgeon* **2** [C,U] the ability to
think clearly; intelligence: *He doesn't have the*
brains to be a doctor. **3** [C] (*informal*) a very
intelligent person: *He's one of the best brains*
in the country. ∘ *Gee, Harriet, you're such a*
brain! **4 the brains** [sing.] the person who
plans or organizes sth : *She's the real brains in*
the organization.

IDM **rack your brains** ⇨ RACK²

brain·child /ˈbreɪntʃaɪld/ *noun* [sing.] the idea
or invention of a particular person: *The fes-*
tival was the brainchild of a young teacher.

brain·storm /ˈbreɪnstɔrm/ *verb* [I,T] to solve
problems or make decisions by asking all the
members of a group to think of as many ideas
as possible

brain·wash /ˈbreɪnwɑʃ; -wɔʃ/ *verb* [T] to force
sb to believe sth by using strong mental pres-
sure: *TV commercials try to brainwash people*
into buying things that they don't need.
—**brain·wash·ing** *noun* [U]

☆ **brake¹** /breɪk/ *noun* [usually pl.] **1** the part of
a vehicle that makes it go slower or stop: *She*
put her foot on the brake and just managed to
stop in time. ∘ *These brakes don't work.* **2** some-
thing that makes sth else slow down or stop:
The government must try to put the brakes on
inflation.

brake² /breɪk/ *verb* [I] to use the brake¹(1) in a
car to stop it or make it go more slowly: *The*
driver braked suddenly.

bran /bræn/ *noun* [U] the brown outer parts of
grains that have been separated from the
flour: *oat/wheat bran*

☆ **branch¹** /bræntʃ/ *noun* [C] **1** one of the main
parts of a tree that grows from its central stem
(**trunk**) and often has leaves, flowers or fruit
on it: *I climbed the tree and sat on a branch.*
☛ picture at **tree**. **2** an office, a store, etc. that
is part of a larger organization: *The company I*
work for has branches in Paris, Milan and
New York. ∘ *the bank's downtown branch* **3** a
part of an academic subject: *Psychiatry is a*
branch of medicine.

branch² /bræntʃ/ *verb*
PHRV **branch off** (used about a road) to leave
a larger road and go off in another direction:
The road branches off to the left ahead.

branch out (into sth) to start doing sth new
and different from the things you usually do:
He started as a poet but branched out into
songwriting.

☆ **brand¹** /brænd/ *noun* [C] **1** the name of a
product that is made by a particular company:
Pepsi is a well-known brand of soft drink. **2** a
particular type of sth: *a strange brand of*
humor

brand² /brænd/ *verb* [T] **1** to mark an animal
with a hot iron to show who owns it **2 brand**
sb (as sth) to say that sb has a bad character
so that people have a bad opinion of him/her:
She was branded as a troublemaker after she
complained about the pay.

bran·dish /ˈbrændɪʃ/ *verb* [T] to wave sth in
the air in an aggressive or excited way: *to*
brandish a knife

ˈbrand name *noun* [C] the name that a com-
pany gives to a product that it produces:
Kleenex is a well-known brand name.

brand-new /ˌbrænˈnu; ˌbrænd-/ *adj.* complete-
ly new

bran·dy /ˈbrændi/ *noun* [C,U] a strong alco-
holic drink that is made from wine

brash /bræʃ/ *adj.* too confident and direct: *a*
brash young salesman

brass /bræs/ *noun* **1** [U] a yellow metal that is
a mixture of a red-colored metal (**copper**) and
a white-colored metal (**zinc**): *brass buttons*
2 [C,U] the group of musical instruments that
are made of brass (1), e.g. the trumpet, the
trombone, etc.: *the brass section in an orches-*
tra ∘ *a brass band* ∘ *The brasses need to play*
more softly in this section.

bras·siere /brəˈzɪr/ *noun* [C] *formal* or *old-*
fashioned = BRA

brat /bræt/ *noun* [C] a child who behaves
badly and annoys you

☆ **brave¹** /breɪv/ *adj.* ready to do things that are
dangerous or difficult without showing fear:
"This might hurt a little, so try and be brave,"
said the dentist. —**brave·ly** *adv.* —**brav·er·y**
/ˈbreɪvəri/ *noun* [U]: *After the war he received*
a medal for bravery.

brave² /breɪv/ verb [T] to face sth dangerous or difficult without showing fear: *She braved the rain and went out into the street.*

bra·vo /ˈbrɑːvəʊ; ˌbrɑːˈvəʊ/ interj. a word that you shout to show that you like sth that sb has done, e.g. an actor's performance in a play

brawl /brɔːl/ noun [C] a noisy fight among a group of people, usually in a public place: *a drunken brawl outside a bar*

breach¹ /briːtʃ/ noun (formal) **1** [C,U] an act that breaks an agreement, a law, etc.: *Giving private information about clients is a breach of confidence.* ○ *She was dismissed from the company for breach of contract.* **2** [C] a break in friendly relations between people, groups, etc.: *a breach between two countries* **3** [C] an opening in a wall, etc. that defends or protects sb/sth: *The waves made a breach in the sea wall.*

breach² /briːtʃ/ verb [T] **1** to break an agreement, a law, etc.: *He accused the corporation of breaching international law.* **2** to make an opening in a wall, etc. that defends or protects sb/sth

bread

French bread

bagel

roll

slice

croissant

crust

loaf of bread

☆ **bread** /brɛd/ noun [U] a type of food. To make bread you mix together flour and water (and often a substance to make the bread rise (**yeast**)) and bake the mixture in an oven: *a piece/slice of bread* ○ *fresh/stale bread* ○ *Would you like some bread and butter?*

☞ A **loaf** of bread is bread that has been shaped and cooked in one piece. **Whole wheat** bread is made from flour that contains all the grain.

breadth /brɛdθ/ noun **1** [C,U] the distance between the two sides of sth: *We measured the length and breadth of the yard.*

☞ **Width** is more common than **breadth** in this meaning. Look at the picture at **length**.

2 [U] the wide range of sth: *I was amazed by the breadth of her knowledge.* ☞ The adjective is **broad**.

bread·win·ner /ˈbrɛdwɪnər/ noun [C, usually sing.] the person who earns the money that his/her family needs

☆ **break¹** /breɪk/ verb (p.t. **broke** /brəʊk/; p.p. **bro·ken** /ˈbrəʊkən/) **1** [I,T] to separate, or

make sth separate, into two or more pieces: *She dropped the vase onto the floor and it broke.* ○ *I'm sorry I broke one of your dinner plates.* ○ *He broke his leg in a car accident.* **2** [I,T] (used about a machine, etc.) to stop working; to stop a machine, etc. from working: *My watch broke last week.* ○ *Be careful with my camera – I don't want you to break it.* **3** [T] to do sth that is against the law, or to not keep a promise, etc.: *A police officer told me that I was breaking the law.* ○ *to break a contract* ○ *Don't worry – I never break my promises.* **4** [T] **break a record** to do sth better or faster than anyone has ever done before: *She broke the world record for the 100 meters.* **5** [I] to stop doing sth for a short time: *to break for lunch* **6** [T] to interrupt sth so that it ends suddenly: *Suddenly, the silence was broken by the sound of a bird singing.* **7** [T] to make sth end by force or strong action: *Smoking is a very difficult habit to break.* ○ *Two days of talks failed to break the deadlock between the countries.* **8** [I] (used about a day or the dawn) to begin: *Dawn was breaking.* **9** [I] (used about a wave) to curl over and fall: *waves breaking on the rocks* **10** [I] (used about a piece of news) to become known: *When the story broke in the newspapers, nobody could believe it.* **11** [I] (used about a boy's voice) to become permanently deeper, usually at about the age of 13 or 14

☞ For idioms containing **break**, look at the entries for nouns, adjectives, etc. For example, **break even** is at **even**.

PHRV break away (from sb/sth) 1 to escape suddenly from sb who is holding you **2** to leave a group, an organization, etc. in order to form a new one: *The region broke away from the rest of the country and declared independence.*

break down 1 (used about a vehicle or machine) to stop working: *My car broke down on the way to work this morning.* **2** (used about a system, discussion, etc.) to fail: *Talks between the two countries have completely broken down.* **3** to lose control of your feelings and start crying: *break down in tears*

break sth down to make a substance separate into parts or change into a different form in a chemical process: *Food is broken down in our bodies by the digestive system.*

break in to enter a building by force, usually in order to steal sth: *The burglars broke in through a window.*

break into sth 1 to enter a building by force, usually in order to steal sth **2** to start doing sth suddenly: *to break into a smile* ○ *to break into a run*

break off to suddenly stop doing or saying sth: *He broke off in the middle of a sentence.*

break (sth) off to remove a part of sth by force; to come off in this way: *Could you break*

B

B

off a piece of chocolate for me? ○ Oh, no! Part of my tooth just broke off!

break sth off to end a relationship suddenly: *They broke off their engagement after a bad argument.* ○ *to break off diplomatic relations with another country*

break out (used about fighting, wars, fires, etc.) to start suddenly

break out (of sth) to escape from a prison, etc.

break up (used about events that involve a group of people) to come to an end: *The meeting broke up just before lunch.*

break up (with sb) to end a relationship with a wife, husband, girlfriend or boyfriend: *My marriage broke up when I was 25.* ○ *She broke up with her boyfriend.*

break (sth) up to separate into parts: *The ship broke up on the rocks.*

break sth up to end an event by separating the people who are involved in it: *The police arrived and broke up the fight.*

break with sth to end a relationship or connection with sb/sth: *to break with tradition, the past, etc.*

☆ **break²** /breɪk/ *noun* [C] **1** a place where sth has been broken: *a break in a pipe* **2** an opening or space in sth: *Wait for a break in the traffic before you cross the street.* **3** a short period of rest: *Let's take a break.* ○ *a lunch/coffee break* ☞ Look at the note at **pause**. **4 break (in sth); break (with sb/sth)** a change from what usually happens or an end to sth: *a break with tradition* ○ *The incident led to a break in diplomatic relations.* **5** an arrangement or a change that is favorable to sb: *tax breaks for small businesses* ○ *Give him a break.* *Everybody makes mistakes when they start a new job.*

IDM give me a break! (*informal*) stop annoying me or making problems for me: *Oh, give me a break. That's not true and you know it.*

break·down /'breɪkdaʊn/ *noun* [C] **1** a time when a vehicle, machine, etc. stops working: *We had a breakdown on the freeway.* **2** the failure or end of sth: *The breakdown of the talks means that a strike is likely.* **3** = NERVOUS BREAKDOWN **4** a list of all the details of sth: *I would like a complete breakdown of how the money was spent.*

☆ **break·fast** /'brɛkfəst/ *noun* [C,U] the meal that you have when you get up in the morning: *to have breakfast* ○ *to eat a big breakfast*

'break-in *noun* [C] the act of entering a building by force, especially in order to steal sth: *The police say there have been several break-ins in this area.*

break·through /'breɪkθru/ *noun* [C] an important discovery or development: *a major breakthrough in cancer research.* ○ *The agreement represents a breakthrough in relations between the two countries.*

break·up /'breɪkʌp/ *noun* [C] **1** the end of a relationship between two people: *the breakup of a marriage* **2** the separation of a group or organization into smaller parts: *the breakup of the Soviet Union*

☆ **breast** /brɛst/ *noun* [C] **1** one of the two soft round parts of a woman's body that can produce milk **2** (used especially in literature) the upper part of the front of your body: *to clasp sb to your breast* **3** the front part of the body of a bird

breast·feed /'brɛstfid/ *verb* [I,T] (*p.t., p.p.* **breast·fed** /'brɛstfɛd/) to feed a baby with milk from the breast (1)

breast·stroke /'brɛststroʊk; 'brɛstroʊk/ *noun* [U] a style of swimming on your front in which you start with your hands together, push both arms forward and then pull them outward and back through the water

☆ **breath** /brɛθ/ *noun* **1** [U] the air that you take into and blow out of your lungs: *to have bad breath* (= breath which smells unpleasant) **2** [C] an act of taking air into or blowing air out of your lungs: *Take a deep breath.*

IDM a breath of fresh air the clean air that you breathe outside, especially when compared to the air inside a room or building: *Let's go for a walk. I need a breath of fresh air.* ○ (*figurative*) *Her happy face is like a breath of fresh air in that miserable place.*

catch your breath ⇨ CATCH¹

hold your breath to stop breathing for a period of time, e.g. when swimming underwater or because of fear or excitement: *We all held our breath as we waited for her reply.*

(be) out of/short of breath to be breathing very quickly, e.g. after physical exercise

say sth, speak, etc. under your breath to say sth very quietly, usually because you do not want people to hear what you are saying

take your breath away to surprise sb very much: *The spectacular view took our breath away.* ☞ The adjective is **breathtaking**.

with bated breath ⇨ BATED

☆ **breathe** /brið/ *verb* [I,T] to take air, etc. into your lungs and blow it out again: *She was unconscious but still breathing.* ○ *to breathe in/out* (= to take air in/to blow air out) ○ *I hate sitting in restaurants breathing other people's cigarette smoke.*

IDM not breathe a word (of/about sth) (to sb) not tell sb about sth that is secret: *If you breathe a word of this to my mother, I'll never speak to you again!* —**breath·ing** /'briðɪŋ/ *noun* [U]: *heavy, irregular, etc. breathing*

breath·er /'briðər/ *noun* [C] (*informal*) a short rest: *to take a breather*

breath·less /'brɛθləs/ *adj.* **1** breathing quickly or with difficulty, e.g. after physical exercise **2** not able to breathe because you are so excited, frightened, etc.: *to be breathless with excitement* —**breath·less·ly** *adv.*

ər	ɪr	ɛr	ɑr	ɔr	ʊr	ʒ	h	ŋ
bird	near	hair	car	north	tour	vision	hat	sing

breath·tak·ing /ˈbrɛθteɪkɪŋ/ *adj.* very exciting, beautiful, etc.: *breathtaking mountain scenery* —**breath·tak·ing·ly** *adv.*

breed¹ /brid/ *verb* (*p.t., p.p.* **bred** /brɛd/) **1** [I] (used about animals or plants) to produce young animals or plants: *Many animals won't breed in zoos.* **2** [T] to keep animals or plants in order to produce young from them: *cattle that are bred to produce high yields of milk* **3** [T] to cause sth: *This kind of thinking breeds intolerance and violence.*

breed² /brid/ *noun* [C] a type of animal: *a breed of cattle*

breed·er /ˈbridər/ *noun* [C] a person who breeds¹(2) animals or plants: *a dog breeder*

breed·ing ground *noun* [C] **1** a place where wild animals go to breed¹(1) **2** a place where sth can develop: *a breeding ground for crime*

breeze /briz/ *noun* **1** [C] a light wind: *A warm breeze was blowing.* **2 a breeze** [C, sing.] something that is very easy to do: *If you study hard enough, the test should be a breeze.*

breez·y /ˈbrizi/ *adj.* (**breez·i·er; breez·i·est**) **1** a little windy **2** informal and cheerful: *a fashion magazine written in a breezy style*

brev·i·ty /ˈbrɛvəti/ *noun* [U] the state of being short or quick ☞ The adjective is **brief.**

brew¹ /bru/ *verb* **1** [T] to make beer **2** [T] to make a drink of tea or coffee by adding hot water: *to brew a pot of coffee*
IDM **be brewing** (used about sth bad) to develop or grow: *There's trouble brewing.*

brew² /bru/ *noun* [C,U] a drink that is made by brewing: *home brew* (= beer that is made at sb's home).

brew·er·y /ˈbruəri/ *noun* [C] (*pl.* **brew·er·ies**) a place where beer is made

bribe /braɪb/ *noun* [C] money, etc. that sb gives to another person, such as an official, to persuade him/her to do sth, especially sth dishonest: *to offer a bribe to sb* ∘ *to accept/take bribes* —**bribe** *verb* [T] **bribe sb (with sth)**: *They got a visa by bribing an official.*

brib·er·y /ˈbraɪbəri/ *noun* [U] the giving or taking of bribes

☆ **brick** /brɪk/ *noun* [C,U] a hard block of baked clay that is used for building houses, etc.: *a house built of red bricks* ∘ *a truck carrying a load of bricks*

brick·lay·er /ˈbrɪkˌleɪər/ *noun* [C] a person whose job is to build walls with bricks

bri·dal /ˈbraɪdl/ *adj.* (only *before* a noun) connected with a bride or a wedding: *the bridal suite in a hotel*

☆ **bride** /braɪd/ *noun* [C] a woman on or just before her wedding day: *the bride and groom* ☞ Look at the note at **wedding.**

bride·groom /ˈbraɪdgrum/ *noun* [C] (*formal*) = GROOM¹

brides·maid /ˈbraɪdzmeɪd/ *noun* [C] a woman or girl who helps the bride at her wedding ☞ Look at the note at **wedding.**

☆ **bridge¹** /brɪdʒ/ *noun* **1** [C] a structure that carries a road, railroad, etc. across a river, valley, road or railroad: *a bridge over the Mississippi River* **2** [C] the high part of a ship where the captain and the people who control the ship stand **3** [U] a card game for four people

bridge² /brɪdʒ/ *verb* [T] to build a bridge¹(1) over sth
IDM **bridge a/the gap** to fill a space between two people, groups or things or to bring them closer together

bri·dle /ˈbraɪdl/ *noun* [C] the leather straps that you put over a horse's head so that you can control it when you are riding it ☞ picture at **horse.**

☆ **brief¹** /brif/ *adj.* short or quick: *a brief phone call* ∘ *Please be brief. We don't have much time.* ☞ The noun is **brevity.**

brief² /brif/ *noun* **1** [C] a short statement or document that gives information and that is often a summary of a longer document: *a news brief* ∘ *Each attorney must submit a brief before the trial.* **2 briefs** [plural] a type of underpants ☞ picture on page A26.

brief³ /brif/ *verb* [T] to give sb information or instructions about sth: *The mayor has been fully briefed on what questions to expect.*

brief·case /ˈbrifkeɪs/ *noun* [C] a flat case that you use for carrying papers, etc., especially when you go to work ☞ picture at **luggage.**

brief·ing /ˈbrifɪŋ/ *noun* [C,U] instructions or information that you are given before sth happens: *a press/news briefing* (= where information is given to journalists)

☆ **brief·ly** /ˈbrifli/ *adv.* **1** for a short time; quickly: *We met briefly to discuss Marsha's report.* **2** using only a few words: *I'd like to comment very briefly on that last statement.*

bri·gade /brɪˈɡeɪd/ *noun* [C] **1** a unit of soldiers in the army **2** a group of people who work together for a particular purpose

☆ **bright** /braɪt/ *adj.* **1** having a lot of light: *a bright, sunny day* ∘ *eyes bright with happiness* **2** (used about a color) strong: *a bright yellow sweater* **3** intelligent, or able to learn things quickly: *a bright idea* ∘ *a bright child* **4** likely to be pleasant or successful: *The future looks bright.* **5** cheerful, happy: *You seem very bright and cheerful today.* —**bright·ly** *adv.*: *brightly-colored clothes* —**bright·ness** *noun* [U]

bright·en /ˈbraɪtn/ *verb* [I,T] **brighten (sth) (up)** to become brighter or happier; to make sth brighter: *His face brightened when he saw her.* ∘ *to brighten up sb's day* (= make it happier)

☆ **bril·liant** /ˈbrɪlyənt/ *adj.* **1** having a lot of light; very bright: *brilliant sunshine* **2** very intelligent; showing a lot of intelligence: *a brilliant young scientist* ∘ *That's a brilliant idea!* —**bril·liance** /-yəns/ *noun* [U] —**bril·liant·ly** *adv.*

tʃ	dʒ	v	θ	ð	s	z	ʃ
chin	June	van	thin	then	so	zoo	she

brim¹ /brɪm/ *noun* [C] **1** the top edge of a cup, glass, etc.: *The cup was filled to the brim.* **2** the bottom part of a hat, that is wider than the rest

brim² /brɪm/ *verb* [I] (**brim·ming; brimmed**) **brim (with sth)** to be full of sth: *His eyes were brimming with tears.*

BRING **bring/take**

"Bring me my newspaper!"

TAKE

"Take it into the kitchen!"

☆ **bring** /brɪŋ/ *verb* [T] (*p.t., p.p.* **brought** /brɔt/) **1** to come to a place with sb/sth: *The weather can be chilly here, so bring a jacket with you.* ○ *Is it all right if I bring a friend to the party?* ○ *Bring us two coffees, please.* ○ *(figurative) He will bring us valuable skills and experience to the team.* **2** to cause or result in sth: *The sight of her brought a smile to his face.* ○ *Money doesn't always bring happiness.* **3** to cause sb/sth to be in a certain place or condition: *Their screams brought people running from all directions.* ○ *Add water to the mixture and bring it to a boil.* ○ *to bring sth to an end* **4** to force yourself to do sth: *The movie was so scary that I could hardly bring myself to watch it.*

PHRV bring about to cause sth to happen: *to bring about changes in people's lives*

bring sb around to cause sb to become conscious again

bring sb/sth back to return sb/sth: *You can borrow the video if you bring it back tomorrow morning.*

bring sth back 1 to cause sth that existed before to be introduced again: *Nobody wants to bring back the days of child labor.* **2** to cause sb to remember sth: *The pictures brought back memories of his childhood.*

bring sb sth back to return with sth for sb: *My sister went to Spain on vacation and brought me back a T-shirt.*

bring sb/sth down to cause sb/sth to be defeated or to lose a position of power: *to bring down a government*

bring sth down to make sth lower in level: *to bring down the price of sth*

bring sth forward to suggest sth for discussion

bring sb in to ask or appoint sb to do a particular job: *A specialist was brought in to set up the new computer system.*

bring sth in to introduce sth: *The government has brought in a new law on seat belts in cars.*

bring sth on to cause sth: *Her headaches are brought on by stress.*

bring sth out to produce sth or cause sth to appear: *When is the company bringing out its next new model?* ○ *A crisis can sometimes bring out the best in people.*

bring sb up to take care of a child until he/she is an adult and to teach him/her how to behave: *After her parents were killed, the child was brought up by her uncle.*

bring sth up to introduce sth into a discussion or conversation: *I intend to bring the matter up at the next meeting.*

brink /brɪŋk/ *noun* [sing.] the edge at the top of a high place: *(figurative) The new president brought the company back from the brink of disaster.*

IDM be on the brink (of sth/of doing sth) to be about to do or experience sth exciting or dangerous

brisk /brɪsk/ *adj.* **1** quick or using a lot of energy; busy: *They set off at a brisk pace.* **2** (used about wind and the weather) cold but pleasantly fresh: *a brisk wind* —**brisk·ly** *adv.*

bris·tle¹ /ˈbrɪsl/ *noun* [C] **1** a short thick hair on an animal **2** one of the short thick hairs of a brush

bris·tle² /ˈbrɪsl/ *verb* [I] **1** (used about hair or an animal's fur) to stand up straight because of fear, anger, cold, etc. **2 bristle (with sth)** to show that you are angry **3 bristle (at sth)** to react (to sth) in an angry way: *The senator bristled at suggestions that he had accepted bribes.*

Brit·ain /ˈbrɪtn/ *noun* = GREAT BRITAIN ☞ Look at the note at **United Kingdom**.

Brit·ish /ˈbrɪtɪʃ/ *adj.* **1** of the United Kingdom, i.e. Great Britain and Northern Ireland: *British culture* **2 the British** *noun* [plural] the people of the United Kingdom

the ˌBritish ˈIsles *noun* [plural] Great Britain and Ireland with all the islands that are near their coasts. The British Isles are a geographical but not a political unit.

brit·tle /ˈbrɪtl/ *adj.* hard but easily broken: *brittle fingernails*

broach /broʊtʃ/ *verb* [T] to start talking about a particular subject, especially one which is difficult or embarrassing: *Have you broached the subject of the money he owes us?*

☆ **broad** /brɔd/ *adj.* **1** large in size from one side to the other; wide: *a broad river valley*

☞ **Wide** is more often used than **broad** when you are talking about the distance between one side of something and the other: *The gate is four yards wide.* ◦ *The table is too wide to go through the door.* **Broad** is often used about geographical features: *a broad expanse of desert* and in particular phrases such as: *broad shoulders.* The noun from **broad** is **breadth**. The opposite is **narrow**.

2 without a lot of detail; general: *Just give me a broad outline of your plan.* **3** felt or believed by a lot of people: *There seems to be broad support for stronger anti-pollution laws.* **IDM** **in broad daylight** during the day, i.e. not at night: *He was attacked in broad daylight.*

☆ **broad·cast¹** /ˈbrɔdkæst/ *verb* (*p.t., p.p.* **broad·cast**) [I,T] to send out radio or television programs: *The local radio station broadcasts 24 hours a day.* ◦ *The Olympics are broadcast live via satellite.*

☆ **broad·cast²** /ˈbrɔdkæst/ *noun* [C] something that is sent out by radio or television: *a news broadcast*

broad·cast·er /ˈbrɔdkæstər/ *noun* [C] **1** a person who speaks on serious subjects on the radio or on television **2** a radio or television station

broad·en /ˈbrɔdn/ *verb* [I,T] to become broader; to make sth broader: *The river broadens beyond the bridge.* (*figurative*) *Travel broadens the mind* (= it makes you understand other people better).

broad·ly /ˈbrɔdli/ *adv.* **1** (used to describe a way of smiling): *to smile broadly* (= to have a very big, wide smile) **2** generally: *Broadly speaking, the plan will work as follows…*

broc·co·li /ˈbrɑkəli/ *noun* [U] a plant with dark green flower heads that can be cooked and eaten as a vegetable ☞ picture at **cabbage**.

bro·chure /broʊˈʃʊr/ *noun* [C] a thin book with pictures in it that gives you information about sth: *a travel brochure*

broil /brɔɪl/ *verb* **1** [T] to cook sth under a heat source in an oven, or on a system of metal bars (**a grill**) over flames: *broiled salmon* ☞ Look at the note at **cook**. **2** [I,T] to become or to make sth very hot: *I'm broiling in this heavy coat!*

broil·er /ˈbrɔɪlər/ *noun* [C] a device in an oven that cooks food with heat from above: *Put the fish under the broiler for eight minutes.*

broke¹ *p.t.* of **BREAK¹**

☆ **broke²** /broʊk/ *adj.* (not before a noun) (*informal*) having no money: *I can't go out tonight. I'm completely broke.*

bro·ken¹ /ˈbroʊkən/ *p.p.* of **BREAK¹**

☆ **bro·ken²** /ˈbroʊkən/ *adj.* **1** damaged or in pieces; not working: *Watch out! There's broken glass on the floor.* ◦ *The washing machine's broken.* ☞ picture at **chip**. **2** not continuous; interrupted: *a broken line* **3** not kept: *a broken*

promise **4** (used about a foreign language) spoken slowly with a lot of mistakes: *to speak in broken English* **5** (used about a family or a home) no longer together: *Many of the kids come from broken homes.* **6** (used about a relationship, etc.) that has ended because the people no longer want to stay together: *a broken marriage*

ˌ**broken-ˈdown** *adj.* in a very bad condition: *a broken-down old pickup truck*

bro·ker /ˈbroʊkər/ *noun* [C] **1** a person who arranges the buying and selling of things such as property, insurance, etc. for other people: *an insurance broker* **2** = STOCKBROKER

bron·chi·tis /brɑŋˈkaɪt̮əs/ *noun* [U] an illness of the tiny tubes in the lungs, that causes a very bad cough

bronze /brɑnz/ *noun* **1** [U] a brown-colored metal that is made from a combination of a red-colored metal (**copper**) and a silver-colored metal (**tin**) **2** [U] the color of bronze (1) **3** [C] = BRONZE MEDAL —**bronze** *adj.*

ˌ**bronze ˈmedal** *noun* [C] a round piece of bronze that you get as a prize for coming third in a race or a competition ☞ Look at **gold medal** and **silver medal**.

brood¹ /brud/ *noun* [C] all the young birds that belong to one mother

brood² /brud/ *verb* [I] **brood (about/over sth)** to worry, or to think a lot about sth that makes you sad: *to brood over a failure*

brook /brʊk/ *noun* [C] a small stream

broom /brum/ *noun* [C] a brush with a long handle that you use for sweeping the floor ☞ picture at **brush**.

broom·stick /ˈbrumstɪk/ *noun* [C] the handle of a broom. In stories witches sometimes fly on broomsticks.

broth /brɔθ/ *noun* [U] thin soup: *chicken broth*

broth·el /ˈbrɑθl; ˈbrɔθl/ *noun* [C] a place where men can go and pay to have sex with a woman (**a prostitute**)

☆ **broth·er** /ˈbrʌðər/ *noun* [C] **1** a man or boy who has the same parents as another person: *Michael and Jim are brothers.* ◦ *Michael is Jim's brother.* ◦ *a younger/an older brother* ☞ Look at **half-brother** and **stepbrother**. Notice that there is not a common English word that means "both brothers and sisters": *Do you have any brothers and sisters?* The word **sibling** is very formal. **2** a man who is a member of a Christian religious community (**a monastery**): *Brother John* **3** (*informal*) boy or man who is your friend or who is from the same social class, race, etc. as you

broth·er·hood /ˈbrʌðərhʊd/ *noun* **1** [U] a feeling of great friendship and loyalty between people: *the brotherhood of all humans* (= a feeling of friendship among all the people in the world) **2** [C] an organization that is formed for a particular, usually religious, purpose

ə	y	w	t̮	eɪ	aɪ	ɔɪ	aʊ	oʊ
about	yes	woman	butter	say	five	boy	now	go

'**brother-in-,law** *noun* [C] (*pl.* **brothers-in-law**) **1** the brother of your husband or wife **2** the husband of your sister

broth·er·ly /'brʌðərli/ *adj.* of or like a brother: *brotherly love*

brought *p.t., p.p.* of BRING

brow /braʊ/ *noun* [C] **1** [usually pl.] = EYEBROW **2** (*formal*) = FOREHEAD: *Sweat was pouring from his brow.*

☆ **brown**[1] /braʊn/ *adj.* having the color of soil or wood: *brown shoes* ○ *dark brown hair*

☆ **brown**[2] /braʊn/ *noun* [C,U] the color of soil or wood: *the yellows and browns of the trees in the fall* ○ *You don't look nice in brown* (= in brown clothes).

brown[3] /braʊn/ *verb* [I,T] to become or cause sth to become brown: *Heat some oil and brown the chicken on both sides.*

brown·ie /'braʊni/ *noun* [C] **1** a type of small, heavy chocolate cake that often contains nuts **2** **Brownie** a young girl who is a member of the junior branch of the Girl Scouts organization

brown·ish /'braʊnɪʃ/ *adj.* slightly or fairly brown: *She has brownish eyes.*

brown·stone /'braʊnstoʊn/ *noun* [C,U] a type of brown-colored stone that is used to make buildings; a house that is made of this type of stone, especially in New York City: *We live in a three-story brownstone.*

browse /braʊz/ *verb* [I] **1** to spend time pleasantly, looking around a store, without a clear idea of what you are looking for: *I spent hours browsing in the local bookstore.* **2 browse through sth** to look through a book or magazine without reading every part or studying it carefully: *I enjoyed browsing through the catalogue, but I didn't order anything.*

brows·er /'braʊzər/ *noun* [C] a computer program that lets you look at words and pictures that you choose from other computer systems by receiving information through telephone wires: *an Internet browser*

☆ **bruise**[1] /bruz/ *noun* [C] a dark mark on the skin caused by a blow that injures but does not break the skin: *He didn't break any bones, but he suffered cuts and bruises on his face.* ○ *These apples are covered in bruises.* ☞ A bruise on your eye is a **black eye**.

bruise[2] /bruz/ *verb* **1** [T] to cause a bruise or bruises: *I fell down and bruised my knee.* ○ *She had a badly bruised face.* **2** [I] to get a bruise or bruises: *I have the sort of skin that bruises easily.*

brunch /brʌntʃ/ *noun* [C,U] a late morning meal that is eaten instead of breakfast and lunch: *The hotel serves Sunday brunch from 10:00 to 12:00.*

brunt /brʌnt/ *noun*

IDM bear/take the brunt of sth to suffer the main force of sth: *The West Coast bore the brunt of the storm.*

hairbrush
nail brush
brush
dustpan
brushes
broom
paintbrushes
toothbrush

☆ **brush**[1] /brʌʃ/ *noun* **1** [C] an object that is used for cleaning things, painting, arranging your hair, etc.: *I scrubbed the kitchen floor with a brush.* ○ *a toothbrush* ○ *a paintbrush* ○ *a hairbrush* **2** [sing.] an act of sweeping, cleaning, etc. with a brush or with your hand: *Give your coat a quick brush.* **3** [U] a thick covering of bushes and small trees; land that is covered in bushes and small trees: *brush fires*

IDM a brush with sth an unexpected and often unpleasant meeting or association with sth: *a brush with death* ○ *This isn't Jill's first brush with the law – she's been arrested before.*

☆ **brush**[2] /brʌʃ/ *verb* **1** [T] to clean, sweep, etc. with a brush: *Make sure you brush your teeth twice a day.* ○ *She was brushing her hair in front of a mirror.* ☞ Look at the note at **clean**[2]. **2** [I,T] to touch sb/sth lightly when passing: *Her hand brushed his cheek.* ○ *Leaves brushed against the car as we drove along the narrow road.*

PHRV brush sb/sth aside 1 to refuse to pay attention to sb/sth: *She brushed aside the protests and continued with the meeting.* **2** to get past sb/sth: *He hurried along, brushing aside the reporters who tried to stop him.*

brush sth away; brush sth off (sth) to remove sth with a brush or with the hand, as if using a brush: *I brushed the dust off my jacket.*

brush sth up/brush up on sth to study or practice sth in order to get back knowledge or skill that you had before and have lost: *She took a course to brush up (on) her Spanish.*

Brussels sprout /'brʌsl spraʊt/ *noun* [C, usually pl.] a green vegetable that looks like a very small cabbage ☞ picture at **cabbage**.

bru·tal /'brutl/ *adj.* very cruel and violent: *a brutal murder* ○ *a brutal dictatorship* —**bru·tal·ly** *adv.*: *The girl had been brutally attacked.* ○ *He was brutally honest and told her that he didn't love her anymore.*

bru·tal·i·ty /bru'tæləti/ *noun* [C,U] (*pl.* **brutal·i·ties**) very cruel and violent behavior: *complaints of police brutality*

ər	ɪr	ɛr	ɑr	ɔr	ʊr	ʒ	h	ŋ
bird	near	hair	car	north	tour	vision	hat	sing

bubbles

☆ **bub·ble¹** /ˈbʌbl/ noun [C] a hollow ball containing air or gas, in liquid or floating in the air: *The kids were blowing soap bubbles.*

bub·ble² /ˈbʌbl/ verb [I] to produce bubbles¹ or to rise with bubbles: *Bake the pizza until the cheese starts to bubble.* ○ *The clear water bubbled up out of the ground.*

'**bubble gum** noun [U] chewing gum that can be blown into bubbles¹ out of the mouth

bub·bly /ˈbʌbli/ adj. **1** full of bubbles¹: *a bubbly drink* **2** (used about a person) lively and happy: *She has a naturally bubbly personality.*

buck¹ /bʌk/ noun [C] **1** (informal) a dollar: *Could you loan me a few bucks?* ○ *I paid 50 bucks for that thing!* **2** (pl. **buck** or **bucks**) a male deer ☞ picture at **deer**. Look at the note at **deer**.

IDM **pass the buck** ⇨ PASS²

buck² /bʌk/ verb **1** [I,T] (used about a horse) to jump into the air with all four feet off the ground, and sometimes throw a rider to the ground: *Wayne's horse suddenly bucked him off.* **2** [T] to resist or oppose sb/sth: *Sales in the Northwest bucked the national downward trend, rising by 5%.*

☆ **buck·et** /ˈbʌkət/ (also **pail**) noun [C] **1** a round, open container, usually made of metal or plastic, with a handle, that is used for carrying or holding liquids or sand **2** the amount that a bucket (1) contains: *How many buckets of cement do you think we'll need?*

bucket

buck·le¹ /ˈbʌkl/ noun [C] a piece of metal or plastic at the end of a belt or strap that is used for fastening it

buck·le² /ˈbʌkl/ verb [I,T] **1** to fasten or be fastened with a buckle **2** to bend because of heat, force, weakness, etc.: *Some train tracks buckled in the heat.*

PHRV **buckle up** to fasten your seat belt in a car or in an airplane. *I want everyone to buckle up before I start the car.*

bud /bʌd/ noun [C] a small lump on a tree or plant that opens and develops into a flower or leaf: *rosebuds*

IDM **nip sth in the bud** ⇨ NIP

Bud·dhism /ˈbudɪzəm; ˈbʊd-/ noun [U] an Asian religion that was founded in India by Buddha

Bud·dhist /ˈbudɪst; ˈbʊd-/ noun [C] a person whose religion is Buddhism —**Bud·dhist** adj.: *a Buddhist temple*

bud·ding /ˈbʌdɪŋ/ adj. wanting or starting to develop and be successful: *Do you have any tips for budding young photographers?*

bud·dy /ˈbʌdi/ noun [C] (pl. **bud·dies**) (informal) a friend, especially a male friend

budge /bʌdʒ/ verb [I,T] **1** to move or cause sth to move a little: *I tried to loosen the screw, but it simply wouldn't budge.* ○ *We couldn't budge the car when it got stuck in the mud.* **2** to change or cause sb to change a firm opinion: *Neither side in the dispute is prepared to budge.* ○ *Once he's made up his mind, nothing will budge him.*

☆ **budg·et¹** /ˈbʌdʒət/ noun [C] a plan of how to spend an amount of money over a particular period of time; the amount of money that is mentioned: *What's your monthly budget for food?* ○ *the country's defense budget* ○ *an advertising budget of $2 million* ○ *to balance a budget*

budg·et² /ˈbʌdʒət/ verb [I,T] **budget (sth) (for sth)** to plan carefully how much money to spend on sth: *Don't forget to budget for possible increased costs.* ○ *Costs for the new building are already far greater than the $10 million originally budgeted.*

budg·et³ /ˈbʌdʒət/ adj. (only before a noun) very cheap: *a budget meal*

buff /bʌf/ noun [C] (informal) a person who knows a lot about a particular subject and is very interested in it: *Civil War buffs*

buf·fa·lo /ˈbʌfəloʊ/ noun [C] (pl. **buf·fa·lo** or **buf·fa·loes**) a large wild animal that looks like a cow with a very large head, curved horns and thick fur on its head and neck: *a herd of buffalo* ☞ Look at **bison**.

buff·er /ˈbʌfər/ noun [C] a thing or person that reduces the unpleasant effects of sth or that protects against sth: *a buffer zone between the two sides in a battle*

buf·fet¹ /bəˈfeɪ; bʊ-/ noun [C] **1** a long table in a restaurant, etc. with food on it, from which people serve themselves: *Help yourself to the salad buffet.* **2** a meal (usually at a party or a special occasion) at which food is placed on a long table and people serve themselves: *a buffet lunch*

buf·fet² /ˈbʌfət/ verb [T] to knock or push sth in a rough way from side to side: *The boat was buffeted by the rough waves.*

bug¹ /bʌg/ noun [C] **1** a small insect **2** an illness that is not very serious and that people get from each other: *I don't feel very well – I think I've got the bug that's going around.* **3** something wrong in a system or machine, especially a computer: *There's a bug in the software.* **4** a tiny hidden microphone that secretly records people's conversations

bug² /bʌg/ verb [T] (**bug·ging; bugged**) **1** (informal) to annoy or worry sb: *You look like something's bugging you. What's wrong?* **2** to

tʃ	dʒ	v	θ	ð	s	z	ʃ
chin	June	van	thin	then	so	zoo	she

B

B

hide a tiny microphone somewhere so that people's conversations can be recorded secretly: *Be careful what you say. This room is bugged.*

IDM **bug off!** (*informal*) (a rude way to tell sb to go away)

bug·gy /ˈbʌgi/ *noun* [C] (*pl.* **bug·gies**) a type of old-fashioned vehicle without an engine, that is pulled by a horse: *a horse-drawn buggy*

☆ **build¹** /bɪld/ *verb* (*p.t., p.p.* **built** /bɪlt/) **1** [T] to make sth by putting pieces, materials, etc. together: *They built a new bridge across the river.* ○ *The house is built of wood.* **2** [I] to put new buildings in a place: *There's plenty of land to build on around here.* **3** [T] to develop or increase sth: *We're trying to build a safer community for our children.* ○ *This book claims to help people to build their self-confidence.*

PHRV **build sth in**; **build sth into sth** to make sth a part of sth else: *A large number of safety features are built into the system.* ☞ Look also at **built-in.**

build on sth to use sth as a base from which you can make further progress: *Now that we're beginning to make a profit, we must build on this success.*

build sth on sth to base sth on sth: *a society built on the principles of freedom and democracy*

build up to become greater in amount or number; to increase: *The traffic starts to build up at this time of day.*

build sth up 1 to make sth seem more important or greater than it really is: *I don't think it's a very serious matter – it's just been built up in the newspapers.* **2** to increase or develop sth over a period: *You'll need to build up your strength again after the operation.*

build² /bɪld/ *noun* [C,U] the shape and size of sb's body: *She has a very athletic build.* ○ *Police are looking for a young man of slim build.*

☞ Compare **build** and **figure**. **Build** usually describes size in connection with strength and muscle and is used for both men and women. **Figure** usually describes shape, especially whether it is attractive or not, and is usually used only for women.

build·er /ˈbɪldər/ *noun* [C] a company that builds houses and other buildings

☆ **build·ing** /ˈbɪldɪŋ/ *noun* **1** [C] a structure, such as a house, church or school, that has a roof and walls: *There are a lot of very old buildings in this town.* **2** [U] the process or business of making buildings (1): *building materials* ○ *the building industry*

build·up /ˈbɪldʌp/ *noun* [C, usually sing.] **1 a buildup (of sth)** an increase of sth over a period: *The buildup of tension in the area has made war seem more likely.* **2 a buildup (to sth)** a period of preparation or excitement

before an event: *The players started to get nervous in the buildup to the big game.*

built *p.t., p.p.* of BUILD¹

-built /bɪlt/ (in compounds) having a body with a particular shape and size: *a tall well-built man*

built-'in *adj.* **1** (used about furniture) built so it is fastened to a wall and cannot be moved: *built-in cupboards* **2** made a part of sth else: *There is built-in unfairness in the system.*

bulb /bʌlb/ *noun* [C] **1** = LIGHT BULB: *The bulb just burned out* (= it no longer works) – *I'll have to put a new one in.* ☞ picture at **light. 2** the round root of certain plants: *a tulip bulb*

bulge¹ /bʌldʒ/ *noun* [C] an outward curve or lump on sth that is usually flat

bulge² /bʌldʒ/ *verb* [I] **1** to stick out from sth that is usually flat; to swell outward: *My stomach is starting to bulge. I ought to get more exercise.* **2 bulge with sth** to be full of sth: *His bags were bulging with presents for the kids.*

bulg·ing /ˈbʌldʒɪŋ/ *adj.* **1** sticking out: *He had a thin face and bulging eyes.* **2** very full: *She came home with bulging grocery bags.*

bulk /bʌlk/ *noun* **1** [U] the large size or amount of sth: *The dresser isn't especially heavy – it's its bulk that makes it hard to move.* **2** [C] a very large body: *He slowly lifted his vast bulk out of the chair.* **3 the bulk (of sth)** [sing.] the main part of sth; most of sth: *The bulk of the work has been done – there's only a little left.*

IDM **in bulk** in large quantities: *If you buy in bulk, it is 10% cheaper.*

bulk·y /ˈbʌlki/ *adj.* (**bulk·i·er**; **bulk·i·est**) large and heavy and therefore difficult to move or carry: *a bulky package*

bull /bʊl/ *noun* [C] **1** an adult male of the cow family ☞ Look at the note and picture at **cow.** **2** the male of certain other animals, e.g. the elephant and the whale

bull·dog /ˈbʊldɔg/ *noun* [C] a strong dog with short legs, a large head and a short, thick neck

bull·doze /ˈbʊldoʊz/ *verb* [T] to make ground flat or knock down a building with a bulldozer: *The old buildings were bulldozed and new ones were built.*

bull·doz·er /ˈbʊldoʊzər/ *noun* [C] a large, powerful tractor with a wide piece of metal at the front, used for clearing ground or knocking down buildings

☆ **bul·let** /ˈbʊlət/ *noun* [C] a small piece of metal with a pointed end that is shot from a gun: *The bullet hit her in the arm.* ○ *a bullet wound*

bul·le·tin /ˈbʊlətɪn/ *noun* [C] **1** a short news report on TV or radio; an official statement about a situation: *a news bulletin* **2** a short newspaper that an organization produces: *the monthly church bulletin*

'bulletin board *noun* [C] a board on a wall for putting papers, signs, etc. on

bul·let·proof /ˈbʊlətpruf/ *adj.* made of a

i	ɪ	ɛ	æ	ɑ	ɔ	ʌ	ʊ	u
see	sit	ten	cat	hot	saw	cup	put	too

strong material that stops bullets from passing through it: *Police officers wear bulletproof vests.*

bull·fight /ˈbʊlfaɪt/ *noun* [C] a traditional public entertainment, especially in Spain, Portugal and Latin America, in which a man makes a bull angry, fights it and often kills it

bull·fight·er /ˈbʊlfaɪtər/ *noun* [C] a man who takes part in a bullfight

bull·fight·ing /ˈbʊlfaɪtɪŋ/ *noun* [U] the public entertainment in which men fight bulls in a special area (**bullring**)

bul·lion /ˈbʊlyən/ *noun* [U] bars of gold or silver: *The price of gold bullion has risen by more than 10%.*

bull's-eye /ˈbʊlzaɪ/ *noun* [C] **1** the center of a target that you aim at when you are shooting or throwing sth ☞ picture at **dart**. **2** a shot that hits this target

bul·ly¹ /ˈbʊli/ *noun* [C] (*pl.* **bul·lies**) a person who uses his/her greater strength or power to hurt or frighten people who are weaker

bul·ly² /ˈbʊli/ *verb* [I,T] (*pres. part.* **bul·ly·ing**; *3rd pers. sing. pres.* **bul·lies**; *p.t., p.p.* **bul·lied**) to use your strength or power to hurt or frighten sb who is weaker: *Tony was bullied a lot in school because he was small.*

PHRV bully sb into doing sth to force sb to do sth by frightening him/her

bum¹ /bʌm/ *noun* [C] (*informal*) **1** a person who has no home and lives by begging ☞ A more polite expression is **a homeless person**. **2** a lazy or useless person

bum² /bʌm/ *verb* [T] (*pres. part.* **bum·ming**; *p.t., p.p.* **bummed**) **bum sth (off sb)** (*informal*) to get sth from sb by begging: *It's too late to catch a bus – we'll have to bum a ride home.* ○ *Can I bum a cigarette off you?*

PHRV bum around (*informal*) to travel around or to spend your time doing nothing in particular: *We spent the summer bumming around (in) Europe.*

bum sb out (*slang*) to make sb feel very disappointed: *It really bums me out when that happens!*

bum·mer /ˈbʌmər/ *noun* [C] (*slang*) an unpleasant situation: *What a bummer! I couldn't get tickets to the concert.*

bump¹ /bʌmp/ *verb* **1** [I] **bump against/into sb/sth** to hit sth solid by accident when you are moving: *She bumped into a lamppost because she wasn't looking where she was going.* **2** [T] **bump sth (against/on sth)** to hit sth against or on sth by accident when moving it: *I bumped my knee on the edge of the table.* **3** [I] to move in an uneven way as if going over bumps: *We bumped along the gravel road.*

PHRV bump into sb to meet sb by chance: *I bumped into a old friend today.*

bump² /bʌmp/ *noun* [C] **1** a sudden strong blow caused by sth hard hitting sth else; the sound of such a blow: *She fell and hit the*

ground with a bump. ○ *We heard a loud bump from upstairs.* **2** a lump on the body, often caused by a blow **3** a part of a flat surface that is raised above the rest of it: *There are a lot of bumps in the road, so drive carefully.*

bump·er¹ /ˈbʌmpər/ *noun* [C] the bar fastened to the front and back of a car, etc. to reduce the effect if it hits sth

bump·er² /ˈbʌmpər/ *adj.* larger than usual: *The unusually good weather has produced a bumper harvest this year.*

bump·y /ˈbʌmpi/ *adj.* (**bump·i·er**; **bump·i·est**) **1** (used about a surface) having a lot of bumps²(3): *a bumpy road* **2** (used about a trip) rough and uncomfortable; not smooth: *Because of the stormy weather, it was a very bumpy flight.*

bun /bʌn/ *noun* [C] **1** a small bread roll: *a hamburger/hot dog bun* **2** hair fastened tightly into a round shape at the back of the head: *She wears her hair in a bun.* **3** (*informal*) one of the two parts of the body which you sit on: *Get up off your buns and do some work!*

☆ **bunch¹** /bʌntʃ/ *noun* [C] **1** a number of things, usually of the same type, fastened or growing together: *a bunch of flowers* ○ *a bunch of bananas* ○ *a bunch of keys* **2** [with sing. or pl. verb] (*informal*) a large group of people or things; a large amount of sth: *A whole bunch of us went out for pizza after work.* ○ *I have a bunch of work to do today.*

☞ We usually use **bunch** with a singular verb when we are thinking of the whole group together. But if we use a phrase like *a bunch of...* with a plural noun or pronoun, we usually use a plural verb: *A bunch of my friends are going to the movies tonight.*

bunch² /bʌntʃ/ *verb* [I,T] **bunch (sth/sb) (up/together)** to stay together in a group; to form sth into a group or bunch: *The runners bunched up as they came around the final bend.* ○ *He kept his papers bunched together in his hand.*

bun·dle¹ /ˈbʌndl/ *noun* [C] a number of things tied or wrapped together: *a bundle of letters with a rubber band around them*

bun·dle² /ˈbʌndl/ *verb* **1** [T] **bundle sth (up)** to make or tie sth into a bundle or bundles: *I bundled up the old newspapers and threw them away.* **2** [I,T] **bundle (sb) (up)** to dress warmly: *It's cold outside – be sure to bundle up.* **3** [T] to put or push sb or sth quickly and in a rough way in a particular direction: *He was arrested and bundled into a police car.*

bun·ga·low /ˈbʌŋgəloʊ/ *noun* [C] a type of house that is usually small and square, with a covered platform (**porch**) in front

bun·gee jump·ing /ˈbʌndʒi ˌdʒʌmpɪŋ/ *noun* [U] a sport in which you jump from a high place, e.g. a bridge, with a thick elastic rope tied around your feet

bun·gle /ˈbʌŋgl/ *verb* [I,T] to do sth badly: *The men fled after bungling a bank robbery.*

bunk /bʌŋk/ *noun* [C] **1** a bed that is fastened to a wall (e.g. on a ship or in a prison) **2** one of a pair of narrow beds built as a unit with one above the other: *I sleep in the top bunk and my brother sleeps in the bottom one.*

ˈ**bunk bed** *noun* [C, usually pl.] a pair of narrow beds built as a unit with one above the other

bun·ker /ˈbʌŋkər/ *noun* [C] **1** a strongly built underground shelter that gives protection in a war **2** an area of sand on a golf course, where it is difficult to hit the ball

bun·ny /ˈbʌni/ *noun* [C] (*pl.* **bun·nies**) (used by and to children) a rabbit

buoy¹ /ˈbui; bɔɪ/ *noun* [C] a floating object, fastened to the bottom of the ocean or a river, that shows ships and boats where dangerous places are

buoy² /ˈbui; bɔɪ/ *verb* [T] **1 buoy sb (up)** to keep sb cheerful: *His encouragement buoyed her up during that difficult period.* **2 buoy sth (up)** to keep sth high by supporting it: *Stock prices were buoyed by news of a takeover.*

buoy·ant /ˈbɔɪənt/ *adj.* **1** (used about a material) floating or able to float **2** (used about economic and business life) successful, with a lot of activity: *Despite the recession, the real estate market remained buoyant.* **3** (used about prices) rising or keeping at a high level **4** happy and cheerful: *The team was in a buoyant mood after their win.* —**buoy·an·cy** /-ənsi/ *noun* [U]: *the buoyancy of the German economy*

☆ **bur·den**¹ /ˈbərdn/ *noun* [C] **1** a heavy load that is difficult to carry **2** a responsibility or difficult task that causes a lot of work or worry: *Having to make all the decisions is a terrible burden for me.* ○ *I don't want to be a burden on my kids when I'm old.*

bur·den² /ˈbərdn/ *verb* [T] **burden sb/ yourself (with sth)** to give sb/yourself a responsibility or task that causes a lot of work or worry: *If I were you, I wouldn't burden myself with other people's problems.*

bu·reau /ˈbyʊroʊ/ *noun* [C] **1** = DRESSER **2** one of certain government departments: *the Federal Bureau of Investigation* **3** an organization or a company that provides information: *a reporter from the magazine's Miami bureau*

bu·reauc·ra·cy /byʊˈrɑkrəsi/ *noun* (*pl.* **bu·reauc·ra·cies**) **1** [C,U] a system of government by a large number of officials in various departments **2** [U] (often used in a critical way) the system of official rules that an organization has for doing sth, that people often think are too complicated: *With all the bureaucracy involved, it takes forever to get a visa.*

bu·reau·crat /ˈbyʊrəkræt/ *noun* [C] (often used in a critical way) an official in an organization or in a government department

bu·reau·crat·ic /ˌbyʊrəˈkrætɪk/ *adj.* connected with a bureaucracy, especially when it follows official rules too closely: *a complex bureaucratic procedure*

burg·er /ˈbərgər/ *noun* [C] = HAMBURGER

-burger /ˈbərgər/ (in compounds) **1** a hamburger with sth else on top: *a cheeseburger* **2** something that is cooked like and looks like a hamburger, but is made of sth else: *a fishburger*

bur·glar /ˈbərglər/ *noun* [C] a person who enters a building illegally in order to steal: *The burglars broke in by smashing a window.* ☛ Look at the note at **thief**.

ˈ**burglar a₁larm** *noun* [C] a piece of equipment, usually fastened on a wall, that makes a loud noise if a thief enters a building

bur·glar·ize /ˈbərgləraɪz/ *verb* [T] to enter a building illegally in order to steal from it: *Our house was burglarized while we were out.*

bur·gla·ry /ˈbərgləri/ *noun* [C,U] (*pl.* **bur·glaries**) the crime of entering a building illegally in order to steal: *There was a burglary at the house next door last week.* ○ *He is in prison for burglary.*

bur·i·al /ˈbɛriəl/ *noun* [C,U] the ceremony when a dead body is put in the ground (**buried**): *The burial took place on Friday.* ○ *The victims of the disaster were flown home for burial.* ☛ Look at the note at **funeral**.

bur·ly /ˈbərli/ *adj.* (used about a person, usually a man, or sb's body) strong and heavy

☆ **burn**¹ /bərn/ *verb* (*p.t., p.p.* **burned** /bərnd/ or **burnt** /bərnt/) **1** [T] to destroy, damage or injure sb/sth with fire or heat: *People who live in town aren't allowed to burn their trash.* ○ *It was a terrible fire and the whole building was burned to the ground* (= was completely destroyed). ○ *The water was so hot that I burned my hands.* ○ *The people inside the building were all burned to death.* **2** [I] to be destroyed, damaged or injured by fire or heat: *If you leave the cake in the oven for much longer, it will burn.* ○ *I can't spend too much time in the sun because I burn easily.* **3** [T] to produce a hole or mark in or on sth by burning: *He dropped his cigarette and it burned a hole in the carpet.* **4** [I] to be on fire: *Firemen raced to the burning building.* **5** [I] to produce light: *I don't think he went to bed at all – I could see his light burning all night.* **6** [I] to feel unpleasantly hot: *You must have a temperature – your forehead's burning.* **7** [I] **burn (with sth)** to be filled with a very strong feeling: *She was burning with indignation.*

PHRV **burn (sth) down** (used about a building) to destroy or be destroyed completely by fire: *The fire could not be brought under control and the school burned down.*

burn (sb/yourself) out to use all your energy or ruin your health, especially by working too hard over a long period of time: *You're going*

to burn yourself out if you don't stop working so hard. ○ She burned out on drugs.

burn sth out (usually passive) to completely destroy sth by burning: the burnt-out wreck of a car

burn up to be destroyed by fire or strong heat: The space capsule burned up when it entered the earth's atmosphere.

burn sth up to destroy sth by fire: She burned up all the letters from her former boyfriend.

burn² /bərn/ noun [C] an injury or piece of damage caused by fire or heat: He has been treated for burns to his face and hands. ○ the burn unit of a hospital

burn·er /'bərnər/ noun [C] one of the round parts on the top of a stove, on which you can put pans ☞ picture at **stove**.

IDM **on the back burner** ⇨ BACK²

burnt¹ p.t., p.p. of BURN¹

burnt² /bərnt/ adj. that has been burned: burnt toast

burp /bərp/ verb [I] to make a noise with the mouth when air rises from the stomach and is forced out: He sat back when he had finished his meal and burped loudly. —**burp** noun [C]: a loud burp

bur·row¹ /'bərou/ noun [C] a hole in the ground made by certain animals (e.g. rabbits) in which they live

bur·row² /'bərou/ verb 1 [I,T] to dig a hole in the ground 2 [I] to search for sth, using your hands as if you were digging: She burrowed in her purse for her keys.

☆ **burst¹** /bərst/ verb (p.t., p.p. **burst**) 1 [I,T] to break open suddenly and violently, usually because there is too much pressure inside; to cause this to happen: My shopping bag burst as I was leaving the grocery store. ○ You'll burst that balloon if you blow it up any more. ○ The balloon burst with a loud bang. [I] (figurative) "Would you like some more to eat?" "No, thanks. If I have any more, I'll burst!" ○ If it rains much more, the river will burst its banks. 2 [I] **burst (with sth)** (only in the -ing forms) to be so full that it is in danger of breaking open: I packed so many clothes that my suitcases were bursting. ○ (figurative) He was bursting with happiness on his wedding day.

PHRV **burst in on sb/sth** to interrupt sb/sth by arriving suddenly: I'm sorry to burst in on you like this, but there's an urgent phone call.

burst into sth to start doing sth suddenly: On hearing the news she burst into tears (= started crying). ○ The truck hit a wall and burst into flames (= started burning).

burst into, out of, through, etc. to move suddenly in a particular direction, often using force: She burst into the manager's office and demanded to speak to him.

burst out 1 to start doing sth suddenly: He looked so ridiculous that I burst out laughing. **2** to say sth suddenly and with strong feeling: Finally she burst out, "I can't stand it anymore!"

burst² /bərst/ noun [C] **1** an occasion when sth bursts or explodes; a crack caused by an explosion: a burst in a water pipe **2** a short period of a particular activity, that often starts suddenly: With a burst of speed, she left the other runners behind. ○ He prefers to work in short bursts. ○ There were several bursts of applause during her speech.

☆ **bur·y** /'bɛri/ verb [T] (pres. part. **bur·y·ing**; 3rd pers. sing. pres. **bur·ies**; p.t., p.p. **bur·ied**) **1** to put a dead body in a grave: She wants to be buried next to her mother. ○ Abraham Lincoln is buried in Springfield, Illinois. **2** to put sth in a hole in the ground to cover it up: Our dog always buries its bones in the yard. ○ All kinds of dangerous materials are buried in garbage dumps. **3** (usually passive) to cover or hide: At last I found the picture, buried at the bottom of a drawer. ○ The state was buried under a foot of snow after yesterday's blizzard. ○ (figurative) Sally's always got her nose buried in a book.

IDM **bury the hatchet** to end a period of being enemies and become friendly: It's time to bury the hatchet and start working together.

☆ **bus¹** /bʌs/ noun [C] (pl. **bus·es**) a big public vehicle that takes passengers from one place to another along a fixed route: to get on/off the bus ○ We'll have to hurry up if we want to catch the 9 o'clock bus. ○ It's too difficult to park your car downtown. It's better to take the bus. ○ I ride the bus to work every day.

☞ You can get on or off a local bus at a **bus stop**. Large cities also have **bus stations** where you can get on a bus to another city. You need to pay the exact **fare** in coins when you get on a city bus. Most **school buses** are orange. Students can ride them to and from school without paying a fare. Note that we travel **by bus** or **on the bus**: "How do you get to work?" "On the bus."

bus² /bʌs/ verb [T] (pres. part. **bus·ing** or **bus·sing**; 3rd pers. sing. pres. **bus·es** or **bus·ses**; p.t., p.p. **bused** or **bussed**) to transport sb by bus: The passengers were bused from the airport terminal to the plane. ○ The city plans to bus students from inner-city neighborhoods to schools in the suburbs.

☞ In many large cities, students are bused to schools that are far away from their own neighborhoods so that students from different races can go to school together.

☆ **bush¹** /bʊʃ/ noun **1** [C] a plant like a small, thick tree with many low branches: a rose bush ○ The house was surrounded by thick bushes. **2** often **the bush** [U, sing.] wild land that is not cultivated, especially in Africa and Australia

IDM **beat around the bush** ⇨ BEAT¹

bush·y /ˈbʊʃi/ (**bush·i·er**; **bush·i·est**) *adj.* growing thickly: *bushy hair* ◦ *bushy eyebrows*

bus·i·er, bus·i·est, bus·i·ly ⇨ BUSY¹

☆**busi·ness** /ˈbɪznəs/ *noun* **1** [U] buying and selling as a way of earning money: *She's interested in a career in international business.* ◦ *They are very easy to do business with.* ◦ *He teaches English for Business.* **2** [U] the work that you do as your job: *The manager will be away on business next week.* ◦ *a business trip* **3** [U] the amount of goods and services that are bought and sold: *Business has been good for this time of year.* **4** [C] a company, a store, a factory, etc. that produces or sells goods or provides a service: *She started a marketing business of her own.* ◦ *Small businesses are finding it hard to survive these days.* **5** [U] something that concerns a particular person: *The friends I choose are my business, not yours.* ◦ *Our business is to collect the information, not to comment on it.* ◦ *"How much did it cost?" "It's none of your business!"* (= I don't want to tell you. It's private.) **6** [sing.] a situation or an event: *The divorce was a messy business.* ◦ *I found the whole business very depressing.*

IDM get down to business to start the work that must be done: *Let's just have a cup of coffee before we get down to business.*

go out of business to have to close because there is no more money available: *The store went out of business because it couldn't compete with the new shopping mall.*

have no business doing sth to have no right to do sth: *You have no business reading my letters without asking me.*

mind your own business ⇨ MIND²

ˈ**business adminiˌstration** *noun* [U] the study of how to control and manage a business (4): *She's studying for a master's degree in business administration.*

busi·ness·like /ˈbɪznəslaɪk/ *adj.* efficient and practical: *She has a very businesslike manner.*

☆**busi·ness·man** /ˈbɪznəsmæn/ (*also* **busi·ness·wom·an** /ˈbɪznəswʊmən/) *noun* [C] (*pl.* **busi·ness·men** /-mən/, **busi·ness·wom·en** /-wɪmən/) **1** a person who works in business (1), especially in a top position **2** a person who is skillful at dealing with money: *My brother can advise you on your investments – he's a better businessman than I am.*

bust¹ /bʌst/ *noun* [C] **1** a model in stone, etc. of a person's head, shoulders and chest **2** a woman's breasts; the measurement around a woman's chest: *That style of blouse doesn't look good on someone with a big bust.* **3** an act of arresting sb by the police, etc.: *a drug bust*

bust² /bʌst/ *verb* [I,T] (*informal*) to break or damage sth so that it cannot be used

bust³ /bʌst/ *adj.*

IDM go bust (*informal*) (used about a business) to have to close because it has lost so much money: *During the recession, thousands of businesses went bust.*

bus·tle¹ /ˈbʌsl/ *verb* [I] **bustle (with sth)** to be full of sth (people, noise, activity, etc.): *It was the week before Christmas and the streets were bustling with shoppers.*

bus·tle² /ˈbʌsl/ *noun* [U] excited and noisy activity: *She loved the hustle and bustle of city life.*

☆**bus·y¹** /ˈbɪzi/ *adj.* (**bus·i·er**; **bus·i·est**) **1 busy (at/with sth); busy (doing sth)** having a lot of work or tasks to do; not free; working on sth: *Mr. Smith is busy until 4 o'clock, but he could see you after that.* ◦ *Don't disturb him. He's busy.* ◦ *She's busy with her preparations for the party.* ◦ *We're busy decorating the guest room before our visitors arrive.* **2** (used about a period of time) full of activity and things to do: *I've had a pretty busy week.* **3** (used about a place) full of people, movement and activity: *Main Street was so busy that I could hardly move.* **4** (used about a telephone) in use: *The line's busy right now. I'll try again later.* ◦ *a busy signal*

IDM get busy start working: *We'll have to get busy if we're going to be ready in time.* —**bus·i·ly** /ˈbɪzəli/ *adv.*: *When I came in she was busily writing something at her desk.*

bus·y² /ˈbɪzi/ *verb* [T] (*pres. part.* **bus·y·ing**; *3rd pers. sing. pres.* **bus·ies**; *p.t., p.p.* **bus·ied**) **busy yourself with sth; busy yourself doing sth** to keep yourself busy; to find sth to do

bus·y·work /ˈbɪziwərk/ *noun* [U] (*informal*) work that has no real purpose and that is just supposed to keep sb busy

☆**but¹** /bət; *strong form* bʌt/ *conj.* **1** (used for introducing an idea that contrasts with or is different from what has just been said): *The weather will be sunny but cold.* ◦ *Theirs is not the first but the second house on the left.* ◦ *James doesn't have a car, but his sister does.* **2** however; and yet: *She's been studying Italian for five years, but she doesn't speak it very well.* ◦ *I'd love to come, but I can't make it until 8 o'clock.* **3** (used with an apology): *I'm sorry, but I can't stay any longer.* **4** (used for introducing a statement that shows that you are surprised or annoyed or that you disagree): *"Here's the money I owe you." "But that's not right – it was only $6."*

IDM but then (again) ⇨ THEN

☆**but²** /bət; *strong form* bʌt/ *prep.* except: *I haven't told anyone but you about this.* ◦ *We've had nothing but trouble with this washing machine!*

IDM but for sb/sth (*formal*) except for or without sb/sth: *We wouldn't have managed but for your help.*

butch·er /ˈbʊtʃər/ *noun* [C] **1** a person who sells meat: *The butcher cut me four lamb chops.* ◦ *She went to the butcher shop for some*

i	ɪ	ɛ	æ	ɑ	ɔ	ʌ	ʊ	u
see	sit	ten	cat	hot	saw	cup	put	too

sausages. **2** a person who kills many people in a cruel way

but·ler /ˈbʌtlər/ *noun* [C] the most important male servant in a big house, especially in former times

☆**butt¹** /bʌt/ *noun* [C] **1** (*informal*) the part of your body that you sit on: *Get up off your butt and do some work! ○ I took two steps on the ice and fell right on my butt. ○ Get your butt in here* (= come in here) *right now!* **2** a person who is often laughed at or talked about in an unkind way: *Fat children are often the butt of other children's jokes.* **3** the thicker, heavier end of a gun: *the butt of a rifle* **4** a short piece of a cigarette or cigar that is left when it has been smoked

butt² /bʌt/ *verb* [T] to hit or push sb/sth with the head

PHRV **butt in (on sb/sth)** (*informal*) to interrupt sb/sth or to join in sth without being asked: *You shouldn't butt in like that when somebody else is talking.*

butt out (*informal*) to stop interfering in other people's affairs: *I'm talking to Molly about something personal, so just butt out, Jerry!*

☆**but·ter¹** /ˈbʌtər/ *noun* [U] a soft yellow fat that is made from cream and is put on bread, etc. or used in cooking: *Would you rather have butter or margarine? ○ First, melt a little butter in the pan.*

but·ter² /ˈbʌtər/ *verb* [T] to spread butter on bread, etc.: *I'll slice the bread and you butter it. ○ hot buttered toast*

butterfly　　　　　　moth

but·ter·fly /ˈbʌtərflaɪ/ *noun* [C] (*pl.* **but·ter·flies**) an insect with a long, thin body and four brightly colored wings: *Caterpillars develop into butterflies.*

IDM **to have butterflies (in your stomach)** (*informal*) to feel very nervous before doing sth

but·ter·milk /ˈbʌtərmɪlk/ *noun* [U] the liquid that is left when butter has been separated from milk

but·tock /ˈbʌtək/ *noun* [C, usually pl.] (*formal*) one of the two parts of the body which you sit on ☞ Look at **bun** (3).

☆**but·ton¹** /ˈbʌtn/ *noun* [C] **1** a small, often round, piece of plastic, wood or metal that you use for fastening your clothes: *One of the buttons on my jacket came off. ○ a coat, shirt, etc. button ○ This blouse is too tight. I can't fasten the buttons.* ☞ picture at **zipper**. **2** a small part of a machine, etc. that you press in order to operate sth: *Press this button to ring the bell. ○ Which button turns the volume down? ○ the buttons on a telephone ○ Position the cursor where you want it and click with the left mouse button.* ☞ picture at **telephone**. **3** a round, flat piece of plastic or metal with pictures, etc. on it that people fasten to their clothes: *The volunteers gave out campaign buttons with the candidate's picture on them. ○ She was wearing a button that said "Have a nice day."* ☞ Look also at **bellybutton**.

but·ton² /ˈbʌtn/ *verb* [T] **button sth (up)** to fasten sth with buttons¹(1) : *He buttoned up his coat.* ☞ The opposite is **unbutton**.

but·ton·hole /ˈbʌtnhoʊl/ *noun* [C] a hole in a piece of clothing that you push a button ¹(1) through in order to fasten it ☞ picture at **zipper**.

☆**buy¹** /baɪ/ *verb* [T] (*p.t., p.p.* **bought** /bɔt/) **1** to get sth by paying money for it: *I'm going to buy a new dress for the party. ○ We bought this book for you in New York. ○ Can I buy you a cup of coffee? ○ He bought the car from a friend. ○ Did you buy this sofa new? ○ He bought the necklace as a present for his wife. ○* (*figurative*) *They made excuses in order to buy time* (= to gain extra time to finish the project). **2** (*informal*) to believe sth: *The boss is never going to buy that excuse!*

PHRV **buy sth up** to buy all or as much as possible of sth: *Foreign investors have bought up most of the real estate in the area.*

buy² /baɪ/ *noun* [C] an act of buying sth or a thing that you can buy: *I think your house was a very good buy* (= worth the money that you paid).

☆**buy·er** /ˈbaɪər/ *noun* [C] **1** a person who is buying sth or may buy sth: *I think we've found a buyer for our house!* **2** a person whose job is to choose and buy goods that are to be sold in a large store

buy·out /ˈbaɪaʊt/ *noun* [C] an act of getting control of a company by buying all of it or a big enough part of it: *Rumors of a possible buyout caused the company's stock price to rise.*

buzz¹ /bʌz/ *verb* [I] to make the sound that bees, etc. make when flying: *A large fly was buzzing against the window.*

buzz² /bʌz/ *noun* **1** [C] the sound that a bee, etc. makes when flying: *the buzz of insects* **2** [sing.] the low sound made by many people talking at the same time: *I could hear the buzz of conversation in the next room.*

buzz·er /ˈbʌzər/ *noun* [C] a piece of equipment that makes a buzzing sound: *Press the buzzer in the lobby and I'll let you in.*

☆**by¹** /baɪ/ *adv.* **1** past: *We stopped to let the ambulance get by. ○ If we sit here, we can watch the boats sail by. ○ Time seemed to be going by very slowly.* **2** near: *There's a nice restaurant close by.*

IDM **by and large** ⇨ LARGE¹

☆ **by²** /baɪ/ *prep.* **1** beside; very near: *Come and sit by me.* ○ *We stayed at a resort by the ocean.* **2** past: *He walked straight by me without speaking.* **3** not later than; before: *I'll be home by 7 o'clock.* ○ *He should have called by now/by this time.* ○ *By this time tomorrow, you'll be married!* **4** (usually without *the*) during a period of time; in particular circumstances: *She attends classes by day and works as a waitress by night.* ○ *The power went off, so we had to work by candlelight.* **5** (after a passive verb) (used for showing who or what did or caused sth): *He was hit by a car.* ○ *The event was organized by local people.* ○ *I was deeply shocked by the news.* ○ *The building was designed by Frank Lloyd Wright.* ○ *Who was the book written by?/Who is the book by?* **6** through doing sth: *You can get hold of me by calling this number.* **7** using sth: *Will you be paying by check?* ○ *The house is heated by electricity.* ○ *"How do you go to work?" "By bus, usually."* ○ *by bus, car, plane, bicycle, etc.* **8** as a result of; due to: *I went to the wrong house by mistake/accident.* ○ *I met an old friend by chance.* **9** according to: *It's 8 o'clock by my watch.* ○ *By law you have to attend school from the age of five.* **10** (used for multiplying or dividing): *4 multiplied by 5 is 20.* ○ *6 divided by 2 is 3.* **11** (used for showing the measurements of an area): *The table is six feet by three feet* (= six feet long and three feet wide). **12** (with *the*) in quantities or periods of: *Gasoline is sold by the gallon.* ○ *I get paid by the hour.* ○ *Copies of the book have sold by the million.* **13** in groups or units of: *They came in one by one.* ○ *Workers cleared away the debris piece by piece.* ○ *Day by day she was getting better.* **14** to the amount of: *Prices have gone up by 10 percent.* ○ *I missed the bus by a few minutes.* **15** (used with a part of the body or an article of clothing) holding: *He grabbed me by the arm.* **16** with regard to: *She's French by birth.* ○ *He's a doctor by profession.* ○ *By nature she's a very gentle person.*

IDM by the way (used for adding sth to the conversation) on a new subject: *Oh, by the way, I saw Cindy downtown yesterday.*

bye /baɪ/ (*also* **bye-bye** /ˈbaɪbaɪ; ˌbaɪˈbaɪ/) *interj.* (*informal*) goodbye: *Bye! See you tomorrow.*

by·pass¹ /ˈbaɪpæs/ *noun* [C] **1** a road that traffic can use to go around a city, instead of through it **2** a medical operation to create a new passage for blood to flow through, especially near the heart: *to have heart bypass surgery*

by·pass² /ˈbaɪpæs/ *verb* [T] to go around or to avoid sth using a bypass¹(1) : *Let's try to bypass the downtown area.* ○ (*figurative*) *It's no good trying to bypass the problem.*

by·prod·uct (*also* **by-product**) /ˈbaɪprɑdʌkt/ *noun* [C] **1** something that is formed during the making of sth else **2** something that happens as the result of sth else

by·stand·er /ˈbaɪstændər/ *noun* [C] a person who is standing near and sees sth that happens, without being involved in it: *Several innocent bystanders were hurt when the two gangs attacked each other.*

byte /baɪt/ *noun* [C] (*computing*) a unit of information that can represent one item, such as a letter or a number. A byte usually consists of a series of eight smaller units (**bits**). ☞ Look at **megabyte**.

Cc

C, c /si/ *noun* [C] (*pl.* **C's; c's** /siz/) **1** the third letter of the English alphabet: *"Come" begins with (a) "C."* **2** a grade that is given for a test or a piece of work that is average in quality. A "C" is lower than a "B": *I got a "C" on my essay.*

c. *abbr.* cup; cups: *Add 2 c. flour and mix well.*

cab /kæb/ *noun* [C] **1** = TAXI¹: *Let's take a cab home.* **2** the part of a truck, etc. where the driver sits

cab·a·ret /ˌkæbəˈreɪ/ *noun* [C,U] an entertainment with singing, dancing, etc. in a restaurant or nightclub

☆ **cab·bage** /ˈkæbɪdʒ/ *noun* [C,U] a large round vegetable with thick green, or sometimes dark

cabbage cauliflower

Brussels sprouts broccoli

red leaves, often eaten cooked: *We're growing cabbages in the garden.* ○ *a head of cabbage*

cab·in /ˈkæbən/ *noun* [C] **1** a small wooden house in the country: *a log cabin in the woods*

ər	ɪr	ɛr	ɑr	ɔr	ʊr	ʒ	h	ŋ
bird	near	hair	car	north	tour	vision	hat	sing

2 one of the parts of an airplane, at the front or where the passengers sit: *A member of the cabin crew will be happy to help you.* ○ *the first-class cabin* **3** a small room on a ship or boat, where a passenger sleeps: *Phil had to stay in our cabin for most of the cruise because he was seasick.*

☆ **cab·i·net** /ˈkæbənət/ *noun* [C] **1** an object like a box with shelves or drawers, used for storing things: *a medicine cabinet* ○ *kitchen cabinets* ○ *a filing cabinet* **2** (*also* usually **the Cabinet**) the most important leaders of departments in the government, who have regular meetings with the President: *The President is meeting with his Cabinet today to discuss the crisis.* ○ *a cabinet meeting, member, etc.*

☆ **ca·ble** /ˈkeɪbl/ *noun* **1** [C] a very strong, thick rope or chain, etc. **2** [C,U] a set of wires covered with plastic, etc. for carrying electricity or signals: *a telephone cable* ○ *underground electrical cable* **3** [C] (*old-fashioned*) = TELEGRAM **4** [U] = CABLE TELEVISION

ˈ**cable car** *noun* [C] a vehicle that runs on tracks and is pulled by a moving cable (1): *We took a ride on a cable car in San Francisco.*

ˌ**cable ˈtelevision** (*also* ˌ**cable TˈV**; **cable**) *noun* [U] a system of sending television programs by cable (2), which you have to pay for every month

cack·le /ˈkækl/ *noun* [C] **1** the loud sound that a chicken makes after laying an egg **2** a loud, unpleasant laugh —**cack·le** *verb* [I]

cac·tus /ˈkæktəs/ *noun* [C] (*pl.* **cac·ti** /ˈkæktaɪ/ or **cac·tus·es**) a type of plant that grows in hot, dry areas, especially deserts. A cactus has a thick stem and sharp points (**spines**) but no leaves.

cactus

ca·det /kəˈdɛt/ *noun* [C] a young person who is training to be in the military forces or the police

Cae·sar·e·an sec·tion *noun* [C] = CESAREAN SECTION

☆ **ca·fé** (*also* **cafe**) /kəˈfeɪ; kæ-/ *noun* [C] a small restaurant that serves drinks and light meals

☆ **caf·e·te·ri·a** /ˌkæfəˈtɪriə/ *noun* [C] a type of restaurant where people choose individual items of food and carry them to their tables: *the school cafeteria*

caf·feine /kæˈfin/ *noun* [U] the substance found in coffee and tea that makes you feel more awake and lively ☞ Look at **decaffeinated**.

☆ **cage** /keɪdʒ/ *noun* [C] a box made of bars or wire, or a space surrounded by wire or metal bars, in which a bird or animal is kept so that

it cannot escape: *The parrot escaped from its cage.* —**caged** /keɪdʒd/ *adj.*: *He felt like a caged animal in the tiny office.*

cake muffin cupcake crackers doughnut (*also* donut) cookies

☆ **cake¹** /keɪk/ *noun* **1** [C,U] a sweet food made by mixing flour, eggs, butter, sugar, etc. together and baking the mixture in the oven: *a birthday cake* ○ *a wedding cake* ○ *a chocolate cake* ○ *a fruit cake* ○ *The bride and groom cut the cake.* ○ *Would you like some more cake?* ○ *a piece of birthday cake*

☞ After **making** or **baking** a cake we often **frost** or **ice** the top and sides of it.

2 [C] a mixture of other food, cooked in a round, flat shape: *fish cakes* ○ *rice cakes*

IDM **have your cake and eat it too** to enjoy the advantages of sth without its disadvantages; to have both things that are available: *Rick thinks he can stay out late every night and still get good grades – he wants to have his cake and eat it too.*

a piece of cake ⇨ PIECE¹

cake² /keɪk/ *verb* [T] (usually passive) to cover sth thickly with a substance that becomes hard when it dries: *boots caked in/with mud*

ca·lam·i·ty /kəˈlæməti/ *noun* [C,U] (*pl.* **ca·lam·i·ties**) a terrible event that causes a lot of damage or harm

cal·ci·um /ˈkælsiəm/ *noun* [U] (*symbol* **Ca**) a chemical substance that is found in foods such as milk and cheese and that helps to make bones and teeth strong

☆ **cal·cu·late** /ˈkælkyəleɪt/ *verb* [T] **1** to find sth out by using mathematics: *I've been calculating the costs involved and it's too expensive.* ○ *It's difficult to calculate how long the project will take.* **2** to consider or expect sth: *We calculated that the advantages would be greater than the disadvantages.*

cal·cu·lat·ed /ˈkælkyəleɪtəd/ *adj.* done on purpose, with careful planning: *a calculated attempt to damage his opponent's reputation*

IDM **be calculated to do sth** to be intended or designed to do sth: *His remark was clearly calculated to annoy me.*

cal·cu·la·tion /ˌkælkyəˈleɪʃn/ *noun* **1** [C,U] finding an answer by using mathematics: *Several of his calculations are wrong.* ○ *Calculation of the exact cost is impossible.* **2** [U] (*formal*) careful thought and planning in

order to achieve your own, selfish aims: *His actions were clearly the result of deliberate calculation.*

cal·cu·la·tor /ˈkælkyəleɪtər/ *noun* [C] a small electronic machine that is used for calculating figures: *a pocket calculator*

☆ **cal·en·dar** /ˈkæləndər/ *noun* [C] **1** a list, often in the form of a book, that shows the days, weeks and months of a particular year: *She had circled the important dates on her calendar in red.* ○ *There was a calendar hanging on the back of the door.* ○ *I'll write that down in my appointment calendar.* **2** a system for dividing time into fixed periods and for marking the beginning and end of a year: *the Muslim calendar* ○ *Our school's academic calendar is divided into four quarters.* **3** a list of dates and events in a year that are important in a particular area of activity: *The party's convention is a major event on the campaign calendar.*

calendar year *noun* [C] = YEAR(2)

calf /kæf/ *noun* [C] (*pl.* **calves** /kævz/) **1** a young cow ☞ The meat from a calf is called **veal**. Look at the note at **meat** and at the picture at **cow**. **2** the young of some other animals, e.g. elephants **3** the back of your leg, below your knee ☞ picture on page A24.

cal·i·ber /ˈkæləbər/ *noun* **1** [C, usually sing.] the width of the inside of a tube, especially the long tube (**barrel**) of a gun: *a .22 caliber rifle* **2** [sing., U] the quality or ability of a person or thing: *The company's employees are of the highest caliber.*

☆ **call¹** /kɔl/ *noun* **1** [C] a loud sound that is made to attract attention; a shout: *a call for help* ○ *That bird's call is easy to recognize.* **2** (*also* **phone call**) [C] an act of telephoning or a conversation on the telephone: *Were there any calls for me while I was out?* ○ *I'll give you a call this weekend.* ○ *The manager is on line 2. Will you take the call?* ○ *a local call* ○ *a long-distance call* **3** [C] a short visit, especially to the house or business of a customer: *Doctors used to make house calls when people were sick.* ○ *I'm sorry, but the technician is out on a call right now.* **4** [C] a request, demand for sth: *There have been calls for the President to resign.* **5** [C,U] **call for sth** a need for sth: *The doctor said there was no call for concern.*

IDM a close call/shave ⇨ CLOSE¹

(be) on call (to be) ready to work if necessary: *Dr. Young will be on call this weekend.*

☆ **call²** /kɔl/ *verb* **1** [I,T] **call (out) to sb; call (sth) (out)** to say sth loudly or to shout in order to attract attention: *"Hello, is anybody there?" she called.* ○ *I could hear a voice calling for help.* ○ *He called out the names and the winners stepped forward.* ○ *Call the kids. Breakfast is ready.* **2** [I,T] to telephone (sb/sth):] *Who's calling, please?* ○ *Thank you for calling.* ○ *I'll call you tomorrow.* ○ *We're right in the middle of dinner. Can I call you back later?*

3 be called to have as a name: *This type of apple is called "Golden Delicious."* ○ *What was that town called?* **4** [T] to name or describe a person or thing in a certain way: *My name is Elizabeth, but my friends call me Liz.* ○ *Can you really call this picture "art"?* ○ *It was mean to call her fat.* ○ *Are you calling me a liar?* **5** [T] to order or ask sb to come to a certain place: *Can you call everybody in for lunch?* ○ *The President called his advisers to the White House.* ○ *I think we had better call the doctor.* **6** [T] to arrange for sth to take place at a certain time: *to call a meeting, an election, a strike, etc.*

IDM call it a day (*informal*) to decide to stop doing sth: *Let's call it a day. I'm exhausted.*

call it quits (*informal*) to decide to stop doing sth: *We finally called it quits when it started raining.*

call/draw sb's attention to sth ⇨ ATTENTION

PHRV call for sth to demand or need: *Critics of the senator are calling for her to resign.* ○ *The crisis calls for immediate action.* ○ *This calls for a celebration!* ○ *His nasty comment was not called for* (= there was no need for it).

call sb in to ask sb to come and help you: *I can't figure out what's wrong with the copier – we'd better call in the technician.*

call sth off to cancel sth: *The baseball game was called off because of rain.*

call on sb to ask sb to speak or answer a question: *I just hope the teacher doesn't call on me – I forgot to read the assignment!*

call sb out to ask or tell sb to go somewhere: *The police were called out to control the riot.*

call sb up 1 to telephone sb: *She called me up to tell me the good news.* **2** to order the army, etc. to go somewhere and work, fight, etc.: *Twenty National Guard units have been called up to help fight the forest fires.*

call sth up to look at sth that is stored in a computer: *The bank teller can call up your balance on screen.*

call·er /ˈkɔlər/ *noun* [C] a person who telephones sb: *I don't know who the caller was. He hung up without giving his name.*

call-in show (*also* **call-in program**) *noun* [C] a radio or television program during which you can ask a question or give your opinion by telephone: *a live radio call-in show*

cal·lous /ˈkæləs/ *adj.* not caring about the suffering of other people

☆ **calm¹** /kɑm/ *adj.* **1** not worried or angry; quiet: *Try to stay calm – there's no need to panic.* ○ *She spoke in a calm voice.* ○ *The city is calm again after last night's riots.* **2** without big waves: *a calm sea* **3** without much wind: *calm weather* —**calm·ly** *adv.*: *Len told the police very calmly exactly what he had seen.* —**calm·ness** *noun* [U]

calm² /kɑm/ *noun* [U, sing.] a period of time or a state when everything is peaceful: *Attacks were reported after months of relative calm.*

i	ɪ	ɛ	æ	ɑ	ɔ	ʌ	ʊ	u
see	sit	ten	cat	hot	saw	cup	put	too

calm³ /kɑm/ *verb* [I,T] **calm (sb/sth) (down)** to become or to make sb quiet or calm: *Calm down! Shouting at everybody won't help.* ○ *She calmed the horses by talking quietly to them.* ○ *He read the kids a story to calm them down.*

☆ **cal·o·rie** /ˈkæləri/ *noun* [C] **1** a unit for measuring the energy that a certain amount of food will produce **2** a unit for measuring heat

calves *pl.* of CALF

cam·cord·er /ˈkæmkɔrdər/ *noun* [C] a camera that you can carry with you and use to record pictures and sound on a video cassette

came *p.t.* of COME

hump camel

☆ **cam·el** /ˈkæml/ *noun* **1** [C] an animal that lives in the desert and has a long neck and either one or two humps on its back. It is used for carrying people and goods. **2** [U] a light brown color

viewfinder flash camera

lens film speed

camera roll of film

☆ **cam·er·a** /ˈkæmrə; -ərə/ *noun* [C] a piece of equipment that you use for taking photographs or moving pictures: *I need more film for my camera.* ○ *a security camera in a bank* ○ *a TV camera* ○ *a video camera*

cam·er·a·man /ˈkæmrəmæn/ *noun* [C] (*pl.* **cam·er·a·men**) a man whose job is to operate a camera for a movie or a television company

☞ Nowadays it is also common to say **camera operator**, especially if the person is a woman.

cam·ou·flage¹ /ˈkæməflɑʒ/ *noun* [U] materials or colors that soldiers use to make themselves and their equipment less easy to see

cam·ou·flage² /ˈkæməflɑʒ/ *verb* [T] to make sb/sth difficult to see in a particular place

☆ **camp** /kæmp/ *noun* [C,U] a place where people live in tents or small houses for a short time: *a summer camp* ○ *a Boy Scout camp* ○ *a training camp* (= for soldiers) ○ *We returned to camp tired after our long hike.* ○ *The climbers set up camp at the foot of the mountain.*

camp² /kæmp/ *verb* [I] **camp (out)** to sleep outdoors, especially in a tent: *The kids like to camp out in the back yard.*

☞ **Go camping** is a common way of talking about camping for pleasure: *They went camping in Colorado last year.*

☆ **cam·paign¹** /kæmˈpeɪn/ *noun* [C] **1** a plan to do a number of things in order to achieve a special aim: *an advertising campaign* ○ *Bill Clinton's presidential campaign* (= his campaign to be elected President) **2** a planned series of attacks in a war

cam·paign² /kæmˈpeɪn/ *verb* [I] **campaign (for/against sb/sth)** to take part in a campaign¹(1) in order to make sth happen or to prevent sth: *She campaigned for Bill Clinton in the 1996 election.* —**cam·paign·er** *noun* [C]: *a campaigner for equal rights for women*

camp·er /ˈkæmpər/ *noun* [C] **1** a person who camps **2** a large vehicle in which you can sleep, cook, etc. and that you can drive around while you are on vacation, or a similar vehicle that can be pulled by a car or small truck ☞ Look also at **trailer** (2) and **RV**.

camp·ground /ˈkæmpgraʊnd/ (*also* **camp·site** /ˈkæmpsaɪt/) *noun* [C] a place where you can camp

camp·ing /ˈkæmpɪŋ/ *noun* [U] sleeping or spending a vacation in a tent: *Camping is cheaper than staying in hotels.* ○ *a camping trip*

☆ **cam·pus** /ˈkæmpəs/ *noun* [C,U] (*pl.* **cam·pus·es**) the area of land where the main buildings of a college or university are: *the college campus* ○ *About half the students live on campus – most of the others have apartments off campus.*

☆ **can¹** /kən; *strong form* kæn/ *modal verb* (*negative* **can·not** /ˈkænɑt; kəˈnɑt/ *short form* **can't** /kænt/; *p.t.* **could** /kəd/ *strong form* /kʊd/; *negative* **could not** *short form* **could·n't** /ˈkʊdnt/) **1** (used for showing that it is possible for sb/sth to do sth or that sb/sth has the ability to do sth): *I can catch a bus from here.* ○ *Can you ride a bike?* ○ *He can't speak French.* ○ *She couldn't answer the question.*

☞ **Can** has no infinitive or participle forms. To make the future and perfect tenses, we use **be able to**: *One day people will be able to travel to Mars.* ○ *He's been able to swim for almost a year.* **Could have** is used when we say that somebody had the ability to do something but did not do it: *She could have passed the test, but she didn't really try.*

2 (asking or giving permission): *Can I have a drink, please?* ○ *He asked if he could have a drink.* ○ *You can't go swimming today.*

☞ When we are talking about general permission in the past, **could** is used: *I could do anything I wanted when I stayed with my grandma.* When we are talking about one particular occasion, we do not use **could**: *They were allowed to visit him in the hospital*

yesterday. Some people do not like the use of **can** in questions asking permission to do something. They prefer to use **may**: *May I go to the bathroom?*

3 (asking sb to do sth): *Can you help me carry these books?* **4** (offering to do sth): *Can I help you find anything?* **5** (talking about sb's typical behavior or of a typical effect): *You can be really annoying sometimes.* ○ *Bee stings can be very painful.* **6** (used in the negative for saying that you are sure sth is not true): *That can't be the last slice of bread – I just bought a fresh loaf today.* ○ *You can't possibly be hungry. You only just had lunch.* **7** (used with the verbs "feel," "hear," "see," "smell," "taste")

☛ These verbs are not used in the continuous tenses. If we want to talk about seeing, hearing, etc. at a particular moment, we use **can**: *I can smell something burning.* NOT *I'm smelling…*

☆ **can²** /kæn/ *noun* [C] **1** a metal container for food that is sealed so that the food stays fresh: *a can of soup* ○ *a can of beer* ○ *an empty soda can* ○ *a can opener* ☛ picture at **container**. **2** a metal or plastic container that is used for holding or carrying liquid: *an oil can* ○ *a can of oil* ○ *a watering can*

can³ /kæn/ *verb* [T] (**can·ning**; **canned**) **1** to put food into a can in order to keep it fresh for a long time: *canned fruit* **2** (*informal*) to say that sb can no longer work for you (because of bad work, bad behavior, etc.): *Joe got canned from his job for stealing from the company.*

☆ **ca·nal** /kə'næl/ *noun* [C] a channel that is cut through land so that boats or ships can travel along it or so that water can flow to an area where it is needed: *the Panama Canal*

ca·nar·y /kə'nɛri/ *noun* [C] (*pl.* **ca·nar·ies**) a small yellow bird that sings and is often kept in a cage as a pet

☆ **can·cel** /'kænsl/ *verb* [T] (**can·cel·ing**; **can·celed** or **can·cel·ling**; **can·celled**) **1** to decide that sth that had been planned or arranged will not happen: *Because of the bad weather, the picnic was canceled.* ☛ Look at **postpone**. **2** to stop sth that you asked for or agreed to: *We need to cancel the reservation.* ○ *I would like to cancel my order for these books.*

PHRV cancel (sth) out to be equal or have an equal effect: *What I owe you is the same as what you owe me, so our debts cancel each other out.*

can·cel·la·tion (*also* **cancelation**) /ˌkænsə-'leɪʃn/ *noun* [C,U] the act of canceling sth: *After the snowstorm, we listened to the list of school cancellations on the radio.* ○ *The cancellation of the game was a great disappointment.*

Can·cer /'kænsər/ *noun* [C,U] the fourth sign of the zodiac, the Crab; a person who was born under this sign ☛ picture at **zodiac**.

☆ **can·cer** /'kænsər/ *noun* [C,U] a very serious disease in which lumps grow in the body in an uncontrolled way: *She has lung cancer.* ○ *He died of cancer.*

can·did /'kændəd/ *adj.* honest and open; saying exactly what you think ☛ The noun is **candor**. —**can·did·ly** *adv.*

can·di·da·cy /'kændədəsi/ *noun* [U] being a candidate

☆ **can·di·date** /'kændədət; -deɪt/ *noun* [C] a person who applies for a job or wants to be elected to or chosen for a particular position: *a candidate for President*

☆ **can·dle** /'kændl/ *noun* [C] a round stick of wax with a piece of string (**a wick**) through the middle that you can burn to give light: *to light/ blow out a candle*

candle
flame
wick
candle
candlestick

can·dle·light /'kændl·laɪt/ *noun* [U] the light that a candle produces: *They had dinner by candlelight.*

can·dle·stick /'kændlstɪk/ *noun* [C] a holder for a candle or candles

can·dor /'kændər/ *noun* [U] the quality of being honest; saying exactly what you think ☛ The adjective is **candid**.

☆ **can·dy** /'kændi/ *noun* [C,U] (*pl.* **can·dies**) (a small piece of) sweet food made with sugar or chocolate: *You eat too much candy.* ○ *a piece of candy*

☆ **'candy bar** *noun* [C] a piece of sweet food, usually made of or covered in chocolate, that is long and thin and that you buy wrapped in paper or plastic

cane /keɪn/ *noun* **1** [C] a stick that you use to lean on if you have difficulty walking: *My grandmother walks with a cane.* ☛ picture at **crutch**. **2** [C,U] the long, hollow stem of certain plants, such as the sugar plant

ca·nine /'keɪnaɪn/ *adj.* connected with dogs or like a dog

can·is·ter /'kænəstər/ *noun* [C] a small metal container

can·na·bis /'kænəbəs/ *noun* [U] (*formal*) a drug made from a plant (**hemp**) that some people smoke for pleasure, but that is illegal in many countries ☛ Look at **marijuana**.

can·ni·bal /'kænəbl/ *noun* [C] a person who eats other people —**can·ni·bal·ism** /-bəlɪzəm/ *noun* [U]

can·non /'kænən/ *noun* [C] (*pl.* **can·nons** or **can·non**) **1** a large old-fashioned gun that was used for firing stone or metal balls (**cannonballs**) **2** a large modern gun on a ship, tank, airplane, etc.

☆ **can·not** /'kænɑt; kə'nɑt/ = CAN NOT

ca·noe¹ /kə'nu/ *noun* [C] a light, narrow boat for one or two people that you can move

through the water using a flat piece of wood (**a paddle**) ☞ Look at **kayak**.

ca·noe² /kə¹nu/ *verb* [I] (*pres. part.* **ca·noe-ing**; *3rd pers. sing. pres.* **ca·noes**; *p.t., p.p.* **ca-noed**) to travel in a canoe ¹ ☞ We can say "He is learning to canoe" or "They canoed down the river," but when we are talking about spending time in a canoe, it is more usual to say **go canoeing**: *We're going canoeing on the Colorado River tomorrow.*

can·o·py /¹kænəpi/ *noun* [C] (*pl.* **can·o·pies**) a cover, often a piece of cloth, that hangs above sth: *a bed with a canopy over it*

can't *short for* CAN NOT

can·vas /¹kænvəs/ *noun* **1** [U] a type of strong cloth that is used for making tents, sails, bags, etc. **2** [C] a piece of canvas (1) for painting a picture on; the painting itself

can·vass /¹kænvəs/ *verb* **1** [T] to find out what people's opinions are about sth: *to canvass voters before an election* **2** [I,T] to go around an area trying to persuade people to vote for a particular person or political party in an election

can·yon /¹kænyən/ *noun* [C] a deep valley with very steep sides: *the Grand Canyon in Arizona*

caps

stocking cap baseball cap

☆ **cap¹** /kæp/ *noun* [C] **1** a type of soft hat: *a baseball cap* **2** a hat that is worn for a particular purpose: *a shower cap* **3** a covering for the end or top of sth: *Please put the cap back on the bottle.* ○ *Take the lens cap off before you take the picture!* ☞ Look at the note at **top¹**.

cap² /kæp/ *verb* [T] (**cap·ping**; **capped**) **1** to cover the top of sth: *mountains capped with snow* **2** to follow sth with sth bigger or better

ca·pa·bil·i·ty /ˌkeɪpə¹bɪləti/ *noun* [C,U] (*pl.* **ca·pa·bil·i·ties**) the quality of being able to do sth: *How many countries have nuclear capability?* (= have a nuclear bomb) ○ *People are often not aware of their own capabilities.*

☆ **ca·pa·ble** /¹keɪpəbl/ *adj.* **1** having a lot of skill; good at doing sth: *She's a very capable teacher.* ○ *We need a capable person to organize the concert.* **2 capable of (doing) sth** able to do sth; having the power to do sth: *He's capable of passing the test if he tries harder.* ○ *That car is capable of 180 miles per hour.* ○ *I do not believe that she's capable of stealing* (= she is not the sort of person who would steal). ☞ The opposite is **incapable**.

☆ **ca·pac·i·ty** /kə¹pæsəti/ *noun* (*pl.* **ca·pac·i·ties**) **1** [sing., U] the greatest amount that a

container or space can hold: *The gas tank has a capacity of 20 gallons.* ○ *The stadium was filled to capacity.* **2** [sing., U] the amount that a factory or machine can produce: *The power plant is working at full capacity.* **3** [sing.] **capacity (for sth)** the ability to understand or do sth: *He has the mental capacity of a three-year-old child.* **4** [C] the official position that a person has: *In his capacity as chairman of the committee, he approved the plan.*

cape /keɪp/ *noun* [C] **1** a piece of clothing with no sleeves that hangs from your shoulders **2** a piece of land that sticks out into the ocean: *the Cape of Good Hope*

☆ **cap·i·tal¹** /¹kæpətl̩/ *noun* **1** [C] the town or city where the government of a country or state is: *Madrid is the capital of Spain.* ○ *Minneapolis is the biggest city in Minnesota, but St. Paul is the state capital.* ☞ Look at **capitol**. **2** [C] (*also* **capital letter**) the large form of a letter that is used at the beginning of a name or sentence: *Write your name in capitals.* **3** [U] an amount of money that you use to start a business or to invest so that you earn more money on it: *When she had enough capital, she bought some new equipment.* ○ *The corporation has been trying to raise extra capital.*

cap·i·tal² /¹kæpətl̩/ *adj.* **1** (only *before* a noun) written in the large form that we use at the beginning of a name, a sentence, etc.: *"David" begins with a capital "D."* **2** connected with punishment by death: *a capital offense* (= a crime for which sb can be sentenced to death) ○ *capital punishment* (= punishment by death)

cap·i·tal·ism /¹kæpətəlɪzəm/ *noun* [U] the economic system in which businesses are owned and run for profit by individuals and not by the government ☞ Look at **communism** and **socialism**. —**cap·i·tal·ist** *noun* [C, *adj.*

cap·i·tal·ize /¹kæpətəlaɪz/ *verb* [T] to write sth as a capital²(1) letter: *Remember to capitalize the first letters of names.*

PHR V capitalize on sth to use sth to your advantage: *We can capitalize on the mistakes that our rivals have made.*

cap·i·tol /¹kæpətl̩/ *noun* [C] **1** (*also* **Capitol**) the building where a state's government meets: *the state capitol building* **2** the Capitol [sing.] the building in Washington, D.C., where the U.S. Congress meets

ca·pit·u·late /kə¹pɪtʃəleɪt/ *verb* [I] (*formal*) to stop fighting and say that you have lost; to give in to sb and do what he/she wants —**ca·pit·u·la·tion** /kəˌpɪtʃə¹leɪʃn/ *noun* [C,U]

Cap·ri·corn /¹kæprɪkɔrn/ *noun* [C,U] the tenth sign of the zodiac, the Goat; a person who was born under this sign ☞ picture at **zodiac**.

cap·size /¹kæpsaɪz; kæp¹saɪz/ *verb* [I,T] (used about boats) to turn over in the water: *The boat capsized.* ○ *She capsized the boat.*

cap·sule /¹kæpsl̩/ *noun* [C] **1** a type of pill,

tʃ	dʒ	v	θ	ð	s	z	ʃ
chin	June	van	thin	then	so	zoo	she

shaped like a very small tube, containing medicine that you swallow whole **2** the part of a spaceship in which the crew live and work

☆ **cap·tain** /'kæptən/ *noun* [C] **1** the person who is in command of a ship or an airplane **2** an officer of middle rank in the military forces **3** a person who is the leader of a group or team: *Who's the captain of the football team?*

cap·tion /'kæpʃn/ *noun* [C] the words that are written above or below a picture, cartoon, etc. to explain what it is about

cap·ti·vate /'kæptəveɪt/ *verb* [T] to attract and hold sb's attention —**cap·ti·vat·ing** *adj.* /-veɪṭɪŋ/

cap·tive¹ /'kæptɪv/ *noun* [C] a prisoner

cap·tive² /'kæptɪv/ *adj.* kept as a prisoner; (of animals) kept in a cage, zoo, etc.

IDM **hold sb captive** to keep sb as a prisoner and not allow him/her to escape

take sb captive to catch sb and hold him/her as your prisoner ☞ It is also possible to say **hold sb prisoner** and **take sb prisoner**.

cap·tiv·i·ty /kæp'tɪvəṭi/ *noun* [U] the state of being kept as a captive: *Wild animals are often unhappy in captivity.*

cap·tor /'kæptər/ *noun* [C] (*formal*) a person who takes or keeps a person as a prisoner

☆ **cap·ture¹** /'kæptʃər/ *verb* [T] **1** to take a person or animal prisoner: *The lion was captured and taken back to the zoo.* **2** to take or win sth from your enemy by force: *The town has been captured by the rebels.* **3** to succeed in representing sth in words, pictures, etc.: *This poem captures the atmosphere of the carnival.*

cap·ture² /'kæptʃər/ *noun* [U] a time when a person, animal or thing is captured

cars

sedan

hatchback

station wagon

☆ **car** /kɑr/ *noun* [C] **1** (*also* **automobile**; **auto**) a vehicle with an engine and four wheels that up to five or six people can ride in: *a new/used car* ○ *Where can I park the car?* ○ *He's having the car serviced tomorrow.* ○ *They had a car accident.* ○ *She gave me a ride in her car.* ○ *to get into/out of a car* ○ *a sports car*

☞ Note that we go **by car**. We can also say **in the car**: *Do you prefer to travel by bus or by car? ○ I come to work in the car.*

2 one of the separate parts of a train: *a dining car* ○ *a subway car* ○ *Some freight trains are over 100 cars long.*

car·a·mel /'kærəml; 'kɑrml/ *noun* **1** [C,U] a type of sticky brown candy that is made from boiled sugar, butter, and cream or milk **2** [U] sugar that has been burned so that it is dark brown. It is used in food because of its color and taste.

car·at /'kærət/ *noun* [C] a unit of measurement used to describe how heavy jewels are: *a 2-carat diamond ring* ☞ Look at **karat**.

car·bo·hy·drate /,kɑrboʊ'haɪdreɪt/ *noun* [C,U] one of the substances in food, e.g. sugar, that gives your body energy: *Athletes need a diet that is high in carbohydrates and low in fat.* ○ *Bread, potatoes and rice all contain carbohydrates.*

car·bon /'kɑrbən/ *noun* [U] (*symbol* **C**) a chemical substance that is found in all living things, and in a pure form in diamonds and in an impure form in coal

car·bon·at·ed /'kɑrbəneɪṭəd/ *adj.* (used about a drink) containing many small bubbles

carbon copy *noun* [C] (*pl.* **carbon copies**) **1** a copy of a letter, etc. that was made by using a special type of paper with a dark substance on one side **2** an exact copy of sth

carbon dioxide /,kɑrbən daɪ'ɑksaɪd/ *noun* [U] (*symbol* CO_2) a gas that has no color or smell that people and animals breathe out of their lungs

carbon monoxide /,kɑrbən mə'nɑksaɪd/ *noun* [U] (*symbol* **CO**) the poisonous gas that is produced when carbon is burned in a small amount of air. Motor vehicles produce a lot of carbon monoxide.

car·bu·re·tor /'kɑrbəreɪṭər/ *noun* [C] the piece of equipment in a car's engine that mixes gasoline and air

car·cass /'kɑrkəs/ *noun* [C] the dead body of an animal ☞ Look at **corpse**.

cards

heart

spade

diamond

club

☆ **card¹** /kɑrd/ *noun* **1** [C] a piece of thick paper or plastic that has information on it: *Here is my business card with my address and telephone number on it.* ○ *a membership card* ○ *an identity card* ○ *a credit card* **2** [C] a piece of thick paper with a picture on it that you use to send greetings or a message to sb: *a Christmas card* ○ *a birthday card* ○ *a get well card* (= one that you send to sb who is sick) ○ *We got a card* (= a postcard) *from Diana in Portugal.*

3 (also **playing card**) [C] one of a set of 52 small pieces of thick paper with shapes or pictures on them that are used for playing games: *a deck of cards* **4 cards** [plural] games that are played with cards: *Let's play cards.* ○ *Let's play a game of cards.* ○ *I never win at cards!*

☞ A **deck** of cards is divided into four **suits**, two red (**hearts** and **diamonds**) and two black (**clubs** and **spades**). Each suit has an **ace**, a **king**, a **queen**, a **jack** and nine other cards, numbered from 2 to 10. Before we play cards we **shuffle** and **deal** the cards.

card² /kɑrd/ *verb* [I,T] (*slang*) to ask sb to show an identification card, especially to prove that they are old enough to buy or drink alcohol: *We got carded outside the club and they wouldn't let us in.* ○ *A lot of students buy their beer at the supermarket because they usually don't card there.*

☆ **card·board** /'kɑrdbɔrd/ *noun* [U] very thick paper that is used for making boxes, etc.: *The computer paper was delivered in large cardboard boxes.*

ₗ**card** ᶥ**catalog** *noun* [C] a set of cards that contain information on names, books, subjects, etc. and that are kept in order in boxes, drawers, etc. especially in a library

car·di·ac /'kɑrdiæk/ *adj.* connected with the heart

car·di·gan /'kɑrdɪɡən/ (also ₗ**cardigan** ᶥ**sweater**) *noun* [C] a piece of clothing for the top part of the body, often made from wool, with long sleeves and buttons or a zipper at the front ☞ picture on page A27. Look at the note at **sweater**.

car·di·nal /'kɑrdn·l/ *noun* [C] **1** a priest of high rank in the Roman Catholic church **2** a type of North American bird. The male has bright red feathers. **3** (also ₗ**cardinal** ᶥ**number**) a whole number, e.g. 1, 2, 3, that shows quantity ☞ Look at **ordinal**.

☆ **care¹** /kɛr/ *verb* **1** [I,T] **care (about sth)** to be worried about or interested in sth; to mind: *I'm going to be late and my mother will be furious, but I don't care.* ○ *Money is the thing that she cares about most.* ○ *I don't care what you do.* **2** [I] **care for sth**; **care to do sth** (*formal*) to like or want: *Would you care for a drink?* ○ *Would you care to leave a message, sir?*

☞ **Care for** in this sense is used in questions and always with "would."

3 care for sb/sth to like: *I don't care for that color very much.* ○ *Do you think she still cares for him even though he married someone else?*

IDM **I, etc. couldn't care less** (*informal*) it does not matter to me, etc. at all: *"Your jacket isn't very clean." "Well, to tell you the truth, I couldn't care less."*

☞ Some people also say **I could care less** in informal situations, but many people consider this form incorrect.

who cares? (*informal*) nobody is interested; it is not important to anyone: *"I wonder who'll win the game." "Who cares?"*

PHRV **care for sb** to help sb who is sick or old and do things for him/her: *Who cared for her while she was sick?*

☆ **care²** /kɛr/ *noun* **1** [U] **care (in doing sth)** thinking about what you are doing so that you do it well or do not have an accident: *This box contains glasses – please handle it with care.* **2** [U] taking care of people so that they have things they need; responsibility for sb/sth: *The children were put into foster care.* ○ *medical care* ○ *She's in intensive care* (= the part of the hospital for people who are very seriously sick or injured). **3** [U] keeping sth in good condition: *information on the care and maintenance of antique furniture* ○ *health care* ○ *skin care products* **4** [C,U] (*formal*) worry, anxiety: *When we were young, we didn't have a care in the world.* ○ *It was a happy life, free from care.*

IDM **(in) care of sb** (*abbr.* **c/o**) words used on an envelope when you are writing to sb at another person's address: *Mary Jenkins, c/o Mrs. Brown, 10 Riverside Drive, Seattle.* ○ *You can write to the author in care of his publisher.*

take care (to do sth) to be careful: *Goodbye and take care!* ○ *Take care not to spill your coffee.*

take care of yourself/sb/sth to keep yourself/sb/sth safe from injury, illness, damage, etc.: *You should take better care of yourself. You look tired.* ○ *Could you take care of the cat while we are away on vacation?* ○ *She always takes great care of her books.*

take care of sb/sth to deal with sb/sth; to organize or arrange sth: *I'll take care of the food for the party.*

☆ **ca·reer** /kə'rɪr/ *noun* [C] **1** a job or profession for which you are trained and which you do for a long time, often with the chance to move to a higher position: *Sarah is considering a career in engineering.* ○ *His career was always more important to him than his family.* ○ *a successful career in politics* **2** your working life: *She spent most of her career working in India.*

care·free /'kɛrfri/ *adj.* happy because you have no problems or worries

☆ **care·ful** /'kɛrfl/ *adj.* **1 careful (with sth)** thinking about what you are doing so that you do not have an accident or make mistakes, etc.: *Be careful! There's a car coming.* ○ *Please be very careful with those glasses.* ○ *That ladder doesn't look very safe. Be careful you don't fall.* ○ *I was careful not to say anything about the money.* ○ *Don't worry – she's a careful driver.* **2** showing care and attention to details: *I'll need to give this matter some careful thought.*

C

—**care·ful·ly** *adv.*: *Please listen carefully.*
—**care·ful·ness** *noun* [U]

☆ **care·less** /'kɛrləs/ *adj.* **careless (about/with sth)** not thinking enough about what you are doing so that you make mistakes, lose or damage things, etc.: *Here's another careless mistake – you forgot the period at the end of the sentence.* ○ *an accident caused by careless driving* —**care·less·ly** *adv.*: *She threw her coat carelessly on the chair.* —**care·less·ness** *noun* [U]

ca·ress /kə'rɛs/ *verb* [T] to stroke sb in a gentle and loving way: *He caressed her hand and looked into her eyes.* —**ca·ress** *noun* [C]

care·tak·er /'kɛrteɪkər/ *noun* [C] a person whose job is to take care of a building, land, etc., especially when the owner is away

☆ **car·go** /'kɑrɡoʊ/ *noun* [C,U] (*pl.* **car·goes** or **car·gos**) the goods that are carried in a ship or an aircraft: *a cargo plane* (= that carries goods, but not passengers)

Car·ib·be·an /ˌkærɪ'biən; kə'rɪbiən/ *noun* [sing.] **the Caribbean** the area in the Caribbean Sea where Jamaica, Puerto Rico and other islands are located —**Car·ib·be·an** *adj.*: *the Caribbean islands*

car·i·bou /'kærəbu/ *noun* [C] (*pl.* **car·i·bou** or **car·i·bous**) a type of large deer that lives in the Arctic regions of North America ☞ Look at **reindeer**.

car·i·ca·ture /'kærəkətʃər; -tʃʊr/ *noun* [C] a picture or description of sb that makes his/her appearance or behavior funnier and more extreme than it really is: *She drew a really funny caricature of our English teacher.* ○ *Many of the people in the book are caricatures of the author's friends.*

car·ing /'kɛrɪŋ/ *adj.* showing that you care about other people: *He is a very caring person and will make a wonderful doctor.*

car·jack·ing /'kɑrdʒækɪŋ/ *noun* [C,U] the crime of taking control of sb's car or forcing him/her to give you his/her car, especially using a gun or other weapon —**car·jack·er** *noun* [C]

car·na·tion /kɑr'neɪʃn/ *noun* [C] a white, pink or red flower with a pleasant smell

car·ni·val /'kɑrnəvl/ *noun* [C] a public festival that may include a parade in the streets, music, dancing, or other types of entertainment: *the carnival in Rio* ○ *The town is holding its annual winter carnival this weekend.*

car·ol /'kærəl/ *noun* [C] a Christian religious song that people sing at Christmas: *to sing Christmas carols*

car·ou·sel /ˌkærə'sɛl/ *noun* [C] **1** = MERRY-GO-ROUND **2** (at an airport) a moving belt that carries luggage for passengers to pick up

☆ **car·pen·ter** /'kɑrpəntər/ *noun* [C] a person whose job is to make and repair wooden objects

car·pen·try /'kɑrpəntri/ *noun* [U] the skill or work of a carpenter

☆ **car·pet** /'kɑrpət/ *noun* **1** [C,U] (a piece of) thick, flat material that is used for covering floors and stairs: *We need new carpet in the bedroom.* ○ *All the carpets in the house had to be replaced.* ☞ Look at **rug**. **2** [C] a thick layer of sth that covers the ground: *The fields were under a carpet of snow.* —**car·pet·ed** *adj.* /'pətəd/: *All the rooms are carpeted.*

car·pet·ing /'kɑrpətɪŋ/ *noun* [U] carpet that has usually been cut to the exact shape of room: *wall-to-wall carpeting* (= that is the exact size and shape of a room and that has been fastened to the floor)

'**car pool** *noun* [C] an arrangement where several people travel together to work, school, etc. in one car and usually share the costs of traveling

'**car-pool** *verb* [I] to travel to work, school, etc. in a car pool: *There would be less traffic if more people car-pooled and used public transportation.*

car·riage /'kærɪdʒ/ *noun* [C] an elegant old-fashioned vehicle with wheels that is pulled by horses ☞ Look also at **baby carriage**.

car·ri·er /'kæriər/ *noun* [C] **1** (in business) a company that transports people or goods: *The airport is served by all the major U.S. airlines and several foreign carriers.* ○ *a long-distance carrier* (= that provides equipment and service for long-distance telephone calls) **2** a military vehicle or ship that is used for transporting soldiers, planes, weapons, etc.: *an armored personnel carrier* ○ *an aircraft carrier* **3** a person or animal that can give an infectious disease to others but does not show the signs of the disease: *Some insects are carriers of tropical diseases.* **4** a box or container that is used for carrying things: *a pet carrier* ☞ Look also at **letter carrier**.

☆ **car·rot** /'kærət/ *noun* [C,U] a long thin orange vegetable that grows under the ground: *a pound of carrots* ○ *half a cup of grated carrot*

☆ **car·ry** /'kæri/ *verb* (*pres. part.* **car·ry·ing**; *3rd pers. sing. pres.* **car·ries**; *p.t., p.p.* **car·ried**) **1** [T] to hold sb/sth in your hand, arms or on your back while you are moving from one place to another: *Could you carry this bag for me? It's really heavy.* ○ *She was carrying a backpack on one shoulder.*

☞ You use **wear**, not **carry**, to talk about having clothes, jewelry, etc. on your body: *He was wearing a black jacket.*

2 [T] to have with you as you go from place to place: *I never carry much cash with me when I go downtown.* ○ *Do the police carry guns in your country?* **3** [T] to transport sb/sth from one place to another: *A plane carrying two hundred passengers crashed yesterday.* ○ *The waves carried the boat to the shore.* **4** [T] to have an infectious disease that can be given to others, usually without showing any signs of

ər	ɪr	ɛr	ɑr	ɔr	ʊr	ʒ	h	ŋ
bird	near	hair	car	north	tour	vision	hat	sing

the disease yourself: *Rats carry all sorts of diseases.* **5** [T] to have sth as a punishment or a result: *The crime carries a penalty of up to 10 years in prison.* **6** [T] (usually passive) to accept a proposal in a meeting because a majority of people vote for it: *The motion was carried by 12 votes to 9.* **7** [I] (used about a sound) to reach a long distance: *You'll have to speak louder if you want your voice to carry to the back of the room.*

IDM **be/get carried away** to be so excited that you forget what you are doing: *I got so carried away watching the game that I forgot how late it was.*

carry weight to have great influence on the opinion of sb else: *Nick's views carry a lot of weight with our manager.*

PHRV **carry it/sth off** to succeed in doing sth difficult: *He felt nervous before he started his speech, but he carried it off very well.*

carry on (with sth); carry sth on to continue: *I know it's hard, but we have to try our best to carry on.* ○ *They ignored me and carried on with their conversation.* ○ *She intends to carry on her father's work after he retires.*

carry sth on to take part in sth: *I can't carry on a normal conversation when you're making that noise.*

carry sth out 1 to do sth that you have been ordered to do: *The soldiers carried out their orders without question.* **2** to do or perform sth, e.g. a test, repair, etc.: *I think we should wait until more tests have been carried out.* ○ *The landlord is responsible for carrying out repairs to the building.*

car·ry·out /ˈkæriaʊt/ *noun* [C,U] = TAKEOUT

carts

luggage cart
(*also* baggage cart) shopping cart

☆ **cart¹** /kɑrt/ *noun* [C] **1** a wooden vehicle with wheels that is used for transporting things: *a horse and cart* **2** a piece of equipment on wheels that you use for moving things: *a shopping cart* ○ *a luggage cart*

cart² /kɑrt/ *verb* [T] (*informal*) to take or carry sth somewhere, often with difficulty: *We left our luggage at the hotel because we didn't want to cart it around all day.* ○ *Six of the women were carted off to the police station.*

car·ti·lage /ˈkɑrṭəlɪdʒ/ *noun* [C,U] a strong substance that surrounds the places where your bones join together

car·ton /ˈkɑrtn/ *noun* [C] a small container, usually made of cardboard: *a carton of milk, eggs, etc.* ☞ picture at **container**.

car·toon /kɑrˈtun/ *noun* [C] **1** a funny drawing, especially one in a newspaper or magazine that makes a joke about a current event **2** a movie or television program that tells a story by using moving drawings instead of real people and places: *a Bugs Bunny cartoon*

car·toon·ist /kɑrˈtunɪst/ *noun* [C] a person who draws cartoons

car·tridge /ˈkɑrtrɪdʒ/ *noun* [C] **1** a closed container that holds a substance such as ink, powder, etc. It is easy to change a cartridge when you want to put in a new one. **2** a small tube that contains explosive powder and a bullet. You put a cartridge into a gun when you want to fire it.

carve /kɑrv/ *verb* **1** [T] **carve sth (out of sth)** to cut wood or stone in order to make an object or to put a pattern or writing on it: *Grandpa enjoys carving miniature animals out of wood.* ○ *He carved his initials into the desk.* ○ *to carve a pumpkin* (= into a jack-o'-lantern) *at Halloween* **2** [I,T] to cut a piece of cooked meat into slices: *Can you carve while I serve the vegetables?* ○ *to carve a turkey*

carv·ing /ˈkɑrvɪŋ/ *noun* [C,U] an object or design that has been carved: *There are ancient carvings on the walls of the cave.*

cas·cade /kæˈskeɪd/ *noun* [C] **1** a waterfall **2** something that hangs or falls in a way that seems similar to a waterfall: *The balcony was covered in a cascade of flowers.* —**cas·cade** *verb* [I]

☆ **case** /keɪs/ *noun* **1** [C] a particular situation or a situation of a particular type: *In some cases, people have had to sell their homes to pay for medical care.* ○ *Most of us can sing pretty well – or, in Susie's case, very well. ○ There's no secret to success in this business. It's just a case of hard work.* **2** **the case** [sing.] the true situation: *The man said he had graduated from Harvard, but we discovered later that this was not the case.* **3** [C] an example of an illness; a person who is suffering from an illness: *Cases of the disease are very unusual in this country.* ○ *The most serious cases were taken to the hospital immediately.* **4** [C] a crime that is being investigated by the police: *a murder case* **5** [C] something that is decided in a court of law; a trial: *The case will come to trial in a few months.* **6** [C, usually sing.] the facts and reasons that support one side in a discussion or legal matter: *She made a case for buying new equipment, but the others disagreed.* **7** [C] (especially in compounds) a container or cover for sth: *a pencil case* ○ *a pillowcase* ○ *She put her sunglasses back in the case.* **8** [C] a large box, and often the things inside it: *They delivered three cases of supplies yesterday.* ○ *It's cheaper to buy them by the case.*

IDM **in any case** whatever happens or has happened: *He didn't say anything about it at the meeting, and in any case, it's too late now.*

tʃ	dʒ	v	θ	ð	s	z	ʃ
chin	June	van	thin	then	so	zoo	she

in case because sth might happen: *I think I'll take an umbrella in case it rains.* ○ *Take my number in case you need to call me.* ○ *I wasn't planning to buy anything, but I took my credit card just in case.*
in case of sth if sth happens: *In case of fire, break this glass.*
in that case if that is the situation: *"I'm busy on Tuesday." "Oh well, in that case we'll have to meet another day."*

ˌcase ˈstudy *noun* [C] (*pl.* case studies) a study of the development of a person, company or group of people

☆ **cash¹** /kæʃ/ *noun* [U] **1** money in the form of coins or paper money and not checks, credit cards, etc.: *How would you like to pay – cash, check or charge?* ○ *How much cash do you have with you?*

☞ picture at **money**. We use **cash** when we are talking about coins and paper money, but **change** when we are talking about coins only.

2 (*informal*) money in any form: *I'm a little short of cash this month, so I can't afford to go out much.*

cash² /kæʃ/ *verb* [T] to exchange a check, traveler's check, etc. for coins and paper money: *I'm just going to the bank to cash my paycheck.*
PHRV **cash in (on sth)** to take advantage of a situation: *They decided to cash in on their boss's absense and go home early.*

☆ **cash·ier** /kæˈʃɪr/ *noun* [C] the person in a store, an office, etc. that customers pay money to or get money from

ˈcash machine *noun* [C] = ATM

cash·mere /ˌkæʒˈmɪr; ˌkæʃ-/ *noun* [U] a type of wool that is very fine and soft

ˈcash ˌregister (*also* register) *noun* [C] a machine in a store that is used to add together the cost of things that you buy. A cash register has a drawer where money is kept.

ca·si·no /kəˈsinoʊ/ *noun* [C] (*pl.* ca·si·nos) a place where people play card games and other types of games in which you can win or lose money

cas·ket /ˈkæskət/ (*also* coffin) *noun* [C] a box in which a dead body is buried ☞ Look at the note at **funeral**.

cas·se·role /ˈkæsəroʊl/ *noun* **1** [C,U] a type of food that you make by cooking meat and vegetables in liquid for a long time in the oven: *chicken casserole* **2** [C] a large dish with a lid for cooking casseroles (1) in.

☆ **cas·sette** /kəˈsɛt/ *noun* [C] a flat case with magnetic tape inside that you use to record and play music and other sounds: *to listen to a cassette* ○ *to record/play a cassette* ○ *Paul Simon's new album is available on CD and cassette.*

☞ Another word for **cassette** is **tape**. When you want to go back to the beginning of a cassette, you **rewind** it. When you want to go forward, you **fast forward** it. The machine that you use for recording and playing cassettes can be called a **cassette player** or a **tape recorder**. ☞ Look at **video**.

cast¹ /kæst/ *noun* [C] **1** all the actors in a play, movie, etc.: *The movie has an all-star cast.* **2** a covering made of soft, wet material that quickly becomes hard (**plaster**), that is kept around a broken bone until it heals: *Her arm is in a cast.* ☞ picture at **Band-Aid**.

cast² /kæst/ *verb* [T] (*p.t., p.p.* cast) **1** (often passive) to choose an actor for a particular role in a play, movie, etc.: *She always seems to be cast in the same sort of role.* **2** to make an object by pouring hot liquid metal into a shaped container (**a mold**): *a statue cast in bronze* **3** (*old-fashioned*) to throw sth: *She cast a stone into the river.*
IDM **cast doubt on sth** to make people unsure about sth: *The newspaper report casts doubts on the truth of the President's statement.*
cast an eye/your eye(s) over sb/sth to read or look at sb/sth quickly in order to check that it is correct, in good condition, etc.: *Can you just cast an eye over my essay before I hand it in?*
cast a shadow (across/over sth) to cause a shadow to appear somewhere: *The tree cast a long shadow across the yard.*
cast a shadow (over sth) to stop people from enjoying sth fully: *The accident cast a shadow over the rest of the trip.*
cast a/your vote to vote: *The senators are casting their votes on the bill today.*
PHRV **cast sb/sth aside** to make yourself free of sb/sth or to leave sb/sth behind because you do not want it anymore: *She cast aside her fear of water and bravely jumped into the pool.*

caste /kæst/ *noun* [C,U] one of the social classes into which Hindus are divided, especially in India, or the system of dividing people in this way

ˌcast-ˈiron *adj.* made of a hard type of iron that has been shaped by pouring hot liquid metal into a hollow form (**mold**): (*figurative*) *a cast-iron alibi* (= one that people cannot doubt)

☆ **cas·tle** /ˈkæsl/ *noun* [C] **1** a large building with high walls and towers that was built in the past to defend people against attack: *a medieval castle* **2** = ROOK

cas·trate /ˈkæstreɪt/ *verb* [T] to remove part of the sexual organs of a male animal or person —**cas·tra·tion** /kæˈstreɪʃn/ *noun* [U]

☆ **ca·su·al** /ˈkæʒuəl/ *adj.* **1** (used about clothes) not formal: *On Fridays we're allowed to wear casual clothes to work.* **2** not involving or showing deep feelings: *She tried to appear casual* (= relaxed and not worried) *as he walked toward her.* ○ *She has a very casual*

i	ɪ	ɛ	æ	ɑ	ɔ	ʌ	ʊ	u
see	sit	ten	cat	hot	saw	cup	put	too

attitude toward her work – I think she should try harder. ○ It was only a casual remark, so I don't know why he got so mad. ○ The two species may appear similar to the casual observer, but in fact they are very different. **3** happening by chance; not planned: The AIDS virus is not spread through casual contact. —**ca·su·al·ly** /ˈkæʒəli/: Dress casually – it won't be a formal party. ○ She walked in casually and said, "I'm not late, am I?"

ca·su·al·ty /ˈkæʒəlti; -ʒuəl-/ noun [C] (pl. **ca·su·al·ties**) **1** a person who is killed or injured in a war or an accident: The army retreated after suffering heavy casualties. **2** a person or thing that suffers as a result of sth else: Many small companies have been casualties of the country's economic problems.

cat
whiskers
tail
paw
kitten

☆ **cat¹** /kæt/ noun [C] **1** a small furry animal with four legs and a tail. People often keep cats as pets. **2** any larger wild animal that is related to a cat, e.g. a lion or tiger: We went to the zoo to see the big cats.

☞ A young cat is called a **kitten**. When a cat makes a soft sound of pleasure, it **purrs**. When it makes a louder sound, it **meows**.

☆ **cat·a·log¹** (also **catalogue**) /ˈkætl̩·ɔg; -lɑg/ noun [C] **1** a book that contains information about all the things you can buy from a company: a mail-order catalog **2** a list, often in the form of a book, of all the courses at a college or university, all the paintings in an art show, etc.: the full course catalog ☞ Look also at **card catalog**. **3** a series, especially of bad things: a catalog of disasters

cat·a·log² (also **catalogue**) /ˈkætl̩·ɔg; -lɑg/ verb [T] (pres. part. **cat·a·log·ing** or **cat·a·log·uing**; p.t., p.p. **cat·a·loged** or **cat·a·logued**) to list things in a catalog¹: She started to catalog all the new library books.

cat·a·lyst /ˈkætəlɪst/ noun [C] **1** (technical) a substance that makes a chemical reaction happen faster, but that is not changed itself **2** a person or thing that causes a change: The newspaper article served as a catalyst for change in the city government.

cat·a·pult /ˈkætəpʌlt/ verb [T] to throw sth/sb suddenly and with great force: When the car crashed, the passengers were catapulted through the windows. ○ (figurative) The success of his first movie catapulted him to fame.

cat·a·ract /ˈkætərækt/ noun [C] a diseased

area that can grow on a person's eye and cause difficulty in seeing

ca·tas·tro·phe /kəˈtæstrəfi/ noun [C] a sudden event that causes great suffering or damage; disaster: Major catastrophes like floods and earthquakes happen regularly in that part of the world. ○ a financial catastrophe —**cat·a·stroph·ic** /ˌkætəˈstrɑfɪk/: The war had a catastrophic effect on the whole country.

☆ **catch¹** /kætʃ/ verb (p.t., p.p. **caught** /kɔt/) **1** [T] to take hold of sth that is moving, usually with your hand or hands: She threw the ball and he caught it in one hand. ○ The dog caught the ball in its mouth. **2** [T] to capture sb/sth that you have been chasing or looking for : Two police officers ran after the thief and caught him at the end of the street. ○ The murderer still hasn't been caught. ○ to catch a fish **3** [T] to discover sb who is doing sth bad: I caught her taking money from my purse. **4** [T] to get on a form of public transportation: I caught the bus into town. ○ to catch a train, plane, etc. **5** [T] to be in time for sth; not to miss sb/sth: We arrived just in time to catch the beginning of the movie. ○ I'll call her now. I might just catch her before she leaves the office. **6** [T] to hear or understand sth that sb says: Sorry, I didn't quite catch what you said. Could you say it again? **7** [I,T] to become or cause sth to become accidentally attached to or trapped in sth: His jacket caught on a nail. ○ I caught my finger in the drawer as I shut it. ○ I'm sorry I'm late. I got caught in the traffic. **8** [T] to get an illness: I've got a bad cold. I must have caught it from somebody at work.

IDM **catch sb's attention/eye** ➪ ATTENTION
catch your breath to rest after physical exercise so that your breathing returns to normal: I just need a minute to catch my breath.
catch fire to start burning, often accidentally: Nobody knows how the building caught fire.
catch sb off guard to surprise and often confuse sb because he/she is not prepared: The question caught me off guard and I didn't know what to say.
catch sb red-handed to find sb just as he/she is doing sth wrong: A police officer noticed the broken window and caught the burglars red-handed.
catch sight/a glimpse of sb/sth to see sb/sth for a moment: I caught sight of the man at the end of the street. ○ We waited outside the theater, hoping to catch a glimpse of the actress.

PHRV **catch on** (informal) **1** to understand or realize sth: Sometimes she's a little slow to catch on. **2** to become popular or fashionable: The idea never really caught on in this country.
catch up (with sb) 1 to reach sb/sth who is ahead of you: Jackie was walking very fast and I had to run to catch up with her. **2** to reach the same level as sb/sth else: Our economy is

C

developing fast and we should soon catch up with other countries in the western world.

catch up on sth to spend time doing sth that you have not been able to do until now: *I'll have to go into the office this weekend to catch up on my work.*

be/get caught up in sth to be or get involved in sth, usually without intending to: *I got caught up in all the excitement about the championship game.*

catch² /kætʃ/ *noun* [C] **1** an act of taking hold of sth that is moving, usually with your hand or hands **2** the amount of fish that sb has caught: *The fishermen brought their catch to the harbor.* **3** a device for fastening sth and keeping it closed: *The catch on my necklace is broken.* **4** a hidden disadvantage to sth that seems attractive: *I can't believe you're selling that for such a low price – what's the catch?*

catch·y /ˈkætʃi/ *adj.* (**catch·i·er; catch·i·est**) (used about a tune or song) easy to remember

cat·e·gor·i·cal /ˌkætəˈgɔrɪkl; -ˈgɑr-/ *adj.* completely definite: *The answer was a categorical "no."* —**cat·e·gor·i·cal·ly** /-kli/: *The spokesperson categorically denied the rumor.*

cat·e·go·rize /ˈkætəgəraɪz/ *verb* [T] to divide people or things into groups; to say that sb/sth belongs to a particular group

☆ **cat·e·go·ry** /ˈkætəˌgɔri/ *noun* [C] (*pl.* **cat·e·go·ries**) a group of people or things that are similar to each other: *There were two categories in the contest: teams and individuals.* ○ *These books are divided into categories according to subject.*

ca·ter /ˈkeɪṭər/ *verb* **1** [I] **cater to sb/sth** to provide what sb/sth needs or wants: *We need a hotel that caters to small children.* ○ *a show that caters to people's love of celebrity gossip* **2** [I,T] **cater (sth); cater (for sb/sth)** to provide and serve food and drinks for a social event: *the company that catered our wedding reception*

ca·ter·er /ˈkeɪṭərər/ *noun* [C] a person or business that provides food and drinks for social events

ca·ter·ing /ˈkeɪṭərɪŋ/ *noun* [U] the activity or business of providing food and drinks for social events: *the hotel and catering industry*

caterpillar

cat·er·pil·lar /ˈkæṭəpɪlər; ˈkæṭər-/ *noun* [C] an animal like a small hairy worm with legs, that changes into a butterfly or moth

cat·fish /ˈkætfɪʃ/ *noun* [C,U] (*pl.* **cat·fish**) a large fish that lives in lakes and rivers and is eaten as food. Catfish have long thin things like hairs near their mouths.

ca·the·dral /kəˈθidrəl/ *noun* [C] a large church that is the most important one in a district

☆ **Cath·o·lic** /ˈkæθəlɪk; -əlɪk/ *noun* [C], *adj.* = ROMAN CATHOLIC —**Ca·thol·i·cism** /kəˈθɑləsɪzəm/ *noun* [U] = ROMAN CATHOLICISM

cat·sup /ˈkætsəp; ˈkɛtʃəp/ *noun* [U] = KETCHUP

cat·tle /ˈkæṭl/ *noun* [plural] male and female cows, e.g. on a farm: *a herd of cattle* (= a group of them) ☛ Look at the note at **cow**.

Cau·ca·sian /kɔˈkeɪʒn/ *noun* [C], *adj.* (of) a member of the race of people who have white or light-colored skin ☛ **White** is more common nowadays.

cau·cus /ˈkɔkəs/ *noun* [C] (*pl.* **cau·cus·es**) a local meeting of the members of a political party, where they choose people for a particular position or choose candidates for an election, etc.: *the Democratic party caucus*

caught *p.t., p.p.* of CATCH¹

cau·li·flow·er /ˈkɔliˌflaʊər; ˈkɑlɪ-/ *noun* [C,U] a large vegetable with green leaves and a round white center that you eat when it is cooked ☛ picture at **cabbage**.

☆ **cause¹** /kɔz/ *noun* **1** [C] a thing or person that makes sth happen: *The police do not know the cause of the accident.* ○ *Smoking is one of the causes of heart disease.* **2** [U] **cause (for sth)** reason: *I don't think you have any real cause for complaint.* **3** [C] an aim or principle that a group of people believe in and support: *We are all committed to the cause of racial equality.* ○ *I don't mind giving money to a good cause.*

IDM **a lost cause** ▷ LOST²

☆ **cause²** /kɔz/ *verb* [T] to make sth happen: *The fire was caused by careless smoking.* ○ *High winds caused many trees to fall during the night.* ○ *Is your leg causing you any pain?*

'cause /kəz/ *conj.* (*informal*) because

☛ This word is common in spoken English, but in formal writing we must use **because**.

caus·tic /ˈkɔstɪk/ *adj.* **1** (used about a substance) able to burn or destroy things by chemical action **2** (used about a comment or type of humor) cruel and unkind

☆ **cau·tion¹** /ˈkɔʃn/ *noun* [U] great care, because of possible danger: *Caution: Dangerous Intersection Ahead* (= on a road sign). ○ *Use caution when working with strong chemicals.*

☆ **cau·tion²** /ˈkɔʃn/ *verb* [I,T] to warn sb about sth: *He cautioned me not to speak to reporters about the case.* ○ *The President's advisers have cautioned against reacting too strongly to the news.* ○ *Dixon was cautioned by his boss for arriving late.*

☆ **cau·tious** /ˈkɔʃəs/ *adj.* taking great care to avoid possible danger: *I'm very cautious about expressing my opinions in public.* ○ *a cautious approach to a difficult problem* ○ *She's a very cautious driver.* —**cau·tious·ly** *adv.*

cav·al·ry /ˈkævlri/ *noun* [sing.] **1** the part of the army that fights in fast, heavily protected

vehicles **2** the group of soldiers who fought on horses in the past

☆ **cave¹** /keɪv/ *noun* [C] a large hole in the side of a cliff or hill, or under the ground: *prehistoric paintings on a cave wall*

cave² /keɪv/ *verb*

PHRV **cave in 1** to fall in: *The roof of the tunnel had caved in and we couldn't go any farther.* **2** to suddenly stop arguing or opposing sth: *He finally caved in and agreed to our plan.*

cav·ern /'kævərn/ *noun* [C] a large, deep cave

cav·i·ar (*also* **caviare**) /'kæviɑr/ *noun* [U] the eggs of a large fish that are eaten as food. Caviar is usually very expensive.

cav·i·ty /'kævəti/ *noun* [C] (*pl.* **cav·i·ties**) **1** a hole in a tooth: *You'll get cavities if you eat too much candy.* **2** an empty space inside sth solid, especially inside your body: *sinus cavities*

cc *abbr.* carbon copy; a copy of a letter that is sent to sb else

CD /ˌsi 'di/ (*also* **compact disc**) *noun* [C] a small, round piece of hard plastic, like a record, on which sound is recorded or information is stored. You play a CD on a special machine: *a CD player*

CD-ROM /ˌsi di 'rɑm/ *noun* [U] compact disc read-only memory; a compact disc that can be used in a computer and has a lot of information recorded on it. The information cannot be changed or removed.

cease /sis/ *verb* [I,T] (*formal*) to stop or end: *Fighting in the area has now ceased.* ○ *That organization has ceased to exist.* ○ *500 people lost their jobs when the company ceased operations.*

'cease-fire *noun* [C] an agreement between two groups to stop fighting each other

ce·dar /'sidər/ *noun* **1** [C] a type of tall tree that has very thin sharp leaves (**needles**) and red wood with a sweet smell **2** [U] the wood from the cedar tree: *a cedar chest*

cede /sid/ *verb* [T] (*formal*) to give land or control of sth to another country or person

☆ **ceil·ing** /'silɪŋ/ *noun* [C] **1** the top surface of the inside of a room: *We painted the walls pink and the ceiling white.* ○ *a room with a high/low ceiling* **2** a top limit on wages, prices, etc.: *to put a ceiling on welfare spending*

☆ **cel·e·brate** /'sɛləbreɪt/ *verb* **1** [I,T] to do sth special and enjoyable on an important day or because of an important event: *When I got the job, we celebrated by opening a bottle of champagne.* ○ *Mrs. Halford celebrated her 80th birthday yesterday.* **2** [T] (used about a priest) to lead a religious ceremony: *to celebrate Mass*

cel·e·brat·ed /'sɛləbreɪtəd/ *adj.* (*formal*) famous: *a celebrated actress*

cel·e·bra·tion /ˌsɛlə'breɪʃn/ *noun* [C,U] the act or occasion of doing sth enjoyable because sth good has happened or because it is a spe-

cial day: *New Year's Eve celebrations* ○ *The governor's visit was cause for celebration.*

ce·leb·ri·ty /sə'lɛbrəti/ *noun* [C] (*pl.* **ce·leb·ri·ties**) a famous person

cel·er·y /'sɛləri/ *noun* [U] a vegetable with long green stems that is eaten raw in salads and sometimes used in cooking: *a stalk of celery*

cel·i·bate /'sɛləbət/ *adj.* (*formal*) remaining unmarried or never having sexual relations, often because of religious beliefs —**cel·i·ba·cy** /'sɛləbəsi/ *noun* [U]: *to practice celibacy*

☆ **cell** /sɛl/ *noun* [C] **1** the smallest living part of an animal or a plant body: *The human body consists of billions of cells.* ○ *red blood cells* **2** a small room in a prison or police station in which a prisoner is locked

cel·lar /'sɛlər/ *noun* [C] an underground room that is used for storing things: *a wine cellar*
☛ Look at **basement**.

cel·list /'tʃɛlɪst/ *noun* [C] a person who plays the cello

cel·lo /'tʃɛloʊ/ *noun* [C] (*pl.* **cel·los**) a musical instrument like a large violin. You sit down to play it and hold it between your knees.

cel·lo·phane /'sɛləfeɪn/ *noun* [U] thin transparent material that is used for wrapping things

cel·lu·lar /'sɛlyələr/ *adj.* consisting of cells (1): *cellular tissue*

ˌ**cellular 'phone** (also *informal* ˈ**cell phone**) *noun* [C] a telephone that you can carry around with you and that works by using radio signals

Cel·si·us /'sɛlsiəs/ (*also* **centigrade**) *adj.* (*abbr.* **C**) the name of a scale for measuring temperatures, in which water freezes at 0° and boils at 100°: *The temperature tonight will fall to 7°C.*

☛ We say "seven degrees Celsius." In the U.S., this system of measuring temperature is mainly used in science. People use the **Fahrenheit** scale to talk about the weather, body temperature, etc.

☆ **ce·ment¹** /sə'mɛnt/ *noun* [U] a gray powder that becomes hard after it is mixed with water and left to dry. It is used in building for sticking bricks or stones together or for making very hard surfaces. ☛ Look at the note at **concrete².**

ce·ment² /sə'mɛnt/ *verb* [T] **1** to stick things together **2** to make a relationship very strong: *This agreement has cemented the relationship between our two companies.*

☆ **cem·e·ter·y** /'sɛməˌtɛri/ *noun* [C] (*pl.* **cem·e·ter·ies**) a place where dead people are buried
☛ Look at **graveyard.**

cen·sor /'sɛnsər/ *noun* [C] an official who examines books, movies, plays, etc. and removes any parts that might offend people, or who examines letters, newspaper reports, etc.

tʃ	dʒ	v	θ	ð	s	z	ʃ
chin	June	van	thin	then	so	zoo	she

and removes any parts which contain secret information: *The network's censors wouldn't allow the comedian to say those words on TV.* —**cen·sor** *verb* [T]: *The journalists said that all the information they sent back to United States was being censored.* —**cen·sor·ship** *noun* [U]: *government censorship of radio and television programs*

cen·sure /'sɛnʃər/ *verb* [T] (*formal*) to tell sb, in a strong and formal way, that he/she has done sth wrong: *The attorney was censured for not revealing the information earlier.* —**cen·sure** *noun* [U] (*formal*): *a letter of censure*

cen·sus /'sɛnsəs/ *noun* [C] (*pl.* **cen·sus·es**) an official count of the people who live in a country, including information about their ages, jobs, etc.: *to take a census*

☆ **cent** /sɛnt/ *noun* [C] (*symbol* ¢) a unit of money that is worth 1/100th of a dollar or of the main unit of money in some other countries

☞ A coin that is worth one cent is called a **penny**. Look also at **nickel**, **dime** and **quarter**, and at Appendix 2.

cen·ten·ni·al /sɛn'tɛniəl/ *noun* [C] the year that comes exactly one hundred years after an important event or the beginning of sth: *1986 was the centennial of the Statue of Liberty.* ○ *centennial celebrations* ☞ Look at **bicentennial**.

☆ **cen·ter¹** /'sɛntər/ *noun* **1** [C, usually sing.] the middle point or part of sth: *There was a vase of flowers in the center of the table.* ○ *The parade went right through the center of town.* ○ *a candy bar with a caramel center* ☞ Look at the note at **middle**. **2** [C] a building or place where a particular activity or service is based: *a shopping center* ○ *the campus health center* ○ *New York is a major financial center.* **3** [C] a person or thing that receives a lot of attention: *She always likes to be the center of attention.* **4 the center** [sing.] a political position that is not extreme: *The candidate's views place her firmly in the center.* **5** [C] (*sports*) a player whose position is in the middle of the field, etc. in sports such as football and basketball

☆ **cen·ter²** /'sɛntər/ *verb*
PHRV **center on/around sb/sth** to have sb/sth as its center: *His life centers on his family.*

cen·ti·grade /'sɛntəgreɪd/ *adj.* = CELSIUS

cen·ti·me·ter /'sɛntə,mitər/ *noun* [C] (*abbr.* **cm**) a measure of length. There are 100 centimeters in a meter: *The insect was about two centimeters long.*

☆ **cen·tral** /'sɛntrəl/ *adj.* **1** (usually *before* a noun) in the center of sth: *a town in central Missouri* ○ *the countries of Central America* (= between Mexico and Colombia) ○ *the building's central staircase* **2** (only *before* a noun) (used about an office, group, etc.) having con-

trol of all other parts of an organization: *All packages are transported to the city's central post office.* **3** controlled from one main point: *central air conditioning* **4** most important; main: *The story's central character is a fifteen-year-old girl.* ○ *This point is central to my argument.*

cen·tral·ize /'sɛntrəlaɪz/ *verb* [T] to make sth come under central control: *We plan to centralize our customer services to make them more efficient.*

cen·tral·ly /'sɛntrəli/ *adv.* in or from the center: *a centrally located city* (= near the center of a region or country) ○ *the centrally planned economies of Communist countries*

☆ **cen·tu·ry** /'sɛntʃəri/ *noun* [C] (*pl.* **cen·tu·ries**) **1** a particular period of 100 years that is used for giving dates: *the 20th century* (= the period between the years 1901 and 2000) **2** any period of 100 years: *People have been making wine in that area for centuries.*

CEO /,si i 'oʊ/ *abbr.* = CHIEF EXECUTIVE OFFICER

ce·ram·ic /sə'ræmɪk/ *adj.* made of clay that has been made hard by baking it: *ceramic tiles*

ce·ram·ics /sə'ræmɪks/ *noun* [U] the art of making and decorating clay pots, etc.

☆ **ce·re·al** /'sɪriəl/ *noun* [C,U] food that is made from plants such as corn or wheat and that is often eaten with milk for breakfast: *a bowl of cereal*

cer·e·bral /sə'ribrəl; 'sɛrəbrəl/ *adj.* connected with the brain: *He died of a cerebral hemorrhage.*

cerebral palsy /,sɛrəbrəl 'pɔlzi/ *noun* [U] a disease that causes a person to lose control of their movements because of brain damage before or during birth

cer·e·mo·ni·al /,sɛrə'moʊniəl/ *adj.* relating to a ceremony: *a ceremonial occasion*

☆ **cer·e·mo·ny** /'sɛrəmoʊni/ *noun* (*pl.* **cer·e·mo·nies**) **1** [C] a formal public or religious event: *the opening ceremony of the Olympic Games* ○ *a wedding ceremony* **2** [U] formal behavior, speech, actions, etc. that are expected on special occasions: *The foreign ambassador was welcomed with great ceremony.*

☆ **cer·tain** /'sərtn/ *adj.* **1** (not before a noun) **certain (that…); certain (of sth)** completely sure; without any doubts: *Police are now certain that the explosion was an accident.* ○ *The events may be connected, but we cannot be certain.* ○ *Scientists are not yet certain what causes this to happen.* ○ *Officials are not absolutely certain of the effects of this decision.*

☞ **Sure** is more common than **certain** in informal speech.

2 certain (that…); certain (to do sth) sure to happen or to do sth; definite: *It is almost certain that unemployment will increase this year.* ○ *The principal is certain to agree.* ○ *Nothing is certain right now. Wait and see.* ○ *If sales do not*

increase, the company will face certain bankruptcy. ☞ Look at the note at **sure**. **3** (only before a noun) (used for talking about a particular thing or person without naming them): You can only contact me at certain times of the day. ○ There are certain reasons why that information is not available. **4** (only before a noun) noticeable but difficult to describe: There was a certain amount of fear in his voice. **IDM** **for certain** without doubt: I don't know for certain how many people will come. **make certain (that…)** to do sth in order to be sure that sth else happens: They're doing everything they can to make certain they win.

☆ **cer·tain·ly** /ˈsərtnli/ adv. **1** without doubt; definitely: The number of students will certainly increase after 1998. ○ I certainly don't think you should tell him now. **2** (formal) (used in answer to questions) of course: "Excuse me, ma'am. Could I ask you a question?" "Certainly." ○ "Senator, could you please comment on this report?" "Certainly not!"

cer·tain·ty /ˈsərtnti/ noun (pl. **cer·tain·ties**) **1** [U] the state of being completely sure about sth: We can't say with certainty that there is life on other planets. ☞ The opposite is **uncertainty**. **2** [C] something that is sure to happen: It's now almost a certainty that Oakland will play in the World Series.

☆ **cer·tif·i·cate** /səˈtɪfəkət/ noun [C] an official piece of paper that says that sth is true or correct: a birth certificate

,**certified** ˈmail noun [U] a postal service that you pay extra for. The person who receives a letter that was sent by certified mail must sign his/her name on a special form (**a receipt**).

cer·ti·fy /ˈsərtəfaɪ/ verb [T] (pres. part. **cer·ti·fy·ing**; 3rd pers. sing. pres. **cer·ti·fies**; p.t., p.p. **cer·ti·fied**) **1** to say formally that sth is true or correct: We need someone to certify that this statement is accurate. **2** to give sb a certificate to show that he/she has successfully completed a course of training for a particular profession: a certified public accountant

Ce·sar·e·an sec·tion (also **Caesarean section**) /sɪˌzɛriən ˈsɛkʃn/ (also **C-section** noun [C] an operation to remove a baby from its mother's body when a normal birth would be impossible or dangerous

☆ **chain¹** /tʃeɪn/ noun **1** [C,U] a line of metal rings that are joined together: They used heavy chains to pull the car out of the snow. ○ a bicycle chain ○ She was wearing a silver chain around her neck. ○ a 4-foot length of chain **2** [C] a number of things in a line: a chain of islands/an island chain **3** [C] a group of stores, hotels, etc. that are owned by the same person or company: a chain of restaurants/a restaurant chain ○ a

chain

padlock

link

chain

chain store (= one store that is part of a chain) **4** [C] a number of connected events that happen one after another: The book examines the complex chain of events that led to the Russian Revolution.

chain² /tʃeɪn/ verb [T] **chain sb/sth (to sth)**; **chain sb/sth (up)** to fasten sb/sth to sth else with a chain: The neighbor's dog has been chained up in the yard all day.

,**chain re·ˈaction** noun [C] a series of events or chemical changes, each of which causes the next one: If the factory closes, it could set off a chain reaction of other business closures in the area.

ˈ**chain ,smoker** noun [C] a person who smokes continuously, lighting one cigarette after another

☆ **chair¹** /tʃɛr/ noun [C] **1** a piece of furniture for one person to sit on. It has a seat, a back and usually four legs. It sometimes has two arms: a kitchen chair ○ an armchair ○ a wheelchair ☞ Look also at **electric chair**. **2** (also **chairman**; **chairperson**; **chairwoman**) [usually sing.] the person who controls a meeting, leads a committee, etc.: Rosa is the new chair of the County Historical Society. **3** a professor who is the head of a department at a college or university: the chair of economics at Princeton University

chair² /tʃɛr/ verb [T] to be the chairman or chairwoman of a meeting, a committee, etc.: Mr. Tran has been appointed to chair the school's finance committee.

☆ **chair·man** /ˈtʃɛrmən/ noun [C] (pl. **chairmen**) **1** the head of a committee, company or other organization: the Chairman of IBM **2** = CHAIR¹(2)

chair·man·ship /ˈtʃɛrmənʃɪp/ noun [sing.] being the chairman of sth; the time during which sb is chairman of sth

☆ **chair·per·son** /ˈtʃɛrpərsn/ noun [C] (pl. **chair·per·sons**) = CHAIR¹(2)

☆ **chair·wom·an** /ˈtʃɛrˌwʊmən/ (pl. **chair·women**) noun [C] = CHAIR¹(2)

cha·let /ʃæˈleɪ/ noun [C] a house or hut that is made of wood, especially in a mountain area

☆ **chalk¹** /tʃɔk/ noun [U] a small stick of white or colored powder that has been pressed together, that is used for writing or drawing on a blackboard: a piece of chalk

chalk² /tʃɔk/ verb

PHRV **chalk sth up** (informal) to succeed in getting sth: The team has chalked up five wins this summer.

chalk·board /ˈtʃɔkbɔrd/ noun [C] = BLACKBOARD

☆ **chal·lenge¹** /ˈtʃælənʤ/ noun **1** [C,U] something new and difficult that forces you to make a lot of effort, but that is often exciting and interesting: Starting my own business was a real challenge. ○ After over 15 years at her old job, Laura wanted a new challenge. ○ The

ə	y	w	ṭ	eɪ	aɪ	ɔɪ	aʊ	oʊ
about	yes	woman	butter	say	five	boy	now	go

President's next big challenge will be to reduce unemployment. **2** [C] **a challenge (to sb) (to do sth)** an invitation from sb to fight, play, argue, etc. against him/her: *She issued her opponents a challenge to find a better solution.*

☆ **chal·lenge²** /'tʃæləndʒ/ *verb* [T] **1 challenge sb (to sth)** to invite sb to fight, play, argue, etc. against you: *They challenged us to a softball game this Saturday.* **2** to question whether sth is true or right: *Several senators challenged the reports of bribery.*

chal·lenged /'tʃæləndʒd/ *adj.* (in compounds) having a particular type of difficulty in doing sth that most other people can do: *to be visually, mentally, physically, etc. challenged* ☞ Look at the note at **handicapped**.

chal·leng·er /'tʃæləndʒər/ *noun* [C] a person who takes part in a competition, because he/she wants to win a title or position that sb else already has

chal·leng·ing /'tʃæləndʒɪŋ/ *adj.* forcing you to make a lot of effort, but often also exciting and interesting: *a challenging job*

☆ **cham·ber** /'tʃeɪmbər/ *noun* [C] **1** a large room that is used for formal meetings: *a city council chamber* ○ *a judge's private chambers* **2** a room that is used for a particular purpose: *a gas chamber* (= where people are killed with poisonous gas)

'chamber ,music *noun* [U] classical music that is written for a small group of instruments

,chamber of 'commerce *noun* [C] (*pl.* **chambers of commerce**) an organization of businesses and store owners in a city or an area, that encourages the development of business

cham·pagne /ʃæm'peɪn/ *noun* [U] a French white wine that has a lot of bubbles in it and is often very expensive

☆ **cham·pi·on¹** /'tʃæmpiən/ *noun* [C] **1** a person, team, etc. that has won a competition: *a world champion* ○ *a champion swimmer* **2** (*formal*) a person who speaks and fights for a particular group, idea, etc.: *a champion of equal rights for women*

cham·pi·on² /'tʃæmpiən/ *verb* [T] (*formal*) to support or fight for a particular group or idea: *to champion the cause of human rights*

☆ **cham·pi·on·ship** /'tʃæmpiən,ʃɪp/ *noun* [C] **1** a competition or series of competitions to find the best player or team in a sport or game: *to win the world championship* **2** the position or title of a champion (1)

☆ **chance¹** /tʃæns/ *noun* **1** [C,U] **chance of (doing) sth; chance (that...)** (a) possibility: *The plan didn't really have a chance of succeeding.* ○ *I think there's a good chance that she'll be the next President.* ○ *He has very little chance of winning.* ○ *Is there any chance of getting tickets for tonight's concert?* **2** [C] **chance (to do sth)** an opportunity: *Could you mail this*

letter for me if you get a chance? ○ *Be quiet and give her a chance to explain.* ○ *I think you should tell him now. You might not get another chance.* ○ *Even though he made a serious mistake, I think he deserves a second chance.* ☞ Look at the note at **occasion**. **3** [C] a risk: *We might lose some money, but that's a chance we'll have to take.* **4** [U] luck or fortune (= sth that you cannot control): *You should plan ahead – don't just leave everything to chance.* ○ *I discovered these old pictures by chance while I was looking for something else in the attic.*

IDM **by any chance** (used for asking sth politely) perhaps or possibly: *Are you by any chance going downtown this afternoon?*

chances are (that)... (*informal*) it is probable that...: *Chances are that it will rain tomorrow.*

stand a chance (of doing sth) to have a possibility of achieving sth: *The other team was a lot better than us – we didn't stand a chance of winning.*

chance² /tʃæns/ *verb* [T] (*informal*) to risk sth: *Should we take umbrellas or should we chance it* (= risk getting wet)?

chan·cel·lor /'tʃænsələr/ *noun* [C] **1** the head of government in some countries: *the German chancellor* **2** the head of some universities or university systems: *the chancellor of the University of California system*

chan·de·lier /,ʃændə'lɪr/ *noun* [C] a large light that hangs from the ceiling and that has many light bulbs or candles

☆ **change¹** /tʃeɪndʒ/ *verb* **1** [I,T] to become different or to make sb/sth different: *This town has changed a lot since I was young.* ○ *Our plans have changed. We leave in the morning.* ○ *His fame has not changed him at all.* **2** [I,T] **change (sb/sth) to/into sth; change (from sth) (to/into sth)** to become sth different; to make sb/sth take a different form: *to change from a caterpillar into a butterfly* ○ *Honestly – I didn't see the traffic light change to red!* ○ *to change water into ice* **3** [T] to take, have or use sth instead of sth else: *to change jobs* ○ *to change a light bulb* ○ *to change direction* ○ *Can I change my appointment from Wednesday to Thursday?* **4** [I,T] to get out of one bus, airplane, etc. and get into another: *Does this bus go all the way to the airport or do we have to change?* ○ *She has to change planes in Dallas.* **5** [I,T] **change (out of sth) (into sth)** to take off your clothes and put different ones on: *He changed his shirt.* ○ *I'm going straight to the party from work, so I'll change when I get there.* ○ *She changed out of her swimsuit and into a dress.* **6** [T] to put clean things onto sb/sth: *It's your turn to change the baby* (= to put a clean diaper on him/her). **7** [T] **change sth (for/into sth)** to give sb money and receive the same amount back in money of a different type: *Can you change a twenty-dollar bill?* ○ *I'd*

like to change a hundred dollars into Swiss francs.
IDM **change hands** to pass from one owner to another
change your mind to change your decision or opinion: *I'll have the green one. No, I changed my mind. I want the red one.*
change/trade places (with sb) ⇨ PLACE¹
change the subject to start talking about sth different
change your tune (*informal*) to change your opinion or feelings about sth
PHRV **change over (from sth) (to sth)** to stop doing or using one thing and start doing or using sth else: *Our office has changed over to a new computer system.*

☆ **change²** /ˈtʃeɪndʒ/ *noun* **1** [C,U] **change (in/to sth)** the process of becoming or making sth different: *There was little change in the patient's condition overnight.* ∘ *After two very cold winters, people were talking about a change in the climate.* **2** [C] **change (of sth)** something that you take, have or use instead of sth else: *We need to notify the bank of our change of address.* **3** [U] coins or bills of lower value that together make up the same value as a larger coin or bill: *Do you have change for a dollar?* **4** [U] coins of low value: *He needs some change for the phone.* **5** [U] the money that you get back if you pay more than the amount sth costs: *If a cake costs $8 and you pay with a $10 bill, you will get $2 in change.*
IDM **a change of heart** a change in your opinion or the way that you feel
for a change in order to do sth different from usual: *We always stay home in the evenings. Let's go out tonight for a change.*

change·o·ver /ˈtʃeɪndʒˌoʊvər/ *noun* [C] a change from one system to another

☆ **chan·nel¹** /ˈtʃænl/ *noun* [C] **1** a television station: *My favorite program is on Channel 10 at 7:30.* ∘ *Go ahead and change the channel.* **2** a narrow area of water between two seas or oceans **3** an open passage along which liquids can flow: *a drainage channel* **4** a way or route along which news, information, etc. is sent: *We are working through diplomatic channels to free the hostages.*

chan·nel² /ˈtʃænl/ *verb* [T] to make sth move along a particular path or route: *Water is channeled from the river to the fields.* ∘ (*figurative*) *You should channel your energies into something constructive.*

chant¹ /tʃænt/ *noun* [C] a word or phrase that is sung or shouted many times: *A chant of "We're number one!" went around the stadium.*

chant² /tʃænt/ *verb* [I,T] to sing or shout a word or phrase many times: *The protestors marched past, chanting slogans.*

Cha·nu·kah /ˈxɑnəkə/ *noun* [C,U] = HANUK-KAH

cha·os /ˈkeɪɑs/ *noun* [U] a state of great dis-

order; confusion: *The meeting ended in chaos when demonstrators burst into the room.* ∘ *The accident has caused total chaos on the freeway.*

cha·ot·ic /keɪˈɑtɪk/ *adj.* in a state of chaos: *With no one in charge the situation became chaotic.*

chap·el /ˈtʃæpl/ *noun* **1** [C] a small part of a large church that can be used for private prayer **2** [C] a small building or room in a prison, hospital, college, etc. that is used as a church **3** [C,U] a church for some Protestant groups: *a Baptist chapel* **4** [C,U] a regular religious meeting for all the students and teachers at some schools: *We have to attend chapel every morning.*

chap·er·one /ˈʃæpəroʊn/ *noun* [C] an older person who goes to social events for young people to watch them and to make sure that they behave correctly —**chap·er·one** *verb* [T]

chap·lain /ˈtʃæplən/ *noun* [C] a priest who works in a hospital, school, prison, in the army, etc.

☆ **chap·ter** /ˈtʃæptər/ *noun* [C] **1** one of the parts into which a book is divided: *Please read Chapter 2 for tomorrow.* ∘ *In the opening chapter, the author sets the scene of the novel.* **2** a local branch of a club, an organization, etc.

☆ **char·ac·ter** /ˈkærəktər/ *noun* **1** [C,U, sing.] the quality that makes sb/sth different from other people or things; the nature of sb/sth: *Although they are twins, their characters are really different.* ∘ *The new shopping center has completely changed the character of downtown.* ∘ *Modern houses often seem to lack character* (= they all seem the same). **2** [U] a person's inner strength: *The game developed into a test of character rather than just physical strength.* ∘ *Dad said that this camping trip would help build my character.* **3** [C] (*informal*) a person: *There was a suspicious-looking character hanging around outside, so I called the police.* **4** [C] a person who is very amusing, or who has an unusual personality: *Neil's a real character.* **5** [C] a person in a book, story, etc.: *The main character in the book is a boy who finds a dead body.* **6** [C] a letter or sign that you use when you are writing or printing: *Chinese characters*
IDM **in character/out of character** typical/ not typical of sb/sth

☆ **char·ac·ter·is·tic¹** /ˌkærəktəˈrɪstɪk/ *noun* [C] a quality that is typical of sb/sth and that makes him/her/it different from other people or things: *The chief characteristic of reptiles is that they are cold-blooded.*

char·ac·ter·is·tic² /ˌkærəktəˈrɪstɪk/ *adj.* **characteristic (of sb/sth)** typical (of sb/sth): *This piece is characteristic of the artist's early paintings.* ☞ The opposite is **uncharacteristic.** —**char·ac·ter·is·ti·cal·ly** /-kli/ *adv.:* *"No,"* he said, *in his characteristically direct manner.*

char·ac·ter·ize /ˈkærəktəraɪz/ *verb* [T]

tʃ	dʒ	v	θ	ð	s	z	ʃ
chin	June	van	thin	then	so	zoo	she

C

1 (often passive) to be typical of sb/sth: *The 1980s were characterized by big business deals.* **2 characterize sb/sth as sth** to describe the nature of sb/sth or to show a person's character in a particular way: *The President characterized the meeting as friendly and positive.*

cha·rade /ʃəˈreɪd/ *noun* **1 charades** [U] a game that is played at a party, etc. in which one person or team acts out a word for others to guess **2** [C] a situation or event that is clearly false but in which people pretend to do or be sth: *They pretend to be friends, but it's all a charade. Everyone knows they hate each other.*

char·coal /ˈtʃɑrkoʊl/ *noun* [U] a black substance that is produced when you burn wood in an oven with very little air. Charcoal can be used for drawing or as a fuel: *a charcoal grill* (= that uses charcoal for fuel)

☆ **charge¹** /tʃɑrdʒ/ *noun* **1** [C,U] the price that you must pay for sth: *There is no charge for our information booklet.* ○ *We deliver free of charge.* ○ *There is a small admission charge.* ☛ Look at the note at **price. 2** [C] = CHARGE CARD: *Will that be cash, check or charge?* **3** [C] an official statement that says that sb has done sth which is against the law: *All the charges against him were dropped and he was free to go.* **4** [C] a sudden attack where sb/sth runs directly at sb/sth else: *The bull made a charge toward the gate.*

IDM in charge (of sb/sth) in control or command (of sb/sth): *Who is in charge of the office while Alan's gone?* ○ *I'd like to speak to the person in charge.*

press charges (against sb) ⇨ PRESS¹

take charge (of sth) to take control of or responsibility for sth

charge² /tʃɑrdʒ/ *verb* **1** [I,T] **charge (sb/sth) for sth** to ask sb to pay a particular amount of money: *Do you charge for delivery?* ○ *We charge $40 per night for a single room.* ○ *How much did they charge you for that?* **2** [T] to buy sth by using a special plastic card (**a credit card**) instead of money: *"Will you be paying cash for this?" "No, I'll charge it."* **3** [T] **charge sb (with sth)** to accuse sb officially of doing sth that is against the law: *Six men have been charged with attempted robbery.* **4** [I,T] to attack sb/sth by running directly at him/her/it: *The bull put its head down and charged.* ○ *(figurative) The kids charged down the stairs and out the back door.* **5** [T] to put electricity into sth: *to charge a battery*

ˈcharge account *noun* [C] an arrangement with a store or business that allows you to pay for goods at a later date: *to open a charge account at a department store*

ˈcharge card (*also* **charge**) *noun* [C] a small plastic card that you can use to get goods or services without using money. You usually receive a bill once a month for what you have bought ☛ Look at **credit card**.

char·i·ot /ˈtʃæriət/ *noun* [C] an open vehicle with two wheels, that was pulled by a horse or horses in ancient times

cha·ris·ma /kəˈrɪzmə/ *noun* [U] the power that some people have to attract and influence people —**char·is·mat·ic** /ˌkærəzˈmætɪk/ *adj.*: *a charismatic politician*

char·i·ta·ble /ˈtʃærətəbl/ *adj.* **1** kind; generous: *Some people accused him of lying, but a more charitable explanation was that he had made a mistake.* ☛ The opposite is **uncharitable. 2** connected with a charity (1): *Charitable contributions can be deducted from your income tax.*

☆ **char·i·ty** /ˈtʃærəti/ *noun* (*pl.* **char·i·ties**) **1** [C,U] an organization that collects money to help people who are poor, sick, etc. or to do work that will be of benefit to society: *to raise money for charity* ○ *He supports a charity that helps the handicapped.* **2** [U] kindness toward other people: *to act out of charity*

☆ **charm¹** /tʃɑrm/ *noun* **1** [C,U] the quality of being pleasant or attractive: *The charm of the island lies in its unspoiled beauty.* ○ *One of his charms was his ability to tell funny stories.* **2** [C] something that you wear because you believe it will bring you good luck: *a necklace with a good-luck charm on it*

☆ **charm²** /tʃɑrm/ *verb* [T] to please sb; to influence people by your power to attract them: *She charmed the judges at the contest with her bright smile.*

charm·ing /ˈtʃɑrmɪŋ/ *adj.* very pleasing or attractive: *He wrote a charming poem for his grandmother's birthday.* ○ *What a charming little boy!*

charred /tʃɑd/ *adj.* black and partly burned by fire

☆ **chart¹** /tʃɑrt/ *noun* **1** [C] a drawing that shows information in the form of a diagram, etc.: *a temperature chart* ○ *This chart shows the company's profits over the last three years.* **2** [C] a map of the ocean or the sky: *navigation charts* **3 the charts** [plural] an official list of the pop and rock songs that have sold the most copies of records, cassettes, etc.

chart² /tʃɑrt/ *verb* [T] **1** to make a map of one area of the ocean or sky: *an uncharted coastline* **2** to follow or record sth carefully and in detail: *Analysts have been charting the company's financial progress.*

char·ter¹ /ˈtʃɑrtər/ *noun* [C,U] **1** an official written statement of the rights, beliefs and purposes of an organization or a particular group of people: *The club's charter does not permit women to become members.* **2** an official document from a government or another authority, that allows a company, university, town, etc. to exist, and that gives it certain rights **3** the renting of a ship, airplane, etc.

for a particular purpose or for a particular group of people: *a charter flight*

char·ter² /ˈtʃɑrtər/ verb [T] **1** to rent a ship, airplane, etc. for a particular purpose or for a particular group of people **2** to give a charter ¹(2) to an organization or a particular group of people

☆ **chase¹** /tʃeɪs/ verb [I,T] to run after sb/sth in order to catch him/her/it: *The dog chased the cat up a tree.* ○ *The police car chased the stolen van down the highway.*

☆ **chase²** /tʃeɪs/ noun [C] the act of following sb/sth in order to catch him/her/it; chasing or being chased: *an exciting car chase*
IDM **give chase** to begin to run after sb/sth in order to try to catch him/her/it: *The robber ran off and the police officer gave chase.*

chasm /ˈkæzəm/ noun [C] **1** a long deep hole in the ground **2** (*figurative*) a wide difference of feelings, interests, etc.

chas·sis /ˈtʃæsi; ˈʃæsi/ noun [C] (*pl.* **chas·sis** /ˈtʃæsiz; ˈʃæsiz/) the metal frame of a vehicle onto which the other parts fit

chas·ti·ty /ˈtʃæstəti/ noun [U] the state of never having had a sexual relationship: *The nuns took a vow of chastity.*

☆ **chat¹** /tʃæt/ noun [C] a friendly informal conversation: *I had a nice chat with Sandy this afternoon.*

☆ **chat²** /tʃæt/ verb [I] (**chat·ting**; **chat·ted**) to talk to sb in a friendly, informal way: *The senator chatted briefly with some visitors in her office.*

chat·ter¹ /ˈtʃætər/ verb [I] **1** to talk quickly or for a long time about sth unimportant: *The kids chattered away continuously.* **2** (used about your teeth) to knock together because you are cold or frightened

chat·ter² /ˈtʃætər/ noun [U] continuous fast talk, usually about sth unimportant: *Most of the stuff on the radio is just idle chatter.*

chauf·feur /ʃouˈfər/ noun [C] a person whose job is to drive a car for sb else: *a chauffeur-driven limousine* —**chauf·feur** verb [T]: *Every Saturday I have to chauffeur the kids around to sports practice.*

chau·vin·ism /ˈʃouvənɪzəm/ noun [U] **1** = MALE CHAUVINISM **2** a strong belief that your country is better and more important than all others

chau·vin·ist /ˈʃouvənɪst/ noun [C] a person who believes in or shows chauvinism

☆ **cheap¹** /tʃip/ adj. **1** low in price; costing little money: *Oranges are cheap at this time of year.* ○ *It's cheaper to buy a round-trip ticket than two one-way tickets.* ☞ The opposite is **expensive**. **2** charging low prices: *There's a cheap restaurant right around the corner.* ☞ Look also at **inexpensive**. It has a less negative meaning than senses 1 and 2 of **cheap**. **3** of low quality: *The cheap thing broke before I even got it home!* **4** (*informal*) not willing to

spend money: *Her boyfriend is so cheap – he never takes her out to eat.*

cheap² /tʃip/ adv. (*informal*) for a low price: *You can eat pretty cheap in the snack bars on campus.*

cheap·ly /ˈtʃipli/ adv. for a low price: *These items can be produced more cheaply in the Far East.*

cheap·skate /ˈtʃipskeɪt/ noun [C] (*informal*) a person who does not like to spend money and often acts in an unreasonable way in order to avoid spending money: *What a cheapskate – Bob bought his girlfriend a fake diamond ring!*

☆ **cheat¹** /tʃit/ verb [I] to act in a dishonest or unfair way in order to get an advantage for yourself: *Len got caught cheating on the test.* ○ *to cheat at cards*
PHRV **cheat sb (out) of sth** to take sth from sb in a dishonest or unfair way: *They tried to cheat the old lady out of her savings.*

cheat² /tʃit/ noun [C] a person who tries to get money, etc. by acting in a dishonest or unfair way: *The government is trying to crack down on tax cheats.*

cheat·er /ˈtʃitər/ noun [C] a person who cheats on a test, etc.: *Cheaters will automatically receive an "F" on the final exam.*

☆ **check¹** /tʃɛk/ verb **1** [I,T] to examine sth in order to make sure that it is safe, correct, in good condition, etc.: *He wasn't sure whether he had locked the door, so he went back to check.* ○ *Check your work carefully for mistakes before you hand it in.* ○ *Don't forget to check your e-mail* (= to see if you have new messages). ○ *Can you check that we have everything on the list?* ○ *She looked at her calendar to check what time her appointment was.* **2** [T] to write a mark (√) on a form, etc. to show your choice, to show that sth is done, etc. *Check the box next to the right answer.* **3** [T] to give sth to sb at an airport, a restaurant, etc. so that it can be kept in a safe place or taken to another place: *All bags must be checked at the counter.* **4** [T] (*formal*) to stop or go more slowly; to make sb/sth stop or go more slowly: *A tight bandage should check the flow of blood from a wound.*
PHRV **check in (at ...); check into ...** to go to a hotel/airline desk and say that you have arrived: *Passengers should check in two hours before their departure time.*

check sth off to put a check mark (√) next to names or items on a list: *The cartons were all checked off as they were unloaded.*

check on sb/sth to find out more information about sb/sth: *Could you please check on the status of my order?* ○ *I'll just check on the baby and make sure he's all right.*

check out (of ...) to pay your bill and leave a hotel

check sb/sth out 1 (*slang*) to look at sb/sth,

ə	y	w	ţ	eɪ	aɪ	ɔɪ	aʊ	oʊ
about	yes	woman	butter	say	five	boy	now	go

especially because it is interesting: *Wow! Check this out, you guys!* ○ *Check out Darla's cool new jacket!* **2** to find out more information about sb/sth, especially to find out if sth is true or not: *We need to check out these rumors about possible pay cuts.*

check sth out 1 to examine or test sth to make sure it works correctly: *The car is back from the repair shop, so let's check it out on the highway!* **2** to record that sth has been borrowed or bought: *to check out a book from the library* ○ *It took a long time for the cashier to check my groceries out.*

check sth over to examine sth to make sure it is correct: *Check your work over carefully before you hand it in.*

check up on sb/sth to make sure sb/sth is working correctly, behaving well, etc., especially if you think they are not: *I wish Mom wouldn't keep checking up on me every five minutes!*

☆ **check²** /tʃɛk/ *noun* **1** [C] **a check (on sth)** a close look at sth to make sure that it is safe, correct, in good condition, etc.: *We conduct regular checks on our products to make sure that they are of high quality.* ○ *a safety check* ○ *a security check* ☞ Look also at **reality check**. **2** [C,U] a piece of paper printed by a bank that you can fill out, sign and use to pay for things: *She wrote a check for $40.* ○ *I went to the bank to cash a check.* ○ *If there isn't enough money in your account, your check will bounce* (= the bank will not pay it). ○ *Can I pay by check?* ☞ picture at **money.** Look also at **paycheck.** **3** [C, usually sing.] a bill for food in a restaurant: *Miss, could I have the check, please?* **4** [C] = CHECK MARK: *Put a check next to the right answer.* **5** [sing.] (in the game of chess) the situation in which a player must move to protect his/her king ☞ Look at **checkmate.** **6** [C] an act of going more slowly or stopping or of making sb/sth go more slowly or stop: *the system of checks and balances among the branches of the federal government*

IDM hold/keep sth in check to stop sth from advancing or increasing too quickly: *government measures to keep inflation in check*

check·book /'tʃɛkbʊk/ *noun* [C] a book of checks²(2) from a bank

checked /tʃɛkt/ (*also* **checkered**) *adj.* with a pattern of squares: *a red-and-white checked tablecloth* ☞ picture at **pattern.**

check·er /'tʃɛkər/ *noun* [C] a person whose job is to use a machine (**a cash register**) to add up the cost of the things that sb is buying, and to take their money: *a supermarket checker*

check·er·board /'tʃɛkərbɔrd/ *noun* [C] a square board with 64 smaller squares in two colors on it, that you play checkers on

check·ered /'tʃɛkərd/ *adj.* = CHECKED

check·ers /'tʃɛkərz/ *noun* [U] a game for two

players that you play on a board with 64 squares on it (**a checkerboard**) using round pieces in two different colors: *to play checkers* ○ *a game of checkers*

check-in *noun* [C] **1** the act of checking in at an airport: *Our check-in time is 10:30 a.m.* **2** the place where you check in at an airport: *the check-in desk*

checking account *noun* [C] a bank account from which you can pay for things or take out money by writing a check²(2) : *to open/close a checking account* ☞ Look at **savings account.**

check·list /'tʃɛklɪst/ *noun* [C] a list of things that you must do or have

☆ **check mark** (*also* **check**) *noun* [C] a mark (√) that shows your choice, that sth has been done, or that sth is not correct: *She put a check mark next to each spelling mistake on the students' quizzes.*

check mark

check·mate /'tʃɛkmeɪt/ (*also* **mate**) *noun* [sing.] (in the game of chess) the situation in which you cannot protect your king and so have lost the game ☞ Look at **check²**(5).

check·out /'tʃɛkaʊt/ *noun* [C] the place in a store where you pay for the things you have bought

check·point /'tʃɛkpɔɪnt/ *noun* [C] a place where all people and vehicles must stop and be checked: *an army checkpoint*

check·up /'tʃɛkʌp/ *noun* [C] a general medical examination to find out whether you are healthy: *You should visit your dentist for a checkup twice a year.*

Ched·dar (*also* **cheddar**) /'tʃɛdər/ *noun* [U] a type of hard cheese that is orange, white, or yellow and that can be eaten cooked or raw

☆ **cheek** /tʃik/ *noun* [C] one of the two parts of your face that are on each side of your nose and mouth and below your eyes: *Their cheeks were red when they came in out of the cold.* ○ *Tears rolled down her cheeks.* ☞ picture on page A24. Look also at **tongue-in-cheek.**

cheek·bone /'tʃikboʊn/ *noun* [C] the bone that is below your eye

☆ **cheer¹** /tʃɪr/ *verb* [I,T] to shout to show that you like sth or to encourage sb who is taking part in a competition, sport, etc.: *The crowd clapped and cheered.* ○ *Everyone cheered the winner as he crossed the finish line.*

PHRV cheer sb on to cheer sb in order to encourage him/her to do better: *As the runners started the last lap, the crowd cheered them on.*

cheer (sb) up to become or to make sb happier: *Cheer up! Things aren't that bad.* ○ *This good news should cheer him up.*

☆ **cheer²** /tʃɪr/ *noun* [C] a loud shout to show that you like sth or to encourage sb who is taking part in a competition, sport, etc.: *There were a lot of cheers when the team came onto the field.*

☆ **cheer·ful** /'tʃɪrfl/ *adj.* happy: *Tom seems very cheerful despite his illness.* ○ *a cheerful smile* —**cheer·ful·ly** *adv.*

cheer·lead·er /'tʃɪrlidər/ *noun* [C] **1** a person who wears a special uniform and who shouts, dances, etc. in front of the audience at a sports game in order to encourage the audience to shout in support of the players **2 cheerleader (for sb/sth)** a person who supports a person, policy, etc. and who encourages others to support the same person or thing: *one of the biggest cheerleaders for the President's economic policies*

cheers /tʃɪrz/ *interj.* (*informal*) (used to express good wishes before you have an alcoholic drink): *"Cheers!" she said, raising her wine glass.*

☆ **cheese** /tʃiz/ *noun* **1** [U] a type of solid food that is made from milk. Cheese is usually white or yellow in color: ○ *a cheese sandwich* ○ *Sprinkle the top of the pizza with grated cheese.* **2** [C] a type of cheese: *a wide selection of cheeses* ☛ Look also at **big cheese.**

cheese·cake /'tʃizkeɪk/ *noun* [C,U] a type of cake that is made from soft white cheese, eggs and sugar on a base made of crushed cookies

chee·tah /'tʃitə/ *noun* [C] a large wild animal of the cat family that comes from Africa and can run very fast

☆ **chef** /ʃɛf/ *noun* [C] a person who works as the chief cook in a hotel, restaurant, etc.

☆ **chem·i·cal¹** /'kɛmɪkl/ *adj.* connected with chemistry; produced by processes that involve changing the structure of a substance: *a chemical reaction* ○ *the chemical industry* ○ *a ban on the use of chemical weapons* ○ *She's being treated for chemical dependency* (= being addicted to drugs). —**chem·i·cal·ly** /-kli/ *adv.*

☆ **chem·i·cal²** /'kɛmɪkl/ *noun* [C] a substance that is used or produced in a chemical process: *You must wear eye protection when handling dangerous chemicals.*

chem·ist /'kɛmɪst/ *noun* [C] **1** a person who is a specialist in chemistry **2** (*BrE*) = PHARMACIST

☆ **chem·is·try** /'kɛməstri/ *noun* [U] **1** the scientific study of the structure of substances and what happens to them in different conditions or when mixed with each other: *We did an experiment in chemistry class today.* ○ *a chemistry laboratory* **2** the structure of a particular substance and the way that it may change under different conditions

cheque /tʃɛk/ *noun* [C] (*BrE*) = CHECK²(2)

cher·ish /'tʃɛrɪʃ/ *verb* [T] **1** to love sb/sth and take care of him/her/it: *The ring was her most cherished possession.* **2** to keep a thought, feeling, etc. in your mind and think about it often:

We cherish the time we spend with our grandchildren.

☆ **cher·ry** /'tʃɛri/ *noun* **1** [C] (*pl.* **cher·ries**) a small round black or red fruit that grows on a tree and that has a small hard part (**pit**) inside it **2** [C] (*also* 'cherry tree') the tree that produces cherries: *a flowering cherry* **3** [U] the wood from a cherry tree: *a table made of cherry*

cherries

☆ **chess** /tʃɛs/ *noun* [U] a game for two people that is played on a board with 64 black and white squares (**a chessboard**). Each player has sixteen pieces which can be moved according to fixed rules.

☆ **chest** /tʃɛst/ *noun* [C] **1** a container, usually with a lid that is fastened on one side, that is used for storing or transporting things: *a jewelry chest* ○ *We'll pack the food for the picnic in the ice chest.* ○ *The aspirin is in the medicine chest* (= the cabinet where you keep the medicines) *in the bathroom.* **2** the upper part of the front of your body: *What is your chest measurement?* ○ *This jacket has a 40-inch chest.* ○ *a hairy chest* ○ *Linda went to the doctor, complaining of chest pains.* ☛ picture on page A24.

IDM get sth off your chest (*informal*) to talk about sth that you have been thinking about or that has been worrying you

chest·nut /'tʃɛsnʌt/ *noun* [C] **1** (*also* 'chestnut tree') a tree with large leaves that produces smooth reddish-brown nuts in shells with sharp points **2** one of the nuts from the chestnut tree. You can eat some chestnuts.

☆ **chew** /tʃu/ *verb* [I,T] to break up food in your mouth with your teeth before you swallow it: *You should chew your food carefully.*

PHRV chew sb out (*slang*) to criticize or speak to sb in an angry way, because he/she has done sth wrong: *The boss really chewed him out for showing up late.*

'**chewing gum** *noun* [U] = GUM(2)

chic /ʃik/ *adj.* fashionable; elegant

chi·ca·no /tʃɪ'kɑnoʊ/ *noun* [C] (*pl.* **chi·ca·nos**) a person in the U.S. whose family came from Mexico —**chi·ca·no** *adj.*

tʃ	dʒ	v	θ	ð	s	z	ʃ
chin	June	van	thin	then	so	zoo	she

chick /tʃɪk/ *noun* [C] **1** a young bird, especially a young chicken **2** (*informal*) a young woman or girl ☞ This word is used by some men. Many women dislike it.

chickens

rooster chick hen

☆**chick·en¹** /'tʃɪkən/ *noun* **1** [C] a bird that people keep for its eggs and its meat **2** [U] the meat of this bird: *roast chicken* ○ *a chicken sandwich*

☞ Notice that chicken is the general word for the bird and its meat. A male chicken is called a **rooster**, a female is called a **hen** and a young bird is called a **chick**.

chick·en² /'tʃɪkən/ *verb*
PHRV **chicken out (of sth)** (*informal*) to decide not to do sth because you are afraid: *Come on! You said you'd give a speech – you can't chicken out now!*

chicken pox /'tʃɪkən pɑks/ *noun* [U] a disease, especially of children. When you have chicken pox you have a high temperature and get red spots on your skin that itch a lot.

☆**chief¹** /tʃif/ *noun* [C] **1** the leader or ruler of a group of people: *Native American tribal chiefs* **2** the person who has command or control over an organization: *the chief of police*

☆**chief²** /tʃif/ *adj.* (only *before* a noun) **1** most important; main: *One of the chief reasons for his decision was money.* **2** of the highest rank: *the Chief Justice of the Supreme Court*

ˌchief exˈecutive *noun* [C] **1** the Chief Executive the President of the United States **2** (*also* ˌchief exˌecutive ˈofficer) (*abbr.* **CEO**) the leader of a large company or organization

chief·ly /'tʃifli/ *adv.* mainly; mostly: *His success was due chiefly to hard work.*

☆**child** /tʃaɪld/ *noun* [C] (*pl.* **chil·dren** /'tʃɪldrən/) **1** a boy or girl; a human who is not yet fully grown: *A group of children were playing in the park.* ○ *a six-year-old child* ○ *child abuse* ☞ **Kid** is more common in informal English. **2** a son or daughter of any age: *She has two children, but both are married and have moved away.* ○ *He is married with three children.*

☞ An **only child** is a child who has no brothers or sisters. A couple may **adopt** a child who is not their own son or daughter (for example if the child's parents are dead). A **foster child** stays for a certain period of time with a family that is not his/her own.

child·birth /'tʃaɪldbərθ/ *noun* [U] the act of giving birth to a baby: *His wife died in childbirth.*

child·care /'tʃaɪldkɛr/ *noun* [U] the service of taking care of children while their parents are at work: *It's difficult to find affordable childcare these days.*

☆**child·hood** /'tʃaɪldhʊd/ *noun* [C,U] the time when you are a child: *Harriet had a very unhappy childhood.* ○ *childhood memories*

child·ish /'tʃaɪldɪʃ/ *adj.* like a child

☞ If you say that people or their behavior are **childlike**, you mean that they are like children in some way: *childlike innocence* ○ *his childlike enthusiasm for the project*. If you say that an adult's behavior is **childish**, you are criticizing it because you think it is silly and that he/she should be more mature: *Don't be so childish! You can't always have everything you want.*

—**child·ish·ly** *adv.*: *to giggle childishly*
child·less /'tʃaɪldləs/ *adj.* having no children: *a childless couple*
child·like /'tʃaɪldlaɪk/ *adj.* like a child ☞ Look at **childish**.
chil·dren /'tʃɪldrən/ *pl.* of CHILD
ˈchild supˌport *noun* [U] money that a parent who does not live with his/her children must pay to support them
chil·i /'tʃɪli/ *noun* [C,U] (*pl.* **chil·ies**) **1** [C,U] (*also* ˈchili pepper) a small green or red vegetable that is used in cooking to give food a strong hot taste **2** (*also* chil·i con car·ne /ˌtʃɪli kɑn 'kɑrni/) [U] a hot-tasting dish of meat and red beans: *a bowl of chili*
chill¹ /tʃɪl/ *verb* [I,T] to become or to make sb/sth colder: *It's better to chill white wine before you serve it.*
chill² /tʃɪl/ *noun* [sing.] an unpleasant coldness: *There's a chill in the air.* ○ (*figurative*) *A chill of fear went down my spine.*
chill·ing /'tʃɪlɪŋ/ *adj.* frightening: *a chilling ghost story*
chill·y /'tʃɪli/ *adj.* (**chill·i·er**; **chill·i·est**) unpleasantly cold: *It's a chilly morning. You need a coat on.* ○ (*figurative*) *The movie got a chilly reception from critics.*
chime¹ /tʃaɪm/ *verb* [I] (used about a bell) to ring
PHRV **chime in (with sth)** (*informal*) to interrupt a conversation and add your own comments
chime² /tʃaɪm/ *noun* [C] the sound of a bell or a clock chiming
☆**chim·ney** /'tʃɪmni/ *noun* [C] (*pl.* **chim·neys**) the passage through which smoke, etc. can get out of a building. A chimney in a house usually goes up from a fire or heating system, behind the walls and to a hole in the roof: *Smoke poured out of the factory chimneys.* ☞ picture on page A28.
chim·pan·zee /ˌtʃɪmpæn'zi/ (*also informal*

chimp /tʃɪmp/) *noun* [C] a type of small ape that lives in Africa

☆ **chin** /'tʃɪn/ *noun* [C] the part of your face that is below your mouth: *He sat listening with his chin in his hand.* ☞ picture on page A24.

chi·na /'tʃaɪnə/ *noun* [U] **1** the substance of which cups, plates, etc. can be made. China is made from fine white baked clay: *a china vase* **2** cups, saucers, plates, etc. that are made from china (1): *The dinner was served on fine china.*

chips

French fries potato chips

☆ **chip¹** /tʃɪp/ *noun* [C] **1** a small piece of wood, stone, glass, etc. that has broken off sth **2** a place where a piece has broken off sth: *This dish has a chip in it.* **3** a thin piece of food that has been fried in oil, dried and covered with salt: *potato chips ∘ tortilla chips ∘ Help yourself to some chips and dip.* **4** a flat round piece of plastic that you use instead of money when you are playing some games **5** (*also* **microchip; computer chip; silicon chip**) a very small piece of a special material (**silicon**) that is used inside a computer, etc. to make it work **6** (*BrE*) = FRENCH FRY

IDM **have a chip on your shoulder** (*informal*) to be angry about sth for a long time, especially because you think you have been treated unfairly

chip
crack

chipped cracked broken

chip² /tʃɪp/ *verb* [I,T] (**chip·ping; chipped**) to lose or to knock a small piece off the edge or surface of sth: *I fell off my bike and chipped my tooth.*

chip·munk /'tʃɪpmʌŋk/ *noun* [C] a small animal with a long tail and brown fur with black and white stripes

chi·ro·prac·tor /'kaɪrəpræktər/ *noun* [C] a person whose job is to treat pain in people's bodies by pressing on and moving their bones, especially in sb's back

chirp /tʃɜrp/ *noun* [C] the short high sound that a small bird makes —**chirp** *verb* [I]

chis·el /'tʃɪzl/ *noun* [C] a tool with a sharp end that is used for cutting or shaping wood, stone, etc. ☞ picture at **tool**.

chives /tʃaɪvz/ *noun* [plural] a plant with purple flowers and long thin leaves that are used in cooking. Chives taste similar to onions.

chlo·rine /'klɔrin; klɔ'rin/ *noun* [U] (*symbol* **Cl**) a greenish-yellow gas with a strong smell, that is used for making water safe to drink or to swim in

☆ **choc·o·late¹** /'tʃɑklət/ *noun* **1** [U] a sweet brown substance that you usually buy in the form of a hard block (**bar**). Chocolate is made from cocoa beans: *milk chocolate* (= sweet and light in color) ∘ *dark chocolate* (= more bitter and darker in color) **2** [C] a small candy that is made from chocolate with a nut or another sweet substance inside: *a box of assorted chocolates* ☞ Look also at **hot chocolate**.

☆ **choc·o·late²** /'tʃɑklət/ *adj.* **1** made with chocolate: *chocolate cake ∘ a chocolate donut* **2** dark brown

☆ **choice¹** /tʃɔɪs/ *noun* **1** [C] **choice (between A and B)** an act of choosing between two or more people or things: *to make the right/ wrong choice ∘ David faced a difficult choice between moving to a different city and losing his job. ∘ You can have first choice of the candy* (= you can choose first). **2** [U] the right or chance to choose: *All the hotels were full so we had no choice but to stay at Lisa's house. ∘ to have freedom of choice* **3** [C,U] two or more things from which you can or must choose: *There's a choice of six different movies every night.* **4** [C] a person or thing that has been chosen: *Who's your choice for governor?*

IDM **by choice** because you want to; of your own free will: *Rick didn't leave his job by choice — he was fired.*

choice² /tʃɔɪs/ *adj.* of good quality: *choice beef*

☆ **choir** /'kwaɪər/ *noun* [C] a group of people who sing together: *Dennis sings in the church choir. ∘ The choir meets on Thursdays to rehearse.*

☆ **choke** /tʃoʊk/ *verb* [I,T] to be or to make sb unable to breathe because sth is stopping air from getting into the lungs: *The child swallowed a pen cap and choked to death. ∘ The smoke was choking us.*

PHRV **choke sth back** to hide or control a strong emotion: *to choke back tears*

chol·er·a /'kɑlərə/ *noun* [U] a serious disease that makes it difficult for you to keep food in your body. Cholera is most common in hot countries and can be carried by water.

cho·les·ter·ol /kə'lɛstərɔl/ *noun* [U] a substance that is found in the bodies of people and animals, and that helps to carry fats. Too much cholesterol is thought to be a cause of heart disease: *to have a high/low cholesterol level*

☆ **choose** /tʃuz/ *verb* [I,T] (*p.t.* **chose** /tʃoʊz/; *p.p.* **cho·sen** /'tʃoʊzn/) **1** **choose (between A and/or B); choose sb/sth as sth** to pick or select the person or thing that you prefer:

C

Choose carefully before you make a final decision. ○ Amy had to choose between getting a job or going to college. ○ You can choose three questions out of the five on the exam. ○ There were too many things to choose from. ○ The viewers chose this program as their favorite. **2** to decide or prefer to do sth: You are free to leave whenever you choose. ○ They chose to resign rather than work for the new manager.

☆ **chop¹** /'tʃɑp/ verb [T] (**chop·ping**; **chopped**) **chop sth (up) (into sth)** to cut sth into small pieces with an ax or knife: They chopped the logs into firewood. ○ finely chopped herbs ○ Chop the onions up into small pieces.

PHRV **chop sth down** to cut a tree, etc. at the bottom so that it falls down

chop sth off (sth) to remove sth from sth by cutting it with an ax or knife: to chop a branch off a tree

chop² /'tʃɑp/ noun [C] **1** an act of chopping sth **2** a thick slice of meat, usually from a pig: a pork chop ☞ Look at **steak**.

chop·per /'tʃɑpər/ noun [C] (informal) = HELICOPTER

chop·py /'tʃɑpi/ adj. (**chop·pi·er**; **chop·pi·est**) **1** (used especially about the ocean, etc.) having a lot of small waves or uneven movement **2** (used about writing or speech) using many very short sentences and changing topics too often

chop·sticks /'tʃɑpstɪks/ noun [plural] two thin sticks that people in China, Japan, etc. use for picking up food

cho·ral /'kɔrəl/ adj. written for or involving a group of singers (**a choir**)

chord /kɔrd/ noun [C] two or more musical notes that are played at the same time

IDM **strike a chord** ⇨ STRIKE²

chore /tʃɔr/ noun [C] a job that is not interesting but that you must do: household chores

cho·re·o·graph /'kɔriəgræf/ verb [T] to design and arrange the movements of a dance

cho·re·og·ra·pher /ˌkɔri'ɑgrəfər/ noun [C] a person whose job is to plan the movements for a dance

cho·re·og·ra·phy /ˌkɔri'ɑgrəfi/ noun [U] the arrangement of movements for a dance

cho·rus /'kɔrəs/ noun [C] **1** a large group of people who sing together **2** (also **refrain**) the part of a song that is repeated at the end of each verse: The audience joined in for the chorus. **3** a piece of music for a large group to sing **4** something that a lot of people say together: a chorus of cheers, boos, criticism, etc. **5** a group of singers and dancers in a show

chose p.t. of CHOOSE

cho·sen p.p. of CHOOSE

chow¹ /tʃaʊ/ noun [U] (slang) food

chow² /tʃaʊ/ verb [I,T] **chow (down) on sth**; **chow (sth) down** (slang) to eat sth quickly because you are very hungry or because you

like it very much: After the game, we chowed down on burgers and hot dogs.

chow·der /'tʃaʊdər/ noun [U] a thick soup made with vegetables and usually fish: clam chowder

Christ /kraɪst/ (also **Jesus**; **Jesus Christ**) noun the man who Christians believe is the son of God and who established the Christian religion

chris·ten /'krɪsn/ verb [T] to give sb/sth a name: Dad christened his new boat "The Wanderer." ○ There have been so many accidents on this road that they've christened it "Suicide Alley." ☞ Look at **baptize**.

☆ **Chris·tian** /'krɪstʃən; 'krɪʃtʃən/ noun [C] a person whose religion is Christianity: Christians all over the world will join in prayers for peace today. —**Chris·tian** adj.: the Christian Church, faith, religion, etc.

Chris·ti·an·i·ty /ˌkrɪstʃi'ænəti/ noun [U] the religion that is based on the teachings of Jesus Christ: to be converted to Christianity

☆ **Christ·mas** /'krɪsməs/ (also informal **Xmas**) noun [C,U] Christmas Day, or the period of time before and after this holiday: Merry Christmas! ○ Where are you spending Christmas this year? ○ the Christmas season

'**Christmas card** noun [C] a card with a picture on the front and a greeting inside that people send to their friends and relatives at Christmas

ˌ**Christmas** '**Day** (also **Christmas**) noun [C] the day on which Christians celebrate the birth of Christ each year. For most Christians Christmas Day is December 25.

ˌ**Christmas** '**Eve** noun [C] the day before Christmas Day, December 24

'**Christmas tree** noun [C] a tree with thin sharp leaves (**an evergreen tree**), or an artificial tree, which people bring into their homes and decorate with bright lights and colored balls

chrome /kroʊm/ noun [U] hard shiny metal that is used for covering other metals: a chrome bumper on a car

chro·mo·some /'kroʊməsoʊm; -zoʊm/ noun [C] the part of the cells of living things that contains the information for producing new cells

chron·ic /'krɑnɪk/ adj. (used about a disease or a problem) that continues for a long time: chronic bronchitis ○ There is a chronic shortage of housing in the city. —**chron·i·cal·ly** /-kli/ adv.

chron·i·cle /'krɑnɪkl/ noun [C] a record of events that happened in the past

chron·o·log·i·cal /ˌkrɑnə'lɑdʒɪkl/ adj. arranged in the order in which the events happened: a list of events arranged in chronological order —**chron·o·log·i·cal·ly** /-kli/ adv.

ər	ɪr	ɛr	ɑr	ɔr	ʊr	ʒ	h	ŋ
bird	near	hair	car	north	tour	vision	hat	sing

chub·by /'tʃʌbi/ adj. (**chub·bi·er**; **chub·bi·est**) slightly fat; round: chubby cheeks

chuck·le /'tʃʌkl/ verb [I] to laugh quietly: Bruce chuckled to himself as he read the letter. —**chuck·le** noun [C]: He put down the phone with a chuckle.

chug /tʃʌg/ verb (**chug·ging**; **chugged**) [T] (slang) to drink sth completely, without stopping: Each of those guys chugged a whole pitcher of beer!

PHRV chug along, down, up, etc. (used about a machine or an engine) to move in a particular direction while making short repeated knocking sounds: The train chugged out of the station.

chum /tʃʌm/ noun [C] (informal, old-fashioned) a friend

chunk /tʃʌŋk/ noun [C] a large or thick piece of sth: chunks of ice floating in the lake ○ (figurative) A big chunk of my income goes toward paying bills.

chunk·y /'tʃʌŋki/ adj. (**chunk·i·er**; **chunk·i·est**) **1** short and slightly fat **2** containing thick pieces: chunky peanut butter

☆ **church** /tʃɔrtʃ/ noun **1** [C,U] a building where Christians go to pray: Services are held in this church every Sunday morning at 10. ○ They are getting married in a beautiful old church. ○ the church steeple ○ Do you go to church regularly? ☞ Notice that when you are talking about going to a ceremony (a service) in a church you say "in church," "to church" or "at church" without " a" or " the": Was Mrs. Stevens in church today?

2 (also **Church**) [C] a particular group of Christians: the Catholic, Methodist, Southern Baptist, etc. church

church·go·er /'tʃɔrtʃgoʊər/ noun [C] a person who goes to church regularly

churn /tʃɔrn/ verb **1** [T] to beat milk or cream so that it turns into butter **2** [I,T] **churn (sth) (up)** to move, or to make sth move with great force: The hurricane churned up huge waves along the coast.

PHRV churn sth out (informal) to produce large numbers of sth very quickly: Some authors of romance novels can churn out a new book every month.

chute /ʃut/ noun [C] a passage down which you can drop or slide things so that you do not have to carry them: a laundry chute

☆ **the CIA** /ˌsi aɪ 'eɪ/ noun [sing.] the Central Intelligence Agency; the government organization that tries to get secret political and military information about other countries ☞ Look at the note at **White House**.

ci·der /'saɪdər/ (also ˌapple 'cider) noun [U] a drink that is made from pressed apples

☆ **ci·gar** /sɪ'gɑr/ noun [C] a roll of dried tobacco leaves that people smoke. Cigars are larger and more expensive than cigarettes: cigar smoke

☆ **cig·a·rette** /ˌsɪgə'rɛt; 'sɪgərɛt/ noun [C] a roll of tobacco in a tube of thin white paper that people smoke: a pack of cigarettes ○ to smoke a cigarette ○ She lit another cigarette. ○ John put out his cigarette.

cin·der /'sɪndər/ noun [C] a very small piece of coal, wood, etc. that has been burning and may still be hot

cin·e·ma /'sɪnəmə/ noun **1** [U] (formal) the art and industry of making movies: one of the most important directors in Latin American cinema ☞ Look also at **movie**. **2** [C] (BrE) = MOVIE THEATER

cin·na·mon /'sɪnəmən/ noun [U] a brown powder that is used for giving flavor to sweet food

cir·ca /'sɔrkə/ prep. (abbr. **ca.**) (formal) (used with dates) about: The vase was made circa 600 B.C.

☆ **cir·cle¹** /'sɔrkl/ noun **1** [C] a line that curves around to form the shape of a ring. Every point on the line is the same distance from the center: The kids were drawing circles and squares on a piece of paper. ○ We all stood in a circle and held hands. ☞ picture at **shape**. **2** [C] a flat, round area: She cut out a circle of paper. **3** [C] a group of people who are friends, or who have the same interest or profession: He has a large circle of friends. ○ Her name was well known in artistic circles.

IDM a vicious circle/cycle ⇨ VICIOUS

cir·cle² /'sɔrkl/ verb **1** [I,T] to move, or to move around sth, in a circle, especially in the air: The plane circled the town several times before it landed. **2** [T] to draw a circle around sth, e.g. on a test: There are three possible answers to each question. Circle the correct one.

cir·cuit /'sɔrkət/ noun [C] **1** a complete circular path that an electric current can flow around ☞ Look also at **closed-circuit television**. **2** a number of events that people take part in, moving around from place to place: Now that Senator Wilson is retired, he's traveling the college lecture circuit (= giving lectures at many different colleges). **3** an area that a judge travels around, hearing court cases in several different cities: the 9th U.S. Circuit Court of Appeals

'**circuit ˌbreaker** noun [C] a small piece of equipment that stops the flow of electricity if there is too much power in a circuit ☞ Look at **fuse¹**(3).

☆ **cir·cu·lar¹** /'sɔrkyələr/ adj. **1** round and flat; shaped like a circle: a circular table **2** (used about a trip, etc.) going around in a circle: The bus will take you on a circular tour of Boston.

cir·cu·lar² /'sɔrkyələr/ noun [C] a printed letter, notice or advertisement that is sent to a large number of people: an advertising circular

tʃ	dʒ	v	θ	ð	s	z	ʃ
chin	June	van	thin	then	so	zoo	she

circulate 118

cir·cu·late /ˈsɚkyəleɪt/ *verb* **1** [I,T] to go from one person to another; to pass information from one person to another: *Stories were circulating about the mayor's private life.* ◦ *We circulated a copy of the report to each department.* **2** [I,T] (used about a substance) to move or make sth move around continuously: *Blood circulates around the body.*

cir·cu·la·tion /ˌsɚkyəˈleɪʃn/ *noun* **1** [U] the passing of sth from one person or place to another: *the circulation of news, information, rumors, etc.* ◦ *Old silver dollar coins are no longer in circulation* (= being used by people). **2** [C] the number of copies of a newspaper, magazine, etc. that are sold each time it is produced: *This newspaper has a circulation of over a million.* **3** [sing.] the movement of blood around the body: *Grandma says she has poor circulation, so her hands and feet get cold easily.*

cir·cum·cise /ˈsɚkəmsaɪz/ *verb* [T] to cut off the skin at the end of a person's sexual organ, for religious or (in the case of a man) medical reasons —**cir·cum·ci·sion** /ˌsɚkəmˈsɪʒn/ *noun* [C,U]

cir·cum·fer·ence /sɚˈkʌmfrəns/ *noun* [C,U] the distance around a circle or sth circular: *The circumference of the moon is about 6,800 miles.* ◦ *The moon is about 6,800 miles in circumference.*

☆ **cir·cum·stance** /ˈsɚkəmstæns/ *noun* **1** [C, usually pl.] the facts and events that affect what happens in a particular situation: *We need to know the exact circumstances surrounding the accident.* ◦ *I'm not sure what I would do under those circumstances.* ◦ *the unusual circumstances surrounding her death* ◦ *We can only make exceptions to the rules in special circumstances.* **2 circumstances** [plural] (*formal*) the amount of money that you have: *The company has promised to repay the money when its financial circumstances improve.*

IDM under no/any circumstances never, for any reason: *Under no circumstances will this government cooperate with terrorists.* ◦ *Late papers will not be accepted under any circumstances.*

under the circumstances as the result of a particular situation: *Well, it's not an ideal solution, but it's the best we can do under the circumstances.*

cir·cus /ˈsɚkəs/ *noun* [C] a show performed in a large tent by a company of people and often animals: *We saw clowns, acrobats, lions and elephants at the circus.*

ci·ta·tion /saɪˈteɪʃn/ *noun* [C] **1** an official warning that you get after you have done sth wrong, that often means that you have to go to court: *Police officers will issue citations to drivers who park here without a permit.* ◦ *a traffic citation* **2** an official report that praises

sb for sth he/she has done: *a citation for bravery*

cite /saɪt/ *verb* [T] (*formal*) to mention sth as an example to support what you are saying: *She cited the high unemployment figures as an example of the government's bad management.*

☆ **cit·i·zen** /ˈsɪtəzn/ *noun* [C] **1** a person who is legally accepted as a member of a particular country: *She was born in Japan, but became an American citizen in 1981.* ◦ *a British citizen* **2** a person who lives in a town or city: *Many of the citizens of New York leave the city for the beach during the summer.* ☞ Look at **senior citizen.**

cit·i·zen·ship /ˈsɪtəzənʃɪp/ *noun* [U] the state of being a citizen of a particular country: *After living in Spain for twenty years, he decided to apply for Spanish citizenship.*

cit·rus /ˈsɪtrəs/ (*also* **citrus fruit**) *noun* [C,U] (a) fruit such as an orange or a lemon

☆ **cit·y** /ˈsɪti/ *noun* (*pl.* **cit·ies**) **1** [C] a large and important town: *Venice is one of the most beautiful cities in the world.* ◦ *Many people are worried about housing conditions in our inner cities* (= the central parts where there are often social problems). **2** [C] a town or city (1) that has specific rights and borders that were decided by the state government: *the city council* ◦ *a bar just outside the city limits* **3 the city** [sing.] the government of a city (2) and the related offices that provide services for the people who live there: *I work for the city.* ◦ *The city picks up our trash once a week.*

city hall (*also* often **City Hall**) *noun* **1** [C] the building where the offices of a city's government are **2** [U] the government of a city: *Our neighborhood is ready to fight city hall in order to get our streets repaired.*

☆ **civ·ic** /ˈsɪvɪk/ *adj.* of a city or town: *civic pride* (= feeling proud because you belong to a particular town or city)

civ·ics /ˈsɪvɪks/ *noun* [U] the study of the rights and responsibilities of citizens and the way government works

☆ **civ·il** /ˈsɪvl/ *adj.* **1** polite, but not very friendly: *I know you don't like the director, but please try and be civil to him.* **2** (only *before* a noun) connected with the public, not with the army or a church: *civil aviation* ◦ *civil engineering* (= the designing and building of roads, railroads, bridges, etc.) ◦ *We got married in a civil ceremony* (= not a religious one). **3** (in law) relating to the rights of ordinary people, and not criminal offenses: *a civil case*

☆ **ci·vil·ian** /səˈvɪlyən/ *noun* [C] a person who is not in the police or military forces: *Two soldiers and one civilian were killed when the bomb exploded.* ◦ *He left the army and returned to civilian life.*

☆ **civ·i·li·za·tion** /ˌsɪvələˈzeɪʃn/ *noun* **1** [C,U] a society that has its own highly developed culture and way of life: *the civilizations of ancient*

i	ɪ	ɛ	æ	ɑ	ɔ	ʌ	ʊ	u
see	sit	ten	cat	hot	saw	cup	put	too

Greece and Rome ◦ *Western civilization* **2** [U] an advanced state of social and cultural development, or the process of reaching this state: *China had reached a higher level of civilization than Europe at that time.* ◦ *The civilization of the human race has taken thousands of years.*

☆ **civ·i·lized** /ˈsɪvəlaɪzd/ *adj.* **1** (used about a society) having a high level of social and cultural development: *In a civilized society there should not be people sleeping on the streets.* **2** polite and reasonable: *a civilized conversation*

ˌ**civil** ˈ**liberties** *noun* [plural] a citizen's legal right to such rights as freedom of speech, freedom of religion, etc.

ˌ**civil** ˈ**rights** *noun* [plural] the legal right to freedom and equality for citizens of every race, sex, religion, etc.: *the continuing struggle for civil rights for black Americans*

ˌ**civil** ˈ**war** *noun* **1 the Civil War** [sing.] the war that was fought from 1861 to 1865 between the northern and the southern states. The two groups of states fought about whether it was right to own slaves. **2** [C,U] a war between different groups of people who live in the same country

clad /klæd/ *adj.* (not before a noun) (*formal*) dressed: *Many people were clad only in pajamas as they escaped from the burning building.*

☆ **claim¹** /kleɪm/ *verb* [T] **1** to say that sth is true, without having any proof. *The bus driver claimed that she had not seen the bike rider.* ◦ *Eric claims the book belongs to him.* ◦ *She claims to be the oldest person in the U.S.* ◦ *No one has claimed responsibility for the bomb attack.* **2** to ask for sth because you think you should have it or that it belongs to you: *The police are keeping the animal until somebody claims it.* ◦ *If you are disabled, you can claim a special deduction on your taxes.* **3** (*formal*) to cause death: *The earthquake claimed thousands of lives.*

☆ **claim²** /kleɪm/ *noun* [C] **1** a statement that sth is true, but that does not have any proof: *I don't believe the President's claim that he can reduce unemployment by the end of the year.* **2 claim (for sth)** a demand for sth that you think you have a right to: *to make an insurance claim* ◦ *After the accident he decided to submit a claim for damages.* **3 claim (on/to sth)** the right to have sth: *You will have to prove your claim to the property in court.*

IDM stake a/your claim ⇨ STAKE²

clam¹ /klæm/ *noun* [C] a type of animal with a hard shell (**shellfish**) that lives in water : *clam chowder*

clam² /klæm/ *verb* **clam·ming; clammed**

PHRV clam up (*informal*) to stop talking and refuse to speak: *She always clams up when I ask her about her past.*

clam·my /ˈklæmi/ *adj.* damp and sticky: *clammy hands*

clam·or¹ /ˈklæmər/ *verb* [I] **clamor for sth** to demand sth in a loud or angry way: *The public is clamoring for answers to all these questions.*

clam·or² /ˈklæmər/ *noun* [sing.] a loud, angry discussion or argument: *We could hear the clamor of angry voices.*

clamp¹ /klæmp/ *noun* [C] a tool that you use to hold two things together very tightly

clamp² /klæmp/ *verb* [T] **1** to fasten two things together with a clamp ¹: *Clamp the two pieces together until the glue dries.* ◦ *Clamp the board to the table so that it doesn't move.* **2** to put or hold sth very firmly in a particular place

PHRV clamp down on sb/sth (*informal*) to take strong action against sb/sth in order to stop or control sth: *The police are clamping down on people who drink and drive.*

clamp·down /ˈklæmpdaʊn/ *noun* [C] strong action in order to stop or control sth: *a clampdown on tax evasion*

clan /klæn/ *noun* [C] **1** a group of families who are related to each other **2** (*informal*) a large family or a group of people with a close relationship: *When the Robinson clan gets together at Thanksgiving, there's a big crowd.*

clan·des·tine /klænˈdestən/ *adj.* (*formal*) secret and often not legal

clang /klæŋ/ *noun* [C] a loud ringing sound that is made when a metal object hits sth: *The huge metal door closed with a clang.* —**clang** *verb* [I,T]

clank /klæŋk/ *noun* [C] a loud sound that is made when a metal object (e.g. a heavy chain) hits sth —**clank** *verb* [I,T]

☆ **clap¹** /klæp/ *verb* (**clap·ping; clapped**) **1** [I,T] to put your hands together quickly in order to make a loud sound, usually to show that you like sth: *The audience clapped as soon as the singer walked onto the stage.* ◦ *Everybody was clapping their hands in time to the music.* **2** [T] to put sth onto sth quickly and firmly: *"Oh no, I shouldn't have said that," she said, clapping a hand over her mouth.*

clap² /klæp/ *noun* [C] a sudden loud noise of thunder: *a clap of thunder*

clap·board /ˈklæbərd; ˈklæpbɔrd/ *noun* [C,U] a long, narrow board that is used to cover the outside walls of a house or other building

clar·i·fi·ca·tion /ˌklærəfəˈkeɪʃn/ *noun* [C,U] an explanation that makes sth clear and easier to understand: *We'd like some clarification on exactly what your company intends to do.*

clar·i·fy /ˈklærəfaɪ/ *verb* [T] (*pres. part.* **clar·i·fy·ing**; *3rd pers. sing. pres.* **clar·i·fies**; *p.t., p.p.* **clar·i·fied**) to make sth become clear and easier to understand: *I hope that what I say will clarify the situation.*

clar·i·net /ˌklærəˈnɛt/ *noun* [C] a musical instrument that is made of wood. You play a clarinet by blowing through it.

clar·i·ty /ˈklærəṭi/ *noun* [U] the quality of

ə	y	w	t	eɪ	aɪ	ɔɪ	aʊ	oʊ
about	yes	woman	butter	say	five	boy	now	go

C

being clear and easy to understand: *clarity of expression*

clash¹ /klæʃ/ *verb* **1** [I] **clash (with sb) (over sth)** to fight or disagree seriously about sth: *A group of demonstrators clashed with police in Washington.* ○ *Congress and the President have clashed again over defense cuts.* **2** [I] **clash (with sth)** (used about colors, etc.) not to match or look nice together: *I don't think you should wear that tie – it clashes with your shirt.* **3** [I,T] (used about two metal objects) to hit together with a loud noise; to cause two metal objects to do this: *Their swords clashed.*

clash² /klæʃ/ *noun* [C] **1** a fight or serious disagreement: *a clash between police and demonstrators* **2** a big difference: *a clash of opinions* ○ *There was a personality clash between the two men.* **3** a loud noise, made by two metal objects hitting each other: *the clash of cymbals*

clasp¹ /klæsp/ *noun* [C] an object, usually of metal, which fastens or holds sth together: *the clasp on a necklace, purse, etc.*

clasp² /klæsp/ *verb* [T] to hold sb/sth tightly: *She clasped her hands together in her lap.*

☆ **class** /klæs/ *noun* **1** [C] a group of students who are taught together: *Jane and I are in the same class at school.* ○ *The whole class is going to the theater tonight.* **2** [C] a group of students who are or were in the same year of their studies at the same time: *the senior class president* ○ *the class of 1997* (= who finished high school, college, etc. in 1997) **3** [C,U] a lesson: *Classes begin at 9 o'clock in the morning.* ○ *We watched an interesting video in class* (= during the lesson) *yesterday.* **4** [C] a course in a particular subject: *I'm taking four classes this semester.* ○ *My cooking class starts next Wednesday evening.* **5** [C,U] a group of people who are at the same social and economic level: *members of the middle class* ○ *middle-class families* **6** [C] a group of things of a similar type: *There are several different classes of insects.* **7** [U] (*informal*) high quality or style: *Barry has absolutely no class.* **8** [C,U] (especially in compounds) of a certain level of quality or comfort: *the most expensive class of service* ☞ Look also at **first-class** and **second-class**.

IDM **cut/skip class** (*informal*) to stay away from class without permission: *Rick skipped math class twice last week.*

clas·sic¹ /'klæsɪk/ *adj.* **1** typical: *This painting is a classic example of the French Impressionist style.* ○ *It was a classic case of bad management.* **2** (used about a book, play, etc.) important and having a value that will last: *classic Hollywood movies from the 1930s and '40s*

clas·sic² /'klæsɪk/ *noun* **1** [C] a famous book, play, etc. which has a value that will last: *All of Charles Dickens' novels are classics.* **2** **Clas-**

sics [U] the study of ancient Greek and Roman language and literature

☆ **clas·si·cal** /'klæsɪkl/ *adj.* **1** (used about music) serious and having a value that lasts: *I prefer classical music to rock or jazz.* **2** traditional, not modern: *classical ballet* ○ *classical scientific methods* **3** relating to ancient Greece or Rome: *classical architecture*

clas·si·cal·ly /'klæsɪkli/ *adv.* **1** in a traditional way: *a classically trained pianist* **2** typically: *These symptoms are classically associated with food poisoning.*

clas·si·fi·ca·tion /ˌklæsəfə'keɪʃn/ *noun* **1** [U] the process of putting sb/sth into a group with other people or things of a similar type: *the classification of different species of butterflies* **2** [C] a group or class (6) into which sb/sth is put

clas·si·fied /'klæsəfaɪd/ *adj.* officially secret: *classified information*

ˌclassified ˈadvertisement (also *informal* ˌ**classified ˈad**; **ˈwant ad**) *noun* [C] a small advertisement that you put in a newspaper if you want to buy or sell sth, employ sb, find an apartment, etc.

☆ **clas·si·fy** /'klæsəfaɪ/ *verb* [T] (*pres. part.* **clas·si·fy·ing**; *3rd pers. sing. pres.* **clas·si·fies**; *p.t., p.p.* **clas·si·fied**) **classify sb/sth (as sth)** to put sb/sth into a group with other people or things of a similar type: *The books in a library are usually classified according to subject.*

class·mate /'klæsmeɪt/ *noun* [C] a person who is in the same class (1, 2) as you in school or college

☆ **class·room** /'klæsrum/ *noun* [C] a room in a school, college, etc. where classes are taught

class·y /'klæsi/ *adj.* (**class·i·er**; **class·i·est**) (*informal*) of high quality or style; expensive: *She took me to a classy restaurant downtown.*

clat·ter /'klætər/ *noun* [sing.] a series of short loud repeated sounds that is made when hard objects hit against each other: *the clatter of computer keyboards in an office* —**clat·ter** *verb* [I]: *The dishes clattered in the cupboard when he slammed the door.*

clause /klɔz/ *noun* [C] **1** a paragraph in a legal document **2** (*grammar*) a group of words that includes a subject and a verb. A clause is usually only part of a sentence: *The sentence, "After we had finished eating, we watched a video," contains two clauses.*

claus·tro·pho·bi·a /ˌklɔstrə'foʊbiə/ *noun* [U] great fear of being in a small or closed space

claus·tro·pho·bic /ˌklɔstrə'foʊbɪk/ *adj.* **1** afraid of being in a small or closed space: *I always feel claustrophobic in elevators.* **2** (used about sth that makes you feel afraid of being in a small or closed space): *a claustrophobic little room*

claw /klɔ/ *noun* [C] **1** one of the pointed nails on the feet of some animals and birds: *Cats have sharp claws.* **2** the part of a leg on some

ər	ɪr	ɛr	ɑr	ɔr	ʊr	ʒ	h	ŋ
bird	near	hair	car	north	tour	vision	hat	sing

types of insects and sea animals that they use to hold things

☆ **clay** /kleɪ/ noun [U] heavy earth that is soft when it is wet and becomes hard when it is baked or dried: *The students were modeling heads out of clay.* ○ *clay pots*

☆ **clean¹** /klin/ adj. **1** not dirty: *Are your hands clean?* ○ *I think I'll put on a clean shirt.* **2** (used about animals and people) having clean habits: *Cats are very clean animals.* **3** (used about humor) not about sex, etc.; not dirty: *a clean joke* **4** having no record of offenses: *a clean driving record* **5** (*informal*) no longer using illegal drugs: *I've been clean for two years now.*

IDM **a clean sweep 1** a complete victory in a sports competition, election, etc. that you get by winning all the different parts of it: *The Russians made a clean sweep of all the gymnastics events.* **2** a complete removal of things or people that you think are no longer necessary: *The new governor plans to make a clean sweep and fire everyone in this department.*

☆ **clean²** /klin/ verb **1** [T] to remove dirt and marks from sth: *to clean the toilet, the windows, the kitchen floor, etc.*

☞ **Clean** is a general word for removing dirt from something. If you **wash** something, you clean it with water and often soap. You can **wipe** a surface by rubbing it with a wet cloth; you **dust** a surface by rubbing it with a dry cloth. If you **brush** something, you clean it with a brush that has a short handle; if you **sweep** the floor, you use a broom with a long handle.

2 [T] to put sth into good order; to make sth neat: *Why don't you ever clean your room? It's a mess!* **3** [I] to make the inside of a house, office, etc. free from dust and dirt: *Mr. Burrows comes in to clean in the evenings.*

PHRV **clean sth out 1** to clean the inside of sth thoroughly: *I'm going to clean out all the kitchen cabinets next week.* **2** to empty sth completely: *We have to clean out our lockers on the last day of school.*

clean (sth) up 1 to remove all the dirt from a place that is very dirty: *I'm going to clean up the kitchen before Mom and Dad get back.* **2** to put sth into good order; to make sth neat: *Will you please clean up all this junk that's on the floor?* **3** to remove sth that has just been spilled: *Oh no, you spilled juice on Mom's new carpet! You'd better clean it up!*

,**clean-**'**cut** adj. (used about men) looking clean, neat and honest: *a clean-cut young man*

clean·er /'klinər/ noun **1** [C] a substance or an instrument that you use for cleaning sth: *liquid floor cleaners* ○ *a carpet cleaner* ☞ Look at **vacuum cleaner. 2** [C] a person whose job is to clean the rooms and furniture inside a house or other building **3 cleaners** (*also* **dry**

cleaners) [plural] a business where you take your clothes to be cleaned, especially with special chemicals instead of water: *Could you take my coat to the cleaners?*

clean·li·ness /'klɛnlinəs/ noun [U] being clean: *High standards of cleanliness are extremely important in a hotel kitchen.*

clean·ly /'klinli/ adv. easily or smoothly: *The knife cut cleanly through the rope.*

cleanse /klɛnz/ verb [T] to make sth thoroughly clean: *to cleanse a cut*

cleans·er /'klɛnzər/ noun [C,U] a substance that you use for cleaning sth: *skin cleanser* ○ *Do not use abrasive cleansers on the bathtub.*

clean-shav·en /,klin 'ʃeɪvn/ adj. (used about men) not having a beard or a mustache

☆ **clear¹** /klɪr/ adj. **1** easy to see through: *clear glass* ○ *The water was so clear that we could see the bottom of the lake.* **2** easy to see, hear or understand: *We get a very clear picture on our new TV set.* ○ *His voice wasn't very clear over the phone.* ○ *She gave me clear directions on how to get there.* **3** free from marks: *a clear sky* (= without clouds) ○ *clear skin* (= without pimples) **4** free from things that are blocking the way: *The highway patrol says that most roads are now clear of snow.* **5 clear (to sb)** easy to see; obvious: *There are clear advantages to the second plan.* ○ *It was clear to me that he was not telling the truth.* ○ *The answer to the problem is absolutely clear.* **6 clear (about/on sth)** sure or definite; without any doubts: *I'm not quite clear about the arrangements for tomorrow.* **7** not confused: *Clear thinking is very important in this job.* ○ *a clear understanding of the situation* **8** free from guilt: *It wasn't your fault. You can have a completely clear conscience.*

IDM **crystal clear** ⇨ CRYSTAL

make yourself clear; make sth clear/plain (to sb) to speak so that there can be no doubt about what you mean: *"I do not want you to go to that concert," said my mother. "Do I make myself clear?"* ○ *He made it very clear that he was not happy with the decision.*

☆ **clear²** /klɪr/ adv. **1** = CLEARLY(1): *We can hear you loud and clear from here.* **2 clear (of sth)** away from sth; not touching sth: *They managed to pull the victims clear of the car wreckage.* **3** (*informal*) completely: *Jim just kicked his foot clear through the door!*

IDM **keep/stay/steer clear (of sb/sth)** to avoid sb/sth: *You'd better steer clear of Vanessa – she's in a bad mood today.*

☆ **clear³** /klɪr/ verb **1** [T] to remove sth that is not wanted or needed: *to clear the roads of snow/to clear snow from the roads* ○ *It's your turn to clear the table* (= to take away the dirty plates, etc. after a meal). ○ *Can I help you clear away the dishes?* **2** [I] (used about fog, smoke, etc.) to disappear: *The fog slowly cleared and the sun came out.* **3** [T] to jump over or get past

tʃ	dʒ	v	θ	ð	s	z	ʃ
chin	June	van	thin	then	so	zoo	she

sth without touching it: *Sara didn't hit the ball very hard, so it barely cleared the net.* **4** [T] to go through a process, especially of getting permission for sth to happen: *The bill has cleared the House and the Senate and will soon be signed into law.* **5** [T] to give permission for sth to happen: *At last the plane was cleared for takeoff.* **6** [I] (used about a check) to go through the system that transfers money from one account to another: *The check will take three days to clear.* **7** [T] **clear sb (of sth)** to prove that sb is not guilty of a crime or mistake: *Hector was finally cleared of murder and has been released from prison.*

IDM clear the air to help people feel better in a difficult situation by talking openly about worries, doubts, etc.: *If you discuss your feelings with her, it will help to clear the air between you.*

clear your throat to cough slightly in order to make it easier to speak: *He cleared his throat and then began his speech.*

PHRV clear sth out to clean sth and throw away things that you do not want: *I really need to clear out the kitchen cabinets.*

clear up (used about the weather or an illness) to get better: *We can go out for a walk if it clears up later on.* ○ *The doctor told him to stay at home until his cold cleared up.*

clear (sth) up to make sth neat and clean: *Make sure you clear up all your stuff before you leave.*

clear sth up to find the solution to a problem, mystery, etc.: *There was a slight misunderstanding, but we've cleared it up now.*

clear·ance /'klɪrəns/ *noun* **1** [U] the removing of sth that is old or not wanted: *The store is having a clearance sale* (= reducing the price of things in order to sell all of them quickly). **2** [U] the distance between an object and something that is passing under or beside it, e.g. a ship or vehicle: *There was not enough clearance for the bus to pass under the bridge safely.* **3** [C,U] official permission for sb/sth to do sth: *Only people with a top-level security clearance may enter the nuclear research lab.*

,**clear-**'**cut** *adj.* definite and easy to see or understand: *It was a clear-cut case of police corruption.*

clear·ing /'klɪrɪŋ/ *noun* [C] a small area without trees in the middle of woods or a forest

☆ **clear·ly** /'klɪrli/ *adv.* **1** in a way that is easy to see, hear or understand: *It was so foggy that we couldn't see the road clearly.* **2** in a way that is not confused: *I'm so tired that I can't think clearly.* **3** obviously; without doubt: *She clearly doesn't want to speak to you anymore.*

cleav·age /'klivɪdʒ/ *noun* [C,U] the space between a woman's breasts

clef /klɛf/ *noun* [C] (in music) a sign (♭,♪) at the beginning of a line of written music that shows the range of the notes

clench /klɛntʃ/ *verb* [T] to close or hold tightly: *He clenched his teeth in pain.* ○ *She clenched her fists and looked as if she were about to hit him.*

cler·gy /'klərdʒi/ *noun* [plural] the people who perform religious ceremonies in the Christian church: *a member of the clergy*

cler·gy·man /'klərdʒimən/ *noun* (pl. **cler·gy·men** /-mɛn/) a man who is a member of the clergy

cler·i·cal /'klɛrɪkl/ *adj.* **1** connected with the work of a clerk in an office: *clerical work* **2** of or concerning the clergy.

☆ **clerk** /klərk/ *noun* [C] **1** (*also* **salesclerk**) a person who sells things to people in a store **2** a person whose job is to do written work or keep records or accounts in an office, a bank, a court of law, etc.

clev·er /'klɛvər/ *adj.* **1** (used about things, ideas, etc.) showing skill or intelligence: *a clever device* ○ *a clever plan* **2** (used about a person) able to find a way of doing sth easily, especially in order to trick people: *a clever criminal* —**clev·er·ly** *adv.*

cli·ché /kli'ʃeɪ/ *noun* [C] a phrase or idea that has been used so many times that it no longer has any real meaning or interest: *the old cliché that life begins at 40*

☆ **click**[1] /klɪk/ *noun* [C] a short sharp sound: *the click of a light switch*

click[2] /klɪk/ *verb* [I,T] to make a short sharp sound; to cause sth to do this: *The door clicked shut.* ○ *He clicked the switch.* ○ *Use the mouse to click on the correct answer.*

☆ **cli·ent** /'klaɪənt/ *noun* [C] someone who receives a service from a professional person

cli·en·tele /ˌklaɪən'tɛl/ *noun* [U] the group of people who regularly go to a particular store, hotel, etc.

☞ This word is more formal than alternatives such as **customers** or **guests**.

☆ **cliff** /klɪf/ *noun* [C] a high, very steep area of rock ☞ picture at **beach**.

☆ **cli·mate** /'klaɪmət/ *noun* [C] **1** the normal weather conditions of a particular region: *a dry, humid, tropical, etc. climate* ○ *What are the effects of global warming on our climate?* **2** the general opinions, etc. that people have at a particular time: *What is the current climate of opinion regarding the death penalty?* ○ *the political climate*

cli·mat·ic /klaɪ'mætɪk/ *adj.* of climate: *a conference to discuss climatic change*

cli·max[1] /'klaɪmæks/ *noun* [C] the most important and exciting part of a book, play, piece of music, event, etc.: *the novel's climax in the final chapter* ○ *The election victory marked the climax of her political career.*

cli·max[2] /'klaɪmæks/ *verb* [I] to reach a climax[1]

i	ɪ	ɛ	æ	ɑ	ɔ	ʌ	ʊ	u
see	sit	ten	cat	hot	saw	cup	put	too

☆ **climb¹** /klaɪm/ verb 1 [I,T] to move up to the top of sth: *The cat climbed to the top of the tree.* ○ *to climb a tree, mountain, rope, etc.* ○ *She climbed the stairs to the attic.* ○ *to climb up a ladder* 2 [I] to move, with difficulty, in the direction mentioned: *I managed to climb out of the window.* 3 [I] to go up mountains, etc. as a sport 4 [I] to rise to a higher position: *The plane climbed steadily.* ○ *The road climbed steeply up the side of the mountain.* ○ *(figurative) The value of the dollar against the British pound has climbed to a record level.*

climb² /klaɪm/ noun [C] 1 an act of climbing up a mountain, etc.: *The cabin could only be reached by a three-hour climb.* 2 an increase in value, amount, or position: *the stock market's rapid climb*

climb·er /klaɪmər/ noun [C] a person who climbs mountains or rocks as a sport

clinch /klɪntʃ/ verb [T] to settle or decide sth finally, e.g. an argument or business agreement: *to clinch a victory*

cling /klɪŋ/ verb [I] (*p.t., p.p.* **clung** /klʌŋ/) 1 **cling (on) to sb/sth; cling together** to hold on tightly to sb/sth: *to cling to a rope* ○ *They clung together for warmth.* 2 to continue to believe that sth is true, often when it is not reasonable to do so: *They were still clinging to the hope that the girl would be found alive.* 3 to stick firmly to sth: *Her wet clothes clung to her.*

☆ **clin·ic** /ˈklɪnɪk/ noun [C] 1 a building where you go to see a doctor for examination or treatment, if you are not sick enough to go to the hospital 2 a medical center or a part of a hospital where you go to receive special medical treatment: *a family planning clinic* ○ *a drug rehabilitation clinic*

clin·i·cal /ˈklɪnɪkl/ adj. connected with the examination and treatment of patients at a clinic or hospital: *Clinical trials of the new drug have proven successful.*

clin·i·cal·ly /ˈklɪnɪkli/ adv. according to medical examination: *to be clinically dead*

clink /klɪŋk/ noun [sing.] the short sharp sound that objects made of glass, metal, etc. make when they touch each other: *the clink of glasses* —**clink** verb [I,T]

clip¹ /klɪp/ noun [C] 1 a small object, usually made of metal or plastic, used for holding things together: *a paper clip* ○ *clip earrings* 2 a short section of a movie or video: *a video clip* ○ *They showed a clip from the governor's speech on the news.*

clip² /klɪp/ verb (**clip·ping; clipped**) 1 [I,T] to be fastened with a clip¹(1) ; to fasten sth to sth else with a clip: *These earrings just clip on.* ○ *Clip the papers together.* 2 [T] to cut sth, especially by cutting small parts off: *to clip the hedge*

clip·pers /ˈklɪpərz/ noun [plural] a small metal tool used for cutting things (e.g. hair or fingernails): *a pair of nail clippers*

clip·ping /ˈklɪpɪŋ/ noun [C] a piece that has been cut out from a newspaper, magazine, etc.: *newspaper clippings*

clique /klik; klɪk/ noun [C] a small group of people with the same interests who do not want others to join their group

cloak /kloʊk/ noun 1 [C] a type of loose coat without sleeves, that was more common in the past 2 [sing.] a thing that hides sth else: *a project hidden under a cloak of secrecy*

clob·ber /ˈklɑbər/ verb [T] (*informal*) to hit sb hard

face digital watch
clock
hands
alarm clock band watch

☆ **clock¹** /klɑk/ noun [C] an instrument that shows you what time it is, often found on the wall of a house or building (not worn like a watch): *an alarm clock* ○ *That clock is five minutes slow* (= it says 10:55 when it is really 11 o'clock). ○ *The clock is five minutes fast* (= it says 6:05 when it is really 6 o'clock). ○ *The clock struck midnight.* ☞ Look also at **time clock**.

IDM **around the clock** all day and all night: *They are working around the clock to repair the bridge.*

clock² /klɑk/ verb [T] **clock sb/sth (at sth)** (usually passive) to measure the speed of sb/sth: *Winds were clocked at 80 miles per hour during the storm.*

clock·wise /ˈklɑkwaɪz/ adv., adj. in the same direction as the hands of a clock: *Turn the handle clockwise.* ○ *to move in a clockwise direction* ☞ The opposite is **counterclockwise**.

clock·work /ˈklɑkwərk/ noun [U] **like clockwork** smoothly and without any problems: *The plan went like clockwork.*

clog¹ /klɑg/ noun [C] a type of shoe made completely of wood or with a thick wooden bottom: *a pair of clogs*

clog² /klɑg/ verb (**clog·ging; clogged**) [I,T] **clog (sth) (up) (with sth)** to block or become blocked: *The drain is clogged up with leaves.* ○ *You clogged up the sink again.* ○ *The roads were clogged with traffic.*

clone¹ /kloʊn/ noun [C] 1 an identical copy of a plant or animal that is produced by artificial methods 2 (*computing*) a computer that is designed to work in the same way as another, usually more expensive, computer: *an IBM clone*

ə	y	w	ţ	eɪ	aɪ	ɔɪ	aʊ	oʊ
about	yes	woman	butter	say	five	boy	now	go

clone² /kloʊn/ *verb* [T] to produce a clone¹ of sth

☆ **close¹** /kloʊs/ *adj.* **1** (not before a noun) **close (to sb/sth); close (together)** near: *Is our hotel close to the beach?* ◦ *It's close to midnight.* ◦ *The edges are fairly close together.* **2** (used about a friend, etc.) known very well and liked: *They invited only close friends to the wedding.* **3** near in a family relationship: *a close relative* **4** (used about a competition, etc.) only won by a small amount: *a close race* **5** careful; thorough: *On close examination, you could see that the 20-dollar bill was a forgery.* **IDM a close call/shave** a bad thing that almost happened: *I wasn't hurt, but it was a pretty close call.*
keep a close eye/watch on sb/sth ⇨ EYE¹ —**close·ly** *adv.: to watch sb closely* ◦ *The insect closely resembles a stick.* —**close·ness** *noun* [U]

☆ **close²** /kloʊs/ *adv.* near: *The child stood close to his mother.* ◦ *to follow close behind someone* ◦ *I held her close* (= tightly).
IDM close by (sb/sth) at a short distance from sb/sth: *She lives close by.*
close to almost: *He was born close to a hundred years ago.*
close up (to sb/sth) at or from a very short distance to sb/sth: *You can't tell it's a forgery until you look at it close up.*

☆ **close³** /kloʊz/ *verb* [I,T] **1** to shut: *The door closed quietly.* ◦ *to close a door, window, cupboard, etc.* ◦ *Close your eyes – I have a surprise for you.* **2** to be, or to make sth, not open to the public: *What time do the banks close?* ◦ *The police closed the street to traffic.* **3** to come or bring sth to an end: *Registration for fall classes closes at 4:00.* ◦ *Detectives have closed the case on the missing girl.*
PHR V close (sth) down to stop all business or work permanently, at a store or factory: *The factory has had to close down because of the recession.* ◦ *Health inspectors have closed the restaurant down.*
close in (on sb/sth) to come nearer and gradually surround sb/sth, especially in order to attack: *The army is closing in on the enemy troops.*

☆ **close⁴** /kloʊz/ *noun* [sing.] the end, especially of a period of time or an activity: *the close of trading on the stock market*
IDM bring sth/come/draw to a close to end: *The chairman brought the meeting to a close.* ◦ *The guests began to leave as the evening drew to a close.*

☆ **closed** /kloʊzd/ *adj.* **1** not open; shut: *Keep your mouth closed.* **2** (usually before a noun) not open to everyone: *a closed meeting of the board of directors*

ˌ**closed-ˌcircuit ˈtelevision** *noun* [C,U] a type of television system that sends signals only to televisions that are directly connected to the system by wires, usually in the same building

close·out /ˈkloʊzaʊt/ *noun* [C] a sale in which a store reduces the prices of things in order to sell all of them quickly: *a closeout sale*

☆ **clos·et** /ˈklɑzət/ *noun* [C] an area for storing things, with a door, that is built behind the wall of a room

ˈ**close-up** *noun* [C] a photograph or movie of sb/sth that you take from a very short distance away

clo·sure /ˈkloʊʒər/ *noun* **1** [C,U] the permanent closing, e.g. of a business: *Auto workers are protesting against plant closures.* ◦ *The company is threatened with closure.* **2** [U] the feeling that a difficult or unhappy period of time is over so that you do not have to think about it anymore

clot¹ /klɑt/ *noun* [C] a lump formed by blood as it becomes thick

clot² /klɑt/ *verb* (**clot·ting; clot·ted**) [I,T] to form or cause sth to form clots¹

☆ **cloth** /klɔθ/ *noun* (*pl.* **cloths** /klɔθs; klɔðz/) **1** [U] a material made of cotton, wool, etc. that you use for making clothes, curtains, etc.: *a yard of cloth* **2** [C] a piece of cloth (1) that you use for a particular purpose: *a tablecloth* ◦ *Where can I find a cloth to wipe this up?* ☞ Look also at **washcloth**.

clothe /kloʊð/ *verb* [T] (*formal*) to provide clothes for sb: *to feed and clothe a child*

clothed /kloʊðd/ *adj.* **clothed (in sth)** dressed: *He was clothed only in his underwear.* ◦ *Luckily I was fully clothed when they came in.*

☆ **clothes** /kloʊz; kloʊðz/ *noun* [plural] the things that you wear, e.g. pants, shirts, dresses, coats, etc. (when thought of all together): *Take off those wet clothes.* ◦ *She was wearing new clothes.* ☞ Remember that clothes is always plural. We can use an **item /piece/article of clothing** to describe a single thing that you wear: *A sweatshirt is an informal item of clothing.* Look also at **garment.**

clothespins
clothesline

clothes·line /ˈkloʊzlaɪn; ˈkloʊðz-/ *noun* [C] a thin rope that you hang clothes on so that they can dry

clothes·pin /ˈkloʊzpɪn; ˈkloʊðz-/ *noun* [C] a type of small wooden or plastic object used for fastening clothes to a clothesline

☆ **cloth·ing** /ˈkloʊðɪŋ/ *noun* [U] the clothes that you wear: *You will need waterproof clothing.* ☞ **Clothing** is more formal than **clothes**.

☆ **cloud¹** /klaʊd/ *noun* [C] **1** a mass of very small drops of water that floats in the sky and

is often gray or white: *The sun disappeared behind a cloud.* ○ *A band of thick clouds is spreading from the west.* **2** a mass of smoke, dust, sand, etc.: *Clouds of smoke were pouring from the burning building.*

cloud² /klaʊd/ *verb* **1** [T] to make sth less clear or easy to understand: *We shouldn't let other factors cloud the issue in our discussion.* **2** [T] to make sth less enjoyable; to spoil: *The festival was clouded by violence between rival gangs.*

PHR V **cloud over 1** (*also* **cloud up**) (used about the sky) to become full of clouds **2** (used about a person's face) to start to look sad

cloud·less /'klaʊdləs/ *adj.* (used about the sky, etc.) clear; without any clouds

☆ **cloud·y** /'klaʊdi/ *adj.* (**cloud·i·er; cloud·i·est**) **1** (used about the sky, etc.) full of clouds **2** (used about liquids, etc.) not clear: *cloudy water*

clout /klaʊt/ *noun* [U] influence and power: *Our senator can use his political clout to bring more industries to our area.*

clove /kloʊv/ *noun* [C] **1** the small dried flower of a tropical plant, used to give a special flavor in cooking **2** a section of a garlic root ☞ picture at **onion**.

clo·ver /'kloʊvər/ *noun* [C] a small plant with pink or white flowers and leaves with three parts to them ☞ Sometimes clover leaves have four parts and it is thought to be very lucky if you find one of these.

clown¹ /klaʊn/ *noun* [C] a person who wears funny clothes and makes people laugh

clown² /klaʊn/ *verb* [I] **clown (around)** to act in a funny or foolish way, like a clown: *Quit clowning around and get some work done!*

☆ **club¹** /klʌb/ *noun* **1** [C] a group of people who meet to share an interest; the place where they meet: *to join a club* ○ *to be a member of a club* ○ *a social club* ○ *the school's chess club* **2** [C] a place where you can go to dance, drink, etc. until late at night **3** [C] a heavy stick, usually with one end that is thicker than the other, used as a weapon **4** [C] a long stick that is specially shaped at one end and used for hitting a ball when playing golf ☞ Look at **bat²**, **racket¹** and **stick¹**(3). **5 clubs** [plural] the group (**suit**) of playing cards with black three-leafed shapes on them: *the two of clubs* ☞ picture at **card**. **6** [C] a playing card from this suit: *Do you have any clubs?*

club² /klʌb/ *verb* (**club·bing; clubbed**) **1** [T] to hit sb/sth hard with a heavy object, especially a club¹(3) : *to club somebody to death* **2** [I] to enjoy yourself, dance, etc. at a club¹(2) ☞ We usually say **go clubbing**.

cluck /klʌk/ *noun* [C] the noise made by a chicken —**cluck** *verb* [I]

clue /klu/ *noun* [C] a piece of information that helps you solve a problem, answer a question,

etc.: *The police were looking for clues to his disappearance.* ○ *the clues for solving a crossword puzzle* ☞ picture at **crossword**.

IDM **not have a clue** (*informal*) to know nothing; to be unable to help or understand: *I don't have a clue where you left your watch.*

clue·less /'kluləs/ *adj.* (*slang*) stupid; not knowing anything about sth: *Fred is totally clueless about music.*

clump /klʌmp/ *noun* [C] a lump of something or a group of things that are stuck together, without a regular shape: *a clump of dirt* ○ *a clump of grass*

clum·sy /'klʌmzi/ *adj.* (**clum·si·er; clum·si·est**) **1** (used about a person) careless or awkward and likely to drop things or do things badly **2** (used about a remark, etc.) not showing enough understanding of the feelings of other people; likely to upset or offend people: *He made a clumsy apology.* ○ *her clumsy attempts at humor* **3** large, awkward to use, and not attractive in design: *a clumsy piece of furniture*

clung *p.t., p.p.* of CLING

clus·ter¹ /'klʌstər/ *noun* [C] a group of people, plants or things that stand or grow close together: *a cluster of buildings* ○ *a cluster of grapes*

clus·ter² /'klʌstər/ *verb*

PHR V **cluster/be clustered around sb/sth** to form a group around sb/sth: *The tourists clustered around their guide.*

clutch /klʌtʃ/ *verb* [T] to hold sth tightly, especially because you are afraid or excited: *He clutched his mother's hand in fear.* ○ *The girl ran off, clutching her prize.*

clutch² /klʌtʃ/ *noun* **1** [C] an act of seizing or clutching: *to make a clutch at sth* **2 clutches** [plural] the power or control of a person or group: *He fell into the enemy's clutches.* **3** [C] the part of some cars that you press with your foot before you change gear; the apparatus that it is connected to: *to press/release the clutch*

clut·ter¹ /'klʌtər/ *noun* [U] things that are where they are not wanted or needed and make a place messy: *Who left all this clutter on the table?*

clut·ter² /'klʌtər/ *verb* [T] **clutter sth (up)** to cover or fill sth with a lot of objects in a messy way: *I think these pictures clutter up the design of the page.* —**clut·tered** *adj.: a cluttered office*

cm *abbr.* = CENTIMETER

Co. *abbr.* = COMPANY

c/o /ˌsi 'oʊ/ *abbr.* (used for addressing a letter to sb who is staying at another person's house) care of: *Jill Wallace, c/o The Schmidts, 245 Walnut Street, Springfield, MO*

☆ **coach¹** /koʊtʃ/ *noun* [C] a person who trains people to compete in certain sports: *a football, basketball, hockey, etc. coach* ☞ Look also at **manager** (3).

tʃ	dʒ	v	θ	ð	s	z	ʃ
chin	June	van	thin	then	so	zoo	she

C

coach² /koʊtʃ/ *verb* [I,T] to train or teach sb, especially to compete in a sport or pass an examination: *She is coached by a former Olympic champion.*

☆ **coal** /koʊl/ *noun* **1** [U] a type of black mineral that is dug (**mined**) from the ground and is burned to give heat and energy: *a lump of coal* ○ *a coal mine* ○ *a coal miner* **2 coals** [plural] burning pieces of coal

☆ **co·a·li·tion** /ˌkoʊə'lɪʃn/ *noun* [C] an association of people, groups, political parties, etc. who are working together, often for a short period of time: *the National Coalition for the Homeless* ○ *a coalition government* (= formed by two or more political parties working together)

coarse /kɔrs/ *adj.* **1** consisting of large, not fine pieces; rough, not smooth: *coarse salt* ○ *coarse fabric* **2** (used about a person or sb's behavior) rude, likely to offend people; having bad manners: *His coarse remarks about women offended her.* —**coarse·ly** *adv.*: *Chop the onion coarsely* (= into pieces which are not too small).

☆ **coast¹** /koʊst/ *noun* [C] the area of land that is next to or close to the ocean: *Vacationers reported seeing sharks just off the coast.* ○ *We went for an afternoon drive along the coast.* ○ *the West Coast* (= next to the Pacific Ocean) ○ *the East Coast* (= next to the Atlantic Ocean)

coast² /koʊst/ *verb* [I] **1** to move (especially down a hill) without using power **2** to achieve sth without much effort: *They coasted to victory.*

coast·al /'koʊstl/ *adj.* at or near a coast: *coastal areas* ○ *fishing in coastal waters*

the ¹Coast Guard *noun* [sing.] the military force that watches the ocean near the coast in order to warn or help ships that are in danger or to stop illegal activities ☞ Look at the note at **White House**.

coast·line /'koʊstlaɪn/ *noun* [C] the edge or shape of a coast: *a rocky coastline*

☆ **coat¹** /koʊt/ *noun* [C] **1** a piece of clothing with long sleeves, that you wear on top of other clothes to keep warm: *Put your winter coat on – it's cold outside.* ○ *Take off your coat and sit down.* ☞ picture on page A27. Look also at **overcoat** and **raincoat**. **2** the fur or hair covering an animal's body: *a dog with a smooth coat* **3** a layer of sth covering a surface: *The walls will probably need two coats of paint.*

coat² /koʊt/ *verb* [T] **coat sth (with/in sth)** to cover sth with a layer of sth: *peanuts coated with milk chocolate*

coat·ing /'koʊtɪŋ/ *noun* [C,U] a thin layer of sth that covers sth else: *caramels with chocolate coating*

coax /'koʊks/ *verb* [T] to persuade sb gently: *They coaxed the cat out of the basket.*

cob /kɑb/ *noun* [C] the long, round, hard part

of the corn plant that grains (**kernels**) of corn grow on: *corn on the cob* (= that has been cooked with the kernels still attached to the cob)

cob·ble·stone /'kɑblstoʊn/ *noun* [C] a rounded stone used (in the past) for covering the surface of streets: *cobblestone streets*

co·bra /'koʊbrə/ *noun* [C] a poisonous snake found in Africa and Asia

cob·web /'kɑbwɛb/ (*also* **spider web**) *noun* [C] a net of threads made by a spider in order to catch insects

Co·ca-Co·la /ˌkoʊkə 'koʊlə/ (*also* **Coke**) *noun* [C,U] (*trademark*) a brown, sweet, nonalcoholic drink

co·caine /koʊ'keɪn/ *noun* [U](*also informal* **coke**) an illegal drug, usually in the form of a white powder, that some people take for pleasure but which it is often difficult to stop using

cock·pit /'kɑkpɪt/ *noun* [C] **1** the part of an aircraft where the pilot sits **2** the part of a racing car in which the driver sits

cock·roach /'kɑkroʊtʃ/ (*also* **roach**) *noun* [C] a large dark brown insect, often found in dirty rooms or damp places

cock·tail /'kɑkteɪl/ *noun* **1** [C] an alcoholic drink made from a mixture of drinks: *a cocktail party* **2** [C,U] a mixture of small pieces of food, usually served as the first part of a meal: *Would you like some fruit cocktail?* ○ *shrimp cocktail*

cock·y /'kɑki/ *adj.* (*informal*) too proud and confident, in a way that annoys other people: *It's great that you won the game, but don't get too cocky about it.*

co·coa /'koʊkoʊ/ *noun* **1** (*also* **cocoa powder**) a dark brown powder made from the seeds of a tropical tree and used in making chocolate **2** (*also* **hot chocolate**) a hot drink made from this powder mixed with milk or water: *a cup of cocoa*

co·co·nut /'koʊkənʌt/ *noun* [C,U] the large brown fruit of a tropical tree. Coconuts have very hard, hairy shells and are filled with a white liquid that you can drink. The white substance inside the shell is often eaten in candy and cakes.

cod /kɑd/ *noun* [C,U] (*pl.* **cod**) a large ocean fish that you can eat

☆ **code¹** /koʊd/ *noun* **1** [C,U] a system of words, letters, numbers, etc. used instead of other words, letters, etc. so that messages, information, etc. can be kept secret: *They succeeded in breaking/cracking/deciphering the enemy code* (= in finding out what it was). ○ *They wrote letters to each other in code.* **2** [C] a group of numbers, letters, etc. that is used for identifying sth: *a bar code* (= a pattern of lines printed on goods, that a computer can read) ☞ Look also at **area code** and **Zip code**. **3** [C] a set of rules for behavior: *a code of practice* (= a set of standards agreed and accepted by a particular

i	ɪ	ɛ	æ	ɑ	ɔ	ʌ	ʊ	u
see	sit	ten	cat	hot	saw	cup	put	too

profession) ○ *the city building code* (= the rules and standards for constructing buildings in a city) ○ *a dress code* (= a set of rules about what clothes sb may wear in a particular place)

code² /koʊd/ *verb* [T] **1** to put or write sth in code¹(1) : *coded messages* **2** to use a particular system for identifying things: *The files are color-coded: blue for North America, green for South America.*

co·ed (*also* **co-ed**) /ˌkoʊˈɛd/ *adj.* for both boys and girls or men and women: *a coed volleyball team* ○ *Oberlin College went coed in 1837.* ☞ Look at **single-sex**.

co·ed·u·ca·tion·al /ˌkoʊˌɛdʒəˈkeɪʃənl/ *adj.* (*formal*) (used about a school) with both boys and girls together in the same classes ☞ Look at **single-sex**.

co·erce /koʊˈərs/ *verb* [T] (*formal*) to force sb to do sth, e.g. by threatening him/her —**co·er·cion** /koʊˈərʒn; -ʃn/ *noun* [U]

co·ex·ist /ˌkoʊɪɡˈzɪst/ *verb* [I] to exist together at the same time or in the same place: *Is it possible for these different ethnic groups to co-exist peacefully?* —**co·ex·is·tence** *noun* [U]

☆**cof·fee** /ˈkɔfi; ˈkɑ-/ *noun* **1** [U] the roasted seeds (**beans**) of a tropical tree, made into powder and used for making a drink: *Coffee is the country's biggest export.* **2** [U] a drink made by adding hot water to coffee beans that have been made into powder: *Would you like tea or coffee?* ○ *a cup of coffee* **3** [C] A cup of this drink: *I'll have a donut and a large coffee with cream and sugar.*

coffee maker

pot

> ☞ **Black coffee** is made without milk. **Decaffeinated coffee** has had the caffeine taken out. Coffee can be **weak** or **strong**. **Instant coffee** is made by pouring hot water onto coffee powder.

ˈcoffee shop *noun* [C] a small restaurant that serves cheap meals, coffee and other drinks (but no alcohol)

ˈcoffee ˌtable *noun* [C] a small low table, usually in a living room

cof·fin /ˈkɔfən/ *noun* [C] = CASKET ☞ Look at the note at **funeral**.

cog /kɑg/ *noun* [C] one of the tooth-shaped parts on the edge of a wheel in a piece of machinery. The cogs fit into those on another wheel so that, as it moves, the other wheel moves too.

co·her·ent /koʊˈhɪrənt/ *adj.* connected in a way that makes sense; clear and easy to understand: *a coherent plan* —**co·her·ence** *noun* [U] —**co·her·ent·ly** *adv.*

co·he·sion /koʊˈhiʒn/ *noun* [U] the ability to

stay or fit together well: *What the team lacks is cohesion – all the players play as individuals.*

coil¹ /kɔɪl/ *verb* [I,T] to wind sth into a round shape: *The snake coiled itself around a tree.* ○ *He coiled up the cord and put it into his tool bag.*

coil² /kɔɪl/ *noun* [C] a length of rope, wire, etc. that has been wound into a round shape: *a coil of rope*

☆**coin¹** /kɔɪn/ *noun* [C] a piece of money made of metal ☞ picture at **money**.

coin² /kɔɪn/ *verb* [T] to invent a new word or phrase: *Who was it who coined the phrase, "a penny saved is a penny earned"?*

co·in·cide /ˌkoʊɪnˈsaɪd/ *verb* [I] **coincide (with sth) 1** (used about events) to happen at the same time as sth else: *The President's visit is timed to coincide with local elections.* **2** to be exactly the same or very similar: *Our views coincide completely.*

co·in·ci·dence /koʊˈɪnsədəns/ *noun* [C,U] the surprising fact of two or more similar things happening at the same time by chance; an occasion when this happens: *By pure coincidence, I found myself sitting next to an old friend from school.* ○ *It's no coincidence that my necklace disappeared the same day Wendy came to visit – I bet she took it!*

co·in·ci·den·tal /koʊˌɪnsəˈdɛntl/ *adj.* resulting from two similar or related events happening at the same time by chance —**co·in·ci·den·tal·ly** *adv.*

coke /koʊk/ *noun* [U] (*slang*) = COCAINE
Coke /koʊk/ *noun* [C,U] (*trademark*) = COCA-COLA

☆**co·la** /ˈkoʊlə/ *noun* [C,U] a brown, sweet non-alcoholic drink such as Coca-Cola or Pepsi-Cola; a glass, can, etc. of this

col·an·der /ˈkɑləndər; ˈkʌl-/ *noun* [C] a metal or plastic bowl with a lot of small holes in it, used for draining water from food

☆**cold¹** /koʊld/ *adj.* **1** having a low temperature; not hot or warm: *If I were you, I'd put a coat on. It's cold outside.* ○ *I'm not going into the lake – the water's too cold.* ○ *Should I turn the heat on? I'm cold.*

> ☞ Compare **cold**, **hot**, **cool**, and **warm**. **Cold** indicates a lower temperature than **cool** and may describe a temperature that is unpleasantly low: *a terribly cold winter.* **Cool** means "fairly cold" and may describe a pleasantly low temperature.: *It's boiling hot outside, but it's nice and cool in here.* **Hot** indicates a higher temperature than warm and may describe a temperature that is unpleasantly high: *I can't drink this yet – it's too hot.* **Warm** means "fairly hot" and may describe a pleasantly high temperature: *You won't need your jacket – it's nice and warm outside.*

2 (used about food or drink) not heated or cooked; having become cool after being heated

ə	y	w	t̬	eɪ	aɪ	ɔɪ	aʊ	oʊ
about	yes	woman	butter	say	five	boy	now	go

C

or cooked: *I don't feel like coffee – I'd rather have a cold drink.* ○ *Eat your soup before it gets cold.* **3** (used about a person or sb's behavior) very unfriendly; not showing kindness, sympathy, etc.: *She gave him a cold, hard look.*

IDM cold turkey suddenly, instead of getting used to sth gradually: *I quit smoking cold turkey.*

get/have cold feet (*informal*) to become/be afraid to do sth: *She started to get cold feet as her wedding day approached.*

in cold blood in a cruel way and without pity: *to kill sb in cold blood*

☆ **cold²** /koʊld/ *noun* **1** [sing., U] lack of heat; low temperature; cold weather: *More bitter cold is forecast for the Northeast today.* ○ *We had to stand out in the cold and wait for the bus.* **2** [C,U] a common illness of the nose and throat. When you have a cold, you have a sore throat and often cannot breathe through your nose: *I think I'm getting a cold – I've been sneezing all day.* ○ *Wear a hat when you go out or you'll catch cold.*

cold-blood·ed /ˌkoʊldˈblʌdəd/ *adj.* **1** having a blood temperature that changes with the temperature of the surroundings: *Reptiles are cold-blooded.* ☞ Look at **warm-blooded**. **2** cruel; having or showing no pity: *cold-blooded killers*

'**cold cuts** *noun* [plural] cooked meat that has been cut into thin slices and is served cold

cold·ly /ˈkoʊldli/ *adv.* in an unfriendly way; in a way that shows no kindness or sympathy: *He looked at her coldly and did not reply.*

cole slaw (*also* **coleslaw**) /ˈkoʊlslɔ/ *noun* [U] a salad made with cabbage that has been cut into very thin pieces

col·lab·o·rate /kəˈlæbəreɪt/ *verb* [I] **1 collaborate (with sb) (on sth)** to work together (with sb), especially to create or produce sth: *She collaborated with another author on the book.* **2 collaborate (with sb)** to help the enemy forces who have taken control of your country ☞ This use of *collaborate* shows disapproval. —**col·lab·o·ra·tion** /kəˌlæbəˈreɪʃn/ *noun* [U]

col·lab·o·ra·tor /kəˈlæbəreɪtər/ *noun* [C] **1** a person who works together with sb else, especially in order to create or produce sth **2** a person who helps the enemy forces who have taken control of his/her country

col·lage /kəˈlɑʒ; koʊ-/ *noun* **1** [C] a picture made by fastening pieces of paper, cloth, photographs, etc. onto a surface **2** [U] the art of making these pictures

☆ **col·lapse¹** /kəˈlæps/ *verb* [I] **1** to fall down or inward suddenly: *A lot of buildings collapsed in the earthquake.* **2** (used about a person) to fall down and perhaps become unconscious: *The winner collapsed at the end of the race.* **3** to fail or break down suddenly or complete-

ly: *Many investors lost millions of dollars when the stock market collapsed.*

col·lapse² /kəˈlæps/ *noun* **1** [sing., U] a sudden fall: *the collapse of the roof under the weight of snow* **2** [C,U] sudden or complete failure: *economic collapse*

☆ **col·lar** /ˈkɑlər/ *noun* **collar** [C] **1** the part of a shirt, coat, dress, etc. that fits around the neck and is often folded over **2** a band of leather that is put around an animal's neck (especially a dog or cat) ☞ Look also at **blue-collar** and **white-collar**.

col·lar·bone /ˈkɑlərboʊn/ *noun* [C] one of the two bones that connect the chest bones to the shoulder

☆ **col·league** /ˈkɑlig/ *noun* [C] (*formal*) a person that you work with in a job, especially in a profession

☞ Nowadays it is more common to say **coworker**, especially among younger people.

☆ **col·lect¹** /kəˈlɛkt/ *verb* **1** [T] to bring a number of things, or a large amount of sth, together: *All the test booklets will be collected at the end of the exam.* ○ *My computer screen collects a lot of dust.* **2** [I] to come together; to gather: *Dirt and leaves always collect in the gutters after a storm.* **3** [I,T] to ask for sth, especially money, from a number of people: *Hello, I'm collecting for a local charity. Would you like to make a contribution?* ○ *We've collected over 200 signatures on our petition so far.* ○ *to collect taxes* **4** [T] to gather a number of objects of a particular type over a period of time as a hobby: *He used to collect stamps.* **5** [T] **collect yourself/sth** to get control of yourself, your feelings, thoughts, etc.: *She collected herself and went back into the room as if nothing had happened.* ○ *I tried to collect my thoughts before the test.*

col·lect² /kəˈlɛkt/ *adj., adv.* (used about a telephone call) to be paid for by the person who receives the call: *a collect call* ○ *She called me collect.*

☆ **col·lec·tion** /kəˈlɛkʃn/ *noun* **1** [C,U] the act of getting sth from a place or from people: *Garbage collection is on Thursdays in this neighborhood.* **2** [C] a group of objects of a particular type that sb has collected as a hobby: *a stamp collection* **3** [C] a number of poems, stories, letters, articles, etc. published in one book: *a collection of modern poetry* **4** [C] the act of asking for money from a number of people (for charity, in church, etc.): *a collection for the homeless* ○ *The department took a collection to buy him a present when he retired.* **5** [C] a group of people or things; a pile: *a large collection of papers on the desk*

col·lec·tive /kəˈlɛktɪv/ *adj.* shared by a group

ər	ɪr	ɛr	ɑr	ɔr	ʊr	ɜ	h	ŋ
bird	near	hair	car	north	tour	vision	hat	sing

of people together; not individual: *collective responsibility* —**col·lec·tive·ly** *adv.*: *We made the decision collectively at a meeting.*

col·lec·tor /kə'lɛktər/ *noun* [C] (often in compounds) a person who collects things: *a stamp collector* ⚬ *a tax collector*

☆ **col·lege** /'kɑlɪdʒ/ *noun* **1** [C,U] a university where you can study for a degree after you finish high school: *a private/public college* ⚬ *college students* ⚬ *He first got interested in politics when he was in college.*

☞ We talk about **college**, without **the**, when we mean that somebody is attending it as a student: *He's away at college in California.* ⚬ *She's going to college in September.* but not if somebody goes there for any other reason: *I went to an art exhibit at the college last night.* Look also at **community college** and at **university**.

2 [C] one of the main divisions of some large universities: *The history department is part of the College of Arts and Sciences.*

col·le·giate /kə'lidʒət/ *adj.* (only *before* a noun) connected with a college or colleges: *collegiate sports teams*

col·lide /kə'laɪd/ *verb* [I] **collide (with sb/sth)** to crash; to hit sb/sth very hard while moving: *Energy is released when the two atoms collide.* ⚬ *The truck collided with a bus, but fortunately nobody was injured.*

col·li·sion /kə'lɪʒn/ *noun* [C] a crash; an occasion when things or people collide: *It was a head-on collision and the driver was killed instantly.*

col·lo·qui·al /kə'loʊkwiəl/ *adj.* (used about words, phrases, etc.) used in conversation, not in formal situations or formal writing —**col·lo·qui·al·ly** /-kwiəli/ *adv.*

co·logne /kə'loʊn/ *noun* [U] a type of perfume that is not very strong

co·lon /'koʊlən/ *noun* [C] **1** a punctuation mark (:) used before a list, an explanation, an example, etc. **2** the large tube below the stomach that carries solid waste material out of the body: *colon cancer*

colo·nel /'kərnl/ *noun* [C] an officer with a high rank in the army

co·lo·ni·al /kə'loʊniəl/ *adj.* **1** (*also* often **Colonial**) connected with the original 13 British colonies (1) that became the United States: *people who lived in Colonial times* (= before 1776, when the U.S. became independent) **2** connected with or owning a colony (1): *Spain used to be a major colonial power.*

co·lo·ni·al·ism /kə'loʊniəlɪzəm/ *noun* [U] the practice of keeping countries as colonies

col·o·nist /'kɑlənɪst/ *noun* [C] **1** a person who lived in one of the 13 original British colonies (1) before the United States became independent in 1776 **2** a person who goes to live in a colony (1) when it is first established as one

col·o·nize /'kɑlənaɪz/ *verb* [T] to take control of a place as a colony (1); to establish a colony in a place —**col·o·ni·za·tion** /ˌkɑlənə'zeɪʃn/ *noun* [U]: *the colonization of Latin America by Spain and Portugal*

col·o·ny /'kɑləni/ *noun* (*pl.* **col·o·nies**) **1** [C] a country or area that is ruled by another, more powerful country: *the 13 original colonies* (= that became the United States) ⚬ *Kenya used to be a British colony.* **2** [C] a group of people with the same interests, profession, etc. living together in the same place: *an artists' colony* **3** [C] a group of the same type of animals, insects or plants living or growing in the same place: *a colony of ants*

☆ **col·or¹** /'kʌlər/ *noun* **1** [C,U] the quality that makes sth red, green, yellow, etc.: *"What color is your car?" "Red."* ⚬ *Brown isn't my favorite color.* ⚬ *a dark/light color* ⚬ *a bright color* ⚬ *a deep/pale color* ⚬ *Those flowers will give the room a little color.* ⚬ *Our school colors are blue and gold.*

☞ We say that a thing **is** a certain color, not that it **has** a color.

2 [U] the use of all the colors, not just black and white: *All the pictures in the book are in color.* ⚬ *a color TV set* **3** [U, sing.] redness in your face, particularly showing how healthy you are: *Playing outdoors in the fresh air sure gave you some color.* **4** [C,U] the color of a person's skin, showing the person's race: *people of all colors and religions* **5** [U] interesting or exciting details: *These descriptions give the story some real color.*

IDM of color (only *after* a noun) (used about a person) belonging to a race that does not have white skin: *Persons of color are especially encouraged to apply for this position.* ⚬ *a collection of poetry by women of color*

with flying colors ⇨ FLYING¹

☆ **col·or²** /'kʌlər/ *verb* [T] **1** to put color on sth, e.g. by painting it: *Color the picture with your crayons.* ⚬ *The area colored yellow on the map is desert.* **2** to influence thoughts, opinions, etc.: *You shouldn't let one bad experience color your attitude toward everything.*

col·or·blind (*also* **color-blind**) /'kʌlərblaɪnd/ *adj.* **1** unable to distinguish between certain colors, especially red and green **2** treating people of all races equally: *the dream of a colorblind society*

☆ **col·ored** /'kʌlərd/ *adj.* **1** having color; a particular color: *She always writes letters on colored paper.* ⚬ *a coffee-colored dress* ⚬ *brightly-colored lights* **2** (used about a person) belonging to a race that does not have white skin

☞ This meaning of **colored** is old-fashioned and is now considered offensive.

☆ **col·or·ful** /'kʌlərfl/ *adj.* **1** with bright colors; full of color: *a colorful shirt* **2** full of interest

tʃ	dʒ	v	θ	ð	s	z	ʃ
chin	June	van	thin	then	so	zoo	she

or excitement: *a colorful story* ○ *He's a pretty colorful character.*

col·or·ing /ˈkʌlərɪŋ/ *noun* [C,U] a substance that is used for giving a particular color to sth, especially food

☆ **col·or·less** /ˈkʌlərləs/ *adj.* **1** without color: *a colorless liquid, like water* **2** dull and uninteresting: *a colorless description*

ˈ**color scheme** *noun* [C] the way in which colors are arranged, especially in a room

co·los·sal /kəˈlɑsl/ *adj.* extremely large; huge: *a colossal building* ○ *a colossal amount*

colt /koʊlt/ *noun* [C] a young male horse

☆ **col·umn** /ˈkɑləm/ *noun* [C] **1** a tall solid vertical post made of stone, supporting or decorating a building or standing alone **2** something that has the shape of a column (1): *a column of smoke* **3** one of the vertical sections into which a printed page, especially in a newspaper, is divided **4** a series of numbers written one under the other: *to add up a column of figures* **5** a piece of writing in a newspaper or magazine that is part of a regular series or written by the same writer: *the gossip column* **6** a long line of people, vehicles, etc., one following behind another: *a column of troops*

col·um·nist /ˈkɑləmnɪst/ *noun* [C] a journalist who writes regular articles in a newspaper or magazine: *a gossip columnist* ○ *a political columnist*

co·ma /ˈkoʊmə/ *noun* [C] a state of deep unconsciousness, often lasting for a long time and caused by serious illness or injury: *She went into a coma and died a few days later.*

☆ **comb¹** /koʊm/ *noun* [C] a piece of metal or plastic with a row of teeth that you use for making your hair neat

comb² /koʊm/ *verb* [T] **1** to make the hair neat using a comb **2 comb (through) sth (for sb/sth)** to search thoroughly: *Police are combing the area for the escaped prisoners.*

☆ **com·bat¹** /ˈkɑmbæt/ *noun* [U] fighting, especially in war: *unarmed combat* (= without weapons) ○ *He got a medal for bravery in combat.*

☆ **com·bat²** /kəmˈbæt; ˈkɑmbæt/ *verb* [T] to fight against sth; to try to stop, reduce or defeat sth: *This government will do everything in its power to combat crime.*

☆ **com·bi·na·tion** /ˌkɑmbəˈneɪʃn/ *noun* [C,U] a number of people or things mixed or joined together; a mixture: *He left the job for a combination of reasons.* ○ *The coach still hasn't found the right combination of players.* ○ *This medication may be dangerous when taken in combination with alcohol.*

☆ **com·bine¹** /kəmˈbaɪn/ *verb* **1** [I,T] **combine (with sb/sth); combine A and B/A with B** to join or mix two or more things together: *The two businesses combined to form one corporation.* ○ *Bad planning, combined with bad luck, led to the company's collapse.* **2** [T] **combine A and B/A with B** to do two or more things at the same time or have two or more qualities at the same time: *to combine business with pleasure* ○ *This car combines speed and reliability.*

com·bine² /ˈkɑmbaɪn/ *noun* [C] a farm machine that both cuts grain and separates the seed from the stem

☆ **com·bined** /kəmˈbaɪnd/ *adj.* done by a number of people joining together, resulting from the joining of two or more things: *The combined efforts of the police and fire departments prevented a major disaster.* ○ *I use that room as a guest bedroom and office combined* (= it can be used as either).

com·bus·tion /kəmˈbʌstʃən/ *noun* [U] the process of burning

☆ **come** /kʌm/ *verb* [I] (*p.t.* **came** /keɪm/; *p.p.* **come**) **1** to move to or toward the person who is speaking or the place that sb is talking about: *Come here!* ○ *Come (and) look at this.* ○ *I hope you can come to my party.* ○ *They're coming to stay for a week.* ○ *The kids came running into the room.* **2** to arrive or reach: *What time are you coming home?* ○ *Did the newspaper come yet?* ○ *The news came as a complete surprise.* ○ *The time has come to say goodbye.* **3** to have a particular position: *March comes after February.* **4** to be available: *This blouse comes in a choice of four colors.* **5** to be produced by or from sth: *Wool comes from sheep.* **6** to become: *My shoelace came untied.* **7 come to do sth** (used for talking about how, why or when sth happened): *How did you come to lose your passport?* **8** (usually used with *to/into* and a noun) to reach a particular state: *We were all sad when summer vacation came to an end.* ○ *My dream of going to Hawaii finally came true last month.*

IDM **come and go** to be present for a short time and then go away: *The pain in my ear comes and goes.*

come easily, etc. to sb to be easy, etc. for sb to do: *Apologizing does not come easily to her.*

how come…? (*informal*) why or how: *How come you're back so early?* ○ *How come I didn't get one too?*

to come (used after a noun) in the future: *You'll regret it in years to come.*

when it comes to sth/to doing sth when it is a question of sth: *When it comes to good cooking, Rick's fried chicken is hard to beat.*

PHRV **come about** to happen: *How did this situation come about?*

come across to make an impression of a particular type: *Elizabeth comes across as being fairly shy.*

come across sb/sth to meet or find sb/sth by chance: *I came across this book at a garage sale.*

come along 1 to arrive or appear: *She won't get married until the right man comes along.*

2 to make progress or improve: *Your English is coming along nicely.*

come apart to break into pieces: *This old coat is coming apart at the seams.*

come around 1 (used about an event that happens regularly) to happen: *The end of summer vacation always comes around very quickly.* **2** = COME TO

come around (to sth) to change your opinion so that you agree with sb/sth: *They finally came around to our way of thinking.*

come back 1 to return: *I don't know what time I'll be coming back.* **2** to become popular or fashionable again: *Flared pants are coming back again.*

come back to sb to be remembered: *At first my mind went blank when she asked me a question, but then everything started to come back to me.*

come before sb/sth to be more important than sb/sth else: *Mark feels his family comes before his career.*

come between sb and sb to damage the relationship between two people: *Arguments over money came between the two brothers.*

come by sth to get sth: *Fresh strawberries are hard to come by in the winter.*

come down 1 to fall down: *The power lines came down in the storm.* **2** to become lower: *The price of land has come down in the past year.*

come down to sth/to doing sth (*informal*) to have as the main feature or most important fact: *It all comes down to having the right experience for the job.*

come down to sth to reach down to a particular point: *Her hair comes down to her waist.*

come down with sth to become sick with sth: *I think I'm coming down with the flu.*

come forward to offer help: *The police are asking witnesses to come forward.*

come from... to live in or have been born in a place: *Where do you come from originally?*

come from (doing) sth to be the result of sth: *"I'm tired." "That comes from all the partying you've done lately."*

come in 1 (used about the tide) to move toward the land **2** (used about news or information) to be received: *Reports are coming in of a shooting downtown.* **3** to finish a race, contest, etc. in a particular position: *Kelly came in first in the 400-meter dash.*

come of sth/of doing sth to be the result of sth: *We've written to several companies asking for help, but nothing has come of it yet.*

come off 1 to be able to be removed: *Does the collar come off?* **2** (*informal*) to be successful: *The deal seems unlikely to come off.*

come off (sth) to become removed from sth: *One of the legs came off this table.* ∘ *This button came off when I was putting on my shirt.*

come on 1 (used about a machine or a piece of equipment) to start to work: *All the lights suddenly came on in the neighbors' house.* **2** (used about a television or radio program, etc.) to start: *The local news comes on at 6:00.* **3** to begin: *I think I feel a sneeze coming on.* **4** to start to act, play in a sports game, etc.: *They played the same music every time the bad guy came on.* ∘ *A substitute came on in the second quarter.* **5 come on!** (*informal*) (used for telling sb to hurry up): *Come on! It's time to go.* **6 come on!** (*informal*) (used for telling sb to stop acting silly, stop telling lies, try harder, etc.): *Oh, come on! Do you expect me to believe that?* ∘ *Come on, you guys! You can do better than that.*

come out 1 to appear: *The rain stopped and the sun came out.* ∘ *The report came out in 1988.* **2** to become known: *It was only after his death that the truth came out.* **3** to be produced or published: *When is her new book coming out?* **4** to tell sb for the first time that you are sexually attracted to people of the same sex as yourself

come out (of sth) to be removed from sth: *Red wine stains don't come out easily.*

come out with sth to say or produce sth: *The committee came out with a new report on the economy.*

come over (to ...) to visit a person or place: *Why don't you come over to our house on Saturday?*

come over (to ...) (from ...) to move from one place to another: *My great-grandfather came over to New York from Germany in 1921.*

come over sb (used about a feeling) to affect sb: *A feeling of despair came over me.*

come through (used about news, information, etc.) to arrive: *Election results are just starting to come through.*

come through (sth) to escape injury or death in a dangerous situation, an illness, etc.: *to come through a heart attack*

come to (*also* **come around**) to become conscious again

come to sth 1 to equal or total a particular amount: *The bill for the meal came to $35.* **2** to reach a bad situation: *We will sell the house to pay our debts if we have to, but we hope it won't come to that.*

come under sth 1 to be included in a particular section, department, etc.: *Serious crimes do not come under the jurisdiction of this court.* **2** to be the object of criticism, an attack, etc.: *Our principal has come under intense pressure to resign.*

come up 1 to be about to happen in the future: *I have an important meeting coming up next week.* **2** to be discussed: *The subject of religion came up.* **3** (used about a plant) to appear above the soil **4** (used about the sun and moon) to rise

come up against sb/sth to find a problem or difficulty that you have to deal with: *We have*

come up against stiff competition from foreign manufacturers.
come up to sth 1 to reach up as far as a particular point: *The water in the pool came up to our knees.* **2** to be as good as usual or as necessary: *This piece of work does not come up to your usual standard.*
come up with sth to find an answer or solution to sth: *Engineers have come up with new ways of saving energy.*

come·back /ˈkʌmbæk/ *noun* [C] a return to a position of strength or importance that you had before: *The former world champion is hoping to make a comeback.*

co·me·di·an /kəˈmidiən/ (*also* **comic**) *noun* [C] a person whose job is to entertain people and make them laugh, e.g. by telling jokes

com·e·dy /ˈkɑmədi/ *noun* (*pl.* **com·e·dies**) **1** [C] an amusing play, movie, etc. that has a happy ending ☛ Look at **tragedy**. **2** [U] the quality of being amusing or making people laugh: *There is a hint of comedy in all her novels.*

com·et /ˈkɑmət/ *noun* [C] an object that looks like a bright star and that moves around the sun

☆ **com·fort¹** /ˈkʌmfərt/ *noun* **1** [U] the state of having everything your body needs, or of having a pleasant life and being relaxed: *to travel in comfort* ○ *This furniture is not designed for comfort.* **2** [U] help or kindness to sb who is suffering: *I tried to offer a few words of comfort.* **3** [sing.] a person or thing that helps you when you are very sad or worried: *You've been a real comfort to me.* **4** [C] something that makes your life easier or more pleasant: *After a week of camping, we really appreciated the comforts of home.* ☛ Look at **discomfort**.

com·fort² /ˈkʌmfərt/ *verb* [T] to try to make sb feel less worried or unhappy: *to comfort a crying child*

☆ **com·fort·a·ble** /ˈkʌmftəbl; ˈkʌmfərṭəbl/ *adj.* **1**(also *informal* **comfy**) allowing you to feel relaxed and providing you with everything your body needs: *Our hotel room was large and comfortable.* ○ *a comfortable temperature* (= not too hot or too cold) ○ *Sit down and make yourselves comfortable.* ☛ The opposite is **uncomfortable**. **2** not having or causing worry, pain, difficulty, etc.: *He did not feel comfortable in the presence of so many women.* **3** having or providing more than enough money for all your needs: *They enjoyed a very comfortable lifestyle.* ○ *a comfortable income* —**com·fort·a·bly** *adv.*: *You can't live comfortably on such low wages.*

com·fort·er /ˈkʌmfərtər/ *noun* [C] a thick cover filled with feathers or another soft material that is placed on top of the sheets and blankets on a bed ☛ picture at **bed**.

com·fy /ˈkʌmfi/ *adj.* (**com·fi·er**; **com·fi·est**) (*informal*) comfortable (1): *a comfy chair*

☆ **com·ic¹** /ˈkɑmɪk/ *adj.* that makes you laugh; funny: *a comic scene in a serious play*

com·ic² /ˈkɑmɪk/ *noun* **1** [C] = COMEDIAN **2** (*also* ˈ**comic book**) [C] a magazine that tells stories through pictures **3 the comics** [plural] the section of a newspaper that contains comic strips

com·i·cal /ˈkɑmɪkl/ *adj.* that makes you laugh

ˈ**comic strip** *noun* [C] a series of pictures that tell a story, e.g. in a newspaper, etc.

com·ing /ˈkʌmɪŋ/ *noun* [sing.] the arrival of sth: *The coming of the railroad meant more trade for these towns.*

IDM **comings and goings** activities that people do in a particular place, such as arriving, leaving, etc.: *Our neighbor sits on her porch and watches all the comings and goings on the block.*

☆ **com·ma** /ˈkɑmə/ *noun* [C] the punctuation mark (,) used for dividing parts of a sentence or items in a list

☆ **com·mand¹** /kəˈmænd/ *verb* **1** [I,T] to tell or order sb to do sth: *The men did as their officer had commanded.* **2** [T] to control or be in charge of sb/sth: *to command a ship, an army, etc.* **3** [T] to deserve and get sth: *The senator commanded great respect.*

☆ **com·mand²** /kəˈmænd/ *noun* **1** [C] an order: *The captain's commands must be obeyed without question.* **2** [C] an instruction that is given to a computer **3** [U] control over sb/sth: *Who is in command of the expedition?* ○ *General Weston has numerous advisers under his command.* ○ *to take command of a situation* **4** [C] a division of an army, a navy, etc. that has a specific function **5** [sing.] the state of being able to do or use sth: *She has a good command of French.*

IDM **at your command** available for you to use: *We'll need all the resources at our command in order to solve this problem.*

com·man·deer /ˌkɑmənˈdɪr/ *verb* [T] to take control or possession of sth for military use

com·mand·er /kəˈmændər/ *noun* [C] a person who controls or is in charge of sb/sth

com·mand·ing /kəˈmændɪŋ/ *adj.* **1** (used about a person who commands¹(2) sb/sth): *Who is your commanding officer?* **2** having or showing power or authority: *to speak in a commanding tone of voice* **3** strong: *Martha holds a commanding lead over her rival in the election polls.*

com·mand·ment (*also* **Commandment**) /kəˈmændmənt/ *noun* [C] (*formal*) one of the ten important rules in the Bible that Christian people should obey

com·man·do /kəˈmændoʊ/ *noun* [C] (*pl.* **com·man·dos** or **com·man·does**) one of a group of soldiers who are trained to make quick attacks in enemy areas

com·mem·o·rate /kəˈmɛməreɪt/ *verb* [T] to keep a special event in people's memories; to

ər	ɪr	ɛr	ɑr	ɔr	ʊr	ʒ	h	ŋ
bird	near	hair	car	north	tour	vision	hat	sing

exist in order to make people remember a special event: *a statue commemorating all the soldiers who died in the Vietnam War* —**com·mem·o·ra·tion** /kə͵mɛmə'reɪʃn/ *noun* [C,U]: *The ceremony was held in commemoration of the 150th anniversary of the town's founding.*

com·mence /kə'mɛns/ *verb* [I,T] (*formal*) **commence sth/doing sth** to start or begin ☞ Look at the note at **begin.**

com·mence·ment /kə'mɛnsmənt/ *noun* **1** [usually sing.] (*formal*) a beginning **2** [C,U] an official ceremony at which students who have finished high school, college, etc. receive their degrees

com·mend /kə'mɛnd/ *verb* [T] (*formal*) to say that sb/sth is very good: *Dean was commended for his excellent work.*

com·mend·a·ble /kə'mɛndəbl/ *adj.* (*formal*) that you must praise: *She played a commendable role in the negotiations.*

☆ **com·ment**[1] /'kɑmɛnt/ *noun* [C,U] **comment (about/on sth)** something that you say or write that gives your opinion or feeling about sth: *The governor was not available for comment.* ○ *Please use the space below to write any additional comments.*
IDM **no comment** (used in reply to a question when you do not want to say anything at all): *"Senator, how do you feel about these latest developments?" "No comment."*

☆ **com·ment**[2] /'kɑmɛnt/ *verb* [I,T] **comment (on sth)** to give your opinion or feeling about sth: *Several people commented on how nice the yard looked.* ○ *Somebody commented that it didn't seem very fair.*

com·men·tar·y /'kɑmən͵tɛri/ *noun* [C,U] (*pl.* **com·men·tar·ies**) **1** a spoken description on the radio or television of sth as it is happening: *the commentary on a football game* **2** a written explanation or discussion of sth: *a magazine containing a mixture of news and commentary*

com·men·tate /'kɑmənteɪt/ *verb* [I] **commentate (on sth)** to give a spoken description on the radio or television of sth as it is happening

com·men·ta·tor /'kɑmənteɪtər/ *noun* [C] **1** a person who commentates on sth: *a sports commentator* **2** a person who gives his/her opinion about sth on the radio, on television or in a newspaper: *a political commentator*

☆ **com·merce** /'kɑmərs/ *noun* [U] the activities that are involved in buying and selling things: *international commerce* ☞ Look also at **chamber of commerce.**

☆ **com·mer·cial**[1] /kə'mərʃl/ *adj.* **1** connected with buying and selling goods: *commercial activities* **2** making a profit: *Although it won a lot of awards, the movie was not a commercial success.* —**com·mer·cial·ly** /-ʃəli/: *These products are still being developed and are not yet commercially available.*

☆ **com·mer·cial**[2] /kə'mərʃl/ *noun* [C] an advertisement on the radio or on television ☞ Look also at **infomercial.**

com·mer·cial·ize /kə'mərʃəlaɪz/ *verb* [T] to try to make a profit out of sth, even if it means spoiling it: *The holidays have become too commercialized in recent years.*

☆ **com·mis·sion**[1] /kə'mɪʃn/ *noun* **1** [C] an official organization that controls or watches an industry or other activity and makes rules for it: *the Federal Trade Commission* **2** [C] a group of people who are elected to manage affairs for a city or county: *the Fulton County Commission* **3** [C,U] money that you get for selling sth: *Agents get 10% commission on everything they sell* (= 10% of the value of the things they sell). **4** [C] an act of asking sb to do a piece of work for you: *He received a commission to write a play for the festival.*

com·mis·sion[2] /kə'mɪʃn/ *verb* [T] to ask sb to do a piece of work: *to commission an architect to design a building*

com·mis·sion·er /kə'mɪʃənər/ *noun* [C] **1** a member of a commission[1] (1, 2) **2** an official who is in charge of a government department: *the city police commissioner* ○ *the state education commissioner*

☆ **com·mit** /kə'mɪt/ *verb* [T] (**com·mit·ting**; **com·mit·ted**) **1** to do sth bad or illegal: *to commit a crime* ○ *After years of mental illness, Frank committed suicide.* **2** (*formal*) to send sb to a prison, mental hospital, etc.: *He was committed to a psychiatric hospital for five years.* **3 commit sb/yourself (to sth/to doing sth)** to promise to do sth: *I can't commit myself to helping you tomorrow. I'm still not sure if I will be free.* **4** to decide to use sth for a particular purpose: *We've already committed over $4 million to the project.* **5 commit yourself (on sth)** to say openly what you think or believe: *When asked for her opinion, she refused to commit herself.* ☞ Look at **noncommittal.**

☆ **com·mit·ment** /kə'mɪtmənt/ *noun* **1** [U] **commitment (to sth)** the state of giving a lot of your time and attention to sth because you believe it is right or important: *We are looking for a teacher with enthusiasm and commitment.* ○ *commitment to an ideal* **2** [C] something that you have promised to do; a responsibility: *Marriage is a great commitment.* ○ *The mayor was unable to attend the ceremony due to a previous commitment.* ○ *Japan has made a commitment to respect the new agreement.*

com·mit·ted /kə'mɪtəd/ *adj.* giving a lot of your time and attention to sth because you believe it is right or important: *a committed supporter of women's rights*

☆ **com·mit·tee** /kə'mɪti/ *noun* [C] a group of people who have been chosen to discuss sth or decide on sth: *They have set up a committee to look into ways of attracting new businesses to*

tʃ	dʒ	v	θ	ð	s	z	ʃ
chin	June	van	thin	then	so	zoo	she

the city. ○ to be/sit on a committee ○ a member of a committee ○ The planning committee meets twice a week.

com·mod·i·ty /kə'mɑdəti/ noun [C] (pl. **com·mod·i·ties**) something that you buy or sell, especially farm products, minerals, etc.: Salt was once a very valuable commodity.

☆ **com·mon**¹ /'kɑmən/ adj. **1** happening or found often or in many places; usual: These days it's fairly common for people to change careers several times. ○ The word is no longer in common use. ○ The daisy is a common wild flower. **2 common (to sb/sth)** shared by or belonging to two or more people or groups, or by most or all people: The Americans and the British share a common language. ○ This type of behavior is common to most children of that age. ○ We have a common interest in computers. **3** (only before a noun) not special; ordinary: The officers had much better living conditions than the common soldiers.

IDM **be common knowledge** to be known by a lot of people: It's common knowledge that he took the money – why does he pretend he didn't?

☆ **com·mon**² /'kɑmən/ noun [C]

IDM **have sth in common (with sb/sth)** to share sth with sb/sth else: They seem to be good friends, although they have few interests in common. ○ to have a lot in common with sb **in common with sb/sth** like sb/sth: This company, in common with many others, is losing a lot of money.

ˌ**common** ˈ**ground** noun [U] beliefs, interests, etc. that two or more people or groups share: We will try to find some common ground during the negotiations.

ˌ**common-law** ˈ**wife** (also ˌ**common-law** ˈ**husband**) noun [C] a person who has been living with a person of the opposite sex for a long time but who is not married to him/her. A common-law wife/husband usually has the same rights as an official wife/husband.

☆ **com·mon·ly** /'kɑmənli/ adv. often; usually: These insects are commonly known as midges.

com·mon·place /'kɑmənpleɪs/ adj. not very exciting or unusual; ordinary: Fax machines have become commonplace in recent years.

ˌ**common** ˈ**sense** noun [U] the ability to make good sensible decisions because of your experience of life, not because of what you have learned at school or from books: Safety precautions are basically just common sense.

com·mon·wealth /'kɑmənwɛlθ/ noun **1** [sing.] **the Commonwealth** the group of countries that once formed the British Empire and that try to work and to trade together in a friendly way **2** [C] (the official legal description of certain U.S. states): the Commonwealth of Virginia **3** [C] (the official legal description of certain regions that are part of the U.S. but are not states): the Commonwealth of Puerto Rico

com·mo·tion /kə'moʊʃn/ noun [sing., U] great noise or excitement: People looked out of their windows to see what all the commotion was about.

com·mu·nal /kə'myunl; 'kɑmyənl/ adj. shared by a group of people: four bedrooms with a communal kitchen and bathroom

com·mune /'kɑmyun/ noun [C] a farm or a small community where a group of people, not from the same family, live together and share their property and responsibilities

☆ **com·mu·ni·cate** /kə'myunəkeɪt/ verb [I,T] to make information or your opinions, feelings, etc. known to sb: Parents often have difficulty communicating with their teenage children (= understanding them and being understood). ○ They communicate by sign language. ○ to communicate news by satellite

☆ **com·mu·ni·ca·tion** /kə,myunə'keɪʃn/ noun **1** [U] the act of communicating: There is little real communication between father and daughter. ○ verbal/nonverbal communication ○ Radio is the only means of communication in remote areas. **2** [C] (formal) a message: a communication from our chairman **3 communications** [sing., U] the study of communicating in an effective way: Toni plans to major in communications when she goes to college. **4 communications** [plural] the methods that are used for traveling to and from a place or for sending messages between places: The phone lines are down, so communications are very difficult.

IDM **be in communication with sb/sth** (formal) to be in regular contact with: The astronauts are in direct communication with the control center in Houston.

com·mu·ni·ca·tive /kə'myunə,keɪtɪv; -kətɪv/ adj. willing to talk or give information: Leslie seems shy and not very communicative. ☞ The opposite is **uncommunicative**.

com·mun·ion /kə'myunyən/ noun **Communion** (also **Holy Communion**) [U] the ceremony in the Christian Church in which people share bread and wine as symbols of Christ's body and blood: to take/go to Communion

com·mu·ni·qué /kə,myunə'keɪ; 'myunəkeɪ/ noun [C] an official statement, especially from a government, a political group, etc.

com·mu·nism /'kɑmyənɪzəm/ noun [U] the political and economic system or theory in which the government owns and controls the means of production and in which everybody is supposed to be equal

com·mu·nist /'kɑmyənɪst/ noun [C] a person who believes in or supports communism —**com·mu·nist** adj.: communist sympathies ☞ When we are talking about a particular society or political party which is organized according to the principles of communism, we often use a capital "C" for **communism** and **communist**: He was a member of the Communist Party.

☆ **com·mu·ni·ty** /kə'myunəţi/ *noun* (*pl.* **com-mu·ni·ties**) **1 the community** [sing.] the group of people who live in a particular place or area: *She was given an award for her work with young people in the community.* ○ *Recent increases in crime have disturbed the whole community.* **2** [C] a town: *The storm caused severe damage in several communities in the region.* **3** [C] a group of people who have sth (e.g. nationality, interests, type of work, etc.) in common: *the Asian community in Los Angeles* ○ *the business community*

com'munity ,center *noun* [C] a building where local people can take part in classes, meetings, etc.

com,munity 'college (*also* 'junior college) *noun* [C] a college that is mainly for students from the local community and that offers programs that are two years long. Some students go to another college or university after they have finished studying at a community college.

com·mute /kə'myut/ *verb* [I] to travel from home to work by car, bus, train or subway every day: *A lot of people commute into Detroit from nearby suburbs.* —**com·mut·er** /kə'myuţər/ *noun* [C]: *The subways are always full of commuters at this time of day.* ○ *a commuter train*

com·pact¹ /'kɑmpækt; kəm'pækt/ *adj.* small, neat and taking up little space: *a compact camera* ○ *The compact design of this iron makes it ideal for travel.*

com·pact² /'kɑmpækt/ *noun* [C] **1** a small car **2** a small flat box that contains a mirror and powder, etc. for the face

,**compact 'disc** *noun* [C] = CD

com·pan·ion /kəm'pænyən/ *noun* [C] a person or animal with whom you spend a lot of time or go somewhere: *a traveling companion* ○ *His dog is his only companion.* ○ *Witnesses saw the victim walking with two female companions shortly before the murder.*

com·pan·ion·ship /kəm'pænyənʃɪp/ *noun* [U] friendship or company: *A lot of people get married for companionship.*

☆ **com·pa·ny** /'kʌmpəni/ *noun* (*pl.* **com·pa-nies**) **1** [C] a business organization selling goods or services: *an insurance company* ○ *You should contact the telephone company to complain about your phone bill.* ○ *She applied to several companies for a job.* ○ *The company is planning to build a new factory in Colorado.* ☛ In names, **company** is written with a capital letter. The abbreviation is **Co.**: *the Walt Disney Company* ○ *Milton & Co.* **2** [U] a visitor or visitors: *Sorry, but I can't talk now. We've got company.* **3** [U] being with a person : *I always enjoy her company because she always has funny stories to tell.* ○ *She was very good company* (= pleasant to be with) *and I really*

enjoyed our evening together. **4** [C] a group of actors, singers, dancers, etc.: *a ballet company* **IDM** **keep sb company** to go or be with sb so that he/she is not alone: *She was nervous, so I went with her to keep her company.* **part company** ⇨ PART³

com·pa·ra·ble /'kɑmpərəbl/ *adj.* **comparable (to/with sb/sth)** of a similar standard or size; that can be compared with sth: *A comparable house in Iowa would be a lot cheaper.*

com·par·a·tive¹ /kəm'pærəţɪv/ *adj.* **1** compared with sth else or with what is usual or normal: *Good soil and a warm climate give this region a comparative advantage over other farming areas.* **2** involving comparing things of the same kind: *a comparative study of government systems* **3** (*grammar*) (used about the form of an adjective or adverb) expressing a greater amount, quality, size, etc.: *"Hotter" is the comparative form of "hot."*

com·par·a·tive² /kəm'pærəţɪv/ *noun* [C] (*grammar*) the form of an adjective or adverb that expresses a greater amount, quality, size, etc.: *"Worse" is the comparative of "bad."*

com·par·a·tive·ly /kəm'pærəţɪvli/ *adv.* as compared with sth else or with what is usual: *The disease is comparatively rare nowadays.* ○ *Most of the houses are old, but this one was built comparatively recently.*

☆ **com·pare** /kəm'pɛr/ *verb* **1** [T] **compare A and B**; **compare A with/to B** to consider people or things in order to find ways in which they are similar or different: *If you compare the old and the new models, you'll see the changes we made.* ○ *When the police compared the two letters, they realized that they had been written by the same person.* ○ *Write an essay comparing the United States in the eighteenth century with the United States today.* **2** [T] **compare A to B** to say that things or people are similar in a way or ways: *When it was built, people compared the stadium to a huge tent.* **3** [I] **compare (with sb/sth)** to be of the same quality as sb/sth: *Her last album was fantastic, but this one just doesn't compare.* ○ *Nothing compares with the taste of bread fresh from the oven.*

com·pared /kəm'pɛrd/ *adj.* **compared to/with** in comparison with; considered in relation to: *Compared to the place where I grew up, this town is exciting.* ○ *I'm a very patient person, compared with him.*

☆ **com·par·i·son** /kəm'pærəsn/ *noun* [C,U] an act of comparing; a statement in which people or things are compared: *Put the new one and the old one side by side for comparison.* ○ *A comparison of this year's figures with last year's shows that the economy is improving.* ○ *It's hard to make comparisons between Jason's painting and Catherine's because he's been learning so much longer.*

ə	y	w	ţ	eɪ	aɪ	ɔɪ	aʊ	oʊ
about	yes	woman	butter	say	five	boy	now	go

C

IDM **by/in comparison (to/with sb/sth)** when compared: *When she told me about her problems I realized that mine were small by comparison.* ◦ *He's pretty tall in comparison to some of the older boys.* ◦ *In comparison with many other people, they're fairly well-to-do.*
draw a comparison/a parallel ▷ DRAW¹

com·part·ment /kəm'pɑrtmənt/ *noun* [C] one of the separate sections into which certain containers are divided: *The drugs were discovered in a secret compartment in his suitcase.* ◦ *the glove compartment* (= the space where you can keep maps, etc. in a car)

com·pass /'kʌmpəs/ *noun* [C] **1** an instrument for finding direction, with a needle that always points north: *a ship's compass* ◦ *They had to find their way back to the camp using a map and a compass.* **2** a V-shaped instrument that is used for drawing circles, etc.

com·pas·sion /kəm'pæʃn/ *noun* [U] **compassion (for sb)** sympathy or pity for sb who is suffering

com·pas·sion·ate /kəm'pæʃənət/ *adj.* having or showing sympathy or pity for sb who is suffering

com·pat·i·ble /kəm'pætəbl/ *adj.* **compatible (with sb/sth)** suitable to live together or to be used together: *As a couple, they are simply not compatible.* ◦ *Is this software compatible with my computer?* ☞ The opposite is **incompatible.** —**com·pat·i·bil·i·ty** /kəm,pætə'bɪləti/ *noun* [U]

com·pa·tri·ot /kəm'peɪtriət/ *noun* [C] a person who comes from the same country as another

com·pel /kəm'pɛl/ *verb* [T] (**com·pel·ling; com·pelled**) *(formal)* to force sb to do sth: *I felt compelled to tell her what I really thought of her.*

com·pel·ling /kəm'pɛlɪŋ/ *adj.* **1** forcing sb to do sth; convincing: *The fingerprints provided compelling evidence of his guilt.* ◦ *I felt that there was no compelling reason to stay, so I left.* ☞ The noun is **compulsion.** **2** very exciting; holding your attention: *a compelling drama*

com·pen·sate /'kɑmpənseɪt/ *verb* **1 compensate (sb) (for sth)** [I,T] to pay sb money because you have injured him/her or lost or damaged his/her property: *To compensate for the loss of my luggage, the airline sent me a check.* **2 compensate (for sth)** [I] to remove or reduce the bad effect of sth; to make up for sth: *His willingness to work hard compensates for his lack of skill.*

☆ **com·pen·sa·tion** /,kɑmpən'seɪʃn/ *noun* **compensation (for sth)** **1** [U] money that you pay to sb, especially because you have injured him/her or lost or damaged his/her property: *She demanded compensation from the company for the injury she suffered while working there.* ◦ *unemployment compensation* **2** [C,U] a fact or action that removes or reduces the bad effect

of sth: *Being a parent can be difficult, but there are compensations* (= good things about it). ◦ *Angie developed a very outgoing personality as compensation for her learning difficulties.*

☆ **com·pete** /kəm'pit/ *verb* [I] **compete (against/with sb) (for sth)** to try to win or achieve sth, or to try to be better than sb else: *The world's best athletes compete in the Olympic Games.* ◦ *The teams are competing for the state championship.* ◦ *When they were kids, they always used to compete with each other.* ◦ *They had to compete against several larger companies to get the contract.*

com·pe·tence /'kɑmpətəns/ *noun* [U] having the ability or skill that is needed: *This job requires competence in several computer applications.* ☞ The opposite is **incompetence.**

com·pe·tent /'kɑmpətənt/ *adj.* **1** having the ability or skill needed for sth: *a highly competent player* ◦ *She is competent at her job.* ◦ *He is not competent to be a manager.* ☞ The opposite is **incompetent.** **2** satisfactory but not excellent: *a competent, but not particularly exciting, performance* —**com·pe·tent·ly** *adv.*

☆ **com·pe·ti·tion** /,kɑmpə'tɪʃn/ *noun* **1** [C] an organized event in which people try to win sth: *She entered a competition in the newspaper and won a car.* ◦ *He finished second in an international piano competition.* **2** [U] a situation where two or more people are trying to achieve the same thing or gain an advantage: *There was fierce competition among the players for places on the team.* ◦ *She is in competition with three other people for the scholarship.* ◦ *Competition from the national chains means that many small stores have had to close.* **3** [U, sing.] the other people, companies, etc. who are trying to achieve the same as you: *If we are going to succeed, we must offer a better product than our competition.* ◦ *laws to protect domestic industries from foreign competition*

☆ **com·pet·i·tive** /kəm'pɛtətɪv/ *adj.* **1** involving people competing against each other: *The travel industry is a highly competitive business.* ◦ *competitive sports* **2** able to be as successful as or more successful than those competing: *They are trying to make the company competitive in the international market.* ◦ *Our prices are highly competitive* (= as low as or lower than those of the others). **3** (used about people) eager to win or to be more successful than others: *She's a very competitive player.* —**com·pet·i·tive·ly** *adv.*

☆ **com·pet·i·tor** /kəm'pɛtətər/ *noun* [C] a person, company, product, etc. that is competing with another or others: *All competitors must wear a number in the race.* ◦ *Two local companies are our main competitors.*

com·pi·la·tion /,kɑmpə'leɪʃn/ *noun* **1** [U] the act of compiling: *The compilation of the encyclopedia took many years.* **2** [C] something that

has been compiled: *The album is a compilation of the band's previous hits.*

com·pile /kəm'paɪl/ *verb* [T] to collect information and arrange it in a list, book, etc.: *to compile a list of addresses*

com·pla·cent /kəm'pleɪsnt/ *adj.* feeling so satisfied with yourself or with the situation that you think (perhaps wrongly) that there is no need to worry: *He had won his matches so easily that he was in danger of becoming complacent.* —**com·pla·cen·cy** /kəm'pleɪsnsi/ *noun* [U]: *We have achieved a high standard but there is no cause for complacency. We can still improve.*

☆ **com·plain** /kəm'pleɪn/ *verb* **1** [I,T] **complain (about sth); complain (that…)** to say that you are not satisfied with or happy about sth: *I wish you would quit complaining.* ○ *People are always complaining about the weather.* ○ *We complained to the hotel manager that the room was too noisy.* ☛ Look at the notes at **grumble** and **protest**. **2** [I] **complain of sth** to say that you have a pain or illness: *He went to the doctor, complaining of chest pains.*

☆ **com·plaint** /kəm'pleɪnt/ *noun* **complaint (about sth); complaint (that…)** **1** [U] an act or acts of complaining: *I wrote a letter of complaint to the manager about the service I had received.* ○ *a cause for complaint* **2** [C] a statement that you are not satisfied with sth: *You should make a complaint to the company that made the machine.* **3** [C] an illness or disease: *a heart complaint* ○ *minor complaints*

com·ple·ment¹ /'kɑmpləmənt/ *noun* [C] **1** a thing that goes together well with sth else: *A light sauce is the perfect complement to this dessert.* **2** the total number that makes a group complete: *Without a full complement of players, the team will not be able to take part in the game.* **3** (*grammar*) a word or words, especially a noun or adjective, used after a verb such as "be" or "become" and describing the subject of that verb: *In "He's friendly" and "He's a fool," "friendly" and "fool" are complements.*

com·ple·ment² /'kɑmpləmənt/ *verb* [T] to go together well with: *The colors of the furniture and the carpet complement each other.*

com·ple·men·ta·ry /ˌkɑmplə'mɛntəri; -'mɛntri/ *adj.* going together well with sth; adding sth which the other thing does not have: *They work well together because their skills are complementary: he's practical and she's creative.*

☆ **com·plete¹** /kəm'plit/ *adj.* **1** having or including all parts; with nothing missing: *I gave a complete list of the stolen items to the police.* ○ *a complete set of Twain's novels* ○ *The book explains the complete history of the place.* **2** (not before a noun) finished or ended: *The investigation should be complete by Friday.* **3** (only *before* a noun) as great as is possible; total; in every way: *the complete reorganiza-*

tion of the department ○ *It was a complete waste of time.*

☆ **com·plete²** /kəm'plit/ *verb* [T] **1** to make sth whole: *We need two more players to complete the team.* ○ *I finally managed to complete my collection.* **2** to finish sth; to bring sth to an end: *When the building has been completed, it will look impressive.* ○ *He completed medical school in June, 1995.* **3** to fill out sth (e.g. a form): *Please complete the following questionnaire in capital letters.* ○ *Completed application forms should be received by December 9.*

☆ **com·plete·ly** /kəm'plitli/ *adv.* as much as is possible; totally; in every way: *The building was completely destroyed by fire.* ○ *We're trying a completely new method.*

com·ple·tion /kəm'pliʃn/ *noun* [U] the act of completing or the state of being complete: *The new freeway is due for completion within two years.*

☆ **com·plex¹** /kəm'plɛks; 'kɑmplɛks/ *adj.* made up of several connected parts and often difficult to understand; complicated: *a complex system of taxation* ○ *You won't find a simple solution when the problem is so complex.*

☆ **com·plex²** /'kɑmplɛks/ *noun* [C] **1** a group or set of things, especially buildings, designed for a particular purpose: *a high-rise apartment complex* **2** a mental problem that causes sb to worry or be upset about sth: *He has a complex about his height.* ○ *an inferiority complex*

com·plex·ion /kəm'plɛkʃn/ *noun* [C] the natural color and quality of the skin or the face: *a dark complexion* ○ *a healthy complexion*

com·plex·i·ty /kəm'plɛksəti/ *noun* (*pl.* **complex·i·ties**) **1** [U] the state of being complex: *an issue of great complexity* **2** [C] one of the many details that make sth complicated: *I don't have time to explain the complexities of the chemical process now.*

com·pli·cate /'kɑmpləkeɪt/ *verb* [T] to make sth difficult to understand: *Let's not complicate things by adding too many details.*

☆ **com·pli·cat·ed** /'kɑmpləkeɪtəd/ *adj.* difficult to understand; made up of many parts: *a novel with a very complicated plot* ○ *a complicated mathematical calculation* ○ *I can't tell you all the details now – it's too complicated.*

com·pli·ca·tion /ˌkɑmplə'keɪʃn/ *noun* [C] **1** something that complicates sth: *Unless there are any unexpected complications, I'll be arriving next month.* ○ *A further complication in the project was the delay in receiving the raw materials.* **2** a new illness that you get when you are already sick

com·plic·i·ty /kəm'plɪsəti/ *noun* [U] being involved, with sb else, in a crime

com·pli·ment¹ /'kɑmpləmənt/ *noun* **1** [C] **a compliment (on sth)** a statement or action that praises or expresses admiration for sb: *People have often paid her compliments on her*

C

piano playing. **2 compliments** [plural] (formal) greetings or good wishes given in a message: *Please help yourself to coffee and donuts, compliments of the hotel management* (= without charge).

com·pli·ment² /ˈkɑmpləmɛnt/ verb [T] **compliment sb (on sth)** to praise or express admiration for sb: *She complimented them on their good manners.*

com·pli·men·ta·ry /ˌkɑmpləˈmɛntəri; -ˈmɛntri/ adj. **1** praising or expressing admiration for sb: *He made several complimentary remarks about her work.* **2** given free of charge: *a complimentary beverage with dinner*

com·ply /kəmˈplaɪ/ verb [I] (pres. part. **com·ply·ing**; 3rd pers. sing. pres. **com·plies**; p.t., p.p. **com·plied**) **comply (with sth)** (formal) to obey an order or request: *All office buildings must comply with fire and safety regulations.*

com·po·nent¹ /kəmˈpoʊnənt/ noun [C] one of the parts that together form sth, especially a machine: *stereo components* ∘ *Fresh fruit and vegetables are essential components of a good diet.*

com·po·nent² /kəmˈpoʊnənt/ adj. being one of the parts that together form sth: *the component parts of an engine*

☆ **com·pose** /kəmˈpoʊz/ verb **1** [I,T] to write music: *Mozart composed 41 symphonies.* **2** [T] to produce a piece of writing, using careful thought: *I sat down and composed a letter to the editor of the paper.* **3** [T] to be the parts that form sth: *the elements that compose the book's central theme* **4** [T] **compose yourself/sth** to make yourself, your feelings, etc. become calm and under control: *The news came as such a shock that it took me a while to compose myself.* ∘ *She tried to compose her thoughts and appear calmly.*

com·posed /kəmˈpoʊzd/ adj. **1 composed of sth** made up of sth; having sth as its parts: *The committee is composed of politicians from both parties.* **2** calm, in control of your feelings: *Although he felt very nervous, he managed to appear composed.*

☆ **com·pos·er** /kəmˈpoʊzər/ noun [C] a person who writes music professionally

com·pos·ite /kəmˈpɑzət/ adj. consisting of different parts, substances or materials

com·po·si·tion /ˌkɑmpəˈzɪʃn/ noun **1** [C] a piece of music that has been written by sb: *"Finlandia" is probably Sibelius's best-known composition.* **2** [U] the act of composing a piece of music or writing **3** [U] the skill or technique of writing music: *She studied both music theory and composition.* **4** [C] (old-fashioned) a short piece of writing done as part of an educational course or exam: *Write a composition of about 500 words on one of the following subjects.* ☛ **Essay** is more common nowadays. **5** [U] the parts that form sth: *the chemical*

composition of a substance ∘ *the composition of the population*

com·post /ˈkɑmpoʊst/ noun [U] a mixture of decaying substances, such as plants and waste material, that is added to soil to help plants to grow: *a compost pile/heap*

com·po·sure /kəmˈpoʊʒər/ noun [U] the state of being calm and having your feelings under control

com·pound¹ /ˈkɑmpaʊnd/ noun [C] **1** something that consists of two or more things or substances combined: *a chemical compound* **2** (grammar) a word or phrase consisting of two or more parts that combine to make a single meaning: *"Roommate" and "round-trip" are compounds.* **3** an area of land with a group of buildings on it, surrounded by a wall or fence

com·pound² /kəmˈpaʊnd/ verb [T] to make sth (a problem, etc.) worse

☆ **com·pre·hend** /ˌkɑmprɪˈhɛnd/ verb [T] (formal) to understand sth completely: *She's too young to comprehend what happened.*

com·pre·hen·si·ble /ˌkɑmprɪˈhɛnsəbl/ adj. easy to understand: *The book is written in clear, comprehensible language.* ☛ The opposite is **incomprehensible**.

com·pre·hen·sion /ˌkɑmprɪˈhɛnʃn/ noun **1** [U] the ability to understand or the act of understanding: *How such a strange thing could happen is beyond my comprehension.* ☛ The opposite is **incomprehension**. **2** [U] an exercise that tests how well you understand spoken or written language: *The first part of the test is reading comprehension.*

☆ **com·pre·hen·sive** /ˌkɑmprɪˈhɛnsɪv/ adj. including everything or nearly everything that is connected with a particular subject: *a guide book giving comprehensive information on the area* ∘ *comprehensive medical insurance*

com·press /kəmˈprɛs/ verb [T] **compress sth (into sth)** **1** to press sth together so that it takes up less space **2** to express sth briefly or in a shorter form —**com·pres·sion** /kəmˈprɛʃn/ noun [U]

com·prise /kəmˈpraɪz/ verb [T] **1** to consist of; to have as parts or members: *The metropolitan area comprises five counties.* ∘ *a committee comprising businesspeople, local politicians and clergy members* **2** to be the parts or members that make up sth; to form: *Women comprise 62% of all employees.*

☆ **com·pro·mise¹** /ˈkɑmprəmaɪz/ noun [C,U] **a compromise (on sth); a compromise (between A and B)** an agreement that is reached when each side allows the other side part of what it wanted: *Unless the union and the management can reach a compromise on pay, there will be a strike.* ∘ *It's difficult to find a compromise between the protection of the environment and our need for more technology.* ∘

"There can be no compromise on the subject of terrorism," a senator said.

☆ **com·pro·mise²** /ˈkɑmprəmaɪz/ *verb* **1** [I] **compromise (with sb) (on sth)** to reach an agreement by which each side gets sth it wants and allows the other side to have sth it wants **2** [T] **compromise yourself** to put yourself in a position in which other people can criticize you for not being honest: *He compromised himself by accepting money from them.* **3** [T] to do sth that is harmful to sth: *She refused to compromise her principles by signing the letter.*

com·pul·sion /kəmˈpʌlʃn/ *noun* **1** [U] forcing sb to do sth or being forced to do sth: *There is no compulsion to take part. You can decide yourself.* ☞ The verb is **compel**. **2** [C] a strong desire that you cannot control, often to do sth that you should not do

com·pul·sive /kəmˈpʌlsɪv/ *adj.* **1** (used about a bad or harmful habit) caused by a strong desire that you cannot control: *compulsive eating* **2** (used about a person) having a bad habit that he/she cannot control: *a compulsive gambler*

com·pul·so·ry /kəmˈpʌlsəri/ *adj.* that must be done, by law, rules, etc.: *Education is compulsory for children under age 16.* ○ *The United States does not have compulsory military service.* ☞ Look also at **mandatory**. It is similar in meaning. Something that you do not have to do is **voluntary**.

☆ **com·put·er** /kəmˈpyuṭər/ *noun* [C] an electronic machine that can store and arrange information, make calculations and control other machinery: *The bills are all processed by computer.* ○ *a computer program* ○ *a computer programmer* ○ *a home computer* ○ *a personal computer* ○ *computer software* ○ *computer games* ○ *She's studying computer science.* ○ *First of all, the details are entered into a computer.* ☞ picture on page A29.

com·put·er·ize /kəmˈpyuṭəraɪz/ *verb* [T] to deal with sth by computer; to store information in a computer: *We have now computerized the library catalog.*

com·put·ing /kəmˈpyuṭɪŋ/ *noun* [U] the skill of using computers: *She took a course in computing.*

com·rade /ˈkɑmræd/ *noun* [C] **1** (used by members of a socialist party when they talk about or to each other): *Comrades, we will fight against injustice!* **2** (*formal*) a friend or companion, especially one with whom you share a difficult experience: *an old army comrade*

con¹ /kɑn/ *verb* [T] (**con·ning; conned**) **con sb (into doing sth/out of sth)** (*informal*) to cheat sb, especially in order to get money: *He conned her into investing in a company that didn't really exist.*

con² /kɑn/ *noun*

IDM **the pros and cons** ⇨ PRO²

con·cave /kɑnˈkeɪv; ˈkɑnkeɪv/ *adj.* (used about a surface) curving inward ☞ Look at **convex**.

con·ceal /kənˈsil/ *verb* [T] **conceal sth/sb (from sb/sth)** to hide sb/sth; to prevent sb/sth from being seen or discovered: *She tried to conceal her anger from her friend.* ○ *The video was recorded with a concealed camera.* —**con·ceal·ment** *noun* [U]: *the concealment of the facts of the case*

con·cede /kənˈsid/ *verb* [T] **1** to admit that sth is true, often unwillingly: *When it was clear that he would lose the election, he conceded defeat.* ○ *She conceded that the problem was mostly her fault.* **2** **concede sth (to sb)** to allow sb to take sth, often unwillingly: *They lost the war and had to concede territory to their enemy.* ○ *Despite conceding two late touchdowns, they still won.* ☞ The noun is **concession**.

con·ceit /kənˈsit/ *noun* [U] too much pride in yourself, too high an opinion of your abilities and importance

con·ceit·ed /kənˈsiṭəd/ *adj.* too proud of yourself, your abilities, your importance, etc.: *He's so conceited – he thinks he's the best at everything!*

con·ceiv·a·ble /kənˈsivəbl/ *adj.* possible to imagine or believe: *I made every conceivable effort to succeed.* ☞ The opposite is **inconceivable**.

con·ceiv·a·bly /-əbli/ *adv.*: *She might just conceivably be telling the truth.*

con·ceive /kənˈsiv/ *verb* **1** [I,T] to form a baby (**fetus**) inside a woman's body: *Tests showed that she was unable to conceive.* ○ *Their first child was conceived soon after they got married.* **2** [T] (*formal*) to form or think of sth (an idea, plan, etc.); to imagine: *He conceived the idea for the novel during his trip through India.* **3** [I,T] **conceive of sb/sth (as sth)** to think of sb/sth in a particular way: *He started to conceive of the world as a dangerous place.* ☞ The noun is **conception**.

☆ **con·cen·trate¹** /ˈkɑnsntreɪt/ *verb* [I,T] **1** **concentrate (sth) (on sth/doing sth)** to give all your attention or effort to sth: *How can you concentrate on your work with so much noise going on?* ○ *It is important to concentrate on the road when you are driving.* ○ *I tried to concentrate my thoughts on the problem.* **2** to come together or to bring people or things together in one place: *The general concentrated most of his tanks on the border.*

con·cen·trate² /ˈkɑnsntreɪt/ *noun* [C,U] a substance that has been made stronger by having water taken out of it: *orange juice concentrate*

con·cen·trat·ed /ˈkɑnsntreɪṭəd/ *adj.* **1** aimed at one particular point: *With another concentrated attack we should break through the*

ə	y	w	ṭ	eɪ	aɪ	ɔɪ	aʊ	oʊ
about	yes	woman	butter	say	five	boy	now	go

C

enemy's defenses. **2** made stronger by the removal of some liquid: *This is concentrated orange juice. You have to add water before you drink it.*

con·cen·tra·tion /ˌkɑnsn̩ˈtreɪʃn/ *noun* **1** [U] **concentration (on sth)** the act of giving all your attention or effort to sth: *This type of work requires total concentration.* ○ *She lost her concentration when she heard a door slam.* **2** [C] **concentration (of sth)** a large amount of people or things in one place: *There are high concentrations of bacteria in the drinking water here.*

ˌ**concenˈtration camp** *noun* [C] a prison (usually a number of buildings inside a high fence) where political prisoners are kept in very bad conditions: *Millions of Jews died in Nazi concentration camps.*

☆ **con·cept** /ˈkɑnsɛpt/ *noun* [C] **concept (of sth/that...)** an idea; a basic principle: *The basic concepts of physics can be difficult to understand.* ○ *The concept that "big is beautiful" is no longer as popular as it was.*

con·cep·tion /kənˈsɛpʃn/ *noun* [C,U] **1** the beginning of a new life inside a female person or animal: *an embryo 14 days after conception* ☞ The verb is **conceive**. **2** an idea or a plan: *We have no real conception of what people suffered during the Middle Ages.*

☆ **con·cern¹** /kənˈsərn/ *verb* [T] **1** to affect or be of importance to sb: *The destruction of the world's forests concerns everybody in some way.* ○ *This doesn't concern you. Just go away.* ○ *The closure of the factory came as a shock to all those concerned.* ○ *It is important that no risks be taken where safety is concerned.* **2 concern yourself with sth** to give your attention to sth: *You don't need to concern yourself with the plans for the party. We'll take care of everything.* **3** to worry sb: *What concerns the experts most is the level of pollution in our cities.*

IDM **as/so far as sb/sth is concerned** ⇨ FAR² **to be concerned with sth** to be about sth: *Tonight's program is concerned with the effects of the law on ordinary people.*

con·cern² /kənˈsərn/ *noun* **1** [U] **concern (for/about/over sb/sth); concern (that...)** worry: *Following the crash there is growing concern over the safety of air travel.* ○ *Don't worry. There is no cause for concern.* **2** [C,U] something that affects you or is important to you: *Edward's family problems are not my concern.* ○ *He showed great concern for the homeless.* **3** [C] a company or business: *a large industrial concern*

☆ **con·cerned** /kənˈsərnd/ *adj.* **concerned (about/for sth); concerned (that...)** worried or anxious: *If you are concerned about your baby's health, you should consult a doctor immediately.* ☞ The opposite is **unconcerned**.

con·cern·ing /kənˈsərnɪŋ/ *prep.* about; on the subject of: *She refused to answer questions concerning her private life.*

☆ **con·cert** /ˈkɑnsərt/ *noun* [C] a performance of music: *a rock concert* ○ *The concert was held in Central Park.* ○ *The orchestra is giving concerts in Cleveland, Columbus and Cincinnati.*

con·cert·ed /kənˈsərtəd/ *adj.* done by a group of people working together: *We must all make a concerted effort.*

con·cer·to /kənˈtʃɛrtoʊ/ *noun* [C] (*pl.* **con·cer·tos**) a piece of music for an orchestra with one instrument playing an important part (**solo**): *Tchaikovsky's piano concerto*

con·ces·sion /kənˈsɛʃn/ *noun* **1** [C,U] **concession (to sb/sth)** something that you agree to do or give up in order to end an argument: *The school district has been forced to make concessions to the teachers' union.* ☞ The verb is **concede**. **2** [C] (*also* **conˈcession stand**) a space in a building, sports center, etc. for providing a service or operating a small business: *a license to operate a food concession at the stadium* **3** [C] a special right to do sth that is given or sold to sb/sth: *The government has granted gambling concessions to several Native American tribes.*

con·cil·i·a·tion /kənˌsɪliˈeɪʃn/ *noun* [U] the process of ending a disagreement: *All attempts at conciliation have failed and civil war seems inevitable.*

con·cil·i·a·to·ry /kənˈsɪliəˌtɔri/ *adj.* intended to end a disagreement: *a conciliatory speech*

con·cise /kənˈsaɪs/ *adj.* giving a lot of information in a few words; short: *He gave a clear and concise summary of what had happened.* —**con·cise·ly** *adv.*

☆ **con·clude** /kənˈklud/ *verb* **1** [I,T] (*formal*) to end or to bring sth to an end: *I'd like to conclude by thanking our guest speaker.* ○ *The orchestra concluded its concert with a piece by Copland.* **2** [T] **conclude sth from sth** to reach a belief or opinion as a result of thought or study: *From their studies the archaeologists concluded that the area was the site of an ancient burial ground.* **3** [T] **conclude sth (with sb)** to arrange or agree to sth formally: *to conclude a treaty, business deal, etc.*

☆ **con·clu·sion** /kənˈkluʒn/ *noun* **1** [C, usually sing.] the end: *The conclusion of the novel was a big surprise.* ○ *to bring sth to a conclusion* ○ *The conclusion is just as important a part of your essay as the introduction.* **2** [C] **the conclusion (that...)** a belief or opinion that you reach after considering sth carefully: *We came to the conclusion that he was right.* ○ *What conclusions can you draw from her remarks?* ○ *The jury reached the conclusion that the defendant was guilty.* **3** [U] an act of arranging or agreeing to sth formally: *The summit ended with the conclusion of a free-trade treaty.*

IDM **a foregone conclusion** ⇨ FOREGONE **in conclusion** finally; lastly: *In conclusion, I*

ər	ɪr	ɛr	ɑr	ɔr	ʊr	ʒ	h	ŋ
bird	near	hair	car	north	tour	vision	hat	sing

would like to wish you continued success in the future.

jump/leap to conclusions to form an opinion about sth without thinking about it carefully enough

con·clu·sive /kən'kluːsɪv/ *adj.* that shows sth is definitely true or real: *conclusive proof of sb's guilt* ☞ The opposite is **inconclusive.** —**con·clu·sive·ly** *adv.*: *Tests can now prove conclusively who is the father of a child.*

con·coct /kən'kɑkt/ *verb* [T] **1** to make sth by mixing different things together **2** to make up or invent sth (an excuse, a story, etc.) —**con·coc·tion** /kən'kɑkʃn/ *noun* [C,U]

con·course /'kɑŋkɔrs/ *noun* [C] a large hall or space inside a building such as a train station or an airport

☆ **con·crete¹** /kɑn'krit; 'kɑŋkrit/ *adj.* **1** that can be touched, felt, etc.; real: *a concrete object* **2** definite; particular: *Can you give me a concrete example of the behavior you're complaining about?* —**con·crete·ly** *adv.*

☆ **con·crete²** /'kɑnkrit; 'kɑŋ-/ *noun* [U] a hard substance made from cement mixed with sand, water, small stones (**gravel**), etc., that is used in building: *a slab of concrete* ☞ Many people also use the word **cement** to refer to this substance: *cement blocks.*

con·cur /kən'kər/ *verb* [I] (**con·cur·ring; con·curred**) (*formal*) **concur (with sb/sth) (in sth)** to agree

con·cur·rent /kən'kərənt/ *adj.* existing or happening at the same time as sth else —**con·cur·rent·ly** *adv.*: *He will serve both his prison sentences concurrently.*

con·cus·sion /kən'kʌʃn/ *noun* [C] an injury to the brain that was caused by a blow to the head: *She suffered a concussion in a car accident.*

☆ **con·demn** /kən'dɛm/ *verb* [T] **1 condemn sb/sth (for/as sth)** to say strongly that you think sb/sth is very bad or wrong: *The President has been condemned for trying to cut funding for education.* ○ *A government spokesman condemned the bombing as a cowardly act of terrorism.* **2 condemn sth (as sth)** to say officially that sth is not good enough to use: *The building was condemned and had to be demolished.* **3 condemn sb (to sth/to do sth)** to say what sb's punishment will be: *The murderer was condemned to die in the electric chair.* ○ (*figurative*) *Their poor education condemns them to a lifetime of poverty.*

con·dem·na·tion /ˌkɑndəm'neɪʃn/ *noun* [C,U] the act of condemning sth; a statement that condemns: *The airport bombing brought condemnation from all around the world.*

con·den·sa·tion /ˌkɑndən'seɪʃn/ *noun* [U] small drops of liquid that are formed when warm air touches a cold surface: *condensation on the windows*

con·dense /kən'dɛns/ *verb* **1** [I,T] to change

from gas to liquid; to make a gas change to liquid: *Steam condenses into water when it touches a cold surface.* ☞ Look at **evaporate.** **2** [I,T] to become or to make sth thicker: *condensed mushroom soup* **3** [T] **condense sth (into sth)** to make a piece of writing shorter: *We'll have to condense these three chapters into one.*

con·de·scend /ˌkɑndə'sɛnd/ *verb* [I] **1** to do sth that you believe is below your level of importance: *Sarah only condescends to speak to me when she wants me to do something for her.* **2 condescend (to sb)** to behave toward sb in a way that shows that you think you are better or more important than him/her: *The teacher must be able to explain things at the right level for the children without condescending to them.* —**con·de·scend·ing** *adj.*: *a condescending smile*

☆ **con·di·tion¹** /kən'dɪʃn/ *noun* **1** [sing., U] the state that sth/sb is in: *The car is five years old, but it is still in very good condition.* ○ *He looks really sick. He is certainly not in a condition to drive home.* **2** [C] something that must happen so that sth else can happen or be possible: *One of the conditions of the job is that you agree to work on Sundays.* ○ *We agreed to the conditions that the negotiators set.* **3 conditions** [plural] a situation or circumstances: *The prisoners were kept in terrible conditions.* ○ *poor housing conditions* ○ *The weather conditions were very favorable for the flight.* **4** [C] an illness: *to have a heart condition*

IDM on the condition (that…) only if: *I agreed to help on the condition that I got half the profit.*

under no condition; not under any condition(s) (*formal*) not at all; for no reason: *Under no condition can the press find out about this new project.*

con·di·tion² /kən'dɪʃn/ *verb* [T] **1** to affect or control the way that sb/sth behaves: *Boys are conditioned to feel that they shouldn't cry in public.* ○ *to be conditioned by your environment* **2** to keep sth in a good condition¹(1) : *a shampoo that moisturizes and conditions your hair*

con·di·tion·al /kən'dɪʃənl/ *adj.* **1 conditional (on/upon sth)** if sth is conditional on sth else, it can only happen if this other thing happens first; the one thing depends on the other: *This job offer is conditional on your graduating from college this spring.* ○ *conditional approval of a business deal* **2** (*grammar*) (used about a phrase or sentence) expressing a condition: *A conditional clause usually begins with "if" or "unless."* —**con·di·tion·al·ly** /-ʃənəli/ *adv.*

con·di·tion·er /kən'dɪʃənər/ *noun* [C,U] a substance that keeps sth in a good condition: *hair conditioner*

con·do /'kɑndoʊ/ *noun* [C] (*pl.* **con·dos**) (*informal*) = CONDOMINIUM

tʃ	dʒ	v	θ	ð	s	z	ʃ
chin	June	van	thin	then	so	zoo	she

C

con·do·lence /kən'doʊləns/ *noun* [C, usually pl., U] an expression of sympathy to sb whose relative or close friend has just died: *Please accept my condolences on your sister's death.*

con·dom /'kɑndəm/ (also *informal* **rubber**) *noun* [C] a rubber covering that a man wears over his penis during sex to prevent his partner from becoming pregnant or as protection against disease

con·do·min·i·um /ˌkɑndə'mɪniəm/(also *informal* **condo** /'kɑndoʊ/) *noun* [C] (*pl.* **con·do·min·i·ums** or (*informal*) **con·dos**) an apartment or apartment building owned by the people who live in it

con·done /kən'doʊn/ *verb* [T] to accept sth; not to consider sth to be wrong: *I can never condone violence – in any circumstances.*

con·dor /'kɑndɔr; -dər/ *noun* [C] a very large bird that lives in the SW United States and in Latin America, and that eats dead animals

con·du·cive /kən'dusɪv/ *adj.* **conducive (to sth)** helping or making sth likely to happen: *This hot weather is not conducive to hard work.*

☆ **con·duct¹** /kən'dʌkt/ *verb* [T] **1** to carry out or organize sth: *Tests are being conducted to find the cause of the accident.* **2** to stand in front of an orchestra and direct the musicians: *The orchestra was conducted by Ozawa.* **3** to allow heat or electricity to pass along or through sth: *Rubber does not conduct electricity.* **4 conduct yourself well, badly, etc.** (*formal*) to behave in a particular way **5** to lead or guide sb/sth: *A tour of the museum is conducted every hour.*

☆ **con·duct²** /'kɑndʌkt/ *noun* [U] **1** a person's behavior: *Ron was fired from the bank for unprofessional conduct.* ○ *a code of conduct* (= a set of rules for behavior) ☞ Look at **misconduct**. **2 conduct of sth** the act of controlling or organizing sth: *She was criticized for her conduct of the bank's financial dealings.*

con·duc·tor /kən'dʌktər/ *noun* [C] **1** a person who stands in front of an orchestra and directs the musicians **2** a person who collects the tickets on a train **3** a substance that allows heat or electricity to pass through or along it: *Water is a good conductor.*

cone /koʊn/ *noun* [C] **1** a solid shape that has a round base and gets narrower, making a point at the top ☞ picture at **cube**. **2** an object of this shape: *an ice cream cone* ○ *orange traffic cones along the side of the road* **3** the hard fruit of a pine or a fir tree: *a pine cone*

the Con·fed·er·a·cy /kən'fɛdərəsi/ *noun* [sing.] the 11 southern states that separated from the United States in 1860-61 and fought against the northern states in the Civil War ☞ Look at the note at **White House**.

Con·fed·er·ate /kən'fɛdərət/ *noun* [C] a supporter of the Confederacy

con·fed·er·a·tion /kənˌfɛdə'reɪʃn/ *noun* [C] an organization of smaller groups which have

joined together: *a confederation of independent republics*

con·fer /kən'fər/ *verb* (**con·fer·ring; con·ferred**) **1** [I] **confer (with sb) (on/about sth)** to discuss sth with sb before making a decision: *The President is conferring with his advisers.* **2** [T] **confer sth (on sb)** to give sb a special right or advantage: *The university plans to confer honorary degrees on two distinguished authors.*

☆ **con·fer·ence** /'kɑnfrəns; -fərəns/ *noun* [C] **1** a meeting for discussion, often one held every year where representatives of a particular profession, organization, etc. meet for several days to hear speeches and vote on the matters discussed: *an international conference on global warming* ○ *a press conference* (= when a politician, etc. talks to reporters) ☞ Look also at **convention**. **2** a group of sports teams that compete against each other: *the eastern conference of the National Basketball Association*

☆ **con·fess** /kən'fɛs/ *verb* [I,T] **1 confess (to sth/to doing sth); confess (sth) (to sb)** to say that you have done sth bad or wrong: *The young woman confessed to the murder of her boyfriend/to murdering her boyfriend.* ○ *Frank confessed that he had stolen the car.* ○ *They confessed to their mother that they had spent all the money.* ○ *I have to confess I didn't understand a word of that speech!* **2 confess (sth) (to sb)** to tell a priest or God what you have done that is bad or wrong: *to confess a sin*

con·fes·sion /kən'fɛʃn/ *noun* [C,U] an act of confessing sth: *The suspect made a full confession to the police.* ○ *She goes to confession* (= with a priest) *twice a year.*

con·fet·ti /kən'fɛti/ *noun* [U] small pieces of colored paper that people throw at parties, festivals or after weddings

con·fide /kən'faɪd/ *verb* [T] **confide sth to sb** to tell sb sth that is secret: *She did not confide her love to anyone – not even to her best friend.* **PHRV** **confide in sb** to talk to sb whom you trust about sth that is secret or private

☆ **con·fi·dence** /'kɑnfədəns/ *noun* **1** [U] **confidence (in sb/sth)** trust or strong belief in sb/sth: *I have every confidence in Kim's ability to do the job.* ○ *They don't have much confidence in him.* ○ *The public is losing confidence in the government's ability to improve the economy.* **2** [U] the feeling that you are sure about your own abilities, opinion, etc.: *I didn't have the confidence to tell her I thought she was wrong.* ○ *to be full of confidence* ○ *"Of course we will win," the coach said with confidence.* ☞ Look at **self-confidence**. **IDM** **in confidence** as a secret: *People with information about the crime can report in confidence to the police.*

☆ **con·fi·dent** /'kɑnfədənt/ *adj.* **confident (about/of sth); confident (that...)** feeling or

showing that you are sure about your own abilities, opinions, etc.: *Kate feels confident about her chances of passing the test.* ○ *to be confident of success* ○ *David has a very confident manner.* ☞ Look at **self-confident.** —**con·fi·dent·ly** *adv.*: *She stepped confidently onto the stage and began to sing.* ○ *We confidently expect an improvement in sales next year.*

con·fi·den·tial /ˌkɑnfəˈdɛnʃl/ *adj.* secret; not to be shown or told to other people: *The letter was marked "private and confidential."* —**con·fi·den·ti·al·i·ty** /ˌkɑnfəˌdɛnʃiˈæləti/ *noun* [U] —**con·fi·den·tial·ly** /ˌkɑnfəˈdɛnʃəli/ *adv.*

con·fine /kənˈfaɪn/ *verb* [T] **1 confine sb/sth (in/to sth)** to keep a person or animal in a particular place, usually a small place: *The prisoners are confined to their cells for long periods at a time.* **2 confine sb/sth/yourself to sth** to stay within the limits of sth: *Please confine your questions and comments to the topic we are discussing.*

con·fined /kənˈfaɪnd/ *adj.* (used about a space) very small : *Sailors on submarines must get used to living in confined spaces.*

con·fine·ment /kənˈfaɪnmənt/ *noun* [U] being kept in a small space: *to be kept in solitary confinement*

con·fines /ˈkɑnfaɪnz/ *noun* [plural] (*formal*) the limits or outer edges of sth: *Patients are not allowed beyond the confines of the hospital grounds.*

☆ **con·firm** /kənˈfərm/ *verb* [T] **1** to say or show that sth is true; to make sth definite: *Please confirm our agreement in writing.* ○ *Seeing the two of them together confirmed our suspicions.* ○ *Can you confirm that you will be able to attend?* **2** to accept sb as a full member of a Christian church: *He was baptized as a baby and confirmed at the age of 13.*

con·fir·ma·tion /ˌkɑnfərˈmeɪʃn/ *noun* **1** [C,U] a statement that confirms sth: *We are waiting for confirmation of the report.* ○ *You will receive a written confirmation of your reservation.* **2** [C] a religious service at which a person is confirmed (2)

con·fis·cate /ˈkɑnfəskeɪt/ *verb* [T] to take sth away from sb as a punishment: *Any cigarettes found in school will be confiscated.* —**con·fis·ca·tion** /ˌkɑnfəˈskeɪʃn/ *noun* [C,U]

☆ **con·flict¹** /ˈkɑnflɪkt/ *noun* [C,U] **1** a fight or an argument: *an armed conflict* ○ *Sheila's aggressive personality often brought her into conflict with her boss.* **2** a difference between two or more ideas, wishes, etc.: *Don't you see any conflict between being a vegetarian and wearing leather shoes?*

IDM conflict of interest a situation in which a person's private interests (for example, his/her own business or company) have an unfair influence on his/her duties in an official position (for example, as a politician)

☆ **con·flict²** /kənˈflɪkt/ *verb* [I] **1 A and B conflict; A conflicts with B** to disagree with or be different from sb/sth: *The statements of the two witnesses conflict.* ○ *John's statement conflicts with yours.* ○ *The two studies came up with conflicting results.* **2 conflict (with sth)** to happen at the same time so that you must choose one thing: *Sorry, I can't come to the meeting on Wednesday. It conflicts with my history class.*

con·form /kənˈfɔrm/ *verb* [I] **conform (to sth) 1** to obey a rule or law; to come up to a particular standard: *This building does not conform to fire regulations.* **2** to behave in the way that other people and society expect you to behave: *Kids are under a lot of pressure to conform when they are in high school.*

con·form·i·ty /kənˈfɔrməti/ *noun* [U] (*formal*) behavior which conforms to rules and customs

con·front /kənˈfrʌnt/ *verb* [T] **1 confront sth; confront sb with sb/sth** to think about, or to make sb think about, sth that is difficult or unpleasant: *to confront a problem, difficulty, etc.* ○ *When the police confronted him with the evidence, he confessed.* **2** to stand in front of sb, e.g. because you want to fight him/her: *The unarmed demonstrators were confronted by a row of soldiers.*

con·fron·ta·tion /ˌkɑnfrənˈteɪʃn/ *noun* [C,U] a fight or an argument

☆ **con·fuse** /kənˈfyuz/ *verb* [T] **1** to make sb unable to think clearly or to know what to do: *He confused everybody with his pages of facts and figures.* **2 confuse A and/with B** to mistake sb/sth for sb/sth else: *I often confuse Lee with his brother. They look very much alike.* ○ *Don't confuse "complement" with "compliment."* **3** to make sth unclear: *The situation is confused by the fact that so many organizations are involved.*

☆ **con·fused** /kənˈfyuzd/ *adj.* **1** not able to think clearly: *When he regained consciousness, he was dazed and confused.* **2** difficult to understand because it is not in good order: *Following the attempted coup, the political situation was confused and unstable.*

☆ **con·fus·ing** /kənˈfyuzɪŋ/ *adj.* difficult to understand: *I can't figure out these instructions – they're too confusing.*

☆ **con·fu·sion** /kənˈfyuʒn/ *noun* [U] **1** the state of not being able to think clearly or to know what to do: *He stared in confusion at the crowd of people in front of his house.* **2** a state of disorder: *In the panic and confusion, two people were trampled to death.* ○ *Their unexpected visit threw all our plans into confusion.* **3** the act of mistaking sb/sth for sb/sth else: *To avoid confusion, all luggage should be labeled with your name and destination.* **4** the state of being uncertain or unclear: *There is*

C

congenial

still a great deal of confusion as to the true facts.

con·gen·ial /kənˈdʒinyəl/ *adj.* (*formal*) pleasant: *We have a very congenial atmosphere in our office.*

con·gen·i·tal /kənˈdʒɛnətl/ *adj.* (used about a disease) beginning at and continuing since birth: *a congenital heart defect*

con·gest·ed /kənˈdʒɛstəd/ *adj.* so full of sth that nothing can move: *The streets of New York are congested with traffic.* ○ *I had a terrible cold last week – my head and chest were all congested.*

con·ges·tion /kənˈdʒɛstʃən/ *noun* [U] the state of being very full of sth: *severe traffic congestion* ○ *medicine to relieve coughing and nasal congestion*

con·glom·er·ate /kənˈglɑmərət/ *noun* [C] a large firm made up of several different companies

☆**con·grat·u·late** /kənˈgrætʃəleɪt/ *verb* [T] **congratulate sb (on sth)** to praise sb or tell sb that you are pleased about sth he/she has done: *I congratulated Sue on graduating from college.* ○ *They sent a card to congratulate the couple on their engagement.*

☆**con·grat·u·la·tions** /kənˌgrætʃəˈleɪʃnz/ *noun* [plural] (used for praising sb or telling sb that you are pleased about sth he/she has done): *Congratulations on the birth of your baby boy!* ○ *Congratulations! Your painting has won first prize.*

con·gre·gate /ˈkɑŋgrəgeɪt/ *verb* [I] to come together in a crowd

con·gre·ga·tion /ˌkɑŋgrəˈgeɪʃn/ *noun* [C] a group of people who go to a particular church

☆**con·gress** /ˈkɑŋgrəs/ *noun* **1 Congress** [sing.] the group of people who are elected to make the laws for the United States: *a member of Congress* ○ *to run for Congress* (= in order to be elected)

☞ The U.S. Congress is made up of the **Senate** and the **House of Representatives**.

2 [C] (in some countries) the group of people who are elected to make the laws: *the Brazilian congress* **3** [C] a large formal meeting or series of meetings: *the Communist Party congress in Beijing* ☞ Look at **conference** and **convention**.

con·gres·sion·al /kənˈgrɛʃənl; kəŋ-/ *adj.* connected with Congress: *a congressional committee*

☆**con·gress·man** /ˈkɑŋgrəsmən/ (*feminine* **con·gress·wom·an** /ˈkɑŋgrəsˌwʊmən/) (*pl.* **con·gress·men; con·gress·wom·en**) *noun* [C] a member of the U.S. Congress, especially the House of Representatives

☞ A member of the Senate is usually called a **senator**.

con·jec·ture /kənˈdʒɛktʃər/ *noun* [C,U] guess-ing or a guess about sth without real proof or evidence

con·ju·gate /ˈkɑndʒəgeɪt/ *verb* [T] to give the different forms of a verb —**con·ju·ga·tion** /ˌkɑndʒəˈgeɪʃn/ *noun* [C,U]

con·junc·tion /kənˈdʒʌŋkʃn/ *noun* [C] a word that is used for joining other words, phrases or sentences: *"And," "but" and "or" are conjunctions.*

IDM in conjunction with sb/sth together with sb/sth: *Various charities are working in conjunction with the United Nations to help the disaster victims.*

con·jure /ˈkɑndʒər/ *verb* [T] **conjure sth (up)** to cause a picture to appear in your mind: *Hawaiian music conjures up images of sunshine, flowers and sandy beaches.*

'con man (*pl.* **con men**) (*also* **'con artist**) *noun* [C] (*informal*) a person who tricks others into giving him money, etc.

☆**con·nect** /kəˈnɛkt/ *verb* **1** [I,T] **connect (sth) (to/with sth)** to be joined or linked to sth; to join or link sth to sth else: *You need the right software to be able to connect to the Internet.* ○ *The printer is connected to the computer.* ○ *The new subway line will connect the southern suburbs directly with downtown.* ○ *The phone company hasn't connected our phone line yet.* ☞ Look at **disconnect**. **2** [T] (usually passive) **connect sb/sth (to/with sb/sth)** to associate sb/sth with sb/sth; to consider sb/sth to be related to sb/sth else: *There was no evidence that she was connected with the crime.* ○ *Doctors believe that the increase in asthma is connected to pollution levels.* **3** [I] **connect (with sth)** (used about a bus, train, plane, etc.) to arrive at a particular time so that passengers can change to another bus, train, plane, etc.: *I hope we won't miss our connecting flight in Chicago!* **4** [T] **connect sb (to/with sb)** to link sb by telephone: *Please stay on the line while we connect you to the next available representative.* **5** [I] **connect (with sb)** to understand sb well and have a good relationship with him/her: *If he wants to win the election, he'll have to connect with middle-class voters.*

☆**con·nec·tion** /kəˈnɛkʃn/ *noun* **1** [C,U] **connection between A and B; connection with/to sth** connecting or being connected: *There is a clear connection between crime and drug addiction.* ○ *Is there any connection between the two organizations?* ○ *What is your connection with the school? Do you work here?* **2** [C] a place where two wires, pipes, etc. join together: *The radio doesn't work. There must be a loose connection somewhere.* **3** [C] a bus, train, plane, etc. that leaves soon after another arrives: *Our plane was late so we missed our connection.* **4** [C, usually pl.] a person that you know who is important or of high rank: *Chris got a good job because of his mother's connections.*

ər	ɪr	ɛr	ɑr	ɔr	ʊr	ʒ	h	ŋ
bird	near	hair	car	north	tour	vision	hat	sing

IDM in connection with sb/sth (*formal*) about or concerning: *I am writing to you in connection with your application.*

con·nois·seur /ˌkɒnəˈsər; -ˈsʊr/ *noun* [C] a person who knows a lot about art, good food, music, etc.: *a connoisseur of modern art*

con·no·ta·tion /ˌkɒnəˈteɪʃn/ *noun* [C] an impression that a word gives in addition to its meaning: *"Spinster" means a single woman, but it has negative connotations.*

☆ **con·quer** /ˈkɒŋkər/ *verb* [T] **1** to take control of an area by winning a war: *Napoleon's ambition was to conquer the whole of Europe.* ○ (*figurative*) *The young singer conquered the hearts of audiences all over the world.* **2** to defeat an enemy, an army, etc.; to overcome sth: *The Spanish conquered the Incas.* ○ *She's trying to conquer her fear of flying.* —**con·quer·or** /ˈkɒŋkərər/ *noun* [C]

con·quest /ˈkɒŋkwest/ *noun* **1** [C, U] an act of conquering sth: *the Spanish conquest of South America* ○ *the conquest of Mount Everest* **2** [C] an area of land that has been taken by war

con·science /ˈkɒnʃəns/ *noun* [C,U] your own feeling about whether what you are doing is right or wrong: *a clear/a guilty conscience*

IDM have sth on your conscience to feel guilty because of sth that you have done that was wrong

con·sci·en·tious /ˌkɒnʃiˈenʃəs/ *adj.* **1** (used about people) careful to do sth correctly and well: *He's a very conscientious worker.* **2** (used about actions) done with great care and attention: *conscientious work* —**con·sci·en·tious·ly** *adv.*

consci,entious ob'jector *noun* [C] a person who refuses to join the army, etc. because he/she believes it is morally wrong to kill other people

☆ **con·scious** /ˈkɒnʃəs/ *adj.* **1** able to see, hear, feel, etc. things; awake: *She was badly injured but conscious and able to tell the doctor what had happened.* ☛ The opposite is **unconscious**. **2 conscious of sth/that…** noticing or aware of sth: *He suddenly became conscious that someone was following him.* ○ *She didn't seem conscious of the danger.* **3** that you do on purpose or for a particular reason: *We made a conscious effort to treat both kids fairly.* ☛ Look at **deliberate**. It has a similar meaning. The opposite is **unconscious**. **4** being particularly interested in or aware of sth: *Teenagers are very fashion-conscious.* —**con·scious·ly** *adv.: I have never consciously harmed another human being.*

☆ **con·scious·ness** /ˈkɒnʃəsnəs/ *noun* **1** [U] the state of being conscious (1); being able to see, hear, feel, etc. things: *As he fell, he hit his head and lost consciousness.* ○ *She regained consciousness after two weeks in a coma.* **2** [U, sing.] the state of being aware of sth: *growing consciousness of the need to save energy*

con·se·crate /ˈkɒnsəkreɪt/ *verb* [T] to make a place, an object or a person holy in a special ceremony: *Four new bishops were consecrated in the cathedral.* —**con·se·cra·tion** /ˌkɒnsəˈkreɪʃn/ *noun* [C,U]

con·sec·u·tive /kənˈsekyətɪv/ *adj.* coming or happening one after the other: *We have had three consecutive rainy weekends.* —**con·sec·u·tive·ly** *adv.*

con·sen·sus /kənˈsensəs/ *noun* [sing., U] agreement among a group of people: *to reach a consensus after a long discussion* ○ *There is no general consensus among experts about the causes of global warming.*

con·sent¹ /kənˈsent/ *verb* [I] **consent (to sth)** to agree to sth; to allow sth to happen

con·sent² /kənˈsent/ *noun* [U] agreement; permission: *The child's parents had to give their consent to the operation.*

☆ **con·se·quence** /ˈkɒnsəkwens/ *noun* **1** [C] something that follows as a result or effect of sth else: *The bridge was unsafe and, as a consequence, was closed and repaired.* ○ *The error had tragic consequences.* **2** [U] (*formal*) importance: *It is of no consequence.*

con·se·quent /ˈkɒnsəkwent/ *adj.* (*formal*) following as the result of sth else: *The economy has benefited from new jobs and the consequent drop in the unemployment rate.* —**con·se·quent·ly** *adv.: She didn't work hard enough and consequently failed the exam.*

con·ser·va·tion /ˌkɒnsərˈveɪʃn/ *noun* [U] **1** not allowing sth to be wasted, damaged or destroyed: *the conservation of energy* **2** the protection of the natural world: *Conservation groups are protesting against the plan to build a road through the forest.* ☛ The verb is **conserve**.

con·ser·va·tion·ist /ˌkɒnsərˈveɪʃənɪst/ *noun* [C] a person who believes in conservation (2)

con·ser·va·tism /kənˈsərvətɪzəm/ *noun* [U] the dislike of new ideas and change

☆ **con·ser·va·tive¹** /kənˈsərvətɪv/ *adj.* **1** not liking change; traditional: *They have very conservative tastes. This design is too modern for them.* **2** supporting a free market, low taxes and traditional ideas about family life, sex, etc. ☛ Look at **liberal**. **3** (used about a guess, estimate, etc.) cautious, not extreme; fairly low: *I would say the damage will cost about $4,000 to repair – and that's a conservative estimate.* —**con·ser·va·tive·ly** *adv.: We have estimated the costs conservatively.*

con·ser·va·tive² /kənˈsərvətɪv/ *noun* [C] a conservative¹(1,2) person

con·ser·va·to·ry /kənˈsərvəˌtɔri/ *noun* [C] (*pl.* **con·ser·va·to·ries**) **1** a building with a glass roof and walls in which plants are grown and shown to the public **2** a school where students can go to study music or acting

con·serve /kənˈsərv/ *verb* [T] to avoid wasting sth: *Higher charges will encourage people*

tʃ	dʒ	v	θ	ð	s	z	ʃ
chin	June	van	thin	then	so	zoo	she

C

to conserve water. ☞ The noun is **conserva-tion.**

☆ **con·si·der** /kənˈsɪdər/ *verb* [T] **1 consider sb/sth (for/as sth); consider doing sth** to think about sb/sth, often before making a decision: *We must consider the matter carefully before we make our choice.* ○ *They are considering him for the part of Romeo.* ○ *She had never considered nursing as a career.* ○ *He is still considering what material to include in the book.* ○ *We're considering going to Hawaii for our vacation.* **2** to have sth as your opinion; to think about sb/sth in a particular way: *He considered that the risk was too great.* ○ *He considered the risk (to be) too great.* **3** to remember or pay attention to sth: *I can't just quit my job. I have to consider my family.* ○ *Be tactful. Consider how other people feel.*

☆ **con·sid·er·a·ble** /kənˈsɪdərəbl/ *adj.* great in amount or size: *We had considerable difficulty in getting tickets for the flights we wanted.* ○ *A considerable number of people preferred the old building to the new one.* —**con·sid·er·a·bly** /-əbli/ *adv.*: *This apartment is considerably larger than our last one.*

con·sid·er·ate /kənˈsɪdərət/ *adj.* careful not to upset people; thinking of others: *It was very considerate of you to offer to drive me home.* ☞ The opposite is **inconsiderate.**

☆ **con·sid·er·a·tion** /kənˌsɪdəˈreɪʃn/ *noun* **1** [U] *(formal)* an act of thinking about sth carefully or for a long time: *I have given some consideration to the idea but I don't think it would work.* ○ *After careful consideration, we regret that we cannot offer you the position.* ○ *Several options are currently under consideration.* **2** [U] **consideration (for sb/sth)** the quality of thinking about other people's wishes and feelings: *You should keep your music turned down low out of consideration for your neighbors.* **3** [C] something that you think about when you are making a decision: *If he changes his job, the salary will be an important consideration.*

IDM **take sth into consideration** to think about sth when you are forming an opinion or making a decision

☆ **con·sid·er·ing** /kənˈsɪdərɪŋ/ *prep., conj.* (used for introducing a surprising fact) when you think about or remember sth: *He coped with the long trip well, considering his age.* ○ *Considering you've only been studying for a year, you speak English very well.*

con·sign /kənˈsaɪn/ *verb* [T] *(formal)* to put sb/sth in, or to send sb/sth to, a particular place

con·sign·ment /kənˈsaɪnmənt/ *noun* [C] goods that are being sent to sb/sth: *We sent a consignment of old books to a used book store.*

☆ **con·sist** /kənˈsɪst/ *verb*

PHRV **consist of sth** to be made up of sth: *The band consists of a singer, two guitarists, a bass player and a drummer.*

con·sis·ten·cy /kənˈsɪstənsi/ *noun* (*pl.* **con·sis·ten·cies**) **1** [U] the quality of being consistent (1); always having the same standard, opinions, etc.: *Your work lacks consistency. Sometimes it's excellent, but at other times it's full of mistakes.* ☞ The opposite is **inconsistency.** **2** [C,U] the degree of thickness or firmness that a substance has: *The mixture should have a thick, sticky consistency.*

☆ **con·sis·tent** /kənˈsɪstənt/ *adj.* **1** always having the same opinions, standard, behavior, etc.; not changing: *You have to be consistent. If you punish Jason, you should punish Paul for doing the same thing.* **2** **consistent (with sth)** agreeing with or similar to sth: *Your statement is not consistent with what the other witnesses said.* —**con·sis·tent·ly** *adv.*: *We must try to maintain a consistently high standard.*

con·so·la·tion /ˌkɑnsəˈleɪʃn/ *noun* **1** [U] making sb feel better when they are sad: *It was some consolation to me to know that I wasn't the only one who had failed the final exam.* ○ *a consolation prize* (= for sb who has lost a contest, game, etc.) **2** [C] a person or thing that consoles you: *Having his children near him was a great consolation when his wife died.*

con·sole¹ /kənˈsoʊl/ *verb* [T] to make sb happier when he/she is very sad or disappointed; to comfort sb

con·sole² /ˈkɑnsoʊl/ *noun* [C] **1** a board or surface that contains the controls for a machine or a piece of electronic equipment: *rows of computer consoles at the space center* **2** a type of cupboard or box for a TV or stereo that stands on the floor

con·sol·i·date /kənˈsɑlədeɪt/ *verb* [I,T] **1** to write or to combine several things into one: *We plan to close several smaller branches and consolidate our operations here in Chicago.* **2** to become or to make sth firmer or stronger: *an attempt by party members to consolidate their power* —**con·sol·i·da·tion** /kənˌsɑləˈdeɪʃn/ *noun* [U]

con·so·nant /ˈkɑnsənənt/ *noun* [C] **1** a sound that you make by partly stopping the air as it comes out through your mouth **2** a letter that represents this sound: *The letters "t," "m," "s" and "b" are all consonants.* ☞ Look at **vowel.**

con·sor·ti·um /kənˈsɔrʃiəm/ -ʃəm; -tiəm/ *noun* [C] (*pl.* **con·sor·ti·ums** or **con·sor·ti·a** /-ʃiə; -ʃə; -tiə/) a group of companies that work closely together for a particular purpose

con·spic·u·ous /kənˈspɪkyuəs/ *adj.* easily seen or noticed: *As a tall, blond American, he was very conspicuous in China.* ☞ The opposite is **inconspicuous.** —**con·spic·u·ous·ly** *adv.*: *She was conspicuously dressed in a large hat.*

i	ɪ	ɛ	æ	ɑ	ɔ	ʌ	ʊ	u
see	sit	ten	cat	hot	saw	cup	put	too

☆ **con·spir·a·cy** /kən'spɪrəsi/ *noun* (*pl.* **conspir·a·cies**) **1** [U] planning sth, especially a crime, together with other people: *They were accused of conspiracy to murder.* **2** [C] a secret plan to do sth bad or illegal: *Investigators have uncovered a conspiracy to defraud the bank of thousands of dollars.*

con·spir·a·tor /kən'spɪrətər/ *noun* [C] a person who plans sth, especially a crime, together with other people

con·spire /kən'spaɪər/ *verb* [I] **1** to plan sth, especially a crime, together with other people: *A group of thieves were conspiring to rob the bank.* **2 conspire (against sb/sth)** to work together to produce a particular, usually bad, result for sb/sth: *When we both lost our jobs in the same week, we felt that everything was conspiring against us.*

☆ **con·stant** /'kɑnstənt/ *adj.* **1** happening or existing all the time or again and again: *The constant noise gave me a headache.* ○ *There were constant interruptions, so we didn't get the work finished.* **2** that does not change: *You use less gas if you drive at a constant speed.*

con·stant·ly /'kɑnstəntli/ *adv.* always; again and again: *The situation is constantly changing.*

con·stel·la·tion /ˌkɑnstə'leɪʃn/ *noun* [C] a number of stars that are considered as a group

con·ster·na·tion /ˌkɑnstər'neɪʃn/ *noun* [U] surprise and worry or fear: *We stared at each other in consternation.*

con·sti·pat·ed /'kɑnstəpeɪṭəd/ *adj.* not able to pass waste material easily from the bowels: *If you are constipated, you should eat more fiber and fresh fruit.* —**con·sti·pa·tion** /ˌkɑnstə'peɪʃn/ *noun* [U]

con·stit·u·en·cy /kən'stɪtʃuənsi/ *noun* [C] (*pl.* **con·stit·u·en·cies**) **1** the people or groups who support a politician: *The President risks offending much of his core* (= main) *constituency if he supports this bill.* **2** a district and the people who are represented by a politician

con·stit·u·ent /kən'stɪtʃuənt/ *noun* [C] **1** a person who lives in the district for which a particular representative in government is responsible **2** one of the parts of sth

con·sti·tute /'kɑnstətut/ *verb* [T] (*formal*) (not in the continuous tenses) to make up or form sth: *Women constitute a high proportion of part-time workers.* ○ *The presence of the troops constitutes a threat to peace.*

☆ **con·sti·tu·tion** /ˌkɑnstə'tuʃn/ *noun* [C] **1** (*also* often **Constitution**) the basic laws or rules of a country, state or organization: *the United States Constitution* ○ *the Tennessee state constitution* **2** (*old-fashioned*) the condition of your body; your health

☆ **con·sti·tu·tion·al** /ˌkɑnstə'tuʃənl/ *adj.* **1** in agreement with or allowed by the constitution (1) of a country or state: *The Supreme Court will decide whether the law is constitutional.* ☞ The opposite is **unconstitutional. 2** connected with a constitution (1): *a constitutional amendment*

con·strain /kən'streɪn/ *verb* [T] (*formal*) to set limits on sth, especially sb's freedom; to force sb to do sth

con·straint /kən'streɪnt/ *noun* [C] a limit on sth, or on your freedom to do sth: *There are always some financial constraints on a project like this.*

con·strict /kən'strɪkt/ *verb* [T] **1** to make sth tighter or narrower; to reduce sth **2** to limit a person's freedom to do sth

☆ **con·struct** /kən'strʌkt/ *verb* [T] to build or make sth: *Early houses were constructed out of logs.* ☞ **Construct** is more formal than **build.**

☆ **con·struc·tion** /kən'strʌkʃn/ *noun* **1** [U] the act or method of building or making sth: *A new bridge is now under construction.* ○ *He works in the construction industry.* ○ *We had to take a detour because of the road construction in town.* **2** [C] something that has been built or made: *The new pyramid was a construction of glass and steel.* **3** [C] the way that words are used together in a phrase or sentence: *a complex sentence construction* ○ *Which of these constructions is more common – "to dress" or "to get dressed"?*

con'struction ˌpaper *noun* [U] a type of heavy paper that comes in bright colors and that can be cut into shapes to make pictures, designs, etc.

con·struc·tive /kən'strʌktɪv/ *adj.* useful or helpful: *She made a number of constructive criticisms to help us to improve our work.* —**con·struc·tive·ly** *adv.*

con·sul /'kɑnsl/ *noun* [C] an official who works in a foreign city helping people from his/her country who are living or visiting there ☞ Look at **ambassador.**

con·su·late /'kɑnsələt/ *noun* [C] the office of a consul

con·sult /kən'sʌlt/ *verb* **1** [T] **consult sb/sth (about sth)** to ask sb or to look sth up in a book, etc. to get information or advice: *You should consult a doctor if the symptoms get worse.* ○ *He consulted the map to find the shortest route.* **2** [I] **consult with sb** to discuss sth with sb

con·sult·ant /kən'sʌltnt/ *noun* [C] a person who gives advice to people on business, law, etc.: *a management consultant* ○ *Diane quit her old job and now works as a computer consultant.*

con·sul·ta·tion /ˌkɑnsl'teɪʃn/ *noun* **1** [U] discussing sth or looking sth up in a book to get information or advice **2** [C,U] a meeting at which sth is discussed: *Diplomats met for consultations on the hostage crisis.* ○ *The measures were introduced without consultation.*

ə	y	w	ṭ	eɪ	aɪ	ɔɪ	aʊ	oʊ
about	yes	woman	butter	say	five	boy	now	go

con·sult·ing /kən'sʌltɪŋ/ *noun* [U] giving advice to people on business, computers, etc.: *I'm thinking about a career in computer consulting.*

☆ **con·sume** /kən'sum/ *verb* [T] (*formal*) **1** to use sth: *The United States imports 45% of the oil it consumes.* **2** to eat or drink sth **3** (used about fire) to destroy sth **4** (used about an emotion) to affect sb very strongly: *She was consumed by grief when her son was killed.*

☆ **con·sum·er** /kən'sumər/ *noun* [C] a person who buys things or uses services: *Consumers should complain if they are not satisfied with the service they receive.* ○ *the rights of the consumer* ○ *Consumer spending has risen in the past few months.*

con·sum·ing /kən'sumɪŋ/ *adj.* (only *before* a noun) that takes up a lot of your time and attention: *Music is her consuming passion.* ☞ Look also at **time-consuming**.

con·sump·tion /kən'sʌmpʃn/ *noun* [U] **1** the act of using, eating, etc. sth: *This fish is unfit for human consumption* (= for people to eat). **2** the amount of fuel, etc. that sth uses: *a car with low fuel consumption*

☆ **con·tact¹** /'kɑntækt/ *noun* **1** [U] the state of touching sb/sth: *Don't let the wires come into contact with each other.* **2** [U] meeting, talking to or writing to sb else: *We are in close contact with our office in New York.* ○ *I've lost contact with most of my old classmates.* ○ *They are trying to make contact with the kidnappers.* ○ *Tom has not been in contact since he moved to Minneapolis.* ○ *Tom broke off contact with his family after an argument.* **3** [C] a person that you know who may be able to help you: *I have some useful business contacts in Canada.* **4** [C] = CONTACT LENS

☆ **con·tact²** /'kɑntækt/ *verb* [T] to call, write to, etc. sb: *Is there a phone number where I can contact you?*

'**contact lens** (*also* **contact**) *noun* [C] a small piece of plastic that fits onto your eye to help you to see better ☞ picture at **glasses**.

con·ta·gious /kən'teɪdʒəs/ *adj.* (used about a disease) that you can catch by touching sb/sth: *Smallpox is a contagious disease.* ○ (*figurative*) *contagious laughter* ☞ Look at **infectious**.

☆ **con·tain** /kən'teɪn/ *verb* [T] **1** to have sth inside (or as part of) itself: *Each box contains 24 cans.* ○ *food containing fiber* **2** to keep sth within limits: *efforts to contain inflation* ○ *The kids couldn't contain themselves – they burst out laughing.* ○ *She found it hard to contain her anger.*

☞ **Contain** or **include**? **Contain** is used when we are talking about objects which have other things inside them: *a jar containing olives* ○ *The package contained six books.* **Include** is used to show that several things are part of a whole or thought to belong to something: *The price of the car does not include sales tax.* ○ *a team of seven people including a cameraman and a doctor*

☆ **con·tain·er** /kən'teɪnər/ *noun* [C] **1** a box, bottle, package, etc. in which sth is kept: *a plastic container* ○ *a watertight container* **2** a large metal box that is used for transporting goods: *The cargo containers were loaded onto the plane.*

contam·i·nate /kən'tæməneɪt/ *verb* [T] to add a substance which will make sth dirty, harmful or dangerous: *The town's drinking water was contaminated with poisonous chemicals.* —**con·tam·i·na·tion** /kən,tæmə'neɪʃn/ *noun* [U]: *There was widespread radioactive contamination after the accident at the nuclear power plant.*

con·tem·plate /'kɑntəmpleɪt/ *verb* [T] **1** to think about sth or the possibility of doing sth: *The idea was too horrible to contemplate.* ○ *Before her illness she had never contemplated retiring.* **2** to look at sb/sth, often quietly or for a long time

con·tem·pla·tion /,kɑntəm'pleɪʃn/ *noun* [U] **1** looking at sth quietly **2** thinking deeply about sth

☆ **con·tem·po·rar·y¹** /kən'tɛmpə,rɛri/ *adj.* **1** of the present time; modern: *contemporary*

containers

boxes · tube · bags · SUGAR · CHIPS · CORN FLAKES · COOKIES · EGGS · JUICE · cartons · cans · jars · BEER · Oil · Cola · MILK · containers · bottles

music, art, etc. **2** belonging to the same time as sb/sth else: *These letters give us a contemporary account of life in colonial America.*

con·tem·po·rar·y² /kən'tɛmpə,rɛri/ *noun* [C] (*pl.* **con·tem·po·rar·ies**) a person who lived or did sth at the same time as sb else: *Telemann, a contemporary of Bach*

con·tempt /kən'tɛmpt/ *noun* [U] **contempt (for sb/sth)** the feeling that sb/sth does not deserve to be respected or is unimportant: *This is just another example of the government's contempt for poorer citizens.*

con·tend /kən'tɛnd/ *verb* **1** [I] **contend with/ against sb/sth; contend for sth** to struggle to overcome sth or to win sth: *She's had a lot of problems to contend with.* ○ *Two athletes are contending for first place.* **2** [T] (*formal*) to declare or argue that sth is true: *He contended that he had never met the murdered girl.*

con·tend·er /kən'tɛndər/ *noun* [C] a person who takes part in a competition: *There were three contenders for the position.*

☆ **con·tent¹** /kən'tɛnt/ *adj.* (not before a noun) **content (with sth); content to do sth** satisfied with what you have: *She is perfectly content to stay home and take care of her children.*

con·tent² /kən'tɛnt/ *verb* [T] **content yourself with sth** to accept sth even though it was not exactly what you wanted: *The museum was closed, so we contented ourselves with a walk around the park.*

☆ **con·tent³** /'kɑntɛnt/ *noun* **1 contents** [plural] the thing or things that are inside sth: *Add the contents of this packet to a quart of cold milk and mix well.* ○ *The table of contents tells you what is inside a book.* **2** [sing.] the main subject, ideas, etc. of a book, article, television program, etc.: *The content of the essay is good, but there are too many grammatical mistakes.* **3** [sing.] the level or amount of a particular substance that sth contains: *Many processed foods have a high sugar content.*

con·tent·ed /kən'tɛntəd/ *adj.* happy or satisfied: *The baby gave a contented smile.* —**content·ed·ly** *adv.*: *The cat purred contentedly.*

con·ten·tion /kən'tɛnʃn/ *noun* **1** [U] the situation of competing for sth: *Four players are still in contention for the championship.* **2** [U] arguing; disagreement **3** [C] your opinion; sth that you declare to be true: *The government's contention is that unemployment will start to fall next year.*

con·ten·tious /kən'tɛnʃəs/ *adj.* likely to cause argument: *a contentious issue*

con·tent·ment /kən'tɛntmənt/ *noun* [U] the state of being happy or satisfied: *a sigh of contentment*

☆ **con·test¹** /'kɑntɛst/ *noun* [C] a competition to find out who is the best, strongest, most beautiful, etc.: *to enter a talent contest* ○ *The election will be a contest between an unpopular senator and an energetic newcomer.*

con·test² /kən'tɛst/ *verb* [T] **1** to say that sth is wrong or that it was not done correctly: *They contested the decision, saying that the judges had not been fair.* **2** to take part in a competition or try to win sth: *a hotly contested championship fight*

con·tes·tant /kən'tɛstənt/ *noun* [C] a person who takes part in a contest: *Four contestants appear on the game show every day.*

☆ **con·text** /'kɑntɛkst/ *noun* [C,U] **1** the words that come before or after a word, phrase, sentence, etc. and that help you to understand its meaning: *You can often guess the meaning of a word from its context.* ○ *Taken out of context, his comment made no sense.* **2** the situation in which sth happens or that caused sth to happen: *The increase in unemployment must be seen in the context of our changing economy.*

☆ **con·ti·nent** /'kɑntənənt; 'kɑntn·ənt/ *noun* [C] one of the seven main areas of land on the Earth: *Asia, Africa and Antarctica are continents.* ○ *ferry service linking Britain and the continent* (= the main part of Europe)

☆ **con·ti·nen·tal** /,kɑntə'nɛntl/ *adj.* **1** connected with or typical of a continent **2** connected with the main part of a continent (1): *Prices are often higher in Alaska and Hawaii than in the continental United States.* ○ *continental Europe* (= not including Britain or Ireland)

,conti,nental 'breakfast *noun* [C] a breakfast of bread or sweet rolls with coffee and fruit juice

con·tin·gen·cy /kən'tɪndʒənsi/ *noun* [C] (*pl.* **con·tin·gen·cies**) a possible future situation or event: *contingency plans*

con·tin·u·al /kən'tɪnyuəl/ *adj.* happening again and again : *His continual phone calls started to annoy her.* —**con·tin·u·al·ly** *adv.*: *She continually criticizes his behavior.*

☞ **Continual** or **continuous?** We use **continuous** to describe an action or state that goes on without stopping: *There has been a continuous improvement in his work.* ○ *After climbing continuously for three hours, we were exhausted.* **Continual** is used to describe something that happens repeatedly, especially something that annoys us: *They have had continual problems with their car.*

con·tin·u·a·tion /kən,tɪnyu'eɪʃn/ *noun* **1** [sing., U] continuing to do sth without stopping; starting to do sth again after you have stopped **2** [sing.] something that continues sth else or makes it longer: *a continuation of recent trends*

☆ **con·tin·ue** /kən'tɪnyu/ *verb* **1** [I,T] **continue (doing/to do sth); continue (with sth)** to go on, or to make sth go on, happening or existing : *If the pain continues, see your doctor.* ○ *They ignored me and continued their conversation.* ○ *He continued working/to work late into the night.* ○ *Are you going to continue with your*

c

music lessons through the summer? **2** [I,T] to begin to do or say sth again after you had stopped: *The meeting will continue after lunch.* ○ *I'm sorry I interrupted. Please continue.* ○ *The next day we continued our trip across the country.* **3** [I,T] to go further or to make sth go further: *We continued along the path until we came to the river.* **4** [I] to remain in a particular situation or condition: *He will continue as principal until the end of the school year.*

☆ **con·tin·ued** /kənˈtɪnyud/ *adj.* going on without stopping: *There are reports of continued fighting near the border.*

con·ti·nu·i·ty /ˌkɑntəˈnuəti/ *noun* [U] the state of continuing without interruption; linking one thing smoothly with the next: *Jean has agreed to remain as manager of the project in order to ensure continuity.*

☆ **con·tin·u·ous** /kənˈtɪnyuəs/ *adj.* happening or existing without stopping: *a period of continuous economic growth* ○ *a continuous process* ○ *There was a continuous line of cars stretching for miles.* —**con·tin·u·ous·ly** *adv.*: *It has rained continuously here for three days.* ☞ Look at the note at **continual**.

con'tinuous tense (*also* **progressive tense**) *noun* [C] (*grammar*) the form of a verb such as "I am waiting" or "It was raining" which is made from a part of "be" and a verb ending in "-ing" and is used to describe an action that continues for a period of time

con·tort /kənˈtɔrt/ *verb* [I,T] to move or to make sth move into an unnatural shape: *His face contorted/was contorted with pain.* —**con·tor·tion** /kənˈtɔrʃn/ *noun* [C]

con·tour /ˈkɑntʊr/ *noun* [C] the outline or shape of the outer surface of sth: *I could just make out the contours of the house in the dark.*

con·tra·cep·tion /ˌkɑntrəˈsɛpʃn/ *noun* [U] the means of preventing a woman from becoming pregnant: *Your doctor will be happy to advise you about contraception.* ○ *a reliable form of contraception*

con·tra·cep·tive /ˌkɑntrəˈsɛptɪv/ *noun* [C] a pill or an object that prevents a woman from becoming pregnant: *an oral contraceptive* —**con·tra·cep·tive** *adj.*: *a contraceptive pill*

☆ **con·tract¹** /ˈkɑntrækt/ *noun* [C] a written legal agreement: *They signed a three-year contract with a major record company.* ○ *The company has just won a contract to supply machinery to the government.* ○ *an employment contract*

con·tract² /kənˈtrækt/ *verb* **1** [I,T] to become or to make sth smaller or shorter: *Metals contract as they cool.* ○ *"I'm" is the contracted form of "I am."* ☞ Look at **expand**. It is the opposite for the first example. **2** [T] to get an illness or a disease: *She contracted pneumonia.*

con·tract³ /ˈkɑntrækt/ *verb* [I,T] to make a written legal agreement with sb to do sth or to have sb work for you: *His company has been*

contracted by the government to produce military uniforms.

con·trac·tion /kənˈtrækʃn/ *noun* **1** [U] the process of getting smaller or of making sth smaller **2** [C] a contracted form of a word or words: *"Mustn't" is a contraction of "must not."* **3** [C] a strong tightening of muscles that happens to a woman as her baby is born

con·trac·tor /ˈkɑntræktər; kənˈtræktər/ *noun* [C] a person or company that does work, especially building work, by contract¹: *The general contractor is in charge of hiring people to remodel our house.*

con·trac·tu·al /kənˈtræktʃuəl/ *adj.* connected with or included in a contract¹

con·tra·dict /ˌkɑntrəˈdɪkt/ *verb* **1** [I,T] to say that sth is wrong or untrue; to say the opposite of sth: *I didn't dare contradict him, but I think he was wrong.* **2** [T] (used about a statement, fact, etc.) to be different from or opposite to sth : *These instructions seem to contradict previous ones.*

con·tra·dic·tion /ˌkɑntrəˈdɪkʃn/ *noun* **1** [C] a statement or fact that is opposite to or different from another: *There were a number of contradictions in what he told the police.* **2** [C,U] **(a) contradiction (between sth and sth)** the fact of two things being opposite to or not matching each other: *There is a contradiction between his public and private personalities.* ○ *This letter is in complete contradiction to their previous one.*

con·tra·dic·to·ry /ˌkɑntrəˈdɪktəri/ *adj.* being opposite to or not matching sth else: *Contradictory reports appeared in the newspapers.*

con·trap·tion /kənˈtræpʃn/ *noun* [C] a strange or complicated piece of equipment

con·trar·y¹ /ˈkɑnˌtrɛri/ *adj.* **contrary to sth** completely different from sth; opposite to sth; against sth: *He's really very nice, contrary to what people say about him.*

con·trar·y² /ˈkɑnˌtrɛri/ *noun*

IDM **on the contrary** the opposite is true; certainly not: *"You look as if you're not enjoying yourself." "On the contrary, I'm having a great time."*

to the contrary saying the opposite: *Unless I hear anything to the contrary, I will assume that the arrangements haven't changed.*

☆ **con·trast¹** /kənˈtræst/ *verb* **1** [T] **contrast (A and/with B)** to compare people or things in order to show the differences between them: *It's interesting to contrast the various styles of architecture here.* ○ *The book contrasts his poor childhood with his later life as a millionaire.* **2** [I] **contrast with sb/sth** to be clearly different when compared: *The red cushions contrast dramatically with the black sofa.* ○ *This comment contrasts sharply with his previous remarks.*

☆ **con·trast²** /ˈkɑntræst/ *noun* **contrast (to/with sb/sth)**; **contrast (between A and B)**

i	ɪ	ɛ	æ	ɑ	ɔ	ʌ	ʊ	u
see	sit	ten	cat	hot	saw	cup	put	too

1 [U] comparison between two people or things that shows the differences between them: *In contrast to previous years, we've had a very successful summer.* ○ *He was friendly and talkative; she, by contrast, said nothing.* **2** [C,U] a clear difference between two things or people that is seen when they are compared: *There is a tremendous contrast between the climate in the valley and the climate in the hills.* **3** [C] something that is clearly different from sth else when the two things are compared: *This house is a real contrast to your old one!*

☆ **con·trib·ute** /kən'trɪbyut/ *verb* **1** [I,T] to give a part of the total, together with others: *Would you like to contribute toward our collection for famine relief?* ○ *He didn't contribute anything to the conversation.* ○ *We contributed $5 each toward a retirement present for her.* **2** [I] to help to produce sth; to play a part in sth: *Every member of the team contributed to the victory.* **3** [I,T] to write articles for a magazine or newspaper

☆ **con·tri·bu·tion** /ˌkɑntrə'byuʃn/ *noun* [C,U] something that you give or do together with others; the act of giving your share: *All contributions to the fund are tax-deductible.* ○ *He made a significant contribution to the country's struggle for independence.*

con·trib·u·tor /kən'trɪbyətər/ *noun* [C] a person who contributes to sth

con·trib·u·to·ry /kən'trɪbyəˌtɔri/ *adj.* helping to cause or produce sth: *a contributory factor*

con·trived /kən'traɪvd/ *adj.* clearly artificial or invented; not natural: *The ending of the movie seemed pretty contrived.*

☆ **con·trol¹** /kən'troʊl/ *noun* **1** [U] **control (of/over sb/sth)** power over sth; the ability to organize, direct or guide sb/sth: *Students took control of the president's office.* ○ *He lost control of the car and crashed.* ○ *There's nothing I can do about the problem – it's outside my control.* ○ *I was late because of circumstances beyond my control.* **2** [C,U] **(a) control (on/over sth)** a limit on sth; a way of keeping sb/sth within certain limits: *price controls* ○ *crowd control* **3** [C] one of the parts of a machine that is used for operating it: *the controls of an airplane* **4** [sing.] the place from which sth is operated or where sth is checked: *We went through passport control and then got onto the plane.* **IDM** **be in control (of sth)** to be in command of sth; to have the power or ability to deal with sth: *Who is in control of the project?* **be/get out of control** to be/become impossible to deal with or guide: *The demonstration got out of control and fighting broke out.* **under control** being dealt with, directed or run successfully: *It took several hours to bring the fire under control.* ○ *She finds it difficult to keep her feelings under control.*

☆ **con·trol²** /kən'troʊl/ *verb* [T] **(con·trol·ling; con·trolled)** **1** to have power over sth or the ability to organize, direct or guide sth: *One family controls the company.* ○ *Police struggled to control the crowd.* ○ *I couldn't control myself any longer and burst out laughing.* **2** to keep sth within certain limits: *measures to control inflation*

☆ **con·trol·ler** /kən'troʊlər/ *noun* [C] a person who directs sth: *air traffic controllers*

☆ **con·tro·ver·sial** /ˌkɑntrə'vərʃl/ *adj.* causing public discussion and disagreement: *a controversial TV program* ○ *a controversial new law*

☆ **con·tro·ver·sy** /'kɑntrəvərsi/ *noun* [C,U] (*pl.* **con·tro·ver·sies**) public discussion and disagreement about sth: *The plans to build a nuclear power plant caused a great deal of controversy.*

con·va·les·cent /ˌkɑnvə'lɛsnt/ *adj.* connected with resting and getting better over a period of time after an illness: *a convalescent home*

con·vene /kən'vin/ *verb* [I,T] to come together or to bring people together for a meeting, etc.

☆ **con·ven·ience** /kən'vinyəns/ *noun* **1** [U] the quality of being suitable or practical for a particular purpose: *For your convenience, we offer a free delivery service.* **2** [C, usually pl.] a piece of equipment or a service that is useful and that makes life easier: *All apartments are equipped with modern conveniences such as dishwashers and cable TV.*

con'venience store *noun* [C] a store that sells food, magazines and other small items, and stays open longer than other stores

☆ **con·ven·ient** /kən'vinyənt/ *adj.* **1** suitable or practical for a particular purpose; not causing difficulty: *I'm willing to meet you on any day that's convenient for you.* ○ *It isn't convenient to talk right now – I'm in the middle of a meeting.* **2** close to sth; in a useful position: *a parking garage convenient to the downtown shopping area* ☞ The opposite is **inconvenient.** —**con·ven·ient·ly** *adv.*: *She had conveniently forgotten that she owed me some money.* ○ *Our offices are conveniently located near two major freeways.*

con·vent /'kɑnvɛnt; -vənt/ *noun* [C] a place where women (**nuns**) live in a religious community ☞ Look at **monastery.**

☆ **con·ven·tion** /kən'vɛnʃn/ *noun* **1** [C] a large meeting or conference: *Dr. Kwan is giving a speech at the association's annual convention.* ○ *the Democratic Party Convention* ○ *a convention center* (= a large building where conventions are held) **2** [C,U] a traditional way of behaving or of doing sth: *A speech by the best man is one of the conventions of a wedding.* ○ *By convention, the top two students give speeches at the*

C

graduation ceremony. **3** [C] a formal agreement, especially between nations: *the Geneva Convention*

☆**con·ven·tion·al** /kən'vɛnʃənl/ *adj.* following what is traditional or considered to be normal, sometimes too closely: *conventional attitudes* ○ *The house was built with conventional materials but in a totally new style.* ○ *I like him, but he's so conventional* (= boring, because of this). ☞ The opposite is **unconventional**. —**con·ven·tion·al·ly** /-ʃənəli/ *adv.*: *He always dresses conventionally.*

con·verge /kən'vərdʒ/ *verb* [I] **converge (on sb/sth)** to move toward or meet at the same point from different directions: *People from the whole state converge on the town during the annual festival.* ○ *The paths converge at the bottom of the hill.*

☆**con·ver·sa·tion** /ˌkɑnvər'seɪʃn/ *noun* [C,U] informal talk: *I had a long conversation with her about her plans for the future.* ○ *His job is his only topic of conversation.* ○ *They sat in the corner, deep in conversation.* ○ *She finds it difficult to make conversation* (= to think of things to say).

con·verse /kən'vərs/ *verb* [I] (*formal*) to talk informally; to have a conversation

con·ver·sion /kən'vərʒn; -ʃn/ *noun* (a) **conversion (from sth) (into/to sth)** **1** [C,U] change from one form, system or use to another: *a conversion table for miles and kilometers* **2** [C,U] becoming a member of a new religion: *conversion to Catholicism*

☆**con·vert¹** /kən'vərt/ *verb* [I,T] **1 convert (sth) (from sth) (into/to sth)** to change from one form, system or use to another: *a sofa that converts into a double bed* ○ *How do you convert pounds into kilograms?* ○ *They're converting the warehouse into an apartment building.* **2 convert (sb) (from sth) (to sth)** to change to, or persuade sb to change to a new religion: *As a young man, he converted to Islam.* ○ *to convert people to Christianity*

con·vert² /'kɑnvərt/ *noun* [C] **a convert (to sth)** a person who has been persuaded to become a member of a particular religion

con·vert·i·ble¹ /kən'vərṭəbl/ *adj.* able to be changed into another form: *convertible currencies* (= those that can be exchanged for other currencies)

con·vert·i·ble² /kən'vərṭəbl/ *noun* [C] a car with a roof that can be folded down or taken off

con·vex /'kɑnvɛks/ *adj.* having a surface that curves outward: *a convex lens* ☞ Look at **concave**.

con·vey /kən'veɪ/ *verb* [T] **convey sth (to sb)** to make ideas, thoughts, feelings, etc. known to sb; to communicate sth: *The video conveys a lot of information, but in a fun way.* ○ *The President tried to convey a message of hope in his speech.*

conveyor belt /kən'veɪər bɛlt/ *noun* [C] a continuous moving belt that carries objects from one place to another, e.g. in a factory

☆**con·vict¹** /kən'vɪkt/ *verb* [T] **convict sb (of sth)** to declare in a court of law that sb is guilty of a crime: *He was convicted of armed robbery and sent to prison.* ○ *a convicted criminal* ☞ The opposite is **acquit**.

con·vict² /'kɑnvɪkt/ (*formal*) *noun* [C] a person who has been found guilty of a crime and put in prison

con·vic·tion /kən'vɪkʃn/ *noun* **1** [C,U] an occasion when sb is found guilty of a crime in a court of law; the act of finding sb guilty in this way: *He has several previous convictions for burglary.* **2** [C] very strong opinion or belief: *religious convictions* **3** [U] being certain and able to convince others about what you are doing: *He played without conviction and lost easily.*

☆**con·vince** /kən'vɪns/ *verb* [T] **1 convince sb (of sth/that…)** to succeed in making sb believe sth: *She convinced him of the need to go back.* ○ *I couldn't convince her that I was right.* **2 convince sb (to do sth)** to persuade sb to do sth: *The salesman convinced them to buy it.*

☆**con·vinced** /kən'vɪnst/ *adj.* completely sure about sth: *He's convinced of his ability to win.* ○ *I'm convinced that she said it, but she denies it.*

☆**con·vinc·ing** /kən'vɪnsɪŋ/ *adj.* **1** able to make sb believe sth: *Her explanation for her absence wasn't very convincing.* **2** (used about a victory) complete; clear: *a convincing win* —**con·vinc·ing·ly** *adv.*: *She argued convincingly that the law should be changed.* ○ *He won the race convincingly.*

con·voy /'kɑnvɔɪ/ *noun* [C] a group of vehicles or ships traveling together: *a convoy of trucks*

con·vul·sion /kən'vʌlʃn/ *noun* [C, usually pl.] a sudden violent movement of the body that you cannot control: *Children sometimes have convulsions when their temperature goes up.*

coo /ku/ *verb* [I] **1** to make the sound that a dove or pigeon makes **2** to speak in a soft, gentle voice: *He went to the crib and cooed over the baby.*

☆**cook¹** /kʊk/ *verb* **1** [I,T] to prepare food for eating by heating it: *My mother taught me how to cook.* ○ *He cooked us a meal.* **2** [I] (used about food) to be prepared for eating by being heated: *I could smell something cooking in the kitchen.*

☞ Food can be cooked in various ways: by **boiling** in a pan of hot water; by **frying** in a frying pan with hot oil or fat; or by **broiling** under a broiler, which heats the food from above. We can **toast** bread in a toaster to make it crisp and brown. Cakes and bread are **baked** in the oven, but we use the word **roast** for cooking meat or potatoes in the oven.

ər	ɪr	ɛr	ɑr	ɔr	ʊr	ʒ	h	ŋ
bird	near	hair	car	north	tour	vision	hat	sing

PHRV **cook sth up** (*informal*) to invent sth that is not true: *She cooked up an excuse for not arriving on time.*

☆**cook²** /kʊk/ *noun* [C] a person who cooks: *My sister is an excellent cook.* ○ *He works as a cook in a hotel restaurant.*

☆**cook·book** /ˈkʊkbʊk/ *noun* [C] a book of recipes and instructions for cooking

☆**cook·ie** /ˈkʊki/ *noun* [C] (*pl.* **cook·ies**) a type of cake that is thin, hard and sweet: *chocolate chip cookies* ☞ picture at **cake.**

☆**cook·ing** /ˈkʊkɪŋ/ *noun* [U] **1** the preparation of food for eating: *Cooking is one of her hobbies.* ○ *a Chinese cooking class*

☞ A common way of talking about the activity of preparing food is **do the cooking**: *In our house, I do the cleaning and my husband does the cooking.*

2 food produced by cooking: *He missed his mother's cooking when he left home.*

cook·out /ˈkʊkaʊt/ *noun* [C] an event where food is cooked and eaten outdoors: *We have a lot of cookouts in our back yard during the summer months.*

☆**cool¹** /kul/ *adj.* **1** fairly cold; not hot or warm: *It was a cool evening, so I put on a sweater.* ○ *This product should be stored in a cool place.* ○ *What I'd like is a nice cool drink.* ☞ Look at the note at **cold. 2** (*informal*) very good; excellent: *What a cool car!* ○ *"There's a party at Dave's tonight." "Cool!"* **3** calm; not excited or affected by strong emotions: *She always manages to remain cool under pressure.* **4** unfriendly; not showing interest: *When we first met, she was fairly cool toward me, but later she became friendlier.* **5** (*informal*) fashionable; popular: *A lot of kids think that smoking makes them look cool.* —**cool·ness** *noun* [U]

☆**cool²** /kul/ *noun* [sing.]
keep/lose your cool to remain calm/to stop being calm and become angry, nervous, etc.

☆**cool³** /kul/ *verb* **1** [I,T] **cool (sth/sb) (down/off)** to lower the temperature of sth; to become cool¹(1): *Let the soup cool (down).* ○ *After the game we needed to cool off.* ○ *A nice cold drink will cool you right down.* **2** [I] (used about feelings) to become less strong: *It took a long time for tensions to cool after the riot.*

IDM **Cool it!** (*informal*) be calm: *Cool it, you guys! There's no reason to fight about this.*

PHRV **cool (sb) down/off** to become or make sb calmer

cool·er /ˈkulər/ *noun* [C] **1** a box with ice in it that is used for keeping food or drinks cool: *We need three coolers to hold all the drinks for the picnic.* **2** a drink with ice and usually wine in it: *a wine cooler*

cool·ly /ˈkulli/ *adv.* in a calm way; without showing much interest or excitement: *At first she was very angry; then she explained the*

problem *coolly.* ○ *Employees reacted coolly to the company's proposal.*

coop /kup/ *verb*
PHRV **coop sb/sth up (in sth)** to keep sb/sth inside a small space: *The kids were cooped up indoors all day because the weather was so bad.*

co·op·er·ate /koʊˈɑpəreɪt/ *verb* [I] **1** to work with sb else to achieve sth: *Our company is cooperating with a Mexican firm on this project.* **2** to be helpful by doing what sb asks you to do: *If everyone cooperates by following the instructions, there will be no problem.* ○ *to cooperate with an investigation* (e.g. by giving information to the police)

co·op·er·a·tion /koʊˌɑpəˈreɪʃn/ *noun* [U] **1 cooperation (with sb)** working together with sb else to achieve sth: *international cooperation to protect the ozone layer* ○ *This device was developed in cooperation with a Korean company.* **2** willingness to be helpful by doing what sb asks you to do: *The police asked the public for their cooperation in the investigation.*

co·op·er·a·tive¹ /koʊˈɑprətɪv/ *adj.* **1** done by people working together: *a cooperative business venture* **2** helpful; doing what sb asks you to do: *My boss was very cooperative and let me take some time off.* ☞ The opposite is **uncooperative.**

co·op·er·a·tive² /koʊˈɑprətɪv/ *noun* [C] a business or organization that is owned and run by all of the people who work for it: *an agricultural cooperative*

co·or·di·nate¹ /koʊˈɔrdənət/ *noun* [C] one of the two sets of numbers and/or letters that are used for finding the position of a point on a map

co·or·di·nate² /koʊˈɔrdəneɪt/ *verb* [T] to organize different things or people so that they work together efficiently: *It is her job to coordinate the various departments.*

co·or·di·na·tion /koʊˌɔrdəˈneɪʃn/ *noun* [U] **1** the organization of different things or people so that they work together efficiently **2** the ability to control the movements of your body properly: *You need good hand-eye coordination to play badminton well.*

co·or·di·na·tor /koʊˈɔrdəneɪt̬ər/ *noun* [C] a person who is responsible for organizing different things or people so that they work together efficiently: *a project coordinator*

☆**cop¹** /kɑp/ *noun* [C] (*informal*) a police officer

cop² /kɑp/ *verb* (**cop·ping; copped**) (*informal*)
cop out (of sth) to avoid sth that you should do, because you are afraid or lazy: *You guys promised you'd help me – you can't cop out now!*

cope /koʊp/ *verb* [I] **cope (with sb/sth)** to deal successfully with a difficult matter or

C

situation: *She sometimes finds it difficult to cope with all the pressure at work.*

☆ **cop·i·er** /ˈkɑpiər/ (*also* ˈ**copy ma‚chine**, *formal* **photocopier**) *noun* [C] a machine that makes copies of documents on paper

ˈ**cop-out** (*also* **copout**) *noun* [C] (*informal*) a way of avoiding sth that you should do: *Using temporary workers is just a cop-out – the company ought to hire more qualified personnel.*

cop·per /ˈkɑpər/ *noun* [U] (*symbol* **Cu**) a common reddish-brown metal: *water pipes made of copper* ○ *copper wire*

cop·u·late /ˈkɑpyəleɪt/ *verb* [I] (*formal*) (used especially about animals) to have sex —**cop·u·la·tion** /‚kɑpyəˈleɪʃn/ *noun* [U]

☆ **cop·y¹** /ˈkɑpi/ *noun* [C] (*pl.* **cop·ies**) **1** something that is made to look exactly like sth else: *The painting isn't an original, of course – it's only a copy.* ○ *to make a copy of a computer file* **2** (*also formal* **photocopy**) a piece of paper that looks exactly like another piece of paper, page in a book, etc., and that is made by a special machine (**a copier**) that can photograph sth quickly: *Can you make 20 copies of this for me?* **3** a book, newspaper, record, etc. of which many have been printed or produced: *I managed to buy the last copy of the book left in the store.*

☆ **cop·y²** /ˈkɑpi/ *verb* (*pres. part.* **cop·y·ing**; *3rd pers. sing. pres.* **cop·ies**; *p.t., p.p.* **cop·ied**) **1** [T] **copy sth (down/out)** to write down sth exactly as it is written somewhere else: *The students copied what was written on the board.* ○ *I copied down the address on the brochure.* ○ *I copied out the letter more neatly.* **2** [T] to make a copy of a video, computer information, etc.: *It is illegal to copy videos.* **3** (*also formal* **photocopy**) [T] to make a copy of a piece of paper, page in a book, etc., using a special machine (**a copier**) **4** [T] to do or try to do the same as sb else; to imitate: *She copies everything her friends do.* **5** [I] **copy (from sb)** to cheat by writing what sb else has written: *He was caught copying from his neighbor during the test.*

ˈ**copy machine** *noun* [C] = COPIER

☆ **cop·y·right** /ˈkɑpiraɪt/ *noun* [C,U] the legal right to be the only person who may print, copy, perform, etc. a piece of original work, such as a book, a song or a computer program

cor·al /ˈkɔrəl; ˈkɑrəl/ *noun* [U] a hard red, pink or white substance formed from the bones of very small sea animals, often used for making jewelry: *a coral reef* (= a line of rock in the ocean formed by coral) ○ *a coral necklace*

☆ **cord** /kɔrd/ *noun* **1** [C,U] (a piece of) strong, thick string **2** [C,U] electric wire inside a plastic tube, used for carrying electricity to electrical equipment

☞ At the end of a cord there is a **plug** which you put into an **outlet**.

cor·dial /ˈkɔrdʒəl/ *adj.* (*formal*) friendly: *a cordial greeting* ○ *a cordial meeting* —**cor·dial·ly** /ˈkɔrdʒəli/ *adv.*

cord·less /ˈkɔrdləs/ *adj.* without a cord (2): *a cordless phone,*

cor·don¹ /ˈkɔrdn/ *noun* [C] a line or ring of police or soldiers that prevents people from entering or leaving an area

cor·don² /ˈkɔrdn/ *verb*

PHR V **cordon sth off** to close an area by surrounding it with a ring of police or soldiers: *The street where the shooting happened was quickly cordoned off.*

cor·du·roy /ˈkɔrdərɔɪ/ *noun* [U] a thick soft cotton cloth with raised lines on it, used for making clothes: *a corduroy jacket*

☆ **core** /kɔr/ *noun* **1** [C] the hard center of certain fruits, containing seeds: *an apple core* **2** [sing.] the central or most important part of sth: *Our core business is installing computer systems, but we also offer computer training.* ○ *the core vocabulary of a language* (= the most common and important words) **3** [C] the central part of a planet: *the earth's core*

IDM **to the core** completely; in every way: *The system is rotten to the core* (= bad in every part).

cork /kɔrk/ *noun* **1** [U] a light but tough substance which comes from the outside of a type of tree. It floats on water. **2** [C] a round piece of cork (1) that you push into the end of a bottle to close it, especially a bottle of wine

cork·screw /ˈkɔrkskru/ *noun* [C] a tool that you use for pulling corks (2) out of bottles

☆ **corn** /kɔrn/ *noun* [U]
1 a tall plant that produces yellow grains (**kernels**) in a large mass (**an ear**) which can be eaten as a vegetable: *corn on the cob* (= that has been cooked with the kernels still attached to the cob) **2** [C] a small, painful area of hard skin on the toe

corn

kernel

an ear of corn

☆ **cor·ner¹** /ˈkɔrnər/ *noun* [C] **1** a place where two lines, edges, surfaces or roads meet: *in a corner of the room* ○ *Write your address in the upper right-hand corner.* ○ *The office is on the corner of Fifth Avenue and 35th Street.* ○ *There's a mailbox around the corner on Walnut Street.* **2** a quiet or secret place or area: *a remote corner of Alaska* **3** a difficult situation which you cannot escape from: *to get yourself into a corner*

IDM **cut corners** ⇨ CUT¹

(just) around the corner (used about an event or a date) very near: *Dad's birthday is just around the corner – have you bought him a present yet?*

The lamp is **in** the **corner**.

The bank is **on** the **corner**.

☆ **cor·ner** ² /ˈkɔrnər/ verb [T] to get a person or an animal into a position from which it is difficult or impossible to escape : *He cornered me at the party and started telling me about his problems.*

IDM **corner the market (on sth)** to get control in some area of business so that there is no room for anybody else to have any success: *We hope to corner the market on healthy snacks.*

corn·flakes /ˈkɔrnfleɪks/ noun [plural] food made of small pieces of dried corn and eaten with milk for breakfast : *a bowl of cornflakes*

corn·y /ˈkɔrni/ adj. (**corn·i·er**; **corn·i·est**) (*informal*) too ordinary or familiar to be interesting or amusing: *a corny joke*

cor·o·nar·y /ˈkɔrəneri/ adj. connected with the heart: *coronary artery disease*

cor·o·na·tion /ˌkɔrəˈneɪʃn/ noun [C] a ceremony at which sb becomes a king or queen

cor·o·ner /ˈkɔrənər/ noun [C] an official whose job is to find out the causes of death of people who have died in violent or unusual ways

corp. abbr. = CORPORATION

cor·po·ral /ˈkɔrpərəl/ noun [C] a person of low rank in the Army or Marine Corps

ˌcorporal ˈpunishment noun [U] the punishment of people by hitting them, especially the punishment of children by parents or teachers

☆ **cor·po·rate** /ˈkɔrpərət/ adj. connected with a large company: *corporate responsibility*

☆ **cor·po·ra·tion** /ˌkɔrpəˈreɪʃn/ noun [C] (abbr. **corp.**) a large business company: *multinational corporations* ☞ Look also at **incorporated**.

corps /kɔr/ noun [C] (pl. **corps** /kɔrz/) **1** a part of an army with special duties: *the medical corps* ☞ Look also at **Marine Corps**. **2** a group of people involved in a special activity: *the White House press corps*

corpse /kɔrps/ noun [C] a dead body, especially of a person

cor·ral /kəˈræl/ noun [C] a piece of land with a fence around it where people keep cows, horses, etc. on a farm

☆ **cor·rect¹** /kəˈrɛkt/ adj. **1** with no mistakes; right or true : *Good job! All your answers were correct.* ○ *Be sure you put the correct address on the envelope.* **2** (used about behavior, manners,

dress, etc.) suitable according to normal customs and ideas: *What's the correct form of address for a priest?* ☞ The opposite is **incorrect**. Look also at **politically correct**. —**correct·ly** adv. —**cor·rect·ness** noun [U]

☆ **cor·rect²** /kəˈrɛkt/ verb [T] **1** to make a mistake, fault, etc. right or better: *to correct a spelling mistake* ○ *to correct a test* (= to mark the mistakes in it) **2** to point out the mistakes or faults of sb: *He's always correcting me when I say something wrong.*

cor·rec·tion /kəˈrɛkʃn/ noun [C,U] (an act of) making sth right or changing sth: *Make your corrections in red ink.* ○ *Some parts of the report needed correction.*

cor·rec·tive /kəˈrɛktɪv/ adj. intended to put right sth that is wrong: *to take corrective action*

cor·re·la·tion /ˌkɔrəˈleɪʃn/; ˌkar-/ noun [C,U] a relationship or connection: *a correlation between salt intake and high blood pressure*

cor·re·spond /ˌkɔrəˈspɑnd/; ˌkar-/ verb [I] **1 correspond (to/with sth)** to be the same as; to match: *Does the name on the envelope correspond with the name on the letter?* **2 correspond (to sth)** to be similar or equal (to sth): *Canadian provinces correspond to American states.* **3 correspond (with sb)** to write letters to and receive them from sb: *They corresponded for a year while he was in prison.*

cor·re·spon·dence /ˌkɔrəˈspɑndəns; ˌkar-/ noun **1** [U] the act of writing letters; the letters that sb writes: *Please address all correspondence to the editor.* **2** [C,U] a close connection or relationship: *There is no correspondence between the two sets of figures.*

cor·res·pon·dent /ˌkɔrəˈspɑndənt; ˌkar-/ noun [C] **1** a person who provides news or writes articles for a newspaper, etc.: *our Middle East correspondent, Andy Jenkins* **2** (*formal*) a person who writes letters

cor·re·spond·ing /ˌkɔrəˈspɑndɪŋ; ˌkar-/ adj. (only *before* a noun) related or similar: *Sales are up 10% compared with the corresponding period last year.* —**cor·re·spond·ing·ly** adv.

☆ **cor·ri·dor** /ˈkɔrədɔr; -dər; ˈkar-/ noun [C] a long narrow passage in a building, with doors that open into rooms, etc.: *to walk along a corridor*

cor·rob·o·rate /kəˈrɑbəreɪt/ verb [T] (*formal*) to support a statement, idea, etc. by providing new evidence: *The witness corroborated her statement about the night of the murder.* —**cor·rob·o·ra·tion** /kəˌrɑbəˈreɪʃn/ noun [U]

cor·rode /kəˈroʊd/ verb [I,T] (used about metals) to become weak or to be destroyed by chemical action; to cause a metal to do this: *Parts of the car were corroded by rust.* —**cor·ro·sive** /kəˈroʊsɪv/ adj.

cor·ro·sion /kəˈroʊʒn/ noun [U] the process of being destroyed by chemical action; the damage caused when sth is corroded

cor·ru·gat·ed /ˈkɔrəgeɪtəd; ˈkɑr-/ *adj.* (used about metal or cardboard) shaped into folds; not smooth and flat: *corrugated iron*

cor·rupt¹ /kəˈrʌpt/ *adj.* not honest, moral or legal: *corrupt business practices* ○ *corrupt politicians who accept bribes*

cor·rupt² /kəˈrʌpt/ *verb* [I,T] to cause sb/sth to become dishonest or to have lower moral standards: *Does television corrupt the minds of young people?*

cor·rup·tion /kəˈrʌpʃn/ *noun* [U] behavior that is not honest or legal, especially by people in official positions: *accusations of corruption among senior police officers*

cos·met·ic¹ /kɑzˈmɛtɪk/ *noun* [C] a substance that you put on your face or hair to make yourself look more attractive: *I only use cosmetics that are not tested on animals.*

cos·met·ic² /kɑzˈmɛtɪk/ *adj.* **1** used or done in order to improve your appearance: *cosmetic products* ○ *cosmetic surgery* **2** done in order to improve only the appearance of sth, without changing it in any other way: *changes in government policies which are purely cosmetic*

cos·mic /ˈkɑzmɪk/ *adj.* of the whole universe

cos·mo·pol·i·tan /ˌkɑzməˈpɑlətn/ *adj.* **1** containing people from all over the world: *a cosmopolitan city* **2** having, or influenced by, wide experience of other countries and cultures: *a cosmopolitan and sophisticated young woman*

cos·mos /ˈkɑzmoʊs; -məs/ *noun* [sing.] **the cosmos** the universe

☆ **cost¹** /kɔst/ *noun* **1** [C,U] the money that you have to pay for sth: *the high cost of healthcare in the U.S.* ○ *the cost of living* (= the general level of prices for things that you need to live a normal life) ○ *The damage will have to be repaired, regardless of cost.* ☛ Look at the note at **price**. **2** [sing., U] what you have to give or lose in order to obtain sth else: *He achieved great success, but only at the cost of a happy family life.*

IDM **at all costs**; **at any cost** using all the means that are necessary to achieve sth: *We must win at all costs.*

☆ **cost²** /kɔst/ *verb* [T] (*p.t., p.p.* **cost**) **1** to have the price of: *These apples cost 80¢ a pound.* ○ *How much does it cost?* ○ *It cost me $10 to have my watch repaired.* **2** to make you lose sth: *That one mistake cost him his job.*

IDM **cost/pay an arm and a leg** ⇨ ARM¹

co·star¹ (*also* **co-star**) /ˈkoʊstɑr/ *verb* (**co·star·ring** or **co-star·ring**; **co·starred** or **co-starred**) **1** [T] (used of a movie, play, etc.) to have two or more famous actors as its stars: *a movie costarring Michael Douglas and Sean Connery* **2** [I] (used of actors) to be one of two or more stars in a movie, play, etc.: *Michael Douglas costars with Sean Connery in the movie.*

co·star² /ˈkoʊstɑr/ *noun* [C] a famous actor or actress who has one of the most important parts in a movie, play, etc. in which another famous actor or actress also appears: *His costar was Marilyn Monroe.*

☆ **cost·ly** /ˈkɔstli/ *adj.* (**cost·li·er**; **cost·li·est**) **1** costing a lot of money; expensive: *a costly repair bill* **2** involving great loss of time, effort, etc.: *a costly mistake*

cos·tume /ˈkɑstum/ *noun* [C,U] special clothes that people wear to a party or in the theater, on television, etc. in order to look like a different person or an animal, etc.: *a Halloween costume* ○ *a costume party* (= where all the guests wear costumes)

co·sy /ˈkoʊzi/ *adj.* (**co·si·er**; **co·si·est**) (*BrE*) = COZY

cot /kɑt/ *noun* [C] a narrow bed, especially one that folds to make it easier to store

cot·tage /ˈkɑtɪdʒ/ *noun* [C] a small and often old house, especially in the country: *We spent the weekend at our summer cottage on the lake.*

cottage cheese *noun* [U] a type of soft white cheese in small lumps

☆ **cot·ton** /ˈkɑtn/ *noun* [U] **1** a natural cloth or thread; the tall plant that produces it: *This shirt is 60% cotton and 40% polyester.* ○ *cotton fields in Mississippi* **2** soft, white hairs of the cotton plant in a mass, used for cleaning the skin or for putting cream, medicine, etc. on the skin: *a cotton ball*

☆ **couch** /kaʊtʃ/ (*also* **sofa**) *noun* [C] a comfortable seat with a back and arms. It is long enough for two or more people to sit on: *Don't let the dog sit on the couch!* ☛ **Sofa** is more formal than **couch**.

couch (*also* **sofa**)

couch po·tato *noun* [C] (*pl.* **couch potatoes**) (*informal*) a person who is very lazy and who watches a lot of television

cou·gar /ˈkugər/ *noun* [C] = MOUNTAIN LION

☆ **cough¹** /kɔf/ *verb* [I] to send air out of your throat and mouth with a sudden loud noise, especially when you have a cold, have sth in your throat, etc.: *I could hear him coughing all night.* ☛ picture at **sneeze**.

PHRV **cough sth up** to send sth out of your throat and mouth with a sudden loud noise: *He was coughing up blood.*

cough (sth) up (*informal*) to give money unwillingly: *Come on, cough up what you owe me!*

☆ **cough²** /kɔf/ *noun* [C] **1** an act or the sound of coughing: *He gave a nervous cough before he started to speak.* **2** an illness or infection that makes you cough a lot: *She's had a bad cough for weeks.* ○ *coughs and colds*

☆ **could** /kəd; *strong form* kʊd/ *modal verb* (*negative* **could not**; *short form* **could·n't** /ˈkʊdnt/) **1** (used as the past form of "can" when you report what sb says): *She said that*

she couldn't come. **2** (used for saying that sth is, will be, or was possible): *I could do it now if you want.* ○ *Couldn't you come earlier?* (= I wish you could) ○ *He could have gone to college, but he didn't want to.* ○ *I can't find my purse. I could have left it at the bank.* ○ *You could have said you were going to be late!* (= I wish that you had)

☛ If something was possible on one occasion in the past, use **was/were able to**: *The firefighters were able to rescue the children.* But in negative sentences **could not** can be used, too: *The firefighters couldn't rescue the children.*

3 (used for saying that sb had the ability in the past to do sth): *I could run two miles without stopping when I was younger.* ○ *My grandma could cook really well.* **4** (used for asking permission politely): *Could I possibly borrow your car?* **5** (used for asking sb politely to do sth for you): *Could you open the door? My hands are full.* **6 I could/could have** I would like/have liked to: *I could scream, I'm so mad.* ○ *I was so mad I could have screamed.* **7** (used with the verbs "feel," "hear," "see," "smell," "taste")

☛ These verbs are not used in the continuous tenses. If we want to talk about seeing, hearing, etc. at a particular moment in the past, we use **could**: *We could hear the birds singing.* (NOT *We were hearing…*)

☆ **coun·cil** /'kaʊnsl/ *noun* [C] **1** a group of people who are elected to manage affairs for a town, city, etc.: *The city council has decided to build a new road.* ○ *council members* **2** a group of people chosen to give advice, manage affairs, etc. for a particular organization or area of activity: *a student council*

coun·cil·or /'kaʊnsələr/ *noun* [C] a member of a council ☛ It is more common to say **council member**.

☆ **coun·sel¹** /'kaʊnsl/ *verb* [T] **1** (*formal*) to advise or recommend: *Mr. Dean's lawyers counseled him against making public statements.* **2** to give professional advice to sb with a problem

coun·sel² /'kaʊnsl/ *noun* **1** [C] (*pl.* **coun·sel**) a lawyer who speaks in a court of law: *the counsel for the defense/prosecution* **2** [U] (*formal*) advice

☆ **coun·sel·ing** /'kaʊnsəlɪŋ/ *noun* [U] professional advice given to people with problems: *Many students come to us for counseling.* ○ *psychiatric counseling*

coun·sel·or /'kaʊnsələr/ *noun* [C] a person whose job is to give advice: *a student counselor*

☆ **count¹** /kaʊnt/ *verb* **1** [I] to say numbers one after another in order: *Close your eyes and count (up) to 20.* ○ *to count from 1 to 100* **2** [T] **count sth (up)** to calculate the total number or amount of sth: *Count up the number of*

mistakes and subtract from 50. **3** [I] **count (for sth)** to be important or valuable: *Your opinion really counts.* **4** [I] **count (as sth)** to be accepted: *"I won!" shouted Tom. "But you cheated, so it doesn't count," replied Sarah.* ○ *Will my driver's license count as identification?* **5** [T] to consider to be: *You should count yourself lucky to have a good job.* **6** [T] to include sb/sth when you are calculating an amount or number: *There should be about 15 people at our party, not counting ourselves.*

PHR V **count against sb** to be considered as a disadvantage: *Do you think my age will count against me?*

count on sb/sth to expect sth with confidence; to rely on sb/sth: *As an artist you can't always count on a steady income.* ○ *Can I count on you to help me?*

count sb/sth out 1 to count things slowly, one by one: *She carefully counted out $100 in five-dollar bills.* **2** (*informal*) to not include sb/sth: *If you're going swimming, you can count me out!*

count² /kaʊnt/ *noun* [C] **1** [usually sing.] an act of counting or a number that you get after counting: *At the latest count, there were nearly 2 million unemployed.* **2** [usually pl.] a point that is made in a discussion, argument, etc.: *I proved her wrong on all counts.* **3** an official statement that sb has done sth which is against the law: *He was charged with two counts of robbery and one count of drug possession.*

IDM **keep/lose count (of sth)** to know/not know how many there are of sth: *I've lost count of the number of times he's told that joke!*

count·a·ble /'kaʊntəbl/ *adj.* that can be counted ☛ The opposite is **uncountable**.

countable noun (*also* **count noun**) *noun* [C] (*grammar*) a noun that can be used in the plural, and with words like "a," "many" and "few": *Countable nouns are marked [C] in this dictionary.*

count·down /'kaʊntdaʊn/ *noun* [C] the act of saying numbers backwards to zero just before sth important happens: *the countdown to takeoff* ○ (*figurative*) *The candidates are making dozens of speeches in the countdown to the election.*

☆ **coun·ter¹** /'kaʊntər/ *noun* [C] a long, flat surface like a table in a kitchen, restaurant, store, etc., where food is prepared or customers are served: *Just put that stuff on the kitchen counter.* ○ *the jewelry counter in a department store*

IDM **over the counter** (used about medicine) that can be bought in a store without a special form (**prescription**) from a doctor: *cough syrup that is available over the counter* ○ *over-the-counter medications*

coun·ter² /'kaʊntər/ *verb* [I,T] to answer or react to sb/sth with a different opinion or a

C

return attack: *He countered our criticism with a powerful defense of his actions.*

coun·ter³ /ˈkaʊntər/ *adv.* **counter to sth** (*formal*) in the opposite direction of sth: *Events seemed to be going counter to our expectations.*

coun·ter·act /ˌkaʊntəˈrækt/ *verb* [T] to reduce the effect of sth by acting against it: *medication to counteract the side effects of cancer treatment*

coun·ter·at·tack /ˈkaʊntərətæk/ *noun* [C] an attack made in reaction to an enemy's attack —**coun·ter·attack** *verb* [I,T]

coun·ter·clock·wise /ˌkaʊntərˈklɑkwaɪz/ *adv., adj.* in the opposite direction of the movement of a clock: *Turn the lid counterclockwise/in a counterclockwise direction.*

coun·ter·feit /ˈkaʊntərfɪt/ *adj.* not genuine, but copied so that it looks like the real thing: *counterfeit money*

coun·ter·part /ˈkaʊntərpɑrt/ *noun* [C] a person or thing that has a similar position or function to sb/sth else: *She's my counterpart in our London office* (= she does the same job there that I do here).

coun·ter·pro·duc·tive /ˌkaʊntərprəˈdʌktɪv/ *adj.* having the opposite effect of the one you want

count·less /ˈkaʊntləs/ *adj.* (*formal*) (only before a noun) very many: *The earthquake killed 2,000 people and left countless others homeless.*

☆ **coun·try** /ˈkʌntri/ *noun* (*pl.* **coun·tries**) **1** [C] an area of land with its own people, government, etc.: *Argentina, Brazil and other South American countries* ○ *There was snow over the northern part of the country last night.*

> ☞ **State** is usually used for one of the 50 parts of the United States: *the state of Oklahoma* ○ *state and federal income taxes.* However, **state** can also be used in more formal situations for talking about a whole country as an organized political unit with one government, or for talking about the government itself. It is not used to talk about the U.S. as a whole: *the member states of the European Union* ○ *state censorship of the news media.* **Land** is more formal or literary: *explorers who set out to discover new lands.* Look also at **nation.**

2 the country [sing.] the people who live in a country (1): *a survey to find out what the country really thinks* **3 the country** [sing.] land which is away from towns and cities: *Do you live in the city or the country?* ○ *country life*

> ☞ The word **country** is used for emphasizing that an area of land is away from towns, etc.: *city workers who like to get out into the country on weekends.* The word **countryside** also refers to areas of land that are away from towns, but it emphasizes the natural features such as hills, rivers, trees, etc. that you find there:

beautiful countryside ○ *the destruction of the countryside by new roads.* **Landscape** refers to everything you see when you look across an area of land either in the town or the country: *a dreary landscape of factories and chimneys* ○ *a landscape of forests and lakes*

4 [U] an area of land (especially considering its physical features): *miles of open country* ○ *hilly country* **5** [U] (*informal*) = COUNTRY MUSIC

ˌcountry and ˈwestern *noun* [U] = COUNTRY MUSIC

coun·try·man /ˈkʌntrimən/ *noun* [C] (*feminine* **coun·try·wom·an** /ˈkʌntriwʊmən/; *pl.* **coun·try·men, coun·try·wom·en**) a person from your own country

ˌcountry ˈmusic (*also* **country; country and western**) *noun* [U] a type of popular music that is based on traditional music from the southern and western parts of the U.S.

☆ **coun·try·side** /ˈkʌntrisaɪd/ *noun* [U, sing.] **the countryside** land which is away from towns and cities, consisting of farms, woods, etc.: *the French countryside* ○ *The countryside in Colorado is very beautiful.* ☞ Look at the note at **country.**

☆ **coun·ty** /ˈkaʊnti/ *noun* [C] (*pl.* **coun·ties**) a district within a state, which has its own government: *the Cook County sheriff* ○ *a county courthouse*

coup /ku/ *noun* [C] (*pl.* **coups** /kuz/) **1** (*also* **coup d'é·tat**) /ˌku deɪˈtɑ/ (*pl.* **coups d'é·tat** /ˌku deɪˈtɑ/) a sudden and often violent change of government organized by a small group of people: *a coup to overthrow the President* ○ *an attempted coup* (= one which did not succeed) **2** a clever and successful thing to do: *It was a real coup for us to get the governor to speak at our school.*

☆ **cou·ple¹** /ˈkʌpl/ *noun* [C] two people who are married, living together, etc.: *A very nice couple moved in next door to us.* ○ *a married couple*

IDM a couple of people/things 1 two people/things: *I need a couple of glasses.* **2** a few (not saying an exact number): *I saw her a couple of months ago.*

cou·ple² /ˈkʌpl/ *verb* [T] (usually passive) to join or link sb/sth to sb/sth else: *The fog, coupled with the amount of traffic on the roads, made driving very difficult.*

cou·pon /ˈkupɑn; ˈkyu-/ *noun* [C] **1** a small piece of paper which you can use to buy goods at a lower price, or which you can collect and then exchange for goods: *a coupon worth $1 off your next purchase* **2** a small form in a newspaper or magazine which you fill out with your name and address and send off, in order to get information or to enter a competition: *To place your order, simply fill out the coupon at the bottom of this page.*

☆ **cour·age** /ˈkərɪdʒ/ *noun* [U] the ability to control fear in a situation that may be dangerous

i	ɪ	ɛ	æ	ɑ	ɔ	ʌ	ʊ	u
see	sit	ten	cat	hot	saw	cup	put	too

or unpleasant: *It took real courage to go back into the burning building.* ○ *She showed great courage through her long illness.*

cou·ra·geous /kə'reɪdʒəs/ *adj.* having or showing courage; brave —**cou·ra·geous·ly** *adv.*

cou·ri·er /'kɔriər; 'kʊr-/ *noun* [C] a person whose job is to carry letters, important papers, etc., especially when they are urgent

☆ **course** /kɔrs/ *noun* **1** [C] **a course (in/on sth)** a complete series of lessons: *I enrolled in an English course.* ○ *a course in self-defense* ○ *How many courses are you taking this semester?* **2** [C] one of the parts of a meal: *a three-course lunch* ○ *I had chicken for the main course.* **3** [C] an area where golf is played or where certain types of race take place: *a golf course* ○ *a racecourse* (= where horse races take place) **4** [C] **a course (of sth)** a series of medical treatments: *The doctor put her on a course of radiation therapy.* **5** [C,U] the route or direction that sth, especially an airplane, ship or river, takes: *We changed course and sailed toward land.* ○ *to be on/off course* (= going in the right/wrong direction) ○ *(figurative) I'm on course* (= making the right amount of progress) *to finish this work by the end of the week.* **6** [sing.] the development of sth over a period of time: *events that changed the course of history* ○ *In the normal course of events* (= the way things normally happen) *such problems do not arise.* **7** (*also* **course of action**) [C] a way of acting in or dealing with a particular situation: *It was the only course left open to us in those circumstances.*

IDM **in the course of sth** during sth: *He mentioned it in the course of conversation.*

in due course ▷ DUE[1]

of course naturally; certainly: *Of course, having children has changed their lives a lot.* ○ *"Can I use your phone?" "Of course you can."* ○ *"You're not mad at me, are you?" "Of course not."*

☆ **court**[1] /kɔrt/ *noun* **1** [C,U] a place where trials take place in front of a judge or a jury, to decide whether a person has broken the law: *a civil/criminal court* ○ *A man has been charged and will appear in court tomorrow.* **2 the court** [sing.] the people in a court, especially the judge or judges: *Only one attorney may address the court at a time.* ○ *The court ruled that the law was unconstitutional.* ☞ Look also at **supreme court**. **3** [C,U] an area where certain ball games are played: *a tennis, basketball, etc. court* ☞ picture at **tennis**.

IDM **take sb to court** to take legal action against sb in a court of law: *She took the company to court for breaking the contract.*

court[2] /kɔrt/ *verb* **1** [T] to try to gain sb's support by paying special attention to them: *Politicians from both parties will be courting voters this week.* **2** [T] to do sth that might lead

to sth bad: *America is courting ecological disaster if it continues to ignore global warming.*

cour·te·ous /'kɔrtiəs/ *adj.* polite and pleasant, showing respect for other people: *The salesclerk was courteous and helpful.* ☞ The opposite is **discourteous**. —**cour·te·ous·ly** *adv.*

cour·te·sy /'kɔrtəsi/ *noun* (*pl.* **cour·te·sies**) **1** [U] polite and pleasant behavior that shows respect for other people: *She didn't even have the courtesy to say that she was sorry.* **2** [C] (*formal*) a polite action or remark: *The two presidents exchanged courtesies before their meeting.*

IDM **courtesy of sb** with the permission or because of the kindness of sb: *These pictures are being shown courtesy of ABC-TV.*

court·house /'kɔrthaʊs/ *noun* [C] a building where courts of law and other offices of a county are located

court-mar·tial[1] /'kɔrt ˌmɑrʃl/ *noun* [C] (*pl.* **courts-martial** or **court-martials**) a military court that deals with matters of military law; a trial that takes place in such a court: *His case will be heard by a court-martial.*

court-mar·tial[2] /'kɔrt ˌmɑrʃl/ *verb* [T] to put sb on trial in a military court

☆ **court of ˈlaw** *noun* [C] (*pl.* **courts of law**) a place where a judge or jury decides legal matters (e.g. whether a person is innocent or guilty)

court·room /'kɔrtrum/ *noun* [C] a room where trials or other law cases are held

court·yard /'kɔrtyɑrd/ *noun* [C] an area of ground, without a roof, that has walls or buildings around it, e.g. in a public building, or between houses or apartment buildings

☆ **cous·in** /'kʌzn/ (*also* ˌ**first ˈcousin**) *noun* [C] the child of your aunt or uncle: *Have you met Ruth? We're cousins.* ☞ The same word is used for both male and female cousins.

cove /koʊv/ *noun* [C] a small bay on the coast: *a sandy cove*

☆ **cov·er**[1] /'kʌvər/ *verb* [T] **1 cover sb/sth (up) (with sth)** to put sth on or in front of sth in order to hide or protect it: *Could you cover the food and put it in the fridge?* ○ *She couldn't look anymore and covered her eyes.* ○ *She was asleep on the couch, so he covered her up with a blanket.* **2** to be across or over the surface of sth: *Snow covered the ground.* **3 cover sb/sth in/with sth** to form a layer on sb/sth: *A car went through the puddle and covered me with mud.* **4** to fill or be spread over a certain area: *The smoke from the fire now covers about 15,000 square miles.* **5** to include or to deal with sth: *Part-time workers are not covered by the law.* ○ *The course covered both North and South American history.* **6** to travel a certain distance: *We covered about 500 miles that day.* **7** to be enough money for sth: *Will $20 cover your expenses?* **8** (used about the media) to

ə	y	w	t̬	eɪ	aɪ	ɔɪ	aʊ	oʊ
about	yes	woman	butter	say	five	boy	now	go

report on or show sth: *All the papers covered the election in depth.* **9 cover sb/sth against/ for sth** to protect sb/sth by insurance: *The insurance policy covers us for any damage to our property.* ○ *The policy even covers your lawn furniture* (= it is insured).

PHRV **cover (sth) up** to prevent people from hearing about a mistake or sth bad: *The police have been accused of trying to cover up the facts of the case.*

cover up for sb to hide a person's mistakes or crimes in order to protect him/her: *His wife covered up for him when the police questioned them.*

☆ **cov·er²** /ˈkʌvər/ *noun* **1** [C] something that is put on or over sth, especially in order to protect it: *a plastic cover for a computer* **2** [C] the outside part of a book or magazine: *I can't remember the title of the book, but I know it has a green cover.* ○ *I read the magazine from cover to cover* (= from beginning to end). **3 the covers** [plural] the blankets, sheets, etc. that cover sb in bed: *She pulled the covers off him and said: "Get up!"* **4** [U] shelter or protection from the weather, damage, etc.: *When the storm started, we took cover in a hotel lobby.* ○ *The soldiers had no cover and were easy targets.* **5** [C, usually sing.] **a cover (for sth)** something that hides the real nature of sth, especially sth illegal: *The whole company was just a cover for all kinds of criminal activities.*
IDM **under cover of sth** hidden by sth; not noticed because of sth: *They attacked under cover of darkness.*

☆ **cov·er·age** /ˈkʌvərɪdʒ; ˈkʌvrɪdʒ/ *noun* [U] **1** the act or amount of reporting on or showing an event in the media: *TV coverage of the Olympic Games* **2 coverage (for sth)** insurance against sth, so that if sth bad happens you get money or help in return: *The policy provides coverage for theft.*

cov·er·alls /ˈkʌvərɔlz/ *noun* [plural] a piece of clothing that covers your body, arms and legs and that you wear over your clothes to keep them clean when you are working ☞ picture at **overalls**.

☆ **cov·ered** /ˈkʌvərd/ *adj.* **1 covered in/with sth** having a layer or a large amount of sth on sb/sth: *The victim was lying on the floor, covered in blood.* ○ *The bookshelves were covered with dust.* **2** having a cover, especially a roof: *The pioneers traveled west in covered wagons.*

☆ **cov·er·ing** /ˈkʌvərɪŋ/ *noun* [C] something that covers the surface of sth: *A thick covering of snow lay on the ground.*

ˈcover ˌletter *noun* [C] a letter that you send with a package or with other documents, explaining them or giving more information about them

cov·ert /ˈkoʊvərt; ˈkʌv-; ˌkoʊˈvərt/ *adj.* done

secretly, not openly: *a covert police operation* —**cov·ert·ly** *adv.*

ˈ**cover-up** (*also* **cov·er-up**) *noun* [C] an act of preventing sth bad or dishonest from becoming known: *Several newspapers claimed that there had been a government cover-up.*

cow / horn / cow / bull / calf

☆ **cow** /kaʊ/ *noun* [C] **1** a large female animal that is kept on farms to produce milk: *to milk a cow* ○ *a herd of cows*

☞ **Cow** is often used for both male and female members of the **cattle** family. The special word for a male is **bull**. A young cow is a **calf**. A number of cows together can be called **cattle**. Look at the note at **meat**.

2 the adult female of certain large animals, e.g. the elephant
IDM **have a cow** (*slang*) to be very anxious, nervous, impatient, etc.: *All right, I'm coming! Don't have a cow!*

cow·ard /ˈkaʊərd/ *noun* [C] (used when disapproving) a person who has no courage and is afraid in dangerous or unpleasant situations: *I was too much of a coward to argue.* —**cow·ard·ly** *adj.*

cow·ard·ice /ˈkaʊərdəs/ *noun* [U] a lack of courage

cowboy / lasso

☆ **cow·boy** /ˈkaʊbɔɪ/ *noun* [C] a man whose job is to take care of cows in certain parts of the U.S.: *cowboy boots*

cow·er /ˈkaʊər/ *verb* [I] to move back or into a low position because of fear: *The dog cowered under the table.*

cow·girl /ˈkaʊgərl/ *noun* [C] a woman whose job is to take care of cows in certain parts of the U.S.

co·work·er (*also* **co-worker**) /ˈkoʊwərkər/ *noun* [C] a person that you work with in a job

coy·o·te /kaɪˈoʊti; ˈkaɪoʊt/ *noun* [C] a wild animal that looks like a dog and lives mainly in western North America

ər	ɪr	ɛr	ɑr	ɔr	ʊr	ʒ	h	ŋ
bird	near	hair	car	north	tour	vision	hat	sing

co·zy /ˈkoʊzi/ *adj.* (**co·zi·er**; **co·zi·est**) warm and comfortable: *a cozy room with a fireplace*

crab /kræb/ *noun* [C] a sea animal with a flat body covered by a shell and five pairs of curved legs. The front two legs have long claws on them. Crabs move sideways. ☞ picture at **shellfish**.

☆**crack¹** /kræk/ *noun* **1** [C] a line on the surface of sth where it has broken, but not into separate pieces: *a pane of glass with a crack in it* ☞ picture at **chip**. **2** [C] a narrow opening: *The wind blew through the cracks in the roof.* **3** [C] a sudden loud, sharp sound: *There was a crack and he realized that he had broken his leg.* **4** [C] an amusing, often critical, remark; a joke: *She made a crack about his clothes.* **5** [U] an illegal drug which is a very strong form of cocaine. It is very difficult to stop using crack: *to smoke crack* ○ *a crack addict*

IDM **at the crack of dawn** very early in the morning

fall/slip through the cracks to not be noticed, helped, or checked by anybody: *We need to make sure that no abused children fall through the cracks in the social services.*

☆**crack²** /kræk/ *verb* **1** [I,T] to break so that a line appears, but without breaking into pieces; to make sth do this: *Don't put boiling water into that glass – it'll crack.* ○ *You can crack this kind of glass, but you can't break it.* ☞ picture at **chip**. **2** [T] to break sth open: *Crack two eggs into a bowl.* **3** [I,T] to make a sudden loud, sharp sound; to cause sth to make this sound. *The cowboy cracked his whip.* **4** [I] to stop being able to deal with pressure and so lose control: *She cracked under the strain of all her problems.* **5** [T] (*informal*) to solve a problem: *Police have finally cracked the murder case.* **6** [T] (*informal*) to reach a difficult goal: *We're hoping to crack the Asian markets with these two new products.* **7** [T] to tell or make a joke

PHRV **crack down (on sb/sth)** (used about people in authority) to start dealing severely with bad or illegal behavior: *The police have started to crack down on drug dealers.*

crack up (*informal*) **1** to suddenly start laughing: *I crack up every time I watch this video.* **2** to be unable to deal with pressure and so lose control and become mentally ill: *He cracked up when his wife left him.*

crack·down /ˈkrækdaʊn/ *noun* [C] action to stop bad or illegal behavior: *a police crackdown on street crime*

☆**crack·er** /ˈkrækər/ *noun* [C] a type of thin flat dry bread that is often salty: *cheese and crackers* ☞ picture at **cake**.

crack·le /ˈkrækl/ *verb* [I] to make a series of short, sharp sounds: *The radio started to crackle and then it stopped working.* —**crack·le** *noun* [sing.]: *the crackle of dry wood burning*

cra·dle¹ /ˈkreɪdl/ *noun* [C] a small bed for a baby. Cradles can often be moved from side to side.

cra·dle² /ˈkreɪdl/ *verb* [T] to hold sb/sth carefully and gently in your arms: *He cradled her head in his arms until the ambulance came.*

craft /kræft/ *noun* [C] **1** a job or activity for which you need skill with your hands: *an arts and crafts exhibition* ○ *the craft of basket making* ☞ Look at **handicraft**. **2** any job or activity for which you need skill: *He regards acting as a craft.* **3** (*pl.* **craft**) a boat, aircraft or spaceship: *There were a few fishing craft in the harbor.*

crafts·man /ˈkræftsmən/ *noun* [C] (*pl.* **craftsmen**) a person who makes things skillfully, especially with the hands: *All the furniture we sell is individually made by craftsmen.*

crafts·man·ship /ˈkræftsmənʃɪp/ *noun* [U] the skill used by sb to make sth of high quality, especially with the hands

craft·y /ˈkræfti/ *adj.* (**craft·i·er**; **craft·i·est**) intelligent and skillful at getting or achieving things by deceiving people or using indirect methods

cram /kræm/ *verb* (**cram·ming**; **crammed**) **1** [T] to push people or things into a small space: *I managed to cram all my clothes into the bag, but I couldn't zip it up.* ○ *We only spent two days in New York, but we crammed in a lot of sightseeing.* **2** [I] to move, with a lot of other people, into a small space: *He only had a small car, but we all crammed into it.* **3** [I] to study very hard and learn a lot in a short time before an examination: *She's cramming for her final exams.*

crammed /kræmd/ *adj.* **crammed (with sth)** very full or too full: *This book is crammed with useful information.* ○ *Orlando is crammed with tourists at that time of year.*

cramp /kræmp/ *noun* [C] a sudden pain that you get in a muscle, that makes it difficult to move: *One of the swimmers got a cramp and we had to pull him out of the water.* ○ *stomach cramps*

cramped /kræmpt/ *adj.* not having enough space: *There were five of us living in a cramped apartment.*

cran·ber·ry /ˈkrænˌbɛri/ *noun* [C] (*pl.* **cran·ber·ries**) a small red berry with a sour taste: *turkey with cranberry sauce*

crane¹ /kreɪn/ *noun* [C] a large machine with a long metal arm that is used for moving or lifting heavy objects

crane² /kreɪn/ *verb* [I,T] to stretch your neck forward in order to see or hear sth: *We all craned forward to get a better view.*

crank¹ /kræŋk/ *verb*

PHRV **crank sth out** (*informal*) to produce large numbers of sth very quickly: *My computer printer can crank out 12 pages a minute.*

crank sth up (*informal*) to make sth stronger, louder, work harder, etc.: *It's too hot in here –*

tʃ	dʒ	v	θ	ð	s	z	ʃ
chin	June	van	thin	then	so	zoo	she

crank up the air conditioner. ○ This is an awesome song – crank it up!

crank² /kræŋk/ noun [C] a person with strange ideas or who behaves in a strange way: Lots of cranks called the police confessing to the murder.

cran·ny /ˈkræni/ noun [C] (pl. **cran·nies**) a small opening in a wall, a rock, etc.
IDM **every nook and cranny** ⇨ NOOK

crap¹ /kræp/ noun [U] (slang) **1** nonsense: I don't want to listen to any more of that crap. **2** something that is of poor quality: This piece of crap broke the first time I used it! **3** solid waste material from the body ☞ Be careful. Some people find this word offensive. —**crap·py** /ˈkræpi/ adj.

crap² /kræp/ verb [I] (**crap·ping**; **crapped**) (slang) to push out solid waste material from the body ☞ Be careful. Some people find this word offensive.

☆ **crash¹** /kræʃ/ noun [C] **1** a sudden loud noise made by sth breaking, hitting sth, etc.: I heard a crash and ran outside. **2** an accident when a car or other vehicle hits sth and is damaged: She was injured in a serious car crash. ○ a plane crash with no survivors **3** an occasion when there is a failure in the business world: the stock market crash of 1987

☆ **crash²** /kræʃ/ verb **1** [I,T] to have an accident in a vehicle; to cause a vehicle to have an accident: He braked too late and crashed into the car in front. **2** [I] to fall or move suddenly, making a loud noise: The tree crashed through the window. ○ waves crashing on the beach **3** [I] (used about a business or a financial organization) to fail suddenly **4** [I] (used about a computer) to stop working suddenly: We lost the data when the computer crashed. **5** [T] (informal) to go to a private party without being invited: to crash a party

ˌ**crash ˈcourse** noun [C] a course in which you learn the basic information about sth in a short period of time: I took a crash course in Japanese before I went to work in Tokyo.

crate /kreɪt/ noun [C] a large box, usually made of wood, in which goods are transported or stored: We had to pack everything into crates when we moved to our new house. ○ a crate of apples

cra·ter /ˈkreɪtər/ noun [C] **1** a large hole in the ground: The bomb left a large crater. ○ craters on the moon **2** the hole in the top of a volcano

crave /kreɪv/ verb [T] to want and need to have sth very much: He craves attention from other people.

crav·ing /ˈkreɪvɪŋ/ noun [C] **craving (for sth)** a strong desire for sth: When she was pregnant, she had cravings for a lot of strange foods.

☆ **crawl¹** /krɔl/ verb [I] **1** to move slowly with the body on or close to the ground, or on the

hands and knees: An insect crawled across the floor. ○ Their baby has just started to crawl. **2** (used about vehicles) to move very slowly: The traffic crawls along the freeway during rush hour.
IDM **be crawling with sth** to be completely full of or covered with sb/sth that is moving and that is considered unpleasant: The kitchen was crawling with insects. ○ The resort is crawling with tourists.

crawl

crawl² /krɔl/ noun [sing.] **1** a very slow speed: The traffic slowed to a crawl. **2** often **the crawl** a style of swimming which you do on your front. When you do the crawl, you move first one arm and then the other over your head, turn your face to one side so that you can breathe and kick up and down with your legs.

☆ **cray·on** /ˈkreɪɑn; -ən/ noun [C,U] a soft, thick, colored pencil made of wax, used for drawing or writing, especially by children

craze /kreɪz/ noun [C] **a craze (for sth) 1** a strong interest in sth, that usually only lasts for a short time: There was a craze for that kind of music years ago. **2** something that a lot of people are very interested in: Beepers are the latest craze among teenagers.

☆ **cra·zy** /ˈkreɪzi/ adj. (**cra·zi·er**; **cra·zi·est**) **1** with a sick mind; mentally ill

☞ It is not polite nowadays to use **crazy** or **insane** to describe a person who is not mentally normal. We use the expression **mentally ill**.

2 very silly or foolish: I think that's a crazy idea. ○ You must be crazy to turn down such a great offer. **3** very angry: These kids are driving me crazy! **4** **crazy about sth** very interested in sth; liking sth very much: He's always been crazy about horses. **5** **crazy about sb** very much in love with sb **6** showing great excitement: The fans went crazy when their team scored the first touchdown.
IDM **like crazy** ⇨ LIKE² —**cra·zi·ness** noun [U]

creak /krik/ verb [I] to make the noise of wood bending or of sth not moving smoothly: The floorboards creaked when I walked across the room. —**creak** noun [C] —**creak·y** adj.: creaky stairs

☆ **cream¹** /krim/ noun **1** [U] the thick yellowish-white liquid that is the fatty part of milk and that rises to the top of it: coffee with cream ○ strawberries and cream ○ whipped cream (= cream that has been beaten) ☞ Look also at **ice cream**. **2** [C,U] a substance that you rub into your skin to keep it soft or as a medical treatment
IDM **the cream of the crop** the best part of sth or the best people in a group

cream² /krim/ adj., noun [U] (of) a yellowish-white color

i	ɪ	ɛ	æ	ɑ	ɔ	─ ʌ	ʊ	u
see	sit	ten	cat	hot	saw	cup	put	too

cream³ /krim/ verb [T] (informal) to defeat sb heavily: The Bulls creamed the Lakers 121-73. ○ Our team got creamed in the tournament.

ˌ**cream ˈcheese** noun [U] a type of soft white cheese that has a mild flavor

cream·y /ˈkrimi/ adj. (**cream·i·er**; **cream·i·est**) 1 containing cream: a creamy sauce 2 thick, smooth and soft; looking or feeling like cream: Beat the mixture until it is light and creamy.

crease¹ /kris/ noun [C] 1 a line on paper, material, a piece of clothing, etc. that is caused by not treating it carefully: When I unrolled the poster, there was a crease in it. 2 a neat line that is put on paper, material, a piece of clothing, etc. intentionally: He had a sharp crease in his pants.

crease² /kris/ verb [I,T] to get creases¹(1,2) ; to make sth get creases: Hang up your jacket or it will crease. ○ Be careful not to crease the paper.

☆ **cre·ate** /kriˈeɪt/ verb [T] to cause sth new to happen or exist: a plan to create new jobs in the area ○ The Bible says that God created the world. ○ All these changes will simply create confusion.

☆ **cre·a·tion** /kriˈeɪʃn/ noun 1 [U] the act of causing sth new to happen or exist: the creation of new independent states 2 usually **the Creation** [sing.] the act of making the whole universe, as described in the Bible 3 [C] some thing that sb has made or produced, especially using skill or imagination: This dish is a new creation – I didn't use a recipe.

☆ **cre·a·tive** /kriˈeɪtɪv/ adj. 1 using skill or imagination to make or do new things: She's a fantastic designer – she's so creative. ○ We need some creative thinking to solve this problem. 2 connected with producing new things, especially works of art: His creative life went on until he was well over 80. —**cre·a·tive·ly** adv.: They don't have a very big house, but they use the space creatively.

cre·a·tiv·i·ty /ˌkrieɪˈtɪvəti/ noun [U] the ability to make or produce new things, especially using skill or imagination: teaching that encourages children's creativity

☆ **cre·a·tor** /kriˈeɪtər/ noun 1 [C] a person who makes or produces sth new, especially using skill or imagination: He was the creator of some of the best-known characters in literature. 2 **the Creator** [sing.] God

☆ **crea·ture** /ˈkritʃər/ noun [C] a living thing such as an animal, a bird, a fish or an insect, but not a plant: a living creature ○ creatures from other planets

cre·den·tials /krəˈdɛnʃlz/ noun [plural] 1 something that shows that a person is qualified or suitable for sth: He has the perfect credentials for the top job. 2 a document that proves that sb is who he/she claims to be, or that he/she is qualified to do sth

cred·i·bil·i·ty /ˌkrɛdəˈbɪləti/ noun [U] the quality of being able to be believed or trusted and taken seriously: The senator had lost all credibility and had to resign.

cred·i·ble /ˈkrɛdəbl/ adj. (formal) 1 that you can believe: a credible witness in a court case 2 that you can trust or take seriously: a credible alternative to nuclear energy ☞ Look at **incredible**. —**cred·i·bly** /-əbli/ adv.

☆ **cred·it¹** /ˈkrɛdət/ noun 1 [U] the system of buying goods or services and not paying for them until later: I bought the television on credit. ○ interest-free credit (= payment over a period of time without any extra charges) 2 [C,U] a sum of money that a bank, etc. lends: The company was not able to get any further credit and went bankrupt. 3 [U] praise for sth good that a person has done: He got all the credit for the success of the project. ○ She didn't do very well, but at least give her credit for trying. ○ Even though your answer wasn't completely correct, I can give you partial credit for it. 4 [C] a unit of study at a school, college or university: My math class is worth three credits. ○ 108 credits are required for graduation. 5 **credits** [plural] the list of the names of the people who made a movie or TV program, shown at the beginning or end of the movie 6 [sing.] **a credit to sb/sth** a person or thing that gives honor: She is a wonderful girl and a credit to her school.
 IDM (**be**) **to sb's credit** (used for showing that you approve of sth that sb has done, although you have criticized sth else): The company, to its credit, apologized and refunded my money.
 have sth to your credit to have finished sth that is successful: She has three best-selling novels to her credit.

cred·it² /ˈkrɛdət/ verb [T] 1 **credit sb/sth for/ with sth** to accept or believe that sb/sth has a particular quality or is responsible for sth: Rap artists are credited with making people aware of the problems in inner cities. 2 **credit sth to sb/sth** to say or believe that sth is the result of sth: She credited her success to a lot of hard work. 3 to record that money has been added to an account: Has the check been credited to my account yet?

☆ ˈ**credit card** noun [C] a small plastic card that allows sb to get goods or services without using money. You usually receive a bill once a month for what you have bought, and you can choose to pay all or part of the bill: Do you take credit cards here? ☞ picture at **money**. Look also at **charge card**.

cred·i·tor /ˈkrɛdətər/ noun [C] a person or company to whom money is owed

creed /krid/ noun [C] a set of beliefs or principles (especially religious ones) that strongly influence sb's life

creek /krik; krɪk/ noun [C] a small river or stream

ə	y	w	t̬	eɪ	aɪ	ɔɪ	aʊ	oʊ
about	yes	woman	butter	say	five	boy	now	go

creep¹ /krip/ *verb* [I] (*p.t., p.p.* **crept** /krɛpt/) **1** to move very quietly and carefully, often with the body in a low position, so that nobody will notice you: *The cat crept silently toward the bird.* **2** to move forward or higher slowly: *Inflation crept up by 0.1% in the last quarter.*

PHRV **creep in** to begin to appear: *I could hear a note of sadness creeping into her voice.*

creep² /krip/ *noun* [C] (*informal*) an annoying or disgusting person

IDM **give sb the creeps** (*informal*) to give sb an unpleasant feeling; to make sb feel frightened: *There's something about the way he laughs that gives me the creeps.*

creep·y /ˈkripi/ *adj.* (**creep·i·er**; **creep·i·est**) (*informal*) that makes you feel nervous and frightened: *a creepy smile*

cre·mate /ˈkrimeɪt; krɪˈmeɪt/ *verb* [T] to burn the body of a dead person as part of a funeral service

cre·ma·tion /krɪˈmeɪʃn/ *noun* [C,U] an act of cremating a dead person ☞ Look at the note at **funeral**.

cre·ma·to·ri·um /ˌkriməˈtɔriəm/ *noun* [C] (*pl.* **cre·ma·to·ri·ums** or **cre·ma·to·ri·a** /-ˈɔriə/) a place where dead people are cremated

crept *p.t., p.p.* of CREEP¹

cres·cen·do /krəˈʃɛndoʊ/ *noun* [C] (*pl.* **cres·cen·dos**) a noise or piece of music that is very loud or that gets louder and louder

cres·cent /ˈkrɛsnt/ *noun* [C] the shape of the moon in its first and last stages; a curved shape that is pointed at both ends ☞ picture at **shape**.

crest /krɛst/ *noun* [C] **1** the white part at the top of a wave **2** the top of a hill **3** a group of attractive feathers on the top of a bird's head

cre·vasse /krəˈvæs/ *noun* [C] a deep crack in thick ice

crev·ice /ˈkrɛvəs/ *noun* [C] a narrow crack in a rock, wall, etc.

☆ **crew** /kru/ *noun* [C] **1** all the people who work on a ship, an airplane, etc.: *The captain and his crew hope you had a pleasant flight.* **2** a group of people who work together: *a camera crew* (= people who film things for television, etc.)

'crew cut (*also* **'crew·cut**) *noun* [C] a very short hairstyle for men

☆ **crib** /krɪb/ *noun* [C] a bed for a baby or young child, with high sides to stop it from falling out

crick /krɪk/ *noun* [sing.] a pain in your neck, back, etc. that makes it difficult for you to move easily: *I have a crick in my neck.*

crick·et /ˈkrɪkət/ *noun* [C] an insect that makes a loud noise by rubbing its wings together

☆ **crime** /kraɪm/ *noun* **1** [C] something which is against the law and which people are punished for, e.g. by being sent to prison: *to com-*

mit a crime ○ *serious crimes such as murder and armed robbery* ☞ Look also at **hate crime**. **2** [U] illegal behavior in general: *an increase in violent crime* ○ *to lead a life of crime* ○ *crime prevention measures* **3** usually **a crime** [sing.] something that is morally wrong: *It is a crime to waste food when people are starving.*

☆ **crim·i·nal¹** /ˈkrɪmənl/ *adj.* **1** (only *before* a noun) connected with crime: *Vandalism is a criminal offense.* ○ *criminal law* **2** morally wrong: *a criminal waste of taxpayers' money*

☆ **crim·i·nal²** /ˈkrɪmənl/ *noun* [C] a person who has committed a crime: *convicted criminals*

crim·son /ˈkrɪmzn/ *adj., noun* [U] (of) a dark red color ☞ Look at **maroon** and **scarlet**.

cringe /krɪndʒ/ *verb* [I] **1** to move away from sb/sth because you are frightened: *The dog cringed in terror when the man raised his arm.* **2** to feel embarrassed: *terrible home videos that make you cringe in embarrassment*

crin·kle /ˈkrɪŋkl/ *verb* [I,T] **crinkle (sth) (up)** (to cause sth) to have thin folds or lines in it: *His face crinkled into a smile.* —**crink·ly** /ˈkrɪŋkli/ *adj.*: *a type of soft crinkly material*

crip·ple¹ /ˈkrɪpl/ *noun* [C] (*old-fashioned*) a person who cannot walk well because his/her legs or back have been injured: *The accident left her a cripple at the age of 20.* ○ (*figurative*) *an emotional cripple*

☞ This is an old-fashioned word and is now considered offensive. A more polite way of expressing the same meaning today is to say that somebody is **disabled** or that he/she has a **disability**.

crip·ple² /ˈkrɪpl/ *verb* [T] **1** (usually passive) (*old-fashioned*) to cause sb to be a cripple¹: *He was crippled in a car accident.* **2** to damage sth badly: *The recession has crippled the automobile industry.*

crip·pling /ˈkrɪplɪŋ/ *adj.* that causes very great damage; that has a very harmful effect: *crippling debts*

☆ **cri·sis** /ˈkraɪsəs/ *noun* [C,U] (*pl.* **cri·ses** /ˈkraɪsiz/) a time of great danger or difficulty; the moment when things change and either improve or get worse: *the international crisis caused by the invasion* ○ *a friend you can rely on in times of crisis*

☆ **crisp¹** /krɪsp/ *adj.* **1** hard and dry: *Store the crackers in an airtight container to keep them crisp.* **2** firm and fresh or new: *a crisp salad* ○ *a crisp apple* ○ *a crisp new $10 bill* **3** (used about the air or weather) cold and dry: *a crisp winter morning* **4** (used about the way sb speaks) quick, clear but not very friendly: *a crisp reply*

crisp² /krɪsp/ *noun* [C] (*BrE*) = CHIP¹(3)

crisp·y /ˈkrɪspi/ *adj.* (**crisp·i·er**; **crisp·i·est**) = CRISP¹(1,2): *crispy onion rings*

criss·cross /ˈkrɪskrɔs/ *adj.* (only *before* a noun) with many lines that cross over each

165

other: *a criss-***cross** **pattern** —**criss·cross** *verb*
[I,T]: *the trails that crisscross the park*

cri·te·ri·on /kraɪˈtɪriən/ *noun* [C] (*pl.* **cri·te·ri·a** /-riə/) the standard that you use when you make a decision or form an opinion about sb/sth: *What are the criteria for deciding who gets financial aid?*

☆**crit·ic** /ˈkrɪtɪk/ *noun* [C] **1** a person who says what he/she thinks is bad or wrong with sb/sth: *He is a long-standing critic of the government's transportation policy.* **2** a person whose job is to give his/her opinion about a play, movie, book, work of art, etc.: *a movie critic* (= in a newspaper, etc.).

☆**crit·i·cal** /ˈkrɪtɪkl/ *adj.* **1 critical (of sb/sth)** saying what is wrong with sb/sth; disapproving: *The report was very critical of the condition of the state's highways.* ○ *to make some critical remarks* **2** (only *before* a noun) describing the good and bad points of a play, movie, book, work of art, etc.: *a critical guide to this month's new movies* **3** dangerous or serious: *The patient is in a critical condition.* **4** very important; at a time when things can suddenly become better or worse: *The talks between the two leaders have reached a critical stage.* —**crit·i·cal·ly** /-ɪkli/ *adv.*: *a critically ill patient* ○ *a critically important decision*

☆**crit·i·cism** /ˈkrɪtəsɪzəm/ *noun* **1** [C,U] (an expression of) what you think is bad about sb/sth: *severe criticism of the city council's plans* ○ *My main criticism is that it is too expensive.* **2** [U] the act of describing the good and bad points of a play, movie, book, work of art, etc.: *literary criticism*

☆**crit·i·cize** /ˈkrɪtəsaɪz/ *verb* [I,T] **criticize (sb/sth) (for sth)** to say what is bad or wrong with sb/sth: *The doctor was criticized for not sending the patient to the hospital.* ○ *Stop criticizing!*

cri·tique¹ /krɪˈtik/ *noun* [C] a piece of writing that describes the good and bad points of sb/sth

cri·tique² /krɪˈtik/ *verb* [T] to describe the good and bad points of sb/sth

crit·ter /ˈkrɪtər/ *noun* [C] (*informal*) a creature; an animal: *Those little critters sure can run fast!*

croak¹ /kroʊk/ *noun* [C] a deep low sound, like the noise that a frog makes

croak² /kroʊk/ *verb* **1** [I,T] to make a noise like a croak, e.g. because you have a cold and are losing your voice **2** (*informal*) to die

cro·chet /kroʊˈʃeɪ/ *verb* [I,T] (*p.t., p.p.* **cro·chet·ed** /-ʃeɪd/) to make clothes, blankets, etc. by using wool or thick cotton and one needle with a hook at one end: *to crochet a shawl* ☞ Look at **knit**.

croc·o·dile /ˈkrɑkədaɪl/ *noun* [C] a large, long animal with hard skin that lives in rivers in hot regions. A crocodile is a dangerous animal because it has a large mouth with a lot of

sharp teeth in it. It is a reptile. ☞ Look at **alligator**.

crois·sant /krəˈsɑnt; krwɑˈsɑn/ *noun* [C] a type of light bread roll, shaped in a curve, that is often eaten with butter ☞ picture at **bread**.

cro·ny /ˈkroʊni/ *noun* [C] (*pl.* **cro·nies**) (*informal*) (often used in a critical way) a friend

crook /krʊk/ *noun* [C] **1** (*informal*) a dishonest person; a criminal **2** a bend or curve in sth: *the crook of your arm* (= the inside of your elbow)

crook·ed /ˈkrʊkəd/ *adj.* **1** not straight or even: *That picture is crooked. I'll straighten it for you.* ○ *crooked teeth* **2** (*informal*) not honest: *a crooked politician*

☆**crop¹** /krɑp/ *noun* **1** [C] all the grain, fruit, vegetables, etc. that grow or are collected at one time or place: *this year's wheat crop* ○ *Another year of crop failure would mean starvation for many people.* **2** [C, usually pl.] plants that are grown on farms for food: *Corn and soybeans are the main crops here.* **3** [sing.] a number of people or things which have appeared at the same time: *the new crop of freshmen*

IDM **the cream of the crop** ➪ CREAM¹

crop² /krɑp/ *verb* [T] (**crop·ping; cropped**) to cut sth very short: *cropped hair*

PHRV **crop up** to appear suddenly, when you are not expecting it: *Some problems have cropped up.*

☆**cross¹** /krɔs/ *noun* [C] **1** a vertical piece of wood with another piece of wood across it, on which people were killed as a punishment in former times, or something shaped like this that is used as a symbol of the Christian religion: *Christ's death on the cross* ○ *The priest made the sign of the cross* (= by moving his right hand in front of his face and chest in the shape of a cross). ☞ Look at **crucifix**. **2** [usually sing.] **a cross (between A and B)** something (especially a plant or an animal) that is a mixture of two different types of things: *a fruit which is a cross between a peach and an apple*

☆**cross²** /krɔs/ *verb* **1** [I,T] **cross (over) (from sth/to sth)** to go from one side of sth to the other: *to cross the street* ○ *Where did you cross the border?* **2** [I] (used about lines, roads, etc.) to pass across each other: *The two roads cross just north of the town.* ○ (*figurative*) *Our letters crossed in the mail.* **3** [T] to put sth across or over sth else: *to cross your legs* **4** [T] **cross yourself** to make the sign of a cross in front of your face and chest as a symbol of the Christian religion **5** [T] to refuse to do what sb wants you to do; to oppose sb: *He's an important man. It could be dangerous to cross him.* **6** [T] **cross sth with sth** to produce a new type of plant or animal by mixing two different types: *If you cross a horse with a donkey, you get a mule.*

tʃ	dʒ	v	θ	ð	s	z	ʃ
chin	June	van	thin	then	so	zoo	she

IDM **cross my heart (and hope to die)** (*informal*) (used for emphasizing that what you are saying is true)

cross your fingers to hope that things will happen in the way that you want; to wish for good luck: *There's nothing more we can do now – just cross our fingers and hope for the best.*

☞ If a person says they are "crossing their fingers" or "keeping their fingers crossed," it doesn't mean that they are really doing this with their hands. It means that they are wishing somebody luck or hoping very much that something good will happen.

cross your mind (used about a thought, idea, etc.) to come into your mind: *It never even crossed my mind that she was lying.*

PHRV **cross sth off (sth)** to remove sth from a list, etc. by drawing a line through it: *Cross Dave's name off the guest list – he can't come.*

cross sth out to draw a line through sth that you have written because you have made a mistake, etc.: *to cross out a spelling mistake*

cross³ /krɔs/ *adj.* angry or annoyed: *I was really cross with her for leaving me with all the work.* ○ *What are you so cross about?*

cross-'country *adj., adv.* across fields, etc.; not using main roads: *a cross-country run* ○ *cross-country skiing*

cross-ex'amine *verb* [T] to ask sb a lot of questions (e.g. in a court) in order to find out the truth about sth: *to cross-examine a witness in court* —**cross-ex,ami'nation** *noun* [C,U]

cross-eyed *adj.* having one or both of your eyes looking toward your nose

cross-fire /'krɔsfaɪər/ *noun* [U] **1** the shooting of guns from two or more places so that the bullets cross each other: *Two children were shot when they were caught in the crossfire between rival gangs.* **2** a situation in which two people or groups are arguing and in which sb else becomes involved against their will

cross-ing /'krɔsɪŋ/ *noun* [C] **1** the act of going or traveling across sth: *Most illegal border crossings are made at night.* **2** a place where roads or railroad tracks cross each other: *Buses must come to a full stop at railroad crossings.* **3** a place where you can cross over sth: *The guards stopped us at the border crossing and searched our car.*

cross-legged with her legs crossed

cross-legged /'krɔs ˌlɛgəd; -lɛgd/ *adj., adv.*

sitting on the floor with your legs pulled up in front of you and with one leg or foot over the other: *to sit cross-legged*

cross-,reference *noun* [C] a note in a book, etc. that tells you to look in another place in the book for more information

cross·roads /'krɔsroʊdz/ *noun* [C] (*pl.* **crossroads**) a place where two or more roads cross each other: *When you come to the next crossroads, turn right.* ○ (*figurative*) *The nation is at a crossroads – the next election will determine the country's future.*

cross ,section (*also* **cross-section**) *noun* [C] **1** a picture of what the inside of sth would look like if you cut through it: *a diagram of a cross section of the human brain* **2** a group of people that are typical of a larger group: *The students in our program represent a cross section of society.*

cross street *noun* [C] a street that crosses another street, usually at an angle of 90°: *Our office is at 198 Madison Avenue – the nearest cross street is 35th St.*

cross·town /'krɔstaʊn/ *adj.* (only *before* a noun) going from one side of a town or city to the other side: *a crosstown bus* ○ *a crosstown highway*

☆ **cross·walk** /'krɔswɔk/ *noun* [C] a place where people can cross a street

crossword puzzle

cross·word /'krɔswərd/ (*also* **crossword ,puzzle**) *noun* [C] a word game with black and white squares where you write the words in the white squares, either across or down. The correct words are the answers to special questions (**clues**): *to do a crossword*

crotch /krɑtʃ/ *noun* [C] the place where a person's legs, or pant legs, join at the top

crouch /kraʊtʃ/ *verb* [I] to bend down so that your body is close to the ground and lean forward slightly: *The cat crouched in front of the hole waiting for the mouse to appear.* ○ *He crouched down behind the couch.* ☞ picture at **kneel**.

crow¹ /kroʊ/ *noun* [C] a large black bird that makes a loud noise

IDM **as the crow flies** (used for describing distances) in a straight line: *It's a mile as the crow flies, but three miles by car.*

crow² /kroʊ/ *verb* [I] **1** to make a loud noise, such as a male chicken (**a rooster**) makes, e.g. early in the morning **2** **crow (about sth)** (*informal*) to speak too proudly about sth

crow·bar /ˈkroʊbɑr/ *noun* [C] a long iron bar that is used for forcing sth open

☆ **crowd¹** /kraʊd/ *noun* **1** [C] a large number of people in one place: *A large crowd gathered to hear the President speak.* ○ *He pushed his way through the crowd.* ○ *There were crowds of people waiting outside the theater.* **2 the crowd** [sing.] most people: *to follow the crowd* (= to do what everybody else does) **3** [C] (*informal*) a group of people who know each other: *John, Linda and Barry will be there – the usual crowd.*

☆ **crowd²** /kraʊd/ *verb* **1** [I] **crowd around (sb)** (used about a lot of people) to come together in one place: *Fans crowded around the singer, hoping to get his autograph.* **2** [T] (used about a lot of people) to fill an area: *Groups of tourists crowded the main streets.*

PHRV **crowd into sth; crowd in** to go into a small place and make it very full: *Somehow we all crowded into our small living room.*

crowd sb/sth into sth; crowd sb/sth in to put a lot of people into a small place: *Ten prisoners were crowded into one small cell.*

☆ **crowd·ed** /ˈkraʊdəd/ *adj.* full of people: *The mall was crowded with holiday shoppers.* ○ *a crowded bus*

☆ **crown¹** /kraʊn/ *noun* **1** [C] a round ornament made of gold and jewels, that a king or queen wears on the head on official occasions **2** [C] an artificial covering for the top part of a tooth that has been damaged **3** [sing.] the top of your head or of a hat

crown² /kraʊn/ *verb* [T] **1** to put a crown¹(1) on the head of a new king or queen in an official ceremony: *Queen Elizabeth of England was crowned in 1952.* ○ (*figurative*) *the newly crowned American champion* **2 crown sth (with sth)** (*formal*) to cover the top of sth: *The mountain was crowned with snow.* **3** to be a good or successful end to sth: *years of hard work that finally crowned with success*

crown·ing /ˈkraʊnɪŋ/ *adj.* (only *before* a noun) the best or most important: *Winning the world championship was the crowning moment of her career.*

☆ **cru·cial** /ˈkruʃl/ *adj.* **crucial (to/for sth)** very important: *Early diagnosis of the illness is crucial for successful treatment.* —**cru·cial·ly** /-ʃəli/ *adv.*: *a crucially important decision, meeting, etc.*

cru·ci·fix /ˈkrusəfɪks/ *noun* [C] a small model of a cross with a figure of Jesus on it

cru·ci·fix·ion /ˌkrusəˈfɪkʃn/ *noun* [C,U] the act of crucifying sb: *the Crucifixion of Christ*

cru·ci·fy /ˈkrusəfaɪ/ *verb* [T] (*pres. part.* **cru·ci·fy·ing**; *3rd pers. sing. pres.* **cru·ci·fies**; *p.t., p.p.* **cru·ci·fied**) to kill sb by nailing or tying him/her to a cross

☆ **crude** /krud/ *adj.* **1** in its natural state: *crude oil* **2** done or made in a simple way; not skillful: *The method was crude but very effective.*

3 rude, talking or acting in a way that would offend many people: *He always tells such crude jokes!* —**crude·ly** *adv.*

☆ **cru·el** /kruəl/ *adj.* (**cru·el·er** or **cru·el·ler**; **cru·el·est** or **cru·el·lest**) causing physical or mental pain or suffering to sb/sth; unkind: *I think it's cruel to keep animals in cages.* ○ *a cruel punishment* —**cru·el·ly** /ˈkruəli/ *adv.*

☆ **cru·el·ty** /ˈkruəlti/ *noun* (*pl.* **cru·el·ties**) **1** [U] **cruelty (to sb/sth)** cruel behavior: *cruelty to children* **2** [C, usually pl.] a cruel act: *the cruelties of war*

☆ **cruise¹** /kruz/ *verb* [I] **1** to travel by boat, visiting a number of places, as a vacation: *to cruise around the Caribbean* **2** to travel by car, plane, etc. staying at the same speed : *cruising at 65 miles an hour* **3** to travel, usually slowly, by car, without intending to go to a particular place: *kids cruising up and down Main Street on Friday night*

cruise² /kruz/ *noun* [C] a vacation in which you travel on a ship and visit a number of different places: *After they retired, they went on a Caribbean cruise.*

ˈcruise conˌtrol *noun* [U] a system in a car that keeps the car going at the same speed, so that the driver does not need to use his/her feet

cruis·er /ˈkruzər/ *noun* [C] **1** a police car **2** a large military ship

crumb /krʌm/ *noun* [C] a very small piece of bread, cake or cookie

crum·ble /ˈkrʌmbl/ *verb* [I,T] **crumble (sth) (into/to sth); crumble (sth) (up)** (to cause sth) to break into very small pieces: *The walls of the old church are beginning to crumble.* (*figurative*) *Support for the policy is starting to crumble.*

crum·my /ˈkrʌmi/ *adj.* (**crum·mi·er; crum·mi·est**) (*informal*) bad or unpleasant: *a crummy little basement apartment*

crum·ple /ˈkrʌmpl/ *verb* [I,T] **crumple (sth) (into sth); crumple (sth) (up)** (to cause sth) to be folded or pressed in a messy way: *The front of the car crumpled when it hit the wall.* ○ *to crumple a piece of paper into a ball*

crunch¹ /krʌntʃ/ *verb* **1** [T] **crunch (on) sth** to make a loud noise when you are eating sth hard: *to crunch on an apple* **2** [I] to make a loud noise like the sound of sth being walked on and crushed: *The snow made a crunching noise under our feet.*

crunch² /krʌntʃ/ *noun* **1** [sing.] an act or noise of crunching¹: *the crunch of their boots on the snow* **2** [C] a situation when there is not enough money, time, etc.: *a financial crunch* ○ *We are experiencing the city's worst housing crunch in 20 years.*

crunch·y /ˈkrʌntʃi/ *adj.* (**crunch·i·er; crunch·i·est**) hard and crisp, so that it makes a noise when you eat it or step on it: *a crunchy apple*

cru·sade /kruˈseɪd/ *noun* [C] **1 Crusade** one

ə	y	w	t	eɪ	aɪ	ɔɪ	aʊ	oʊ
about	yes	woman	butter	say	five	boy	now	go

of the wars that European Christians fought with Muslims in the Middle Ages to win back land in the area that is now Israel **2** a fight for sth that you believe to be good or against sth that you believe to be bad: *a crusade against drugs*

cru·sad·er /kru'seɪdər/ *noun* [C] a person who takes part in a crusade

☆ **crush¹** /krʌʃ/ *verb* [T] **1** to press sb/sth hard so that he/she/it is broken, damaged or injured: *Don't pack the eggs at the bottom of the bag or they'll get crushed.* ○ *to be crushed to death* **2 crush sth (up)** to break sth hard into very small pieces or a powder: *First, crush the garlic and fry in olive oil.* **3** to defeat sb/sth completely : *The army was sent in to crush the rebellion.*

crush² /krʌʃ/ *noun* **1** [C] **a crush (on sb)** (*informal*) a strong feeling of love and admiration for sb that does not usually last for a long time: *to have a crush on your teacher* **2** [sing.] a large group of people in a small space: *There was a crush of reporters in the lobby of the courthouse.*

crush·ing /'krʌʃɪŋ/ *adj.* (only *before* a noun) that defeats sb/sth completely or upsets sb/sth a lot: *a crushing defeat* ○ *a crushing blow to the country's economy*

☆ **crust** /krʌst/ *noun* [C,U] **1** the hard part on the outside of a loaf of bread, pie, etc.: *I cut the crusts off the bread.* ☛ picture at **bread**. **2** [C] a hard layer on the outside of sth: *the earth's crust*

crust·y /'krʌsti/ *adj.* (**crust·i·er**; **crust·i·est**) **1** having a hard crust (1): *crusty bread* **2** (*informal*) bad-tempered and impatient: *a crusty old professor*

crutch
cane

crutch /krʌtʃ/ *noun* [C] a type of stick that you put under your arm to help you walk when you have hurt your leg or foot: *to be on crutches* (= to walk using crutches)

crux /krʌks/ *noun* [sing.] the most important or difficult part of a problem: *Now we come to the crux of the problem.*

☆ **cry¹** /kraɪ/ *verb* (*pres. part.* **cry·ing**; *3rd pers. sing. pres.* **cries**; *p.t., p.p.* **cried**) **1** [I] to make a noise and produce tears in your eyes, e.g. because you are unhappy or have hurt yourself: *The baby never stops crying.* ○ *The child was crying for* (= because she wanted) *her mother.* ○ *to cry yourself to sleep* **2** [I,T] **cry**

(out) to shout or make a loud noise: *"Look!" he cried. "There they are!"* ○ *to cry out in pain*

PHR V **cry out for sth** to need sth very much: *The school district is crying out for good teachers.*

☆ **cry²** /kraɪ/ *noun* (*pl.* **cries**) **1** [C] a shout or loud noise: *the cry of a seagull* ○ *a cry of pain, fear, joy, etc.* **2** [sing.] an act of crying¹(1) : *After a good cry, I felt much better.*

IDM **a far cry from sth/from doing sth** ➪ **FAR¹**

cry·ing /'kraɪɪŋ/ *adj.* (only *before* a noun) very great (usually used when talking about a bad situation, etc.): *There's a crying need for more doctors.* ○ *It's a crying shame that so many people can't find jobs.*

cryp·tic /'krɪptɪk/ *adj.* having a hidden meaning that is not easy to understand; mysterious: *a cryptic message, remark, etc.*

crys·tal /'krɪstl/ *noun* **1** [U] a transparent rock or mineral **2** [U] very high-quality glass: *a crystal vase* **3** [C] a regular shape that some mineral substances form when they are solid: *salt crystals*

IDM **crystal clear** very easy to understand: *The meaning is crystal clear.*

crystal 'ball *noun* [C] a glass ball in which some people believe you can see what is going to happen in the future

C-section /'si ˌsɛkʃn/ *noun* [C] = CESAREAN SECTION

cu. *abbr.* = CUBIC

cub /kʌb/ *noun* [C] a young fox, bear, lion, tiger or wolf

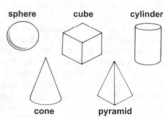

sphere cube cylinder

cone pyramid

cube¹ /kyub/ *noun* [C] **1** a solid shape that has six equal square sides: *ice cubes* **2** the number that you get if you multiply a number by itself twice: *the cube of 5 (5^3) is 125 (= 5 x 5 x 5).*

cube² /kyub/ *verb* [T] (usually passive) to multiply a number by itself twice: *Four cubed (4^3) is 64 (= 4 x 4 x 4).*

cu·bic /'kyubɪk/ *adj.* (*abbr.* **cu.**) measured by multiplying the length by the width by the height of sth: *If a box is 2 ft. long, 2 ft. wide and 2 ft. high, its volume is 8 cubic feet.*

cu·bi·cle /'kyubɪkl/ *noun* [C] a small separate section of a larger room, e.g. part of an office with low walls around it

'Cub Scout *noun* [C] a younger member of the Boy Scouts organization

☆ **cu·cum·ber** /ˈkyukʌmbər/ *noun* [C,U] a long, thin vegetable with dark green skin and a soft white part inside that is often used in salads ☞ picture at **salad**. Look also at **pickle**.

cud·dle /ˈkʌdl/ *verb* [I,T] to hold (sb/sth/each other) closely in your arms as a sign of love

cud·dly /ˈkʌdli/ (**cud·dli·er; cud·dli·est**) *adj.* soft and pleasant to hold close to you: *a cuddly teddy bear*

cue /kyu/ *noun* [C] **1** a word or gesture that is the signal for sb else to say or do sth, especially in a play: *When Julia puts the tray on the table, that's your cue to come on stage.* **2** an example of how to behave: *I wasn't sure how to behave at a Japanese wedding, so I took my cue from my hosts.* **3** a long, thin wooden stick, used to hit the ball in games like pool and billiards ☞ picture at **pool**.

IDM (right) on cue at exactly the moment expected

cuff /kʌf/ *noun* [C] **1** the end part of a sleeve, which often fastens at the wrist ☞ picture on page A26. **2** the bottom part of a pants leg that is folded up on the outside ☞ Look also at **handcuffs**.

cui·sine /kwəˈzin/ *noun* [U] a style of cooking: *Italian cuisine* ☞ A less formal word is **cooking**.

cul-de-sac /ˈkʌl də sæk/ *noun* [C] (*pl.* **cul-de-sacs**) a street that is closed at one end

cu·li·nar·y /ˈkʌlə,nɛri/ *adj.* connected with cooking

cull /kʌl/ *verb* [T] to gather or select information, ideas, etc., from different sources

cul·mi·nate /ˈkʌlməneɪt/ *verb* [I] (*formal*) **cul·minate in sth** to reach a final result or high point: *The team's efforts culminated in victory in the national championships.* —**cul·mi·na·tion** /ˌkʌlməˈneɪʃn/ *noun* [sing.]: *The joint space mission was the culmination of years of research.*

cul·prit /ˈkʌlprət/ *noun* [C] a person who has done sth wrong

cult /kʌlt/ *noun* [C] **1** a type of religion or religious group, especially one that is considered unusual **2** (usually used before another noun) a person or thing that has become popular with a particular group of people: *His books have become cult favorites among young people.*

cul·ti·vate /ˈkʌltəveɪt/ *verb* [T] **1** to prepare and use land for growing crops: *to cultivate the soil* **2** to grow crops: *Olives have been cultivated for centuries in Mediterranean countries.* **3** to try hard to develop sth that could be useful to you: *He cultivated links with colleagues in Europe.* —**cul·ti·va·tion** /ˌkʌltəˈveɪʃn/ *noun* [U]

cul·ti·vat·ed /ˈkʌltəveɪtəd/ *adj.* well educated, with good manners

☆ **cul·tur·al** /ˈkʌltʃərəl/ *adj.* **1** connected with the customs, ideas, art, etc. of a society: *cul-*

tural identities ○ *the nation's cultural diversity* **2** connected with art, music, literature, etc.: *The city has a rich cultural life, with many theaters, concert halls and art galleries.* ☞ Look also at **multicultural**. —**cul·tur·al·ly** /-rəli/ *adv.*

☆ **cul·ture** /ˈkʌltʃər/ *noun* **1** [C,U] the customs, ideas, civilization, etc. of a particular society or group of people: *the language and culture of the Aztecs* ○ *The international conference aims to bring together people from many different cultures.* **2** [U] achievement in or understanding of art, literature, ideas, etc.: *New York has always been a center of culture.*

cul·tured /ˈkʌltʃərd/ *adj.* well-educated, showing a good knowledge of the arts, etc.: *a cultured manner, mind, person, etc.*

ˈ**culture shock** *noun* [U] a feeling of confusion, etc. that you may experience when you go to a country that is very different from your own

cum·ber·some /ˈkʌmbərsəm/ *adj.* **1** heavy and difficult to carry, use, wear, etc. **2** (used about a system, etc.) slow; too complicated to be efficient: *cumbersome rules and regulations*

cu·mu·la·tive /ˈkyumyələtɪv/ *adj.* increasing steadily in amount, degree, etc.: *a cumulative effect*

cun·ning /ˈkʌnɪŋ/ *adj.* skillful at deceiving people: *a cunning liar* ○ *a cunning trick* —**cunningly** *adv.*

☆ **cup**[1] /kʌp/ *noun* [C] **1** a small deep container with a round base and usually a handle, used for drinking liquids: *a cup and saucer* ○ *a cup of coffee* **2** (*abbr.* **c.**) a unit of measurement used in cooking. A cup of liquid is equal to 0.237 liter: *Add half a cup of sugar and two cups of flour.* **3** (in sports) a large metal cup (1) given as a prize; the competition for such a cup: *the World Cup soccer tournament* **4** an object shaped like a cup (1): *a set of measuring cups*

cup and saucer mug

IDM not sb's cup of tea not what sb likes or is interested in: *Horror movies just aren't my cup of tea.*

cup[2] /kʌp/ *verb* (**cup·ping; cupped**) [T] to form sth, especially your hands, into the shape of a cup: *I cupped my hands to take a drink from the stream.* ○ *to cup your hand behind your ear*

☆ **cup·board** /ˈkʌbərd/ *noun* [C] a piece of furniture, usually with shelves inside and a door or doors at the front, used for storing food, etc.: *a kitchen cupboard* ☞ Look also at **cabinet** and **closet**.

cup·cake /ˈkʌpkeɪk/ *noun* [C] a small round cake for one person ☞ picture at **cake**.

cur·a·ble /ˈkyʊrəbl/ *adj.* that can be cured: *a curable disease* ☞ The opposite is **incurable**.

tʃ	dʒ	v	θ	ð	s	z	ʃ
chin	**June**	**van**	**thin**	**then**	**so**	**zoo**	**she**

C

cu·ra·tor /kyʊˈreɪtər; ˈkyʊrətər/ *noun* [C] a person whose job is to take care of the things that are kept in a museum, an art gallery, etc.

☆ **curb¹** /kərb/ *noun* [C] **1** a line of stones or cement that forms a raised border along the side of a street: *kids sitting on the curb* ☞ picture on page A28. **2 a curb (on sth)** something that controls or puts a limit on sth else: *to put a curb on government spending*

curb² /kərb/ *verb* [T] to control or set a limit on sth: *a plan to curb inflation*

☆ **cure¹** /kyʊr/ *verb* [T] **1 cure sb (of sth)** to make sb healthy again: *The treatment cured him of cancer.* ○ *The doctors couldn't cure her.* **2** to make an illness, injury, etc. end or disappear: *It is still not possible to cure the common cold.* **3** to make certain types of food last longer by drying, smoking or salting them: *cured ham*

☆ **cure²** /kyʊr/ *noun* [C] **1** a medicine or treatment that can cure an illness, etc.: *There is no known cure for AIDS.* **2** a return to good health; the process of being cured: *The new drug brought about a miraculous cure.*

cur·few /ˈkərfyu/ *noun* [C] a time after which sb is not allowed to go outside his/her home: *The government imposed a curfew.* ○ *Mom and Dad set a curfew of 10:00 for my brother and me.*

cu·ri·os·i·ty /ˌkyʊriˈɑsəti/ *noun* [C,U] (*pl.* **cu·ri·os·i·ties**) **1** [U] a desire to know or learn: *I was full of curiosity about their plans.* ○ *Out of curiosity, he opened her letter.* **2** [C] an unusual and interesting person or thing: *As the only girl who played football for the school team, she was a real curiosity.*

☆ **cu·ri·ous** /ˈkyʊriəs/ *adj.* **1** eager to know or learn as much as you can: *He was curious to know how the machine worked.* ○ *I've always been curious about politics.* **2** unusual or strange: *As I was walking home, a curious thing happened.* —**cu·ri·ous·ly** *adv.*: *Curiously enough, we discovered that we had exactly the same name.*

☆ **curl¹** /kərl/ *noun* [C] **1** a piece of hair that curves around: *Her hair fell in curls around her face.* **2** a thing that has a curved round shape: *a curl of blue smoke*

curl² /kərl/ *verb* **1** [I,T] to form or to make sth form into a curl or curls: *The pages had curled with age.* ○ *to curl your hair* **2** [I] to move around in a curve: *The snake curled around his arm.*

PHRV curl up to pull your arms, legs and head close to your body: *I like to curl up on the couch and watch TV.* ○ *The animal curled up into a ball to protect itself.*

curl·er /ˈkərlər/ (*also* **roller**) *noun* [C] a small plastic or metal tube that you wrap hair around in order to make it curly

☆ **curl·y** /ˈkərli/ *adj.* (**curl·i·er; curl·i·est**) full of curls; shaped like a curl: *curly hair* ☞ picture at **hair**. The opposite is **straight**.

☆ **cur·ren·cy** /ˈkərənsi/ *noun* (*pl.* **cur·ren·cies**) **1** [C,U] the system or type of money that a particular country uses: *foreign currency* ○ *a weak, strong, stable, etc. currency* **2** [U] (*formal*) the state of being believed, accepted or used by many people: *new ideas that soon gained currency*

☆ **cur·rent¹** /ˈkərənt/ *adj.* of the present time; happening now: *current fashions* ○ *current events*

cur·rent² /ˈkərənt/ *noun* **1** [C] a continuous flowing movement of water, air, etc.: *to swim against/with the current* ○ (*figurative*) *a current of anti-government feeling* **2** [U] the flow of electricity through a wire, etc.: *electrical current*

ˌcurrent afˈfairs *noun* [plural] important political or social events that are happening at the present time

☆ **cur·rent·ly** /ˈkərəntli/ *adv.* now: *He is currently working in Spain.*

☆ **cur·ric·u·lum** /kəˈrɪkyələm/ *noun* [C] (*pl.* **cur·ric·u·lums** or **cur·ric·u·la** /-lə/) all the subjects that are taught in a school, college or university: *Latin is not part of the curriculum at our school.* ○ *The school's science curriculum includes biology, chemistry and physics.*

cur·ry /ˈkəri/ *noun* [C,U] (*pl.* **cur·ries**) a hot-tasting dish of meat, vegetables, etc. usually served with rice: *some Indian vegetable curry* ○ *a hot/mild curry*

ˈcurry ˌpowder *noun* [C] a mixture of strongly flavored substances (**spices**) in powder form, that is used to make curry

curse¹ /kərs/ *noun* [C] **1** a word used for expressing anger; a swear word **2** a word or words expressing the wish that sth terrible will happen to sb: *In the story, the witch put a curse on the prince.* ○ *The family seemed to be under a curse* (= lots of bad things happened to them). **3** something that causes great harm: *the curse of drug addiction*

curse² /kərs/ *verb* **1** [I,T] to swear at sb/sth; to use rude language to express your anger: *He dropped the box, cursed, and started to pick up the contents.* **2** [T] to use a curse¹(2) against sb/sth: *She cursed her family.*

cur·sor /ˈkərsər/ *noun* [C] a small sign on a computer screen that you can move to indicate a particular position

cur·so·ry /ˈkərsəri/ *adj.* quick and brief; done in a hurry: *a cursory glance at the newspaper*

cur·tail /kərˈteɪl/ *verb* [T] (*formal*) to make sth shorter or smaller; to reduce

i	ɪ	ɛ	æ	ɑ	ɔ	ʌ	ʊ	u
see	sit	ten	cat	hot	saw	cup	put	too

shade — curtain —

windowsill

☆ **cur·tain** /ˈkərtn/ *noun* [C] **1** a piece of material that you can move sideways to cover a window, etc.: *Could you close the curtains?* ○ *a shower curtain* ○ *The curtain goes up at 7 p.m.* (= in a theater, the play begins). ☞ Look also at **drapery**. **2** a thing that covers or hides sth: *a curtain of mist*

curt·sy[1] (*also* **curtsey**) /ˈkərtsi/ *noun* [C] (*pl.* **curt·sies** or **curt·seys**) a movement made by a woman as a sign of respect, done by bending the knees, with one foot behind the other

curt·sy[2] /ˈkərtsi/ (*also* **curtsey**) *verb* (*pres. part.* **curt·sy·ing** or **curt·sey·ing**; *3rd pers. sing. pres.* **curt·sies** or **curt·seys**; *p.t., p.p.* **curt·sied** or **curt·seyed**) [I] to make a curtsy[1]

☆ **curve**[1] /kərv/ *noun* [C] **1** a line that bends around: *a curve on a graph* **2** [usually sing.] a system in which letter grades are given to students based on how well they have done in comparison with other students, not based on a fixed standard: *Prof. Jenkins grades on a curve.*

☆ **curve**[2] /kərv/ *verb* [I,T] to bend or to make sth bend in a curve1: *The bay curved around to the south.* ○ *a curved line*

cush·ion[1] /ˈkʊʃn/ *noun* [C] **1** a thick pad or a bag filled with soft material that you can sit on: *I found my keys under the cushions on the couch.* ☞ A cushion on a bed is a **pillow**. **2** something that acts or is shaped like a cushion (1): *a cushion of air*

cush·ion[2] /ˈkʊʃn/ *verb* [T] **1** to make a blow, etc. less painful: *The snow cushioned his fall.* **2** to reduce the bad effect of sth: *government programs that help to cushion the blow of unemployment*

cus·tard /ˈkʌstərd/ *noun* [U] a soft, sweet food made from milk, eggs and sugar, that is baked in an oven

cus·to·di·an /kəˈstoʊdiən/ (*also* **janitor**) *noun* [C] a person whose job is to clean a large building and to do small repairs: *a school custodian*

cus·to·dy /ˈkʌstədi/ *noun* [U] **1** the legal right or duty to take care of sb/sth: *After the divorce, the mother was given custody of the children.* **2** the state of being guarded, or kept in prison temporarily, especially by the police: *The man was arrested and kept in police custody until his trial.*

☆ **cus·tom**[1] /ˈkʌstəm/ *noun* [C,U] a way of behaving which a particular group or society has had for a long time: *the Native American custom of smoking a peace pipe at ceremonies* ○

according to local custom ☞ Look at the note at **habit**.

cus·tom[2] /ˈkʌstəm/ *adj.* (only *before* a noun) specially made or built for a particular customer: *custom kitchen cabinets*

custom- /ˈkʌstəm-/ (in compounds) specially done for a particular customer: *a custom-made suit* ○ *custom-designed furniture*

cus·tom·ar·y /ˈkʌstəˌmɛri/ *adj.* according to custom; usual: *Is it customary to send Christmas cards in your country?* —**cus·tom·ar·i·ly** /ˌkʌstəˈmɛrəli/ *adv.*

☆ **cus·tom·er** /ˈkʌstəmər/ *noun* [C] a person who buys goods or services: *a regular customer* ○ *The salesclerk was helping a customer.*

☆ **cus·toms** (*also* **Customs**) /ˈkʌstəmz/ *noun* [U] the place at an airport, etc. where government officials check your luggage to see whether you are bringing goods into the country illegally: *We went straight through customs with nothing to declare.* ○ *a customs officer*

☆ **cut**[1] /kʌt/ *verb* (*pres. part.* **cut·ting**; *p.t., p.p.* **cut**) **1** [I,T] to make an opening, wound or mark in sth using a sharp tool, e.g. a pair of scissors or a knife: *Be careful not to cut yourself on that broken glass!* ○ *This knife doesn't cut very well.* **2** [T] to remove sth or a part of sth, using a knife, etc.: *She cut two slices of bread.* **3** [T] **cut sth (in/into sth)** to divide sth into pieces with a knife, etc.: *She cut the cake into eight pieces.* ○ *He cut the rope in two.* ○ *Cut the sandwich in half* (= into two equal pieces). **4** [T] to make sth shorter by using scissors, etc.: *I cut my own hair.* ○ *to have your hair cut* (= at the salon). ○ *to cut the grass* **5** [T] to make or form sth by removing material with a sharp tool: *She cut a hole in the card and pushed the string through.* ○ *They cut a path through the jungle.* **6** [T] to reduce sth or make it shorter; to remove sth: *to cut taxes* ○ *Several employees' hours have been cut because of budget problems.*

IDM **cut/skip class** ⇨ CLASS

cut corners to do sth quickly and not as well as you should

cut in line to go to the front of a line of people without waiting for your turn, or to join a line of people in the middle and not at the end

have your work cut out for you ⇨ WORK[1]

PHRV **cut across sth** to go beyond the limits of: *The question of aid for the earthquake victims cuts across national boundaries.*

cut across, along, through, etc. (sth) to go across, etc. sth, in order to shorten your trip: *It's a lot quicker if we cut across the field.*

cut sth back; cut back (on sth) to reduce sth: *to cut back on public spending*

cut sth down 1 to make sth fall down by cutting it: *to cut down a tree* **2** to shorten sth: *I have to cut my essay down to 2,000 words.*

cut sth down; cut down (on sth) to reduce

C

ə	y	w	t̬	eɪ	aɪ	ɔɪ	aʊ	oʊ
about	yes	woman	butter	say	five	boy	now	go

the quantity or amount of sth; to do sth less often: *You should cut down on fatty foods.*

cut in (on sb/sth); cut into sth to interrupt sb/sth: *to cut into a conversation*

cut sb off (often passive) to stop or interrupt sb's telephone conversation: *We were cut off before I could give her my message.*

cut sb/sth off (often passive) to stop the supply of sth to sb: *If you don't pay your gas bill, they'll cut you off.* ○ *The electricity was cut off.*

cut sth off to block a road, etc. so that nothing can pass: *We must cut off all possible escape routes.*

cut sb/sth off (from sb/sth) (often passive) to prevent sb/sth from moving from a place or contacting people outside: *The farm was cut off from the highway by heavy snow.*

cut sth open to open sth by cutting: *She fell and cut her head open.*

cut sth out 1 to remove sth or to form sth into a particular shape by cutting: *to cut out a dress from a piece of cloth* **2** to leave sth out: *Cut out the boring details!* **3** (*informal*) (often in orders) to stop saying or doing sth, usually sth annoying: *Cut that out and leave me alone!* ○ *Cut it out! That hurts!* **4** (*informal*) to stop doing or using sth: *You'll only lose weight if you cut out junk food from your diet.*

cut sth out (of sth) to remove sth from sth larger by cutting: *He cut the advertisement out of the newspaper.*

be cut out for sth; be cut out to be sth to have the qualities to be able to do sth; to be suitable for sth/sb: *You're not cut out to be a soldier.* ○ *David and Janet are cut out for each other.*

cut sth up to cut sth into small pieces with a knife, etc.

☆ **cut²** /kʌt/ *noun* [C] **1** a wound or an opening made with a knife, etc.: *He had a deep cut on his forehead.* **2** an act of cutting: *to have a cut and blow-dry* (= at a hair salon) **3 a cut (in sth)** a reduction in size, amount, etc.: *a cut in government spending* ○ *tax cuts* **4** a piece of meat from a particular part of an animal **5** (*informal*) a share, especially in profits

cut·back /'kʌtbæk/ *noun* [C] a reduction in amount or number: *budget cutbacks* ○ *The management had to make cutbacks in personnel.*

☆ **cute** /kyut/ *adj.* attractive; good-looking: *Your little girl is so cute!* ○ *Check out those cute guys over there!* ○ *a cute dress* ☞ Look at the note at **pretty¹**.

cut·ler·y /'kʌtləri/ *noun* [U] the instruments, especially sharp knives, that you use to cut and eat food

cut·let /'kʌtlət/ *noun* [C] a small, flat piece of meat that is usually covered in flour or very small bits of bread (**crumbs**) and fried or baked

cut·off (*also* **cut-off**) /'kʌtɔf/ *noun* [C] the level or time at which sth stops: *The cutoff date for applications is May 12.*

'cut-rate *adj.* sold at a reduced price; selling goods that are often of poor quality at low prices: *cut-rate plane fares* ○ *a cut-rate store*

cut·ter /'kʌtər/ *noun* [C] (*also* **cut·ters** [plural]) a tool that you use for cutting through sth, e.g. metal: *a pair of wire cutters*

cut·throat /'kʌtθrout/ *adj.* caring only about success and not worried about hurting anybody: *cutthroat business practices*

cut·ting /'kʌtɪŋ/ *noun* [C] a piece cut off from a plant that you use for growing a new plant

‚cutting 'edge *noun* [sing.] the most advanced position in a field of study: *Our firm is right at the cutting edge of cancer research.* ○ *cutting-edge technology*

cy·a·nide /'saɪənaɪd/ *noun* [U] a poisonous chemical

☆ **cy·cle¹** /'saɪkl/ *noun* [C] **1** a series of events, etc. that happen repeatedly in the same order: *the life cycle of a frog* **2** a bicycle or motorcycle: *a cycle shop*
IDM **a vicious circle/cycle** ⇨ VICIOUS

cy·cle² /'saɪkl/ *verb* [I] to ride a bicycle, especially as a sport

☞ **Ride a bike** is a common way of talking about cycling for pleasure: *We like to ride our bikes on weekends.*

cy·cli·cal /'saɪklɪkl; sɪk-/ (*also* **cy·clic** /'saɪklɪk; sɪk-/) *adj.* following a repeated pattern

cy·clist /'saɪklɪst/ *noun* [C] a person who rides a bicycle, especially as a sport

cy·clone /'saɪkloʊn/ *noun* [C] a violent wind that moves in a circle, causing a storm ☞ Look at the note at **storm**. Look also at **tornado**.

cyl·in·der /'sɪləndər/ *noun* [C] **1** a shape or an object with circular ends and straight sides ☞ picture at **cube**. **2** a cylinder-shaped part of an engine, e.g. in a car: *a six-cylinder engine*

cy·lin·dri·cal /sə'lɪndrɪkl/ *adj.* having the shape of a cylinder

cym·bal /'sɪmbl/ *noun* [C, usually pl.] one of a pair of round metal plates used as a musical instrument. Cymbals make a loud ringing sound when you strike them together or hit them with a stick.

cy·nic /'sɪnɪk/ *noun* [C] a person who believes that people only do things for selfish reasons: *Don't be such a cynic. He did it to help us, not for the money.* —**cyn·i·cal** /'sɪnɪkl/ *adj.*: *She has a cynical view of politics.* ○ *a cynical remark* —**cyn·i·cal·ly** /-kli/ *adv.* **cyn·i·cism** /'sɪnəsɪzəm/ *noun* [U]

Cy·ril·lic /sɪ'rɪlɪk/ *adj.* the Cyrillic alphabet is used in languages such as Russian

cyst /sɪst/ *noun* [C] a swelling filled with liquid in the body or under the skin

ər	ɪr	ɛr	ɑr	ɔr	ʊr	ʒ	h	ŋ
bird	near	hair	car	north	tour	vision	hat	sing

Dd

D, d /di/ *noun* [C] (*pl.* **D's**; **d's** /diz/) **1** the fourth letter of the English alphabet: *"David" begins with (a) "D."* **2** a grade that is given for a test or piece of work that is not very good. A "D" is the lowest grade with which you can pass: *I got a "D" on my essay.*

D (*also* **D.**) *abbr.* = DEMOCRAT

D.A. (*also* **DA**) /ˌdi ˈeɪ/ *abbr.* = DISTRICT ATTORNEY

dab¹ /dæb/ *verb* (**dab·bing**; **dabbed**) [I,T] to touch sth lightly, usually several times: *He dabbed the cut with a cotton ball.*

PHRV dab sth on/off (sth) to put sth on or to remove sth with a light stroke or strokes: *to dab some antiseptic on a wound*

dab² /dæb/ *noun* [C] **1** a light touch: *She gave her eyes a dab with a handkerchief.* **2** a small quantity of sth that is put on a surface: *a dab of paint, perfume, etc.*

dab·ble /ˈdæbl/ *verb* [I] to become involved in sth in a manner that is not very serious: *to dabble in politics*

☆**dad** /dæd/ *noun* [C] (*informal*) father: *Is that your dad?* ○ *Come on, Dad!*

☆**dad·dy** /ˈdædi/ *noun* (*pl.* **dad·dies**) (*informal*) (used by children) father: *I want my daddy!* ○ *Give Daddy a kiss.*

daf·fo·dil /ˈdæfədɪl/ *noun* [C] a tall yellow flower that grows early in the spring

dag·ger /ˈdæɡər/ *noun* [C] a type of knife with a point and two sharp edges used as a weapon, especially in former times: *He plunged a dagger into her heart.*

☆**dai·ly¹** /ˈdeɪli/ *adj., adv.* done, made or happening every day: *a daily routine, delivery, newspaper, etc.* ○ *Our airline flies to Japan daily.*

dai·ly² /ˈdeɪli/ *noun* [C] (*pl.* **dai·lies**) a newspaper that is published every day, or every day except Saturday and Sunday

dai·ry /ˈdɛri/ *noun* [C] (*pl.* **dai·ries**) a company which buys milk from farms and puts it into containers for sale, and makes butter, cheese, etc.: *dairy products such as butter, cheese and ice cream*

'dairy cattle *noun* [plural] cows which are kept for their milk, not their meat

'dairy farm *noun* [C] a farm that produces mainly milk and milk products

dai·sy /ˈdeɪzi/ *noun* [C] (*pl.* **dai·sies**) a small white flower with a yellow center, which usually grows wild on grass, or a larger flower grown in gardens

dam /dæm/ *noun* [C] a wall built across a river to hold back the water and form a lake (**reservoir**) behind it

☆**dam·age¹** /ˈdæmɪdʒ/ *noun* **1** [U] **damage (to sth)** harm or injury caused when sth is broken or spoiled: *The earthquake caused widespread damage.* ○ *The driver suffered severe brain damage in the accident.* **2 damages** [plural] money that you can claim from sb if he/she damages sth of yours or hurts you: *The jury awarded him $2 million in damages.*

☆**dam·age²** /ˈdæmɪdʒ/ *verb* [T] to spoil or harm sth, e.g. by breaking it: *The roof was damaged by the storm.*

dam·ag·ing /ˈdæmədʒɪŋ/ *adj.* having a bad or harmful effect

dame /deɪm/ *noun* [C] (*old-fashioned*, *slang*) a woman ☞ Nowadays many people consider this word offensive because it does not show respect toward women.

damn¹ /dæm/ *verb* **1** [I,T] (*informal*) (used to show that you are angry or annoyed): *Damn that stupid driver!* ○ *Damn! I left my wallet at home.*

☞ **Darn** is not as strong as **damn**.

2 [T] to describe sth as very bad: *The movie was damned by all the critics.* **3** [T] (used about God) to send sb to hell

damn² /dæm/ *noun*

IDM not give a damn (about sb/sth) (*informal*) to not care at all: *I don't give a damn what he thinks about me.*

☞ Some people find this expression offensive. Look also at **darn²**.

damned¹ /dæmd/ (*also* **damn** /dæm/) *adj.* (only *before* a noun) (*informal*) (used for showing that you are angry or annoyed): *Some damned fool parked too close to me.*

☞ **Darned** is not as strong as **damned**.

damned² /dæmd/ (*also* **damn** /dæm/) *adv.* (*informal*) (used for emphasizing that sth is good or bad) very: *Don't be so damned dumb!* ○ *You guys played pretty damn well today.*

☞ **Darned** is not as strong as **damned**.

damn·ing /ˈdæmɪŋ/ *adj.* very unfavorable; showing that sb/sth is bad or guilty: *The most damning evidence against her was a fingerprint on the weapon.*

☆**damp** /dæmp/ *adj.* a little wet: *The grass is a little damp. Sit on the blanket.* ○ *Wipe the surface with a damp cloth.* —**damp·ness** /ˈdæmpnəs/ *noun* [U]

damp·en /ˈdæmpən/ *verb* [T] **1** to make sth less strong or urgent: *Even the bad weather did not dampen their enthusiasm for the trip.*

tʃ	dʒ	v	θ	ð	s	z	ʃ
chin	June	van	thin	then	so	zoo	she

2 to make sth a little wet: *He dampened his hair to try to stop it from sticking up.*

☆ **dance¹** /dæns/ *noun* **1** [C] a series of steps and movements which you do to music: *What type of dance is this? A waltz.* **2** [C] a social meeting at which people dance with each other: *There's usually a dance at the end of the semester.* **3** [U] dancing as a form of art or entertainment: *She's very interested in modern dance.*

☆ **dance²** /dæns/ *verb* **1** [I,T] to move around to the rhythm of music by making a series of steps: *to dance the waltz* **2** [I] to move in a lively way, usually up and down: *She was dancing up and down with excitement.*

☆ **danc·er** /'dænsər/ *noun* [C] a person who dances, often as a job: *a ballet dancer* ○ *She's a good dancer.*

☆ **danc·ing** /'dænsɪŋ/ *noun* [U] moving to music: *Will there be dancing at the party?* ○ *ballet dancing*

dan·de·li·on /'dændəlaɪən/ *noun* [C] a small wild plant with a bright yellow flower, that often grows in grass around people's houses

dan·druff /'dændrəf/ *noun* [U] small pieces of dead skin in the hair, which look like white dust

☆ **dan·ger** /'demdʒər/ *noun* **1** [U] the chance that sb/sth may be hurt, killed or damaged or that sth bad may happen: *Danger! Falling rocks!* (= on a sign) ○ *The men kept on running until they thought they were out of danger.* **2** [C] **a danger (to sb/sth)** a person or thing that can cause injury, pain or damage: *Drunk drivers are a danger to everyone on the road.*

☆ **dan·ger·ous** /'demdʒərəs/ *adj.* likely to cause injury or damage: *a dangerous animal, road, illness, etc.* ○ *The strong currents in the ocean here are extremely dangerous for swimmers.* —**dan·ger·ous·ly** *adv.*: *He was standing dangerously close to the edge of the cliff.*

dan·gle /'dæŋgl/ *verb* [I,T] to hang or swing freely; to hold sth so that it hangs in this way: *She sat on the dock with her legs dangling over the water.*

Dan·ish /'demɪʃ/ (*also* ,Danish 'pastry) (*pl.* Danish pastries) *noun* [C] a type of round, sweet bread, usually with fruit, jam or sweet cheese in the center

☆ **dare¹** /dɛr/ *verb* **1** (usually in negative sentences) to be brave enough to do sth: *I don't dare ask her to loan me any more money.* ○ *We were so scared that we didn't dare go into the room.* ○ *Who would dare to criticize her in public?* ○ *Nobody dared (to) speak.*

☞ In this sense, **dare** can be followed by an infinitive with or without "to."

2 [T] to try to persuade sb to do sth in order to prove how brave he/she is: *Can you jump off that wall? Go on, I dare you!* ○ *He dared his friend to put a worm on the teacher's desk.*

☞ In this sense, **dare** is used with an infinitive with "to."

IDM **don't you dare** (used for telling sb very strongly not to do sth): *Don't you dare tell my parents about this!*

how dare you (used when you are angry about sth that sb has done): *How dare you speak to me like that!*

☆ **dare²** /dɛr/ *noun* [C, usually sing.] something you do because sb asks you to, to prove how brave you are: *"Why did you try to swim across the river?" "It was a dare."*

dare·dev·il /'dɛrdɛvl/ *noun* [C] a person who is willing to take risks, often foolishly

dar·ing /'dɛrɪŋ/ *adj.* willing to take risks or to do or say things which other people might not; brave; bold: *a daring attack*

☆ **dark¹** /dɑrk/ *noun* [sing.] **the dark** the state of having no light: *He's afraid of the dark.* ○ *Why are you sitting alone in the dark?*

IDM **before/after dark** before /after the sun goes down

(be/keep sb) in the dark (about sth) (be/keep sb) in a position of not knowing (about sth): *Don't keep me in the dark. Tell me!*

☆ **dark²** /dɑrk/ *adj.* **1** with no light or very little light: *It was a dark night, with no moon.* **2** (used about a color) nearer black than white; not light: *dark blue* **3** (only *before* a noun) sad; without hope: *the dark days leading up to the start of the war* **4** (only *before* a noun) mysterious or slightly threatening: *He seemed friendly, but there was a dark side to his character.*

dark·en /'dɑrkən/ *verb* [I,T] to become or to make sth darker: *The sky suddenly darkened and it looked like it was going to rain.*

,**dark 'glasses** *noun* [plural] = SUNGLASSES

☆ **dark·ness** /'dɑrknəs/ *noun* [U] the state of being dark: *We sat in complete darkness, waiting for the lights to come back on.*

dar·ling /'dɑrlɪŋ/ *noun* [C] (used for speaking to sb that you love): *Darling, I'm home!* ○ *How was your day at school, darling?*

darn ¹ /dɑrn/ *verb* **1** [I,T] (*informal*) (used to show that you are angry or annoyed): *Darn it! I can't make this stupid thing work.* ○ *There's no milk for my coffee. Darn!* **2** [T] to fix a hole in clothes by sewing across it in one direction and then in the other

darn² /dɑrn/ *noun*

IDM **not give a darn (about sb/sth)** (*informal*) to not care at all: *I don't give a darn what the neighbors say.*

darned¹ /dɑrnd/ (*also* darn /dɑrn/) *adj.* (only *before* a noun) (*informal*) (used for showing that you are angry or annoyed): *Those darned kids stole my garbage can!*

darned² /dɑrnd/ (*also* darn /dɑrn/) *adv.* (*informal*) (used for emphasizing that sth is good

or bad) very: *You did a darned good job today.* ○ *It's just too darn hot!*

dartboard dart **darts**

bull's eye

dart¹ /dɑrt/ *noun* **1** [C] an object like a small arrow. It is thrown or shot as a weapon or in a game: *First, they tranquilize the tiger with a special dart.* **2 darts** [U] a game in which you throw darts at a round board with numbers on it (**a dartboard**): *to play darts*

dart² /dɑrt/ *verb* [I] to move suddenly and quickly in a certain direction: *A rabbit darted across the field.*

dash¹ /dæʃ/ *noun* **1** [sing.] a short, quick act of running: *We made a dash for the bus and just got on.* ○ *Tonya finished third in the 200-meter dash.* **2** [C, usually sing.] a small amount of sth that you add to sth else: *a dash of lemon juice* **3** [C] a small horizontal line (–) used in writing, especially for adding extra information ☞ Look at **hyphen**. **4** [C] = DASHBOARD

dash² /dæʃ/ *verb* **1** [I] to go or run suddenly and quickly: *We all dashed for shelter when it started to rain.* **2** [T] to ruin or destroy sb's hopes, dreams, etc.: *The accident dashed his hopes of becoming a pianist.* **3** [I,T] to hit sth with great force; to throw sth so that it hits sth else very hard: *She dashed her racket to the ground.*
PHRV dash sth off to write or draw sth very quickly

dash·board /'dæʃbɔrd/ (*also* **dash**) *noun* [C] the part in a car in front of the driver where most of the switches, etc. are

☆ **da·ta** /'deɪtə; 'dæt̬ə/ *noun* [U, plural] facts or information: *to collect data* ○ *The data is/are still being analyzed.*

☞ Data was originally the plural form of a Latin noun, but it is now often used as an uncountable noun: *The data we have is not very interesting.*

da·ta·base /'deɪt̬əbeɪs; 'dæt̬ə-/ *noun* [C] a large amount of data that is stored in a computer and can easily be used, added to, etc.

☆ **date¹** /deɪt/ *noun* **1** [C] a particular day of the month or year: *What's the date today?* ○ *What date is it today?* ○ *What's your date of birth/your birth date?* **2** [sing.] a particular time: *We can discuss this at a later date.* **3** [C] an appointment to meet sb, especially a boy-

friend or girlfriend: *I'm going out on a date with Tom Friday night.* ☞ Look also at **blind date**. **4** [C] (*old-fashioned*) a person that you have made an appointment to meet, especially a boyfriend or girlfriend: *Sarah introduced us to her date at the party.* **5** [C] a small, sweet, dark brown fruit that comes from a tree which grows in hot countries
IDM out of date unfashionable; no longer useful: *out-of-date methods, machinery, etc.* ○ *This textbook is completely out of date.*
to date (*formal*) until now: *We've had very few complaints to date.*
up to date with all the latest information: *In this report, we'll bring you up to date with the latest news from the area.* ○ *We need to keep our records up to date.* ☞ Look also at **up-to-date**.

☆ **date²** /deɪt/ *verb* **1** [T] to discover or guess how old sth is: *to date a skeleton, a rock, etc.* **2** [T] to write the day's date on sth: *The letter is not dated, so we can't tell when it was written.* **3** [I,T] to seem, or to make sb/sth seem, unfashionable: *We chose a simple style so that it wouldn't date as quickly.* **4** [I,T] (*old-fashioned*) to meet a girlfriend or boyfriend regularly **5** [I] **date back to...; date from...** to have existed since...: *The house dates back to the Revolutionary War.*

dat·ed /'deɪt̬əd/ *adj.* unfashionable: *a very dated hairstyle*

☆ **daugh·ter** /'dɔt̬ər/ *noun* [C] a female child: *I have two sons and one daughter.* ○ *Janet's daughter is a doctor.*

'daughter-in-law *noun* [C] (*pl.* **daughters-in-law**) the wife of your son

daunt /dɔnt/ *verb* [T] (*usually passive*) to frighten or to worry sb by being too big or difficult: *I was daunted by the sudden responsibility.*

daunt·ing /'dɔnt̬ɪŋ/ *adj.* making you feel frightened or making you worry by being too big or difficult: *We faced the daunting task of cleaning up after the flood.*

dawn¹ /dɔn/ *noun* **1** [C,U] the early morning, when light first appears in the sky: *before/at dawn* **2** [sing.] the beginning: *the dawn of civilization*
IDM the crack of dawn ⇨ CRACK¹

dawn² /dɔn/ *verb* [I] to begin to grow light, after the night: *The day dawned bright and cold.* ○ (*figurative*) *A new era of peace is dawning.*
PHRV dawn on sb to become clear to sb: *Suddenly it dawned on her. "Of course!" she said. "You're Mike's brother!"*

☆ **day** /deɪ/ *noun* **1** [C] a period of 24 hours, of which seven make up a week: *"What day is it today?" "Tuesday."* ○ *We went to Hawaii for ten days.* ○ *I saw that movie a few days ago.* ○ *The next day was Saturday.* ○ *the day before* ○ *New Year's Day* **2** [C,U] the period of time after the sun rises and before it sets: *The days were*

D

D

warm, but the nights were freezing. ∘ *Have a nice day! See you tonight.* ∘ *It's been raining all day.* ☞ Look at **daily. 3** [C] the hours of the day when you work: *She has to work an eight-hour day.* **4** [C] (*also* **days**) a particular period of time: *in Shakespeare's day* ∘ *in the days of Shakespeare* ∘ *In the old days, most houses didn't have electricity.*

IDM by day/night during the day/night: *These animals sleep by day and hunt by night.*

call it a day ⇨ CALL²

the day after tomorrow not tomorrow, but the next day

the day before yesterday not yesterday, but the day before

day by day every day; as time passes: *Day by day, she was getting a little bit stronger.*

day in, day out every day, without any change: *He sits at his desk working, day in, day out.*

from day to day; from one day to the next within a short period of time: *Things change so quickly that we never know what will happen from one day to the next.*

have a field day ⇨ FIELD DAY

make sb's day (*informal*) to make sb very happy

one day; some day at some time in the future: *Some day we'll go back and see all our old friends.*

the other day a few days ago; recently: *I bumped into him in town the other day.*

the present day ⇨ PRESENT¹

these days in the present age; nowadays: *More and more couples are getting divorced these days.*

day·break /ˈdeɪbreɪk/ *noun* [U] the time in the early morning when light first appears: *at daybreak*

day·care (*also* **day care**) /ˈdeɪkɛr/ *noun* [U] the service of taking care of small children while their parents are working; a place that offers this service: *a daycare center* ∘ *My husband takes the kids to day care every morning.*

☆ **day·dream** /ˈdeɪdrim/ *noun* [C] thoughts that are not connected with what you are doing; often pleasant scenes in your imagination: *He stared out of the window, lost in a daydream.* —**day·dream** *verb* [I]

☆ **day·light** /ˈdeɪlaɪt/ *noun* [U] the light that there is during the day: *The colors look a lot different in daylight.* ∘ *daylight hours*

IDM in broad daylight ⇨ BROAD

daylight-ˈsaving time *noun* [U] the period of time from April to October when clocks in most parts of the U.S. are set one hour later than standard time

☆ **day·time** /ˈdeɪtaɪm/ *noun* [U] the period of time after the sun rises and before it sets: *These flowers open in the daytime and close up again at night.*

daze /deɪz/ *noun*

IDM in a daze in a confused state

dazed /deɪzd/ *adj.* confused; not showing normal reactions: *He had a dazed expression on his face.*

daz·zle /ˈdæzl/ *verb* [T] (usually passive) to impress sb very much: *He had been dazzled by her beauty.*

daz·zling /ˈdæzlɪŋ/ *adj.* very bright or impressive: *a dazzling light* ∘ *a dazzling performance*

dea·con /ˈdikən/ (*feminine* **dea·con·ess**) *noun* [C] an official who has a rank below a priest, or a person who helps a priest, in some Christian churches

☆ **dead¹** /dɛd/ *adj.* **1** no longer alive: *They rushed him to the hospital, but he was dead on arrival.* ∘ *There's a dead spider in the bathtub.* **2** (not before a noun) no longer working (used about a piece of equipment): *I picked up the phone, but the line was dead.* ∘ *a dead battery* **3** (only *before* a noun) complete: *There was dead silence when she finished speaking.* **4** without movement, activity or interest: *This town is completely dead after 11 o'clock at night.* **5** no longer used; over and finished: *Latin is a dead language.*

IDM a dead end 1 a street that is only open at one end **2** a point, situation, etc. from which you can make no further progress: *a dead-end job* (= one that offers no chance of promotion)

drop dead ⇨ DROP¹

dead² /dɛd/ *noun* **the dead** [plural] people who have died: *A church service was held in memory of the dead.*

IDM in the dead of night in the middle of the night, when it is very dark and quiet

dead·en /ˈdɛdn/ *verb* [T] to make sth less strong, painful, etc.: *They gave her drugs to try and deaden the pain.*

ˌ**dead ˈheat** *noun* [C] a situation in a race or contest when two or more people are at the same level: *The two candidates are in a dead heat in the polls.*

☆ **dead·line** /ˈdɛdlaɪn/ *noun* [C] a time or date before which sth must be done: *A journalist is used to having to meet deadlines.* ∘ *The deadline for our history paper is Friday.*

dead·lock /ˈdɛdlɑk/ *noun* [C,U] a situation in which an agreement between two sides cannot be reached

☆ **dead·ly¹** /ˈdɛdli/ *adj.* (**dead·li·er; dead·li·est**) **1** causing or likely to cause death: *a deadly poison* **2** very great : *They're deadly enemies.*

dead·ly² /ˈdɛdli/ *adv.* extremely; very: *I'm not joking – I'm deadly serious!*

☆ **deaf** /dɛf/ *adj.* **1** unable to hear anything or unable to hear very well: *You'll have to speak louder. My father's going deaf.* ☞ We often describe a person as **hearing-impaired** rather than **deaf. 2 the deaf** *noun* [plural] deaf people: *sign language for the deaf* —**deaf·ness** *noun* [U]

ər	ɪr	ɛr	ɑr	ɔr	ʊr	ʒ	h	ŋ
bird	near	hair	car	north	tour	vision	hat	sing

deaf·en·ing /'dɛfənɪŋ/ adj. very loud: a deaf-ening noise

☆**deal**[1] /dil/ verb [I,T] (p.t., p.p. **dealt** /dɛlt/)
1 deal sth (out); deal (sth) (to sb) to give cards to players in a game of cards: Start by dealing seven cards to each player. **2** to sell illegal drugs: He was arrested for dealing heroin.
IDM deal sb/sth a blow; deal a blow to sb/sth to give sb a shock, etc.: This news dealt a terrible blow to my father.
PHRV deal in sth to buy and sell sth; to trade in sth: She deals in antique furniture.
deal with sb to behave toward sb; to handle sb: He's a difficult man. Nobody really knows how to deal with him.
deal with sth 1 to act in a suitable way in order to solve a problem, complete a task, etc.; to handle sth: I'm not sure how to deal with the situation at work. **2** to have sth as its subject: This chapter deals with writing letters.

☆**deal**[2] /dil/ noun **1** [C] an agreement or ar-rangement, especially in business: We made a deal with a Korean company. ○ I got a terrific deal on these tires today (= I bought them for a low price). **2** [sing.] (informal) a situation: What's the deal with Bob? He's in a rotten mood. ○ Here's the deal: Diane says she can help us, but only for a short time.
IDM big deal ⇨ BIG[1]
a good/great deal (of sth) (used with un-countable nouns) a lot (of sth): I spent a great deal of time on this report.
strike a deal (with sb) ⇨ STRIKE[2]

☆**deal·er** /'dilər/ noun [C] **1** a person whose business is buying and selling things: a dealer in gold and silver ○ a drug dealer **2** the person who gives the cards to the players in a game of cards

deal·er·ship /'dilərʃɪp/ noun [C] a business that sells a particular type of product: a used car dealership

☆**deal·ing** /'dilɪŋ/ noun **1** [U] buying and sell-ing: drug dealing **2 dealings** [plural] rela-tions, especially in business: We are investigating his financial dealings with known criminals.

dealt p.t., p.p. of DEAL[1]

dean /din/ noun [C] an important official at a college or university: the dean of students

'dean's list noun [C] a list of the names of students at a college or university who have earned high grades: Susan made the dean's list (= her name was put on the list) every semester.

☆**dear**[1] /dɪr/ adj. **1** (used at the beginning of a letter before the name or title of the person you are writing to): Dear Sarah,... ○ Dear Sir or Madam,... **2 dear (to sb)** loved by or im-portant to sb: She's one of my dearest friends. ○ It was a subject that was very dear to him.

dear[2] /dɪr/ noun [C] (old-fashioned) (used for speaking to sb you know well or love): Did you have a nice day, dear?

dear[3] /dɪr/ interj. (old-fashioned) (used for ex-pressing disappointment, sadness, surprise, etc.): Oh dear! I spilled the wine.

dear·ly /'dɪrli/ adv. **1** very much: He loves her dearly. **2** (formal) at great cost: I've already paid dearly (= suffered a lot) for that mistake.

☆**death** /dɛθ/ noun **1** [C,U] the end of sb/sth's life; dying: He continued to write until his death. ○ There were two deaths and many other people were injured. ○ The police do not know the cause of death. ○ There was no food and people were starving to death. **2** [U] the end (of sth): the death of communism
IDM put sb to death (usually passive) to kill sb, usually as a punishment: The general had ordered the prisoners to be put to death.
sick to death of sb/sth ⇨ SICK

the 'death penalty noun [sing.] the punish-ment of being killed

death 'row noun [U] the part of a prison for people who will be killed as a punishment for crimes they have committed: prisoners on death row

'death toll noun [C] the number of people killed in a disaster, war, etc.

de·bat·a·ble /dɪ'beɪtəbl/ adj. not certain; something that you could argue about

☆**de·bate**[1] /dɪ'beɪt/ noun **1** [C] a formal argu-ment or discussion of a question at a public meeting or in Congress, etc. At the end there may be a vote: a debate in the state legislature on tax reform **2** [C,U] a discussion; talk ex-pressing different opinions: There's been a lot of debate about the cause of acid rain.

☆**de·bate**[2] /dɪ'beɪt/ verb [I,T] **1** to discuss sth in a formal way or at a public debate1 **2** to think about or discuss sth before deciding what to do: They debated (about) whether to go or not.

de·bris /də'bri; 'deɪ-/ noun [U] pieces from sth that has crashed to the ground or been de-stroyed: debris from the plane crash

☆**debt** /dɛt/ noun **1** [C] a sum of money that you owe sb: She borrowed a lot of money and she's still paying off the debt. ○ the national debt (= that the government owes to other countries and organizations) **2** [U] the state of owing money: After he lost his job, he got into debt. **3** [C, usually sing.] (formal) something that you owe sb, e.g. because they have helped or been kind to you: He acknowledged his debt to his family and friends for their support.
IDM be in debt/out of debt to owe/not owe money
be in sb's debt (formal) to feel grateful to sb for sth that he/she has done for you

debt·or /'dɛtər/ noun [C] a person who owes money

de·but (also **début**) /deɪ'bju/ noun [C] a first

decade

appearance in public of an actor, etc.: *She made her debut at Carnegie Hall in 1989.*

☆ **de·cade** /ˈdɛkeɪd/ *noun* [C] a period of ten years

de·caf /ˈdikæf/ *noun* [U] coffee that has had most or all of the caffeine removed: *Regular or decaf?*

de·caf·fein·at·ed /ˌdiˈkæfəneɪtəd/ *adj.* (used about coffee or tea) with most or all of the caffeine removed

de·cap·i·tate /dɪˈkæpəteɪt/ *verb* [T] (*formal*) to cut off a person's head

☆ **de·cay¹** /dɪˈkeɪ/ *verb* [I] **1** to become bad or fall apart: *The old farm buildings had been left to decay.* ○ *Children's teeth will decay if they eat too much candy.* **2** to become weaker or less efficient: *The Roman Empire had by then begun to decay.*

de·cay² /dɪˈkeɪ/ *noun* [U] the process of decaying, or the state reached after decaying: *tooth decay.* ○ *Many of the old houses had fallen into decay.*

de·ceased /dɪˈsist/ *adj.* (*formal*) **1** dead: *He inherited the house from his deceased parents.* **2 the deceased** *noun* [sing.] a person who has died, especially one who has died recently: *Many friends of the deceased were present at the funeral.*

de·ceit /dɪˈsit/ *noun* [U] dishonest behavior; trying to make sb believe sth that is not true

de·ceit·ful /dɪˈsitfl/ *adj.* dishonest, and intending to make sb believe sth that is not true —**de·ceit·ful·ly** *adv.* **de·ceit·ful·ness** *noun* [U]

☆ **de·ceive** /dɪˈsiv/ *verb* [T] **deceive sb/ yourself (into doing sth)** to try to make sb believe sth that is not true: *Her story didn't deceive me – I knew it was a lie.* ○ *You're deceiving yourself if you think there's an easy solution to the problem.* ☞ The noun is **deception** or **deceit.**

☆ **De·cem·ber** /dɪˈsɛmbər/ *noun* [C,U] (*abbr.* **Dec.**) the twelfth month of the year, coming before January ☞ For examples of the use of the months in sentences, look at **January.**

de·cen·cy /ˈdisənsi/ *noun* [U] moral or correct behavior: *She had the decency to admit that it was her fault.*

de·cent /ˈdisənt/ *adj.* **1** satisfactory; of an acceptable standard: *All she wants is a decent job with decent pay.* **2** (used about people or behavior) honest and respectable: *All decent people are appalled by such terrible crimes.* **3** not likely to embarrass or offend sb: *I can't come to the door – I'm not decent* (= I'm not dressed). ☞ The opposite is **indecent.** —**decent·ly** *adv.*

de·cep·tion /dɪˈsɛpʃn/ *noun* [C,U] deceiving or being deceived; a trick: *He had obtained the secret papers by deception.*

de·cep·tive /dɪˈsɛptɪv/ *adj.* likely to give a false impression or to make sb believe sth that is not true: *The water is deceptive. It's much*

deeper than it looks. —**de·cep·tive·ly** *adv.*: *She made the task sound deceptively easy.*

de·ci·bel /ˈdɛsəbl; -bɛl/ *noun* [C] a measurement of how loud a sound is

☆ **de·cide** /dɪˈsaɪd/ *verb* **1** [I,T] to think about two or more possibilities and choose one of them: *There are so many to choose from – I can't decide!* ○ *She decided against borrowing the money.* ○ *They decided on a name for the baby.* ○ *He decided that it was too late to go.* ○ *You'll have to decide what to do.* ○ *We decided not to invite Isabel.* **2** [T] to influence sth so that it produces a particular result: *Your votes will decide the winner.* ☞ The noun is **decision.** The adjective is **decisive.**

de·cid·ed /dɪˈsaɪdəd/ *adj.* clear; definite: *There has been a decided improvement in his work.* —**de·cid·ed·ly** *adv.*: *The new office is decidedly better than the old one.*

de·cid·u·ous /dɪˈsɪdʒuəs/ *adj.* (used about a tree) of a type that loses its leaves every year ☞ Look at **evergreen.**

dec·i·mal¹ /ˈdɛsəml/ *adj.* based on or counted in units of ten

dec·i·mal² /ˈdɛsəml/ *noun* [C] part of a number, written after a dot (**decimal point**) and expressed in tenths, hundredths, etc.: *Three quarters expressed as a decimal is 0.75.*

de·ci·pher /dɪˈsaɪfər/ *verb* [T] to succeed in reading or understanding sth that is not clear: *It's impossible to decipher his handwriting.*

☆ **de·ci·sion** /dɪˈsɪʒn/ *noun* **1** [C,U] **a decision (on/about sth); a decision (to do sth); a decision (that…)** a choice or judgment that you make after thinking about various possibilities: *"Have you made a decision yet?" "No, I'm still thinking about it!"* ○ *I realize now that I made the wrong decision.* ○ *It took us several hours to reach a decision.* ○ *There were good reasons for his decision to leave.* **2** [U] being able to decide clearly and quickly

de·ci·sive /dɪˈsaɪsɪv/ *adj.* **1** making sth certain or final: *the decisive battle of the war* **2** having the ability to make clear decisions quickly: *It's no use hesitating. Be decisive.* —**de·ci·sive·ly** *adv.*

deck /dɛk/ *noun* [C] **1** one of the floors of a ship: *The restaurant is on the upper deck.* **2** a complete set of playing cards ☞ Look at the note at **card.** **3** a platform, usually made of wood, that is attached to the back of a house: *Let's go sit out on the deck.* ☞ Look also at **patio, porch** and **veranda.**

IDM **on deck** on the floor of a ship which is in the open air: *I'm going out on deck for some fresh air.*

i	ɪ	ɛ	æ	ɑ	ɔ	ʌ	ʊ	u
see	sit	ten	cat	hot	saw	cup	put	too

☆ **dec·la·ra·tion** /ˌdɛkləˈreɪʃn/ *noun* **1** [C,U] a statement: *a strong declaration of support* ○ *Fighting has started without declaration of war.* ○ *the Declaration of Independence* (= the official document, written in 1776, that said that the U.S. was an independent country) **2** [C] a written statement giving information on goods or income on which you have to pay tax: *If you're sending a package abroad, you have to fill out a customs declaration form.*

☆ **de·clare** /dɪˈklɛr/ *verb* [T] **1** to announce or to make sth known, especially in an official or forceful way: *to declare war on another country* ○ *The republic has declared its independence.* ○ *"I've had enough of this," she declared.* **2** to give information about goods or income on which you have to pay taxes: *You must declare all your income on this form.*

☆ **de·cline¹** /dɪˈklaɪn/ *verb* **1** [I,T] (*formal*) to refuse, usually politely: *Thank you for the invitation, but unfortunately I have to decline.* ○ *The candidate declined to make a statement.* **2** [I] to become weaker, smaller or less good: *declining profits* ○ *The standard of education has declined in this country.*

de·cline² /dɪˈklaɪn/ *noun* [C,U] **(a) decline (in sth)** a process or period of becoming weaker, smaller or less satisfactory: *a decline in sales* ○ *As an industrial power, the country is in decline.*

de·code /ˌdiˈkoʊd/ *verb* [T] to find the meaning of sth that is in code ☞ The opposite is **encode**.

de·com·pose /ˌdikəmˈpoʊz/ *verb* [I,T] to decay or to make sth decay: *The body was so badly decomposed that it couldn't be identified.*

dé·cor (*also* **decor**) /deɪˈkɔr; ˈdeɪkɔr/ *noun* [U, sing.] the furniture and decoration in a place

☆ **dec·o·rate** /ˈdɛkəreɪt/ *verb* [T] **decorate sth (with sth)** to add sth in order to make a thing more attractive to look at: *Decorate the cake with cherries and nuts.* ○ *to decorate a Christmas tree*

☆ **dec·o·ra·tion** /ˌdɛkəˈreɪʃn/ *noun* **1** [C,U] something that is added to sth in order to make it look more attractive: *We put up decorations for Jason's birthday party.* **2** [C] a military award that sb wears on his/her uniform

dec·o·ra·tive /ˈdɛkərətɪv/ *adj.* attractive to look at; added to sth to make it prettier: *The cloth had a decorative lace edge.*

de·coy /ˈdikɔɪ/ *noun* [C] a person or object that is used to lead sb/sth in the wrong direction

☆ **de·crease¹** /dɪˈkris; ˈdikris/ *verb* [I,T] to become or to make sth smaller or less: *Profits have decreased by 15%.* ○ *Decrease your speed when you are approaching an intersection.* ☞ The opposite is **increase**.

☆ **de·crease²** /ˈdikris/ *noun* [C,U] **(a) decrease (in sth)** a process of becoming or making sth smaller or less; a reduction: *a decrease in the number of students* ○ *a 10% decrease in sales*

de·cree¹ /dɪˈkri/ *noun* [C] an official order given by a government, a ruler, etc.

de·cree² /dɪˈkri/ *verb* [T] (*p.t., p.p.* **de·creed**) (used about a government, a ruler, etc.) to give an official order

de·crep·it /dɪˈkrɛpɪt/ *adj.* old and in very bad condition

ded·i·cate /ˈdɛdəkeɪt/ *verb* [T] **1** to give all your energy, time, efforts, etc. to sth: *He dedicated his life to helping the poor.* **2 dedicate sth to sb** to say that sth is in honor of sb: *She dedicated the book she had written to her brother.*

☆ **ded·i·cat·ed** /ˈdɛdəkeɪtəd/ *adj.* **1** giving a lot of your energy, time, efforts, etc. to sth that you believe to be important: *dedicated nurses and doctors* **2** (only *before* before a noun) made or used for only one specific task: *a dedicated fax line*

ded·i·ca·tion /ˌdɛdəˈkeɪʃn/ *noun* **1** [U] being willing to give your time and energy to sth: *I admire her dedication to her career.* **2** [C] a message at the beginning of a book or before a piece of music is played, saying that it is for a particular person

de·duce /dɪˈdus/ *verb* [T] to form an opinion using the facts that you already know: *From his name, I deduced that he was Polish.* ☞ The noun is **deduction**.

de·duct /dɪˈdʌkt/ *verb* [T] **deduct sth (from sth)** to take sth such as money or points away from a total amount: *Social Security payments are deducted from your salary.* ○ *Points will be deducted for sloppy work.*

de·duct·i·ble¹ /dɪˈdʌktəbl/ *adj.* that can be taken away from a total amount or number: *tax-deductible business expenses*

de·duct·i·ble² /dɪˈdʌktəbl/ *noun* [C] an amount of money that sb must pay before his/her insurance pays the rest of the cost of sth: *My health insurance policy has a $500 deductible.*

de·duc·tion /dɪˈdʌkʃn/ *noun* [C,U] **1** something that you work out from facts that you already know; the skill of reasoning in this way: *It was a brilliant piece of deduction by the detective.* **2 deduction (from sth)** taking away an amount or number from a total; the amount or number taken away from the total: *What is your total income after deductions?* (= when taxes, insurance, etc. are taken away)

deed /did/ *noun* [C] (*formal*) something that you do; an action: *Deeds are more important than words.*

deem /dim/ *verb* [T] (*formal*) to consider sth: *He did not even deem it necessary to apologize.*

☆ **deep¹** /dip/ *adj.* **1** going a long way down from top to bottom: *the deep end of a swimming pool* ○ *to dig a deep hole* ○ *a coat with deep pockets* ☞ The noun is **depth**. **2** going a long

ə	y	w	t̬	eɪ	aɪ	ɔɪ	aʊ	oʊ
about	yes	woman	butter	say	five	boy	now	go

D

way from front to back: *deep shelves* **3** measuring a particular amount from top to bottom or from front to back: *The water is only three feet deep at this end of the pool.* **4** (used about sounds) low: *a deep voice* **5** (used about colors) dark; strong: *a deep red* **6** strongly felt; serious: *Please accept my deepest sympathy on this sad occasion.* ○ *The country is in a deep recession.* **7** (used about a breath) taking in or letting out a lot of air: *Take a few deep breaths.* **8** concentrating on or involved in sth: *She was deep in thought.* ○ *deep sleep* **9** thorough, able to deal with the difficult parts of sth: *His books show a deep understanding of human nature.* —**deep·ly** *adv.*: *a deeply unhappy person* ○ *to breathe deeply* ☞ The noun is **depth**.

☆ **deep²** /dip/ *adv.* a long way down or inside sth: *The ship sank deep into the sea.* ○ *They talked deep into the night.*

IDM **deep down** in what you really think or feel: *I tried to appear optimistic, but deep down I knew there wasn't any hope.*

☆ **deep·en** /ˈdipən/ *verb* [I,T] to become or to make sth deep or deeper: *The river deepens here.* ○ *This bad news deepened the atmosphere of depression.*

deep-'rooted (*also* **deep-'seated**) *adj.* strongly felt or believed and therefore difficult to change: *deep-seated prejudices*

the ,Deep 'South *noun* [sing.] an area in the southeastern United States, including Louisiana, Mississippi, Alabama, Georgia and South Carolina ☞ Look at the note at **White House.**

deer

antlers

buck

doe

☆ **deer** /dɪr/ *noun* [C] (*pl.* **deer**) a large wild grass-eating animal. The male has horns shaped like branches (**antlers**).

☞ A male deer is called a **buck**. The female is a **doe** and a young deer a **fawn**. **Venison** is the meat from deer.

de·face /dɪˈfeɪs/ *verb* [T] to spoil the way sth looks by writing on or marking the surface of it: *Vandals defaced the statue with graffiti.*

de·fault¹ /dɪˈfɔlt/ *noun* **1** [sing.] (*computing*) a course of action taken by a computer when it is not given any other instruction **2** [C,U] not doing sth that you should do by law: *Defaults on student loans* (= people failing to pay them back) *have increased in recent years.*

IDM **by default** because nothing happened, not because of successful effort: *They won by default because the other team didn't show up.*

de·fault² /dɪˈfɔlt/ *verb* [I] not to do sth that you should do by law: *If you default on the loan payments* (= you don't pay them), *the car will be taken back.*

☆ **de·feat¹** /dɪˈfit/ *verb* [T] **1** to win a game, a fight, a vote, etc. against sb: *In the last game, Ohio State defeated Michigan by 14 points to 6.* **2** to prevent sth from succeeding: *The local residents are determined to defeat the city's building plans.* **3** to be too difficult for sb to do or understand: *I've tried to figure out what's wrong with the car, but it defeats me.*

de·feat² /dɪˈfit/ *noun* **1** [C] an occasion when sb is defeated: *This season they have had two victories and three defeats.* **2** [U] defeating or being defeated: *She refused to admit defeat and kept on trying.*

def·e·cate /ˈdɛfəkeɪt/ *verb* [I] (*formal*) to pass solid waste materials from the bowels ☞ It is more common to say **go to the bathroom.** Look also at **poop.**

de·fect¹ /ˈdifɛkt; dɪˈfɛkt/ *noun* [C] something that is wrong with or missing from sb/sth: *a speech defect* ○ *defects in the education system* —**de·fec·tive** /dɪˈfɛktɪv/ *adj.*: *The accident was caused by a defective bolt.*

de·fect² /dɪˈfɛkt/ *verb* [I] to leave your country, a political party, etc. and go to or join an opposing one: *a spy who defected from a communist country* —**de·fec·tion** *noun* [C,U]

☆ **de·fend** /dɪˈfɛnd/ *verb* **1** [T] **defend sb/sth (against sb/sth)** to act, especially to fight, to protect sb/sth: *Would you be able to defend yourself if someone attacked you on the street?* **2** [T] **defend sb/sth (against sb/sth)** to say or write sth to support sb/sth: *The candidate went on television to defend her policy.* **3** [T] (in law) to speak for sb who is accused of sth in a court of law **4** [I,T] to try to stop the other team or player from scoring: *They defended well and managed to hold onto their lead.* **5** [T] to try to win a game so that you remain champion: *She successfully defended her title.*

☆ **de·fen·dant** /dɪˈfɛndənt/ *noun* [C] a person who is accused of sth in a court of law

de·fend·er /dɪˈfɛndər/ *noun* [C] a person who defends sb/sth, especially in sports ☞ Look also at **public defender.**

☆ **de·fense¹** /dɪˈfɛns/ *noun* **1** [U] **defense (against sth)** action to protect sb/sth from attack: *Would you fight in defense of your country?* **2** [C] **a defense (against sth)** something that protects sb/sth from sth or that is used for fighting against attack: *to build up a country's defenses* ○ *the body's defenses against disease* **3** [U] the military equipment, forces, etc. for protecting a country: *the Defense Department* ○ *Defense spending can be cut if fewer weapons are needed.* **4** [C,U] something that

you say or write to support sb/sth that is being attacked or accused: *He made a strong defense of the President's policy.* ○ *I must say in her defense that I have always found her very reliable.* **5** [C] (in law) an argument in support of the accused person in a court of law: *His defense was that he was only carrying out orders.* **6 the defense** [sing.] (in law) the accused person in a court of law and the lawyer or lawyers who are acting for him/her: *The defense claims that many of the witnesses were lying.* ○ *a defense attorney*

de·fense² /'difɛns; dɪ'fɛns/ *noun* [C,U, usually sing.] (in sports) the players who try to prevent the other team from scoring points; the action of these players: *The Vikings' defense was unable to stop Jackson's spectacular touchdown pass.*

de·fense·less /dɪ'fɛnsləs/ *adj.* unable to defend yourself against attack

☆ **de·fen·sive¹** /dɪ'fɛnsɪv/ *adj.* **1** used or intended for protecting sb/sth from attack: *The troops took up a defensive position.* **2** showing that you feel that sb is accusing or criticizing you: *When I asked him about his new job, he became very defensive and tried to change the subject.*

de·fen·sive² /dɪ'fɛnsɪv/ *noun*
IDM **on the defensive** ready to defend yourself against attack or criticism

de·fer /dɪ'fər/ *verb* [T] (**de·fer·ring; de·ferred**) (*formal*) to leave sth until a later time

def·er·ence /'dɛfərəns/ *noun*
IDM **in deference to sb/sth** (*formal*) because you respect and do not wish to upset sb: *In deference to her father's wishes, she didn't mention the subject again.*

de·fi·ance /dɪ'faɪəns/ *noun* [U] open refusal to obey: *As an act of defiance, they continued to play loud music.*
IDM **in defiance of sb/sth** openly refusing to obey sb/sth

de·fi·ant /dɪ'faɪənt/ *adj.* showing open refusal to obey —**de·fi·ant·ly** *adv.*

de·fi·cien·cy /dɪ'fɪʃənsi/ *noun* (*pl.* **de·fi·cien·cies**) **1** [C,U] a condition of not having enough of sth; a lack: *a vitamin C deficiency* **2** [C] something that is not good enough or that is wrong with sb/sth: *The problems were caused by deficiencies in the design.*

de·fi·cient /dɪ'fɪʃənt/ *adj.* **1 deficient (in sth)** not having enough of sth: *food that is deficient in minerals* **2** not good enough or not complete

def·i·cit /'dɛfəsɪt/ *noun* [C] the amount by which the money you receive is less than the money you have spent: *a trade deficit*

de·fine /dɪ'faɪn/ *verb* [T] **1** to say exactly what a word or idea means: *How would you define "happiness"?* **2** to explain the exact nature of sth clearly: *Something is worrying me, but I can't define exactly what it is.*

☆ **def·i·nite** /'dɛfənət/ *adj.* **1** fixed and unlikely to change; certain: *I'll give you a definite answer in a couple of days.* **2** clear; easy to see or notice: *There has been a definite change in her attitude recently.*

definite 'article *noun* [C] (*grammar*) the name used for the word "the" ☞ Look at **indefinite article.**

☆ **def·i·nite·ly** /'dɛfənətli/ *adv.* certainly; without doubt: *We definitely can't afford such a high price.* ○ *This is definitely not what I expected!* ○ *"Are you coming along tonight?" "Definitely!"*

☆ **def·i·ni·tion** /,dɛfə'nɪʃn/ *noun* [C,U] a statement of the exact meaning of a word or idea

de·fin·i·tive /dɪ'fɪnətɪv/ *adj.* in a form that cannot be changed or that cannot be improved: *This is the definitive version of the document.* —**de·fin·i·tive·ly** *adv.*

de·flate /dɪ'fleɪt; di-/ *verb* **1** [I,T] to become or to make sth smaller by letting the air or gas out: *The balloon slowly deflated and began to come down.* ☞ The opposite is **inflate.** **2** [T] to make sb feel less confident, proud or excited

de·flect /dɪ'flɛkt/ *verb* **1** [I,T] to change direction after hitting sb/sth; to make sth change direction in this way: *The ball was deflected off the rim and into the hoop.* **2** [T] to turn sb or sb's attention away from sth: *The senator hoped to deflect criticism of his financial dealings.*

de·for·es·ta·tion /di,fɔrə'steɪʃn; -,far-/ *noun* [U] cutting down trees over a large area: *Deforestation is a major cause of global warming.*

de·form /dɪ'fɔrm/ *verb* [T] to change the shape of sth so that it is unnatural

de·formed /dɪ'fɔrmd/ *adj.* having an unnatural or ugly shape

de·for·mi·ty /dɪ'fɔrməti/ *noun* (*pl.* **de·for·mi·ties**) [C,U] the state of being deformed; a part of the body that is deformed: *The drug caused women to give birth to babies with severe deformities.*

de·fraud /dɪ'frɔd/ *verb* [T] to get sth from sb by cheating

de·frost /,dɪ'frɔst/ *verb* **1** [T] to remove the ice from sth: *to defrost a fridge* (= by turning it off so that the ice melts) **2** [I,T] (used about frozen food) to return to a normal temperature; to make food do this: *Defrost the chicken thoroughly before cooking.*

deft /dɛft/ *adj.* (used especially about movements) skillful and quick —**deft·ly** *adv.*

de·funct /dɪ'fʌŋkt/ *adj.* no longer existing or in use

de·fuse /,dɪ'fyuz/ *verb* [T] **1** to remove the part of a bomb that would make it explode: *Army experts defused the bomb safely.* **2** to make a situation calmer or less dangerous: *She defused the tension by changing the subject.*

de·fy /dɪ'faɪ/ *verb* [T] (*p.p.* **de·fy·ing**; *3rd pers.*

D

sing. pres. **de·fies**; *p.t.*, *p.p.* **de·fied**) **1** to openly refuse to obey sb/sth: *She defied her parents and continued seeing him.* ☞ The adjective is **defiant** and the noun **defiance**. **2 defy sb to do sth** to tell sb to do sth that you believe to be impossible: *I defy you to prove me wrong.* **3** to make sth impossible or very difficult: *It's such a beautiful place that it defies description.*

de·gen·er·ate /dɪˈdʒɛnəreɪt/ *verb* [I] to fall to a less satisfactory standard; to become worse: *It degenerated from a pleasant discussion into an ugly argument.*

deg·ra·da·tion /ˌdɛgrəˈdeɪʃn/ *noun* [U] **1** degrading sb or being degraded: *the degradation of women* **2** causing the condition of sth to become worse: *environmental degradation*

de·grade /dɪˈgreɪd/ *verb* [T] to make people respect sb less: *It's the type of movie that really degrades women.* —**de·grad·ing** *adj.*: *Having to ask other people for money is degrading.*

☆ **de·gree** /dɪˈgri/ *noun* **1** [C] a measurement of temperature: *Water boils at 212 degrees Fahrenheit (212°F) or 100 degrees Celsius (100° C).* ○ *three degrees below zero/minus three degrees (-3°)* **2** [C] a measurement of angles: *a 45-degree (45°) angle* ○ *An angle of 90 degrees is called a right angle.* **3** [C,U] (used about feelings or qualities) a certain amount or level: *There is always some degree of risk involved in mountain climbing.* ○ *Our lives have changed to a considerable degree.* ○ *I sympathize with her to some degree.* **4** [C] a qualification gained by successfully completing a program at a college or university: *A college degree is one of the requirements for the job.* ○ *He has a bachelor's degree in economics.*

☞ There are many different types of degrees given by U.S. colleges and universities. The first degree that most people receive is a **bachelor's degree**, which is usually given after four years of study. Community colleges also award **associate's degrees** to students who have studied for two years. The official document that students receive when they have finished studying is a **diploma**. Look also at **master's degree** and **Ph.D.**

de·hy·drate /ˌdiˈhaɪdreɪt/ *verb* **1** [T] (usually passive) to remove all the water from food so that it can be kept longer: *dehydrated vegetables* **2** [I,T] to lose or to take water from the body: *If you run for a long time in the heat, you start to dehydrate.* —**de·hy·dra·tion** /ˌdihaɪˈdreɪʃn/ *noun* [U]

de·i·ty /ˈdeɪəṭi; ˈdiəṭi/ *noun* [C] (*pl.* **de·i·ties**) (*formal*) a god or goddess

☆ **de·lay¹** /dɪˈleɪ/ *verb* **1** [T] to make sb/sth slow or late: *The plane was delayed for several hours because of bad weather.* **2** [I,T] **delay (sth/doing sth)** to decide not to do sth until a later time: *I was forced to delay the trip until the following week.*

☆ **de·lay²** /dɪˈleɪ/ *noun* [C,U] a situation or period of time where you have to wait: *Delays are likely on the roads because of heavy traffic.* ○ *Because of the storm, all flights are subject to delay.*

del·e·gate¹ /ˈdɛləgət/ *noun* [C] a person who has been chosen to speak or make decisions for a group of people, especially at a meeting: *delegates at the party's national convention*

del·e·gate² /ˈdɛləgeɪt/ *verb* [I,T] to give sb with a lower job or rank a particular task to carry out: *You can't do everything yourself. You need to learn how to delegate.*

del·e·ga·tion /ˌdɛləˈgeɪʃn/ *noun* **1** [U] giving sb with a lower job or rank a particular task to perform **2** [C] a group of people who have been chosen to speak or make decisions for a larger group of people, especially at a meeting: *The American delegation walked out of the meeting in protest.*

de·lete /dɪˈlit/ *verb* [T] **1** to cross out or leave out part of sth that is written: *If you do not attend class during the first week, your name will be deleted from the class list.* **2** (*computing*) to remove sth (e.g. a word, a sentence, a document, etc.) that is stored in a computer: *Don't delete that file!*

de·le·tion /dɪˈliʃn/ *noun* **1** [U] the act of deleting **2** [C] part of sth written or printed (e.g. a word, a sentence, a paragraph, etc.) that is deleted

del·i /ˈdɛli/ *noun* [C] (*informal*) = DELICATESSEN: *the deli counter at the grocery store*

☆ **de·lib·er·ate¹** /dɪˈlɪbərət; -brət/ *adj.* **1** done on purpose; planned: *Was it an accident or was it deliberate?* **2** done slowly and carefully, without hurrying: *She spoke in a calm, deliberate voice.*

de·lib·er·ate² /dɪˈlɪbəreɪt/ *verb* [I,T] (*formal*) to think about or discuss sth thoroughly before making a decision: *The jury deliberated for two days before announcing their verdict.*

☆ **de·lib·er·ate·ly** /dɪˈlɪbərəṭli; -brəṭli/ *adv.* **1** on purpose; intentionally: *I didn't break it deliberately – it was an accident.* **2** slowly and carefully, without hurrying

de·lib·er·a·tion /dɪˌlɪbəˈreɪʃn/ *noun* **1** [C,U] discussion or thinking about sth: *After much deliberation, I decided to reject the offer.* **2** [U] slowness and carefulness; lack of hurry: *He spoke with great deliberation.*

del·i·ca·cy /ˈdɛlɪkəsi/ *noun* (*pl.* **del·i·ca·cies**) **1** [C] a type of food that is considered particularly good: *Try this dish – it's a local delicacy.* **2** [U] using or needing particular care or skill so as not to offend sb: *She approached the issue with great delicacy.* **3** [U] the quality of being fine, light or detailed: *the delicacy of the antique china cups*

☆ **del·i·cate** /ˈdɛlɪkət/ *adj.* **1** fine or thin; easy to damage or break: *delicate skin* ○ *delicate china teacups* **2** (used about colors, flavors, etc.)

i	ɪ	ɛ	æ	ɑ	ɔ	ʌ	ʊ	u
see	sit	ten	cat	hot	saw	cup	put	too

light and pleasant; not strong: *a delicate shade of pale blue* **3** requiring skillful treatment and care: *a very delicate operation* **4** (*old-fashioned*) frequently sick or easily made sick: *He was a delicate child and often in the hospital.*

del·i·cate·ly /ˈdɛlɪkətli/ *adv.* **1** lightly, gently or finely: *delicately painted vases* **2** with skillful and careful movement: *She stepped delicately over the broken glass.* **3** carefully so as not to offend sb or to cause problems: *a delicately balanced agreement*

del·i·ca·tes·sen /ˌdɛlɪkəˈtɛsn/(also *informal* **deli**) *noun* [C] a store that sells foods such as meat, cheese and salads that are ready to eat and do not need to be cooked

☆ **de·li·cious** /dɪˈlɪʃəs/ *adj.* having a very pleasant taste or smell: *What are you cooking? It smells delicious.*

de·light¹ /dɪˈlaɪt/ *noun* **1** [U] great pleasure; joy: *She laughed with delight as she opened the present.* **2** [C] something that gives sb great pleasure: *The story is a delight to read.*

☆ **de·light²** /dɪˈlaɪt/ *verb* [T] to give sb great pleasure: *She delighted the audience by singing all her old songs.*

PHRV **delight in sth/in doing sth** to get great pleasure from sth: *He delights in playing tricks on people.*

☆ **de·light·ed** /dɪˈlaɪtəd/ *adj.* **delighted (about/at/with sth); delighted (to do sth/that ...)** extremely pleased: *"How do you feel about winning today?" "Delighted."* ○ *She was delighted about getting the job/that she got the job.* ○ *"Would you like to come for dinner?" "Thanks – I'd be delighted to."*

de·light·ful /dɪˈlaɪtfl/ *adj.* giving sb great pleasure: *a delightful view* ○ *He has a delightful sense of humor.* —**de·light·ful·ly** *adv.*

de·lin·quen·cy /dəˈlɪŋkwənsi/ *noun* [U] bad or criminal behavior, usually among young people

de·lin·quent /dəˈlɪŋkwənt/ *adj.* (usually used about a young person) behaving badly and often breaking the law: *delinquent children* —**de·lin·quent** *noun* [C]: *a juvenile delinquent*

de·lir·i·ous /dɪˈlɪriəs/ *adj.* **1** speaking or thinking in a crazy way, often because of a fever **2** extremely happy —**de·lir·i·ous·ly** *adv.*

☆ **de·liv·er** /dɪˈlɪvər/ *verb* **1** [I,T] to take sth (goods, letters, etc.) to the place requested or to the address on it: *Your order will be delivered within five days.* **2** [T] to help a mother to give birth to her baby: *The doctor who delivered the baby said she was lucky to be alive.* **3** [T] to give sth (a speech, a warning, etc.): *She delivered a long lecture to the employees about efficiency.* **4** [I] **deliver (on sth)** (*informal*) to do or give sth that you have promised: *He's made a lot of promises, but can he deliver?*

de·liv·er·y /dɪˈlɪvəri/ *noun* (*pl.* **de·liv·er·ies**) **1** [U] the act of taking sth (goods, letters, pack-

ages, etc.) to the place or person who has ordered it or whose address is on it: *Please allow 28 days for delivery.* ○ *a delivery truck* **2** [C] an occasion when sth is delivered: *Mail deliveries may be delayed because of the blizzard.* **3** [C] something (letters, packages, etc.) that is delivered **4** [C] the process of giving birth to a baby: *an easy delivery*

del·ta /ˈdɛltə/ *noun* [C] an area of flat land shaped like a triangle where a river divides into smaller rivers flowing toward the ocean

del·uge¹ /ˈdɛlyudʒ/ *noun* [C] **1** a sudden very heavy fall of rain; a flood **2** a very large number of things that happen or arrive at the same time: *The program was followed by a deluge of complaints from the public.*

del·uge² /ˈdɛlyudʒ/ *verb* [T] (usually passive) to send or give sb/sth a very large quantity of sth, all at the same time: *They were deluged with applications for the job.*

de·lu·sion /dɪˈluʒn/ *noun* [C,U] a false belief: *He seems to be under the delusion that he's popular.*

de·luxe /dɪˈlʌks/ *adj.* of extremely high quality and more expensive than usual: *a deluxe hotel*

delve /dɛlv/ *verb* [I] **delve into sth** to search inside sth: *She delved into the bag and brought out a tiny box.*

☆ **de·mand¹** /dɪˈmænd/ *noun* **1** [C] **a demand (for sth/that ...)** a strong request or order that must be obeyed: *a demand for changes in the law* ○ *I was amazed by their demand that I leave immediately.* ☞ Look at the note at **recommend** (2). **2** [U, sing.] **demand (for sth/sb)** the desire or need for sth among a group of people: *We don't stock that product anymore because there is no demand for it.* ○ *the effects of supply and demand on retail prices*

IDM **in demand** wanted by a lot of people: *Air conditioners are always in demand at the beginning of summer.*

make demands on sb/sth to require a large amount of effort from sb or a lot of sth: *Being the club leader makes a lot of demands on my free time.*

☆ **de·mand²** /dɪˈmænd/ *verb* [T] **1** to ask for sth in a way that shows you expect to get it: *I walked into the office and demanded to see the manager.* ○ *She demanded that I pay her immediately.* ○ *Your behavior was disgraceful and I demand an apology.* ☞ Look at the note at **recommend** (2). **2** to ask a question in a rude way: *"What are you doing here?" he demanded.* **3** to require or need: *a sport that demands skill as well as strength*

☆ **de·mand·ing** /dɪˈmændɪŋ/ *adj.* **1** (used about a job, task, etc.) requiring a great deal of effort, care, skill, etc.: *It will be a demanding schedule – I have to go to six cities in six days.* **2** (used about a person) constantly wanting

D

ə	y	w	t̬	eɪ	aɪ	ɔɪ	aʊ	oʊ
about	yes	woman	butter	say	five	boy	now	go

attention or expecting very high standards of people: *a demanding child* ○ *a demanding boss*

de·mise /dɪ'maɪz/ *noun* [sing.] **1** (*formal*) the death of a person: *the President's demise* **2** the unsuccessful end of sth: *Poor business decisions led to the company's demise.*

dem·o /'dɛmoʊ/ *noun* [C] (*pl.* **dem·os**) (*informal*) = DEMONSTRATION(2): *This is just a demo version of the software – the real program will have even more functions.*

☆ **de·moc·ra·cy** /dɪ'mɑkrəsi/ *noun* (*pl.* **de·moc·ra·cies**) **1** [U] a system in which the government of a country is elected by its citizens **2** [C] a country that has this system: *How long has that country been a democracy?* **3** [U] the right of everyone in an organization, etc. to vote on matters that affect them and to be treated equally: *There is a need for more democracy in the company.*

☆ **Dem·o·crat** /'dɛməkræt/ *noun* [C] (*abbr.* **D**) a member or supporter of the Democratic Party of the United States ☞ Look at **Republican**.

☆ **dem·o·crat·ic** /,dɛmə'krætɪk/ *adj.* **1** based on the system of democracy: *democratic elections* ○ *a democratic government* **2** having or supporting equality for all members: *a fully democratic society* **3** **Democratic** connected with the Democratic Party of the United States: *the Democratic senator from Illinois* —**dem·o·crat·i·cal·ly** /-kli/ *adv.*: *a democratically elected government*

☆ **the ˌDemoˌcratic 'Party** *noun* [sing.] one of the two main political parties in the United States

☞ The other main party is the **Republican Party**. Look at the note at **White House**.

de·mol·ish /dɪ'mɑlɪʃ/ *verb* [T] **1** to knock sth down (e.g. a building): *The old houses were demolished and a shopping mall was built in their place.* **2** to destroy sth (an idea, a belief, etc.): *She demolished his argument in one sentence.*

dem·o·li·tion /,dɛmə'lɪʃn/ *noun* [C,U] the act of knocking down or destroying sth

de·mon /'dimən/ *noun* [C] an evil spirit

☆ **dem·on·strate** /'dɛmənstreɪt/ *verb* **1** [T] to show clearly that sth exists or is true; to prove: *The prison escape demonstrates the need for greater security.* **2** [T] to show and explain to sb how to do sth or how sth works: *The crew demonstrated the use of lifejackets just after takeoff.* **3** [I] **demonstrate (against/for sb/sth)** to take part in a public protest or march in which a crowd of people express their opposition to, or support of, sb/sth: *Enormous crowds have been demonstrating for human rights.*

☆ **dem·on·stra·tion** /,dɛmən'streɪʃn/ *noun* **1** [C,U] something that shows clearly that sth exists or is true: *This accident is a clear demonstration of the system's faults.* **2** (also *infor-*

mal **demo**) [C,U] an act of showing or explaining to sb how to do sth or how sth works: *The salesclerk gave me a demonstration of what the computer could do.* **3** [C] **a demonstration (against/for sb/sth)** a public protest or march in which a crowd of people show how they oppose or support sb/sth: *Thousands took part in demonstrations for greater political freedom.*

de·mon·stra·tive /də'mɑnstrətɪv/ *adj.* (used about a person) showing feelings, especially affection, openly

dem·on·stra·tor /'dɛmənstreɪtər/ *noun* [C] a person who takes part in a public protest or march

de·mor·al·ize /dɪ'mɔrəlaɪz; -'mɑr-/ *verb* [T] to make sb lose confidence or the courage to continue doing sth: *Repeated defeats demoralized the team.* —**de·mor·al·iz·ing** *adj.*: *The layoffs had a demoralizing effect on the whole company.*

de·mure /dɪ'myʊr/ *adj.* (used especially about a girl or young woman) shy, quiet and well behaved

den /dɛn/ *noun* [C] **1** the hidden home of certain wild animals, e.g. lions **2** a secret meeting place: *a den of thieves* **3** a room in a house where people go to relax, watch television, etc.

de·ni·al /dɪ'naɪəl/ *noun* **1** [C] a statement that sth is not true: *The mayor issued a denial about his involvement in the scandal.* **2** [U] refusing to believe that sth is true: *I think Mary's still in denial about her son's drug use.* **3** [C,U] **(a) denial (of sth)** refusing to allow sb to have or do sth: *a denial of personal freedom* ☞ The verb is **deny**.

den·im /'dɛnəm/ *noun* [U] a thick cotton material (often blue) that is used for making clothes, e.g. jeans

de·nom·i·na·tion /dɪ,nɑmə'neɪʃn/ *noun* [C] a religious group that is part of a larger religious organization; a particular type of religious group: *Various denominations hold services in the hospital chapel.*

de·note /dɪ'noʊt/ *verb* [T] to indicate or be a sign of sth; to mean: *What does* [U] *denote in this dictionary?*

de·nounce /dɪ'naʊns/ *verb* [T] to say publicly that sth is wrong; to be very critical of a person in public: *The President denounced the bombing as a cowardly act of terrorism.* ☞ The noun is **denunciation**.

dense /dɛns/ *adj.* **1** containing a lot of things or people close together: *dense forests* ○ *areas of dense population* **2** difficult to see through: *dense fog* **3** (*informal*) unintelligent; stupid: *How can you be so dense?* —**dense·ly** *adv.*: *densely populated*

den·si·ty /'dɛnsəti/ *noun* (*pl.* **den·si·ties**) **1** [U] the number of things or people in a place in relation to its area: *the density of population*

ər	ɪr	ɛr	ɑr	ɔr	ʊr	ʒ	h	ŋ
bird	near	hair	car	north	tour	vision	hat	sing

2 [C,U] (*technical*) the relation of the weight of a substance to the space it occupies

dent¹ /dɛnt/ *noun* [C] a hollow place in the surface of sth hard, especially metal, that is the result of sth hitting or pressing against it: *This can has a dent in it.*

dent² /dɛnt/ *verb* [T] to damage sth by hitting it and making a hollow place in it: *I hit a wall and dented the front of the car.*

den·tal /ˈdɛntl/ *adj.* connected with teeth: *dental care*

☆ **den·tist** /ˈdɛntɪst/ *noun* [C] a person whose job is to take care of people's teeth: *You should go to the dentist for a checkup.* ○ *I have a dentist's appointment tomorrow.*

den·tures /ˈdɛntʃərz/ *noun* [plural] teeth that are made of plastic, etc., worn by a person who has lost his/her natural teeth

de·nun·ci·a·tion /dɪˌnʌnsiˈeɪʃn/ *noun* [C,U] an expression of strong disapproval of sb/sth in public: *a strong denunciation of the invasion* ☞ The verb is **denounce.**

☆ **de·ny** /dɪˈnaɪ/ *verb* [T] (*pres. part.* **de·ny·ing**; *3rd pers. sing. pres.* **de·nies**; *p.t., p.p.* **de·nied**) **1 deny sth/doing sth/that ...** to state that sth is not true: *The mayor denied reports that he had accepted bribes.* ○ *She denied telling lies/that she had told lies.* **2 deny sb sth; deny sth (to sb)** to refuse to allow sb to have sth: *She was denied permission to remain in the country.* ☞ The noun is **denial.**

☆ **de·o·dor·ant** /diˈoʊdərənt/ *noun* [C,U] a chemical substance that you put onto your body to destroy or prevent bad smells

de·part /dɪˈpart/ *verb* [I] (*formal*) to leave a place, usually at the beginning of a trip: *Tour buses depart from Kennedy Plaza every hour.* ☞ The noun is **departure.** Look at the note at **leave¹.**

☆ **de·part·ment** /dɪˈpartmənt/ *noun* [C] (*abbr.* **dept.**) **1** one of the sections into which an organization (e.g. a school or a business) is divided: *The book department is on the second floor.* ○ *She works in the personnel department.* **2** a division of the government responsible for a particular area of activity: *the Department of Defense*

de·part·men·tal /ˌdipartˈmɛntl/ *adj.* concerning a department: *a departmental meeting*

☆ **de'partment store** *noun* [C] a large store that is divided into departments selling many different types of goods

☆ **de·par·ture** /dɪˈpartʃər/ *noun* [C,U] **1** leaving or going away from a place: *Arrivals and departures are shown on screens around the airport.* ○ *Passengers should check in at least one hour before departure.* **2** an action which is different from what is usual or expected: *a departure from normal practice*

☆ **de·pend** /dɪˈpɛnd/ *verb*
IDM **it/that depends** (used alone or at the beginning of a sentence) it is not certain; it is

influenced or decided by sth: *"Can you loan me some money?" "That depends. How much do you want?"* ○ *I don't know whether I'll see him. It depends what time he gets here.*

PHRV **depend on sb/sth** to be sure that sb/sth will help you; to trust sb/sth to do sth: *If you ever need any help, you know you can depend on me.* ○ *You can't depend on the buses. They're always late.*

depend on sb/sth (for sth) to need sb/sth to provide sth: *I depend on my parents for advice.* ○ *Our organization depends on donations from the public.*

depend on sth to be decided or influenced by sb/sth: *His whole future depends on these exams.* ○ *The starting salary will be between $25,000 and $30,000, depending on education and experience.*

de·pend·a·ble /dɪˈpɛndəbl/ *adj.* that can be trusted: *The bus service is usually very dependable.*

de·pend·ence /dɪˈpɛndəns/ *noun* [U] **dependence on sb/sth** the state of needing sb/sth : *The country wants to reduce its dependence on imported oil.*

de·pend·en·cy /dɪˈpɛndənsi/ *noun* [U] the state of being dependent on sb/sth; the state of being unable to live without sth, especially a drug: *a drug dependency clinic*

de·pend·ent¹ /dɪˈpɛndənt/ *noun* [C] a person who depends on sb else for money, a home, food, etc.: *The insurance provides coverage for you and all your dependents.*

de·pend·ent² /dɪˈpɛndənt/ *adj.* **dependent (on sb/sth)** needing sb/sth to support you: *The industry is heavily dependent on government contracts.* ○ *dependent children*

de·pict /dɪˈpɪkt/ *verb* [T] **1** to show sb/sth in a painting or drawing: *a painting depicting a country scene* **2** to describe sb/sth in words: *The novel depicts rural life a century ago.*

de·plete /dɪˈplit/ *verb* [T] to reduce the amount of sth: *We are depleting the world's natural resources.* —**de·ple·tion** /dɪˈpliʃn/ *noun* [U]: *the depletion of the ozone layer*

de·plor·a·ble /dɪˈplɔrəbl/ *adj.* morally bad and deserving disapproval —**de·plor·a·bly** /-əbli/ *adv.*

de·plore /dɪˈplɔr/ *verb* [T] (*formal*) to feel or state that sth is morally bad: *I deplore such dishonest behavior.*

de·ploy /dɪˈplɔɪ/ *verb* [T] **1** to put soldiers or weapons in a position where they can be used **2** to arrange people or things so that they can be used efficiently —**de·ploy·ment** *noun* [U]: *the deployment of troops*

de·port /dɪˈpɔrt/ *verb* [T] to send a foreigner out of a country officially: *A number of illegal immigrants have been deported.* —**de·por·ta·tion** /ˌdipɔrˈteɪʃn/ *noun* [C,U]: *The illegal immigrants face deportation.*

de·pose /dɪˈpoʊz/ *verb* [T] to remove a ruler

tʃ	dʒ	v	θ	ð	s	z	ʃ
chin	June	van	thin	then	so	zoo	she

or leader from power: *There was a revolution and the dictator was deposed.*

☆**de·pos·it¹** /dɪˈpɑzət/ *verb* [T] **1** to put money into an account at a bank: *She deposited $20 a week into her savings account.* **2** to put sth valuable in an official place where it is safe until needed again: *Valuables can be deposited in the hotel safe.* **3** to put sth down somewhere: *He deposited his bags on the floor and sat down.* **4** to leave sth lying on a surface, as the result of a natural or chemical process: *mud deposited by a flood*

de·pos·it² /dɪˈpɑzət/ *noun* [C] **1** a sum of money put into a bank account; the paying of a sum of money into a bank account: *to make a deposit* **2** **a deposit (on sth)** a sum of money which is the first payment for sth, with the rest of the money to be paid later: *Once you have paid a deposit, the merchandise will be held for you.* **3** **a deposit (on sth)** a sum of money that you pay when you rent sth and that you get back when you return it or finish using it without damage: *The rent is $500 a month, plus a $500 deposit.* **4** a substance that has been left on a surface or has developed in the ground as the result of a natural or chemical process: *mineral deposits*

de·pot /ˈdipoʊ/ *noun* [C] **1** a place where military supplies are stored **2** (*old-fashioned*) a small bus or train station, especially in the country or a small town

de·pre·ci·ate /dɪˈpriʃieɪt/ *verb* [I] to lose value, especially as a result of use or age —**de·pre·ci·a·tion** /dɪˌpriʃiˈeɪʃn/ *noun* [C,U]

de·press /dɪˈprɛs/ *verb* [T] **1** to make sb unhappy: *The thought of going to work tomorrow really depresses me.* **2** (used especially in connection with business) to cause sth to become less successful or profitable: *The reduction in the number of tourists has depressed local business.*

☆**de·pressed** /dɪˈprɛst/ *adj.* very unhappy, often for a long period. If you are depressed, you may be suffering from the medical condition of depression: *He's been very depressed ever since he lost his job.*

de·press·ing /dɪˈprɛsɪŋ/ *adj.* making sb feel sad or without hope: *The outlook for the future of the company is very depressing.*

☆**de·pres·sion** /dɪˈprɛʃn/ *noun* **1** [U] a feeling of unhappiness and lack of hope that lasts for a long time. Depression can be a medical condition and may have physical symptoms. **2** [C] a period when the economic situation is bad, with little business activity and many people without a job: *the Great Depression of the 1930s* **3** [C] a hollow part in the surface of sth: *a depression in the ground*

de·prive /dɪˈpraɪv/ *verb* [T] **deprive sb/sth of sth** to prevent sb/sth from having sth; to take away sth from sb: *to deprive people of their rights as citizens* ○ *The prisoners were deprived*

of food. —**dep·ri·va·tion** /ˌdɛprəˈveɪʃn/ *noun* [C,U]: *people suffering from sleep deprivation*

de·prived /dɪˈpraɪvd/ *adj.* not having enough of the basic things in life, such as food, money, etc.: *He came from a deprived background.*

dept. *abbr.* = DEPARTMENT

☆**depth** /dɛpθ/ *noun* **1** [C,U] the distance down from the top surface of sth; the measurement of how deep sth is: *What's the depth of the swimming pool?* ○ *The hole should be one inch in depth.* ☞ picture at **length**. **2** [C,U] the distance from the front to the back: *the depth of a shelf* ☞ picture at **length**. **3** [U] (used about emotions, knowledge, etc.) the amount that a person has: *the depth of his feelings for her* **IDM** **in depth** looking at all the details: *to discuss a problem in depth*
out of your depth in a situation that is too difficult for you: *When they started discussing politics, I felt totally out of my depth.*

dep·u·ty /ˈdɛpyəti/ *noun* [C] (*pl.* **dep·u·ties**) a person with the second-highest rank in a particular organization. A deputy does the work of his/her boss if the boss is absent: *the deputy chief of police* ○ *Sheriff's deputies are investigating a series of thefts from farms.*

de·rail /dɪˈreɪl/ *verb* [I,T] (used about a train) to come off a railroad track; to cause a train to do this —**de·rail·ment** *noun* [C,U]: *Several people were injured in a derailment near Springfield this morning.*

de·ranged /dɪˈreɪndʒd/ *adj.* thinking and behaving in a way that is not normal, especially because of mental illness

der·e·lict /ˈdɛrəlɪkt/ *adj.* no longer used and in bad condition: *a derelict house*

de·ride /dɪˈraɪd/ *verb* [T] (*formal*) to say that sb/sth is ridiculous; to laugh at sth in a cruel way —**de·ri·sion** /dəˈrɪʒn/ *noun* [U]: *Her comments were met with howls of derision.*

de·riv·a·tive¹ /dəˈrɪvətɪv/ *adj.* copied from sth or influenced by sth and therefore not new or original: *a derivative action movie*

de·riv·a·tive² /dəˈrɪvətɪv/ *noun* [C] **1** a form of sth (especially a word) that has developed from the original form: *"Sadness" is a derivative of "sad."* **2** a substance that has been developed from another substance: *The new medication is a derivative of Vitamin A.*

de·rive /dɪˈraɪv/ *verb* **1** [T] (*formal*) to get sth (especially a feeling or an advantage) from sth: *I derive great satisfaction from my work.* **2** [I,T] to come from sth; to have sth as its origin: *The town derives its name from a Native American word for "clear water."*

de·rog·a·to·ry /dəˈrɑgəˌtɔri/ *adj.* expressing a lack of respect for, or a low opinion of sth: *derogatory comments about the standard of my work*

de·scend /dɪˈsɛnd/ *verb* [I,T] (*formal*) to go down to a lower place; to go down sth: *The plane started to descend, and a few minutes*

later we landed. ○ *She descended the stairs slowly.* ☞ The opposite is **ascend.**

IDM **be descended from sb** to have as a relative or relatives in the distant past: *He says he's descended from a Russian prince.*

de·scen·dant /dɪ'sɛndənt/ *noun* [C] a person who is related to sb who lived a long time ago: *She's a descendant of freed slaves.* ☞ Look at **ancestor.**

de·scent /dɪ'sɛnt/ *noun* **1** [C] a movement down to a lower place: *The pilot informed us that we were about to begin our descent.* **2** [U] family origins, especially in connection with a particular country: *He is of Italian descent.*

☆ **des·cribe** /dɪ'skraɪb/ *verb* [T] **describe sb/sth (as sth)** to say what sb/sth is like, or what happened: *Can you describe the bag you lost?* ○ *It's impossible to describe how I felt.* ○ *The thief was described as tall, thin and about twenty years old.* ○ *Would you describe yourself as confident?*

☆ **des·crip·tion** /dɪ'skrɪpʃn/ *noun* **1** [C,U] a picture in words of sb/sth or an account of sth that happened; the ability to describe sb/sth: *The man gave the police a detailed description of the burglar.* **2** [C] a type or kind of sth: *There were animals of every description at the fair.*

des·crip·tive /dɪ'skrɪptɪv/ *adj.* **1** that describes sb/sth: *a piece of descriptive writing* **2** that describes sb/sth in a skillful and interesting way: *She gave a highly descriptive account of the trip.*

de·seg·re·gate /,di'sɛgrəgeɪt/ *verb* [T] to end a system of separating people of different races in a place: *a plan to desegregate the city's public schools* ☞ Look also at **segregate** and **integrate.** —**des·e·gre·ga·tion** /di,sɛgrə-'geɪʃn/ *noun* [U]

de·sert¹ /dɪ'zərt/ *verb* **1** [T] to leave sb/sth, usually forever: *He deserted his wife and went to live with another woman.* **2** [I,T] (used especially about sb in the armed forces) to leave without permission: *He deserted from the army because he didn't want to fight.*

☆ **des·ert²** /'dɛzərt/ *noun* [C,U] a large area of land, usually covered with sand, that has very little water and very few plants: *the Gobi Desert*

de·sert·ed /dɪ'zərtəd/ *adj.* empty, because all the people have left: *The streets are practically deserted on Sunday nights.*

de·sert·er /dɪ'zərtər/ *noun* [C] a person who leaves military duty without permission

☆ **de·serve** /dɪ'zərv/ *verb* [T] (not used in the continuous tenses) to earn sth, especially a suitable reward or punishment, for sth that you have done: *We've done a lot of work and we deserve a break.* ○ *He deserves to be punished severely for such a crime.*

de·serv·ing /dɪ'zərvɪŋ/ *adj.* that deserves

help: *The scholarship will be awarded to a deserving student with good grades.*

☆ **de·sign¹** /dɪ'zaɪn/ *noun* **1** [C] a drawing that shows how sth should be made: *The architect showed us her design for the new theater.* **2** [U] the way in which sth is planned and made or in which the parts of sth are arranged: *Design flaws have been discovered in the car.* **3** [U] the process and skill of making drawings that show how sth should be made: *to study industrial design* ○ *graphic design* **4** [C] a pattern of lines, shapes, etc. that decorate sth: *a T-shirt with a geometric design on it*

☆ **de·sign²** /dɪ'zaɪn/ *verb* **1** [I,T] to plan and make a drawing of how sth will be made: *She designs the interiors of office buildings.* **2** [T] to invent, plan and develop sth for a particular purpose: *The bridge wasn't designed for such heavy traffic.*

des·ig·nate /'dɛzɪgneɪt/ *verb* [T] (*formal*) **1** to give sth a name to show that it has a particular purpose: *This has been designated a historic site.* **2** to choose sb for a particular job or task **3** to show or mark sth: *These arrows designate the emergency exits.*

de·sign·er /dɪ'zaɪnər/ *noun* [C] a person whose job is to make drawings showing how sth will be made: *a fashion designer* ○ *designer clothing* (= made by a famous designer)

de·sir·a·ble /dɪ'zaɪrəbl/ *adj.* **1** wanted, often by many people; worth having: *a desirable neighborhood* (= one that many people would like to live in) ○ *Experience is desirable but not essential for this job.* **2** sexually attractive

☆ **de·sire¹** /dɪ'zaɪər/ *noun* [C,U] **(a) desire (for sth/to do sth) 1** the feeling of wanting sth very much; a strong wish: *the desire for a peaceful solution to the crisis* ○ *I have no desire to visit that place again.* **2** the wish for sexual relations with sb

☆ **de·sire²** /dɪ'zaɪər/ *verb* [T] **1** (*formal*) to want: *They have everything they could possibly desire.* **2** to find sb/sth sexually attractive

☆ **desk** /dɛsk/ *noun* [C] **1** a type of table, often with drawers, that you sit at to write or work: *The students took their books out of their desks.* ○ *a computer that fits easily onto any desk* **2** a table or place in a building where a particular service is provided: *Brochures are available at the information desk.*

desk·top /'dɛsktɑp/ *noun* [C] **1** the flat surface on the top of a desk: *a desktop computer* (= one that fits on the top of a desk) **2** (*computing*) the background picture on a computer screen: *Use the mouse to move the icons on the desktop.*

des·o·late /'dɛsələt/ *adj.* **1** (used about a place) sad, empty and depressing: *desolate wasteland* **2** (used about a person) lonely, very unhappy and without hope

des·o·la·tion /,dɛsə'leɪʃn/ *noun* [U] **1** the state of being empty because all the people have

ə	y	w	t	eɪ	aɪ	ɔɪ	aʊ	oʊ
about	yes	woman	butter	say	five	boy	now	go

left: *All the factories closed, leaving the town in a state of desolation.* **2** the feeling of being lonely and without hope: *He felt utter desolation when his wife died.*

de·spair¹ /dɪˈspɛr/ *noun* [U] the state of having lost all hope: *I felt like giving up in despair.* ○ *Despair drove him to attempt suicide.*

de·spair² /dɪˈspɛr/ *verb* [I] **despair (of sb/sth)** to lose all hope and to feel that there will be no improvement: *We began to despair of ever getting out of debt.*

☆ **des·per·ate** /ˈdɛspərət; -prət/ *adj.* **1** out of control and willing to do anything to change the situation you are in because it is so terrible: *I only took this job because I was desperate.* **2** done with little hope of success, as a last thing to try when everything else has failed: *I made a desperate attempt to persuade her to change her mind.* **3 desperate (for sth/to do sth)** wanting or needing sth very much: *Let's go into a coffee shop. I'm desperate for something to drink.* **4** terrible, very serious: *There is a desperate shortage of doctors in rural areas.* —**des·per·ate·ly** *adv.*: *She desperately needs a heart transplant in order to survive.*

des·per·a·tion /ˌdɛspəˈreɪʃn/ *noun* [U] the feeling or state of being desperate: *She wanted to scream in desperation.*

des·pi·ca·ble /dəˈspɪkəbl/ *adj.* deserving to be hated: *a despicable liar* ○ *a despicable act of terrorism*

de·spise /dɪˈspaɪz/ *verb* [T] to hate sb/sth; to consider sb/sth worthless: *I despise him for lying about me to other people.*

☆ **de·spite** /dɪˈspaɪt/ *prep.* (used to show that sth happened although you would not expect it): *Despite having very little money, they enjoy life.* ○ *The project went ahead despite public opposition.*

de·spon·dent /dɪˈspɑndənt/ *adj.* without hope; expecting no improvement

☆ **des·sert** /dɪˈzɜrt/ *noun* [C,U] something sweet that is eaten after the main part of a meal: *What would you like for dessert – ice cream or fresh fruit?*

des·ti·na·tion /ˌdɛstəˈneɪʃn/ *noun* [C] the place where sb/sth is going or being sent: *I finally reached my destination two hours late.*

des·tined /ˈdɛstənd/ *adj.* **1 destined for sth/ to do sth** sure to or intended to be, have or do sth: *I think she is destined for success.* ○ *He was destined to become one of the country's leading politicians.* **2 destined for ...** on a trip or moving toward a particular place: *They were destined for a new life in a new country.*

des·ti·ny /ˈdɛstəni/ *noun* (*pl.* **des·ti·nies**) **1** [U] a power that people believe influences their lives; fate **2** [C] the things that happen to you in your life, especially things that you do not control: *She felt that it was her destiny to be a great singer.*

des·ti·tute /ˈdɛstətut/ *adj.* not having

things that are necessary in life, such as money, food, a home, etc. —**des·ti·tu·tion** /ˌdɛstəˈtuʃn/ *noun* [U]

☆ **de·stroy** /dɪˈstrɔɪ/ *verb* [T] **1** to damage sth so badly that it can no longer be used or no longer exists: *The building was destroyed by fire.* ○ *The defeat destroyed his confidence.* **2** to kill an animal, especially because it is injured or dangerous: *The horse broke its leg and had to be destroyed.*

de·stroy·er /dɪˈstrɔɪər/ *noun* [C] **1** a person or thing that destroys sth **2** a small warship

☆ **de·struc·tion** /dɪˈstrʌkʃn/ *noun* [U] destroying or being destroyed: *the destruction of the rainforests*

de·struc·tive /dɪˈstrʌktɪv/ *adj.* causing a lot of damage : *destructive weapons* ○ *the destructive effects of alcohol and drugs*

de·tach /dɪˈtætʃ/ *verb* [T] **detach sth (from sth)** to separate sth from sth it is attached to: *Detach the form at the bottom of the page and send it to this address:...*

de·tached /dɪˈtætʃt/ *adj.* not being or not feeling personally involved

de·tach·ment /dɪˈtætʃmənt/ *noun* **1** [U] the fact or feeling of not being personally involved **2** [C] a group of soldiers who have been given a particular task away from the main group

☆ **de·tail¹** /ˈditeɪl; dɪˈteɪl/ *noun* [C,U] a small individual fact, point or piece of information: *Just give me the basic facts. Don't worry about the details.* ○ *For more details on how to join the club, call this number:...* ○ *The work involves close attention to detail.*

IDM **go into detail(s)** to talk or write about the details of sth: *I can't go into detail now because it would take too long.*

in detail including the details; thoroughly: *We haven't discussed the matter in detail yet.*

de·tail² /dɪˈteɪl; ˈditeɪl/ *verb* [T] to give a full list of sth; to describe sth fully: *He detailed all the equipment he needed for the job.*

☆ **de·tailed** /dɪˈteɪld; ˈditeɪld/ *adj.* having many details or giving a lot of attention to details: *a detailed description of the accident*

de·tain /dɪˈteɪn/ *verb* [T] (*formal*) to stop sb from leaving a place; to delay sb: *He was detained by immigration officials at the airport.* ☞ The noun is **detention.**

de·tect /dɪˈtɛkt/ *verb* [T] to notice or discover sth that is difficult to see, feel, etc.: *Traces of blood were detected on his clothes.* —**de·tec·tion** /dɪˈtɛkʃn/ *noun* [U]: *The crime escaped detection for many years.*

☆ **de·tec·tive** /dɪˈtɛktɪv/ *noun* [C] a person, especially a police officer, who tries to solve crimes and find the person who is guilty

de·tec·tor /dɪˈtɛktər/ *noun* [C] an instrument that is used for detecting sth: *a smoke detector*

de·ten·tion /dɪˈtɛnʃn/ *noun* [U] **1** the act of stopping a person from leaving a place, especially by keeping him/her in prison, often for

political reasons ☞ The verb is **detain**. **2** the punishment of having to stay at school after the school day is finished: *I got three hours' detention for skipping class.*

de·ter /dɪˈtər/ *verb* [T] (**de·ter·ring**; **de·terred**) **deter sb (from doing sth)** to make sb decide not to do sth: *Even the high prices didn't deter people from buying tickets.*

de·ter·gent /dɪˈtərdʒənt/ *noun* [C,U] a chemical liquid or powder that is used for cleaning things

de·te·ri·o·rate /dɪˈtɪriəreɪt/ *verb* [I] to become worse: *The political tension is deteriorating into civil war.* —**de·te·ri·o·ra·tion** /dɪˌtɪriəˈreɪʃn/ *noun* [C,U]

de·ter·mi·na·tion /dɪˌtərməˈneɪʃn/ *noun* **1** [U] the quality of having firmly decided to succeed in doing sth, even if it is very difficult or people are against you: *You need great determination to succeed in business.* **2** (*formal*) [C,U] the act of deciding or calculating sth: *The board will make a determination today as to which students will be awarded scholarships.* ○ *the determination of payments on insurance claims*

☆ **de·ter·mine** /dɪˈtərmən/ *verb* [T] **1** to decide or calculate sth: *The results of the tests will determine what treatment you need.* **2** to find sth out: *an attempt to determine the exact position of the enemy submarine*

☆ **de·ter·mined** /dɪˈtərmənd/ *adj.* having firmly decided to succeed in doing sth, even if it is difficult or people are against you: *He is determined to drop out of school, even though his parents want him to stay.*

de·ter·min·er /dɪˈtərmənər/ *noun* [C] (*grammar*) a word that comes before a noun to show how the noun is being used: *"Her," "most" and "those" are all determiners.*

de·ter·rent /dɪˈtərənt/ *noun* [C] something that is intended to stop you from doing sth: *Their punishment will be a deterrent to others.* —**de·ter·rent** *adj.*

de·test /dɪˈtɛst/ *verb* [T] (*formal*) to hate or dislike sb/sth very much: *They absolutely detest each other.*

det·o·nate /ˈdɛtn·eɪt/ *verb* [I,T] to explode or to make sth explode

☆ **de·tour** /ˈditʊr/ *noun* [C] **1** a different route which traffic can take when a road is closed **2** a longer route that you take from one place to another in order to avoid sth or in order to see or do sth: *On our way to the lake, we made a detour to visit Aunt Joan.*

de·tract /dɪˈtrækt/ *verb* [I] **detract from sth** to make sth seem less good or important: *These criticisms in no way detract from the team's achievements.*

det·ri·ment /ˈdɛtrəmənt/ *noun*
IDM **to the detriment of sb/sth** harming or damaging sb/sth: *The new law will be to the detriment of public safety.*

det·ri·men·tal /ˌdɛtrəˈmɛntl/ *adj.* harmful: *Too much alcohol is detrimental to your health.*

de·val·ue /ˌdiˈvælyu/ *verb* [T] to reduce the value of the money of one country in relation to the value of the money of other countries: *The peso has been devalued against the dollar.* —**de·val·u·a·tion** /ˌdivælyuˈeɪʃn/ *noun* [U]

dev·as·tate /ˈdɛvəsteɪt/ *verb* [T] to destroy sth or damage it badly: *a land devastated by war* —**dev·as·ta·tion** /ˌdɛvəˈsteɪʃn/ *noun* [U]: *a scene of total devastation*

dev·as·tat·ed /ˈdɛvəsteɪt̬əd/ *adj.* **1** completely destroyed **2** shocked or very upset: *The community was devastated by the killings.*

dev·as·tat·ing /ˈdɛvəsteɪt̬ɪŋ/ *adj.* **1** that destroys sth completely: *a devastating explosion* **2** that shocks or upsets sb very much: *The factory shutdown was a devastating blow to the workers.*

☆ **de·vel·op** /dɪˈvɛləp/ *verb* **1** [I,T] to grow slowly, increase, or change into sth else; to make sb/sth do this: *to develop from a child into an adult* ○ *a plan to help children develop their natural talents* **2** [T] to begin to have sth: *to develop cancer* **3** [I] to begin to happen or be noticeable: *His symptoms developed soon after we got home.* ○ *Trouble is developing at the border.* **4** [T] to make pictures from a piece of film by using special chemicals: *to develop a roll of film* **5** [T] to build houses, stores, factories, etc. on a piece of land: *This site is being developed for offices.*

☆ **de·vel·oped** /dɪˈvɛləpt/ *adj.* having advanced political and economic systems and a high standard of living: *a highly developed economy*

de·vel·op·er /dɪˈvɛləpər/ *noun* [C] a person or company that plans new projects, such as buildings: *a real estate developer* ○ *a software developer*

de·vel·op·ing /dɪˈvɛləpɪŋ/ *adj.* (used about a country, an area, etc.) trying to develop or improve its economy: *assistance to developing nations*

☆ **de·vel·op·ment** /dɪˈvɛləpmənt/ *noun* **1** [U] developing or being developed: *the history of Japan's development from a feudal to an industrial society* ○ *a child's intellectual development* **2** [C] a new event: *a number of new developments in the situation in the Middle East* **3** [C,U] a new product or the act of making a new product: *a technological development* ○ *research and development* **4** [C] a piece of land on which houses, stores, factories, etc. have been built: *a new housing development*

de·vi·ate /ˈdivieɪt/ *verb* [I] to change the way you think or behave, or to start to behave in a way that is not acceptable to other people: *He never deviated from his principles.*

de·vi·a·tion /ˌdiviˈeɪʃn/ *noun* [C,U] a difference from what is usual or expected, or from what is approved of by society: *a deviation from our usual way of doing things*

D

tʃ	dʒ	v	θ	ð	s	z	ʃ
chin	June	van	thin	then	so	zoo	she

D

☆**de·vice** /dɪˈvaɪs/ *noun* [C] **1** a tool or piece of equipment made for a particular purpose: *a security device which detects movement* ◦ *labor-saving devices such as washing machines and vacuum cleaners* ☞ Look at the note at **tool**. **2** a trick or plan: *Critics dismissed the speech as a political device for winning support.*

☆**dev·il** /ˈdɛvl/ *noun* [C] **1 the Devil** the most powerful evil being, according to the Christian religion ☞ Look at **Satan**. **2** an evil being or spirit **3** (*informal*) a person, especially a child, who behaves badly and causes trouble: *Those little devils threw an egg at my car!*

de·vi·ous /ˈdiviəs/ *adj.* intelligent but not honest or direct: *I wouldn't trust him – he can be very devious.*

de·vise /dɪˈvaɪz/ *verb* [T] to invent a plan, system, etc.: *Scientists have devised a new method of preserving vitamins in foods.*

de·void /dɪˈvɔɪd/ *adj.* (*formal*) **devoid of sth** not having a particular quality; without sth: *to be devoid of hope*

de·vote /dɪˈvoʊt/ *verb* [T] **devote yourself/ sth to sb/sth** to give a lot of time, energy, etc. to sb/sth: *She wanted to devote herself full-time to her music.* ◦ *Schools should devote more time to science.*

☆**de·vot·ed** /dɪˈvoʊt̮əd/ *adj.* loving sb/sth very much: *a devoted husband*

dev·o·tee /ˌdɛvəˈti; -teɪ/ *noun* [C] a person who likes sb/sth very much: *Devotees of science fiction will enjoy this new movie.*

de·vo·tion /dɪˈvoʊʃn/ *noun* [U] **devotion (to sb/sth)** **1** great love: *a mother's devotion to her children* **2** the act of giving a lot of your time, energy, etc. to sb/sth: *devotion to duty* **3** great religious feeling

de·vour /dɪˈvaʊər/ *verb* [T] to eat sth quickly and with enjoyment

de·vout /dɪˈvaʊt/ *adj.* very religious: *a devout Muslim family*

dew /du/ *noun* [U] small drops of water that form on plants, leaves, etc. during the night

di·a·be·tes /ˌdaɪəˈbit̮iz; -ˈbit̮əs/ *noun* [U] a serious disease in which a person's body cannot control the level of sugar in the blood

di·a·bet·ic /ˌdaɪəˈbɛt̮ɪk/ *noun* [C] a person who suffers from diabetes —**di·a·bet·ic** *adj.*: *diabetic children*

di·ag·nose /ˌdaɪəgˈnoʊs/ *verb* [T] to find out what is wrong or what illness a person has: *His illness was diagnosed as bronchitis.*

di·ag·no·sis /ˌdaɪəgˈnoʊsəs/ *noun* [C,U] (*pl.* **di·ag·no·ses** /-ˈnoʊsiz/) an act of diagnosing sth: *The doctor's diagnosis turned out to be right.* ◦ *What's your diagnosis of the situation?*

di·ag·o·nal /daɪˈægənl/ *adj.* **1** (used about a straight line) not vertical or horizontal; sloping ☞ picture at **vertical**. **2** going from one corner to the opposite corner of a square, rectangle, etc. —**di·ag·o·nal·ly** /-nəli/ *adv.*: *I*

was sitting diagonally across from Diane at the table.

☆**di·a·gram** /ˈdaɪəgræm/ *noun* [C] a simple picture that is used to explain how sth works or what sth looks like: *a diagram of the body's digestive system*

di·al¹ /ˈdaɪəl/ *noun* [C] **1** the round part of a clock, watch or other piece of equipment that gives you information about the time or about a measurement. A dial has numbers and an arrow on it: *a dial for showing air pressure* **2** the round part on a piece of equipment that you turn to change sth **3** the round part with holes in it on some telephones. You put your finger in one of the holes and turn the dial to call a number.

di·al² /ˈdaɪəl/ *verb* [I,T] to move the dial¹(3) or push the buttons on a telephone in order to call a particular telephone number: *to dial the wrong number*

di·a·lect /ˈdaɪəlɛkt/ *noun* [C,U] a form of a language that is spoken in one part of a country: *a local dialect*

☆**di·a·logue** (*also* **dialog**) /ˈdaɪəlɔg; -lɑg/ *noun* [C,U] **1** (a) conversation between people in a book, play, etc. **2** (a) discussion between people who have different opinions: *a dialogue between the political parties*

ˈ**dial tone** *noun* [C] the sound that you hear when you pick up a telephone before you begin to dial

di·am·e·ter /daɪˈæmət̮ər/ *noun* [C] (the length of) a straight line that goes from one side to the other of a circle, passing through the center ☞ Look at **radius**.

☆**di·a·mond** /ˈdaɪmənd; ˈdaɪə-/ *noun* **1** [C,U] a hard, bright precious stone which is very expensive and is used for making jewelry and in industry. A diamond usually has no color. **2** [C] a flat shape that has four sides of equal length and points at two ends ☞ picture at **shape**. **3** [C] a field where baseball is played **4 diamonds** [plural] the group (**suit**) of playing cards with red shapes like diamonds (2) on them: *the seven of diamonds* ☞ picture at **card**. **5** [C] one of the cards from this suit: *If you don't have any diamonds, you can play a trump.*

ˌ**diamond ˌanniˈversary** *noun* [C] the 60th anniversary of a wedding ☞ Look at **golden anniversary** and **silver anniversary**.

☆**di·a·per** /ˈdaɪpər; ˈdaɪə-/ *noun* [C] a piece of soft, thick cloth or paper that a baby or very young child wears around its bottom and between its legs: *Does her diaper need to be changed?* ◦ *disposable diapers* (= that you throw away when they have been used)

di·a·phragm /ˈdaɪəfræm/ *noun* [C] **1** the muscle between your lungs and your stomach that helps you to breathe **2** a thin piece of rubber that a woman puts inside her body

i	ɪ	ɛ	æ	ɑ	ɔ	ʌ	ʊ	u
see	sit	ten	cat	hot	saw	cup	put	too

before having sex to stop her from becoming pregnant

di·ar·rhe·a /ˌdaɪəˈriə/ *noun* [U] an illness that causes you to pass waste material (**feces**) from your bowels very often and in a more liquid form than usual: *diarrhea and vomiting*

☆ **di·a·ry** /ˈdaɪəri/ *noun* [C] (*pl.* **di·a·ries**) a book in which you write down what happens to you each day: *Do you keep a diary?*

dice /daɪs/ (*also* **die** /daɪ/) *noun* [C] (*pl.* **dice**) a small cube with a different number of spots (from one to six) on each side, used in certain games: *Throw the dice to see who goes first.*

dice

dic·tate /ˈdɪkteɪt/ *verb* **1** [I,T] to say sth aloud so that sb else can write or type it: *to dictate a letter to a secretary* **2** [I,T] to tell or order sb to do sth: *Parents can't dictate to their children how they should run their lives.* **3** [T] to decide or influence sth: *an attempt by large corporations to dictate the country's economic policy*

dic·ta·tion /dɪkˈteɪʃn/ *noun* [C,U] spoken words that sb else must write or type: *We had a dictation test in English today* (= in which we had to write down what the teacher said).

☆ **dic·ta·tor** /ˈdɪkteɪtər/ *noun* [C] a ruler who has total power in a country, especially one who used force to gain power and who rules the country unfairly

dic·ta·tor·ship /dɪkˈteɪtərʃɪp; ˈdɪkteɪtər-/ *noun* [C,U] government by a dictator; a country that is ruled by a dictator: *a military dictatorship*

☆ **dic·tion·ar·y** /ˈdɪkʃəˌnɛri/ *noun* [C] (*pl.* **dic·tion·ar·ies**) a book that lists the words of a language in alphabetical order and that tells you what they mean in the same or another language: *to look up a word in a dictionary* ∘ *a bilingual/monolingual dictionary* ∘ *a French-English dictionary*

did *p.t.* of DO[1,2]

did·n't *short for* DID NOT

☆ **die[1]** /daɪ/ *verb* (*pres. part.* **dy·ing**; *3rd pers. sing. pres.* **dies**; *p.t., p.p.* **died**) **1** [I] to stop living: *Thousands of people have died from this disease.* ∘ *to die of a heart attack* ∘ *to die for what you believe in* ∘ (*figurative*) *Our love will never die.* **2** [I] (used about a machine) to stop working: *The pilot managed to land the plane safely after one of the engines died.* **3** [T] to have a particular kind of death: *to die a natural death*

IDM **be dying for sth/to do sth** to want sth/to do sth very much: *I'm dying for a cup of coffee.*

die hard to change or disappear only slowly or with difficulty: *Old attitudes toward women die hard.*

PHRV **die away** to slowly become weaker before stopping or disappearing: *The sound of the engine died away as the car drove off.*

die down to slowly become less strong: *Let's wait until the storm dies down before we go out.*

die out to disappear: *The use of horses on farms died out a long time ago.*

die[2] /daɪ/ *noun* [C] (*pl.* **dice** /daɪs/) = DICE

die·sel /ˈdizl; ˈdisl/ *noun* **1** (*also* ˈ**diesel engine**) [C] an engine in buses, trucks, and some cars that uses heavy oil **2** [U] the heavy oil that is used in these engines: *a taxi that runs on diesel* ☞ Look at **gasoline**.

☆ **di·et[1]** /ˈdaɪət/ *noun* **1** [C,U] the food that a person or animal usually eats: *The peasants live on a diet of rice and vegetables.* ∘ *Poor diet is a cause of ill health.* **2** [C] certain foods that a person is allowed to eat for a special reason: *a low-fat diet* ∘ *a kosher diet* ∘ *diet cola* (= that has no sugar in it)

IDM **be/go on a diet** to eat only certain foods or a small amount of food because you want to lose weight: *I won't have any cake today. I'm on a diet.*

di·et[2] /ˈdaɪət/ *verb* [I] to be trying to lose weight by eating less food or only certain kinds of food: *You've lost some weight. Have you been dieting?*

☆ **dif·fer** /ˈdɪfər/ *verb* [I] **1** **differ (from sb/sth)** to be different: *How does this car differ from the other model?* **2** **differ (with sb) (about/on sth)** to have a different opinion: *Although I differ with Sue on some issues, we get along well.*

☆ **dif·fer·ence** /ˈdɪfrəns/ *noun* **1** [C] **difference (between A and B)** the way that people or things are not the same or the way that sb/sth has changed: *the differences between men and women* **2** [C,U] **difference (in sth) (between A and B)** the amount by which people or things are not the same or by which sb/sth has changed: *There's not much difference in price between the two brands.* ∘ *We put down a 30% deposit and have to pay the difference* (= the rest of the money) *when the work is finished.* **3** [C] a disagreement that is not very serious: *All couples have their differences from time to time.*

IDM **make a, some, etc. difference (in/to sb/sth)** to have an effect (on sb/sth): *A week of vacation made a big difference to her health.*

not make any difference (to sb/sth); make no difference to not be important (to sb/sth): *"Do you want the red one or the blue one?" "Oh, it doesn't make any difference."*

☆ **dif·fer·ent** /ˈdɪfrənt/ *adj.* **1** **different (from/than sb/sth)** not the same: *Football is very different from soccer.* ∘ *We always stay home on Saturdays – let's do something different this weekend.*

☞ Some people do not like the use of **different than**, especially in formal writing. However, **different...than** is often used with longer phrases: *The company shipped me a different item than what I had ordered.*

2 separate; individual: *This coat is available*

D

in three different colors. —**dif·fer·ent·ly** *adv.: I think you'll feel differently about it tomorrow.*

dif·fer·en·ti·ate /ˌdɪfəˈrenʃieɪt/ *verb* **1** [I,T] **differentiate between A and B**; **differentiate A (from B)** to see how things are different: *It is hard to differentiate between these two species of fungus.* **2** [T] **differentiate sth (from sth)** to make one thing different from another: *What differentiates him from previous presidents?* **3** [T] to treat one person or group differently from another: *We don't differentiate between the two groups – we treat everybody alike.*

☆ **dif·fi·cult** /ˈdɪfɪkəlt/ *adj.* **1** not easy to do or understand: *a difficult test* ∘ *Dean found it difficult to pass the driving test.* ∘ *It was difficult for Dean to pass the driving test.* ∘ *I'm in a difficult situation.* **2** (used about a person) not friendly, reasonable or helpful: *a difficult customer*

☆ **dif·fi·cul·ty** /ˈdɪfɪkəlti/ *noun* (*pl.* **dif·fi·cul·ties**) **1** [U] **difficulty (doing sth/in doing sth)** the state of being difficult or of not being able to do sth easily: *We didn't have any difficulty selling our car.* **2** [C, usually pl.] (*formal*) something that is difficult to do or understand; a problem: *Students who encounter difficulties in applying for financial aid should speak to a counselor.*

☆ **dig¹** /dɪg/ *verb* (*pres. part.* **dig·ging**; *p.t., p.p.* **dug** /dʌg/) [I,T] to move earth and make a hole using your hands, a tool, a machine, etc.: *The kids are busy digging in the sand.* ∘ *to dig a hole* ∘ *to dig for gold*

dig

shovel

PHRV dig in (*informal*) to begin to eat sth in an enthusiastic way: *The food's ready – let's dig in!*

dig sth in; **dig sth into sth** to push sth into sb/sth: *She dug her fingernails into my arm.*

dig sb/sth out (of sth) 1 to get sb/sth out of sth by digging: *Rescue workers dug the survivors out of the rubble.* **2** to get or find sb/sth by searching: *Bill went into the attic and dug out some old pictures.*

dig sth up 1 to remove sth from the earth by digging: *to dig up potatoes* **2** to make a hole or take away soil by digging: *Workers are digging up the road in front of our house.* **3** to find information by searching or studying: *Newspapers dug up some embarrassing facts about his private life.*

dig² /dɪg/ *noun* **1** [C] a hard push: *to give sb a dig in the ribs* (= with your elbow, etc.) **2** [C] something that you say to upset sb: *The others kept making digs at him because of the way he spoke.*

☆ **di·gest** /daɪˈdʒɛst; dɪ-/ *verb* [T] to change food in your stomach so that it can be used by the body —**di·ges·tive** /daɪˈdʒɛstɪv; dɪ-/ *adj.: the digestive system*

di·ges·tion /daɪˈdʒɛstʃən; dɪ-/ *noun* [C,U] the process of digesting food

dig·it /ˈdɪdʒət/ *noun* [C] any of the numbers from 0 to 9: *a four-digit code number* ∘ *a six-digit salary* (= $100,000 or more) ☛ Look also at **double-digit**.

☆ **dig·i·tal** /ˈdɪdʒətl/ *adj.* **1** showing information, e.g. time, by numbers alone: *a digital clock/watch* ∘ *a digital display screen* ☛ picture at **clock**. **2** using information in the form of many separate electronic signals: *digital sound recordings on CD*

dig·ni·fied /ˈdɪgnəfaɪd/ *adj.* behaving in a calm, serious way that makes other people respect you: *dignified behavior* ☛ The opposite is **undignified**.

dig·ni·ty /ˈdɪgnəti/ *noun* [U] **1** calm, serious behavior that makes other people respect you: *to behave with dignity* **2** the quality of being serious or formal: *the quiet dignity of the funeral service*

di·gress /daɪˈgrɛs; dɪ-/ *verb* [I] (*formal*) to stop talking or writing about the main subject under discussion and start talking or writing about another, possibly less important, one

dike /daɪk/ *noun* [C] a wall made of earth, etc. used for preventing a river or an ocean from flooding

di·lap·i·dat·ed /dəˈlæpədeɪtəd/ *adj.* (used about a building, furniture, etc.) old and broken: *a dilapidated apartment building* —**di·lap·i·da·tion** /dəˌlæpɪˈdeɪʃn/ *noun* [U]

di·lem·ma /dəˈlɛmə/ *noun* [C] a situation in which you have to make a difficult choice between two or more things: *to face a moral dilemma*

di·lute /dɪˈlut; daɪ-/ *verb* [T] **dilute sth (with sth)** to make a liquid weaker by adding water or another liquid ☛ Look at **concentrate**.

dim¹ /dɪm/ *adj.* (**dim·mer**; **dim·mest**) **1** not bright or easily seen; not clear: *The light was too dim to read by.* ∘ *dim memories* **2** not favorable or likely to succeed: *The team's chances of winning the championship appear very dim.* ∘ *the dim prospects for this year's harvest* —**dim·ly** *adv.: a dimly lit room*

dim² /dɪm/ *verb* [I,T] (**dim·ming**; **dimmed**) to become or make sth dim¹(1) : *to dim the lights*

☆ **dime** /daɪm/ *noun* [C] a coin used in the United States and Canada that is worth ten cents

IDM a dime a dozen (*informal*) very common and so not interesting or special: *Aspiring actors are a dime a dozen in Los Angeles.*

di·men·sion /dəˈmɛnʃn/ *noun* **1** [C,U] a measurement of the length, width or height of sth **2 dimensions** [plural] the size of sth including its length, width and height: *to measure the dimensions of a room* ○ *(figurative) the full dimensions of a problem* **3** [C] something that affects the way you think about a problem or situation: *Global warming has added a new dimension to the problem of hunger in the world.*

-di·men·sion·al /dəˈmɛnʃənəl/ (in compounds) with the number of dimensions mentioned: *a three-dimensional object*

di·min·ish /dəˈmɪnɪʃ/ *verb* [I,T] *(formal)* to become or to make sth smaller or less important: *The bad news did nothing to diminish her enthusiasm for the plan.*

di·min·u·tive /dəˈmɪnyətɪv/ *adj. (formal)* very small

dim·ple /ˈdɪmpl/ *noun* [C] a small round hollow area on your chin, cheek, etc. which can often be seen when you smile

din /dɪn/ *noun* [sing.] *(formal)* a loud unpleasant noise that continues for a long time: *We had to shout over the din of the helicopters.*

dine /daɪn/ *verb* [I] *(formal)* to eat dinner: *We dined at an exclusive French restaurant.*
PHRV **dine out** to eat in a restaurant

din·er /ˈdaɪnər/ *noun* [C] **1** *(formal)* a person who is eating at a restaurant **2** a restaurant which serves simple, cheap food in an informal atmosphere

din·ghy /ˈdɪŋi/ *noun* [C] *(pl.* **din·ghies**) a small open boat, often used to take people to or from a larger boat

din·gy /ˈdɪndʒi/ *adj.* (**din·gi·er**; **din·gi·est**) dirty and not bright or cheerful: *a dark and dingy room*

ˈdining room *noun* [C] a room where you eat meals

☆ **din·ner** /ˈdɪnər/ *noun* **1** [C,U] the main meal of the day, eaten either at noon or in the evening: *What's for dinner, Mom?* ○ *That was a great dinner you cooked.* ○ *It's dinnertime/time for dinner.*

☞ People from different parts of the country and different backgrounds have different ways of talking about their meals. People may call the meal they eat around noon **lunch** or **dinner**. If people eat their main meal of the day in the evening, they may call this meal **dinner**. Some people who eat a lighter meal in the evening prefer to call this meal **supper**. On certain holidays, people may eat a large formal meal called **dinner** in the afternoon: *Thanksgiving dinner.*

2 [C] a formal occasion in the evening during which a meal is served: *A dinner was given for the President.*

di·no·saur /ˈdaɪnəsɔr/ *noun* [C] a very large animal that disappeared from the earth (**became extinct**) before the appearance of human beings

dinosaur

di·o·cese /ˈdaɪəsɪs; -sis/ *noun* [C] an area containing a number of churches, for which a bishop is responsible

dip¹ /dɪp/ *verb* (**dip·ping**; **dipped**) **1** [T] **dip sth (into sth)**; **dip sth (in)** to put sth into liquid for a short time: *Julie dipped her toe into the pool to see how cold it was.* **2** [I,T] to go down; to lower sth: *The road suddenly dipped down to the river.* ○ *The temperature dipped below freezing last night.*
PHRV **dip into sth 1** to take money out of sth: *Tim had to dip into his savings to pay for his new suit.* **2** to read parts, but not all, of sth: *I've only dipped into the book. I haven't read it all the way through.*

dip² /dɪp/ *noun* **1** [C] a drop; a downward movement: *a dip in sales* **2** [C] *(informal)* a quick swim: *We went for a dip in the pool before breakfast.* **3** [C,U] a thick sauce that you eat by dipping pieces of vegetable, etc. into it: *Help yourselves to some chips and dip.* **4** [C] an area of lower ground: *Careful – there's a dip in the road ahead.*

diph·the·ri·a /dɪfˈθɪriə; dɪp-/ *noun* [U] a serious disease of the throat that makes it difficult to breathe

diph·thong /ˈdɪfθɔŋ; ˈdɪp-/ *noun* [C] two vowel sounds pronounced together, making one sound: *The /aɪ/ sound in "fine" is a diphthong.*

☆ **di·plo·ma** /dəˈploʊmə/ *noun* [C] the official piece of paper which shows that you have completed a course of study: *a high school diploma* ☞ Look at the note at **degree**.

di·plo·ma·cy /dəˈploʊməsi/ *noun* [U] **1** the management of the relations between countries **2** skill in dealing with people: *He handled the awkward situation with tact and diplomacy.*

dip·lo·mat /ˈdɪpləmæt/ *noun* [C] one of the officials who represent their country abroad: *a diplomat at the embassy in Rome*

dip·lo·mat·ic /ˌdɪpləˈmætɪk/ *adj.* **1** connected with diplomacy (1): *Diplomatic relations between the two countries have been restored.* **2** clever at dealing with people: *He searched for a diplomatic reply so as not to offend her.* —**dip·lo·mat·i·cal·ly** /-kli/ *adv.*

dire /ˈdaɪər/ *adj. (formal)* very bad or serious: terrible: *dire consequences* ○ *dire poverty*

☆ **di·rect¹** /dəˈrɛkt; daɪ-/ *adj.* **1** going from one place to another without turning or stopping; straight: *The most direct route is through the center of town.* ○ *a direct flight to Hong Kong*

D

tʃ	dʒ	v	θ	ð	s	z	ʃ
chin	June	van	thin	then	so	zoo	she

2 with nobody/nothing in between; not involving anybody/anything else: *The President is in direct contact with his Cabinet.* ○ *Keep the plant away from direct sunlight.* **3** saying what you mean; clear: *Politicians never give a direct answer to a direct question.* ☞ The opposite for senses 1, 2 and 3 is **indirect**. **4** (only *before* a noun) complete; exact: *What she did was in direct opposition to my orders.*

di·rect² /dəˈrɛkt; daɪ-/ *adv.* **1** not turning or stopping; straight: *Our airline flies direct to Tokyo.* **2** not involving anybody/anything else: *I always deal direct with the manager.*

☆ **di·rect³** /dəˈrɛkt; daɪ-/ *verb* [T] **1 direct sb (to...)** to tell or show sb how to get somewhere: *I was directed to an office at the end of the corridor.* ☞ Look at the note at **lead³**(1). **2** to manage or control sb/sth: *a police officer directing traffic* ○ *to direct a play, movie, etc.* **3 direct sth to/toward sb/sth; direct sth at sb/sth** to turn or aim your attention or actions toward sb/sth: *In recent weeks, the media's attention has been directed toward events in Washington.* ○ *The ad is directed at young people.* **4** (*formal*) to tell or order sb to do sth: *Take the medication as directed by your doctor.*

☆ **di·rec·tion** /dəˈrɛkʃn; daɪ-/ *noun* **1** [C] the path or line along which a person or thing is moving, looking or pointing: *A woman was seen running in the direction of Seventh Avenue.* ○ *The wind changed direction.* ○ *Wait! We're going in the wrong direction.* **2** [C, usually pl.] information or instructions about how to do sth or how to get to a place: *I can give you directions to our house.* **3** [U] management or control: *This department is under the direction of Mrs. Walters.* ○ *the direction of a play, movie, etc.*

di·rec·tive /dəˈrɛktɪv; daɪ-/ *noun* [C] an official order to do sth: *a government directive on safety at work*

☆ **di·rect·ly** /dəˈrɛktli; daɪ-/ *adv.* **1** exactly; in a direct way: *The bank is directly across from the grocery store.* ○ *He refused to answer my question directly.* ☞ The opposite is **indirectly**. **2** (especially in the southern U.S.) immediately; very soon: *Wait where you are. I'll return directly.*

di·rect ˈobject *noun* [C] (*grammar*) a noun or phrase that is directly affected by the action of a verb: *In the sentence "Anne bought a book," "a book" is the direct object.* ☞ Look at **indirect object**.

☆ **di·rec·tor** /dəˈrɛktər; daɪ-/ *noun* [C] **1** a person who manages or controls a company or organization: *the Director of Operations of the CIA* **2** a person who tells the actors, camera crew, etc., what to do in a movie, play, etc.

di·rec·to·ry /dəˈrɛktəri; daɪ-/ *noun* [C] (*pl.* **di·rec·to·ries**) **1** an alphabetical list of names, addresses and telephone numbers **2** (*comput-*

ing) a place where a group of files is stored in some types of computers ☞ Look also at **folder**.

☆ **dirt** /dərt/ *noun* [U] **1** a substance that is not clean: *Wipe that dirt off your face.* **2** earth or soil: *Pack some more dirt around the plant's roots.* ○ *a dirt road*

ˌdirt-ˈpoor *adj.* extremely poor; not having many of the things necessary for life

☆ **dirt·y¹** /ˈdərti/ *adj.* (**dirt·i·er; dirt·i·est**) **1** not clean: *Your hands are dirty. Go and wash them!* ○ *Fixing the car can be a dirty job* (= it makes you dirty). **2** referring to sex in a way that may upset or offend people: *to tell a dirty joke* **3** unkind and not honest; intended to harm sb: *That's a dirty lie!* ○ *a dirty trick*

IDM a dirty word an idea or thing that you do not like or agree with or that you find offensive: *Students aren't allowed to use dirty words in class.* ○ (*figurative*) *"Socialism" is a dirty word to many Americans.*

dirt·y² /ˈdərti/ *verb* [I,T] (*pres. part.* **dirt·y·ing**; *3rd pers. sing. pres.* **dirt·ies**; *p.t., p.p.* **dirt·ied**) to become or to make sth dirty

dis (*also* **diss**) /dɪs/ *verb* [T] (**dis·sing; dissed**) (*slang*) to say sth unkind to sb, showing that you do not respect them; to insult sb: *If you keep dissing those guys, you're going to get beaten up!* ☞ Look also at **disrespect²**.

☆ **dis·a·bil·i·ty** /ˌdɪsəˈbɪləti/ *noun* (*pl.* **dis·a·bil·i·ties**) **1** [U] the state of being unable to use a part of your body properly: *physical/mental disability* **2** [C] something that makes you unable to use a part of your body properly: *Because of his disability, he needs constant care.*

dis·a·ble /dɪsˈeɪbl/ *verb* [T] **1** (often passive) to make sb unable to use a part of his/her body properly: *Many soldiers were disabled in the Vietnam War.* **2** to do sth in order to stop a machine or part of a machine from working: *to disable a function in a computer program*

☆ **dis·a·bled** /dɪsˈeɪbld/ *adj.* **1** unable to work or use a part of the body properly: *The car has been adapted for disabled drivers.* **2 the disabled** *noun* [plural] people who are disabled (1): *The hotel has improved facilities for the disabled.*

☆ **dis·ad·van·tage** /ˌdɪsədˈvæntɪdʒ/ *noun* [C] **1** something that may make you less successful than other people: *Your qualifications are good. Your main disadvantage is your lack of experience.* **2** something that is not good or that causes problems: *What are the advantages and disadvantages of nuclear energy?*

IDM put sb/be at a disadvantage to put sb/be in a situation where he/she/you may be less successful than other people: *The fact that you don't speak Spanish will put you at a disadvantage in Mexico.*

to sb's disadvantage (*formal*) not good or helpful for sb: *The agreement will be to your disadvantage – don't accept it.*

i	ɪ	ɛ	æ	ɑ	ɔ	ʌ	ʊ	u
see	sit	ten	cat	hot	saw	cup	put	too

dis·ad·van·taged /ˌdɪsəd'væntɪdʒd/ adj. in a bad social or economic situation; poor: extra help for the most disadvantaged members of society

☆**dis·a·gree** /ˌdɪsə'gri/ verb [I] **1 disagree (with sb/sth) (about/on sth)** to have a different opinion from sb/sth; not agree: Bill often disagrees with his father about politics. ○ They strongly disagreed with the idea. **2** to be different: These two sets of statistics disagree.

dis·a·gree·a·ble /ˌdɪsə'griəbl/ adj. (formal) unpleasant

☆**dis·a·gree·ment** /ˌdɪsə'grimənt/ noun **1** [U] **disagreement (about/on sth)** having a different opinion from sb or not agreeing with sb/sth: There's a lot of disagreement about what causes people to turn to crime. **2** [C] an argument: Diane resigned after a disagreement with her boss.

dis·al·low /ˌdɪsə'laʊ/ verb [T] to not allow or accept sth: The touchdown was disallowed because the player stepped out of bounds.

☆**dis·ap·pear** /ˌdɪsə'pɪr/ verb [I] **1** to become impossible to see; to go away: He walked away and disappeared into a crowd of people. ○ My purse was here a second ago, and now it's disappeared. **2** to go to a place where you cannot be found: She disappeared five years ago and hasn't been heard from since. **3** to stop existing: Plant and animal species are disappearing at an alarming rate. —**dis·ap·pear·ance** /ˌdɪsə'pɪrəns/ noun [C,U]: The mystery of her disappearance was never solved.

☆**dis·ap·point** /ˌdɪsə'pɔɪnt/ verb [T] to make sb sad because what he/she had hoped for has not happened or because sb/sth is less good, interesting, etc than he/she had hoped: I'm sorry to disappoint you, but you didn't win the prize.

☆**dis·ap·point·ed** /ˌdɪsə'pɔɪntəd/ adj. **disappointed (about/at sth); disappointed (in/ with sb/sth)** sad because you/sb/sth did not succeed or because sth was not as good, interesting, etc. as you had hoped: They are very disappointed that they can't stay longer. ○ Connie was deeply disappointed at not being chosen for the team. ○ I'm disappointed in you. I thought you could do better.

☆**dis·ap·point·ing** /ˌdɪsə'pɔɪntɪŋ/ adj. making you feel sad because sth was not as good, interesting, etc. as you had hoped: It has been a disappointing year for the company. —**dis·ap·point·ing·ly** adv.: The amount of money they collected was disappointingly small.

☆**dis·ap·point·ment** /ˌdɪsə'pɔɪntmənt/ noun **1** [U] the state of being disappointed: To his great disappointment, he failed to get the job. **2** [C] **a disappointment (to sb)** a person or thing that disappoints you: Our vacation was a big disappointment.

dis·ap·prov·al /ˌdɪsə'pruvl/ noun [U] a feeling

that sth is bad or that sb is behaving badly: to shake your head in disapproval

☆**dis·ap·prove** /ˌdɪsə'pruv/ verb [I] **disapprove (of sb/sth)** to think that sb/sth is bad, foolish, etc.: His parents strongly disapproved of his dropping out of college. —**dis·ap·prov·ing** adj.: After he had told the joke there was a disapproving silence. —**dis·ap·prov·ing·ly** adv.: David frowned disapprovingly when I lit a cigarette.

dis·arm /dɪs'ɑrm/ verb [T] **1** to take weapons away from sb: The police caught and disarmed the terrorists. **2** [T] to make a bomb or wepon safe and unable to explode

dis·ar·ma·ment /dɪs'ɑrməmənt/ noun [U] reducing the number of weapons that a country has: nuclear disarmament

dis·arm·ing /dɪs'ɑrmɪŋ/ adj. making sb feel less angry: a disarming smile

dis·as·so·ci·ate /ˌdɪsə'soʊsieɪt; -ʃieɪt/ verb = DISSOCIATE

☆**dis·as·ter** /dɪ'zæstər/ noun **1** [C] an event that causes a lot of harm or damage: earthquakes, floods and other natural disasters **2** [C] a person or thing that is very bad, harmful or unsuccessful: The school play was a total disaster. Everything went wrong. **3** [U] failure; a terrible situation: The drought brought disaster to the area.

dis·as·trous /dɪ'zæstrəs/ adj. very bad, harmful or unsuccessful: Our mistake had disastrous results.

dis·band /dɪs'bænd/ verb [I,T] to stop existing as a group; to break up

dis·be·lief /ˌdɪsbɪ'lif/ noun [U] not believing sb/sth: "It can't be true!" he shouted in disbelief.

disc /dɪsk/ noun [C] = DISK ☞ Look also at compact disc.

dis·card /dɪ'skɑrd/ verb [T] (formal) to throw sth away because it is not useful

dis·cern /dɪ'sərn/ verb [T] (formal) to see or notice sth with difficulty: I discerned a note of anger in his voice.

dis·cern·i·ble /dɪ'sərnəbl/ adj. (formal) that can only be seen or noticed with difficulty: The shape of a house was just discernible through the mist.

dis·cern·ing /dɪ'sərnɪŋ/ adj. (formal) able to recognize the quality of sb/sth: The discerning music lover will appreciate the excellence of this recording.

dis·charge¹ /dɪs'tʃɑrdʒ/ verb **1** [T] to send sth out (a liquid, gas, etc.): Smoke and fumes are discharged from the factory and cause air pollution. **2** [I] to shoot a bullet or explode, especially by accident: The rifle accidentally discharged, and a bullet struck Andy in the chest. **3** [T] to allow sb officially to leave; to send sb away: to discharge sb from the hospital, the army, etc.

ə	y	w	t̬	eɪ	aɪ	ɔɪ	aʊ	oʊ
about	yes	woman	butter	say	five	boy	now	go

D

dis·charge² /ˈdɪstʃɑrdʒ/ *noun* **1** [C,U] the action of sending sb/sth out or away: *The discharge of oil from the leaking tanker could not be prevented.* ○ *The wounded soldier was given a medical discharge.* **2** [C,U] a substance that has come out of somewhere: *yellowish discharge from a wound*

dis·ci·ple /dɪˈsaɪpl/ *noun* [C] **1** (*also* **Disciple**) a person who follows a teacher, especially a religious one: *the twelve Disciples of Jesus* **2** a person who follows and believes strongly in a particular idea or set of ideas: *disciples of free-market capitalism*

dis·ci·pli·nar·y /ˈdɪsəpləˌnɛri/ *adj.* connected with punishment for breaking rules

☆ **dis·ci·pline** /ˈdɪsəplɪn/ *noun* **1** [U] a way of training your mind and body so that you control your actions and obey rules: *military discipline* ○ *It takes a lot of self-discipline to practice for three hours a day.* **2** [U] the result of such training: *A good teacher must be able to maintain discipline in the classroom.* **3** [C] a subject of study: *academic disciplines*

dis·ci·pline² /ˈdɪsəplɪn/ *verb* [T] **1** to train sb to obey and to behave in a controlled way: *You should discipline yourself to practice the piano every morning.* **2** to punish sb

dis·claim·er /dɪsˈkleɪmər/ *noun* [C] **1** an official statement that sb has no knowledge of, or responsibility for, sth: *The TV program carried a disclaimer saying that it was not based on actual events.* **2** an official document that says that sb has no right to do sth: *I had to sign a disclaimer which said that I couldn't sue the hospital if anything went wrong.*

dis·close /dɪsˈkloʊz/ *verb* [T] (*formal*) to tell sth to sb or to make sth known publicly: *The newspapers did not disclose the victim's name.*

dis·clo·sure /dɪsˈkloʊʒər/ *noun* [C,U] making sth known; the facts that are made known: *the disclosure of secret information* ○ *He resigned following disclosures about his private life.*

dis·co /ˈdɪskoʊ/ *noun* (*pl.* **dis·cos**) **1** [U] a type of music that was popular in the 1970s. Disco music has a strong, fast beat and people dance to it. **2** [C] (*old-fashioned*) a place where people dance to popular music on records, etc. Discos usually have loud music and bright colored lights. ☞ The word that we usually use nowadays is **club**.

dis·col·or /dɪsˈkʌlər/ *verb* **1** [I] to change color (often by the effect of light, age or dirt) **2** [T] to change or spoil the color of sth

dis·com·fort /dɪsˈkʌmfərt/ *noun* **1** [U] a slight feeling of pain: *You may have some discomfort from the wound after the operation.* **2** [C] something that makes you feel uncomfortable or that causes a slight feeling of pain: *The beauty of the scenery made up for the discomforts of the long trip.* **3** [U] a feeling of embarrassment

dis·con·cert·ing /ˌdɪskənˈsərtɪŋ/ *adj.* making

sb feel confused or worried: *disconcerting news from the war zone*

dis·con·nect /ˌdɪskəˈnɛkt/ *verb* [T] to undo two things that are joined or connected together: *If you don't pay your gas bill, your supply will be disconnected.* ○ *Disconnect the appliance from the power supply before cleaning it.*

dis·con·tent /ˌdɪskənˈtɛnt/ *noun* [U] (*formal*) the state of being unhappy or not satisfied with sth

dis·con·tent·ed /ˌdɪskənˈtɛntəd/ (*also* **dis·content**) *adj.* unhappy or not satisfied

dis·con·tin·ue /ˌdɪskənˈtɪnyu/ *verb* [T] (*formal*) to stop sth or stop producing sth

dis·cord /ˈdɪskɔrd/ *noun* (*formal*) **1** [U] disagreement or argument **2** [C] two or more musical notes that do not sound pleasant when they are played together

☆ **dis·count¹** /ˈdɪskaʊnt/ *noun* [C,U] a reduction in the price or cost of sth: *Employees get a 20% discount on all merchandise.* ○ *discount prices*

dis·count² /dɪsˈkaʊnt; ˈdɪskaʊnt/ *verb* [T] to consider sth not true or not important: *I think we can discount that idea. It's just not practical.*

¹discount store *noun* [C] a large store that sells many different types of items at reduced prices

☆ **dis·cour·age** /dɪsˈkərɪdʒ/ *verb* [T] **1 discourage sb (from doing sth)** to make sb lose hope or feel less confident about sth: *Don't let these little problems discourage you.* **2 discourage sb from doing sth** to try to stop sb doing sth: *Consumers should be discouraged from throwing glass and cans in the garbage.* ☞ The opposite is **encourage**.

dis·cour·aged /dɪsˈkərɪdʒd/ *adj.* having lost hope; not feeling confident about sth: *After failing the final exam, Paul felt very discouraged.*

dis·cour·age·ment /dɪsˈkərɪdʒmənt/ *noun* [C,U] discouraging or being discouraged; something that discourages you

☆ **dis·cov·er** /dɪsˈkʌvər/ *verb* [T] **1** to find or learn sth that nobody knew or had found before: *Who discovered the source of the Mississippi?* ○ *Scientists are hoping to discover the cause of the epidemic.* **2** to find or learn sth new or unexpected or sth that you did not know before: *I think I discovered why the computer won't print out.* ○ *We recently discovered that a famous writer used to live in this house.*

dis·cov·er·er /dɪsˈkʌvərər/ *noun* [C] a person who discovers sth

☆ **dis·cov·er·y** /dɪsˈkʌvəri/ *noun* (*pl.* **dis·cov·er·ies**) **1** [U] finding sth: *The discovery of X-rays changed the history of medicine.* **2** [C] something that has been discovered: *scientific discoveries*

dis·cred·it /dɪsˈkrɛdət/ *verb* [T] to cause

sb/sth to lose people's trust; to damage the reputation of sb/sth

dis·creet /dɪˈskrit/ *adj.* careful not to attract attention and so cause embarrassment or difficulty for sb: *She was too discreet to mention the argument in front of Neil.* —**dis·creet·ly** *adv.* ☛ The noun is **discretion**. The opposite is **indiscreet**.

dis·crep·an·cy /dɪˈskrɛpənsi/ *noun* [C,U] (*pl.* **dis·crep·an·cies**) a difference between two things that should be the same: *There is a discrepancy between these two sets of figures.*

dis·cre·tion /dɪˈskrɛʃn/ *noun* [U] **1** care not to attract attention and so cause embarrassment or difficulty for sb: *This is confidential, but I know I can rely on your discretion.* ☛ The adjective is **discreet**. **2** the freedom and ability to make decisions by yourself: *You need to decide what is best. Use your discretion.* **IDM** **at sb's discretion** depending on what sb thinks or decides: *Pay raises are awarded at the discretion of the manager.*

dis·crim·i·nate /dɪˈskrɪməneɪt/ *verb* **1** [I] **discriminate (against sb)** to treat one person or group worse than others: *It is illegal to discriminate against any ethnic or religious group.* **2** [I,T] **discriminate (between A and B)** to see or make a difference between two people or things: *Does the tax law discriminate between commercial and residential properties?*

☆ **dis·crim·i·na·tion** /dɪˌskrɪməˈneɪʃn/ *noun* [U] **1 discrimination (against sb)** treating one person or group worse than others: *sexual, racial, religious, etc. discrimination* **2** the state of being able to judge what is good, true, etc.

dis·cus /ˈdɪskəs/ *noun* [C] a heavy round flat object that is thrown as a sport

☆ **dis·cuss** /dɪˈskʌs/ *verb* [T] **discuss sth (with sb)** to talk or write about sth seriously or formally: *I need to discuss the matter with my parents before I make a decision.* ○ *The article discusses the need for a change in the law.*

☆ **dis·cus·sion** /dɪˈskʌʃn/ *noun* [C,U] a time when you talk about sth: *After a great deal of discussion, we all agreed to share the cost.* ○ *a long discussion on the meaning of life* **IDM** **under discussion** being talked about: *The proposal is still under discussion in Congress.*

dis·dain /dɪsˈdeɪn/ *noun* [U] (*formal*) the feeling that sb/sth is not good enough and does not deserve to be respected

☆ **dis·ease** /dɪˈziz/ *noun* [C,U] an illness of the body in humans, animals or plants: *an infectious disease* ○ *Rats and flies spread disease.* —**dis·eased** *adj.*: *His diseased kidney had to be removed.*

☛ **Illness** and **disease** can be used in a similar way. However, we use **disease** to describe a type of illness which has a name and is recognized by certain symptoms. Diseases may be caused by bacteria, viruses, etc., and you can often catch and pass them on to others. **Illness** is used to describe the general state of being sick and the time during which you are not well.

dis·en·chant·ed /ˌdɪsənˈtʃæntəd/ *adj.* having lost your good opinion of sb/sth —**dis·en·chant·ment** *noun* [U]: *There is increasing disenchantment among voters with the government's policies.*

dis·fig·ure /dɪsˈfɪɡyər/ *verb* [T] to spoil the appearance of sb/sth

dis·grace¹ /dɪsˈɡreɪs/ *noun* **1** [U] the state of not being respected by other people, usually because you have behaved badly: *There is no disgrace in finishing third in the race.* **2** [sing.] **a disgrace (to sb/sth)** a person or thing that gives such a bad impression that other people feel ashamed: *The sidewalks are covered with trash. It's a disgrace!* **IDM** **(be) in disgrace** (to be) in a position where other people do not respect you, usually because you have behaved badly

dis·grace² /dɪsˈɡreɪs/ *verb* [T] **1** to cause disgrace to sb/yourself **2** to cause sb to lose his/her position of power: *the disgraced leader*

dis·grace·ful /dɪsˈɡreɪsfl/ *adj.* very bad, making other people feel ashamed: *Your behavior last night was absolutely disgraceful.* —**dis·grace·ful·ly** *adv.*

dis·grun·tled /dɪsˈɡrʌntld/ *adj.* fairly angry; disappointed and annoyed

dis·guise¹ /dɪsˈɡaɪz/ *verb* [T] **disguise sb/sth (as sb/sth)** to change the appearance, sound, etc. of sb/sth so that people cannot recognize him/her/it: *They disguised themselves as fishermen and escaped in a boat.* ○ *to disguise your voice* ○ (*figurative*) *His smile disguised his anger.*

dis·guise² /dɪsˈɡaɪz/ *noun* [C,U] clothes or items such as false hair, glasses, etc. that you wear to change your appearance so that nobody recognizes you **IDM** **in disguise** wearing or using a disguise

☆ **dis·gust¹** /dɪsˈɡʌst/ *noun* [U] a strong feeling of dislike or disapproval: *She looked around the filthy room with disgust.* ○ *The movie was so bad that we walked out in disgust.*

dis·gust² /dɪsˈɡʌst/ *verb* [T] to cause a strong feeling of dislike or disapproval: *Cruelty toward animals really disgusts me.*

dis·gust·ed /dɪsˈɡʌstəd/ *adj.* feeling strong dislike or disapproval: *We were disgusted at the standard of service we received.*

☆ **dis·gust·ing** /dɪsˈɡʌstɪŋ/ *adj.* causing a strong feeling of dislike or disapproval: *What a disgusting smell!*

☆ **dish¹** /dɪʃ/ *noun* **1** [C] a shallow container for food. You can use a dish to cook sth in the oven, to serve food on the table or to eat from: *I'll have a dish of ice cream for dessert.*

D

☞ picture at **plate**. **2** [C] a type of food prepared in a particular way: *The main dish was lasagna. It was served with a selection of side dishes.* **3 the dishes** [plural] all the plates, cups, etc. that you use during a meal: *Will you put the dishes away in the cupboard?* **4** [C] (*also* **satellite dish**) a large round object that you place outside your house or another building in order to receive television pictures by satellite

IDM do/wash the dishes to wash the plates, cups, etc. that you used during a meal

dish² /dɪʃ/ *verb*

PHRV dish sth out (*informal*) to give away a lot of sth

dish sth up (*informal*) to serve food

dis·heart·en·ing /dɪsˈhɑrtənɪŋ/ *adj.* making you feel sad or disappointed

di·shev·eled /dɪˈʃɛvld/ *adj.* (used about a person's appearance) messy

dis·hon·est /dɪsˈɑnəst/ *adj.* not honest or truthful —**dis·hon·est·ly** *adv.* —**dis·hon·es·ty** *noun* [U]

dis·hon·or /dɪsˈɑnər/ *noun* [U, sing.] (*formal*) the state of no longer being respected; shame —**dis·hon·or·a·ble** /-nərəbl/ *adj.*

dish·wash·er /ˈdɪʃwɑʃər; -wɔʃ-/ *noun* [C] **1** an electric machine that washes plates, cups, knives, forks, etc. **2** a person whose job is to wash the plates, cups, knives, forks, etc. in a restaurant

dis·il·lu·sion /ˌdɪsəˈluʒn/ *verb* [T] to destroy sb's belief in or good opinion of sb/sth

dis·il·lu·sioned /ˌdɪsəˈluʒnd/ *adj.* disappointed because sb/sth is not as good as you first thought: *She's disillusioned with law school.*

dis·il·lu·sion·ment /dɪsəˈluʒnmənt/ *noun* [U] disappointment because sb/sth is not as good as you first thought

dis·in·fect /ˌdɪsənˈfɛkt/ *verb* [T] to clean sth with a liquid that destroys bacteria: *to disinfect a toilet* ∘ *to disinfect a wound*

dis·in·fec·tant /ˌdɪsənˈfɛktənt/ *noun* [C,U] a substance that destroys bacteria and is used for cleaning: *to mop the floor with disinfectant*

dis·in·te·grate /dɪsˈɪntəɡreɪt/ *verb* [I] to break into many small pieces: *The plate hit the floor and disintegrated.*

dis·in·te·gra·tion /dɪsˌɪntəˈɡreɪʃn/ *noun* [U] the act of breaking or dividing into many parts: *the disintegration of families*

dis·in·ter·est·ed /dɪsˈɪntrəstəd; -ˈɪntərɛstəd/ *adj.* fair; not influenced by personal feelings: *disinterested advice* ☞ Look at **uninterested**. It has a different meaning.

dis·joint·ed /dɪsˈdʒɔɪntəd/ *adj.* (used especially about ideas, writing or speech) not clearly linked and therefore difficult to follow

disk /dɪsk/ *noun* [C] **1** (*also* **disc**) a round flat object **2** (*computing*) a flat piece of plastic that stores information for use by a computer

☞ Look at **floppy disk** and **hard disk**. **3** (*also* **disc**) one of the pieces of thin strong material (**cartilage**) between the bones in your back

disk drive *noun* [C] a piece of electrical equipment, often a part of a computer, that passes information to or from a computer disk

disk·ette /dɪsˈkɛt/ *noun* [C] (*old-fashioned*) = FLOPPY DISK

disk jockey *noun* [C] = DJ

☆ **dis·like¹** /dɪsˈlaɪk/ *verb* [T] to think that sb/sth is unpleasant: *I really dislike flying.* ∘ *What is it that you dislike about living here?*

dis·like² /dɪsˈlaɪk/ *noun* [U, sing.] **dislike (of/ for sb/sth)** the feeling of not liking sth: *She couldn't hide her dislike for him.* ∘ *He seems to have a strong dislike of hard work.*

IDM likes and dislikes ⇨ LIKE⁵

dis·lo·cate /dɪsˈloʊkeɪt; ˈdɪsloʊkeɪt/ *verb* [T] to put a bone out of its correct position: *He dislocated his shoulder.* —**dis·lo·ca·tion** /ˌdɪsloʊˈkeɪʃn/ *noun* [C,U]

dis·lodge /dɪsˈlɑdʒ/ *verb* [T] to make sb/sth move from a fixed position

dis·loy·al /dɪsˈlɔɪəl/ *adj.* doing or saying sth that is against sb/sth that you should support; not loyal —**dis·loy·al·ty** /-ˈlɔɪəlti/ *noun* [C,U] (*pl.* **dis·loy·al·ties**)

dis·mal /ˈdɪzməl/ *adj.* **1** depressing; causing sadness: *dismal surroundings* ∘ *a dismal failure* **2** of low quality; poor: *the team's dismal record of 2 wins and 15 losses*

dis·man·tle /dɪsˈmæntl/ *verb* [T] to separate sth into the parts it is made from: *The photographer dismantled his equipment and packed it away.*

dis·may¹ /dɪsˈmeɪ/ *noun* [U] a strong feeling of worry and shock: *Several people expressed dismay at the news of the murder.*

dis·may² /dɪsˈmeɪ/ *verb* [T] (usually passive) to give sb a strong feeling of worry and shock: *I am dismayed by the growing use of drugs in our nation's cities.*

dis·mem·ber /dɪsˈmɛmbər/ *verb* [T] to tear or cut a body apart

☆ **dis·miss** /dɪsˈmɪs/ *verb* [T] **1** (*formal*) to order an employee to leave his/her job: *He was dismissed for refusing to obey orders.* ☞ **Fire** is a less formal word for **dismiss**. **2** to allow sb to leave: *The lecture ended and the professor dismissed the class.* **3** to remove sb/sth from your mind; to stop thinking about sb/sth completely: *Dismiss any thoughts of failure from your mind.* **4 dismiss sb/sth (as sth)** to say or think that sb/sth is not important or is not worth considering seriously: *He dismissed the idea as nonsense.*

dis·miss·al /dɪsˈmɪsl/ *noun* **1** [C,U] ordering sb or being ordered to leave a job: *a case of unfair dismissal* **2** [U] refusing to consider sb/sth seriously: *She was hurt at their dismissal of her suggestion.*

dis·mis·sive /dɪsˈmɪsɪv/ *adj.* saying or show-

i	ɪ	ɛ	æ	ɑ	ɔ	ʌ	ʊ	u
see	sit	ten	cat	hot	saw	cup	put	too

ing that you think that sb/sth is not important or is not worth considering seriously: *The boss was dismissive of my efforts.*

dis·o·be·di·ent /ˌdɪsəˈbidiənt/ *adj.* not willing to obey; refusing to do what you are told to do —**dis·o·be·di·ence** /-iəns/ *noun* [U]

dis·o·bey /ˌdɪsəˈbeɪ/ *verb* [I,T] to refuse to do what you are told to do; not to obey: *He was punished for disobeying orders.*

☆ **dis·or·der** /dɪsˈɔrdər/ *noun* **1** [U] a messy, confused or disorganized state: *His financial affairs are in complete disorder.* **2** [U] violent behavior by a large number of people **3** [C,U] an illness in which the mind or part of the body is not working correctly: *a stomach disorder*

dis·or·dered /dɪsˈɔrdərd/ *adj.* messy, confused or disorganized

dis·or·der·ly /dɪsˈɔrdərli/ *adj.* **1** very messy **2** (used about people or behavior) out of control and violent; causing trouble in public: *They were arrested for disorderly conduct.*

dis·or·gan·i·za·tion /dɪsˌɔrgənəˈzeɪʃn/ *noun* [U] a lack of organization

☆ **dis·or·gan·ized** /dɪsˈɔrgənaɪzd/ *adj.* not organized; badly organized

dis·o·ri·ent /dɪsˈɔriənt/ *verb* [T] (usually passive) to make sb lose all sense of direction or become confused about where he/she is: *The street signs were very confusing and I soon became disoriented.* —**dis·o·ri·en·ta·tion** /dɪsˌɔriənˈteɪʃn/ *noun* [U]

dis·own /dɪsˈoʊn/ *verb* [T] to decide or say that you are no longer associated with sb/sth: *When he was arrested, his family disowned him.*

dis·par·age /dɪˈspærɪdʒ/ *verb* [T] (*formal*) to talk about sb/sth in a critical way or to say that sb/sth is of little value or importance

dis·par·ag·ing /dɪˈspærɪdʒɪŋ/ *adj.* very critical of sth: *disparaging remarks*

dis·patch¹ /dɪˈspætʃ/ *verb* [T] (*formal*) to send: *Medical workers and supplies have been dispatched to the area.*

dis·patch² /dɪˈspætʃ; ˈdɪspætʃ/ *noun* [C] an official message or news report

dis·pel /dɪˈspɛl/ *verb* [T] (**dis·pel·ling**; **dis·pelled**) to make sth disappear; to remove sth from sb's mind: *His reassuring words dispelled all her fears.*

dis·pen·sa·ble /dɪˈspɛnsəbl/ *adj.* not necessary: *I suppose I'm dispensable. Anybody could do my job.* ☞ The opposite is **indispensable**.

dis·pense /dɪˈspɛns/ *verb* [T] **1** (*formal*) to give out: *a machine that dispenses hot and cold drinks* **2** (*formal*) to prepare and give out medicines

PHRV **dispense with sb/sth** to get rid of sb/sth that is not necessary: *They decided to dispense with luxuries and live a simple life.*

dis·pen·ser /dɪˈspɛnsər/ *noun* [C] a machine

or container from which you can get sth: *a paper towel dispenser*

dis·perse /dɪˈspərs/ *verb* [I,T] to separate and go in different directions; to break sth up : *When the meeting was over, the group dispersed.* ○ *Police arrived and quickly dispersed the crowd.*

dis·pir·it·ed /dɪˈspɪrətəd/ *adj.* having lost confidence or hope; depressed

dis·place /dɪsˈpleɪs/ *verb* [T] **1** to force sb/sth to move from the usual or correct place: *Thousands of people were displaced from their homes by the flood.* **2** to remove and take the place of sb/sth: *She hoped to displace Hingis as the top player in the world.*

☆ **dis·play¹** /dɪˈspleɪ/ *verb* [T] **1** to put sth in a place where people will see it or where it will attract attention: *Posters for the concert were displayed all over the city.* **2** to show sth (e.g. a feeling or personal quality): *She displayed no interest in the discussion.*

☆ **dis·play²** /dɪˈspleɪ/ *noun* [C] **1** a public event in which sth is shown in action: *a fireworks display* **2** an arrangement of things for people to see: *We're going to set up a display of our new products at the convention.* **3** behavior that shows a particular feeling or quality: *a display of aggression* **4** (*computing*) words, pictures, etc. that can be seen on a computer screen

IDM **on display** in a place where people will see it and where it will attract attention: *The bones were put on display at the museum.*

dis·please /dɪsˈpliz/ *verb* [T] (*formal*) to annoy sb or to make sb angry or upset

dis·pleas·ure /dɪsˈplɛʒər/ *noun* [U] (*formal*) the feeling of being annoyed or not satisfied

dis·pos·a·ble /dɪˈspoʊzəbl/ *adj.* intended to be thrown away after being used once or for a short time: *a disposable razor*

dis·pos·al /dɪˈspoʊzl/ *noun* [U] the act of getting rid of sth: *the disposal of chemical waste*
IDM **at sb's disposal** available for sb's use at any time: *We are using all the means at our disposal to develop a cure for this disease.*

dis·pose /dɪˈspoʊz/ *verb*
PHRV **dispose of sb/sth** to throw away or sell sth; to get rid of sb/sth that you do not want

dis·pro·por·tion·ate /ˌdɪsprəˈpɔrʃənət/ *adj.* larger or smaller than is acceptable or expected —**dis·pro·por·tion·ate·ly** *adv.*

dis·prove /ˌdɪsˈpruv/ *verb* [T] to show or prove that sth is not true

☆ **dis·pute¹** /dɪˈspyut/ *noun* [C,U] disagreement or argument between people: *There was some dispute about whose fault it was.* ○ *a pay dispute*
IDM **in dispute** in a situation of arguing or being argued about: *The exact number of victims is still in dispute.*

dis·pute² /dɪˈspyut/ *verb* [T] to argue about

D

sth or to suggest that sth is not true: *The coach disputed the referee's call.*

dis·qual·i·fy /dɪsˈkwɑləfaɪ/ *verb* [T] (*pres. part.* **dis·qual·i·fy·ing**; *3rd pers. sing. pres.* **dis·qual·i·fies**; *p.t., p.p.* **dis·qual·i·fied**) **disqualify sb (from sth/from doing sth)** to officially forbid sb to do sth or to take part in sth, usually because he/she has broken a rule or law: *The runner was disqualified for taking illegal drugs.* —**dis·qual·i·fi·ca·tion** /dɪsˌkwɑləfəˈkeɪʃn/ *noun* [C,U]

dis·re·gard¹ /ˌdɪsrɪˈɡɑrd/ *verb* [T] to pay no attention to sb/sth: *These are the latest instructions. Please disregard any you received before.*

dis·re·gard² /ˌdɪsrɪˈɡɑrd/ *noun* [U, sing.] **(a) disregard (for/of sb/sth)** lack of attention to, interest in or care for sb/sth: *He rushed into the burning building with complete disregard for his own safety.*

dis·re·pair /ˌdɪsrɪˈpɛr/ *noun* [U] a bad condition, existing because repairs have not been made: *Over the years the building fell into a state of disrepair.*

dis·rep·u·ta·ble /dɪsˈrɛpyətəbl/ *adj.* not deserving to be trusted; having a bad reputation

dis·re·pute /ˌdɪsrɪˈpyut/ *noun* [U] the situation when people no longer respect sb/sth: *Such unjust jury verdicts bring the legal system into disrepute.*

dis·re·spect¹ /ˌdɪsrɪˈspɛkt/ *noun* [U] behavior or words that show that you do not respect sb/sth —**dis·re·spect·ful** /-fl/ *adj.* —**dis·re·spect·ful·ly** *adv.*

dis·re·spect² /ˌdɪsrɪˈspɛkt/ *verb* [T] (*informal*) to say or do sth which shows that you do not respect sb/sth: *Why do so many kids disrespect their parents these days?* ☞ Look also at **dis**.

dis·rupt /dɪsˈrʌpt/ *verb* [T] to disturb a process or system: *The strike severely disrupted flights.* —**dis·rup·tion** /dɪsˈrʌpʃn/ *noun* [C,U] —**dis·rup·tive** /dɪsˈrʌptɪv/ *adj.*: *The child was taken out of class because of his disruptive behavior.*

diss /dɪs/ *verb* [T] (*slang*) = DIS

dis·sat·is·fac·tion /dɪˌsætəsˈfækʃn; dɪs-/ *noun* [U] the feeling of not being satisfied or pleased: *There is some dissatisfaction among teachers with their workload.*

dis·sat·is·fied /dɪˈsætəsfaɪd/ *adj.* **dissatisfied (with sb/sth)** not satisfied or pleased: *complaints from dissatisfied customers*

dis·sect /dɪˈsɛkt; daɪ-/ *verb* [T] to cut up a dead body, a plant, etc. in order to examine its structure —**dis·sec·tion** /dɪˈsɛkʃn; daɪ-/ *noun* [C,U]

dis·sent¹ /dɪˈsɛnt/ *noun* [U] (*formal*) disagreement with official or generally agreed ideas or opinions: *There is some dissent among Republicans on these issues.*

dis·sent² /dɪˈsɛnt/ *verb* [I] **dissent (from sth)** (*formal*) to have opinions that are different from those that are officially held

dis·sent·ing /dɪˈsɛntɪŋ/ *adj.* showing or feeling dissent¹: *the dissenting opinion given by one of the judges*

dis·ser·ta·tion /ˌdɪsərˈteɪʃn/ *noun* [C] a long piece of writing on sth that you have studied, as part of the highest university degree (**Ph.D.**) ☞ Look at **thesis**.

dis·serv·ice /dɪˈsərvəs; dɪs-/ *noun* [U, sing.] **(a) disservice to sb/sth** an action that is unhelpful or has a negative effect

dis·si·dent /ˈdɪsədənt/ *noun* [C] a person who expresses disagreement with the actions or ideas of a government or an organization

dis·sim·i·lar /dɪˈsɪmələr; dɪs-/ *adj.* **dissimilar (from/to sb/sth)** unlike; not similar; different

dis·so·ci·ate /dɪˈsoʊsieɪt; -ʃieɪt/ (*also* **disassociate** /ˌdɪsəˈsoʊsieɪt; -oʊʃi-/) *verb* [T] **dissociate sb/sth/yourself from sth** to say or believe that a thing or a person is not connected with another, or that you do not agree with sth: *She dissociated herself from the views of the extremists in her party.*

☆ **dis·solve** /dɪˈzɑlv/ *verb* [I,T] to become liquid or to make sth become liquid: *Sugar dissolves in water.* ○ *Dissolve two tablets in cold water.*

dis·suade /dɪˈsweɪd/ *verb* [T] **dissuade sb (from doing sth)** to persuade sb not to do sth: *I tried to dissuade her from calling him.*

☆ **dis·tance¹** /ˈdɪstəns/ *noun* **1** [C,U] the amount of space between two places or points: *It's only a short distance from my home to work.* ○ *The map tells you the distances between the major cities.* ○ *We still have some distance to go.* ○ *The house is within walking distance of the stores.* **2** [sing.] a point that is a long way from sb/sth: *At this distance I can't read the sign.* ○ *From a distance, the farm looks very nice.*

IDM **in the distance** far away: *I could hear voices in the distance.*

keep your distance (from sb/sth) 1 to avoid going too close to sb/sth: *Remember to keep your distance from the car in front of you.* **2** to avoid becoming too friendly with sb or too involved in a situation: *I tried to keep my distance from the gangs at school.*

dis·tance² /ˈdɪstəns/ *verb* [T] **1** to make sb feel less friendly toward sb/sth: *Her wealth and success have distanced her from her old friends.* **2 distance yourself from sb/sth** to show that you are not involved or connected with sb/sth: *She was careful to distance herself from the views of her colleagues.*

☆ **dis·tant** /ˈdɪstənt/ *adj.* **1** a long way away in space or time: *to travel to distant parts of the world* ○ *in the not too distant future* (= quite soon) **2** (used about a relative) not closely related: *a distant cousin* **3** (used about a competition, etc.) losing by a large amount: *Lopez won the race, with Wilson finishing a distant second.* **4** not very friendly: *He can sometimes seem very cold and distant.* **5** seeming to be

ər	ɪr	ɛr	ɑr	ɔr	ʊr	ʒ	h	ŋ
bird	near	hair	car	north	tour	vision	hat	sing

thinking about sth else: *She had a distant look in her eyes.*

dis·taste /dɪsˈteɪst/ *noun* [U, sing.] **(a) distaste (for sb/sth)** dislike; the feeling that sb/sth is unpleasant or unacceptable: *She viewed politics with distaste.* ◦ *He seems to have a distaste for hard work.*

dis·taste·ful /dɪsˈteɪstfl/ *adj.* causing the feeling of dislike; unpleasant or unacceptable

dis·till /dɪˈstɪl/ *verb* [T] to heat a liquid until it becomes steam and then collect the liquid that forms when the steam cools: *distilled water*

☆ **dis·tinct** /dɪˈstɪŋkt/ *adj.* **1** clear; easily seen, heard or understood: *There has been a distinct improvement in your work recently.* ◦ *I had the distinct impression that she was lying.* **2 distinct (from sth)** clearly different: *Her books fall into two distinct groups: the novels and the travel stories.* ◦ *This region, as distinct from other parts of the state, relies heavily on tourism for its income.*

☆ **dis·tinc·tion** /dɪˈstɪŋkʃn/ *noun* [C,U] **1 (a) distinction (between A and B)** a clear or important difference between things or people: *We must make a distinction between classical and popular music here.* **2** the quality of being excellent; fame for what you have achieved: *a violinist of great distinction* ◦ *She has the distinction of being the only player to win the championship five times.* ◦ *Becky graduated from high school with distinction.*
IDM draw/make a distinction between A and B to show how two things are different: *It's important to draw a distinction between legal and illegal drugs.*

dis·tinc·tive /dɪˈstɪŋktɪv/ *adj.* clearly different from others and therefore easy to recognize: *the U.N. forces wearing their distinctive light blue helmets* —**dis·tinc·tive·ly** *adv.*

☆ **dis·tinct·ly** /dɪˈstɪŋktli/ *adv.* **1** clearly: *I distinctly heard her say that she couldn't come.* **2** very; particularly: *The town has a distinctly southern atmosphere.*

☆ **dis·tin·guish** /dɪˈstɪŋgwɪʃ/ *verb* **1** [I,T] **distinguish between A and B; distinguish A from B** to recognize the difference between things or people: *He doesn't seem able to distinguish between what's important and what isn't.* ◦ *People who are colorblind often can't distinguish red from green.* **2** [T] **distinguish A (from B)** to make sb/sth different from others; to show the difference between people or things: *Each zebra's unique pattern of stripes distinguishes it from others in the herd.* ◦ *distinguishing features* (= things by which sb/sth can be recognized) **3** [T] to see, hear or recognize with effort: *I heard voices, but I couldn't distinguish what they were saying.* **4** [T] **distinguish yourself** to do sth which causes you to be noticed and admired: *She distinguished herself in track and field events.*

dis·tin·guish·a·ble /dɪˈstɪŋgwɪʃəbl/ *adj.*

1 possible to distinguish as different from sb/sth else: *The male bird is distinguishable from the female by the color of its beak.* **2** possible to see, hear or recognize with effort: *The letter is so old that the signature is barely distinguishable.*

dis·tin·guished /dɪˈstɪŋgwɪʃt/ *adj.* important and respected: *distinguished guests*

dis·tort /dɪˈstɔrt/ *verb* [T] **1** to change the shape or sound of sth so that it seems unnatural: *Her face was distorted with grief.* **2** to change sth and show it falsely: *People in other countries are often given a distorted view of the U.S.* —**dis·tor·tion** /dɪˈstɔrʃn/ *noun* [C,U]

dis·tract /dɪˈstrækt/ *verb* [T] to take sb's attention away from sth: *Could you please stop talking? You're distracting me (from my work).*

dis·trac·tion /dɪˈstrækʃn/ *noun* [C,U] something that takes your attention away from what you were doing or thinking about: *I find it hard to work at home because there are so many distractions.*

dis·traught /dɪˈstrɔt/ *adj.* extremely sad and upset

dis·tress¹ /dɪˈstrɛs/ *noun* [U] **1** the state of being very upset or unhappy or of suffering great pain: *Their distress on hearing the bad news was obvious.* ◦ *He was in such distress that I didn't want to leave him on his own.* **2** the state of being in great danger and needing immediate help: *The ship's captain radioed that it was in distress.*

dis·tress² /dɪˈstrɛs/ *verb* [T] (often passive) to make sb very upset or unhappy: *She was too distressed to talk.*

dis·tress·ing /dɪˈstrɛsɪŋ/ *adj.* causing sb to be very upset or unhappy

☆ **dis·trib·ute** /dɪˈstrɪbyut/ *verb* [T] **1 distribute sth (to/among sb/sth)** to give things to a number of people; to divide sth up and give the parts to people or place them in various positions: *Protesters were distributing leaflets in the street.* ◦ *Tickets will be distributed to all club members.* ◦ *Make sure that the weight is evenly distributed.* **2 distribute sth (to sb/sth)** to transport and supply sth to various people or places: *They distributed emergency food supplies to the areas that were most in need.*

☆ **dis·tri·bu·tion** /ˌdɪstrəˈbyuʃn/ *noun* **1** [sing., U] the act of giving sth: *the distribution of food packages to needy families* **2** [sing., U] the way sth is divided among people; the pattern in which sth is found: *the uneven distribution of wealth* ◦ *a map to show the distribution of rainfall in India* **3** [U] the transport and supply of goods, etc. to various people or places: *The country produces enough food, but distribution is a problem.*

dis·trib·u·tor /dɪˈstrɪbyətər/ *noun* [C] a person or company that transports and supplies goods to a number of stores and companies

☆ **dis·trict** /'dɪstrɪkt/ *noun* [C] **1** an official division of a city, state, country etc.: *a school district* ○ *Congressional districts* **2** a part of a town or city that is of a particular type: *a business district* ○ *the city's financial district*

☞ A **district** may be part of a town, city, state or country, and it may have fixed boundaries: *a judicial district*. A **region** is larger, usually part of a country or state and may not have fixed boundaries: *the industrial regions of the country*. An **area** is also a general term and is used with the same meaning as **region**: *the poorer areas of a town* ○ *an agricultural area of the state*. We use **part** more often when we are talking about a specific section of a town, city, state or country: *Which part of St. Louis do you live in?* ○ *The rain will affect mainly the northern and western parts of the state.*

ˌdistrict at'torney (*abbr.* **D.A.** or **DA**) *noun* [C] a lawyer who works for the government of a city, county, etc. and whose job is to prove in a court of law that sb is guilty of a crime

ˌdistrict 'court *noun* [C,U] a court of law for a particular area in which cases involving national (**federal**) laws, and not state or local laws, are considered

dis·trust /dɪs'trʌst/ *noun* [U, sing.] **(a) distrust (of sb/sth)** the feeling that you cannot believe sb/sth; lack of trust —**dis·trust** *verb* [T]: *She distrusts him because he lied to her once before.*

☆ **dis·turb** /dɪ'stərb/ *verb* [T] **1** to interrupt and possibly annoy sb while he/she is doing sth or sleeping; to spoil a peaceful situation: *I'm sorry to disturb you, but there's a phone call for you.* ○ *Keep the noise down! You'll disturb the neighbors.* **2** to cause sb to worry: *It disturbed her to think that he might be unhappy.* **3** to change sth from its normal position or condition: *I noticed a number of things had been disturbed and realized that there had been a burglary.*

dis·tur·bance /dɪ'stərbəns/ *noun* **1** [C,U] an interruption; something that stops you from concentrating, sleeping, etc. **2** [C] an occasion when people behave violently or make a lot of noise in public: *Further disturbances have been reported in the downtown area.*

dis·turbed /dɪ'stərbd/ *adj.* having mental or emotional problems: *The suspect was described as mentally disturbed.*

dis·turb·ing /dɪ'stərbɪŋ/ *adj.* causing sb to worry: *These disturbing developments suggest that war is a possibility.*

dis·use /dɪs'yus/ *noun* [U] the state of not being used anymore: *The farm buildings had fallen into disuse.*

ditch¹ /dɪtʃ/ *noun* [C] a long narrow hole that has been dug into the ground, especially along the side of a road or field for water to flow through: *The car left the road and ended up in a ditch.*

ditch² /dɪtʃ/ *verb* [T] (*informal*) to get rid of or leave sb/sth: *The suspect ditched his gun in a field before he fled.*

dit·to /'dɪtoʊ/ *adv.* (*informal*) (used to say that something is the same as sth that you have already mentioned): *We should get rid of those old chairs – ditto the couch in the basement.*

☆ **dive¹** /daɪv/ *verb* [I] (*p.t.* **dived** or **dove** /doʊv/; *p.p.* **dived**) **1** to jump into water with your head first: *to dive off rocks into the ocean* ○ *A passerby dived in and saved the drowning man.* **2 dive (for sth)** to go under water, often to search for sth: *people diving for pearls* **3** to move downward steeply and quickly through the air: *The engines failed and the plane dived.* **4** to move quickly in a particular direction, especially downward: *He dove under the table and hid there.*

dive

dive² /daɪv/ *noun* [C] **1** an act of diving into the water **2** a quick movement in a particular direction, especially down or across: *a desperate dive to catch the ball*

IDM **take a dive** (*informal*) to fall or go down suddenly: *Stock prices took a huge dive yesterday.*

div·er /'daɪvər/ *noun* [C] a person who goes under water using special equipment: *Police divers searching the lake found the body.*

☆ **di·verse** /də'vərs; daɪ-/ *adj.* very different from each other: *people with diverse social backgrounds*

di·ver·si·fy /də'vərsəfaɪ; daɪ-/ *verb* [I,T] (*pres. part.* **di·ver·si·fy·ing**; *3rd pers. sing. pres.* **di·ver·si·fies**; *p.t., p.p.* **di·ver·si·fied**) (used especially about a business) to increase the range of activities, products, etc.: *To remain successful in the future, the company will have to diversify.* ○ *to diversify your investments* —**di·ver·si·fi·ca·tion** /də,vərsəfə'keɪʃn/ *noun* [C, U]

di·ver·sion /də'vərʒn; daɪ-/ *noun* **1** [C,U] the act of changing the direction or purpose of sth: *the diversion of a river to prevent flooding* ○ *the illegal diversion of government funds to terrorist groups* **2** [C] something that takes your attention away from sth: *Two girls created a diversion while the third stole several necklaces.*

di·ver·si·ty /də'vərsəti; daɪ-/ *noun* [U] the wide range or variety of sth: *the racial and ethnic diversity of the population*

di·vert /də'vərt; daɪ-/ *verb* [T] **divert sb/sth (from sth) (to sth)** to change the direction or purpose of sb/sth: *All traffic is being diverted around the accident site.* ○ *Government money*

i	ɪ	ɛ	æ	ɑ	ɔ	ʌ	ʊ	u
see	sit	ten	cat	hot	saw	cup	put	too

was diverted from defense to education and training.

☆ **di·vide** /dəˈvaɪd/ verb 1 [I,T] **divide (sth) (up) (into sth)** to separate into different parts: *The egg divides into two cells.* ○ *a book divided into ten sections* ○ *The house was divided into apartments.* 2 [T] **divide sth (up) (between/among sb)** to separate sth into parts and give a share to each of a number of people: *The robbers divided the money among themselves.* ○ *When he died, his property was divided up among his children.* 3 [T] **divide sth (between A and B)** to use different parts or amounts of sth for different purposes: *They divide their time between their two homes.* 4 [T] to separate two places by being a boundary or area between them: *The Charles River divides Boston from Cambridge.* 5 [T] to cause people to disagree: *The question of immigration has divided the country.* 6 [T] **divide sth by sth** to calculate how many times a number will go into another number: *10 divided by 5 is 2.*

di̩vided ˈhighway noun [C] a road that has an area of grass or a fence down the middle to separate the traffic that is going in one direction from the traffic that is going in the other direction

div·i·dend /ˈdɪvədɛnd/ noun [C] a part of a company's profits that is paid to the people who own stock in it

di·vine /dəˈvaɪn/ adj. connected with God or a god —**di·vine·ly** adv.

div·ing /ˈdaɪvɪŋ/ noun [U] the activity or sport of diving into water or swimming under water: *The resort has facilities for sailing, water skiing and diving.* ☞ Look also at **scuba diving**.

ˈdiving board noun [C] a board at the side of a swimming pool from which people can dive into the water

di·vis·i·ble /dəˈvɪzəbl/ adj. that can be divided: *9 is divisible by 3.*

☆ **di·vi·sion** /dəˈvɪʒn/ noun 1 [U] the dividing of sth into separate parts: *the division of the class into two teams* 2 [U, sing.] the sharing of sth: *a fair/unfair division of the profits* 3 [U] dividing one number by another: *the teaching of multiplication and division* 4 [C] a disagreement or difference in thought, way of life, etc.: *deep divisions within the Democratic Party* 5 [C] something that divides or separates: *There is no great division between being a teenager and being an adult.* 6 [C] a part or section of an organization: *the company's sales division*

di·vi·sive /dəˈvaɪsɪv/ adj. (formal) likely to cause disagreements or arguments between people: *a divisive policy*

☆ **di·vorce¹** /dəˈvɔrs/ noun [C,U] the legal end of a marriage: *to get a divorce* ○ *One in three marriages ends in divorce.*

☆ **di·vorce²** /dəˈvɔrs/ verb [T] 1 to legally end your marriage to sb ☞ It is more common to say **to get divorced** than **to divorce**: *My parents got divorced when I was three.* However when only one partner wants a divorce, we say **to divorce**: *She divorced her first husband after suffering years of abuse.* 2 **divorce sb/sth from sth** to separate sb/sth from sth: *His ideas are divorced from reality.* —**di·vorced** adj.: *No, I'm not married – I'm divorced.*

di·vulge /dəˈvʌldʒ; daɪ-/ verb [T] (formal) to tell sth secret: *The reporter refused to divulge her sources.*

Dix·ie /ˈdɪksi/ noun [sing.] (informal) the southeastern states of the U.S.

diz·zy /ˈdɪzi/ adj. (**diz·zi·er**; **diz·zi·est**) feeling as if everything is spinning around and that you might fall: *to feel/get dizzy* —**diz·zi·ness** noun [U]: *He had been to the doctor complaining of headaches and dizziness.*

DJ /ˈdidʒeɪ/ (also **ˈdisk jockey**) noun [C] a person who plays and introduces music on the radio or in a dance club

present tense	past tense
I **do**	I **did**
you **do**	you **did**
he/she/it **does**	he/she/it **did**
we **do**	we **did**
you **do**	you **did**
they **do**	they **did**
past participle	**done**
present participle	**doing**
negative short forms	**don't**, **doesn't**, **didn't**

☆ **do¹** /du/ auxiliary verb (negative **do not**; short form **don't** /doʊnt/; 3rd pers. sing. pres. **does** /dəz; strong form dʌz/; negative **does not**; short form **does·n't** /ˈdʌznt/; p.t. **did** /dɪd/; negative **did not**; short form **did·n't** /ˈdɪdnt/) 1 (used with other verbs to form questions and negative sentences, also in short answers and tag questions): *Do you know John?* ○ *He doesn't live in Portland.* ○ *"Do you agree?" "No, I don't/yes, I do."* ○ *She works in Montreal, doesn't she?* ○ *He didn't say that, did he?* 2 (used for emphasizing the main verb): *"Why didn't you buy any milk?" "I did buy some – it's in the fridge."* 3 (used to avoid repeating the main verb): *He earns a lot more than I do.* ○ *She's feeling a lot better than she did last week.*

☆ **do²** /du/ verb (pres. part. **do·ing**; 3rd pers. sing. pres. **does** /dʌz/; p.t. **did** /dɪd/; p.p. **done** /dʌn/) 1 [T] to perform an action: *What are you doing?* ○ *We didn't do much yesterday.* ○ *Please do as you're told.* ○ *It's not fair, but what can we do about it (= how can we change it)?* ○ *What is the government doing about the national debt?* ○ *What do you do (= what is your job)?* ○ *I don't know what I did with the keys (= where I put them).* 2 [T] to carry out a

particular activity: *Barbara always does* (= styles) *my hair.* ○ *Did he do his homework?* ○ *Who does the cooking in your house?* ○ *I do the laundry every Saturday.* ○ *Did you get your essay done* (= finished)? **3** [I] to make progress or develop: *How are you doing* (= how are you)? ○ *"How's your daughter doing at school?" "She's doing well* (= she is successful)*."* **4** [T] to travel at a certain speed: *This car can do 120 miles per hour.* **5** [T] to produce sth: *The copy machine does 60 copies a minute.* **6** [T] to have a particular effect: *A vacation will do you good.* ○ *The storm did a lot of damage.* **7** [I,T] to be good enough: *I don't need much money – $10 will do.*

IDM do/wash the dishes ⇨ DISH[1]

have to do with sb/sth to be connected with sb/sth: *Don't ask me about the accident. I had nothing to do with it.* ○ *This report has to do with the effects of pollution on the environment.*

could do with sth to want or need sth: *I could do with a cold beer right now.* ○ *The house could do with a fresh coat of paint.*

how do you do? ⇨ HOW[1]

make do with sth ⇨ MAKE[1]

PHRV do away with sth to get rid of sth: *It's time to do away with old stereotypes about women drivers.*

do sb in (*informal*) to kill sb: *All those cigarettes he smoked throughout his life finally did him in.*

do sth over to do sth again, usually because you did not do it well enough the first time: *The camera broke during the filming, so they had to do the whole scene over.* ○ *If I had to do it all over again* (= repeat my life), *I wouldn't change a thing.*

do without (sth) to manage without having sth: *If there isn't any coffee left, we'll just have to do without.*

do[3] /du/ *noun*

IDM do's and don'ts (*informal*) rules that tell you what you should do and what you should not do in a particular situation: *Here are some basic do's and don'ts for successful job interviews:...*

doc·ile /'dɑsl/ *adj.* (used about a person or animal) quiet and easy to control

dock[1] /dɑk/ *noun*
1 [C] a wooden platform at the edge of a lake, river, etc. that you can walk on and tie a boat to: *Fishing from the dock is not allowed.* **2** [C,U] an area of a port where ships stop to be loaded, unloaded, repaired, etc.

dock dock

dock[2] /dɑk/ *verb* **1** [I,T] (used about a ship) to sail into a dock [1](2) : *The ship had docked/was docked at Tampa.* **2** [I] **dock (with sth)** (used

about a spacecraft) to join together with another spacecraft in space **3** [T] to take away part of sb's wages, especially as a punishment: *They docked $20 from my paycheck for taking the morning off without asking.*

dock·et /'dɑkət/ *noun* [C] a list of the cases that will take place in a court of law

☆ **doc·tor[1]** /'dɑktər/ *noun* [C] (*abbr.* **Dr.**) **1** a person who has been trained in medical science and who treats people who are sick: *Our family doctor is Dr. Young.* ○ *I have a doctor's appointment at 10 o'clock.*

☞ We can say **go to the doctor** or **go to the doctor's** (= the doctor's office or clinic). A doctor **sees**, **examines** or **treats** his/her **patients**. He/she may **prescribe** treatment or **medication**. This is written on a **prescription**. We also use the title "Doctor" when we speak to dentists.

2 a person who has received the highest degree from a university: *Doctor of Philosophy* ☞ Look also at **Ph.D.**

doc·tor[2] /'dɑktər/ *verb* [T] **1** to change sth that should not be changed in order to gain some advantage: *The police were accused of doctoring evidence.* **2** to add sth harmful to food or drink

doc·tor·ate /'dɑktərət/ *noun* [C] the highest university degree ☞ Look also at **Ph.D.**

doc·trine /'dɑktrən/ *noun* [C,U] a belief or a set of beliefs that is taught by a church, political party, etc.

☆ **doc·u·ment** /'dɑkyəmənt/ *noun* [C] **1** an official piece of writing which gives information, proof or evidence: *Her lawyer asked her to read and sign a number of documents.* **2** (*computing*) a file such as a letter, a picture, etc., that is stored in a computer or on a disk

doc·u·men·ta·ry /ˌdɑkyə'mɛntəri; -'mɛntri/ *noun* [C] (*pl.* **doc·u·men·ta·ries**) a movie or television or radio program that gives facts or information about a particular subject: *a documentary on/about life in Alaska*

dodge /dɑdʒ/ *verb* **1** [I,T] to move quickly in order to avoid sb/sth: *I ran across the road, dodging the traffic.* **2** [T] to avoid doing or thinking about sth such as a duty, etc.: *He was accused of dodging* (= not paying) *his income taxes for years.*

doe /doʊ/ *noun* [C] a female deer or rabbit ☞ picture at **deer**.

does ⇨ DO[1,2]

☆ **dog[1]** /dɔg/ *noun* [C] an animal that many people keep as a pet, or for working on farms, hunting, etc.

☞ A dog can **bark**, **growl**, **whine** and **wag** its tail. Look also at **hot dog**.

dog[2] /dɔg/ *verb* [T] (**dog·ging**; **dogged**) (often passive) to follow closely and often cause

problems for sb: *Her career has been dogged by bad luck.*

dog-eared /'dɔgɪrd/ *adj.* (used about a book or piece of paper) in bad condition and having the corners of the pages turned down because it has been used a lot

dog-ged /'dɔgəd/ *adj.* refusing to give up even when sth is difficult: *I was impressed by his dogged determination to succeed.* —**dog-ged-ly** *adv.: She doggedly refused all offers of help.*

dog-gy bag (*also* **doggie bag**) /'dɔgi bæg/ *noun* [C] a small bag or box for food that you do not finish eating at a restaurant, that you can take home with you

dog-ma /'dɔgmə/ *noun* [C,U] a belief or set of beliefs that people are expected to accept as true without questioning

dog-mat-ic /dɔg'mætɪk/ *adj.* insisting that sth is true or right; not prepared to consider other opinions

dol-drums /'doʊldrəmz/ *noun* [plural]
in the doldrums (*informal*) **1** not active or busy: *Business has been in the doldrums but should improve later in the year.* **2** sad or depressed

dole /doʊl/ *verb* (*informal*)
dole sth out to give sth, especially food, money, etc. to a number of people, in small amounts

☆ **doll** /dɑl/ *noun* [C] a child's toy that looks like a small person or a baby

☆ **dol-lar** /'dɑlər/ *noun* **1** [C] (*symbol* $) a unit of money in the U.S., Canada, Australia, etc.: *Melissa earns $24,000 a year.* ○ *a five-dollar bill* ○ *Grandpa sent me a check for $25.* ☞ There are 100 **cents** in a dollar. For more information, look at Appendix 2. **2** [C] a bill or coin that is worth one dollar (1): *I found a dollar lying on the sidewalk.* **3 the dollar** [sing.] the value of the U.S. dollar on international money markets: *The dollar has fallen against the yen.*

doll-house /'dɑlhaʊs/ *noun* [C] a small toy house that children use when they play with dolls

dolphin

dol-phin /'dɑlfən/ *noun* [C] an intelligent animal that lives in the ocean and looks like a large fish. Dolphins usually swim in large groups.

do-main /doʊ'meɪn/ *noun* [C] an area of knowledge or activity: *I don't know the answer – that's really outside my domain.* ○ *This issue is*

now in the public domain (= the public knows about it).

dome /doʊm/ *noun* [C] a round roof on a building

☆ **do-mes-tic** /də'mɛstɪk/ *adj.* **1** connected with the home or family: *domestic responsibilities* **2** (used about a person) enjoying doing things in the home, such as cooking and cleaning: *No, I don't know how to bake cookies – I'm not really very domestic.* **3** not international; of or inside a particular country: *domestic flights* (= within one country) **4** (used about animals) kept as pets or on farms; not wild: *domestic animals such as cats and dogs*

do-mes-ti-cat-ed /də'mɛstəkeɪṭəd/ *adj.* (used about animals) used to living near people and being controlled by them

dom-i-nance /'dɑmənəns/ *noun* [U] control or power: *Japan's dominance of the car industry*

dom-i-nant /'dɑmənənt/ *adj.* the strongest or most important: *Norman's mother was the dominant influence in his life.*

☆ **dom-i-nate** /'dɑməneɪt/ *verb* **1** [I,T] to have strong control or influence; to be the most important person or thing in sth: *The Raiders' offense dominated throughout the second half of the game.* ○ *She always tends to dominate the conversation at dinner parties.* **2** [T] (used about a building or place) to look down on or over: *The Space Needle dominates Seattle's skyline.*

dom-i-na-tion /ˌdɑmə'neɪʃn/ *noun* [U] strong control, power or influence

dom-i-neer-ing /ˌdɑmə'nɪrɪŋ/ *adj.* having a very strong character and wanting to control other people

dominoes

dom-i-no /'dɑmənoʊ/ *noun* [C] (*pl.* **dom-i-noes**) one of a set of small flat pieces of wood or plastic that are used for playing a game (**dominoes**). Each domino has a different number of spots on one side of it.

☆ **do-nate** /'doʊneɪt; doʊ'neɪt/ *verb* [T] to give money or goods to an organization, especially one for people or animals who need help: *She donated a large sum of money to the American Cancer Society.*

do-na-tion /doʊ'neɪʃn/ *noun* [C] a gift of money or goods to an organization, especially one for people or animals who need help: *Would you like to make a small donation to the Red Cross?*

done¹ *p.p.* of DO²

☆ **done²** /dʌn/ *adj.* (not before a noun) **1** finished: *I have to go out as soon as this job is*

D

done. **2** (used about food) cooked enough: *The meat's ready, but the vegetables still aren't done.* ☞ Look also at **well-done**.

IDM **over (and done) with** ⇨ OVER[2]

☆ **don·key** /'dɑŋki; 'dɔŋ-/ *noun* [C] (*pl.* **don·keys**) an animal like a small horse, with long ears

donkey

do·nor /'doʊnər/ *noun* [C] **1** a person who gives blood or a part of his/her own body for medical use: *a blood donor* ∘ *a kidney donor* **2** a person who gives money or goods to an organization that needs it, especially an organization for helping other people

don't ⇨ DO[1,2]

do·nut = DOUGHNUT

doo·dle /'dudl/ *verb* [I] to draw lines, patterns, etc. without concentrating, especially when you are bored or thinking about sth else —**doo·dle** *noun* [C]

doom /dum/ *noun* [U] death or a terrible event in the future which you cannot avoid: *a sense of doom* (= that something bad is going to happen)

doomed /dumd/ *adj.* certain to fail or to suffer sth bad: *The plan was doomed from the start.* ∘ *a doomed love affair*

☆ **door** /dɔr/ *noun* [C] **1** a piece of wood, glass, etc. that you open and close to get in or out of a room, building, car, etc.: *to open/shut/close the door* ∘ *Don't forget to lock the door when you leave the house.* ∘ *Please don't slam the door.* ∘ *Can you get the door* (= open it and see who is there) *for me?* ∘ *I could hear someone knocking on the door.* ∘ *Go and see who's at the door.* ∘ *the front/back door* **2** the entrance to a building, room, car, etc.: *I peeked through the door and saw her sitting there.*

IDM **door to door** from house to house: *The candidate went door to door to ask people to vote for her.* ∘ *a door-to-door salesperson* (= a person who visits people in their homes to try and sell them things)

next door (to sb/sth) in the next house, room, etc.: *Do you know the people (who) live next door?* ∘ *You'll find the bathroom next door to your bedroom.*

door·bell /'dɔrbɛl/ *noun* [C] a bell on the outside of a house which you ring when you want to go in

door·knob /'dɔrnɑb/ *noun* [C] a round handle on a door that you turn to open the door

door·mat /'dɔrmæt/ *noun* [C] **1** a piece of material in front of a door which you can wipe your shoes on to clean them before going inside **2** (*informal*) a person who allows other people to treat him/her badly without complaining

door·step /'dɔrstɛp/ *noun* [C] a step in front of a door, usually outside a building

IDM **on your doorstep** very near to you: *The beach was practically on our doorstep.*

door·way /'dɔrweɪ/ *noun* [C] an entrance into a building, room, etc.: *She was standing in the doorway.*

dope[1] /doʊp/ *noun* (*informal*) **1** [U] a drug that is not legal, especially marijuana: *to smoke dope* **2** [C] a stupid person: *What a dope!*

dope[2] /doʊp/ *verb* [T] to give a drug secretly to a person or animal, especially to make him/her/it sleep

dop·ey (*also* **dopy**) /'doʊpi/ *adj.* (**dop·i·er**; **dop·i·est**) **1** tired and not able to think clearly, especially because of drugs, alcohol or lack of sleep **2** (*informal*) stupid; not very intelligent

dork /dɔrk/ *noun* [C] (*slang*) a person who you think is boring and stupid because he/she behaves in a strange way and wears unfashionable clothes —**dork·y** /'dɔrki/ *adj.*

dorm /dɔrm/ *noun* [C] (*informal*) = DORMITORY: *a dorm room*

dor·mant /'dɔrmənt/ *adj.* not active for some time: *a dormant volcano*

☆ **dor·mi·to·ry** /'dɔrmə,tɔri/ (*also informal* **dorm**, *formal* **residence hall**) *noun* [C] (*pl.* **dor·mi·to·ries**) a building at a college or university where students live

dos·age /'doʊsɪdʒ/ *noun* [C, usually sing.] the amount of a medicine you should take over a period of time: *The recommended dosage is one tablet every four hours.*

dose /doʊs/ *noun* [C] **1** an amount of medicine that you take at one time: *How large a dose should I take?* **2** (*informal*) an amount of sth, especially sth bad: *Rick got a dose of reality when his first credit card bill arrived in the mail.* ∘ *I can only stand my mother-in-law in small doses.*

☆ **dot**[1] /dɑt/ *noun* [C] **1** a small, round mark: *The letters i and j have dots over them.* ☞ Look also at **polka dot**. **2** something that looks like a dot (1): *The airplane was just a dot in the sky.*

IDM **on the dot** (*informal*) at exactly the right time or at exactly the time mentioned: *Classes start at 9 o'clock on the dot.*

dot[2] /dɑt/ *verb* [T] (**dot·ting**; **dot·ted**) to mark with a dot1

IDM **be dotted with** to have many things or people in or on it: *a hillside dotted with sheep*

dote /doʊt/ *verb* [I] **dote on sb/sth** to have or show too much love for sb/sth and think they are perfect: *He dotes on his youngest son.*

dot·ing /'doʊtɪŋ/ *adj.* very or too loving: *doting parents*

dot·ted line /,dɑtəd 'laɪn/ *noun* [C] a line of dots which show where sth is to be written on a form, etc.: *Just sign your name on the dotted line.* ☞ picture at **line**.

☆ **dou·ble¹** /'dʌbl/ *adj.* **1** twice as much or as many (as usual): *a double helping of ice cream* **2** having two equal or similar parts: *double doors* ∘ *a double burger* (= with two pieces of meat in it) **3** made for or used by two people or things: *a double garage* ∘ *a double bed*

☆ **dou·ble²** /'dʌbl/ *det.* twice as much or as many (as usual, as sb/sth, etc.): *His income is double hers.* ∘ *We'll need double the amount of food.*

☆ **dou·ble³** /'dʌbl/ *adv.* in twos or two parts: *When I saw her with her twin sister, I thought I was seeing double.*

☆ **dou·ble⁴** /'dʌbl/ *noun* **1** [U] twice the (usual) number or amount: *I only ordered you a small serving of French fries, but they gave me double.* **2** [C] a person who looks very much like another: *I thought it was you I saw at the grocery store. You must have a double.* **3** doubles [plural] (in some sports, e.g. tennis) with two pairs of people playing: *the men's doubles championship* ☞ Look at **singles²**(3).

☆ **dou·ble⁵** /'dʌbl/ *verb* **1** [I,T] to become or to make sth twice as much or as many: *The price of houses has almost doubled.* ∘ *Think of a number and double it.* **2** [I] **double as sth** to have a second use or function: *The small room doubles as a study.*

PHRV **double (sb) over/up** (to cause sb) to bend the body: *to be doubled up in pain* ∘ *to double over with laughter*

ˌ**double** ˈ**bass** (*also* **bass**) *noun* [C] the largest instrument of the violin family, that you play standing up or sitting down

ˌ**double-**ˈ**breasted** *adj.* (used about a coat or jacket) having the front parts cross over each other, with two rows of buttons

ˌ**double-**ˈ**check** *verb* [I,T] to check sth again, or with great care

ˌ**double-**ˈ**cross** *verb* [T] to cheat sb who believes that he/she can trust you

ˌ**double-**ˌ**decker** ˈ**bus** (*also* ˌ**double-**ˈ**deck-er**) *noun* [C] (*pl.* **double-decker buses**) a bus with two floors

ˌ**double-**ˈ**digit** *adj.* (only *before* a noun) connected with a number from 10 to 99: *double-digit inflation*

ˌ**double** ˈ**negative** *noun* [C] the use of two negative words, such as "no" or "not," in one sentence. This is considered incorrect according to the rules of English: *The sentence, "She doesn't have no friends," contains a double negative.*

ˌ**double-**ˈ**park** *verb* [I,T] to park (a car) illegally in the middle of a street, beside another car that is already parked at the edge of the street

dou·bly /'dʌbli/ *adv.* **1** in two ways: *He was doubly blessed with both good looks and talent.* **2** more than usually: *I made doubly sure that the door was locked.*

☆ **doubt¹** /daʊt/ *noun* [C,U] (a feeling of) being uncertain: *I am starting to have some serious doubts about my relationship with Jeff.* ∘ *You'll definitely pass. There's no doubt about it.* ∘ *There was some doubt as to whether she was the right person for the job.*

☞ Be careful – **doubt** is not the same as **question**. We use **doubt** when we are not certain about sth: *I have some doubts about the fairness of this new policy.* We use **question** when we are asking for information about sth: *I have some questions about the homework assignment.*

IDM **beyond/without a shadow of a doubt** ⇨ SHADOW¹

cast doubt on sth ⇨ CAST²

give sb the benefit of the doubt ⇨ BENEFIT¹

in doubt not sure or definite

no doubt (used when you expect sth to happen but you are not sure that it will) probably: *No doubt she'll write when she has time.*

without (a) doubt definitely: *It was without doubt the coldest winter for many years.*

☆ **doubt²** /daʊt/ *verb* [T] to think that sth is unlikely or to feel uncertain (about sth): *She never doubted* (= she was always sure) *that he was telling the truth.* ∘ *I doubt whether/if I'll have time to go shopping today* (= I don't think I'll be able to go). ∘ *He had never doubted her support.*

doubt·ful /'daʊtfl/ *adj.* **1** unlikely or uncertain: *It's doubtful whether/if we'll finish in time for the meeting.* ∘ *It was doubtful that he was still alive.* **2** doubtful (about sth/about doing sth) (used about a person) not sure: *He still felt doubtful about his decision.* —**doubt-ful·ly** *adv.*: *"I suppose it'll be all right," she said doubtfully.*

doubt·less /'daʊtləs/ *adv.* (*formal*) almost certainly: *The talks will doubtless promote better relations between the two countries.*

dough /doʊ/ *noun* [U] **1** a thick mixture of flour, water and sometimes fat and sugar. It is used for baking into bread, etc.: *cookie dough* ☞ Look also at **batter²**. **2** (*informal, old-fashioned*) money

dough·nut (*also* **donut**) /'doʊnʌt/ *noun* [C] a small cake in the shape of a ring or a ball, made from sweet dough cooked in fat ☞ picture at **bread**.

dour /'daʊər; dʊr/ *adj.* (used about a person's manner or expression) cold and unfriendly

douse /daʊs/ *verb* [T] **1** to cover sb/sth with liquid: *to douse yourself in perfume* (= wear too much of it) **2** (*formal*) to stop a fire, etc. from burning: *The firemen managed to douse the blaze.*

dove¹ /dʌv/ *noun* [C] a type of white or gray bird that is often used as a sign of peace

dove² /doʊv/ *p.t.* of DIVE¹

dow·dy /'daʊdi/ *adj.* (**dow·di·er**; **dow·di·est**)

D

(used about a person or the clothes he/she wears) dull and unfashionable

☆ **down¹** /daʊn/ adv. **1** to or at a lower level or place; not up: *We sat and watched the sun go down.* ∘ *Can you get that book down from the top shelf?* ∘ *"Where's Mary?" "She's down in the basement."* **2** from a standing or vertical position to a sitting or horizontal one: *I think I'll sit/lie down.* **3** to or in the south: *We went down to Florida on our vacation.* **4** (used for showing that the level, amount, strength, etc. of sth is less or lower): *Do you mind if I turn the heat down a little?* **5** (written) on paper: *Put these dates down in your calendar.* **6** as a first payment: *We bought the car for just $500 down.* **7 down to sb/sth** even including: *Everybody was invited, from the president down to the custodians.*

IDM be/come down to sb to be sb's responsibility: *It's all down to you, Pat – if you make this basket, we'll win the game!* ∘ *When my father died, it came down to me to take care of the family's affairs.*

be down to sth to have only the amount mentioned left: *I can't loan you any money – I'm down to my last $5.*

come down with sth to be or become sick with sth: *I think I'm coming down with the flu.*

down and out having no money, job or home

down under (*informal*) (in) Australia: *He comes from down under.*

☆ **down²** /daʊn/ prep. **1** along: *"Where's the nearest gas station?" "Go down this road and take the first right."* **2** from the top toward the bottom of sth: *Her hair hung down her back.* ∘ *The snow began to slide down the mountain.* **3** at or to a lower or further part of sth: *We sailed down the river.*

down³ /daʊn/ verb [T] (*informal*) to finish a drink quickly: *He downed two beers and left.*

down⁴ /daʊn/ noun [U] very soft feathers: *a down comforter*

IDM ups and downs ⇨ UP³

down⁵ /daʊn/ adj. **1** sad: *You're looking a little down today.* **2** lower than before: *Unemployment figures are down for the third month in a row.* **3** (used about computers) not working

down·cast /ˈdaʊnkæst/ adj. **1** (used about eyes) looking down **2** (used about a person) sad and without hope

down·fall /ˈdaʊnfɔl/ noun [sing.] **1** a loss of power or success: *The senator's downfall seemed inevitable.* **2** a thing that causes a loss of power or success: *Alcohol proved to be her downfall.*

down·grade /ˈdaʊngreɪd/ verb [T] to reduce sb/sth to a lower level or position of importance

down·hill /ˌdaʊnˈhɪl/ adj., adv. (going) down a slope; toward the bottom of a hill: *It's an easy walk. The road runs downhill most of the way.* ∘ *Do you go downhill or cross-country skiing?*

IDM go downhill to get worse: *Their relationship has been going downhill for quite a while.*

down·load /ˈdaʊnloʊd/ verb [T] to copy a computer file, etc. from a large computer system to a smaller one

down ·payment noun [C] a first payment for sth that you buy, with the rest of the price to be paid later: *I finally saved enough money to make a down payment on a new car.*

down·pour /ˈdaʊnpɔr/ noun [C, usually sing.] a heavy, sudden fall of rain

down·right¹ /ˈdaʊnraɪt/ adj. (only *before* a noun) (used about sth bad or unpleasant) complete: *Our trip was a downright disaster.*

down·right² /ˈdaʊnraɪt/ adv. completely or thoroughly: *That road is downright dangerous!*

down·size /ˈdaʊnsaɪz/ verb [I,T] (used about a large company) to reduce the number of people working, in order to save money: *Several hundred jobs were lost when the company downsized its operations.* —**down·siz·ing** noun [U]: *the era of corporate downsizing*

Down's syn·drome /ˈdaʊnz ˌsɪndroʊm/ noun [U] a condition that a person is born with. People with this condition have a flat, wide face and lower than average intelligence.

☆ **down·stairs** /ˌdaʊnˈstɛrz/ adv. **1** down the stairs: *He fell downstairs and broke his arm.* **2** to a lower floor: *Dad's downstairs in the basement.* ☞ The opposite is **upstairs**. —**down·stairs** /ˈdaʊnstɛrz/ adj.: *the downstairs bathroom*

down·stream /ˌdaʊnˈstrim/ adv. in the direction in which a river flows: *The boat floated downstream.* ☞ The opposite is **upstream**.

down-to-ˈearth adj. sensible and practical; not too silly

☆ **down·town** /ˌdaʊnˈtaʊn/ adj., adv. in or to the central area of a city or large town, especially where there are many stores and businesses: *downtown Milwaukee* ∘ *I need to go downtown and get some stuff for the party.* ☞ In New York City, **downtown** is used to describe the southern part of Manhattan, where the streets have low numbers in their names. Look also at **uptown**.

down·trod·den /ˈdaʊntrɑdn/ adj. (used about a person) made to suffer bad treatment or living conditions by people in power, but being too tired, poor, ill, etc. to change things

☆ **down·ward¹** /ˈdaʊnwərd/ adj. (only *before* a noun) toward the ground or a lower level: *a downward movement* ∘ *There is still a downward trend in the stock market.*

☆ **down·ward²** /ˈdaʊnwərd/ (*also* **downwards** /ˈdaʊnwərdz/) adv. toward the ground or a lower level: *They stood a few feet apart, staring downward and refusing to speak.* ☞ The opposite is **upward(s)**.

dow·ry /ˈdaʊri/ noun [C] (*pl.* **dow·ries**) an amount of money or property which, in some

countries, a woman's family gives to the man she is marrying

doz. *abbr.* = DOZEN: *3 doz. eggs*

doze /douz/ *verb* [I] to sleep lightly and/or for a short time: *He was dozing in front of the television.*
PHRV **doze off** to go to sleep, without meaning to: *I'm sorry – I must have dozed off for a minute.*

☆**doz·en** /'dʌzn/ *noun* (*abbr.* **doz.**) **1** [C] (*pl.* **dozen**) twelve or a group of twelve: *I need to buy a dozen eggs.* ○ *half a dozen* (= six) ○ *two dozen sheep* **2 dozens** [plural] (*informal*) very many: *I've tried calling her dozens of times.*
IDM **a dime a dozen** ⇨ DIME

Dr. *abbr.* **1** = DOCTOR¹ **2** = DRIVE²(3)

drab /dræb/ *adj.* (**drab·ber**; **drabbest**) dull and not interesting or attractive: *a drab gray office building*

☆**draft¹** /dræft/ *noun* **1** [C] a piece of writing, etc. which will probably be changed and improved; not the final copy: *the first draft of a speech* ○ *a rough draft of an essay* **2** [C] a current of air that comes into a room: *Can you shut the door? There's a draft in here.* **3 the draft** [sing.] the system of making sb join the army, etc.: *young men who tried to avoid the draft during the Vietnam War*

☆**draft²** /dræft/ *verb* [T] **1** to make a first or an early copy of a piece of writing: *I'll draft a letter and show it to you before I type it.* **2** (usually passive) to order sb to join the armed forces: *He was drafted into the army.*

draft·y /'dræfti/ *adj.* (**draft·i·er**; **draft·i·est**) having currents of air blowing through it: *a drafty old house*

drag¹ /dræg/ *noun* **1** [sing.] (*informal*) a thing that is boring or annoying: *Having to stay home on a Saturday night is a real drag.* **2 a drag on sth** [sing.] something that slows the progress of sth else: *High interest rates continue to be a drag on the economy.* **3** [C] (*informal*) an act of breathing in cigarette smoke: *He took a long drag on his cigarette.* **4** [U] (*informal*) the wearing of women's clothes by a man, especially as part of a show, etc.
☞ Look also at **main drag**.

☆**drag²** /dræg/ *verb* (**drag·ging**; **dragged**) **1** [T] to pull sb/sth along with difficulty: *The box was so heavy we had to drag it along the floor.* **2** [T] to force or to make sb come or go somewhere: *She dragged the child up the steps by her arm.* ○ *Can I drag you away from your desk for a minute?* **3** [I] **drag (on)** to be boring or to seem to last a long time: *The speeches dragged on for hours.*
PHRV **drag sth out** to make sth last longer than necessary: *Let's not drag this decision out – should we go or not?*
drag sth out (of sb) to force or persuade sb to give you information that you want

drag·on /'drægən/ *noun* [C] (in stories, etc.)

an imaginary animal with wings, which can breathe out fire

☆**drain¹** /dreɪn/ *noun* [C] a pipe or hole that dirty water, etc. goes down to be carried away: *Just pour the rest of that stuff down the drain.*
IDM **a drain on sb/sth** something that uses up time, money, strength, etc.: *The cost of college tuition is a big drain on our budget.*
(go) down the drain (*informal*) (to be) wasted: *All that hard work has gone down the drain.*

drain² /dreɪn/ *verb* **1** [I,T] to flow away; to make a liquid flow: *The sink's clogged – the water won't drain away at all.* ○ *The mechanic drained the oil from the engine.* **2** [I,T] to become dry as liquid flows away; to make sth dry in this way: *Drain the spaghetti and serve.* **3** [T] to drink all the liquid (in a glass, etc.): *She drained her glass in one gulp.* **4** [I] (used about a feeling) to become weaker and weaker until it disappears: *He felt his anger drain away.* **5** [T] **drain sb/sth (of sth)** to make sb/sth weaker, poorer, etc. by slowly using all the strength, money, etc. available

drain·age /'dreɪnɪdʒ/ *noun* [U] a system used for draining water, etc. away from a place: *a drainage ditch*

drake /dreɪk/ *noun* [C] a male duck

dra·ma /'drɑmə/ *noun* **1** [C] a play for the theater, radio or television: *a contemporary drama* **2** [U] plays as a form of writing; the performance of plays: *He wrote some drama as well as poetry.* ○ *a drama student* **3** [C] an exciting event **4** [U] excitement: *...and to add to all the drama, the lights went out!*

☆**dra·mat·ic** /drə'mætɪk/ *adj.* **1** noticeable or sudden: *a dramatic change* **2** exciting or impressive: *a dramatic scene.* **3** (used about a person, a person's behavior, etc.) showing feelings, etc. in a very obvious way because you want other people to notice you or pay attention to you: *Calm down. There's no need to be so dramatic about everything!* **4** connected with plays or the theater: *Shakespeare's dramatic works* —**dra·mat·ic·al·ly** /drə'mætɪkli/ *adv.*: *"I can't go on," she said dramatically.*

dram·a·tist /'drɑmətɪst; 'dræ-/ *noun* [C] a person who writes plays

dram·a·tize /'drɑmətaɪz; 'dræ-/ *verb* **1** [T] to make a book, an event, etc. into a play: *The novel has been dramatized for television.* **2** [I,T] to make sth seem more exciting or important than it really is: *The newspaper was accused of dramatizing the situation.* —**dram·a·ti·za·tion** /ˌdrɑmətə'zeɪʃn; ˌdræ-/ *noun* [C,U]

drank *p.t.* of DRINK¹

drape /dreɪp/ *verb* [T] **1 drape sth around/over sth** to put a piece of cloth, clothing, etc. loosely on sth: *He quickly draped a towel around his waist.* **2 drape sb/sth (in/with sth)** (usually passive) to cover sb/sth (with cloth,

tʃ	dʒ	v	θ	ð	s	z	ʃ
chin	June	van	thin	then	so	zoo	she

etc.): *The stadium was draped with red, white and blue flags.*

drap·er·y /ˈdreɪpəri/ (*also* **drape** /dreɪp/) *noun* [C, usually pl.] (*pl.* **drap·er·ies**) a long curtain that is made of heavy cloth

dras·tic /ˈdræstɪk/ *adj.* **1** strong, effective and usually quick: *The situation requires drastic action.* **2** very noticeable or serious: *a drastic rise in crime* —**dras·tic·al·ly** /-kli/ *adv.*: *Home prices have fallen drastically over the last two years.*

D

draught /drɑːft/ *noun* [C] (*BrE*) = DRAFT¹(2)

☆ **draw¹** /drɔ/ *verb* (*p.t.* **drew** /dru/; *p.p.* **drawn** /drɔn/) **1** [I,T] to make a picture or diagram of sth with a pencil, pen, etc.: *I'll draw you a map of how to get there.* **2** [T] **draw sth out of/from sth** to pull sth smoothly out of its present position: *She drew the letter out of her pocket and handed it to me.* **3** [T] to pull sb/sth gently into a new position: *He drew me by the hand into the room.* **4** [T] (used about horses, etc.) to pull sth along: *The carriage was drawn by six horses.* **5** [T] to close curtains, etc.: *I couldn't see inside the window because the curtains were drawn.* **6** [T] to pull a gun, sword or knife out of its holder, quickly and in order to attack sb: *The police officer drew his gun.* **7** [I] (*formal*) to move in the direction mentioned: *The President's limousine drew into/out of the White House grounds.* **8** [T] **draw sth from sb/sth** to gain sth from sb/sth: *This information has been drawn from a number of sources.* **9** [T] **draw sth (from sth)** to learn sth from study, experience, etc.: *Can we draw any conclusions from this survey?* **10** [T] **draw sth (from sb)** to produce a reaction or response to the thing mentioned: *The advertisement has drawn interest from people all over the country.* **11** [T] **draw sb (to sb/sth)** to attract or interest sb: *The musicians drew a fairly large crowd.*

IDM **bring sth/come/draw to an end** ⇨ END¹

call/draw sb's attention to sth ⇨ ATTENTION

draw a blank to fail to find an answer: *Detectives investigating the case have drawn a blank so far.*

draw a comparison/a parallel to show how two things compare or are similar: *The program drew an interesting comparison between education in Japan and in the U.S.*

draw/make a distinction between sth and sth ⇨ DISTINCTION

draw the line at sth to say "no" to sth even though you are prepared to be helpful in other ways: *I do most of the cooking, but I draw the line at doing the dishes afterward!*

draw straws to decide sth by chance: *They drew straws to see who should stay behind.*

PHRV **draw sth out** to make sth last longer than usual or necessary: *There's no need to draw this discussion out any longer.*

draw up (used about a car, etc.) to drive up and stop in front of or near sth: *A police car drew up outside the building.*

draw sth up to prepare a document, list, etc. and write it out: *Our lawyer is going to draw up the contract.*

draw² /drɔ/ *noun* [C] **1** a person or thing that attracts interest or attention: *The young star is a big draw at the box office.* **2** a result of a game or competition in which both players or teams get the same score so that neither of them wins: *The game ended in a draw.* ☞ It is more common to say **tie**.

draw·back /ˈdrɔbæk/ *noun* [C] a disadvantage or problem: *His lack of experience is a major drawback.*

☆ **draw·er** /drɔr/ *noun* [C] a container which forms part of a piece of furniture, such as a desk, that you can pull out to put things in or take things out: *There's some paper in the top drawer of my desk.*

☆ **draw·ing** /ˈdrɔɪŋ/ *noun* **1** [C] a picture made with a pencil, pen, etc. **2** [U] the art of drawing pictures: *She's good at drawing and painting.*

drawl /drɔl/ *verb* [I,T] to speak slowly, making the vowel sounds very long —**drawl** *noun* [sing.]

drawn¹ /drɔn/ *adj.* (used about a person or his/her face) looking tired, worried or sick: *He looked pale and drawn after the long journey.*

drawn² *p.p.* of DRAW¹: *The curtains were drawn.*

dread¹ /drɛd/ *noun* [U, sing.] great fear: *He lived in dread of the same thing happening to him one day.* ○ *a secret dread of what might happen*

dread² /drɛd/ *verb* [T] to be very afraid of or worried about sth: *I'm dreading my final exams.* ○ *She dreaded having to tell him what had happened.* ○ *I dread to think what my dad will say.*

dread·ed /ˈdrɛdəd/ *adj.* terrible; causing you to feel afraid or worried

dread·ful /ˈdrɛdfl/ *adj.* (*formal* or *old-fashioned*) very bad, unpleasant or poor in quality: *There's been a dreadful* (= very serious) *mistake.* —**dread·ful·ly** *adv.*

dread·locks /ˈdrɛdlɑks/ *noun* [plural] hair worn in long curled pieces, especially by some black people

☆ **dream¹** /drim/ *noun* **1** [C] a series of events or pictures which happen in your mind while you are asleep: *I had a strange dream last night.* ○ *In my dream I was flying a helicopter...* ☞ Look at **nightmare**. **2** [C] an event or situation that you want very much to happen, although it is not very likely that it will: *His dream was to give up his job and live on an island.* ○ *a dream house* (= one that you would like very much to own)

☆ **dream²** /drim/ *verb* [I,T] (*p.t., p.p.* **dreamed** /drimd/ or **dreamt** /drɛmt/) **1** to see or experience pictures and events in your mind

i	ɪ	ɛ	æ	ɑ	ɔ	ʌ	ʊ	u
see	sit	ten	cat	hot	saw	cup	put	too

while you are asleep: *I dreamed about the house that I lived in as a child.* ○ *I woke up to find that I wasn't really rich. I had only dreamed it.* ○ *I dreamed that I was running but I couldn't get away.* **2** to imagine sth that you would like to happen: *I've always dreamed about winning lots of money.* ○ *I never dreamed that I would be so lucky!* ☞ Look at **day-dream**.

IDM **I, etc. would not dream of sth** I, etc. would definitely not do sth, under any circumstances: *"Don't tell anybody." "Of course not. I wouldn't dream of it."*

PHRV **dream sth up** (*informal*) to think of sth such as a plan, etc. especially sth unusual or slightly foolish: *Which one of you dreamed up that idea?*

dream·er /ˈdrimər/ *noun* [C] a person who thinks a lot about ideas, plans, etc. which may never happen instead of concentrating on what is really happening

dream·y /ˈdrimi/ *adj.* (**dream·i·er**; **dream·i-est**) (used about a person or his/her expression) having or showing thoughts that are far away from the real world: *a dreamy look, expression, etc.*

drea·ry /ˈdrɪri/ *adj.* (**drea·ri·er**; **drea·ri·est**) dull, boring or depressing: *dreary weather*

dredge /drɛdʒ/ *verb* [T] to clear the mud, etc. from the bottom of a river or harbor using a special machine

PHRV **dredge sth up** to mention again sth bad from the past that it would be better to forget: *The newspaper had dredged up all sorts of embarrassing details about her private life.*

drench /drɛntʃ/ *verb* [T] (usually passive) to make sb/sth completely wet: *We got totally drenched in the storm.*

☆ **dress¹** /drɛs/ *noun* **1** [C] a piece of clothing worn by a girl or a woman. It covers the body from the shoulders to the knees or below and often covers the arms. ☞ picture on page A26. **2** [U] clothes for either men or women: *formal/informal dress* ○ *evening dress*

☆ **dress²** /drɛs/ *verb* **1** [I,T] to put clothes on sb or yourself: *He dressed quickly and left the house with a minute to spare.* ○ *If you don't get dressed soon, we'll be late.* ○ *My husband dressed the kids while I got breakfast ready.* ○ *Hurry up, Kelly! Aren't you dressed yet?* ☞ It is more common to say **get dressed** than **dress**. **2** [I] to put or have clothes on, in the way or style mentioned: *to dress well, badly, etc.* ○ *to be well dressed, badly dressed, etc.* **3** [I] to put on formal clothes for the evening: *In the past, wealthy families always dressed for dinner.* **4** [T] to clean and put a bandage, etc. on a wound: *to dress a wound*

IDM **(be) dressed in sth** wearing sth: *The people at the funeral were all dressed in black.*

PHRV **dress up 1** to put on special or unusual clothes for fun or for a play: *The kids decided*

to dress up as pirates. **2** to put on nice clothes, usually for a special occasion: *You don't need to dress up for the party.*

¹**dress code** *noun* [C] a set of rules explaining what types of clothes people are allowed to wear in a particular place: *Our company's dress code requires all employees to wear business suits.*

dress·er /ˈdrɛsər/ *noun* [C] a piece of furniture with drawers in it that is used for storing clothes

dress·ing /ˈdrɛsɪŋ/ *noun* **1** [C,U] a sauce for food, especially for salads **2** [U] = STUFFING(1) **3** [C] a covering that you put on a wound to protect it and keep it clean

drew *p.t.* of DRAW¹

drib·ble /ˈdrɪbl/ *verb* **1** [I,T] (used about a liquid) to move downward in a thin stream; to make a liquid move in this way: *The paint dribbled down the side of the can.* **2** [I,T] (used in basketball or soccer) to make a ball move forward by using many short hits or kicks: *to dribble a basketball*

dried¹ *p.t., p.p.* of DRY²

dried² /draɪd/ *adj.* (used about food) with all the liquid removed from it: *dried fruit*

dri·er *adj.* ⇨ DRY¹

drift¹ /drɪft/ *verb* [I] **1** to be carried or moved along by wind or water: *The boat drifted out to sea.* **2** (used about snow or sand) to be moved into piles by wind or water: *The snow drifted up to six feet deep in some places.* **3** to move slowly or without any particular purpose: *She drifted into acting almost by accident.* ○ *At one time they were close friends, but over the years they drifted apart.*

drift² /drɪft/ *noun* **1** [C] a slow movement toward sth: *the country's drift into economic decline* **2** [sing.] the general meaning of sth: *I couldn't understand every word, but I got the drift of what he was saying.* **3** [C] = SNOWDRIFT

drill¹ /drɪl/ *noun* **1** [C] a tool or machine that is used for making holes in things: *a dentist's drill* ☞ picture at **tool**. **2** [U] exercise in marching, etc. that soldiers do **3** [C] something that you repeat many times in order to learn sth **4** [C,U] practice for what you should do in an emergency: *a fire drill*

drill² /drɪl/ *verb* [I,T] **1** to make a hole in sth with a drill ¹(1) : *to drill a hole in sth* ○ *to drill for oil* **2** to teach sb by making him/her repeat sth many times

☆ **drink¹** /drɪŋk/ *verb* (*p.t.* **drank** /dræŋk/; *p.p.* **drunk** /drʌŋk/) **1** [I,T] to take liquid into your body through your mouth: *You've lost a lot of fluid. You need to keep drinking.* ○ *I never drink coffee.* **2** [I] to drink alcohol: *Don't drink and drive.*

PHRV **drink to sb/sth** to wish sb/sth good luck by raising your glass before you drink: *We all drank to the future of the bride and groom.* ☞ Look at **toast²(2)**.

D

☆**drink²** /drɪŋk/ *noun* [C,U] **1** liquid for drink-ing: *Can I have a drink?* ○ *a drink of milk* ○ *food and drink* **2** alcoholic drink: *a strong drink* ○ *He turned to drink when his problems became too much for him.*

drink·er /'drɪŋkər/ *noun* [C] a person who drinks alcohol: *a heavy drinker*

☆**drink·ing** /'drɪŋkɪŋ/ *noun* [U] drinking alco-hol: *Her drinking became a problem.*

drinking ˌfountain (*also* **water fountain**; **fountain**) *noun* [C] a piece of equipment con-nected to the water supply in a public build-ing, that produces a stream of water that you can drink from

drinking ˌwater *noun* [U] water that is safe to drink

drip¹ /drɪp/ *verb* (**drip·ping**; **dripped**) **1** [I] (used about a liquid) to fall in small drops: *Water was dripping down through the roof.* **2** [I,T] to have drops of liquid falling: *The faucet is dripping.* ○ *Her finger was dripping blood.*

drip² /drɪp/ *noun* **1** [C] a drop of liquid that falls down from sb/sth: *Be sure to wipe up any paint drips immediately.* **2** [sing.] the act or sound of water dripping: *the drip of a leaky faucet*

☆**drive¹** /draɪv/ *verb* (*p.t.* **drove** /droʊv/; *p.p.* **driv·en** /'drɪvn/) **1** [I,T] to control or operate a car, train, bus, etc.: *Can you drive?* ○ *to drive a car, train, bus, truck, etc.* **2** [I,T] to go or take sb somewhere in a car, etc.: *I usually drive to work.* ○ *We drove Nancy to the airport.* **3** [T] to force people or animals to move in a particu-lar direction: *The farmer drove the sheep into the pen.* **4** [T] to force sth into a particular position by hitting it: *to drive a post into the ground* **5** [T] to cause sb to be in a particular state or to do a particular thing: *That noise is driving me crazy.* ○ *to drive sb to despair* ○ *His loneliness drove him to commit suicide.* **6** [T] to make sb/sth work very hard: *You shouldn't drive yourself so hard.* **7** [T] to make a ma-chine work, by giving it power: *What drives the wheels in this engine?*

IDM **drive sb up the wall** (*informal*) to make sb extremely angry: *These kids have been driv-ing me up the wall all day!*

PHRV **drive off** (used about a car, driver, etc.) to leave

drive sb/sth off to force sb/sth to go back or away: *The defenders drove off each attack.*

☆**drive²** /draɪv/ *noun* **1** [C] a trip in a car: *The shopping mall is only a five-minute drive away.* ○ *Let's go out for a drive through the country.* **2** [C] a private road that leads to a large house **3** (*abbr.* **Dr.**) [sing.] (used in the name of some streets): *We live at 1120 Lakeside Drive.* **4** [U] the position of the gears of a car, etc. with automatic transmission in which the engine is sending power to the wheels so that the car can move forward: *Don't turn off the ignition*

while the car is still in drive. ☞ Look at **neu-tral²**, **park¹**(4) and **reverse²**(2). **5** [U] the en-ergy and determination you need to succeed in doing sth **6** [C,U] a strong natural need or desire: *a strong sex drive* **7** [C] a strong effort by a group of people in order to achieve sth: *a sales drive* ☞ Look also at **disk drive**.

drive-by *adj.* (only *before* a noun) (used about an attack, etc.) done by sb who is going past in a car: *drive-by shootings, killings, etc.*

drive-in *noun* [C] a place where you can go to eat, watch a movie, etc. in your car

driv·en *p.p.* of DRIVE¹

☆**driv·er** /'draɪvər/ *noun* [C] a person who drives a vehicle: *One passenger died in the accident, but the driver was unhurt.*

☆**driver's ˌlicense** *noun* [C] an official card that says you are allowed to drive a car, etc. You get this card after you have passed a written examination and a driver's test.

drive-through (*also* informal **drive-thru**) *noun* [C] a part of a restaurant, bank, or other business where you can buy sth or receive a service without getting out of your car

drive·way /'draɪvweɪ/ *noun* [C] a small pri-vate road or an area with a hard surface that goes from a street to sb's house: *I see Ann's car in the driveway – she must be home.* ☞ picture on page A28.

☆**driv·ing¹** /'draɪvɪŋ/ *noun* [U] the act of con-trolling a car, etc.: *She was arrested for reck-less driving.*

driv·ing² /'draɪvɪŋ/ *adj.* very strong: *driving rain* ○ *Who's the driving force behind this plan?*

driz·zle /'drɪzl/ *noun* [U] light rain that has many small drops —**driz·zle** *verb* [I] ☞ Look at the note at **weather**.

drone¹ /droʊn/ *verb* [I] **1** to make a continu-ous low sound: *I could hear the TV droning in the background.* **2** to talk in a flat or boring voice

drone² /droʊn/ *noun* [C] **1** [usually sing.] a continuous low sound **2** a person who does a lot of boring work and who other people think is not very important: *low-paid office drones*

drool /drul/ *verb* [I] **1** to let liquid (**saliva**) come out from your mouth: *Oh, no – the baby just drooled on my new blouse!* **2** **drool (over sb/sth)** to show in a foolish way how much you like or admire sb/sth: *teenagers drooling over pictures of their favorite rock stars*

droop /drup/ *verb* [I] to bend or hang down-ward, e.g. because of weakness: *The flowers were drooping without water.* —**droop·ing** /'drupɪŋ/ *adj.*: *droop-ing shoulders* ○ *a drooping mustache*

drop¹ /drɑp/ *verb* (**drop·ping**; **dropped**) **1** [T] to allow sth to fall: *That vase was*

drop

very expensive. Whatever you do, don't drop it!
2 [I] to fall: *The soldier climbed over the wall and dropped safely to the ground.* **3** [I] to become weaker or lower; to make sth weaker or lower: *The temperature will drop below freezing overnight.* **4** [T] to no longer include sb/sth in sth: *Joe has been dropped from the team.* **5** [T] to not continue sth: *I'm going to drop my geography course* (= stop studying it). ○ *Drop everything – I need your help right now!* ○ *All the charges against you have been dropped – you're free to go home.*

IDM **drop dead** (*informal*) to die suddenly
drop sb a line to write a letter to sb: *I hope you'll drop us a line when you get a chance.*

PHRV **drop back; drop behind (sb)** to move into a position behind sb else, because you are moving more slowly: *Toward the end of the race, she dropped behind the other runners.*

drop by/in; drop in on sb to visit sb informally or without having told them you were coming: *We were in the area, so we thought we'd drop in and see you.*

drop off (*informal*) to fall into a light sleep: *I must have dropped off in front of the television.*

drop sb/sth off to stop your car, etc. so that sb can get out, or in order to take sth out: *Drop me off at the corner, please.* ○ *I'll drop off the package at your house.*

drop out (of sth) to leave or stop doing sth before you have finished: *His injury forced him to drop out of the tournament.* ○ *to drop out of college*

☆ **drop²** /drɑp/ *noun* **1** [C] a small round mass of liquid: *I thought I felt a drop of rain.* **2 drops** [plural] liquid medicine that you put into your eyes, ears or nose **3** [C] a small piece of candy or a small, sweet piece of medicine: *cough drops* **4** [sing.] a vertical distance down from a place: *It's a drop of 100 feet from the top of the cliff.* **5** [sing.] a smaller amount or level of sth: *We were forced to accept a drop in salary.*

drop·out /'drɑpaʊt/ *noun* [C] **1** a person who leaves school, college, university, etc. before finishing his/her studies: *high school dropouts* **2** a person who does not accept the rules of society and who wants to live in a way that is different from one that most people consider is acceptable

drop·pings /'drɑpɪŋz/ *noun* [plural] waste material from the bodies of small animals or birds: *rabbit droppings*

drought /draʊt/ *noun* [C,U] a long period of weather which is too dry: *Drought has affected many countries in Africa.*

drove *p.t.* of DRIVE¹

☆ **drown** /draʊn/ *verb* [I,T] to die in water because it is not possible to breathe; to make sb die in this way: *The girl fell into the river and drowned.* ○ *Twenty people were drowned in the floods.*

PHRV **drown sb/sth out** (used about a sound) to be so loud that you cannot hear sb/sth else: *His answer was drowned out by the music.*

drow·sy /'draʊzi/ *adj.* (**drow·si·er; drow·si·est**) very sleepy: *The heat made me feel drowsy.* —**drow·si·ly** /-əli/ *adv.* —**drow·si·ness** *noun* [U]

☆ **drug¹** /drʌg/ *noun* [C] **1** a chemical which is used as a medicine: *Some drugs can only be obtained with a prescription from a doctor.* **2** a chemical which people use to give them pleasant or exciting feelings. It is against the law in many countries to use drugs: *illegal drugs such as heroin and cocaine* ○ *a drug dealer* ○ *I think Rob is on drugs* (= I think he uses drugs). ○ (*slang*) *to do drugs* (= to use illegal drugs)

drug² /drʌg/ *verb* [T] (**drug·ging; drugged**) to give a person or animal a chemical to make them tired or unconscious: *The lion was drugged before the start of the trip.*

'drug addict *noun* [C] a person who cannot stop taking drugs

'drug ad·dic·tion (*also* **'drug de·pen·dency**) *noun* [U] the state of being a drug addict

☆ **drug·store** /'drʌgstɔr/ *noun* [C] a store that sells medicine, soap, shampoo, film, etc.

☆ **drum¹** /drʌm/ *noun* [C] **1** a round hollow musical instrument, with plastic or skin stretched across the ends. You play a drum by hitting it with your hands or with sticks: *She plays the drums in a band.* ☞ picture at **rock band**. **2** a round hollow container: *an oil drum*

drum² /drʌm/ *verb* (**drum·ming; drummed**) **1** [I] to play a drum¹(1) or drums **2** [I,T] to make a noise like a drum¹(1) by hitting sth many times: *to drum your fingers on the table* (= because you are annoyed, impatient, etc.)

PHRV **drum sth into sb** to make sb remember sth by repeating it many times: *Safety rules should be drummed into children from an early age.*

drum sth up to try to get more of sth: *to drum up more support for a candidate*

drum·mer /'drʌmer/ *noun* [C] a person who plays a drum¹(1) or drums

drunk¹ *p.p.* of DRINK¹

☆ **drunk²** /drʌŋk/ *adj.* having drunk too much alcohol: *You're drunk!* ○ *drunk drivers*

drunk³ /drʌŋk/ *noun* [C] (*informal*) a person who is drunk, or who often gets drunk

drunk·en /'drʌŋkən/ *adj.* (only *before* a noun) **1** showing the effects of too much alcohol: *drunken singing* **2** having drunk too much alcohol: *drunken drivers* —**drunk·en·ness** *noun* [U]

☆ **dry¹** /draɪ/ *adj.* (**dri·er; dri·est**) **1** without liquid in it or on it; not wet: *The laundry isn't dry yet.* ○ *The paint is dry now.* ○ *Rub your hair dry with a towel.* ○ *In the hot weather, the stream ran dry.* **2** having little or no rain: *a*

hot, dry summer **3** (used about wine) not sweet **4** dull or boring **5** (used of a remark, etc.) amusing, although it sounds serious: *a dry sense of humor* **6** (used about a place) not allowing alcohol to be sold or drunk: *a dry college campus* —**dry·ness** *noun* [U]

☆**dry²** /draɪ/ *verb* [I,T] (*pres. part.* **dry·ing**; *3rd pers. sing. pres.* **dries**; *p.t., p.p.* **dried**) **dry (off)**; **dry sth (off)** to become dry; to make sth dry: *Leave your swimsuit in the sun to dry.* ○ *to dry your hands on a towel* ○ *to dry yourself off after a bath*

PHRV **dry (sth) out** (to cause sth wet) to become very dry or too dry: *Don't allow the soil to dry out.*

dry up 1 (used about a river, etc.) to have no more water in it **2** to stop being available: *Because of the recession a lot of construction work has dried up.*

'dry-clean *verb* [T] to clean clothes using special chemicals, without using water

'dry ˌcleaners *noun* = CLEANER(3)

dry·er /'draɪər/ *noun* [C] a machine that you use for drying sth: *a hair dryer* ○ *a clothes dryer*

ˌdry 'land *noun* [U] land, not the ocean

dry·ly (*also* **drily**) /'draɪli/ *adv.* in a dry¹ (5) way: *"I can hardly contain my excitement,"* Peter said dryly (= he was not excited at all).

ˌdry 'run *noun* [C] (*informal*) = TRIAL RUN

du·al /'duəl/ *adj.* (only *before* a noun) having two parts; double: *the dual role of mother and working woman* ○ *to have dual citizenship*

dub /dʌb/ *verb* [T] (**dub·bing**; **dubbed**) **1** to give sb/sth a new or amusing name (**a nickname**): *Ronald Reagan was dubbed "The Great Communicator."* **2** to change the sound in a movie so that what the actors said originally is spoken by actors using a different language: *I don't like foreign movies when they're dubbed into English. I prefer subtitles.*

du·bi·ous /'dubiəs/ *adj.* **1 dubious (about sth/about doing sth)** not sure or certain: *I'm very dubious about whether we're doing the right thing.* **2** (only *before* a noun) having little value: *They have the dubious distinction of being the first team to lose 15 games in a row.* **3** that may not be honest or safe: *dubious financial dealings*

duch·ess (*also* **Duchess**) /'dʌtʃəs/ *noun* [C] **1** the wife of a duke **2** a woman who is of the same rank as a duke

☆**duck¹** /dʌk/ *noun* **duck** **1** [C] a common bird that lives on or near water. Ducks have short legs, special (**webbed**) feet for swimming and a wide beak.

☞ A male duck is called a **drake** and a young duck is a **duckling**. A duck **waddles** and **quacks**.

2 [U] the meat of a duck ☞ Look also at **lame duck**.

duck² /dʌk/ *verb* **1** [I,T] to move your head down quickly so that you are not seen or hit by sb/sth: *I saw the ball coming toward me and ducked.* **2** [T] (*informal*) to try to avoid sth difficult or unpleasant: *The governor ducked several important questions during the interview.*

duct /dʌkt/ *noun* [C] a tube that carries liquid, gas, etc.: *They got into the building through the air duct.*

dud /dʌd/ *noun* [C] (*informal*) a thing that is useless or that does not work correctly

dude /dud/ *noun* [C] (*slang*) a boy or young man: *Hey, dude, what's happening?* ○ *Do you know those dudes over there?*

☆**due¹** /du/ *adj.* **1** (not *before* a noun) expected or planned to happen or arrive: *What time is the plane due?* ○ *Their first child is due* (= is expected to be born) *in August.* **2** (not *before* a noun) having to be paid, finished, etc.: *The rent is due on the first of each month.* ☞ Look also at **due date**. **3** that is owed to you because it is your right to have it: *Make sure you claim any refund that is due to you.* **4 due to sb/sth** caused by or because of sb/sth: *His illness is probably due to stress.*

☞ Some careful speakers only use **due to** after the verb **to be**: *The strike was due to poor working conditions.* However, **due to** is often used in the same way as **owing to** and **because of**: *Due to/Owing to/Because of the bad weather, many flights have been canceled.*

5 due for sth deserving or expecting to have sth: *I think I'm due for a raise.* **6** (only *before* a noun) (*formal*) suitable or right: *With all due respect, ma'am, I can't let you into the chairman's office.*

IDM **in due course** (*formal*) at some time in the future: *All applicants will be informed of our decision in due course.*

due² /du/ *adv.* (used before "north," "south," "east" and "west") exactly: *The airplane was flying due east.*

du·el¹ /'duəl/ *noun* [C] **1** a fight or an angry competition **2** a formal type of fight with guns or swords which was used in the past to settle an argument between two men: *to challenge sb to a duel*

du·el² /'duəl/ *verb* [I,T] **duel (with sb/sth)** to fight or compete (against sb/sth): *Environmentalists are dueling with real estate developers over plans to build a new shopping mall.*

ˌdue 'process *noun* [U] the correct way in which action should be taken in a court of law, by the police, etc. in order to protect sb's rights

dues /duz/ *noun* [plural] money that you must pay to be a member of an organization, a club, etc.: *to pay your union dues*

i	ɪ	ɛ	æ	ɑ	ɔ	ʌ	ʊ	u
see	sit	ten	cat	hot	saw	cup	put	too

du·et /duˈet/ noun [C] a piece of music for two people to sing or play

duf·fle bag (also **duf·fel bag**) /ˈdʌfl bæg/ noun [C] a bag made of cloth with two round ends, that you can carry clothes, etc. in ☞ picture at **luggage**.

dug p.t., p.p. of DIG¹

dug·out /ˈdʌgaʊt/ noun [C] 1 (in baseball) an area at the side of the field that is partly underground, with a roof, where the players can wait for their turn to play 2 (also ˌdugout ˈcanoe) a small, narrow boat that is made by cutting out a long space in a thick, round part of a tree (a log)

duke (also **Duke**) /duk/ noun [C] (in some countries) a man with a very high social rank: the Duke of York ☞ Look at **duchess**.

☆ **dull** /dʌl/ adj. 1 not interesting or exciting: Life is never dull in the city. 2 not loud, sharp or strong: Her head hit the floor with a dull thud. ○ a dull pain 3 not bright: dull, drab colors —**dull·ness** noun [U]

du·ly /ˈduli/ adv. (formal) (only before a verb or a participle) in the correct or official way: a duly authorized government representative

☆ **dumb** /dʌm/ adj. 1 stupid: What a dumb thing to do! 2 (old-fashioned) not able to speak: to be deaf and dumb ○ (figurative) They were struck dumb with amazement. ☞ This use of **dumb** is considered offensive nowadays. If a person is unable to speak, we can say that he/she is **mute** or **speech-impaired**.

dumb·found·ed /dʌmˈfaʊndəd/ adj. very surprised

dum·my¹ /ˈdʌmi/ noun [C] (pl. **dum·mies**) 1 a model of the human body used for showing clothes in a store window or while you are making clothes: a department store dummy 2 (informal) a stupid person: You dummy! What did you do that for? ○ Of course I know how to program the VCR – I'm no dummy! 3 something that is made to look like sth else but that is not the real thing

dum·my² /ˈdʌmi/ adj. (only before a noun) made to look like sth else but not the real thing

☆ **dump¹** /dʌmp/ verb [T] 1 to take sth that you do not want to a place, especially a place which is not suitable, and leave it there: Nuclear waste should not be dumped in the ocean. 2 to put something down quickly or in a careless way: The kids dumped their coats and bags in the hall and ran off to play. 3 (informal) to leave sb in a rude and sudden way: Jill dumped her boyfriend after they'd been together for two years.

☆ **dump²** /dʌmp/ noun [C] 1 a place where garbage or waste material from factories, etc. is left: the municipal garbage dump 2 (informal) a place that is very dirty, messy or unpleasant: Your room is a total dump!

dump·ling /ˈdʌmplɪŋ/ noun [C] a small ball of fat and flour (dough) that is cooked and usually eaten with meat

dumps /dʌmps/ noun [plural] (informal) **down in the dumps** unhappy or depressed

Dump·ster (also **dumpster**) /ˈdʌmpstər/ noun [C] (trademark) a very large metal container for garbage, that is usually used outdoors

dune /dun/ (also **ˈsand dune**) noun [C] a low hill of sand by the ocean or in the desert ☞ picture at **beach**.

dung /dʌŋ/ noun [U] waste material from the bodies of large animals

dun·geon /ˈdʌndʒən/ noun [C] an underground prison, e.g. in a castle

dunk /dʌŋk/ verb 1 [T] to push sb's head under water for a short time, especially when playing 2 [T] to put sth into liquid for a short time: to dunk a cookie in your coffee 3 [I,T] (in basketball) to jump very high and put the ball through the basket with great force from above ☞ Look also at **slam-dunk**.

du·o /ˈduoʊ/ noun [C] (pl. **du·os**) two people who do sth together, especially playing music or singing

dupe /dup/ verb [T] to trick sb: The woman was duped into carrying the drugs.

du·plex /ˈdupleks/ noun [C] a house that is divided into two separate homes, usually with a separate door for each one

du·pli·cate¹ /ˈdupləkət/ adj. (only before a noun) exactly the same as sth else: a duplicate key (= a copy of another key)

du·pli·cate² /ˈdupləkət/ noun [C] something that is exactly the same as sth else **[IDM] in duplicate** with two copies (e.g. of an official piece of paper) that are exactly the same: The form must be submitted in duplicate.

du·pli·cate³ /ˈdupləkeɪt/ verb [T] 1 to make an exact copy of sth 2 to do sth that has already been done: We don't want to duplicate the work of other departments. —**du·pli·ca·tion** /ˌdupləˈkeɪʃn/ noun [U]

du·ra·ble /ˈdʊrəbl/ adj. that is able to last a long time: a durable fabric —**du·ra·bil·i·ty** /ˌdʊrəˈbɪləti/ noun [U]

du·ra·tion /dʊˈreɪʃn/ noun [U] the time that sth lasts: Please remain seated for the duration of the flight.

du·ress /dʊˈres/ noun [U] **under duress** because of the threat of force being used; not willingly: He signed the confession under duress.

☆ **dur·ing** /ˈdʊrɪŋ/ prep. 1 for all of a period of time: The audience must remain seated during the performance. 2 on more than one occasion in a period of time: During the summer vacation we went swimming every day. 3 at some point in a period of time: Grandpa had a stroke during the night. ☞ Notice that you use **during** to say when something happens and **for** to say how long something lasts: I went

ə	y	w	t̬	eɪ	aɪ	ɔɪ	aʊ	oʊ
about	yes	woman	butter	say	five	boy	now	go

shopping during my lunch break. I was out for about 25 minutes.

dusk /dʌsk/ *noun* [U] the time in the evening when the sun has already gone down and it is nearly dark ☞ Look at **dawn**.

☆ **dust¹** /dʌst/ *noun* [U] a fine dry powder that is made of very small pieces of earth, dirt, etc.: *There is dust everywhere in our house.* ○ *chalk dust* ○ *The truck drove off in a cloud of dust.* ○ *a speck* (= small piece) *of dust*

dust² /dʌst/ *verb* [I,T] to remove dust¹ from furniture, etc. with a cloth: *Let me dust those shelves before you put the books on them.* ☞ Look at the note at **clean²**.

dust·pan /'dʌstpæn/ *noun* [C] a flat container with a handle into which you brush dust or dirt from the floor ☞ picture at **brush**.

dust·y /'dʌsti/ *adj.* (**dust·i·er**; **dust·i·est**) having a lot of dust¹: *This shelf has gotten very dusty.*

Dutch /dʌtʃ/ *adj.* from the Netherlands ☞ Look at Appendix 3.

☆ **du·ty** /'duti/ *noun* (*pl.* **du·ties**) **1** [C,U] something that you have to do because people expect you to do it or because you think it is right: *a sense of moral duty* ○ *It's your duty to take care of your parents when they get older.* **2** [C,U] the tasks that you do when you are at work: *the duties of a police officer* ○ *Colonel Hamilton is retired from active military duty.* **3** [C] a tax that you pay, especially on goods that you bring into a country **IDM** **on/off duty** (used about doctors, nurses, police officers, etc.) to be working/not working: *Sergeant Smith is on duty from 8 to 4.* ○ *What time does she go off duty?* ☞ Look also at **heavy-duty**.

duty-'free *adj., adv.* (used about goods) that you can bring into a country without paying tax: *a duty-free shop at the airport* ○ *How much wine can you bring into the U.S. duty-free?*

dwarf¹ /dwɔrf/ *noun* [C] (*pl.* **dwarfs** or **dwarves** /dwɔrvz/) **1** a person, animal or plant that is much smaller than the usual size **2** (in children's stories) a very small person, often with special powers: *Snow White and the Seven Dwarfs*

dwarf² /dwɔrf/ *verb* [T] (used about a large object) to make sth seem very small in comparison: *The skyscraper dwarfs all the other buildings around it.*

dwell /dwɛl/ *verb* [I] (*p.t., p.p.* **dwelt** /dwɛlt/ or **dwelled**) (*old-fashioned, formal*) to live or stay in a place

PHRV **dwell on/upon sth** to think, speak or write about sth for a long time: *I don't want to dwell on the past. Let's think about the future.*

dwell·er /'dwɛlər/ *noun* [C] (often in compounds) a person or animal that lives in the place mentioned: *apartment dwellers*

dwell·ing /'dwɛlɪŋ/ *noun* [C] (*formal*) the place where a person lives; a house

dwin·dle /'dwɪndl/ *verb* [I] to become smaller or weaker: *Their savings dwindled away to nothing.*

dye¹ /daɪ/ *verb* [T] (*pres. part.* **dye·ing**; *3rd pers. sing. pres.* **dyes**; *p.t., p.p.* **dyed**) to color sth, especially by putting it into a liquid: *Does she dye her hair?* ○ *I'm going to dye this blouse black.*

dye² /daɪ/ *noun* [C,U] a substance, usually added to a liquid, that changes the color of sth, e.g. cloth, hair

dy·ing ⇨ DIE

dyke /daɪk/ *noun* [C] (*slang*) a woman who is sexually attracted to other women

☞ This word is extremely offensive. Look at **lesbian**.

dy·nam·ic /daɪ'næmɪk/ *adj.* **1** (used about a person) full of energy and ideas; active **2** (used about a force or power) that causes movement —**dy·na·mism** /'daɪnəmɪzəm/ *noun* [U]

dy·na·mite /'daɪnəmaɪt/ *noun* [U] a type of explosive substance, used especially in mining: *a stick of dynamite*

dy·na·mo /'daɪnəmoʊ/ *noun* [C] (*pl.* **dy·na·mos**) (*informal*) a person who is full of energy

dy·nas·ty /'daɪnəsti/ *noun* [C] (*pl.* **dy·nas·ties**) a series of rulers who are from the same family: *the Ming dynasty*

dys·en·ter·y /'dɪsənˌtɛri/ *noun* [U] a serious disease which causes a severe form of diarrhea

dys·func·tion /dɪs'fʌŋkʃn/ *noun* [C,U] failure to work correctly; a time when sth does not work correctly

dys·func·tion·al /dɪs'fʌŋkʃənl/ *adj.* (used about a family, a relationship between people, etc.) not happy or behaving according to the normal rules of society: *children growing up in dysfunctional families*

dys·lex·i·a /dɪs'lɛksiə/ *noun* [U] a problem in sb's brain that causes difficulties in reading and spelling —**dys·lex·ic** /dɪs'lɛksɪk/ *noun* [C], *adj.*

ər	ɪr	ɛr	ɑr	ɔr	ʊr	ʒ	h	ŋ
bird	near	hair	car	north	tour	vision	hat	sing

Ee

E, e /i/ *noun* [C] (*pl.* **E's**; **e's**) the fifth letter of the English alphabet: *"Egg" begins with (an) "E."*

E (*also* **E.**) *abbr.* = EAST, EASTERN

☆ **each** /itʃ/ *det., pron.* every one of two or more things or people in a group, when you think about them individually: *Each class lasts an hour.* ○ *Each of the classes lasts an hour.* ○ *The classes each last an hour.* ○ *He gave each child a present.* ○ *He gave each of the children a present.* ○ *He gave the children a present each.*

each other

He's looking at himself. They're looking at **each other.**

each 'other *pron.* (used for saying that sb feels, does or has the same thing as another person/other people in the group): *They loved each other very much.* ○ *We looked at each other.*

☆ **ea·ger** /ˈigər/ *adj.* full of desire or interest: *He is eager to meet you.* ○ *eager for success* —**ea·ger·ly** *adv.* —**ea·ger·ness** *noun* [U]

beak

eagle

☆ **ea·gle** /ˈigl/ *noun* [C] a very large bird that can see very well. It eats small birds and animals. ☞ Look also at **bald eagle.**

☆ **ear** /ɪr/ *noun* **1** [C] one of the two parts of the body of a person or an animal that are used for hearing: *Elephants have large ears.* ○ *He pulled his hat down over his ears.* ○ *Whisper in my ear!* **2** [sing.] **an ear (for sth)** an ability to recognize or appreciate sounds, especially in music or language: *an ear for music* **3** [C] the part of a grain plant, especially a corn plant, where the grains grow ☞ picture at **corn.**

IDM **play (sth) by ear** to play a piece of music, etc. from memory and without using written notes

play it by ear (*informal*) to decide what to do as things happen, instead of planning in advance

be up to your ears/eyes/neck in sth ⇨ UP¹

ear·ache /ˈɪreɪk/ *noun* [C] a pain in your ear: *I have an earache.*

ear·drum /ˈɪrdrʌm/ *noun* [C] a thin piece of skin inside the ear that is tightly stretched and that allows you to hear sound

ear·lobe /ˈɪrloʊb/ (*also* **lobe**) *noun* [C] the round soft part at the bottom of your ear

☆ **ear·ly** /ˈərli/ (**ear·li·er**; **ear·li·est**) *adj., adv.* **1** near the beginning of a period of time, a piece of work, a series, etc.: *Come in the early afternoon.* ○ *I have to get up early on weekday mornings.* ○ *He died in his early twenties.* ○ *The project is still in its early stages.* ○ *The tunnel should be finished early next year.* **2** before the usual or expected time: *She arrived five minutes early for her interview.* ○ *Spring is early this year.*

IDM **at the earliest** not before the date or time mentioned: *I can fix it by Friday at the earliest.*

the early hours very early in the morning, i.e. the hours after midnight: *The burglary occurred in the early hours of Tuesday, May 10.*

early on soon after the beginning: *He achieved fame early on in his career.*

ear·mark /ˈɪrmɑrk/ *verb* [T] **earmark sth (for sth/sb)** to choose or keep sth, especially money, for a particular purpose: *$17 million has been earmarked for highway improvements.*

ear·muffs /ˈɪrmʌfs/ *noun* [plural] coverings for your ears that are made of thick material connected by a curved band, that you wear in cold weather to keep your ears warm: *a pair of earmuffs* ☞ picture on page A27.

☆ **earn** /ərn/ *verb* [T] **1** to get money by working: *How much does a dentist earn?* ○ *I earn $30,000 a year.* ○ *He earns his living as an artist.* ○ *How much interest will my savings earn* (= produce) *in the bank?* **2** to get sth that you deserve: *You've earned a vacation.*

ear·nest¹ /ˈərnəst/ *adj.* serious or determined: *They were having a very earnest discussion.* —**ear·nest·ly** *adv.*

ear·nest² /ˈərnəst/ *noun*

IDM **in earnest** happening more seriously or with more force than before: *Work began in earnest on the project.*

E

tʃ	dʒ	v	θ	ð	s	z	ʃ
chin	**J**une	**v**an	**th**in	**th**en	**s**o	**z**oo	**sh**e

E

☆ **earn·ings** /'ərnɪŋz/ *noun* [plural] the money that a person earns by working: *Average earnings have increased by 5%.*

ear·phones /'ɪrfoʊnz/ *noun* [plural] a piece of equipment that fits over or in the ears and is used for listening to music, the radio, etc.

ear·ring /'ɪrɪŋ/ *noun* [C] a piece of jewelry that is worn in or on the lower part of the ear: *Do these earrings clip on or are they for pierced ears?* ☞ picture at **jewelry**.

ear·shot /'ɪrʃɑt/ *noun* [U]
(be) out of/within earshot where a person cannot/can hear: *Wait until he's out of earshot before you say anything about him.*

northern hemisphere **the earth**

axis, North Pole, tropic of Cancer, Arctic Circle, line of longitude, tropic of Capricorn, equator, South Pole, line of latitude, Antarctic Circle

southern hemisphere

☆ **earth** /ərθ/ *noun* **1** (*also* **the earth; the Earth**) [sing.] the world; the planet on which we live: *life on earth* ○ *The earth is protected by the ozone layer.* **2** [sing., U] the surface of the world; land: *The satellite fell toward earth.* ○ *The earth shook.* **3** [U] soil: *The bulldozer piled up a huge mound of earth.* ☞ Look at the note at **ground**.
IDM how, why, where, who, etc. on earth (*informal*) (used for emphasizing sth or expressing surprise): *Where on earth have you been?*

earth·ly /'ərθli/ *adj.* connected with this world, not heaven: *The monks gave up all their earthly possessions.*

☆ **earth·quake** /'ərθkweɪk/ (*also informal* **quake**) *noun* [C] a sudden violent movement of the earth's surface: *Thousands of people were left homeless by the earthquake.*

earth·worm /'ərθwərm/ *noun* [C] a common type of worm that lives in the soil

ear·wax /'ɪrwæks/ *noun* [U] = WAX(2)

☆ **ease¹** /iz/ *noun* [U] a lack of difficulty: *She answered the questions with ease.* ☞ Look at **easy.**
IDM (be/feel) at ease to be/feel comfortable, relaxed, etc.: *They were all so kind and friendly that I felt completely at ease.*

ease² /iz/ *verb* **1** [I,T] to become or make sth

less painful or severe: *These pills will help ease the pain.* ○ *The tension between the two countries has eased.* **2** [T] to cause sth to move slowly and gently: *He eased his truck into a narrow parking space.*
PHRV ease up 1 to work less hard: *Ease up a little or you'll make yourself sick!* **2** to become less severe: *Let's wait until the rain eases up.*

ea·sel /'izl/ *noun* [C] a wooden frame that holds a blackboard or a picture that is being painted

☆ **eas·i·ly** /'izəli/ *adv.* **1** without difficulty: *I can easily call up and check the time.* **2** without doubt: *It's easily his best novel.*

☆ **east¹** /ist/ *noun* [sing.] (*abbr.* **E; E.**) **1** (*also* **the east**) one of the four main points of the compass; the direction you look toward in order to see the sun rise: *Which way is east?* ○ *a cold wind from the east* ○ *Which state is to the east of Indiana?* ☞ picture at **north**. **2 the east; the East** the part of any country, city, etc. that lies further to the east (1) than the other parts: *The oldest American universities are in the East.* ☞ Look at **Far East** and **Middle East**.

☆ **east²** /ist/ (*also* **East**) *adj.* in or toward the east, or from the east: *the East Coast* (= next to the Atlantic Ocean) ○ *an east wind* ○ *East Los Angeles*

☆ **east³** /ist/ *adv.* to or toward the east: *They headed east.* ○ *We live east of the city.*

east·bound /'istbaʊnd/ *adj.* traveling or leading toward the east: *The eastbound lanes of the freeway are closed.*

☆ **Eas·ter** /'istər/ *noun* [U] the Sunday in March or April when Christians celebrate Christ's return to life

'Easter egg *noun* [C] an egg that has been boiled inside its shell and decorated, that you give as a present at Easter

east·er·ly /'istərli/ *adj.* **1** to, toward or in the east: *They traveled in an easterly direction.* **2** (used about winds) coming from the east: *cold easterly winds*

☆ **east·ern** /'istərn/ *adj.* **1** of, in or from the east of a place: *eastern Canada* ○ *the eastern shore of the lake* **2** (*also* **Eastern**) from or connected with the countries of Asia: *Eastern philosophy*

east·ward¹ /'istwərd/ *adj.* toward the east: *to travel in an eastward direction*

east·ward² /'istwərd/ (*also* **eastwards** /'istwərdz/) *adv.* toward the east: *The Amazon flows eastwards.*

☆ **eas·y¹** /'izi/ *adj.* (**eas·i·er; eas·i·est**) **1** not difficult: *an easy question* ○ *It isn't easy to explain the system.* ○ *The system isn't easy to explain.* **2** without any pain, trouble or worry: *an easy drive to work* ○ *Life is easy when you've got plenty of money.* ☞ Look at **ease** and **easily.**

☆ **eas·y²** /'izi/ *adv.* **eas·i·er; eas·i·est**
IDM easier said than done more difficult to do than to talk about: *"You should get her to help you." "That's easier said than done."*

i	ɪ	ɛ	æ	ɑ	ɔ	ʌ	ʊ	u
see	sit	ten	cat	hot	saw	cup	put	too

go easy on sb/sth (*informal*) **1** to be gentle or less strict with sb: *Go easy on him; he's just a child.* **2** to avoid using too much of sth: *Go easy on the salt; it's bad for your heart.*

over easy/medium/hard ⇨ OVER²

take it easy (*informal*) to relax and not work too hard or worry too much: *My doctor advised me to take it easy for a while.*

'easy chair *noun* [C] a large comfortable chair with arms

eas·y·go·ing /ˌizi'goʊɪŋ/ *adj.* (used about a person) calm, relaxed and not easily worried: *Her parents are very easygoing. They let her do what she wants.*

☆ **eat** /it/ *verb* (*p.t.* **ate** /eɪt/; *p.p.* **eat·en** /'itn/) **1** [I,T] to put food into your mouth, then chew and swallow it: *Did you eat all the cookies?* ○ *Eat up your lunch, Joe* (= Finish it all). ○ *She doesn't eat right. No wonder she's so thin.* **2** [I] to have a meal: *What time should we eat?*

IDM **eat your heart out!** (*informal*) (used to say that sb, especially a famous person, should be jealous because sb else thinks that he/she can do sth better): *I scored 42 points in one game – eat your heart out, Michael Jordan!*

have your cake and eat it too ⇨ CAKE

PHRV **eat sth away/eat away at sth** to damage or destroy sth gradually: *The ocean waves had eaten away at the cliff.*

eat out to have a meal in a restaurant: *Would you like to eat out tonight?*

eat·er /'itər/ *noun* [C] a person who eats in a particular way: *My uncle's a big eater* (= he eats a lot).

eat·er·y /'itəri/ *noun* [C] (*pl.* **eat·er·ies**) (*informal*) a restaurant

eaves·drop /'ivzdrɑp/ *verb* [I] (**eaves·drop·ping**; **eaves·dropped**) to listen secretly to other people talking: *They caught her eavesdropping on their conversation.*

ebb /ɛb/ *verb* [I] **1** (used about the water in the ocean) to flow away from the land **2** (used about a feeling, etc.) to become weaker: *My enthusiasm for the idea began to ebb.*

eb·on·y /'ɛbəni/ *noun* [U] a hard black wood

ec·cen·tric¹ /ɪk'sɛntrɪk/ *adj.* (used about people or their behavior) strange or unusual: *People said he was crazy, but I think he was just slightly eccentric.* —**ec·cen·tric·i·ty** /ˌɛksɛn'trɪsəṭi/ *noun* [C,U] (*pl.* **ec·cen·tric·i·ties**)

ec·cen·tric² /ɪk'sɛntrɪk/ *noun* [C] an eccentric person: *She is quite an eccentric.*

ec·cle·si·as·ti·cal /ɪˌklizi'æstɪkl/ *adj.* connected with the Christian church: *ecclesiastical law*

ech·o¹ /'ɛkoʊ/ *noun* [C] (*pl.* **ech·oes**) a sound that is repeated as it is sent back off a surface such as the wall of a cave: *If you shout across the valley, you'll hear an echo of your own voice.*

ech·o² /'ɛkoʊ/ *verb* **1** [I] (used about a sound)

to be repeated; to come back as an echo: *Their footsteps echoed in the empty church.* **2** [T] to repeat sth that sb else has said: *Citizens' groups have echoed the governor's call for tougher drug laws.* **3** [I] **echo (with sth)** (used about places) to be full of a particular sound: *The valley echoed with their laughter.*

e·clipse¹ /ɪ'klɪps/ *noun* [C] **1** an occasion when the moon passes between the earth and the sun or the earth's shadow falls on the moon, cutting off all or some of the light: *a total/partial eclipse of the sun* **2** the loss of a person's importance, success, etc.

e·clipse² /ɪ'klɪps/ *verb* [T] **1** (used about the moon, etc.) to cause an eclipse of the sun, etc. **2** (used about a person) to make another person seem less interesting, important, etc.

e·col·o·gist /ɪ'kɑlədʒɪst/ *noun* [C] a expert in ecology

e·col·o·gy /ɪ'kɑlədʒi/ *noun* [U] the relations between living things and their surroundings; the study of this subject —**ec·o·log·i·cal** /ˌikə'lɑdʒɪkl/ *adj.*: *an ecological disaster* ○ *Environmentalists have tried to make people aware of ecological issues.* —**ec·o·log·i·cal·ly** *adv.*

☆ **ec·o·nom·ic** /ˌɛkə'nɑmɪk; ˌikə-/ *adj.* (only *before* a noun) connected with the supply of money, trade, industry, etc.: *the government's economic policy* ○ *The country faces growing economic problems.* ☛ Look at **economical**. It has a different meaning. —**ec·o·nom·i·cal·ly** /-kli/ *adv.*: *The country was very underdeveloped economically.*

ec·o·nom·i·cal /ˌɛkə'nɑmɪkl; ˌikə-/ *adj.* not costing much time, money, fuel, etc.; using sth carefully: *an economical car to drive* ○ *The company felt it wouldn't be economical to expand.* ☛ Look at **economic**. It has a different meaning. —**ec·o·nom·i·cal·ly** /-kli/ *adv.*: *The business could be run more economically.*

ec·o·nom·ics /ˌɛkə'nɑmɪks; ˌikə-/ *noun* [U] the study or principles of the way money, trade and industry are organized: *a bachelor's degree in economics* ○ *the economics of a company* ☛ Look also at **home economics**.

e·con·o·mist /ɪ'kɑnəmɪst/ *noun* [C] an expert in economics

e·con·o·mize /ɪ'kɑnəmaɪz/ *verb* [I] **economize (on sth)** to save money, time, resources, etc.; to use sth carefully

☆ **e·con·o·my¹** /ɪ'kɑnəmi/ *noun* (*pl.* **e·con·o·mies**) **1** [C] (*also* **the economy**) the operation of a country's money supply, trade and industry: *The economy of the country is based on agriculture.* ○ *There are signs of improvement in the economy.* ○ *the economies of the United States and Japan* **2** [U] careful spending of money, time, resources, etc.; trying to save, not waste sth: *For reasons of economy, please turn off all unnecessary lights.*

e·con·o·my² /ɪ'kɑnəmi/ *adj.* (only *before* a

ə	y	w	t̬	eɪ	aɪ	ɔɪ	aʊ	oʊ
about	yes	woman	butter	say	five	boy	now	go

E

noun) that helps you to save money because it is cheaper to use: *You should buy the large economy-size box of detergent – it costs less per ounce than the small box.* ○ *an economy car* ○ *an economy-class airline ticket*

ec·sta·sy /ˈɛkstəsi/ *noun* [U] a feeling or state of great happiness: *to be in ecstasy*

ec·stat·ic /ɪkˈstætɪk/ *adj.* extremely happy

ec·u·men·i·cal /ˌɛkyəˈmɛnɪkl/ *adj.* connected with the idea of uniting all the different parts of the Christian Church

ec·ze·ma /ˈɛksəmə; ˈɛgzəmə; ɪgˈzimə/ *noun* [U] a disease which makes the skin red and sore

ed·dy /ˈɛdi/ *noun* [C] (*pl.* **ed·dies**) a circular movement of water, wind, dust, etc.

☆ **edge¹** /ɛdʒ/ *noun* [C] **1** the place where sth, especially a surface, ends; the limit: *the edge of a table* ○ *The leaves were brown and curling at the edges.* ○ *I stood at the water's edge.* **2** the sharp cutting part of a knife, etc. ☞ Look also at **cutting edge**.

IDM **an/the edge on/over sb/sth** a slight advantage over sb/sth: *She knew she had an edge over the other candidates.*

(be) on edge to be nervous, excited or quick to become angry: *I'm a little on edge because I get my report card today.* ☞ Look at **edgy**. It has a similar meaning.

edge² /ɛdʒ/ *verb* **1** [I,T] **edge (sth/your way) across, along, away, back, etc.** to move slowly and carefully across, etc.: *The burglar edged his way along the roof.* ○ *We edged closer to get a better view.* ○ *She edged her chair up to the window.* **2** [I] to increase or decrease by a small amount: *Unemployment edged up by 0.2% to 4.6% in January.* **3** [T] (usually passive) **edge sth (with sth)** to arrange sth along the edge of sth else: *The cloth was edged with lace.*

edge·wise /ˈɛdʒwaɪz/ *adv.*

IDM **get a word in edgewise** ⇨ WORD¹

edg·y /ˈɛdʒi/ *adj.* (*informal*) nervous, worried or quick to become upset: *You seem awfully edgy. What's bothering you?*

ed·i·ble /ˈɛdəbl/ *adj.* good or safe to eat: *Are these mushrooms edible?* ☞ The opposite is **inedible**.

ed·it /ˈɛdət/ *verb* [T] **1** to prepare a piece of writing to be published, making sure that it is correct, the right length, etc. **2** to prepare a movie or a television or radio program by arranging filmed material in a particular order **3** to be in charge of a newspaper, magazine, etc.

e·di·tion /ɪˈdɪʃn/ *noun* [C] **1** the form in which a book is published: *a paperback/hardcover edition* **2** one of a series of television or radio programs: *And now for this week's edition of the nation's top news program…* **3** the number of copies of a book, etc. that are printed at the same time: *the morning edition of a newspaper*

☆ **ed·i·tor** /ˈɛdətər/ *noun* [C] **1** a person whose job is to prepare a book, television or radio program **2** the person who is in charge of a newspaper or part of a newspaper: *Who is the editor of the school newspaper?*

☆ **ed·i·to·ri·al¹** /ˌɛdəˈtɔriəl/ *noun* [C] an article in a newspaper, usually written by the editor, giving an opinion on an important subject

ed·i·to·ri·al² /ˌɛdəˈtɔriəl/ *adj.* connected with the work of an editor, especially in a newspaper: *the editorial pages*

☆ **ed·u·cate** /ˈɛdʒəkeɪt/ *verb* [T] to teach or train sb, especially in school: *Young people should be educated to care for their environment.* ○ *All their children were educated at private schools.*

ed·u·cat·ed /ˈɛdʒəkeɪtəd/ *adj.* having learned a lot of things to a high standard: *a highly educated woman*

☆ **ed·u·ca·tion** /ˌɛdʒəˈkeɪʃn/ *noun* [C, usually sing., U] the teaching or training of people, especially in schools, etc. to improve their knowledge and develop their skills: *elementary and secondary education* ○ *She received an excellent education.*

☆ **ed·u·ca·tion·al** /ˌɛdʒəˈkeɪʃənl/ *adj.* connected with or providing education: *an educational toy, visit, experience, etc.*

ed·u·ca·tor /ˈɛdʒəkeɪtər/ *noun* [C] (*formal*) a teacher

eel /il/ *noun* [C] a long fish that looks like a snake

ee·rie /ˈɪri/ *adj.* strange and frightening —**ee·ri·ly** *adv.*

☆ **ef·fect¹** /ɪˈfɛkt/ *noun* **1** [C,U] **(an) effect (on sb/sth)** a change that is caused by sth; a result: *the effects of acid rain on the lakes and forests* ○ *His words had a strong effect on me.* ○ *Her shouting had little or no effect on him.* ☞ Look at **aftereffect** and **side effect**. **2** [C,U] the impression that a speaker, book, movie, etc. gives: *How does the artist create the effect of moonlight?* ○ *He likes to say things just for effect* (= to impress people). **3 effects** (*formal*) your personal possessions

IDM **come into effect** (used especially about laws or rules) to begin to be used; to come into operation

in effect 1 (used to describe how a situation really is, especially if it appears to be different): *Although they haven't made an official announcement, she is, in effect, the new director.* **2** (used about a rule, a law, etc.) in operation; in use: *The new rules will be in effect starting next season.*

take effect 1 (used about a drug, etc.) to begin to work; to produce the desired result: *The anesthetic took effect immediately.* **2** (used about a law, etc.) to come into operation: *The cease-fire takes effect at midnight.*

to this/that effect with this/that meaning: *I told him to leave her alone, or words to that effect.*

ər	ɪr	ɛr	ɑr	ɔr	ʊr	ʒ	h	ŋ
bird	near	hair	car	north	tour	vision	hat	sing

ef·fect² /ɪˈfɛkt/ *verb* [T] (*formal*) to cause sth to happen; to have sth as a result: *to effect a change* ☞ Look at **affect**. It has a different meaning.

☆ **ef·fec·tive** /ɪˈfɛktɪv/ *adj.* **1** producing the result that you want: *Scientists are looking for an effective way to reduce energy consumption.* ○ *a medicine that is effective against the common cold* ☞ The opposite is **ineffective**. **2** real or actual, although perhaps not official: *The soldiers gained effective control of the town.* —**ef·fec·tive·ness** *noun* [U]

ef·fec·tive·ly /ɪˈfɛktɪvli/ *adv.* **1** in an effective way: *She dealt with the situation effectively.* **2** (used to describe how a situation really is, especially if it appears to be different): *It meant that, effectively, they had lost.*

ef·fem·i·nate /ɪˈfɛmənət/ *adj.* (used about a man or his behavior) like a woman

☆ **ef·fi·cient** /ɪˈfɪʃnt/ *adj.* able to work well without making mistakes or wasting time and energy: *Our secretary is very efficient.* ○ *You need to find a more efficient way of organizing your time.* ○ *a fuel-efficient car* (= one that does not use much fuel) ☞ The opposite is **inefficient**. —**ef·fi·cien·cy** /ɪˈfɪʃnsi/ *noun* [U] —**ef·fi·cient·ly** *adv.*

☆ **ef·fort** /ˈɛfərt/ *noun* **1** [U] the use of strength or energy: *They have put a lot of effort into their group project.* ○ *He made no effort to contact his parents.* **2** [C] something that is done with difficulty or the use of energy: *It was a real effort to stay awake during class.*

ef·fort·less /ˈɛfərtləs/ *adj.* (apparently) needing little or no effort —**ef·fort·less·ly** *adv.*

☆ **EFL** /ˌi ɛf ˈɛl/ *abbr.* English as a Foreign Language; (the subject of) the English language when it is taught in countries where most people do not speak English ☞ Look at **ESL**.

e.g. /ˌi ˈdʒi/ *abbr.* for example

e·gal·i·tar·i·an /ɪˌɡæləˈtɛriən/ *adj.* (used about a person, system, society, etc.) following the principle that everyone should have equal rights

eggshell **eggs**

yolk white a fried egg

☆ **egg¹** /ɛɡ/ *noun* **1** [C] an oval object with a hard shell that contains a young bird, reptile or insect

☞ A female bird **lays** her eggs and then **sits** on them until they **hatch**.

2 [C,U] an egg from a chicken, etc., used as food: *We had bacon and eggs for breakfast.*

☞ Eggs may be **hard-boiled** (until the yolk is solid), **soft-boiled** (so that the yolk is still soft), **fried**, **poached** (cooked in water without their shells) or **scrambled**. Eggs can be

fried in several different ways. Look at **over easy/medium/hard** and **sunny-side up**.

3 [C] the small cell in a female animal or a woman that can join with a male cell (a **sperm**) to make a baby

IDM **put all your eggs in one basket** to risk everything by depending completely on one thing, plan, etc.

egg² /ɛɡ/ *verb*

PHRV **egg sb on (to do sth)** to encourage sb to do sth (bad or dangerous)

egg·plant /ˈɛɡplænt/ *noun* [C,U] a long vegetable with dark purple skin

egg·shell /ˈɛɡʃɛl/ *noun* [C,U] the hard outside part of an egg

e·go /ˈiɡoʊ/ *noun* [C] (*pl.* **e·gos**) the (good) opinion that you have of yourself: *It was a blow to her ego when she lost her job.*

e·go·cen·tric /ˌiɡoʊˈsɛntrɪk/ *adj.* interested only in yourself; selfish

e·go·tism /ˈiɡətɪzəm/ *noun* [U] thinking about yourself too much; selfishness —**e·go·tis·ti·cal** /ˌiɡəˈtɪstɪkl/ *adj.*

eh /eɪ/ *interj.* (*informal*) (used for asking sb to agree with you): *"Good party, eh?"*

☆ **eight** /eɪt/ *number* 8; one more than seven ☞ For examples of how to use numbers in sentences, look at **six**. Look also at Appendix 2.

eight- /eɪt/ (in compounds) having eight of sth: *an eight-hour workday*

☆ **eight·een** /eɪˈtin/ *number* 18; one more than seventeen ☞ For examples of how to use numbers in sentences, look at **six**. Look also at Appendix 2. —**eight·eenth** /ˌeɪˈtinθ/ *pron., det., adv.* ☞ Look at the examples at **sixth**.

☆ **eighth¹** /eɪtθ/ *pron., det., adv.* 8th; next after seventh ☞ Look at the examples at **sixth**. For more information, look at Appendix 2.

☆ **eighth²** /eɪtθ/ *noun* [C] the fraction 1/8; one of eight equal parts of sth ☞ For more information, look at Appendix 2.

☆ **eight·y** /ˈeɪti/ *number* 80; one more than seventy-nine ☞ For examples of how to use numbers in sentences, look at **sixty**. Look also at Appendix 2. —**eight·i·eth** /ˈeɪtiəθ/ *pron., det., adv.* ☞ Look at the examples at **sixth**.

☆ **ei·ther¹** /ˈiðər/ ˈaɪðər/ *det., pron.* **1** one or the other of two; it does not matter which: *There's cake or ice cream. You can have either.* ○ *You can ask either of us for advice.* ○ *Either of us is willing to help.*

☞ **Either** is used with a singular verb, but in spoken informal English a plural verb can be used after **either of** and a plural noun: *Either of us are willing to help.*

2 both: *It is a pleasant road, with trees on either side.*

☆ **ei·ther²** /ˈiðər/ ˈaɪðər/ *conj.* **either...or...** (used when you are giving a choice, usually of two things): *You can get the jacket in either*

E

black or blue. ○ *Either you leave or I do.* ○ *You can either write or call.*

☆ **ei·ther³** /ˈiðər/ ˈaɪðər/ *adv.* **1** (used after two negative statements) also: *I don't like Pat and I don't like Nick very much either.* ○ *"I can't remember his name." "I can't either."*

☞ We can also say **neither can I** or **me neither**. In very informal situations, some people also say **me either**.

2 (used for emphasizing a negative statement): *The restaurant is pretty good – and it's not too expensive either.*

e·jac·u·late /ɪˈdʒækyəleɪt/ *verb* [I] to send out liquid (**semen**) from the male sex organ (**penis**) —**e·jac·u·la·tion** /ɪˌdʒækyəˈleɪʃn/ *noun* [C,U]

e·ject /ɪˈdʒɛkt/ *verb* **1** [T] to push or send sb/sth out of a place (usually with force): *The protesters were ejected from the building.* **2** [I] to make an emergency exit from an airplane

eke /ik/ *verb*

IDM eke out a living to manage to live with very little money

e·lab·o·rate¹ /ɪˈlæbərət; -brət/ *adj.* very complicated; done or made very carefully: *elaborate plans*

e·lab·o·rate² /ɪˈlæbəreɪt/ *verb* [I] **elaborate (on sth)** (*formal*) to give details about sth

e·lapse /ɪˈlæps/ *verb* [I] (*formal*) (used about time) to pass

e·las·tic¹ /ɪˈlæstɪk/ *noun* [U] material with rubber in it which can stretch

e·las·tic² /ɪˈlæstɪk/ *adj.* **1** (used about material, etc.) able to return to its original size after being stretched **2** (*figurative*) able to be changed; not fixed: *Our rules are fairly elastic.*

e·lat·ed /ɪˈleɪtəd/ *adj.* (*formal*) very happy and excited —**e·la·tion** /ɪˈleɪʃn/ *noun* [U]

☆ **el·bow¹** /ˈɛlboʊ/ *noun* [C] **1** the place where the arm bends in the middle ☞ picture on page A24. **2** the part of the sleeve of a coat, jacket, etc. that covers the elbow (1)

IDM rub elbows/shoulders with sb ⇨ RUB¹

el·bow² /ˈɛlboʊ/ *verb* [T] to push with the elbows: *She elbowed me out of the way to get to the food first.*

el·bow·room /ˈɛlboʊrum/ *noun* [U] enough space to move freely

eld·er¹ /ˈɛldər/ *adj.* (*formal*) (only *before* a noun) older (of two members of a family): *my elder sister* ☞ **Older** is more common and less formal than **elder**.

eld·er² /ˈɛldər/ *noun* **1** [sing.] (*formal*) the older of two people: *Who is the elder of the two?* ☞ **Older** is more common and less formal than **elder**. **2 elders** [plural] older people

☆ **eld·er·ly** /ˈɛldərli/ *adj.* (used about a person) old

☞ This is a polite way of saying "old." You can use **the elderly** to refer to old people in general: *health care for the elderly*

eld·est /ˈɛldəst/ *adj., noun* [C] (*formal*) oldest (of three or more members of a family): *Their eldest child is a boy.* ☞ **Oldest** is more common and less formal than **eldest**.

☆ **e·lect** /ɪˈlɛkt/ *verb* [T] **1 elect sb (to sth); elect sb (as sth)** to choose a President, senator, representative, etc. by voting: *He was elected to Congress in 1970.* ○ *The committee elected her as their representative.* **2 elect to do sth** (*formal*) to decide to do sth

☆ **e·lec·tion** /ɪˈlɛkʃn/ *noun* [C,U] (the time of) choosing a member of Congress, President, etc. by voting: *I will not be running for election again.* ○ *After many years of dictatorship, the government finally allowed free elections.*

☞ In the United States, **presidential elections** are held every four years in November. Sometimes state and local elections are held at other times. Voters choose from a list of **candidates** who are usually members of **political parties**.

e·lec·tive¹ /ɪˈlɛktɪv/ *noun* [C] a school or college course that you can choose to take if you want to: *I'm taking three core courses plus two electives this semester.*

e·lec·tive² /ɪˈlɛktɪv/ *adj.* (used about a job, position, etc.) for which there is an election

e·lec·tor·al /ɪˈlɛktərəl/ *adj.* connected with elections or an election: *the electoral process*

the E,lectoral 'College *noun* [sing.] a group of people who represent all the people that vote in each state, who meet to choose the next President and Vice President ☞ Look at the note at **White House**.

e·lec·tor·ate /ɪˈlɛktərət/ *noun* [C] all the people who can vote in a district, state, country, etc.

☆ **e·lec·tric** /ɪˈlɛktrɪk/ *adj.* **1** producing or using electricity: *an electric current* ○ *an electric drill* **2** (*figurative*) very emotional: *The atmosphere in the room was electric.*

☆ **e·lec·tri·cal** /ɪˈlɛktrɪkl/ *adj.* of or about electricity: *an electrical appliance* (= a machine that uses electricity) ○ *an electrical engineer* (= a person who produces electrical systems and equipment)

the e'lectric chair *noun* [sing.] a special chair that is used for putting criminals to death with a very strong electric current: *to be sent to the electric chair*

☆ **e·lec·tri·cian** /ɪˌlɛkˈtrɪʃn/ *noun* [C] a person whose job is to install and repair electrical systems and equipment

☆ **e·lec·tric·i·ty** /ɪˌlɛkˈtrɪsəti/ *noun* [U] a type of energy that provides heat, light and power to work machines, etc.: *Turn that light off. We don't want to waste electricity.*

i	ɪ	ɛ	æ	ɑ	ɔ	ʌ	ʊ	u
see	sit	ten	cat	hot	saw	cup	put	too

elephant

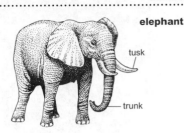

☞ Electricity is usually **generated** in **power plants**. It may also be produced by **generators** or by **batteries** (e.g. in portable radios or flashlights).

e₁lectric 'shock (*also* **e₁lectrical 'shock**; **shock**) *noun* [C] the effect on the body when an electric current goes through it: *That light switch isn't safe. I got a shock when I touched it.*

e·lec·tri·fy /ɪˈlɛktrəfaɪ/ *verb* [T] (*pres. part.* **e·lec·tri·fy·ing**; *3rd pers. sing. pres.* **e·lec·tri·fies**; *p.t.*, *p.p.* **e·lec·tri·fied**) **1** to supply sth with electricity: *an electrified fence* **2** (*figurative*) to make sb excited

e·lec·tro·cute /ɪˈlɛktrəkyut/ *verb* [T] (usually passive) to kill sb with an electric current that passes through the body: *A worker was electrocuted while trying to repair a power cable.* —**e·lec·tro·cu·tion** /ɪˌlɛktrəˈkyuʃn/ *noun* [U]

e·lec·trode /ɪˈlɛktroʊd/ *noun* [C] one of two points (**terminals**) where an electric current enters or leaves a battery, etc.

☆ **e·lec·tron·ic** /ɪˌlɛkˈtranɪk; ˌilɛk-/ *adj.* using electronics: *electronic equipment* ○ *This dictionary is available in electronic form* (= on a computer disk). —**e·lec·tron·i·cal·ly** /-kli/ *adv.*

elec₁tronic 'mail *noun* [U] = E-MAIL

☆ **e·lec·tron·ics** /ɪˌlɛkˈtranɪks/ *noun* [U] the technology of using electricity and very small parts (**chips**) in equipment such as computers, radios, etc.: *the electronics industry*

☆ **el·e·gant** /ˈɛləgənt/ *adj.* showing style or good design: *She looked very elegant in her new dress.* ○ *an elegant coat* —**el·e·gance** /ˈɛləgəns/ *noun* [U] —**el·e·gant·ly** *adv.*

☆ **el·e·ment** /ˈɛləmənt/ *noun* **1** [C] one important part of sth: *Cost is an important element when we're thinking about our vacation.* **2** [C, usually sing.] **an element of sth** a small amount of sth: *There was an element of truth in what he said.* **3** [C] people of a certain type: *the criminal element in our society* **4** [C] one of the most basic chemical substances, e.g. iron, oxygen, gold, etc. **5** [C] the part of an electric oven, an electric heater, etc. that produces heat **6 the elements** [plural] (*formal*) (bad) weather

IDM **in your element/out of your element** in a situation where you feel comfortable/uncomfortable

☆ **el·e·men·ta·ry** /ˌɛləˈmɛntəri; -ˈmɛntri/ *adj.* **1** at or in the beginning stages: *an elementary course in English* **2** basic; not difficult: *elementary physics*

☆ **ele'mentary school** (*also* **'grade school**, *old-fashioned* **'grammar school**) *noun* [C] a school for children who are about six to twelve years old

tusk

trunk

☆ **el·e·phant** /ˈɛləfənt/ *noun* [C] a very large gray animal with two long curved teeth (**tusks**) and a long nose (**a trunk**)

el·e·vate /ˈɛləveɪt/ *verb* [T] (*formal*) to raise sb/sth to a higher place or position: *an elevated freeway* ○ *He was elevated to the Board of Directors.*

el·e·va·tion /ˌɛləˈveɪʃn/ *noun* **1** [C,U] (*formal*) elevating or being elevated **2** [C] the height of a place (above sea level): *The city is at an elevation of 5,000 feet.*

☆ **el·e·va·tor** /ˈɛləveɪtər/ *noun* [C] a machine in a large building that is used for carrying people or goods from one floor to another: *It's on the fifth floor, so we'd better take the elevator.*

☆ **e·lev·en** /ɪˈlɛvən/ *number* 11, one more than ten ☞ For examples of how to use numbers in sentences, look at **six**. Look also at Appendix 2. —**e·lev·enth** /ɪˈlɛvənθ/ *pron., det., adv.* ☞ Look at the examples at **sixth**.

elf /ɛlf/ *noun* [C] (*pl* **elves** /ɛlvz/) (in stories) a small creature with pointed ears who has magic powers

e·lic·it /ɪˈlɪsət/ *verb* [T] **elicit sth (from sb)** (*formal*) to get information, facts, a reaction, etc. from sb

☆ **e·li·gi·ble** /ˈɛlɪdʒəbl/ *adj.* **eligible (for sth/to do sth)** having the right qualifications for sth; suitable: *In the United States, you are eligible to vote when you are eighteen.* ○ *an eligible young man* (= a man who might be a suitable husband)

☆ **e·lim·i·nate** /ɪˈlɪməneɪt/ *verb* [T] **1** to remove sb/sth that is not wanted or needed: *We must try and eliminate waste.* **2** (often passive) to stop sb from going further in a competition, etc.: *The team was eliminated in the first round of the playoffs.* —**e·lim·i·na·tion** /ɪˌlɪməˈneɪʃn/ *noun* [U]

☆ **e·lite** (*also* **élite**) /ɪˈlit; eɪ-/ *noun* [C, with sing. or pl. verb] a social group that is thought to be the best or most important because of its power, money, intelligence, etc.: *the ruling elite* ○ *an intellectual elite* —**e·lite** (*also* **élite**) *adj.* (only *before* a noun): *an elite military unit*

e·lit·ism /ɪˈlitɪzəm; eɪ-/ *noun* [U] the belief that elites should be treated in a special way

e·lit·ist /-tɪst/ *noun* [C], *adj.*

moose

elk

E

elk /ɛlk/ *noun* [C] (*pl.* **elk** or **elks**) a large deer that lives in North America

elm /ɛlm/ (*also* **'elm tree**) *noun* [C] a tall tree with broad leaves

e·lon·gat·ed /ɪˈlɔŋɡeɪṭəd/ *adj.* long and thin

e·lope /ɪˈloʊp/ *verb* [I] **elope (with sb)** to run away secretly to get married

el·o·quent /ˈɛləkwənt/ *adj.* (*formal*) able to speak well and influence other people —**el·o·quence** /ˈɛləkwəns/ *noun* [U] —**el·o·quent·ly** *adv.*

☆ **else** /ɛls/ *adv.* (used after words formed with *any-, no-, some-* and after question words) **1** in addition: *What else would you like?* ○ *Does anybody else* (= any other person) *know about this?* **2** different: *There's nothing on TV. Let's find something else to do.* ○ *This isn't mine. It must be somebody else's* (= belong to another person). ○ *You'll have to pay. Nobody else* (= no other person) *will.* **3** apart from: *Everybody else* (= everybody apart from me) *has gone.*
IDM **or else 1** otherwise; if not: *You'd better go to bed now or else you'll be tired in the morning.* ○ *He either forgot or else decided not to come.* **2** (*informal*) (used to express a threat or a warning): *Give us the money or else!*

☆ **else·where** /ˈɛlswɛr/ *adv.* (*formal*) in or to another place: *If she doesn't like it here, she can go elsewhere.* ○ *He's traveled a lot – in Europe and elsewhere.*

e·lude /ɪˈlud/ *verb* [T] (*formal*) **1** to escape (from sb/sth) (sometimes by using a trick) **2** to be difficult or impossible to remember: *I remember his face, but his name eludes me.*

e·lu·sive /ɪˈlusɪv/ *adj.* not easy to find, catch or remember

elves *pl.* of ELF

'em /əm/ *pron.* (*informal*) = THEM

e·ma·ci·at·ed /ɪˈmeɪʃieɪṭəd/ *adj.* (used about a person) thin and weak because of illness, lack of food, etc.

☆ **e·mail** (*also* **email**) /ˈimeɪl/ (*also* **ˌelecˌtronic 'mail**) *noun* [U] the system of sending mes-sages from one computer to another: *an e-mail message*

e·man·ci·pate /ɪˈmænsəpeɪt/ *verb* [T] to give sb the same legal, social and political rights as other people —**e·man·ci·pa·tion** /ɪˌmænsəˈpeɪʃn/ *noun* [U]

em·bank·ment /ɛmˈbæŋkmənt/ *noun* [C] a thick wall of earth, stone, etc. that is built to stop a river from overflowing or to carry a road or railroad

em·bar·go /ɛmˈbɑrɡoʊ/ *noun* [C] (*pl.* **em·bar·goes**) an official order to stop trade with an-other country: *to impose an oil embargo* ○ *to lift/remove the embargo on foreign oil*

em·bark /ɛmˈbɑrk/ *verb* I
PHRV **embark on sth** (*formal*) to start sth (new): *I'm embarking on a completely new career.*

☆ **em·bar·rass** /ɛmˈbærəs/ *verb* [T] to make sb feel ashamed or uncomfortable: *Why do you always embarrass me in front of my friends?* —**em·bar·rass·ing** *adj.*: *an embarrassing mis-take* —**em·bar·rass·ing·ly** *adv.*

☆ **em·bar·rassed** /ɛmˈbærəst/ *adj.* feeling ashamed or uncomfortable: *He was too embar-rassed to talk about what had happened.*

em·bar·rass·ment /ɛmˈbærəsmənt/ *noun* **1** [U] the feeling you have when you are em-barrassed **2** [C] a person or thing that makes you embarrassed

☆ **em·bas·sy** /ˈɛmbəsi/ *noun* [C] (*pl.* **em·bas·sies**) (the official building of) a group of people (**diplomats**) headed by an ambassador, who are sent to live in a foreign country and represent their government there ☞ Look at **consulate**.

em·bed /ɛmˈbɛd/ *verb* [T] (**em·bed·ding; em·bed·ded**) (usually passive) to fix sth firmly and deeply (in sth else): *The ax was embedded in the piece of wood.*

em·bez·zle /ɛmˈbɛzl/ *verb* [T] to steal money, etc. that you are responsible for (e.g. in a business or an organization)

em·blem /ˈɛmbləm/ *noun* [C] an object or a symbol that represents sth: *a T-shirt with the team's emblem on it*

em·bod·y /ɛmˈbɑdi/ *verb* [T] (*pres. part.* **em·bod·y·ing**; *3rd pers. sing. pres.* **em·bod·ies**; *p.p., p.t.* **em·bod·ied**) (*formal*) **1** to be a very good example of sth: *To me she embodies all the best qualities of a teacher.* **2** (often passive) to include or contain sth: *the ideas and values embodied in the U.S. Constitution*

em·brace¹ /ɛmˈbreɪs/ *verb* **1** [I,T] (*formal*) to take sb into your arms as a sign of love or affection ☞ **Hug** is less formal. **2** [T] (*formal*) to accept sth eagerly: *She embraced Christian-ity in her later years.*

em·brace² /ɛmˈbreɪs/ *noun* [C] the act of em-bracing¹(1) : *a warm embrace*

em·broi·der /ɛmˈbrɔɪdər/ *verb* [T] to decorate cloth by sewing with small stitches

ər	ɪr	ɛr	ɑr	ɔr	ʊr	ʒ	h	ŋ
bird	near	hair	car	north	tour	vision	hat	sing

em·broi·der·y /ɛmˈbrɔɪdəri/ *noun* [U] decorative sewing with small stitches; something that has been embroidered

em·bry·o /ˈɛmbrioʊ/ *noun* [C] (*pl.* **em·bry·os** /-oʊz/) an animal or a plant in the early stages of development before birth ☞ Look at **fetus.** —**em·bry·on·ic** /ˌɛmbriˈɑnɪk/ *adj.*

em·cee¹ /ˌɛmˈsi/ *noun* [C] a person who introduces the different performers in a show at a theater or on television and talks to the audience

em·cee² /ˌɛmˈsi/ *verb* [T] (*pres. part.* **em·cee·ing**; *p.t., p.p.* **em·ceed**) to act as an emcee¹ at a show

em·er·ald¹ /ˈɛmərəld/ *noun* [C] a bright green precious stone

em·er·ald² /ˈɛmərəld/ (*also* ˌemerald ˈgreen) *adj.* bright green

e·merge /ɪˈmərdʒ/ *verb* [I] **emerge (from sth)** **1** to appear or come from somewhere (unexpectedly): *A man emerged from the shadows.* ○ (*figurative*) *She is likely to emerge as the top candidate for the job.* **2** to become known: *During investigations, it emerged that he was lying about his age.* —**e·mer·gence** /-dʒəns/ *noun* [U]

☆ **e·mer·gen·cy** /ɪˈmərdʒənsi/ *noun* [C,U] (*pl.* **e·mer·gen·cies**) a serious event that needs immediate action: *In an emergency, dial 911 for help.* ○ *The government has declared a state of emergency.* ○ *an emergency exit*

eˈmergency brake *noun* [C, usually sing.] **1** (*also* **parking brake**) a device in a car, etc. that is used when the car is not moving to prevent it from rolling down a hill **2** a device in a train, etc. that you can pull in an emergency to stop the train from moving

☆ **eˈmergency room** *noun* [C] (*abbr.* **ER**) the part of a hospital where people who have been injured in accidents or who are very sick are taken for immediate treatment

em·i·grant /ˈɛməgrənt/ *noun* [C] a person who has gone to live in another country ☞ Look also at **immigrant.**

☆ **em·i·grate** /ˈɛməgreɪt/ *verb* [I] to leave your own country to go and live in another one: *They emigrated to Australia twenty years ago.* —**em·i·gra·tion** /ˌɛməˈgreɪʃn/ *noun* [C,U] ☞ Look at **immigrate** and **immigration.**

em·i·nent /ˈɛmənənt/ *adj.* (*formal*) (used about a person) famous and important: *an eminent scientist*

em·i·nent·ly /ˈɛmənəntli/ *adv.* (*formal*) obviously; very: *She is eminently qualified for the job.*

e·mit /ɪˈmɪt/ *verb* [T] (**e·mit·ting**; **e·mit·ted**) (*formal*) to send out sth (a smell, a sound, smoke, heat, light, etc.) —**e·mis·sion** /ɪˈmɪʃn/ *noun* [C,U]: *controls on hazardous emissions from factories*

☆ **e·mo·tion** /ɪˈmoʊʃn/ *noun* **1** [C] a strong feeling such as love, anger, fear, jealousy, etc.

2 [U] strength of feeling: *His voice was filled with emotion.*

☆ **e·mo·tion·al** /ɪˈmoʊʃənl/ *adj.* **1** connected with the emotions: *emotional problems* **2** causing strong feelings: *He gave an emotional speech.* **3** having strong emotions and showing them openly: *She always gets really emotional when I leave.* ○ *He's a very emotional person* (= his moods change suddenly). —**e·mo·tion·al·ly** /-ʃənəli/ *adv.*

em·pa·thy /ˈɛmpəθi/ *noun* [U] the ability to imagine how another person is feeling and so understand his/her mood

em·per·or /ˈɛmpərər/ (*feminine* **em·press**) *noun* [C] the ruler of an empire

☆ **em·pha·sis** /ˈɛmfəsəs/ *noun* [C,U] (*pl.* **em·pha·ses** /-əsiz/) **1** the force that you give to a word or phrase when you are speaking to show that it is important **2** **emphasis (on sth)** (giving) special importance or attention (to sth): *There's a lot of emphasis on science at our school.* ○ *We should really put a greater emphasis on getting our facts right.*

☆ **em·pha·size** /ˈɛmfəsaɪz/ *verb* [T] **emphasize (that…)** to put emphasis on sth; stress: *They emphasized that healthy eating is important.* ○ *They emphasized the importance of healthy eating.*

em·phat·ic /ɛmˈfætɪk/ *adj.* having or using emphasis: *an emphatic refusal* —**em·phat·i·cal·ly** /-kli/ *adv.*

em·pire /ˈɛmpaɪər/ *noun* [C] **1** a group of countries that is governed by one country: *the Roman Empire* ☞ Look at **emperor** and **empress.** **2** a group of companies or businesses that is controlled by one parent company or by one person or group: *a publishing empire*

☆ **em·ploy** /ɛmˈplɔɪ/ *verb* [T] **1** **employ sb (in/on sth); employ sb (as sth)** to pay sb to work for you: *He is employed in a chocolate factory.* ○ *She is employed as a truck driver.* ○ *They employ 600 workers.* ☞ Look at **unemployed.** **2** **employ sb/sth (in/on) sth** (*formal*) to use: *a factory that employs modern techniques in the manufacturing process*

☆ **em·ploy·ee** /ɛmˈplɔɪi; ˌɛmplɔɪˈi/ *noun* [C] a person who works for sb: *These restrooms are for employees only.* ○ *federal and state employees* (= of the federal and state governments)

☆ **em·ploy·er** /ɛmˈplɔɪər/ *noun* [C] a person or company that employs other people: *My health insurance is paid for by my employer.*

☆ **em·ploy·ment** /ɛmˈplɔɪmənt/ *noun* [U] **1** the state of having a paid job: *She is looking for employment.* ○ *It is difficult to find employment in rural areas.* ☞ Look at **unemployment** and at the note at **work¹.** **2** (*formal*) the use of sth: *the employment of force*

emˈployment agency *noun* [C] (*pl.* **employment agencies**) a business that helps people to find work

em·pow·er /ɛmˈpaʊər/ *verb* [T] to give sb

E

power or authority (to do sth), or to make sb feel that he/she can do more things —**em·pow·er·ment** *noun* [U]

em·press /ˈɛmprəs/ *noun* [C] **1** a woman who rules an empire **2** the wife of an emperor

☆ **emp·ty¹** /ˈɛmpti/ *adj.* **1** having nothing or nobody inside it : *an empty box* ○ *The bus was half empty.* ○ *That house has been empty for months.* **2** without meaning or value: *It was an empty threat* (= it was not meant seriously). ○ *My life feels empty now that the kids have left home.* —**emp·ti·ness** *noun* [U]

☆ **emp·ty²** /ˈɛmpti/ *verb* (*pres. part.* **emp·ty·ing**; *3rd pers. sing. pres.* **emp·ties**; *p.t., p.p.* **emp·tied**) **1** [T] **empty sth (out)** to make sth empty: *Just empty your cup into the sink.* ○ *Empty your pockets out.* **2** [T] **empty sth (out) (into/onto sth)** to take sth from a container and put it somewhere else: *Empty that milk into the sink. It's sour.* ○ *The boy emptied out all his toys onto the floor.* **3** [I] to become empty: *The theater emptied very quickly once the movie was over.*

ˌempty-ˈhanded *adj.* bringing or taking nothing: *She went out to buy a new dress but returned empty-handed.*

☆ **en·a·ble** /ɛˈneɪbl/ *verb* [T] **enable sb/sth to do sth** to make sb/sth able to do sth (by giving him/her/it power, authority, etc.): *Computer technology has enabled us to predict the weather more accurately.*

e·nam·el /ɪˈnæml/ *noun* [U] **1** a hard, shiny substance used for protecting or decorating metal, etc.: *enamel paint* **2** the hard white outer covering of a tooth

en·chant·ed /ɛnˈtʃæntəd/ *adj.* **1** (especially in children's stories) under the influence of special magic words (**a spell**): *an enchanted forest* **2** pleased or delighted: *The little girl was completely enchanted with the dollhouse.*

en·chant·ing /ɛnˈtʃæntɪŋ/ *adj.* very nice or pleasant; delightful

en·cir·cle /ɛnˈsərkl/ *verb* [T] (*formal*) to make a circle around sth; to surround: *The building was completely encircled by police.*

☆ **en·close** /ɛnˈkloʊz/ *verb* [T] **1 enclose sth (in/with sth)** to surround sth with a wall, fence, etc.: *The yard is enclosed by a tall fence.* ○ *He gets very nervous in enclosed spaces.* **2** to put sth in an envelope, package, etc.: *Can I enclose a letter with this package?*

en·clo·sure /ɛnˈkloʊʒər/ *noun* [C] **1** a piece of land that is enclosed by a wall, fence, etc. **2** something that is enclosed in an envelope, package, etc.

en·core¹ /ˈɑnkɔr/ *interj.* (called out by an audience that wants the performers in a play, concert, etc. to perform sth extra)

en·core² /ˈɑnkɔr/ *noun* [C] an extra performance at the end of a play, concert, etc.

en·coun·ter¹ /ɛnˈkaʊntər/ *verb* [T] **1** (*formal*) to meet sb unexpectedly **2** to experience sth (a danger, difficulty, etc.): *I've never encountered any discrimination at work.* ☞ **Meet with** is used as a synonym for encounter in this sense.

en·coun·ter² /ɛnˈkaʊntər/ *noun* [C] an unexpected (often unpleasant) meeting

☆ **en·cour·age** /ɛnˈkərɪdʒ/ *verb* [T] **1** encourage sb/sth (in sth/to do sth) to give hope, support or confidence to sb: *The teacher encouraged her students to ask questions.* ○ *His friends encouraged him in his attempt to stop smoking.* ☞ The opposite is **discourage**. Note that we say **discourage sb from doing sth**: *The teacher discouraged her students from asking questions.* **2** to make sth happen more easily: *The government wants to encourage investment in the area.* —**en·cour·age·ment** *noun* [C,U] —**en·cour·ag·ing** *adj.*

☆ **en·cy·clo·pe·di·a** /ɛnˌsaɪkləˈpidiə/ *noun* [C] (*pl.* **en·cy·clo·pe·di·as**) a book or set of books that gives information about many subjects, arranged in alphabetical order (i.e. from A to Z). Some encyclopedias are also available on CD-ROM so they can be used in a computer.

☆ **end¹** /ɛnd/ *noun* [C] **1** the furthest or last part of sth; the place or time where sth stops: *the end of a road, room, piece of string, etc.* ○ *Go to the end of the line.* ○ *My house is at the end of the street.* ○ *The man on the other end of the phone spoke so quietly that I didn't catch his name.* ○ *There are some seats at the far end of the room.* ○ *I'm going on vacation at the end of October.* ○ *He promised to give me an answer by the end of the week.* ○ *She couldn't wait to hear the end of the story.*

☞ **End** is sometimes used before another noun: *the end house* ○ *the end seat*. Look at the noun **finish**. It is used to mean **end** only in connection with races and competitions. Look also at **rear end**.

2 (*formal*) an aim or purpose: *They were prepared to do anything to achieve their ends.*

IDM **at an end** (*formal*) finished or used up: *Her career is at an end.*

at the end of your rope having no more patience or strength

bring sth/come/draw to an end (to cause sth) to finish: *The summer is coming to an end.*

a dead end ⇨ DEAD¹

end to end in a line with the ends touching: *They put the tables end to end.*

in the end at last; finally: *He wanted to get home early, but in the end it was midnight before he left.*

loose ends ⇨ LOOSE

make ends meet to have enough money for your needs: *It's hard for us to make ends meet.*

odds and ends ⇨ ODDS

on end (used about time) continuously: *He sits and reads for hours on end.*

put an end to sth to stop sth from happening any more

the short end of the stick ⇨ SHORT¹

☆ **end²** /ɛnd/ *verb* [I,T] **end (in/with sth)** (to cause sth) to finish: *The road ends here.* ○ *How does this story end?* ○ *Most adverbs in English end in "-ly".* ○ *I think we'd better end this conversation now.*

PHRV **end up (as sth)**; **end up (doing sth)** to find yourself in a place/situation that you did not intend or expect: *We got lost and ended up in a bad part of town.* ○ *She had always wanted to be a writer but ended up as a teacher.* ○ *There was nothing to eat at home, so we ended up ordering a pizza.*

en·dan·ger /ɛn'deɪndʒər/ *verb* [T] to cause danger to sb/sth: *Smoking endangers your health.*

en·dan·gered /ɛn'deɪndʒərd/ *adj.* (used about animals, plants, etc.) in danger of disappearing from the world (**becoming extinct**): *The panda is an endangered species.*

en·dear·ing /ɛn'dɪrɪŋ/ *adj.* very pleasing and easy to like: *Mike's playful sense of humor is one of his most endearing qualities.*

en·deav·or¹ /ɛn'dɛvər/ *verb* [I] (*formal*) **endeavor (to do sth)** to try: *She endeavored to make the best of a very difficult situation.*

en·deav·or² /ɛn'dɛvər/ *noun* [C,U] (*formal*) effort, or an act of trying to do sth: *remarkable advances in every area of human endeavor* ○ *We wish you every success in your future endeavors.*

☆ **end·ing** /'ɛndɪŋ/ *noun* [C] **1** the end (of a story, play, movie, etc.): *a story with a happy ending* **2** (*grammar*) the last part of a word, which can change: *When nouns end in -ch or -sh or -x, the plural ending is -es, not -s.*

☆ **end·less** /'ɛndləs/ *adj.* without end: *Our plane was delayed for hours and the wait seemed endless.* —**end·less·ly** *adv.*

en·dorse /ɛn'dɔrs/ *verb* [T] **1** to give (official) support or agreement to a candidate or a plan, statement, decision, etc.: *The auto workers' union has endorsed the Democratic candidate for President.* **2** to say in an advertisement that you use and like a product: *professional athletes who endorse sneakers on TV* **3** to sign your name on the back of a check —**en·dorse·ment** *noun* [C,U]

en·dur·ance /ɛn'dʊrəns/ *noun* [U] the ability to endure(1) sth: *The competition will test your strength and endurance.*

en·dure /ɛn'dʊr/ *verb* (*formal*) **1** [T] to suffer sth painful or uncomfortable: *She endured ten years of loneliness.* **2** [I] to last; continue: *Mozart died long ago, but his music endures.*

'end zone *noun* [C] an area at each end of a football field, where players must carry the ball in order to score points (**touchdowns**) ☞ picture at **football**.

☆ **en·e·my** /'ɛnəmi/ *noun* (*pl.* **en·e·mies**) **1** [C] a person who hates and tries to harm sb/sth: *The former friends became bitter enemies.* ○ *He*

has made several enemies since his arrival at the school. ☞ The noun is **enmity**. **2 the enemy** the army or country that your country is fighting against: *The enemy is attacking at dawn.*

en·er·get·ic /ˌɛnər'dʒɛtɪk/ *adj.* full of or needing energy (1): *Running is a very energetic form of exercise.* —**en·er·get·i·cal·ly** /-kli/ *adv.*

en·er·gize /'ɛnərdʒaɪz/ *verb* [T] to give energy to sb/sth: *Her speech energized the audience members.*

☆ **en·er·gy** /'ɛnərdʒi/ *noun* (*pl.* **en·er·gies**) **1** [U] the ability to be very active or do a lot of work without getting tired: *Children are usually full of energy.* ○ *This flu has left me with no energy at all.* **2 energies** [plural] the effort and attention which you give to doing sth: *She devoted all her energies to helping the homeless.* **3** [U] the power that comes from coal, electricity, gas, etc. that is used for driving machines, etc.: *nuclear energy*

☆ **en·force** /ɛn'fɔrs/ *verb* [T] **1** to make sure that laws, etc. are obeyed: *How will they enforce the new law?* **2** to force sth to be done or to happen: *Enforcing discipline by using threats is not often successful.* —**en·force·ment** *noun* [U] ☞ Look also at **law enforcement**.

en·gage /ɛn'geɪdʒ/ *verb* [T] **1** to fill sb's thoughts, time, interest, etc.: *You need to engage the students' attention right from the start.* **2** to make parts of a machine fit together: *Be sure that the emergency brake is engaged before leaving the car.*

PHRV **engage in sth** to take part in sth: *to engage in illegal activities*

☆ **en·gaged** /ɛn'geɪdʒd/ *adj.* **1 engaged (to sb)** having agreed to get married: *We just got engaged.* ○ *Susan is engaged to Jim.* **2** (*formal*) (used about a person) busy or occupied with sth: *Sorry, I can't come. I'm otherwise engaged.*

en·gage·ment /ɛn'geɪdʒmənt/ *noun* [C] **1** an agreement to get married; the time when you are engaged: *Their engagement was announced in the paper.* ○ *Their engagement only lasted for six months.* ○ *He broke off their engagement.* **2** (*formal*) an arrangement to go somewhere or do sth at a fixed time; an appointment

en'gagement ring *noun* [C] a ring, usually with precious stones in it, that a man gives to a woman when they get engaged (1)

☆ **en·gine** /'ɛndʒən/ *noun* [C] **1** the part of a machine that changes energy (from oil, electricity, etc.) into movement: *This engine runs on diesel.* ○ *an automobile engine* ☞ Look at the note at **motor**. **2** (*also* **locomotive**) a machine that pulls a train

☆ **en·gi·neer¹** /ˌɛndʒə'nɪr/ *noun* [C] **1** a person whose job is to use science and maths in practical ways, e.g. to design machines, roads, bridges, etc., or to plan processes in factories, etc.: *a civil, chemical, mechanical, etc. engineer* **2** a person whose job is to drive a train

ə	y	w	t̬	eɪ	aɪ	ɔɪ	aʊ	oʊ
about	yes	woman	butter	say	five	boy	now	go

en·gi·neer² /ˌɛndʒəˈnɪr/ *verb* [T] **1** (*formal*) to arrange for sth to happen by careful (secret) planning: *Her promotion was engineered by her father.* **2** (often passive) to change the structure of sth, often in order to make it work or develop in a different way: *strawberry plants that have been genetically engineered to produce bigger fruit*

en·gi·neer·ing /ˌɛndʒəˈnɪrɪŋ/ *noun* [U] (the study of) the work that is done by an engineer¹(1): *a degree in engineering* ☞ Look also at **genetic engineering**.

☆ **En·glish¹** /ˈɪŋglɪʃ/ *noun* **1** [U] the language that is spoken in the United States, Canada, Britain and in some other countries: *Do you speak English?* ○ *I've been learning English for five years.* ○ *How do you say "perro" in English?* **2 the English** [plural] the people of England

En·glish² /ˈɪŋglɪʃ/ *adj.* from or connected with England: *My friend Simon is English.* ○ *English history*

☞ Be careful. The people of Scotland (the Scots) and of Wales (the Welsh) are **British**, not English. Look at the note at **United Kingdom**.

en·grave /ɛnˈgreɪv/ *verb* [T] **engrave B on A/ engrave A with B** to cut patterns or words on metal, stone, etc.: *His name is engraved on the plaque.* ○ *The plaque is engraved with his name.*

en·grav·ing /ɛnˈgreɪvɪŋ/ *noun* [C] a picture that is printed from an engraved metal plate

en·grossed /ɛnˈgroʊst/ *adj.* **engrossed (in sth)** very interested in sth so that you forget other things: *She was completely engrossed in her book.*

en·gulf /ɛnˈgʌlf/ *verb* [T] **engulf sb/sth (in sth)** to surround or cover sb/sth completely (with sth): *Flames quickly engulfed the entire house.*

en·hance /ɛnˈhæns/ *verb* [T] (*formal*) to improve sth or to make sth look better —**en·hance·ment** *noun* [C,U]

e·nig·ma /ɪˈnɪgmə/ *noun* [C] (*pl.* **e·nig·mas**) a person, thing or situation that is strange or difficult to understand —**en·ig·ma·tic** /ˌɛnɪgˈmætɪk/ *adj.*

☆ **en·joy** /ɛnˈdʒɔɪ/ *verb* [T] **1 enjoy sth/enjoy doing sth** to get pleasure from: *I really enjoyed that meal.* ○ *Do you enjoy your work?* ○ *He enjoys listening to music while he's driving.* **2 enjoy yourself** to be happy; to have a good time: *I enjoyed myself at Sue's party last night – did you?*

☆ **en·joy·a·ble** /ɛnˈdʒɔɪəbl/ *adj.* giving pleasure: *We spent an enjoyable few days at the beach.*

en·joy·ment /ɛnˈdʒɔɪmənt/ *noun* [C,U] pleasure, or a thing which gives pleasure: *She gets a lot of enjoyment from traveling.*

en·large /ɛnˈlɑrdʒ/ *verb* [I,T] (to cause sth) to become larger: *I'm going to have this picture enlarged.*

en·large·ment /ɛnˈlɑrdʒmənt/ *noun* [C,U] making sth larger or sth that has been made larger: *an enlargement of a picture*

en·light·en /ɛnˈlaɪtn/ *verb* [T] to give sb more information about sth so that he/she knows the truth

en·list /ɛnˈlɪst/ *verb* **1** [I,T] to join the army, navy or air force; to make sb a member of the army, etc. **2** [T] to get help, support, etc.: *We need to enlist the support of everybody who works here.*

en·mi·ty /ˈɛnməti/ *noun* [U] the feeling of hatred toward an enemy

e·nor·mi·ty /ɪˈnɔrməti/ *noun* [sing.] (*formal*) the level of seriousness of sth; how bad sth is

☆ **e·nor·mous** /ɪˈnɔrməs/ *adj.* very large or very great: *an enormous building* ○ *enormous pleasure* ○ *There is an enormous amount of work involved in this.* —**e·nor·mous·ly** *adv.*

☆ **e·nough¹** /ɪˈnʌf/ *det., pron.* **1** as much or as many of sth as necessary: *We've saved enough money to buy a computer.* ○ *Not everybody can have a book – there aren't enough.* ○ *Are there enough chairs?* ○ *If enough of you are interested, we'll arrange a trip to the theater.* **2** as much or as many as you want: *Don't give me any more work. I have enough already.*

IDM have had enough (of sth) to be tired of sth and annoyed by it: *I've had enough of living in the city* (= I don't want to live in the city anymore).

☆ **e·nough²** /ɪˈnʌf/ *adv.* (used *after* verbs, adjectives and adverbs) to the necessary degree; sufficiently: *You don't practice enough.* ○ *He's not old enough to travel alone.* ○ *Does she speak Italian well enough to get the job?* ○ *Are those shoes big enough for you, or do you need a larger size?* ☞ picture at **too**.

IDM fair enough ⇨ FAIR²

funnily, strangely, etc. enough it is funny, etc. that…: *Funnily enough, I thought exactly the same thing myself.*

sure enough ⇨ SURE²

en·raged /ɛnˈreɪdʒd/ *adj.* very angry

en·rich /ɛnˈrɪtʃ/ *verb* [T] to improve the quality, flavor, etc. of sth: *These cornflakes are enriched with vitamins.*

☆ **en·roll** /ɛnˈroʊl/ *verb* [I,T] **enroll (sb) (in/as sth)** to become or to make sb a member of a club, school, etc.: *I enrolled in my local swimming class.* ○ *They enrolled 100 new students last year.*

en·roll·ment /ɛnˈroʊlmənt/ *noun* [C,U] the number of people who are members of a school, club, etc.: *Enrollment in this course is limited to twenty people.*

en route /ˌɑnˈrut; ˌɛn-/ *adv.* **en route (from …) (to …)** on the way: *The car broke down when we were en route to Seattle.*

en·sue /ɛnˈsu/ *verb* [I] (*formal*) to happen after (and often as a result of) sth else

☆ **en·sure** /ɛnˈʃʊr/ (*also* **insure**) *verb* [T] (*formal*) to make sth certain to happen: *regulations to ensure that water supplies are safe to drink* ○ *a plan that would ensure a victory in the election*

☞ A less formal expression is **make sure (that)**....

en·tail /ɛnˈteɪl/ *verb* [T] (*formal*) to make sth necessary; to involve: *This is going to entail a lot of hard work.* ○ *What exactly does the job entail?*

en·tan·gled /ɛnˈtæŋɡəld/ *adj.* caught in sth else: *The bird was entangled in the net.*

☆ **en·ter¹** /ˈɛntər/ *verb* **1** [I,T] (*formal*) to come or go into a place: *Don't enter without knocking.* ○ *They all stood up when he entered the room.* ○ (*figurative*) *We have just entered a new phase in international relations.*

☞ Note that **enter** is used without a preposition. **Come into** and **go into** are much more common. Look also at **entrance**, **entrant** and **entry**.

2 [T] **enter sth** to put your name on the list for an exam, a race, a competition, etc.: *I entered the Boston Marathon last year, but I didn't finish.* **3** [T] **enter sth (in/into/on sth)** to put names, numbers, etc. in a list, book, computer, etc.: *Your name has not been entered in our records.* ○ *Enter your 4-digit code and press the "return" key.* **4** [T] to become a member of a school, a college, a profession, an institution, etc.: *She entered politics in 1980.*

PHRV **enter into sth (with sb)** to begin sth: *to enter into an agreement with another company*

en·ter² /ˈɛntər/ *noun* = RETURN²(5)

en·ter·prise /ˈɛntərpraɪz/ *noun* **1** [C] something (e.g. a plan or a project) that is new and difficult: *It's a very exciting new enterprise.* **2** [U] the courage that you need to start a new and difficult project: *We need men and women of enterprise and energy.* **3** [C,U] a business; the way business is organized: *a new industrial enterprise* ○ *The government supports private enterprise.*

en·ter·pris·ing /ˈɛntərpraɪzɪŋ/ *adj.* having enterprise (2): *an enterprising young manager* ☞ The opposite is **unenterprising**.

☆ **en·ter·tain** /ˌɛntərˈteɪn/ *verb* **1** [T] to interest and amuse sb: *He entertained us with jokes all evening.* ○ *I find it very hard to keep my class entertained on a Friday afternoon.* **2** [I,T] to welcome sb as a guest; to give sb food and drink: *They entertain a lot./They do a lot of entertaining.*

en·ter·tain·er /ˌɛntərˈteɪnər/ *noun* [C] a person who entertains (1) as a job

☆ **en·ter·tain·ing** /ˌɛntərˈteɪnɪŋ/ *adj.* interesting and amusing

☆ **en·ter·tain·ment** /ˌɛntərˈteɪnmənt/ *noun* [U] things to do that interest and amuse people: *There isn't much entertainment for young people in this town.* ○ *live entertainment* (= people singing, dancing, etc. in front of an audience)

en·thrall /ɛnˈθrɔl/ *verb* [T] to hold sb's interest and attention completely: *He was enthralled by her story.* —**en·thrall·ing** *adj.*

☆ **en·thu·si·asm** /ɛnˈθuziæzəm/ *noun* [U] **enthusiasm (for/about sb/sth)** a strong feeling of eagerness or interest: *Jan showed great enthusiasm for the new project.*

en·thu·si·ast /ɛnˈθuziæst/ *noun* [C] a person who is very interested in an activity or a subject: *She is a jazz enthusiast.*

☆ **en·thu·si·as·tic** /ɛnˌθuziˈæstɪk/ *adj.* full of enthusiasm —**en·thu·si·as·ti·cal·ly** /-kli/ *adv.*

en·tice /ɛnˈtaɪs/ *verb* [T] to persuade sb to do sth by offering something nice: *Advertisements try to entice people into buying more things than they need.* —**en·tice·ment** *noun* [C,U]

en·tic·ing /ɛnˈtaɪsɪŋ/ *adj.* attractive and making you want to do sth

☆ **en·tire** /ɛnˈtaɪər/ *adj.* (only *before* a noun) whole or complete: *the entire world* ○ *We invited the entire class to the party.* ☞ **Entire** is stronger than **whole**.

☆ **en·tire·ly** /ɛnˈtaɪərli/ *adv.* completely: *I entirely agree with you.*

en·tire·ty /ɛnˈtaɪrəti; ɛnˈtaɪərti/ *noun* [U]
in its entirety; in their entirety (*formal*) as a whole: *We need to consider the problem in its entirety.*

en·ti·tle /ɛnˈtaɪtl/ *verb* [T] to give sb the right to have or do sth: *I think I'm entitled to a day off – I've worked hard enough.*

en·ti·tled /ɛnˈtaɪtld/ *adj.* (used about books, plays, etc.) with the title: *The first song on the album is entitled "Common People."*

en·ti·tle·ment /ɛnˈtaɪtlmənt/ *noun* **1** [C,U] **entitlement (to sth/to do sth)** a person's right to have or do sth: *employees' entitlements to paid vacation time* **2** (*also* **en'titlement ‚program**) [C] a government system or plan that makes money, food, etc. available to people because they are poor, over a certain age, etc.

en·ti·ty /ˈɛntəti/ *noun* [C] (*pl.* **en·ti·ties**) something that exists separately from sth else: *The city and county governments are separate entities.*

☆ **en·trance** /ˈɛntrəns/ *noun* **1** [C] the door, gate or opening where you go into a place: *I'll meet you at the entrance to the theater.* ☞ Look also at **entry** (3). It has a similar meaning. **2** [C] **entrance (into/onto sth)** the act of coming or going in: *He made a dramatic entrance onto the stage.* ☞ **Entry** can be used with the same meaning. **3** [U] **entrance (to sth)** the right to enter a place: *They were refused entrance to the nightclub.* ○ *an entrance fee* ☞ **Entry** is also possible. Look at **admission** and **admittance**.

E

4 [U] **entrance (into/to sth)** the right to join a club, an institution, etc.: *You may not need to take an entrance exam to get into a state university.* ☞ Look at **admission**.

'entrance ramp (*also* **'on-ramp**) *noun* [C] a road that leads onto a freeway ☞ Look at the note at **freeway**.

en·trant /ˈɛntrənt/ *noun* [C] a person who enters a competition, etc.

en·trée (*also* **entree**) /ˈɑntreɪ/ *noun* [C] the main course of a meal, especially in a restaurant

en·tre·pre·neur /ˌɑntrəprəˈnər; -ˈnʊr/ *noun* [C] a person who starts a business and often takes risks in order to become successful —**en·tre·pre·neur·i·al** /ˌɑntrəprəˈnʊriəl/ *adj.*: *entrepreneurial talent*

en·trust /ɛnˈtrʌst/ *verb* [T] **entrust A with B/ entrust B to A** (*formal*) to make sb responsible for sth that is given to him/her: *I entrusted Rachel with the arrangements for the party./I entrusted the arrangements for the party to Rachel.*

☆ **en·try** /ˈɛntri/ *noun* (*pl.* **en·tries**) **1** [C] **entry (into sth)** the act of coming or going in; entering(1): *The thieves forced an entry into the building.* ☞ **Entrance** is also possible. **2** [U] **entry (to sth)** the right to enter a place: *an entry visa* ☞ **Entrance** is also possible. Look at **admission** and **admittance**. **3** [C] a door, gate, passage, etc. where you enter a building, etc.; an entrance hall: *We stood in the entry of the building until the rain stopped.* ☞ **Entrance** and **entryway** have similar meanings. **4** [C] **entry (in sth)** one item that is written down in a list, calendar, account book, dictionary, etc.: *You'll find "briskly" at the entry for "brisk."* **5** [C] **entry (for sth)** a person or thing that is entered for a competition, etc.: *There were 50 entries for the best apple pie at the state fair.*

'entry-,level *adj.* (only *before* a noun) for people who are just beginning their career or some such activity: *an entry-level job*

en·try·way /ˈɛntriweɪ/ *noun* [C] an area, usually with a roof or a covering, that you go through to enter a place

en·vel·op /ɛnˈvɛləp/ *verb* [T] (*formal*) to cover or surround sb/sth completely (in sth): *The hills were enveloped in mist.*

☆ **en·ve·lope** /ˈɛnvəloʊp; ˈɑn-/ *noun* [C] the paper cover for a letter

☞ After writing a letter, you **address** the envelope, **seal** it and stick a stamp in the top right-hand corner. Sometimes when you answer an advertisement you are asked to send a "self-addressed stamped envelope," i.e. an envelope that is addressed to yourself with a stamp on it.

en·vi·ous /ˈɛnviəs/ *adj.* **envious (of sb/sth)**

feeling or showing that you want sth that sb else has: *She was envious of her sister's success.*

☆ **en·vi·ron·ment** /ɛnˈvaɪərnmənt/ *noun* **1** [C,U] the conditions in which you live, work, etc.: *A bad home environment can affect a child's progress in school.* **2 the environment** [sing.] the natural world, e.g. land, air, water, etc. in which people, animals and plants live: *We need stronger laws to protect the environment.* —**en·vi·ron·men·tal** /ɛnˌvaɪərnˈmɛntl/ *adj.*: *environmental science* —**en·vi·ron·men·tal·ly** /-ˈmɛntəli/ *adv.*: *environmentally friendly products*

en·vi·ron·men·tal·ist /ɛnˌvaɪərnˈmɛntəlɪst/ *noun* [C] a person who wants to protect the environment (2)

en·vi·sion /ɛnˈvɪʒən/ *verb* [T] (*formal*) to think of sth as being possible in the future; to imagine: *I don't envision any problems.*

en·voy /ˈɛnvɔɪ; ˈɑn-/ *noun* [C] a person who is sent by a government with a message to another country

☆ **en·vy¹** /ˈɛnvi/ *noun* [U] **envy (of sb/sth)** the feeling that you have when sb else has sth that you want: *It was difficult for her to hide her envy of her friend's success.* ☞ Look at **envious**.

IDM the envy of sb the thing that causes sb to feel envy: *The city's school system is the envy of many of its neighbors.*

green with envy ⇨ GREEN¹

☆ **en·vy²** /ˈɛnvi/ *verb* [T] (*pres. part.* **en·vy·ing**; *3rd pers. sing. pres.* **en·vies**; *p.t., p.p.* **en·vied**) **envy sb/sth** to want sth that sb else has; to feel envy¹: *I've always envied your good luck.* ○ *I don't envy the people who have to clean up after the party* (= I'm glad that I don't have to clean up).

ep·ic¹ /ˈɛpɪk/ *noun* [C] a long book, poem, movie, etc. that describes exciting adventures

ep·ic² /ˈɛpɪk/ *adj.* of or like an epic¹: *an epic struggle*

ep·i·cen·ter /ˈɛpəˌsɛntər/ *noun* [C, usually sing.] the point on the Earth's surface that is directly over the point inside the Earth where a sudden, violent movement (**an earthquake**) begins

ep·i·dem·ic /ˌɛpəˈdɛmɪk/ *noun* [C] a large number of cases of people or animals suffering from the same disease at the same time: *A flu epidemic broke out in February.*

ep·i·lep·sy /ˈɛpəlɛpsi/ *noun* [U] a disease of the brain that can cause a person to become unconscious (sometimes with violent uncontrolled movements)

ep·i·lep·tic¹ /ˌɛpəˈlɛptɪk/ *adj.* connected with or suffering from epilepsy: *an epileptic seizure* ○ *She's epileptic.*

ep·i·lep·tic² /ˌɛpəˈlɛptɪk/ *noun* [C] a person who suffers from epilepsy

the E·pis·co·pal Church /ɪˌpɪskəpl ˈtʃərtʃ/

i	ɪ	ɛ	æ	ɑ	ɔ	ʌ	ʊ	u
see	sit	ten	cat	hot	saw	cup	put	too

noun [sing.] a Protestant church that is connected with the official church of England

E·pis·co·pa·lian /ɪˌpɪskəˈpeɪliən/ *adj.* connected with the Episcopal Church —**E·pis·co·pa·lian** *noun* [C]

☆ **ep·i·sode** /ˈɛpəsoʊd/ *noun* [C] **1** one separate event in sb's life, a novel, etc.: *That's an episode in my life I'd rather forget.* **2** one part of a TV or radio drama that is broadcast in several parts (**a series**): *Don't miss tomorrow's exciting episode!*

ep·i·taph /ˈɛpətæf/ *noun* [C] words that are written or said about a dead person, especially words written on a gravestone

e·pit·o·me /ɪˈpɪtəmi/ *noun* [sing.] a perfect example of sth: *Paula is the epitome of the successful businesswoman.*

e·pit·o·mize /ɪˈpɪtəmaɪz/ *verb* [T] to be typical of sth

ep·och /ˈepək/ *noun* [C] a period of time in history (that is important because of special events, features, etc.)

☆ **e·qual¹** /ˈikwəl/ *adj.* the same in size, amount, value, number, status, etc.: *They are equal in weight.* ○ *They are of equal weight.* ○ *Divide it into two equal parts.* ○ *Employees will receive a bonus equal to one week's salary.* ○ *Women are demanding equal pay for equal work.* ○ *Our company adopted an Equal Opportunities policy* (= rules to make sure that people are treated equally). ☞ The opposite is **unequal**.

IDM **on equal terms (with sb)** with the same advantages and disadvantages as sb else

e·qual² /ˈikwəl/ *noun* [C] a person who has the same ability, rights, etc. as you do: *to treat sb as an equal*

☆ **e·qual³** /ˈikwəl/ *verb* [T] **1** to be or mean the same as sth: *44 plus 17 equals 61 is written: 44 + 17 = 61.* ○ *Some people believe that money equals happiness.* **2** **equal sb/sth (in sth)** to be as good as sb/sth: *He ran an excellent race, equaling the club record in the 400 meters.*

☆ **e·qual·i·ty** /ɪˈkwɑləṭi/ *noun* [U] the situation in which everybody has the same rights and advantages; being equal: *Absolute equality is probably impossible to achieve.* ○ *racial equality* (= between people of different races) ☞ The opposite is **inequality**.

e·qual·ize /ˈikwəlaɪz/ *verb* [I] to make things equal in size, level, etc.: *efforts to equalize the academic performance of boys and girls*

☆ **e·qual·ly** /ˈikwəli/ *adv.* **1** to the same degree or extent: *They both worked equally hard.* **2** in equal parts: *His money was divided equally among his three children.*

e·quate /ɪˈkweɪt/ *verb* [T] **equate sth (with sth)** to consider one thing as being the same as sth else: *It is a mistake to equate wealth with happiness.*

e·qua·tion /ɪˈkweɪʒn/ *noun* [C] (in mathematics) a statement that two quantities are equal: *Solve the equation 2x + 5 = 11.*

the e·qua·tor (*also* **the Equator**) /ɪˈkweɪṭər/ *noun* [sing.] the imaginary line around the earth at an equal distance from the North and South Poles: *on the equator* ☞ picture at **earth**.

e·ques·tri·an /ɪˈkwɛstriən/ *adj.* (*formal*) connected with horse riding

e·quip /ɪˈkwɪp/ *verb* [T] (**e·quip·ping**; **e·quipped**) **equip sb/sth (with sth) 1** (usually passive) to supply sb/sth with what is needed (for a particular purpose): *We will equip all schools with new computers in the next year.* ○ *The schools in the suburbs are much better equipped than the ones in large cities.* ○ *The car comes equipped with air conditioning and automatic transmission.* **2** to prepare sb for a particular task: *We were just not equipped to deal with the problem.*

☆ **e·quip·ment** /ɪˈkwɪpmənt/ *noun* [U] things that are needed for carrying out a particular activity: *office equipment* ○ *sports equipment* ○ *Standard equipment in the car includes power steering and an airbag.*

☞ Note that **equipment** is uncountable. We have to say "a piece of equipment" if we are talking about one item: *a very useful piece of kitchen equipment.*

☆ **e·quiv·a·lent¹** /ɪˈkwɪvələnt/ *adj.* **equivalent (to sth)** equal in value, amount, meaning, importance, etc.: *The price of imported cars is higher than that of equivalent American models.* ○ *Is the Canadian House of Commons roughly equivalent to the House of Representatives?* —**e·quiv·a·lence** /-ləns/ *noun* [U] —**e·quiv·a·len·cy** /-lənsi/ *noun* [C,U] (*pl.* **e·quiv·a·len·cies**)

e·quiv·a·lent² /ɪˈkwɪvələnt/ *noun* [C] something that is equivalent¹: *There is no English equivalent to the French "bon appetit."*

ER /ˌi ˈɑr/ *abbr.* = EMERGENCY ROOM

e·ra /ˈɪrə; ˈɛrə/ *noun* [C] a period of time in history (that is special for some reason): *We are living in the era of the computer.* ○ *the Civil War era*

e·rad·i·cate /ɪˈrædəkeɪt/ *verb* [T] (*formal*) to destroy sth completely —**e·rad·i·ca·tion** /ɪˌrædəˈkeɪʃn/ *noun* [U]

☆ **e·rase** /ɪˈreɪs/ *verb* [T] to remove sth (a pencil mark, a recording on tape, etc.): *Be sure to erase any mistakes completely.*

☆ **e·ras·er** /ɪˈreɪsər/ *noun* [C] a piece of rubber or other material that you use to remove writing made with a pencil, chalk, etc.

e·rect¹ /ɪˈrɛkt/ *adj.* **1** standing straight up; upright: *He stood with his head erect.* **2** (used about the male sexual organ) stiff and upright because of sexual excitement

e·rect² /ɪˈrɛkt/ *verb* [T] (*formal*) to build sth or to put sth in an upright position: *to erect a statue* ○ *Huge TV screens were erected so that everybody could see what was going on.*

ə	y	w	ṭ	eɪ	aɪ	ɔɪ	aʊ	oʊ
about	yes	woman	butter	say	five	boy	now	go

E

e·rec·tion /ɪˈrɛkʃn/ *noun* **1** [U] (*formal*) the act of putting sth in an upright position or of building sth **2** [C] the hardening of the male sexual organ in sexual excitement: *to get/have an erection*

e·rode /ɪˈroʊd/ *verb* [T] (usually passive) (used about the ocean, the weather, etc.) to destroy sth slowly: *The cliff has been eroded by the ocean waves.* ○ (*figurative*) *Freedom of speech is being eroded.* —**e·ro·sion** /ɪˈroʊʒn/ *noun* [U]: *the erosion of the coastline by the ocean*

e·rot·ic /ɪˈrɑtɪk/ *adj.* causing sexual excitement: *an erotic video, poem, etc.*

err /ɛr; ər/ *verb* [I] (*formal*) to be or do wrong; to make mistakes: *It is better to err on the side of caution* (= it is better to be too careful rather than not careful enough).

er·rand /ˈɛrənd/ *noun* [C] a short trip to take or get sth for sb, e.g. to buy sth from a store: *to run an errand*

er·rat·ic /ɪˈrætɪk/ *adj.* (used about a person's behavior, or about the quality of sth) changing without reason; that you cannot rely on: *Phil's moods became more erratic when he was under a lot of stress.* —**er·rat·i·cal·ly** /-kli/ *adv.*

☆ **er·ror** /ˈɛrər/ *noun* **1** [C] a mistake: *an error of judgment* ○ *to make an error*

☞ **Error** is more formal than **mistake**. There are some expressions, e.g. *error of judgment, human error* where only **error** can be used.

2 [U] the state of being wrong in behavior or belief: *The letter was sent to you in error.* ○ *The accident was the result of human error.*

IDM **trial and error** ➪ TRIAL

e·rupt /ɪˈrʌpt/ *verb* [I] **1** (used about a volcano) to explode and throw out fire, rock that has melted (**lava**), etc. **2** (used about violence, anger, etc.) to start suddenly: *The demonstration erupted into violence.* **3** (used about people) to suddenly become very angry —**e·rup·tion** /ɪˈrʌpʃn/ *noun* [C,U]

es·ca·late /ˈɛskəleɪt/ *verb* [I,T] **1** (to cause sth) to become stronger or more serious: *The demonstrations are escalating into violent protest in several cities.* **2** (to cause sth) to become greater or higher; to increase: *The cost of housing has escalated in recent years.* —**es·ca·la·tion** /ˌɛskəˈleɪʃn/ *noun* [C,U]

es·ca·la·tor /ˈɛskəleɪtər/ *noun* [C] a moving staircase in a store, etc.

☆ **es·cape¹** /ɪˈskeɪp/ *verb* **1** [I] **escape (from sb/sth)** to get away from a place where you do not want to be; to get free: *to escape from prison* **2** [I] (used about gases or liquids) to find a way out of a container, etc. **3** [I,T] to be safe from sth; to avoid sth: *The two passengers were killed, but the driver escaped unhurt.* ○ *to escape criticism* **4** [T] to be forgotten or not noticed by sb: *Her name escapes me.* ○ *to escape sb's notice* (= not be noticed by sb)

☆ **es·cape²** /ɪˈskeɪp/ *noun* **1** [C,U] **escape (from sth)** the act of escaping¹ (1,2,3): *Escape from Alcatraz Prison was impossible.* ○ *She had a narrow escape when a truck crashed into her car* (= she was nearly killed or seriously hurt). **2** [C] a way, or sth that you can use, to escape: *a fire escape* **3** [U, sing.] something that helps you forget your daily life: *For him, listening to music is a means of escape.* ○ *an escape from reality*

es·caped /ɪˈskeɪpt/ *adj.* having escaped¹(1) from a place: *The escaped prisoners have not been recaptured.*

es·cort¹ /ˈɛskɔrt/ *noun* [C] **1** a person or vehicle (or group of people and vehicles) that goes with and protects sb/sth, or that goes with sb/sth as an honor: *a police escort* ☞ Note the phrase **under escort**: *He arrived under military escort.* **2** (*formal*) a companion for a particular social event

es·cort² /ɛsˈkɔrt/ *verb* [T] **1** to go with sb as an escort: *The governor's limousine was escorted by several police cars.* **2** to take sb somewhere: *Philip escorted her to the door.*

Es·ki·mo /ˈɛskəmoʊ/ *noun* [C] (*pl.* **Es·ki·mo** or **Es·ki·mos**) (*old-fashioned*) a member of a race of people who live in the Arctic regions of North America

☞ Nowadays the native people of Alaska prefer to be called **Alaska Natives**. Look also at **Inuit**.

☆ **ESL** /ˌi ɛs ˈɛl/ *abbr.* English as a Second Language; (the subject of) the English language when it is taught in countries where most people speak English, e.g. the United States, Canada, or Britain, to people whose native language is not English ☞ Look at **EFL**.

☆ **es·pe·cial·ly** /ɪˈspɛʃəli/ *adv.* **1** (*abbr.* **esp.**) to an unusual degree; in particular: *She loves animals, especially dogs.* ○ *The car is pretty small, especially if you have a big family.* **2** for a particular purpose: *I made this especially for you.* ☞ **Specially** is also possible with this meaning. It is less formal. **3** very (much): *Donna gave me an especially large piece of cake.* ○ *"Do you like jazz?" "Not especially."*

es·pi·o·nage /ˈɛspiənɑʒ/ *noun* [U] the system of finding out secret information about another country or organization ☞ Look at **spy**.

☆ **es·say** /ˈɛseɪ/ *noun* [C] a short piece of writing about one subject: *Your assignment for Monday is to write a 250-word essay on this painting.* ☞ A **paper** is usually longer than an essay.

es·sence /ˈɛsns/ *noun* [sing.] the basic or most important quality of sth: *The essence of the problem is that there is not enough money available.*

☆ **es·sen·tial¹** /ɪˈsɛnʃl/ *adj.* absolutely necessary; that you must have or do: *Essential medical supplies will be delivered to the area by*

plane. ○ *Math is essential for a career in computers.* ○ *It is essential that you have a high school diploma for this job.* ○ *It is absolutely essential to have a passport to travel outside the U.S.*

☆ **es·sen·tial²** /ɪˈsɛnʃl/ *noun* [C, usually pl.] something that is necessary or very important: *food and other essentials such as clothing and heating*

☆ **es·sen·tial·ly** /ɪˈsɛnʃəli/ *adv.* basically; really: *The problem is essentially one of money.*

☆ **es·tab·lish** /ɪˈstæblɪʃ/ *verb* [T] **1** to start sth (especially an organization or institution): *The school was established in 1875.* **2** to make sth exist: *We need to establish good relations with the local residents.* **3 establish sb/sth (as sth)** to place sb/sth in a position permanently: *She has been trying to get/become established as a novelist for several years.* **4** to decide sth: *We need to establish our aims before we can go any further.* **5** to make certain of sth; to prove: *The police are not able to establish where he was at the time of the murder.*

☆ **es·tab·lish·ment** /ɪˈstæblɪʃmənt/ *noun* **1** [U] the act of starting sth such as an organization or institution: *the establishment of a new government department* **2** [C] a store or business **3 the establishment** [sing.] the people in positions of power in a country, who usually do not support change

es·tate /ɪˈsteɪt/ *noun* [C] **1** a large area of land in the country that is owned by one person or family: *We visited George Washington's estate, Mount Vernon.* **2** all the money and property that sb leaves when he/she dies ☞ Look also at **real estate**.

es·teem /ɪˈstim/ *noun* [U] (*formal*) great respect; a good opinion of sb: *to hold sb in high esteem*

es·thet·ic = AESTHETIC

☆ **es·ti·mate¹** /ˈɛstəmət/ *noun* [C] **1** a guess or judgment about the size, cost, etc. of sth, before you have all the facts and figures: *Can you give me a rough estimate of how many people will be at the meeting?* **2** a written statement giving a price for a particular job that sb will do, e.g. building or fixing sth

☆ **es·ti·mate²** /ˈɛstəmeɪt/ *verb* [T] to calculate the size, cost, etc. of sth approximately, before you have all the facts and figures: *She estimated that the work would take three months.* ○ *The police estimated the crowd at 10,000.* ○ *Work on the new bridge will cost an estimated five million dollars.*

es·ti·ma·tion /ˌɛstəˈmeɪʃn/ *noun* [U] (*formal*) opinion or judgment

es·tranged /ɪˈstreɪndʒd/ *adj.* **1** no longer living with your husband/wife: *He's estranged from his wife.* ○ *her estranged husband* **2** no longer friendly toward sb who used to be close to you, especially a member of your family

etc. *abbr.* et cetera; and so on, and other things of a similar kind: *cars, trucks, vans, etc.*

e·ter·nal /ɪˈtɜrnl/ *adj.* without beginning or end; lasting forever: *eternal life* (= after death) —**e·ter·nal·ly** /-əli/ *adv.*: *I'll be eternally grateful if you could help me.*

e·ter·ni·ty /ɪˈtɜrnəti/ *noun* **1** [U] time that has no end; the state or time after death **2 an eternity** [sing.] (*informal*) a period of time that seems endless: *It seemed like an eternity before the ambulance came.*

eth·i·cal /ˈɛθɪkl/ *adj.* **1** connected with ethics (2): *an ethical problem* **2** morally correct: *She did not break the law, but her behavior was not ethical.* ☞ The opposite is **unethical**.

eth·ics /ˈɛθɪks/ *noun* **1** [U] the study of what is right and wrong in human behavior: *Ethics is a branch of philosophy.* **2** [plural] beliefs about what is morally right and wrong: *The medical profession has its own code of ethics.*

☆ **eth·nic** /ˈɛθnɪk/ *adj.* connected with or typical of a racial group or groups, or of a group from a particular country or region: *ethnic minorities* ○ *ethnic food, music, etc.* ○ *areas that have been devastated by ethnic cleansing* (= forcing certain ethnic groups to leave an area)

et·i·quette /ˈɛtɪkɛt; -kət/ *noun* [U] the rules of polite and correct behavior

et·y·mol·o·gy /ˌɛtəˈmɑlədʒi/ *noun* (*pl.* **et·y·mol·o·gies**) **1** [U] the study of the origins and history of words and their meanings **2** [C] an explanation of the origin and history of a particular word

eu·phe·mism /ˈyufəmɪzəm/ *noun* [C,U] (using) a polite word or expression instead of a more direct one when you are talking about sth that is unpleasant or embarrassing: *"Go to the bathroom" is a euphemism for "urinate."*

eu·pho·ri·a /yuˈfɔriə/ *noun* [U] (*formal*) a strong feeling of happiness

Eu·ro·pe·an¹ /ˌyʊrəˈpiən/ *adj.* of or from Europe: *European languages*

Eu·ro·pe·an² /ˌyʊrəˈpiən/ *noun* [C] a person from a country in Europe

eu·tha·na·sia /ˌyuθəˈneɪʒə/ *noun* [U] the painless killing of sb who is very old or suffering from a disease that cannot be cured

e·vac·u·ate /ɪˈvækyueɪt/ *verb* [T] (often passive) to move people from a dangerous place to somewhere safer; to leave a place because it is dangerous: *The town had to be evacuated when the river flooded its banks.* —**e·vac·u·a·tion** /ɪˌvækyuˈeɪʃn/ *noun* [C,U]

e·vade /ɪˈveɪd/ *verb* [T] **1** to get out of the way of or to escape from sb/sth: *They managed to evade capture and escaped to Canada.* **2** to avoid sth: *He was accused of evading income tax.* ☞ The noun is **evasion**.

e·val·u·ate /ɪˈvælyueɪt/ *verb* [T] (*formal*) to study the facts and then give your opinion about the meaning of sth or about how good sth is: *We evaluated the situation very carefully*

E

before we made our decision. —**e·val·u·a·tion** /ɪˌvælyuˈeɪʃn/ *noun* [C,U]

e·van·gel·i·cal /ˌivænˈdʒɛlɪkl/ *adj.* (of certain Protestant churches) believing that religious ceremony is not as important as faith in Jesus Christ and study of the Bible

e·van·gel·ist /ɪˈvændʒəlɪst/ *noun* [C] a person who tells other people about Jesus Christ and the Bible and tries to persuade them to become Christians —**e·van·gel·ism** /ɪˈvændʒəlɪzm/ *noun* [U]

e·vap·o·rate /ɪˈvæpəreɪt/ *verb* [I] **1** (used about a liquid) to change into steam or a gas and disappear: *The water evaporated in the sunshine.* ☞ Look at **condense**. **2** (used about feelings) to disappear: *All her hopes evaporated when she heard the news.* —**e·vap·o·ra·tion** /ɪˌvæpəˈreɪʃn/ *noun* [U]

e·va·sion /ɪˈveɪʒn/ *noun* [C,U] an action, statement, etc. that is used for avoiding sth unpleasant: *He has been sentenced to two years' imprisonment for income tax evasion.* ☞ The verb is **evade**.

e·va·sive /ɪˈveɪsɪv/ *adj.* trying to avoid sth; not direct: *Ann gave an evasive answer.*

eve /iv/ *noun* [C] the day or evening before a religious festival, important event, etc.: *Christmas Eve* (= December 24)

☆ **e·ven¹** /ˈivən/ *adj.* **1** flat, level or smooth: *an even surface* **2** not changing; regular: *This wine must be stored at an even temperature.* **3** (used about a competition, etc.) with one side being as good as the other: *an even contest* ☞ The opposite for senses **1,2,3** is **uneven**. **4** (used about numbers) that can be divided by two: *4, 6, 8, 10, etc. are even numbers.* ☞ The opposite is **odd**.

IDM **be/get even (with sb)** to hurt or harm sb who has hurt or harmed you

break even to make neither a loss nor a profit —**e·ven·ly** *adv.*: *The game was very evenly balanced.*

☆ **e·ven²** /ˈivən/ *adv.* **1** (used for emphasizing sth that is surprising): *It isn't very warm here even in the summer.* ○ *Even the kids helped in the yard.* ○ *He didn't even open the letter* (= so he certainly didn't read it). ○ *I have been so busy that I haven't even had time to read the newspaper.* ○ *I like her a lot even though she can be really annoying.* ☞ Look at the note at **although**. **2** (used when you are comparing things, to make the comparison stronger): *It is even more difficult than I expected.* ○ *We are even busier than we were yesterday.*

IDM **even if** (used for saying that what follows "if" makes no difference): *I wouldn't do it, even if you paid me a thousand dollars.*

even so (used for introducing a new idea, fact, etc. that is surprising) in spite of that; nevertheless: *There are a lot of spelling mistakes; even so, it's a very good essay.*

☆ **eve·ning** /ˈivnɪŋ/ *noun* [C,U] the part of the day between the afternoon and the time that you go to bed: *What are you doing this evening?* ○ *We were out yesterday evening.* ○ *I went to the movies Saturday evening.* ○ *Tom usually goes swimming Wednesday evenings.* ○ *Most people watch television in the evening.* ○ *an evening class* (= a course for adults that takes place in the evening)

IDM **good evening** (*formal*) (used when you see sb for the first time in the evening): *Good evening, ladies and gentlemen, and welcome to the show.*

☞ When you use the adjectives *early* or *late* before "evening" you must use the preposition *in*: *It started to rain in the early evening.* ○ *They arrived in the late evening.* With other adjectives, we often use *on*: *After sunset on a clear evening, the temperature can drop quickly.* But with days of the week, we do not usually use *on*: *My Spanish class starts Monday evening.* No preposition is used before *this*, *tomorrow*, *last* or *yesterday*: *I'll wash the dishes this evening.* ○ *I'll call Liz tomorrow evening.* ○ *We went to Omar's house last evening.* ○ *They weren't home yesterday evening.* Look also at the notes at **morning** and **night**.

☆ **e·vent** /ɪˈvɛnt/ *noun* [C] **1** something that happens, especially sth important or unusual: *a historic event* ○ *The events of the past few days have made things very difficult for the governor.* **2** one of the races, competitions, etc. in a sports program: *The next event is the 800 meters.*

IDM **in any event** whatever happens: *I hope to see you soon, but in any event I'll call you on Sunday.*

in the event of sth (*formal*) if sth happens: *In the event of fire, leave the building as quickly as possible.*

e·vent·ful /ɪˈvɛntfl/ *adj.* full of interesting or important events ☞ The opposite is **uneventful**.

e·ven·tu·al /ɪˈvɛntʃuəl/ *adj.* (only *before* a noun) happening as a result; happening at last: *It is impossible to say what the eventual cost will be.*

e·ven·tu·al·ly /ɪˈvɛntʃəli/ *adv.* in the end; at last: *He eventually persuaded his parents to buy him a motorcycle.*

☆ **ev·er** /ˈɛvər/ *adv.* **1** (used in questions and negative sentences, when you are comparing things, and in sentences with "if") at any time: *Do you ever wish you were famous?* ○ *She hardly ever* (= almost never) *goes out.* ○ *Today is hotter than ever.* ○ *This is the best meal I've ever had.* ○ *If you're ever in Dallas, give me a call.* **2** (used in questions with verbs in the perfect tenses) at any time up to now: *Have you ever been to Spain?*

i	ɪ	ɛ	æ	ɑ	ɔ	ʌ	ʊ	u
see	sit	ten	cat	hot	saw	cup	put	too

☞ Notice that when you answer a question like this, you do not use "ever." You say, "Yes, I have" or "No, I haven't" (or "No, never"). Look also at **whatever, whenever, however**, etc.

3 ever- (in compounds) always; continuously: *the ever-growing problem of pollution*
IDM **(as) bad, good, etc. as ever** (as) bad, good, etc. as usual or as you expected: *In spite of his problems, Andrew is as cheerful as ever.*
ever after (used especially at the end of stories) from that moment on for always: *The prince married the princess and they lived happily ever after.*
ever since (...) all the time from (...) until now: *She has had a car ever since she was in college.*

ev·er·green /ˈɛvərɡrin/ *noun* [C], *adj.* (a tree, etc.) with green leaves all year ☞ Look at **deciduous**.

ev·er·last·ing /ˌɛvərˈlæstɪŋ/ *adj. (formal)* lasting forever: *everlasting life*

☆ **eve·ry** /ˈɛvri/ *det.* **1** (used with singular nouns) all the people or things in a group of three or more: *She knows every student in the school.* ○ *There are 400 students in the school, and she knows every one of them.* ○ *I've read every book in this house.* ○ *You were out every time I called.* **2** all that is possible: *You have every chance of success.* ○ *She had every reason to be angry.* **3** (used for saying how often sth happens): *We see each other every day.* ○ *Take the medicine every four hours* (= at 8:00, 12:00, 4:00, etc.). ○ *Our team practices every other day* (= on Monday, Wednesday, Friday, etc.). ○ *One in every three marriages ends in divorce.*
IDM **every last; every single** (used to emphasize the importance of each individual unit): *I can't believe you ate every last cookie in the box!* ○ *The candidate shook hands with every single person in the room.*
(every) now and then ⇨ NOW¹
(every) once in a while ⇨ ONCE¹
every so often occasionally

☆ **eve·ry·bod·y** /ˈɛvriˌbadi/ -ˌbʌdi/ *(also* **everyone** /ˈɛvriwʌn/) *pron.* [with sing. verb] every person; all people: *Is everybody here?* ○ *The police questioned everyone who was at the party.* ○ *I'm sure everybody else* (= all the other people) *will agree with me.*

☞ **Everyone** is only used about people and is not followed by "of." **Every one** means "each person or thing" and is often followed by "of": *Every one of his records has been successful.* Look also at the note at **somebody**.

eve·ry·day /ˈɛvrideɪ/ *adj.* (only *before* a noun) normal and usual: *The computer is now part of everyday life.*

eve·ry·place /ˈɛvripleɪs/ *adv. (informal)* = EVERYWHERE

☆ **eve·ry·thing** /ˈɛvriθɪŋ/ *pron.* [with sing. verb] **1** each thing; all things: *Sam lost everything in the fire.* ○ *Everything is very expensive in this store.* ○ *We can leave everything else* (= all the other things) *at my parents' house.* **2** the most important thing: *Money isn't everything.*

☆ **eve·ry·where** /ˈɛvriwɛr/ *adv.* in or to every place: *I've looked everywhere, but I still can't find it.*

e·vict /ɪˈvɪkt/ *verb* [T] to force sb (officially) to leave the house or land where he/she is living: *They were evicted for not paying the rent.* —**e·vic·tion** /ɪˈvɪkʃn/ *noun* [C,U]

☆ **ev·i·dence** /ˈɛvədəns/ *noun* [U] something that gives a reason for believing sth: *There was no evidence of a struggle in the room.* ○ *There was not enough evidence to prove him guilty.* ○ *Her statement to the police was used in evidence against him.*

☞ Note that **evidence** is uncountable. We use **piece** if we are talking about single items that are evidence: *One piece of evidence is not enough to prove that somebody is guilty.*

IDM **be in evidence** *(formal)* to be seen; to be noticeable: *The effects of last year's flood are still in evidence.*

ev·i·dent /ˈɛvədənt/ *adj.* clear (to the eye or mind); obvious: *It was evident that the damage was very serious.*

ev·i·dent·ly /ˈɛvədəntli/ *adv.* **1** it appears that: *Evidently he has decided to leave.* **2** it is obvious that: *She was evidently extremely shocked at the news.*

☆ **e·vil¹** /ˈivl/ *adj.* very bad; causing trouble or harm: *evil crimes*

☆ **e·vil²** /ˈivl/ *noun* [C,U] *(formal)* something that is very bad: *The play is about the good and evil in all of us.* ○ *Drugs and alcohol are two of the evils of modern society.*
IDM **the lesser of two evils** ⇨ LESSER

e·voke /ɪˈvoʊk/ *verb* [T] *(formal)* to produce a memory, feeling, etc.: *For me, that music always evokes long summer evenings.* ○ *Her article evoked a lot of interest.*

ev·o·lu·tion /ˌɛvəˈluʃn/ *noun* [U] **1** the development of living things over many thousands of years from simple early forms: *Darwin's theory of evolution* **2** the process of change and development: *Political evolution is a slow process.*

e·volve /ɪˈvalv/ *verb* **1** [I] (used about living things) to develop from simple early forms **2** [I,T] *(formal)* to develop or to make sth develop: *His style of painting has evolved gradually over the past 20 years.* ○ *The twins have evolved a language of their own.*

ewe /yu/ *noun* [C] a female sheep ☞ Look at the note and picture at **sheep**.

ex /ɛks/ *noun* [C] *(informal)* a former husband, wife, partner in a relationship, etc.: *My ex and I are still good friends.*

E

ex- /ɛks/ (in compounds) former; of an earlier time: *Monica's ex-husband* ○ *an ex-girlfriend* ○ *an ex-employee*

☆ **ex·act¹** /ɪgˈzækt/ *adj.* **1** (completely) correct; accurate: *He's in his mid-fifties. Well, 56 to be exact.* ○ *I can't tell you the exact number of people who are coming.* ○ *She's the exact opposite of her sister.* **2** able to work in a way that is completely accurate: *You need to be very exact when you calculate the costs.*

ex·act² /ɪgˈzækt/ *verb* [T] (*formal*) to demand and get sth

ex·act·ing /ɪgˈzæktɪŋ/ *adj.* needing or demanding a lot of care and attention; difficult: *Our product must meet the client's exacting standards.*

☆ **ex·act·ly** /ɪgˈzæktli; -ˈzækli/ *adv.* **1** (used for emphasizing sth) just: *You arrived at exactly the right moment.* ○ *I found exactly what I wanted.* **2** (used when you are asking for, or giving, completely correct information): *Where exactly do you live?* ○ *He took exactly one hour to finish.* **3** (used for agreeing with a statement) yes; you are right: *"But I don't think she's old enough to travel on her own." "Exactly."*

IDM **not exactly** (*informal*) **1** not really; not at all: *He's not exactly the most careful driver I know.* **2** (used as an answer to say that sth is almost true): *"So you think I'm wrong?" "No, not exactly, but…"*

☆ **ex·ag·ger·ate** /ɪgˈzædʒəreɪt/ *verb* [I,T] to make sth seem larger, better, worse, etc. than it really is: *Don't exaggerate. I was only two minutes late, not twenty.* ○ *The problems have been greatly exaggerated.*

ex·ag·ger·a·tion /ɪgˌzædʒəˈreɪʃn/ *noun* [C,U] making sth seem bigger, etc. than it really is; sth that does this: *It's an exaggeration to say that all the students are lazy.*

☆ **ex·am** /ɪgˈzæm/ *noun* [C](also *informal* **examination**) a written, spoken or practical test of what you know or can do, especially at the end of a course: *a final exam* ○ *the exam scores* ☞ A **test** is less formal and usually less important than an exam.

☆ **ex·am·i·na·tion** /ɪgˌzæməˈneɪʃn/ *noun* **1** [C,U] the act of looking at sth carefully: *They made a thorough examination of the car before buying it.* ○ *On close examination, it was found that the passport was false.* **2** (*formal*) = EXAM

☆ **ex·am·ine** /ɪgˈzæmən/ *verb* [T] **1 examine sb/sth (for sth)** to look at sb/sth carefully in order to find out sth: *The detective examined the room for clues.* ○ *I'm going to have my teeth examined next week.* **2 examine sb (in/on sth)** (*formal*) to test what sb knows or can do: *You will be examined on everything that has been studied in the course.*

ex·am·in·er /ɪgˈzæmənər/ *noun* [C] a person whose job is to check business records, etc. to

make sure that they are correct: *a bank examiner* ☞ Look also at **medical examiner.**

☆ **ex·am·ple** /ɪgˈzæmpl/ *noun* [C] **1** a thing that shows a general rule about what sth is like: *I don't quite understand you. Can you give me an example of what you mean?* ○ *This is a typical example of a Picasso painting.* **2** a person or thing or a type of behavior that is good and should be copied: *Joe's bravery should be an example to us all.*

IDM **follow sb's example/lead** ⇨ FOLLOW

for example (used for giving an illustration of what you are talking about): *In many countries – Italy, for example – family life is much more important than here.* ○ *There are lots of ways to lose weight. For example, use skim milk instead of whole milk.* ☞ The short form, which is always used *before* the illustration you are giving, is **e.g.**

set a good, bad, etc. example (for sb) to behave in a way that should/should not be copied: *Professional athletes who use drugs set a bad example for kids.*

ex·as·per·ate /ɪgˈzæspəreɪt/ *verb* [T] to make sb angry; to annoy: *She was exasperated by the lack of progress.* —**ex·as·per·at·ing** /-reɪtɪŋ/ —**ex·as·per·a·tion** /ɪgˌzæspəˈreɪʃn/ *noun* [U]: *She finally threw the book across the room in exasperation.*

ex·ca·vate /ˈɛkskəveɪt/ *verb* [I,T] **1** to dig a hole in the ground **2** to uncover objects or buildings from the past by digging in an area of land: *The remains of a Native American village have been excavated in a valley near the river.* —**ex·ca·va·tion** /ˌɛkskəˈveɪʃn/ *noun* [C,U]: *Excavations on the site have revealed several ancient burial grounds.*

ex·ceed /ɪkˈsid/ *verb* [T] **1** to be greater than sth: *The price must not exceed $100.* **2** to go beyond what is allowed or necessary: *to exceed the speed limit* ☞ Look at **excess** and **excessive.**

ex·ceed·ing·ly /ɪkˈsidɪŋli/ *adv.* very: *an exceedingly difficult problem*

ex·cel /ɪkˈsɛl/ *verb* [I] (**ex·cel·ling**; **ex·celled**) (*formal*) **excel in/at sth** to be very good at sth

ex·cel·lence /ˈɛksələns/ *noun* [U] the quality of being very good: *The school is a center of academic excellence.*

☆ **ex·cel·lent** /ˈɛksələnt/ *adj.* very good; of high quality: *He speaks excellent French.* —**ex·cel·lent·ly** *adv.*

☆ **ex·cept¹** /ɪkˈsɛpt/ *prep.* **except (for) sb/sth; except (that…)** not including sb/sth; apart from the fact that : *The museum is open every day except Tuesdays.* ○ *Everyone except Tony is going on the trip.* ○ *I can answer all of the questions except for the last one.* ○ *It was a good hotel except that it was a little noisy.*

ex·cept² /ɪkˈsɛpt/ *verb* [T] (often passive) **except sb/sth (from sth)** (*formal*) to leave sb/sth out; to not include sb/sth

ər	ɪr	ɛr	ɑr	ɔr	ʊr	ʒ	h	ŋ
bird	near	hair	car	north	tour	vision	hat	sing

☆ **ex·cep·tion** /ɪkˈsɛpʃn/ noun [C] a person or thing that is not included: *Most of his songs are terrible, but this one is an exception.* ◦ *There's an exception to every rule.*

IDM **to make an exception (for sb/sth)** to treat sb/sth differently: *We don't usually allow kids under 14 in, but we'll make an exception in your case.*

with the exception of except for; apart from: *He has won every major tennis championship with the exception of Wimbledon.*

without exception in every case; including everybody/everything: *Everybody without exception must take the test.*

ex·cep·tion·al /ɪkˈsɛpʃənl/ adj. very unusual; unusually good: *You will only be allowed to leave early in exceptional circumstances.* ◦ *exceptional skill* —**ex·cep·tion·al·ly** /-ʃənəli/ adv.: *exceptionally difficult*

ex·cerpt /ˈɛksərpt/ noun [C] a short piece taken from a book, movie, piece of music, etc.

ex·cess¹ /ɪkˈsɛs; ˈɛksɛs/ noun **1** [sing.] more of sth than is needed or usual; too much of sth: *An excess of fat in your diet can lead to heart disease.* **2** excesses [plural] behavior or actions that people think are too harmful or extreme

IDM **in excess of** more than: *Her debts are in excess of $1,000.*

to excess too much; much more than people think is normal or acceptable: *After his wife left him, he began drinking to excess.*

ex·cess² /ˈɛksɛs/ adj. (only *before* a noun) more than is usual or allowed; extra: *There are high charges for excess baggage on planes.*

ex·ces·sive /ɪkˈsɛsɪv/ adj. too much; too great: *I think $200 for a dress is excessive.* —**ex·ces·sive·ly** adv.: *I think you are being excessively pessimistic about this.*

☆ **ex·change¹** /ɪksˈtʃeɪndʒ/ noun **1** [C,U] giving or receiving sth in return for sth else: *a useful exchange of information* ◦ *We can offer free room and board in exchange for some help in the house.* **2** [C] an (angry) conversation or argument **3** [U] the relation in value between kinds of money used in different countries: *What's the exchange rate/rate of exchange for dollars?* ◦ *The exchange rate is one dollar to one hundred yen.* **4** [C] a visit by a person or group of people to another country and often a return visit by a similar group from that country: *an exchange student* ☞ Look at **foreign exchange** and **stock exchange**.

☆ **ex·change²** /ɪksˈtʃeɪndʒ/ verb [T] **exchange A for B**; **exchange sth (with sb)** to give or receive sth in return for sth else: *I would like to exchange this skirt for a bigger one.* ◦ *Kari and Linda exchanged addresses with the boys.* ◦ *They exchanged glances* (= they looked at each other).

ex·cit·a·ble /ɪkˈsaɪtəbl/ adj. easily excited

ex·cite /ɪkˈsaɪt/ verb [T] **1** to cause strong feel-

ings (e.g. of happiness or nervousness): *Don't excite the baby too much or we'll never get him to sleep.* **2** to cause a reaction in sb: *The program excited great interest.*

☆ **ex·cit·ed** /ɪkˈsaɪṭəd/ adj. feeling very happy because you are looking forward to sth happening; not calm: *Are you getting excited about your vacation?* ◦ *We're all really excited to be moving into our new house.* —**ex·cit·ed·ly** adv.

☆ **ex·cite·ment** /ɪkˈsaɪtmənt/ noun [U] the state of being excited; a feeling of pleasure, especially because sth interesting is happening or will happen: *The children could not hide their excitement before the trip.* ◦ *There was a lot of excitement in the room as the winner's name was announced.*

☆ **ex·cit·ing** /ɪkˈsaɪtɪŋ/ adj. causing strong feelings of pleasure and interest: *That's very exciting news.* ◦ *San Francisco is one of the most exciting cities in America.* ☛ The opposite is **unexciting**.

ex·claim /ɪkˈskleɪm/ verb [I,T] to say sth suddenly because you are surprised, angry, etc.: *"I just don't believe it!" he exclaimed.*

☆ **ex·cla·ma·tion** /ˌɛkskləˈmeɪʃn/ noun [C] a sound or word that expresses sudden pain, anger, surprise, etc.: *"Ouch!" is an exclamation.*

exclamation point noun [C] a mark (!) that is written after an exclamation

☆ **ex·clude** /ɪkˈsklud/ verb [T] **1** exclude sb/sth (from sth) to prevent sb/sth from getting in: *Women are excluded from the temple.* ◦ *Many health insurance companies exclude people with previous illnesses from coverage.* **2** to decide that sth is not true: *The police had excluded the possibility that the child had run away.* **3** to leave out; not include: *These statistics exclude people over 70.*

☆ **ex·clud·ing** /ɪkˈskludɪŋ/ prep. not including: *The price of the car is $14,995, excluding taxes and registration.*

ex·clu·sion /ɪkˈskluʒn/ noun [U] keeping or leaving sb/sth out

ex·clu·sive¹ /ɪkˈsklusɪv/ adj. **1** expensive and not welcoming people who are thought to be from a low social class: *an exclusive restaurant* ◦ *a home in an exclusive neighborhood* **2** (only *before* a noun) for only one person, group, etc.; not to be shared: *an exclusive interview with Tom Cruise* (= on only one television or radio station).

ex·clu·sive² /ɪkˈsklusɪv/ noun [C] a newspaper story that is given to and published by only one newspaper

ex·clu·sive·ly /ɪkˈsklusɪvli/ adv. only; not involving anybody/anything else: *The swimming pool is reserved exclusively for members of the club.*

ex·cre·ment /ˈɛkskrəmənt/ noun [U] (*formal*) the solid waste matter that is passed from the

tʃ	dʒ	v	θ	ð	s	z	ʃ
chin	June	van	thin	then	so	zoo	she

body through the bowels ☞ Look at **feces**. An informal word is **poop**.

ex·cru·ci·at·ing /ɪkˈskruʃieɪtɪŋ/ *adj.* (used about pain, etc.) very bad

ex·cur·sion /ɪkˈskɚʒn/ *noun* [C] a short trip (that a group of people make for pleasure): *to go on a weekend excursion to Atlantic City*

ex·cus·a·ble /ɪkˈskyuzəbl/ *adj.* that can be forgiven ☞ The opposite is **inexcusable**.

☆ **ex·cuse¹** /ɪkˈskyus/ *noun* [C] **excuse (for sth/ for doing sth)** a reason (that may be true or untrue) that you give in order to explain your behavior: *There's no excuse for bad manners.* ○ *He always finds a good excuse for not helping with the housework.*

☆ **ex·cuse²** /ɪkˈskyuz/ *verb* [T] **1 excuse sb/sth (for sth/for doing sth)** to forgive sb/sth: *Please excuse the mess – I haven't had time to clean up.* **2** to explain sb's bad behavior and make it seem less bad: *Nothing can excuse such behavior.* **3 excuse yourself** to say politely that you need to leave a place: *She excused herself and got up from the table.* **4 excuse sb (from sth)** to free sb from a duty, responsibility, etc.: *I was excused from gym class today because I hurt my knee.*

☞ The expression **excuse me** is used when you interrupt somebody or when you want to start talking to somebody that you don't know: *Excuse me, can you tell me the way to the post office?* We can also use **excuse me** to apologize for something, such as sneezing, yawning, etc.: *Did I step on your toe? Excuse me.* **Excuse me** can be used as a question, for asking sb to repeat what he/she just said because you did not hear or understand it: *"Is this your bag?" "Excuse me?" "I asked if this was your bag."* Look also at **pardon³** and **sorry**.

ex·e·cute /ˈɛksəkyut/ *verb* [T] **1** to kill sb as an official punishment: *He was executed for murder.* **2** (*formal*) to perform a task, etc. or to carry out a plan

ex·e·cu·tion /ˌɛksəˈkyuʃn/ *noun* **1** [C,U] the act of killing sb as an official punishment **2** [U] (*formal*) carrying out a plan, order, etc.

ex·e·cu·tion·er /ˌɛksəˈkyuʃənər/ *noun* [C] a person whose job is to execute (1) criminals

☆ **ex·ec·u·tive¹** /ɪɡˈzɛkyətɪv/ *adj.* **1** (used in connection with people in business, government, etc.) concerned with managing, making decisions, carrying out plans, etc.: *an executive vice president of the company* ○ *The President is the head of the executive branch of the federal government.* **2** (used about goods, buildings, etc.) designed to be used by important businesspeople: *an executive briefcase*

☆ **ex·ec·u·tive²** /ɪɡˈzɛkyətɪv/ *noun* [C] a person who has an important position in a business: *She's a senior executive in a computer company.*

ex·em·pla·ry /ɪɡˈzɛmpləri/ *adj.* very good; that can be an example to other people: *exemplary behavior*

ex·em·pli·fy /ɪɡˈzɛmpləfaɪ/ *verb* (*pres. part.* **ex·em·pli·fy·ing**; *3rd pers. sing. pres.* **ex·em·pli·fies**; *p.t., p.p.* **ex·em·pli·fied**) [T] to be a typical example of sth

ex·empt¹ /ɪɡˈzɛmpt/ *adj.* **exempt (from sth)** free from having to do sth or pay sth: *Are city employees exempt from the new law?* ○ *tax-exempt contributions to charity*

ex·empt² /ɪɡˈzɛmpt/ *verb* [T] **exempt sb/sth (from sth)** (*formal*) to say officially that sb does not have to do sth or pay sth —**ex·emp·tion** /ɪɡˈzɛmpʃn/ *noun* [C,U]

☆ **ex·er·cise¹** /ˈɛksərsaɪz/ *noun* **1** [U] use of the body in a way that will keep you healthy: *The doctor advised him to get regular exercise.* ○ *Swimming is a good form of exercise.* **2** [C] (often plural) a movement or activity that you do in order to keep healthy or to train sth: *You need to do some exercises to improve your technique.* **3** [C] a piece of work that is intended to help you learn or practice sth: *an exercise on phrasal verbs* ○ *a grammar exercise* **4** [C] an action or a series of actions that have a particular aim: *The senator's speech was really just an exercise in public relations.* **5** [U] (*formal*) the use of sth (e.g. a power, right, etc.) **6** [C] a series of activities by soldiers to practice fighting: *military exercises*

☆ **ex·er·cise²** /ˈɛksərsaɪz/ *verb* **1** [I] to do some form of physical movement in order to stay fit and healthy: *It is important to exercise regularly.* **2** [T] to make use of sth (e.g. a power, right, etc.): *You should exercise your right to vote.*

ex·ert /ɪɡˈzɚt/ *verb* [T] **1** to make use of sth (e.g. influence, strength, etc.): *Parents exert a powerful influence on their children's opinions.* **2 exert yourself** to make an effort: *You won't make any progress if you don't exert yourself a little more.*

ex·er·tion /ɪɡˈzɚʃn/ *noun* [C,U] using your body in a way that takes a lot of effort; sth that you do that makes you tired: *At his age physical exertion was dangerous.*

ex·haust¹ /ɪɡˈzɔst/ *noun* **1** [C] a pipe (especially at the back of a car) through which waste gas escapes from an engine or machine **2** [U] the waste gas that escapes from an engine or machine

ex·haust² /ɪɡˈzɔst/ *verb* [T] **1** to make sb very tired: *Getting up so early every morning exhausted him.* **2** to use sth up completely; to finish sth: *All the supplies of food have been exhausted.* **3** to say everything you can about a subject, etc.: *Well, I think we've exhausted that topic.*

☆ **ex·haust·ed** /ɪɡˈzɔstəd/ *adj.* very tired

i	ɪ	ɛ	æ	ɑ	ɔ	ʌ	ʊ	u
see	sit	ten	cat	hot	saw	cup	put	too

☆ **ex·haust·ing** /ɪɡˈzɔstɪŋ/ *adj.* making sb very tired: *Teaching young children is exhausting work.*

ex·haus·tion /ɪɡˈzɔstʃən/ *noun* [U] great tiredness

ex·haus·tive /ɪɡˈzɔstɪv/ *adj.* including everything possible: *an exhaustive list*

☆ **ex·hib·it¹** /ɪɡˈzɪbət/ *noun* [C,U] an object or a collection of objects that is shown in a museum, etc.: *a special exhibit of works by local artists* ○ *The kids loved the panda exhibit at the zoo.* ☞ Notice the expression **on exhibit**: *Her paintings will be on exhibit in San Diego through April 30.*

ex·hib·it² /ɪɡˈzɪbət/ *verb* [T] **1** to show sth to the public: *His paintings have been exhibited in the local art gallery.* **2** (*formal*) to show sth (e.g. a feeling or quality): *The refugees are exhibiting signs of exhaustion and stress.*

☆ **ex·hi·bi·tion** /ˌɛksəˈbɪʃn/ *noun* [C] a collection of objects that are shown to the public: *Have you seen the Picasso exhibition?*

ˌexhiˈbition game *noun* [C] a sports game that is not part of a serious competition

ex·hib·i·tor /ɪɡˈzɪbətər/ *noun* [C] a person who shows his/her work to the public

ex·hil·a·rate /ɪɡˈzɪləreɪt/ *verb* [T] (usually passive) to make sb feel very happy, excited, etc.: *We felt exhilarated by our walk along the beach.* —**ex·hil·a·rat·ing** *adj.* —**ex·hil·a·ra·tion** /ɪɡˌzɪləˈreɪʃn/ *noun* [U]

ex·ile¹ /ˈɛɡzaɪl; ˈɛks-/ *noun* **1** [U] the state of being forced to live outside your own country (especially for political reasons): *to go into exile* ○ *They lived in exile in Canada for many years.* **2** [C] a person who is forced to live outside his/her own country (especially for political reasons): *political exiles* ☞ Look at **refugee**.

ex·ile² /ˈɛɡzaɪl; ˈɛks-/ *verb* [T] (usually passive) to send sb to live in another country (especially for political reasons): *The king was exiled after the revolution.*

☆ **ex·ist** /ɪɡˈzɪst/ *verb* [I] **1** to be real; to be found in the real world; to live: *Does God exist?* ○ *I don't think that word exists, does it?* ○ *Fish cannot exist out of water.* **2** **exist (on sth)** to manage to live: *I don't know how she exists on so little money.*

☆ **ex·is·tence** /ɪɡˈzɪstəns/ *noun* **1** [U] the state of existing: *This is the oldest human skeleton in existence.* ○ *The country of Liberia came into existence in 1821.* **2** [sing.] a way of living; life: *They lead a miserable existence in a tiny shack in the mountains.*

☆ **ex·ist·ing** /ɪɡˈzɪstɪŋ/ *adj.* (only *before* a noun) that is already there or being used; present: *Under the existing law, you are not allowed to work in this country.*

☆ **ex·it¹** /ˈɛɡzət; ˈɛksət/ *noun* [C] **1** a door or way out of a public building: *an emergency exit* **2** the act of leaving sth: *When he saw her*

coming, he made a quick exit. **3** a place where traffic can turn off a freeway, etc.: *Take Exit 3 off Interstate 90 and go south on Lake Shore Drive.*

ex·it² /ˈɛɡzət; ˈɛksət/ *verb* [I] to go out or away

ˈexit poll *noun* [C] a process of predicting who will win an election by asking some people who they have voted for when they leave the buildings where they voted

ˈexit ramp (*also* ˈoff-ramp) *noun* [C] a road that leads off a freeway ☞ Look at the note at **freeway**.

ex·on·er·ate /ɪɡˈzɑnəreɪt/ *verb* [T] (often passive) (*formal*) to free sb from blame, responsibility etc.

ex·or·bi·tant /ɪɡˈzɔrbətənt/ *adj.* (*formal*) (used about the cost of sth) much more expensive than it should be

ex·ot·ic /ɪɡˈzɑtɪk/ *adj.* unusual or interesting because it comes from a different country or culture: *exotic plants, animals, etc.*

☆ **ex·pand** /ɪkˈspænd/ *verb* [I,T] to become bigger or to make sth bigger: *Metals expand when they are heated.* ○ *We hope to expand our business this year.* ☞ The opposite is **contract**.

PHR V **expand on sth** to give more details of a story, plan, point of view, etc.

ex·panse /ɪkˈspæns/ *noun* [C] a large open area (of land, ocean, sky, etc.)

☆ **ex·pan·sion** /ɪkˈspænʃn/ *noun* [U] the action of expanding or the state of being expanded: *The rapid expansion of the university has caused a lot of problems.*

ex·pan·sive /ɪkˈspænsɪv/ *adj.* **1** broad in size or range: *the university's expansive campus* ○ *an expansive survey of American music* **2** (*formal*) (used about a person) willing to talk a lot; friendly

ex·pa·tri·ate /ˌɛksˈpeɪtriət/ *noun* [C] a person who lives outside his/her own country

☆ **ex·pect** /ɪkˈspɛkt/ *verb* [T] **1** to think or believe that sb/sth will come or that sth will happen: *She was expecting a letter from the bank this morning, but it didn't come.* ○ *We expect that more people will buy computers this year.* ○ *He expected it to be hot in Washington and it was.* ○ *"I'm really disappointed – she forgot my birthday." "Well, what did you expect?"* (= it's not surprising) ○ *She's expecting a baby in the spring* (= she's pregnant). ☞ Look at the note at **wait¹**. **2** **expect sth (from sb)**; **expect sb to do sth** to hope that you will get sth from sb or that he/she will do what you want: *He expects a high standard of work from everyone.* ○ *Factory workers are often expected to work at night.*

ex·pec·tan·cy /ɪkˈspɛktənsi/ *noun* [U] the state of expecting sth to happen; hope: *a look, feeling, etc. of expectancy* ☞ Look at **life expectancy**.

ex·pec·tant /ɪkˈspɛktənt/ *adj.* **1** expecting sth

ə	y	w	t̬	eɪ	aɪ	ɔɪ	aʊ	oʊ
about	yes	woman	butter	say	five	boy	now	go

good; hopeful: *an expectant audience* ○ *expectant faces* **2** pregnant; waiting for a baby: *Expectant mothers should drink plenty of milk.* —**ex·pec·tant·ly** *adv.*

☆ **ex·pec·ta·tion** /ˌɛkspɛkˈteɪʃn/ *noun* (*formal*) **1** [C,U] the belief that sth will happen: *There's no expectation of any increase in our profits yet.* **2** [C, usually pl.] hope for the future: *They had high expectations for their daughter, but she didn't really live up to them.*

ex·pe·di·tion /ˌɛkspəˈdɪʃn/ *noun* [C] a long trip for a special purpose: *a scientific expedition to Antarctica*

ex·pel /ɪkˈspɛl/ *verb* [T] (**ex·pel·ling; expelled**) **1** to force sb to leave a school, country, club, etc.: *The boy was expelled for smoking in the school restroom.* ○ *The government has expelled all foreign journalists from the country.* ☞ Look also at **suspend** (3). **2** to send sth out by force: *to expel air from the lungs* ☞ The noun is **expulsion**.

ex·pend /ɪkˈspɛnd/ *verb* [T] (*formal*) to spend or use money, time, care, etc. in doing sth: *I have expended a lot of time and energy on that project.*

ex·pend·a·ble /ɪkˈspɛndəbl/ *adj.* (*formal*) not considered important or worth saving: *In a war, human life is expendable.*

ex·pen·di·ture /ɪkˈspɛndətʃər/ *noun* [C,U] (*formal*) the act of spending or using money, etc.; an amount of money, etc. which is spent: *Government expenditure on education is very low in this state.* ○ *The President has cut military expenditure by 5%.* ○ *an expenditure of $2,000*

☆ **ex·pense** /ɪkˈspɛns/ *noun* **1** [C,U] the cost of sth in time or money: *Maintaining a second home is a great expense.* ○ *Expense wasn't important when they were deciding where to go on vacation.* ☞ Note the expressions: **at great expense** (= at a high cost) and **at no expense** (= at no cost). **2 expenses** [plural] money that is spent for a particular purpose: *You can deduct your business travel expenses from your income tax.*

IDM at sb's expense 1 with sb paying; at sb's cost: *My trip is at the company's expense.* **2** against sb, so that he/she looks silly: *They were always making jokes at Paul's expense.*

at the expense of sth harming or damaging sth: *He was a successful businessman, but it was at the expense of his family life.*

☆ **ex·pen·sive** /ɪkˈspɛnsɪv/ *adj.* costing a lot of money: *Houses are very expensive in this area.* ○ *It's too expensive.* ☞ The opposite is **inexpensive** or **cheap.** —**ex·pen·sive·ly** *adv.*

☆ **ex·pe·ri·ence¹** /ɪkˈspɪriəns/ *noun* **1** [U] the things that you have done; the knowledge or skill that you get from seeing or doing sth: *She has five years' teaching experience.* ○ *You need a lot of experience in this job.* ○ *I know from experience what will happen.* **2** [C] something

that has happened to you (often something unusual or exciting): *She wrote a book about her experiences in Africa.* ○ *It's an experience that shouldn't be missed.*

ex·pe·ri·ence² /ɪkˈspɪriəns/ *verb* [T] to have experience ¹(1) of sth; to feel: *It was the first time I had ever experienced failure.* ○ *to experience pleasure, pain, difficulty, etc.*

☆ **ex·pe·ri·enced** /ɪkˈspɪriənst/ *adj.* having the knowledge or skill that is necessary for sth: *He's not a very experienced driver.* ☞ The opposite is **inexperienced.**

☆ **ex·per·i·ment¹** /ɪkˈspɛrəmənt/ *noun* [C] a scientific test that is done in order to prove sth or to get new knowledge: *a chemistry experiment* ○ *Researchers often perform experiments on animals.* ○ *It's difficult to conduct experiments on how people learn languages.* ○ *I'm going to try riding my bike to work – it's just part of an experiment in ways to save energy.*

ex·per·i·ment² /ɪkˈspɛrəmənt/ *verb* [I] **experiment (on sth) /(with sth)** to do an experiment or to test: *Is it really necessary to experiment on animals?* ○ *teenagers who experiment with* (= try) *illegal drugs*

ex·per·i·men·tal /ɪkˌspɛrəˈmɛntl/ *adj.* connected with experiments or new ideas: *experimental treatments for AIDS* ○ *The government approved the new drug for use on an experimental basis.* —**ex·per·i·men·tal·ly** /-təli/ *adv.*

☆ **ex·pert¹** /ˈɛkspərt/ *noun* [C] **an expert (at/in/on sth)** a person who has special knowledge or skill: *He's an expert on the history of rock music.* ○ *She's a computer expert.* ○ *Let me try – I'm an expert at parking cars in small spaces.*

ex·pert² /ˈɛkspərt/ *adj.* **expert (at/in/on sth)** with special knowledge or skill: *He's an expert cook.* ○ *I think we should get expert advice on the problem.* —**ex·pert·ly** *adv.*

ex·per·tise /ˌɛkspərˈtiz/ *noun* [U] special knowledge or skill: *She has shown real expertise in dealing with difficult customers.*

ex·pi·ra·tion /ˌɛkspəˈreɪʃn/ *noun* [U] the end of a period when you can use sth: *The expiration date on this yogurt was November 20.*

ex·pire /ɪkˈspaɪər/ *verb* [I] (*formal*) (used about sth that only lasts for a certain period of time) to come to the end of the time when you can use it: *My passport expired. I'll have to get it renewed.*

☆ **ex·plain** /ɪkˈspleɪn/ *verb* [I,T] **1** to make sth clear or easy to understand: *A dictionary explains the meaning of words.* ○ *She explained how I should fill out the form.* ○ *I don't understand this. Can you explain it to me?* **2** to give a reason for sth: *I know I'm half an hour late, but please let me explain.* ○ *That explains why she was looking so miserable.* ○ *The manager explained to the customers why the goods were not available.*

☆ **ex·pla·na·tion** /ˌɛkspləˈneɪʃn/ *noun* **1** [U] making sth clear or giving a reason for sth:

That idea doesn't need much explanation. **2** [C] something that makes a situation clear or understandable: *He could not give a satisfactory explanation for his behavior.*

ex·plan·a·to·ry /ɪkˈsplænəˌtɔri/ *adj.* giving an explanation: *There are some explanatory notes at the back of the book.* ∘ *The instructions are self-explanatory* (= they don't need explaining).

ex·plic·it /ɪkˈsplɪsət/ *adj.* **1** clear, not making anything difficult to understand: *I gave you explicit instructions not to touch anything.* ∘ *She was very explicit about her feelings on the subject.* **2** not hiding anything: *a sexually explicit movie* —**ex·plic·it·ly** *adv.*: *The law explicitly states which kinds of drugs are illegal.*

☆ **ex·plode** /ɪkˈsploʊd/ *verb* [I,T] to burst with a loud noise: *The bomb exploded without warning.* ∘ *The bomb was taken away and the police exploded it at a safe distance from the houses.* ∘ *(figurative) My dad exploded* (= became very angry) *when I told him how much the car would cost to repair.* ☞ The noun is **explosion**.

☆ **ex·ploit¹** /ɪkˈsplɔɪt/ *verb* [T] **1** to use sth or to treat sb unfairly or selfishly: *Developing countries are often exploited by the richer nations.* **2** to develop sth or make the best use of sth: *Solar energy is a source of power that needs to be exploited more fully.*

ex·ploit² /ˈɛksplɔɪt/ *noun* [C] a brave or adventurous action

ex·ploi·ta·tion /ˌɛksplɔɪˈteɪʃn/ *noun* [U] exploiting or being exploited: *They're only paying $3 an hour? That's exploitation!*

ex·plo·ra·tion /ˌɛkspləˈreɪʃn/ *noun* [C,U] the act of exploring: *space exploration*

ex·plor·a·to·ry /ɪkˈsplɔrəˌtɔri/ *adj.* done in order to find sth out: *The doctors are doing some exploratory tests to try and find out what's wrong.*

☆ **ex·plore** /ɪkˈsplɔr/ *verb* [I,T] to travel around a place, etc. in order to learn about it: *They went on an expedition to explore the Amazon River.* ∘ *scientists exploring near the base of the volcano* ∘ *(figurative) We need to explore* (= look carefully at) *all the possibilities before we decide.*

ex·plor·er /ɪkˈsplɔrər/ *noun* [C] a person who travels around a place in order to find out about it

☆ **ex·plo·sion** /ɪkˈsploʊʒn/ *noun* [C] the sudden and violent bursting and loud noise that happen when sth like a bomb explodes: *The explosion may have been caused by a gas leak.* ∘ *(figurative) the population explosion* (= the sudden increase in the number of people in a country or in the world)

ex·plo·sive¹ /ɪkˈsploʊsɪv/ *adj.* **1** capable of exploding and therefore dangerous: *Hydrogen is extremely explosive.* **2** causing strong feelings or having dangerous effects: *The situation is* explosive. *We need to do everything we can to calm people down.*

ex·plo·sive² /ɪkˈsploʊsɪv/ *noun* [C] a substance that can explode: *Dynamite is a powerful explosive.*

☆ **ex·port¹** /ɪkˈspɔrt; ˈɛkspɔrt/ *verb* [I,T] to send goods, etc. to another country, usually for sale: *India exports tea and cotton.* ☞ The opposite is **import**.

☆ **ex·port²** /ˈɛkspɔrt/ *noun* **1** [U] sending goods to another country for sale: *Most of our products are manufactured for export.* ∘ *the export trade* **2** [C, usually pl.] something that is sent to another country for sale: *What are the main exports of Brazil?* ☞ The opposite is **import**.

ex·port·er /ɪkˈspɔrtər; ˈɛkspɔrtər/ *noun* [C] a person, company or country that exports goods: *Japan is the largest exporter of electronic products.* ☞ The opposite is **importer**.

☆ **ex·pose** /ɪkˈspoʊz/ *verb* [T] **1** to make it possible to see sth that is usually hidden: *He liked to wear his shirt open to expose his chest.* ∘ *The rocks are exposed at low tide.* ∘ *He was arrested for exposing himself* (= showing his sexual organs) *in the park.* **2** to put sb/sth or yourself in a situation that could be difficult or dangerous: *Thousands of people were exposed to radiation when the nuclear reactor exploded.* **3** to make the truth about a bad person or situation known to the public: *This is an injustice which needs to be exposed.* ∘ *The letter has been exposed as a forgery.* **4** (in photography) to allow light to reach the film in a camera

ex·posed /ɪkˈspoʊzd/ *adj.* not covered or protected: *The cord had been damaged, leaving the wires exposed.* ∘ *High winds and blowing snow are likely in exposed areas tonight.*

ex·po·si·tion /ˌɛkspəˈzɪʃn/ *noun* [C] an occasion when new products are shown to the public

ex·po·sure /ɪkˈspoʊʒər/ *noun* **1** [U] **exposure to sth** seeing or being in contact with sth, and possibly being affected by it: *Does exposure to violence on TV make children more aggressive?* **2** [U] a harmful condition when a person becomes very cold because he/she has been outside in very bad weather: *The mountain climbers all died of exposure.* **3** [C,U] the act of making sth public; the thing that is made public: *The congressman resigned because of the exposures about his private life.* **4** [U] attention from newspapers, television, etc., publicity: *The President's visit has been given a lot of exposure in the media.* **5** [C] the amount of film that is exposed (4) when you take one photograph: *How many exposures are there on this film?* (= how many photographs can I take?)

☆ **ex·press¹** /ɪkˈsprɛs/ *verb* [T] **1** to show sth such as a feeling or an opinion by words or actions: *I found it very hard to express what I felt about her.* **2 express yourself** to speak or

write: *I don't think she expresses herself very well in that article.*

ex·press² /ɪkˈsprɛs/ *adj.* (only *before* a noun) **1** going or sent quickly: *express delivery* ○ *an express bus* **2** (used about a wish, command, etc.) clearly and openly stated: *It was her express wish that they have the picture after her death.*

ex·press³ /ɪkˈsprɛs/ *adv.* by a special service that does sth faster than usual: *We'd better send the package express if we want it to get there on time.*

☆ **ex·pres·sion** /ɪkˈsprɛʃn/ *noun* **1** [C] a number of words that belong together: *You don't quite have the right expression here.* ○ *a slang expression* ○ *"Ballpark figure" is often a difficult expression for foreign students to understand.* **2** [C] the look on a person's face that shows what he/she is thinking or feeling: *He had a puzzled expression on his face.* **3** [C,U] putting feelings or thoughts into words or actions; an example of doing this: *Freedom of expression* (= freedom to say what you think) *is a basic human right.* ○ *These flowers are an expression of our gratitude.* ○ *She read the poem with a great deal of expression* (= showing feeling for the meaning of it).

ex·pres·sive /ɪkˈsprɛsɪv/ *adj.* showing feelings or thoughts: *That is a very expressive piece of music.* —**ex·pres·sive·ly** *adv.*

ex·press·ly /ɪkˈsprɛsli/ *adv.* (*formal*) **1** clearly; definitely: *The law expressly prohibits the sale of alcohol to people under 21.* **2** for a special purpose; specially: *These scissors are expressly designed for left-handed people.* ☞ A less formal word is **specifically**.

ex·press·way /ɪkˈsprɛsweɪ/ *noun* [C] = FREE-WAY

ex·pul·sion /ɪkˈspʌlʃn/ *noun* [C,U] making sb leave a place or an institution (when he/she does not want to go): *There have been three expulsions from school this year.* ☞ The verb is **expel**.

ex·qui·site /ɪkˈskwɪzət; ˈɛkskwəzət/ *adj.* very beautiful and pleasing: *an exquisite diamond ring* ○ *The dancers' costumes were absolutely exquisite.*

☆ **ex·tend** /ɪkˈstɛnd/ *verb* **1** [T] to make sth longer or larger (in space or time): *They are planning to extend the expressway as far south as New Orleans.* ○ *Could you extend your visit for a few days?* **2** [I] (usually used about space, land, time, etc.) to continue or stretch: *How far does your property extend?* ○ *This project will extend well into next year.* **3** [T] to stretch out a part of the body: *She extended her hand to her new colleague.* **4** [T] (*formal*) to offer or give sth (such as an invitation or a welcome): *The whole town extended a warm welcome to the President.*

ex·tend·ed ˈfamily *noun* [C] (*pl.* **extended families**) a family group that includes par-

ents, children, grandparents, aunts, uncles, etc., who often live together or very near each other and have a close relationship

ex·ten·sion /ɪkˈstɛnʃn/ *noun* [C] **1** a part which is added to a building, road, etc.: *A four-mile extension to Route 7 is planned.* **2** an extra period of time that is given to you, especially by an official: *I applied for an extension of my work permit.* ○ *I asked the professor for an extension on my English paper.* **3** a telephone that is connected to a central phone in a house or to a central point (**switchboard**) in a large office building: *What's your extension number?* ○ *My phone number is 555-1800, extension 342.*

☆ **ex·ten·sive** /ɪkˈstɛnsɪv/ *adj.* large in area or amount: *an extensive search for the missing boy* ○ *Most of the buildings suffered extensive damage in the earthquake.* —**ex·ten·sive·ly** *adv.*

☆ **ex·tent** /ɪkˈstɛnt/ *noun* [U] the area or size of sth: *I was amazed at the extent of his knowledge.* ○ *The full extent of the damage is not yet known.*

IDM **to a certain/to some extent** (used to show that sth is only partly true): *I agree with you to a certain extent, but there are still a lot of points I disagree on.*

to a great/large extent (used to show that sth is mostly true): *The increase in crime has been caused to a large extent by gangs and drugs.*

to what extent how much: *I'm not sure to what extent I believe her.*

ex·te·ri·or¹ /ɪkˈstɪriər/ *adj.* (only *before* a noun) on the outside: *the exterior walls of a house* ☞ The opposite is **interior**.

ex·te·ri·or² /ɪkˈstɪriər/ *noun* [C, usually sing.] the appearance of sb/sth; the outside of sth: *The exterior of the house is fine, but inside it isn't in very good condition.* ☞ The opposite is **interior**.

ex·ter·mi·nate /ɪkˈstɜrməneɪt/ *verb* [T] to kill a large group of people, animals, insects, etc. —**ex·ter·mi·na·tion** /ɪkˌstɜrməˈneɪʃn/ *noun* [U]

☆ **ex·ter·nal** /ɪkˈstɜrnl/ *adj.* **1** connected with the outside of sth: *The cream is for external use only* (= to be used on the skin). **2** coming from another place: *Several external factors were blamed for the company's failure.* ☞ The opposite is **internal**.

ex·tinct /ɪkˈstɪŋkt/ *adj.* **1** (used about a type of animal, plant, etc.) no longer existing: *Tigers are nearly extinct in the wild.* **2** (used about a volcano) no longer active —**ex·tinc·tion** /ɪkˈstɪŋkʃn/ *noun* [U]: *The panda is in danger of extinction.*

ex·tin·guish /ɪkˈstɪŋgwɪʃ/ *verb* [T] (*formal*) to cause sth to stop burning: *The fire was extinguished very quickly.* ○ *The flight attendant asked everyone to extinguish their cigarettes.* ☞ A less formal expression is **put out**.

i	ɪ	ɛ	æ	ɑ	ɔ	ʌ	ʊ	u
see	sit	ten	cat	hot	saw	cup	put	too

ex·tin·guish·er /ɪkˈstɪŋgwɪʃər/ *noun* [C] = FIRE EXTINGUISHER

ex·tort /ɪkˈstɔrt/ *verb* [T] **extort sth (from sb)** to get sth, especially money, by using threats, violence, etc.

ex·tor·tion /ɪkˈstɔrʃn/ *noun* [U] getting sth, especially money, by using threats, violence, etc.

☆ **ex·tra¹** /ˈɛkstrə/ *adj., adv.* more than is usual: *I'll need some extra money for the weekend.* ∘ *"What size is this sweatshirt?" "Extra large."* ∘ *The bed costs $495, and delivery is extra.* ∘ *They charge $1 extra if you pay by credit card.* ∘ *I tried to be extra nice to him yesterday because it was his birthday.*

☆ **ex·tra²** /ˈɛkstrə/ *noun* [C] **1** something that is or costs extra: *All these fancy little extras added a lot to the price of the car.* **2** a person in a movie, etc. who has a small unimportant part, for example in a crowd

ex·tract¹ /ɪkˈstrækt/ *verb* [T] to take or get sth out (with force or difficulty): *to extract gold and other precious metals from rock* ∘ *I wasn't able to extract an apology from her.*

ex·tract² /ˈɛkstrækt/ *noun* **1** [C] a part of a book, piece of music, etc. An extract has often been specially chosen to show sth: *We're reading extracts from modern American novels this semester.* **2** [U] a substance (usually a liquid) that is taken from a plant or food and that has a strong smell or taste of that plant or food: *Add 1 teaspoon of vanilla extract.*

ex·trac·tion /ɪkˈstrækʃn/ *noun* **1** [U] the act of taking or getting sth out **2** [C] the removal of a tooth **3** [U] (*formal*) family origin: *He's an American of Italian extraction.*

ex·tra·cur·ric·u·lar /ˌɛkstrəkəˈrɪkyələr/ *adj.* not part of the normal program of studies (**curriculum**) in a school or college: *The school offers many extracurricular activities such as sports, music, drama, etc.*

ex·tra·dite /ˈɛkstrədaɪt/ *verb* [T] to send a person who may be guilty of a crime from the country or state in which he/she is living to the country or state which wants to put him/her on trial for the crime: *The suspected terrorists were captured in Mexico and extradited to the United States.* —**ex·tra·di·tion** /ˌɛkstrəˈdɪʃn/ *noun* [C,U]

☆ **ex·traor·di·nar·y** /ɪkˈstrɔrdəˌnɛri/ *adj.* **1** unusually good, large, etc.: *She had an extraordinary ability to learn new languages.* ∘ *They spent an extraordinary amount of time on the project.* **2** very strange (and not what you would expect in a particular situation): *The law allows special actions to be taken under extraordinary circumstances.* —**ex·traor·di·nar·i·ly** /ɪkˈstrɔrdəˌnɛrəli/ *adv.*: *He was an extraordinarily talented musician.*

ex·trav·a·gant /ɪkˈstrævəgənt/ *adj.* **1** spending or costing too much money: *He stole from the company in order to finance his extrava-*

gant lifestyle. ∘ *an extravagant present* **2** (used about ideas, behavior, etc.) not controlled, not realistic: *The advertisements made extravagant claims about the product.* —**ex·trav·a·gance** /-gəns/ *noun* [C,U] —**ex·trav·a·gant·ly** *adv.*

☆ **ex·treme¹** /ɪkˈstrim/ *adj.* **1** (only *before* a noun) as far away as possible; at the very beginning or at the very end: *Barrow is in the extreme north of Alaska.* **2** (only *before* a noun) the greatest or strongest possible: *Use extreme caution when driving on icy roads.* **3** (used about a person and his/her political opinions) not usual or moderate: *She holds extreme views on immigration.* ∘ *the extreme left/right* ☞ This word is used in a disapproving way in this sense.

ex·treme² /ɪkˈstrim/ *noun* [C] something that is completely different from or opposite to sth else: *Alex used to be very shy, but now he's gone to the opposite extreme.*

☆ **ex·treme·ly** /ɪkˈstrimli/ *adv.* very: *It was an extremely difficult decision.*

ex·trem·ist /ɪkˈstrimɪst/ *noun* [C] a person who has extreme¹ (3) political opinions —**ex·trem·ism** *noun* [U]

ex·trem·i·ty /ɪkˈstrɛməṭi/ *noun* [C] (*pl.* **ex·trem·i·ties**) **1** the furthest point of sth **2** **extremities** [plural] the hands and feet: *Her heart was not pumping enough blood to her extremities.*

ex·tri·cate /ˈɛkstrəkeɪt/ *verb* [T] to free sb/sth /yourself from a difficult situation or position: *I finally managed to extricate myself from the meeting by saying that I had to pick up my kids from school.*

ex·tro·vert /ˈɛkstrəvərt/ *noun* [C] a person who is enthusiastic and cheerful and who prefers being with other people to being alone ☞ The opposite is **introvert**. —**ex·tro·vert·ed** /-vərṭəd/ *adj.*

ex·u·ber·ant /ɪgˈzubərənt/ *adj.* (used about a person and his/her behavior) full of energy and excitement —**ex·u·ber·ance** /-rəns/ *noun* [U]

☆ **eye¹** /aɪ/ *noun* [C] **1** one of the two organs of the body that we use to see with: *She opened/closed her eyes.* ∘ *He is blind in one eye.* ∘ *She has blue eyes.* ∘ *an eye operation*

☞ If somebody hits you in the eye you might get a **black eye**. When you close both eyes very quickly and open them again, you **blink**. To close one eye quickly and open it again is to **wink**.

2 the power of seeing: *He has sharp eyes* (= he can see very well). ∘ *She has an eye for detail* (= she notices small details). **3** the part at one end of a needle that the thread passes through **4** the center of a large tropical storm (**a hurricane**), where the winds are calm

IDM be up to your ears/eyes/neck in sth ⇨ UP¹

cast an eye/your eye(s) over sb/sth ⇨ CAST²

catch sb's attention/eye ⇨ ATTENTION

in the eyes of sb/in sb's eyes in the opinion of sb: *She was still a child in her mother's eyes.*

keep a close eye/watch on sb/sth; keep an eye on sb/sth to make sure that sb/sth is safe; to watch sb/sth carefully: *Could you please keep an eye on the house while we are away?*

keep an eye open/out (for sb/sth); keep your eyes open (for sb/sth) to watch or look out for sb/sth: *I lost my ring – could you keep an eye out for it?*

the naked eye ⇨ NAKED

not bat an eye ⇨ BAT²

see eye to eye with sb to agree with sb; to have the same opinion as sb: *We're good friends, but we don't always see eye to eye on political matters.*

set eyes on sb/sth to see sb/sth: *He loved the house the moment he set eyes on it.*

turn a blind eye ⇨ BLIND¹

eye² /aɪ/ *verb* [T] (*pres. part.* **eye·ing** or **ey·ing**; *p.t., p.p.* **eyed**) to look at sb/sth closely: *She eyed him with suspicion.*

eye·ball /ˈaɪbɔl/ *noun* [C] the whole of the eye (including the part which is hidden inside the head)

eye·brow /ˈaɪbraʊ/ (*also* **brow**) *noun* [C] the line of hair that is above your eye: *to pluck your eyebrows* ☛ picture on page A24.

IDM raise your eyebrows ⇨ RAISE¹

eye-ˌcatching *adj.* interesting or attractive to look at: *an eye-catching design*

eye·glass·es /ˈaɪɡlæsəz/ *noun* [plural] = GLASSES

eye·lash /ˈaɪlæʃ/ (*also* **lash**) *noun* [C] one of the hairs that grow on the edges of your eyelids

eye·lid /ˈaɪlɪd/ (*also* **lid**) *noun* [C] the piece of skin that you can move to close your eye

eye·lin·er /ˈaɪlaɪnər/ *noun* [U] makeup that you use to draw a line around your eyes

eye ˌopener *noun* [C] something that makes you realize the truth about sth: *That TV program about the greenhouse effect was a real eye opener.*

eye ˌshadow *noun* [U] colored powder that you use to decorate your eyelids

eye·sight /ˈaɪsaɪt/ *noun* [U] the ability to see: *good/poor eyesight*

eye·sore /ˈaɪsɔr/ *noun* [C] something that is ugly and unpleasant to look at: *All this garbage in the streets is a real eyesore.*

eye·wit·ness /ˌaɪˈwɪtnəs; ˈaɪwɪtnəs/ *noun* [C] = WITNESS¹(1)

Ff

F, f /ɛf/ *noun* [C] (*pl.* **F's; f's**) **1** the sixth letter of the English alphabet: *"Father" begins with (an) "F."* **2** the lowest grade that is given for a test or a piece of work. An "F" means that the person has failed: *I got an "F" on my last history test.*

F *abbr.* = FAHRENHEIT: *98.6° F*

fa·ble /ˈfeɪbl/ *noun* [C] a short story that teaches a lesson (**a moral**) and that often has animals as speaking characters: *Aesop's fables*

fab·ric /ˈfæbrɪk/ *noun* **1** [C,U] (a type of) cloth: *cotton fabrics* **2** [sing.] the basic structure of sth: *The Industrial Revolution changed the fabric of society.*

fab·u·lous /ˈfæbyələs/ *adj.* **1** (*informal*) very good; excellent **2** (used about beauty, wealth, etc.) very great

fa·çade (*also* **facade**) /fəˈsad/ *noun* [C] **1** the front wall of a large building that you see from the outside **2** something that gives you the wrong impression about a situation: *His good mood was just a façade.*

☆ **face¹** /feɪs/ *noun* [C] **1** the front part of your head and the expression on it: *Go and wash your face.* ○ *She has a very pretty face.* ○ *He came in with a smile on his face.* ○ *the children's happy faces* **2** the front or one side of sth: *the north face of the mountain* ○ *He put the cards face up/down on the table.* ○ *a clock face*

IDM face to face (with sb/sth) close to and looking at sb/sth: *She turned the corner and came face to face with the principal.*

keep a straight face ⇨ STRAIGHT¹

lose/save face to lose/keep yourself from losing the respect of other people: *He did not want to lose face by making a mistake in front of his boss.*

make faces/a face (at sb) to make an expression that shows that you dislike sb/sth: *When she saw what was for dinner, she made a face.*

make faces to make rude expressions with your face: *The children made faces behind the teacher's back.*

to sb's face openly and directly: *I wanted to*

ər	ɪr	ɛr	ɑr	ɔr	ʊr	ʒ	h	ŋ
bird	near	hair	car	north	tour	vision	hat	sing

say that I was sorry to her face, not on the phone. ☞ The opposite is **behind sb's back**.

☆ **face²** /feɪs/ verb [T] **1** to have or turn the face or front toward sb/sth: *The porch faces south.* ○ *Can you all face the front, please?* **2** to have to deal with sth unpleasant; to deal with sb in a difficult situation: *They faced a lot of problems when they moved to a new house.* ○ *I can't face another argument.* ○ *Face it – you're never going to be a professional athlete.* ○ *He couldn't face going to work yesterday – he felt too sick.* ○ *I didn't know how to face my mother after I'd wrecked her car.* **3** to need attention from sb: *There are several problems facing the country.* **4** (often passive) to force somebody to deal with a situation, etc.: *We are faced with a difficult decision.*

IDM **let's face it** (informal) we must accept it as true: *Let's face it – not everybody is going to pass the test.*

PHRV **face up to sth** to accept a difficult or unpleasant situation and do sth about it: *She faced up to the fact that she had no money and went out and got a job.*

-faced /feɪst/ (in compounds) with a particular type of face: *red-faced*

face·less /ˈfeɪsləs/ adj. without individual character: *faceless government employees*

ˈface·lift (also **ˈface-lift**) noun [C] a medical operation that makes your face look younger: (figurative) *The monument is scheduled for a $5 million facelift next year.*

ˈface-ˌsaving adj. done to stop yourself from looking silly or losing other people's respect: *to make a face-saving excuse*

fac·et /ˈfæsət/ noun [C] **1** one part of sth: *There are many facets to this argument* (= points that must be considered). **2** one side of a precious stone

fa·ce·tious /fəˈsiʃəs/ adj. trying to be amusing at an unsuitable time or about an unsuitable subject: *He kept making facetious remarks during the lecture.* —**fa·ce·tious·ly** adv.

ˌface ˈvalue noun [C,U] the cost or value that is shown on stamps, coins, etc.

IDM **take sb/sth at face value** to accept sb/sth as it, he, etc. appears to be: *Don't take his story at face value.*

fa·cial /ˈfeɪʃl/ adj. of or for the face: *a facial expression*

fa·cil·i·tate /fəˈsɪləteɪt/ verb [T] (formal) to make sth possible or easier

☆ **fa·cil·i·ty** /fəˈsɪləti/ noun (pl. **fa·cil·i·ties**) **1** **facilities** [plural] a service, piece of equipment, etc. that makes it possible to do sth: *Our town has excellent sports facilities (a big stadium, swimming pool, etc.).* **2** [C] a building where a particular type of service is provided: *a health care facility* ○ *a storage facility* **3** [C] an extra feature that a machine, etc. may have: *This*

word processor has a facility for checking spelling.

fac·sim·i·le /fækˈsɪməli/ noun [C,U] an exact copy of a picture, piece of writing, etc. ☞ Look at **fax**.

☆ **fact** /fækt/ noun **1** [C] something that you know has happened or is true: *It is a scientific fact that light travels faster than sound.* ○ *We need to know all the facts before we can decide.* ○ *I know for a fact that Peter wasn't sick yesterday.* ○ *The fact that I am older than you makes no difference at all.* ○ *You need to face the facts and accept that he has gone.* **2** [U] true things; reality: *The movie is based on fact.* ☞ The opposite is **fiction**.

IDM **as a matter of fact** ➪ MATTER¹

the fact (of the matter) is (that)… the truth is that…: *I would love a car, but the fact is that I just can't afford one.*

facts and figures (informal) detailed information: *Here are some facts and figures on the state of Oregon:…*

a fact of life a true situation that you cannot ignore, even if it is unpleasant: *It's just a fact of life that some children come from poor families.*

the facts of life the details of sexual behavior and how babies are born

hard facts ➪ HARD¹

in fact 1 (used for emphasizing that sth is true) really; actually: *I thought the lecture would be boring, but in fact it was pretty interesting.* **2** (used for introducing more detailed information): *It was cold. In fact, it was freezing.*

☆ **fac·tor** /ˈfæktər/ noun [C] **1** one of the things that influences a decision, situation, etc.: *His unhappiness at home was a major factor in his decision to move away.* **2** (in mathematics) a whole number by which a larger number can be divided: *2, 3, 4 and 6 are factors of 12.*

☆ **fac·to·ry** /ˈfæktəri; -tri/ (pl. **fac·to·ries**) noun [C] a large building or group of buildings where goods are manufactured or put together in large quantities (by machine): *a car factory* ○ *factory workers*

fac·tu·al /ˈfæktʃuəl/ adj. based on or containing facts: *a factual account of the events* ☞ Look at **fictional**.

☆ **fac·ul·ty** /ˈfæklti/ (pl. **fac·ul·ties**) noun [C] **1** [usually sing.] the people who teach at a school, college, or university: *This dining room is only for members of the faculty, staff and administration.* ○ *a faculty meeting* **2** one of the natural abilities of a person's body or mind: *At 85, he still had all his mental faculties.*

fad /fæd/ noun [C] (informal) a fashion, interest, etc. that will probably not last long

☆ **fade** /feɪd/ verb **1** [I] to become lighter in color or less strong or fresh: *Jeans fade when you wash them.* ○ *The sun was setting and the light*

tʃ	dʒ	v	θ	ð	s	z	ʃ
chin	June	van	thin	then	so	zoo	she

was fading fast. **2** [T] to make sth fade: *Look how the sun has faded these curtains.* **3** [I] **fade (away)** to disappear slowly (from sight, hearing, memory, etc.): *The cheering of the crowd faded away.* ○ *The smile faded from his face.*

fag /fæg/ *noun* (*slang*) a man who is sexually attracted to other men

☛ This word is extremely offensive. Look at **gay**.

☆ **Fahr·en·heit** /'færənhaɪt/ *noun* [U] (*abbr.* **F**) the name of a scale which measures temperatures: *Water freezes at 32 degrees Fahrenheit (32°F).*

☛ In everyday situations, temperatures are almost always given in Fahrenheit. Look at **Celsius.**

F ☆ **fail¹** /feɪl/ *verb* **1** [I,T] to be unsuccessful in sth: *She failed her driving test.* ○ *I feel that I've failed – I'm 25 and I still don't have a steady job.* ☛ Look at **pass** and **succeed**. **2** [T] (used about a teacher, etc.) to decide that sb is unsuccessful in a test, on a piece of work, etc.: *The teachers failed 10 percent of the students who took the exam.* ☛ The opposite is **pass**. **3** [I] **fail to do sth** to not do sth: *Jimmy failed to arrive on time.* ○ *She never fails to do her homework.* **4** [I,T] to not be enough or not do what people are expecting or wanting: *If the crops fail, people will starve.* ○ *Words fail me!* (= I don't know how to express my feelings) ○ *I think the government has failed us.* **5** [I] (used about health, eyesight, etc.) to become weak: *His health is failing.* **6** [I] to stop working: *My brakes failed on the hill, but I managed to stop the car.*

fail² /feɪl/ *noun* [U]
without fail always, even if there are difficulties: *The schoolbus always comes at 8 o'clock without fail.*

fail·ing¹ /'feɪlɪŋ/ *noun* [C] a weakness or fault: *She's not very patient – that's her only failing.*

fail·ing² /'feɪlɪŋ/ *adj.* showing that sb/sth has failed; no longer functioning correctly: *Five students received failing grades on the test.*

fail·ing³ /'feɪlɪŋ/ *prep.* (*formal*) if sth is not possible: *We hope to solve the problem today, or, failing that, to develop a plan to solve it soon.*

☆ **fail·ure** /'feɪlyər/ *noun* **1** [U] lack of success: *All my efforts ended in failure.* **2** [C] a person or thing that is unsuccessful: *I was a failure as a mother.* **3** [C,U] **failure to do sth** not doing sth that people expect you to do: *I was very disappointed at his failure to come to the meeting.* **4** [C,U] an example of sth not working or functioning properly: *She died of heart failure.* ○ *a power failure*

☆ **faint¹** /feɪnt/ *adj.* **1** (used about things that you can see, hear, feel, etc.) not strong or clear: *a faint light in the distance* ○ *There is still a faint hope that they will find more people*

alive. **2** (used about people) on the point of losing consciousness; very weak: *I feel faint – I'd better sit down.* **3** (used about actions, etc.) done without much effort: *He made a faint protest.*

IDM **not have the faintest idea** not to know at all: *I don't have the faintest idea where they went.*

faint² /feɪnt/ *verb* [I] to lose consciousness: *She fainted from shock and loss of blood.*

☆ **fair¹** /fɛr/ *adj.* **1** **fair (to sb)** treating each person or side equally, according to the law or the rules, etc.: *That's not fair – he made the same number of mistakes as I did and he got a better grade.* ○ *It wasn't fair to her to ask her to stay so late.* ○ *a fair trial* **2** right, according to what people generally accept as right: *a fair price* ○ *I think it's fair to say that the number of homeless people is increasing.* ☛ The opposite for senses **1** and **2** is **unfair**. **3** not better, bigger, etc. than average: *They have a fair chance of success.* ○ *It is a fair-sized house.* ○ *How would you describe the service here: excellent, good, fair or poor?* **4** (used about the skin or hair) light in color: *He has a fair complexion and gets sunburned easily.* **5** (used about the weather) good, without rain

IDM **fair game** a person or thing that is easy to criticize or that people think should be criticized: *The silly behavior of celebrities makes them fair game for comedians.*

fair play equal treatment of both/all sides according to the rules: *Special privileges for some people violate our sense of fair play.*

have (more than) your (fair) share of sth ⇨ SHARE¹ —**fair·ness** *noun* [U]

☆ **fair²** /fɛr/ *adv.* in a fair¹(1) way: *You have to play fair in all team games.*

IDM **fair and square** in an honest and fair¹(1) way: *Quit complaining – she won the game fair and square.*

fair enough (used for showing that you think that what sb has said is right, even if you do not like it): *"I washed the dishes every night last week – I'm not doing them again." "Okay, fair enough. I'll do them tonight."*

fair³ /fɛr/ *noun* [C] **1** a public event which is organized by people who live in a particular area. At a fair you can ride on machines, look at farm animals and products that people have made, or try and win prizes at games: *My pumpkin pie won first prize at the county fair.* **2** a large exhibition of commercial or industrial goods: *a trade fair*

fair·ground /'fɛrgraʊnd/ *noun* [C] a large outdoor area where fairs³(1) are held

☆ **fair·ly** /'fɛrli/ *adv.* **1** in a fair¹(1) way: *I felt that the teacher didn't treat us fairly.* ☛ The opposite is **unfairly**. **2** more than a little, but not extremely: *fairly tall* ○ *We need to leave fairly soon.* ☛ Look at the note at **rather**.

i	ɪ	ɛ	æ	ɑ	ɔ	ʌ	ʊ	u
see	sit	ten	cat	hot	saw	cup	put	too

fair·y /ˈfɛri/ *noun* [C] (*pl.* **fair·ies**) (in stories) a small creature with magical powers

fairy / wing

ˈ**fairy tale** *noun* [C] a story that is about fairies, magic, etc.: *Grimm's fairy tales*

☆**faith** /feɪθ/ *noun* **1** [U] **faith (in sb/sth)** strong belief (in sb/sth); trust: *I have great faith in your ability to do the job* (= I'm sure that you can do it). ○ *I have lost faith in him.* **2** [U] strong religious belief **3** [C] a religion: *the Christian faith*
IDM **in good faith** with honest reasons for doing sth: *I bought the car in good faith. I didn't know it was stolen.*

☆**faith·ful** /ˈfeɪθfl/ *adj.* **1** not changing; loyal: *a faithful friend* ○ *He was always faithful to his wife* (= he didn't have sex with anyone else). ☞ The opposite is **unfaithful**. **2** true to the facts; accurate: *a faithful description* —**faith·ful·ly** *adv.* —**faith·ful·ness** *noun* [U]

fake¹ /feɪk/ *noun* [C] **1** a work of art, etc. that seems to be real or genuine but is not: *That's not a real diamond necklace. It's just a fake!* **2** a person who pretends to be sb/sth else in order to deceive people

fake² /feɪk/ *adj.* not real or genuine: *a fake passport*

fake³ /feɪk/ *verb* [T] **1** to copy sth in order to deceive people: *He faked his father's signature.* **2** to pretend that you are feeling sth that you are not: *I faked surprise when he told me the news.*

fal·con /ˈfælkən; ˈfɔl-/ *noun* [C] a bird that kills and eats other animals. Falcons can be trained to hunt.

☆**fall¹** /fɔl/ *verb* [I] (*p.t.* **fell** /fɛl/; *p.p.* **fall·en** /ˈfɔlən/) **1** to drop down toward the ground: *He fell off the ladder onto the grass.* ○ *Don't walk along that ledge – you might fall.* ○ *October came and the leaves started to fall.* ○ *The rain was falling steadily.* **2** **fall (down/over)** to suddenly stop standing: *She slipped on the ice and fell.* ○ *The little boy fell down and hurt his knee.* ○ *The tree fell over onto my car.* **3** (*formal*) to come or happen: *My birthday falls on a Sunday this year.* ○ *In the word "interesting," the stress falls on the first syllable.* **4** to hang down: *Her hair fell down over her shoulders.* **5** to become lower or less: *The temperature is falling.* ○ *The price of coffee has fallen again.* **6** to be killed (in battle) **7** to be defeated: *The senator fell from power because of the scandal.* **8** to change into a different state; to become: *He fell asleep on the sofa.* ○ *I need to get some new shoes – these ones are falling to pieces.* **9** to belong to a particular group, type, etc.: *Animals fall into two groups: those with backbones and those without.*
IDM **fall flat** ➪ FLAT²

fall in love ➪ LOVE¹
fall short (of sth) ➪ SHORT²
fall/slip through the cracks ➪ CRACK¹
PHR V **fall apart** to break (into pieces): *My car is falling apart.*
fall back on sb/sth to use sb/sth when you are in difficulty: *If my new business isn't a success, we can always fall back on my wife's income.*
fall for sb (*informal*) to fall in love with sb
fall for sth (*informal*) to be tricked into believing sth that is not true: *He makes excuses and she falls for them every time.*
fall out (with sb) to argue or fight (with sb)
fall through to fail or not happen: *Our trip to Japan fell through.*

☆**fall²** /fɔl/ *noun* **1** [C] an act of falling¹(1,2): *She had a bad fall while she was skiing.* **2** [C] **a fall (of sth)** the amount of sth that has fallen or the distance that sth has fallen: *a heavy fall of snow* **3** [C] a decrease (in value, quantity, etc.): *There has been a sharp fall in the price of oil.* ☞ The opposite is **rise**. **4** [sing.] **the fall of sth** a (political) defeat: *the fall of the Roman Empire* **5** [C, usually sing.] (also *formal* **autumn**) the season of the year that comes between summer and winter: *I visited Europe in the fall of 1993.* ○ *fall weather* **6** [C, usually pl.] a waterfall: *Niagara Falls*

fal·la·cy /ˈfæləsi/ *noun* (*pl.* **fal·la·cies**) [C,U] (*formal*) a false or mistaken belief or argument: *It's a fallacy to believe that money brings happiness.*

fall·en *p.p.* of FALL¹

fall·out /ˈfɔlaʊt/ *noun* [U] dangerous waste matter that is carried in the air after a nuclear explosion: (*figurative*) *the political fallout* (= bad effects) *from the scandal*

☆**false** /fɔls/ *adj.* **1** not true; incorrect: *I think the information you were given is false.* **2** not real; artificial: *false hair, teeth, eyelashes, etc.* **3** based on wrong information or belief: *I got a completely false impression of him from our first meeting.* **4** made or done incorrectly in order to deceive people: *This suitcase has a false bottom.* ○ *a false name* **5** not faithful; not loyal: *a false friend*
IDM **a false alarm** a warning about a danger that does not happen
under false pretenses pretending to be or to have sth in order to deceive people: *The journalist got the information under false pretenses – she claimed to be the senator's secretary.*

fal·si·fy /ˈfɔlsəfaɪ/ *verb* [T] (*pres. part.* **fal·si·fy·ing**; *3rd pers. sing. pres.* **fal·si·fies**; *p.t., p.p.* **fal·si·fied**) (*formal*) to change a document, information, etc. in order to deceive other people

fal·ter /ˈfɔltər/ *verb* [I] **1** to become weak or move in a weak, unsteady way: *As she began*

F

to speak, her voice faltered. ○ *The engine faltered and stopped.* **2** to lose confidence and hesitate: *Agassi faltered and missed the ball.*

☆**fame** /feɪm/ *noun* [U] being known or talked about by many people: *She achieved fame at a young age.* ☞ Look also at **hall of fame.**

famed /feɪmd/ *adj.* well-known (for sth): *Colorado is famed for its ski resorts.* ☞ Look at **famous,** which is the more usual word.

☆**fa·mil·iar** /fəˈmɪlyər/ *adj.* **1** (not before a noun) **familiar with sth** having a good knowledge of sth: *Are you familiar with Chinese music?* **2 familiar (to sb)** well-known (to sb): *Chinese music isn't very familiar to people in America.* ○ *It was a relief to see a familiar face in the crowd.* ☞ The opposite for both senses is **unfamiliar.**

fa·mil·iar·i·ty /fəˌmɪliˈærəti; fəˌmɪlˈyærəti/ *noun* [U] good knowledge of sth: *His familiarity with the area was an advantage.*

fa·mil·iar·ize /fəˈmɪlyəraɪz/ *verb* [T] to inform sb/yourself about sth: *I want to familiarize myself with the plans before the meeting.*

☆**fam·i·ly** /ˈfæmli; ˈfæməli/ *noun* (*pl.* **fam·i·lies**) **1** [C] a group of people who are closely related to each other and who usually live together: *There are four people in my family.* ○ *the Wilson family* ○ *We are planning to start a family next year* (= to have our first baby).

☞ Sometimes we use "family" to mean "parents and their children" (a **nuclear family**); sometimes we use it to include other relatives, e.g. grandparents, aunts, uncles, etc. (an **extended family**). **Family** can be used before another noun to describe things that are suitable for or that can be used by the whole family: *family entertainment* ○ *the family car*

2 [C,U] (a group of) people who are related to sb: *Do you have any family in the area?* ○ *a family reunion* **3** [C] a group of animals, plants, etc. that are related to each other: *Lions belong to the cat family.*

IDM **run in the family** to be found very often in a family (2): *Red hair runs in the family.*

ˌfamily ˈdoctor (*also* ˌfamily phyˈsician; ˌfamily pracˈtitioner) *noun* [C] a doctor who treats common health problems in people of all ages

ˈfamily ˈname *noun* [C] the name that is shared by members of a family; last name ☞ Look at the note at **name.**

ˌfamily ˈplanning *noun* [U] controlling the number of children in a family by using birth control ☞ Look at **contraception.**

ˈfamily ˈroom *noun* [C] a room in a house, usually with informal furniture, where a family can watch television, listen to music, etc.

ˌfamily ˈtree *noun* [C] a diagram that shows the relationships between different members of a family

ˌfamily ˈvalues *noun* [plural] qualities such as

hard work, strong religious belief, strict discipline, moral behavior and traditional roles for men and women

fam·ine /ˈfæmən/ *noun* [C,U] a lack of food in a large area that can cause the death of many people: *There is a severe famine in many parts of Africa.* ○ *The long drought was followed by famine.*

☆**fa·mous** /ˈfeɪməs/ *adj.* **famous (for sth)** well-known to many people: *a famous singer* ○ *New York is famous for its museums and art galleries.* ☞ Look at **infamous** and **notorious,** which mean "famous for being bad."

 fans

☆**fan¹** /fæn/ *noun* [C] **1** something that is used for making a (cool) wind, e.g. an object made of paper, feathers, etc. in the shape of half a circle, or an electric machine with large blades that turn around very quickly **2** a person who admires and is very enthusiastic about a sport, a movie star, a singer, etc.: *football fans* ○ *He's a Mariah Carey fan.* ○ *I'm not a big fan of modern jazz* (= I don't like it very much).

fan² /fæn/ *verb* [T] (**fan·ning; fanned**) **1** to cool sb/sth by moving the air with a fan¹(1) or sth like a fan: *She used a newspaper to fan her face.* **2** to make a fire burn more strongly: *The strong wind really fanned the flames.*

PHRV **fan out** to spread out: *The police fanned out across the field.*

fa·nat·ic /fəˈnætɪk/ *noun* [C] a person who is too enthusiastic about sth (especially about religion or politics): *a religious fanatic* ○ *She's a health food fanatic.*

fa·nat·i·cal /fəˈnætɪkl/ *adj.* feeling very strongly or being too enthusiastic about sth: *He's fanatical about keeping things neat.* —**fa·nat·i·cal·ly** /-kli/ *adv.* —**fa·nat·i·cism** /-təsɪzəm/ *noun* [C,U]

☆**fan·cy** /ˈfænsi/ *adj.* not simple or ordinary: *a fancy restaurant* ○ *I just want a regular pair of blue jeans – nothing fancy.*

fan·fare /ˈfænfɛr/ *noun* **1** [C] a short loud piece of music played on trumpets that is used for introducing sb/sth **2** [C,U] an exciting event or behavior that attracts poeple's attention: *The tax cut was announced in Washington with a great deal of fanfare.*

fang /fæŋ/ *noun* [C] a long sharp tooth of a dog, poisonous snake, etc.

fan·ny /ˈfæni/ *noun* [C] (*pl.* **fan·nies**) (*informal*) the part of your body that you sit on

ər	ɪr	ɛr	ɑr	ɔr	ʊr	ʒ	h	ŋ
bird	near	hair	car	north	tour	vision	hat	sing

fan·ta·size /ˈfæntəsaɪz/ *verb* [I,T] to imagine sth that you would like to happen: *He liked to fantasize about winning a gold medal in the Olympics.*

☆ **fan·tas·tic** /fænˈtæstɪk/ *adj.* **1** very good; excellent: *She's a fantastic swimmer.* ○ *You passed your test. Fantastic!* **2** strange and difficult to believe: *fantastic creatures from other worlds* —**fan·tas·ti·cal·ly** /-kli/ *adv.*

fan·ta·sy /ˈfæntəsi/ *noun* [C,U] (*pl.* **fan·ta·sies**) a situation that is not true, that you just imagine: *My fantasy is to become a famous actress.* ○ *They live in a world of fantasy.* ☞ Look at the note at **imagination.**

☆ **far¹** /fɑr/ *adj.* (**far·ther** /ˈfɑrðər/ or **fur·ther** /ˈfərðər/, **far·thest** /ˈfɑrðəst/ or **fur·thest** /ˈfərðəst/) (only *before* a noun) more distant (used about one of two ends, sides, etc.): *My friend lives at the far end of the street.* ○ *In the far north, days are short during the winter.*

IDM **a far cry from sth/from doing sth** an experience that is very different from sth/doing sth

☆ **far²** /fɑr/ *adv.* (**far·ther** /ˈfɑrðər/ or **fur·ther** /ˈfərðər/, **far·thest** /ˈfɑrðəst/ or **fur·thest** /ˈfərðəst/) **1** (at) a distance: *Do you live far from Seattle?* ○ *How far did we walk yesterday?* ○ *Call me if you need me; I won't be far away.*

☞ **Far** in this sense is usually used in negative sentences and questions. In positive sentences we say **a long way**: *It's a long way from here to the ocean.* Some sentences have a negative meaning although they are positive in form. **Far** can be used in them: *Let's drive there. It's way too far to walk.*

2 a long time: *This story began far back in 1850.* ○ *We danced far into the night.* **3** (before comparative adjectives) very much: *She's far more intelligent than I thought.* ○ *It's far wetter in Oregon than in Arizona.*

IDM **as far as** to the place mentioned but not farther: *We walked as far as the river and then turned back.*

as/so far as to the degree that: *As far as I know, she's not coming, but I may be wrong.*

as far as I can see/tell (used for introducing your opinion): *As far as I can tell, the accident was John's fault, not Ann's.*

as far as sb is concerned in sb's opinion: *As far as I'm concerned, there's nothing left to say on the subject.*

as/so far as sth is concerned; as far as sth goes on the subject of sth; as sth is affected or influenced by sth: *As far as school work goes, he's not very good.*

by far (used for emphasizing comparative or superlative words) by a large amount: *Jane is by far the best student in the class.*

far afield far away, especially from where you live or from where you are staying: *We decided to rent a car in order to explore farther afield.*

far from sth/from doing sth almost the opposite of sth: *The future of the company is far from certain* (= it's very uncertain).

far from it (*informal*) certainly not; just the opposite: *"Were there a lot of people at the concert?" "Far from it – the place was almost empty."*

few and far between ⇨ FEW¹

go too far to be too extreme: *He's always been mean, but this time he's gone too far.*

so far until now: *So far the weather has been good, but it might change.*

far·a·way /ˈfɑrəˌweɪ/ *adj.* **1** distant: *He told us stories of faraway countries.* **2** (used about a look in a person's eyes) as if you are thinking of sth else: *She stared out of the window with a faraway look in her eyes.*

farce /fɑrs/ *noun* [C] **1** something important or serious that is not organized well or treated with respect: *The election was a farce. Everybody already knew what the result would be.* **2** a funny play for the theater that is full of silly situations

☆ **fare¹** /fɛr/ *noun* **1** [C] the amount of money you pay to travel by bus, plane, taxi, etc.: *How much is the fare to Toledo?* ○ *He didn't even have enough money for the bus fare into town.* **2** [U] food, especially food served in a restaurant

fare² /fɛr/ *verb* [I] (*formal*) to be successful/unsuccessful in a particular situation: *How did you fare on the test?* (= did you do well or badly?)

the ˌFar ˈEast *noun* [sing.] China, Japan and other countries in eastern Asia ☞ Look at the note at **White House.**

fare·well /ˌfɛrˈwɛl/ *interj.* (*old-fashioned*) goodbye

IDM **bid sb farewell** ⇨ BID¹ —**fare·well** *noun* [C]: *a farewell party*

ˌfar-ˈfetched *adj.* not easy to believe: *It's a good book, but the story's too far-fetched.*

☆ **farm¹** /fɑrm/ *noun* [C] an area of land with fields and buildings that is used for growing crops and keeping animals: *My grandparents live on a farm.* ○ *farm buildings* ○ *a pig farm*

☆ **farm²** /fɑrm/ *verb* [I,T] to use land for growing crops or keeping animals: *They farm 1,200 acres south of town.*

☆ **farm·er** /ˈfɑrmər/ *noun* [C] a person who owns or manages a farm

ˌfarmers' ˈmarket *noun* [C] a place in a town or city where farmers and other people bring food that they have grown or made and sell it directly to other people

farm·house /ˈfɑrmhaʊs/ *noun* [C] the house on a farm where the farmer lives

☆ **farm·ing** /ˈfɑrmɪŋ/ *noun* [U] managing a farm or working on it: *Farming is extremely hard work.*

ˌfar-ˈreaching *adj.* having, or going to have, a great influence on a lot of other things: *far-reaching changes*

F

tʃ	dʒ	v	θ	ð	s	z	ʃ
chin	June	van	thin	then	so	zoo	she

far·sight·ed /ˈfɑrˌsaɪtəd/ *adj.* **1** able to see things clearly only when they are far away ☞ The opposite is **nearsighted**. **2** being able to see what will be necessary and making plans for it ☞ The opposite is **shortsighted**.

☆ **far·ther** /ˈfɑrðər/ *adj., adv.* more distant in space or time; a greater distance: *Los Angeles is farther from New York than Boston is.* ○ *I can swim farther than you.*

☞ **Farther** is the comparative of **far**. Look at the note at **further**.

☆ **far·thest** /ˈfɑrðəst/ (*also* **furthest**) *adj., adv.* most distant in space or time; the greatest distance: *the farthest corner of the country* ○ *Who can swim farthest?*

☞ **Farthest** is the superlative of **far**.

☆ **fas·ci·nate** /ˈfæsəneɪt/ *verb* [T] to attract or interest sb very much: *He fascinated the kids with his magic tricks.* ○ *I was fascinated by that movie.* —**fas·ci·nat·ing** *adj.* —**fas·ci·na·tion** /ˌfæsəˈneɪʃn/ *noun* [C,U]

fas·cism (*also* **Fascism**) /ˈfæʃɪzəm/ *noun* [U] an extreme political system in which one very powerful ruler (**dictator**) controls the social and economic systems of a country and often expresses hatred of people from other countries or races: *the rise of fascism in the 1930s* —**fas·cist** (*also* **Fascist**) /ˈfæʃɪst/ *noun* [C], *adj.*

☆ **fash·ion** /ˈfæʃn/ *noun* **1** [C,U] the style of dressing or behaving that is the most popular at a particular time: *men's fashions* ○ *a fashion show, model, etc.* **2** [U, sing.] the way you do sth: *It should be possible to connect the parts in some fashion.* ○ *Over 60% of women approved of the plan, and men responded in a similar fashion.*

IDM **come into/be in fashion** to become or to be popular as a style: *Jeans are always in fashion.*

go/be out of fashion to become or to be unpopular as a style: *This simple blazer will never go out of fashion.*

☆ **fash·ion·a·ble** /ˈfæʃn·əbl; ˈfæʃnəbl/ *adj.* following the latest popular style: *a fashionable woman, suit, restaurant, idea, etc.* ☞ The opposite is **unfashionable** or **old-fashioned**. —**fash·ion·a·bly** /-əbli/ *adv.*

☆ **fast¹** /fæst/ *adj.* **1** able to move or act at great speed: *a fast car, horse, worker, etc.*

☞ There is no noun formed from **fast**. Use **speed**: *The car was traveling very fast./The car was traveling at a high speed.* Look at the note at **quick**.

2 (used about a clock or watch) showing a time that is later than the real time: *I'm early – my watch must be fast.* ○ *The clock is five minutes fast.* ☞ The opposite is **slow**.

☆ **fast²** /fæst/ *adv.* **1** quickly: *Don't drive so fast.* **2** firmly or deeply: *fast asleep* ○ *Our car was stuck fast in the mud.*

fast³ /fæst/ *verb* [I] to eat no food for a certain time, usually for religious reasons or in order to lose weight: *Muslims fast during Ramadan.* —**fast** *noun* [C]

☆ **fas·ten** /ˈfæsn/ *verb* **1** [T] to connect, join or shut and lock sth firmly: *Please fasten your seat belts.* **2** [I] to become closed or connected: *My blouse fastens at the back.* **3** [T] **fasten sth (on/to sth)**; **fasten A and B (together)** to attach sth to sth, or two things together: *Fasten this tag onto your suitcase.* ○ *How can I fasten these pieces of wood together?*

fas·ten·er /ˈfæsn·ər; ˈfæsnər/ *noun* [C] something that fastens things together

☆ **fast ʹfood** *noun* [U] food that can be cooked and eaten quickly in a restaurant or taken away from the restaurant: *a fast-food restaurant*

ˌ**fast-ʹforward** *verb* [I,T] (used about a tape or video) to go forward or to make sth go forward quickly, without playing it ☞ Look at the note at **cassette**.

ʹ**fast lane** *noun* [C] the part of a wide road or freeway that is for the fastest cars

IDM **life in the fast lane** ⇨ LIFE

☆ **fat¹** /fæt/ *adj.* (**fat·ter; fat·test**) **1** (used about bodies) covered with too much flesh: *You'll get fat if you eat too much.*

☞ It is not polite to describe a person as **fat**. Less direct words are **plump**, **heavy** or **overweight**. Look also at **obese**. The opposite is **thin**.

2 (used about a thing) thick or full: *a fat wallet, book, etc.*

☆ **fat²** /fæt/ *noun* **1** [U] the greasy substance under the skins of animals and people: *I don't like meat with too much fat on it.* ☞ The adjective is **fatty**. **2** [C,U] the greasy substance we obtain from animals, plants or seeds and use for cooking: *You have too much fat in your diet.* ○ *Vegetable fats are healthier than animal fats.*

☆ **fa·tal** /ˈfeɪtl/ *adj.* **1** causing or ending in death: *a fatal accident* **2** causing trouble or a bad result: *the fatal flaw in his plan* —**fa·tal·ly** *adv.*

fa·tal·i·ty /feɪˈtæləti; fə-/ *noun* [C] (*pl.* **fa·tal·i·ties**) a person's death caused by an accident or in war, etc.: *There were no fatalities in the fire.*

☆ **fate** /feɪt/ *noun* **1** [U] the power that some people believe controls everything that happens: *It was fate that brought them together again after 20 years.* **2** [C] your future or something that happens to you: *Both men suffered the same fate – they both lost their jobs.*

fate·ful /ˈfeɪtfl/ *adj.* having an important effect on the future: *a fateful decision*

i	ɪ	ɛ	æ	ɑ	ɔ	ʌ	ʊ	u
see	sit	ten	cat	hot	saw	cup	put	too

☆ **fa·ther** /ˈfɑðər/ noun [C] 1 a person's male parent: *John looks exactly like his father.* 2 a man who starts something important: *The Wright brothers are the fathers of air travel.* 3 **Father** the title of certain priests: *Father O'Reilly*

fa·ther·hood /ˈfɑðərhʊd/ noun [U] the state of being a father: *How are you enjoying father-hood?*

ˈ**father-in-law** noun [C] (*pl.* **fathers-in-law**) the father of your husband or wife

fa·ther·ly /ˈfɑðərli/ adj. like or typical of a father: *a piece of fatherly advice*

fath·om /ˈfæðəm/ verb [T] to understand sth: *I can't fathom why she did that.*

fa·tigue /fəˈtig/ noun [U] 1 great tiredness 2 weakness in metals caused by a lot of use

fat·ten /ˈfætn/ verb [T] **fatten sb/sth (up)** to make sb/sth fatter: *He's fattening the pigs up for slaughter.*

fat·ten·ing /ˈfætn·ɪŋ; ˈfætnɪŋ/ adj. (used about food) that makes people fat: *You shouldn't eat too much chocolate. It's very fattening.*

☆ **fat·ty** /ˈfæti/ adj. (**fat·ti·er; fat·ti·est**) (used about food) having a lot of fat in or on it

☆ **fau·cet** /ˈfɔsət/ (*also* **tap**) noun [C] a type of handle that you turn to let water out of a pipe: *Go and turn the bathroom faucet off – I can hear it dripping.* ☞ picture at **plug.**

☆ **fault¹** /fɔlt/ noun 1 [C] something wrong or not perfect in a person's character or in a thing: *One of my faults is that I'm always late.* ○ *a fault in the car's brakes* ☞ Look at the note at **mistake.** 2 [U] responsibility for a mistake: *"We're going to be late." "Well, it's not my fault – I was ready on time."* ○ *It will be your own fault if you don't pass your test.* 3 [C] a large crack in the surface of the Earth: *earthquakes near the San Andreas fault*

IDM **be at fault** be wrong or responsible for a mistake: *The other driver was at fault – he didn't stop at the traffic light.*

find fault ⇨ FIND¹

fault² /fɔlt/ verb [T] to find a fault or mistake in sb/sth: *It was impossible to fault her English.*

☆ **fault·y** /ˈfɔlti/ adj. (used especially about electricity or machinery) not working correctly; having a fault¹(1) : *a faulty switch* ○ *faulty reasoning*

fau·na /ˈfɔnə/ noun [U] all the animals of an area or a period of time: *the flora and fauna of South America* ☞ Look at **flora.**

faux pas /ˌfoʊ ˈpɑ/ noun [C] (*pl.* **faux pas** /ˌfoʊ ˈpɑz/) something you say or do that is embarrassing or offends people

☆ **fa·vor¹** /ˈfeɪvər/ noun 1 [C] something that helps sb: *Would you do me a favor and mail this letter for me?* ○ *Can I ask you a favor – could you babysit for us tonight?* 2 [U] liking or approval: *In the end, the politician won the crowd's favor.* 3 [C] = PARTY FAVOR

IDM **be/fall out of favor (with sb)** to have/lose the approval of sb: *The politician fell out of favor with the voters after he made a racist comment.*

in favor of sb/sth in agreement with sb/sth: *Are you in favor of gun control?*

in sb's favor to the advantage of sb: *The committee decided in their favor.*

☆ **fa·vor²** /ˈfeɪvər/ verb [T] 1 to support sb/sth; to prefer: *Which suggestion did they favor?* 2 to treat one person very well and so be unfair to others: *Does the legal system favor wealthy citizens?*

fa·vor·a·ble /ˈfeɪvərəbl; ˈfeɪvrəbl/ adj. 1 showing liking or approval: *Did you get a favorable report on your work?* ○ *He made a favorable impression on his new boss.* 2 (often used about the weather) suitable or helpful: *Conditions are favorable for skiing today.* ☞ The opposite for both senses is **unfavorable.** —**fa·vor·a·bly** /-əbli/ adv.

☆ **fa·vor·ite¹** /ˈfeɪvrət; ˈfeɪvərət/ adj. liked more than any other: *What is your favorite color?* ○ *My favorite singer is Whitney Houston.*

fa·vor·ite² /ˈfeɪvrət; ˈfeɪvərət/ noun [C] 1 a person or thing that you like more than any others: *This restaurant is a big favorite of mine.* ○ *That sweater is my husband's favorite.* 2 **the favorite** (especially in sports) the person, team, or thing that is expected to win

fa·vor·it·ism /ˈfeɪvrətɪzəm; ˈfeɪvərət-/ noun [U] giving unfair advantages to the people that you like best

fawn /fɔn/ noun [C] a young deer ☞ Look at the note at **deer.**

☆ **fax¹** /fæks/ noun 1 [C,U] a copy of a letter, etc. which you can send by telephone lines using a special machine: *I need an answer today. Send them a fax!* ○ *They contacted us by fax.* 2 [C] (*also* ˈ**fax machine**) the machine that you use for sending faxes (1): *Do you have a fax?* ○ *What's your fax number?*

fax² /fæks/ verb [T] **fax sth (to sb); fax sb (sth)** to send sb a fax: *We will fax our order to you tomorrow.* ○ *I faxed her a copy of the letter.*

faze /feɪz/ verb [T] to make sb anxious or nervous: *Jeff always stays calm – nothing seems to faze him.*

the FBI /ˌɛf bi ˈaɪ/ noun [sing.] the Federal Bureau of Investigation; the department of the U.S. government which investigates serious crimes that are against national (**federal**) law ☞ Look at the note at **White House.**

☆ **fear¹** /fɪr/ noun [C,U] the feeling that you have when sth dangerous, painful or frightening might happen: *He was shaking with fear after the accident.* ○ *She showed no fear.* ○ *My fears for his safety were unnecessary.*

☆ **fear²** /fɪr/ verb 1 [I,T] to be afraid of sb/sth great or important: *We all fear illness and death.* ○ *We'll get there in time – never fear!* (= don't worry). 2 [T] to feel that something

F

bad might happen: *The senator fears that she will lose the next election.* ☞ Look at **afraid** and at the note at **frightened**.

PHRV **fear for sb/sth** to be worried about sb/sth: *Parents often fear for the safety of their children.*

fear·ful /ˈfɪrfl/ *adj.* **fearful (of sth/of doing sth); fearful (that)** anxious or afraid about sth: *You should never be fearful of starting something new.* ☞ Look at **frightened** and the note at **afraid**. These words are much more common. —**fear·ful·ly** *adv.*

fear·less /ˈfɪrləs/ *adj.* not afraid; brave —**fear·less·ly** *adv.* —**fear·less·ness** *noun* [U]

fea·si·ble /ˈfizəbl/ *adj.* possible to do: *a feasible plan* —**fea·si·bil·i·ty** /ˌfizəˈbɪləti/ *noun* [U]

feast /fist/ *noun* [C] a large, special meal (sometimes to celebrate sth) —**feast** *verb* [I]

feat /fit/ *noun* [C] something you do that shows great strength, skill or courage: *That new bridge is a real feat of engineering.*

☆**feath·er** /ˈfɛðər/ *noun* [C] one of the light, soft things that grow in a bird's skin and cover its body

IDM **ruffle (sb's) feathers** ⇨ RUFFLE[1]

☆**fea·ture¹** /ˈfitʃər/ *noun* [C] **1** an important or noticeable part of sth: *Lakes are a main feature of the landscape of Minnesota.* ○ *Noise is a feature of city life.* ○ *improved safety features on a car* **2** a part of the face: *Her eyes are her best feature.* **3** an important newspaper or magazine article, especially one that is meant to be interesting or entertaining: *a feature on popular pets* **4** (*also* **feature film**) a full-length movie with a story

fea·ture² /ˈfitʃər/ *verb* **1** [T] to include sb/sth as an important part: *Tonight's program features an interview with actor Brad Pitt.* **2** [I] **feature in sth** to have a part in sth: *Does marriage feature in your future plans?*

☆**Feb·ru·ar·y** /ˈfɛbyuˌɛri; ˈfɛbru-/ *noun* [C,U] (*abbr.* **Feb.**) the second month of the year, coming before March ☞ For examples of the use of the months in sentences, look at **January**.

fe·ces /ˈfisiz/ *noun* [plural] (*formal*) solid waste matter that is passed from the body through the bowels ☞ Feces is used mainly in a medical context. Look at **excrement**. An informal word is **poop**.

fed *p.t.*, *p.p.* of FEED[1]

☆**fed·er·al** /ˈfɛdərəl/ *adj.* relating to the national government of a country such as the United States: *state and federal income taxes* ○ *a federal judge*

fed·er·a·tion /ˌfɛdəˈreɪʃn/ *noun* [C] a group of people, organizations, states, etc. that have joined together: *The American Federation of Teachers*

fed up /ˌfɛdˈʌp/ *adj.* (not before a noun) (*informal*) bored or unhappy; tired of sth: *What's the*

matter? *You look really fed up.* ○ *I'm fed up with waiting for the phone to ring.*

☆**fee** /fi/ *noun* [C] **1** (usually plural) the money you pay for professional advice or services from doctors, lawyers, universities, etc.: *Some attorneys charge extremely high fees for their services.* **2** the cost of an examination, club membership, entrance etc.: *How much is the entrance fee?* ☞ Look at the note at **pay¹**.

fee·ble /ˈfibl/ *adj.* **1** with no energy or power; weak: *a feeble old man* **2** not able to convince sb: *a feeble argument*

☆**feed¹** /fid/ *verb* (*p.t.*, *p.p.* **fed** /fɛd/) **1** [T] to give food to a person or an animal: *Don't forget to feed the dog.* ○ *I can't come yet. I haven't fed the baby.* ○ *I cooked enough to feed us all week.* ☞ Look also at **fed up**. **2** [I] (used about animals) to eat: *What do horses feed on in the winter?* **3** [T] to put sth, such as supplies or information, into sth else: *Can you feed this information into the computer?*

feed² /fid/ *noun* [U] food for animals: *cattle feed*

feed·back /ˈfidbæk/ *noun* [U] information about sth that you have done or made which tells you how good or successful it is: *We need some more feedback from the people who use our textbooks.*

feed·ing /ˈfidɪŋ/ *noun* [C] a meal for an animal or a baby: *It's almost time for the baby's feeding.*

☆**feel¹** /fil/ *verb* (*p.t.*, *p.p.* **felt** /fɛlt/) **1** [I] (usually with an adjective) to be in the state that is mentioned: *to feel cold, sick, tired, happy, etc.* ○ *How are you feeling today?* ○ *You'll feel better in the morning.* **2** [I] **feel (to sb) (like sth/sb)** to give an impression of sth: *The cavity in my tooth feels a lot bigger than it is.* ○ *My new coat feels like leather, but it's not.* **3** [T] to learn about sth by touching it with your hands: *Feel this material. Is it silk or cotton?* ○ *I felt her forehead and knew that she had a temperature.* **4** [T] to be aware of sth: *I felt something crawling up my back.* ○ *I could feel myself dropping off to sleep.* **5** [T] to believe or think: *I felt (that) it was a mistake not to ask her advice.* **6** [T] to suffer from sth: *Do you feel the cold in winter?* ○ *She felt the loss badly when her mother died.* **7** [I] **feel (around) (for sb/sth)** to try to find something with your hands instead of your eyes: *She felt around in the dark for the light switch.* **8** [I] **feel as if/as though/like** to have or give the impression that: *He felt as if he had been there before.* ○ *My head feels as though it will burst.* ○ *I feel like I'm going to throw up!*

☞ **It** is often used as the subject of **feel** in this sense: *It feels as if it is going to snow soon.* **Feel like** is very common in informal English, but some people do not like to use this phrase in formal writing.

ər	ɪr	ɛr	ɑr	ɔr	ʊr	ʒ	h	ŋ
bird	near	hair	car	north	tour	vision	hat	sing

IDM be/feel sorry for sb ⇨ SORRY¹
feel like sth/doing sth to want sth or to want to do sth: *Do you feel like going out?*

☆**feel²** /fil/ *noun* [sing.] **1** the feel the impression something gives you when it is touched; the impression an experience gives you: *You can tell it's wool by the feel.* **2** an act of touching sth in order to learn about it: *Let me have a feel.*

IDM get/have a feel for sth to get or have a natural understanding or ability for sth: *Barbara has a good feel for trends in business.*

☆**feel·ing** /'filɪŋ/ *noun* **1** [C] **a feeling (of sth)** something that you feel in your mind or body: *a feeling of hunger, happiness, fear, success, etc.* **2** feelings [plural] a person's emotions: *I don't want to hurt his feelings* (= make him unhappy). ∘ *to show/hide your feelings.* **3** [U] the ability to feel in your body: *After the accident, he lost all feeling in his legs.* **4** [sing.] a belief or idea that you cannot explain exactly: *I had a feeling that something terrible would happen.* **5** [U] sympathy or understanding: *She doesn't have much feeling for music.*

IDM bad/ill feeling(s) unhappy relations between people: *The decision caused a lot of bad feelings at the factory.*

have mixed feelings about sb/sth ⇨ MIXED

feet *pl.* of FOOT¹

feist·y /'faisti/ *adj.* (**feist·i·er; feist·i·est**) (used about a person) having a lot of energy and liking to argue or fight

fe·line /'filaɪn/ *adj.* of or like a cat

fell¹ *p.t.* of FALL¹

fell² /fɛl/ *verb* [T] (*formal*) to cut down a tree

☆**fel·low¹** /'fɛloʊ/ *noun* [C] **1** (*informal*) a man: *What's that fellow over there doing?* **2** a person who has received an award of money in order to study at a university, etc.: *Jill is a research fellow in the biology department.*

☆**fel·low²** /'fɛloʊ/ *adj.* (only *before* a noun) another or others like yourself in the same situation: *Her fellow students were all older than she was.*

fel·low·ship /'fɛloʊʃɪp; 'fɛlə-/ *noun* **1** [U] friendly relations with others **2** [C] a group or society, especially a Christian religious group **3** [C] an award of money that makes it possible for sb to study at a university, etc.

fel·on /'fɛlən/ *noun* [C] a person who is guilty of a felony: *a convicted felon*

fel·o·ny /'fɛləni/ *noun* [C] (*pl.* **fel·o·nies**) a serious crime, e.g. murder: *to be charged with a felony* ☛ Look at misdemeanor.

felt¹ *p.t., p.p.* of FEEL¹

felt² /fɛlt/ *noun* [U] a type of soft cloth made from wool, etc. which has been pressed flat

felt-tip ˌpen (*also* ˌfelt-tip) *noun* [C] a type of pen with a tip made of felt²

☆**fe·male¹** /'fimeɪl/ *adj.* of the sex that can give birth to young: *Please state sex: male or female* (e.g. on a form).

fe·male² /'fimeɪl/ *noun* [C] a female animal: *Is your dog a male or a female?*

☛ **Female** and **male** are used only to describe the sex of a creature. To describe the qualities we think of as typical of females and males, we use **feminine** and **masculine**.

☆**fem·i·nine** /'fɛmənən/ *adj.* **1** of or like a woman: *My daughter always dresses like a boy. She hates looking feminine.* ☛ Look at masculine and the note at female. **2** (*grammar*) (*abbr.* **fem.**) (in English) of the forms of words used to describe females: *"Lioness" is the feminine form of "lion."* **3** (*grammar*) (*abbr.* **fem.**) (in certain languages) belonging to a certain grammatical class: *The German word "Blume" is feminine.* ☛ Look at masculine and neuter. —**fem·i·nin·i·ty** /ˌfɛmə'nməti/ *noun* [U]

fem·i·nism /'fɛmənɪzəm/ *noun* [U] the belief that women should have the same rights and opportunities as men

fem·i·nist /'fɛmənɪst/ *noun* [C] a person who believes in and supports the aims of feminism

☆**fence¹** /fɛns/ *noun* [C] a line of wooden or metal posts joined by wood, wire, metal, etc. to divide land or to keep animals in or out: *a fence around the back yard* ∘ *an electric fence* ∘ *a barbed-wire fence*

IDM be/sit on the fence to be unwilling or unable to decide between two things

fence² /fɛns/ *verb* **1** [T] to surround land with a fence **2** [I] to fight with a long thin sword as a sport

PHRV fence sb/sth in to surround sb/sth with a fence: *They fenced in their back yard to make it more private.*
fence sth off to separate one area from another with a fence: *Several streets were fenced off while police searched for the bomb.*

fenc·ing /'fɛnsɪŋ/ *noun* [U] the sport of fighting with swords

fend /fɛnd/ *verb*

PHRV fend for yourself to take care of yourself without having to rely on help from other people: *It's time Ben left home and learned to fend for himself.*
fend sth/sb off to defend yourself from sth/sb: *He fended off the dog with a stick.*

tʃ	dʒ	v	θ	ð	s	z	ʃ
chin	June	van	thin	then	so	zoo	she

fend·er /ˈfɛndər/ *noun* [C] the part of the outside of a car, truck, etc. that is over the top of the wheels

ˈfender-ˌbender (*also* ˈfender ˌbender) *noun* [C] (*informal*) a car accident that does not cause much damage

fer·ment¹ /fərˈmɛnt/ *verb* [I,T] to (make sth) change chemically: *The wine is starting to ferment.*

fer·ment² /ˈfərmɛnt/ *noun* [U] (*formal*) a state of uncertainty and change: *Central African nations are in ferment and no one is sure what will happen next.*

fern /fərn/ *noun* [C] a green plant with no flowers and a lot of long thin leaves

fe·ro·cious /fəˈroʊʃəs/ *adj.* very fierce and violent —**fe·ro·cious·ly** *adv.*

fe·roc·i·ty /fəˈrɑsəti/ *noun* [U] violent cruelty

Fer·ris wheel /ˈfɛrəs wil/ *noun* [C] (at an outdoor festival, etc.) a machine like a large vertical wheel with seats attached to its outside edge, that people can sit in and ride as it goes around

fer·ry¹ /ˈfɛri/ *noun* [C] (*pl.* **fer·ries**) a boat that transports people and goods over short distances: *You can take the ferry from Vancouver Island to the mainland.* ○ *a ferry terminal*

fer·ry² /ˈfɛri/ *verb* [T] (*pres. part.* **fer·ry·ing**; *3rd pers. sing. pres.* **fer·ries**; *p.t., p.p.* **fer·ried**) to carry people or goods by boat, airplane, car, etc. from one place to another: *We share the job of ferrying the kids to school.*

fer·tile /ˈfərtl/ *adj.* **1** (used about land, plants, animals and people) able to produce crops, fruit or young ☞ The opposite is **infertile**. Look at **sterile**. **2** (used about a person's mind) full of ideas: *a fertile imagination*

fer·til·i·ty /fərˈtɪləti/ *noun* [U] the state of being fertile: *drugs that can increase a woman's fertility* (= her chances of having a child) ☞ The opposite is **infertility**.

fer·til·ize /ˈfərtl·aɪz/ *verb* [T] **1** to put a male seed into an egg, a plant or a female animal so that it starts to develop fruit or young **2** to put natural or artificial substances on soil in order to make it more fertile —**fer·til·i·za·tion** /ˌfərtl·əˈzeɪʃn/ *noun* [U]

fer·til·iz·er /ˈfərtl·aɪzər/ *noun* [C,U] a natural or chemical substance that is put on land to make plants grow better

fer·vent /ˈfərvənt/ *adj.* showing strong feelings: *She's a fervent believer in women's rights.* —**fer·vent·ly** *adv.*

fer·vor /ˈfərvər/ *noun* [U] strong feeling

fest /fɛst/ *noun* [C] (*informal*) = FESTIVAL(2)

fes·ter /ˈfɛstər/ *verb* [I] **1** (used about a cut or wound) to become infected **2** (used about a bad situation, feeling or thought) to become worse or more painful

☆ **fes·ti·val** /ˈfɛstəvl/ *noun* [C] **1** a day or time when people celebrate sth (especially a religious event): *Hanukkah is an important Jewish festival.* **2** (*also informal* **fest**) a large public celebration that is often held regularly in one place: *a jazz festival*

fes·tive /ˈfɛstɪv/ *adj.* happy, because people are enjoying themselves: *a festive occasion*

fes·tiv·i·ty /fɛˈstɪvəti/ *noun* (*pl.* **fes·tiv·i·ties**) **1** [U] being happy and celebrating **2 festivities** [plural] happy events when people celebrate sth: *The festivities went on until dawn.*

fetch /fɛtʃ/ *verb* **1** [I,T] (usually used about a dog) to go for and bring back sth that sb has thrown: *If I throw this ball, my dog will fetch it.* ○ *I taught my dog to fetch.* **2** [T] (*formal or old-fashioned*) to go for and bring back sb/sth: *Residents of the village still have to fetch their water from a well.* **3** [T] (used about goods) to be sold for the price mentioned: *The painting could fetch up to $2 million at the auction.*

fe·tus /ˈfitəs/ *noun* [C] (*pl.* **fe·tus·es**) a young human or animal that is still developing in its mother's body ☞ An **embryo** is at an earlier stage of development.

feud /fyud/ *noun* [C] a long and serious argument between two people or groups —**feud** *verb* [I]

feu·dal /ˈfyudl/ *adj.* relating to the system of feudalism

feu·dal·ism /ˈfyudl·ɪzəm/ *noun* [U] the social system which existed in the Middle Ages in Europe, in which people worked and fought for a person who owned the land, and received land and protection from him

☆ **fe·ver** /ˈfivər/ *noun* **1** [C,U] a condition of the body when it is too hot because of illness: *A high fever can be dangerous, especially in small children.* ○ *Symptoms include dizziness, fever and diarrhea.* ☞ When somebody's body is very hot, we can also say he/she **has a temperature**. **2** [sing.] (*figurative*) a state of nervous excitement

fe·ver·ish /ˈfivərɪʃ/ *adj.* **1** showing the signs of a fever **2** showing great excitement: *to work at a feverish pace*

fe·ver·ish·ly /ˈfivərɪʃli/ *adv.* very quickly and excitedly

☆ **few¹** /fyu/ *det., adj., pron.* (used with a plural noun and a plural verb) not many: *Few people live to be 100.* ○ *There are fewer cars here today than yesterday.* ○ *The few people I asked thought the same as I do.* ○ *Few of the players played really well.* ○ *Very few of the books were new.*

IDM few and far between (*informal*) not happening very often; not very common: *Our visits to the theater are few and far between.* ○ *Real gentlemen are few and far between these days.*

☆ **few²** /fyu/ **a few** *det., pron.* (used with a plural noun and a plural verb) a small number of; some: *a few people* ○ *a few letters* ○ *Only a few of the people who applied were suitable.* ○ *She's written lots of books, but I've only read a few*

i	$ɪ$	$ɛ$	$æ$	$ɑ$	$ɔ$	$ʌ$	$ʊ$	u
see	sit	ten	cat	hot	saw	cup	put	too

fiery

255

(of them). ○ *I knew a few* (= some) *of the people there.* ☞ Compare with: *I knew few of the people* (= not many).

IDM quite a few ⇨ QUITE

fi·an·cé /ˌfiɑnˈseɪ; fiˈɑnseɪ/ *noun* [C] a man to whom a woman is engaged to be married: *This is my fiancé Dave. We got engaged a few weeks ago.*

fi·an·cée /ˌfiɑnˈseɪ; fiˈɑnseɪ/ *noun* [C] a woman to whom a man is engaged to be married: *Can I introduce you to my fiancée?*

fi·as·co /fiˈæskoʊ/ *noun* [C] (*pl.* **fi·as·coes** or **fi·as·cos**) the ridiculous failure of an organized event: *Our last party was a complete fiasco.*

fib¹ /fɪb/ *noun* [C] (*informal*) something you say that is not true; a small lie: *to tell a fib*

fib² /fɪb/ *verb* [I] (**fib·bing; fibbed**) (*informal*) to say untrue things; to tell a fib¹: *to fib about your age* ☞ Look at lie¹. Fib is used when the lie does not seem very important.

fi·ber /ˈfaɪbər/ *noun* **1** [C] one of the thin threads which form a natural or artificial substance: *cotton fibers* ○ *a muscle fiber* **2** [C,U] material or a substance made from fibers

☞ **Natural** fibers are, for example, cotton and wool. **Man-made** or **synthetic** fibers are nylon, polyester, etc.

3 [U] the part of plants (used as food) that your body cannot digest and that are thought to be good for it: *Whole wheat bread is high in fiber.*

fi·ber·glass /ˈfaɪbərglæs/ *noun* [U] a hard material made from plastic and glass fibers, used for making small boats, parts of cars, etc.

fick·le /ˈfɪkl/ *adj.* always changing your mind or your feelings

☆ **fic·tion** /ˈfɪkʃn/ *noun* [U] stories, novels, etc. which describe events and people that do not really exist: *I don't read much fiction.*

☞ Fiction is one type of **literature**. Look at **drama** and **poetry**. The opposite is **non-fiction**. Look also at **fact**.

fic·tion·al /ˈfɪkʃənl/ *adj.* only existing in fiction: *The book gave a fictional account of a doctor's life.* ☞ Look at **factual**.

fic·ti·tious /fɪkˈtɪʃəs/ *adj.* invented; not real: *They used fictitious names in the newspaper article.*

fid·dle¹ /ˈfɪdl/ *noun* [C] (*informal*) a violin

☞ We use **fiddle** especially when we are talking about country music.

fid·dle² /ˈfɪdl/ *verb* [I] **fiddle (around) (with sth)** to play with sth carelessly, nervously or without thinking: *He sat nervously, fiddling with a paper clip.*

fi·del·i·ty /fɪˈdɛləti/ *noun* [U] (*formal*) the quality of being faithful ☞ The opposite is **infidelity**. A less formal word is **faithfulness**.

fidg·et /ˈfɪdʒət/ *verb* [I] **fidget (with sth)** to move about or play with sth in a restless way because you are nervous, bored, etc.: *Stop fidgeting!* ○ *The students were fidgeting with their pens while they waited for the bell to ring.* —**fidg·et·y** *adj.*

☆ **field¹** /fild/ *noun* **1** [C] an area of land on a farm that is used for growing crops or for feeding animals: *a cornfield* ○ *a field of corn* ○ *farmers working in the fields* **2** [C] an area of land used for sports, games or some other activity: *a baseball, football, soccer, etc. field* ○ *an airfield* (= where airplanes land and take off) ○ *a battlefield* ☞ Look also at **track and field**. **3** [C] an area of land where oil, coal or other minerals are found: *an oil field* **4** [C] an area of study or knowledge: *He's an expert in the field of economics.* ○ *That question is outside my field.* **5** [C] an area affected by or included in sth: *a magnetic field* ○ *It's outside my field of vision* (= I can't see it). **6 the field** [sing.] all the people, animals, companies, etc. who are competing against each other in a race, in business, etc.: *We have a huge lead over the rest of the field.*

field² /fild/ *verb* **1** [I,T] (to be ready) to catch and throw back the ball (in baseball) ☞ When one team is **fielding**, the other is **batting**. **2** [T] to choose a group of candidates for an election, a team for a sports game, soldiers for an army, etc.: *In spite of injuries, they managed to field a good team.* **3** [T] to answer a difficult question, a telephone call, etc. without having time to prepare your answer: *The governor spoke about taxes and then fielded questions from the audience.*

¹field day *noun* [C] a special day at a school when there are no classes and students compete in sports activities

IDM have a field day to have a time of great excitement, especially because you have an opportunity to make sb appear silly or stupid: *The newspapers always have a field day when there's a political scandal.*

¹field ˌhockey *noun* [U] a game that is played on a field by two teams of eleven players who try to hit a small hard ball into a goal, using a curved wooden stick

¹field trip *noun* [C] a trip that a group of people, especially a class, go on in order to learn about sth: *Our class is going on a field trip to the state capitol building.*

fiend /find/ *noun* [C] **1** a devil or a very cruel person **2** (*informal*) a person who is unusually interested in one particular thing: *a sports fiend*

fiend·ish /ˈfindɪʃ/ *adj.* **1** very fierce or cruel **2** clever and complicated: *a fiendish plan*

☆ **fierce** /fɪrs/ *adj.* **1** angry and aggressive: *a fierce dog* **2** very strong: *fierce competition for jobs* ☞ The noun is **ferocity**. —**fierce·ly** *adv.*

fier·y /ˈfaɪəri/ *adj.* **1** looking like fire **2** (used

ə	y	w	t̬	eɪ	aɪ	ɔɪ	aʊ	oʊ
about	yes	woman	butter	say	five	boy	now	go

about a person's character or temper) quick to become angry

☆ **fif·teen** /ˌfɪfˈtiːn/ *number* 15, one more than fourteen ☞ For examples of how to use numbers in sentences, look at **six**. Look also at Appendix 2. —**fif·teenth** /ˌfɪfˈtiːnθ/ *pron.*, *det.*, *adv.* ☞ Look at the examples at **sixth**.

☆ **fifth¹** /fɪfθ/ *pron.*, *det.*, *adv.* 5th, next after fourth ☞ Look at **five** and at the examples at **sixth**. For more information on numbers, look at Appendix 2.

☆ **fifth²** /fɪfθ/ *noun* [C] the fraction 1/5; one of five equal parts of sth ☞ Look at the examples at **sixth**. For more information on numbers, look at Appendix 2.

☆ **fif·ty** /ˈfɪfti/ *number* 50, one more than forty-nine ☞ For examples of how to use numbers in sentences, look at **sixty**. Look also at Appendix 2. —**fif·ti·eth** /ˈfɪftiəθ/ *pron.*, *det.*, *adv.* ☞ Look at the examples at **sixth**.

ˌfifty-ˈfifty *adj.*, *adv.* (*informal*) equal or equally (between two people, groups, etc.): *You have a fifty-fifty chance of winning.* ○ *We'll split the money fifty-fifty.*

fig /fɪg/ *noun* [C] (a type of tree with) a soft sweet fruit full of small seeds that grows in warm areas and is often eaten dried

fig. *abbr.* **1** = FIGURE¹(7): *See diagram in fig. 2.* **2** = FIGURATIVE

☆ **fight¹** /faɪt/ *verb* (*p.t.*, *p.p.* **fought** /fɔːt/) **1** [I,T] **fight (against/with sb/sth) (about/over sth)** to use physical strength, guns, weapons etc. against sb/sth: *What were the boys fighting each other about?* ○ *Have you been fighting with your sister again?* **2** [I] **fight (about/over sth)** to argue: *It's not worth fighting about money.* **3** [I,T] **fight (against sth)** to try very hard to stop or prevent sth: *to fight a fire, a decision, etc.* ○ *to fight against crime, disease, etc.* **4** [I] **fight (for sth/to do sth)** to try very hard to get or keep sth: *to fight for your rights*

PHRV **fight back** to protect yourself by fighting with actions or with words: *If he hits you again, fight back!*

☆ **fight²** /faɪt/ *noun* **1** [C] an act of fighting or a struggle: *Don't get into a fight at school, okay?* ○ *the administration's fight against inflation* **2** [C] a very angry argument: *I had a big fight with my parents last night.* **3** [U] the desire to continue trying or struggling: *I've had some bad luck, but I've still got plenty of fight left in me.*

IDM **pick a fight** ⇨ PICK¹

fight·er /ˈfaɪtər/ *noun* [C] **1** a person who fights in war or in sports (especially a boxer) **2** (*also* **fighter plane**) a small fast aircraft that is used for shooting down enemy aircraft

☆ **fight·ing** /ˈfaɪtɪŋ/ *noun* [U] an occasion when people fight: *The fighting between the two gangs continued past midnight.*

fig·u·ra·tive /ˈfɪgyərətɪv/ *adj.* (*abbr.* **fig.**) (used about a word or an expression) not used with its exact meaning but used for giving an imaginative description or a special effect: *"He exploded when he heard the news" is a figurative use of the verb "to explode."* ☞ The opposite is **literal**. —**fig·u·ra·tive·ly** *adv.*

☆ **fig·ure¹** /ˈfɪgyər/ *noun* [C] **1** a written sign for a number (0 to 9): *Write the numbers in figures, not words.* **2** an amount (in numbers) or a price: *The unemployment figures are lower this month.* ○ *That figure of $10,000 is just a rough estimate.* **3** a well-known or important person: *an important political figure* **4** a person (that you cannot see very clearly): *Two figures were coming toward us in the dark.* **5** a person (in a picture or photograph): *There were two figures on the right of the picture that I didn't recognize.* **6** the shape of the human body, especially a woman's body: *She's almost 50, but she still has the figure of a teenager.* ○ *I'll lose my figure* (= I'll get fat) *if I eat too much chocolate.* ☞ Look at the note at **build**. **7** (*abbr.* **fig.**) a diagram or illustration used in a book to explain sth: *Figure 3 shows the major cities of Italy.*

IDM **facts and figures** ⇨ FACT

☆ **fig·ure²** /ˈfɪgyər/ *verb* **1** [T] **figure (that)** (*informal*) to think or guess sth: *I figured he was here because I saw his car outside.* **2** [T] to calculate: *to figure your income taxes* **3** [I] **figure (in sth)** to be included in sth; to be an important part of sth: *Women don't figure much in his novels.*

IDM **it/that figures** (*informal*) that is what I expected

PHRV **figure sb/sth out** to find an answer to sth or to understand sb

ˌfigure ˈeight *noun* [C] something in the shape of an 8

ˌfigure of ˈspeech *noun* [C] (*pl.* **figures of speech**) a word or expression used not with its original meaning but in an imaginative way to make a special effect ☞ Look at **figurative**.

☆ **file¹** /faɪl/ *noun* [C] **1** a collection of papers or information kept in a box or a cover: *Which file is that letter in?* **2** a collection of information or material on one subject that is stored in a computer or on a disk: *to open/close a file* **3** a metal tool with a rough surface that is used for making rough surfaces smooth: *a nail file*

IDM **in single file** ⇨ SINGLE¹

on file kept in a file: *We have all the information you need on file.*

the rank and file ⇨ RANK¹

☆ **file²** /faɪl/ *verb* **1** [T] **file sth (away)** to put in a file¹(1) : *File these letters under "Job Applications."* **2** [T] to send a form, report, etc. to a place where it is officially recorded: *to file criminal charges against sb* ○ *Your income tax return must be filed by April 15.* **3** [I,T] to use a file¹(3) to cut sth or make sth smooth: *to file*

your fingernails **4** [I] **file in, out, past, etc.** to walk or march in a line

IDM **file suit (against sb)** to send an official document to a court of law, saying that you intend to ask for money from sb because he/she did sth bad to you or said sth bad about you: *She filed suit against her former employer for discrimination.*

fi·let (*also* **fillet**) /fɪˈleɪ/ *noun* [C,U] (a piece of) fish with no bones in it

☆ **fill** /fɪl/ *verb* **1** [I,T] **fill (sth/sb) (with sth)** to make sth full or to become full: *The candidate's supporters completely filled the auditorium.* ○ *The news filled him with excitement.* ○ *The room filled with smoke within minutes.* **2** [T] to occupy a position or time: *That teaching position has just been filled* (= somebody has gotten the job).

PHRV **fill sth in** to write information on a form, etc.: *Please fill in your name and address here.* ○ *to fill in the blanks on a quiz*
fill sth out to complete a form, etc. by writing information on it: *to fill out a questionnaire*
fill (sth) up to become or to make sth completely full: *There weren't many people at first, but then the room filled up.* ○ *I need to fill up the car* (= with gasoline) *before we start on our trip.*

fil·let = FILET

fill·ing /ˈfɪlɪŋ/ *noun* **1** [C] the material that a dentist uses to fill a hole in a tooth: *a gold filling* **2** [C,U] food put inside a sandwich, pie, cake, etc. to make it taste good

ᶥ**filling ˌstation** *noun* [C] (*old-fashioned*) = GAS STATION

☆ **film¹** /fɪlm/ *noun* **1** [C,U] a roll of thin plastic that you use in a camera to take photographs: *a 35 millimeter film* ○ *I need to buy a new roll of film.* ○ *black-and-white film* ○ *color film* ○ *Fast film is better in this light.*

☞ picture at **camera**. You **load** a film into a camera and **rewind** it when it is finished. When the film is **developed**, you can have **prints** made from the **negatives**.

2 [C] a movie

☞ **Film** is usually used for serious works with important artistic value. **Movie** is usually used for more popular works: *a French avant-garde film* ○ *the latest action movie starring Sylvester Stallone.*

3 [usually sing.] a thin layer of a substance or material: *a film of oil*

☆ **film²** /fɪlm/ *verb* [I,T] to make a movie of an event, story, etc. with a camera: *A lot of westerns are filmed in Spain.*

fil·ter¹ /ˈfɪltər/ *noun* [C] **1** a piece of paper or other material with many small holes in it that is used for holding back solid substances from a liquid or gas that passes through it: *a coffee filter* ○ *an oil filter* **2** a piece of colored

glass that is used with a camera to hold back some types of light

fil·ter² /ˈfɪltər/ *verb* **1** [T] to pass a liquid through a filter¹(1) : *Do you filter your water?* **2** [I] **filter in, out, through, etc.** to move slowly: (*figurative*) *News of her illness filtered through to her friends.*

filth /fɪlθ/ *noun* [U] **1** disgusting dirt: *The room was covered in filth.* **2** extremely offensive words, pictures, etc. usually in books, magazines or movies

filth·y /ˈfɪlθi/ *adj.* (**filth·i·er**; **filth·i·est**) **1** very dirty: *They got completely filthy playing football in the rain.* **2** (used about language, books, movies, etc.) extremely unpleasant, often about sex

fin /fɪn/ *noun* [C] a part of a fish, shaped like a thin wing. Fish use fins for swimming.

☆ **fi·nal¹** /ˈfaɪnl/ *adj.* **1** (only *before* a noun) last (in a series): *This will be the final lesson of our course.* ○ *I don't want to miss the final episode of that series.* **2** not to be changed: *The judge's decision is always final.*

IDM **the last/final straw** ➪ STRAW

fi·nal² /ˈfaɪnl/ *noun* [C] **1** (*also* **finals**) the last game or match in a series of competitions or sports events: *Do you think the Lakers will make it to the NBA finals this year?* ○ *The finals of the swimming championship will be held in Chicago.* ☞ Look at **semifinal. 2** (*also* **final exam**) an examination that you take at the end of a course: *I'm studying hard for my finals.* ○ *I'm taking my history final tomorrow.*

fi·nal·e /fɪˈnæli; -ˈnɑli/ *noun* [C] the last part of a piece of music, an opera, a show, etc.

fi·nal·ist /ˈfaɪnl·ɪst/ *noun* [C] a person who is in the final²(1) of a competition ☞ Look at **semifinalist.**

fi·nal·ize /ˈfaɪnl·aɪz/ *verb* [T] to make firm decisions about plans, dates, etc.: *Have you finalized your vacation, plans yet?*

☆ **fi·nal·ly** /ˈfaɪnl·i/ *adv.* **1** after a long time or delay: *It was getting dark when the plane finally took off.* **2** (*formal*) (used at the beginning of a sentence when you have a list of things to say, especially in a speech) as a last point: *Finally, I would like to say how much we all enjoyed this evening.*

☆ **fi·nance¹** /ˈfaɪnæns; fəˈnæns/ *noun* **1** [U] the management of (public) money: *the Senate Finance Committee* ○ *an expert in finance* **2** **finances** [plural] the money a person, company, country, etc. has available to spend: *What are our finances like right now?* (= how much money do we have?)

☆ **fi·nance²** /ˈfaɪnæns; fəˈnæns/ *verb* [T] to provide the money to pay for sth: *Your trip will be financed by the company.*

☆ **fi·nan·cial** /fəˈnænʃl; faɪ-/ *adj.* connected with

F

tʃ	dʒ	v	θ	ð	s	z	ʃ
chin	June	van	thin	then	so	zoo	she

F

money: *The business got into financial difficulties.* ○ *If you plan to go to college, you'll probably have to apply for financial aid.* —**fi·nan·cial·ly** *adv.*

☆**find¹** /faɪnd/ *verb* [T] (*p.t., p.p.* **found** /faʊnd/) **1** to get back sth that you have lost: *Did you find the pen you lost?* ○ *I can't find my new sweater anywhere.* **2** to discover sth or get sth that you want (after a search): *After six months, she finally found a job.* ○ *Did you manage to find a good hotel?* ○ *Scientists still haven't found a cure for colds.* ○ *I hope you find an answer to your problem.* ☞ Notice the expressions **find time, find the money:** *I never seem to find time to write letters these days.* ○ *We'd like to go on vacation, but we can't find the money.* **3** to discover sth by chance: *Tom found a $20 bill in the park.* ○ *We went into the house and found her lying on the floor.* **4** to think or to have an opinion about sth (because of your own experience): *I find that book very difficult to understand.* ○ *We didn't find the movie at all funny.* ○ *How are you finding life as a student?*

☞ When we are expressing an opinion, we say **I think that…** NOT **I find that…**

IDM **find fault (with sb/sth)** to look for things that are wrong with sb/sth and complain about them

PHRV **find (sth) out** to get some information by asking or studying: *Did you find out how much the tickets cost?*

find sb out to discover that sb has done sth wrong: *He used a false name for years before he was found out.*

find² /faɪnd/ *noun* [C] a thing or a person that is unusually good or valuable: *This little gadget was a real find.*

find·er /ˈfaɪndər/ *noun* [C] a person who finds sth

find·ing /ˈfaɪndɪŋ/ *noun* [C] (usually plural) something that is discovered by research or investigation: *the findings of a survey, a report, a committee, etc.*

☆**fine¹** /faɪn/ *adj.* **1** (only *before* a noun) of very good quality, beautiful: *a fine piece of work* ○ *That's the finest painting I've ever seen by that artist.* **2** good enough: *"Do you want some more cream in your coffee?" "No, thanks, that's fine."* ○ *Don't cook anything special – a sandwich will be fine.* ○ *The hotel rooms were fine, but the food was terrible.* **3** in good health, or happy and comfortable: *"How are you?" "Fine, thanks."* ○ *"Do you want to trade places?" "No, thanks. I'm fine here."*

☞ We do not use meanings 2 and 3 in questions or in the negative form, so you CANNOT say *"Are you fine?"* or *"This isn't fine."*

4 thin: *shampoo for fine hair* ○ *a fine pencil* ☞ The opposite is **thick. 5** made of very small pieces, grains, etc.: *Salt is finer than sugar.* ☞

The opposite is **coarse. 6** difficult to see; very detailed: *The difference in meaning between those two words is very fine.* ○ *I couldn't understand the finer points of his argument.*

☆**fine²** /faɪn/ *adv.* (*informal*) very well: *Don't worry – you'll do just fine.*

☆**fine³** /faɪn/ *noun* [C] a sum of money that you have to pay for breaking a law or rule: *a parking fine* ○ *You'll get a fine if you park your car there.* ○ *He'll have to either pay a heavy fine or go to prison.*

fine⁴ /faɪn/ *verb* [T] **fine sb (for sth/for doing sth)** to make sb pay a sum of money because he/she has broken a law or rule: *He was fined $50 for speeding.*

fine ˈarts *noun* [plural] subjects such as painting, drawing, music, or making movies that you study at a school, college or university

fine·ly /ˈfaɪnli/ *adv.* **1** into small pieces: *finely chopped onions* **2** very delicately: *a finely tuned instrument*

fine ˈprint *noun* [U] a part or parts of a legal contract, document, etc. that contain important details that you might not notice: *Make sure you read the fine print before you sign anything.*

☆**fin·ger** /ˈfɪŋgər/ *noun* [C] one of the five parts at the end of each hand (or a glove): *little finger, ring finger, middle finger, index finger, thumb* ○ *Children learn to count on their fingers.*

☞ Sometimes we think of the thumb as one of the fingers; sometimes we contrast it: *Hold the pen between your finger and thumb.* The "fingers" on our feet are called **toes.**

IDM **give sb the finger** (*informal*) to make an offensive sign to sb by holding up your middle finger, to show that you are angry at him/her

keep your fingers crossed to hope that sb/sth will be successful or lucky: *Good luck on the test – I'll keep my fingers crossed for you!* ☞ Look also at **cross your fingers** at **cross². point a/the finger at sb/sth** ⇨ POINT²

snap your fingers ⇨ SNAP¹

fin·ger·nail /ˈfɪŋgərneɪl/ (*also* **nail**) *noun* [C] the hard parts on the ends of the fingers: *Your fingernails are filthy!*

fin·ger·print /ˈfɪŋgərprɪnt/ *noun* [C] **1** the mark made by the skin of a finger, used for identifying people: *The burglar left his fingerprints all over the house.* ○ *The police took the suspect's fingerprints.* **2** a mark on a wall, door, book, etc. made by a dirty finger

fin·ger·tip /ˈfɪŋgərtɪp/ *noun* [C] the end of a finger

IDM **have sth at your fingertips** to have sth ready for quick and easy use: *They asked some difficult questions but luckily I had all the facts at my fingertips.*

☆**fin·ish¹** /ˈfɪnɪʃ/ *verb* **1** [I,T] **finish (sth/doing sth)** to come or bring sth to an end or to reach

i	ɪ	ɛ	æ	ɑ	ɔ	ʌ	ʊ	u
see	sit	ten	cat	hot	saw	cup	put	too

the end of sth: *The U.S. sprinters finished first, second and third.* ○ *Finish your work quickly!* ○ *Did you finish typing that letter?* **2** [T] **finish sth (off/up)** to eat, drink or use the last part of sth: *Finish your milk, Tommy!* **3** [T] **finish sth (off/up)** to complete the last details of sth or make sth perfect: *She stayed up all night to finish up the article she was writing.*

PHRV **finish sb/sth off** (*informal*) to kill sb/sth: *The cat pounced and finished off the mouse.* ○ (*figurative*) *It was losing his job that really finished him off* (= depressed him).

fin·ish² /ˈfɪnɪʃ/ *noun* [C] **1** (used especially about a race) the end: *The last race was a very close finish* (= the runners at the front were close together at the end of the race). ☞ The opposite is **start**. **2** (used especially about wood and furniture) the feel or look that sth has when it has been polished, etc.: *This table has a beautiful finish.*

☆ **fin·ished** /ˈfɪnɪʃt/ *adj.* **1** (not before a noun) **finished (with sb/sth)** having stopped doing sth, using sth or dealing with sb/sth: *Aren't you finished in there yet? Hurry up!* ○ *I'll borrow that book when you're finished with it.* **2** (not before a noun) not able to continue: *The business is finished – there's no more money.* **3** made; completed: *the finished product, article, etc.*

fir /fər/ (*also* **ˈfir tree**) *noun* [C] a straight tree that keeps its thin sharp leaves (**needles**) in the winter

☆ **fire¹** /ˈfaɪər/ *noun* **1** [U] hot bright flames produced by sth that is burning: *Many animals are afraid of fire.* **2** [C,U] burning that destroys and is out of control: *Fire fighters struggled for three hours to put out the fire.* ○ *forest fires.* ○ *You need to insure your house against fire.* ○ *The furniture caught fire within seconds* (= started burning). ○ *Did someone set fire to that pile of wood?* ○ *Help! The frying pan's on fire!* **3** [C] burning wood or coal to warm people or cook food: *They lit a fire to keep warm.* ○ *It's cold – don't let the fire go out!* ○ *Let's roast hot dogs over the fire.* **4** [U] shooting from guns: *The soldiers were under fire from all sides.*

IDM **open fire** ⇨ OPEN³

☆ **fire²** /ˈfaɪər/ *verb* **1** [I,T] **fire (sth) (at sb/sth); fire (sth) into sth** to shoot with a gun or shoot bullets, etc. from a gun: *"Fire!" shouted the officer.* ○ *Can you hear the guns firing?* ○ *He fired his gun at the ceiling.* ○ *They fired rubber bullets into the crowd.* **2** [T] to say that sb can no longer work for you (because of bad work, bad behavior, etc.): *He was fired for always being late.* **3** [T] **fire sth at sb** to ask questions, or make remarks, quickly and aggressively: *If you stop firing questions at me, I might be able to answer!* **4** [T] **fire sb with sth** to produce a strong feeling in sb: *Her speech fired me with determination.*

ˈfire aˌlarm *noun* [C] a bell or other signal to warn people that there is a fire: *If the fire alarm goes off, leave the building immediately.*

fire·arm /ˈfaɪərɑrm/ *noun* [C, usually pl.] a gun that you can carry: *The prison guards carry firearms.*

fire·crack·er /ˈfaɪərˌkrækər/ *noun* [C] a very small container filled with chemicals, that explodes with a sudden loud noise when you set fire to it

☆ **ˈfire deˌpartment** *noun* [C] an organization of people trained to put out (= stop) fires: *Dial 911 to call the fire department.*

ˈfire ˌengine (*also* **ˈfire truck**) *noun* [C] a special truck that carries equipment for fighting large fires

ˈfire esˌcape *noun* [C] a special staircase on the outside of a building that people can run down if there is a fire

ˈfire exˌtinguisher (*also* **extinguisher**) *noun* [C] a metal container with water or chemicals inside that you use for fighting small fires

☆ **fire·fight·er** /ˈfaɪərˌfaɪtər/ *noun* [C] a person whose job is to fight fires

☞ People of both sexes now work in most jobs, so nowadays it is usually not necessary to use different words for men and women doing the same job. Some people, especially women, consider names of jobs that mention a person's sex old-fashioned or offensive. For example, instead of **policeman** or **policewoman** we can say **police officer**. Instead of **mailman** we can say **letter carrier**, and instead of **stewardess** we can say **flight attendant**.

ˈfire ˌhydrant (*also* **hydrant**) *noun* [C] a piece of metal equipment on a sidewalk, connected to a pipe from which water can be taken for putting out fires

fire·man /ˈfaɪərmən/ *noun* [C] (*pl.* **fire·men** /-mən/) a man whose job is to fight fires ☞ Look at the note at **firefighter**.

fireplace

knickknacks

mantel

poker

fire·place /ˈfaɪərpleɪs/ *noun* [C] the open place in a room (at the bottom of a chimney) where you light a fire

ˈfire ˌstation *noun* [C] a building where fire

F

engines are kept and firefighters wait to be called

fire·wood /ˈfaɪərwʊd/ *noun* [U] wood used for burning on fires

fire·work /ˈfaɪərwərk/ *noun* [C, usually pl.] a small container with chemicals inside that burns or explodes with colored lights and loud noises, used for entertainment: *a fireworks display*

fireworks

ˈfiring squad *noun* [C]
a group of soldiers who have been ordered to shoot and kill a prisoner

☆ **firm¹** /fərm/ *noun* [C] a business company: *a law firm* (= that lawyers work for)

☆ **firm²** /fərm/ *adj.* **1** able to stay the same shape when pressed; fairly hard: *a firm mattress* **2** strong or steady or not likely to change: *She kept a firm grip on her mother's hand.* ○ *Do you have a firm date for your wedding yet?* ○ *We made a firm decision – we're not going to change it now.* ○ *I have a firm offer of a job in New York.* **3 firm (with sb)** insisting that people do what you want: *He's very firm with his kids.* —**firm·ly** *adv.* —**firm·ness** *noun* [U]

☆ **first¹** /fərst/ *det.* coming before all others; that has not happened before: *his first day at school* ○ *their first baby* ○ *You won first prize!* ○ *first impressions* ○ *The first time she went skiing, she broke her leg.* ○ *King Charles I* (= King Charles the First)

IDM at first glance/sight when first seen or examined: *At first glance, it looked like solid gold.* ○ *When I met Rob, it was love at first sight.*

first thing as early as possible: *I'll call her first thing tomorrow morning.*

☆ **first²** /fərst/ *adv.* **1** before any others: *Sue arrived first at the party.* ○ *Our team finished first in the race* (= we won). ○ *Do you want to go first or second?* **2** before doing anything else: *I'll come out later. I have to finish my homework first.* **3** for the first time: *Where did you first meet your husband?* **4** at the beginning: *When I first started my job, I hated it.* **5** (used for introducing the first thing in a list): *There are several people I would like to thank: first, my mother.*

IDM at first at the beginning: *At first I thought he was joking, but then I realized he was serious.*

come first to be more important (to sb) than anything else: *Her family has always come first.*

first and foremost more than anything else; most importantly: *He worked in television, but he was a stage actor first and foremost.*

first of all as the first thing (to be done or

said): *First of all, make sure your hands are clean.*

☆ **first³** /fərst/ *noun, pron.* **1** [C] (*pl.* **first**) the first person or thing, people or things: *Are we the first to arrive?* ○ *They enjoyed the vacation – their first in ten years.* **2** [sing.] an important event that is happening for the first time: *This operation is a first in medical history.*

☆ **first ˈaid** *noun* [U] medical help that you give to sb who is hurt or sick before the doctor arrives

first ˈbase *noun* [sing.] **1** (in baseball) the first point (**base**) on the field that a player must touch after hitting the ball **2** (*informal*) the first part of a project, process, etc.: *If the boss is in a bad mood, you won't even get to first base with your proposal.*

first ˈclass *noun* [U] **1** the most comfortable and expensive area on a plane, train, etc.: *The seats in first class are a lot bigger than these.* **2** the class of mail, especially for letters, that is delivered most quickly ☞ Look at **parcel post.**

first-ˈclass *adj.* (usually *before* a noun) **1** excellent, of the best quality: *a first-class player* **2** giving or using the best or most expensive type of service: *the first-class section of an airplane* ○ *How much does a first-class stamp cost?* —**first class** *adv.*: *to travel first class* ○ *If you send the package first class, it will get there sooner.*

first ˈcousin *noun* [C] = COUSIN

first-deˈgree *adj.* (only *before* a noun) (used about crimes) of the worst or most serious kind: *He was charged with first-degree murder.*

first ˈfloor (*also* **ground floor**) *noun* [C] the floor of a building on street level: *I live in an apartment on the first floor/a first-floor apartment.*

first·hand /ˌfərstˈhænd/ *adj., adv.* (used about information, experience, a story, etc.) heard, seen or learned directly, not from other people: *He gave me a firsthand account of the accident* (= he had seen it). ○ *I've experienced the problem firsthand, so I know exactly how you feel.*

first ˈlady (*also* **First Lady**) *noun* [C] (*pl.* **first ladies**) the wife of the President of the U.S. or of the governor of a state

☆ **first name** *noun* [C] the name that is given to a person when he/she is born: *"What's Mrs. Brown's first name?" "Alice, I think."* ☞ Look at the note at **name¹.**

IDM be on a first-name basis (with sb) to know sb well enough to call them by their first name

the ˌfirst ˈperson *noun* [sing.] **1** (*grammar*) the words such as "I," "me," "we," and the verb forms that go with them: *"I am" is the first person singular of the verb "to be."* **2** the style of telling a story as if it happened to you: *The author writes in the first person* (= he/she

writes, "I..."). ☞ Look at the note at **White House**.

,**first-**'**rate** *adj.* excellent; of the best quality

fis·cal /'fɪskl/ *adj.* (only *before a noun*) connected with money that the government receives and spends: *the government's fiscal policies*

,**fiscal** '**year** *noun* [C] a period of twelve months that a company or government uses to calculate its accounts, taxes, etc.

☆**fish¹** /fɪʃ/ *noun* (*pl.* **fish** or **fish·es**) **1** [C] an animal that lives, breathes and swims in water: *How many fish did you catch?* ○ (*formal*) *exotic fishes* (= types or species of fish) *of the Caribbean.*

☞ The plural form **fish** is more common. **Fishes** is used in formal or technical English when we are talking about different types of fish.

2 [U] fish (1) as food: *fresh fish*

☆**fish²** /fɪʃ/ *verb* [I] **1 fish (for sth)** to try to catch fish with rods, nets, etc.: *He's fishing for trout.*

☞ When we are talking about spending time fishing, we usually say **go fishing**: *They often go fishing on weekends.*

2 fish (around) for sth to search for sth in water or in a deep or hidden place: *She fished (around) for her keys in the bottom of her bag.*
PHRV **fish for sth** to try to get sth you want in an indirect way: *to fish for a compliment*
fish sth out (of sth) to take or pull sth out (of sth) especially after searching for it: *After the accident, they fished the car out of the river.* ○ *She fished a pair of socks out of the bottom of the drawer.*

fish·er·man /'fɪʃərmən/ *noun* [C] (*pl.* **fish·er·men** /'fɪʃərmən/) a person who catches fish as a job or as a sport

fish·ing /'fɪʃɪŋ/ *noun* [U] catching fish as a job, sport or hobby: *Fishing is a major industry in New England.*

'**fishing rod** (*also* '**fishing pole**) *noun* [C] a long thin stick with a long string and a hook on it for catching fish

'**fish stick** *noun* [C] a small square or long piece of fish that is covered in very small pieces of dried bread: *a box of frozen fish sticks*

fish·y /'fɪʃi/ *adj.* (**fish·i·er**; **fish·i·est**) **1** (*informal*) seeming suspicious or untrue: *The police thought his story sounded pretty fishy.* **2** of or like a fish, especially in taste or smell: *a fishy smell*

☆**fist** /fɪst/ *noun* [C] a hand with the fingers closed together tightly: *She clenched her fists.*

☆**fit¹** /fɪt/ *adj.* (**fit·ter**; **fit·test**) **1 fit for sb/sth; fit to do sth** good enough; suitable: *These houses are not fit (for people) to live in.* ○ *a meal fit for a king* **2** in good physical health (especially because of exercise): *He keeps physically fit by*

jogging five miles a day. ☞ The expression **in (good) shape** is more common than fit in this sense.

☆**fit²** /fɪt/ *verb* (*pres. part.* **fit·ting**; *p.t., p.p.* **fit** or, especially in the passive **fit·ted**) **1** [I,T] to be the right size or shape for sb/sth: *These jeans don't fit.* ○ *This dress doesn't fit me anymore.* ○ *This key doesn't fit the lock.* ○ *My car won't fit into your garage.* **2** [T] **fit sb/sth in/into/on/ onto sth** to find enough space for sb/sth: *Can you fit one more person in the car?* ○ *I can't fit all these books onto the shelf.* **3** [T] to put or fasten sth in the right place: *I can't fit these pieces of the model together.* **4** [T] **fit sth with sth** (often passive) to put or attach sth, such as a part or a piece of equipment, onto or into sth: *a car that has been fitted with an alarm* **5** [T] to be or make sb/sth right or suitable: *The punishment should fit the crime.*
PHRV **fit sb/sth in; fit sb/sth in/into sth** to find time to see sb or to do sth: *The doctor managed to fit me in this morning.* ○ *You're tired because you're trying to fit too much into one day.*
fit in (with sb/sth) to be able to live, work, etc. in an easy and natural way (with sb/sth): *The new girl found it difficult to fit in (with the other kids) at school.* ○ *I can easily change my plans to fit in with yours.*

fit³ /fɪt/ *noun* **1** [sing.] (usually after an adjective) the way in which sth (e.g. a piece of clothing) fits: *a good, bad, tight, etc. fit* **2** [C] (*old-fashioned*) a sudden loss of consciousness with movements that are not controlled and sometimes violent ☞ **Seizure** is more common nowadays. **3** [C] a sudden (usually short) attack of illness: *a fit of coughing* **4** [C] a sudden period of activity or violent feeling: *a fit of laughter, energy, etc.* ○ *a fit of anger*
IDM **have/throw a fit** (*informal*) to suddenly become very angry, shocked, etc.: *Dad'll have a fit when he finds out we got arrested!*

☆**fit·ness** /'fɪtnəs/ *noun* [U] **1** the condition of being fit(2) : *physical fitness* **2 fitness for sth/ to do sth** the quality of being suitable: *The managers were not sure about his fitness for the job.*

fit·ting /'fɪtɪŋ/ *adj.* (*formal*) right; suitable

☆**five** /faɪv/ *number* 5; one more than four ☞ Look also at **fifth** (= 5th). For examples of how to use numbers in sentences, look at **six**. Look also at Appendix 2.

five- /faɪv/ (used in compounds) having five of the thing mentioned: *a five-day week* ○ *a five-hour flight*

☆**fix¹** /fɪks/ *verb* [T] **1** to repair: *The electrician's coming to fix the light switch.* **2** to decide or arrange sth: *The price has been fixed at $30.* ○ *Have you fixed a date for the party?* **3 fix sth (for sb)** to prepare sth (especially food or drink) for sb: *Can I fix you a drink/a drink for you?* **4** (usually passive) (*informal*) to arrange

the result of sth in a way that is not honest or fair: *The race was fixed* (= the result was arranged before it happened).

IDM **be fixing to do sth** (*informal*) (used especially in the southern U.S.) to get ready to do sth: *I'm fixing to go to the post office. Do you need any stamps?*

fix your hair to arrange your hair so that it looks attractive

PHR V **fix sth up** to repair or improve sth so that it is suitable to use: *My brother likes to fix up old cars.*

fix sb up (with sth) (*informal*) to arrange for sb to have sth: *I can fix you up with a job and a place to stay.*

fix² /fɪks/ *noun* [C] **1** [usually sing.] (*informal*) a difficult situation: *I was in a real fix – I'd locked my keys inside the car.* **2** (*slang*) an injection of a drug such as heroin

fix·a·tion /fɪkˈseɪʃn/ *noun* [C] a feeling (about sb/sth) that is too strong and not normal

☆ **fixed** /fɪkst/ *adj.* **1** firmly attached in a place so that it will not move: *All the seats are fixed to the floor.* **2** already decided: *a fixed date, rent, price, etc.* **3** not changing: *He has such fixed ideas that you can't discuss anything with him.* ○ *a fixed income*

fix·ture /ˈfɪkstʃər/ *noun* [C] **1** [usually pl.] a piece of furniture or equipment that is attached inside a house or building and sold with it: *a light fixture* **2** a person or thing that always seems to be at a particular place and has become connected with that place in people's minds: *Mr. Carlson is a permanent fixture in the coffee shop.*

fizz¹ /fɪz/ *verb* [I] to produce many small bubbles and/or make a soft sound

fizz² /fɪz/ *noun* [U] the bubbles in a liquid and the sound they make: *This cola has lost its fizz.*

fiz·zle /ˈfɪzl/ *verb*

PHR V **fizzle out** to end in a weak or disappointing way: *The party started well, but it fizzled out around 11:00.*

fizz·y /ˈfɪzi/ *adj.* (**fiz·zi·er**; **fiz·zi·est**) (used about a drink) containing many small bubbles

flab·ber·gast·ed /ˈflæbərgæstəd/ *adj.* (*informal*) extremely surprised

flab·by /ˈflæbi/ *adj.* (**flab·bi·er**; **flab·bi·est**) **1** (used about a person) having too much soft loose flesh **2** (used about muscles, arms, legs, etc.) too soft

☆ **flag¹** /flæg/ *noun* [C] a piece of cloth with a pattern or picture on it, often attached to a pole (**flagpole**) or rope and used as a symbol of a country, club, etc. or as a signal: *a flag flying over the state capitol* ○ *All the kids were waving flags.*

flag² /flæg/ *verb* [I] (**flag·ging**; **flagged**) to become tired or less strong or active

fla·grant /ˈfleɪɡrənt/ *adj.* (only *before* a noun) easily seen to be bad and shocking: *a flagrant violation of the law*

flag·ship /ˈflæɡʃɪp/ *noun* [C] **1** the most important ship in a group of military ships **2** [usually sing.] the most important in a group of products, stores, etc.: *Macy's flagship store in New York City*

flail /fleɪl/ *verb* [I,T] to wave or swing around without control: *The insect's legs were flailing in the air.* ○ *The drowning child flailed his arms above his head.*

flair /flɛr/ *noun* **1 (a) flair for sth** [sing.] a natural ability to do sth well: *She has a flair for languages* (= she's good at learning them). **2** [U] the quality of being interesting or having style: *a poster designed with her usual flair*

flake¹ /fleɪk/ *noun* [C] **1** a small thin piece of sth: *snowflakes* ○ *corn flakes* **2** (*slang*) a person who acts in a strange or crazy way and forgets things easily

flake² /fleɪk/ *verb* [I] **flake (off)** to come off in flakes¹(1) : *The paint is flaking off the wall.*

flak·y /ˈfleɪki/ *adj.* (**flak·i·er**; **flak·i·est**) **1** made of flakes¹(1) or that can easily break into flakes: *flaky pie crust* ○ *dry, flaky skin* **2** (*slang*) behaving in a strange or crazy way and forgetting things easily

flam·boy·ant /flæmˈbɔɪənt/ *adj.* **1** (used about a person) acting in a loud, confident way so that other people will notice **2** very easily noticed: *flamboyant colors* —**flam·boy·ance** /-ˈbɔɪəns/ *noun* [U] —**flam·boy·ant·ly** *adv.*

☆ **flame** /fleɪm/ *noun* [C,U] an area of bright burning gas that comes from sth that is on fire: *the flame of a candle* ○ *The house was in flames when the fire engine arrived.* ○ *The car rolled down a hill and burst into flames* (= suddenly began to burn strongly). ○ *a huge ball of flame* ☞ picture at **candle**.

flam·ing /ˈfleɪmɪŋ/ *adj.* (only *before* a noun) burning brightly: *a flaming torch*

fla·min·go /fləˈmɪŋɡoʊ/ *noun* [C] (*pl.* **fla·min·gos** or **fla·min·goes**) a large bird that lives near water in warm areas and has long thin legs, a long neck and bright pink feathers

flam·ma·ble /ˈflæməbl/ *adj.* able to burn easily ☞ The opposite is **nonflammable**. **Inflammable** has the same meaning as flammable.

flank¹ /flæŋk/ *noun* [C] (used about an animal or an army ready for battle) the side

flank² /flæŋk/ *verb* [T] (often passive) to be at the side or sides of: *The governor was flanked by bodyguards.*

flan·nel /ˈflænl/ *noun* [U] a type of soft wool or cotton cloth

flap¹ /flæp/ *noun* [C] **1** a piece of material that is attached to sth at one side only, often covering an opening: *a tent flap* ○ *a pocket flap* **2** [usually sing.] (*informal*) a state of worry or nervous excitement: *the latest flap over tax increases*

flap² /flæp/ *verb* (**flap·ping**; **flapped**) [I,T] to move sth up and down or from side to side; to

move in this way, especially in the wind: *The sails were flapping in the wind.* ○ *The bird flapped its wings and flew away.*

flap·jack /'flæpdʒæk/ *noun* [C] = PANCAKE

flare¹ /flɛr/ *verb* [I] **1** to burn with a sudden bright flame **2** (used about a person's temper, anger, violence, etc.) to start suddenly or become worse: *Tempers flared at Tuesday's school board meeting.*

PHRV flare up 1 (used about a fire) to suddenly burn more fiercely **2** (used about violence, anger, pain, a person's temper, etc.) to start suddenly or become worse: *My arthritis is flaring up again.*

flare² /flɛr/ *noun* [C] **1** a sudden bright light or flame **2** a thing that produces a bright light or flame, used especially as a signal

flared /flɛrd/ *adj.* (used about pants and skirts) becoming wider toward the bottom

☆ **flash¹** /flæʃ/ *noun* [C] **1** a sudden bright light that comes and goes quickly: *a flash of lightning* **2** a sudden ability to guess, understand or imagine sth): *In a flash of inspiration, I saw what the answer must be.* **3** a bright light that you use with a camera for taking photographs when the light is not good; the apparatus for producing this light: *The light's not very good. You'll need the flash.* ○ *My new camera has a built-in flash.* ☞ picture at **camera**.

☆ **flash²** /flæʃ/ *verb* **1** [I,T] to produce a sudden bright light or to make sth produce it: *The neon lights were flashing on and off all night.* ○ *That truck driver's flashing his lights at us* (in order to tell us sth) **2** [I] to move very fast: *I saw something flash past the window.* ○ *Thoughts kept flashing through my mind and I couldn't sleep.* **3** [T] to show sth quickly: *The detective flashed his card and went straight in.* **4** [T] to send a particular look toward sb (suddenly, and only for a moment): *He flashed a smile at her and drove away.*

PHRV flash back (used about a person's thoughts) to return suddenly to a time in the past: *Something he said made my mind flash back to my childhood.*

flash·back /'flæʃbæk/ *noun* **1** [C,U] a part of a movie, play, etc. that shows sth that happened before the main story **2** [C] a time when a person's thoughts return suddenly to an event in the past, especially one that was very frightening

'**flash card** (*also* '**flashcard**) *noun* [C] a card with a word or words, numbers, or a picture on it that you look at to help you learn or remember sth

,**flash** '**flood** *noun* [C] a sudden flood of water, usually caused by heavy rain

☆ **flash·light** /'flæʃlaɪt/ *noun* [C] a small electric light that you carry in your hand. A flashlight runs on batteries: *Shine the flashlight under the couch and see if you can find my ring.* ☞ picture at **light**.

flash·y /'flæʃi/ *adj.* (**flash·i·er**; **flash·i·est**) too bright or big and intended to attract attention, especially to make people think that the owner is rich: *a flashy car* ○ *flashy clothes*

flask /flæsk/ *noun* [C] **1** a bottle with a narrow neck that is used in a laboratory **2** a small flat bottle that is used for carrying alcohol in a pocket

"Oh, no! I've got a **flat tire!**"

flat

☆ **flat¹** /flæt/ *adj.* (**flat·ter**; **flat·test**) **1** smooth and level, with no parts that are raised above the rest: *The countryside in Kansas is extremely flat* (= there are no hills). ○ *I need a flat surface to write this letter on.* ○ *a flat roof* **2** not high or deep: *You need flat shoes for walking.* **3** (used about a tire) without enough air in it: *I drove over some glass and got a flat tire.* **4** (used about a drink) not fresh because it has lost its bubbles: *Open a new bottle. This cola is flat.* **5** (*symbol* b) (in music) half a tone lower than the stated note: *a symphony in B flat* ☞ Look at **sharp¹**(10). **6** (in music) lower than the correct note: *That last note was flat. Can you sing it again?* ☞ Look at **sharp¹**(11). **7** that will not change; firm (used about sth that you say or decide) : *He answered our request with a flat "No."* **8** (used about the cost of sth) that is the same for everybody; that is fixed: *We charge a flat fee of $20, however long you stay.* **9** (used about business, trade, etc.) not increasing or active: *Sales have been flat for the last three months.*

☆ **flat²** /flæt/ *adv.* **1** in a level position: *She lay flat on her back in the sunshine.* ○ *He fell flat on his face in the mud.* **2** lower than the correct note: *You're singing flat.* ☞ Look at **sharp²**(2). **3** (used for emphasizing how quickly sth is done) in exactly the time mentioned and no longer: *She can get up and out of the house in ten minutes flat.*

IDM fall flat (used about a joke, a story, an event, etc.) to fail to produce the effect that you wanted

flat out 1 (*informal*) in a direct way; absolutely: *I told the boss flat out that I quit.* ○ *That's just flat out wrong!* **2** as fast as possible; without stopping: *He's been working flat out for two weeks and he needs a break.*

flat³ /flæt/ *noun* [C] **1** (*symbol* b) (in music) a note which is half a step lower than the note with the same letter ☞ Look at **sharp³**. **2** a tire on a car, etc. that has no air in it: *I had a*

F

flat on the way to work yesterday. **3** (*BrE*) = APARTMENT

flat·ly /'flætli/ *adv.* **1** in a way that shows no interest **2** in a direct way; absolutely: *He flatly denied the allegations.*

flat·ten /'flætn/ *verb* [I,T] **flatten (sth) (out)** to become flat or to make sth flat: *The country-side flattens out as you drive west.* ○ *The storms flattened crops all over the state.*

flat·ter /'flætər/ *verb* [T] **1** to praise sb too much because you want to please him/her or because you want to get an advantage for yourself **2** (*usually passive*) to give pleasure or honor to sb: *I felt very flattered when they gave me the job.*

flat·ter·ing /'flætərɪŋ/ *adj.* making sb look or sound more attractive or important than he/ she really is

flat·ter·y /'flætəri/ *noun* [U] praise that you do not really mean

flaunt /flɔnt/ *verb* [T] to show sth that you are proud of so that other people will admire it

☆ **fla·vor**[1] /'fleɪvər/ *noun* [C,U] **1** the taste and smell (of food): *Do you think a little salt would improve the flavor?* ○ *ten different flavors of yogurt* ○ *yogurt in ten different flavors* **2** the particular quality or character of sth: *The hotel's architecture gives it a real Southern flavor.*

fla·vor[2] /'fleɪvər/ *verb* [T] to give flavor to sth: *a strawberry-flavored milkshake* ○ *I flavored the soup with pepper and parsley.*

☆ **fla·vor·ing** /'fleɪvərɪŋ/ *noun* [C,U] something that you add to food or drink to give it a particular taste

flaw /flɔ/ *noun* [C] **1** a mark or crack in an object that means that it is not perfect **2** a mistake in sth that makes it not satisfactory: *a flaw in an argument* **3** a bad quality in sb's character

flawed /flɔd/ *adj.* with a fault or weakness so that it is not perfect

flaw·less /'flɔləs/ *adj.* perfect

flea /fli/ *noun* [C] a very small jumping insect without wings that lives on animals, e.g. cats and dogs. Fleas bite people and animals and make them scratch.

'flea ,market *noun* [C] a sale, often in an outdoor place, where people sell old and used goods

fleck /flɛk/ *noun* [C] a tiny mark on sth; a tiny piece of sth

flee /fli/ *verb* [I,T] (*p.t., p.p.* **fled** /flɛd/) to run away or escape from sth: *When the hunter fired his gun, the deer turned and fled.* ○ *The man whom the police want to interview has fled the country.*

fleet /flit/ *noun* [C] **1** a group of ships or boats that are sailing together **2** a group of vehicles (especially taxis, buses or aircraft) that are traveling together or owned by one person or company

fleet·ing /'flitɪŋ/ *adj.* passing quickly; lasting only a short time: *I just caught a fleeting glimpse of the burglar.*

☆ **flesh** /flɛʃ/ *noun* [U] **1** the soft part of a human or animal body (around the bones and under the skin) ☞ Flesh that we eat is called **meat**. **2** the part of a fruit or vegetable that is soft and can be eaten

flew *p.t.* of FLY[2]

flex /flɛks/ *verb* [T] to bend or move a leg, arm, muscle, etc. in order to exercise it

flex·i·ble /'flɛksəbl/ *adj.* **1** able to bend easily without breaking **2** that can change or be changed in order to suit different situations or conditions ☞ The opposite is **inflexible**. —**flex·i·bil·i·ty** *noun* [U]

flick[1] /flɪk/ *verb* **1** [I,T] to move, or to make sth move, with a quick sudden movement: *The frog's tongue flicked out and caught the fly.* ○ *She flicked the switch and the light came on.* **2** [T] to hit sb/sth lightly and quickly

PHRV flick sth away; flick sth off sth to remove sth with a quick movement of your hand or finger

flick/flip through sth to turn over the pages of a book, magazine, etc. quickly

flick[2] /flɪk/ *noun* [C] **1** a quick sudden movement or light hit **2** (*informal*) a movie

flick·er[1] /'flɪkər/ *verb* [I] **1** (used about a light or a flame) to burn or shine in a weak or unsteady way: *The candle flickered and went out.* **2** to move lightly and quickly up and down or backwards and forwards: *His eyelids flickered for a second and then he lay still.*

flick·er[2] /'flɪkər/ *noun* [C, *usually sing.*] **1** a flickering movement **2** a slight feeling of sth: *a flicker of hope*

flies /flaɪz/ *pl.* of FLY[2]

☆ **flight** /flaɪt/ *noun* **1** [C] a trip in an airplane, etc.: *The captain and crew hope that you enjoyed the flight.* ○ *a direct flight* ○ *a scheduled flight* ○ *a charter flight* ○ *a manned space flight to Mars* **2** [C] an airplane that takes you on a particular trip: *Flight number 340 to New York is boarding now* (= is ready for passengers to get on it). **3** [U] the action of flying: *It's unusual to see swans in flight* (= when they are flying). **4** [C,U] the act of running away or escaping **5** [C] a number of stairs or steps leading up or down: *a flight of stairs*

☆ **'flight at,tendant** *noun* [C] a person whose job is to help the passengers on an airplane and serve them drinks, etc. ☞ Look at the note at **firefighter**.

flim·sy /'flɪmzi/ *adj.* (**flim·si·er; flim·si·est**) **1** (used about material) too light and thin **2** (used about an object) not strong; easily broken **3** weak; not convincing you that it is true: *He gave a flimsy excuse for his absence.*

flinch /flɪntʃ/ *verb* [I] to make a slight movement backwards because of sth painful or frightening

ər	ɪr	ɛr	ɑr	ɔr	ʊr	ʒ	h	ŋ
bird	near	hair	car	north	tour	vision	hat	sing

fling¹ /flɪŋ/ verb [T] (p.t., p.p. **flung** /flʌŋ/) to throw sb/sth suddenly or with great force: *She flung her book on the floor and rushed out.*

fling² /flɪŋ/ noun [C] (*informal*) a short period of fun and pleasure

flint /flɪnt/ noun [U] very hard gray stone that produces small flames (**sparks**) when you strike it against metal or other stone

flip /flɪp/ verb (**flip·ping; flipped**) **1** [I,T] to turn with a quick movement: *She flipped the book open and started to read.* **2** [T] to throw sth into the air and make it turn over: *Let's flip a coin to see who starts.* **3** (*also* **flip out**) [I] (*informal*) to become very angry or excited
PHRV **flick/flip through sth** ➪ FLICK¹

flip·pant /ˈflɪpənt/ adj. not serious or respectful enough about things that are important

flip·per /ˈflɪpər/ noun [C] **1** a flat limb that some sea animals use for swimming **2** a rubber shoe shaped like an animal's flipper (1) that people wear so that they can swim better (especially underwater): *a pair of flippers*

flirt¹ /flərt/ verb [I] **1** to behave in a way that suggests you find sb attractive and are trying to attract him/her: *Who was that guy Suzy was flirting with at the party?* **2 flirt with sth** to think about doing sth (but not very seriously)

flirt² /flərt/ noun [C] a person who often flirts¹(1)

flit /flɪt/ verb [I] (**flit·ting, flit·ted**) to fly or move quickly from one place to another

float/sink

floating sinking

☆**float¹** /floʊt/ verb [I] **1** to stay on the surface of a liquid and not sink; to move gently on the surface of a liquid: *Cork floats in water.* ○ *There was something floating near the bank of the river.* **2** to move slowly through the air: *A leaf floated gently down to the ground.*

float² /floʊt/ noun [C] **1** a truck or other vehicle that is decorated and used in a procession (**a parade**) **2** a drink that has a ball (**scoop**) of ice cream floating in it: *a root beer float* **3** a light floating object used on a fishing line or net

flock¹ /flɑk/ noun [C] **1** a group of birds, sheep or goats ☛ Look at **herd**. **2** a large number of people: *Flocks of tourists visit Florida every summer.*

flock² /flɑk/ verb [I] to gather or go somewhere in large numbers: *People áre flocking to the state fair this weekend.*

flog·ging /ˈflɑgɪŋ; ˈflɔgɪŋ/ noun [C,U] hitting sb with a whip or stick as a punishment

☆**flood¹** /flʌd/ verb **1** [I,T] to fill a place with water; to be filled or overflow with water: *The river burst its banks and flooded the valley.* ○ *Our basement flooded after last week's storm.* **2** [T] **flood sb/sth (with sth)** to go or send sth somewhere in large numbers: *The station has been flooded with complaints from angry viewers.* ○ *Angry viewers flooded the station with complaints.* **3** [I] **flood across, in, into, through, etc.** to arrive in large numbers: *Entries for the contest have been flooding in.* ○ *Refugees flooded across the border.* **4** [I,T] (used about a thought, feeling, etc.) to fill sb's mind suddenly: *At the end of the day, all his worries came flooding back.*

☆**flood²** /flʌd/ noun [C] **1** (*also* **floods** [plural]) a large amount of water (from a river, the ocean, etc.) that covers an area which should be dry: *Many people have been forced to leave their homes because of the floods.* ☛ Look also at **flash flood**. **2** a large number or amount: *She received a flood of letters after the accident.*

flood·light /ˈflʌdlaɪt/ noun [C] a powerful light that is used for lighting sports grounds, the outside of public buildings, etc.

flood·lit /ˈflʌdlɪt/ adj. lit by floodlights: *a floodlit stadium*

☆**floor** /flɔr/ noun **1** [C, usually sing.] the flat surface that you walk on indoors: *Don't come in – there's broken glass on the floor!* ○ *There aren't enough chairs so some people will have to sit on the floor.* ○ *to sweep the floor* ○ *a wooden floor* ☛ Look at the note at **ground**. **2** [C, usually sing.] the ground or surface at the bottom of the ocean, a forest, etc.: *the ocean floor* **3** [C] a level in a building: *The restrooms are on the second floor.*

☛ In the U.S., the floor that is at street level is called the **first floor** or the **ground floor**.

4 the floor [sing.] the area in a large room where the members of an official committee, etc. sit: *a fierce debate on the Senate floor*

flop /flɑp/ verb [I] (**flop·ping; flopped**) **1** to move or fall in a heavy or an awkward way: *I was so tired that all I could do was flop down onto the couch and watch TV.* **2** (used about a book, movie, album, etc.) to be unsuccessful with the public

flop² /flɑp/ noun [C] something that is not a success; a failure: *Her first novel was very successful, but her second was a flop.*

flop·py /ˈflɑpi/ adj. (**flop·pi·er; flop·pi·est**) soft, loose and hanging downward; not stiff: *a floppy hat*

floppy 'disk (*also* **floppy; diskette**) noun [C] a square piece of plastic that can store information for a computer: *Don't forget to back up your files onto a floppy disk.* ☛ Look also at **hard disk**.

F

flo·ra /'flɔrə/ noun [plural] all the plants growing in a particular area: *He's studying the flora and fauna* (= the plants and animals) *of South America.* ☞ Look at **fauna**.

flo·ral /'flɔrəl/ adj. decorated with a pattern of flowers, or made with flowers

flo·rist /'flɔrɪst; 'flɑr-/ noun [C] a person who has a store that sells flowers

floss /flɔs; flɑs/ (*also* **dental floss**) noun [U] a kind of special thread that you use for cleaning between your teeth —**floss** verb [I,T]: *Be sure to brush and floss regularly.*

floun·der¹ /'flaʊndər/ verb [I] **1** to move with difficulty or to struggle (e.g. when you are trying not to sink in water) **2** to find it difficult to speak or act in a suitable way (usually in an awkward situation)

floun·der² /'flaʊndər/ noun [C,U] (*pl.* **flounder** *or* **floun·ders**) a type of flat fish that you can eat

☆ **flour** /'flaʊər/ noun [U] a fine powder made from wheat or other grain and used for making breads, cakes, cookies, etc.

flour·ish¹ /'flərɪʃ/ verb **1** [I] to be strong and healthy; to develop in a successful way: *These plants flourish in a sunny position.* ○ *a flourishing new community* **2** [T] to wave sth in the air so that people will notice it

flour·ish² /'flərɪʃ/ noun [C, usually sing.] a movement that you make to attract attention

flout /flaʊt/ verb [T] (*formal*) to refuse to obey or accept sth: *to flout the rules of the organization* ○ *to flout sb's advice*

☆ **flow¹** /floʊ/ verb [I] **1** to move in a smooth and continuous way (like water): *This river flows south into the Gulf of Mexico.* ○ *a fast-flowing stream* ○ *It was three hours before the traffic began to flow normally after the accident.* ○ *People have been steadily flowing out of the country since the trouble began.* **2** (used about hair and clothes) to hang down in a loose way: *a long flowing dress*

flow² /floʊ/ noun [sing.] **1** a steady, continuous movement of sth/sb: *There's a steady flow of young people from rural areas to urban areas.* **2** a supply of sth: *Press hard on the wound to stop the flow of blood.* ○ *a flow of information between the school and the parents*

☆ **flow·er¹** /'flaʊər/ noun [C] **1** the beautiful colored part of a plant or tree from which seeds or fruit grow

☞ A flower consists of several **petals**. It grows from a **bud** on the end of a **stem**.

2 a plant that is grown for its flowers; a flower (1) and its stem: *She grows a lot of flowers but no vegetables.* ○ *a beautiful bunch of flowers*

☞ We **pick** flowers and **arrange** them in a vase. Flowers that are given or carried on a special occasion are called a **bouquet**.

flow·er² /'flaʊər/ verb [I] to produce flowers¹(1) : *This plant flowers in late summer.*

'flower bed noun [C] a piece of ground where flowers are grown

flow·ered /'flaʊərd/ adj. covered or decorated with flowers: *a flowered dress, hat, tablecloth, etc.* ☞ picture at **pattern**.

flow·er·pot /'flaʊərpɑt/ noun [C] a pot in which a plant can be grown

flow·er·y /'flaʊəri/ adj. (used about a style of speaking or writing) using long, difficult words

flown p.p. of FLY²

☆ **flu** /flu/ usually **the flu** (*also formal* **influenza**) noun [sing., U] an illness that is like a bad cold but more serious. You usually have a fever and your arms and legs are sore: *The whole family has the flu.* ○ *They're in bed with the flu.* ○ *The flu is going around* (= a lot of people have it).

fluc·tu·ate /'flʌktʃueɪt/ verb [I] **fluctuate (between A and B)** (used about prices and numbers, or people's feelings) to change frequently from one thing to another: *The number of students fluctuates between 100 and 150.* ○ *Many people find that their moods fluctuate with the weather.* —**fluc·tu·a·tion** /ˌflʌktʃuˈeɪʃn/ noun [C,U]

flu·ent /'fluənt/ adj. **1** **fluent (in sth)** able to speak or write a language easily and accurately: *After a year in France she was fluent in French.* **2** (used about speech, reading or writing) expressed in a smooth and accurate way: *He speaks fluent German.* —**flu·en·cy** /-ənsi/ noun [U] —**flu·ent·ly** adv.

fluff /flʌf/ noun [U] **1** the soft new fur on young animals or birds **2** material in an article, essay, etc. that is not necessary or important: *The report was mostly fluff.*

fluff·y /'flʌfi/ adj. (**fluff·i·er**; **fluff·i·est**) very soft and light: *a fluffy kitten* ○ *fluffy snow*

flu·id¹ /'fluəd/ noun [C] a substance that can flow; a liquid: *The doctor told her to drink plenty of fluids.* ○ *body fluids*

flu·id² /'fluəd/ adj. **1** able to flow like a liquid **2** (used about plans, etc.) able or likely to be changed

fluid 'ounce (*also* **ounce**) noun [C] (*abbr.* **fl oz; fl. oz.**) a measure of liquid; 0.0296 of a liter. There are 16 fluid ounces in a pint and 32 fluid ounces in a quart.

fluke /fluk/ noun [C, usually sing.] (*informal*) something good that happens by accident, not because you have been intelligent or skillful: *The result was not a fluke. The better team won.*

flung p.t., p.p. of FLING¹

flunk /flʌŋk/ verb (*informal*) **1** [I,T] to fail a test or a course: *Carl flunked math and now he has to go to summer school.* ○ *I thought I was going to flunk, but I got a B!* **2** [T] to give sb a failing grade on a test, in a course, etc.: *Prof. Hall flunks about three students every semester.*

PHRV **flunk out (of sth)** (*informal*) to be forced to leave a school, college, etc. because your grades are not good enough: *to flunk out of college*

fluo·res·cent /flɔ'rɛsnt; flʊ-/ *adj.* **1** shining with a particular kind of hard white light: *a fluorescent light fixture* **2** very bright; seeming to shine: *fluorescent pink socks*

fluor·ide /'flɔraɪd; 'flʊ-/ *noun* [U] a chemical substance that can be added to water or toothpaste to help keep teeth strong and healthy

flur·ry /'fləri/ *noun* [C] (*pl.* **flur·ries**) **1** a small amount of snow that comes suddenly **2** a short sudden burst of activity or feelings: *a flurry of excitement*

flush /flʌʃ/ *verb* **1** [T] to clean a toilet by pressing or pulling a handle that sends a stream of water into the toilet: *Please remember to flush the toilet.* **2** [I] (used about a toilet) to be cleaned with a stream of water: *The toilet won't flush.* **3** [T] **flush sth away, down, etc.** to get rid of sth in a stream of water, especially in the toilet: *You can't flush diapers down the toilet – they'll clog it.* **4** [I] (used about a person or his/her face) to become red: *Susan flushed and could not hide her embarrassment.*

flus·ter /'flʌstər/ *verb* [T] (usually passive) to make sb feel nervous and confused (because there is too much to do or not enough time): *Don't get flustered – there's plenty of time.*

flute recorder

flute /flut/ *noun* [C] a musical instrument like a pipe that you hold sideways and play by blowing over a hole at one side

flut·ist /'flutɪst/ *noun* [C] a person who plays the flute

flut·ter¹ /'flʌt̮ər/ *verb* **1** [I,T] to move up and down or from side to side quickly and lightly; to make sth move in this way: *The flags were fluttering in the wind.* ○ *The bird fluttered its wings and tried to fly.* **2** [I] to move lightly through the air: *The dead leaves fluttered to the ground.* **3** [I] when your heart or stomach flutters, you are feeling nervous and excited

flut·ter² /'flʌt̮ər/ *noun* [C, usually sing.] a quick, light movement

☆ **fly¹** /flaɪ/ *verb* (*pres. part.* **fly·ing**; *3rd pers. sing. pres.* **flies**; *p.t.* **flew** /flu/; *p.p.* **flown** /floʊn/) **1** [I] (used about a bird, insect, airplane, etc.) to move through the air: *Penguins can't fly.* ○ *a plane flying overhead* **2** [I,T] to

travel in or to carry sth in an airplane, etc.: *My daughter is flying (out) to Singapore next week.* ○ *Supplies of food were flown (in) to the starving people.* **3** [I,T] (used about a pilot) to control an airplane, etc.: *You have to have special training to fly a jumbo jet.* **4** [T] to travel over an area of land or ocean by flying: *How long does it take to fly the Atlantic?* **5** [I] to move quickly or suddenly: *A brick came flying through the window.* **6** [I] (used about time) to pass quickly: *The weekend just flew by, and now it's Monday again.* ○ *Time flies when you're having fun!* **7** [I,T] to move around in the air; to make sth move around in the air: *The flags are flying.* ○ *to fly a kite* ☞ The noun from fly is **flight**.

IDM **as the crow flies** ⇨ CROW¹

fly off the handle (*informal*) to become very angry

☆ **fly²** /flaɪ/ *noun* [C] (*pl.* **flies**) **1** a small insect with two wings: *flies buzzing around a dead animal* ☞ picture at **insect**. **2** the zipper or buttons on the front of a pair of pants: *Henry, your fly is open.* ○ *jeans with a button fly* **3** (*also* **'fly ball**) (in baseball) a ball that is hit high into the air: *to hit a fly*

fly·ing¹ /'flaɪɪŋ/ *adj.* able to fly: *flying insects*

IDM **with flying colors** with great success; very well: *Shelley passed the test with flying colors.*

get off to a flying start to begin sth well and so get some advantage

fly·ing² /'flaɪɪŋ/ *noun* [U] traveling in an airplane, etc.: *I don't like flying.*

‚flying 'saucer *noun* [C] a round, flat spacecraft that some people say they have seen and that they believe comes from another planet

FM /‚ɛf 'ɛm/ *abbr.* frequency modulation; one of the systems of broadcasting radio signals ☞ Look at **AM**.

foal /foʊl/ *noun* [C] a young horse ☞ Look at the note at **horse**.

☆ **foam¹** /foʊm/ *noun* [U] **1** a mass of small white bubbles that are formed when air and a liquid are mixed together: *white foam on the tops of the waves* ○ *The firefighters sprayed chemical foam onto the fire.* **2** (*also* **‚foam 'rubber**) soft rubber or plastic that is used inside seats, cushions, etc. —**foam·y** *adj.*

foam² /foʊm/ *verb* [I] to produce foam: *The dog was foaming at the mouth.*

fo·cal point /'foʊkl pɔɪnt/ *noun* **1** [C] = FOCUS¹(1) **2** [sing.] the center of interest or activity

☆ **fo·cus¹** /'foʊkəs/ *noun* [C] (*pl.* **fo·cus·es**) **1** the point at which rays of light meet or from which they appear to come **2** [usually sing.] the center of interest or attention; special attention that is given to sb/sth: *The mayor has been the focus of a lot of media attention recently.*

ə	y	w	t̮	eɪ	aɪ	ɔɪ	aʊ	oʊ
about	yes	woman	butter	say	five	boy	now	go

IDM **in focus/out of focus** (used about a photograph or sth in a photograph) clear/not clear: *It's too bad that Tony's face is out of focus in this picture.*

fo·cus² /'foʊkəs/ *verb* **focus (sth) (on sth)** **1** [T] to direct rays of light onto one particular point **2** [I,T] to be or become able to see clearly; to adjust your eyes so that you can see clearly: *Gradually his eyes focused.* ○ *She focused her eyes on the page.* **3** [I,T] to adjust a camera so that the picture that you are taking will be clear: *I focused on the person in the middle of the group.* **4** [I,T] to give all your attention to sth: *to focus on a problem* ○ *to focus attention on a problem*

fod·der /'fɑdər/ *noun* [U] food that is given to farm animals

foe /foʊ/ *noun* [C] (*formal*) an enemy

☆**fog** /fɔg; fɑg/ *noun* [U] a mass of thick clouds that forms close to or just above the land or ocean. Fog makes it difficult for us to see: *Dense fog is making driving dangerous.* ○ *The fog had lifted/cleared by noon.*

☞ **Fog** is thicker than **mist**. **Haze** is caused by heat. **Smog** is caused by pollution. Look at the note at **weather**.

fog·gy /'fɔgi; 'fɑgi/ *adj.* (**fog·gi·er**; **fog·gi·est**) used to describe the weather when there is fog: *a foggy morning*

IDM **not have the foggiest idea/notion** not to know at all: *He doesn't have the foggiest notion of what's going on.*

foil¹ /fɔɪl/ *noun* [U] metal that has been rolled or beaten into very thin sheets, often used when you are wrapping or cooking food: *aluminum foil*

foil² /fɔɪl/ *verb* [T] to prevent sb from succeeding or from carrying out his/her plans; to prevent a plan from succeeding: *The escape attempt was foiled.*

folding a letter

fold

folding a chair

☆**fold¹** /foʊld/ *verb* **1** [T] **fold sth (up)** to bend one part of sth over another part in order to make it smaller, neater, etc.: *He folded the letter into thirds before putting it into the envelope.* ○ *Fold up the blanket and put it away.* ☞ The opposite is **unfold**. **2** [I] **fold (up)** to be

able to be folded in order to be easier to carry or to store: *This picnic table folds up flat.* ○ *a folding chair* **3** [I] (used about a business, a play in the theater, etc.) to close because it is unsuccessful

IDM **cross/fold your arms** ⇨ ARM¹

fold² /foʊld/ *noun* [C] **1** the mark or line where sth has been folded: *Tear the paper along the fold.* **2** a curved shape that is made by a piece of material, etc. that has been folded: *the folds of a dress*

fold·er /'foʊldər/ *noun* [C] **1** a cardboard or plastic cover that is used for holding papers, etc. **2** a collection of information or files on one subject that is stored in some computers or on some disks ☞ Look at **directory**.

fo·li·age /'foʊliɪdʒ/ *noun* [U] (*formal*) all the leaves of a tree or plant

☆**folk¹** /foʊk/ *noun* **1** [plural] (*also* **folks**) (*informal*) people in general: *Folk around here don't often see foreigners.* ○ *Some folks are never satisfied.* **2** [plural] (*also* **folks**) a particular type of people: *country folk* ○ *Old folks often don't like change.* **3 folks** [plural] (*informal*) your parents: *How are your folks?*

folk² /foʊk/ *adj.* traditional in a community; of a traditional style: *Daniel Boone is an American folk hero.* ○ *an English folk dance*

☞ **Folk music** is used to describe a type of music which became popular in the United States in the 1960's. **Folk singers** who perform this type of music often play guitars and sing about political topics, especially about peace.

folk·lore /'foʊklɔr/ *noun* [U] (the study of) the traditional stories and beliefs of a community

☆**fol·low** /'fɑloʊ/ *verb* **1** [I,T] to come, go or happen after sb/sth: *You go first and I'll follow later.* ○ *The dog followed her wherever she went.* ○ *The crash was followed by a scream and then there was silence.* ○ *We had steak followed by fresh fruit.* **2** [T] to go after sb in order to catch him/her: *Go faster! I think the cops are following us!* **3** [T] to go along a road, etc.; to go in the same direction as sth: *Follow this road for a mile and then turn right at the stoplight.* **4** [T] to accept advice, instructions, an example, etc. and do what you have been told or shown to do: *It is important to follow the instructions carefully.* ○ *She always follows the latest trends.* **5** [I,T] to understand the meaning of sth: *Then the molecules join to form a new compound. Do you follow?* ○ *Sorry, I don't follow you there.* ○ *The kids couldn't follow the plot of that movie.* **6** [T] to watch or listen to sb/sth very carefully: *You'll have to follow what he says very carefully if you want to understand it.* **7** [T] to take an active interest in sth: *Have you been following the tennis tournament?* **8** [I] **follow (from sth)** to happen as a result (of sth); to be the necessary result (of

sth): *It doesn't follow that old people can't lead active lives.* **9** [T] to happen in the planned or expected way: *The day's events followed the usual pattern.*

IDM **as follows** (used for introducing a list): *The names of the winning candidates are as follows:...*

follow sb's example/lead to do what sb else has done or decided to do

follow suit to do the same thing that sb else has just done

PHRV **follow through on sth** to continue doing sth until it is finished

follow sth up 1 to take further action about sth: *You should follow up your letter with a phone call.* **2** to find out more about sth: *We need to follow up the story about the school.*

fol·low·er /ˈfɑloʊər/ *noun* [C] a person who follows or supports a person, belief, etc.

☆ **fol·low·ing¹** /ˈfɑloʊɪŋ/ *adj.* **1** next (in time): *He had a heart attack on Sunday and died the following week.* **2** (in a list) that I will mention now: *Please bring the following items to the meeting:...*

☛ We can also use **the following** as a noun: *The following are the winners of the competition:...*

fol·low·ing² /ˈfɑloʊɪŋ/ *noun* [sing.] a group of people who support or admire sth: *Baseball has a large following in Japan.*

☆ **fol·low·ing³** /ˈfɑloʊɪŋ/ *prep.* after; as a result of: *Following the riots, many students were arrested.*

follow-up *noun* [C] something that is done to continue sth: *a follow-up to last year's report*

fol·ly /ˈfɑli/ *noun* [C,U] (*pl.* **fol·lies**) (*formal*) a foolish act: *It would be folly to throw away all our hard work because of one setback.*

☆ **fond** /fɑnd/ *adj.* **1** (not before a noun) **fond of sb/sth**; **fond of doing sth** liking a person or a thing, or liking doing sth: *We're all very fond of Mrs. Simpson.* ○ *I grew very fond of Turkish food while I was living in Istanbul.* **2** (only before a noun) kind and loving: *I have fond memories of both my aunts.*

fon·dle /ˈfɑndl/ *verb* [T] to touch or stroke sb/sth in a loving or sexual way: *She accused her boss of trying to fondle her in the hallway.*

fond·ly /ˈfɑndli/ *adv.* in a loving way

fond·ness /ˈfɑndnəs/ *noun* [U] a liking for sb/sth

☆ **food** /fud/ *noun* **1** [U] something that people, animals or plants take into their bodies in order to keep them alive and healthy: *Plants get food from the soil.* ○ *a shortage of food* **2** [C,U] a particular type of food (1) that you eat: *baby food* ○ *frozen foods* ○ *health foods*

food ˌpoisoning *noun* [U] an illness that is caused by eating food that is bad

food ˌprocessor *noun* [C] an electric ma-

chine that can mix food and also cut or slice food into small pieces ☛ picture at **mixer**.

food stamp *noun* [C] a small piece of paper (**a coupon**) that is given to poor people by the government and used instead of money to buy food

food·stuff /ˈfudstʌf/ *noun* [C, usually pl.] (*formal*) a substance that is used as food: *There has been a sharp rise in the cost of basic food-stuffs.*

☆ **fool¹** /ful/ *noun* [C] a person who is silly or stupid or who acts in a silly or stupid way: *I felt like such a fool when I realized my mistake.* ○ *Only a fool would go out in weather like this.*

☛ Look at **April Fool's Day**.

IDM **make a fool of sb/yourself** to make sb/yourself look foolish or silly

fool² /ful/ *verb* **1** [T] to trick sb: *Don't be fooled into believing everything the salesman says.* **2** [I] to speak without being serious: *I was only fooling when I said I loved you.*

PHRV **fool around** to behave in a silly or stupid way: *Stop fooling around with that knife or someone will get hurt!*

fool·har·dy /ˈfulhɑrdi/ *adj.* taking unnecessary risks

☆ **fool·ish** /ˈfulɪʃ/ *adj.* **1** silly; not sensible: *I was foolish enough to trust him.* **2** looking silly or feeling embarrassed: *He felt pretty foolish when he couldn't start his motorcycle in front of his friends.* —**fool·ish·ly** *adv.* —**fool·ish·ness** *noun* [U]

fool·proof /ˈfulpruf/ *adj.* not capable of going wrong or being wrongly used: *Our security system is absolutely foolproof.*

☆ **foot¹** /fʊt/ *noun* [C] (*pl.* **feet** /fit/) **1** the lowest part of the leg, below the ankle, on which a person or animal stands: *She rose to her feet* (= she stood up). ○ *I've been on my feet* (= standing and walking around) *all day.* ○ *What size feet do you have?* ○ *big/small feet* ○ *wide/narrow feet* ○ *She sat by the fire and the dog sat at her feet.*

☛ When you walk somewhere you go **on foot**. The nails on your feet are called **toe-nails**. If you have no shoes or socks on, you are **barefoot** or **in your bare feet**.

2 the part of a sock, etc. into which you put your foot **3** the lowest part on which a piece of furniture, etc. stands: *a typewriter with rubber feet* **4** (*abbr.* **ft.**) a measure of length; 30.48 centimeters. There are 12 inches in a foot, and 3 feet in a yard: *"How tall are you?" "Five foot two (inches)."* ○ *a six-foot-high wall* ○ *We need enough paint to cover 120 square feet.*

☛ The plural for **4** can be **feet** or **foot**. For more information, look at Appendix 2.

5 [sing.] the bottom of sth: *There's a note at the foot of the page.* ○ *sitting at the foot of the stairs*
☛ The opposite is **top**. **6** [sing.] the end of a bed where the feet go ☛ The opposite is **head**.

IDM **get/have cold feet** ⇨ **COLD¹**

tʃ	dʒ	v	θ	ð	s	z	ʃ
chin	**June**	**van**	**thin**	**then**	**so**	**zoo**	**she**

football

scoreboard

| HOME | 14 | VISITORS | 7 |
| DOWN | 2 | QUARTER | 3 |

stands

field

50-yard line

goal post

end zone

F

put your foot down (*informal*) to say firmly that sth must (not) happen: *Susan finally put her foot down and said that the kids could only watch an hour of TV each evening.*

put your foot in your mouth (*informal*) to say or do sth that upsets or embarrasses sb

set foot in/on sth to visit, enter or arrive at/ in a place: *I hope he never sets foot in my house again!*

stand on your own two feet to take care of yourself without help; to be independent

foot² /fʊt/ *verb*

IDM foot the bill (for sth) to pay (for sth)

☆ **foot·ball** /'fʊtbɔl/ *noun* **1** [U] a game that is played by two teams of eleven players who wear special protective equipment and try to carry or kick an oval ball to the end of a field: *a football field ○ a football player ○ a football game*

football player

helmet
shoulder pad
jersey
football

☞ Football players wear **helmets** and **pads** to protect themselves. The most important player on a football team is the **quarterback** who tries to **pass** (= throw) the ball to other players on his team. Players try to score **touchdowns** by catching the ball in the **end zone** or by carrying it into the **end zone**. A **touchdown** is worth six points. The game which is called "football" in British English and is played with a round ball is called **soccer** in American English.

2 [C] the large, usually brown, oval ball that is used in this game

foot·bridge /'fʊtbrɪdʒ/ *noun* [C] a narrow

bridge for people who are walking and not for cars

foot·hold /'fʊthoʊld/ *noun* [C] a place where you can safely put your foot when you are climbing: (*figurative*) *We hope to gain a foothold in the European market.*

foot·ing /'fʊtɪŋ/ *noun* [sing.] **1** being able to stand firmly on a surface: *He lost his footing on the wet floor and fell.* **2** the basis on which sth is established: *The company is now on a solid financial footing and will soon be making a profit.* **3** the level or position of sb/sth (in relation to sb/sth else): *to be on equal footing with sb*

foot·note /'fʊtnoʊt/ *noun* [C] an extra piece of information that is added at the bottom of a page in a book

footprints

foot·print /'fʊtprɪnt/ *noun* [C] a mark that is left by a foot or a shoe

foot·step /'fʊtstɛp/ *noun* [C] the sound of sb walking: *I heard his footsteps in the hall.*

foot·wear /'fʊtwɛr/ *noun* [U] boots or shoes

☆ **for¹** /fər; *strong form* fɔr/ *prep.* **1** (showing the person who will receive sth): *Here is a letter for you.* ○ *Save a piece of cake for Mary.* ○ *He made lunch for them.* ○ *She bought some candy for the kids.* **2** (showing purpose or use): *What's this gadget for?* ○ *Let's go for a walk.* ○ *a*

i	ɪ	ɛ	æ	ɑ	ɔ	ʌ	ʊ	u
see	sit	ten	cat	hot	saw	cup	put	too

shampoo for dry hair ○ *Let's have eggs for breakfast.* **3** (showing where sb/sth is going to): *passengers on board a flight for Miami* ○ *They set out for home.* **4** intended to be used by a particular group or in a particular way: *It's a book for children.* ○ *That chair is for guests.* ○ *Is that house for sale?* **5** in order to help sb/sth : *What can I do for you?* ○ *You should take some medicine for your cold.* ○ *Doctors are fighting for his life.* ○ *Take care of her for my sake.* **6** (showing the price of sth): *I bought this car for $2,000.* ○ *She gave me their old TV for nothing.* **7** (showing a reason): *He was sent to prison for murder.* ○ *The city is famous for its beautiful lakes and parks.* ○ *"Greg got suspended from school today." "What for?"* ○ *What did you do that for?* (= Why did you do that?) **8** on the occasion of: *What did they give you for your birthday?* **9** in support of (sb/sth): *Three cheers for the winner!* ○ *Are you for or against the death penalty?* **10** as a representative of (sb/sth): *Who's the lawyer for the defense?* ○ *She plays basketball for Boston College.* **11** meaning or representing (sb/sth): *What's the "C" for in "NBC"?* ○ *What's the Russian word for "window"?* **12** (after a verb) in order to have or get sth: *She asked me for help.* **13** (after an adjective) when you consider what you could expect: *She's tall for her age.* ○ *It's quite warm for January.* **14** (used when you give one thing and get sth else back): *I want to exchange this sweater for a larger one.* **15** (showing a length of time): *I'm going away for a few days.* ○ *He was a teacher for 20 years* (= he is not a teacher now). ○ *He has been a teacher for 20 years* (= he is still a teacher).

☞ **Since** is used with a point in time for showing when something began: *He has been a teacher since 1977.* **Ago** is also used for showing when something began: *He became a teacher 20 years ago.*

16 (showing that sth has been arranged to happen at a particular time): *The appointment is for 10:30.* ○ *We're planning our vacation for the second week in July.* **17** (showing when sth happens): *I'm warning you for the last time.* ○ *I met her for the second time yesterday.* **18** (showing a distance): *He walked for ten miles.*
IDM **for all** in spite of: *For all his talk, he really doesn't know what's going on.*
for good permanently: *They have left town for good* (= they will never return).

for² /fər; *strong form* fɔr/ *conj.* (*formal*) because: *The children could not enter the castle, for they did not know the magic words.*

☆ **for·bid** /fərˈbɪd/ *verb* [T] (*pres. part.* **for·bid·ding**; *p.t.* **for·bade** /fərˈbeɪd/ or **for·bad** /fərˈbæd/; *p.p.* **for·bid·den** /fərˈbɪdn/) (*formal*) **1** forbid sb to do sth; forbid sb from doing sth to order sb not to do sth: *My father forbade me to smoke.* **2** to not allow sth: *Eating pork is*

forbidden by some religions. ☞ Look at **prohibit** and **permit**.

for·bid·ding /fərˈbɪdɪŋ/ *adj.* looking unfriendly or frightening: *The steep, rocky path looked very forbidding.*

☆ **force¹** /fɔrs/ *noun* **1** [U] physical strength or power: *The force of the explosion knocked them to the ground.* ○ *The police used force to break up the demonstration.* **2** [U] power and influence: *His arguments lost some of their force when they were translated into French.* **3** [C] a person or thing that has power or influence: *The United States is still a major force in international affairs.* **4** [C,U] (*technical*) a power that can cause change or movement: *the force of gravity* **5** [C, usually *sing.*] a measure of wind strength: *hurricane-force winds* **6** [C] a group of people who are trained for a particular purpose: *a highly trained workforce* ○ *a UN peacekeeping force* ○ *the police force*
IDM **bring sth/come into force** to start using a new law, etc.; to start being used: *The government wants to bring new anti-drug legislation into force next year.*
in force 1 (used about people) in large numbers: *The police were out in force at the protest march.* **2** (used about a law, rule, etc.) being used: *The new laws about seat belts in cars are now in force.*
join forces (with sb) ⇨ JOIN

☆ **force²** /fɔrs/ *verb* [T] **1** to make sb do sth that he/she does not want to do: *The bank robber forced us to lie on the floor.* ○ *She forced herself to speak to him.* **2** to use physical strength to do sth or to move sth: *The window had been forced open.* ○ *We had to force our way through the crowd.*

☆ **force·ful** /ˈfɔrsfl/ *adj.* strong; powerful: *He has a very forceful personality.* ○ *a forceful speech* —**force·ful·ly** *adv.*

for·ceps /ˈfɔrsɛps; -səps/ *noun* [plural] a special instrument that looks like a pair of scissors but is not sharp. Forceps are used by doctors and dentists for holding things firmly: *a pair of forceps*

forc·i·ble /ˈfɔrsəbl/ *adj.* (only *before* a noun) **1** done using (physical) force: *The police made a forcible entry into the building.* **2** (used about ideas, an argument, etc.) strong; convincing: *a forcible reminder*

forc·i·bly /ˈfɔrsəbli/ *adv.* using force: *The protesters were forcibly removed from the building.*

fore /fɔr/ *noun*
IDM **come to the fore** to get into an important position so that you are noticed by people
bring sth to the fore to cause sth to be noticed by people; to emphasize: *to bring an issue to the fore*

fore·arm /ˈfɔrɑrm/ *noun* [C] the lower part of your arm between your elbow and your wrist

fore·bod·ing /fɔrˈboʊdɪŋ/ *noun* [U, *sing.*] a

ə	y	w	t̬	eɪ	aɪ	ɔɪ	aʊ	oʊ
about	yes	woman	butter	say	five	boy	now	go

strong feeling that danger or trouble is coming: *a sense of foreboding*

☆**fore·cast** /ˈfɔrkæst/ *verb* [T] (*p.t., p.p.* **forecast** or **fore·cast·ed**) to say (with the help of information) what will probably happen in the future: *The market analyst did not forecast the sudden rise in inflation.* ○ *Rain has been forecast for tomorrow.* —**fore·cast** *noun* [C]: *The weather forecast said it would be sunny tomorrow.*

fore·close /fɔrˈkloʊz/ *verb* [I,T] **foreclose on sth** (used about a bank, etc.) to take control of sb's property, usually because they have not paid back a loan on time —**fore·clo·sure** /fɔrˈkloʊʒər/ *noun* [C]

fore·fin·ger /ˈfɔrˌfɪŋgər/ *noun* [C] = INDEX FINGER

fore·front /ˈfɔrfrʌnt/ *noun* [sing.] the leading position; the position at the front: *Our department is right at the forefront of scientific research.*

fore·go /fɔrˈgoʊ/ *verb* [T] (*p.t.* **fore·went**; *p.p.* **fore·gone**) = FORGO

fore·gone /ˈfɔrgɔn/ *-gən/ adj.*
IDM **a foregone conclusion** a result that is or was certain to happen

fore·ground /ˈfɔrgraʊnd/ *noun* [sing.] **the foreground 1** the part of a view, picture, etc. that appears closest to the person looking at it: *Notice the artist's use of color in the foreground of the picture.* **2** a position where you will be noticed most: *He likes to be in the foreground at every meeting.* ☞ Look at **background**.

fore·hand /ˈfɔrhænd/ *noun* [C] a stroke in tennis, etc. that is made with the inside of your hand facing forward ☞ Look at **backhand**.

☆**fore·head** /ˈfɔrɛd; ˈfɑrəd; ˈfɔrhɛd; ˈfɑrhɛd/ (*also* **brow**) *noun* [C] the flat part of a person's face above the eyes and below the hair ☞ picture on page A24.

☆**for·eign** /ˈfɔrən; ˈfɑr-/ *adj.* **1** belonging to or connected with a country that is not your own: *a foreign country* ○ *to learn a foreign language* ○ *a foreign coin* **2** dealing with or involving other countries: *foreign policy* (= government decisions concerning other countries) ○ *the French Foreign Minister* ☞ Look at the note at **secretary**. **3** (used about an object or a substance) not belonging where it is: *The X-ray showed a foreign body* (= object) *in her stomach.*

for·eign·er /ˈfɔrənər; ˈfɑr-/ *noun* [C] a person who comes from a country that is not your own

☞ This word is often used to show disrespect toward sb from another country, e.g. because you do not approve of his/her customs, etc. A polite way to talk about sb from another country is to mention his/her nationality: *a woman from Mexico* ○ *students from Asia.* We

can also use the phrase **people from other countries** to talk about people who come from countries outside our own.

foreign ex·change *noun* **1** [C,U] the system of buying and selling money from a different country; the place where it is bought and sold: *The dollar dropped against the British pound on the foreign exchange yesterday.* **2** [C] a visit to another country to learn about its culture, language, etc.: *We have a foreign exchange student staying at our house.*

fore·man /ˈfɔrmən/ *noun* [C] (*pl.* **fore·men** /ˈfɔrmən/) **1** a worker who is in charge of other workers **2** the person on a jury who speaks for all the members

☞ Nowadays many people prefer to say **foreperson**, especially when referring to a woman.

fore·most /ˈfɔrmoʊst/ *adj.* most famous or important; best: *Robert De Niro is among the foremost actors of his generation.*
IDM **first and foremost** ⇨ FIRST²

fo·ren·sic /fəˈrɛnsɪk; -zɪk/ *adj.* connected with the law and finding out about a crime: *The police are gathering forensic evidence to try and find out the cause of death.* ○ *forensic medicine*

fore·run·ner /ˈfɔrˌrʌnər/ *noun* [C] a person or thing that is an early example or a sign of sth that appears or develops later

fore·see /fɔrˈsi/ *verb* [T] (*p.t.* **fore·saw** /fɔrˈsɔ/; *p.p.* **fore·seen** /fɔrˈsin/) to know or guess that sth is going to happen in the future: *Nobody could have foreseen the result of the election.* ☞ Look at **predict** and at **unforeseen**.

fore·see·a·ble /fɔrˈsiəbl/ *adj.* that can be expected: *These problems were foreseeable.* ○ *The weather won't change in the foreseeable future* (= as far ahead as we can see).

fore·sight /ˈfɔrsaɪt/ *noun* [U] the ability to see what will probably happen in the future (and to make wise plans): *My neighbor had the foresight to move to a new house before the new freeway was built.* ☞ Look at **hindsight**.

fore·skin /ˈfɔrskɪn/ *noun* [C] the loose piece of skin that covers the end of the male sexual organ

☆**for·est** /ˈfɔrəst; ˈfɑr-/ *noun* [C,U] a large area of land that is covered with trees: *tropical rain forests* ○ *A large part of Canada is covered in forest.* ○ *a forest fire*

☞ Forests are generally larger than **woods**. **Forest** is used in official names: *Black Hills National Forest.* **The woods** is used as a general expression for an area that is covered with trees: *We went for a walk in the woods.* A **jungle** is a forest in a tropical part of the world.

for·est·ry /ˈfɔrəstri; ˈfɑr-/ *noun* [U] the science of planting and taking care of trees in forests

ər	ɪr	ɛr	ɑr	ɔr	ʊr	ʒ	h	ŋ
bird	near	hair	car	north	tour	vision	hat	sing

fore·tell /fɔrˈtɛl/ verb [T] (p.t., p.p. **fore·told** /fɔrˈtoʊld/) (formal) to say what will happen in the future ☞ A more common word is **predict**.

fore·thought /ˈfɔrθɔt/ noun [U] careful thought about, or preparation for, the future

fore·told p.t., p.p. of FORETELL

☆ **for·ev·er** /fəˈrɛvər/ adv. for all time; permanently: I wish summer would last forever! ○ I realized that our relationship had ended forever. ○ My sister always takes forever (= a very long time) in the bathroom.

fore·word /ˈfɔrwərd/ noun [C] a piece of writing at the beginning of a book that introduces the book and/or its author

for·feit /ˈfɔrfət/ verb [T] to lose sth or no longer have sth because you have done sth wrong or because you want to achieve an aim: Because of his violent behavior, he forfeited the right to visit his children. ○ Their team was late, so they had to forfeit the game.

for·gave p.t. of FORGIVE

forge /fɔrdʒ/ verb [T] **1** to make a copy of sth in order to deceive people: to forge a signature **2** to create a relationship with sb/sth: Our university has forged links with several businesses in the community.
PHR V **forge ahead** to go forward steadily and gradually: Despite the problems, we managed to forge ahead and finish the project on time.

for·ger·y /ˈfɔrdʒəri/ noun (pl. **for·ger·ies**) **1** [U] the crime of copying a document, signature, painting, etc. in order to deceive people **2** [C] a document, signature, picture, etc. that has been forged: The painting that had been sold as a Rembrandt was discovered to be a forgery.

☆ **for·get** /fərˈgɛt/ verb (p.t. **for·got** /fərˈgɑt/; p.p. **for·got·ten** /fərˈgɑtn/) **1** [I,T] **forget about sth** to fail to remember sth; to lose the memory of sth: "Why didn't you come to the party?" "Oh, no! I completely forgot about it!" ○ You never forget how to ride a bicycle. ○ I forgot what I was going to say. ○ I forgot the telephone number. ○ He forgot that he had invited her to the party. ○ I'll never forget meeting my husband for the first time. **2** [I,T] to fail to remember to do sth: Try not to forget about feeding the cat! ○ Don't forget to do your homework! **3** [T] to fail to bring sth with you: When my father got to the airport, he realized he'd forgotten his passport. ☞ When we are talking about where we have forgotten something, we have to use the word **leave**. We CANNOT say: "My father forgot his passport at home." We have to say: "He left his passport at home." **4** [I,T] to stop thinking about sth: Forget about your work and enjoy yourself! ○ "I'm sorry I shouted at you." "Forget it." (= don't worry about it)

for·get·ful /fərˈgɛtfl/ adj. often forgetting things: My mother's almost 80 and she's starting to get a little forgetful.

for·giv·a·ble /fərˈgɪvəbl/ adj. that can be forgiven ☞ The opposite is **unforgivable**.

☆ **for·give** /fərˈgɪv/ verb [T] (p.t. **for·gave** /fərˈgeɪv/; p.p. **for·given** /fərˈgɪvn/) **1** forgive sth; **forgive sb (for sth/for doing sth)** to stop being angry with sb or about sth: I can't forgive his behavior last night. ○ I can't forgive him for his behavior last night. ○ I can't forgive him for behaving like that last night. **2** (used for apologizing politely): Forgive me for asking, but where did you get that dress?

for·give·ness /fərˈgɪvnəs/ noun [U] the act of forgiving

for·giv·ing /fərˈgɪvɪŋ/ adj. ready and willing to forgive

for·go (also **forego**) /fɔrˈgoʊ/ verb [T] (p.t. **for·went** /fɔrˈwɛnt/; p.p. **for·gone** /fɔrˈgɔn; -ˈgɑn/) (formal) to be willing not to have sth nice or sth that you have a right to: The defendant has decided to forgo his right to a jury trial.

for·got p.t. of FORGET

for·got·ten p.p. of FORGET

☆ **fork¹** /fɔrk/ noun [C] **1** a small implement with a handle and two or more points. You use a fork for lifting food to your mouth when eating: knives, forks and spoons **2** a place where a road, river, etc. divides into two parts: When you come to a fork in the road, take the right branch . ☞ Look also at **pitchfork**.

fork² /fɔrk/ verb [I] (used about a road, river, etc.) to divide into two parts
PHR V **fork out** (informal) to pay: I forked out $20 for that book.
fork sth over (informal) to give sth (often money) when you do not want to: I had to fork over the $10 that I owed her.

fork·lift /ˈfɔrklɪft/ noun [C] a vehicle with a mechanical device on the front for lifting and moving heavy objects

forklift

for·lorn /fərˈlɔrn; fɔr-/ adj. lonely and unhappy; not cared for

☆ **form¹** /fɔrm/ noun **1** [C] a particular type of sth or way of doing sth: Swimming is an excellent form of exercise. ○ We never eat meat in any form. ○ What form will the meeting take? (= How will it be organized?) **2** [C,U] the shape of sb/sth: The articles will be published in book form. **3** [C] a piece of paper with questions on it and spaces where you give answers and personal information: a tax form ○ an entry form for a contest ○ to fill out an application form ○ Please fill in your name and address on this form. **4** [C] (grammar) a way of spelling or changing a word in a sentence: the irregular forms of the verbs ○ The plural form of "mouse" is "mice."

F

F

☆ **form²** /fɔrm/ *verb* **1** [T] to make or organize sth: *They formed an organization called "Citizens for Nature."* ○ *In English we usually form the past tense by adding "-ed."* **2** [T] to take the shape of sth: *The two roads join to form a "Y."* **3** [I,T] to move into the shape or order mentioned: *The police formed a circle around the house.* **4** [T] to be the thing mentioned: *Seminars form the main part of the course* (= The main part of the course consists of seminars). **5** [I,T] to begin to exist or to make sth exist; to begin to have sth: *Buds form on trees in the early spring.* ○ *The rain had formed a huge puddle on the street.* ○ *We formed a very good impression of the school on our first visit.*

☆ **for·mal** /ˈfɔrml/ *adj.* **1** (used about language or behavior) used when you want to appear serious or official and when you are in a situation in which you do not know the other people very well: *"Yours sincerely" is a formal way of ending a letter.* ○ *a formal occasion* (= one where you must behave politely and wear the clothes that people think are suitable)

☞ In this dictionary some words and phrases are marked *(formal)* or *(informal)*. This will help you to choose the right word for a particular situation. Often there is an informal or neutral word with a similar meaning to a more formal one.

2 public and official: *I am going to make a formal complaint to the hospital about the way I was treated.* **3** (only *before* a noun) obtained in a school or college: *My grandfather only had eight years of formal education.* —**for·mal·ly** *adv.*

for·mal·i·ty /fɔrˈmælət̮i/ *noun* (*pl.* **for·mal·i·ties**) **1** [C] an action that is necessary according to custom or law: *There are certain formalities to go through before we can give you a visa.* ☞ If an action is **just a formality**, we mean that people think that it is necessary according to custom or law but that it has no real importance or effect otherwise. **2** [U] careful attention to rules of language and behavior

for·mat¹ /ˈfɔrmæt/ *noun* [C] the shape of sth or the way it is arranged or produced: *It's the same book but in a different format.*

for·mat² /ˈfɔrmæt/ *verb* [T] (**format·ting**; **format·ted**) to arrange sth in a particular format, usually for a computer: *to format a floppy disk*

for·ma·tion /fɔrˈmeɪʃn/ *noun* **1** [U] the making or developing of sth: *the formation of a new corporation* **2** [C,U] an arrangement or pattern (especially of soldiers, airplanes, ships, etc.): *Several military planes flew over in formation.* **3** [C] a thing that is formed; the particular way in which it is formed: *rock formations* ○ *cloud formations*

form·a·tive /ˈfɔrmət̮ɪv/ *adj.* having an important and lasting influence (on sb's character and opinions): *A child's early years are thought to be the most formative ones.*

☆ **for·mer¹** /ˈfɔrmər/ *adj.* (only *before* a noun) of an earlier time; previous: *Jimmy Carter, the former President* ○ *Their new neighbor is a former teacher.* ○ *In former times people often had larger families.*

for·mer² /ˈfɔrmər/ *adj., noun* the first (of two people or things just mentioned): *Of the two hospitals in town, the General and the County, the former* (= the General) *has the better reputation.* ☞ The opposite is **the latter**.

☆ **for·mer·ly** /ˈfɔrmərli/ *adv.* in the past; previously: *the country of Myanmar (formerly Burma)* ○ *The hotel was formerly a private house.*

☞ **Used to** is a more common way of expressing the same meaning: *The hotel used to be a private house.*

for·mi·da·ble /ˈfɔrmədəbl; fərˈmɪdəbl/ *adj.* **1** causing you to be nervous or frightened: *His mother is a very formidable lady.* **2** difficult to deal with; needing a lot of effort: *Reforming the education system will be a formidable task.*

☆ **for·mu·la** /ˈfɔrmyələ/ *noun* (*pl.* **for·mu·las** or **for·mu·lae** /ˈfɔrmyəli/) **1** [C] a group of signs, letters or numbers used in science or mathematics to express a general law or fact: *The formula for carbon monoxide is CO.* ○ *What is the formula for converting miles to kilometers?* **2** [C] a list of substances used for making sth; the instructions necessary for making sth: *The formula for the new vaccine has not been made public yet.* **3** [C] a plan of how to get sth or how to do sth: *What is her formula for success?* **4** [U] a liquid food for babies that is similar to milk

for·mu·late /ˈfɔrmyəleɪt/ *verb* [T] **1** to prepare and organize a plan or ideas for doing sth: *The Republican Party still has not formulated its policy on defense spending.* **2** to express sth (clearly and exactly)

for·sake /fərˈseɪk; fɔr-/ *verb* [T] (*p.t.* **for·sook** /fərˈsʊk; fɔr-/; *p.p.* **for·sak·en** /fərˈseɪkən; fɔr-/) (*formal*) to leave a person or a place forever (especially when you should stay)

fort /fɔrt/ *noun* [C] **1** a strong building that is used for military defense **2** (often used in proper names) a place with houses, offices, stores, military equipment, etc. where members of the army, etc. live and work: *Fort Bragg* ☞ Look at **base¹(5)**.

forth /fɔrθ/ *adv.*

IDM and so forth and other things like those just mentioned: *The kind of job that you'll be doing is taking messages, making coffee and so forth.*

back and forth ⇨ BACK³

i	ɪ	ɛ	æ	ɑ	ɔ	ʌ	ʊ	u
see	sit	ten	cat	hot	saw	cup	put	too

forth·com·ing /ˌfɔrθˈkʌmɪŋ/ *adj.* **1** going to happen or appear in the near future: *Look in the local paper for a list of forthcoming events.* **2** (not before a noun) offered or given: *If no money is forthcoming, we will not be able to continue the project.* **3** (not before a noun) willing to be helpful, give information, etc.: *Rob was not very forthcoming when his parents asked him about his grades.*

forth·right /ˈfɔrθraɪt/ *adj.* saying clearly and honestly what you think

☆ **for·ti·eth** /ˈfɔrtiəθ/ *pron., det., adv.* 40th, next after thirty-ninth ☞ Look at the examples at **sixth**.

for·ti·fy /ˈfɔrtəfaɪ/ *verb* [T] (*pres. part.* **for·ti·fy·ing**; *3rd pers. sing. pres.* **for·ti·fies**; *p.t., p.p.* **for·ti·fied**) **1** to make a place stronger and ready for an attack: *to fortify a city* **2** to improve sth by adding extra substances to it: *This cereal is fortified with vitamins.*

fort·night /ˈfɔrtnaɪt/ *noun* [C, usually sing.] (*BrE*) two weeks

for·tress /ˈfɔrtrəs/ *noun* [C] a castle or other large building that has been made strong so that it is not easy to attack

☆ **for·tu·nate** /ˈfɔrtʃənət/ *adj.* lucky: *You were fortunate to have such good weather for your vacation.* ○ *It was fortunate that he was at home when you called.* ☞ The opposite is **unfortunate**.

☆ **for·tu·nate·ly** /ˈfɔrtʃənətli/ *adv.* by good luck; luckily: *Fortunately the traffic wasn't too bad.* ○ *Jane arrived late but, fortunately for her, everybody was too busy to notice.*

☆ **for·tune** /ˈfɔrtʃən/ *noun* **1** [C] what is going to happen to a person in the future: *Show me your hand and I'll try to tell your fortune.* **2** [C] a very large amount of money: *I always spend a fortune on birthday presents.* **3** [C, usually pl.] the things (both good and bad) that happen to a person, family, country, etc.: *The country's fortunes depend on its industry being successful.* **4** [U] the power that affects what happens in a person's life; luck: *Fortune was not on our side that day* (= we were unlucky).

ˈfortune ˌteller *noun* [C] a person who tells people's fortunes (3)

☆ **for·ty** /ˈfɔrti/ *number* 40, one more than thirty-nine ☞ Look at **fortieth**. For examples of how to use numbers in sentences, look at **sixty**. Look also at Appendix 2.

fo·rum /ˈfɔrəm/ *noun* [C] a place or meeting where people can exchange and discuss ideas

☆ **for·ward¹** /ˈfɔrwərd/ *adv.* **1** (*also* **forwards**) in the direction that is in front of you; toward the front, end or future: *Keep going forward and try not to look back.* ○ *We seem to be going backwards, not forwards.* **2** in the direction of progress; ahead: *The new drug is a big step forward in the fight against AIDS.*

☞ **Forward** is used after many verbs, e.g. **bring, come, look, put**. For the meaning of the expressions, look at the verb entries.

☆ **for·ward²** /ˈfɔrwərd/ *adj.* **1** (only *before* a noun) toward the front or future: *forward planning* **2** direct and confident: *I don't want to seem too forward, but could I buy you a drink?*

for·ward³ /ˈfɔrwərd/ *verb* [T] to send a letter, etc. to a new address: *The post office is forwarding all our mail.*

for·ward⁴ /ˈfɔrwərd/ *noun* [C] a player in a sport such as basketball or soccer who tries to score points

ˌfor·ward·ing adˈdress *noun* [C] a new address to which mail should be sent

ˈforward-ˌlooking *adj.* thinking about or planning for the future; having modern ideas

for·went *p.t.* of FORGO

fos·sil /ˈfɑsl/ *noun* [C] the remains, or a mark, of a prehistoric animal or plant that has been buried in rock for a very long time and that has become hard

fos·ter /ˈfɔstər; ˈfɑs-/ *verb* [T] **1** to take a child who needs a home into your family and to care for him/her without becoming the legal parents: *to foster a homeless child*

☞ The people who do this are **foster parents**. Their home is a **foster home**. The child is a **foster child**. Look at **adopt**.

2 to help or encourage the development of sth (especially feelings or ideas)

fought *p.t., p.p.* of FIGHT¹

foul¹ /faʊl/ *adj.* **1** disgusting and dirty (often with a bad smell or taste): *foul city air* **2** very bad or unpleasant: *Careful what you say – he's got a foul temper* (= he becomes angry very easily). ○ *What's in this drink? It tastes foul.* **3** (used about weather) very bad; stormy **4** (used about language) very rude; full of swearing: *That guy's got a really foul mouth* (= he uses a lot of swear words).

foul² /faʊl/ *verb* **1** [T] to make sth dirty (with garbage, waste, etc.): *rivers fouled by industrial waste* **2** [I,T] (*sports*) to be guilty of a foul³ (1) (against another player)

PHRV foul sth up to spoil sth: *The weather really fouled up our vacation.*

foul³ /faʊl/ *noun* [C] (*sports*) **1** an action that is against the rules: *to commit a foul on another player* **2** (*also* **ˈfoul ball**) (in baseball) a ball that is hit too far to the left or to the right: *to hit a foul*

ˌfoul ˈplay *noun* [U] **1** action that is against the rules of a sport **2** violent crime that leads to murder

☆ **found¹** *p.t., p.p.* of FIND¹ ☞ Look also at **lost and found**.

ə	y	w	ţ	eɪ	aɪ	ɔɪ	aʊ	oʊ
about	yes	woman	butter	say	five	boy	now	go

found² /faʊnd/ *verb* [T] **1** to start an organization, institution, etc. especially by providing money: *The university was founded in 1867.* **2** to begin to build a town or establish a country: *Liberia was founded by freed slaves.* **3** (usually passive) to base sth on sth: *a relationship founded on trust*

☆ **foun·da·tion** /faʊnˈdeɪʃn/ *noun* **1** [U] the act of founding sth (a building, town, organization, etc.) **2** [C,U] the part of a building beneath the ground that forms its base: *The construction workers have just started to lay the foundation of the new school.* **3** [C,U] the idea, principle or fact on which sth is based: *That rumor is completely without foundation* (= it is not true). **4** [C] an organization that provides money for a special purpose, e.g. for research or to help people who have a particular problem: *The National Kidney Foundation* (= researching the causes of kidney disease)

foun·der /ˈfaʊndər/ *noun* [C] a person who founds or establishes sth

foun·dry /ˈfaʊndri/ *noun* [C] (*pl.* **foun·dries**) a place where metal or glass is melted and shaped into objects

☆ **foun·tain** /ˈfaʊntn/ *noun* [C] **1** an ornament (in a yard, park, etc.) that shoots a stream of water into the air. The water that comes out is also called a fountain. **2** = DRINKING FOUNTAIN

fountain *(caption)*

ˈ**fountain pen** *noun* [C] a type of pen that you fill with ink

☆ **four** /fɔr/ *number* 4, one more than three ☛ For examples of how to use numbers in sentences, look at **six** and at Appendix 2.
IDM **on all fours** ⇨ ALL¹

four- /fɔr/ (in compounds) having four of the thing mentioned: *four-legged animals*

ˌ**four-letter** ˈ**word** *noun* [C] one of a type of word (often with four letters) that people think is very rude

☆ **four·teen** /ˌfɔrˈtin/ *number* 14, one more than thirteen ☛ For examples of how to use numbers in sentences, look at **six**. Look also at Appendix 2. —**four·teenth** /ˌfɔrˈtinθ/ *pron.*, *det.*, *adv.* ☛ Look at the examples at **sixth**.

☆ **fourth** /fɔrθ/ *pron.*, *det.*, *adv.* 4th, next after third ☛ For ¼ we often use the word **quarter**: *a quarter of an hour* (= fifteen minutes). Look at the examples at **sixth**. Look also at Appendix 2.

fourth·ly /ˈfɔrθli/ *adv.* (used to introduce the fourth point in a list): *Fourthly, you must speak clearly.*

ˌ**four-wheel** ˈ**drive** *adj.* having an engine that turns all four wheels

fowl /faʊl/ *noun* [plural] birds, especially ones that are kept on a farm

fox *(caption)*

☆ **fox** /fɑks/ *noun* [C] a wild animal with reddish fur that looks like a dog
☛ A young fox is a **pup**.

fox·hole /ˈfɑkshoʊl/ *noun* [C] a hole in the ground that soldiers dig and use for shelter in a battle

foy·er /ˈfɔɪər/ *noun* [C] an entrance hall in a house, hotel, theater, etc. where people can meet or wait

frac·tion /ˈfrækʃn/ *noun* [C] **1** a small part or amount: *For a fraction of a second, I thought the car was going to crash.* **2** an exact part of a number: *½ and ¼ are fractions.*

frac·tion·al·ly /ˈfrækʃənl·i/ *adv.* to a very small degree; slightly

frac·ture¹ /ˈfræktʃər/ *verb* [T] to break sth (especially a bone): *She fell and fractured her ankle.* ○ *a fractured ankle*

frac·ture² /ˈfræktʃər/ *noun* [C] a break in sth hard, especially in a bone: *a fracture of the arm*

frag·ile /ˈfrædʒl/ *adj.* easily damaged or broken: *This bowl is very fragile. Please handle it carefully.*

frag·ment¹ /ˈfrægmənt/ *noun* [C] a small piece (that has broken off sth bigger): *fragments of ancient pottery* ○ (*figurative*) *I only heard a fragment of their conversation.*

frag·ment² /ˈfrægmɛnt; frægˈmɛnt/ *verb* [I,T] (*formal*) to be broken into small pieces; to break sth into small pieces: *The country is becoming increasingly fragmented by civil war.*

fra·grance /ˈfreɪgrəns/ *noun* [C,U] a pleasant smell

fra·grant /ˈfreɪgrənt/ *adj.* having a pleasant smell

frail /freɪl/ *adj.* not strong or healthy: *My Grandmother is getting very old and frail.*

frail·ty /ˈfreɪlti/ *noun* [C,U] (*pl.* **frail·ties**) moral or physical weakness

☆ **frame¹** /freɪm/ *noun* [C] **1** a border of wood or metal that goes around the outside of a door, picture, window, etc.: *a window frame* **2** [usually pl.] a structure made of plastic or metal that holds the lenses of a pair of glasses ☛ picture at **glasses**. **3** the basic structure of a piece of furniture, building, vehicle, etc. onto which other pieces are added: *the frame of a bicycle* **4** [usually sing.] the shape of a

ər	ɪr	ɛr	ur	ɔr	ʊr	ʒ	h	ŋ
bird	near	hair	car	north	tour	vision	hat	sing

human or animal body: *He has a large frame, but he is not fat.*

IDM **frame of mind** a particular state or condition of your feelings; mood: *I'm not in the right frame of mind for a party. I'd rather be on my own.*

frame² /freɪm/ *verb* [T] **1** to put a border around sth (especially a picture or photograph): *Let's have this picture framed.* **2** (*formal*) to express sth in words, in a particular way: *The question was very carefully framed.* **3** (usually passive) to give false evidence against sb in order to make him/her seem guilty of a crime: *The man claimed that he had been framed by the police.*

☆ **frame·work** /'freɪmwərk/ *noun* [C] **1** the basic structure of sth that gives it shape and strength: *A greenhouse is made of glass panels fixed in a metal framework.* **2** a system of rules or ideas which help you decide what to do: *The plan may be changed, but it will provide a framework on which we can build.*

franc /fræŋk/ *noun* [C] the unit of money that is used in France, Belgium, Switzerland and several other countries

fran·chise /'fræntʃaɪz/ *noun* [C] **1** a branch of a chain of restaurants, stores, etc.: *A new burger franchise is going to open on the outskirts of town.* **2** official permission from a company to sell its goods or services in a particular area: *a franchise for a fast-food restaurant*

frank /fræŋk/ *adj.* showing your thoughts and feelings openly; saying what you mean; honest: *To be perfectly frank with you, I don't think you'll pass your driver's test.* —**frank·ness** *noun* [U]: *She spoke with great frankness about her past life.*

frank·furt·er /'fræŋkfərtər; -fətər/ (*also* **wiener**) *noun* [C] a type of sausage usually made from beef or pork ☛ Look at **hot dog.**

frank·ly /'fræŋkli/ *adv.* **1** in a frank manner: *Please tell me frankly what you think about my idea.* **2** speaking openly and honestly: *Quite frankly, I'm not surprised at what happened.*

fran·tic /'fræntɪk/ *adj.* **1** in a very emotional state because you are extremely worried or frightened: *The mother was frantic because she couldn't find her child.* ○ *frantic cries for help* **2** very busy or rushed; without organization: *a frantic search for the keys* —**fran·ti·cal·ly** /-kli/ *adv.*: *They have been working frantically all week trying to get things ready in time.*

frat /fræt/ *noun* [C] = FRATERNITY(1)

fra·ter·nal /frə'tərnl/ *adj.* (*formal*) of or like brothers; friendly

fra·ter·ni·ty /frə'tərnəti/ *noun* (*pl.* **fra·ter·ni·ties**) **1** [C](also *informal* **frat**) a social organization for male students at some colleges and universities

☛ A similar student organization for women is called a **sorority.** The names of frater-

nities and sororities are usually combinations of Greek letters.

2 [U] the feeling of friendship between people (like that between brothers) **3** [C] a group of people who share the same work or interests: *the legal fraternity*

fraud /frɔd/ *noun* **1** [C,U] (an act of) deceiving or tricking sb in order to get money, etc. in a way that is against the law: *The accountant was sent to prison for fraud.* ○ *credit card frauds* **2** [C] a person who deceives or tricks sb by pretending to be sb else

fraud·u·lent /'frɔdʒələnt/ *adj.* (*formal*) done in order to deceive sb; dishonest: *the fraudulent use of stolen checks*

fraught /frɔt/ *adj.* **fraught with sth** filled with sth (bad): *The situation was fraught with danger.*

fray /freɪ/ *verb* [I,T] (used about cloth, etc.) to become worn so that some threads are loose; to cause cloth to do this: *This shirt is beginning to fray at the cuffs.* ○ *a frayed cuff* ○ (*figurative*) *Nerves began to fray toward the end of the game* (= the players started to get nervous).

freak¹ /frik/ *noun* [C] **1** a very strange or unusual event: *By some strange freak of nature, we had snow in June.* ○ *a freak accident, storm, etc.* **2** (*informal*) a person who has a very strong interest in sth: *a health freak* **3** a person or animal that is physically abnormal in some way; a person who behaves in a strange way: *Disabled people should never be treated as freaks.*

freak² /frik/ (*also* **freak out**) *verb* [I] (*slang*) to become suddenly very excited, upset, angry, etc.: *Mom really freaked out when she saw that her favorite vase was broken!*

freck·le /'frɛkl/ *noun* [C, usually pl.] a small brown spot on a person's skin: *A lot of people with red hair have freckles.* —**freck·led** *adj.*: *a freckled face*

☆ **free¹** /fri/ *adj.* **1** not in prison or in a cage, etc.: *After twenty years in prison, he was finally set free in 1989.* **2** **free (to do sth)** not controlled by the government, rules, etc.: *a free press* ○ *You're free to do anything you want.* **3** costing nothing: *Admission to the museum is free (of charge).* ○ *a free sample* **4** **free from/of sth** not having sth dangerous, bad, etc.: *free from all worries and responsibilities* ○ *free from pain* **5** not being used: *Do you have a room free for Saturday night?* **6** without appointments; not busy: *I'm sorry, but Mr. Spencer is not free this afternoon.* ○ *I don't have much free time.*

IDM **of your own free will** because you want to, not because sb forces you

free² /fri/ *adv.* **1** in a free manner: *There is no place around here where dogs can run free.* **2** without cost or payment: *Children under five usually travel free on the subway.*

F

tʃ	dʒ	v	θ	ð	s	z	ʃ
chin	June	van	thin	then	so	zoo	she

☆**free³** /fri/ *verb* [T] **1 free sb/sth (from sth)** to let sb/sth go; to set sb/sth free: *to free a prisoner* ○ *The protesters freed the animals from their cages.* **2 free sb/sth of/from sth** to take away from sb sth that is bad: *The medicine freed her from pain for a few hours.* **3 free sb/sth (from sth)** to move sb/sth that is stuck or caught: *The fire department took three hours to free the man from the wreckage of his car.* **4 free sb/sth for sth** to make sth available so that it can be used; to put sb in a position in which he/she can do sth: *Cuts in defense spending would free money to spend on education.*

-free /fri/ (used in compounds to form adjectives) without sth: *sugar-free cola*

☆**free·dom** /'fridəm/ *noun* **1** [U] the state of being free, i.e. of not being in prison or under the control of sb else: *The slaves were granted their freedom after the Civil War.* **2** [C,U] the right to do or say what you want: *You have the freedom to come and go as you please.* ○ *freedom of speech* ○ *the rights and freedoms of the individual* ☛ Look at **liberty**. **3 freedom from sth** the state of not having sth bad: *freedom from fear, hunger, pain, etc.*

ˌfree ˈenterprise *noun* [U] the operation of trade and business without government control

free·hand /'frihænd/ *adj., adv.* (done) by hand, without the help of an instrument, e.g. a ruler: *a freehand sketch*

free·lance /'frilæns/ *adj., adv.* working for several different employers and being paid separately for each piece of work: *a freelance journalist* ○ *She works freelance.* —**free·lance** *verb* [I]: *She freelances for the local paper.* —**free·lanc·er** *noun* [C]

free·ly /'frili/ *adv.* **1** in a way that is not controlled or limited: *He is the country's first freely elected president for 40 years.* ○ *Traffic is flowing freely this morning.*

☛ Note that if you travel **free**, it means that you do not have to pay anything. If you can travel **freely**, it means that you can go wherever you want.

2 willingly, without hesitating: *I freely admit that I made a mistake.*

ˌfree-ˈrange *adj.* from animals that are allowed to move around freely: *free-range eggs* ○ *free-range beef*

ˌfree ˈspeech *noun* [U] the right to express any opinion in public

☆**free·way** /'friweɪ/ (also **expressway**) *noun* [C] a wide road that is specially built for fast traffic

☛ A freeway has at least two **lanes** going in each direction. There are no **traffic lights** or **intersections** on freeways. Cars can use **exit ramps** to leave a freeway, and **entrance ramps** to join it. **Interstate** freeways form a

system which was built in the United States in the 1960s and 1970s to connect all the states (except Alaska and Hawaii). Look also at the note at **road**.

☆**freeze¹** /friz/ *verb* (*p.t.* **froze** /froʊz/; *p.p.* **frozen** /'froʊzn/) **1** [I,T] to become hard (and often change into ice) because of extreme cold; to make sth do this: *Water freezes at 32° Fahrenheit.* ○ *Leave the heat on when you're away or the pipes will freeze.* ○ *The ground is frozen solid.* ○ *I froze the raspberries that we picked.* ○ *Raspberries freeze well.* ○ *frozen peas* **2** [I] (used with "it" to describe extremely cold weather, when water turns into ice): *I think it's going to freeze tonight.* **3** [I,T] (to cause a person) to be very cold or to die from cold: *The two men froze to death on the mountain.* ○ *Turn the heat up a little – my hands are frozen.* **4** [I] to stop suddenly or become still: *The terrible scream made her freeze with terror.* ○ *"Freeze!" shouted the gunman and everybody stood completely still.* **5** [T] to keep wages, prices, fares, etc. at a fixed level for a certain period of time: *Spending on defense has been frozen for one year.*

freeze² /friz/ *noun* [C] **1** a period of weather when the temperature stays below 0°C or 32°F (the freezing point) **2** the fixing of wages, prices, fares, etc. at a certain level for a certain period of time

☆**freez·er** /'frizər/ *noun* [C] a piece of electrical equipment in which you can store food for a long time at a temperature below 0°C or 32°F (the freezing point) so that it stays frozen ☛ Look at **refrigerator**.

freez·ing /'frizɪŋ/ *adj.* (*informal*) very cold (not necessarily below 32° F or 0° C): *Can we turn the heat on? I'm freezing.* ○ *It's freezing outside.*

ˈfreezing point (also **freezing**) *noun* [C,U] the temperature at which water, etc. freezes: *Last night the temperature fell to six degrees below freezing.*

☆**freight** /freɪt/ *noun* [U] **1** the method of carrying goods from one place to another: *freight costs* **2** things that are carried by train or truck: *a freight train* ☛ Look at **cargo**.

freight·er /'freɪtər/ *noun* [C] a ship that carries only freight

☆**French fry** /'frɛntʃ fraɪ/ *noun* [C] (*pl.* **French fries**) (also **fry**) a long, thin piece of potato that is fried in hot fat or oil: *a hamburger and French fries* ○ *Would you like ketchup with your fries?* ☛ picture at **chip**.

French toast /ˌfrɛntʃ 'toʊst/ *noun* [U] bread that has been covered with a mixture of eggs and milk and then fried: *a slice/piece of French toast*

fren·zied /'frɛnzid/ *adj.* wild and excited: *a frenzied attack*

fren·zy /'frɛnzi/ *noun* [sing., U] a state of great excitement; a period when a person cannot

control his/her actions: *The speaker worked the crowd up into a frenzy.*

fre·quen·cy /ˈfrikwənsi/ *noun* (*pl.* **fre·quen·cies**) 1 [U] the rate at which sth happens (= the number of times sth happens in a particular period): *Fatal accidents have decreased in frequency in recent years* (= there are fewer of them). 2 [U] the fact that sth happens often: *The frequency of deaths from cancer near the nuclear power plant is being investigated.* 3 [C,U] the rate at which a sound wave or radio wave vibrates: *high-frequency/low-frequency sounds* ○ *Which frequency does the radio station broadcast on?*

☆ **fre·quent**[1] /ˈfrikwənt/ *adj.* happening often: *a frequent bus service* ☞ The opposite is **infrequent.** —**fre·quent·ly** *adv.*: *Buses run frequently from downtown to the airport.*

fre·quent[2] /friˈkwɛnt; ˈfrikwənt/ *verb* [T] (*formal*) to go to a place often: *Many famous writers frequented this bar.*

☆ **fresh** /frɛʃ/ *adj.* 1 new or different: *They decided to make a fresh start in a different town.* ○ *a fresh approach to a problem* 2 not old (so there has been no time for any change): *There was fresh blood all over the walls.* ○ *Write down a few notes while the lecture is still fresh in your mind.* 3 (used about food, flowers, etc.) made or picked not long ago: *fresh bread* ☞ The opposite (for food) is **stale.** 4 (used about food) not frozen or from a can: *fresh fruit and vegetables* 5 (used about water) not salty; not sea water ☞ A fish that lives in this type of water is a **freshwater** fish. 6 (used about the air) clean and cool: *Open the window and let some fresh air in.* 7 (used about colors, or a person's skin) bright or clear: *a fresh complexion* 8 not tired: *I'll think about the problem again in the morning when I'm fresh.* 9 impolite; not showing respect: *Don't you get fresh with me, young man!* 10 **fresh from/out of sth** having just finished sth: *Life isn't easy for a young teacher fresh out of college.*

IDM **be fresh out (of sth)** (*informal*) to have just finished your supply of sth: *Sorry. We're fresh out of strawberries.* —**fresh·ness** *noun* [U]

fresh·en /ˈfrɛʃn/ *verb* [T] **freshen sth (up)** to make sth cleaner or brighter: *Some new curtains would freshen up this room.*

PHRV **freshen (yourself) up** to wash and make yourself clean and neat

fresh·ly /ˈfrɛʃli/ *adv.* newly; recently: *freshly baked bread*

☆ **fresh·man** /ˈfrɛʃmən/ *noun* [C] (*pl.* **fresh·men** /ˈfrɛʃmən/) a student who is in the ninth grade in school or in his/her first year at college ☞ Look at **sophomore, junior** and **senior.**

fret /frɛt/ *verb* [I] (*old-fashioned*) (**fret·ting; fret·ted**) **fret (about/at/over sth)** to be unhappy or worried about sth: *Don't fret. Everything will be all right.*

fric·tion /ˈfrikʃn/ *noun* [U] 1 the rubbing of one surface or thing against another 2 disagreement between people or groups

☆ **Fri·day** /ˈfraideɪ; -di/ *noun* [C,U] (*abbr.* **Fri.**) the day of the week after Thursday and before Saturday ☞ For examples of the use of the days of the week in sentences, look at **Monday.**

fridge /frɪdʒ/ *noun* [C] = REFRIGERATOR

☆ **friend** /frɛnd/ *noun* [C] 1 a person that you know and like (not a member of your family): *Steve and I are old friends. We went to the same school.* ○ *We're only inviting close friends and relatives to the funeral.* ○ *Do you know Irene Pearse? She's my best friend.* ○ *A friend of mine told me about this restaurant.* ○ *One of my friends told me about this restaurant.* ☞ Look at **boyfriend** and **girlfriend.** 2 **a friend of/to sth** a helper or supporter of sth: *the friends of the poor*

IDM **be/make friends (with sb)** to be/become a friend (of sb): *Tony is very shy and finds it hard to make friends.*

friend·less /ˈfrɛndləs/ *adj.* without friends

☆ **friend·ly** /ˈfrɛndli/ *adj.* (**friend·li·er; friend·li·est**) 1 behaving in a kind and pleasant way; showing kindness and pleasantness: *Everyone here has been very friendly toward us.* ○ *a friendly smile* ○ *a small friendly hotel* 2 **friendly with sb** being the friend of sb: *Nick's gotten quite friendly with the boy next door.* —**friend·li·ness** *noun* [U]

-friendly /ˈfrɛndli/ (in compounds) supporting or helping sb/sth: *Our computer is extremely user-friendly.*

☆ **friend·ship** /ˈfrɛndʃɪp/ *noun* 1 [U] the state of being friends: *Our relationship is based on friendship not love.* 2 [C] a relationship between people who are friends: *lifelong friendships*

fright /fraɪt/ *noun* [C,U] a sudden feeling of fear: *That loud bang gave me a real fright.* ○ *The child cried out in fright.*

☆ **fright·en** /ˈfraɪtn/ *verb* [T] to fill sb with fear: *Sorry, I didn't mean to frighten you.*

PHRV **frighten sb/sth away/off** to cause a person or animal to go away by frightening him/her/it: *The cat frightened the birds away.*

☆ **fright·ened** /ˈfraɪtnd/ *adj.* 1 full of fear or worry: *Frightened children were calling for their mothers.* ○ *He was frightened at the thought of being alone.* ○ *I was frightened that they would think I was being rude.* 2 **frightened of sb/sth** fearing a particular person, thing or situation: *When I was little, I was frightened of cats.* ☞ Look at the note at **afraid.**

☆ **fright·en·ing** /ˈfraɪtn·ɪŋ; ˈfraɪtnɪŋ/ *adj.* causing fear: *It was a very frightening situation to be in.* ○ *It's frightening how quickly time passes.* ○ *It's frightening that time passes so quickly.*

fright·ful /ˈfraɪtfl/ *adj.* very bad; causing great

F

fear: *She described the mugging as a frightful experience.*

frig·id /ˈfrɪdʒəd/ adj. **1** very cold: *There will be frigid air coming from the north tomorrow.* **2** (usually used about a woman) disliking sexual activity

frill /frɪl/ noun [C] **1** a special edge for a dress, shirt, etc. which is made by forming many folds in a narrow piece of cloth **2** [usually pl.] something that is not necessary but is decorative or pleasant: *We just want a plain, simple meal – no frills.*

frill·y /ˈfrɪli/ (**frill·i·er; frill·i·est**) adj. having many frills (1): *a frilly dress*

fringe /frɪndʒ/ noun [C] **1** a decorative edge on a rug, etc. or on clothes, that is made of loose or hanging threads **2** a place, part or position that is a long way from the center or from what is usual: *the outer fringes of Los Angeles*

fringe 'benefit noun [C] = BENEFIT²(4)

Fris·bee /ˈfrɪzbi/ noun (*trademark*) **1** [C] a light plastic disk, shaped like a plate, which is thrown between players in a game **2** [U] a game in which players throw and catch a Frisbee: *to play a game of Frisbee*

frisk /frɪsk/ verb **1** [T] to touch sb's body and clothes in order to search for hidden weapons, drugs, etc.: *to frisk a prisoner* **2** [I] (used about an animal or child) to play and jump around in a lively and happy way

frisk·y /ˈfrɪski/ adj. (**frisk·i·er; frisk·i·est**) lively and playful

frit·ter¹ /ˈfrɪt̮ər/ verb

PHRV **fritter sth away (on sth)** to waste time or money on things that are not important

frit·ter² /ˈfrɪt̮ər/ noun [C] a piece of fruit, meat, etc. that has been covered with a mixture of flour and egg and then fried in hot fat or oil: *a banana fritter*

friv·o·lous /ˈfrɪvələs/ adj. not serious; silly: *This is a serious issue. Please don't make frivolous remarks.* —**friv·o·lous·ly** adv.

friz·zy /ˈfrɪzi/ adj. (used about hair) with a lot of very small curls

fro /froʊ/ adv.

IDM **to and fro** ⇨ TO³

frog

toad

frog /frɔg; frɑg/ noun [C] a small animal with smooth skin and long legs that are used for jumping. Frogs live in or near water: *the croaking of frogs*

from /frəm; *strong forms* frʌm; frɑm/ prep. **1** (showing the place where sb/sth starts or started): *Has the plane from Chicago arrived yet?* ∘ *She comes home from work at 7 o'clock.* ∘ *A child fell from the seventh floor of an apart-*

ment building. **2** (showing the time when sth starts or started): *Peter will be on vacation from Wednesday through Friday.* ∘ *The store is open from 8 a.m. until 8 p.m. every day.* ∘ *We lived in Oregon from 1979 to 1986.* **3** (showing the person who sent, gave, said, etc. sth): *Did you get a birthday card from John?* ∘ *I borrowed this jacket from my sister.* ∘ *a phone call from my father* **4** (showing the origin of sb/sth): *"Where do you come from?" "I'm from Australia."* ∘ *There's a man from the bank here to see you.* **5** (showing the material with which sth is made): *Paper is made from wood.* **6** (showing the distance between two places): *The house is fifty yards from the lake.* **7** (showing the lower limit in a range of prices, figures, etc.): *Our prices start from $2.50 a bottle.* ∘ *Tickets cost from $3 to $11.* **8** (showing the state of sb/sth before a change): *The bus fare has gone up from 75¢ to 85¢.* ∘ *The article was translated from Russian into English.* ∘ *Things have gone from bad to worse.* **9** (showing that sb/sth is taken away): *She borrowed the book from the library.* ∘ *If you subtract 8 from 12, it leaves 4.* **10** (showing sth that you want to avoid): *There was no shelter from the wind.* ∘ *This game will keep you from getting bored.* **11** (showing the reason for sth): *People in the camps are suffering from hunger and cold.* **12** (showing the difference between two people, places or things): *Is Portuguese very different from Spanish?* **13** (showing your position or point of view): *There's a great view from the top of the tower.* ∘ *He always looks at things from his own point of view.*

IDM **from...on** starting at a particular time and continuing forever: *She never spoke to him again from that day on.* ∘ *From now on, you will have to help with the housework.*

in the front of the bus • on the front of the bus • front • in front of the bus

☆ **front¹** /frʌnt/ noun **1** [C, usually sing.] the side or surface of sth that is most usually seen or that is most important: *a dress with buttons down the front* ∘ *the front of a building* (= the front wall) **2** [C, usually sing.] the most forward part of sth or the area that is just outside of or before sb/sth: *Young children should not ride in the front of the car.* ∘ *There is a small porch at the front of the house.*

☞ **On the front of** means "on the front surface of sth": *The number is shown on the front of the bus.* **In front of** means "farther forward than another person or thing": *A car stopped in front of the bus.* **At/In the front of**

across from **in front of**

"means in the most forward part inside sth": *The driver sits at the front of the bus.* Look at these sentences too: *The teacher usually stands in front of the class.* ○ *The noisy students had to sit at the front of the class* (= in the front seats).

3 the front [sing.] the line or area where fighting takes place in a war: *to be sent to the front* **4** [sing.] a way of behaving that hides your true feelings: *His brave words were just a front. He was really feeling very nervous.* **5** [C, usually sing.] a person, group, or thing that hides an illegal or secret activity: *The Mafia set up an export company as a front for its illegal activities.* **6** [C] (*technical*) (used when talking about the weather) a line or area where warm air and cold air meet **7** [C] a particular area of activity: *Things are difficult on the domestic front right now.*

IDM **in front** ahead of or further forward than sb/sth: *After three miles, the Kenyan runner was in front.*

in front of 1 in a position further forward than but close to sb/sth: *The bus stops right in front of our house.* ○ *Don't stand in front of the TV.* ○ *The book was open in front of her on the desk.* ☞ **In front of** does not mean the same as **across from**. **2** in the presence of: *I couldn't talk about that in front of my parents.*

up front (*informal*) as payment before sth is done: *I want half the money up front and half when the job is finished.*

☆**front²** /frʌnt/ *adj.* (only *before* a noun) of or at the front¹ (1,2): *the front door, yard, room, etc.* ○ *front teeth*

fron·tal /ˈfrʌntl/ *adj.* (only *before* a noun) from the front: *a frontal attack*

fron·tier /frʌnˈtɪr/ *noun* **1** [usually sing.] land that people are just beginning to live on, especially in the western U.S. in the 1800s: *frontier towns of the Wild West* ☞ Look at the note at **border¹**. **2 the frontiers** [plural] the border between what we know and what we do not know: *Scientific research is constantly pushing back the frontiers of our knowledge about the world.*

☆**frost¹** /frɔst/ *noun* **1** [C,U] the weather conditions when the temperature falls below the freezing point: *There was a hard frost last night.* **2** [U] a very thin layer of little pieces of

ice that is formed on surfaces when the temperature is below the freezing point: *The ground was white with frost.*

frost² /frɔst/ *verb* [T] to decorate the top of a cake, cookies, etc. with a mixture containing sugar (**frosting**)

PHRV **frost over/up** to become covered with frost¹(2) : *The window frosted over/up during the night.*

frost·bite /ˈfrɔstbaɪt/ *noun* [U] injury to the fingers, toes, etc. that is caused by very low temperatures

frost·ed /ˈfrɔstəd/ *adj.* (used about glass or a window) with a special surface so you cannot see through it

frost·ing /ˈfrɔstɪŋ/ *noun* [U] a mixture of powdered sugar, butter, flavoring, etc. that is used for decorating cakes, cookies, etc.: *chocolate frosting* ☞ Look at **icing**.

frost·y /ˈfrɔsti/ *adj.* (**frost·i·er; frost·i·est**) **1** very cold, with frost: *a cold and frosty morning* **2** cold and unfriendly: *a frosty welcome*

froth¹ /frɔθ/ *noun* [U] a mass of small white bubbles on the top of a liquid, etc. —**froth·y** *adj.*: *a frothy drink*

froth² /frɔθ/ *verb* [I] to have or produce froth: *The mad dog was frothing at the mouth.*

frown¹ /fraʊn/ *verb* [I] to bring your eyebrows together so that you make lines appear on your forehead. You frown when you are angry, worried, or thinking very hard: *"You're late," he said, frowning.*

PHRV **frown on/upon sth** to think that sth is not good; to disapprove: *Smoking is very much frowned upon these days.*

frown² /fraʊn/ *noun* [C] an act of frowning: *She looked at me with a frown.*

froze *p.t.* of FREEZE¹

fro·zen /ˈfroʊzn/ *p.p.* of FREEZE¹: *The pond is frozen. Let's go skating.* ○ *frozen vegetables* ○ *I'm frozen* (= very cold).

fru·gal /ˈfrugl/ *adj.* careful not to spend too much money or buy too much

☆**fruit** /frut/ *noun* **1** [C,U] the part of a plant or tree that contains seeds and that is used as food: *Try and eat more fresh fruit and vegetables.* ○ *citrus fruit* (= oranges, lemons, grapefruit, etc.) ○ *Is a tomato a fruit or a vegetable?* ○ *fruit juice*

☞ When we say "a fruit" we mean "a type of fruit": *Most big supermarkets sell many different tropical fruits.* When we are talking about one individual piece, e.g. a single apple, pear, banana, etc. we must say "a piece of fruit": *What would you like for dessert: ice cream or a piece of fruit?* It is more usual to use the uncountable form: *Would you like some fruit?*

2 [C] the part of any plant in which the seed is formed **3 the fruits** [plural] a good result or a reward for what you have done

fruit·ful /ˈfrutfl/ *adj.* producing good results; useful: *fruitful discussions*

F

fru·i·tion /fru'ɪʃn/ *noun* [U] the time when a plan, etc. starts to be successful: *After months of hard work, our efforts were coming to fruition.*

fruit·less /'frutləs/ *adj.* producing poor or no results; unsuccessful: *a fruitless search*

frus·trate /'frʌstreɪt/ *verb* [T] **1** to prevent sb from doing sth or sth from happening: *The rescue work has been frustrated by bad weather conditions.* **2** to cause a person to feel angry or dissatisfied because things are not happening as he/she wants: *It's the lack of money that really frustrates him.*

frus·trat·ed /'frʌstreɪtəd/ *adj.* angry or dissatisfied, e.g. because you cannot have or do what you want: *He felt very frustrated at his lack of progress in learning Chinese.*

frus·trat·ing /'frʌstreɪtɪŋ/ *adj.* making you angry or dissatisfied: *I spent a frustrating morning trying to reach Sandy on the phone.*

frus·tra·tion /frʌ'streɪʃn/ *noun* [C,U] a feeling of anger or dissatisfaction, or sth that causes it: *He felt anger and frustration at not being able to help the starving children.* ○ *Every job has its frustrations.*

☆ **fry** /fraɪ/ *verb* [I,T] (*pres. part.* **fry·ing**; *3rd pers. sing. pres.* **fries**; *p.t., p.p.* **fried** /fraɪd/) to be cooked in hot fat or oil; to cook sth in this way: *to fry an egg* ○ *a fried egg* ○ *There was a smell of bacon frying in the kitchen.* ☞ Look at the note at **cook**.

'frying pan (*also* **fry pan**; **skillet**) *noun* [C] a flat shallow pan with a long handle that is used for frying food ☞ picture at **pan**.

fudge /fʌdʒ/ *noun* [U] a type of soft candy made with milk, butter, sugar and another flavoring

☆ **fuel¹** /'fyuəl; fyul/ *noun* **1** [U] material that is burned to produce heat or power: *What's the car's fuel consumption?* ○ *Our fuel bills are very high.* **2** [C] a type of fuel: *I think natural gas is the best fuel for home heating.*

fuel² /'fyuəl; fyul/ *verb* [T] to provide fuel for sth: (*figurative*) *Her comments fueled speculation that she was going to resign.*

fu·gi·tive /'fyudʒətɪv/ *noun* [C] a person who is running away or escaping (e.g. from the police) ☞ Look at **refugee**.

ful·fill /fʊl'fɪl/ *verb* [T] **1** to perform or carry out a duty, task, etc.: *She fulfills an advisory role on the committee.* **2** to make sth that you wish for, or have promised, happen: *to fulfill an ambition* ○ *The government has not yet fulfilled its promises to improve education.* **3** to do, have, or provide what is needed or necessary, especially according to a contract, a rule, etc.: *to fulfill the requirements for a job*

ful·filled /fʊl'fɪld/ *adj.* completely satisfied and happy

ful·fill·ing /fʊl'fɪlɪŋ/ *adj.* making you feel happy and satisfied: *I find my work very fulfilling.*

ful·fill·ment /fʊl'fɪlmənt/ *noun* [U] **1** the act of fulfilling or the state of being fulfilled: *Moving into our own home was the fulfillment of a dream.* **2** the feeling of satisfaction that you have when you have done sth: *Some men find fulfillment in raising a family.*

☆ **full¹** /fʊl/ *adj.* **1** **full (of sb/sth)** holding or containing as much or as many as possible: *The garbage can needs to be emptied. It's full.* ○ *a full bottle* ○ *The bus was full so we had to wait for the next one.* ○ *"Is there any coffee left?" "Yes, the pot's still half full."* ○ (*figurative*) *The kids are full of energy.* ○ (*figurative*) *We need a good night's sleep because we have a full (= busy) day tomorrow.* **2** **full (of sb/sth)** with a lot of people or things in it: *The room was full of people.* ○ *His work was full of mistakes.* **3** **full (up)** having had enough to eat and drink: *No dessert for me. I'm full (up).* **4** (only *before* a noun) complete; not leaving anything out: *I would like a full report on the accident.* ○ *Full details of today's TV programs are on page 20.* ○ *He took full responsibility for what had happened.* ○ *Please give your full address.* **5** (only *before* a noun) the highest or greatest possible: *The roses are in full bloom.* ○ *a train traveling at full speed* **6** round in shape: *a full figure* **7** (used about clothes) made with plenty of material: *a full skirt* **8** (used about a bed) big enough for two people ☞ Look at the note at **bed¹**.

IDM **be full of yourself** to think that you are very important: *He's been very full of himself ever since he was promoted.*

have your hands full ⇨ **HAND¹**

in full with nothing missing; completely: *Your money will be refunded in full (= you will get all your money back).* ○ *Please write your name in full.*

in full swing at the stage when there is a lot of activity: *When we arrived, the party was already in full swing.*

in full view (of sb/sth) in a place where you can easily be seen: *In full view of the guards, he tried to escape over the prison wall.* ○ *in full view of the front windows*

to the full as much as possible: *to enjoy life to the full*

full² /fʊl/ *adv.* completely; directly: *All the hotel rooms in town were booked full.* ○ *You know full well why I asked that question.*

full-'blown *adj.* fully developed: *to have full-blown AIDS*

full-fledged /ˌfʊl'flɛdʒd/ *adj.* completely trained or completely developed: *Media studies is now a full-fledged academic subject.*

full-'length *adj.* **1** (used about a picture, mirror, etc.) showing a person from head to foot **2** (used about a dress, skirt, etc.) reaching the ankles: *a full-length ball gown* **3** not shorter than normal: *a full-length movie, book, etc.*

full 'moon *noun* [sing.] the moon when it

appears as a circle ☞ The opposite is a **new moon**.

ˌfull-ˈscale *adj.* **1** (used about a plan, drawing, etc.) of the same size as the original object **2** using every means that is available: *a full-scale murder investigation*

☆ˌfull-ˈtime *adj., adv.* for a whole of the normal period of work: *He has a full-time job.* ○ *He works full-time.* ○ *We have 800 full-time and 500 part-time employees.* ☞ Look at **part-time**.

☆ful·ly /ˈfʊli/ *adv.* completely; to the highest possible degree: *I'm fully aware of the problem.* ○ *All our engineers are fully trained.* ○ *a fully automatic camera*

fum·ble /ˈfʌmbl/ *verb* [I] to use your hands in an awkward way, especially when you are looking for sth: *She was fumbling in her pocket for her key.*

fume /fyum/ *verb* [I] to feel or express anger: *By the time they arrived, I was absolutely fuming.* ○ *"They're almost two hours late," she fumed.*

fumes /fyumz/ *noun* [plural] smoke or gases that smell bad and that can be harmful if you breathe them in: *Six people died in the fire when they were overcome by smoke and fumes.*

☆fun¹ /fʌn/ *noun* [U] pleasure and enjoyment; an activity or a person that gives you pleasure and enjoyment. *There isn't much fun In staying home on your own.* ○ *Staying home on your own isn't much fun.* ○ *We had a lot of fun at the party last night.* ○ *The party was a lot of fun.* ○ *Have fun!* (= enjoy yourself!) ○ *Sailing can be good fun if you don't mind getting wet.* ○ *He was extremely intelligent, but he was also a lot of fun.*

IDM **(just) for fun/for the fun of it** (just) for amusement or pleasure; not seriously: *I don't need English for my work. I am just learning it for fun.*

(just) in fun as a joke: *It was said in fun. They didn't mean to upset you.*

make fun of sb/sth to laugh at sb/sth in an unkind way; to make other people do this: *The older kids are always making fun of him because of his accent.*

poke fun at sb/sth ⇨ POKE

☆fun² /fʌn/ *adj.* **1** amusing and enjoyable: *a fun evening*

☞ Be careful. **Funny** describes something that makes you laugh or that is strange. It is not the same as **fun**: *The party was fun* (= it was enjoyable). ○ *The movie was funny* (= it made us laugh).

2 (used about people) amusing and enjoyable to be with: *He's a really fun guy.*

☆func·tion¹ /ˈfʌŋkʃn/ *noun* [C] **1** the purpose or special duty of a person or thing: *One function of the school board is to appoint new teachers.* ○ *The function of the heart is to pump blood through the body.* **2** an important social event,

ceremony, etc.: *The Vice President attends hundreds of official functions every year.*

☆func·tion² /ˈfʌŋkʃn/ *verb* [I] to work; to be in action: *My new computer isn't functioning very well.* ○ *Only one engine was still functioning.*

func·tion·al /ˈfʌŋkʃənl/ *adj.* **1** practical and useful rather than attractive: *cheap, functional furniture* **2** working; being used: *The system is now fully functional.*

☆fund¹ /fʌnd/ *noun* **1** [C] a sum of money that is collected for a particular purpose: *They contributed $30 to the disaster relief fund.* **2 funds** [plural] money that is available and can be spent

fund² /fʌnd/ *verb* [T] to provide a project, etc. with money: *The government is funding a new project to help inner-city children.*

☆fun·da·men·tal /ˌfʌndəˈmɛntl/ *adj.* important or basic; from which everything else develops: *There will be fundamental changes in the way the school is run.* ○ *There is a fundamental difference between your opinion and mine.* —**fun·da·men·tal·ly** *adv.*: *The two candidates have fundamentally different views on the issue.*

fun·da·men·tal·ist /ˌfʌndəˈmɛntəlɪst/ *noun* **1** a person who follows all the teaching of a religion very strictly **2** a Christian who believes that everything in the Bible is absolutely true —**fun·da·men·tal·ist** *adj.*

fun·da·men·tals /ˌfʌndəˈmɛntlz/ *noun* [plural] basic facts or principles

☆fu·ner·al /ˈfyunərəl/ *noun* [C] a ceremony (often in a church or a funeral home) connected with burying or burning (**cremating**) a dead person: *The funeral will be held next week.* ○ *The mourners at the funeral were all in black.*

☞ The body of the dead person is carried in a **casket** or **coffin**, on which there are often **wreaths** of flowers. The coffin is buried in a **grave** or is burned (**cremated**).

ˈfuneral diˌrector (*also* **mortician**, *old-fashioned* **undertaker**) *noun* [C] a person whose job is to prepare dead people's bodies to be buried and to arrange funerals

ˈfuneral home (*also* ˈfuneral parlor) *noun* [C] a place where dead people's bodies are prepared to be buried or burned and where visitors can look at the body

fun·gus /ˈfʌŋgəs/ *noun* [C,U] (*pl.* **fun·gi** /ˈfʌndʒaɪ; ˈfʌŋgaɪ/ *or* **fun·gus·es**) a plant that is not green and that does not have leaves or flowers. One type has a thick stem and a big flat top, another type is like a powder. Fungi grow on other plants, decaying wood or food, etc.: *mushrooms and other edible fungi.* ○ *The roses are covered in fungus.* ☞ Look at **mold** and **toadstool**.

fun·nel¹ /ˈfʌnl/ *noun* [C] an object that is wide at the top and narrow at the bottom, used for

ə	y	w	t̮	eɪ	aɪ	ɔɪ	aʊ	oʊ
about	yes	woman	butter	say	five	boy	now	go

pouring liquid, powder, etc. into a small opening

fun·nel² /'fʌnl/ *verb* [I,T] to move or make sth move through a funnel or a narrow space: *People funneled slowly through the stadium exits.*

funnel cloud *noun* [C] a type of dangerous storm with very strong winds that blow in a circle (**a tornado**) that is not touching the ground

fun·ni·ly /'fʌnl·i/ *adv.* **1** (used for expressing surprise at sth strange that has happened): *Funnily enough, my parents weren't at all angry about it.* **2** in a funny way: *She's breathing very funnily.*

☆ **fun·ny** /'fʌni/ *adj.* (**fun·ni·er**; **fun·ni·est**) **1** that makes you smile or laugh: *She told us a funny story about taking a cow to church.* ○ *He's a really funny person* (= he can make people laugh). **2** strange or unusual: *The engine is making a funny noise.* ○ *It's funny how people never talk in elevators.* ○ *What a funny little chair!* ○ *That's funny – he was here a minute ago and now he's gone.* ○ *Can I sit down for a minute? I feel a little funny* (= a little sick).

☆ **fur** /fər/ *noun* **1** [U] the soft thick hair that covers the bodies of some animals **2** [C,U] the skin and hair of an animal that is used for making clothes, etc.; a piece of clothing that is made from this: *These boots are lined with fur.* ○ *a fur coat* —**fur·ry** /'fəri/ *adj.*: *a small furry animal*

fu·ri·ous /'fyʊriəs/ *adj.* **1 furious (with sb)/ (about/at sth)** very angry: *He was furious with her.* ○ *He was furious at her behavior.* ☞ The noun is **fury**. **2** very strong; violent: *a furious argument* —**fu·ri·ous·ly** *adv.*

fur·nace /'fərnəs/ *noun* [C] **1** a piece of equipment in which fuel is burned in order to heat a building: *an oil furnace* ○ *a gas furnace* **2** = BLAST FURNACE

fur·nish /'fərnɪʃ/ *verb* [T] to put furniture in a room, house, etc.: *The room was comfortably furnished.*

fur·nished /'fərnɪʃt/ *adj.* having furniture: *a furnished apartment* ☞ The opposite is **unfurnished**.

fur·nish·ings /'fərnɪʃɪŋz/ *noun* [plural] the furniture, carpets, curtains, etc. in a room, house, etc.

☆ **fur·ni·ture** /'fərnɪtʃər/ *noun* [U] the movable things, e.g. tables, chairs, beds, etc. in a room, house or office: *modern/antique/secondhand furniture*

☞ Be careful. "Furniture" is an uncountable noun: *We need some new furniture.* If we are talking about an individual item, we must say "a piece of furniture": *The only nice piece of furniture in the room was an antique desk.*

fur·row /'fəroʊ/ *noun* [C] **1** a line in a field

that is made by a plow **2** a line in a person's face, especially on the forehead

fur·ry ⇨ FUR

☆ **fur·ther¹** /'fərðər/ *adj.* **1** more; additional: *Are there any further questions?* ○ *Let us know if you require any further information.* ○ *The museum is closed until further notice* (= until another announcement is made). **2** more distant or far; farther: *Which is further from school: my house or yours?* ☞ Look at the note at **further²(3).**

fur·ther² /'fərðər/ *adv.* **1** more; to a greater degree: *The board needs time to consider the matter further.* **2** at or to a greater distance in time: *I can't remember any further back than 1970.* **3** at or to a greater distance in space; farther: *It's not safe to go any further.* ○ *The hospital is further down the road on the left.*

☞ Some speakers of American English believe that only **farther** should be used when you are talking about distance in space: *I jumped farther than you did.* However, many people also use **further** when talking about distances, especially in informal conversation: *Boston is further/farther from New York than New Haven is.* Only **further** can be used in other senses: *We need a further week to finish the project.*

IDM further afield ⇨ FAR AFIELD

fur·ther³ /'fərðər/ *verb* [T] (*formal*) to help sth to be successful: *to further the cause of peace*

fur·ther·more /'fərðərmɔr/ *adv.* (*formal*) in addition; also: *We are donating $6 million to the disaster fund. Furthermore, we will send medical supplies immediately.*

☆ **fur·thest** /'fərðəst/ *adj., adv.* **1** to the greatest degree: *Anne has progressed the furthest of all the children in her class.* **2** = FARTHEST

fur·tive /'fərtɪv/ *adj.* secret, acting as though you are trying to hide sth because you feel guilty: *a furtive glance* —**fur·tive·ly** *adv.*: *He crept furtively out the front door.*

fu·ry /'fyʊri/ *noun* [U] very great anger: *She was speechless with fury.* ☞ The adjective is **furious.**

fuse¹ /fyuz/ *noun* [C] **1** a (long) piece of rope, string, etc. that is used for lighting a bomb, etc. **2** a device that makes a bomb, etc. explode at a particular time **3** a small piece of wire in an electrical system, machine, etc. that melts and breaks if there is too much power. This stops the flow of electricity and prevents fire or damage: *You'll blow a fuse if you turn on all the appliances at once.* ○ *Do you know how to change a fuse?* ☞ Look at **circuit breaker.**

fuse² /fyuz/ *verb* [I,T] to join together: *Sadness and joy are fused in her poems.*

fu·se·lage /'fyusəlaʒ/ *noun* [C] the main outer part of an airplane (not the engines, wings or tail)

fu·sion /'fyuʒn/ *noun* [C,U] the joining to-

ər	ɪr	ɛr	ɑr	ɔr	ʊr	ʒ	h	ŋ
bird	near	hair	car	north	tour	vision	hat	sing

gether of different things: *the fusion of two political systems* ∘ *nuclear fusion* (= a method of releasing nuclear energy)

fuss¹ /fʌs/ *noun* **1** [sing., U] unnecessary nervous excitement or activity: *The kids brushed their teeth and went to bed without any fuss at all.* ∘ *What's all the fuss about?* **2** [sing.] a time when people are angry: *There will be an awful fuss if my parents find out that I borrowed the car.*

IDM **make, raise, etc. a fuss (about/over sth)** to complain strongly

make a fuss over sb/sth to pay a lot of attention to sb/sth

fuss² /fʌs/ *verb* [I] **1** to be worried or excited about small things: *Quit fussing. We're not going to be late.* **2 fuss over sb/sth** to pay too much attention to sb/sth: *to fuss over details*

fuss·y /ˈfʌsi/ *adj.* (**fuss·i·er**; **fuss·i·est**) (used about people) giving too much attention to small details and therefore difficult to please: *He is a very fussy eater* (= there are many things which he does not eat).

fu·tile /ˈfyutl̩/ *adj.* (used about an action) having no effect or result; useless: *They made a*

last futile attempt to persuade him. —**fu·til·i·ty** /fyuˈtɪləti/ *noun* [U]: *the futility of war*

☆**fu·ture¹** /ˈfyutʃər/ *noun* **1** [sing.] the time that will come after the present: *Who knows what will happen in the future?* ∘ *in the near/distant future* (= soon/not soon) ∘ *in the immediate future* (= very soon) **2** [C] what will happen to sb/sth in the time after the present: *The company's future does not look very hopeful.* **3** [U] the possibility of being successful: *I could see no future in this country, so I left to work abroad.* **4** [sing.] (*also* **future tense**) (*grammar*) the tense of a verb that expresses what will happen after the present

☆**fu·ture²** /ˈfyutʃər/ *adj.* (only *before* a noun) of or happening in the time after the present: *She met her future husband when she was still in school.* ∘ *You can keep that book for future reference* (= to look at again later). ∘ *What are your future plans?*

fuzz /fʌz/ *noun* [U] short, thin hairs or threads: *You have some fuzz on your shirt.*

fuzz·y /ˈfʌzi/ *adj.* (**fuzz·i·er**; **fuzz·i·est**) **1** covered with fuzz: *a fuzzy teddy bear* **2** not clear: *Can you adjust the TV? The picture's kind of fuzzy.*

Gg

G, g /dʒi/ *noun* [C] (*pl.* **G's**; **g's**) the seventh letter of the English alphabet: *"Girl" begins with (a) "G."*

g *abbr.* = GRAM

ga·ble /ˈgeɪbl̩/ *noun* [C] the pointed part at the top of an outside wall between two parts of a roof

gadg·et /ˈgædʒət/ *noun* [C] (*informal*) a small tool or machine

gag¹ /gæg/ *noun* [C] **1** a piece of cloth, etc. that is put in or over sb's mouth in order to stop him/her from talking **2** a joke or funny story

gag² /gæg/ *verb* (**gag·ging**; **gagged**) **1** [T] to put a gag in or over sb's mouth: (*figurative*) *The new laws are an attempt to gag the press.* **2** [I] **gag (on sth)** to feel as if you cannot swallow and as if you are going to bring food from your stomach into your throat: *to gag on a piece of raw fish*

gag order *noun* [C] an official document which forbids lawyers, journalists, etc. to speak about sth in public: *The judge issued a gag order.*

gai·e·ty /ˈgeɪəti/ *noun* [U] a feeling of happiness and fun ☞ The adjective is **gay**.

gai·ly /ˈgeɪli/ *adv.* in a gay (2) manner

☆**gain¹** /geɪn/ *noun* **1** [C,U] an increase in money; (a) profit or advantage: *Shares in software companies have made big gains on the stock market.* ∘ *Everything he did was for personal gain.* **2** [C] an increase in size, amount or power: *a gain in weight of one pound*

☆**gain²** /geɪn/ *verb* **1** [T] to get or win sth (especially sth that is wanted or needed): *They managed to gain access to secret information.* ∘ *He has gained an international reputation as an artist.* **2** [T] to get more of sth: *The train was gaining speed.* ∘ *I've gained a lot of weight recently.* **3** [I] **gain by/from (doing) sth** to get an advantage from sth/from doing sth: *Many people will gain from the changes in the law.* ∘ *I have nothing to gain by staying in this job.* **4** [T] (used about a clock or watch) to go too fast and show the incorrect time: *My watch gains five minutes a day.* ☞ When a clock gains time we say it is **fast**. ☞ The opposite for 2, 3 and 4 is **lose**.

IDM **gain ground** to make progress; to become stronger or more popular: *The Republican Party gained some ground in the recent elections.*

tʃ	dʒ	v	θ	ð	s	z	ʃ
chin	June	van	thin	then	so	zoo	she

PHRV **gain in sth** to get more of sth: *He's gained in confidence in the past year.*

gain on sb/sth to get closer to sb/sth that you are trying to catch

gait /geɪt/ *noun* [sing.] the way that a person or an animal walks

gal. *abbr.* = GALLON

ga·la /ˈgeɪlə; ˈgælə/ *noun* [C] a special social occasion: *a gala performance for charity*

gal·ax·y /ˈgæləksi/ *noun* [C] (*pl.* **gal·ax·ies**) a large group of stars and planets in outer space

gale /geɪl/ *noun* [C] a very strong wind ☞ Look at the note at **storm**.

gal·lant /ˈgælənt/ *adj.* (*formal*) **1** brave: *a gallant soldier* **2** /gəˈlænt; -ˈlɑnt; ˈgælənt/ (used about men) polite to and showing special respect for women

gal·ler·y /ˈgæləri/ *noun* [C] (*pl.* **gal·ler·ies**) **1** a building or room where works of art are shown to the public: *an art gallery* **2** a raised area around the sides or at the back of a large hall, theater, etc. People can sit in the gallery and watch what is happening below: *the public gallery in the Senate*

☆ **gal·lon** /ˈgælən/ *noun* [C] (*abbr.* **gall.**) a measure of liquid; 3.8 liters. There are 4 quarts in a gallon. ☞ For more information on measurements, look at Appendix 2.

gal·lop[1] /ˈgæləp/ *verb* [I] (used about a horse or a rider) to go at the fastest speed, when the horse's four feet all leave the ground together

gal·lop[2] /ˈgæləp/ *noun* [sing., C] the fastest speed of a horse, etc.; a time when you ride at this speed: *They went for a gallop over the fields.*

gal·lows /ˈgælouz/ *noun* [C] (*pl.* **gal·lows**) a wooden framework on which criminals are hanged

ga·lore /gəˈlɔr/ *adv.* (only *after* a noun) in large numbers: *There will be bargains galore at our super sale on Saturday.*

☆ **gam·ble**[1] /ˈgæmbl/ *verb* [I,T] to risk money on the result of a card game, horse race, etc.: *He spent every evening gambling at poker.* ○ *She gambled $25 on the last race.*

PHRV **gamble on sth/on doing sth** to act in the hope that sth will happen although it is possible that it will not: *I wouldn't gamble on the weather staying nice like this.*

gam·ble[2] /ˈgæmbl/ *noun* [C] something you do that is a risk (i.e. you might win sth but you might also lose): *Setting up this business was a real gamble.*

IDM **take a gamble (on sth)** to take a chance (on sth or on sth happening) —**gam·bler** *noun* [C]: *He's always been a gambler.* —**gam·bling** *noun* [U]: *an addiction to gambling*

☆ **game**[1] /geɪm/ *noun* **1** [C] a form of play or a sport with rules; a time when you play it: *Let's have a game of chess.* ○ *a game of football, baseball, tennis, etc.* ○ *Our next game is against the Boston Eagles.* ○ *Tonight's game is between*

Chicago and Detroit. ○ *What an exciting game!* ○ *The game ended in a tie.* **2** [C] a unit in a match of tennis, etc.: *Hingis won the first game of the second set.* **3** [C] the set of equipment that you need in order to play a particular (indoor) game: *We usually buy a new board game each year.*

IDM **the name of the game** ➪ NAME[1]

game[2] /geɪm/ *adj.* (used about a person) ready and willing to do sth new, unusual, difficult, etc.: *I have never been sailing, but I'm game to try.*

game[3] /geɪm/ *noun* [U] wild animals or birds that are hunted for sport or food: *Shooting game is popular in Montana.* ○ *big game* (= lions, tigers, etc. that are hunted)

ˈgame show *noun* [C] a television program in which people play games or answer questions in order to win prizes: *a game show host*

☆ **gang**[1] /gæŋ/ *noun* [C] **1** an organized group of criminals, especially young men: *a gang member* ○ *to join a gang* ○ *inner-city gang warfare* **2** a group of prisoners who work together as a team: *a chain gang* (= prisoners who are connected by a chain around their legs) **3** (*informal*) a group of (young) friends: *The whole gang is here tonight.*

gang[2] /gæŋ/ *verb* (*informal*)

gang up on sb to join together with other people in order to act against sb: *I felt like all my friends were ganging up on me.*

gan·grene /ˈgæŋgrin; gæŋˈgrin/ *noun* [U] the decay of a part of the body because the blood supply to it has been stopped

gang·ster /ˈgæŋstər/ *noun* [C] a member of an organization of criminals

☆ **gap** /gæp/ *noun* [C] **a gap (in/between sth)** **1** an empty space in sth or between two things: *The sheep got out through a gap in the fence.* ○ *He has a gap between his two front teeth.* **2** a space where sth should be: *There were several gaps in his story.* ○ *I think our new product should fill a gap in the market.* ○ *Her husband's death left a big gap in her life.* **3** a period of time that is not filled or when you are not doing what you normally do: *I returned to teaching after a gap of about five years.* ○ *a gap in the conversation* **4** a difference between people or their ideas: *The gap between the rich and the poor is getting wider.* ○ *the generation gap* (= the difference in opinions between parents and their children)

IDM **bridge a/the gap** ➪ BRIDGE[2]

gape /geɪp/ *verb* [I] to stare at sb/sth with your mouth open

gap·ing /ˈgeɪpɪŋ/ *adj.* (used about a hole) wide open: *There was a gaping hole in the wall after the explosion.*

☆ **ga·rage** /gəˈrɑʒ; -ˈrɑdʒ/ *noun* [C] **1** a building or a part of a house where cars, etc. are kept: *The house has a two-car garage.* ☞ picture on

G

page A28. **2** a place where you can have your car checked or repaired. It may also sell gasoline, etc.: *to take your car to the garage* ☞ Look at **gas station**.

ga'rage sale *noun* [C] a sale, held in sb's garage, of used things that people do not want anymore ☞ Look also at **yard sale** and **rummage sale**.

☆ **gar·bage** /'gɑrbɪdʒ/ (*also* **trash**) *noun* [U] **1**(also *formal* **rubbish**) things that you do not want anymore; waste material: *Our garbage is picked up every Monday.* ○ *It's only garbage – throw it away.* **2** the place where you put waste material: *Throw it in the garbage.* **3** (*informal*) something that you think is bad, stupid or wrong: *I don't know why you watch that garbage on TV.*

garbage cans

garbage can

wastebasket

garbage (*also* trash)

trash

trash can

garbage can (*also* trash can)

☆ **'garbage can** (*also* **trash can**) *noun* [C] a container that you put waste material in ☞ picture at **can**.

☆ **'garbage man** (*pl.* **garbage men**) *noun* [C] a man whose job is to take away the garbage that people put in their garbage cans

gar·bled /'gɑrbld/ *adj.* (used about a message, story, etc.) difficult to understand; not clear

☆ **gar·den¹** /'gɑrdn/ *noun* [C] **1** a small piece of land (usually near a house) where vegetables or flowers are grown: *My grandfather planted some onions in his garden.* ○ *a vegetable/flower garden* ○ *a garden hose* (= that you use in the garden) ☞ Look at **yard** and **lawn**. **2** a public place with flowers, trees and other plants: *the Botanical Garden* **3** (*BrE*) = YARD(1)

gar·den² /'gɑrdn/ *verb* [I] to work in a garden: *She's been gardening all afternoon.*

gar·den·er /'gɑrdnər/ *noun* [C] a person who works in a garden: *to hire a gardener*

gar·den·ing /'gɑrdnɪŋ; 'gɑrdnɪŋ/ *noun* [U] taking care of a garden, e.g. planting flowers, digging, etc.: *to do some gardening*

gar·gle /'gɑrgl/ *verb* [I] to wash your throat with a liquid (which you do not swallow)

gar·ish /'gɛrɪʃ/ *adj.* too bright or highly decorated

gar·lic /'gɑrlɪk/ *noun* [U] a plant with a strong taste and smell that looks like a small onion and is used in cooking: *a clove of garlic* ☞ picture at **onion**.

gar·ment /'gɑrmənt/ *noun* [C] (*formal*) one piece of clothing: *This garment must be dry cleaned.*

gar·nish¹ /'gɑrnɪʃ/ *verb* [T] **garnish sth (with sth)** to decorate food or a plate, dish, etc. with small additional amounts of food: *a drink garnished with a slice of lemon*

gar·nish² /'gɑrnɪʃ/ *noun* [C] a small amount of food that is used to decorate food or a plate, dish, etc.: *Top the potatoes with a garnish of chopped parsley.*

gar·ri·son /'gærəsn/ *noun* [C] a group of soldiers who are living in and guarding a town or building

☆ **gas¹** /gæs/ *noun* (*pl.* **gas·es**) **1** [C,U] a substance that is like air (i.e. not solid or liquid): *Hydrogen and oxygen are gases.* **2** [U] a gas (1) or mixture of gases that is used for heating, cooking, etc.: *Does your clothes dryer run on gas or electricity?* ○ *a gas stove* ○ *natural gas* ○ *The explosion was caused by a gas leak.* **3** [U] a poisonous gas (1) that is used in war ☞ Look also at **tear gas**. **4** [U] (*also* **gasoline**) the liquid that is used as fuel for motor vehicles such as cars, trucks, and motorcycles: *a gas pump* ○ *to fill up the gas tank* **5** [U] gas (1) that forms in your stomach: *I've got terrible gas.*

gas² /gæs/ *verb* [T] (**gas·sing**; **gassed**) to poison or kill sb with gas

'gas ˌchamber *noun* [C] a room that can be filled with poisonous gas in order to kill animals or people

gash /gæʃ/ *noun* [C] a long deep cut or wound: *He had an awful gash in his arm.*

'gas mask *noun* [C] a piece of equipment that you wear over your face to protect you against poisonous gas

☆ **gas·o·line** /ˌgæsə'lin; 'gæsəlin/ *noun* [U] = GAS¹(4)

gasp¹ /gæsp/ *verb* **1** [I] to breathe quickly and noisily (e.g. when you have been running fast): *At the end of the race, some of the runners were gasping for breath.* **2** [I] **gasp (at sth)** to breathe in suddenly and noisily because you are surprised or in pain: *She gasped in surprise as she read the letter.* **3** [T] to say sth while you are finding it difficult to breathe: *"I can't go on," he gasped. "I've got to sit down."*

gasp² /gæsp/ *noun* [C] a quick breath (when you are surprised, in pain, etc.): *Suddenly she gave a gasp of surprise.*

'gas ˌpedal *noun* [C] (*informal*) = ACCELERATOR: *to step on the gas pedal*

☆ **'gas ˌstation** *noun* [C] a place where you can buy gasoline and other things for your car

gas·tro·nom·ic /ˌgæstrə'nɑmɪk/ *adj.* connected with (good) food: *the gastronomic delights of Italy*

☆ **gate** /geɪt/ *noun* [C] **1** a movable structure (like a door) that closes an opening in a wall, fence, etc.: *Please keep the front gate closed.* ☞ picture at **fence**. **2** (*also* **'gateway**) an

G

ə	y	w	t̬	eɪ	aɪ	ɔɪ	aʊ	oʊ
about	yes	woman	butter	say	five	boy	now	go

opening in a wall, fence, hedge, etc. that is closed by a gate (1): *Drive through the gates and you'll find the parking lot on the right.* **3** an entrance or exit at an airport: *Flight 139 to Geneva is now boarding at gate 16.*

gate·way /ˈgeɪtweɪ/ *noun* [C] **1** = GATE(2) **2** [sing.] **gateway to sth** the place through which you have to pass through in order to get to somewhere else: (*figurative*) *A good education can be the gateway to success.*

☆ **gath·er** /ˈgæðər/ *verb* **1** [I,T] **gather around (sb/sth); gather sb/sth around (sb/sth)** (used about people) to come together in a group; to make people come together: *A crowd soon gathered at the scene of the accident.* ○ *The kids were gathered in a group around the teacher's desk.* **2** [T] **gather sth (together/up)** to bring many things together; to collect: *They gathered up all their picnic things and headed home.* ○ *They have gathered together a lot of information on the subject.* ○ *I need some time to gather my thoughts before I can give you an answer.* **3** [T] to collect plants, fruits, etc. **4** [T] to understand or find out sth (from sb/sth): *I gather from your letter that you have several years' experience in this kind of work.* ○ *"She's been very sick recently." "So I gather."* **5** [T] to pull material together into small folds and sew it: *a gathered skirt* **6** [I,T] to become greater or to make greater; to increase: *The train is gathering speed.* ○ *In the gathering darkness, it was hard to see the ball.*

gath·er·ing /ˈgæðərɪŋ/ *noun* [C] a time when people come together; a meeting: *a family gathering*

gaud·y /ˈgɔdi/ *adj.* (**gaud·i·er**; **gaud·i·est**) too bright or highly decorated

gauge¹ /geɪdʒ/ *noun* [C] **1** an instrument for measuring the amount of sth: *a gas gauge on a car* (= to show how much gasoline is left) **2** a measurement of the width of certain things: *a narrow-gauge railroad* ○ *a 12-gauge shotgun* **3** a fact that you can use to judge a situation, sb's feelings, etc.

gauge² /geɪdʒ/ *verb* [T] **1** to measure sth **2** to judge a situation, sb's feelings, etc.: *It was difficult to gauge the mood of the audience.*

gaunt /gɔnt/ *adj.* (used about a person) very thin because of hunger, illness, etc.

gauze /gɔz/ *noun* [U] thin material (often used for covering wounds)

gave *p.t.* of GIVE¹

gawk /gɔk/ *verb* [I] (*informal*) **gawk (at sb/sth)** to look or stare (at sb/sth) in a stupid way (with your mouth open)

☆ **gay** /geɪ/ *adj.* **1** sexually attracted to people of the same sex; homosexual: *He told me he was gay.* ○ *the gay community* **2** (*old-fashioned*) happy and full of fun ☞ The noun for this meaning is **gaiety** and the adverb **gaily**.

gays /geɪz/ *noun* [plural] people, especially men, who are sexually attracted to people of

the same sex; homosexuals: *a club for lesbians and gays*

☞ It is considered very rude and offensive to use the noun form **gay** to refer to a particular person. We use the adjective form instead: *a gay man*

gaze¹ /geɪz/ *verb* [I] to look steadily for a long time: *Stop gazing out the window.*

gaze² /geɪz/ *noun* [sing.] a long steady look: *The cat kept its gaze fixed on the bird.*

☆ **gear¹** /gɪr/ *noun* **1** [C] one of a set of wheels that fits into another set in order to pass power from one part of a machine to another, e.g. from a car's engine to its wheels: *My bike chain slipped off the gears.* **2** [U] a particular position of the gears (1) (on a bicycle, in a car, etc.): *You can't pedal up that hill in fifth gear!*

☞ A car can be **in** or **out of** gear. You use a **low** gear (**first** gear) when you first start moving and then **shift** gears as you go faster. For the fastest speeds, you use **high** gear. Look also at the note at **transmission**.

3 [U] equipment or clothing that you need for a particular activity, etc.: *camping gear* **4** [sing.] (in compounds) an instrument or part of a machine that is used for a particular purpose: *the landing gear of an airplane*

☆ **gear²** /gɪr/ *verb*

PHRV **gear sth for/to/toward sth** (often passive) to make sth suitable for a particular purpose: *There is a special course geared toward older students.*

gear up (for sb/sth); gear sb/sth up (for sb/sth) to get ready or to make sb/sth ready: *I was all geared up for the party, but it was canceled at the last minute.*

gear·shift /ˈgɪrʃɪft/ *noun* [C] a stick that is used for changing gears ¹(2) (in a car, etc.)

GED /ˌdʒi i ˈdi/ *noun* [C] general equivalency diploma; an official certificate that people who did not finish high school can get, after taking classes and passing an examination: *I'm going to night school so I can get my GED.*

gee /dʒi/ *interj.* (*informal*) (used for expressing surprise, pleasure, etc.): *Gee, I'm sorry. I didn't know your dad died.*

geek /gik/ *noun* [C] (*slang*) a person who is not popular because he/she behaves in a strange way: *Clarence is such a total geek – he never bathes and he picks his nose in class!* ☞ Look at **nerd**. —**geek·y** *adj.*

geese *pl.* of GOOSE

gel /dʒɛl/ *noun* [C,U] (often in compounds) a thick substance like jelly that is between a liquid and a solid: *hair gel*

gel·a·tin (*also* **gelatine**) /ˈdʒɛlətn; -tən/ *noun* [U] **1** = JELL-O **2** a powder that is used in making desserts, etc. It is added to liquids to make them firm: *Dissolve one packet of unflavored gelatin in a cup of boiling water.*

ər	ɪr	ɛr	ɑr	ɔr	ʊr	ʒ	h	ŋ
bird	near	hair	car	north	tour	vision	hat	sing

gem /dʒɛm/ noun [C] **1** a jewel or precious stone **2** a person or thing that has great value

Gem·i·ni /'dʒɛmənaɪ; -ni/ noun [C,U] the third sign of the Zodiac, the Twins; a person who was born under this sign ☞ picture at **zodiac**.

Gen. abbr. = GENERAL²

gen·der /'dʒɛndər/ noun [C,U] **1** (formal) the classification of people into two sexes: male and female **2** (grammar) (in some languages) the classification of nouns, pronouns, etc. into masculine, feminine and neuter; one of these divisions: There are three genders in German. ○ In French the adjective must agree with the noun in number and gender.

gene /dʒin/ noun [C] one of the parts of a cell of a living thing which decide its development. Genes are passed from parents to children. In human beings they decide, for example, the size of a child or the color of his/ her eyes. ☞ Look at **genetic**.

☆ **gen·er·al¹** /'dʒɛnərəl; 'dʒɛnrəl/ adj. **1** affecting all or most people, places, things, etc.: a matter of general interest ○ The general feeling is that the situation is improving (= most people think so). ○ the general public (= most ordinary people) **2** (only before a noun) not limited to, or describing, one particular part; not detailed: Your general health is very good. ○ The introduction gives you a general idea of what the book is about. ○ Let's talk in general terms at first and then get down to details. **3** not limited to one subject or area of study; not specialized: Children need a good general education. ○ The quiz tests your general knowledge. ○ a general hospital **4** (often in compounds) with responsibility for the whole of an organization: The Secretary General of the United Nations ○ the United States Surgeon General (= the chief medical officer for the government) ○ a general manager

IDM in general in most cases; usually: In general, test scores are improving

gen·er·al² /'dʒɛnərəl; 'dʒɛnrəl/ noun [C] (abbr. **Gen.**) an army officer of very high rank: General Roberts

general anes'thetic noun [C,U] a substance that is given to a patient in the hospital before an operation so that he/she becomes unconscious and does not feel any pain ☞ Look at **local anesthetic**.

gen·er·al·i·za·tion /,dʒɛnrələ'zeɪʃn; ,dʒɛnərəl-/ noun [C] a general statement about sth that does not consider details

gen·er·al·ize /'dʒɛnrəlaɪz; 'dʒɛnərəl-/ verb [I] **1** generalize (about sth) to form an opinion using only a small amount of information: You can't generalize about American food after only two meals. **2** generalize (about sth) to make a general statement about sth and not look at the details: You're generalizing. Every case is different.

gen·er·al·ized /'dʒɛnrəlaɪzd; 'dʒɛnərəl-/ adj.

found or happening over a large area; affecting a large number of people: a generalized effort to reduce poverty

☆ **gen·er·al·ly** /'dʒɛnərəli; 'dʒɛnrəli/ adv. **1** usually: She generally drives to work. **2** by most people: He is generally considered a good doctor. **3** in a general sense, without looking at the details: Generally speaking, houses in America have big back yards.

general 'store noun [C] a small store, especially in a very small town or in the country, that sells many different types of things

gen·er·ate /'dʒɛnəreɪt/ verb [T] **1** to produce power, heat, electricity, etc. **2** to cause sth to exist: I think this new product will generate a lot of income for the company.

☆ **gen·er·a·tion** /,dʒɛnə'reɪʃn/ noun **1** [U] the act of generating: the generation of electricity by burning coal **2** [C] one stage in a family history: This picture shows three generations of my family (= children, parents and grandparents). ○ the generation gap (= the difference in behavior between young people and older people) **3** [C] all the people in a group or country who were born at about the same time: My grandmother's generation didn't have TV when they were young. ○ future generations ○ The younger generation only seems to be interested in money. **4** [C] a period of about 25 or 30 years (i.e. the time that a person takes to become an adult): A generation ago, foreign travel was still only possible for a few people.

gen·er·a·tor /'dʒɛnəreɪtər/ noun [C] a machine that produces electricity

ge·ner·ic /dʒə'nɛrɪk/ adj. **1** (used about a product) without a special name that was given by the company that made it: It's cheaper to buy the generic pills. **2** describing a general type of sth, not one thing in particular: a diagram of a generic engine

gen·er·os·i·ty /,dʒɛnə'rɑsəṭi/ noun [U] the quality of being generous

☆ **gen·er·ous** /'dʒɛnərəs/ adj. **1** willing to give more money, help, etc. than is usual or necessary: It was very generous of your parents to loan us all that money. **2** larger than usual: The recipe makes four generous servings. —**gen·er·ous·ly** adv.: Please give generously.

ge·net·ic /dʒə'nɛtɪk/ adj. connected with the parts of cells in living things that decide their development (**genes**) or genetics: The disease is caused by a genetic defect. —**ge·net·i·cal·ly** /-kli/ adv.

ge,netic engi'neering noun [U] changes made by scientists in the genetic structure of plants and animals

ge·net·ics /dʒə'nɛtɪks/ noun [U] the scientific study of the way that the development of living things is controlled by features that have been passed on from parents to children ☞ Look at **gene**.

tʃ	dʒ	v	θ	ð	s	z	ʃ
chin	June	van	thin	then	so	zoo	she

gen·ial /ˈdʒinyəl; ˈdʒiniəl/ *adj.* (used about a person) pleasant and friendly

gen·i·tals /ˈdʒɛnətlz/ *noun* [plural] (*formal*) the external sex organs —**gen·i·tal** /ˈdʒɛnətl/ *adj.*

gen·ius /ˈdʒinyəs/ *noun* (*pl.* **gen·ius·es**) **1** [U] very great and unusual ability: *Shakespeare's tragedies show true genius.* **2** [C] a person who has very great and unusual ability, especially in a particular subject: *Einstein was a mathematical genius.* **3** [sing.] **a genius for (doing) sth** great natural ability for (doing) sth: *Our teacher had a genius for explaining difficult things in a simple way.*

gen·o·cide /ˈdʒɛnəsaɪd/ *noun* [U] the murder of a nation or race

gen·re /ˈʒɑnrə/ *noun* [C] a particular type of literature, art, etc.

gent /dʒɛnt/ *noun* [C] (*informal*) a gentleman

gen·teel /dʒɛnˈtil/ *adj.* paying great (perhaps too much) attention to polite manners —**gen·til·i·ty** /dʒɛnˈtɪləti/ *noun* [U]

☆ **gen·tle** /ˈdʒɛntəl/ *adj.* **1** (used about people) kind; calm; touching or treating people or things in a careful way so that they are not hurt: *He was a gentle, patient man who loved playing with his grandchildren.* ○ *"I'll be as gentle as I can," the dentist said.* **2** not rough or violent: *A gentle breeze was blowing through the trees.* ○ *a gentle* (= not sharp) *curve in the road* —**gen·tle·ness** *noun* [U] —**gen·tly** /ˈdʒɛntli/ *adv.*: *He touched her gently on the shoulder.* ○ *The beach slopes gently down to the ocean.*

gen·tle·man /ˈdʒɛntəlmən/ *noun* [C] (*pl.* **gen·tle·men** /-mən/) **1** a man who is polite and who behaves well toward other people and (especially in former times) who is rich and has a high social position: *He is a real gentleman.* **2** (*formal*) (used when speaking to or about a man or men in a polite way): *Ladies and gentlemen!* (e.g. at the beginning of a speech)

☆ **gen·u·ine** /ˈdʒɛnyuən/ *adj.* **1** a person or thing that is genuine is exactly what he/she/it seems to be; real: *He thought that he had bought a genuine Rolex watch, but it was a cheap fake.* **2** (used about a person or his/her feelings or behavior) honest; real: *She seems genuine enough, but can I trust her?* —**gen·u·ine·ly** *adv.*: *I'm genuinely interested in a career in teaching.*

ge·og·ra·pher /dʒiˈɑgrəfər/ *noun* [C] a student of or an expert in geography

☆ **ge·og·ra·phy** /dʒiˈɑgrəfi/ *noun* [U] **1** the study of the countries of the world, of their natural and physical features and of the cities, industries, etc. that have been made by people **2** the way in which the features of a particular country or place are arranged: *We're studying the geography of Asia.* —**ge·o·graph·ic**

/ˌdʒiəˈgræfɪk/ (*also* **ge·o·graph·i·cal** /-ɪkl/) *adj.* —**ge·o·graph·i·cal·ly** /-kli/ *adv.*

ge·ol·o·gist /dʒiˈɑlədʒɪst/ *noun* [C] a student of or an expert in geology

ge·ol·o·gy /dʒiˈɑlədʒi/ *noun* [U] the study of rocks and soil, and of their development —**ge·o·log·i·cal** /dʒiəˈlɑdʒɪkl/ *adj.*

☆ **ge·o·met·ric** /dʒiəˈmɛtrɪk/ (*also* **ge·o·met·ri·cal** /-ɪkl/) *adj.* **1** of geometry **2** consisting of regular shapes and lines: *a geometric design/pattern* —**ge·o·met·ri·cal·ly** /-kli/ *adv.*

ge·om·e·try /dʒiˈɑmətri/ *noun* [U] the study in mathematics of lines, shapes, curves, etc.

ger·i·at·ric /ˌdʒɛriˈætrɪk; ˌdʒɪri-/ *adj.* connected with very old people

☆ **germ** /dʒərm/ *noun* [C] a very small living thing that causes disease. Germs can only be seen with a microscope: *This disinfectant kills most germs.* ☞ Look at **bacteria** and **virus**.

Ger·man mea·sles /ˌdʒərmən ˈmizlz/ (*also* **rubella**) *noun* [U] a mild disease that causes red spots all over the body. It may damage an unborn baby if the mother catches it.

Ger·man shep·herd /ˌdʒərmən ˈʃɛpərd/ *noun* [C] a large dog with thick black and brown hair, that is often trained to work with the police, as a guard dog or as a guide dog for blind people

ger·mi·nate /ˈdʒərməneɪt/ *verb* [I,T] (used about a seed of a plant) to start growing; to cause a seed to do this —**ger·mi·na·tion** /ˌdʒərməˈneɪʃn/ *noun* [U]

ger·und /ˈdʒɛrənd/ *noun* [C] (*grammar*) a noun, ending in -ing, that has been made from a verb: *In the sentence "His hobby is collecting stamps," "collecting" is a gerund.*

ges·tic·u·late /dʒɛˈstɪkyəleɪt/ *verb* [I] to make movements with your hands and arms in order to express sth

☆ **ges·ture¹** /ˈdʒɛstʃər; ˈdʒɛʃtʃər/ *noun* [C] **1** a movement of the hand, head, etc. that expresses sth: *The kid made an obscene gesture and ran away.* **2** something that you do that shows other people what you think or feel: *It would be a nice gesture to invite the neighbors over for dinner.*

ges·ture² /ˈdʒɛstʃər; ˈdʒɛʃtʃər/ *verb* [I,T] to point at sth, to make a sign to sb: *We saw the manager speak to the boys and gesture toward the door.*

☆ **get** /gɛt/ *verb* (*pres. part.* **get·ting**; *p.t.* **got** /gɑt/; *p.p.* except in sense 1 **got·ten** /ˈgɑtn/) **1** [T] **have/has got** to have sth: *I've got a headache.*

☞ We generally do not use **have got** in questions. We usually use **have got** to emphasize the fact that sb has one thing instead of another: *"Does your brother have brown hair?" "No, he's got blond hair."* In very informal spoken English, it is possible to use **got** in questions without **have** or **has**: *"You got any money?" "Yeah, I do./No, I don't."* However,

G

this use is not considered correct in more formal English.

2 [I] to become: *It's getting dark.* ∘ *She got angry.* **3** [T] to receive or obtain sth: *I got a letter from my sister.* ∘ *He went shopping and got a suit.* ∘ *She got a job in a travel agency.* ∘ *I'll do it if I get time.* ∘ *Nina gets $10 an hour for working in her family's business.* **4** [T] to go and bring sth back: *Go (and) get me a pen.* ∘ *I'll get the kids from school today.* **5** [T] to hear or understand sth: *Sorry, I didn't get that. Can you repeat it?* ∘ *I don't get it. Why did he buy a car when he can't drive?* **6** [T] to catch a disease: *You can get cancer from smoking.* **7** [T] to use a form of transportation: *I didn't walk – I got a taxi.* **8** [I] to move somewhere; to reach a place: *We got to San Diego at about 10.* ∘ *What time will we get there?* ☞ Look at **get in, on,** etc. **9** [T] to cause sth to be in a particular place: *We couldn't get the piano upstairs.* **10** [T] (*informal*) to hurt sb as punishment for sth that he/she did to you: *I'll get you guys for making a fool of me!* **11** [I] (used with a past participle) to do sth that you are responsible for: *I'm getting dressed.* ∘ *They got divorced.* **12** [I] to be in a certain situation: *He got into trouble with the police.* **13** [I] (used in a similar way to the passive) to have sth happen to you: *She got bitten by a dog.* **14** [T] to cause sb/sth to do sth or to happen: *I got him to agree to the plan.* ∘ *I can't get the TV to work.* ∘ *She finally got the assignment finished.* ☞ Note that we also use **get** when we arrange for somebody else to do something: *You need to get the car serviced every 10,000 miles* (at a service station). **15** [I] **get to do sth** to have the opportunity to do sth: *Did you get to go to the concert?*

IDM get it (*informal*) to be punished: *You're gonna get it when Mom sees this mess!*

get somewhere/nowhere (with sb/sth) to make some/no progress: *I'm not getting anywhere with my research.*

☞ For other idioms containing **get**, look at the noun and adjective entries, e.g. for **get rid of** look at **rid**.

PHRV get sth across (to sb) to succeed in making people understand sth: *The candidate failed to get his policies across to the voters.*

get ahead to progress and be successful in sth, especially a career

get along 1 to make progress: *How are you getting along at college?* **2** to perform in a particular way or to have a good or bad experience in a particular situation: *How did you get along at your interview?*

get along with sb; get along (together) to have a friendly relationship with sb: *Do you get along well with your coworkers?* ∘ *We're not close friends, but we get along pretty well together.*

get around 1 to move or travel to and from many places: *Chicago this week, Dallas next week – you sure get around!* **2** (used about news, a story, etc.) to spread; to become known by many people

get around sth to find a way of avoiding or overcoming a problem

get around to sth/doing sth to find the time to do sth, after a delay: *I've been meaning to reply to that letter, but I haven't gotten around to it yet.*

get at sb to say unkind or critical things to sb

get at sb/sth to succeed in reaching sb/sth: *You'll need to stand on a chair to get at the top shelf.*

get at sth (used only in the continuous tenses) to suggest sth indirectly; to mean sth but not to state it directly: *I'm not quite sure what you're getting at – am I doing something wrong?*

get away (from…) to succeed in leaving or escaping from sb or a place: *He kept talking to me and I couldn't get away from him.* ∘ *The thieves got away in a stolen car.*

get away with sth/with doing sth to do sth bad and not be punished for it: *He lied, but he got away with it.* ∘ *I don't know how they get away with charging such high prices.*

get back to return to the place where you live or work: *When did you get back from vacation?*

get sth back to be given sth that you had lost or lent: *Can I borrow this book? You'll get it back next week, I promise.*

get back to sb to speak to, write to or call sb later, especially in order to give an answer or deal with sth: *I'll get back to you when I have some more information.*

get back to sth to return to doing sth or talking about sth: *I woke up early and couldn't get back to sleep.* ∘ *Let's get back to the point you raised earlier.*

get behind (on/with sth) to fail to do or produce sth on time: *We got behind on our rent.*

get by (on sth) to manage, often with difficulty, to live, using a certain income: *It's very hard to get by on such a low income.*

get by (on/with sth) to manage by doing or having as little of sth as possible: *I can get by on just five hours' sleep.*

get sb down to make sb miserable: *These cold winter days get me down.*

get sth down to make a note of sth; to write sth down: *Did you get the address for the contest down?*

get down to sth/doing sth to start doing or concentrating on sth: *That's enough small talk – let's get down to business.*

get in to reach a place: *What time does your flight get in?*

get in; get into sth to climb into a car: *We all got in and Tim drove off.*

get into sb (*informal*) (used about a feeling or attitude) to start affecting sb strongly, causing

G

the person to behave in an unusual way: *I wonder what's gotten into him – he isn't usually that mean.*

get into sth 1 to start a particular activity; to become involved in sth: *How did you first get into the music business?* ○ *She has gotten into the habit of turning up late.* ○ *We got into an argument about politics.* **2** (*informal*) to become interested in sth: *She doesn't usually like sports, but recently she's been getting into basketball.*

get off (sth) 1 to leave a bus, plane, bicycle, etc.; to climb down from a horse **2** to leave work with permission at a particular time: *I might be able to get off early today.*

get sth off (sth) to remove sth from sth: *Can you help me get these boots off?*

get off on sth/doing sth (*slang*) to get great pleasure or satisfaction from sth/doing sth: *For some reason, he gets off on criticizing people.*

get (sb) off (with sth) to receive little or no punishment; to help sb to receive little or no punishment: *If you're lucky, you'll get off with a small fine.* ○ *Her lawyer was confident that he would get her off.*

get on 1 to be getting old: *He's getting on – I'm sure he's over 60.* **2** to be getting late: *Time's getting on – we don't want to be late.*

☞ **Get on** is only used in the continuous tenses.

get on/onto sth to climb onto a bus, plane, bicycle, horse, etc.: *I got onto the wrong bus by mistake.*

get sth on to put on a piece of clothing: *Get your shoes on – we're going out now.*

get onto sb (about sth) (*informal*) to speak or write to sb about a particular matter, especially because you want them to do sth for you: *You should get onto the city council about that hole in the sidewalk.*

get on with sth to continue doing sth, especially after an interruption: *Stop talking and get on with your work!*

get out (used about a piece of information) to become known, having previously been secret

get sth out (of sth) to take sth from its container: *I got my keys out of my bag.*

get out (of sth) to leave or escape from a place: *My grandmother doesn't get out of the house much.*

get out of sth/doing sth to avoid a duty or doing sth that you have said you will do: *I said I'd go to their party, and I can't get out of it now.*

get sth out of sb to obtain sth from sb by force or by persuading him or her: *His parents finally got the truth out of him.*

get sth out of sb/sth to gain sth from sb/sth: *I get a lot of pleasure out of music.*

get over sth to recover from sth bad, or from an illness: *He still hasn't gotten over his wife's*

death. ○ *It took her a long time to get over her operation.* ○ *I can't get over how mean he was!* (= I still find it surprising)

get sth over with (*informal*) to do and complete sth unpleasant that has to be done: *I'll be glad to get my visit to the dentist over with.*

get (sb) through (sth) to be successful in sth (often sth unpleasant); to help sb to be successful: *She got through her final exams easily.* ○ *Her kindness got me through those awful days.*

get through (to sb) 1 to succeed in making a telephone connection with sb: *I couldn't get through to them because their phone was busy all day.* **2** to succeed in making sb understand what you are saying: *They couldn't get through to him that he was completely wrong.*

get to sb (*informal*) to affect sb in a bad way: *Don't let their comments get to you – just do your best.*

get together (with sb) to meet socially or in order to discuss or do sth: *Let's get together and talk about it.*

get up to rise to a standing position; to stand up: *He got up to let an elderly woman sit down.*

get (sb) up to get out of bed or make sb get out of bed: *What time do you have to get up in the morning?* ○ *Could you get me up at 6 tomorrow?*

get up to sth 1 to reach a particular point or stage in sth: *We've gotten up to the last section in our grammar book.* **2** to do sth, especially sth bad: *I wonder what the kids are getting up to.*

get·a·way /ˈgɛt̬əweɪ/ *noun* [C] an escape (after a crime): *to make a getaway* ○ *a getaway car*

get-to·geth·er *noun* [C] (*informal*) an informal social meeting or party: *We're having a little get-together Saturday evening.*

gey·ser /ˈgaɪzər/ *noun* [C] a natural hole in the ground that suddenly sends hot water and steam up into the air with great force

ghast·ly /ˈgæstli/ *adj.* (**ghast·li·er; ghast·li·est**) **1** causing fear or shock: *a ghastly accident* **2** very bad, ugly or unpleasant: *a ghastly mistake*

ghet·to /ˈgɛtoʊ/ *noun* [C] (*pl.* **ghet·toes**) a part of a city where many poor people of the same race live in crowded conditions

☆ **ghost** /goʊst/ *noun* [C] the spirit of a dead person that is seen or heard by sb who is still living: *I don't believe in ghosts.* ○ *a ghost story* —**ghost·ly** /ˈgoʊstli/ *adj.*: *ghostly noises*

ghost town *noun* [C] a town whose inhabitants have all left

ghost·wri·ter /ˈgoʊstˌraɪt̬ər/ *noun* [C] a person who writes a book, etc. for a famous person (whose name appears as the author)

☆ **gi·ant¹** /ˈdʒaɪənt/ *noun* [C] **1** (in children's stories) a person of human shape but very great size and strength **2** something that is very large: *the multinational oil giants* (= very large companies)

ər	ɪr	ɛr	ɑr	ɔr	ʊr	ʒ	h	ŋ
bird	near	hair	car	north	tour	vision	hat	sing

gi·ant² /ˈdʒaɪənt/ *adj.* extremely large: *a giant new shopping center*

☆ **gift** /gɪft/ *noun* [C] **1** something that you give to a person; a present: *wedding gifts* ○ *Their teacher was presented with a gift of flowers and candy.* ○ *They often give away a free gift with the magazine.* ☞ Look at the note at **present**. **2 a gift (for sth/doing sth)** [sing.] natural ability: *She has a gift for languages.*

ˈgift cerˌtificate *noun* [C] a piece of paper that is often given as a gift, that you can exchange at a particular store for goods or services with a certain value

gift·ed /ˈgɪftəd/ *adj.* having natural ability or great intelligence: *a gifted musician*

gig /gɪg/ *noun* [C] a performance by rock or jazz musicians

gi·gan·tic /dʒaɪˈgæntɪk/ *adj.* extremely large

gig·gle¹ /ˈgɪgl/ *verb* [I] to laugh in a silly way because you are amused or nervous

gig·gle² /ˈgɪgl/ *noun* [C] a silly laugh: *I have the giggles* (= I can't stop laughing).

gim·mick /ˈgɪmɪk/ *noun* [C] something unusual or amusing that is used to attract people's attention (usually so that they buy sth): *They're looking for a new gimmick to advertise the restaurant.*

gin /dʒɪn/ *noun* [C,U] a colorless alcoholic drink that is made from grain and a particular type of berry: *I'll have a gin and tonic.*

gin·ger /ˈdʒɪndʒər/ *noun* [U] the hot-tasting root of a plant (used in cooking): *ground ginger*

ˈginger ale *noun* [U] a non-alcoholic drink that is flavored with ginger, sometimes mixed with alcoholic drinks

gin·ger·ly /ˈdʒɪndʒərli/ *adv.* very slowly and carefully so as not to cause harm, make a noise, etc.

gi·raffe /dʒəˈræf/ *noun* [C] (*pl.* **gi·raffe** or **gi·raffes**) an African animal with a very long neck and legs and dark spots on its skin

gird·er /ˈgərdər/ *noun* [C] a long iron or steel bar that is used in the construction of bridges, large buildings, etc.

☆ **girl** /gərl/ *noun* [C] **1** a female child: *the little girl who lives next door* ○ *There are more boys than girls in the class.* **2** a daughter: *They have two boys and a girl.* **3** a young woman: *He was 18 before he became interested in girls.* ○ *The girl at the checkout was very helpful.*

☞ Some people find **girl** offensive when it is used about an adult woman.

4 the girls [plural] female friends of any age: *a night out with the girls*

☆ **girl·friend** /ˈgərlfrɛnd/ *noun* [C] **1** a girl or woman with whom sb has a romantic and/or sexual relationship **2** a girl or woman's female friend

ˈGirl Scout *noun* [C] a member of an organization for girls that encourages helpfulness and teaches practical skills ☞ Look at **Boy Scout**.

the gist /dʒɪst/ *noun* [sing.] the general meaning of sth rather than all the details: *I know a little Spanish, so I was able to get the gist of what he said.*

☆ **give¹** /gɪv/ *verb* (*p.t.* **gave** /geɪv/; *p.p.* **giv·en** /ˈgɪvn/) **1** [T] **give sb sth; give sth to sb** to hand sth to sb as a present; to allow sb to have sth as a present: *My parents gave me a watch for my birthday.* ○ *to give money to charity* **2** [T] **give sb sth; give sth to sb** to hand sth to sb so that he/she can look at it, use it or keep it for a time: *Can you give me that book over there?* ○ *I gave my ticket to the woman at the check-in desk.* **3** [T] **give sb sth; give sth to sb** to provide sb with sth he/she wants, asks for or pays for: *He was thirsty, so I gave him a drink.* ○ *I hope the doctor will give me some new pills.* ○ *Can you give me some help with my homework?* **4** [T] **give sth to sb/sth** to spend time, etc. on sb/sth: *I can only give you ten minutes.* ○ *We'll have to give some more thought to the matter* (= think about it more). **5** [T] **give (sb) sth for sth** to pay: *How much would you give me for my old car?* **6** [T] **give sb sth** to cause sb/sth to have or feel sth: *The news about his father gave him a big shock.* ○ *Hard work gives you an appetite.* ○ *That noise is giving me a headache.* **7** [T] **give sth; give sb sth; give sth to sb/sth** to perform an action: *She gave my hand a squeeze* (= she squeezed it). ○ *They gave us a warm welcome.* ○ *He gave me a very long answer.* ○ *She gave him a kiss.* **8** [T] to perform sth in public: *He gave a very interesting lecture on India.* ○ *They're giving* (= having) *a party for their son's tenth birthday.* **9** [I] to bend or stretch under pressure: *The branch began to give under his weight.*

IDM **give or take** more or less the number mentioned: *It took us two hours to get here, give or take five minutes.*

☞ For other idioms containing **give**, look at the entries for the nouns, adjectives, etc., e.g. **give way** is at **way**.

PHRV **give sb away** (at a wedding in a church) to go with the bride into the church and officially give her to the groom during the marriage ceremony: *Her father gave her away.*

give sth away to give sth, often sth that you no longer want, to sb without asking for or receiving money in return: *When she got older, she gave all her toys away.* ○ *We are giving a shirt away with every suit purchased.*

give sth away to show or tell the truth about sth which was secret: *He smiled politely and didn't give away his real feelings.*

give sb sth back; give sth back (to sb) to return sth to the person from whom you took or borrowed it: *I should give you back those books you loaned me.*

G

tʃ	dʒ	v	θ	ð	s	z	ʃ
chin	**June**	**van**	**thin**	**then**	**so**	**zoo**	**she**

give in (to sb/sth) to stop fighting against sb/sth; to accept that you have been defeated

give sth off to send sth (e.g. a smell, heat) out into the air

give out (used about a machine, etc.) to stop working

give sth out to hand or pass sth to people: *Could you give out these worksheets to the class?*

give up to stop trying to do sth; to accept that you cannot do sth: *Don't give up now – you're improving all the time.* ○ *I give up. What's the answer?*

give up on sb to stop expecting sb to arrive, succeed, improve or recover: *If he doesn't come by noon, we'll give up on him.* ○ *The doctors had given up on her when she suddenly started to get better.*

give up sth to stop doing or having sth that you had done or had regularly before: *to give up smoking* ○ *Don't give up hope. Things are bound to improve.*

give yourself/sb up (to sb) to go to the police when they are trying to catch you: *The suspect gave himself up to the police.*

give sth up (to sb) to give sth to sb who needs or asks for it: *He gave up his seat on the bus to an elderly woman.*

give² /gɪv/ *noun* [U] the quality of being able to bend or stretch a little: *These pants don't have enough give in the waist.*

IDM give and take the willingness, within a relationship, to move toward another person's point of view because he/she is willing to move toward your point of view: *This dispute can only be settled if there is give and take on both sides.*

giv·en¹ /ˈgɪvn/ *adj.* (only *before* a noun) already stated or fixed: *At any given time, over 10% of students are absent from class.*

giv·en² /ˈgɪvn/ *prep.* taking sth into consideration: *Given that you had very little help, I think you did pretty well.*

ˈgiven name *noun* [C] = FIRST NAME ☞ Look at the note at **name**.

gla·cial /ˈgleɪʃl/ *adj.* caused by ice or a glacier: *a glacial valley*

gla·cier /ˈgleɪʃər/ *noun* [C] a mass of ice that moves slowly across land

☆ **glad** /glæd/ *adj.* (**glad·der; glad·dest**) (not before a noun) **glad (to do sth/that…)** happy; pleased: *I'm glad to hear he's feeling better.* ○ *I'm glad (that) he's feeling better.* ○ *We'd be glad to see you if you're in the area.*

☞ **Glad** is not used before a noun, but **happy** can be used before the noun it describes: *This kind of music always makes me feel happy.* ○ *She's such a happy child – she's always laughing.*

glad·i·a·tor /ˈglædieɪṭər/ *noun* [C] (in ancient Rome) a man who fought against another man or a wild animal in a public show

☆ **glad·ly** /ˈglædli/ *adv.* happily; willingly: *She gladly accepted the invitation to stay at our house.* ○ *I would gladly give up my job if I could afford to.*

glam·or·ize /ˈglæməraɪz/ *verb* [T] to make sth appear more attractive or exciting than it really is: *Television tends to glamorize violence.*

glam·or·ous /ˈglæmərəs/ *adj.* attractive or full of glamour: *She didn't look very glamorous without her makeup.* ○ *a glamorous job* —**glam·or·ous·ly** *adv.*

glam·our (*also* **glamor**) /ˈglæmər/ *noun* [U] the quality of seeming to be exciting or attractive: *Young people are often attracted by the glamour of city life.*

☆ **glance¹** /glæns/ *verb* [I] to take a quick look: *She glanced around the room to see if they were there.* ○ *He glanced at her and smiled.* ○ *The receptionist glanced down the list of names.*

PHRV glance off (sth) to hit sth at an angle and move off again in another direction: *Luckily, the bullet glanced off his big belt buckle.*

glance² /glæns/ *noun* [C] a quick look: *I only had time for a glance at the newspaper.* ○ *They exchanged glances when no one was looking.* ○ *She stole* (= sneaked) *a glance at her watch.*

IDM at a glance in a form that can be understood by looking quickly at sth: *Here, at a glance, is a summary of the key issues in the election:…*

at first glance/sight ➪ FIRST¹

gland /glænd/ *noun* [C] a small part (**an organ**) of the body that produces a substance that your body uses: *sweat glands* ○ *the poison glands of a snake* ○ *swollen glands* (e.g. in your throat)

glare¹ /glɛr/ *noun* **1** [U] strong light that hurts your eyes: *the glare of the sun on snow* ○ *the glare of a car's headlights* **2** [C] a (long) angry look

glare² /glɛr/ *verb* [I] **1** to shine with strong light that hurts your eyes **2 glare (at sb/sth)** to stare at sb angrily: *They stood glaring at each other.*

glar·ing /ˈglɛrɪŋ/ *adj.* **1** (used about a light, etc.) too strong and bright **2** angry: *glaring eyes* **3** great or very noticeable: *a glaring mistake*

☆ **glass** /glæs/ *noun* **1** [U] a hard, usually transparent, substance that windows, bottles, etc. are made of: *He cut himself on broken glass.* ○ *a sheet/pane of glass* ○ *In case of emergency, break the glass and press the button.* ○ *a glass jar, dish, etc.* **2** [C] a drinking container, usually made of glass (1), with no handle; the amount of liquid it contains: *a wine glass, champagne glass, etc.* ○ *Could I have a glass of water, please?* **3** [U] a collection of objects made of glass (1)

i	ɪ	ɛ	æ	ɑ	ɔ	ʌ	ʊ	u
see	sit	ten	cat	hot	saw	cup	put	too

glasses (*also* eyeglasses) contact lens

☆ **glass·es** /ˈglæsəz/ (*also* **eyeglasses**) *noun* [plural] two pieces of glass in a frame that a person wears in front of his/her eyes (in order to be able to see better): *My sister has to wear glasses.* ○ *I lost my glasses.* ○ *reading glasses* ○ *sunglasses*

☞ **Glasses** is always plural so we cannot use it with the article *a*. We cannot say: *I need a new glasses.* We can say: *I need a new pair of glasses.*

glass·y /ˈglæsi/ *adj.* (**glass·i·er**; **glass·i·est**) **1** looking like glass: *a glassy lake* **2** (used about the eyes) showing no interest or expression: *a glassy stare*

glaze¹ /gleɪz/ *verb* [T] **1 glaze sth (with sth)** to cover a pot, brick, etc. with a shiny substance (before it is put into an oven) **2** to put a thin, usually sweet sauce on food: *a glazed doughnut* ○ *glazed carrots*

PHRV **glaze over** (used about the eyes) to show no interest or expression

glaze² /gleɪz/ *noun* [C,U] **1** (a substance that gives) a shiny surface on a pot, brick, etc. **2** a thin, usually sweet sauce for food

gleam¹ /glim/ *noun* [C, sing.] a soft or bright light (that shines for a short time): *the gleam of moonlight on the water*

gleam² /glim/ *verb* [I] to shine softly or brightly: *The water of the lake gleamed in the moonlight.*

gleam·ing /ˈglimɪŋ/ *adj.* shining: *gleaming white teeth*

glee /gli/ *noun* [U] a feeling of joy or happiness (at sth good that has happened to you or at sth bad that has happened to sb else): *The kids laughed with glee at the clown's tricks.* —**glee·ful** /-fl/ *adj.* —**glee·ful·ly** *adv.*

glib /glɪb/ *adj.* **1** (used about a person) speaking quickly and cleverly, in a way that will persuade people, but not always telling the truth: *a glib salesman, politician, etc.* **2** spoken quickly and without hesitating, but not always true: *a glib answer, excuse, etc.* —**glib·ly** *adv.*

glide /glaɪd/ *verb* [I] **1** to move smoothly without noise or effort: *The dancers glided across the floor.* ○ *The yachts went gliding past.* **2** to fly in a glider, or in another aircraft without using an engine

glid·er /ˈglaɪdər/ *noun* [C] a light airplane without an engine that flies using air currents
☞ Look at **hang glider**.

glim·mer¹ /ˈglɪmər/ *noun* [C] **1** a weak unsteady light **2** a weak sign of sth: *a glimmer of hope*

glim·mer² /glɪmər/ *verb* [I] to give out a weak unsteady light

glimpse¹ /glɪmps/ *noun* [C] **a glimpse (at/of sth)** a quick incomplete view of sb/sth

☞ **Glimpse** is most often used in the phrase **catch a glimpse of**: *I caught a glimpse of myself in the mirror as I walked past.*

glimpse² /glɪmps/ *verb* [T] to get a quick look at sb/sth (often by chance): *I glimpsed Cathy in the crowd, but I don't think she saw me.*

glis·ten /ˈglɪsn/ *verb* [I] (used about wet surfaces) to shine: *Her eyes glistened with tears.* ○ *Tears glistened in her eyes.*

glit·ter /ˈglɪtər/ *verb* [I] to give out many little flashes of light: *The stars glittered in the frosty sky.* —**glit·ter** *noun* [U]: *the glitter of jewelry* ○ (*figurative*): *the glitter of Broadway*

glit·ter·ing /ˈglɪtərɪŋ/ *adj.* **1** shining brightly with many little flashes of light: *a glittering Christmas tree* **2** very successful, exciting, etc.: *a glittering career, performance, etc.*

glitz /glɪts/ *noun* [U] (*informal*) the quality of seeming to be exciting and attractive, often in an exaggerated way: *Hollywood glitz and glamour* —**glitz·y** /ˈglɪtsi/ *adj.*

gloat /gloʊt/ *verb* [I] **gloat (about/over sth)** to feel or express pleasure at sth good that has happened to you or at sth bad that has happened to sb else: *Don't gloat – you might be in the same position yourself sometime*

glob /glɑb/ *noun* [C] (*informal*) a drop or ball of a liquid or melted solid: *There was a big glob of fat in my soup.*

☆ **glob·al** /ˈgloʊbl/ *adj.* **1** affecting the whole world: *the global effects of pollution* ○ *global warming* **2** affecting the whole of a group of facts, possibilities, etc.: *We need to take a global view of the problem.* —**glob·al·ly** /-bəli/ *adv.*

globe /gloʊb/ *noun* **1** [C] a model of the earth, in the shape of a ball, with the continents, etc. painted on it **2 the globe** [sing.] the earth: *to travel (all) over the globe* ○ *With the help of television, we can see things that are going on on the other side of the globe.*

globe·trot·ter /ˈgloʊbˌtrɑtər/ *noun* [C] (*informal*) a person who travels to many countries

gloom /glum/ *noun* [U] **1** a feeling of sadness or hopelessness: *The news brought deep gloom to the community.* **2** (near) darkness: *It was hard to see anything in the gloom.*

gloom·y /ˈglumi/ *adj.* (**gloom·i·er**; **gloom·i·est**) **1** dark (and depressing): *What a gloomy day!* ○ *This dark paint makes the room very gloomy.* **2** (making sb feel) sad or depressed: *For many young people graduating from high school, the prospects of finding a job are gloomy.* ○ *Don't be so gloomy all the time –*

G

ə	y	w	t̬	eɪ	aɪ	ɔɪ	aʊ	oʊ
about	yes	woman	butter	say	five	boy	now	go

cheer up!—**gloom·i·ly** /-əli/ *adv.* —**gloom·i·ness** *noun* [U]

glo·ri·fied /ˈglɔrəfaɪd/ *adj.* (only *before* a noun) described in a way that makes sb/sth seem better, bigger, more important, etc. than he/she/it really is: *The "luxury hotel" turned out to be a glorified motel.*

glo·ri·fy /ˈglɔrəfaɪ/ *verb* (*pres. part.* **glo·ri·fy·ing**; *3rd pers. sing. pres.* **glo·ri·fies**; *p.t., p.p.* **glo·ri·fied**) [T] **1** to make sb/sth appear better or more important than he/she/it really is: *Critics claimed that the movie glorified drug abuse.* **2** (*formal*) to praise sb/sth highly

glo·ri·ous /ˈglɔriəs/ *adj.* **1** having or deserving fame or glory: *a glorious victory* **2** wonderful or excellent: *What glorious weather!* ○ *a glorious day, view, etc.* —**glo·ri·ous·ly** *adv.*

☆ **glo·ry** /ˈglɔri/ *noun* [U] **1** fame or honor that is won by great achievements: *The winning team was welcomed home in a blaze of glory.* **2** great beauty: *October is the best time to see the New England foliage in all its glory.*

gloss¹ /glɔs; glɑs/ *noun* [U, sing.] (a substance that gives) brightness or shine on a surface: *the gloss on wood, hair, silk, etc.* ○ *gloss paint*

gloss² /glɔs; glɑs/ *verb*

PHRV **gloss over sth** to avoid talking about a problem, mistake, etc. in detail

☆ **glos·sa·ry** /ˈglɑsəri; ˈglɔs-/ *noun* [C] (*pl.* **glos·sa·ries**) a list of special or unusual words and their meanings (at the end of a book)

gloss·y /ˈglɔsi; ˈglɑsi/ *adj.* (**gloss·i·er**; **gloss·i·est**) **1** smooth and shiny: *glossy hair* ○ *glossy photographs* ☞ Look at **matte**. **2** (used about a magazine, etc.) printed on good quality paper and having many color photographs

☆ **glove** /glʌv/ *noun* [C] a piece of clothing that covers your hand (and has separate parts for the thumb and each finger): *I need a new pair of gloves for the winter.*

☞ picture on page A27. Common types of gloves are *baseball gloves, boxing gloves, leather gloves, rubber gloves* and *winter gloves.* Look also at **mitten**.

☆ **glow¹** /gloʊ/ *verb* [I] **1** to give out light and/or heat without smoke or flames: *The TV screen glowed in the dark room.* **2 glow (with sth)** to be warm or red because of excitement, exercise, etc.: *to glow with health, enthusiasm, pride, etc.*

glow² /gloʊ/ *noun* [sing.] **1** a warm light: *the glow of the sky at sunset* **2** a feeling or look of warmth or satisfaction: *a rosy glow on the children's cheeks*

glow·ing /ˈgloʊɪŋ/ *adj.* giving high praise; favorable: *His teacher wrote a glowing report about his work.* —**glow·ing·ly** *adv.*

glu·cose /ˈglukoʊs/ *noun* [U] a type of sugar that is found in fruit

☆ **glue¹** /glu/ *noun* [U] a thick sticky liquid that is used for joining things together: *You can*

make glue from flour and water. ○ *Stick the photo in with glue.*

☆ **glue²** /glu/ *verb* [T] (*pres. part.* **glu·ing**) **glue A (to/onto B)**; **glue A and B (together)** to join a thing or things together with glue¹: *Do you think you can glue the handle back onto the mug?*

IDM **glued to sth** (*informal*) giving all your attention to sth and unwilling to leave it: *He just sits there every evening glued to the TV set.*

glum /glʌm/ *adj.* (*informal*) sad or disappointed: *What are you looking so glum about?* —**glum·ly** *adv.*

glut /glʌt/ *noun* [C, usually sing.] more of sth than is needed: *The oil glut has forced down the price of gasoline.*

glut·ton /ˈglʌtn/ *noun* [C] **1** a person who eats too much **2 a glutton for sth** (*informal*) a person who is willing to have or do more of sth difficult, unpleasant, etc.: *She's a glutton for punishment – she always takes the hardest jobs.*

GMAT /ˌdʒi ɛm eɪ ˈti/ *noun* [sing.] (*trademark*) Graduate Management Admissions Test; an examination that people who have a first (**bachelor's**) degree take in order to study for another degree in business

gnarled /nɑrld/ *adj.* rough and twisted, because of old age or hard work: *The old man had gnarled fingers.* ○ *a gnarled oak tree*

gnarl·y /ˈnɑrli/ *adj.* (**gnarl·i·er**; **gnarl·i·est**) (*slang*) **1** very good; excellent: *"Mike's parents are away this weekend." "Gnarly, dudes! Let's party!"* **2** difficult to deal with: *We had this really gnarly homework assignment for math today.*

gnash /næʃ/ *verb*

IDM **gnash your teeth** to make a noise with your teeth because of anger, pain, worry, etc.

gnat /næt/ *noun* [C] a very small flying insect that bites

gnaw /nɔ/ *verb* [I,T] **1 gnaw (at/on) sth** to bite a bone, etc. many times: *The dog lay on the carpet gnawing on a bone.* **2 gnaw (at) sb/sth** to cause sb/sth to feel nervous, worried, etc. all the time: *Fear of the future gnawed away at her all the time.*

gnome /noʊm/ *noun* [C] (in children's stories, etc.) a little old man with a beard and a pointed hat who lives under the ground

☆ **go¹** /goʊ/ *verb* (*pres. part.* **go·ing**; *3rd pers. sing. pres.* **goes**; *p.t.* **went** /wɛnt/; *p.p.* **gone** /gɔn; gɑn/) **1** [I] to move or travel from one place to another: *We're going downtown.* ○ *"Is Anita here?" "No, she went home."* ○ *We still have fifty miles to go.* ○ *How fast does this car go?*

☞ **Been** is often used as the past participle of **go** in this meaning: *Have you ever been to Arizona?*

2 [I] to travel to a place to take part in an

activity or do sth: *Are you going to Dave's party?* ○ *Do you want to go swimming this afternoon?* ○ *They went on vacation.* ○ *We went to watch the game.* ○ *I'll go make some coffee.* **3** [I] to visit or attend a place regularly: *Does Jacob go to school yet?* **4** [I] to leave a place: *I have to go now. It's almost 4 o'clock.* **5** [I] to lead to or reach a place or time: *Where does this road go to?* ○ *This cut on my hand goes pretty deep.* **6** [I] to have as its usual place: *Where does this vase go?* **7** [I] to fit into a space: *My clothes won't all go in one suitcase.* **8** [I] to happen in a particular way; to develop: *Hi, Mark. How's it going* (= How are you)*?* ○ *My work's going pretty well.* **9** [I] to become; to reach a particular state: *Her hair is going gray.* ○ *He went blind when he was 20.* ○ *The baby just went to sleep.* **10** [I] to remain in the state mentioned: *Many mistakes go unnoticed.* **11** [I] to become worse or stop working correctly: *The brakes on the car suddenly went yesterday.* **12** [I] to have certain words or a certain tune: *How does that song go?* **13** [T] to make a sound: *Cats go "meow."* **14** [T] (*informal*) (usually used in the present tense) to say or ask: *...So then I go, "I have to work tonight," and he goes, "How come?"*

☞ Many people, especially older people, do not like this use of the word **go**. However, it is very common in informal speech.

15 [I] (used about time) to pass: *The last hour went very slowly.* ○ *There's only one minute left to go.*

IDM **as people, things, etc. go** compared to the average person or thing: *As Chinese restaurants go, it wasn't bad.*

be going to do sth 1 (used for showing what you plan to do in the future): *We're going to sell our car.* **2** (used for saying that you are sure sth will happen): *It's going to rain soon.* ○ *Oh no! He's going to fall!*

go all out to do sth to make a great effort to do sth

Here goes! (said just before you start to do sth difficult or exciting)

to go (used about food) ready to be taken from a restaurant and eaten in another place: *I'll have a cheeseburger and fries to go.*

☞ For other idioms containing **go**, look at the entries for nouns, adjectives, etc.; for example, **go astray** is at **astray**.

PHRV **go about sth** to continue to do what you usually do: *We went about our normal routine.*

go about sth/doing sth to start trying to do sth difficult: *I wouldn't have any idea how to go about building a house.*

go against sb to be unfavorable to sb: *The referee's decision went against him.*

go against sb/sth to do sth that is opposed to sb/sth: *She went against her parents' wishes and married him.*

go against sth to be opposed or opposite to sth; not to be in agreement with sth: *It goes against my principles to use violence.*

go ahead 1 to take place after being planned: *Although several members were missing, the meeting went ahead without them.* **2** to walk, move, etc. in front of sb else: *Go ahead – I still have to button my coat.*

go ahead (and do sth) (used to encourage sb to do sth): *Go ahead and have another piece of cake – there's plenty.*

go ahead (with sth) to begin to do sth that you have planned

go along to continue: *The course gets more difficult as you go along.*

go along with sb/sth to agree with sb/sth: *I'm happy to go along with whatever you suggest.*

go around 1 (used about a story, a belief, etc.) to pass from person to person: *There's a rumor going around that he's going to resign.* **2** (used about an illness) to pass from person to person in a group or area: *There's a virus going around at work.* **3** (used especially after "enough") to be shared among all the people: *In this area, there aren't enough jobs to go around.*

go around (doing sth) to go from place to place in a certain way or while you are doing sth, especially sth that people do not approve of: *You can't go around in your pajamas all day!* ○ *She's been going around accusing me of stealing the money.*

go away 1 to leave a person or place: *Go away! Just leave me alone!* **2** to leave the place where you live (e.g. for a vacation) for a period of time of at least one night: *We're going away this weekend and we'll be back on Sunday evening.* **3** to disappear: *I tried to remove the stain in the carpet, but it won't go away.*

go back (to ...) to return (to a place): *It's a wonderful city and I'd like to go back there some day.*

go back (to sth) 1 to return to a previous matter or situation: *Let's go back to the subject we were discussing a few minutes ago.* **2** to have its origins in a previous period of time: *A lot of buildings on the East Coast go back to colonial times.*

go back on sth to break a promise, an agreement, etc.: *I promised to help them and I can't go back on it now.*

go back to sth/to doing sth to start doing again sth that you had stopped doing: *When the kids got a little older, she went back to full-time work.*

go by 1 (used about time) to pass: *As time went by, her confidence grew.* **2** to pass a place: *She stood at the window watching people go by.*

G

tʃ	dʒ	v	θ	ð	s	z	ʃ
chin	June	van	thin	then	so	zoo	she

go by sth to obey, follow or be guided by sth: *I wouldn't go by what politicians say.*

go down 1 (used about an aircraft) to crash: *A military helicopter went down 10 miles from the Air Force base.* **2** (used about a ship, etc.) to sink **3** (used about the sun) to disappear from the sky **4** to become lower in price, level, etc.; to fall: *The price of these computers has gone down in the last two years.* ○ *The number of people out of work went down last month.*

go down (with sb) (used with adverbs, especially "well" or "badly," or in questions beginning with "how") (used about sth that is said, a performance, etc.) to be received by sb: *The play went down well with the critics.*

go for sb to attack sb

go for sb/sth to be true for a particular person or thing: *We have financial problems, but I suppose the same goes for a lot of people.*

go for sth to make a great effort to reach a particular goal: *We know we can win this race, so let's go for it!*

go into sth 1 to start working in a certain type of job: *After she graduated, she went into nursing.* **2** to look at or describe sth in detail: *I don't have time to go into all the details now.*

go off 1 to explode: *The soldiers were injured when a bomb went off near them.* **2** to make a sudden loud noise: *I woke up when my alarm clock went off.* **3** (used about lights, heating, etc.) to stop working: *There was a power outage and all the lights went off.*

go off with sth to take sth that belongs to sb else: *Who went off with my cup?*

go on 1 (used about lights, heating, etc.) to start working: *I saw the lights go on in the house across the street.* **2** (used about time) to pass: *As time went on, she became more and more successful.* **3** (used especially in the continuous tenses) to happen or take place: *Can anybody tell me what's going on here?* **4** (used about a situation) to continue without changing: *This is a difficult period, but it won't go on forever.* **5** to continue speaking after stopping briefly: *Go on. What happened next?* **6** (used as an order for encouraging sb to do sth): *Go on, ask her!*

go on sth to use sth as information so that you can understand a situation: *There were no witnesses to the crime, so the police had very little to go on.*

go on (about sb/sth) to talk about sb/sth for a long time in a boring or annoying way: *She went on and on about the people she works with.*

go on (with sth) to continue doing sth, perhaps after a pause or break: *She ignored me and went on with her dinner.*

go on doing sth to continue doing sth without stopping or changing: *We don't want to go on living here for the rest of our lives.*

go out 1 to leave the place where you live or work for a short time, returning on the same day: *Let's go out for a meal tonight* (= to a restaurant). ○ *I'm going out for a walk, but I won't be long.* **2** (used about the ocean) to move away from the land: *The water was a long way away because the tide had gone out.* **3** to stop being fashionable or in use: *That kind of music went out in the seventies.* ○ *Teaching methods like that went out years ago.* **4** to stop shining or burning: *Suddenly all the lights went out.*

go out with sb; go out (together) to spend time regularly with sb, having a romantic and/or sexual relationship: *He's going out with Jill Brown now.* ○ *They went out together for five years before they got married.*

go over sth to look at, think about or discuss sth carefully from beginning to end: *Go over your work carefully before you hand it in.*

go over (to …) to visit sb's home, usually a short distance away: *I'm going over to Jo's for dinner tonight.*

go through to be completed successfully: *The deal went through as we had agreed.*

go through sth 1 to look in or at sth carefully, especially in order to find sth: *I went through all my pockets, but I couldn't find my wallet.* **2** to look at, think about or discuss sth carefully from beginning to end: *Let's go through the arrangements for the trip again.* ○ *We'll start class by going through your homework.* **3** to suffer a bad experience: *I'd hate to go through such a terrible ordeal again.*

go through with sth to do sth bad or difficult that you have decided, agreed or threatened to do: *Do you think she'll go through with her threat to leave him?*

go together (used about two or more things) **1** to belong to the same set or group **2** to look good together

go toward(s) sth to be used as part of the payment for sth: *The money I got for my birthday went toward my new bike.*

go under 1 to sink below the surface of water **2** (*informal*) (used about a company) to go out of business: *A lot of businesses are going under in the recession.*

go up 1 to start burning suddenly and strongly: *The car crashed into a wall and went up in flames.* **2** to become higher in price, level, amount, etc.; to rise: *Gas went up again yesterday.* ○ *The birthrate has gone up by 10%.*

go with sth 1 to be included with sth; to happen as a result of sth: *Pressure goes with the job.* **2** to match or be suitable with sth: *What color carpet would go with the walls?*

go without (sth) to manage without having sth: *They went without sleep many nights when the baby was sick.*

go² /goʊ/ *noun*

IDM **be on the go** (*informal*) to be very active or busy: *I'm exhausted. I've been on the go all day.*

to have a go (at sth/doing sth) (*informal*) to try to do sth: *I'm not sure if I can fix it, but I'll have a go.*
make a go of sth (*informal*) to be successful in sth: *They're struggling to make a go of their small store.*

'**go-ahead** *noun* [sing.] permission to do sth: *We've been given the go-ahead for the new building.*

☆ **goal** /ɡoʊl/ *noun* [C] **1** your purpose or aim: *I've finally achieved my goal of getting a college degree.* **2** (in soccer, hockey, etc.) the area between two posts which the ball or puck must enter for a point to be scored ☞ picture at **soccer**. **3** a point that is scored when the ball goes into the goal (2): *The Bruins won by three goals to two.* ○ *to score a goal*

goal·keep·er /'ɡoʊlˌkipər/ (*also* **goal·tend·er** /'ɡoʊlˌtɛndər/ *or informal* **goal·ie** /'ɡoʊli/) *noun* [C] the player who stands in front of the goal (2) and tries to stop the other team from scoring a goal (3): *The goalkeeper made a terrific save.* ☞ picture at **soccer**.

'**goal post** *noun* [C] one of the two posts that form the sides of a goal. They are joined together by a bar (**the crossbar**). ☞ picture at **football**.

horn　　**goat**
kid　　bell　　**goat**

goat /ɡoʊt/ *noun* [C] a small animal with horns which lives in mountainous areas or is kept on farms for its milk and meat

gob /ɡɑb/ *noun* [C] (*informal*) **1** a small piece of a thick liquid or of sth soft: *Yuck! There's a gob of toothpaste in the sink.* **2 gobs (of sth)** [plural] a large amount of sth: *a businessman with gobs of cash*

gob·ble /'ɡɑbl/ *verb* [I,T] (*informal*) **gobble sth (up)** to eat quickly and noisily: *He had gobbled up all his food before I even started mine.*

gob·ble·dy·gook (*also* **gobbledegook**) /'ɡɑbldiɡʊk/ *noun* [U] (*informal*) official language that is hard to understand

'**go-be·tween** *noun* [C] a person who takes messages between two people or groups who do not or cannot meet: *He acted as a go-between in the peace negotiations.*

gob·lin /'ɡɑblən/ *noun* [C] (in stories) a small ugly creature who plays tricks on people

'**go-cart** *noun* [C] a very small racing car with no roof

☆ **god** /ɡɑd/ *noun* **1** (*feminine* **god·dess**) [C] a being or force who is worshiped by a group

of people and who is believed to have the power to control nature and human affairs: *Mars was the Roman god of war and Venus was the goddess of love.* **2 God** [sing.] (in Christianity, Islam and Judaism) the creator and ruler of all things: *Do you believe in God?* ○ *Muslims worship God in a mosque.* ○ *Dear God, please help us...*

☞ **God** is used in a number of expressions. (However, some people think that it is wrong to use God's name in this way.) *Oh my God!* expresses surprise or shock: *Oh my God! I won $1,000!* We use **thank God** when we are happy and relieved about something: *Thank God you're here – I was beginning to think you'd had an accident.* The expression **God forbid!** is used when we say that we don't want something to happen: *If, God forbid, anything should happen to us, our children will take over the family business.* We use **for God's sake** when we are asking somebody to do something and want to sound more urgent or when we are angry with somebody: *For God's sake, shut up!* **God (only) knows** is used when we don't know an answer or when we don't understand something: *"What ever happened to our old neighbors?" "God knows!"*

god·child /'ɡɑdtʃaɪld/ *noun* [C] (*pl.* **god·chil·dren** /'ɡɑdˌtʃɪldrən/) a person for whom a godparent takes responsibility at a Christian baptism

☞ A male godchild is a **godson**, and a female godchild is a **goddaughter**.

god·dess /'ɡɑdəs/ *noun* [C] a female god

god·for·sak·en (*also* **Godforsaken**) /'ɡɑdfərˌseɪkən/ *adj.* (used about a place) depressing or having nothing of interest

god·par·ent /'ɡɑdˌpɛrənt; -ˌpær-/ *noun* [C, sing.] a person who promises to take responsibility for a child (at his/her baptism) and to make sure that he/she is educated as a Christian

☞ A male godparent is a **godfather**, and a female godparent is a **godmother**.

god·send /'ɡɑdsɛnd/ *noun* [C, sing.] something unexpected that is a great help to you because it comes just when it is needed: *The lottery win was a real godsend just after I lost my job.*

gog·gles /'ɡɑɡlz/ *noun* [plural] special glasses that you wear to protect your eyes from water, wind, dust, etc. ☞ Look at **mask**.

go·ing¹ /'ɡoʊɪŋ/ *noun* [U] the rate or speed of travel, progress, etc.: *It's been pretty slow going lately.*

IDM comings and goings ⇨ COMING

go·ing² /'ɡoʊɪŋ/ *adj.*

IDM the going rate (for sth) the usual cost (of sth): *The going rate for a cleaner is about $6 an hour.*

G

,goings-'on *noun* [plural] (*informal*) unusual things that are happening: *The old lady was shocked by the goings-on in the house next door.*

☆ **gold¹** /goʊld/ *noun* **1** [U] a precious yellow metal that is used for making coins, jewelry, etc.: *Is your bracelet made of gold?* ○ *solid, pure, 22-karat, etc. gold* ○ *a gold chain, ring, watch, etc.* **2** [C] = GOLD MEDAL

IDM **(as) good as gold** very well-behaved: *The children were as good as gold while you were out.*

gold² /goʊld/ *adj.* the color of gold: *The invitation was written in gold letters.*

☆ **gold·en** /'goʊldən/ *adj.* made of gold or like gold: *a golden crown* ○ *golden hair* ○ (*figurative*) *a golden* (= excellent) *opportunity*

,golden ,anni'versary *noun* [C] the 50th anniversary of a wedding ☞ Look at **diamond anniversary** and **silver anniversary**.

gold·fish /'goʊldfɪʃ/ *noun* [C] (*pl.* **gold·fish**) a small orange fish that is kept as a pet in a bowl or pond

,gold 'medal (*also* **gold**) *noun* [C] the prize for first place in a sports competition: *How many gold medals did we win in the 1996 Olympics?* ☞ Look at **silver medal** and **bronze medal**.

,gold 'medalist *noun* [C] the winner of a gold medal

'gold mine *noun* [C] **1** a place where gold is taken from the earth **2** (*informal*) a business that makes a lot of profit

'gold rush *noun* [C] a situation in which many people hurry to an area where gold has just been discovered in the earth: *the California gold rush of 1849*

☆ **golf** /gɑlf; gɔlf/ *noun* [U] a game that is played outdoors on a large area of grass (**a golf course**) and in which you use a stick (**a golf club**) to hit a small hard ball (**a golf ball**) into a series of holes (usually 18): *to play a round of golf*

golf·er /'gɑlfər; 'gɔlfər/ *noun* [C] a person who plays golf

gol·ly /'gɑli/ *interj.* (*old-fashioned, informal*) (used for expressing surprise)

gone¹ *p.p.* of GO¹

☆ **gone²** /gɔn; gɑn/ *adj.* (not before a noun) not present any longer; completely used up: *He stood at the door for a moment, and then he was gone.* ○ *Is the milk all gone?*

gon·na /'gənə; 'gɔnə/ (*informal*) (only used before a verb) a way of writing "going to" to show that sb is speaking in an informal way

☞ Do not write "gonna" yourself (unless you are copying somebody's speech) because it might be marked as a mistake. **Wanna** (= want to) and **gotta** (= got to) are similar

goo /gu/ *noun* [U] (*informal*) a sticky wet substance —**goo·ey** /'gui/ (**goo·i·er**; **goo·i·est**) *adj.* (*informal*)

☆ **good¹** /gʊd/ *adj.* (**bet·ter** /'bɛtər/, **best** /bɛst/) **1** of a high quality or standard: *a good book, movie, concert, etc.* ○ *The hotel was really good.* ○ *"Why don't you apply for the job?" "I don't think my English is good enough."* ○ *The car was in very good condition.* **2 good at sth**; **good with sb/sth** able to do sth or deal with sb/sth well; successful: *Jane's good at chemistry.* ○ *He's very good with children.* **3** pleasant or enjoyable: *It's good to be home again.* ○ *good news, weather, etc.* ○ *Have a good time!* **4** morally right or well behaved: *She was a very good person – she spent her whole life trying to help other people.* ○ *Were the kids good while we were out?* **5 good (to sb)** kind; helpful: *They were good to me when I was sick.* **6 good (for sb/sth)** having a positive effect on your health: *Green vegetables are very good for you.* **7** suitable or favorable: *This beach is very good for surfing.* ○ *I think Paul would be a good person for the job.* ○ *"When should we meet?" "Thursday would be a good day for me."* **8** (only used before an adjective or noun) great in number, size, length, etc.: *a good many people* (= a lot of people) ○ *Take a good* (= long and careful) *look at this picture.* **9** (only before a noun) at least: *We waited for a good ten minutes.* ○ *It's a good three miles to the post office.* **10** (used when you are pleased about sth): *"Tom invited us to dinner next week." "Oh, good!"*

IDM **a good/great many** ⟹ MANY

as good as almost: *The project is as good as finished.*

in good faith ⟹ FAITH

good for you (*informal*) (used for congratulating sb): *Good for you! You should be really proud.*

good grief, good heavens, etc. (used for expressing surprise) ☞ Look at the entries for **grief**, etc.

good morning / afternoon / evening / night (used for greeting sb) ☞ Look at the entries for **morning**, etc.

☆ **good²** /gʊd/ *noun* [U] **1** the quality of being morally right: *the difference between good and evil* ○ *I'm sure there's some good in everybody.* **2** something that will help sb/sth; advantage: *I know you don't want to go to the hospital, but it's for your own good.* ○ *What's the good in learning French if you have no chance of using it?* ☞ Look also at **goods**.

IDM **be no good** to be of no use or value: *This work is just no good – you'll have to do it again.* ○ *These shoes are no good for walking through snow.*

do you good to help or be useful to you: *It'll do you good to meet some new people.*

for good forever: *I hope they're gone for good this time.*

good³ /gʊd/ *adv.* (*informal*) well; in a good way: *You guys did pretty good today.*

G

ər	ɪr	ɛr	ɑr	ɔr	ʊr	ʒ	h	ŋ
bird	near	hair	car	north	tour	vision	hat	sing

☞ Careful speakers do not use **good** as an adverb, but it is common in very informal speech. We use **well** in writing and in more formal, careful speaking.

the ,Good 'Book *noun* [sing.] (*informal*) the Christian Bible

☆ **good·bye** (*also* **good-bye**) /,gʊd'baɪ; gə'baɪ/ *interj.* (said when sb goes or when you go): *Goodbye! See you tomorrow!* ○ *We said goodbye to Steven at the airport.*

☞ **Bye** has the same meaning and is more informal than **goodbye**. **Goodbye** can also be used as a noun: *a sad goodbye at the airport.*

,Good 'Friday *noun* [C] the Friday before Easter when Christians remember the death of Christ

'good guy *noun* [C] (*informal*) a good person in a movie, book, etc.

good·ies /'gʊdiz/ *noun* [plural] (*informal*) small things that are good, especially good things to eat

,good-'looking *adj.* (usually used about a person) attractive ☞ Look at the note at **beautiful**.

good-na·tured /,gʊd 'neɪtʃərd/ *adj.* friendly or cheerful

☆ **good·ness** /'gʊdnəs/ *noun* [U] **1** the quality of being good **2** the quality that helps sb/sth to grow: *This new product has all the goodness of regular yogurt, but only half the fat.*

☞ **Goodness** is used in a number of expressions. We say **Goodness!** or **My goodness!** to show that we are surprised. *Thank goodness* expresses happiness and relief: *Thank goodness it stopped raining!* We say **For goodness' sake** when we are asking somebody to do something and want to sound more urgent or when we are angry with somebody: *For goodness' sake, hurry up!*

'good old boy (*also* **good ol' boy** /'gʊd oʊl bɔɪ/) *noun* [C] (*informal*) a white man, usually from a small town or the countryside in the southern U.S., who does not like people of other races and who often drinks a lot of alcohol and is not well educated

☆ **goods** /gʊdz/ *noun* [plural] things that are for sale: *a wide range of consumer goods* ○ *stolen goods* ☞ Look also at **product** and **merchandise**. They are similar in meaning.

good-tem·pered /,gʊd 'tɛmpərd/ *adj.* not easily made angry

good·will /,gʊd'wɪl/ *noun* [U] friendly, helpful feelings toward other people: *There is a new atmosphere of goodwill in international politics.*

goo·ey ⇨ GOO

goof¹ /guf/ *verb* [I] (*informal*) to make a stupid mistake

PHR V goof around (*informal*) to spend time doing silly, unimportant things: *We spent most of the summer just goofing around at the beach.* **goof off** (*informal*) to avoid doing sth that you should be doing: *Quit goofing off and get back to work!*

goof² /guf/ *noun* [C] (*informal*) a stupid mistake: *The government's goof could cost taxpayers $10 million.*

goof·y /'gufi/ *adj.* (**goof·i·er**; **goof·i·est**) (*informal*) silly; stupid

goose /gus/ *noun* (*pl.* **geese** /gis/) [C] a large bird that is like a duck, but larger. Some geese are kept on farms for their meat and eggs.

☞ A male goose is called a **gander** and a young goose is a **gosling**.

'goose bumps *noun* [plural] (*also* **'goose pimples**) small points or lumps which appear on your skin because you are cold or frightened

the GOP /,dʒi oʊ 'pi/ *abbr.* Grand Old Party; the Republican Party: *a GOP presidential candidate* ☞ Look at the note at **White House**.

go·pher /'goʊfər/ *noun* [C] a small animal with brown fur that lives in areas where the land is flat, and that digs holes in the ground

gore /gɔr/ *noun* [U] the blood that comes from a cut or wound: *His new movie is full of gore* (= there are many violent scenes in it). ☞ The adjective is **gory**.

gorge¹ /gɔrdʒ/ *noun* [C] a narrow valley with steep sides and a stream or river running through it

gorge² /gɔrdʒ/ *verb* [I,T] **gorge (yourself) (on/with sth)** to eat a lot of food: *At Thanksgiving, people gorge themselves on rich food.*

gor·geous /'gɔrdʒəs/ *adj.* beautiful; wonderful: *You look gorgeous in that dress.* —**gorgeous·ly** *adv.*

go·ril·la /gə'rɪlə/ *noun* [C] a very large black African monkey that is the largest of the monkeys (**apes**) that are closely related to people

go·ry /'gɔri/ *adj.* (**go·ri·er**; **go·ri·est**) full of violence and blood: *a gory movie* ○ (*figurative*) *He told me all the gory details about the divorce.*

gosh /gaʃ/ *interj.* (*informal*) (used for expressing surprise, shock, etc.)

gos·ling /'gazlɪŋ/ *noun* [C] a young goose

gos·pel /'gaspl/ *noun* **1** **Gospel** [C] one of the four books in the Bible that describe the life and teachings of Jesus Christ: *St. Matthew's/Mark's/Luke's/John's Gospel* **2** [U] the truth: *You can't take what he says as gospel.* **3** (*also* **'gospel music**) [U] a style of religious music that is especially popular among African-American Christians

G

tʃ	dʒ	v	θ	ð	s	z	ʃ
chin	June	van	thin	then	so	zoo	she

☆ **gos·sip** /ˈgɑsəp/ *noun* [U] informal talk about other people and their private lives: *Don't believe all the gossip you hear.* ◦ *He loves spreading gossip about his neighbors.* —**gos·sip** *verb* [I]: *I can't stand here gossiping all day.*

got *p.t.* of GET

got·ta /ˈgɑtə/ (*informal*) (only used before a verb) a way of writing "got to" to show that sb is speaking in an informal way

☞ Do not write "gotta" yourself (unless you are copying somebody's speech) because it might be marked as a mistake. **Gonna** and **wanna** are similar.: *I gotta go* (= I've got to go).

got·ten *p.p.* of GET

gouge /gaʊdʒ/ *verb* [T] to charge sb too much money for sth, especially in a way that is not honest or legal: *laws to prevent stores from gouging consumers*
PHRV **gouge sth out** to take sth out with force (usually with a tool or with your fingers)

gour·met /gʊrˈmeɪ; ˈgʊrmeɪ/ *noun* [C] a person who enjoys food and wine and knows a lot about them: *a gourmet restaurant*

☆ **gov·ern** /ˈgʌvərn/ *verb* **1** [I,T] to rule or control the public affairs of a country, city, etc.: *A group of rebels overthrew the governing party.* **2** [T] (often passive) to influence or control: *Our decision will be governed by the amount of money we have to spend.*

☆ **gov·ern·ment** /ˈgʌvərmənt; ˈgʌvərnmənt/ *noun* **1** [C] the group of people who govern a country, state, city, etc.: *the federal government* (= the national government of the United States) ◦ *government policy, committees, etc.* **2** [usually sing.] the offices, services, etc. that belong to the government (1) and are not part of a company: *government employees* ◦ *I work for the state government.* **3** [U] the act or method of governing: *Six years of weak government had left the economy in ruins.* —**gov·ern·men·tal** /ˌgʌvərˈmɛntəl; ˌgʌvərn-/ *adj.*: *governmental affairs* ◦ *different governmental systems*

☆ **gov·er·nor** /ˈgʌvənər; ˈgʌvərnər/ *noun* [C] a person who is elected to govern a state: *the governor of California* ☞ The adjective is **gubernatorial**.

gown /gaʊn/ *noun* [C] **1** a long woman's dress for a special occasion: *a wedding gown* **2** a loose piece of clothing that is worn by judges or students during official ceremonies, or by doctors and nurses during medical operations

GPA /ˌdʒi pi ˈeɪ/ *abbr.* = GRADE POINT AVERAGE

☆ **grab** /græb/ *verb* (**grab·bing**; **grabbed**) [I,T] to take sth suddenly or roughly: *Jenny grabbed the toy car from her little brother.* ◦ *Don't grab – there's plenty for everybody.* ◦ (*figurative*) *He grabbed the opportunity of a free trip to Hawaii.* ◦ (*figurative*) *I don't have much time, so I'll just grab a burger for lunch.* ☞ Look at **snatch**. It is similar in meaning. —**grab** /græb/ *noun* [C]: *A man suddenly made a grab for my necklace.*

grace /greɪs/ *noun* [U] **1** the ability to move in a smooth and attractive way: *to walk, dance, move, etc. with grace* **2** good or favorable treatment of sb, especially by God **3** a short prayer of thanks to God before or after a meal: *Dad always says grace.*

☆ **grace·ful** /ˈgreɪsfl/ *adj.* having grace (1) and beauty: *a graceful dancer* ☞ Look at **gracious**. Its meaning is different. —**grace·ful·ly** *adv.*: *She accepted the decision gracefully* (= without showing her disappointment). —**grace·ful·ness** *noun* [U]

gra·cious /ˈgreɪʃəs/ *adj.* (used about a person or his/her behavior) pleasant, kind or polite (to sb of a lower social position): *Mrs. Lowell is always a warm, gracious hostess.* —**gra·cious·ly** *adv.* —**gra·cious·ness** *noun* [U]

grad /græd/ *adj., noun* [C] = GRADUATE[1,3]

☆ **grade[1]** /greɪd/ *noun* [C] **1** a letter or number that is given for school work, etc. or in an examination to show how good the work is: *He got good/bad grades this semester.*

☞ In American schools and universities, grades are usually given as letters of the alphabet. The letters used are A (the best grade), B, C, D and F (a failing grade). Sometimes a plus or a minus sign is added after the letter. For example, a B+ is slightly better than a B, and a B– is slightly worse than a B.

2 one of the levels in a school. Most students begin a new grade each year in the fall: *My daughter is in (the) third grade.*

☞ There are 12 numbered grades in American schools. Look also at **kindergarten**.

3 the quality or place in a series that sb/sth has: *We need to use high-grade materials for this job.* ◦ *grade A fresh eggs*
IDM **make the grade** (*informal*) to reach the expected standard; succeed

☆ **grade[2]** /greɪd/ *verb* [T] **1** to look at school, etc. work that sb has done, mark where there are mistakes and give it a number or letter to show how good it is: *I spent the whole weekend grading papers.* **2** (often passive) to divide things into groups, according to their quality or size: *The books are graded according to level of difficulty.* ◦ *Meat is graded by quality.*

grade point average *noun* [C, usually sing.] (*abbr.* **GPA**) a number that is calculated from the average of all the grades1 that a student has gotten in his/her courses over a period of time: *I graduated with a 3.7 GPA.*

☞ A student's grade point average is usually calculated using these numbers: A = 4.0, B = 3.0, C = 2.0, D = 1.0 and F = 0.0.

grad·er /ˈgreɪdər/ *noun* [C] **1** (used after *first, second, third*, etc.) a student who is in the grade[1](2) mentioned: *The play is open to all*

G

seventh and eighth graders. **2** a person who grades²(1) students' papers, tests, etc.: *Prof. Cohen is a really tough grader* (= he/she does not give many high grades).

'**grade school** *noun* [C,U] = ELEMENTARY SCHOOL

'**grad school** *noun* [C,U] (*informal*) = GRADUATE SCHOOL

☆ **grad·u·al** /'grædʒuəl/ *adj.* happening slowly or over a long period of time; not sudden: *There has been a gradual increase in the number of people without jobs.* —**grad·u·al·ly** /-dʒuəli/ *adv.*: *After the storm, things gradually got back to normal.*

☆ **grad·u·ate¹** /'grædʒuət/ (also *informal* **grad**) *noun* [C] a person who has completed his/her studies at a school, college, university, etc.: *a college graduate* ○ *She's a graduate of Jefferson High School.*

☆ **grad·u·ate²** /'grædʒueɪt/ *verb* [I] **1 graduate (from sth)** to finish your studies at a school, college, university, etc. and receive an official piece of paper (**a diploma**) that shows that you have finished: *I graduated from Florida State University with a degree in biology in 1992.* **2 graduate (from sth) to sth** to change (from sth) to sth more difficult, important, expensive, etc.

grad·u·ate³ /'grædʒuət/ (also *informal* **grad**) *adj.* (only *before* a noun) for or connected with students who already have a first (**bachelor's**) degree and are studying for a further degree: *graduate students* ○ *graduate courses* ☞ Look at **undergraduate**.

'**graduate school** (also *informal* '**grad school**) *noun* [C,U] the part of a university that is for students who already have a first (**bachelor's**) degree and are studying for a further degree

☆ **grad·u·a·tion** /ˌgrædʒu'eɪʃn/ *noun* **1** [U] graduating from a school, university, etc. **2** [C] a ceremony in which official pieces of paper (**diplomas**) are given to people who have finished their studies at a school, university, etc.

graf·fi·ti /grə'fiti/ *noun* [U] pictures or writing on a wall, etc. in a public place that are rude, funny or political: *The wall was covered in graffiti.*

graft¹ /græft/ *noun* [C] **1** a piece of living skin, bone, etc. that is attached onto a damaged part of a body in a medical operation: *a skin graft* **2** a piece of a living plant that is attached inside another plant so that it will grow

graft² /græft/ *verb* [T] **graft sth onto sth** to attach sth as a graft¹ onto a plant, body, etc. ☞ Look at **transplant**.

☆ **grain** /greɪn/ *noun* **1** [U] the seeds of wheat, rice, etc. as a product: *The U.S. is a major producer of grain.* ○ *grain exports* **2** [C] a single seed of wheat, rice, etc. **3** [C] a very small piece of sth: *a grain of sand, salt, sugar, etc.* ○

(*figurative*) *There isn't a grain of truth in what you say.* **4** the natural pattern of lines that can be seen or felt in wood, rock, stone, etc.: *to cut a piece of wood with/against the grain*

IDM **take sth with a grain of salt** to believe that sth is probably not true or not completely accurate

gram /græm/ *noun* [C] (*abbr.* **g**) a measure of weight. There are 1,000 grams in a kilogram.

☆ **gram·mar** /'græmər/ *noun* **1** [U] the rules of language, e.g. for forming words or joining words together in sentences: *Russian grammar can be difficult for foreign students.* **2** [U] the way in which sb uses the rules of language: *Your vocabulary is good, but your grammar needs improvement.*

'**grammar school** *noun* [C] = ELEMENTARY SCHOOL

gram·mat·i·cal /grə'mætɪkl/ *adj.* **1** connected with grammar: *grammatical rules* **2** following the rules of grammar ☞ The opposite is **ungrammatical**. —**gram·mat·i·cal·ly** /-kli/ *adv.*: *a grammatically correct sentence*

☆ **grand¹** /grænd/ *adj.* looking impressive in size or appearance (also used in names): *the grand opening of a new store* (= a special ceremony) ○ *the Grand Canyon* ○ *the Grand Hotel* ☞ The noun is **grandeur**. —**grand·ly** *adv.*

grand² /grænd/ *noun* [C] (*pl.* **grand**) (*slang*) 1,000 dollars: *It'll cost you 50 grand!*

☆ **grand·child** /'græntʃaɪld/ *noun* [C] (*pl.* **grand·chil·dren** /'græntʃɪldrən/) the daughter or son of your child

☆ **grand·daugh·ter** /'grændɔtər/ *noun* [C] the daughter of your child

gran·deur /'grændʒər; -dʒʊr/ *noun* [U] (*formal*) **1** the quality of being large and impressive: *the grandeur of the Swiss Alps* **2** the feeling of being important

☆ **grand·fa·ther** /'grænˌfɑðər/ *noun* [C] the father of one of your parents ☞ Look at the note at **grandparent**.

ˌ**grandfather** '**clock** *noun* [C] a clock that stands on the floor in a tall wooden case

gran·di·ose /'grændioʊs; ˌgrændi'oʊs/ *adj.* bigger or more complicated than necessary: *Their grandiose scheme was completely impractical.*

☞ Using this word about something shows that you do not have a good opinion of it.

ˌ**grand** '**jury** *noun* [C] (*pl.* **grand juries**) a group of people who are chosen to decide whether there is enough evidence against an accused person for a trial

grand·ma /'grænmɑ; 'græmɑ/ *noun* [C] (*informal*) = GRANDMOTHER

ə	y	w	t̬	eɪ	aɪ	ɔɪ	aʊ	oʊ
about	yes	woman	butter	say	five	boy	now	go

☆ **grand·moth·er** /ˈɡrænˌmʌðər/ *noun* [C] the mother of one of your parents ☞ Look at the note at **grandparent**.

grand·pa /ˈɡrænpɑ; ˈɡræmpɑ/ *noun* [C] (*informal*) = GRANDFATHER

☆ **grand·par·ent** /ˈɡrænˌpɛrənt; -ˌpær-/ *noun* [C] the father or mother of one of your parents

☞ If you need to distinguish between one of your mother's parents and one of your father's parents, you can say, for example: *my maternal/paternal grandfather* or *my grandfather on my mother's/father's side*.

ˌ**grand piˈano** *noun* [C] a large flat piano (with horizontal strings)

☆ **grand·son** /ˈɡrænsʌn/ *noun* [C] the son of your child

grand·stand /ˈɡrændstænd/ *noun* [C] rows of seats (covered by a roof) from which you get a good view of a sports competition, etc.

ˌ**grand ˈtotal** *noun* [C] the amount that you get when you add several totals together

gran·ite /ˈɡrænət/ *noun* [U] a hard gray rock

gran·ny /ˈɡræni/ *noun* [C] (*pl.* **gran·nies**) (*informal*) = GRANDMOTHER

gra·no·la /ɡrəˈnoʊlə/ *noun* [U] food made of grains, nuts, dried fruit, etc. that you eat with milk for breakfast

grant¹ /ɡrænt/ *verb* [T] **1** (*formal*) to give sb what he/she has asked for: *He was granted permission to leave early.* **2** to agree (that sth is true): *I grant you that New York is an interesting place, but I still wouldn't want to live there.*

IDM **take sb/sth for granted** to show too little attention to sb/sth; not be grateful enough to a person or thing : *In developed countries, we take running water for granted.* ○ *She never says thank you – she just takes me for granted.*
take sth for granted to accept sth as being true: *We can take it for granted that the new students will have at least an elementary knowledge of English.*

grant² /ɡrænt/ *noun* [C] money that is given (by the government, etc.) for a particular purpose: *a college grant* (= to help pay for a college education) ☞ Look also at **scholarship**.

grant·ed /ˈɡræntəd/ *adv.* (used for saying that sth is true, before you make a comment about it): *"We've never had any problems before." "Granted, but this year there are 200 more people coming."*

gran·u·lat·ed /ˈɡrænyəleɪtəd/ *adj.* in the form of small hard pieces or grains: *granulated sugar*

gran·ule /ˈɡrænyul/ *noun* [C] a small hard piece or grain of sth

a bunch of grapes

☆ **grape** /ɡreɪp/ *noun* [C] a green or purple berry that grows in bunches on a climbing plant (**a vine**) and that is used for making wine: *a bunch of grapes* ○ *seedless grapes*

☞ Grapes that have been dried are called **raisins**.

IDM **sour grapes** ⇨ SOUR

grape·fruit /ˈɡreɪpfrut/ *noun* [C] (*pl.* **grapefruit** or **grape·fruits**) a large round yellow fruit with a thick skin that is like a big orange but with a sour taste

☞ **Grapefruit** is more common than **grapefruits** as a plural form.

grape·vine /ˈɡreɪpvaɪn/ *noun*

IDM **hear sth through the grapevine** to hear news that has been passed from one person to another: *"How did you find that out?" "Oh, I just heard it through the grapevine."*

☆ **graph** /ɡræf/ *noun* [C] a mathematical diagram in which a line or a curve shows the relationship between two quantities, measurements, etc.: *a graph showing the number of cars sold each month* ○ *a bar graph* ○ *a line graph* ○ *graph paper* ☞ Look also at **chart**.

graph — Number of items sold — Mar Apr May

graph·ic¹ /ˈɡræfɪk/ *adj.* **1** (only *before* a noun) connected with drawings, letters, diagrams, etc.: *graphic design* **2** (used about descriptions) clear and giving a lot of detail: *She described the accident in graphic detail.* ○ *I think there's too much graphic violence on TV.* —**graph·i·cal·ly** /-kli/ *adv.*

graph·ic² /ˈɡræfɪk/ *noun* [C] a picture or diagram, especially in a computer document or in a book: *a CD-ROM with text and graphics*

grap·ple /ˈɡræpl/ *verb* [I] **grapple (with sb/sth)** to struggle or fight with a person or a difficult problem: *We have been grappling with this issue all day.*

☆ **grasp¹** /ɡræsp/ *verb* [T] **1** to take hold of sb/sth suddenly and firmly: *Lisa grasped the child firmly by the hand.* ○ (*figurative*) *to grasp an opportunity* **2** to understand sth: *I don't think you've grasped how serious this is.*

ər	ɪr	ɛr	ɑr	ɔr	ʊr	ʒ	h	ŋ
bird	near	hair	car	north	tour	vision	hat	sing

G

PHRV **grasp at sth** to try to take hold of sth: *He grasped at the swinging rope but missed.*

grasp² /græsp/ *noun* [usually sing.] **1** a firm hold or control over sb/sth: *a strong grasp* **2** the ability to get or achieve sth: *Finally their dream was within their grasp.* **3** understanding: *He has a good grasp of English grammar.*

☆ **grass** /græs/ *noun* **1** [U] the common green plant with thin leaves which covers fields and which often grows around people's houses. Cows, sheep, horses, etc. eat grass: *She lay on the grass and listened to the birds singing.* ○ *Keep off the grass* (on a sign). ○ *to mow the grass* ○ *a blade* (= one leaf) *of grass* ☞ An area of grass around a house is called a **lawn** or a **yard**. Look also at **bluegrass**. **2** [C] one type of grass (1): *an arrangement of dried flowers and grasses*

grass·hop·per /'græsˌhɑpər/ *noun* [C] an insect that lives in long grass and that can jump high in the air

ˌ**grass 'roots** (*also* **grassroots**) *noun* [plural] the ordinary people in an organization and not those who make decisions: *a grassroots political movement*

grass·y /'græsi/ *adj.* covered with grass

grate¹ /greɪt/ *noun* [C] a framework of metal bars in front of a window, over a hole in the street, etc.: *a sewer grate*

grate² /greɪt/ *verb* **1** [T] to rub food into small pieces using a metal tool (**a grater**): *Grate the cheese and sprinkle it over the top of the pizza.* **2** [I] to make a sharp unpleasant sound (when two surfaces rub against each other): *The gate grated against the sidewalk as it opened.* **3** [I] **grate (on sb)** to annoy or irritate: *Her voice really grates on me!*

☆ **grate·ful** /'greɪtfl/ *adj.* **grateful (to sb) (for sth)**; **grateful (that...)** feeling or showing thanks (to sb): *We are extremely grateful to you for all the help you have given us.* ○ *I know you wrecked my car, but I'm just grateful you're not hurt.* ○ *I would be very grateful if you could send me a copy of your brochure.* ☞ The opposite is **ungrateful**. The noun is **gratitude**. —**grate·ful·ly** *adv.*

grat·er /'greɪtər/ *noun* [C] a piece of kitchen equipment with a rough surface that is used for grating food

grat·i·fi·ca·tion /ˌgrætəfəˈkeɪʃn/ *noun* [U] the state of being pleased or satisfied

grat·i·fy /'grætəfaɪ/ *verb* [T] (*pres. part.* **grat·i·fy·ing**; *3rd pers. sing. pres.* **grat·i·fies**; *p.t., p.p.* **grat·i·fied**) (*formal*) (often passive) to give sb pleasure: *I was gratified to hear that you enjoyed my book.* —**grat·i·fy·ing** *adj.*

grat·i·tude /'grætətud/ *noun* [U] **gratitude (to sb) (for sth)** the feeling of being grateful or thankful: *We would like to express our gratitude to David Stewart for all his help and advice.* ☞ The opposite is **ingratitude**.

☆ **grave¹** /greɪv/ *noun* [C] the place where a dead body is buried: *The casket was lowered into the grave.* ○ *I put some flowers on the grave.*

grave² /greɪv/ *adj.* (*formal*) **1** bad or serious: *These events could have grave consequences for us all.* ○ *a matter of grave concern* **2** (used about people) sad or serious: *He had a very grave expression on his face.* ☞ The noun is **gravity**. **Serious** is much more common for both senses.

grav·el /'grævl/ *noun* [U] very small stones that are used for making roads, paths, etc.

grave·stone /'greɪvstoʊn/ *noun* [C] = HEADSTONE

grave·yard /'greɪvyɑrd/ *noun* [C] an area of land (often near a church) where dead people are buried ☞ Look at **cemetery**.

grav·i·ty /'grævəti/ *noun* [U] **1** the natural force that makes things fall to the ground when you drop them: *the force of gravity* **2** (*formal*) importance or seriousness: *Politicians are just beginning to realize the gravity of the situation.* ☞ **Seriousness** is more common than gravity in this sense. The adjective is **grave**.

gra·vy /'greɪvi/ *noun* [U] a sauce that is made from the juices that come out of meat while it is cooking. Gravy is served with meat, potatoes, etc. ☞ Look at **sauce**.

☆ **gray¹** (*also* **grey**) /greɪ/ *adj.* **1** of the color between black and white: *dark/light/pale gray* ○ *He was wearing a gray suit.* **2** with gray hair: *He's going gray.*

☆ **gray²** (*also* **grey**) /greɪ/ *noun* [C,U] the color between black and white

gray·ish (*also* **greyish**) /'greɪɪʃ/ *adj.* slightly gray

graze /greɪz/ *verb* **1** [I] (used about cows, sheep, etc.) to eat grass (that is growing in a field) **2** [T] to pass sth and touch it lightly, perhaps causing slight damage: *Luckily the bullet just grazed his head..*

☆ **grease¹** /gris/ *noun* [U] **1** a thick oily substance used, for example, in engines: *engine grease* ○ *grease marks* **2** oil or fat that has been left in a pan after meat has been cooked: *You'll need very hot water to get all the grease off those pans.*

grease² /gris/ *verb* [T] to put grease on or in sth: *Grease the pan thoroughly to stop the cake from sticking.*

greas·y /'grisi/ *adj.* (**greas·i·er**; **greas·i·est**) covered with or containing a lot of grease: *greasy fingers* ○ *greasy food* ○ *greasy hair*

☆ **great¹** /greɪt/ *adj.* **1** large in amount, degree, size, etc.; a lot of: *We had great difficulty in solving the problem.* ○ *The party was a great success.* ○ *It gives me great pleasure to introduce tonight's guest.* ☞ Look at the note at **big**. **2** particularly important; of unusually high

tʃ	dʒ	v	θ	ð	s	z	ʃ
chin	June	van	thin	then	so	zoo	she

quality: *one of the greatest scientists of the 20th century* ○ *a great moment in history* **3** (*informal*) good; wonderful: *We had a great time in Florida.* ○ *It's great to see you again.*

☞ We sometimes use **great** in a sarcastic way, that is, when something is not good at all: *Oh great! I spilled coffee all over my homework!*

4 (*informal*) (used to emphasize sth) very; very good: *There was a great big dog in the back yard.* ○ *They were great friends.*
IDM **go to great lengths to do sth** ⇨ LENGTH
a good/great deal ⇨ DEAL[1]
a good/great many ⇨ MANY —**great·ness** *noun* [U]
great² /greɪt/ *noun* [C, usually pl.] (*informal*) a person or thing of special ability or importance: *He's one of the all-time greats in baseball.*
great- /greɪt/ (used before a noun to show a family relationship)

☞ **Great-** can be added to other words for family members to show another generation: *your great-aunt* (= the aunt of your mother or father) ○ *your great-nephew* (= the son of your nephew or niece) ○ *your great-great-grandfather* (= the grandfather of one of your grandparents) .

Great 'Britain (*also* Britain) *noun* the island that includes England, Wales and Scotland
☞ Look at the note at **United Kingdom**.
great-'grandchild *noun* [C] the daughter or son of your grandchild
great-'grand,daughter *noun* [C] the daughter of one of your grandchildren
great-'grand,father *noun* [C] the father of one of your grandparents
great-'grand,mother *noun* [C] the mother of one of your grandparents
great-'grand,parent *noun* [C] the father or mother of one of your grandparents
great-'grandson *noun* [C] the son of one of your grandchildren
☆ great·ly /ˈgreɪtli/ *adv.* very much: *She will be greatly missed by friends and family.*
☆ greed /grid/ *noun* [U] greed (for sth) a strong desire for more food, money, power, etc. than you really need
greed·y /ˈgridi/ *adj.* (greed·i·er; greed·i·est) greedy (for sth) wanting more food, money, power, etc. than you really need: *Don't be so greedy – you've already had three pieces of cake.* —greed·i·ly /-əli/ *adv.*
☆ green¹ /grin/ *adj.* **1** of the color of grass or leaves: *dark/light/pale green* ○ *olive green* ○ *These bananas aren't ripe yet – they're still green.* **2** (*informal*) (used about a person) with little experience
IDM **give sb/get the green light** (*informal*) to give sb/get permission to do sth
green with envy (*informal*) wanting to have

what sb else has: *She was green with envy when she found out how much money I make!*
have a green thumb (*informal*) to be able to grow plants well
☆ green² /grin/ *noun* **1** [C,U] the color of grass and leaves: *They were dressed in green.* ○ *The room was decorated in greens and blues.* **2** greens [plural] green vegetables whose leaves are usually eaten cooked **3** [C] a flat area of very short grass used in games such as golf: *the green at the 18th hole*
green·back /ˈgrinbæk/ *noun* [C] (*informal*) a U.S. dollar
green 'bean *noun* [C] = STRING BEAN
green card *noun* [C] an official card that shows that sb from another country is allowed to live and work in the United States: *to apply for a green card*
green·house /ˈgrinhaʊs/ *noun* [C] a building made of glass in which plants are grown
the 'greenhouse ef,fect *noun* [sing.] the warming of the earth's atmosphere as a result of pollution
green·ish /ˈgrinɪʃ/ *adj.* slightly green
☆ greet /grit/ *verb* [T] **1** to welcome sb when you meet him/her; to say hello to sb: *He greeted me with a friendly smile.* **2** greet sth with sth (usually passive) to receive sth in a particular way: *The news was greeted with a loud cheer.*
☆ greet·ing /ˈgritɪŋ/ *noun* [C] **1** the first words you say when you meet sb: *Jan mumbled a quick greeting as she walked past us.* **2** [usually pl.] a good wish: *Greetings from sunny Arizona!*
IDM **season's greetings** ⇨ SEASON[1]
'greeting card *noun* [C] a card that you send to sb on his/her birthday, on holidays, etc.
gre·gar·i·ous /grɪˈgɛriəs/ *adj.* liking to be with other people
gre·nade /grəˈneɪd/ *noun* [C] a small bomb that is thrown by hand or fired from a gun: *a hand grenade*
grew *p.t.* of GROW
grey /greɪ/ *adj.* = GRAY[1,2]
grey·hound /ˈgreɪhaʊnd/ *noun* [C] a large thin dog that can run very fast and that is used for racing: *greyhound racing*
grid /grɪd/ *noun* [C] **1** a pattern of lines that cross each other to form squares **2** a system of squares that are drawn on a map so that the position of any place can be described or found: *a grid reference* **3** the system of cables, etc. taking electricity to all parts of a region
grid·dle /ˈgrɪdl/ *noun* [C] a type of flat pan that is used for cooking food on top of a stove
grid·i·ron /ˈgrɪdaɪərn/ *noun* [C] the field that football is played on
grid·lock /ˈgrɪdlɑk/ *noun* [U] **1** a situation in which there is so much traffic on a city's streets that no cars can move **2** a situation in which no progress can be made because

i	ɪ	ɛ	æ	ɑ	ɔ	ʌ	ʊ	u
see	sit	ten	cat	hot	saw	cup	put	too

people are not willing to work together or change their opinions: *The President blamed members of the other party for the gridlock in Congress.*

grief /grif/ *noun* [U] great sadness (especially because of the death of sb you love)
IDM good grief (*informal*) (used for expressing surprise or shock): *Good grief! Look at that!*

griev·ance /ˈgrivns/ *noun* [C] **a grievance (against sb)** something that you think is unfair and that you want to complain or protest about: *The workers aired* (= expressed) *their grievances at the meeting.*

grieve /griv/ *verb* [I] **grieve (for sb)** to feel great sadness (especially about the death of sb you love): *He is still grieving for his wife.*

☆ **grill¹** /grɪl/ *noun* [C] a framework of metal bars that you put food on to cook over a fire: *Dad's cooking burgers on the grill outside.*

☆ **grill²** /grɪl/ *verb* **1** [I,T] to cook on a grill¹: *grilled steak* ☞ Look at the note at **cook**. **2** [T] (*informal*) to question sb for a long time: *When she got home her parents grilled her about where she had been.*

grim /grɪm/ *adj.* (**grim·mer**; **grim·mest**) **1** (used about a person) very serious; not smiling: *His face was grim as he announced the bad news.* **2** (used about a situation, news, etc.) unpleasant or worrying: *We face the grim prospect of even higher inflation.* ○ *The news is pretty grim.*

grim·ace¹ /ˈgrɪməs; grɪˈmeɪs/ *noun* [C] an expression on your face that shows that you are angry or that sth is hurting you: *a grimace of pain*

grim·ace /ˈgrɪməs; grɪˈmeɪs/ *verb* [I] to make a grimace¹: *She grimaced with pain.*

grime /graɪm/ *noun* [U] a thick layer of dirt

grim·y /ˈgraɪmi/ *adj.* (**grim·i·er**; **grim·i·est**) very dirty

☆ **grin** /grɪn/ *verb* [I] (**grin·ning**; **grinned**) to smile broadly (so that you show your teeth): *She grinned at me as she came into the room.* —**grin** *noun* [C]: *He came in with a big grin on his face and told us the good news.*

grind¹ /graɪnd/ *verb* [T] (*p.t., p.p.* **ground** /graʊnd/) **1** to crush sth into very small pieces or into a powder, using a machine: *Wheat is ground into flour.* ○ *ground pepper* ☞ Look also at **ground beef**. **2** to press sth together or into sth firmly: *Some people grind their teeth while they're sleeping.*
IDM grind to a halt to stop slowly: *Traffic ground to a halt on I-35 yesterday.*

grind² /graɪnd/ *noun* **1** [sing.] something that you must do, that is boring, makes you feel tired, etc.: *Riding the subway to work is a real grind.* ○ *the daily grind* (= the boring things that you must do every day) *at the office* **2** [C] (*informal*) a person who studies too hard

grind·er /ˈgraɪndər/ *noun* [C] a machine for grinding: *a coffee grinder*

☆ **grip¹** /grɪp/ *verb* [T] (**grip·ping**; **gripped**) to take and keep hold of sb/sth firmly: *Don't grip the bat too tight.* ○ *It's important that the car's tires grip the road well.* ○ (*figurative*) *The story really gripped my imagination.*

☆ **grip²** /grɪp/ *noun* [sing.] **a grip (on sb/sth)** a firm hold (on sb/sth): *I relaxed my grip and he ran away.* ○ (*figurative*) *a dictator's grip on power*
IDM come to grips with sth to start dealing with a problem in an effective way: *We are trying to come to grips with a difficult period in our history.*

grip·ping /ˈgrɪpɪŋ/ *adj.* exciting; holding your attention: *a gripping drama*

gris·ly /ˈgrɪzli/ *adj.* (used for describing sth that is concerned with death) horrible; terrible: *a series of grisly murders* ☞ Look at **gruesome**. It is similar in meaning.

grit¹ /grɪt/ *noun* [U] **1** small hard bits of dirt or stone: *Be sure to rinse the grit out of the clams.* **2** (*informal*) courage; determination

grit² /grɪt/ *verb* [T] (**grit·ting**; **grit·ted**)
IDM grit your teeth to have courage or determination in a difficult situation: *If things get difficult, you'll have to grit your teeth and keep going.*

grits /grɪts/ *noun* [with sing. or pl. verb] a soft white or yellow food that is made from corn. Grits are popular in the southern U.S. and are eaten warm, often with butter or cheese on top.

griz·zly bear /ˈgrɪzli bɛr/ (*also* **grizzly**) (*pl.* **griz·zlies**) *noun* [C] a type of North American bear that has brown fur

groan /groʊn/ *verb* [I] to make a deep sad sound because you are in pain, or to show that you are unhappy or do not approve of sth: *He groaned with pain.* ○ *The audience groaned at his terrible jokes.* —**groan** *noun* [C]

☆ **gro·cer·ies** /ˈgroʊsəriz; ˈgroʊsriz/ *noun* [plural] food and other small things for the home that are sold in a store

gro·cer·y store /ˈgroʊsəri stɔr; ˈgroʊsri-/ *noun* [C] a store where groceries are sold ☞ Look at **supermarket**.

grog·gy /ˈgrɑgi/ *adj.* (**grog·gi·er**; **grog·gi·est**) (*informal*) weak and unable to walk steadily because you feel sick, have not had enough sleep, etc.

groin /grɔɪn/ *noun* [C] the place where the tops of the legs join the body

groom¹ /grum/ (*also formal* **bridegroom**) *noun* [C] a man on, or just before, his wedding day ☞ Look at the note at **wedding**.

groom² /grum/ *verb* [T] **1** to clean or take care of an animal by brushing it, etc. **2** (usually passive) to choose and prepare sb for a particular career or job: *He is clearly being groomed for the manager's job.*

ə	y	w	t̬	eɪ	aɪ	ɔɪ	aʊ	oʊ
about	yes	woman	butter	say	five	boy	now	go

groom·ing /'grumɪŋ/ *noun* [U] the way you take care of your appearance, e.g. by brushing your hair, washing, etc.

groove /gruv/ *noun* [C] a long deep line that is cut in the surface of sth

grope /group/ *verb* [I] **grope (around) (for sth)** to search for sth using your hands, as you do in the dark: *He groped for the light switch.*

gross¹ /grous/ *adj.* **1** (*slang*) very bad; disgusting: *Yuck! This stuff smells really gross.* ○ *Don't be so gross – keep your mouth closed when you're eating.* **2** (*formal*) obvious or serious: *gross violations of human rights* **3** total: *gross income* (= before taxes, etc. are taken away) ☞ The opposite is **net**.

gross² /grous/ *verb* [T] to earn an amount of money before taxes, etc. are taken away: *The movie grossed over $12 million last weekend.*
PHR V **gross sb out** (*slang*) to behave in a way that sb finds bad or disgusting: *Could you change the subject? You're really grossing me out.*

gross·ly /'grousli/ *adv.* very, in a way that people think is wrong: *That is grossly unfair.*

gro·tesque /grou'tɛsk/ *adj.* strange or unnatural in a way that is funny or frightening

☆**ground¹** /graund/ *noun* **1 the ground** [sing.] the solid surface of the earth: *We sat on the ground to eat our picnic.* ○ *He slipped off the ladder and fell to the ground.* **2** [U] an area or type of soil: *rocky ground*

☞ The **Earth** is the name of the planet where we live. **Land** is the opposite of sea or ocean: *The sailors sighted land./The astronauts returned to Earth.* **Land** is also something that you can buy or sell: *The price of land in Tokyo is extremely high.* When you are outside, the surface under your feet is called **the ground**. When you are inside it is called **the floor**: *Don't sit on the ground. You'll get wet.* ○ *Don't sit on the floor. I'll get another chair.* Plants grow in **earth**, **soil** or **dirt**.

3 [C] a piece of land that is used for a particular purpose: *a burial ground* ○ *a playground* **4 grounds** [plural] land surrounding a large building: *Smoking is not allowed on the school grounds.* **5** [U] an area of interest, study, discussion, etc.: *The lecture went over the same old ground/covered a lot of new ground.* **6** [C, usually pl.] a reason for sth: *She retired on medical grounds.* ○ *grounds for divorce* **7** [C, usually sing.] a wire that makes a piece of electrical equipment safer by connecting it to the ground (1)
IDM **above/below ground** above/below the surface of the earth ☞ Look also at **underground**.
break new ground to make a discovery or introduce a new method or activity: *Scientists*

are breaking new ground in the field of genetic engineering.
gain ground ⇨ GAIN²
get off the ground (used about a business, plan, etc.) to make a successful start

ground² /graund/ *verb* [T] **1** to force an airplane, etc. to stay on the ground: *to be grounded by fog* **2** to make a piece of electrical equipment safer by connecting it to the ground¹(1) with a wire **3** to punish a child by not allowing him/her to leave the house for a period of time: *My parents grounded me for two weeks.* ○ *Get to your room – you're grounded!*

ground³ /graund/ *p.t., p.p.* of GRIND¹: *ground black pepper* ○ *Our burgers are made with 100% pure ground beef.*

ground floor *noun* [usually sing.] = FIRST FLOOR

ground·hog /'graundhɔg; -hɑg/ *noun* [C] = WOODCHUCK

Groundhog Day *noun* [C] February 2. On this day, people in Pennsylvania hold a festival and watch a groundhog come out of its hole in the ground. There is a story that says that if the groundhog does not see its shadow, spring will come early that year. But if the groundhog sees its shadow, there will be six more weeks of winter.

ground·ing /'graundɪŋ/ *noun* [sing.] knowledge of the basic facts or principles of a subject: *This book provides a good grounding in English grammar.*

ground·less /'graundləs/ *adj.* without reason: *Our fears were groundless.* —**groundless·ly** *adv.*

ground·work /'graundwərk/ *noun* [U] work that is done in preparation for further work or study

☆**group¹** /grup/ *noun* [C] **1** [with sing. or pl. verb] a number of people or things that are together or that are connected : *A group of students are going bowling tonight.* ○ *Groups of people were standing around in the streets.* ○ *He is in the 40-50 age group.* ○ *people of many different social groups* ○ *a pressure group* (= a political group that tries to influence the government) ○ *Divide the class into groups.*

☞ We usually use **group** with a singular verb when we are thinking of the whole group together: *Our drama group meets every Tuesday.* But if we use a phrase like *a group of...* with a plural noun or pronoun, we usually use a plural verb: *A group of students are planning a Halloween party.*

2 a number of people who play music together: *a jazz group* ☞ Look at **band**.

group² /grup/ *verb* [I,T] to form or put into one or more groups¹(1) : *Group these words according to their meaning.*

☆**grow** /grou/ *verb* (*p.t.* **grew** /gru/; *p.p.* **grown** /groun/) **1** [I] to increase in size or number; to

develop into an adult form: *Look at how much Billy has grown!* ○ *a growing child* ○ *You need to invest if you want your business to grow.* ○ *Kittens soon grow into cats.* **2** [I] (used about plants) to be alive in a particular place: *Palm trees don't normally grow in Canada.* **3** [T] to cause or allow something to grow: *to grow a beard/mustache* ○ *My grandfather grows a lot of vegetables in his garden.* **4** [I] to become (gradually): *It began to grow dark.* ○ *to grow older, wiser, etc.* ☞ **Get** is also possible and is less formal. **5** [I] (used about a feeling, etc.) to develop or become strong: *A close friendship has grown between them.*

PHRV **grow into sth 1** to become (gradually): *She has grown into a very attractive child.* **2** to become big enough to fit clothes, etc.: *The coat is too big for him now, but he will grow into it.*

grow on sb to become more pleasing: *I didn't like it at first, but it's a taste that grows on you.*

grow out of sth to become too big or too old for sth: *She has grown out of that dress.*

grow up to become mature or adult: *What do you want to be when you grow up?* (= what job do you want to do later?) ○ *Oh, grow up!* (= don't be silly!)

growl /graʊl/ *verb* [I] (used about dogs and other animals) to make a low noise in the throat to show anger or to give a warning —**growl** *noun* [C]

grown /groʊn/ *adj.* physically adult or mature: *a full-grown elephant*

grown-up (*also* **grown-up**) /ˈgroʊnʌp/ *noun* [C] an adult person: *Don't use the stove unless a grownup is there to help you.*

grown-up *adj.* (usually before a noun) **1** physically or mentally adult or mature: *They have two grown-up daughters.* **2** for or connected with adults: *My son is too young to watch grown-up movies.*

☆**growth** /groʊθ/ *noun* **1** [U] growing or development: *A good diet is very important for children's growth.* ○ *a growth industry* (= one that is growing) **2** [U, sing.] an increase (in sth): *population growth* ○ *There has been a sudden growth in the candidate's popularity.* **3** [C] a lump that is not normal, that grows in a person's or an animal's body

grub·by /ˈgrʌbi/ *adj.* (**grub·bi·er; grub·bi·est**) (*informal*) dirty

grudge /grʌdʒ/ *noun* [C] **a grudge (against sb)** unfriendly feelings toward sb, because you are angry about what has happened in the past: *She still bears a grudge against me for what happened in high school.* ○ *to have/hold a grudge against sb*

gru·el·ing /ˈgruəlɪŋ; ˈgrulɪŋ/ *adj.* difficult and tiring: *a grueling 26-mile race*

grue·some /ˈgrusəm/ *adj.* (used about sth concerned with death or injury) very bad or shocking: *A gruesome sight awaited the police*

officers when they arrived at the accident. ☞ Look at **grisly**. It is similar in meaning.

gruff /grʌf/ *adj.* (used about a person or a voice) rough and unfriendly —**gruff·ly** *adv.*

grum·ble /ˈgrʌmbl/ *verb* [I] to complain or protest in a slightly angry way; to keep saying that you do not like sth: *The students were always grumbling about food in the cafeteria.*

grump·y /ˈgrʌmpi/ *adj.* (**grump·i·er; grump·i·est**) (*informal*) in a bad mood

grunt /grʌnt/ *verb* [I,T] to make a noise like a pig (a short low sound in the throat). People grunt when they do not like sth or are not interested and do not want to talk: *She just grunted when I asked her about it.* —**grunt** *noun* [C]

☆**guar·an·tee¹** /ˌgærənˈti/ *noun* [C] **1** a written promise by a company that it will repair or replace a product if it breaks or stops working in a certain period of time: *The watch comes with a two-year money-back guarantee* (= you can get your money back if it stops working within two years). ☞ Look also at **warranty**. **2** a promise that sth will be done or that sth will happen: *There is no guarantee that the treatment will be effective.*

guar·an·tee² /ˌgærənˈti/ *verb* [T] **1** to give a guarantee¹(1) on a product: *This washing machine is guaranteed for three years.* **2** to promise that sth will be done or that sth is true: *They guaranteed delivery within one week.* ○ *The food is guaranteed to be free of additives.* ○ *I can guarantee that you will have a good time.*

☆**guard¹** /gɑrd/ *verb* [T] **1** to keep sb/sth safe from other people; protect: *The building was guarded by men with dogs.* ○ *agents guarding the President* **2** to watch over sb and prevent him/her from escaping: *The prisoner was closely guarded on the way to the courthouse.*

PHRV **guard against sth** to try to prevent sth or stop sth from happening: *A good diet helps to guard against disease.*

☆**guard²** /gɑrd/ *noun* **1** [C] a person who guards sb/sth: *a border guard* ○ *a security guard* ☞ Look also at **bodyguard.** **2** [U] the state of being ready to prevent attack or danger: *Who is on guard?* ○ *The prisoner arrived under armed guard.* ○ *a guard dog* **3** [sing.] a group of soldiers, police officers, etc. who guard sb/sth ☞ Look also at **Coast Guard** and **National Guard.** **4** [C] something that covers sth dangerous or protects sth: *a shin guard*

IDM **catch sb off guard** ⇨ CATCH¹

on guard (against sth) prepared for an attack, a surprise, a mistake, etc.: *Visitors to the city should be on guard against pickpockets.*

guard·ed /ˈgɑrdəd/ *adj.* (used about an answer, a statement, etc.) not saying very much; careful —**guard·ed·ly** *adv.*

guard·i·an /ˈgɑrdiən/ *noun* [C] **1** a person who is responsible for a child who does not

tʃ	dʒ	v	θ	ð	s	z	ʃ
chin	June	van	thin	then	so	zoo	she

live with his/her parents **2** a person or institution that guards or protects sth: *The police are the guardians of law and order.*

gu·ber·na·to·ri·al /ˌgubərnəˈtɔriəl/ *adj.* (usually before a noun) connected with a governor or the position of a governor of a state

guer·ril·la (*also* **guerilla**) /gəˈrɪlə/ *noun* [C] a member of a small group of fighters (not an army) who make surprise attacks on the enemy: *guerrilla warfare*

☆ **guess¹** /gɛs/ *verb* **1** [I,T] to give an answer or opinion about sth without being sure of all the facts: *Can you guess how much this cost?* ○ *to guess at an answer* ○ *I'd guess that he's about 45.* **2** [T] to give the correct answer when you are not sure about it; to guess correctly: *He guessed the weight of the package exactly.* ○ *"You passed the test!" "How did you guess?"*
IDM **I guess** (*informal*) (used when you think that sth is probably true, or when you are not sure about sth) I suppose: *Nobody else is here yet – I guess we'll just have to wait.* ○ *"Are you ready to go?" "Yeah, I guess so."*

☆ **guess²** /gɛs/ *noun* [C] an attempt to give the right answer when you are not sure what it is: *If you don't know the answer, then take a guess!* ○ *My guess is that they're stuck in traffic.* ○ *Your guess is as good as mine* (= I don't know).

guess·work /ˈgɛswərk/ *noun* [U] an act of guessing: *I arrived at the answer by pure guesswork.*

☆ **guest** /gɛst/ *noun* [C] **1** a person that you invite to your home or to a party, etc.: *We are having guests at our house this weekend.* ○ *wedding guests* ○ *an unexpected guest* ○ *an uninvited guest* ☞ Look at **host. 2** a person that you invite out and pay for at a restaurant, theater, etc. **3** a person who is staying at a hotel, etc.: *This hotel can accomodate 500 guests.* **4** a person who is invited to appear on a television or radio show: *tonight's special guest* ○ *a guest speaker*

guid·ance /ˈgaɪdns/ *noun* [U] help or advice: *We need expert guidance on this problem.*

ˈguidance ˌcounselor *noun* [C] a person who works in a school and whose job it is to give students advice about jobs, further education and personal problems

☆ **guide¹** /gaɪd/ *noun* [C] **1** a person whose job is to show cities, museums, etc. to tourists: *a tour guide* **2** a person who shows the way to others where it is difficult or dangerous: *We found a guide who knew the mountains well.* **3** something that helps you plan what you are going to do: *As a rough guide, use twice as much water as rice.* **4** = GUIDEBOOK **5** a book that gives information about a subject: *a guide to French wines*

☆ **guide²** /gaɪd/ *verb* [T] **1** to help a person or a group of people to find the right way or direction to go: *He guided us through the busy*

streets to our hotel. **2** to have an influence on sb/sth: *I was guided by your advice.* ☞ Look at the note at **lead³**(1).

guide·book /ˈgaɪdbʊk/ (*also* **guide**) *noun* [C] a book for tourists, etc. that gives information about interesting places, etc.

guid·ed /ˈgaɪdəd/ *adj.* led by a guide¹(1) : *a guided tour*

☆ **guide·line** /ˈgaɪdlaɪn/ *noun* [C, usually pl.] advice on what to do about sth (that is given by sb in authority): *The government has issued new guidelines on food safety.*

guil·lo·tine /ˈgɪlətin; ˈgiətin; ˌgiəˈtin/ *noun* [C] a machine with a heavy sharp blade that is dropped from a great height. The guillotine was used (especially in France) for killing criminals by cutting their heads off.

☆ **guilt** /gɪlt/ *noun* [U] **1** the feeling that you have when you know that you have done sth wrong: *Now that he was dead, she felt terrible guilt at the way she had behaved.* **2** the fact of having broken a law: *His guilt was not proven, and so he went free.* ☞ The opposite is **innocence. 3** blame or responsibility for doing sth wrong: *It's difficult to say whether the guilt lies with the parents or the children.*

☆ **guilt·y** /ˈgɪlti/ *adj.* (**guilt·i·er**; **guilt·i·est**) **1 guilty (of sth)** having broken a law; being responsible for doing sth wrong: *She pleaded guilty/not guilty to the crime.* ○ *to be found guilty of murder* ☞ The opposite is **innocent. 2** showing or feeling guilt (1): *I feel really guilty about not writing to you for so long.* ○ *a guilty conscience* —**guilt·i·ly** /-əli/ *adv.*

guin·ea pig /ˈgɪni pɪg/ *noun* [C] **1** a small furry animal with no tail that is often kept as a pet **2** a person who is used in an experiment

☆ **gui·tar** /gɪˈtɑr/ *noun* [C] a type of musical instrument with strings that you play with the fingers or with a piece of plastic (**a pick**): *an acoustic guitar* (= wooden, with a hollow body) ○ *an electric guitar* (= using electricity, with a solid plastic body) ☞ picture at **rock band.** Note that we usually say "play **the** guitar."

gui·tar·ist /gɪˈtɑrɪst/ *noun* [C] a person who plays the guitar

gulf /gʌlf/ *noun* [C] **1** a part of the ocean that is almost surrounded by land: *the Gulf of Mexico* **2** an important or serious difference between people or their opinions: *a wide gulf between people of different generations*

gull /gʌl/ (*also* **ˈsea gull**) *noun* [C] a white or gray sea bird with a loud cry

gul·li·ble /ˈgʌləbl/ *adj.* (used about a person) easily tricked or deceived

gulp¹ /gʌlp/ *verb* **1** [T] **gulp sth (down)** to eat or drink sth quickly **2** [I] to make a swallowing movement because you are afraid, surprised, etc.

gulp² /gʌlp/ *noun* [C] **1** an act of gulping¹ **2** the amount that you can swallow when you

gulp¹(1) : *He took a gulp of coffee and rushed out.*

gum /gʌm/ *noun* **1** [C, usually pl.] the hard pink part of the mouth that holds the teeth **2** (*also* **chewing gum**) [U] a sweet, sticky substance that you chew in your mouth but do not swallow ☞ Look also at **bubble gum.**

☆ **gun¹** /gʌn/ *noun* [C] a weapon that is used for shooting. A gun fires bullets from a metal tube (**a barrel**): *The robber held a gun to my head.* ○ *activists campaigning for gun control* (= laws that restrict the sale and use of guns)

☞ Verbs often used with "gun" are **load, unload, point, aim, fire.** Different types of gun include a **machine gun, rifle** and **shotgun. Pistols** and **revolvers** are types of **handguns.**

gun² /gʌn/ *verb* [T]**gun·ning; gunned**
PHRV gun sb down (*informal*) to shoot sb and kill or seriously injure him/her

gun·boat /ˈgʌnboʊt/ *noun* [C] a small military ship that carries heavy guns

gun·fire /ˈgʌnˌfaɪər/ *noun* [U] the act of firing a gun or several guns; the sound that it makes: *the distant sound of gunfire*

gun·man /ˈgʌnmən/ *noun* [C] (*pl.* **gun·men** /-mən/) a man who uses a gun to rob or kill people

gun·point /ˈgʌnpɔɪnt/ *noun*
IDM at gunpoint threatening to shoot: *He held the hostages at gunpoint* (= he said that he would shoot them if they did not obey him).

gun·pow·der /ˈgʌnˌpaʊdər/ *noun* [U] an explosive powder that is used in guns

☆ **gun·shot** /ˈgʌnʃɑt/ *noun* [C] the firing of a gun or guns or the sound that it makes: *gunshot wounds*

gur·gle /ˈgərgl/ *noun* [C] a sound like water draining out of a large container —**gur·gle** *verb* [I]: *The baby gurgled with delight.*

gu·ru /ˈguru; ˈgʊru/ *noun* [C] **1** a spiritual leader or teacher in the Hindu religion **2** (*informal*) a person whose ideas are followed by many people: *a fitness guru*

gush /gʌʃ/ *verb* [I] **1 gush (out) (from sth)** (used about a liquid) to flow out suddenly and in great quantities: *Blood gushed from the wound.* **2 gush (about/over sb/sth)** to express pleasure or admiration in an exaggerated way —**gush** *noun* [C, usually sing.]: *a sudden gush of water*

gust¹ /gʌst/ *noun* [C] a sudden rush of wind: *A sudden gust of wind blew my hat off.*

gust² /gʌst/ *verb* [I] (used about the wind) to blow in gusts

gus·to /ˈgʌstoʊ/ *noun*
IDM with gusto with great enthusiasm: *We all joined in the singing with gusto.*

gut¹ /gʌt/ *noun* (*informal*) **1 guts** [plural] the organs inside your body (especially the stomach and the organs below it) **2** [C] the part of the body between the chest and the legs: *Phil punched him right in the gut.* ○ *a huge beer gut* (=from drinking too much beer) **3 guts** [plural] courage and determination: *It takes guts to admit that you are wrong.* ○ *She didn't have the guts to tell them the truth.*

gut² /gʌt/ *verb* [T] (**gut·ting; gut·ted**) **1** to remove the guts¹(1) from an animal, fish, etc. **2** to destroy the inside of a building (in a fire): *The warehouse was gutted by fire.*

gut³ /gʌt/ *adj.* (only *before* a noun) based on emotion or feeling rather than on reason: *a gut feeling/reaction*

gut·ter /ˈgʌtər/ *noun* [C] **1** a long metal or plastic pipe that is attached under the edge of a roof to carry away water **2** a channel between the road and the sidewalk that carries away water

☆ **guy** /gaɪ/ *noun* [C] (*informal*) a man or a boy: *He's a nice guy.*
IDM you guys ⇨ YOU

☆ **gym** /dʒɪm/ *noun* **1** [C] (*informal*) = GYMNASIUM **2** [U] a class in school in which you do physical exercises and play sports: *gym shoes* ○ *I hurt my knee yesterday during gym.*

gym·na·si·um /dʒɪmˈneɪziəm/(*also informal* **gym**) *noun* [C] a large room that contains equipment, e.g. bars, ropes, etc. for doing physical exercises

gym·nast /ˈdʒɪmnəst; -næst/ *noun* [C] a person who is an expert at gymnastics

gym·nas·tics /dʒɪmˈnæstɪks/ *noun* [U] physical exercises that are done indoors, often using special equipment such as bars and ropes

gy·ne·col·o·gist /ˌgaɪnəˈkɑlədʒɪst/ *noun* [C] a doctor who has special training in gynecology

gy·ne·col·o·gy /ˌgaɪnəˈkɑlədʒi/ *noun* [U] the study and treatment of diseases and medical problems that only women have

gyp·sy /ˈdʒɪpsi/ *noun* [C] (*pl.* **gyp·sies**) a member of a race of people from eastern Europe who spend their lives traveling around from place to place

ə	y	w	t	eɪ	aɪ	ɔɪ	aʊ	oʊ
about	yes	woman	butter	say	five	boy	now	go

Hh

H, h /eɪtʃ/ *noun* [C] (*pl.* **H's; h's**) the eighth letter of the English alphabet: *"Hat" begins with (an) "H."*

ha /hɑ/ *interj.* **1** (*also* **hah**) (used for showing that you are surprised or pleased) **2** (*also* **ha! ha!**) (used in written language to show that sb is laughing)

☆ **hab·it** /'hæbət/ *noun* **1** [C] something that sb does very often (sometimes almost without thinking about it): *Biting your nails is a bad habit.* ∘ *He has an annoying habit of tapping his pen on his desk.* ☞ The adjective is **habitual.**

> ☞ A **habit** is usually something that is done by one person. A **custom** is something that is done by a group, community or nation: *the custom of giving presents at Christmas.*

2 [U] doing sth regularly: *I think I only smoke out of habit now – I don't really enjoy it.* **IDM be in/get into the habit of doing sth; make a habit of sth** to do sth regularly: *I've gotten into the habit of going for a jog every morning.* ∘ *I don't make a habit of talking to strange men at parties.*

hab·i·tat /'hæbətæt/ *noun* [C] the natural home of a plant or an animal

ha·bit·u·al /hə'bɪtʃuəl/ *adj.* doing sth very often: *a habitual criminal* (= who commits many crimes) —**ha·bit·u·al·ly** *adv.*

hack /hæk/ *verb* [I,T] **1** to cut sth using rough strokes with a tool such as a large knife: *He hacked (away) at the branch of the tree until it fell.* ∘ *The explorers hacked their way through the jungle.* **2 hack (into) (sth)** (*informal*) to use a computer to look at (and change) information that is stored on another computer

hack·er /'hækər/ *noun* (*informal*) a person who hacks (2) into other people's computers without permission

had¹ *p.t., p.p.* of HAVE[1,2]

had² /hæd/ *adj.* **be had** (*informal*) to be tricked or deceived: *I've been had. This watch I bought doesn't work.*

hag·gard /'hægərd/ *adj.* (used about a person) looking tired or worried

hag·gle /'hægl/ *verb* [I] **haggle (with sb) (over/about sth)** to argue about the price of sth

hah /hɑ/ *interj.* = HA(1)

hail¹ /heɪl/ *noun* [U] frozen rain that falls in small hard balls ☞ Look at the note at **weather.**

hail² /heɪl/ *verb* [T] **1** to call or wave to sb/sth: *She raised her arm to hail the taxi.* **2 hail**

sb/sth as sth to say in public that sth is very good: *The book was hailed as a masterpiece.*

bangs

She has straight hair. He has curly hair.

She has wavy hair. He's bald.

☆ **hair** /hɛr/ *noun* **1** [C] one of the long thin things that grow on the skin of people and animals: *There's a hair in my soup.* ∘ *The dog left hairs all over the furniture.* **2** [U] the mass of hairs (1) on a person's head: *He has short black hair.*

> ☞ Some special words for the color of hair are: **auburn, blond** and **red.** In order to take care of or style your hair, you may **brush, comb, wash** (or **shampoo**) it and then **blow-dry** it. You may **part** it (or have a **part**) in the middle or on one side. When you go to the **salon,** you have your hair **cut, styled** or **permed.**

IDM fix your hair ⇨ FIX¹
let your hair down (*informal*) to relax and enjoy yourself (after being formal): *After the wedding, you can let your hair down at the reception.*

hair·brush /'hɛrbrʌʃ/ *noun* [C] a brush that you use on your hair ☞ picture at **brush.**

☆ **hair·cut** /'hɛrkʌt/ *noun* [C] **1** the cutting of your hair, usually by sb else: *You need a haircut.* **2** the style in which your hair has been cut: *That haircut really looks good on you.*

hair·do /'hɛrdu/ *noun* [C] (*pl.* **hair·dos**) = HAIRSTYLE

hair·dress·er /'hɛrdrɛsər/ (*also* **hairstylist**) *noun* [C] a person whose job is to cut and style people's hair ☞ A **barber** is a hairdresser who only cuts men's hair.

'hair ,dryer *noun* [C] a machine that dries hair by blowing hot air through it ☞ Look also at **blow-dry.**

-haired /hɛrd/ *adj.* (in compounds) having hair of the stated type: *a long-haired rabbit*

hair·piece /'hɛrpis/ *noun* = TOUPEE

'hair-,raising *adj.* that makes you very frightened

'hair spray (*also* **hairspray**) *noun* [U] a substance that you spray on your hair to hold it in place

☆ **hair·style** /'hɛrstaɪl/ (*also* **hairdo**) *noun* [C] the style in which your hair has been cut or arranged

hair·styl·ist /'hɛrstaɪlɪst/ *noun* = HAIRDRESSER

hair·y /'hɛri/ *adj.* (**hair·i·er; hair·i·est**) **1** having a lot of hair: *a hairy chest* **2** (*informal*) dangerous or worrying: *We had a pretty hairy drive down the freeway in freezing rain.*

☆ **half¹** /hæf/ *noun* [C] (*pl.* **halves** /hævz/) one of two equal parts of sth: *Two halves make a whole.* ○ *The second half of the book is more exciting.* ○ *O'Neal scored twelve points in the first half* (= of a game). ☞ The verb is **halve**.
IDM break, cut, etc. sth in half to break, etc. sth into two parts

☆ **half²** /hæf/ *det., pron.* forming one of two equal parts: *Half of this money is yours.* ○ *He got half his aunt's money when she died.* ○ *half a gallon/a half-gallon* ○ *half an hour* ○ *Half the people in the office leave at 5.*
IDM half past ... (*formal*) 30 minutes past an hour on the clock: *half past six* (= 6:30)
☞ It is much more common to say **six-thirty**, etc.

☆ **half³** /hæf/ *adv.* to the extent of half; not completely: *half full* ○ *The hotel was only half finished.* ○ *I half thought she might come, but she didn't.* ○ *He's half German.*

half-and-half /'hæf n hæf/ *noun* [U] a mixture that contains half milk and half cream, that is often used in coffee

'half ,brother *noun* [C] a brother with whom you share one parent

half-heart·ed /,hæf'hartəd/ *adj.* without interest or enthusiasm —,**half-'heart·ed·ly** *adv.*

'half ,sister *noun* [C] a sister with whom you share one parent

half·time /'hæftaɪm/ *noun* [U] (in sports) the period of time between the two halves of a game

half·way /,hæf'weɪ/ *adj., adv.* at an equal distance between two places; in the middle of a period of time: *We live halfway between Columbus and Cincinnati.* ○ *They take a break halfway through the morning.* ○ *We've reached the halfway point in our project.*

☆ **hall** /hɔl/ *noun* [C] **1** (*also* **'hallway**) a room or passage that leads to other rooms in a house or public building: *The restrooms are at the end of the hall, on the right.* ○ *There is a pay phone in the entrance hall of this building.* ○ *She ran down the hall and into the classroom.* **2** a building or large room in which meetings, concerts, classes, etc. can be held: *a lecture*

hall ○ *a concert hall* ☞ Look at **city hall**, **residence hall** and **study hall**.

,**hall of 'fame** *noun* [C] (*pl.* **halls of fame**) a list of people who are very successful in a certain type of activity such as a sport, or a place, similar to a museum, where you can see things connected with these people: *the Baseball Hall of Fame*

☆ **Hal·low·een** /,hælə'win; ,hɑ-/ *noun* [sing.] October 31

☞ Halloween is the time when people say that witches and ghosts appear. Children dress up in costumes and go to other houses in their neighborhood. At each house they say, "Trick or treat!" and the people in the houses give them candy.

hal·lu·ci·na·tion /hə,lusə'neɪʃn/ *noun* [C,U] seeing sth that is not really there (because you are sick or have taken a drug)

hall·way /'hɔlweɪ/ *noun* = HALL(1)

ha·lo /'heɪloʊ/ *noun* [C] (*pl.* **ha·los** or **hal·oes**) the circle of light that is drawn around the head of a holy person in a painting

halt¹ /hɔlt/ *noun* [sing.] a stop (that does not last very long): *Work came to a halt when the machine broke down.* ○ *to bring sth to a halt*
IDM grind to a halt ⟹ GRIND¹

halt² /hɔlt/ *verb* [I,T] to stop for a short time; to make sth stop

halve /hæv/ *verb* [T] **1** to divide sth into two equal parts: *First halve the peach and then remove the pit.* **2** to make sth half as big as it was before: *We aim to halve the unemployment rate.*

☆ **ham** /hæm/ *noun* [C,U] meat from a pig's back leg that has been smoked, etc. to keep it fresh: *a slice of ham* ○ *a ham sandwich* ☞ Look at **bacon** and **pork** and at the note at **meat**.

☆ **ham·burg·er** /'hæmbərgər/ *noun* **1** (*also* **burger**) [C] a sandwich that is made with chopped meat that has been formed into a flat round shape, in a soft round bread roll (a **bun**) **2** [U] meat from cows that has been cut into very small pieces with a special machine

☆ **ham·mer¹** /'hæmər/ *noun* [C] a tool with a heavy metal head that is used for hitting nails, etc. ☞ picture at **tool**.

ham·mer² /'hæmər/ *verb* **1** [I,T] to hit with a hammer¹: *She hammered the nail into the wall.* **2** [I] to hit sth, making a loud noise: *He kept hammering on the door across the hall.*
PHRV hammer (away) at sb/sth to repeat a criticism, etc. many times in a very forceful way: *The candidate kept hammering away at her opponent's voting record.*
hammer sth into sb to force sb to remember sth by repeating it many times
hammer sth out (*figurative*) to succeed in making a plan or agreement after a lot of difficulty: *Eventually a solution was hammered out.*

H

tʃ	dʒ	v	θ	ð	s	z	ʃ
chin	**June**	**van**	**thin**	**then**	**so**	**zoo**	**she**

ham·mer·ing /ˈhæmərɪŋ/ *noun* [U] the noise that is made by sb using a hammer or by sb knocking sth many times

ham·mock /ˈhæmək/ *noun* [C] a bed, made of strong cloth or net, which is hung up at both ends. Hammocks are used on ships or outdoors.

ham·per¹ /ˈhæmpər/ *noun* [C] a large basket with a lid that you can put dirty clothes in

ham·per² /ˈhæmpər/ *verb* [T] to make sth difficult: *The construction work was hampered by bad weather.*

ham·ster /ˈhæmstər/ *noun* [C] a small animal that is kept as a pet. Hamsters are like mice but are fatter and do not have a tail. They store food in the sides of their mouths.

☆ **hand¹** /hænd/ *noun*
1 [C] the part of a person's arm below the wrist: *He took the child by the hand.* ○ *She lifted the hot pan out of the oven with her bare hands.* ○ *He held the bird gently in the palm of his hand.*
2 a hand [sing.] some help: *I'll give you a hand with the dishes.* **3** [C] one of the parts on a clock or watch that points to the numbers: *the hour/minute/second hand* ☛ picture at **clock**. **4** [C] a person who works with his/her hands: *All hands (= all sailors) on deck!* ○ *He works as a hired hand on a dairy farm.* **5** [C] the set of playing cards that sb has been given in a game of cards

holding hands

IDM at hand 1 near in space or time: *Help is close at hand.* **2** being dealt with at this time: *We need to focus on the task at hand.*
be an old hand (at sth) ⇨ OLD
by hand 1 done by a person and not by machine: *I had to do all the sewing by hand.* **2** not by mail: *The letter was delivered by hand.*
change hands ⇨ CHANGE¹
get, etc. the upper hand ⇨ UPPER
give sb/get a big hand ⇨ BIG
hand in hand 1 holding each other's hands **2** (*figurative*) usually happening together; closely connected
hands off (sb/sth) (*informal*) (used for ordering sb not to touch sth or to leave sth alone)
hands up 1 (used in a classroom, etc. for asking people to raise one hand and give an answer): *Hands up, who wants to go on the trip this afternoon?* **2** (used by a person with a gun to tell other people to put their hands in the air)
have your hands full to be very busy so that you cannot do anything else
a helping hand ⇨ HELP¹
hold sb's hand to give help or comfort to sb in a difficult situation

hold hands (with sb) (used about two people) to hold each other's hands (because you like each other)
in your/sb's hands in your/sb's possession, control or care: *The document is no longer in my hands.* ○ *The matter is in the hands of an attorney.*
on hand available to help or to be used: *Several artists will be on hand to discuss their work.*
on your hands being your responsibility: *We seem to have a problem on our hands.*
on the one hand…on the other (hand) (used for showing opposite points of view): *On the one hand, of course, cars are very useful. But on the other, they cause a huge amount of pollution.*
out of hand not under control: *This whole situation has gotten totally out of hand.* ☛ Look at **in hand**.
out of your/sb's hands not in your/sb's control: *I can't help you – the problem is out of my hands.*
shake sb's hand/shake hands (with sb) ⇨ SHAKE¹
take sth off sb's hands to help sb by taking a responsibility away from him/her: *I was so glad when Connie offered to take that project off my hands!*
wash your hands of sb/sth ⇨ WASH¹

☆ **hand²** /hænd/ *verb* [T] to give or pass sth to sb: *Please hand me the scissors.* ○ *Please hand the scissors to me.* ○ *Let's hand the picture around the class so everybody can see it.*
PHRV hand sth down (to sb) 1 to pass customs, traditions, etc. from older people to younger ones: *These stories have been handed down from generation to generation.* **2** to pass clothes, toys, etc. from older children to younger ones in the family ☛ Look also at **hand-me-down. 3** (used about a judge, etc.) to give an official decision in a court of law: *The Supreme Court handed down its ruling on the case yesterday.*
hand sth in (to sb) to give sth to sb in authority: *Time's up. Hand in your tests now.* ○ *Your papers must be handed in by Friday.*
hand sth out (to sb) to give sth to many people in a group: *Food was handed out to the starving people.*
hand sb/sth over (to sb) to give sb/sth (to sb): *People were tricked into handing over large sums of money.*

hand·bag /ˈhændbæg/ *noun* [C] = PURSE¹

☆ **hand·book** /ˈhændbʊk/ *noun* [C] a small book that gives useful information and advice about sth

hand·cuffs /ˈhændkʌfs/ *noun* [plural] a pair of metal rings that are joined together by a chain and put around the wrists of prisoners

-hand·ed /ˈhændəd/ (in compounds) having,

using or made for the stated type of hand(s)[1,2]: *right-handed* ○ *left-handed scissors*

☆ **hand·ful** /ˈhændfʊl/ *noun* **1** [C] **a handful (of sth)** as much or as many of sth as you can hold in one hand: *a handful of sand* **2** [sing.] a small number (of sb/sth): *a handful of people* **3 a handful** [sing.] (*informal*) a person or an animal that is difficult to control: *The little girl is quite a handful.*

☆ **hand·gun** /ˈhændɡʌn/ *noun* [C] a gun that is small enough to hold in one hand ☞ Look at the note at **gun**[1].

hand·i·cap[1] /ˈhændikæp/ *noun* [C] **1** a physical or mental problem that makes it difficult for you to do some things that other people can do: *people with mental handicaps* ☞ **Disability** is more common nowadays. **2** something that makes doing sth more difficult; a disadvantage: *Not speaking Spanish is going to a real handicap in my new job.* **3** a disadvantage that is given to a strong competitor in a sports event, etc. so that the other competitors have a better chance

hand·i·cap[2] /ˈhændikæp/ *verb* (**handicapping; handicapped**) [T] (usually passive) to give or be a disadvantage to sb: *They were handicapped by their lack of education.*

hand·i·capped /ˈhændikæpt/ *adj.* **1** having sth serious wrong with you (either physically or mentally) that means that you have difficulties doing things that other people can do: *a handicapped child* ○ *mentally, visually, etc. handicapped*

☞ Some people do not like the word **handicapped** and prefer to use expressions such as **disabled people** or **people with disabilities**. We can also use **challenged** or **impaired** in compounds to talk about a specific difficulty that sb has: *physically challenged* ○ *visually impaired.*

2 for or connected with handicapped (1) people: *a handicapped parking space*

hand·i·crafts /ˈhændikræfts/ *noun* objects that are made with skillful use of the hands as well as artistic ability, e.g. by sewing

hand·ker·chief /ˈhæŋkərtʃɪf; -tʃif/ *noun* (*pl.* **hand·ker·chiefs** or **hand·ker·chieves** /-tʃivz/) a square piece of cloth that you use for blowing your nose

☞ picture at **sneeze**. The informal word is **hankie**. A handkerchief that is made of soft thin paper is called a **Kleenex** or a **tissue**.

☆ **han·dle**[1] /ˈhændl/ *noun* [C] a part of sth that is used for holding or opening it: *the door handle* ○ *the handle of a frying pan* ☞ picture at **pan**.

IDM **fly off the handle** ⇨ **FLY**[1]

☆ **han·dle**[2] /ˈhændl/ *verb* [T] **1** to touch sth with, or hold sth in, your hand(s): *Wash your hands before you handle food.* ○ *Handle with care!* **2** to deal with or to control sb/sth: *This*

port handles 100 million tons of cargo each year. ○ *I have a problem at work and I don't really know how to handle it.*

☆ **han·dle·bar** /ˈhændlbɑr/ *noun* [C, usually pl.] the curved metal bar at the front of a bicycle that you hold when you are riding it ☞ picture at **bicycle**.

hand·made /ˌhændˈmeɪd/ *adj.* made by hand, not by machine

[1]**hand·me·down** *noun* [C] (*pl.* **hand·me·downs**) a thing, such as a piece of clothing, that you no longer want and that you give to sb else in your family: *When I was little, I had to wear my brother's hand-me-downs.* —[1]**hand·me·down** *adj.* (only *before* a noun): *a hand-me-down sweater*

hand·out /ˈhændaʊt/ *noun* [C] **1** food, money, etc. that is given to people who need it badly **2** a printed sheet of paper that is given to a lot of people, e.g. to explain sth in a class

hand·picked /ˌhændˈpɪkt/ *adj.* carefully chosen: *the chairman's handpicked successor*

hand·shake /ˈhændʃeɪk/ *noun* [C] the act of shaking sb's right hand with your right hand as a greeting

☆ **hand·some** /ˈhænsəm/ *adj.* **1** (used about a man) good-looking; attractive ☞ Look at the note at **beautiful**. **2** (*formal*) large or generous: *The company made a handsome profit.* —**hand·some·ly** *adv.*: *Her efforts were handsomely rewarded.*

[1]**hands·on** *adj.* learned by you doing sth yourself, not watching sb else do it; practical: *hands-on computer experience*

hand·writ·ing /ˈhændraɪtɪŋ/ *noun* [U] a person's style of writing by hand: *I can't read Joe's handwriting.*

☆ **hand·written** /ˈhændrɪtn/ *adj.* written by hand, not typed or printed

hand·y /ˈhændi/ *adj.* (**hand·i·er; hand·i·est**) **1** useful; easy to use: *a handy tip* ○ *a handy gadget* **2** nearby or easy to reach: *Always keep a first-aid kit handy.* ○ *Put the printer over there so that it will be handy for everyone.*

IDM **come in handy** to be useful at some time: *Don't throw that box away. It may come in handy.*

hand·y·man /ˈhændimæn/ *noun* (*pl.* **hand·y·men** /-mɛn/) a person who is good at making or repairing things

☆ **hang**[1] /hæŋ/ *verb* (*p.t., p.p.* **hung** /hʌŋ/)

☞ The past tense and past participle **hanged** is only used in sense 2.

1 [I,T] to fasten sth or be fastened at the top so that the lower part is free or loose: *Hang your coat on the hook.* ○ *I hung the wash on the line.* ○ *I left the wash hanging on the line all day.* ○ (*figurative*) *People were hanging out of windows to see the parade go past.* **2** [I,T] to kill sb by putting a rope around his/her neck and allowing him/her to drop, or to die in this

H

way: *She hanged herself in the attic.* ○ *He was hanged for murder.* ○ *He was sentenced to hang for murder.* **3** [I] **hang (above/over sb/sth)** to stay in the air (above/over sb/sth): *Smog hung in the air over the city.* ○ *(figurative) That paper I've got to write is hanging over me.*

IDM hang in there (*informal*) to have courage in a difficult situation and not stop trying to do sth: *The worst part is over – just hang in there and be patient.*

PHRV hang around (*informal*) to stay in or near a place not doing very much: *a bunch of kids hanging around at the mall*

hang on 1 to not stop making an effort or trying to do sth: *Keep hanging on. We'll get you to the hospital in a few minutes.* **2** to wait for a short time: *Hang on a minute. I'm almost ready.* ○ *The line is busy. Would you like to hang on or call back later?*

hang on to sth 1 to hold sth tightly **2** (*informal*) to keep sth: *Let's hang on to the car for another year.*

hang out (*slang*) to spend time in a place, often without doing very much: *I usually just hang out with my friends after school.*

hang sth out to put wet clothes, etc. outdoors so that they can dry

hang up (on sb) to end a telephone conversation by putting down the telephone or pushing a button ☞ Look at the note at **telephone**.

hang² /hæŋ/ *noun*

IDM get the hang of sth (*informal*) to learn how to use or do sth: *It took me a long time to get the hang of this computer.*

han·gar /'hæŋər; 'hæŋgər/ *noun* [C] a big building where airplanes are kept

hanger hooks

hang·er /'hæŋər/ (*also* '**clothes hanger**; '**coat hanger**) *noun* [C] a metal, plastic or wooden object with a hook that is used for hanging up clothes in a closet

hang glid·er /'hæŋ ˌglaɪdər/ *noun* [C] a type of frame with cloth on it, like wings, from which a person can hang and fly through the air —'**hang ˌglid·ing** *noun* [U]: *to go hang gliding*

hang·o·ver /'hæŋoʊvər/ *noun* [C] a pain in the head and a feeling of sickness that is caused by drinking too much alcohol the night before

'**hang-up** *noun* [C] (*informal*) something that worries you a lot: *He has a real hang-up about his height.*

hankie /'hæŋki/ *noun* [C] (*informal*) = HAND-KERCHIEF

Ha·nuk·kah (*also* **Chanukah**) /'hɑnəkə; 'xɑ-/ *noun* [U] a Jewish religious festival that lasts for eight days in December

hap·haz·ard /hæp'hæzərd/ *adj.* without any order or organized plan: *Her system of filing seems to be completely haphazard.* —**hap·haz·ard·ly** *adv.*

☆ **hap·pen** /'hæpən/ *verb* [I] **1** (of an event or situation) to take place: *Can you describe to the police what happened after you left the party?* ○ *How did the accident happen?*

☞ **Happen** and **occur** are usually used with events that are not planned. **Occur** is more formal than **happen**. **Take place** suggests that an event is planned: *The wedding took place on Saturday, June 13.*

2 happen to sb/sth to be what sb/sth experiences: *What do you think happened to Julie? She should have been here an hour ago.* ○ *What will happen to the business when your father retires?* **3 happen to do sth** to do sth by chance: *I happened to see him downtown yesterday.* ○ *She happened to be there yesterday too.*

IDM as it happens/happened (used when you are adding to what you have said) actually: *The deadline for my project is June 5, which, as it happens, is also my birthday.*

it (just) so happens ⇨ SO¹

what's happening? (*slang*) (used as a friendly greeting to sb that you know very well): *Hey, dudes, what's happening?*

☆ **hap·pen·ing** /'hæpənɪŋ; 'hæpnɪŋ/ *noun* [C, usually pl.] a thing that happens; an event (that is usually strange or difficult to explain): *Strange happenings have been reported in that old hotel.*

☞ A **happening** is usually something that happens by chance. An **event** is usually something that is planned and suggests something special or important.

☆ **hap·pi·ly** /'hæpəli/ *adv.* **1** in a happy way: *They all lived happily ever after.* ○ *I would happily give up my job if I didn't need the money.* **2** it is lucky that; fortunately: *The police found my purse and, happily, nothing had been stolen.*

☆ **hap·py** /'hæpi/ *adj.* (**hap·pi·er**; **hap·pi·est**) **1** feeling, showing or giving pleasure or satisfaction: *a happy childhood* ○ *a happy family* ○ *a happy smile* ○ *The movie is sad, but it has a happy ending.* ○ *She doesn't feel happy about the salary she was offered.* ○ *Are you happy with your work?* ○ *Congratulations! I'm really happy for you.* ☞ The opposite is **unhappy**. Look at the note at **glad**. **2** (not before a noun) **happy to do sth** willing; pleased: *I'll be happy to see you any day next week.* **3 Happy** (used in greetings to wish sb an enjoyable time): *Happy Birthday!* ○ *Happy New Year!* —**hap·pi·ness** *noun* [U]: *Money can't buy happiness.*

ər	ɪr	ɛr	ɑr	ɔr	ʊr	ʒ	h	ŋ
bird	near	hair	car	north	tour	vision	hat	sing

ha·rass /həˈræs; ˈhærəs/ *verb* [T] to annoy or put pressure on sb, especially continuously or on many different occasions: *The court ordered him to stop harassing his ex-wife.* —**ha·rass·ment** /-mənt/ *noun* [U]: *She accused her boss of sexual harassment.*

☆ **har·bor¹** /ˈhɑrbər/ *noun* [C,U] a place on the coast where ships can be tied up to shelter from the ocean: *The weather was too rough for the fishing boats to leave the harbor yesterday.*

har·bor² /ˈhɑrbər/ *verb* [T] **1** to hide or give shelter to sb/sth bad: *They were accused of harboring criminals.* **2** to keep sth secret in your mind for a long time: *She harbored a deep dislike of him for years.*

☆ **hard¹** /hɑrd/ *adj.* **1** not soft to touch; not easy to break or bend; very firm: *The bed was so hard that I couldn't sleep.* ○ *Diamonds are the hardest known mineral.* **2 hard (for sb) (to do sth)** difficult to do or understand; not easy: *The first question on the test was really hard.* ○ *This book is hard to understand./It is a hard book to understand.* ○ *It's hard for young people to find good jobs these days.* **3** needing or using a lot of effort: *It's a hard climb to the top of the hill.* ○ *They say that hard work is good for you.* ○ *She's a hard worker.* **4 hard (on sb)** (used about a person) not feeling or not showing kindness or pity; not gentle: *He's way too hard on his kids.* **5** (used about conditions) bad or unhappy: *He had a hard time when his parents died.* **6** (used about the weather) very cold: *The forecast is for a hard winter.* ☞ The opposite is **mild**. **7** (used about water) containing particular minerals so that soap does not make many bubbles ☞ The opposite is **soft**.

IDM **be hard on sb/sth** to hurt sb/sth or to make things difficult: *Living on very little money can be hard on students.*

give sb a hard time (*informal*) to criticize sb or make jokes about him/her, usually in order to make him/her feel embarrassed: *Don't give Bobby such a hard time about being short – he can't help it.*

hard facts information that you know is correct: *Reporters still have very few hard facts on this story.*

hard of hearing unable to hear well

have a hard/rough time ⇨ TIME¹ —**hard·ness** *noun* [U]

☆ **hard²** /hɑrd/ *adv.* **1** with great effort, energy or attention: *He worked hard all his life.* ○ *You'll have to try harder than that.* ○ *She looked hard at the man, but she didn't recognize him.* **2** with great force; heavily: *It was snowing hard.* ○ *He hit her hard across the face.*

IDM **be hard up (for sth)** (*informal*) to want or need sth, e.g. money, very much: *You must be pretty hard up for entertainment if you're watching that dumb show.*

die hard ⇨ DIE¹

hard-ˈboiled *adj.* (used about an egg) boiled inside its shell until it is hard inside

☆ **hard·cov·er** /ˈhɑrdkʌvər/ *noun* [C] a book that has a hard stiff cover ☞ Note the phrase **in hardcover**: *I'm sorry, this book is only available in hardcover.* Look at **paperback**.

hard ˈcurrency *noun* [U] money of a particular country that is easy to exchange for money from another country

ˈhard drive (*also* **hard ˈdisk**) *noun* [C] a piece of hard plastic used for storing information inside a computer. It can hold more information than a floppy disk.

☆ **hard·en** /ˈhɑrdn/ *verb* **1** [I,T] to become or to make sth hard or less likely to change: *Put the mixture in the freezer to harden.* ○ *The senator hardened her opposition to the proposal.* **2** [T] (usually passive) **harden sb (to sth)** to make sb less sensitive: *a hardened reporter* ○ *a hardened criminal*

☞ **Harden** is only used when hard means "firm" or "unkind": *The concrete will harden in 24 hours.* ○ *He hardened himself to the feelings of other people.* **Get harder** is used when hard has another meaning such as "difficult": *Learning a foreign language gets harder as you get older.*

hard ˈline *noun* [sing.] a way of thinking or a plan which will not be changed or influenced by anything: *The police take a very hard line against people who drink and drive.*

☆ **hard·ly** /ˈhɑrdli/ *adv.* **1** almost not; with difficulty: *Speak up – I can hardly hear you.* ○ *She'd hardly gone to sleep when the alarm went off.* ○ *I can hardly wait for the holidays.* ○ *It hardly matters whether you are there or not.* ○ *Winning this money could hardly have come at a better time.*

☞ We usually use **hardly** before the main verb in a sentence. Note that **hardly** is *not* the adverb form of **hard**. Look at **hard²**.

2 (used especially before "any," "ever," "anybody," etc.) almost none, never, nobody, etc.: *There's hardly any* (= almost no) *coffee left.* ○ *We hardly ever* (= almost never) *go to the theater these days.* ○ *Hardly anybody I knew was at the party.*

☞ Note that we do not use **hardly** with a negative word.

3 (used when you are saying that sth is not probable or that it is unreasonable): *She hasn't written for two years – she's hardly likely to write now* (= it's very improbable that she will write now).

hard·ship /ˈhɑrdʃɪp/ *noun* [C,U] difficulty or problems, e.g. because you do not have enough money; the situation in which these difficulties exist: *families suffering severe financial hardship* ○ *Not having a car for a week is going to be a real hardship for us.*

H

tʃ	dʒ	v	θ	ð	s	z	ʃ
chin	June	van	thin	then	so	zoo	she

☆ **hard·ware** /ˈhɑrdwɛr/ noun [U] **1** tools and equipment that are used to build or repair things in the house: *a hardware store* **2** the machinery of a computer, not the programs written for it ☞ Look at **software**.

☆ **hard-ˈworking** adj. working with effort and energy: *a hard-working student*

har·dy /ˈhɑrdi/ adj. (**har·di·er; har·di·est**) (used about people, animals and plants) able to live through cold weather or difficult conditions

hare /hɛr/ noun [C] an animal like a rabbit but bigger, faster and with longer ears and legs

har·em /ˈhɛrəm; ˈhær-/ noun [C] a number of women living with one man, especially in Muslim societies. The part of the building the women live in is also called a harem.

☆ **harm¹** /hɑrm/ noun [U] hurt or damage: *Peter ate some of those berries, but they didn't do him any harm.* ○ *The scandal caused a great deal of harm to the company.* ○ *It was just a joke – she meant no harm.*

☆ **harm²** /hɑrm/ verb [T] to cause injury or damage; hurt: *Too much sunshine can harm your skin.* ○ *It wouldn't harm him to work a little harder!*

☆ **harm·ful** /ˈhɑrmfl/ adj. causing harm¹: *The new drug has no harmful side effects.*

☆ **harm·less** /ˈhɑrmləs/ adj. not able to cause harm; safe: *a harmless snake* —**harm·less·ly** adv.

har·mon·i·ca /hɑrˈmɑnɪkə/ noun [C] a small musical instrument that you play by moving it across your lips while you are blowing

har·mo·nize /ˈhɑrmənaɪz/ verb [I,T] to fit in well with other things or to make sth fit in: *That new house was designed to harmonize with the older homes in the street.* —**har·mo·ni·za·tion** /ˌhɑrmənəˈzeɪʃn/ noun [U]

har·mo·ny /ˈhɑrməni/ noun (pl. **har·mo·nies**) **1** [U] a state of agreement (of feelings, interests, opinions, etc.): *There is a lack of harmony within Congress.* **2** [C,U] the pleasant combination of different musical notes played or sung together: *They sang in harmony.* —**har·mo·ni·ous** /hɑrˈmoʊniəs/ adj. —**har·mo·ni·ous·ly** adv.

har·ness¹ /ˈhɑrnəs/ noun [C] **1** a set of leather straps with which a horse is fastened to a cart, etc. and controlled **2** a set of straps that fasten sth to a person's body: *a safety harness*

har·ness² /ˈhɑrnəs/ verb [T] **1** to put a harness¹(1) on a horse or to attach a horse to a cart **2** to control sth so that you can use it to produce electricity

harp /hɑrp/ noun [C] a large musical instrument which has many strings stretching from the top to the bottom of a frame. You play the harp with your fingers.

har·poon /hɑrˈpun/ noun [C] a long thin weapon with a sharp pointed end and a rope attached to it that is thrown or fired when hunting large animals in the ocean

har·row·ing /ˈhæroʊɪŋ/ adj. making people feel very upset: *The program showed harrowing scenes of life in the refugee camps.*

☆ **harsh** /hɑrʃ/ adj. **1** not thinking of people's feelings; severe or cruel: *a harsh punishment* ○ *harsh criticism* ○ *The judge had some harsh words for the attorney's behavior.* **2** not pleasant to be in: *a harsh climate* **3** (used about light or sound or the way sth feels) too bright, loud or rough: *a harsh light* —**harsh·ly** adv. —**harsh·ness** noun [U]

har·vest¹ /ˈhɑrvəst/ noun **1** [C,U] the cutting and picking of crops when they are ripe; the time when this is done: *Farmers always need extra help with the harvest.* ○ *A storm destroyed the crops a month before harvest.* **2** [C] the crops that have been gathered in; the amount or quality of them: *This year's wheat harvest was very bad.*

har·vest² /ˈhɑrvəst/ verb [I,T] to cut, pick or gather a crop

has ⇨ HAVE¹,²

ˈhas-been noun [C] (informal) a person or thing that is no longer as famous, successful or important as before

hash browns /ˈhæʃ braʊnz/ noun [plural] a food made from potatoes that have been cut into very small pieces, pressed together into a flat shape and then fried

hash·ish /ˈhæʃiʃ; hæˈʃiʃ/(also slang **hash**) noun [U] an illegal drug that is made from a part of the same plant as marijuana and is usually smoked or chewed for pleasure

hasn't short for HAS NOT

has·sle¹ /ˈhæsl/ noun [C,U] (informal) a thing or situation that is difficult or that causes problems: *It's going to be a real hassle getting to the airport with all this luggage.*

has·sle² /ˈhæsl/ verb [T] (informal) to bother or annoy sb by telling him/her to do sth: *I wish she'd quit hassling me about cleaning the house.*

haste /heɪst/ noun [U] (formal) doing things too quickly: *In their haste to publish the story, the journalists did not check all the facts.*
IDM in haste (formal) quickly; in a hurry: *He reacted in haste and was very sorry later on.*

has·ten /ˈheɪsn/ verb (formal) **1** [T] to make sth happen or be done earlier or more quickly **2** [I] **hasten to do sth** to be quick to do or say sth

hast·y /ˈheɪsti/ adj. (**hast·i·er; hast·i·est**) (formal) **1** hasty (in doing sth/to do sth) (used about a person) acting or deciding sth too quickly or without enough thought: *Don't be too hasty. This is an important decision.* **2** said or done too quickly: *He said a hasty "good-bye" and left.* —**hast·i·ly** /-əli/ adv.

☆ **hat** /hæt/ *noun* [C] a covering that you wear on your head, usually when you are outside: *to wear a hat*

IDM **old hat** ⇨ OLD

hatch¹ /hætʃ/ *noun* [C] **1** an opening in the deck of a ship for loading and unloading cargo **2** a door in an airplane or spaceship

hatch² /hætʃ/ *verb* **1** [I] (used about a baby bird, insect, fish, etc.) to come out of an egg **2** [T] to make a baby bird, etc. come out of an egg **3** [I] (used about an egg) to break open and allow the baby bird, etc. inside to get out **4** [T] to think of a plan (usually to do sth bad): *He hatched a plan to avoid paying any income tax.*

hatch·back /'hætʃbæk/ *noun* [C] a small car with a large door at the back that opens upward ☞ picture at **car**.

hatch·et /'hætʃət/ *noun* [C] a small tool with a wooden handle and a metal blade used for cutting wood, etc.

IDM **bury the hatchet** ⇨ BURY

☆ **hate¹** /heɪt/ *verb* [T] **1** to have a very strong feeling of dislike (for sb/sth): *I hate grapefruit.* ○ *I hate to see the countryside ruined.* ○ *He hates driving at night.* ○ *I just hate it when she does that!* ☞ Look at **detest** and **loathe**. They express an even stronger feeling. **2** (used as a polite way of apologizing for sth you are going to say) to be sorry: *I hate to disappoint you, but I don't think Val wants to go out with you.*

hate² /heɪt/ *noun* [U] a very strong feeling of dislike ☞ Another word for hate is **hatred**.

'hate crime *noun* [C] a crime that sb commits against another person because he/she has a strong dislike of that person's race, religion, etc., or because he/she does not approve of the way that person lives

hate·ful /'heɪtfl/ *adj.* showing or feeling hate: *a hateful remark*

☆ **ha·tred** /'heɪtrəd/ *noun* [U] **hatred (for/of sb/sth)** a very strong feeling of dislike ☞ Another word for hatred is **hate**.

'hat trick *noun* [C] (especially in hockey or soccer) three goals scored by the same person in one game: *to score a hat trick*

haul¹ /hɔl/ *verb* [T] **1** to pull or drag sth with great effort: *I don't want to haul all that stuff upstairs.* **2** to transport sth in a truck, usually over a long distance

haul² /hɔl/ *noun* [C, usually sing.] an amount gained, especially of fish in a net or stolen goods in a robbery: *Police seized the largest cocaine haul ever today.*

IDM **the long haul** ⇨ LONG¹

haunt¹ /hɔnt/ *verb* [T] **1** (often passive) (used about a ghost of a dead person) to appear in a place regularly: *The ghost of a woman haunts the castle.* ○ *People say the house is haunted.* **2** (used about sth unpleasant or sad) to be always in your mind: *That memory has haunted me for years.*

haunt² /hɔnt/ *noun* [C] a place that a person visits regularly: *This bar has always been one of my favorite haunts.*

haunt·ing /'hɔntɪŋ/ *adj.* having a quality that stays in your mind: *a haunting song*

present tense	past tense
I **have** (I**'ve**)	I **had** (I**'d**)
you **have** (you**'ve**)	you **had** (you**'d**)
he/she/it **has** (he**'s**/she**'s**/it**'s**)	he/she/it **had** (he**'d**/she**'d**/it**'d**)
we **have** (we**'ve**)	we **had** (we**'d**)
you **have** (you**'ve**)	you **had** (you**'d**)
they **have** (they**'ve**)	they **had** (they**'d**)
past participle	**had**
present participle	**having**
negative short forms	**haven't, hasn't, hadn't**

☆ **have¹** /həv; əv; v; *strong form* hæv/ *auxiliary verb* (used for forming perfect tenses): *I've already seen this program.* ○ *She's been in the U.S. for six months.* ○ *Jim hasn't written to me yet.* ○ *Have you been waiting long?* ○ *They had already told us the news.*

☆ **have²** /hæv/ *verb* (3rd pers. sing. pres. **has**; p.t., p.p. **had**) **1** **have to** (*also* **have got to**) (used for saying that sb must do sth or that sth must happen): *I usually have to work on Saturday mornings.* ○ *Do you have to get a visa to go to Canada?* ○ *She's got to go to the bank this afternoon.*

☞ We generally do not use **have got to** in questions or in negative sentences. We usually use **have got to** to emphasize the fact that sb must do sth: *I've really got to finish my paper tonight!*

2 (*also* **have got**) to own or possess: *I have a new camera.* ○ *They don't have a car.* ○ *The apartment has two bedrooms.* ○ *He's got short dark hair.* ○ *Do you have any brothers or sisters?*

☞ We generally do not use **have got** in questions or in negative sentences. We usually use **have got** to emphasize the fact that sb has one thing instead of another: *She doesn't have much money, but at least she's got a steady job.* Look also at the note at **get**.

3 (*also* **have got**) to be sick with sth: *She's got a bad cold.* ○ *to have the flu, a headache, etc.* ○ *to have AIDS, cancer, etc.* ☞ Look at the note in sense 2. **4** (in a restaurant) to order sth: *I'll have a cheeseburger and a Coke.* ○ *Okay, who had the chicken?* **5** (used with many nouns to talk about doing sth): *What time do you have breakfast?* ○ *to have a drink, a cigarette, a cup of coffee, a sandwich, etc.* ○ *to have an argument, a talk, a conversation, etc.* ○ *We're having a meeting next week.* **6** (used with many nouns to talk about experiencing sth): *Have a nice day!* ○ *to have fun, a good time, etc.* ○ *to have*

H

problems, difficulties, etc. ○ *to have an accident, a heart attack, an operation, etc.* **7** to give birth to a baby: *Guess what, honey? We're going to have a baby!* ○ *They kept me in the hospital for a week after I had Josh.* **8** (*also* **have got**) (used with many abstract nouns): *I have no patience with little kids.* ○ *to have time to do sth* ○ *to have power, authority, etc.* ☞ Look at the note in sense 2. **9 have sth done** to arrange for sth to be done, usually for payment: *I have my hair cut every six weeks.* ○ *You should have your eyes tested.* **10 have sb do sth** to arrange for or tell sb to do sth: *I'll have Gwen send you a copy of the report.* **11 have sth done** (used when sth bad happens to you): *She had her bag stolen on the subway.* ○ *He had his driver's license taken away.*

IDM **have had it** (*informal*) (used about things that are completely broken, or dead): *This TV set has had it. We'll have to buy a new one.*

have had it (with sb/sth) (*informal*) to have no more patience for sb/sth: *I've had it with this stupid job! I'm quitting!*

PHR V **have (got) sth on** to be wearing sth: *She has a green sweater on.* ○ *What did the man have on?* ☞ Look at the note in sense 2.

haven /ˈheɪvn/ *noun* [C] a place where people feel safe or where they can rest and be quiet ☞ A **tax haven** is a country where income tax is low.

hav·oc /ˈhævək/ *noun*
IDM **wreak havoc (on sth)** ⇨ WREAK

hawk /hɔk/ *noun* [C] **1** a type of bird that catches and eats small animals and birds. Hawks can see small things from very far away. **2** (in politics) a person who supports strong action and the use of force rather than peaceful solutions

hay /heɪ/ *noun* [U] grass that has been cut and dried for use as food for animals: *a bale of hay*

hay ˌfever *noun* [U] an illness like a bad cold, that especially affects your nose

☞ People get hay fever if they are **allergic** to the **pollen** of plants.

hay·wire /ˈheɪwaɪər/ *adj.*
IDM **go haywire** (*informal*) to become out of control

haz·ard /ˈhæzərd/ *noun* [C] a danger or risk: *Smoking is a serious health hazard.*

☆ **haz·ard·ous** /ˈhæzərdəs/ *adj.* dangerous

haze /heɪz/ *noun* [U] a thin, low cloud caused by heat, dust or smoke ☞ Look at the note at **fog**.

ha·zel /ˈheɪzl/ *adj.* (used especially about eyes) light brown in color

ha·zel·nut /ˈheɪzlnʌt/ *noun* [C] a small nut that you can eat ☞ picture at **nut**.

haz·y /ˈheɪzi/ *adj.* (**haz·i·er**; **haz·i·est**) **1** not clear; covered by a thin, low cloud: (*figurative*) *I have only a hazy memory of the vacation we spent in France.* **2** (used about a person) uncer-

tain, not expressing things clearly: *She's a little hazy about the details of the trip.*

☆ **he¹** /i; *strong form* hi/ *pron.* (the subject of a verb) the male person or animal mentioned earlier: *I talked to John before he left.* ○ *Look at that little boy – he's going to fall!*

☞ **He**, **him** and **his** are often used to refer to a member of a group that includes both males and females: *A good teacher prepares his lessons well.* Many people think that this is not fair to women and the use of **he or she**, **him or her**, etc. is becoming more common. In writing **he/she**, **s/he** or **(s)he** can be used: *Ask your doctor. He/she can give you further information.* ○ *When a baby cries, it means that s/he is tired, hungry or just unhappy.* In informal language **they**, **them** or **their** can be used: *Everybody knows what they want.* ○ *When somebody asks me a question, I always try to give them a quick answer.* Or the sentence can be made plural: *A baby cries when he/she is tired* becomes: *Babies cry when they are tired.*

he² /hi/ *noun* [sing.] a male animal: *Is your cat a he or a she?*

☆ **head¹** /hɛd/ *noun* [C] **1** the part of the body above the neck which has your eyes, nose, mouth and brain in it: *She turned her head to look at him.* ○ *serious head injuries*

☞ In English-speaking countries, when you **nod** your head, it means "yes" or shows agreement. When you **shake** your head, it means "no" or shows disagreement.

2 a person's mind, brain or mental ability: *Use your head!* (= think!) ○ *A terrible thought entered my head…* ○ *He has a good head for numbers.* **3** the top, front or most important part or end: *to sit at the head of the table* ○ *Put your name at the head of the paper.* ○ *Julia graduated at the head of her class.* **4** something that is like a head (1) in shape or position: *the head of a hammer* **5** the chief or most important person (in a family, company, country, etc.): *the head of the family* ○ *The President is welcoming heads of state from all over the world.* ○ *the head waiter* **6 heads** the side of a coin with the head of a person on it: *Heads or tails? Heads I go first, tails you do.* **7 a head** [sing.] the height or length of one head: *a head taller* **8 a head** [sing.] (for) one person: *Admission is $12 a head.* ☞ We also say **per head**.

IDM **from head to toe/foot** over your whole body: *He was covered in mud from head to toe.*

go to sb's head 1 to make sb drunk: *Wine always goes straight to my head.* **2** to make sb too proud: *If you keep telling him how smart he is, it will go to his head!*

head over heels (in love) 2 completely in love: *Jane's head over heels in love with her new boyfriend.*

hit the nail on the head ⇨ HIT¹
laugh, scream, etc. your head off to laugh, scream, etc. loudly
off the top of your head ⇨ TOP¹
shake your head ⇨ SHAKE¹
head² /hɛd/ verb 1 [T] to be in charge of or to lead sth: *Do you think that he has the experience necessary to head a department?* 2 [T] to be at the front of a line, top of a list, etc.: *to head a procession* ○ *Two names headed the list of possible suspects.* 3 [T] (often passive) to give a title or some instructions at the top of a piece of writing: *The report was headed "Private."* 4 [I] to move in the direction mentioned: *The ship headed toward the harbor.* ○ *Let's head out.*
PHRV head for to move toward a place: *It's getting late – I think it's time to head for home.* ○ *(figurative) You're heading for trouble if you go on behaving like that.*
☆**head·ache** /'hɛdeɪk/ noun [C] 1 a pain in your head: *I have a splitting* (= very bad) *headache.* ☞ Look at the note at **ache.** 2 a person or thing that causes worry or difficulty: *Paying the bills is a constant headache.*
head·first /ˌhɛd'fərst/ adv. 1 with your head before the rest of your body: *Don't go down the slide headfirst.* 2 too quickly or suddenly: *Don't rush headfirst into a decision.*
head·ing /'hɛdɪŋ/ noun [C] the words written as a title at the top of a page or a piece of writing
head·light /'hɛdlaɪt/ (also **headlamp** /'hɛdlæmp/) noun [C] one of the two large bright lights at the front of a car, truck, etc.: *Turn your headlights on – it's getting dark.*
☆**head·line** /'hɛdlaɪn/ noun 1 [C] the title of a newspaper article printed in large letters above the story 2 **the headlines** [plural] the main news stories that are read on television or the radio
head·long /'hɛdlɔŋ/ adv., adj. 1 with your head before the rest of your body 2 too quickly; without enough thought: *He rushed headlong into buying the business.*
head·mas·ter /'hɛdˌmæstər/ (feminine **head·mis·tress** /'hɛdˌmɪstrəs/) noun [C] a man or woman who is in charge of a private school ☞ Look at **principal²**.
ˌhead-'on adj., adv. with the front of one car, etc. hitting the front of another: *There's been a head-on collision between two trucks on the interstate.*

headphones

head·phones /'hɛdfoʊnz/ noun [plural] a piece of equipment with two round parts that fit over your ears, connected by a band over the top of your head. Headphones are used for listening to the radio, music, etc.
☆**head·quar·ters** /'hɛdˌkwɔrtərz; -ˌkwɔtərz/ noun [with sing. or pl. verb] (abbr. **HQ**) the central office, etc. of an organization: *Where is/are the company's headquarters?*
ˌhead 'start noun [sing.] an advantage that you have from the beginning of a race or competition
head·stone /'hɛdstoʊn/ (also **gravestone**) noun [C] a large stone used to mark the head of a grave, usually with the dead person's name, etc. on it
head·way /'hɛdweɪ/ noun
IDM make headway to go forward or make progress in a difficult situation: *It was impossible for the boat to make any headway against the wind.*
☆**heal** /hil/ verb [I,T] **heal (up)** to become healthy again; to make sth healthy again: *The cut will heal up in a few days if you keep it clean and dry.* ○ *It takes time to heal a broken leg.* ○ *(figurative) Nothing he said could heal the damage done to their relationship.*
☆**health** /hɛlθ/ noun [U] 1 the condition of a person's body or mind: *Fresh fruit and vegetables are good for your health.* ○ *in good/poor health* ○ *health insurance* ○ *Cigarette packs carry a health warning.* 2 the state of being well and free from illness: *Would you have health, wealth or beauty?*
▲ˈhealth care (also ˈhealthcare) noun [U] the services that doctors, nurses, etc. give to people in order to keep them healthy or to make them well if they are sick: *the rising cost of health care* ○ *the health care industry*
ˈhealth ˌcenter noun [C] a place where doctors, nurses, etc. treat people, that is not part of a hospital: *the campus health center*
ˈhealth club noun [C] a place where people pay to exercise, swim, play sports, etc.
ˈhealth food noun [C,U] natural food that many people think is especially good for your health because it has been made or grown without adding chemicals
health·ful /'hɛlθfl/ adj. helping to produce good health: *a healthful diet* ☞ **Healthy** is often used with the same meaning.
ˈhealth ˌmaintenance ˌorganiˌzation noun = HMO
☆**health·y** /'hɛlθi/ adj. (**health·i·er; health·i·est**) 1 not often sick; strong and well: *a healthy child, animal, plant, etc.* 2 showing good health (of body or mind): *healthy skin and hair* 3 helping to produce good health: *a healthy climate* ☞ **Healthful** is often used with the same meaning. ☞ The opposite for all senses is **unhealthy.** —**health·i·ly** /-əli/ adv.
heap¹ /hip/ noun [C] a large number or

H

tʃ	dʒ	v	θ	ð	s	z	ʃ
chin	June	van	thin	then	so	zoo	she

amount of sth which is piled up in a messy way: *All his clothes are in a heap on the floor!* ○ (figurative) *a heap of trouble* ☞ Look at the note at **pile**.

heap² /hip/ *verb* [T] **heap sth (up)** to put things in a pile: *I'm going to heap all the leaves up over there.* ○ (figurative) *to heap praise on sb* (= to give sb a lot of praise)

☆ **hear** /hɪr/ *verb* (p.t., p.p. **heard** /hərd/) **1** [I,T] (not in the *-ing* forms) to receive sounds with your ears: *Can you speak a little louder? I don't hear very well.* ○ *Sorry I'm late – I didn't hear my alarm clock this morning.*

☞ Compare **hear** and **listen**. To **hear** is to receive a sound by chance or in a passive way with your ears; to **listen** is to make a conscious or active effort to hear something: *I always wake up when I hear the neighbors' dog barking.* ○ *I love listening to music in the evenings.* ○ *Listen! I have something to tell you.*

2 [T] (not in the *-ing* forms) to be told or informed about sth: *I hear that you've been offered a job in Canada.* ○ *Did you hear about Ken? He got fired yesterday!* **3** [T] (used about a judge, a court, etc.) to listen to the evidence in a trial in order to make a decision about it: *Your case will be heard this afternoon.*

IDM won't/wouldn't hear of sth to refuse to allow sth: *I wanted to go to art school, but my parents wouldn't hear of it.*

PHR V hear from sb to receive a letter, telephone call, etc. from sb

hear of sb/sth (used especially in questions and negatives) to know or receive information about the existence of a person, place, thing, etc.: *Have you ever heard of the Bermuda Triangle?*

hear·ing /ˈhɪrɪŋ/ *noun* **1** [U] the ability to hear: *Her hearing isn't very good, so you need to speak louder.* **2** [C] a trial in a court of law: *Will there be TV cameras at the hearing?* **3** [C] a chance to give your opinion or explain your position: *If everybody comes to the meeting, it will give all points of view a fair hearing.*

IDM hard of hearing ⇨ HARD¹

hearing aid *noun* [C] a small device that makes sound louder, that sb who cannot hear well wears in his/her ear

hearing-im·paired *adj.* unable to hear very well or unable to hear anything

hear·say /ˈhɪrseɪ/ *noun* [U] things you have heard another person or other people say, which may or may not be true: *Hearsay is not admissable as evidence in court.*

hearse /hərs/ *noun* [C] a large car used for carrying a dead body in a box (**casket**) to the funeral

☆ **heart** /hart/ *noun* **1** [C] the organ inside the chest that sends blood around the body: *When you exercise, your heart beats faster.* ○ *heart disease* **2** [C] the center of a person's feelings:

She has a kind heart (= she is kind and gentle). ○ *In my heart, I knew she was right.* **3** [sing.] the most central part of sth; the middle: *Rare plants can be found in the heart of the forest.* ○ (figurative) *Let's get straight to the heart* (= to the most important part) *of the matter.* **4** [C] a symbol that is shaped like a heart (1), often red or pink and used to show love: *He sent her a card with a big red heart on it.* **5 hearts** [plural] the group (**suit**) of playing cards with red shapes like hearts (4) on them: *I know you have the queen of hearts!* ☞ picture at **card**. **6** [C] one of the cards from this suit: *Play a heart, if you have one.* **7** [U] complete interest or attention: *He's not working well because his heart isn't in the job.*

IDM at heart really; in fact: *My father seems strict, but he's a very kind man at heart.*

break sb's heart to make sb very sad

by heart by remembering exactly; from memory: *to learn a poem by heart* ○ *I can play three songs by heart.*

a change of heart ⇨ CHANGE²

cross my heart ⇨ CROSS²

lose heart ⇨ LOSE

not have the heart (to do sth) to be unable to do sth unkind: *I didn't have the heart to say no.*

take sth to heart to be greatly affected or upset by sth

young at heart ⇨ YOUNG¹

heart·ache /ˈhartˌeɪk/ *noun* [C,U] great sadness or worry; emotional pain

heart at·tack *noun* [C] a sudden serious illness when the heart stops working correctly, sometimes causing death: *She had a heart attack.*

heart·beat /ˈhartbit/ *noun* [C] the regular movement of the heart or the sound it makes

heart·break /ˈhartbreɪk/ *noun* [U] very great unhappiness

heart·break·ing /ˈhartˌbreɪkɪŋ/ *adj.* very sad

heart·bro·ken /ˈhartˌbroʊkən/ *adj.* extremely sad: *Mary was heartbroken at the news of her friend's death.*

heart·en /ˈhartn/ *verb* [T] (usually passive) to encourage sb; to make sb feel more cheerful ☞ The opposite is **dishearten**.

heart·felt /ˈhartfɛlt/ *adj.* deeply felt; sincere: *a heartfelt apology*

heart·i·ly /ˈhartl i/ *adv.* **1** in a loud cheerful way: *He laughed heartily.* **2** very much; completely: *I heartily recommend that you approve this proposal.*

heart·land /ˈhartlænd/ *noun* [C] the most central or important part of a country, area, etc.: *The Midwest is America's heartland.*

heart·y /ˈharti/ *adj.* (**heart·i·er**; **heart·i·est**) **1** showing warm and friendly feelings: *a hearty laugh* **2** large: *a hearty breakfast* ○ *a hearty appetite*

☆ **heat¹** /hit/ *noun* **1** [U] the feeling of sth hot: *the heat of the sun* ○ *This fire doesn't give out*

much heat. **2** [sing.] (often with *the*) hot weather: *I like the Alaskan climate because I can't stand the heat.* **3** [sing.] a thing that produces heat (1): *Remove the pan from the heat* (= the stove). **4** [U] a system for heating a house or a building: *Our house has electric heat.* ○ *Turn the heat up – I'm freezing!* **5** [U] a state or time of anger or excitement: *In the heat of the argument, he said a lot of things he didn't mean.* **6** [C] one of the first parts of a race or competition. The winners of the heats compete against other winners until the final result is decided: *He won his heat and went through to the finals.*

☆ **heat²** /hit/ *verb* [I,T] **heat (sth) (up)** to become or to make sth hot or warm: *Wait for the oven to heat up before you put the cake in.* ○ *Old houses are more difficult to heat than newer ones.* ○ *a heated swimming pool* ○ *The meal is already cooked, but you'll need to heat it up.*

heat·ed /'hitəd/ *adj.* (used about a discussion) angry or excited —**heat·ed·ly** *adv.*

☆ **heat·er** /'hitər/ *noun* [C] a piece of equipment used for heating water or the air in a room, car, etc.: *an electric heater* ○ *a water heater*

'**heat wave** *noun* [C] a period of time when the weather is much hotter than usual

heave /hiv/ *verb* **1** [I,T] to lift or pull sth heavy, using a lot of effort: *Take hold of this rope and heave!* ○ *We heaved the couch up the stairs.* **2** [T] to throw sth heavy **3** [I] to move up and down or in and out in a heavy but regular way: *His chest was heaving with the effort of carrying the cabinet.*

IDM **heave a sigh** to let out a long, deep breath that shows you are sad, tired, relieved, etc.: *He heaved a sigh of relief when he heard the good news.*

☆ **heav·en** /'hɛvn/ *noun* **1** [sing.] the place where it is believed that God lives and good people go when they die: *to go to/be in heaven* ☞ Look at **hell.** ☞ **Heaven** (often with a capital H) is used in a number of expressions to mean "God." For the meaning of *for Heaven's sake, Heaven forbid,* etc. look at the entry for **God. 2 the heavens** [plural] (*formal*) the sky: *The stars shone brightly in the heavens that night.*

IDM **(good) heavens!** (used to express surprise): *Good heavens! I didn't expect to see you!*

thank heaven ⇨ THANK

heav·en·ly /'hɛvnli/ *adj.* **1** (only *before* a noun) connected with heaven or the sky: *heavenly music* ○ *heavenly bodies* (= the sun, moon, stars, etc.) **2** (*informal*) very pleasant; wonderful

☆ **heav·y¹** /'hɛvi/ *adj.* (**heav·i·er; heav·i·est**) **1** weighing a lot, and difficult to lift or move: *This box is too heavy for me to carry.* **2** (used when asking or stating how much sb/sth weighs): *How heavy do you think this bag is?* **3** larger or stronger than usual: *heavy rain* ○

heavy traffic ○ *He felt a heavy blow on the back of his head.* ○ *a heavy smoker/drinker* (= a person who smokes/drinks a lot) ○ *The sound of his heavy* (= loud and deep) *breathing told her that he was asleep.* **4** (used about a person) fat: *Donna's gotten a little heavier since the last time I saw her.* **5** (used about a material or substance) solid or thick: *a heavy coat* **6** (used about food) difficult for the body to absorb: *He had a heavy meal and dropped off to sleep in the afternoon.* **7** full of hard work; (too) busy: *I have a heavy schedule this week.* **8** serious, difficult or boring: *This book is very heavy reading.* **9 heavy on sth** using a lot of sth: *The traditional American diet was heavy on red meat and fried foods.* **10 heavy with sth** containing a lot of sth: *an airplane heavy with fuel* ○ *a speech heavy with symbolism* —**heav·i·ly** /-əli/ *adv.* —**heav·i·ness** *noun* [U]

heav·y² /'hɛvi/ *adv.*

IDM **to go heavy on sth** (*informal*) to use a lot of sth: *I think you went a little too heavy on the perfume.*

'**heavy-'duty** *adj.* (only *before* a noun) (used about materials, machines, etc.) strong and able to last for a long time: *a heavy-duty truck* ○ *heavy-duty gloves*

'**heavy 'industry** *noun* [C,U] (*pl.* **heavy industries**) an industry that produces materials such as steel or that makes large, heavy objects

'**heavy 'metal** *noun* [U] a style of very loud rock music that is played on electric instruments

heav·y·weight /'hɛviweɪt/ *noun* [C] **1** (in some sports) a person in the heaviest weight group: *a heavyweight boxer/wrestler* **2** (*informal*) an important person who has a lot of power

heck /hɛk/ *interj., noun* [sing.] (*informal*) (used to express or emphasize annoyance or surprise or to emphasize the amount or size of sth): *Oh heck! I missed the bus!* ○ *How the heck did you know where I was?* ○ *It's a heck of a long way to drive in one day.*

heck·le /'hɛkl/ *verb* [I,T] to interrupt a speaker at a public meeting with difficult questions or rude remarks —**heck·ler** /'hɛklər/ *noun* [C] —**heck·ling** /'hɛklɪŋ/ *noun* [U]

hec·tic /'hɛktɪk/ *adj.* very busy and full of a lot of things that you have to do quickly: *We had a hectic day at the office.*

he'd /hid; *weak form also* id/ *short for* HE HAD; HE WOULD

hedge /hɛdʒ/ *noun* [C] a row of bushes that are planted close together: *I need to trim the hedge.* ☞ picture at **fence.**

heed¹ /hid/ *verb* [T] (*formal*) to pay attention to advice, a warning, etc.

heed² /hid/ *noun* (*formal*)

take heed (of sth) (*formal*) to pay careful

H

attention to what sb says: *You should take heed of your doctor's advice.*

☆ **heel** /hil/ *noun* [C] **1** the back part of the foot: *These shoes rub against my heels.* ☞ picture on page A24. **2** the part of a sock that covers your heel (1) **3** the raised part of a shoe under the heel (1) of your foot: *High heels* (= shoes with high heels) *are not practical for long walks.* ☞ picture at **shoe.**

IDM head over heels (in love) ⇨ HEAD¹

heft·y /'hɛfti/ *adj.* (**heft·i·er**; **heft·i·est**) (*informal*) strong, heavy or big: *a hefty young man* ○ *a hefty increase in food prices*

☆ **height** /haɪt/ *noun* **1** [C,U] the measurement from the bottom to the top of a person or thing: *The nurse is going to check your height and weight.* ○ *She's of medium height.* ○ *We need a fence that's about six feet in height.* ☞ picture at **length.** The adjective is **high.** Look at the note at **tall. 2** [U] being tall: *He's only ten, but he looks older because of his height.* **3** [C,U] the distance that sth is above the ground or sea level: *She survived a fall from a height of 20 feet.* **4** [C, usually pl.] a high place or area: *I can't go up there. I'm afraid of heights.* **5** [U] the strongest or most important part of sth: *the height of summer* ○ *At its height in the 1970s, the company had over 500 employees.* ○ *He joined the army during the height of the war.*

height·en /'haɪtn/ *verb* [I,T] to become or to make sth greater or stronger: *I'm using yellow paint to heighten the sunny effect of the room.*

heir /ɛr/ *noun* [C] the person with the legal right to receive (**inherit**) money, property or a title when the owner dies: *He's the heir to a large fortune.* ○ *Who is the heir to the throne?* (= Who will become king or queen?) ☞ A female heir is often called an **heiress**, especially when we are talking about somebody who has inherited a very large amount of money.

heir·loom /'ɛrlum/ *noun* [C] something valuable that has belonged to the same family for many years

heist /haɪst/ *noun* [C] (*informal*) a crime of stealing sth from a bank, business, etc.: *a jewelry heist*

held *p.t., p.p.* of HOLD¹

☆ **hel·i·cop·ter** /'hɛləkɑptər/ (also *informal* **chopper**) *noun* [C] a small aircraft that can go straight up into the air. Helicopters fly with the help of large spinning blades.

☆ **hell** /hɛl/ *noun* **1** [sing.] the place that some religions say bad people will go to when they die: *to go to/be in hell* ☞ Look at **heaven. 2** [C,U] (*informal*) a situation or place that is very unpleasant, painful or miserable: *He went through hell when his wife left him.* **3** [U] (*informal*) (used as a swear word to show anger or surprise or to make another expression stronger): *Oh hell, I forgot my money!* ○ *Go*

to hell! (= go away!) ○ *Who the hell is that at the front door?*

IDM a/one hell of a... (*informal*) (used to make an expression stronger or to mean "very"): *That was one hell of a surprise!* ○ *She's a hell of a nice girl.*

give sb hell (*informal*) to speak to sb very angrily or to treat sb severely

like hell (*informal*) (used to make an expression stronger): *I'm working like hell* (= very hard) *these days.*

☞ Be careful. Some people find **hell** offensive when it is used in informal expressions. **Heck** is not as strong as **hell.**

he'll /hil; hɪl; *weak form also* il; ɪl/ *short for* HE WILL

☆ **hel·lo** /hə'loʊ; hɛ'loʊ/ *interj.* (used for greeting sb, to attract sb's attention, or when you are using the telephone): *Hello, how are you?* ○ *Hello, is anybody there?*

☞ We usually use **hi**, not **hello**, in less formal situations: *"Rob, this is my friend, Laura Kwan." "Hi, nice to meet you."* However, we always use **hello** when we answer the telephone.

helm /hɛlm/ *noun* [C] the part of a boat or ship that is used to guide it. The helm can be a handle or a wheel.: (*figurative*) *Mr. Perkins has been at the helm* (= in charge) *of the company for 17 years.*

hel·met /'hɛlmət/ *noun* [C] a type of hard hat that you wear to protect your head: *a crash helmet* ○ *a football helmet*

☆ **help¹** /hɛlp/ *verb* **1** [I,T] to do sth for sb in order to be useful or to make a person's work easier: *Can I do anything to help?* ○ *Could you help me with the cooking?* ○ *I helped her to organize the party.* ○ *to help sb off the bus, out of a car, across the street, etc.* (= to help sb move in the direction mentioned) **2** [I,T] to make sth better or easier: *If you apologize to him, it might help* (= it might make the situation better). ○ *These pills should help your headache.* **3** [T] (in a store) to take a customer's order; to show sth to a customer or sell goods, etc.: *Can I help you?* ○ *Is somebody helping you?* ○ *Sorry, I'm helping another customer right now.* **4** [T] **help yourself (to sth)** to take or give sth (especially food and drink): *Help yourself to a drink!* ○ *"Can I borrow your pen?" "Yes, help yourself."* **5** [T] **help yourself to sth** to take sth without asking permission: *Don't just help yourself to my money!* **6** [I] (used to get sb's attention when you are in danger or difficulty): *Help! I'm going to fall!*

IDM can/can't/couldn't help sth to be able/not be able to stop or avoid doing sth: *Try not to move your arm if you can help it.* ○ *He can't help being so small* (= it's not his fault). ○ *The accident couldn't be helped* (= it couldn't be avoided, so we must accept that). ○ *I just*

ər	ɪr	ɛr	ɑr	ɔr	ʊr	ʒ	h	ŋ
bird	near	hair	car	north	tour	vision	hat	sing

couldn't help myself – I had to laugh. ○ *It was so funny I couldn't help laughing.*

☞ It is also possible to say **can't/couldn't help but do sth**: *It was so funny I couldn't help but laugh.*

a helping hand some help: *My neighbor is always ready to give me a helping hand.*

PHRV help (sb) out to help sb in a difficult situation or to give money to help sb: *My parents promised to help us out with buying the car.*

☆**help²** /hɛlp/ *noun* **1** [U] the act of helping: *Do you need any help?* ○ *I'll give you all the help I can.* **2** [U, sing.] a person or thing that helps: *This map isn't much help.* ○ *Your directions were a big help – we found the place easily.*

help·er /'hɛlpər/ *noun* [C] a person who helps (especially with work)

☆**help·ful** /'hɛlpfl/ *adj.* giving help: *helpful advice* ○ *Ask Mr. Brown. He's always very helpful.* ☞ The opposite is **unhelpful**. —**help·ful·ly** *adv.* —**help·ful·ness** *noun* [U]

help·ing /'hɛlpɪŋ/ *noun* [C] an amount of food that sb serves: *Sarah ate two big helpings of mashed potatoes.*

'helping verb *noun* [C] = AUXILIARY²

☆**help·less** /'hɛlpləs/ *adj.* needing help from other people: *a helpless baby* —**help·less·ly** *adv.* —**help·less·ness** *noun* [U]

hem¹ /hɛm/ *noun* [C] the edge of a piece of cloth (especially on a skirt, dress or pants) that has been turned under and sewn down

hem² /hɛm/ *verb* [T] **(hem·ming; hemmed)** to sew a hem¹ on sth

PHRV hem sb in to surround sb and prevent him/her from moving away: *We were hemmed in by the crowd and couldn't leave.*

hem·i·sphere /'hɛməsfɪr/ *noun* [C] **1** the shape of half a ball; half a sphere **2** one half of the earth: *the northern/southern/eastern/western hemisphere* ☞ picture at **earth**.

he·mo·phil·i·a /ˌhiməˈfɪliə; -ˈfɪlyə/ *noun* [U] a disease that causes a person to bleed very heavily from small injuries because the blood does not thicken (**clot**) properly

he·mo·phil·i·ac /ˌhiməˈfɪliæk; -ˈfɪlyæk/ *noun* [C] a person who suffers from hemophilia

hem·or·rhage /'hɛmrɪdʒ; 'hɛmərɪdʒ/ *noun* [C,U] very heavy bleeding —**hem·or·rhage** *verb* [I]

hem·or·rhoids /'hɛmrɔɪdz; 'hɛmərɔɪdz/ *noun* [plural] painful swellings near the hole in your body where solid waste comes out (**the anus**)

hemp /hɛmp/ *noun* [U] a plant that is used for making rope and rough cloth and for producing the illegal drug marijuana

☆**hen** /hɛn/ *noun* [C] a female bird that is often kept on farms for its eggs or its meat: *Our hens haven't laid many eggs this week.* ☞ Look at the note at **chicken**.

hence /hɛns/ *adv.* for this reason: *(formal) The town was founded by William Clark – hence the name Clarksville.*

hench·man /'hɛntʃmən/ *noun* [C] *(pl.* **hench·men** /-mən/*)* a person who follows sb or works for sb and who may do things for him/her that are illegal or violent: *the dictator and his henchmen*

hep·a·ti·tis /ˌhɛpəˈtaɪtəs/ *noun* [U] a serious disease of the liver

☆**her¹** /hər; *weak form also* ər/ *pron.* (the object of a verb or preposition) a female person or animal that was mentioned earlier: *He told Sue that he loved her.* ○ *I have a letter for your mother. Could you give it to her for me?* ○ *(informal) That must be her now.* ☞ Look at **she** and the note at **he**.

☆**her²** /hər; *weak form also* ər/ *det.* belonging to a female person or animal that was mentioned earlier: *That's her book. She left it there this morning.* ○ *Lynn broke her leg.*

her·ald /'hɛrəld/ *verb* [T] to be a sign that sb/sth is coming: *The senator's speech heralded a change in policy.*

herb /ərb/ *noun* [C] a plant whose leaves, seeds, etc. are used for giving food more flavor or in some types of traditional medicine ☞ Look at **spice**.

herb·al /'ərbl; 'hərbl/ *adj.* made of or using herbs: *herbal tea* ○ *herbal medicine*

herd¹ /hərd/ *noun* [C] a large number of animals that live and eat together: *a herd of cattle, deer, elephants, etc.*

herd² /hərd/ *verb* [T] to move people or animals forward as if they were in a herd: *The prisoners were herded onto the train.*

☆**here¹** /hɪr/ *adv.* **1** (after a verb or a preposition) in, at or to the place where you are or which you are pointing to: *I live here.* ○ *Come (over) here.* ○ *The school is a mile from here.* ○ *Please sign here.* **2** (used for introducing or drawing attention to sb/sth): *Here is the ten o'clock news.* ○ *Here comes the bus.* ○ *Here we are* (= we have arrived). ○ *"Are the others coming?" "Yes, here they are now."*

☞ Note the word order in the last two examples. We say: *Here are the children* and: *Here they are.* Note also the expression: *Here you are* which is used when we are giving something to somebody: *Here you are – this is that book I was talking about.*

3 at this point: *Here the speaker stopped and looked around the room.* **4** (used for emphasizing a noun): *My friend here saw it happen.* ○ *I think you'll find this book here very useful.*

IDM here and there in various places: *We could see small groups of people here and there along the beach.*

here goes *(informal)* (used before doing sth exciting, dangerous, etc.): *I've never done a backward dive before, but here goes!*

here's to sb/sth (used for drinking to the health, success, etc. of sb/sth): *Here's to your future happiness!*

here² /hɪr/ *interj.* (used when offering help or when giving sth to sb): *Here, let me help!* ◦ *Here, take this and buy yourself a candy bar.*

he·red·i·tar·y /hə'rɛdə,tɛri/ *adj.* passed on from parent to child: *a hereditary disease* ◦ *Do you think intelligence is hereditary?* ☞ Look at **inherit**.

he·red·i·ty /hə'rɛdəti/ *noun* [U] the passing on of physical or mental features from parent to child ☞ Look at **inherit**.

her·e·sy /'hɛrəsi/ *noun* [C,U] (*pl.* **her·e·sies**) (*formal*) a (religious) opinion or belief that is against what is generally accepted as true in the group you belong to

her·e·tic /'hɛrətɪk/ *noun* [C] a person who believes a heresy —**he·ret·i·cal** /hə'rɛtɪkl/ *adj.*

her·i·tage /'hɛrətɪdʒ/ *noun* [C, usually sing.] the traditions, qualities and cultural achievements of a country that have existed for a long time and that have great importance for the country: *Wildlife in an important part of our national heritage.* ◦ *We need to preserve our cultural heritage for future generations.*

her·mit /'hərmət/ *noun* [C] a person who prefers to live alone, without contact with other people.

her·ni·a /'hərniə/ (*also* **rupture**) *noun* [C,U] the medical condition when an organ inside your body, especially below the stomach, pushes through the wall of muscle which surrounds it

☆ **he·ro** /'hɪroʊ; 'hiroʊ/ *noun* [C] (*pl.* **he·roes**) **1** a person who has done sth brave or good and who is admired and remembered for it: *sports heroes* **2** the most important male character in a book, play, movie, etc. ☞ Look at **villain**. **3** = SUBMARINE(2)

he·ro·ic /hə'roʊɪk/ *adj.* (used about people or their actions) very brave: *a heroic effort* —**he·ro·i·cal·ly** /-kli/ *adv.*

her·o·in /'hɛroʊən/ *noun* [U] a very powerful illegal drug that people take especially by putting it directly into their blood with a type of needle (**a syringe**). It is very difficult to stop using heroin.

her·o·ine /'hɛroʊən/ *noun* [C] **1** a woman who has done sth brave or good and who is admired and remembered for it **2** the most important female character in a book, play, movie, etc.

her·o·ism /'hɛroʊɪzəm/ *noun* [U] great courage; being very brave

her·ring /'hɛrɪŋ/ *noun* [C] (*pl.* **her·ring** or **her·rings**) a small silver fish that swims in large groups in the ocean and that is used for food

IDM a red herring ⇨ RED¹

hers /hərz/ *pron.* of or belonging to her: *I didn't have a pencil, but Jill let me borrow hers.*

☆ **her·self** /hər'sɛlf; *weak form also* ər'sɛlf/ *pron.* **1** (used as the object of a verb or preposition when the female person or animal who does an action is also affected by it): *She hurt herself pretty badly.* ◦ *Val bought herself a burger for lunch.* ◦ *Kim looked at herself in the mirror.* **2** (used for emphasis): *She told me the news herself.* ◦ *Did Sara do this herself?* (= or did sb else do it for her?) **3** in her normal state; healthy: *She's just not herself today* (= she's feeling sick).

IDM (all) by herself 1 alone: *She lives by herself.* ☞ Look at the note at **alone**. **2** without help: *I don't think she needs any help – she can change a tire by herself.*

he's short for HE IS, HE HAS

hes·i·tant /'hɛzətənt/ *adj.* **hesitant (to do/ about doing sth)** slow to speak or act because you are not sure whether you should or not: *I'm very hesitant about criticizing him too much.* —**hes·i·tan·cy** /-ənsi/ *noun* [U] —**hes·i·tant·ly** *adv.*

☆ **hes·i·tate** /'hɛzəteɪt/ *verb* [I] **1** to pause before you do sth or before you make a decision, usually because you are uncertain or worried: *He hesitated before going into the room.* **2** **hesi·tate (to do sth)** to be unwilling to do sth because you are not sure that it is right: *Don't hesitate to call if you have any problems.*

☆ **hes·i·ta·tion** /,hɛzə'teɪʃn/ *noun* [C,U] a time when you wait because you are not sure: *He continued speaking after a slight hesitation.*

het·er·o·sex·u·al /,hɛtərə'sɛkʃʊəl/ *adj.* (*formal*) sexually attracted to a person of the other sex (= a man to a woman or a woman to a man) ☞ A less formal word is **straight**. Look also at **bisexual** and **homosexual**. —**het·er·o·sex·u·al** *noun* [C]

hex·a·gon /'hɛksəgən/ *noun* [C] a shape with six sides —**hex·ag·o·nal** /hɛk'sægənl/ *adj.*

hey /heɪ/ *interj.* (*informal*) (used when you want to attract sb's attention or to show that you are surprised or interested): *Hey, what are you doing?* ◦ *Hey, I like your bike!*

hey·day /'heɪdeɪ/ *noun* [sing.] the period when sb/sth was most powerful, successful, rich, etc.

☆ **hi** /haɪ/ *interj.* (*informal*) (used as a greeting when you meet sb) ☞ Look at the note at **hello**.

hi·ber·nate /'haɪbərneɪt/ *verb* [I] (used about animals) to spend the winter in a state like deep sleep —**hi·ber·na·tion** /,haɪbər'neɪʃn/ *noun* [U]

hic·cup /'hɪkʌp/ *noun* **1** [C] a sudden stopping of the breath with a noise like a cough, usually caused by eating or drinking too quickly **2 (the) hiccups** [plural] a series of hiccups: *Don't eat so fast, or you'll get the hiccups!* ◦ *I had the hiccups.* ◦ *Do you know of a cure for hiccups?* **3** [C] a small problem or difficulty:

i	ɪ	ɛ	æ	ɑ	ɔ	ʌ	ʊ	u
see	sit	ten	cat	hot	saw	cup	put	too

There was a slight hiccup in our plans, but everything's okay now. —**hic·cup** verb [I]

hick /hɪk/ noun [C] (informal) a person from the countryside or a small town who does not know much about the rest of the world and is not well educated ☞ This word is used in a negative way.

☆ **hide¹** /haɪd/ verb (p.t. **hid** /hɪd/; p.p. **hid·den** /ˈhɪdn/) **1** [T] to put or keep sb/sth in a place where he/she/it cannot be seen: Where should I hide the money? ○ The scar is partially hidden by hair. ○ The trees hid the house from view. **2** [I] to be or get in a place where you cannot be seen or found: Quick, run and hide! ○ Tammy was hiding under the bed. **3** [T] **hide sth (from sb)** to keep sth secret so that other people do not know about it: She tried to hide her disappointment from them.

hide² /haɪd/ noun [C,U] the skin of an animal that will be used for making leather, etc.

hide-and-seek /ˌhaɪd n ˈsik/ (also **hide-and-go-seek** /ˌhaɪd n goʊ ˈsik/) noun [U] a children's game in which one person hides and the others try to find him/her

hid·e·ous /ˈhɪdiəs/ adj. very ugly or unpleasant: a hideous sight ○ a hideous crime ○ (informal) a hideous orange dress —**hid·e·ous·ly** adv.

hid·ing /ˈhaɪdɪŋ/ noun [U]
be in/go into hiding to be in or go into a place where you cannot be found: She escaped from prison and went into hiding.

hi·er·ar·chy /ˈhaɪərɑrki; ˈhaɪrɑrki/ noun [C] (pl. **hi·er·ar·chies**) a system or organization that has many grades or ranks from the lowest to the highest —**hi·er·ar·chi·cal** /ˌhaɪəˈrɑrkɪkl; haɪˈrɑr-/ adj.

hi·er·o·glyph·ics /ˌhaɪərəˈglɪfɪks; ˌhaɪrə-/ noun [plural] the system of writing that was used in ancient Egypt in which a type of picture represents a word or sound

☆ **high¹** /haɪ/ adj. **1** (used about things) measuring a great amount from the bottom to the top: high cliffs ○ What's the highest mountain in the world? ○ high heels (= on shoes) ○ The fence was so high that we couldn't see over it. ☞ Look at **height**, **low** and the note at **tall**. **2** having a particular height: The hedge is three feet high. ○ knee-high boots **3** at a level which is a long way from the ground, or from sea level: Keep all medications on a high shelf where children cannot reach them. ○ The fort was built on high ground. **4** above the usual or normal level or amount: high prices ○ at high speed ○ a high level of unemployment ○ high-quality goods ○ He has high blood pressure. ○ Oranges are high in vitamin C. **5** good or favorable: Her work is of a very high standard. ○ He has a high opinion of you. **6** having an important position or rank: We will have to refer the matter to a higher authority. **7** morally good: high ideals **8** (used about a sound or voice) not deep or

low: She sang the high notes beautifully. **9 high (on sth)** (informal) under the influence of drugs, etc. **10** (used about a gear in a car) that allows a faster speed

☆ **high²** /haɪ/ adv. **1** at or to a high¹(3) position or level: The sun was high in the sky. ○ I can't jump any higher. ○ The plane flew high overhead. ○ You should aim high. **2** (used about a sound) at a high¹(8) level: How high can you sing?
IDM **high and low** everywhere: We searched high and low for the keys.

☆ **high³** /haɪ/ noun [C] **1** a high level or point: Profits reached an all-time high last year. **2** (used about the weather) the highest temperature in a certain place during a certain time: Highs tomorrow will be in the mid-80s. **3** (slang) a feeling of great pleasure or happiness that may be caused by a drug, etc. **4 High** (informal) (used in the names of schools) short for HIGH SCHOOL: We both went to Central High.

high·brow /ˈhaɪbraʊ/ adj. connected with people who are interested in serious intellectual things

higher edu·ca·tion noun [U] education at a college or university

the **high jump** noun [sing.] the sport in which people try to jump over a bar in order to find out who can jump the highest ☞ Look at **long jump**.

high-level adj. (only before a noun) involving important people: high-level talks

high·light¹ /ˈhaɪlaɪt/ noun **1** [C] the best or most interesting part of sth: Highlights of the game will be shown on TV tonight. **2 highlights** [plural] areas of lighter color that are put in a person's hair

high·light² /ˈhaɪlaɪt/ verb [T] **1** to give special attention to sth: The report highlighted the need for improved safety in inner cities. **2** to mark important parts of a book, document, etc. with a brightly colored pen

☆ **high·ly** /ˈhaɪli/ adv. **1** to a high degree; very: The movie was highly entertaining. ○ The disease is highly contagious. **2** (very) well or favorably: I think highly of your work (= I have a good opinion of it).

High·ness /ˈhaɪnəs/ noun [C] (pl. **High·ness·es**) a title used when speaking about or to a member of a royal family: Good evening, Your Highness. ○ His Royal Highness Prince Charles

high-powered adj. (only before a noun) **1** (used about things) having great power: a high-powered engine **2** (used about people) important and successful: high-powered executives

high-profile adj. (only before a noun) that attracts a lot of attention in the news, on television, etc.: a high-profile lawsuit

high-rise adj. (only before a noun) (used about a building) tall, with many levels: a high-rise

H

apartment block —**'high-rise** (*also* **highrise**) *noun* [C]: *a 22-story high-rise*

☆ **'high school** *noun* [C,U] a school that is for children who are about 14 to 18 years old: *Our daughter is already in college, and our son is in high school now.* ○ *high school students* ○ *a high school graduate* ○ *a high school diploma* ☞ Look also at **junior high school** and **senior high school**.

,**high-'strung** *adj.* (used about a person) very nervous or becoming excited very easily

,**high-'tech** *adj.* (*informal*) **1** using a lot of modern equipment, especially computers **2** using designs or styles taken from industry, etc.; very modern

,**high 'tide** *noun* [U] the time when the ocean comes closest to the land

☆ **high·way** /'haɪweɪ/ *noun* [C] a main road (especially between towns or cities) ☞ Look at the note at **road**. Look also at **divided highway**.

'**highway pa,trol** *noun* [U] the police force that is in charge of the main roads in a particular state: *a highway patrol officer*

hi·jack /'haɪdʒæk/ *verb* [T] to take control of a plane, etc. by force, usually for political reasons: *The plane was hijacked on its flight to Miami.* —**hi·jack·er** *noun* [C] —**hi·jack·ing** *noun* [C,U]

hike¹ /haɪk/ *noun* [C] **1** a long walk in the mountains or the country **2** (*informal*) a sudden large increase: *a price hike*

hike² /haɪk/ **1** *verb* [I] to go for a long walk in the mountains or the country

☞ **Go hiking** is used when you are talking about spending time hiking: *They went hiking in the Rocky Mountains last summer.*

2 [T] (*informal*) to increase a price, etc. suddenly: *The legislature plans to hike state income taxes.* —**hik·er** *noun* [C]

hi·lar·i·ous /hɪ'lɛriəs/ *adj.* very funny —**hi·lar·i·ous·ly** *adv.*

☆ **hill** /hɪl/ *noun* [C] a high area of land that is not as high as a mountain: *There was a wonderful view from the top of the hill.* ○ *Tim enjoys walking in the hills.* ○ *I had to push my bike up the hill – it was too steep to ride.* ☞ Note the words **uphill** and **downhill** (*adj., adv.*) : *an uphill climb* ○ *I like riding downhill on my bike.*

hill·bil·ly /'hɪlbɪli/ *noun* [C] (*pl.* **hill·bil·lies**) (*informal*) a person who is usually not well educated and who comes from a part of the countryside in the southern U.S. where there are many hills

hill·side /'hɪlsaɪd/ *noun* [C] the sloping side of a hill: *a house built on the hillside*

hill·top /'hɪltɑp/ *noun* [C] the top of a hill

hill·y /'hɪli/ *adj.* (**hill·i·er**; **hill·i·est**) having many hills: *The landscape is very hilly around here.*

☆ **him** /ɪm; *strong form* hɪm/ *pron.* (the object of a verb or preposition) a male person or animal that was mentioned earlier: *Louise told Joe that she loved him.* ○ *I have a letter for your father – can you give it to him for me?* ○ *That must be him now.* ☞ Look at the note at **he**.

☆ **him·self** /hɪm'sɛlf; *weak form also* ɪm'sɛlf/ *pron.* **1** (used as the object of a verb or preposition when the male person or animal who does an action is also affected by it): *He hurt himself pretty badly.* ○ *He bought himself a new sweater.* ○ *John looked at himself in the mirror.* ☞ picture at **each other**. **2** (used for emphasis): *He told me the news himself.* ○ *The governor himself came to see the damage.* ○ *Did he write this himself?* (= or did sb else do it for him?) **3** in his normal state; healthy: *He's just not himself today* (= he's feeling sick).

IDM (all) by himself 1 alone: *He lives by himself.* ☞ Look at the note at **alone**. **2** without help: *He should be able to cook a meal by himself.*

hind /haɪnd/ *adj.* (only *before* a noun) (used about an animal's legs, etc.) at the back ☞ We also say **back legs**. The legs at the front are **front legs**.

hin·der /'hɪndər/ *verb* [T] to make it more difficult for sb/sth to do sth: *A lot of scientific work is hindered by lack of money.*

hin·drance /'hɪndrəns/ *noun* [C] a person or thing that makes it difficult for you to do sth: *Mark wanted to help me, but he was more of a hindrance than a help.*

hind·sight /'haɪndsaɪt/ *noun* [U] knowing afterwards why sth bad happened and how you could have stopped it happening: *It's very easy to criticize with the benefit of hindsight.* ☞ Look at **foresight**.

Hin·du /'hɪndu/ *noun* [C] a person whose religion is Hinduism —**Hin·du** *adj.*: *Hindu beliefs*

Hin·du·ism /'hɪnduɪzəm/ *noun* [U] the main religion of India, which includes a belief in many gods and the belief that, after death, people will return to life in a different form

hinge¹ /hɪndʒ/ *noun* [C] a piece of metal that joins two sides of a box, door, etc. together and allows it to be opened or closed

hinge

hinge² /hɪndʒ/ *verb*

PHR V hinge on sth to depend on sth: *The future of the project hinges on the meeting today.*

hint¹ /hɪnt/ *noun* [C] **1** something that you suggest in an indirect way: *She kept looking at her watch as a hint that it was time to go.* ○ *I don't know the answer – can you give me a hint?* **2** a piece of advice or information: *The magazine had some helpful hints about how to lose weight.* **3** a small amount of sth: *There was a hint of sadness in his voice.*

hint² /hɪnt/ verb [I,T] to suggest sth in an indirect way: *They only hinted at their great disappointment.* ◦ *He hinted that he might be moving to Florida.*

hip¹ /hɪp/ noun [C] the part of the side of your body above your legs and below your waist: *He stood there angrily with his hands on his hips.* ◦ *She broke her hip* (= the bone inside her hip) *when she fell.* ☞ picture on page A24.

hip² /hɪp/ adj. (**hip·per**; **hip·pest**) (*slang*) very fashionable or knowing a lot about fashionable clothes, music, etc.

hip³ /hɪp/ interj.
IDM **hip, hip, hooray** (used when a group wants to show that it is pleased with sb or with sth that has happened): *"Three cheers for David. He did a great job. Hip, hip..." "Hooray!"*

'hip-hop noun [U] (*informal*) a culture that is popular among young people in large cities. People who are interested in hip-hop often wear loose clothes and like to listen to loud music that has a strong beat (**rap music**).

hip·pie (*also* **hippy**) /'hɪpi/ noun [C] (*pl.* **hippies**) a person who does not share the same ideas and values as most people in society. Hippies show that they are different by wearing long hair, colorful clothes, etc. and sometimes by living in groups.

hip·po·pot·a·mus /ˌhɪpə'pɑṭəməs/ noun [C] (*pl.* **hip·po·pot·a·mus·es** /-məsəz/ *or* **hip·po·pot·a·mi** /-maɪ/) (*also informal* **hip·po** /'hɪpoʊ/ *pl.* **hip·pos**) a large African river animal with a large head and short legs and thick dark skin

☆ **hire** /'haɪər/ verb [T] to give sb a job: *We hired a new secretary.*

☆ **his¹** /ɪz; *strong form* hɪz/ det. belonging to a male person or animal that was mentioned earlier: *That's his book. He left it there this morning.* ◦ *Matthew hurt his shoulder.*

his² /hɪz/ pron. of or belonging to him: *This is my book, so that one must be his.* ◦ *My dad has a lot of neckties, so I borrowed one of his.* ☞ Look at the note at **he**.

☆ **His·pan·ic¹** /hɪ'spænɪk/ adj. connected with or coming from a place where Spanish is spoken, especially Latin America: *the Hispanic population of the U.S.*

☆ **His·pan·ic²** /hɪ'spænɪk/ noun [C] a person who is from a place where Spanish is spoken, especially Latin America, or whose ancestors came from a place where Spanish is spoken: *an effort to hire more Blacks and Hispanics*

hiss /hɪs/ verb **1** [I] to make a sound like a very long "s" to show that you are angry or do not like sth: *The cat hissed at me.* **2** [T] to say sth in an angry hissing voice: *"Stay away from me!" she hissed.* —**hiss** noun [C]

his·to·ri·an /hɪ'stɔriən/ noun [C] a person who is an expert in history

his·tor·ic /hɪ'stɔrɪk; -'stɑr-/ adj. famous or im-

portant in history: *The astronauts' landing on the moon was a historic occasion.*

☆ **his·tor·i·cal** /hɪ'stɔrɪkl; -'stɑr-/ adj. **1** connected with history or the study of history: *There is very little historical evidence about the life of Christ.* ◦ *This house is of great historical interest.* **2** that really lived or happened: *Was Daniel Boone really a historical figure?* ◦ *historical events* —**his·tor·i·cal·ly** /-kli/ adv.

☆ **his·to·ry** /'hɪstəri; 'hɪstri/ noun (*pl.* **his·to·ries**) **1** [U] the study of past events and social, political and economic developments: *She has a bachelor's degree in history.* ◦ *History was my favorite subject in school.* ◦ *a history teacher* **2** [U] events of the past (when you are thinking of them as a whole): *History often repeats itself.* ◦ *an important moment in history* ☞ Look at **natural history**. **3** [C] a written description of past events: *a new history of Europe* **4** [C, usually sing.] the series of events or facts that is connected with a person, place or thing: *There is a history of heart disease in our family.*

☞ **History** is something true that really happened. A **story** is a description of a series of events that may or may not have happened.

H

☆ **hit¹** /hɪt/ verb [T] (*pres. part.* **hit·ting**; *p.t., p.p.* **hit**) **1** to touch sb/sth with a lot of force: *"Don't hit me," she begged.* ◦ *The old man was hit by a car while he was crossing the street.* ◦ *to hit a ball with a bat* ◦ *(figurative) The smell of burning hit her as she entered the room.* ◦ *(figurative) Things were going really well until we hit this problem.* ☞ **Strike** is a more formal word than **hit**. **Beat** means to hit many times: *He was badly beaten in the attack.* **2** **hit sth (on/against sth)** to knock a part of your body, etc. against sth: *Peter hit his head on the low beam.* **3** to have a bad effect upon sb/sth: *Inner-city areas have been badly hit by unemployment.* ◦ *Her father's death hit her very hard.* **4** to find or reach sth: *If you follow this road, you should hit the freeway in about ten minutes.* ◦ *The price of oil hit a new high yesterday.*
IDM **hit it off (with sb)** (*informal*) to like sb when you first meet him/her: *When I first met Tony's parents, we didn't really hit it off.*
hit the jackpot 1 to win a lot of money or a big prize **2** to be very successful or lucky: *We really hit the jackpot with our latest product.*
hit the nail on the head to say sth that is exactly right
PHRV **hit back (at sb/sth)** to attack (with words) sb who has attacked you: *The President hit back at his critics.*

☆ **hit²** /hɪt/ noun [C] **1** the act of hitting sth; a blow: *The ship took a direct hit and sank.* ◦ *What a great hit!* (e.g. in a game of baseball) ☞ Look at **miss**. **2** a person or thing that is

very popular or successful: *He was a big hit in his last movie.* ○ *The album was a smash hit.*

hit-and-run /ˌhɪt n ˈrʌn/ *adj.* **1** (used about a car driver) causing an accident and not stopping to see if anybody is hurt **2** (used about a car accident) caused by a hit-and-run (1) driver

hitch¹ /hɪtʃ/ *verb* **1** [I,T] (*informal*) to get free rides in other people's cars as a way of traveling cheaply: *They hitched a ride in a truck to the next state.* **2** [T] to fasten sth to sth else: *The horses were hitched to the fence.* ○ *to hitch a trailer to the back of a car*

hitch² /hɪtʃ/ *noun* [C] a small problem or difficulty: *The wedding went off without a hitch.*

hitch·hike /ˈhɪtʃhaɪk/ *verb* [I] to travel by getting free rides in other people's cars: *He hitchhiked across Europe.* —**hitch·hik·er** *noun* [C]

☆ **HIV** /ˌeɪtʃ aɪ ˈvi/ *noun* [U] human immunodeficiency virus; a very small living thing (**a virus**) that is believed to cause the disease AIDS: *to be HIV-positive* (= to have HIV in your body) ○ *to be HIV-negative* (= not to have HIV in your body)

hive /haɪv/ *noun* [C] = BEEHIVE

hmm /hm; m/ *interj.* (used when you are not sure or when you are thinking about sth)

☆ **HMO** /ˌeɪtʃ ɛm ˈoʊ/ (*also* **health maintenance organization**) *noun* [C] (*pl.* **HMOs**) a company that gives medical care to people who pay money every month to be members. HMOs control costs by limiting the amount and types of treatment that their doctors and nurses can give to patients.

hoard¹ /hɔrd/ *verb* [I,T] to collect and store large quantities of sth (often secretly)

hoard² /hɔrd/ *noun* [C] a quantity of money, food, etc. that sb has collected and stored (often secretly): *a hoard of treasure*

hoarse /hɔrs/ *adj.* **1** (used about a voice) sounding rough and quiet, e.g. because you have a cold: *a hoarse whisper* **2** (used about people) with a hoarse voice: *The fans shouted themselves hoarse.* —**hoarse·ly** *adv.*

hoax /hoʊks/ *noun* [C] a trick that is played on sb: *The firefighers answered the call, but it turned out to be a hoax.*

hob·ble /ˈhɑbl/ *verb* [I] to walk with difficulty because your feet or legs are hurt: *He hobbled home on his twisted ankle.*

☆ **hob·by** /ˈhɑbi/ *noun* [C] (*pl.* **hob·bies**) something that you do regularly for pleasure in your free time: *Do you have any hobbies?* ○ *My favorite hobby is stamp collecting.*

hock·ey /ˈhɑki/ *noun* [U] a game that is played on an area of ice (**a rink**) by two teams that try to hit a small round, flat rubber object (**a puck**) into a goal with long wooden sticks ☞ Look also at **field hockey**.

hoe /hoʊ/ *noun* [C] a garden tool with a long handle that is used for turning the soil and for removing weeds

hog¹ /hɔg; hɑg/ *noun* [C] a pig that is kept for its meat ☞ Look at the note at **pig**.

hog² /hɔg; hɑg/ *verb* [T] (**hog·ging**; **hogged**) (*informal*) to take or keep too much or all of sth in a selfish way: *Don't hog the bathroom when everyone's getting ready to go out!* ○ *The red car was hogging the middle of the road so no one could pass it.*

hoist /hɔɪst/ *verb* [T] to raise or lift sth by using ropes, etc.: *to hoist a flag, sail, etc.*

☆ **hold¹** /hoʊld/ *verb* (*p.t., p.p.* **held** /hɛld/) **1** [T] to take sb/sth and keep him/her/it in your hand, etc.: *He held a gun in his hand.* ○ *The woman was holding a baby in her arms.* ○ *He manages to write by holding the pen between his teeth.* ○ *Hold my hand. This is a busy street.* **2** [T] to keep sth in a certain position: *Hold your head up straight.* ○ *Hold the camera still or you'll spoil the picture.* ○ *These two screws hold the shelf in place.* **3** [T] to keep a person in a position or place by force: *The hijackers are holding three men hostage.* ○ *A suspect is being held at the police station.* **4** [I,T] to contain or have space for a particular amount: *The car holds five people.* ○ *How much does this bottle hold?* **5** [T] to have sth (usually in an official way): *Does she hold an American passport?* ○ *She holds the world record in the 100 meters.* **6** [T] to have an opinion, etc.: *They hold the view that we shouldn't spend any more money.* **7** [I] to remain the same: *I hope this weather holds until the weekend.* ○ *What I said still holds; nothing has changed.* **8** [T] to believe that sth is true about a person: *I hold the parents responsible for the child's behavior.* **9** [T] to organize an event: *They're holding a party for his fortieth birthday.* ○ *Elections are held every November.* **10** [I,T] (when you are telephoning) to wait until the person you are calling is ready: *That extension is busy right now. Can you hold?* **11** [T] to have a conversation: *It's impossible to hold a conversation with all this noise.*

IDM Hold it! Wait! Don't move!

☞ For other idioms containing **hold**, look at the entries for the nouns, adjectives, etc., e.g. **hold your own** is at **own**.

PHRV hold sb/sth back 1 to prevent sb from making progress **2** to prevent sb/sth from moving forward: *The police tried to hold the crowd back.*

hold sth back not give information: *The police are sure that she is holding something back. She knows a lot more than she is saying.*

hold on 1 to wait: *Hold on. I'll be with you in a minute.* **2** to manage in a difficult or dangerous situation: *They managed to hold on until an ambulance arrived.*

hold onto sb/sth not let go of sb/sth: *The*

child held onto his mother; he didn't want her to go.

hold onto sth not give or sell sth: *They offered me a lot of money for this painting, but I'm going to hold onto it.*

hold out to last (in a difficult situation): *How long will our supply of water hold out?*

hold sth out to offer sth by moving it toward sb: *He held out a piece of candy and offered it to the girl.*

hold out for sth to continue to ask for sth

hold sb/sth up to make sb/sth late: *We were held up by the traffic.*

hold up sth to rob sth, using a gun, etc.: *Masked men held up a bank on Main Street yesterday.*

☆**hold²** /hoʊld/ *noun* **1** [C, sing.] the act or manner of holding sb/sth: *to have a firm hold on the rope* ○ *judo holds*

☞ "Hold" is often used with the verbs **catch**, **get**, **grab**, **seize**, **take**, etc.: *Take hold of the other side of this sheet and help me to fold it.* ○ *I can touch it, but I can't quite get hold of it. It's too far away.*

2 [sing.] **a hold (on/over sb/sth)** influence or control: *The party has strengthened its hold on Congress.* **3** [C] a place where a climber can put his/her hand or foot when climbing ☞ Look at **foothold. 4** [C] the part of a ship or an airplane where goods are carried

IDM **get (a) hold of sb/sth 1** to find sth (that will be useful): *Where can I get hold of a good dictionary?* **2** to find sb or make contact with sb: *I've been trying to get hold of the customer service department all morning.*

on hold 1 (on the telephone) waiting to talk to sb or to continue a conversation: *to put sb on hold* ○ *They kept me on hold for ten minutes!* **2** (used about a project, etc.) in a state of delay for an uncertain length of time: *Plans to build a new stadium are on hold until we can find more funding.*

☆**hold·er** /ˈhoʊldər/ *noun* [C] (often in compounds) **1** a person who has or holds sth: *the world record holder in the 100 meters* ○ *holders of U.S. passports* **2** something that contains or holds sth: *a cup holder in the car*

hold·up /ˈhoʊldʌp/ *noun* [C] **1** a delay: *What's the holdup?* **2** an act of robbing sb/sth, by people with guns

☆**hole** /hoʊl/ *noun* [C] **1** a hollow space in sth solid: *The sidewalk is full of holes.* ○ *to dig a hole in the ground* **2** an opening or an empty space in sth solid: *There are holes in my socks.* ○ *(figurative) There was a big hole in my life after Jim left.* **3** the place where an animal lives in the ground or in a tree: *a rabbit hole* **4** (in golf) the hole (1) in the ground that you must hit the ball into. Each section of a golf course is also called a hole: *an eighteen-hole golf course* ○ *Barbara won the seventh hole.*

IDM **in the hole** (*informal*) owing more money then you have: *The company is over $5 million in the hole.*

☆**hol·i·day** /ˈhɑlədeɪ/ *noun* **1** [C] a special day when government offices, schools, banks and some businesses are closed: *The post office will be closed Monday because it's a holiday.* ○ *New Year's Day is a holiday in every state.* **2 the holidays** [plural] the time in late December and early January that includes Christmas, Hanukkah, New Year's Day, etc.: *Airports across the country are full of people heading home for the holidays.*

☞ We say "*Happy holidays!*" to people in December to wish them a nice Christmas, Hanukkah, New Year, etc.

3 [C,U] (*BrE*) = VACATION

hol·ler /ˈhɑlər/ *verb* [I,T] (*informal*) to shout: *"You kids get out of here!" he hollered.* ○ *The fans were all screaming and hollering.* —**holler** *noun* [C]

☆**hol·low¹** /ˈhɑloʊ/ *adj.* **1** with a hole or empty space inside: *a hollow tree* **2** (used about a sound) seeming to come from a hollow (1) place: *hollow footsteps in the empty house* **IDM** **ring hollow** ⇨ RING²

hol·low² /ˈhɑloʊ/ *noun* [C] an area that is lower than the surrounding land

hol·low³ /ˈhɑloʊ/ *verb* **PHRV** **hollow sth out** to take the inside part of sth out in order to make sth else: *They hollowed out a tree trunk to make a canoe.*

hol·ly /ˈhɑli/ *noun* [U] a plant that has shiny dark green leaves with sharp points and red berries in the winter. It is often used as a Christmas decoration.

hol·o·caust /ˈhɑləkɔst; ˈhoʊlə-/ *noun* **1 the Holocaust** [sing.] the killing of large numbers of Jews and other people in central Europe by the Nazis in World War II: *Holocaust victims/survivors* **2** [C] a situation where a great many things are destroyed and a great many people die: *a nuclear holocaust*

hol·ster /ˈhoʊlstər/ *noun* [C] a leather case for a gun that is attached to a belt or worn under the arm

☆**ho·ly** /ˈhoʊli/ *adj.* (**ho·li·er; ho·li·est**) connected with God or with religion and therefore very special or sacred: *the Holy Bible* ○ *holy water* ○ *The Koran is the holy book of the Muslims.*

IDM **holy cow** (*informal*) (used to express surprise): *Holy cow! Cruz just scored another goal!*

Holy Com·mun·ion *noun* [U] = COMMUNION(1)

the Holy Ghost (*also* **the Holy Spirit**) *noun* [sing.] one of the three parts of God that Christians believe in. The other two parts are the Father and the Son (Jesus Christ).

☆**home¹** /hoʊm/ *noun* **1** [C,U] the place where you live (with your family) or where you feel that you belong: *She left home at the age of 21.* ○

ə	y	w	t	eɪ	aɪ	ɔɪ	aʊ	oʊ
about	yes	woman	butter	say	five	boy	now	go

Children from broken homes (= whose parents are divorced) *sometimes have learning difficulties.*

☞ Be careful. The preposition *to* is not used before "home": *It's time to go home.* ∘ *She's usually tired when she gets home.* If you want to talk about somebody else's home, you have to say: *at Jane and Andy's* or: *at Jane and Andy's place/house.* Look at the note at **house**.

2 [C] a house, an apartment, etc.: *Sales of new homes rose by 3% last year.* ☞ Look also at **mobile home**. **3** [C] a place that provides care for a particular type of person: *a retirement home* (= for people who are retired) ☞ Look also at **nursing home**. **4** [sing.] the place where sth began: *Nashville is the home of country music.* **5** [U] = HOME PLATE

IDM at home 1 in your house, apartment, etc.: *We bought a computer so that Jackie can work at home.* ∘ *Nick is 28 years old, but he still lives at home* (= with his parents).

☞ With the verbs *be* and *stay*, we usually use **home** without the preposition *at*: *Is anybody home?* ∘ *I think I'll just stay home tonight.*

2 as if you were in your own home; comfortable: *Please make yourself at home.* ∘ *They were warm and welcoming and I felt at home right away.*

☆ **home²** /hoʊm/ *adj.* (only *before* a noun) **1** connected with home¹: *home cooking* ∘ *a happy home life* **2** (used in sports) connected with your own sports team or field: *The home team is wearing white, and the visiting team is in red.* ∘ *The team won all of their home games but lost most of their away games.*

IDM the home stretch the last part of a long and often difficult activity, process, competition, etc.: *Both candidates are making a large number of speeches in the home stretch of the campaign.*

☆ **home³** /hoʊm/ *adv.* at, in or to your home¹ or home country: *We stopped at Jack and Terri's house, but they weren't home.* ∘ *We should go home soon.* ∘ *She'll be flying home for the holidays.*

IDM bring sth home to sb to make sb understand sth fully: *Looking at those pictures of hungry children really brought home to me how lucky we are.*

home·com·ing /ˈhoʊmˌkʌmɪŋ/ *noun* [C,U] **1** the arrival home (especially of sb who has been away for a long time) **2** a festival at a high school, college or university which takes place on a weekend in the fall. Many former students return to their old school to watch an important football game and to join in other social events.

ˌ**home eco'nomics** (also *informal* ˌ**home 'ec**) *noun* [U] a school subject that includes cooking, sewing, etc.

home·land /ˈhoʊmlænd/ *noun* [C] the country where you were born or that your parents came from, or to which you feel you belong

☆ **home·less** /ˈhoʊmləs/ *adj.* **1** having no home **2 the homeless** *noun* [plural] people without a home —**home·less·ness** *noun* [U]

ˌ**home 'loan** *noun* [C] = MORTGAGE

home·ly /ˈhoʊmli/ *adj.* (**home·li·er; home·li·est**) (used about a girl or woman) not very attractive

home·made /ˌhoʊmˈmeɪd/ *adj.* made at home; not bought in a store: *homemade soup*

home·mak·er /ˈhoʊmˌmeɪkər/ *noun* [C] a person, usually a woman, who cooks, cleans, etc. in his/her own home and does not have another job

home·own·er /ˈhoʊmˌoʊnər/ *noun* [C] a person who owns his/her home

ˈ**home page** *noun* [C] (*computing*) the first page of information about a company, an organization, a person, etc. that can be read on a computer screen when it is connected to an international system of computers (**the World Wide Web**). A home page usually has links to other pages with more information: *Visit our home page at www.oup-usa.org.*

ˌ**home 'plate** (*also* **home**) *noun* [U] (in baseball) the place (**base**) where a player stands when he/she hits the ball and which he/she must touch in order to gain a point (**run**) ☞ picture at **baseball**.

hom·er /ˈhoʊmər/ *noun* [C] (*informal*) = HOME RUN

home·room /ˈhoʊmrum/ *noun* [C,U] a room in a school where a group of students must go at the beginning of each day and where a teacher gives them general information about school events and rules

ˌ**home 'run** (also *informal* **homer**) *noun* [C] (in baseball) a hit that goes so far that the player who hit the ball is allowed to run around all four corners (**bases**) and score a point (**run**): *to hit a home run* ☞ Look at the note at **baseball**.

home·sick /ˈhoʊmsɪk/ *adj.* sad because you are away from home: *She was very homesick for Japan.* —**home·sick·ness** *noun* [U]

home·town /ˌhoʊmˈtaʊn/ *noun* [C] the town or city where you were born or where you lived when you were a child

☆ **home·work** /ˈhoʊmwərk/ *noun* [U] the work that teachers give to students to do away from school: *to do your homework* ∘ (*figurative*) *The mayor had not done his homework and there were several questions that he couldn't answer.* ☞ Look at the note at **housework**.

hom·i·cide /ˈhɑməsaɪd/ *noun* [C,U] the illegal killing of one person by another; murder —**hom·i·cid·al** /ˌhɑməˈsaɪdl/ *adj.*

hom·o·nym /ˈhɑmənɪm/ *noun* [C] a word that is spelled or pronounced like another word but that has a different meaning

ər	ɪr	ɛr	ɑr	ɔr	ʊr	ʒ	h	ŋ
bird	near	hair	car	north	tour	vision	hat	sing

ho·mo·sex·u·al /ˌhoʊməˈsɛkʃuəl/ *adj.* (*formal*) sexually attracted to people of the same sex ☞ A less formal word is **gay**. Look also at **heterosexual, bisexual** and **lesbian**. —**ho·mo·sex·u·al** *noun* [C] —**ho·mo·sex·u·al·i·ty** /ˌhoʊməsɛkʃuˈæləti/ *noun* [U]

hon·cho /ˈhɑntʃoʊ/ *noun* [C] (*pl.* **hon·chos**) (*slang*) a manager or person who is in charge of sb/sth: *the record company's head honcho*

☆ **hon·est** /ˈɑnəst/ *adj.* **1** (used about a person) telling the truth; not cheating or stealing: *Just be honest – do you like this skirt or not?* ○ *We need somebody who's completely honest for this job.* **2** showing honest (1) qualities: *an honest face* ○ *I'd like your honest opinion.* ☞ The opposite for both senses is **dishonest**.

☆ **hon·est·ly** /ˈɑnəstli/ *adv.* **1** in an honest way: *He tried to answer the lawyer's questions honestly.* **2** (used for emphasizing sth): *I honestly don't know where she went.* **3** (used for expressing disapproval): *Honestly! What a mess!*

☆ **hon·es·ty** /ˈɑnəsti/ *noun* [U] the quality of being honest ☞ The opposite is **dishonesty**.

hon·ey /ˈhʌni/ *noun* **1** [U] the sweet sticky yellow substance that is made by bees and that people eat: *Would you like honey on your bread?* **2** [C] (*informal*) (a way of speaking to sb that you love): *Honey, I'm home!*

hon·ey·moon /ˈhʌnimun/ *noun* [C] a vacation that is taken by a man and a woman who have just gotten married: *We went to Hawaii on our honeymoon.*

honk /hɑŋk; hɔŋk/ *verb* [I,T] to sound the horn of a car; to make this sound

☆ **hon·or¹** /ˈɑnər/ *noun* **1** [sing.] something that gives pride or pleasure: *It was a great honor to give a speech at the convention.* ○ *He did me the honor of mentioning my name in the book.* **2** [U] the respect from other people that a person, country, etc. gets because of high standards of behavior and moral character: *a man of honor* ○ *to fight for the honor of your country* ☞ Look at **dishonor**. **3** [C] an award that is given to a person officially, to show great respect or to recognize sth important that he/she has achieved: *She graduated with honors* (= because she had gotten very good grades) *from Madison High School in 1993.* **4 Honor** [U] (used after *Your, His* or *Her*) (a title that is used when speaking about or to a judge, mayor, or some other official person)

IDM in honor of sb/sth; in sb/sth's honor out of respect for sb/sth: *A party was given in honor of the guests from Japan.*

☆ **hon·or²** /ˈɑnər/ *verb* [T] **1** honor sb/sth (with sth) to show great (public) respect for sb/sth or to give sb pride or pleasure: *I am very honored by the confidence you have shown in me.* **2** to keep a promise to do sth

hon·or·a·ble /ˈɑnərəbl/ *adj.* acting in a way that makes people respect you; having or

showing honor: *The only honorable thing to do was to resign.* ○ *an honorable person* ☞ Look at **dishonorable**. —**hon·or·a·bly** *adv.*

hon·or·ar·y /ˈɑnərɛri/ *adj.* **1** given as an honor (without the person needing the usual qualifications): *to be awarded an honorary degree* **2** not getting any money for doing a job, and often not doing any real work: *an actor chosen to be the charity's honorary chairman*

'honor roll *noun* [C, usually sing.] a list of the names of students in a school who have earned high grades

hood /hʊd/ *noun* [C] **1** the part of a coat, etc. that you use to cover your head and neck in bad weather **2** the front part of a car that covers the engine

 hood

hoof /hʊf; huf/ *noun* [C] (*pl.* **hoofs** or **hooves** /huvz; hʊvz/) the hard part of the foot of horses and some other animals ☞ picture at **horse**.

☆ **hook¹** /hʊk/ *noun* [C] **1** a curved piece of metal, plastic, etc. that is used for catching sth or hanging sth on: *a fish hook* ○ *Put your coat on the hook over there.* ☞ picture at **hanger**. **2** (used in boxing) a hit or punch that is given with the elbow bent: *a right hook* (= with the right arm)

IDM off the hook 1 with the part of the telephone that you speak into (**the receiver**) not in position so that telephone calls cannot be received: *Martha's number is still busy – maybe she left the phone off the hook.* **2** (*informal*) out of a difficult situation: *My dad paid the money I owed and got me off the hook.*

ring off the hook ➪ RING²

hook² /hʊk/ *verb* **1** [I,T] to fasten sth or to be fastened with a hook¹(1) or sth like a hook **2** [T] to catch hold of sth with a hook¹(1) or with sth shaped like a hook

IDM be/get hooked (on sth) (*slang*) **1** to like (doing) sth very much: *Brian is hooked on computer games.* **2** to be unable to stop using (**addicted to**) drugs, alcohol, etc.: *to be hooked on gambling*

PHRV hook (sth) up (to sth) to connect a machine, etc. to a larger system so that it can work: *You can't call me at my new apartment – the phone isn't hooked up yet.*

hook·er /ˈhʊkər/ *noun* [C] (*informal*) = PROSTITUTE

hoop /hup/ *noun* [C] **1** a large metal or plastic ring **2** (in basketball) the metal ring that the net (**basket**) hangs from: *Let's go out and shoot some hoops* (= practice our basketball). ☞ picture at **basketball**.

hoo·ray /hʊˈreɪ/ *interj.* (used for expressing great pleasure, approval, etc.): *Hooray, we won!*

tʃ	dʒ	v	θ	ð	s	z	ʃ
chin	June	van	thin	then	so	zoo	she

IDM hip, hip, hooray ⇨ HIP³

hoot¹ /hut/ *noun* **1** [C] a loud shout, especially to show disapproval **2** [sing.] (*informal*) something that is very funny: *The party was a real hoot!*

IDM can't/don't give a hoot (*informal*) not to care at all about sth: *I don't give a hoot what he thinks.*

hoot² /hut/ *verb* [I] to make a loud noise : *They hooted with laughter at the suggestion.*

hooves *pl.* of HOOF

hop¹ /hɑp/ *verb* (**hop·ping; hopped**) [I] **1** (used about a person) to jump on one leg ☞ picture at **bounce**. **2** (used about an animal or bird) to jump with both or all feet together

PHRV hop in/into sth; hop out/out of sth (*informal*) to get in or out of a car, etc. (quickly): *Hop in! I'll give you a ride downtown.*

hop on/onto sth; hop off sth to get onto/off a bus, etc. (quickly)

hop² /hɑp/ *noun* [C] **1** an act of hopping¹(1,2) **2** (*informal*) a short trip: *It's just a short hop from the island to the mainland.*

☆ **hope¹** /hoʊp/ *noun* **1** [C,U] **hope (of/for sth); hope (of doing sth/that…)** the feeling of wanting sth to happen and thinking that it will: *What hope is there for the future?* ○ *There is no hope of finding anybody else alive.* ○ *David has high hopes of becoming a doctor.* ○ *She never gave up hope that he would come back.* **2** [C, usually sing.] a person or thing that gives you hope (1): *You've got to help me – you're my only hope.*

IDM in the hope of sth/that… because you want sth to happen: *I came here in the hope that we could talk privately.*

a ray of hope ⇨ RAY

☆ **hope²** /hoʊp/ *verb* [I,T] **hope (for sth); hope to do sth; hope (that) sth will happen** to want sth to happen or be true: *We're hoping for sunny weather tomorrow.* ○ *I hope (that) you feel better soon.* ○ *I'm hoping to buy a car this summer.* ○ *"Is it raining?" "I hope not.* ○ *"Are you coming to New York with us?" "I'm not sure yet, but I hope so."*

☆ **hope·ful** /ˈhoʊpfl/ *adj.* **1** thinking that sth that you want to happen will happen: *He's very hopeful about the success of the business.* ○ *The strikers seem hopeful of an improved pay offer.* **2** making you think that sth good will happen: *a hopeful sign*

☆ **hope·ful·ly** /ˈhoʊpfl i/ *adv.* **1** in a hopeful way: *She smiled hopefully at me, waiting for my answer.* **2** I/We hope; if everything happens as planned: *Hopefully, we'll be finished by six o'clock.* ☞ Some people think this use is not correct.

☆ **hope·less** /ˈhoʊpləs/ *adj.* giving no hope that sth will be successful or get better: *This is a hopeless situation. There is nothing we can do.*

—**hope·less·ly** *adv.*: *They were hopelessly lost.*
—**hope·less·ness** *noun* [U]

horde /hɔrd/ *noun* [C] a very large number of people: *hordes of shoppers*

☆ **ho·ri·zon** /həˈraɪzn/ *noun* [C] the line where the earth and sky appear to meet: *The ship appeared on/disappeared over the horizon.*

☆ **hor·i·zon·tal** /ˌhɔrəˈzɑntl; ˌhɑr-/ *adj.* going from side to side, not up and down; flat or level ☞ picture at **vertical**. —**hor·i·zon·tal·ly** *adv.*

hor·mone /ˈhɔrmoʊn/ *noun* [C] a substance in the body that influences growth and development

☆ **horn** /hɔrn/ *noun* [C] **1** one of the hard pointed things that cows, goats, etc. have on their heads ☞ picture at **cow**. **2** the thing in a car, etc. that gives a loud warning sound: *Don't blow your horn late at night.* ○ *a fog horn* **3** one of the family of brass musical instruments that you play by blowing into them: *a French horn*

horn·y /ˈhɔrni/ *adj.* (**horn·i·er; horn·i·est**) (*slang*) sexually excited

hor·o·scope /ˈhɔrəskoʊp; ˈhɑr-/ *noun* [C] a statement about what is going to happen to a person in the future, based on the position of the stars and planets when he/she was born: *What does my horoscope say for next week?* ☞ Look at **astrology** and **zodiac**.

hor·ren·dous /həˈrɛndəs/ *adj.* very bad or unpleasant: *a horrendous crime* —**hor·ren·dous·ly** *adv.*

☆ **hor·ri·ble** /ˈhɔrəbl; ˈhɑr-/ *adj.* **1** causing fear or shock: *a horrible murder* **2** very bad or unpleasant: *I've got a horrible feeling that I forgot something.* —**hor·ri·bly** /-əbli/ *adv.*

hor·rif·ic /həˈrɪfɪk/ *adj.* causing fear or shock: *a horrific road accident*

hor·ri·fy /ˈhɔrəfaɪ; ˈhɑr-/ *verb* [T] (*pres. part.* **hor·ri·fy·ing;** *3rd pers. sing. pres.* **hor·ri·fies;** *p.t., p.p.* **hor·ri·fied**) to shock sb greatly: *I was horrified by the conditions they were living in.* —**hor·ri·fy·ing** *adj.*

hor·ror /ˈhɔrər; ˈhɑr-/ *noun* **1** [U] a feeling of great fear or shock: *They watched in horror as the building collapsed.* ○ *a horror movie* (= that shows frightening or shocking things) ○ (*figurative*) *Jan told us some horror stories about life in her school.* **2** [C] something that makes you feel frightened or shocked: *I'll never forget the horror of what I saw that day.* ○ *the horrors of war*

☆ **horse¹** /hɔrs/ *noun* [C] a large animal that is used for riding on or for pulling or carrying heavy loads

☞ A male horse is a **stallion**, a female horse is a **mare** and a young horse is a **foal**.

horse² /hɔrs/ *verb*

i	ɪ	ɛ	æ	ɑ	ɔ	ʌ	ʊ	u
see	sit	ten	cat	hot	saw	cup	put	too

saddle · mane · **horse** · bridle · tail · reins · stirrup · hoof

PHRV **horse around** (*informal*) to play or act in a silly, rough way: *Quit horsing around with those knives!*

horse·back /ˈhɔrsbæk/ *noun* [U]
on horseback sitting on a horse: *Police on horseback were controlling the crowds.* ☞ Police on horseback are also called **mounted police.**

ˈ**horseback ˌriding** *noun* [U] the sport or hobby of riding a horse: *to go horseback riding*

horse·pow·er /ˈhɔrspaʊər/ *noun* [C] (*pl.* **horse·pow·er**) (*abbr.* **hp**) a measure of the power of an engine, etc.: *a ten-horsepower engine*

horse·shoe /ˈhɔrʃʃu; ˈhɔrsʃu/ *noun* **1** [C] a U-shaped piece of metal that is fastened to the bottom of a horse's foot. People believe that horseshoes bring good luck. **2 horseshoes** [U] a game that people play outdoors, in which they throw U-shaped pieces of metal at a small post in the ground

☆ **hose** /hoʊz/ *noun* [C,U] a long rubber or plastic tube that is used for getting water from one place to another, in the yard or when there is a fire ☞ Look at **pantyhose.**

hos·pice /ˈhɑspəs/ *noun* [C] a special hospital where people who are dying are cared for

hos·pi·ta·ble /hɑˈspɪtəbl; ˈhɑspɪtəbl/ *adj.* (used about a person) friendly and helpful to visitors ☞ Look at **inhospitable.**

☆ **hos·pi·tal** /ˈhɑspɪtl/ *noun* [C] a place where sick or injured people are treated: *He was rushed to the hospital in an ambulance.* ○ *to be admitted to/discharged from the hospital*

☞ A person who is being treated in a hospital by **doctors** and **nurses** is a **patient**. If you have an accident, you are taken first to the **emergency room**.

hos·pi·tal·i·ty /ˌhɑspəˈtæləti/ *noun* [U] being friendly and helpful to guests: *We're very grateful for your hospitality.*

hos·pi·tal·ize /ˈhɑspɪtl·aɪz/ *verb* [T] (usually passive) to take sb to a hospital for treatment: *Two men were hospitalized with gunshot wounds.* —**hos·pi·tal·i·za·tion** /ˌhɑspɪtl· əˈzeɪʃn/ *noun* [C,U]

☆ **host¹** /hoʊst/ *noun* [C] **1** a person who receives and entertains visitors: *It's polite to write a thank-you note to your host.* ○ *the host country for the next Olympic Games* ○ *We need more host families for international students.* ☞ Look at **hostess.** **2** a person who introduces a television or radio show and talks to the guests

host² /hoʊst/ *verb* [T] to act as a host or hostess: *a game show hosted by Alex Trebek*

☆ **hos·tage** /ˈhɑstɪdʒ/ *noun* [C] a person who is caught and kept prisoner by a person or group. The hostage may be killed or injured if that person or group does not get what it is asking for: *The hijackers released the women and children but kept the men as hostages.*
IDM **take/hold sb hostage** to catch/keep sb as a hostage

hos·tel /ˈhɑstl/ *noun* [C] ⇨ YOUTH HOSTEL

host·ess /ˈhoʊstəs/ *noun* [C] **1** a woman who receives and entertains visitors **2** a woman who introduces a television or radio show and talks to the guests **3** a woman whose job is to take you to your table in a restaurant

hos·tile /ˈhɑstl; -taɪl/ *adj.* very unfriendly toward sb/sth; not having a good opinion of sb/sth: *a hostile crowd* ○ *They are very hostile to any change.*

hos·til·i·ty /hɑˈstɪləti/ *noun* **1** [U] being unfriendly toward sb/sth: *She didn't say anything, but I could sense her hostility* **2** [U] thinking that sth is bad: *They didn't try to hide their hostility toward the police.* **3 hostilities** [plural] fighting in a war: *Negotiations have led to an end to hostilities.*

☆ **hot** /hɑt/ *adj.* (**hot·ter; hot·test**) **1** having a high degree of heat; not cold: *Can I open the window? I'm really hot.* ○ *Be careful. The plates are hot.* ○ *It's hot today, isn't it?* ○ *Do you like this hot weather?* ○ *a hot meal*

☞ You can describe the temperature of sth as **freezing (cold), cold, cool, lukewarm** (used about water), **warm, hot** or **boiling (hot).**

2 (used about food) causing a burning feeling in your mouth: *hot sauce* **3** (*informal*) very popular with the public, especially because of being new, exciting or interesting: *one of Hollywod's hottest stars* **4** (*slang*) sexually attractive: *I think Keanu's really hot!*
IDM **be hot at sth** (often used with a negative) to know a lot about sth, or to be good at doing sth: *Don't ask me. I'm not very hot at history.*

ˌ**hot-ˈair balˌloon** *noun* [C] = BALLOON(2)

ˌ**hot ˈchocolate** *noun* [U] = COCOA(2)

☆ ˈ**hot dog** *noun* [C] a food, like a type of sandwich, that consists of warm meat in the shape of a tube (a **frankfurter**) inside a long, soft piece of bread (a **bun**)

☆ **ho·tel** /hoʊˈtɛl/ *noun* [C] a place where you pay to sleep (and perhaps eat your meals) when you are on vacation or traveling: *to stay at/in a hotel* ○ *to reserve a hotel room*

H

ə	y	w	t̪	eɪ	aɪ	ɔɪ	aʊ	oʊ
about	yes	woman	butter	say	five	boy	now	go

☞ You reserve a **single room**, a **double room** or a **suite** at a hotel. When you arrive, you **check in** or **register** and when you leave, you **check out**.

hot·line /ˈhɑtlam/ *noun* [C] a direct telephone line

hot·ly /ˈhɑtli/ *adv.* **1** angrily or with force: *They hotly denied the newspaper reports.* **2** closely: *The dog ran off, hotly pursued by its owner.*

hot tub (*also* **Jacuzzi** (*trademark*)) *noun* [C] a large container, big enough for several people to sit in, that is filled with warm water which is pumped around to make your body feel relaxed

hound /haʊnd/ *verb* [T] to follow and disturb sb: *Movie stars are always being hounded by the press.*

☆ **hour** /ˈaʊər/ *noun* **1** [C] a period of 60 minutes: *He worked for three hours after supper.* ○ *The program lasts about half an hour.* ○ *I've been waiting here for hours.* ○ *I'm going shopping now. I'll be back in about an hour.* ○ *a four-hour drive* **2 the hour** [sing.] the time when a new hour starts (i.e. 1 o'clock, 2 o'clock, etc.): *The next traffic report is at ten minutes after the hour.* **3 hours** [plural] the period of time when sb is working or a store, etc. is open: *Office hours are usually from 9 a.m. to 5 p.m.* ○ *Visiting hours in the hospital are from 2 to 3 p.m.* ○ *The employees are demanding shorter working hours.* **4** [C,U] a period of time: *I'm going shopping on my lunch hour.* ○ *The traffic is very bad during rush hour.*

IDM (**at/until) all hours** (at/until) any time: *People come and go at all hours of the day and night next door.* ○ *I've been working all hours* (= very late) *recently.*

the early hours ⇨ EARLY

on the hour at exactly 1, 2, 3, etc. o'clock: *The buses to downtown leave on the hour.*

the wee hours ⇨ WEE

hour·ly¹ /ˈaʊərli/ *adv.* every hour: *This medication must be taken hourly.*

hour·ly² /ˈaʊərli/ *adj.* **1** done or happening every hour: *an hourly news bulletin* **2** for an hour: *What is your hourly fee?*

☆ **house¹** /haʊs/ *noun* [C] (*pl.* **hous·es** /ˈhaʊzəz/) **1** a building that is made for one family to live in: *a three-bedroom house*

☞ Your **home** is the place where you live, even if it is not a house: *Let's go home to my apartment.* Your home is also the place where you feel that you belong. A house is just a building: *We just moved into our new house, so it doesn't feel like home yet.* You can **build**, **fix up**, **remodel** or **add on to** a house. You may **rent** a house or **rent** it **out** to somebody else. If you want to **move** to a new house, you go to a **Realtor**.

2 [usually sing.] all the people who live in one house: *Don't shout. You'll wake the whole house up.* **3** a building that is used for a particular purpose: *an apartment house* (= that contains several apartments) ○ *a warehouse* ☞ Look also at **White House**. **4** a group of people who meet to make laws for a country or state: *The Senate is the upper house in the U.S. Congress.* ☞ Look at the note at **Congress**. **5 the House** [sing.] = THE HOUSE OF REPRESENTATIVES: *Republicans in the House and Senate voted against the bill.*

IDM **on the house** paid for by the bar, restaurant, etc. that you are visiting; free: *Your first drink is on the house.*

house² /haʊz/ *verb* [T] **1** to provide sb with a place to live: *The city is unable to house all homeless families.* **2** to contain or keep sth: *Her office is housed in a separate building.*

house·boat /ˈhaʊsboʊt/ *noun* [C] a large boat on a river, etc. that sb can live in

☆ **house·hold** /ˈhaʊshoʊld/ *noun* [C] all the people who live in one house and the housework, money, organization, etc. that is needed to take care of them: *Almost all households have a television.* ○ *the head of the household* ○ *household expenses* ○ *household cleaning products*

house·keep·er /ˈhaʊsˌkipər/ *noun* [C] a person who is paid to clean sb else's house and often cook food, etc.

house·keep·ing /ˈhaʊsˌkipɪŋ/ *noun* [U] **1** work that is done in a house, such as cleaning, etc. **2** the department in a hotel, a hospital, an office building, etc. that is responsible for cleaning the building, etc.: *Call housekeeping and tell them to bring us some clean towels.*

☆ **the ˌHouse of ˌRepreˈsentatives** (*also* **the House**) *noun* [sing.] one of the two groups of people who are elected to make new laws for the U.S. or for an individual state ☞ Look at **Congress** and **Senate**, and at the note at **White House**.

ˌhouse-to-ˈhouse *adj.* going to each house: *The police are making a house-to-house search.*

house·warm·ing /ˈhaʊsˌwɔrmɪŋ/ *noun* [C] a party that you give when you have just moved into a new home

house·wife /ˈhaʊswaɪf/ *noun* [C] (*pl.* **house·wives** /-waɪvz/) a woman who spends her time doing housework, cooking, taking care of her family, etc. and who does not have another job ☞ A man who does this is called a **househusband**. A more modern word which can be used for men and women is **homemaker**.

house·work /ˈhaʊswərk/ *noun* [U] the work that is needed to keep a house clean

☞ Be careful. The word for work that is given to students by teachers to be done after school hours is **homework**.

ər	ɪr	ɛr	ɑr	ɔr	ʊr	ʒ	h	ŋ
bird	near	hair	car	north	tour	vision	hat	sing

☆**hous·ing** /'haʊzɪŋ/ *noun* [U] houses, apartments, etc. for people to live in: *low-income housing* (= for people with low incomes)

'**housing de,velopment** *noun* [C] an area where a large number of private houses are planned and built at the same time

'**housing ,project** (*also* ,**public** '**housing ,project**, *informal* **project**) *noun* [C] an area with a large number of apartments, usually in tall buildings, which are owned by the government for people with low incomes to live in

hov·er /'hʌvər/ *verb* [I] **1** (used about a bird, etc.) to stay in the air in one place **2** to stay at or near one place, level, etc.: *Temperatures hovered around 100° all week.* ○ *The storm is hovering off the eastern coast of Florida.*

☆**how**[1] /haʊ/ *adv.* **1** (used in questions) in what way: *How do you spell your name?* ○ *Can you show me how to use this machine?* **2** (used when you are asking about sb's health): *"How is your mother?" "She's feeling a lot better now."*

☞ You use "how" only when you are asking about a person's health. When you are asking about a person's character or appearance you say **what ... like?**: *"What is your sister like?" "Well, she's taller than I am and she has dark hair."*

3 (used when you are asking about a thing or a situation): *How was the weather?* ○ *How is your meal?* **4** (used in questions before an adjective or adverb when you are asking about the degree, amount, age, etc. of sb/sth): *How old are you?* ○ *How much is that?* ○ *How long did it take to get here?* **5** (used for expressing surprise, shock, thanks, pleasure, etc.): *How nice of you to remember my birthday!* ○ *How could he have lied to me?*

IDM **how/what about ...?** ⇨ ABOUT[2]

how come ...? ⇨ COME

how do you do? (*formal*) (used when meeting sb for the first time)

☞ Be careful. **How are you?** and **How do you do?** are answered very differently.: *"How do you do?"* is a very formal old-fashioned greeting and it is answered with the same words: *"How do you do?"* The answer to: *"How are you?"* depends on how you are feeling: *"I'm fine."/"Okay."/"A lot better."*

how in the world (used in questions for expressing surprise) in what way; how: *How in the world did you manage to find me here?* ○ *How in the world can he afford a car like that?*

☆**how**[2] /haʊ/ *conj.* the way in which: *I can't remember how to get there.*

how·dy /'haʊdi/ *interj.* (*informal, old-fashioned*) (used as an informal greeting, especially by people in the southern and western U.S.): *Howdy, folks!*

☆**how·ev·er**[1] /haʊ'ɛvər/ *adv.* **1** (used for adding a comment on what you have just said) although sth is true: *Sales are low this month. There may, however, be an increase before Christmas.* **2** (*formal*) (before an adjective or adverb) to whatever degree: *We are grateful for any donation, however large or small.* ○ *They could not succeed however hard they tried.*

☞ The phrase *no matter how ...* is more common.

how·ev·er[2] /haʊ'ɛvər/ *conj.* in whatever way: *You can dress however you want.*

howl /haʊl/ *noun* [C] a long loud cry made by a dog or a wolf: (*figurative*) *The governor's statement was greeted with howls of protest.* —**howl** *verb* [I,T]: *The wind howled across the prairie.*

hub /hʌb/ *noun* [C] the round central part of a wheel

hud·dle[1] /'hʌdl/ *verb* [I] **1** to get close to other people because you are cold or frightened: *The campers huddled (together) around the fire.* **2** to curl your body up and wrap your arms around yourself because you are cold or frightened: *Some of us slept in sleeping bags, while others huddled under blankets.* —**huddled** *adj.*: *We found the children lying huddled together on the ground.*

hud·dle[2] /'hʌdl/ *noun* [C] a small group of people or things that are close together: *They all sat in a huddle in front of the computer.*

☆**hug**[1] /hʌg/ *verb* [T] (**hug·ging; hugged**) **1** to put your arms around sb to show that you love him/her: *There was a lot of hugging and kissing at the airport before Grandma and Grandpa left.* **2** (used about a ship, car, etc.) to keep close to sth: *to hug the coast*

☆**hug**[2] /hʌg/ *noun* [C] an act of hugging: *She gave the child a hug and he stopped crying.*

☆**huge** /hyudʒ/ *adj.* very large: *There is a huge amount of work left to be done.* ○ *a huge building* —**huge·ly** *adv.*: *The play was hugely successful.*

huh /hʌ/ *interj.* (*informal*) **1** (used for asking sb to agree with you): *"Good party, huh?"* **2** (used for asking sb to repeat sth): *"Are you ready?" "Huh?" "I asked if you were ready!"*

hull /hʌl/ *noun* [C] the body of a ship

hum[1] /hʌm/ *verb* (**hum·ming; hummed**) **1** [I] to make a continuous low noise like the noise bees make: (*figurative*) *The classroom was humming with activity.* **2** [I,T] to sing with your lips closed: *You can hum the tune if you don't know the words.*

hum[2] /hʌm/ *noun* [C, usually sing.] a humming sound: *the hum of distant traffic*

☆**hu·man**[1] /'hyumən/ *adj.* connected with people, not with animals or machines; typical of people: *the human body* ○ *The famine caused a terrible loss of human life.* ○ *A human skeleton was found by the construction workers.* ○ *The disaster was caused by human error.* ○ *It's*

tʃ	dʒ	v	θ	ð	s	z	ʃ
chin	June	van	thin	then	so	zoo	she

only human to be upset in a situation like that. —**hu·man·ly** *adv.*: *They did all that was humanly possible to rescue him* (= everything that a human being could possibly do).

☆ **hu·man²** /ˈhyumən/ (*also* ˌhuman ˈbeing) *noun* [C] a person; a man, woman or child

hu·mane /hyuˈmeɪn/ *adj.* having or showing kindness or understanding especially to a person or animal that is suffering: *A civilized society treats mentally handicapped people in a humane way.* ☞ The opposite is **inhumane**. —**hu·mane·ly** *adv.*

hu·man·i·tar·i·an /hyuˌmænəˈtɛriən/ *adj.* concerned with trying to make people's lives better and reduce suffering

hu·man·i·ty /hyuˈmænəṭi/ *noun* [U] **1** all the people in the world, thought of as a group; the human race: *crimes against humanity* **2** the quality of being kind and understanding: *The prisoners were treated with humanity.* ☞ The opposite is **inhumanity**. **3 humanities** [plural] subjects such as history or languages that you study at a school, college or university: *courses in the arts and humanities*

ˌhuman ˈnature *noun* [U] feelings, behavior, etc. that are common to all people: *It's only human nature to want the best for yourself and your family.*

the ˌhuman ˈrace *noun* [sing.] all the people in the world (when you are thinking of them as a group)

ˌhuman ˈresources (*also* **personnel**) *noun* [U] the department in a company that is in charge of employing new workers and taking care of all the workers in the company

ˌhuman ˈrights *noun* [plural] the basic freedoms that all people should have, e.g. the right to say what you think, travel freely

hum·ble¹ /ˈhʌmbl/ *adj.* **1** not thinking that you are better or more important than other people; not proud: *He became very rich and famous, but he always remained a very humble man.* ☞ The noun is **humility**. **2** low in social status; unimportant: *She comes from a humble background.* —**hum·bly** *adv.*: *He apologized very humbly for his behavior.*

hum·ble² /ˈhʌmbl/ *verb* [T] to make sb humble¹(1) : *He felt humbled by the experience.* —**hum·bling** /ˈhʌmblɪŋ/ *adj.*: *a humbling defeat*

☆ **hu·mid** /ˈhyuməd/ *adj.* (used about the air or climate) containing a lot of water; damp: *Florida is hot and humid in the summer.* —**hu·mid·i·ty** /hyuˈmɪdəṭi/ *noun* [U]

hu·mil·i·ate /hyuˈmɪlieɪt/ *verb* [T] to make sb feel ashamed: *Did you have to humiliate me in front of all those people?* —**hu·mil·i·at·ing** *adj.*: *a humiliating defeat* —**hu·mil·i·a·tion** /hyuˌmɪliˈeɪʃn/ *noun* [C,U]

☆ **hu·mor¹** /ˈhyumər/ *noun* [U] **1** the funny or amusing quality or qualities of sb/sth: *It's an awful situation, but at least you can see the*

humor in it. ○ *It is sometimes hard to understand the humor* (= the jokes) *of another country.* **2** being able to see when sth is funny and to laugh at things: *Rose has a good sense of humor.*

hu·mor² /ˈhyumər/ *verb* [T] to keep sb happy by doing what he/she wants: *I'm only doing this to humor Dad.*

hu·mor·ous /ˈhyumərəs/ *adj.* amusing and funny: *It's a very humorous book.* ○ *a humorous speaker* —**hu·mor·ous·ly** *adv.*

hump /hʌmp/ *noun* [C] a round lump, e.g. on an animal's back ☞ picture at **camel**.

hunch¹ /hʌntʃ/ *noun* [C] (*informal*) a thought or an idea that is based on a feeling rather than on facts or information: *I'm not sure, but I have a hunch that she's got a new job.*

hunch² /hʌntʃ/ *verb* [I,T] to bend your back and shoulders forward in a round shape: *They sat there, hunched over their desks.*

☆ **hun·dred** /ˈhʌndrəd/ *number* 100; one more than ninety-nine: *two hundred* ○ *There were a/ one hundred people in the room.* ○ *She's a hundred* (= a hundred years old) *today.*

☞ Note that when we are saying a number, e.g. 420, we often put "and" after the word **hundred**: *four hundred (and) twenty.* The plural **hundreds** is used when we mean "many" or "a lot": *The doll cost hundreds of dollars.* ○ *hundreds of people.* Look at Appendix 2.

hun·dredth¹ /ˈhʌndrədθ; -ətθ/ *pron., det., adv.* 100th; next after ninety-ninth

hun·dredth² /ˈhʌndrədθ; -ətθ/ *noun* [C] the fraction 1/100th; one of a hundred equal parts of sth

hung *p.t., p.p.* of HANG¹

☆ **hun·ger** /ˈhʌŋgər/ *noun* [U] **1** the wish or need for food: *Hunger is one reason why babies cry.* **2** a lack of food: *to die of hunger* ☞ Look at **thirst**.

☞ Be careful. You cannot say *I have hunger* in English. You must say: *I am hungry.*

ˈhunger strike *noun* [C,U] a time when people (especially prisoners) refuse to eat because they are protesting about sth

☆ **hun·gry** /ˈhʌŋgri/ *adj.* (**hun·gri·er**; **hun·gri·est**) wanting to eat: *I'm hungry. Let's eat soon.* ☞ Look at **thirsty**.

IDM **go hungry** not have any food: *I'd rather go hungry than eat that!* —**hun·gri·ly** /-əli/ *adv.*

hunk /hʌŋk/ *noun* [C] **1** a large piece of sth: *a hunk of bread* **2** (*informal*) a man who is considered to be sexually attractive because he is big and strong: *What a hunk!*

☆ **hunt¹** /hʌnt/ *verb* [I,T] **1** to chase wild animals, etc. in order to catch or kill them either for sport or for food: *Owls hunt at night.* ○ *Are tigers still hunted in India?*

i	ɪ	ɛ	æ	ɑ	ɔ	ʌ	ʊ	u
see	sit	ten	cat	hot	saw	cup	put	too

☛ We often use the expression **go hunting** when we are talking about spending time hunting: *to go duck hunting.*

2 hunt (for) (sb/sth) to look or search for sb/sth: *I hunted everywhere for my gloves, but I still can't find them.* ○ *The police are still hunting the murderer.*

☆ **hunt²** /hʌnt/ *noun* [C] **1** [usually sing.] the act of searching or looking for sb/sth: *a job hunt* ○ *The police have launched a hunt for the missing child.* **2** the act of hunting wild animals, etc.: *a fox hunt*

☆ **hunt·er** /'hʌntər/ *noun* [C] a person or animal that hunts: *(figurative) a bargain hunter*

hunt·ing /'hʌntɪŋ/ *noun* [U] the chasing and killing of wild animals: *Hunting and fishing are Dan's favorite hobbies.* ☛ Look at **shoot**.

hur·dle /'hərdl/ *noun* **1** [C] a type of light fence that you jump over in a race **2 hurdles** [plural] a race over hurdles (1): *the 200-meter hurdles* **3** [C] a problem or difficulty that you must overcome

hurl /hərl/ *verb* [T] to throw sth with force

☆ **hur·ri·cane** /'hərəkən/ *noun* [C] a storm with very strong winds and heavy rain, over or near the ocean ☛ Look at the note at **storm**.

hur·ried /'hərid/ *adj.* done (too) quickly: *a hurried meal* ☛ The opposite is **unhurried**. —**hur·ried·ly** *adv.*

☆ **hur·ry¹** /'həri/ *noun* [U] a need or wish to do sth quickly: *Take your time. There's no hurry.* ○ *What's the hurry?*

IDM in a hurry 1 quickly: *She got up late and left in a hurry.* **2** wanting to do sth soon: *They are in a hurry to get the job done before winter.*

in no hurry; not in any hurry 1 not needing or wishing to do sth quickly: *We weren't in any hurry, so we stopped to admire the view.* **2** unwilling: *I am in no hurry to repeat that experience.*

☆ **hur·ry²** /'həri/ *verb* (*pres. part.* **hur·ry·ing**; *3rd pers. sing. pres.* **hur·ries**; *p.t., p.p.* **hur·ried**) **1** [I] to move or do sth quickly: *Don't hurry. There's plenty of time.* ○ *They hurried back home after school.* **2** [T] to cause sb/sth to do or to happen more quickly: *He was hurried into a decision.*

PHRV hurry up (*informal*) to move or do sth more quickly: *Hurry up or we'll miss our flight.*

☆ **hurt¹** /hərt/ *verb* (*p.t., p.p.* **hurt**) **1** [T] to cause pain or injury: *Did he hurt himself?* ○ *I fell and hurt my arm.* ○ *No one was seriously hurt in the accident.* ○ *(figurative) The tax increase will hurt families on low incomes.*

☛ Compare **hurt, injure** and **wound**. A person may be **wounded** by a knife, sword, gun, etc., usually as a result of fighting: *a wounded soldier.* People are usually **injured** in an accident: *Five people were badly injured in the crash.* **Hurt** and **injured** are similar in meaning but **hurt** is more often used when

the damage is not very great: *I hurt my leg when I fell off my bike.*

2 [I] to produce a feeling of pain: *My leg hurts.* ○ *It hurts when I lift my leg.* ○ *These shoes hurt; they're too tight.* **3** [T] to make sb unhappy; to upset sb: *His unkind remarks hurt her deeply.*

IDM it won't/wouldn't hurt (sb/sth) (to do sth) (*informal*) it would be a good thing for sb/sth (to do): *It wouldn't hurt you to get some exercise.*

hurt² /hərt/ *noun* [U] (*formal*) mental pain or suffering

hurt·ful /'hərtfl/ *adj.* unkind; upsetting: *to say hurtful things*

☆ **hus·band** /'hʌzbənd/ *noun* [C] a man that a woman is married to: *a good husband and father* ○ *Her ex-husband sees the kids once a month.*

hush /hʌʃ/ *noun* [sing.] silence: *As he rose to speak, a hush fell over the audience.*

husk·y¹ /'hʌski/ *adj.* (**husk·i·er; husk·i·est**) **1** (used about a voice) sounding rough and quiet as if your throat were dry **2** (used about a man or boy) having a strong, wide body

husk·y² (*also* **huskie**) /'hʌski/ *noun* [C] (*pl.* **hus·kies**) a strong dog with thick fur that is used in teams for pulling heavy loads over snow

hus·tle /'hʌsl/ *verb* **1** [I] (*informal*) to move or do sth quickly and with a lot of energy: *We've got to hustle if we want to win this game!* **2** [T] to push or move sb roughly: *The demonstrators were hustled into police cars.*

hut /hʌt/ *noun* [C] a small building with one room, usually made of wood or metal

hy·drant /'haɪdrənt/ *noun* [C] = FIRE HYDRANT

hy·drau·lic /haɪ'drɔlɪk/ *adj.* worked by water or another liquid moving through pipes, etc.: *hydraulic brakes*

hy·dro·e·lec·tric /ˌhaɪdroʊɪ'lɛktrɪk/ *adj.* **1** using the power of water to produce electricity: *a hydroelectric dam* **2** (used about electricity) produced by the power of water: *hydroelectric power*

hy·dro·gen /'haɪdrədʒən/ *noun* [U] (*symbol* **H**) a light colorless gas. Hydrogen and oxygen form water (H_2O).

hy·giene /'haɪdʒin/ *noun* [U] (the rules of) keeping yourself and things around you clean, in order to prevent illness: *High standards of hygiene are essential when you are preparing food.* ○ *personal hygiene*

hy·gi·en·ic /ˌhaɪdʒi'ɛnɪk; haɪ'dʒɛnɪk; haɪ'dʒinɪk/ *adj.* clean, without the germs that cause disease: *hygienic conditions* ☛ The opposite is **unhygienic**. —**hy·gi·en·i·cal·ly** /-kli/ *adv.*

hymn /hɪm/ *noun* [C] a song of praise to God that Christians sing together in church, etc.

ə	y	w	t̬	eɪ	aɪ	ɔɪ	aʊ	oʊ
about	yes	woman	butter	say	five	boy	now	go

hype /haɪp/ *noun* [U] (*informal*) advertisements or statements that make sth seem better or more important than it really is: *media hype surrounding the Internet*

hy·phen /ˈhaɪfən/ *noun* [C] the punctuation mark (-) used for joining two words together (e.g. *so-called*, *red-hot*) or to show that a word has been divided and continues on the next line

hy·phen·ate /ˈhaɪfəneɪt/ *verb* [T] to write with a hyphen: *"Red-hot" is hyphenated.* —**hy·phen·a·tion** /ˌhaɪfəˈneɪʃn/ *noun* [U]

hyp·no·sis /hɪpˈnoʊsəs/ *noun* [U] (the producing of) a state that is like deep sleep where sb's mind and actions can be controlled by another person: *She was questioned under hypnosis.* —**hyp·not·ic** /hɪpˈnɑtɪk/ *adj.*: *The rhythmic dance had a hypnotic effect on the audience.*

hyp·no·tize /ˈhɪpnətaɪz/ *verb* [T] to use hypnosis on sb

hy·poc·ri·sy /hɪˈpɑkrəsi/ *noun* [U] pretending to feel, believe, etc. sth that is different from what you really feel, etc.; saying one thing and doing another

hyp·o·crite /ˈhɪpəkrɪt/ *noun* [C] a person who pretends to have feelings and opinions which he/she does not really have —**hy·po·crit·i·cal** /ˌhɪpəˈkrɪtɪkl/ *adj.* —**hyp·o·crit·i·cal·ly** /-kli/ *adv.*

hy·po·der·mic /ˌhaɪpəˈdərmɪk/ *adj.* used for putting drugs into the body through the skin: *a hypodermic needle/syringe*

hy·poth·e·sis /haɪˈpɑθəsəs/ *noun* [C] (*pl.* **hy·poth·e·ses** /-siz/) an idea that is suggested as the possible explanation for sth: *to test a scientific hypothesis*

hy·po·thet·i·cal /ˈhaɪpəˈθɛtɪkl/ *adj.* based on situations that have not yet happened, not on facts: *That's a hypothetical question because we don't know what the situation will be next year.* —**hy·po·thet·i·cal·ly** /-kli/ *adv.*

hys·ter·i·a /hɪˈstɛriə; -ˈstɪr-/ *noun* [U] a state of excitement in which a person or a group of people cannot control their emotions, e.g. cannot stop laughing, crying, shouting, etc.: *mass hysteria*

hys·ter·i·cal /hɪˈstɛrɪkl/ *adj.* **1** caused by or suffering from hysteria: *hysterical crying* ○ *She was hysterical with grief.* **2** (*informal*) very funny —**hys·ter·i·cal·ly** /-kli/ *adv.*

Ii

I, i¹ /aɪ/ *noun* [C] (*pl.* **I's**; **i's**) the ninth letter of the English alphabet: *"Island" begins with (an) "I."*

☆ **I²** /aɪ/ *pron.* (the subject of a verb) the person who is speaking or writing: *I called and said that I was busy.* ○ *I'm not going to fall, am I?* ○ *I'm taller than you, aren't I?* ○ *She and I are planning to go out later.*

I³ /aɪ/ *abbr.* = INTERSTATE¹: *Head east on I-90 for about 25 miles.*

☆ **ice¹** /aɪs/ *noun* [U] water that has frozen solid: *Do you want ice in your drink?* ○ *I slipped on a patch of ice.* ○ *The ice on the lake isn't thick enough to walk on.* ○ *The ice quickly melted in the sunshine.* ○ *black ice* (= ice on roads, that cannot be seen easily)

ice² /aɪs/ *verb* [T] to cover a cake with a thin sweet mixture (**icing**)

ice·berg /ˈaɪsbɜrg/ *noun* [C] a very large block of ice that is floating in the ocean: *The ship hit an iceberg and sank.*

IDM **the tip of the iceberg** ⇨ TIP¹

ice·box /ˈaɪsbɑks/ *noun* [C] (*old-fashioned*) = REFRIGERATOR

ice-'cold *adj.* very cold: *ice-cold beer* ○ *Your hands are ice-cold.*

☆ **ice cream** *noun* [U] a frozen sweet food that is made from cream

ice cube *noun* [C] a small block of ice that you put in a drink to make it cold

iced /aɪst/ *adj.* (used about drinks) served very cold, with ice: *iced tea* ○ *iced coffee*

ice skate¹ (*also* **skate**) *noun* [C] a boot with a thick metal blade on the bottom that is used for ice skating

ice skate² (*also* **skate**) *verb* [I] to move over ice on ice skates

☞ **Go ice skating** is a common way of talking about ice skating for pleasure: *We go ice skating every weekend.*

i·ci·cle /ˈaɪsɪkl/ *noun* [C] a pointed piece of ice that is formed by water freezing as it falls or runs down from sth

ic·ing /ˈaɪsɪŋ/ *noun* [U] a thin mixture of powdered sugar, water or milk and sometimes butter and flavoring, etc. that is used for decorating cakes: *chocolate icing* ☞ Look at **frosting**.

i·con /ˈaɪkɑn/ *noun* [C] **1** a person or thing that is considered to be a symbol of sth: *Elvis Presley and other icons of 1950s popular culture* **2** (*computing*) a small picture or symbol on a computer screen that represents a computer program: *Click on the "print" icon and select the correct paper size.* ☞ picture on page A29.

ər	ɪr	ɛr	ɑr	ɔr	ʊr	ʒ	h	ŋ
bird	near	hair	car	north	tour	vision	hat	sing

ic·y /ˈaɪsi/ adj. (**ic·i·er**; **ic·i·est**) **1** very cold: an icy wind **2** covered with ice: icy roads

ID /ˌaɪˈdi/ noun [C,U] (informal) = IDENTIFICATION(2)

I'd /aɪd/ short for I HAD, I WOULD

I'D card noun [C] (informal) = IDENTITY CARD

☆ **i·de·a** /aɪˈdiə/ noun **1** [C] a plan or suggestion: That's a good idea! ○ He has an idea for a new play. ○ I had the bright idea of getting Jane to help me with my homework. ○ Does anyone have any ideas about how to tackle this problem? ○ It was your idea to invite so many people to the party. **2** [U, sing.] a picture or thought in your mind: Do you have any idea how much this cost? ○ You have no idea (= you can't imagine) how difficult it was! ○ The program gave a good idea of what life was like back then. **3** [C] an opinion or belief: She has her own ideas about how to bring up children. ○ If that's your idea of a joke, I don't think it's funny. **4 the idea** [sing.] the aim or purpose of sth: The idea of the course is to help people communicate.

IDM get the idea to understand: It was a mess! Piles of trash everywhere, empty beer bottles... you get the idea.

get the idea (that)... to get the feeling or impression that...: Where did you get the idea that I was paying for this meal?

not have the faintest idea ⇨ FAINT[1]

☆ **i·de·al¹** /aɪˈdiəl/ adj. the best possible; perfect: In an ideal world, there would be no poverty.

i·de·al² /aɪˈdiəl/ noun [C] **1** an idea or principle that seems perfect to you and that you want to achieve: She finds it hard to live up to her parents' high ideals. ○ Christian ideals **2** [usually sing.] a perfect example of a person or thing: Fashion magazines present very thin models as the ideal of beauty.

i·de·al·ism /aɪˈdiəlɪzəm/ noun [U] the belief that people should have high ideals and live according to them, or that the world can be made perfect: Young people are usually full of idealism. ☞ Look at realism.

i·de·al·ist /aɪˈdiəlɪst/ noun [C] a person who has high ideals (but who is sometimes not very practical) —**i·de·al·is·tic** /ˌaɪdiəˈlɪstɪk/ adj.

i·de·al·ly /aɪˈdiəli/ adv. **1** perfectly: She's ideally suited to the job. **2** in an ideal situation: Ideally, no class should have over 25 students.

i·den·ti·cal /aɪˈdɛntɪkl/ adj. identical (to/with sb/sth) exactly the same as: I can't see any difference between these two pens – they look identical to me. —**i·den·ti·cal·ly** /-kli/ adv.

i,dentical 'twin noun [C, usually pl.] one of two children who come from the same egg of the mother and so are of the same sex and look exactly alike

☆ **i·den·ti·fi·ca·tion** /aɪˌdɛntəfəˈkeɪʃn/ noun [C,U] **1** the act of identifying or being identified: We cannot name the victim until a positive identification of the body has been made. **2**

(also informal **ID**) an official card, paper, etc. that proves who you are: Do you have any identification? ○ They're checking IDs at the door.

☆ **i·den·ti·fy** /aɪˈdɛntəfaɪ/ verb [T] (pres. part. **i·den·ti·fy·ing**; 3rd pers. sing. pres. **i·den·ti·fies**; p.t., p.p. **i·den·ti·fied**) **identify sb/sth (as sb/sth)** to recognize or say who or what sb/sth is: The police need someone to identify the body. ○ to identify the cause of a problem ○ She has been identified as the main suspect in the case.

PHRV identify with sb to feel that you understand and share what sb else is feeling: I found it hard to identify with the woman in the movie.

identify (yourself) with sb/sth to be connected with sb/sth

☆ **i·den·ti·ty** /aɪˈdɛntəti/ noun [C,U] (pl. **i·den·ti·ties**) who or what a person or a thing is: There are few clues to the identity of the killer. ○ The region has its own cultural identity. ○ The arrest was a case of mistaken identity (= the wrong person was arrested by the police). ○ Children of immigrants often suffer from a loss of identity (= they are not sure which culture they belong to).

i'dentity card (also informal **I'D card**) noun [C] a card, usually with your picture on it, that proves who you are

i·de·ol·o·gy /ˌaɪdiˈɑlədʒi/ noun [C,U] (pl. **i·de·ol·o·gies**) a set of ideas which form the basis for a political or economic system: Marxist ideology —**i·de·o·log·i·cal** /ˌaɪdiəˈlɑdʒɪkl/ adj.

☆ **id·i·om** /ˈɪdiəm/ noun [C] a expression with a meaning that you cannot guess from the meanings of the separate words: The idiom "twist sb's arm" means "force sb to do sth."

id·i·o·mat·ic /ˌɪdiəˈmætɪk/ adj. **1** containing an idiom or idioms: an idiomatic expression **2** using language in a way that sounds natural: She speaks good idiomatic English.

id·i·ot /ˈɪdiət/ noun [C] (informal) a stupid or foolish person: I was an idiot to believe what he said. —**id·i·ot·ic** /ˌɪdiˈɑtɪk/ adj. – **id·i·ot·i·cal·ly** /-kli/ adv.

i·dle /ˈaɪdl/ adj. **1** not doing anything; not being used: The factory stood idle while the machines were being repaired. **2** not wanting to work hard; lazy **3** (formal) (only before a noun) not to be taken seriously because it will not have any result: an idle promise —**i·dle·ness** noun [U] —**i·dly** /ˈaɪdli/ adv.

i·dol /ˈaɪdl/ noun [C] **1** a statue that people worship as a god **2** a person (such as a movie star or pop musician) who is admired or loved: When I was 14, Madonna was my idol.

i·dyl·lic /aɪˈdɪlɪk; ɪˈd-/ adj. very pleasant and peaceful: an idyllic Caribbean resort

i.e. /ˈaɪ i/ abbr. that is; in other words: a study of people who are obese, i.e. more than 30% overweight

☆ **if** /ɪf/ conj. **1** (used in sentences in which one thing happens or is true, depending on

whether another thing happens or is true): *If you see him, give him this letter.* ○ *We won't go to the beach if it rains.* ○ *If I had more time, I would learn another language.* ○ *If I had known about the accident, I would have gone to see her in the hospital.* ○ *I might see her tomorrow. If not, I'll see her this weekend.* **2** (used after verbs such as "ask," "know," "remember"): *They asked if we wanted to go too.* ○ *I can't remember if I mailed the letter or not.* ☛ Look at the note at **whether**. **3** (used when you are asking sb to do sth or suggesting sth very politely): *If you would just come this way, sir.* ○ *If I could add something…*

IDM as if ⇨ AS

even if ⇨ EVEN[2]

if I were you (used when you are giving sb advice): *If I were you, I'd leave now.*

if only (used for expressing a strong wish): *If only I had a decent car!* ○ *If only he'd call!*

ig·loo /'ɪglu/ *noun* [C] (*pl.* **ig·loos**) a traditional type of small house that is built from blocks of ice by people in the Arctic regions of North America

ig·nite /ɪg'naɪt/ *verb* [I,T] (*formal*) to start burning or to make sth start burning: *A spark from the engine ignited the fuel.*

ig·ni·tion /ɪg'nɪʃn/ *noun* **1** [U] starting to burn or making sth start burning: *accidental ignition of a gas tank* **2** [C] the electrical system that starts the engine of a car: *to turn the ignition on/off* ○ *He had left his key in the ignition.*

ig·no·rance /'ɪgnərəns/ *noun* [U] lack of information or knowledge (about sth): *The mistake was due to ignorance.* ○ *widespread ignorance of the new regulations*

ig·no·rant /'ɪgnərənt/ *adj.* **1** not knowing about sth: *Many people are ignorant of their rights.* ○ *I'm pretty ignorant about modern technology.* **2** not educated; stupid

☆ **ig·nore** /ɪg'nɔr/ *verb* [T] to pay no attention to sb/sth: *I said hi to Debby, but she totally ignored me* (= acted as if she hadn't seen me). ○ *George ignored his doctor's advice about smoking less.*

☛ Be careful. **Ignore** and **be ignorant** are very different in meaning.

☆ **ill¹** /ɪl/ *adj.* **1** (not usually before a noun) not in good health; not well; sick: *I became ill after eating shellfish.* ○ *terminally ill patients* ○ *mentally ill*

☛ **Ill** is more formal than **sick**. We usually use **ill** with an adverb to describe how sick a person is: *seriously ill*

2 (only *before* a noun) bad or harmful: *There should be no ill will* (= bad feelings) *between friends.* ○ *We suffered no ill effects from all that rich food.*

ill² /ɪl/ *adv.* **1** (often in compounds) badly or wrongly: *You would be ill-advised to drive*

until you have fully recovered. **2** (*formal*) only with difficulty; not easily: *They could ill afford the extra money for college tuition.*

IDM bode well/ill (for sb/sth) ⇨ BODE

I'll /aɪl/ *short for* I WILL, I SHALL

☆ **il·le·gal** /ɪ'lig l/ *adj.* not allowed by the law; not legal: *It is illegal to own a gun without a license.* ○ *illegal drugs* ○ *illegal immigrants* (= people who enter a country illegally) —**il·le·gal·ly** *adv.*

il·leg·i·ble /ɪ'lɛdʒəbl/ *adj.* difficult or impossible to read: *The doctor's handwriting is completely illegible.* ☛ The opposite is **legible**. —**il·leg·i·bly** /-əbli/ *adv.*

il·le·git·i·mate /ˌɪlə'dʒɪtəmət/ *adj.* **1** (used about a child) born to parents who are not married to each other **2** not allowed by law; against the rules: *the sale of weapons for illegitimate purposes* —**il·le·git·i·ma·cy** /ˌɪlə'dʒɪtəməsi/ *noun* [U]

ill-fat·ed /ˌɪl 'feɪtəd/ *adj.* unlucky; having an unlucky or unsuccessful result: *a list of the victims aboard the ill-fated flight*

il·lic·it /ɪ'lɪsət/ *adj.* (used about an activity or substance) not allowed by law or by the rules of society: *the illicit trade in drugs* ○ *They were having an illicit affair.* ☛ The usual opposite of illicit is **legal**.

il·lit·er·ate /ɪ'lɪtərət/ *adj.* **1** not able to read or write **2** showing that you have little education or knowledge, especially in a particular subject: *computer illiterate* —**il·lit·er·a·cy** /ɪ'lɪtərəsi/ *noun* [U]: *adult illiteracy*

☆ **ill·ness** /'ɪlnəs/ *noun* **1** [U] the state of being physically or mentally ill: *There is a history of mental illness in the family.* **2** [C] a type or period of physical or mental ill health: *Although it is serious, cancer is not always a fatal illness.* ○ *She died after a long illness.* ☛ Look at the note at **disease**.

il·log·i·cal /ɪ'ladʒɪkl/ *adj.* not sensible or reasonable; not logical: *It seems illogical to pay somebody for doing work that you could do yourself.* —**il·log·i·cal·ly** /-kli/ *adv.*

il·lu·mi·nate /ɪ'luməneɪt/ *verb* [T] (*formal*) **1** to give light to sth or to decorate sth with lights: *The church was illuminated by floodlights.* **2** to explain sth or make sth clear —**il·lu·mi·na·tion** /ɪˌlumə'neɪʃn/ *noun* [U]

il·lu·mi·nat·ing /ɪ'luməneɪtɪŋ/ *adj.* helping to explain sth or make sth clear: *an illuminating discussion*

il·lu·sion /ɪ'luʒn/ *noun* **1** [C,U] a false idea, belief or impression: *I have no illusions about the situation – I know it's serious.* **2** [C] something that your eyes tell you is there or is true but in fact is not: *That plane seems to be flying very slowly, but that's just an optical illusion.*

IDM be under an/the illusion (that) to believe wrongly: *I think he's under the illusion that we're rich.*

☆ **il·lus·trate** /'ɪləstreɪt/ verb [T] **1** to explain or make sth clear by using examples, pictures or diagrams: *These statistics illustrate the point that I was making.* **2** to add pictures, diagrams, etc. to a book or magazine: *an illustrated cookbook*

☆ **il·lus·tra·tion** /ˌɪlə'streɪʃn/ noun **1** [C] a drawing, diagram or picture in a book or magazine: *color illustrations* **2** [C] an example that makes a point or an idea clear **3** [U] the activity or art of illustrating

I'm /aɪm/ short for I AM

☆ **im·age** /'ɪmɪdʒ/ noun [C] **1** the general impression that a person or an organization gives to the public: *Advertising has to create a positive image of the product it is selling.* **2** a mental picture or idea of sb/sth: *Many people have an image of Canada as being cold all the time.* **3** a picture or description that appears in a book, movie or painting: *horrific images of war* **4** a copy or reflection: *A perfect image of the building was reflected in the lake.*

im·age·ry /'ɪmɪdʒri/ noun [U] the use of descriptions and comparisons in language in order to have a strong effect on people's imagination and emotions

i·mag·i·na·ble /ɪ'mædʒənəbl/ adj. (often after a noun) that you can think of: *The deli has every imaginable kind of cheese.* ○ *It was the worst day imaginable!*

☆ **i·mag·i·nar·y** /ɪ'mædʒəˌnɛri/ adj. existing only in the mind; not real: *Many children have imaginary friends.*

☆ **i·mag·i·na·tion** /ɪˌmædʒə'neɪʃn/ noun **1** [C,U] the ability to create mental pictures or new ideas: *He has a lively imagination.* ○ *She's very intelligent, but she doesn't have much imagination.*

☞ **Imagination** is a creative quality that a person has. **Fantasy** consists of daydreams about stories and situations that are not related to reality.

2 [C] the part of the mind that uses this ability: *to use your imagination*

i·mag·i·na·tive /ɪ'mædʒənətɪv/ adj. having or showing imagination: *She's always full of imaginative ideas.* ○ *His writing is highly imaginative.* ☞ The opposite is **unimaginative**. —**i·mag·i·na·tive·ly** adv.

☆ **i·mag·ine** /ɪ'mædʒən/ verb [T] **1** to form a picture or idea of sth in the mind: *Imagine the colors of the forest in the fall.* ○ *Imagine that you're lying on a beach.* ○ *It's not easy to imagine your brother as a doctor.* ○ *I can't imagine myself working in an office.* ○ *I can imagine how you felt.* **2** to see, hear or think sth that is not true or does not exist: *There's nobody at the door – you're just imagining things.* **3** to think of sth as probable; to suppose: *I imagine he'll be tired when he gets home.*

im·bal·ance /ˌɪm'bæləns/ noun [C] a difference or lack of equality: *an imbalance between our import and export trade*

im·i·tate /'ɪmətɪt/ verb [T] **1** to copy the behavior of sb/sth: *Small children learn by imitating their parents.* **2** to copy the speech or actions of sb/sth, often in order to be amusing: *She could imitate her mother perfectly.*

☆ **im·i·ta·tion** /ˌɪmə'teɪʃn/ noun **1** [C] a copy (of a real thing): *Some artificial flowers are good imitations of real ones.* ○ *This suitcase is made of imitation leather* (= of material that is made to look like leather). ☞ Look at **genuine**. **2** [C] a copy (of a person's speech or behavior): *He can do a very good imitations of the teacher.* **3** [U] the act of copying sth: *Good pronunciation of a language is best learned by imitation.*

im·mac·u·late /ɪ'mækyələt/ adj. perfectly clean and neat: *His house is always immaculate.* ○ *immaculate white shirts* —**im·mac·u·late·ly** adv.

im·ma·ture /ˌɪmə'tʃʊr; -'tʊr/ adj. **1** not fully grown or developed; not mature: *an immature body* **2** (used about a person) not behaving in a way that is as sensible as you would expect for a person of that age: *Some students are very immature when they go to college.*

☆ **im·me·di·ate** /ɪ'midiət/ adj. **1** happening or done without delay: *I'd like an immediate answer to my proposal.* **2** (only before a noun) existing now and needing attention: *Tell me what your immediate needs are.* **3** (only before a noun) nearest in time, position or relationship: *They won't make any changes in the immediate future.* ○ *He has left most of his money to his immediate family* (= parents, children, brothers and sisters).

☆ **im·me·di·ate·ly** /ɪ'midiətli/ adv. **1** now; without delay: *We need an ambulance immediately!* **2** directly; very closely: *He wasn't immediately involved in the crime.* **3** (formal) nearest in time or position: *Who's the girl immediately in front of Dan?* ○ *What did you do immediately after college?* ☞ It is more common to use **right** with this meaning: *She was sitting right in front of me.*

im·mense /ɪ'mɛns/ adj. very large or great: *immense difficulties* ○ *She gets immense pleasure from her job.*

im·mense·ly /ɪ'mɛnsli/ adv. extremely; very much: *immensely enjoyable*

im·men·si·ty /ɪ'mɛnsəti/ noun [U] very large size or extent

im·merse /ɪ'mɜrs/ verb [T] **1 immerse yourself (in sth)** to involve yourself deeply in sth so that you give it all your attention: *Rachel's usually immersed in a book.* **2 immerse sth (in sth)** to put sth into a liquid so that it is covered

☆ **im·mi·grant** /'ɪməgrənt/ noun [C] a person who has come into a foreign country to live there permanently: *recent immigrants to the*

United States ○ *illegal immigrants* (= people who come to live in a country without permission) ○ *New York has a high immigrant population.* ☞ The United States has many immigrant communities which make it a **multicultural society**. Look also at **emigrant**.

☆ **im·mi·grate** /ˈɪməgreɪt/ *verb* [I] to enter a country in order to live there: *His family immigrated to the United States from Taiwan in 1982.* ☞ Look also at **emigrate**.

☆ **im·mi·gra·tion** /ˌɪməˈɡreɪʃn/ *noun* [U] **1** entering a country in order to live there: *There are more controls on immigration than there used to be.* ○ *the Immigration and Naturalization Service* **2** the control point at an airport, port, etc. where the documents of people who want to come into a country are checked: *When you leave the plane, you have to go through customs and immigration.*

im·mi·nent /ˈɪmənənt/ *adj.* (usually used about sth bad) almost certain to happen very soon: *Heavy rainfall in the Ohio Valley means that flooding is imminent.* —**im·mi·nent·ly** *adv.*

im·mo·bile /ɪˈmoʊbl/ *adj.* not moving or not able to move —**im·mo·bil·i·ty** /ˌɪməˈbɪləti/ *noun* [U]

im·mo·bi·lize /ɪˈmoʊbəlaɪz/ *verb* [T] to prevent sb/sth from moving or working normally: *The airport was completely immobilized by the blizzard.*

im·mor·al /ɪˈmɔrəl; -ˈmɑr-/ *adj.* wrong according to the accepted rules of behavior; not moral: *I think experiments on animals are immoral.* —**im·mor·al·i·ty** /ˌɪməˈræləti/ *noun* [U] —**im·mor·al·ly** *adv.*

im·mor·tal /ɪˈmɔrtl/ *adj.* living or lasting for ever: *Nobody is immortal – we all have to die sometime.* ○ (*figurative*) *Shakespeare's immortal plays* —**im·mor·tal·i·ty** /ˌɪmɔrˈtæləti/ *noun* [U]

im·mor·tal·ize /ɪˈmɔrtl aɪz/ *verb* [T] to give lasting fame to sb/sth (especially in a book, movie or painting): *The historic occasion was immortalized in a poem.*

im·mune /ɪˈmyun/ *adj.* **1 immune (to sth)** protected against a certain disease or illness because you have a resistance to it: *You should be immune to measles if you've had it already.* **2 immune (to sth)** not affected by sth: *You can say what you want – I'm immune to criticism!* **3 immune (from sth)** protected from a danger or punishment: *Are young children immune from prosecution?*

imˈmune ˌsystem *noun* [C] the system in your body that protects you from diseases

im·mu·ni·ty /ɪˈmyunəti/ *noun* [U] the ability to avoid or be unaffected by disease, criticism, court cases, etc.: *immunity to disease* ○ *Ambassadors to other countries receive diplomatic immunity* (= protection from being tried in a court of law, etc.).

im·mu·nize /ˈɪmyənaɪz/ *verb* [T] to make sb immune to a disease, usually by giving an injection of a substance (**vaccine**): *Before visiting certain countries, you will need to be immunized against cholera.* ☞ Look at **vaccinate**. —**im·mu·ni·za·tion** (*also* **immunisation**) /ˌɪmyənəˈzeɪʃn/ *noun* [C,U]

☆ **im·pact¹** /ˈɪmpækt/ *noun* **1** [C, usually sing.] **an impact (on/upon sb/sth)** an effect or impression: *Her speech made a great impact on the audience.* **2** [U] the action or force of one object hitting another: *The impact of the crash threw the passengers out of their seats.* ○ *The bomb exploded on impact* (= when it hit something).

im·pact² /ˈɪmpækt/ *verb* [I,T] **impact (on) sb/sth** to have a strong effect on sb/sth, especially in a bad or negative way: *How will the new shopping center impact the businesses downtown?*

☞ Many people do not like the use of **impact** as a verb. They prefer to use the verb **affect**.

im·pair /ɪmˈpɛr/ *verb* [T] to damage or weaken sth: *Ear infections can result in impaired hearing.* ☞ Look at **hearing-impaired** and at the note at **handicapped**.

im·part /ɪmˈpɑrt/ *verb* [T] (*formal*) **1 impart sth (to sb)** to tell or teach: *What kind of values are we imparting to our children?* **2 impart sth (to sth)** to give: *Grilling will impart a smoky flavor to the fish.*

im·par·tial /ɪmˈpɑrʃl/ *adj.* fair or neutral; not preferring one to another: *A referee must be impartial.* —**im·par·ti·al·i·ty** /ˌɪmˌpɑrʃiˈæləti/ *noun* [U] —**im·par·tial·ly** /-ʃəli/ *adv.*

im·pass·a·ble /ɪmˈpæsəbl/ *adj.* (used about a road, etc.) impossible to travel on because it is blocked: *Flooding and fallen trees have made many roads impassable.*

im·passe /ˈɪmpæs/ *noun* [usually sing.] a situation in which it is impossible to make any more progress: *Negotiations have reached an impasse.*

☆ **im·pa·tient** /ɪmˈpeɪʃnt/ *adj.* **1 impatient (with sb/sth)** not able to wait for sb/sth calmly; easily annoyed by sb/sth that seems slow; not patient: *Don't be so impatient – it's your turn next.* ○ *The passengers are getting impatient due to the delay.* ○ *It's no good being impatient with small children.* **2 impatient (to do sth); impatient (for sth)** (not before a noun) wanting sth to happen soon: *By the time they are seniors, many young people are impatient to leave high school.* ○ *At the end of winter, we are often impatient for spring to come.* —**im·pa·tience** /ɪmˈpeɪʃns/ *noun* [U]: *He began to explain for the third time with growing impatience.* —**im·pa·tient·ly** *adv.*

im·peach /ɪmˈpitʃ/ *verb* [T] to accuse a politician, judge, etc. formally of breaking the law or acting wrongly in his/her job: *The state*

ər	ɪr	ɛr	ɑr	ɔr	ʊr	ʒ	h	ŋ
bird	near	hair	car	north	tour	vision	hat	sing

House of Representatives voted to impeach the governor. —**im·peach·ment** /-mənt/ noun [U]

im·pec·ca·ble /ɪmˈpɛkəbl/ adj. perfect; without any mistakes: impeccable behavior ○ His accent is impeccable. —**im·pec·ca·bly** /-bli/ adv.

im·pede /ɪmˈpid/ verb [T] (formal) to make it difficult for sb/sth to move or make progress: The completion of the new expressway has been impeded by bad weather conditions.

im·ped·i·ment /ɪmˈpɛdəmənt/ noun [C] (formal) 1 something that makes it difficult for a person or thing to move or progress: The high tax rate will be a major impediment to new businesses. 2 something that makes speaking difficult: a speech impediment

im·pend·ing /ɪmˈpɛndɪŋ/ adj. (only before a noun) (usually used about sth bad) that will happen soon: There was a feeling of impending disaster in the air.

im·per·a·tive[1] /ɪmˈpɛrətɪv/ adj. (formal) very important or urgent: It's imperative that you see a doctor immediately.

im·per·a·tive[2] /ɪmˈpɛrətɪv/ noun [C, sing.] (grammar) the form of the verb that is used for giving orders: In "Shut the door!" the verb is in the imperative.

im·per·fect /ɪmˈpərfɪkt/ adj. 1 with mistakes or faults; not perfect: This is a very imperfect system. 2 (only before a noun) (grammar) used for expressing action in the past that is not completed: In "While I was taking a bath," the verb is in the imperfect tense.

☞ We can also use **imperfect** as a noun and say: The verb is in the imperfect. It is more usual to call this tense the **past continuous** or **past progressive**.

—**im·per·fect·ly** adv.

im·pe·ri·al /ɪmˈpɪriəl/ adj. connected with an empire or its ruler: the imperial palace ○ imperial power

im·pe·ri·al·ism /ɪmˈpɪriəlɪzəm/ noun [U] a political system in which a rich and powerful country controls other countries (**colonies**) which are not so rich and powerful as itself —**im·pe·ri·al·ist** /ɪmˈpɪriəlɪst/ adj.

im·per·son·al /ɪmˈpərsənl/ adj. 1 not showing friendly human feelings; cold in feeling or atmosphere: A large organization can be very impersonal to work for. ○ The hotel room was very impersonal. 2 not referring to any particular person: Can we try to keep the discussion as impersonal as possible, please?

im·per·son·ate /ɪmˈpərsəneɪt/ verb [T] to copy the actions and way of speaking of a person or to pretend to be a different person: He was arrested for impersonating a medical doctor. —**im·per·son·a·tion** /ɪmˌpərsəˈneɪʃn/ noun [C,U] —**im·per·son·a·tor** noun [C]

im·per·vi·ous /ɪmˈpərviəs/ adj. 1 not allow-

ing water, etc. to pass through 2 not affected or influenced by sth: impervious to criticism

im·pe·tus /ˈɪmpətəs/ noun [sing., U] something that encourages sth else to happen: I need a fresh impetus to start working on this essay again.

im·pinge /ɪmˈpɪndʒ/ verb [I] **impinge on/upon sth** (formal) to have an effect on sth; to interfere with sth: I'm not going to let my job impinge on my family life.

im·plant[1] /ɪmˈplænt/ verb [T] to put sth into the body, usually in a medical operation: Surgeons implanted an artificial heart into a 64-year-old patient.

im·plant[2] /ˈɪmplænt/ noun [C] something that is implanted into the body: breast implants (= that make the breasts larger)

im·plau·si·ble /ɪmˈplɔzəbl/ adj. not easy to believe: an implausible excuse

im·ple·ment[1] /ˈɪmpləmənt/ noun [C] a tool or instrument (especially for work outdoors): farm implements ☞ Look at the note at **tool**.

im·ple·ment[2] /ˈɪmpləmɛnt/ verb [T] to start using a plan, system, etc.: The tax reforms will be implemented next year. —**im·ple·men·ta·tion** /ˌɪmpləmənˈteɪʃn/ noun [U]

im·pli·cate /ˈɪmpləkeɪt/ verb [T] **implicate sb (in sth)** (formal) (often passive) to show that sb is involved in sth bad, especially a crime: The mayor's brother was implicated in the scandal.

im·pli·ca·tion /ˌɪmpləˈkeɪʃn/ noun 1 [C] the effect that sth will have on sth else in the future: The new law will have serious implications for our work. 2 [C,U] something that is suggested but that is not said openly: The implication of her comments was that we had made a bad mistake. ☞ The verb is **imply**. Look also at **infer**.

im·plic·it /ɪmˈplɪsət/ adj. not expressed directly but understood by the people involved: an implicit agreement ☞ Look at **explicit**. —**im·plic·it·ly** adv.

im·plore /ɪmˈplɔr/ verb [T] (formal) to ask sb for sth or to do sth. You implore sb when the situation is very serious and you need sth very much: She implored him not to leave her alone. ○ "Don't leave me alone," she implored. ☞ Look at **beg**. It is similar in meaning.

im·ply /ɪmˈplaɪ/ verb [T] (pres. part. **im·ply·ing**; 3rd pers. sing. pres. **im·plies**; p.t., p.p. **im·plied**) to suggest sth in an indirect way or without actually saying it: The article implied that the senator was involved in the scandal. ☞ The noun is **implication**.

im·po·lite /ˌɪmpəˈlaɪt/ adj. rude; not polite: I think it was impolite of him to ask you to leave. —**im·po·lite·ly** adv.

☆ **im·port**[1] /ɪmˈpɔrt/ verb [T] **import sth (from ...)**; **import sth (into ...)** to buy goods, etc. from a foreign country and bring them into your own country: This country has to

tʃ	dʒ	v	θ	ð	s	z	ʃ
chin	June	van	thin	then	so	zoo	she

import most of its raw materials. ○ imported goods ○ America imports cars from Japan, Germany, South Korea, etc. **—im·port·er** noun [C]: Is America the world's largest importer of oil? ☞ The opposites are **export** and **exporter**.

☆ **im·port²** /ˈɪmpɔrt/ noun **1** [C, usually pl.] goods bought from a foreign country for sale or use in your own country: What are your country's major imports? ☞ The opposite is **export**. **2** [U] = IMPORTATION: new import quotas on agricultural products

☆ **im·por·tance** /ɪmˈpɔrtns/ noun [U] the state of being important; value: The decision was of great importance to the future of the business.

☆ **im·por·tant** /ɪmˈpɔrtnt/ adj. **1** having great value or influence; very necessary: an important meeting, decision, etc. ○ Tomorrow will be the most important day of my life! ○ Is money important for happiness? ○ It's important not to be late. ○ It's important that people learn at least one foreign language. ○ It's important for people to see the results of what they do. ○ It was important to me that you were there. **2** (used about a person) having great influence or authority: He was one of the most important writers of his time. ○ I soon got to know who was important in the company and who wasn't. ☞ The opposite is **unimportant**. **—im·por·tant·ly** adv.

im·por·ta·tion /ˌɪmpɔrˈteɪʃn/ (also **import**) noun [U] the action of bringing goods from a foreign country to sell or use in your own country: a ban on the importation of automatic weapons

im·pose /ɪmˈpoʊz/ verb **1** [T] to make sth be accepted because you are the person with power: to impose a tax increase on cigarettes ○ The government should impose restrictions on the use of harmful chemicals. ○ Parents should try not to impose their own ideas on their children. **2** [I] **impose (on/upon sb/sth)** to ask or expect sb to do sth that may cause extra work or trouble: I hope I'm not imposing – but could I come and stay at your house next week? ○ I hate to impose on you, but can you loan me $20?

im·pos·ing /ɪmˈpoʊzɪŋ/ adj. making an impression on people because it is big or important: I work in a large, imposing building in the center of town.

im·po·si·tion /ˌɪmpəˈzɪʃn/ noun **1** [U] the action of imposing: I'm against the imposition of unnecessary rules and regulations on people. **2** [C] an unfair or bad thing that sb has to accept; sth that causes extra work or trouble: "Please stay for supper." "Are you sure it's not an imposition?"

☆ **im·pos·si·ble** /ɪmˈpɑsəbl/ adj. **1** not able to be done or to happen; not possible: It's impossible for me to be there before 12. ○ I find it almost impossible to get up in the morning! ○ That horse is impossible to control. ○ That's impossible! (= I don't believe it!) **2** very difficult to

deal with or to make better: These kids are just impossible! ○ This is an impossible situation! **—im·pos·si·bil·i·ty** /ɪmˌpɑsəˈbɪləti/ noun [C,U] (pl. **im·pos·si·bil·i·ties**) [U]: the impossibility of reaching an agreement [C]: What you are suggesting is a complete impossibility! **—im·pos·si·bly** /-əbli/ adv.: impossibly high standards

the im'possible noun [sing.] something that cannot be done: Don't attempt the impossible, you'll never succeed!

im·pos·tor /ɪmˈpɑstər/ noun [C] a person who pretends to be sb else in order to trick other people

im·po·tent /ˈɪmpətənt/ adj. **1** without enough power or influence ☞ The opposite is **powerful**. **2** (used about men) not capable of having sex **—im·po·tence** /-əns/ noun [U]

im·pov·er·ished /ɪmˈpɑvərɪʃt/ adj. extremely poor: impoverished inner-city neighborhoods

im·prac·ti·cal /ɪmˈpræktɪkl/ adj. **1** not sensible or reasonable; not practical: an impractical suggestion ○ It would be impractical to take our bikes on vacation. **2** (used about a person) not good at doing ordinary everyday jobs: He's intelligent but completely impractical.

im·pre·cise /ˌɪmprɪˈsaɪs/ adj. not clear or exact; not precise: imprecise instructions

☆ **im·press** /ɪmˈprɛs/ verb [T] **1** **impress sb (with sth)** to make sb feel admiration and respect: She's always trying to impress people with her new outfits. ○ It impressed me that he understood immediately what I meant. **2** (formal) **impress sth on/upon sb** to make sth very clear to sb: I wish you could impress the importance of these tests on John.

☆ **im·pres·sion** /ɪmˈprɛʃn/ noun [C] **1** the effect that a person or thing produces on sb else: She gives the impression of being older than she really is. ○ I want to create an impression of light and space in the house. ○ Do you think I made a good impression on your parents? **2** an opinion about sb/sth (that is sometimes unclear or wrong): What's your impression of the new manager? ○ I'm not sure, but I have the impression that Jane is unhappy. ○ I was under the impression that you were married. **3** an amusing imitation of the behavior or speech of a well-known person: My brother does some marvelous impressions of TV stars. **4** a mark made by pressing an object hard into a surface

☆ **im·pres·sive** /ɪmˈprɛsɪv/ adj. causing a feeling of admiration and respect because of importance, size, excellent quality, etc.: an impressive building, speech, etc. ○ The way he handled the situation was very impressive. ☞ The opposite is **unimpressive**.

im·print /ˈɪmprɪnt/ noun [C] the mark made by pressing an object on a surface: the imprint of a foot in the sand

im·pris·on /ɪmˈprɪzn/ verb [T] (often passive) to put or keep in prison: He was imprisoned for assault with a deadly weapon. **—im·pris·on-**

ment /-mənt/ *noun* [U]: *She was sentenced to five years' imprisonment.* ∘ *life imprisonment*

im·prob·a·ble /ɪm'prɑbəbl/ *adj.* not likely to be true or to happen; not probable: *an improbable explanation* ∘ *an improbable result* ∘ *It is highly improbable that she will arrive tonight.* ☞ Look at **unlikely.** —**im·prob·a·bil·i·ty** /ɪmˌprɑbə'bɪlṭi/ *noun* [U] —**im·prob·a·bly** /-əbli/ *adv.*

im·promp·tu /ɪm'prɑmptu/ *adj., adv.* (done) without being prepared or organized : *an impromptu speech*

im·prop·er /ɪm'prɑpər/ *adj.* **1** illegal or not honest: *It seems that she had been involved in improper business deals.* **2** not correct or suitable for the situation: *The explosion was caused by improper storage of gasoline.* **3** rude (in a sexual way): *He lost his job for making improper suggestions to several of the female employees.* —**im·prop·er·ly** *adv.*

im·pro·pri·e·ty /ˌɪmprə'praɪəṭi/ *noun* [C,U] (*pl.* **im·pro·pri·e·ties**) (*formal*) the state of being improper; an improper act: *We are certain there were no improprieties in the handling of the deal.*

☆**im·prove** /ɪm'pruv/ *verb* [I,T] to become or to make sth better: *I hope the weather will improve later on.* ∘ *Your vocabulary is excellent, but you could improve your pronunciation.*

PHRV improve on/upon sth to produce sth that is better than sth else: *I think the movie improved on the book* (= the movie was better than the book). ∘ *Nobody will be able to improve on that score* (= nobody will be able to get a higher score).

☆**im·prove·ment** /ɪm'pruvmənt/ *noun* [C,U] **improvement (on/in/over sth)** (a) change which makes the quality or condition of sb/sth better: *There's been a considerable improvement in your mother's condition.* ∘ *These grades are a big improvement over your previous ones.* ∘ *Housing and public transportation are areas which need improvement.* ∘ *Even minor home improvements such as painting can increase the value of your house.*

im·pro·vise /'ɪmprəvaɪz/ *verb* [I,T] **1** to make, do, or manage sth quickly or without preparation, using what you have: *If you're short of workers today, you'll just have to improvise* (= manage somehow with the people who are there). **2** to play music, speak or act using your imagination instead of written or remembered material: *I can read music, but I can't improvise, so I can't play jazz.* ∘ *a hilarious improvised comedy act* —**im·prov·i·sa·tion** /ɪmˌprɑvə'zeɪʃn/ *noun* [C,U]

im·pulse /'ɪmpʌls/ *noun* [C] **1** a sudden desire to do sth without thinking about the results: *She felt a terrible impulse to steal something.* **2** a single push or signal in a nerve, wire, etc. that causes a reaction: *electrical impulses*

IDM on impulse without thinking or planning: *I just bought this cake on impulse when I saw it in the store..*

im·pul·sive /ɪm'pʌlsɪv/ *adj.* likely to act suddenly and without thinking; done without careful thought: *an impulsive shopper* ∘ *impulsive behavior* —**im·pul·sive·ly** *adv.* —**im·pul·sive·ness** *noun* [U]

im·pure /ɪm'pyʊər/ *adj.* **1** consisting of more than one substance (and therefore not of good quality); not pure: *impure metals* **2** (*old-fashioned*) (used about thoughts and actions connected with sex) not moral; bad

im·pu·ri·ty /ɪm'pyʊərəṭi/ *noun* (*pl.* **im·pu·ri·ties**) **1** [C, usually pl.] a substance that is present in another substance, making it of poor quality: *impurities in the water* **2** [U] the state of being impure

☆**in¹** /ɪn/ *adv.*

☞ For special uses with many verbs, e.g. **give in,** look at the verb entries.

1 to a position within a particular area: *She opened the door and went in.* ∘ *My suitcase is full. I can't get any more in.* ∘ *When does the plane get in?* (= to the airport). **2** at home or at work: *She won't be in until late today.* **3** (used about the movements of the ocean) at the highest point, when the water is closest to the land: *The tide's coming in.* **4** received by sb official: *Entries should be in by March 20.*

IDM be in for sth to be going to experience sth bad: *He's going to be in for a shock when he gets the bill.*

be/get in on sth to have a share in sth; to know about sth that is happening: *I'd like to be in on the new project.*

have (got) it in for sb (*informal*) to be unkind to sb because he/she has done sth to upset you

☆**in²** /ɪn/ *prep.*

☞ For special uses with many nouns, e.g. **in time,** look at the noun entries.

1 (showing place) within the area of sth; enclosed by sth: *a country in Africa* ∘ *a town in Mexico* ∘ *an island in the Pacific* ∘ *in a box* ∘ *I read about it in the newspaper.* ∘ *in bed* ∘ *She put the keys in her pocket.* ∘ *They were working in the garden.* ∘ *His wife's in the hospital.* **2** (showing time) during a period of time: *My birthday is in August.* ∘ *He was born in 1980.* ∘ *You could walk there in about an hour* (= it would take that long to walk there). **3** (showing time) after a period of time: *I'll be finished in ten minutes.* **4** contained in; forming the whole or part of sth: *There are 366 days in a leap year.* **5** (used for giving the rate of sth): *One family in four owns a dishwasher.* **6** wearing sth: *They were all dressed in black for the funeral.* ∘ *I've never seen you in a suit before.* **7** (used for saying how things are arranged): *We sat in a circle.* **8** (used for saying how sth is written or expressed): *Please write in pen.* ∘

ə	y	w	ṭ	eɪ	aɪ	ɔɪ	aʊ	oʊ
about	yes	woman	butter	say	five	boy	now	go

They were talking in Italian. **9** (used with feel-ings): *He looked at me in horror.* **10** (showing the condition or state of sb/sth): *My parents are in poor health.* ○ *This room is in a mess!* ○ *Richard's in love.* **11** (showing sb's job or the activity sb is involved in): *He's got a good job in advertising.* ○ *Her whole family is in politics.* ○ *He's in the army.*

in³ /ɪn/ *adj.* (*informal*) fashionable and popu-lar: *Short skirts are going to be in this spring.* ○ *This is the in place to hang out.*

in⁴ /ɪn/ *noun*

IDM **the ins and outs (of sth)** the details and difficulties (involved in sth): *Will somebody explain the ins and outs of the situation to me?*

in. *abbr.* = INCH(ES): *It's 4 ft. 2 in. long.*

in·a·bil·i·ty /ˌɪnəˈbɪləti/ *noun* [U] **inability (to do sth)** lack of ability, power or skill: *He has a complete inability to listen to other people's opinions.* ☞ The adjective is **unable.**

in·ac·ces·si·ble /ˌɪnækˈsɛsəbl/ *adj.* very diffi-cult or impossible to reach or contact: *That beach is inaccessible by car.* ○ (*figurative*) *His books are inaccessible to* (= cannot be under-stood by) *the average reader.* —**in·ac·ces·si·bil·i·ty** /ˌɪnækˌsɛsəˈbɪləti/ *noun* [U]

in·ac·cu·ra·cy /ɪnˈækyərəsi/ *noun* (*pl.* **in·ac·cu·ra·cies**) **1** [U] being inaccurate: *The in-accuracy of the statistics was immediately obvi-ous.* **2** [C] an inaccurate statement; a written or spoken mistake: *There are always some inaccuracies in newspaper reports.*

in·ac·cu·rate /ɪnˈækyərət/ *adj.* not correct; not accurate: *an inaccurate report, description, etc.*

in·ac·tion /ɪnˈækʃn/ *noun* [U] doing nothing; lack of action: *The crisis was blamed on the government's earlier inaction.*

in·ac·tive /ɪnˈæktɪv/ *adj.* doing nothing; not active: *The virus remains inactive in the body.* —**in·ac·tiv·i·ty** /ˌɪnækˈtɪvəti/ *noun* [U]

in·ad·e·quate /ɪnˈædɪkwət/ *adj.* **1** not suffi-cient; not good enough: *the problem of inad-equate housing* **2** (used about a person) not able to deal with a problem or situation, etc.; not confident: *There was so much to learn in the new job that for a while I felt totally inad-equate.* —**in·ad·e·qua·cy** /ɪnˈædɪkwəsi/ *noun* [C,U] (*pl.* **in·ad·e·qua·cies**): *his inadequacy as a parent* ○ *The inadequacies in police protection are the result of budget cuts.* —**in·ad·e·quate·ly** /ɪnˈædɪkwətli/ *adv.*

in·ad·ver·tent /ˌɪnədˈvərtənt/ *adj.* (used about actions) done without thinking, not on pur-pose; not intentional —**in·ad·ver·tent·ly** *adv.*: *She had inadvertently left the letter where he could find it.*

in·al·ien·a·ble /ɪnˈeɪliənəbl; -ˈeɪlyən-/ *adj.* (*formal*) (used about a right) that cannot be taken away from sb

in·ap·pro·pri·ate /ˌɪnəˈproʊpriət/ *adj.* not

suitable: *Her dress was totally inappropriate for the occasion.* ☞ Look at **unsuitable.**

in·at·ten·tion /ˌɪnəˈtɛnʃn/ *noun* [U] lack of attention: *inattention to detail*

in·at·ten·tive /ˌɪnəˈtɛntɪv/ *adj.* not paying at-tention: *One inattentive student can disturb the whole class.*

in·au·di·ble /ɪnˈɔdəbl/ *adj.* not loud enough to be heard —**in·au·di·bly** /ɪnˈɔdəbli/ *adv.*

in·au·gu·ral /ɪˈnɔgyərəl/ *adj.* (only *before* a noun) (used about a speech or meeting that marks the beginning of a new organization, leadership, etc.) first: *the President's inaugural speech*

in·au·gu·rate /ɪˈnɔgyəreɪt/ *verb* [T] **1** to intro-duce a new official, leader, etc. at a special ceremony: *He will be inaugurated as President next month.* **2** (*formal*) to start, introduce or open sth new (often at a special ceremony) —**in·au·gu·ra·tion** /ɪˌnɔgyəˈreɪʃn/ *noun* [C,U]

inc. (*also* **Inc.**) *abbr.* = INCORPORATED

in·cal·cu·la·ble /ɪnˈkælkyələbl/ *adj.* very great; too great to calculate: *an incalculable risk* ○ *incalculable damage*

in·ca·pa·ble /ɪnˈkeɪpəbl/ *adj.* **incapable of sth/doing sth** not able to do sth; not capable of sth/doing sth: *She is incapable of hard work/working hard.*

in·ca·pac·i·tate /ˌɪnkəˈpæsɪteɪt/ *verb* [T] to make sb unable (to work, live normally, etc.): *incapacitated by the tropical heat*

in·car·cer·ate /ɪnˈkɑrsəreɪt/ *verb* [T] (usually passive) to put or keep in prison —**in·car·cer·a·tion** /ɪnˌkɑrsəˈreɪʃn/ *noun* [U]

in·car·na·tion /ˌɪnkɑrˈneɪʃn/ *noun* [C] a life on earth in a particular form

in·cen·di·ar·y /ɪnˈsɛndiˌɛri/ *adj.* that causes a fire: *an incendiary device*

in·cense /ˈɪnsɛns/ *noun* [U] a substance that produces a sweet smell when burned, used especially in religious ceremonies

in·cen·tive /ɪnˈsɛntɪv/ *noun* [C,U] **incentive (to do sth)** something that encourages you (to do sth): *The company is offering cash incentives to its employees to boost productivity.* ○ *I get my meals for free, so I have no incentive to cook.*

in·ces·sant /ɪnˈsɛsnt/ *adj.* never stopping: *in-cessant rain, noise, etc.* ☞ Look at **continual.** —**in·ces·sant·ly** *adv.*

in·cest /ˈɪnsɛst/ *noun* [U] sex between close members of a family, e.g. brother and sister —**in·ces·tu·ous** /ɪnˈsɛstʃuəs/ *adj.*: *an incestu-ous relationship*

☆ **inch¹** /ɪntʃ/ *noun* [C] (*abbr.* **in.**) a measure of length; 2.54 centimeters. There are 12 inches in a foot: *He's 5 feet, 10 inches tall.* ○ *Three inches of rain fell last night.* ☞ For more infor-mation on measurements, look at Appendix 2.

inch² /ɪntʃ/ *verb*

PHRV **inch forward, past, through, etc.** to

move slowly and carefully in the direction mentioned: *I inched the car into the space.*

in·ci·dence /ˈɪnsədəns/ *noun* [sing.] the number of times sth (usually sth bad) happens; the rate of sth: *a high incidence of crime, disease, unemployment, etc.*

☆ **in·ci·dent** /ˈɪnsədənt/ *noun* [C,U] (*formal*) an event (especially one that involves violence, danger, something strange, etc.): *There were a number of violent incidents during the demonstration.* ○ *We believe the burglary was an isolated incident* (= not part of a series of crimes).

in·ci·den·tal /ˌɪnsəˈdɛntəl/ *adj.* happening as part of sth more important; minor: *Take enough money for food and incidental expenses.*

in·ci·den·tal·ly /ˌɪnsəˈdɛntəli/ *adv.* (used to introduce extra news, information, etc. that the speaker has just thought of): *Incidentally, that new restaurant you told me about is excellent.* ☞ A more informal expression is **by the way**.

in·cin·er·ate /ɪnˈsɪnəreɪt/ *verb* [T] (*formal*) to destroy sth completely by burning

in·cin·er·a·tor /ɪnˈsɪnəreɪtər/ *noun* [C] a container or machine for burning garbage, etc.

in·ci·sion /ɪnˈsɪʒn/ *noun* [C,U] (*formal*) a cut carefully made into sth (especially into a person's body as part of a medical operation)

in·cite /ɪnˈsaɪt/ *verb* [T] **incite sb (to sth)**; **incite sth** to encourage sb to do sth by making him/her very angry or excited: *He was accused of inciting the crowd to violence.* ○ *to incite a riot* —**in·cite·ment** *noun* [C,U]

in·cli·na·tion /ˌɪnkləˈneɪʃn/ *noun* [C,U] a feeling that makes sb want to behave in a particular way: *My inclination is to say "no," but what do you think?*

in·cline /ˈɪnklaɪn/ *noun* [C, usually sing.] a slope; an area of sloping ground: *a steep incline*

in·clined /ɪnˈklaɪnd/ *adj.* (not before a noun) **1 inclined to do sth** likely to do sth: *She's inclined to change her mind very easily.* **2 inclined (to do sth)** wanting to behave in a particular way: *I know Andrew well, so I'm inclined to believe what he says.* **3 inclined to do sth** (used to make what is said sound less sure) holding a particular opinion: *I'm inclined to say "yes," but I'll have to ask Molly first.* **4** having a natural ability in the subject mentioned: *to be musically inclined*

☆ **in·clude** /ɪnˈklud/ *verb* [T] **1** to have as one part; to contain (among other things): *The price of the room includes one drink in the hotel bar.* ○ *The crew included one woman.* ☞ Look at **exclude** and at the note at **contain**. **2** to make sb/sth part (of another group, etc.): *We should include the other departments in our discussions.* ○ *Everyone was disappointed, myself included.* —**in·clu·sion** /ɪnˈkluʒn/ *noun* [U]:

The inclusion of all that violence in the show was unnecessary.

☆ **in·clud·ing** /ɪnˈkludɪŋ/ *prep.* having as a part: *It costs $17.99, not including sales tax.*

in·clu·sive /ɪnˈklusɪv/ *adj.* including as many types of people or things as possible: *The candidate said his party was aiming to become more friendly and inclusive.*

in·cog·ni·to /ˌɪnkɑɡˈnitoʊ/ *adj., adv.* hiding your real name and identity (especially if you are famous and do not want to be recognized): *to travel incognito*

in·co·her·ent /ˌɪnkoʊˈhɪrənt/ *adj.* not clear or easy to understand; not expressing yourself clearly —**in·co·her·ence** /-əns/ *noun* [U] —**in·co·her·ent·ly** *adv.*

☆ **in·come** /ˈɪnkʌm/ *noun* [C,U] the money you receive regularly as payment for your work or from other sources: *It's sometimes difficult for a family to live on one income.*

☞ We can talk about a **yearly** or an **annual** income. An income may be **high** or **low**. Your **gross** income is the amount you earn before paying taxes. Your **net** income is your income after taxes. Look at the note at **pay**.

income tax *noun* [C,U] the tax that you pay on the money you earn: *federal and state income taxes*

in·com·ing /ˈɪnkʌmɪŋ/ *adj.* (only *before* a noun) **1** coming in: *incoming telephone calls* ○ *incoming missiles* **2** new; recently elected: *incoming freshmen* ○ *the incoming administration*

in·com·pat·i·ble /ˌɪnkəmˈpætəbl/ *adj.* **incompatible (with sb/sth)** not able to live or work happily with sb; not able to exist in harmony with sb/sth else: *Their marriage won't last; they're completely incompatible.* ○ *This software is incompatible with our computer system.* —**in·com·pat·i·bil·i·ty** /ˌɪnkəmˌpætəˈbɪləti/ *noun* [C,U] (*pl.* **in·com·pat·i·bil·i·ties**)

in·com·pe·tent /ɪnˈkɑmpətənt/ *adj.* lacking the necessary skill to do sth well: *There are too many incompetent people working there.* ○ *The defendant was found mentally incompetent to stand trial* (= because he/she could not tell the difference between right and wrong). —**in·com·pe·tence** /-əns/ *noun* [U] —**in·com·pe·tent·ly** *adv.*

in·com·plete¹ /ˌɪnkəmˈplit/ *adj.* having a part or parts missing; not total or complete: *The witness could only give an incomplete account of what had happened.* ○ *Her last novel was left incomplete when she died.* —**in·com·plete·ly** *adv.*

in·com·plete² /ˌɪnkəmˈplit/ *noun* [C] a grade that you get in a course when you have not done all of the work for the course

in·com·pre·hen·si·ble /ɪnˌkɑmprɪˈhɛnsəbl/

tʃ	dʒ	v	θ	ð	s	z	ʃ
chin	**J**une	**v**an	**th**in	**th**en	**s**o	**z**oo	**sh**e

adj. impossible to understand: *an incomprehensible explanation* ○ *I find her attitude incomprehensible.*

in·con·ceiv·a·ble /ˌɪnkənˈsivəbl/ *adj.* impossible or very difficult to believe or imagine

in·con·clu·sive /ˌɪnkənˈklusɪv/ *adj.* not leading to a definite decision or answer: *an inconclusive discussion* ○ *Results of the tests were inconclusive* (= they didn't prove anything). —**in·con·clu·sive·ly** *adv.*

in·con·sid·er·ate /ˌɪnkənˈsɪdərət/ *adj.* (used about a person) not thinking or caring about the feelings, or needs of other people: *It was inconsiderate of you not to offer her a ride.* ☞ Another word for inconsiderate is **thoughtless.** The opposite is **considerate.**

in·con·sis·tent /ˌɪnkənˈsɪstənt/ *adj.* **1** likely to change (in attitude, behavior, etc.); not reliable: *She's so inconsistent – sometimes her work is good and sometimes it's really awful.* ○ *inconsistent enforcement of a law* **2 inconsistent (with sth)** not in agreement with sth: *These new facts are inconsistent with the earlier information.* —**in·con·sis·ten·cy** /-ənsi/ *noun* [C, U] (*pl.* **in·con·sis·ten·cies**) —**in·con·sis·tent·ly** *adv.*

in·con·spic·u·ous /ˌɪnkənˈspɪkyuəs/ *adv.* not easily noticed: *inconspicuous colors* ○ *I tried to make myself as inconspicuous as possible so that no one would ask me a question.* —**in·con·spic·u·ous·ly** *adv.*

in·con·ti·nent /ɪnˈkɑntn·ənt/ *adj.* unable to control the passing of waste materials from the body —**in·con·ti·nence** /-əns/ *noun* [U]

in·con·ven·ience /ˌɪnkənˈvinyəns/ *noun* [C,U] (something that causes) difficulty or problems: *We apologize for any inconvenience caused by the delays this afternoon.* —**in·con·ven·ience** *verb* [T]

in·con·ven·ient /ˌɪnkənˈvinyənt/ *adj.* causing difficulty or problems; not convenient: *It's inconvenient for me to drive so far just to pick up a few items.* —**in·con·ven·ient·ly** *adv.*

in·cor·po·rate /ɪnˈkɔrpəreɪt/ *verb* [T] **incorporate sth (in/into sth)** to make sth part of sth else or to have sth as a part; to include: *I'd like you to incorporate this information into your report.* ○ *The new car incorporates all the latest safety features.*

☆**in·cor·po·rat·ed** /ɪnˈkɔrpəreɪţəd/ *adj.* (*abbr.* **Inc.**) (following the name of a company) formed into a legal organization (**corporation**)

☆**in·cor·rect** /ˌɪnkəˈrɛkt/ *adj.* not right or true; not correct: *an incorrect answer* —**in·cor·rect·ly** *adv.*: *The envelope was incorrectly addressed.*

☆**in·crease¹** /ɪnˈkris/ *verb* [I,T] to become or to make sth larger in number or amount: *The number of people working from home will increase steadily during the next decade.* ○ *The rate of inflation has increased by 1% to 7%.* ○

She increased her speed to pass the truck. ☞ The opposite is **decrease** or **reduce.**

☆**in·crease²** /ˈɪnkris/ *noun* [C,U] **increase (in sth)** a rise in the number, amount or level of sth: *a steady increase in the number of people taking vacations abroad* ○ *There has been a sharp increase of nearly 50% over last year's figures.* ○ *Doctors expect some further increase in the spread of the disease.* ○ *a huge tax increase* ☞ The opposite is **decrease** or **reduction.**

IDM on the increase becoming larger or more frequent; increasing: *Attacks by dogs on children are on the increase.*

in·creas·ing·ly /ɪnˈkrisɪŋli/ *adv.* more and more: *increasingly difficult, important, unhappy, etc.*

☆**in·cred·i·ble** /ɪnˈkrɛdəbl/ *adj.* **1** wonderful or fantastic; very great: *He earns an incredible salary.* **2** impossible or very difficult to believe: *It seemed incredible to us that something like that could happen.*

in·cred·i·bly /ɪnˈkrɛdəbli/ *adv.* extremely: *incredibly strong*

in·crim·i·nate /ɪnˈkrɪməneɪt/ *verb* [T] to provide evidence that sb is guilty of a crime: *She refused to answer in order to avoid incriminating herself.* —**in·crim·i·nat·ing** /-neɪţɪŋ/ *adj.*: *The police found several incriminating documents in his desk.*

in·cu·bate /ˈɪŋkyəbeɪt/ *verb* [I,T] **1** (used about eggs) to keep or be kept warm until the young birds come out (**hatch**) **2** (used about an infectious disease, etc.) to develop: *Some viruses take weeks to incubate.*

in·cu·ba·tion /ˌɪŋkyəˈbeɪʃn/ *noun* **1** [U] the process of incubating eggs **2** [C] (*also* **incuˈbation period**) the period between catching a disease and the time when signs of it (**symptoms**) appear

in·cu·ba·tor /ˈɪŋkyəbeɪţər/ *noun* [C] **1** a heated piece of equipment shaped like a box, that is used in hospitals for keeping small or weak babies alive **2** a similar piece of equipment for keeping eggs warm until they break open (**hatch**)

in·cum·bent /ɪnˈkʌmbənt/ *noun* [C] a person who is currently in a particular position or job, especially a political one —**in·cum·bent** *adj.* (only *before* a noun): *the incumbent vice president*

in·cur /ɪnˈkər/ *verb* [T] (**incurred; incur·ring**) (*formal*) to cause or suffer sth unpleasant as a result of your own actions: *to incur debts/sb's anger, etc.*

in·cur·a·ble /ɪnˈkyʊrəbl/ *adj.* not able to be cured or changed: *an incurable disease* —**in·cur·a·bly** *adv.*: *incurably ill*

in·debt·ed /ɪnˈdɛţəd/ *adj.* **indebted to sb (for sth)** very grateful to sb: *I am deeply indebted to my family for all their help and support.*

in·de·cent /ɪnˈdisnt/ *adj.* offending against

accepted sexual, moral or social standards of behavior —**in·de·cen·cy** /-nsi/ *noun* [C,U] (*pl.* **in·de·cen·cies**) —**in·de·cent·ly** *adv.*

in·de·ci·sion /ˌɪndɪˈsɪʒn/ *noun* [U] being unable to decide: *indecision about the future*

in·de·ci·sive /ˌɪndɪˈsaɪsɪv/ *adj.* **1** (used about a person) not able to make decisions **2** (used about a thing) not having a clear result or a strong effect: *an indecisive election that left no party with an absolute majority* —**in·de·ci·sive·ly** *adv.*

in·deed /ɪnˈdid/ *adv.* (*formal*) **1** (used for agreeing with sth that has just been said or for emphasis) really; certainly: *"Have you found out what happened?" "Yes, indeed."* **2** (used for emphasizing a point that has just been made) in fact: *It's important that you come at once. Indeed, it's essential.*

in·de·fen·si·ble /ˌɪndɪˈfɛnsəbl/ *adj.* (used about behavior, etc.) completely wrong; that cannot be defended or excused

in·de·fin·a·ble /ˌɪndɪˈfaɪnəbl/ *adj.* difficult or impossible to describe: *an indefinable atmosphere of hostility* —**in·de·fin·a·bly** /-əbli/ *adv.*

in·def·i·nite /ɪnˈdɛfənət/ *adj.* not having clear limits or a certain end: *Our plans are still pretty indefinite.*

in,definite 'article *noun* [C] (*grammar*) the name used for the words "a" and "an" ☞ Look at **definite article.**

in·def·i·nite·ly /ɪnˈdɛfənətli/ *adv.* for an indefinite period of time (= you do not know how long it will last): *The meeting was postponed indefinitely.*

in·del·i·ble /ɪnˈdɛləbl/ *adj.* that cannot be removed or washed out: *indelible ink* ○ (*figurative*) *an indelible impression* —**in·del·i·bly** /-əbli/ *adv.*

in·dent /ɪnˈdɛnt/ *verb* [I,T] to start a line of writing further from the left side of the page than the other lines: *to indent the first line of a paragraph*

☆ **in·de·pend·ence** /ˌɪndɪˈpɛndəns/ *noun* [U] **independence (from sb/sth)** (used about a person, country, etc.) the state of being free or not controlled by another person, country, etc.: *In 1776 the United States declared its independence from Britain.* ○ *financial independence*

Inde'pendence Day *noun* [U] July 4; a national holiday in the U.S. on which Americans celebrate the day in 1776 when America declared itself independent from Britain

☆ **in·de·pend·ent** /ˌɪndɪˈpɛndənt/ *adj.* **1 independent (of sb/sth)** not dependent on or controlled by another person, country, etc.: *Many former colonies are now independent nations.* ○ *to be independent of your parents* **2** not needing or wanting help: *My son likes traveling on his own – he's very independent for his age.* **3** not influenced by or connected with sb/sth: *an independent candidate for governor* (= one who is not a member of a political party) ○ *an*

independent inquiry —**in·de·pend·ent·ly** *adv.*: *Scientists working independently of each other have had very similar results in their experiments.*

'in-depth *adj.* (only before a noun) very thorough; done with a lot of attention to details: *an in-depth discussion, report, analysis, etc.*

in·de·scrib·a·ble /ˌɪndɪˈskraɪbəbl/ *adj.* too good or bad to be described: *indescribable poverty, luxury, etc.* —**in·de·scrib·a·bly** /-əbli/ *adv.*

in·de·struc·ti·ble /ˌɪndɪˈstrʌktəbl/ *adj.* that cannot be easily damaged or destroyed

☆ **in·dex¹** /ˈɪndɛks/ *noun* [C] **1** (*pl.* **in·dex·es**) a list of names or subjects at the end of a book, arranged in the order of the alphabet **2** (*pl.* **dex·es** or **in·dic·es**) a way of showing how the price, value, rate, etc. of sth has changed: *the consumer price index*

in·dex² /ˈɪndɛks/ *verb* [T] to make an index¹ or include sth in an index

'index finger (*also* **forefinger**) *noun* [C] the finger next to your thumb

☆ **In·di·an** /ˈɪndiən/ *noun* [C, *adj.* **1** = NATIVE AMERICAN: *an Indian tribe* **2** (a person) from the Republic of India: *Indian food is hot and spicy.*

,Indian 'summer *noun* [C,U] a period of warm weather in late fall

☆ **in·di·cate** /ˈɪndəkeɪt/ *verb* **1** [T] to show or point to sth: *The receptionist indicated where I should sign.* ○ (*figurative*) *The report indicates a need for more spending on research.* **2** [T] to be or give a sign about sth: *If a horse has its ears forward, that indicates that it is happy.* **3** [T] to say sth briefly and in a general way: *The spokesman indicated that an agreement was likely soon.*

in·di·ca·tion /ˌɪndəˈkeɪʃn/ *noun* [C,U] something that shows sth; a sign: *There was no indication of a struggle.* ○ *There is every indication that he will make a full recovery.*

in·dic·a·tive /ɪnˈdɪkətɪv/ *adj.* (*formal*) **indicative (of sth)** being or giving a sign of sth: *Is the unusual weather indicative of fundamental changes in the climate?*

in·di·ca·tor /ˈɪndəkeɪtər/ *noun* [C] something that gives information or shows sth; a sign: *The leading economic indicators point to a strong recovery.*

in·di·ces *pl.* of INDEX¹(2)

in·dict /ɪnˈdaɪt/ *verb* [T] (often passive) (in a court of law) to accuse sb officially of committing a crime: *He was indicted for murder.* ○ *The grand jury indicted them on charges of theft.*

in·dict·ment /ɪnˈdaɪtmənt/ *noun* [C] **1** a written paper that officially accuses sb of a crime **2** (*figurative*) something that shows how bad sth is: *The fact that some young people leave school without knowing how to read or write is an indictment of our educational system.*

in·dif·fer·ence /ɪnˈdɪfrəns/ *noun* [U] a lack of

interest or feeling (toward sb/sth): *He treated our suggestion with complete indifference.*

in·dif·fer·ent /ɪnˈdɪfrənt/ *adj.* **indifferent (to sb/sth)** not interested in or caring about sb/sth: *How can you remain indifferent when children are suffering?* —**in·dif·fer·ent·ly** *adv.*

in·dig·e·nous /ɪnˈdɪdʒənəs/ *adj.* (used about people, animals or plants) living or growing in the place where they are from originally

in·di·gent /ˈɪndɪdʒənt/ *adj.* (formal) poor; not having enough money to pay for many things: *medical care for indigent patients*

in·di·ges·tion /ˌɪndəˈdʒɛstʃən/ *noun* [U] pain in the stomach that is caused by difficulty in digesting food: *Onions give me terrible indigestion.*

in·dig·nant /ɪnˈdɪɡnənt/ *adj.* shocked or angry (because sb has said or done sth that you do not like and do not agree with): *They were indignant that they had to pay more for worse services.* —**in·dig·nant·ly** *adv.*

in·dig·na·tion /ˌɪndɪɡˈneɪʃn/ *noun* [U] shock and anger: *The brutal crime aroused public indignation.* ○ *to express indignation*

in·di·rect /ˌɪndɪˈrɛkt; -daɪ-/ *adj.* **1** not going in a straight line or using the shortest route; not direct: *We took the indirect route to avoid driving through Los Angeles.* **2** not directly caused by or connected with sth: *an indirect result* **3** not mentioning sth openly: *She gave only an indirect answer to my question.* —**in·di·rect·ly** *adv.* —**in·di·rect·ness** *noun* [U]

indirect ˈobject *noun* [C] (grammar) an additional object[1](4) that is used after some verbs: *In the sentence, "I wrote her a letter," "her" is the indirect object.*

indirect ˈspeech *noun* [U] = REPORTED SPEECH

in·dis·cre·tion /ˌɪndɪˈskrɛʃn/ *noun* [C,U] behavior that is not careful or polite

in·dis·crim·i·nate /ˌɪndɪˈskrɪmənət/ *adj.* not carefully chosen or done with careful thought: *the indiscriminate shooting of civilians* —**in·dis·crim·i·nate·ly** *adv.*

in·dis·pen·sa·ble /ˌɪndɪˈspɛnsəbl/ *adj.* very important so that it is not possible to be without it; essential or necessary: *A car is indispensable in most parts of the U.S.*

in·dis·put·a·ble /ˌɪndɪˈspyuṭəbl/ *adj.* definitely true; that cannot be proved wrong

in·dis·tinct /ˌɪndɪˈstɪŋkt/ *adj.* not clear; not distinct: *indistinct figures, sounds, memories, etc.* —**in·dis·tinct·ly** *adv.*

in·dis·tin·guish·a·ble /ˌɪndɪˈstɪŋɡwɪʃəbl/ *adj.* **indistinguishable (from sth)** appearing to be the same: *From a distance, the two colors are indistinguishable.*

☆ **in·di·vid·u·al**[1] /ˌɪndəˈvɪdʒuəl/ *adj.* **1** (only before a noun) single or particular: *Each individual battery is tested before being packaged.* **2** for or from one person: *Children need indi-*

vidual attention when they are learning to read.

☆ **in·di·vid·u·al**[2] /ˌɪndəˈvɪdʒuəl/ *noun* [C] **1** one person: *Are the needs of society more important than the rights of the individual?* ○ *Two individuals were arrested in connection with the robbery.* **2** (informal) a person of the type that is mentioned: *She's a strange individual.*

in·di·vid·u·al·i·ty /ˌɪndəˌvɪdʒuˈæləṭi/ *noun* [U] the qualities that make sb/sth different from other people/things: *Young people often try to express their individuality by the way they dress.*

in·di·vid·u·al·ly /ˌɪndəˈvɪdʒuali/ *adv.* separately; one by one: *The teacher talked to each member of the class individually.*

in·di·vis·i·ble /ˌɪndəˈvɪzəbl/ *adj.* not able to be divided or split into smaller pieces

in·doc·tri·nate /ɪnˈdɑktrəneɪt/ *verb* [T] to put ideas or beliefs into sb's mind so that they are accepted without criticism: *For 20 years, the people have been indoctrinated by the government.* ☞ Using the word **indoctrinate** shows that you disapprove of what is happening. —**in·doc·tri·na·tion** /ɪnˌdɑktrəˈneɪʃn/ *noun* [U]: *the indoctrination of political prisoners*

☆ **in·door** /ˈɪndɔr/ *adj.* (only before a noun) done or used inside a building: *indoor sports* ○ *an indoor swimming pool* ○ *In those days, many houses had no indoor plumbing* (= water pipes, toilets, etc.). ☞ The opposite is **outdoor**.

☆ **in·doors** /ˌɪnˈdɔrz/ *adv.* in or into a building: *Let's go/stay indoors.* ○ *I left my sunglasses indoors.* ☞ Look at **outdoors** and **out of doors**.

in·duce /ɪnˈdus/ *verb* [T] (formal) **1 induce sb to do sth** to make or persuade sb to do sth: *Nothing could induce him to change his mind.* **2** to cause or produce: *a drug that induces sleep*

in·duct /ɪnˈdʌkt/ *verb* [T] (usually passive) to make sb a member of a group or to give sb a special position or title during an official ceremony: *He was inducted into the baseball hall of fame.* —**in·duc·tion** /ɪnˈdʌkʃn/ *noun* [C,U]: *an induction ceremony*

in·dulge /ɪnˈdʌldʒ/ *verb* **1** [I] **indulge (in sth)** to allow yourself to have or do sth for pleasure: *There's still some cake left – go ahead and indulge!* ○ *to indulge in self-pity* **2** [T] satisfy a strong desire for or interest in sth: *After she retired, she had time to indulge her passion for traveling.*

in·dul·gence /ɪnˈdʌldʒəns/ *noun* **1** [U] the state of having or doing whatever you want: *a life of indulgence* **2** [C] something that you have or do because it gives you pleasure: *A cigar after dinner is my only indulgence.*

☆ **in·dus·tri·al** /ɪnˈdʌstriəl/ *adj.* **1** (only before a noun) connected with industry (1): *industrial development* ○ *industrial workers* **2** having a

lot of factories, etc.: *an industrial region, country, etc.*

in·dus·tri·al 'arts (*also* **shop**; **'shop class**) *noun* [U] a school subject in which students learn to use tools and machines, and to make things out of wood or metal

in·dus·tri·al·ist /mˌdʌstriəlɪst/ *noun* [C] a person who owns or manages a large industrial company

in·dus·tri·al·ize /mˌdʌstriəlaɪz/ *verb* [T] to develop industries (2) in a country: *the industrialized nations of the world* —**in·dus·tri·al·i·za·tion** /mˌdʌstriələ'zeɪʃn/ *noun* [U]

in'dustrial park *noun* [C] an area of land that has small factories and other businesses on it

in·dus·tri·ous /m'dʌstriəs/ *adj.* hard-working

☆ **in·dus·try** /'ɪmdəstri/ *noun* (*pl.* **in·dus·tries**) **1** [U] the work of making things in factories: *a good year for American industry* ○ *heavy/light industry* **2** [C] all the people, buildings, etc. that are involved in producing sth, providing a service, etc.: *The new high-tech industries are replacing manufacturing industries in many areas.* ○ *the tourist, catering, entertainment, etc. industry*

in·ef·fec·tive /ˌmɪ'fɛktɪv/ *adj.* not producing the effect or result that you want

in·ef·fi·cient /ˌmɪ'fɪʃnt/ *adj.* not working or producing results in the best way, so that time and money are wasted: *an inefficient way of working* ○ *an inefficient use of space* ○ *Our furnace is very old and extremely inefficient.* ○ *The new manager is very nice, but he's very inefficient.* —**in·ef·fi·cien·cy** /-nsi/ *noun* [U] —**in·ef·fi·cient·ly** *adv.*

in·el·i·gi·ble /m'ɛlɪdʒəbl/ *adj.* ineligible (for sth/to do sth) without the necessary qualifications to do or get sth: *She was ineligible for financial aid because her family's income was too high.* ○ *ineligible to vote* —**in·el·i·gi·bil·i·ty** /mˌɛlɪdʒə'bɪləti/ *noun* [U]

in·ept /ɪ'nɛpt/ *adj.* not able to do sth well; having no skill: *weak, inept leadership*

in·e·qual·i·ty /ˌmɪ'kwɑləti/ *noun* [C,U] (*pl.* **in·e·qual·i·ties**) (a) difference between groups in society because one has more money, advantages, etc. than the other: *inequality between the sexes*

in·er·tia /ɪ'nərʃə/ *noun* [U] the physical force that tends to keep things in the position they are in or to keep them moving in the direction they are traveling: (*figurative*) *The inertia of the system makes change very difficult.*

in·es·cap·a·ble /ˌmɪ'skeɪpəbl/ *adj.* (*formal*) that cannot be avoided: *an inescapable conclusion*

in·ev·i·ta·ble /m'ɛvətəbl/ *adj.* **1** that cannot be avoided or prevented from happening: *With more cars on the road, traffic jams are inevitable.* ○ *It was inevitable that she would find out the truth one day.* **2 the inevitable** *noun* [sing.] something that cannot be avoided or

stopped from happening —**in·ev·i·ta·bil·i·ty** /mˌɛvətə'bɪləti/ *noun* [U] —**in·ev·i·ta·bly** *adv.*: *Construction projects on major highways inevitably create huge problems* (= they cannot be avoided).

in·ex·cus·a·ble /ˌmɪk'skyuzəbl/ *adj.* that cannot be allowed or forgiven: *Their behavior was quite inexcusable.* ○ *inexcusable delays*

in·ex·haust·i·ble /ˌmɪg'zɔstəbl/ *adj.* that cannot be finished or used up: *Our energy supplies are not inexhaustible.*

☆ **in·ex·pen·sive** /ˌmɪk'spɛnsɪv/ *adj.* low in price; not expensive: *an inexpensive camping vacation* —**in·ex·pen·sive·ly** *adv.*

in·ex·pe·ri·ence /ˌmɪk'spɪriəns/ *noun* [U] not knowing how to do sth because you have not done it before; lack of experience: *The mistakes were all due to inexperience.*

in·ex·pe·ri·enced /ˌmɪk'spɪriənst/ *adj.* not having the knowledge that you get from having done sth before; lacking experience: *He's too young and inexperienced to be given such responsibility.*

in·ex·pli·ca·ble /ˌmɪk'splɪkəbl/ *adj.* that cannot be explained: *Her sudden disappearance is completely inexplicable.* —**in·ex·pli·ca·bly** *adv.*

in·fal·li·ble /m'fæləbl/ *adj.* **1** (used about a person) never making mistakes or being wrong: *Even the most careful typist is not infallible.* **2** always doing what you want it to do; never failing: *There is no infallible method of birth control.* —**in·fal·li·bil·i·ty** /mˌfælə'bɪləti/ *noun* [U]

in·fa·mous /'ɪmfəməs/ *adj.* (usually before a noun) famous for being bad: *an infamous dictator* ○ *The area is infamous for drugs and prostitution.*

in·fan·cy /'ɪmfənsi/ *noun* [U] the period when you are a baby: (*figurative*) *Research in this field is still in its infancy.*

☆ **in·fant** /'ɪmfənt/ *noun* [C] a baby: *There is a high rate of infant mortality* (= many children die when they are still babies).

☞ **Baby** is more common in spoken or informal English.

in·fan·try /'ɪmfəntri/ *noun* [U] soldiers who fight on foot: *The infantry was supported by heavy gunfire.*

in·fat·u·at·ed /m'fætʃueɪtəd/ *adj.* having a strong but foolish feeling of love for sb/sth that usually does not last long: *The boy was infatuated with one of his teachers.* —**in·fat·u·a·tion** /mˌfætʃu'eɪʃn/ *noun* [C,U]

☆ **in·fect** /m'fɛkt/ *verb* [T] (usually passive) to cause sb/sth to have a disease or illness or to become dirty: *We need to clean the wound before it becomes infected.* ○ *Many thousands of people have been infected with the virus.*

☆ **in·fec·tion** /m'fɛkʃn/ *noun* **1** [U] making sb sick: *A dirty water supply can be a source of infection.* **2** [C] a disease or illness that is

caused by very small living things: *She is suffering from a chest infection.* ○ *an ear infection*

☞ Infections can be caused by **bacteria** or **viruses**. An informal word for these is **germs**.

☆ **in·fec·tious** /ɪnˈfɛkʃəs/ *adj.* (used about a disease, illness, etc.) that can be easily passed on to another person: *The flu is very infectious.* ○ (*figurative*) *infectious laughter* ☞ Look at **contagious**.

in·fer /ɪnˈfər/ *verb* [T] (**infer·ring; inferred**) **infer sth (from sth)** to reach a conclusion from the information you have: *I inferred from our conversation that he was unhappy with his job.* ☞ Look also at **imply**.

in·fe·ri·or /ɪnˈfɪriər/ *adj.* **inferior (to sb/sth)** low or lower in social position, importance, quality, etc.: *I don't like the way he treats new staff as inferior.* ○ *Cheaper products are generally of inferior quality.* ☞ The opposite is **superior**. —**in·fe·ri·or·i·ty** /ɪnˌfɪriˈɔrəti; -ˈɑr-/ *noun* [U]

in·feri·or·i·ty ,complex *noun* [C] a feeling that you are less important, intelligent, successful, etc. than other people

in·fer·tile /ɪnˈfərtl; -tail/ *adj.* **1** (used about a person or animal) not able to have a baby or young animal **2** (used about land) not able to grow strong healthy plants —**in·fer·til·i·ty** /ˌɪnfərˈtɪləti/ *noun* [U]: *treatment for infertility*

in·fest·ed /ɪnˈfɛstəd/ *adj.* **infested (with sth)** (used about a building) with large numbers of unpleasant animals or insects in it: *The warehouse was infested with rats.*

in·fil·trate /ˈɪnfəltreɪt/ *verb* [T] to enter an organization, etc. secretly so that you can find out what it is doing: *The police managed to infiltrate the terrorist group.* —**in·fil·tra·tion** /ˌɪnfəlˈtreɪʃn/ *noun* [C,U] —**in·fil·tra·tor** /ˈɪnfəltreɪtər/ *noun* [C]

in·fi·nite /ˈɪnfənət/ *adj.* **1** without end or limits: *Supplies of oil are not infinite.* **2** very great: *You need infinite patience for this job.*

in·fi·nite·ly /ˈɪnfənətli/ *adv.* (used before an adjective or adverb) very much: *Compact discs sound infinitely better than audio cassettes.*

in·fin·i·tive /ɪnˈfɪnətɪv/ *noun* [C] (*grammar*) the basic form of a verb

☞ In English the infinitive is sometimes used with and sometimes without *to*: *He can sing.* ○ *He wants to sing.*

in·fin·i·ty /ɪnˈfɪnəti/ *noun* [U] **1** endless space or time **2** (in mathematics) the number that is larger than any other that you can think of

in·firm /ɪnˈfərm/ *adj.* sick or weak, e.g. because of old age

in·fir·ma·ry /ɪnˈfərməri/ *noun* [C] (*pl.* **in·fir·ma·ries**) a part of a university, prison, etc.

where sick or injured people can go for treatment

in·fir·mi·ty /ɪnˈfərməti/ *noun* [C,U] (*pl.* **in·fir·mi·ties**) (*formal*) weakness or illness

in·flamed /ɪnˈfleɪmd/ *adj.* (used about a part of the body) red and swollen because of some infection

in·flam·ma·ble /ɪnˈflæməbl/ *adj.* that burns easily: *Natural gas is highly inflammable.*

☞ The opposite is **nonflammable**. Look also at **flammable**. It has the same meaning and is more common than **inflammable**.

in·flam·ma·tion /ˌɪnfləˈmeɪʃn/ *noun* [C,U] redness and swelling in a part of the body, because of infection

in·flat·a·ble /ɪnˈfleɪtəbl/ *adj.* that can or must be filled with air: *an inflatable boat*

in·flate /ɪnˈfleɪt/ *verb* [I,T] (*formal*) to fill sth with air; to become filled with air ☞ The opposite is **deflate**.

☆ **in·fla·tion** /ɪnˈfleɪʃn/ *noun* [U] a general rise in prices: *High increases in wages cause inflation.* ○ *the inflation rate/rate of inflation* ○ *Annual inflation remains at 10%.* ○ *The government is taking measures to control inflation.* ○ *They've reduced inflation by 2%.*

in·flec·tion /ɪnˈflɛkʃn/ *noun* **1** [U] the rise and fall of your voice when you are talking ☞ Look at **intonation**. **2** [U] the act of changing the ending or form of a word to show its grammatical function **3** [C] something that is added to a word that changes its grammatical function, e.g. *-ed, -est*

in·flex·i·ble /ɪnˈflɛksəbl/ *adj.* not able to bend or be bent easily: (*figurative*) *an inflexible attitude* —**in·flex·i·bil·i·ty** /ɪnˌflɛksəˈbɪləti/ *noun* [U] —**in·flex·i·bly** *adv.*

in·flict /ɪnˈflɪkt/ *verb* [T] **inflict sth (on/upon sb)** to force sb to have sth bad or unwanted: *to inflict severe injuries on sb*

,in-'flight *adj.* happening or provided during a trip in a plane: *an in-flight movie*

☆ **in·flu·ence¹** /ˈɪnfluəns/ *noun* **1** [U] **influence (on/over sb/sth)** the power to affect, change or control sb/sth: *I used my influence with the boss to get things changed.* ○ *The fact that he's rich and famous had no influence on our decision.* ○ *Nobody should drive while they are under the influence of alcohol.* **2** [C] **influence (on sb/sth)** a person or thing that affects or changes sb/sth: *His new girlfriend has been a good influence on him.*

☆ **in·flu·ence²** /ˈɪnfluəns/ *verb* [T] to have an effect or influence on sb/sth: *You have to decide for yourself. Don't let anyone else influence you.* ○ *Her style of painting has been influenced by Japanese art.*

☞ **Affect** and **influence** are often very similar in meaning. **Affect** is usually used when the change is physical and **influence** is more often used to describe a change of feeling or

attitude: *Drinking alcohol can affect your ability to drive.* ○ *Those TV commercials have influenced my attitude toward drinking and driving.*

in·flu·en·tial /ˌɪnfluˈɛnʃl/ *adj.* having power or influence: *an influential politician* ○ *He was influential in getting the hostages set free.*

in·flu·en·za /ˌɪnfluˈɛnzə/ *noun* [U] (*formal*) = FLU

in·flux /ˈɪnflʌks/ *noun* [C] a sudden arrival of people or things in large numbers: *the influx of tourists from the cities during the summer*

info /ˈɪnfoʊ/ *noun* [U] (*informal*) information: *Here's some more info on that concert:...*

in·fo·mer·cial /ˈɪnfoʊmərʃl/ *noun* [C] an advertisement on television that is as long as a regular program

☆ **in·form** /ɪnˈfɔrm/ *verb* [T] **inform sb (of/about sth)** to give sb information (about sth): *You should inform the police about the accident.* ○ *Everyone has been informed of the changes.*

PHRV inform on sb to give information, etc. to the police, etc. about what sb has done wrong: *The wife of the killer informed on her husband.*

☆ **in·for·mal** /ɪnˈfɔrml/ *adj.* relaxed and friendly or suitable for a relaxed occasion; not formal: *Don't get dressed up for the party – it'll be very informal.* ○ *an informal survey* ○ *informal discussions*

☞ Some words and expressions in this dictionary are described as *(informal)*. This means that you can use them when you are speaking to friends or people that you know well but that you should not use them in written work, official letters, etc..

—**in·for·mal·i·ty** /ˌɪnfɔrˈmæləti/ *noun* [C,U] (*pl.* **in·for·mal·i·ties**) [U]: *an atmosphere of informality* —**in·for·mal·ly** *adv.*: *Managers met informally* (= unofficially) *with a few employees.*

in·form·ant /ɪnˈfɔrmənt/ *noun* [C] a person who gives sb knowledge or information: *undercover agents and informants*

☆ **in·for·ma·tion** /ˌɪnfərˈmeɪʃn/ *noun* [U] **information (on/about sb/sth)** knowledge or facts: *For further information, please send for our brochure.* ○ *Can you give me some information about Spanish classes?* ○ *to feed information into a computer*

☞ The word **information** is uncountable so you CANNOT say: *I need an information.* You can, however, talk about **a bit** or **piece** of information.

infor·mation tech·nology *noun* [U] the study or use of computer systems, etc. for collecting, storing and sending out all kinds of information

in·form·a·tive /ɪnˈfɔrmətɪv/ *adj.* giving useful knowledge or information ☞ The opposite is **uninformative**.

☆ **in·formed** /ɪnˈfɔrmd/ *adj.* having knowledge or information about sth: *The radio keeps me well informed about what is happening.* ○ *Consumers cannot make informed choices unless they are told all the facts.*

in·form·er /ɪnˈfɔrmər/ *noun* [C] a person who gives the police, etc. information about what sb has done wrong

in·fra·struc·ture /ˈɪnfrəstrʌkʃər/ *noun* [C,U, usually sing.] the basic structures and systems that are needed so that a country or an organization can work well, e.g. roads, transportation, etc.

in·fre·quent /ɪnˈfrikwənt/ *adj.* not happening often: *infrequent visits* —**in·fre·quent·ly** *adv.*

in·fringe /ɪnˈfrɪndʒ/ *verb* (*formal*) **infringe on/upon sth** to reduce or limit sb's rights, freedom, etc. —**in·fringe·ment** /-mənt/ *noun* [C,U]

in·fu·ri·ate /ɪnˈfyʊrieɪt/ *verb* [T] to make sb very angry —**in·fu·ri·at·ing** /-eɪtɪŋ/ *adj.*: *an infuriating habit* —**in·fu·ri·at·ing·ly** *adv.*

in·gen·ious /ɪnˈdʒinyəs/ *adj.* **1** (used about a person) good at finding answers to problems or at thinking of new things **2** (used about a thing or an idea) that has been made or planned in an intelligent way, with new ideas: *an ingenious plan* —**in·gen·ious·ly** *adv.* —**in·ge·nu·i·ty** /ˌɪndʒəˈnuəti/ *noun* [U]

in·grained /ɪnˈɡreɪnd/ *adj.* deeply fixed; difficult to change: *an ingrained attitude*

☆ **in·gre·di·ent** /ɪnˈɡridiənt/ *noun* [C] one of the items of food you need to make sth to eat: *The main ingredient of this drink is sugar.* ○ (*figurative*) *The movie has all the ingredients of success.*

in·hab·it /ɪnˈhæbət/ *verb* [T] to live in a place: *Are the Aleutian Islands inhabited?*

in·hab·i·tant /ɪnˈhæbətənt/ *noun* [C, usually pl.] (*formal*) a person or animal that lives in a place: *the original inhabitants of North America* ☞ Look also at **population**.

in·hale /ɪnˈheɪl/ *verb* [I,T] to breathe in: *to inhale smoke*

in·hal·er /ɪnˈheɪlər/ *noun* [C] a small tube containing medicine that sb breathes in through his/her mouth in order to help him/her breathe more easily

in·her·it /ɪnˈhɛrət/ *verb* [T] **inherit sth (from sb) 1** to receive property, money, etc. from sb who has died: *I inherited $12,000 from my grandmother.* **2** to receive a quality, disease, etc. from your parents or family: *She has inherited her father's gift for languages.*

in·her·i·tance /ɪnˈhɛrətəns/ *noun* [C,U] property, money, etc. that you receive from sb who has died: *inheritance tax*

in·hib·it /ɪnˈhɪbət/ *verb* [T] to prevent sth or make sth happen more slowly: *a drug to inhibit the growth of tumors*

in·hib·it·ed /ɪnˈhɪbətəd/ *adj.* not able to express your feelings freely or naturally; not

relaxed: *I feel inhibited if everyone watches me.* ○ *inhibited about sex* ☞ The opposite is **uninhibited**.

in·hi·bi·tion /ˌɪnhɪˈbɪʃn; ˌɪnɪ-/ *noun* [C,U] a feeling of being unable to express your feelings freely or naturally or to relax: *She has no inhibitions about speaking in front of a large group of people.*

ˌin·ˈhouse *adj., adv.* inside a company, an organization, etc.: *an in-house design studio* ○ *The designs are all done in-house.*

in·hu·man /ɪnˈhyumən/ *adj.* very cruel, not seeming to be human: *inhuman treatment*

in·hu·mane /ˌɪnhyuˈmeɪn/ *adj.* very cruel; not caring if people or animals suffer: *the inhumane conditions in which animals are kept in some zoos*

☆ **in·i·tial¹** /ɪˈnɪʃl/ *adj.* (only *before* a noun) that is at the beginning; first: *My initial reaction was to refuse, but I later changed my mind.* ○ *the initial stages of our survey*

☆ **in·i·tial²** /ɪˈnɪʃl/ *noun* [C, usually pl.] the first letter of a name: *Patricia Anne Morgan's initials are P. A. M.*

in·i·tial³ /ɪˈnɪʃl/ *verb* [T] to mark or sign sth with your initials²

in·i·tial·ly /ɪˈnɪʃl·i/ *adv.* at the beginning; at first: *I liked the job initially, but it soon got pretty boring.*

in·i·ti·ate /ɪˈnɪʃieɪt/ *verb* [T] **1** (*formal*) to start sth: *to initiate a new training program* **2 initiate sb (into sth)** to bring sb into a group by means of a special ceremony or by giving him/her special knowledge: *to initiate somebody into a secret club* —**in·i·ti·a·tion** /ɪˌnɪʃiˈeɪʃn/ *noun* [C,U]

☆ **in·i·tia·tive** /ɪˈnɪʃətɪv/ *noun* **1** [C] official action that is taken to solve a problem or improve a situation: *a new government initiative to help people start small businesses* **2** [U] the ability to see and do what needs to be done without help from others: *He'll never get the project started. He has no initiative.*

IDM seize/take the initiative to be first to do sth: *Let's take the initiative and start organizing things now.*

☆ **in·ject** /ɪnˈdʒɛkt/ *verb* [T] **1** to put a substance into sb/sth with a needle (**syringe**) : *Scientists injected cancer cells into the mice.* **2** to add sth: *They injected a lot of money into the business.* —**in·jec·tion** /ɪnˈdʒɛkʃn/ *noun* [C,U] **injection (of sth) (into sb/sth)** *an injection of $2 million into the company*

in·junc·tion /ɪnˈdʒʌŋkʃn/ *noun* [C] an official order from a court of law to do/not do sth

☆ **in·jure** /ˈɪndʒər/ *verb* [T] to harm or hurt a person, animal or part of the body: *David was badly injured in the accident.* ○ *Three people were seriously injured.* ○ *She fell and injured her back.* ☞ Look at the note at **hurt**.

☆ **in·jured** /ˈɪndʒərd/ *adj.* **1** physically or mentally hurt: *an injured leg* **2 the injured** *noun*

[plural] people who have been hurt: *The injured were rushed to the hospital.*

☆ **in·ju·ry** /ˈɪndʒəri/ *noun* [C,U] (*pl.* **in·ju·ries**) harm or hurt done to a person, animal or part of the body: *They escaped from the accident with only minor injuries.* ○ *Injury to the head can be extremely dangerous.*

in·jus·tice /ɪnˈdʒʌstəs/ *noun* [C,U] **1** unfairness; a lack of justice: *People are protesting about the injustice of the jury's verdict.* **2** an unfair action or situation: *economic and social injustices* ☞ The noun is **unjust**.

☆ **ink** /ɪŋk/ *noun* [C,U] a colored liquid that is used for writing, drawing, etc.: *Please write in ink, not pencil.*

in·kling /ˈɪŋklɪŋ/ *noun* [sing.] a slight feeling (about sth): *I had an inkling that something was wrong.*

in·land¹ /ˈɪnlənd/ *adj.* in the middle of a country away from the coast: *inland areas*

in·land² /ˌɪnˈlænd/ *adv.* in or toward the middle of a country: *The hurricane will weaken as it moves farther inland.*

ˈin-laws *noun* [plural] (*informal*) your husband's or wife's mother and father or other relatives: *My in-laws are coming to lunch on Sunday.*

ˌin-line ˈskate *noun* [C] = ROLLERBLADE

☆ **in·mate** /ˈɪnmeɪt/ *noun* [C] one of the people living in an institution such as a prison or mental hospital

inn /ɪn/ *noun* [C] a small hotel, usually in the country, that often also serves food and drinks

in·nate /ɪˈneɪt/ *adj.* being a natural quality of sb/sth: *innate ability*

☆ **in·ner** /ˈɪnər/ *adj.* (only *before* a noun) **1** (of the) inside: *The inner ear is very delicate.* ☞ The opposite is **outer**. **2** (used about a feeling, etc.) that you do not express or show to other people: *Everyone has inner doubts.*

☆ **ˌinner ˈcity** *noun* [C] (*pl.* **inner cities**) the poor parts of a large city that often have a lot of social problems: *inner-city schools*

in·ner·most /ˈɪnərmoʊst/ *adj.* (only *before* a noun) **1** farthest from the outside **2** (used about a feeling, etc.) most secret or private: *She never told anyone her innermost thoughts.*

in·ning /ˈɪnɪŋ/ *noun* [C] one of nine periods in a game of baseball in which each team has a turn to hit the ball (**to bat**) ☞ Look at the note at **baseball**.

☆ **in·no·cent** /ˈɪnəsnt/ *adj.* **1 innocent (of sth)** not having done wrong; not guilty: *An innocent man was arrested by mistake.* ○ *to be innocent of a crime* **2** not causing harm or intended to upset sb: *He got very aggressive when I asked an innocent question about his past.* **3** not knowing the bad things in life; believing everything you are told: *young and innocent* ○ *She was so innocent as to believe that politicians never lie.* —**in·no·cence** /-sns/ *noun* [U]: *The accused man protested his innocence*

throughout his trial. ☞ The opposite is **guilt.**
—**in·no·cent·ly** *adv.*

in·noc·u·ous /ɪˈnɑkyuəs/ *adj.* (*formal*) not causing harm or intended to upset sb: *I thought it was an innocuous remark, but she got really upset.*

in·no·vate /ˈɪnəveɪt/ *verb* [I] to introduce sth new; to change

in·no·va·tion /ˌɪnəˈveɪʃn/ *noun* [C,U] the introduction of new things, ideas, etc., or something new that has been introduced: *technological innovations in industry* ○ *a company with a reputation for innovation*

in·no·va·tive /ˈɪnəveɪṭɪv/ *adj.* **1** (used about a company, etc.) introducing many new products and ideas **2** (used about a product, an idea, etc.) new; developed using new ways of thinking

in·no·va·tor /ˈɪnəveɪṭər/ *noun* [C] a person, company, etc. that introduces changes

in·nu·mer·a·ble /ɪˈnumərəbl/ *adj.* too many to be counted

in·oc·u·late /ɪˈnɑkyəleɪt/ *verb* [T] (*formal*) **inoculate sb (with sth) (against sth)** to inject sb with a mild form of a disease. This protects him/her from getting the serious form: *to be inoculated against tetanus* ☞ Look at **immunize** and **vaccinate.** —**in·oc·u·la·tion** /ɪˌnɑkyəˈleɪʃn/ *noun* [C,U]

in·or·di·nate /ɪnˈɔrdn·ət/ *adj.* (*formal*) much greater than usual or expected: *an inordinate amount of time* —**in·or·di·nate·ly** *adv.*

in·or·gan·ic /ˌɪnɔrˈgænɪk/ *adj.* not made of or coming from living things: *Rocks and metals are inorganic substances.*

in·pa·tient /ˈɪnpeɪʃnt/ *noun* [C] a person who goes to a hospital for medical treatment and stays in the hospital for at least one night ☞ Look at **outpatient.**

in·put¹ /ˈɪnpʊt/ *noun* [U] **1 input (into/to sth)** what you add to sth to make it better; what you put into sth: *We need some creative input from teachers into this book.* **2** information that is put into a computer: *The computer can process the input in just a few seconds.* ☞ Look at **output.**

in·put² /ˈɪnpʊt/ *verb* [T] (*pres. part.* **in·put·ting**; *p.t., p.p.* **in·put** or **in·put·ted**) to put information into a computer

in·quest /ˈɪŋkwɛst/ *noun* [C] an official investigation that is held when the reason for sb's death is not clear: *to hold an inquest*

in·quire /ɪnˈkwaɪər/ *verb* (*formal*) [I,T] to ask for information about sth: *I inquired whether the plane had arrived yet.* ○ *I am writing to inquire about your latest product.*
PHRV **inquire into sth** to study or investigate sth to find out all the facts: *The journalist inquired into the politician's financial affairs.*

in·quir·ing /ɪnˈkwaɪərɪŋ/ *adj.* interested in learning new things: *We should encourage children to have inquiring minds.*

☆ **in·quir·y** /ˈɪŋkwəri; ɪnˈkwaɪəri/ *noun* (*pl.* **inquir·ies**) **1** [C] **inquiry (about/concerning sb/sth)** (*formal*) a question that you ask about sth: *Thank you for your inquiry about our English language programs.* **2** [C] **inquiry (into sth)** an official investigation to find out about sth or why sth happened: *an inquiry into a plane crash* **3** [U] the act of asking about sth: *His financial dealings are our main area of inquiry.*

in·quis·i·tive /ɪnˈkwɪzəṭɪv/ *adj.* very interested in learning about a lot of different things: *He's a very inquisitive child who loves to read.*

the INS /ˌaɪ ɛn ˈɛs/ *noun* [sing.] the Immigration and Naturalization Service; the government department that gives people permission to enter the U.S. ☞ Look at the note at **White House.**

in·sane /ɪnˈseɪn/ *adj.* **1** mentally ill or crazy **2** (*informal*) very foolish or stupid; not sensible: *You must be insane to leave your job before you've found another one.* ○ *$4.00 for a cup of coffee? That's totally insane!* ☞ Look at the note at **crazy.** —**in·sane·ly** *adv.*: *insanely jealous* —**in·san·i·ty** /ɪnˈsænəṭi/ *noun* [U]

in·sa·tia·ble /ɪnˈseɪʃəbl/ *adj.* not able to be satisfied; very great: *an insatiable desire for knowledge* ○ *an insatiable appetite*

in·scribe /ɪnˈskraɪb/ *verb* [T] (*formal*) **inscribe A (on/in B); inscribe B (with A)** to write or cut (**carve**) words on sth. You inscribe sth when you want it to be a permanent record: *The book was inscribed with the author's name.* ○ *names inscribed on a trophy*

in·scrip·tion /ɪnˈskrɪpʃn/ *noun* [C] words that are written or cut on sth: *There was a Latin inscription on the tombstone.*

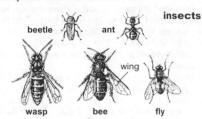

insects

beetle ant wing

wasp bee fly

☆ **in·sect** /ˈɪnsɛkt/ *noun* [C] a small animal with six legs and a body which is divided into three parts: *Ants, flies, beetles, butterflies and mosquitoes are all insects.* ○ *an insect bite/sting*

☞ Some other small animals, e.g. spiders, are often also called insects although this is technically incorrect. A more informal word for **insect** is **bug.**

in·sec·ti·cide /ɪnˈsɛktəsaɪd/ *noun* [C,U] a substance that is used for killing insects ☞ Look at **pesticide.**

in·se·cure /ˌɪnsɪˈkyʊr/ *adj.* **1** not supported very well; not safe or secure: *That ladder looks*

I

insecure. ○ *The future of the company looks very insecure.* **2 insecure (about sb/sth)** feeling anxious and not sure of yourself; not confident: *Some small children feel insecure away from their parents.* —**in·se·cu·ri·ty** /ˌɪnsɪˈkyʊrəti/ *noun* [C,U] (*pl.* **in·se·cu·ri·ties**) *Their aggressive behavior is really a sign of insecurity.* ○ *fears and insecurities*

in·sem·i·na·tion /ɪnˌsɛməˈneɪʃn/ *noun* [U] the act of putting a male's cells (**sperm**) into a female in order to produce a baby ☞ Look also at **artificial insemination**.

in·sen·si·tive /ɪnˈsɛnsətɪv/ *adj.* **1** not knowing or caring how another person feels and whether you have hurt or upset him/her: *to make an insensitive remark* **2 insensitive (to sth)** not able to feel sth: *insensitive to pain, cold, etc.* —**in·sen·si·tive·ly** *adv.* —**in·sen·si·tiv·i·ty** /ɪnˌsɛnsəˈtɪvəti/ *noun* [U]

in·sep·a·ra·ble /ɪnˈsɛpərəbl/ *adj.* not able to be separated from sb/sth: *inseparable friends*

in·sert¹ /ɪnˈsərt/ *verb* [T] (*formal*) to put sth into sth or between two things: *Insert your money and then select an item.* —**in·ser·tion** /ɪnˈsərʃn/ *noun* [C,U]

in·sert² /ˈɪnsərt/ *noun* [C] something that is put into sth else: *an advertising insert in a newspaper*

☆ **in·side¹** /ɪnˈsaɪd/ *adv.* in or to the inner part or surface of sth: *We'd better stay inside until the rain stops.* ○ *It's getting cold. Let's go inside.* ○ *Take a look inside and see what's in it.*

inside out

☆ **in·side²** /ɪnˈsaɪd; ˈɪnsaɪd/ (also *informal* **inside of**) *prep.* **1** in or on the inner part or surface of sb/sth: *Is there anything inside the box?* ○ *inside a building* **2** (used about time) in less than: *Your photos will be ready inside of an hour.*

☆ **in·side³** /ˈɪnsaɪd; ɪnˈsaɪd/ *noun* **1** [C] the inner part or surface of sth: *The insides of the windows need a good cleaning.* ○ *The door was locked from the inside.* **2** [sing.] (also **insides** [plural]) (*informal*) the inner parts of sth, especially a body or a machine: *Have you ever seen the insides of a computer?*

IDM **inside out 1** with the inner surface on the outside: *You've got your shirt on inside out.* **2** very well, in great detail: *She knows these streets inside out.*

☆ **in·side⁴** /ˈɪnsaɪd/ *adj.* (only *before* a noun) **1** in or on the inner part or surface of sth: *the inside pocket of a jacket* ○ *the inside pages of a newspaper* **2** (used about information, etc.) told secretly by sb who belongs to a group, organization, etc.: *The robbers had some inside information about the bank's security system.*

in·sid·er /ɪnˈsaɪdər; ˈɪnsaɪdər/ *noun* [C] a person who is a member of a group or an organization

in·sight /ˈɪnsaɪt/ *noun* [C,U] **insight (into sth)** (an example of) understanding the true nature of sb/sth: *The book gives a good insight into the lives of the poor.* ○ *You need insight into human nature for this job.*

in·sig·nif·i·cant /ˌɪnsɪɡˈnɪfɪkənt/ *adj.* of little value or importance: *an insignificant detail* —**in·sig·nif·i·cance** /-kəns/ *noun* [U] —**in·sig·nif·i·cant·ly** *adv.*

in·sin·cere /ˌɪnsɪnˈsɪr/ *adj.* not meaning what you say; not truthful; not sincere: *His apology sounded insincere.* —**in·sin·cere·ly** *adv.* —**in·sin·cer·i·ty** /ˌɪnsɪnˈsɛrəti/ *noun* [U]

in·sin·u·ate /ɪnˈsɪmyueɪt/ *verb* [T] to suggest sth unkind in an indirect way: *She seemed to be insinuating that our work was below average.* —**in·sin·u·a·tion** /ɪnˌsɪmyuˈeɪʃn/ *noun* [C,U]: *to make insinuations about sb's honesty*

☆ **in·sist** /ɪnˈsɪst/ *verb* **1** [I,T] **insist (on sth/on doing sth)** to say or demand that you must have or do sth or that sb else must do sth: *He always insists on the best.* ○ *Her parents insist that she come home before midnight.* ○ *Dick insisted on coming too.* ○ *"Have another piece of cake." "Oh all right, if you insist."* **2** [I,T] **insist (on sth)** to say firmly that sth is true (when sb does not believe you): *She insisted on her innocence.* ○ *James insisted that the accident wasn't his fault.*

in·sis·tent /ɪnˈsɪstənt/ *adj.* saying or demanding that you must have or do sth or that sb else must do sth: *Local residents are insistent on having the hazardous waste moved out of the area.* ○ (*figurative*) *We could not ignore the insistent ringing of the telephone.* —**in·sis·tence** /-əns/ *noun* [U] —**in·sis·tent·ly** *adv.*

in·sol·vent /ɪnˈsɑlvənt/ *adj.* (*formal*) (used about a bank, etc.) not having enough money to pay its debts: *Several savings and loan associations have been declared insolvent.* —**in·sol·ven·cy** /ɪnˈsɑlvənsi/ *noun* [C,U] (*pl.* **in·sol·ven·cies**)

in·som·ni·a /ɪnˈsɑmniə/ *noun* [U] if you suffer from insomnia you find it difficult to get to sleep and to sleep well

☆ **in·spect** /ɪnˈspɛkt/ *verb* [T] **1 inspect sb/sth (for sth)** to look at sth closely or in great detail: *to inspect a machine for faults* **2** to make an official visit to make sure that rules are being obeyed, work is being done correctly, etc.: *All restaurants should be inspected regularly.* —**in·spec·tion** /ɪnˈspɛkʃn/ *noun* [C,U]: *Officials carried out inspections of all the airline's planes.* [U]: *On inspection, the passport turned out to be false.*

☆ **in·spec·tor** /ɪnˈspɛktər/ *noun* [C] **1** an official who inspects(2) sth: *a health and safety inspector* **2** a police officer of middle rank

in·spi·ra·tion /ˌɪnspəˈreɪʃn/ *noun* [C,U] **inspiration (to/for sb); inspiration (to do sth)** (a

person or thing that causes) a feeling of wanting and being able to do sth good, create a work of art, etc.: *The beauty of the mountains was a great source of inspiration to the writer.* ∘ *Her example has been an inspiration to many younger women.*

in·spire /ɪnˈspaɪər/ *verb* [T] **1** to give sb a feeling of wanting and being able to do sth good, create a work of art, etc.: *His novel was inspired by his relationship with his first wife.* **2 inspire sb (with sth); inspire sth (in sb)** to make sb feel, think, etc. sth: *to be inspired with enthusiasm* ∘ *The guide's nervous manner did not inspire much confidence in us.* —**in·spir·ing** /ɪnˈspaɪərɪŋ/ *adj.*: *It was not a very inspiring speech.* ☞ The opposite is **uninspiring.**

in·spired /ɪnˈspaɪərd/ *adj.* produced with the help of inspiration: *The pianist gave an inspired performance.* ☞ The opposite is **uninspired.**

in·sta·bil·i·ty /ˌɪnstəˈbɪləti/ *noun* [U] the state of being likely to change: *political instability* ☞ The adjective is **unstable.**

☆ **in·stall** /ɪnˈstɔl/ *verb* [T] **1** to put a piece of equipment, etc. in place so that it is ready to be used: *We are waiting to have our new washing machine installed.* ∘ *to install software on a computer* **2** put sb/sth or yourself in a position or place: *He was installed as chairperson yesterday.* —**in·stal·la·tion** /ˌɪnstəˈleɪʃn/ *noun* [C,U]

in·stall·ment /ɪnˈstɔlmənt/ *noun* [C] **1** one of the regular payments that you make for sth. People buy sth in installments when they cannot or do not want to pay the whole amount at once. **2** a single part of a book, television show, etc. that is published or shown regularly over a period of time: *Don't miss next week's exciting installment.*

☆ **in·stance** /ˈɪnstəns/ *noun* [C] an example or case (of sth): *There have been several instances of racial attacks in the area.* ∘ *In most instances the drug has no side effects.*

IDM **for instance** for example: *There are several interesting places to visit around here. Georgetown, for instance, has a lot of historic buildings.*

☆ **in·stant¹** /ˈɪnstənt/ *adj.* **1** happening suddenly or at once; immediate: *The movie was an instant success.* **2** (used about food) able to be prepared quickly and easily: *instant coffee*

in·stant² /ˈɪnstənt/ *noun* [usually sing.] **1** a particular point in time: *At that instant I realized I had been tricked.* ∘ *Stop doing that this instant* (= now)*!* **2** a very short period of time: *Alex thought for an instant and then agreed.*

in·stan·ta·ne·ous /ˌɪnstənˈteɪniəs/ *adj.* happening at once or immediately: *Death was instantaneous.* —**in·stan·ta·ne·ous·ly** *adv.*

☆ **in·stant·ly** /ˈɪnstəntli/ *adv.* without delay; immediately: *I asked him a question and he replied instantly.*

instant ˈreplay *noun* [C] a short part of a sports game on television that is shown again, often at a slower speed, so that people can see an exciting or important moment again

☆ **in·stead** /ɪnˈstɛd/ *adv.* **instead (of sb/sth)** in the place of sb/sth: *I couldn't go so my husband went instead.* ∘ *There's nothing on TV, so let's play a game instead.* ∘ *You should play tennis instead of just watching it on TV.* ∘ *Could I come at 8:00 instead of 7:30?*

in·sti·gate /ˈɪnstəɡeɪt/ *verb* [T] (*formal*) to make sth start to happen —**in·sti·ga·tion** /ˌɪnstəˈɡeɪʃn/ *noun* [U]

in·still /ɪnˈstɪl/ *verb* [T] **instill sth (in/into sb)** to make sb think or feel sth: *Parents should try to instill a sense of responsibility into their children.*

in·stinct /ˈɪnstɪŋkt/ *noun* [C,U] the natural force that causes a person or animal to behave in a certain way without thinking or learning about it: *Birds learn to fly by instinct.* ∘ *I didn't stop to think. I just acted on instinct.* —**in·stinc·tive** /ɪnˈstɪŋktɪv/ *adj.*: *Your instinctive reaction is to run from danger.* —**in·stinc·tive·ly** *adv.*

☆ **in·sti·tute¹** /ˈɪnstətut/ *noun* [C] an academic, etc. organization: *the Massachusetts Institute of Technology*

in·sti·tute² /ˈɪnstətut/ *verb* [T] (*formal*) to set up or start a system, course of action, etc.: *The government has instituted a new job training program.*

☆ **in·sti·tu·tion** /ˌɪnstəˈtuʃn/ *noun* [C] **1** a large organization such as a bank, a university, etc.: *the financial institutions on Wall Street* ∘ *an educational institution* **2** a building where certain people with special needs live and are taken care of: *a mental institution* (= a hospital for the mentally ill) **3** a social custom or habit that has existed for a long time: *the institution of marriage* —**in·sti·tu·tion·al** /-ʃənl/ *adj.*

☆ **in·struct** /ɪnˈstrʌkt/ *verb* [T] **1 instruct sb (to do sth)** to give an order to sb; to tell sb to do sth: *The soldiers were instructed to shoot above the heads of the crowd.* **2 instruct sb (in sth)** (*formal*) to teach: *Children should be instructed in traffic safety.*

☆ **in·struc·tion** /ɪnˈstrʌkʃn/ *noun* **1** [U] **instruction (in sth)** teaching or being taught: *We offer instruction in all styles of dance.* **2** [C, usually pl.] an order or direction that tells you what to do or how to do sth: *The guard was under strict instructions not to let anyone in.* **3 instructions** [plural] information on how you should use sth, do sth, etc.: *Read the instructions carefully.* ∘ *to follow the instructions*

in·struc·tive /ɪnˈstrʌktɪv/ *adj.* giving useful information —**in·struc·tive·ly** *adv.*

☆ **in·struc·tor** /ɪnˈstrʌktər/ *noun* [C] a person who teaches: *a driving instructor* ∘ *an instructor at the college*

☆ **in·stru·ment** /ˈɪnstrəmənt/ *noun* [C] **1** a tool that is used for doing a particular job or task:

surgical instruments ☞ Look at the note at **tool**. **2** something that is used for playing music: *"What instrument do you play?" "The violin."*

☞ **Musical instruments** may be **stringed** (*violins, guitars*, etc.), **brass** (*horns, trumpets,* etc.) or **woodwind** (*flutes, clarinets,* etc.). **Percussion** instruments include *drums* and *cymbals*.

3 something that is used for measuring speed, fuel levels, etc. in a car, plane or ship: *the instrument panel of an airplane*

☆ **in·stru·men·tal** /ˌɪnstrəˈmɛntl/ *adj.* **1** (not before a noun) **instrumental in doing sth** helping to make sth happen: *She was instrumental in getting him the job.* **2** for musical instruments, without voices: *instrumental music*

in·sub·or·di·na·tion /ˌɪnsəˌbɔrdnˈeɪʃn/ *noun* [U] refusing to obey orders or instructions, especially in the army, etc.

in·suf·fi·cient /ˌɪnsəˈfɪʃnt/ *adj.* **insufficient (for sth/to do sth)** not enough: *We were given insufficient time for the test.*

in·su·lar /ˈɪnsələr; ˈɪnsyələr/ *adj.* not interested in, or able to accept, new people or different ideas —**in·su·lar·i·ty** /ˌɪnsəˈlærəti; ˌɪnsyə-/ *noun* [U]

in·su·late /ˈɪnsəleɪt/ *verb* [T] to protect or cover sth with a material that prevents electricity, heat or sound from passing through: *You can save a lot of money on heating if your house is well insulated.*

in·su·la·tion /ˌɪnsəˈleɪʃn/ *noun* [U] **1** the material used for insulating sth **2** the process of insulating or the state of being insulated: *Foam rubber provides good insulation.*

☆ **in·sult¹** /ɪnˈsʌlt/ *verb* [T] to speak or act rudely to sb: *I felt very insulted when I didn't even get an answer to my letter.*

☆ **in·sult²** /ˈɪnsʌlt/ *noun* [C] a rude remark or action: *The drivers were yelling insults at each other.* ○ *Some television commercials are an insult to people's intelligence.*

in·sult·ing /ɪnˈsʌltɪŋ/ *adj.* rude or offensive: *A lot of women find his behavior very insulting.*

☆ **in·sur·ance** /ɪnˈʃʊrəns/ *noun* **1** [U] a contract in which, in return for regular payment, a company or the state agrees to pay a sum of money if sth (e.g. illness, death, loss of or damage to property) happens to sb: *Farmers should always have insurance against crop damage.* ○ *They had no insurance on their house when it burned down.* ○ *Our roof was blown off in the storm, but our insurance paid for it.*

☞ We **take out** an **insurance policy.** An **insurance premium** is the regular amount you pay to the insurance company. We can take out **life**, **health** (or **medical**), **car** (or **auto**), **travel** and **homeowners' insurance.**

2 [U] the business of providing insurance (1) contracts: *He works in insurance.*

☆ **in·sure** /ɪnˈʃʊr/ *verb* [T] **1 insure sb/sth (against sth)** to take out or to provide insurance: *They insured the painting for $10,000 against damage or theft.* ○ *Are you insured against accident and medical expenses on your trip?* **2** = ENSURE

in·sur·rec·tion /ˌɪnsəˈrɛkʃn/ *noun* [C,U] violent action against the rulers of a country or the government

☆ **in·tact** /ɪnˈtækt/ *adj.* complete; not damaged: *Very few of the buildings remained intact after the earthquake.*

in·take /ˈɪnteɪk/ *noun* [C, usually sing.] (used about food, liquid, air, etc.) the amount that sb/sth takes in or the process of taking it in: *If you're driving, you should watch your alcohol intake carefully.*

in·tan·gi·ble /ɪnˈtændʒəbl/ *adj.* (used about a quality or an idea) difficult to describe, understand or explain

in·te·gral /ˈɪntəgrəl; ɪnˈtɛgrəl/ *adj.* essential (in order to make sth complete): *Lab work is an integral part of the course.*

☆ **in·te·grate** /ˈɪntəgreɪt/ *verb* **1** [T] to end a system of separating people of different races in a place: *plans to integrate public housing in the city* ☞ Look also at **segregate** and **desegregate**. **2** [I,T] **integrate (sb) (into sth/with sth)** to join in and become part of a group or community or to make sb do this: *The school aims to integrate hearing-impaired students into regular classes.* ☞ Look at **segregate**. **3** [T] **integrate sth (into sth); integrate A and B/integrate A with B** to join things so that they become one thing or fit together: *The architect integrated our ideas into the plans for the house.* —**in·te·gra·tion** /ˌɪntəˈgreɪʃn/ *noun* [U]: *racial integration* ☞ Look at **segregation** and **desegregation.**

in·teg·ri·ty /ɪnˈtɛgrəti/ *noun* [U] the quality of being honest and having firm moral ideas: *He's a person of courage and integrity.*

in·tel·lect /ˈɪntəlɛkt/ *noun* [C,U] the power of the mind to think and to learn

☆ **in·tel·lec·tu·al¹** /ˌɪntəˈlɛktʃuəl/ *adj.* (usually before a noun) using or able to use the power of the mind: *The boy's intellectual development was very advanced for his age.* ○ *intellectual people, interests, discussions, etc.* —**in·tel·lec·tu·al·ly** *adv.*

in·tel·lec·tu·al² /ˌɪntəˈlɛktʃuəl/ *noun* [C] a person who is interested in ideas, literature, art, etc.: *The café was a well-known meeting place for artists and intellectuals.*

☆ **in·tel·li·gence** /ɪnˈtɛlədʒəns/ *noun* [U] **1** the ability to understand, learn and think: *Examinations are not necessarily the best way to measure intelligence.* ○ *a person of normal intelligence* ○ *an intelligence test* **2** important information about an enemy country: *The army*

gathered intelligence about the enemy's strength.

☆**in·tel·li·gent** /ɪnˈtɛlədʒənt/ adj. having or showing intelligence: *All their kids are very intelligent.* ○ *an intelligent question* ☞ The opposite is **unintelligent**. A more informal word for intelligent is **smart**. —**in·tel·li·gent·ly** adv.

in·tel·li·gi·ble /ɪnˈtɛlədʒəbl/ adj. (used especially about speech or writing) possible or easy to understand ☞ The opposite is **unintelligible**.

☆**in·tend** /ɪnˈtɛnd/ verb [T] **1 intend (to do sth)** to plan or mean to do sth: *I spent more money than I had intended.* ○ *I intended to call, but I totally forgot.* ○ *I certainly don't intend to wait here all day!* ☞ The noun is **intention**. **2 intend sth for sb/sth; intend sth as sth** (often passive) to plan, mean or make sth for a particular person or purpose: *You shouldn't have read that letter – it wasn't intended for you.* ○ *This dictionary is intended for intermediate learners of English.* ○ *His remark was not intended as an insult.* **3 intend sth to do sth; intend for sb to do sth** to plan or mean that sb/sth should do sth: *The show was not the success its writers had intended it to be.* ○ *I never intended for you to do all the work.*

☆**in·tense** /ɪnˈtɛns/ adj. very great, strong or serious: *intense heat* ○ *intense anger* ○ *an intense* (= very serious) *young man* —**in·tense·ly** adv.: *They obviously dislike each other intensely.* —**in·ten·si·ty** /-səṭi/ noun [U]: *I wasn't prepared for the intensity of his reaction to the news.*

in·ten·si·fy /ɪnˈtɛnsəfaɪ/ verb (pres. part. **in·ten·si·fy·ing**; 3rd pers. sing. pres. **in·ten·si·fies**; p.t., p.p. **in·ten·si·fied**) [I,T] to become or to make sth greater or stronger: *The government has intensified its anti-smoking campaign.*

in·ten·sive /ɪnˈtɛnsɪv/ adj. concentrated on a particular activity or area within a limited amount of time: *an intensive investigation* ○ *The course only lasted a week, but it was very intensive.* —**in·ten·sive·ly** adv.

in,tensive ˈcare noun [U] special care for patients who are very seriously sick or injured (or the department that gives this care): *Your son has been seriously hurt and is in intensive care.*

in·tent[1] /ɪnˈtɛnt/ noun [C,U] (formal) what sb intends or plans to do; intention: *He was arrested and charged with assault with intent to murder.*

in·tent[2] /ɪnˈtɛnt/ adj. **1** showing great attention: *He listened to the whole story with an intent expression on his face.* **2 intent on/upon sth/doing sth** determined to do sth or concentrating on sth: *He's always been intent on making a lot of money.* ○ *She was so intent upon her*

work that she didn't hear Phoebe come in. —**in·tent·ly** adv.

☆**in·ten·tion** /ɪnˈtɛnʃn/ noun [C,U] what sb intends or means to do; a plan or purpose: *It's not clear what the enemy's intentions are.* ○ *Our intention was to leave early in the morning.* ○ *I have no intention of staying indoors on a nice sunny day like this.*

☆**in·ten·tion·al** /ɪnˈtɛnʃənl/ adj. done on purpose, not by chance: *It was an intentional attempt to manipulate the news media.* ○ *victims of intentional discrimination* ☞ The opposite is **unintentional**. Look at **deliberate**. It is similar in meaning. —**in·ten·tion·al·ly** adv.: *I can't believe the boys broke the window intentionally.*

in·ter·act /ˌɪntərˈækt/ verb [I] **1** (used about people) to communicate or mix in a way that has an influence or effect on sb else: *She is studying the way babies interact with each other.* **2** (of two things) to have an effect on each other

in·ter·ac·tion /ˌɪntərˈækʃn/ noun [C,U] (an example of) working together or mixing: *An interaction of two chemicals produced the explosion.* ○ *There is a need for greater interaction among the different departments.*

in·ter·ac·tive /ˌɪntərˈæktɪv/ adj. (technical) (used about computers) involving or allowing direct two-way communication between the computer and the person using it: *interactive computer games*

in·ter·cept /ˌɪntərˈsɛpt/ verb [T] to stop or catch sb or sth that is moving from one place to another: *Agents intercepted several messages from the drug dealer to his supplier.* —**in·ter·cep·tion** /ˌɪntərˈsɛpʃn/ noun [C,U]

in·ter·change·a·ble /ˌɪntərˈtʃeɪmdʒəbl/ adj. able to be used in place of each other without making any difference: *Are these two words interchangeable?* —**in·ter·change·a·bly** adv.

in·ter·com /ˈɪntərkɑm/ noun [C] an electrical system for communication between people in different parts of a factory, an airplane, etc.: *Please try to contact Mr. Pearson on/over the intercom.*

in·ter·con·nect /ˌɪntərkəˈnɛkt/ verb [I] to be connected or linked —**in·ter·con·nect·ed** adj.

in·ter·con·ti·nen·tal /ˌɪntərˌkɑntəˈnɛntl; -ˌkɑntnˈɛntl/ adj. between continents: *intercontinental flights*

in·ter·course /ˈɪntərkɔrs/ noun [U] = SEX(3)

in·ter·de·pend·ent /ˌɪntərdɪˈpɛndənt/ adj. depending on each other: *Exercise and good health are generally interdependent.* —**in·ter·de·pend·ence** /-əns/ noun [U]

☆**in·ter·est**[1] /ˈɪntrəst; ˈɪntrɛst/ noun **1** [U, sing.] **an interest (in sb/sth)** a desire to learn or hear more about sb/sth or to be involved with sb/sth: *She's starting to show a great interest in politics.* ○ *I wish he'd take more interest in*

his kids. ○ *Don't lose interest now!* **2** [C] something that you enjoy doing or learning about: *Tell me about your interests and hobbies.* **3** [U] the quality that makes sb curious or attracts sb's attention: *I thought this article might be of interest to you.* **4** [C] something that gives a benefit, profit or advantage to sb: *We have your interests at heart.* **5** [C] a legal right to share in a business, etc., especially in its profits: *When he retired, he sold his interests in the company.* **6** [U] **interest (on sth)** the money that you earn from investments or that you pay for borrowing money: *If you invest your capital wisely, it will earn a lot of interest.* ○ *We're paying 10% interest on our mortgage right now.* ○ *The interest rate has never been so high/low.* ○ *Some companies offer interest-free loans.*

IDM conflict of interest ⇨ CONFLICT¹

in sb's interest(s) to sb's advantage: *He claimed to be acting in the public interest when he lied in court.*

in the interest(s) of sth in order to achieve or protect sth: *In the interest(s) of safety, please fasten your seat belts.*

☆ **in·ter·est²** /ˈɪntrəst; ˈɪntrɛst/ *verb* [T] **1** to make sb want to learn or hear more about sth or to become involved in sth: *Politics is a subject that interests me greatly.* **2** to make sb want to buy, have or do sth: *Can I interest you in our new product line?*

☆ **in·ter·est·ed** /ˈɪntrəstəd; ˈɪntərəstəd/ *adj.* **1** (not before a noun) **interested (in sth/sb)** wanting to know or hear about sth/sb; or to do or achieve sth: *They weren't interested in my news at all!* ○ *I was interested to hear that you have a new job. Where is it?* ○ *All he's interested in is money.* ☛ The opposite is **uninterested. 2** (only before a noun) involved in or affected by (a particular situation, etc.): *I think they should have talked to the interested parties* (= people, groups, etc.) *before they made that decision.* ☛ The opposite is **disinterested.**

☆ **in·ter·est·ing** /ˈɪntrəstɪŋ; ˈɪntərəstɪŋ/ *adj.* enjoyable and entertaining to do, think about, talk to, etc.; holding your attention: *an interesting person, book, idea, job, etc.* ○ *It's always interesting to hear about other cultures.* ☛ The opposite is **uninteresting.** —**in·ter·est·ing·ly** *adv.*

☆ **in·ter·fere** /ˌɪntərˈfɪr/ *verb* [I] **1 interfere (in sth)** to try to take part in sb's affairs, etc. when you and your help are not wanted: *You shouldn't interfere – let your kids make their own decisions.* **2 interfere (with sb/sth)** to prevent sth or slow down the progress that sb/sth makes: *Every time the telephone rings, it interferes with my work.* **3 interfere (with sth)** to touch or alter sth without permission: *Many people feel that scientists shouldn't interfere with nature.*

in·ter·fer·ence /ˌɪntərˈfɪrəns/ *noun* [U]

1 interference (in/with sth) the act of interfering: *I left home because I couldn't stand my parents' interference in my life.* **2** something, such as other signals, that prevents equipment from receiving clear radio, television or telephone signals

in·ter·im¹ /ˈɪntərəm/ *noun*

IDM in the interim in the time between two things happening

in·ter·im² /ˈɪntərəm/ *adj.* (only *before* a noun) not final or lasting; temporary: *an interim arrangement* (= before sth definite can be decided)

☆ **in·te·ri·or¹** /ɪnˈtɪriər/ *adj.* (only *before* a noun) inner; on the inside: *interior walls* ○ *interior decoration* (= decorating the rooms in a house)

☆ **in·te·ri·or²** /ɪnˈtɪriər/ *noun* [C, usually sing.] the inner part; inside: *I'd love to see the interior of their house.* ☛ The opposite is **exterior.**

the In·te·ri·or De·part·ment *noun* [sing.] the U.S. government department that is in charge of the country's natural resources and the land that the government owns ☛ Look at the note at **White House.**

in·ter·jec·tion /ˌɪntərˈdʒɛkʃn/ *noun* [C] **1** (*formal*) something you say that interrupts sb else **2** (*grammar*) a word or phrase that is used as an expression of surprise, pain, pleasure, etc. (e.g. Oh!, Hey! or Wow!) ☛ Look at **exclamation.**

in·ter·lude /ˈɪntərlud/ *noun* [C] a short period of time when an entertainment or activity stops for a break; an interval: *There was a brief interlude in the fighting.*

in·ter·mar·riage /ˌɪntərˈmærɪdʒ/ *noun* [U] marriage between people of different races, religions, etc.

in·ter·me·di·ar·y /ˌɪntərˈmidiˌɛri/ *noun* [C] (*pl.* **in·ter·me·di·ar·ies**) a person who passes communications between two people or groups, usually in order to help them reach an agreement

☆ **in·ter·me·di·ate** /ˌɪntərˈmidiət/ *adj.* **1** coming between two people or things in position, level, etc. **2** between two stages (beginning and advanced): *an intermediate student, class, course, book, level, etc.*

in·ter·mis·sion /ˌɪntərˈmɪʃn/ *noun* [C] a break during a play, concert, etc.

in·ter·mit·tent /ˌɪntərˈmɪtnt/ *adj.* stopping for a while and then starting again: *There will be intermittent showers.* —**in·ter·mit·tent·ly** *adv.*

in·tern¹ /ˈɪntərn/ *noun* [C] **1** a doctor who is finished studying in medical school and is receiving practical training in a hospital **2** a person, especially a student, who is working somewhere for a short time in order to learn about a particular job or career

in·tern² /ɪnˈtərn/ *verb* [T] (*formal*) to keep sb in prison, especially for political reasons or during a war —**in·tern·ment** /ɪnˈtərnmənt/ *noun* [U]

i	ɪ	ɛ	æ	ɑ	ɔ	ʌ	ʊ	u
see	sit	ten	cat	hot	saw	cup	put	too

☆ **in·ter·nal** /m'tərnl/ *adj.* **1** of or on the inside (of a place, person or object): *He was rushed to the hospital with internal injuries.* **2** happening or existing inside a particular organization, country, etc.: *The police department conducted an internal investigation.* ○ *Internal documents showed evidence of bribery.* ☞ The opposite for all senses is **external**.

in·ter·nal·ly /m'tərnl·i/ *adv.* on the inside: *This medication is not to be taken internally* (= not to be swallowed).

the In₁ternal 'Revenue ₁Service *noun* [sing.] = IRS ☞ Look at the note at **White House**.

☆ **in·ter·na·tion·al** /₁mtər'næʃənl/ *adj.* involving two or more countries: *an international agreement, flight, competition, etc.* ○ *international trade, law, etc.* —**in·ter·na·tion·al·ly** *adv.*

the In·ter·net /'mtərnɛt/(also *informal* **the Net**) *noun* [sing.] the international system of computers that makes it possible for you to see information from around the world on your computer and to send information to other computers: *I read about this on the Internet.* ☞ Look at the note at **White House**.

in·tern·ship /'mtərnʃɪp/ *noun* [C] a period of time when sb, especially a student, works in order to learn about a particular career, or the job that he/she does during that time: *I'm applying for an internship at a software company.* ○ *a paid/an unpaid internship*

☆ **in·ter·pret** /m'tərprət/ *verb* **1** [T] **interpret sth (as sth)** to explain or understand the meaning of sth: *I don't know how to interpret her behavior.* ○ *How would you interpret this part of the poem?* **2** [I] to translate what sb is saying into another language: *He'll need somebody to interpret for him.*

in·ter·pre·ta·tion /m₁tərprə'teɪʃn/ *noun* [C,U] **1** an explanation or understanding of sth: *What's your interpretation of these statistics?* **2** the way an actor or a musician chooses to perform or understand a character or piece of music: *The actor's interpretation of Hamlet was severely criticized.*

in·ter·pret·er /m'tərprətər/ *noun* [C] a person whose job is to translate what sb is saying immediately into another language: *The president spoke through an interpreter.* ☞ Look at **translator**.

in·ter·ra·cial /₁mtər'reɪʃl/ *adj.* involving people of different races: *interracial dating and marriage*

in·ter·re·lat·ed /₁mtərrɪ'leɪtəd/ *adj.* connected with each other

in·ter·ro·gate /m'tɛrəgeɪt/ *verb* [T] **interrogate sb (about sth)** to ask sb questions in a thorough and sometimes aggressive way (in order to get information): *The prisoner was interrogated for six hours.* —**in·ter·ro·ga·tor** *noun* [C]

in·ter·ro·ga·tion /m₁tɛrə'geɪʃn/ *noun* [C,U] the time when a person is interrogated: *The interrogations took place in a small underground room.* ○ *The prisoner was led away for interrogation.*

☆ **in·ter·rupt** /₁mtə'rʌpt/ *verb* **1** [I,T] **interrupt (sb/sth) (with sth)** to make sb stop speaking or doing sth by saying or doing sth yourself: *I'm sorry to interrupt, but there's a phone call for you.* ○ *Quit interrupting me when I'm talking.* **2** [T] to stop sth or make a break in it: *The program was interrupted by a news bulletin.*

☆ **in·ter·rup·tion** /₁mtə'rʌpʃn/ *noun* **1** [C] something that prevents an activity or situation from continuing: *I've had so many interruptions this morning that I haven't gotten anything done!* **2** [U] the act of interrupting sb/sth: *I need one whole day without any interruption.*

in·ter·sect /₁mtərsɛkʃn; ₁mtər'sɛkt/ *verb* [I,T] (used about roads, lines, etc.) to meet and go across each other

☆ **in·ter·sec·tion** /₁mtər'sɛkʃn/ *noun* [C] the place where two or more roads, lines, etc. meet and cross each other: *The accident happened at the intersection of Fifth Avenue and Jefferson Street.*

in·ter·sperse /₁mtər'spərs/ *verb* [T] (usually passive) to put things at various points in sth: *His speech was interspersed with jokes.*

☆ **in·ter·state¹** /'mtərsteɪt/ *noun* [C] (*abbr.* I) a wide road for fast traffic that is part of a national system of these roads: *Head south on Interstate 95 until you see the sign for Providence.* ☞ Look at the note at **freeway**.

☆ **in·ter·state²** /'mtərsteɪt/ *adj.* (only *before* a noun) between different states: *interstate commerce*

☆ **in·ter·val** /'mtərvl/ *noun* [C] a period of time between two events: *I'm trying to leave longer intervals between cigarettes.* ○ *There were only a few intervals of silence during the discussion.* ☞ Look at the note at **pause¹**.

IDM **at intervals (of...)** with time or with spaces between: *I always write home at regular intervals.* ○ *The trees should be planted at intervals of two yards.*

in·ter·vene /₁mtər'vin/ *verb* [I] **1 intervene (in sth/between A and B)** to act in a way that prevents sth from happening or influences the result of sth: *The police had to intervene between the two groups.* ○ *to intervene in a dispute* **2** (used about time) to come between: *During the months that intervened, they wrote to each other nearly every day.*

in·ter·ven·ing /₁mtər'vinm/ *adj.* (only *before* a noun) coming or existing between (two events, dates, objects, etc.): *the intervening years*

in·ter·ven·tion /₁mtər'vɛnʃn/ *noun* [C,U] an act of intervening, especially to prevent sth

ə	y	w	ṭ	eɪ	aɪ	ɔɪ	aʊ	oʊ
about	yes	woman	butter	say	five	boy	now	go

from happening: *military intervention in the crisis*

☆ **in·ter·view¹** /ˈɪntərvyu/ *noun* [C] **1** a meeting at which a journalist asks sb questions in order to find out his/her opinion, etc. (often shown on television or printed in a newspaper): *an exclusive interview with a popular TV star* ○ *The actress refused to give an interview.* ○ *The mayor criticized his opponent in an interview on the local news.* **2** a meeting at which sb is asked questions to find out if he/she is suitable for a job: *Interviews will be held on June 10.* ○ *They called me for an interview for that job in Washington!*

☆ **in·ter·view²** /ˈɪntərvyu/ *verb* [T] **1 interview sb (about sth)** (used about a journalist, etc.) to ask sb questions in an interview (to find out his/her opinions, etc.) **2 interview sb (for sth)** to ask sb questions in an interview (to find out if he/she is suitable for a job, etc.): *How many applicants did you interview for the job?*

☆ **in·ter·view·er** /ˈɪntərvyuər/ *noun* [C] a person who asks the questions in an interview

in·tes·tine /ɪnˈtɛstən/ *noun* [C, usually pl.] the long tube in your body that carries food from your stomach —**in·tes·ti·nal** /ɪnˈtɛstənl/ *adj.*

in·ti·ma·cy /ˈɪntəməsi/ *noun* [U] **1** the state of being very close: *Their intimacy grew with the years.* **2** a sexual relationship

in·ti·mate /ˈɪntəmət/ *adj.* **1** having a very close relationship: *They're intimate friends.* **2** private and personal: *They told each other their most intimate thoughts and secrets.* **3** connected with sex: *She had had an intimate relationship with the senator.* **4** very detailed: *He has an intimate knowledge of the area.* **5** (used about a place, an atmosphere, etc.) quiet and friendly or small: *a chance to see top Broadway stars in a more intimate setting*

in·ti·mate·ly /ˈɪntəmətli/ *adv.* in a close or personal way: *Do you know him intimately?*

in·tim·i·date /ɪnˈtɪmədeɪt/ *verb* [T] **intimidate sb (into sth/doing sth)** to frighten sb (often in order to make him/her do sth) —**in·tim·i·da·tion** /ɪnˌtɪməˈdeɪʃn/ *noun* [U]: *The rebel troops controlled the area by intimidation.*

in·tim·i·dat·ing /ɪnˈtɪmədeɪṭɪŋ/ *adj.* frightening (because of size or difficulty)

☆ **in·to** /ˈɪntə; *strong form and before vowels* ˈɪntu/ *prep.* **1** moving to a position inside or in sth: *Come into the house.* ○ *I'm going into town.* **2** in the direction of sth: *Please speak into the microphone.* **3** to a point at which you hit sth: *I backed the car into a wall.* **4** (showing a change): *We're turning the spare room into a study.* ○ *She changed into her jeans.* ○ *The new rules will come into force next year.* **5** (used when you are dividing numbers): *7 goes into 28 four times.*

IDM be into sth (*informal*) to be very interested in sth (e.g. as a hobby): *I'm really into canoeing.*

in·tol·er·a·ble /ɪnˈtɑlərəbl/ *adj.* too bad or severe to stand or accept: *The living conditions were intolerable.* ○ *intolerable pain* ☞ The verb is **tolerate**. —**in·tol·er·a·bly** /-əbli/ *adv.*

in·tol·er·ant /ɪnˈtɑlərənt/ *adj.* **intolerant (of sb/sth)** not able to accept behavior or opinions that are different from your own —**in·tol·er·ance** /-əns/ *noun* [U]

in·to·na·tion /ˌɪntəˈneɪʃn/ *noun* [C,U] the rise and fall of the level of your voice while you are speaking

in·tox·i·cat·ed /ɪnˈtɑksəkeɪṭəd/ *adj.* (*formal*) **1** having had too much alcohol to drink; drunk: *He was arrested for driving while intoxicated.* **2** very excited: *She was intoxicated by her success.* —**in·tox·i·ca·tion** /ɪnˌtɑksəˈkeɪʃn/ *noun* [U]

in·tran·si·tive /ɪnˈtrænsəṭɪv; -ˈtrænz-/ *adj.* (*grammar*) (used about a verb) used without an object

☞ Intransitive verbs are marked [I] in this dictionary.

—**in·tran·si·tive·ly** *adv.*

in·tra·ve·nous /ˌɪntrəˈvinəs/ *adj.* directly into the body's blood system through a vein: *intravenous drug users* (= who use special needles to put drugs directly into their veins) ☞ Look also at **IV**.

in·trep·id /ɪnˈtrɛpəd/ *adj.* (*formal*) (used about people and their actions) brave and without any fear

in·tri·ca·cy /ˈɪntrɪkəsi/ *noun* **1 intricacies** [plural] the complicated details (of sth): *It's difficult to understand all the intricacies of the situation.* **2** [U] the quality of being intricate: *I was impressed by the intricacy of the design.*

in·tri·cate /ˈɪntrɪkət/ *adj.* having many small parts put together in a complicated way: *an intricate pattern* ○ *an intricate plot to the story* —**in·tri·cate·ly** *adv.*

in·trigue¹ /ɪnˈtrig/ *verb* [T] (often passive) to make sb very interested or curious: *I was intrigued by some of the unusual objects in the exhibit.*

in·trigue² /ˈɪntrig; ɪnˈtrig/ *noun* [C,U] the making of a secret plan to do sth bad: *a story of political intrigue and corruption*

in·tri·guing /ɪnˈtrigɪŋ/ *adj.* very interesting; fascinating

in·trin·sic /ɪnˈtrɪnzɪk; -sɪk/ *adj.* (only *before* a noun) (*formal*) (used about the value or quality of sth) belonging to sth as part of its nature; basic: *The object has no intrinsic value* (= the material it is made of is not worth anything). —**in·trin·si·cal·ly** /-kli/ *adv.*

☆ **in·tro·duce** /ˌɪntrəˈdus/ *verb* [T] **1 introduce sb (to sb)** to tell two or more people who have not met before what each others' names are so

that they can get to know each other: *"Who's that girl over there?" "Come with me and I'll introduce you to her."* **2 introduce yourself (to sb)** to tell sb what your name is so that you can get to know him/her: *He just walked over and introduced himself to me.* **3** to tell an audience the name of the person, who is going to speak, perform, entertain, etc.: *And now it's time to introduce my next guest on the show...* **4** to announce and give details of a radio or television program: *The program was introduced by Charles Kuralt.* **5 introduce sth (in/into sth)** to bring in, use, or take sth to a place for the first time: *The new law was introduced in 1991.* **6 introduce sb to sth** to make sb begin to learn about sth or do sth for the first time: *This pamphlet will introduce you to the basic aims of our society.*

☛ There are a number of different ways of introducing one person to another, depending on the occasion: (*informal*) *"John, this is my friend Mary."* ○ *"Mrs. Smith, this is my daughter, Jane."* ○ (*formal*) *"Let me introduce you. Dr. Gordon, this is Prof. Phil Jones. Prof. Jones, Dr. Joan Gordon."* An informal response to an introduction is "Hi" or "Nice to meet you." In a more formal situation you can say "Hello" or "I'm pleased to meet you." A very formal response is "How do you do?" The other person then also replies: "How do you do?" When people are introduced, they often shake hands.

☆ **in·tro·duc·tion** /ˌɪntrəˈdʌkʃn/ *noun* **1** [U] bringing in or using sth for the first time: *the introduction of computers into the classroom* **2** [sing.] **introduction to sth** first experience of sth: *My first job – in a factory – was not a pleasant introduction to work.* **3** [C] the first part of a book or a talk which gives an explanation of the rest of it **4** [C] a book for people who are beginning to study a subject: *An Introduction to English Grammar* **5** [C] the act of telling two or more people each others' names for the first time: *I think I'll get my husband to make the introductions – he's better at remembering names!* ○ *You don't need an introduction, do you?* (= you already know each other)

in·tro·duc·to·ry /ˌɪntrəˈdʌktəri/ *adj.* happening or said at the beginning in order to give a general idea of what will follow: *an introductory speech, chapter, remark, etc.*

in·tro·vert /ˈɪntrəvərt/ *noun* [C] a quiet, shy person who is concerned with his/her own thoughts or feelings ☛ The opposite is **extrovert**.

in·tro·vert·ed /ˈɪntrəvərt̬əd/ *adj.* quiet and shy

in·trude /ɪnˈtrud/ *verb* [I] **intrude (on/upon sb/sth)** to enter a place or situation without permission or when you are not wanted: *I'm sorry to intrude on your lunch break, but...*

in·trud·er /ɪnˈtrudər/ *noun* [C] a person who enters a place without permission and often secretly: *an alarm system to protect your home against intruders*

in·tru·sion /ɪnˈtruʒn/ *noun* [C,U] **intrusion (on/upon/into sth)** something that disturbs you or your life when you want to be private —**in·tru·sive** /ɪnˈtrusɪv/ *adj.*

in·tu·i·tion /ˌɪntuˈɪʃn/ *noun* [C,U] the feeling or understanding that makes you believe or know sth without any reason or proof: *My intuition tells me something's wrong here.* —**in·tu·i·tive** /ɪnˈtuət̬ɪv/ *adj.* —**in·tu·i·tive·ly** *adv.*

in·u·it /ˈɪnuɪt/ *noun* [C] (*pl.* **in·u·it** or **in·u·its** a member of a race of people who live in the Arctic regions of North America.

in·un·date /ˈɪnəndeɪt/ *verb* [T] (usually passive) **1 inundate sb (with sth)** to give or send sb so many things that he/she can hardly deal with them all: *We were inundated with applications for the job.* **2** (*formal*) to cover with water; to flood

☆ **in·vade** /ɪnˈveɪd/ *verb* **1** [I,T] to enter a country with an army in order to attack, conquer it, etc.: *They invaded the country with tanks and troops.* **2** [T] to enter in large numbers: *College students invade the Florida beaches every spring.* **3** [T] to come in and disturb: *Door-to-door salespeople invade my privacy.* —**in·vad·er** *noun* [C, usually pl.]: *They forced back the invaders.* ☛ Look at **invasion**.

in·va·lid¹ /ˈɪnvələd/ *noun* [C] a person who has been very sick for a long time and needs sb else to take care of him/her

in·va·lid² /ɪnˈvæləd/ *adj.* **1** not able to be accepted by law; not valid (1,2): *Your driver's license is invalid.* **2** not correct according to reason; not valid (3): *an invalid argument*

in·val·u·a·ble /ɪnˈvælyəbl, ɪnˈvælyuəbl/ *adj.* very useful or valuable: *She has made an invaluable contribution to the project.* ☛ Be careful. Invaluable is not the opposite of valuable. The opposite is **worthless**.

☆ **in·va·sion** /ɪnˈveɪʒn/ *noun* [C,U] a time when the armed forces of one country enter another country in order to attack it: *Germany's invasion of Poland in 1939* ○ (*figurative*) *Such questions are an invasion of privacy.* ☛ The verb is **invade**.

☆ **in·vent** /ɪnˈvɛnt/ *verb* [T] **1** to think of or make sth for the first time: *Who invented the sewing machine?* ○ *When was the camera invented?* **2** to make up a story, excuse, etc. that is not true

☆ **in·ven·tion** /ɪnˈvɛnʃn/ *noun* **1** [C] a thing that has been made or designed by sb for the first time: *The microwave oven is a very useful invention.* **2** [U] the act or process of making or designing sth for the first time: *Books had to be written by hand before the invention of printing.*

in·ven·tive /ɪnˈvɛntɪv/ *adj.* having new and original ideas

☆**in·ven·tor** /ɪnˈvɛntər/ *noun* [C] a person who invents (1) sth for the first time

in·ven·to·ry /ˈɪnvəntɔri/ *noun* [C] (*pl.* **in·ven·to·ries**) a detailed list, e.g. of all the items in a store

in·vert /ɪnˈvərt/ *verb* [T] (*formal*) to put sth in the opposite order or position of the way it should be or usually is

☆**in·vest** /ɪnˈvɛst/ *verb* **1** [I,T] to buy property or stock in a business, etc. in the hope that you will make a profit: *We invested in the new software company.* ○ *I usually invest my money in the stock market.* (*figurative*) *You have to invest a lot of time to learn a language well.* **2** [I] to buy sth (usually sth expensive): *Maybe we should invest in a new lawnmower.*

☆**in·ves·ti·gate** /ɪnˈvɛstəgeɪt/ *verb* [I,T] to try to find out all the facts about sth: *A murder was reported and the police were sent to investigate.* ○ *A group of experts are investigating the cause of the crash.* —**in·ves·ti·ga·tor** /-geɪtər/ *noun* [C]

☆**in·ves·ti·ga·tion** /ɪnˌvɛstəˈgeɪʃn/ *noun* [C,U] **investigation (into sth)**: *The airlines are carrying out a thorough investigation into security at airports.* ○ *The matter is still under investigation.*

·**in·ves·ti·ga·tive** /ɪnˈvɛstəgeɪtɪv/ *adj.* trying to find out all the facts about sb/sth: *investigative journalism*

☆**in·vest·ment** /ɪnˈvɛstmənt/ *noun* **1** [U] **investment (in sth)** the act of putting money in a property, business, etc.: *The industry needs new capital investment.* ○ *foreign investment in the state's economy* **2** [C] **investment (in sth)** an amount of money that has been put in a business, etc.: *We got a good return on our original investment of $10,000.* **3** [C] a thing that you have bought, especially in order to save money or to make a profit: *Those stocks were a good long-term investment.* ○ *This coat has been a good investment – I've worn it for three years.*

☆**in·ves·tor** /ɪnˈvɛstər/ *noun* [C] a person who invests (1) in sth

in·vig·or·ate /ɪnˈvɪgəreɪt/ *verb* [I,T] to give new strength or energy to sb/sth: *efforts to invigorate the state's tourist industry* —**in·vig·or·at·ing** *adj.*: *an invigorating early-morning run*

in·vin·ci·ble /ɪnˈvɪnsəbl/ *adj.* too strong or powerful to be defeated or beaten

in·vis·i·ble /ɪnˈvɪzəbl/ *adj.* not able to be seen: *bacteria that are invisible to the naked eye* ○ *Frodo put on the magic ring and became invisible.* ○ (*figurative*) *Children from low-income families are the nation's invisible poor.* —**in·vis·i·bil·i·ty** /ɪnˌvɪzəˈbɪləti/ *noun* [U] —**in·vis·i·bly** *adv.*

☆**in·vi·ta·tion** /ˌɪnvəˈteɪʃn/ *noun***1** [C] **an invitation to sb/sth (to sth/to do sth)** a written or spoken request to go somewhere or do sth: *He has been sent an invitation to the opening ceremony.* **2** [U] inviting or being invited: *Admission is by invitation only.* ○ *a letter of invitation*

☞ You can **accept** an invitation or **turn it down**. (**Decline** and **refuse** are more formal.)

☆**in·vite** /ɪnˈvaɪt/ *verb* [T] **invite sb (to/for sth)** to ask sb to come (to a party, etc.): *We invited the whole family to the wedding.* ○ *Shall we invite Louise and Pete to the party on Saturday?* ○ (*figurative*) *You're just inviting trouble if you criticize the boss.*

PHRV **invite sb in** to ask sb to come into your home

invite sb over to ask sb to come to your home: *I invited Trevor and his family over for dinner on Sunday.* ☞ Note that **ask** can be used instead of invite in all senses.

in·vit·ing /ɪnˈvaɪtɪŋ/ *adj.* attractive and pleasant: *The log fire and smell of cooking were very inviting.*

in·voice /ˈɪnvɔɪs/ *noun* [C] an official paper that lists goods or services that you have received and says how much you must pay for them

in·vol·un·tar·y /ɪnˈvɑlənteri/ *adj.* done without wanting or meaning to: *She was charged with involuntary manslaughter.* —**in·vol·un·tar·i·ly** /ɪnˌvɑlənˈterəli/ *adv.*

☆**in·volve** /ɪnˈvɑlv/ *verb* [T] **1** to make necessary: *The job involves a lot of traveling.* **2 involve sb/sth in (doing) sth** to cause sb/sth to take part in or be concerned with sth: *a project involving more than 100 people* ○ *Please don't involve me in your family arguments.* ○ *I don't want to get involved – figure it out for yourself.* —**in·volve·ment** *noun* [C,U]

in·volved /ɪnˈvɑlvd/ *adj.* **1 involved (in sth)** taking part in sth because you are very interested in it: *I'm involved in local politics.* **2** difficult to understand; complicated: *The book has a very involved plot.* **3 involved (with sb)** to be emotionally or sexually connected with sb: *She is involved with an older man.*

in·ward /ˈɪnwərd/ *adj.* (only *before* a noun) inside your mind, not shown to other people: *my inward feelings* ☞ The opposite is **outward**.

in·ward /ˈɪnwərd/ (*also* **inwards**) *adv.* toward the inside or center: *Stand in a circle facing inwards.* ☞ The opposite is **outward**.

IOU /ˌaɪ oʊ ˈyu/ *noun* [C] (*pl.* **IOU's** or **IOUs**) I owe you; a piece of paper that you sign to show that you owe sb some money

IQ /ˌaɪ ˈkyu/ *noun* [C] intelligence quotient; a number that shows how intelligent sb is, according to his/her score on a certain test: *to have a high/low IQ* ○ *an IQ of 120*

IRA /ˌaɪ ɑr ˈeɪ; ˈaɪrə/ *noun* [C] individual retire-

ment account; a special type of bank account in which you can save money without paying taxes on it until you stop working (**retire**) when you are older

i·rate /aɪˈreɪt/ adj. (formal) very angry

i·ris /ˈaɪrəs/ noun [C] the colored part of the eye

I·rish /ˈaɪrɪʃ/ adj. **1** of Ireland or its people, language, culture, etc.: *Irish folk music* ○ *Irish whiskey* **2 the Irish** noun [plural] the people of Ireland

iron
ironing board
iron

☆ **i·ron¹** /ˈaɪərn/ noun **1** [U] (symbol **Fe**) a common hard gray metal. Iron is used for making steel and is found in small quantities in food and in blood: *an iron bar* ○ *wrought-iron railings* ○ *The roof of the shack was made of corrugated iron.* ○ *a pot made of cast iron* ○ *iron ore* ○ (*figurative*) *The general has an iron* (= very strong) *will.* **2** [C] an electrical instrument with a flat bottom that is heated and used to smooth clothes after you have washed and dried them: *Use a hot iron on cotton and a cool iron on polyester.* ○ *a steam iron*

☆ **i·ron²** /ˈaɪərn/ verb [I,T] to use an iron¹(2) to get the folds out of clothes. *Could you iron this dress for me?* ○ *That shirt needs ironing.*

☞ **Do the ironing** is often used instead of iron: *I usually do the ironing on Sunday.*

i·ron·ic /aɪˈrɑnɪk/ adj. **1** meaning the opposite of what you say: *"Oh, I'm so pleased," she said in an ironic way.* ☞ Look at **sarcastic**. **2** (used about a situation) strange or amusing because it is unusual or unexpected: *It is ironic that the busiest people are often the most willing to help.* —**i·ron·i·cal·ly** /-kli/ adv.

ˈ**ironing board** noun [C] a special table that is used for ironing clothes on

i·ro·ny /ˈaɪrəni; ˈaɪərni/ noun (pl. **i·ro·nies**) **1** [U] the way of speaking that shows you are joking or that you mean the opposite of what you say: *"Gee, what a generous tip," she said with heavy irony.* **2** [C,U] the unusual or unexpected side of a situation, etc. that seems strange or amusing: *The irony was that he was killed in a car accident soon after the end of the war.*

ir·ra·tion·al /ɪˈræʃənl/ adj. not based on reason or clear thought: *an irrational fear of worms* —**ir·ra·tion·al·i·ty** /ɪˌræʃəˈnæləti/ noun [U] **ir·ra·tion·al·ly** adv.

☆ **ir·reg·u·lar** /ɪˈrɛgyələr/ adj. **1** having parts or sides of different sizes or lengths; not even or regular: *an irregular shape* **2** happening at

unequal intervals; not regular: *His visits became more and more irregular.* ○ *an irregular pulse* **3** not allowed according to the rules or social customs: *It is highly irregular for a doctor to give information about patients without their permission.* **4** not following the usual rules of grammar; not regular: *"Caught" is an irregular past tense form.* —**ir·reg·u·lar·i·ty** /ɪˌrɛgyəˈlærəti/ noun [C,U] (pl. **ir·reg·u·lar·i·ties**) —**ir·reg·u·lar·ly** adv.

ir·rel·e·vant /ɪˈrɛləvənt/ adj. not connected with sth or important to it: *That's completely irrelevant to the subject under discussion.* —**ir·rel·e·vance** /-əns/ noun [U] —**ir·rel·e·van·cy** /-ənsi/ noun [C,U] (pl. **ir·rel·e·van·cies**)

ir·rep·a·ra·ble /ɪˈrɛpərəbl/ adj. not able to be repaired or made better: *Acid rain has caused irreparable damage to many forests and lakes.* —**ir·rep·a·ra·bly** adv.

ir·re·place·a·ble /ˌɪrɪˈpleɪsəbl/ adj. (used about sth very valuable or special) not able to be replaced

ir·re·sis·ti·ble /ˌɪrɪˈzɪstəbl/ adj. **1** very strong or powerful so that you cannot stop yourself from doing or agreeing with sth: *Their arguments were irresistible – I had to agree.* ○ *an irresistible urge to laugh* **2** very attractive: *The swimming pool is irresistible on a hot day like this.* ☞ The verb is **resist**. —**ir·re·sis·ti·bly** /-əbli/ adv.

ir·re·spon·si·ble /ˌɪrɪˈspɑnsəbl/ adj. (used about a person of his/her actions) not thinking about the effect your actions will have; not responsible: *It is irresponsible to let small children go out alone when it's dark.* —**ir·re·spon·si·bil·i·ty** /ˌɪrɪˌspɑnsəˈbɪləti/ noun [U] —**ir·re·spon·si·bly** /-əbli/ adv.

ir·rev·er·ent /ɪˈrɛvərənt/ adj. not feeling or showing respect for traditions, important people, etc. —**ir·rev·er·ence** /-əns/ noun [U] —**ir·rev·er·ent·ly** adv.

ir·re·vers·i·ble /ˌɪrɪˈvərsəbl/ adj. not able to be stopped or changed: *Once made, the decision is irreversible.*

ir·ri·gate /ˈɪrəgeɪt/ verb [T] to supply land and crops with water by using pipes, equipment, etc. —**ir·ri·ga·tion** /ˌɪrəˈgeɪʃn/ noun [U]

ir·ri·ta·ble /ˈɪrətəbl/ adj. easily made angry —**ir·ri·ta·bil·i·ty** /ˌɪrətəˈbɪləti/ noun [U] —**ir·ri·ta·bly** /-əbli/ adv.

☆ **ir·ri·tate** /ˈɪrəteɪt/ verb [T] **1** to make sb angry; to annoy: *It really irritates me the way he keeps repeating himself.* **2** to cause a part of the body to be painful or sore: *Very bright sunlight can irritate your eyes.* —**ir·ri·ta·tion** /ˌɪrəˈteɪʃn/ noun [C,U]

the IRS /ˌaɪ ɑr ˈɛs/ (also **the Internal Revenue Service**) noun [sing.] the department of the U.S. government that deals with taxes ☞ Look at the note at **White House**.

is ⇨ BE¹,²

☆ **Is·lam** /ɪsˈlɑm; ɪz-/ *noun* [U] the religion of Muslim people. Islam teaches that there is only one God and that Muhammad is His Prophet. —**Is·lam·ic** /ɪsˈlɑmɪk; ɪz-/ *adj.*: *Islamic law*

☆ **is·land** /ˈaɪlənd/ *noun* [C] a piece of land that is surrounded by water: *the tropical islands of the Caribbean* ○ *Robinson Crusoe spent many years living on a desert island.*

is·land·er /ˈaɪləndər/ *noun* [C] a person who lives on a small island

is·n't /ˈɪznt/ *short for* IS NOT: *It isn't far now.* ○ *This is enough, isn't it?*

i·so·late /ˈaɪsəleɪt/ *verb* [T] **isolate sb/sth (from sb/sth)** to put or keep sb/sth apart or separate from other people or things: *Some farms were isolated by the heavy snowfalls.* ○ *We need to isolate all the animals with the disease so that the others don't catch it.*

☆ **i·so·lat·ed** /ˈaɪsəleɪtəd/ *adj.* **1** not connected with others; separate: *Is this an isolated case or part of a general pattern?* **2** alone or apart from other people or things: *an isolated farmhouse*

i·so·la·tion /ˌaɪsəˈleɪʃn/ *noun* [U] away from other people or things; a feeling of being alone and lonely: *She lived in complete isolation from the outside world.*

IDM **in isolation (from sb/sth)** alone or separately: *Acting in isolation is not very effective. We need to work together as a team.*

☆ **is·sue¹** /ˈɪʃu/ *noun* **1** [C] a problem or subject for discussion: *I want to raise the issue of overtime pay at the meeting.* ○ *The government cannot avoid the issue of homelessness any longer.* **2** [C] one in a series of things that are published or produced: *Do you have last week's issue of this magazine?*

IDM **make an issue (out) of sth** to give too much importance to a small problem: *OK, we disagree on this but let's not make a big issue out of it.*

☆ **is·sue²** /ˈɪʃu/ *verb* **1** [T] to make sth known or give out sth to the public: *The United Nations issued a report yesterday on the Brazilian rainforests.* **2** [T] to give or supply sth to sb: *The new employees were issued with uniforms.* ○ *to issue a visa*

☆ **it** /ɪt/ *pron.* **1** (used as the subject or object of a verb, or after a preposition) an animal or thing mentioned earlier or that is being talked about now: *Look at that car. It's going way too fast.* ○ *The kids went up to the dog and patted it on the head.* ○ *This box is heavy. What's inside it?*

☞ It can also refer to a baby whose sex you do not know: *Is it a boy or a girl?*

2 (used for identifying a person): *It's your mom on the phone.* ○ *"Who's that?" "It's the mailman."* ○ *It's me!* ○ *It's him!* **3** (used in the position of the subject or object of a verb when

the real subject or object is at the end of the sentence): *It's hard for them to talk about their problems.* ○ *I think it doesn't really matter what time we arrive.* **4** (used in the position of the subject of a verb when you are talking about time, the date, distance, the weather, etc): *It's almost 8:00.* ○ *It's Tuesday today.* ○ *It's about 50 miles north of New York City.* ○ *It was very cold last weekend.* ○ *It's raining.* **5** (used when you are talking about a situation): *It gets very crowded here in the summer.* ○ *I'll come at 7 o'clock if it's convenient.* ○ *It's too bad they can't come to the party.* **6** (used for emphasizing a part of a sentence): *It's John who's good at cooking, not me.* ○ *It's your health I'm worried about, not the cost.*

IDM **that's it 1** (used for saying that you have had enough of a situation): *That's it. I'm leaving and I'm not coming back.* **2** that's right: *Just move it a little bit higher – that's it, right there.*

i·tal·ics /ɪˈtælɪks/ *noun* [U, plural] the type of writing or printing in which the letters slope to the right: *This sentence and all the example sentences in the dictionary are printed in italics.*

☆ **itch¹** /ɪtʃ/ *noun* [C] the feeling on your skin that makes you want to rub or scratch it

☆ **itch²** /ɪtʃ/ *verb* [I] to have or cause an itch¹: *My nose is itching.* ○ *Mosquito bites really itch.* —**itch·y** *adj.*: *an itchy wool sweater* —**itch·i·ness** *noun* [U]

it'd /ˈɪtəd/ *short for* IT HAD, IT WOULD

☆ **i·tem** /ˈaɪtəm/ *noun* [C] **1** one single thing on a list or in a collection: *Some items arrived too late to be included in the catalog.* ○ *What is the first item on the agenda?* ○ *an item of luggage* **2** a single piece of news: *There was an interesting item about Cuba in yesterday's news.*

i·tem·ize /ˈaɪtəmaɪz/ *verb* [T] to make a list of all the items (1) in sth: *an itemized bill*

i·tin·er·ar·y /aɪˈtɪnəreri/ *noun* [C] (*pl.* **i·tin·er·ar·ies**) a plan of a trip, route, etc.

it'll /ˈɪtl/ *short for* IT WILL

its /ɪts/ *det.* belonging to a thing, animal, etc.: *The cat's had its dinner.* ○ *The swimming club held its annual meeting last night.*

it's /ɪts/ *short for* IT IS; IT HAS

☞ Be careful. **It's** is a short way of saying *it is* or *it has*. **Its** means "belonging to it": *The bird has broken its wing.*

☆ **it·self** /ɪtˈsɛlf/ *pron.* **1** (used as the object of a verb or preposition when the animal or thing that does an action is also affected by it): *The cat was washing itself.* ○ *The company has gotten itself into financial difficulties.* **2** (used for emphasis): *The town itself is pretty dull, but the surrounding area has spectacular scenery.*

IDM **(all) by itself 1** without being controlled by a person; automatically: *The furnace comes*

on by itself before we get up. **2** alone: *The house stood all by itself on top of the hill.* ☞ Look at the note at **alone**.

IV /ˌaɪ ˈviː/ *noun* [C] a piece of medical equipment, like a tube, that is used for putting liquid food or medicine directly into a sick person's blood: *She's on an IV in the hospital.*

I've /aɪv/ *short for* I HAVE

i·vo·ry /ˈaɪvri; ˈaɪvəri/ *noun* [U] the hard white substance that an elephant's long teeth (**tusks**) are made of

i·vy /ˈaɪvi/ *noun* [U] a climbing plant that has dark leaves with three or five points ☞ Look also at **poison ivy**.

the ˈIvy League *noun* [sing.] a group of eight private universities in the northeastern United States which are very old and are respected for their high social and academic status ☞ Look at the note at **White House**.

Jj

J, j /dʒeɪ/ *noun* [C] (*pl.* **J's; j's**) the tenth letter of the English alphabet: *"Jam" begins with (a) "J."*

jab /dʒæb/ *verb* [I,T] **1 jab (at sb/sth) (with sth); jab sb/sth (with sth)** to push at sb/sth roughly, usually with sth sharp: *He kept jabbing at his potato with his fork.* ○ *She jabbed me in the ribs with her elbow.* **2 jab sth into sb/sth** to push sth roughly into sb/sth: *He jabbed his finger into my stomach.* —**jab** *noun* [C]

jack¹ /dʒæk/ *noun* [C] **1** a piece of equipment for lifting a car, etc. off the ground, e.g. so that you can change its wheel **2** the card between the ten and the queen in a deck of cards: *the jack of hearts* ☞ Look at the note at **card**. **3** a place where you can connect a telephone or other electronic equipment to the system of telephone wires in a building

jack² /dʒæk/ *verb*

PHRV **jack sth up 1** to lift a car, etc. using a jack¹(1) **2** (*informal*) to increase prices, etc. suddenly by a large amount: *Airlines always jack up their fares during the holidays.*

☆**jack·et** /ˈdʒækət/ *noun* [C] **1** a short coat with sleeves: *a tweed sports jacket* ○ *It's getting chilly – you'd better wear your jacket.* ☞ picture on page A27. Look also at **life jacket**. **2** a cover for a book or record

jack·knife¹ /ˈdʒæknaɪf/ *noun* [C] (*pl.* **jackknives**) = POCKET KNIFE

jack·knife² /ˈdʒæknaɪf/ *verb* [I] (used about a truck that is in two parts) to bend in the middle in an uncontrolled way

jack-o'-lan·tern /ˈdʒæk ə ˌlæntərn/ *noun* [C] a large round orange vegetable (**a pumpkin**) that has shapes cut into it so that it looks like a face, usually with a light inside. Jack-o'-lanterns are a traditional type of decoration for Halloween.

jack·pot /ˈdʒækpɑt/ *noun* [C] the largest prize that you can win in a game

IDM **hit the jackpot** ⇨ HIT¹

Ja·cuz·zi /dʒəˈkuzi/ *noun* [C] (*trademark*) = HOT TUB

jad·ed /ˈdʒeɪdəd/ *adj.* no longer finding things interesting or exciting because you have done or seen them too much

jag·ged /ˈdʒægəd/ *adj.* rough and uneven with sharp points: *Be careful not to cut yourself – that metal has a jagged edge.* ○ *jagged rocks*

jag·uar /ˈdʒægwɑr/ *noun* [C] a large spotted wild cat that comes from Central and South America

☆**jail¹** /dʒeɪl/ *noun* [C,U] (a) prison: *She was sent to jail for ten years.*

jail² /dʒeɪl/ *verb* [T] to put sb in prison: *She was jailed for ten years.*

☆**jam¹** /dʒæm/ *noun* **1** [U] a sweet substance that you spread on bread, made by boiling fruit and sugar together: *I put jam on my toast.* ○ *a jar of raspberry jam*

☞ Note that jam made from oranges is called **marmalade**. Look also at **jelly**.

2 [C] a lot of people or things that are crowded together making it difficult to move: *a traffic jam* **3** [C] a situation in which sth is stuck in one position: *There's a paper jam in the copier.* **4** [C] (*informal*) a difficult situation: *We're really in a financial jam.*

jam² /dʒæm/ *verb* (**jam·ming; jammed**) **1** [T] **jam sb/sth in, under, between, etc. sth** to push or force sb/sth into a place where there is not much room: *There were three of us jammed into a phone booth.* ○ *She managed to jam everything into her suitcase.* **2** [I,T] **jam (sth) (up)** to be stuck in one position or to cause sth to be stuck: *Something is jamming up the machine.* ○ *Don't stick that pin into the keyhole, or the lock will jam.* **3** [T] **jam sth (up)** to fill sth so that it is difficult to move: *All the fans jammed the stadium exits after the game.* **4** [T] to send out signals in order to stop radio

tʃ	dʒ	v	θ	ð	s	z	ʃ
chin	June	van	thin	then	so	zoo	she

programs, etc. from being received or heard clearly

jammed /dʒæmd/ adj. (not before a noun) stuck in one position or completely full, so that nothing can move: *The parking lot was jammed with shoppers yesterday.*

jan·i·tor /'dʒænəṭər/ noun [C] = CUSTODIAN

☆ **Jan·u·ar·y** /'dʒænyuɛri/ noun [C,U] (pl. **Jan·u·ar·ies**) (abbr. **Jan.**) the first month of the year, coming before February: *We're going skiing in January.* ○ *We go skiing every year in January.* ○ *last/next January* ○ *the January before last* ○ *the January after next* ○ *Christine's birthday is (on) January 17* (we say, "January seventeenth" or sometimes, "the seventeenth of January"). ○ *The last two Januaries have been extremely cold.* ○ *January mornings can be very dark.*

☆ **jar¹** /dʒɑr/ noun [C] **1** a container with a lid, usually made of glass and used for keeping food, etc. in: *a jam jar* ○ *Can you open this jar for me?* ☞ picture at **container**. **2** the food that a jar (1) contains: *a jar of honey*

jar² /dʒɑr/ verb (**jar·ring**; **jarred**) [T] to shock or surprise sb by making a sudden movement, noise, etc.: *A mild earthquake jarred local residents awake yesterday.*

jar·gon /'dʒɑrgən/ noun [U] special or technical words that are used by a particular group of people and that other people do not understand: *scientific, legal, computer, etc. jargon*

jaun·dice /'dʒɔndəs/ noun [U] a disease that makes the skin and eyes yellow

jave·lin /'dʒævlən; 'dʒævələn/ noun [C] a long pointed pole that is thrown in sports competitions

jaw /dʒɔ/ noun **1** [C] either of the bones in your face that contain the teeth: *the lower/upper jaw* ☞ picture on page A24. **2 jaws** [plural] the mouth (especially of an animal): *The lion was coming toward him with its jaws open.*

☆ **jazz¹** /dʒæz/ noun [U] a style of popular music with a strong rhythm, originally played by black Americans: *a jazz band*

jazz² /dʒæz/ verb
PHRV **jazz sth up** (informal) to make sth brighter, more interesting or lively

☆ **jeal·ous** /'dʒɛləs/ adj. **1** feeling upset because you think that sb loves another person more than you: *Tim gets jealous whenever Sue talks to another boy!* **2 jealous (of sb/sth)** feeling angry or sad because you want to be like sb else or because you want what sb else has: *He's always been jealous of his older brother.* ○ *I'm really jealous of your new car – how much did it cost?* —**jeal·ous·ly** adv. —**jeal·ous·y** /'dʒɛləsi/ noun [C,U] (pl. **jeal·ous·ies**)

☆ **jeans** /dʒinz/ noun [plural] pants made of strong, usually blue, cotton cloth (**denim**):

These jeans are a little too tight. ○ *a pair of jeans* ☞ picture on page A27.

Jeep /dʒip/ noun [C] (trademark) a small, strong vehicle that is suitable for traveling over rough ground

jeer¹ /dʒɪr/ verb [I,T] **jeer (at sb/sth)** to laugh or shout rudely at sb/sth: *The audience jeered the losing team.*

jeer² /dʒɪr/ noun [C] an unkind or rude remark or shout

jeez /dʒiz/ interj. (slang) (used for expressing surprise, shock, etc.) ☞ Be careful. Some people find this word offensive because it is similar to the name of Jesus Christ.

Jell-O (also **Jello**) /'dʒɛloʊ/ (also **gelatin**) noun [U] (trademark) a soft, solid, brightly-colored food that shakes when it is moved. Jell-O usually has a fruit flavor and is often eaten as a dessert.

jel·ly /'dʒɛli/ noun [U] **1** a type of jam made of fruit juice and sugar: *grape jelly* ○ *a peanut butter and jelly sandwich* **2** a soft solid substance that shakes when it is moved: *My legs felt like jelly before the test* (= not steady because of fear, etc.).

jel·ly·fish /'dʒɛlifɪʃ/ noun [C] (pl. **jel·ly·fish** or **jel·ly·fish·es**) a sea animal with a body that looks like colorless jelly (2). Jellyfish sometimes sting.

jeop·ard·ize /'dʒɛpərdaɪz/ verb [T] to do sth that may damage sth or put it in a dangerous position

jeop·ard·y /'dʒɛpərdi/ noun
IDM **in jeopardy** in danger of losing, failing, being injured or damaged, etc.

jerk¹ /dʒərk/ noun [C] **1** (informal) a person, especially a man or boy, who is stupid, rude or annoying: *Adam's such a jerk!* **2** a sudden pull, push or other movement: *Give the rope a good jerk.*

jerk² /dʒərk/ verb **1** [T] to pull sb/sth suddenly and quickly: *She jerked the door open.* **2** [I] to move with a sudden movement or a series of sudden movements: *The truck jerked from one side to the other over the bumpy road.* —**jerk·y** adj.: *jerky movements* —**jerk·i·ly** /-əli/ adv.

jer·sey /'dʒərzi/ noun [C] (pl. **jer·seys**) a shirt that is part of a sports uniform: *a football jersey* ☞ picture at **football player**.

Je·sus /'dʒizəs; 'dʒizəz/ noun = CHRIST

☆ **jet** /dʒɛt/ noun [C] **1** a fast modern airplane with an engine that pushes out a stream of hot air and gases at the back **2** a fast, thin stream of water, gas, etc. coming out of a small hole

jet 'black adj. very dark black in color

'**jet lag** noun [U] the tired feeling that people often have after a long trip in an airplane to a place where the local time is different —'**jet-lagged** adj.

jet·ty /'dʒɛti/ noun [C] (pl. **jet·ties**) a stone

i	ɪ	ɛ	æ	ɑ	ɔ	ʌ	ʊ	u
see	sit	ten	cat	hot	saw	cup	put	too

wall built out into the ocean to protect boats from large waves

☆**Jew** /dʒu/ *noun* [C] a person whose family was originally from the ancient land of Israel or whose religion is Judaism —**Jew·ish** /'dʒuɪʃ/ *adj.*: *He's Jewish.* ○ *the Jewish New Year*

☆**jew·el** /'dʒuəl/ *noun* [C] a valuable stone (e.g. a diamond) or a necklace, ring, etc. with such a stone in it

jew·el·er /'dʒuələr/ *noun* [C] a person whose job is to buy, sell, make or repair jewelry and watches

jewelry

ring

earrings

pierced earrings

pin

clip earrings

bracelet

bangle

necklaces

beads

chain

☆**jew·el·ry** /'dʒuəlri/ *noun* [U] rings and other things made from gold, silver, jewels, etc. that are worn to decorate your body: *a piece of jewelry* ○ *a jewelry store*

jif·fy /'dʒɪfi/ *noun*
> **IDM** **in a jiffy** (*informal*) very soon: *I'll be ready in a jiffy.*

jig·gle /'dʒɪgl/ *verb* [T] to move sth quickly from side to side

jigsaw puzzle

jig·saw puzzle /'dʒɪgsɔ ˌpʌzl/ (*also* **puzzle**) *noun* [C] a picture on cardboard or wood that is cut into small pieces. The pieces are then put together again as a game.

jin·gle¹ /'dʒɪŋgl/ *noun* **1** [sing.] a noise that sounds like metal objects gently hitting each other: *the jingle of coins* **2** [C] a short simple tune or song, especially one that is used in an advertisement on television or on the radio

jin·gle² /'dʒɪŋgl/ *verb* **1** [I] to make a gentle noise that sounds like metal objects hitting each other **2** [T] to move sth so that it makes a

gentle ringing sound: *He jingled the coins in his pockets.*

jinx /dʒɪŋks/ *noun* [C, usually sing.] bad luck; a person or thing that is thought to bring bad luck

jinxed /dʒɪŋkst/ *adj.* having or bringing bad luck

jit·ters /'dʒɪtərz/ *noun* [plural] (*informal*) extremely nervous or anxious feelings: *Just thinking about the test gives me the jitters!*

jit·ter·y /'dʒɪtəri/ *adj.* (*informal*) nervous or anxious

☆**job** /dʒɑb/ *noun* **1** [C] the work that you do to earn money: *My dad told me to go out and get a job.*

> ☞ We **look for, apply for** or **find** a job. A job can be **well-paid / highly-paid** or **badly-paid / low-paid**. A job can be **full-time** or **part-time**, **permanent** or **temporary**. Look at the note at **work¹**.

2 [C] a task or a piece of work that may be paid or unpaid: *I always have a lot of jobs to do around the house on weekends.* **3** [C, usually sing.] a function or responsibility: *It's not his job to tell us what we can and can't do.*
> **IDM** **do a good, bad, etc. job (on sth)** to do or finish sth in a particular way: *The garage did a great job on our car.*
> **do the job/trick** (*informal*) to get the result that is wanted
> **good/nice job!** (*informal*) (used to praise sb after he/she has done sth very well): *Good job, Amy! You should be proud of yourself.*
> **on the job** while working; at work: *He was fired for being drunk on the job.* ○ *on-the-job training*
> **out of a job** without paid work ☞ A more formal word is **unemployed**.

job·less /'dʒɑbləs/ **1** *adj.* (used about large numbers of people) without paid work **2 the jobless** *noun* [plural] the people who are without work —**job·less·ness** *noun* [U]

jock /dʒɑk/ *noun* [C] (*slang*) a person, especially a student, who plays a lot of sports

jock·ey /'dʒɑki/ *noun* [C] (*pl.* **jock·eys**) a person who rides in horse races, especially as a profession ☞ Look at **disc jockey**.

jog¹ /dʒɑg/ *verb* (**jog·ging**; **jogged**) [I] to run slowly, especially as a form of exercise

> ☞ We often say **go jogging** rather than **jog**: *I go jogging most evenings.*

> **IDM** **jog sb's memory** to make sb remember sth: *I have a picture here that should jog your memory.*

jog² /dʒɑg/ *noun* [sing.] a slow run as a form of exercise: *She goes for a jog before breakfast.*

jog·ger /'dʒɑgər/ *noun* [C] a person who goes jogging for exercise

☆**join** /dʒɔɪn/ *verb* **1** [T] to become a member of a club or organization: *James is going to join*

J

the army when he leaves school. **2** [T] to take your place in sth or to take part in sth: *We joined the crowd outside the club.* **3** [I,T] to meet or unite (with sb/sth): *Do the two rivers join at any point?* ○ *Where does this road join the main highway?* ○ *Would you like to join us for a drink?* **4** [T] **join A with B**; **join A and B (together)** to fasten or connect one thing to another: *The Golden Gate Bridge joins San Francisco with Marin County.* ○ *The door is made of several sections that are joined together.* **5** [I,T] **join (with) sb in doing sth/to do sth**; **join together in doing sth/to do sth** to take part with sb (in doing sth for sb else): *I know that everybody here joins me in wishing you the best of luck in your new job.* ○ *The whole class joined together to buy a present for the teacher.*

IDM **join forces (with sb)** to work together in order to achieve sth: *Neighborhood residents have joined forces with the police to get rid of drug dealers.*

PHRV **join in (sth/doing sth)** to take part in an activity: *Steve wouldn't join in when everybody else was playing football.*

☆**joint¹** /dʒɔɪnt/ *noun* [C] **1** a part of the body where two bones fit together and are able to bend **2** the place where two or more things are fastened or connected **3** (*informal*) a place such as a bar or restaurant, especially one that is not expensive or elegant: *The band just plays at local beer joints.* **4** (*informal*) a cigarette that contains an illegal drug (**marijuana**)

☆**joint²** /dʒɔɪnt/ *adj.* (only *before* a noun) shared or owned by two or more people: *Do you and your husband have a joint account?* (= at a bank) ○ *a joint decision* ○ *the joint chairpersons of the committee* —**joint·ly** *adv.*

joint 'venture *noun* [C] an agreement between two companies, especially in different countries, to do business together

☆**joke¹** /dʒoʊk/ *noun* **1** [C] something said or done to make you laugh, especially a funny story: *Have you heard the joke about the three men in a taxi?* ○ *to tell a joke* ○ *a dirty joke* (= about sex) ○ *I laughed at her joke even though I didn't get* (= understand) *it.* ☞ A **practical joke** is something you do, not just say. **2** [sing.] a ridiculous person, thing or situation: *The salary he was offered was a joke!*

IDM **play a joke on sb** to trick sb in order to amuse yourself or other people

take a joke to accept a trick or sth said about you in fun without getting angry

joke² /dʒoʊk/ *verb* [I] to say things that are not meant to be serious: *I never joke about religion.*

jok·er /'dʒoʊkər/ *noun* [C] **1** a person who likes to make jokes or play tricks **2** an extra playing card in a deck which can be used instead of any card in some games

jol·ly /'dʒɑli/ *adj.* (**jol·li·er**; **jol·li·est**) (*old-fashioned*) happy and cheerful

jolt /dʒoʊlt/ *verb* [T] to shake sth or make it move suddenly: *The crash jolted all the passengers forward.*

jolt² /dʒoʊlt/ *noun* [usually sing.] **1** a sudden movement: *The train stopped with a jolt.* **2** a surprise or shock: *His sudden anger gave her quite a jolt.*

jos·tle /'dʒɑsl/ *verb* [I,T] to push against sb in a rough way (often in a crowd)

jot /dʒɑt/ *verb* **jot·ting**; **jot·ted**

PHRV **jot sth down** to make a quick short note of sth: *Let me jot down your address.*

☆**jour·nal** /'dʒɜrnl/ *noun* [C] **1** a magazine, especially one in which all the articles are about a particular subject: *a medical journal* **2** a written account of what you have done each day: *to keep a journal* (= to write regularly in one)

jour·nal·ism /'dʒɜrnl·ɪzəm/ *noun* [U] the profession of collecting, writing and publishing news in newspapers and magazines and on television and radio

☆**jour·nal·ist** /'dʒɜrnl·ɪst/ *noun* [C] a person whose job is to collect, write or publish news, in newspapers and magazines or on television and radio: *a job as a journalist with the local paper* ☞ Look at **reporter**.

☆**jour·ney** /'dʒɜrni/ *noun* [C] (*pl.* **jour·neys**) a long trip from one place to another: *He wrote a book describing his journey through South America.* ☞ Look at the note at **travel**.

jo·vi·al /'dʒoʊviəl/ *adj.* (used about a person) very cheerful and friendly

☆**joy** /dʒɔɪ/ *noun* **1** [U] a feeling of great happiness: *We'd like to wish you joy and success in your life together.* ○ *to jump, shout, etc. for joy* (= because you feel so happy) **2** [C] a person or thing that gives you great pleasure: *That class is a joy to teach.*

joy·ful /'dʒɔɪfl/ *adj.* very happy: *a joyful occasion* —**joy·ful·ly** *adv.* —**joy·ful·ness** *noun* [U]

joy·ride /'dʒɔɪraɪd/ *noun* [C] (*informal*) a drive or ride (usually in a stolen car) just for fun and excitement '**joy·rid·er** *noun* [C] '**joy·rid·ing** *noun* [U]

joy·stick /'dʒɔɪstɪk/ *noun* [C] a handle used for controlling movement on a computer, an airplane, etc.

Jr. *abbr.* = JUNIOR¹(2)

ju·bi·lant /'dʒubələnt/ *adj.* (*formal*) extremely happy, especially because of a success: *The fans were jubilant at their team's victory.*

ju·bi·la·tion /,dʒubə'leɪʃn/ *noun* [U] great happiness because of a success

Ju·da·ism /'dʒudiɪzəm; -dəɪzəm/ *noun* [U] the religion of the Jewish people, which is based on the Old Testament of the Bible

☆**judge¹** /dʒʌdʒ/ *noun* [C] **1** a person whose job is to apply the law and decide what punishment should be given to sb found guilty in a court of law: *The judge sentenced the man to*

ər	ɪr	ɛr	ɑr	ɔr	ʊr	ʒ	h	ŋ
bird	near	hair	car	north	tour	vision	hat	sing

three years in prison. **2** a person who decides who has won a competition: *The judges included several local celebrities.* ○ *The judges' decision is final* (= it cannot be changed). **3** a person who has the ability or knowledge to give an opinion about sth: *You're a good judge of character – what do you think of him?*

☆**judge²** /dʒʌdʒ/ *verb* **1** [I,T] to form or give an opinion about sb/sth; to consider: *Judging from what he said, his work is going well.* ○ *It's hard to judge how long the project will take.* ○ *The movie was judged to be too violent for young children.* **2** [T] to decide the result or winner (in a competition): *The principal will judge the contest.* **3** [T] to be critical about sb; to form an unfair opinion about sb: *I wish you'd quit judging my friends!* **4** [I,T] to act as a judge¹(1) , in court: *He said it was the hardest case he had ever had to judge.*

☆**judg·ment** /'dʒʌdʒmənt/ *noun* **1** [C] an opinion: *What, in your judgment, would be the best course of action?* **2** [C,U] an official decision made by a judge or a court of law: *The man collapsed when the judgment was read out in court.* **3** [U] the ability to form sensible opinions or to make wise decisions

☆**ju·di·cial** /dʒu'dɪʃl/ *adj.* of a judge, a judgment or a court of law: *the judicial branch of the federal government* ○ *judicial powers*

ju·di·cious /dʒu'dɪʃəs/ *adj.* (used about a decision or an action) sensible —**ju·di·cious·ly** *adv.*

jug /dʒʌg/ *noun* [C] a large container with a small opening and a handle, used for holding liquids: *a jug of cider* ☞ picture at **pitcher.**

jug·gle /'dʒʌgl/ *verb* **1** [I,T] to keep several objects in the air at the same time by throwing and catching them quickly: *He can dance, sing, juggle – whatever you like!* **2** [T] to try to keep two or more activities, etc. in progress at the same time: *I'll have to juggle my work schedule around so that I'm free on Mondays.* ○ *She's trying to juggle a career with raising a family.* —**jug·gler** /'dʒʌglər/ *noun* [C]

☆**juice** /dʒus/ *noun* [C,U] **1** the liquid that comes from fruit and vegetables: *lemon juice* ○ *I'll have a large orange juice.* **2** [usually pl.] the liquid that comes from a piece of meat when it is cooked

☆**juic·y** /'dʒusi/ *adj.* (**juic·i·er**; **juic·i·est**) **1** containing a lot of juice: *juicy oranges* **2** (*informal*) interesting because it is connected with sth bad: *Tell me all the juicy details!*

juke·box /'dʒukbɑks/ *noun* [C] a machine in a cafe or bar that plays music when a coin is put into it

☆**Ju·ly** /dʒʊ'laɪ/ *noun* [C,U] (*pl.* **Ju·lys**) (*abbr.* **Jul.**) the seventh month of the year, coming before August ☞ For examples of the use of the months in sentences, look at **January.**

jum·ble /'dʒʌmbl/ *noun* [sing.] a messy group of things; a mess: *a jumble of shoes in the closet*

—**jum·bled** /'dʒʌmbld/ *adj.*: *a jumbled heap of toys*

jum·bo /'dʒʌmboʊ/ *adj.* (*informal*) (only *before* a noun) very large

☆**jump¹** /dʒʌmp/ *verb* **1** [I] to move quickly off the ground by pushing yourself up with your legs and feet: *to jump into the air, over a stream, onto a chair, etc.* ○ *How high can you jump?* ○ *Jump up and down to keep warm.* ☞ picture at **bounce. 2** [I] to let your body drop from a high place to a lower place: *She killed herself by jumping off a bridge.* ☞ Look also at **bungee jumping. 3** [T] to get over sth by jumping (1): *The dog jumped the fence and ran off down the road.* **4** [I] to move quickly and suddenly: *The telephone rang and she jumped up to answer it.* ○ *He jumped out of bed when he realized what time it was.* **5** [I] to make a sudden movement because of surprise, fear or excitement: *"Oh, it's only you – you made me jump," he said.* **6** [I] **jump (from sth) to sth**; **jump (by) (sth)** to increase suddenly by a very large amount: *His salary jumped from $30,000 to $50,000 last year.* ○ *Prices jumped (by) 50% in the summer.* **7** [I] **jump from sth to sth** to change suddenly from one subject to another: *The book kept jumping from the present to the past.*

IDM **jump on the bandwagon** to copy what other people are doing because it is fashionable or successful

jump the gun (*informal*) to do sth or start sth too soon: *Don't jump the gun on this – make sure you get permission first.*

jump/leap to conclusions ⇨ CONCLUSION

PHRV **jump at sth** to accept an opportunity or an offer eagerly: *I jumped at the chance to be on the committee.*

☆**jump²** /dʒʌmp/ *noun* [C] **1** an act of jumping: *With a huge jump the horse cleared the fence.* ☞ Look at **high jump** and **long jump. 2 a jump (in sth)** a sudden increase in amount, price or value

jump·er /'dʒʌmpər/ *noun* [C] **1** a type of dress without sleeves, that is usually worn over a shirt **2** a person or animal that jumps

jump rope *noun* [C] a long piece of rope, often with a handle at each end, that is used for jumping over again and again as a game or as a form of exercise

jump-start *verb* [T] **1** to start the engine of a car that does not work by using wires to connect its battery to the battery of a car that works **2** (*informal*) to start a process, an activity, etc., or to make sth happen more quickly: *an effort to jump-start the senator's campaign for re-election*

jump·y /'dʒʌmpi/ *adj.* (*informal*) nervous or anxious: *Why are you so jumpy today?*

junc·tion /'dʒʌŋkʃn/ *noun* [C] a place where roads or railroads meet or join: *There was an accident at the junction of routes 17 and 21.*

tʃ	dʒ	v	θ	ð	s	z	ʃ
chin	June	van	thin	then	so	zoo	she

☆ **June** /dʒun/ *noun* [C,U] (*abbr.* **Jun.**) the sixth month of the year, coming before July ☞ For examples of the use of the months in sentences, look at **January**.

☆ **jun·gle** /'dʒʌŋgl/ *noun* [C,U] a thick forest in a hot tropical country: *the jungles of Africa and South America* ☞ Look at the note at **forest**.

☆ **jun·ior¹** /'dʒunyər/ *adj.* **1** connected with students who are in their eleventh year of school or in their third year of college: *the junior class play* **2 Junior** (*abbr.* **Jr.**) (used after the name of a son who has the same first name as his father): *Sammy Davis, Jr.* **3 junior (to sb)** having a low or lower position (than sb) in an organization, etc.: *a junior officer* ○ *A lieutenant is junior to a captain in the army.* ☞ The opposite is **senior**. **4** of or for younger children: *the winner of the junior tournament*

☆ **jun·ior²** /'dʒunyər/ *noun* **1** [C] a student who is in his/her eleventh year in school or his/her third year in college ☞ Look at **freshman**, **sophomore** and **senior**. **2** [sing.] (with *his, her, your,* etc.) a person who is younger than sb else by the number of years mentioned: *She's two years his junior/his junior by two years.* ☞ Look at **senior**.

,junior 'college *noun* [C] = COMMUNITY COLLEGE

,junior 'high school (also *informal* ,junior 'high) *noun* [C,U] a school for students who are about 12 to 15 years old

junk /dʒʌŋk/ *noun* [U] (*informal*) things that are old or useless or do not have much value: *There's an awful lot of junk up in the attic – we ought to clean it out.*

'junk food *noun* [U] (*informal*) food that is not healthy but that is ready to eat or easy to prepare: *junk food like potato chips and candy*

junk·ie /'dʒʌŋki/ *noun* [C] (*informal*) **1** a person who takes a lot of illegal drugs and is unable to stop **2** a person who is extremely interested in sth and does, uses, etc. it a lot: *a sports junkie*

'junk mail *noun* [U] mail, usually advertisements, that is sent to people but that they do not want

Ju·pi·ter /'dʒupətər/ *noun* [sing.] the planet that is fifth in order from the sun

ju·ris·dic·tion /,dʒʊrəs'dɪkʃn/ *noun* [U] legal power or authority; the area in which this power can be used: *That matter is outside the jurisdiction of this court.*

ju·ror /'dʒʊrər/ *noun* [C] a member of a jury

☆ **ju·ry** /'dʒʊri/ *noun* [C] (*pl.* **ju·ries**) a group of twelve people in a court of law who listen to the facts about a crime and decide whether the accused person is guilty or not guilty: *Does the jury have to reach a unanimous decision?* ○ *The jury returned a guilty verdict.* ☞ Look also at **grand jury**.

☆ **just¹** /dʒʌst/ *adv.* **1** exactly: *That's just what I meant.* ○ *You're just as smart as he is.* **2** only:

She's just a child. ○ *It's not just the money; it's the principle of the thing, too.* ○ *It was worth it just to see her face as she opened the present.* ○ *Just a minute! I'm almost ready.* **3** a very short time ago: *She's just been offered a new job.* ○ *He'd just returned from the Bahamas when I saw him.* ○ *I just ate a candy bar, so I'm not hungry.* **4 just (about to do sth); just (going to do sth)** at this/that moment; now or very soon: *We were just finishing supper when the phone rang.* ○ *I was just about to call my mother when she got here.* **5** at exactly the same time (as); when: *Just as I was beginning to enjoy myself, John said it was time to go.* ○ *Just then the door opened.* **6** (often before *barely*) almost not; hardly: *I could just barely hear what she was saying.* **7** (often with the imperative) (used for getting attention or for emphasis): *Just let me talk for a minute, will you?* ○ *I just don't want to go to the party.* ○ *Just imagine how awful she must feel!* **8** really; absolutely: *Our trip was just great.*

IDM **all/just the same** ⇨ SAME²

it is just as well (that) it is a good thing: *It's just as well that he never found out about it.*

just about almost; very nearly: *I'm just about finished.*

just in case in order to be completely prepared or safe: *It might be hot in Washington – take your shorts just in case.*

just now a very short time ago: *There was a call for you just now.* ○ *We are just now starting to realize* (= since a very short time ago) *how serious the situation is.*

just so neat and correct; exactly as it should be

would just as soon do sth (used to say that sb would prefer to do sth): *I'd just as soon forget about that whole evening!*

just² /dʒʌst/ *adj.* (*formal*) fair and right; reasonable: *I don't think that was a very just decision.* ○ *a just punishment* ☞ The opposite is **unjust**.

☆ **jus·tice** /'dʒʌstəs/ *noun* **1** [U] fair behavior or treatment: *a struggle for justice* **2** [U] the law and the way it is used: *a miscarriage of justice* (= a wrong legal decision) **3** [C] a judge in the highest court (**the Supreme Court**) of the U.S. or a particular state

IDM **do justice to sb/sth; do sb/sth justice** to treat sb/sth fairly or to show the real quality of sb/sth: *The photograph doesn't do you justice* (= make you look as nice as you are). ○ *The band couldn't do justice to that difficult piece.*

,justice of the 'peace *noun* [C] an official in some states who judges less serious cases in a court of law and performs marriage ceremonies, etc.

jus·ti·fi·a·ble /'dʒʌstəfaɪəbl; ,dʒʌstə'faɪəbl/ *adj.* possible to accept because there is a good reason for it: *His action was entirely justifiable.* ☞ The opposite is **unjustifiable**. —**jus·ti·**

i	ɪ	ɛ	æ	ɑ	ɔ	ʌ	ʊ	u
see	sit	ten	cat	hot	saw	cup	put	too

fi·a·bly /-əbli/ adv.: She was justifiably angry and upset.

jus·ti·fi·ca·tion /ˌdʒʌstəfəˈkeɪʃn/ noun [C,U] **justification (for sth/doing sth)** (a) good reason

☆ **jus·ti·fy** /ˈdʒʌstəfaɪ/ verb [T] (pres. part. **jus·ti·fy·ing**; 3rd pers. sing. pres. **jus·ti·fies**; p.t., p.p. **jus·ti·fied**) to give or be a good reason for sth: Can you justify your decision? ○ Nothing can justify child abuse.

just·ly /ˈdʒʌstli/ adv. (formal) fairly or correctly

jut /dʒʌt/ verb **jut·ting**; **jut·ted**
PHRV **jut out** to stand out from sth; to be out of line with the surroundings: rocks that jut out into the ocean

☆ **ju·ve·nile¹** /ˈdʒuːvənaɪl; -nl/ noun [C] (formal) a child or young person who is not yet an adult

☆ **ju·ve·nile²** /ˈdʒuːvənaɪl; -nl/ adj. **1** (formal) connected with young people who are not yet adults: juvenile crime **2** like a child: Don't be so juvenile!

ˌ**juvenile deˈlinquent** noun [C] a young person who has committed a crime or who behaves like a criminal

jux·ta·pose /ˈdʒʌkstəpoʊz; ˌdʒʌkstəˈpoʊz/ verb [T] (formal) to put two people, things, etc. very close together, especially in order to show a contrast: The artist achieves a special effect by juxtaposing light and dark. —**jux·ta·po·si·tion** /ˌdʒʌkstəpəˈzɪʃn/ noun [U]

Kk

K, k /keɪ/ noun [C] (pl. **K's; k's**) the eleventh letter of the English alphabet: "Kate" begins with (a) "K."

K /keɪ/ abbr. **1** (informal) thousand: She earns $60K a year. **2** (computing) = KILOBYTE, KILO-BYTES: This disk only has 12K of memory free on it. **3** = KARAT: a 14K gold ring

ka·lei·do·scope /kəˈlaɪdəskoʊp/ noun [C] a toy that consists of a tube containing mirrors and small pieces of colored plastic. When you look into one end of the tube and turn it, you see changing patterns of colors.

kan·ga·roo /ˌkæŋgəˈruː/ noun [C] (pl. **kan·ga·roos**) an Australian animal that moves by jumping on its strong back legs and that carries its young in a pocket of skin (**a pouch**) on its stomach

kangaroo

kar·at /ˈkærət/ noun [C] (abbr. **K**) a unit of measurement used to describe how pure gold is: a 18-karat gold ring

ka·ra·te /kəˈrɑːti/ noun [U] a style of fighting originally from Japan in which the hands and feet are used as weapons

kay·ak /ˈkaɪæk/ noun [C] a small narrow boat with a small opening in the top for one person to sit in ☞ Look also at **canoe**.

keel¹ /kiːl/ noun [C] the wooden or metal bar at the bottom of a boat

keel² /kiːl/ verb
PHRV **keel over** to fall over sideways: Several people keeled over in the heat.

keen /kiːn/ adj. (used about one of the senses,

a feeling, etc.) good or strong: Foxes have a keen sense of smell.
IDM **keen on sb/sth** (often used with a negative) very interested in or having a strong desire for sb/sth: I'm not very keen on opera music. —**keen·ly** adv.: We are keenly aware of the problems there. —**keen·ness** noun [U]

☆ **keep¹** /kiːp/ verb (p.t., p.p. **kept** /kɛpt/) **1** [T] to continue to have sth, permanently or for a period of time: You can keep that pen – I don't need it anymore. ○ Can I keep the car until next week? **2** [T] to make sb/sth remain in a particular state, place or condition: Please keep this door closed. ○ He kept his hands in his pockets. ○ It's hard to keep the kids entertained when they can't go outside. ○ I'm sorry to keep you waiting. **3** [I] to continue to be in a particular state or position: You need to keep warm. ○ That boy can't keep still. ○ Keep close to me and we won't get separated. **4** [T] to have sth in a particular place: Where do you keep the matches? **5** [T] **keep doing sth** to continue doing sth; to do sth again and again: Keep going until you get to the church and then turn left. ○ She keeps asking me dumb questions. **6** [T] to delay sb/sth; to prevent sb from leaving: Finally – you're here! What kept you? **7** [T] to have and take care of animals: They keep ducks on their farm. **8** [T] to do what you promised or arranged: Can you keep a promise? ○ She didn't keep her appointment at the dentist. ○ to keep a secret (= not tell it to anyone) **9** [T] to write down sth that you want to remember: Keep a record of how much you spend. **10** [I] (used about food) to stay fresh: Onions will keep for months if you store them in a cool place.

K

IDM **keep it up** to continue doing sth as well as you are doing it now: *You made very good progress this year. Keep it up!*

☞ For other expressions using **keep**, look at the entries for the nouns and adjectives, e.g. **keep count** is at **count**.

PHRV **keep at it/sth** to continue to work on/at sth: *Keep at it – we'll be finished soon.*

keep away from sb/sth to not go near sb/sth, especially to avoid danger: *Keep away from the neighbors' dog.*

keep sb/sth back to prevent sb/sth from moving forward: *The police tried to keep the crowd back.*

keep sth back (from sb) to refuse to tell sb sth: *I know he's keeping something back; he knows a lot more than he says.*

keep sth down to make sth remain at a low level, to stop sth from increasing: *Keep your voice down.* ○ *We're trying to keep our electricity bill down.* ○ *Keep it down* (= be quiet) *in there – I'm trying to sleep!*

keep sb from sth/from doing sth to prevent sb from doing sth: *His injury kept him from playing in the game yesterday.*

keep sth from sb to refuse to tell sb sth

keep off sth to not approach or go on sth: *Keep off the grass!*

keep sth off (sb/sth) to stop sth from touching or going on sb/sth: *Keep your hands off me!*

keep on (doing sth) to continue doing sth; to do sth again and again: *He keeps on interrupting me.*

keep out (of sth) to not enter sth: *The sign said "Danger – Keep out!"*

keep to sth to continue doing sth: *He didn't keep to the subject* (= he started talking about sth else).

keep sth up 1 to continue doing sth: *How long can the baby keep up that crying?* ○ *Your last essay was excellent. Keep up the good work!* **2** to prevent sth from falling down **3** to cause sth to remain at a high level: *We want to keep up standards of education.*

keep up (with sb) to move at the same speed as sb: *Can't you walk a little slower? I can't keep up.*

keep up (with/on sth) to know about what is happening: *You have to read the latest magazines if you want to keep up.*

keep² /kip/ *noun* [U] (*old-fashioned*) food and other things that you need for life: *to earn your keep*

IDM **for keeps** (*informal*) forever: *Take it. It's yours for keeps.*

keep·er /'kipər/ *noun* [C] **1** a person who guards or takes care of sth: *a keeper at the zoo* **2** (*informal*) something that is worth keeping, especially a fish that you have just caught: *Wow! This one's a keeper!*

keep·ing /'kipɪŋ/ *noun*

IDM **in keeping with sth** correct or expected according to a rule, belief, etc.: *The manager's decision is in keeping with company policy.*

keg /kɛg/ *noun* [C] a round metal container with curved sides and a flat top and bottom, that is used for holding beer: *a keg party* (= where beer is served from a keg)

ken·nel /'kɛnl/ *noun* [C] a place where dogs can stay while their owners are on vacation

kept *p.t.*, *p.p.* of KEEP¹

kerb /kɜrb/ *noun* [C] (*BrE*) = CURB¹(1)

ker·nel /'kɜrnl/ *noun* [C] a single piece of grain, especially corn ☞ picture at **corn**.

ker·o·sene /'kɛrəsin; ˌkɛrə'sin/ *noun* [U] a type of oil that is used in old-fashioned lamps, heaters, etc.

☆ **ketch·up** /'kɛtʃəp; 'kætʃəp/ (also *old-fashioned* **catsup**) *noun* [U] a sauce made from tomatoes that is eaten cold with hot or cold food

ket·tle /'kɛtḷ/ *noun* [C] = TEAKETTLE

lock key key ring

☆ **key¹** /ki/ *noun* [C] **1** a metal object that is used for locking or unlocking a door, etc.: *Have you seen my car keys anywhere?* ○ *We need a spare key to the front door.* ○ *a bunch of keys* **2** a set of musical notes that is based on one particular note: *The piece is in the key of A minor.* **3** one of the parts of a piano, typewriter, etc. that you press with your fingers to make it work **4** a set of answers to exercises or problems: *The key to the crossword will appear in next week's issue.* **5** a list of the symbols and signs used in a map or book, showing what they mean **6** [usually sing.] something that helps you achieve or understand sth: *A good education is the key to success.* ○ *This letter holds the key to the mystery.*

key² /ki/ *verb* [T] **key sth (in)** to put information into a computer or give it an instruction by typing on the keyboard: *to key in some data* ○ *First, key in your password.*

key³ /ki/ *adj.* very important: *Tourism is a key industry in Florida.* ○ *When you're writing a paper, organization is key.*

☆ **key·board** /'kibɔrd/ *noun* [C] **1** the set of keys¹(3) on a piano, computer, etc. **2** an electrical musical instrument like a small piano ☞ picture at **rock band**.

key·hole /'kihoʊl/ *noun* [C] the hole in a lock where you put the key

key·note /'kinoʊt/ *adj.* (only *before* a noun) (used about a speech or a speaker) introducing the most important topic at a large meet-

K

ing, etc.: *The governor of Texas gave the keynote address at the party's convention.*

¹key ring *noun* [C] a ring on which you keep keys ☞ picture at **key¹**.

khak·i /ˈkæki/ *adj., noun* [U] (of) a dull greenish-brown color: *khaki pants*

☆ **kick¹** /kɪk/ *verb* **1** [T] to hit or move sb/sth with your foot: *She was knocked to the ground and kicked in the stomach.* ○ *He kicked the ball over the top of the net.* **2** [I,T] to move your foot or feet: *You have to kick your legs harder if you want to swim faster.* ○ *The protesters were dragged kicking and screaming into the police vans.* **3** [T] (*informal*) to stop doing sth, especially a dangerous habit: *I've smoked for over twenty years, but I want to kick the habit* (= to stop smoking). ○ *to kick a drug addiction*

PHRV **kick sth off** to start sth, especially with an exciting event: *The candidate kicked off her election campaign with an appearance at the state capitol building.*

kick sb out (of sth) (*informal*) to force sb to leave a place: *He was kicked out of college.*

☆ **kick²** /kɪk/ *noun* **1** [C] an act of kicking¹(1,2) : *She gave the door a kick and it closed.* **2** [C] (*informal*) a feeling of great pleasure, excitement, etc.: *He gets a real kick out of rock climbing.* ○ *Some teenagers steal things just for kicks.*

kick·off /ˈkɪkɔf/ *noun* [C] the start of a game of football: *Kickoff is at 2:30.*

☆ **kid¹** /kɪd/ *noun* [C] **1** (*informal*) a child or young person: *How are your kids?* ☞ **Kid** is much more common than **child** in informal and spoken English. **2** (*informal*) a son or daughter of any age: *Our kids are all grown up and married now.* **3 kid brother/sister** (*informal*) younger brother/sister **4** a young goat ☞ picture at **goat**.

kid² /kɪd/ *verb* [I,T] (**kid·ding**; **kid·ded**) (*informal*) to trick or deceive sb/yourself; to make a joke about sth: *I didn't mean it. I was only kidding.* ○ *Don't kid yourself, Martin – she doesn't really love you.*

kid·die /ˈkɪdi/ *adj.* (*informal*) (only *before* a noun) for or connected with children: *We only went on the kiddie rides at the fair.*

kid·nap /ˈkɪdnæp/ *verb* [T] (**kid·nap·ping**; **kid·napped**) to take sb away by force and demand money for his/her safe return: *The child was kidnapped and $50,000 was demanded for her release.* ☞ Look at **hijack**. —**kid·nap·per** *noun* [C] —**kid·nap·ping** *noun* [C,U]: *The kidnapping took place just outside his home.*

kid·ney /ˈkɪdni/ *noun* [C] (*pl.* **kid·neys**) one of the two parts of the body that separate waste liquid from the blood

☆ **kill¹** /kɪl/ *verb* **1** [I,T] to make sb/sth die: *Smoking kills.* ○ *She was killed instantly in the crash.*

☞ **Murder** means to kill a person on purpose: *This was no accident. The old lady was*

murdered. **Assassinate** means to kill for political reasons: *President Kennedy was assassinated.* **Slaughter** and **massacre** mean to kill a large number of people: *Hundreds of people were massacred when the army opened fire on the crowd.* **Slaughter** is also used to talk about killing an animal for food.

2 [T] (*informal*) to cause sb pain; hurt: *My feet are killing me.* **3** [T] to cause sth to end or fail: *The committee killed the proposal during yesterday's meeting.*

IDM **have an hour, etc. to kill** to have some time when you have nothing to do, usually when you are waiting for sb/sth

kill time to do sth uninteresting or unimportant to pass the time

kill two birds with one stone to do one thing which will achieve two results

kill² /kɪl/ *noun* [sing.] the act of killing (an animal): *The lion watched its prey, then moved in for the kill.* ☞ Look also at **road kill**.

☆ **kill·er¹** /ˈkɪlər/ *noun* [C] a person, animal or thing that kills: *He's a dangerous killer who may strike again.* ○ *a serial killer* (= sb who has killed many people) ☞ Look also at **painkiller**.

kill·er² /ˈkɪlər/ *adj.* (*slang*) (only *before* a noun) extremely difficult to deal with or to do: *We had a killer math test today.*

☆ **kill·ing** /ˈkɪlɪŋ/ *noun* [C,U] the act of killing a person or an animal on purpose; a murder: *There have been a number of brutal killings in the area recently.* ○ *a ban on the killing of whales* ☞ Look also at **mercy killing**.

IDM **make a killing** (*informal*) to make a large amount of money very quickly: *They made a killing on the stock market.*

kil·o·byte /ˈkɪləbaɪt/ *noun* [C] (*abbr.* **K**) (*computing*) a unit of computer memory. One kilobyte is equivalent to 1,024 (= 2^{10}) bytes.

kil·o·gram /ˈkɪləɡræm/ *noun* [C] (*abbr.* **kg.**) a measure of weight; 1,000 grams, or about 2.2 pounds

kil·o·me·ter /kɪˈlɑmɪətər; ˈkɪləmiˌtər/ *noun* [C] (*abbr.* **km**) a measure of length; 1,000 meters, or about 0.62 miles

kilt /kɪlt/ *noun* [C] a skirt, usually made of wool, with many folds (**pleats**) and a pattern of colored squares and stripes that cross each other (**plaid**). Kilts are worn by men in Scotland as part of their traditional national costume. ☞ picture at **bagpipes**.

kin /kɪn/ *noun* [plural] members of your family; relatives ☞ **Kin** is now a formal or oldfashioned word and is rarely used. **Next of kin** however, is still common. It means your closest family member, including your husband or wife, who should be told first if you are injured or killed.

☆ **kind¹** /kaɪnd/ *noun* [C] a group whose members all have the same qualities: *The concert*

attracted people of all kinds. ○ *The concert attracted all kinds of people.* ○ *Many kinds of plants and animals are being lost every year.*

☞ *Kinds of* may be followed by a plural noun or an uncountable noun: *There are so many kinds of cameras on the market that it's hard to know which is best.* ○ *I'm interested in all different kinds of music.* Sometimes you may hear people say something like: *Those kind/sort of dogs are really dangerous,* but this is still thought by many people not to be correct English.

IDM a kind of; kind of a (*informal*) (used for describing sth in a way that is not very clear): *There's a funny kind of smell in here.* ○ *I had kind of a weird feeling that something was wrong.*

kind of (*informal*) a little bit: *I'm kind of worried about the interview.* ○ *I kind of expected him to come late.*

one of a kind ⇨ ONE¹

☆ **kind²** /kaɪnd/ *adj.* friendly and thoughtful about what other people want or need: *A present! How kind of you!* ○ *to be kind to children and animals* ☞ The opposite is **mean** or **unkind** (which is more formal). —**kind·ness** *noun* [U]: *an act of kindness*

☆ **kin·der·gar·ten** /'kɪndərgɑrtn; -gɑrdn/ *noun* [C,U] the first year of school for children, before first grade. Children usually begin kindergarten when they are five years old. ☞ Look at **nursery school**. —**kin·der·gart·ner** (*also* **kindergartener**) *noun* [C]

☆ **kind·ly¹** /'kaɪndli/ *adv.* **1** in a kind² way: *The nurse smiled kindly.* **2** (used for asking sb to do sth, especially when you are annoyed) please: *Would you kindly leave me alone?*

kind·ly² /'kaɪndli/ *adj.* (**kind·li·er; kind·li·est**) (only *before* a noun) kind and friendly: *a kindly old man*

☆ **king** /kɪŋ/ *noun* [C] **1** (the title of) a man who rules a country. A king is usually the son or close relative of the previous ruler: *the king of Sweden* ○ (*figurative*) *The lion is the king of the jungle.*

☞ We say *King Henry VIII* as "King Henry the Eighth." Look also at **queen**.

2 one of the four playing cards in a deck with a picture of a king on it: *the king of spades* ☞ Look at the note at **card**. **3** one of the pieces used in the game of chess ☞ picture at **chess**.

☆ **king·dom** /'kɪŋdəm/ *noun* [C] **1** a country that is ruled by a king or queen: *the Kingdom of Saudi Arabia* **2** one of the parts of the natural world: *the animal kingdom*

'king-size (*also* **'king-sized**) *adj.* very large: *a king-size bed* ☞ Look at the note at **bed¹**.

kink /kɪŋk/ *noun* [C] a turn or bend in sth that should be straight: *There's a kink in the hose so the water won't come out.*

kink·y /'kɪŋki/ *adj.* (**kink·i·er; kink·i·est**) (*informal*) **1** connected with strange or unusual sexual activities **2** (used about hair) having many very small curls

☆ **kiss¹** /kɪs/ *verb* [I,T] to touch sb with your lips as a greeting or to show love or affection: *They sat in the back row of the movie theater, kissing and giggling.* ○ *He kissed her tenderly on the cheek.* ○ *They kissed each other goodbye.*

☆ **kiss²** /kɪs/ *noun* [C] a touch with the lips: *Give Daddy a goodnight kiss.* ○ *a kiss on the lips*

kit /kɪt/ *noun* [C] **1** equipment that you need for a particular activity, situation, etc.: *a first-aid kit* ○ *a tool kit* **2** a set of parts that you buy and put together in order to make sth: *a kit for a model airplane*

☆ **kitch·en** /'kɪtʃən/ *noun* [C] a room where food is prepared and cooked: *We usually eat in the kitchen.* ○ *a kitchen cupboard*

kite /kaɪt/ *noun* [C] a toy which is made of a light frame covered with paper or cloth. Kites are flown in the wind on the end of a long piece of string: *Several people were flying kites on the hill.*

☆ **kit·ten** /'kɪtn/ *noun* [C] a young cat ☞ picture at **cat**.

kit·ty /'kɪti/ *noun* [C] (*pl.* **kit·ties**) (used especially by children) a cat

ki·wi /'kiwi/ (*also* **'kiwi fruit**) *noun* [C] a fruit with brown skin that is green inside with black seeds

☆ **Kleen·ex** /'klinɛks/ (*also* **tissue**) *noun* [C,U] (*trademark*) a thin piece of soft paper that you use for wiping or blowing your nose and throw away after you have used it

klutz /klʌts/ *noun* [C] (*informal*) a person who often drops things, is not good at sports, etc. —**klutz·y** /'klʌtsi/ *adj.*

knack /næk/ *noun* [sing.] the ability to do sth (difficult): *Knitting isn't difficult once you get the knack of it.*

knead /nid/ *verb* [T] to press and squeeze sth with your hands: *Knead the bread dough for ten minutes, then let it rise.*

☆ **knee** /ni/ *noun* [C] **1** the place where your leg bends in the middle: *Angie fell and hurt her knee.* ○ *Come and sit on my knee.* ☞ picture on page A24. **2** the part of a pair of pants, etc. that covers the knee (1): *There's a hole in the knee of those jeans.*

knee·cap /'nikæp/ *noun* [C] the bone that covers the front of the knee

,knee-'deep *adj.* **1** deep enough to reach the knees: *We had to wade through knee-deep water.* **2 knee-deep in sth** (*informal*) very deeply involved in sth: *He was knee-deep in the company's illegal business deals.*

i	ɪ	ɛ	æ	ɑ	ɔ	ʌ	ʊ	u
see	sit	ten	cat	hot	saw	cup	put	too

kneel/crouch

kneeling crouching

☆ **kneel** /nil/ *verb* [I] (*p.t.*, *p.p.* **knelt** /nɛlt/ or **kneeled**) **kneel (down)** to go down on one or both knees; to be in this position: *Kneel down while I comb your hair.* ○ *to kneel in prayer*

knew *p.t.* of KNOW

knick-knack /ˈnɪknæk/ *noun* [C] an object that you have because it is attractive, not because it is useful. Knickknacks are used to decorate rooms, etc. ☞ picture at **fireplace**.

☆ **knife¹** /naɪf/ *noun* [C] (*pl.* **knives** /naɪvz/) a sharp flat piece of metal (**a blade**) with a handle. A knife is used for cutting things or as a weapon: *Be careful. That bread knife is very sharp.* ○ *a blunt/dull knife* ○ *Don't use your fingers. Use a knife and fork.* ○ *a pocket knife*

knife² /naɪf/ *verb* [T] to injure sb with a knife¹: *The young man had been knifed in the chest.*

knife-point /ˈnaɪfpɔɪnt/ *noun*
IDM at knifepoint threatening to injure or kill sb with a knife: *He robbed the old woman at knifepoint.*

knight /naɪt/ *noun* [C] **1** a soldier who fought while riding a horse in the Middle Ages **2** one of the pieces used in the game of chess ☞ picture at **chess**.

☆ **knit** /nɪt/ *verb* [I,T] (**knit·ting**; *p.t.*, *p.p.* **knit** or **knit·ted**) to make sth (e.g. an article of clothing) with yarn using long needles or a special machine: *Grandma loves knitting.* ○ *I'm knitting a sweater for my nephew.* ☞ Look also at **close-knit**. —**knit·ting** *noun* [U]: *She put down her knitting and yawned.* ○ *a knitting machine*

stitches **knit**

yarn knitting needle

'**knitting** ,**needle** *noun* [C] = NEEDLE(2)

knives *pl.* of KNIFE¹

knob /nɑb/ *noun* [C] **1** a round handle on a door, etc. **2** a round button on a machine that controls a part of it

☆ **knock¹** /nɑk/ *noun* [C] a sharp hit or the sound it makes: *I thought I heard a knock at the door.* ○ (*figurative*) *She has suffered some hard knocks in her life.*

☆ **knock²** /nɑk/ *verb* **1** [T] to hit sb/sth with a sharp blow: *He knocked the vase onto the floor.* ○ *She fell off her bike and knocked two teeth loose.* ○ *to knock sb unconscious* **2** [I] to make a noise by hitting sth: *Someone is knocking on the door.* **3** [T] (*informal*) to say bad or

unfavorable things about sb/sth: *It's not the best food in the world, but it's free – so don't knock it!*
IDM knock it off! (*informal*) (used to tell sb to stop doing sth)
knock on wood (an expression that people use, often while knocking on sth made of wood, to prevent good luck from becoming bad luck): *I've been driving for 15 years without an accident – knock on wood!*
knock your/sb's socks off (*informal*) to surprise and impress sb: *This new show is really going to knock your socks off.*
PHRV knock sb down to cause sb to fall to the ground/floor: *The old lady got knocked down by a car.*
knock sth down to destroy a building, etc.: *The old houses will be knocked down to make way for an apartment complex.*
knock off (sth) (*informal*) to stop doing work, etc.: *What time do you knock off?*
knock sb off (*slang*) to kill or defeat sb: *Two of the main characters get knocked off in the last scene of the movie.*
knock sth off (sth) (*informal*) to reduce a price by a certain amount: *He agreed to knock $10 off the price.*
knock sb out 1 to hit sb so that he/she becomes unconscious or cannot get up again for a while: *The punch on the nose knocked him out.* **2** (used about a drug, alcohol, etc.) to cause sb to sleep: *Three glasses of vodka knocked her out.*
knock sth out to break sth or make sth useless by using force: *The tornado knocked out all power supplies to the town.*
knock sb out (of sth) to beat a person or team in a competition so that they do not play any more games in it: *Our team was knocked out of the playoffs in the semifinals.*
knock sb/sth over to cause sb/sth to fall over: *Be careful not to knock over the drinks.*

knock·out /ˈnɑkaʊt/ *noun* [C] **1** a blow that causes sb to become unconscious or to be unable to get up again for a while **2** (*informal*) a very attractive woman

knot bow

string ribbon

☆ **knot¹** /nɑt/ *noun* [C] **1** a place where two ends or pieces of rope, string, etc. have been tied together firmly: *to tie/untie a knot* ○ *a tight/loose knot* **2** a measure of the speed of a ship or an airplane; 1.15 or 1.85 kilometers per hour

knot² /nɑt/ *verb* [T] (**knot·ting**; **knot·ted**) (usually passive) to tie a knot in sth: *She wore her jacket knotted around her waist.*

ə	y	w	t̬	eɪ	aɪ	ɔɪ	aʊ	oʊ
about	yes	woman	butter	say	five	boy	now	go

K

☆ **know** /noʊ/ *verb* (*p.t.* **knew** /nu/; *p.p.* **known** /noʊn/) (not in the continuous tenses) **1** [I,T] to have knowledge or information in your mind: *I don't know much about sports.* ∘ *Do you know their telephone number?* ∘ *"You've got a flat tire." "I know."* ∘ *Did you know that Jonathan enjoyed painting?* ∘ *Do you know the whole poem by heart?* ∘ *Knowing Barbara, she'll be out with her friends.* **2** [T] to have met or seen sb before: *We've known each other for years.* ☞ Notice the expression **get to know sb**: *I'd like to get to know Kevin better.* **3 know sb/sth (to do sth)** [T] to have seen, heard, etc. sth: *I've known him to go a whole day without eating.* ∘ *It's been known to snow in June.* **4** [T] to be familiar with a place: *I don't know this part of the city well.* **5** [T] (often passive) to give sth a particular name; to recognize sb/sth as sth: *Istanbul was previously known as Constantinople.* ∘ *She's known as an excellent manager.* ∘ *He knows a genuine antique when he sees one.* **6** [T] to speak or understand a language: *I don't know much Spanish.* **7** [T] to be able to do sth: *Do you know how to swim?*

☞ Be careful. You must use **how to**; you CANNOT say: *I know swim.*

8 [T] to have experience of sth: *They have known both wealth and poverty.* ∘ *Many people in western countries don't know what it's like to be hungry.* **IDM God/goodness/Heaven (only) knows 1** I don't know: *They ordered a new car, but goodness only knows how they're going to pay for it.* **2** (used for emphasizing sth): *I hope I get an answer soon. Goodness knows, I've waited long enough.*
know better (than that/than to do sth) to have enough sense (not to do sth): *I thought you knew better than to go out in the rain with no coat on.*
know sth inside out/like the back of your hand (*informal*) to be very familiar with sth: *I grew up here. I know these woods like the back of my hand.*
know what you are talking about (*informal*) to have knowledge of sth from your own experience
know what's what (*informal*) to have all the important information about sth
let sb know ⇨ LET

you know (*informal*) **1** (used when the speaker is thinking of what to say next): *Well, you know, it's kind of hard to explain.* **2** (used when the speaker wants to check whether sb understands what he/she is saying): *It just makes me really mad, you know?* ∘ *I bought one of those new bread machines – you know, like the one Mike has.*
PHRV know of sb/sth to have information about or experience of sb/sth: *Do you know of a good restaurant nearby?*

know² /noʊ/ *noun*
IDM in the know (*informal*) having information that other people do not have: *People in the know say that the governor is going to resign.*

know-how *noun* [U] (*informal*) knowledge of or skill in sth: *We are looking for someone with technical know-how in this field.*

know·ing /ˈnoʊɪŋ/ *adj.* showing that you know a lot about sth: *a knowing look*

know·ing·ly /ˈnoʊɪŋli/ *adv.* **1** on purpose: *I've never knowingly lied to you.* **2** in a way that shows that you understand: *He smiled knowingly.*

☆ **knowl·edge** /ˈnɑlɪdʒ/ *noun* [U, sing.] information or facts that you have in your mind about sth: *He has extensive knowledge of ancient Egypt.* ∘ *I have a working knowledge of French.* ∘ *To my knowledge they are still living there.* ∘ *She did it without my knowledge.*
IDM be common knowledge ⇨ COMMON¹

☆ **knowl·edge·a·ble** /ˈnɑlɪdʒəbl/ *adj.* having a lot of knowledge; well-informed: *She's very knowledgeable about history.* —**knowl·edge·ably** *adv.*

knuck·le /ˈnʌkl/ *noun* [C] one of the places where the fingers join the rest of the hand, or between the bones in a finger ☞ picture on page A24.

ko·a·la /koʊˈɑlə/ (*also* **koala bear**) *noun* [C] an Australian animal with thick gray fur that lives in trees and looks like a small bear

Ko·ran /kəˈræn; -ˈrɑn/ *noun* [sing.] **the Koran** the holy book of the Muslims

ko·sher /ˈkoʊʃər/ *adj.* (used about food) suitable to be eaten by religious Jews

Kwan·zaa /ˈkwɑnzə/ *noun* [U] a cultural festival that is celebrated by some African-Americans from December 26 through January 1

LI

L, l /ɛl/ *noun* [C] (*pl.* **L's; l's**) the twelfth letter of the English alphabet: *"Lake" begins with (an) "L."*

L *abbr.* large

l *abbr.* **1** liter **2 l.** left **3 l.** line

lab /læb/ *noun* [C] (*informal*) = LABORATORY

☆ **la·bel¹** /ˈleɪbl/ *noun* [C] a piece of paper, etc. on an object which gives information about it: *There is a list of all the ingredients on the label.* ○ (*figurative*) *She hated the label "housewife."*

la·bel² /ˈleɪbl/ *verb* [T] **1** to put a label¹ or labels on sth: *All items of clothing should be clearly labeled with your name.* **2** label sb/sth (as) sth to describe sb/sth as sth: *The press had labeled him an extremist.*

☆ **la·bor¹** /ˈleɪbər/ *noun* **1** [C,U] work, especially of a hard, physical kind: *manual labor* [C] (*formal*) *These changes are a direct result of her labors.* **2** [U] workers, when thought of as a group: *skilled labor* ○ *Labor relations* (= between workers and managers) *have improved in recent years.* **3** [U] the process of giving birth: *She was in labor for ten hours.*

la·bor² /ˈleɪbər/ *verb* [I] (*formal*) to work hard, especially on sth that is difficult: *She labored on her book for two years.*

☆ **lab·o·ra·to·ry** /ˈlæbrətɔri/ *noun* [C] (*pl.* **lab·o·ra·to·ries**) (also *informal* **lab**) a room or building that is used for scientific work or for teaching about science: *a physics laboratory* ☞ Look at **language laboratory**.

'Labor Day *noun* [C,U] a holiday on the first Monday in September, when banks, schools and many businesses are closed: *Labor Day weekend* (= the weekend before Labor Day, when many people go on vacation)

la·bor·er /ˈleɪbərər/ *noun* [C] a person whose job needs hard physical work: *unskilled laborers*

la·bo·ri·ous /ləˈbɔriəs/ *adj.* needing a lot of effort —**la·bo·ri·ous·ly** *adv.*

'labor ˌunion *noun* [C] = UNION(3)

lab·y·rinth /ˈlæbərɪnθ/ *noun* [C] a complicated set of paths and passages, through which it is difficult to find your way: *a labyrinth of corridors* ☞ Look at **maze**.

lace

lace /leɪs/ *noun* [U] cloth that is made of very fine threads in beautiful patterns: *lace curtains* ○ *a collar made of lace* ☞ Look also at **shoelace**.

☆ **lack¹** /læk/ *verb* [T] to have too little or none of sth: *She seems to lack the will to succeed.*
IDM **be lacking** to be needed: *Money is still lacking for the new school building.*
be lacking in sth to not have enough of sth: *He's certainly not lacking in intelligence.*

☆ **lack²** /læk/ *noun* [U, sing.] an absence of sth that is needed: *A lack of food forced many people to leave their homes.*

lac·quer /ˈlækər/ *noun* [U] a type of transparent paint that is put on wood, metal, etc. in order to protect it and make it shiny

lac·y /ˈleɪsi/ *adj.* of or like lace

ladders
stepladder
ladder
rung
step

☆ **lad·der** /ˈlædər/ *noun* [C] a piece of equipment that is used for climbing up sth. A ladder consists of two long pieces of metal, wood or rope with steps fastened between them: (*figurative*) *to climb the ladder of success*

lad·en /ˈleɪdn/ *adj.* **laden with sth** having or carrying a lot of sth: *The guests arrived, laden with gifts.* ○ (*figurative*) *to be laden with guilt*

'ladies' room *noun* [C] a room with toilets in it for women in a public building ☞ Look at **men's room**, **restroom** and at the note at **toilet**.

☆ **la·dy** /ˈleɪdi/ *noun* [C] (*pl.* **la·dies**) **1** a woman who is polite and who behaves well to other people: *A real lady does not scream and shout.* ☞ Look at **gentleman**. **2** (a formal or very polite way of saying "woman"): *The old lady next door lives alone.*

☞ Many women, especially younger women, do not like this use of **lady** because it seems old-fashioned. They prefer the word **woman**. Look also at **first lady**.

3 (*informal*) (a rude way of talking to a woman who you do not know): *Hey, lady, why don't you hurry up?*
IDM **ladies and gentlemen** (used when you start making a speech to a large group of people)

L

la·dy·bug /ˈleɪdibʌg/ *noun* [C] a small insect that is red or orange with black spots

lag¹ /læg/ *verb* [I] (**lag·ging; lagged**) **lag (behind sb/sth); lag (behind)** to go more slowly than sb/sth: *I always lag behind when we go walking.* ○ (*figurative*) *Tyler has missed a lot of school and is lagging behind the rest of his class.*

lag² /læg/ *noun* [C] a period of time between two events: *There will be a nine-month lag between the opening of the first part of the highway and its completion.* ☞ Look also at **jet lag**.

laid *p.t., p.p.* of LAY¹

laid-back /ˌleɪd ˈbæk/ *adj.* (*informal*) having a relaxed, casual personality or atmosphere: *He's a really laid-back kind of guy.* ○ *a laid-back style of management*

lain *p.p.* of LIE²

☆ **lake** /leɪk/ *noun* [C] a large area of water that is surrounded by land: *They went swimming in the lake.* ○ *Lake Michigan* ○ *the Great Lakes* ☞ A **pond** is smaller than a lake.

☆ **lamb** /læm/ *noun* **1** [C] a young sheep ☞ Look at the note and picture at **sheep**. **2** [U] the flesh of a lamb (1) when eaten as meat: *lamb chops* ☞ Look at the note at **meat**.

lame /leɪm/ *adj.* **1** not able to walk well because of an injury to the leg: *The horse is lame and cannot work.* ☞ **Lame** is not often used about a person. The verb and noun **limp** are more often used: *He walks with a limp.* ○ *You're limping. Did you hurt your leg?* **2** (used about an excuse, argument, etc.) not easily believed; weak **3** (*slang*) not interesting, exciting or fashionable: *What a lame party!*

ˌ**lame** ˈ**duck** *noun* [C] a politician who does not have much real power because his/her period in a political position will end soon

la·ment /ləˈmɛnt/ *verb* [I,T] (*formal*) to feel or express great sadness (about sth)

☆ **lamp** /læmp/ *noun* [C] a piece of equipment that uses electricity, gas or oil to produce light: *a table lamp* ☞ picture at **light**.

lamp·shade /ˈlæmpʃeɪd/ *noun* [C] a cover for a lamp that makes it look more attractive and makes the light softer ☞ picture at **light**.

☆ **land¹** /lænd/ *noun* **1** [U] the solid part of the surface of the earth (= not water): *After three months on a ship, she was glad to reach dry land.* ☞ Look at the note at **ground**. **2** [C,U] a piece of ground: *They own over 2,000 acres of land.* ○ *federal lands* (= owned by the federal government) **3** [U] ground, soil or earth of a particular kind: *The land is rich and fertile.* ○ *barren land* **4** [C] (*formal*) a country: *She died far from her native land.* ☞ Look at the note at **country**. **5** [U, sing.] (*informal*) an area or region that is connected with sth particular in people's minds: *California, the land of sun, sea and fun*

☆ **land²** /lænd/ *verb* **1** [I,T] to come down from the air or bring sth down to the ground: *The bird landed on the roof.* ○ *The pilot landed the airplane safely.* ○ *He is due to land at 3 o'clock.* ☞ Look at **take off**. **2** [I,T] to go onto land or put sth onto land from a ship or boat: *Thousands of immigrants landed on Ellis Island in the early 1900s.* ○ *Dave landed a 5-pound fish.* **3** [T] (*informal*) to get sth after a long effort: *The company just landed a big contract.*

land·fill /ˈlændfɪl/ *noun* [C] a place where large amounts of garbage or other waste materials are put into the ground and covered with earth

☆ **land·ing** /ˈlændɪŋ/ *noun* [C] **1** coming down onto the ground (in an airplane): *to make an emergency landing* ○ *a crash landing* ○ *a safe landing* ☞ Look at **takeoff**. **2** the area at the top of a staircase or between one staircase and another

land·la·dy /ˈlændˌleɪdi/ *noun* [C] (*pl.* **land·la·dies**) a woman who rents a house or an apartment to people for money

☆ **land·lord** /ˈlændlɔrd/ *noun* [C] a person or company that rents a house or an apartment to people for money

land·mark /ˈlændmɑrk/ *noun* [C] **1** an object (often a building) that can be seen easily from a distance: *The Empire State Building is one of the landmarks on New York's skyline.* **2** an important stage or change in the development of sth: *The American Revolution was a landmark in world history.*

ˈ**land mine** *noun* [C] a device that is put under the surface of the ground, that explodes when sb walks on it or drives a car over it

☆ **land·scape** /ˈlændskeɪp/ *noun* [C] **1** an area of country (when you are thinking about what it looks like): *The prairie landscape is very flat.* ○ *an urban landscape* ☞ Look at the note at **scenery**. **2** a picture that shows a view of the countryside: *one of Van Gogh's landscapes*

land·slide /ˈlændslaɪd/ *noun* [C] **1** a sudden fall of earth, rocks, etc. down the side of a mountain **2** a result, especially in a political election, in which one person or party receives many more votes than anyone else: *The governor was re-elected in a landslide.*

☆ **lane** /leɪn/ *noun* [C] **1** (*abbr.* **Ln.**) (used in the names of some streets in towns and cities): *We live at 1015 Beech Lane.* **2** a part of a wide road for one line of traffic: *You should signal before you change lanes.* ○ *a four-lane highway* ☞ Look also at **fast lane**. **3** a part of a sports track, swimming pool, etc. for one competitor in a race: *The American runner is in lane two.* **4** a route or path that is regularly used by ships or airplanes: *shipping lanes*

☆ **lan·guage** /ˈlæŋgwɪdʒ/ *noun* **1** [U] the system of sounds and writing that human beings use to express their thoughts, ideas and feelings: *written language* ○ *the spoken language* **2** [C] a

L

form of language that is used by a particular group (usually in one country): *a foreign language* ○ *Latin is a dead language.* **3** [C,U] any system of signs, symbols, movements, etc. that is used to express sth: *sign language* **4** [U] words of a particular type, or words that are used by a particular person or group: *bad language* (= swearing) ○ *legal language*

ˈlanguage ˌlaboratory *noun* [C] (*pl.* **language laboratories**) (also *informal* **language lab**) a room that has special equipment, e.g. tape recorders, to help you learn a foreign language

lank·y /ˈlæŋki/ *adj.* (used about a person) very tall and thin

lan·tern /ˈlæntərn/ *noun* [C] a type of light that can be carried. A lantern usually consists of a metal frame with glass sides and a lamp or candle inside. ☞ Look also at **jack-o'-lantern.**

lap¹ /læp/ *noun* [C] **1** the flat area that is formed by the upper part of your legs when you are sitting down: *Come and sit on my lap.* **2** one trip around a race track, etc.: *There are three more laps to go in the race.*

lap² /læp/ *verb* (**lap·ping; lapped**) **1** [T] **lap sth (up)** (usually used about an animal) to drink sth using the tongue: *The cat lapped up the cream.* **2** [I,T] (used about water) to make gentle sounds as it splashes against sth: *The waves lapped against the side of the boat.* **PHRV lap sth up** (*informal*) to listen to or read sth eagerly and accept it as true

la·pel /ləˈpɛl/ *noun* [C] one of the two parts of the front of a coat or jacket that are folded back

lapse¹ /læps/ *noun* [C] **1** a short time when you cannot remember sth or you are not thinking about what you are doing: *a lapse of memory* ○ *The accident was the result of a temporary lapse in concentration.* **2** a short period of bad behavior that is unlike a person's usual behavior **3** a period of time in which you do not do sth, go somewhere, etc.: *She returned to work after a lapse of ten years.* ☞ Look at the verb **elapse.**

lapse² /læps/ *verb* **PHRV lapse into sth** to go into a particular state: *to lapse into silence, a coma, etc.*

lap·top /ˈlæptɑp/ (*also* **ˌlaptop comˈputer**) *noun* [C] a small computer that is easy to carry around and that can use batteries for power

lard /lɑrd/ *noun* [U] a white fat from pigs, that is used in cooking

☆ **large¹** /lɑrdʒ/ *adj.* greater in size or amount than is usual: *I'll have a cheeseburger and a large Coke.* ○ *Large amounts of money are spent on advertising.* ☞ Look at the note at **big. IDM by and large** mostly; in general: *By and large, the school is very efficient.*

large² /lɑrdʒ/ *noun* [C] (*abbr.* **L**) something

that is large¹ or larger than average: *Do you have this shirt in a large?* **IDM at large 1** (used about a criminal, animal, etc.) free: *The escaped prisoner is still at large.* **2** as a whole; in general: *Society at large is becoming more concerned about the environment.*

☆ **large·ly** /ˈlɑrdʒli/ *adv.* mostly: *His success was largely due to hard work.*

ˈlarge-scale *adj.* (only *before* a noun) happening over a large area or affecting a lot of people

lar·yn·gi·tis /ˌlærənˈdʒaɪtəs/ *noun* [U] a mild disease of the throat that makes it difficult to speak

la·ser /ˈleɪzər/ *noun* [C] (a piece of equipment that produces) a very strong beam of light. Laser beams are used in weapons and medical operations and can also cut hard substances such as metals.

ˈlaser ˌprinter *noun* [C] a machine that is connected to a computer and that can print documents very clearly

lash¹ /læʃ/ *noun* [C] **1** an act of hitting sb/sth with a whip: *The prisoner was given twenty lashes.* **2** = EYELASH

lash² /læʃ/ *verb* **1** [I,T] to hit (as if) with a whip: *The rain lashed against the windows.* **2** [T] **lash A to B; lash A and B together** to tie two things together firmly with rope, etc.: *The two boats were lashed together.* **PHRV lash out (at/against sb/sth)** to suddenly attack sb/sth (with words or by hitting them): *When he came home drunk his wife lashed out at him.*

las·so /ˈlæsoʊ/ *noun* [C] (*pl.* **las·sos** or **las·soes**) a long rope with a circle at one end that is used for catching cows and horses ☞ picture at **cowboy.** – **las·so** *verb* [T] (*pres. part.* **las·so·ing;** *3rd pers. sing. pres.* **las·sos** or **las·soes;** *p.t., p.p.* **las·soed**)

☆ **last¹** /læst/ *det.* **1** coming at the end; final: *December is the last month of the year.* ○ *Would the last person to leave please turn off the lights?* ○ *She lived alone for the last years of her life.* **2** (only *before* a noun) (used about a time, period, event, etc. in the past that is nearest to the present): *I went shopping last Saturday.* ○ *The last time I saw her was in San Francisco.*

☞ The **latest** means "most recent" or "new." The **last** means the one before the present one: *His last novel was a huge success, but the latest one is much less popular.*

3 (only *before* a noun) only remaining: *This is my last chance to take the test.* ○ *Who's going to have the last piece of cake?* **4** (only *before* a noun) most unlikely; not suitable: *She's on a diet. Chocolate is the last thing she wants.* **IDM (have) the last word 1** (to make) the final comment in a discussion or argument

2 (to make) the final decision about sth after a discussion

(as) a last resort when everything else has failed; the person or thing that helps when everything else has failed: *As a last resort we can always walk home.*

the last/final straw ⇨ STRAW

the last minute/moment the final minute/moment before sth happens: *We arrived at the last minute to catch the plane.* ○ *a last-minute change of plan*

next, second, third, etc. to last the next, second, third, etc. one from the end: *Y is the second-to-last letter of the alphabet.*

☆ **last²** /læst/ *adv.* **1** at the end; after all the others: *The British athlete came in last.* ○ *Put the eggs in last so they won't get crushed.* **2** on the occasion in the past that is nearest to the present: *When did you last have your eyes checked?*

IDM last but not least (used before the final item in a list) just as important as all the other items: *And last but not least, I'd like to thank you all very much.*

☆ **last³** /læst/ *verb* [I,T] **1** to continue for a period of time: *Do you think this weather will last until the weekend?* ○ *The meeting lasted for an hour.* **2** to remain in a good condition: *It's only a cheap radio, but it'll probably last a year or so.* **3** (used about the quantity, condition, etc. of sth) to be good enough or sufficient for what sb needs: *The coffee won't last until next week.* ○ *This old coat will have to last another winter.* ○ *I only have ten dollars to last me until Saturday.*

last⁴ /læst/ *noun* [C] (*pl.* **last**) **1** a person or thing that is after all the others: *Alex was the last to arrive.* **2 the last (of sb/sth)** the only remaining part of sth: *We finished the last of the milk at breakfast.*

IDM at (long) last in the end; finally: *After months of separation they were together at last.*

last·ing /ˈlæstɪŋ/ *adj.* continuing for a long time: *The children's faces left a lasting impression on me.*

last·ly /ˈlæstli/ *adv.* finally; last of all: *Lastly, I would like to wish you all a happy new year.*

☆ **last ˈname** *noun* [C] the name that you share with other people in your family: *"What's your last name?" "Jones."* ☞ Look at the note at **name**.

latch /lætʃ/ *noun* [C] a small metal bar that is used for fastening a door or a gate. You have to lift the latch in order to open the door.

☆ **late** /leɪt/ *adj., adv.* **1** after the usual or expected time: *She was ten minutes late for school.* ○ *The ambulance arrived too late to save him.* ○ *to be late with the rent* ○ *to stay up late* ○ *The buses are running late today.* **2** near the end of a period of time: *the late nineteenth century* ○ *His mother's in her late fifties* (= between 55 and 60). ○ *We got back home late at night.* **3** happen-

ing at night: *a late movie* **4** (*formal*) (only *before* a noun) no longer alive; dead: *his late wife*

IDM a late night a time when you go to bed very late at night: *I've been spending a lot of late nights in front of the computer.*

☆ **late·ly** /ˈleɪtli/ *adv.* in the period of time up to now; recently: *I've been feeling really tired lately.* ☞ Look at the note at **recently**.

☆ **lat·er¹** /ˈleɪtər/ *adv.* at a time in the future, or more recently than sth in the past: *I'll call you back later.* ○ *Later, he got a job as a salesman.*

IDM later (on) at a later time or in the future: *Later on, you'll probably wish that you'd worked harder in school.*

see you later (*informal*) goodbye (until some time in the future)

sooner or later ⇨ SOON

lat·er² /ˈleɪtər/ *adj.* (only *before* a noun) coming at a time in the future, or after sth else in the past: *We can discuss that at a later date.* ○ *The artist's later paintings consist mainly of landscapes.*

lat·est¹ /ˈleɪtəst/ *noun* [U] **the latest** the most recent (fashion, news, etc.): *Here is the latest* (= news) *on the space shuttle launch:...* ○ *They have the very latest in software.*

IDM at the latest no later than: *I need your report by Friday at the latest.*

lat·est² /ˈleɪtəst/ *adj.* very recent or new: *the latest fashion* ○ *the latest news* ○ *the terrorists' latest attack* ☞ Look at the note at **last¹**.

la·tex /ˈleɪtɛks/ *noun* [U] an artificial substance like rubber, that is used in products such as gloves, paints, etc.

lath·er /ˈlæðər/ *noun* [U] white bubbles that you get when you mix soap with water

Lat·in¹ /ˈlætn/ *noun* [U] the language that was used in ancient Rome

Lat·in² /ˈlætn/ *adj.* **1** of or in Latin¹: *Latin poetry* **2** connected with, or typical of, Mexico, Central America, or South America

La·ti·na /ləˈtinə/ *noun* [C] a woman or girl in the U.S. whose family came from Latin America

☆ **Latin Aˈmerica** *noun* [U] Mexico, Central America and South America —**Latin Aˈmerican** *noun* [C], *adj.*

La·ti·no /ləˈtinoʊ/ *noun* [C] (*pl.* **La·ti·nos**) a person in the U.S. whose family came from Latin America —**La·ti·no** *adj.*: *Latino culture*

lat·i·tude /ˈlætətud/ *noun* [U] the distance of a place north or south of the imaginary line around the middle of the earth (**the equator**) ☞ picture at **earth**. Latitude is measured in **degrees**. Look at **longitude**.

lat·ter /ˈlætər/ *adj.* (*formal*) **1** (only *before* a noun) nearer to the end of a period of time; later: *Interest rates should fall in the latter half of the year.* **2 the latter** *noun* [sing.], *pron.* the second of two people or things that are mentioned: *We offer both standard and express delivery – the latter costs $5 extra.* ☞ The first

ər	ɪr	ɛr	ɑr	ɔr	ʊr	ʒ	h	ŋ
bird	near	hair	car	north	tour	vision	hat	sing

of two people or things that are mentioned is **the former.**

☆ **laugh¹** /læf/ *verb* [I] to make the sounds that show you are happy or amused: *His jokes always make me laugh.* ○ *to laugh out loud*

PHRV **laugh at sb/sth 1** to show, by laughing, that you think sb/sth is funny: *The kids laughed at the clown.* **2** to show that you think sb is ridiculous: *Don't laugh at him. He can't help the way he speaks.*

☆ **laugh²** /læf/ *noun* [C] the sound or act of laughing: *Her jokes got a lot of laughs.* ○ *She has a really irritating laugh.*

laugh·a·ble /ˈlæfəbl/ *adj.* deserving to be laughed at; foolish or ridiculous

☆ **laugh·ter** /ˈlæftər/ *noun* [U] the sound or act of laughing: *Everyone roared with laughter.*

launch /lɔntʃ/ *verb* [T] **1** to send a ship into the water or a rocket, etc. into the sky **2** to start sth new or to show sth for the first time: *The enemy launched an attack at midnight.* ○ *to launch a new product*

PHRV **launch into sth** to start talking about sth in an enthusiastic or aggressive way: *She launched into an attack on her opponent's policies.* —**launch** *noun* [C, usually sing.]: *The shuttle launch has been delayed.*

Laun·dro·mat /ˈlɔndrəmæt/ (*also* **laundromat**) *noun* [C] (*trademark*) a type of store where you pay to wash and dry your clothes in machines

☆ **laun·dry** /ˈlɔndri/ *noun* [U] clothes, etc. that need washing or that are being washed: *a laundry basket* ○ *to do the laundry* (= to wash clothes, etc.)

¹**laundry room** *noun* [C] a room in an apartment building, etc., with machines for washing and drying clothes

la·va /ˈlɑvə/ *noun* [U] hot liquid rock that comes out of a volcano

lav·a·to·ry /ˈlævətɔri/ *noun* [C] (*pl.* **lav·a·to·ries**) a small room, especially in an airplane, that contains a toilet, sink, etc. ☞ Look at the note at **toilet.**

lav·en·der /ˈlævəndər/ *noun* [U] **1** a garden plant with purple flowers that smells very pleasant **2** a pale purple color —**lav·en·der** *adj.*

lav·ish /ˈlævɪʃ/ *adj.* **1** giving or spending generously or in large quantities: *She is very lavish with her presents.* **2** large in amount or number, and often expensive: *a lavish meal*

☆ **law** /lɔ/ *noun* **1** [C] an official rule of a country, a state, etc. that says what a person, company, etc. may or may not do: *a law banning the sale of certain automatic weapons* **2** **the law** [U] a law or the system of laws in a country, etc.: *Stealing is against the law.* ○ *to break the law* ○ *to obey the law* ☞ Look at **legal.** **3** **the law** [U] the police: *This isn't the first time Dan has been in trouble with the law.* **4** [U] the law(2) as a subject of study or as a

profession: *She is studying law.* ○ *My brother works for a law firm in Cleveland.* ☞ Look at **legal.** **5** [C] (in science) a statement of what always happens in certain circumstances: *the laws of mathematics*

IDM **law and order** a situation in which the law is obeyed: *a breakdown of law and order*

¹**law·a·biding** *adj.* (used about a person) obeying the law: *We are all respectable law-abiding citizens.*

¹**law en·force·ment** *noun* [U] making sure that people obey the laws of a country, etc.: *Law enforcement officials arrested the suspects yesterday.*

law·ful /ˈlɔfl/ *adj.* (*formal*) allowed or recognized by law: *We will use all lawful means to obtain our demands.* ○ *his lawful wife* ☞ Look at **legal.** The opposite is **unlawful.**

law·less /ˈlɔləs/ *adj.* (used about a person or his/her actions) breaking the law: *a gang of lawless youths* —**law·less·ness** *noun* [U]

law·mak·er /ˈlɔˌmeɪkər/ *noun* [C] (*formal*) a person, e.g. a member of Congress, etc., who makes new laws

☆ **lawn** /lɔn/ *noun* [C,U] an area of grass in a yard or park that is cut regularly ☞ picture on page A28.

lawn mower (*also* **lawn·mow·er**) /ˈlɔnˌmoʊər/ *noun* [C] a machine that is used for cutting the grass in a yard

☆ **law·suit** /ˈlɔsut/ (*also* **suit**) *noun* [C] a legal argument in a court of law that is between two people or groups, usually because one person or group thinks the other did sth wrong to them and wants money in order to reduce the bad effect: *to file a lawsuit against sb*

☆ **law·yer** /ˈlɔyər/ *noun* [C] a person who has studied law and whose job is to give advice on legal matters and/or to speak for you in a court of law: *to consult a lawyer* ☞ A more formal word for **lawyer** is **attorney**, which is used especially in job titles: *a defense attorney*

lax /læks/ *adj.* not having high standards; not strict: *Their security checks are fairly lax.*

☆ **lay¹** /leɪ/ *verb* [T] (*p.t., p.p.* **laid** /leɪd/) **1** to put sb/sth carefully in a particular position or on a surface: *He laid the child gently down on his bed.* ○ *"Don't worry," she said, laying her hand on my shoulder.* **2** to put sth in the correct position, especially on a flat surface or under the ground, for a particular purpose: *They're laying new sewer pipes on our block.* **3** to produce eggs: *Does a snake lay eggs?* **4** (used with some nouns to give a meaning similar to a verb): *They laid all the blame on him* (= they blamed him). ○ *lay emphasis on sth* (= emphasize it)

PHRV **lay sth down** to give sth as a rule: *It's all laid down in the employee handbook.*

lay off (sb) (*informal*) to stop annoying sb: *Can't you lay off me for a little while?*

lay sb off to stop sb's job, usually because

there is not enough work to do: *They laid off 500 workers at the automobile factory.*

lay sth out to spread out sth or a group of things so that you can see it/them easily or so that they look nice: *All the food was laid out on a table in the back yard.*

lay² /leɪ/ *adj.* (only *before* a noun) without special training in a particular subject: *a lay preacher*

☆ **lay³** *p.t.* of LIE²

☆ **lay·er** /ˈleɪər/ *noun* [C] a thickness or quantity of sth that is on sth else or between other things: *A thin layer of dust covered everything in the room. ○ It's very cold. You'll need several layers of clothing. ○ the top/bottom layer ○ the inner/outer layer*

lay·man /ˈleɪmən/ *noun* [C] (*pl.* **lay·men** /-mən/) a person who does not have special training in or knowledge of a particular subject: *It's difficult to explain the system in layman's terms* (= in a way that average people can understand).

☆ **lay·off** /ˈleɪɔf/ *noun* [C, usually pl.] an act of stopping sb's job because there is not enough work for him/her

lay·out /ˈleɪaʊt/ *noun* [C, usually sing.] **1** the way in which the parts of sth, such as a building or an area, are arranged **2** the way in which words and pictures, etc., are arranged on a page

☆ **la·zy** /ˈleɪzi/ *adj.* (**la·zi·er**; **la·zi·est**) **1** (used about a person) not wanting to work: *Don't be lazy. Come and give me a hand.* **2** moving slowly or without much energy: *a lazy river* **3** making you feel that you do not want to do very much: *a lazy summer day* —**la·zi·ly** *adv.* —**la·zi·ness** *noun* [U]

lb. *abbr.* = POUND¹(1)

☆ **lead¹** /lɛd/ *noun* **1** [U] (*symbol* **Pb**) a soft heavy gray metal. Lead is used in pipes, etc. **2** [C,U] the black substance inside a pencil that makes a mark when you write

☆ **lead²** /lid/ *noun* **1** [sing.] a position ahead of other people, organizations, etc.: *America has taken the lead in developing computer software.* **2 the lead** [sing.] the first place or position: *The Canadian athlete has just gone into the lead. ○ Who is in the lead?* **3** [sing.] the distance or amount by which sb/sth is in front of another person or thing: *The company has a lead of several years in the development of the new technology.* **4** [C] the main part or role in a play or show: *Who's playing the lead in the new movie?* **5** [C] a piece of information that may help to give the answer to a problem: *The police are following all possible leads to track down the killer.*

IDM **follow sb's example/lead** ⇨ FOLLOW

☆ **lead³** /lid/ *verb* (*p.t., p.p.* **led** /lɛd/) **1** [T] to go with or in front of a person or animal to show the way or to make them go in the right direction: *The teacher led the class back to the*

classroom. *○ The receptionist led the way to the office. ○ to lead sb by the hand* ☞ You usually **guide** or **show** a tourist or somebody who needs special help: *He guided the blind woman to her seat. ○ to show visitors around the city* **2** [I] (used about a road or path) to go to a place: *I don't think this path leads anywhere.* **3** [I] **lead to sth** to have sth as a result: *Eating too much sugar can lead to all kinds of health problems.* **4** [T] to have a particular type of life: *They lead a very busy life. ○ to lead a life of crime* **5** [I,T] **lead (sb/sth) (in sth)** to be the best at sth or to be in first place: *Sampras is leading by two sets to love. ○ Sampras is leading Chang by two sets to love.* **6** [I,T] to be in control or the leader of sth: *Who is going to lead the discussion?* **7** [T] to influence what sb does or thinks: *He led me to believe he really meant what he said.*

PHRV **lead up to sth** to be an introduction to or cause of sth: *What were the events that led up to the First World War?*

☆ **lead·er** /ˈlidər/ *noun* [C] **1** a person who is the head of sth or in charge of sth: *a weak/strong leader ○ She is a natural leader* (= she knows how to tell other people what to do). **2** the person or team that is best or in first place: *The leader has just finished the third lap.*

☆ **lead·er·ship** /ˈlidərʃɪp/ *noun* **1** [U] the qualities that a leader(1) should have **2** [U] the state of being a leader(1): *The company has done well under Mrs. Brown's leadership.* **3** [sing.] a group of leaders(1): *Has the leadership of our country lost touch with ordinary people?*

☆ **lead·ing** /ˈlidɪŋ/ *adj.* **1** best or very important: *He's one of the leading experts in this field.* **2** in front or first in place: *Jordan has been the leading point scorer this season. ○ the leading brand of shampoo* (= that sells the most)

☆ **leaf¹** /lif/ *noun* [C] (*pl.* **leaves** /livz/) one of the thin, flat parts of a plant or tree. Leaves are usually green and grow from a branch, but different plants have different shaped leaves: *autumn leaves* ☞ picture at **tree.**

leaf² /lif/ *verb*

PHRV **leaf through sth** to turn the pages of a book, etc. quickly and without looking at them carefully

leaf·let /ˈliflət/ *noun* [C] a small printed piece of paper that advertises or gives information about sth. Leaflets are usually given free of charge: *I picked up a leaflet about museums in the downtown area.*

leaf·y /ˈlifi/ *adj.* (**leaf·i·er**; **leaf·i·est**) having many leaves: *cabbage, spinach, lettuce and other leafy vegetables*

☆ **league** /lig/ *noun* [C] **1** a group of sports clubs that compete with each other for a prize: *the National Football League* **2** a group of people, countries, etc. that join together for a particular purpose: *the League of Nations* **3** (*informal*)

i	ɪ	ɛ	æ	ɑ	ɔ	ʌ	ʊ	u
see	sit	ten	cat	hot	saw	cup	put	too

a standard of quality or achievement: *He is so much better than the others. They're just not in the same league.*

☆ **leak¹** /lik/ *verb* **1** [I,T] to allow liquid or gas to get through a hole or crack: *The boat was leaking badly.* **2** [I] (used about liquid or gas) to get out through a hole or crack: *Water is leaking in through the window frame.* **3** [T] **leak sth (to sb)** to give secret information: *The committee's findings were leaked to the press.*

PHRV **leak out** (used about secret information) to become known: *The White House did not want the details to leak out.*

☆ **leak²** /lik/ *noun* [C] **1** a small hole or crack that liquid or gas can get through: *There's a leak in the pipe.* ○ *The roof has sprung a leak.* **2** the liquid or gas that gets through such a hole: *There are oil leaks all over the garage.* **3** the act of giving away information that should be kept secret or secret information that is given out

leak·age /'likɪdʒ/ *noun* [C,U] an example of leaking; sth that has been leaked: *a leakage of dangerous chemicals*

leak·y /'liki/ *adj.* having a hole or holes through which liquid or gas can get in or out

lean

leaning against a tree

leaning out of a window

lean¹ /lin/ *adj.* **1** (used about a person or animal) thin and in good health **2** (used about meat) having little or no fat **3** not producing much: *a lean harvest*

☆ **lean²** /lin/ *verb* **1** [I] to be in a position that is not straight or upright: *He leaned across the table to pick up the phone.* ○ *to lean forward, backward, over to one side, etc.* **2** [I] **lean against/on sth** to rest against sth so that it gives support: *She had to stop and lean on the gate.* ○ *(figurative) You can rely on me. I'll always be there for you to lean on.* **3** [T] to put sth against sth: *Please don't lean bicycles against this window.*

leap¹ /lip/ *verb* (*p.t., p.p.* **leaped** /lipt/ or **leapt** /lɛpt; lipt/) [I] **1** to jump high or a long way: *The horse leaped over the wall.* **2** to move quickly: *I leaped upstairs when I heard the scream.*

IDM **jump/leap to conclusions** ➪ CONCLUSION

PHRV **leap at sth** to accept a chance or offer with enthusiasm: *She leapt at the chance to be on TV.*

leap² /lip/ *noun* [C] **1** a big jump: *He took a flying leap at the wall but didn't get over it.* **2** a great change (for the better) or an increase in sth: *Penicillin was a great leap forward in the field of medicine.* ○ *a leap in the price of land*

leap·frog /'lipfrɔg; -frɑg/ *noun* [U] a children's game in which one person bends over and another person jumps over him/her

'**leap year** *noun* [C] one year in every four, in which February has 29 days instead of 28

☆ **learn** /lərn/ *verb* **1** [I,T] **learn (sth) (from sb/sth)** to get knowledge, a skill, etc. (from sb/sth): *What did you learn about in school today?* ○ *Debby is learning to play the piano.* ○ *to learn a foreign language* ○ *Where did you learn how to swim?* **2** [I] **learn (of/about) sth** (*formal*) to get some information about sth; to find out: *I was sorry to learn of your father's death.* **3** [T] to understand or realize: *We should have learned by now that we can't rely on her.*

learn·er /'lərnər/ *noun* [C] a person who is learning: *a dictionary for learners of English*

lease¹ /lis/ *noun* [C] an official written agreement (**a contract**) in which land, a building, etc. is rented to sb else for a certain period of time in return for money, usually paid every month

lease² /lis/ *verb* [T] to pay rent in order to use sth for a certain length of time, or to let sb use sth in this way: *to lease a car*

leash /liʃ/ *noun* [C] a long chain or piece of leather, rope, etc. that is attached to the collar around a dog's neck and used for keeping the dog under control: *All dogs must be kept on a leash.*

☆ **least¹** /list/ *det., pron.* (used as the superlative of *little*) smallest in size, amount, extent, etc.: *He has the least experience of all of us.* ○ *Sherrie did the most work and John did the least.*

☆ **least²** /list/ *adv.* to the smallest extent or degree; less than anybody/anything else: *He's the person who needs help least.* ○ *I bought the least expensive tickets.*

IDM **at least 1** not less than, and probably more: *It'll cost at least $200.* **2** even if other things are wrong: *It may not be beautiful but at least it's cheap.* **3** (used for correcting sth that you have just said): *I saw him – or at least I think I saw him.* **4** (used for saying that sth is the minimum you expect sb to do): *You could at least say you're sorry!*

last but not least ➪ LAST²

least of all especially not: *Nobody should be worried, least of all you.*

not in the least (*formal*) not at all: *It doesn't matter in the least.*

to say the least ➪ SAY¹

☆**leath·er** /'lɛðər/ *noun* [U] the skin of animals which has been specially treated. Leather is used to make shoes, bags, coats, etc.: *a leather jacket*

☆**leave¹** /liv/ *verb* (*p.t., p.p.* **left** /lɛft/) **1** [I,T] to go away from sb/sth: *When should we leave for the airport?* ○ *The train leaves Providence at just after ten.* ○ *He left his mother in tears.* ○ *Barry left his wife for another woman.*

☞ Notice that if you leave sb/sth it may be permanently or just for a short time: *He leaves home at 8:00 every morning.* ○ *He left home and went to live with his girlfriend.* **Depart** is a more formal word and is used about boats, trains, airplanes, etc.: *The 6:15 train for Washington, D.C., departs from Track 3.*

2 [T] to cause or allow sb/sth to stay in a particular place or condition: *Leave the door open, please.* ○ *Don't leave the iron on when you are not using it.* ○ *Don't leave your friend outside. Ask him in.* **3** [T] to forget to bring sth with you: *I can't find my glasses. I must have left them at work.* **4** [T] to cause sth to remain as a result: *Don't put that cup on the table. It'll leave a mark.* **5** [T] to not use sth: *Leave some cake for me, please.* ○ *Is there any bread left?* **6** [T] to put sth somewhere: *Val left a message on her answering machine.* ○ *I left him a note.* **7** [T] to wait until later to do sth: *Let's leave the dishes until tomorrow.* **8** [T] to give sth to sb when you die: *In his will he left everything to his three sons.* **9** [T] to give the care of sb/sth to another person: *I'll leave it to you to organize the food.* ○ *He left his assistant in charge when he went on vacation.*

IDM leave sb/sth alone to not touch, bother or speak to sb/sth: *She's very upset. Leave her alone for a few minutes.*

leave sb in the lurch to leave sb without help in a difficult situation

PHRV leave sb/sth behind to forget to bring sth with you: *I left my gloves behind, and now my hands are cold.*

leave sb/sth out (of sth) to not include sb/sth: *This doesn't make sense. I think the typist left out a line.*

☆**leave²** /liv/ *noun* [C,U] a period of time when you do not go to work, usually for a particular reason: *Peggy has been away on sick leave since her operation.* ○ *maternity leave* (= for a woman who has just had a baby) ○ *I'm taking a six-week leave of absence from work.* ☞ Look at the note at **vacation**.

leaves *pl.* of LEAF¹

☆**lec·ture¹** /'lɛktʃər/ *noun* [C] **1 a lecture (on/ about sth)** a talk or speech to a group of people on a particular subject: *He gave a lecture on the geology of the Pacific.* ○ *a series of lectures* **2** a serious talk to sb that explains what he/she has done wrong or how he/she should behave

lec·ture² /'lɛktʃər/ *verb* **1** [I] **lecture (on sth)** to give a lecture¹ or lectures (on a particular subject) **2** [T] **lecture sb (about sth)** to talk seriously to sb about what he/she has done wrong or how he/she should behave: *The police officer lectured the boys about the dangers of playing in the street.*

lec·tur·er /'lɛktʃərər/ *noun* [C] a person who gives lectures

led *p.t., p.p.* of LEAD³

ledge /lɛdʒ/ *noun* [C] a narrow shelf under a window, or a narrow piece of rock that sticks out on the side of a cliff or mountain

☆**left¹** /lɛft/ *adj., adv.* on or to the side (of your body) that is toward the west when you face north: *Turn left just past the post office.* ○ *I hurt my left arm.*

☆**left²** /lɛft/ *noun* **1** [U] the left side: *Our house is the next one on the left.* ○ *...and to your left, you can see the statue of Abraham Lincoln.* **2** [C] a turn to the left, or a street or road on the left: *Make a left at the stoplight.* ○ *Go past the school and then take the next left.* **3 the left** political parties or groups that support socialism: *The left is losing popularity.*

☆**left³** *p.t., p.p.* of LEAVE¹

☆**left⁴** /lɛft/ *adj.* (not before a noun) remaining; available to use, sell, etc.: *There's only one piece of cake left.* ○ *We have 50 tickets left to sell.*

IDM left over remaining; extra: *After I pay my bills each month, I hardly have any money left over.*

left-hand *adj.* (only *before* a noun) of or on the left: *the left-hand side of the road*

left-'handed *adj.* **1** (used about a person) using the left hand more easily than the right: *Are you left-handed?* **2** made for left-handed people to use: *left-handed scissors*

left·o·vers /'lɛft͵oʊvərz/ *noun* [plural] food that has not been eaten when a meal has finished

left-wing *adj.* (only *before* a noun) having political ideas that support government ownership of industries, social change to make everyone more financially equal, etc.: *left-wing politicians*

☆**leg** /lɛg/ *noun* [C] **1** the part of the body on which a person or animal stands or walks: *A spider has eight legs.* ○ *long/short legs* ○ *She sat down and crossed her legs.* **2** one of the parts that support a table, chair, etc. **3** the part of a pair of pants, etc. that covers your leg (1) **4** one part or section of a trip, competition, etc.

IDM cost/pay an arm and a leg = ARM¹

pull sb's leg ⇨ PULL¹

stretch your legs ⇨ STRETCH¹

leg·a·cy /'lɛgəsi/ *noun* [C] (*pl.* **leg·a·cies**) a situation that exists because of events that happened in the past: *racial discrimination that is the legacy of slavery*

☆ **le·gal** /ˈligl/ adj. **1** allowed by law: *It is not legal to own a gun without a license.* ☞ The opposite is **illegal**. Look also at **lawful** and **legitimate**. **2** (only *before* a noun) using or connected with the law: *legal advice* ○ *to take legal action against sb* ○ *the legal system* —**le·gal·ly** adv.: *Schools are legally responsible for the safety of their students.* —**le·gal·i·ty** /liˈgæləti/ noun [U]: *The legality of the agreement is not certain.*

le·gal·ize /ˈligəlaɪz/ verb [T] to make sth legal (1)

ˈ**legal pad** noun [C] a number of sheets of paper with lines on them, fastened together at one end

ˈ**legal-size** (also **legal**) adj. (used about paper) 8½ inches (215.9 mm) wide and 14 inches (355.6 mm) long ☞ Look also at **letter-size**.

☆ **leg·end** /ˈlɛdʒənd/ noun **1** [C] an old story that may or may not be true: *the legend of Paul Bunyan* **2** [U] old stories, thought of as a group: *According to legend, Paul Bunyan had an ox named Babe.* **3** [C] a person who is famous for doing sth extremely well: *baseball legend Mickey Mantle*

leg·en·dar·y /ˈlɛdʒəndɛri/ adj. **1** from a legend or legends: *the legendary heroes of Greek myths* **2** very famous: *Bjorn Borg, the legendary tennis star*

leg·gings /ˈlɛgɪŋz/ noun [plural] a piece of clothing, usually worn by women, that fits tightly over your legs and reaches from your waist to your ankles ☞ picture on page A27.

leg·i·ble /ˈlɛdʒəbl/ adj. (used about writing or things that are printed) clear enough to be read easily ☞ The opposite is **illegible**. —**leg·i·bil·i·ty** /ˌlɛdʒəˈbɪləti/ noun [U] —**leg·i·bly** /-əbli/ adv.

leg·is·late /ˈlɛdʒəsleɪt/ verb [I,T] to make a law or laws (about sth): *It is impossible to legislate morality.*

leg·is·la·tion /ˌlɛdʒəsˈleɪʃn/ noun [U] **1** the act of making laws **2** a law or a group of laws: *The government is introducing new legislation to help small businesses.*

leg·is·la·tive /ˈlɛdʒəsleɪtɪv/ adj. **1** connected with the act of making laws: *the legislative powers of Congress* **2** connected with the part of the government that makes laws: *the legislative branch of the U.S. government*

leg·is·la·tor /ˈlɛdʒəsleɪtər/ noun [C] a person who has been elected to an official government position to make laws

☆ **leg·is·la·ture** /ˈlɛdʒəsleɪtʃər/ noun [C] an official group of people who have been elected to the government to make laws: *the Kansas state legislature*

le·git·i·mate /lɪˈdʒɪtəmət/ adj. **1** reasonable or acceptable: *This program is not a legitimate use of taxpayers' money.* **2** allowed by law: *Could he earn so much from legitimate busi-*

ness activities? ☞ Look at **lawful** and **legal**. —**le·git·i·mate·ly** adv.

☆ **lei·sure** /ˈliʒər/ noun [U] the time when you do not have to work; spare time: *leisure activities*

lei·sure·ly /ˈliʒərli/ adj. without hurry: *to walk at a leisurely pace*

☆ **lem·on** /ˈlɛmən/ noun [C,U] a yellow fruit with sour juice that is used for giving flavor to food and drinks: *a slice of lemon*

lem·on·ade /ˌlɛməˈneɪd/ noun [C,U] a drink that is made from fresh lemon juice, sugar and water

☆ **lend** /lɛnd/ verb [T] (p.t., p.p. **lent** /lɛnt/) **1** to allow sb to use sth for a short time or to give sb money that must be paid back after a certain period of time: *Could you lend me $5 until Friday?* ○ *He lent me his bicycle.* ○ *He lent his bicycle to me.*

☞ picture at **borrow**. In informal spoken English, many people use **loan** with this meaning: *He loaned me his bike.* However, some people do not like this use of **loan**, especially in formal or written English. If a bank, etc. lends you money, you must **pay** it **back/repay** it over a fixed period of time with extra payments (called **interest**).

2 lend sth (to sth) (formal) to add or give: *to lend advice, support, etc.* ○ *The flowers lent a touch of color to the room.* —**lend·er** noun [C]

☆ **length** /lɛŋkθ/ noun **1** [U] the distance or amount that sth measures from one end to the other; how long sth is: *to measure the length of a room* ○ *It took an hour to walk the length of Rodeo Drive.* ○ *The tiny insect is only one millimeter in length.* **2** [U] the amount of time that sth takes or lasts: *Many people complained about the length of time they had to wait.* **3** [C] the length (1) of a swimming pool: *I can swim a length in twenty seconds.* **4** [C] a piece of sth (that is long and thin): *a length of material, rope, string, etc.*

IDM **at length** for a long time or in great detail: *We discussed the matter at great length.*

go to great lengths to do sth to make more effort than usual in order to achieve sth

length·en /ˈlɛŋkθən/ verb [I,T] to become longer or to make sth longer

length·wise /ˈlɛŋkθwaɪz/ adv. in a direction along the length of sth: *Fold the paper lengthwise.*

length·y /ˈlɛŋkθi/ adj. (**length·i·er**; **length·i·est**) very long: *lengthy discussions* ○ *Recovery from the illness will be a lengthy process.*

tʃ	dʒ	v	θ	ð	s	z	ʃ
chin	June	van	thin	then	so	zoo	she

le·ni·ent /ˈliniənt; ˈlinyənt/ *adj.* (used about a punishment or person who punishes) not strict or severe —**le·ni·en·cy** /-ənsi/ *noun* [U] —**le·ni·ent·ly** *adv.*

lens /lɛnz/ *noun* [C] (*pl.* **lens·es**) a piece of glass, etc. that has one or more curved surfaces. Lenses are used in glasses, cameras, telescopes, microscopes, etc.

☞ picture at **glasses** and **camera**. You may wear **contact lenses** to help you see better. You may use a **zoom** or **telephoto lens** on your camera.

lent *p.t., p.p.* of LEND

Lent /lɛnt/ *noun* [U] the period of 40 days before Easter, when some Christians stop doing or eating certain things in order to remember how Jesus Christ suffered during his life

len·til /ˈlɛntl/ *noun* [C] the small orange or brown seed of a plant that is like a bean. Lentils are dried and then cooked and eaten

Le·o /ˈlioʊ/ *noun* [C,U] (*pl.* **Le·os**) the fifth sign of the zodiac, the Lion; a person who was born under this sign ☞ picture at **zodiac**.

leop·ard /ˈlɛpərd/ *noun* [C] a large wild animal of the cat family that has yellow fur with dark spots. Leopards live in Africa and southern Asia. ☞ picture at **lion**.

le·o·tard /ˈliətard/ *noun* [C] a piece of clothing that fits close to the body and arms but does not cover the legs. Leotards are worn by dancers, people doing exercises, etc.

les·bi·an /ˈlɛzbiən/ *noun* [C] a woman who is sexually attracted to other women —**les·bi·an** *adj.*: *a lesbian relationship* —**les·bi·an·ism** *noun* [U] ☞ Look at **gay** and **homosexual**.

☆**less¹** /lɛs/ *det., pron.* (used with uncountable nouns) a smaller amount (of): *It took less time than I thought.* ○ *I'm too fat – I should try to eat less.*

☞ Many people use **less** with plural nouns: *less cars*, but **fewer** is the form which is still considered to be correct: *fewer cars.*

☆**less²** /lɛs/ *adv.* to a smaller extent; not so much (as): *He's less intelligent than his brother.* ○ *It rains less in Arizona than in Oregon.* ○ *People work less well when they're tired.* **ᴵᴰᴹ less and less** becoming smaller and smaller in amount or degree: *I seem to have less and less time for my hobbies.* **more or less** ⇨ MORE²

☆**less·en** /ˈlɛsn/ *verb* [I,T] to become less; to make sth less: *This medicine will lessen the pain.*

less·er /ˈlɛsər/ *adj., adv.* (only *before* a noun) not as great/much as: *He is guilty, and so, to a lesser extent, is his wife.* ○ *a lesser-known artist* **ᴵᴰᴹ the lesser of two evils** the better of two bad things

☆**les·son** /ˈlɛsn/ *noun* [C] **1** a period of time when you learn or teach sth, usually not in school: *She teaches piano lessons.* ○ *a driving lesson*

☞ We usually use **class** to talk about a period of time in school: *This class is over at 9:55.*

2 something that you have learned or that must be learned: *I hope we can learn some lessons from this disaster.*

☆**let** /lɛt/ *verb* [T] (*pres. part.* **let·ting**; *p.t., p.p.* **let**) **1** to allow or permit sb/sth to do sth; to allow sth to happen: *My parents let me stay out until 11 o'clock.* ○ *He wanted to take the day off, but his boss wouldn't let him.*

☞ You cannot use **let** in the passive here. You must use **allow** or **permit** and **to**: *They let her take the test again.* ○ *She was allowed to take the test again.* Look at the note at **allow**.

2 (used for offering help to sb): *Let me help you carry your bags.* **3** (used for making requests or giving instructions): *Don't help him. Let him do it himself.* ○ *If she refuses to come home with us now, let her walk home.* **4** to allow sb/sth to move in a particular direction: *Open the windows and let some fresh air in.* ○ *They let him out of prison yesterday.* **5 let's** (used for making suggestions about what you and other people can do): *Let's go to the movies tonight.*

☞ The negative is **let's not**: *Let's not go to that awful restaurant again.*

ᴵᴰᴹ let alone and certainly not: *We haven't decided where we're going yet, let alone made any reservations.*

let sb go to make sb leave his/her job, usually because there is not enough work: *We're going to have to let 20 people go.*

let sb/sth go; let go of sb/sth to stop holding sb/sth: *Let me go. You're hurting me!* ○ *I tried to take the book, but he wouldn't let go of it.*

let it go (*informal*) to decide not to argue or worry about sth

let sb know to tell sb sth: *If you need any help, let me know.* ○ *I'll let you know how much the bill is.*

let me see; let's see (used when you are thinking or trying to remember sth): *Where did I put the car keys? Let's see. I think I left them by the phone.*

let's say for example: *You could work two mornings a week, let's say Tuesday and Friday.*

let yourself go to allow yourself to behave as you wish; to feel free: *Just relax. Let yourself go!*

let yourself/sth go to allow yourself/sth to become messy, dirty, fat, etc.: *She used to be so pretty, but after her husband died she just let herself go.*

ᴾᴴᴿⱽ let sb down not to do sth that you promised to do for sb; to disappoint sb

i	ɪ	ɛ	æ	ɑ	ɔ	ʌ	ʊ	u
see	sit	ten	cat	hot	saw	cup	put	too

let sb off not to punish sb, or to give sb a lighter punishment than usual: *He expected to go to prison, but they let him off with a fine.*

let sth out to tell people sth that was secret: *Who let the story about the mayor's debts out?* '

let sth out/down to make clothes larger/longer: *These pants are too tight. I'll have to let them out.*

let up to become less strong: *We'd better wait until the rain lets up.*

le·thal /ˈliθl/ *adj.* able to cause death or great damage —**le·thal·ly** *adv.*

☆**let·ter** /ˈlɛtər/ *noun* [C] **1** a written or printed sign that represents a sound in a language: *"Z" is the last letter of the English alphabet.*

☞ Letters may be written or printed as **capitals**, (also **upper case**), or **small** letters (also **lower case**): *Is "east" written with a capital or a small "e"?*

2 a written or printed message. A letter is usually put in an envelope and sent to sb by mail: *I wrote Denise a letter, but I haven't mailed it yet.*

☞ When you have written a letter you put it in an **envelope**, **address** it, **put/stick** a **stamp** on it and then **mail** it.

ˈletter ˌcarrier *noun* [C] a person whose job is to collect and deliver letters, packages, etc.

ˈletter-size (*also* **letter**) *adj.* (used about paper) 8½ inches (215.9 mm) wide and 11 inches (279.4 mm) long ☞ Look also at **legal-size**.

☆**let·tuce** /ˈlɛtəs/ *noun* [U] a plant with large green leaves that are eaten raw in salads: *a head of lettuce* ☞ picture at **salad**.

leu·ke·mi·a /luˈkimiə/ *noun* [U] a serious disease of the blood which often results in death

☆**lev·el¹** /ˈlɛvl/ *adj.* **1** with no part higher than any other; flat: *Make sure the shelves are level before you nail them to the wall.* ○ *a level teaspoon of sugar* **2 level (with sth)** at the same height, standard or position: *The boy's head was level with his father's shoulder.*

☆**lev·el²** /ˈlɛvl/ *noun* [C] **1** the height or position of sth in relation to sth else: *We are at 500 feet above sea level.* ○ *at ground level* ○ *an intermediate-level student* ○ *top-level discussions* **2** the amount, size or number of sth (compared to sth else): *a high level of unemployment* ○ *low levels of pollution* **3** one of several floors in a building: *The new shopping mall has 180 stores on three levels.*

lev·el³ /ˈlɛvl/ *verb* [T] to destroy a building, etc., by knocking it to the ground: *The tornado leveled several barns in the county.*

PHRV **level sth against/at sb/sth** to make a serious criticism of sb or accuse sb of doing sth wrong: *Several criminal charges have been leveled against the mayor.*

level off/out to become flat, equal or level:

Stock prices rose sharply yesterday, but today they have leveled off (= stayed at one level).

lev·el·head·ed /ˈlɛvlˌhɛdəd/ *adj.* able to act calmly in a difficult situation

☆**lev·er** /ˈlɛvər; ˈlivər/ *noun* [C] **1** a bar or tool that is used to lift or open sth when you put pressure or force on one end **2** a handle that you pull or push in order to make a machine, etc. work: *a gear shift lever in a car*

lev·er·age /ˈlɛvərɪdʒ; ˈli-/ *noun* [U] power or influence over other people or groups

lev·y /ˈlɛvi/ *verb* [T] (*p.t., p.p.* **lev·ied**) **levy sth (on sb)** to officially demand and collect money, etc.: *The new tax will be levied on chemical manufacturers.* —**lev·y** *noun* [C] (*pl.* **lev·ies**): *an additional property tax levy*

li·a·bil·i·ty /ˌlaɪəˈbɪləti/ *noun* (*pl.* **li·a·bil·i·ties**) **1** [U] **liability (for sth)** the state of being responsible (for sth): *The airline admitted liability for the crash.* **2** [C] a person or thing that can cause a lot of problems, cost a lot of money, etc.: *The senator's stupid comments have made him a real liability to the party.*

li·a·ble /ˈlaɪəbl/ *adj.* (not before a noun) **1 liable (for sth)** responsible (in law) (for sth): *Should tobacco companies be held liable for smokers' health problems?* **2 liable to do sth** likely to do sth, especially sth bad: *We're all liable to have accidents when we are very tired.*

li·aise /liˈeɪz/ *verb* [I] **liaise (with sb/sth)** to work closely with a person, group, etc. and give him/her/it regular information about what you are doing

li·ai·son /liˈeɪzɑn; ˈliəˌzɑn/ *noun* **1** [U] communication between two or more people or groups that work together **2** [C] a person who helps to pass information between two or more people or groups that are working together **3** [C] a sexual relationship between two people who are not married to each other

li·ar /ˈlaɪər/ *noun* [C] a person who tells lies (= who says or writes things that are not true): *She called me a liar.* ☞ Look at the verb and noun **lie**.

li·bel /ˈlaɪbl/ *noun* [C,U] something false that is written or printed about sb that would make other people think badly of him/her: *The singer is suing the newspaper for libel.* ☞ Look at **slander**.

☆**lib·er·al¹** /ˈlɪbərəl; ˈlɪbrəl/ *adj.* **1** willing to accept different opinions or kinds of behavior; tolerant **2** supporting political and social changes to make people more equal, and willing to accept different ideas about family life, sex, etc. ☞ Look at **conservative**. **3** generous; large: *We were given liberal quantities of food and drink.* —**lib·er·al·ism** /-ɪzəm/ *noun* [U]

lib·er·al² /ˈlɪbərəl; ˈlɪbrəl/ *noun* [C] a person who is liberal¹(1,2) in his/her way of thinking

ˌliberal ˈarts *noun* [plural] subjects such as history, languages, literature, etc. (and not technical subjects) that you study in college

ə	y	w	t̬	eɪ	aɪ	ɔɪ	aʊ	oʊ
about	yes	woman	butter	say	five	boy	now	go

lib·er·al·ly /ˈlɪbərəli; ˈlɪbrəli/ *adv.* freely or generously

lib·er·ate /ˈlɪbəreɪt/ *verb* [T] **liberate sb/sth (from sth)** (*formal*) to set sb/sth free: *France was liberated in 1945.* ○ *to liberate people from poverty* —**lib·er·a·tion** /ˌlɪbəˈreɪʃn/ *noun* [U]: *the women's liberation movement wants equal rights for women.*

lib·er·at·ed /ˈlɪbəreɪṭəd/ *adj.* not sharing traditional opinions or ways of behaving

☆ **lib·er·ty** /ˈlɪbərṭi/ *noun* [C,U] (*pl.* **lib·er·ties**) the freedom to go where you want, do what you want, etc.: *religious liberty* ○ *We must defend our civil liberties* (= the rights we have as citizens).

IDM **be at liberty to do sth** to be free or allowed to do sth: *I am not at liberty to tell you how I got this information.*

Li·bra /ˈlibrə/ *noun* [C,U] the seventh sign of the zodiac, the Balance; a person who was born under this sign ☞ picture at **zodiac.**

li·brar·i·an /laɪˈbrɛriən/ *noun* [C] a person who works in or is in charge of a library

☆ **li·brar·y** /ˈlaɪbrɛri/ *noun* [C] (*pl.* **li·brar·ies**) **1** a room or building that contains a collection of books, etc. that can be looked at or borrowed: *My library books are due back tomorrow.*

☞ Most cities in the United States have a **public library** where you can borrow books, usually without having to pay anything, and read magazines and newspapers.

2 a private collection of books, etc.

lice *pl.* of LOUSE

☆ **li·cense**[1] /ˈlaɪsns/ *noun* **1** [C] an official paper, card, etc. that shows you are allowed to do or have sth: *a driver's license* ○ *a fishing license* **2** [U] (*formal*) freedom to do sth: *The soldiers were given license to kill if they were attacked.*

li·cense[2] /ˈlaɪsns/ *verb* [T] to give official permission for sth: *a licensed gun owner*

☆ **license plate** *noun* [C] a sign on the front and back of a car, truck, etc. with numbers and letters on it ☞ Look also at **vanity plate.**

lick/bite/swallow

licking biting swallowing

lick /lɪk/ *verb* [T] to move your tongue across sth: *The child licked the spoon clean.* —**lick** *noun* [C]: *Let me have a lick of your ice cream.*

lic·o·rice /ˈlɪkərɪʃ; -rɪs/ *noun* [U] a type of black candy with a strong flavor

☆ **lid** /lɪd/ *noun* [C] **1** the top part of a box, pot, etc. that can be lifted up or taken off ☞ picture at **pan.** Look at the note at **top. 2** = EYELID

☆ **lie**[1] /laɪ/ *verb* [I] (*pres. part.* **ly·ing**; *p.t., p.p.* **lied**) **lie (to sb) (about sth)** to say or write sth that you know is not true: *He lied about his age in order to join the army.* ○ (*figurative*) *The camera cannot lie.*

☆ **lie**[2] /laɪ/ *noun* [C] a statement that you know is not true: *to tell a lie*

☞ You tell a **white lie** in order not to hurt sb's feelings. Look at **liar** and **fib.**

☆ **lie**[3] /laɪ/ *verb* [I] (*pres. part.* **ly·ing**; *p.t.* **lay** /leɪ/; *p.p.* **lain** /leɪn/) **1** to be or put yourself in a flat or horizontal position (so that you are not standing or sitting): *He lay on the sofa and went to sleep.* ○ *to lie on your back/side/front* ○ *The book lay open in front of her.*

☞ Remember that **lie** cannot be used with an object. If you put an object in a flat position, you **lay** it down.

2 to be or remain in a certain state or position: *Snow lay thick on the ground.* ○ *The hills lie to the north of the town.* ○ *The final decision lies with the chief executive officer.* ○ *They are young and their whole lives lie ahead of them.*

PHRV **lie around** to relax and do nothing: *Don't just lie around all day – do some work!*

lie back to relax and do nothing while sb else works, etc.

lie down (used about a person) to be or put yourself in a flat or horizontal position so that you can rest: *I'm feeling dizzy – I have to lie down.*

'lie de·tector *noun* [C] = POLYGRAPH

lieu·ten·ant /luˈtɛnənt/ *noun* [C] a junior officer in the army or navy, or a police officer of middle rank

☆ **life** /laɪf/ *noun* (*pl.* **lives** /laɪvz/) **1** [U] the quality that people, animals or plants have when they are not dead: *Life on earth began in a very simple form.* ○ *Do you believe in life after death?* **2** [U] living things: *No life was found on the moon.* ○ *There was no sign of life in the deserted house.* ○ *plant life* **3** [C] the existence of an individual person: *He risked his life to save the child.* ○ *Doctors fought all night to save her life.* ○ *Three lives were lost in the fire.* **4** [U] the state of being alive as a human being: *The hostages were rescued without loss of life.* ○ *to bring sb back to life* **5** [C] the period between your birth and death or between your birth and the present: *He worked as a doctor all his life.* ○ *to ruin sb's life* **6** [U] the things that you may experience during your life (5): *Life can be hard for a single parent.* **7** [U] the period between the present and your death: *She was sent to prison for life.* ○ *life membership in a club* **8** [C,U] a way of living: *They came to America to start a new life.* ○ *They lead a busy*

STUDY PAGES

Dictionary Quiz

This quiz shows how the *American Wordpower Dictionary* can help you. You'll find the answers to all these questions in the dictionary.

1 What are **hash browns** made of?

2 Who would wear a **diaper**?

3 What doesn't a **cheapskate** like to do?

MEANINGS
The dictionary explains what words mean in language that is easy to understand, and the example sentences show you how to use the word correctly.

4 What's the name of the part of a **telephone** that you pick up when you want to make a phone call?

5 What's the opposite of **honest**?

6 *I could see the **shade** of a man outside the window.*
In this sentence, the word **shade** is wrong. What's the correct word?

VOCABULARY
There are notes (shown by the ☞ symbol) that give useful extra vocabulary associated with a word and explain the difference between words that people often confuse.

7 Which word in this sentence would you NOT use in an informal situation: *What time does the meeting commence?*

STYLE
The dictionary tells you if a word is formal or informal, and it often suggests another word that you can use in most situations.

8 Is the word **meek** a noun, a verb or an adjective?

9 Is the word **luggage** countable or uncountable?

10 What's the past tense form of **swear**?

GRAMMAR
The dictionary tells you whether a word is a noun, verb, adjective, etc. and whether nouns are countable or uncountable. It also gives irregular forms (e.g. irregular past tenses of verbs).

11 How do you spell the plural of **factory**?

12 How do you spell the *-ing* form of the verb **occur**?

13 Which letter is silent in the word **receipt**?

14 Which part of **hot dog** receives the main stress?

15 How many idioms are there that have the word **kill** in them?

16 How many phrasal verbs can you make with the word **burn**?

17 What two nouns can you form from the word **smuggle**?

18 What's the noun formed from **elegant**?

19 What do you call a person who comes from **Norway**?

20 How many **quarts** are there in a gallon?

SPELLING
You can use the dictionary to check how a word is spelled. It also tells you about small spelling changes in other forms of the word (e.g. irregular plurals).

PRONUNCIATION
This dictionary gives the pronunciation of words, and at the bottom of each page there is a key that shows you how to read the phonetic spelling. Look also at the ' marks that show you where the main stress of the word is.

IDIOMS AND PHRASAL VERBS
These are given in two separate sections after the main meanings of the word. (Look also at the "Phrasal verbs" page – page A16.)

WORDS FORMED FROM OTHER WORDS
Derivatives (**loudly** and **loudness** are derivatives of **loud**) are given after the main meanings of the word.

EXTRA INFORMATION
At the back of the dictionary you will find a list of irregular verbs, a list of expressions using numbers, maps and a list of geographical names.

Now turn the page upside down and check your answers.

Words that go together

In addition to explaining the meaning of a word, the *American Wordpower Dictionary* shows you how to use it correctly in a phrase or sentence.

THE EXAMPLE SENTENCES

Do we talk about **stale** bread or **rotten** bread? Do you **say** a joke or **tell** a joke? (It's **stale** and **tell**.) If you look up a word in the dictionary, the example sentences show you which other words are often used with it:

> ☆ **mon·ey** /ˈmʌni/ *noun* [U] the means of paying for sth or buying sth, especially in the form of coins or bills: *How much money do you earn a year?* ∘ *Teenagers spend a lot of money on clothes.* ∘ *Our trip cost an awful lot of money.* ∘ *to borrow/lend money*

Earn, **spend**, **cost** and **save** are verbs that are often used with the word **money**.

> ☆ **wind¹** /wɪnd/ *noun* **1** [C,U] (*also* **the wind**) air that is moving across the surface of the earth: *There was a strong wind blowing.* ∘ *A gust of wind blew his hat off.* ∘ *high winds* ∘ *a cold north wind*

Strong, **high**, **cold** and **north** are adjectives that are often used with the word **wind**.

EXERCISE 1

Match a word in group A with a word in group B. Find the words in group B in the dictionary and look at the example sentences.

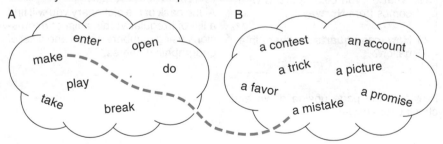

A

make · enter · open · do · play · take · break

B

a contest · an account · a trick · a picture · a favor · a promise · a mistake

EXERCISE 2

What's the opposite of...

a) a high salary? *a low salary*

b) a wide street? ...

c) a short tree? ...

d) the right answer? ...

e) a thin slice of bread? ...

f) an even number? ...

g) a light meal? ...

h) a serious offense? ...

PREPOSITIONS AND VERB PATTERNS
The dictionary also shows you which preposition to use after a noun, verb or adjective and which construction to use after a verb:

> ☆ **mar·ried** /ˈmærid/ *adj.* **1 married (to sb)** having a husband or wife: *Jenny's married to Mark.*

This shows that the preposition which goes with **married** is **to**.

> ☆ **en·joy** /ɛnˈdʒɔɪ/ *verb* [T] **1 enjoy sth/enjoy doing sth** to get pleasure from: *I really enjoyed that meal.* ○ *Do you enjoy your work?* ○ *He enjoys listening to music while he's driving.*

You can say that you **enjoy something** or that you **enjoy doing something**.

EXERCISE 3
Use the dictionary to complete these sentences with the right preposition.

a) Everybody laughed _ _ _ _ _ the joke.

b) I don't agree _ _ _ _ _ him at all.

c) She has found a solution _ _ _ _ _ the problem.

d) It took her a long time to recover _ _ _ _ _ the accident.

e) Do you believe _ _ _ _ _ life after death?

f) I apologized _ _ _ _ _ Sam _ _ _ _ _ breaking the chair.

g) She's very proud _ _ _ _ _ her new car.

h) The house is fairly close _ _ Kari's school.

EXERCISE 4
Fill in the blanks with the correct form of the verb in parentheses.

a) I want you to finish _ _ _ _ _ _ _ _ (clean) your room.

b) He keeps _ _ _ _ _ _ _ _ _ (call) me late at night.

c) I persuaded Jan _ _ _ _ _ _ _ _ (come) to the party.

d) Try to avoid _ _ _ _ _ _ _ _ (make) mistakes.

e) You're not allowed _ _ _ _ _ _ _ _ (smoke) in here.

f) The bank agreed _ _ _ _ _ _ _ _ (loan) me the money.

Checking your work

If you make a lot of mistakes in a letter, a paper or any other piece of written work, people will find it difficult to understand. You'll also lose a lot of points on your homework and tests! So it's important to check your work carefully when you're finished with it and try to correct as many mistakes as you can. Your dictionary can help you with this.

Look at this piece of work that was written by a student. There are a lot of mistakes in it. Read through it carefully and, with the help of your dictionary, correct the mistakes. Use the checklist on the next page and put a check mark in the box ☑ when you have dealt with each point.

Last summer I went to Boston to study english in a langage school. I stayed with an american family during two months. They dwell in a suburb close to the city. Mrs. Taylor works as an atorney, and her spouse has a good work with an insuranse company.

I enjoyed to be at the langage school. I meeted students of many diferent nationalitys — Japanesse, Brazilien, swis and mexico. The professors were very sympathetic and teached me a lot, but I didn't like making so many homeworks!

CHECKLIST

☐ 1 Did I use the right word?

The dictionary has notes that explain the difference between words that people often confuse, so check words like **work** and **sympathetic**, and any others that you're not sure about.

☐ 2 What about style?

Did you use any words that might be too formal or too informal in this situation? Check in the dictionary if you're not sure.

☐ 3 Did I use the right word combinations?

Is it "**make** homework" or "**do** homework"? If you're not sure about this type of word combination, look up the main word (**homework**) in the dictionary and see which word is used with it in the example sentences.

☐ 4 What about prepositions?

Is it "close **to**" or "close **from**"? Everyone knows how easy it is to use the wrong preposition after a noun, verb or adjective – they always seem to be different in English! Check these carefully in the dictionary.

☐ 5 Did I use the correct verb patterns?

Is it "enjoy **to do** something" or "enjoy **doing** something"? The example sentences for **enjoy** will show you which construction to use. Make sure you get things like this right.

☐ 6 What about spelling?

Be careful of words that are very similar to words in your language – often the spelling is different. Watch out for countries and nationalities – there's a list of these at the back of the dictionary. Check the spelling of plurals, past tenses, -*ing* forms and comparative and superlative adjectives.

☐ 7 Is the grammar OK?

Did you check the nouns to see if they're countable or uncountable? Are the past tenses and past participles of irregular verbs right? The list of irregular verbs at the back of the dictionary will help you.

Now turn the page upside down and check your answers.

ANSWERS

Last summer I went to Boston to study **English** in a language school. I stayed with an **American** family **for** two months. They **live** in a suburb close to the city. Mrs. Taylor works as an **attorney**, and her **husband** has a good **job** with an insurance company.
I enjoyed **being** at the language school. I **met** students of many different nationalities – Japanese, **Swiss**, Brazilian, and **Mexican**. The **teachers** were very **nice** and **taught** me a lot, but I didn't like **doing** so **much** homework!

Word Formation

When you find a new word in English, what do you do? Look it up in a **mono**lingual or a **bi**lingual dictionary? Ask a teach**er** or another stud**ent**? Try to **pre**dict the meaning from the rest of the sentence or paragraph – the **con**text? There is another way to try to simpl**ify** difficult words. Often, long words are made from shorter words that you know, combined with a few letters added to the beginning (a prefix) or to the end (a suffix). Look at the prefixes and suffixes (in **dark** type) in this paragraph. They can all be used with many other words, so when you know their meaning, you have the key to a large number of new words. These pages show you some important groups of prefixes and suffixes. There is a longer alphabetical list on the next pages which will help you with the quiz questions.

Numbers Many common words have prefixes that tell us about numbers. A word that begins with *bi-* shows that there are two of something. A *bicycle* has two wheels (but a *tricycle* has three). Words for metric measurements are often made with the prefixes **cent-**, **kilo-**, etc. 100 *centimeters* = 1 meter, 1 *kilogram* = 1,000 grams, and so on.

1 How many sides does an **octagon** have?
2 If 1976 was the **bicentennial** of Mozart's death, in which year did he die?
3 Which word is a **monosyllable**, "but," "although," or "however?"
4 Does a **multinational** company exist in only one country?

Time A number of prefixes are connected with time, for example **pre-** (before) and **ex-** (former). A *prearranged* meeting was arranged beforehand. A divorced man might talk about his *ex-wife*. The *ex-president* is no longer president.

5 If a house was built in the **postwar** period, was it built before or after the war?
6 Would a woman go to **prenatal** classes before or after her baby was born?
7 If your teacher told you to **rewrite** your essay, why would you be angry?

Size and degree Some common prefixes tell us "how big" or "how much." A word that begins with **maxi-** is large or the greatest; **mini-** refers to something small (*miniskirt*). **extra-** means "more" - *extra-strong glue* is stronger than usual.

8 Which flies faster than the speed of sound, a **subsonic** plane or a **supersonic** plane?
9 If something is **microscopic**, is it very large or very small?
10 How do you feel if you have **overeaten** – very full or still hungry?

Negative Many prefixes change the meaning of a word to its opposite or make it negative. A *nonsmoker* does not smoke; the opposite of happy is *unhappy*. Besides **non-** and **un-** we also use **in-** (or before certain letters **im-**, **il-**, or **ir-**) in this way. It is important to learn which is the correct prefix to make the opposite of a word.

11 Which of the prefixes **un-**, **in-**, **im-**, **il-**, **ir-** would you use to make the opposites of these words?
**correct certain possible
regular sure legal valid
relevant patient legible**
If you are not sure, use the list to help you.

Position These prefixes tell us where something is or happens. For example, sub- gives the idea of "under": a *subway* goes under the road; we read the *subtitles* under the pictures of a foreign movie.

12 Is an activity that is **extracurricular** part of the curriculum of a school?
13 Is a flight from New York to London **transatlantic**?
14 Is an **interstate** a road within one state or a road that links two or more states?

A **suffix** is added to the end of a word, and it often changes the function of the word. There is one suffix that you probably use very often: **-ly** to make an adjective into an adverb. (*He sings beautifully. The car was badly damaged.*) A suffix can also be added to a noun to make it into an adjective: you can change the noun *Japan* into an adjective describing the nationality of the people who live there by adding **-ese**: *Japanese*.

To make nouns that describe a **state**, an **action** or a **quality** you can add a suffix such as **-ation**. e.g. *inform + ation = information*; *examine + ation = examination*. There may be small changes in the spelling, e.g. the second "e" is dropped in *examination*.

15 Use one of the suffixes **-ation, -ment, -ness** to make nouns from these verbs and adjectives:
develop kind arrange imagine happy organize
What happens to the spelling of "happy?"

Other suffixes are used **to make nouns** that describe **people**, for example, **-er, -or, -ist, -ian, -ee, -ant, -ent.** They may be added to a verb to describe the person who does the action, e.g. *rider, sailor, cyclist,* or we can add them to nouns to describe someone who works on a particular subject (*artist, historian*).

16 Fill the gaps to make words that describe people and their jobs:
a _ _ or (works in a theater)
t _ _ _ _ er (works in a school)
c _ _ _ _ _ _ or (stands in front of an orchestra)
e _ _ _ _ _ er (goes out to discover new countries)

We can also make a noun or an adjective into a **verb** by adding a suffix such as **-en, -ify** or **-ize.** If we make something wider, simpler or more modern, we *widen, simplify* or *modernize* it.

17 Which verbs can you make from these words, using one of the suffixes **-ize, -en** and **-ify**?
magnet beauty sharp general loose pure
(You may need to change the spelling a little.)

Adjectives can be made with many different suffixes. Some very common ones are **-able** (or sometimes **-ible** or just **-ble**), which often means "possible to" (*acceptable, avoidable*), **-y** and **-ful**, which often describe qualities: *cloudy, helpful, beautiful.* To show that something is missing, we can add **-less**: a situation where there is no hope is *hopeless*.

18 Solve the clues to find these adjectives: (They all end in one of the suffixes mentioned)
a) practical, that can be used a lot
b) having no friends
c) easy to see or notice
d) needing something to drink

Now turn the page upside down and check your answers:

1 eight **2** 1776 **3** but **4** no **5** after **6** before **7** because you have to write it again **8** supersonic **9** very small **10** very full **11** incorrect uncertain impossible irregular unsure illegal invalid irrelevant impatient illegible **12** no **13** yes **14** a road that links two or more states **15** development kindness arrangement imagination happiness organization (the "y" of "happy" becomes an "i") **16** actor teacher conductor explorer **17** magnetize beautify sharpen generalize loosen purify **18** useful friendless noticeable thirsty

List of Prefixes and Suffixes

PREFIXES

a- not: *atypical*

anti- against: *anti-American, antisocial*

auto- self: *autobiography* (= the story of the writer's own life)

bi- two: *bicycle, bilingual* (= using two languages), *bimonthly* (= twice a month or every two months)

cent-, centi- hundred: *centennial* (= the hundredth anniversary), *centimeter* (= one hundredth of a meter)

circum- around: circumnavigate (= sail around)

co- with; together: *copilot, coexist, co-operation*

con- with; together: *context* (= the words or sentences that come before and after a particular word or sentence)

contra- against; opposite: *contradict* (= say the opposite)

counter- against; opposite: *counter-revolution, counterproductive* (= producing the opposite of the desired effect)

de- taking sth away; the opposite: *defrost* (= removing the layers of ice from a fridge, etc.), *decentralize*

deci- one tenth: *deciliter*

dis- reverse or opposite: *displeasure, disembark, discomfort*

ex- former: *ex-wife, ex-president*

extra- **1** very; more than usual: *extra-thin, extra-special* **2** outside; beyond: *extraordinary, extraterrestrial* (= coming from somewhere beyond the earth)

fore- **1** before; in advance: *foretell* (= say what is going to happen), *foreword* (= at the beginning of a book) **2** front: *foreground* (= the front part of a picture), *forehead*

in- (**il-, im-, ir-**) not: *incorrect, invalid, illegal, illegible, immoral, impatient, impossible, irregular, irrelevant*

inter- between; from one to another: *international, interracial*

kilo- thousand: *kilogram, kilowatt*

maxi- most; very large: *maximum*

mega- million; very large: *megabyte, megabucks* (= a lot of money)

micro- millionth; very small: *microchip, microclimate* (= the climate of a small area)

mid- in the middle of: *mid-afternoon, midair*

milli- thousandth: *millisecond, millimeter*

mini- small: *miniskirt, miniseries*

mis- bad or wrong; not: *misbehave, miscalculate, misunderstand*

mono- one; single: *monolingual* (= using one language), *monorail*

multi- many: *multinational* (= involving many countries)

non- not: *nonalcoholic, nonsense, non-smoker, nonstop*

out- more; to a greater degree: *outdo, outrun* (= run faster or better than sb)

over- more than normal; too much: *overeat, oversleep* (= sleep too long), *overestimate* (= guess too high)

post- after: *postwar*

pre- before: *prepay, preview*

pro- for; in favor of: *pro-democracy, pro-hunting*

quad- four: *quadruple* (= multiply by four), *quadruplet* (= one of four babies born at the same time)

re- again: *rewrite, rebuild*

semi- half: *semicircle, semiconscious*

sub- **1** below; less than: *subzero, subsonic* (= less than the speed of sound) **2** under: *subway, subtitles* (= translations under the pictures in a movie)

super- extremely; more than: *superhuman* (= having greater power than humans normally have), *supersonic* (= faster than the speed of sound)

tele- far; over a long distance: *telecommunications, telephoto lens*

trans- across; through: *transatlantic, transcontinental*

tri- three: *triangle, tricycle*

ultra- extremely; beyond a certain limit: *ultramodern, ultraviolet* (= light that is beyond what we can normally see)

un- not; opposite; taking sth away: *uncertain, uncomfortable, unsure, undo, undress*

uni- one; single: *uniform* (= having the same form)

SUFFIXES

-able, -ible, -ble to make adjectives; possible to ~: *acceptable, noticeable, convertible, divisible* (= possible to divide), *irresistible* (= that you cannot resist)

-age to make nouns; a process or state: *storage, shortage*

-al to make adjectives; connected with: *experimental, accidental, environmental*

-ance, -ence, (-ancy, -ency) to make nouns; an action, process or state: *appearance, performance, importance, existence, intelligence, patience*

-ant, -ent to make nouns; a person who does sth: *assistant, immigrant, student*

-ation to make nouns; a state or action: *examination, imagination, organization*

-ble look at **-able**

-ee to make nouns; a person to whom sth is done: *employee* (= sb who is employed), *trainee* (= sb who is being trained)

-en to make verbs; to give sth a particular quality; to make sth more ~: *shorten, widen, blacken, sharpen, loosen,* (but note: *lengthen*)

-ence (-ency) look at **-ance**

-ent look at **-ant**

-er to make nouns; a person who does sth: *rider, painter, baker, banker, driver, teacher*

-ese to make adjectives; from a place: *Japanese, Chinese, Viennese*

-ess to make nouns; a woman who does sth as a job: *waitress, actress*

-ful to make adjectives; having a particular quality: *helpful, useful, thankful, beautiful*

-hood to make nouns; **1** a state, often during a particular period of time: *childhood, motherhood* **2** a group with sth in common: *sisterhood, neighborhood*

-ian to make nouns; a person who does sth as a job or hobby: *historian, comedian, politician*

-ible look at **-able**

-ical to make adjectives from nouns ending in -y or -ics; connected with: *economical, mathematical, physical*

-ify to make verbs; to produce a state or quality: *beautify, simplify, purify*

-ish to make adjectives; **1** describing nationality or language: *English, Swedish, Polish* **2** like sth: *babyish, foolish* **3** fairly, sort of: *longish, youngish, brownish*

-ist to make nouns; **1** a person who has studied sth or does sth as a job: *artist, scientist, economist* **2** a person who believes in sth or belongs to a particular group: *capitalist, pacifist, feminist*

-ion to make nouns; a state or process: *action, connection, exhibition*

-ive to make adjectives; able to ~, having a particular quality: *attractive, effective*

-ize to make verbs; actions producing a particular state: *magnetize, standardize, modernize, generalize*

-less to make adjectives; not having sth: *hopeless, friendless*

-like to make adjectives; similar to: *childlike*

-ly to make adverbs; in a particular way: *badly, beautifully, completely*

-ment to make nouns; a state, action or quality: *development, arrangement, excitement, achievement*

-ness to make nouns; a state or quality: *kindness, happiness, weakness*

-ology to make nouns; the study of a subject: *biology, psychology, zoology*

-or to make nouns; a person who does sth, often as a job: *actor, conductor, sailor*

-ous to make adjectives; having a particular quality: *dangerous, religious, ambitious*

-ship to make nouns; showing status: *friendship, membership, citizenship*

-ward, -wards to make adverbs; in a particular direction: *backward, upward*

-wise to make adverbs; in a particular way: *clockwise, edgewise*

-y to make adjectives; having the quality of the thing mentioned: *cloudy, rainy, fatty, thirsty*

Prepositions

The lamp is **above** the table.

The meat is **on** the table.

The cat in **under** the table.

The truck is **in front of** the car.

The car is **behind** the truck.

Sam is **between** Tom and Kim.

Kim is **next to/beside** Sam.

The bird is **in/inside** the cage.

The temperature is **below** zero.

The house is **among** the trees.

Tom is **across from** Kim.

The girl is leaning **against** the wall.

Phrasal verbs

Phrasal verbs are verbs that consist of two (or three) parts – an ordinary verb and another word (or words) like **in**, **for**, or **off**. They are very common in English. Here are some examples:

lie down give up look for get along with

Some of them are easy to understand (you can guess the meaning of **lie down** if you know the words **lie** and **down**), but many phrasal verbs are more difficult because they have special meanings (you cannot guess that "**give up** smoking" means "stop smoking" even if you know the words **give** and **up**).

If you want to find a phrasal verb in the dictionary, look under the first word (to find **give up**, look under **give**). The "phrasal verbs" section comes after the ordinary meanings of the verb.

EXERCISE 1
Use the dictionary to fill in the blanks with the correct word.

a) Business is pretty bad these days. A lot of workers have been laid _ _ _ _ _ .
 (over, off, down)
b) "U.S." stands _ _ _ _ _ United States.
 (out, to, for)
c) I can't figure _ _ _ _ _ how to use this gadget.
 (up, out, for)
d) Sue came _ _ _ _ _ the letter while she was cleaning her room.
 (to, across, for)
e) I'm sure that story wasn't true. I think Pete made it _ _ _ _ _ .
 (up, for, in)
f) She was offered a job in Dallas, but she decided to turn it _ _ _ _ _ .
 (over, up, down)
g) Alex dropped out _ _ _ _ _ school when he was 16 years old.
 (for, of, from)
h) Please write _ _ _ _ _ your address and phone number.
 (down, over, away)

Answers: a) off b) for c) out d) across e) up f) down g) of h) down

THE FOUR TYPES
There are four main types of phrasal verbs:

TYPE 1 – phrasal verbs *without* an object

> The fire **went out**.
> My car **broke down** on the highway.

In the dictionary, these verbs are written like this:

> **go out**
> **break down**

TYPE 2 – phrasal verbs that can be separated by an object

a If the object is a noun, it can go either *after* both parts of the phrasal verb or *between* them:

She **tried on** the red sweater.
She **tried** the red sweater **on**.

b If the object is a pronoun, it must go between the two parts of the phrasal verb:

She **tried** it **on**. (NOT She tried on it.)

In the dictionary, this verb is written like this: **try sth on**. When you see **sth** or **sb** between the two parts of the phrasal verb, you know that they can be separated by an object.

TYPE 3 – phrasal verbs that cannot be separated by an object

The two parts of the phrasal verb must go together:

The teacher **called on** Doug.
(NOT The teacher called Doug on.)

The teacher **called on** him.
(NOT The teacher called him on.)

In the dictionary, this verb is written like this: **call on sb**. When you see **sb** or **sth** *after* the two parts of the phrasal verb, you know that they *cannot* be separated by an object.

TYPE 4 – phrasal verbs with three parts

The three parts of the phrasal verb must go together:

I can't **put up with** this noise anymore.

In the dictionary, this verb is written like this: **put up with sb/sth**. Again, when you see **sb** or **sth** after the three parts of the phrasal verb, you know that they *cannot* be separated by an object.

EXERCISE 2
Fill in the blanks by putting the word "it" in the correct place. In each sentence you will have to leave one blank empty.

a) You must be hot with your coat on. Why don't you take _ _ off _ _ ?

b) If you don't understand this word, look _ _ up _ _ in your dictionary.

c) He had a very bad illness, and it will take him a long time to get _ _ over _ _ .

d) I was going to do my homework last night, but I didn't get around _ _ to _ _ .

e) I thought you were finished reading the newspaper, so I threw _ _ away _ _ .

f) Jill can't come to the meeting tomorrow, so we'll have to put _ _ off _ _ until next week.

Answers: a) take it off b) look it up c) get over it d) get around to it e) threw it away f) put it off

Punctuation

A **period (.)** is used at the end of a sentence, unless the sentence is a question or an exclamation:
We went shopping. ○ *He tried to go.* ○ *That's enough.*
It is also used after an abbreviation:
Mr. Smith ○ *Emerdale St.* ○ *etc.* ○ *a.m.*

A **question mark (?)** is used at the end of a direct question:
How old are you? ○ *"When did they go?" Todd asked.*
It is not used after an indirect question:
Todd asked when they went.

An **exclamation point (!)** is used with sentences that express strong emotion, such as surprise, enthusiasm, excitement, shock or horror:
I can't believe it! ○ *That man stole my purse!* ○ *Oh no!* ○ *That's wonderful!*
or after an interjection:
Bye! ○ *Ouch!*

A **comma (,)** separates items in a series. When *and* is used before the last item in a series, the comma that comes before *and* is optional:
He liked to hunt, fish, hike, and climb. ○ *I would like to visit France, Spain and Portugal.*
Commas are always used between three or more adjectives where *and* is not used:
It was a warm, balmy, starlit night.
Commas are also used to separate different parts of a sentence:
He wanted to go, but didn't have time. ○ *Although she is small, she is very strong.*
Commas appear before or around extra information in a relative clause or in a sentence:
They don't like our dog, which barks constantly. ○ *Shakespeare, the English playwright, is well-known throughout the world.*
A comma also usually comes before or after a quotation:
David said, "I'll see you on Saturday." ○ *"I'll see you on Saturday," David said, "at about 8 o'clock."*
and goes before or after a name when a person is being spoken to directly:
Stuart, would you like to go? ○ *I'm sorry, Mark.*
It also comes before tag questions:
You don't have any, do you? ○ *She's a doctor, isn't she?*
Commas also separate cities and towns from states:
Des Moines, Iowa ○ *Juneau, Alaska* ○ *San Francisco, California*

A **colon (:)** is used to introduce explanations, long quotations or a series:
The girl had four pets: a dog, a cat, a horse, and a turtle. ○ *The school offered several language courses: French, German, Spanish, and Russian.*
It is also used after the salutation in a formal letter:
Dear Mr. Howard: ○ *Dear Ms. Leigh:* ○ *Dear Sir/Madam:*

A **semicolon (;)** is used to separate two contrasting parts of a sentence:
Humans use moral judgment; animals do not.
It is also used in a series that already has commas within it:
The menu featured hamburger, potato, and carrot casserole; and pecan pie.

,

An **apostrophe (')** shows that one or more letters are missing in a short form:
we've ○ don't ○ he's ○ I'm ○ they're
It also shows that a person or thing belongs to someone:
Janet's car ○ Cynthia's keys ○ John's sister
With names that end in "s", you do can choose whether to add another "s" after the apostrophe to show possession:
James' teacher or *James's teacher* (both are correct)
Note that with possessives, the apostrophe goes after the "s" if the noun is plural:
the student's apartment (the apartment belonging to one student)
the students' apartment (the apartment shared by several students)

" "

Quotation marks (" ") are used to show what someone said:
"Let's see a movie," Roger suggested. ○ Sylvia said, "I don't remember her name."
or thoughts that are presented like speech:
"Where did I put my keys?" I wondered. ○ "I should leave now," she thought.
Quotation marks are also used around the titles of essays, songs, poems, etc. that are part of other works:
They always play "The Star-Spangled Banner" before baseball games.
They are also used to draw attention to a word or a phrase that is intended to be ironic:
The "new" bride was recently married – to her seventh husband.

-

A **hyphen (-)** connects two or more words that form one idea:
a twelve-year-old boy ○ a well-known politician
It sometimes, but not always, joins a prefix to a word:
pro-Communist ○ anti-American ○ pre-packaged food
A hyphen is also used with compound numbers:
ninety-nine ○ twenty-seven ○ sixty-two
You can also use a hyphen at the end of a line if you need to divide a word and write part of it on the next line:
Though I had known her since we were children, I was hard-ly able to recognize her after ten years.

—

A **dash (–)** separates a word or phrase from the rest of a sentence. It is often used near the end of a sentence to sum up or emphasize an idea:
I lost my keys, forgot my homework, and missed a class – it was an awful day. ○ Art is about creativity, magic, dreams, illusion – and money.
A dash can also be used before and after a phrase that gives extra information:
I ran into her in – of all places – Denmark. ○ I got married – against my family's wishes – to Jim last June.
It also shows that an idea has been interrupted mid-sentence or mid-thought:
If only she would love me, I would – Oh, what's the use? It will never happen.

()

Parentheses () separate extra information from the rest of the sentence:
The recipe calls for 1 pound (450 grams) of flour. ○ Howard (the smallest boy in his class) was hurt playing football.
Numbers and letters used in sentences, particularly with lists or choices, may have a parenthesis after them or parentheses around them:
Airplanes have revolutionized travel by: 1) cutting travel time drastically, 2) providing a relatively cheap form of transportation, and 3) reducing the dangers of long-distance travel. ○ If you had a choice, would you rather live in (a) China, (b) Russia, (c) America or (d) France?

Letter Writing

FORMAL LETTERS

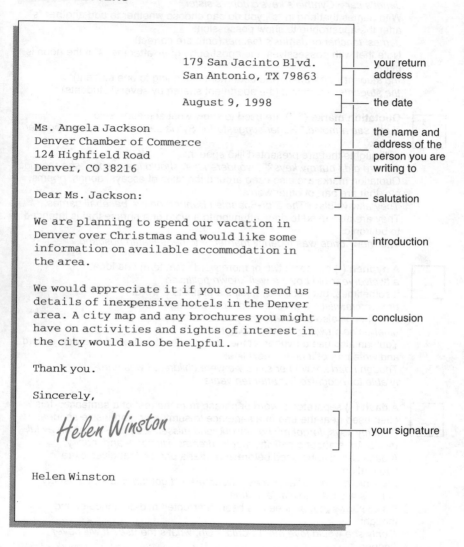

179 San Jacinto Blvd.
San Antonio, TX 79863 — your return address

August 9, 1998 — the date

Ms. Angela Jackson
Denver Chamber of Commerce
124 Highfield Road
Denver, CO 38216 — the name and address of the person you are writing to

Dear Ms. Jackson: — salutation

We are planning to spend our vacation in Denver over Christmas and would like some information on available accommodation in the area. — introduction

We would appreciate it if you could send us details of inexpensive hotels in the Denver area. A city map and any brochures you might have on activities and sights of interest in the city would also be helpful. — conclusion

Thank you.

Sincerely,

Helen Winston

Helen Winston — your signature

1 If you don't know the name of the person you are writing to, begin the letter with *Dear Sir/Madam:*.

2 You can end the letter by signing off with *Sincerely, Sincerely yours* or *Yours truly*.

3 You should not use short forms, such as *I'm* or *don't*, or informal phrases in formal letters.

INFORMAL LETTERS

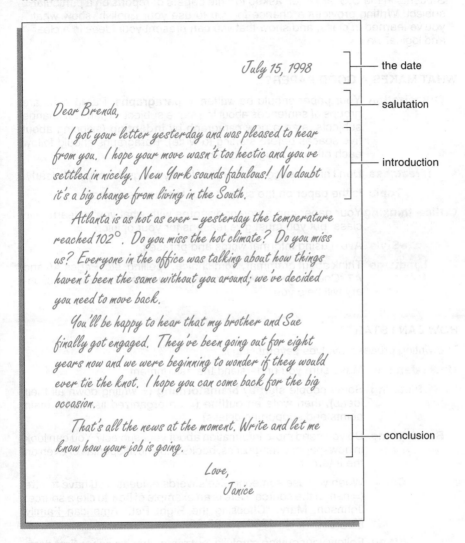

July 15, 1998 — the date

Dear Brenda, — salutation

I got your letter yesterday and was pleased to hear from you. I hope your move wasn't too hectic and you've settled in nicely. New York sounds fabulous! No doubt it's a big change from living in the South. — introduction

Atlanta is as hot as ever – yesterday the temperature reached 102°. Do you miss the hot climate? Do you miss us? Everyone in the office was talking about how things haven't been the same without you around; we've decided you need to move back.

You'll be happy to hear that my brother and Sue finally got engaged. They've been going out for eight years now and we were beginning to wonder if they would ever tie the knot. I hope you can come back for the big occasion.

That's all the news at the moment. Write and let me know how your job is going. — conclusion

Love,
Janice

1 Your return address is not included in the letter, but written on the front of the envelope in the upper left-hand corner.

2 As this is an informal letter, the writer can use short forms and informal phrases such as *tie the knot* (get married) and *going out* (dating).

3 Depending on your relationship with the person you are writing to, you can sign off with *Best wishes* instead of the more informal *Love*.

WRITING A PAPER

Students in the U.S. are often asked to write papers or reports on a particular subject. Writing provides a chance for you to use your English, show what you've learned in class, and show that you can present your ideas in a clear and logical way.

WHAT MAKES A GOOD PAPER?

Organization Your paper should be written in **paragraphs**. Paragraphs are groups of sentences about the same subject. When you change subjects, start a new paragraph by **indenting** (skipping about five spaces before starting to write). Paragraphs should follow each other in a logical order.

Directness Don't hint or suggest. You should say things directly and clearly.

Topic Is the paper on the subject your teacher assigned?

Critical thinking Your paper can agree or disagree with what you've learned in class, but you must give reasons for your opinion.

Style Avoid using informal words and phrases.

Language Think about grammar, word choice, spelling, etc. Pages **A6** and **A7** "Checking your Work" in your *American Wordpower* Dictionary will help you.

HOW CAN I START?

The writing process involves several stages.

Understanding Make sure you understand the assignment.

Planning Some people start by **brainstorming** (= writing down all their ideas), then write an **outline** (= an organized list of the main points and supporting details).

Researching Do you need more information about your subject? You can look in newspapers, magazines, books and encyclopedias or even on the Internet.

Citing When you use someone else's words or ideas, you have to **cite** (= name) the source. Here is an example of how to cite a source: Johnson, Mary. "Choosing the Right Pet." American Family Magazine Feb. 1998: pp. 23-26.

Writing Follow your outline carefully, but remember it's only a **first draft** (= version) and you can change and improve it afterward if necessary.

Revising Read your draft, thinking about the things that make a paper good. Check the meaning, spelling and grammar of any difficult words in *American Wordpower*. Once you are happy with your text, you are ready to write your **final draft**.

Your name, class, and the date

Title

Introduction
The first paragraph should tell the reader what the subject of the paper is. (The reader can guess that this paper is about the relationship between dogs and people.)

Jun Watanabe
English 103
Prof. Rosen
September 14, 1998

Dogs – are they
"man's best friend"?

As pets and as working animals, dogs have kept humans company for a long time.

Topic sentence
usually the first sentence in a paragraph. It tells the reader what the paragraph is about. (This paragraph will probably be about dogs who help disabled people.)

Some dogs help people who are blind or have other disabilities.

The paragraphs between the introduction and conclusion make up the **body** of the text.

true.[1]

Reference to the footnote

indent

Footnote
This is where you cite your sources.

[1] Johnson, Mary, "Choosing the Right Pet." <u>American Family Magazine</u> Feb. 1998: pp. 23-26.

Conclusion
The last paragraph goes over the main points of the essay and gives a statement or opinion based on them.

Keeping vocabulary records

It's important to organize your vocabulary learning by keeping a record of all the new words that you want to remember.

VOCABULARY NOTEBOOKS

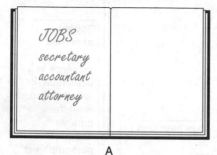

JOBS
secretary
accountant
attorney

A

H
honey
hairstyle
however

B

Many people like to buy a special notebook for vocabulary. You can divide your notebook into topic pages (as in picture A) or organize the pages alphabetically (as in picture B). Write in a few words when you first buy the book and then keep adding more words as you encounter them.

VOCABULARY CARDS

SHALLOW

(front of card)

not deep

EXAMPLE
The river is very shallow here.

(back of card)

Another way of recording vocabulary is to write each new word on a card and keep all the cards in a box. Write the word on one side of the card and the meaning and an example sentence on the other. Later, you can test yourself: look at the word on the front of the card and try to remember what it means, or look at the information on the back of the card and see if you can remember the word!

RECORDING MEANINGS

There are several different ways of recording the meaning of a new word:

You can draw a picture

snake

You can explain the word in English

salary = the money you get from your job

You can give the word
in your own language

tired = cansado

Or you can show the word
in an example sentence

*Although it was late, we didn't want
to go to bed.*

EXERCISE 1

How would you record the meaning of these words? Choose the best way for each word.

banana summer since above museum rich

RECORDING OTHER INFORMATION

There may be other important things that you want to remember about a new word. Find it in your dictionary and decide what you need to write down about it. Always try to write an example sentence, because this will help you remember how the word is used in English.

part of speech

lazy (adjective) = not wanting to work

Don't be so lazy. Come and help us! —— example sentence

adverb — lazily noun — laziness —— related words

EXERCISE 2

Now write down the things that you think are most important about these words. Use the dictionary to help you.

bleed deaf on the ball fluent trade

TABLES AND DIAGRAMS

Sometimes it is helpful to write down words in groups. Look at these two ways of recording groups of words:

a) WORD TABLE

SPORT	EQUIPMENT	PLACE
baseball	bat	field
football	football	field
tennis	racket	court
golf	club	course

b) WORD DIAGRAM

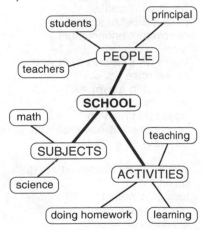

EXERCISE 3

a) Make a word table, using words for JOBS, PLACES OF WORK and THINGS PEOPLE USE IN THEIR JOBS.

b) Draw a word diagram showing vocabulary connected with VACATIONS. You could divide the words into "places to stay," "ways of traveling" and "activities."

Health and Fitness

HEAD

hair
ear
cheek
jaw

forehead
eyebrow
eyelash
eye
nose
nostril
mouth
lips
chin
throat

FACE

HAND

thumb
fingernail
fingers
wrist
knuckle
palm

neck
shoulder
armpit
chest
stomach
back
waist
hip
buttocks
thigh

ARM

elbow

LEG

calf
knee
shin

toenail
big toe
toes
sole
heel

ankle

FOOT

WAYS OF DESCRIBING YOUR BODY
healthy/unhealthy
in shape/out of shape
overweight/underweight

WAYS OF KEEPING IN SHAPE
do exercise
work out in a gym
do aerobics
go jogging/running
play basketball/baseball/tennis/golf
ride your bike

WAYS OF BECOMING HEALTHIER
go on a diet
lose/gain weight
quit smoking/drinking
cut down on snacks
eat more fresh fruit and vegetables

For more information about these expressions, look them up in the main part of the dictionary.

The Family

This is Sarah's family tree. All the people in the pictures are Sarah's relations.

(grandparents)

grandmother | grandfather

(parents)

aunt | uncle | mother | father | mother-in-law | father-in-law

cousin | cousin | sister-in-law | brother | SARAH | husband | sister-in-law | brother-in-law

(children)

niece | nephew | daughter-in-law | son | daughter | son-in-law

granddaughter | grandson

(grandchildren)

OTHER RELATIONSHIPS

If you have a girlfriend or boyfriend you say you are **going out with** him/her. If you want to be married to somebody, you **get engaged** first and then **get married**. Some people decide to **live with** somebody without getting married. You say you are **living together**. If you decide that you want to end your marriage, you **get divorced**.

If your father dies, or if your parents get divorced, your mother may decide to marry again, and her new husband will be your **stepfather**. If your father remarries, his new wife will be your **stepmother**. If your stepfather or stepmother already has children from an earlier marriage, those children become your **stepsisters** and **stepbrothers**, and your mother's or father's **stepchildren**. If your mother and stepfather or your father and stepmother have children, they are your **half brothers** and **half sisters**.

Clothes

T-shirt

hood

sweatshirt

USA

blouse

cuff

collar

SWEATS

sweatpants

shirt

sleeve

dress

skirt

nightgown

bathrobe

pantyhose/nylons

socks

stockings

pajamas

underpants/briefs

bra

panties

undershirt

slip

shorts/boxers

USEFUL EXPRESSIONS
to be wearing sth
to have sth on
to be dressed in sth

to get dressed/undressed
to dress/undress
to put sth on
to take sth off
to change your clothes
to change into sth
to try sth on
to dress well/badly/casually
to dress up

Clothes can **fit** you or **look good on** you

For more information about how to use these expressions, look them up in the main part of the dictionary.

raincoat

jacket

scarf

coat

gloves mittens earmuffs

jacket

tie/necktie

leggings

round neck

vest

belt

pocket

sweaters

turtleneck

jeans

V neck

pants pants

shorts

cardigan

SUIT

Houses

A HOUSE

antenna
chimney
skylight
roof
siding
screen
shutter
shingles
porch
front door
screen door
bay window
garage
mailbox
lawn — front yard
driveway
sidewalk
front walk
curb

AN APARTMENT

hallway
closet
bathroom
kitchen
hall
closet
closet
living room
bedroom
bedroom

Computers

menu bar buttons

menu

window

toolbar

mouse pointer/arrow

icons

mouse buttons

mouse pad

mouse

A computer can **store** and **process** information. This information is called **data** and can be words, numbers or **graphics** (pictures/images). To process data, the computer uses a **program**, which is a set of instructions stored on the computer's **hard drive**.

To **input** data, you can **enter** it using the keyboard. If you want to store this data, you **save** it in the computer's **memory** or onto a **floppy disk**. Large amounts of information, such as books, can be stored on a **CD-ROM**.

On the screen, **Icons** (special symbols) and **menus** show you what programs and data are stored on the computer and what jobs the computer can do. You use the **mouse** to tell the computer what job you want it to do and which part of the screen you want to work on. A small symbol called a **cursor** shows your position on the screen.

Computers can be connected to other computers to form a **network**. This allows different people to have access to the same information and to communicate with each other using **e-mail** (electronic mail). To communicate with someone using e-mail, you send your message to their **e-mail address**. For example, John_Jones@aol.com is a typical e-mail address. To say this address, you say "John underscore Jones at A O L dot com."

The Internet or **the Net** is an enormous network that covers the world. People who want to make information available to the whole world can pay for their own space on the Internet. This is called a **Web site**. **The Web** or **the World Wide Web** is the system which lets you **download** (look at) information on the Internet. You can also enter a subject and find all the Web sites that have information about it. This is called **surfing** the Net.

The Educational System

SCHOOLS
Most American children go to **public schools** which are free. There are also **private schools** where students have to pay. Parochial schools are supported by religious organizations.

ASSESSMENT
Generally examination is by continuous assessment, which means that teachers **grade** (assess) students throughout the year on how well they do in tests, classroom discussions, homework, and written and oral work. At the end of a semester students must have achieved at least 70% **GPA** (grade point average) or they have to repeat the class. If students choose to go on to higher education, most colleges and universities require them to take the **SAT** (**Scholastic Aptitude Test**).

GRADUATION
Students must collect units in the core courses – math, English, science, history, and government - in their first years of high school. They can then move on to **electives** (specialized subjects) in the last two years. Students can **graduate** from high school if they have collected enough **credits** in the core and elective subjects.

HIGHER EDUCATION
To receive a **degree** most students study for four years. Students have to pay to go to a private or a state university. There are examinations at the end of each course; students graduate if they have collected enough credits in their **major**.

If students wish to continue their education after receiving a **Bachelor's degree**, they can do a **Master's degree**, which usually takes two years. Then they can go on to do a **Ph.D.** (a doctorate), which can take any number of years to complete.

This chart shows how education is generally organized in the U.S., although in some states the system may be different.

Government

The White House

THE FEDERAL GOVERNMENT

The **United States Constitution** divides power between the **federal government** and the governments of the individual states. The federal government, which is based in Washington, DC, deals with national issues such as economic and foreign policy. There are three branches of the federal government: the Legislative, Executive and Judicial.

The Legislative branch is the **Congress** which meets in the **Capitol** and is made up of the **Senate** and the **House of Representatives**. The Senate has 100 **senators,** two from each state. The House of Representatives has 435 **representatives**; the number of representatives from each state depends on its population. Members of Congress introduce new laws.

The Executive branch is led by the **President**, who lives and works in the **White House**. The President is assisted by a **Cabinet**, which consists of the heads of the departments of the federal government. The President signs laws passed by Congress. The President can also **veto** a law, but Congress can **override** the veto with the votes of more than two thirds of its members.

The Judicial branch consists of the **Supreme Court** and other federal courts. The Supreme Court is made up of nine **justices**, led by a **chief justice**, who are appointed by the President. The Supreme Court decides whether laws passed by Congress or decisions made by other courts are **constitutional**.

ELECTIONS

The members of the House of Representatives are elected every two years. One third of senators are elected every two years for a six-year term. **Presidential elections** are held every four years. In each state, the candidates for President and Vice President who get the most votes win the state's **electoral votes**. The candidates who get the most electoral votes win the election. Most candidates in elections belong to one of two **political parties**, the **Democrats** and the **Republicans**.

STATE GOVERNMENT

Each state has its own laws and system of government. The head of every state government is the **governor** who is elected by the state's voters. The officials in state governments are chosen every two or four years.

The Environment

heat from the sun

some heat escapes back into space

but CO_2 traps heat in the atmosphere

CO_2

THE EARTH

ultraviolet radiation

the ozone layer

CFCs

THE EARTH

GLOBAL WARMING

Scientists say the temperature of the earth could rise 4-5° Fahrenheit in the future. This is called **global warming** and may cause droughts in some parts of the world and floods in others as ice at the North and South Poles begins to melt and sea levels rise. Global warming is caused by the **greenhouse effect**. Normally heat from the sun warms the earth and then escapes back into space. However, **carbon dioxide** and other gases trap the sun's heat and this is making the earth warmer.

THE OZONE LAYER

The **ozone layer** is a layer of gas high above the surface of the earth that helps to protect the earth from the sun's **ultraviolet radiation**, which can cause skin **cancer**. Scientists have discovered holes in the ozone layer, caused by substances called **CFCs** (chlorofluorocarbons). CFCs are used in air conditioners, refrigerators, and aerosol cans. Today many countries are trying to reduce the amount of CFCs they use.

DEFORESTATION

Rainforests help to control global warming because they absorb carbon dioxide. However, large areas have been destroyed as trees are cut down for wood or burned to clear land for farming.

POLLUTION

Factories, power stations, and motor vehicles are a major source of air pollution which increases the greenhouse effect. To reduce air pollution, factories and power stations are continually checked. City governments are also encouraging people to use **public transportation** or to **car-pool** (have two or more people ride to work in one car).

RECYCLING

Recycling is the processing of used objects and materials so that they can be used again. Glass, paper, and aluminum cans can be recycled very easily. Most cities have recycling centers and services that collect trash for recycling.

life. ○ *married life* **9** [U] activity; liveliness: *Young kids are full of life.* ○ *This town comes to life in the evenings.*

IDM the facts of life ⇨ FACT

get a life (*slang*) (often imperative) to stop being boring and annoying

life in the fast lane (*informal*) a way of living that involves exciting activities and spending a lot of money

lose your life ⇨ LOSE

real life ⇨ REAL¹

take your (own) life to kill yourself

a walk of life ⇨ WALK²

a/sb's way of life ⇨ WAY¹

life-and-'death (*also* **life-or-'death**) *adj.* (only *before* a noun) very serious or dangerous: *a life-or-death situation*

life·boat /'laɪfboʊt/ *noun* [C] **1** a small boat that is carried on a large ship and that is used by people to escape from the ship if it is in danger of sinking **2** a special boat that is used for rescuing people who are in danger in the ocean

'life cycle *noun* [C] the series of forms or stages of development that a plant, animal, etc. goes through from the beginning of its life to the end

'life ex·pectancy *noun* [C,U] (*pl.* **life expectancies**) the number of years that a person is likely to live

life·guard /'laɪfɡɑrd/ *noun* [C] a person at a beach or swimming pool whose job is to rescue people who are in difficulties in the water

'life in·surance *noun* [U] a type of insurance that pays a certain amount of money to sb's family after he/she dies

'life jacket (*also* **'life vest**) *noun* [C] a plastic or rubber jacket with no sleeves that can be filled with air. A life-jacket is worn by sb to stop him/her from sinking in water.

life·less /'laɪfləs/ *adj.* **1** dead: *Police pulled her lifeless body from the river.* **2** without life (9) or energy

life·like /'laɪflaɪk/ *adj.* looking like the real person or thing: *a lifelike baby doll*

life·line /'laɪflaɪn/ *noun* [C] something that sb needs in order to survive in a difficult situation: *For many old people, their telephone is a lifeline.*

life·long /'laɪflɔn/ *adj.* (only *before* a noun) for all of your life: *a lifelong friend*

'life pre·server *noun* [C] an object, shaped like a ring, that is made from light material which will float. A life preserver is thrown to a person who has fallen into water to stop him/her from sinking.

'life-size (*also* **'life-sized**) *adj.* (only *before* a noun) of the same size as the real person or thing: *a life-size statue*

'life span *noun* [C] the length of time that sb/sth lives, works, lasts, etc.

life·style /'laɪfstaɪl/ *noun* [C] the way that you

live: *After I got divorced, my whole lifestyle changed.*

'life sup·port *noun* [U] medical equipment that keeps sb alive when he/she cannot breathe, etc. alone: *She spent two weeks in the hospital on life support.*

☆ **life·time** /'laɪftaɪm/ *noun* [C] the period of time that sb is alive: *It's a chance of a lifetime. Don't miss it!*

'life vest *noun* [C] = LIFE JACKET

☆ **lift¹** /lɪft/ *verb* **1** [T] **lift sb/sth (up)** to move sb/sth to a higher level or position: *He lifted the child up onto his shoulders.* ○ *Lift your arm very gently and see if it hurts.* **2** [T] to take hold of sb/sth and move him/her/it to a different position: *She lifted the suitcase down from the rack.* **3** [T] to end or remove a rule, law, etc.: *The ban on imports has been lifted.* **4** [T] **lift sth (from sb/sth)** (*informal*) to steal or copy sth: *Most of his essay was lifted straight from the textbook.* ☞ Look at **shoplift.** **5** [I] (used about clouds, fog, etc.) to rise up or disappear: *The mist lifted toward the end of the morning.*

PHRV lift off (used about a rocket or spacecraft) to rise straight up from the ground

☆ **lift²** /lɪft/ *noun* **1** [sing.] a feeling of happiness or excitement: *Her words of encouragement gave the whole team a lift.* **2** [C] a free ride in a car, etc.: *Can you give me a lift to the store?* **3** [sing.] an act of lifting or being lifted **4** [C] (*BrE*) = ELEVATOR

lift·off /'lɪftɔf/ *noun* [C] the start of the flight of a rocket or spacecraft: *Only ten seconds to liftoff!*

lig·a·ment /'lɪɡəmənt/ *noun* [C] a strong band in a person's or an animal's body that holds the bones, etc. together

light lampshade **lights**

light bulb spotlight

lampshade

battery **flashlight**

table lamp

☆ **light¹** /laɪt/ *noun* **1** [U] the brightness that allows you to see things: *the light of the sun* ○ *The light was too bad for us to read by.*

☞ You may see things by **sunlight, moonlight, firelight, candlelight, lamplight,** etc.

2 [C] something that produces light (1), e.g. a lamp: *the lights of the city in the distance* ○ *a neon light* ○ *That car's lights aren't on.*

☞ A light can be **on** or **off.** You **turn** or **switch** a light **on, off** or **out**: *Should I turn the light on? It's getting dark in here.* ○ *Please switch the lights off before you leave.*

3 [C] one of three colored lights, or a set of these lights (red, yellow and green) that control traffic: *Slow down – there's a red light ahead.* **4** [C] something, e.g. a match, that can be used to light a cigarette, start a fire, etc.: *Can you give me a light?*

IDM **come to light** to be found or become known

give sb/get the green light ⇨ GREEN¹

in a good, bad, etc. light (used about the way that sth is seen or described by other people) well, badly, etc.: *The newspapers often portray his behavior in a bad light.*

in the light of because of; considering: *We might have to change our decision in the light of what you just said.*

set light to sth to cause sth to start burning

☆ **light²** /laɪt/ *adj.* **1** having a lot of light¹(1) ; not dark: *In the summer it's still light at 9 o'clock.* ∘ *a light room* **2** (used about a color) pale; not dark: *a light blue sweater* **3** not of great weight; not heavy: *Carry this bag – it's the lightest.* ∘ *I've lost weight – I'm five pounds lighter than I used to be.* ∘ *light clothes* (= for summer) **4** not great in amount, degree, etc.: *Traffic downtown is light on Sundays.* ∘ *a light prison sentence* ∘ *a light wind* ∘ *a light breakfast* **5** not using much force; gentle: *a light touch on the shoulder* **6** (used about work, etc.) easy to do: *light exercise* **7** not very serious or hard to understand: *light reading* **8** (used about sleep) not deep —**light·ness** *noun* [U]

☆ **light³** /laɪt/ *verb* (*p.t.*, *p.p.* **lit** or **light·ed**) **1** [I,T] to begin to burn or to make sb do this: *This match won't light.* ∘ *to light a fire*

☞ **Lighted** is usually used as an adjective before the noun. **Lit** is used as the past participle of the verb: *Candles were lit in memory of the dead.* ∘ *The church was full of lighted candles.*

2 [T] to give light to sth: *The room was lit with one 40-watt bulb.*

PHRV **light up** (used about sb's face, eyes, etc.) to become bright with happiness or excitement

☆ **light⁴** /laɪt/ *adv.* **1** without much luggage: *to travel light* **2** without a lot of fat or oil: *to cook/eat light*

light bulb (*also* **bulb**) *noun* [C] the glass part of an electric lamp that gives out light: *a 60-watt light bulb*

☆ **light·en** /ˈlaɪtn/ *verb* [I,T] **1** to become lighter in weight or to make sth lighter: *to lighten a load* **2** to become brighter or to make sth brighter

light·er /ˈlaɪtər/ *noun* [C] an object which produces a small flame for lighting cigarettes, etc.

light·heart·ed /ˈlaɪtˌhɑrtəd/ *adj.* **1** without problems; happy **2** funny; amusing

light·house /ˈlaɪthaʊs/ *noun* [C] a tall build-ing with a light at the top that guides ships or warns them of dangerous rocks, etc.

light·ing /ˈlaɪtɪŋ/ *noun* [U] the quality or type of lights used in a room, building, etc.: *Soft lighting helps to make people more relaxed.*

☆ **light·ly** /ˈlaɪtli/ *adv.* **1** in a light² way: *He touched her lightly on the arm.* **2** not seriously; without serious thought: *We should not take her remarks lightly – this is an important matter.*

☆ **light·ning** /ˈlaɪtnɪŋ/ *noun* [U] a bright flash of light that appears in the sky during a thunderstorm: *The tree was struck by lightning.*

light·weight /ˈlaɪtweɪt/ *noun* [C], *adj.* **1** (a boxer) weighing between 126 and 135 pounds **2** (a person or thing) weighing less than usual: *a lightweight suit for the summer*

lik·a·ble (*also* **likeable**) /ˈlaɪkəbl/ *adj.* (used about a person) easy to like; pleasant

☆ **like¹** /laɪk/ *verb* [T] (not in the continuous tenses) **1** to find sb/sth pleasant; to be fond of sb/sth: *He's nice. I like him a lot.* ∘ *Do you like their new house?* ∘ *I like my coffee with milk.* ∘ *I like playing tennis./I like to play tennis.* ∘ *She didn't like it when I shouted at her.* ☞ The opposite is **dislike**. **2** to want: *How do you like your steak done, sir?*

☞ **Would like** is a more polite way to say "want": *Would you like to come to lunch on Sunday?* ∘ *I would like some more cake, please.* ∘ *I'd like to speak to the manager.* **Would like** is always followed by the infinitive (to + verb), never by the -ing form.

IDM **like the look/looks/sound of sb/sth** to have a good impression of sb/sth after seeing or hearing about him/her/it

☆ **like²** /laɪk/ *prep.* **1** similar to sb/sth: *He looks like his father.* ∘ *Their car is like ours.* ∘ *With a coat of paint it will look like new.*

☞ Look also at **unlike**. If you want somebody to give a description of something you ask: **"What's it like?"**: *Tell me about your town. What's it like?* ∘ *What's your town like?*

2 showing what is usual or typical for sb: *It was just like him to be late.*

☞ Notice the difference in meaning between "as" and "like" when used about a person's job, occupation, etc.: *Jeff acted as our leader* (= he was our leader). ∘ *Jeff acted like our leader* (= but he was not really our leader).

3 in the same way or manner as sb/sth: *Stop behaving like kids.* ∘ *That's not right. Do it like this.* **4** for example: *They enjoy most team games, like football and baseball.*

IDM **like crazy** (*informal*) very much, fast, hard, etc.: *We had to pedal like crazy to get up the hill.*

☆ **like³** /laɪk/ *conj.* **1** in the same way or manner as: *She can't draw like her sister can.* ∘ *Well, like I said before, it's not going to be easy.*

L

2 (*informal*) as if: *She acts like she's the boss.* ○ *I felt like I was going to die.*

☆ **like⁴** /laɪk/ *adv.* (*informal*) (used to fill a pause while the speaker is thinking of what to say next, or before an example): *It was, like, really scary, you know?*

IDM **be like ...** (not in the continuous tenses) (used to tell what sb said or thought): *I asked Paul if he could help us and he was like, forget it.*

☞ Many people, especially older people, do not like this use of **like**. However, it is very common in informal spoken English.

like⁵ /laɪk/ *noun* [sing.] a person or thing that is similar to sb/sth else: *to compare like with like*

IDM **...and the like** (*formal*) and other similar things: *pollution from farms, factories and the like*

likes and dislikes the things that you like or do not like

like⁶ /laɪk/ *adj.* (*formal*) similar: *We're of like mind* (= we have the same opinion).

-like /laɪk/ (in compounds) in the manner of; similar to: *ladylike* ○ *lifelike*

like·li·hood /'laɪklihʊd/ *noun* [U] probability: *There seems very little likelihood of success.*

☆ **like·ly¹** /'laɪkli/ *adj.* (**like·li·er; like·li·est**) **1** probable or expected: *Do you think it's likely to rain?* ○ *The boss is not likely to agree.* ○ *It's not likely that the boss will agree.* **2** probably suitable: *a likely candidate for the job*

like·ly² /'laɪki/ *adv.*

IDM **most/very likely** very probably: *They left very late. They'll most likely miss the start of the movie.*

lik·en /'laɪkən/ *verb* [T] (*formal*) **liken sth to sth** to compare sth with sth else: *She likened the process to "using a hammer to crack an egg."*

like·ness /'laɪknəs/ *noun* [C,U] (an example of) being alike or similar in appearance: *There is a strong family likeness.* ○ *The portrait is a very good likeness of Grandpa.*

like·wise /'laɪkwaɪz/ *adv.* (*formal*) the same: *I intend to send a letter of apology and suggest that you do likewise.*

lik·ing /'laɪkɪŋ/ *noun*

IDM **to your liking** (*formal*) the way that you like sth: *I hope that everything is to your liking.*

li·lac /'laɪlɑk; -læk; -lək/ *noun* **1** [C,U] a tree or large bush that has large purple or white flowers in spring. The flowers are also called lilacs. **2** [U] a pale purple color

lil·y /'lɪli/ *noun* [C] (*pl.* **lil·ies**) a type of plant that grows from a bulb and that has large white or colored flowers

li·ma bean /'laɪmə bin/ *noun* [C] a type of light green flat bean

limb /lɪm/ *noun* [C] **1** a leg or an arm of a person **2** one of the main branches of a tree

☆ **lime** /laɪm/ *noun* **1** [C] a small green fruit that tastes like a lemon **2** [U] (*also* ,**lime 'green**) a bright yellowish-green color

lime·light /'laɪmlaɪt/ *noun*

IDM **in the limelight** getting a lot of attention from the public: *The singer was in the limelight wherever he went.*

☆ **lim·it¹** /'lɪmət/ *noun* [C] **1** a point or line that marks the end or edge of sth: *No alcohol is sold within the city limits* (= inside the city). **2** the greatest amount of sth that is possible, allowed, etc.: *What's the speed limit on this road?* ○ *a limit on government spending*

IDM **off limits** not to be entered, touched, discussed, etc.: *My desk is off limits to my kids.* ○ *We only talk about work – her personal life is off limits.*

within limits as long as it is not too much, great, etc.: *I don't mind how much it costs – within limits.*

☆ **lim·it²** /'lɪmət/ *verb* [T] **limit sb/sth (to sth)** to keep sb/sth within or below a certain amount, size, degree or area: *laws to limit pollution by manufacturers* ○ *In China, families are limited to just one child.*

lim·i·ta·tion /,lɪmə'teɪʃn/ *noun* **1** [C,U] controlling sth or making sth smaller; a condition that puts a limit on sth: *There are certain limitations on what we can do.* **2** [plural] **limitations** what you cannot do: *It is important to know your own limitations.*

☆ **lim·it·ed** /'lɪmətəd/ *adj.* small in number or amount: *Reserve early because there are only a limited number of seats available.*

lim·ou·sine /'lɪməzin; ,lɪmə'zin/(also *informal* **limo** /'lɪmoʊ/ *pl.* **lim·os**) *noun* [C] a long expensive car that usually has a sheet of glass between the driver and the passengers in the back

limp¹ /lɪmp/ *adj.* not stiff or strong: *a limp handshake*

limp² /lɪmp/ *verb* [I] to walk in an uneven way, e.g. because you have hurt your leg or foot: (*figurative*) *After the accident the ship limped back to the harbor.* —**limp** *noun* [sing.]: *to walk with a bad limp*

☆ **line¹** /laɪn/ *noun* **1** [C] a long thin mark on the surface of sth: *A solid line in the middle of the road means "no passing."* ○ *to draw a line*

a straight line

a wavy line

a dotted line

☞ A line may be **horizontal**, **vertical**, **diagonal** or **parallel** to sth

2 [C] a line (1) on the ground that marks the side or end of a sports field, etc.: *The ball was definitely over the line.* ○ *the finish line of a race* **3** [C] an imaginary line (1) that marks the

L

ə	y	w	t̬	eɪ	aɪ	ɔɪ	aʊ	oʊ
about	yes	woman	butter	say	five	boy	now	go

boundary between two states, counties, etc.: *the Montana-Idaho state line* ○ *The neighbors built a brick wall right on our property line.* **4** [C] a row of things, words on a page, etc.: *a neat line of china dolls on a shelf* ○ *a five-line poem* ○ *Start each paragraph on a new line.* **5** a row of people, cars, etc. that are waiting for sth or to do sth: *We had to wait in line for hours to get tickets.* ○ *The line stretched around the block.* **6** [C] a piece of rope or string: *He hung out the clothes on the line.* ○ *a fishing line* **7** [C] a telephone or electricity wire or connection: *I'm sorry – the line is busy. Can I take a message?* ○ *The strong winds blew down many power lines.* **8** **lines** [plural] the words that are spoken by an actor in a play, etc.: *to learn your lines* **9** [sing.] a direction or course of thought or action: *a line of argument* ○ *He can't even walk in a straight line.* **10** [C] a company that provides transportation by air, ship, etc.: *a Greek shipping line* **11** [sing.] a type of product in a store, etc.: *a new line of environmentally-friendly detergents* **12** [C] a route that people move along or send messages, goods, etc. along: *lines of communication* ○ *Before you travel on the subway, check which line you need.* **13** [C] the place where an army is fighting: *a spy working behind enemy lines*

IDM **along the same lines** in the way that is mentioned: *We both think along the same lines, so we work well together.*

the bottom line ⇨ BOTTOM²

cut in line ⇨ CUT¹

draw the line at sth/doing sth ⇨ DRAW¹

drop sb a line ⇨ DROP¹

in line for sth likely to get sth: *She's next in line for promotion.*

in line with sth similar to sth and fitting in with it

on line connected to a computer system

out of line (used about sb's behavior) not acceptable or polite: *That remark was totally out of line!*

stand in line ⇨ STAND¹

line² /laɪn/ *verb* [T] **1** (often passive) to mark sth with lines¹(1): *lined paper* ○ *a face lined with age* **2** to make or form a line¹(4) along sth: *Crowds lined the streets to see the parade.* ○ *a tree-lined avenue* **3** (often passive) to cover the inside surface of sth with a different material: *fur-lined boots*

PHRV **line up (for sth)** to form a line (for sth) **line sth up** to arrange or plan sth: *What do you have lined up for the weekend?*

lin·en /'lɪnən/ *noun* **1** [U] a type of strong cloth that is made from a natural substance (**flax**) **2** **linens** [plural] sheets, tablecloths, etc. (which often used to be made of linen (1)): *bed linens*

lin·er /'laɪnər/ *noun* [C] a large ship that carries people, etc. long distances

lin·ger /'lɪŋɡər/ *verb* [I] **1** to stay somewhere for a long time: *lingering effects of the floods* **2** (*formal*) to take a long time doing sth: *to linger over a meal*

lin·ge·rie /ˌlɑnʒə'reɪ; ˌlɑndʒə'reɪ/ *noun* [U] women's underwear that is usually very delicate and elegant

lin·guist /'lɪŋɡwɪst/ *noun* [C] a person who studies or teaches language(s); a person who is good at learning foreign languages

lin·guis·tic /lɪŋ'ɡwɪstɪk/ *adj.* of language or linguistics

lin·guis·tics /lɪŋ'ɡwɪstɪks/ *noun* [U] the scientific study of language

lin·ing /'laɪnɪŋ/ *noun* [C,U] material that covers the inside surface of sth: *I tore the lining of my coat.*

☆**link¹** /lɪŋk/ *noun* [C] **1** one ring in a chain ☛ picture at **chain**. **2** a person or thing that connects two other people or things: *There is a strong link between smoking and heart disease.* ○ *Economic links with South Africa were broken for many years.*

☆**link²** /lɪŋk/ *verb* [T] **link A to/with B; link A and B (together)** to make or suggest a connection between two or more people or things: *Air pollution has been linked to asthma.* ○ *This evidence could link him with several robberies.*

PHRV **link up (to/with sb/sth)** to join together (with sb/sth), especially by computer

li·no·le·um /lɪ'noʊliəm/ *noun* [U] a type of smooth, hard covering for floors

lint /lɪnt/ *noun* [U] small pieces of thread that come off clothing, etc. and form into balls

leopard / tiger / lioness / lion

☆**li·on** /'laɪən/ *noun* [C] a large animal of the cat family that lives in Africa and parts of southern Asia. Male lions have a large amount of hair around their head and neck (**a mane**).

☛ A female lion is called a **lioness** and a young lion is called a **cub**. The noise a lion makes is a **roar**.

☆**lip** /lɪp/ *noun* [C] **1** one of the two soft red parts above and below your mouth: *to kiss somebody on the lips*

☞ picture on page A24. You have a **top/upper** lip and a **bottom/lower** lip.

2 the edge of a cup or of sth that is shaped like a cup

IDM **purse your lips** ⇨ PURSE²

'lip-read verb [I,T] (p.t., p.p. **lip-read** /-rɛd/) to understand what sb is saying by looking at the movements of his/her lips

lip·stick /'lɪpstɪk/ noun [C,U] a substance that is used for giving color to your lips: to put on some lipstick ○ a new lipstick

li·queur /lɪ'kər; -'kʊr/ noun [U] a strong alcoholic (usually sweet) drink that is often drunk in small quantities after a meal

☆ **liq·uid** /'lɪkwəd/ noun [C,U] a substance, e.g. water, that is not solid and that can flow or be poured —**liq·uid** adj.: The patient can only be given liquid food.

liq·ui·date /'lɪkwədeɪt/ verb [T] to close down a business because it has no money left —**liq·ui·da·tion** /ˌlɪkwə'deɪʃn/ noun [U]: to go into liquidation (= of a business)

liq·uor /'lɪkər/ noun [U] (also **spirits** [plural]) strong alcoholic drinks

'liquor store noun [C] a store where you can buy alcohol, including beer and wine

lisp /lɪsp/ noun [C] an incorrect way of speaking in which "s" sounds like "th": He speaks with a slight lisp. —**lisp** verb [I,T]

☆ **list¹** /lɪst/ noun [C] a series of names, figures, items, etc. that are written or printed one after another: a shopping list ○ an alphabetical list ○ Your name is third on the waiting list.

☆ **list²** /lɪst/ verb [T] to make a list of sth; to put or include sth on a list: to list items in alphabetical order ○ Her number is not listed in the phone book.

☆ **lis·ten** /'lɪsn/ verb [I] **1 listen (to sb/sth)** to pay attention to sb/sth in order to hear him/her/it: Now please listen carefully to what I have to say. ○ to listen to the radio, music, etc. ☞ Look at the note at hear. **2 listen (to sb/sth)** to pay attention to or believe what sb says, etc.: I try to give them advice but they never listen to what I tell them. ○ Now, listen, you two – I want you to behave!

PHRV **listen for sth** to wait to hear sth: to listen for a knock on the door

listen up (informal) (used to tell people to pay attention to what you are going to say): Okay, listen up, everybody – I have an important announcement to make.

lis·ten·er /'lɪsn·ər; 'lɪsnər/ noun [C] a person who listens: He is a good listener (= he pays attention to you when you are speaking).

list·less /'lɪstləs/ adj. tired and without energy —**list·less·ly** adv.

lit p.t., p.p. of LIGHT²

lite /laɪt/ adj. (informal) (used especially on food packages, in restaurants, etc.) light; having less fat, alcohol, or other unhealthy substances than usual: lite cheesecake

li·ter /'litər/ noun [C] (abbr. **l**) a measure of liquid, used especially in science: One liter of fluid evaporated.

☞ It is more common in the U.S. to measure liquids in **quarts**. One quart is equal to 0.946 liter.

☆ **lit·er·a·cy** /'lɪtərəsi/ noun [U] the ability to read and write ☞ Look at illiteracy.

lit·er·al /'lɪtərəl/ adj. **1** (used about the meaning of a word or phrase) original or basic: The word "gay" isn't used very much in its literal sense anymore. ☞ Look at figurative and metaphorical. **2** (used about a translation, etc.) translating each word separately without looking at the general meaning

lit·er·al·ly /'lɪtərəli/ adv. **1** in a literal (2) way: You shouldn't take his comments literally. **2** (informal) (used for emphasizing sth): We were literally frozen to death (= we were very cold). ☞ Many people consider this use of **literally** incorrect.

lit·er·ar·y /'lɪtərɛri/ adj. of or concerned with literature: a literary journal

lit·er·ate /'lɪtərət/ adj. **1** able to read and write ☞ The opposite is illiterate. **2** well-educated

☆ **lit·er·a·ture** /'lɪtərətʃər; -tʃʊr/ noun [U] **1** writing that is considered to be a work of art. Literature includes novels, plays and poetry: French literature **2** printed material on a particular subject: the senator's campaign literature

lit·i·ga·tion /ˌlɪtə'geɪʃn/ noun [U] the process of bringing a legal case to a court of law, especially when one person or group is trying to get money from another

lit·ter¹ /'lɪtər/ noun **1** [U] pieces of paper, cans, etc. that are left in a public place **2** [C] all the young animals that are born to one mother at the same time: a litter of six puppies

lit·ter² /'lɪtər/ verb [I,T] to make sth messy with litter¹: The streets were littered with beer bottles. ○ Do Not Litter (= on a sign)

lit·ter·bug /'lɪtərbʌg/ noun [C] (informal) a person who drops litter in a public place

☆ **lit·tle¹** /'lɪtl/ adj. **1** not big; small: There's a little hole in my sock. ○ your little finger/toe (= the smallest one on your hand/foot)

☞ **Little** is often used with another adjective: a little old lady ○ a sweet little kitten Look at the note at **small**.

2 (used about distance or time) short: Do you mind waiting a little while? ○ It's only a little farther. **3** young: a little girl/boy ○ my little brother **4** not important: a little problem

☆ **lit·tle²** /'lɪtl/ det. (with uncountable [U] nouns) **1** not much or not enough: They have very little money. ○ There is little hope that she will

tʃ	dʒ	v	θ	ð	s	z	ʃ
chin	June	van	thin	then	so	zoo	she

recover. ☞ Look at **less** and **least**. **2 a little** (*also* **a little bit of**) by a small amount of sth: *I like a little sugar in my coffee.*

☆ **lit·tle³** /ˈlɪtl/ *pron.* **1** (also as a noun after *the*) a small amount; not enough: *We studied Latin in school, but I remember very little.* ○ *The little I know of him has given me a good impression.* **2 a little** (*also* **a little bit**) a small amount: *"Is there any butter left?" "Yes, just a little."*
IDM **after/for a little (bit)** after/for a short distance or time: *You should rest for a little.*

☆ **lit·tle⁴** /ˈlɪtl/ *adv.* **1** not much or not enough: *I slept very little last night.* ○ *a little-known author* **2 a little** (*also* **a little bit**) by a small amount: *This skirt is a little (bit) too tight.*
IDM **little by little** slowly: *After the accident, her strength returned little by little.*

☆ **live¹** /lɪv/ *verb* **1** [I] to be or remain alive: *You can't live without water.* ○ *She doesn't have long to live.* ○ *to live to the age of 100* **2** [I] to have your home: *Where do you live?* ○ *I lived in Texas for three years.* **3** [I,T] to spend your life in a certain way: *to live a quiet life* ○ *They have plenty of money and live well.* **4** [I] to be able to buy the things that you need: *Many families don't have enough to live.* **5** [I] to enjoy all the opportunities of life fully: *I want to live a little before settling down and getting married.*
PHRV **live sth down** to make people forget sth bad or embarrassing that has happened to you: *They lost 10 – 0? They'll never live it down!*
live on to continue to exist: *Mozart is dead, but his music lives on.*
live on sth 1 to have sth as your only food: *to live on bread and water* **2** to have sth as your income: *I don't know how they live on $8,000 a year!*
live together 1 to live in the same house as sb **2** to live in the same house, etc. as sb and have a sexual relationship with him/her
live up to sth to be as good as expected: *Children sometimes find it hard to live up to their parents' expectations.*
live with sb = LIVE TOGETHER: *He's 30 years old and still lives with his parents.*
live with sth to accept sth unpleasant that you cannot change: *I know it's not the best solution, but we'll just have to live with it.*

☆ **live²** /laɪv/ *adj.* **1** having life; not dead: *Have you ever touched a real live snake?* ☞ Look at **alive** and **living**. **2** (used about a bomb, etc.) that has not yet exploded, or that can explode: *The police used live ammunition when they fired on the crowd.* **3** (used about a wire, etc.) carrying electricity. If you touch sth that is live you will get an electric shock. **4** (used about a radio or TV program) seen or heard as it is happening: *live coverage of the championships* **5** recorded from a concert, etc., i.e. not made in a studio: *a live recording of Bob Dylan's last concert*

☆ **live³** /laɪv/ *adv.* appearing on television or on the radio at the same time as it is happening: *The concert will be broadcast live from New York.*

live·li·hood /ˈlaɪvlihʊd/ *noun* [C, usually sing.] the way that you earn money: *to lose your livelihood*

☆ **live·ly** /ˈlaɪvli/ *adj.* (**live·li·er**; **live·li·est**) full of energy, interest, excitement, etc.: *lively kids* ○ *There was a lively debate on the route of the new highway.* ○ *a lively imagination*

li·ven /ˈlaɪvn/ *verb*
PHRV **liven (sb/sth) up** to become lively or to make sb/sth lively: *Once the band started to play, the party livened up.*

liv·er /ˈlɪvər/ *noun* **1** [C] the part of your body that cleans your blood **2** [U] the liver of an animal when it is cooked and eaten as food

lives *pl.* of LIFE

live·stock /ˈlaɪvstɑk/ *noun* [U] animals that are kept on a farm, e.g. cows, pigs, sheep, etc.

☆ **liv·ing¹** /ˈlɪvɪŋ/ *adj.* **1** alive now: *He has no living relatives.* **2** (used about a language, etc.) still used ☞ The opposite for both meanings is **dead**.

☆ **liv·ing²** /ˈlɪvɪŋ/ *noun* **1** [C, usually sing.] a means of earning money to buy the things you need: *What do you do for a living?* **2** [U] your way or quality of life: *The cost of living has risen in recent years.* ☞ Look at **standard of living**.

☆ **living room** *noun* [C] the room in a house where people sit, relax, watch TV, etc. together

lizard

liz·ard /ˈlɪzərd/ *noun* [C] a small reptile with four legs, rough skin and a long tail. A lizard has a long tongue that it uses to catch insects.

Ln. *abbr.* = LANE

☆ **load¹** /loʊd/ *noun* [C] **1** something (heavy) that is being or is going to be carried: *The ship was carrying a full load of oil.* **2** (often in compounds) the quantity of sth that can be carried in a machine, car, etc.: *a truckload of sand* ○ *busloads of tourists* **3 loads (of sth)** [plural] (*informal*) a lot (of sth): *loads of cash*
IDM **a load of crap, garbage, etc.** (*informal*) nonsense
get a load of sb/sth (*informal*) (used to tell sb to look at sb/sth that is funny, surprising, etc.): *Hey guys, get a load of that dude's hat!*

☆ **load²** /loʊd/ *verb* **1** [I,T] to put or have a load¹ or large quantity of sth in or on sb/sth: *Are you finished loading yet?* ○ *Uncle Tim arrived loaded down with presents.* ○ *They loaded the plane with supplies for the refugees.* [T] **2** [I] to receive a load¹: *The ship is still loading.* **3** [I,T]

L

(*computing*) to put a program or disk into a computer, or to move onto another computer or disk: *The graphics may take a while to load.* **4** [T] to put a roll of film in a camera or a bullet in a gun

load·ed /'loʊdəd/ *adj.* **1** carrying a load, or filled with sth: *a loaded gun* **2** giving an unfair advantage: *That's a loaded question – I can't give you an accurate answer.*

IDM loaded with sth containing a lot of sth: *a cereal loaded with vitamins*

☆ **loaf** /loʊf/ *noun* [C] (*pl.* **loaves** /loʊvz/) bread shaped and baked in one piece: *a loaf of bread*

☆ **loan¹** /loʊn/ *noun* [C] money, etc. that sb/sth lends you: *to take out a bank loan ∘ to make a loan to sb ∘ to pay off a loan*

IDM on loan (from sb/sth) borrowed from sb/sth: *This painting is on loan from a museum in Italy.* ☞ Look also at **savings and loan.**

☆ **loan²** /loʊn/ *verb* [T] **loan sth (to sb)** to lend sth; to let sb borrow sth: *I loaned him $15 to buy gas. ∘ Can you loan me your pen for a minute?* ☞ picture at **borrow.**

loaves *pl.* of LOAF

☆ **lob·by¹** /'labi/ *noun* (*pl.* **lob·bies**) **1** [C] the area that is inside the entrance to a large building. A lobby often has a reception desk and doors, stairs, elevators, etc. that lead to other parts of the building: *a hotel lobby* **2** [C] a group of people who try to persuade the government to do or not to do sth: *the anti-abortion lobby*

☆ **lob·by²** /'labi/ *verb* [I,T] (*pres. part.* **lob·by·ing**; *3rd pers. sing. pres.* **lob·bies**; *p.t., p.p.* **lob·bied**) to try to persuade the government that sth should or should not be done: *A group of victims lobbied Congress to vote for tighter gun control.*

lob·by·ist /'labiist/ *noun* [C] a person who works for a lobby¹(2) : *environmental lobbyists*

lobe /loʊb/ *noun* [C] = EARLOBE

lob·ster /'labstər/ *noun* **1** [C] a large shellfish that has eight legs. A lobster is bluish-black, but it turns red when it is cooked. ☞ picture at **shellfish. 2** [U] a lobster (1) when it is cooked and eaten as food

☆ **lo·cal¹** /'loʊkl/ *adj.* of or in a particular place (near you): *local newspapers ∘ The local high school is the center of the community. ∘ a local phone call* —**lo·cal·ly** *adv.*: *These potatoes were grown locally.*

lo·cal² /'loʊkl/ *noun* [C, usually pl.] a person who lives in a particular place: *One of the locals showed us around the town.*

local anes'thetic *noun* [C,U] medicine that is put into one part of your body so that you do not feel pain there ☞ Look at **general anesthetic.**

lo·cal·ized /'loʊkl·aɪzd/ *adj.* (*formal*) limited to a particular place or area: *localized flooding*

local time *noun* [U] the time at a particular place in the world: *We arrive in Los Angeles at 2 o'clock in the afternoon, local time.*

lo·cate /'loʊkeɪt/ *verb* **1** [T] to find the exact position of sb/sth: *The missing ship has been located.* **2 be located** to be in a particular place: *The new mall is located to the west of the city.* **3** [I,T] to put or build sth, especially a business, in a particular place: *The bank is planning to locate its new headquarters in Springfield.* ☞ Look at **relocate.**

☆ **lo·ca·tion** /loʊ'keɪʃn/ *noun* **1** [C] a place or position: *Several locations have been suggested for the new stadium.* **2** [U] finding where sb/sth is: *The police investigation led to the location of the smuggled drugs.*

IDM on location (used about a movie, television program, etc.) made in a suitable place (= not in a studio): *The series was filmed on location in Baltimore.*

☆ **lock¹** /lak/ *noun* [C] **1** something that is used to fasten a door, lid, etc. so that you need a key or a group of numbers to open it again: *to turn the key in the lock ∘ a combination lock* (= a lock that you can only open using a particular set of numbers) ☞ picture at **key.** Look also at **padlock. 2** a part of a river or a canal where the level of water changes. Locks have gates at each end and are used to allow boats to move to a higher or lower part of the canal or river.

☆ **lock²** /lak/ *verb* **1** [I,T] to close or fasten with a lock: *Did you lock the car? ∘ The door won't lock.* ☞ Look at **unlock. 2** [T] to put sb/sth inside sth that is locked: *Lock your passport in a safe place.* **3** [I,T] to stick sth or be stuck in one position: *The wheels locked and the car crashed into the wall.*

PHRV lock sth away to keep sth in a safe or secret place (that is locked)

lock sb in/out to lock a door so that a person cannot get in/out: *All the prisoners are locked in for the night. ∘ to lock yourself out of your house*

lock (sth) up to lock all the doors, windows, etc. of a building: *Make sure that you lock up before you leave.*

lock sb up to put sb in prison

☆ **lock·er** /'lakər/ *noun* [C] a small cupboard or closet with a lock where personal things can be kept or left. Lockers are found in schools, sports centers, etc.

locker room *noun* [C] a room where people can change their clothes and leave them in lockers, especially before and after playing sports

lock·et /'lakət/ *noun* [C] a piece of jewelry that is worn around the neck on a chain. A locket is a small case that often contains a photograph.

lo·co·mo·tive /'loʊkəmoʊtɪv/ *noun* [C] = ENGINE(2)

lodge¹ /ladʒ/ *noun* [C] the main building at a

hotel in the country, where people stay especially to do sports or outdoor activities: *a ski lodge*

lodge² /lɑdʒ/ *verb* **1** [I,T] to become firmly attached or stuck, or to make sth do this: *The bullet lodged in her shoulder.* ☞ Look at **dislodge**. **2** [T] (*formal*) to make an official statement complaining about sth: *to lodge a complaint*

lodg·ing /'lɑdʒɪŋ/ *noun* [U] a place where you can stay, especially when you are on vacation: *The tour package includes all meals and lodging.*

loft /lɔft/ *noun* [C] **1** a raised platform over part of a room or building, that is used for storing things, for sleeping, etc. **2** a large apartment that does not have many walls inside it, usually in a bulding that was a factory, etc. in the past

☆ **log¹** /lɔg; lɑg/ *noun* [C] **1** the trunk or large branch of a tree that has been cut or has fallen down: *a log cabin* **2** a small piece of wood for a fire **3** (*also* **logbook**) an official written record of sth, written over a period of time: *to keep a log of visitors to a building*

log² /lɔg; lɑg/ *verb* [T] (**log·ging**; **logged**) to write sth in a log¹(3)

PHRV **log in/on** to start using a computer that is part of a larger system

log off/out to finish using a computer that is part of a larger system

log·ging /'lɔgɪŋ; 'lɑg-/ *noun* [U] the industry of cutting down trees to be used for buildings, paper, etc.

log·ic /'lɑdʒɪk/ *noun* [U] **1** the science of using reason **2** the use of reason or good sense: *There is no logic in your argument.*

☆ **log·i·cal** /'lɑdʒɪkl/ *adj.* **1** according to the rules of logic; reasonable: *As I see it, there is only one logical conclusion.* **2** able to use logic: *a logical mind* ☞ The opposite is **illogical**. —**log·i·cal·ly** /-kli/ *adv.*

lo·go /'loʊgoʊ/ *noun* [C] a symbol or design that is used as an advertisement by a company or organization. A logo appears on the things the company owns and produces.

lol·li·pop /'lɑlipɑp/ (*also* **sucker**) *noun* [C] a piece of hard candy on a stick

lone /loʊn/ *adj.* (only *before* a noun) without any other people; alone: *a lone swimmer*

☆ **lone·ly** /'loʊnli/ *adj.* (**lone·li·er**; **lone·li·est**) **1** unhappy because you are not with other people: *to feel sad and lonely* **2** (only *before* a noun) far from other people and places where people live: *a lonely house in the hills* ☞ Look at the note at **alone**. —**lone·li·ness** *noun* [U]

lon·er /'loʊnər/ *noun* [C] a person who likes to be alone or who has no friends

lone·some /'loʊnsəm/ *adj.* lonely or making you feel lonely ☞ Look at the note at **alone**.

☆ **long¹** /lɔŋ/ *adj.* (**long·er** /'lɔŋgər/, **long·est** /'lɔŋgəst/) **1** measuring a great amount in dis-

tance or time: *She has beautiful long hair.* ○ *We had to wait a long time.* ○ *a long dress* (= down to the floor) ☞ Look at **length**.

☞ **Long** is also used when you are asking for or giving information about how much something measures in length, distance or time: *How long is the movie?* ○ *The insect was only 2 millimeters long.* ○ *a five-mile-long traffic jam*

2 having or seeming to have a greater length than usual: *It was a long day at work today.* ○ *long, cold winter nights* ○ *We're going to spend a long weekend in New York* (= Saturday and Sunday, plus one or two more days).

IDM **go a long way** (used about money, food, etc.) to be used for buying a lot of things, feeding a lot of people, etc.: *to make a little money go a long way*

in the long run after a long time; in the end: *We ought to buy a new car – it'll be cheaper in the long run.*

the long haul (*informal*) the entire time of an event, a process, etc.: *I don't plan to quit this project – I'm in it for the long haul.*

in the long/short term ⇨ TERM¹

☆ **long²** /lɔŋ/ *noun* [U] a long time: *They won't be gone for long.* ○ *It shouldn't take long.*

☆ **long³** /lɔŋ/ *adv.* **1** for a long¹ time: *She didn't stay long.* ○ *You shouldn't have to wait long.* ○ *I hope we don't have to wait much longer.*

☞ **Long** and **a long time** are both used as expressions of time. In positive sentences **a long time** is usually used: *They stood there for a long time.* **Long** is only used in positive sentences with another adverb, e.g. "too," "enough," "ago," etc.: *We lived here long ago.* ○ *I've put up with this noise long enough.* ○ *I'm going to complain.* Both **long** and **a long time** can be used in questions: *Were you away long/a long time?* In negative sentences there is sometimes a difference in meaning between **long** and **a long time**: *I haven't been here long* (= I arrived only a short time ago). ○ *I haven't been here for a long time* (= it has been a long time since I was last here).

2 at a time that is distant from a particular point in time: *All that happened long ago.* ○ *We got married long before we moved here.* **3** for the whole of the time that is mentioned: *The baby cried all night long.*

IDM **as/so long as** on condition that: *As long as there are no problems, we should get the job done by Friday.*

no/not any longer not anymore: *They no longer live here.* ○ *They don't live here any longer.*

so long (*informal*) goodbye

long⁴ /lɔŋ/ *verb* [I] **long for sth**; **long (for sb) to do sth** (*formal*) to want sth very much: *He longed to hold her in his arms.*

'long-,distance *adj.* (only *before* a noun)

ər	ɪr	ɛr	ɑr	ɔr	ʊr	ʒ	h	ŋ
bird	near	hair	car	north	tour	vision	hat	sing

(used about travel or communication) between places that are far from each other: *a long-distance truck driver* —,**long** '**distance** *adv.*: *to call long distance*

long·ing /'lɔŋɪŋ/ *noun* [C,U] (*formal*) a great desire (for sb/sth) —**long·ing·ly** *adv.*: *She gazed longingly at the cakes in the bakery window.*

lon·gi·tude /'lɑndʒətud / *noun* [U] the distance of a place east or west of a line from the North Pole to the South Pole that passes through Greenwich, England. Longitude is measured in degrees. ☞ picture at **earth**. Look also at **latitude**.

long johns /'lɔŋ dʒɑnz/ *noun* [plural] (*informal*) = LONG UNDERWEAR

the '**long jump** *noun* [sing.] the sport in which people try to jump as far as possible ☞ Look at **high jump**.

long-lived /,lɔŋ 'lɪvd; -'laɪvd/ *adj.* living or lasting for a long time: *a long-lived dispute*

'**long-range** *adj.* (only *before* a noun) **1** of or for a long period of time starting from the present: *the long-range weather forecast* **2** that can go or be sent over long distances: *long-range nuclear missiles*

,**long-**'**standing** *adj.* that has lasted for a long time: *a long-standing arrangement*

'**long-term** *adj.* (usually *before* a noun) of or for a long period of time: *long-term planning*

'**long-time** (*also* **longtime**) *adj.* (only *before* a noun) having existed or done sth for a long period of time: *a long-time Seattle resident*

,**long** '**underwear** *noun* [U] (also *informal* **long johns**) [plural] a piece of warm underwear that covers your legs from your waist to your ankles

long-wind·ed /,lɔŋ'wɪndəd/ *adj.* (used about sth that is written or spoken) boring because it is too long

☆ **look**[1] /lʊk/ *verb* **1** [I,T] to turn your eyes in a particular direction (in order to pay attention to sb/sth): *Look carefully at these pictures.* ○ *She blushed and looked away.* ○ *to look out of the window* ○ *Look who's here!* ○ *Look where you are going!*

☞ You can **see** something without paying attention to it: *I saw a girl riding past on a horse.* If you **look** at something, you pay attention to it with your eyes: *Look carefully. Can you see anything strange?*

2 [I] **look (like sb/sth) (to sb)**; **look (to sb) as if.../as though.../like...** to seem or appear: *You look very nice in that shirt.* ○ *to look tired, sick, sad, well, happy, etc.* ○ *The boy looks like his father.* ○ *The room looks (to me) like it needs a coat of paint.* ○ *It looks like rain* (= as if it is going to rain). **3** [I] **look (for sb/sth)** to try to find (sb/sth): *We looked for you everywhere. Where were you?* ○ *"Did you find your watch?" "No, I'm still looking."* ○ *to look for work* **4** [I]

to face a particular direction: *Our hotel room looks out onto the beach.*

IDM **look good** to seem to be encouraging: *This year's sales figures are looking good.*

PHRV **look after sb/sth/yourself** to be responsible for or take care of sb/sth/yourself: *The old lady's son looked after all her financial affairs.*

look ahead to think about or plan for the future: *Looking ahead a few years, there's going to be a shortage of skilled workers.*

look around 1 to turn your head in order to see sb/sth **2** to look at many things (before buying sth): *She looked around but couldn't find anything she liked.*

look around sth to visit a place of interest, etc.: *to look around the museum*

look at sth 1 to examine sth (closely): *My tooth aches. I think a dentist should look at it.* **2** to think about or study sth: *Management is looking at ways of cutting costs.* **3** to read sth: *Could I look at the newspaper when you're finished with it?* **4** to consider sth: *People from different cultures look at life differently.*

look back (on sth) to think about sth in your past

look down on sb/sth to think that you are better than sb/sth: *Don't look down on them just because they aren't as successful as you.*

look forward to sth/doing sth to wait with pleasure for sth to happen (because you expect to enjoy it): *The kids are really looking forward to going on vacation.*

look into sth to study or investigate sth: *A committee was set up to look into the causes of the accident.*

look on to watch sth happening: *All we could do was look on as the house burned.*

look out to be careful or to pay attention to sth dangerous, etc.: *Look out! There's a bike coming.*

look through sth to read sth quickly

look to sb for sth; **look to sb to do sth** to expect sb to do or to provide sth: *He always looked to his father for advice.*

look up 1 to raise your eyes: *She looked up and smiled.* **2** (*informal*) to improve: *Business is looking up.*

look sth up to search for information in a book: *to look up a word in a dictionary*

look up to sb to respect or admire sb

☆ **look**[2] /lʊk/ *noun* **1** [C] the act of looking: *Take a look at this article.* ○ *I knew something was wrong – everybody was giving me funny looks* (= looking at me strangely). **2** [C, usually sing.] a search: *I had a good look, but I couldn't find it.* **3** [C] the expression or appearance of sb/sth: *He had a worried look on his face.* **4** [C] a fashion or style: *The store has a new look to appeal to younger customers.* **5 looks** [plural] a person's appearance: *He's lucky – he's got good looks and intelligence.*

L

tʃ	dʒ	v	θ	ð	s	z	ʃ
chin	June	van	thin	then	so	zoo	she

IDM **like the look/looks/sound of sb/sth** ⇨ LIKE¹

look³ /lʊk/ *interj.* (used for asking sb to listen to what you are saying, especially when you are annoyed): *Look, I don't want to explain this again – so pay attention!*

-look·ing /'lʊkɪŋ/ (used in compounds to form adjectives) having the type of appearance mentioned: *an odd-looking building* ○ *He's very good-looking.*

look·out /'lʊkaʊt/ *noun* [C] a person who watches out for danger

IDM **be on the lookout for sb/sth** to pay attention in order to see, find or be careful of sb/sth

loom¹ /lum/ *noun* [C] a machine that is used for making (**weaving**) cloth by passing pieces of thread across and under other pieces

loom² /lum/ *verb* [I] to appear as a shape that is not clear and in a way that seems frightening: *The mountain loomed in the distance.* ○ (*figurative*) *The threat of war loomed over the country.*

loon·y /'luni/ *noun* [C, adj. (pl. **loon·ies**) (slang) (a person who is) crazy

loop¹ /lup/ *noun* [C] a curved or circular shape, e.g. in a piece of rope or string

loop

loop² /lup/ *verb* [T] **1** to make sth into a loop **2** to fasten or connect sth with a loop

loop·hole /'luphoʊl/ *noun* [C] a way of avoiding sth because the words of a rule or law are badly chosen: *a loophole in the tax law*

☆ **loose** /lus/ *adj.* **1** not tied up or shut in sth: *The dog broke loose and ran away.* ○ *She wore her long hair loose.* **2** not firmly attached: *a loose tooth* **3** not contained in sth or connected together: *loose change* ○ *some loose sheets of paper* **4** not fitting closely; not tight: *These pants are way too loose around the waist.*

IDM **loose ends** small parts of a project, etc. that are not finished yet: *We just have a few loose ends to tie up on that report.* —**loose·ly** *adv.*

loos·en /'lusn/ *verb* [I,T] to become or make sth loose or looser: *to loosen your tie*

PHRV **loosen (sb/sth) up** to relax or make sb move more easily: *These exercises will help you to loosen up.*

loot¹ /lut/ *noun* [U] (*informal*) goods or money that have been stolen

loot² /lut/ *verb* [I,T] to steal things during a war or period of fighting: *Many stores were looted during yesterday's riots.* —**loot·er** /'lutər/ *noun* [C]

lop·sid·ed /'lɑp,saɪdəd/ *adj.* with one side lower or smaller, etc. than the other: *a lopsided smile*

lord /lɔrd/ *noun* **1 Lord** (*also* **the Lord**) [sing.] God; Christ **2** [C] (in some countries) a man who has been given the title "Lord," e.g. by a king or queen

IDM **(Good) Lord** (used for expressing surprise, worry, etc.)

the ˌLord's ˈPrayer *noun* [sing.] a very important Christian prayer that was first taught by Christ to his followers

lor·ry /'lɔri/ *noun* [C] (pl. **lor·ries**) (*BrE*) = TRUCK¹

☆ **lose** /luz/ *verb* (*p.t., p.p.* **lost** /lɑst; lɔst/) **1** [T] to be unable to find sth: *I lost my purse. I can't find it anywhere.* **2** [T] to no longer have sb/sth: *She lost a leg in the accident.* ○ *He lost his wife last year* (= she died). ○ *to lose your job* **3** [T] to have less of sth: *to lose weight, interest, patience, etc.* ○ *Downtown stores are losing business to the large malls.* **4** [I,T] not to win; to be defeated: *to lose a court case* ○ *Michigan lost to Ohio State in their last football game.* ○ *to lose an argument* **5** [T] to waste time, a chance, etc.: *Hurry up! There's no time to lose.* **6** [I,T] to become poorer (as a result of sth): *The company lost on the deal.* **7** [T] (used about a clock, watch, etc.) to go too slowly: *My watch loses two minutes a day.* ☞ The opposite is **gain**. **8** [T] (*informal*) to cause sb not to understand sth: *You totally lost me! Try to explain it again.*

IDM **keep/lose your balance** ⇨ BALANCE²

lose your bearings to become confused about where you are

keep/lose your cool ⇨ COOL²

keep/lose count ⇨ COUNT²

lose/save face ⇨ FACE¹

lose heart to believe that you will be unsuccessful

lose it (*informal*) to suddenly be unable to control your emotions because sth is very funny, shocking, etc.: *I just about lost it when that guy's pants fell down!*

lose your life to be killed

lose your marbles (*informal*) to go crazy

lose your place to be unable to find the place in a book, etc. where you stopped reading

lose sight of sb/sth 1 to no longer be able to see sb/sth **2** to forget sb/sth: *Don't lose sight of your original aim.*

keep/lose your temper ⇨ TEMPER

lose your touch to lose a special skill or ability to do sth

lose touch (with sb/sth) to no longer have contact (with sb/sth): *I've lost touch with a lot of my old friends from high school.*

keep/lose track of sb/sth ⇨ TRACK¹

a losing battle a competition, struggle, etc. in which it seems that you will be unsuccessful

PHRV **lose out (on sth)** (*informal*) to be at a disadvantage: *If a teacher pays too much attention to the bright students, the others lose out.*

☆ **los·er** /'luzər/ *noun* [C] **1** a person who is defeated: *He is a bad loser. He always gets upset if I beat him.* **2** (*slang*) a person who is not successful or popular: *What a total loser!*

☆ **loss** /lɔs/ *noun* **1** [U] no longer having sth or not having as much as before; the act of losing sth: *loss of blood, money, etc.* ○ *The loss (= death) of his wife was very sad for him.* ○ *The plane crashed with great loss of life.* **2** [C, usually pl.] people who are killed or things that are destroyed, usually in a war: *The government troops suffered heavy losses in the fighting.* **3** [C] a disadvantage: *If she leaves, it will be a big loss to the department.* **4** [C] the amount of money which is lost by a business: *The company announced a loss of $5 million.*
IDM **at a loss (for sth/to do sth)** not knowing what to do or say: *She was at a loss for words.* ○ *The police were at a loss to explain how the accident happened.*

lost¹ *p.t., p.p.* of LOSE

☆ **lost²** /lɔst/ *adj.* **1** (used about a person or an animal) unable to find the way: *This isn't the right road – we're completely lost!* ○ *Don't get lost!* **2** difficult or impossible to find; missing: *The kids were looking for their lost dog.* **3 lost (without)** not able to work in an efficient way or to live happily: *I'm lost without my watch!* ○ *He would be lost without his pets for company.* **4 lost on sb** not noticed or understood by sb: *The humor of the situation was completely lost on Joe and he got really upset.*
IDM **get lost** (*informal*) go away: *"Get lost!"* she shouted and walked off.
a lost cause an ambition or aim that cannot be achieved

☆ **lost and 'found** *noun* [sing.] a special office where things that people have lost or left in a public place are kept for the owners to collect

☆ **lot¹** /lɑt/ *pron.* **a lot; lots** (*informal*) a large amount or number: *"How many people are coming to the party?" "I'm not sure, but a lot!"* ○ *Have another piece of cake. There's lots left.*
IDM **a lot of sb/sth; lots of sb/sth** a large amount or number of (sb/sth): *There's been a lot of rain this year.* ○ *We ate lots of cake at the birthday party.*

☆ **lot²** /lɑt/ *adv.* (*informal*) **1 a lot; lots** (before adjectives and adverbs in the comparative form) very much: *It's a lot faster now that there's a freeway.* ○ *He plays tennis lots better than his brother does.* **2 a lot** very much or often: *Thanks a lot – that's very nice of you.* ○ *It generally rains a lot at this time of year.*

☆ **lot³** /lɑt/ *noun* **1** [C] an area of land used for a particular purpose: *a parking lot* ○ *We're going to build a house on this lot.* **2** [sing.] the quality or state of a person's life; your fate: *Women's lot in life has not always been easy.* **3** [C] a group of objects that were produced at the same time: *The defective packages all had the same lot number on their labels.* **4** [C] an object or group of objects that are for sale at an auction (= a sale at which the object goes to the person who offers the highest price): *Lot 27: 6 chairs*

☆ **lo·tion** /'louʃn/ *noun* [C,U] liquid or cream that you use on your skin: *suntan lotion*

☆ **lot·ter·y** /'lɑtəri/ *noun* [C] (*pl.* **lot·ter·ies**) a way of raising money by selling tickets with numbers on them and giving prizes to the people who have bought certain numbers which are chosen by chance

☆ **loud¹** /laʊd/ *adj.* **1** making a lot of noise; not quiet: *He has a very loud laugh.* ○ *Can you turn the TV down? It's too loud.*

☞ **Loud** is usually used to describe the sound itself or the thing producing the sound: *a loud noise, a loud bang, loud music.* **Noisy** is used to describe a person, an animal, a place, an event, etc. that is very or too loud: *a noisy street, party, etc./noisy neighbors, children, etc.*

2 (used about clothes, colors, behavior, etc.) too bright or noticeable: *Isn't that shirt a little loud for a formal dinner?* —**loud·ly** *adv.* —**loud·ness** *noun* [U]

☆ **loud²** /laʊd/ *adv.* making a lot of noise: *Could you speak a little louder? The people at the back can't hear.*
IDM **out 'loud** ⇨ OUT¹

loud·speak·er /'laʊd,spikər/ *noun* [C] **1** an apparatus for making sounds, voices, etc. louder: *The winner of the competition was announced over the loudspeaker.* **2** = SPEAKER(2)

☆ **lounge¹** /laʊndʒ/ *noun* [C] **1** a room in a hotel, office building, etc. where you can sit comfortably: *Let's go and have coffee in the lounge.* **2** a room at an airport where passengers wait: *the departure lounge*

lounge² /laʊndʒ/ *verb* [I] **lounge (around)** to sit or stand in a lazy way; to relax: *We spent the afternoon lounging in the sun.*

louse /laʊs/ *noun* [C] (*pl.* **lice** /laɪs/) a small insect that lives on the bodies of animals and people

lous·y /'laʊzi/ *adj.* (**lous·i·er; lous·i·est**) (*informal*) very bad: *We had lousy weather on vacation.* ○ *You'll feel lousy tomorrow if you drink too much.*

lov·a·ble /'lʌvəbl/ *adj.* easy to love because attractive and pleasant

☆ **love¹** /lʌv/ *noun* **1** [U] a very strong feeling of affection for sb/sth: *It was love at first sight.* ○ *I don't think she's marrying him for love!* ○ *his love for his country* ☞ The opposite is **hate** or **hatred**. **2** [U, sing.] a strong feeling of interest in or enjoyment of sth: *a love of adventure* **3** [C] a thing in which you are very interested: *Computers are the love of his life these days.* **4** [C] a person who is loved: *Of course, my love.* **5** [U] (used in tennis) a score of zero: *"15-love," called the umpire.* **6** [U] (*informal*) (a way of ending a letter to a friend or a member of your family): *Lots of love from us all, Denise.*

IDM **be in love (with sb)** to have a strong feeling of affection and sexual attraction (for sb): *They're very much in love (with each other).*

fall in love (with sb) to start to feel a strong affection and attraction for sb: *They fell in love and were married within two months.*

make love (to sb) to have sex

☆ **love²** /lʌv/ *verb* [T] **1** to have a strong feeling of affection for sb/sth: *"Do you love him?" "Yes, very much."* ○ *It's wonderful to be loved.* **2** to like very much or to enjoy: *I love summertime!* ○ *My father loves to listen/listening to music.* ○ *"Would you like to come?" "I'd love to."* ○ *The cat just loves it when you pet her right here.*

'**love af·fair** *noun* [C] a (usually sexual) relationship between two people who love each other but are not married

☆ **love·ly** /'lʌvli/ *adj.* (**love·li·er**; **love·li·est**) **1** beautiful or attractive: *a lovely room* ○ *You look lovely with your hair short.* **2** very nice, enjoyable or pleasant: *What a lovely day!* ○ *It's lovely to see you again.* —**love·li·ness** *noun* [U]

☆ **lov·er** /'lʌvər/ *noun* [C] **1** a person who is having a sexual relationship outside marriage ☞ Look at **mistress**. **2 lovers** [plural] (*old-fashioned*) two people who are in love or are having a sexual relationship without being married: *In the evening the park was full of young lovers walking hand in hand.* **3** a person who likes or enjoys the thing mentioned: *a music lover* ○ *an animal lover*

'**love story** *noun* [C] (*pl.* **love stories**) a story or novel that is mainly about love

lov·ing /'lʌvɪŋ/ *adj.* feeling or showing love or care —**lov·ing·ly** *adv.*

☆ **low¹** /loʊ/ *adj.* **1** not high: *The dog will be able to jump over that fence – it's way too low.* **2** close to the ground or to the bottom of sth: *Hang that picture a little higher – it's still too low!* **3** below the usual or normal level or amount: *Temperatures were very low last winter.* ○ *The price of fruit is lower in the summer.* ○ *low wages* **4** below what is normal in quality, importance or development: *a low standard of living* ○ *low status* **5** (used about a sound or voice) deep or soft and quiet: *I need some practice in order to sing those low notes.* ○ *She spoke in a low voice so her boss couldn't hear her.* **6** not cheerful or bright: *He's been feeling awfully low since his wife died.*

IDM **keep a low profile** to act in a way that does not attract attention from other people

☆ **low²** /loʊ/ *adv.* **1** in or to a low position, level, etc.; near the ground or bottom; not high: *The helicopter flew low over the buildings.* ○ *"Where is the pain? Here?" "A little lower down," she replied.* **2** (in music) with deep notes: *Jim can sing a lot lower than I can.*

IDM **high and low** ⇨ HIGH²

run low (used about supplies, etc.) to be or

become almost finished: *Food and medical supplies were running low.*

run low on sth to have used almost all of sth: *We're running low on milk – could you buy some more today?*

low³ /loʊ/ *noun* [C] a low point, level, figure, etc.: *The peso has fallen to a new low against the dollar.*

'**low-down** *adj.* (*informal*) (used about behavior, etc.) not respectable or honest: *a low-down trick*

☆ **low·er¹** /'loʊər/ *adj.* at the bottom of sth; being the bottom part of sth: *She bit her lower lip.* ○ *in the lower left-hand corner of the page* ☞ The opposite is **upper**.

☆ **low·er²** /'loʊər/ *verb* [T] **1** to move sb/sth down: *They lowered the boat into the water.* **2** to make sth less in amount or quality: *The virus lowers resistance to other diseases.* ☞ The opposite for 1 and 2 is **raise**.

low·er·case /,loʊər'keɪs/ *adj., noun* [U] (in) small letters, not capitals: *A lowercase R looks like this: r.* ☞ The opposite is **uppercase**.

,**lower-'class** *adj.* belonging to a low social and economic class ☞ Look at **middle-class**, **upper-class** and **working-class**.

,**low-'key** *adj.* (used about the style of sth) quiet, without a lot of preparation or fuss: *The wedding will be very low-key. We're only inviting ten people.*

,**low-'lying** *adj.* (used about land) near to sea level; not high

,**low-'paid** *adj.* not paying or earning much money: *low-paid workers*

,**low 'tide** *noun* [U] the time when the ocean is at its lowest level: *At low tide, you can walk out to the island.* ☞ The opposite is **high tide**.

☆ **loy·al** /'lɔɪəl/ *adj.* (used about a person) not changing in your friendship or beliefs; faithful: *a loyal friend* ○ *Will you remain loyal to the Republicans in the next election?* ☞ The opposite is **disloyal**. —**loy·al·ly** *adv.*

☆ **loy·al·ty** /'lɔɪəlti/ *noun* (*pl.* **loy·al·ties**) **1** [U] the quality of being loyal: *a dog's loyalty to its owner* **2** [C, usually pl.] a feeling of friendship that makes you faithful toward sth/sb: *I know where my loyalties lie.*

loz·enge /'lɑzndʒ/ *noun* [C] a candy that you suck if you have a cough or sore throat

lu·bri·cant /'lubrɪkənt/ *noun* [C,U] a substance like oil used for making a machine, etc. work smoothly

lu·bri·cate /'lubrɪkeɪt/ *verb* [T] to put oil, etc. onto or into sth so that it works smoothly —**lu·bri·ca·tion** /,lubrɪ'keɪʃn/ *noun* [U]

lu·cid /'lusəd/ *adj.* (*formal*) **1** (used about sth that is said or written) clear and easy to understand **2** (used about a person's mind) not confused; clear and normal —**lu·cid·ly** *adv.* —**lucidity** /lu'sɪdəti/ *noun* [U]

☆ **luck** /lʌk/ *noun* [U] **1** the fact of something happening by chance: *There's no skill in this*

game – it's all luck. ○ to have good, bad, etc. luck **2** success or good things that happen by chance: We'd like to wish you lots of luck in your new career.

IDM **be in luck/out of luck** to be lucky/unlucky: I was in luck – the store had the book I wanted.

good luck (to sb) (used to wish that sb is successful): Good luck! I'm sure you'll get the job.

tough (luck)! ⇨ TOUGH

☆ **luck·i·ly** /ˈlʌkəli/ adv. fortunately: Luckily, I remembered to bring my umbrella.

☆ **luck·y** /ˈlʌki/ adj. (luck·i·er; luck·i·est) **1** (used about a person) having good luck: We were very lucky with the weather on vacation (= it was nice). ○ I'm very lucky to have such good friends. **2** (used about a situation, an event, etc.) having a good result: It's lucky you reminded me (= or I would have forgotten). ○ a lucky escape **3** (used about a thing) bringing success or good luck: a lucky number ○ It was not my lucky day. ☞ The opposite for all senses is **unlucky**.

lu·cra·tive /ˈlukrətɪv/ adj. (formal) producing a lot of money

lu·di·crous /ˈludɪkrəs/ adj. very silly; ridiculous: What a ludicrous idea! —**lu·di·crous·ly** adv.

lug /lʌɡ/ verb [T] (**lug·ging; lugged**) (informal) to carry or pull sth with great difficulty

duffle bag luggage

briefcase suitcase

trunk backpack

☆ **lug·gage** /ˈlʌɡɪdʒ/ noun [U] bags, suitcases, etc. used for carrying a person's things on a trip: We can fit one more piece of luggage in the trunk!

luggage rack noun [C] a structure that you fasten to the roof of a car and use for carrying luggage or other large objects

luke·warm /ˌlukˈwɔrm/ adj. **1** (used about liquids) only slightly warm **2 lukewarm (about sb/sth)** not showing much interest; not eager: John's fairly lukewarm about going to Iowa on vacation.

lull¹ /lʌl/ verb [T] **1** to make sb/sth quiet or sleepy: She sang a song to lull the children to sleep. **2** to make sb/sth feel safe, especially by deceiving them: Our first success lulled us into a false sense of security.

lull² /lʌl/ noun [C, usually sing.] a short period of quiet; a pause in activity: When she entered the room, there was a lull in the conversation.

lull·a·by /ˈlʌləbaɪ/ noun [C] (pl. **lull·a·bies**) a gentle song that you sing to help a child to go to sleep

☆ **lum·ber¹** /ˈlʌmbər/ noun [U] wood that is going to be used for building

lum·ber² /ˈlʌmbər/ verb [I] to move in a slow, heavy way: He heaved himself out of bed and lumbered into the bathroom.

lum·ber·jack /ˈlʌmbərdʒæk/ noun [C] a person whose job is to cut down trees

lum·ber·yard /ˈlʌmbəryard/ noun [C] a store that sells wood, etc. for building. The wood is usually kept outdoors or under a roof.

lu·mi·nous /ˈlumənəs/ adj. shining, especially in the dark: a watch with luminous hands

☆ **lump¹** /lʌmp/ noun [C] **1** a piece of sth solid of any size or shape: a lump of coal ○ The sauce was full of lumps. **2** a hard swelling on or in the body: You'll have a little lump on your head where you hit it.

lump² /lʌmp/ verb [T] **lump sb/sth together; lump sb/sth into sth** to put people or things together; to consider or treat them as being all alike: Don't just lump everybody into one category.

lump ˈsum noun [C] an amount of money that is paid all at once, rather than in several smaller amounts

lump·y /ˈlʌmpi/ adj. (**lump·i·er; lump·i·est**) full of or covered with lumps

lu·na·cy /ˈlunəsi/ noun [U] very foolish behavior: It was lunacy to swim so far from the shore.

lu·nar /ˈlunər/ adj. connected with the moon: lunar dust ○ a lunar spacecraft

lu·na·tic /ˈlunətɪk/ noun [C] **1** (informal) a person who behaves in a crazy or dangerous way **2** (old-fashioned) a person who is crazy ☞ Look at the note at **crazy**.

☆ **lunch¹** /lʌntʃ/ noun [C,U] a meal that you have in the middle of the day: What would you like for lunch?

☞ You might take a **bag lunch** or a **picnic lunch** if you're out for the day. If you're working, you might have a **business lunch** (= working at the same time as having lunch). Look at the note at **dinner**.

lunch² /lʌntʃ/ verb [I] (formal) to eat lunch: We will lunch with the ambassador next week.

lunch·box /ˈlʌntʃbaks/ noun [C] a metal or plastic box with a handle that you use to carry your lunch to school or to work

lunch·eon /ˈlʌntʃən/ noun [C] a formal meal eaten in the middle of the day: The Ladies'

Association will hold its annual luncheon next Wednesday.

☆ **lunch·time** /ˈlʌntʃtaɪm/ noun [C,U] the time around the middle of the day when lunch is eaten: I'll meet you at lunchtime.

☆ **lung** /lʌŋ/ noun [C] one of the two parts of the body that are inside your chest and are used for breathing: lung cancer

lunge /lʌndʒ/ noun [C, usually sing.] a sudden forward movement of the body, especially when trying to attack sb —**lunge** verb [I]: The man lunged toward me with a knife in his hand.

lurch¹ /lərtʃ/ noun [C] a sudden movement: a sudden lurch forward

IDM **leave sb in the lurch** ⇨ LEAVE¹

lurch² /lərtʃ/ verb [I] to move suddenly, especially when out of control: The truck lurched forward and hit a tree.

lure¹ /lʊr/ noun [C] **1** a thing that is used to attract people or animals: a fishing lure **2** the power of attracting sb: the lure of money, fame, adventure, etc.

lure² /lʊr/ verb [T] to attract or tempt sb/sth: It's such a nice day – can I lure you away from your work?

lu·rid /ˈlʊrəd/ adj. **1** shocking, especially because violent or unpleasant: The newspaper was criticized for its lurid description of the murder. **2** having colors that are very or too bright: a lurid dress in purple and orange —**lurid·ly** adv.

lurk /lərk/ verb [I] to wait where you cannot be seen, especially when intending to do sth bad: I thought I saw somebody lurking among the trees.

lush¹ /lʌʃ/ adj. (used about plants) growing very thickly and well

lush² /lʌʃ/ noun [C] (informal) a person who often gets drunk

lust¹ /lʌst/ noun **1** [U] strong sexual desire **2** [C,U] (a) very strong desire to possess or get sth: a lust for power

lust² /lʌst/ verb [I] **lust after/for sb/sth** to have a very strong desire for sb/sth: to lust for power, success, fame, etc.

Lu·ther·an /ˈluθərən/ noun [C], adj. (a member) of a Protestant church that is based on the ideas of Martin Luther

lux·u·ri·ous /lʌgˈʒʊriəs/ adj. very comfortable; full of luxury: a luxurious seaside hotel —**lux·u·ri·ous·ly** adv.

☆ **lux·u·ry** /ˈlʌkʃəri; ˈlʌgʒəri/ noun (pl. **lux·u·ries**) **1** [U] great comfort and pleasure, often including the use and enjoyment of expensive and beautiful things: Somebody said she was living in luxury in Barbados. ○ to lead a life of luxury ○ a luxury hotel, car, yacht, etc. **2** [C] something that is enjoyable and expensive that you do not really need: A vacation is a luxury we just can't afford this year. **3** [U, sing.] a pleasure which you do not often have: It was a real luxury to do nothing all weekend.

lynch /lɪntʃ/ verb [T] (used about a crowd of people) to kill sb (usually by hanging) who is thought to be guilty of a crime, without a legal trial

lyr·ic /ˈlɪrɪk/ adj. (used about poetry) expressing personal feelings

lyr·i·cal /ˈlɪrɪkl/ adj. like a song or a poem, expressing strong personal feelings

lyr·ics /ˈlɪrɪks/ noun [plural] the words of a song: Who wrote the lyrics?

Mm

M, m /ɛm/ noun [C] (pl. **M's; m's**) the thirteenth letter of the English alphabet: "Montana" begins with (an) "M."

M (also **med.**) abbr. medium (size)

m abbr. = METER¹(1)

M.A. abbr. Master of Arts ☞ Look at **master's degree.**

ma'am /mæm/ noun [sing.] (used when speaking to a woman, as a short form for "madam")

ma·ca·bre /məˈkɑbrə/ adj. horrible and frightening because connected with death

ma·ca·ro·ni /ˌmækəˈroʊni/ noun [U] a type of Italian food made from dried flour and water (**pasta**) in the shape of curved hollow tubes

ma·chet·e /məˈʃɛt̬i/ noun [C] a large knife with a heavy curved blade, used as a weapon and for cutting down plants

☆ **ma·chine** /məˈʃin/ noun [C] **1** (often in compounds) a piece of equipment with several moving parts, made to perform a particular task: a washing machine ○ Can you operate/work this machine? ○ One of the machines broke down. ☞ Look at the note at **tool.** **2** a system or organization carefully controlled and organized by a group of people: It's hard to understand the workings of the party machine (= a political party).

ma·chine gun noun [C] a gun that fires bullets very quickly and continuously

i	ɪ	ɛ	æ	ɑ	ɔ	ʌ	ʊ	u
see	sit	ten	cat	hot	saw	cup	put	too

☆ **ma·chin·er·y** /məˈʃinəri/ *noun* [U] machines in general or the moving parts of a machine: *farm machinery* ○ *the delicate machinery of a watch*

ma·cho /ˈmɑtʃoʊ/ *adj.* (*informal*) (used about a man or his behavior) very masculine in an aggressive way

mac·ro /ˈmækroʊ/ *noun* [C] (*pl.* **mac·ros**) an instruction that can tell a computer to perform a series of tasks

☆ **mad** /mæd/ *adj.* (**mad·der**; **mad·dest**) **1 mad (at sb)** very angry: *His laziness really makes me mad!* ○ *Don't get mad at him. He didn't mean to do it.* **2** not controlled; wild or very excited: *We're always in a mad rush to get ready in the morning.* ○ *The audience was cheering and clapping like mad* (= very hard). **3 mad about sb/sth** (*informal*) extremely interested in sb/sth: *He's mad about basketball.* ○ *Steve's mad about Jane* (= he likes her very much). **4** with a sick mind; crazy: *a mad scientist*

Mad·am /ˈmædəm/ *noun* [sing.] **1** used for beginning a formal letter to a woman when you do not know her name: *Dear Madam, I am writing in reply…* **2** (*formal*) a polite way of speaking to a woman, especially to a leader of an organization or a politician: *Good morning, Madam President.* ☞ Look at **ma'am** and **sir**.

mad·den /ˈmædn/ *verb* [T] to make sb very angry or annoyed —**mad·den·ing** /ˈmædn·ɪŋ/ *adj.*: *She has some really maddening habits.* —**mad·den·ing·ly** *adv.*

made¹ *p.t., p.p.* of MAKE¹

☆ **made²** /meɪd/ *adj.*

IDM **be made of sth** to have been built from sth, or to consist of sth (a particular material, etc.): *The desk is made of solid wood.*

be made for sb/sth/each other to be very suitable for sb/sth/each other: *Jim and Alice are just made for each other.*

have (got) it made (*informal*) (often used about sb whom you envy) to have an easy life with everything you need or want: *Bob has a new sports car, and he just won a trip to Hawaii – he's got it made!*

mad·ly /ˈmædli/ *adv.* **1** extremely: *They're madly in love.* **2** in a wild or crazy way: *She rushed around madly looking for her keys.*

mad·man /ˈmædmæn; -mən/ *noun* [C] (*pl.* **mad·men**) a person who is mad(4) or who behaves in a crazy, dangerous way: *He was running around like a madman!*

mad·ness /ˈmædnəs/ *noun* [U] **1** the state of being mad(4) **2** a situation that is wild or not controlled: *It was sheer madness at the mall today – there were crowds everywhere.* **3** crazy, dangerous behavior: *It would be madness to take a boat out in such stormy weather.*

ma·fi·a /ˈmɑfiə/ usually **the Mafia** *noun* [sing.] a secret criminal organization that influences some business activities

☆ **mag·a·zine** /ˈmægəzin; ˌmægəˈzin/ *noun* [C] a type of book with a paper cover which is published every week or month and contains articles, advertisements, photographs and stories by various writers: *a women's, computer, fashion, etc. magazine* ○ *a magazine article*

mag·got /ˈmægət/ *noun* [C] an insect that looks like a small worm. Maggots grow from the eggs of flies, which have been laid in meat, cheese, etc.

☆ **mag·ic¹** /ˈmædʒɪk/ *noun* [U] **1** (in stories) a power that can make extraordinary or impossible things happen: *The witch had used her magic to turn the children into frogs.* ☞ Look at **black magic**. **2** the art of performing tricks to entertain people **3** a special or fascinating quality, or sth that has this quality: *I'll never forget the magic of that moment.* ○ *The whole trip was magic from beginning to end.*

mag·ic² /ˈmædʒɪk/ *adj.* **1** used in or using magic¹: *a magic spell* **2** wonderful; excellent: *The way she sings is absolutely magic.*

mag·i·cal /ˈmædʒɪkl/ *adj.* **1** that seems to use magic or to produce it: *a magical box that makes things disappear* **2** mysterious and exciting: *Santa Claus has a magical fascination for many children.* —**mag·i·cal·ly** /ˈmædʒɪkli/ *adv.*

ma·gi·cian /məˈdʒɪʃn/ *noun* [C] **1** a person who performs magic tricks to entertain people **2** (in stories) a man who has magic power ☞ Look at **wizard**.

mag·is·trate /ˈmædʒəstreɪt; -strət/ *noun* [C] a judge in the lowest rank of court that deals especially with less serious crimes

mag·ne·si·um /mægˈniziəm/ *noun* (*symbol* **Mg**) a silver-colored metal that burns with a bright white light

mag·net /ˈmægnət/ *noun* [C] a piece of iron that can attract and pick up iron and steel

magnet

magnet

mag·net·ic /mægˈnɛtɪk/ *adj.* **1** having the ability of a magnet to attract iron and steel: *Is this metal magnetic?* ○ *a magnetic field* (= an area around a magnet where there is a magnetic force) **2** having a quality that strongly attracts people: *a magnetic personality*

mag·netic ˈtape *noun* [C,U] plastic tape covered with a magnetic substance and used for recording computer data

mag·net·ism /ˈmægnətɪzəm/ *noun* [U] **1** the power of magnets to attract **2** strong personal attraction: *His personal magnetism made him a powerful and dangerous political figure.*

mag·net·ize /ˈmægnətaɪz/ *verb* [T] to make sth become magnetic: *a magnetized identification card*

mag·nif·i·cent /mægˈnɪfəsənt/ *adj.* extremely good or beautiful: *What a magnificent castle!*

M

—**mag·nif·i·cent·ly** *adv.* —**mag·nif·i·cence** /-səns/ *noun* [U]

magnifying glass

magnify

mag·ni·fy /'mægnəfaɪ/ *verb* [T] (*pres. part.* **mag·ni·fy·ing**; *3rd pers. sing. pres.* **mag·ni·fies**; *p.t., p.p.* **mag·ni·fied**) **1** to make sth look bigger than it is: *to magnify sth under a microscope* **2** to make sth seem more important than it really is: *to magnify a problem* —**mag·ni·fi·ca·tion** /,mægnəfə'keɪʃn/ *noun* [U]

magnifying glass *noun* [C] a lens that is held in your hand, and used for making things look bigger than they are

mag·ni·tude /'mægnətud/ *noun* [U] the great size or importance of sth: *the magnitude of the problem*

mag·no·lia /mæg'noʊlyə/ *noun* [C] a tree that has large, sweet-smelling, usually pink or white flowers. The flowers are also called magnolias.

ma·hog·a·ny /mə'hɑgəni/ *noun* [U] hard reddish-brown wood (from a tropical tree) that is used for making expensive furniture

maid /meɪd/ *noun* [C] a woman whose job is to clean, etc. in a hotel or in sb else's house: *a luxury apartment with maid service*

maid·en name /,meɪdn 'neɪm/ *noun* [C] the family name that a woman had before she got married

maid·en voyage /,meɪdn 'vɔɪdʒ/ *noun* [C] the first trip made by a new ship or spacecraft

maid of hon·or *noun* [C] (*pl.* **maids of honor**) in a wedding ceremony, the woman who helps the bride (usually her best friend or else a close family member) ☞ Look at the note at **wedding**.

☆ **mail¹** /meɪl/ *noun* [U] **1** the system for collecting and delivering letters and packages: *to send a package by airmail/first-class mail* ○ *The check is in the mail.* **2** letters, packages, etc. that are collected or delivered: *Is there any mail for me?* ○ *to open the mail* ○ *junk mail* (= letters, usually advertising sth, that are sent to people although they have not asked for them)

☆ **mail²** /meɪl/ *verb* [T] to send a letter, package, etc. to sb by putting it in a mailbox or taking it to a post office: *to mail a letter* ○ *I'll mail it to you tomorrow.* ○ *I'll mail you a copy of my report.*

PHRV **mail sth in** to send sth by mail to a place where it will be officially dealt with: *Don't forget to mail in your entry form for the contest!*

mail sth out to send sth by mail, usually from

a central place to various other places: *We've mailed out 10,000 copies of our new catalog to our customers.*

mailboxes

☆ **mail·box** /'meɪlbɑks/ *noun* [C] **1** a private box outside a house or building or a hole in a door which letters can be put into when they are delivered **2** a container in a public place where you put letters, etc. that you want to send

mailing list *noun* [C] a list of the names and addresses of people to whom advertising material or information is sent

☆ **mail·man** /'meɪlmæn; -mən/ *noun* [C] (*pl.* **mail·men**) a man whose job is to collect and deliver letters, packages, etc. ☞ Look at **letter carrier**.

mail order *noun* [U] a method of shopping. You choose what you want from a special book (**a catalog**) and the products are then sent to you by mail.

maim /meɪm/ *verb* [T] to hurt sb so badly that part of the body can no longer be used

☆ **main¹** /meɪn/ *adj.* (only *before* a noun) most important; chief: *My main reason for wanting to learn English is to get a better job.* ○ *the main road into town* ○ *the main course (of a meal)* ○ *He doesn't earn very much, but he's happy. That's the main thing.*

main² /meɪn/ *noun* [C] a large pipe that carries water or natural gas to a building or that takes waste water away from it: *The water main burst.* ○ *There's a crack in the sewer main.*

main drag *noun* [sing.] (*informal*) the main street of a city or town: *restaurants on Springfield's main drag*

main·land /'meɪnlænd; -lənd/ *noun* [sing.] the main part of a country or continent, not including the islands around it: *Taiwan and mainland China* ○ *the ferry between the island and the mainland*

☆ **main·ly** /'meɪnli/ *adv.* mostly: *The students here are mainly from Japan.*

main·stay /'meɪnsteɪ/ *noun* [C] (*figurative*) a thing or person that helps sb/sth to work well or to continue: *Rice production is the mainstay of the country's economy.*

ər	ɪr	ɛr	ɑr	ɔr	ʊr	ʒ	h	ŋ
bird	near	hair	car	north	tour	vision	hat	sing

main·stream /'meinstrim/ *noun* [sing.] the way that most people think or behave: *The Green Party is not in the mainstream of American politics.* —**main·stream** *adj.*: *That politician is completely out of touch with mainstream views.*

☆ **main·tain** /mein'tem/ *verb* [T] **1** to continue to have sth; to keep sth at the same level or standard: *We need to maintain the quality of our goods but not increase the price.* ○ *to maintain law and order* **2** to support sb/sth by paying for the things he/she/it needs: *She works hard to maintain her family.* ○ *Our company also maintains an office in Moscow.* **3** to keep sth in good condition: *to maintain a road, building, machine, etc.* **4** to say that sth is true: *In the Middle Ages, people maintained that the sun went around the Earth.* ○ *The defendant maintained his innocence* (= that he was innocent) *during the trial.*

☆ **main·te·nance** /'meintn·əns/ *noun* [U] keeping sth in good condition: *This house needs a lot of maintenance.* ○ *car maintenance*

'**maintenance man** *noun* [C] (*pl.* **maintenance men**) a man whose job is to repair and maintain buildings, machines, etc.

maize /meiz/ *noun* [U] (*BrE*) = CORN(1)

ma·jes·tic /mə'dʒestik/ *adj.* making a strong impression because it is dignified or beautiful: *a majestic mountain landscape* —**ma·jes·ti·cal·ly** /-kli/ *adv.*

maj·es·ty /'mædʒəsti/ *noun* (*pl.* **maj·es·ties**) **1** [U] the quality of being grand or dignified like a king or queen: *the splendor and majesty of the Grand Canyon* **2 Majesty** [C] (used when speaking to or about a royal person): *Her Majesty Queen Elizabeth II*

☆ **ma·jor¹** /'meidʒər/ *adj.* (only *before* a noun) great in size, importance, seriousness, etc.: *The patient needs major heart surgery.* ○ *a major road* ○ *There haven't been any major problems.* ☞ The opposite is **minor**.

☆ **ma·jor²** /'meidʒər/ *noun* **1** the main subject that you study at a college or university: *Her major is chemistry.* **2** a person who studies sth as his/her main subject at a college or university: *She's a chemistry major.* **3** an officer of middle rank in the army

☆ **major³** /'meidʒər/ *verb*

PHRV **major in sth** to study sth as your main subject at a college or university: *She's majoring in chemistry.* ☞ Look at **minor³**.

☆ **ma·jor·i·ty** /mə'dʒɔrəti; -'dʒɑr-/ *noun* (*pl.* **major·i·ties**) **1** [sing.] more than half of sth: *The majority of students in the class come from Japan.*

☞ **Majority** can be used in the singular with either a singular or a plural verb. If we are thinking of the members of the group individually, we use a plural verb: *The majority has the power to create new laws.* ○ *A majority*

of the residents are in favor of building the new road. Look also at **minority**.

2 [C] **majority (over sb)** the difference in the number of votes in an election between the person/party who came first and the person/party who came second: *He was elected by a majority of only 50 votes.*

IDM **be in the/a majority** to form more than half of sth: *Will the Republicans still be in the majority in Congress after the next election?*

ma·jor·ly /'meidʒərli/ *adv.* (*slang*) very; extremely: *We were, like, majorly disappointed when we found out.*

☆ **make¹** /meik/ *verb* [T] (*p.t., p.p.* **made** /meid/) **1** to produce sth or to cause sth to appear: *I'll make some coffee.* ○ *They make VW cars in Wolfsburg.* ○ *made in Japan* (= on a label) ○ *What's that shirt made of?* (= what material) ○ *The blood made a stain on the carpet.* **2** (used with nouns) to perform a certain action: *to make a mistake, a noise, a statement, a suggestion, etc.* ○ *to make progress*

☞ Often there is a verb with a similar form, e.g. **decide/make a decision**. If you use "make" + noun, you can use an adjective with it: *He made the right decision.* ○ *They made a generous offer.*

3 to cause a particular action, feeling or situation: *The movie made me cry.* ○ *That dress makes you look thin.* ○ *Flying makes him nervous.* **4** to force sb/sth to do sth: *They made him wait at the police station all day.*

☞ In the passive we must use **to**: *He was made to wait at the police station.*

5 (used with *clear, certain, plain* and *sure*): *She made it clear that she didn't agree.* ○ *Make sure you lock the car.* ○ *I made certain I had enough money.* **6** (used with money and numbers): *He makes* (= earns) *$40,000 a year.* ○ *to make a lot of money* ○ *5 and 7 make 12.* **7** to have the right qualities to be sth; to make sth perfect: *She'll make a good teacher.* ○ *The beautiful weather really made our trip.* **8** to give sb a job or elect sb to a position: *She was made assistant manager.* **9** to reach a place; to be able to go somewhere: *We should make Seattle by about 10.* ○ *I'm afraid I can't make the meeting next week.*

IDM **make do with sth** to use sth that is not good enough because nothing better is available: *If we can't get limes, we'll have to make do with lemons.*

make it 1 to get to a place (in time); to go to a place you have been invited to: *The train leaves in five minutes. We'll never make it!* ○ *I'm afraid I can't make it to your party.* **2** to be successful: *She'll never make it as an actress.*

make the most of sth to get as much pleasure, profit, etc. as possible from sth: *You won't*

M

tʃ	dʒ	v	θ	ð	s	z	ʃ
chin	June	van	thin	then	so	zoo	she

get another chance – make the most of it!
☞ For other expressions with **make**, look at the noun and adjective entries, e.g. for **make love** look at **love**.

PHRV **make for sb/sth** to move toward sb/sth: *As soon as the lecture was finished, they made for the door.*

make for sth to help or allow sth to happen: *Arguing all the time doesn't make for a happy marriage.*

make sb/sth into sth to change sb/sth into sb/sth: *She made her other bedroom into an office.*

make sth of sb/sth to understand sb/sth: *I don't know what to make of my boss* (= I can't understand him).

make off (*informal*) to leave or escape in a hurry

make off with sth (*informal*) to steal sth and leave quickly with it: *The thieves made off with $5 million in cash.*

make sb/sth out 1 to understand sb/sth: *I just can't make him out.* ○ *Can you make this form out?* **2** to be able to see or hear sb/sth; to manage to read sth: *I could just make out her signature.*

make sth out to write or complete sth: *She made out a check for $100.* ○ *He made out a will shortly before he died.*

make sb/sth out to be sth to say that sth is true and try to make people believe it: *The crime problem may not be as bad as it's been made out to be.* ○ *She's not as smart as she makes herself out to be.*

make (sb) up to put powder, lipstick, etc. on the face

make sth up 1 to form: *the different groups that make up our society* **2** to invent sth, often sth that is not true: *to make up an excuse* **3** to make a number or an amount complete: *We need one more person to make up our team.*

make up for sth to do sth that corrects a bad situation: *Her enthusiasm makes up for her lack of experience.* ○ *You'll have to work longer today to make up for the hours you missed yesterday.*

make it up to sb (*informal*) to do sth that shows you are sorry for what you have done to sb or that you are grateful for what they have done for you: *You've done me a big favor. How can I make it up to you?*

make up (with sb) to become friends again after an argument: *Has she made up with him yet?*

☆ **make²** /meɪk/ *noun* [C] the name of the company that produced sth: *"What make is your new car?" "It's a Toyota."*

make-be‚lieve *noun* [U] pretending or imagining sth; the things that are imagined: *I don't believe his stories – they're all make-believe.*

☆ **mak·er** /ˈmeɪkər/ *noun* [C] (in compounds) a

person or company that makes sth: *a dressmaker*

make·shift /ˈmeɪkʃɪft/ *adj.* used for a short time until there is sth better: *The refugees built makeshift shelters out of old cardboard boxes.*

☆ **make·up** /ˈmeɪkʌp/ *noun* **1** [U] powder, cream, etc. that you put on your face to make yourself more attractive. Actors use makeup to change their appearance when they are acting: *to put on/take off makeup* ○ *She wears a lot of makeup.* ☞ Look at **cosmetics**. The verb is **make up** / **make yourself up**. **2** [sing.] the things or people that form sth: *the makeup of the board of directors* **3** [sing.] a person's character: *He can't help his temper. It's part of his makeup.* **4** [C] a special test, piece of work, etc. given to students who failed or missed an earlier one: *Students who were absent yesterday should write a book report as a makeup.* ○ *There will be a makeup quiz on Thursday.*

mak·ing /ˈmeɪkɪŋ/ *noun* [sing.] the act of doing or producing sth: *breadmaking*

IDM **have the makings of sth** to have the necessary qualities for sth: *The book has the makings of a good movie.*

in the making in the process of developing or being made: *What we're seeing is history in the making.* ○ *Tonight's celebration has been three years in the making.*

ma·lar·i·a /məˈlɛriə/ *noun* [U] a serious disease that you may get when you have been bitten by a small flying insect (**a mosquito**) that lives in hot countries

☆ **male** /meɪl/ *adj.* belonging to the sex that does not give birth to babies or lay eggs: *A male deer is called a buck.* ☞ Look at the note at **female**. —**male** *noun* [C]: *a white male in his 40s* ○ *What a cute puppy! Is it a male or a female?*

male 'chau·vin·ism *noun* [U] the belief that men are better than women —**male 'chau·vin·ist** *noun* [C]

mal·func·tion /ˌmælˈfʌŋkʃn/ *verb* [I] (used about machines, etc.) not to work normally or correctly: *The explosion was caused by a malfunctioning fuel valve.* —**mal·func·tion** *noun* [C,U]: *a malfunction in the computer system* ○ *to suffer from kidney malfunction*

mal·ice /ˈmæləs/ *noun* [U] a wish to hurt other people —**ma·li·cious** /məˈlɪʃəs/ *adj.* —**ma·li·cious·ly** *adv.*

ma·lig·nant /məˈlɪɡnənt/ *adj.* (used to describe tumors in the body) likely to cause death if not controlled ☞ The opposite is **benign**.

☆ **mall** /mɔl/ (*also* **shopping mall**) *noun* [C] a large building that has many stores, restaurants, etc. inside it: *teenagers hanging out at the mall*

M

i	ɪ	ɛ	æ	ɑ	ɔ	ʌ	ʊ	u
see	sit	ten	cat	hot	saw	cup	put	too

mal·let /ˈmælət/ noun [C] a heavy wooden hammer ☞ picture at **tool**.

mal·nu·tri·tion /ˌmælnuˈtrɪʃn/ noun [U] bad health that is the result of not having enough food or enough of the right kind of food

mal·prac·tice /ˌmælˈpræktəs/ noun [U] wrong or bad treatment or service, especially by a doctor or a lawyer: *He sued his doctor for malpractice.*

malt /mɔlt/ noun [U] **1** grain that has been left in water for a long time and then dried. Malt is used for making beer and whiskey. **2** (*also* ˌmalt·ed ˈmilk) [C] a thick drink made of milk, ice cream, flavoring and usually malt (1) powder: *a strawberry malt* ☞ Look at **milk shake**.

ma·ma /ˈmɑmə/ noun [C] (*informal*) mother

mam·mal /ˈmæml/ noun [C] an animal of the type that gives birth to live animals and does not lay eggs. Mammals feed their babies with milk from their bodies: *Birds and fish are not mammals, but whales and dolphins are.*

mam·moth /ˈmæməθ/ adj. very big; huge: *a mammoth construction project* ○ *a mammoth tax increase*

☆ **man¹** /mæn/ noun (*pl.* **men** /mɛn/) **1** [C] an adult male person: *a handsome man in his mid-twenties* ○ *men, women and children* **2** [C] a person of either sex, male or female: *All men are equal.* ○ *No man could survive long in such conditions.* **3** [sing.] the human race; human beings: *Early man lived by hunting and gathering.* ○ *Why is man so destructive?*

☞ Some people do not like the way **man** is used in senses 2 and 3 (or the use of **mankind** to mean "all men and women") because it seems that women are not included. They prefer to use **humanity, the human race,** or **people**.

4 [C] a husband, boyfriend or male lover: *There's a new man in her life.* **5** [C, usually pl.] a man of low rank in the army, etc. who takes orders from an officer: *officers and men* **6** (*slang*) (used when you are talking to sb): *Hey, man, can you lend me a quarter?*
IDM **man to man** (used about speaking) honestly and directly, between two men: *Let's talk man to man.* ○ *to have a man-to-man talk*

man² /mæn/ interj. (*informal*) (used when you are annoyed or surprised): *Oh, man! Why does this always happen to me?* ○ *Man! That's a great car!*

man³ /mæn/ verb [T] (**man·ning; manned**) to operate sth or to provide people to operate sth: *to man a boat, gun, telephone, etc.* ○ *When was the first manned space flight?*

☆ **man·age** /ˈmænɪdʒ/ verb **1** [T] to be in charge or control of sth: *She manages a small advertising business.* **2** [I,T] (often with *can* or *could*) to be able to do sth or to deal with sth: *I'm sorry I didn't manage to write that report last week.* ○ *I can't manage this suitcase. It's too*

heavy. ○ *How in the world did you manage to find us here?* **3** [I] **manage (on sth); manage (without sb/sth)** to have a reasonable way of life: *They live in the country and couldn't manage without a car.* ○ *It's hard for a family to manage on just one income.*

man·age·a·ble /ˈmænɪdʒəbl/ adj. not too big or too difficult to control or take care of: *a yard of manageable size* ○ *This shampoo makes your hair shiny and more manageable.*

☆ **man·age·ment** /ˈmænɪdʒmənt/ noun **1** [U] the control or organization of sth: *Good management is the key to success in business.* ○ *financial/risk management* **2** [C] the people who control a business or company: *The hotel is now under new management.* ○ *The management is considering laying off some workers.*

☆ **man·ag·er** /ˈmænɪdʒər/ noun [C] **1** a man or woman who controls an organization or part of an organization: *Martha is the new manager of the bookstore.* ○ *a sales manager* **2** a person who takes care of the business affairs of a singer, an actor, etc. **3** a person who is in charge of training a baseball team: *the Yankees' manager* ☞ Look at **coach**.

man·da·rin /ˈmændərɪn/ (*also* **mandarin orange**) noun [C] a type of small orange whose skin comes off easily

Man·da·rin /ˈmændərɪn/ (*also* **Mandarin Chinese**) noun [U] the official spoken language of mainland China

man·date /ˈmændeɪt/ noun [usually sing.] the power that a group of people has to do sth as a result of winning an election: *The members of Congress had a clear mandate from the voters to reduce taxes.*

man·da·to·ry /ˈmændəˌtɔri/ adj. that must be done by laws, rules, etc.: *mandatory drug testing for Olympic athletes*

mane /meɪn/ noun [C] the long hair on the neck of a horse or male lion ☞ picture at **horse**.

ma·neu·ver¹ /məˈnuvər/ noun **1** [C] a movement that needs care or skill: *In the driving test you will have to perform several maneuvers such as parallel parking.* **2** [C] something clever that you do in order to win sth, trick sb, etc. **3** [usually pl.] a way of training soldiers when large numbers of them practice fighting in battles: *large-scale military maneuvers*

ma·neu·ver² /məˈnuvər/ verb [I,T] to move to a different position using skill: *to maneuver into a parking space*

man·gle /ˈmæŋgl/ verb [T] **1** to damage sth greatly so that it is difficult to see what it used to look like: *Oh, no! The VCR mangled my new tape!* ○ *The highway was covered with the mangled wreckage of cars and trucks.* **2** to ruin sth such as a song, speech, etc. by performing it badly: *a mangled translation, speech, etc.*

man·go /ˈmæŋgoʊ/ noun [C] (*pl.* **man·goes** or

M

man·gos) a tropical fruit that has yellowish-red skin and is yellow inside

man·hole /'mænhoʊl/ *noun* [C] a hole in the street with a lid over it through which sb can go to look at the pipes, wires, etc. that are underground

man·hood /'mænhʊd/ *noun* [U] the state of being a man rather than a boy: *to reach manhood*

ma·ni·a /'meɪniə/ *noun* **1** [U] a serious mental illness that may cause a person to be very excited or violent **2** [C] (*informal*) a very great love (for sth) or interest (in sth): *My mom remembers the rock 'n' roll mania of the sixties.* —**man·ic** /'mænɪk/ *adj.*

ma·ni·ac /'meɪniæk/ *noun* [C] **1** a person who is crazy and dangerous: (*figurative*) *to drive like a maniac* **2** a person who has a great love for sth: *a golf maniac*

man·i·cure /'mænəkyʊr/ *noun* [C,U] treatment to make your hands and fingernails look nice: *to have/get a manicure*

man·i·fest /'mænəfɛst/ *verb* [T] (*formal*) **1** to show sth clearly **2 manifest itself/themselves** to appear: *Mental illness can manifest itself in many forms.*

man·i·fes·ta·tion /ˌmænəfə'steɪʃn/ *noun* [C,U] (*formal*) a sign that sth is happening

man·i·fes·to /ˌmænə'fɛstoʊ/ *noun* [C] (*pl.* **man·i·fes·tos** or **man·i·fes·toes**) a written statement by a political party or group that explains its beliefs or what it hopes to do

ma·nip·u·late /mə'nɪpyəleɪt/ *verb* [T] **1** to use or control sth with skill **2** to influence sb so that he/she does or thinks what you want: *Clever politicians know how to manipulate public opinion.* —**ma·nip·u·la·tion** /məˌnɪpyə'leɪʃn/ *noun* [C,U]

man·kind /ˌmæn'kaɪnd/ *noun* [U] all the people in the world: *A nuclear war would be a threat to all mankind.* ☛ Look at the note at **man**.

man·ly /'mænli/ *adj.* typical of or suitable for a man: *He had a deep manly voice.* —**man·li·ness** *noun* [U]

ˌ**man-'made** *adj.* made by people, not formed in a natural way; artificial: *man-made fabrics such as nylon and polyester* ☛ The opposite is **natural.**

man·ne·quin /'mænəkən/ *noun* [C] a figure shaped like a person's body, used to show clothes in a store

☆ **man·ner** /'mænər/ *noun* **1** [sing.] (*formal*) the way that you do sth or that sth happens: *They hoped to resolve the crisis in a peaceful manner.* **2** [sing.] (*formal*) the way that sb behaves toward other people: *He charmed the voters with his easy-going manner.* ☛ A less formal word is **way.** **3 manners** [plural] the way of behaving that is thought to be polite in your society or culture: *In some countries it is bad manners*

to show the soles of your feet. ○ *Their kids have excellent table manners.*

IDM all manner of ... (*formal*) every kind of...

man·ner·ism /'mænərɪzəm/ *noun* [C] a way of speaking or a movement of part of the body that is typical for a particular person

man·pow·er /'mænpaʊər/ *noun* [U] the people that you need to do a particular job: *There is a shortage of skilled manpower in the computer industry.*

man·sion /'mænʃn/ *noun* [C] a very large, expensive house

man·slaugh·ter /'mænslɔtər/ *noun* [U] the crime of killing sb without intending to do so ☛ Look at **murder.**

man·tel /'mæntl/ (*also* **mantelpiece** /'mæntlpis/) *noun* [C] a shelf that is above a fireplace ☛ picture at **fireplace.**

man·u·al¹ /'mænyuəl/ *adj.* using your hands; operated by hand: *manual work* ○ *a car with manual transmission* ○ *a skilled manual worker*

man·u·al² /'mænyuəl/ *noun* [C] a book that explains how to do or operate sth: *a training manual* ○ *Full instructions are given in the owner's manual.*

man·u·al·ly /'mænyuəli/ *adv.* by hand, not automatically

☆ **man·u·fac·ture** /ˌmænyə'fæktʃər/ *verb* [T] to make sth in large quantities using machines: *a local factory that manufactures high-quality furniture* ○ *manufacturing industries* —**man·u·fac·ture** *noun* [U]: *The manufacture of chemical weapons should be illegal.* —**man·u·fac·tur·er** *noun* [C]: *Faulty goods should be returned to the manufacturer.*

ma·nure /mə'nʊr/ *noun* [U] the waste matter from animals that is put on the ground in order to make plants grow better ☛ Look at **fertilizer.**

man·u·script /'mænyəskrɪpt/ *noun* [C] **1** a very old book or document that was written by hand **2** a typed or hand-written copy of a book that has not yet been printed

☆ **man·y** /'mɛni/ *det., pron.* (used with plural nouns or verbs) **1** a large number of people or things: *Many people do not get enough to eat.* ○ *There are too many mistakes in this essay.* ○ *Many of the people at the meeting left early.* **2** (used with "how" to ask about the number of people or things): *How many kids do you have?* ○ *How many mistakes did you make?* ○ *How many came to the meeting?*

IDM a good/great many very many

Mao·ri /'maʊri/ *noun* [C] a member of the race of people who were the original inhabitants of New Zealand —**Mao·ri** *adj.*

☆ **map¹** /mæp/ *noun* [C] a drawing or plan of (part of) the surface of the earth that shows countries, rivers, mountains, roads, etc.: *a map of the world* ○ *a road map* ○ *a street map of Chicago* ○ *I can't find Portland on the map.* ○ *to*

ər	ɪr	ɛr	ɑr	ɔr	ʊr	ʒ	h	ŋ
bird	near	hair	car	north	tour	vision	hat	sing

read a map ☞ A book of maps is called an atlas.

☆**map²** /mæp/ *verb* [T] (**map·ping; mapped**) to make a map of a place

PHRV **map sth out** to plan sth in detail: *We need to map out our strategy for winning the election.*

ma·ple /'meɪpl/ *noun* [C] a tree that has leaves with five points and that produces a very sweet liquid: *pancakes with maple syrup*

Mar. *abbr.* = MARCH

mar·a·thon /'mærəθɑn/ *noun* [C] a long-distance running race in which people run about 26 miles: *Have you ever run a marathon?* ○ the *New York City Marathon* ○ (*figurative*) *a marathon meeting* (= one that lasts a very long time)

mar·ble /'mɑrbl/ *noun* **1** [U] a hard attractive stone that is used to make statues and parts of buildings: *a marble statue* ○ *This staircase is made of marble.* **2** [C] a small ball of colored glass that children play with **3 marbles** [plural] the children's game that you play by rolling marbles along the ground trying to hit other marbles

IDM **lose your marbles** ▷ LOSE

☆**March** /mɑrtʃ/ *noun* [C,U] (*abbr.* **Mar.**) the third month of the year, coming before April ☞ For examples of the use of the months in sentences, look at **January**.

☆**march¹** /mɑrtʃ/ *verb* **1** [I] to walk with regular steps (like a soldier): *The President saluted as the troops marched past.* ○ *He marched in and demanded an explanation.* **2** [I] to walk in a large group to protest about sth: *The demonstrators marched through the center of town.* **3** [T] to cause sb to walk or march (1) somewhere: *The prisoner was marched away.*

march² /mɑrtʃ/ *noun* [C] **1** an act of marching: *The soldiers were tired after their long march.* **2** an organized walk by a large group of people who are protesting about sth: *a peace march* ☞ Look at **demonstration**.

Mardi Gras /'mɑrdi grɑ/ *noun* [U] a festival before the beginning of a period called Lent

☞ Mardi Gras is celebrated mainly in the southern U.S., especially in and around New Orleans, Louisiana. People go to parties and march in parades wearing fancy costumes.

mare /mɛr/ *noun* [C] a female horse or donkey ☞ Look at the note at **horse**.

☆**mar·ga·rine** /'mɑrdʒərən/ *noun* [U] a food that looks like butter, made of vegetable fats. Margarine is used for spreading on bread and in cooking.

☆**mar·gin** /'mɑrdʒən/ *noun* [C] **1** the empty space at the side of a page in a book, etc.: *notes in the margin* ○ *a wide/narrow margin* **2** the amount of space, time, votes, etc. by which you win sth: *He won the race by a comfortable margin.* **3** an amount of space, time, etc. that

is more than you need: *a safety margin* **4** (*also* **profit margin**) the amount of profit that a company makes on sth

mar·gin·al /'mɑrdʒənl/ *adj.* small in size or importance: *The differences are marginal.*

mar·gin·al·ly /'mɑrdʒənəli/ *adv.* a little; slightly: *In most cases costs will increase only marginally.*

,**margin of** '**error** *noun* [C, usually sing.] an amount allowed for the possibility that numbers, calculations, etc. are not entirely correct: *The poll has a margin of error of plus or minus 4%.*

mar·i·jua·na /,mærə'wɑnə/ *noun* [U] an illegal drug that is smoked in cigarettes (**joints**)

ma·ri·na /mə'rinə/ *noun* [C] an area of water where people can leave their boats

Ma·rine /mə'rin/ *noun* [C] a soldier who has been trained to fight on land or at sea

☆**ma·rine** /mə'rin/ *adj.* **1** connected with the sea: *a marine biologist* ○ *the study of marine life* **2** connected with ships or sailing: *marine insurance*

the Ma'rine Corps *noun* [sing.] (*also* **the Marines** [plural]) the branch of the U.S. military forces whose soldiers have been trained to fight on land or at sea: *My son's in the Marines.* ☞ Look at the note at **White House**.

mar·i·tal /'mærətl/ *adj.* (only *before* a noun) connected with marriage: *marital problems*

'**marital ,status** *noun* [U] (*formal*) whether you are married, single, widowed or divorced

mar·i·time /'mærətaɪm/ *adj.* connected with the ocean or ships

☆**mark¹** /mɑrk/ *noun* [C] **1** a spot or line that spoils the appearance of sth: *There's a dirty mark on the front of your shirt.* ○ *If you press your nose against the window, it will leave a mark.* ☞ Look at **birthmark**. **2** something that shows who or what sb/sth is or that gives information about sb/sth: *Did the bank robber have any identifying marks on his face?* **3** a written or printed symbol that is a sign of sth: *a question, punctuation, check, etc. mark* ○ *quotation marks* **4** a sign of a quality or feeling: *They stood in silence for two minutes as a mark of respect.* **5** a judgment of sb/sth's work or performance: *Voters gave the governor high marks for his ability to improve the state's economy.* ○ *to earn top marks for honesty* **6** the level of sth: *The company's sales have now reached the million-dollar mark.* **7** the unit of money in Germany

IDM **make your mark** to become famous and successful or to leave a strong impression: *an actor who made his mark in action movies*

on your mark(s), get set, go! (used at the start of a sports race)

☆**mark²** /mɑrk/ *verb* [T] **1** to put a sign on sth: *We marked the price on all items in the sale.* ○ *The route is marked with a red line.* ○ *Why did you mark that answer wrong?* **2** to show where

M

tʃ	dʒ	v	θ	ð	s	z	ʃ
chin	June	van	thin	then	so	zoo	she

sth is or where sth happened: *Flowers mark the spot where he died.* **3** to celebrate sth: *The ceremony marked the fiftieth anniversary of the opening of the school.*

mark·down /'mɑrkdaʊn/ *noun* [C] a reduction in the price of sth in a store

marked /mɑrkt/ *adj.* clear; noticeable: *There has been a marked increase in vandalism in recent years.*

mark·er /'mɑrkər/ *noun* [C] **1** something that shows the position of sth: *A historical marker shows where the battle took place.* **2** (*also* **Magic Marker** (*trademark*)) a type of pen that draws thick lines

☆ **mar·ket¹** /'mɑrkət/ *noun* **1** [C] a place where people go to buy and sell things: *The farmers are taking their cattle to the livestock market today.* ○ *an open-air/covered market* ○ *a market square* ☞ Look at **flea market**, **farmers' market** and **supermarket**. **2** [U, sing.] the people who want to buy a particular thing: *There's no market for lawnmowers in the middle of winter.* **3** [C] the business of buying and selling a particular thing: *High interest rates can have a significant effect on the automobile market.* **4** [C] a country, an area or a group of people that may want to buy sth: *The company is hoping to expand into the European market.* ○ *the domestic/international market* ☞ Look at **black market**. **5** [C] = STOCK MARKET

IDM **be in the market for sth** to be interested in buying sth: *I'm in the market for a used car.*

on the market for sale: *This is one of the best automatic cameras on the market.*

☆ **mar·ket²** /'mɑrkət/ *verb* [T] to sell sth with the help of advertising

mar·ket·a·ble /'mɑrkətəbl/ *adj.* able to be sold easily, because people want it

☆ **mar·ket·ing** /'mɑrkətɪŋ/ *noun* [U] deciding how sth can be sold most easily, e.g. what price it should be or how it should be advertised: *Effective marketing will lead to increased sales.* ○ *the marketing department*

ˌ**market** ˈ**research** *noun* [U] the study of what people want to buy and why

mark·ing /'mɑrkɪŋ/ *noun* [C, usually pl.] a pattern of color on an animal or a bird

marks·man /'mɑrksmən / *noun* [C] (*pl.* **marks·men**) a man who can shoot very well with a gun

mar·ma·lade /'mɑrməleɪd/ *noun* [U] a type of jam that is made from oranges: *toast and marmalade for breakfast*

ma·roon /mə'run/ *adj.* dark brownish-red in color ☞ Look at **crimson** and **scarlet**.

ma·rooned /mə'rund/ *adj.* in a place that you cannot leave: *The sailors were marooned on a desert island.*

mar·quee /mɑr'ki/ *noun* [C] a sign over the entrance to a theater that shows the names of the movies being shown or the play being performed

☆ **mar·riage** /'mærɪdʒ/ *noun* **1** [C,U] the state of being husband and wife: *They are getting divorced after five years of marriage.* ○ *a happy/ an unhappy marriage* ○ *an arranged marriage* (= one where your partner is chosen for you by your parents) ○ *a mixed marriage* (= one between people of different races or religions) **2** [C] a wedding ceremony: *The marriage took place in the bride's parents' home.* ☞ The verb is **marry**. Look at the note at **wedding**.

☆ **mar·ried** /'mærid/ *adj.* **1 married (to sb)** having a husband or wife: *a married man/ woman/couple* ○ *They've been married for almost 50 years.* ○ *Jenny's married to Mark.* ○ *They're getting married in June.* ☞ Look also at **divorced**, **unmarried**, **single** and **widowed**. **2** (only *before* a noun) of marriage (1): *How do you like married life?*

mar·row /'mæroʊ/ *noun* [U] = BONE MARROW

☆ **mar·ry** /'mæri/ *verb* (*pres. part.* **mar·ry·ing**; *3rd pers. sing. pres.* **mar·ries**; *p.t., p.p.* **married**) **1** [I,T] to take sb as your husband or wife: *They married when they were very young.* ○ *When did Roger ask you to marry him?* ☞ **Get married** is more commonly used than **marry**: *When are Sue and Jack getting married?* ○ *They got married in 1982.* ○ *Many people live together without getting married.* **2** [T] to join two people together as husband and wife: *We asked John's priest to marry us.* ☞ The noun is **marriage**.

Mars /mɑrz/ *noun* [sing.] the planet that is fourth in order from the sun and second nearest to the Earth ☞ Look at **Martian**.

marsh /mɑrʃ/ *noun* [C,U] an area of soft wet land —**marshy** *adj.*

mar·shal /'mɑrʃl/ *noun* [C] **1** an officer whose job is to carry out court orders: *Federal marshals brought the defendant into the courtroom.* **2** an officer of high rank in some police or fire departments: *a deputy fire marshal* **3** a military officer of high rank in some countries: *Field Marshal Montgomery of the British army*

marsh·mal·low /'mɑrʃmɛloʊ/ *noun* [C,U] a soft, sweet, white food that comes in small round pieces and is often used to decorate other foods

mar·tial /'mɑrʃl/ *adj.* (*formal*) connected with war

ˌ**martial** ˈ**art** *noun* [usually pl.] a type of fighting sport, originally from Asia, in which you use your hands and feet as weapons

ˌ**martial** ˈ**law** *noun* [U] military government of a country, especially during a war or other emergency: *The country has been under martial law for three years.* ○ *to declare martial law*

Mar·tian /'mɑrʃn/ *noun* [C] (in stories) a creature that comes from the planet Mars

mar·tyr /'mɑrtər/ *noun* [C] **1** a person who is killed because of what he/she believes **2** a person who does not do or have what he/she wants in order to help other people or to be

admired by them: *Don't be such a martyr! You don't have to do all the housework.* —**mar·tyr·dom** /-dəm/ *noun* [U]

mar·vel[1] /ˈmɑrvl/ *noun* [C] a person or thing that surprises you because it is wonderful: *the marvels of modern technology*

mar·vel[2] /ˈmɑrvl/ *verb* [I] (*formal*) to be very surprised at how good, beautiful, etc. sb/sth is: *We marveled at how much they had been able to do in a short time.*

mar·vel·ous /ˈmɑrvl·əs/ *adj.* very good; wonderful: *Studying abroad is a marvelous opportunity to learn about another culture.* ○ *It was marvelous to come home again after being in the hospital.*

Marx·ism /ˈmɑrksɪzəm/ *noun* [U] the political and economic thought of Karl Marx, who said that important changes in history were caused by the struggle between social classes ☞ Look at **communism** and **socialism**. —**Marx·ist** /ˈmɑrksɪst/ *noun* [C], *adj.*: *Their president was a Marxist.* ○ *Marxist ideology*

mas·car·a /mæˈskærə/ *noun* [U] a type of make-up that is used to make your eyelashes look darker and thicker

mas·cot /ˈmæskɑt/ *noun* [C] a person, animal or thing that is thought to bring good luck, especially as a symbol of a sports team or other organization

mas·cu·line /ˈmæskyələn/ *adj.* with the qualities that people think are typical of men

☞ In English grammar, **masculine** words refer to male people or animals: *"He" is a masculine pronoun.* In some other languages all nouns are given a gender, either **masculine**, **feminine** or **neuter**. Look also at **male** and **manly**, and at **feminine** and the note at **female**.

—**mas·cu·lin·i·ty** /ˌmæskyəˈlɪnəṭi/ *noun* [U]

mash /mæʃ/ *verb* [T] to mix or crush sth until is it soft: *mashed potatoes*

masks

ski mask surgeon's mask Halloween mask

mask[1] /mæsk/ *noun* [C] something that you wear that covers your face or part of your face. People wear masks in order to hide or protect their faces or to make themselves look different: *The bank robbers wore stocking masks. The kids wore animal masks to the party.* ☞ Look at **gas mask** and **goggles**.

mask[2] /mæsk/ *verb* [T] **1** to cover or hide your face with a mask: *a masked gunman* **2** to

hide your feelings: *He masked his anger with a smile.*

mas·och·ism /ˈmæsəkɪzəm/ *noun* [U] getting (sexual) pleasure from feeling pain ☞ Look at **sadism**. —**mas·o·chist** /ˈmæsəkɪst/ *noun* [C] —**mas·och·is·tic** /ˌmæsəˈkɪstɪk/ *adj.*

ma·son /ˈmeɪsn/ *noun* [C] **1** a person who makes things from stone or brick **2 Mason** (*also* **Freemason**) a man who belongs to an international secret society whose members help each other and who recognize each other by secret signs

ma·son·ry /ˈmeɪsənri/ *noun* [U] the parts of a building that are made of stone or brick: *The building is old and the masonry is crumbling.*

mas·quer·ade[1] /ˌmæskəˈreɪd/ *noun* [C] a party at which people dress up to look like a different person (e.g. from history or a story): *I'm going to the masquerade ball dressed as Napoleon.*

mas·quer·ade[2] /ˌmæskəˈreɪd/ *verb* [I] to pretend to be sb/sth: *Two people, masquerading as doctors, knocked on the door and asked to see the child.*

☆**mass[1]** /mæs/ *noun* **1** [C] a large amount or number of sth: *The garden was a mass of flowers.* ○ *a dense mass of smoke* **2** [U] (in physics) the amount of material that sth contains; weight **3 the masses** [plural] ordinary people when considered as a political group

☆**mass[2]** /mæs/ *adj.* (only *before* a noun) involving a large number of people: *a mass murderer* ○ *a mass meeting*

mass[3] /mæs/ *verb* [I,T] to gather together in a mass1 : *The students massed in the center of campus.*

Mass (*also* **mass**) /mæs/ *noun* [C,U] the ceremony in some Christian churches, especially Roman Catholic churches, when people eat bread and drink wine in order to remember the last meal that Christ had before he died: *to go to Mass* ○ *Fifty people attended Mass.*

mas·sa·cre /ˈmæsəkər/ *noun* [C] the killing of a large number of people or animals —**mas·sa·cre** *verb* [T] ☞ Look at the note at **kill**.

mas·sage /məˈsɑʒ/ *noun* [C,U] rubbing or pressing sb's body in order to reduce pain or to help the person move more easily: *to give sb a massage* —**mas·sage** *verb* [T]

mas·sive /ˈmæsɪv/ *adj.* very big: *a massive increase in prices*

ˌmass ˈmedia *noun* [plural] the means of communicating with large numbers of people, i.e. newspapers, television and radio

ˌmass-proˈduce *verb* [T] to make large numbers of similar things by machine in a factory —**ˌmass proˈduction** *noun* [U]

mast /mæst/ *noun* [C] a tall wooden or metal pole for a flag, ship's sails, etc. ☞ picture at **boat**.

☆**mas·ter[1]** /ˈmæstər/ *noun* [C] **1** a man who has people or animals in his control: *The dog ran*

M

to its master. ☞ Look at **mistress**. **2** a person who has great skill at doing sth: *a master carpenter* ○ *a master of disguise* ○ *He's a master at manipulating the news media.* **3** a tape, document, etc from which copies can be made

☆ **mas·ter²** /ˈmæstər/ *verb* [T] **1** to learn how to do sth well: *It takes a long time to master a foreign language.* **2** to control sth: *to master a situation*

ˌmaster ˈkey *noun* [C] a key that can open many different locks, each of which can be opened by its own separate key

mas·ter·mind /ˈmæstərmaɪnd/ *noun* [C] a very clever person (who planned or organized sth) —**mas·ter·mind** *verb* [T]: *The police failed to catch the man who masterminded the whole operation.*

☆ **mas·ter·piece** /ˈmæstərpis/ *noun* [C] a work of art, music, literature, etc. that is of the highest quality

ˌmaster ˈplan *noun* [C, usually sing.] a detailed plan for success in a complex operation: *It was all part of my master plan for taking over the company.*

ˈmaster's deˌgree (*also* **master's**) *noun* [C] a second or higher university degree. You usually get a master's degree by studying for one or two years after your first degree: *Master of Arts (M.A.)* ○ *Master of Science (M.S.)* ○ *She has a master's in chemistry.* ☞ Look at **bachelor's degree**.

mas·ter·y /ˈmæstəri/ *noun* [U] **1 mastery (of sth)** great skill at doing sth: *His mastery of the violin was exceptional for a child of his age.* **2 mastery (of/over sb/sth)** control over sb/sth: *The battle was fought for mastery of the territory near the border.*

mas·tur·bate /ˈmæstərbeɪt/ *verb* [I] to make yourself feel sexually excited by touching and rubbing your sex organs —**mas·tur·ba·tion** /ˌmæstərˈbeɪʃn/ *noun* [U]

M

mat /mæt/ *noun* [C] a piece of thick material that you put on the floor: *a welcome mat* (= a mat in front of the door to a house, usually with the word "welcome" on it) ○ *an exercise mat for gymnasts* ○ *a straw mat* ☞ Look at **rug**.

☆ **match¹** /mætʃ/ *noun* **1** [C] a short piece of wood or cardboard with a tip that catches fire when it is rubbed against another surface: *to light/strike a match* ○ *a box/book of matches* **2** [C] an organized game or sports event: *a tennis, boxing, etc. match* **3** [sing.] a person or thing that is as good as or better than sb/sth else: *Carol is no match for her mother when it comes to cooking* (= she doesn't cook as well as her mother). ○ *Jason had thought he was the best chess player in the school, but he finally met his match in Valerie* (= she could beat him). **4** [sing.] **a match (for/with sb/sth)** something that looks good with sth else, e.g. because it has the same color or pattern:

Those shoes aren't a very good match with your dress. ○ (*figurative*) *Bill and Sue are a good match. They should be very happy together.*

☆ **match²** /mætʃ/ *verb* **1** [I,T] to have the same color or pattern as sth else, or to look nice with sth else: *That blouse doesn't match your skirt.* ○ *We've chosen the curtains, but now we need a carpet to match.* **2** [T] to find sb/sth that is like or suitable for sb/sth else: *The agency tries to match single people with suitable partners.* **3** [T] to be as good as or better than sb/sth else: *The two teams are very evenly matched.* ○ *Taiwan produces the goods at a price that the U.S. cannot match.*

PHRV **match up** to be the same: *The statements of the two witnesses don't match up.*

match sth up (with sth) to fit or put sth together (with sth else): *What you have to do is match up each celebrity with his or her pet.*

match·book /ˈmætʃbʊk/ *noun* [C] a small container made of folded paper, with matches attached inside

match·box /ˈmætʃbɑks/ *noun* [C] a small box for matches

match·stick /ˈmætʃstɪk/ *noun* [C] the thin wooden part of a match

☆ **mate¹** /meɪt/ *noun* [C] **1** (especially in compounds) a friend or sb you live or work with: *a roommate* (= sb with whom you share a house, an apartment or a room) ○ *a classmate* ☞ Look at **running mate**. **2** one of a male and female pair of animals, birds, etc.: *The female sits on the eggs while her mate hunts for food.* **3** an officer on a ship: *the captain and his first mate* **4** = CHECKMATE

mate² /meɪt/ *verb* **1** [I] (used about animals and birds) to have sex and produce young: *Pandas rarely mate in zoos.* **2** [T] to bring two animals together so that they can have sex and produce young

☆ **ma·te·ri·al¹** /məˈtɪriəl/ *noun* **1** [C,U] a substance that can be used for making or doing sth: *Many African countries export raw materials* (= natural substances that are used to make things in factories, etc.). ○ *writing materials* (= pens, paper, etc.) **2** [C,U] cloth (for making clothes, etc.): *Is there enough material for a dress?* **3** [U] facts or information that you collect before you write a book, article, etc.

☆ **ma·te·ri·al²** /məˈtɪriəl/ *adj.* **1** connected with real or physical things rather than the spirit or emotions: *We should not value material comforts too highly.* ☞ Look at **spiritual**. **2** important: *material evidence* ☞ This word is not common, but look at **immaterial**.

ma·te·ri·al·ism /məˈtɪriəlɪzəm/ *noun* [U] the belief that money and possessions are the most important things in life —**ma·te·ri·al·ist** /məˈtɪriəlɪst/ *noun* [C] —**ma·te·ri·al·is·tic** /məˌtɪriəˈlɪstɪk/ *adj.*

ma·te·ri·al·ize /məˈtɪriəlaɪz/ *verb* [I] to be-

come real; to happen: *The pay raise that they had promised never materialized.*

ma·ter·nal /məˈtərnl/ *adj.* **1** of or like a mother: *maternal love* **2** related through your mother's side of the family: *your maternal grandfather* ☞ Look at **paternal**.

ma·ter·ni·ty /məˈtərnəṭi/ *adj.* connected with women who are going to have or have just had a baby: *maternity clothes* ○ *Our manager had her baby at the end of June, so she's on maternity leave until September.*

☆ **math** /mæθ/ (also *formal* **mathematics**) *noun* [U] the science or study of numbers, quantities or shapes: *Math is my favorite subject.* ○ *a math teacher*

math·e·ma·ti·cian /ˌmæθəməˈtɪʃn/ *noun* [C] a person who studies or is an expert in mathematics

math·e·mat·ics /ˌmæθəˈmæṭɪks/ *noun* [U] (*formal*) = MATH —**math·e·mat·i·cal** /ˌmæθəˈmæṭɪkl/ *adj.* —**math·e·mat·i·cal·ly** /-kli/ *adv. It is now mathematically impossible for him to win.*

mat·i·née /ˌmætn·ˈeɪ/ *noun* [C] an afternoon performance of a play, movie, etc.

mat·ri·mo·ny /ˈmætrəmoʊni/ *noun* [U] (*formal*) the state of being married —**mat·ri·mo·ni·al** /ˌmætrəˈmoʊniəl/ *adj.*

ma·tron /ˈmeɪtrən/ *noun* [C] an older married woman or widow, usually from a high social class: *wealthy society matrons*

ma·tron·ly /ˈmeɪtrənli/ *adj.* (a polite word used about an older woman) fat: *a matronly figure*

ˌ**matron of** ˈ**honor** *noun* [C] (*pl.* **matrons of honor**) in a wedding ceremony, the married woman who helps the bride (usually her best friend or a close family member) ☞ Look at the note at **wedding**.

matte /mæt/ *adj.* not shiny: *This paint gives a matte finish.* ☞ Look at **glossy**.

☆ **mat·ter**[1] /ˈmæṭər/ *noun* **1** [C] a subject or situation that you must think about and give your attention to: *It's a personal matter and I don't want to discuss it with you.* ○ *They should try to settle matters between themselves before going to court.* ○ *to simplify/complicate matters* **2** [U] all physical substances; a substance of a particular kind: *waste matter* ○ *reading matter*

IDM **as a matter of fact** to tell the truth; in reality: *I like him very much, as a matter of fact.*

for that matter in addition; as well: *Mick is fed up with his classes. I am too, for that matter.*

make matters/things worse ⇨ WORSE[1]

(be) the matter (with sb/sth) to be the reason for unhappiness, pain, problems, etc.: *She looks so sad. What's the matter with her?* ○ *There seems to be something the matter with the car.* ○ *Eat that food! There's nothing the matter with it.*

a matter of opinion a subject on which people do not agree: *"I think the governor is doing a good job." "That's a matter of opinion."*

a matter of sth/doing sth something that needs or requires sth: *Learning a language is largely a matter of practice.*

no matter who, what, where, etc. whoever, whatever, wherever, etc.: *They never listen no matter what you say.*

☆ **mat·ter**[2] /ˈmæṭər/ *verb* [I] to be important: *It doesn't really matter how much it costs.* ○ *Does it matter if we're a little late?* ○ *What matters most is giving the kids a good start in life.*

☞ **Matter** is often used in negative sentences, questions and sentences containing *what, who, when, if,* etc. It is not used in the *-ing* forms.

mat·tress /ˈmætrəs/ *noun* [C] a large soft thing that you lie on to sleep, usually on a bed ☞ picture at **bed**.

☆ **ma·ture**[1] /məˈtʃʊr; -ˈtʊr/ *adj.* **1** fully grown or fully developed: *a mature tree, bird, animal, etc.* ☞ Look at **immature**. **2** behaving in a sensible adult way: *Is she mature enough to stay home alone this weekend?* ☞ Look at **immature**. —**ma·tur·i·ty** /məˈtʃʊrəti; -ˈtʊr-/ *noun* [U]

ma·ture[2] /məˈtʃʊr; -ˈtʊr/ *verb* [I] to become mature: *He matured a lot during his four years at college.*

maul /mɔl/ *verb* [T] (usually used about a wild animal) to attack and injure sb

mauve /moʊv/ *adj., noun* [U] pinkish purple

mav·er·ick /ˈmævərɪk/ *noun* [C] **1** a young animal, especially a cow, that has become separated from its mother and does not have its owner's mark (**a brand**) on it **2** a person with independent or unusual views: *a political maverick*

max /mæks/ *noun* [sing.] (*informal*) = MAXIMUM: *I can fit six people in my car – that's the absolute max.* —**max** *adv. I can afford to pay $200 a month max.*

max·im /ˈmæksəm/ *noun* [C] a few words that express a rule for good or sensible behavior: *Their maxim is: "If a job's worth doing, it's worth doing well."*

max·i·mize /ˈmæksəmaɪz/ *verb* [T] to increase sth as much as possible: *to maximize profits* ☞ Look at **minimize**.

☆ **max·i·mum** /ˈmæksəməm/ *noun* [sing.] (*abbr.* **max.**) the greatest amount or level of sth that is possible, allowed, recorded, etc.: *The bus can carry a maximum of 40 people.* ○ *$500 is the maximum we can afford.* ☞ The opposite is **minimum**. —**max·i·mum** *adj.* (only *before* a noun): *a maximum speed of 120 miles per hour* ○ *a maximum security prison*

☆ **May** /meɪ/ *noun* [C,U] the fifth month of the year, coming before June ☞ For examples of

M

the use of the months in sentences, look at **January**.

☆ **may** /meɪ/ *modal verb* (*negative* **may not**) **1** (*formal*) (used for saying that sth is possible): *You may be right.* ○ *They may have forgotten the meeting.* ○ *He may have been driving too fast.* ☞ Look at **might**[1](2). **2** (*formal*) (used as a polite way of asking for and giving permission): *May I use your phone?* ○ *You may only borrow books for two weeks.* ☞ It is more common to say **can**. **3** (used in the negative as a way of forbidding sb to do sth): *You may not take photographs in the museum.* **4** (used for contrasting two facts): *He may be smart, but he can't do anything practical.* **5** (*formal*) (used for expressing wishes and hopes): *May God be with you.*

IDM may/might as well (do sth) ⇨ WELL[1]

☆ **may·be** /ˈmeɪbi/ *adv.* perhaps; possibly: *"Are you going to come?" "Maybe."* ○ *There were three, maybe four armed men.* ○ *Maybe I'll go to the party and maybe I won't.* ☞ Look at the note at **perhaps**.

ˈ**May Day** *noun* [C] May 1st

☞ **May Day** is traditionally celebrated as a spring festival and in some countries it is also a day for socialist groups to hold meetings and demonstrations.

may·on·naise /ˌmeɪəˈneɪz; ˈmeɪəneɪz/(also *informal* **mayo** /ˈmeɪoʊ/) *noun* [U] a thick white sauce made with eggs and oil, often eaten in sandwiches

☆ **may·or** /ˈmeɪər/ *noun* [C] a person who is elected to be the leader of the group of people (**a council**) who manage the affairs of a town or city

maze /meɪz/ *noun* [C] **1** a complicated pattern of paths, in which it is difficult to find your way: *a maze of winding streets* **2** a puzzle in which you draw a line through a complex group of lines without touching any of them

maze

M.B.A. /ˌɛm bi ˈeɪ/ *abbr.* Master of Business Administration; an advanced degree for people who study how to run a business

M.D. /ˌɛm ˈdi/ *abbr.* Doctor of Medicine

☆ **me** /mi/ *pron.* (used as an object or after the verb *be*) the person who is speaking or writing: *He called me yesterday.* ○ *She wrote to me last week.* ○ *"Somebody spilled the wine." "Sorry, it was me."* ○ *"Who's this picture of?" "Me."*

☞ It **is/was me** is much more common than it **is/was I**, although this can be used in formal speech or writing.

mead·ow /ˈmɛdoʊ/ *noun* [C] a field of grass: *sheep grazing in a meadow*

mea·ger /ˈmigər/ *adj.* too small in amount: *a meager income* ○ *The refugees carried their meager belongings across the border.*

☆ **meal** /mil/ *noun* [C] a certain time when you eat or the food that is eaten at that time: *Do you have your main meal at lunchtime or in the evening?* ○ *a heavy/light meal*

☞ The main meals of the day are **breakfast**, **lunch** and **dinner**. **Brunch** is a meal that people often eat late in the morning on weekends, instead of breakfast and lunch. **Supper** is usually a smaller meal (but look at the note at **dinner**). A very small meal is called a **snack**.

meal·time /ˈmiltaɪm/ *noun* [C] a time at which a meal is usually eaten

☆ **mean**[1] /min/ *verb* [T] (*p.t., p.p.* **meant** /mɛnt/) **1** (not in the *-ing* forms) to express, show or have as a meaning: *What does this word mean?* ○ *The bell means that class is over.* ○ *"What does that symbol mean?"* ○ *Does the name "Charles Bell" mean anything to you?* **2** to want or intend to say sth; to refer to sb/sth: *I don't understand what you mean.* ○ *She said "yes," but I think she really meant "no."* ○ *What do you mean by "a lot of money?"*

☞ Note that **mean** cannot be used with the meaning "to have the opinion that." We say: *I think (that)…* or *In my opinion…: I think she'd be silly to buy that car.* **I mean** is often used in conversation when you want to explain something you have just said or to add more information: *I think I'm falling in love with Rick – I mean, he's so cute!* ○ *I could hear their conversation – I mean, they were standing right next to me.* **I mean** is also used to correct something you have just said: *We went there on Tuesday, I mean Thursday.*

3 (not in the *-ing* forms) to be important to sb: *This job means a lot to me.* **4** (not in the *-ing* forms) to make sth likely; to cause: *The shortage of teachers means that classes are larger.* ○ *The new law means higher taxes for businesses.* **5** (not in the *-ing* forms) to be serious or sincere about sth: *He said he loved me, but I don't think he meant it!* **6** to want or plan to do sth; to intend sth: *I'm sure she didn't mean to upset you.* ○ *They didn't mean any harm.* ○ *I didn't mean you to cook the whole meal!* **7** (usually passive) to intend or expect sth to be or do sth: *It was only meant as a joke.* ○ *What's this picture meant to be?* ○ *This dessert is meant to be served chilled.*

IDM mean well to want to be kind and helpful but usually without success: *My mother means well, but I wish she'd stop treating me like a child.*

☆ **mean**[2] /min/ *adj.* **1 mean (to sb)** (used about people or their behavior) unkind; not nice: *It*

M

was mean of him not to invite you, too. ○ *Don't be mean to your little sister!* **2** (only *before* a noun) average: *What is the mean annual temperature in California?*

mean³ /min/ *noun* [C] (*technical*) average

me·an·der /miˈændər/ *verb* [I] **1** (used about a river, road, etc.) to have a lot of curves and bends **2** (used about a person or animal) to walk or travel slowly or without any definite direction

☆ **mean·ing** /ˈminɪŋ/ *noun* **1** [C,U] what sth means or expresses; its sense or intention: *This word has two different meanings in English.* ○ *What do you think is the meaning of the last line of the poem?* **2** [U] purpose or importance: *With his daughter dead, there seemed to be no meaning in life.*

mean·ing·ful /ˈminɪŋfl/ *adj.* **1** useful, important or interesting: *Most people need a meaningful relationship with another person.* **2** (used about a look, expression, etc.) trying to express a certain feeling or idea: *They kept giving each other meaningful glances across the table.* —**mean·ing·ful·ly** *adv.*

mean·ing·less /ˈminɪŋləs/ *adj.* without meaning, reason or sense: *The figures are meaningless if we have nothing to compare them with.*

☆ **means** /minz/ *noun* (*pl.* **means**) **1** [C, with sing. or pl. verb] a method of doing sth: *buses, cars, and other means of transportation* ○ *Is there any means of contacting your husband?* **2** [plural] (*formal*) money or wealth: *a family of modest means*

IDM **by means of** by using: *We got out of the hotel by means of the fire escape.*

by no means; not by any means (*formal*) (used for emphasis) not at all: *I'm by no means sure that this is the right thing to do.*

meant *p.t., p.p.* of MEAN¹

mean·time /ˈmintaɪm/ *noun*

IDM **in the meantime** in the time between two things happening: *Our new house isn't finished yet, so in the meantime we're living with my mother.*

☆ **mean·while** /ˈminwaɪl/ *adv.* during the same time or during the time between two things happening: *Peter was at home studying. Tony, meanwhile, was out with his friends.* ○ *The new computer will arrive next week. Meanwhile you'll have to manage without one.*

mea·sles /ˈmizlz/ *noun* [U] (*also* **the measles**) a common infectious disease, especially among children. You have a fever and your skin is covered in small red spots

☞ **Measles** looks like a plural noun, but it is used with a singular verb: *In many countries, measles is a very dangerous disease.*

mea·sly /ˈmizli/ *adj.* (*informal*) much too small in size, amount or value: *He paid me a measly three bucks to mow his lawn.*

☆ **meas·ure¹** /ˈmɛʒər/ *verb* **1** [I,T] to find the size, weight, etc. of sb/sth often by using an instrument such as a ruler: *Could you measure the table to see if it will fit into our dining room?* ○ *Height is measured in feet and inches.* ○ *Most countries use the metric system for measuring.* **2** [I] to be a certain height, width, length, etc.: *The pool measures 25 meters by 5 meters.* **3** [T] to show or judge the size, amount, etc. of sth: *A speedometer measures speed.* ○ (*figurative*) *How do you measure a person's success?*

PHRV **measure up (to sth)** to be as good as you need to be or as sb expects you to be: *Did the trip measure up to your expectations?*

☆ **meas·ure²** /ˈmɛʒər/ *noun* **1** [C] a way of describing the size, amount, etc. of sth: *A yard is a measure of length.* **2** [sing.] (*formal*) a certain amount or quantity; some but not much: *The play achieved a measure of success.* **3** [sing.] a way of understanding or judging sth: *The school's popularity is a measure of the teachers' success.* **4** [C, usually pl.] an action that is done for a special reason: *The government is taking new measures to reduce inflation.* ○ *As a temporary measure, the road will have to be closed.* ○ *emergency measures* ○ *safety measures*

☆ **meas·ure·ment** /ˈmɛʒərmənt/ *noun* **1** [C] a size, amount, etc. that is found by measuring: *What are the exact measurements of the room?* (= how wide, long, etc. is it?) ○ *What's your waist measurement?* ○ *Let's start by taking your measurements* (= measuring the size of your chest, waist and other parts of the body). **2** [U] the act of measuring: *I'm not sure how accurate his measurement of the area was.*

measuring cup *noun* [C] a glass, plastic or metal container with marks on it used for measuring food

☆ **meat** /mit/ *noun* [U] the flesh of animals or birds that people eat: *She doesn't eat meat – she's a vegetarian.*

☞ Some types of meat have different names from the animals they come from. We get **pork**, **ham** or **bacon** from a pig, **beef** from a cow, **veal** from a calf and **venison** from a deer. **Mutton** comes from a sheep, but we get **lamb** from a lamb. For specific types of birds and fish there is not a different word, but the meat from birds in general is called **poultry**. We often call beef, mutton and lamb **red meat**. We can **fry**, **grill**, **broil**, **roast** or **stew** meat. We **carve** a turkey, for example, or **slice** a ham or a **roast**. Meat can be described as **tough** or **tender**, **lean** or **fatty**. Uncooked meat is **raw**. Look also at **cook** and **rare**.

meat·ball /ˈmitbɔl/ *noun* [C] a thick ball made of meat that has been cut (**ground**) into very small pieces: *spaghetti and meatballs*

M

Mec·ca /ˈmɛkə/ *noun* **1** the city in Saudi Arabia where Muhammad was born, which is the center of Islam **2** [C, usually .sing.] **mecca** a place that many people wish to visit because of a particular interest: *Italy is a mecca for art lovers.*

me·chan·ic /məˈkænɪk/ *noun* [C] a person whose job is to repair and work with machines and tools: *a car mechanic*

☆ **me·chan·i·cal** /məˈkænɪkl/ *adj.* **1** connected with, worked by or produced by machines: *a mechanical pump* ○ *mechanical engineering* ○ *a mechanical mind* (= a mind that understands machines) **2** (used about a person's behavior) done like a machine as if you are not thinking about what you are doing: *He played the piano in a dull and mechanical way.* —**me·chan·i·cal·ly** /-kli/ *adv.*

me·chan·ics /məˈkænɪks/ *noun* **1 the mechanics** [plural] the way in which sth works or is done: *Don't ask me – I don't understand the mechanics of the legal system.* **2** [U] the science of how machines work

mech·a·nism /ˈmɛkənɪzəm/ *noun* [C] **1** a part of a piece of equipment or a machine that does a certain task: *Our car has an automatic locking mechanism.* **2** the way in which sth works or the process by which sth is done: *the mechanism of the heart* ○ *The new committee will provide a mechanism for investigating complaints.*

mech·a·nize /ˈmɛkənaɪz/ *verb* [I,T] to use machines instead of people to do work: *We have mechanized the entire production process.* —**mech·a·ni·za·tion** /ˌmɛkənəˈzeɪʃn/ *noun* [U]: *Increased mechanization has led to unemployment.*

med /mɛd/ (*informal*) = MEDICAL: *She's in med school.* ○ *a med student*

med·al /ˈmɛdl/ *noun* [C] a flat piece of metal, usually with a design and words on it, which is given to sb for bravery or as a prize in a sports event: *He was awarded a medal for bravery.* ○ *to win a gold/silver/bronze medal in the Olympics*

med·al·ist /ˈmɛdəlɪst/ *noun* [C] a person who has won a medal, especially in a sport: *an Olympic gold medalist*

me·dal·lion /məˈdælyən/ *noun* [C] a small round piece of metal on a chain which is worn as jewelry around the neck

med·dle /ˈmɛdl/ *verb* [I] **meddle (in/with sth)** to take too much interest in sth that you should not: *She criticized her mother for meddling in her personal life.*

☆ **me·di·a** /ˈmidiə/ *noun* [plural] **the media** television, radio and newspapers used as a means of communication: *The reports in the media have been greatly exaggerated.*

☞ Sometimes **media** is used with a singular verb, although it is a plural noun: *The media always take/takes a great interest in Holly-* wood stars' lives. Look also at **mass media** and **the press**.

me·di·ate /ˈmidieɪt/ *verb* [I,T] to try to settle a disagreement between two or more people or groups: *As a supervisor, she had to mediate between her colleagues and the management.* —**me·di·a·tion** /ˌmidiˈeɪʃn/ *noun* [U] —**me·di·a·tor** *noun* [C]

Med·i·caid (*also* **medicaid**) /ˈmɛdɪkeɪd/ *noun* [U] the system that provides medical care for poor people in the U.S. and that is paid for by taxes

☆ **med·i·cal** /ˈmɛdɪkl/ *adj.* connected with medicine and the treatment or prevention of illness: *a medical school/student* ○ *Have you had any medical treatment during the last three years?* ○ *medical research*

'**medical examiner** *noun* [C] an official person, usually a doctor, whose job is to examine a dead body in order to find out how the person died

Med·i·care (*also* **medicare**) /ˈmɛdɪkɛr/ *noun* [U] the system that provides medical care for old people in the U.S. and that is paid for by taxes

med·i·cat·ed /ˈmɛdɪkeɪṭəd/ *adj.* containing a substance like a medicine: *medicated shampoo*

☆ **med·i·ca·tion** /ˌmɛdɪˈkeɪʃn/ *noun* [C,U] pills, liquids, etc. that you take in order to treat an illness: *Are you currently taking any medication?* ○ *Many flu medications are available without a prescription.*

☆ **med·i·cine** /ˈmɛdɪsn/ *noun* **1** [U] the science of preventing and treating illness: *to study/practice medicine* **2** [C,U] pills, liquids, etc. that you take in order to treat an illness: *Medicines should be kept out of the reach of children.* ○ *to take medicine* ○ *Did the doctor prescribe any medicine?* ○ *cough medicine*

me·di·e·val /ˌmɛdˈivl; mɪd-; ˌmid-/ *adj.* of the Middle Ages in European history; i.e. between about 1100 and 1500 AD: *medieval art*

me·di·o·cre /ˌmidiˈoʊkər/ *adj.* of not very high quality: *a mediocre performance* —**me·di·oc·ri·ty** /ˌmidiˈakrəṭi/ *noun* [U]

med·i·tate /ˈmɛdəteɪt/ *verb* [I] **2** to spend time thinking deeply in a special way so that you become calm and peaceful, often as part of religious training **2** to think carefully and deeply (about sth): *I've been meditating on what you said last week.* —**med·i·ta·tion** /ˌmɛdəˈteɪʃn/ *noun* [U]: *Meditation is practiced by certain Eastern religions.*

the Med·i·ter·ra·ne·an /ˌmɛdətəˈremiən/ *noun* [sing.] the Mediterranean Sea or the countries around it ☞ Look at the note at **White House.** —**Med·i·ter·ra·ne·an** *adj.*: *Mediterranean cuisine*

☆ **me·di·um¹** /ˈmidiəm/ *noun* [C] **1** (*pl.* usually **me·di·a**) a means you can use to express or communicate sth: *Many actors feel that the*

M

theater is a more rewarding medium than tele-
vision. ○ He tried to keep the story out of the
media (= television, radio and newspapers).
☞ Look at media and mass media. 2 (pl.
me·di·ums) a person who says that he/she
can speak to and take messages from the
spirits of dead people

☆me·di·um² /ˈmidiəm/ adj. of a size or amount
that is neither very large nor very small; aver-
age: She was of medium height and weight. ○
Would you like a small, medium or large
drink? ○ a medium-sized dog

meek /mik/ adj. (used about people) quiet,
and doing what other people say without ask-
ing questions or arguing: a meek and humble
servant —**meek·ly** adv. —**meek·ness** noun [U]

☆**meet** /mit/ verb (p.t., p.p. **met** /mɛt/) 1 [I,T] to
come together by chance or because you have
arranged it: You'll never guess who I met
today! ○ What time should we meet for lunch?
2 [I,T] to see and know sb for the first time:
Have you two met before? ○ Where did you first
meet your husband? 3 [T] to go to a place and
wait for sb/sth to arrive: I'll come and meet
you at the bus station. ○ A limousine will meet
your plane and take you to your hotel. 4 [I]
(used about a group of people) to come to-
gether for a special purpose: Representatives
from both countries will meet for talks in New
York. ○ How often does the city council meet?
5 [T] to be enough for sth; to be able to deal
with sth: The money that I earn is enough to
meet our basic needs. ○ I'm afraid this piece of
work doesn't meet our requirements (= it's not
good enough). ○ This year is going to be diffi-
cult, but I'm sure that we can meet the chal-
lenge. 6 [I,T] to touch, join or make contact
with: The rivers meet in St. Louis. ○ Can you see
where the road meets the freeway on the map? ○
His eyes met hers.
IDM **make ends meet** ➭ END¹
there is more to sb/sth than meets the eye
sb/sth is more interesting or complex than
you might think at first: Do you think there's
more to their relationship than meets the eye?
PHRV **meet up (with sb)** to meet sb, espe-
cially after first going in different directions
or doing different things: Let's both do our
own shopping and meet up with each other for
coffee.
meet with sb to meet sb, especially for discus-
sion: The President met with his advisors early
this morning.
meet with sth to get a certain answer, reac-
tion or result: The mayor's proposal met with a
great deal of resistance.

☆**meet·ing** /ˈmitɪŋ/ noun [C] an organized occa-
sion when a number of people come together
in order to discuss or decide sth: The next
committee meeting will be held on August 19. ○
What's on the agenda for the department meet-
ing? ○ to attend a meeting

☞ We call, set up, arrange or organize a
meeting. We can also cancel or postpone a
meeting.

mega- /ˈmɛgə/ (in compounds) 1 a million: a
power plant with a capacity of 600 megawatts
2 (informal) very large or great: I bet she's
making megabucks in her new job.

meg·a·byte /ˈmɛgəbaɪt/(also informal **meg**)
noun [C] (abbr. **MB**) (computing) a unit of
computer memory. One megabyte is equal to
1,048, 576 (= 2²⁰) bytes: a 250-megabyte hard
drive

meg·a·phone /ˈmɛgəfoʊn/ noun [C] a piece of
equipment that you speak through to make
your voice sound louder, especially outside

mel·an·chol·y /ˈmɛlənkɑli/ noun [U] (formal)
a feeling of sadness that lasts for a long time
—**mel·an·chol·y** adj.

mel·low /ˈmɛloʊ/ adj. 1 (used about colors,
flavors or sounds) soft and pleasant 2 (infor-
mal) (used about people) calm and relaxed,
especially because of age —**mel·low** verb [I,T]:
Experience had mellowed her views about
many things.

mel·o·dra·ma /ˈmɛlədrɑmə/ noun [C,U] a
type of play or novel in which a lot of exciting
things happen and in which people's emotions
are stronger than in real life

mel·o·dra·mat·ic /ˌmɛlədrəˈmætɪk/ adj.
(used about a person's behavior) making
things seem more exciting and serious than
they really are

mel·o·dy /ˈmɛlədi/ noun [C] (pl. **mel·o·dies**)
1 a song or tune: to play a melody 2 the main
tune in a piece of music that is played by
several instruments or sung by several voices:
The tenors have the melody here.

mel·on /ˈmɛlən/ noun [C,U] a large round fruit
with a thick yellow or green skin and many
seeds: a slice of melon ☞ Look at watermelon

☆**melt** /mɛlt/ verb 1 [I,T] to change from solid to
liquid by means of heat: When we got up in the
morning the snow had melted. ○ First melt the
butter in a saucepan. 2 [I] (used about sb's
feelings, etc.) to become softer or less strong:
My heart melted when I saw the tiny puppy.
PHRV **melt away** to disappear: The crowd
melted away when the speaker had finished.
melt sth down to heat a metal or glass object
until it becomes soft

melt·down /ˈmɛltdaʊn/ noun [C,U] a serious
accident in which the central part of a nuclear
power plant (a reactor) becomes much too
hot, causing the release of a dangerous form of
energy (radiation)

'melting pot noun [C] a place where large
numbers of people from different countries
live together: New York is a melting pot of
different nationalities.

☆**mem·ber** /ˈmɛmbər/ noun [C] a person, ani-
mal or thing that belongs to a group, club,

M

organization, etc.: *All the members of the family were there.* ○ *a staff member* ○ *a member of Congress* ☞ Look at **congressman** and **congresswoman**.

☆ **mem·ber·ship** /ˈmɛmbərʃɪp/ *noun* **1** [U] the state of being a member of a group, organization, etc.: *To apply for membership, please complete the enclosed form.* ○ *Annual membership costs $200.* **2** [C,U] the people who belong to a group, organization, etc.: *Membership* (= the number of members) *has fallen in the past year.*

mem·brane /ˈmɛmbreɪn/ *noun* [C] (*formal*) a thin skin which covers or connects parts inside a person's or an animal's body

me·men·to /məˈmɛntoʊ/ *noun* [C] (*pl.* **me·men·tos** or **me·men·toes**) something that you keep to remind you of a person, a place or of sth that has happened

mem·o /ˈmɛmoʊ/ *noun* [C] (*pl.* **mem·os**) (also *formal* **memorandum**) a note sent from one person or office to another within an organization

mem·oirs /ˈmɛmwɑrz/ *noun* [plural] a person's written account of his/her own life and experiences

mem·o·ra·ble /ˈmɛmrəbl/ *adj.* worth remembering or easy to remember because it is special in some way: *The concert was a memorable experience.* —**mem·o·ra·bly** /-bli/ *adv.*

mem·o·ran·dum /ˌmɛməˈrændəm/ *noun* [C] (*pl.* **mem·o·ran·da** /ˌmɛməˈrændə/ or **mem·o·ran·das**) (*formal*) = MEMO

☆ **me·mo·ri·al** /məˈmɔriəl/ *noun* [C] **memorial (to sb/sth)** something that is built or done to remind people of an event or a person: *a war memorial* (= a statue or cross) ○ *a memorial service*

Me·morial Day *noun* [C] a holiday in the U.S. on the last Monday in May, for remembering soldiers who died in war

mem·o·rize /ˈmɛməraɪz/ *verb* [T] to learn sth so that you can remember it exactly: *Actors have to memorize their lines.*

☆ **mem·o·ry** /ˈmɛməri/ *noun* (*pl.* **mem·o·ries**) **1** [C] a person's ability to remember things: *a good/bad memory* ○ *A teacher needs to have a good memory for names.* **2** [C,U] the part of your mind in which you store things that you remember: *That day remained firmly in my memory for the rest of my life.* ○ *The appointment completely slipped my memory* (= I forgot it). ○ *He recited the whole poem from memory.* **3** [C] something that you remember: *That is one of my happiest memories.* ○ *I have no memories of that time at all.* ○ *childhood memories* **4** [U] the part of a computer where information is stored so that it can be changed or removed: *This computer has 32MB of memory.* ☞ Look at **RAM**.

IDM **in memory of sb/to the memory of sb** in order to remind people of sb who has died: *A service was held in memory of the dead.*

refresh your/sb's memory ➩ REFRESH

men *pl.* of MAN[1]

men·ace[1] /ˈmɛnəs/ *noun* **1** [C] a danger or threat: *The escaped prisoner is a menace to public safety.* **2** [U] a quality, feeling, etc. that is threatening or frightening: *He spoke with menace in his voice.*

men·ace[2] /ˈmɛnəs/ *verb* [T] to be likely to hurt sb/sth; to threaten

men·ac·ing /ˈmɛnəsɪŋ/ *adj.* threatening or frightening

☆ **mend**[1] /mɛnd/ *verb* [T] to repair a hole in a piece of clothing: *to mend a sock* ○ (*figurative*) *The management tried to mend relations with the unions.*

IDM **mend fences (with sb)** (especially in politics) to improve relations with sb after an argument: *The governor hopes to mend fences with the opposing party.*

mend[2] /mɛnd/ *noun*

IDM **on the mend** to be getting better after an illness or injury; to be recovering: *She's been in bed for a week, but she's on the mend now.*

me·ni·al /ˈminiəl/ *adj.* (used about work) not skilled or important: *a menial job*

men·in·gi·tis /ˌmɛnənˈdʒaɪtəs/ *noun* [U] a serious illness which affects the brain and the spine

men·o·pause /ˈmɛnəpɔz/ *noun* [U] the time when a woman stops losing blood once a month (**menstruating**). This usually happens around the age of 50.

men's room *noun* [C, usually sing.] a room with toilets in it for men in a public building: *go to the men's room* ➩ Look at **ladies' room**, **restroom** and at the note at **toilet**.

men·stru·ate /ˈmɛnstrueɪt; -streɪt/ *verb* [I] (*formal*) to lose blood from the uterus about once a month ➩ A less formal way of saying this is **to have your period**. —**men·stru·a·tion** /ˌmɛnstruˈeɪʃn; -ˈstreɪʃn/ *noun* [U]

☆ **men·tal** /ˈmɛntl/ *adj.* (only *before* a noun) **1** of or in the mind: *He has the mental capacity of a 7-year-old.* ○ *I'm not very good at mental arithmetic.* ○ *mental health* **2** connected with illness of the mind: *a mental hospital* —**men·tal·ly** /ˈmɛntəli/ *adv.*: *a home for mentally ill people*

men·tal·i·ty /mɛnˈtæləti/ *noun* [C] (*pl.* **men·tal·i·ties**) a type of mind or way of thinking: *Grandma says that kids today have a herd mentality – nobody wants to be independent.* ○ *the criminal mentality*

☆ **men·tion**[1] /ˈmɛnʃn/ *verb* [T] to say or write sth about sb/sth; to talk about sb/sth: *I wouldn't mention her exams to her – she's feeling nervous.* ○ *Did she mention what time the movie starts?* ○ *Whenever I mention going out together, she makes an excuse.* ○ *She mentioned Freeport as a good place for shopping.*

i	ɪ	ɛ	æ	ɑ	ɔ	ʌ	ʊ	u
see	sit	ten	cat	hot	saw	cup	put	too

IDM **don't mention it** (used as an informal polite reply when sb thanks you for sth) I'm pleased to help; not at all: *"Thanks for all your help." "Don't mention it."*
not to mention (used for emphasis) and also; as well as: *She's a mother and a doctor, not to mention being a state senator.*

men·tion² /ˈmɛnʃn/ *noun* [C,U] a brief remark about sb/sth: *There wasn't even a mention of the riots in the newspaper.* ○ *The candidate made no mention of her opponent in her speech.*

men·tor /ˈmɛntɔr; -tər/ *noun* [C] a person who gives advice to a younger or less experienced person

☆ **men·u** /ˈmɛnyu/ *noun* [C] **1** a list of the food that you can choose in a restaurant: *Could we have/see the dessert menu, please?* ○ *I hope there's some pizza on the menu.* **2** a list of choices in a computer program which is shown on the screen

me·ow /miˈaʊ/ *noun* [C] one of the sounds that a cat makes —**me·ow** *verb* [I] ☞ Look at **purr.**

mer·ce·nar·y /ˈmərsəˌnɛri/ *noun* [C] (*pl.* **mer·ce·nar·ies**) a person who fights for any group or country that will pay him/her

mer·chan·dise /ˈmərtʃəndaɪz; -daɪs/ *noun* [U] goods that are for sale

mer·chant /ˈmərtʃənt/ *noun* [C] a person whose job is to buy and sell goods, usually of one particular type: *a wine merchant*

mer·ci·ful /ˈmərsəfl/ *adj.* feeling or showing kindness to sb: *His death was a merciful release from pain.*

mer·ci·ful·ly /ˈmərsəfəli/ *adv.* luckily: *It was bitterly cold, but mercifully it was not snowing.*

mer·ci·less /ˈmərsələs/ *adj.* showing no kindness —**mer·ci·less·ly** *adv.*

Mer·cu·ry /ˈmərkyəri/ *noun* [sing.] the planet that is nearest to the sun

mer·cu·ry /ˈmərkyəri/ *noun* [U] (*symbol* Hg) a heavy silver-colored metal that is usually in liquid form. Mercury is used in thermometers.

☆ **mer·cy** /ˈmərsi/ *noun* [U] kindness or forgiveness (that is shown to sb who has done sth wrong): *The prisoners begged for mercy from the king.* ○ *The rebels were shown no mercy.*
IDM **at the mercy of sb/sth** having no power against sb/sth strong: *We spent the night on the mountain at the mercy of the wind and rain.*

mercy killing *noun* [C,U] = EUTHANASIA

☆ **mere** /mɪr/ *adj.* (only *before* a noun) (used for emphasizing how small or unimportant sth is) nothing more than: *Our market share has been reduced to a mere 10%.*

☆ **mere·ly** /ˈmɪrli/ *adv.* (*formal*) only; just: *The President can stop a bill from becoming law merely by refusing to sign it.*

merge /mərdʒ/ *verb* [I,T] **merge (sth) (with/into sth)** to join together or to join things together so that they become one: *Three small companies merged into one large one.* ○ *This creek merges with the Missouri River a few miles downstream.* ○ *Those colors seem to merge into each other.* ○ *The story merges fact and fantasy.* ○ *We have merged the two classes into one.*

merg·er /ˈmərdʒər/ *noun* [C,U] the act of joining two or more companies together

me·ringue /məˈræŋ/ *noun* [U] a mixture of sugar and egg whites that is beaten together and cooked in the oven

mer·it¹ /ˈmɛrət/ *noun* **1** [U] high quality; excellence: *There is a lot of merit in her ideas.* ○ *a certificate of merit* ○ *a novel of great artistic merit* **2** [C, usually pl.] an advantage or a good quality of sb/sth: *What are the merits of this new proposal?* ○ *Each case must be judged separately on its own merits* (= not according to general principles).

mer·it² /ˈmɛrət/ *verb* [T] (*formal*) to be good enough for sth; to deserve: *This suggestion certainly merits further discussion.*

mer·maid /ˈmərmeɪd/ *noun* [C] (in stories) a woman who has the tail of a fish instead of legs and who lives in the ocean

mer·ri·ment /ˈmɛrəmənt/ *noun* [U] (*formal*) laughter and enjoyment

☆ **mer·ry** /ˈmɛri/ *adj.* (**mer·ri·er**; **mer·ri·est**) happy and cheerful: *merry laughter* ○ *Merry Christmas!* —**mer·ri·ly** /ˈmɛrəli/ *adv.*

merry-go-round *noun* [C] (*also* **carousel**) a big round platform at a fair, etc. that turns around and around by the use of a motor. It has model horses, etc. on it for children to ride on: *to have a ride on a merry-go-round*

mesh /mɛʃ/ *noun* [C,U] material that is like a net (= made of plastic, wire or rope threads with holes in between): *a wire mesh fence*

mes·mer·ize /ˈmɛzməraɪz/ *verb* [T] to hold sb's attention completely: *The audience seemed to be mesmerized by the speaker's voice.*

☆ **mess¹** /mɛs/ *noun* **1** [sing.] a thing or place that is dirty or not organized: *Who spilled flour on the kitchen floor? Come here and clean up your mess!* ○ *My hair is a mess.* **2** [C, usually sing.] the state of being dirty or not organized: *The kitchen's in a real mess!* ☞ The adjective is **messy.** **3** [sing.] the state of having problems or troubles: *The company is in a financial mess.* ○ *to make a mess of your life* **4** [C] (*also* **mess hall**) the room or building where soldiers eat together: *the officers' mess*

mess² /mɛs/ *verb*
PHRV **mess around** to behave in a foolish way: *We were just messing around when Greg broke the lamp.*
mess around with sth to touch or use sth in a careless or foolish way: *Stop messing around with those tools before somebody gets hurt!*

ə	y	w	t̬	eɪ	aɪ	ɔɪ	aʊ	oʊ
about	yes	woman	butter	say	five	boy	now	go

mess sth up 1 to make sth dirty or not organized **2** to do sth badly or spoil sth: *I really messed up the last question on the test.*

mess with sb (*informal*) to treat sb in a way that is not fair or reasonable: *Don't mess with Big John – he's got a pretty bad temper!*

☆ **mes·sage** /ˈmɛsɪdʒ/ *noun* **1** [C] a written or spoken piece of information that is passed from one person to another: *Mr. Thomas is not here right now. Can I take a message?* ○ *to get/ receive a message from sb* ○ *Please leave a message after the beep.* **2** [sing.] the main idea of a book, speech, etc.: *It was a funny movie, but it also had a serious message.*

IDM **get the message** (*informal*) to understand what sb means even if it is not said directly: *He finally got the message and left Dick and Sarah alone together.*

mes·sen·ger /ˈmɛsəndʒər/ *noun* [C] a person who carries a message

Mes·si·ah (*also* messiah) /məˈsaɪə/ *noun* [C] a person, e.g. Jesus Christ, who is expected to come and save the world

☆ **mess·y** /ˈmɛsi/ *adj.* (**mess·i·er**; **mess·i·est**) **1** dirty or not neat: *a messy room* **2** needing a lot of cleaning up: *Painting the ceiling is a messy job.* **3** having or causing problems or trouble: *a messy divorce*

met *p.t., p.p.* of MEET

☆ **met·al** /ˈmɛtl/ *noun* [C,U] a type of solid mineral substance, e.g. tin, iron, gold, steel, etc.: *Aluminum is a non-magnetic metal.* ○ *to recycle scrap metal* ○ *a metal bar*

me·tal·lic /məˈtælɪk/ *adj.* looking like metal or making a noise like one piece of metal hitting another: *a metallic blue car* ○ *harsh metallic sounds*

met·a·mor·pho·sis /ˌmɛtəˈmɔrfəsəs/ *noun* [C] (*pl.* **met·a·mor·pho·ses** /-fəsiz/) (*formal*) a complete change of form (as part of natural development): *the metamorphosis of a tadpole into a frog*

met·a·phor /ˈmɛtəfɔr/ *noun* [C,U] a way of describing sth by comparing it to sth else which has the same qualities (but without using the words "as" or "like"). For example, if you say sb is a "parrot," you are using a metaphor to express the fact that the person just repeats things without thinking. ☞ Look also at **simile**. —**met·a·phor·i·cal** /ˌmɛtəˈfɔrɪkl/ *adj.*: *a metaphorical expression* —**met·a·phor·i·cal·ly** /-kli/ *adv.*

me·te·or /ˈmitiər/ *noun* [C] a small piece of rock, etc. in space. When a meteor enters the earth's atmosphere, it makes a bright line in the night sky.

me·te·or·ic /ˌmitiˈɔrɪk; -ˈɑr-/ *adj.* very fast or successful: *a meteoric rise to fame*

me·te·or·ol·o·gist /ˌmitiəˈrɑlədʒɪst/ *noun* [C] a person who studies the weather in order to produce a report on what will happen (**a forecast**)

me·te·or·ol·o·gy /ˌmitiəˈrɑlədʒi/ *noun* [U] the study of the weather and climate —**me·te·or·o·log·i·cal** /ˌmitiərəˈlɑdʒɪkl/ *adj.*: *meteorological data*

☆ **me·ter¹** /ˈmitər/ *noun* [C] **1** (*abbr.* **m**) a measure of length; 100 centimeters: *A meter is about 39 inches.* ○ *Who holds the record in the 100 meters?* (= the race). **2** a piece of equipment that measures the amount of gas, water, electricity, time, etc. that you have used: *to read the gas meter* ○ *a parking meter*

me·ter² /ˈmitər/ *verb* [T] to measure sth with a meter¹(2)

☆ **meth·od** /ˈmɛθəd/ *noun* [C] a way of doing sth: *modern methods of teaching languages* ○ *a simple method for calculating loan payments*

me·thod·i·cal /məˈθɑdɪkl/ *adj.* having or using a well-organized and careful way of doing sth: *Paul is a very methodical worker.* —**me·thod·i·cal·ly** /-kli/ *adv.*

Meth·od·ist /ˈmɛθədɪst/ *noun* [C, adj.] (a member) of a Protestant Church that was started by John Wesley in the 18th century

me·tic·u·lous /məˈtɪkyələs/ *adj.* giving or showing great attention to detail; very careful —**me·tic·u·lous·ly** *adv.*

met·ric /ˈmɛtrɪk/ *adj.* using the system of measurement that is based on meters, grams, liters, etc. (**the metric system**) ☞ Look at Appendix 2.

met·ro /ˈmɛtroʊ/ *adj.* = METROPOLITAN

me·trop·o·lis /məˈtrɑpələs/ *noun* [C] a very large city

☆ **met·ro·pol·i·tan** /ˌmɛtrəˈpɑlətn/ (*also* **metro**) *adj.* connected with a large city: *the population of metropolitan Detroit* (= the city and its suburbs) ○ *the six-county metro area*

mg *abbr.* = MILLIGRAM

mi. *abbr.* = MILE

mice *pl.* of MOUSE

mi·cro·chip /ˈmaɪkroʊtʃɪp/ = CHIP¹

mi·cro·cosm /ˈmaɪkrəkazəm/ *noun* [C] something that is a small example of sth larger: *Some people say a college is a microcosm of society as a whole.*

mi·cro·film /ˈmaɪkroʊfɪlm/ *noun* [C,U] a piece of film on which information is stored in very small print

mi·cro·phone /ˈmaɪkrəfoʊn/ (*also informal* **mike**) *noun* [C] a piece of electrical equipment that is used for making sounds louder or for recording them: *Speak into the microphone so that everyone can hear you.*

mi·cro·scope /ˈmaɪkrəskoʊp/ *noun* [C] a piece of equipment that makes very small objects look large enough for you to be able to see them: *to examine sth under a microscope*

mi·cro·scop·ic /ˌmaɪkrəˈskɑpɪk/ *adj.* too small to be seen without a microscope

mi·cro·wave /ˈmaɪkrəweɪv/ *noun* [C] **1** a short electric wave that is used for sending radio messages and for cooking food **2** (*also*

ər	ɪr	ɛr	ɑr	ɔr	ʊr	ʒ	h	ŋ
bird	near	hair	car	north	tour	vision	hat	sing

M

microwave oven) a type of oven that cooks or heats food very quickly using microwaves

mid- /mɪd/ (in compounds) in the middle of: *a mid-air collision* ○ *the mid-1950s* ○ *in mid-June*

mid·day /ˌmɪdˈdeɪ/ *noun* [U] the middle of the day: *the midday temperature* ○ *The stock market had fallen three points by midday.* ☞ Look at **midnight**.

☆ **mid·dle¹** /ˈmɪdl/ *noun* **the middle** [sing.] the part, point or position that is at about the same distance from the two ends of sth: *There was a broken bottle lying in the middle of the road.* ○ *Here's a picture of me with my two brothers. I'm the one in the middle.*

☞ **Center** and **middle** are often very similar in meaning, but center is used when you mean the exact middle of something: *How do you find the center of a circle?* ○ *There was a large table in the middle of the room.* When you are talking about a period of time, only **middle** may be used: *The baby woke up in the middle of the night.* ○ *the middle of July*

IDM **be in the middle of sth/of doing sth** to be busy doing sth: *We were right in the middle of supper when the phone rang.*

the middle of nowhere (*informal*) a place that is far away from big cities

☆ **mid·dle²** /ˈmɪdl/ *adj.* (only *before* a noun) in the middle¹: *I wear my mother's ring on my middle finger.* ○ *Unfortunately, I had a middle seat on the plane.*

ˌ**middle ˈage** *noun* [U] the time when you are about 40 to 60 years old: *in late middle age* —ˌ**middle-ˈaged** *adj.*: *middle-aged people*

the ˌMiddle ˈAges *noun* [plural] the period of European history from about AD1100 to AD1500

the ˌmiddle ˈclass *noun* [sing.] the people in society who are in the middle income group. Middle-class people include business people, managers, teachers, etc.: *taxpayers who belong to the middle class* ○ *students from middle-class families*

☆ **the ˌMiddle ˈEast** *noun* [sing.] the group of countries that are situated at the point where Europe, Africa and Asia meet ☞ Look at the note at **White House**.

mid·dle·man /ˈmɪdlmæn/ *noun* [C] (*pl.* **middle-men**) a person who buys sth in order to sell it to sb else for more money

ˌ**middle ˈname** *noun* [C] the second of two given names

ˈ**middle school** *noun* [C] a school for children in grades 5 or 6 through 8

midg·et /ˈmɪdʒət/ *noun* [C] an offensive word for a very small person

☆ **mid·night** /ˈmɪdnaɪt/ *noun* [U] twelve o'clock at night: *They left the party at midnight.* ○ *The clock struck midnight.* ☞ Look at **noon**.

midst /mɪdst/ *noun* [U] **in the midst of** in the

middle of sth: *The police department is in the midst of a murder investigation.*

mid·sum·mer /ˌmɪdˈsʌmər/ *noun* [U] the time around the middle of summer

mid·term /ˈmɪdtərm/ *noun* [C] an examination that you take in the middle of a course: *a biology midterm* —**mid·term** *adj.*: *a midterm exam*

mid·way /ˌmɪdˈweɪ/ *adj., adv.* **midway (between sth and sth)** in the middle or halfway (between sth and sth): *Our farm is midway between Lincoln and Omaha.*

mid·week /ˌmɪdˈwik/ *noun* [U] the middle of the week (= Tuesday, Wednesday and Thursday) —**mid·week** *adv.*: *If you travel midweek, it will be less crowded.*

☆ **the Mid·west** /ˌmɪdˈwɛst/ *noun* [sing.] the northern central part of the United States. The Midwest includes the states of Minnesota, Wisconsin, Illinois, Michigan, Indiana, Nebraska, Iowa, Kansas and Missouri. —**Mid·west·ern** /ˌmɪdˈwɛstərn/ *adj.*

mid·wife /ˈmɪdwaɪf/ *noun* [C] (*pl.* **mid·wives** /-waɪvz/) a person who has been trained to help women give birth to babies

mid·win·ter /ˌmɪdˈwɪntər/ *noun* [U] the time around the middle of winter

☆ **might¹** /maɪt/ *modal verb* (*negative* **might not**) **1** (used for saying that sth is possible): *"Where's William?" "He might be upstairs."* ○ *We might be going to Spain on vacation this year.* ○ *She might not come if she's very busy.* ○ *If I had known the movie was about dinosaurs, I might have gone to see it* (= but I didn't know, so I didn't go). **2** (used as the past form of "may" when you report what sb has said): *He said he might be late* (= his words were, "I may be late"). **3** (used to suggest sth politely): *If you need more information, you might try the library.*

IDM **may/might as well (do sth)** ☞ WELL¹

I might have known (used for saying that you are not surprised that sth has happened): *I might have known he wouldn't help.*

might² /maɪt/ *noun* [U] (*formal*) great strength or power: *We pushed with all our might, but the rock did not move.*

might·y¹ /ˈmaɪti/ *adj.* (**might·i·er; might·i·est**) very strong or powerful

might·y² /ˈmaɪti/ *adv.* (*informal*) very: *That's mighty kind of you.*

mi·graine /ˈmaɪɡreɪn/ *noun* [C,U] a very bad headache that makes you feel sick

mi·grant /ˈmaɪɡrənt/ *noun* [C] a person who goes from place to place in search of work: *migrant farm workers*

mi·grate /ˈmaɪɡreɪt/ *verb* [I] **1** (used about animals and birds) to travel from one part of the world to another at the same time every year **2** to move from one place to go and live and work in another: *Many of the poorer people were forced to migrate to the cities to look for*

M

tʃ	dʒ	v	θ	ð	s	z	ʃ
chin	June	van	thin	then	so	zoo	she

work. ☞ Look at **emigrate.** —**mi·gra·tion** /maɪˈɡreɪʃn/ *noun* [C,U]: *the annual migration south*

mike /maɪk/ *noun* [C] (*informal*) = MICRO-PHONE

☆ **mild** /maɪld/ *adj.* **1** gentle, not strong or severe: *a mild soap that is gentle to your skin* ○ *a mild winter* ○ *a mild punishment* **2** (used about food) not having a strong taste: *mild cheese* ○ *mild, medium or hot chili sauce* —**mild·ness** *noun* [U]

mil·dew /ˈmɪldu/ *noun* [U] a substance (**a fungus**) that grows in warm, damp places

mild·ly /ˈmaɪldli/ *adv.* **1** in a mild way **2** not very; slightly: *The audience was only mildly enthusiastic.*

☆ **mile** /maɪl/ *noun* [C] **1** a measure of length; 1.6 kilometers. There are 1,760 yards in a mile: *The nearest beach is seven miles away.* ○ *It's a seven-mile drive to the lake.* ○ *My car gets 35 miles to the gallon.* ☞ For more information on measurements, look at Appendix 2. **2** (*also* **miles**) a lot: *to miss a target by a mile* **3 miles** a long way: *How much farther is it? We've walked miles already.*

mile·age /ˈmaɪlɪdʒ/ *noun* [U] **1** the distance that has been traveled (measured in miles): *The car is five years old, but it has very low mileage.* **2** the distance that a car, etc. can travel using a certain amount of fuel: *Our car gets good gas mileage* (= it can go a long way on each gallon of gasoline). **3** [U] (*informal*) the amount of use or benefit you get from sth: *You've gotten a lot of mileage out of that coat – it's five years old and still looks good.*

mile·stone /ˈmaɪlstoʊn/ *noun* [C] **1** (*old-fashioned*) a stone at the side of the road that shows how far it is to the next town **2** a very important event: *Jenny's first day of kindergarten was a real milestone.*

mil·i·tant¹ /ˈmɪlətənt/ *adj.* using or willing to use force or strong pressure to get what you want: *Members of a militant group placed a bomb near police headquarters.* —**mil·i·tan·cy** /-tənsi/ *noun* [U]

mil·i·tant² /ˈmɪlətənt/ *noun* [C] a militant person

☆ **mil·i·tar·y¹** /ˈmɪləˌtɛri/ *adj.* (only *before* a noun) of or for soldiers, the army, navy, etc.: *Do you have military service in your country?* ○ *to take military action*

☆ **mil·i·tar·y²** /ˈmɪləˌtɛri/ **the military** *noun* the army, navy, etc.: *Our son's in the military.* ○ *to join the military*

mi·li·tia /məˈlɪʃə/ *noun* [C] a group of people who are not regular soldiers but who have had some military training

☆ **milk¹** /mɪlk/ *noun* [U] **1** a white liquid that is produced by women and animals to feed their babies. People drink cows', goats', etc. milk and use it to make butter and cheese: *whole, skim, powdered, condensed, lowfat, etc. milk* ○

2% milk (= milk which contains two percent fat) ○ *Don't use that milk – it's sour.* ○ *coffee with milk and sugar* ○ *a carton of milk* ○ *a milk carton* **2** the juice of some plants or trees that looks like milk: *coconut milk*

milk² /mɪlk/ *verb* **1** [I,T] to take milk from a cow, goat, etc. **2** [T] to get as much money, information, etc. as you can from sb/sth: *The colonists milked the country of its natural resources.*

milk chocolate *noun* [U] chocolate that is made with milk

milk·man /ˈmɪlkmæn/ *noun* [C] (*pl.* **milkmen**) a person who delivers milk to your house

milk·shake /ˈmɪlkʃeɪk/ (*also* **shake**) *noun* [C] a drink made of milk, ice cream and flavoring ☞ Look at **malt.**

milk·y /ˈmɪlki/ *adj.* (**milk·i·er; milk·i·est**) **1** made with milk: *a hot milky drink* **2** of a pale white color

the Milky Way *noun* [sing.] the system of stars that contains our sun and its planets

mill¹ /mɪl/ *noun* [C] **1** a building that contains a large machine that is used for grinding grain into flour: *a water mill* ☞ Look also at **windmill. 2** a factory that is used for making certain kinds of material: *a paper mill* ○ *a steel mill*

mill² /mɪl/ *verb* [T] to grind sth in a mill¹(1)

PHRV **mill around** (*informal*) (used about a large number of people or animals) to move around in one place with no real purpose

mil·len·ni·um /məˈlɛniəm/ *noun* [C] (*pl.* **millennia** /məˈlɛniə/ or **mil·len·ni·ums**) a period of 1,000 years

mil·li·gram /ˈmɪləɡræm/ *noun* [C] (*abbr.* **mg**) a measure of weight. There are 1,000 milligrams in a gram.

mil·li·li·ter /ˈmɪləlitər/ *noun* [C] (*abbr.* **ml**) a measure of liquid. There are 1,000 milliliters in a liter.

mil·li·me·ter /ˈmɪləmitər/ *noun* [C] (*abbr.* **mm**) a measure of length. There are 1,000 millimeters in a meter.

☆ **mil·lion** /ˈmɪlyən/ *number* 1,000,000: *Almost 250 million people live in the United States.* ○ *Millions are at risk from the disease.*

☞ Notice that when you are counting, you use million without s: *six million dollars.* For more information about numbers, look at Appendix 2.

☆ **mil·lion·aire** /ˌmɪlyəˈnɛr/ *noun* [C] a person who has a million dollars, etc.; a very rich person

mil·lionth¹ /ˈmɪlyənθ/ *det.* 1,000,000th: *the store's millionth customer*

mil·lionth² /ˈmɪlyənθ/ *noun* [C] one of a million equal parts of sth: *a millionth of a second*

mime¹ /maɪm/ *noun* **1** [C,U] (*also* **pantomime**) acting or telling a story without

M

speaking, by using your hands, body and the expressions on your face **2** [C] an actor who performs using mime

mime² /maɪm/ *verb* [I,T] to act or express sth using mime¹(1)

mim·ic¹ /'mɪmɪk/ *verb* [T] (*pres. part.* **mim·ick·ing**; *p.t., p.p.* **mim·icked**) to copy sb's behavior in an amusing way

mim·ic² /'mɪmɪk/ *noun* [C] a person who can mimic other people

min. *abbr.* = MINIMUM, MINUTE

mince /mɪns/ *verb* [T] to cut sth into very small pieces: *half a cup of minced onion*

☆ **mind¹** /maɪnd/ *noun* [C,U] the part of your brain that thinks and remembers; your thoughts and intelligence: *He has a very sharp mind.*

IDM **be out of your mind** (*informal*) to be crazy: *He must be out of his mind to give up a good job like that.*

bear in mind (that) ⇨ BEAR²

blow your mind ⇨ BLOW¹

change your mind ⇨ CHANGE¹

cross your mind ⇨ CROSS²

frame of mind ⇨ FRAME¹

give sb a piece of your mind ⇨ PIECE¹

have/keep an open mind ⇨ OPEN¹

in mind in your/sb's thoughts: *I understand your concern and I'll keep it in mind for the future.*

in the back of your mind ⇨ BACK¹

keep your mind on sth to continue to pay attention to sth: *Stop talking and try to keep your mind on your work!*

make up your mind to decide: *I can't make up my mind which sweater to buy.*

on your mind worrying you: *Don't bother her with that. She's got enough on her mind already.*

slip your mind ⇨ SLIP¹

state of mind ⇨ STATE¹

take your/sb's mind off sth to help you/sb not to think or worry about sth

☆ **mind²** /maɪnd/ *verb* **1** [I,T] (especially in questions, answers and negative sentences) to feel annoyed, unhappy or uncomfortable: *"Do you mind if I smoke?" "No, not at all."* ○ *I'm sure Frank won't mind if you don't invite him.* ○ *We have four kids so I hope you won't mind about the mess!* ○ *Do you mind having to travel so far to work every day? I wouldn't mind a vacation in the Caribbean this year!* (= I would like it.) **2** [T] (used in a question as a polite way of asking sb to do sth) could you ...?: *Would you mind closing the window for me?* ○ *Do you mind driving? I'm feeling pretty tired.*

IDM **mind your own business** (*informal*) to pay attention to your own affairs, not other people's: *Mom, tell Todd to mind his own business and stop listening to my private phone calls!*

never mind don't worry; it doesn't matter: *"I*

forgot to mail your letter." "Never mind, I'll do it later."

-mind·ed /'maɪndəd/ *adj.* **1** (in compounds) having the type of mind mentioned: *a independent-minded person* ☞ Look at **open-minded**. **2** (in compounds) interested in the thing mentioned: *career-minded*

mind·less /'maɪndləs/ *adj.* not having or not needing thought or intelligence: *mindless violence* ○ *mindless factory work*

☆ **mine¹** /maɪn/ *pron.* of or belonging to me: *"Whose jacket is this?" "It's mine."* ○ *Don't take your car – you can come in mine.* ○ *May I introduce a friend of mine?* (= one of my friends) ☞ Look at **my**.

☆ **mine²** /maɪn/ *noun* [C] **1** a hole, or system of holes and passages, that people dig under the ground in order to obtain coal, tin, gold, etc.: *a coal mine* **2** a bomb that is hidden under the ground or under water: *to step on a land mine*

mine³ /maɪn/ *verb* **1** [I,T] to dig in the ground for coal, gold, etc.; to get coal, etc. by digging: *Diamonds are mined in South Africa.* ☞ Look at **mining**. **2** [T] to put hidden mines²(2) in an area of land or ocean

mine·field /'maɪnfild/ *noun* [C] **1** an area of land or ocean where mines²(2) have been hidden **2** a situation that is full of hidden dangers or difficulties: *The question of raising taxes was a political minefield.*

min·er /'maɪnər/ *noun* [C] a person whose job is to work in a mine²(1) to get coal, etc.

☆ **min·er·al** /'mɪnərəl/ *noun* [C] a natural substance such as coal, salt, iron, etc., especially one that is dug out of the ground for people to use: *a country rich in minerals* ○ *Vegetables are excellent sources of vitamins and minerals.*

'mineral ˌwater *noun* [U] water that comes directly from the ground, contains minerals and is thought to be good for your health: *a bottle of mineral water*

min·gle /'mɪŋgl/ *verb* [I,T] to mix with another thing or with other people: *His excitement was mingled with fear.* ○ *She was too shy to mingle with the other party guests.*

min·i- /'mɪni/ (in compounds) very small: *a miniskirt* (= a very short skirt)

min·i·a·ture /'mɪnətʃʊr; -tʃər/ *adj.* very small; much smaller than usual: *a collection of miniature cars*

min·i·mal /'mɪnəməl/ *adj.* very small in amount or level: *The project has had minimal support.*

min·i·mize /'mɪnəmaɪz/ *verb* [T] to make sth as small as possible (in amount or level): *We will try to minimize the risks to the public.* ☞ The opposite is **maximize**.

☆ **min·i·mum¹** /'mɪnəməm/ *noun* [sing.] the smallest amount or level that is possible or allowed: *I need a minimum of seven hours' sleep.* ○ *The minimum he will accept is $20,000 a year.* ○ *We will try and keep the cost of the*

M

ə	y	w	t	eɪ	aɪ	ɔɪ	aʊ	oʊ
about	yes	woman	butter	say	five	boy	now	go

tickets to a minimum. ☞ The opposite is **max-imum**.

☆ **min·i·mum²** /ˈmɪnəməm/ *adj.* (only *before* a noun) the smallest possible or allowed: *What's the minimum age for leaving school in your country?* ○ *the minimum wage* (= the lowest rate of pay that is allowed by law) ☞ The opposite is **maximum**.

min·ing /ˈmaɪnɪŋ/ *noun* [U] (often in compounds) the process or industry of getting coal, metals, salt, etc. out of the ground by digging: *tin mining* ○ *a mining town*

☆ **min·is·ter** /ˈmɪnəstər/ *noun* [C] **1** a religious leader, especially in a Protestant church ☞ Look at **pastor** and at the note at **priest**. **2** (in some countries) a senior member of the government who is often the head of a department ☞ Look at **Prime Minister** and **secretary**.

min·is·try /ˈmɪnəstri/ *noun* (*pl.* **min·is·tries**) **1 the ministry** [sing.] the profession of being a priest (in Protestant churches): *to enter the ministry* (= to become a minister) **2** (in some countries) a division of the government responsible for a particular subject ☞ Look at **department**.

min·i·van /ˈmɪnivæn/ *noun* a large car that can carry five to seven people

mink /mɪŋk/ *noun* [C] a small wild animal whose fur is used for expensive coats: *a mink coat*

☆ **mi·nor¹** /ˈmaɪnər/ *adj.* **1** not very big, serious or important (when compared with others): *It's only a minor problem. Don't worry.* ○ *She's in the hospital for a minor operation.* **2** of one of the two types of key¹(2) in which music is usually written: *a symphony in F minor* ☞ The opposite for both senses is **major**.

☆ **mi·nor²** /ˈmaɪnər/ *noun* [C] **1** a person who is not old enough to do sth legally: *The purchase of cigarettes by minors is strictly prohibited.* ○ *He was arrested for providing alcohol to minors.*

☞ In the United States, you must be at least 16 years old in order to buy tobacco products and at least 21 in order to buy and drink alcohol. Your parents are legally responsible for taking care of you until you are 18.

2 a subject that you study at a college or university and that is less important than your main subject: *He's studying French with a minor in art history.* **3** a person who is studying sth as a less important subject: *He's an art history minor.* ☞ Look at **major²**.

☆ **mi·nor³** /ˈmaɪnər/ *verb*

PHRV **minor in sth** to study sth as a less important subject at a college or university: *He's minoring in art history.* ☞ Look at **major³**.

☆ **mi·nor·i·ty** /məˈnɔrəti; maɪ-; -ˈnɑr-/ *noun* [C] (*pl.* **mi·nor·i·ties**) **1** [usually sing., with sing.

or pl. verb] the smaller number or part of a group; less than half: *Most women continue to work when they are married. Only a minority stays/stay at home.* ○ *to hold a minority interest in a company* (= to own less than half of a company) ○ *the Senate minority leader*

☞ Note that if we are thinking of the members of the group individually, we use a plural verb. The opposite is **majority**.

2 a group of people who are of a different race or religion from most of the people in the country where they live: *children from racial and ethnic minorities* ○ *minority neighborhoods* ○ *minority-owned businesses*

IDM **be in a/the minority** to be the smaller of two groups: *Smokers are in the minority in our company.* ☞ Look at **in a/the majority**.

mint /mɪnt/ *noun* **1** [U] a small plant (**an herb**) whose leaves are used for giving a fresh flavor to food, drinks, toothpaste, etc.: *mint-flavored mouthwash* ○ *a candy bar with mint filling* **2** [C] a candy with a strong fresh flavor ☞ Look also at **peppermint**. **3** [sing.] a place where paper money and coins are made by the government

mint·y /ˈmɪnti/ *adj.* tasting like mint

mi·nus¹ /ˈmaɪnəs/ *prep.* **1** less; subtract; take away: *Six minus two is four.* ☞ The opposite is **plus**. **2** (used about a number) below zero: *The temperature will fall to minus 10.* **3** (*informal*) without: *The police found my car – minus the radio – shortly after it had been stolen.*

mi·nus² /ˈmaɪnəs/ *adj.* (only *after* a noun) (used with grades given for school work) slightly lower than: *I got an A minus (A–) on the test.* ☞ Look at **plus**.

mi·nus³ /ˈmaɪnəs/ (*also* **ˈminus sign**) *noun* [C] the sign (–) which is used in mathematics to show that a number is below zero or that you should subtract the second number from the first

min·us·cule /ˈmɪnəskyul/ *adj.* very small; tiny

☆ **min·ute¹** /ˈmɪnət/ *noun* **1** [C] (*abbr.* **min.**) one of the 60 parts that make up one hour; 60 seconds: *It's five minutes to/after nine.* ○ *He called ten minutes ago.* ○ *Hurry up! The plane leaves in twenty minutes!* ○ *The show lasts for about 50 minutes.* **2** [sing.] a very short time; a moment: *Wait a minute! You forgot your notes.* ○ *Do you have a minute to spare? I want to talk to you.* **3 the minutes** [plural] a written record of what is said and decided at a meeting: *to take (the) minutes* (= to write them down)

IDM **(at) any minute/moment (now)** (*informal*) very soon: *The plane will be landing any minute now.*

in a minute very soon: *I'll be with you in a minute – I'm almost finished.*

just a minute (*informal*) (used for stopping a person, pausing to think, etc.) to wait for a

ər	ɪr	ɛr	ɑr	ɔr	ʊr	ʒ	h	ŋ
bird	near	hair	car	north	tour	vision	hat	sing

short time: *Just a minute. Is that your book or mine?*
the last minute/moment ⇨ LAST¹
the minute/moment (that) as soon as: *I'll tell him you called the minute (that) he gets here.*
wait a minute/second ⇨ WAIT¹

mi·nute² /maɪˈnut/ adj. (**mi·nu·ter**; **mi·nu·test**) **1** very small; tiny: *I just have one minute criticism.* **2** very exact or accurate: *She was able to describe the man in minute detail.*

mir·a·cle /ˈmɪrəkl/ noun [C] a wonderful and very unusual event that is impossible to explain and that is thought to be caused by God or a god: *Christ performed many miracles, even bringing dead people back to life.* ○ *She's doing her best, but nobody can work miracles!* ○ *It will be a miracle if he passes his driving test.*

mi·rac·u·lous /məˈrækyələs/ adj. extremely lucky, impossible to explain or understand: *She made a miraculous recovery from her illness.* —**mi·rac·u·lous·ly** adv.

mi·rage /məˈrɑʒ/ noun [C] something that you think you see in very hot weather but that does not really exist, especially water in a desert

☆ **mir·ror¹** /ˈmɪrər/ noun [C] a piece of special glass that you can look into in order to see yourself or what is behind you: *That dress looks great on you. Take a look in the mirror.* ○ *Check your rear view mirror before you change lanes.*

☞ A mirror **reflects** images. What you see in a mirror is a **reflection**.

mir·ror² /ˈmɪrər/ verb [T] to reflect sth as if in a mirror: *The trees were mirrored in the lake.*

mis·be·have /ˌmɪsbɪˈheɪv/ verb [I] to behave badly —**mis·be·hav·ior** /ˌmɪsbɪˈheɪvyər/ noun [U]

misc. *abbr.* = MISCELLANEOUS

mis·cal·cu·late /ˌmɪsˈkælkyəleɪt/ verb [I,T] to make a mistake in calculating or estimating (a situation or an amount, a distance, etc.): *The driver miscalculated the speed at which the other car was traveling.* —**mis·cal·cu·la·tion** /ˌmɪsˌkælkyəˈleɪʃn/ noun [C,U]

mis·car·riage /ˈmɪskærɪdʒ; mɪsˈkærɪdʒ/ noun [C,U] giving birth to a baby before it is ready to be born, with the result that it cannot live: *She's had several miscarriages.* ☞ Look at **abortion**.

mis·carriage of ˈjustice noun [C] a situation in which a court of law treats a person unfairly

mis·car·ry /ˈmɪsˌkæri; ˌmɪsˈkæri/ verb [I] (*pres. part.* **mis·car·ry·ing**; *3rd pers. sing. pres.* **mis·car·ries**; *p.t., p.p.* **mis·car·ried**) to give birth to a baby before it is ready to be born, with the result that it cannot live

mis·cel·la·ne·ous /ˌmɪsəˈleɪniəs/ adj. (*abbr.* **misc.**) of various, different types; mixed: *a box of miscellaneous items for sale*

mis·chief /ˈmɪstʃəf/ noun [U] (*old-fashioned*) bad behavior (usually of children) that is not very serious: *You can go and see your friends, but keep out of mischief this time.*

mis·chie·vous /ˈmɪstʃəvəs/ adj. (*old-fashioned*) (usually used about children) liking to have fun by doing things that are not allowed —**mis·chie·vous·ly** adv.

mis·con·cep·tion /ˌmɪskənˈsɛpʃn/ noun [C] a wrong idea or understanding of sth: *It is a popular misconception (= many people wrongly believe) that snakes have slimy skin.*

mis·con·duct /ˌmɪsˈkɑndʌkt/ noun [U] (*formal*) bad behavior, especially by a professional person

mis·de·mean·or /ˌmɪsdɪˈminər/ noun [C] something slightly bad or wrong that a person does; a minor crime: *to be charged with a misdemeanor*

mis·er /ˈmaɪzər/ noun [C] a person who loves having a lot of money but hates spending any

☆ **mis·er·a·ble** /ˈmɪzərəbl; ˈmɪzrəbl/ adj. **1** very unhappy; sad: *You look miserable. What's wrong?* **2** unpleasant (because difficult or uncomfortable): *It's miserable working in such an unfriendly atmosphere.* —**mis·er·a·bly** /-bli/ adv.: *I stared miserably out of the window.* ○ *Our first business venture failed miserably* (= in a disappointing way).

☆ **mis·er·y** /ˈmɪzəri/ noun [C,U] (*pl.* **mis·er·ies**) great unhappiness or lack of comfort; suffering: *There was an expression of pain and misery on his face.* ○ *The period after the war was a time of economic misery.* ○ *the miseries of poverty*

mis·fit /ˈmɪsfɪt/ noun [C] a person who is or feels different from other people: *a couple of social misfits with no friends or hobbies*

mis·for·tune /ˌmɪsˈfɔrtʃən/ noun [C,U] (an event, accident, etc. that brings) bad luck or disaster: *Various misfortunes had made her sad and bitter.* ○ *I hope I don't ever have the misfortune of meeting him again.*

mis·giv·ing /ˌmɪsˈgɪvɪŋ/ noun [U, usually pl.] a feeling of doubt, worry or suspicion: *I had serious misgivings about leaving him on his own in that condition.*

mis·guid·ed /ˌmɪsˈgaɪdəd/ adj. **1** (used about a person) acting in a way that is not sensible **2** (used about behavior or opinions) based on wrong ideas or information

mis·hap /ˈmɪshæp/ noun [C,U] an unlucky accident or bad luck that does not have serious results: *to have a slight mishap*

mis·in·form /ˌmɪsənˈfɔrm/ verb [T] to give sb the wrong information: *It seems that the public has been misinformed about the cause of the disease.*

mis·in·ter·pret /ˌmɪsənˈtɜrprət/ verb [T] to understand sth wrongly —**mis·in·ter·pre·ta·tion** /ˌmɪsənˌtɜrprəˈteɪʃn/ noun [C,U]: *Parts of*

M

tʃ	dʒ	v	θ	ð	s	z	ʃ
chin	June	van	thin	then	so	zoo	she

the speech were open to misinterpretation (= easy to misunderstand).

mis·judge /ˌmɪsˈdʒʌdʒ/ *verb* [T] to form a wrong opinion of sb/sth or to estimate sth wrongly —**mis·judg·ment** *noun* [C,U]

mis·lead /ˌmɪsˈlid/ *verb* [T] (*p.t., p.p.* **mis·led** /ˌmɪsˈlɛd/) to make sb have the wrong idea or opinion: *Don't be misled by his smile – he's not really very friendly.*

mis·lead·ing /ˌmɪsˈlidɪŋ/ *adj.* giving a wrong idea or impression: *a misleading advertisement*

mis·man·age /ˌmɪsˈmænɪdʒ/ *verb* [T] to manage or organize sth badly or without skill —**mis·man·age·ment** *noun* [U]

mis·place /ˌmɪsˈpleɪs/ *verb* [T] to lose sth, usually for a short time because you cannot remember where you left it: *I seem to have misplaced my checkbook – have you seen it anywhere?*

mis·placed /ˌmɪsˈpleɪst/ *adj.* given to sb/sth that does not deserve to have it: *misplaced loyalty*

mis·print /ˈmɪsprɪnt/ *noun* [C] a mistake in printing

mis·pro·nounce /ˌmɪsprəˈnaʊns/ *verb* [T] to pronounce a word or letter wrongly: *Be careful not to mispronounce "live" as "leave."* —**mis·pro·nun·ci·a·tion** /ˌmɪsprəˌnʌnsiˈeɪʃn/ *noun* [C,U]

mis·read /ˌmɪsˈrid/ *verb* [T] (*p.t., p.p.* **mis·read** /ˌmɪsˈrɛd/) to read or understand sth wrongly: *I misread the bus schedule and missed the last bus home.* ∘ *He misread my silence as a refusal.*

mis·rep·re·sent /ˌmɪsˌrɛprɪˈzɛnt/ *verb* [T] (usually passive) to give a wrong description of sb/sth —**mis·rep·re·sen·ta·tion** /ˌmɪsˌrɛprɪzɛnˈteɪʃn/ *noun* [C,U]: *That's a misrepresentation of what was actually said.*

☆ **miss¹** /mɪs/ *verb* **1** [T] to not see, hear, understand, etc. sb/sth: *The house is on the corner, so you can't miss it.* ∘ *There was so much noise that I missed a lot of what the speaker said.* ∘ *They completely missed the point of what I was saying.* **2** [I,T] to not hit, catch, etc. sth: *She tried hard to hit the ball but missed.* ∘ *Drive more carefully. You just barely missed that car.* **3** [T] to feel sad because sb is not with you anymore, or because you do not have or cannot do sth that you once had or did: *I'll really miss you when you go away.* ∘ *I don't miss teaching at all. I prefer my new job.* **4** [T] to arrive too late for sth or to fail to be at sth: *Hurry up or you'll miss the bus!* ∘ *She'll be really upset if you miss her birthday party.*

PHRV **miss out (on sth)** to lose a chance to gain sth/enjoy yourself, etc.: *You'll miss out on all the fun if you stay home.*

miss² /mɪs/ *noun* [C] a failure to hit, catch, etc. sth that you are aiming at: *After several misses, he finally managed to hit the target.*

IDM **a near miss** ⇨ NEAR¹

☆ **Miss** /mɪs/ **1** (used as a title before the name of a girl or unmarried woman): *Our math teacher is Miss Lopez.* ∘ *"Dear Miss Harris," the letter began.*

☞ In the southern United States it is considered polite to speak to a woman using **Miss** with her first name, whether she is married or not: *Good morning, Miss Dorothy.* However, this form is used mostly by older people and it is not used at all in other parts of the U.S. Look at the note at **Ms.**

2 (*also* **miss**) (used as a polite way of speaking to a woman, especially a young one, whose name you do not know): *Miss, could I please have some more coffee?* ∘ *Can I help you, miss?*

☆ **mis·sile** /ˈmɪsl/ *noun* [C] a powerful exploding weapon that can be sent long distances through the air: *nuclear missiles*

☆ **mis·sing** /ˈmɪsɪŋ/ *adj.* lost, or not in the right or usual place: *Some of my books are missing – have you seen them?* ∘ *The roof has some shingles missing.* ∘ *The little girl has been missing from home for two days.* ∘ *a missing person*

☆ **mis·sion** /ˈmɪʃn/ *noun* [C] **1** an important task or purpose that a person or group of people are sent somewhere to do: *Your mission is to send back information about the enemy.* **2** a group of people who are sent to another country to perform a special task: *a U.S. trade mission to China* **3** a special trip made by a space rocket or military airplane: *a mission to the moon* **4** a particular task or duty which you feel that you should do: *Her work with the poor was more than just a job – it was her mission in life.* **5** a place where the local people are taught about religion, given medical help, etc. by people who are sent to do this (**missionaries**).

mis·sion·ar·y /ˈmɪʃəˌnɛri/ *noun* [C] (*pl.* **mis·sion·ar·ies**) a person who is sent abroad to teach about religion

mis·spell /ˌmɪsˈspɛl/ *verb* [T] to spell sth wrongly

mis·spent /ˌmɪsˈspɛnt/ *adj.* (used about time or money) used in a foolish way; wasted

☆ **mist¹** /mɪst/ *noun* [C,U] clouds made of small drops of water, close to the ground, which make it difficult to see very far; a thin fog: *The fields were covered in mist.* ☞ Look at the notes at **fog** and **weather**.

mist² /mɪst/ *verb*

PHRV **mist (sth) up** to cover or be covered with mist: *The bathroom mirror always mists up when I take a hot shower.*

☆ **mis·take¹** /mɪˈsteɪk/ *noun* [C,U] something that you think or do that is wrong: *The teacher corrected my mistakes.* ∘ *a spelling mistake* ∘ *I must have made a mistake in adding these numbers together.* ∘ *I think there must be some mistake. My name is Sedgley, not Selley.* ∘ *It*

was a big mistake not to reserve our seats earlier. ○ *We made the mistake of asking Paul to take care of our plants while we were away.* **IDM** **by mistake** as a result of a mistake or carelessness: *The terrorists shot the wrong man by mistake.*

☞ **Error** is more formal than **mistake**: *(formal) Please accept my apologies. I opened your letter in error.* ○ *(informal) I'm sorry. I opened your letter by mistake.* There are some expressions, e.g. *error of judgment, human error, computer error* where only **error** can be used. **Fault** indicates who is to blame: *The accident wasn't my fault. The other driver pulled out in front of me.* **Fault** is also used to describe something that is wrong with, or not good about, a person or a thing: *a technical fault* ○ *Laziness is not one of her faults.*

☆ **mis·take²** /mɪˈsteɪk/ *verb* [T] *(p.t.* **mis·took** /mɪˈstʊk/; *p.p.* **mis·tak·en** /mɪˈsteɪkən/) **mistake sb/sth for sb/sth** to think (wrongly) that sb/sth is sb/sth else: *Police mistook my car for one that had been used in a bank robbery.*

mis·tak·en /mɪˈsteɪkən/ *adj.* wrong; not correct: *I thought I saw Jackie sitting over there, but I must have been mistaken.* ○ *a case of mistaken identity* —**mis·tak·en·ly** *adv.*

mis·ter /ˈmɪstər/ ➪ MR.

mis·tle·toe /ˈmɪsl̩ˌtoʊ/ *noun* [U] a plant with white berries and leaves that are green at all times of the year. Mistletoe grows on trees.

☞ Mistletoe is used as a decoration inside houses in the United States at Christmas time. There is a tradition of kissing people "under the mistletoe."

mis·took *p.t.* of MISTAKE²

mis·treat /ˌmɪsˈtrit/ *verb* [T] to behave badly or cruelly toward a person or animal —**mis·treat·ment** *noun* [U]

mis·tress /ˈmɪstrəs/ *noun* [C] a man's mistress is a woman who is having a (secret) sexual relationship with him ☞ Look at **lover.**

mis·trust /ˌmɪsˈtrʌst/ *noun* [U, sing.] a lack of belief or confidence in sb/sth; a lack of trust: *She has a deep mistrust of strangers.* —**mis·trust** *verb* [T]

mist·y /ˈmɪsti/ *adj.* (**mist·i·er; mist·i·est**) full of or covered with mist: *a misty day* ☞ Look at **foggy.**

☆ **mis·un·der·stand** /ˌmɪsʌndərˈstænd/ *verb* [T] *(p.t., p.p.* **mis·un·der·stood** /ˌmɪsʌndərˈstʊd/) to understand sb/sth wrongly: *Don't misunderstand me. I'm only trying to help.* ○ *I misunderstood the instructions and answered three questions instead of four.*

mis·un·der·stand·ing /ˌmɪsʌndərˈstændɪŋ/ *noun* [C,U] not understanding sb/sth correctly; an example of this: *There must have been some misunderstanding. I ordered spaghetti, not pizza.* ○ *It was all a misunderstand-*

ing, but we've got it straightened out now.

mis·use /ˌmɪsˈyuz/ *verb* [T] to use sth in the wrong way or for the wrong purpose: *These chemicals can be dangerous if misused.*

mis·use /ˌmɪsˈyus/ *noun* [C,U] using sth in the wrong way or for the wrong purpose: *The former mayor was on trial for misuse of public funds.*

mit·i·gate /ˈmɪṱəgeɪt/ *verb* [T] *(formal)* to make sth less serious, painful, unpleasant, etc. —**mit·i·gat·ing** /-geɪṱɪŋ/ *adj.*: *Because of the mitigating circumstances* (= that made the crime seem less bad), *the judge gave her a lighter sentence.*

mitt /mɪt/ *noun* [C] a type of large, thick glove that you wear to protect your hand ☞ picture at **baseball.**

☆ **mit·ten** /ˈmɪtn/ *noun* [C] a type of glove that has one part for the thumb and another part for the other four fingers: *a pair of mittens* ☞ picture on page A27.

☆ **mix¹** /mɪks/ *verb* **1** [T] to put two or more substances together and shake or stir them until they form a new substance: *to mix oil and vinegar together to make a salad dressing* ○ *Mix yellow and blue together to make green.* **2** [I] to join together to form a separate substance: *Oil and water don't mix.* **3** [T] to make sth (by mixing two or more substances together): *to mix cement* **4** [T] to do or have two or more things at the same time: *to mix business and pleasure* **5** [I] to be with and talk to other people: *He mixes with all types of people at work.* ○ *She is very shy and doesn't mix well.* **IDM** **be/get mixed up in sth** *(informal)* to be/ become involved in sth bad or unpleasant **PHRV** **mix sb up** *(informal)* to confuse sb: *Don't mix me up when I'm trying to count all these pennies.*

mix sth up to get something in the wrong order: *He dropped his folder and got the papers all mixed up.*

mix sb/sth up (with sb/sth) to confuse sb/sth with sb/sth else: *I think you've got us mixed up. I'm Jane and she's Sally.*

mix² /mɪks/ *noun* **1** [C, usually sing.] a group of different types of people or things: *We need a good ethnic mix in the police force.* **2** [C,U] a special powder that contains most of the substances needed to make a cake, bread, etc. You add water or another liquid, eggs, etc. to this powder: *Did you make these muffins from a mix?* ○ *a box of cake mix*

☆ **mixed** /mɪkst/ *adj.* made or consisting of different types of sth: *mixed vegetables* ○ *The reaction to our suggestion has been very mixed.* **IDM** **have mixed feelings (about sb/sth)** to have some good and some bad feelings about sb/sth; not to be sure about what you think: *I have very mixed feelings about graduating.*

ˌmixed-ˈup *adj.* *(informal)* confused or unsure

M

ə	y	w	t̬	eɪ	aɪ	ɔɪ	aʊ	oʊ
about	yes	woman	butter	say	five	boy	now	go

about sth/yourself: *He has been very mixed-up
since his parents' divorce.*

mixer

blender

food processor

mix·er /ˈmɪksər/ *noun* [C] a machine that is
used for mixing sth: *a cement mixer*

☆ **mix·ture** /ˈmɪkstʃər/ *noun* **1** [C] something
that is made by mixing together two or more
substances: *Put the mixture into a baking pan
and bake for half an hour.* **2** [sing.] something
that consists of several things that are differ-
ent from one another: *I stood and stared with
a mixture of amazement and horror.*

mix-up (*also* **mix·up**) *noun* [C] (*informal*) a
mistake in the planning or organization of
sth: *Because of a mix-up at the travel agency,
we didn't get our tickets on time.*

ml *abbr.* = MILLILITER

mm *abbr.* = MILLIMETER

mo. *abbr.* (*pl.* **mos.**) = MONTH

moan¹ /moʊn/ *noun* [C] a low sound that you
make if you are in pain or very sad

moan² /moʊn/ *verb* [I] **1** to make the sound of
a moan¹: *to moan with pain* **2** (*informal*) to
keep saying what is wrong about sth; to com-
plain: *People always moan about the weather,
even though they can't change it.*

moat /moʊt/ *noun* [C] a deep ditch that was
dug around a castle and filled with water in
order to protect the castle

mob¹ /mɑb/ *noun* [C] **1** a large crowd of
people that may become violent or cause
trouble: *The police used tear gas to disperse the
angry mob.* **2** [sing.] **the mob** = MAFIA

mob² /mɑb/ *verb* [T] (**mob·bing**; **mobbed**) to
gather around sb, with a large crowd of
people, because you are angry or are very
interested in him/her: *The rock singer was
mobbed as he left the hotel.*

mo·bile /ˈmoʊbl/ *adj.* able to move or be
moved easily ☞ Look at **immobile.** —**mo·bil·
i·ty** /moʊˈbɪləti/ *noun* [U]

mobile ˈhome (*also* **trailer**) *noun* [C] a long,
narrow house that is built in a factory and can
be moved with a truck

mo·bi·lize /ˈmoʊbəlaɪz/ *verb* [I,T] to get ready
or to organize sb/sth for a particular purpose:
Police officers mobilized in anticipation of fur-

ther riots. ◦ *They mobilized the local residents
to oppose the new development.*

moc·ca·sin /ˈmɑkəsn/ *noun* [C] a type of soft
leather shoe, especially one that is tradition-
ally worn by Native American people
☞ picture at **shoe.**

mock¹ /mɑk/ *verb* [I,T] (*formal*) to laugh at
sb/sth in an unkind way or to make other
people laugh at him/her ☞ **Laugh at** and
make fun of are less formal.

mock² /mɑk/ *adj.* (only *before* a noun) not
real or genuine: *The soldiers staged a mock
battle to test the new equipment.*

mo·dal /ˈmoʊdl/ (*also* **modal ˈverb**; **modal
auˈxiliary**) *noun* [C] a verb, e.g. "might," "can"
or "must" that is used with another verb for
expressing possibility, permission, necessity,
etc.

mode /moʊd/ *noun* [C] **1** (*formal*) a type of sth
or way of doing sth: *a mode of transportation*
2 (used about machines, etc.) a way of operat-
ing: *I put the generator in standby mode, so it
will be ready in case we need it.*

☆ **mod·el¹** /ˈmɑdl/ *noun* [C] **1** a copy of sth that
is usually smaller than the real thing: *a scale
model of an antique car* ◦ *a model airplane*
2 one of the machines, vehicles, etc. that is
made by a particular company: *This has been
a very popular model of car.* **3** a person or
thing that is a good example to copy: *Our city's
school system could serve as a model for other
communities.* ◦ *a role model* **4** a person who is
employed to wear clothes at a fashion show or
for magazine photographs: *a male fashion
model* **5** a person who is painted, drawn or
photographed by an artist

☆ **mod·el²** /ˈmɑdl/ *verb* **1** [T] to try to copy or be
like sb/sth: *He modeled himself after his favor-
ite teacher.* ◦ *The house is modeled on the Pal-
ace of Versailles.* **2** [I,T] to wear and show
clothes as a model¹(4): *to model swimsuits*
3 [I,T] to make a model¹(1) of sth

mod·el·ing /ˈmɑdl·ɪŋ/ *noun* [U] working as a
model¹(4) : *a career in modeling*

mo·dem /ˈmoʊdəm/ *noun* [C] a piece of equip-
ment that connects two or more computers
together by means of a telephone line so that
information can go from one to the other

☆ **mod·er·ate¹** /ˈmɑdərət/ *adj.* **1** average or not
very great in size, amount or degree: *a moder-
ate speed* ◦ *The change will affect thousands of
people on moderate incomes.* **2** (used about a
person's political opinions) not very different
from those of most other people; not extreme:
a moderate position on an issue ◦ *disagreement
between conservative and moderate Republic-
ans* ☞ Look at **extreme** and **radical.**

mod·er·ate² /ˈmɑdərət/ *noun* [C] a person
who has moderate political, etc. opinions
☞ Look at **extremist.**

mod·er·ate³ /ˈmɑdəreɪt/ *verb* [I,T] (*formal*) to
become or to make sth less strong or extreme

ər	ɪr	ɛr	ɑr	ɔr	ʊr	ʒ	h	ŋ
bird	near	hair	car	north	tour	vision	hat	sing

☆ **mod·er·ate·ly** /ˈmɑdərətli/ adv. not very; a little: *His career has been moderately successful.*

mod·er·a·tion /ˌmɑdəˈreɪʃn/ noun [U] the quality of being able to control your feelings or actions: *The people reacted violently, but their leaders called for moderation.*
IDM in moderation within limits that are sensible: *Alcohol can harm fetuses even if it's drunk in moderation.*

☆ **mod·ern** /ˈmɑdərn/ adj. **1** of the present or recent times: *Pollution is one of the major problems in the modern world.* ○ *to study modern history* ☞ Look at **ancient** and **traditional**. **2** with all the newest methods, equipment, buildings, etc.: *It is one of the most modern hospitals in the country.* ☞ Look at **old-fashioned**.

mod·ern·ize /ˈmɑdərnaɪz/ verb [I,T] to become or to make sth suitable for what is needed today: *We need to modernize our production line in order to manufacture the new model.* —**mod·ern·i·za·tion** /ˌmɑdərnəˈzeɪʃn/ noun [U]: *The factory equipment requires extensive modernization.*

ˌ**modern** ˈ**language** noun [C] a language that is spoken now

mod·est /ˈmɑdəst/ adj. **1** not having or expressing a high opinion of your own qualities or abilities: *She got the best grade on the test, but she was too modest to tell anybody.* ☞ Look at **humble** and **proud**. **2** shy and easily embarrassed by anything that is connected with sex **3** (formal) not very large: *a modest salary* ○ *a modest increase in price* **4** (formal) ordinary and plain; not expensive: *They live in a modest suburb north of the city.* —**mod·est·ly** adv.

mod·es·ty /ˈmɑdəsti/ noun [U] the quality of being modest (1,2)

mod·i·fi·ca·tion /ˌmɑdəfəˈkeɪʃn/ noun [C,U] a small change: *There have been some minor modifications to our original design.*

mod·i·fy /ˈmɑdəfaɪ/ verb [T] (pres. part. **mod·i·fy·ing**; 3rd pers. sing. pres. **mod·i·fies**; p.t., p.p. **mod·i·fied**) to change sth slightly: *We will need to modify the existing plan.*

mod·ule /ˈmɑdʒul/ noun [C] a unit that forms part of sth bigger: *The lunar module separated from the spacecraft.*

mo·hair /ˈmoʊhɛr/ noun [U] very soft wool that comes from a type of goat

moist /mɔɪst/ adj. slightly wet; damp: *Her eyes were moist with tears.* ○ *Keep the soil moist, but be careful not to water the plant too much.* ☞ Look at the note at **wet**.

mois·ten /ˈmɔɪsn/ verb [I,T] to become or to make sth moist

mois·ture /ˈmɔɪstʃər/ noun [U] water in small drops on a surface, in the air, etc.

mo·lar /ˈmoʊlər/ noun [C] one of the large teeth in the back of your mouth

mo·las·ses /məˈlæsəz/ noun [U] a thick, dark,

sticky liquid that is made from sugar ☞ Look at **syrup**.

mold¹ /moʊld/ noun **1** [C] a hollow container that you use to make sth into a particular shape. You put a liquid substance into a mold and wait for it to become solid (**set**) in the shape of the mold. **2** [sing.] a particular type of person: *You can't force every student to fit the same mold.* **3** [U] a soft green substance (a type of fungus) that grows in warm, damp places or on food that has been kept too long —**mold·y** /ˈmoʊldi/ adj.: *moldy cheese/bread* ☞ Look also at **rotten, sour** and **stale**.

mold² /moʊld/ verb [T] to make sth into a particular shape or form

mole /moʊl/ noun [C] **1** a small dark spot on a person's skin that never goes away ☞ Look at **freckle**. **2** a small animal with dark fur that lives underground and is almost blind **3** (informal) a person who works in one organization and gives secret information to another organization or country ☞ Look at **spy**.

mol·e·cule /ˈmɑləkyul/ noun [C] the smallest unit into which a substance can be divided without changing its chemical nature. A molecule consists of one or more atoms. —**mo·lec·u·lar** /məˈlɛkyələr/ adj.

mo·lest /məˈlɛst/ verb [T] to attack sb (especially a child) in a sexual way ☞ Look at **rape**. —**mo·lest·er** /məˈlɛstər/ noun [C]

mol·ten /ˈmoʊltn/ adj. (used about metal or rock) made liquid by very great heat: *molten lava*

☆ **mom** /mɑm/ noun [C] (informal) mother: *My mom works in a bank.* ○ *Hi Mom, I'm home!* ☞ Look also at **mommy**.

☆ **mo·ment** /ˈmoʊmənt/ noun **1** [C] a very short period of time: *Would you mind waiting for a moment?* ○ *He hesitated for a few moments and then knocked on the door.* **2** [sing.] a particular point in time: *Just at that moment my mother arrived.* ○ *the moment of birth/death*
IDM (at) any minute/moment (now) ⇨ MINUTE¹
at the moment now: *She's busy at the moment. Can I take a message?*
for the moment/present for a short time; for now: *I'm not very happy at work but I'll stay there for the moment.*
in a moment very soon: *Just wait here. I'll be back in a moment.*
the last minute/moment ⇨ LAST¹
the minute/moment (that) ⇨ MINUTE¹
on the spur of the moment ⇨ SPUR¹

mo·men·tar·i·ly /ˌmoʊmənˈtɛrəli/ adv. **1** for a very short time **2** in a very short time; very soon: *We will be landing in Dallas momentarily.*

mo·men·tar·y /ˈmoʊmənˌtɛri/ adj. lasting for a very short time: *a momentary lack of concentration*

M

tʃ	dʒ	v	θ	ð	s	z	ʃ
chin	June	van	thin	then	so	zoo	she

mo·men·tous /moʊˈmɛntəs; mə-/ *adj.* very important: *The birth of our daughter was a momentous occasion for us.*

mo·men·tum /moʊˈmɛntəm; mə-/ *noun* [U] strength or speed: *The ball gained momentum as it rolled downhill.* ○ *The environmental movement is gathering momentum.*

☆ **mom·my** /ˈmɑmi/ *noun* [C] (*pl.* **mom·mies**) (*informal*) (used by or to children) mother: *I want my mommy!*

Mon. *abbr.* = MONDAY

mon·arch /ˈmɑnərk; -ɑrk/ *noun* [C] a king or queen

mon·ar·chy /ˈmɑnərki/ *noun* (*pl.* **mon·ar·chies**) **1** [sing., U] the system of government or rule by a monarch: *Should Britain abolish its monarchy?* **2** [C] a country that is governed by a monarch ☞ Look at **republic**.

mon·as·ter·y /ˈmɑnəˌstɛri/ *noun* [C] (*pl.* **mon·as·ter·ies**) a place where men (**monks**) live in a religious community ☞ Look at **convent**.

☆ **Mon·day** /ˈmʌndeɪ; -di/ *noun* [C,U] (*abbr.* **Mon.**) the day of the week after Sunday and before Tuesday : *I'm going to see her (on) Monday.* ○ *We usually play tennis on Mondays.* ○ *They have piano lessons every Monday.* ○ *Monday morning/afternoon/evening/night* ○ *last/next Monday* ○ *this coming Monday* ○ *a week from Monday* (= not next Monday, but the Monday after that) ○ *The museum is open Monday through Friday, 10 to 4:30.* ○ *Did you see that article about Italy in Monday's paper?*

mon·e·tar·y /ˈmɑnəˌtɛri/ *adj.* connected with money: *the government's monetary policy*

check money

credit card

cash

coin

bill

☆ **mon·ey** /ˈmʌni/ *noun* [U] the means of paying for sth or buying sth, especially in the form of coins or bills: *How much money do you earn a year?* ○ *Teenagers spend a lot of money on clothes.* ○ *Our trip cost an awful lot of money.* ○ *to borrow/lend money* ○ *My father invested his money in stocks and bonds.* ○ *Is this picture worth a lot of money?* ☞ Look also at **allowance**.

IDM get your money's worth to get full value for the money you have spent: *The meal was expensive, but we got our money's worth because there were five courses.*

make money to earn money or to make a profit on a business

ˈmoney ˌorder *noun* [C] an official piece of paper, similar to a check, that you can use to send money to sb, e.g. through the mail

☆ **mon·i·tor¹** /ˈmɑnətər/ *noun* [C] **1** a machine, often a part of a computer, that shows information or pictures on a screen like a television **2** a machine that records or checks sth: *A monitor checks the baby's heartbeat.* **3** a person who checks, records or watches sth and reports the information to sb in authority: *human rights monitors in a war zone* ○ *a playground monitor*

☆ **mon·i·tor²** /ˈmɑnətər/ *verb* [T] to check, record or watch sth regularly for a period of time: *Pollution levels in the lake are being monitored closely.* ○ *to monitor foreign radio broadcasts*

monk /mʌŋk/ *noun* [C] a man who has decided to leave the ordinary world and live a religious life in a community (**monastery**) ☞ Look at **nun**.

☆ **mon·key** /ˈmʌŋki/ *noun* [C] (*pl.* **mon·keys**) a small, usually brown, animal with a long tail that lives in hot countries and can climb trees ☞ Look at **ape**. Chimpanzees and **gorillas** are apes, although people often call them monkeys.

monkey

mo·nog·a·my /məˈnɑgəmi/ *noun* [U] being married to, or having a sexual relationship with only one person at a time —**mo·nog·a·mous** /məˈnɑgəməs/ *adj.*

mon·o·lin·gual /ˌmɑnəˈlɪŋgwəl/ *adj.* using only one language: *This is a monolingual dictionary.* ☞ Look at **bilingual**.

mon·o·logue (*also* **monolog**) /ˈmɑnəlɔg; -lɑg/ *noun* [C] a long speech by one person, e.g. in a play

mo·nop·o·lize /məˈnɑpəlaɪz/ *verb* [T] to control sth so that other people cannot have or use it: *She completely monopolized the conversation. I couldn't get a word in.*

mo·nop·o·ly /məˈnɑpəli/ *noun* [C] (*pl.* **mo·nop·o·lies**) **1** the control of an industry or service by one company: *Standard Oil had a monopoly on supplying kerosene for lamps in the 19th century.* **2** a company or organization that controls an industry: *Congress passed a law to prohibit monopolies in the telephone industry.*

mon·o·rail /ˈmɑnəreɪl/ *noun* [C] a train that runs on a single track

mon·o·syl·la·ble /ˈmɑnəsɪləbl/ *noun* [C] a

short word, such as "leg," that has only one syllable

mo·not·o·nous /məˈnɑtn·əs/ *adj.* boring and uninteresting because it does not change: *monotonous work* ∘ *a monotonous voice* —**mo·not·o·nous·ly** *adv.* —**mo·not·o·ny** /məˈnɑtn·i/ *noun* [U]: *The monotony of the speaker's voice made us all feel sleepy.*

mon·soon /ˌmɑnˈsun/ *noun* [C] the season of heavy rain in Southern Asia, or the wind which brings the rain

☆ **mon·ster** /ˈmɑnstər/ *noun* [C] (in stories) a type of animal that is large, ugly and frightening: *a story about dragons, goblins and other monsters* ∘ (*figurative*) *The murderer was described as a dangerous monster.*

☆ **month** /mʌnθ/ *noun* [C] (*abbr.* **mo.**) **1** one of the twelve periods of time into which the year is divided, e.g. January: *They are starting work next month.* ∘ *The rent is $500 a month.* ∘ *"When are the final exams?" "Later in the month."* ∘ *at the beginning/end of the month* ∘ *on the 15th of every month* **2** a period of about four weeks: *"How long will you be gone?" "For about a month."* ∘ *"When will Sue be back?" "About a month from now."* ∘ *a three-month course* ∘ *The window cleaner will come again in a month.* ∘ *Little Eric will be eighteen months old on Sunday.*

☆ **month·ly** /ˈmʌnθli/ *adj., adv.* (happening or produced) once a month or every month: *a monthly meeting* ∘ *a monthly magazine* ∘ *Are you paid weekly or monthly?*

mon·u·ment /ˈmɑnyəmənt/ *noun* [C] **1** a building or statue that is built to remind people of a famous person or event: *the Washington Monument* **2** an old building or other place that is of historical importance: *The pyramids in Eygpt are famous monuments from ancient times.*

mon·u·men·tal /ˌmɑnyəˈmɛntl/ *adj.* **1** (used about a building) very large and impressive **2** very great: *a monumental success*

moo /mu/ *noun* [C] the sound that a cow makes —**moo** *verb* [I]

☆ **mood** /mud/ *noun* **1** [C,U] the way that you feel at a particular time, i.e. if you are happy, sad, etc.: *Leave Dad alone for a while. He's in a really bad mood.* ∘ *You're in a good mood today!* ∘ *a sudden change of mood* ∘ *Turn that music down – I'm not in the mood for it.* **2** [C] a time when you are angry or bad-tempered: *Debby's in one of her moods again.* **3** [sing.] the way that a group of people feel about sth: *After a year of record-breaking sales, the mood at company headquarters is very optimistic.*

mood·y /ˈmudi/ *adj.* (**mood·i·er; mood·i·est**) **1** having moods (1) that change often **2** bad-tempered or unhappy —**mood·i·ly** /ˈmudəli/ *adv.* **mood·i·ness** *noun* [U]

☆ **moon** /mun/ *noun* **1 the moon** [sing.] the object that shines in the sky at night and that

moves around the earth once every 28 days: *The moon's very bright tonight.* ∘ *When was the first landing on the moon?*

☞ You may see a **new moon**, a **full moon** or a **crescent moon**.

2 [C] an object like the moon that moves around another planet: *How many moons does Neptune have?*

IDM **once in a blue moon** ⇨ ONCE¹

moon·light¹ /ˈmunlaɪt/ *noun* [U] light that comes from the moon: *The lake looked beautiful in the moonlight.*

moon·light² /ˈmunlaɪt/ *verb* [I] (*informal*) to work at a second job in addition to your main job: *police officers who moonlight as private security guards* —**moon·light·ing** /-laɪtɪŋ/ *noun* [U]

moon·lit /ˈmunlɪt/ *adj.* having light from the moon: *a moonlit evening*

moor¹ /mʊr/ *noun* [C,U] a wild open area of high land that is covered with grass and other low plants

moor² /mʊr/ *verb* [I,T] to fasten a boat to the land or to an object in the water, with a rope or chain

moor·ing /ˈmʊrɪŋ/ *noun* [C] a place where a boat is moored

moose /mus/ *noun* [C] (*pl.* **moose**) a type of very large deer with broad flat horns (**antlers**) that comes from North America ☞ picture at **elk**. In northern Europe the same animal is called an **elk**.

mop¹ /mɑp/ *noun* [C] a tool that is used for washing floors. A mop has a long handle and a bunch of thick strings or a sponge at the end.

mop² /mɑp/ *verb* [T] (**mop·ping; mopped**) **1** to clean sth with a mop¹ **2** to remove liquid from sth using a dry cloth: *to mop your forehead with a handkerchief*

PHRV **mop sth up** to clean unwanted liquid with a mop or dry cloth: *Mop up that grape juice you spilled or it'll leave a stain!*

mope /moʊp/ *verb* [I] to feel unhappy and not try to do anything to make yourself feel better: *Why don't you quit moping around the house and go out for a walk?*

mo·ped /ˈmoʊpɛd/ *noun* [C] a type of small, not very powerful, motorcycle with pedals ☞ picture at **motorcycle**.

☆ **mor·al¹** /ˈmɔrəl; ˈmɑrəl/ *adj.* **1** concerned with what you believe is the right way to behave: *Some people refuse to eat meat on moral grounds* (= because they believe that it is wrong). ∘ *the moral dilemma of whether or not animals should be used in laboratory tests* **2** having high standards of behavior: *She has always led a very moral life.* ☞ The opposite is **immoral**.

☆ **mor·al²** /ˈmɔrəl; ˈmɑrəl/ *noun* **1** [C] a lesson in the right way to behave that can be learned from a story or from sth that happens: *The*

M

moral of the play is that friendship is more important than money. **2 morals** [plural] standards or principles of good behavior

mo·rale /məˈræl/ *noun* [U] the way that a group of people feel at a particular time: *The team's morale was high before the game* (= they were confident that they would win). ○ *Low pay in recent years has led to low morale among blue-collar workers.*

☆ **mo·ral·i·ty** /məˈræləti/ *noun* [U] principles and standards relating to whether sth is right or wrong: *There was a lively debate about the morality of the death penalty.* ☞ The opposite is **immorality**.

mor·al·ly /ˈmɔrəli; ˈmɑr-/ *adv.* **1** in a way that is good or right: *to behave morally* **2** connected with standards of what is right or wrong: *to be morally responsible for sb* (e.g. because it is your duty to take care of him/her) ○ *What he did wasn't illegal, but it was morally wrong.*

ˌ**moral supˈport** *noun* [U] help or encouragement that you give to sb (by being with him/her or saying that you agree with him/her): *I went to the dentist with him just to give him some moral support.*

mor·bid /ˈmɔrbəd/ *adj.* having or showing great interest in unpleasant things, e.g. disease and death

☆ **more¹** /mɔr/ *det., pron.* a larger number of people/things or larger amount of sth; sth in addition to what you already have: *There were more people than I expected.* ○ *I bought some more plants for the garden.* ○ *There's enough room for three more people.* ○ *Tell me more about your job.* ○ *There's no more milk in the fridge.* ○ *I couldn't eat any more cake.* ☞ Look also at **anymore**.

IDM more and more an increasing amount or number: *There are more and more cars on the road.*

☆ **more²** /mɔr/ *adv.* **1** (used to form the comparative of adjectives and adverbs with two or more syllables): *He was more frightened than I was.* ○ *Please write more carefully.* **2** to a greater extent: *I like him more than I like his wife.* ○ *This one costs more.*

IDM no more (*formal*) not any longer: *The last remaining barrier to peace in the region exists no more.*

more or less approximately; almost: *We are more or less the same age.*

what's more (used for adding another fact): *Joanna and her mother look very much alike. What's more, they even sound alike.*

more·o·ver /mɔrˈoʊvər/ *adv.* (*formal*) (used, especially in writing, when you are giving some extra information that supports what you are saying) in addition; also: *The value of this stock rose 17% last year. Moreover, analysts say it should continue to increase this year.*

morgue /mɔrg/ *noun* [C] a building or a place

in a hospital, etc. where dead bodies are kept until they are buried or burned ☞ Look at **mortuary**.

Mor·mon /ˈmɔrmən/ *adj., noun* [C, adj. (a member of) a religious group founded in the United States in 1830, officially called "The Church of Jesus Christ of Latter-day Saints"

☆ **morn·ing** /ˈmɔrnɪŋ/ *noun* [C,U] **1** the early part of the day between the time when the sun rises and noon: *Pat's going to Chicago tomorrow morning.* ○ *Pat stayed with us on Sunday night and went to Chicago the next/the following morning.* ○ *I've been studying hard all morning.* ○ *Dave makes breakfast every morning.* ○ *She only works in the mornings.* ○ *the morning paper* **2** the part of the night that is after midnight: *I was woken by a strange noise in the the early hours of the morning.*

IDM good morning (used when you see sb for the first time in the morning)

☞ Often we just say **Morning**: *"Good morning, Mrs. Stevenson." "Morning, Mr. Chang."*

in the morning 1 during the morning of the next day; tomorrow morning: *I'll try to talk to her about it in the morning.* **2** not in the afternoon or evening: *The time of death was about 10:30 in the morning.*

☞ When you use the adjectives *early* or *late* before "morning" or "afternoon," you must use the preposition **in**: *The accident happened in the early morning.* ○ *We arrived in the late afternoon.* With other adjectives, use **on**: *School starts on Monday morning.* ○ *They set out on a cold, windy afternoon.* No preposition is used before *this, tomorrow or yesterday*: *Let's go swimming this morning.* ○ *We went to the zoo yesterday afternoon.* Look also at the notes at **evening** and **night**.

mo·ron /ˈmɔrɑn/ *noun* [C] (*informal*) a very foolish or stupid person —**mo·ron·ic** /məˈrɑnɪk/ *adj.*

mor·phine /ˈmɔrfin/ *noun* [U] a very strong drug that is used for reducing pain

mor·sel /ˈmɔrsl/ *noun* [C] a very small piece of food

mor·tal¹ /ˈmɔrtl/ *adj.* **1** not living forever: *We are all mortal.* ☞ The opposite is **immortal**. **2** that will result in death: *a mortal wound* ☞ Look at **fatal**, which is more common. **3** very great or extreme: *They were in mortal fear of the enemy.*

mor·tal² /ˈmɔrtl/ *noun* [C] a human being

mor·tal·i·ty /mɔrˈtæləti/ *noun* [U] **1** the fact that nobody can live forever **2** the number of deaths in a certain period of time or in a certain place: *Infant mortality is high in the region.*

mor·tal·ly /ˈmɔrtəli/ *adv.* **1** in a way that will result in death: *to be mortally wounded* **2** very; extremely: *to be mortally offended*

M

ər	ɪr	ɛr	ɑr	ɔr	ʊr	ʒ	h	ŋ
bird	near	hair	car	north	tour	vision	hat	sing

mor·tar /'mɔrṭər/ noun 1 [U] a mixture of cement, sand and water that you put between bricks when you are building sth 2 [C] a type of heavy gun

☆ **mort·gage** /'mɔrgɪdʒ/ (also **home loan**) noun [C] money that you borrow in order to buy a house: *We took out a $60,000 mortgage.* ○ *mortgage payments*

☞ You usually borrow money from a **bank** or a **savings and loan association**, which decides what **rate** of **interest** you must pay on the **loan**.

mor·ti·cian /mɔr'tɪʃn/ noun [C] = FUNERAL DIRECTOR

mor·tu·ar·y /'mɔrtʃuˌɛri/ noun [C] (pl. **mor·tu·ar·ies**) a building or a place in a hospital, etc. where dead bodies are kept before they are buried or burned ☞ Look at **morgue**.

mo·sa·ic /moʊ'zeɪk/ noun [C,U] a picture or pattern that is made by placing together small colored stones, pieces of glass, etc.

Mos·lem /'mɑzləm/ noun [C], adj. = MUSLIM

mosque /mɑsk/ noun [C] a building where Muslims worship

☆ **mos·qui·to** /mə'skiṭoʊ/ noun [C] (pl. **mos·qui·toes**) a small flying insect. Mosquitoes bite people and animals in order to suck their blood, and some types of mosquito spread a very serious disease (**malaria**).

moss /mɔs/ noun [C,U] a small green plant, with no flowers, that grows in a flat mass in damp places, especially on rocks or trees

☆ **most¹** /moʊst/ det., pron. (used as the superlative of *many, much*) 1 greatest in number or amount: *Who picked the most apples?* ○ *The kids had the most fun.* ○ *We all worked hard, but I did the most.* 2 nearly all of a group of people or things: *Most families in this country have a TV set.* ○ *I like most Italian food.*

☞ When **most** is followed by a noun which has **the, this, my**, etc. before it, we must use **most of**: *Most of our friends were able to come to the party.* ○ *It rained most of the time we were in Ireland.*

IDM **at (the) most** not more than a certain number, and probably less: *There were 20 people there, at the most.*
make the most of sth ⇨ MAKE¹

☆ **most²** /moʊst/ adv. 1 (used to form the superlative of adjectives and adverbs that have two or more syllables): *It's the most beautiful house I've ever seen.* ○ *I think this machine works the most efficiently.* 2 more than anybody/ anything else: *What do you miss most when you're away from home?* 3 (formal) very: *We heard a most interesting talk about Japan.* 4 (informal) = ALMOST: *most everyone*

☆ **most·ly** /'moʊstli/ adv. 1 almost all: *The people at work are mostly very nice.* 2 usually: *We mostly go shopping in Seattle, not Tacoma.*

mo·tel /moʊ'tɛl/ noun [C] a hotel for people who are traveling by car. At a motel you can usually park your car near your room.

moth /mɔθ/ noun [C] an insect like a butterfly that usually flies at night. Moths do not have such bright colors as butterflies. ☞ picture at **butterfly**.

moth·ball /'mɔθbɔl/ noun [C] a small white ball made of a chemical substance with a strong smell that protects clothes in closets from moths

☆ **moth·er¹** /'mʌðər/ noun [C] the female parent of a person or animal: *an expectant mother* ○ *a single mother* ○ *a foster mother* ○ *Working mothers need good daycare facilities.* ○ *a mother cow and her calf* ☞ Look at **mom, mommy** and **stepmother**.

moth·er² /'mʌðər/ verb [T] to care for sb as a mother does: *Tim complained that his girlfriend tried to mother him too much.*

moth·er·hood /'mʌðərhʊd/ noun [U] the state of being a mother

mother-in-law noun [C] (pl. **mothers-in-law**) the mother of your husband or wife

moth·er·ly /'mʌðərli/ adj. of a mother or like a mother: *She's a motherly type of person.*

mother tongue noun [C] the first language that you learned to speak as a child

mo·tif /moʊ'tif/ noun [C] a picture or pattern on sth: *The blouse has a butterfly motif on each sleeve.*

☆ **mo·tion¹** /'moʊʃn/ noun 1 [U] movement or a way of moving: *The swaying motion of the ship made us all feel sick.* ○ *Pull the lever to set the machine in motion.* ☞ Look at **slow motion**. 2 [C] a suggestion that you discuss and vote on at a meeting: *The motion was carried/rejected by a majority of eight votes.*

mo·tion² /'moʊʃn/ verb [I,T] to make a movement that shows sth or tells sb what to do: *She was motioning to us that she couldn't breathe.*

mo·tion·less /'moʊʃnləs/ adj. not moving

motion picture noun [C] (formal) a movie

mo·ti·vate /'moʊṭəveɪt/ verb [T] 1 to cause sb to act in a particular way: *Her reaction was motivated by fear.* ○ *The attack was politically motivated.* 2 to make sb want to do sth (by making it interesting): *Our new teacher certainly knows how to motivate his classes.* —**mo·ti·vat·ed** /-veɪṭəd/ adj.: *highly motivated students*

mo·ti·va·tion /ˌmoʊṭə'veɪʃn/ noun [C,U] the need or reason for doing sth; a feeling of interest in doing sth: *I'm suffering from a lack of motivation. My new job is really boring.*

mo·tive /'moʊṭɪv/ noun [C,U] a reason for doing sth: *Nobody seemed to have a motive for the murder.*

IDM **an ulterior motive** ⇨ ULTERIOR

M

tʃ	dʒ	v	θ	ð	s	z	ʃ
chin	June	van	thin	then	so	zoo	she

☆ **mo·tor¹** /ˈmouṭər/ noun [C] a machine that changes power into movement: *The washing machine doesn't work. I think something is wrong with the motor.* ○ *to start/turn off a motor*

☞ **Engine**, not **motor**, is usually used in connection with cars and motorcycles, but sometimes **motor** is also used. In fact, cars used to be called **motor cars**. **Engines** generally use gasoline and **motors** use electricity.

mo·tor² /ˈmouṭər/ adj. (only *before* a noun) connected with vehicles that have an engine or a motor: *motor vehicles* (= cars, trucks, vans, etc.) ○ *motor oil*

| motorcycle | moped |

mo·tor·bike /ˈmouṭərbaɪk/ noun [C] a light, two-wheeled vehicle with a small engine

mo·tor·boat /ˈmouṭərbout/ noun [C] a small fast boat that has an engine ☞ picture at **boat**.

☆ **mo·tor·cy·cle** /ˈmouṭərsaɪkl/ noun [C] a two-wheeled vehicle with a powerful engine

mo·tor·cy·clist /-saɪklɪst/ noun [C] a person who rides a motorcycle

motor home noun [C] = RV

mo·tor·ist /ˈmouṭərɪst/ noun [C] a person who drives a car ☞ Look at **pedestrian**.

mo·tor·ized /ˈmouṭəraɪzd/ adj. having an engine or a motor: *a motorized wheelchair*

mo·tor·way /ˈmouṭərweɪ/ noun [C] (*BrE*) = FREEWAY

mot·to /ˈmɑtou/ noun [C] (*pl.* **mot·toes**) a short sentence that expresses a rule for a person's or an organization's behavior: *Our company has adopted the motto, "The customer is always right."*

mound /maund/ noun [C] **1** a large pile of earth; a small hill **2** a pile or heap of things: *Look at this mound of dirty clothes on the floor!*

mount¹ /maunt/ noun [C] (*abbr.* **Mt.**) (used in names) a mountain: *Mt. Everest*

☆ **mount²** /maunt/ verb **1** [T] (*formal*) to go to the top of sth: *The conductor mounted the podium.* **2** [I] to increase in level or amount: *The tension mounted as the end of the game approached.* **3** [T] to attach sth on or in sth else : *A video camera was mounted above the cash register in the store.* **4** [T] to organize sth: *to mount an exhibition* ○ *to mount an attack* **5** [I,T] to get on a horse ☞ The opposite is **dismount**.

☆ **moun·tain** /ˈmauntn/ noun [C] **1** a very high hill: *What's the name of the highest mountain in the world?* ○ *Have you ever climbed a moun-*

tain? ○ *a steep mountain road* ○ *a range of mountains* **2** a large amount of sth: *There is a mountain of unanswered letters on her desk.*

ˈmountain bike noun [C] a strong bicycle that you can ride over rough ground

moun·tain·eer /ˌmauntn·ˈɪr/ noun [C] a person who climbs mountains

moun·tain·eer·ing /ˌmauntn·ˈɪrɪŋ/ noun [U] the sport of climbing mountains

ˈmountain ˌlion (*also* **cougar**; **puma**) noun [C] a large wild cat that lives in western North America

moun·tain·ous /ˈmauntn·əs/ adj. **1** having many mountains: *mountainous terrain* **2** very large: *The mountainous waves made sailing impossible.*

moun·tain·side /ˈmauntnsaid/ noun [C] one of the steep sides of a mountain

mount·ed /ˈmauntəd/ adj. riding a horse: *mounted police*

mount·ing /ˈmauntɪŋ/ adj. increasing: *mounting unemployment*

mourn /mɔrn/ verb [I,T] **mourn (for/over sb/sth)** to feel great sadness, especially because sb has died: *She is still mourning for her child.* ○ *They are mourning the death of her father.*

mourn·er /ˈmɔrnər/ noun [C] a person who goes to a funeral as a friend or relative of the person who has died

mourn·ful /ˈmɔrnfl/ adj. sad: *a mournful song* —**mourn·ful·ly** adv.

mourn·ing /ˈmɔrnɪŋ/ noun [U] a time when people feel or show great sadness because sb has died: *He wore a black armband to show he was in mourning.*

☆ **mouse** /maus/ noun [C] (*pl.* **mice** /mais/) **1** a small furry animal with a long tail: *a field mouse* ☞ **Mice**, like **rats**, **hamsters**, etc. are members of the **rodent** family. **2** a piece of equipment, attached to a computer, for entering commands without using the keyboard ☞ picture on page A29. The mouse controls the **cursor** when you **click** its **buttons**.

mousse /mus/ noun **1** [C,U] a type of food that is made by beating together cream and eggs with sth else: *a chocolate mousse* ○ *salmon mousse* **2** [U] a white substance with a lot of air in it that you put in your hair to shape it and hold it in place: *a can of styling mousse*

mous·tache = MUSTACHE

☆ **mouth¹** /mauθ/ noun [C] (*pl.* **mouths** /mauðz/) **1** the part of your face that you use for eating and speaking: *Don't talk with your mouth full.* ○ *Open your mouth, please!* ○ *You can close your mouth now.* ○ *Keep your mouth closed when you're eating.* ○ (*figurative*) *They have a low income and five mouths to feed.* ○ (*figurative, informal*) *Don't tell him any secrets – he's got a big mouth* (=he says things he should not say). **2** the place where a river enters the ocean

M

mouth² /maʊð/ *verb* [I,T] to move your mouth as if you were speaking but without making any sound: *Don't worry if you can't sing – you can just mouth the words.*

-mouthed /maʊðd/ (in compounds) **1** having a particular type of mouth: *We stared open-mouthed in surprise.* **2** having a particular way of speaking: *He's loud-mouthed and obnoxious.*

mouth·ful /ˈmaʊθfʊl/ *noun* **1** [C] the amount of food or drink that you can put in your mouth at one time **2** [sing.] a word or phrase that is long or difficult to say

mouth·piece /ˈmaʊθpis/ *noun* [C] **1** the part of a telephone, musical instrument, etc. that you put in or near your mouth **2** a person, newspaper, etc. that a particular group uses to express its opinions: *The paper was the mouthpiece of the Soviet government.*

mouth·wash /ˈmaʊθwɑʃ; -wɔʃ/ *noun* [U] liquid that you use for cleaning your mouth and making it smell nice

mouth·wa·ter·ing /ˈmaʊθˌwɑt̬ərɪŋ/ *adj.* (used about food) that looks or smells very good

☆ **mov·a·ble** /ˈmuvəbl/ *adj.* that can be moved ☞ Look at **portable**.

☆ **move¹** /muv/ *noun* [C] **1** a change of place or position: *She sat and watched every move I made.* ○ *One false move and I'll shoot!* **2** a change in the place where you live or work: *a move to a bigger house* ○ *I've been in the same job for six years and think it's time for a move.* **3** action that you take because you want to achieve a particular result: *Moves are being made to secure the release of the hostages.* ○ *Both sides want to negotiate, but neither is prepared to make the first move.* ○ *Asking him to help me was a good move.* **4** a change in the position of a piece in a game like chess: *It's Lori's move.*

IDM **get a move on** (*informal*) to hurry : *I'm late. I'll have to get a move on.*

☆ **move²** /muv/ *verb* **1** [I,T] to change position or to put sth in a different position: *Don't move – there's a bee on your arm.* ○ *Move your car. It's blocking the driveway.* ○ *I thought I heard something moving in the bushes over there.* ○ *They are moving the patient to another hospital.* **2** [I] to go and live in another house, etc.: *Our neighbors have sold their house and are moving next week.* **3** [I] to change or make progress: *When the new team of construction workers arrived things started moving very quickly.* **4** [T] to cause sb to have strong feelings (often of sadness): *The reports about the starving children moved many people to tears.* **5** [I] to take action: *Unless we move quickly, lives will be lost.* **6** [I,T] to change the position of a piece in a game like chess

IDM **get moving** to go, leave or do sth quickly
get sth moving to cause sth to make progress

PHRV **move aside/down/over/up** to move further in a particular direction in order to make space for sb/sth else: *Move over so I can sit down!* ○ *Could you please move down a seat?*
move away to stop living in one house and go to live in another: *Jeff was very sad when his best friend moved away.*
move in to start living in a new house
move out to stop living in a house

☆ **move·ment** /ˈmuvmənt/ *noun* **1** [C,U] an action that involves changing position or place or using the body in some way: *The dancer's movements were smooth and beautifully controlled.* ○ *The man lay still in the long grass, knowing that any movement would be seen by the police.* ○ *the slow movement of the clouds across the sky* **2** [C, usually sing.] **a movement (away from/toward sth)** a general change in the way people think or behave: *There's been a slight movement away from the materialism of the 1980s.* **3 movements** [plural] a person's actions or plans during a period of time: *Investigators have been watching the man's movements for several days.* **4** [C] a group of people who have the same aims or ideas (and who want to persuade other people that they are right): *I support the animal rights movement.* **5** [C] one of the main parts of a long piece of music: *a symphony in four movements*

mov·er /ˈmuvər/ *noun* [C] a person or business that moves sb's furniture, etc. to a new house

☆ **mov·ie** /ˈmuvi/ *noun* **1** [C] a story, play, etc. shown in moving pictures in a theater or on television: *Would you like to go and see a movie?* ○ *We stayed home last night and watched a movie on TV.* ○ *a science fiction movie* ○ *a movie director* ☞ Look at the note at **film¹**(2). **2 the movies** [plural] a building where movies are shown: *Let's go to the movies.*

'movie ˌtheater *noun* [C] = THEATER(2)

mov·ing /ˈmuvɪŋ/ *adj.* **1** (only *before* a noun) that moves: *It's an electronic system with few moving parts.* **2** causing strong feelings: *a moving story about a young boy's fight against cancer*

'moving van a truck that is used for transporting furniture, etc. from one house to another

mow /moʊ/ *verb* [I,T] (*p.t.* **mowed**; *p.p.* **mown** /moʊn/ or **mowed**) to cut grass using a machine or an instrument: *You need to mow the lawn at least once a week.*

mow·er /ˈmoʊər/ *noun* [C] a machine for cutting grass or crops: *a lawnmower*

mpg (*also* **m.p.g.**) /ˌɛm pi ˈdʒi/ *abbr.* miles per gallon (of fuel)

mph (*also* **m.p.h.**) /ˌɛm pi ˈeɪtʃ/ *abbr.* miles per hour

M

ə	y	w	t̬	eɪ	aɪ	ɔɪ	aʊ	oʊ
about	yes	woman	butter	say	five	boy	now	go

☆ **Mr.** /'mɪstər/ *abbr.* (used as a title before the name of a man): *Mr. (John) Brown*

☆ **Mrs.** /'mɪsəz/ *abbr.* (used as a title before the name of a married woman): *Mrs. (Jane) Brown*

☆ **Ms.** /mɪz/ *abbr.* (used as a title before the name of a woman, either married or unmarried): *Ms. (Joan) Smith*

☞ We can use the title **Ms.** when we do not know whether or not a woman is married. Some women also prefer it to **Mrs.** or **Miss.**

mt. (*also* **Mt.**) *abbr.* = MOUNT, MOUNTAIN

☆ **much¹** /mʌtʃ/ *det., pron.* (used with uncountable nouns, mainly in negative sentences and questions, or after *as, how, so, too*) a large amount of sth: *I don't have much money.* ○ *Did you have much difficulty finding the house?* ○ *You've given me too much food.* ○ *How much time do you have?* ○ *I didn't write much.* ○ *Did she say much?* ○ *How much do you want?* ○ *Eat as much as you can.* ○ *"Is there any mail?" "Not much."*

☞ In statements we usually use **a lot of**, not **much** (which is extremely formal): *I have a lot of experience.*

IDM **not much of a...** not very good: *Bob's not much of a cook.*

☆ **much²** /mʌtʃ/ *adv.* **1** to a great extent or degree: *I don't like her very much.* ○ *Thank you very much for a wonderful weekend.* ○ *We are very much looking forward to meeting you.* ○ *Do you go to the opera much?* (= very often) ○ *Their house is much nicer than ours.* ○ *You ate much more than I did.* **2** (with past participles used as adjectives) to a great extent or degree: *a much-needed rest* ○ *Katie was much loved by all her friends.* ☞ Compare: *Katie was **very** popular.*

IDM **much the same** very similar: *Polish food is much the same as German.*
not much good (at sth) not very good: *I'm not much good at singing.*

muck /mʌk/ *noun* [U] (*informal*) a thick, wet, dirty substance, such as mud

mu·cus /'myukəs/ *noun* [U] (*formal*) a sticky substance that is produced in some parts of the body, especially the nose ☞ Look at **phlegm** and **snot.**

☆ **mud** /mʌd/ *noun* [U] soft, wet earth: *He came home from the football game covered in mud.* —**mud·dy** /'mʌdi/ *adj.*: *Take those muddy boots off by the door!* ○ *It's very muddy down by the river.*

mud·dle /'mʌdl/ *verb*
PHRV **muddle through (sth)** to achieve a goal even though you do not act efficiently, have the right equipment, etc.: *I don't speak Spanish very well, but I managed to muddle through during my vacation in Mexico.*

mud·dle /'mʌdl/ *noun* [C,U] a state of disorder or confusion, in a place or in the mind: *We need to organize this information – it's all in a muddle right now.*

mud·dled /'mʌdld/ *adj.* not clear; confused: *His thoughts were all muddled because he was very sleepy.*

mud·slide /'mʌdslaɪd/ *noun* [C] the sudden fall of wet earth down the side of a hill or mountain

muf·fin /'mʌfən/ *noun* [C] a small sweet cake, often with fruit in it: *fresh blueberry muffins* ☞ picture at **cake.**

muf·fle /'mʌfl/ *verb* [T] to make a sound quieter and more difficult to hear: *He put his hand over her mouth to muffle her cries.*

muf·fled /'mʌfld/ *adj.* (used about sounds) difficult to hear; quiet or not clear: *I could hear muffled voices outside, but I couldn't tell what they were saying.*

muf·fler /'mʌflər/ *noun* [C] **1** the part of a car which reduces the engine noise coming from the back of a car **2** = SCARF(1)

mug¹ /mʌg/ *noun* [C] a deep cup with straight sides, used without a saucer; the contents of a mug: *Would you rather have a cup or a mug?* ○ *a mug of coffee* ☞ picture at **cup.**

mug² /mʌg/ *verb* [T] (**mug·ging; mugged**) to attack and rob sb in a public place —**mug·ging** *noun* [C,U]: *an increase in the number of muggings and other violent crimes*

mug·ger /'mʌgər/ *noun* [C] a person who attacks and robs sb in a public place

mug·gy /'mʌgi/ *adj.* (used about the weather) too warm and damp

mule /myul/ *noun* [C] an animal that has a horse and a donkey as its parents: *to be as stubborn as a mule*

☞ We say that a mule is a **cross** between a horse and a donkey.

mull /mʌl/ *verb*
PHRV **mull sth over** to think about sth carefully and for a long time: *Don't ask me for a decision right now. I'll have to mull it over.*

multi- /'mʌlti/ (in compounds) having several or many of: *a multinational corporation* ○ *a multi-billion-dollar deal* (= one that costs several billion dollars) ○ *a multimedia computer presentation* (= one that uses video, sound, pictures and text)

☆ **mul·ti·cul·tur·al** /ˌmʌltiˈkʌltʃərəl/ *adj.* for or including people from several different races, religions, languages or traditions: *a multicultural society* ○ *the college's Office of Multicultural Affairs*

mul·ti·mil·lion·aire /ˌmʌltiˌmɪlyəˈnɛr/ *noun* [C] a person who has several million dollars, etc.; an extremely rich person

mul·ti·ple¹ /'mʌltəpl/ *adj.* involving many people or having many parts, types, etc.: *a multiple crash on the freeway* ○ *to receive multiple injuries*

M

ər	ɪr	ɛr	ɑr	ɔr	ʊr	ʒ	h	ŋ
bird	near	hair	car	north	tour	vision	hat	sing

mul·ti·ple² /ˈmʌltəpl/ *noun* [C] a number that contains another number an exact number of times: *12, 18 and 24 are multiples of 6.*

ˌmultiple-ˈchoice *adj.* (used about test questions) showing several different answers from which you have to choose the right one

multiple sclerosis /ˌmʌltəpl sklǝˈroʊsǝs/ *noun* [U] (*abbr.* **MS**) a serious disease which slowly causes you to lose control of your body and of the ability to move

mul·ti·pli·ca·tion /ˌmʌltǝpləˈkeɪʃn/ *noun* [U] the process of multiplying a number: *The students will be tested on addition, subtraction, multiplication and division.*

☆ **mul·ti·ply** /ˈmʌltǝplaɪ/ *verb* (*pres. part.* **mul·ti·ply·ing**; *3rd pers. sing. pres.* **mul·ti·plies**; *p.t., p.p.* **mul·ti·plied**) **1** [I,T] **multiply A by B**; **multiply A and B (together)** to increase a number by the number of times mentioned: *to learn to multiply and divide* ○ *2 multiplied by 4 makes 8 (2 x 4 = 8)* ○ *What do you get if you multiply 13 and 11?* ○ *Multiply the two numbers together and you should get the answer.* **2** [I,T] to become bigger or greater; to make sth bigger or greater; to increase: *Our profits have multiplied over the last two years.* ○ *Using this method, you can multiply your profit in a very short time.* **3** [I] (used especially about animals) to increase in number by producing large numbers of young

mul·ti·tude /ˈmʌltǝtud/ *noun* [C] (*formal*) a very large number of people or things: *a multitude of difficulties*

mum /mʌm/ *noun* [C] (*BrE*) (*informal*) = MOM

mum·ble /ˈmʌmbl/ *verb* [I,T] to speak quietly without opening your mouth enough so that people cannot really hear the words: *I can't hear if you mumble – speak up!* ○ *Last night you kept mumbling something about a car crash in your sleep.* ☞ Look at **mutter**.

mum·my /ˈmʌmi/ *noun* [C] (*pl.* **mum·mies**) a dead body of a person or animal which has been preserved by rubbing it with special oils and wrapping it in cloth: *an Egyptian mummy*

mumps /mʌmps/ *noun* [U] an infectious disease, especially of children. Mumps causes the neck and lower face to swell: *to have/catch the mumps*

munch /mʌntʃ/ *verb* [I,T] **munch (sth)**; **munch (on) sth** to eat steadily, especially with pleasure: *He sat there munching (on) his sandwich and didn't say a word.*

mun·dane /mʌnˈdeɪn/ *adj.* ordinary; not interesting or exciting: *a mundane life, job, conversation, etc.*

mu·nic·i·pal /myuˈnɪsǝpl/ *adj.* connected with a town or city that has its own local government: *municipal employees*

mu·ni·tions /myuˈnɪʃnz/ *noun* [plural] military supplies, especially bombs and guns

mu·ral /ˈmyʊrǝl/ *noun* [C] a large picture which is painted on a wall

☆ **mur·der¹** /ˈmǝrdǝr/ *noun* **1** [C,U] the crime of killing a person illegally and on purpose: *Police believe that both murders were committed by the same person.* ○ *He was sentenced to life imprisonment for murder.* ○ *the murder victim* ○ *the murder weapon* **2** [U] (*informal*) a very difficult or bad experience: *It's murder trying to work when it's as hot as this.*

☆ **mur·der²** /ˈmǝrdǝr/ *verb* [T] to kill a person illegally and on purpose: *It seems that she was murdered with a knife.* ☞ Look at the note at **kill**.

☆ **mur·der·er** /ˈmǝrdǝrǝr/ *noun* [C] a person who has murdered sb

mur·der·ous /ˈmǝrdǝrǝs/ *adj.* likely to murder, or capable of murder

murk·y /ˈmǝrki/ *adj.* (**murk·i·er**; **murk·i·est**) dark and unpleasant or dirty: *They couldn't see anything in the murky water of the lake.*

mur·mur¹ /ˈmǝrmǝr/ *noun* **1** [C] the sound of words that are spoken quietly: *A murmur of disagreement ran through the room.* **2** [sing.] a low, gentle, continuous sound that is often not very clear: *the murmur of the wind in the trees*

mur·mur² /ˈmǝrmǝr/ *verb* [I,T] to say sth in a low quiet voice: *"Thank you," he murmured.* ○ *Samantha murmured an answer.*

☆ **mus·cle** /ˈmʌsl/ *noun* **1** [C,U] a piece of flesh inside the body which you can tighten or relax to produce movement: *Do some stretching before you run or you'll pull a muscle.* ○ *Riding a bicycle is good for developing the leg muscles.* ○ *The heart is made of muscle.* **2** [U] strength or power: *political muscle*

muscle

mus·cu·lar /ˈmʌskyǝlǝr/ *adj.* **1** connected with muscles: *muscular pain* **2** having large strong muscles: *a muscular body*

☆ **mu·se·um** /myuˈziǝm/ *noun* [C] a building where collections of valuable and interesting objects are kept and shown to the public: *Have you been to the Science Museum in St. Paul?*

mush·room /ˈmʌʃrum/ *noun* [C] a type of plant (**a fungus**) which grows very quickly, has a flat rounded top on a short stem and can be eaten as a vegetable: *mushrooms with garlic* ○ *mushroom soup*

☞ A **mushroom** is a type of **fungus**. Some, but not all, **fungi** can be eaten. **Toadstool** is another name for some types of poisonous fungi.

☆ **mu·sic** /ˈmyuzɪk/ *noun* [U] **1** an arrangement of sounds in patterns to be sung or played on instruments: *What sort of music do you like?* ○ *classical, folk, pop, rock, etc. music* ○ *Who composed this piece of music?* ○ *That poem has been*

M

tʃ	dʒ	v	θ	ð	s	z	ʃ
chin	June	van	thin	then	so	zoo	she

set to music. ○ a music lover ○ a music lesson **2** the written signs that represent the sounds of music; the sheet or book where these signs are printed: *Can you read music?* ○ *I forgot my music – can I share yours?*

☆**mu·si·cal¹** /ˈmyuzɪkl/ *adj.* **1** connected with music: *musical instruments* (= the piano, the violin, the trumpet, etc.) ○ *Would you like our program of this month's musical events?* **2** interested in or good at music: *He's very musical.* ○ *a musical child* **3** pleasant to listen to because it is like music: *a musical voice*

mu·si·cal² /ˈmyuzɪkl/ *noun* [C] a play or movie which has singing and dancing in it: *a Broadway musical*

☆**mu·si·cian** /myuˈzɪʃn/ *noun* [C] **1** a person whose job is to play a musical instrument: *The band consists of ten musicians.* **2** a person who is good at writing or playing music: *At the age of ten, he was already a fine musician.*

☆**Mus·lim** /ˈmʌzləm; ˈmʊz-; ˈmʊs-/ (*also* **Moslem** /ˈmɑzləm/) *noun* [C] a person whose religion is Islam —**Mus·lim** (*also* **Moslem**) *adj.*: *Muslim traditions, beliefs, etc.*

mus·sel /ˈmʌsl/ *noun* [C] a type of sea animal that lives inside a black shell and can be eaten ☞ picture at **shellfish**.

☆**must¹** /məst; *strong form* mʌst/ *modal verb* (*negative* **must not**; *short form* **mustn't** /ˈmʌsnt/) **1** (*formal*) (used for saying that it is necessary for sth to happen): *All visitors must report to the security desk.* ○ *Cars must not park in front of the entrance.*

☞ In more informal English, it is more common to use **have (got) to** to express this meaning. To tell people not to do sth, we usually use **can't** or **cannot**: *You can't park in front of the entrance – it's prohibited.*

2 (used for giving sb advice): *You really must come and see us sometime.*

☞ It is more common to use **should** or **ought to** when giving advice: *You really ought to come and see us sometime.*

3 (used for saying that you are sure that sth is true): *Have something to eat. You must be hungry.* ○ *I can't find my checkbook. I must have left it at home.* ○ *It must have been a great shock when your mother died.* ○ *That car that passed us must have been going 100 miles an hour.*

must² /məst; *strong form* mʌst/ *noun* [C] a thing that is absolutely necessary, or that must be seen, done, etc.: *This book is a must for all science fiction fans.*

mustache

beard

☆**mus·tache** (*also* **moustache**) /ˈmʌstæʃ; məˈstæʃ/ *noun* [C] hair that grows on the top lip, between the mouth and the nose: *My dad has a mustache.*

☆**mus·tard** /ˈmʌstərd/ *noun* [U] a yellow or brown sauce which is made from the seeds of the mustard plant. The sauce has a strong taste and is eaten in small amounts, usually with meat: *a large hot dog with ketchup and mustard*

must·y /ˈmʌsti/ *adj.* having an unpleasant stale or damp smell: *The rooms in the old house were dark and musty.*

mu·tant /ˈmyutnt/ *noun* [C] a living thing that is different from other living things of the same type because of a change in its basic (**genetic**) structure

mu·ta·tion /myuˈteɪʃn/ *noun* [C,U] a change in the basic structure of a living or developing thing; an example of such a change: *genetic mutations caused by radiation*

mut·ed /ˈmyutəd/ *adj.* **1** (used about colors or sounds) not bright or loud; soft **2** (used about a feeling or reaction) not strong or not openly expressed: *muted criticism* ○ *a muted response*

mu·ti·late /ˈmyutəleɪt/ *verb* [T] (usually passive) to damage sb's body very badly, often by cutting off parts: *The body was too badly mutilated to be identified.* —**mu·ti·la·tion** /ˌmyutəˈleɪʃn/ *noun* [C,U]

mu·ti·ny¹ /ˈmyutn·i/ *noun* [C,U] (*pl.* **mu·ti·nies**) an act that involves a group of people, especially sailors or soldiers, refusing to obey the person who is in command: *There'll be a mutiny if conditions don't improve.*

mu·ti·ny² /ˈmyutn·i/ *verb* [I] (*pres. part.* **mu·ti·ny·ing**; *3rd pers. sing. pres.* **mu·ti·nies**; *p.t., p.p.* **mu·ti·nied**) **mutiny (against sb/sth)** to refuse to obey your leader or to accept sth

mutt /mʌt/ *noun* [C] a dog which has parents of different types (**breeds**)

mut·ter /ˈmʌtər/ *verb* [I,T] to speak in a low, quiet and sometimes rather angry voice that is difficult to hear: *He muttered something about being late for an appointment and left the room.*

mut·ton /ˈmʌtn/ *noun* [U] the meat from an adult sheep: *a leg of mutton* ○ *a mutton chop* ☞ Look at the note at **meat**.

mu·tu·al /ˈmyutʃuəl/ *adj.* **1** (used about a feeling or an action) felt or done by both or all the people involved: *Harry left the company by mutual agreement* (both Harry and the company agreed). ○ *I just can't stand her and I'm sure the feeling is mutual* (= she doesn't like me either). **2** shared by two or more people: *We get along very well together because we have so many mutual interests.* ○ *It seems that Jane is a mutual friend of ours.* —**mu·tu·al·ly** /ˈmyutʃuəli; -tʃəli/ *adv.*: *The statements of the two witnesses were mutually exclusive* (= they could not both be true).

i	ɪ	ɛ	æ	ɑ	ɔ	ʌ	ʊ	u
see	sit	ten	cat	hot	saw	cup	put	too

muz·zle /'mʌzl/ *noun* [C] **1** the nose and mouth of an animal (e.g. a dog or fox) **2** a cover made of leather or wire that is put over an animal's nose and mouth so that it cannot bite **3** the open end of a gun where the bullets come out

☆ **my** /maɪ/ *det.* **1** of or belonging to me: *This is my husband, Jim.* ○ *It's my turn, not yours!* ○ *My favorite color is blue.* **2** (used before a noun or adjective as a way of talking to sb): *My dear Anne,...* ○ *Goodbye, my darling.* **3** (used in exclamations): *My goodness! Look at the time.*

☆ **my·self** /maɪ'sɛlf/ *pron.* **1** (used as the object of a verb or preposition when the person who does an action is also affected by it): *I saw myself in the mirror.* ○ *I felt pretty pleased with myself.* **2** (used for emphasis): *I'll speak to her myself.* ○ *I myself don't agree.* ○ *I'll do it myself* (= if you don't want to do it for me).

IDM (all) by myself 1 alone: *I live by myself.* ☞ Look at the note at **alone**. **2** without help: *I painted the house all by myself.*

☆ **mys·te·ri·ous** /mɪ'stɪriəs/ *adj.* **1** that you do not know about or cannot explain; strange: *Several people reported seeing mysterious lights in the sky.* **2** (used about a person) keeping sth secret or refusing to explain sth: *They're being very mysterious about where they're going this evening.* —**mys·te·ri·ous·ly** *adv.*

☆ **mys·ter·y** /'mɪstəri/ *noun* (*pl.* **mys·ter·ies**) **1** [C] a thing that you cannot understand or explain: *The police are still trying to solve the mystery of his disappearance.* ○ *It's a mystery to me what my daughter sees in her boyfriend.* ○ *It's one of the great mysteries of the natural world.* ○ *a mystery guest, person, etc.* (= one that you don't know anything about) **2** [U] the quality of being strange and secret and full of things that are difficult to explain: *novels full of mystery and suspense* ○ *a mystery story* **3** [C] a book or story about a crime, etc. that seems difficult to explain: *a mystery by Agatha Christie*

mys·tic /'mɪstɪk/ *noun* [C] a person who spends his/her life developing the spirit and communicating with God or a god

mys·ti·cal /'mɪstɪkl/ (*also* **mystic** /'mɪstɪk/) *adj.* of the spirit; involving hidden meaning, powers and feelings that are outside our normal everyday experience: *a mystical experience*

mys·ti·cism /'mɪstəsɪzəm/ *noun* [U] the belief that you can reach complete truth and knowledge of God or gods by prayer, thought and development of the spirit

mys·ti·fy /'mɪstəfaɪ/ *verb* [T] (*pres. part.* **mys·ti·fy·ing**; *3rd pers. sing. pres.* **mys·ti·fies**; *p.t., p.p.* **mys·ti·fied**) to make sb puzzled or confused: *I was mystified by the strange note. What did it mean?*

myth /mɪθ/ *noun* [C] **1** a very old story, especially one about gods and heroes. Myths often explain natural or historical events. **2** an idea, belief or story which is untrue or impossible: *The idea that money makes you happy is a complete myth.*

myth·i·cal /'mɪθɪkl/ *adj.* **1** existing only in myths (1): *mythical heroes* **2** not real; existing only in the imagination

my·thol·o·gy /mɪ'θɑlədʒi/ *noun* [U] very old stories and the beliefs contained in them: *Greek and Roman mythology*

Nn

N, n /ɛn/ *noun* [C] (*pl.* **N's** or **n's**) the fourteenth letter of the English alphabet: *"Nicholas" begins with (an) "N."*

N (*also* **N.**) *abbr.* north: *N. American*

nag /næg/ *verb* (**nag·ging**; **nagged**) **1** [I,T] **nag (at) sb** to talk to sb continuously in a complaining or critical way: *Quit nagging! I'll do it as soon as I can.* ○ *My parents are always nagging me to clean my room.* **2** [T] to worry or hurt sb continuously: *a nagging doubt in my mind* ○ *a nagging backache*

☆ **nail¹** /neɪl/ *noun* [C] **1** a small thin piece of metal with a point at one end. It is used for holding pieces of wood together, hanging pictures on, etc.: *to hammer a nail into a wall* ☞ picture at **tool**. **2** the thin hard layer that covers the ends of your fingers and toes: *fin-*gernails ○ *toenails* ○ *I still bite my nails sometimes when I'm nervous.* ☞ picture on page A24.

IDM hit the nail on the head ⇨ HIT¹

nail² /neɪl/ *verb* [T] to fasten sth with a nail¹(1) or nails: *Do you think we should nail these pieces together or use glue?*

PHRV nail sb down (to sth) to make a person say clearly what he/she wants or intends to do: *She says she'll visit us in the summer, but I can't nail her down to a definite date.*

'nail brush *noun* [C] a small brush for cleaning your fingernails ☞ picture at **brush**.

'nail file *noun* [C] a small tool with a rough surface that you use for shaping your nails

'nail ,pol·ish *noun* [U] a liquid that people

N

paint on their nails to give them color or to make them shine

na·ive (*also* **naïve**) /nɑˈiːv; naɪ-/ *adj.* without enough experience of the world and too ready to believe what other people say: *I was too naive to really understand what was going on.* ○ *a naive remark* —**na·ive·ly** (*also* **naïvely**) *adv.*: *She naively accepted the first price he offered.* —**na·ive·te** (*also* **naïveté** /nɑˌiˈvteɪ; nɑˈiːvətər; naɪ-/) *noun* [U]: *He showed complete naivete in financial matters.*

☆ **na·ked** /ˈneɪkəd/ *adj.* **1** without any clothes on: *He came to the door naked except for a towel.* ☞ Look at **bare** (1) and **nude**. **2** (*only before* a noun) not covered (used about sth that is usually covered): *a naked flame* **3** (*only before* a noun) openly shown or expressed; easy to see and often shocking: *naked aggression*

IDM **the naked eye** the eye without the help of a microscope or telescope: *Bacteria are too small to be seen with the naked eye.*

stark naked ➪ STARK²

☆ **name¹** /neɪm/ *noun* **1** [C] a word or words by which a person, an animal, a place or a thing is known: *What's your name?* ○ *Do you know the name of this flower?* ○ *Does this kind of sauce have a name?*

☞ Your **first name** (also **given name**) is the name your parents choose for you when you are born. Most people in the United States also have a **middle name** which is also chosen by their parents, but they may not use it very often. Some people use their **middle initial** on forms, documents, etc. (such as "Steven N. Palmer"). **Last name** is the expression usually used for your family name which you are born with. When a woman gets married, she may change her last name to be the same as her husband's. Her last name before marriage is then called her **maiden name**.

2 [sing.] an opinion that people have of a person or thing; reputation: *That area of Miami has a pretty bad name.* ○ *The company needs to build up a good name for itself.* **3** [C] a famous person: *All the big names in show business were invited to the party.*

IDM **by name** using the name of sb/sth: *It's a big school, but the principal knows all the students by name.*

in the name of sth because you believe in sth; for the sake of: *They acted in the name of democracy.*

in the name of sb representing a certain group of people: *Could you write a letter in the name of our class at school?*

make a name for yourself; make your name to become well known and respected: *an actor who made his name in comedies*

the name of the game the most important thing in a particular activity, business, etc.:

Staying ahead of our competitors is the name of the game here.

☆ **name²** /neɪm/ *verb* [T] **1 name sb/sth (after/ for sb)** to give sb/sth a name: *What are you going to name your baby?* ○ *The boy was named for his grandfather Harold.* ○ *Washington, D.C., was named after George Washington.*

☞ Be careful. When you are talking about being known by a particular name, **be named** or **be called** is used: *The baby is named Dan and his brother is Joe.*

2 to say what the name of sb/sth is: *The journalist refused to name the person who had given her the information.* ○ *Can you name all the planets in order?* **3** to state a date, price, etc.: *Have Alex and Julie named a date for their wedding?*

name·less /ˈneɪmləs/ *adj.* **1** without a name or with a name that you do not know or want to say: *the nameless slaves who built the pyramids* **2** not easily described or explained, e.g. because it is so terrible: *the nameless horrors of war*

name·ly /ˈneɪmli/ *adv.* (used for giving more detail about what you are saying) that is to say: *We both reached the same conclusion – namely, that it was time to sell the business.*

name·sake /ˈneɪmseɪk/ *noun* [C] a person who has the same name as another

nan·ny /ˈnæni/ *noun* [C] (*pl.* **nan·nies**) a woman whose job is taking care of young children. A nanny usually works at or lives in the child's home.

nap¹ /næp/ *noun* [C] a short sleep that you have during the day

nap² /næp/ *verb* [I] (**nap·ping**; **napped**) to have a short sleep

nape /neɪp/ *noun* [sing.] the back part of the neck

☆ **nap·kin** /ˈnæpkən/ *noun* [C] a piece of cloth or paper that you use when you are eating to protect your clothes or for wiping your hands and mouth: *a paper/cloth napkin*

nap·py /ˈnæpi/ *noun* [C] (*pl.* **nap·pies**) (*BrE*) = DIAPER

nar·cot·ic /nɑrˈkɑtɪk/ *noun* [C] a drug that makes you feel sleepy or stops you from feeling pain. Many types of narcotics are illegal. Some people take narcotics for pleasure and then cannot stop taking them (= they become addicted). —**nar·cot·ic** *adj.*

nar·rate /ˈnæreɪt; næˈreɪt/ *verb* [T] (*formal*) to tell a story

nar·ra·tion /næˈreɪʃn/ *noun* [C,U] telling a story; the story that you tell

nar·ra·tive /ˈnærətɪv/ *noun* [C] (*formal*) a story or an account

nar·ra·tor /ˈnæreɪtər/ *noun* [C] the person who tells a story or explains what is happening in a play, movie, etc.

ər	ɪr	ɛr	ɑr	ɔr	ʊr	ʒ	h	ŋ
bird	near	hair	car	north	tour	vision	hat	sing

☆ **nar·row¹** /ˈnærəʊ/ *adj.* **1** having only a short distance from side to side: *The bridge is too narrow for two cars to pass.* ☞ The opposite is **wide** or **broad**. **2** not large: *a narrow circle of friends* **3** by a small amount: *That was a very narrow escape. You were lucky.* ○ *a narrow defeat/victory* —**nar·row·ness** *noun* [U]

nar·row² /ˈnærəʊ/ *verb* [I,T] to become narrow or to make sth narrow: *The road narrows ahead.*

PHRV **narrow sth down** to make a list of things smaller: *We had a huge list of places we wanted to visit on vacation, but we managed to narrow it down to three.*

nar·row·ly /ˈnærəʊli/ *adv.* only by a small amount: *The driver swerved and narrowly missed hitting the boy.*

ˌnarrow-ˈminded *adj.* not willing to accept new ideas or the opinions of other people if they are not the same as your own

NASA /ˈnæsə/ *abbr.* National Aeronautics and Space Administration; the department of the government that is responsible for space exploration

na·sal /ˈneɪzl/ *adj.* connected with the nose

☆ **nas·ty** /ˈnæsti/ *adj.* (**nas·ti·er; nas·ti·est**) **1** angry or aggressive: *When she was asked to leave, she got really nasty.* **2** very unkind: *Nick said some pretty nasty things about his ex-wife.* **3** very bad: *nasty weather* ○ *That sounds like a nasty cough.* **4** (*informal*) bad or ugly: *Yuck! This stuff tastes nasty!* —**nas·ti·ly** /ˈnæstəli/ *adv.* —**nas·ti·ness** *noun* [U]

☆ **na·tion** /ˈneɪʃn/ *noun* [C] a country or all the people in a country: *The President is going to speak to the nation on television.* ○ *a summit of the leaders of seven nations*

☆ **na·tion·al¹** /ˈnæʃənl/ *adj.* concerning all of a nation or country; typical of a particular nation: *Here is today's national and international news.* ○ *a national newspaper* ○ *a young Swede dressed in his national costume* ○ *a national holiday* ☞ Look at **international** and **local**. —**na·tion·al·ly** *adv.*: *to advertise sth nationally*

na·tion·al² /ˈnæʃənl/ *noun* [C] (*formal*) a person who comes from a particular country: *There are many Algerian nationals working in France.*

ˌnational ˈanthem *noun* [C] the official song of a country that is played at public events

the ˌNational ˈGuard *noun* [sing.] a type of army in each state of the U.S. Most members of the National Guard are only part-time soldiers: *The governor called in the National Guard to prevent further riots.*

☆ **na·tion·al·ism** /ˈnæʃənl·ɪzəm/ *noun* [U] **1** the strong feeling of love or pride that you feel for your own country. Nationalism often makes people think that their own country is better than others. ☞ Look at **patriotism**. **2** the desire of a group of people to form an independent country: *Nationalism is very strong in Quebec.*

na·tion·al·ist /ˈnæʃənl·ɪst/ *noun* [C] a person who wants a particular group of people to be able to form an independent country: *a Quebec nationalist*

na·tion·al·is·tic /ˌnæʃənəˈlɪstɪk/ *adj.* having or showing strong feelings of love for or pride in your own country

☞ **Nationalistic** is usually used in a critical way, meaning that a person's feelings of pride are too strong. Look also at **patriotic**.

☆ **na·tion·al·i·ty** /ˌnæʃəˈnæləti/ *noun* [C,U] (*pl.* **na·tion·al·i·ties**) being a member of a particular nation or country: *students of many nationalities* ○ *to have dual nationality* (= of two countries) ☞ Look at **citizenship**.

na·tion·al·ize /ˈnæʃənəlaɪz/ *verb* [T] to put a company or organization under the control of the government: *The new prime minister wanted to nationalize the country's oil industry.* ☞ Look at **privatize**. —**na·tion·al·i·za·tion** /ˌnæʃənələˈzeɪʃn/ *noun* [U]

ˌnational ˈpark *noun* [C] a large area of beautiful land that is protected by the federal government so that the public can enjoy it

☆ **na·tion·wide** /ˌneɪʃnwaɪd/ *adj., adv.* over the whole of a country: *The police launched a nationwide hunt for the killer.*

☆ **na·tive¹** /ˈneɪtɪv/ *noun* [C] **1** a person who was born in a particular place: *She lives in Arizona but she's a native of New York.* **2** (usually used by white people about non-white people) a person who lives in a particular place: *When explorers first arrived in South America, they were given a warm welcome by the natives.*

☞ This sense of **native** is used by people who feel that they are better than the local people and it is becoming rare.

3 an animal or plant that lives or grows naturally in a particular place: *The koala is a native of Australia.*

na·tive² /ˈneɪtɪv/ *adj.* **1** (only *before* a noun) connected with the place where you were born: *Tadeusz's native land is Poland, but he left in 1938.* **2** (used about an animal or plant) living or growing naturally in a particular place: *The koala is native to Australia.*

ˌNative Aˈmerican (*also* **American Indian; Indian**) *adj., noun* [C] (of) a member of the race of people who were the original inhabitants of North America; especially the area that is now the United States (but not Alaska or Hawaii)

☞ Some people do not like the names **American Indian** and **Indian**.

ˌnative ˈspeaker *noun* [C] a person who learned a particular language as a very young child: *Are you a native speaker of Dutch?*

NATO /ˈneɪtoʊ/ *abbr.* North Atlantic Treaty

Organization; a group of European countries, Canada and the U.S., who agree to give each other military help if necessary

☆ **nat·u·ral** /'nætʃərəl/ *adj.* **1** connected with things that were not made by people: *natural disasters such as earthquakes and floods* ○ *We use only natural flavorings in our products.* ○ *I prefer to see animals in their natural surroundings rather than in zoos.*

☞ If somebody dies of **natural causes**, he/she dies because he/she was sick or old, not because he/she was killed in an accident.

2 usual or normal; what you would expect: *It's natural to feel nervous before an interview.* ○ *It's only natural for people to be nervous.* ☞ The opposite is **unnatural**. **3** that you had from birth or that was easy for you to learn: *a natural gift for languages* ○ *natural charm*

ˌnatural ˈgas *noun* [U] a mixture of gases taken from the earth that is used for heating, cooking, etc.: *We heat our home with natural gas.* ○ *a natural gas pipeline*

ˌnatural ˈhistory *noun* [U] the study of plants and animals

nat·u·ral·ist /'nætʃrəlɪst/ *noun* [C] a person who studies plants and animals

nat·u·ral·ize /'nætʃrəlaɪz/ *verb* [T] (usually passive) to make sb a citizen of a country where he/she was not born: *a naturalized American citizen* —**nat·u·ral·i·za·tion** /ˌnætʃrələ'zeɪʃn/ *noun* [U]

☆ **nat·u·ral·ly** /'nætʃrəli/ *adv.* **1** in a natural (3) way: *Vera is naturally a very cheerful person.* ○ *Working with computers comes naturally to Nick.* **2** of course; as you would expect: *Naturally, the team was upset about its defeat.* **3** in a way that is normal: *You look very stiff and tense. Try to stand naturally.* ○ *Don't try and impress people. Just act naturally.* **4** in a way that is not made or done by people: *naturally wavy hair*

☆ **na·ture** /'neɪtʃər/ *noun* **1** [U] all the things in the world that were not made or caused by people: *the forces of nature* (e.g. volcanoes, hurricanes, etc.) ○ *If we destroy too many forests, we may upset the balance of nature.* ○ *the wonders of nature* **2** [C,U] the qualities or features of a person or thing: *He's basically honest by nature.* ○ *It's not in Shelley's nature to tell lies.* ○ *The nature of my work is secret and I cannot discuss it.* ○ *human nature* **3** [sing.] the type or sort of sth: *I'm not very interested in things of that nature.*

IDM **second nature** ⇨ SECOND¹

-natured /'neɪtʃərd/ (in compounds) having a particular quality or feature: *good-natured*

naugh·ty /'nɔti/ *adj.* (**naugh·ti·er; naugh·ti·est**) (used when you are talking to or about a child) not doing what an adult says; badly-behaved; causing trouble: *one of the naughtiest*

children in the class —**naugh·ti·ly** /'nɔtəli/ *adv.* **naugh·ti·ness** *noun* [U]

nau·se·a /'nɔziə; 'nɔʒə/ *noun* [U] the feeling that you are going to vomit (= bring up food from your stomach): *A wave of nausea came over him at the sight of all the blood.* ☞ Look at **sick** (2).

nau·se·ate /'nɔzieɪt/ *verb* [T] to cause sb to feel nausea or strong dislike —**nau·se·at·ing** /-eɪtɪŋ/ *adj.*

nau·ti·cal /'nɔtɪkl/ *adj.* connected with ships, sailors or sailing

na·val /'neɪvl/ *adj.* connected with the navy: *a naval battle*

na·vel /'neɪvl/ *noun* [C] (*formal*) the small hollow in the middle of your stomach ☞ Look at **belly button** and **umbilical cord**.

nav·i·ga·ble /'nævɪɡəbl/ *adj.* that boats can sail along: *a navigable river*

nav·i·gate /'nævəɡeɪt/ *verb* **1** [I] to use a map, etc. to find out which way a car, ship, plane, etc. should go: *Early explorers used the stars to navigate.* ○ *If you drive, I'll navigate.* **2** [T] to move or guide a ship, etc. in a particular direction; to find a way through a difficult place: *We managed to navigate the yacht through the rocks.* ○ *Nobody had navigated the Amazon until then.* —**nav·i·ga·tion** /ˌnævə'ɡeɪʃn/ *noun* [U]

nav·i·ga·tor /'nævəɡeɪtər/ *noun* [C] a person who navigates

☆ **na·vy** /'neɪvi/ *noun* [C] (*pl.* **na·vies**) **1** the **Navy** the organization that controls the warships of a country and the people that work on them: *to join the Navy* ☞ Look at **army**, **air force**, **Marine Corps** and **merchant marine**. **2** a group of warships belonging to a country: *Does Switzerland have a navy?*

ˌnavy ˈblue (*also* **navy**) *adj.*, *noun* [U] dark blue

NBA /ˌɛn bi 'eɪ/ *abbr.* National Basketball Association; the organization of professional basketball teams in the U.S.

NC-17 /ˌɛn si ˌsɛvən'tin/ *adj.* (used about movies that children under age 17 are not allowed to see)

NE *abbr.* northeast; northeastern

☆ **near¹** /nɪr/ *adj.* **1** not far in time or distance (from sb/sth): *We're hoping to move to Arizona in the near future.* ○ *Our new house is very near to Kara's school.* ○ *Where's the nearest post office?*

☞ **Close** and **near** are often the same in meaning, but in some phrases only one of them may be used: *a close friend* ○ *the near future* ○ *a close contest.* Look at the note at **next**.

2 closely related to you: *My nearest relative who's still alive is my cousin.*

IDM **a near miss** a situation where sth nearly hits sth else or where sth bad nearly happens:

Two military planes were involved in a near miss over the desert yesterday.

☆**near²** /nɪr/ *adv., prep.* not far in time or distance; close to: *It's a little town near the Oklahoma border.* ○ *I don't want to sit near the window.* ○ *Her birthday is near mine.* ○ *I wasn't sitting near enough to see.* ○ *They live very near.*
IDM **nowhere near** far from: *We've sold nowhere near enough tickets to make a profit.*

near³ /nɪr/ *verb* [I,T] to get closer to sth in time or distance: *The day was nearing when we would have to decide.* ○ *The job is nearing completion.*

☆**near·by¹** /'nɪrbaɪ/ *adj.* (only *before* a noun) not far away in distance: *We went out to a nearby restaurant.*

☞ Notice that **nearby** is only used before the noun. **Near** cannot be used before a noun in this way: *We went out to a restaurant near our house.* ○ *The restaurant is pretty near there.*

☆**near·by²** /ˌnɪr'baɪ/ *adv.* not far away in distance: *A new restaurant has opened nearby.*

☆**near·ly** /'nɪrli/ *adv.* almost; not completely or exactly: *It's been nearly five years since the last time I saw him.* ○ *Linda was so badly hurt she nearly died.* ○ *It's not far now. We're nearly there.* ○ *He earns nearly $50,000 a year.*
IDM **not nearly** far from: *It's not nearly as warm as it was yesterday.*

near-sight·ed /'nɪrˌsaɪtəd/ *adj.* only able to see things clearly when they are close ☞ The opposite is **far-sighted**.

☆**neat** /nit/ *adj.* **1** with everything arranged in its place or done carefully: *Please keep your room neat and clean.* ○ *neat handwriting* (= with all the letters carefully formed) **2** (used about a person) liking things to be done or arranged carefully **3** (*informal*) good; nice; interesting: *We saw a lot of neat stuff at the Science Museum.* —**neat·ly** *adv.* **neat·ness** *noun* [U]

☆**nec·es·sar·i·ly** /ˌnɛsə'sɛrəli/ *adv.* in all cases; always: *Shouting is not necessarily the best way to make yourself understood.*

☆**nec·es·sar·y** /'nɛsəˌsɛri/ *adj.* needed in order to get sth or to do sth: *A good diet is necessary for a healthy life.* ○ *Don't spend more than $20 unless it's absolutely necessary.* ○ *It's not necessary for you all to come.*

ne·ces·si·tate /nə'sɛsəteɪt/ *verb* [T] (*formal*) to make sth necessary

☆**ne·ces·si·ty** /nə'sɛsəti/ *noun* (*pl.* **ne·ces·si·ties**) **1** [U] (*formal*) **necessity (for sth/to do sth)** being necessary; need: *Is there any necessity for change?* ○ *There's no necessity to write every single name down.* **2** [C] something that you must have: *Clean water is an absolute necessity.* ○ *Food, clothing and shelter are all necessities of life.*

☆**neck** /nɛk/ *noun* [C] **1** the part of the body that joins your head to your shoulders: *She wrapped a scarf around her neck.* ○ *Giraffes have long necks.* **2** the part of a piece of clothing that goes around your neck: *The neck on this sweater is too tight.* ○ *a V-neck sweater* ☞ picture on page A27. **3** the narrow part of sth that looks like a neck: *the neck of a bottle*
IDM **neck and neck (with sb/sth)** equal or level: *At the halfway point, the two cars were neck and neck.*
pain in the neck ⇨ PAIN¹
be up to your ears/eyes/neck in sth ⇨ UP¹.

☆**neck·lace** /'nɛkləs/ *noun* [C] a piece of jewelry that you wear around your neck ☞ picture at **jewelry**.

neck·tie /'nɛktaɪ/ (*also* **tie**) *noun* [C] a long thin piece of cloth that you wear around your neck with a shirt ☞ Look at **bow tie**.

☆**need¹** /nid/ *verb* [T] (not usually used in the continuous forms) **1** to require sth; to think that sth is necessary: *All living things need water.* ○ *I need a new roll of film for my camera.* ○ *Does Bob need any help?* ○ *Can I borrow your dictionary or do you need it?* ○ *She needs three volunteers to bring the food.* ○ *This sweater needs washing/to be washed.* ○ *He needed his eyes tested.* **2** to have to; to be obliged to: *Do we need to buy the tickets in advance?* ○ *I need to ask some advice.* ○ *You didn't need to bring any food, but it was very kind of you.*

☞ Note that the question form of the main verb **need** is **do I need?**, etc. and the past tense is **needed** (question form **did you need?**, etc.; negative **didn't need**).

☆**need²** /nid/ *noun* **1** [U, sing.] a situation in which sth is wanted or required: *We are all in need of a rest.* ○ *There is a growing need for low-cost housing in this area.* ○ *There's no need for you to come if you don't want to.* ○ *Is there any need for all that noise?* ○ *Please call me if you feel the need to talk.* **2 needs** [plural] the things that you must have: *He doesn't earn enough to pay for his basic needs.* ○ *Parents must consider their children's emotional as well as their physical needs.* **3** [U] the state of not having enough money: *a campaign to help families in need*

☆**nee·dle** /'nidl/ *noun* [C] **1** a small thin piece of metal with a point at one end and a hole (**an eye**) at the other that is used for sewing: *to thread a needle* ☞ picture at **sew**. **2** (*also* **knitting needle**) a long thin piece of metal, plastic or wood with a point at one end that is used for knitting ☞ picture at **knit**. **3** the thin hollow part of a syringe that is used for injecting liquids into your body **4** something that looks like a needle : *a pine needle* ○ *the needle of a compass* ☞ Look also at **pins and needles**.

need·less /'nidləs/ *adj.* that is not necessary: *We had gone through a lot of needless worry.*

ə	y	w	t̬	eɪ	aɪ	ɔɪ	aʊ	oʊ
about	yes	woman	butter	say	five	boy	now	go

N

He was safe at home. ☞ Look at **unneces-sary**. —**need·less·ly** *adv.*

need·le·work /ˈnidlwərk/ *noun* [U] work that you do by hand using a needle (1). Needlework includes sewing and embroidery.

need·y /ˈnidi/ *adj.* (**need·i·er**; **need·i·est**) not having enough money, etc.; poor

☆ **ne·ga·tive**[1] /ˈnɛɡəṭɪv/ (*abbr.* **neg.**) *adj.* **1** (used about a word, phrase or sentence) saying or meaning "no" or "not": *a negative sentence* ○ *"Don't you like Maryland?" is a negative question.* ☞ Look at **affirmative**. **2** only thinking about the bad qualities of sb/sth: *I wish you wouldn't be so negative about everything – try to look on the bright side.* ☞ The opposite is **positive**. **3** (used about a medical or scientific test) showing that sth has not happened or has not been found: *The results of the pregnancy test were negative.* ☞ The opposite is **positive**. **4** (used about a number) less than zero ☞ The opposite is **positive**.

☆ **ne·ga·tive**[2] /ˈnɛɡəṭɪv/ *noun* [C] **1** a word, phrase or sentence that says or means "no" or "not": *Carol answered in the negative* (= she said no). ○ *"Never," "neither" and "nobody" are all negatives.* **2** a piece of film from which we can make a photograph. The light areas of a negative are dark on the final photograph and the dark areas are light: *If you give me the negative, I can have another print made.*

☆ **ne·glect**[1] /nɪˈɡlɛkt/ *verb* [T] to give too little or no attention or care to sb/sth: *to neglect your studies*

ne·glect[2] /nɪˈɡlɛkt/ *noun* [U] giving too little care to sb/sth; the state of being neglected: *The house was empty and in a state of total neglect.* ○ *The parents were arrested and charged with child neglect.*

ne·glect·ed /nɪˈɡlɛkṭəd/ *adj.* having or showing a lack of care and attention: *Neglected children often have trouble in school.*

neg·li·gence /ˈnɛɡlɪdʒəns/ *noun* [U] not being careful enough; lack of care: *The accident was a result of human negligence.*

neg·li·gent /ˈnɛɡlɪdʒənt/ *adj.* not giving enough care or attention to sth (that you are responsible for) —**neg·li·gent·ly** *adv.*

neg·li·gi·ble /ˈnɛɡlɪdʒəbl/ *adj.* not important because it is too small

ne·go·tia·ble /nəˈɡoʊʃəbl/ *adj.* that can be decided or changed by discussion: *The price is not negotiable* (= it can't be changed).

☆ **ne·go·ti·ate** /nəˈɡoʊʃieɪt/ *verb* **1** [I] to talk to sb in order to decide or agree about sth: *Union leaders are still negotiating with the management about this year's pay increase.* **2** [T] **negotiate sth (with sb)** to decide or agree sth by talking about it: *to negotiate an agreement* **3** [T] to get over, past or along sth difficult: *The bike racers had to negotiate several difficult turns along the route.*

☆ **ne·go·ti·a·tion** /nəˌɡoʊʃiˈeɪʃn/ *noun* [C,U] discussions at which people try to decide or agree on sth: *The salary is now open to negotiation.* ○ *The negotiations were extremely difficult.* ○ *to enter/break off negotiations*

ne·go·ti·a·tor /nəˈɡoʊʃieɪṭər/ *noun* [C] a person who negotiates (1, 2)

Ne·gro /ˈnigroʊ/ *noun* [C] (*pl.* **Ne·groes**) (*old-fashioned*) a black person

☞ This word is now considered offensive. Look at **African-American**.

neigh /neɪ/ *noun* [C] the long high sound that a horse makes —**neigh** *verb* [I]

☆ **neigh·bor** /ˈneɪbər/ *noun* [C] **1** a person who lives near you: *Don't make too much noise, or you'll wake the neighbors.* ○ *our next-door neighbors* **2** a person or thing that is near or next to another: *The United States is Canada's neighbor.* ○ *Try not to look at what your neighbor is writing.*

☆ **neigh·bor·hood** /ˈneɪbərhʊd/ *noun* [C] a particular part of a town or city and the people who live there: *We just moved into the neighborhood and don't know our way around yet.* ○ *a friendly neighborhood*

neigh·bor·ing /ˈneɪbərɪŋ/ *adj.* (only *before* a noun) near or next to: *Kids from all the neighboring towns will attend the new school.*

neigh·bor·ly /ˈneɪbərli/ *adj.* friendly and helpful

☆ **nei·ther**[1] /ˈniðər; ˈnaɪ-/ *det., pron.* (used about two people or things) not one and not the other: *Neither team played very well.* ○ *Neither of the teams played very well.* ○ *"Would you like a sandwich? Or a piece of cake?" "Neither, thank you. I'm not hungry."* ○ *I asked both Jamal and Terry, but neither one wanted to come along.*

☞ Notice that **neither** is followed by a singular noun and verb: *Neither day was suitable.* The noun or pronoun that follows **neither of** is in the plural, but the verb may be singular or plural: *(formal) Neither of the days is suitable.* ○ *(informal) Neither of the days are suitable.*

☆ **nei·ther**[2] /ˈniðər; ˈnaɪ-/ *adv., conj.* **1** also not; not either: *I don't eat meat and neither does Tom.* ○ *Stella didn't attend the meeting and neither did Jane.* ○ *"I haven't seen that play." "Neither have I."*

☞ In this sense **nor** can be used in the same way in formal English: *"I haven't seen that play." "Nor have I."* Notice that when you use **not ... either** the order of words is different: *I don't eat meat and Tom doesn't either.* ○ *"I haven't seen that play." "I haven't either."*

2 neither ... nor not ... and not: *Neither Tom nor I eat meat.*

ər	ɪr	ɛr	ɑr	ɔr	ʊr	ʒ	h	ŋ
bird	near	hair	car	north	tour	vision	hat	sing

N

☞ **Neither** ... **nor** can be used with a singular or a plural verb: *(formal) Neither Stella nor Jane was at the meeting.* ○ *(informal) Neither Stella nor Jane were at the meeting.*

ne·on /'niɑn/ *noun* [U] (*symbol* **Ne**) a type of gas that is used for making bright lights and signs: *the neon lights of the city*

☆ **neph·ew** /'nɛfyu/ *noun* [C] the son of your brother or sister, or the son of your husband's or wife's brother or sister ☞ Look at **niece**.

Nep·tune /'nɛptun/ *noun* [sing.] the planet that is eighth in order from the sun

nerd /nɜrd/ *noun* [C] (*slang*) a person who is boring and unfashionable and who is often very interested in science and computers: *a computer nerd* ☞ This word is used in a critical way. **—nerd·y** *adj.*

☆ **nerve** /nɜrv/ *noun* **1** [C] one of the long thin threads in your body that carry feelings or other messages to and from your brain **2 nerves** [plural] the ability to stay calm and not get worried: *You need strong nerves for this job.* **3 nerves** [plural] the state of being very nervous or worried: *Breathing deeply should help to calm your nerves.* **4** [U] the courage that you need to do sth difficult or dangerous: *Race car drivers need a lot of nerve.* ○ *He didn't have the nerve to ask Mandy to go out with him.* ○ *She climbed to the highest diving board but lost her nerve and couldn't jump.* **5** [U] the rudeness that is needed to do sth: *He had the nerve to ask me to loan him some money, and he still owes me $20.*

IDM get on sb's nerves (*informal*) to annoy sb or make sb angry: *Turn that music down – it's getting on my nerves.*

nerve-racking (*also* **nerve-wracking**) /'nɜrv,rækɪŋ/ *adj.* making you very nervous or worried: *Waiting for test scores can be very nerve-racking.*

☆ **nerv·ous** /'nɜrvəs/ *adj.* **1** connected with the nerves of the body: *a nervous disorder* **2** worried or afraid: *I'm a little nervous about traveling on my own.* ○ *I always get nervous just before a game.* ○ *nervous laughter* **—nerv·ous·ly** *adv.*: *He sat there, biting his fingernails nervously.* **—nerv·ous·ness** *noun* [U]

ˌ**nervous ˈbreakdown** (*also* **breakdown**) *noun* [C] a time when sb is so depressed that he/she cannot continue living and working normally: *to have a nervous breakdown*

ˈ**nervous ˌsystem** *noun* [C] your brain and all the nerves in your body

☆ **nest¹** /nɛst/ *noun* [C] **1** a round hollow structure that a bird builds to lay its eggs in ☞ picture at **bird**. **2** the home of certain animals or insects: *a wasps' nest*

nest² /nɛst/ *verb* [I] to use or build a nest[1]

nes·tle /'nɛsl/ *verb* [I,T] to move yourself or a part of your body into a comfortable position, against a person or sth soft: *The child nestled up against his mother.* ○ *The baby nestled her*

head *on her mother's shoulder.* (*figurative*) *a beautiful town nestled in a river valley*

☆ **net¹** /nɛt/ *noun* **1** [U] material that is made of long pieces of string, thread, etc. that are tied together, with spaces between them: *a piece of nylon net* ☞ Look also at **netting**. **2** [C] a piece of net that is used for a particular purpose: *a tennis net* (= in the center of the court) ○ *a fishing net* ○ *a hairnet* ☞ picture at **tennis**. Look also at **safety net**. **3 the Net** [sing.] (*informal*) = INTERNET

☆ **net²** /nɛt/ *adj.* (only *before* a noun) from which nothing more needs to be taken away: *What is your net income?* (= after taxes, etc. have been paid) ○ *The net weight of the jam is 12 ounces* (= not including the jar). ○ *net profit* ☞ The opposite is **gross**.

net³ /nɛt/ *verb* [T] (**net·ting**; **net·ted**) **1** to gain sth as a profit: *The sale of the land netted the county $2 million.* **2** to catch sth using a net[1](2)

net·ting /'nɛtɪŋ/ *noun* [U] material that is made of long pieces of string, thread, wire, etc. that are tied together with spaces between them: *a bridal veil made of white netting*

☆ **net·work** /'nɛtwərk/ *noun* [C] **1** a group of people or companies, etc. that work together closely: *We have a network of agents who sell our products all over the country.* **2** a group of television or radio companies that broadcasts the same programs in different parts of a country **3** a complicated system of roads, train tracks, etc.: *The subway network covers all areas of the capital.* **4** a system of computers that are connected by cables or telephone lines

neu·ro·sis /nʊ'roʊsəs/ *noun* [C] (*pl.* **neu·ro·ses** /-siz/) a mental illness that causes strong feelings of fear and worry

neu·rot·ic /nʊ'rɑtɪk/ *adj.* **1** suffering from neurosis **2** worried about things in a way that is not normal

neu·ter¹ /'nutər/ *adj.* (used about a word) not masculine or feminine according to the rules of grammar

neu·ter² /'nutər/ *verb* [T] to remove the sexual parts of an animal

☆ **neu·tral¹** /'nutrəl/ *adj.* **1** not supporting or belonging to either side in an argument, war, etc.: *Switzerland remained neutral during the war.* ○ *The two sides agreed to meet on neutral ground.* **2** having or showing no strong qualities, feelings or color: *a blouse in a neutral color that will go with anything*

neu·tral² /'nutrəl/ *noun* [U] the position that the gears of a car, etc. are in when no power is sent from the engine to the wheels, but the wheels can still turn: *Make sure the car is in neutral before you turn on the engine.* ☞ Look also at **drive²(4)**, **park¹(4)** and **reverse²(2)**.

neu·tral·i·ty /nu'trælə̭ti/ *noun* [U] the state of being neutral1 in an argument, war, etc.

tʃ	dʒ	v	θ	ð	s	z	ʃ
chin	June	van	thin	then	so	zoo	she

N

neu·tral·ize /'nutrəlaɪz/ *verb* [T] to take away the effect of sth

☆ **nev·er** /'nɛvər/ *adv.* at no time; not ever: *I never start work before 9 o'clock.* ○ *I've never been to Portugal.* ○ *We'll never go back to that hotel.* ○ *You should never leave valuables in your car.* ○ *He never ever eats meat.* ○ *(formal) Never before has such a high standard been achieved.*

IDM **never mind** ⇨ MIND²

nev·er·the·less /,nɛvərðə'lɛs/ *adv.* *(formal)* in spite of that: *It was a cold, rainy day. Nevertheless, more people came than we had expected.* ○ *She knew that the accident wasn't her fault. She still felt guilty, nevertheless.*

☆ **new** /nu/ *adj.* **1** that has recently been built, made, invented, etc.: *We went shopping at the new mall yesterday.* ○ *There have been record sales of new cars this month.* ○ *Have you seen Tom Cruise's new movie?* ○ *a new method of treating mental illness* ○ *Paula came to show us her new baby.* **2** different; other; changed from what was before: *Our new house is a lot bigger than the old one.* ○ *I've just started reading a new book.* ○ *to make new friends* **3 new (to sb)** that has not been seen, learned, etc. before: *This type of machine is new to me.* ○ *to learn a new language* ○ *We just moved here, so the area is still new to us.* **4 new (to sth)** having just started being or doing sth: *We are new to the area.* ○ *a new parent* ○ *She's new to the job and needs a lot of help.* ○ *a new member of the club*

IDM **break fresh/new ground** ⇨ GROUND¹

—**new·ness** *noun* [U]

new- /nu/ (in compounds) recently: *a newborn baby*

New 'Age *noun* [U] a set of beliefs connected with religion, health and the environment that are not part of any traditional Western religion —**New Age** *adj.*: *New Age philosophy*

new·com·er /'nukʌmər/ *noun* [C] a person who has just arrived in a place

new·fan·gled /'nufæŋgld/ *adj.* new or modern in a way that the speaker dislikes or refuses to accept: *I don't need all these newfangled gadgets in the kitchen.*

☆ **new·ly** /'nuli/ *adv.* (usually before a past participle) recently: *the newly appointed Secretary of Defense*

new·ly·wed /'nuliwɛd/ *noun* [C, usually pl.] a person who has recently gotten married

new 'moon *noun* [sing.] the moon when it appears as a thin line ☞ Look at **full moon**.

☆ **news** /nuz/ *noun* **1** [U] information about sth that has happened recently: *Have you heard the latest news? Mary and Joe are getting married!* ○ *That's news to me* (= I didn't know that). ○ *News is coming in of a plane crash in Thailand.* ○ *There will be another news bulletin at 1 o'clock.* ○ *Our town has been in the news a lot recently* (= a lot has been written in newspapers, etc.).

☞ **News** is an uncountable noun. If we are talking about an individual item, we must say "a piece of news": *We had a piece of good news yesterday.*

2 the news [sing.] a regular broadcast of the latest news (1) on the radio and TV: *We always watch the six o'clock news on TV.* ○ *I heard on the news that there was a plane crash in Thailand.* ○ *the local/national news*

IDM **break the news (to sb)** to be the first to tell sb about sth important that has happened

news·cast·er /'nuzkæstər/ *noun* [C] a person who reads the news on TV or radio

news·let·ter /'nuzlɛtər/ *noun* [C] a printed report about a club or organization that is sent regularly to members and other people who may be interested

☆ **news·pa·per** /'nuzpeɪpər/ *noun* **1** *(also* **paper)** [C] large folded pieces of paper printed with news, advertisements and articles on various subjects. Newspapers are usually printed and sold either daily or weekly: *a national/local newspaper* ○ *a morning/evening paper* ○ *a newspaper article* ○ *a newspaper headline* **2** *(also* **paper)** [C] an organization that produces a newspaper: *Which paper is he from?* **3** [U] the paper on which newspapers are printed: *Wrap those glasses in some newspaper so they won't break.*

☞ **Journalists** and **reporters** collect news for newspapers. The **editor** decides what is printed.

news·stand /'nuzstænd/ *noun* [C] a type of small store which is open at the front and sells newspapers, magazines, and sometimes books

the ,New 'Testament *noun* [sing.] the second part of the Christian Bible, that tells the story of the life of Jesus Christ and later events ☞ Look at **Old Testament** and at the note at **White House**.

new 'year *noun* [sing.] the first few days of January: *Happy New Year!* ○ *We will get in touch in the new year.*

☆ **,New Year's 'Day** *noun* [U] January 1

,New Year's 'Eve *noun* [U] December 31

☆ **next¹** /nɛkst/ *adj.* **1** (usually with *the*) coming immediately after sth in order, space or time; closest: *The next bus leaves in 20 minutes.* ○ *She went into the hospital on a Sunday and the next day she died.* ○ *the next name on the list* ○ *I will be on vacation for the next two weeks.* ○ *How far is it to the next gas station?* ○ *Go past the post office and take the next left.*

☞ Compare **nearest** and **next. The next** means "the following" in a series of events or places: *When is your next appointment?* ○ *Turn left at the next intersection.* **(The) nearest** means "the closest" in time or place: *Where's the nearest grocery store?*

2 (used without *the* before days of the week,

months, seasons, years, etc.) the one immediately following the present one: *See you again next Monday.* ○ *Let's go camping next weekend.* ○ *We are going to Florida next spring.* ○ *Rachel hopes to get a job as a teacher next year.* **3 the next** *noun* [sing.] the person or thing that is next (1): *If we miss this train, we'll have to wait two hours for the next.*

IDM **next/second/third to last** ⇨ LAST¹

☆ **next²** /nɛkst/ *adv.* **1** after this or that; then: *I wonder what will happen next.* ○ *I know Joe finished first, but who came next?* ○ *First brown half a pound of ground beef. Next add one chopped onion.* **2 next to sb/sth** at the side of sb/sth; beside: *He sat down next to Pam.* ○ *There's a mailbox next to the phone booth over there.* **3 next to sb/sth** in a position after sb/sth: *Next to San Francisco, I think my favorite city is Santa Fe.*

IDM **next to nothing** almost nothing: *We took $50, but we've got next to nothing left.*

ˌ**next** ˈ**best** *adj.* not the best, but good enough if you cannot have the best

☆ ˌ**next** ˈ**door** *adj., adv.* in or into the next house or building: *our next-door neighbors* ○ *Who lives next door?* ○ *The school is next door to a nursing home.*

ˌ**next of** ˈ**kin** *noun* [plural, U] your closest living family member or members

☞ **Next of kin** is used to mean both a single relative and a group of relatives: *My husband is my next of kin.* ○ *Her next of kin have been informed of her death.*

NFL /ˌɛn ɛf ˈɛl/ *abbr.* National Football League; the organization of professional football teams in the U.S.

NHL /ˌɛn eɪtʃ ˈɛl/ *abbr.* National Hockey League; the organization of professional hockey teams in the U.S.

nib·ble /ˈnɪbl/ *verb* [I,T] to eat sth by taking small bites —**nib·ble** *noun* [C]

☆ **nice** /naɪs/ *adj.* **1** pleasant; good: *The weather was really nice yesterday.* ○ *Have a nice day!* ○ *You look very nice today.* ○ *Go and pick out some nice bananas.* **2** kind; friendly: *What a nice girl!* ○ *Try and be nice to Julie. She's not feeling well.*

IDM **nice and...** (*informal*) (used for saying that you like sth): *It's nice and warm by the fire.*

nice·ly /ˈnaɪsli/ *adv.* **1** in a pleasant way: *You can have a cookie if you ask nicely.* **2** (*informal*) very well: *Things are coming along very nicely on our project.*

niche /nɪtʃ; niːʃ/ *noun* [C] **1** a hollow place in a wall, often with a shelf **2** a job, position, etc. that is suitable for you: *to find your niche in life*

nick¹ /nɪk/ *noun* [C] a small cut in sth

IDM **in the nick of time** just barely in time: *The ambulance arrived in the nick of time.*

nick² /nɪk/ *verb* [T] to make a small cut in sb/sth

☆ **nick·el** /ˈnɪkl/ *noun* **1** [C] an American or Canadian coin that is worth five cents **2** [U] (*symbol* **Ni**) a hard silver-white metal that is often mixed with other metals

☆ **nick·name** /ˈnɪkneɪm/ *noun* [C] an informal name that is used instead of your own name, usually by your family or friends

nic·o·tine /ˈnɪkətin/ *noun* [U] the poisonous chemical substance in tobacco

☆ **niece** /nis/ *noun* [C] the daughter of your brother or sister; the daughter of your husband's or wife's brother or sister ☞ Look at **nephew**.

nig·ger /ˈnɪgər/ *noun* [C] a black person

☞ This word is extremely offensive.

☆ **night** /naɪt/ *noun* [C,U] **1** the part of the day when it is dark and when most people sleep: *a dark night* ○ *We will be away for a few nights.* ○ *Did you sleep well last night?* ○ *a sleepless night* ○ *The baby cried all night long.* ○ *It's a long way home. Why don't you stay the night?* ○ *Owls come out at night.* **2** the time between late afternoon and when you go to bed: *Let's go out on Saturday night.* ○ *He doesn't get home until 8 o'clock at night.* ○ *I tried to call Walter last night, but he was out.*

☞ Note the use of different prepositions with **night**. **At** is most common: *I'm not allowed out after 11 o'clock at night.* **By** is used about something that you usually do in the daytime: *They slept by day and traveled by night.* **In/during** the night is used for the night that has just passed, but it is also common to use **last night** to talk about that night: *I woke up twice in the night.* ○ *I woke up twice last night.* **On** is used when we are talking about one particular night: *On the night of Saturday, June 30.* **Tonight** means the night or evening that will come next: *Where are you staying tonight?*

IDM **a night on the town/out** an evening that you spend away from home enjoying yourself

in the dead of night ⇨ DEAD²

good night (said late in the evening, before you go home or before you go to sleep)

night·club /ˈnaɪtklʌb/ *noun* [C] a place where you can go to eat, drink, dance, listen to sb singing, etc. until late at night

night·gown /ˈnaɪtgaʊn/ (also *informal* **nightie** /ˈnaɪti/) *noun* [C] a loose dress that a girl or woman wears in bed ☞ picture on page A27.

night·in·gale /ˈnaɪtn̩ˌgeɪl; ˈnaɪtɪŋgeɪl/ *noun* [C] a small brown European bird that sings very beautifully

night·life /ˈnaɪtlaɪf/ *noun* [U] the entertainment that is available at night in a particular place: *It's a small town with very little nightlife.*

ə	y	w	t̬	eɪ	aɪ	ɔɪ	aʊ	oʊ
about	yes	woman	butter	say	five	boy	now	go

N

☆ **night·ly** /ˈnaɪtli/ *adj.*, *adv.* (done or happening) every night: *The band will be appearing nightly at the Cavern Club.*

☆ **night·mare** /ˈnaɪtmɛr/ *noun* [C] **1** a dream that is frightening: *I had a terrible nightmare last night.* **2** something that is very unpleasant or frightening: *Driving in rush-hour traffic can be a real nightmare.*

ˈ**night school** *noun* [C] a place where adults can go to classes in the evening

☆ **night·time** /ˈnaɪt taɪm/ *noun* [U] the time when it is dark: *Many old people are afraid to go out at nighttime.*

nil /nɪl/ *noun* [U] nothing: *Our chances of success are virtually nil.*

nim·ble /ˈnɪmbl/ *adj.* able to move quickly and lightly: *For a large person she's very nimble on her feet.* —**nim·bly** /-bli/ *adv.*

☆ **nine** /naɪn/ *number* 9; one more than eight ☞ For examples of how to use numbers in sentences, look at **six**. Look also at Appendix 2.

IDM **nine to five** the hours that you work in most offices: *a nine-to-five job*

☆ **nine·teen** /ˌnaɪnˈtin/ *number* 19; one more than eighteen ☞ For examples of how to use numbers in sentences, look at **six**. Look also at Appendix 2. —**nine·teenth** /ˌnaɪnˈtinθ/ *pron.*, *det.*, *adv.* ☞ Look at the examples at **sixth**.

☆ **nine·ty** /ˈnaɪnti/ *number* 90; one more than 89 ☞ For examples of how to use numbers in sentences, look at **sixty**. Look also at Appendix 2. —**nine·ti·eth** /ˈnaɪntiəθ/ *pron.*, *det.*, *adv.* ☞ Look at the examples at **sixth**.

ninth¹ /naɪnθ/ *pron.*, *det.*, *adv.* 9th; next after eighth ☞ Look at the examples at **sixth**. For more information on numbers, look at Appendix 2.

ninth² /naɪnθ/ *noun* [C] the fraction 1/9; one of nine equal parts of sth ☞ Look at the examples at **sixth**. For more information on numbers, look at Appendix 2.

nip /nɪp/ *verb* (**nip·ping**; **nipped**) [I,T] to bite or pinch sb/sth lightly: *The dog nipped him on the ankle.*

IDM **nip sth in the bud** to stop or destroy sth at an early stage in its development: *Federal agents managed to nip the consipiracy in the bud.*

PHRV **nip sth off (sth)** to remove a part of sth, usually with your fingers: *to nip off some dead leaves*

nip·ple /ˈnɪpl/ *noun* [C] **1** the dark hard part in the center of a woman's breast from which a baby drinks milk **2** one of the similar parts on a man's chest **3** a rubber part with a small hole in it through which a baby can drink milk, etc. from a bottle

ni·tro·gen /ˈnaɪtrədʒən/ *noun* [U] (*symbol* **N**) a gas that has no color, taste or smell. Nitrogen forms about 80% of the air around the earth.

nitty-gritty /ˌnɪtiˈɡrɪti/ *noun* [U] **the nitty-gritty** (*informal*) the most important facts, not the small or unimportant details

☆ **no¹** /noʊ/ *det.* **1** not any; not a: *I have no time to talk now.* ○ *No visitors may enter without a ticket.* ○ *He's no friend of mine.* ○ *There are no jobs for high school drop-outs in this town.* **2** (used for saying that sth is not allowed): *No smoking.* ○ *No children under 16.* ○ *No parking.*

☆ **no²** /noʊ/ *interj.* **1** (used for giving a negative reply or statement): *"Are you ready?" "No, I'm not."* ○ *"Would you like something to eat?" "No, thank you. I'm not hungry."* ○ *"Can I borrow the car?" "No, you can't."* ○ *It's about 70 – no, I'm wrong – 80 miles from Topeka.* ○ *No! Don't touch it. It's very hot.*

☞ You can also use **no** when you want to agree with a negative statement: *"This program's not very good." "No, you're right. It isn't."*

2 (used for expressing surprise or shock): *"Mike's been in an accident." "Oh, no!"*

no³ /noʊ/ *adv.* not any: *There will be no more talking during the test.* ○ *Applications must be returned no later than July 31.*

No. *abbr.* north

no·bil·i·ty /noʊˈbɪləti/ *noun* **1** [U] the quality of being noble **2 the nobility** [sing.] the group of people who belong to the highest social class, with titles: *Members of the nobility and other wealthy people were invited to the duke's wedding.*

no·ble /ˈnoʊbl/ *adj.* **1** belonging to the highest social class, with a title: *a noble family* **2** honest; brave; that other people should admire: *They made a noble effort in the face of many difficulties.*

no·bly /ˈnoʊbli/ *adv.* in a way that is honest, brave, or that other people should admire: *He nobly sacrificed his own happiness for that of his family.*

☆ **no·bod·y¹** /ˈnoʊbʌdi; -badi/ (*also* **no one** /ˈnoʊ wʌn/) *pron.* no person; not anybody: *He screamed, but nobody came to help him.* ○ *No one else was around.* ○ *There was nobody home.*

☞ **None of**, not **nobody**, must be used before words like *the, his, her, those*, etc. or before a pronoun: *Nobody remembered my birthday.* ○ *None of my friends remembered my birthday.* ○ *I asked all my classmates, but nobody is free.* ○ *None of them are free.*

no·bod·y² /ˈnoʊbʌdi; -badi/ *noun* [C] (*pl.* **no·bod·ies**) a person who is not very important: *Do you want to be a nobody all your life?*

no-brain·er /ˌnoʊˈbreɪmər/ *noun* [C, usually sing.] (*slang*) a project, problem, question, etc. that is very easy to finish or solve: *The issue of whether to build a new stadium is a real no-brainer for most fans.*

noc·tur·nal /nɑkˈtərnl/ *adj.* **1** happening in

ər	ɪr	ɛr	ɑr	ɔr	ʊr	ʒ	h	ŋ
bird	near	hair	car	north	tour	vision	hat	sing

the night: *a nocturnal adventure* **2** (used about animals and birds) awake and active at night: *Owls are nocturnal birds.*

☆ **nod** /nɑd/ *verb* (**nod·ding; nod·ded**) [I,T] to move your head down and then up again quickly as a way of saying "yes" or as a greeting or a sign: *"Would you like to come too?" he asked. She nodded and got up.* ○ *Everybody at the meeting nodded in agreement.* ○ *Nod your head if you understand what I'm saying.* ○ *We nodded to each other across the room.* —**nod** *noun* [C]: *She gave him a quick nod.*

☆ **noise** /nɔɪz/ *noun* [C,U] something that you hear; a sound, especially one that is loud, unpleasant or unwanted: *Did you hear a noise downstairs?* ○ *Why is the engine making so much noise?*

noise·less /ˈnɔɪzləs/ *adj.* making no sound —**noise·less·ly** *adv.*

☆ **nois·y** /ˈnɔɪzi/ *adj.* (**nois·i·er; nois·i·est**) making a lot of or too much noise; full of noise: *Are small boys noisier than girls?* ○ *We live on a very noisy street.* ☞ Look at the note at **loud**. —**nois·i·ly** /ˈnɔɪzəli/ *adv.*

no·mad /ˈnoʊmæd/ *noun* [C] a member of a tribe that travels around to find grass for its animals instead of living in one place —**no·mad·ic** /noʊˈmædɪk/ *adj.*

'no man's land *noun* [U] land between two armies in a war, between two borders, etc.

nom·i·nal /ˈnɑmənl/ *adj.* **1** being sth in name only but not in reality: *the nominal leader of the country* (= sb else is really in control) **2** (used about a price, sum of money, etc.) very small; less than is normal: *Because we were friends, he only charged us a nominal fee.*

☆ **nom·i·nate** /ˈnɑməneɪt/ *verb* [T] **1 nominate sb/sth (for/as sth)** to suggest that sb/sth should be considered for an official position, prize, etc.: *I would like to nominate Don Jones as chairman.* ○ *The movie was nominated for an Oscar for best soundtrack.* **2 nominate sb (to/as sth) (to do sth)** to choose sb/sth for a position: *You may nominate a representative to speak for you.*

☆ **nom·i·na·tion** /ˌnɑməˈneɪʃn/ *noun* [C,U] a formal suggestion that sb/sth should be considered for an official position, prize, etc.; the appointment of sb/sth to such a position: *The closing date for nominations is September 8th.* ○ *The movie received 10 Oscar nominations.* ○ *His nomination as the party's candidate was announced at the convention.*

nom·i·nee /ˌnɑməˈni/ *noun* [C] a person who is suggested or chosen for a position

non·cha·lant /ˌnɑnʃəˈlɑnt/ *adj.* not feeling or showing interest or excitement; seeming calm —**non·cha·lance** /-ˈlɑns/ *noun* [U] —**non·cha·lant·ly** *adv.*

non·com·mit·tal /ˌnɑnkəˈmɪtl/ *adj.* not saying or showing exactly what you think, or what you are going to do

non·con·form·ist /ˌnɑnkənˈfɔrmɪst/ *noun* [C] a person who behaves or thinks differently from most other people in society —**non·con·form·ist** *adj.*

non·count noun /ˌnɑnkaʊnt ˈnaʊn/ *noun* [C] (*grammar*) = UNCOUNTABLE NOUN

non·de·script /ˈnɑndəskrɪpt/ *adj.* not very interesting; dull

☆ **none¹** /nʌn/ *pron.* not any, not one (of a group of three or more): *"Could you pour me some more juice?" "Sorry, there's none left."* ○ *They gave me a lot of information, but none of it was very helpful.* ○ *I went to several stores, but none had what I was looking for.* ○ *I have four brothers, but none of them live/lives nearby.*

☞ When we use **none of** with a plural noun, the verb can be singular, which is formal, or plural, which is informal: *None of the buses is/are going downtown.* When we are talking about two people or things we use **neither** not **none**: *Neither of my brothers lives nearby.* Note the difference between **none** and **no**: *I told him that I had no money left.* ○ *When he asked me how much money I had left, I told him that I had none.*

☆ **none²** /nʌn/ *adv.* (with *the* and a comparative adjective) not at all: *We talked for a long time, but I'm still none the wiser* (= I don't know any more than before).

☆ **none·the·less** /ˌnʌnðəˈlɛs/ *adv.* anyway; in spite of what has just been said: *It won't be easy, but they're going to try nonetheless.* ☞ **Nevertheless** has the same meaning.

non·ex·ist·ent /ˌnɑnɪɡˈzɪstənt/ *adj.* not existing or not available: *In some areas public transportation is completely nonexistent.*

non·fic·tion /ˌnɑnˈfɪkʃn/ *noun* [U] writing that is about real people, events and facts

non·plussed /ˌnɑnˈplʌst/ *adj.* very surprised or confused

☆ **non·prof·it** /ˌnɑnˈprɑfət/ *adj.* (used about a company, organization, etc.) that does not aim to make a profit. *Nonprofit organizations usually offer services to help people*

☆ **non·sense** /ˈnɑnsɛns; -səns/ *noun* [U] **1** something that sb says or writes that is not true or is just silly: *What you're saying is nonsense.* ○ *Any rumors about my resignation are a lot of nonsense.* ○ *"I'm no good at sports," said Tim. "Nonsense!" said his mother, "You're very good."* **2** foolish or bad behavior: *Mr. Davidson doesn't allow any nonsense in his classroom.*

non·sen·si·cal /nɑnˈsɛnsɪkl/ *adj.* not intelligent or sensible; stupid: *That was a completely nonsensical thing to say.*

☆ **non·smok·er** /ˌnɑnˈsmoʊkər/ *noun* [C] a person who does not smoke —**non·smok·ing** /ˌnɑnˈsmoʊkɪŋ/ *adj.*: *Would you like a table in the smoking or the nonsmoking section?*

non·stick /ˌnɑnˈstɪk/ *adj.* (used about a pan,

tʃ	dʒ	v	θ	ð	s	z	ʃ
chin	June	van	thin	then	so	zoo	she

N

etc.) covered with a substance that prevents food from sticking to it

non·stop /ˌnɑnˈstɑp/ *adj., adv.* without a stop or a break: *a nonstop flight to London* ○ *He talked nonstop for two hours about his trip.*

non·vi·o·lence /ˌnɑnˈvaɪələns/ *noun* [U] the refusal to use violence against the government, police, etc. in order to bring about political or social change —**non·vi·o·lent** /-lənt/ *adj.*

☆ **noo·dle** /nudl/ *noun* [C, usually pl.] food (*pasta*) made of flour, water and usually egg that is cut into long thin pieces and cooked in boiling water or used in soups

nook /nʊk/ *noun* [C] a small quiet place or corner (in a house, garden, etc.)

IDM **every nook and cranny** every part of a place

☆ **noon** /nun/ *noun* [U] 12 o'clock in the middle of the day: *At noon the sun is at its highest point in the sky.* ○ *They arrived around noon and stayed all afternoon.* ☞ Look at **midnight.**

☆ **'no one** *pron.* = NOBODY

noose /nus/ *noun* [C] a circle that is tied in the end of a rope and that can be made tighter or looser. A noose is used for killing people by hanging.

nope /noʊp/ *interj.* (*informal*) no: *"Hey, Mike! Are you coming with us?" "Nope."*

☆ **nor** /nɔr/ *conj., adv.* **1** (used after *neither* or *not*) and not: *I received neither a telephone call nor a letter during the whole six months.* ○ (*formal*) *Not a building nor a tree was left standing.* **2** (used after a negative statement to add some further information) also not: *The sun hardly shone at all during the first week. Nor during the second, for that matter.*

norm /nɔrm/ *noun* [C] (often with *the*) a pattern of behavior that is normal or expected: *Is it the norm in your country for young people to leave home before they get married?*

☆ **nor·mal¹** /ˈnɔrml/ *adj.* **1** usual, ordinary or what you expect: *I'll pick you up at the normal time.* ○ *I just want to lead a normal life again.* ○ *We're just a normal middle-class family.* ○ *It's quite normal to feel angry in a situation like this.* ○ *Under normal circumstances, the meeting would only have lasted an hour.* **2** (used about a person or animal) formed or developed in the usual way: *The child was completely normal at birth.* ☞ Look at **abnormal.**

☆ **nor·mal²** /ˈnɔrml/ *noun* [U] the usual or average state, level, standard, etc.: *Your temperature is slightly above normal.* ○ *I hope the situation will soon return to normal.* ○ *Things are back to normal at work now.*

nor·mal·cy /ˈnɔrmlsi/ (*also* **normality** /nɔrˈmæləti/) *noun* [U] the state of being normal

nor·mal·ize /ˈnɔrmlˌaɪz/ *verb* [I,T] (*formal*) to become or make sth normal, good or friendly again

☆ **nor·mal·ly** /ˈnɔrməli/ *adv.* **1** usually: *I normally leave the house at 8 o'clock.* ○ *We don't normally have people over for dinner.* ○ *Normally, he takes the bus.* **2** in a usual or an ordinary way: *The man wasn't behaving normally.*

☆ **north¹** /nɔrθ/ *noun* [sing.] (*abbr.* **N.**; **No.**) **1** (*also* **the north**) one of the four main points of the compass; the direction that is on your left when you face the sunrise: *cold winds from the north* ○ *Which way is north?* **2 the north** the part of any country, city, etc. that lies farther toward the north than other parts: *Rebels have taken control of several towns in the north.*

☆ **north²** /nɔrθ/ *adj.* in or toward the north, or from the north¹: *The new offices will be in North Minneapolis.* ○ *The north wing of the school was destroyed by a tornado.* ○ *a cold north wind*

☆ **north³** /nɔrθ/ *adv.* to or toward the north¹: *We got onto the freeway going north instead of south.* ○ *The house faces north.* ○ *Is Phoenix north of Tucson?*

IDM **up north** in or to the north: *We're going up north on vacation.*

north·bound /ˈnɔrθbaʊnd/ *adj.* traveling or leading toward the north: *the northbound lanes of the freeway*

☆ **north·east¹** /ˌnɔrθˈist/ *noun* [sing.] (*abbr.* **NE**) **1** (*also* **the northeast**) the direction or point of the compass that is between north and east **2 the northeast; the Northeast** a region that is toward the northeast: *the Northeast of France*

☆ **north·east²** /ˌnɔrθˈist/ *adj., adv.* in, from or to the northeast of a place or country: *the northeast coast of Florida* ○ *If you look northeast, you can see the ocean.*

north·east·er·ly /ˌnɔrθˈistərli/ *adj.* **1** toward the northeast: *in a northeasterly direction* **2** (used about a wind) coming from the northeast

north·east·ern /ˌnɔrθˈistərn/ *adj.* in or from the northeast of a place or country: *northeastern Africa*

north·east·ward /ˌnɔrθˈistwərd/ *adv.* toward the northeast: *Follow Interstate 94 northeastward.*

i	ɪ	ɛ	æ	ɑ	ɔ	ʌ	ʊ	u
see	sit	ten	cat	hot	saw	cup	put	too

north·er·ly /ˈnɔrðərli/ *adj.* **1** to, toward or in the north: *Keep going in a northerly direction.* **2** (used about a wind) coming from the north

☆ **north·ern** /ˈnɔrðərn/ *adj.* of, in or from the north of a place: *in northern Australia* ○ *the northern hemisphere*

north·ern·er (*also* **Northerner**) /ˈnɔrðərnər/ *noun* [C] a person who was born in or who lives in the northern part of a country

north·ern·most /ˈnɔrðərnmoʊst/ *adj.* farthest north

the ˌNorth ˈPole *noun* [sing.] the point on the Earth's surface which is farthest north ☞ picture at **earth**.

north·ward /ˈnɔrθwərd/ *adj., adv.* toward the north: *in a northward direction* ○ *Continue northward out of the city for about five miles.*

☆ **north·west¹** /ˌnɔrθˈwɛst/ *noun* [sing.] (*abbr.* **NW**) **1** (*also* **the northwest**) the direction or point of the compass that is between north and west **2** **the northwest**; **the Northwest** a region that is toward the northwest: *the Northwest of France*

☆ **north·west²** /ˌnɔrθˈwɛst/ *adj., adv.* in, from or to the northwest of a place or country: *the northwest coast of Canada* ○ *If you look northwest you can see the ocean.*

north·west·er·ly /ˌnɔrθˈwɛstərli/ *adj.* **1** toward the northwest: *in a northwesterly direction* **2** (used about a wind) coming from the northwest

north·west·ern /ˌnɔrθˈwɛstərn/ *adj.* in or from the northwest of a place or country: *northwestern Australia*

north·west·ward /ˌnɔrθˈwɛstwərd/ *adv.* toward the northwest: *Follow Interstate 94 northwestward.*

☆ **nose¹** /noʊz/ *noun* [C] **1** the part of the face, above the mouth, that is used for breathing and smelling: *a broken nose* ○ *The baseball hit him on the nose.* ○ *This medicine should help your runny nose.* ○ *Breathe in through your nose and out through your mouth.* ☞ The adjective is **nasal**. **2** the front part of sth, especially an airplane: *The nose of the plane was badly damaged.*

IDM **blow your nose** ➪ BLOW¹

look down your nose at sb/sth to think that you are better than sb; to think that sth is of poor quality

poke/stick your nose into sth to interfere in sth when you should not: *He's always poking his nose into other people's business!*

turn your nose up at sth to refuse sth because you do not think it is good or do not like it

nose² /noʊz/ *verb* [I] to go forward slowly and carefully: *The bus nosed out into the line of traffic.*

PHRV **nose around** (*informal*) to look around a private place trying to find sth interesting

nose·bleed /ˈnoʊzblid/ *noun* [C] a time when

a lot of blood comes from your nose: *to have a nosebleed*

-nosed /noʊzd/ (in compounds) having a nose of the type mentioned: *red-nosed* ○ *runny-nosed*

¹nose job *noun* [C] (*informal*) an operation to improve the appearance of sb's nose: *Do you think she's had a nose job?*

nos·tal·gi·a /nəˈstældʒə; nɑ-/ *noun* [U] a feeling of affection, mixed with sadness, for things that are in the past —**nos·tal·gic** /-dʒɪk/ *adj.* —**nos·tal·gi·cal·ly** /-kli/ *adv.*

nos·tril /ˈnɑstrəl/ *noun* [C] one of the two openings at the end of the nose ☞ picture on page A24.

nos·y (*also* **nosey**) /ˈnoʊzi/ *adj.* (**nos·i·er; nos·i·est**) too interested in other people's affairs

☆ **not** /nɑt/ *adv.* **1** (used to form the negative with verbs like *be, can, do, have, must, will,* etc. and often shortened to *n't* in speech and informal writing): *It's not/it isn't raining now.* ○ *He's not coming/He isn't coming.* ○ *I cannot/ can't see from here.* ○ *You shouldn't have said that.* ○ *He didn't invite me.* ○ *Don't you like spaghetti?* ○ *I hope she will not/won't be late.* ○ *You're German, aren't you?* **2** (used to give the following word or phrase a negative meaning or to reply in the negative): *He told me not to call after 10:00.* ○ *I remember her but not her sister.* ○ *Not everybody was able to come.* ○ *"Whose turn is it to do the dishes?" "Not mine."* ○ *"Do you see each other a lot?" "No, not often."* **3** (used after *be afraid, believe, expect, guess, hope, suppose,* etc., to give a negative reply): *"Do you think they'll get married?" "I hope not."* (= I hope that they will not.) ○ *"You can't drive all that way alone." "I suppose not."* ○ *"Did you see her?" "I'm afraid not."* **4** (used with *or* to give a negative possibility): *Should we tell her or not?* ○ *I don't know if he's telling the truth or not.* **5** (used for saying that sth is not possible or that you do not want to do sth): *"Can I borrow $20?" "Absolutely not!"* ○ *"Are you coming to the movie with us?" "I'd rather not, if you don't mind."* **6** (used for showing that you mean the opposite of the word or phrase that follows): *It's not easy* (= it's difficult).

IDM **not at all 1** (a way of saying "no" or "not"): *"Do you mind if I come too?" "Not at all."* ○ *The instructions are not at all clear.* **2** (*formal*) (a way of replying when sb has thanked you): *"Thanks for the present." "Not at all – it was my pleasure."*

not only... (but) also (used for emphasizing the fact that there is something more): *They not only have two houses in the U.S., they also have one in France.*

no·ta·ble /ˈnoʊtəbl/ *adj.* deserving to be noticed; interesting or important: *The area is notable for its scenery and wildlife.*

no·ta·bly /ˈnoʊtəbli/ *adv.* (used for giving an especially important example of what you are

N

talking about): *Many countries, notably Denmark, have refused to sign the agreement.*

notch¹ /nɑtʃ/ *noun* [C] **1** a cut in an edge or surface in the shape of a V **2** a level on a scale of quality: *This meal is certainly a notch above the last one we had here.*

notch² /nɑtʃ/ *verb*
PHR V **notch sth up** to achieve sth or to record sth you have achieved: *It's time to notch up another victory for the Springfield baseball team!*

☆ **note¹** /noʊt/ *noun* **1** [C] a short letter: *This is just a note to thank you for letting us stay at your house.* **2** [C] some words that you write down quickly to help you remember sth: *I'd better make a note of your name and address.* ○ *Keep a note of who has paid and who hasn't.* ○ *The professor advised the students to take* (= write down) *notes while he was speaking.* **3** [C] a short explanation or extra piece of information that is given at the back of a book, etc. or at the bottom or side of a page: *See note 5, page 340.* ☞ Look at **footnote. 4** [C] a single musical sound made by a voice or an instrument: *I can only remember the first few notes of the song.* ○ *high/low notes* **5** [C] a written sign that represents a musical sound **6** [sing.] (something that suggests) a certain quality or feeling: *There was a note of embarrassment in her voice.* ○ *The meeting ended on a fairly negative note.*

☆ **note²** /noʊt/ *verb* [T] **1** to notice or be aware of sth: *He noted a slight change in her attitude toward him.* **2** to mention sth: *I'd like to note that the project has been extremely successful so far.*
PHR V **note sth down** to write sth down so that you remember it: *The police officer noted down the girl's description of the man.*

☆ **note·book** /'noʊtbʊk/ *noun* [C] a book with plain paper in which you write things

notebook com·pu·ter *noun* [C] a small computer that you can carry with you

not·ed /'noʊtəd/ *adj.* **noted (for/as sth)** (*formal*) well-known; famous: *The hotel is noted for its gourmet cuisine.*

note·wor·thy /'noʊtwərði/ *adj.* deserving to be noticed; interesting or important: *a noteworthy development*

'nother /'nʌðər/ *adj.* = ANOTHER: *Now that's a whole 'nother question.*

☞ **'Nother** is an incorrect form which some people use instead of **another.**

☆ **noth·ing** /'nʌθɪŋ/ *pron.* not anything; no thing: *There's nothing in this suitcase.* ○ *Nothing exciting ever happens to me.* ○ *There was nothing else to say.* ○ *"What's the matter?" "Oh, nothing."* ○ *"Thank you so much for all your help." "It was nothing."* (= nothing of any importance) ☞ Look at the note at **zero.**

IDM **have nothing to do with sb/sth** to have no connection with sb/sth: *That question has nothing to do with what we're discussing.*

for nothing 1 for no good reason or with no good result: *His hard work was all for nothing.* **2** for no payment; free: *Children under four are allowed in for nothing.*

nothing but only: *He was wearing nothing but a pair of swimming trunks.*

(there's) nothing to it (it's) very easy: *You just need to practice – there's nothing to it really.*

☆ **no·tice¹** /'noʊtəs/ *noun* **1** [C] a written statement giving information or news that is put where everybody can read it: *There's a notice on the board saying that the meeting has been canceled.* **2** [U] a warning that sth is going to happen: *I can't produce a meal at such short notice!* ○ *I wish you had given me more notice that you were going on vacation.* ○ *The swimming pool is closed until further notice* (= until we are told that it will open again). ○ *We've been given a month's notice to move out* (= we have been told we must leave in a month).
IDM **on notice** having been told or warned that sth is going to happen: *The police have put the public on notice that drugs will not be tolerated.*

take notice (of sth) to act in a way that shows that you know sth is important: *The protests are finally making the government take notice.*

not take any notice (of sb/sth) to pay no attention (to sb/sth): *Some people don't take any notice of speed limits.*

☞ If you **don't notice** something, e.g. a speed limit, it means that you don't see it at all. However if you **don't take any notice** of it, it means that you see it but you choose to ignore it.

☆ **no·tice²** /'noʊtəs/ *verb* [I,T] to see and be aware of sth: *"What kind of car was the man driving?" "I didn't notice."* ○ *Did you notice her eyes?* ○ *I noticed (that) he was carrying a black briefcase.* ○ *Did you notice which direction she went in?* ○ *We didn't notice him leave/leaving.*

no·tice·a·ble /'noʊtəsəbl/ *adj.* easy to see or notice: *The scar from the accident was hardly noticeable.* ○ *a noticeable difference* —**no·tice·a·bly** /-bli/ *adv.*: *The crowds at this year's event were noticeably smaller than at last year's.*

☆ **no·ti·fy** /'noʊtəfaɪ/ *verb* [T] (*pres. part.* **no·ti·fy·ing**; *3rd pers. sing. pres.* **no·ti·fies**; *p.t., p.p.* **no·ti·fied**) **notify sb (of sth)** to inform sb (about sth) officially: *The police should be notified of the theft.* ○ *You must notify your landlady that you intend to move out.* —**no·ti·fi·ca·tion** /ˌnoʊtəfəˈkeɪʃn/ *noun* [C,U]

no·tion /'noʊʃn/ *noun* [C] something that you have in your mind; an idea: *I had a vague*

notion that I had seen her before. ○ *You seem to have no notion of how difficult it is going to be.*

no·to·ri·e·ty /ˌnoʊtəˈraɪəti/ *noun* [U] the state of being famous for sth bad

no·to·ri·ous /noʊˈtɔriəs/ *adj.* **notorious (for/ as sth)** well-known for sth bad: *a notorious drug dealer* ○ *This road is notorious for the number of accidents on it.* —**no·to·ri·ous·ly** *adv.*: *English cuisine is notoriously bad.*

not·with·stand·ing¹ /ˌnɑtwɪθˈstændɪŋ/ *prep.* (*formal*) without being affected by; in spite of: *The plane landed on time, notwithstanding the terrible weather conditions.*

not·with·standing² /ˌnɑtwɪθˈstændɪŋ/ *adv.* (*formal*) anyway; in spite of this: *He was advised against the deal, but went ahead notwithstanding.*

☆ **noun** /naʊn/ *noun* [C] (*grammar*) a word that is the name of a person, place, thing or idea: *"Jane," "London," "table" and "happiness"* are all nouns. ☛ Look at **proper noun**, **countable** and **uncountable**.

nour·ish /ˈnərɪʃ/ *verb* [T] **1** to give a person or animal the right kind of food so that they can grow and be healthy **2** (*formal*) to allow a feeling or belief to grow stronger

nour·ish·ment /ˈnərɪʃmənt/ *noun* [U] food that you need to stay healthy

Nov. *abbr.* = NOVEMBER

☆ **nov·el¹** /ˈnɑvl/ *noun* [C] a book that tells a story about people and events that are not real: *the novels of Charles Dickens* ○ *a romantic novel*

nov·el² /ˈnɑvl/ *adj.* new and different: *That's a novel idea! Let's try it.*

nov·el·ist /ˈnɑvəlɪst/ *noun* [C] a person who writes novels

nov·el·ty /ˈnɑvlti/ *noun* (*pl.* **nov·el·ties**) **1** [U] the quality of being new and different: *The novelty of her new job soon wore off.* **2** [C] something new and unusual: *It was quite a novelty not to have to get up at 7 o'clock.* **3** [C] a small, cheap object that is sold as a toy or souvenir

☆ **No·vem·ber** /noʊˈvɛmbər/ *noun* [C,U] (*abbr.* **Nov.**) the eleventh month of the year, coming before December ☛ For examples of the use of the months in sentences, look at **January**.

nov·ice /ˈnɑvəs/ *noun* [C] a person who is new and without experience in a certain job, situation, etc.; a beginner

☆ **now¹** /naʊ/ *adv.* **1** (at) the present time: *Where are you living now?* ○ *It's too late now to do anything about it.* ○ *From now on, the nights will be getting longer.* ○ *I've been living with my parents until now.* ○ *Up to now, we haven't been able to afford a house of our own.* ○ *He should be on his way home by now.* **2** because of what has happened: *I lost my pen. Now I'll have to buy a new one.* **3** (used to introduce a new subject or to emphasize a request, command, etc., or while pausing to think): *Now, this is*

how it all began. ○ *Now listen to what he's saying.* ○ *Now, let me think.* ☛ **Now then** is also used: *Now then, are there any questions?* ○ *Now then, what was I saying?*

IDM **now and again/then**; **(every) now and then** occasionally: *We see each other now and then, but not very often.*

just now ⇨ JUST¹

right now ⇨ RIGHT²

☆ **now²** /naʊ/ *conj.* **now (that)** ... because of the fact that: *Now (that) the kids have left home, we can move to a smaller house.*

☆ **now·a·days** /ˈnaʊədeɪz/ *adv.* at the present time (when compared with the past): *Kids don't get much exercise nowadays* (= but they did in the past).

☆ **no·where** /ˈnoʊwɛr/ *adv.* not anywhere; (in or to) no place: *There's nowhere to stay in this town.* ○ *There's nowhere interesting to go around here.* ○ *It's so hot I'm getting nowhere with this work* (= making no progress). ○ *"Don't leave the car there!" "There's nowhere else to park it."*

IDM **in the middle of nowhere** ⇨ MIDDLE¹

nowhere near ⇨ NEAR²

nox·ious /ˈnɑkʃəs/ *adj.* (*formal*) harmful or poisonous: *noxious gases*

noz·zle /ˈnɑzl/ *noun* [C] a narrow tube that is put on the end of a pipe, etc. to control the liquid or gas coming out

nu·ance /ˈnuɑns/ *noun* [C] a very small difference in meaning, feeling, sound, etc.

☆ **nu·cle·ar** /ˈnukliər/ *adj.* **1** connected with the nucleus of an atom: *nuclear physics* **2** connected with the energy that is produced when the nucleus of an atom is split: *nuclear energy* ○ *a nuclear power plant* ○ *nuclear weapons* ○ *nuclear disarmament* (= stopping the use and development of nuclear weapons) ☛ The opposite is **non-nuclear**. Look also at **atomic**.

nuclear re·ac·tor (*also* **reactor**) *noun* [C] a very large machine that produces nuclear energy

nu·cle·us /ˈnukliəs/ *noun* [C] (*pl.* **nu·cle·i** /ˈnukliaɪ/) **1** the central part of an atom **2** the central or most important part of sth

nude¹ /nud/ *adj.* not wearing any clothes ☛ Look at **bare** and **naked**.

nude² /nud/ *noun* [C] a picture or photograph of a person who is not wearing clothes

IDM **in the nude** not wearing any clothes

nudge /nʌdʒ/ *verb* [T] to touch or push sb/sth with your elbow —**nudge** *noun* [C]: *to give sb a nudge*

nu·dist /ˈnudɪst/ *noun* [C] a person who likes to be nude, often in groups with other people: *a nudist beach*

nu·di·ty /ˈnudəti/ *noun* [U] the state of being nude

nug·get /ˈnʌgət/ *noun* [C] a lump of a valuable metal that is found in the earth: *a gold nugget*

tʃ	dʒ	v	θ	ð	s	z	ʃ
chin	June	van	thin	then	so	zoo	she

N

☆ **nui·sance** /ˈnusns/ *noun* [C] a person, thing or situation that annoys you or causes you trouble: *The neighbors' dog has been causing a real nuisance.*

nuke¹ /nuk/ *noun* [C] (*slang*) a weapon that uses nuclear energy

nuke² /nuk/ *verb* [T] (*slang*) **1** to attack a place using nuclear weapons **2** to cook sth in a microwave oven

numb¹ /nʌm/ *adj.* not able to feel anything; not able to move: *My fingers were numb with cold.* ○ *I'll give you an anesthetic and the tooth will go completely numb.* ○ *He was numb with fear.* —**numb·ness** *noun* [U]: *The numbness should wear off after a few hours.*

numb² /nʌm/ *verb* [T] to make sb/sth numb: *The whole family was numbed and shocked by the news.*

☆ **num·ber¹** /ˈnʌmbər/ *noun* **1** [C] a word or symbol that indicates a quantity: *Pick a number between ten and twenty.* ○ *2 is an even number and 3 is an odd number.* ○ *a three-digit number* (= more than 99 and less than 1,000) ○ *high/low numbers* ○ *cardinal/ordinal numbers* **2** [C] a group of numbers that is used to identify sb/sth: *What's your car's license plate number?* ○ *a telephone number* ○ *"Hello, could I talk to Julie?" "Sorry, you've got the wrong number."* **3** [C,U] a quantity or amount: *a large number of visitors* ○ *Part-time students have doubled in number in recent years.* ○ *a number of* (= several) *questions* ○ *We're trying to reduce the number of accidents in the home.*

☞ When **number** has an adjective before it, it is always followed by a plural verb: *A small number of students study Latin.*

4 [C] (*abbr.* **No.; no.**) (*symbol* #) (used before a number to show the position of sth in a series): *I live in apartment number 5C.* ○ *room no. 347* ○ *Example #3* **5** [C] (*informal*) a song or dance: *Our next number will be a classic love song.*

IDM **any number of** very many: *We've given the workers any number of offers, but they still voted to strike.*

☆ **num·ber²** /ˈnʌmbər/ *verb* **1** [T] to give a number to sth: *We keep our photos in numbered boxes.* **2** [I] (used for expressing how many people or things there are): *Our forces number 40,000.*

nu·mer·al /ˈnumərəl/ *noun* [C] a sign or symbol that represents a quantity: *Roman numerals*

nu·mer·i·cal /nuˈmɛrɪkl/ *adj.* of or shown by numbers : *to put sth in numerical order*

☆ **nu·mer·ous** /ˈnumərəs/ *adj.* (*formal*) very many; existing in large quantities

nun /nʌn/ *noun* [C] a woman who has gone to live in a religious community (**convent**) and who is not allowed to get married or own property ☞ Look at **monk**.

☆ **nurse¹** /nərs/ *noun* [C] a person whose job is to take care of sick or injured people: *a trained nurse* ○ *a male nurse* ○ *Nurse Mills*

nurse² /nərs/ *verb* **1** [T] to take care of sb who is sick or injured: *She nursed her mother until she died in 1969.* ○ *The boys found a sick puppy and nursed it back to health.* **2** [I,T] to feed a baby with milk from the breast: *nursing mothers* ☞ Look at **breastfeed**. **3** [I] (used about a baby) to suck milk from a woman's breast

☆ **nurs·e·ry** /ˈnərsəri/ *noun* [C] (*pl.* **nurs·e·ries**) **1** a baby's bedroom in a house **2** a room in a hospital for babies **3** a place where parents can leave their children for a short time while the parents do sth else **4** a place where young trees and plants are grown and sold ☞ Look at **greenhouse**.

ˈ**nursery rhyme** *noun* [C] a traditional poem or song for children

ˈ**nursery school** *noun* [C] = PRESCHOOL

nurs·ing /ˈnərsɪŋ/ *noun* [U] the job of being a nurse: *She has decided to go into nursing.*

ˈ**nursing home** *noun* [C] a small private hospital, usually for old people

almond • nuts • shell • Brazil nut • hazelnut • walnut • pecan • peanut • cashew

☆ **nut** /nʌt/ *noun* [C] **1** a dry fruit that consists of a hard shell with a seed (**kernel**) inside. Many types of nut may be eaten: *chopped hazelnuts and almonds* **2** a six-sided piece of metal with a round hole in the middle through which you screw a long round piece of metal (**bolt**). Nuts and bolts are used for fastening things together: *Tighten the nut with a wrench.* **3** (*informal*) a crazy or foolish person ☞ Look at **nuts** and **nutty**.

nut·crack·er /ˈnʌtkrækər/ *noun* [C] a tool that you use to break open the shell of a nut

nut·meg /ˈnʌtmɛg/ *noun* [C,U] a type of spice, used for giving flavor to food

☆ **nu·tri·tion** /nuˈtrɪʃn/ *noun* [U] the food that you eat and the way that it affects your health: *Good nutrition is essential for children's growth.*

nu·tri·tious /nuˈtrɪʃəs/ *adj.* (used about a food) very good for you

nuts /nʌts/ *adj.* (not before a noun) (*informal*)

1 crazy or foolish: *You're completely nuts!* **2** very interested in and excited about sth: *She's nuts about ice skating.*

nut·shell /ˈnʌtʃɛl/ *noun*

IDM **in a nutshell** using few words: *That, in a nutshell, is the answer to your question.*

nut·ty /ˈnʌti/ *adj.* (**nut·ti·er; nut·ti·est**) **1** containing or tasting like nuts **2** (*informal*) crazy

or foolish: *a nutty idea*

nuz·zle /ˈnʌzl/ *verb* [T] to press or rub sb/sth gently with the nose

NW *abbr.* northwest; northwestern

☆ **ny·lon** /ˈnaɪlɑn/ *noun* **1** [U] a very strong artificial material that is used for making clothes, rope, brushes, etc.: *a nylon raincoat* **2 nylons** [plural] = PANTYHOSE

Oo

O, o /oʊ/ *noun* [C] (*pl.* **O's; o's**) **1** the fifteenth letter of the English alphabet: *"Orange" begins with (an) "O."* **2** (used when you are speaking) zero: *My number is seven three one, O two nine three* (=731-0293). ☞ Look at the note at **zero**.

oak /oʊk/ *noun* **1** (*also* ˈ**oak tree**) [C] a type of large tree with hard wood that is common in many northern parts of the world **2** [U] the wood from the oak tree: *a solid oak table*

☞ The fruit of the oak is an **acorn**.

oar /ɔr/ *noun* [C] a long pole that is flat at one end and that is used for moving a small boat through water (**rowing**) ☞ Look at **paddle**.

o·a·sis /oʊˈeɪsəs/ *noun* [C] (*pl.* **o·a·ses** /-siz/) a place in the desert where there is water and where plants grow

oat /oʊt/ *noun* [usually pl.] a type of grain that is used as food for people and animals: *oat bran* ○ *The horses were eating oats and hay.*

oath /oʊθ/ *noun* [C] a formal promise: *They have to swear an oath of loyalty.* ○ *She took the oath of office as the country's new president.*

IDM **under oath** having made a formal promise to tell the truth in a court of law: *He was accused of lying under oath.*

oat·meal /ˈoʊtmil/ *noun* [U] a food that is made from oats mixed with hot milk or water and usually eaten for breakfast: *instant oatmeal*

o·be·di·ent /oʊˈbidiənt/ *adj.* doing what you are told to do: *He was an obedient child and never caused any problems.* ☞ The opposite is **disobedient**. —**o·be·di·ence** /-əns/ *noun* [U]: *They acted out of obedience to their leader.* —**o·be·di·ent·ly** *adv.*

o·bese /oʊˈbis/ *adj.* (used about people) extremely fat —**o·be·si·ty** /oʊˈbisəti/ *noun* [U]: *Obesity among children is on the increase in the U.S.*

☆ **o·bey** /oʊˈbeɪ/ *verb* [I,T] to do what you are told to do: *Soldiers are trained to obey orders.* ☞ The opposite is **disobey**.

o·bit·u·ar·y /oʊˈbɪtʃuˌɛri/ *noun* [C] (*pl.* **o·bit·u-**

ar·ies) an article about a person's life that is printed in a newspaper soon after he/she has died

☆ **ob·ject¹** /ˈɑbdʒɛkt; -dʒɪkt/ *noun* [C] **1** a thing that can be seen and touched: *The shelves were filled with objects of all shapes and sizes.* **2 the object of sth** a person or thing that causes a feeling, interest, thought, etc. **3** an aim or a purpose: *Making money is his sole object in life.* **4** (*grammar*) the noun or phrase describing the person or thing that is affected by the action of a verb

☞ In the sentences: *I sent a letter to Melanie* ○ *I sent Melanie a letter,* "a letter" is the **direct** object of the verb and "Melanie" is the **indirect** object.

IDM **money, etc. is no object** money, etc. is not important or is no problem: *She only buys the best clothes – money is no object for her.*

☆ **ob·ject²** /əbˈdʒɛkt/ *verb* **1** [I] **object (to sb/sth)** to not like or to be against sth/sb: *Many people object to the new tax.* **2** [T] to say that you do not like sth or to say that sth is wrong: *"I think that's unfair," he objected.*

☆ **ob·jec·tion** /əbˈdʒɛkʃn/ *noun* [C,U] a statement or feeling that you do not like or are against sb/sth: *We listed our objections to the proposed new road and sent them to the city council.* ○ *My parents have no objection to our marriage.*

ob·jec·tion·a·ble /əbˈdʒɛkʃənəbl/ *adj.* very unpleasant

☆ **ob·jec·tive¹** /əbˈdʒɛktɪv/ *adj.* not influenced by your own personal feelings (= based only on facts): *Please try and give an objective report of what happened.* ○ *It's hard to be objective about your own strengths and weaknesses.*

☞ The opposite is **subjective**. —**ob·jec·tive·ly** *adv.*: *He is too upset to see things objectively.* —**ob·jec·tiv·i·ty** /ˌɑbdʒɛkˈtɪvəti/ *noun* [U]

☆ **ob·jec·tive²** /əbˈdʒɛktɪv/ *noun* [C] your aim or purpose: *Our objective is to finish by the end of the year.* ○ *to achieve your objective*

ə	y	w	t̬	eɪ	aɪ	ɔɪ	aʊ	oʊ
about	yes	woman	butter	say	five	boy	now	go

ob·jec·tor /əbˈdʒɛktər/ *noun* [C] a person who objects to sth ☞ Look also at **conscientious objector**.

ob·li·gate /ˈɑbləɡeɪt/ *verb* [T] **obligate sb (to do sth)** (often passive) to force sb to do sth

ob·li·ga·tion /ˌɑbləˈɡeɪʃn/ *noun* **1** [C] something that you must do because it is your duty or because you promised to do it: *We have a moral obligation to help people who are in need.* **2** [U] having to do sth because it is is your duty: *The company is under no obligation to give out that information* (= they do not have to give the information).

o·blig·a·to·ry /əˈblɪɡəˌtɔri/ *adj.* (*formal*) that you must do: *obligatory military service*

o·blige /əˈblaɪdʒ/ *verb* **1** [T] (usually passive) to force sb to do sth: *You are not obliged to answer these questions, but it would be a great help if you did.* **2** [I,T] (*formal*) to do what sb asks; to be helpful: *The service there is excellent. They are always happy to oblige.*

o·bliged /əˈblaɪdʒd/ *adj.* grateful: *Thank you, ma'am. I'm much obliged to you.*

o·blig·ing /əˈblaɪdʒɪŋ/ *adj.* friendly and helpful

o·blit·er·ate /əˈblɪtəreɪt/ *verb* [T] (*formal*) to destroy or ruin sth completely

o·bliv·i·on /əˈblɪviən/ *noun* [U] **1** the state of having forgotten sth or of not being aware of sth: *I was in a state of complete oblivion.* **2** the state of being forgotten: *His work faded into oblivion after his death.*

o·bliv·i·ous /əˈblɪviəs/ *adj.* not noticing or being aware of sth: *The baby slept, oblivious to everything that was going on around him.*

ob·long /ˈɑblɔŋ/ *adj., noun* [C] (of) a shape with two long sides and two short sides ☞ Look at **rectangle**.

ob·nox·ious /əbˈnɑkʃəs/ *adj.* very unpleasant

o·boe /ˈoʊboʊ/ *noun* [C] a musical instrument that is made of wood. You play an oboe by blowing through a very narrow piece (**reed**) at the top.

ob·scene /əbˈsin/ *adj.* (used about words, thoughts, books, pictures, etc.) shocking or disgusting (usually because of the way they talk about or show sex): *an obscene book* ○ (*figurative*) *It's obscene to spend so much on food when millions are starving.*

ob·scen·i·ty /əbˈsɛnəti/ *noun* (*pl.* **ob·scen·i·ties**) **1** [U] the state of being obscene **2** [C] an obscene word or act

ob·scure¹ /əbˈskyʊr/ *adj.* **1** not easy to see or understand: *The reasoning behind his comments was somewhat obscure.* **2** not well-known: *an obscure Spanish poet* —**ob·scu·ri·ty** /əbˈskyʊrəti/ *noun* [U]: *The artist died penniless and in obscurity.*

ob·scure² /əbˈskyʊr/ *verb* [T] to make sth difficult to see or understand: *Our view was obscured by a high fence.*

ob·ser·vance /əbˈzɜrvəns/ *noun* [U] (*formal*) the practice of obeying or following a law, custom, ceremony, etc.

ob·ser·vant /əbˈzɜrvənt/ *adj.* quick at noticing things: *An observant witness gave the police a description of the men.* ☞ The opposite is **unobservant**.

☆ **ob·ser·va·tion** /ˌɑbzərˈveɪʃn; -sər-/ *noun* **1** [U] the act of watching sb/sth carefully or the state of being watched carefully: *the observation of animals in their natural surroundings* **2** [U] the ability to notice things: *Scientists need good powers of observation.* **3** [C] something that you say or write; a remark: *to make an observation about the weather* ☞ Look at **remark** and **comment**. These words are more common.

IDM **under observation** being watched carefully: *After his car accident, Mick was kept under observation in the hospital overnight.* ☞ Look at **surveillance**.

ob·ser·va·to·ry /əbˈzɜrvəˌtɔri/ *noun* [C] (*pl.* **ob·ser·va·to·ries**) a building from which scientists can look at the stars, the moon, etc. with telescopes

☆ **ob·serve** /əbˈzɜrv/ *verb* [T] **1** to notice sb/sth or watch sb/sth carefully: *A man and a woman were observed leaving by the back door.* ○ *We observed the birds throughout the breeding season.* **2** (*formal*) to say or remark: *"The bus is running late," she observed.* **3** (*formal*) to obey a law, rule, etc.: *to observe the speed limit*

☆ **ob·serv·er** /əbˈzɜrvər/ *noun* [C] **1** a person who watches sb/sth: *Political observers have been predicting trouble for quite a while.* **2** a person who attends a meeting, lesson, etc. to watch and listen but who does not say anything

ob·sess /əbˈsɛs/ *verb* [T] (usually passive) to fill sb's mind all the time: *He became obsessed with getting good grades in college.* ○ *Alison is obsessed with an older man.*

ob·ses·sion /əbˈsɛʃn/ *noun* **1** [U] the state of being obsessed **2** [C] a person or thing that obsesses you: *Football is an obsession to some people.*

ob·ses·sive /əbˈsɛsɪv/ *adj.* having or showing a way of thinking or behaving that you cannot stop: *He's obsessive about not being late.* ○ *obsessive cleanliness*

ob·so·lete /ˌɑbsəˈlit/ *adj.* no longer used because it is out of date

ob·sta·cle /ˈɑbstəkl/ *noun* [C] something that makes it difficult for you to go somewhere or do sth: *Not speaking a foreign language was a major obstacle to her career.*

ob·ste·tri·cian /ˌɑbstəˈtrɪʃn/ *noun* [C] a doctor who treats women who are pregnant

ob·sti·nate /ˈɑbstənət/ *adj.* not willing to change your mind if you have decided sth: *an obstinate refusal to apologize* ☞ This word is usually used in a critical way. Look at **stub-**

ər	ɪr	ɛr	ɑr	ɔr	ʊr	ʒ	h	ŋ
bird	near	hair	car	north	tour	vision	hat	sing

born, which has the same meaning. —**ob·sti-na·cy** /ˈɑbstɪnəsi/ *noun* [U] —**ob·sti·nate·ly** *adv.*

ob·struct /əbˈstrʌkt/ *verb* [T] to stop sb/sth from happening or moving: *You're obstructing traffic if you park there.*

ob·struc·tion /əbˈstrʌkʃn/ *noun* **1** [U] stopping sth from happening or making progress: *obstruction of justice* **2** [C] a thing that stops sb/sth from moving: *This car is causing an obstruction.*

ob·struc·tive /əbˈstrʌktɪv/ *adj.* trying to stop sth from happening

☆**ob·tain** /əbˈtem/ *verb* [T] (*formal*) to get sth: *This book can now be obtained in paperback.*

ob·tain·a·ble /əbˈtemabl/ *adj.* that can be obtained: *That brand of vacuum cleaner is no longer obtainable.* ☛ The opposite is **unobtainable.**

☆**ob·vi·ous** /ˈɑbviəs/ *adj.* easily seen or understood; clear: *It was obvious that he was not well.* ◦ *His disappointment was obvious to everyone.* ◦ *an obvious lie*

☆**ob·vi·ous·ly** /ˈɑbviəsli/ *adv.* as can easily be seen or understood; clearly: *There has obviously been a mistake.* ◦ *Obviously we don't want to spend too much money if we can avoid it.*

☆**oc·ca·sion** /əˈkeɪʒn/ *noun* **1** [C] a particular time when sth happens: *I have met Bill on two occasions.* **2** [sing.] **occasion (for sth)** the suitable or right time (for sth): *I'll tell her what I think if the occasion arises.*

☛ You use **occasion** when you mean the time is right or suitable for something: *I saw them at the funeral, but it was not a suitable occasion for discussing vacation plans.* You use **opportunity** or **chance** when you mean that it is possible to do something: *I was only in Paris for one day, and I didn't get the opportunity/chance to visit the Louvre.*

3 [C] a special event, ceremony, etc.: *Their wedding was a memorable occasion.* ◦ *an official, special, great, etc. occasion*
IDM on occasion sometimes

☆**oc·ca·sion·al** /əˈkeɪʒənl/ *adj.* done or happening from time to time but not very often: *I rarely drink alcohol – just an occasional glass of wine.* —**oc·ca·sion·al·ly** *adv.*: *We see each other occasionally.*

oc·cult /əˈkʌlt/ *adj.* connected with magic or supernatural powers

oc·cu·pant /ˈɑkyəpənt/ *noun* [C] (*formal*) a person who lives in or uses a room, house, etc.

☆**oc·cu·pa·tion** /ˌɑkyəˈpeɪʃn/ *noun* **1** [C] a job: *Please state your occupation on the form.* ☛ Look at the note at **work¹**. **2** [U] the control of a country by the army of another country

oc·cu·pa·tion·al /ˌɑkyəˈpeɪʃənl/ *adj.* connected with your work: *Accidents are an occupational hazard on construction sites.*

oc·cu·pied /ˈɑkyəpaɪd/ *adj.* **1** being used: *Is this seat occupied?* **2** busy: *Taking care of the kids keeps me fully occupied.* **3** (used about a country or a piece of land) under the control of another country: *occupied territory*

☆**oc·cu·py** /ˈɑkyəpaɪ/ *verb* [T] (*pres. part.* **oc·cu·py·ing**; *3rd pers. sing. pres.* **oc·cu·pies**; *p.t., p.p.* **oc·cu·pied**) **1** to live in or use a house, piece of land, etc.: *The house next door has not been occupied for some months.* **2** to take control of a building, country, etc. by force: *The rebel forces have occupied the parliament building.* **3** to fill a space or period of time: *The large table occupied most of the room.* **4** **occupy sb/yourself (in doing sth/with sth)** to keep sb/yourself busy: *How does he occupy himself now that he's retired?*

☆**oc·cur** /əˈkər/ *verb* [I] (**occur·ring**; **occurred**) **1** (*formal*) to happen: *The accident occurred late last night.* ☛ Look at the note at **happen**. **2** to be or exist: *Child abuse occurs in all classes of society.* **3** **occur to sb** to come into sb's mind: *It never occurred to John that his wife might be unhappy.*

oc·cur·rence /əˈkərəns/ *noun* [C] something that happens: *Car theft is now a very common occurrence.*

☆**o·cean** /ˈoʊʃn/ *noun* **1** [sing.] the mass of salt water that covers most of the surface of the earth: *Did you ever go swimming in the ocean?* ◦ *the ocean floor* **2** [C] **Ocean** one of the five main areas into which the sea is divided: *the Atlantic Ocean*

☆**o'clock** /əˈklɑk/ *adv.* (used after the numbers one to twelve for saying what the time is): *Lunch is at twelve o'clock.*

☛ Be careful. **O'clock** can only be used with full hours: *We arranged to meet at 5 o'clock. It's 5:30 already and he's still not here.*

Oct. *abbr.* = OCTOBER

oc·ta·gon /ˈɑktəgɑn/ *noun* [C] a shape that has eight straight sides —**oc·tag·o·nal** /ɑkˈtægənl/ *adj.*

oc·tave /ˈɑktɪv/ *noun* [C] the set of eight musical notes that western music is based on

☆**Oc·to·ber** /ɑkˈtoʊbər/ *noun* [C,U] (*abbr.* **Oct.**) the tenth month of the year, coming before November ☛ For examples of the use of the months in sentences, look at **January**.

oc·to·pus /ˈɑktəpəs/ *noun* [C] (*pl.* **oc·to·pus·es** or **oc·to·pi** /ˈɑktəpaɪ/) a sea animal with a soft body and eight long arms (**tentacles**)

OD /ˌoʊˈdi/ *verb* [I] (*pres. part.* **OD'ing**; *3rd pers. sing. pres.* **OD's**; *p.t., p.p.* **OD'd**) (*informal*) **OD (on sth)** = OVERDOSE² (*figurative*) *Ugh! I think I OD'd on Halloween candy.*

☆**odd** /ɑd/ *adj.* **1** strange; unusual: *There's something odd about him.* ◦ *It's kind of odd that she didn't call to say she couldn't come.* **2** (used about a number) that cannot be divided by two: *One, three, five and seven are all odd*

tʃ	dʒ	v	θ	ð	s	z	ʃ
chin	**June**	**van**	**thin**	**then**	**so**	**zoo**	**she**

O

O

numbers. ☞ The opposite is **even. 3** (only *before* a noun) that remains after other similar things have been used: *He made the bookshelves out of a few odd pieces of wood.* **4** (usually used after a number) a little more than: *There must have been 30-odd people at the meeting.* **5** not regular or fixed: *My neighbor seems to work odd hours.* —**odd·ness** *noun* [U]

odd·i·ty /ˈɑdəti/ *noun* (*pl.* **odd·i·ties**) **1** [U] the quality of being strange or unusual **2** [C] a person or thing that is unusual

‚odd 'jobs *noun* [plural] small jobs of various kinds: *Our son does a few odd jobs for the neighbors like raking leaves and shoveling snow.*

odd·ly /ˈɑdli/ *adv.* in a strange way: *He's behaving very oddly.*

☆ **odds** /ɑdz/ *noun* [plural] the chance or probability that sth will or will not happen: *The odds that he'll survive are very slim.* ∘ *The odds are against you.* ∘ *The odds against winning the lottery are fourteen million to one* (= there are fourteen million combinations of numbers which are possible).

IDM **against all the odds; against the odds** happening although it seemed impossible; in spite of problems or disadvantages: *Dave passed his exam against all the odds.*

odds and ends (*informal*) small things of little value or importance

o·dom·e·ter /oʊˈdɑmətər/ *noun* [C] a piece of equipment that measures the distance you have traveled: *My car only has 12,000 miles on the odometer.*

☆ **o·dor** /ˈoʊdər/ *noun* [C] (*formal*) a smell (often a bad one)

☆ **of** /əv; *strong form* ʌv; *informal* ə/ *prep.* **1** belonging to, relating to, or part of sth: *the result of the survey* ∘ *the back of the book* ∘ *the leader of the party* **2** relating to a person: *a friend of mine* (= one of my friends) ∘ *the poems of Milton* ∘ *That was nice of her* (= she was nice to do that). **3** (used for saying what sb/sth is or what a thing contains or consists of): *a woman of intelligence* ∘ *the city of Paris* ∘ *a glass of milk* ∘ *a crowd of people* ∘ *It's made of silver.* ∘ *a feeling of anger* **4** showing sth: *a map of New York* **5** (showing that sb/sth is part of a larger group): *some of the people* ∘ *three of the houses* **6** (with measurements and expressions of time): *five miles north of Bismarck* ∘ *a gallon of milk* ∘ *the fourth of August* **7** (with some adjectives): *I'm proud of you.* ∘ *She's jealous of her.* **8** (with some verbs): *They accused him of espionage.* ∘ *Think of a number.* ∘ *It reminds me of you.* **9** (used after a noun which is connected with a verb. The noun after "of" can be either the subject or the object): *the arrival of the President* (= he arrives) ∘ *the murder of the President* (= he is murdered) **10** (used about time) before: *It's*

five minutes of two. ∘ *The movie starts at a quarter of eight.* ☞ Look at **to¹**(5).

☆ **off¹** /ɔf; ɑf/ *adv., prep.* ☞ For special uses with many verbs and nouns, e.g. **turn off, off the record**, look at the verb and noun entries. **1** down or away from a place: *He fell off the ladder.* ∘ *We got off the bus.* ∘ *I shouted to him, but he just walked off.* ∘ *When are you off to Brazil?* ∘ (*figurative*) *We've gotten off the subject.* **2** (used with verbs that mean "remove"): *She took her coat off.* ∘ *He shook the rain off his umbrella.* ∘ *Don't leave the cap off the toothpaste.* **3** at a distance from sth: *Key West is just off the southern tip of Florida.* ∘ *Summer is still a long way off* (= it is a long time until then). **4** joined to and leading from: *My office is off the central corridor.* **5** (used about a machine, a light, etc.) not working or being used: *Please make sure the lights are off.* **6** when you do not work: *I'm taking a day off next week.* **7** no longer happening: *The meeting next Monday is off.* **8** cheaper; costing a certain amount less: *Today only: 20% off all red-tagged items* ∘ *This jacket was on sale for $10 off.*

☞ Some people say **off of** before a noun in conversation, but it is not considered correct in written English: *Hey! You kids stay off of my lawn!*

IDM **(be) better off** ⇨ **BETTER²**

off and on; on and off sometimes, but not all the time

well/badly off having/not having a lot of money

☆ **off²** /ɔf; ɑf/ *adj.* (not before a noun) **1** not as good as usual or normal: *The team's playing seems a little off today.* **2** not correct: *Their estimate for the job was off by about $500.*

☆ **of·fend** /əˈfɛnd/ *verb* **1** [T] (often passive) to hurt sb's feelings; to upset sb: *I hope they won't be offended if I don't come.* ∘ *He felt offended that she hadn't written for so long.* **2** [I,T] to be wrong or act wrongly according to law, usual behavior, certain beliefs, etc.: *Wilson offended* (= committed a crime) *again within days of his release from prison.* ∘ *Parts of the book offended their religious beliefs.*

of·fend·er /əˈfɛndər/ *noun* [C] **1** (*formal*) a person who commits a crime: *juvenile offenders who are sent to adult prisons* ∘ *a first-time/ repeat offender* **2** a person or thing that causes harm or trouble: *When it comes to polluting the environment, heavy industry is by far the worst offender.*

☆ **of·fense¹** /əˈfɛns/ *noun* **1** [C] **offense (against sth)** (*formal*) a crime; breaking the law: *to commit an offense* ∘ *The new law makes it a criminal offense to drink alcohol in public places.* ∘ *a minor/serious offense* ∘ *She pleaded guilty to five traffic offenses.* **2** [U] **offense (to sb/sth)** annoyance, anger or sadness or sth

i	ɪ	ɛ	æ	ɑ	ɔ	ʌ	ʊ	u
see	sit	ten	cat	hot	saw	cup	put	too

that causes these feelings: *I didn't mean to cause you any offense.*

IDM **take offense (at sth)** to feel upset or hurt: *Be careful what you say – she takes offense very easily.*

of·fense² /ˈɔfɛns; ˈɑf-/ *noun* [C,U, usually sing.] the part of a sports team that is responsible for scoring points: *The Bears' offense is the best in the league this year.* ☞ The opposite is defense.

of·fen·sive¹ /əˈfɛnsɪv/ *adj.* **1** unpleasant; insulting: *an offensive remark* ◦ *offensive behavior* ☞ Look at **inoffensive**. **2** (*formal*) used for or connected with attacking: *offensive weapons* ☞ The opposite is **defensive**.

☆ **of·fen·sive²** /əˈfɛnsɪv/ *noun* [C] an attack

IDM **take the offensive** to be the first to attack

☆ **of·fer¹** /ˈɔfər; ˈɑf-/ *verb* **1** [T] **offer sth (to sb)** to ask if sb would like sth or to give sb the opportunity to have sth: *He offered his seat on the bus to an old lady.* ◦ *I've been offered a job in Denver.* ◦ *She offered me a cigarette.* **2** [I,T] to say or show that you are willing to do sth: *I don't want to do it, but I suppose I'll have to offer.* ◦ *My brother offered to help me paint the house.* **3** [T] to give or provide sth: *The brochure offers very little information about the surrounding area.* ◦ *The job offers plenty of opportunity for travel.* **4** [T] to say that you will pay a certain amount: *He offered (me) $6,000 for the car and I took it.*

☆ **of·fer²** /ˈɔfər; ˈɑf-/ *noun* [C] **1** a statement offering to do sth or give sth to sb: *She accepted my offer of help.*

☞ We can **make**, **accept**, **refuse** or **withdraw** an offer.

2 a low price for sth in a store, or sth extra that you get when buying sth: *"Fantastic offers," the advertisement said. "Buy now!"* ◦ *See below for details of our special offer.* **3** an amount of money that you say you will give for sth: *They made an offer on the house.* ◦ *We turned down* (= refused) *an offer of $90,000.*

of·fer·ing /ˈɔfərɪŋ; ˈɑf-/ *noun* [C] something that is given or produced: *He gave me a bouquet of flowers as a peace offering.* ◦ *to give an offering in church*

off·hand¹ /ˌɔfˈhænd; ˌɑf-/ *adj.* (used about statements, comments, etc) without thought or preparation: *an offhand remark*

off·hand² /ˌɔfˈhænd; ˌɑf-/ *adv.* without having time to think; immediately: *I can't tell you what it's worth offhand.*

☆ **of·fice** /ˈɔfəs; ˈɑf-/ *noun* **1** [C] a room or building where written work is done, especially work connected with a business: *The company's main office is in Philadelphia.* ◦ *office furniture, equipment, etc.* ◦ *Please call again during office hours.* ◦ *a doctor's/dentist's office* **2** **Office** [sing.] (often in compounds) a gov-

ernment department, including the people who work there and the work they do: *the Office of Management and Budget* ☞ Look at **box office** and **post office**. **3** [U] an official position, often as part of a government or other organization: *to run for office* ◦ *to be voted into/out of office*

☆ **of·fi·cer** /ˈɔfəsər; ˈɑf-/ *noun* [C] **1** a person who gives the orders to others in the army, navy, etc.: *an army officer* **2** (often in compounds) a person with a position of authority or responsibility in the government or other organization: *a loan officer at a bank* **3** = POLICE OFFICER: *Excuse me, officer, is this the way to the stadium?* ☞ Look at the note at **official**.

☆ **of·fi·cial¹** /əˈfɪʃl/ *adj.* **1** accepted and approved by the government or some other authority: *official documents* ◦ *The project has not yet received official approval.* **2** connected with a position of authority: *official duties* ◦ *Her official title is now "Vice President for Finance."* **3** known publicly: *Their engagement is not yet official.* ◦ *The official reason for his resignation* (= but maybe not the real reason) *was that he wanted to spend more time with his family.* ☞ The opposite is **unofficial**.

of·fi·cial² /əˈfɪʃl/ *noun* [C] a person who has a position of authority: *The reception was attended by members of Congress and other high-ranking officials.* ◦ *a council official*

☞ An **office worker** is a person who works in an office, at a desk. An **official** is a person who has a position of responsibility in an organization, often the government: *senior government officials.* An **officer** is either a person who gives orders to others in the army, navy, etc. or a policeman or -woman. However the word is sometimes used like **official**: *She's an executive officer on the board of directors.*

☆ **of·fi·cial·ly** /əˈfɪʃəli/ *adv.* **1** as announced publicly but perhaps not strictly true: *Officially we don't accept children under six, but we'll make an exception in this case.* **2** in an official way: *The new school was officially opened last week.*

ˌoff-ˈkey *adj., adv.* (used about music) slightly too high or too low: *to sing off-key*

ˌoff-ˈlimits *adj.* forbidden; not to be entered by sb: *The teachers' lounge is off-limits to students.*

ˌoff-ˈpeak *adj.* available or used at a less popular or busy time: *Off-peak plane fares have been reduced.*

ˈoff-ramp *noun* [C] = EXIT RAMP

off·set /ˌɔfˈsɛt; ˌɑf-; ˈɔfsɛt; ˈɑf-/ *verb* [T] (**off·setting**; *p.t., p.p.* **off·set**) to make the effect of sth less strong or noticeable; to balance: *The disadvantages of the project are more than offset by the advantages.*

off·shore /ˌɔfˈʃɔr; ˌɑf-/ *adj., adv.* in the ocean, away from the land: *offshore oil drilling*

ə	y	w	t̬	eɪ	aɪ	ɔɪ	aʊ	oʊ
about	yes	woman	butter	say	five	boy	now	go

off·spring /ˈɔfsprɪŋ; ˈɑf-/ *noun* [C] (*pl.* **off-spring**) (*formal*) a child or children; the young of an animal: *Parents can pass many diseases on to their offspring.*

off-'stage (*also* **offstage**) *adj., adv.* away from or not on the stage: *to walk off-stage* ○ *off-stage laughter*

off-'white *adj.* not pure white

☆ **of·ten** /ˈɔfn; ˈɔftn; ˈɑf-/ *adv.* **1** many times; frequently: *We often go swimming on weekends.* ○ *I'm sorry I didn't write very often.* ○ *How often should you go to the dentist?* ○ *Write as often as you can.* **2** in many cases: *Women often go back to work after they have had a baby.*

IDM **more often than not** usually: *More often than not, the buses are late in the morning.*

every so often occasionally; from time to time

o·gre /ˈoʊɡər/ *noun* [C] **1** (in children's stories) a cruel and frightening giant **2** a person who is unkind and frightening

☆ **oh** /oʊ/ *interj.* **1** (used for introducing a reply or remark, for attracting sb's attention or when pausing to think): *"What time should we leave?" "Oh, early, I think."* ○ *"I'm a teacher." "Oh really? Where?"* ○ *Oh, Jill, could you mail this letter for me?* **2** (used for expressing surprise, fear, etc.): *Oh, no! Look what happened!*

☆ **oil¹** /ɔɪl/ *noun* [U] **1** a thick liquid that comes from under the ground and is used as a fuel or to make machines work smoothly: *The United States relies heavily on imported oil.* ○ *Your bicycle chain needs a little oil.* ○ *Crude oil* (= the raw material) *is transported by tanker to the refinery.* **2** a thick liquid that comes from plants and is used in cooking: *cooking, vegetable, olive, etc. oil*

oil² /ɔɪl/ *verb* [T] to put oil on or into sth, to make it work smoothly

oil·field /ˈɔɪlfild/ *noun* [C] an area where oil is found under the ground or the ocean

'oil painting *noun* [C] a painting that has been done using paint made with oil

'oil slick *noun* [C] an area of oil that floats on the ocean, usually when a ship carrying oil has leaked

'oil well (*also* **well**) *noun* [C] a hole that is made deep in the ground or under the ocean in order to obtain oil

☆ **oil·y** /ˈɔɪli/ *adj.* (**oil·i·er; oil·i·est**) covered with oil or like oil

oint·ment /ˈɔɪntmənt/ *noun* [C,U] a smooth substance that you put on sore skin or on an injury to help it to heal: *The doctor gave me an ointment to rub in twice a day.*

☆ **OK¹** (*also* **okay**) /ˌoʊˈkeɪ/ *adj., adv.* (*informal*) all right; good or well enough: *"How's your mom doing?" "OK."* ○ *If it's okay with you, I'll come around 7.*

☆ **OK²** (*also* **okay**) /ˌoʊˈkeɪ/ *interj.* yes; all right: *"Do you want to go to the movies?" "OK."*

OK³ (*also* **okay**) /ˌoʊˈkeɪ/ *noun* [sing.] agree-

ment or permission: *My parents have given me the OK to stay out late.* —**OK** (*also* **okay**) *verb* [T] (*p.p.* **OK'ing** *or* **okaying**; *3rd pers. sing. pres.* **OK's** *or* **okays**; *p.t., p.p.* **OK'd** *or* **okayed**): *The boss okayed my request to take some time off.*

o·kra /ˈoʊkrə/ *noun* a vegetable with long green seed containers (**pods**) that are cooked and eaten

☆ **old** /oʊld/ *adj.* **1** (used about people, animals, etc.) having lived a long time; not young: *My mother wasn't very old when she died.* ○ *He's only 50, but he looks older.* ○ *to get, grow, become old* **2** having existed for a long time; not modern: *a beautiful old stone house* ○ *old ideas, traditions, etc.* **3** having been used a lot; not new: *My younger brother gets all my old clothes.* ○ *I'm going to trade in my old car for a new one.* **4** (only *before* a noun) former; previous: *I earn more now than I did in my old job.* **5** (used with a period of time or with *how*) of a particular age: *Our car is only a year old.* ○ *They have a two-year-old* (= a child who is two years old). ○ *How old are you?* ○ *Are you older or younger than your sister?* ○ *my older sister* ☛ Look at the note at **age¹**. **6** (only *before* a noun) known for a long time (but maybe not old in years): *She's a very old friend of mine.* **7** (only *before* a noun) (*informal*) (used for expressing friendship and affection): *Good old Tom solved the problem!* **8** (only *before* a noun) (*informal*) (used for emphasizing that sth is not important): *"What time should I come?" "Oh, any old time – it doesn't matter."* **9 the old** *noun* [plural] old people

☛ Nowadays it is more acceptable to use the expression **senior citizens** to talk about old people.

IDM **be an old hand (at sth)** to be good at sth because you have done it often before

old hat (*informal*) no longer interesting or exciting because it has been done, seen, etc. too many times: *Staying in fancy hotels soon becomes old hat when you travel a lot on business.*

plain old ⇨ PLAIN¹

old 'age *noun* [U] the part of your life when you are old: *He's enjoying life in his old age.* ☛ Look at **youth**.

☆ **old-fash·ioned** /ˌoʊld ˈfæʃənd/ *adj.* **1** not modern; not commonly worn, used, etc. now: *an old-fashioned record player* **2** (used about people) believing in old ideas, customs, etc.: *My parents are pretty old-fashioned about some things.*

the ˌOld 'Testament *noun* [sing.] the first part of the Bible, that tells the history of the Jewish people ☛ Look at **New Testament** and at the note at **White House**.

ol·ive¹ /ˈɑlɪv/ *noun* [C] a small green or black fruit with a bitter taste, used for food and oil

ol·ive² /'ɑlɪv/ (also **olive green**) adj. of a dark color between yellow and green

'olive oil noun [U] oil obtained from olives and used in cooking or on salads

O·lym·pic /ə'lɪmpɪk/ adj. connected with the Olympic Games: *Who holds the Olympic record for the 1,500 meters?*

the O,lympic 'Games (also **the Olympics**) noun [plural] the international sports competitions which are organized every four years in a different country: *to win a medal at/in the Olympics* ○ *the 1994 Winter Olympics*

om·buds·man /'ɑmbʌdzmən; -mæn/ noun [C] (pl. **om·buds·men** /-mən/) an official who reports on complaints made by ordinary people against public authorities, newspapers, etc.

om·e·let (also **omelette**) /'ɑmlət/ noun [C] a mixture of eggs and milk which is beaten, fried, and usually folded over other foods. In the U.S., omelettes are usually eaten at breakfast: *a mushroom and cheese omelette*

o·men /'oʊmən/ noun [C] a sign of sth that will happen in the future: *a good/bad omen*

om·i·nous /'ɑmənəs/ adj. suggesting that sth bad is going to happen: *Those black clouds look ominous.*

o·mis·sion /oʊ'mɪʃn; ə-/ noun **1** [C] something that has not been included: *There were several omissions from the list of names.* **2** [U] the act of not including sb/sth: *The program was criticized for its omission of certain important details.*

o·mit /oʊ'mɪt; ə-/ verb [T] (**omit·ting**; ~~omit·ted~~) **1** to not include sth: *Several verses of the song can be omitted.* **2** (formal) to not do sth: *He omitted to mention the man's name.*

☆ **on** /ɑn; ɔn/ adv., prep. ☞ For special uses with many verbs and nouns, e.g. **get on**, **on vacation**, look at the verb and noun entries. **1** supported by a surface: *The plates are on the table.* ○ *We sat on the floor.* ○ *Make sure you put the lid on.* **2** touching or forming part of sth: *There's a mark on your skirt.* ○ *paintings on the wall* ○ *Write it down on a piece of paper.* **3** at a place: *on the farm* ○ *I live on Walnut Street.* ○ *a house on the banks of the river* **4** (showing direction): *on the right/left* **5** (used with means of transportation): *on the bus, train, plane* ○ *"I took the bus." "Where did you get on?"* ○ *We came on foot* (= walking). ○ *on a bicycle* ☞ Note that we say **in** a car, truck, van, or taxi. **6** (with expressions of time): *on August 19th* ○ *on Monday* ○ *on Thanksgiving* ○ *What are you doing on your birthday?* **7** immediately or soon after: *He called her on his return from New York.* ○ *She began to sob on hearing the news.* **8** (showing that sth continues): *The man shouted at us, but we walked on.* ○ *The war went on for five years.* **9** about sth: *We have a test on irregular verbs tomorrow.* ○ *a lecture on Japan* **10** working; being used: *All the lights were on.* ○ *Turn the TV on.*

11 happening: *There's a great play on in town next week.* ○ *Is the party still on for tonight?* **12** using sth; by means of sth: *I spoke to her on the phone.* ○ *There's a good movie on TV tonight.* ○ *I heard it on the radio.* **13** wearing sth: *What did she have on?* **14** having sth with you: *I don't have any money on me.* **15** using drugs or medicine: *I've been on antibiotics for two weeks.* **16** receiving a certain amount of money: *I can't support a family on the salary I earn.* **17** (showing the way sth is spent): *He spends a lot on clothes.* ○ *Don't waste your time on that.* **18** paid for by sb: *The drinks are on me!*

IDM **from now/then on** starting from this/that time and continuing: *From then on he never smoked another cigarette.*

off and on; **on and off** ➩ OFF¹

on and on without stopping: *He just went on and on about his work.*

☆ **once¹** /wʌns/ adv. **1** one time only; on one occasion: *I've only been to Mexico once.* ○ *once a week, month, year, etc.* ○ *I have the car serviced once every six months.* **2** at some time in the past; formerly: *This house was once the general store.*

IDM **all at once** all at the same time or suddenly: *People began talking all at once.* ○ *All at once she got up and left the room.*

at once 1 (formal) immediately; now: *The treaty requires all fighting to cease at once.* **2** at the same time: *I can't understand anything if you all talk at once.*

just this once on this occasion only: *"Have a glass of wine." "Oh, all right. Just this once."*

once again again, as before: *Spring will soon be here once again.*

once and for all now and for the last time: *You've got to make a decision once and for all.*

once in a blue moon (informal) very rarely; almost never: *We live in Amarillo, so I only go to Dallas once in a blue moon.*

(every) once in a while occasionally, but not often: *We like to order Chinese food every once in a while.*

once more 1 one more time: *All right. We'll read the story once more, but then it's time for bed.* **2** again, as before: *The valuable painting is once more in the hands of its rightful owner.*

once upon a time (used at the beginning of a children's story) a long time ago; in the past: *Once upon a time, there was a beautiful princess...*

☆ **once²** /wʌns/ conj. as soon as; when: *Once you've practiced a little, you'll find that it's fairly easy.* ○ *Once the meal was finished, the discussions began.*

on·com·ing /'ɑnkʌmɪŋ; 'ɔn-/ adj. (only before a noun) coming toward you: *oncoming traffic*

☆ **one¹** /wʌn/ pron., det., noun [C] **1** the number 1: *There's only one cookie left.* ○ *The trip takes one hour.* ○ *If you take one from ten, it leaves*

O

nine. ☞ Look at **first**. For more information on numbers, look at Appendix 2. **2** (used for emphasizing sth) only: *She's the one person I trust.* **3** (used when you are talking about a time in the past or future without actually saying which one) a certain: *He came to see me one evening last week.* ○ *We ought to go and visit them one day.* **4** (*formal*) (used in front of sb's name to show that you do not know the person) a certain: *I believe that one Wanda Smith is the person you need to see.* **5** (used with *the other, another* or *other(s)*) to make a contrast): *The twins are so much alike that it's hard to tell one from the other.* **6** the same: *We can't all get in this one car.*

IDM **(all) in one** all together or combined: *It's a shampoo and a conditioner all in one.*

one after another/the other first one, then the next, etc.: *One after another, the winners went up to get their prizes.*

one by one individually or separately: *One by one, the boys were called in to the principal's office.*

one of a kind not similar to anything or anyone else: *I miss my grandpa – he was really one of a kind.*

one or two a few: *I borrowed one or two new books from the library.* ○ *Just take one or two – not too many.*

☆ **one²** /wʌn/ *pron.* **1** (used instead of repeating a noun): *I think I'll have an apple. Would you like one?* **2 one of** one member (of a certain group): *One of the plates is broken.* ○ *He's staying with one of his friends.* ○ *One of the kids is crying.*

☞ **One of** is always followed by a plural noun. The verb is singular because the subject is **one**: *One of our assistants is sick.* ○ *One of the buses was late.*

3 (*formal*) (used for referring to people in general, including the speaker or writer): *One should try not to get annoyed.* ○ *Plenty of exercise makes one physically fit.*

☞ It is very formal to use **one** in this way. In everyday English it is more common to use **you**. Note that the possessive form is **one's**: *One must be sure of one's facts before criticizing other people.* **One's** is also the short form of "one is" or "one has."

IDM **one another** each other: *We exchanged news with one another.* ○ *You should listen to one another more often.*

☆ **one³** /wʌn/ *noun* [C] **1** (used after *this, that, which* or after an adjective which cannot stand alone): *"Which dress do you like?" "This one."* ○ *"Can I borrow some books of yours?" "Yes. Which ones?"* ○ *This coat's a little too small. You need a bigger one.* ○ *That idea is a very good one.* **2** (used before a group of words that show which person or thing you are talking about): *My house is the one after the post*

office. ○ *The girl he's going out with is the one with red hair.* ○ *If you find some questions difficult, leave out the ones you don't understand.* **3** someone: *She's not one to get upset easily.*

ˌ**one-on-ˈone** (*also* ˌ**one-to-ˈone**) *adj., adv.* between only two people: *one-on-one English lessons* (= one teacher with one student)

one·self /wʌnˈsɛlf/ *pron.* (*formal*) **1** (used for referring to people in general when *one* is the subject of the sentence): *One can teach oneself to play the piano, but it is easier to have lessons.* **2** (used for emphasizing *one*): *One could easily arrange it all oneself.*

IDM **(all) by oneself 1** alone **2** without help

☞ **Oneself** is very formal. It is much more common to say **yourself** when talking about people in general.

ˌ**one-ˈsided** *adj.* **1** involving one person more than the other: *Her feelings for him seem to be kind of one-sided* (= he doesn't feel the same). **2** unfair; seeing only one side (of an argument, etc): *I think you're being very one-sided. Think of my point of view.*

ˌ**one-ˈway** *adv., adj.* **1** (used about roads) that you can only drive along in one direction: *a one-way street* **2** (used about a ticket) that you can use to travel somewhere but not back again: *I'd like to buy a one-way ticket to the Caribbean!* ☞ Look at **round-trip**.

on·go·ing /ˈɑŋgoʊɪŋ; ˈɔn-/ *adj.* (only *before* a noun) continuing to exist now: *It's an ongoing problem.* ○ *an ongoing relationship*

☆ **on·ion** /ˈʌnyən/ *noun* [C,U] a small white vegetable with many layers and a brown skin. Onions have a strong smell and taste, and are often used in cooking: *onion soup*

onion
garlic
clove
of garlic

ˌ**on-ˈline** (*also* **online**) *adj.* (*technical*) connected to and controlled by a computer: *an on-line ticket reservation system*

on·look·er /ˈɑnlʊkər; ˈɔn-/ *noun* [C] a person who watches sth happening without taking part in it: *The police were questioning several onlookers about the incident.*

☆ **on·ly¹** /ˈoʊnli/ *adj.* (only *before* a noun) **1** with no others existing or present: *I was the only woman in the bar.* ○ *This is the only dress we have in your size.* **2** the most suitable or the best: *It's so cold that the only thing to do is to sit by the fire.*

☆ **on·ly²** /ˈoʊnli/ *adv.* and no one or nothing else; no more than: *She only likes rock music.* ○ *I only asked a few friends to the party.* ○ *It was only a little spider.* ○ *It's only one o'clock. There's plenty of time.*

☞ In written English **only** is usually placed before the word it refers to. In spoken English we can use stress to show which word it refers to and so **only** can have different positions.: *I only kissed 'Jane* (= I kissed Jane and no one else). ○ *I only 'kissed Jane* (= I kissed Jane, but I didn't do anything else).

IDM **if only** ⇨ IF

not only...but also both...and: *He not only did the shopping, but he also cooked the meal.*

☆ **on·ly³** /'oʊnli/ *conj.* (*informal*) except that; but: *The movie was really good, only it was a little too long.*

only 'child *noun* [C] a child who has no brothers or sisters

on-ramp *noun* [C] = ENTRANCE RAMP

on·set /'ɑnsɛt; 'ɔn-/ *noun* [sing.] the beginning (often of sth bad): *the onset of winter*

on·slaught /'ɑnslɔt; 'ɔn-/ *noun* [C] **onslaught (on sb/sth)** a fierce attack: *an onslaught on government policy*

☆ **on·to** (*also* **on to**) /'ɑntə; 'ɔn-*; before vowels* 'ɑntu; 'ɔn-/ *prep.* to a position on sth: *The cat jumped onto the sofa.* ○ *The bottle fell onto the floor.*

IDM **be onto sb/sth** (*informal*) to have some information about sb/sth that could lead to an important discovery, etc.: *The police were onto the car thieves.* ○ *I think you may be onto something big here.*

on·ward /'ɑnwərd; 'ɔn-/ (*also* **onwards** /'ɑnwərdz; 'ɔn-/) *adv.* **1** and after: *From September onward it usually begins to get colder.* **2** forward or toward progress: *The road stretched onward into the distance.* ○ *The President said the economy would soon be moving onward and upward.*

oops /ʊps; ups/ (*also* **whoops** /wʊps/) *interj.* (*informal*) (used when you have, or almost have, a small accident): *Oops! I almost spilled my juice.*

ooze /uz/ *verb* [I,T] to flow slowly out or to allow sth to flow slowly out: *Blood was oozing from a cut on his head.* ○ *The container started to ooze a strange green liquid.* (*figurative*) *She was oozing confidence* (= she was very confident).

o·paque /oʊ'peɪk/ *adj.* **1** that you cannot see through; not transparent: *opaque glass in the door* **2** (*formal*) difficult to understand; not clear

☆ **o·pen¹** /'oʊpən/ *adj.* **1** not closed: *Don't leave the door open.* ○ *an open window* ○ *I can't get this carton of milk open.* ○ *She stared at me with her eyes wide open.* ○ *The diary was lying open on her desk.* ○ *The curtains were open so that we could see into the room.* **2** honest and willing to talk: *Jane will tell you exactly what happened at the meeting – she's a very open person.* **3** not hidden or secret: *He looked at him with open dislike.* **4** with its doors unlocked so that customers can enter: *The bank*

isn't open until 9:30. **5** (used about a new building, public area, etc.) ready to be used for the first time: *The new shopping mall will soon be open.* **6 open (to sb/sth)** (used about a road, a course of action, etc.) possible to use, do, etc.: *After the heavy snow many minor roads were not open to traffic.* **7** (used about clothes) with the buttons not fastened: *His shirt was open at the neck.* **8** (only *before* a noun) with few buildings, towns, etc. near (used about an area of land): *open country* **9** (only *before* a noun) at a distance from the land (used about an area of ocean): *Once we were out in the open sea, the wind got stronger.* **10** (only *before* a noun) not covered: *an open fire* **11 open (to sb/sth)** that anyone can enter, visit, etc.: *The competition is open to everyone.* ○ *The building is open to the public in the summer.* **12** not finally decided; still being considered: *Let's leave the details open.*

IDM **have/keep an open mind (about/on sth)** to be willing to listen to or consider new ideas and suggestions

in the open air outside: *Somehow, food eaten in the open air tastes much better.*

open to sth willing to receive sth: *I'm always open to suggestions.*

with open arms in a friendly way that shows that you are pleased to see sb or have sth

☆ **o·pen²** /'oʊpən/ **the open** *noun* [sing.] outside: *After working in an office I like to be out in the open on weekends.*

IDM **bring sth out into the open; come out into the open** to make sth known publicly; to be known publicly: *I'm glad our secret has come out into the open at last.*

☆ **o·pen³** /'oʊpən/ *verb* **1** [I,T] to become open or to make sth open: *This window won't open – it's stuck.* ○ *Do you mind if I open this window?* ○ *When I opened my eyes, she was gone.* ○ *Can I open my presents now?* **2** [I,T] to fold out, back, etc.: *The book opened at the very page I needed.* ○ *Open your hand – what have you got inside?* ○ *She opened the curtains and looked out.* **3** [I,T] **open (sth) (out)** (used about a map, etc.) to fold out: *Open the map out and let's all take a look.* **4** [I,T] (used about a store, an office, etc.) to be unlocked so that business, work, etc. can start; to unlock sth: *The store hasn't opened yet.* ○ *They open the museum an hour later on Sundays.* **5** [T] to say officially that a new building, etc. is ready for use: *The mayor will open the stadium next week.* **6** [I,T] to start: *The play opens on Broadway next month.* ○ *The chairman opened the meeting by welcoming everybody.* ○ *I'd like to open a bank account.* **7** [T] to make a road, etc. available for use again: *Snowplows have opened many major roads.*

IDM **open fire (at/on sb/sth)** to start shooting: *He ordered his men to open fire on the advancing enemy troops.*

O

ə	y	w	t̮	eɪ	aɪ	ɔɪ	aʊ	oʊ
about	yes	woman	butter	say	five	boy	now	go

PHRV **open into/onto sth** to lead straight to sth: *This door opens onto the lawn.*

open (sth) up 1 to become available or to make sth available: *After I graduated from college, all sorts of opportunities opened up for me.* ○ *Parts of the desert may soon be opened up for farming.* **2** to open a door: *"Open up!" shouted the police to the man inside.*

ˌopen-ˈair *adj.* outside; not indoor: *an open-air concert*

☆ **o·pen·er** /ˈoʊpənər/ *noun* [C] (in compounds) a thing that takes the lid, etc. off sth: *a can opener*

ˌopen ˈhouse *noun* [C, usually sing.] a day when the public can visit a place that is usually closed to them: *to have/hold an open house*

☆ **o·pen·ing¹** /ˈoʊpənɪŋ/ *noun* **1** [sing.] beginning: *The book is famous for its dramatic opening.* **2** [C] a hole; a way in or out: *We were able to get through an opening in the hedge.* **3** [C] an opportunity: *There are many new openings for trade with Eastern Europe.* **4** [C] a job which is available: *We currently have an opening for a sales manager.* **5** [C] the occasion when a public building, etc. is officially opened or ready for use: *the opening of the new theater*

o·pen·ing² /ˈoʊpənɪŋ/ *adj.* (only *before* a noun) first: *the opening chapter of a book* ○ *His opening remarks were very witty.*

o·pen·ly /ˈoʊpənli/ *adv.* not secretly; honestly: *I think you should discuss your feelings openly with each other.*

ˌopen-ˈminded *adj.* willing to consider new ideas and opinions

o·pen·ness /ˈoʊpənəs/ *noun* [U] the quality of being honest and willing to talk: *I was surprised by her openness about her relationship with Jerry.*

☆ **o·pe·ra** /ˈɑprə; ˈɑpərə/ *noun* **1** [C] a play in which the actors (**opera singers**) sing the words to music: *an opera by Wagner* ○ *a comic opera* **2** [U] works of this kind: *Do you like opera?* ○ *grand* (= serious) *opera* ○ *light* (= not serious) *opera* ☞ Look at **soap opera**. —**op·er·at·ic** /ˌɑpəˈrætɪk/ *adj.*: *operatic music*

ˈopera house *noun* [C] a theater where operas are performed

☆ **op·er·ate** /ˈɑpəreɪt/ *verb* **1** [I,T] to work, or to make sth work: *I don't understand how this machine operates.* ○ *These controls here operate the air conditioning.* **2** [I] to act or to have an effect: *Several factors were operating to our advantage.* **3** [I,T] to do business; to manage or direct sth: *The corporation operates from its headquarters in Atlanta.* ○ *Many companies operate mail order services now.* **4** [I] **operate (on sb) (for sth)**; **operate (on sth)** to cut open a patient's body in order to deal with a part that is damaged, diseased, etc.: *The surgeon is going to operate on her in the morning.* ○ *He was operated on for appendicitis.*

ˈoperating room *noun* [C] a room in a hospital where operations (3) are performed

ˈoperating ˌsystem *noun* [C] a computer program that organizes a number of other programs at the same time

☆ **op·er·a·tion** /ˌɑpəˈreɪʃn/ *noun* **1** [C] an activity, often highly organized, that involves many people, actions, days, etc.: *A rescue operation was launched to find the missing children.* ○ *military operations* ○ *Putting up the new wallpaper was a very tricky operation.* **2** [C] a business company: *a huge international operation* **3** [C] **operation (on sb/sth) (for sth)** cutting open a patient's body in order to deal with a part inside: *The surgeon performed an operation on her for a kidney problem.* ○ *He had an operation to remove some damaged lung tissue.* **4** [U] the way in which sth works; working: *The operation of these machines is quite simple.*

IDM **in operation** working or having an effect: *The water heater should be back in operation in the next few hours.*

op·er·a·tion·al /ˌɑpəˈreɪʃənl/ *adj.* **1** connected with an operation (1,4) **2** ready for use: *The new factory is now fully operational.*

☆ **op·er·a·tor** /ˈɑpəreɪtər/ *noun* [C] **1** a person whose job is to connect telephone calls, for the public or in a particular building: *Dial 0 for the operator.* ○ *a switchboard operator* **2** a person whose job is to work a particular machine or piece of equipment: *a computer operator* **3** a person or company that does certain types of business: *a tour operator*

☆ **o·pin·ion** /əˈpɪnyən/ *noun* **1** [C] **opinion (of sb/sth)**; **opinion (on/about sth)** what you think about sb/sth: *She asked me for my opinion of her new hairstyle and I told her.* ○ *He has very strong opinions on almost everything.* **2** [U] what people in general think about sth: *Public opinion is in favor of a change in the law.*

IDM **be of the opinion that…** (*formal*) to think or believe that…: *In this case we are of the opinion that you made the right decision.*

have a high, low, etc. opinion of sb/sth to think that sb/sth is good, bad, etc.

in my, your, etc. opinion I, you, etc. think that…: *In my opinion, you're making a terrible mistake.*

a matter of opinion ⇨ MATTER¹

oˈpinion poll *noun* [C] = POLL¹(1)

o·pi·um /ˈoʊpiəm/ *noun* [U] a drug that is made from the seeds of the poppy flower

o·pos·sum /əˈpɑsəm/ (*also* **possum**) *noun* [C] a type of small furry animal that lives in trees and carries its young in a pocket of skin (a **pouch**) on its stomach. When they are afraid, opossums act as if they are dead.

☆ **op·po·nent** /əˈpoʊnənt/ *noun* [C] **1** (in sports or games) a person who plays against sb **2 an opponent (of sth)** a person who disagrees

with sb's actions, plans or beliefs and tries to stop or change them

☆ **op·por·tu·ni·ty** /ˌɑpərˈtunəti/ *noun* [C,U] (*pl.* **op·por·tu·ni·ties**) a chance to do sth that you would like to do; a situation or a time in which it is possible to do sth that you would like to do: *There will be plenty of opportunity for asking questions later.* ○ *The trip gave me a great opportunity to use my Spanish.* ○ *I'd like to take this opportunity to thank you for all your help.* ○ *an equal opportunity employer* (= an employer who employs people regardless of sex, race, etc.) ☞ Look at the note at **occasion**.

☆ **op·pose** /əˈpoʊz/ *verb* [T] to disagree with sb's beliefs, actions or plans and to try to change or stop them: *They opposed the plan to widen the main road through their town.*

op·posed /əˈpoʊzd/ *adj.* **opposed to sth** disagreeing with a plan, action, etc.; believing that sth is morally wrong: *I'm not opposed to the idea, but I need more details.* ○ *She has always been opposed to experiments on animals.*

IDM **as opposed to** (used to emphasize the difference between two things) in contrast with: *Your work will be judged on the basis of quality, as opposed to quantity.*

☆ **op·po·site¹** /ˈɑpəzət/ *adj., adv.* **1** as different as possible: *I can't walk with you because I'm going in the opposite direction.* ○ *the opposite sex* (= men for women, women for men) **2** in a position directly on the other side of sb/sth; facing: *The two farms are on opposite sides of the river.* ○ *The two families sat at opposite ends of the room to each other.*

☞ Sometimes **opposite** is used after the noun: *Write your answer in the space opposite.*

☆ **op·po·site²** /ˈɑpəzət/ *noun* [C] the word, thing or person that is as different as possible from sb/sth: *"Hot" is the opposite of "cold."* ○ *She's very friendly, whereas her brother is the complete opposite.*

op·po·site³ /ˈɑpəzət/ *prep.* directly on the other side of a space between sth and sth else; facing sb/sth: *I always buy my paper from the store opposite our house.*

op·po·si·tion /ˌɑpəˈzɪʃn/ *noun* **1** [U] **opposition (to sb/sth)** the feeling of disagreeing with sth and the action of trying to change it: *Despite strong opposition from local people, the new prison was built on the edge of town.* ○ *to express your opposition to sth* **2 the opposition** [sing.] the person or team who plays against sb in sports or games: *Their coach told them not to underestimate the opposition.* **3 the opposition** [sing.] (used about the political system of some countries) the politicians or the political parties that are in Parliament, but do not control the country's government

op·press /əˈprɛs/ *verb* [T] (usually passive) to

rule sb (especially a nation or a part of society) in a way that allows the people no freedom; to control sb in an unjust way, using force

op·pressed /əˈprɛst/ *adj.* unfairly ruled or treated; not free: *an oppressed minority*

op·pres·sion /əˈprɛʃn/ *noun* [U] the system or act of oppressing; the state of being oppressed: *a struggle against oppression*

op·pres·sive /əˈprɛsɪv/ *adj.* **1** allowing no freedom; controlling by force; unjust: *The military government announced oppressive new laws.* **2** (used especially about heat or the atmosphere) causing you to feel very uncomfortable

op·pres·sor /əˈprɛsər/ *noun* [C] a person who oppresses sb

opt /ɑpt/ *verb* [T] **opt to do sth** to choose or decide to do sth after thinking about it

PHRV **opt for sb/sth** to choose sth after you have decided that you do not want the other possibilities

opt out (of sth) to choose not to take part in sth; to decide to stop being involved in sth: *Several employees have opted out of the strike which was called by the union last week.*

op·ti·cal /ˈɑptɪkl/ *adj.* connected with the sense of sight: *optical instruments*

optical il·lu·sion *noun* [C] something that tricks the eye and makes you believe sth is there or is true when it is not

op·ti·cian /ɑpˈtɪʃn/ *noun* [C] a person who is qualified to make and sell eyeglasses ☞ Look at **optometrist**.

op·ti·mism /ˈɑptəmɪzəm/ *noun* [U] the feeling that the future or sth in the future will be good or successful: *There is considerable optimism that the economy will improve.* ☞ The opposite is **pessimism**.

op·ti·mist /ˈɑptəmɪst/ *noun* [C] a person who is always hopeful that things will be good or successful in the future ☞ The opposite is **pessimist**.

op·ti·mis·tic /ˌɑptəˈmɪstɪk/ *adj.* hoping or believing that what happens in the future will be good or successful: *I applied for the job, but I'm not very optimistic about my chances of getting it.* ☞ The opposite is **pessimistic**. —**op·ti·mis·ti·cal·ly** /-kli/ *adv.*

☆ **op·tion** /ˈɑpʃn/ *noun* **1** [U, sing.] the freedom to choose; choice: *If you're late again, you will give us no option but to fire you.* **2** [C] a thing that you choose or can choose; choice: *She looked carefully at all her options before deciding on a college.* **3** [C] something, especially a piece of equipment, that you can choose to have in a new car, truck, etc. but must pay for: *Options like a CD player and leather seat covers can add quite a bit to the price of a car.*

op·tion·al /ˈɑpʃənl/ *adj.* that you can choose or not choose: *an optional subject at school* ○ *an optional extra* (= sth that you can have as*

tʃ	dʒ	v	θ	ð	s	z	ʃ
chin	**June**	**van**	**thin**	**then**	**so**	**zoo**	**she**

O

an extra thing but must pay for) ☞ The opposite is **compulsory** or **mandatory**.

op·tom·e·trist /ɑpˈtɑmətrɪst/ *noun* [C] a person who is qualified to test your eyes and tell you which glasses, etc. you need ☞ Look at **optician.**

☆ **or** /ər; *strong form* ɔr/ *conj.* **1** (used before another possibility or the last of a series of possibilities): *Would you like to sit here or next to the window?* ○ *Are you interested or not?* ○ *You can have chicken, beef or fish.* ☞ Look at **either…or. 2** if not; otherwise: *Don't drive so fast or you'll have an accident!* ○ *She must have loved him, or she wouldn't have married him.* ☞ **Or else** and **otherwise** can be used with this meaning. **3** (after a negative) and neither; and not: *She hasn't called or written to me for weeks.* ○ *I've never been to Chile or Peru.* ☞ Look at **neither…nor. 4** (used before a word or phrase that explains or comments on what has been said before): *20% of the population, or one out of every five* ○ *Minneapolis and St. Paul, or the "Twin Cities" as they are sometimes known*

IDM or else ⇨ ELSE

or so about: *I would think the repairs will cost you $100 or so.*

or sb/sth/someplace/somewhere (*informal*) (used for showing that you are not sure, cannot remember or do not know which person, thing or place): *She's a computer programmer or something.* ○ *The movie was set in Sweden or somewhere.* ☞ Another phrase that shows that you are not sure is **…or other:** *He muttered something or other about not having any time and disappeared.*

☆ **o·ral¹** /ˈɔrəl/ *adj.* **1** spoken, not written: *an oral exercise* **2** concerning or using the mouth: *oral hygiene*

o·ral² /ˈɔrəl/ *noun* [C] a spoken examination: *I have my German oral next week.*

o·ral·ly /ˈɔrəli/ *adv.* **1** using speech, not writing: *Orally her English is good.* **2** through the mouth and swallowed

☆ **or·ange¹** /ˈɔrɪndʒ; ˈɑr-/ *noun* **1** [C] a round fruit with a thick skin, that is divided into sections (**segments**) inside, and is a color between red and yellow: *orange juice* **2** [U] the color of this fruit, between red and yellow

☆ **or·ange²** /ˈɔrɪndʒ; ˈɑr-/ *adj.* having the color orange¹(2): *orange paint*

or·a·tor /ˈɔrətər; ˈɑr-/ *noun* [C] (*formal*) a person who is good at making public speeches

or·bit¹ /ˈɔrbət/ *noun* [C,U] the path taken by sth (a planet, moon, spacecraft, etc.) going around sth else in space: *to put a satellite into orbit*

or·bit² /ˈɔrbət/ *verb* [I,T] to move around sth (the moon, the sun, a planet etc.) in orbit

or·chard /ˈɔrtʃərd/ *noun* [C] a piece of land in which fruit trees are grown: *a cherry orchard*

☆ **or·ches·tra** /ˈɔrkəstrə/ *noun* [C] a large group of musicians who play different musical instruments together: *a symphony orchestra*

☞ An orchestra usually plays classical music. Rock music, jazz, etc. are played by a **group** or **band.**

or·ches·tral /ɔrˈkɛstrəl/ *adj.* played by or written for an orchestra

or·chid /ˈɔrkəd/ *noun* [C] a plant that has flowers of unusual shapes and bright colors

or·deal /ɔrˈdil/ *noun* [C] a very bad experience: *The woman who was attacked last night is in the hospital recovering from her ordeal.*

☆ **or·der¹** /ˈɔrdər/ *noun* **1** [U] the way in which people or things are arranged in relation to each other: *a list of names in alphabetical order* ○ *a list of dates in chronological order* **2** [U] an organized state, when everything is in its right place: *Make sure your notes are in order before you start your speech.* **3** [U] the situation in which laws, rules, authority, etc. are obeyed: *Police have restored order on the streets following last week's violence.* ☞ Look at **disorder. 4** [C] an instruction or demand that sb must do sth, given by sb who has power over that person: *In the army, you have to obey orders at all times.* ○ *Frank's ex-wife obtained a court order allowing her to keep their children.* **5** [C] a request asking for sth to be made, supplied or delivered: *The company has just received a major export order.* **6** [C] a request for food, drink, etc. in a hotel, restaurant, etc.: *Can I take your order now, sir?*

IDM in order to do sth with the purpose or intention of doing sth; so that sth can be done: *In order to obtain a passport, you need a birth certificate and two photographs.* ○ *We left early in order to avoid the traffic.*

in working order (used about machines, etc.) working correctly, not broken: *It's an old fridge, but it's still in good working order.*

law and order ⇨ LAW

out of order ⇨ OUT²

☆ **or·der²** /ˈɔrdər/ *verb* **1** [T] **order sb (to do sth)** to tell sb to do sth in a strong way which does not permit him/her to refuse, and without saying "please": *I'm not asking you to do your homework – I'm ordering you!* ○ *The police ordered the demonstrators to stop.* **2** [T] to ask for sth to be made, supplied or delivered: *The store didn't have the book I wanted, so I ordered it.* ○ *We ordered some new chairs for the living room.* **3** [I,T] to ask for food, drink, etc. in a restaurant, hotel, etc.: *Are you ready to order yet, ma'am?*

PHRV order sb around to keep telling sb what to do and how to do it: *Quit ordering me around! You're not my boss.*

or·der·ly¹ /ˈɔrdərli/ *adj.* **1** well-arranged; well-organized; neat and clean: *an orderly office*

i	ɪ	ɛ	æ	ɑ	ɔ	ʌ	ʊ	u
see	sit	ten	cat	hot	saw	cup	put	too

2 well-behaved; peaceful: *The teacher told the class to form an orderly line.*

or·der·ly² /'ɔrdərli/ *noun* [C] (*pl.* **or·der·lies**) a hospital assistant who has not had special training

or·di·nal /'ɔrdənl/ (*also* **ordinal 'number**) *noun* [C] a number that shows the order or position in a series: *"First," "second," and "third" are ordinals.* ☞ Look at **cardinal¹**(4).

or·di·nar·i·ly /ˌɔrdn·'ɛrəli/ *adv.* usually; generally: *I don't ordinarily work as late as this.*

☆ **or·di·nar·y** /'ɔrdn·ˌɛri/ *adj.* normal; not special or unusual or different from others: *It's interesting to see how ordinary people live in other countries.* ◦ *For my next magic trick, I'll need an ordinary handkerchief.*

IDM **out of the ordinary** unusual; different from normal

ore /ɔr/ *noun* [C,U] rock or earth from which metal can be obtained: *iron ore*

☆ **or·gan** /'ɔrgən/ *noun* [C] **1** a part of the body that has a particular function: *vital organs* (= those such as the heart which help to keep you alive) ◦ *sexual organs* **2** a large musical instrument of the piano family which you play with your hands and feet. Many organs have pipes through which air is forced in order to make sounds, and they are often found in churches: *a church organ* ◦ *a pipe organ* ◦ *organ music* ☞ Note that you play **the** organ: *When did you learn to play the organ?*

or·gan·ic /ɔr'gænɪk/ *adj.* **1** produced by or existing in living things: *You need to add a lot of organic matter to the soil.* ☞ The opposite is **inorganic.** **2** (used about food or agricultural methods) produced by or using natural materials, not chemicals: *organic vegetables* ◦ *organic farming* **3** connected with substances which contain carbon: *organic chemistry* —**or·gan·i·cal·ly** /-kli/ *adv.*: *organically grown vegetables*

or·gan·ism /'ɔrgənɪzəm/ *noun* [C] an animal or plant, especially one that is so small that you can only see it with a special instrument (**microscope**)

or·gan·ist /'ɔrgənɪst/ *noun* [C] a person who plays the organ

☆ **or·gan·i·za·tion** /ˌɔrgənə'zeɪʃn/ *noun* **1** [C] an organized group of people who do sth together: *She works for a volunteer organization helping homeless people.* **2** [U] the activity of organizing or arranging: *An enormous amount of organization went into the festival.* **3** [U] the way in which sth is organized : *The students all complained about the poor organization of the course.* —**or·gan·i·za·tion·al** /-ʃənl/ *adj.*: *The job requires a high level of organizational ability.*

☆ **or·gan·ize** /'ɔrgənaɪz/ *verb* **1** [T] to plan or arrange an event, an activity, etc.: *The school organizes trips to various historic sites.* **2** [I,T] to put things in order; to arrange into a

system or logical order: *Can you decide what needs to be done? I'm terrible at organizing.*

☆ **or·gan·ized** /'ɔrgənaɪzd/ *adj.* **1** planned or arranged: *My department is badly organized.* **2** having a good system; working well: *Jenny's always very organized.*

or·gan·iz·er /'ɔrgənaɪzər/ *noun* [C] a person who organizes an event, etc.: *The organizers of the concert said that it had been a great success.*

or·gasm /'ɔrgæzəm/ *noun* [C,U] the point of greatest sexual pleasure: *to have an orgasm*

or·gy /'ɔrdʒi/ *noun* [C] (*pl.* **or·gies**) **1** a wild party, involving a lot of sex and/or alcohol or drugs **2** **an orgy (of sth)** a period of doing sth in an uncontrolled way: *an orgy of violence*

o·ri·ent /'ɔriənt/ *verb* [T] **1** to put sth in the correct place or position: *A computer sensor is used to orient the spacecraft in orbit.* **2** **orient yourself** to find out where you are; to become familiar with a place: *When I came out of the airport, I couldn't orient myself at first.*

the O·ri·ent /'ɔriənt; -ɛnt/ *noun* [sing.] (*old-fashioned*) the countries of the Far East (China, Japan, etc.) ☞ Nowadays most people prefer to say **Asia** or **the Far East.**

O·ri·en·tal /ˌɔri'ɛntl/ *adj.* (*old-fashioned*) coming from or belonging to the Far East: *Oriental languages* ☞ This word is sometimes considered offensive. Nowadays most people prefer to say **Asian.**

o·ri·en·ta·tion /ˌɔriən'teɪʃn/ *noun* [U] **1** the direction in which sth is pointing: *the orientation of the radar* **2** the process of becoming familiar with sth new: *a two-week orientation course for new employees* **3** the kind of interests or aims that a person or organization has: *sexual orientation* (= whether sb is attracted to people of the opposite sex, the same sex, or both sexes) ◦ *the theme park's family orientation*

o·ri·ent·ed /'ɔriɛntəd/ *adj.* aimed or directed at a particular type of person or thing: *Our products are male-oriented.* ◦ *She's very career-oriented.*

☆ **or·i·gin** /'ɔrədʒɪn; 'ɑr-/ *noun* [C,U] **1** the time when or place where sth first comes into existence; the reason why sth starts: *Could you explain to me the origins of this tradition to me?* ◦ *Many English words are of Latin origin.* **2** the family, race, class, etc. that a person comes from: *people of African origin* ◦ *middle-class origins*

☆ **o·rig·i·nal¹** /ə'rɪdʒənl/ *adj.* **1** first; earliest (before changes or developments): *The original meaning of this word is different from the meaning it has nowadays.* **2** new and interesting; different from others of its type: *There are no original ideas in his work.* **3** made or created first, before copies: *"Is that an original painting?" "No, it's a copy."*

ə	y	w	t̬	eɪ	aɪ	ɔɪ	aʊ	oʊ
about	yes	woman	butter	say	five	boy	now	go

☆ **o·rig·i·nal**[2] /əˈrɪdʒənl/ noun [C] the first one made or created; not a copy: *Could you make a copy and give the original back to me?*

o·rig·i·nal·i·ty /əˌrɪdʒəˈnæləṭi/ noun [U] the quality of being new and interesting

☆ **o·rig·i·nal·ly** /əˈrɪdʒənəli/ adv. **1** in the beginning; in the first form (before changes or developments): *I'm originally from Ohio, but we moved to Iowa when I was very young.* **2** in a way or style that is unlike others: *She has a talent for expressing simple ideas originally.*

o·rig·i·nate /əˈrɪdʒəneɪt/ verb (formal) **1** [I] to start or be caused to start: *This game originated in the nineteenth century.* **2** [T] to start or create first: *I wonder who originated the custom of sending birthday cards.*

o·ri·ole /ˈɔrioʊl; ˈɔriəl/ noun [C] a small bird with black and yellow or orange feathers

or·na·ment /ˈɔrnəmənt/ noun [C] an object that you have because it is attractive, not because it is useful. Ornaments are used to decorate rooms, etc.: *Christmas tree ornaments*

or·na·men·tal /ˌɔrnəˈmɛntl/ adj. made or put somewhere in order to look attractive, not for any practical use

or·nate /ɔrˈneɪt/ adj. having a lot of decoration: *an ornate building*

or·ni·thol·o·gist /ˌɔrnəˈθɑlədʒɪst/ noun [C] a person whose job is to study birds

or·ni·thol·o·gy /ˌɔrnəˈθɑlədʒi/ noun [U] the study of birds

or·phan[1] /ˈɔrfən/ noun [C] a child whose parents are dead

or·phan[2] /ˈɔrfən/ verb [T] (usually passive) to cause a child to become an orphan[1]: *She was orphaned when she was three and went to live with her grandparents.*

or·phan·age /ˈɔrfənɪdʒ/ noun [C] an institution where orphans live and are taken care of

or·tho·dox /ˈɔrθədɑks/ adj. **1** generally believed, done or accepted: *orthodox opinions* ○ *orthodox methods* ☞ The opposite is **unorthodox**. **2** practicing the old, traditional beliefs, ceremonies, etc. of certain religions: *an orthodox Jew* ○ *the Greek Orthodox Church*

os·ten·ta·tious /ˌɑstɛnˈteɪʃəs/ adj. showing wealth, importance, etc. very openly in order to attract attention and impress other people —**os·ten·ta·tious·ly** adv.

os·trich /ˈɑstrɪtʃ; ˈɔ-/ noun [C] a very large African bird with a long neck and long legs, which can run very fast but which cannot fly

☆ **oth·er** /ˈʌðər/ det., pron. **1** in addition to or different from the one or ones that have already been mentioned or understood: *I didn't have any other plans that evening, so I accepted their invitation.* ○ *How many other students are there in your class?* ○ *If you're busy now, I'll come back some other time.* ○ *Some of my friends went to college, others didn't.* ○ *She doesn't care what other people think.*

☞ **Other** cannot be used after "an." Look at **another**.

2 (after *the* or a possessive with a singular noun) second of two: *I can only find one sock. Have you seen the other one?* ○ *My glasses broke, but fortunately I had my other pair with me.* **3** (after *the* or a possessive with a plural noun) the rest of a group or number of people or things: *Their youngest son still lives with them, but the other kids have left home.* ○ *I'll have to wear this shirt because all my others are dirty.*

IDM **in other words** saying sth in a different way

(on the one hand...) on the other hand (used for showing opposite points of view): *It's cheaper to travel by bus. On the other hand, flying is so much faster.*

one after another/the other ⇨ ONE[1]

other than 1 (usually after a negative) apart from; except (for): *The plane was a little bit late, but other than that the trip was fine.* **2** different(ly) from; not: *Justin is never anything other than a perfect gentleman.*

the other day, morning, week, etc. recently, not long ago: *An old friend called me the other day.*

sb/sth/someplace/somewhere or other ⇨ OR

☆ **oth·er·wise** /ˈʌðərwaɪz/ adv. **1** in all other ways; apart from that: *I'm a little tired, but otherwise I feel fine.* **2** in a different or another way: *Follow these instructions exactly unless the boss tells you otherwise.* **3** (used for stating what would happen if you do not do sth or if sth does not happen) if not: *You have to press the red button; otherwise it won't work.*

IDM **or otherwise** (indicating another possibility or a contrast to what has just been mentioned): *I have no opinion, good or otherwise, on this subject.*

ot·ter /ˈɑṭər/ noun [C] an animal with brown fur that lives in water and eats fish

☆ **ouch** /aʊtʃ/ interj. (used when reacting to a sudden feeling of pain): *Ouch! You're hurting me.* ☞ Look also at **ow**.

☆ **ought to** /ˈɔṭə; before vowels and in final position ˈɔt tu/ modal verb (negative **ought not to**; short form **oughtn't to** /ˈɔtnt tə; before vowels and in final position ˈɔtnt tu/) **1** (used for asking for and giving advice about what to do): *You ought to read this book. It's really interesting.* ○ *Do you think I ought to call her before we go?* ○ "Should I tell her what happened?" "Yes, I think you ought to." **2** (used for telling sb what his/her duty is): *You ought to visit your parents more often.* ○ *She oughtn't to make private phone calls in work time.* ○ *I ought to have helped. I'm sorry.* **3** (used for saying that you expect sth is true, or that you expect sth to happen/to have happened): *She ought to pass her test.* ○ *They ought to be here*

ər	ɪr	ɛr	ɑr	ɔr	ʊr	ʒ	h	ŋ
bird	near	hair	car	north	tour	vision	hat	sing

by now. They left at six. ○ I bought six loaves of bread. That ought to have been enough.

☞ We usually use **should** instead of **ought to** in questions. Many people leave out **to** after **oughtn't**: *You oughtn't do that.* However, some people consider this use incorrect.

☆ **ounce** /aʊns/ *noun* **1** [C] (*abbr.* **oz.**) a measure of weight; 28.35 grams. There are 16 ounces in a pound: *Our daughter weighed seven pounds, four ounces when she was born.* **2** [C] = FLUID OUNCE: *a 12-ounce can of pop* **3** [sing.] **an ounce of sth** a very small amount of sth: *He doesn't have an ounce of imagination.*

☆ **our** /ɑr; ˈaʊər/ *det.* belonging to or connected with us: *Our house is on the corner.* ○ *Our teacher is excellent.* ○ *This is our first visit to Britain.*

☆ **ours** /ɑrz; ˈaʊərz/ *pron.* the one or ones belonging to, connected with or done by us: *Your stereo system is exactly the same as ours.* ○ *Their new car is nice, but I like ours better.* ○ *That clock was a gift from a friend of ours.*

☆ **our·selves** /ɑrˈsɛlvz; aʊərˈsɛlvz/ *pron.* **1** (used as the object of a verb or preposition when "we" do an action and are also affected by it): *We should be angry with ourselves for making such a stupid mistake.* ○ *They asked us to wait, so we sat down and made ourselves comfortable.* **2** (used for emphasis): *We don't have any kids ourselves, but many of our friends do.* ○ *Do you think we should paint the house ourselves?* (= or should we ask sb else to do it for us?)

IDM **(all) by ourselves 1** without help from anyone else: *We managed to move the piano by ourselves.* **2** not with anyone else; alone: *Now that we're by ourselves, can I ask you a personal question?* ☞ Look at the note at **alone**.

☆ **out¹** /aʊt/ *adj., adv.* ☞ For special uses with many verbs, e.g. **try sb/sth out**, look at the verb entries. **1** (used for showing movement away from a place): *He opened the case and took a gun out.* ○ *I threw out that old shirt of yours.* ○ *He opened the window and put his head out.* **2** not at home or in your place of work: *I was out when she called.* ○ *We usually eat out on Saturdays.* ○ *They took me out for dinner when I was in New Orleans.* **3** outside a house, building, etc.: *You should be out in the fresh air.* **4** (used for showing that sth is no longer hidden): *Oh look! The sun's out.* **5** not in fashion: *Short skirts are completely out.* **6** (used about electric power, a light or a fire) not on; not burning: *The lights are out. They must be in bed.* **7** not possible or acceptable: *I'm afraid Friday is out. I have a meeting that day.* **8** in a loud voice; clearly: *She cried out in pain.* **9** (used about the tide) away from the shore: *Don't swim when the tide is going out.* **10** (in sports, especially baseball) no longer allowed to play in a game or a part of a game: *Strike three – you're out!*

IDM **be out for sth; be out to do sth** to try hard to get or do sth

out-and-out complete: *It was out-and-out war between us.*

ˌout ˈloud in a normal speaking voice that other people can hear, not silently

☆ **out²** /aʊt/ **out of** /ˈaʊtəv/ *prep.* **1** (used with verbs expressing movement away from the inside of sth): *She took her wallet out of her purse.* ○ *to get out of bed* **2** away from, or no longer in, a place or situation: *He's out of the country on business.* ○ *The doctors say she's out of danger.* **3** at a distance from a place: *We live a long way out of Boise.* **4** (used for saying what you use to make sth): *You could make a table out of this wood.* **5** from among a number: *Nine out of ten people prefer this model.* **6** (used for saying that you no longer have sth): *We're out of milk.* ○ *I'm out of breath.* ○ *out of work* **7** (used for saying which feeling causes you to do sth): *I only helped them out of pity.* **8** from: *I copied the recipe out of a book.* ○ *I'd rather drink coffee out of a cup, not a mug.*

IDM **be/feel out of it** (*informal*) to be/feel unable to think clearly because you are tired, not feeling well, etc.: *I felt really out of it at the meeting and decided to go home early.*

out of order (used about a machine, etc.) not working correctly or not working at all

out·age /ˈaʊtɪdʒ/ *noun* [C] a period of time when sth (especially electricity) is cut off temporarily: *widespread power outages due to a severe storm*

out·back /ˈaʊtbæk/ *noun* [sing.] the part of a country (especially Australia) which is a long way from where most people live

out·board mo·tor /ˌaʊtbɔrd ˈmoʊtər/ *noun* [C] an engine that can be attached to a boat

out·break /ˈaʊtbreɪk/ *noun* [C] the sudden beginning or appearance of sth bad (especially disease or violence): *an outbreak of cholera* ○ *outbreaks of fighting*

out·burst /ˈaʊtbərst/ *noun* [C] a sudden expression of a strong feeling, especially anger: *an angry outburst*

out·cast /ˈaʊtkæst/ *noun* [C] a person who is no longer accepted by society or by a group of people: *a social outcast*

☆ **out·come** /ˈaʊtkʌm/ *noun* [C, usually sing.] how an event, an action or a situation ends; the result of sth: *We will inform you of the outcome of the interview within a week.*

out·cry /ˈaʊtkraɪ/ *noun* [C, usually sing.] (*pl.* **out·cries**) a strong protest by a large number of people because they disagree with sth: *The public outcry forced the government to change its mind.*

out·dat·ed /ˌaʊtˈdeɪtəd/ *adj.* not useful or common anymore; old-fashioned: *A lot of the computer equipment is getting outdated.*

out·do /ˌaʊtˈdu/ *verb* [T] (*pres. part.* **out·do·ing**; *3rd pers. sing. pres.* **out·does** /-ˈdʌz/; *p.t.*

O

out·did /-'dɪd/; *p.p.* **out·done** /-'dʌn/) to do sth better than another person; to be more successful than sb else: *He doesn't want to be outdone by his brother.*

☆ **out·door** /'aʊtdɔr/ *adj.* (only *before* a noun) happening, done or used in the open air (not in a building): *an outdoor concert* ○ *outdoor furniture* ☞ The opposite is **indoor**.

☆ **out·doors** /ˌaʊt'dɔrz/ *adv.* in the open air; outside a building: *It's such a nice evening – why don't we sit outdoors?* ☞ The opposite is **indoors**.

☆ **out·er** /'aʊtər/ *adj.* **1** on the outside: *the outer layer of skin* **2** far from the inside or the center: *the outer suburbs of a city* ☞ The opposite is **inner**.

out·er·most /'aʊtərmoʊst/ *adj.* farthest from the inside or center; most distant: *the outermost planet in the solar system* ☞ The opposite is **innermost**.

,outer 'space *noun* [U] = SPACE¹(2)

out·fit /'aʊtfɪt/ *noun* [C] **1** a set of clothes that are worn together **2** (*informal*) an organization, a company, etc.: *He works for a computer outfit I've never heard of.*

out·go·ing *adj.* **1** /ˌaʊt'goʊɪŋ/ friendly and interested in other people and new experiences **2** /'aʊtgoʊɪŋ/ (only *before* a noun) leaving a job or a place: *The outgoing mayor gave a short speech.* ○ *Put all the outgoing mail in a pile there.* ☞ The opposite is **incoming**.

out·grow /ˌaʊt'groʊ/ *verb* [T] (*p.t.* **out·grew** /-'gru/; *p.p.* **out·grown** /-'groʊn/) to become too old or too big for sth (especially clothes): *Kids outgrow their shoes so quickly.*

out·house /'aʊthaʊs/ *noun* [C] (*pl.* **out·houses** /'aʊthaʊzɪz/) (especially in former times) a very small building, separate from a house, with a type of toilet inside

out·ing /'aʊtɪŋ/ *noun* [C] a short trip for pleasure: *to go on an outing to the zoo*

out·land·ish /aʊt'lændɪʃ/ *adj.* very strange or unusual: *outlandish clothes*

out·last /ˌaʊt'læst/ *verb* [T] to last or live longer than sb/sth

out·law¹ /'aʊtlɔ/ *noun* [C] (especially in former times) a criminal who is living outside society and trying to avoid being captured: *The movie is about a band of outlaws in the Wild West.*

out·law² /'aʊtlɔ/ *verb* [T] to make sth illegal

out·lay /'aʊtleɪ/ *noun* [C, usually sing.] (*formal*) money that is spent, especially in order to start a business or a project

out·let /'aʊtlɛt; -lət/ *noun* [C] **1** a place in a wall where an electrical appliance can be connected to the electricity supply ☞ picture at **plug**. **2** a hole or a place through which a gas or liquid can escape: (*figurative*) *Gary found an outlet for his energy in playing football.* **3** a store or a branch of a large company: *We found some real bargains at the factory outlet*

(= a store that sells products directly from a factory at cheaper prices).

☆ **out·line¹** /'aʊtlaɪn/ *noun* [C] **1** a line that shows the shape or outside edge of sb/sth: *She could see the outline of a person through the mist.* **2** the most important facts or ideas about sth: *a brief outline of Mexican history* **3** a list or diagram that shows how sth is to be organized: *Before you start writing an essay, it's a good idea to make a brief outline.*

out·line² /'aʊtlaɪn/ *verb* [T] to give the most important facts or ideas about sth

out·live /ˌaʊt'lɪv/ *verb* [T] to live or exist longer than sb/sth: *This bridge has outlived its usefulness and should be replaced.* ☞ Look at **outlast**.

☆ **out·look** /'aʊtlʊk/ *noun* [C] **1** your attitude to or feeling about life: *an optimistic outlook on life* **2 outlook (for sth)** what will probably happen: *The outlook for the economy is not good.*

out·ly·ing /'aʊtlaɪɪŋ/ *adj.* (only *before* a noun) far from the center of a town or city

out·mod·ed /ˌaʊt'moʊdəd/ *adj.* no longer common or fashionable

out·num·ber /ˌaʊt'nʌmbər/ *verb* [T] (often passive) to be greater in number than sb/sth: *The enemy troops outnumbered us by three to one.* ○ *We were completely outnumbered.*

out·pa·tient /'aʊtpeɪʃənt/ *noun* [C] a person who goes to see a doctor for treatment but who does not stay in the hospital overnight ☞ Look at **inpatient**.

out·put /'aʊtpʊt/ *noun* [U] **1** the amount that a person or machine produces: *Output has increased in the past year.* **2** the information that is given by a computer ☞ Look at **input**.

out·rage¹ /'aʊtreɪdʒ/ *noun* **1** [C] something that is very bad or wrong and that causes you to feel great anger: *It's an outrage that they show things like that on TV.* **2** [U] great anger: *a feeling of outrage*

out·rage² /'aʊtreɪdʒ/ *verb* [T] (often passive) to make sb feel very angry or upset: *His parents were outraged when he dyed his hair green.*

out·ra·geous /aʊt'reɪdʒəs/ *adj.* **1** making you very angry: *I refuse to pay such outrageous prices.* **2** very strange or unusual; shocking —**out·ra·geous·ly** *adv.*

out·reach /'aʊtritʃ/ *noun* [U] the activity of providing help or a service to particular people in a community, usually not in regular offices, schools, health centers, etc.: *educational outreach programs for families in rural areas*

out·right¹ /aʊt'raɪt/ *adv.* **1** without hiding anything; openly: *She told them outright what she thought about it.* **2** immediately or completely: *to be killed outright* ○ *They were able to buy the house outright.*

out·right² /'aʊtraɪt/ *adj.* (only *before* a noun)

complete and clear, without any doubt: *an outright lie*

out·set /ˈaʊtsɛt/ *noun*

IDM **at/from the outset (of sth)** at/from the beginning (of sth): *There have been difficulties with this supplier right from the outset.*

☆ **out·side¹** /ˈaʊtsaɪd; ˌaʊtˈsaɪd/ *noun* **1** [C, usually sing.] the outer side or surface of sth: *There is a list of all the ingredients on the outside of the package.* ○ *to paint the outside of a house* **2** [sing.] **the outside** the area that is near or around a building, etc.: *We've only seen the church from the outside.*

☆ **out·side²** /ˈaʊtsaɪd/ *adj.* **1** of or on the outer side or surface of sth: *the outside walls of a building* **2** not connected with or belonging to a particular group or organization: *We can't do all the work by ourselves. We'll need outside help.* ○ *She spends so much time studying that she has no time for outside interests.* **3** (used about a chance, possibility, etc.) very small

IDM **the outside world** ⇨ WORLD

☆ **out·side³** /ˌaʊtˈsaɪd; ˈaʊtsaɪd/ *prep.* **1** in, at or to a place that is not in but close to a building, etc.: *Leave your muddy boots outside the door.* **2** (*also* **outside of**) not in: *You can do whatever you want outside of office hours.* ○ *a suburb just outside Miami* **3** **outside of** (*informal*) except; other than: *I don't know what else we can do, outside of starting all over again.*

☆ **out·side⁴** /ˌaʊtˈsaɪd/ *adv.* **1** in or to a place that is not in a room: *Please wait outside for a few minutes.* **2** in or to a place that is not in a building: *Let's eat outside. The weather is just perfect.* ○ *Go outside and see if it's raining.* ☞ Look at **outdoors** and **out of doors** (at the entry for **door**).

out·sid·er /ˌaʊtˈsaɪdər/ *noun* [C] **1** a person who is not accepted as a member of a particular group **2** a person or animal in a race or competition that is not expected to win

out·skirts /ˈaʊtskərts/ *noun* [plural] **the outskirts** the parts of a town or city that are farthest from the center

out·spo·ken /ˌaʊtˈspoʊkən/ *adj.* saying exactly what you think or feel: *Linda is very outspoken in her criticism.* —**out·spo·ken·ness** *noun* [U]

☆ **out·stand·ing** /ˌaʊtˈstændɪŋ/ *adj.* **1** very good; excellent: *Your work in this course has been outstanding.* **2** not yet paid or done: *outstanding debts*

out·stand·ing·ly /ˌaʊtˈstændɪŋli/ *adv.* very well: *Jeff played outstandingly.*

out·stretched /ˌaʊtˈstrɛtʃt/ *adj.* spread out as far as possible: *outstretched arms*

out·ward¹ /ˈaʊtwərd/ *adj.* (only *before* a noun) of or on the outside: *She showed no outward signs of emotion when she heard the bad news.*

out·ward² /ˈaʊtwərd/ (*also* **outwards** /ˈaʊtwərdz/) *adv.* toward the outside or away

from the place where you are: *This door opens outward.*

out·ward·ly /ˈaʊtwərdli/ *adv.* on the outside or surface: *He remained outwardly calm so as not to frighten the children.*

out·weigh /ˌaʊtˈweɪ/ *verb* [T] to be more important than sth: *The advantages outweigh the disadvantages.*

o·val /ˈoʊvl/ *adj., noun* [C] shaped like an egg; a shape like that of an egg: *an oval mirror* ☞ picture at **shape**.

o·va·ry /ˈoʊvəri/ *noun* [C] (*pl.* **o·va·ries**) one of the two parts of the female body that produce eggs

o·va·tion /oʊˈveɪʃn/ *noun* [C] a long period of clapping: *The dancers were given a standing ovation* (= people stood up and clapped).

☆ **ov·en** /ˈʌvən/ *noun* [C] a piece of equipment with a door that you use to cook food: *Bake in a 375° oven for 50 minutes.* ○ *a microwave oven* ☞ picture at **stove**. Note that you **roast** or **bake** food in an oven.

over/above

a painting **above/over** a bookcase

a dog jumping **over** a fence

a cover **over** an armchair

☆ **o·ver¹** /ˈoʊvər/ *adv., prep.* ☞ For special uses with many verbs, e.g. **get over sth**, look at the verb entries. **1** directly above sth, but not touching: *There's a painting over the bookcase.* ○ *We watched the plane fly over.* **2** on, and partly or completely covering or touching: *There's a cover over the chair.* ○ *She hung her coat over the back of the chair.* **3** down or sideways from an upright position: *He leaned over to speak to the woman next to him.* ○ *I knocked my glass over during supper.* **4** across to the other side of sth: *The dog is jumping over the fence.* ○ *a bridge over the river* **5** on or to the other side: *a town just over the border* ○ *Turn the mattress over.* **6** (used for expressing distance): *He's over in Japan right now.* ○ *Sit down over there.* **7** above or more than a number, price, etc.: *She lived in Juno for over ten years.* ○ *suitable for children ages 10 and over* **8** (used with *all*) in every part or place: *There was blood all over the place.* ○ *I can't find my glasses. I've looked all over for them.* **9** (used for saying that sth is repeated): *You'll have to start all over again* (= from the beginning). ○ *She kept saying the same thing over and over*

ə	y	w	t	eɪ	aɪ	ɔɪ	aʊ	oʊ
about	yes	woman	butter	say	five	boy	now	go

O

again. **10** about; on the subject of: *We had an argument over money.* **11** during: *What did you do over the weekend?*

IDM **left over** ⇨ LEFT[4]

over the counter ⇨ COUNTER[1]

☆ **o·ver**[2] /ˈoʊvər/ *adj.* finished: *Summer vacation will be over soon.*

IDM **over (and done) with** (*informal*) (used about a bad situation, etc.) finished: *"Are you ready to start the test?" "OK, let's get it over with."* ○ *I'm glad that's over and done with!*

over easy/medium/hard (used about eggs) fried on both sides for a short time/for a moderate length of time/for a longer time: *I'll have two eggs over easy and a cup of coffee, please.*

☆ **o·ver·all**[1] /ˈoʊvərɔl/ *adj.* (only *before* a noun) including everything: *The overall cost of the work will be about $200.*

☆ **o·ver·all**[2] /ˌoʊvərˈɔl/ *adv.* **1** speaking generally about sth: *Overall, I can say that we are pleased with your work.* **2** including everything or everybody: *Denise finished third overall in the 100-meter dash.*

overalls aprons coveralls

o·ver·alls /ˈoʊvərɔlz/ (*also* **bib overalls**) *noun* [plural] a piece of clothing, similar to jeans, but also covering your chest and with straps that go over your shoulders: *a pair of overalls*

o·ver·board /ˈoʊvərbɔrd/ *adv.* over the side of a boat or ship into the water: *Man overboard!* ○ *She fell overboard and drowned.*

IDM **go overboard (about sb/sth)** to react in a way that is extreme, often when you are too excited about sb/sth

o·ver·cast /ˈoʊvərkæst/ *adj.* (used about the sky) covered with clouds

o·ver·charge /ˌoʊvərˈtʃɑrdʒ/ *verb* [I,T] to ask sb to pay too much money: *The man in the post office overcharged me by 50¢.*

o·ver·coat /ˈoʊvərkoʊt/ *noun* [C] a long thick coat that you wear in cold weather

☆ **o·ver·come** /ˌoʊvərˈkʌm/ *verb* [T] (*p.t.* **o·ver·came** /-ˈkeɪm/; *p.p.* **o·ver·come**) **1** to control or succeed in defeating sb/sth: *She tried hard to overcome her fear of flying.* **2** (usually passive) to cause sb to become weak or sick or to lose control: *He was overcome with emotion and had to leave the room.* ○ *to be overcome by smoke*

o·ver·crowd·ed /ˌoʊvərˈkraʊdəd/ *adj.* (used about a place) with too many people: *The subway is always overcrowded during rush hour.*

o·ver·do /ˌoʊvərˈdu/ *verb* [T] (*p.t.* **o·ver·did** /-ˈdɪd/; *p.p.* **o·ver·done** /-ˈdʌn/) **1** to use or show too much of sth: *You look nice, but you overdid the makeup a little.* **2** to cook sth too long: *The meat was overdone.*

IDM **overdo it** to work, etc. too hard: *Exercise is fine, but don't overdo it.*

o·ver·dose[1] /ˈoʊvərdoʊs/ *noun* [C] an amount of a drug or medicine that is too large and so is not safe: *Jake killed himself by taking an overdose.*

o·ver·dose[2] /ˈoʊvərdoʊs/ (also *informal* **OD**) *verb* [I] **overdose (on sth)** to become very sick or die from taking too much of a drug or medicine

o·ver·drawn /ˌoʊvərˈdrɔn/ *adj.* having spent more money than you have in your bank account: *Darren is $50 overdrawn.*

o·ver·due /ˌoʊvərˈdu/ *adj.* late in arriving, happening, being paid, being returned, etc.: *I had to pay a fine because my library book was two weeks overdue.* ○ *Change is long overdue (= it should have happened before now).*

o·ver·es·ti·mate /ˌoʊvərˈɛstəmeɪt/ *verb* [T] to think that sb/sth is bigger, better, more expensive, etc. than he/she/it really is: *I overestimated how much we could paint in a day.* ☞ The opposite is **underestimate**.

overflow

"Oh, no! The bathtub's overflowing!"

o·ver·flow /ˌoʊvərˈfloʊ/ *verb* [I,T] to be so full that the contents go over the sides or beyond the limits; to go over the sides or beyond the limits of sth: *The water was left on and the bathtub overflowed.* ○ *shopping bags overflowing with clothes and gifts* ○ *After the heavy rains, the river overflowed its banks.*

o·ver·grown /ˌoʊvərˈgroʊn/ *adj.* covered with plants that have not been taken care of and that have grown too big: *The vegetable garden is neglected and overgrown with weeds.*

o·ver·haul /ˌoʊvərˈhɔl; ˈoʊvərhɔl/ *verb* [T] to look at sth carefully and change or repair it if necessary: *to overhaul an engine* —**o·ver·haul** /ˈoʊvərhɔl/ *noun* [C]: *a complete overhaul of the welfare system*

o·ver·head[1] /ˈoʊvərhɛd/ *adj.* above your head: *an overhead luggage compartment in an airplane* —**o·ver·head** /ˌoʊvərˈhɛd/ *adv.*: *A helicopter flew overhead.*

o·ver·head[2] /ˈoʊvərhɛd/ *noun* [C,U] money

that a company must spend on things like salaries, heat, light, rent, etc.

overhead pro·jec·tor *noun* [C] a piece of equipment that uses an electric light to show words, pictures, etc. in a larger size on a wall or screen

o·ver·hear /ˌoʊvərˈhɪr/ *verb* [T] (*p.t., p.p.* **o·ver·heard** /-ˈhərd/) to hear what sb is saying when he/she is speaking to sb else and not to you

o·ver·joyed /ˌoʊvərˈdʒɔɪd/ *adj.* (not before a noun) **overjoyed (at sth/to do sth)** very happy: *We were overjoyed at the news.*

o·ver·lap /ˌoʊvərˈlæp/ *verb* [I,T] (**overlapping**; **overlapped**) **1** when two things overlap, part of one covers part of the other: *Make sure that the two pieces of material overlap.* **2** to be partly the same as sth: *Our jobs overlap to some extent.* —**o·ver·lap** *noun* [C,U]: *There will be some overlap between my duties in my old job and in my new one.*

overlap

overlapping shingles

o·ver·load /ˌoʊvərˈloʊd/ *verb* [T] **1** (often passive) to put too many people or things into or onto sth: *an overloaded vehicle* ∘ (*figurative*) *to be overloaded with work* **2** to put too much electricity through sth: *If you use too many electrical appliances at one time, you could overload the circuit.*

☆ **o·ver·look** /ˌoʊvərˈlʊk/ *verb* [T] **1** to fail to see, notice or remember sth: *to overlook a spelling mistake* ∘ *The local residents felt that their opinions had been completely overlooked.* **2** to take no action about sth that sb has done wrong: *I will overlook your behavior this time, but don't let it happen again.* **3** to have a view over sth: *a hotel room overlooking the river*

o·ver·ly /ˈoʊvərli/ *adv.* (only before an adjective) too; too much; very: *I'm not overly optimistic about our chances of success.*

☆ **o·ver·night** /ˌoʊvərˈnaɪt/ *adj., adv.* **1** for or during the night: *an overnight bag* ∘ *Why don't you stay overnight?* **2** (happening) very suddenly: *an overnight success* ∘ *She became a star overnight.*

o·ver·pass /ˈoʊvərpæs/ *noun* [C] a type of bridge that carries a road over another road ☞ Look at **underpass**.

o·ver·pow·er /ˌoʊvərˈpaʊər/ *verb* [T] to be too strong for sb; to defeat sb because you are stronger than he/she is: *The police overpowered the gunman.* ∘ *The firefighter was overpowered by the heat and smoke.*

o·ver·pow·er·ing /ˌoʊvərˈpaʊərɪŋ/ *adj.* very strong: *an overpowering smell*

o·ver·rate /ˌoʊvərˈreɪt/ *verb* [T] (often passive) to have too high an opinion of sb/sth: *I think this movie is greatly overrated* (= people

think that it is better than it really is). ☞ The opposite is **underrate**.

o·ver·ride /ˌoʊvərˈraɪd/ *verb* [T] (*p.t.* **o·ver·rode** /-ˈroʊd/; *p.p.* **o·ver·rid·den** /-ˈrɪdn/) **1** (used about sb/sth with authority) to pay no attention to a person's decisions or actions: *Congress can vote to override the President's veto.* **2** to be more important than sth: *Corporate profits should not override environmental concerns.* **3** to interrupt an automatic machine, process, etc. and control it yourself: *Press this key to override the "print" command.*

o·ver·rid·ing /ˌoʊvərˈraɪdɪŋ/ *adj.* (only before a noun) more important than anything else

o·ver·rule /ˌoʊvərˈrul/ *verb* [T] (used about sb/sth with authority) to decide that another person's decisions or actions are not valid: *The judge overruled the defense attorney's objection.*

o·ver·run /ˌoʊvərˈrʌn/ *verb* (*p.t.* **o·ver·ran** /-ˈræn/; *p.p.* **o·ver·run** /-ˈrʌn/) [T] to spread all over an area in great numbers: *The city was overrun by rats.* ∘ *Army troops overran the rebel camp.*

☆ **o·ver·seas¹** /ˌoʊvərˈsiz/ *adj.* (only before a noun) in, to or from another country (especially one that you have to cross the ocean to get to): *We have lost some important clients to our overseas competitors.*

o·ver·seas² /ˌoʊvərˈsiz/ *adv.* in or to another country (especially one that you have to cross the ocean to get to): *It's cheaper to produce these goods overseas.* ∘ *People overseas will be able to vote in the election.*

o·ver·see /ˌoʊvərˈsi/ *verb* [T] (*p.t.* **o·ver·saw** /-ˈsɔ/; *p.p.* **o·ver·seen** /-ˈsin/) to watch sth to make sure that it is done correctly

o·ver·shad·ow /ˌoʊvərˈʃædoʊ/ *verb* [T] **1** to cause sth to be less happy: *The holiday celebrations were overshadowed by her illness.* **2** to cause sb/sth to seem less important or successful: *Doug always seemed to be overshadowed by his sister.*

☆ **o·ver·sight** /ˈoʊvərsaɪt/ *noun* [C,U] something that you do not notice or do (that you should have noticed or done): *Through an oversight Leroy's name did not appear on the list.*

o·ver·sim·pli·fy /ˌoʊvərˈsɪmpləfaɪ/ *verb* [I,T] (*pres. part.* **o·ver·sim·pli·fy·ing**; *3rd pers. sing. pres.* **o·ver·sim·pli·fies**; *p.t., p.p.* **o·ver·sim·pli·fied**) to explain sth in such a simple way that its real meaning is lost

o·ver·sized /ˈoʊvərsaɪzd/ *adj.* (often used about clothes) larger than usual

o·ver·sleep /ˌoʊvərˈslip/ *verb* [I] (*p.t., p.p.* **o·ver·slept** /-ˈslɛpt/) to sleep longer than you should have

o·ver·take /ˌoʊvərˈteɪk/ *verb* (*p.t.* **o·ver·took** /-ˈtʊk/; *p.p.* **o·ver·tak·en** /-ˈteɪkən/) [T] to increase or develop and become bigger, better, etc. than sb/sth else: *Our company has now overtaken all its competitors.*

O

o·ver·throw /ˌouvər'θrou/ *verb* [T] (*p.t.* **o·ver·threw** /-'θru/; *p.p.* **o·ver·thrown** /-'θroun/) to remove a leader or government from power, by using force: *The dictator was overthrown in a military coup.* —**o·ver·throw** /'ouvərθrou/ *noun* [sing.]: *the overthrow of the French monarchy in 1789*

☆ **o·ver·time** /'ouvərtaɪm/ *noun* [U] **1** time that you spend at work after your usual working hours: *Betty did ten hours of overtime last week.* ○ *Do you get paid extra for overtime?* **2** (*sports*) an extra period of play at the end of a football, basketball, etc. game when the scores are equal at the end of the normal period: *The game went into overtime.* —**o·ver·time** *adv.*: *I have been working overtime for weeks.*

o·ver·tone /'ouvərtoun/ *noun* [C, usually pl.] something that is suggested but not expressed openly: *It's a funny play, but it has serious overtones.*

o·ver·ture /'ouvərtʃər; -tʃʊr/ *noun* **1** [C, usually pl.] (*formal*) an act of being friendly toward sb (perhaps because you want sth): *The government's peace overtures to the rebels were rejected.* **2** [C] a piece of music that is the introduction to an opera, a ballet, etc.

o·ver·turn /ˌouvər'tərn/ *verb* [I,T] to turn over so that the top is at the bottom: *The car overturned, but the driver escaped unhurt.* ○ (*figurative*) *to overturn a decision* (= to change it)

o·ver·weight /ˌouvər'weɪt/ *adj.* too heavy or fat: *You're a little overweight. Maybe you should go on a diet.* ☞ Look at the note at **fat**.

o·ver·whelm /ˌouvər'wɛlm/ *verb* [T] (usually passive) **1** to cause sb to feel a very strong emotion: *The new world champion was overwhelmed by all the publicity.* **2** to defeat sb/sth because you have more people

o·ver·whelm·ing /ˌouvər'wɛlmɪŋ/ *adj.* very great or strong: *Anna had an overwhelming desire to return home.* —**o·ver·whelm·ing·ly** *adv.*: *The city council voted overwhelmingly against the plan.*

o·ver·work /ˌouvər'wərk/ *verb* [I,T] to work too hard or to make sb work too hard: *They are overworked and underpaid.* —**o·ver·work** /ˌouvər'wərk/ *noun* [U]

ow /au/ *interj.* (used when reacting to a sudden feeling of pain): *Ow! That hurts!* ☞ Look also at **ouch**.

☆ **owe** /ou/ *verb* [T] **1 owe sth (to sb) (for sth); owe sb for sth** to have to pay money to sb for sth that they have done or given: *We owe the bank $5,000.* ○ *We owe $5,000 to the bank.* ○ *I still owe you for that coffee you bought me yesterday.* ○ (*figurative*) *Claudia owes me an explanation.* **2** to feel grateful to sb for sth: *I owe you a lot for all you did for me when I was young.* **3 owe sth (to sb/sth)** to have sth (for the reason given): *I owe my life to the firefighters who rescued me.*

IDM owe it to yourself/sb (to do sth) to feel that you should do sth for yourself/sb because it is your duty or because you want to: *We owe it to our children to protect the environment.* ○ *Let's eat out tonight – we owe it to ourselves after a week of hard work!*

¹**owing to** /'ouɪŋ tə; *strong form* 'ouɪŋ tu/ *prep.* because of: *The game was canceled owing to the severe weather.*

owl /aul/ *noun* [C] a bird that flies at night and that catches and eats small animals. Owls are used as a symbol of wisdom.

owl

☆ **own¹** /oun/ *det., pron.* **1** (used to emphasize that sth belongs to a particular person): *I saw him do it with my own eyes.* ○ *Use your own pen. I need mine.* ○ *This is his own house.* ○ *This house is his own.* ○ *Rachel would like her own room* (= she doesn't want to share one).

☞ **Own** cannot be used after "an" or "the." You CANNOT say: *I would like an own car.* Say: *I would like my own car* or *I would like a car of my own.*

2 (used to show that sth is done or made without help from another person): *The kids are old enough to get their own breakfast.* ○ *They grow all their own vegetables.*

IDM hold your own (against sb/sth) to be as strong, good, etc. as sb/sth else

of your, etc. own belonging to you and not to anyone else: *Kate has always wanted a pony of her own.*

(all) on your, etc. own 1 alone: *John lives on his own.* ☞ Look at the note at **alone**. **2** without help: *I managed to fix the car all on my own.*

☆ **own²** /oun/ *verb* [T] to have sth belonging to you; possess: *We don't own the house. We just rent it.* ○ *Who is this land owned by?*

PHRV own up (to sth) (*informal*) to tell sb that you have done sth wrong: *None of the kids owned up to breaking the window.* ☞ Look at **confess**. It is more formal.

☆ **own·er** /'ounər/ *noun* [C] a person who owns sth: *a dog owner*

own·er·ship /'ounərʃɪp/ *noun* [U] the state of owning sth

ox /ɑks/ *noun* [C] (*pl.* **ox·en** /'ɑksn/) a male cow that has been castrated. Oxen are sometimes used for pulling or carrying heavy loads. ☞ Look at **bull**.

☆ **ox·y·gen** /'ɑksɪdʒən/ *noun* [U] (*symbol* **O**) a gas that you cannot see, taste or smell. Plants and animals cannot live and fire cannot burn without oxygen.

oys·ter /'ɔɪstər/ *noun* [C] a shellfish that is eaten as food. Some oysters produce pearls. ☞ picture at **shellfish**.

i	ɪ	ɛ	æ	ɑ	ɔ	ʌ	ʊ	u
see	sit	ten	cat	hot	saw	cup	put	too

oz. *abbr.* = OUNCE: *net weight 12 oz.*
o·zone /ˈoʊzoʊn/ *noun* [U] (*symbol* O₃) a form of oxygen
ˈozone ˌlayer *noun* [sing.] the layer of ozone

high above the surface of the earth that helps to protect it from the dangerous rays of the sun: *a hole in the ozone layer*

Pp

P, p /pi/ *noun* [C] (*pl.* **P's**; **p's**) the sixteenth letter of the English alphabet: *"Pencil" begins with (a) "P."*

P *abbr.* (on a sign) parking

p *abbr.* (*also* **p.**) (*pl.* **pp.**) = PAGE¹: *See p. 94.* ∘ *pp. 63 – 96*

PA /ˌpi ˈeɪ/ *abbr.* = PUBLIC ADDRESS SYSTEM

☆ **pace¹** /peɪs/ *noun* **1** [C] the distance that you move when you take one step: *Take two paces forward and then stop.* **2** [sing.] the speed at which you do sth or at which sth happens: *Run at a steady pace and you won't get tired so quickly.* ∘ *I can't stand the pace of life in New York.*
IDM keep pace (with sb/sth) to move or do sth at the same speed as sb/sth else; to change as quickly as sth else is changing: *Incomes are not keeping pace with inflation.*
set the pace to move or do sth at the speed that others must follow

pace² /peɪs/ *verb* [I,T] to walk with slow regular steps: *Fran paced nervously up and down the room, waiting for news.*

pace·mak·er /ˈpeɪsmeɪkər/ *noun* [C] a small machine that helps to make a person's heart beat regularly or more strongly

pac·i·fi·er /ˈpæsəfaɪər/ *noun* [C] a plastic or rubber object that you put in a baby's mouth to keep him/her quiet and happy

pac·i·fism /ˈpæsəfɪzəm/ *noun* [U] the belief that all wars are wrong and that you should not fight in them

pac·i·fist /ˈpæsəfɪst/ *noun* [C] a person who believes in pacifism

pac·i·fy /ˈpæsəfaɪ/ *verb* [T] (*pres. part.* **pac·i·fy·ing**; *3rd pers. sing. pres.* **pac·i·fies**; *p.t., p.p.* **pac·i·fied**) to cause sb who is angry or upset to be calm or quiet

☆ **pack¹** /pæk/ *noun* [C] **1** a number of things that are wrapped or tied together: *The donkey had a heavy pack on its back.* ∘ *She put an ice pack on her forehead to ease the pain.* ∘ *(figurative) Everything she told me was a pack of lies.* ☞ Look at **backpack**. **2** a package or group of things that are sold together: *a pack of cigarettes* ∘ *a pack of chewing gum* ∘ *a six-pack of*

soda ☞ Look at **package¹** and **packet**. **3** a group of animals that hunt together: *a pack of wolves*

☆ **pack²** /pæk/ *verb* **1** [I,T] to put your things into a suitcase, etc. before you go away or go on a trip: *I'll pack my suitcase in the morning.* ∘ *Have you packed yet?* ∘ *Did you pack your toothbrush?* **2** [I,T] to put things into boxes, containers, etc. so that they can be stored, transported, etc.: *The moving van is already here, but I'm not finished packing!* ∘ *Be sure to pack those glasses in plenty of newspaper.* ☞ The opposite for 1 and 2 is **unpack**. **3** [T] **pack sth (with sth)** to fill sth that is going to be stored, transported, etc.: *to pack a box* ∘ *Pack the carton with tissue paper first.* **4** [T] to press sth so that it forms a hard, thick mass: *Pack the dirt firmly around the roots of the plant.* ∘ *Add one cup of packed brown sugar.* **5** [T] (often passive) to fill or crowd: *The bus was totally packed. We couldn't get a seat.* ∘ *an action-packed movie*
PHRV pack it in (*informal*) to stop doing sth: *I'm getting too old for this kind of work – it's time to pack it in.*
pack sth in; pack sth in/into sth to do a lot in a short time: *They packed an awful lot into their three days in Boston.*
pack up (*informal*) to finish working or doing sth: *There was nothing else to do, so we packed up and went home.*

☆ **pack·age¹** /ˈpækɪdʒ/ *noun* [C] **1** something, or a number of things, in a box or wrapped up in paper and sent by mail, or carried: *to send/mail a package* **2** something, or a number of things, wrapped up, or in a bag, etc., to be sold in a store: *a package of hamburger buns* ☞ Look at **pack¹** and **packet**. **3** a box, bag, etc. in which things are wrapped or packed: *Check the list of ingredients on the side of the package.* ∘ *Don't throw the package away after you open your present!* **4** a number of things that must be bought or accepted together: *a software package* ∘ *Congress voted to approve the tax reform package.* ∘ *a financial aid package*

☆ **pack·age²** /ˈpækɪdʒ/ *verb* [T] to wrap sth or put sth into a box, etc. before it is sold or sent

P

somewhere: *Products that are attractively packaged sell more quickly.*

package tour *noun* [C] a vacation that is organized by a company that arranges your transportation and hotel room, etc. for you

pack·ag·ing /ˈpækɪdʒɪŋ/ *noun* [U] all the materials that are used to wrap sth before it is sold or sent somewhere: *Cookies and crackers often have two or three layers of packaging.*

pack·et /ˈpækət/ *noun* [C] a small flat bag that is closed on all four sides, in which things are packed to be sold in a store: *a packet of instant cocoa mix* ○ *to tear open a foil packet.*

pack·ing /ˈpækɪŋ/ *noun* [U] putting things into a suitcase, box, package, etc.: *I haven't done any packing yet and we're going away this evening.* ○ *the meat packing industry*

pact /pækt/ *noun* [C] a formal agreement between two people, groups or countries

☆ **pad¹** /pæd/ *noun* [C] **1** a thick piece of soft material, used for protecting sth or giving sth a full, round shape: *Soccer players wear shin pads to protect their legs.* ○ *a jacket with shoulder pads* ○ *Press the gauze pad onto the wound to stop the bleeding.* **2** a number of pieces of paper that are fastened together at one end: *a note pad* **3** the place from which helicopters and space rockets take off: *a launch pad* **4** the soft part on the bottom of the foot of some animals, e.g. dogs, cats, etc. **5** a piece of material, like thick soft paper, that women use to absorb blood during their monthly period (3)

pad² /pæd/ *verb* (**pad·ding; pad·ded**) **1** [T] (usually passive) to fill or cover sth with soft material in order to protect it, make it larger or more comfortable, etc.: *a padded bra* ○ *Violent patients in mental hospitals are put in padded cells.* **2** [T] **pad sth (out)** to make a book, speech, etc. longer by adding things that are not necessary **3** [I] **pad along, around, etc.** to walk quickly and quietly

pad·ding /ˈpædɪŋ/ *noun* [U] material that you use to pad² sth

pad·dle¹ /ˈpædl/ *noun* [C] **1** a short pole that is wide at one or both ends and that you use for moving a small boat through water ☞ Look at **oar**. **2** a round flat piece of wood with a handle that is used for hitting the ball in table tennis **3** a flat piece of wood with a handle that is used for hitting sb's buttocks as a punishment

pad·dle² /ˈpædl/ *verb* **1** to move a small boat through water using a paddle¹(1) : *to paddle a canoe* ☞ Look at **row**. **2** [I] **paddle along, around, etc.** to swim with short quick movements of the arms and legs **3** [T] to hit sb's buttocks with a paddle¹(3) as a punishment

pad·lock¹ /ˈpædlɑk/ *noun* [C] a type of lock that is used for fastening gates, bicycles, etc. ☞ picture at **chain**.

pad·lock² /ˈpædlɑk/ *verb* [T] to fasten sth with a padlock¹

pa·gan /ˈpeɪɡən/ *adj.* having religious beliefs that do not belong to any of the main religions: *Hallowe'en is an ancient pagan festival.*

☆ **page¹** /peɪdʒ/ *noun* [C] (*abbr.* **p.**) **1** one side of a piece of paper: *The letter was three pages long.* ○ *Full details are given on page 63.* ○ *the front page of a newspaper* ○ *the sports page* **2** one piece of paper in a book, etc.: *One page had been torn from her address book.* ○ *to turn the page*

page² /peɪdʒ/ *verb* [T] to call sb's name over a loudspeaker in a place where there are a lot of people so that you can give him/her a message

pag·eant /ˈpædʒənt/ *noun* [C] **1** a competition in which girls or young women are judged according to their beauty, and sometimes also according to other qualities: *a beauty pageant* **2** a type of outdoor public entertainment at which there is a procession of people, often dressed up in historical costume

pag·eant·ry /ˈpædʒəntri/ *noun* [U] the feeling and appearance of a grand ceremony when people are dressed in colorful costumes: *The Olympic Games began in a blaze of pageantry.*

pag·er /ˈpeɪdʒər/ (*also* **beeper**) *noun* [C] a small piece of equipment that makes noises to let a person know when sb is trying to contact him/her

paid *p.t., p.p.* of PAY²

pail /peɪl/ *noun* [C] = BUCKET

☆ **pain¹** /peɪn/ *noun* **1** [C,U] the unpleasant feeling that you have when a part of your body has been hurt or when you are sick: *to be in pain* ○ *I have a terrible pain in my back.* ○ *to scream with pain* ○ *chest pains* ○ *After I took the pills the pain wore off.* ○ *The pills relieved the pain.*

☞ Look at **ache**. Notice that we usually say: *I have a headache,* etc. instead of using an expression with "pain."

2 [U] unhappiness that you feel because sth bad has happened or because sb has been unkind: *It took me years to get over the pain of my mother's death.*

IDM **a pain (in the neck)** (*informal*) a person, thing or situation that causes you to be angry or annoyed: *Having to scrape the ice off the windshield every morning is a real pain in the neck.*

be at/go to (great) pains to do sth to make a special effort to do sth: *He went to great pains to hide his true feelings.*

take great pains (with/to do sth) to take great care with sth or to make a special effort to do sth: *She always takes great pains with her writing.*

pain² /peɪn/ *verb* [T] to cause sb to feel unhappy or upset

pained /peɪnd/ *adj.* showing that you are unhappy or upset: *a pained expression*

ər	ɪr	ɛr	ɑr	ɔr	ʊr	ʒ	h	ŋ
bird	near	hair	car	north	tour	vision	hat	sing

☆ **pain·ful** /'peɪnfl/ *adj.* that causes pain: *A wasp sting can be very painful.* ○ *The breakup of their marriage was very painful for the kids.* —**pain·ful·ly** *adv.*: *Progress is still painfully slow.*

pain·kill·er /'peɪnkɪlər/ *noun* [C] a medicine that is used for reducing or removing pain

pain·less /'peɪnləs/ *adj.* that does not cause pain: *The animals' death is quick and painless.* —**pain·less·ly** *adv.*

pains·tak·ing /'peɪmzteɪkɪŋ/ *adj.* very careful: *The painstaking search of the wreckage gave us clues as to the cause of the crash.* —**pains·tak·ing·ly** *adv.*

paint

painting a wall painting a picture

☆ **paint¹** /peɪnt/ *noun* **1** [C,U] a liquid that you put onto a surface with a brush in order to give it color or to protect it: *The door will need two more coats of paint.* ○ *Wet paint!* ○ *The paint was peeling off the walls.* ○ *chemicals used in paints* **2** [C,U] colored liquid that you can use to make a picture: *red paint* ○ *oil paints* **3** **paints** [plural] a collection of tubes, blocks, etc. of paint (2) that an artist uses

☆ **paint²** /peɪnt/ *verb* [I,T] **1** to put paint¹(1) onto sth: *The bathroom needs to be painted.* ○ *Wear old clothes when you're painting.* ○ *The walls were painted pink.* **2** to make a picture of sb/sth using paints: *Vicky paints well.* ○ *to paint a self-portrait*

☆ **paint·brush** /'peɪntbrʌʃ/ *noun* [C] a brush that you use to paint ☞ picture at **brush**.

☆ **paint·er** /'peɪntər/ *noun* [C] **1** a person whose job is to paint buildings, walls, etc. **2** a person who paints pictures ☞ Look at **artist**.

☆ **paint·ing** /'peɪntɪŋ/ *noun* **1** [U] the act of painting pictures or buildings **2** [C] a picture that sb has painted: *a famous painting by Van Gogh* ☞ Look at **drawing**.

☆ **pair¹** /pɛr/ *noun* **1** [C] two things that are the same or almost the same and that are used together: *a pair of shoes* ○ *a pair of gloves* ○ *a pair of earrings* **2** [C] a thing that consists of two parts that are joined together: *a pair of scissors* ○ *a pair of glasses* ○ *two pairs of pants*

☞ In informal speech, some people also use **pair** as a plural form: *three pair of socks.* However, this is not considered correct in written English.

3 [C, with sing. or pl. verb] two people or animals that are closely connected with each other: *Tony and his wife make a wonderful*

pair. ○ *A pair of blackbirds are nesting in the apple tree.* ☞ Look at **couple**.

IDM **in pairs** two at a time: *These earrings are only sold in pairs.*

pair² /pɛr/ *verb*

PHRV **pair (sb/sth) off (with sb)** to form a pair or pairs: *Stop trying to pair me off with your brother – I'm not interested.*

pair up (with sb) to join together with another person or group

☆ **pa·ja·mas** /pə'dʒæməz/ *noun* [plural] loose pants and a loose jacket or shirt that you wear in bed: *a pair of pajamas*

☞ picture on page A27. Notice that you use **pajama** (without an "s") before another noun: *pajama pants*. Look also at the note at **pants**.

pal /pæl/ *noun* [C] (*informal*) a friend

☆ **pal·ace** /'pæləs/ *noun* [C] a large house that is or was the home of a king or queen

pal·ate /'pælət/ *noun* [C] the top part of the inside of your mouth

☆ **pale** /peɪl/ *adj.* **1** (used about a person or his/her face, etc.) having less color than usual; very light in color: *Are you OK? You look a little pale.* ○ *She has a very pale complexion.* **2** not bright or strong in color: *pale yellow*

☆ **palm¹** /pɑm/ *noun* [C]
1 the flat part of the front of your hand: *Laura held the bird in the palm of her hand.*
☞ picture on page A24. **2** (*also* **'palm tree**) a type of tree that grows in hot regions. Palms have no branches and a mass of large leaves at the top: *a date/coconut palm*

palm trees

palm² /pɑm/ *verb*

PHRV **palm sth off as sth** (*informal*) to pretend that sth is what it is not, especially in order to sell it

pal·sy /'pɔlzi/ ➪ CEREBRAL PALSY

pal·try /'pɔltri/ *adj.* very small and so not worth very much

pam·per /'pæmpər/ *verb* [T] to treat sb very or too kindly

pam·phlet /'pæmflət/ *noun* [C] a thin book with a paper cover that gives you information about sth

pans

frying pan (*also* **skillet**)
handle
cake pan
lid
wok
saucepan (*also* **pan**)

tʃ	dʒ	v	θ	ð	s	z	ʃ
chin	June	van	thin	then	so	zoo	she

P

☆ **pan** /pæn/ *noun* [C] a metal container that is used for cooking or baking

pan·cake /'pænkeɪk/ *noun* [C] a type of very thin round cake that is made by frying a mixture of flour, milk and eggs (**batter**). Pancakes are usually eaten for breakfast: *pancakes with maple syrup*

pan·da /'pændə/ *noun* [C] a large black and white animal that looks like a bear and that comes from China. Pandas are very rare nowadays.

pan·de·mo·ni·um /,pændə'moʊniəm/ *noun* [U] a state of great noise and confusion

pan·der /'pændər/ *verb*

PHR V **pander to sb/sth** to do or say what sb wants even if it is wrong or unpleasant: *The government cannot go on pandering to the rich and powerful.*

pane /peɪn/ *noun* [C] a piece of glass in a window, etc.: *a pane of glass ∘ a window pane*

☆ **pan·el** /'pænl/ *noun* [C] **1** a group of people who are chosen to discuss sth, decide sth, answer questions, etc.: *All the candidates were interviewed by a panel of four judges. ∘ a panel of experts ∘ an advisory panel* **2** a piece of wood, metal or glass that forms part of a door, wall, etc. or that is attached to it: *They smashed the glass panel in the front door.* **3** a surface that contains the equipment for controlling a car, machine, etc.: *the instrument panel ∘ a control panel*

pan·el·ist /'pænl·ɪst/ *noun* [C] a member of a panel (1)

pang /pæŋ/ *noun* [C, usually pl.] a sudden strong feeling (of pain, hunger, guilt, etc.)

pan·han·dle¹ /'pænhændl/ *noun* [C] a narrow part of a state extending from the wider part of the state: *the Oklahoma panhandle*

pan·han·dle² /'pænhændl/ *verb* [I] (*informal*) to beg for money from strangers on the street —**pan·han·dler** *noun* [C]

☆ **pan·ic¹** /'pænɪk/ *noun* [C,U] a sudden feeling of fear that makes you do things without thinking carefully about them: *The rumors of war spread panic on the stock market. ∘ to be in a state of panic ∘ There was a terrible panic when the alarm went off.*

☆ **pan·ic²** /'pænɪk/ *verb* [I] (**pan·ick·ing**; **pan·icked**) to have a sudden feeling of fear that makes you act without thinking carefully: *Stay calm and don't panic.*

'panic-,stricken *adj.* very frightened

pan·o·ram·a /,pænə'ræmə; -'rɑmə/ *noun* [C] a view over a wide area of land —**pan·o·ram·ic** /,pænə'ræmɪk/ *adj.*: *a panoramic view from the top of the hill*

pant /pænt/ *verb* [I] to take short quick breaths, e.g. after running or because the weather is very hot ☞ Look also at the note at **pants**.

pan·ther /'pænθər/ *noun* [C] a large wild cat (usually black)

pant·ies /'pæntiz/ *noun* [plural] a small piece of clothing that women and girls wear under their other clothes (from their waists to the top of their legs) ☞ picture on page A26. Look also at **underpants**.

pan·to·mime /'pæntəmaɪm/ *noun* [C,U] = MIME¹(1)

pan·try /'pæntri/ *noun* [C] (*pl.* **pan·tries**) a small room where food is kept

☆ **pants** /pænts/ *noun* [plural] (also *formal* **trousers**) a piece of clothing that covers both legs and reaches from your waist to your ankles

☞ picture on page A27. Note that, because **pants** is a plural word, we cannot say, for example, "a new pants." The following are possible: *I need some new pants. ∘ I need a new pair of pants.* Before another noun, the form **pant** is usually used: *a pant leg.*

pant·y·hose /'pæntihoʊz/ (*also* **nylons**) *noun* [plural] a piece of thin clothing worn by women, that fits tightly from the waist over the legs and feet: *a pair of pantyhose* ☞ picture on page A26. Look also at **tights**.

☆ **pa·per** /'peɪpər/ *noun* **1** [U] a material that consists of thin sheets that you use to wrap things in, write or draw on, etc.: *a blank piece/ sheet of paper ∘ Waste paper can be recycled. ∘ a brown paper bag ∘ a paper napkin ∘ paper money* (= money that is made of paper, i.e. not coins)

☞ Types of paper include **tissue, toilet, typing, wrapping** and **writing** paper.

2 [C] = NEWSPAPER: *Where's today's paper? ∘ a daily paper ∘ I read it in the local paper.* **3 papers** [plural] pieces of paper that have information written on them. Papers are usually important: *If you don't have all your papers with you, you won't be allowed to cross the border. ∘ The file you want is somewhere in the pile of papers on her desk.* **4** [C] a piece of writing on a particular subject: *We have to write a ten-page paper for history.*

IDM **on paper 1** in writing: *I won't make any commitment until I see something on paper.* **2** from what appearances show; in theory: *The project sounds fine on paper, but would it work in practice?*

☆ **pa·per·back** /'peɪpərbæk/ *noun* [C,U] a book that has a paper cover: *The novel is available in paperback. ∘ a cheap paperback*

pa·per·boy /'peɪpərbɔɪ/ (*feminine* **pa·per·girl**) *noun* [C] a boy or girl who delivers newspapers to people's houses

'paper clip *noun* [C] a piece of wire or plastic that is used for holding pieces of paper together

paper clip

☆ **pa·per·work** /'peɪpərwərk/ *noun* [U] the written work that you do in an office, including writing letters and reports, filling out forms, etc.

i	ɪ	ɛ	æ	ɑ	ɔ	ʌ	ʊ	u
see	sit	ten	cat	hot	saw	cup	put	too

pa·pri·ka /pæˈprikə; pə-/ *noun* [U] red powder that is made from a type of sweet pepper¹(2) and is used to flavor and sometimes also to decorate food

Pap smear /ˈpæp smɪr/ *noun* [C] a medical test in which a few cells are removed from inside a woman's sexual organs in order to examine them for signs of disease

par /pɑr/ *noun*

IDM **below par** (*informal*) not as good or as well as usual

on a par with sb/sth of an equal level, standard, etc. to sb/sth else

par·a·ble /ˈpærəbl/ *noun* [C] a short story (especially in the Bible) that teaches a lesson

par·a·chute /ˈpærəʃut/ *noun* [C] a large piece of strong cloth that is folded and fastened with thin ropes to a person's body. A parachute lets the person fall to the ground slowly when he/she jumps from an airplane: *a parachute jump* —**par·a·chute** *verb* [I]

parachute

pa·rade /pəˈreɪd/ *noun* [C] an occasion when people, bands, vehicles, etc. go down the street so that people can watch them: *our town's Fourth of July parade* ○ *to march in a parade*

par·a·dise /ˈpærədaɪs/ *noun* **1 Paradise** [sing.] (without *a* or *the*) the place where some people think good people go after they die; heaven **2** [C] a perfect place: *This beach is a paradise for surfers.*

par·a·dox /ˈpærədɑks/ *noun* [C] **1** a statement that seems to be impossible but that is or may be true: *"A deafening silence" is a paradox.* **2** a situation that has two or more qualities that you would not expect to find together: *It's a paradox that some countries produce too much food while in other countries people are starving.* —**par·a·dox·i·cal** /ˌpærəˈdɑksɪkl/ *adj.*

par·af·fin /ˈpærəfɪn/ *noun* [U] a type of white wax that is used for making candles

☆ **par·a·graph** /ˈpærəgræf/ *noun* [C] a part of a piece of writing that consists of one or more sentences. A paragraph always starts on a new line.

par·a·keet /ˈpærəkit/ *noun* [C] a small, brightly-colored bird that people often keep as a pet in a cage

par·al·lel¹ /ˈpærəlɛl/ *adj., adv.* **1** (used about two lines, etc.) with the same distance between them for all their length: *parallel lines* ○ *The train tracks run parallel to the road.* **2** similar: *The two brothers followed parallel careers in different companies.*

parallel

parallel lines

par·al·lel² /ˈpærəlɛl/ *noun* **1** [C] (*also* **parallel**

line) a line, etc. that is parallel to another **2** [C,U] a person, thing or situation that is similar to sb/sth else: *Japan's economic success is without parallel in the postwar period.* **3** [C] an act of comparing sb/sth with sb/sth else: *He drew a parallel between George Washington and Simon Bolivar.*

pa·ral·y·sis /pəˈræləsəs/ *noun* **1** [U] the state of being unable to move your body or a part of it **2** [C,U] being unable to work in a normal way: *There has been a complete paralysis of the subway system.*

par·a·lyze /ˈpærəlaɪz/ *verb* [T] **1** to make a person unable to move his/her body or a part of it: *Mary Ann is paralyzed from the waist down.* **2** to make sb/sth unable to work in a normal way: *The automobile plant was completely paralyzed by the strike.*

par·a·med·ic /ˌpærəˈmɛdɪk/ *noun* [C] a person who has had special training in caring for sick or injured people, but who is not a doctor or nurse

par·a·mil·i·tar·y /ˌpærəˈmɪləˌtɛri/ *adj.* organized in the same way as, but not belonging to, an official army

par·a·mount /ˈpærəmaʊnt/ *adj.* (*formal*) most important

par·a·noi·a /ˌpærəˈnɔɪə/ *noun* [U] a type of mental illness in which sb wrongly believes that other people are trying to hurt him/her

par·a·noid /ˈpærənɔɪd/ *adj.* wrongly believing that other people are trying to hurt you

par·a·pher·na·lia /ˌpærəfəˈneɪliə; -fər-/ *noun* [U] a large number of different objects that you need for a particular purpose

par·a·phrase /ˈpærəfreɪz/ *verb* [T] to express sth again using different words so that it is easier to understand —**par·a·phrase** *noun* [C]

par·a·site /ˈpærəsaɪt/ *noun* [C] a plant or an animal that lives in or on another plant or animal and gets its food from it

par·a·troop·er /ˈpærətrupər/ *noun* [C] a soldier who is trained to drop from an airplane by parachute

par·cel /ˈpɑrsl/ *noun* [C] **1** a piece of land: *a 20-acre parcel of land* **2** = PACKAGE¹(1)

parcel post *noun* [U] one of the post office's systems for sending packages in the U.S. It is cheaper and slower than first-class mail.

parched /pɑrtʃt/ *adj.* very hot, dry or thirsty: *Can I have a drink? I'm parched!* ○ *parched fields during a drought*

☆ **par·don¹** /ˈpɑrdn/ *noun* [C,U] an act of forgiving sb. If a prisoner receives a pardon, he/she is released from prison. ☞ **I beg your pardon** is a formal way of saying "sorry": *Oh, I beg your pardon. I had no idea this was your seat.* It can also be used when you want to ask somebody to repeat what they said because you did not understand.

par·don² /ˈpɑrdn/ *verb* [T] **pardon sb (for**

tʃ	dʒ	v	θ	ð	s	z	ʃ
chin	June	van	thin	then	so	zoo	she

P

sth/for doing sth) to forgive sb or to say that sb will not be punished

par·don³ /ˈpɑrdn/ (*also* ˌpardon ˈme) *interj.* (a very polite way of asking sb to repeat what he/she has just said because you did not hear or understand it, or of saying that you are sorry for sth that you have done) ☞ Look at **excuse me** and **sorry**.

par·don·a·ble /ˈpɑrdn·əbl/ *adj.* (*formal*) that can be forgiven or excused

☆ **par·ent** /ˈpɛrənt/ *noun* [C] a mother or father: *Most parents try to bring up their kids to be good citizens.*

☞ A **single parent** is a mother or father who is bringing up his/her child or children alone, without the other parent. A **foster parent** is a person who takes care of a child who is not legally his/her own.

pa·ren·tal /pəˈrɛntl/ *adj.* (only *before* a noun) of a parent or parents: *parental support*

☆ **pa·ren·the·ses** /pəˈrɛnθəsiz/ *noun* [plural] a pair of marks, (), that you put around extra information in a piece of writing or around part of a math problem: *Add the numbers in parentheses first.* ☞ Look at **bracket**.

par·ent·hood /ˈpɛrənthʊd/ *noun* [U] the state of being a parent: *the joys and sorrows of parenthood*

par·ish /ˈpærɪʃ/ *noun* [C] **1** an area or district which has its own church and priest **2** (in Louisiana) a county

☆ **park¹** /pɑrk/ *noun* **1** [C] a piece of beautiful land with grass and trees, where anybody can go to walk, play, etc.: *a walk in the park* ○ *a park ranger* ○ *Central Park* ☞ Look also at **national park.** **2** [C] (in compounds) a large area of land that is open to the public and is used for special purposes: *an amusement park* ○ *a business park* ○ *an industrial park* **3** [C] a field or stadium where people play baseball **4** [U] the position of the gears of a car, etc. with automatic transmission in which the engine is not sending power to the wheels and the brakes are on, so that the car cannot move: *Put the car in park before you turn off the ignition.* ☞ Look at **drive²**(4), **neutral²** and **reverse²**(2).

☆ **park²** /pɑrk/ *verb* [I,T] to stop and leave a car, truck, etc. somewhere for a time: *You can't park in front of the exit.* ○ *Somebody parked their car in front of my driveway.*

par·ka /ˈpɑrkə/ *noun* [C] a warm jacket or coat with a hood that has fur around its edge

☆ **park·ing** /ˈpɑrkɪŋ/ *noun* [U] **1** leaving a car, truck, etc. somewhere for a time: *The sign said, "No Parking."* **2** an area where you can leave a car, truck, etc. for a time: *There is parking for employees behind the office buildings.* ○ *These parking spaces are reserved for customers.*

ˈparking gaˌrage *noun* [C] a building, usually with more than one level, where people can park their cars, trucks, etc.

☆ ˈparking lot *noun* [C] an area for parking cars

ˈparking ˌmeter *noun* [C] a metal post that you put coins into to pay for parking a car in the space beside it

ˈparking ˌticket *noun* [C] a piece of paper that orders you to pay money (**a fine**) for parking your car where it is not allowed

park·way /ˈpɑrkweɪ/ *noun* [C] **1** a wide street in a town or city with trees along the sides and often with an area of grass in the middle **2 Parkway** [sing.] (*abbr.* **Pkwy.**) (used in the names of some streets): *1200 Bay State Parkway*

par·lia·ment /ˈpɑrləmənt/ *noun* [C] the group of people who discuss and make the laws in some countries: *The German parliament is called the "Bundestag."* ○ *When we were in London, we saw the Houses of Parliament* (= the buildings where the British parliament meets).

par·lia·men·ta·ry /ˌpɑrləˈmɛntəri/ *adj.* (only *before* a noun) connected with parliament: *parliamentary debates*

par·o·dy¹ /ˈpærədi/ *noun* [C,U] (*pl.* **par·o·dies**) (a piece of) writing, speech or music that copies a writer's or musician's style, often as a joke: *His first novel,* Snow White, *is a parody of a traditional fairy tale.*

par·o·dy² /ˈpærədi/ *verb* [T] (*pres. part.* **par·o·dy·ing**; *3rd pers. sing. pres.* **par·o·dies**; *p.t., p.p.* **par·o·died**) to make a parody of sb/sth

pa·role /pəˈroʊl/ *noun* [U] allowing a prisoner to go free before the official end of his/her time (**sentence**) in prison on condition that he/she continue to behave well: *She's hoping to get parole.* ○ *He's going to be released on parole.*

par·rot /ˈpærət/ *noun* [C] a type of tropical bird with a curved beak and usually with very bright feathers. Parrots that are kept as pets often copy what people say.

pars·ley /ˈpɑrsli/ *noun* [U] a plant (**an herb**) with small curly leaves that are used for flavoring or decorating food

☆ **part¹** /pɑrt/ *noun* **1** [C] (often without *a/an*) **part (of sth)** one of the pieces, areas, periods, divisions, etc. of sth; some, but not all: *Which part of Chile do you come from?* ○ *I enjoyed some parts of the movie.* ○ *A large part of my job involves dealing with the public.* ○ *Part of the problem is lack of information.* ○ *a part of the body* ○ *Getting up in the morning is always the hardest part of the day.* **2** [C] one of the essential pieces that make up a machine: *They couldn't find the right spare part for my car at the repair shop.* **3** [C] an amount or quantity (of a liquid or substance): *Use one part (of) juice concentrate to three parts (of) water.* **4** [C] a role or character in a play, movie, etc.: *He played the part of Macbeth.* ○ *a small part in*

the school play **5** [C,U] **part (in sth)** a person's share in an activity, event, etc.: *Did you have any part in the decision?* **6** [C] the line on your head where you divide your hair and comb it in different directions: *a center/side part* ☞ picture at **braid**
IDM the better part of sth most of sth; more than half of sth, often a period of time: *They've lived here for the better part of forty years.*
for the most part usually or mostly: *The countryside is, for the most part, flat and uninteresting.*
for my, your, etc. part as far as it concerns me, you, etc.: *I, for my part, am willing to go.*
in part not completely; to some extent: *The accident was, at least in part, the fault of the driver.*
on the part of sb/on sb's part made, done or felt by sb: *I'm sorry. It was a mistake on my part.* ○ *There is concern on the part of the teachers that class size will increase.*
play a part (in sth) to have a share in sth or to have an effect on sth
take part (in sth) to join with other people in an activity: *He was unable to take part in the race because of his recent accident.* ○ *Everybody took part in the discussion.*

☆ **part²** /pɑrt/ *adv.* not completely one thing and not completely another: *A mule is part donkey and part horse.*

part³ /pɑrt/ *verb* **1** [I,T] **part (from sb); part sb (from sb)** to leave or go away from sb; to separate people or things: *We exchanged telephone numbers when we parted.* ○ *She parted from her husband several years ago.* ○ *He hates being parted from his kids.* **2** [I,T] to divide or separate: *The curtains parted and a face looked out.* **3** [T] to separate the hair on the head with a comb so as to make a clear line: *Don't part your hair in the middle. It looks awful.*
IDM part company (with sb/sth) to go different ways or to separate after being together
PHRV part with sth to give or sell sth to sb else: *When we went to live in Japan, we had to part with our horses and dogs.*

par·tial /ˈpɑrʃl/ *adj.* **1** not complete: *The outing was only a partial success.* **2 partial to sb/sth** *(old-fashioned)* liking sth very much: *He's very partial to a glass of wine.*

par·ti·al·i·ty /ˌpɑrʃiˈæləti/ *noun* [U] acting unfairly toward one person or side: *The judge was accused of partiality toward the defendant.* ☞ Look at **impartial**.

par·tial·ly /ˈpɑrʃəli/ *adv.* partly; not completely: *The road was partially blocked by a fallen tree.*

par·tic·i·pant /pɑrˈtɪsəpənt/ *noun* [C] a person who takes part in an activity, etc.

par·tic·i·pate /pɑrˈtɪsəpeɪt/ *verb* [I] **participate (in sth)** to share or join (in an activity); to take part: *Students are encouraged to par-*

ticipate in extracurricular activities. —**par·tic·i·pa·tion** /pɑrˌtɪsəˈpeɪʃn/ *noun* [U]

par·ti·ci·ple /ˈpɑrtəsɪpl/ *noun* [C] *(grammar)* a word that is formed from a verb and that ends in *-ing* *(present participle)* or *-ed, -en,* etc. *(past participle).* Participles are used to form tenses of the verb, or as adjectives: *"Hurrying"* and *"hurried"* are the present and past participles of *"hurry."*

par·ti·cle /ˈpɑrtɪkl/ *noun* [C] **1** a very small piece; a bit: *Particles of the substance were examined under a microscope.* **2** *(grammar)* a minor word that is not as important as a noun, a verb or an adjective: *In the phrasal verb "break down," "down" is an adverbial particle.*

☆ **par·tic·u·lar** /pərˈtɪkyələr/ *adj.* **1** (only *before* a noun) (used to make it clear that you are talking about one person, thing, time, etc. and not about others): *At that particular time I was working in Washington.* ○ *One particular school, which I won't name, is having a lot of problems.* **2** (only *before* a noun) special or more than usual: *Are you going to Pittsburgh for any particular reason?* ○ *This article is of particular interest to you.* **3** connected with one person or thing and not with others: *Everybody has their own particular problems.* **4** (not before a noun) **particular (about sth)** difficult to please: *Some people are extremely particular about the food they eat.* ☞ Look at **fussy**.
IDM in particular 1 especially: *Is there anything in particular you'd like to do this weekend?* **2** (used for giving more detail about sth that you have said): *You have to be careful about what you eat. In particular, avoid anything fatty.*

☆ **par·tic·u·lar·ly** /pərˈtɪkyələrli/ *adv.* especially: *I'm particularly interested in European history.* ○ *The meal was excellent, particularly the dessert.*

par·tic·u·lars /pərˈtɪkyələrz/ *noun* [plural] *(formal)* details; facts: *The police took down all the particulars about the missing child.*

part·ing /ˈpɑrtɪŋ/ *noun* [C,U] saying goodbye to, or being separated from, another person (usually for quite a long time): *the sadness of parting*

par·ti·tion /pɑrˈtɪʃn/ *noun* **1** [C] something that divides a room, etc. into two parts, especially a thin or temporary wall in a house. **2** [U] the division of a country into two or more countries: *the partition of Germany after World War II* —**par·ti·tion** *verb* [T]

☆ **part·ly** /ˈpɑrtli/ *adv.* to some extent; not completely: *She was only partly responsible for the mistake.* ○ *I love Italy – partly because of the food, but mostly because of the people.*

☆ **part·ner** /ˈpɑrtnər/ *noun* [C] **1** a person that you are dancing with or playing a game with **2** one of the people who own a business: *a partner in a law firm* ○ *business partners* ○ *a*

P

junior/senior partner **3** the person that you are married to or have a sexual relationship with **4** a country or organization that has an agreement with another: *the United States' trading partners*

☆ **part·ner·ship** /ˈpɑrtnərʃɪp/ *noun* **1** [U] the state of being a partner or partners, especially in business: *Mary went into partnership with her sister and opened a toy store in Springfield.* **2** [C] an arrangement or a business with two or more partners: *"Does your husband own the company?" "Well, it's a partnership."*

ˌpart of ˈspeech *noun* [C] (*pl.* **parts of speech**) (*grammar*) one of the groups that words are divided into, e.g. noun, verb, adjective, etc.

☆ ˌpart-ˈtime *adj., adv.* for only a part of the working day or week: *She has a part-time job.* ○ *I work part-time, about 20 hours a week.* ☞ Look at **full-time**.

☆ **par·ty**[1] /ˈpɑrṭi/ *noun* [C] (*pl.* **par·ties**) **1** a social occasion to which people are invited in order to eat, drink and enjoy themselves: *to have a party* ○ *to go to a party* ○ *a birthday party* ○ *When they moved into the new house, they had a housewarming party.* ○ *a farewell party* ○ *a dinner party* **2** (*also* **Party**) a group of people who have the same political aims and ideas and who are trying to win elections to Congress, etc.: *the Republican Party platform* ○ *a member of the Democratic Party* ○ *the party's national convention* ○ *the party chairman*

☞ The two main political parties in the United States are the **Democrats** and the **Republicans**. The symbol of the Democratic Party is a donkey, and the symbol of the Republican Party is an elephant.

3 (often in compounds) a group of people who are working, traveling, etc. together: *A search party has set out to try and find the missing child.* ○ *a party of tourists* ○ *I'd like to reserve a table for a party of five.* **4** (*formal*) a person or group of people forming one side of a legal agreement or argument: *the guilty party* ☞ Look at **third party**.

par·ty[2] /ˈpɑrṭi/ *verb* [I] (*pres. part.* **par·ty·ing**; *3rd pers. sing. pres.* **par·ties**; *p.t., p.p.* **par·tied**) (*informal*) to have or attend a party1 : *Hey, dudes – let's party!* ○ *We partied all night long at Dave's house.*

ˈparty ˌfavor (*also* **favor**) *noun* [C] a small gift that is given to guests at a party

☆ **pass**[1] /pæs/ *noun* [C] **1** the act of kicking, hitting or throwing the ball to sb on your own team in various sports **2** an official card or piece of paper that gives you permission to enter or leave a building, travel on a bus or train, etc.: *Visitors must obtain a pass from the reception desk.* ○ *a bus pass* **3** a road or way over or through mountains: *The pass was blocked by snow.* **4** a successful result on an

examination, etc.: *There are no letter grades in this course. Students will receive a "pass" or a "fail."*

☆ **pass**[2] /pæs/ *verb* **1** [I,T] to move forward or to the other side of sb/sth; to leave sth behind or on one side as you go past: *The kids waved to the clowns as they passed in the parade* ○ *They passed a police checkpoint.* ○ *Do we pass a mailbox on the way to the store?* ○ (*figurative*) *The number of students at the school has passed 500.*

☞ The past tense of **pass** is **passed**. It sounds like **past**, which is an adjective or a preposition: *The summer months passed slowly.* ○ *The past week was very hot.* ○ *Our house is just past the church.*

2 [I,T] to go past another person, car, etc. because you are moving faster: *DO NOT PASS* (= on a sign) ○ *The car that passed us must have been going 80 miles an hour.* **3** [I] **pass along, down, etc. (sth)** to go or move in the direction mentioned: *Which towns do we pass through on the way to Boston?* ○ *You pass over a bridge, and then the restaurant is on the right.* **4** [T] **pass sth (to sb)** to pick sth up and give it to sb; to hand sth: *Could you pass (me) the salt, please?* ○ *He passed the bottle to his father.* **5** [T] **pass sth across, around, through, etc. sth** to put or move sth in the direction mentioned: *We'll have to pass the cord behind the couch.* **6** [I,T] **pass (sth) (to sb)** to kick, hit or throw the ball to sb on your own team in various sports **7** [I] (used about time) to go by: *At least a year has passed since I last saw them.* ○ *The time passed very quickly.* **8** [T] to spend time: *I'll have to think of something to do to pass the time in the hospital.* **9** [I,T] to achieve the necessary standard on an examination, test, etc.: *Good luck on the exam! I'm sure you'll pass.* **10** [T] to test sb/sth and say that they are good enough: *The professor passed most of the people in her course.* **11** [T] to officially approve a law, proposal, etc.: *One of the functions of Congress is to pass new laws.* **12** [T] **pass sth (on sb/sth)** to give an opinion, a judgment, etc.: *The judge passed sentence on the young man* (= said what his punishment would be). **13** [I] to be allowed or accepted: *I didn't like what they were saying, but I let it pass without comment.*

IDM **pass the buck (to sb)** to give the responsibility or the blame for sth to sb else

pass water (*old-fashioned, formal*) to urinate

PHRV **pass sth along/on (to sb)** to give sth (to sb else) especially after you have been given it or used it yourself: *Could you pass along the message to Eli, please?*

pass away a polite way of saying "die": *The old man passed away in his sleep.*

pass by (sb/sth) to go past: *I pass by your house on the way to work.*

pass sth down to give sth (to people who live

i	\imath	ε	æ	ɑ	ɔ	ʌ	ʊ	u
see	sit	ten	cat	hot	saw	cup	put	too

after you have died): *The family home has been passed down from one generation to the next.*
pass for sb/sth to be accepted as sb/sth, but without really being that person or thing: *You'll never pass for a real cowboy in that ridiculous hat.*
pass sb/sth off (as sb/sth) to say that a person or a thing is sth that he/she/it is not: *He managed to pass the work off as his own.*
pass out to become unconscious; to faint
pass sth up to choose not to take or make use of sth, especially an opportunity: *The offer was too good to pass up.*
pass·a·ble /ˈpæsəbl/ *adj.* **1** (not before a noun) (used about roads, rivers, etc.) possible to use or cross; not completely blocked ☞ The opposite is **impassable**. **2** good enough but not very good: *My French is not great, but it's passable.*
☆ **pas·sage** /ˈpæsɪdʒ/ *noun* **1** [C] (*also* ˈpassageway) a long, narrow way through sth, especially one in a building that leads to other rooms; a corridor: *We had to go down a dark passage to reach the bathroom.* **2** [C] a tube in your body which air, liquid, etc. can pass through: *the nasal passages* **3** [C] a short part of a book, speech or piece of music: *The students were given a passage from the novel to study in detail.* **4** [U] the movement or progress of sb/sth from one place or stage to another: *We watched the ants' slow passage across the road.* **5** [U] (used about time) the passing: *With the passage of time, these seeds will grow into beautiful flowers.*
☆ **pas·sen·ger** /ˈpæsəndʒər/ *noun* [C] a person who is traveling in a car, bus, train, plane, etc. but who is not driving it or working on it: *Passengers are asked to remain seated until the plane has come to a complete standstill.* ○ *the passenger seat of a car*
pas·ser·by /ˌpæsərˈbaɪ/ *noun* [C] (*pl.* **passers·by** /ˌpæsərzˈbaɪ/) a person who is walking past sb/sth (by chance): *None of the passersby had seen how the accident happened.*
pass·ing¹ /ˈpæsɪŋ/ *adj.* lasting for only a short time; brief: *No, I wasn't serious about going to Hawaii. It was only a passing thought.*
pass·ing² /ˈpæsɪŋ/ *noun* [U] the process of going by: *the passing of time*
IDM in passing done or said quickly, while you are thinking or talking about sth else: *He mentioned the house in passing, but he didn't give any details.*
pas·sion /ˈpæʃn/ *noun* **1** [U] very strong sexual love or attraction: *They loved each other, but there was no passion in their relationship.* **2** [C,U] (a) very strong feeling, especially of love, hate or anger: *He was a violent man, controlled by his passions.* ○ *She argued her case with passion.* **3** [sing.] **a passion for sth** a very strong liking for or interest in sth: *He has a passion for chocolate.*

pas·sion·ate /ˈpæʃn·ət/ *adj.* showing or caused by very strong, sometimes sexual feelings: *a passionate believer in democracy* ○ *a passionate speech* ○ *a passionate relationship* ○ *a passionate kiss* —**pas·sion·ate·ly** *adv.*
pas·sive /ˈpæsɪv/ *adj.* **1** showing no reaction, feeling or interest; not active: *Television encourages people to be passive.* **2** (used about the form of a verb or a sentence when the subject of the sentence is affected by the action of the verb): *In the sentence "He was bitten by a dog," the verb is passive.* ☞ You can also say: "The verb is in the passive." Look at **active**. —**pas·sive·ly** *adv.*
Pass·o·ver /ˈpæsoʊvər/ *noun* [U] the Jewish religious festival which celebrates the freeing of the Jews from being slaves in Egypt
☆ **pass·port** /ˈpæspɔrt/ *noun* [C] **1** an official document that identifies you and that you have to show when you enter or leave a country: *Do you have to show your passport at the check-in counter?* **2 a passport to sth** a thing that makes it possible to achieve sth: *a passport to success*
pass·word /ˈpæswɔrd/ *noun* [C] **1** a secret word or phrase that you need to know in order to be allowed into a place **2** a secret word that you must type in order to use a computer system: *Please enter your password.*
☆ **past¹** /pæst/ *adj.* **1** already gone; belonging to a time before the present: *in past years, centuries, etc.* ○ *I'd rather forget some of my past mistakes.* ○ *Mr. Garcia is a past president of the city council.* **2** (only *before* a noun) just finished; last: *He had to work very hard during the past year.* ○ *The past few weeks have been very difficult.* **3** (not before a noun) over; finished; no longer existing: *Suddenly his childhood was past and he was a young man.*
☆ **past²** /pæst/ *noun* **1 the past** [sing.] the time before the present; the things that happened in that time: *The story was set in the distant past.* ○ *We spent the evening talking about the past.* **2** [C] a person's life before now: *May I ask you a few questions about your past?* **3 the past** [sing.] = PAST TENSE
☆ **past³** /pæst/ *prep.* **1** from one side to the other of sb/sth; further than or on the other side of sb/sth: *He walked straight past me.* ○ *Go past the school and our house is the second on the right.* ○ *The telephone booth is just past the gas station.* **2** beyond the limits or age when you can do sth: *She was past the age when she could have children.* **3** older than: *She's past 40.* **4** (used when telling the time) after; later than: *It's ten (minutes) past three.* ○ *It's a quarter past seven.*
IDM not put it past sb (to do sth) ⇨ PUT
☆ **past⁴** /pæst/ *adv.* by; from one side of sb/sth to another: *The bus went right past without stopping.* ○ *He waved as he drove past.*
pas·ta /ˈpɑstə/ *noun* [U] a type of food made

P

from a mixture of flour, water and sometimes eggs which is cut into various shapes and cooked: *Macaroni is a type of pasta.*

paste¹ /peɪst/ *noun* **1** [C,U] a soft, wet mixture, usually made of a powder and a liquid and sometimes used for sticking things together: *wallpaper paste* ○ *Mix the flour and milk into a paste.* **2** [U] (usually in compounds) a soft mixture of food that has been cut into very small pieces to make it smooth: *tomato paste*

paste² /peɪst/ *verb* [T] to stick sth to sth else using glue or paste: *He pasted the picture into his book.*

pas·tel /pæˈstɛl/ *adj.* (used about colors) pale; not strong

pas·teur·ized /ˈpæstʃəraɪzd/ *adj.* (used about milk or milk products) free from bacteria because it has been heated

pas·time /ˈpæstaɪm/ *noun* [C] something that you enjoy doing when you are not working: *What are your favorite pastimes?* ☞ Look at **hobby**.

pas·tor /ˈpæstər/ *noun* [C] a religious leader in some Protestant churches ☞ Look at **minister** and at the note at **priest**.

pas·tor·al /ˈpæstərəl/ *adj.* **1** connected with the work of a pastor **2** (*formal*) connected with the countryside and country life: *a pastoral scene*

the ˌpast ˈperfect (*also* **the pluperfect**) *noun* [sing.] (*grammar*) the tense of a verb that describes an action that was finished before another event happened: *In the sentence "After they had finished the meal, they went for a walk," "had finished" is in the past perfect.*

☆ **pas·try** /ˈpeɪstri/ *noun* (*pl.* **pas·tries**) **1** [U] a mixture of flour, fat and water that is used for making pies, etc. and is baked in an oven **2** [C] a small cake made with pastry: *Danish pastries*

the ˌpast ˈtense (*also* **the past**; **the simple past**) *noun* [sing.] (*grammar*) a form of a verb used to describe actions in the past²(1): *The past tense of the verb "come" is "came."*

pas·ture /ˈpæstʃər/ *noun* [C,U] a field or land covered with grass, where farm animals can eat

ˌPˈA ˌsystem (also *formal* **public-address system**) *noun* [C, usually sing.] an electronic system that makes sb's voice louder or carries it into many rooms of a large building, such as an airport, a school, etc.

pat¹ /pæt/ *verb* [T] (**pat·ting**; **pat·ted**) to tap sb/sth very gently with a flat hand or with sth flat: *"Good dog," she said, patting him.*

pat² /pæt/ *noun* [C] a gentle tap with a flat hand or with sth flat: *Jerry gave his friend a pat on the shoulder to congratulate him.*

IDM a pat on the back congratulations for sth good that a person has done

pat³ /pæt/ *adj.* (only *before* a noun) too quick (used about an answer, comment, etc.)

☆ **patch¹** /pætʃ/ *noun* [C] **1** a piece of material that you use to cover a hole in clothes, etc.: *an old pair of jeans with patches on both knees* ○ *to sew a patch on* **2** a small piece of material that you wear over one eye: *an eye patch* **3 a patch (of sth)** a part of a surface that is different in some way from the area around it: *Drive carefully. There are patches of ice on the roads.* ○ *a damp patch on the ceiling* **4** a small piece of land: *a vegetable patch*

patch² /pætʃ/ *verb* [T] to put a piece of material over a hole in clothes, etc. or to repair sth by doing this: *to patch a hole in sth* ○ *to patch an old pair of pants*

PHRV patch sth up 1 to repair sth quickly or not very carefully: *The car had been patched up after an accident.* **2** to settle an argument: *It's time the boys patched up their differences and made friends.*

patch·work /ˈpætʃwərk/ *noun* **1** [U] a type of sewing in which small pieces of cloth of different colors and patterns are sewn together: *a patchwork quilt* **2** [sing.] a thing that is made of many different pieces or parts

patch·y /ˈpætʃi/ *adj.* (**patch·i·er**; **patch·i·est**) **1** not all the same or not complete: *His work is patchy* (= some, but not all, of it is good). ○ *We have only patchy* (= not complete) *information on the accident.* **2** in small quantities, not everywhere: *patchy fog*

☆ **pat·ent¹** /ˈpætnt/ *noun* [C] an official license from the government that gives one person or company the right to make or sell a certain product and prevents others from copying it: *a patent on a new invention*

pat·ent² /ˈpætnt/ *verb* [T] to obtain a patent¹ for sth

pat·ent³ /ˈpætnt/ *adj.* (*formal*) clear; obvious: *a patent lie*

ˌpatent ˈleather *noun* [U] a type of leather with a hard, shiny surface

pat·ent·ly /ˈpætntli/ *adv.* clearly: *She was patently very upset.* ○ *He was patently honest.*

pa·ter·nal /pəˈtərnl/ *adj.* (only *before* a noun) **1** of a father: *the importance of paternal interest and support* **2** related through the father's side of the family: *my paternal grandparents* ☞ Look at **maternal**.

pa·ter·ni·ty /pəˈtərnəti/ *noun* [U] the state of being a father

☆ **path** /pæθ/ *noun* [C] (*pl.* **paths** /pæðz; pæðz/) **1** a way across a piece of land that is made by or used for people walking: *a path through the woods* ○ *Stay on the path or you could get lost.* ○ *Where does this path lead to?* ○ (*figurative*) *We're on the path to victory!* ☞ **Pathway** is similar in meaning: *There was a narrow pathway leading down the cliff.* Look also at **trail**. **2** the line along which sb/sth moves: *the flight path of an airplane* ○ *The grasshoppers moved*

ər	ɪr	ɛr	ɑr	ɔr	ʊr	ʒ	h	ŋ
bird	near	hair	car	north	tour	vision	hat	sing

across the country eating everything in their path.

IDM **off the beaten path/track** ⇨ BEAT¹

pa·thet·ic /pə'θεtɪk/ *adj.* **1** causing you to feel pity or sadness: *the pathetic cries of the hungry children* **2** *(informal)* very bad, weak or useless: *What a pathetic performance! The team deserved to lose.* —**pa·thet·i·cal·ly** /-kli/ *adv.*

path·o·log·i·cal /ˌpæθə'lɑdʒɪkl/ *adj.* **1** connected with pathology **2** *(informal)* caused by feelings that you cannot control; not reasonable: *He's a pathological liar.* ○ *a pathological fear of water* —**path·o·log·i·cal·ly** /-kli/ *adv.*

pa·thol·o·gist /pə'θɑlədʒɪst/ *noun* [C] a person who is an expert in pathology, especially one who tries to find out why a person has died

pa·thol·o·gy /pə'θɑlədʒi/ *noun* [U] the scientific study of the diseases of the body

☆ **pa·tience** /'peɪʃns/ *noun* [U] **patience (with sb/sth)** the quality of being able to remain calm and not get angry, especially when there is a difficulty or you have to wait a long time: *I have no patience with people who don't even try.* ○ *to lose your patience with sb* ○ *After three hours of waiting, our patience was wearing thin.* ☛ The opposite is **impatience**.

☆ **pa·tient¹** /'peɪʃnt/ *adj.* able to remain calm and not get angry, especially when there is a difficulty or you are waiting for sth: *It's hard to be patient with a screaming child.* ○ *It won't be long now. Just sit there and be patient.* ☛ The opposite is **impatient**. —**pa·tient·ly** *adv.*: *to wait patiently*

☆ **pa·tient²** /'peɪʃnt/ *noun* [C] a person who is receiving medical treatment: *a hospital patient* ○ *a specialist who treats patients with heart problems*

pat·i·o /'pætioʊ/ *noun* [C] *(pl.* **pat·i·os** /-oʊz/*)* an area with a hard surface next to a house where people can sit, eat, etc. outdoors ☛ Look at **deck**, **porch** and **veranda**.

pa·tri·ot /'peɪtriət/ *noun* [C] a person who loves his/her country: *the patriots who fought for American independence*

pa·tri·ot·ic /ˌpeɪtri'ɑtɪk/ *adj.* having or showing a love for your country —**pa·tri·ot·i·cal·ly** /-kli/ *adv.*

pa·tri·ot·ism /'peɪtriətɪzəm/ *noun* [U] love of your country ☛ Look at **nationalism**.

☆ **pa·trol¹** /pə'troʊl/ *verb* [I,T] **(patrol·ling; pa·trolled)** to go around a town, building, etc. to make sure that there is no trouble and that nothing is wrong: *Guards patrol the grounds at regular intervals.*

☆ **pa·trol²** /pə'troʊl/ *noun* [C] **1** the act of patrolling: *The army makes hourly patrols of the area.* **2** a person or group of people that patrols sth: *a police patrol* ○ *a patrol car*
IDM **on patrol** patrolling sth

pa·trol·man /pə'troʊlmən/ *(feminine* **pa·trol·wom·an** /-wʊmən/*) noun* [C] a police officer

who goes around a particular part of a town to make sure that there is no trouble and to prevent crime

pa·tron /'peɪtrən/ *noun* [C] **1** a person who gives money to artists, musicians, etc. or who supports a good cause: *a patron of the arts* ○ *She is a patron of the Metropolitan Opera.* **2** a person who goes to a store, theater, restaurant, etc.: *This parking lot is reserved for store patrons.*

pa·tron·ize /'peɪtrənaɪz/ *verb* [T] **1** to go regularly to a store, theater, restaurant, etc. **2** to treat sb in a friendly way but as if you were better than him/her

pa·tron·iz·ing /'peɪtrənaɪzɪŋ/ *adj.* treating sb in a friendly way but as if you were better than him/her: *I really hate that patronizing smile of hers.* —**pa·tron·iz·ing·ly** *adv.*

patron 'saint *noun* [C] a saint who is believed to give help and protection to a particular place or to people doing a particular activity: *St. Patrick is the patron saint of Ireland.*

patterns

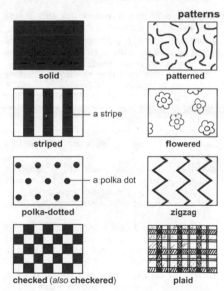

solid

patterned

a stripe

striped

flowered

a polka dot

polka-dotted

zigzag

checked *(also* checkered*)*

plaid

☆ **pat·tern** /'pæṭərn/ *noun* [C] **1** an arrangement of lines, shapes, colors, etc. Patterns are often used to decorate clothes, wallpapers, carpets, etc.: *Our new china has a flower pattern on it.* ○ *a geometrical pattern* **2** the way in which sth happens, develops, is arranged, etc.: *Her periods of mental illness all followed the same pattern.* ○ *patterns of behavior* **3** something that helps you to make sth, e.g. a piece of clothing, by showing the shape it should be: *a paper pattern*

pat·terned /'pæṭərnd/ *adj.* having a pattern(1): *patterned curtains*

tʃ	dʒ	v	θ	ð	s	z	ʃ
chin	June	van	thin	then	so	zoo	she

P

pat·ty /ˈpæti/ *noun* [C] (*pl.* **pat·ties**) food, especially meat, that has been cut into very small pieces and then formed into a round flat shape: *a hamburger patty*

☆ **pause¹** /pɔz/ *noun* [C] a short stop in sth: *He continued playing for twenty minutes without a pause.* ○ *a pause in the conversation*

☞ **Pause**, **break**, **recess** and **intermission** have similar meanings. A **pause** is a short period of time when you stop speaking or doing sth: *After a brief pause, she answered.* A **break** is especially used in connection with periods of work or study, e.g. **a lunch/coffee break** in an office, a factory or a school: *We've been working pretty hard – let's take a break.* ○ *college students spending their spring break in Florida.* A break during the school day, especially after lunch, is called **recess**. A **recess** is also a longer period of time when work in Congress or in a court of law stops: *senators returning from the Memorial Day recess.* We use **intermission** for a break in a concert or performance.

pause² /pɔz/ *verb* [I] **pause (for sth)** to stop for a short time: *to pause for breath*

pave /peɪv/ *verb* [T] (often passive) to cover an area of ground with a hard surface: *There were no paved roads through the jungle.*

IDM **pave the way (for sb/sth)** to create a situation in which sb will be able to do sth or sth will be possible: *The President's visit helped to pave the way for better relations between the two countries.*

pave·ment /ˈpeɪvmənt/ *noun* **1** [U] the hard surface of a street, sidewalk, etc. **2** [C] (*BrE*) = SIDEWALK

pa·vil·ion /pəˈvɪlyən/ *noun* [C] a building, often in a park, which has a roof but usually no walls, where people can rest or look at things: *a demonstration about making quilts in the craft pavilion*

☆ **paw¹** /pɔ/ *noun* [C] the foot of animals such as dogs, cats, bears, etc. ☞ picture at **cat**. Paws have sharp **claws** and soft **pads** underneath. Look also at **hoof**.

paw² /pɔ/ *verb* [I,T] **paw (at) sth** (used about an animal) to touch sb/sth with a paw or foot

pawn¹ /pɔn/ *noun* [C] **1** one of the eight pieces in the game of chess that are of least value and importance ☞ picture at **chess**. **2** a person who is used or controlled by another person

pawn² /pɔn/ *verb* [T] to give sth of value to a person who lends you money (**a pawn-broker**). If you cannot pay back the money after a certain period, the pawnbroker can keep or sell the thing that you gave him/her.

pawn·bro·ker /ˈpɔnbroʊkər/ *noun* [C] a person who lends money to people when they leave sth of value with him/her

☆ **pay¹** /peɪ/ *noun* [U] money that you get regularly for work that you have done: *It's a tough job, but the pay is good.* ○ *a pay increase*

☞ **Pay** is the general word for money that you get regularly for work that you have done. **Wages** are paid every week or every two weeks, based on how many hours you have worked. A **salary** is a fixed amount that is paid every week, every two weeks or every month, depending on a company's system. You pay a **fee** for professional services, e.g. to a doctor, lawyer, etc. **Payment** is money that you get for work that you do once or not regularly.

☆ **pay²** /peɪ/ *verb* (*p.t., p.p.* **paid**) **1** [I,T] **pay (sb) (for sth)**; **pay sth (to sb) (for sth)** to give sb money for sth: *She is very well paid.* ○ *Do you want to pay by check or by credit card?* ○ *The work's finished, but we haven't paid the plumber yet.* ○ *to be paid by the hour* ○ *We paid the dealer $5,000 for the car.* **2** [T] **pay sth (to sb)** to give the money that you owe for sth: *Did you pay the gas bill?* **3** [I,T] to make a profit; to be worth doing: *The factory closed down because the owners couldn't make it pay.* ○ *I've learned that it pays to be prepared.* **4** **pay (for sth)** to suffer or be punished for sth you believe in or have done: *I'll make him pay for embarrassing me like that!*

IDM **cost/pay an arm and a leg** ⇨ ARM¹

pay attention (to sb/sth) to listen carefully to or to take notice of sb/sth

pay sb a compliment; pay a compliment to sb to say that you like sth about sb; to praise sb

pay your respects (to sb) (*formal*) to visit sb, especially sb who is dead or very sick, as a sign of respect

pay tribute to sb/sth to praise and show your respect for sb/sth, especially sb who is dead

PHRV **pay sb back (sth)**; **pay sth back** to give money back to sb that you borrowed from him/her: *Can you lend me $10? I'll pay you back/I'll pay it back to you on Friday.*

pay sb back (for sth) to do sth unkind to sb who did sth unkind to you: *What a mean trick! I'll pay you back one day.*

pay sth down to pay back money that you owe: *to pay down a debt*

pay off (*informal*) to be successful: *All their hard work has paid off! The house is finished at last.*

pay sth off to pay all the money that you owe for sth: *to pay off a debt*

pay up (*informal*) to pay the money that you owe: *If you don't pay up, we'll take you to court.*

pay·a·ble /ˈpeɪəbl/ *adj.* that should or must be paid: *This bill is payable immediately.* ○ *Make the check payable to Diane Weller.*

☆ **pay·check** /ˈpeɪtʃɛk/ *noun* [C] a special printed form that an employee receives regularly as

i	ɪ	ɛ	æ	ɑ	ɔ	ʌ	ʊ	u
see	sit	ten	cat	hot	saw	cup	put	too

payment for work that he/she has done: *I need to go to the bank to cash my paycheck.*

☆ **pay·ment** /'peɪmənt/ *noun* **payment (for sth)** **1** [U] paying or being paid: *You get a 5% discount for prompt payment.* ○ *payment of a bill* ○ *I did the work last month, but I haven't had any payment yet.* ☞ Look at the note at **pay¹**. **2** [C] an amount of money that you must pay: *They asked for a payment of $100 as a deposit.*

'pay phone *noun* [C] a telephone in a public place, which you can use by putting in money or using a special card

pay·roll /'peɪroʊl/ *noun* [C] a list of people who work for a company and the amount of money to be paid to each person: *Our company has over 250 people on the payroll.*

PC¹ /ˌpiˈsi/ (*pl.* **PCs**) *noun* [C] personal computer; a small computer that is designed for home or business use ☞ The term **PC** is usually used to refer to a specific type of computer manufactured by IBM, or to other computers that work in a similar way: *The software is available in both PC and Macintosh versions.*

PC² /ˌpiˈsi/ *adj.* (*informal*) = POLITICALLY CORRECT

P.E. /ˌpiˈi/ *noun* [U] = PHYSICAL EDUCATION

☆ **pea** /pi/ *noun* [C] a small round green seed that is eaten as a vegetable

☞ A number of peas grow together in a **pod**.

☆ **peace** /pis/ *noun* [U] **1** the state of not being at war or of not having fighting, disorder, etc.: *fifty years of peace in Europe* ○ *a peace treaty* **2** the state of being calm or quiet: *He longed to escape from the city to the peace of the countryside.* ○ *I'm tired – can't you just leave me in peace?* ○ *The noise of lawnmowers disturbed the peace of the afternoon.*

the 'Peace Corps *noun* [sing.] a U.S. government organization that sends young people to other countries to work on projects to help local people: *to join the Peace Corps* ○ *a Peace Corps volunteer* ☞ Look at the note at **White House**.

☆ **peace·ful** /'pisfl/ *adj.* **1** not wanting or involving war, fighting or disorder: *a peaceful demonstration* ○ *Nuclear power can be used for peaceful or military purposes.* ○ *a peaceful solution to the conflict* **2** calm and quiet: *a peaceful spot near the river* —**peace·ful·ly** *adv.* —**peace·ful·ness** *noun* [U]

'peace pipe *noun* [C] a holy pipe which some Native Americans use to smoke tobacco during ceremonies. It is passed from one person to another as a sign of peace.

peace·time /'pistaɪm/ *noun* [U] a period when a country is not at war

peach /pitʃ/ *noun* [C] a soft round fruit with

peach

orange-red skin. A peach is soft inside and has a large hard part (**pit**) in its center: *canned peaches*

peacock

pea·cock /'pikɑk/ *noun* [C] a large bird with beautiful long blue and green tail feathers that it can lift up and spread out like a fan

peak¹ /pik/ *noun* [C] **1** the pointed top of a mountain: *snow-covered peaks in the distance* **2** the highest level, value, rate, etc.: *In the early evening demand for electricity is at its peak.* ○ *a man at the peak of his career* ☞ Look at **off-peak**.

peak² /pik/ *verb* [I] to reach the highest level, value, rate, etc.: *Sales usually peak just before the holidays.*

peal /pil/ *noun* [C] the loud ringing of a bell or of a set of bells that all have different notes: (*figurative*) *peals of laughter*

pea·nut /'pinʌt/ *noun* [C] a nut that grows in a shell under the ground: *roasted and salted peanuts* ☞ picture at **nut**.

'peanut ˌbutter *noun* [U] a thick soft food made from crushed peanuts. It is usually eaten on bread: *a peanut butter and jelly sandwich*

pear /pɛr/ *noun* [C] a fruit that has yellow or green skin and is white inside. Pears are thinner at the top than at the bottom.

pear

☆ **pearl** /pərl/ *noun* [C] a small, hard, round, white object that grows inside the shell of an oyster (a type of shellfish). Pearls are used to make jewelry: *a pearl necklace*

peas·ant /'pɛznt/ *noun* [C] (especially in former times or in poorer countries) a poor person who owns or rents a small piece of land on which he/she grows food and keeps animals in order to feed his/her family

peat /pit/ *noun* [U] a natural substance that is made of decayed plants. Peat is formed underground in cool, wet places. It can be burned as a fuel or put on the garden to make plants grow better.

peb·ble /'pɛbl/ *noun* [C] a smooth round stone that is usually found in or near water

pe·can /pəˈkɑn; -ˈkæn/ *noun* [C] a nut that you can eat, with a smooth reddish-brown shell. It grows on trees in the southern U.S.: *pecan pie* ☞ picture at **nut**.

peck /pɛk/ *verb* [I,T] **peck (at sth)** (used about a bird) to eat or bite sth with the beak: *The sparrows were pecking around for food.* ○ *Don't touch the bird – it might peck you.* —**peck** *noun* [C] (*figurative*): *She gave him a quick peck* (= kiss) *on the cheek and then left.*

pe·cu·liar /pɪˈkyulyər/ *adj.* **1** odd or strange: *Warren has some very peculiar habits.* ○ *Our new neighbor seems a little peculiar.* **2** only belonging to a particular person or thing or found in a particular place: *a problem peculiar to this type of car*

pe·cu·li·ar·i·ty /pɪˌkyuliˈærəṭi/ *noun* (*pl.* **pe·cu·li·ar·i·ties**) **1** [U] the quality of being strange or odd **2** [C] something that is strange or odd: *One of his peculiarities is that he never wears socks.* **3** [C] sth that only belongs to or is only found in sb/sth

pe·cu·liar·ly /pɪˈkyulyərli/ *adv.* **1** in a peculiar (1) way: *Luke is behaving very peculiarly.* **2** in a way that is especially typical of sb/sth: *Is talking about the weather a peculiarly American habit?*

☆ **ped·al**[1] /ˈpɛdl/ *noun* [C] the part of a bicycle or other machine that you push with your foot in order to make it move or work ☞ picture at **bicycle**. Look also at **accelerator**.

ped·al[2] /ˈpɛdl/ *verb* [I,T] to push the pedals of a bicycle: *She had to pedal hard to get up the hill.*

pe·dan·tic /pəˈdæntɪk/ *adj.* too worried about rules or small details —**pe·dan·ti·cal·ly** /-kli/ *adv.*

ped·es·tal /ˈpɛdəstl/ *noun* [C] the base on which a column, statue, etc. stands

☆ **pe·des·tri·an**[1] /pəˈdɛstriən/ *noun* [C] a person who is walking on or near the street (not traveling in a vehicle): *Motorists must yield to pedestrians in crosswalks.*

pe·des·tri·an[2] /pəˈdɛstriən/ *adj.* **1** of or for pedestrians: *a pedestrian bridge* **2** (*formal*) ordinary; not interesting; dull

pe·di·a·tri·cian /ˌpidiəˈtrɪʃn/ *noun* [C] a doctor who specializes in treating sick babies and children

ped·i·gree /ˈpɛdəgri/ *noun* [C] **1** the parents, grandparents and other previous family members of an animal. The names of the ancestors are recorded on a document which is also called a "pedigree." **2** a person's background

ped·i·greed /ˈpɛdəgrid/ *adj.* (used about an animal) of high quality because the parents, grandparents, etc. are all of the same breed and specially chosen

pee /pi/ *verb* [I] (*informal*) to send out waste water from your body; to urinate

☞ It is more polite to say **go to the bathroom.**

—**pee** *noun* [sing.] (*informal*): *I'm going to take a pee.*

peek /pik/ *verb* [I] (*informal*) **peek (at sth)** to look at sth quickly or secretly: *No peeking at the presents before Christmas.* —**peek** *noun* [sing.]: *to take a quick peek at the answers*

☆ **peel**[1] /pil/ *verb* **1** [T] to take the skin off a fruit or vegetable: *Could you peel the potatoes for me?* **2** [I] to come off in one piece or in small pieces: *Soak the envelope in water and the stamp will peel off easily.* ○ *My nose got sunburned and now it is peeling* (= the skin is coming off). ○ *The paint is starting to peel.*

☆ **peel**[2] /pil/ *noun* [C,U] the skin of a fruit or vegetable: *apple peel* ☞ Look at **rind**.

peep[1] /pip/ *verb* [I] **1 peep (at sth)** to look at sth quickly and secretly: *to peep through a keyhole* **2** (used about part of sth) to appear: *The moon is peeping out from behind the clouds.* **3** to make a weak high sound, like a young bird makes

peep[2] /pip/ *noun* [sing.] **1** a quick or secret look: *Take a peep in the bedroom and see if the baby is asleep.* **2** the weak high sound that is made, for example, by a young bird: *There hasn't been a peep out of the kids for hours.*

peer[1] /pɪr/ *noun* [C] a person who is of the same age or rank: *A lot of teenagers worry about being accepted by their peers.* ○ *peer pressure* (= the feeling that young people have that they must do what others of their age do)

peer[2] /pɪr/ *verb* [I] **peer (at sb/sth)** to look closely or carefully at sb/sth, e.g. because you cannot see very well: *I peered outside, but it was too dark to see much.* ○ *I had to peer very hard at the handwriting to make out what it said.*

peg[1] /pɛg/ *noun* [C] a round piece of wood, metal, etc. that you can hang things on or use to fasten things together: *Most of the tools were hanging on pegs on the wall.* ○ *To assemble the bookcase, insert a wooden peg into each hole as shown in the diagram.* ○ *a tent peg*

peg[2] /pɛg/ *verb* [T] (**peg·ging; pegged**) **1** to fasten sth with a peg **2** to fix or keep sth at a certain level; often in relation to sth else: *Inflation was pegged at 7% last year.* ○ *Some countries' currencies are pegged to the dollar.*

IDM **peg sb/sth as sth**; **have sb/sth pegged as sth** (*informal*) to regard sb/sth in a particular way: *I had him pegged as a real jerk, but he's actually a nice guy.*

pel·i·can /ˈpɛlɪkən/ *noun* [C] a large water bird that lives in warm countries. A pelican has a large beak that it uses for catching and holding fish.

pel·let /ˈpɛlət/ *noun* [C] a small hard ball that is made from mud, metal, etc.: *shotgun pellets*

pelt[1] /pɛlt/ *verb* **1** [T] to attack sb/sth by throwing things: *The speaker was pelted with tomatoes.* **2** [T] (used about rain, etc.) to hit sth or to fall very heavily: *Much of Nebraska was pelted by hail yesterday.*

pelt[2] /pɛlt/ *noun* [C] the skin of an animal,

ər	ɪr	ɛr	ɑr	ɔr	ʊr	ʒ	h	ŋ
bird	near	hair	car	north	tour	vision	hat	sing

especially with the fur or hair still on it: *beaver pelts*

pel·vis /ˈpɛlvəs/ *noun* [C] (*pl.* **pel·vis·es**) the set of wide bones at the bottom of your back, to which your leg bones are joined —**pel·vic** /ˈpɛlvɪk/ *adj.*

☆ **pen** /pɛn/ *noun* [C] **1** an instrument that you use for writing in ink: *a fountain pen* ○ *a ballpoint pen* ○ *a felt-tip pen* **2** a small piece of ground with a fence around it that is used for keeping animals in ☞ Look also at **playpen**.

pe·nal /ˈpinl/ *adj.* (only *before* a noun) connected with punishment by law

pe·nal·ize /ˈpinl·aɪz; ˈpɛn-/ *verb* [T] **1** to punish sb for breaking a law or rule: *Players must be penalized if they touch the ball with their hands.* ○ *Motorists who drink and drive should be heavily penalized.* **2** to cause sb to suffer a disadvantage: *The new tax unfairly penalizes single parents.*

☆ **pen·al·ty** /ˈpɛnlti/ *noun* [C] (*pl.* **pen·al·ties**) **1** a punishment for breaking a law or rule: *We need stiffer penalties for people who litter.* ○ *the death penalty* ○ *The judge ordered him to pay a penalty of $50.* **2** a disadvantage or sth bad that happens as the result of sth: *I didn't work hard enough and I paid the penalty. I failed all my final exams.* **3** (in sports) a punishment for one team and an advantage for the other team because a rule has been broken: *The goalie was fouled and the referee awarded a penalty.*

☞ In soccer and hockey, a penalty is a free shot at the goal.

penalty box *noun* [C] (in hockey) a small area off the ice where a player who has broken a rule must sit for a certain length of time

pen·ance /ˈpɛnəns/ *noun* [C,U] a punishment that you give yourself to show you are sorry for doing sth wrong

☆ **pen·cil¹** /ˈpɛnsl/ *noun* [C,U] an object that you use for writing or drawing. Pencils are usually made of wood and contain a thin stick of a black or colored substance: *colored pencils for children* ○ *Write in pen, not pencil.*

pen·cil² /ˈpɛnsl/ *verb* [T] to write or draw with a pencil

pencil case *noun* [C] a small bag or box that you keep pens, pencils, etc. in

pencil ˌsharpener *noun* [C] an instrument that you use for making pencils sharp

pen·dant /ˈpɛndənt/ *noun* [C] an ornament that you wear on a chain around your neck

pend·ing¹ /ˈpɛndɪŋ/ *adj.* (*formal*) waiting to be done or decided: *The judge's decision is still pending.*

pend·ing² /ˈpɛndɪŋ/ *prep.* (*formal*) until: *Roberts was set free pending an appeal in the state Supreme Court.*

pen·du·lum /ˈpɛndʒələm; -dələm/ *noun* [C] a

string or stick with a heavy weight at the bottom. Some large clocks are worked by a swinging pendulum.

pen·e·trate /ˈpɛnətreɪt/ *verb* [I,T] to make or force a way into or through sth: *The bullet hadn't penetrated his lung.* ○ *The car's headlights could not penetrate the thick fog.* ○ *The troops managed to penetrate into enemy territory.* —**pen·e·tra·tion** /ˌpɛnəˈtreɪʃn/ *noun* [U]

pen·e·trat·ing /ˌpɛnəˈtreɪtɪŋ/ *adj.* **1** showing the ability to think and understand quickly and well: *a penetrating question* **2** (used about a voice or sound) loud and carrying for a long way: *a penetrating scream* **3** (used about sb's eyes or the way sb looks at sth) very powerful and direct, making you feel uncomfortable: *a penetrating stare*

pen·guin /ˈpɛŋgwən/ *noun* [C] a black and white sea bird that lives in the Antarctic. Penguins cannot fly.

penguin

pen·i·cil·lin /ˌpɛnəˈsɪlən/ *noun* [U] a substance that is used as a medicine for preventing and treating diseases caused by tiny living things (**bacteria**)

pen·in·su·la /pəˈnɪmsələ/ *noun* [C] an area of land that is almost surrounded by water

pe·nis /ˈpinəs/ *noun* [C] the male sex organ that is used for passing waste water and having sex

pen·i·ten·tia·ry /ˌpɛnəˈtɛnʃəri/ *noun* [C] (*pl.* **pen·i·ten·tia·ries**) a prison

pen·knife /ˈpɛnnaɪf/ *noun* [C] (*pl.* **pen·knives**) = POCKET KNIFE

pen name *noun* [C] = PSEUDONYM

pen·ni·less /ˈpɛnɪləs/ *adj.* having no money; poor

☆ **pen·ny** /ˈpɛni/ *noun* [C] (*pl.* **pen·nies**) a small brown American or Canadian coin that is worth one cent

pen pal *noun* [C] a person that you become friendly with by sending and receiving letters

pen·sion /ˈpɛnʃn/ *noun* [C] money that sb who has stopped working (**retired**) because of old age receives regularly from the company or organization where he/she used to work: *to pay money into a pension fund* ☞ Look also at **Social Security**.

pen·ta·gon /ˈpɛntəgɑn/ *noun* **1** [C] a shape that has five straight sides **2 the Pentagon** [sing.] a large government building near Washington, D.C., that contains the main offices of the U.S. military forces; the military officials who work here

pent·house /ˈpɛnthaʊs/ *noun* [C] an expensive apartment at the top of a tall building

pent up /ˌpɛntˈʌp/ *adj.* (used about feelings) that you do not express: *pent-up anger and frustration*

tʃ	dʒ	v	θ	ð	s	z	ʃ
chin	June	van	thin	then	so	zoo	she

P

☆ **peo·ple** /'pipl/ noun **1** [plural] more than one person: *How many people are coming to the party?* ○ *Young people often rebel against their parents.* ○ *What will people say if you go out looking like that?* ○ *He meets a lot of famous people in his job.*

☞ Be careful. **People** is almost always used instead of the plural form **persons**. **Persons** is very formal and is usually used in legal language, etc.: *Persons under the age of twenty-one are not permitted to buy alcohol.* **Folk(s)** is an informal word for people. It is often used when you are talking about older people or people who live in the country: *The old folks have seen many changes in the town over the years.*

2 [C] (*pl.* **peoples**) (*formal*) a nation, race, etc.: *The Japanese are a hard-working people.* ○ *the French-speaking peoples of the world* **3 the people** [plural] the ordinary citizens of a country: *a man of the people*

pep¹ /pɛp/ noun [U] (*informal*) energy and positive attitude

pep² /pɛp/ verb **pep·ping; pepped**
PHR V **pep sb/sth up** (*informal*) to make sb/sth more lively, interesting, etc.: *A spoonful of curry powder should pep up the sauce.*

☆ **pep·per¹** /'pɛpər/ noun **1** [U] a powder with a hot taste that is used for flavoring food: *salt and pepper* **2** (*also* **bell 'pepper**) [C] a hollow green, red or yellow vegetable: *stuffed green peppers*

pep·per² /'pɛpər/ verb [T] **1** to put pepper (1) on sth **2 pepper sb/sth with sth** to hit sb/sth many times with sth: *The wall had been peppered with bullets.*

pep·per·mint /'pɛpərmɪnt/ noun [U] a natural substance with a strong flavor that is used in candy

'pep ˌrally noun [C] (*pl.* **pep rallies**) a meeting for all the students in a school before a sports game in which the students shout, sing songs, etc. in order to encourage their team to win

'pep talk noun [C] a speech that is given to encourage people or to make them work harder

☆ **per** /pər/ prep. for each: *The speed limit is 30 miles per hour.* ○ *It costs $10 per hour to rent a boat.*

per·ceive /pər'siv/ verb [T] (*formal*) **1** to notice or realize sth: *Scientists failed to perceive how dangerous the levels of pollutants had become.* **2** to see or think of sth in a particular way: *I perceived his comments as a criticism.*
☞ The noun is **perception**.

☆ **per·cent¹** /pər'sɛnt/ adj., adv. (*symbol* **%**) in or of each hundred: *There is a ten percent service charge.* ○ *a two percent fall in the price of oil*

☆ **per·cent²** /pər'sɛnt/ noun [C, with sing. or pl. verb] (*pl.* **percent**) (*symbol* **%**) one part in every hundred: *Nearly ten percent of all chil-*

dren attend private schools. ○ *95% of the population owns a television.* ○ *The price of bread has gone up by 50 percent in two years.*

☞ We usually use **percent** and **percentage** with a singular verb when we are talking about a singular or an uncountable noun: *About 75 percent of the population owns a VCR.* But we use a plural verb when we are talking about a plural noun: *About 75 percent of all households own a VCR.*

☆ **per·cent·age** /pər'sɛntɪdʒ/ noun [C, with sing. or pl. verb] a part of an amount, expressed as a number of parts in every hundred of that amount: *"What percentage of the voters chose Bill Clinton?" "About 43 percent."* ○ *Please express your answer as a percentage.*

☞ If we say **the percentage of sth**, we must use a singular verb: *The percentage of people with college degrees is increasing.* Look also at the note at **percent²**.

per·cen·tile /pər'sɛntaɪl/ noun [C, usually sing.] (*technical*) a number that expresses how well sb did on an exam, etc., in comparison to the other people who took the same exam: *I scored in the 85th percentile on the TOEFL* (= I did better than 85% of the other people).

per·cep·ti·ble /pər'sɛptəbl/ adj. (*formal*) that can be seen or felt: *a barely perceptible change in color* ☞ The opposite is **imperceptible**. —**per·cep·ti·bly** /-əbli/ adv.

per·cep·tion /pər'sɛpʃn/ noun **1** [U] the ability to notice or understand sth **2** [C] a particular way of looking at or understanding sth; an opinion: *What is your perception of the situation?* ☞ The verb is **perceive**.

per·cep·tive /pər'sɛptɪv/ adj. (*formal*) quick to notice or understand things —**per·cep·tive·ly** adv.

perch¹ /pərtʃ/ noun [C] **1** a branch (or a bar in a cage) where a bird sits **2** a high position where sb can sit: *From our perch on the hill, we had a good view of the parade.*

perch² /pərtʃ/ verb **1** [I] (used about a bird) to rest on a branch, etc. **2** [I,T] to sit, or be put, on a high place or on the edge of sth: *The house was perched on the edge of a cliff.* ○ *He perched on a stool at the end of the bar.*

per·cus·sion /pər'kʌʃn/ noun [U, sing.] the section of an orchestra that consists of the drums and other instruments that you play by hitting them

per·en·ni·al /pə'rɛniəl/ adj. that happens often or that lasts for a long time: *the perennial problem of poverty in the inner cities*

☆ **per·fect** /'pərfɪkt/ adj. **1** as good as can be; without fault: *The car is two years old, but it is still in perfect condition.* ○ *Nobody is perfect!* ○ *These shoes are a perfect fit.* ○ *What perfect weather!* ○ *a perfect score on a quiz* **2 perfect (for sb/sth)** very suitable or right: *Ken would*

i	ɪ	ɛ	æ	ɑ	ɔ	ʌ	ʊ	u
see	sit	ten	cat	hot	saw	cup	put	too

be perfect for the job. ○ Orlando is the perfect place for a family vacation. ○ the perfect solution to a problem **3** (used to describe the tense of a verb that is formed with has/have/had and the past participle) **4** (only before a noun) complete; total: What he was saying made perfect sense to me. ○ a perfect stranger

per·fect² /pərˈfɛkt/ verb [T] to make sth perfect¹: Derek is spending a year in France to perfect his French.

the per·fect /ˈpərfɪkt/ noun [sing.] the perfect¹(3) tense: the present/past perfect

per·fec·tion /pərˈfɛkʃn/ noun [U] the state of being perfect¹ or without fault: Perfection is impossible to achieve. ○ The steak was cooked to perfection.

per·fec·tion·ist /pərˈfɛkʃn·ɪst/ noun [C] a person who always does things as well as he/she possibly can and who expects others to do the same

☆ **per·fect·ly** /ˈpərfɪktli/ adv. **1** in a perfect¹(1) way: He played the piece of music perfectly. **2** very; completely: Laura understood perfectly well what I meant.

per·fo·rate /ˈpərfəreɪt/ verb [T] to make a hole or holes in sth: Tear along the perforated line.

☆ **per·form** /pərˈfɔrm/ verb **1** [T] to do a piece of work or sth that you have been ordered to do: Doctors performed an emergency operation. ○ to perform a task **2** [I,T] to take part in a play, or to sing, dance, etc. in front of an audience: She is currently performing on Broadway. ○ Children performed square dances for the visiting president. ○ This play has never been performed previously. **3** [I] (used about a machine, etc.) to work: The car performs badly in cold weather.

☆ **per·form·ance** /pərˈfɔrməns/ noun **1** [sing.] (formal) doing sth: the performance of your duties **2** [C] sth that you perform (2) in front of an audience: a live performance by Whitney Houston ○ a performance of one of Shakespeare's plays **3** [C] the way in which you do sth, especially how successful you are: The company's performance was disappointing last year. ○ The Yankees' fine performance in the World Series **4** [U] (used about a machine, etc.) the ability to work well: This car has a high-performance engine.

☆ **per·form·er** /pərˈfɔrmər/ noun [C] a person who performs (2) in front of an audience

☆ **per·fume** /ˈpərfyum/ noun [C,U] **1** a liquid with a sweet smell that women put on their bodies to make themselves smell nice: You're wearing too much perfume. **2** a pleasant smell

☆ **per·haps** /pərˈhæps/ adv. (formal) (used when you are not sure about sth) maybe; possibly: She was, perhaps, one of the most famous writers of the time. ○ This is an excellent restaurant, though perhaps not the best in the city.

☞ Perhaps and maybe are similar in meaning. They are often used to make what you are saying sound more polite. Perhaps is

more formal than **maybe**: Perhaps you would like to join us for dinner sometime? ○ Maybe I ought to go.

per·il /ˈpɛrəl/ noun (formal) **1** [U] great danger **2** [C] sth that is very dangerous: the perils of drug use ☞ **Danger** is more common.

per·il·ous /ˈpɛrələs/ adj. (formal) dangerous ☞ **Dangerous** is more common.

pe·rim·e·ter /pəˈrɪmətər/ noun [C] the outside edge or boundary of an area of land: the perimeter fence of the army camp

☆ **pe·ri·od** /ˈpɪriəd/ noun [C] **1** a length of time: The plan will be in effect for a six-month trial period. ○ Her son is going through a difficult period right now. ○ The play is set in the colonial period in New England. ○ Camels can go for long periods without water. **2** one of the equal lengths of time that the school day is divided into: I have English during second period. **3** the monthly loss of blood from a woman's body: My period started this morning. **4** a mark (.) that is used when you are writing to show the end of a sentence, etc.

IDM ...period. (used when you are speaking to emphasize a fact or an opinion that you are not willing to discuss anymore): No late papers will be accepted, period.

pe·ri·od·ic /ˌpɪriˈɑdɪk/ adj. happening fairly regularly —**pe·ri·od·i·cal·ly** /-kli/ adv.: All machines need to be checked periodically.

pe·ri·od·i·cal /ˌpɪriˈɑdɪkl/ noun [C] (formal) a magazine that is produced at regular intervals

per·ish /ˈpɛrɪʃ/ verb [I] (formal) to die or be destroyed: Thousands perished in the war.

per·ish·a·ble /ˈpɛrɪʃəbl/ adj. (used about food) that will go bad quickly

per·ju·ry /ˈpərdʒəri/ noun [U] the crime of telling a lie (in a court of law)

perk¹ /pərk/ verb
PHRV **perk up** to become more cheerful or lively
perk sb/sth up to make sb/sth more cheerful or lively

perk² /pərk/ noun [C] something extra that you get from your employer in addition to your salary: International travel is one of the perks of the job.

perk·y /ˈpərki/ adj. (perk·i·er; perk·i·est) lively and cheerful: a perky TV show host

perm /pərm/ (also old-fashioned **permanent**) noun [C] a treatment of the hair with special chemicals in order to give it curls or waves —**perm** verb [T]: She had her hair permed.

☆ **per·ma·nent¹** /ˈpərmənənt/ adj. lasting for a long time or forever; that will not change: The accident left him with a permanent scar. ○ Are you looking for a permanent or a temporary job? —**per·ma·nence** /-nəns/ noun [U] —**per·ma·nent·ly** adv.: Is she gone permanently?

per·ma·nent² /ˈpərmənənt/ noun [C] (old-fashioned) = PERM

ə	y	w	t̬	eɪ	aɪ	ɔɪ	aʊ	oʊ
about	yes	woman	butter	say	five	boy	now	go

P

per·mis·si·ble /pərˈmɪsəbl/ *adj.* (*formal*) that is allowed (by the rules): *They have been exposed to radiation above the permissible level.*

☆ **per·mis·sion** /pərˈmɪʃn/ *noun* [U] the act of allowing sb to do sth: *You can't leave without permission.* ◦ *Children under 18 need their parents' permission to attend.* ◦ *to ask permission for sth* ◦ *to give permission for sth* ◦ *The refugees have been refused permission to stay in this country.*

☞ Be careful. **Permission** is uncountable. A piece of paper that says that you are allowed to do something is a **permit**.

per·mis·sive /pərˈmɪsɪv/ *adj.* having, allowing or showing a lot of freedom, especially in sexual matters: *the permissive society of the 1960s*

☆ **per·mit¹** /pərˈmɪt/ *verb* (*formal*) (**per·mit·ting**; **per·mit·ted**) **1** [T] to allow sth: *Food and drink are not permitted in this building.* ◦ *You are not permitted to smoke in the hospital.* ◦ *His visa does not permit him to work.* ☞ Look at the note at **allow**. **2** [I,T] to make possible: *The game will start at 2:00, weather permitting.*

☆ **per·mit²** /ˈpərmɪt/ *noun* [C] an official piece of paper that says you are allowed to do sth: *a work permit* ◦ *a parking permit*

per·pen·dic·u·lar /ˌpərpənˈdɪkyələr/ *adj.* **1 perpendicular (to sth)** at an angle of 90° to sth ☞ Look at **horizontal**, **vertical** and **parallel**. **2** pointing straight up; not leaning to either side

per·pe·trate /ˈpərpətreɪt/ *verb* [T] (*formal*) to do sth that is wrong or illegal —**per·pe·tra·tor** /-treɪt̬ər/ *noun* [C]: *The police have arrested the perpetrators.*

per·pet·u·al /pərˈpɛtʃuəl/ *adj.* (*formal*) not stopping or changing: *They lived in perpetual fear of losing their jobs.* ◦ *the perpetual roar of traffic*

per·pet·u·al·ly /pərˈpɛtʃuəli; -tʃəli/ *adv.* always: *a company that is perpetually in debt*

per·pet·u·ate /pərˈpɛtʃueɪt/ *verb* [T] (*formal*) to cause sth to continue

per·plexed /pərˈplɛkst/ *adj.* not understanding sth; confused

per·se·cute /ˈpərsəkyut/ *verb* [T] to cause sb to suffer, especially because of what he/she believes —**per·se·cu·tion** /ˌpərsəˈkyuʃn/ *noun* [C,U]: *the persecution of minorities* —**per·se·cu·tor** /ˈpərsəkyut̬ər/ *noun* [C]

per·se·vere /ˌpərsəˈvɪr/ *verb* [I] **persevere (in/with sth)** to continue trying or having sth that is difficult: *The treatment is painful, but I'm going to persevere with it.* —**per·se·ver·ance** /ˌpərsəˈvɪrəns/ *noun* [U]: *It takes a lot of perseverance to become a champion at any sport.*

per·sist /pərˈsɪst/ *verb* [I] **1** to continue to exist: *If your symptoms persist, you should consult your doctor.* **2** persist (**in sth/in doing sth**) (*formal*) to continue doing sth even though other people say that you are wrong or that you cannot do it: *We will persist in our efforts to get rid of gangs in our neighborhood.*

per·sist·ent /pərˈsɪstənt/ *adj.* **1** continuing to do sth even though people say that you are wrong or that you cannot do it: *Some salespeople can be very persistent.* **2** lasting for a long time or happening often: *a persistent cough* ◦ *persistent rain* —**per·sist·ence** /-əns/ *noun* [U]: *Thanks to her patience and persistence, she finally got what she wanted.* ◦ *the persistence of unemployment* —**per·sist·ent·ly** *adv.*

☆ **per·son** /ˈpərsn/ *noun* (*pl.* **peo·ple** or **persons**) ☞ Look at the note at **people**. **1** [C] a man, woman or child: *I would like to speak to the person in charge.* **2** [C] (*informal*) (usually *after* another noun) somebody who likes or is interested in the thing mentioned: *I'm not really much of a sports person.* ◦ *a computer person* **3** [sing.] one of the three types of pronoun in grammar. *I/we* are the first person, *you* is the second person and *he/she/it/they* are the third person.

IDM **in person** seeing or speaking to sb face to face (not speaking on the telephone or writing a letter): *I went to apologize to her in person.*

☆ **-per·son** /ˈpərsn/ (in compounds) someone who has a particular job or role, especially when it could be either a man or a woman: *a salesperson* ◦ *the chairperson of a committee* ◦ *a pizza delivery person*

☆ **per·son·al** /ˈpərsn·l/ *adj.* **1** (only *before* a noun) of or belonging to a particular person: *Judges should not let their personal feelings influence their decisions.* ◦ *a personal savings account* **2** connected with your feelings, health, relations with other people, etc.: *I would like to speak to you in private. I have something personal to discuss.* ◦ *The letter was marked "personal," so I did not open it.* **3** (only *before* a noun) connected with your private life and not with your work: *Employees are not allowed to make personal calls during office hours.* ◦ *Maybe Julie can arrange a meeting with the senator – she's a personal friend of his.* ◦ *Do you have a good personal relationship with your boss?* **4** (only *before* a noun) done or made by a particular person: *The president made a personal visit to the victims in the hospital.* **5** speaking about sb's appearance or character in an unkind or unfriendly way: *It started as a general discussion, but then people started making personal remarks and an argument began.* **6** (only *before* a noun) connected with the body: *personal hygiene*

‚personal com'puter *noun* [C] = PC¹

☆ **per·son·al·i·ty** /ˌpərsəˈnæləti/ *noun* (*pl.* **person·al·i·ties**) **1** [C] the qualities and features of a person: *Joe has a very forceful personality.* **2** [C] a famous person (especially in sports, on

television, etc.): *a television personality* **3** [U] the quality of having a strong, interesting and attractive character: *A good entertainer needs a lot of personality.*

per·son·al·ize /ˈpərsənəlaɪz/ *verb* [T] (often passive) **1** to mark sth with your name, etc. to show that it belongs to you: *a car with personalized license plates* **2** to make sth suitable for a particular person: *a computer service that offers personalized vacation planning*

☆ **per·son·al·ly** /ˈpərsənəli/ *adv.* **1** in person, not with sb else acting for you: *I would like to deal with this matter personally.* **2** (used for expressing your own opinions): *Personally, I think that nurses deserve more money.* **3** as a person: *I wasn't talking about you personally – I meant all teachers.* ○ *The ship's captain was held personally responsible for the accident.*

ˌ**personal** ˈ**pronoun** *noun* [C] (*grammar*) any of the pronouns *I, me, she, her, he, him, we, us, you, they, them*

per·son·i·fy /pərˈsɑnəfaɪ/ *verb* [T] (*pres. part.* **per·son·i·fy·ing**; *3rd pers. sing. pres.* **per·son·i·fies**; *p.t., p.p.* **per·son·i·fied**) **1** to be an example in human form of a particular quality **2** to describe sth as if it were a person, e.g. in a poem

per·son·nel /ˌpərsəˈnɛl/ *noun* **1** [plural] the people who work for a large company or organization: *The army cannot afford to lose qualified personnel.* **2** [U] (*also* **person'nel department**) = HUMAN RESOURCES

per·spec·tive /pərˈspɛktɪv/ *noun* **1** [U] the art of drawing on a flat surface so that some objects appear to be farther away than others: *the laws of perspective* **2** [C,U] the way that you think about sth; your point of view: *If you go away for a few days, you will see everything from a new perspective.*

IDM **keep/put sth in perspective** to recognize what is really important and what is not important in a particular situation: *Let's try to keep things in perspective here – it's not a complete disaster.*

per·spi·ra·tion /ˌpərspəˈreɪʃn/ *noun* [U] (*formal*) **1** the act of perspiring **2** the liquid that you lose through your skin: *a drop of perspiration* ☞ **Sweat** is more common. Look also at **antiperspirant**.

per·spire /pərˈspaɪər/ *verb* [I] (*formal*) to lose liquid through your skin ☞ **Sweat** is more common.

☆ **per·suade** /pərˈsweɪd/ *verb* [T] **1 persuade sb (to do sth)** to cause sb to do sth by giving him/her good reasons: *It was difficult to persuade Louise to change her mind.* ☞ Look at **dissuade**. **2 persuade sb (of sth); persuade sb (that...)** to cause sb to believe sth: *The jury was persuaded of her innocence.* ○ *The attorney persuaded the jury that she was innocent.* ☞ Look at **convince**.

per·sua·sion /pərˈsweɪʒn/ *noun* **1** [U] per-

suading or being persuaded: *It took a lot of persuasion to get Alan to agree.* **2** [C] (*formal*) a religious or political belief: *There were people of every political persuasion at the meeting.*

per·sua·sive /pərˈsweɪsɪv/ *adj.* able to make sb do or believe sth: *The arguments were very persuasive.* —**per·sua·sive·ly** *adv.* —**per·sua·sive·ness** *noun* [U]

per·tain /pərˈteɪn/ *verb* [I] **pertain to sth** (*formal*) to be directly connected with sth: *documents pertaining to a court case*

per·ti·nent /ˈpərtn·ənt/ *adj.* **pertinent (to sth)** directly connected with sth: *to ask a pertinent question*

per·va·sive /pərˈveɪsɪv/ *adj.* that is present in all parts of sth: *a pervasive mood of pessimism and gloom*

per·verse /pərˈvərs/ *adj.* (*formal*) having or showing behavior that is not reasonable or that upsets other people: *Derek gets perverse pleasure from shocking his parents.* —**per·verse·ly** *adv.* —**per·ver·si·ty** *noun* [U]

per·ver·sion /pərˈvərʒn/ *noun* [C,U] **1** the changing of sth from right to wrong or good to bad: *That statement is a perversion of the truth.* **2** sexual behavior that is unnatural or not acceptable

per·vert¹ /ˈpərvərt/ *noun* [C] a person whose sexual behavior is not natural or normal

per·vert² /pərˈvərt/ *verb* [T] to change sth so that it becomes bad or is used wrongly: *to pervert the original meaning of a document*

pes·ky /ˈpɛski/ *adj.* (**pes·ki·er**; **pes·ki·est**) (*informal*) annoying and not going away: *These pesky mosquitoes won't leave me alone!*

pes·si·mism /ˈpɛsəmɪzəm/ *noun* [U] the state of expecting or believing that bad things will happen

pes·si·mist /ˈpɛsəmɪst/ *noun* [C] a person who always thinks that what is going to happen will be bad —**pes·si·mis·tic** /ˌpɛsəˈmɪstɪk/ *adj.* —**pes·si·mis·ti·cal·ly** /-kli/ *adv.* ☞ Look at **optimism, optimist**, and **optimistic**.

pest /pɛst/ *noun* [C] **1** an insect or animal that destroys plants, food, etc.: *pest control* **2** (*informal*) a person or thing that annoys you

pes·ter /ˈpɛstər/ *verb* [T] to annoy or bother sb, e.g. by asking him/her sth many times: *to pester sb for money*

pes·ti·cide /ˈpɛstəsaɪd/ *noun* [C,U] a chemical substance that is used for killing animals or insects that eat food crops ☞ Look at **insecticide**.

☆ **pet¹** /pɛt/ *noun* [C] an animal that you keep in your home for company or for pleasure: *a pet guinea pig* ○ *to have/own a pet* ☞ Look also at **teacher's pet**.

pet² /pɛt/ *verb* (**pet·ting**; **pet·ted**) [T] to rub an animal in a loving way: *Can I pet your dog?*

pet·al /ˈpɛtl/ *noun* [C] one of the thin soft colored parts of a flower

tʃ	dʒ	v	θ	ð	s	z	ʃ
chin	June	van	thin	then	so	zoo	she

pe·ter /ˈpitər/ *verb*
PHRV **peter out** to finish or come to an end gradually: *The flow of water slowed down and finally petered out.*

pe·ti·tion /pəˈtɪʃn/ *noun* [C] a written document, signed by many people, that asks a government, etc. to do sth: *More than 50,000 area residents signed the petition protesting against the new waste dump.*

pe·tri·fied /ˈpɛtrəfaɪd/ *adj.* very frightened

pet·rol /ˈpɛtrəl/ *noun* [U] (*BrE*) = GASOLINE

pe·tro·le·um /pəˈtroʊliəm/ *noun* [U] oil that is found under the surface of the earth and that is used for making gasoline and other types of chemical substances

pet·ty /ˈpɛti/ *adj.* **1** small or not important: *He didn't want to get involved with the petty details.* ○ *petty crime* **2** unkind or unpleasant (for a reason that does not seem very important): *He tried so hard that it would be petty to criticize him now.*

pew /pyu/ *noun* [C] one of the long seats in a church

PG /ˌpi ˈdʒi/ *abbr.* parental guidance (used about movies that may not be suitable for young children to see)

PG-13 /ˌpi dʒi ˌθərˈtin/ *abbr.* (used about movies that may not be suitable for children under age 13 to see): *a PG-13 movie*

phan·tom /ˈfæntəm/ *noun* [C] **1** something with the shape of a dead person that seems to appear on earth and behave as if it were alive ☞ **Ghost** is a more common word. **2** something that you think exists, but that is not real: *phantom aircraft on a radar screen*

phar·ma·ceu·ti·cal /ˌfɑrməˈsutɪkl/ *adj.* connected with the production of medicines

phar·ma·cist /ˈfɑrməsɪst/ *noun* [C] a person whose job is to prepare and sell medicines

☆ **phar·ma·cy** /ˈfɑrməsi/ *noun* [C] (*pl.* **pharmacies**) a place where medicines are prepared and sold

☆ **phase¹** /feɪz/ *noun* [C] a period in the development of sth: *the final phase of construction* ○ *to enter a new phase.*

phase² /feɪz/ *verb*
PHRV **phase sth in** to introduce sth slowly or over a period of time: *The wage increases were phased in over three years.*
phase sth out to take away or remove sth slowly or over a period of time: *The older machines are gradually being phased out and replaced by new ones.*

Ph.D. /ˌpi eɪtʃ ˈdi/ *abbr.* Doctor of Philosophy; the highest university degree that you can earn: *She has a Ph.D. in history.* ○ *Richard Cruz, Ph.D.*

pheas·ant /ˈfɛznt/ *noun* [C,U] (*pl.* **pheasants** or **pheasant**) a type of bird with a long tail. The males have brightly colored feathers. Pheasants are often hunted and eaten as food. The meat of this bird is also called pheasant.

phe·nom·e·nal /fəˈnɑmənl/ *adj.* unusual because it is so good or so great: *phenomenal success* —**phe·nom·e·nal·ly** /-nəli/ *adv.*

phe·nom·e·non /fəˈnɑmənən; -nɑn/ *noun* [C] **1** (*pl.* **phe·nom·e·na** /-ənə/) something that happens or exists (often sth unusual): *Acid rain is not a natural phenomenon. It is caused by pollution.* **2** (*pl.* **phe·nom·e·nons**) (*informal*) a person or thing that has a lot of ability or is very successful: *golfing phenomenon Tiger Woods*

phi·los·o·pher /fəˈlɑsəfər/ *noun* [C] a person who has developed a set of ideas and beliefs about the meaning of life

phil·o·soph·i·cal /ˌfɪləˈsɑfɪkl/ *adj.* **1** of or concerning philosophy: *a philosophical debate* **2 philosophical (about sth)** having or showing a calm, quiet attitude when you are in danger or are suffering or disappointed: *The team captain was philosophical about their loss and praised the other team's skill.* —**phil·o·soph·i·cal·ly** /-kli/ *adv.*

☆ **phi·los·o·phy** /fəˈlɑsəfi/ *noun* (*pl.* **phi·los·o·phies**) **1** [U] the study of ideas and beliefs about the meaning of life **2** [C] a belief or set of beliefs that tries to explain the meaning of life or give rules about how to behave: *the philosophy of Nietzsche* ○ *Her philosophy is "If a job's worth doing, it's worth doing well."*

phlegm /flɛm/ *noun* [U] the thick yellow substance that is produced in your nose and your throat when you have a cold

pho·bi·a /ˈfoʊbiə/ *noun* [C] a very strong fear or dislike that you cannot explain

☆ **phone¹** /foʊn/ *noun* (*informal*) **1** [U] = TELEPHONE¹(1): *to make a phone call* ○ *What's your phone number?* ○ *You can buy the tickets by phone.* **2** [C] = TELEPHONE¹(2): *to answer the phone* ○ *The phone is ringing – can you get* (= answer) *it?* ☞ Look also at **cellular phone.**
IDM **on the phone/telephone** using the telephone: *"Where's Rob?" "He's on the phone."*

phone² /foʊn/ *verb* [I,T] = TELEPHONE²: *Could you phone the restaurant and make a reservation?* ☞ **Call** is more common than **phone.**

phone book *noun* [C] = TELEPHONE BOOK

pho·net·ic /fəˈnɛtɪk/ *adj.* **1** connected with the sounds of human speech **2** using a system for writing a language that has a different sign for each sound: *the phonetic alphabet* —**pho·net·i·cal·ly** /-kli/ *adv.*

pho·net·ics /fəˈnɛtɪks/ *noun* [U] the study of the sounds of human speech

pho·ny¹ /ˈfoʊni/ *adj.* not real; false

pho·ny² /ˈfoʊni/ *noun* [C] (*pl.* **pho·nies**) a person who is not what he/she pretends to be

☆ **pho·to** /ˈfoʊtoʊ/ *noun* [C] (*pl.* **pho·tos** /-toʊz/) (*informal*) = PHOTOGRAPH¹

pho·to·cop·i·er /ˈfoʊtəkɑpiər/ *noun* [C] (*formal*) = COPIER

pho·to·cop·y /ˈfoʊtəkɑpi/ *noun* [C] (*pl.* **pho·to·cop·ies**) (*formal*) = COPY¹(2) —**pho·to·cop·y**

i	ɪ	ɛ	æ	ɑ	ɔ	ʌ	ʊ	u
see	sit	ten	cat	hot	saw	cup	put	too

verb [I,T] (*pres. part.* **pho·to·cop·y·ing**; *3rd pers. sing. pres.* **pho·to·cop·ies**; *p.t., p.p.* **pho·to·cop·ied**)

☆ **pho·to·graph**[1] /'foʊt̬əgræf/ (*also* **photo**) *noun* [C] a picture that is taken with a camera: *to take a photo ∘ a color photograph ∘ to have a photo enlarged* ☞ Look at **picture, negative** and **slide**. We use **photograph** and **photo** especially when it is necessary to show a difference between pictures that were made with a camera and other types of pictures: *an exhibit of the artist's paintings and photographs.*

pho·to·graph[2] /'foʊt̬əgræf/ *verb* [T] (*formal*) (often passive) to take a photograph of sb/sth: *Suzanne was never photographed with her glasses on.*

☆ **pho·tog·ra·pher** /fə'tɑgrəfər/ *noun* [C] a person who takes photographs ☞ Look at **cameraman**.

pho·to·graph·ic /ˌfoʊt̬ə'græfɪk/ *adj.* connected with photographs or photography: *photographic equipment*

☆ **pho·tog·ra·phy** /fə'tɑgrəfi/ *noun* [U] the skill or process of taking photographs: *wildlife photography*

'**photo ˌoppor'tunity** *noun* [C] (*pl.* **photo opportunities**) (*also informal* '**photo op**) an event at which a politician or some other famous person appears, with the main purpose of allowing journalists to take photographs which show that person in a favorable or attractive way

phras·al verb /ˌfreɪzl 'vərb/ *noun* [C] a verb that is combined with an adverb or a preposition to give a new meaning, such as "take over" or "call sb up"

☆ **phrase**[1] /freɪz/ *noun* [C] a group of words that are used together. A phrase does not contain a full verb: *"First of all" and "a cup of coffee" are phrases.*

phrase[2] /freɪz/ *verb* [T] to express sth in a particular way: *The statement was phrased so that it would not offend anyone.*

phys. ed. (*also* **phys ed**) /ˌfɪz 'ɛd/ *noun* [U] = PHYSICAL EDUCATION

☆ **phys·i·cal**[1] /'fɪzɪkl/ *adj.* **1** of or for your body: *physical exercise ∘ Parents must consider their children's physical and emotional needs.* **2** connected with real things that you can touch, or with the laws of nature: *physical geography ∘ It is a physical impossibility to be in two places at once.* **3** connected with physics —**phys·i·cal·ly** /-kli/ *adv.*: *to be physically fit ∘ It will be physically impossible to fit all this stuff into the car.*

phys·i·cal[2] /'fɪzɪkl/ *noun* [C] an examination of your body by a doctor to check the condition of your general health: *to go for a physical*

ˌ**physical edu'cation** *noun* [U] (*formal*) (*also* **P.E.**; **phys. ed.**) a class in school in which you do physical exercises and play sports

ˌ**physical 'therapy** *noun* [U] the treatment of

disease or injury by exercise, heat, etc. —ˌphysical 'therapist *noun* [C]

phy·si·cian /fə'zɪʃn/ *noun* [C] (*formal*) a medical doctor

phys·i·cist /'fɪzəsɪst/ *noun* [C] a person who is an expert in physics

☆ **phys·ics** /'fɪzɪks/ *noun* [U] the scientific study of natural forces such as light, sound, heat, electricity, pressure, etc.

phy·sique /fə'zik/ *noun* [C] the size and shape of a person's body: *a strong muscular physique*

pi·an·ist /pi'ænɪst; 'piənɪst/ *noun* [C] a person who plays the piano

☆ **pi·an·o** /pi'ænoʊ/ *noun* [C] (*pl.* **pi·an·os** /-noʊz/) a large musical instrument that you play by pressing down black and white bars (**keys**). This causes small hammers to hit strings inside the instrument: *an upright piano ∘ a grand piano*

☆ **pick**[1] /pɪk/ *verb* [T] **1** to choose sb/sth from a group of people or things: *She picked her words carefully so she wouldn't upset anybody. ∘ to be picked to play for the team ∘ We picked a good day to go to the beach.* **2** to take a flower, fruit or vegetable from the place where it is growing: *I picked a bunch of flowers for you. ∘ Don't pick wild flowers. ∘ a freshly picked apple* **3** to remove a small piece or pieces from sth with your fingers: *Don't pick your nose! ∘ Don't pick all the nuts off the top of the cake. ∘ She picked a hair off her jacket.* **4** to open a lock without a key, e.g. with a piece of wire

IDM **pick a fight (with sb)** to start a fight with sb deliberately

pick sb's pocket to steal money, etc. from sb's pocket or bag

PHRV **pick on sb** to behave unfairly or unkindly toward sb

pick sb/sth out to choose or recognize sb/sth from a number of people or things: *You can go to the video store and pick out a movie to watch. ∘ I immediately picked Jean out in the picture.*

pick up to become better; to improve

pick sb up 1 (*informal*) to start talking to sb you do not know and try to start a sexual relationship with him/her **2** (used about the police) to stop and question him/her: *The drug dealers were picked up downtown.*

pick sb/sth up 1 to take hold of and lift sb/sth: *The phone stopped ringing just as I picked up the receiver. ∘ Lucy picked up the child and gave him a hug.* **2** to go and get sb/sth in a car, etc.: *My sister is coming to pick me up at 10:00. ∘ Can you pick up some stuff for supper on your way home?* **3** to hear or see sth by means of a radio, television, etc.: *You can't pick up many stations on this cheap radio.*

pick sth up 1 to put sth in its correct place, or to make a place clean and neat by doing this: *to pick up your toys ∘ Pick up your room before Grandma comes!* **2** to learn sth without formal

ə	y	w	t̬	eɪ	aɪ	ɔɪ	aʊ	oʊ
about	yes	woman	butter	say	five	boy	now	go

lessons: *Joe picked up a lot of Spanish by playing with the neighborhood kids.*

pick up on sth to notice and understand sth and change your behavior based on this: *TV comedians were quick to pick up on the President's mistake and make jokes about him.*

pick² /pɪk/ *noun* **1** [sing.] the one that you choose: *You can have whichever piece you want. Take your pick.* **2** [C, usually sing.] an act of choosing sth: *Jill got the first pick of the seats in the classroom.* **3** [C] a small piece of plastic that you use for playing a guitar **4** [C] (*also* **pickax** /ˈpɪkæks/) a tool that consists of a curved iron bar with sharp points at both ends, attached to a wooden handle. Picks are used for breaking rocks or hard ground.

pick·er /ˈpɪkər/ *noun* [C] a person whose job is to pick fruits or vegetables from trees, in fields, etc.: *tomato pickers*

pick·et /ˈpɪkət/ (*also* ˈ**picket line**) *noun* [C] a group of workers who stand or walk around, holding signs, in front of a factory, etc. during a protest (**a strike**) and try to persuade other people not to go in —**pick·et** *verb* [I,T]

ˌ**picket ˈfence** *noun* [C] a fence made from vertical sticks of wood that are pointed at the top

pick·le /ˈpɪkl/ *noun* [C,U] a cucumber that is put in vinegar or salt water to give it a sour taste: *a jar of pickles* —**pick·le** *verb* [T]: *pickled onions*

pick·pock·et /ˈpɪkpɑkət/ *noun* [C] a person who steals things from other people's pockets or bags in public places

☆ **pick·up** /ˈpɪkʌp/ *noun* **1** (*also* ˈ**pickup truck**) [C] a type of light truck that has a large open part with low sides in the back ☞ picture at **truck**. **2** [C,U] an act of taking sth from a place in order to transport it to another place: *The mayor promised to increase trash pickups and improve street maintenance.* ○ *We offer free pickup and delivery in the local area.* **3** [C] an increase or improvement in sth: *a pickup in exports*

pick·y /ˈpɪki/ *adj.* (**pick·i·er**; **pick·i·est**) (*informal*) difficult to please: *a picky eater* ☞ Look at **fussy**.

☆ **pic·nic** /ˈpɪknɪk/ *noun* [C] a meal that you eat outdoors (in the country or on a beach, etc.): *a picnic lunch* ○ *We had a picnic on the beach.*
IDM be no picnic (*informal*) to be difficult or unpleasant: *Being in the army is definitely no picnic!* —**pic·nic** *verb* [I] (*pres. part.* **pic·nick·ing**; *p.t., p.p.* **pic·nicked**)

pic·to·ri·al /pɪkˈtɔriəl/ *adj.* expressed in pictures

☆ **pic·ture¹** /ˈpɪktʃər/ *noun* **1** [C] a painting, drawing or photograph: *Here's a picture of my brother.* ○ *to draw/paint a picture* ○ *Look at the picture on page 96 and describe what you see.* ○ *Come and have your picture (= photograph) taken.* **2** [C] an idea or memory of sth in your

mind: *Jack London's novels give a good picture of what life was like in the Alaskan wilderness.* **3** [C] the quality of what you see on a television: *I can't get a good picture on this TV.* ☞ Look also at **motion picture**.
IDM get the picture (*informal*) to understand a situation: *He just doesn't seem to get the picture.*

in the picture/out of the picture (*informal*) involved in a situation/no longer involved in a situation: *Now that Jenkins is out of the picture, Yamada will probably be chosen as the next manager.*

☆ **pic·ture²** /ˈpɪktʃər/ *verb* [T] **1** to imagine sth in your mind: *Kevin used to be so wild. I can't picture him as a father.* **2** to make a picture of sb/sth: *The happy couple, pictured above, left for a honeymoon in Bali.*

pic·tur·esque /ˌpɪktʃəˈrɛsk/ *adj.* (usually used about a place) attractive and interesting: *a picturesque town on the coast*

☆ **pie** /paɪ/ *noun* [C,U] a type of food made of a pastry case or shell which is filled with fruit and then baked: *apple pie* ○ *a piece of pie*

pie

☆ **piece¹** /pis/ *noun* [C] **1** an amount or example of sth: *a piece of paper* ○ *a nice piece of furniture* ○ *Would you like another piece of cake?* ○ *a piece of advice* ○ *a very interesting piece of information* **2** one of the parts that sth is made of: *a 500-piece jigsaw puzzle* **3** one of the parts into which sth breaks: *The plate fell to the floor and smashed to pieces.* **4** one of the small objects that you use when you are playing indoor board games: *chess pieces* **5** an article in a newspaper or magazine **6** a single work of art, music, etc.: *He played a piece by Chopin.*
IDM give sb a piece of your mind (*informal*) to criticize sb in an angry way

go to pieces to be unable to control yourself: *When his wife died, he seemed to go to pieces.*

in one piece not injured or broken: *He was in a car accident, but he came out of it in one piece.*

a piece of cake (*informal*) something that is very easy

☆ **piece²** /pis/ *verb*
PHRV piece sth together 1 to put sth together from several pieces **2** to discover the truth about sth from different pieces of information

pier /pɪr/ *noun* [C] a large wooden, metal or concrete structure that is built out into the ocean. Boats can stop at piers so that people can get on or off and goods can be loaded or unloaded.

pierce /pɪrs/ *verb* [T] **1** to make a hole in sth with a sharp point: *Paul has had one ear pierced.* ○ *The sharp thorns pierced the ball.*

ər	ɪr	ɛr	ɑr	ɔr	ʊr	ʒ	h	ŋ
bird	near	hair	car	north	tour	vision	hat	sing

2 (used about light or a sound) to be seen or heard suddenly: *A scream pierced the air.*

pierc·ing /ˈpɪrsɪŋ/ *adj.* **1** (used about the wind, pain, a loud noise, etc.) strong and unpleasant **2** (used about eyes or a look) seeming to know what you are thinking

☆ **pig** /pɪg/ *noun* [C] **1** a fat animal with short legs and a curly tail that is kept on farms for its meat (**pork**)

☞ A male pig is called a **hog** or a **boar**, a female pig is a **sow** and a young pig is a **piglet**. When they make a noise, pigs **grunt**. Look at the note at **meat**.

2 (*informal*) a dirty person, or a person who eats too much ☞ Look also at **guinea pig**.

pig² /pɪg/ *verb* [T] **pig·ging; pigged**
PHRV pig out (on sth) (*informal*) to eat or drink too much

pi·geon /ˈpɪdʒən/ *noun* [C] a fat gray bird that often lives in cities

pig·gy·back /ˈpɪgibæk/ *adj., adv.* (used about a way of carrying sb) on sb's back: *to give sb a piggyback ride*

pig·gy bank /ˈpɪgi bæŋk/ *noun* [C] a small box, often shaped like a pig, that children use for saving money

pig·let /ˈpɪglət/ *noun* [C] a young pig

pig·ment /ˈpɪgmənt/ *noun* [C,U] a substance that gives color to things: *The color of your skin depends on the amount of pigment in it.*

pig·tail /ˈpɪgteɪl/ *noun* [C] one of two pieces of hair that is tied together at the sides of sb's head ☞ picture at **braid**.

☆ **pile¹** /paɪl/ *noun* [C] **1** a number of things lying on top of one another, or an amount of sth that is in a large mass: *He always left his books in a neat pile.* ○ *The truck dumped a large pile of sand in the road.*

☞ A **pile** may be neat or messy. A **heap** is not neat.

2 (*informal*) a lot of sth: *I have piles of work to do this evening.* ○ *She won a pile of money in the lottery.*

☆ **pile²** /paɪl/ *verb* [T] **1 pile sth (up)** to put things one on top of the other to form a pile¹: *Pile them on top of each other.* **2 pile A on(to) B; pile B with A** to put a lot of sth on sth: *She piled the papers on the desk.* ○ *The desk was piled with papers.*
PHRV pile into sth/out of sth (*informal*) to go in or out of sth in a disorganized way: *All the students tried to pile into the bus at the same time.*
pile up 1 to increase in quantity: *The problems really piled up while I was away.* **2** (used about several cars, etc.) to crash into each other

pile·up /ˈpaɪlʌp/ *noun* [C] a crash that involves several cars, etc.

pil·grim /ˈpɪlgrəm/ *noun* [C] **1 Pilgrim** one of

the group of people who came from England to the area that is now Massachusetts in 1620 **2** a person who travels to a holy place for religious reasons: *Many pilgrims visit Mecca every year.*

pil·grim·age /ˈpɪlgrəmɪdʒ/ *noun* [C,U] a trip that is made by a pilgrim (2): *to make a pilgrimage to Lourdes*

☆ **pill** /pɪl/ *noun* **1** [C] a small round piece of medicine that you swallow: *Take one pill, three times a day after meals.* ○ *a sleeping pill* ☞ Look at **tablet**. **2 the pill** [sing.] a pill that some women take regularly so that they do not become pregnant: *She is on the pill.*

pil·lar /ˈpɪlər/ *noun* [C] **1** a column of stone, wood or metal that is used for supporting part of a building **2** an important and active member of sth, who usually has strong moral values: *He is a real pillar of the community.*

☆ **pil·low** /ˈpɪloʊ/ *noun* [C] a large cushion that you put under your head when you are in bed ☞ picture at **bed**.

pil·low·case /ˈpɪloʊkeɪs/ *noun* [C] a cover for a pillow, that can be removed

☆ **pi·lot¹** /ˈpaɪlət/ *noun* [C] a person who flies an aircraft: *Philip is an airline pilot.*

pi·lot² /ˈpaɪlət/ *adj.* (only *before* a noun) done as an experiment or to test sth: *The pilot program will run for six months, and then we will judge how successful it was.*

pi·lot³ /ˈpaɪlət/ *verb* [T] **1** to act as the pilot¹ of a vehicle **2** to guide or help sb/sth (through sth)

pimp /pɪmp/ *noun* [C] a man who controls prostitutes, finds customers for them and takes part of the money they earn

pim·ple /ˈpɪmpl/ (also *slang* **zit**) *noun* [C] a small red spot on your skin

safety pin **pins**

pin pin

☆ **pin¹** /pɪn/ *noun* [C] **1** a short thin piece of metal with a round head at one end and a sharp point at the other. Pins are used for fastening together pieces of cloth, paper, etc. ☞ Look at **clothespin**, **rolling pin** and **safety pin**. **2** a small piece of wood or metal that is used to fasten things together **3** a small piece of jewelry with a pin (1) on the back that you wear on your shirt, jacket, etc. as a decoration **4** a wooden object, shaped like a bottle, that you try to knock over in the sport of bowling

☆ **pin²** /pɪn/ *verb* [T] (**pin·ning; pinned**) **pin sth to/on sth; pin sth together** to fasten sth with a pin¹ or pins: *to pin a notice on the bulletin board* ○ *The dress is just pinned together. I haven't sewn it yet.* ○ (*figurative*) *The police officer held him with his arms pinned to his*

P

sides. ○ (*figurative*) *All our hopes are pinned on her.*

PHRV **pin sb/sth against/under sth** to keep sb/sth in one position so that it is impossible to move: *He was pinned under the fallen tree.* ○ *to be pinned against a wall*

pin sb down 1 to cause sb to be unable to move **2** to make sb decide sth or say exactly what he/she is going to do: *Can you pin her down and find out what time she will be coming?*

pin sth down to describe or explain exactly what sth is

PIN /pɪn/ (*also* **'PIN number**) *noun* [C] personal identification number; a secret number that you use with a special card to get money from a cash machine

pinch¹ /pɪntʃ/ *verb* [T] to squeeze a piece of sb's skin tightly between your thumb and finger, or between two hard surfaces: *The lecture was so boring I had to pinch myself to stay awake.* ○ *Paul pinched his finger in the car door.*

pinch² /pɪntʃ/ *noun* [C] **1** an act of pinching¹: *She gave him a little pinch on the arm.* **2** the amount of sth that you can pick up with your thumb and finger: *a pinch of salt*

IDM **in a pinch** if necessary but with some difficulty: *We really need three, but we could manage with two in a pinch.*

pine /paɪn/ *noun* **1** [C] (*also* **'pine tree**) a tall tree that has thin sharp leaves (**needles**) and woody fruit (**pine cones**): *a northern pine forest*

☛ Trees, like the pine, that do not lose their leaves in winter are called **evergreen**.

2 [U] the wood from pine trees (which is often used for making furniture): *a pine table*

pine·ap·ple /'paɪnæpl/ *noun* [C,U] a large juicy fruit that is yellow inside and has a thick brown skin with sharp points. Pineapples grow in hot regions: *pineapple juice*

pineapple

Ping-Pong /'pɪŋpɔŋ; -pɑŋ/ *noun* [U] (*trademark*) = TABLE TENNIS

☆ **pink** /pɪŋk/ *adj.* pale red in color: *Baby girls are often dressed in pink clothes.* —**pink** *noun* [U]: *The bedroom was decorated in pink.*

pink·ie (*also* **pinky**) /'pɪŋki/ (*pl.* **pink·ies**) *noun* [C] the smallest finger on the hand

pin·na·cle /'pɪnəkl/ *noun* [C] **1** [usually sing.] the highest point of sth: *Mary is at the pinnacle of her career.* **2** a high rock on a mountain **3** a pointed stone ornament on the top of a church or castle

pin·point /'pɪnpɔɪnt/ *verb* [T] **1** to find the exact position of sth: *to pinpoint a place on the map* **2** to describe or explain exactly what sth

is: *Once the cause of the failure has been pinpointed, we can decide what to do about it.*

pins and 'needles *noun* [plural] (*informal*) the little pains that you get in a part of your body after it has been in one position for too long and when the blood is returning to it: *I've got pins and needles in my hand.*

IDM **on pins and needles** (*informal*) very nervous, worried or anxious: *Everybody was on pins and needles waiting for the results.*

pin·stripe /'pɪnstraɪp/ *noun* [C,U] a thin, usually light-colored line on cloth; a type of cloth with a pattern of these lines on it: *a pinstripe suit*

☆ **pint** /paɪnt/ *noun* [C] (*abbr.* **pt.**) a measure of liquid; 0.47 of a liter. There are eight pints in a gallon: *a pint of whipping cream* ☛ For more information on measurements, look at Appendix 2.

pi·o·neer¹ /ˌpaɪəˈnɪr/ *noun* [C] **1** a person who is one of the first to go and live in a particular area: *the pioneers of the American West* **2** a person who is one of the first to go somewhere or do sth: *Yuri Gagarin was one of the pioneers of space exploration.*

pi·o·neer² /ˌpaɪəˈnɪr/ *verb* [I,T] to be one of the first people or organizations to go somewhere, do sth or develop sth: *The hospital is famous for its pioneering work in open heart surgery.*

pi·ous /'paɪəs/ *adj.* having or showing a deep belief in and love of religion —**pi·ous·ly** *adv.*

☆ **pipe¹** /paɪp/ *noun* [C] **1** a hollow tube that carries gas or liquid: *a gas pipe* ○ *The hot water pipe burst.* **2** a small tube with a bowl at one end that is used for smoking tobacco: *Does Don smoke a pipe?*

pipe² /paɪp/ *verb* [T] to carry liquid or gas in pipes (1): *Water has to be piped.* ○ (*figurative*) *Many supermarkets have piped music playing all the time.*

PHRV **pipe up** (*informal*) to start speaking suddenly: *Just then Alex piped up, "No way!"*

pipe·line /'paɪplaɪn/ *noun* [C] a line of pipes ¹(1) that are used for carrying liquid or gas: *The oil pipeline stretches across Alaska.*

pi·ra·cy /'paɪrəsi/ *noun* [U] **1** robbery by pirates **2** illegal copying of books, videos, etc.

pi·rate¹ /'paɪrət/ *noun* [C] **1** a sailor who attacks and robs ships on the oceans **2** a person who copies books, videos, computer programs, etc. in order to sell them illegally

pi·rate² /'paɪrət/ *verb* [T] to copy a book, video, etc. in order to sell it illegally: *pirated software*

Pi·sces /'paɪsiz/ *noun* [C,U] the twelfth sign of the zodiac, the Fish; a person who was born under this sign ☛ picture at **zodiac**.

☆ **pis·tol** /'pɪstl/ *noun* [C] a small gun that you hold in one hand: *She aimed the pistol and fired.* ○ *a water pistol* (= a children's toy that shoots water) ☛ Look at the note at **gun**.

i	ɪ	ɛ	æ	ɑ	ɔ	ʌ	ʊ	u
see	sit	ten	cat	hot	saw	cup	put	too

pis·ton /ˈpɪstən/ *noun* [C] a piece of metal in an engine, etc. that fits tightly inside a tube. The piston is moved up and down inside the tube and itself causes other parts of the engine to move.

pit¹ /pɪt/ *noun* [C] **1** a large hole that is made in the ground: *a gravel pit* **2** the large hard seed in some fruits: *a peach, cherry, plum, etc. pit* ☞ picture at **peach**. **3** (*also* **the pits** [plural]) the place near a race track where cars stop for fuel, new tires, etc. during a race **IDM** **be the pits** (*informal*) to be very bad: *The food in that restaurant is the pits!*

pit² /pɪt/ *verb* [T] (**pit·ting; pit·ted**) to make shallow holes in the surface of sth: *The front of the building was pitted with bullet marks.* **PHRV** **pit A against B** to test sb/sth against sb/sth else in a fight or competition: *The two best teams were pitted against each other in the championship.*

☆ **pitch¹** /pɪtʃ/ *verb* **1** [T] to throw sth, especially with force and/or careful aim: *Doug pitched his empty can into the bushes.* **2** [I,T] (in baseball) to throw the ball to a person from the other team who tries to hit it: *Clemens pitched a near-perfect game against the Dodgers on Friday.* **3** [T] to set sth at a particular level: *The talk was pitched at people with far more experience than I have.* ○ *a high-pitched voice* **4** [T] to try and persuade sb to buy or use sth, such as a product or an idea: *companies that hire Hollywood stars to pitch their products on TV* **5** [I,T] (to cause sb/sth) to fall in a particular direction: *His bike hit a rock and he was pitched forward over the handlebars.* **6** [I] (used about a ship or an airplane) to move up and down or from side to side **7** [T] to put up a tent or tents: *They pitched their tents in the valley.* **PHRV** **pitch in** (*informal*) to join in and work together with other people: *Everybody has to pitch in at home when Mom's sick.*

☆ **pitch²** /pɪtʃ/ *noun* **1** [C] (in baseball) an act of throwing the ball to the player who tries to hit it, or a particular way of throwing: *Ripken hit the first pitch of the game deep into center field.* ○ *a wild pitch* **2** [C] a speech or statement, etc., that you make in order to persuade sb to buy, use, or do sth: *a sales pitch for a new soft drink* ○ *The senator made a pitch for his proposed tax cut.* **3** [U] the degree of how high or low a musical note or a voice is **4** [sing.] the level of sth: *The crowd's excitement reached fever pitch* (= they were very excited).

,**pitch-'black** *adj.* completely dark; with no light at all

pitch·er /ˈpɪtʃər/ *noun* [C] **1** a container with a handle, used for holding and pouring liquids **2** (in baseball) the player who throws the ball to players from the other team, who try to hit it ☞ picture at **baseball**.

jug pitcher

pitch·fork /ˈpɪtʃfɔrk/ *noun* [C] a tool that looks like a large fork, that is used on farms for lifting and moving cut grass, etc.

pit·fall /ˈpɪtfɔl/ *noun* [C, usually pl.] an unexpected danger; a mistake that you might easily make

pit·i·ful /ˈpɪtɪfl/ *adj.* causing you to feel pity or sadness: *the pitiful groans of the wounded soldiers* ☞ Look at **pathetic**. —**pit·i·ful·ly** *adv.*: *The children were pitifully thin.*

pit·i·less /ˈpɪtɪləs/ *adj.* having or showing no pity for other people's suffering

pit·y¹ /ˈpɪti/ *noun* **1** [U] a feeling of sadness that you have for sb/sth that is suffering or in trouble: *He showed no pity at the way they had been treated.* ○ *All I feel for her now is pity – I'm not mad anymore.* **2** [sing.] something that makes you feel sad or disappointed: *It's a pity that he never took good care of her.* **IDM** **take pity on sb** to help sb who is suffering or in trouble because you feel sorry for him/her

pit·y² /ˈpɪti/ *verb* [T] (*pres. part.* **pit·y·ing**; *3rd pers. sing. pres.* **pit·ies**; *p.t., p.p.* **pit·ied**) to feel pity¹ or sadness for sb who is suffering or in trouble: *It is not enough to pity these people; we should try to help them.* ○ *I pity the person who has to clean his room!*

piv·ot¹ /ˈpɪvət/ *verb* [I] to balance or turn on a central point

piv·ot² /ˈpɪvət/ *noun* [C] the central point on which sth balances or turns

☆ **piz·za** /ˈpitsə/ *noun* [C,U] a round flat piece of bread that is covered with tomatoes, cheese, onions, etc. and cooked in an oven

Pkwy. *abbr.* = PARKWAY(2)

Pl. *abbr.* = PLACE¹(10)

plac·ard /ˈplækərd; -kɑrd/ *noun* [C] a large notice that is hung on a wall or carried (in a demonstration, etc.)

☆ **place¹** /pleɪs/ *noun* [C] **1** a particular position or area: *No one can be in two places at once.* ○ *This is a good place for a picnic.* ○ *The wall was damaged in several places.* ○ *I lost my place in my book* (= where I was reading) *when the phone rang.* ○ *Do you think that lamp is in the right place?* **2** a building, town, country, etc.: *Monterey is a very beautiful place.* ○ *Do you know of a good place to eat* (= a restaurant) *around here?* **3** a seat or position for sb/sth: *If you get there early, save me a place in line.*

☞ A **place** [C] is a seat or position for sb/sth: *If you get there first, can you save a place for me?* A **place** where you can park your car is also called a **space** [C]. You use **space** [U] and **room** [U] when you are talking about area in general: *This piano takes up a lot of space/room.* ○ *There is enough space/room for three people in the back of the car.*

place

4 your rank or position in society; your role: *I feel it is not my place to criticize my boss.* **5** an opportunity to study at a college, play for a team, etc.: *There were many applicants for places in the freshman class.* ○ *Lucy is now sure of a place on the Olympic team.* **6** the usual or proper position or occasion for sth: *The room was neat. Everything had been put away in its place.* ○ *I saw him at the funeral, but it was not the place to discuss business.* **7** the position of a number after the decimal point: *Your answer should be correct to three decimal places.* **8** the position that you have at the end of a race, competition, etc.: *Claire finished in second place.* **9** (*informal*) the house, etc. where you live: *Why not spend the night at our place?* **10** Place (*abbr.* **Pl.**) (used in the names of some streets): *We live at 220 Jefferson Place.*

IDM **all over the place** ⇨ ALL²

change/trade places (with sb) to take sb's seat, position, etc. and let him/her have yours: *Let's change places so that you can look out of the window.*

come, fall, fit, etc. into place (used about sth that is complicated or difficult to understand) to become organized or clear in your mind: *Pete spent two hours working on the schedule before it all fell into place.*

in the first, second, etc. place (used when you are explaining or giving reasons for sth) first, second, etc.: *He should never have been given such responsibility in the first place.*

in place in the correct position; ready for sth: *Everything is in place for the governor's visit tomorrow.*

in place of sb/sth; in sb/sth's place instead of sb/sth: *You can use milk in place of the cream in the recipe.* ○ *Prof. Brown was too sick to travel, but she sent one of her colleagues in her place.*

put yourself in sb else's/sb's place to imagine that you are sb else: *Put yourself in Steve's place and you will realize how worried he must be.*

out of place 1 not in the correct or usual place **2** not suitable for a particular situation: *I felt totally out of place around all those smart people.*

take place to happen: *The ceremony took place outdoors.*

take sb's/sth's place; take the place of sb/sth to replace sb/sth: *The President died and the Vice-President took his place.* ○ *Computers have taken the place of typewriters in most offices.*

☆ **place²** /pleɪs/ *verb* [T] **1** to put sth in a particular position or in its usual or correct position: *Dominic placed the cup on the table.* ○ *The chairs had all been placed in neat rows.* ○ *to place an ad in a newspaper* ○ (*figurative*) *We placed our trust in you, and you failed us.* ○ (*figurative*) *The blame for the disaster was*

placed firmly on the company. **2** to put sb in a particular position or situation: *His behavior placed me in a difficult situation.* ○ *to place sb in charge* **3** to remember who sb is or where you have seen them before **4** to give an order for sth to a person or company: *We placed an order for 150 T-shirts with a company in New York.*

place mat (*also* **place-mat**) *noun* [C] a piece of cloth, plastic, paper, etc. that you put on a table under one person's plate, bowl, etc.

plac·id /ˈplæsəd/ *adj.* calm or not easily excited —**plac·id·ly** *adv.*

pla·gia·rize /ˈpleɪdʒəraɪz/ *verb* [T] **plagiarize sth (from sb/sth)** to take sb else's ideas or words and use them as if they were your own: *Most of his essay was plagiarized from articles in other journals.* ☞ This word shows disapproval. —**pla·gia·rism** /ˈpleɪdʒərɪzəm/ *noun* [U]: *to be accused of plagiarism*

plague¹ /pleɪg/ *noun* **1** [C,U] a disease that spreads quickly and kills many people **2** [C] a large number of unpleasant animals or insects that come into an area at one time: *a plague of ants*

plague² /pleɪg/ *verb* [T] to cause sb/sth trouble or discomfort: *The project was plagued by a series of disasters.*

plaid /plæd/ *adj.* a pattern on material with colored squares and stripes that cross each other: *a plaid flannel shirt* ☞ picture at **pattern**.

☆ **plain¹** /pleɪn/ *adj.* **1** ordinary; not special or unusual: *plain country folks* ○ *You can use plain soap and water to remove that stain.* **2** simple in style; without any decoration, etc.: *a plain black dress* ○ *My father likes plain, hearty food.* ○ *The documents will be delivered in a plain brown envelope.* **3** without any extra flavors, etc.: *plain yogurt* ○ *Which kind of candy bar do you want: plain or with nuts?* **4** easy to see, hear or understand; clear: *It was plain that he didn't want to talk about it.* ○ *She made it plain that she didn't want to see me again.* ○ *The mugging took place in plain view of the police station.* **5** (used about people, thoughts, actions, etc.) saying what you think; direct and honest: *The senator has a reputation for plain speaking.* **6** (used especially about the appearance of a woman or girl) not beautiful: *She has very plain features.*

IDM **plain old** (*informal*) (only *before* a noun) ordinary; basic: *What that boy needs is some plain old common sense.*

☆ **plain²** /pleɪn/ *adv.* (*informal*) completely: *That is just plain wrong.*

☆ **plain³** /pleɪn/ *noun* [C] a large area of flat land with few trees: *a coastal plain* ○ *snowstorms moving across the central plains* ○ *the Great Plains of the central United States*

plain clothes *noun* [plural] (used in con-

ər	ɪr	ɛr	ɑr	ɔr	ʊr	ʒ	h	ŋ
bird	near	hair	car	north	tour	vision	hat	sing

nection with the police) ordinary clothes; not uniform: *The detectives were in plain clothes.* —**'plain·clothes** *adj.*: *a plainclothes detective*

plain·ly /ˈpleɪmli/ *adv.* clearly: *Smoke was plainly visible nearly 20 miles away.* ○ *He was plainly very upset.*

plain·tiff /ˈpleɪntəf/ *noun* [C] a person who starts a legal action against sb in a court of law ☞ Look at **defendant**.

plait /plæt/ *noun* [C] (*BrE*) = BRAID²(1) —**plait** *verb* [T]

☆ **plan¹** /plæn/ *noun* [C] **1** an idea or arrangement for doing or achieving sth in the future: *Do you have any plans for the weekend?* ○ *We usually make our vacation plans in January.* ○ *The company has no plans to hire more people.* ○ *The best plan is to ask him to meet us on Monday.* ○ *I wrote down my plan for the project – take a look.* **2** a drawing, diagram, etc. that shows how sth such as a building, part of a building, machine, etc. is arranged: *This brochure contains a floor plan of the museum.* ○ *We're having an architect draw up some plans for an addition to the house.*

IDM **go according to plan** to happen as planned

☆ **plan²** /plæn/ *verb* (**plan·ning; planned**) **1** [I,T] to decide, organize or prepare for sth: *to plan for the future* ○ *You need to plan your work more carefully.* **2** [I,T] **plan (on sth)** to intend to do sth: *I'm planning on taking a vacation in July.* ○ *We're planning to arrive at about 4 o'clock.* **3** [T] to make a plan of or for sth; to design sth: *You need an expert to help you plan your financial investments.* ○ *The new shopping center seems to be very poorly planned.*

☆ **plane** /pleɪn/ *noun* [C] **1** = AIRPLANE: *We boarded the plane in Atlanta.* ○ *a plane ticket* ○ *Has her plane landed yet?* ○ *a Lufthansa plane* ○ *a plane crash* **2** (*technical*) a flat surface **3** a tool used for making the surface of wood smooth by taking very thin pieces off it

☆ **plan·et** /ˈplænət/ *noun* [C] a large body in space that moves around the sun or another star: *The planets of our solar system are Mercury, Venus, Earth, Mars, Jupiter, Saturn, Uranus, Neptune and Pluto.* ○ *the natural resources of our planet* (= of the Earth)

plan·e·tar·i·um /ˌplænəˈtɛriəm/ *noun* [C] (*pl.* **plan·e·tar·i·ums** or **plan·e·tar·i·a**) a building that contains equipment for showing the positions and movements of the planets and stars

plank /plæŋk/ *noun* [C] **1** a long flat piece of wood (that is used for making floors, etc.) **2** an idea that is one of a set of political plans

☆ **plan·ning** /ˈplænɪŋ/ *noun* [U] making plans or arrangements: *The project requires careful planning.* ○ *Family planning* (= using contraception) *enables people to control the number of children they have.*

☆ **plant¹** /plænt/ *noun* **1** [C] a living thing that grows in soil and has a stem, leaves and roots: *a tomato plant* ○ *a house plant* (= one that grows in a pot inside a house) ○ *to water the plants* **2** [C] a building where an industrial process takes place; a large factory: *a power plant* (= where electricity is produced)

☆ **plant²** /plænt/ *verb* [T] **1** to put plants, seeds, etc. in the ground to grow: *Bulbs should be planted in the fall.* **2** **plant sth (with sth)** to cover or supply a garden, area of land, etc. with plants: *It takes a lot of hard work to plant a vegetable garden.* ○ *The field was planted with wheat this year.* **3** to put sb/sth firmly in a certain position: *He planted himself in the best seat.* **4** **plant sth (on sb)** to hide sth somewhere for a secret and usually criminal purpose (sometimes in order to make sb seem guilty of a crime): *The police think that terrorists may have planted the bomb.* ○ *The women claimed that the drugs had been planted on them.*

plan·ta·tion /plænˈteɪʃn/ *noun* [C] a large farm, especially in a tropical country or formerly in the southern U.S., where tea, cotton, tobacco, etc. are grown: *Some slaves managed to escape from plantations before the Civil War.*

plaque /plæk/ *noun* **1** [C] a flat piece of stone or metal with writing on it that is attached to a wall as a way of remembering a famous person or past event: *a memorial plaque* **2** [U] a harmful substance that forms on teeth

plas·ma /ˈplæzmə/ *noun* [U] the liquid part of blood, in which the blood cells are carried

plas·ter¹ /ˈplæstər/ *noun* **1** [U] a soft mixture of sand, water, etc. that becomes hard when it is dry. Plaster is put on walls and ceilings to form a smooth surface. **2** [U] a white substance that becomes hard when dry and is used to make figures, decorations, etc. and for putting around broken bones, etc. until they heal: *We'll have to put a plaster cast on your arm.*

plas·ter² /ˈplæstər/ *verb* [T] **1** to cover a wall, etc. with plaster¹(1) **2** to cover sth thickly with sth; to put things onto a surface: *The car was plastered with mud.* ○ *She had plastered her room with posters.* ○ *She plastered pictures of the singer all over her room.*

☆ **plas·tic** /ˈplæstɪk/ *noun* [C,U] a light, artificial material which does not break easily and is used for making many different sorts of objects: *A lot of kitchen utensils are made of plastic.* ○ *plastics and other synthetic materials* —**plas·tic** *adj.*: *plastic cups and spoons* ○ *a plastic bag*

plastic 'surgery *noun* [U] doing a surgical operation to repair or replace damaged skin or to improve the appearance of a person's face or body: *facelifts and other types of plastic surgery*

tʃ	dʒ	v	θ	ð	s	z	ʃ
chin	June	van	thin	then	so	zoo	she

bowl (*also* **dish**) **plate**

☆ **plate** /pleɪt/ *noun* **1** [C] a flat, usually round, dish that you eat or serve food from: *Put the cake on a plate.* ○ *a china plate* ○ *a paper plate*
☞ You eat your main course from a **dinner plate.** You may put your cup on a **saucer.** You usually eat cereal, soup or ice cream from a **bowl** or a **dish.**

2 [C] a thin flat piece of metal or glass **3** [C] a flat piece of metal with sth written on it: *I couldn't read the car's license plate.* **4** [U] a thin covering of gold, silver, etc. on another metal: *gold plate* **5** [C] a picture or photograph in a book that takes up a whole page: *color plates* **6** [C] a piece of plastic with artificial teeth attatched to it that fits inside a person's mouth: *an upper/a lower plate*

pla·teau /plæˈtoʊ/ *noun* [C] **1** a large area of high, flat land **2** a state where there is little development or change: *House prices seem to have reached a plateau.*

plate·ful /ˈpleɪtfʊl/ *noun* [C] the amount of food that a plate (1) can hold: *a plateful of spaghetti*

☆ **plat·form** /ˈplætfɔrm/ *noun* [C] **1** a raised floor in a public place, where people stand to make speeches or to perform: (*figurative*) *The newspaper's editor uses his column as a platform for his conservative views.* **2** a flat raised surface, especially the area beside the track at a train station where passengers get on and off trains: *a subway platform* **3** a flat raised surface on which equipment stands: *an offshore oil platform* (= for drilling oil) **4** a particular type of computer system and the way it operates: *This software operates on a UNIX platform.* **5** the ideas and aims of a political party, especially as expressed before an election: *The Democratic party platform*

plat·i·num /ˈplætn·əm/ *noun* [U] (*symbol* **Pt**) a valuable grayish-white metal that is often used for making jewelry: *a platinum ring*

pla·ton·ic /pləˈtɑnɪk/ *adj.* (used about a relationship between two people) not sexual

pla·toon /pləˈtun/ *noun* [C] a small group of soldiers

plat·ter /ˈplætər/ *noun* [C] a large, shallow, usually oval dish that is used for serving food

plau·si·ble /ˈplɔzəbl/ *adj.* sounding as if it is true; reasonable: *a plausible excuse* ☞ The opposite is **implausible.**

☆ **play¹** /pleɪ/ *verb* **1** [I] to do sth to enjoy yourself; to have fun: *They've been playing on the beach all day.* ○ *He's playing with his new toy.* ○ *Jane found a new friend to play with.* **2** [I,T] to take part in a sport or game: *"How about a game of chess?" "Sorry, but I don't know how*

to play." ○ *Who's playing in the game tonight?* ○ *I play football on Saturdays.* **3** [I,T] **play (sth) (with/against sb); play sb (at sth)** to compete against sb in a game or sport: *I usually play against Bob.* ○ *Our team plays baseball against other schools nearby.* ○ *She played him at cards and won!* **4** [T] **play sth (on sb)** to do sth which may surprise or annoy sb for your own amusement: *The kids decided to play a trick on their teacher.* **5** [I,T] to act a part in a play²(1) : *Steve is going to play Romeo.*
☞ **Play a part, role,** etc. is often used in a figurative way: *The United States has played an active part in the recent discussions.* ○ *Sarah played a key role in organizing the protest.*

6 [I,T] to make music with a musical instrument: *My son's learning the piano. He plays very well.* ○ *She played a few notes on the violin.* ○ *Could you play that piece of music again?*
☞ We usually use the definite article **the** before the names of musical instruments: *to play the piano* ○ *to learn the trumpet, etc.*

7 [T] to turn on a CD, tape, etc. so that it produces sound: *Should I play the tape for you again?* **8** [I] (*formal*) to move quickly and lightly: *A smile played on her lips.*
IDM **play ball 1** to play a ball game, especially baseball **2** to agree to do what sb wants you to do

play possum (*informal*) to pretend you are asleep or dead: *Neil was just playing possum when his mom knocked on his door.*
PHRV **play along (with sb/sth) 1** to pretend to agree or work together with sb/sth: *I decided to play along with her idea for a while.* **2** to play a game that sb else is also playing, without competing against them: *This game show has a lot of viewers who like to play along at home.*

play sth back (to sb) to turn on a tape or a movie after recording the material on it: *We made a video of the party and played it back to all the guests before they left.*

play sth down/up to make sth seem less/more important than it really is: *to play down a crisis*

☆ **play²** /pleɪ/ *noun* **1** [C] a story which is written to be performed by actors in the theater, on television or on the radio: *Would you like to go to a Broadway play while you're in New York?* ○ *a radio play* ○ *to have a part in the school play* ○ *the opening night of the play*
☞ Actors and actresses **rehearse** a play. A director **directs.** A play is usually performed on a **stage.**

2 [U] activities that are done for enjoyment only, especially by children: *Young children learn through play.* ○ *Everybody needs a balance of work and play.* **3** [U] the playing of a

game or sport; the way it is played: *Bad weather stopped play yesterday.* ○ *rough play*

☞ We **play** tennis, football, etc. but we CANNOT say **a play** of tennis. We play **a game** of tennis.

IDM **fair play** ⇨ FAIR¹

play·boy /ˈpleɪbɔɪ/ *noun* [C] a rich man who spends his time enjoying himself and spending money

☆ **play·er** /ˈpleɪər/ *noun* [C] **1** a person who plays a game: *a game for four players* ○ *She's an excellent tennis player.* **2** a person who plays a musical instrument: *a piano player* **3** *(old-fashioned)* an actor

☆ **play·ful** /ˈpleɪfl/ *adj.* **1** done or said in fun; not serious: *a playful remark* **2** full of fun; lively: *a playful puppy*

☆ **play·ground** /ˈpleɪgraʊnd/ *noun* [C] a public area of land where children can play: *the school playground*

ˈ**playing card** *noun* [C] = CARD¹(3)

ˈ**playing field** *noun* [C] a large field used for sports such as football and soccer

play·off /ˈpleɪɔf/ *noun* [C] a series of sports games that are played by the best teams or players in a particular sport, in order to find the overall winner

play·pen /ˈpleɪpɛn/ *noun* [C] a small movable platform with wooden bars or a net around its sides in which a baby or small child can play safely

play·wright /ˈpleɪraɪt/ *noun* [C] a person who writes plays

pla·za /ˈplɑzə; ˈplæzə/ *noun* [C] **1** an open space in a town or city that has buildings around it: *The demonstrators gathered on the plaza in front of the state capitol building.* **2** *(also* **shopping plaza)** a row of stores with an open area for parking in front

plea /pli/ *noun* [C] **1** a strong request; an appeal: *a last plea for mercy* **2** a statement made by sb in a court of law in which he/she claims to be guilty or not guilty of a certain crime: *to enter a plea of guilty/not guilty*

ˈ**plea-ˌbargain** *verb* [I] to say, in a court of law, that you are guilty of a less serious crime in order to get a lighter punishment and avoid a trial for a more serious crime

plead /plid/ *verb* (*p.t., p.p.* **plead·ed** or **pled** /plɛd/) **1** [I] **plead (with sb) (for sth)** to ask sb for sth in a very strong and emotional or serious way: *She pleaded with him not to leave her.* ○ *The hostages' families pleaded for their release.* **2** [T] *(formal)* to give sth as an excuse or explanation for sth: *He pleaded family problems as the reason for his lack of concentration.* **3** [T] *(formal)* (used about sb accused of a crime in a court of law) to say that you are guilty or not guilty: *The defendant pleaded not guilty to the charge of theft.*

☆ **pleas·ant** /ˈplɛznt/ *adj.* nice, enjoyable or friendly: *The weather was very pleasant.* ○ *What a pleasant surprise!* ○ *It must be pleasant to live in such a peaceful place.* ○ *He's not a very pleasant young man.* ○ *Mr. Lee is always very pleasant to me when I'm in his store.* ☞ The opposite is **unpleasant**. —**pleas·ant·ly** *adv.*

☆ **please¹** /pliz/ *verb* **1** [I,T] to make sb happy; to satisfy: *Our customer service department always aims to please.* ○ *I'll put on my best clothes to please my mother.* ○ *That teacher's very hard to please.* ○ *We were very pleased by the judge's decision.* **2** [I] (not used as the main verb in a sentence; used after words like *as, what, whatever, anything,* etc.) to want; to choose: *You can't always do exactly as you please.* ○ *She has so much money she can buy anything she pleases.*

☆ **please²** /pliz/ *interj.* (used as a polite way of making a request, an inquiry or giving an order): *Come in, please.* ○ *Could you help me, please?* ○ *Please don't touch the paintings.* ○ *Sit down, please.* ○ *Two cups of coffee, please.* ○ *"Would you like something to drink?" "Yes, please."*

☞ We do not use **please** in English when we are giving something to somebody.

☆ **pleased** /plizd/ *adj.* (not before a noun) **pleased (at sth); pleased (with sb/sth); pleased to do sth** happy or satisfied: *We were quite pleased at the outcome of the investigation.* ○ *John seems very pleased with his new car.* ○ *My parents weren't at all pleased with me when I came home late.* ○ *We were very pleased to hear your wonderful news.* ○ *I'm pleased that you've decided to stay another week.* ☞ Look at the note at **glad**. The opposite is **displeased**.

pleas·ing /ˈplizɪŋ/ *adj.* giving pleasure: *The results of our research are very pleasing.* ☞ The opposite is **displeasing**.

☆ **pleas·ure** /ˈplɛʒər/ *noun* **1** [U] the feeling of being happy or satisfied: *Parents get a lot of pleasure out of watching their children grow up.* ○ *She expressed pleasure at the judge's decision.* ○ *It gives me great pleasure to introduce our next speaker.* **2** [U] enjoyment (rather than work): *Are you in Paris on business, or is it for pleasure?* **3** [C] an event or activity that you enjoy or that makes you happy: *It's been a pleasure to work with you.* ○ *This car is a pleasure to drive.* ○ *"Thanks for your help." "It's a pleasure."*

IDM **take (no) pleasure in sth/doing sth** to enjoy/not enjoy (doing) sth: *Billy seems to take great pleasure in teasing his little sister.*

pleat /plit/ *noun* [C] a fold that is sewn or pressed into a piece of cloth: *a skirt with pleats at the front*

pled *p.t., p.p.* of PLEAD

pledge¹ /plɛdʒ/ *noun* [C] a promise or agreement, especially a promise to give money: *The*

P

government made a pledge to reduce unemployment.

pledge² /plɛdʒ/ verb [T] **pledge (sth) (to sb/sth)** to promise to give or do sth: *They pledged their support to us.* ○ *The government has pledged $250,000 to help the victims of the crash.* ○ *The President pledged to find a peaceful solution.*

plen·ti·ful /ˈplɛntɪfl/ adj. available in large amounts or numbers: *Strawberries are plentiful at this time of year.* ☞ Look at **scarce**.

☆ **plen·ty¹** /ˈplɛnti/ pron. as much or as many as you need; a lot: *"Should I get some more coffee?" "No, we've still got plenty."* ○ *Make sure you take plenty of warm clothes with you.* ○ *There's still plenty of time to get there.* ○ *You and your friends will have plenty to talk about tonight.*

plen·ty² /ˈplɛnti/ adv. **1** (before more) a lot: *There's plenty more ice cream.* **2** (informal) (with big, long, tall, etc. followed by enough): *"This shirt's too small." "Well, it looks plenty big enough to me."*

pli·a·ble /ˈplaɪəbl/ adj. **1** easy to bend or shape: *Plastic is more pliable than wood.* **2** (used about a person or a person's mind) easy to influence

pli·ers /ˈplaɪərz/ noun [plural] a tool that is used for holding things tightly, pulling nails out of wood, bending things, etc.: *Do you have the/any pliers?* ○ *a pair of pliers* ☞ picture at **tool**.

plight /plaɪt/ noun [sing.] (formal) a bad or difficult state or situation: *the plight of America's homeless people*

plod /plɑd/ verb [I] (**plod·ding**; **plod·ded**) **plod (along, through, etc.)** **1** to walk slowly and in a heavy or tired way: *We plodded along in the rain for nearly an hour.* **2** to do sth or to work slowly and with difficulty: *I spent the whole day plodding through the pile of paperwork on my desk.*

plop /plɑp/ noun [usually sing.] a sound like that of a small, smooth object dropping into water: *With a tiny plop the ring disappeared into the water.* —**plop** verb [I] (**plop·ping**; **plopped**): *The fish plopped back into the water.*

☆ **plot¹** /plɑt/ noun [C] **1** a secret plan made by several people, to do sth that is wrong: *a plot to kill the Pope* **2** the events in a story, movie, etc. and how they develop: *The play had a very strong plot, but the acting was terrible.* ○ *I can't follow the plot of this novel.* **3** a piece of land (usually small), used for a special purpose: *a garden plot* ○ *a burial plot in a cemetery* ○ *a 20-acre plot of land*

plot² /plɑt/ verb [I,T] **1** to make a secret plan to do sth: *They were accused of plotting against the government.* ○ *The terrorists had been plotting this campaign for years.* **2** to mark sth on a map, diagram, graph, etc.: *to plot the ship's*

course on the map ○ *to plot the figures on a graph*

plough /plaʊ/ noun [C] (BrE) = PLOW¹ —**plough** verb [I,T]

☆ **plow¹** /plaʊ/ noun [C] a large tool which is used on a farm and is pulled by a tractor or by an animal. A plow turns the soil over and is used especially before seeds are planted. ☞ Look also at **snowplow**.

☆ **plow²** /plaʊ/ verb [I,T] to break up or move soil, snow, etc. using a plow¹: *to plow the fields*
PHRV **plow into sb/sth** (informal) (used about a car, truck, etc.) to hit sb/sth with great force: *His car went out of control and plowed into a tree.*

plow through sth (informal) to finish reading something or doing some work, even though it is long and boring

ploy /plɔɪ/ noun [C] something that you say or do in order to get what you want or to persuade sb to do sth: *He realized that her kindness had been a ploy to get him to stay.*

pluck /plʌk/ verb [T] **1** to pull sth in order to pick or remove it: *He plucked the letter from my hands.* ○ *to pluck your eyebrows* (= to pull out the hairs you do not want) **2** to pull the feathers out of a chicken, etc. in order to prepare it for cooking **3** to pull the strings of a musical instrument and let them go again, in order to make music

pluck·y /ˈplʌki/ adj. (**pluck·i·er**; **pluck·i·est**) brave; having a lot of courage

☆ **plug¹** /plʌg/ noun [C] **1** a plastic or rubber object with two or three metal pins, which connects the wire on a piece of electrical equipment to a point in the wall where there is electricity (**an outlet**): *If the plug is damaged, do not attempt to use the appliance.* **2** a piece of rubber, metal or plastic that fits tightly into a hole (e.g. in a bathtub, sink, etc.) **3** a favorable reference to a book, record, etc. made in public in order to make people buy the thing mentioned
IDM **pull the plug (on sb/sth)** ⇨ PULL¹

☆ **plug²** /plʌg/ verb [T] (**plug·ging**; **plugged**) **1** to fill or block a hole with sth: *He managed to plug the leak in the pipe with a piece of plastic.* **2** (informal) to praise a book, record, etc. in public in order to make people buy the thing mentioned: *He went on the talk show in order to plug his new book.*

PHRV **plug sth in** to connect sth to the supply of electricity with a plug¹(1) : *The VCR isn't plugged in.* ☞ The opposite is **unplug.**

plum /plʌm/ *noun* [C] a soft, round fruit with red or purple skin and a large hard part (**pit**) in the middle

plumb·er /ˈplʌmər/ *noun* [C] a person whose job is to put in and repair water pipes, bathtubs, sinks, etc.

plumb·ing /ˈplʌmɪŋ/ *noun* [U] **1** all the pipes, water tanks, etc. in a building: *The plumbing in this house is very old.* **2** the work of a person who puts in and repairs the water pipes, tanks, etc.

plume /plum/ *noun* [C] a quantity of smoke, gas, etc. that rises in the air

plump /plʌmp/ *adj.* (used about a person or an animal) a little bit fat, but looking nice: *the baby's plump cheeks* ○ *a nice, plump chicken*

plun·der /ˈplʌndər/ *verb* [I,T] to steal things from a place, especially during war or fighting: *They captured the city, killing and plundering as they advanced.*

plunge¹ /plʌndʒ/ *verb* **1** [I] **plunge (into sth)** to go, jump, dive, fall, etc. suddenly and with force into sth: *He turned and plunged into the crowd.* ○ *A woman plunged to her death from a downtown skyscraper yesterday.* **2** [T] **plunge sth in/into sth** to push sth suddenly and with force into sth: *He plunged the knife into the woman's arm and·ran off.* **3** [T] to cause sb/sth to be in the state mentioned: *The state has been plunged into chaos by the hurricane.* **4** [I] **plunge into sth** to suddenly start or become involved in sth: *She plunged into her new job with enthusiasm.* **5** [I] to move suddenly downward; to decrease: *The value of the dollar plunged overnight.*

plunge² /plʌndʒ/ *noun* [C] a sudden forward or downward movement; a dive, fall or decrease: *a quick plunge into cold water* ○ *the plunge in house prices*

IDM **take the plunge** to decide to do sth difficult after thinking about it for a long time

plunk /plʌŋk/ *verb*

PHRV **plunk sth down** (*informal*) **1** to put sth down or drop sth heavily: *He plunked his suitcase down on my foot.* **2** to spend (a lot of) money on sth: *Some people plunk down $20 every week for lottery tickets.*

plu·per·fect /ˌpluˈpərfɪkt/ *noun* [sing.] (*grammar*) = PAST PERFECT

☆ **plu·ral** /ˈplʊrəl/ *noun* [C] (*grammar*) the form of a noun, verb, etc. which refers to more than one person or thing: *The plural of "man" is "men."* ○ *The verb should be in the plural.* —**plu·ral** *adj.* (*grammar*): *A plural noun must be followed by a plural verb.* ☞ Look at **singular.**

plu·ral·i·ty /plʊˈræləti/ *noun* [C] (in an election with more than two candidates) the number of votes received by the winner, if this

number is less than 50% of all the votes ☞ Look also at **majority.**

☆ **plus¹** /plʌs/ *prep.* **1** and; added to: *Two plus two is four (2 + 2 = 4).* ☞ Look at **minus. 2** and; in addition to: *I have a paper to write tonight, plus some reading.*

plus² /plʌs/ *conj.* (*informal*) and; in addition: *Ron has to take a test tomorrow, plus his science project is due Friday.*

plus³ /plʌs/ *adj.* **1** (used after a number) or more: *He must earn $100,000 plus.* **2** (used before a number) higher than zero: *Low temperatures could go down to plus 5 degrees tonight.* **3** (used after a letter grade on students' work) slightly above: *I got a B plus (written "B+") on my homework.* ☞ Look at **minus.**

plus⁴ /plʌs/ *noun* [C] **1** (*also* **ˈplus sign**) the sign (+): *He mistook a plus for a minus.* **2** an advantage: *The job involves a lot of travel, which is a big plus.* ☞ Look at **minus.**

plush /plʌʃ/ *adj.* fashionable and expensive: *a plush hotel*

Plu·to /ˈplutoʊ/ *noun* [sing.] the planet that is farthest from the sun

plu·to·ni·um /pluˈtoʊniəm/ *noun* [U] a dangerous substance that is used especially as a fuel in nuclear power plants

ply /plaɪ/ *verb* (*pres. part.* **ply·ing**; *3rd pers. sing. pres.* **plies**; *p.t., p.p.* **plied** /plaɪd/) [I,T] (*formal*) (used about ships, boats, etc.) to travel regularly on a certain route: *ships that ply the Atlantic*

ply·wood /ˈplaɪwʊd/ *noun* [U] a type of board that is made by sticking thin layers of wood on top of each other

P.M. (*also* **p.m.**) /ˌpi ˈɛm/ *abbr.* after noon: *2 p.m. (= 2 o'clock in the afternoon)* ○ *10:30 p.m. (= 10:30 in the evening)*

pneu·mo·nia /nuˈmoʊnyə/ *noun* [U] a serious illness of the lungs which makes breathing difficult

poach /poʊtʃ/ *verb* **1** [T] to cook an egg without its shell in boiling water: *poached eggs* **2** [T] to cook food (especially fish) in water or liquid that is boiling gently **3** [I,T] to catch or kill birds, animals or fish illegally, especially on sb else's land **4** [T] to take an idea from sb else and use it in an unfair way

poach·er /ˈpoʊtʃər/ *noun* [C] a person who kills birds, animals or fish illegally

PO Box (*also* **P.O. Box**) /ˌpi ˈoʊ bɑks/ *noun* [C] = POST OFFICE BOX

pocket

pocket

☆ **pock·et¹** /ˈpɑkət/ *noun* [C] **1** a small bag that is sewn inside or on sth you wear and that you

can carry things in: *He always walks with his hands in his pants pockets.* ○ *a pocket dictionary, calculator, etc.* (= one small enough to fit in your pocket) **2** a bag or flap that is fastened to the inside of a car door, suitcase, etc. and that you can put things in: *There are safety instructions in the pocket of the seat in front of you.* **3** a small area or group of sth: *pockets of unemployment* ○ *a pocket of warm air*
IDM **pick sb's pocket** ➪ PICK¹

pock·et² /'pɑkət/ *verb* [T] **1** to put sth in your pocket¹(1): *He took the letter and pocketed it quickly.* **2** to steal sth or to keep money for yourself

pock·et·book /'pɑkətbʊk/ *noun* [C] (*old-fashioned*) = PURSE¹ (*figurative*) *Most people worry about how government policies will affect their pocketbooks* (= how much money they have).

pock·et·ful /'pɑkətfʊl/ *noun* [C] the amount that a pocket¹(1) holds

pocket knife *noun* [C] (*pl.* **pocket knives**) (*also* **penknife**; **jack-knife**) a small knife with one or more blades that fold down into the handle

pocket knife
blade

pod /pɑd/ *noun* [C] the long, green part of some plants, such as peas and beans, that holds the seeds

po·di·um /'poʊdiəm/ *noun* [C] a tall, narrow desk that sb stands behind when speaking formally to a large group of people

☆ **po·em** /'poʊəm/ *noun* [C] a piece of writing, often arranged in short lines with similar sounds at the ends of lines. Poems try to express thoughts and feelings with the help of sound and rhythm: *a Robert Frost poem* (= written by him) ○ *to write a poem*

☆ **po·et** /'poʊət/ *noun* [C] a person who writes poems

po·et·ic /poʊ'ɛt̮ɪk/ *adj.* **1** beautiful and full of imagination **2** of or like poets and poetry: *poetic language* —**po·et·i·cal·ly** /-kli/ *adv.*

☆ **po·et·ry** /'poʊətri/ *noun* [U] poems, thought of as a group or a form of literature: *Shakespeare's poetry and plays* ○ *poetry and prose*

poign·ant /'pɔmyənt/ *adj.* causing sadness or pity: *a poignant memory* —**poign·an·cy** /-yənsi/ *noun* [U] (*formal*) —**poign·ant·ly** *adv.*

☆ **point¹** /pɔmt/ *noun* [C, sing.] **1** [C] something that you say as part of a discussion; a particular fact, idea or opinion: *During the meeting, she made some interesting points.* ○ *I see your point, but I don't agree with you.* ○ *"How are we going to pay for everything?" "That's a good point."*

☛ We **bring up, raise, make, emphasize** and **illustrate** a point.

2 the point [sing.] the most important part of what is being said; the main piece of informa-

tion: *The point is that we can't go on vacation until the car is fixed.* ○ *She always talks and talks and takes forever to get to the point.* ○ *You're still missing* (= not understanding) *the point here.* **3** [C] a detail, single item, quality of sb/sth: *What would you say are your strong and weak points?* (= good and bad qualities) **4** [sing.] the meaning, reason, purpose, etc. of sth: *What's the point of calling her again?* ○ *There's no point in telling my parents all my problems.* **5** [C] (often in compounds) a particular place or position: *We should be reaching the point where the road joins the freeway.* ○ *The library is a good starting point for that sort of information.* ○ *He aimed the gun at a point just above the man's head.* **6** [C] the thin, sharp end of sth: *the point of a pin, needle, pencil, etc.* **7** [C] a small round dot used when writing parts of numbers **8** [C] a particular time or moment; a stage of progress, development, etc.: *At one point I thought I was going to laugh.* ○ *He has reached the high point of his career.* ○ *the boiling/freezing point of water* **9** [C] a single unit in some games, sports, etc. that you add to others to get the score: *to score a point* ○ *Kari won the game by one point over Mark.* **10** [C] a unit of measurement for certain things: *The stock market gained 27 points today.*

IDM **beside the point** not connected with the subject you are discussing

make a point of doing sth to be especially careful to do sth: *I'll make a point of inviting them to our next party.*

point of view a way of looking at a situation; an opinion: *You should try to understand other people's points of view.* ○ *From my point of view, it would be better to wait a little longer.*

☛ Do not confuse **from my point of view** with **in my opinion**. The first means "from my position in life" i.e. as a woman, child, teacher, etc. The second means "I think": *From an advertiser's point of view, television is a wonderful medium.* ○ *In my opinion, people watch too much television.*

a sore point ➪ SORE¹

to the point connected with what is being discussed: *His speech was short and to the point.*

up to a point partly: *I agree with you up to a point.*

☆ **point²** /pɔmt/ *verb* **1** [I] **point (at/to sb/sth)** to show where sth is or to draw attention to sth using your finger, a stick, etc.: *"I'll take that one," she said, pointing to a big chocolate cake.* **2** [T] **point sth (at/toward sb/sth)** to aim sth in the direction of sb/sth: *The farmer pointed his gun at the rabbit and fired.* **3** [I] to face in a particular direction or to show that sth is in a particular direction: *Go down this road and you'll see the sign pointing toward the highway.* **4** [I] **point to sth** to show that sth is

i	ɪ	ɛ	æ	ɑ	ɔ	ʌ	ʊ	u
see	sit	ten	cat	hot	saw	cup	put	too

likely to exist, happen, be true, etc.: *Research points to a connection between smoking and cancer.*

IDM **point a/the finger at sb/sth** to blame sb/sth for sth; to accuse sb/sth: *It's too easy to point the finger at somebody else when things go wrong.*

PHR V **point sth out (to sb)** to direct attention to sth; to make sth clear to sb: *The guide pointed out all the places of interest to us on the way.* ○ *I'd like to point out that we don't have much time left to make a decision.*

point-'blank *adj., adv.* **1** (used about sth that is said) in a way that is very direct and often not polite; not allowing any discussion: *He told her point-blank to get out of the house.* **2** (used about a shot) from a very close position: *The shot was fired at point-blank range.*

point-ed /'pɔɪntəd/ *adj.* **1** (also *informal* **point-y**) having a point[1](6) at one end: *She has a pointed nose.* **2** done or spoken in a way that makes it clear that you are being critical: *She made a pointed comment about people who are always late.* —**point-ed-ly** *adv.*

point-er /'pɔɪntər/ *noun* [C] **1** a piece of helpful advice or information: *Could you give me some pointers on the best way to tackle the problem?* **2** a stick or rod which is used to point to things on a map, etc.

point-less /'pɔɪntləs/ *adj.* without any use or purpose: *It's pointless to try and make him agree.* ○ *My whole life seemed pointless after my husband died.* —**point-less-ly** *adv.* —**point-less-ness** *noun* [U]

point-y /'pɔɪnti/ *adj.* (*informal*) = POINTED (1)

poise /pɔɪz/ *noun* [U] a calm, confident way of behaving: *The job requires poise and an ability to deal with people.*

poised /pɔɪzd/ *adj.* **1** poised (to do sth) ready to act; about to do sth: *The Red Cross is poised to take action if the crisis continues.* **2** not moving but ready to move: *"Should I call the doctor or not?" he asked, his hand poised above the telephone.* **3** calm and confident

☆**poi-son¹** /'pɔɪzn/ *noun* [C,U] a substance that kills or harms you if you eat or drink it: *The label on the bottle said, "Poison. Do not take internally."* ○ *rat poison* ○ *poison gas*

poi-son² /'pɔɪzn/ *verb* [T] **1** to give poison to sb/sth; to kill, harm or damage sb/sth with poison: *The police confirmed that the murder victim had been poisoned.* **2** to put poison in sth: *The cup of coffee had been poisoned.* ○ *a poisoned drink* **3** to spoil or ruin sth: *The fight had poisoned their relationship.*

poi-son-ing /'pɔɪzn·ɪŋ/ *noun* [U] the giving or taking of poison or a dangerous substance: *His death was the result of poisoning.* ○ *food poisoning* (= illness as a result of eating bad food)

poison 'ivy *noun* [U] a wild plant with a

substance on its leaves that makes your skin red and painful if you touch it

☆**poi-son-ous** /'pɔɪzn·əs/ *adj.* **1** causing death or illness if you eat or drink it: *a poisonous plant* **2** (used about animals, etc.) producing and using poison to attack its enemies: *poisonous snakes, insects, etc.*

poke /pouk/ *verb* [T] **1** to push sb/sth with a finger, stick or other long, thin object: *He poked the insect with his finger to see if it was alive.* **2 poke sth into, through, out of, down, etc.** to push sth quickly into sth or in a certain direction: *"Hi Jane," she said, poking her head through the doorway.* ○ *He poked the stick into the hole to see how deep it was.*

IDM **poke fun at sb/sth** to make jokes about sb/sth, often in an unkind way

poke/stick your nose into sth ⇨ NOSE[1]

PHR V **poke around** (*informal*) to try to find sth by looking behind, under, etc. things: *I noticed that somebody had been poking around in my desk.*

poke out of/through sth; poke out/through/up to be visible coming through a hole, an open space, etc.: *A pen was poking out of her bag.* —**poke** *noun* [C]: *I gave him a poke in the side to wake him up.*

pok-er /'poukər/ *noun* **1** [U] a type of card game usually played to win money: *to play poker* ○ *a game of poker* **2** [C] a metal stick for moving the coal or wood in a fire ☞ picture at **fireplace**.

po-lar /'poulər/ *adj.* (only *before* a noun) of or near the North or South Pole: *the polar regions*

polar bear *noun* [C] a large white bear that lives in the area near the North Pole

Po-lar-oid /'poulərɔɪd/ *noun* [C] (*trademark*) a special type of photograph that comes directly out of the camera and develops by itself in just a few minutes, or a camera that takes these photographs

☆**pole** /poul/ *noun* [C] **1** a long, thin piece of wood or metal: *a fishing pole* ○ *a tent pole* **2** either of the two points at the exact top and bottom of the earth: *the North/South Pole* ☞ picture at **earth**.

the 'pole vault *noun* [sing.] the sport of jumping over a high bar with the help of a long pole

☆**po-lice¹** /pə'lis/ *noun* [plural] the official organization whose job is to make sure that people obey the law, and to prevent and solve crime, etc.: *Did you call the police when your car was stolen?* ○ *a police car* ○ *a police report*

☞ **Police** is a plural noun, always used with a plural verb. You cannot say "a police" meaning one man or woman. When we are talking about the organization, we always use **the**: *The police are investigating the murder.*

po·lice² /pə'lis/ *verb* [T] to keep control in a place by using the police or by making people follow the rules: *The cost of policing the neighborhood is extremely high.* ○ *One of the teachers' jobs is policing the student cafeteria.*

☆**po'lice de,partment** *noun* [C] the official organization of the police in a town or city

po'lice force *noun* [C] all the police officers in a town or an area: *the campus police force*

po·lice·man /pə'lismən/ *noun* [C] (*pl.* **po·lice·men** /-mən/) a man who is a member of the police

☆**po'lice officer** (*also* **officer**) *noun* [C] a person who is a member of the police: *a plainclothes police officer* (= one who is not wearing a uniform) ☞ Look at **detective**.

☆**po'lice station** *noun* [C] an office of a local police department

po·lice·wo·man /pə'liswʊmən/ *noun* [C] (*pl.* **-wo·men**) (*old-fashioned*) a woman who is a member of the police ☞ **Police officer** is more common nowadays.

☆**pol·i·cy** /'pɑləsi/ *noun* [C,U] (*pl.* **pol·i·cies**) **1** policy (on sth) a plan of action or statement of aims and ideas, especially that of a government, company or other organization: *the administration's new policy on women in the military* ○ *Company policy does not allow smoking in the building.* ☞ Look at the note at **politics**. **2** a document that shows an agreement that you have made with an insurance company: *an insurance policy*

po·li·o /'poʊlioʊ/ *noun* [U] a serious disease which can cause you to lose the power in certain muscles

poli sci /ˌpɑli 'saɪ/ *noun* [U] (*informal*) = POLITICAL SCIENCE

☆**pol·ish¹** /'pɑlɪʃ/ *verb* [T] **1** to make sth shine by rubbing it and often by putting a special cream or liquid on it: *Don't forget to polish your shoes!* **2** to spend time in order to improve sth: *She spent the whole weekend polishing her big speech.*
PHR V **polish sth off** (*informal*) to finish sth, especially food, quickly: *The kids polished off a whole carton of ice cream.*

pol·ish² /'pɑlɪʃ/ *noun* [U] a cream, liquid, wax, etc. that you put on sth to clean it and make it shine: *a can of shoe polish* ☞ Look also at **nail polish**.

pol·ished /'pɑlɪʃt/ *adj.* **1** shiny because of polishing: *polished wood floors* **2** (used about a performance, etc.) of a high standard: *a polished performance on television* **3** (used a person) confident and skillful: *a polished political speaker*

☆**po·lite** /pə'laɪt/ *adj.* having or showing good manners, e.g. that you are helpful and thoughtful toward other people and do not say or do things that might upset them; not rude: *The clerks in that store are always very helpful and polite.* ○ *It's polite to say thank you.* ○ *He*
gave me a polite smile. ☞ The opposite is **impolite** or **rude**. —**po·lite·ly** *adv.* —**po·lite·ness** *noun* [U]

☆**po·lit·i·cal** /pə'lɪtɪkl/ *adj.* **1** connected with politics and government: *The two main political parties are the Republicans and the Democrats.* ○ *She has very strong political opinions.* ○ *a political prisoner* (= one who has been put in prison for criticizing the government) ○ *an important local political figure* **2** (used about people) interested or active in politics: *I'm not really very political.* —**po·lit·i·cal·ly** /-kli/ *adv.*: *Politically, he's pretty right wing.*

po,litically cor'rect (*also* **PC**) *adj.* (used about words, behavior, etc.) that many people consider polite and acceptable and not likely to offend women, people of other races, etc.: *It is no longer politically correct to call young women "girls."* —**po,litical cor'rectness** *noun* [U]

☞ These terms are sometimes used in a critical way by people who believe it is not necessary to find new words for ones that may be unacceptable to some people.

po,litical 'science (*also informal* **poli sci**) *noun* [U] the study of politics and systems of government

☆**pol·i·ti·cian** /ˌpɑlə'tɪʃn/ *noun* [C] a person who works in an official government job to which he/she has been elected, or who is trying to be elected: *Politicians from both parties supported the war.*

☆**pol·i·tics** /'pɑlətɪks/ *noun* **1** [U] the work and ideas that are connected with governing a country, a town, etc.: *Are you interested in politics?* ○ *My son wants to go into politics* (= become a politician). ○ *local politics* ○ *Politics has never been a big interest of mine.* **2** [plural] a person's political opinions and beliefs: *She is well-known for her liberal politics.* ☞ A government's **policy** (= plan of action or aim) will depend on its **politics** (= its ideas and beliefs). **3** [plural] actions within a group that are done in order to gain power or control: *office politics*

pol·ka dot /'poʊkə dɑt/ *noun* [C] one of a pattern of round spots on fabric, etc.: *a blue scarf with white polka dots* —**pol·ka·dot·ted** /'poʊkə dɑtəd/ *adj.* ☞ picture at **pattern**.

☆**poll¹** /poʊl/ *noun* **1** [C] (*also* **opinion poll**) a way of finding out public opinion by asking a number of people what they think about sth: *The Democratic candidate had a five point lead over the Republican in the latest poll.* ☞ Look also at **exit poll**. **2 the polls** [plural] voting in a political election: *The state will go to the polls to choose a new governer tomorrow.* ○ *The polls close at 8:00.*

poll² /poʊl/ *verb* [T] to ask sb his/her opinion on a subject: *Of those polled, only 20 percent were in favor of changing the law.*

pol·len /'pɑlən/ *noun* [U] a fine, usually yel-

low, powder which is formed in flowers. It makes other flowers of the same type produce seeds when it is carried to them by the wind, insects, etc.

'polling place (also **'polling ,station**) *noun* [C] a place where people go to vote in an election

pol·lut·ant /pə'lutnt/ *noun* [C] a substance that pollutes air, water, etc.

☆ **pol·lute** /pə'lut/ *verb* [T] to make air, rivers, etc. dirty and dangerous: *Many East Coast beaches are polluted.*

☆ **pol·lu·tion** /pə'luʃn/ *noun* [U] **1** the act of polluting: *Major steps are being taken to control the pollution of beaches.* **2** substances that pollute: *Five years after the disaster, the pollution on the coast of Alaska had still not been cleaned up.*

po·lo /'poʊloʊ/ *noun* [U] a game for two teams of horses and riders. The players try to score points by hitting a ball with long wooden hammers.

'polo shirt *noun* [C] a shirt made of a light, knit fabric, with short sleeves, a collar and two or three buttons in the front

☆ **pol·y·es·ter** /,pɑli'ɛstər; 'pɑliɛstər/ *noun* [U] a type of artificial material that is used for making clothes, etc.: *The sheets are 50% cotton and 50% polyester.*

pol·y·graph /,pɑligræf/ (also **lie detector**) *noun* [C] a piece of equipment that can show whether a person is lying or not

pom·pom /'pɑmpɑm/ (also **pompon** /'pɑmpɑn/) *noun* [C] a large ball made of thin strips of paper, fabric or plastic tied together, that people wave around in the air to show enthusiasm at football games, etc.

pom·pous /'pɑmpəs/ *adj.* feeling or showing that you think you are more important than other people, e.g. by using long and important-sounding words. ☛ This word is used in a critical way.

pond /pɑnd/ *noun* [C] an area of water that is smaller than a lake

pon·der /'pɑndər/ *verb* [I,T] **ponder (on/over sth)** to think about sth carefully or for a long time

po·ny /'poʊni/ *noun* [C] (*pl.* **po·nies**) a type of small horse

po·ny·tail /'poʊniteɪl/ *noun* [C] long hair that is tied at the back of the head and that hangs down like the tail of a horse: *She wore her hair in a ponytail.* ☛ picture at **braid**.

poo·dle /'pudl/ *noun* [C] a type of dog with thick curly hair which is often cut into a special pattern

☆ **pool¹** /pul/ *noun* **1** [C] = SWIMMING POOL: *a heated indoor pool* ○ *He swam ten lengths of the pool.* **2** [C] a small area of water or another liquid, or of light: *They found her lying in a pool of blood.* ○ *a pool of light* **3** [C] a quantity of money, goods, workers, etc. that is shared

pool

cushion
cue
pocket
ball
pool table

between a group of people: *a great pool of talent* ○ *a pool of potential jurors* ☛ Look also at **car pool**. **4** [U] an indoor game that is played on a table with 15 colored and numbered balls and a white (**cue**) ball. Two players try to hit these balls into holes (**pockets**) in the table with long thin sticks (**cues**): *to play/shoot pool* ○ *a pool table* ○ *a pool hall* (= a building where people can go to play pool)

pool² /pul/ *verb* [T] to collect money, ideas, etc. from a number of people and share them: *If we pool our ideas, we should come up with a good plan.*

poop¹ /pup/ *noun* [U] (*informal*) solid waste material that is passed out of the body through the bowels: *Careful – don't step in that dog poop!* ☛ **Excrement** and **feces** are formal words with the same meaning.

poop² /pup/ *verb* [I] (*informal*) to push solid waste material out of the body through the bowels ☛ **Defecate** is a more formal word with the same meaning. A polite expression is **go to the bathroom**.

pooped /pupt/ (also **,pooped 'out**) *adj.* (*informal*) (not before a noun) very tired

☆ **poor** /pʊr; pɔr/ *adj.* **1** having very little money and a very low standard of living: *The family was too poor to buy good food.* ○ *We ought to help poorer countries.* ☛ The opposite is **rich**. **2** of low quality or in a bad condition: *Paul is in very poor health.* ○ *The airline has a poor safety record.* ○ *Attendance at the meeting was poor* (= not as many people came as had been expected). **3** (used when you are showing that you feel sorry for somebody): *That poor child lost both her parents.* ○ *Poor Don! His car got stolen yesterday.* **4 the poor** *noun* [plural] people who have little money

> ☛ Note that we use **the poor** in the plural. It always means "poor people" and CANNOT mean "the poor person."

☆ **poor·ly** /'pʊrli; 'pɔrli/ *adv.* not well; badly: *a poorly paid job* ○ *The science lab is very poorly equipped.*

pop¹ /pɑp/ *noun* **1** [C] a short sharp sound like a small explosion: *There was a loud pop as the champagne cork came out of the bottle.* **2** [U] = SODA **3** (also **'pop music**) [U] a type of modern music that is most popular among young

people: *I like to listen to rock, pop and jazz.*
4 [C] (*old-fashioned*) father

pop² /pɑp/ *verb* (**pop·ping; popped**) [I,T] (to
cause sth) to make a short sharp sound like a
small explosion: *The balloon popped.* ○ *He
popped the balloon.*

PHRV **pop out** to come out (of sth) suddenly
or quickly: (*figurative*) *Her eyes almost popped
out of her head in surprise.*

pop up (*informal*) to appear or happen sud-
denly: *There are new fast-food restaurants pop-
ping up everywhere.* ○ *If you click here, another
window will pop up on the screen.*

pop³ /pɑp/ *adj.* (*informal*) (only *before* a noun)
connected with the culture of ordinary people;
not for experts: *pop culture* ○ *You shouldn't
rely on advice from those pop psychology books.*

pop·corn /'pɑpkɔrn/ *noun* [U] a type of corn
that is heated until it bursts and becomes
light and full of air

☆ **pope** /poʊp/ *noun* [C] the head of the Roman
Catholic Church: *Pope John Paul II*

pop·py /'pɑpi/ *noun* [C] (*pl.* **pop·pies**) a bright
red wild flower that has small black seeds: *a
roll with poppy seeds on top*

ˌ**pop 'quiz** *noun* [C] (*pl.* **pop quiz·zes**) a short
test that a teacher gives in class without
warning, in order to check whether students
have been studying

Pop·si·cle /'pɑpsɪkl/ *noun* [C] (*trademark*) a
piece of flavored ice on a stick

☆ **pop·u·lar** /'pɑpyələr/ *adj.* **1** liked by many
people or by most people in a group: *Computer
games are popular with kids.* ○ *Niagara Falls
is a popular place to go for a honeymoon.* ○ *He's
very popular with his students.* ☞ The oppo-
site is **unpopular**. **2** for ordinary people (=
not for specialists or people with a high level
of education): *People were surprised that such
a respected scientist had written a popular book
on astronomy.* **3** (only *before* a noun) of or for
a lot of people: *The program is being repeated
by popular demand.*

☆ **pop·u·lar·i·ty** /ˌpɑpyə'lærəti/ *noun* [U] the
quality or state of being liked by many people:
*A presidential campaign should be more than a
popularity contest.* ○ *to lose popularity*

pop·u·lar·ize /'pɑpyələraɪz/ *verb* [T] to make
sth popular with, or known to, a lot of people:
The movie did a lot to popularize her novels.

pop·u·lar·ly /'pɑpyələrli/ *adv.* by many
people; generally: *The Republican Party is
popularly known as the GOP.*

pop·u·late /'pɑpyəleɪt/ *verb* [T] (usually pas-
sive) to fill a particular area with people: *Mon-
tana is very thinly populated.* ○ *Most of New
England is very densely populated.*

☆ **pop·u·la·tion** /ˌpɑpyə'leɪʃn/ *noun* **1** [C,U] a
number of people who live in a particular
place: *What is the population of Iowa?* ○ *a town
with a population of over 10,000* ○ *an increase/a
fall in population* **2** [C] all the people who live

in a particular area: *The report examines the
effects of the changes on the local population.*
3 [C] all the people or animals of a particular
type that live in an area: *The prison popula-
tion has increased a lot in recent years.* ○ *the
civilian population* (= the people who are not
soldiers) ○ *the penguin population of the island*

por·ce·lain /'pɔrsələn/ *noun* [U] a hard white
substance that is made by baking clay in an
oven. Porcelain is used for making expensive
cups, plates, etc.

porch /pɔrtʃ/ *noun* [C] an area attached to a
house, usually at the front, with a roof and a
floor but no outside walls: *On warm summer
evenings, we sit out on the porch and talk.*
☞ picture on page A28. Look also at **deck**,
patio and **veranda**.

por·cu·pine /'pɔrkyəpaɪn/ *noun* [C] a small
brown or black animal that is covered with
stiff, sharp needles which point out from its
body when it is angry or afraid

pore¹ /pɔr/ *noun* [C] one of the small holes in
your skin through which sweat can pass

pore² /pɔr/ *verb*
PHRV **pore over sth** to study or read sth very
carefully

pork /pɔrk/ *noun* [U] meat from a pig: *roast
pork* ○ *pork sausages* ☞ Look at **bacon** and
ham and at the note at **meat**.

por·nog·ra·phy /pɔr'nɑgrəfi/ (also *informal*
porn /pɔrn/) *noun* [U] books, magazines,
movies, etc. that describe or show sexual acts
in order to cause sexual excitement — **por·no-
graph·ic** /ˌpɔrnə'græfɪk/ *adj.*: *pornographic
movies*

po·rous /'pɔrəs/ *adj.* allowing liquid or air to
pass through slowly: *Sand is a porous mate-
rial.*

por·poise /'pɔrpəs/ *noun* [C] a sea animal
that looks like a large fish. It is very similar to
a dolphin and also lives in groups.

☆ **port** /pɔrt/ *noun* **1** [C,U] an area where ships
load and unload goods and passengers: *a fish-
ing port* ○ *The ship spent two days in port.* **2** [C]
a town or city that has a harbor: *Baltimore is
a major port.*

port·a·ble /'pɔrtəbl/ *adj.* that can be moved or
carried easily: *a portable TV set*

por·ter /'pɔrtər/ *noun* [C] a person whose job
is to carry suitcases, etc. at a train station

port·fo·li·o /pɔrt'foʊlioʊ/ *noun* [C] (*pl.* **port-
fo·li·os**) **1** a collection of pieces of work by an
artist, a student, etc.: *50% of your final grade
will be based on your homework portfolio.* **2** a
collection of shares in companies that are
owned by a person or another company: *a
stock portfolio*

port·hole /'pɔrthoʊl/ *noun* [C] a small round
window in a ship: *Anna spent the entire voyage
staring out of a porthole at the sea.*

☆ **por·tion** /'pɔrʃn/ *noun* [C] **1** a part or share of
sth: *What portion of your salary is deducted for
taxes?* ○ *We both have to accept a portion of the*

i	ɪ	ɛ	æ	ɑ	ɔ	ʌ	ʊ	u
see	sit	ten	cat	hot	saw	cup	put	too

blame. **2** an amount of food for one person (especially in a restaurant): *They don't serve very large portions here.* ☞ Look at **helping** and **serving**.

por·trait /ˈpɔrtrət/ *noun* [C] **1** a picture, painting or photograph of a person: *to paint sb's portrait* **2** a description of sb/sth in words

por·tray /pɔrˈtreɪ/ *verb* [T] **1** to describe sb/sth in words; to show sb/sth in a particular way: *The attorney portrayed her client as an honest family man.* **2** to act the part of sb in a play or movie: *It's hard for a young actress to portray a very old woman.* —**por·tray·al** /pɔrˈtreɪəl/ *noun* [C]: *He won an award for his portrayal of Abraham Lincoln.*

pose¹ /poʊz/ *verb* **1** [I] to sit or stand in a particular position for a painting, photograph, etc.: *After the wedding, we all posed for pictures.* **2** [I] **pose as sb/sth** to pretend to be sb/sth: *The thieves got into the house by posing as salesmen.* **3** [T] to set, cause or create sth: *The rise in the cost of living is posing problems for many families.* ○ *to pose a question*

pose² /poʊz/ *noun* [C] a position in which you pose, e.g. for a painting or photograph: *The kids struck a silly pose for the camera.*

posh /pɑʃ/ *adj.* fashionable and expensive: *a posh neighborhood*

☆ **po·si·tion** /pəˈzɪʃn/ *noun* **1** [C,U] the place where sb/sth is or should be: *The enemy's position was marked on the map.* ○ *That plant's in the wrong position. It's getting too much sun.* ○ *All the dancers were in position waiting for the music to begin.* **2** [C,U] the way in which sb/sth sits, stands or is placed: *I have a stiff neck. I must have been sitting in an awkward position.* ○ *Turn the switch to the "off" position.* ○ *He woke up in pain every time he changed position.* **3** [C] **a position (on sth)** what you think about sth; your opinion: *What is the government's position on the refugee crisis?* **4** [C, usually sing.] a state or situation: *What would you do if you were in my position?* ○ *I'm sorry, I'm not in a position to help you financially.* **5** [C,U] your place or rank in society, in a group, or in a race or competition: *He's always been in a respected position in the community.* **6** [C] (*formal*) a job: *I am writing to apply for the position which was advertised in yesterday's newspaper.* **7** [C] the part you play in a team game: *"What position do you play?" "Catcher."*

☆ **po·si·tion²** /pəˈzɪʃn/ *verb* [T] to put sb/sth in a particular place or position¹(1) : *Mary positioned herself near the door so she could get out quickly.*

☆ **pos·i·tive** /ˈpazətɪv/ *adj.* **1 positive (about sth/that ...)** certain; sure: *Are you positive that this is the woman you saw?* **2** clear; definite: *There is no positive evidence that he is guilty.* ○ *We have to take positive action to keep the situation from getting worse.* **3** helpful or en-

couraging: *The teacher tried to make positive suggestions.* ○ *Their reaction to my idea was pretty positive.* **4** hopeful or confident: *I feel very positive about our team's chances this season.* ○ *Positive thinking will help you succeed.* **5** (used about a medical or scientific test) showing that sth has happened or is present: *The result of the pregnancy test was positive.* **6** (used about a number) more than zero ☞ In senses 3–6 the opposite is **negative**.

pos·i·tive·ly /ˈpazətɪvli; ˌpazəˈtɪvli/ *adv.* **1** in a helpful or encouraging way: *Our customers have reacted positively to the changes.* **2** (used for emphasizing sth) really; extremely: *A lot of the people in the audience looked positively ancient!* **3** certainly or firmly: *I was positively convinced that I was doing the right thing.*

pos·se /ˈpasi/ *noun* [C] **1** (in the past) a group of people who were brought together by a law officer (a **sheriff**) to find a criminal, etc. **2** (*slang*) a group of friends who spend a lot of time together and do things together

☆ **pos·sess** /pəˈzɛs/ *verb* [T] **1** (*formal*) to have or own: *They lost everything they possessed in the fire.* ○ *It is illegal to possess a gun without a license.* **2** to influence sb or to make sb do sth: *What in the world possessed you to say a thing like that?*

☆ **pos·ses·sion** /pəˈzɛʃn/ *noun* **1** [U] the state of having or owning sth: *Enemy forces took possession of the hill.* ○ *He was arrested for possession of an illegal weapon.* **2** [C, usually pl.] something that you have or own: *Bob packed all his possessions into a suitcase and left.*

IDM **in possession (of sth)** having or owning sth: *Two teenagers were caught in possession of stolen property.*

pos·ses·sive /pəˈzɛsɪv/ *adj.* **1** not wanting to share sb/sth: *Dan is so possessive with his toys – he won't let anyone else play with them.* **2** (used in grammar to describe words that show who or what a person or thing belongs to): *"My," "your" and "his" are possessive adjectives.* ○ *"Mine," "yours" and "his" are possessive pronouns.*

☆ **pos·si·bil·i·ty** /ˌpasəˈbɪləti/ *noun* (*pl.* **pos·si·bil·i·ties**) **1** [U] **possibility (of sth/of doing sth); possibility (that ...)** the situation when sth might happen or be true; the state of being possible: *There's not much possibility of the letter reaching you before Saturday.* ○ *Is there any possibility that I can see you this weekend?*

☞ Be careful. We CANNOT say "a/the possibility to do sth" in English. To say that something is possible, we can use the verb **can**: *You can learn about American culture by staying with a host family.* We can use **opportunity** to talk about something that is possible in a certain situation: *The exchange trip gave us a unique opportunity to learn about American culture.*

P

2 [C] something that might happen or be true; sth that is possible: *There is a strong possibility that the fire was started deliberately.* ○ *One possibility would be for you to take the bus and for me to come later by car.*

☆ **pos·si·ble** /ˈpasəbl/ *adj.* **1** that can happen or be done: *I'll call you back as soon as possible.* ○ *It is now possible to use the Internet for shopping.* ○ *The doctors did everything possible to save his life.* ○ *You were warned of all the possible dangers.* ☞ Look at **impossible**. **2** that may be true or suitable: *There are several possible explanations for her strange behavior.* ○ *There are four possible candidates for the job.* ☞ Look at **probable**.

☆ **pos·si·bly** /ˈpasəbli/ *adv.* **1** perhaps; maybe: *Tomorrow's weather will be cloudy with showers or possibly heavy rain.* ○ *We will have to postpone the meeting until Thursday or possibly even Friday.* **2** (used for emphasizing sth) according to what is possible: *I will leave as soon as I possibly can.*

pos·sum /ˈpasəm/ *noun* [C] = OPOSSUM
IDM play possum ⇨ PLAY¹

☆ **post¹** /poʊst/ *noun* **1** [C] an upright piece of metal or wood that is put in the ground to mark a position or to support sth: *a goal post* ○ *a fence post* **2** [C] an important job, especially with the government or in the military forces: *She was given a diplomatic post in Paris.* **3** [C] a place where sb is on duty or is guarding sth: *The soldiers had to remain at their posts all night.* **4** [U] (*BrE*) = MAIL¹

☆ **post²** /poʊst/ *verb* [T] **1** to put a sign, notice, etc. on a wall or in a public place so that everyone can see it: *The notice was posted on every bulletin board on campus.* **2** to send sb to go and work somewhere, especially in an official government job or in the military forces: *After two years in Germany, Rosa was posted to an Air Force base in Texas.* **3** to put sb on guard or on duty in a particular place: *Police officers were posted at the front door of the building.* **4** (*BrE*) = MAIL²

☆ **post·age** /ˈpoʊstɪdʒ/ *noun* [U] the amount that it costs to send a letter, package, etc.: *The cost of postage and handling is $2.*

postage stamp *noun* [C] = STAMP¹

☆ **post·al** /ˈpoʊstl/ *adj.* connected with the collecting and delivering of letters, packages, etc.: *postal workers* ○ *the U.S. Postal Service*

☆ **post card** (*also* **postcard**) *noun* [C] a card that you write a message on and send to sb. Post cards often have a picture on one side and are usually sent without an envelope.

post·doc·tor·al /ˌpoʊstˈdaktərəl/(also *informal* **postdoc** /ˈpoʊstdak/) *adj.* connected with work or studying that sb does after he/she has received the highest university degree (**a Ph.D.**): *postdoctoral research*

☆ **post·er** /ˈpoʊstər/ *noun* [C] a large printed picture or a notice that is used to advertise sth or to decorate a room

pos·ter·i·ty /paˈstɛrəti/ *noun* [U] the future and the people who will be alive then: *We should protect our environment for the sake of posterity.*

post·grad·u·ate /ˌpoʊstˈgrædʒuət/ *adj.* (*formal*) connected with further studies that sb does at a university after he/she has received his/her first (**bachelor's**) degree ☞ Look at **graduate³**, **undergraduate** and **postdoctoral**.

post·hu·mous /ˈpastʃəməs/ *adj.* given or happening after sb has died: *a posthumous medal for bravery* —**post·hu·mous·ly** *adv.*: *Her last novel was published posthumously.*

post·mark /ˈpoʊstmark/ *noun* [C] an official mark over a stamp on a letter, package, etc. that says when and where it was mailed

post·mas·ter /ˈpoʊstmæstər/ *noun* [C] a person who is in charge of a post office

☆ **post office** *noun* [C] a building where you can buy stamps, send packages, etc.

post office box (*also* **PO box**) *noun* [C] a place in a post office where letters, packages, etc. are kept until they are picked up by the person they were sent to

☆ **post·pone** /poʊstˈpoʊn; poʊsˈpoʊn/ *verb* [T] to arrange that sth will happen at a later time than the time you had planned; to delay: *The wedding was postponed until August because the bride's mother was in the hospital.* ○ *Because of illness, the concert is postponed until further notice* (= no date for it can be given now). ☞ Look at **cancel**. —**post·pone·ment** *noun* [C,U]

pos·ture /ˈpastʃər/ *noun* [U] the way that a person sits, stands, walks, etc.: *Poor posture can lead to backache.*

post·war /ˌpoʊstˈwɔr/ *adj.* existing or happening in the period after the end of a war, especially after World War II: *postwar reconstruction*

☆ **pot¹** /pat/ *noun* **1** [C] a round container that is used for cooking food: *pots and pans* **2** [C] a container that you use for a particular purpose: *That plant needs a larger pot.* ○ *a flowerpot* ○ *a coffee pot* ☞ picture at **coffee**. **3** [C] the amount that a pot (2) contains: *We drank two pots of coffee.* **4** [U] (*informal*) the illegal drug marijuana: *to smoke pot*

pot² /pat/ *verb* [T] (**pot·ting; pot·ted**) to put a plant into a container

☆ **po·ta·to** /pəˈteɪtoʊ; -tə/ *noun* [C,U] (*pl.* **po·ta·toes**) a round vegetable with a brown, yellow or red skin. Potatoes are white or yellow inside. They grow under the ground on the roots of the potato plant: *mashed potatoes with gravy* ○ *baked potatoes* (= baked in the oven inside their skins) ○ *potato salad* ○ *Linda peeled*

ər	ɪr	ɛr	ɑr	ɔr	ʊr	ʒ	h	ŋ
bird	near	hair	car	north	tour	vision	hat	sing

the potatoes for supper. ☛ Look also at **couch potato**.

☆ **po'tato chip** *noun* [C] a very thin piece of potato that is fried in oil, dried and then sold in bags. Potato chips usually have salt on them.

po·tent /'poʊtnt/ *adj.* strong or powerful: *a potent force* —**po·ten·cy** /-nsi/ *noun* [U]

☆ **po·ten·tial¹** /pə'tɛnʃl/ *adj.* (only *before* a noun) that may possibly become sth, happen, be used, etc.: *Wind power is a potential source of energy.* ○ *potential customers* —**po·ten·tial·ly** /-ʃəli/ *adv.*: *That machine is very rusty and is potentially very dangerous.*

☆ **po·ten·tial²** /pə'tɛnʃl/ *noun* [U] the qualities or abilities that sb/sth has but that may not be fully developed yet: *That boy has great potential as a pianist.* ○ *to realize your full potential*

pot·hole /'pɑthoʊl/ *noun* [C] a hole in the surface of a road, etc.

pot·ter /'pɑtər/ *noun* [C] a person who makes pots, dishes, etc. (**pottery**) from baked clay

pot·ter·y /'pɑtəri/ *noun* [U] pots, dishes, etc. that are made from baked clay

pot·ty /'pɑti/ *noun* [C] (*pl.* **pot·ties**) (*informal*) (used especially by and to small children) a toilet: *Do you need to go potty* (= use the toilet) *before we leave?*

pouch /paʊtʃ/ *noun* [C] **1** a small bag, usually with one main part inside for carrying things in **2** a pocket of skin in which some animals, e.g. kangaroos, carry their babies ☛ picture at **kangaroo**.

☆ **poul·try** /'poʊltri/ *noun* **1** [plural] birds, e.g. chickens, ducks, turkeys, etc. that are kept on farms for their eggs or their meat: *to raise poultry* **2** [U] the meat from these birds ☛ Look at the note at **meat**.

pounce /paʊns/ *verb* [I] **pounce (on sb/sth)** to jump or spring on sb/sth suddenly in order to attack: *The cat sat motionless, waiting to pounce on the mouse.* ○ (*figurative*) *He was quick to pounce on any mistakes I made.*

☆ **pound¹** /paʊnd/ *noun* **1** [C] (*abbr.* **lb.**) a measure of weight; 0.454 of a kilogram. There are 16 ounces in a pound: *The carrots cost 49¢ a pound.* ○ *The baby weighed six pounds at birth.* ○ *I lost 15 pounds on my diet.* ○ *Get a pound of coffee if you're going to the grocery store.* ○ *a five-pound bag of flour* ☛ For more information on measurements, look at Appendix 2. **2** [C] (*symbol* £) the unit of money in Britain

pound² /paʊnd/ *verb* **1** [T] to beat sth with a heavy tool to make it soft or like powder **2** [I] **pound (away) (at/against/on sth)** to hit or beat sth many times: *Giant waves pounded against the rocks.* ○ *to pound on a door* ○ (*figurative*) *My heart was pounding with excitement.* **3** [T] (*informal*) to attack sb fiercely, or to defeat sb: *The Panthers pounded the Sharks in their game Friday, beating them 8-1.*

☆ **pour** /pɔr/ *verb* **1** [I] (used about a liquid) to flow out of or into sth, quickly and steadily, and in large quantities: *Water poured through the hole in the ceiling.* ○ *Tears were pouring down her cheeks.* ○ *There was blood pouring out of the wound.* ○ (*figurative*) *People were pouring out of the stadium.* **2** [T] to make sth flow steadily out of or into a container: *I spilled some of the oil when I tried to pour it back into the bottle.* ○ *Pour the sugar into a bowl.* **3** [T] **pour sth (for sb)** to serve drinks to sb: *Pour me another glass of wine.* **4** [I] to rain heavily: *I'm not going out. It's pouring.*

PHRV **pour sth out** to speak freely about what you think or feel about sth that has happened to you: *to pour out all your troubles*

pout /paʊt/ *verb* [I] to push your lips, or your bottom lip, forward to show that you are unhappy about sth

☆ **pov·er·ty** /'pɑvərti/ *noun* [U] the state of having very little money; the state of being poor: *to live in poverty*

the 'poverty ,line *noun* [sing.] a minimum level of income, below which the government says it is impossible to buy the things that sb needs to live: *families living above/below the poverty line*

'poverty-,stricken *adj.* very poor

POW /,pi oʊ 'dʌbl yu; -'dʌbəyu/ *abbr.* (*pl.* **POW's** or **POWs**) = PRISONER OF WAR

☆ **pow·der** /'paʊdər/ *noun* **1** [C,U] a dry substance that is in the form of very small grains: *This new scouring powder doesn't get the bathtub very clean.* ○ *baking powder* ☛ Look also at **gunpowder**. **2** [U] powder (1) that you use on your skin: *face powder* ○ *baby powder*

pow·dered /'paʊdərd/ *adj.* (used about a substance that is usually a liquid) dried in the form of a powder: *powdered milk*

'powder room *noun* [C] a room in a public building with toilets for women

☆ **pow·er¹** /'paʊər/ *noun* **1** [C,U] the ability to do sth: *The ambassador promised to do everything in her power to make sure the hostages were not harmed.* ○ *He has great powers of observation.* **2** [U] force or strength: *The ship was helpless against the power of the storm.* **3** [U] control or influence over other people: *The military government came to power after a long struggle.* ○ *the power of the unions* ○ *He sacrificed everything for power and money.* ○ *to have sb in your power* **4** [C] the right or authority to do sth: *Do the police have the power to stop cars without a good reason?* **5** [C] a person, an organization or a country that controls or influences others: *a meeting of the world's major economic powers* **6** [U] energy that is used for making machines work, giving light, heat, etc.: *nuclear power* ○ *the power supply*

pow·er² /'paʊər/ *verb* [T] to supply energy to sth so that it can work: *a portable generator*

tʃ	dʒ	v	θ	ð	s	z	ʃ
chin	**June**	**van**	**thin**	**then**	**so**	**zoo**	**she**

P

that can power several pieces of equipment ○ *vehicles powered by electricity or natural gas*

☆ **pow·er·ful** /ˈpaʊərfl/ *adj.* **1** very strong in a physical way: *That car has a very powerful engine.* ○ *Sue is a powerful swimmer.* **2** having a strong effect: *The senator made a powerful speech.* **3** having a lot of influence over other people: *There was a meeting of some of the most powerful people in the country.* —**pow·er·ful·ly** *adv.*

pow·er·less /ˈpaʊərləs/ *adj.* **1** without strength or influence **2** not able to do sth: *I stood and watched him struggle, powerless to help.*

ˈpower ˌoutage (*also* **ˈpower ˌfailure**) *noun* [C] a time when the supply of electricity is cut off, especially by accident, such as during a storm

☆ **ˈpower plant** *noun* [C] a place where electricity is made (**generated**)

pow·wow /ˈpaʊwaʊ/ *noun* [C] a traditional Native American ceremony or meeting, often with dancing

pp. *abbr.* pages: *See pp. 10-12.*

PR /ˌpi ˈɑr/ *abbr.* public relations

☆ **prac·ti·cal** /ˈpræktɪkl/ *adj.* **1** concerned with actually doing sth rather than ideas or theory: *A degree in agriculture is not very useful without practical experience working on a farm.* ☛ Look at **theoretical**. **2** very suitable for a particular purpose; useful: *Plastic tablecloths are practical, but they're not very elegant.* **3** (used about people) making sensible decisions and good at dealing with problems: *We have to be practical. There's no point in looking at a house we can't afford to buy.* **4** that is likely to succeed: *Your plan just isn't practical.* ☛ The opposite in senses 2, 3, 4 is **impractical.** —**prac·ti·cal·i·ty** /ˌpræktɪˈkæləṭi/ *noun* [U]: *Price and practicality are more important factors for us than style.*

ˌpractical ˈjoke *noun* [C] a trick that you play on sb (that involves doing sth that will make him/her look silly)

☆ **prac·ti·cal·ly** /-kli/ *adv.* **1** almost; nearly: *The streets downtown are practically deserted on Sundays.* ○ *He practically begged me not to go.* **2** in a practical way

☆ **prac·tice¹** /ˈpræktəs/ *noun* **1** [U] the actual doing of sth rather than ideas or theory: *Your suggestion sounds fine in theory, but would it work in practice?* ○ *I can't wait to put what I've learned into practice.* **2** [C,U] (a period of) doing sth many times so that you become good at it: *You need plenty of practice when you're learning how to drive.* ○ *His accent should improve with practice.* ○ *Our team's first practice is tomorrow.* **3** [C,U] (*formal*) the usual way of doing sth; sth that is done regularly: *It is standard practice to check the accuracy of our data.* ○ *Working more than 40 hours a week is a common practice in many U.S. companies.* **4** [C]

the business of a doctor or lawyer: *Sarah wants to leave her father's law firm and set up her own practice.*

IDM **out of practice** not having spent a lot of time practicing sth recently: *I'm not playing very well right now. I'm really out of practice.*

☆ **prac·tice²** /ˈpræktəs/ *verb* **1** [I,T] to do sth many times so that you become very good at it: *to practice the piano every day* ○ *The team is practicing for their big game on Friday.* ○ *They practiced the dance until it was perfect.* ○ *You need to practice saying "th" in front of a mirror.* **2** [T] to do sth or take part in sth regularly or openly: *For many years people were not allowed to practice their religion.* **3** [I,T] to work as a doctor or lawyer: *She's practicing medicine in Philadelphia.*

IDM **practice what you preach** to follow the advice that you give to other people: *Dr. Rosen always tells me to get plenty of exercise, but he doesn't always practice what he preaches* (= he is often lazy).

prac·ti·tion·er /prækˈtɪʃənər/ *noun* [C] (*formal*) a person who works in a particular profession, especially as a doctor or a lawyer

prag·mat·ic /prægˈmæṭɪk/ *adj.* dealing with problems in a practical way rather than by following theory or principles

☆ **prai·rie** /ˈprɛri/ *noun* [C] a very large area of flat land covered in grass with few trees (especially in the middle of North America)

☆ **praise¹** /preɪz/ *verb* [T] **1** **praise sb/sth (for sth)** to say that sb/sth is good and should be admired: *Her new novel has been highly praised.* ○ *The mayor praised the efforts of the firefighters.* ○ *The police officer was praised for his courage.* **2** to express thanks or honor to God: *Praise the Lord!*

☆ **praise²** /preɪz/ *noun* [U] what you say when you are expressing admiration for sb/sth: *His new play has received a lot of praise.* ○ *Children respond better to praise than to criticism.*

pram /præm/ *noun* [C] (*BrE*) = BABY CARRIAGE

prance /præns/ *verb* [I] to walk as if you were jumping or dancing, often because you feel proud of yourself or happy

☆ **pray** /preɪ/ *verb* [I,T] **1** **pray (to sb) (for sb/sth)** to speak to God or a god in order to give thanks or to ask for sth: *Let us pray.* ○ *They knelt down and prayed for peace.* ○ *to pray to Allah* ○ *They prayed that the war would end soon.* **2** **pray (for sth)** to hope for sth very strongly: *Cubs fans are praying for a big win against the Mets tonight.*

☆ **prayer** /prɛr/ *noun* **1** [C] the words that you use when you speak to God or a god: *The priest said a prayer for all the people who were sick.* **2** [U] the act of praying: *to kneel in prayer*

preach /pritʃ/ *verb* **1** [I,T] to give a talk (a **sermon**) on a religious subject: *The minister preached a sermon on the meaning of love.* ○ *Jesus preached that we should love our neigh-*

bors as ourselves. **2** [I] to tell sb in an annoying way what he/she should do: *Quit preaching at me!* **3** [T] to say that sth is good and to persuade others to accept it: *I always preach caution in situations like this.*

IDM practice what you preach ⇨ PRACTICE²

preach·er /ˈpritʃər/ *noun* [C] a person who gives religious talks (**sermons**) and often performs religious ceremonies, e.g. in a church ☞ Look at the note at **priest**.

pre·car·i·ous /priˈkɛriəs/ *adj.* not safe or certain; dangerous: *The construction workers were in a very precarious position on the roof of the building.* —**pre·car·i·ous·ly** *adv.*: *They lived precariously on his small income.*

pre·cau·tion /priˈkɔʃn/ *noun* [C] something that you do in order to avoid danger or problems: *We took the precaution of locking our valuables in the hotel safe.* ○ *precautions against fire* —**pre·cau·tion·ar·y** /priˈkɔʃəˌnɛri/ *adj.*: *I'm going to copy all these documents as a precautionary measure.*

pre·cede /priˈsid/ *verb* [I,T] (*formal*) to come or go before sb/sth: *The program was preceded by a warning about the strong language and violence in it.* ○ *Look at the diagram on the preceding page.*

prec·e·dence /ˈprɛsədəns/ *noun* [U] **precedence (over sb/sth)** the right that sb/sth has to come before sb/sth else because of greater importance: *In business, making a profit seems to take precedence over everything else.*

prec·e·dent /ˈprɛsədənt/ *noun* [C,U] something that is considered as an example or rule for what happens later: *We don't want to set a precedent by allowing one person to come in late, or else they'll all want to do it.* ○ *an event without precedent anywhere in the world* ☞ Look at **unprecedented**.

pre·cinct /ˈprisɪŋkt/ *noun* [C] **1** a part of a city that has its own police station **2** one of the parts into which a city or town is divided in order to organize voting in an election

☆ **pre·cious** /ˈprɛʃəs/ *adj.* **1** of great value (usually because there is not very much of it available): *Gold and silver are precious metals.* ○ *our precious natural resources* **2** loved very much: *My mother's old ring is one of my most precious possessions.* ○ *my precious little daughter*

ˌ**precious ˈstone** *noun* [C] a stone which is very rare and valuable and often used in jewelry: *diamonds, rubies and other precious stones*

pre·cip·i·ta·tion /prɪˌsɪpəˈteɪʃn/ *noun* [U] (*formal*) rain, snow, etc. that falls to the ground

☆ **pre·cise** /priˈsaɪs/ *adj.* **1** clear and accurate; giving a lot of details: *Try to be precise in your measurements.* ○ *I gave them precise instructions on how to get here.* ○ *The answer was 10, or 9.98 to be precise.* ○ *She couldn't be very precise about what her attacker was wearing.* **2** (only *before* a noun) exact; particular: *It is*

difficult to determine the precise moment when the crime occurred. **3** (used about a person) taking care to get small details right: *He's very precise.* ☞ In senses **1** and **3** the opposite is **imprecise**.

☆ **pre·cise·ly** /prɪˈsaɪsli/ *adv.* (*formal*) **1** clearly or exactly: *That's precisely what I mean.* ○ *I mean precisely what I say.* **2** (used for agreeing with a statement) yes, that is right: *"So, if we don't make a reservation now, we probably won't get seats?" "Precisely."* ☞ A less formal word with the same meaning as senses **1** and **2** is **exactly**. **3** (used before "because" to emphasize that the reason you are giving is different from the reason that people might expect): *"But he was so friendly." "I didn't trust him precisely because he was so friendly."*

pre·ci·sion /prɪˈsɪʒn/ *noun* [U] the quality of being clear or exact: *The plans were drawn with great precision.*

pre·co·cious /prɪˈkoʊʃəs/ *adj.* (used about children) acting in a way that makes them seem older or more intelligent than they really are ☞ This word is often used in a critical way.

pre·con·ceived /ˌprikənˈsivd/ *adj.* (used about an idea or opinion) formed before you have knowledge or experience: *When I visited Russia last year, I soon forgot all my preconceived ideas about the country.*

pred·a·tor /ˈprɛdətər/ *noun* [C] an animal that kills and eats other animals

pred·e·ces·sor /ˈprɛdəsɛsər/ *noun* [C] **1** the person who was formerly in the job or position that sb else is in now: *The new principal is much better than her predecessor.* **2** something that is no longer used and has been replaced by sth else: *Our new car is more reliable than most of its predecessors.* ☞ Look at **successor**.

pre·dic·a·ment /prɪˈdɪkəmənt/ *noun* [C] a difficult situation

pred·i·cate /ˈprɛdɪkət/ *noun* [C] (*grammar*) the part of a sentence that contains the main verb and often describes the subject: *In the sentence "The cat sat on the mat," "sat on the mat" is the predicate.*

☆ **pre·dict** /prɪˈdɪkt/ *verb* [T] to say that sth will happen (often because you have special knowledge): *to predict the results of the election* ○ *Scientists still cannot predict when earthquakes will happen.* ○ *Mrs. Jones predicted that all the students would pass the test, and they did.*

☆ **pre·dict·a·ble** /prɪˈdɪktəbl/ *adj.* **1** that was or could be expected **2** (used about a person) always behaving in the way that is expected: *I knew you were going to say that – you're so predictable.* ☞ The opposite is **unpredictable**. —**pre·dict·a·bly** *adv.*: *Predictably, all the applause came from his own supporters.*

☆ **pre·dic·tion** /prɪˈdɪkʃn/ *noun* [C,U] saying what will happen; what sb thinks will happen:

ə	y	w	t̬	eɪ	aɪ	ɔɪ	aʊ	oʊ
about	yes	woman	butter	say	five	boy	now	go

new technology to improve the prediction of earthquakes ○ *to make a prediction about the future*

pre·dom·i·nant /prɪˈdɑmənənt/ *adj.* most noticeable, powerful or important : *The predominant color was yellow.*

pre·dom·i·nant·ly /prɪˈdɑmənəntli/ *adv.* mostly; mainly: *The population of this neighborhood is predominantly Hispanic.*

pre·dom·i·nate /prɪˈdɑməneɪt/ *verb* [I] **predominate (over sb/sth)** *(formal)* to be most important or greatest in number: *Pine trees predominate in the north of the state.*

pre·ex·ist·ing (*also* **pre-existing**) /ˌpriɪgˈzɪstɪŋ/ *adj.* existing before sth else, or existing already: *My health insurance does not cover any preexisting medical conditions (= that I had before I took out the insurance).*

pref·ace /ˈprɛfəs/ *noun* [C] a written introduction to a book that explains what it is about or why it was written

☆ **pre·fer** /prɪˈfər/ *verb* [T] (**pre·fer·ring**; **pre·ferred**) **prefer sth (to sth)** *(formal)* to choose sth rather than sth else; to like sth better: *Would you prefer tea or coffee?* ○ *I prefer skating to skiing.* ○ *Marianne prefers not to walk home on her own at night.*

☞ Notice the different ways that **prefer** can be used: *Helen prefers going by bus to flying.* ○ *Helen prefers to go by bus rather than to fly.* ○ *My parents would prefer it if I went to law school.* The last sentence is more formal. Note that **prefer** is generally used in formal English. Instead of: *Would you prefer coffee or tea?* we can say: *Would you rather have coffee or tea?* Instead of: *I prefer skating to skiing* we can say: *I like skating better than skiing.*

☆ **pref·er·a·ble** /ˈprɛfərəbl/ *adj.* **preferable (to sth/to doing sth)** better or more suitable: *Going anywhere is preferable to staying home all weekend.* ○ *Cold drinks are preferable in hot weather.* —**pref·er·a·bly** /ˈprɛfərəbli/ *adv.*: *Give me a call Sunday morning but preferably not before 10:00!*

☆ **pref·er·ence** /ˈprɛfərəns; -frəns/ *noun* **1** [sing., U] **preference (for sth)** a liking for sth rather than for sth else: *What you wear is a matter of personal preference.* ○ *We have both red and white wine. Do you have a preference for one or the other?* **2** [U] **preference (to sb)** special, better treatment that you give to one person or group but not to others: *When assigning seats, we will give preference to families with young children.* ○ *Please list your choices in order of preference (= put the thing you want most at the top of the list, and so on).*

pref·er·en·tial /ˌprɛfəˈrɛnʃl/ *adj.* giving or showing better treatment to one person or group than to others: *I don't see why he should get preferential treatment – I've worked here just as long!*

pre·fix /ˈprifɪks/ *noun* [C] a word or group of letters that you put at the beginning of a word to change its meaning: *The prefix "im-" means "not," e.g. "impossible."* ☞ Look at **suffix**.

☆ **preg·nan·cy** /ˈprɛgnənsi/ *noun* (*pl.* **preg·nan·cies**) **1** [U] the state of being pregnant: *You should be sure to get plenty of exercise during pregnancy.* ○ *a pregnancy test* **2** [C] the period of time when a woman or female animal is pregnant: *to have a difficult pregnancy*

☆ **preg·nant** /ˈprɛgnənt/ *adj.* (used about a woman or female animal) having a baby developing in her body: *Elizabeth is five months pregnant.*

☞ It is also common to say: *She's expecting a baby* or: *She's going to have a baby.*

pre·his·tor·ic /ˌprihɪˈstɔrɪk; -ˈstɑrɪk/ *adj.* of the time before history was written down: *prehistoric cave paintings*

☆ **prej·u·dice¹** /ˈprɛdʒədɪs/ *noun* [C,U] a strong feeling of like or dislike toward sb/sth that is not based on reason: *racial prejudice* ○ *He has a prejudice against female doctors.*

prej·u·dice² /ˈprɛdʒədɪs/ *verb* [T] **1 prejudice sb (against/in favor of sb/sth)** to influence sb; to cause sb to have a prejudice¹: *The media coverage had prejudiced the jury against him.* **2** *(formal)* to have an influence on sth that will cause it to be unfair: *Discussing these matters could prejudice the outcome of the trial.*

☆ **prej·u·diced** /ˈprɛdʒədɪst/ *adj.* having or showing prejudice¹: *Why is he so prejudiced against women?*

pre·lim·i·nar·y /prɪˈlɪməˌnɛri/ *adj.* coming before sth else that is more important: *After a few preliminary remarks, the discussions began.*

prel·ude /ˈpreɪlud; ˈprɛlyud/ *noun* [C] **1** something that comes before sth else or that forms an introduction to sth: *The buildup of troops seemed to be a prelude to war.* **2** a piece of music that forms the first part of a longer piece of serious music

pre·ma·ture /ˌpriməˈtʃʊr; -ˈtʊr/ *adj.* **1** coming or happening before the right or expected time: *Premature babies (= babies who are born before the expected time) need special care.* **2** acting or happening too soon: *I think our decision was premature. We should have thought about it for longer.* —**pre·ma·ture·ly** *adv.*: *The shock caused her hair to go prematurely gray.*

pre·med·i·tat·ed /ˌpriˈmɛdəteɪtəd/ *adj.* planned in advance: *Was the attack premeditated?*

pre·mier¹ /prɪˈmɪr; -ˈmyɪr/ *noun* [C] = PRIME MINISTER

pre·mier² /prɪˈmɪr; -ˈmyɪr/ *adj.* (only *before* a noun) most important; best: *He's the premier performer of his time.*

pre·miere (*also* **première**) /prɪˈmɪr; -ˈmyɪr;

-'myɛr/ *noun* [C] the first performance of a play, movie, etc.

pre·mis·es /'prɛməsəz/ *noun* [plural] (*formal*) a building and the land that surrounds it: *Smoking is not allowed on the premises.*

pre·mi·um /'primiəm/ *noun* [C] **1** an amount of money that you pay regularly to a company for insurance: *monthly premiums of $150* **2** an extra amount of money: *You pay a premium for the convenience of shopping close to home.*

pre·na·tal /ˌpriˈneɪt̬l/ *adj.* happening or existing before a baby is born: *a prenatal checkup*

pre·oc·cu·pa·tion /priˌɑkyəˈpeɪʃn/ *noun* **1** [U] **preoccupation (with sth)** the state of thinking or being worried about sth all the time **2** [C] a thing that you think or worry about all the time: *The family's main preoccupation at that time was finding somewhere to live.*

pre·oc·cu·pied /priˈɑkyəpaɪd/ *adj.* (not before a noun) **preoccupied (with sb/sth)** not paying attention because you are thinking or worrying about sb/sth else

☆ **prep·a·ra·tion** /ˌprɛpəˈreɪʃn/ *noun* **1** [U] the act of getting sb/sth ready: *Hygiene is essential during the preparation of food.* **2** [C, usually pl.] **preparation (for sth/to do sth)** something that you do to get ready for sth: *The wedding preparations are almost complete.*

IDM in preparation (for sth) in order to get ready for sth: *Get a good night's sleep in preparation for the trip.*

pre·par·a·to·ry /prɪˈpærəˌtɔri; -'pɛr-; 'prɛprəˌtɔri/ *adj.* (*formal*) done in order to get ready for sth: *preparatory discussions before an important meeting*

preparatory school *noun* [C] (*formal*) = PREP SCHOOL

☆ **pre·pare** /prɪˈpɛr/ *verb* [I,T] **prepare (sb/sth) (for sb/sth)** to get ready or to make sb/sth ready: *Bob helped me prepare for the party.* ○ *I didn't leave myself enough time to prepare for the test.* ○ *to prepare a meal* ○ *The spokesman read out a prepared statement but refused to answer any questions.* ○ *You'd better prepare yourself for a shock.*

IDM be prepared for sth to be ready for sth difficult or unpleasant

be prepared to do sth (*formal*) to be willing to do sth: *I am not prepared to answer that question at this time.*

prep·o·si·tion /ˌprɛpəˈzɪʃn/ *noun* [C] a word or phrase that is used before a noun or pronoun to show place, time, direction, etc.: *"In," "for," "to," "out of" and "from" are all prepositions.*

prep·py (*also* **preppie**) /'prɛpi/ *adj.* (*informal*) connected with or typical of people who go to expensive private schools: *preppy clothes*

prep school /'prɛp skul/ (also *formal* **preparatory school**) *noun* [C] a private school that prepares students for college

pre·req·ui·site /ˌpriˈrɛkwəzɪt/ *noun* [C] **prerequisite (for/to sth)** something that is necessary before sth else can happen, exist, or be done: *English 101 is a prerequisite for all higher-level courses.*

Pres·by·te·ri·an /ˌprɛsbəˈtɪriən; ˌprɛz-/ *noun* [C], *adj.* (a member) of a Protestant church that was started by John Knox in Scotland in the 16th century

pre·school /'priskul/ (*also* **nursery school**) *noun* [C] a school for children who are about three to five years old ☛ Look also at **kindergarten**. —**pre·school** *adj.* —**pre·school·er** /'priskulər/ *noun* [C]

pre·scribe /prɪˈskraɪb/ *verb* [T] **1** to say what medicine or treatment you should have; to order medicine on a special form (**prescription**): *The doctor prescribed some medication for the pain.* **2** (*formal*) (used about a person or an organization with authority) to say that sth must be done: *a procedure prescribed by the company's handbook*

☆ **pre·scrip·tion** /prɪˈskrɪpʃn/ *noun* **1** [C,U] a form on which a doctor has written the name of the medicine that you need. You take your prescription to a drugstore and get the medicine there: *a prescription for sleeping pills* ○ *Some medicines are only available by prescription* (= with a prescription from a doctor). **2** [U] the act of prescribing sth

☆ **pres·ence** /'prɛzns/ *noun* **1** [U] being in a place or with sb: *He apologized to her in the presence of the whole family.* ○ *to request sb's presence at a meeting* ☛ The opposite is **absence**. **2** [sing.] a number of soldiers or police officers who are in a place for a special reason: *There was a huge police presence at the demonstration.*

☆ **pres·ent¹** /'prɛznt/ *adj.* **1** (not before a noun) being in a particular place: *There were 200 people present at the meeting.* ☛ The opposite is **absent**. **2** (only *before* a noun) existing or happening now: *We hope to solve our present problems very soon.*

IDM the present day modern times: *In some countries, traditional methods of farming have survived to the present day.* ○ *present-day attitudes toward women*

☆ **pres·ent²** /'prɛznt/ *noun* **1** [C] something that you give to sb or receive from sb; a gift: *The tie was a present from my sister.* ○ *a birthday, wedding, Christmas, etc. present* ○ *I have to buy a present for my friend.* ☛ **Gift** has the same meaning and is often used in stores, catalogs, etc. **2 the present** [sing.] the time now: *We live in the present, but we must learn from the past.* **3 the present** [sing.] = PRESENT TENSE

IDM for the moment/present ⇨ MOMENT

☆ **pre·sent³** /prɪˈzɛnt/ *verb* [T] **1 present sb with sth; present sth (to sb)** to give sth to sb, e.g. at a formal ceremony: *All the dancers were presented with flowers.* ○ *Flowers were presented*

P

to all the dancers. ○ *The principal presented a trophy to the winner.* **2** to give or show sth: *Good teachers try to present their material in an interesting way.* ○ *to present a report to the board of directors* **3** to cause or provide sth: *Learning English presented no problem to him.* ○ *The course aims to present each participant with new challenges.* **4** to show a play, etc. to the public: *The local theater company is presenting a musical this summer.* **5** (*formal*) **present sb (to sb)** to introduce sb in a formal situation, especially to a person of higher social rank: *Ladies and gentlemen, allow me to present my associate, Mr. Steve Jackson.*

pre·sent·a·ble /prɪˈzɛntəbl/ *adj.* good enough, and suitable to be seen in public: *This dress is a few years old – do I still look presentable?*

☆ **pres·en·ta·tion** /ˌprɛznˈteɪʃn; ˌprizn-/ *noun* **1** [U] presenting sth or being presented: *the presentation of new material in a textbook* **2** [U] the appearance of sth or the impression that it makes on other people: *Contest entries will be judged on content and artistic presentation.* **3** [C] a formal ceremony at which a prize, etc. is given to sb **4** [C] a talk that gives information on a particular subject: *to give a presentation on sth*

pres·ent·ly /ˈprɛzntli/ *adv.* (*formal*) now: *She is presently employed as the manager of our Denver branch.*

present participle *noun* [C] (*grammar*) the form of the verb that ends in *-ing*: *"Going," "walking" and "trying" are all present participles.*

the present perfect *noun* [sing.] (*grammar*) the tense of a verb that describes an action that happened from a time in the past up to now: *In the sentence "We have lived in Colorado for three years," "have lived" is in the present perfect.*

the present tense (*also* **the present**; **the simple present**) *noun* [sing.] (*grammar*) the tense of the verb that you use when you are talking about what is true or what exists now

☆ **pres·er·va·tion** /ˌprɛzərˈveɪʃn/ *noun* [U] keeping sth in the same or in good condition: *the preservation of law and order* ○ *The society is working for the preservation of wildlife.*

pre·ser·va·tive /prɪˈzərvətɪv/ *noun* [C,U] a substance that is used for keeping food, etc. in good condition

☆ **pre·serve** /prɪˈzərv/ *verb* [T] to keep sth safe or in good condition: *They have managed to preserve most of the wall paintings in the caves.* ○ *Before people had refrigerators, they used salt to preserve meat.* ○ *Efforts to preserve peace have failed.*

pre·side /prɪˈzaɪd/ *verb* [I] to be in charge of a discussion, meeting, etc.: *District Judge Gerhard Gesell presided at some of the Watergate trials.*

PHRV **preside over sth** to be in control of or responsible for sth: *Mr. Wender has presided over a period of expansion at the company.*

pres·i·den·cy /ˈprɛzədənsi/ *noun* (*pl.* **pres·i·den·cies**) **1 the presidency** [sing.] the position of being president: *to be nominated for the presidency* **2** [C] the period of time that sb is president

☆ **pres·i·dent** /ˈprɛzədənt/ *noun* [C] **1** (*also* **President**) the leader of the country and head of the government in many countries. A president is usually chosen in an election: *May I ask you a question, Mr. President?* ○ *President Chirac of France* ☞ Look also at **vice president**. **2** the person with the highest position in some companies and organizations —**pres·i·den·tial** /ˌprɛzəˈdɛnʃl/ *adj.*

'Presidents' Day *noun* [C] a holiday that is held on the third Monday in February to celebrate the birthdays of George Washington and Abraham Lincoln

☆ **press¹** /prɛs/ *verb* **1** [I,T] to push firmly: *Just press that button, and the door will open.* ○ *Don't press too hard on the brakes.* ○ *The girl pressed her nose against the window.* **2** [T] to make a piece of clothing smooth by using an iron **3** [T] to put weight onto sth, e.g. in order to get juice out of it: *to press grapes* **4** [T] to hold sb/sth firmly as a sign of love, etc.: *She pressed his hand to her heart.* **5** [I,T] **press (sb) (for sth/to do sth)** to try to get sth or to make sb do sth: *to press sb for an answer* ○ *Their lobbyists are pressing Congress to take action quickly.*

IDM **be pressed for sth** to not have enough of sth, especially time or money: *I have to hurry. I'm really pressed for time.*

press charges (against sb) to make an official statement that sb has done sth illegal so that he/she must go to court

PHRV **press against, around, etc. (sth)** (used about people) to move in a particular direction by pushing: *The crowd pressed up against the fence.*

press ahead/forward/on (with sth) to continue doing sth even though it is difficult or hard work: *They pressed on with their efforts to find the killer.*

☆ **press²** /prɛs/ *noun* **1 the press** [sing.] newspapers, and the journalists who work for them. The news departments of television and radio are also part of the press: *The candidate refused to speak to the press.* ○ *members of the local press* ○ *The law ensures the freedom of the press in this country.* **2** [C] a company that publishes books: *Oxford University Press* **3** = PRINTING PRESS

IDM **good/bad press** favorable/unfavorable attention in newspapers, on television or the radio, etc.: *The governor's tax proposals have gotten a lot of bad press recently.*

'press conference *noun* [C] a meeting in

i	ɪ	ɛ	æ	ɑ	ɔ	ʌ	ʊ	u
see	sit	ten	cat	hot	saw	cup	put	too

which a famous or important person answers questions from newspaper and television journalists: *to hold a press conference*

press·ing /ˈprɛsɪŋ/ *adj.* that you must do or deal with immediately: *the nation's most pressing economic problem*

☆ **pres·sure¹** /ˈprɛʃər/ *noun* **1** [U] the force that is produced when you press on or against sth: *Apply pressure to the cut and it will stop bleeding.* **2** [C,U] the force that a gas or liquid has when it presses against sth: *high/low blood pressure* ○ *You should check your tire pressure regularly.* ○ *Low air pressure often brings rain.* **3** [C,U] a situation that causes you to be worried or unhappy : *financial pressures* ○ *They moved to the suburbs to escape the pressure of city life.*

IDM put pressure on sb (to do sth) to persuade or force sb to do sth: *The press is putting pressure on the mayor to resign.*

under pressure 1 (used about liquid or gas) having great force: *Water is forced out through the hose under pressure.* **2** being forced to do sth: *The workers were under a lot of pressure to get the job finished as quickly as possible.*

☆ **pres·sure²** /ˈprɛʃər/ *verb* [T] **pressure sb into sth/into doing sth** to use force or influence to make sb do sth: *Her parents pressured her into going to a college near home.*

ˈpressure ˌcooker *noun* [C] a large pan with a lid in which you can cook things quickly using steam under high pressure: *(figurative) The atmosphere on campus is like a pressure cooker during finals week.*

pres·sur·ized /ˈprɛʃəraɪzd/ *adj.* (used about air in an airplane, or air or another gas in a tank) kept under pressure

pres·tige /prɛˈstiʒ; -ˈstidʒ/ *noun* [U] the respect and admiration that people feel for sb/sth, especially because of success, wealth, etc.: *He had always wanted a job with a lot of power and prestige.*

pres·ti·gious /prɛˈstidʒəs; -ˈstidʒ-/ *adj.* respected or admired because of success, wealth, high quality, etc.: *a prestigious private college*

pre·sum·a·bly /prɪˈzuməbli/ *adv.* I imagine; I suppose: *Presumably, this rain means the parade will be canceled.*

pre·sume /prɪˈzum/ *verb* [T] (*formal*) to think that sth is true even if you do not know for sure; to suppose: *The soldiers were missing, presumed dead.*

☆ **pre·tend** /prɪˈtɛnd/ *verb* [I,T] to appear to do or be sth, in order to trick or deceive sb: *Frances walked past, pretending (that) she didn't see me.* ○ *Paul's not really asleep. He's just pretending.* ○ *The kids are pretending to be astronauts.*

pre·tense /ˈpritɛns; prɪˈtɛns/ *noun* [C, sing.] an action that makes people believe sth that is not true: *He kept up the pretense that he was sick.*

IDM under false pretenses ⇨ FALSE

pre·text /ˈpritɛkst/ *noun* [C] a reason that you give for doing sth that is not the real reason: *Tom left on the pretext of having a doctor's appointment.*

☆ **pret·ty¹** /ˈprɪti/ *adj.* (**pret·ti·er; pret·ti·est**) pleasant to look at; attractive: *Rachel looks really pretty in that dress, doesn't she?* ○ *very pretty material with yellow and blue flowers on it* —**pret·ti·ly** *adv.*

☞ When we are talking about people, we use **pretty** to describe girls and women. To describe men we use **good-looking** or **handsome**. We can use **cute** in informal English to describe children and young women and men. Look also at **beautiful**.

☆ **pret·ty²** /ˈprɪti/ *adv.* (*informal*) **1** very, but not completely: *You should wear a heavier coat – it's pretty cold outside.* ○ *I'm pretty sure that Alex will agree.* **2** a little; fairly: *It was a pretty good concert, but not the best I've ever seen.*

☞ In spoken English, we use different stress and intonation for these two meanings of **pretty**. For example, if someone asks, *"How was the movie?"* we can say: *"ˌPretty ˈgood!"* (= really good) or: *"ˈPretty good."* (= not really good).

IDM pretty much/near/well almost: *I won't be long. I'm pretty much finished.*

pret·zel /ˈprɛtsl/ *noun* [C] a type of bread which is rolled thin and twisted into a special shape, then baked and covered with salt. Some pretzels are thin and hard like crackers.

pre·vail /prɪˈveɪl/ *verb* [I] (*formal*) **1** to win or gain control: *Justice prevailed and the killer was sent to prison for life.* **2** to exist or be common in a particular area: *Dry, sunny weather usually prevails in the eastern region.*

pre·vail·ing /prɪˈveɪlɪŋ/ *adj.* (only *before* a noun) most common or general in a particular area: *the prevailing opinion among residents*

prev·a·lent /ˈprɛvələnt/ *adj.* (*formal*) common in a particular place at a particular time: *The prevalent atmosphere was one of fear.*

☆ **pre·vent** /prɪˈvɛnt/ *verb* [T] **prevent sb/sth (from doing sth)** to stop sth from happening or to stop sb from doing sth: *Everyone hopes the negotiations will prevent a war.* ○ *Her parents tried to prevent her from going to live with her boyfriend.* ☞ **Prevent** is more formal than **stop**. —**pre·vent·a·ble** *adj.*: *Many accidents are preventable.*

☆ **pre·ven·tion** /prɪˈvɛnʃn/ *noun* [U] the act of preventing sth: *fire prevention tips*

pre·ven·tive /prɪˈvɛntɪv/ (*also* **preventative** /prɪˈvɛntətɪv/) *adj.* intended to stop or prevent sth (especially crime or disease) from happening: *preventive measures to reduce crime* ○ *preventative medicine*

pre·view /ˈprivyu/ *noun* [C] a chance to see a

ə	y	w	t̬	eɪ	aɪ	ɔɪ	aʊ	oʊ
about	yes	woman	butter	say	five	boy	now	go

P

play, movie, etc. before it is shown to the general public

☆ **pre·vi·ous** /ˈpriviəs/ *adj.* coming or happening before or earlier: *Do you have previous experience in this type of work?* ○ *Frank has one daughter from his previous marriage.* ○ *The previous owners of our house moved to Ohio.* —**pre·vi·ous·ly** *adv.*: *Before I got this job, I had previously worked in a department store.*

prey¹ /preɪ/ *noun* [U] an animal or bird that is killed and eaten by another animal or bird: *The lion silently watched its prey.* ○ *The eagle is a bird of prey* (= it kills and eats other birds or small animals).

prey² /preɪ/ *verb*
PHRV **prey on sb/sth** to watch sb/sth carefully and then attack him/her/it: *Cats prey on rats and mice.* ○ *a killer who preys on young women*

☆ **price¹** /praɪs/ *noun* [C] the amount of money that you must pay in order to buy sth: *What's the price of gas now?* ○ *to charge high/low prices* ○ *We can't afford to buy the car at that price.* ○ *There's no price tag on this jacket.* ○ *This shirt was on sale for half price.* ○ *(figurative) Is pollution the price we have to pay for progress?*

☞ A **charge** is the amount of money that you must pay for using something: *Is there a charge for parking here?* ○ *service charges.* You use **cost** when you are talking about paying for services or about prices in general without mentioning an actual sum of money: *The cost of electricity is going up.* ○ *the cost of living.* The **price** of something is the amount of money that you must pay in order to buy it. A store may **raise** / **increase** or **reduce** / **lower** its prices. The prices **rise** / **go up** or **fall** / **go down**.

IDM **at any price** even if the cost is very high or if it will have bad results: *Richard was determined to succeed at any price.*

price² /praɪs/ *verb* [T] **1** to set the price¹ of sth: *The books were priced between $15 and $20.* **2** to mark the price on goods in a store

price·less /ˈpraɪsləs/ *adj.* of very great value: *priceless jewels and antiques* ☞ Look at **worthless**, **valuable** and **invaluable**.

pric·ey /ˈpraɪsi/ *adj.* (**pric·i·er**; **pric·i·est**) (*informal*) expensive

prick¹ /prɪk/ *verb* [T] to make a small hole in sth or to cause sb pain with a sharp point: *You should prick the pie crust before you bake it.* ○ *Ouch! I pricked myself on that needle.*

prick² /prɪk/ *noun* [C] the sharp pain that you feel when sth pricks you: *the sharp prick of a needle*

prick·ly /ˈprɪkli/ *adj.* covered with sharp points: *a prickly bush*

☆ **pride¹** /praɪd/ *noun* **1** [U] **pride (in sb/sth)** the feeling of pleasure that you have when you (or

people who are close to you) do sth good or own sth good: *Her parents watched with pride as Mary went up to get her diploma.* ○ *her pride in her achievement* ☞ The adjective is **proud**. **2** [sing.] **the pride of sth** a person or thing that is very important or of great value to sb: *The new stadium was the pride of the whole town.* **3** [U] the feeling that you are better than other people: *the sin of pride* **4** [U] the sense of your own worth or value; self-respect: *You'll hurt his pride if you don't accept the gift.*

IDM **take pride in sb/sth** to feel pleased and proud about sth good that sb has done: *The coach took great pride in his team's success.*

take pride in sth/in doing sth to do sth very well or carefully: *I wish you took more pride in your work.*

pride² /praɪd/ *verb*
PHRV **pride yourself on sth/on doing sth** to feel pleased about sth that you can do well: *Henry prides himself on his ability to cook.*

☆ **priest** /prist/ *noun* [C] a person (usually a man) who performs religious ceremonies in a Christian church

☞ **Priest** is a general word and is used in many churches but especially in the Roman Catholic Church. A priest in a Protestant church is usually called a **minister**, a **pastor** or a **preacher**. A general term which can also be used for other religions is **clergyman** or (for a man or a woman) **member of the clergy**.

prim /prɪm/ *adj.* (used about a person) always behaving very correctly and easily shocked by swearing, talking about sex, etc. —**prim·ly** *adv.*

pri·mar·i·ly /praɪˈmɛrəli/ *adv.* more than anything else; mainly: *The course will be aimed primarily at people who have no previous experience.*

☆ **pri·mar·y¹** /ˈpraɪˌmɛri/ *adj.* most important; main: *Smoking is one of the primary causes of lung cancer.* ○ *A high standard of quality should be of primary importance.*

pri·mar·y² /ˈpraɪˌmɛri/ (*also* **primary e'lection**) *noun* [C] (*pl.* **pri·mar·ies**) an election in which people vote for the person who will be a political party's candidate in a later important election, e.g. for President

primary 'care *noun* [U] the general medical care that you get from your family doctor (not from a doctor with special skills in a specific area)

primary 'color *noun* [C] any of the colors red, yellow or blue. You can make any other color by mixing primary colors in different ways.

☆ **prime¹** /praɪm/ *adj.* (only *before* a noun) **1** most important; main: *The prime cause of the company's bankruptcy was high interest rates.* **2** of very good quality; best: *prime pieces of beef* **3** having all the typical qualities:

ər	ɪr	ɛr	ɑr	ɔr	ʊr	ʒ	h	ŋ
bird	near	hair	car	north	tour	vision	hat	sing

P

That's a prime example of what I was talking about.

prime² /praɪm/ noun [sing.] the time when sb is strongest, most beautiful, most successful, etc.: *Agassi is past his prime as a tennis player.* ○ *to be in the prime of life*

prime³ /praɪm/ verb [T] **prime sb/sth for sth/ to do sth** to prepare sb/sth for a situation or to do sth: *The candidate had been primed for the interview with all the facts.*

ˌprime ˈminister (*also* **premier**) noun [C] the leader of the government in some countries

ˌprime ˈrate noun [C] the lowest amount of interest that a bank charges its best customers at a particular time for borrowing money

ˌprime ˈtime noun [U] the time in the evening, usually from 7:00 to 10:00 or from 8:00 to 11:00, when the largest number of people watch television

prim·i·tive /ˈprɪmətɪv/ adj. **1** (only *before* a noun) connected with a very early stage of development (particularly of human life): *Primitive humans lived in caves and hunted wild animals.* **2** very simple; not developed: *The bathroom facilities at the campground were very primitive.* ○ *a primitive shelter made out of pieces of wood and cloth*

prince /prɪns/ noun [C] **1** a son or other close male relative of a king or queen: *Prince Charles* **2** the male ruler of a small country

prin·cess /ˈprɪnsəs; -sɛs/ noun [C] **1** a daughter or other close female relative of a king or queen: *Princess Anne* **2** the wife of a prince

☆**prin·ci·pal¹** /ˈprɪnsəpl/ adj. (only *before* a noun) most important; main: *The principal aim of the talks is to reduce the numbers of weapons.* ○ *the principal characters in a play*

☆**prin·ci·pal²** /ˈprɪnsəpl/ noun [C] the person who is in charge of a school

prin·ci·pal·ly /ˈprɪnsəpli/ adv. mainly; mostly: *Our products are designed principally for the American market.*

☆**prin·ci·ple** /ˈprɪnsəpl/ noun **1** [C] a basic general rule or truth about sth: *We believe in the principle of equal opportunity for everyone.* ○ *The class teaches the basic principles of car maintenance.* **2** [C,U] a rule for good behavior, based on what each person believes is right: *She refuses to wear fur. It's a matter of principle.* ○ *a person of high moral principles* **3** [sing.] a law of science: *The system works on the principle that heat rises.*

IDM **in principle** in general, but possibly not in detail: *His proposal sounds fine in principle, but there are a few points I'm not happy about.*

on principle because of your moral beliefs or principles (2): *Helen refuses to wear leather on principle.*

☆**print¹** /prɪnt/ noun **1** [U] the letters, words, etc. in a book, newspaper, etc.: *The print is too small for me to read without my glasses.*
☞ Look also at **fine print. 2** [C] a mark that is

made by sth pressing onto sth else: *The neighbors' dog left paw prints in our fresh cement!*
☞ Look also at **fingerprint** and **footprint.**
3 [C] a picture that was made by printing **4** [C] a photograph (when it has been printed from a negative): *I'd like an extra set of prints from this film.* **5** [C,U] cloth with a colored pattern on it, or the pattern itself: *a floral print blouse*

IDM **out of print** (used about a book, etc.) that is not available from the publisher; not being printed anymore: *I'm sorry, the book you ordered is out of print.*

☆**print²** /prɪnt/ verb **1** [T] to put words, pictures, etc. onto paper by using a metal or wood surface covered with ink: *How much did it cost to print the posters?* **2** [I,T] **print (sth) (off/out)** (*computing*) to put information from a computer onto paper: *Can you print that file for me?* ○ *I can't get this document to print out.* **3** [I,T] to produce a book, newspaper, etc.: *50,000 copies of the textbook were printed.* **4** [T] to include sth in a book, newspaper, etc.: *The newspaper printed a photograph of the killer.* **5** [I,T] to write with letters that are not joined together: *Please print your name and address on this form.* **6** [T] to put a pattern onto cloth, paper, etc.: *printed cotton, wallpaper, etc.* **7** [T] to make a photograph from a piece of film —**print·ing** noun [U]: *the invention of printing by Gutenberg*

☆**print·er** /ˈprɪntər/ noun [C] **1** a machine that prints out information from a computer onto paper: *a laser printer* **2** a person or company that prints books, newspapers, etc.

ˈprint·ing press noun [C] a machine that is used for printing books, newspapers, etc.

print·out /ˈprɪntaʊt/ noun [C,U] information from a computer that is printed onto paper

pri·or /ˈpraɪər/ adj. (only *before* a noun) coming before or earlier: *Ms. Parker was unable to attend the ceremony because of a prior commitment.*

IDM **prior to sth** (*formal*) before: *Passengers are asked to report to the check-in desk prior to departure.*

☆**pri·or·i·ty** /praɪˈɔrəti; -ˈɑr-/ noun (pl. **pri·or·i·ties**) **1** [U] **priority (over sb/sth)** the state of being more important than sb/sth or of coming before sb/sth else: *Families with small children will be given priority.* ○ *Emergency cases take priority over other patients in the hospital.* **2** [C] something that is most important or that you must do before anything else: *Our top priority is to get food and water to the refugee camps.* ○ *You have to decide what your priorities are.*

☆**pris·on** /ˈprɪzn/ noun [C,U] a building where criminals are kept as a punishment: *She was sent to a maximum-security federal prison.* ○ *The terrorists were sent to prison for twenty-five years.* ○ *to escape from prison* ○ *He will be*

tʃ	dʒ	v	θ	ð	s	z	ʃ
chin	June	van	thin	then	so	zoo	she

released from prison next month. ○ *a prison guard*

☞ You talk about **prison** (without " **the**") when you are talking about somebody going or being there as a prisoner: *He's in prison.* You talk about **the prison** if you are talking about people going there for a different reason: *The governor will visit the prison tomorrow.* You also use **a** or **the** when more information is given: *a high-security prison.* Look also at **imprison** and **jail**.

☆ **pris·on·er** /ˈprɪzn̩ ·ər/ *noun* [C] a person who is being kept in a prison: *In many prisons, there are three prisoners in a cell.* ○ *a political prisoner*

ˌ**prisoner of** ˈ**war** *noun* [C] (*pl.* **prisoners of war**) (*abbr.* **POW**) a soldier, etc. who is caught by the enemy during a war and who is kept in a prison until the end of the war

☆ **pri·va·cy** /ˈpraɪvəsi/ *noun* [U] the state of being alone or away from other people who may disturb you: *He locked the bathroom door so he could have some privacy.*

☆ **pri·vate¹** /ˈpraɪvət/ *adj.* **1** belonging to one particular person or group and not to be used by others: *This is private property. You can't park here.* **2** secret; not to be shared by other people: *a private letter* **3** with no one else present: *I'd like to have a private talk with you.* **4** not connected with work or business: *He never discusses his private life with his coworkers.* **5** owned, done or organized by a person or company, and not by the government: *investment in the private sector of the economy* ○ *a private school* ○ *a private detective* (= one who is not in the police) ○ *an attorney in private practice* ☞ Look at **public**. —**pri·vate·ly** *adv.*: *She said she agreed, but privately she had her doubts.* ○ *privately-owned businesses*

pri·vate² /ˈpraɪvət/ *noun* [C] a person of the lowest rank in some branches of the military forces

IDM **in private** with no one else present: *Can I talk to you in private?*

pri·va·tize /ˈpraɪvətaɪz/ *verb* [T] to change the ownership of an organization from the government to a private company: *a proposal to privatize the Social Security system* —**pri·va·ti·za·tion** /ˌpraɪvətəˈzeɪʃn/ *noun* [U]

☆ **priv·i·lege** /ˈprɪvlɪdʒ; -vəlɪdʒ/ *noun* **1** [C,U] a special right or advantage that only one person or group has: *Prisoners who behave well have special privileges.* ○ *the wealth and privilege of certain families* **2** [C] a special advantage or opportunity that gives you great pleasure: *It was a great privilege to hear her sing in person.*

priv·i·leged /ˈprɪvlɪdʒd; -vəlɪdʒd/ *adj.* having an advantage or opportunity that most people do not have: *I feel very privileged to be attending this university.* ☞ Look at **underprivileged**.

☆ **prize¹** /praɪz/ *noun* [C] something of value that is given to sb who is successful in a race, competition, game, etc.: *He won first prize in the competition.* ○ *Her pickles were awarded second prize in the state fair.* ○ *a prize-winning novel*

prize² /praɪz/ *adj.* (only *before* a noun) winning, or good enough to win, a prize: *a prize flower display*

prize³ /praɪz/ *verb* [T] to consider sth to be very valuable: *This picture is one of my most prized possessions.*

pro¹ /proʊ/ *adj.* (*informal*) = PROFESSIONAL¹(3,4): *a pro basketball player*

pro² /proʊ/ *noun* [C] (*pl.* **pros**) (*informal*) = PROFESSIONAL²(2,3): *a golf pro*

IDM **the pros and cons** the reasons for and against doing sth: *We should consider all the pros and cons before making a final decision.*

prob·a·bil·i·ty /ˌprɑbəˈbɪləti/ *noun* (*pl.* **prob·a·bil·i·ties**) **1** [U, sing.] the state of being probable or likely: *At that time, there seemed to be little probability of success.* **2** [C] something that is probable or likely: *It might happen, but it's not a real probability.*

☆ **prob·a·ble** /ˈprɑbəbl/ *adj.* that you expect to happen or to be true; likely: *It's possible that they might still come, but it doesn't seem very probable.*

☞ The opposite is **improbable**. Notice that **probable** and **likely** mean the same but are used differently: *It's probable that he will be late.* ○ *He is likely to be late.*

☆ **prob·a·bly** /ˈprɑbəbli/ *adv.* almost certainly: *I'll call you next week, probably on Wednesday.* ○ *"Are you going to the mall with us?" "Probably not."*

pro·ba·tion /proʊˈbeɪʃn/ *noun* [U] **1** the system of keeping an official check on a person who has broken the law instead of sending him/her to prison or after he/she has left prison: *The prisoner was released on probation.* ○ *He was sentenced to two years' probation.* **2** a period of time at the start of a new job when you are tested to see if you are really suitable: *a three-month probation period* **3** a period of time when a student who has behaved badly or has received bad grades must try to improve his/her performance: *Daryl's on academic probation this quarter – if he doesn't pass all his classes, he'll get kicked out.*

pro·ba·tion ·of·fi·cer *noun* [C] a person who keeps an official check on people who are on probation (1)

probe¹ /proʊb/ *noun* [C] **1** a long thin tool that you use for examining sth that is difficult to reach, especially a part of the body **2** asking questions, collecting facts, etc. in order to find

out all the information about sth: *a police probe into illegal gambling*

probe² /proʊb/ *verb* **1** [T] to examine sth carefully with a probe¹(1) or sth similar **2** [I,T] **probe (into sth)** to try to find out all the facts about sth —**prob·ing** *adj.*: *to ask probing questions*

☆ **prob·lem** /ˈprɑbləm/ *noun* [C] **1** a difficult situation that you must deal with: *Unemployment causes a lot of social problems.* ○ *The problem of racial discrimination is very difficult to solve.* ○ *I'm facing a lot of big problems at work these days.* ○ *to have financial problems* ○ *There's a problem with the washing machine. It won't work.* ○ *He has a drinking problem* (= he drinks too much alcohol). ○ *Finding a good plumber is a real problem these days.* ○ *Bruce had a lot of stomach problems when we were on vacation.* **2** a question that you have to solve by thinking about it: *Vicky had ten physics problems to do for homework.*

IDM **no problem** (*informal*) **1** (used to say that sth is very easy to do and you are willing to do it): *"Can you fix this for me?" "Sure, no problem."* **2** (used as a friendly, very informal response after sb has said "thank you" or "sorry," to say that sth was not important): *"Thanks a lot for helping us out." "Hey, no problem."* ○ *"Oops! Sorry I stepped on your toe." "No problem."*

prob·lem·at·ic /ˌprɑbləˈmætɪk/ *adj.* causing a lot of problems, or full of problems

☆ **pro·ce·dure** /prəˈsidʒər/ *noun* [C,U] the action or series of actions that you must take in order to do sth in the usual or correct way: *If you want to make a complaint, please follow the correct procedure.*

☆ **pro·ceed** /prəˈsid; proʊ-/ *verb* [I] (*formal*) **1** to go on to do sth else: *After getting an estimate, we can decide whether or not to proceed with the work.* ○ *Once he had calmed down, he proceeded to tell us what had happened.* **2** to continue or go on in a particular way or direction: *The construction work was proceeding according to schedule.* ○ *The marchers proceeded over the bridge toward City Hall.*

pro·ceed·ings /prəˈsidɪŋz; proʊ-/ *noun* [plural] **1** **proceedings (against sb/for sth)** legal action in court: *to start divorce proceedings* **2** events that happen, especially at a formal meeting, ceremony, etc.: *The proceedings of the city council were interrupted by the demonstrators.*

pro·ceeds /ˈproʊsidz/ *noun* [plural] **proceeds (from/of sth)** money that you get when you sell sth, or for sth that you have organized: *The proceeds from the sale will benefit the Red Cross.*

☆ **proc·ess¹** /ˈprɑsɛs; ˈproʊ-/ *noun* [C] **1** a series of actions that you do for a particular purpose: *the process of producing steel* ○ *Foreign residents who want to work in the U.S. have to go*

through the complicated process of getting a work permit. **2** a series of changes that happen naturally: *Trees go though the process of growing and losing leaves every year.*

IDM **in the process** while you are doing sth else: *We washed the dog yesterday – and we all got very wet in the process.*

in the process of sth/doing sth in the middle of doing sth: *They are in the process of selling their house.*

☆ **proc·ess²** /ˈprɑsɛs; ˈproʊ-/ *verb* [T] **1** to change a raw material, e.g. with chemicals, before it is sold or used: *Cheese is processed so that it lasts longer.* ○ *to process a film* (= to develop it so that you can print photographs from it) **2** to deal with information, e.g. on a computer: *When we have collected all the data, it will be processed by computer.* ○ *It will take about ten days to process your application.*

pro·ces·sion /prəˈsɛʃn/ *noun* [C,U] a number of people, vehicles, etc. that move slowly in a line, e.g. as part of a ceremony: *a funeral procession*

proc·es·sor /ˈprɑsɛsər/ *noun* [C] (used in compounds) a machine that processes food or information: *a food processor* ○ *a word processor*

pro·claim /prəˈkleɪm; proʊ-/ *verb* [T] (*formal*) to make sth known officially or publicly: *Environmentalists have proclaimed the oil spill the worst disaster in recent times.* ○ *to proclaim a state of emergency* —**proc·la·ma·tion** /ˌprɑkləˈmeɪʃn/ *noun* [C,U]

prod /prɑd/ *verb* [I,T] (**prod·ding**; **prod·ded**) to push or press sb/sth with your finger or some other pointed object: (*figurative*) *I had to prod him to give me some information about the project.* —**prod·ding** *noun* [U] (*figurative*): *Harold needs a lot of prodding before he will go and see a doctor.*

prod·i·gy /ˈprɑdədʒi/ *noun* [C] (*pl.* **prod·i·gies**) a person (especially a child) who is unusually good at sth: *a 14-year-old tennis prodigy* ☞ Look at **genius**.

☆ **pro·duce¹** /prəˈdus/ *verb* [T] **1** to make or grow sth: *Some VW cars are produced here in the U.S.* ○ *The Midwest produces most of the country's wheat.* ○ *The students have produced some beautiful pictures for the exhibit.* ○ *Burning coal produces carbon dioxide.* **2** to cause sth to happen: *Her remarks produced roars of laughter.* **3** (*formal*) to show sth so that sb else can look at or examine it: *to produce evidence in court* **4** to organize a play, movie, etc. so that it can be shown to the public: *She is producing a Shakespeare play at the local theater.*

pro·duce² /ˈprɑdus; ˈproʊ-/ *noun* [U] food that comes from a farm, especially fresh fruit and vegetables ☞ Look at the note at **production**.

☆ **pro·duc·er** /prəˈdusər/ *noun* [C] **1** a person, company or country that makes or grows sth:

product

Brazil is a major producer of coffee. **2** a person who deals with the business side of organizing a play, movie, etc.

☆ **prod·uct** /ˈprɑdʌkt/ *noun* [C] **1** something that is made in a factory or that is formed naturally: *Coal is an important product of West Virginia.* ○ *waste products* ○ *We have to find the right product for the market.* ○ *The finished product should look a lot like this design.* ☞ Look at the note at **production**. **2 a/the product of sth** the result of sth: *The industry's problems are the product of a lack of investment.* **3** the amount that you get if you multiply one number by another: *The product of three and five is fifteen.*

☆ **pro·duc·tion** /prəˈdʌkʃn/ *noun* **1** [U] the act of making or growing sth: *This farm specializes in the production of organic vegetables.* ○ *mass production* ○ *The price increases were the result of rising production costs.* **2** [U] the amount of sth that is made or grown: *Saudi Arabia is increasing its oil production.* **3** [C] a play, movie, etc.

☞ Notice that **produce** means food, etc. that comes from a farm and a **product** is something that was made in a factory. A **production** is a play, movie, etc.: *fresh organic produce* ○ *The company's main products are plastic toys.* ○ *the local theater's production of a Broadway comedy*

IDM **in production** being made: *That model is no longer in production.*

pro·duc·tive /prəˈdʌktɪv/ *adj.* **1** that can make or grow sth well or in large quantities: *productive workers* ○ *productive farmland* **2** useful (because results come from it): *a productive discussion* ☞ The opposite is **unproductive**.

pro·duc·tiv·i·ty /ˌprɑdʌkˈtɪvəti; ˌproʊ-/ *noun* [U] the state of being productive (1) or the amount that sb/sth produces (1): *More efficient methods will lead to greater productivity.*

prof /prɑf/ *noun* [C] (*informal*) = PROFESSOR

Prof. *abbr.* = PROFESSOR

pro·fess /prəˈfɛs/ *verb* [T] (*formal*) **1** to say that sth is true (even if it is not): *The government professes concern about homelessness, but does little to help homeless people.* **2** to say openly that you think or believe sth: *He professed his hatred of war.*

☆ **pro·fes·sion** /prəˈfɛʃn/ *noun* **1** [C] a job that requires a lot of training and that is respected by other people: *the medical, legal, teaching, etc. profession* ☞ Look at the note at **work**[1]. **2 the profession** [sing.] all the people who work in a particular profession: *The legal profession is trying to resist the reforms.*

☆ **pro·fes·sion·al**[1] /prəˈfɛʃənl/ *adj.* **1** (only before a noun) of or concerning sb who has a profession: *The apartment would be ideal for a professional couple.* ○ *Get professional advice*

from your lawyer before you take any action. **2** doing sth in a way that shows skill, training or care: *The police are trained to deal with every situation in a calm and professional manner.* ○ *Her application was neatly typed and looked very professional.* ☞ The opposite is **unprofessional**. **3** (also *informal* **pro**) doing a job or for money: *After his success at the Olympic Games, he turned professional.* **4** (also *informal* **pro**) (used about a sport, etc.) done by people who are paid: *professional football* ☞ The opposite for **3** and **4** is **amateur**.

☆ **pro·fes·sion·al**[2] /prəˈfɛʃənl/ *noun* [C] **1** a person who works in a profession (1): *medical professionals* **2** (also *informal* **pro**) a person who plays or teaches a sport, etc. for money **3** (also *informal* **pro**) a person who does his/her work with skill and care

pro·fes·sion·al·ism /prəˈfɛʃənlˌɪzəm/ *noun* [U] the quality of showing great skill or care when you are doing a job: *Although they were students, they performed with great professionalism.*

pro·fes·sion·al·ly /prəˈfɛʃənli/ *adv.* **1** in a professional[1](1,2) way **2** for money, by a professional person: *Rob plays the saxophone professionally.* ○ *to have your photograph taken professionally*

☆ **pro·fes·sor** /prəˈfɛsər/ (also *informal* **prof**) *noun* [C] (*abbr.* **Prof.**) a teacher at a college or university: *Professor Rosen* ○ *Professor Sally Thomas* ○ *My French professor says that my accent needs work.* ☞ Look also at **assistant professor** and **associate professor**.

pro·fi·cien·cy /prəˈfɪʃnsi/ *noun* [U] **proficiency (in sth/doing sth)** the ability to do sth well; skill: *students with limited English proficiency*

pro·fi·cient /prəˈfɪʃnt/ *adj.* **proficient (in/at sth/doing sth)** able to do a particular thing well; skilled: *We are looking for someone who is proficient in French.*

pro·file /ˈproʊfaɪl/ *noun* [C] **1** a person's face or head seen from the side, not the front **2** a short description of sb's life, character, etc.

IDM **keep a low profile** ⇨ LOW[1] ☞ Look also at **high-profile**.

☆ **prof·it**[1] /ˈprɑfət/ *noun* [C,U] the money that you make when you sell sth for more than it cost you: *Did you make a profit on your house when you sold it?* ○ *an annual profit of $25,000* ○ *We fixed up an old car and sold it at a profit.* ○ *We won't make much profit in the first year.* ☞ Look at **loss**.

☆ **prof·it**[2] /ˈprɑfət/ *verb*

PHRV **profit from sth** (*formal*) to get some advantage from sth: *We hope to profit from our competitors' mistakes.*

prof·it·a·ble /ˈprɑfətəbl/ *adj.* **1** that makes a profit: *a profitable business* **2** helpful or useful: *We had a very profitable discussion yesterday.*

ər	ɪr	ɛr	ɑr	ɔr	ʊr	ʒ	h	ŋ
bird	near	hair	car	north	tour	vision	hat	sing

—**prof·it·a·bil·i·ty** /ˌprɑfətəˈbɪləti/ *noun* [U]
—**prof·it·a·bly** /-əbli/ *adv.*: *to invest money profitably* ○ *to spend your time profitably*

pro·found /prəˈfaʊnd/ *adj.* **1** great; that you feel very strongly: *The experience had a profound influence on her.* **2** serious; showing knowledge or thought: *profound statements about the meaning of life*

pro·found·ly /prəˈfaʊndli/ *adv.* (*formal*) very; extremely: *an invention that profoundly changed people's lives*

prog·no·sis /prɑgˈnoʊsəs/ *noun* [C] (*pl.* **prog·no·ses** /-siz/) a judgment that predicts how sth, especially a disease, will develop in the future

☆ **pro·gram¹** /ˈproʊgræm/ *noun* [C] **1** a show or other item that is broadcast on the radio or on television: *a TV program* ○ *Do you want to watch that program on Channel 4 at 8 o'clock?* ○ *We just missed an interesting program about the Gold Rush.* **2** an official plan or system of services or activities for doing sth: *the state's proposed welfare-to-work program* ○ *an intense training program* ○ *plans to expand the university's graduate programs* **3** a set of instructions that you give to a computer so that it will carry out a particular task: *to write a program* **4** a little book or piece of paper which you get at a play, concert, etc. that gives you information about what you are going to see

☆ **pro·gram²** /ˈproʊgræm; -grəm/ *verb* [T] (**pro·gram·ming; pro·grammed**) **1** to give a set of instructions to a computer **2** to make a piece of equipment work or act automatically in a particular way: *The lights are programmed to come on as soon as it gets dark.*

pro·gram·mer /ˈproʊgræmər/ *noun* [C] a person whose job is to write programs¹(3) for a computer: *a computer programmer*

☆ **pro·gress¹** /ˈprɑgrɛs; -grəs/ *noun* [U] **1** movement forward or toward achieving sth: *The heavy traffic meant that we made very slow progress.* ○ *Anna's making steady progress in school.* ○ *The talks made very little progress toward solving the problem.* ○ *a progress report* **2** change or improvement in society: *scientific progress* ○ *People who oppose new technologies are accused of holding back progress.*

IDM in progress happening now: *Quiet! Examination in progress.*

☆ **prog·ress²** /prəˈgrɛs/ *verb* [I] **1** to become better; to develop (well): *Medical knowledge has progressed rapidly in the last twenty years.* **2** to move forward; to continue: *I got more and more tired as the evening progressed.*

pro·gres·sion /prəˈgrɛʃn/ *noun* [C,U] **pro·gression (from sth) (to sth)** movement forward or a development from one stage to another: *I can't see any logical progression in your thoughts in this paper.*

pro·gres·sive /prəˈgrɛsɪv/ *adj.* **1** using or

agreeing with modern methods and ideas: *a progressive school* **2** happening or developing steadily: *a progressive reduction in the number of workers*

pro·gres·sive·ly /prəˈgrɛsɪvli/ *adv.* steadily; a little at a time: *The situation got progressively worse.*

the pro·gressive tense *noun* [sing.] = CONTINUOUS TENSE

☆ **pro·hib·it** /proʊˈhɪbət; prə-/ *verb* [T] (*formal*) **prohibit sb/sth (from doing sth)** to say that sth is not allowed by law; to forbid: *Federal law prohibits smoking on all domestic airline flights.* ○ *That sign means that parking is prohibited here.*

pro·hi·bi·tion /ˌproʊəˈbɪʃn/ *noun* **1** [C,U] (*formal*) a law or rule that forbids sth, or the act of forbidding sth **2 Prohibition** [U] the period between 1920 and 1933, when it was illegal to produce and sell alcoholic drinks in the U.S.

☆ **proj·ect¹** /ˈprɑdʒɛkt; -dʒɪkt/ *noun* [C] **1** a piece of work, often involving many people, that is planned and organized carefully; a plan for some work: *a major project to reduce pollution in our rivers* ○ *His latest project is fixing up an old car.* **2** a piece of school work in which a student has to collect information about a certain subject and then write about it: *The whole class is doing a project on rainforests.* **3** (*informal*) = HOUSING PROJECT

pro·ject² /prəˈdʒɛkt/ *verb* **1** [T] (usually passive) to plan: *the President's projected tour of Europe* **2** [T] (usually passive) to estimate or calculate: *a projected increase of 10%* **3** [T] **project sth (on/onto sth)** to make sth (light, a shadow, a picture from a movie, etc.) fall on a surface: *Colored lights were projected onto the dance floor.* **4** [T] to show or represent sb/sth/yourself in a certain way: *The candidate's advisers told him to project a more conservative image.* **5** [I] (*formal*) to stick out: *The porch projects three yards from the front of the house.*

pro·jec·tion /prəˈdʒɛkʃn/ *noun* **1** [C] a guess about a future amount, situation, etc. based on the information you have now: *sales projections for the next five years* **2** [U] the act of making light, a picture from a movie, etc. fall on a surface: *film projection*

pro·jec·tor /prəˈdʒɛktər/ *noun* [C] an apparatus that projects pictures or movies onto a screen or wall: *a movie projector* ○ *a slide projector* ○ *an overhead projector*

pro·lif·er·ate /prəˈlɪfəreɪt/ *verb* [I] (*formal*) to increase quickly in number —**pro·lif·er·a·tion** /prəˌlɪfəˈreɪʃn/ *noun* [U]

pro·lif·ic /prəˈlɪfɪk/ *adj.* (used especially about a writer, an artist, etc.) producing a lot: *a prolific writer of short stories*

pro·long /prəˈlɔŋ; -ˈlɑŋ/ *verb* [T] to make sth last longer: *Careful treatment will prolong the life of the furniture.*

pro·longed /prəˈlɔŋd; -ˈlɑŋd/ *adj.* (only *before*

tʃ	dʒ	v	θ	ð	s	z	ʃ
chin	**June**	**van**	**thin**	**then**	**so**	**zoo**	**she**

a noun) continuing for a long time: *There was a prolonged silence before anybody spoke.*

prom /prɑm/ *noun* [C] a formal dance that is held for high school students near the end of a school year

prom·i·nent /'prɑmənənt/ *adj.* (usually *before a noun*) **1** important or famous: *a prominent political figure* ○ *The First Lady often plays a prominent role in charity work.* **2** noticeable; easy to see: *The Space Needle is the most prominent feature of Seattle's skyline.* —**prom·i·nence** /-əns/ *noun* [U]: *She gained national prominence after appearing in a popular commercial.* —**prom·i·nent·ly** *adv.*: *The Chinese leader's visit was prominently featured on the TV news.*

pro·mis·cu·ous /prə'mɪskyuəs/ *adj.* (*formal*) having sexual relations with many people —**prom·is·cu·i·ty** /ˌprɑmə'skyuəti/ *noun* [U]

☆ **prom·ise¹** /'prɑməs/ *noun* **1** [C] a written or spoken statement or agreement that you will or will not do sth: *He made a promise not to tell anyone what he had seen.* ○ *Her parents kept their promise to buy her a dog for her birthday.* ○ *He said he would help us, but he broke his promise.* ○ *They both gave me a promise of their complete support.* **2** [U] signs that you will be able to do sth well or be successful: *He showed great promise as a musician.*

☆ **prom·ise²** /'prɑməs/ *verb* **1** [I,T] to say definitely that you will or will not do sth: *I'll try to be back at 6 o'clock, but I can't promise.* ○ *"I'll pay you back tomorrow," his friend promised.* ○ *She promised that she would write every week.* ○ *Tom promised me that he'd never be late again.* ○ *The mayor has promised to clean up local government.* **2** [T] **promise sth (to sb)** to say definitely that you will give sth to sb: *My father has promised me a new bike.* ○ *Can you promise your support?* **3** [T] to show signs of sth, so that you expect it to happen: *The picnic promises to be a lot of fun.*

prom·is·ing /'prɑməsɪŋ/ *adj.* showing signs of being very good or successful: *a promising young writer*

☆ **pro·mote** /prə'moʊt/ *verb* [T] **1** (often passive) to give sb a higher position, more important job, etc.: *He's been promoted from assistant manager to manager.* **2** to encourage sth; to help sth to happen or develop: *The meetings of the leaders have helped to promote good relations between the two countries.* **3** to advertise sth (in order to increase its sales or popularity): *In order to sell a new product, you need to promote it in the right way.*

pro·mot·er /prə'moʊtər/ *noun* [C] a person who organizes or provides the money for an event

☆ **pro·mo·tion** /prə'moʊʃn/ *noun* **1** [C,U] (the giving or receiving of) a higher position or more important job: *She's hoping to receive a promotion this year.* ○ *The job offers a good*

salary and excellent chances of promotion. **2** [U] making sth successful or popular: *We need to work on the promotion of health, not the treatment of disease.* **3** [C,U] things that you do in order to advertise a product: *It's all part of a special promotion of the new book.* ○ *Millions of dollars were spent on advertising and promotion.*

☆ **prompt¹** /prɑmpt/ *adj.* **1** quick; done without delay: *I received a prompt reply from my lawyer.* ○ *We need a prompt decision on this matter.* **2 prompt (in doing sth/to do sth)** (used about a person) quick; acting without delay: *We are always prompt in paying our bills.* ○ *She was prompt to point out my mistake.*

prompt² /prɑmpt/ *verb* **1** [T] to cause sth; to make sb decide to do sth: *What prompted that remark?* ○ *What prompted you to give up your job?* **2** [I,T] to help sb to continue speaking or to remind an actor of his/her words: *"And can you tell the court what happened next?" the lawyer prompted.* ○ *The speaker had to be prompted several times.* —**prompt·ing** *noun* [C,U]: *He apologized without any prompting.*

prompt³ /prɑmpt/ *noun* [C] (*computing*) a special symbol that appears on a computer screen when the computer is ready to receive an instruction

☆ **prompt·ly** /'prɑmptli/ *adv.* **1** immediately; without delay: *I invited her to dinner and she promptly accepted.* **2** punctually; at the time that you have arranged: *We arrived promptly at 12 o'clock.*

prone /proʊn/ *adj.* (not before a noun) **prone to sth** likely to suffer from sth or to do sth: *Young people are especially prone to this disease.* ○ *to be accident-prone* (= to have a lot of accidents)

prong /prɔŋ; prɑŋ/ *noun* [C] a short, thin piece of metal, plastic, etc. that sticks out of sth ☛ picture at **plug**.

pro·noun /'proʊnaʊn/ *noun* [C] (*grammar*) a word that is used in place of a noun or a phrase that contains a noun: *"He," "it," "hers," "me" and "them" are all pronouns.*

☆ **pro·nounce** /prə'naʊns/ *verb* **1** [T] to make the sound of a word or letter: *You don't pronounce the "b" at the end of "comb."* ○ *How do you pronounce your last name?* **2** [T] (*formal*) to say in a formal or official way that sb/sth is in a particular condition: *The doctors pronounced him dead on arrival at the hospital.*

pro·nounced /prə'naʊnst/ *adj.* very noticeable: *to walk with a pronounced limp*

☆ **pro·nun·ci·a·tion** /prəˌnʌnsi'eɪʃn/ *noun* **1** [C,U] the way in which a language or a word is pronounced: *The dictionary gives two different pronunciations for this word.* ○ *standard pronunciation* **2** [U] a person's way of speaking a language: *His grammar is good, but his pronunciation is awful!*

i	ɪ	ɛ	æ	ɑ	ɔ	ʌ	ʊ	u
see	sit	ten	cat	hot	saw	cup	put	too

☆ **proof¹** /pruf/ *noun* [U] a fact or piece of information which shows that sth is true: *Keep your receipt as proof of purchase.* ○ *What proof do we have that what he is saying is true?* ☞ The verb is **prove**.

proof² /pruf/ *adj.* (in compounds) able to protect from or to be protected against the thing mentioned: *a soundproof room* ○ *bulletproof glass*

prop¹ /prɑp/ *verb* [T] (**prop·ping**; **propped**) **1** to support sth or keep sth in the correct position: *I'll use this book to prop the window open.* **2** to lean sth against sth else: *He propped his bicycle against the wall.*
PHRV **prop sb/sth up** to put an object under or behind sb/sth in order to give support
prop sth up to support sth that would otherwise fail: *to prop up a corrupt administration*

prop² /prɑp/ *noun* [C, usually pl.] a piece of furniture or another object that is used in a play, movie, etc.

prop·a·gan·da /ˌprɑpəˈgændə/ *noun* [U] information and ideas, especially ones that are not true, that are made public by a government or large organization, in order to influence people or persuade them about sth: *political propaganda* ○ *anti-immigrant propaganda*

pro·pel /prəˈpɛl/ *verb* [T] (**propel·ling**; **pro·pelled**) to move, drive or push sb/sth forward

pro·pel·ler /prəˈpɛlər/ *noun* [C] a piece of equipment with several blades, which turns around very fast in order to make a ship or an aircraft move

☆ **prop·er** /ˈprɑpər/ *adj.* **1** (only *before* a noun) right or correct: *information on the proper use of chemicals* ○ *It is important to use the proper tool for the job.* **2** (*formal*) accepted as socially correct or appropriate: *Is it considered proper to wear a hat indoors?* ☞ The opposite for **2** is **improper**. **3** (only *after* a noun) real or main: *We traveled through miles of suburbs before we got to the city proper.*

prop·er·ly /ˈprɑpərli/ *adv.* **1** correctly: *a lock that was not properly installed* **2** in a way that is socially correct; politely ☞ The opposite is **improperly**.

ˌ**proper ˈnoun** (also ˌ**proper ˈname**) *noun* [C] (*grammar*) a word which is the name of a particular person or place and begins with a capital letter: *"Mary," "Rome" and "the White House" are all proper nouns.*

☆ **prop·er·ty** /ˈprɑpərti/ *noun* (pl. **prop·er·ties**) **1** [U] something that belongs to sb; all the things that belong to sb: *"Is this your property?" the police officer asked, pointing to a small suitcase.* ○ *The bag contained stolen property.* **2** [C,U] land and/or a building or buildings on it: *property tax* ○ *private/public property* ○ *to invest your money in property* ○ *They own several commercial properties in Florida.* **3** [C] a special quality that a substance, etc. has: *Some plants have healing properties.*

proph·e·cy /ˈprɑfəsi/ *noun* [C] (pl. **proph·e·cies**) a statement about what is going to happen in the future: *His prophecy that there would be a disaster came true.*

proph·et /ˈprɑfət/ *noun* [C] **1** (*also* **Prophet**) a person who is chosen by God to give his message to people: *the Prophet Mohammed* ○ *the prophets of the Old Testament* **2** a person who tells or claims to tell what will happen in the future —**pro·phet·ic** /prəˈfɛtɪk/ *adj.*

☆ **pro·por·tion** /prəˈpɔrʃn/ *noun* **1** [C] a part or share of a whole: *A large proportion of the earth's surface is covered by oceans.* **2** [C] **proportion (of sth to sth)** the relationship between the size or amount of two things: *The proportion of teachers to students was too low* (= there were not enough teachers for the number of students). **3** **proportions** [plural] the size and shape of sth: *He stood and gazed at the magnificent proportions of the cathedral.* ○ *Violent crime is reaching alarming proportions.*
IDM **in proportion** in the correct relation to other things: *to draw sth in proportion* (= so that the parts are balanced as they are in reality) ○ *She's so upset that she can't see the problem in proportion anymore* (= it seems more important than it really is).
in proportion to sth 1 by the same amount or number as sth else: *Salaries have not risen in proportion to inflation.* **2** compared with: *In proportion to the number of students as a whole, there are very few women.*
out of proportion (to sth) 1 too big, small, etc. in relation to other things **2** too great, serious, important, etc. in relation to sth: *His reaction was completely out of proportion to the situation.* ○ *Aren't you getting this thing completely out of proportion* (= you think it's more important than it really is)?

pro·por·tion·al /prəˈpɔrʃn·l/ *adj.* directly linked in size, amount, etc.: *The cost will be proportional to the amount used.*

☆ **pro·pos·al** /prəˈpoʊzl/ *noun* [C] **1** a plan that is suggested: *to submit a new proposal for raising money* ○ *The recent proposal was rejected.* **2** an act of asking sb to marry you

☆ **pro·pose** /prəˈpoʊz/ *verb* **1** [T] to suggest sth officially as a possible plan or action: *The idea will be proposed at the next committee meeting.* ○ *I propose that we wait until next week to discuss it.* **2** [T] to intend; to have as a plan: *And just how do they propose to pay for all this?* **3** [I] **propose (to sb)** to ask sb to marry you: *We've been going out for a long time, but he still hasn't proposed.*

prop·o·si·tion /ˌprɑpəˈzɪʃn/ *noun* [C] **1** an idea or opinion that sb expresses about sth: *That's a very interesting proposition. But can*

you prove it? **2** an arrangement or offer, especially in business; a suggestion: *He made me a proposition to buy my share of the company.* **3** (*also* **Proposition**) a plan for a new law that people vote on in order to decide whether it becomes a law or not: *California voters approved Proposition 187 in 1994.*

pro·pri·e·tor /prəˈpraɪətər/ *noun* [C] (*formal*) the owner of a business

prose /proʊz/ *noun* [U] written or spoken language that is not poetry: *to write in prose* ○ *a prose writer*

pros·e·cute /ˈprɑsəkyut/ *verb* [I,T] **prosecute sb (for sth)** to accuse sb of a crime and to try to prove it in a court of law: *the prosecuting attorney in the murder trial* ○ *He was prosecuted for theft.* ☛ Look at **defend**.

☆**pros·e·cu·tion** /ˌprɑsəˈkyuʃn/ *noun* **1** [sing.] a person or group of people who try to prove in a court of law that sb is guilty of a crime: *a witness for the prosecution* ○ *The prosecution claims that Thompson was driving at 100 miles per hour.* ☛ Look at **defense**. **2** [C,U] (an example of) accusing sb of a crime and trying to prove it in a court of law: *Failure to pay your parking ticket will result in prosecution.*

☆**pros·pect** /ˈprɑspɛkt/ *noun* **1** [C,U] **prospect (of sth/of doing sth)** the chance or hope that sth will happen: *There's not much prospect of better weather before next week.* ○ *Prospects for peace do not look good.* **2** [C,U] an idea of what may or will happen: *the awful prospect of the air conditioning breaking in July* **3 prospects** [plural] chances of being successful: *A college degree will improve your job prospects.*

pro·spec·tive /prəˈspɛktɪv/ *adj.* likely to be or to happen; possible: *prospective changes to the law* ○ *a prospective car buyer*

pros·per /ˈprɑspər/ *verb* [I] to be successful, especially financially

pros·per·i·ty /prɑˈspɛrəti/ *noun* [U] the state of being financially successful: *Tourism has brought prosperity to central Florida.* ○ *economic prosperity*

pros·per·ous /ˈprɑspərəs/ *adj.* rich and successful: *the prosperous counties of northern California*

pros·ti·tute /ˈprɑstətut/ (*also informal* **hooker**, *old-fashioned* **whore**) *noun* [C] a person, especially a woman, who earns money by having sex with people —**pros·ti·tu·tion** /ˌprɑstəˈtuʃn/ *noun* [U]

☆**pro·tect** /prəˈtɛkt/ *verb* [T] **protect sb/sth (against/from sth)** to keep sb/sth safe; to defend sb/sth: *It was interesting to watch the bird trying to protect its young.* ○ *basic rights that are protected by the U.S. Constitution* ○ *Politicians always try to protect themselves against criticism.* ○ *Parents try to protect their children from danger.* ○ *Alligators are a protected species in Florida* (= they must not be killed). —**pro·tec·tor** /prəˈtɛktər/ *noun* [C]

☆**pro·tec·tion** /prəˈtɛkʃn/ *noun* [U] **protection (against/from sth)** (a way of) keeping sb/sth safe so that he/she/it is not harmed or damaged: *the protection of the environment* ○ *Vaccination against measles gives you protection against the disease.* ○ *A good sunblock provides protection from the sun's harmful rays.*

pro·tec·tive /prəˈtɛktɪv/ *adj.* **1** that prevents sb/sth from being damaged or harmed: *All employees must wear protective clothing in this area.* **2 protective (of sb)** wanting to protect sb and keep him/her safe: *parents who are overly protective of their college-age children*

pro·tein /ˈproʊtin/ *noun* [C,U] a substance found in food such as meat, fish and beans. It is important for helping people and animals to grow and be healthy.

☆**pro·test¹** /ˈproʊtɛst/ *noun* [C,U] the showing of disagreement; a statement or action that shows that you do not like or agree with sth: *The union organized a protest against the layoffs.* ○ *The planned site for the prison was moved after protests from local residents.* ○ *We received thousands of letters of protest.* ○ *He resigned in protest against the decision.* ○ *a protest march*

IDM **under protest** not happily or willingly: *Carol finally agreed to pay, but only under protest.*

☆**pro·test²** /ˈproʊtɛst; prəˈtɛst/ *verb* **1** [I,T] **protest (about/against/at sth)** to say or show that you do not like or agree with sth: *Thousands gathered to protest against the new tax.* ○ *The kids protested loudly at being taken home early.* ○ *Several customers protested about the poor service in the restaurant.* ○ *They protested the government's handling of the situation.* **2** [T] to say sth firmly: *He protested a total lack of knowledge of the affair.* ○ *He protested that he hadn't been in the area when the robbery took place.* ○ *"That's just not true," she protested.*

☛ **Protest** is stronger and usually used about more serious things than **complain**. You **protest** about something that you feel is not right or fair; you **complain** about the quality of something or about a less serious action: *to protest about the tax increase* ○ *to complain about the weather.*

—**pro·test·er** *noun* [C]: *Protesters lined the sidewalk as the President's car drove up.*

☆**Prot·es·tant** /ˈprɑtəstənt/ *noun* [C] a member of the Christian church that separated from the Catholic church in the 16th century —**Prot·es·tant** *adj.*: *a Protestant church* ☛ Look at **Catholic**.

pro·to·col /ˈproʊtəkɔl; -kɑl/ *noun* **1** [U] the system of rules for correct behavior in formal, official situations **2** [C] the first or original version of an official written agreement **3** [C] (*computing*) a set of signals and rules that

ər	ɪr	ɛr	ɑr	ɔr	ʊr	ʒ	h	ŋ
bird	near	hair	car	north	tour	vision	hat	sing

control how information is sent from one computer to another

pro·to·type /ˈproʊtətaɪp/ noun [C] the first model or design of sth from which other forms will be copied or developed

pro·trude /proʊˈtrud; prə-/ verb [I] to stick out from a surface: *protruding teeth*

☆ **proud** /praʊd/ adj. **1** proud (of sb/sth); proud (to do sth/that…) feeling pleased and satisfied about sth that you own or have done, or are connected with: *a proud father of twins* ○ *They are very proud of their new house.* ○ *I feel extremely proud to be part of such a successful organization.* ○ *You should feel proud that you were chosen.* **2** not wanting help from other people: *He was too proud to ask for help.* **3** feeling that you are better than other people: *a proud, impatient man* ☞ The noun is **pride**. —**proud·ly** adv.: *"I did all the work myself," he said proudly.*

☆ **prove** /pruv/ verb (p.p. **prov·en** or **proved**) **1** [T] prove sth (to sb) to show that sth is true: *It will be difficult to prove that she was lying.* ○ *to prove sb's innocence to the court* ☞ The noun is **proof**. **2** [I,T] (formal) to be found to be sth: *The job proved more difficult than we'd expected.* ○ *He was proven innocent.* ○ *Lisa proved herself to be just as strong as the men.*

prov·en /ˈpruvn/ adj. that has been shown to be true: *a proven fact*

prov·erb /ˈprɑvərb/ noun [C] a short well-known sentence or phrase that gives advice or a general truth about life: *Benjamin Franklin's proverb, "a penny saved is a penny earned"*

☆ **pro·vide** /prəˈvaɪd/ verb [T] provide sb (with sth); provide sth (for sb) to give or supply sth to sb: *This book will provide you with all the information you need.* ○ *The university cannot provide housing for all students.* ○ *The seminar lasts all day and lunch will be provided.*

PHRV provide for sb to give sb all that he/she needs to live: *Robin has four children to provide for.*

provide for sth to make arrangements to deal with sth that might happen in the future: *We did not provide for such a large increase in prices.*

☆ **pro·vid·ed** /prəˈvaɪdəd/ (also **provided that**; **providing**; **providing that**) conj. only if: *She agreed to go and work abroad provided that her family could go with her.*

prov·ince /ˈprɑvəns/ noun [C] one of the main parts into which some countries are divided: *Canada has ten provinces.* ☞ Look at **county** and **state**. —**pro·vin·cial** /prəˈvɪnʃl/ adj. (only before a noun): *the Ontario provincial government*

☆ **pro·vi·sion** /prəˈvɪʒn/ noun **1** [C] one of the parts of an official agreement or document: *The rebels violated several key provisions of the*

peace treaty. **2** [U] (formal) the act of giving or supplying sth to sb: *The state is responsible for the provision of education.* **3 provisions** [plural] (formal) supplies of food and drink **4** [C,U] provision(s) for/against sth arrangements that you make to deal with sth that might happen in the future: *The budget makes no provision for the effects of inflation.*

pro·vi·sion·al /prəˈvɪʒn·l/ adj. only for the present time, that may be changed: *UN troops helped to set up a provisional government in the region.*

prov·o·ca·tion /ˌprɑvəˈkeɪʃn/ noun **1** [U] the act of trying to make sb angry: *The guards fired their weapons without provocation.* **2** [C] something that sb does to make you angry: *The attack was a response to deliberate provocations.*

pro·voc·a·tive /prəˈvɑkətɪv/ adj. **1** intending to cause anger or argument: *a provocative question* **2** intending to cause sexual excitement

pro·voke /prəˈvoʊk/ verb [T] **1** to make a person or an animal angry by annoying him/her/it: *The cat will scratch if you provoke it.* ○ *Stop trying to provoke me!* **2** to cause a feeling or reaction: *The judge's remarks provoked a storm of controversy.*

pro·vost /ˈproʊvoʊst/ noun [C] an important official at some colleges and universities

prow·ess /ˈpraʊəs/ noun [U] (formal) skill at doing sth

prowl /praʊl/ verb [I,T] prowl (around) (used about an animal that is hunting or a person who is waiting for a chance to steal sth, etc.) to move quietly so that you are not seen or heard: *I could hear someone prowling around outside, so I called the police.* ☞ A person or animal that is prowling is **on the prowl**. —**prowl·er** noun [C]: *The police arrested a prowler outside the hospital.*

prox·im·i·ty /prɑkˈsɪməti/ noun [U] (formal) the state of being near to sth: *One advantage is the town's proximity to the beach.*

prox·y /ˈprɑksi/ noun [U] the right that you give to sb to act for you: *to vote by proxy*

prude /prud/ noun [C] a person who does not like to see or hear anything connected with sex —**prud·ish** /ˈprudɪʃ/ adj.

pru·dent /ˈprudnt/ adj. (formal) having or showing careful thought; wise and sensible: *It would be prudent to find out more before you decide.* ☞ The opposite is **imprudent**. —**pru·dence** noun [U] —**pru·dent·ly** adv.

prune¹ /prun/ noun [C] a dried plum

prune² /prun/ verb [T] to cut branches or parts of branches off a tree or bush in order to make it a better shape or improve its growth

pry /praɪ/ verb (pres. part. **pry·ing**; 3rd pers. sing. pres. **pries**; p.t., p.p. **pried**) **1** [T] to use force to open sth, remove a lid, etc.: *He pried the door open with a steel bar.* **2** [I] pry (into

P

sth) to try to find out about other people's private affairs: *I don't want to pry – but is everything all right?*

P.S. *abbr.* (used at the end of a letter to add extra information): *...Love, Deanna. P.S. I'll meet you Thursday at 7:00.*

pseu·do·nym /ˈsudənɪm/ (*also* **pen name**) *noun* [C] a name used by an author, etc. that is not his/her real name: *to write under a pseudonym*

psych¹ /saɪk/ *verb*

PHRV **psych sb out** (*informal*) to convince sb that you will defeat him/her by acting in a very confident way

psych yourself up (for sth) (*informal*) to prepare yourself in your mind for sth difficult, e.g. by telling yourself that you will be successful

psych² /saɪk/ *noun* [U] (*informal*) = PSYCHOLOGY(1): *Cindy's majoring in psych and art history.*

psyched /saɪkt/ *adj.* (*slang*) (not before a noun) **be/get psyched** to be prepared or to prepare yourself mentally for sth and to be or become excited: *Wow! You must be totally psyched about getting into college! ○ Let's get psyched for tonight's game!*

psy·chi·at·ric /ˌsaɪkiˈætrɪk/ *adj.* connected with psychiatry: *a psychiatric hospital*

☆ **psy·chi·a·trist** /saɪˈkaɪətrɪst; sə-/ *noun* [C] a medical doctor who is trained to treat people with mental illness

psy·chi·a·try /saɪˈkaɪətri; sə-/ *noun* [U] the study and treatment of mental illness ☞ Look at **psychology**.

psy·chic /ˈsaɪkɪk/ *adj.* (used about a person or his/her mind) having unusual powers, e.g. knowing what sb else is thinking or being able to see into the future

psy·cho /ˈsaɪkoʊ/ *noun* [C] (*pl.* **psy·chos**) (*slang*) a person who is crazy or dangerous —**psy·cho** *adj.*

psy·cho·a·nal·y·sis /ˌsaɪkoʊəˈnæləsəs/ *noun* [U] a way of treating sb with a mental illness by asking about his/her past life and dreams in order to find out what is causing his/her illness

psy·cho·an·a·lyst /ˌsaɪkoʊˈænl·ɪst/ *noun* [C] a person who uses psychoanalysis to treat people

psy·cho·an·a·lyze /ˌsaɪkoʊˈænl·aɪz/ *verb* [T] to treat sb who has a mental illness using psychoanalysis

psy·cho·log·i·cal /ˌsaɪkəˈlɑdʒɪkl/ *adj.* **1** connected with the mind or the way that it works: *Did her ordeal cause her long-term psychological damage?* **2** connected with psychology: *psychological tests* —**psy·cho·log·i·cal·ly** /-kli/ *adv.*: *Psychologically, it was a bad time to be starting a new job.*

☆ **psy·chol·o·gist** /saɪˈkɑlədʒɪst/ *noun* [C] a person who is trained in psychology

psy·chol·o·gy /saɪˈkɑlədʒi/ *noun* **1**(also *informal* **psych**) [U] the study of the mind and the way that people behave: *child psychology* ☞ Look at **psychiatry**. **2** [sing.] the type of mind that a person or group of people has: *If we understood the psychology of the killer, we would have a better chance of catching him.*

psy·cho·path /ˈsaɪkəpæθ/ *noun* [C] a person who has a serious mental illness and who may hurt or kill other people —**psy·cho·path·ic** /ˌsaɪkəˈpæθɪk/ *adj.*

psy·cho·ther·a·py /ˌsaɪkoʊˈθerəpi/ *noun* [U] the treatment of people with mental illness by psychological methods rather than with drugs

pu·ber·ty /ˈpyubərti/ *noun* [U] the time when a child's body is changing and becoming physically like that of an adult: *to reach puberty*

pu·bic /ˈpyubɪk/ *adj.* of the area around the sexual organs: *pubic hair*

☆ **pub·lic¹** /ˈpʌblɪk/ *adj.* **1** of or concerning all the people in a country or area: *The town's old sewage system is a danger to public health. ○ How much public support is there for the administration's policy? ○ to increase public awareness* **2** connected with the government and not with private companies: *public employees ○ budget cuts in the public sector ○ public spending* (= money that the government spends on education, roads, etc.) **3** provided for the use of people in general; not private: *a public library ○ a public park* **4** known by many people: *We're going to make the news public soon.* ☞ Compare **keep sth secret**. —**pub·lic·ly** /-kli/ *adv.*: *The company refused to admit publicly that it had made a mistake.*

☆ **pub·lic²** /ˈpʌblɪk/ *noun* [sing.] **the public** people in general: *Is the White House open to the public? ○ The police have asked for information from members of the public. ○ The public is mostly in favor of the new law.*

IDM **in public** when other people are present: *This is the first time that Jane has spoken about her experience in public.*

public-adˈdress ˌsystem *noun* [C, usually sing.] (*formal*) = PA SYSTEM

public asˈsistance *noun* [U] money, food, etc. that the government gives to poor people: *families living on public assistance*

☆ **pub·li·ca·tion** /ˌpʌbləˈkeɪʃn/ *noun* **1** [U] the act of printing a book, magazine, etc. and making it available to the public: *His latest book has just been accepted for publication.* **2** [C] a book, magazine, etc. **3** [U] the act of making sth known to the public: *the publication of the company's annual report*

public deˈfender *noun* [C] a lawyer who works for the government of a city, county, etc. and who defends people who cannot pay for a lawyer themselves in court cases

public ˈhousing ˌproject *noun* [C] = HOUSING PROJECT

i	ɪ	ɛ	æ	ɑ	ɔ	ʌ	ʊ	u
see	sit	ten	cat	hot	saw	cup	put	too

☆ **pub·lic·i·ty** /pʌbˈlɪsəti/ *noun* [U] **1** notice or attention from the newspapers, television, etc.: *to seek/avoid publicity* **2** giving information about sth in order to attract people's attention; advertising: *There has been a lot of publicity for Brad Pitt's latest movie.* ○ *a publicity campaign*

pub·li·cize /ˈpʌbləsaɪz/ *verb* [T] to attract people's attention to sth or to give people information about sth: *The event has been well publicized and should attract a lot of people.*

ˌ**public oˈpinion** *noun* [U] what people in general think about sth: *Public opinion was in favor of the war.*

ˌ**public reˈlations** *noun* (*abbr.* **PR**) **1** [plural] the state of the relationship between an organization and the public: *Giving money to local charities is good for public relations.* **2** [U] the job of making a company, an organization, etc. popular with the public

☆ˌ**public ˈschool** *noun* [C] a local school that any child can go to, that provides free education

ˌ**public ˈtelevision** (*also* ˌ**public ˌTˈV**) *noun* [C] a television service that shows mainly educational programs and is paid for by the government, the public and some companies

☆ˌ**public ˌtransporˈtation** *noun* [U] (the system of) buses, trains, etc. that run according to a schedule and that anybody can use: *to use public transportation*

ˌ**public uˈtility** *noun* [C] a company that is controlled by the government, that provides sth important such as water or electricity to the public

☆ **pub·lish** /ˈpʌblɪʃ/ *verb* **1** [I,T] to prepare and print a book, magazine, etc. and make it available to the public: *This dictionary was published by Oxford University Press.* **2** [T] (used about a writer, etc.) to have your work put in a book, magazine, etc.: *Dr. Fraser has published several articles on the subject.* **3** [T] to make sth known to the public: *Large companies must publish a report every year.*

☆ **pub·lish·er** /ˈpʌblɪʃər/ *noun* [C] a person or company that publishes books, magazines, etc.

☆ **pub·lish·ing** /ˈpʌblɪʃɪŋ/ *noun* [U] the business of preparing books, magazines, etc. to be printed and sold

puck /pʌk/ *noun* [C] a hard round flat rubber object that players hit with sticks in the sport of hockey

☆ **pud·ding** /ˈpʊdɪŋ/ *noun* [U] a soft, sweet food that is made from a special powder mixed with milk, or from milk, eggs, sugar, flavoring, etc. and baked or cooked at a low temperature until it becomes firmer: *chocolate pudding*

pud·dle /ˈpʌdl/ *noun* [C] a small amount of water (especially rain) that has gathered on the ground ☞ Look at **pool**.

puff¹ /pʌf/ *noun* [C] **1** a small amount of air, smoke, wind, etc. that is blown or sent out: *a puff of smoke* **2** one breath that you take when you are smoking a cigarette or pipe: *to take a puff on a cigarette* **3** a type of light food with a lot of air in it: *a cream puff*

puff² /pʌf/ *verb* **1** [I,T] (to cause air, smoke, wind, etc.) to blow or come out in puffs: *Smoke was puffing out of the chimney.* ○ *Stop puffing smoke in my face.* **2** [I,T] to smoke a cigarette, pipe etc.: *to puff away at a cigarette* ○ *He sat puffing his pipe.* **3** [I] to breathe loudly or quickly, e.g. when you are running: *He was puffing hard as he ran up the hill.*

PHR V **puff sth out/up** to cause sth to become larger by filling it with air

puff·y /ˈpʌfi/ *adj.* looking soft and round: *Your eyes look a little puffy. Have you been crying?* ○ *puffy clouds*

puke /pyuk/ *verb* [I,T] (*slang*) to bring food up from the stomach and out of the mouth; to vomit ☞ A more polite expression is **throw up**. —**puke** *noun* [U]

☆ **pull¹** /pʊl/ *verb* **1** [I,T] to use force to move or try to move sb/sth toward yourself: *Wendy pulled at the rope to make sure that it was secure.* ○ *to pull sb's hair* ○ *to pull a door open* ○ *You push and I'll pull.* ○ *to pull the trigger of a gun* ○ *They managed to pull the child out of the water just in time.* **2** [T] to move sth in the direction that is described: *She pulled her sweater on/She pulled on her sweater.* ○ *He pulled up his pants/He pulled his pants up.* ○ *Pull your chair a little bit closer to the table.* ○ *Pull the sheets off the bed.* **3** [T] to move sth behind you in the direction that you are moving: *The little boy pulled his wagon behind him.* ○ *That cart is too heavy for one horse to pull.* **4** [T] to damage a muscle, etc. by using too much force

IDM **pull sb's leg** (*informal*) to make fun of sb by trying to make him/her believe sth that is not true

pull strings to use your influence to gain an advantage

pull the plug (on sb/sth) (*informal*) to force a plan, project, etc. to end: *The network pulled the plug on the series after only three episodes.*

pull your weight to do your fair share of the work

PHR V **pull (sth) away** to move your body or part of it away with force: *She pulled away as he tried to kiss her.*

pull in (to sth); pull into sth (used about a car, etc.) to leave the road and enter another place in order to stop there: *He pulled into a gas station.*

pull sth off (*informal*) to succeed in sth: *to pull off a business deal*

pull out (used about a car, etc.) to move away from the side of the road: *I braked as a car suddenly pulled out in front of me.*

pull (sb/sth) out (of sth) (to cause sb/sth) to leave sth: *The President has decided to pull all U.S. troops out of the region.* ○ *We pulled out of the deal.*

pull sth out to take sth out of a place suddenly or with force: *She walked into the bank and pulled out a gun.*

pull (sb/sth) over (used about a car, etc.) to move to the side of the road in order to stop, or to order sb in a car to do this: *Paul was pulled over by the police for speeding on Route 128.*

pull yourself together to control your feelings and behave in a calm way: *Pull yourself together and stop crying.*

pull up (used about a car, etc.) to stop: *to pull up to the traffic lights*

☆ **pull²** /pʊl/ *noun* [C] **a pull (at/on sth)** an act of pulling: *Give the handle a good pull.* ○ *He took a long pull on his cigarette.*

pul·ley /ˈpʊli/ *noun* [C] (*pl.* **pul·leys**) a piece of equipment, consisting of a wheel and a rope, that is used for lifting heavy things

pull·o·ver /ˈpʊloʊvər/ (*also* ˌpullover ˈsweater**) *noun* [C] a piece of clothing that is usually made of wool and that covers the top part of your body and your arms. You put a pullover on by pulling it over your head. ☞ The word that we usually use is **sweater**.

pulp /pʌlp/ *noun* **1** [U] the soft inner part of some fruits or vegetables **2** [U] a soft substance made from wood that is used for making paper **3** [sing., U] a soft substance that you make by pressing and mixing sth for a long time: *Crush the strawberries to a pulp.*

pul·pit /ˈpʊlpɪt; ˈpʌl-/ *noun* [C] a raised platform in a church where the priest stands when he/she is speaking to the people there

pul·sate /ˈpʌlseɪt/ *verb* [I] to move or shake with strong regular movements: *a pulsating rhythm*

pulse¹ /pʌls/ *noun* [C, usually sing.] the regular beating in your body as blood is pumped through it by your heart. You can feel your pulse in your wrist, neck, etc.: *Your pulse rate increases after exercise.* ○ *to have a strong/weak pulse* ○ *to feel/take sb's pulse* (= to count how many times it beats in one minute)

pulse² /pʌls/ *verb* [I] **pulse (through sth)** to move with strong regular movements

pu·ma /ˈpumə/ *noun* [C] = MOUNTAIN LION

☆ **pump¹** /pʌmp/ *noun* [C] **1** a machine that is used for forcing a gas or liquid in a particular direction: *Do you have a bicycle pump? My tire's flat.* ○ *a gasoline pump* **2** a type of formal shoe for women, usually with a high heel ☞ picture at **shoe**.

☆ **pump²** /pʌmp/ *verb* [I,T] to force a gas or liquid to go in a particular direction: *Your heart pumps blood around your body.*

PHR V **pump sth up** to fill sth with air, e.g. by using a pump¹: *to pump up a car tire*

pump·kin /ˈpʌmpkɪn/ *noun* [C,U] a very large round fruit with thick orange-colored skin that is cooked and eaten like a vegetable: *pumpkin pie* ☞ Look also at **jack-o'-lantern** and at the note at **Halloween**.

pun /pʌn/ *noun* [C] **pun (on sth)** an amusing use of a word that can have two meanings or of different words that sound the same: *Mr. Stevens, who likes making puns, said after a very long meeting that he was "the chairman of the bored (= board)."*

punch¹ /pʌntʃ/ *verb* [T] **1** to hit sb/sth hard with your closed hand (**fist**): *Annie punched him hard in the stomach and ran away.* **2** to make a hole in sth with a special tool: *He punched a hole in the ticket.* ○ *He punched the ticket.*

PHR V **punch in** to put a card into a special machine that records the time you arrive at work

punch out to put a card into a special machine that records the time you leave work

punch² /pʌntʃ/ *noun* **1** [C] a hard hit with your closed hand (**fist**) **2** [C] a machine or tool that you use to make holes in sth: *a paper punch* **3** [U] a drink, often served at parties, made from fruit juice, sugar and, sometimes, alcohol

ˈ**punch line** *noun* [C] the last and most important words of a joke or story

punc·tu·al /ˈpʌŋktʃuəl/ *adj.* (*formal*) doing sth or happening at the right time; not late ☞ The phrase **on time** is more common than punctual. —**punc·tu·al·i·ty** /ˌpʌŋktʃuˈæləti/ *noun* [U]

punc·tu·ate /ˈpʌŋktʃueɪt/ *verb* **1** [I,T] to use punctuation marks when you are writing **2** [T] **punctuate sth (with sth)** (often passive) to interrupt sth many times: *Her speech was punctuated with bursts of applause.*

punc·tu·a·tion /ˌpʌŋktʃuˈeɪʃn/ *noun* [U] the use of punctuation marks when you are writing

☆ ˌ**punctu'ation mark** *noun* [C] one of the signs that you use when you are writing in order to divide the words into sentences, show that sb is speaking, etc.: *Punctuation marks include periods, commas, question marks and quotation marks.*

punc·ture /ˈpʌŋktʃər/ *verb* [T] to make a small hole in sth with sth sharp: *That nail must have punctured the tire.*

pun·gent /ˈpʌndʒənt/ *adj.* having a very strong smell

☆ **pun·ish** /ˈpʌnɪʃ/ *verb* [T] **punish sb (for sth) (by/with sth)** to cause sb to suffer because he/she has done sth wrong: *They broke the law and they deserve to be punished.* ○ *The boys were severely punished for shoplifting.* ○ *Petty criminals should be punished by having to do community service.* ○ *Drunk driving should be punished with imprisonment.*

pun·ish·a·ble /ˈpʌnɪʃəbl/ *adj.* **punishable by sth** (used about a crime, etc.) that you can be punished for doing: *In some countries, drug smuggling is punishable by death.*

pun·ish·ing /ˈpʌnɪʃɪŋ/ *adj.* that makes you very tired or weak: *The band had a punishing schedule of nine concerts in one week.*

☆ **pun·ish·ment** /ˈpʌnɪʃmənt/ *noun* **1** [U] the act of punishing or the state of being punished: *Most Southern states have capital punishment* (= punishment by death). **2** [C] a way in which sb is punished: *Ideally, the punishment should fit the crime.*

pu·ni·tive /ˈpyunətɪv/ *adj.* intended as a punishment: *The jury awarded the victim $2 million in punitive damages against the company.*

punk /pʌŋk/ *noun* **1** (*also* **punk music**) [U] a type of rock music that was popular in the late 1970s and early 1980s. Punk music often protests strongly about the way that society is organized. **2** [C] a person who likes punk music and often has brightly-colored hair and unusual clothes: *punks wearing torn jeans and safety pins in their ears* **3** [C] (*informal*) a boy or a young man who you think is unimportant, especially one who is often involved in fights, illegal activities, etc.: *What do you think you're looking at, punk?*

pu·ny /ˈpyuni/ *adj.* (**pu·ni·er; pu·ni·est**) small and weak

pup /pʌp/ *noun* [C] **1** = PUPPY **2** the young of some animals, e.g. seals

pu·pil /ˈpyupl/ *noun* [C] **1** (*formal or old-fashioned*) a child in school: *There are 28 pupils in the class.* ☞ **Student** is more common than **pupil**. **2** the round black hole in the middle of the eye

pup·pet /ˈpʌpət/ *noun* [C] **1** a model of a person or animal that you can move by pulling the strings which are attached to it or by putting your hand inside it and moving your fingers **2** a person or organization that is controlled by sb else

☆ **pup·py** /ˈpʌpi/ *noun* [C] (*pl.* **pup·pies**) (*also* **pup**) a young dog

☆ **pur·chase¹** /ˈpərtʃəs/ *noun* (*formal*) **1** [U] the act of buying sth: *to make a purchase* (= to buy sth) ○ *Please state the date and place of purchase.* **2** [C] something that you buy: *Employees will help you carry your purchases to your car.*

☆ **pur·chase²** /ˈpərtʃəs/ *verb* [T] (*formal*) to buy sth: *advice for people planning to purchase a new home*

pur·chas·er /ˈpərtʃəsər/ *noun* [C] (*formal*) a person who buys sth: *a law requiring security checks on handgun purchasers*

☆ **pure** /pyʊr/ *adj.* **1** not mixed with anything else: *a pure silk blouse* ○ *She was dressed in pure white.* ○ *pure Florida orange juice* **2** not containing any harmful substances: *the pure mountain air* **3** (*old-fashioned*) not doing or knowing anything evil or anything that is connected with sex: *to remain spiritually pure* ☞ The opposite for 2 and 3 is **impure**. **4** (only *before* a noun) complete: *We met by pure chance.* ○ *a pure waste of time* **5** (used about a sound) clear **6** (only *before* a noun) (used about an area of learning) concerned only with theory rather than practical uses: *pure mathematics* ☞ The opposite for 6 is **applied**.

pu·rée /pyʊˈreɪ/ *noun* [C,U] a food that you make by cooking a fruit or vegetable and then pressing and mixing it until it is a smooth liquid: *apple purée*

pure·ly /ˈpyʊrli/ *adv.* only or completely: *It's not purely a question of money.*

purge /pərdʒ/ *verb* [T] to remove people that you do not want from a political party or other organization —**purge** *noun* [C]

pu·ri·fy /ˈpyʊrəfaɪ/ *verb* [T] (*pres. part.* **pu·ri·fy·ing**; *3rd pers. sing. pres.* **pu·ri·fies**; *p.t., p.p.* **pu·ri·fied**) to remove dirty or harmful substances from sth: *purified water*

pu·ri·tan /ˈpyʊrɪtn/ *noun* [C] **1 Puritan** a member of a Christian religious group in England and N. America in the 1600s and 1700s who had very strict moral beliefs **2** a person who has strong religious beliefs and strict, traditional attitudes toward moral behavior, sex, etc.

pu·ri·tan·i·cal /ˌpyʊrəˈtænɪkl/ *adj.* having strict, traditional attitudes toward moral behavior, sex, etc. ☞ This word is often used in a critical way.

pu·ri·ty /ˈpyʊrəti/ *noun* [U] the state of being pure: *to test the purity of the air* ☞ Look at **impurity**.

☆ **pur·ple** /ˈpərpl/ *adj.* of a reddish-blue color: *a purple plum* —**pur·ple** *noun* [U]

☆ **pur·pose** /ˈpərpəs/ *noun* **1** [C] the reason for doing or making sth: *The main purpose of this meeting is to decide on a name for our new product.* ○ *You may only use the telephone for business purposes.* ○ *These complicated rules serve no useful purpose.* **2** [U] (*formal*) having

tʃ	dʒ	v	θ	ð	s	z	ʃ
chin	**June**	**van**	**thin**	**then**	**so**	**zoo**	**she**

an aim or plan and acting according to it: *A good leader inspires people with a sense of purpose.*

IDM on purpose not by accident; with a particular intention: *"You tore a page out of my book!" "Sorry, I didn't do it on purpose."* ∘ *I came a little early on purpose, to see if I could help you.*

pur·pose·ly /ˈpərpəsli/ *adv.* with a particular intention: *I purposely waited until everyone was gone so that I could talk to you in private.*

purr /pər/ *verb* [I] (used about a cat) to make a continuous low sound that shows pleasure

☆ **purse¹** /pərs/ (*also* **handbag**, *old-fashioned* **pocketbook**) *noun* [C] a small bag in which a woman carries money, keys, etc.

purse² /pərs/ *verb*
IDM purse your lips to press your lips together to show that you do not like sth

☆ **pur·sue** /pərˈsu/ *verb* [T] (*formal*) **1** to follow sb/sth in order to catch him/her/it: *The robber ran off, pursued by two police officers.* ∘ (*figurative*) *He is pursuing a completely unrealistic goal.* ☞ **Pursue** is more formal than **chase**. **2** to continue with sth; to find out more about sth: *to pursue a career in banking* ∘ *She didn't seem to want to pursue the discussion, so I changed the subject.*

pur·suit /pərˈsut/ *noun* **1** [U] the act of pursuing sb/sth: *the pursuit of pleasure* **2** [C] something that you spend your time doing, either for work or for pleasure: *outdoor pursuits* ∘ *leisure pursuits*
IDM in pursuit (of sb/sth) trying to catch or get sb/sth: *a dog in pursuit of a cat* ∘ *He neglected his family in pursuit of his own personal ambitions.*

pus /pʌs/ *noun* [U] a thick yellowish liquid that may form in a part of your body that has been hurt

push

pushing somebody in a wheelchair pushing somebody into the water

☆ **push¹** /pʊʃ/ *verb* **1** [I,T] to use force to move or try to move sb/sth forward or away from you: *You push and I'll pull.* ∘ *You can pull a rope, but you can't push it!* ∘ *Christine pushed him into the water.* ∘ *to push sb in a wheelchair* ∘ *to push a baby carriage* ∘ *She pushed the door*

shut with her foot. **2** [I,T] to move forward by pushing sb/sth: *John pushed his way through the crowd.* ∘ *to push past sb* **3** [I,T] to press or use force, e.g. with your finger, to move sth: *Push this button to call the nurse.* **4** [T] (*informal*) to try to make sb do sth, e.g. by asking or telling him/her many times: *Kim will not work hard unless you push her.* ∘ *to push sb for an answer* **5** [T] (*informal*) to try to make sth seem attractive, e.g. so that people will buy it: *They are launching a major advertising campaign to push their new product.* ∘ *dealers pushing drugs on street corners*
PHRV push ahead (with sth) to continue with sth: *The government will push ahead with plans to reduce its spending in some areas.*
push sb around (*informal*) to give sb orders in a rude way: *You shouldn't let your husband push you around like that.*
push for sth to try hard to get sth: *Journalists are always pushing for greater freedom of information.*

☆ **push²** /pʊʃ/ *noun* **1** [C] an act of pushing: *Paul gave the door a push and it opened.* ∘ *The car windows opened at the push of a button.* **2** [usually sing.] a strong effort to do or finish sth: *the company's big push to improve customer service* ∘ *a push for increased government spending on education*

push-button (*also* **pushbutton**) *adj.* (only before a noun) (used about a machine, etc.) that you work by pushing a button: *a push-button phone*

push·er /ˈpʊʃər/ *noun* [C] (*informal*) a person who sells illegal drugs

push·o·ver /ˈpʊʃoʊvər/ *noun* [C] (*informal*) a person who is easy to persuade, convince, or defeat

push·up /ˈpʊʃʌp/ *noun* [C] a type of exercise in which you lie on your front on the floor and push your body up with your arms

push·y /ˈpʊʃi/ *adj.* (**push·i·er**; **push·i·est**) (*informal*) (used about a person) behaving in a rude, forceful way in order to get an advantage or to make people notice you: *a pushy mother-in-law*

puss·y·cat /ˈpʊsikæt/ *noun* [C] (*informal*) (used by and to small children) a cat

☆ **put** /pʊt/ *verb* [T] (*pres. part.* **put·ting**; *p.t., p.p.* **put**) **1** to move sb/sth so that it is in a particular place or position: *She put the book on the table.* ∘ *I put the knife back in the drawer.* ∘ *Did you put sugar in my coffee?* ∘ *When do you put your kids to bed?* **2** to fasten sth to or in sth else: *Can you put* (= sew) *a button on this shirt?* ∘ *We're going to put new carpeting in this room.* **3** to make sb feel or experience sth: *This kind of weather always puts me in a bad mood.* ∘ *Your decision puts me in a difficult position.*

i	ɪ	ɛ	æ	ɑ	ɔ	ʌ	ʊ	u
see	sit	ten	cat	hot	saw	cup	put	too

4 to say or express sth: *I don't know exactly how to put this, but…* **5** to write sth: *12:30 on Friday? I'll put it on my calendar.* ○ *What did you put for question 2?*

IDM **be put off (by sb/sth)** to feel uncomfortable or uncertain because of sb/sth: *Don't be put off by the restaurant's ugly exterior – they serve excellent food.*

would not put it past sb (to do sth) to think sb is capable of doing sth bad: *I wouldn't put it past him to do a thing like that.*

put together (used after a noun or nouns referring to a group of people or things) combined: *You got more presents than the rest of the family put together.*

☞ For other idioms containing **put**, look at the entries for the nouns, adjectives, etc., e.g. **put an end to sth** is at **end**.

PHRV **put sth across** to say sth clearly, so that people can understand it: *He didn't put his ideas across very well at the meeting.*

put sth aside to save sth, especially money, to use later

put sb away (*informal*) to send sb to prison

put sth away 1 to put sth where you usually keep it, e.g. in a cupboard: *Put your toys away – our guests are coming soon.* **2** to save money to use later: *Her grandparents had put some money away for her education.* **3** (*informal*) to eat or drink a lot of sth: *I saw him put away an entire ham once!*

put sth back to return sth to its correct place: *to put books back on the shelf*

put sb down (*informal*) to say things to make sb seem stupid or foolish: *He's always putting his wife down.*

put sth down 1 to place sth, e.g. on the floor, a table, etc.: *The police officer persuaded him to put the gun down.* **2** to write sth: *I can tell you exactly what she said – I put it all down in my notebook.* **3** (used about a government, an army or the police) to stop sth by force: *to put down a rebellion*

put sth forward to suggest sth: *a proposal put forward by one of the school board members*

put sth in; **put sth into sth/into doing sth** to spend time, etc. on sth: *I put in 10 hours at work yesterday.* ○ *She puts all her time and energy into her business.*

put in for sth to make an official request for sth: *She put in for a transfer to the company's California office.*

put sth off; **put off doing sth** to delay doing sth: *"I've got to go to the store." "Can't you put it off?"* ○ *She put off writing her paper until the last minute.*

put sth on 1 to place clothes on your body: *Put on your coat!* ○ *I'll have to put my glasses on.* **2** to make a piece of electrical equipment, etc. start working, usually by pressing a switch: *It's not hot enough to put the air condi-*

tioning on yet. **3** to begin cooking food in a pan: *I'll put the carrots on while you set the table.* **4** to make sth (e.g. a CD, a tape, etc.) begin to play: *Let's put some music on.* **5** to become fatter or heavier (by the amount mentioned): *I put on weight very easily.* ○ *She's put on several pounds since the last time I saw her.*

put sb out to give sb trouble or extra work: *I really don't want to put you out – I'll take a taxi home.*

put sth out 1 to make sth stop burning: *to put out a fire* **2** to give or tell the public sth, often by using the television, radio or newspapers: *The police put out a warning about the escaped prisoner.* **3** to move your hand, foot, etc. away from the rest of your body: *If you want a piece of candy, put your hand out and I'll give you one.*

put sb through sth to make sb experience sth bad

put sb/sth through to make a telephone connection that allows sb to speak to sb: *Hold on while I put you through to Mr. Weber's voice mail.*

put sth to sb (*formal*) to suggest sth to sb; to ask sb sth: *She put a proposal to the chairman of the board.*

put sth together to build or repair sth by joining its parts together: *The furniture comes with instructions on how to put it together.*

put up sth to offer or give resistance in a fight, etc.: *The old lady put up a struggle against her attacker.*

put sb up to give sb food and a place to stay: *Her car wouldn't start, so I offered to put her up for the night.*

put sth up 1 to build sth: *to put up a fence* **2** to fasten sth to a wall, etc. so that everyone can see it: *to put up a notice*

put up with sb/sth to suffer sb/sth bad and not complain about it: *I don't know how they put up with this noise.*

putt /pʌt/ *verb* [I,T] (used in golf) to hit the ball gently when it is near the hole

put·ter /ˈpʌtər/ *verb* [I] **putter (around)** to spend your time doing small jobs in a relaxed way: *Grandpa spends most of the day puttering around in the back yard.*

put·ty /ˈpʌti/ *noun* [U] a substance that is used for fastening things together, filling in cracks, etc. Putty is soft when you use it, but it turns hard later.

☆ **puz·zle¹** /ˈpʌzl/ *noun* [C] **1** a game or toy that tests your knowledge, skill, intelligence, etc.: *to do a crossword puzzle* ○ *The solution to the puzzle is on page 27.* **2** = JIGSAW PUZZLE **3** [usually sing.] something that is difficult to understand or explain; a mystery: *The reasons for his action have remained a puzzle to historians.*

puz·zle² /ˈpʌzl/ *verb* **1** [T] to cause sb to think hard about sth he/she cannot understand or

ə	y	w	t̬	eɪ	aɪ	ɔɪ	aʊ	oʊ
about	yes	woman	butter	say	five	boy	now	go

explain: *Scientists are puzzled by the recent changes in weather patterns.* **2** [I] **puzzle over sth** to think hard about sth in order to understand or explain it: *to puzzle over a mathematical problem*

puz·zled /ˈpʌzld/ *adj.* not able to understand or explain sth: *a puzzled expression*

py·ja·mas /pəˈdʒæməz/ *noun* [plural] (*BrE*) = PAJAMAS

pyr·a·mid /ˈpɪrəmɪd/ *noun* [C] a shape with a flat base and three or four triangular sides ☞ picture at **cube**.

py·thon /ˈpaɪθən/ *noun* [C] a large snake that kills animals by squeezing them very hard

Qq

Q, q /kyu/ *noun* [C] (*pl.* **Q's**; **q's** /kyuz/) the seventeenth letter of the English alphabet: *"Queen" begins with (a) "Q."*

Q *abbr.* question: *a Q & A* (= question and answer) *column in the newspaper*

qt. *abbr.* quart(s)

Q-Tip /ˈkyu tɪp/ *noun* [C] (*trademark*) a small thin stick with soft material such as cotton at each end, that is used for cleaning small places such as your ears

quack /kwæk/ *noun* [C] the sound that a duck makes —**quack** *verb* [I]

quad /kwɑd/ (also *formal* **quad·ran·gle** /ˈkwɑdræŋgl/) *noun* [C] a square open area with buildings around it, in a school, college, etc.

quad·ru·ple /kwɑˈdrupl/ *verb* [I,T] to multiply or be multiplied by four: *Profits have quadrupled in the past ten years.*

quaint /kweɪnt/ *adj.* attractive or unusual because it seems to belong to the past: *New England has many quaint old towns.*

quake¹ /kweɪk/ *verb* [I] to shake: *to quake with fear, cold, etc.*

quake² /kweɪk/ *noun* [C] (*informal*) = EARTHQUAKE

☆ **qual·i·fi·ca·tion** /ˌkwɑləfəˈkeɪʃn/ *noun* **1** [C] a skill or quality that makes you suitable to do sth, such as a job: *She has all the right qualifications for the manager's job.* ○ *He does not meet the qualifications for U.S. citizenship.* **2** [C,U] success in one part of a competition so that you can go on to the next part: *the team's qualification for the state tournament* ○ *the world championship qualification match* **3** [C,U] (*formal*) something that limits or weakens the meaning of a general statement: *These attacks must be condemned without qualification.*

qual·i·fied /ˈkwɑləfaɪd/ *adj.* **1** having the skill, knowledge or quality that you need to do sth: *I don't feel qualified to comment – I know nothing about the subject.* ○ *Since he passed the bar exam, he's a fully qualified lawyer.* **2** (*formal*) not complete; limited: *My boss gave only*

qualified approval to the plan. ☞ The opposite is **unqualified**.

☆ **qual·i·fy** /ˈkwɑləfaɪ/ *verb* (*pres. part.* **qual·i·fy·ing**; *3rd pers. sing. pres.* **qual·i·fies**; *p.t., p.p.* **qual·i·fied**) **1** [I] to have the qualities that are necessary for sth: *To qualify for the scholarship, you have to be a resident of the state of Texas.* ○ *A cup of coffee and a sandwich doesn't really qualify as a meal.* **2** [T] to give sb the right to do a particular job: *This certificate will qualify me to teach music.* **3** [I] to be successful in one part of a competition and to go on to the next part: *Our team has qualified for the final round.* **4** [I,T] to have or give sb the right to have or do sth: *How many years do you have to work to qualify for a company pension?* ○ *Residence in this country does not qualify you to vote.* **5** [T] to limit or weaken the meaning of a general statement: *I should qualify what I said earlier – it wasn't quite true.*

☆ **qual·i·ty¹** /ˈkwɑləti/ *noun* (*pl.* **qual·i·ties**) **1** [U] how good or bad sth is: *This paper isn't very good quality.* ○ *These photos are of poor quality.* ○ *a high-quality magazine* ○ *the quality of life in our cities* **2** [U] a high standard or level: *We aim to provide quality at a reasonable price.* **3** [C] something that is typical of a person or thing: *Vicky has all the qualities of a good manager.* ○ *One quality of oil is that it floats on water.*

qual·i·ty² /ˈkwɑləti/ *adj.* (only *before* a noun) of a high standard or level: *We want employees who can produce quality work.* ○ *I ought to spend more quality time with my kids* (= paying attention to them, doing special activities together, etc.).

qualm /kwɑm; kwɔm/ *noun* [C, usually pl.] a feeling of doubt or worry about whether what you are doing is right: *I don't have any qualms about asking them to loan us some money.*

quan·da·ry /ˈkwɑndəri; -dri/ *noun* [C] (*pl.* **quan·da·ries**) a state of not being able to decide what to do; a difficult situation: *to be in a quandary*

☆ **quan·ti·ty** /ˈkwɑntəti/ *noun* (*pl.* **quan·ti·ties**) **1** [U] the measurement of sth by stating how

ər	ɪr	ɛr	ɑr	ɔr	ʊr	ʒ	h	ŋ
bird	near	hair	car	north	tour	vision	hat	sing

much of it there is: *Don't write too much in your essay – quality is more important than quantity.* **2** [C,U] a number or an amount: *Add a small quantity of salt.* ○ *It's cheaper to buy goods in quantity* (= in large amounts). ○ *It's cheaper to buy goods in large quantities.*

quar·an·tine /ˈkwɔrəntin; ˈkwɑr-/ *noun* [U] a period of time when a person or animal that has or may have a disease must be kept away from other people or animals: *to keep a dog in quarantine*

quar·rel¹ /ˈkwɔrəl; ˈkwɑrəl/ *noun* [C] (*formal*) an angry argument or disagreement: *Several people pulled out knives during a quarrel on Elm Street last night.* ☛ Look at **argument** and **fight**.

IDM **have no quarrel with sb/sth** to have no reason for complaining about or disagreeing with sb/sth: *I have no quarrel with what has just been said.*

quar·rel² /ˈkwɔrəl; ˈkwɑrəl/ *verb* [I] (*formal*) **1 quarrel (with sb) (about/over sth)** to have an angry argument or disagreement: *Politicians quarreled bitterly over whether to send U.S. troops to the area.* ☛ Look at **argue** and **fight**. **2 quarrel with sth** to disagree with sth: *I wouldn't quarrel with Mary's description of what happened.*

quar·ry /ˈkwɔri; ˈkwɑri/ *noun* [C] (*pl.* **quar·ries**) a place where sand, stone, etc. is dug out of the ground ☛ Look at **mine²**(1).

☆ **quart** /kwɔrt/ *noun* [C] (*abbr.* **qt.**) a measure of liquid; 0.95 liter. There are two pints in a quart: *a quart of milk* ☛ For more information on measurements, look at Appendix 2.

☆ **quar·ter** /ˈkwɔrtər/ *noun* **1** [C] one of four equal parts into which sth is divided: *The program lasts for three quarters of an hour.* ○ *a mile and a quarter* ○ *to cut an apple into quarters* **2** [sing.] fifteen minutes before or after every hour: *I'll meet you at a quarter after six.* ○ *It's a quarter to three.* **3** [C] a coin that is worth 25 cents (¼ dollar) **4** [C] a period of three months: *The company had record profits for the last quarter.* **5** [C] (at some schools, colleges and universities) one of the four equal parts that the academic year is divided into: *I'm going to take chemistry next quarter.* **6 quarters** [plural] a place that is provided for a person to live in, usually not in a private house: *The White House living quarters are not open to the public.*

IDM **in some quarters** among people who have certain opinions: *Racist attitudes still exist in some quarters.*

quar·ter·back /ˈkwɔrtərbæk/ *noun* [C] the player on a football team who tells the other players what to do and throws the ball to them ☛ Look at the note at **football**.

quar·ter·fi·nal /ˌkwɔrtərˈfaml/ *noun* [C] one of the four games between the eight remaining players or teams in a competition. The players that win in the quarterfinals go on to the semifinals.

quar·ter·ly /ˈkwɔrtərli/ *adj., adv.* (produced or happening) once every three months: *a quarterly magazine* ○ *The committee meets quarterly.*

quar·tet /kwɔrˈtɛt/ *noun* [C] **1** four people who sing or play music together **2** a piece of music for four people to sing or play together

quartz /kwɔrts/ *noun* [U] a type of hard rock that is used in making very accurate clocks or watches

quash /kwɑʃ/ *verb* [T] (*formal*) **1** to stop or defeat sth by force: *to quash a rebellion* **2** to declare that an official decision, judgment, etc. is no longer true or legal: *The Supreme Court quashed the verdict of the lower court.*

☆ **queen** /kwin/ *noun* [C] **1** (*also* **Queen**) the female ruler of a country that has a royal family, or the wife of a king: *Queen Elizabeth II* ☛ Queen Elizabeth II is pronounced "Queen Elizabeth **the Second**." Look at **king** and **princess**. **2** the largest and most important female in a group of insects: *the queen bee* **3** one of the four playing cards in a deck with a picture of a queen (1) on it: *the queen of hearts* ☛ Look at the note at **card**. **4** one of the pieces used in the game of chess ☛ picture at **chess**.

¹queen-size *adj.* larger than usual: *queen-size pantyhose* ○ *a queen-size bed* ☛ Look at the note at **bed**.

queer¹ /kwɪr/ *adj.* **1** (*old-fashioned*) strange; odd **2** (*slang*) homosexual ☛ Look at **gay**. **Queer** is often used in an offensive way, but some homosexual people use it about themselves.

queer² /kwɪr/ *noun* [C] (*slang*) a homosexual man ☛ Look at the note at **queer¹**.

quell /kwɛl/ *verb* [T] to put an end to sth: *to quell a rebellion*

quench /kwɛntʃ/ *verb* [T] to satisfy your feeling of thirst by drinking: *to quench your thirst*

que·ry¹ /ˈkwɪri/ *noun* [C] (*pl.* **que·ries**) (*formal*) a question: *The White House spokesperson answered reporters' queries about the policy.*

que·ry² /ˈkwɪri/ *verb* [T] (*pres. part.* **que·ry·ing**; *3rd pers. sing. pres.* **que·ries**; *p.t., p.p.* **que·ried**) (*formal*) to ask sb a question about sth: *1,000 people were queried about their eating habits for the survey.*

quest /kwɛst/ *noun* [C] (*formal*) a long search for sth that is difficult to find: *the quest for eternal youth*

☆ **ques·tion¹** /ˈkwɛstʃən/ *noun* **1** [C] a sentence or phrase that asks for an answer: *Are there any questions about what I just said?* ○ *Raise your hand if you want to ask a question.* ○ *On the test, you have to answer five questions in one hour.* ○ *What's the answer to question 5?* ☛ Look at the note at **doubt¹**. Look also at **tag question**. **2** [C] a problem or difficulty that

tʃ	dʒ	v	θ	ð	s	z	ʃ
chin	June	van	thin	then	so	zoo	she

needs to be discussed or dealt with: *His resignation raises the question of who will take over from him.* ○ *It's not difficult. It's just a question of finding the time to do it.* ○ *We all agree that more money should be spent on education. The question is where that money is going to come from.* **3** [U] doubt or uncertainty: *There is no question about Brenda's enthusiasm for the job.* ○ *His honesty is beyond question.*

IDM **in question** (*formal*) that is being considered or talked about: *The lawyer asked where she was on the night in question.*

no question of sth/doing sth no possibility of sth/doing sth: *There was no question of any illegal activity in the company.*

out of the question impossible: *A new car is out of the question. It's just too expensive.*

☆ **ques·tion²** /ˈkwɛstʃən/ *verb* [T] **1** to ask sb a question or questions, especially in a formal situation or in an aggressive way: *The police questioned him for several hours.* ○ *The interviewers questioned me about my previous experience.* **2** to express or feel doubt about sth: *She told me she was an employee, so I didn't question her right to be there.* ○ *to question sb's sincerity*

☆ **ques·tion·a·ble** /ˈkwɛstʃənəbl/ *adj.* **1** that is not certain: *It's questionable whether we'll be able to finish in time.* **2** that may not be true, suitable or honest: *A lot of money has been spent on very questionable projects.* ○ *questionable motives*

'**question mark** *noun* [C] the sign (?) that you use when you write a question

ques·tion·naire /ˌkwɛstʃəˈnɛr/ *noun* [C] a list of questions that are answered by many people. A questionnaire is used to collect information about a particular subject: *to complete/fill out a questionnaire*

queue /kyu/ *noun* [C] (*BrE*) = LINE¹(5)

quiche /kiʃ/ *noun* [C,U] a pie without a top that is filled with a mixture of eggs and milk with cheese, ham, etc. and cooked in the oven.

☆ **quick¹** /kwɪk/ *adj.* **1** doing sth at a high speed or in a short time: *It's quicker to travel by plane.* ○ *Nick is a quick worker.* ○ *She was quick to point out all the mistakes I had made.* **2** done in a short time: *Could I make a quick phone call?*

☞ **Fast** is more often used for describing a person or thing that moves or can move at great speed: *a fast horse, car, runner, etc.*. **Quick** is more often used for describing sth that is done in a short time: *a quick decision, breakfast, visit, etc.*.

☆ **quick²** /kwɪk/ *adv.* (*informal*) quickly: *to get rich quick* ○ *The stove's on fire – do something quick!*

☆ **quick·ly** /ˈkwɪkli/ *adv.* at a high speed or in a short time: *Tom undressed quickly and got into*

bed. ○ *I'd like you to get here as quickly as possible.*

☆ **qui·et¹** /ˈkwaɪət/ *adj.* **1** with very little or no noise: *Be quiet!* ○ *His voice was quiet but firm.* ○ *Please keep the kids quiet when I'm on the phone.* ○ *Go into the library if you want to work. It's a lot quieter in there.* ☞ The opposite is **loud**. **2** without many people or much activity; without anything very exciting happening: *It's very quiet downtown on Sundays.* ○ *"Have you been busy?" "No, it was a very quiet day today."* ○ *a quiet suburb* ○ *a quiet life* **3** (used about a person) not saying very much; not attracting other people's attention: *You're very quiet today. Is anything wrong?*

IDM **keep quiet about sth; keep sth quiet** to say nothing about sth: *Can you keep quiet about my new job until I tell the boss?* —**qui·et·ly** *adv.*: *Try and close the door quietly!* ○ *"She was my best friend," Rose said quietly.* ○ *He quietly got up and left the room.* —**qui·et·ness** *noun* [U]

☆ **qui·et²** /ˈkwaɪət/ *noun* [U] the state of being quiet¹(1,2) : *the peace and quiet of the countryside*

☆ **qui·et³** /ˈkwaɪət/ *verb* [T] to make sb/sth quiet¹(1) : *to quiet a crowd*

PHRV **quiet (sb/sth) down** to become quiet or to make sb/sth quiet: *Quiet down! I want to listen to the radio.*

quilt /kwɪlt/ *noun* [C] a cover for a bed that has a thick warm material, e.g. cotton or feathers, inside it. Some quilts are made with pieces of colored cloth that have been sewn together to make a design.

quin·tet /kwɪnˈtɛt/ *noun* [C] **1** a group of five people who sing or play music together **2** a piece of music for five people to sing or play together

quirk /kwərk/ *noun* [C] **1** a strange habit or type of behavior **2** a strange happening: *By a quirk of fate, they met again several years later.*

quirk·y /ˈkwərki/ *adj.* (used about a person's behavior) unusual

quit /kwɪt/ *verb* (*pres. part.* **quit·ting**; *p.t., p.p.* **quit**) **1** [I,T] to leave a job, etc.: *I've had enough of this stupid company – I quit!* ○ *Joe quit his job to go back to college.* **2** [T] (*informal*) to stop doing sth: *to quit smoking* **3** [I,T] (*computing*) to close a computer program

☆ **quite** /kwaɪt/ *adv.* (used before an adjective or adverb) (*formal*) very, but not completely or extremely: *We are quite pleased with the results of our experiments.* ○ *She shouldn't be so modest – she really speaks English quite well.*

IDM **not quite** (used for showing that sth is nearly suitable or almost happens): *There's not quite enough bread for breakfast.* ○ *I can't quite reach it – can you give it to me?* ○ *These shoes don't quite fit.*

quite a (used for emphasizing that sth is unusual, or larger, longer, etc. than usual):

i	ɪ	ɛ	æ	ɑ	ɔ	ʌ	ʊ	u
see	sit	ten	cat	hot	saw	cup	put	too

race

That's quite a hairstyle, Ben! ∘ That's quite a big problem. ∘ We'll have to wait quite a while. **quite a bit (of sth); quite a few; quite a lot (of sth)** a lot, but not an extremely large amount or number of sth: *I learned quite a bit during the tour of the museum. ∘ We received quite a few responses to our ad. ∘ They've worked hard, but there's still quite a lot left to do.*

quits /kwɪts/ *adj.*
IDM call it quits ⇨ CALL²

quit·ter /ˈkwɪt̬ər/ *noun* [C] (*informal*) a person who becomes discouraged too easily when a job, etc. becomes difficult and is likely to stop doing it

quiv·er /ˈkwɪvər/ *verb* [I] to tremble or shake: *to quiver with rage, excitement, fear, etc.*

☆ **quiz** /kwɪz/ *noun* [C] (*pl.* **quiz·zes**) a short, informal test: *We have a quiz in math class today.* ☛ Look also at **pop quiz**.

quo·ta /ˈkwoʊt̬ə/ *noun* [C] the number or amount of sth that is allowed or that you must do: *There is a quota on the number of cars that can be imported each year. ∘ We have a fixed quota of work to get through each day.*

quo·ta·tion /kwoʊˈteɪʃn/ (*also informal*

quote) *noun* [C] **1** a group of words from a book, speech, play, etc., that you repeat exactly: *That's a quotation from a poem by Longfellow. ∘ Please include quotations from the text to support your argument.* **2** the amount that sb thinks a piece of work will probably cost: *You should get a quotation from three mechanics.* ☛ Look at **estimate**.

☆ **quo·tation marks** (also *informal* **quotes**) *noun* [plural] the signs (" ... ") that you use at the beginning and end of words that were spoken or that are being quoted, or that you are using in an unusual way

☆ **quote** /kwoʊt/ *verb* **1** [I,T] **quote (sth) (from sb/sth)** to repeat exactly sth that sb else has said or written before: *The journalist quoted a statement that the senator had made several years earlier. ∘ to quote from the Bible ∘ She was quoted as saying that she disagreed with the decision. ∘ The mayor asked the newspaper not to quote him.* **2** [T] to give sth as an example to support what you are saying: *She quoted several reasons why she was unhappy about the decision.* **3** [T] to say what the cost of a piece of work, etc. will probably be: *The insurance company quoted us a rate for insuring our car.* — **quote** *noun* [C]

Rr

R, r /ɑr/ *noun* [C] (*pl.* **R's; r's**) the eighteenth letter of the English alphabet: *"Rabbit" begins with (an) "R."*

R *abbr.* **1** restricted (used about movies that children under age 17 are not allowed to see without a parent) **2** (*also* **R.**) = REPUBLICAN

rab·bi /ˈræbaɪ/ *noun* [C] (*pl.* **rab·bis**) a Jewish religious leader and teacher of Jewish law

☆ **rab·bit** /ˈræbət/ *noun* [C] a small animal with long ears: *a wild rabbit ∘ a pet rabbit* ☛ The children's word for rabbit is **bunny**.

ra·bies /ˈreɪbiz/ *noun* [U] a serious, usually fatal, disease that can be given to humans by the bite of an animal that has the disease

rac·coon /ræˈkun/ *noun* [C] a small wild animal with brownish-gray fur on its body, black fur around its eyes and a thick tail with rings of black and white fur on it

☆ **race¹** /reɪs/ *noun* **1** [C] **race (against/with sb/sth)** a competition between people, animals, cars etc. to see which is the fastest: *to run/win/lose a race ∘ to come first, second, last, etc. in a race ∘ a five-mile race ∘ a horse race ∘ Let's have a race to the end of the road. ∘ (figurative) the race to find a cure for AIDS ∘ (figurative) the nuclear arms race* ☛ Look also at **rat race**. **2** [C] an election and the speeches, meetings, etc. that come before it: *Officials have now announced the winner in the race for governor. ∘ the 1996 presidential race* **3** [C,U] one of the groups into which people can be divided according to the color of their skin, their hair type, the shape of their face, etc.: *the different races of South Africa ∘ a child of mixed race ∘ People should not be discriminated against on grounds of race, religion or gender.* ☛ Look at **human race**.

☆ **race²** /reɪs/ *verb* **1** [I,T] **race (against/with sb/sth)** to have a competition with sb/sth to find out who is the fastest: *I'll race you home. ∘ In the 5,000 meters he'll be racing against some of the finest runners in the country.* **2** [I,T] to go very fast or to move sb/sth very fast: *We raced*

ə	y	w	t̬	eɪ	aɪ	ɔɪ	aʊ	oʊ
about	yes	woman	butter	say	five	boy	now	go

to catch the bus. ○ *The child had to be raced to the hospital.*

☆ **ra·cial** /'reɪʃl/ *adj.* connected with people's race[1](3) ; happening between people of different races: *racial tension* ○ *racial discrimination* —**ra·cial·ly** *adv.*: *a racially integrated neighborhood*

rac·ing /'reɪsɪŋ/ *noun* [U] the sport of taking part in races: *car racing* ○ *horse racing* ○ *bike racing*

☆ **ra·cism** /'reɪsɪzəm/ *noun* [U] the belief that some races are better than others and people of other races are not as good as people of your own race; ways of treating people that show this belief: *to take measures to combat racism* —**rac·ist** /'reɪsɪst/ *noun* [C], *adj.*: *He's a racist.* ○ *a racist remark*

wine rack

racks

coat rack

luggage rack

rack[1] /ræk/ *noun* [C] (often in compounds) a type of shelf, made of bars, that you can put things in or on: *a towel rack* ○ *racks of clothing in a department store*

rack[2] /ræk/ *verb*

IDM **rack your brains** to try hard to think of sth or remember sth: *Steve racked his brains trying to remember where they'd met before.*

rack·et /'rækət/ *noun* **1** [C] (*also* **racquet**) a piece of sports equipment that you use to hit the ball in games such as tennis ☞ picture at **tennis**. Rackets are different from **bats** because they have **strings**. Look also at **club[2]**(2) and **stick[1]**(3). **2** [sing.] (*informal*) a loud noise: *Quit making that racket!* **3** [C] an illegal way of making money: *a drug racket*

☆ **ra·dar** /'reɪdɑr/ *noun* [U] the system for finding out the position of sth that you cannot see, with the help of radio waves

ra·di·ant /'reɪdiənt/ *adj.* **1** sending out light or heat: *radiant energy* **2** showing great happiness: *a radiant smile*

ra·di·ate /'reɪdieɪt/ *verb* **1** [T] to send out heat or light: (*figurative*) *to radiate health* **2** [I] **ra·diate (out) from sth** to go out in all directions from a central point: *several corridors which radiate out from the lobby*

ra·di·a·tion /ˌreɪdi'eɪʃn/ *noun* [U] powerful and very dangerous rays of energy that are sent out from certain substances. You cannot see or feel radiation, but it can cause serious illness or death: *High levels of radiation have* been recorded near the power plant. ○ *to be exposed to radiation* ☞ Look at **radioactive**.

ra·di·a·tor /'reɪdieɪţər/ *noun* [C] **1** a piece of equipment that is used for heating a room. Radiators are made of metal and filled with hot water: *Turn the radiator down a little!* **2** a piece of equipment that is used for keeping an engine cool

rad·i·cal[1] /'rædɪkl/ *adj.* **1** (used about changes in sth) very great: *radical reforms in the welfare system* ○ *radical change* **2** wanting great social or political change: *radical feminists* ○ *to hold radical views* ☞ Look at **moderate**. —**rad·i·cal·ly** /-kli/ *adv.*: *two radically different views on the subject*

rad·i·cal[2] /'rædɪkl/ *noun* [C] a person who wants great social or political change: *antiwar radicals of the 1960s*

ra·di·i *pl.* of RADIUS

☆ **ra·di·o[1]** /'reɪdioʊ/ *noun* (*pl.* **ra·di·os**) **1** [C] a piece of equipment that is used for receiving and/or sending messages or broadcasts that you listen to (on a ship, airplane, etc. or in the house): *a portable radio* ○ *A radio cassette player was stolen from the car.*

☞ You may **turn** or **switch** a radio **on** or **off**. You may also **turn** it **up** or **down** to make it louder or quieter.

2 often **the radio** [U, sing.] the broadcasting of programs for people to listen to on their radios (1): *I always listen to the radio in the car.* ○ *I heard an interesting report on the radio this morning.* ○ *a radio station, show, etc.* **3** [U] the process of sending or receiving messages through the air by electrical signals: *The yachtsman was in contact with the coast by radio.* ○ *a radio signal*

ra·di·o[2] /'reɪdioʊ/ *verb* [I,T] (*p.t., p.p.* **ra·di·oed**) to send a message by radio[1]: *to radio for help*

ra·di·o·ac·tive /ˌreɪdioʊ'æktɪv/ *adj.* sending out powerful and very dangerous rays of energy that are produced when atoms are broken up. These rays cannot be seen or felt but can cause serious illness or death: *the problem of the disposal of radioactive waste from power plants* ☞ Look at **radiation**.

ra·di·o·ac·tiv·i·ty /ˌreɪdioʊækˈtɪvəţi/ *noun* [U] **1** the state of being radioactive **2** the energy that is produced by radioactive substances

rad·ish /'rædɪʃ/ *noun* [C] a small red vegetable with a strong taste that you eat raw, especially in salads. A radish is the root of a radish plant.

ra·di·us /'reɪdiəs/ *noun* [C] (*pl.* **ra·di·i** /-diaɪ/) **1** the distance from the center of a circle to the outside edge ☞ Look at **diameter**. **2** a circular area that is measured from a point in its center: *The wreckage of the plane was scattered over a radius of several miles.*

raf·fle /'ræfl/ *noun* [C] a way of making money

for a charity, church, etc. by selling tickets with numbers on them. Later some numbers are chosen and the tickets with these numbers on them win prizes.

raft /ræft/ *noun* [C] a type of simple flat boat that you make by tying pieces of wood together

raft·er /ˈræftər/ *noun* [C] one of the long pieces of wood that support a roof

rag¹ /ræg/ *noun* **1** [C,U] a small piece of old cloth that you use for cleaning **2 rags** [plural] clothes that are very old and torn: *to be dressed in rags*

rag² /ræg/ *verb* **rag·ging; ragged**
PHRV **rag on sb** (*slang*) to criticize sb in order to make him/her feel embarrassed or because you are angry at him/her: *Everybody was totally ragging on me at school today.*

rage¹ /reɪdʒ/ *noun* [C,U] great anger: *He was trembling with rage.* ○ *to fly into a rage* (= to suddenly become very angry)

rage² /reɪdʒ/ *verb* [I] (used about a battle, disease, storm, etc.) to continue with great force: *The fire raged out of control.*

rag·ged /ˈrægəd/ *adj.* (used about clothes, etc.) old and torn

raid¹ /reɪd/ *noun* [C] **raid (on sth) 1** a surprise attack on an enemy: *an air raid* **2** an attack in order to steal sth: *a bank raid* **3** a surprise visit by the police: *Police found large supplies of cocaine during a raid on a hotel last night.*

raid² /reɪd/ *verb* [T] to make a raid¹ on a place: *Police raided the bar looking for drugs.*

☆ **rail** /reɪl/ *noun* **1** (*also* **railing**) [C] a bar, usually of metal or wood, which protects people from falling (on stairs, from a building, etc.): *Hold on to the hand rail – these steps are very slippery.* **2** [C, usually pl.] the tracks that trains run on **3** [U] the railroad system; trains as a means of transportation: *commuter rail lines* ○ *The goods were shipped by rail.*

rail·ing /ˈreɪlɪŋ/ *noun* [C] = RAIL(1)

☆ **rail·road** /ˈreɪlroʊd/ *noun* [C] the system of trains, the metal lines (**tracks**) that they run on, and the companies that own them: *railroad tracks* ○ *This town got a lot bigger after the railroad came in the 1860s.*

ˈrailroad ˌcrossing *noun* [C] a place where a railroad track crosses the surface of a road

rail·way /ˈreɪlweɪ/ *noun* [C] (*BrE*) = RAILROAD

☆ **rain¹** /reɪn/ *noun* **1** [U] the water that falls from the sky: *Seattle gets a lot of rain.* ○ *Take your umbrella – it looks like rain.* ○ *Half an inch of rain fell on the city yesterday.* ☞ Look at **shower¹**(3) and **acid rain** and at the note at **weather. 2** [C] an occasion when rain (1) falls: *Everything smells fresh after a good rain.* ○ *recent heavy rains* **3 the rains** [plural] (in tropical countries) the time of the year when there is a lot of rain (1): *When the rains come in July, the people move their houses to higher ground.*

☆ **rain²** /reɪn/ *verb* [I] (used with *it*) to fall as rain¹(1) : *Oh no! It's raining again!* ○ *Is it raining hard?* ○ *We'll go out when it stops raining.*
PHRV **rain (sth) out** (usually passive) to stop sth from happening because it is raining: *I'm sorry, but the picnic has been rained out.*

rain·bow /ˈreɪnboʊ/ *noun* [C] an arch of many colors that sometimes appears in the sky when the sun shines through rain: *all the colors of the rainbow*

ˈrain check *noun*
IDM **take a rain check (on sth)** (*informal*) to refuse an invitation or offer, but say that you might accept it later

☆ **rain·coat** /ˈreɪnkoʊt/ *noun* [C] a special coat that you wear when it is raining ☞ picture on page A27.

☆ **rain·drop** /ˈreɪndrɑp/ *noun* [C] a single drop of rain

☆ **rain·fall** /ˈreɪnfɔl/ *noun* [U] the total amount of rain that falls in a particular place during a month, year, etc.: *The annual rainfall in Cairo is less than 2 inches.*

ˈrain forest *noun* [C] a forest in a tropical part of the world

rain·y /ˈreɪni/ (**rain·i·er; rain·i·est**) *adj.* having a lot of rain: *the rainy season*
IDM **keep/save sth for a rainy day** to save money or sth valuable or useful so that you can use it at a later time when you really need to

☆ **raise¹** /reɪz/ *verb* [T] **1** to lift sth: *If you want to leave the room, raise your hand.* ○ *The captain of the winning team raised the trophy in the air.* **2** to increase sth or to make sth better or stronger: *They've raised their prices a lot since last year.* ○ *The hotel needs to raise its standards.* ○ *There's no need to raise your voice* (= speak angrily). **3** to get sth; obtain: *We managed to raise nearly $100 for the school at the bake sale.* **4** to take care of a child until he/she is an adult: *You can't raise a family on what I earn.* **5** to make a plant or animal grow so that you can use it: *In New Zealand, sheep are raised for meat and wool.* **6** to introduce a subject that needs to be talked about: *I would like to raise the subject of money.* ○ *This raises the question of why nothing was done before.*
IDM **raise your eyebrows** to show that you are surprised or that you do not approve of sth
raise/sound the alarm ⇨ ALARM¹

raise² /reɪz/ *noun* [C] an increase in pay: *I'm going to ask the boss for a raise.*

rai·sin /ˈreɪzn/ *noun* [C] a dried grape

rake¹ /reɪk/ *noun* [C] a garden tool with a long handle, used for collecting leaves or making the earth smooth

rake² /reɪk/ *verb* [T] to use a rake¹ on sth: *to rake the leaves*

R

R

PHRV **rake sth in** (*informal*) to earn a lot of money, especially without working hard: *Spielberg's new movie raked in $10 million during its first week.*

ral·ly¹ /ˈræli/ *noun* [C] (*pl.* **ral·lies**) a meeting of people to express support for a person, a political idea, etc.: *20,000 people attended the rally for the presidential candidate.* ☞ Look also at **pep rally**.

ral·ly² /ˈræli/ *verb* (*pres. part.* **ral·ly·ing**; *3rd pers. sing. pres.* **ral·lies**; *p.t.*, *p.p.* **ral·lied**) **1** [I] to get stronger: *The dollar rallied against the yen late yesterday.* ○ *The Sharks rallied in the third period to win the game 2-1.* **2** [I,T] to come together or to bring people together: *Gore has rallied the party behind him.*

PHRV **rally around (sb/sth)** to come together to help or support sb/sth: *When I was in trouble, my family rallied around me.*

ram¹ /ræm/ *noun* [C] a male sheep ☞ Look at the note and picture at **sheep**.

ram² /ræm/ *verb* [I,T] (**ram·ming**; **rammed**) **ram (into) sth** to crash into sth or push sth with great force: *The stolen car rammed into the side of a bus.*

RAM /ræm/ *noun* [U] (*computing*) random-access memory; the part of a computer where information is used or changed: *a computer with 32 megabytes of RAM* ☞ Look at **ROM**.

Ram·a·dan /ˈrɑmədɑn/ *noun* [U] the ninth month of the Muslim year, when Muslims do not eat or drink anything between the time when the sun rises and the time when it sets

ram·ble /ˈræmbl/ *verb* [I] to talk for a long time in a confused way: *Grandpa has a tendency to ramble.*

ram·bling /ˈræmblɪŋ/ *adj.* (usually *before* a noun) **1** (used about writing or speech) not saying things in a clear way; confused: *a long, rambling speech* **2** (used about a building) spreading in many directions

ramp /ræmp/ *noun* [C] a sloping path which people can use instead of steps to get from one place to another higher or lower place: *a wheelchair ramp at the side of a building* ☞ Look also at **entrance ramp** and **exit ramp**.

ram·page¹ /ˈræmpeɪdʒ/ *noun* [C, usually sing.] a period of wild, violent behavior: *Five people were injured in a shooting rampage at the Glenville Mall yesterday.*

IDM **be/go on the rampage** to rush around breaking things and attacking people

ram·page² /ˈræmpeɪdʒ; ræmˈpeɪdʒ/ *verb* [I] to rush from one place to another, breaking things and attacking people: *The elephant escaped and rampaged through the zoo.*

ram·pant /ˈræmpənt/ *adj.* very common and very difficult to control: *rampant crime and drug abuse*

ram·shack·le /ˈræmʃækl/ *adj.* (used about a building or a car, etc.) old and needing repair

ran *p.t.* of RUN¹

☆ **ranch** /ræntʃ/ *noun* [C] a large farm in the western U.S. or Canada, usually where cows, horses or sheep are raised

ranch·er /ˈræntʃər/ *noun* [C] a person who owns or manages a ranch: *a cattle/sheep rancher*

ˈranch house *noun* [C] a type of house for one family, that usually has only one level above the ground and a low roof

ran·dom /ˈrændəm/ *adj.* happening or chosen by chance: *random drug testing* ○ *a random number, selected by a computer*

IDM **at random** not in any special order or for any special reason: *He ran through the town shooting people at random.* ○ *The competitors were chosen at random from the audience.* —**ran·dom·ly** *adv.*

ˌrandom-ˌaccess ˈmemory *noun* [U] = RAM

rang *p.t.* of RING²

☆ **range¹** /reɪndʒ/ *noun* **1** [C] different things that belong to the same group: *The course will cover a whole range of topics.* ○ *We offer a full range of services to meet all your needs.* **2** [C] the amount between certain limits: *There's a very wide range of ability in the class.* ○ *That car is outside my price range.* ○ *I'm looking for a bike in the $200-250 range.* **3** [C] a line of mountains or hills **4** [C,U] the distance that it is possible for sb or sth to travel, see or hear, etc.: *The gunman shot the police officer at close range.* ○ *They can pick up signals at a range of 400 yards.* **5** [C] = STOVE

range² /reɪndʒ/ *verb* [I] **range from A to B** to stretch from one thing to another, within certain limits: *The students range in age from 18 to 24.*

rang·er /ˈreɪndʒər/ *noun* [C] a person who works in a public park or forest and takes care of the land and animals in it

☆ **rank¹** /ræŋk/ *noun* **1** [C,U] the level of importance that sb has in an organization, especially the military forces: *General is one of the highest ranks in the army.* ○ *She's much higher in rank than I am.* **2 ranks** [plural] the ordinary members of a large group or organization: *the ranks of the unemployed*

IDM **the rank and file** the ordinary members of an organization

☆ **rank²** /ræŋk/ *verb* [I,T] to have or to give a place in an order of importance: *She's ranked first among U.S. tennis players.* ○ *I think Tokyo ranks as one of the world's most expensive cities.* ○ *a high-ranking police officer*

ran·som /ˈrænsəm/ *noun* [C,U] the money that you must pay to free sb who has been captured by criminals: *The kidnappers demanded a ransom of $500,000 for the boy's release.*

IDM **hold sb for ransom** to capture sb and say that you will not free them until you have received some money ☞ Look at **hostage**.

i	ɪ	ɛ	æ	ɑ	ɔ	ʌ	ʊ	u
see	sit	ten	cat	hot	saw	cup	put	too

rap¹ /ræp/ *noun* **1** [C] a knock, on a door or window, etc., which is quick and fairly loud **2** [C,U] a style or piece of music with a strong beat, in which the words of a song are spoken, not sung: *a rap artist*

rap² /ræp/ *verb* (**rap·ping**; **rapped**) **1** [I,T] to hit sth quickly and lightly, making a noise **2** [I] to speak the words of a song (**a rap**) that has music with a very strong beat

☆ **rape¹** /reɪp/ *verb* [T] to force a person to have sex when he/she does not want to

☆ **rape²** /reɪp/ *noun* [C,U] **1** the act of forcing sb to have sex: *to commit rape ∘ a rape victim* **2** the destruction of sth beautiful: *Industry has been responsible for the rape of the countryside.*

☆ **rap·id** /ˈræpəd/ *adj.* happening very quickly or moving with great speed: *She made rapid progress and was soon the best in the class. ∘ After leaving the hospital, he made a rapid recovery and was soon back at work.* —**ra·pid·i·ty** /rəˈpɪdəṭi/ *noun* [U] (*formal*) —**rap·id·ly** *adv.*

rap·ids /ˈræpədz/ *noun* [plural] the part of a river where the water flows very fast over rocks

ˌ**rapid ˈtransit** *noun* [U] a system of public transportation in a city that uses trains which run above or under the ground

rap·ist /ˈreɪpɪst/ *noun* [C] a person who has forced sb to have sex

rap·port /rəˈpɔr; ræ-/ *noun* [U, sing.] a friendly situation in which people understand each other very well: *to establish a good rapport with your coworkers*

☆ **rare** /rɛr/ *adj.* **1** not found or seen very often: *a rare bird, flower, etc. ∘ It's very rare to have hot weather like this in April.* **2** (used about meat) not cooked for very long: *a rare steak* ☞ Look at the note at **meat**.

☆ **rare·ly** /ˈrɛrli/ *adv.* not often: *We rarely eat out because it's too expensive.*

rar·i·ty /ˈrɛrəṭi/ *noun* (*pl.* **rar·i·ties**) **1** [C] a thing or a person that is not found very often: *Women truck drivers are still quite a rarity.* **2** [U] being unusual or difficult to find: *The rarity of this stamp increases its value a lot.*

rash¹ /ræʃ/ *noun* [C, usually sing.] an area of small red spots that appear on your skin when you are sick or have been stung by an insect, plant, etc.: *He broke out in a rash where the plant had touched him.*
IDM **a rash of sth** a series of bad events of the same kind happening close together: *There has been a rash of attacks on senior citizens this month.*

rash² /ræʃ/ *adj.* **1** done without much thought: *a rash decision ∘ a rash promise* (= one which you cannot keep easily) **2** doing things that might be dangerous without thinking about it: *There's no need to be rash or irresponsible.*

rasp·ber·ry /ˈræzˌbɛri/ *noun* [C] (*pl.* **rasp·ber·**

ries) a small, soft, red fruit which grows on bushes: *raspberry jam*

☆ **rat** /ræt/ *noun* [C] **1** an animal like a large mouse ☞ Rats belong to the family of animals that are called **rodents**. **2** (*informal*) a person who is not honest or loyal: *You dirty rat!* ☞ Look also at **rat race**.

☆ **rate¹** /reɪt/ *noun* [C] **1** a measurement of one amount or of how fast or how often sth is happening in relation to another amount: *The birth rate is falling. ∘ a rise in the annual rate of inflation from 6 to 7% ∘ The population increased at a rate of less than 0.5% a year. ∘ an exchange rate of 112 yen to the dollar* **2** the amount that sth costs or that sb is paid: *The bank raised the interest rate on our loan to 6.25%. ∘ We offer reliable service at affordable rates.* ☞ Look at **first-rate** and **second-rate**.
IDM **at any rate 1** (used when you are giving more exact information about sth): *He said that they would be here by ten. At any rate, I think that's what he said.* **2** regardless of anything else that might happen: *Well, that's one good piece of news at any rate.*
at this/that rate if this/that situation continues in the same way: *At this rate, we won't be finished before next summer!*
the going rate (for sth) ⇨ GOING²

rate² /reɪt/ *verb* [T] **1** to say how good you think sb/sth is: *She's rated among the best tennis players of all time.* **2** (often passive) to put sth into an official group or class, for example in order to show that it is suitable for a certain group of people: *This movie is rated PG-13.* **3** to deserve or to get sth: *The accident wasn't very serious – it didn't rate a mention in the local newspaper.*

☆ **rath·er** /ˈræðər/ *adv.* **1** (*formal*) to some extent; very but not extremely: *The paintings seemed rather traditional and unoriginal.* ☞ **Fairly** and **pretty** are less formal words with the same meaning. **2** (*formal*) (used to show that sth contrasts with sth that was mentioned earlier): *The damage was not caused by vandals, but rather by some curious wild animals.*
IDM **or rather** (a way of correcting sth you have said, or making it more exact): *She lives in Los Angeles, or rather a suburb of Los Angeles.*
rather than in the place of; instead of: *I think I'll just have a sandwich rather than a full meal.*
would rather ... (than) would prefer to: *"How old are you?" "I'd rather not say." ∘ Would you rather eat at home tonight or go out?*

rat·i·fy /ˈræṭəfaɪ/ *verb* [T] (*pres. part.* **ratifying**; *3rd pers. sing. pres.* **ratifies**; *p.t., p.p.* **ratified**) to make a document, a decision, etc. official and legal, especially by signing it: *to ratify an amendment to the Constitution*

rat·ing /ˈreɪṭɪŋ/ *noun* [C] a measurement of how popular, good, difficult, etc. sth is: *The*

R

senator's popularity rating has fallen sharply. o a movie with an "R" rating o The network's ratings soared during the broadcasts of the Olympics.

ra·tio /ˈreɪʃiou; ˈreɪʃou/ noun [C] the relation between two numbers which shows how much bigger one quantity is than another: The ratio of students to books in this class is two to one (= there are two times as many students as books).

ra·tion¹ /ˈræʃn; ˈreɪʃn/ noun [C] the amount of food, gasoline, etc. that you get when there is not enough for everybody to get as much as they want: emergency food rations

ra·tion² /ˈræʃn/ verb [T] to give people only a small amount of sth, not as much as they want, because there is not enough or because it is too expensive: Will we have to start rationing health care? —**ra·tion·ing** noun [U]: gasoline rationing

ra·tion·al /ˈræʃənl/ adj. **1** (used about a person) able to use thought to make decisions, not just feelings: We're both rational human beings – let's sit down and talk about the problem. ☞ The opposite is **irrational**. **2** based on reason; sensible or logical: There must be a rational explanation for his behavior. —**ra·tion·al·ly** adv.

ra·tion·al·ize /ˈræʃənl·aɪz/ verb [I,T] to find reasons that explain why you have done sth (perhaps because you do not like the real reason): She rationalized her theft from the office by saying that the company had plenty of money and wouldn't miss a few things. —**ra·tion·al·i·za·tion** /ˌræʃənl·əˈzeɪʃn/ noun [C,U]

the ˈrat race noun [sing.] (informal) the situation in which everybody is competing with each other in order to be better, more successful, etc.

rat·tle¹ /ˈræt̮l/ verb **1** [I,T] to make a noise like things hitting each other, or to shake sth so that it makes this noise: The windows were rattling all night in the wind. o He rattled the ice cubes in his glass. **2** [T] (informal) to make sb unsure and afraid: The news of his arrival really rattled her.

PHRV **rattle sth off** to say a list of things very quickly: She rattled off the names of every player on the team.

rat·tle² /ˈræt̮l/ noun **1** [C, sing.] a noise made by things hitting each other: There's a funny rattle coming from the back of the car. **2** [C] a toy that a baby can shake to make a noise

rat·tle·snake /ˈræt̮lsneɪk/ noun [C] a poisonous snake that makes a noise with its tail when it is angry or afraid

rau·cous /ˈrɔkəs/ adj. (used about people's voices) loud and rough: The raucous laughter in the bar could be heard across the road.

rav·age /ˈrævɪdʒ/ verb [T] to damage sth very badly: The forests were ravaged by the winter storms.

rave /reɪv/ verb [I] **1 rave (about sb/sth)** to praise sb/sth very much: Critics raved about the new restaurant. **2** to speak angrily or wildly

ra·ven /ˈreɪvən/ noun [C] a large black bird that has a loud voice

ˌrave reˈview noun [C] an article in a newspaper, etc. that praises a book, movie, record, etc. very much

ra·vine /rəˈvin/ noun [C] a narrow deep valley with steep sides

rav·ing /ˈreɪvɪŋ/ adj. (informal) (only before a noun) acting in a wild, uncontrolled way: He's a raving lunatic!

☆ **raw** /rɔ/ adj. **1** not cooked: Have you ever eaten raw fish? o Raw vegetables are good for your teeth. **2** (used about an injury where the skin has been rubbed away): I scratched this mosquito bite until my skin was red and raw. **3** in the natural state: raw sugar o raw materials (= that are used to make things, in factories, etc.)

☆ **ray** /reɪ/ noun [C] a line of light, heat or energy: A single ray of light came through a hole in the roof. o the rays of the sun ☞ Look at **X-ray**.

IDM **a ray of hope** a small chance that things will get better

☆ **ra·zor** /ˈreɪzər/ noun [C] a sharp instrument which people use to cut off the hair from their skin (= **to shave**): an electric razor

ˈrazor blade (also **razorblade**) noun [C] the thin sharp piece of metal that you put in a razor

Rd. abbr. = ROAD(2)

re /ri/ prep. (formal) (used in formal letters or messages to introduce the topic) connected with; about: Re: your memo dated May 3

☆ **reach¹** /ritʃ/ verb **1** [T] to arrive at a place or condition: The letter should reach you on Wednesday. o We won't reach the airport in time. o Tell me when you have reached the end of the book. o Anyone who has reached the age of 60 knows something about the world. o Sometimes the temperature reaches 100°F. o We finally reached an agreement after hours of discussion. o to reach a decision **2** [I,T] **reach (out) (for sb/sth)** to stretch out your arm to try and touch sth or get sth: The child reached for her mother. o The monkey reached out its hand for the banana. o She reached into her bag for her wallet. **3** [I,T] to be able to touch sth: Can you get me that book off the top shelf? I can't reach that high. o He couldn't reach the light switch. o I need a longer ladder. This one won't reach. **4** [T] to contact sb: You can reach me at this number. o She can't be reached until Monday morning.

PHRV **reach out (to sb)** to make an effort to help or communicate with sb: We need to reach out to elderly people in our community.

reach² /ritʃ/ noun [U] the distance that you

ər	ɪr	ɛr	ɑr	ɔr	ʊr	ʒ	h	ŋ
bird	near	hair	car	north	tour	vision	hat	sing

can stretch your hand: *Keep this medication out of the reach of children.*

IDM beyond/out of (sb's) reach not able to be gotten or done by sb: *A job like that is completely beyond his reach.*

within (sb's) reach 1 inside the distance that you can stretch your arm: *Always keep a glass of water within reach.* **2** able to be gotten or done by sb: *Sampras led by five games to two – victory was almost within reach!*

☆ **re·act** /riˈækt/ *verb* [I] **1 react (to sb/sth)** to do or say sth because of sth that has happened or been said: *I haven't told her about the problem yet – I don't know how she'll react.* ○ *He wasn't sure how to react to the news.* **2 react (against sb/sth)** to behave or talk in a way that shows that you do not like the influence of sb/sth (e.g. authority, your family, etc.): *She reacted against the strict way she had been brought up.*

☆ **re·ac·tion** /riˈækʃn/ *noun* **1** [C,U] **(a) reaction (to sb/sth)** sth that you do or say because of sth that has happened or been said: *Can we have your reaction to the latest news, Senator?* ○ *a hostile reaction* ○ *I shook him to try and wake him up, but there was no reaction.* **2** [C,U] **(a) reaction (against sb/sth)** behavior that shows that you do not like the influence of sb/sth (e.g. authority, your family, etc.): *Her strange clothes are a reaction against the conservative way she was brought up.* **3** [C, usually pl.] the physical ability to act quickly when sth happens: *If the other driver's reactions hadn't been so good, there would have been an accident.*

re·ac·tion·ar·y /riˈækʃəˌnɛri/ *noun* [C] (*pl.* **re·ac·tion·ar·ies**) a person who tries to prevent (political) progress or change: *The reactionaries in the party oppose any form of gun control.* —**re·ac·tion·ar·y** *adj.*

re·ac·tor /riˈæktər/ *noun* [C] = NUCLEAR REACTOR

☆ **read** /rid/ *verb* (*p.t., p.p.* **read** /rɛd/) **1** [I,T] to look at words and understand them: *In their first years in school, children learn to read and write.* ○ *Don't bother me – I'm reading.* ○ *Have you read any good books lately?* ○ *I read an interesting article about Japan recently.* ○ *I read in the paper that they found a cure for migraines.* **2** [I,T] **read (sb) (sth); read sth (to sb)** to say written words to sb: *My father used to read me stories when I was little.* ○ *Read that sentence to me again – I didn't understand it.* ○ *I hate reading out loud.* **3** [T] to be able to see and understand sth: *Can you read music?* ○ *(figurative) She doesn't know what you're thinking. She can't read your mind.* **4** [T] to show sth; to have sth written on it: *The sign read "Keep Right."* ○ *What does the thermometer read?*

PHRV read sth into sth to think that there is meaning in sth that it may not really have:

Don't read too much into the letter. They're only asking you for an interview, not offering you the job.

read sth out to read sth to other people

read·a·ble /ˈridəbl/ *adj.* easy or pleasant to read: *a highly readable overview of the Civil War*

☆ **read·er** /ˈridər/ *noun* [C] **1** a person who reads sth (a particular newspaper, magazine, type of book, etc.) **2** (with an adjective) a person who reads (in a particular way): *a fast/slow reader*

read·er·ship /ˈridərʃɪp/ *noun* [sing.] the number of people who regularly read a particular newspaper, magazine, etc.

read·i·ly /ˈrɛdl·i/ *adv.* **1** easily, without difficulty: *Most vegetables are readily available at this time of year.* **2** without hesitating: *He readily admitted that he was wrong.*

read·i·ness /ˈrɛdnəs/ *noun* [U] **1** the state of being ready or prepared **2** willingness: *The bank has indicated its readiness to loan him the money.*

☆ **read·ing** /ˈridɪŋ/ *noun* [U] **1** what you do when you read sth: *I haven't had time to do much reading lately.* ○ *On the form she described her interests as reading and tennis.* ○ *This report makes for interesting reading* (= reading it is an interesting thing to do). **2** the figure or measurement that is shown on a piece of equipment: *a reading of 20°*

re·ad·just /ˌriəˈdʒʌst/ *verb* **1** [I,T] **readjust (to sth)** to get used to being in a situation again that you have been in before: *After her divorce, it took her a long time to readjust to being alone again.* **2** [T] to change the position or organization of sth again in order to make it correct —**re·ad·just·ment** *noun* [C,U]

☆ **read·y¹** /ˈrɛdi/ *adj.* **1 ready (for sb/sth); ready (to do sth)** prepared and able to be used or to do sth: *Dinner will be ready in ten minutes.* ○ *The car will be ready for you to pick up Friday.* ○ *He isn't ready for his driving test – he hasn't had enough practice.* ○ *I can't talk now – I'm getting ready to go out.* **2 ready to do sth** willing to do sth: *You know me – I'm always ready to help.* **3** in a place which makes it possible for you to use or reach it easily and quickly: *Have your ticket ready before you get on the bus.*

read·y² /ˈrɛdi/ *adv.* (before a past participle) already; previously: *ready-mixed concrete*

ˌready-ˈmade *adj.* already prepared and ready for use, not made especially for you: *You can buy ready-made reading glasses now.* ○ *(figurative) He always has a ready-made answer to every question.*

☆ **real¹** /ril/ *adj.* **1** actually existing, not imagined: *The program contained interviews with real people* (= not actors). ○ *This isn't a real word – I made it up.* **2** actually true, not what may appear to be true: *The name he gave to the police wasn't his real name.* ○ *She said she had*

tʃ	dʒ	v	θ	ð	s	z	ʃ
chin	**J**une	**v**an	**th**in	**th**en	**s**o	**z**oo	**sh**e

missed the bus, but that's not the real reason why she was late. **3** natural, not artificial: *This shirt is real silk.* **4** (used when you are making what you say stronger, usually when you are saying how bad sth is) big; complete: *The meal I cooked was a real disaster.* ○ *Money is a real problem for us right now.*

IDM **be for real** (*informal*) to be genuine and not imagined or pretended: *OK, that was just for practice – but this time it's for real!* ○ *How could Darren say a thing like that – is he for real?* (= I am shocked and surprised by what he said.)

real life; the real world the way that things in general actually are, not the way sb imagines they are: *He looks shorter in real life than he does on TV.* ○ *That's not how things work in the real world.*

the real thing 1 something genuine, not artificial: *This painting is just a copy. The real thing is in a museum.* **2** the best example of sth: *She's had boyfriends before, but this time she says it's the real thing* (= real love).

real² /riːl/ *adv.* (*informal*) very; really: *It was real nice of you to help me.*

☆ **real e‚state** (*also* **realty**) *noun* [U] property that cannot be moved, such as land and buildings

'real e‚state ‚agent (*also* **Realtor**) *noun* [C] a person who buys and sells houses and land for other people

re·al·ism /'riːəlɪzəm/ *noun* [U] **1** behavior that shows that you accept the facts of a situation and are not too influenced by your feelings **2** (in art, literature, etc.) showing things as they really are

re·al·ist /'riːəlɪst/ *noun* [C] a person who accepts the facts of life and situations, and who thinks and behaves according to them: *I'm a realist – I don't expect the impossible.*

☆ **re·al·is·tic** /ˌriːə'lɪstɪk/ *adj.* **1** accepting the facts of a situation (not believing or making yourself believe that they are different): *Be realistic! You're not going to get a job like that without any experience.* ○ *a realistic price* **2** showing things as they really are: *a realistic description of the lives of ordinary people in rural Alaska* **3** not real but appearing to be real: *The monsters in the movie were very realistic.* ☞ The opposite for **1**, **2** and **3** is **unrealistic**. —**re·al·is·ti·cal·ly** /-kli/ *adv.*: *Think about your future realistically.*

☆ **re·al·i·ty** /riˈæləti/ *noun* (*pl.* **re·al·i·ties**) **1** [U] the way life really is, not the way it may appear to be or what you would like it to be: *It was a great vacation, but now it's back to reality.* **2** [C] the way sth really is when you experience it: *We had hoped that things would get easier, but the reality was very different.* ○ *The realities of living in a foreign country were too much for Susan and she went home.* **3** [C] something that really exists, not sth that is

imagined: *Death is a reality that everyone has to face eventually.*

IDM **in reality** in fact, really (not the way sth appears and has been described): *People say this is an exciting city, but in reality it's pretty boring.*

re'ality check *noun* [C, usually sing.] (*informal*) a time when you stop working, talking, etc. in order to consider what is really important in a situation, and not what you think is important: *I think those politicians in Washington are in need of a reality check.*

☆ **re·al·ize** /'riːəlaɪz/ *verb* [T] **1** to know and understand that sth is true or that sth has happened: *I'm sorry I mentioned the subject – I didn't realize how much it upset you.* ○ *Do you realize how much work I did today?* **2** to become aware of sth or that sth has happened, usually some time later: *When I got home, I realized that I had left my keys at the office.* ○ *I'm starting to realize that this job isn't as easy as I thought it was.* **3** to make sth (an ambition, hope, etc.) become reality: *She finally realized her ambition to see the Taj Mahal.* —**re·al·i·za·tion** /ˌriːələ'zeɪʃn/ *noun* [U]: *He was suddenly hit by the realization that he might die.* ○ *Becoming Chief Executive Officer was the realization of all her dreams.*

☆ **re·al·ly** /'riːli; 'rɪli/ *adv.* **1** actually; in fact; truly: *I couldn't believe it was really happening.* ○ *He said that he was sorry, but I don't think he really meant it.* ○ *She wasn't really mad – she was only pretending.* ○ *Is it really true?* **2** very; very much: *I'm really tired.* ○ *He really enjoys his job.* ○ *Are you really sure?* ○ *I really tried, but I couldn't do it.* **3** (used as a question for expressing surprise, interest, doubt, etc.): *"She left her husband." "Really? When did that happen?"* ○ *"He's a very happy person." "Really? I've never seen him smile."* **4** (used in questions when you are expecting sb to answer "No"): *You don't really expect me to believe that, do you?* **5** (*informal*) (used to agree with sth that sb has just said): *"Kevin's such a jerk." "Yeah, really."*

IDM **not really** not completely: *I'm not really sure this is the right way.* ○ *"Did you have to wait a long time?" "No, not really."*

realm /rɛlm/ *noun* [C, usually sing.] an area of activity, interest or knowledge: *These beliefs are completely outside the realm of science.*

'real-time *adj.* (only *before* a noun) (used about computer systems and information) able to respond immediately so that the user is not aware of a delay: *real-time Internet video games* —**'real time** *noun* [U]: *The Web site shows images taken from the space shuttle in real time.*

Re·al·tor /'riːltər/ *noun* [C] (*trademark*) = REAL ESTATE AGENT

re·al·ty /'riːlti/ *noun* [U] = REAL ESTATE

reap /riːp/ *verb* [T] to cut and pick up a crop

i	ɪ	ɛ	æ	ɑ	ɔ	ʌ	ʊ	u
see	sit	ten	cat	hot	saw	cup	put	too

(corn, wheat, etc.): (*figurative*) *Work hard now and you'll reap the benefits later on.*

re·ap·pear /ˌriəˈpɪr/ *verb* [I] to appear again or be seen again: *If any symptoms reappear, see your doctor immediately.* —**re·ap·pear·ance** /-rəns/ *noun* [C,U]

☆ **rear¹** /rɪr/ *noun* [sing.] **1 the rear** the back part: *There are some empty seats in the rear of the bus.* ○ *I only saw him from the rear* (= from behind). **2** (*also* **rear end**) (*informal*) the part of your body that you sit on; buttocks
IDM **bring up the rear** to be the last one in a race, a line of people, etc.: *The fastest runners are nearing the finish line now, with Ben Smith bringing up the rear.*

☆ **rear²** /rɪr/ *adj.* (only *before* a noun) (used especially about parts of a car) placed at the back: *the rear window* ○ *rear lights*

rear³ /rɪr/ *verb* **1** [T] to care for and educate a child until it is an adult: *She was born and reared in Kentucky.* **2** [I] **rear (up)** (used about horses) to stand on the back legs

‚**rear ¹end** *noun* [sing.] = REAR¹(2)

‚**rear-¹end** *verb* [T] (*informal*) to hit the back of another car while you are driving: *We got rear-ended on Lake Street today.*

re·ar·range /ˌriəˈreɪndʒ/ *verb* [T] to change the way that sth is organized or arranged: *We rearranged the living room to make more space.* ○ *I'll have to rearrange my schedule for next week.*

☆ **rea·son¹** /ˈrizn/ *noun* **1** [C,U] **reason (for sth/for doing sth); reason (why…/that…)** the cause of sth; sth that explains why sth happens or exists: *What's your reason for being so late?* ○ *Is there any reason why you couldn't tell me this before?* ○ *The main reason that I'm calling you is to ask for a favor.* ○ *For some reason or other, they can't give us an answer until next week* (= I don't know what the reason is). ○ *She quit her job for personal reasons.* **2** [C,U] **reason (for sth); reason (to do sth)** something that shows that it is right or logical to do sth: *There is a reason for doing things this way – it's cheaper.* ○ *I chose this color for a reason* (= the reason was important). ○ *He had no reason to be mean to me – I never did anything to him.* ○ *You have every reason* (= you are completely right) *to be upset, considering what happened to you.* ○ *I have reason to believe that you lied to me.* **3** [U] the ability to think and to make sensible decisions: *Any new law must be based on reason, not emotion.*
IDM **(do anything) within reason** if it is not too extreme or completely unacceptable: *I'll pay anything within reason for a ticket.*

rea·son² /ˈrizn/ *verb* [I,T] to form a judgment or opinion, after thinking about sth in a logical way
PHRV **reason with sb** to talk to sb in order to persuade him/her to behave or think in a more reasonable or less extreme way: *The police tried to reason with the gunman, but he refused to put down his rifle.*

☆ **rea·son·a·ble** /ˈriznˌəbl/ *adj.* **1** (used about people) willing to listen to other people's opinions; not asking too much; fair: *I tried to be reasonable even though I was really mad.* **2** (used about actions, decisions, etc.) resulting from good reasons; logical: *That seems like a reasonable decision under the circumstances.* **3** (used about opinions or about what you expect people to do) not expecting too much; fair: *I think it's reasonable to expect people to keep their promises.* **4** (used about a price) not too high; not higher than it should be: *It was great food and the prices were very reasonable!* ☞ The opposite for 1, 2, 3 and 4 is **unreasonable.** **5** fairly good; not bad: *His work is of a reasonable standard.* **6** (used about amounts or numbers) not very large: *They have a reasonable amount of money, but they certainly aren't rich.*

rea·son·a·bly /ˈriznˌəbli/ *adv.* **1** fairly or quite (but not very): *The weather was reasonably good but not terrific.* **2** in a reasonable way: *If you think about my suggestion reasonably, you'll see that I'm right.*

rea·son·ing /ˈriznˌɪŋ/ *noun* [U] **reasoning (behind sth)** the process of thinking and making a judgment or decision: *What's the reasoning behind his sudden decision to quit?*

re·as·sur·ance /ˌriəˈʃʊrəns/ *noun* [C,U] an act of reassuring or being reassured: *I need some reassurance that I'm doing things the right way.* ○ *The government issued reassurances that the area is safe.*

re·as·sure /ˌriəˈʃʊr/ *verb* [T] to say or do sth in order to make sb feel less frightened, worried or nervous: *I keep trying to reassure my parents that my friends don't take drugs, but they just don't believe me.*

re·as·sur·ing /ˌriəˈʃʊrɪŋ/ *adj.* causing sb to feel less worried, frightened or nervous —**re·as·sur·ing·ly** *adv.*

re·bate /ˈribeɪt/ *noun* [C] a sum of money that is given back to you because of a special offer or because you have paid too much: *a $500 rebate on a new car*

re·bel¹ /ˈrɛbl/ *noun* [C] **1** a person who fights against his/her country's government because he/she wants things to change: *Rebels have taken control of the capital.* **2** a person who fights against or refuses to cooperate with authority, society, an order, a law, etc.: *He had a reputation as a rebel in high school.*

re·bel² /rɪˈbɛl/ (**re·bel·ling; re·belled**) *verb* [I] **rebel (against sb/sth) 1** to fight against authority, society, an order, a law, etc.: *She rebelled against her parents by dropping out of high school.* **2** to fight against the government in order to bring change

re·bel·lion /rɪˈbɛlyən/ *noun* [C,U] fighting

against authority or the government: *The rebellion ended in failure when all the leaders were shot.* ○ *Burning the flag was an act of open rebellion.*

re·bel·lious /rɪˈbɛlyəs/ *adj.* not doing what authority, society, etc. wants you to do: *rebellious teenagers*

re·bound[1] /ˈribaʊnd; rɪˈbaʊnd/ *verb* **1** [I] to hit sth and then go in a different direction: *The puck rebounded off a defender and went into the goal.* **2** [I,T] (in basketball) to catch and control the ball after sb has tried unsuccessfully to throw it through the basket: *Rodman quickly rebounded and scored the winning basket.*

re·bound[2] /ˈribaʊnd/ *noun* [C] **1** a sudden increase or improvement after a period of decreasing or getting worse: *last month's rebound in home prices* **2** (in sports) a ball or puck that hits sth and then goes in a different direction **3** (in basketball) an act of catching the ball after sb has tried unsuccessfully to throw it through the basket

IDM on the rebound 1 increasing or improving again, after a period of getting worse: *California's economy is on the rebound.* **2** (*informal*) upset, sad and confused because of the end of a romantic relationship: *I'd never go out with a guy who's on the rebound!*

re·build /ˌriˈbɪld/ *verb* [T] (*p.t., p.p.* **re·built** /ˌriˈbɪlt/) to build again: *Following the storm, dozens of houses will have to be rebuilt.* ○ (*figurative*) *She's trying to rebuild her life now that her husband is dead.*

re·call[1] /rɪˈkɔl/ *verb* [T] **1** to remember sth (a fact, event, action, etc.) from the past: *I don't recall exactly when I first met her.* ○ *She couldn't recall meeting him before.* **2** to ask people to bring a product back to the store where they bought it because of a possible problem: *The manufacturer is recalling all washing machines made in 1995.*

re·call[2] /ˈrikɔl/ *noun* [C] a request or an order from a company for people to return a particular type of product to the store where they bought it because of a possible problem: *a voluntary recall of all 1998 station wagons*

re·cap /ˈrikæp; riˈkæp/ (*informal*) *noun* [C, usually sing.] a short summary which repeats the main points of sth: *Here is a brief recap of the events leading up to the trial:...*

re·cap·ture /ˌriˈkæptʃər/ *verb* [I,T] **1** to capture again a person or an animal that has escaped **2** to create or experience again a feeling or period from the past: *The movie magnificently recaptures the lives of ordinary people in the 1930s.*

re·cede /rɪˈsid/ *verb* [I] to move away or seem to move away and begin to disappear: *Flood waters have now begun to recede in most areas.* ☛ If a person's **hairline is receding**, he is losing his hair from the front of his head.

☆ **re·ceipt** /rɪˈsit/ *noun* **1** [C] a piece of paper that is given to show that you have paid for sth: *Keep the receipt in case you want to exchange the sweater.* ○ *Can I get a receipt for that?* **2** [U] **receipt (of sth)** (*formal*) the act of receiving: *Payment must be made within seven days of receipt of the shipment.*

☆ **re·ceive** /rɪˈsiv/ *verb* [T] **1 receive sth (from sb/sth)** (*formal*) to get or take sth that sb sends or gives to you: *The independent candidate received only 210 votes in the election.* ○ *We received hundreds of cards and letters from our supporters.* ○ *Mrs. DeAngelis received her master's degree in 1979.* ☛ **Get** is less formal than **receive** in this sense. **2** (*formal*) to have medical treatment: *Stan received a liver transplant last year.* ☛ **Have** is less formal than **receive** in this sense. **3** (often passive) to react to sth (news, ideas, work, etc.) in a particular way: *My suggestions at the meeting were received in silence.*

re·ceiv·er /rɪˈsivər/ *noun* [C] the part of a telephone that is used for listening and speaking

☛ To answer or make a telephone call you **pick up** or **lift** the receiver. To end a telephone call you **put down** the receiver or you **hang up**. Picture at **telephone**.

☆ **re·cent** /ˈrisənt/ *adj.* (usually *before* a noun) having happened, been done or produced a short time ago: *There have been many changes in recent years.* ○ *In a recent interview, the mayor promised to hire more police.* ○ *This is a recent picture of my daughter.*

☆ **re·cent·ly** /ˈrisəntli/ *adv.* **1** a short time ago: *I don't know her very well – I only met her recently.* ○ *She worked here until fairly recently.* **2** during a period between not long ago and now: *Have you seen Paul recently?* ○ *She hasn't been feeling well recently.*

☛ **Recently** can refer to both a point in time and a period of time. If it refers to a point in time, use the past simple tense: *He died recently.* If it refers to a period of time, use the present perfect or present perfect continuous tense: *I haven't done anything interesting recently.* ○ *She's been working hard recently.* **Lately** can only refer to a period of time. Use only the present perfect or present perfect continuous tense: *I've seen a lot of movies lately.* ○ *I've been spending too much money lately.*

re·cep·ta·cle /rɪˈsɛptəkl/ *noun* [C] (*formal*) a container: *a trash receptacle*

☆ **re·cep·tion** /rɪˈsɛpʃn/ *noun* **1** [C] a formal party to celebrate sth (especially a wedding) or to welcome an important person: *Their wedding reception was held at a local hotel.* ○ *There will be an official reception at the embassy for the visiting ambassadors.* **2** [sing.] the way people react to sth: *The play got a*

mixed reception (= some people liked it, some people didn't). ○ *The President received a warm reception during his visit to the state* (= people showed that they liked him). **3** [U] the quality of radio or television signals: *We can't get good TV reception here in the valley.*

re·cep·tion·ist /rɪ'sɛpʃn·ɪst/ *noun* [C] a person who works in a hotel, an office, etc. answering the telephone, dealing with guests, customers, visitors, etc.

re·cep·tive /rɪ'sɛptɪv/ *adj.* **receptive (to sth)** willing to listen to new ideas, suggestions, etc.

re·cess /'risɛs; rɪ'sɛs/ *noun* **1** [U] a period of free time during the day at school, especially after lunch: *We'll finish the story after recess.* ☛ Look at the note at **pause**. **2** [C,U] a period of time when a government, a court of law, etc. stops its work: *The judge will take a short recess to consider his decision.*

re·ces·sion /rɪ'sɛʃn/ *noun* [C] a period of time when the businesses and industries of a country are not successful: *The country is now in a recession.* ☛ Look also at **depression**.

☆ **rec·i·pe** /'rɛsəpi/ *noun* [C] **1 a recipe (for sth)** the instructions for cooking or preparing sth to eat. A recipe tells you what to use (**the ingredients**) and what to do. **2 a recipe for sth** the way to get or produce sth: *What's the recipe for a happy marriage?*

re·cip·i·ent /rɪ'sɪpiənt/ *noun* [C] (*formal*) a person who receives sth

re·cip·ro·cal /rɪ'sɪprəkl/ *adj.* both given and received: *The arrangement is reciprocal. They help us and we help them.*

re·cit·al /rɪ'saɪtl/ *noun* [C] a public performance of music or poetry, by one person or a small group: *a piano recital* ☛ Look at **concert**.

re·cite /rɪ'saɪt/ *verb* [I,T] to say a piece of writing (especially a poem) or a list from memory: *He can recite the names and dates of all the Presidents of the United States.*

reck·less /'rɛkləs/ *adj.* not thinking about whether what you are doing is dangerous or might have bad results: *reckless driving* —**reck·less·ly** *adv.*

reck·on /'rɛkən/ *verb* [T] **1** (*informal*) (used especially in the southern U.S.) to think, suppose or believe: *Billy Joe reckons we'd better start heading home.* **2** to calculate approximately or guess: *The plant's annual production is reckoned to be around 50 million units.*

PHRV **reckon with sb/sth** to expect sth; to think about sth as a possible problem: *When they decided to buy a bigger house, they didn't reckon with the enormous cost involved.*

re·claim /rɪ'kleɪm/ *verb* [T] **1 reclaim sth (from sb/sth)** to get back sth that you have lost, or to get back control of sth that you controlled in the past: *We hope to reclaim our position as the nation's number one auto manufacturer.* **2** to make land suitable for use: *farm-*

land that has been reclaimed from the spreading desert

re·cline /rɪ'klaɪn/ *verb* [I] to lie back or down in order to be more comfortable: *If you want to recline, press the button on the side of your seat.*

re·clin·ing /rɪ'klaɪnɪŋ/ *adj.* lying back; able to be adjusted so that you can lie back: *The car has reclining front seats.*

☆ **rec·og·ni·tion** /,rɛkəg'nɪʃn/ *noun* [U] the act of recognizing sth or of showing or receiving respect: *He showed no sign of recognition when he passed me in the street.* ○ *She has received public recognition for her services to the community.*

☆ **rec·og·nize** /'rɛkəgnaɪz/ *verb* [T] **1 recognize sb/sth (by/from sth)** to know again sb/sth that you have seen or heard before: *I recognized him, but I couldn't remember his name.* ○ *This neighborhood has changed so much since the last time I was here that I hardly recognize it now.* **2** to accept or admit that sth is true: *I recognize that some of my ideas are unrealistic.* **3** to accept sth officially (usually done by institutions or governments): *My degree is not recognized in other countries.* **4** to show that you think sth that sb has done is good: *The company gave her a special gift to recognize her long years of service.* —**rec·og·niz·a·ble** /'rɛkəgnaɪzəbl; ,rɛkəg'naɪzəbl/ *adj.* —**rec·og·niz·a·bly** /-əbli/ *adv.*

rec·ol·lec·tion /,rɛkə'lɛkʃn/ *noun* **1** [U] recollection (of sb/sth) the ability to remember: *I have no recollection of promising to loan you any money.* **2** [C, usually pl.] something that you remember: *I have only vague recollections of my grandfather.*

☆ **rec·om·mend** /,rɛkə'mɛnd/ *verb* [T] **1** to say that sb/sth is good and that it would be liked or useful: *Which movie would you recommend?* ○ *We hope that you'll recommend this restaurant to all your friends.* ○ *The manager of her department recommended her for a promotion.* ○ *Doctors don't always recommend medication as the best treatment for every illness.*

☛ Notice that we cannot use **recommend** with an indirect object immediately after it. So we CANNOT say e.g.: *Can you recommend me a good hotel?* or: *I can recommend you a very nice restaurant.* We must say instead: *Can you recommend a good hotel?* or: *I can recommend a very nice restaurant.*

2 to strongly suggest sth; to tell sb what you strongly believe he/she should do: *My doctor recommended a long period of rest.* ○ *I recommend that you get some legal advice.* ○ *I wouldn't recommend traveling on your own. It could be dangerous.*

☛ Note the form of the verb which must be used after **recommend/recommendation that ...**, **suggest/suggestion that ...**, etc.: *We*

tʃ	dʒ	v	θ	ð	s	z	ʃ
chin	June	van	thin	then	so	zoo	she

recommend that Susan's proposal *be approved.* ○ *I suggest that he* see *a doctor.* ○ *They requested that the newspaper* not print *their real names.* ○ *The salesclerk ignored our demand that she* give *us our money back.*

☆ **rec·om·men·da·tion** /ˌrɛkəmənˈdeɪʃn/ *noun* [C] **1** a statement about what should be done in a particular situation: *After the train crash, an independent commission made several recommendations on how safety could be improved.* **2** an official letter from an employer, a teacher, etc. that says that sb is suitable for a job, etc.: *I asked my former boss to write a recommendation for me.*

rec·on·cile /ˈrɛkənsaɪl/ *verb* **1** [I,T] (often passive) **reconcile (with sb)** (to cause people) to become friendly with or close to each other again: *After years of not speaking to each other, she and her parents were eventually reconciled.* **2** [T] **reconcile sth (with sth)** to find a way to make two things (ideas, situations, statements, etc.) be possible together, when in fact they seem to oppose each other: *She finds it difficult to reconcile her career ambitions with her responsibilities to her children.*

rec·on·cil·i·a·tion /ˌrɛkənˌsɪliˈeɪʃn/ *noun* [C,U] becoming friendly or close again (after an argument, etc.): *to bring about a reconciliation between the two sides*

re·con·nais·sance /rɪˈkɑnəsəns; -zəns/ *noun* [C,U] the study of a place or area for military reasons

re·con·sid·er /ˌrikənˈsɪdər/ *verb* [I,T] to think again about sth (a decision, situation, etc.): *Public protests have forced the government to reconsider its policy.*

re·con·struct /ˌrikənˈstrʌkt/ *verb* [T] **1** to build again sth that has been destroyed or damaged: *The cathedral was reconstructed after the fire.* **2** to get a full description or picture of sth using the facts that are known: *The police are trying to reconstruct the victim's movements on the day of the murder.* —**re·con·struc·tion** /-ˈstrʌkʃn/ *noun* [C,U]: *the reconstruction of the city after the earthquake* ○ *a reconstruction of the crime using actors*

☆ **re·cord¹** /ˈrɛkərd/ *noun* [C] **1 record (of sth)** a written account of what has happened, been done, etc.: *The teachers keep records of the students' progress.* ○ *medical records* **2** (*also* **album**) a large, thin, round, usually black piece of plastic which can store music and other sound so that you can play it when you want: *to listen to/play some records* ○ *a record player* ○ *a record collection* **3** the best performance or the highest or lowest level, etc. ever reached in sth, especially in sports: *Who holds the world record for the high jump?* ○ *to set a new record* ○ *to break a record* ○ *We've had so little rain this year – I'm sure it must be a record* (= the lowest amount ever). ○ *He did it in record time* (= very fast). **4** [sing.] the facts,

events, etc. that are known (and sometimes written down) about sb/sth: *The police said that the man had a criminal record* (= he had been found guilty of crimes in the past). ○ *This airline has a poor safety record.*

IDM **off the record** (used about sth that sb says) not officially; not intended to be published: *She told me off the record that the school was going to close.*

on the record (used about sth that sb says) officially; intended to be published: *The senator was not willing to speak to us on the record.*

set the record straight to correct a misunderstanding by telling sb the true facts

☆ **re·cord²** /rɪˈkɔrd/ *verb* **1** [T] to write sth down, put it into a computer, film it, etc. so that it can be used later and will not be forgotten: *All property sales are recorded in the county courthouse.* **2** [I,T] to put music, a movie, a program, etc. onto a cassette or record so that it can be listened to or watched again later: *Quiet, everybody! We're recording.* ○ *The band recently recorded a new album.* ○ *I forgot to record my favorite TV show last night.*

ˈ**record-ˌbreaking** *adj.* (only *before* a noun) the best, fastest, highest, etc. ever: *She finished the race in record-breaking time.*

re·cord·er /rɪˈkɔrdər/ *noun* [C] **1** a machine for recording sound and/or pictures: *a tape recorder* ○ *a video recorder* **2** a type of musical instrument that is often played by children. You play it by blowing through it and covering the holes in it with your fingers. ☞ picture at **flute**.

☆ **re·cord·ing** /rɪˈkɔrdɪŋ/ *noun* **1** [C] sound or pictures that have been put onto a cassette, record or movie: *I taped the concert last week, but it's not a very good recording.* **2** [U] the process of making cassettes, records or movies: *a recording studio*

☆ **re·cov·er** /rɪˈkʌvər/ *verb* **1** [I] **recover (from sth)** to become well again after you have been sick: *It took him two months to recover from the operation.* **2** [I] **recover (from sth)** to get back to normal again after a bad experience, etc.: *It took her a long time to recover from her father's death.* **3** [T] **recover sth (from sb/sth)** to find or get back sth that has been lost or stolen: *Police recovered the stolen goods from a warehouse in South Chicago.* **4** [T] to get back a state of health, an ability to do sth, etc.: *He needs daily exercise if he's going to recover the use of his legs.* ○ *She recovered consciousness in the ambulance.*

☆ **re·cov·er·y** /rɪˈkʌvəri/ *noun* **1** [sing., U] **recovery (from sth)** a return to good health after an illness or to a normal condition after a difficult period of time: *to make a good, quick, slow, etc. recovery* ○ *Nobody is optimistic about the prospects of economic recovery this year.* **2** [U] **recovery (of sth/sb)** getting sth

back: *He offered a reward for the recovery of the paintings.*

☆ **rec·re·a·tion** /ˌrɛkriˈeɪʃn/ *noun* [U] doing activities that you enjoy when you are not working: *What do you do for recreation?* ○ *The county Recreation and Parks Department offers swimming lessons in the summer.* —**rec·re·a·tion·al** /ˌrɛkriˈeɪʃn·l/ *adj.*

ˌrecre·ational ˈvehicle *noun* [C] = RV

re·cruit¹ /rɪˈkrut/ *noun* [C] a person who has just joined the army or another organization; a new member

re·cruit² /rɪˈkrut/ *verb* [I,T] to get sb to work as sth, to help with sth or to join sth, such as the military forces or a sports team: *to recruit young people into the army* —**re·cruit·er** /rɪˈkruṭər/ *noun* [C] —**re·cruit·ment** *noun* [U]

☆ **rec·tan·gle** /ˈrɛktæŋgl/ *noun* [C] a shape with four straight sides and four angles of 90 degrees (**right angles**). Two of the sides are usually longer than the other two. ☞ picture at **shape.** —**rec·tan·gu·lar** /rɛkˈtæŋgyələr/ *adj.*

rec·ti·fy /ˈrɛktəfaɪ/ *verb* [T] (*pres. part.* **rec·ti·fy·ing**; *3rd pers. sing. pres.* **rec·ti·fies**; *p.t., p.p.* **rec·ti·fied**) (*formal*) to change sth so that it is right: *All these errors will need to be rectified.*

re·cu·per·ate /rɪˈkupəreɪt/ *verb* [I] to get well again after an illness or injury —**re·cu·per·a·tion** /rɪˌkupəˈreɪʃn/ *noun* [U]

re·cur /rɪˈkər/ *verb* [I] (**re·cur·ring; re·curred**) to happen again or many times: *a recurring problem* ○ *It was a theme that recurred in many of her books.* —**re·cur·rence** /rɪˈkərəns/ *noun* [C,U] —**re·cur·rent** /-ənt/ *adj.*

☆ **re·cy·cle** /riˈsaɪkl/ *verb* [T] **1** to process used objects and materials so that they can be used again: *recycled paper* ○ *Aluminum cans can be recycled.* ○ *We return our empty bottles to the store for recycling.* **2** to keep used objects and materials and use them again: (*figurative*) *She just keeps recycling the same old jokes.* —**re·cy·cla·ble** /riˈsaɪkləbl/ *adj.*: *Most plastics are recyclable.*

☆ **red¹** /rɛd/ *adj.* (**red·der; red·dest**) **1** of the color of blood: *red wine* ○ *The berries on that bush turn bright red in October.* ☞ We use **crimson, maroon** and **scarlet** to describe different shades of red. **2** (used about a person's face) a darker color than usual because of anger, sadness, shame, etc.: *He turned bright red when she talked to him.* **3** (used about a person's hair or an animal's fur) of a color between red, orange and brown: *She has red hair and freckles.*

IDM **a red herring** an idea or subject which takes people's attention away from what is really important

☆ **red²** /rɛd/ *noun* [C,U] the color of blood: *She was dressed in red* (= in red clothes).

IDM **(be) in the red** to have spent more money than you have in the bank, etc.: *The airline*

ended the year $40 million in the red. ☞ Look at **in the black** at **black².**

ˌred ˈcarpet *noun* [sing.] a piece of red carpet that is put out for an important visitor; a special welcome for an important visitor

red·dish /ˈrɛdɪʃ/ *adj.* slightly red

re·deem /rɪˈdim/ *verb* [T] **1** to exchange sth for money, products, etc. with an equal value: *This gift certificate can be redeemed in any one of our stores.* **2** to prevent sth from being completely bad: *The only redeeming feature of the job is the good salary.* **3 redeem yourself** to say or do sth in order to remove the bad effect of sth you did: *It was all his fault. There's nothing he can say to redeem himself.*

re·demp·tion /rɪˈdɛmpʃn/ *noun* [U] (*formal*) being saved or redeemed

re·de·vel·op·ment /ˌridəˈvɛləp/ *noun* [U] new building work, especially more modern buildings which will replace older ones: *There's a lot of redevelopment going on downtown.*

ˌred-ˈhand·ed *adj.*

IDM **catch sb red-handed** ⇨ CATCH¹

red·head /ˈrɛdhɛd/ *noun* [C] a person, especially a woman, who has red hair

ˌred-ˈhot *adj.* (used about a metal) so hot that it turns red

re·dis·trib·ute /ˌridɪˈstrɪbyut/ *verb* [T] to share sth among people, groups, etc. in a different way —**re·dis·tri·bu·tion** /ˌridɪstrə-ˈbyuʃn/ *noun* [U]

red·neck /ˈrɛdnɛk/ *noun* [C] (*informal*) a person from a small town or the countryside, especially in the southern U.S., who comes from a low social class, is not well educated and often does not like people of other races

red·skin /ˈrɛdskɪn/ *noun* [C] (*old-fashioned*) a Native American

☞ This word is considered offensive nowadays.

ˌred ˈtape *noun* [U] official rules that seem unnecessary and often cause delay and difficulty in achieving sth

☆ **re·duce** /rɪˈdus/ *verb* [T] **1** to make sth less: *Doctors have advised us to reduce the amount of fat in our diets.* ☞ The opposite is **increase.** **2 reduce sb/sth (from sth) to sth** (often passive) to make sb/sth be in the (usually bad) state mentioned: *One of the older boys reduced the little child to tears.* ○ *They were reduced from wealth to poverty almost overnight.*

☆ **re·duc·tion** /rɪˈdʌkʃn/ *noun* [C,U] making sth less or becoming less; an example of this happening: *a reduction in the numbers of unemployed people* ○ *a reduction in the rate of inflation*

re·dun·dant /rɪˈdʌndənt/ *adj.* more than is wanted; not needed, especially because sth else has the same function: *"Revert back" is a*

ə	y	w	t̮	eɪ	aɪ	ɔɪ	aʊ	oʊ
about	yes	woman	butter	say	five	boy	now	go

redundant expression. —**re·dun·dan·cy** /-ənsi/ *noun* [U]

,**red 'wine** *noun* [U] wine that is made from purple grapes ☞ Look at **white wine** and **rosé**.

red·wood /'rɛdwʊd/ (*also* **sequoia**) *noun* [C] an extremely large, tall tree that grows near the west coast of the U.S.

reed /rid/ *noun* [C] **1** a tall plant, like grass, that grows in or near water **2** a very small, thin piece of wood in some types of musical instruments (**woodwinds**) that you blow over or through in order to make a sound

reef /rif/ *noun* [C] a long line of rocks, sand, etc. just below or above the surface of the ocean: *a coral reef*

reek /rik/ *verb* [I] to have a very strong, bad smell: *His breath reeked of alcohol.*

reel[1] /ril/ *noun* [C] a round object that film for movies, a fishing line, etc. is wound around: *a fishing rod and reel*

reel[2] /ril/ *verb* [T] **reel sth in/out** to wind sth on or off a reel or to pull it toward you using a reel: *to reel out the hose* ○ *to reel in a fish*

IDM **be reeling (from sth)** to be shocked and confused because of sth that has happened: *The Florida coast is still reeling from the effects of the hurricane.*

PHRV **reel sth off** to say or repeat sth from memory quickly and without effort: *She reeled off a list of all the people she invited to the party.*

ref /rɛf/ *noun* [C] (*informal*) = REFEREE

☆ **re·fer** /rɪ'fər/ *verb* (**re·fer·ring**; **re·ferred**) **1** [I] **refer to sb/sth** to mention or talk about sb/sth: *When he said "some students," do you think he was referring to us?* ○ *Many people still refer to Russia as the Soviet Union.* **2** [I] **refer to sb/sth** to be used to describe sb/sth: *The term "adolescent" refers to young people between the ages of 12 and 17.* **3** [I] to be connected with or important for: *The numbers in parentheses refer to diagrams at the end of the chapter.* **4** [I] **refer to sb/sth** to go to sb/sth or to look at sth for information: *If you don't understand a particular word, you can refer to your dictionaries.* **5** [T] **refer sb/sth to sb/sth** to send or direct sb/sth to sb/sth for help or to be dealt with: *My doctor referred me to a specialist.* ○ *The dispute was referred to the United Nations.*

ref·e·ree /,rɛfə'ri/ *noun* [C](*also informal* **ref**) the person in football, basketball, etc. who controls the game and prevents the rules from being broken ☞ Look at **umpire**. —**ref·e·ree** *verb* [I,T]: *Who refereed the boxing match?*

☆ **ref·er·ence** /'rɛfrəns/ *noun* **1** [C,U] **reference (to sb/sth)** a statement that mentions sb/sth; the act of mentioning sb/sth: *The article made a direct reference to a certain member of the White House staff.* ○ *Don't make any reference to his behavior last night.* **2** [C] a note, especially

in a book, etc., that tells you where certain information has been or can be found **3** [C] a person who gives a statement or writes a letter describing a person's character and ability to do a job, etc.: *Would you be willing to be a reference for me?*

IDM **in/with reference to sb/sth** (*formal*) about or concerning sb/sth: *I am writing in reference to your letter dated April 10th…*

'**reference book** *noun* [C] a book that is used for obtaining information, not for reading straight through

ref·er·en·dum /,rɛfə'rɛndəm/ *noun* [C] (*pl.* **ref·er·en·dums** or (*formal*) **ref·er·en·da** /-də/) an occasion when all the people of a state, county, etc. are able to vote on a particular political question

re·fill /,ri'fɪl/ '**rifɪl**/ *verb* [T] to fill sth again: *I need to go to the drugstore to refill my prescription.* —**re·fill** /'rifɪl/ *noun* [C]: *They charge $1.50 for a cup of coffee, but refills are free.*

re·fine /rɪ'faɪn/ *verb* [T] **1** to make a substance pure and free from other substances: *to refine sugar, oil, etc.* **2** to improve sth by changing little details: *to refine a theory* —**re·fine·ment** *noun* [C,U]

re·fined /rɪ'faɪnd/ *adj.* **1** (used about a person) having extremely good manners and knowing a lot about art, literature, etc. **2** that has been improved or made pure: *refined sugar* ☞ The opposite for **1** and **2** is **unrefined**.

re·fin·er·y /rɪ'faɪnəri/ *noun* [C] (*pl.* **re·fin·er·ies**) a factory where a certain substance is refined: *an oil refinery*

☆ **re·flect** /rɪ'flɛkt/ *verb* **1** [T] to show or express sth: *The increase in the cost of paper will be reflected in higher prices for books and newspapers.* **2** [I,T] to send back light, heat, sound or an image, or to be sent back off a surface: *She saw herself reflected in the store window.* ○ *The fireworks lit up the sky and reflected off the skyscrapers downtown.* **3** [I,T] **reflect (on/upon sth)** to think, especially deeply: *I really need some time to reflect on what you've said.*

PHRV **reflect (well, badly, etc.) on sb/sth** to give a particular impression of sb/sth: *It reflects badly on the whole school if some of the students get involved in crime.*

☆ **re·flec·tion** /rɪ'flɛkʃn/ *noun* **1** [C] a thing that shows or expresses sth: *His success is a reflection of all the hard work he puts into his job.* **2** [C] an image that you see in a mirror or in water **3** [U] (*technical*) the process of sending light, heat or sound back from a surface **4** [C,U] **reflection (on sth)** thinking deeply about sth, or a deep thought or thoughts that you express: *She wrote about her reflections on being an immigrant in a small town.* **5** [sing.] **a reflection on/upon sb/sth** a thing that causes a bad impression of sb/sth: *Parents often feel that their children's behavior is a reflection on themselves.*

ər	ɪr	ɛr	ɑr	ɔr	ʊr	ʒ	h	ŋ
bird	near	hair	car	north	tour	vision	hat	sing

re·flec·tive /rɪˈflɛktɪv/ *adj.* **1 reflective of sth** showing a good example of sth; typical of sth: *His insulting remarks are not reflective of the whole group's opinions.* **2** (used about a surface) reflecting light: *Wear reflective clothing when you're riding your bike at night.* **3** (used about a person, mood, etc.) thoughtful: *a reflective expression*

re·flec·tor /rɪˈflɛktər/ *noun* [C] a thing, usually made of plastic, that reflects light

re·flex /ˈriflɛks/ *noun* **1** [C] a sudden movement or action that you make automatically: *"I'm going to tap your knee to test your reflexes," said the doctor.* **2 reflexes** [plural] the ability to act quickly when necessary: *A good tennis player needs to have excellent reflexes.*

re·flex·ive /rɪˈflɛksɪv/ *adj., noun* [C] (*grammar*) (a word or verb form) showing that the action of a sentence is done to the subject of the sentence: *In the sentence "He cut himself," "himself" is a reflexive pronoun.*

☆ **re·form¹** /rɪˈfɔrm/ *verb* **1** [T] to change sth in order to make it better: *to reform the welfare system* **2** [I,T] to behave better or fit into society better; to make sb do this: *He's done wrong in the past, but he has made serious efforts to reform.* ○ *a reformed criminal*

☆ **re·form²** /rɪˈfɔrm/ *noun* [C,U] (a) change in sth in order to make it better: *major economic reforms* ○ *political reform in Mexico*

re·form·er /rɪˈfɔrmər/ *noun* [C] a person who tries to change society and make it better

re·frain¹ /rɪˈfrem/ *verb* [I] **refrain (from sth/ doing sth)** (*formal*) to stop yourself from doing sth; not do sth: *Please refrain from smoking in the hospital.*

re·frain² /rɪˈfrem/ *noun* [C] = CHORUS(2)

re·fresh /rɪˈfrɛʃ/ *verb* [T] to make sb/sth feel fresh, strong or full of energy again: *A good night's sleep will refresh you.*

IDM **refresh your/sb's memory (about sb/sth)** to remind yourself/sb about sth: *Could you refresh my memory about what we said on this point last week?*

re·fresh·ing /rɪˈfrɛʃɪŋ/ *adj.* **1** interesting, different and enjoyable: *It's refreshing to meet somebody who is so enthusiastic.* **2** making you feel fresh and strong again: *a refreshing swim*

re·fresh·ment /rɪˈfrɛʃmənt/ *noun* **1 refreshments** [plural] light food and drinks that are available at a concert, theater or other public event: *Refreshments will be sold during the intermission.* **2** [U] (*formal*) being refreshed, or the food and drink that makes you feel refreshed: *There will be two stops for refreshment on the trip.*

re·frig·er·ate /rɪˈfrɪdʒəreɪt/ *verb* [T] to put food, etc. in a refrigerator in order to keep it fresh and cool

☆ **re·frig·er·a·tor** /rɪˈfrɪdʒəreɪtər/ (also *informal* **fridge**, *old-fashioned* **icebox**) *noun* [C] a piece of electrical equipment in which food, etc. is

kept cold so that it stays fresh ☞ Look at **freezer**.

ref·uge /ˈrɛfyudʒ/ *noun* [C,U] **refuge (from sb/sth)** a place that is safe; the protection that this place gives you against sth bad: *a wildlife refuge* (= where wild animals cannot be hunted) ○ *They took refuge in foreign embassies.*

☆ **ref·u·gee** /ˌrɛfyuˈdʒi/ *noun* [C] a person who has been forced to leave his/her country for political or religious reasons or because there is a war, not enough food, etc.: *political refugees* ○ *a refugee camp*

re·fund¹ /rɪˈfʌnd; ˈrifʌnd/ *verb* [T] to pay back money: *Your travel expenses will be refunded.* —**re·fund·a·ble** *adj.*: *The deposit is not refundable.*

re·fund² /ˈrifʌnd/ *noun* [C] a sum of money that is returned to you, for example if you take sth back to the store where you bought it

☆ **re·fus·al** /rɪˈfyuzl/ *noun* [C,U] **refusal (to do sth)** an act of saying or showing that you will not do or accept sth: *Did they give a reason for their refusal to offer you the job?* ○ *So far we've had ten replies to the invitation: eight acceptances and two refusals.*

☆ **re·fuse¹** /rɪˈfyuz/ *verb* [I,T] to say or show that you do not want to do, give, accept, etc. sth: *I asked her to come but she refused.* ○ *He refused to listen to what I was saying.* ○ *My application for a loan has been refused.* ○ *We offered her a lift, but she refused it.*

ref·use² /ˈrɛfyus/ *noun* [U] (*formal*) things that you throw away; garbage: *a refuse dump*

re·gain /rɪˈgem/ *verb* [T] to get sth back that you have lost: *to regain your freedom* ○ *to regain consciousness*

re·gal /ˈrigl/ *adj.* very grand; like or suitable for a king or queen

☆ **re·gard¹** /rɪˈgɑrd/ *verb* [T] **regard sb/sth (as sth); regard sb/sth (with sth)** to think of sb/sth (in the way mentioned): *I regard him as my best friend.* ○ *Do you regard this issue as important?* ○ *Her work is highly regarded* (= people have a very good opinion of it). ○ *In some neighborhoods, newcomers are regarded with suspicion.*

re·gard² /rɪˈgɑrd/ *noun* **1** [U] **regard (for sb/sth)** a feeling of admiration for sb/sth: respect: *She obviously has great regard for your ability.* **2** [U] **regard to/for sb/sth** care or consideration for sb/sth: *He shows little regard for other people's feelings.* **3 regards** [plural] (used especially at the end of a letter) kind thoughts and greetings: *Please give my regards to your parents.*

IDM **in/with regard to sb/sth; in this/that/one regard** (*formal*) about sb/sth; concerning this or that: *With regard to the details – these will be finalized later.* ○ *It has been a successful year financially, so in this regard we have been fortunate.*

R

tʃ	dʒ	v	θ	ð	s	z	ʃ
chin	June	van	thin	then	so	zoo	she

R

☆ **re·gard·ing** /rɪˈgɑrdɪŋ/ *prep.* (*formal*) about or concerning: *Please write if you require further information regarding this matter.*

☆ **re·gard·less** /rɪˈgɑrdləs/ *adv.* **regardless of sb/sth** paying no attention to sb/sth: *Everyone wil receive the same bonus, regardless of how long they have been working here.*

reg·gae /ˈrɛgeɪ/ *noun* [U] a type of Caribbean popular music with a strong rhythm

re·gime /reɪˈʒim/ *noun* [C] a method or system of government: *a military regime* ☞ This word is used to show disapproval.

reg·i·ment /ˈrɛdʒəmənt/ [C] a large group of soldiers in the military forces —**reg·i·men·tal** /ˌrɛdʒəˈmɛntl/ *adj.*

☆ **re·gion** /ˈridʒən/ *noun* [C] **1** a part of the country or the world; a large area of land: *desert, tropical, polar, etc. regions* ○ *This region of the Midwest is very flat.* ○ *She is responsible for sales in the West Coast region.* ☞ Look at the note at **district. 2** an area of your body: *He's been having pains in his abdominal region.*
IDM in the region of sth about or approximately: *It must have cost somewhere in the region of $1,000.*

☆ **re·gion·al** /ˈridʒənl/ *adj.* connected with a particular region (1): *regional accents*

☆ **reg·is·ter¹** /ˈrɛdʒəstər/ *noun* [C] **1** = CASH REGISTER **2** an official list of names, etc. or a book that contains such a list: *Be sure to record each check that you write in your checkbook register.*

☆ **reg·is·ter²** /ˈrɛdʒəstər/ *verb* **1** [I,T] to put a name or other information on an official list: *I'd like to register for the course in June.* ○ *to register to vote* ○ *All births, deaths and marriages must be registered.* **2** [I,T] to show on a measuring instrument: *The thermometer registered 32°F.* **3** [T] (*formal*) to show feelings, opinions, etc.: *Her face registered intense dislike.*

ˌ**registered ˈmail** *noun* [U] a postal service that you pay extra for, in which the post office records when you sent the letter or package and each point that it passes until it arrives at the correct place

ˌ**registered ˈnurse** *noun* [C] (*abbr.* **RN**) a person who has passed a special state examination and has received official permission to work as a nurse

reg·is·trar /ˈrɛdʒəstrɑr/ *noun* [C] **1** a person who is responsible for official records, etc. at a college or university **2** a person whose job is to keep official lists, especially in a government office

☆ **reg·is·tra·tion** /ˌrɛdʒəˈstreɪʃn/ *noun* **1** [U] the act of putting sth or sb's name on an official list: *Registration for evening classes will take place on September 8th.* **2** [C] an official piece of paper with information about a car, truck, etc. and the name of its owner: *Can I see your license and registration, please?*

reg·is·try /ˈrɛdʒəstri/ *noun* [C] (*pl.* **reg·is·tries**) a place where official lists are kept: *the Massachusetts Registry of Motor Vehicles*

re·gret¹ /rɪˈgrɛt/ *noun* [C,U] a feeling of sadness about sth that cannot now be changed: *Do you have any regrets that you didn't go to college?* ○ *I accepted his decision to leave with great regret.*

☆ **re·gret²** /rɪˈgrɛt/ *verb* [T] (**re·gret·ting; re·gret·ted**) **1** to feel sorry or sad about sth; to wish that you had not done sth: *I hope you won't regret your decision later.* ○ *I really regretted not saying goodbye to her.* ○ *Do you regret what you said to him?* **2** (*formal*) (used as a way of saying that you are sorry for sth): *I regret to inform you that your application has not been approved.*

re·gret·ful /rɪˈgrɛtfl/ *adj.* feeling or expressing sadness —**re·gret·ful·ly** *adv.*

re·gret·ta·ble /rɪˈgrɛtəbl/ *adj.* that you should feel sorry or sad about

re·gret·ta·bly /rɪˈgrɛtəbli/ *adv.* (*formal*) **1** in a way that makes you feel sad or sorry **2** it is to be regretted that: *Regrettably, some hotels are not well-equipped for disabled people.*

☆ **reg·u·lar¹** /ˈrɛgyələr/ *adj.* **1** having the same amount of space or time between each thing or part: *regular breathing* ○ *Nurses checked her blood pressure at regular intervals.* **2** happening at the same time each day, week, etc. (as a result of an arrangement or a plan): *We have regular meetings every Thursday.* **3** going somewhere or doing sth often: *a regular customer* ○ *We're regular passengers of the airline.* **4** normal or usual: *Who is your regular dentist?* **5** evenly shaped: *regular teeth* ○ *a regular geometric pattern* **6** of a medium size: *I'll have a cheeseburger and a regular Coke.* **7** ordinary; without any special or extra features: *Do you want regular or diet cola?* ○ *I just want to buy a regular white shirt – nothing fancy.* **8** (*grammar*) (used about a noun, verb, etc.) having the usual or expected plural, verb form, etc.: *"Walk" is a regular verb.* ☞ Look at **irregular. —reg·u·lar·i·ty** /ˌrɛgyəˈlærəti/ *noun* [U]

reg·u·lar² /ˈrɛgyələr/ *noun* [C] (*informal*) a person who goes to a particular store, bar, etc. very often

☆ **reg·u·lar·ly** /ˈrɛgyələrli/ *adv.* **1** at regular times or in a regular way: *to have a car serviced regularly* **2** often: *Mr. Davis regularly takes part in contests, but this is the first one that he has won.*

reg·u·late /ˈrɛgyəleɪt/ *verb* [T] **1** to control sth by using laws: *a strict law to regulate pollution from factories* **2** to control a machine, piece of equipment, etc.: *Individual controls allow you to regulate the temperature in each room.*

☆ **reg·u·la·tion** /ˌrɛgyəˈleɪʃn/ *noun* **1** [U] control of sth: *government regulation of agriculture* **2** [C, usually pl.] a law or rule that controls how sth is done: *to observe/obey the safety*

i	ɪ	ɛ	æ	ɑ	ɔ	ʌ	ʊ	u
see	sit	ten	cat	hot	saw	cup	put	too

regulations ○ *It is against fire regulations to smoke at a gas station.* ○ *The plans must comply with the new federal regulations.* ○ *to enforce a regulation*

re·hab /'rihæb/ *noun* [U] (*informal*) the process of helping sb to stop using drugs or alcohol: *Brett is in drug rehab.*

re·ha·bil·i·tate /,riə'bɪləteɪt; ,rihə-/ *verb* [T] to help sb to live a normal life again after an illness, being in prison, etc. —**re·ha·bil·i·ta·tion** /,riə,bɪlə'teɪʃn; ,rihə-/ *noun* [U]

re·hears·al /rɪ'hərsl/ *noun* [C,U] the time when you practice a play, dance, piece of music, etc. before you perform it for other people: *a dress rehearsal* (= when all the actors wear their stage clothes)

re·hearse /rɪ'hərs/ *verb* [I,T] to practice a play, dance, piece of music, etc. before you perform it for other people

reign¹ /reɪn/ *noun* [C] the period of time that a king or queen rules a country: *the long reign of Queen Victoria*

reign² /reɪn/ *verb* [I] **1 reign (over sb/sth)** (used about a king or queen) to rule a country: (*figurative*) *the reigning world champion* **2** to be present as the most important feature of a particular situation: *Chaos reigned after the first snow of the winter.*

re·im·burse /,rim'bərs/ *verb* [T] (*formal*) to pay money back to sb: *The company will reimburse you in full for your traveling expenses.* ○ *Your expenses will be reimbursed in full.*

rein /reɪn/ *noun* [C, usually pl.] a long thin piece of leather that you use to control a horse ☞ picture at **horse**.

rein·deer /'reɪndɪr/ *noun* [C] (*pl.* **rein·deer**) a type of large deer that lives in Arctic regions

☞ According to tradition, reindeer pull Santa Claus's sleigh on the night before Christmas when he brings presents to children.

re·in·force /,rim'fɔrs/ *verb* [T] to make sth stronger: *Concrete can be reinforced by putting steel bars inside it.* ○ *evidence to reinforce her argument*

re·in·force·ment /,rim'fɔrsmənt/ *noun* **1** [U] the act of supporting or strengthening sth: *The roof is weak in places and needs reinforcement.* **2 reinforcements** [plural] extra people who are sent to make an army, navy, etc. stronger

re·in·state /,rim'steɪt/ *verb* [T] to bring sb/sth back into his/her/its previous job, position or condition: *The Supreme Court reinstated the county court's original decision.* —**re·in·state·ment** *noun* [U]

☆ **re·ject¹** /rɪ'dʒɛkt/ *verb* [T] to refuse to accept sb/sth: *The plan was rejected as being impractical.* ○ *I rejected all the applicants for the job except one.* —**re·jec·tion** *noun* [C,U]: *Penny got*

a rejection letter from Harvard. [U]: *There has been total rejection of the new policy.*

re·ject² /'ridʒɛkt/ *noun* [C] a person or thing that is not accepted because he/she/it is not good enough: *Rejects are sold at half price.*

re·joice /rɪ'dʒɔɪs/ *verb* [I] **rejoice (at/in/over sth)** (*formal*) to feel or show great happiness: *The people rejoiced at the news of the victory.* —**re·joic·ing** *noun* [U]

re·ju·ve·nate /rɪ'dʒuvəneɪt/ *verb* [T] to cause sb/sth to feel or look younger —**re·ju·ve·na·tion** /rɪ,dʒuvə'neɪʃn/ *noun* [U]

re·lapse /rɪ'læps; 'rilæps/ *noun* [C] a time when sb/sth becomes worse again after an improvement: *The patient suffered a relapse and then died.*

☆ **re·late** /rɪ'leɪt/ *verb* **1** [T] **relate sth to/with sth** to show a connection between two or more things: *The report relates heart disease to high levels of stress.* **2** [T] **relate sth (to sb)** (*formal*) to tell a story to sb

PHRV **relate to sb/sth 1** to be concerned with; to have sth to do with: *That question is very interesting, but it doesn't really relate to the subject that we're discussing.* **2** to be able to understand how sb feels: *Some teenagers find it hard to relate to their parents.*

☆ **re·lat·ed** /rɪ'leɪtəd/ *adj.* **related (to sb/sth) 1** connected with sb/sth: *The rise in the cost of living is directly related to the price of oil.* **2** of the same family: *We are related by marriage.* ○ *Are you related to Joe Garcia?* ○ *to be closely/distantly related*

☆ **re·la·tion** /rɪ'leɪʃn/ *noun* **1** [U] **relation (between sth and sth); relation (to sth)** the connection between two or more things: *There seems to be no relation between the cost of the houses and their size.* ○ *The movie bears no relation to the book* (= it is very different). **2** [C] a member of your family: *a close/distant relation* **3 relations** [plural] the way that people, groups, countries, etc. feel about or behave toward each other: *The police officer stressed that good relations with the community were essential.* ○ *to break off diplomatic relations*

IDM **in/with relation to sb/sth 1** concerning sb/sth: *Many questions were asked, particularly in relation to the cost of the new buildings.* **2** compared with: *Prices are low in relation to those in other parts of the country.*

☆ **re·la·tion·ship** /rɪ'leɪʃnʃɪp/ *noun* [C] **1** the way that people, groups, countries, etc. feel about or behave toward each other: *The police have a poor relationship with the local people.* ○ *The relationship between the parents and the school has improved greatly.* **2** a friendship or love affair: *to have a relationship with sb* ○ *Are you currently in a relationship?* ○ *The movie describes the relationship between a young man and an older woman.* ○ *a close relationship* **3** a family connection: *"What is your relationship*

ə	y	w	t̬	eɪ	aɪ	ɔɪ	aʊ	oʊ
about	yes	woman	butter	say	five	boy	now	go

to Bruce?" "He is married to my cousin." **4** the connection between two or more things: *Is there a relationship between violence on TV and the increase in crime?*

☆ **rel·a·tive**[1] /ˈrɛlətɪv/ *noun* [C] a member of your family: *a close/distant relative*

☆ **rel·a·tive**[2] /ˈrɛlətɪv/ *adj.* **1** when compared to sb/sth else: *They live in relative luxury.* ○ *We're in a period of relative calm after the winds of the past few days.* ○ *It's hard to assess the relative importance of the two jobs.* **2** (*grammar*) referring to an earlier noun, phrase or sentence: *In the phrase "the woman who lives next door," "who" is a relative pronoun.*

☆ **rel·a·tive·ly** /ˈrɛlətɪvli/ *adv.* to a certain degree; fairly: *Spanish is a relatively easy language to learn.* ○ *It's a small house, but the back yard is relatively large.*

☆ **re·lax** /rɪˈlæks/ *verb* **1** [I,T] to make or become less worried or tense; to spend time not doing very much: *This vacation will give you a chance to relax.* ○ *A hot bath will relax you after a hard day's work.* ○ *They spent the evening relaxing in front of the TV.* **2** [I,T] to make or become less stiff or tight: *You should be able to feel all your muscles relaxing.* **3** [T] to make rules or laws less strict: *The regulations on importing animals have been relaxed.*

re·lax·a·tion /ˌrilækˈseɪʃn/ *noun* [U] **1** the act of relaxing (1,2,3): *the relaxation of a rule* **2** sth that you do in order to rest or relax (1): *Everyone needs time for rest and relaxation.*

☆ **re·laxed** /rɪˈlækst/ *adj.* not worried or anxious: *The relaxed atmosphere made everyone feel at ease.*

☆ **re·lax·ing** /rɪˈlæksɪŋ/ *adj.* pleasant, helping you to rest and become less worried: *a quiet, relaxing vacation*

re·lay[1] /ˈrileɪ/ (*also* **relay race**) *noun* [C] a race in which each member of a team runs, swims, etc. one part of the race: *the 4 x 100-meter relay*

re·lay[2] /ˈrileɪ; rɪˈleɪ/ *verb* [T] (*p.t., p.p.* **relayed**) to receive and send on a signal or message

☆ **re·lease**[1] /rɪˈlis/ *verb* [T] **1** to allow sb/sth to be free: *The hostages will be released before Christmas.* ○ *He was released from prison.* ○ *The driver of the wrecked car had to be released by firefighters.* **2** to stop holding sth: *She released his hand and walked off.* **3** to move sth from a fixed position: *Pull this lever to release the hood latch.* **4** to allow sth to be known by the public: *The identity of the victim has not been released.* **5** to make a movie, record, etc. available so the public can see or hear it: *Their new compact disc is due to be released next week.* **6** to let substances escape into the air, ocean, etc.: *The new power plant would release 230,000 tons of carbon dioxide into the atmosphere every year.*

☆ **re·lease**[2] /rɪˈlis/ *noun* **1** [C,U] **release (from sth)** the act of freeing or the state of being freed: *The release of the hostages took place this morning.* ○ *I had a great feeling of release when my final exams were over.* **2** [C] a book, movie, record, piece of news, etc. that has been made available to the public: *a press release* ○ *The band played their latest release.*

re·lent /rɪˈlɛnt/ *verb* [I] (*formal*) to become less strict or hard, e.g. by allowing sth that you had previously forbidden: *Her parents finally relented and let her go to the party.* ☞ A less formal expression is **give in**.

re·lent·less /rɪˈlɛntləs/ *adj.* not stopping or changing: *the relentless fight against crime* —**re·lent·less·ly** *adv.*: *The sun beat down relentlessly.*

☆ **rel·e·vant** /ˈrɛləvənt/ *adj.* **relevant (to sb/sth)** **1** connected with what is happening or being talked about: *Please enclose all the relevant documents with your visa application.* ○ *Much of what they said was not directly relevant to my case.* **2** important and useful: *Many people feel that poetry is no longer relevant in today's world.* ☞ The opposite is **irrelevant**. —**rel·e·vance** /-əns/ *noun* [U]: *I honestly can't see the relevance of what he said.* ○ *Does the Bible have any relevance to life today?*

☆ **re·li·a·ble** /rɪˈlaɪəbl/ *adj.* that you can trust: *Japanese cars are usually very reliable.* ○ *I'm surprised she didn't call back – she's usually very reliable.* ○ *reliable information* ○ *Is he a reliable witness?* ☞ The opposite is **unreliable**. Look at the verb **rely**. —**re·li·a·bil·i·ty** /rɪˌlaɪəˈbɪləti/ *noun* [U]: *These cars have a good reputation for reliability.* —**re·li·a·bly** /-əbli/ *adv.*

re·li·ance /rɪˈlaɪəns/ *noun* [U] **1 reliance on sb/sth** being able to trust sb/sth: *Don't place too much reliance on her promises.* **2** not being able to live or work without sb/sth; being dependent on sb/sth: *the nation's reliance on fossil fuels*

re·li·ant /rɪˈlaɪənt/ *adj.* **reliant on sb/sth** (not before a noun) not being able to live or work without sb/sth: *She is totally reliant on her parents for financial support.* ☞ The verb is **rely**. Look also at **self-reliant**.

rel·ic /ˈrɛlɪk/ *noun* [C] something from the past that still exists today

☆ **re·lief** /rɪˈlif/ *noun* **1** [U, sing.] **relief (from sth)** the feeling that you have when sth unpleasant stops or becomes less strong: *The medication brought him some relief from the pain.* ○ *What a relief! That terrible noise finally stopped.* ○ *It was a great relief to know they were safe.* ○ *to breathe a sigh of relief* ○ *To my relief, he didn't argue with my suggestion at all.* **2** [U] money or food that is given to help people who are in trouble: *disaster relief for the flood victims*

ər	ɪr	ɛr	ɑr	ɔr	ʊr	ʒ	h	ŋ
bird	near	hair	car	north	tour	vision	hat	sing

☆ **re·lieve** /rɪˈliv/ verb [T] to make a bad feeling or situation better: *These pills should relieve the pain.* ○ *Four new prisons are being built to relieve overcrowding.*
PHRV **relieve sb of sth** (formal) to take sth away from sb

re·lieved /rɪˈlivd/ adj. pleased because your fear or worry has been taken away: *I was very relieved to hear that you weren't seriously hurt.*

☆ **re·lig·ion** /rɪˈlɪdʒən/ noun 1 [U] the belief in a god or gods who made the world and who can control what happens in it: *I never discuss politics or religion with them.* 2 [C] one of the systems of worship that is based on this belief: *the Christian, Hindu, Muslim, etc. religion*

☆ **re·lig·ious** /rɪˈlɪdʒəs/ adj. 1 connected with religion: *religious faith* 2 having a strong belief in a religion: *I'm not very religious, but I do go to church at Easter.*

re·lig·ious·ly /rɪˈlɪdʒəsli/ adv. 1 in a religious way 2 regularly: *They brush their teeth religiously, every night and every morning.*

re·lin·quish /rɪˈlɪŋkwɪʃ/ verb [T] (formal) to stop having or doing sth ☞ **Give up** is more common.

rel·ish¹ /ˈrɛlɪʃ/ verb [T] to enjoy sth or to look forward to sth very much

rel·ish² /ˈrɛlɪʃ/ noun [U] 1 a cold sauce, usually made with chopped pickles, that is eaten with meat: *a hot dog with mustard and relish* 2 great enjoyment: *They all sang with great relish.*

re·live /ˌriˈlɪv/ verb [T] to remember sth and imagine that it is happening again

re·lo·cate /ˌriˈloʊkeɪt/ verb [I,T] to move (sb/sth) to a new place: *The company plans to relocate to North Carolina.* —**re·lo·ca·tion** /ˌriloʊˈkeɪʃn/ noun [U]

☆ **re·luc·tant** /rɪˈlʌktənt/ adj. **reluctant (to do sth)** slow to agree to do sth, because you are unwilling: *I was reluctant to loan him my car because he's such a fast driver.* —**re·luc·tance** /-əns/ noun [U] **reluctance (to do sth)**: *the President's reluctance to raise taxes* —**re·luc·tant·ly** adv.

☆ **re·ly** /rɪˈlaɪ/ verb [I] (pres. part. **re·ly·ing**; 3rd pers. sing. pres. **re·lies**; p.t., p.p. **re·lied**) **rely on/upon sb/sth (to do sth)** 1 to need sb/sth and not be able to live or work well without them: *The old lady had to rely on other people to go shopping for her.* ○ *Many students have to rely on their parents for money.* 2 to trust sb/sth to work or behave well: *You can't rely on the weather in the springtime.* ○ *Can I rely on you to keep a secret?* ☞ The noun is **reliance**. Look at the adjectives **reliable** and **reliant**.

☆ **re·main** /rɪˈmeɪn/ verb [I] 1 to be left after other people or things have gone: *Today only a few veterans of the First World War remain.* ○ *They spent the two remaining days of their vacation buying presents to take home.* ○ *The*

Giants scored a touchdown with five minutes of the game remaining. 2 to stay or continue in the same place or condition: *They remained silent throughout the trial.* ○ *They're divorced but they remain friends.* ○ *Officials refused to allow him to remain in the United States.* ○ (figurative) *Although he seems very pleasant, the fact remains that I don't trust him.*

re·main·der /rɪˈmeɪndər/ noun [sing., with sing. or pl. verb] (formal) **the remainder (of sth)** the people, things, etc. that are left after the others have gone away or been dealt with; the rest: *Fifty percent of local residents are in favor of the proposal, 45% are against it and the remainder are undecided.* ○ *The remainder of the week is expected to be warm and sunny.* ☞ **Rest** is less formal then **remainder**.

☆ **re·mains** /rɪˈmeɪnz/ noun [plural] 1 what is left behind after other parts have been used or taken away: *The construction workers found the remains of a Native American burial ground.* 2 (formal) a dead body (sometimes one that has been found somewhere a long time after death): *Human remains were discovered in the woods.*

☆ **re·mark¹** /rɪˈmɑrk/ verb [I,T] **remark (on/upon sb/sth)** to say or write sth; to comment: *"What a strange movie," he remarked.* ○ *Millie remarked that she had found the movie very interesting.* ○ *A lot of people have remarked on the similarity between them.*

☆ **re·mark²** /rɪˈmɑrk/ noun [C] something that you say or write; a comment: *a few personal remarks at the end of the letter* ○ *to make a nasty remark*

☆ **re·mark·a·ble** /rɪˈmɑrkəbl/ adj. unusual or noticeable: *She certainly is a remarkable woman.* ○ *That is a remarkable achievement for someone so young.* —**re·mark·a·bly** /-əbli/ adv.

re·me·di·al /rɪˈmidiəl/ adj. 1 helping people who are slow at learning sth: *remedial English classes* 2 used to improve sth (e.g. a difficult situation)

rem·e·dy¹ /ˈrɛmədi/ noun [C] (pl. **rem·e·dies**) **remedy (for sth)** 1 something that makes you better when you are sick or in pain: *Hot tea with honey is a good remedy for colds.* 2 a way of solving a problem: *There is no easy remedy for unemployment.*

rem·e·dy² /ˈrɛmədi/ verb [T] (pres. part. **rem·e·dy·ing**; 3rd pers. sing. pres. **rem·e·dies**; p.t., p.p. **rem·e·died**) to change or improve sth that is wrong or bad: *to remedy an injustice*

☆ **re·mem·ber** /rɪˈmɛmbər/ verb 1 [I,T] to have sth in your mind or to bring sth back into your mind: *When did they move to Texas? I just don't remember.* ○ *I'm sorry. I don't remember your name.* ○ *Do you remember the night we first met?* ○ *Remember that we're having company tonight.* ○ *I know her face, but I can't remember what her name is.* ○ *Can you remember when we bought the stereo?*

tʃ	dʒ	v	θ	ð	s	z	ʃ
chin	**June**	**van**	**thin**	**then**	**so**	**zoo**	**she**

R

☞ If you remember **to do** something, you don't forget to do it: *I remembered to buy the coffee.* ○ *Remember to turn the lights off before you leave.* If you remember **doing** something, you have a picture or memory in your mind of doing it: *Polly remembers seeing her keys on the table yesterday.*

2 [T] to give money, etc. to sb/sth: *to remember sb in your will* ☞ Look at the note at **remind**.

re·mem·brance /rɪˈmɛmbrəns/ *noun* [U] (*formal*) the act of remembering and showing respect for sb who is dead: *a service in remembrance of those killed in the war*

☆ **re·mind** /rɪˈmaɪnd/ *verb* [T] **1** to say sth to help sb remember sth: *"Christmas is in two weeks!" "Don't remind me – I haven't bought any presents yet."* ○ *She reminded him of his appointment at two o'clock.* ○ *He reminded the kids to wash their hands.* ○ *The doctor reminded me that I should see her again in two months.* **2 remind sb of sb/sth** to cause sb to remember sb/sth: *This song reminds me of Paris.* ○ *You remind me of your father.*

☞ You **remember** something by yourself. If somebody or something **reminds** you of something, he/she/it causes you to remember it: *Kristi remembered to say thank you after the party.* ○ *Mom reminded Kristi to say thank you after the party.*

re·mind·er /rɪˈmaɪndər/ *noun* [C] something that makes you remember sth: *We received a reminder that we hadn't paid the electric bill.* ○ *Eddie kept the ring as a reminder of happier days.*

rem·i·nisce /ˌrɛməˈnɪs/ *verb* [I] **reminisce (about sb/sth)** to talk about (pleasant) things that happened in the past

rem·i·nis·cent /ˌrɛməˈnɪsnt/ *adj.* **reminiscent of sb/sth** that makes you remember sb/sth; similar: *I think that painting is very reminiscent of one by Monet.*

re·mis·sion /rɪˈmɪʃn/ *noun* [C,U] a period of time when a serious disease improves or seems to go away: *Rebecca's cancer has been in remission for two years.*

rem·nant /ˈrɛmnənt/ *noun* [C] a piece of sth that remains after the rest is gone

re·mod·el /ˌriˈmɑdl/ *verb* [I,T] to change the structure or appearance of sth, especially a building: *Our neighbors are remodeling their house.* ○ *We're thinking of remodeling, but we're not sure we can afford it.*

re·morse /rɪˈmɔrs/ *noun* [U] a feeling of sadness because you have done sth wrong: *She was filled with remorse for what she had done.* ☞ Look at **guilt**. —**re·morse·ful** /-fl/ *adj.*

☆ **re·mote** /rɪˈmoʊt/ *adj.* **1** far away from where other people live: *a cabin in a remote area of the state* **2** far away in time: *the remote past/*

future **3** not very great: *a remote possibility* —**re·mote·ness** *noun* [U]

re·mote con·trol *noun* **1** [C] (also *informal* **remote**) a piece of equipment for controlling sth, such as a television, toy, etc. from a distance **2** [U] a system for controlling sth from a distance: *You can open the garage door by remote control.*

re·mote·ly /rɪˈmoʊtli/ *adv.* (used in negative sentences) to a very small degree; at all: *I'm not remotely interested in your problems.*

☆ **re·mov·al** /rɪˈmuvl/ *noun* [U] taking sb/sth away: *I demanded the removal of my name from the list.* ○ *the city's budget for snow removal*

☆ **re·move** /rɪˈmuv/ *verb* [T] (*formal*) **1 remove sb/sth (from sth)** to take sb/sth off or away: *Please remove your shoes before entering the temple.* ○ *This detergent will remove most stains.* ○ *to remove doubts, fears, problems, etc.* ○ *I would like you to remove my name from your mailing list.* ☞ **Take off**, **take out**, etc. are less formal. **2 remove sb (from sth)** to make sb leave his/her job, especially an official position: *Citizens voted to remove the senator from office.*

re·moved /rɪˈmuvd/ *adj.* (not before a noun) **removed (from sth)** far or different from sth: *Hospitals today are far removed from what they were fifty years ago.*

re·mov·er /rɪˈmuvər/ *noun* [C,U] a substance that cleans off paint, stains, etc.: *a stain remover*

ren·der /ˈrɛndər/ *verb* [T] (*formal*) to cause sb/sth to be in a certain condition: *She was rendered speechless by the attack.*

ren·dez·vous /ˈrɑndeɪvu/ *noun* [C] (*pl.* **ren·dez·vous** /-z/) **1 rendezvous (with sb)** a meeting that you have arranged with sb **2** a place where people often meet

re·new /rɪˈnu/ *verb* [T] **1** to give new strength or energy: *After a break, he went to work with renewed enthusiasm.* **2** to start sth again: *renewed outbreaks of violence* ○ *to renew a friendship* **3** to make sth valid for a further period of time: *to renew your driver's license* —**re·new·al** /-ˈnuəl/ *noun* [C,U]

re·new·a·ble /rɪˈnuəbl/ *adj.* that can be continued or replaced so that it is never finished or used completely: *renewable energy sources such as solar power and wind*

ren·o·vate /ˈrɛnəveɪt/ *verb* [T] to repair an old building and put it back into good condition —**ren·o·va·tion** /ˌrɛnəˈveɪʃn/ *noun* [C,U]: *The house is in need of complete renovation.*

☆ **rent¹** /rɛnt/ *noun* [C,U] money that you pay regularly for the use of land, a house or a building: *a high/low rent* ○ *How much rent do you pay?*

IDM for rent offered for sb to rent: *apartment for rent* (= on a sign)

i	ɪ	ɛ	æ	ɑ	ɔ	ʌ	ʊ	u
see	sit	ten	cat	hot	saw	cup	put	too

☆ **rent²** /rɛnt/ verb 1 [I,T] to pay money for the use of sth, usually for a fixed period of time: *Let's rent a movie tonight.* ○ *We rented a car to go on vacation.* ○ *"Do you own your home?" "No, we're just renting."* 2 [T] **rent sth (out) (to sb)** to allow sb to use sth for money, usually for a fixed period of time: *We could rent out the basement apartment to somebody.* ○ *Does the video store also rent VCRs?*

☆ **rent·al¹** /ˈrɛntl/ noun 1 [C,U] the system of renting sth: *The travel agency can arrange your car rental before you go on your trip.* 2 [U] money that you pay when you rent sth: *Video rental is $2.75 for 24 hours.*

rent·al² /ˈrɛntl/ adj. that is being rented or available to rent: *a rental car*

re·or·gan·ize /ˌriˈɔrgənaɪz/ verb [I,T] to organize sth again or in a new way so that it works better —**re·or·gan·i·za·tion** /riˌɔrgənəˈzeɪʃn/ noun [C,U]

rep /rɛp/ (informal)(also formal **representative**) noun [C] a person whose job is to travel around a particular area and visit companies, etc., to sell the products of the company for which he/she works: *a sales rep*

Rep. abbr. = REPRESENTATIVE¹(1): *Rep. James T. Walsh of New York*

☆ **re·pair¹** /rɪˈpɛr/ verb [T] to put sth old or damaged back into good condition: *How much will it cost to repair the car?* ○ (figurative) *It's difficult to see how their marriage can be repaired.* ☞ Look at **irreparable**.

re·pair² /rɪˈpɛr/ noun [C,U] something that you do to fix sth that is damaged: *The bridge is under repair.* ○ *The swimming pool is closed for repairs to the roof.* ○ *to be damaged beyond repair*

IDM in good, bad, etc. repair (formal) in a good, bad, etc. condition

☆ **re·pay** /rɪˈpeɪ/ verb [T] (p.t., p.p. **re·paid** /rɪˈpeɪd/) 1 **repay sth (to sb)** to pay back money that you owe to sb: *to repay a debt* 2 **repay sb (for sth)** to give sth to sb in return for help, kindness, etc.: *How can I ever repay you for all you have done for me?* —**re·pay·ment** noun [C,U]: *the repayment of a loan*

re·peal /rɪˈpil/ verb [T] (e.g. in Congress) to make a law no longer valid

☆ **re·peat¹** /rɪˈpit/ verb 1 [I,T] to say, write or do sth more than once: *Can you repeat what you said? I didn't catch it.* ○ *"I really don't want to do it," he repeated.* ○ *Your essay is pretty good, but you repeat yourself several times* (= you say the same thing more than once). ○ *Billy may have to repeat third grade.* ○ *History often seems to repeat itself.* 2 [T] to say or write sth that sb else has said or written or that you have learned: *Repeat each sentence after me.* ○ *Please don't repeat what you've heard here.* ☞ The noun is **repetition**.

☆ **re·peat²** /rɪˈpit/ noun [C] something that is done, shown, given, etc. again, especially a program on television

☆ **re·peat·ed** /rɪˈpitəd/ adj. (only before a noun) done or happening many times: *There have been repeated accidents on this stretch of road.*

☆ **re·peat·ed·ly** /rɪˈpitədli/ adv. many times; often

re·pel /rɪˈpɛl/ verb [T] (**re·pel·ling; re·pelled**) 1 to send or push sb/sth back or away: *The army repelled the enemy attack.* 2 to cause sb to feel strong dislike or disgust: *The dirt and smell repelled her.* ☞ The noun is **repulsion**.

re·pel·lent /rɪˈpɛlənt/ noun [U] a chemical substance that is used to keep insects, etc. away: *mosquito repellent*

re·pent /rɪˈpɛnt/ verb [I,T] (formal) to be very sorry about sth bad that you have done: *to repent your sins* —**re·pen·tance** /-əns/ noun [U] —**re·pen·tant** /-ənt/ adj.

re·per·cus·sion /ˌripərˈkʌʃn/ noun [C, usually pl.] the bad effect or result of sth that you do: *His resignation will have serious repercussions.*

rep·er·toire /ˈrɛpərtwar/ noun [C] all the plays or music that an actor or a musician knows and can perform

rep·e·ti·tion /ˌrɛpəˈtɪʃn/ noun [C,U] doing sth again; sth that you do or that happens again: *We don't want any repetition of what happened on Friday.* ○ *We're trying to avoid a repetition of what happened on Friday.* ☞ The verb is **repeat**.

re·pet·i·tive /rɪˈpɛtətɪv/ adj. not interesting because the same thing is repeated many times: *repetitive factory work*

☆ **re·place** /rɪˈpleɪs/ verb [T] 1 to put sth back in the right place: *Please replace the books on the shelves when you are finished with them.* ☞ **Put back** is more common and less formal. 2 to take the place of sb/sth: *Credit cards have replaced cash in many situations.* 3 **replace sb/sth (with sb/sth)** to exchange sb/sth for sb/sth that is better or newer: *We will replace any goods that are damaged.* —**re·place·a·ble** /-əbl/ adj. ☞ The opposite is **irreplaceable**.

☆ **re·place·ment** /rɪˈpleɪsmənt/ noun 1 [U] exchanging sb/sth for sb/sth that is better or newer: *The carpets are in need of replacement.* 2 [C] a person or thing that will take the place of sb/sth: *Mary is leaving next month, so we need to advertise for a replacement for her.*

re·play¹ /ˌriˈpleɪ/ verb [T] to play again sth that you have recorded

re·play² /ˈripleɪ/ noun [C] something on television, on a video or a cassette that you watch or listen to again: *Now let's see a replay of that incredible home run!* ☞ Look also at **instant replay**.

rep·li·ca /ˈrɛplɪkə/ noun [C] an exact copy of sth

ə	y	w	t̬	eɪ	aɪ	ɔɪ	aʊ	oʊ
about	yes	woman	butter	say	five	boy	now	go

R

☆ **re·ply**[1] /rɪ'plaɪ/ *verb* [I,T] (*pres. part.* **re·ply·ing**; *3rd pers. sing. pres.* **re·plies**; *p.t., p.p.* **replied**) to give an answer: *I wrote to Sue, but she hasn't replied.* ∘ *"Yes, I will," she replied.* ∘ *I asked Matthew if he was sorry, and he replied that he was.* ∘ *to reply to a question* ☞ Look at the note at **answer**.

☆ **re·ply**[2] /rɪ'plaɪ/ *noun* [C,U] (*pl.* **re·plies**) (an) answer: *Alison nodded in reply to my question.* ∘ *How many replies did you get to your ad?*

☆ **re·port**[1] /rɪ'pɔrt/ *verb* **1** [I,T] **report (on sb/sth)(to sb/sth); report sth (to sb)** to say or write what you have seen, heard, done, etc.: *All accidents must be reported to the police.* ∘ *Several people reported having seen the boy.* ∘ *Several people reported that they had seen the boy.* **2** [I,T] (in a newspaper or on the television or radio) to write or speak about sth that has happened: *Kate reported on the events in China for the network news.* ∘ *The strike was not reported in the newspapers.* **3** [T] **report sb (to sb) (for sth)** to tell a person in authority about sth wrong that sb has done: *She was reported to the principal for smoking.* **4** [I] **report (to sb/sth) (for sth)** to tell sb in authority that you have arrived in a place: *All visitors must report to the school office.* ∘ *Team members reported for their first practice session today.*

☆ **re·port**[2] /rɪ'pɔrt/ *noun* [C] a written or spoken description of what you have seen, heard, done, studied, etc.: *a report of an earthquake in California* ∘ *newspaper reports* ∘ *Your assignment is to write a report on the state's economy.* ∘ *a book report* (= about a book that you have read) ∘ *an eyewitness report* (= from the person who saw what happened)

re'port card *noun* [C] a written statement about the work of a student: *He had four A's and two B's on his report card.*

re·port·ed·ly /rɪ'pɔrtədli/ *adv.* according to what people say or what has been reported: *The mayor was taken to the hospital after reportedly suffering chest pains.*

re,ported 'speech (*also* **indirect speech**) *noun* [U] (*grammar*) reporting what sb said earlier, not using the actual words

☞ For example, Tim's words were, *"I'll call back later."* In reported speech this becomes *"Tim said that he would call back later."*

☆ **re·port·er** /rɪ'pɔrtər/ *noun* [C] a person who writes about the news in a newspaper or speaks about it on television or on the radio ☞ Look at **journalist**.

☆ **rep·re·sent** /ˌrɛprɪ'zɛnt/ *verb* [T] **1** to be a picture, sign, example, etc. of sb/sth: *The yellow lines on the map represent gravel roads.* ∘ *an abstract painting that represents pain* ∘ *Which sound does this phonetic symbol represent?* **2** to describe sb/sth in a particular way: *Susan is represented as a very ordinary*

person in the book. **3** to be equal to: *A 3% raise represents a drop in real income if you take inflation into account.* **4** to act or speak in the place of sb else; to be the representative of a group or country: *You will need an attorney to represent you in court.* ∘ *The ambassador represented the President at the funeral.*

☆ **rep·re·sen·ta·tion** /ˌrɛprɪzɛn'teɪʃn; -zən-/ *noun* **1** [U] representing or being represented: *Minority groups are demanding better representation in Congress.* **2** [C] (*formal*) a picture, sign, etc. of sb/sth

☆ **rep·re·sen·ta·tive**[1] /ˌrɛprɪ'zɛntətɪv/ *noun* [C] **1 Representative** (*abbr.* **Rep.**) a member of the House of Representatives in the U.S. Congress, or of a similar group in the government of a particular state **2** a person who has been chosen to act or speak for sb else or for a group **3** (*formal*) = REP

☆ **rep·re·sen·ta·tive**[2] /ˌrɛprɪ'zɛntətɪv/ *adj.* **representative (of sb/sth)** typical of a larger group to which it belongs: *Tonight's audience is not representative of the entire nation.* ∘ *a representative sample of the student population* ☞ The opposite is **unrepresentative**.

re·press /rɪ'prɛs/ *verb* [T] **1** to prevent an action or a protest **2** to control an emotion or to try to prevent it from being shown or felt —**re·pres·sion** /rɪ'prɛʃn/ *noun* [U]: *memories of political repression in Eastern Europe*

re·pressed /rɪ'prɛst/ *adj.* **1** (used about a person) not able to show feelings, especially about sex **2** (used about an emotion) that you do not show

re·pres·sive /rɪ'prɛsɪv/ *adj.* allowing very little freedom: *a repressive government*

re·prieve /rɪ'priv/ *noun* [C] an act of stopping or delaying the punishment of a prisoner who has been condemned to death: *to grant sb a last-minute reprieve*

rep·ri·mand /'rɛprəmænd/ *verb* [T] **reprimand sb (for sth)** to tell sb officially that he/she has done sth wrong —**rep·ri·mand** *noun* [C]: *a severe reprimand*

re·print /'riprɪnt/ *noun* [C] a copy of sth, especially a photograph or a magazine article: *I'd like to get two reprints of this picture.*

re·pri·sal /rɪ'praɪzl/ *noun* [C,U] punishment, especially by military force, for harm that one group of people did to another: *The army carried out reprisals on the village that had sheltered the rebels.* ∘ *Civilian targets were bombed in reprisal.*

re·proach /rɪ'proʊtʃ/ *noun* [U] (*formal*) blame or criticism: *His behavior is beyond reproach* (= cannot be criticized).

☆ **re·pro·duce** /ˌriprə'dus/ *verb* **1** [T] to produce a copy of sth: *It is very hard to reproduce a natural environment in the laboratory.* **2** [I,T] (used about people, animals and plants) to produce young: *Fish reproduce by laying eggs.*

ər	ɪr	ɛr	ɑr	ɔr	ʊr	ʒ	h	ŋ
bird	near	hair	car	north	tour	vision	hat	sing

☆ **re·pro·duc·tion** /ˌriprəˈdʌkʃn/ *noun* **1** [U] the act or process of reproducing or being reproduced: *The sound reproduction on a CD is better than on a cassette.* ○ *sexual reproduction* **2** [C] a copy of a painting, etc.: *That painting is a reproduction, not an original.*

re·pro·duc·tive /ˌriprəˈdʌktɪv/ *adj.* connected with the production of young animals, plants, etc.: *the male reproductive organs*

rep·tile /ˈreptaɪl; -tl/ *noun* [C] an animal, such as a snake or a crocodile, that has rough skin, lays eggs, and whose body temperature changes with the temperature around it

☆ **re·pub·lic** /rɪˈpʌblɪk/ *noun* [C] a country that has an elected government and is not ruled by a king or queen: *the Republic of Ireland*

☆ **re·pub·li·can** /rɪˈpʌblɪkən/ *adj.* **1** Republican connected with the Republican Party of the United States: *Republican Congressmen* **2** connected with or supporting a republic

☆ **Re·pub·li·can** /rɪˈpʌblɪkən/ *noun* [C] (*abbr.* **R**) a member or supporter of the Republican Party of the United States

☆ **the Re·publican Party** *noun* [sing.] one of the two main political parties in the United States

> ☞ The other main party is the Democratic Party, whose members are called **Democrats**. Look at the note at **White House**.

re·pul·sive /rɪˈpʌlsɪv/ *adj.* that causes a strong feeling of dislike; disgusting

rep·u·ta·ble /ˈrepyəṭəbl/ *adj.* that is known to be good: *Make sure you take your car to a reputable mechanic.* ☞ Look at **disreputable**.

☆ **rep·u·ta·tion** /ˌrepyəˈteɪʃn/ *noun* [C] **reputation (for sth)** the opinion that people in general have about what sb/sth is like: *to have a good/bad reputation* ○ *The restaurant has a reputation for serving some of the finest food in the city.* ○ *an international reputation* ○ *She began to make her reputation as a novelist in the 1960s.*

re·put·ed /rɪˈpyuṭəd/ *adj.* generally said to be sth, although it is not certain: *He's reputed to earn more than $1 million a year.* ○ *a reputed gang leader* —**re·put·ed·ly** *adv.*

☆ **re·quest¹** /rɪˈkwest/ *noun* [C] **request (for sth/that…)** an act of asking for sth: *a request for help* ○ *to make an official request* ○ *to grant/turn down a request* ○ *The judge denied the attorney's request that Nelson be released from jail.* ☞ Look at the grammar note at **recommend**.

IDM **at sb's request/at the request of sb** because sb asked for it: *This report was prepared at the request of the Millville School Board.*

on/upon request if you ask: *Nonsmoking rooms are available on request.*

☆ **re·quest²** /rɪˈkwest/ *verb* [T] **request sth (from/of sb); request that…** (*formal*) to ask

for sth: *to request a brochure from a resort* ○ *We request that all passengers remain seated.*
☞ **Request** is more formal than **ask**. Look at the grammar note at **recommend**.

☆ **re·quire** /rɪˈkwaɪər/ *verb* [T] **1** to need: *Please contact us if you require further information.* ○ *a situation that requires tact and diplomacy* ☞ **Require** is more formal than **need**. **2** **require sth; require that…** (often passive) to demand or order sth: *Passengers are required by law to wear seat belts.* ○ *State law requires that all drivers have adequate auto insurance.* ☞ Look at the grammar note at **recommend**.

☆ **re·quire·ment** /rɪˈkwaɪərmənt/ *noun* [C] something that you need or that is demanded: *I'm sorry, but you do not meet the requirements for the job that was advertised.* ○ *college entrance requirements*

re·run /ˈriːrʌn/ *noun* [C] (*informal*) a television program that is being shown again: *"Is there anything good on TV tonight?" "No, just reruns."*

☆ **res·cue¹** /ˈreskyu/ *verb* [T] **rescue sb/sth (from sb/sth)** to save sb/sth from a situation that is dangerous or unpleasant: *to rescue sb from drowning* ○ *You rescued me from an embarrassing situation.* —**res·cu·er** *noun* [C]

☆ **res·cue²** /ˈreskyu/ *noun* [C,U] an act of rescuing or the state of being rescued: *The attempted rescue of the mountain climber failed when snow began to fall.*

IDM **come to the/sb's rescue** to try to help or rescue sb: *She was attacked on the street and no one came to her rescue.*

☆ **re·search¹** /ˈrisərtʃ; rɪˈsərtʃ/ *noun* [U] **research (into/on sth)** a detailed and careful study of sth to find out more information about it: *Bob is doing research into the practical applications of solar power.* ○ *scientific, medical, historical, etc. research* ○ *Market research has shown that many people now prefer low-fat foods.*

☆ **re·search²** /rɪˈsərtʃ; ˈrisərtʃ/ *verb* [I,T] to study sth carefully and in detail: *Scientists are still researching the possible causes of so many cases of childhood cancer in the area.* —**re·search·er** *noun* [C]

re·sem·ble /rɪˈzembl/ *verb* [T] to be or look like sb/sth else: *Laura closely resembles her brother.* —**re·sem·biance** /rɪˈzembləns/ *noun* [C,U] **resemblance (between A and B); resemblance (to sth)** [C]: *a family resemblance* [U]: *The movie bears no resemblance to the novel* (= it is very different).

re·sent /rɪˈzent/ *verb* [T] to feel angry about sth because you think it is unfair: *Louise bitterly resented being treated differently from the men.* —**re·sent·ful** /-fl/ *adj.*: *William felt very resentful at being criticized unfairly.* —**re·sent·ment** *noun* [sing., U]: *Do you feel any resentment toward her new husband?*

tʃ	dʒ	v	θ	ð	s	z	ʃ
chin	June	van	thin	then	so	zoo	she

R

☆ **res·er·va·tion** /ˌrɛzərˈveɪʃn/ *noun* **1** [C] an arrangement in which a seat, table, room, etc. is kept available for you to use: *I made a reservation for a table for two in the name of Morgan.* ○ *Do you have a reservation?* **2** [C,U] a feeling of doubt about sth (such as a plan or an idea): *I still have some reservations about Jerry's proposal.* **3** [C] an area of land where the U.S. government forced Native Americans to live in the past, and where some Native Americans still live

☆ **re·serve**¹ /rɪˈzərv/ *verb* [T] **reserve sth (for sb/sth)** **1** to arrange for a seat, table, room, etc. to be kept available for you to use: *I reserved a table in the nonsmoking section.* **2** to keep sth for a special reason or to use at a later time: *The parking lot is reserved for hotel guests only.*

re·serve² /rɪˈzərv/ *noun* **1** [C, usually pl.] something that you keep for a special reason or to use at a later date: *The Middle East still has huge oil reserves.* **2** [C] an area of land where the plants, animals, etc. are protected by law: *a nature reserve* **3** [U] the quality of being shy or keeping your feelings hidden: *It took a long time to break down her reserve and get her to relax.* **4 the reserve** [sing.] (*also* **the reserves** [plural]) extra military forces that a country can use in addition to the regular army, etc. in an emergency

IDM **in reserve** that you keep and do not use unless you need to: *Keep some money in reserve for emergencies.*

re·served /rɪˈzərvd/ *adj.* shy and keeping your feelings hidden: *Fred is very reserved until you get to know him well.*

res·er·voir /ˈrɛzərvwɑr; -vwɔr/ *noun* [C] a large lake where water to be used in a town or city is stored

re·side /rɪˈzaɪd/ *verb* [I] (*formal*) **reside (in/at…)** to have your home in or at a particular place

res·i·dence /ˈrɛzədəns/ *noun* **1** [C] (*formal*) the place where sb lives: *The President's official residence is the White House.* **2** [U] the state of having your home in a particular place: *The family applied for permanent residence in the United States.*

ˈresidence hall *noun* [C] (*formal*) = DORMITORY

☆ **res·i·dent** /ˈrɛzədənt/ *noun* [C] **1** a person who lives in a place: *Local residents have complained about the smell from the factory.* **2** a doctor who has finished medical school and is continuing his/her training in a hospital

☆ **res·i·den·tial** /ˌrɛzəˈdɛnʃl/ *adj.* **1** (used about a place or an area) that has houses rather than offices, large stores or factories: *residential suburbs* **2** where you live or stay: *This home provides residential care for the elderly.*

res·i·due /ˈrɛzədu/ *noun* [C,U, usually sing.] what remains of sth after the main part is taken or used

☆ **re·sign** /rɪˈzaɪn/ *verb* **1** [I,T] **resign (from sth)** to leave your job or position: *She's threatening to resign if she doesn't get a raise.* ○ *He resigned as chairman of the committee.* ○ *I wonder why she resigned from her job.* **2** [T] **resign yourself to sth/doing sth** to accept sth that is bad but that cannot be changed: *Larry resigned himself to the fact that she was not coming back to him.*

☆ **res·ig·na·tion** /ˌrɛzɪgˈneɪʃn/ *noun* **1** [C,U] **resignation (from sth)** a letter or statement that says you want to leave your job or position: *to hand in your resignation* ○ *a letter of resignation* **2** [U] the state of accepting sth bad that you cannot change

re·signed /rɪˈzaɪnd/ *adj.* accepting sth that is bad but that cannot be changed: *a resigned sigh*

IDM **be resigned to sth/doing sth** to accept sth that is bad but that cannot be changed: *Ben was resigned to the fact that he would never be a pro basketball player.*

re·sil·ient /rɪˈzɪlyənt/ *adj.* strong enough to recover quickly from damage, illness, a shock, change, etc. —**re·sil·ience** /-əns/ *noun* [U]

☆ **re·sist** /rɪˈzɪst/ *verb* [I,T] **1** to try to stop sth from happening or to stop sb from doing sth; to fight against sb/sth: *The unions are resisting the proposal to move the factory to Mexico.* ○ *If the enemy attacks, we will not resist.* ○ *to resist arrest* **2** to stop yourself from having or doing sth that you want to have or do: *The cake looked so delicious that I couldn't resist it.* ○ *I couldn't resist opening my present.* ○ *"Are you coming to the party?" "How could I resist?"*

☆ **re·sis·tance** /rɪˈzɪstəns/ *noun* [U] **1** **resistance (to sb/sth)** trying to stop sth from happening or to stop sb from doing sth; fighting against sb/sth: *The government troops overcame the resistance of the rebel army.* ○ *There is strong resistance to the plan for a new freeway in the area.* **2** **resistance (to sth)** the power in a person's body not to be affected by disease: *People with AIDS have very little resistance to infection.*

re·sis·tant /rɪˈzɪstənt/ *adj.* **resistant (to sth)** **1** not wanting sth and trying to prevent it from happening: *resistant to change* **2** not harmed by sth: *This watch is water-resistant.*

☆ **res·o·lu·tion** /ˌrɛzəˈluʃn/ *noun* **1** [U] the quality of being firm and determined **2** [C] a firm decision to do or not to do sth: *Rose made a New Year's resolution to quit smoking.* **3** [C] a formal decision that is made after a vote by a group of people: *The UN resolution condemned the invasion.*

re·solve /rɪˈzɑlv/ *verb* (*formal*) **1** [T] to find a solution to a problem: *Most of the difficulties have been resolved.* **2** [I,T] to decide sth and be determined not to change your mind: *Ray re-*

i	ɪ	ɛ	æ	ɑ	ɔ	ʌ	ʊ	u
see	sit	ten	cat	hot	saw	cup	put	too

solved never to let the same thing happen again. **3** [I,T] **resolve (to do sth)**; **resolve (that ...)** to make a formal decision after a vote by a group of people

☆ **re·sort**[1] /rɪˈzɔrt/ *verb* [I] **resort to sth** to do or use sth bad or unpleasant because you feel you have no choice: *People who owe huge amounts of money have had to resort to selling their houses.*

☆ **re·sort**[2] /rɪˈzɔrt/ *noun* [C] a place in the country, in the mountains, near the ocean, etc. where people can stay when they are on vacation and do activities such as swimming and golf: *a ski resort*

IDM (as) a last resort ⇨ LAST[1]

re·sound·ing /rɪˈzaʊndɪŋ/ *adj.* (only *before* a noun) **1** very loud: *resounding cheers* **2** (used about a success, etc.) very great: *a resounding victory*

☆ **re·source** /ˈrisɔrs; rɪˈsɔrs/ *noun* [C, usually pl.] something that a person, country, etc. has or can use: *Russia is rich in natural resources such as oil and minerals.* ○ *The video is an excellent resource for teachers.* ☞ Look also at **human resources**.

re·source·ful /rɪˈsɔrsfl/ *adj.* good at finding ways of doing things

☆ **re·spect**[1] /rɪˈspɛkt/ *noun* **1** [U] **respect (for sb/sth)** the feeling that you have when you admire or have a very high opinion of sb/sth: *I don't have much respect for politicians.* ○ *to win/lose sb's respect* ☞ Look at **self-respect**. **2** [U] **respect (for sb/sth)** the quality of being polite to sb: *We should all treat older people with more respect.* ☞ The opposite is **disrespect**. **3** [U] **respect (for sb/sth)** care for or attention to sb/sth: *The military regime shows little respect for human rights.* **4** [C] a detail or point: *In what respects do you think things have changed in the last ten years?* ○ *Her performance was outstanding in every respect.*

IDM with respect to sth (*formal*) about or concerning: *I am writing with respect to your recent letter.*

pay your respects ⇨ PAY[2]

☆ **re·spect**[2] /rɪˈspɛkt/ *verb* [T] **1 respect sb/sth (for sth)** to admire or have a high opinion of sb/sth: *I respect him for his honesty.* **2** to show care for or pay attention to sb/sth: *We should respect other people's cultures and values.* ○ *to respect sb's wishes* (= do what they want)

re·spect·a·ble /rɪˈspɛktəbl/ *adj.* **1** considered by society to be good, proper or correct: *a respectable, hard-working family* ○ *Wear something respectable to the party!* **2** fairly good or large: *a respectable salary* —**re·spect·a·bil·i·ty** /rɪˌspɛktəˈbɪləti/ *noun* [U]

re·spect·ful /rɪˈspɛktfl/ *adj.* **respectful (to/ toward sb)** showing respect[1](2) or politeness toward sb/sth: *The crowd listened in respectful silence.* ☞ The opposite is **disrespectful**. —**re·spect·ful·ly** *adv.*

re·spec·tive /rɪˈspɛktɪv/ *adj.* (only *before* a noun) belonging separately to each of the people who have been mentioned: *After lunch, we all went back to our respective offices.*

re·spec·tive·ly /rɪˈspɛktɪvli/ *adv.* in the same order that sb/sth was mentioned: *German and Italian courses are offered in Munich and Rome respectively.*

res·pi·ra·tion /ˌrɛspəˈreɪʃn/ *noun* [U] (*formal*) the act of breathing —**res·pi·ra·to·ry** /ˈrɛsprəˌtɔri/ *adj.*

res·pite /ˈrɛspət/ *noun* [sing., U] **respite (from sth)** a short period of rest from sth that is difficult or unpleasant: *There was a brief respite from the fighting.*

☆ **re·spond** /rɪˈspɑnd/ *verb* [I] **1 respond (to sb/sth) (with/by sth)** (*formal*) to say or do sth as an answer or reaction to sth: *I wrote to them last week, but they haven't responded yet.* ○ *He responded to my question with a nod.* ○ *The administration has responded to criticism by promising to spend more on education.* ☞ **Respond** is more formal than **answer** or **reply**. **2 respond (to sb/sth)** to have or show a good or quick reaction to sb/sth: *The patient did not respond well to the new treatment.*

☆ **re·sponse** /rɪˈspɑns/ *noun* [C,U] **response (to sb/sth)** an answer or reaction to sb/sth: *I've sent my resume to 20 companies, but I haven't received any responses yet.* ○ *Congress acted in response to economic pressure.* ○ *He knocked on the door, but there was no response.* ○ *Sharon Stone's new movie has received a positive response.*

☆ **re·spon·si·bil·i·ty** /rɪˌspɑnsəˈbɪləti/ *noun* (*pl.* **re·spon·si·bil·i·ties**) **1** [U] **responsibility (for sb/sth)** the state of being responsible; having to make decisions about sth so that you are blamed if sth goes wrong: *The new job means taking on more responsibility.* ○ *I refuse to take responsibility if anything goes wrong.* ○ *A terrorist group claimed responsibility for planting the bomb.* **2** [U] the quality of being sensible: *I wish you would show a little more responsibility.* **3** [C] a job or duty that you must do: *It is John's responsibility to make sure the orders are sent out on time.* ○ *I feel that I have a responsibility to help them – after all, they did help me.* ○ *the responsibilities of parenthood* ○ *The kids are my responsibility* (= I am responsible for them).

☆ **re·spon·si·ble** /rɪˈspɑnsəbl/ *adj.* **1** (not *before* a noun) **responsible (for sb/sth)**; **responsible (for doing sth)** having the job or duty of doing or taking care of sb/sth (so that you are blamed if sth goes wrong): *The school is responsible for the safety of the children between 9 a.m. and 3 p.m.* ○ *The manager is responsible for making sure the store is run according to company policy.* **2** (not *before* a noun) **responsible (for sth)** being the cause of or to blame for sth: *Who was responsible for the accident?* ○

If anything goes wrong, the boss will hold me responsible! **3** (not before a noun) **responsible (to sb/sth)** having to report to sb/sth with authority or in a higher position about what you have been doing: *Members of Congress are responsible to their voters.* **4** (used about a person) that you can trust to behave well and sensibly: *All children must be accompanied by a responsible adult.* ☞ The opposite is **irresponsible**.

☆ **re·spon·si·bly** /rɪˈspɑnsəbli/ *adv.* in a sensible and responsible (4) way: *I hope you will behave responsibly while I am out.*

re·spon·sive /rɪˈspɑnsɪv/ *adj.* paying attention to sb/sth and reacting in a suitable or positive way: *The company has achieved success by being responsive to sudden changes in the market.*

☆ **rest¹** /rɛst/ *verb* **1** [I] to relax, sleep or do nothing after a period of activity or because of illness: *We've been walking for hours. Let's rest here for a while.* ○ *The nurse said we couldn't visit him because he was resting.* **2** [T] to allow sb/sth to rest (1): *Your knee will get better if you rest it as much as you can.* **3** [I,T] **rest (sth) on/against sth** to place sth in a position where it is supported by sth else; to be in such a position: *She rested her head on his shoulder and went to sleep.*

PHRV **rest on/upon sb/sth** to depend or be based on sth: *The whole theory rests on a very simple idea.*

rest with sb to be sb's responsibility: *We can make some recommendations, but the final decision rests with the manager.*

☆ **rest²** /rɛst/ *noun* **1 the rest (of sth)** [sing.] the part that is left: *We ate lunch and spent the rest of the day at the beach.* ○ *If you don't want the rest, I'll eat it.* ○ *She takes no interest in what happens in the rest of the world.* **2 the rest** [plural] the ones that are left; the others: *One of the questions was tough, but the rest were pretty easy.* ○ *They were the first people to arrive. The rest came later.* **3** [C,U] a period or the action of relaxing, sleeping or doing nothing: *I can't walk any farther! I need a rest.* ○ *Try not to worry now. Get some rest and think about it again tomorrow.*

IDM **at rest** (formal) not moving: *Do not open the door until the vehicle is at rest.*

come to (a) rest to stop moving: *The car crashed through a fence and came to rest in a field.*

put sth to rest to show that a belief, an idea, etc. is not true: *We want to put to rest people's fears about the new power plant.*

☆ **res·tau·rant** /ˈrɛstrɑnt; -tərɑnt; -tərənt/ *noun* [C] a place where you can buy and eat a meal: *a fast-food restaurant* ○ *Andy took me out to lunch at a Chinese restaurant.* ○ *She works as a waitress in a local restaurant.* ☞ Look at **cafe** and **cafeteria**.

rest·less /ˈrɛstləs/ *adj.* unable to relax or sit still because you are bored, nervous or impatient: *The kids always get restless on long car trips.* —**rest·less·ly** *adv.*

☆ **re·store** /rɪˈstɔr/ *verb* [T] **restore sb/sth (to sb/sth)** **1** to bring sth back into existence or use, or to put sb/sth back into a previous condition or position: *The police have restored law and order following the riots.* ○ *Winning their last two games has restored the team's confidence.* ○ *The former leader has been restored to power.* **2** to put sth (a building, a painting, a piece of furniture, etc.) back into a condition that is as close as possible to its original condition: *I'm restoring my grandmother's antique dresser.* —**res·to·ra·tion** /ˌrɛstəˈreɪʃn/ *noun* [U]: *a campaign for the restoration of democracy*

re·strain /rɪˈstreɪn/ *verb* [T] **restrain sb/sth (from sth/from doing sth)** to keep sb or sth under control; to prevent sb or sth from doing sth: *Can't you restrain your dog?* ○ *I had to restrain myself from saying something nasty.*

re·strained /rɪˈstreɪnd/ *adj.* not showing strong feelings; calm

re·straint /rɪˈstreɪnt/ *noun* **1** [U] the quality of behaving in a calm or moderate way: *It took a lot of restraint on my part not to hit him.* **2** [C] **restraint (on sb/sth)** a limit or control on sth: *Are there any restraints on what newspapers are allowed to publish?* **3** [C] a piece of equipment in a car, plane, etc. that helps to hold sb/sth in place: *The use of child safety restraints is required in automobiles.*

☆ **re·strict** /rɪˈstrɪkt/ *verb* [T] to limit the number, amount, size, freedom, etc. of sb/sth: *I'm trying to restrict myself to two cups of coffee a day.* ○ *Having small children tends to restrict your freedom.* ○ *There is a plan to restrict the use of cars on the college campus.*

☆ **re·strict·ed** /rɪˈstrɪktəd/ *adj.* controlled or limited in some way: *The junior tournament is restricted to players under age 16.* ○ *The land around the military base is a restricted area.*

☆ **re·stric·tion** /rɪˈstrɪkʃn/ *noun* **restriction (on sth)** **1** [U] the act of limiting the freedom of sb/sth: *He is opposed to any restriction on people's right to free speech.* **2** [C] something (sometimes a rule or law) that limits the number, amount, size, freedom, etc. of sb/sth: *parking restrictions in the downtown area* ○ *The government has imposed restrictions on the number of immigrants permitted to enter this country.*

re·stric·tive /rɪˈstrɪktɪv/ *adj.* limiting; preventing people from doing what they want

☆ **rest·room** /ˈrɛstrum/ *noun* [C] a room with toilets in it in a public building ☞ Look also at **men's room, ladies' room** and at the note at **toilet**.

☆ **re·sult¹** /rɪˈzʌlt/ *noun* **1** [C,U] **result (of sth)** something that happens because of sth else;

ər	ɪr	ɛr	ɑr	ɔr	ʊr	ʒ	h	ŋ
bird	near	hair	car	north	tour	vision	hat	sing

the final situation at the end of a series of actions: *The result of our argument was that we never spoke to each other again.* ○ *The traffic was very heavy, and as a result, I arrived late.* ○ *This wasn't really the result that I was expecting.* **2** [C,U] a good effect of an action: *He has tried very hard to find a job, but with no result.* ○ *The treatment is beginning to show results.* **3** [C] the score or final position at the end of a game, competition or election: *Stay tuned for today's playoff results.* ○ *The results of the contest will be published next week.* ○ *The result of the election was a gain for the Democrats in the House* **4** [C] something that is discovered by a medical test: *I'm still waiting for the result of my X-ray.*

☆ **re·sult²** /rɪˈzʌlt/ *verb* [I] **result (from sth)** to happen or exist because of sth: *Ninety percent of the deaths resulted from injuries to the head.* **PHRV** **result in sth** to cause sth to happen or exist; to produce as an effect: *There has been an accident on the freeway, resulting in long delays.*

re·sume /rɪˈzum/ *verb* [I,T] to begin again or continue after a pause or interruption: *The meeting resumed after a short break.* ○ *After the birth of the baby, she resumed her career.* —**re·sump·tion** /rɪˈzʌmpʃn/ *noun* [sing., U] (*formal*): *a resumption of diplomatic relations between the two countries*

☆ **ré·su·mé** (*also* **re·su·me**) /ˈrɛzəmeɪ; ˌrɛzəˈmeɪ/ *noun* [C] a written account of your education and work experience, often used when you are applying for a new job: *Applicants should send a résumé and cover letter to the following address:...*

res·ur·rect /ˌrɛzəˈrɛkt/ *verb* [T] to bring sth that has not been used or has not existed for a long time back into use or existence: *From time to time, they resurrect classic TV programs and show them again on cable.*

res·ur·rec·tion /ˌrɛzəˈrɛkʃn/ *noun* **1 the Resurrection** [sing.] (in the Christian religion) the return to life of Jesus Christ **2** [U] the act of resurrecting sth: *the resurrection of the nation's auto industry*

re·sus·ci·tate /rɪˈsʌsəteɪt/ *verb* [T] to bring sb who has stopped breathing back to life: *All efforts to resuscitate the patient failed.* —**re·sus·ci·ta·tion** /rɪˌsʌsəˈteɪʃn/ *noun* [U]

☆ **re·tail¹** /ˈriteɪl/ *noun* [U] the selling of goods to the public in stores, etc. (for personal use, not to be sold again): *the recommended retail price* ☞ Look at **wholesale**.

re·tail² /ˈriteɪl/ *verb* [I] **retail at/for sth** to be for sale in a store at a particular price: *This camera retails for $99.95.*

re·tail·er /ˈriteɪlər/ *noun* [C] a person or company that sells products in a store

re·tain /rɪˈteɪn/ *verb* [T] (*formal*) to keep or continue to have; not to lose: *Despite all her problems, she has managed to retain a sense of*

humor. ○ *The Democrats retained control of the Senate after the election.* ○ *The house has retained much of its original character.* ○ *These cups retain the heat.* ☞ The noun is **retention**.

re·tal·i·ate /rɪˈtælieɪt/ *verb* [I] **retaliate (against sb/sth)** to react to sth bad that sb does to you by doing sth bad in return: *They have announced that they will retaliate against anyone who attacks their country.* —**re·tal·i·a·tion** /rɪˌtæliˈeɪʃn/ *noun* [U] **retaliation (against sb/sth); retaliation (for sth)**: *He was shot in retaliation for his attack on a gang member.*

re·tard·ed /rɪˈtardəd/ *adj.* (*old-fashioned*) (used about people) less advanced mentally than other people of the same age

☞ This word is often considered offensive nowadays. If a person has difficulties in learning things, we can say that he/she has **special needs**, has a **learning disability** or is **mentally disabled.**

re·ten·tion /rɪˈtɛnʃn/ *noun* [U] the act of keeping sth or of being kept: *Many experts are against the retention of this law.*

re·think /ˌriˈθɪŋk/ *verb* [I,T] (*p.t., p.p.* **rethought** /-ˈθɔt/) to think about sth again because you probably need to change it: *The administration has been forced to rethink its economic policy.*

☆ **re·tire** /rɪˈtaɪr/ *verb* [I] **retire (from sth)** to leave your job and stop working, usually because you have reached a certain age: *She's worried that she won't have enough money to live on when she retires.* ○ *Michael Stich retired from professional tennis when he was still a young man.* ○ *He retired as the team's coach in 1995.*

☆ **re·tired** /rɪˈtaɪərd/ *adj.* having stopped work permanently, usually because of having reached a certain age: *a retired teacher* ○ *He's retired, but his wife is still working.*

re·tir·ee /rɪˌtaɪəˈri/ *noun* [C] a person who is retired

☆ **re·tire·ment** /rɪˈtaɪərmənt/ *noun* **1** [C,U] the act of stopping or being forced to stop working permanently, usually because of reaching a certain age: *Is there a mandatory retirement age at your company?* ○ *There have been a number of retirements in our department this year.* ○ *She decided to take early retirement.* ○ *The former world champion has announced his retirement* (= that he is not going to play, etc. again). **2** [sing., U] the situation or period after retiring from work: *We all wish you a long and happy retirement.*

re·tort /rɪˈtɔrt/ *verb* [T] to reply quickly to what sb says, in an angry or amusing way: *"Who asked you for your opinion?" she retorted.* ○ *He retorted that there was no such thing as an honest politician.* —**re·tort** *noun* [C]: *an angry retort*

tʃ	dʒ	v	θ	ð	s	z	ʃ
chin	**J**une	**v**an	**th**in	**th**en	**s**o	**z**oo	**sh**e

re·trace /riˈtreɪs/ *verb* [T] to repeat a past trip, series of events, etc.: *I retraced my steps* (= I went back the way I had come) *in an attempt to find my wallet.*

☆ **re·treat**[1] /rɪˈtrit/ *verb* [I] **1** (of an army, etc.) to move backward in order to leave a battle or in order not to become involved in a battle: *The general gave an order to retreat from the area.* ☞ Look at **advance**. **2** to move backward; to go to a safe or private place: *Firefighters were forced to retreat by the intense heat.* ○ *(figurative) She seems to retreat into a world of her own sometimes.*

☆ **re·treat**[2] /rɪˈtrit/ *noun* **1** [C,U] the act of retreating: *The invading forces are now in retreat.* ○ *the candidate's retreat from his original position* **2** [C] a private place where you can go when you want to be quiet or to rest

re·tri·al /ˈritraɪl; ˌriˈtraɪl/ *noun* [C] a process in which a case is presented again in a court of law, usually because there was a problem the first time

ret·ri·bu·tion /ˌrɛtrəˈbyuʃn/ *noun* [U] **retribution (against sb) (for sth)** (*formal*) punishment for a crime or sth that you have done: *The witnesses did not want their real names to be used for fear of retribution.*

re·trieve /rɪˈtriv/ *verb* [T] **1 retrieve sth (from sb/sth)** to get sth back from the place where it was left or lost: *The police retrieved the body from the river.* **2** (*computing*) to find information that has been stored: *The computer can retrieve all the data about a particular customer.* —**re·triev·al** /-vl/ *noun* [U]: *Retrieval of the bodies from the wreckage of the plane took several hours.*

ret·ro·ac·tive /ˌrɛtrouˈæktɪv/ *adj.* (used about laws, decisions, payments, etc.) applying to the past, as well as to the present and the future: *a tax increase that is retroactive to January 1* —**ret·ro·ac·tive·ly** *adv.*

ret·ro·spect /ˈrɛtrəspɛkt/ *noun*
IDM **in retrospect** thinking about sth that happened in the past (and often seeing it differently from the way you saw it at the time): *In retrospect, I can see what a stupid mistake it was.*

☆ **re·turn**[1] /rɪˈtɚn/ *verb* **1** [I] **return (to…)**; **return (from…)** to come or go back to a place: *I will be returning to this country in six months.* ○ *When did you return from Japan?* ○ *He left his hometown when he was 18 and never returned.* ☞ **Return** is more formal than **come/go back**. **2** [I] **return (to sth)** to start doing a previous activity or talking about a previous subject again: *The strike is over and they will be returning to work on Monday.* ○ *We'll return to this subject in next week's lecture.* **3** [I] **return (to sth/to doing sth)** to come or go back to a previous situation or condition: *Telephone services should return to normal soon.* **4** [I] to come back; to happen again: *If the pain re-*

turns, make another appointment to see me.* **5** [T] **return sth (to sb/sth)** to give, send, put or take sth back: *I stopped loaning him things because he never returns them.* ○ *If that shirt doesn't fit your husband, you can always return it* (= take it back to the store where you bought it). **6** [T] to react to sth that somebody does, says or feels by doing, saying, or feeling sth similar: *I called them several times and left messages, but they haven't returned any of my calls.* ○ *Thanks a lot for helping me – I hope I can return the favor sometime.*

☆ **re·turn**[2] /rɪˈtɚn/ *noun* **1** [sing.] **a return (to/ from…)** the act of coming or going back to a place, a previous activity, a previous situation or a previous condition: *the return of warm summer weather* ○ *a former leader's return to power* ○ *Our return flight is at 3 o'clock in the morning.* **2** [U] the act of giving, sending, putting or taking sth back: *I demand the return of my passport immediately.* **3** [C] an official form that you send to the government with information about how much money you have earned and how much tax you must pay: *Federal income tax returns must be filed by April 15.* **4** [C,U] (*also* **returns** [plural]) the profit from a business or an investment: *They're not expecting any return on their new restaurant for at least a year.* ○ *This account offers high returns on your savings.* **5** [U] (*also* **enter**) (*computing*) the key on a computer that you press in order to begin writing on a new line or to tell the computer to do sth: *Type in your password and press return.*
IDM **in return (for sth)** as payment or in exchange (for sth); as a reaction to sth: *Please accept this gift in return for all your help.*

re·turn adˈdress *noun* [C] the address written on a letter or package of the person who sent it

re·un·ion /riˈyunyən/ *noun* **1** [C] a party or occasion when friends or colleagues meet again after they have not seen each other for a long time: *The college holds an annual reunion for alumni.* ○ *a family reunion* **2** [C,U] the act of coming together again after a separation: *The released hostages had an emotional reunion with their families at the airport.*

re·u·nite /ˌriyuˈnaɪt/ *verb* [I,T] **reunite (sb/sth) (with sb/sth)** to come together again; to cause sb/sth to come together again: *The original band members have reunited for a national tour.* ○ *The missing child was reunited with his parents.*

rev /rɛv/ *verb* [T] (**rev·ving**; **revved**) **rev sth (up)** to increase the speed of an engine (usually before driving the car): *Rev the engine for a while to warm it up.*

Rev. *abbr.* = REVEREND

☆ **re·veal** /rɪˈvil/ *verb* [T] **1 reveal sth (to sb)** to make sth known that was previously secret or

i	ɪ	ɛ	æ	ɑ	ɔ	ʌ	ʊ	u
see	sit	ten	cat	hot	saw	cup	put	too

unknown: *She revealed that she had serious financial problems.* ○ *He refused to reveal any names to the police.* **2** to allow sth to be seen that was previously hidden: *Close inspection of the photograph revealed the identity of the gunman.* ○ *In a moment, the curtains will open to reveal tonight's grand prize.*

re·veal·ing /rɪˈvilɪŋ/ *adj.* **1** allowing sth (facts previously unknown, secrets, etc.) to be known: *This book provides a revealing insight into the world of politics.* **2** allowing sth to be seen that is usually hidden: *a very revealing swimsuit*

rev·el /ˈrɛvl/ *verb*

PHRV **revel in sth/in doing sth** to enjoy sth very much: *He likes being famous and revels in the attention he gets.*

rev·e·la·tion /ˌrɛvəˈleɪʃn/ *noun* [C] something that is made known, that was previously secret or unknown (especially sth surprising): *This magazine is full of revelations about the private lives of famous people.*

re·venge /rɪˈvɛndʒ/ *noun* [U] something that you do to punish sb who has hurt you, made you suffer, etc.: *He made a fool of me and now I want revenge.* ○ *The attack was an act of revenge.*

IDM **take/get revenge (on sb) (for sth)** to punish sb in return for sth bad that he/she has done to you: *He wants to take revenge on the judge who sent him to prison.*

out of revenge (for sth); in revenge (for sth) as a way of punishing sb in return for sth bad he/she has done to you: *The shooting was in revenge for an attack on the drug dealer's family.*

☆ **rev·e·nue** /ˈrɛvənu/ *noun* [U, plural] income received by a government, company, etc.: *Revenue from income tax rose last year.* ○ *Oil revenues are a vital part of the country's economy.* ☞ Look also at **IRS**.

rev·er·ence /ˈrɛvərəns/ *noun* [U] a feeling of great respect: *She has great reverence for classical literature.*

Rev·er·end /ˈrɛvərənd; ˈrɛvrənd/ *adj.* (also *formal* **the Reverend**) (*abbr.* **Rev.**) the title of a Christian minister: *(the) Reverend Charles Gray*

re·ver·sal /rɪˈvɜrsl/ *noun* [C,U] the act of changing sth to the opposite; an occasion when sth changes to the opposite of what is usual or expected: *The administration insists that there will be no reversal of policy.* ○ *The decision announced yesterday was a complete reversal of last week's decision.* ○ *a reversal of roles* (= when each person does what the other person was doing)

☆ **re·verse¹** /rɪˈvɜrs/ *adj.* opposite to what is expected or has just been described: *In Brazil, the reverse situation is true.*

☆ **re·verse²** /rɪˈvɜrs/ *noun* **1** [sing.] **the reverse (of sth)** the complete opposite of the previous

statement or of what is expected: *This should have been a relaxing trip, but it was just the reverse.* **2** [U] the position of the gears in a car, etc. that makes it move backward: *Put the car in reverse and back into that parking space.* ☞ Look also at **drive²(4)**, **neutral²** and **park¹(4)**.

IDM **in reverse** in the opposite order, starting at the end and going backward to the beginning; in the opposite way of the previous direction

☆ **re·verse³** /rɪˈvɜrs/ *verb* [T] **1** to change a decision, a process, etc. to the opposite: *It's too late to reverse your decision now; you've already signed the contract.* ○ *Some experts say that exercise and good nutrition can reverse the early signs of aging.* ○ *to reverse a trend* **2** **reverse yourself** to change your opinion to the opposite: *The city council reversed itself and approved the proposal to build a new fire station.* **3** to put sth in the opposite position: *Writing is reversed in a mirror.* ○ *My husband and I have reversed roles – he stays home now and I go to work.*

re·vers·i·ble /rɪˈvɜrsəbl/ *adj.* **1** (used about clothes) that can be worn with either side on the outside: *a reversible coat* **2** that can be undone: *Some of the harmful effects of smoking may be reversible if you quit early enough.* ☞ The opposite for this sense is **irreversible**.

re·vert /rɪˈvɜrt/ *verb* [I] **revert (to sth)** to return to a previous state or to sth that you did previously: *The land will soon revert to jungle if it is not farmed.*

☆ **re·view¹** /rɪˈvyu/ *noun* **1** [C,U] the act of examining or considering sth again in order to decide whether changes are necessary: *There will be a review of your performance after the first six months.* ○ *The system is in need of review.* **2** [C] the act of looking back at sth in order to check, remember, or be clear about sth: *a review of the major events of the year* **3** [C] a newspaper or magazine article, or an item on television or radio, in which sb gives an opinion on a new book, movie, play, etc.: *The show got bad reviews.* ○ *a book review*

☆ **re·view²** /rɪˈvyu/ *verb* **1** [T] to examine or consider again in order to decide whether changes are necessary: *Your progress will be reviewed after one year.* **2** [I,T] to look at or think about sth again to make sure that you understand it, especially when preparing for a test: *Let's review what we've covered in this chapter so far.* **3** [T] to write an article or to talk on television or radio, giving an opinion on a new book, movie, play, etc.: *A movie critic reviews the latest releases.*

re·view·er /rɪˈvyuər/ *noun* [C] a person who writes reviews ¹(3) of books, movies, etc.

re·vise /rɪˈvaɪz/ *verb* [T] to make changes to sth in order to correct or improve it: *The book has been revised for this new edition.* ○ *a revised*

estimate of the cost of the project —**re·vi·sion** /rɪˈvɪʒn/ noun [C,U]: The whole system is in need of revision.

re·vi·tal·ize /ˌriˈvaɪtl̩ˌaɪz/ verb [T] to make sth stronger or more active: plans to revitalize inner-city neighborhoods

re·viv·al /rɪˈvaɪvl/ noun **1** [C,U] the act of becoming or making sth strong or popular again: economic revival ○ a revival of interest in traditional farming methods **2** [C] a new performance of a play that has not been performed for some time: a revival of a popular musical on Broadway

re·vive /rɪˈvaɪv/ verb [I,T] **1** to become or make sb/sth strong or healthy again; to come or to bring sb back to life or consciousness: Hopes have revived for an early end to the fighting. ○ I'm awfully tired, but I'm sure a cup of coffee will revive me. ○ Attempts were made to revive him, but he was already dead. **2** to become or make sth popular again; to begin to do or use sth again: Attendance at games has revived since the team started winning. ○ to revive an old custom

re·volt /rɪˈvoʊlt/ verb **1** [I] **revolt (against sb/sth)** to protest in a group (often violently) against the person or people in power: A group of generals revolted against the government. **2** [T] to make sb feel disgusted or sick: The sight and the smell revolted him. ☞ The noun for this meaning is **revulsion.** —**re·volt** noun [C,U]: The revolt was quickly put down by the army. What started as a small protest has turned into widespread revolt.

re·volt·ing /rɪˈvoʊltɪŋ/ adj. extremely bad; disgusting: a revolting smell of fish

☆ **rev·o·lu·tion** /ˌrɛvəˈluʃn/ noun **1** [C,U] changing or trying to change the political system by violent action, etc.: the French Revolution of 1789 ○ Student leaders are calling for revolution. **2** [C] **a revolution (in sth)** a complete change in methods, opinions, etc., often as a result of progress: a revolution in the treatment of diseases such as cancer ○ the Industrial Revolution **3** [C,U] a movement around sth; one complete turn around a central point (e.g. in a car engine): 400 revolutions per minute

rev·o·lu·tion·ar·y¹ /ˌrɛvəˈluʃn̩ˌɛri/ adj. **1** connected with or supporting political revolution: Revolutionary forces have attacked the country's capital. ○ the revolutionary leaders **2** producing great changes; very new and different: a revolutionary new method of treating cancer

rev·o·lu·tion·ar·y² /ˌrɛvəˈluʃn̩ˌɛri/ noun [C] (pl. **rev·o·lu·tion·ar·ies**) a person who takes part in and supports a revolution

the Revolutionary War noun [sing.] the war (1775-1783) in which the United States won its independence from Britain ☞ Look at the note at **White House.**

rev·o·lu·tion·ize /ˌrɛvəˈluʃn̩ˌaɪz/ verb [T] to change sth completely: a discovery that could revolutionize the treatment of mental illness

re·volve /rɪˈvɑlv/ verb [I] to move in a circle around a central point; to go around: The earth revolves around the sun.

PHRV **revolve around sb/sth** to have sth as the most important part: Her life revolves around her career.

re·volv·er /rɪˈvɑlvər/ noun [C] a type of small gun with a container for bullets that goes around ☞ Look at the note at **gun.**

re·vul·sion /rɪˈvʌlʃn/ noun [U] a feeling of disgust (because sth is extremely bad)

☆ **re·ward¹** /rɪˈwɔrd/ noun **1** [C,U] something that is given in return for work, effort, etc.: She feels that she has done a lot of work for little or no reward. ○ Being a parent is often hard work but it has its rewards. **2** [C] an amount of money that is given in exchange for helping the police, returning sth that was lost, etc.: The police are offering a $5,000 reward for information leading to a conviction.

☆ **re·ward²** /rɪˈwɔrd/ verb [T] **reward sb (for sth/for doing sth)** to give a reward¹(1,2) to sb: Eventually her efforts were rewarded and she got a job. ○ His parents bought him a bicycle to reward him for getting straight A's on his report card.

re·ward·ing /rɪˈwɔrdɪŋ/ adj. giving satisfaction: She finds her work with disabled children very rewarding.

re·wind /ˌriˈwaɪnd/ verb [T] (p.t., p.p. **re·wound**) to make a tape go backward: Please rewind the tape before you return it.

re·write /ˌriˈraɪt/ verb [T] (p.t. **re·wrote** /-ˈroʊt/; p.p. **re·writ·ten** /-ˈrɪtn/) to write sth again in a different or better way

rhet·o·ric /ˈrɛtərɪk/ noun [U] speech or writing that is intended to impress or influence people —**rhe·tor·i·cal** /rɪˈtɔrɪkl; -ˈtɑr-/ adj. —**rhe·tor·i·cal·ly** /-kli/ adv.

rhe·torical question noun [C] a question that is not really a question because it does not expect an answer

rhine·stone /ˈraɪnstoʊn/ noun [C] a cheap artificial jewel that is made to look like a diamond

rhi·no /ˈraɪnoʊ/ noun [C] (pl. **rhi·nos**) (informal) = RHINOCEROS

rhi·noc·er·os /raɪˈnɑsərəs/ noun [C] (pl. **rhi·noc·er·os** or **rhi·noc·er·os·es**) a large animal from Africa or Asia, with thick skin and either one or two horns on its nose

rhu·barb /ˈrubɑrb/ noun [U] a plant with long red stems and very large leaves. The stems can be cooked and eaten as fruit.

☆ **rhyme¹** /raɪm/ noun **1** [U] the technique of using words that have the same sound as each other, especially at the ends of lines: All of his poetry was written in rhyme. **2** [C] a word that has the same sound as another: Can you think of a rhyme for "peace"? **3** [C] a short piece of

ər	ɪr	ɛr	ɑr	ɔr	ʊr	ʒ	h	ŋ
bird	near	hair	car	north	tour	vision	hat	sing

writing, or something spoken, in which the words at the end of each line sound the same as the words at the end of previous lines ☞ Look at **nursery rhyme**.

☆**rhyme²** /raɪm/ *verb* **1** [I] to have the same sound as another word; to consist of lines that end with words that sound the same: *"Tough" rhymes with "stuff."* ○ *"Book" and "look" rhyme.* ○ *He thinks that all poetry should rhyme.* **2** [T] to put together words that have the same sound: *You can't rhyme "face" with "stays."*

☆**rhythm** /ˈrɪðəm/ *noun* [C,U] a regular repeated pattern of sound or movement: *the rhythms of jazz* ○ *I don't care for the tune, but I love the rhythm.* ○ *He's a terrible dancer because he has no sense of rhythm.*

rhyth·mic /ˈrɪðmɪk/ *adj.* having rhythm: *the rhythmic qualities of African music* —**rhyth·mi·cal·ly** /-kli/ *adv.*

rib /rɪb/ *noun* [C] **1** one of the curved bones that go around the chest: *He's so thin that you can see his ribs.* **2** [usually pl.] meat, especially from a cow or pig, that contains an animal's rib (1): *barbecued ribs*

rib·bon /ˈrɪbən/ *noun* **1** [C,U] a long, thin piece of material that is used for tying or decorating sth ☞ picture at **knot**. **2** [C] a piece of ribbon (1), often folded into the shape of a flower, that is given as a prize in a competition: *Carol's apple pie won a blue ribbon* (= the first prize) *at the county fair.* **3** [C] a long, thin piece of material that contains ink: *a typewriter ribbon*

☆**rice** /raɪs/ *noun* [U] the grain from a plant grown in hot, wet countries, that we cook and eat: *a bowl of rice* ○ *brown rice* ○ *boiled rice*

☆**rich** /rɪtʃ/ *adj.* **1** having a lot of money or property; not poor: *a rich family* ☞ Look at **wealthy**. **2 the rich** *noun* [plural] rich people: *The rich are getting richer and the poor are getting poorer.* **3** (not before a noun) **rich in sth** containing a lot of sth: *Oranges are very rich in vitamin C.* **4** able to produce sth in large amounts: *rich soil* **5** (used about food) containing a lot of fat, oil, sugar, cream, etc.: *a rich sauce* ○ *a rich chocolate cake* **6** (used about colors, sounds or smells) strong and deep: *a rich purple* —**rich·ness** *noun* [U]

rich·es /ˈrɪtʃəz/ *noun* [plural] (*formal*) a lot of money or property; wealth: *Despite all his riches, he was a deeply unhappy man.*

rich·ly /ˈrɪtʃli/ *adv.* **1** extremely well: *She was richly rewarded for her hard work.* **2** fully: *His promotion was richly deserved.* **3** in a beautiful way that looks very expensive: *a richly decorated palace*

rick·et·y /ˈrɪkəti/ *adj.* likely to fall or break; not strongly made: *a rickety old fence*

ric·o·chet /ˈrɪkəʃeɪ; ˌrɪkəˈʃeɪ/ *verb* [I] **ricochet (off sth)** (used about a bullet, etc.) to fly away from a surface after hitting it

☆**rid** /rɪd/ *verb* [T] (*pres. part.* **rid·ding**; *p.t., p.p.* **rid**) **rid sb/sth of sb/sth** (*formal*) to make sb/sth free from sb/sth that is bad or unwanted: *They have managed to rid the world of smallpox.* ○ *He was unable to rid himself of his fears and suspicions.*

IDM get rid of sb/sth to become free of sb/sth or to remove sb/sth: *I didn't enjoy having my family stay at my place. In fact, I was glad to get rid of them.* ○ *I can't get rid of this stain on the carpet.* ○ *Let's get rid of that old chair and buy a new one.*

rid·dance /ˈrɪdns/ *noun*
IDM good riddance (*informal*) (used for expressing pleasure or relief that sb/sth that you do not like has gone)

rid·den¹ *p.p.* of **RIDE²**

rid·den² /ˈrɪdn/ *adj.* (usually in compounds) full of sth (usually sth bad): *She was ridden with guilt.* ○ *She was guilt-ridden.*

rid·dle /ˈrɪdl/ *noun* [C] **1** a type of question that you ask people for fun that has a clever or amusing answer **2** a person, a thing or an event that you cannot understand

rid·dled /ˈrɪdld/ *adj.* **riddled with sth** full of: *The car was was riddled with bullet holes.* ○ *This essay is riddled with mistakes.*

☆**ride¹** /raɪd/ *noun* [C] **1** a trip on a horse or bicycle, or in a car, bus, etc.: *They went for a bike ride through the park.* ○ *She gave me a ride home after the party.* **2** a large machine with small trains or moving seats that people ride for fun: *We went on every single ride at the amusement park!*

IDM take sb for a ride (*informal*) to cheat or deceive sb

☆**ride²** /raɪd/ *verb* [I,T] (*p.t.* **rode** /roʊd/; *p.p.* **rid·den** /ˈrɪdn/) **1** to sit on a bicycle, horse, etc. and be carried along, controlling its movements: *I've never ridden on a horse.* ○ *She jumped onto her motorcycle and rode away.* ○ *I usually ride my bike to school.* **2** to travel as a passenger in a bus, car, etc.: *He's been riding the city bus to work for years.*

☆**rid·er** /ˈraɪdər/ *noun* [C] a person who rides a horse, bicycle, etc.

☆**ridge** /rɪdʒ/ *noun* [C] **1** a long, narrow piece of high land along the top of hills or mountains **2** a line where two sloping surfaces meet

rid·i·cule¹ /ˈrɪdəkyul/ *noun* [U] unkind laughter or behavior that is meant to make sb/sth appear silly

rid·i·cule² /ˈrɪdəkyul/ *verb* [T] to laugh at sb/sth in an unkind way: *The idea was ridiculed by everybody at the meeting.*

☆**ri·dic·u·lous** /rɪˈdɪkyələs/ *adj.* very silly or stupid; foolish: *Take that hat off – you look ridiculous!* ○ *I knew things were going to be bad, but this is ridiculous* (= much worse than I expected). ○ *They're asking a ridiculous*

tʃ	dʒ	v	θ	ð	s	z	ʃ
chin	June	van	thin	then	so	zoo	she

(= very high) *price for that house.* —**ri·dic·u·lous·ly** *adv.*: *She gets paid a ridiculously low salary for the work she does.*

rife /raɪf/ *adj.* (not before a noun) (*formal*) **1 rife with sth** full of sth unpleasant or bad: *a department rife with corruption* **2** (used especially about bad things) very common: *The drug use was rife among certain groups of students.*

☆ **ri·fle** /ˈraɪfl/ *noun* [C] a long gun that you hold against your shoulder to shoot with

☞ We **load**, **aim** and **fire** a rifle. Look at the note at **gun**.

R **rift** /rɪft/ *noun* [C] **1** a serious disagreement between friends, groups, etc.: *a growing rift between the brothers* **2** a crack or split in sth

rig¹ /rɪg/ *verb* [T] (**rig·ging**; **rigged**) **1** to arrange or control an event, etc. in an unfair way, in order to get the result you want: *They claimed that the election had been rigged.* **2 rig sth (up)** to make sth simple or change the way sth works, using any materials you can find: *a car that was rigged with explosives*

rig² /rɪg/ *noun* [C] **1** (usually in compounds) a large platform, with special equipment for bringing oil and natural gas out of the ground: *an oil rig* **2** (*informal*) a large truck

☆ **right¹** /raɪt/ *adj.* **1** on or of the side of the body that faces east when a person is facing north; not left: *Do you write with your right hand or your left?* ○ *Your seats are on the right side of the plane.* **2** correct; true: *Sorry, that's not the right answer.* ○ *Do you have the right time?* ○ *You're absolutely right – the movie does start at 7 o'clock.* ○ *You were right about the weather – it did rain.* **3** best; most suitable: *I don't think this is the right color for the walls.* ○ *I hope I made the right decision.* ○ *We wouldn't have missed the flight if we'd left at the right time.* ○ *You have to know the right people if you want to join that golf club.* **4** normal; satisfactory: *Her voice didn't sound quite right on the phone.* **5** (used about behavior, actions, etc.) good; fair or what the law allows: *It's not right to pay people so little.* ○ *It was right of her to give you the news at once.* ○ *It's never right to steal.* **6** (*informal*) (used as a question at the end of a sentence to check whether sb agrees with you or whether what you said is correct): *We want to be the best company in the business, right?* ○ *Let's see – you ordered a cheeseburger and fries, right?* **7** (*informal*) (used to tell sb that you agree with or understand what he/she has just said, or that you will do what he/she has asked you to do): *"…And then we went to that new restaurant on Sunset Drive." "Right."* ○ *"Take this package down to the post office." "Right."*

IDM **all right** ⇨ ALL²

right side up with the top part turned to the top; in the correct, normal position: *Fortunately, my toast landed right side up when I dropped it on the floor.* ☞ The opposite is **upside down**.

on the right/wrong track ⇨ TRACK¹ —**right·ness** *noun* [U]

☆ **right²** /raɪt/ *adv.* **1** to the right¹(1) side; not left: *Turn right at the traffic light.* **2** correctly; in a satisfactory way: *Did I spell your name right?* ○ *Nothing seems to be going right for me these days.* ○ *These shoes don't fit right.* **3** exactly: *The bus was right on time.* ○ *The accident happened right here.* **4** all the way: *He kicked his foot right through the door!* **5** immediately: *He left right after dinner.* ○ *Wait here a minute – I'll be right back.*

IDM **right away** immediately; without any delay: *I'll take care of that right away.* ○ *I understood right away what she wanted me to do.*

right now 1 at this moment; exactly now: *We can't discuss this right now.* **2** at the present time (when compared with the past or the future): *Interest rates are relatively low right now.*

right off the bat (*informal*) without delay; at the beginning: *We both liked each other right off the bat.*

serve sb right ⇨ SERVE

☆ **right³** /raɪt/ *noun* **1** [U] the right¹(1) side or direction; not left: *We live in the first house on the right.* ○ *If you look slightly to your right, you will see the Rocky Mountains in the distance.* **2** [C] a turn to the right, or a street or road on the right: *Make a right at the next intersection.* ○ *Take the first right after the gas station.* **3** [U] what is morally good and fair: *Children learn about right and wrong from a very early age.* **4** [C] a thing that you are allowed to do according to the law: *In the U.S., citizens have the right to vote at 18.* ○ *Freedom of speech is one of the basic human rights.* ○ *civil rights* (= the rights each person has to political and religious freedom, etc.) **5** [U] **right to sth/to do sth** a moral authority to do sth: *You have no right to tell me what to do.* **6 the right** (*also* **the Right**) [sing.] the people or political parties who support low taxes, very little government control over businesses and strict, traditional moral behavior

IDM **in your own right** because of what you are yourself and not because of other people: *She's a very wealthy woman in her own right* (= not only because she married somebody who is rich).

within your rights (to do sth) acting in a reasonable or legal way: *You are perfectly within your rights to demand to see your lawyer.*

right⁴ /raɪt/ *verb* [T] **1** to return to a normal position: *The boat tipped over and then righted itself again.* **2** to correct sth

i	ɪ	ɛ	æ	ɑ	ɔ	ʌ	ʊ	u
see	sit	ten	cat	hot	saw	cup	put	too

☛ This verb is almost always used in this sense with the noun **wrong**: *There are many wrongs that need to be righted.* You do not "right" a mistake; you **correct** it.

,right 'angle *noun* [C] an angle of 90°: *A square has four right angles.* ☛ picture at **angle**.

right·eous /'raɪtʃəs/ *adj.* (*formal*) morally good or fair ☛ Look at **self-righteous**.

right·ful /'raɪtfl/ *adj.* (only *before* a noun) (*formal*) fair, proper or legal: *You have a rightful claim to your father's property.* —**right·ful·ly** *adv.*

'right-hand *adj.* (only *before* a noun) of or on the right of sb/sth: *The mailbox is on the right-hand side of the road.* ○ *a sharp right-hand turn*

,right-'hand·ed *adj.* using the right hand more than the left for writing, etc.

,right-hand 'man *noun* [C] (*pl.* **right-hand men**) the person you rely on most to help and support you in your work

right·ly /'raɪtli/ *adv.* correctly or fairly: *As you rightly said, it's time to decide what we want.*

,right of 'way *noun* [U, sing.] (used in road traffic) the right³(4) to continue while other traffic must stop: *Pedestrians always have the right of way at intersections.*

,right 'wing *noun* [sing.] the people in a political party who support ideas such as low taxes, very little government control over businesses and strict, traditional moral behavior: *the right wing of the Republican party* —,**right-'wing** *adj.*: *a right-wing talk show host* ☛ The opposite is **left-wing**.

rig·id /'rɪdʒɪd/ *adj.* **1** not able or willing to change or be changed; strict: *rigid rules and regulations* **2** stiff; not easy to bend: *For air travel, a rigid suitcase is better than a soft bag.* ○ *She was rigid with fear.* —**ri·gid·i·ty** /rɪ'dʒɪdəṭi/ *noun* [U] —**rig·id·ly** *adv.*: *regulations that are rigidly enforced*

rig·or /'rɪgər/ *noun* (*formal*) **1** [C, usually pl.] severe conditions; difficulties: *the rigors of a harsh climate* **2** [U] care and attention to detail

rig·or·ous /'rɪgərəs/ *adj.* thorough and careful: *Rigorous tests have been carried out on the drinking water.* —**rig·or·ous·ly** *adv.*

rim /rɪm/ *noun* [C] an edge at the top or outside of sth that is round: *the rim of a cup* ○ *glasses with silver rims*

rind /raɪnd/ *noun* [C,U] the thick hard skin on the outside of some fruits and some types of cheese, etc.

☛ **Rind** is hard and is not usually removed with the fingers. We say the **rind** or **peel** of a lemon or an orange, but only the **rind** of a watermelon. A fruit with a thinner or softer covering has a **skin**. So apples, pears, etc. all have **skins**. We usually say that a banana has a **peel**.

☆**ring**¹ /rɪŋ/ *noun* [C] **1** a piece of jewelry, a round piece of metal, often of silver or gold, that you wear on your finger: *a wedding ring* ○ *an engagement ring* ○ *a gold, diamond, etc. ring* ☛ picture at **jewelry**. **2** (usually in compounds) a round object of any material with a hole in the middle: *a key ring* (= for holding keys) ☛ picture at **key**. **3** a circle: *His coffee cup left an ugly ring on the table.* ○ *The house was surrounded by a ring of police officers.* **4** the sound made by a bell: *I thought I heard a ring at the door.* **5** the space with seats all around it where a performance, sports match, etc. takes place: *a circus ring* ○ *a boxing ring* **6** a number of people who are involved together in sth that is secret or not legal: *a smuggling ring*

☆**ring**² /rɪŋ/ *verb* (*p.t.* **rang** /ræŋ/; *p.p.* **rung** /rʌŋ/) **1** [I,T] to make a sound like a bell or to cause sth to make this sound: *Is that the phone ringing?* ○ *We rang the doorbell again and again, but nobody answered.* **2** [I] **ring (for sb/sth)** to ring a bell in order to call sb, ask for sth, etc.: *"Did you ring?" asked the nurse.* **3** [I] to be filled with loud sounds: *My ears were still ringing an hour after the concert.*

IDM **ring a bell** to sound familiar or to remind you, not very clearly, of sth: *"Do you know Jane Sykes?" "Well, the name rings a bell."*

ring off the hook (used about a telephone) to ring all the time because many people are calling: *I haven't had a break yet – the phone's been ringing off the hook all morning!*

ring true/hollow to sound as if you should/ should not believe it: *Her words just didn't ring true.*

PHRV **ring out** to sound loudly and clearly: *A pistol shot rang out.*

ring sth up to add together the costs of things, e.g. prices of things that sb is buying in a store: *When the cashier rang up my total, I was shocked.*

ring³ /rɪŋ/ *verb* (*p.t., p.p.* **ringed** /rɪŋd/) [T] to surround sb/sth: *The whole area was ringed by police.*

ring·lead·er /'rɪŋlidər/ *noun* [C] a person who leads a group of people who are doing sth wrong or causing trouble: *Who is the ringleader of the group?*

rink /rɪŋk/ *noun* [C] a large area of ice, or a building containing a large area of ice, that people can skate or play hockey on

☆**rinse** /rɪns/ *verb* [T] to wash sth in water in order to remove soap or dirt, etc.: *Rinse your hair thoroughly after each shampoo.* ○ *You should rinse the apples before you eat them.* —**rinse** *noun* [C]: *Give the paintbrush a good rinse after using it.*

☆**ri·ot** /'raɪət/ *noun* [C] fighting and noisy violent behavior by a crowd of people: *Further riots have broken out in the downtown area.* ○ *Police have been brought in to deal with the*

R

riots. —**ri·ot** verb [I]: *There is a danger that the prisoners will riot if conditions don't improve.* —**ri·ot·er** noun [C]

ri·ot·ous /ˈraɪətəs/ adj. (formal) wild or violent; lacking in control: *The crowd was becoming increasingly riotous.*

☆ **rip¹** /rɪp/ verb (**rip·ping; ripped**) **1** [I,T] to tear quickly and sharply: *My jeans ripped when I was climbing over the fence.* ○ *He ripped the letter in two and threw it in the trash.* ○ *The blast of the bomb ripped the house apart.* **2** [T] to pull sth quickly and violently: *He ripped the poster from the wall.* ○ *The roof was ripped off by the tornado.* **3** [I] to move very quickly: *The house was badly damaged when fire ripped through the roof and second floor.*

PHRV **rip sb off** (informal) to steal from sb, or to cheat sb by asking too much money for sth
rip sth up to tear sth into small pieces

rip² /rɪp/ noun [C] a long tear or cut (in material, etc.)

☆ **ripe** /raɪp/ adj. (used about fruit, grain, etc.) ready to be picked and eaten
IDM **be ripe for sth** to be ready for sth or in a suitable state for sth: *Conditions in the area are ripe for hurricane formation.*

rip·en /ˈraɪpən/ verb [I,T] to make sth ripe or to become ripe

rip-off noun [C] (informal) something that costs too much money: *$2 for a cup of coffee is a total rip-off!*

rip·ple¹ /ˈrɪpl/ noun [C] **1** a very small wave or movement on the surface of water: *The breeze sent tiny ripples across the lake.* **2** a gentle sound: *A ripple of laughter ran around the room.*

rip·ple² /ˈrɪpl/ verb [I,T] to move gently: *The branches of the trees rippled in the wind.* ○ *The wind rippled the surface of the ocean.*

☆ **rise¹** /raɪz/ noun **1** [C] an increase: *There has been a rise in the number of people out of work.* ○ *a sharp price rise* ☞ Look at **drop²**(4) and **fall¹**(1). **2** [sing.] the process of becoming more powerful or important: *His rise in the world of politics was remarkable.*
IDM **be on the rise** to be increasing: *Violent crime is on the rise in several major cities.*
give rise to sth to cause sth: *The news gave rise to considerable anxiety among many people.*

☆ **rise²** /raɪz/ verb [I] (p.t. **rose** /roʊz/; p.p. **ris·en** /ˈrɪzn/) **1** to move upward, to become higher or to increase: *Smoke was rising from the chimney.* ○ *Her voice rose in anger* (= became louder). ○ *Do you think inflation will continue to rise?* ○ *The temperature has risen to nearly ninety degrees.* ○ *Let the dough rise for an hour.* ☞ Look at **fall**. **2** to stand up: *The audience rose and applauded the singers.* **3** (formal) to get out of bed: *They rose at dawn in order to be in Washington by eight.* ☞ In this sense **get up** is more common. **4** (used about the sun,

moon, etc.) to appear above the horizon: *The sun rises in the east and sets in the west.* **5** to show (as sth tall above the surroundings): *A range of mountains rose in the distance.* **6** to come from: *Shouts of protest rose from the crowd.* **7 rise (up) (against sb/sth)** to start opposing or fighting people in authority: *The people were afraid to rise up against the dictator.* **8** to move to a higher position (in rank, society, career, etc.): *He rose rapidly within the company.*
IDM **rise to the occasion, challenge, task, etc.** to be successful in dealing with sth by working harder or doing things better than you normally do: *Do you think she will rise to the demands of the job?*

☆ **risk** /rɪsk/ noun **1** [C,U] **risk (of sth/that ...)** a possibility (that sth dangerous or bad could happen): *There's always a risk that the price will go up if you wait too long.* ○ *Do you think there's any risk of fire?* **2** [C] a dangerous or stupid thing to do: *It was an unnecessary risk to pass that truck on the hill.* **3** [C] a person or thing that might cause danger: *That open window is a real security risk.*
IDM **at your own risk** having the responsibility for whatever may happen: *This building is in a dangerous condition – enter at your own risk.*
at risk in danger: *Small children are most at risk from the disease.*
at the risk of sth/doing sth with the possibility of sth bad: *At the risk of sounding pushy, can I give you some advice?*
run the risk of (doing sth) to do sth knowing that the result might be bad or unpleasant; to risk: *If we don't leave early, we run the risk of missing the plane.*
take a risk; take risks to do sth that you know might fail or be dangerous, etc.: *You shouldn't take risks when driving.* ○ *He's very young, but I'm prepared to take a risk and give him a job.*

☆ **risk²** /rɪsk/ verb [T] **1** to take the chance that sth bad could happen: *If you don't study hard now, you risk failing your final exams.* **2** to put sth or yourself in a dangerous position: *The man risked his life to save the little boy.*

☆ **risk·y** /ˈrɪski/ adj. (**risk·i·er; risk·i·est**) dangerous; involving a chance that sth bad could happen: *risky business investments*

rit·u·al¹ /ˈrɪtʃuəl/ noun [C,U] an action, ceremony or process which is usually repeated in the same pattern: *priests performing a ritual in a temple*

rit·u·al² /ˈrɪtʃuəl/ adj. (only before a noun) done according to a particular pattern or tradition —**rit·u·al·ly** adv.

ritz·y /ˈrɪtsi/ adj. (**ritz·i·er; ritz·i·est**) (informal) fashionable and expensive: *a ritzy hotel*

☆ **ri·val¹** /ˈraɪvl/ noun [C] a person or thing that is competing with another: *They're business*

ər	ɪr	ɛr	ɑr	ɔr	ʊr	ʒ	h	ŋ
bird	near	hair	car	north	tour	vision	hat	sing

rivals. ○ The top candidate has a 3% lead over her closest rival. ○ a gun battle between rival gangs

☆ **ri·val²** /ˈraɪvl/ verb [T] **rival sb/sth (for sth)** to be as good as sb/sth: This novel doesn't rival his earlier writing. ○ Nothing rivals skiing for sheer excitement.

ri·val·ry /ˈraɪvlri/ noun [C,U] (pl. **ri·val·ries**) competition between people, groups, etc.: There was a lot of rivalry between the sisters.

☆ **riv·er** /ˈrɪvər/ noun [C] a large natural stream of water that flows across the land: the Mississippi River ○ a picnic on the bank of the river

☞ A river **flows** into a lake or an ocean. The **mouth** of the river is the place where it joins the lake or ocean. A boat travels **on** the river. We walk, sail, etc. **up** or **down** the river. A small river is a **creek** or **stream**.

riv·er·front /ˈrɪvərfrʌnt/ noun [sing.] the land or property by the side of a river: People were strolling along the riverfront. ○ a riverfront restaurant

riv·et¹ /ˈrɪvət/ noun [C] a metal pin for fastening two pieces of metal together

riv·et² /ˈrɪvət/ verb [T] (usually passive) to interest sb very much: I was riveted by her story.

riv·et·ing /ˈrɪvətɪŋ/ adj. extremely interesting: His speech was absolutely riveting.

roach /roʊtʃ/ noun [C] = COCKROACH

☆ **road** /roʊd/ noun **1** [C] a way between places, with a hard surface which cars, buses, etc. can drive on: Route 27 is the main road into town. ○ The traffic was terrible because of all the road construction. ○ a few miles up/down the road (= farther along the road) ○ a dirt/gravel road ○ back roads (= small, minor roads) ○ road signs

☞ **Highways** are roads that connect cities and towns. A road in a town or city that has buildings at the side is usually called a **street**. **Street** is not used for roads outside towns: a street map of San Francisco. However, streets in cities or towns may have the word **Road** as part of their names. Look also at the note at **freeway**.

2 Road (abbr. **Rd.**) [sing.] (used in names of roads): 60 Stone Road

IDM **on the road 1** traveling: We were on the road for 14 hours. **2** (used about a sports team) playing in another team's city: The Cubs have lost all their games on the road so far this season.

on the road to sth on the way to achieving sth: The nation's economy is on the road to recovery.

road·block /ˈroʊdblɑk/ noun [C] a barrier put across the road by the police or army to stop traffic

road·kill /ˈroʊdkɪl/ noun [U] (informal) animals that have been killed by cars on a road

road·side /ˈroʊdsaɪd/ noun [C, usually sing.] the edge of a road: cars parked along the roadside ○ a roadside vegetable stand

road·way /ˈroʊdweɪ/ noun [C] the part of the road used by cars, etc.; not the side of the road

roam /roʊm/ verb [I,T] to walk or travel with no particular plan or aim: There were several dogs roaming the neighborhood last night.

roar¹ /rɔr/ noun [C] a loud, deep sound like that made by a lion: the roar of a jet plane overhead ○ roars of laughter

roar² /rɔr/ verb **1** [I] to make a loud, deep sound: We watched as a jet roared overhead. ○ She roared with laughter at the joke. ○ 50,000 fans roared as the Cowboys won the Super Bowl. **2** [I] to make the sound that is typical of a lion: The lion opened its huge mouth and roared. **3** [T] **roar sth (out)** to express sth very loudly: The audience roared its approval.

PHRV **roar along, down, past, etc.** to move in the direction mentioned, making a loud, deep sound: A motorcycle roared past us.

roar·ing /ˈrɔrɪŋ/ adj. **1** making a very loud noise: the roaring waves **2** (used about a fire) burning very well **3** very great: a roaring success

☆ **roast¹** /roʊst/ verb **1** [I,T] to cook or be cooked in an oven or over a fire: a smell of roasting meat ○ to roast a chicken ☞ Look at the note at **cook**. **2** [T] to heat and dry sth: roasted peanuts **3** [I] (informal) to be very hot: Turn on the air conditioner – I'm roasting in here!

☆ **roast²** /roʊst/ adj. (only before a noun) cooked by roasting: roast beef

☆ **roast³** /roʊst/ noun **1** [C,U] a piece of meat that has been roasted **2** [C] an outdoor meal at which food is roasted: a hot dog roast ☞ Look at **barbecue** and **cookout**.

☆ **rob** /rɑb/ verb [T] (**rob·bing; robbed**) **rob sb/sth (of sth) 1** to take sth (money, property, etc.) from a person or place illegally: to rob a bank ○ Several people on the bus were robbed of their money and jewelry. ☞ Look at the note at **steal**. **2** to take sth away from sb/sth that he/she/it should have: His injury robbed him of the chance to play in the Super Bowl.

rob·ber /ˈrɑbər/ noun [C] a person who steals from a bank, etc. ☞ Look at the note at **thief**.

☆ **rob·ber·y** /ˈrɑbəri/ noun [C,U] (pl. **rob·ber·ies**) the crime of stealing from a bank, etc.: They were accused of armed robbery. ○ There's been a robbery. They took half a million dollars.

robe /roʊb/ noun [C] **1** a long, loose piece of clothing: a judge's black robe **2** = BATHROBE

rob·in /ˈrɑbən/ noun [C] a small brown bird with a bright red breast. Robins are thought to be a sign of spring.

☆ **ro·bot** /ˈroʊbɑt/ noun [C] a machine that can move and that can be made to do some of the work that a person does. Some robots are made to look like people.

tʃ	dʒ	v	θ	ð	s	z	ʃ
chin	**June**	**van**	**thin**	**then**	**so**	**zoo**	**she**

ro·bust /rouˈbʌst/ *adj.* strong and healthy: (*figurative*) *a robust economy*

rock band
drums
bass guitar
keyboard
electric guitar

☆**rock¹** /rɑk/ *noun* **1** [U] the very hard substance that forms part of the earth's surface: *layers of rock formed over millions of years* **2** [C] a piece or an area of stone: *The ship hit the rocks and started to sink.* ○ *to go rock climbing* ○ *The boy threw a rock at the dog.* **3** [U] (*also* **ˈrock music**) a type of popular music with a very strong beat, played on electric guitars, etc.: *I like jazz better than rock.* ○ *a rock singer* ○ *a rock band*

☆**rock²** /rɑk/ *verb* **1** [I,T] to move backward and forward or from side to side; to make sb/sth do this: *sailboats rocking gently on the waves* ○ *The baby won't go to sleep unless you rock her for a while.* **2** [T] to shake sth violently: *San Francisco was rocked by an earthquake.* **3** [T] to cause shock to sb/sth: *Riots rocked downtown Los Angeles.*

ˌ**rock and ˈroll** *noun* [U] = ROCK 'N' ROLL

ˌ**rock ˈbottom** *noun* [U] the lowest or worst point: *Jerry hit rock bottom when he went to jail.*

rock·et /ˈrɑkət/ *noun* [C] **1** a vehicle shaped like a tube, that is used for travel into space: *to launch a rocket* ○ *a rocket engine* **2** an object shaped like a tube that is used as a weapon and that carries a bomb

ˈ**rocking chair** *noun* [C] a type of chair with two curved pieces of wood attached to the bottom of the legs

rock 'n' roll (*also* **rock and roll**) /ˌrɑknˈroul/ *noun* [U] a type of music with a strong beat that was most popular in the 1950s: *Elvis Presley was the king of rock 'n' roll.*

rock·y /ˈrɑki/ *adj.* (**rock·i·er; rock·i·est**) **1** full of rocks or not level and smooth: *a rocky beach* ○ *rocky hills* **2** (*informal*) difficult and full of problems: *a rocky marriage*

rod /rɑd/ *noun* [C] (often in compounds) a thin straight piece of wood or metal: *a fishing rod*

rode *p.t.* of RIDE²

ro·dent /ˈroudnt/ *noun* [C] a type of small animal (such as a rat, a rabbit, a mouse, etc.) that has strong sharp front teeth

ro·de·o /ˈroudiou; rouˈdeiou/ *noun* [C] (*pl.* **ro·de·os**) a contest or performance in which people show their skill in riding wild horses, catching cows, etc.

rogue /roug/ *adj.* (only *before* a noun) causing trouble by not following official rules: *an attack by a rogue nation*

☆**role** /roul/ *noun* [C] **1** a person's part in a play, movie, etc.: *Many actresses have played the role of Cleopatra.* ○ *a leading role in the next James Bond movie* **2** the position or importance of sb/sth: *Parents play a vital role in their children's education.*

ˈ**role-play** *noun* [C,U] (*also* **role-playing** [U]) an activity, used especially in teaching, in which a person acts a part

☆**roll¹** /roul/ *noun* [C] **rolls**
1 something made into the shape of a tube by winding it around itself: *a roll of toilet paper* ○ *a roll of film* **2** bread that has been baked in a round shape, small enough for one person: *a basket of warm rolls* ○ *I'll have a cinnamon roll and a cup of coffee.* ☞ picture at **bread**. **3** an official list of names: *The teacher called the roll (= read the names of the students in the class).* **4** a long, low sound: *a roll of drums*

roll of toilet paper
roll of film

☆**roll²** /roul/ *verb* **1** [I,T] to move by turning over and over; to make sth move in this way: *The apples fell out of the bag and rolled everywhere.* ○ *We couldn't stop the ball from rolling into the river.* ○ *It was Michael's turn to roll the dice.* **2** [I,T] to move smoothly (on wheels or as if on wheels); to make sth move in this way: *The car began to roll back down the hill.* ○ *Tears were rolling down her cheeks.* ○ *Workers rolled the airplane out of the hangar.* **3** [I,T] to turn over or upward; to make sb/sth do this: *We taught the dog to roll over and play dead.* ○ *The medical team rolled the patient onto her back.* **4** [I,T] **roll (sth) (up)** to make sth into the shape of a ball or tube; to be made into this shape: *He rolls his own cigarettes.* ○ *Beth rolled up her sleeves.* ○ *The insect rolled up when I touched it.* ☞ The opposite is **unroll**. **5** [T] **roll sth (out)** to make sth become flat by moving sth heavy over it: *Roll out the dough (= using a rolling pin).* **6** [I] to rock or swing from side to side: *The ship began to roll in the storm.* ○ *She was rolling with laughter.*

PHRV **roll in** (*informal*) to arrive in large numbers or quantities: *Offers of help have been rolling in.*

roll·er /ˈroulər/ *noun* [C] **1** a long object in the shape of a tube, which can be rolled over a surface or which can turn over and over as part of a machine: *He used a roller to paint the wall.* **2** = CURLER

Roll·er·blade /ˈroulərbleid/ *noun* [C] (*trademark*) (*also* **in-line skate**) a kind of boot with one row of narrow wheels on the bottom. It allows you to move quickly over a smooth

surface: *a pair of Rollerblades* ☞ picture at skate. —**Roll·er·blade** *verb* [I]

'roller ˌcoaster *noun* [C] a type of train track with small open trains, sharp bends and very steep slopes. People go on roller coasters for fun at fairs, etc.

'roller skate (*also* **skate**) *noun* [C] a type of shoe with two pairs of small wheels on the bottom. It allows you to move quickly over a smooth surface: *a pair of roller skates* ☞ picture at skate. —**'roller-skate** *verb* [I]

'rolling pin *noun* [C] a piece of wood, etc. in the shape of a tube, that you use for making cookies, etc. flat and thin before baking

ROM /rɑm/ *noun* [U] (*computing*) read-only memory; the part of a computer where information is stored but cannot be changed ☞ Look at **RAM** and **CD-ROM**.

Ro·man /'roʊmən/ *adj.* connected with ancient Rome: *the remains of a Roman villa* ○ *a Roman soldier*

the ˌRoman ˈalphabet *noun* [sing.] the letters A to Z, used especially in West European languages

ˌRoman ˈCatholic (*also* **Catholic**) *noun* [C], *adj.* (a member) of the Christian church which has the Pope as its head: *She's (a) Roman Catholic.* ☞ Look at **Protestant**.

ˌRoman ˈCatholicism (*also* **Catholicism**) *noun* [U] the beliefs of the Roman Catholic Church

ro·mance /'roʊmæns; roʊ'mæns/ *noun* **1** [C] a love affair: *The movie was about a teenage romance.* **2** [U] a feeling or atmosphere of love or of sth new, special and exciting: *The stars were out, the night was warm and romance was in the air.* **3** [C] a novel about a love affair: *She writes historical romances.*

ˌRoman ˈnumeral *noun* [C] one of the letters that were used by the ancient Romans as numbers

☞ Roman numerals, e.g. IV=4 and X=10, are still used sometimes. For example, they may be found numbering the pages and chapters of books or on some clocks.

☆ **ro·man·tic** /roʊ'mæntɪk/ *adj.* **1** having a quality that strongly affects your emotions or makes you think about love; showing feelings of love: *a romantic dinner by candlelight* ○ *He isn't very romantic – he never says he loves me.* **2** involving a love affair; describing situations involving love: *Reports of a romantic involvement between the two movie stars have been strongly denied.* ○ *a romantic comedy* **3** having or showing ideas about life and love that are emotional rather than real or practical: *Now that I've been here for a while, I have a much less romantic view of life in the city.* —**ro·man·ti·cal·ly** /-kli/ *adv.*

ro·man·ti·cize /roʊ'mæntəsaɪz/ *verb* [I,T] to make sth seem more interesting, exciting, etc. than it really is

☆ **roof** /ruf; rʊf/ *noun* [C] (*pl.* **roofs**) **1** the part of a building, vehicle, etc. which covers the top of it: *the roof of the school* ○ *a hole in the roof* ○ *The library and the gymnasium are under one roof* (= in the same building). ○ *A couple of shingles have fallen off the roof.* ☞ picture on page A28. **2** the highest part inside sth: *The roof of the cave collapsed.* ○ *the roof of your mouth*

roof·top /'ruftɑp; 'rʊf-/ *noun* [C] the outside of the roof of a building: *From the plane we could see the rooftops of our town.*

rook /rʊk/ (*also* **castle**) *noun* [C] one of the pieces used in the game of chess ☞ picture at **chess**.

rook·ie /'rʊki/ *noun* [C] a person who has just started doing a job or playing a professional sport: *a rookie cop, quarterback, pitcher, etc.*

☆ **room** /rum; rʊm/ *noun* **1** [C] a part of a house or building that is separated from the rest by its own walls, floor and ceiling: *The house has three rooms downstairs and four bedrooms upstairs.* ○ *a dining room* ○ *a hotel room* ○ *a conference room* **2** [U] **room (for sb/sth)**; **room (to do sth)** space; enough space: *There isn't room for any more furniture in here.* ○ *The table takes up too much room.* ○ *They're tearing down those old factories to make room for a new development.* ○ *There were so many people that there wasn't any room to move.* **3** [U] **room (for sth)** the opportunity or need for sth: *There's room for improvement in your work* (= it could be much better). ☞ Look at the note at **place**[1].

room·ful /'rumfʊl/ *noun* [C, usually sing.] **a roomful of sb/sth** the amount or number that a room can contain: *There was a roomful of reporters waiting to interview him.*

☆ **room·mate** /'rumeɪt/ *noun* [C] a person that you share a room or an apartment, a house, etc. with

'room ˌservice *noun* [U] a service in some hotels in which food or drinks are brought to guests in their rooms

room·y /'rumi/ *adj.* (**room·i·er**; **room·i·est**) having plenty of space: *a roomy house, car, etc.*

roost·er /'rustər/ *noun* [C] an adult male chicken: *The rooster crowed at dawn.* ☞ picture at **chicken**.

☆ **root**[1] /rut; rʊt/ *noun* **1** [C] the part of a plant that grows under the ground and takes in water and food from the soil **2** [C] the part of a hair or tooth that is under the skin and that attaches it to the rest of the body **3 roots** [plural] the place where you feel that you belong, because you grew up there, live there or your relatives once lived there: *Sam is proud of his African roots.* **4** [C] the cause, source or main part of sth: *Let's try and get to*

R

the root of the problem. ☞ Look at **grass roots** and **square root**.

root² /rut; rʊt/ *verb*

IDM **be rooted in sth** to have origins in sth and so be influenced by it: *These attitudes are deeply rooted in the nation's history.*

PHRV **root for sb/sth** to give support to sb who is in a game, contest, etc.: *The crowd was rooting for the home team.*

root sb/sth out to find and destroy sth bad completely: *to root out corruption in the city government*

'root beer *noun* [U] a type of sweet brown drink with a lot of small bubbles in it, but no alcohol

☆ **rope¹** /roʊp/ *noun* [C,U] very thick, strong cord, that is used for tying or lifting heavy things, climbing up, etc.: *We need some rope to tie up the boat.* ○ *The victim was found with a rope tied around her neck.* ☞ Look also at **jump rope**.

IDM **at the end of your rope** ⇨ END¹

rope² /roʊp/ *verb*

PHRV **rope sth off** to put ropes around or across an area in order to keep people out of it

ro·sa·ry /'roʊzəri/ *noun* [C] (*pl.* **ro·sa·ries**) a string of beads used by Roman Catholics for counting prayers

rose¹ *p.t.* of RISE²

☆ **rose²** /roʊz/ *noun* [C] a flower with a sweet smell, that grows on a bush and usually has sharp points (**thorns**) on its stem

ro·sé /roʊ'zeɪ/ *noun* [U] pink wine

Rosh Ha·sha·nah (*also* **Rosh Hashana**) /ˌrɑʃ hə'ʃɑnə/ *noun* [U] the Jewish new year, which is celebrated in September or early October

ros·ter /'rɑstər/ *noun* [C] a list of people's names, often showing the jobs that they must do and when they must do those jobs: *a flight/duty roster* ○ *There are ten new players on the team's roster.*

ros·y /'roʊzi/ *adj.* (**ros·i·er**; **ros·i·est**) **1** deep pink in color and (used about a person) healthy-looking: *rosy cheeks* **2** (used about a situation) full of good possibilities: *The future was looking rosy.* ○ *The President painted a rosy picture of the economy* (= described it in a very positive way).

rot /rɑt/ *verb* (**rot·ting**; **rot·ted**) **1** [I] to go bad (as part of a natural process); to decay: *Wood will rot in damp conditions.* **2** [T] to make sth go bad or decay: *Too much candy will rot your teeth!*

ro·tate /'roʊteɪt/ *verb* [I,T] **1** to turn in circles around a central point; to make sth do this: *The earth rotates around the sun.* ○ *You can see the parts that rotate the hands of the clock.* **2** to happen in a particular order; to make sth do this: *Employees are rotated among all the work shifts.*

ro·ta·tion /roʊ'teɪʃn/ *noun* **1** [U] movement in

circles: *the earth's rotation* **2** [C] one complete turn around sth: *one rotation every 24 hours* **3** [C,U] the regular changing around of people or things, or of the order of events: *a planned rotation of troops in the area* ○ *crop rotation*

rote /roʊt/ *noun* [U] a way of learning sth in which you remember information after repeating it many times, but do not understand it: *to learn sth by rote* ○ *This class focuses on critical thinking skills rather than rote learning.*

☆ **rot·ten** /'rɑtn/ *adj.* **1** (used about food and other substances) old and not fresh enough or good enough to use: *rotten vegetables* ○ *Some of the stairs were rotten and unsafe.* **2** (*informal*) very bad: *We had rotten weather all week.* **3** (*informal*) unfair, unkind or bad: *What a rotten thing to say!*

☆ **rough¹** /rʌf/ *adj.* **1** not smooth or level: *It's not easy to walk over such rough terrain.* ○ *Her hands were rough from too much work.* **2** moving or behaving with too much force and not enough care; not gentle or calm: *Football is a rough game.* ○ *The ferry was canceled because the ocean was too rough* (= because of a storm). ○ *He grew up in a rough neighborhood* (= where there is a lot of crime or violence). **3** made or done quickly or without much care; approximately correct: *a rough draft of an essay* ○ *a rough estimate of what the work would cost* ○ *Can you give me a rough idea of what time you'll be arriving?* **4** not easy; full of difficulty: *She's had a rough life.*

IDM **a hard/rough time** ⇨ TIME¹ —**rough·ness** *noun* [U]

rough² /rʌf/ *adv.* (*informal*) in a rough¹(2) way: *One of the boys was told to leave because he was playing too rough.*

rough³ /rʌf/ *verb*

IDM **rough it** to live without the usual comforts of life: *The girls love roughing it when they go camping in the summer.*

PHRV **rough sb up** (*informal*) to attack sb by hitting him/her: *He claimed he had been roughed up by a police officer.*

☆ **rough·ly** /'rʌfli/ *adv.* **1** in a violent way; not gently: *He grabbed her roughly by the arm.* **2** not exactly; approximately: *It took roughly three hours, I think.*

☆ **round¹** /raʊnd/ *adj.* **1** having the shape of a circle or a ball: *a round table* ○ *People used to think the earth was flat, not round.* ○ *He had a round face and white hair.* **2** (used about a number) given to the nearest 10, 100, 1,000, etc.; not exact: *In round numbers, we've sold a quarter of a million of these gadgets so far.*

☆ **round²** /raʊnd/ *noun* [C] **1** a number or set of events, etc.: *a further round of talks between the company and the union* **2** a regular series of visits, etc., often as part of a job: *The mail carrier's round takes him about three hours.* **3** one part of a game or competition: *the third*

ər	ɪr	ɛr	ɑr	ɔr	ʊr	ʒ	h	ŋ
bird	near	hair	car	north	tour	vision	hat	sing

round of the boxing match ○ *The winners of the first round will go on to the second stage of the tournament.* **4** (in golf) one game: *to play a round of golf* **5** a bullet or a number of bullets, fired from a gun: *He fired several rounds at us.*

IDM **a round of applause** a time when people clap after a performance, etc.: *to give sb a round of applause*

round³ /raʊnd/ *verb* [T] to go around sth: *The police car rounded the corner at high speed.*

PHRV **round sth off** to increase or decrease a number, price, etc. to the nearest whole number or to the nearest 10, 100, 1,000, etc.: *The price has been rounded off to the nearest dollar.* **round sb/sth up** to gather sb/sth in one place: *The teacher rounded up the kids.*

round⁴ /raʊnd/ *adv.*

IDM **all year round** ⇨ YEAR

round·a·bout /ˈraʊndəbaʊt/ *adj.* not direct: *He answered in a roundabout way.*

ˈround-the-ˌclock *adj.* (only *before* a noun) happening continuously, 24 hours a day: *round-the-clock news*

ˌround ˈtrip *noun* [C] a trip that you take from one place to another and back again

ˈround-trip (*also* **ˈroundtrip**) *adj.* (only *before* a noun) for traveling to a place and back again: *a round-trip ticket* ○ *a round-trip fare of $50* ☛ Look at **one-way** (2).

rouse /raʊz/ *verb* [T] **1** to make sb/sth very angry, excited, interested, etc.: *a fiery speech that roused voters* **2** (*formal*) to make sb wake up: *She was sleeping so soundly that I couldn't rouse her.*

rous·ing /ˈraʊzɪŋ/ *adj.* exciting and powerful: *a rousing speech*

rout /raʊt/ *noun* [C] a complete defeat —**rout** *verb* [T]

☆**route** /rut; raʊt/ *noun* **1** [C] a way from one place to another: *We took the fastest and most direct route to New York.* ○ *My apartment is close to a major bus route.* ○ *Thousands of people were waiting along the parade route.* ☛ Look also at **en route**. **2** a way of achieving sth: *Hard work is the best route to success.* **3 Route** (*abbr.* **Rte.**) [sing.] (used in the names of some roads, especially major roads in the country): *Route 66*

☆**rou·tine¹** /ruˈtin/ *noun* [C,U] the fixed and usual way of doing things: *If you work out a routine, you will get things done more quickly.* ○ *Children like routine.*

☆**rou·tine²** /ruˈtin/ *adj.* normal and regular; not unusual or special: *My doctor discovered the cancer after a routine medical test.*

☆**rou·tine·ly** /ruˈtinli/ *adv.* very often; regularly; as part of a routine: *The machines are routinely checked for signs of wear and tear.*

☆**row¹** /roʊ/ *noun* [C] **1** a line of people or things: *a row of books* ○ *The kids were standing in a row at the front of the classroom.* **2** a line

of seats in a theater, etc.: *Our seats were in the back row.* ○ *a front-row seat*

IDM **in a row** one after another; without a break: *It rained steadily for four days in a row.*

☆**row²** /roʊ/ *verb* [I,T] to move a boat through the water using long wooden poles with wide, flat ends (**oars**): *Jill and I took turns rowing.* ○ *He rowed the boat slowly down the river.*

row³ /raʊ/ *noun* [C] (*BrE*) = FIGHT²(2) —**row** *verb* [I]

row·boat /ˈroʊboʊt/ *noun* [C] a small boat that you move through the water using long wooden poles with wide, flat ends (**oars**)

row·dy /ˈraʊdi/ *adj.* (**row·di·er**; **row·di·est**) noisy and uncontrolled: *The crowd were getting rowdy.* —**row·di·ness** *noun* [U]

☆**roy·al** /ˈrɔɪəl/ *adj.* connected with a king, queen or a member of their family: *the British royal family*

ˌroyal ˈblue *adj.* deep bright blue in color

roy·al·ty /ˈrɔɪəlti/ *noun* (*pl.* **roy·al·ties**) **1** [U] members of a royal family **2** [C, usually pl.] an amount of money that is paid to the person who wrote a book, piece of music, etc. every time his/her work is sold or performed

Rte. *abbr.* = ROUTE(3)

☆**rub¹** /rʌb/ *verb* (**rub·bing**; **rubbed**) **1** [I,T] to move your hand, a cloth, etc. backward and forward on the surface of sth while pressing firmly: *Ralph rubbed his hands together to keep them warm.* ○ *If you rub hard, the mark should come out.* ○ *The cat rubbed against my leg.* ○ *The cat rubbed its head against my leg.* ○ *He rubbed his face with his hand.* ○ *He rubbed his hand across his face.* ○ *He rubbed the sweat off his face with his hand.* **2** [T] to put a cream, liquid, etc. onto a surface by rubbing (1): *Apply a little of the lotion and rub it into the skin.* **3** [I,T] **rub (on/against sth)** to press on/against sth (often causing pain or damage): *These new shoes are rubbing my heels.*

IDM **rub elbows/shoulders with sb** to spend time at parties and social events with sb, especially famous people

rub it in (*informal*) to remind sb of sth bad, in order to make him/her feel stupid or embarrassed: *I know I'm the one who screwed up – don't rub it in.*

PHRV **rub off (on/onto sb)** (used about a good quality) to be transferred from one person to another: *Let's hope some of her enthusiasm rubs off onto her brother.*

rub² /rʌb/ *noun* [C] an act of rubbing (1): *to give sb a back rub*

☆**rub·ber** /ˈrʌbər/ *noun* **1** [U] a strong substance that is made chemically or from the juice of a tropical tree. Rubber is elastic (= it can stretch and then return to its original shape) and water cannot pass through it: *Car tires are made of rubber.* ○ *foam rubber* ○ *The surgeon put on a pair of rubber gloves.* **2** [C] (*slang*) = CONDOM

tʃ	dʒ	v	θ	ð	s	z	ʃ
chin	**J**une	**v**an	**th**in	**th**en	**s**o	**z**oo	**sh**e

R

rubber 'band *noun* [C] a thin circular piece of rubber that is used for holding things together: *Her hair was tied back with a rubber band.*

rubber 'stamp *noun* [C] a piece of equipment with rubber letters and numbers on it that you use for printing a name, date, etc. on a document

rubber-'stamp *verb* [T] (usually used about sb with authority) to agree to sth without thinking about it carefully

rub·ber·y /ˈrʌbəri/ *adj.* like rubber

☆ **rub·bish** /ˈrʌbɪʃ/ *noun* [U] *formal* or *BrE* = GARBAGE

rub·ble /ˈrʌbl/ *noun* [U] pieces of broken brick, stone, etc., especially from a damaged building

ru·bel·la /ruˈbɛlə/ *noun* [U] = GERMAN MEASLES

ru·by /ˈrubi/ *noun* [C] (*pl.* **ru·bies**) a type of precious stone that is red

ruck·us /ˈrʌkəs/ *noun* [sing.] (*informal*) a noisy argument or disturbance

rud·der /ˈrʌdər/ *noun* [C] a piece of wood or metal that is used for controlling the direction of a boat or an airplane

☆ **rude** /rud/ *adj.* **1** not polite: *It's rude to interrupt when other people are speaking.* ○ *You shouldn't be so rude to your parents.* ☞ Look at **impolite**. **2** sudden and unpleasant: *If you're expecting any help from him, you're in for a rude surprise.* —**rude·ly** *adv.* —**rude·ness** *noun* [U]

ru·di·men·ta·ry /ˌrudəˈmɛntəri/ *adj.* basic or very simple

ruf·fle¹ /ˈrʌfl/ *verb* [T] **1** to make sth messy or no longer smooth: *to ruffle sb's hair* **2** (often passive) to make sb annoyed or confused

IDM ruffle sb's feathers to annoy or upset sb: *He certainly ruffled a few feathers at the meeting with that comment.*

ruf·fle² /ˈrʌfl/ *noun* [C] a narrow piece of cloth with many folds in it which is used to decorate the edge of a curtain, a cover for a bed, etc.

☆ **rug** /rʌg/ *noun* [C] **1** a piece of thick material that covers a small part of a floor ☞ Look at **carpet**. **2** (*slang*) = TOUPEE: *That's quite a rug he's got on!*

Rug·by /ˈrʌgbi/ *noun* [U] a game similar to football that is played by two teams of 13 or 15 players with an oval ball that can be carried or kicked

rug·ged /ˈrʌgəd/ *adj.* **1** (used about land) rough and rocky with few plants: *a rugged coastline* **2** (used about a man) looking strong and attractive

☆ **ru·in¹** /ˈrum/ *verb* [T] **1** to damage sth badly, to destroy: *the ruined city* ○ *The crops were ruined by the late frost.* **2** to change sth so that it is no longer good: *My dress was ruined when I spilled wine over it.* ○ *The scandal ruined his chances for re-election.* **3** to cause sb to lose all

his/her money, hope of being successful, etc.: *The cost of the court case nearly ruined them.*

☆ **ru·in²** /ˈrum/ *noun* **1** [U] a state of destruction, when sth is very badly damaged: *The city was in a state of ruin.* **2** [U] the cause or state of having lost all your money, hope of being successful, etc.: *Many small companies are facing financial ruin.* **3** [C] a building, town, etc. that has been badly damaged or destroyed; the parts of a building, town, etc. that are left when it has been almost completely destroyed: *The old house is now a ruin.* ○ *We went to look at the ruins of the old fort.* ○ *the ruins of the ancient city of Pompeii*

IDM in ruins badly damaged or destroyed: *After the accident, her life seemed to be in ruins.* ○ *The city of Berlin was in ruins at the end of World War II.*

☆ **rule¹** /rul/ *noun* **1** [C] an official statement that tells you what you can or cannot do, say, etc.: *to obey/break a rule* ○ *If you want to be on the team, you'll have to follow the rules.* ○ *Do you know the rules of chess?* ○ *It's against the rules to touch the ball with your hands.* ○ *rules and regulations*

☞ A **law** is stronger. You can be officially punished if you break it.

2 [C] (in a language) a description of what is usual or correct: *What is the rule for forming the past tense?* **3** [sing.] what is usual: *Large families are the exception rather than the rule nowadays.* **4** [U] government; control: *the collapse of Communist rule.* ○ *the rule of law*

IDM as a (general) rule (*formal*) usually: *Women, as a rule, live longer than men.*

bend the rules ⇨ BEND¹

☆ **rule²** /rul/ *verb* **1** [I,T] **rule (over sb/sth)** to have the power over a country, etc.: *Great Britain once ruled over a vast empire.* ○ *A military government ruled the country for over a decade.* ○ *(figurative) His whole life was ruled by his ambition to become a millionaire.* **2** [I,T] **rule (on) sth** to make an official decision: *The Supreme Court ruled that the law was unconstitutional.* **3** [I] (*slang*) to be excellent and much better than anything or anybody else: *The Dallas Cowboys rule!* ☞ The opposite for this meaning is **suck**.

PHRV rule sb/sth out to say that sb/sth is not thought to be possible: *The President has not ruled out sending troops to the area.* ○ *She has been ruled out as a suspect in the murder investigation.*

☆ **rul·er** /ˈrulər/ *noun* [C] **1** a person who rules a country, etc. **2** a straight piece of wood, plastic, etc. marked with inches or centimeters, that you use for measuring sth or for drawing straight lines

☆ **rul·ing¹** /ˈrulɪŋ/ *adj.* (only *before* a noun) with the most power in an organization, a country, etc.: *the nation's ruling party*

i	ɪ	ɛ	æ	ɑ	ɔ	ʌ	ʊ	u
see	sit	ten	cat	hot	saw	cup	put	too

☆ **rul·ing²** /ˈrulɪŋ/ noun [C] an official decision: *the first major Supreme Court ruling on* (= about) *the Internet*

rum /rʌm/ noun [U] a strong alcoholic drink that is made from sugar

rum·ble /ˈrʌmbl/ verb [I] to make a deep heavy sound: *Thunder was rumbling in the distance.* ○ *The truck rumbled past us.* —**rum·ble** noun [sing.]: *the distant rumble of thunder*

rum·mage /ˈrʌmɪdʒ/ verb [I] to move things and make them messy while you are looking for sth: *Nina rummaged through the drawer, looking for a spoon.*

ˈ**rummage sale** noun [C] a sale of old things that people do not want anymore. Clubs, churches, schools and other organizations hold rummage sales in order to get money.
☞ Look also at **garage sale** and **yard sale**.

☆ **ru·mor** /ˈrumər/ noun [C,U] (a piece of) news or information that many people are talking about but that is possibly not true: *There's a rumor going around that the plant is going to close.* ○ *Rumor has it* (= people are saying) *that Len has resigned.* ○ *to confirm/deny a rumor* (= to say that it is true/not true)

ru·mored /ˈrumərd/ adj. said in an unofficial way (but perhaps not true): *It is rumored that they are getting divorced.* ○ *They are rumored to be getting divorced.*

rump /rʌmp/ noun [C] **1** the back end of an animal **2** (*informal*) the part of the body that you sit on

☆ **run¹** /rʌn/ verb [I,T] (*pres. part.* **run·ning**; *p.t.* **ran** /ræn/; *p.p.* **run**) **1** [I,T] to move using your legs, going faster than when you walk: *I had to run to catch the bus.* ○ *The children came running to meet us.* ○ *She's running in the relay race.* ○ *I ran almost five miles this morning.* **2** [I,T] to move, or move sth, quickly in a particular direction: *The car ran downhill and crashed into a wall.* ○ *She ran her finger down the list of passengers.* **3** [I] **run (across, down, out, over, etc.)** (*informal*) to go somewhere quickly: *Can you run to the store and get a quart of milk?* ○ *I'm just going to run across to the neighbors' house for a while.* **4** [I] to go in a particular direction: *The road runs along the side of a lake.* **5** [I] (used about water, a liquid, or a river, etc.) to flow: *When it's really cold, my nose runs.* ○ *I can hear a faucet running somewhere* (= the water from a faucet). **6** [T] to start water flowing, e.g. for a bath: *Run some more hot water into the tub.* **7** [I] (used about the color in material, etc.) to spread (e.g. when the material is washed): *Don't put that red shirt in the washing machine. It might run.* **8** [I] (used about buses, trains, etc.) to travel at regular times: *The school bus is running late this morning.* **9** [I] (used about a machine, an organization, a system, etc.) to work or function: *The engine is running very smoothly now.* **10** [T] to start a machine, etc. and make it

work: *Run the engine for a few minutes before you start off.* ○ *We're running a new computer program today.* **11** [T] to organize or be in charge of sth: *They run a restaurant in Buffalo.* **12** [I] to be one of the people to be chosen (**a candidate**) in an election: *He's running for President.* **13** [I] to continue for a time: *The play ran for almost two years on Broadway.* **14** [T] to publish sth in a newspaper or magazine: *The local paper is running a series of articles on pollution.*

IDM **be running at** to be at a certain level: *The interest rate is now running at 10%.*

up and running ⇨ UP²

☞ For other idioms containing **run**, look at the entries for the nouns, adjectives, etc., e.g. **run in the family** is at **family**.

PHRV **run across sb/sth** to meet or find sb/sth by chance

run away to escape from somewhere: *The dog jumped over the fence and ran away.* ○ *This is the second time Angie has run away from home.* ☞ Look also at **runaway¹**.

run sb/sth down to hit sb/sth with a car, etc.: *Somebody ran him down in the parking lot.*

run into sb to meet sb by chance

run into sth to have difficulties or a problem: *If you run into any problems, just let me know.*

run into sb/sth to hit sb/sth with a car, etc.: *He ran his car into a brick wall.*

run sth off to copy sth, using a machine: *Can you run off ten copies of this, please?*

run off with sth to take or steal sth: *They ran off with his jacket.*

run out (of sth) to finish your supply of sth; to come to an end: *We've run out of coffee.* ○ *Time is running out.*

run sb/sth over; run over sb/sth to hit sb or drive over sb/sth with a car, etc.: *The boy was run over as he was crossing the street.*

run through sth to discuss or read sth quickly: *She ran through the names on the list.*

run sth up to make a bill, cost, etc. greater: *She ran up a huge phone bill when her boyfriend was away at college.*

☆ **run²** /rʌn/ noun **1** [C] an act of running on foot: *Kate goes for a three-mile run every morning.* ○ *a cross-country run* **2** [C] a regular trip that a bus, truck, train, etc. makes: *The school bus was on its last morning run when the accident occurred.* **3** [C] a point in the game of baseball ☞ Look also at **home run** and at the note at **baseball**. **4** [C] an attempt to win a political position in an election: *his unsuccessful run for the state senate* **5** [C] a continuous series of performances of a play, movie, etc.: *The play had a successful run off Broadway.* **6** [sing.] a series of similar events or sth that continues for a very long time: *We've had a run of bad luck recently.* **7** [sing.] **a run on sth** a sudden great demand for sth: *There's always a run on ice cream in the hot weather.* **8** a long

R

ə	y	w	t	eɪ	aɪ	ɔɪ	aʊ	oʊ
about	yes	woman	butter	say	five	boy	now	go

hole that forms from a small tear in a pair of pantyhose

IDM **in the long run** ⇨ LONG¹(2)

on the run hiding or trying to escape from sb/sth: *The escaped prisoner is still on the run.*

run·a·way¹ /ˈrʌnəweɪ/ *noun* [C] a child or young person who has left his/her home without permission, especially in order to avoid problems there: *teenage runaways*

run·a·way² /ˈrʌnəweɪ/ *adj.* (only *before* a noun) **1** out of control: *a runaway train* **2** happening very easily: *His first novel was a runaway success.*

run·down¹ (*also* **run-down**) /ˌrʌnˈdaʊn/ *adj.* **1** in bad condition: *a rundown section of town* **2** tired and not healthy: *You look very rundown.*

run·down² /ˈrʌndaʊn/ *noun* [C, usually sing.] **a rundown (of sth)** a short list or explanation of the way sth is happening or organized: *Here's a rundown of the events at the county fair this weekend:...*

rung¹ /rʌŋ/ *noun* [C] one of the bars that form the steps of a ladder ☞ picture at **ladder**.

rung² *p.p.* of RING²

☆ **run·ner** /ˈrʌnər/ *noun* [C] **1** a person who runs, especially in a race: *a long-distance runner* **2** a person who takes guns, drugs, etc. illegally from one country to another

runner-'up *noun* [C] (*pl.* **runners-up** /ˌrʌnərzˈʌp/) the person or team that finished second in a race or competition

☆ **run·ning¹** /ˈrʌnɪŋ/ *noun* [U] **1** the act or sport of running: *Scott goes running every morning.* ○ *running shoes* **2** the management of a business or other organization: *Jackie's in charge of the day-to-day running of the project.*

IDM **in the running/out of the running (for sth)** (*informal*) having/not having a good chance of getting or winning sth

run·ning² /ˈrʌnɪŋ/ *adj.* (only *before* a noun) **1** not stopping; continuous: *a running battle between two rival gangs* **2** flowing or available from a faucet (used about water): *Her grandparents lived in a one-room shack with no running water.*

run·ning³ /ˈrʌnɪŋ/ *adv.* (used after a number and a noun) one after another, without a break: *Our school has won the championship for four years running.*

'running mate *noun* [C] a person who is chosen to be the candidate for the second-highest position in the government of the U.S. or of a particular state. In an election, people give one vote to a candidate and his/her running mate together.

run·ny /ˈrʌni/ *adj.* (**run·ni·er**; **run·ni·est**) (*informal*) **1** containing more liquid than is usual or than you expected: *The cake batter is very runny.* **2** (used about your eyes or nose) producing too much liquid: *Their kids always seem to have runny noses.*

run-on 'sen·tence *noun* [C] (*grammar*) a sentence that contains two or more parts (**clauses**) which could stand alone as sentences, and which have not been joined together correctly. For example, *"Barry is a good student, he always does his homework."* is a run-on sentence.

run·way /ˈrʌnweɪ/ *noun* [C] a long piece of ground with a hard surface where aircraft take off and land

rup·ture¹ /ˈrʌptʃər/ *noun* [C,U] **1** a sudden breaking or tearing **2** = HERNIA

rup·ture² /ˈrʌptʃər/ *verb* [I,T] to break or tear

☆ **ru·ral** /ˈrʊrəl/ *adj.* connected with the country, not large towns or cities: *He comes from rural Georgia.* ○ *a lack of adequate health care in rural areas* ☞ The opposite is **urban**.

☆ **rush¹** /rʌʃ/ *verb* **1** [I] to go or come very quickly: *Don't rush – take your time.* ○ *The doctor rushed down the hallway.* ○ *I rushed back home when I got the news.* ○ *Don't rush off – I want to talk to you.* **2** [I] **rush to do sth** to do sth without delay: *People rushed to buy stock in the new software company.* **3** [T] to take sb/sth to a place very quickly: *He suffered a heart attack and was rushed to the hospital.* **4** [I,T] **rush (sb) (into sth/into doing sth)** to do sth in a hurry or without enough thought; to make sb act in this way: *We rushed into buying the house – it turned out to be a mistake.* ○ *Don't rush your project – there's plenty of time.* ○ *Don't let yourself be rushed into marriage.*

☆ **rush²** /rʌʃ/ *noun* **1** [sing.] a sudden quick movement: *At the end of the game there was a mad rush for the exits.* **2** [sing., U] (a need for) hurry: *I can't stop now. I'm in a big rush.* ○ *You can give it to me when you finish. There's no rush.* **3** [sing.] a time when many people try to get or do sth in a hurry: *There's been a rush to buy gas before the price goes up.* ○ *You should do your shopping now to avoid the holiday rush.* ☞ Look also at **gold rush**. **4** [C, usually sing.] (*slang*) a sudden, strong feeling that you get especially from taking a drug or doing sth exciting: *Wow, what a rush – let's go on the roller coaster again!*

☆ **'rush hour** *noun* [C,U] the time each day when the traffic is busy because people are traveling to or from work: *rush-hour traffic*

☆ **rust¹** /rʌst/ *noun* [U] a reddish-brown substance that forms on the surface of iron, etc., caused by the action of air and water

rust² /rʌst/ *verb* [I,T] to (cause sth to) be attacked by rust¹: *Some parts of the machine had rusted pretty badly.* ○ *Road salt had rusted the car pretty badly.*

rus·tic /ˈrʌstɪk/ *adj.* typical of the country (and therefore simple and old-fashioned): *The rooms are decorated in a rustic style.* ☞ Look at **rural** and **urban**.

rus·tle /ˈrʌsl/ *verb* [I,T] to make a sound like dry leaves moving together; to cause sth to

ər	ɪr	ɛr	ɑr	ɔr	ʊr	ʒ	h	ŋ
bird	near	hair	car	north	tour	vision	hat	sing

make this sound: *There was a rustling noise in the bushes.* ○ *Somebody behind me was rustling his newspaper all through the concert.*

PHRV **rustle sb/sth up** (*informal*) to find sb or prepare sth in a short time: *to rustle up a quick snack* —**rus·tle** *noun* [sing.]: *the rustle of leaves in the woods*

☆**rust·y** /ˈrʌsti/ *adj.* (**rust·i·er**; **rust·i·est**) **1** covered with rust[1]: *rusty cans* **2** (used about a skill) of poor quality because you have not used it for a long time: *I can speak French well, but my Spanish is pretty rusty.*

rut /rʌt/ *noun* [C] a deep track that a wheel makes in soft ground

IDM **be (stuck) in a rut** to have a boring way of life that is difficult to change

ruth·less /ˈruθləs/ *adj.* showing no pity or sympathy toward other people; thinking first about yourself and what you want: *You have to be ruthless to succeed in politics.* —**ruth·less·ly** *adv.* —**ruth·less·ness** *noun* [U]

RV /ˌɑr ˈvi/ (*also* **motor home**) *noun* [C] recreational vehicle; a large vehicle that you can sleep, cook, etc. in when you are traveling or on vacation

rye /raɪ/ *noun* [U] a plant that is grown for its grain, which is used to make flour and also whiskey

Ss

S, s /ɛs/ *noun* [C] (*pl.* **S's**; **s's**) the nineteenth letter of the English alphabet: *"School" begins with (an) " S."*

S (*also* **S.**) *abbr.* south

the Sab·bath /ˈsæbəθ/ *noun* [sing.] the day of the week for rest and worship in certain religions (Sunday for most Christians, Saturday for Jews)

sab·bat·i·cal /səˈbætɪkl/ *noun* [C,U] a long paid break that teachers, especially at colleges and universities, take in order to study, write books, etc.: *Prof. Ramos is on sabbatical this quarter.*

sab·o·tage[1] /ˈsæbətɑʒ/ *noun* [U] the act of damaging or destroying machinery, roads, bridges, etc. or of ruining plans on purpose and secretly, in order to prevent an enemy or a competitor from being successful: *The explosion at the oil refinery was caused by sabotage.*

sab·o·tage[2] /ˈsæbətɑʒ/ *verb* [T] to destroy or damage sth by using sabotage[1]: *There are rumors that the plane which crashed had been sabotaged.*

sac·cha·rin /ˈsækərɪn/ *noun* [U] a very sweet artificial substance that can be used instead of sugar

☆**sack[1]** /sæk/ *noun* [C] a large bag made from paper, plastic or rough, heavy material, used for carrying or storing things (e.g. vegetables, coal, etc.): *a paper sack* ○ *sacks of onions* ○ *They carried several sacks of groceries in from the car.*

sack[2] /sæk/ *verb* [T] (*BrE*) = FIRE2

sa·cred /ˈseɪkrəd/ *adj.* **1** connected with God, a god or religion; having a special religious meaning: *sacred music* (= music played in religious services) ○ *The Koran is the sacred book of Islam.* **2** too important and special to be changed or harmed: *a sacred tradition*

sac·ri·fice[1] /ˈsækrəfaɪs/ *noun* **1** [U] the act of offering sth, e.g. an animal that has been killed, to a god **2** [C] a thing, e.g. an animal that has been killed, that is offered to a god **3** [C,U] the act of giving up sth that is important or valuable in order to achieve sth; the thing that you give up in this way: *If we're going to take a trip this year, we'll have to make some sacrifices.* ○ *He was willing to make any sacrifice in order to succeed.*

sac·ri·fice[2] /ˈsækrəfaɪs/ *verb* **1** [I,T] to offer sth to a god, often by killing it **2** [T] to give up sth important or valuable in order to achieve sth: *to sacrifice your life for your country* ○ *She is not willing to sacrifice her career in order to have children.*

sac·ri·le·gious /ˌsækrəˈlɪdʒəs/ *adj.* treating sth that is considered holy or very special without the respect that it deserves

☆**sad** /sæd/ *adj.* (**sad·der**; **sad·dest**) **1** unhappy or causing unhappiness: *I was sad to hear of the death of your father.* ○ *She felt terribly sad when her friend moved away.* ○ *That's one of the saddest stories I've ever heard!* **2** bad or unsatisfactory: *It's a sad state of affairs when your best friend doesn't trust you.* —**sad·ness** *noun* [C,U]

sad·den /ˈsædn/ *verb* [T] (often passive) to cause sb to feel sad: *We were deeply saddened by the news of your mother's death.*

sad·dle[1] /ˈsædl/ *noun* [C] **1** a seat, usually made of leather, that you put on a horse so that you can ride it ☞ picture at horse. **2** a seat on a bicycle or motorcycle

sad·dle[2] /ˈsædl/ *verb* [I,T] to put a saddle1 on a horse, etc.

PHRV **saddle sb with sth** to give sb a responsibility or task that he/she does not want: *I've been saddled with organizing the office party.*

tʃ	dʒ	v	θ	ð	s	z	ʃ
chin	**June**	**van**	**thin**	**then**	**so**	**zoo**	**she**

sa·dism /ˈseɪdɪzəm/ noun [U] getting enjoyment or sexual pleasure from being cruel or causing pain —**sa·dist** /ˈseɪdɪst/ noun [C] —**sa·dis·tic** /səˈdɪstɪk/ adj. —**sa·dis·ti·cal·ly** /-kli/ adv.

☆ **sad·ly** /ˈsædli/ adv. **1** in a way that shows unhappiness: He spoke sadly about the death of his father. **2** unfortunately, in a way that makes you feel sad or sorry: Sadly, Morgan died before his book was published. **3** in a way that is wrong: If you think that I've forgotten what you did, you're sadly mistaken.

sa·fa·ri /səˈfɑri/ noun [C,U] (pl. **sa·fa·ris**) a trip, especially in Africa, for hunting or looking at wild animals

☆ **safe¹** /seɪf/ adj. **1 safe (from sb/sth)** free from danger; not able to be hurt: You shouldn't walk home alone at night. You won't be safe. ○ Do you think my car will be safe on this street? ○ Keep the papers where they will be safe from fire. **2** not causing danger, harm or risk: Don't sit on that chair – it isn't safe. ○ I left my suitcase in a safe place and went for a cup of coffee. ○ Is this drug safe for children? ○ He hid from the police until it was safe to come out. ○ She's a very safe driver. ○ I thought it would be a safe investment, but I lost everything. ○ Is it safe to drink the water here? ○ I think it's safe to say that the situation is unlikely to change for quite a while. **3** not hurt or damaged: After the accident, he made sure that all the passengers were safe.

IDM **be on the safe side** to avoid taking risks; to be very careful: I think this is enough money to pay for the meal, but I'll take a little more just to be on the safe side.

safe and sound not hurt or damaged: The missing child was found safe and sound by the police. —**safe·ly** adv.: I called my parents to tell them I had arrived safely.

☆ **safe²** /seɪf/ noun [C] a strong metal box or cabinet with a special lock where you can keep money, jewelry, documents, etc.

safe-de·pos·it box noun [C] a box or drawer in a special room in a bank where you can keep valuable things such as documents, jewelry, etc.

safe·guard¹ /ˈseɪfgɑrd/ noun [C] **a safeguard (against sb/sth)** something that protects against possible dangers: Make a copy of all your computer disks as a safeguard against accidents.

safe·guard² /ˈseɪfgɑrd/ verb [T] **safeguard sb/sth (against sb/sth)** to keep sth safe; to protect: When parents get divorced, the children's rights must be safeguarded.

safe sex (also **safer sex**) noun [U] ways of having sex that can reduce the chance of passing a sexual disease such as AIDS from one person to another, e.g. using a condom

☆ **safe·ty** /ˈseɪfti/ noun [U] the state of being safe; not being dangerous or in danger: In the

interests of safety, all employees must wear hard hats. ○ safety regulations ○ She has been missing for several days, and the police are very concerned about her safety. ○ The new law will improve the quality and safety of these products.

safety belt noun [C] = SEAT BELT

safety net noun [C] **1** a net that is placed to catch sb who is performing high above the ground if he/she falls **2** something that will help you (usually with money) in a difficult situation

safety pin noun [C] a metal pin that is used for fastening things together. The pin is bent around and the point goes under a cover so that it cannot be dangerous. ☞ picture at pin.

sag /sæg/ verb [I] (**sag·ging**; **sagged**) to hang loosely or to sink down, especially in the middle: The skin on your face starts to sag as you get older.

sa·ga /ˈsɑgə/ noun [C] a very long story; a long series of events

sage·brush /ˈseɪdʒbrʌʃ/ noun [U] a small bush that grows in dry areas of western North America

Sag·it·tar·i·us /ˌsædʒəˈtɛriəs/ noun [C,U] the ninth sign of the zodiac, the Hunter; a person who was born under this sign ☞ picture at zodiac.

said p.t., p.p. of SAY¹

☆ **sail¹** /seɪl/ noun [C] a large piece of strong material that is fastened onto a ship or boat. The wind blows against the sail and drives the ship along. ☞ picture at boat.

IDM **set sail** to begin a trip by sea: Columbus set sail for India.

☆ **sail²** /seɪl/ verb **1** [I] to travel on water in a ship or boat of any type; to move on water: On the cruise, we sailed into the Caribbean. ○ I stood at the window and watched the ships sailing by. **2** [I,T] to travel in and control a boat with sails, especially as a sport: I've never sailed this kind of boat before.

☞ When you are talking about spending time sailing a boat, the form **go sailing** is very common: We often go sailing on weekends.

3 [I] to begin a trip on water: When does the ship sail? ○ We sail for the Bahamas at six o'clock tomorrow morning. **4** [I] to move somewhere quickly in a smooth or confident way: The ball sailed over the fence and into the neighbor's yard. ○ Mary sailed into the room and sat down at the head of the table.

IDM **sail through (sth)** to get through a test or a difficult process easily: He studied hard and sailed through all his exams.

sail·board /ˈseɪlbɔrd/ noun [C] a board with a sail that you hold while standing, as the wind moves it across the surface of the water ☞ picture at windsurfing.

i	ɪ	ɛ	æ	ɑ	ɔ	ʌ	ʊ	u
see	sit	ten	cat	hot	saw	cup	put	too

☆**sail·boat** /ˈseɪlboʊt/ *noun* [C] a boat that uses a sail or sails ☞ picture at **boat**.

sail·ing /ˈseɪlɪŋ/ *noun* [U] the sport of being in, and controlling, small boats with sails: *They do a lot of sailing.*

☆**sail·or** /ˈseɪlər/ *noun* [C] a member of the crew of a ship (usually not an officer)

☆**saint** /seɪnt/ *noun* [C] **1** a very good or holy person who is given special respect after death by the Christian church

☞ When it is used as a title, **saint** is written with a capital letter: *Saint Patrick.* In the names of places, churches, etc., the short form **St.** is usually used: *St. Louis, Missouri.* Look also at **patron saint**.

2 a very good, kind person

☆**sake** /seɪk/ *noun* [C]
for Christ's, God's, goodness', Heaven's, Pete's sake (used as part of a question or order, to make it stronger or to show that you are angry): *What took you so long, for God's sake? ○ For Christ's sake, don't be so stupid! ○ For goodness' sake, hurry up!*

☞ **For Christ's sake** and **for God's sake** are stronger and may offend some people.

for the sake of sb/sth; for sb's/sth's sake in order to help sb/sth: *Don't go to any trouble for my sake. ○ They only stayed together for the sake of their children/for their children's sake.*
for the sake of sth/of doing sth in order to get or keep sth; for the purpose of sth: *It's not worth complaining for the sake of a few pennies. ○ You're just arguing for the sake of arguing* (= because you like arguing).

salad salad

lettuce

cucumber

tomato

☆**sal·ad** /ˈsæləd/ *noun* [C,U] a mixture of vegetables, usually uncooked, often with spices and sometimes small pieces of meat: *potato salad ○ What kind of dressing do you want on your salad? ○ I don't feel like a big meal – I think I'll just have a salad.*

ˈsalad bar *noun* [C] a place in a restaurant where you can choose several kinds of salads and put them on your plate yourself

sa·la·mi /səˈlɑmi/ *noun* [C,U] a type of large sausage with a strong flavor, usually eaten in thin slices

☆**sal·a·ry** /ˈsæləri/ *noun* [C,U] (*pl.* **sal·a·ries**) the money that a person receives regularly for the work he/she has done: *My salary is de-*

posited directly into my bank account. ○ *a high/low salary* ☞ Look at the note at **pay¹**.

☆**sale** /seɪl/ *noun* **1** [C,U] the act of selling or being sold; the exchange of an item for money; the occasion when sth is sold: *The sale of alcohol to anyone under the age of 21 is against the law. ○ Business is bad. I haven't made a sale all week. ○ a sale of used toys* ☞ Look also at **garage sale, rummage sale** and **yard sale**. **2 sales** [plural] the amount sold: *Sales of personal computers have increased rapidly.* **3** [C] a time when stores sell things at prices that are lower than usual: *Sale! All week! Everything half price! ○ I'm not going to buy a coat now – I'll wait until there's a sale.*

IDM for sale offered for sb to buy: *This painting is not for sale.*

on sale 1 offered at a lower price than usual: *I bought this jacket on sale at the mall.* **2** available for sb to buy, especially in stores: *Tickets for the concert go on sale Saturday morning at 10:00.*

☆**sales·clerk** /ˈseɪlzklərk/ (*also* **clerk**) *noun* [C] a person whose job is to sell things to people in a store

☆**sales·man** /ˈseɪlzmən/ (*also* **sales·wom·an, sales·per·son**) *noun* [C] a person whose job is to sell things to people: *an insurance salesman*

☆**ˈsales tax** *noun* [C,U] a tax that is added to the price of sth that you buy

sa·li·va /səˈlaɪvə/ *noun* [U] the liquid that is produced in the mouth

salm·on /ˈsæmən/ *noun* [C,U] (*pl.* **salm·on**) a large fish with silver skin and pink flesh: *smoked salmon*

sal·mo·nel·la /ˌsælməˈnɛlə/ *noun* [U] a type of very small living thing (**bacteria**) that causes food poisoning

sa·lon /səˈlɑn/ *noun* [C] a store where you can have your hair cut or have beauty treatments: *a hair salon ○ a beauty salon*

sa·loon /səˈlun/ *noun* [C] a bar where alcoholic drinks were sold in the western U.S. in the 1800s

sal·sa /ˈsɔlsə/ *noun* [U] **1** a type of Mexican sauce with a hot taste, made from tomatoes, onions, red or green peppers, and sometimes other vegetables or fruit **2** a type of Latin American dance music with a strong beat

☆**salt¹** /sɔlt/ *noun* [U] a common white substance that is found in ocean water and the earth, that is used especially for flavoring and preserving food: *Season with salt and pepper. ○ Could you please pass the salt? ○ Add a pinch* (= a small amount) *of salt.*

IDM take sth with a grain of salt ⇨ **GRAIN**

salt² /sɔlt/ *verb* [T] to put salt on or in sth: *salted peanuts*

salt³ /sɔlt/ *adj.* having the taste of or containing salt: *salt water*

salt·wa·ter /ˈsɔltwɔtər; -wɑ-/ *adj.* living in the

ocean: *a saltwater fish* ☞ Fish in rivers and lakes are **freshwater** fish.

☆ **salt·y** /ˈsɔlti/ *adj.* (**salt·i·er**; **salt·i·est**) having the taste of, or containing, salt: *I didn't like the meat – it was too salty.*

sa·lute¹ /səˈlut/ *noun* [C] **1** a sign that a soldier, etc. makes to show respect, by raising his/her hand to the forehead: *to give a salute* **2** an action that shows respect for sb: *The next program is a salute to one of Hollywood's greatest stars.*

sa·lute² /səˈlut/ *verb* [I,T] to show respect with a salute¹(1,2) : *The soldiers saluted as they marched past the general.* ◦ *The soldiers saluted the general.* ◦ *This is the day on which we salute those who died in the war.*

sal·vage /ˈsælvɪdʒ/ *verb* [T] to rescue sth from a damaged building or ship; to rescue sth from a disaster: *They salvaged as much as they could from the house after the fire.* ◦ (*figurative*) *The team have only 5 minutes left to salvage something from the game.* —**sal·vage** *noun* [U]: *a salvage operation*

sal·va·tion /sælˈveɪʃn/ *noun* **1** [U, sing.] a thing or a person that saves sb/sth from danger or a difficult situation **2** [U] (in the Christian religion) the state of being saved from evil

☆ **same¹** /seɪm/ *adj.* **1 the same … (as sb/sth …); the same … (that…)** not different, not another or other; exactly the one or ones that you have mentioned before: *My brother and I had the same teacher in school.* ◦ *She comes from the same town as I do.* ◦ *I'm going to wear the same clothes as I wore yesterday.* ◦ *Are you the same person (that) I talked to on the phone yesterday?* **2 the same … (as sb/sth …); the same … (that…)** exactly like the one already mentioned: *I wouldn't buy the same car again* (= the same model of car). ◦ *We both came to the party wearing the same outfit.* ◦ *I had the same experience as you some time ago.* ◦ *I've had the same experience (that) you had.*

☞ We cannot say **a same** … To express this idea we use **the same kind/sort/type of:** *I'd like the same type of job my dad has.*

IDM **at the same time 1** together; at one time: *I can't concentrate on two things at the same time.* ◦ *Can he really watch TV and study at the same time?* **2** on the other hand; however: *It's a really good idea, but at the same time it's pretty risky.*

be in the same boat to be in the same difficult situation as sb else: *Nobody's happy about the boss's decision – we're all in the same boat here.*

by the same token in a similar way; using the same reasons: *I agree that Dad shouldn't have gotten so mad at you. But, by the same token, you should try not to aggravate him so much.*

on the same wavelength able to understand sb because you have similar ideas and opinions

☆ **same²** /seɪm/ *pron.* **the same (as sb/sth/…)** the same thing, person, situation, etc.: *Is there another word that means the same as this?* ◦ *Look at what I'm doing and then do the same.* ◦ *Things will never be the same again now that my mom has passed away.*

IDM **all/just the same** even though sth is true; in spite of this/that: *I understand your point of view. All the same, it doesn't change my opinion.* ◦ *They tried to act naturally, but I knew just the same that something was wrong.*

much the same ⇨ MUCH²

same here (*informal*) the same thing is also true for me: *"I'm bored." "Same here."*

(the) same to you (*informal*) (used as an answer when sb says sth rude to you or wishes you sth): *"You jerk!" "Same to you!"* ◦ *"Have a nice weekend." "The same to you."*

the same *adv.* in the same way; not differently: *We treat everyone in the class the same.*

☆ **sam·ple¹** /ˈsæmpl/ *noun* [C] **1** a small quantity of sth that is typical of the rest of it: *She sent a sample of her work in an attempt to get a job.* ◦ *a blood sample* **2** a small number of people who are asked questions in order to find out information about a larger group **3** a small amount of a product, that is given free to the public in order to show what it is like: *They were giving out free samples of candy at the store.*

☆ **sam·ple²** /ˈsæmpl/ *verb* [T] to taste or use a small amount of sth (in order to find out what it is like or to decide whether you like it or not): *Let me sample a little of your cake.*

sanc·tion¹ /ˈsæŋkʃn/ *noun* **1** [C, usually pl.] an action, especially the stopping of trade, that is taken by other countries against a country that has broken an international law: *The United Nations imposed economic sanctions against South Africa during the 1980s.* **2** [U] (*formal*) official permission to do sth

sanc·tion² /ˈsæŋkʃn/ *verb* [T] (*formal*) to give official permission for sth: *an officially sanctioned protest march*

sanc·tu·ar·y /ˈsæŋktʃuˌɛri/ *noun* (*pl.* **sanc·tu·ar·ies**) **1** [C] a place where birds or animals are protected from hunters and other dangers: *a wildlife sanctuary* **2** [C,U] a place where sb can be safe from enemies, the police, etc.

☆ **sand¹** /sænd/ *noun* [U] a powder consisting of very small grains of rock, found in deserts and on beaches: *You need sand to make concrete.* ◦ *Wait a minute – I have some sand in my shoe.* ◦ *When we go on vacation, all we want is sun, sea and sand.*

sand² /sænd/ *verb* [T] **1** to make sth, especially wood, smooth by rubbing it with sandpaper **2** to put sand¹ onto a road, sidewalk, etc.

ər	ɪr	ɛr	ɑr	ɔr	ʊr	ʒ	h	ŋ
bird	near	hair	car	north	tour	vision	hat	sing

which is covered in ice and snow in the winter in order to make it safer to walk or drive on

san·dal /ˈsændl/ *noun* [C] a type of light, open shoe with straps that people wear when the weather is warm ☞ picture at **shoe**.

sand·cas·tle /ˈsændkæsl/ *noun* [C] a pile of sand that looks like a castle, made by children playing on a beach

ˈsand dune *noun* [C] = DUNE

sand·pa·per /ˈsændpeɪpər/ *noun* [U] strong paper with sand on it that is used for rubbing surfaces in order to make them smoother

☆ **sand·wich¹** /ˈsænwɪtʃ/ *noun* [C] two slices of bread with food between them: *a ham and cheese sandwich* ○ *It's going to be a long trip, so let's take some sandwiches.* ○ *What's in that sandwich?*

sand·wich² /ˈsænwɪtʃ/ *verb* [T] **sandwich sb/sth (between sb/sth)** to place sb/sth in a very narrow space between two other things or people: *I wasn't very comfortable during the flight, sandwiched between two very large people.*

sand·y /ˈsændi/ *adj.* (**sand·i·er; sand·i·est**) covered with sand or with a lot of sand in it: *miles of sandy beach* ○ *sandy soil*

sane /seɪn/ *adj.* **1** (used about a person) mentally normal; not crazy: *With a job like mine, it's incredible that I'm still sane!* **2** (used about a person or an idea, a decision, etc.) sensible; showing good judgment: *I had to accept the offer. It was the only sane thing to do.* ☞ The opposite is **insane**. The noun is **sanity**.

sang *p.t.* of SING

san·i·tar·y /ˈsænəˌtɛri/ *adj.* **1** for or connected with the protection of health, e.g. how human waste is removed: *a refugee camp with no sanitary facilities or clean drinking water* **2** clean; without any tiny living things (**germs**) that can cause disease: *Don't let the dog lick your face – it's not sanitary!*

san·i·ta·tion /ˌsænəˈteɪʃn/ *noun* [U] a system for protecting public health, especially by removing waste and garbage

san·i·ty /ˈsænəti/ *noun* [U] **1** the ability to think and behave in a normal way **2** sensible or normal thought or behavior ☞ The opposite is **insanity**.

sank *p.t.* of SINK¹

San·ta Claus /ˈsæntə klɔz/ (*also* **Santa**) *noun* [sing.] an old man with a red coat and a long white beard who, some children believe, brings presents in the night before Christmas

☞ Children believe that Santa Claus lives at the North Pole. He rides in a **sleigh** which is pulled by **reindeer** that can fly through the air.

sap¹ /sæp/ *noun* [U] the liquid in a plant or tree

sap² /sæp/ *verb* [T] (**sap·ping; sapped**) to make sth weak or to destroy it

sap·ling /ˈsæplɪŋ/ *noun* [C] a young tree

sap·phire /ˈsæfaɪər/ *noun* [C,U] a bright blue precious stone

sar·casm /ˈsɑrkæzəm/ *noun* [U] the use of words or expressions to mean the opposite of what they actually say. People use sarcasm in order to criticize other people or to make them look stupid: *"No, you didn't take long to get ready. Only two hours," she said with heavy sarcasm.* —**sar·cas·tic** /sɑrˈkæstɪk/ *adj.*: *a sarcastic comment* —**sar·cas·ti·cal·ly** /-kli/ *adv.*

sar·dine /sɑrˈdin/ *noun* [C] a type of very small fish, usually sold packed very tightly in cans

SASE *abbr.* = SELF-ADDRESSED STAMPED ENVELOPE

sash /sæʃ/ *noun* [C] a long piece of material that is worn around the waist or over the shoulder, often as part of a uniform, etc.

sat *p.t., p.p.* of SIT

SAT /ˌɛs eɪ ˈti/ *noun* [C] (*trademark*) Scholastic Assessment Test; an exam that students in high school take before they go to college: *to take the SAT* ○ *SAT scores*

Sat. *abbr.* = SATURDAY

Sa·tan /ˈseɪtn/ the Devil —**satanic** /səˈtænɪk/ *adj.*

☆ **sat·el·lite** /ˈsætlˌaɪt/ *noun* [C] **1** a natural object in space that goes around a bigger object, usually a planet **2** an artificial object that has been sent into space and that moves around a planet for a particular purpose: *satellite pictures of today's weather*

ˌsatellite ˈtelevision (*also* ˌsatellite ˌTˈV) *noun* [U] a system of broadcasting television programs by satellite ☞ In order to receive satellite TV, you need a satellite **dish**. Look also at **cable television**.

sat·in /ˈsætn/ *noun* [U] a type of cloth that is smooth and shiny

sat·ire /ˈsætaɪər/ *noun* **1** [U] the use of humor to attack a person, an idea or behavior that you think is bad or foolish **2** [C] **satire (on sb/sth)** a piece of writing or a play, movie, etc. that uses satire (1): *a political satire* —**sa·tir·i·cal** /səˈtɪrɪkl/ *adj.*: *a satirical magazine* —**sa·tir·i·cal·ly** /-kli/ *adv.*

☆ **sat·is·fac·tion** /ˌsætəsˈfækʃn/ *noun* **1** [U] the feeling of pleasure that you have when you have done, gotten or achieved what you wanted: *Gwen stood back and looked at her work with a sense of satisfaction.* ○ *We finally made a decision that was to everyone's satisfaction* (= that everyone was pleased with). ☞ The opposite is **dissatisfaction**. **2** [C] something that gives you a feeling of pleasure: *It was a great satisfaction to me to know that I had done the job well.*

☆ **sat·is·fac·to·ry** /ˌsætəsˈfæktəri/ *adj.* **1** good enough (but not very good): *This piece of work is not satisfactory. Please do it again.* ○ *She is in the hospital in satisfactory condition.* **2** good

tʃ	dʒ	v	θ	ð	s	z	ʃ
chin	June	van	thin	then	so	zoo	she

enough for a particular purpose: *a satisfactory solution to a conflict* ☞ The opposite is **unsatisfactory**. —**sat·is·fac·to·ri·ly** /-tərəli/ *adv.*: *Work is progressing satisfactorily.*

☆ **sat·is·fied** /ˈsætəsfaɪd/ *adj.* **satisfied (with sb/sth)** pleased because you have had or done what you wanted: *a satisfied smile* ○ *a satisfied customer* ○ *I hope you're satisfied with what you did!* ☞ The opposite is **dissatisfied**.

☆ **sat·is·fy** /ˈsætəsfaɪ/ *verb* [T] (*pres. part.* **sat·is·fy·ing**; *3rd pers. sing. pres.* **sat·is·fies**; *p.t., p.p.* **sat·is·fied**) **1** to make sb pleased by doing or giving him/her what he/she wants: *Nothing satisfies him – he's always complaining.* **2** to have or do what is necessary for sth: *She satisfied all the requirements for her bachelor's degree.* ○ *I had a quick look inside the package just to satisfy my curiosity.* **3 satisfy sb (that ...)** to show or prove to sb that sth is true or has been done: *The jury were not satisfied that she was telling the truth.* ○ *She checked the room once again to satisfy herself that everything was ready.*

sat·is·fy·ing /ˈsætəsfaɪɪŋ/ *adj.* pleasing; giving satisfaction: *It was a very satisfying feeling, knowing that we'd finished the job on time.*

sat·u·rate /ˈsætʃəreɪt/ *verb* [T] **1** to make sth very wet: *Her clothes were completely saturated.* **2** to fill sth completely: *The market is saturated with cheap imports.* —**sat·u·ra·tion** /ˌsætʃəˈreɪʃn/ *noun* [U]: *The market for VCRs has reached saturation point* (= there can be no more increases in sales).

☆ **Sat·ur·day** /ˈsætərdeɪ; -di/ *noun* [C,U] (*abbr.* **Sat.**) the day of the week after Friday and before Sunday ☞ For examples of the use of the days of the week in sentences, look at **Monday**.

Sat·urn /ˈsætərn/ *noun* [sing.] the planet that is sixth in order from the sun and that has rings around it

☆ **sauce** /sɔs/ *noun* [C,U] a thick liquid (that can be hot or cold) that you eat on or with other food: *The chicken was served in a delicious sauce.* ○ *tomato sauce* ○ *I opened a jar of spaghetti sauce.* ☞ **Gravy** is a type of thin sauce that is made from meat juices and eaten hot with meat. **Dressing** is a type of sauce that is eaten cold on salads.

sauce·pan /ˈsɔspæn/ *noun* [C] a round metal pot that is used for cooking things on top of a stove. A saucepan usually has a lid and one or more handles. ☞ picture at **pan**.

☆ **sau·cer** /ˈsɔsər/ *noun* [C] a small round plate that you put under a cup: *a cup and saucer* ☞ picture at **cup**.

sau·na /ˈsɔnə/ *noun* [C] a room or building that is very hot and full of steam, where you can sit to relax: *The health club has a swimming pool and sauna.*

sausages

☆ **sau·sage** /ˈsɔsɪdʒ/ *noun* [C,U] a mixture of chopped meat, spices, etc. that is made into a long thin shape. Some sausage is eaten cold in slices; other types are cooked and then served whole: *Italian sausage* ○ *sausage and eggs*

sav·age¹ /ˈsævɪdʒ/ *adj.* very cruel or fierce: *a savage attack by a big dog* ○ *The book has received some savage criticism.* —**sav·age·ly** *adv.*

sav·age² /ˈsævɪdʒ/ *verb* [T] to attack sb/sth fiercely

sav·age·ry /ˈsævɪdʒri/ *noun* [U] very cruel or violent behavior

☆ **save¹** /seɪv/ *verb* **1** [T] **save sb/sth (from sth/ from doing sth)** to make or keep sb/sth safe from death, loss, changes, etc.: *to save sb's life* ○ *to save sb from drowning* ○ *a campaign to save the whales* ○ *We are trying to save the school from closing.* **2** [I,T] **save (sth) (up) (for sth)** to keep or not spend money, etc. so that you can use it later: *Carol is saving up for a new car.* ○ *We try and save $100 a month.* **3** [T] to keep sth for future use: *I'll be home late, so save me some dinner.* ○ *Save that box. It might come in handy.* ○ *If you get there first, save me a seat.* **4** [T] to store information in a computer by giving it a special instruction: *Don't forget to save the file before you close it.* **5** [I,T] to prevent the spending or waste of time or money: *You can save on gas by getting a smaller car.* ○ *This car will save you a lot on gas.* ○ *I saved over $5 on groceries by using coupons today.* **6** [T] to make sth unnecessary; to make it unnecessary for sb to use sth, spend sth, etc.: *You could save yourself a lot of time and effort if you organized your work better.* ○ *Can you give me a ride? It'll save me having to walk.* **7** [T] to stop a goal from being scored in soccer, hockey, etc.

IDM **keep/save sth for a rainy day** ⇨ RAINY
lose/save face ⇨ FACE¹

save² /seɪv/ *noun* [C] (in soccer, hockey, etc.) an act of preventing a goal from being scored: *The goalie made a great save.*

sav·er /ˈseɪvər/ *noun* [C] a person who saves money in a bank: *The increase in interest rates is good news for savers.*

☆ **sav·ing** /ˈseɪvɪŋ/ *noun* **1** [C] an amount of time, money, etc. that you do not have to use or spend: *The sale price represents a saving of 25%.* **2 savings** [plural] money that you have saved for future use: *He used his life savings to buy the business.*

S

'savings ac,count *noun* [C] a type of bank account where your money earns interest ☞ Look at **checking account**.

,savings and 'loan *noun* [C] a business like a bank where people can save money in order to earn interest and borrow money in order to buy houses, etc.

sav·ior /'seɪvyər/ *noun* **1** [C] a person who rescues or saves sb/sth from danger, loss, death, etc. **2** often **Savior** [sing.] (in the Christian religion) Jesus Christ

sa·vor·y /'seɪvəri/ *adj.* (used about food) having a very good taste or smell

☆ **saw¹** *p.t.* of SEE

☆ **saw²** /sɔ/ *noun* [C] a tool that is used for cutting wood, etc. A saw has a long metal blade with sharp teeth on it: *a power saw* ☞ picture at **tool**.

saw³ /sɔ/ *verb* [I,T] (*p.t.* **sawed**; *p.p.* **sawed** or **sawn** /sɔn/) to cut sth with a saw²: *to saw through the trunk of a tree* ○ *Paula sawed the branch off the tree.* ○ *He sawed the log up into firewood.*

saw·dust /'sɔdʌst/ *noun* [U] very small pieces of wood that fall like powder when you are sawing

sax /sæks/ *noun* [C] (*informal*) = SAXOPHONE

sax·o·phone
/'sæksəfoʊn/(also *informal* **sax**) *noun* [C] a metal musical instrument that you play by blowing into it. Saxophones are usually used for playing jazz.

saxophone

☆ **say¹** /seɪ/ *verb* (*3rd pers. sing. pres.* **says** /sɛz/; *p.t., p.p.* **said** /sɛd/) **1** [T] **say sth (to sb)** to speak words: *"Please come back," she said.* ○ *The teacher said we should hand in our papers by Friday.* ○ *to say goodbye* ○ *to say your prayers* ○ *He said to his mother that he would call back later.* ○ *They just sat there without saying anything.* ○ *"This isn't going to be easy," she said to herself* (= she thought).

☞ **Say** or **tell**? **Say** is often used with the actual words that were spoken or before **that** in indirect speech: *"I'll catch the 9 o'clock flight," he said.* ○ *He said that he would catch the 9 o'clock flight.* Notice that you say sth **to** sb: *He said to me that he would catch the 9 o'clock flight.* **Tell** is always followed by a noun or pronoun, showing who you were speaking to: *He told me that he would catch the 9 o'clock flight.* **Tell**, not **say**, can also be used when you are talking about giving orders or advice: *I told them to hurry up.* ○ *She's always telling me what I ought to do.*

2 [T] (used about a book, notice, etc.) to give information: *What time does it say on that*

clock? ○ *The map says the hotel is just a couple of blocks away.* **3** [I,T] to express a thought, feeling, answer, opinion, etc.: *"What time is she coming?" "I don't know – she didn't say."* ○ *I would like to say how happy I am to be here today.* ○ *He is said to be very rich* (= people say that he is very rich). ○ *What is the artist trying to say in this painting?* ○ *Don't get mad at me – all I'm saying is that we should wait a little longer.* ○ *Well, what do you say? Do you think it's a good idea?* **4** [T] to suppose sth: *We will need, say, $10,000 for a new car.* ○ *Say you don't get into college – what will you do then?*

IDM **go without saying** to be clear, so that you do not need to say it: *It goes without saying that the children will be taken care of at all times.*

that is to say... (*formal*) which means...: *A car which cost $15,000 two years ago now costs $16,500. That is to say, the price has gone up by 10%.*

to say the least (used to say that you are describing a situation in a very mild way): *Mom was pretty upset, to say the least* (= she was really very angry).

say² /seɪ/ *noun* [sing., U] **say (in sth)** the power or right to decide sth: *I'd like to have some say in the arrangements for the party.*

IDM **have your say** to express your opinion: *Thank you for your comments. Now let somebody else have their say.*

say³ /seɪ/ *interj.* (*informal*) (used in order to get sb's attention or to introduce a new topic in a conversation): *Say, Kelly – how about going to see a movie tonight?*

☆ **say·ing** /'seɪɪŋ/ *noun* [C] a well-known phrase that gives advice about sth: *"A stitch in time saves nine" is an old saying.* ☞ Look at **proverb**.

scab /skæb/ *noun* [C,U] a mass of dried blood that forms over a part of the body where the skin has been cut or broken ☞ Look at **scar**.

scaf·fold /'skæfəld; -foʊld/ *noun* [C] = SCAFFOLDING

scaffolding

scaf·fold·ing /'skæfəldɪŋ/ *noun* [U] (*also* **scaffold** [C]) a structure made of long metal poles and wooden boards, that is put next to a building, high wall, etc. for people to stand on while they repair, clean or paint the building or wall

ə	y	w	t	eɪ	aɪ	ɔɪ	aʊ	oʊ
about	yes	woman	butter	say	five	boy	now	go

S

scald /skɔld/ *verb* [T] to burn sb/sth with very hot liquid —**scald·ing** *adj., adv.*: *scalding hot water*

☆ **scale¹** /skeɪl/ *noun*

bathroom scale

1 [C] a series of numbers, amounts, etc. that are used for measuring or setting the level of sth: *The earthquake measured 6.5 on the Richter scale.* ◦ *the new pay scale for city employees* ◦ *The test is graded on a scale of 1 to 100.* **2** [C,U] the size or extent of sth when compared to other things: *We will be making the product on a large scale next year.* ◦ *I think we have just begun to realize the scale of the problem* (= how serious it is). **3** [C] a piece of equipment that is used for weighing sb/sth: *I put the box on the bathroom scale.* **4** [C] a series of marks on a tool or piece of equipment that you use for measuring sth: *The ruler has one scale in centimeters and one scale in inches.* **5** [C] the relationship between the actual size of sth and its size on a map or plan: *The map has a scale of one inch to the one mile.* ◦ *a scale of 1: 50,000* ◦ *The plan of the building is not drawn to scale* (= the parts of the drawing do not have the same relationship to each other as the parts of the actual building do). **6** [C] a series of musical notes which go up or down in a fixed order. People play or sing scales to practice their musical technique **7** [C] one of the small flat pieces of hard material that cover the bodies of some fish and animals: *the scales of a snake*

scale² /skeɪl/ *verb* [T] to climb up a high wall, steep cliff, etc.

PHRV **scale sth back/down** to reduce the size or amount of sth: *The company plans to scale back its workforce by 10%.*

scalp¹ /skælp/ *noun* [C] the skin on the top of your head that is under your hair

scalp² /skælp/ *verb* [T] (*informal*) to sell a ticket for a sports game, a concert, etc. at a price that is much higher than the original price —**scalp·er** *noun* [C]

scal·pel /ˈskælpəl/ *noun* [C] a small knife that is used by doctors (**surgeons**) when they are doing operations

scam·per /ˈskæmpər/ *verb* [I] (often used about a child or small animal) to run quickly

scan /skæn/ *verb* [T] (**scan·ning**; **scanned**) **1** to examine sth carefully because you are looking for sth: *The sailors scanned the horizon for signs of land.* **2** to look at or read sth quickly: *Matt scanned the list until he found his own name.* **3** (used about a machine) to use beams of light or energy to examine what is inside a person's body or inside an object such as a suitcase, or to examine the surface of an object: *All luggage will be scanned before it is loaded onto the plane.* ◦ *to scan groceries at the* supermarket checkout **4** (*computing*) to copy a picture, etc. from a piece of paper into a computer —**scan** *noun* [C]: *Doctors performed a brain scan on the accident victim.*

☆ **scan·dal** /ˈskændl/ *noun* [C,U] an action or a situation or behavior that shocks people; the public feeling that is caused by such behavior: *another government scandal involving illegal campaign contributions* ◦ *There was no suggestion of scandal in his private life.* ◦ *If this information is published, it will cause a huge scandal!*

scan·dal·ous /ˈskændələs/ *adj.* very shocking or wrong: *It is scandalous that murderers are allowed to go free.*

Scan·di·na·vi·a /ˌskændɪˈneɪviə/ *noun* [U] the group of countries in northern Europe that consists of Denmark, Norway and Sweden. Finland and Iceland are also usually considered to be part of Scandinavia. —**Scan·di·na·vi·an** *adj.*

scan·ner /ˈskænər/ *noun* [C] a machine that scans (3,4)

scant /skænt/ *adj.* (*formal*) (only *before* a noun) not very much; not as much as necessary: *They paid scant attention to my advice.*

scape·goat /ˈskeɪpgoʊt/ *noun* [C] a person who is blamed for sth that sb else has done

scar¹ /skɑr/ *noun* [C] a mark on the skin that is caused by a cut or wound that has now healed: *The operation didn't leave a very big scar.* ◦ (*figurative*) *Parts of the city still bear the scars of the riots.* ☞ Look at **scab**.

scar² /skɑr/ *verb* [I,T] (**scar·ring**; **scarred**) to leave a scar on sb/sth: *Will's face was scarred for life in the accident.*

☆ **scarce** /skɛrs/ *adj.* not existing in large quantities; hard to find: *Food for birds and animals is scarce in the winter.* ☞ The opposite is **plentiful.** —**scar·ci·ty** /ˈskɛrsəti/ *noun* [C,U] (*pl.* **scar·ci·ties**) *There will be food scarcities in most regions.* ◦ *The scarcity of qualified workers is a serious problem for business.*

scarce·ly /ˈskɛrsli/ *adv.* almost not; just: *There was scarcely a car in sight.* ◦ *She's not a friend of mine. I scarcely know her.* ☞ Look at **hardly.**

☆ **scare¹** /skɛr/ *verb* [T] to make a person or an animal frightened: *The sudden noise scared us all.*

PHRV **scare sb/sth away/off** to make a person or animal leave or stay away by frightening him/her/it: *Don't make any noise or you'll scare the birds away.*

scare² /skɛr/ *noun* [C] **1** a feeling of being frightened: *It wasn't a serious heart attack, but it gave him a scare.* **2** a situation where many people are afraid or worried about sth: *Last night there was a bomb scare at Union Station.*

scare·crow /ˈskɛrkroʊ/ *noun* [C] a model of a person that is dressed in old clothes and put in a field to frighten away the birds

ər	ɪr	ɛr	ɑr	ɔr	ʊr	ʒ	h	ŋ
bird	near	hair	car	north	tour	vision	hat	sing

☆**scared** /skɛrd/ *adj.* **scared (of sb/sth)**; **scared (of doing sth/to do sth)** frightened: *Are you scared of the dark?* ○ *She's scared of walking home alone.* ○ *Everyone was too scared to move.*

☆**scarf** /skɑrf/ *noun* [C] (*pl.* **scarfs** /skɑrfs/ or **scarves** /skɑrvz/) **1** a long thin piece of cloth, usually made of wool, that you wear around your neck to keep warm: *He wrapped a scarf around his neck.* ☞ picture on page A27. **2** a square piece of cloth that (usually) women wear around their neck or shoulders or over their heads to keep warm or for decoration: *She tied a scarf around her neck and went out.*

scar·let /'skɑrlət/ *adj., noun* [U] (of) a bright red color ☞ Look at **crimson** and **maroon**.

scar·y /'skɛri/ *adj.* (**scar·i·er**; **scar·i·est**) (*informal*) frightening: *a scary ghost story* ○ *It was pretty scary driving in the mountains at night.*

scath·ing /'skeɪðɪŋ/ *adj.* expressing a very strong negative opinion about sb/sth; very critical: *a scathing attack on the candidate* ○ *scathing criticism*

scat·ter /'skæt̮ər/ *verb* **1** [I] (used about a group of people or animals) to move away quickly in different directions: *The deer scattered when they heard us approaching.* **2** [T] to drop or throw things in different directions over a wide area: *The wind scattered the papers all over the room.*

scat·tered /'skæt̮ərd/ *adj.* spread over a large area or over a period of time: *The weather will be partly cloudy with scattered showers today.*

scav·enge /'skævɪndʒ/ *verb* [I,T] to look for food, etc. among waste and garbage —**scav·en·ger** *noun* [C]

'scavenger hunt *noun* [C] a game or competition in which people are given a list of things that they must find and bring to a particular place

sce·nar·i·o /sə'nɛrioʊ; -'nær-/ *noun* [C] (*pl.* **sce·nar·i·os**) **1** one way that things may happen in the future: *The doctor described a scenario in which the disease spread rapidly across the whole country.* **2** a description of what happens in a play or movie

☆**scene** /sin/ *noun* **1** [C] the place where sth happened: *the scene of a crime, an accident, etc.* **2** [C] an occasion when sb expresses great anger or another strong emotion in public: *She made a real scene when the waiter brought the wrong drinks.* ○ *There were emotional scenes at the airport as the students boarded the plane.* **3** [C] one part of a book, play, movie, etc. in which the events happen in one place: *His character appears in Act IV, Scene 2.* ○ *There are too many sex scenes in that movie.* **4** [C,U] what you see around you in a particular place: *Remington painted many scenes of life in the West.* ○ *Her new job was no better, but at least it would be a change of scene.* **5 the scene** [sing.] the way of life or present situation in a particular area of activity: *The political scene in the region is very confused.* ○ *the fashion scene*

IDM **behind the scenes** in secret; without the knowledge of most people: *Several people have been working behind the scenes to destroy the mayor's reputation.*

☆**scen·er·y** /'sinəri/ *noun* [U] **1** the natural features that you see around you in the country: *The scenery is fantastic in the mountains.*

☞ We say that an area of the country has beautiful **scenery** when it is attractive to look at. The **landscape** of a particular area is the way the natural features of it are arranged: *Rugged mountains are a typical feature of the landscape in Colorado.* You have a **view** of something when you look out of a window or down from a tower: *There was a terrific view of the ocean from our hotel room.*

2 the furniture, painted cloth, boards, etc. that are used on the stage in a theater: *The scenery is changed during intermission.*

sce·nic /'sinɪk/ *adj.* having beautiful scenery: *a scenic route along the coast*

scent /sɛnt/ *noun* [C,U] **1** a pleasant smell: *This flower has no scent.* **2** the smell that an animal leaves behind and that some other animals can follow —**scent·ed** /'sɛntəd/ *adj.*

☆**sched·ule¹** /'skɛdʒəl; -dʒul/ *noun* **1** [C,U] a plan of things that will happen or of work that must be done: *Max has a busy schedule for the next few days.* ○ *to be ahead of/behind schedule* (= to have done more/less than was planned) ○ *to be on schedule* (= to have done the amount that was planned) **2** a list that shows when planes, buses, etc. arrive at and leave a particular place

sched·ule² /'skɛdʒəl; -dʒul/ *verb* [T] **schedule sth (for sth/to do sth)** (often passive) to arrange for sth to happen or be done at a particular time: *The hearing has been scheduled for Monday morning.* ○ *The train was scheduled to arrive at 10:07.* ○ *This concludes our special news bulletin – we now return to our regularly scheduled program.*

scheme¹ /skim/ *noun* [C] a plan to do sth, especially sth that is morally wrong or illegal: *an elaborate scheme to influence the outcome of the election* ☞ Look at **color scheme**.

scheme² /skim/ *verb* [I] to make a secret or dishonest plan

schiz·o·phre·ni·a /ˌskɪtsə'friniə/ *noun* [U] a serious mental illness in which a person confuses the real world and the world of the imagination and often behaves in strange and unexpected ways —**schiz·o·phren·ic** /ˌskɪtsə'frɛnɪk/ *adj., noun* [C]

schlep /ʃlɛp/ *verb* [I,T] (**schlep·ping**; **schlepped**) **schlep (sth) (across, around, down, up, etc.)** (*informal*) to carry sth or go

tʃ	dʒ	v	θ	ð	s	z	ʃ
chin	June	van	thin	then	so	zoo	she

somewhere, using a lot of effort: *I don't want to schlep your suitcase all the way upstairs!*

schlock /ʃlɑk/ *noun* [U] (*informal*) something that is of low quality —**schlock·y** *adj.*: *a schlocky horror movie*

schmooze /ʃmuz/ *verb* [I] (*informal*) to talk about unimportant things at a social event, e.g. a party

schol·ar /ˈskɑlər/ *noun* [C] **1** a person who studies and has a deep knowledge of a particular subject: *a leading Shakespeare scholar* **2** a person who has received an amount of money (**a scholarship**) to help pay for his/her studies or for travel or research connected with his/her studies: *a Fulbright scholar*

☆ **schol·ar·ship** /ˈskɑlərʃɪp/ *noun* **1** [C] an amount of money that is given to a person by an organization or a school or college, in order to help pay for his/her studies or for travel or research connected with his/her studies: *to win a full scholarship to Yale* **2** [U] serious study; the work of scholars

☆ **school** /skul/ *noun* **1** [C] the place where children go to be educated: *They're building a new school in our area.* ○ *Paula goes to Kennedy High School.* ○ *Do you have to wear a school uniform?* ○ *We go on the school bus.* ○ *a public/private/parochial school* ☞ Look also at **elementary school**, **middle school** and **high school**. **2** [U] the time you spend at a school; the process of being educated in a school: *Children start school at age 5 in the U.S. and can quit school when they are 16.* ○ *School starts at 8:30 and finishes at about 3 o'clock.* ○ *After school we usually have homework to do.* ○ *Because of the snow, there will be no school today.*

☞ You talk about **school** (without "**the**") when you are talking about going there for the usual reason (that is, as a student or teacher): *Where do your kids go to school?* ○ *I enjoyed being in school.* ○ *Do you walk to school?* You talk about **the school** if you are talking about going there for a different reason (for example, as a parent): *I have to go to the school on Thursday to talk to John's teacher.* You must also use **a** or **the** when more information about the school is given: *Pat goes to the neighborhood school.* ○ *She teaches at a school in Atlanta.*

3 [sing.] all the students and teachers in a school: *The whole school cheered the winner.* **4** [C] a place where you go to learn a particular subject: *a driving school* ○ *a language school* **5** [C,U] a college or university: *Jack had to pay his own way through school.* **6** [C,U] a department of some colleges or universities that teaches a particular subject or group of subjects: *the School of Arts and Sciences* ○ *She's in law school.* **7** [C] a group of writers, painters, etc. who have the same ideas or style **IDM a school of thought** the ideas or

opinions that one group of people share: *There are various schools of thought on this matter.*
at school in the school building: *Kristy stayed at school until 4:30 to finish her science project.*
in school being a student; attending a school, college, or university: *I wasn't happy in school, so I got a job.*

ˈschool board *noun* [C] a group of people who have been elected to be in charge of the public schools in a city or an area

school·boy /ˈskulbɔɪ/ (*also* **schoolgirl** /ˈskulgərl/ **schoolchild** /ˈskultʃaɪld/) *noun* [C] (*formal*) a boy/girl/child who goes to school ☞ **Student** is more common.

ˈschool ˌdistrict *noun* [C] an area in which all the public schools are governed by one group of people (**school board**)

school·ing /ˈskulɪŋ/ *noun* [U] the time that you spend in school; your education: *Her grandfather had only six years of schooling.*

school·teach·er /ˈskultitʃər/ *noun* [C] (*old-fashioned*) a person who teaches in a school

☆ **sci·ence** /ˈsaɪəns/ *noun* **1** [U] the study of and knowledge about the physical world and natural laws: *science and technology* ○ *Modern science has discovered a lot about the origin of life.* ○ *Fewer young people are studying science in college.* ○ *a science teacher* (= one who teaches biology, chemistry or physics) **2** [C,U] one of the subjects into which science can be divided: *Biology, chemistry and physics are all sciences.* ○ *Is mathematics a science?* ☞ Subjects connected with the study of people and society are called **social sciences**. Look also at **political science**.

ˌscience ˈfiction (also *informal* **sci-fi**) *noun* [U] books, movies, etc. about events that take place in the future, especially connected with travel in space

☆ **sci·en·tif·ic** /ˌsaɪənˈtɪfɪk/ *adj.* **1** connected with science: *We need more funding for scientific research.* **2** using the methods that are used in science (1) (= observing facts and testing ideas with experiments): *a scientific study of the way people use language* —**sci·en·tif·i·cal·ly** /-kli/ *adv.*: *It will be hard to prove the idea scientifically* (= using the methods of science).

☆ **sci·en·tist** /ˈsaɪəntɪst/ *noun* [C] a person who studies or teaches science, especially biology, chemistry or physics

sci-fi /ˌsaɪˈfaɪ/ *noun* [U] (*informal*) = SCIENCE FICTION

scissors

☆ **scis·sors** /ˈsɪzərz/ *noun* [plural] a tool for cutting things that consists of two flat sharp blades that are joined together

☞ **Scissors** is a plural noun: *These scissors are* blunt. We CANNOT say "a scissors"; we must use the word **pair**: *I need a new pair of scissors.*

scoff /skɔf; skɑf/ *verb* [I] **scoff (at sb/sth)** to speak about sb/sth without respect

scold /skoʊld/ *verb* [I,T] **scold sb (for sth/for doing sth)** to speak angrily to sb because he/she has done something bad or wrong: *The teacher scolded her for being late.*

scoop¹ /skup/ *noun* [C] **1** a tool like a spoon used for picking up ice cream, sugar, etc. **2** the amount that one scoop (1) contains: *apple pie served with a scoop of ice cream* **3** an exciting piece of news that is reported by one newspaper, television or radio station before it is reported anywhere else

scoop² /skup/ *verb* [T] **scoop sth (out/up)** to make a hole in sth or to take sth out by using a scoop (1) or sth similar: *Scoop out the middle of the pineapple.* ○ *He scooped up a handful of change for the parking meter.*

scope /skoʊp/ *noun* **1** [sing.] the range of subjects that are being discussed or considered: *The government was unwilling to extend the scope of the investigation.* **2** [U] **scope (for sth/to do sth)** the chance or opportunity to do sth: *The job offers plenty of scope for creativity.*

scorch /skɔrtʃ/ *verb* [T] to burn sth slightly so that its color changes but it is not destroyed: *I scorched my blouse when I was ironing it.* ○ *the scorched landscape of the Arizona desert*

scorch·ing /ˈskɔrtʃɪŋ/ *adj.* very hot: *scorching temperatures*

☆ **score¹** /skɔr/ *noun* **1** [C] the number of points that sb/sth gets in a game, a competition, on an examination, etc.: *What was the final score?* ○ *The score is Indians 5, Yankees 2.* ○ *I don't know who won – nobody kept score* (= recorded the scores). ○ *The highest score on the test was 80%.* ○ *SAT scores* **2 scores** [plural] very many: *Scores of people have written to offer their support.* **3** [C] the written form of a piece of music
IDM **on that score** about that: *I have no concerns on that score.*

☆ **score²** /skɔr/ *verb* **1** [I,T] to get points in a game, a competition, on an examination, etc.: *The team still hadn't scored by halftime.* ○ *The Orioles scored two runs in the third inning.* **2** [T] to give a number that shows how well sb does on an examination, in a competition, etc.: *The written driving test is scored by computer.* **3** [I,T] (*slang*) to succeed in getting sth, especially sex or illegal drugs

score·board /ˈskɔrbɔrd/ *noun* [C] a large

board that shows the score¹(1) during a game, competition, etc. ☞ picture at **football**.

scorn¹ /skɔrn/ *noun* [U] the strong feeling that you have when you do not respect sb/sth: *She looked at him with scorn.* —**scorn·ful** /-fl/ *adj.*: *a scornful look, smile, etc.* —**scorn·ful·ly** *adv.*

scorn² /skɔrn/ *verb* [T] to show that you do not respect sb/sth by making unkind comments, etc.: *The candidate scorned his rival.*

Scor·pi·o /ˈskɔrpioʊ/ *noun* [C,U] (*pl.* **Scor·pi·os**) the eighth sign of the zodiac, the Scorpion; a person who was born under this sign ☞ picture at **zodiac**.

scor·pi·on /ˈskɔrpiən/ *noun* [C] a creature that looks like a large insect and lives in warm climates. A scorpion has a long tail with a poisonous sting in it.

Scotch /skɑtʃ/ *noun* [C,U] a strong alcoholic drink (**whiskey**) that is made in Scotland, or a glass of this drink ☞ Look at the note at **Scottish**.

Scotch tape *noun* [U] (*trademark*) a type of clear tape that is sticky on one side. It is sold in rolls and is used for sticking things together.

Scot·tish /ˈskɑtɪʃ/ *adj.* of or connected with Scotland, its people, culture, etc. ☞ **Scottish** is used about Scotland and about both people and things that come from Scotland: *She speaks with a strong Scottish accent.* ○ *the Scottish Highlands.* **Scotch** is used for a type of whiskey that comes from Scotland and for some kinds of food. You should not use it for Scottish people.

scoun·drel /ˈskaʊndrəl/ *noun* [C] (*old-fashioned*) a man who behaves very badly toward other people, especially by being dishonest

scour /ˈskaʊər/ *verb* [T] **1** to search a place very carefully because you are looking for sb/sth: *A search party scoured the area, looking for the missing boy.* **2** to clean sth by rubbing it hard with sth rough: *to scour dirty pots and pans*

scout¹ /skaʊt/ *noun* [C] **1** a soldier who is sent out in front of the rest of the group to find out where the enemy is or which is the best route to take **2** a person whose job is to find people who are good at sports, music, etc. in order to give them jobs: *a football scout* ☞ Look at **Boy Scout** and **Girl Scout**.

scout² /skaʊt/ *verb* [I] **scout around (for sth)**; **scout for sth** to search for sth in a particular place: *Go scout around for some firewood.*

scowl /skaʊl/ *noun* [C] a look on your face that shows you are angry or in a bad mood ☞ Look at **frown**. —**scowl** *verb* [I]

scram·ble¹ /ˈskræmbl/ *verb* **1** [I] to move or do something quickly because you are in a hurry: *Rescue workers scrambled to find survivors in the wreckage.* **2** [I] **scramble (for sth)**

to struggle to get sth which a lot of people want: *Everyone was scrambling to get the best bargains.* **3** [T] to change a television, radio, etc. signal so that it cannot be understood without a special machine

scram·ble² /ˈskræmbl/ *noun* [sing.] a situation in which a lot of people are in a hurry and struggling to get or do sth: *There was a mad scramble as everyone rushed for the best seats.*

ˌscrambled ˈeggs *noun* [plural] eggs that are mixed together and then cooked in a pan

scrap¹ /skræp/ *noun* **1** [C] a small piece or amount of sth: *a scrap of paper* ○ *scraps of food* **2** [U] something that you do not want anymore but that is made of material that can be used again: *scrap metal*

scrap² /skræp/ *verb* [T] (**scrap·ping**; **scrapped**) (*informal*) to get rid of sth that you do not want anymore: *I think we should scrap that idea.*

scrap·book /ˈskræpbʊk/ *noun* [C] a large book with blank pages that you can stick pictures, newspaper articles, etc. in

scrape¹ /skreɪp/ *verb* **1** [T] **scrape sth (off)** to make sth clean or smooth by moving a sharp edge across it firmly: *Scrape your plate into the garbage can.* **2** [T] to remove sth by moving a sharp edge across a surface: *Scrape all the mud off your boots before you come in.* **3** [T] **scrape sth (against/along/on sth)** to damage or hurt sth by rubbing it against sth rough or hard: *Mark fell and scraped his knee.* ○ *Jenny scraped the car against a tree.* **4** [I,T] **scrape (sth) against/along/on sth** to rub (sth) against sth and make a sharp unpleasant noise: *The branch scraped against the window.*
PHR V **scrape by** to have just enough money to buy the things that you need: *We're just able to scrape by on my welfare checks.*
scrape sth together/up to get enough money together with difficulty: *We barely managed to scrape together enough money for a week's vacation.*

scrape² /skreɪp/ *noun* [C] **1** a mark or small wound on your skin from scraping it against sth: *Tom only suffered minor scrapes and bruises in the accident.* **2** (*informal*) a difficult situation or problem, often that was caused by your own behavior: *She had several scrapes with the law, but managed to stay out of prison.*

☆ **scratch¹** /skrætʃ/ *verb* **1** [I,T] to rub a part of the body with your fingernails: *Your mosquito bites will become infected if you don't stop scratching.* ○ *to scratch an itch* ○ *Could you scratch my back for me?* **2** [I,T] to make a mark on a surface or a small wound on a person's skin with sth sharp: *The cat will scratch if you make her mad.* ○ *The paint is badly scratched on the car door.* **3** [T] to put sth somewhere or

to take it away by scratching (2): *He scratched his name on the top of his desk.*

☆ **scratch²** /skrætʃ/ *noun* [C] a cut, mark or sound that was made by sb/sth scratching sb/sth else: *There's a scratch on the car door.* ○ *They survived the accident without even a scratch.*
IDM **from scratch** from the very beginning: *to start from scratch* ○ *to make a cake from scratch*

scrawl /skrɔl/ *verb* [I,T] to write in a messy and careless way —**scrawl** *noun* [sing.]: *Her signature was just a scrawl.* ☞ Look at **scribble**.

☆ **scream** /skrim/ *verb* [I,T] **scream (sth) (out) (at sb)** to cry out loudly in a high voice because you are afraid, excited, angry, in pain, etc.: *She saw a rat hiding in the corner of the room and screamed.* ○ *"Don't touch that!" he screamed.* ○ *She screamed at the girls to stop fighting.* ○ *When the car hit him, he screamed with pain.* ○ *He clung to the edge of the cliff, screaming for help.* ☞ Look at **shout**. —**scream** *noun* [C]: *We heard a scream from the apartment next door.*

screech /skritʃ/ *verb* [I,T] to make an unpleasant loud high sound: *The car's brakes screeched as it came to a halt.* ☞ Look at **shriek**. —**screech** *noun* [sing.]

☆ **screen** /skrin/ *noun* **1** [C] the glass surface of a television or computer where the picture or information appears **2** [C] the white surface on which movies are shown **3** [C] a wire or plastic net that is held in a frame and fastened on a door or an open window to let in air but keep out insects: *a window screen* ○ *Don't leave the screen door open* ☞ picture on page A28. **4** [C] a flat vertical surface that is used for dividing a room or keeping sb/sth out of sight **5** [sing., U] movies: *a star of stage and screen* (= a famous actor who appears in both plays and movies) ☞ Look also at **sunscreen**.

screen² /skrin/ *verb* [T] **1 screen sb (for sth)** to examine or test sb to find out if he/she has a particular disease or if he/she is suitable for a particular job: *All children are screened for vision problems in school.* ○ *The Department of Defense carefully screens all job applicants.* **2 screen sb/sth (off) (from sb/sth)** to hide or protect sb/sth from sb/sth: *The bed was screened off while the doctor examined him.* ○ *to screen your eyes from the sun* **3** to show sth on TV or in a movie theater: *The program was too violent to be screened before 9 o'clock.*

screen·play /ˈskrinpleɪ/ *noun* [C] a story that is written to be performed by actors in a movie

☆ **screw¹** /skru/ *noun* [C] a small piece of metal with a sharp end and a round head used for fastening two things, e.g. pieces of wood, together. A screw is like a nail, but you fasten it

ər	ɪr	ɛr	ɑr	ɔr	ʊr	ʒ	h	ŋ
bird	near	hair	car	north	tour	vision	hat	sing

into sth by turning it around with a special tool (**a screwdriver**). ☞ picture at **tool**.

screw[2] /skru/ *verb* **1** [T] to fasten sth with a screw[1] or screws: *The bookcase is screwed to the wall.* **2** [I,T] to fasten sth, or to be fastened, by turning: *The legs screw into holes on the underside of the table.* ○ *to screw in a lightbulb* **IDM** **be screwed** (*slang*) to be in trouble; to be in a very difficult situation with no hope: *If my dad finds out we took his car, we're screwed!*
PHRV **screw up** (*slang*) to make a mistake: *You really screwed up this time, Jeff!*
screw sth up (*slang*) to ruin sth or cause sth to fail: *You'd better not screw up this deal.*

screw·dri·ver /'skrudraɪvər/ *noun* [C] a tool that you use for turning screws ☞ picture at **tool**.

scrib·ble /'skrɪbl/ *verb* [I,T] to write sth quickly and carelessly: *to scribble down a note on a pad* ☞ Look at **scrawl**. —**scrib·ble** *noun* [C,U]

script /skrɪpt/ *noun* **1** [C] the written form of a play, movie, speech, etc. **2** [C,U] a system of writing: *Arabic, Roman, etc. script* **3** [U] a style of writing with letters that are joined together

Scrip·ture /'skrɪptʃər/ *noun* [U] (*also* **the Scriptures** [plural]) the holy books of religion, such as the Bible

scroll[1] /skroʊl/ *noun* [C] a long roll of paper with writing on it

scroll[2] /skroʊl/ *verb* [I,T] to move text up or down on a computer screen until you find the part you want

scrub[1] /skrʌb/ *noun* [U] small trees and bushes that grow in an area that has poor soil or low rainfall

scrub[2] /skrʌb/ *verb* (**scrub·bing**; **scrubbed**) **1** [I,T] to clean sth with soap and water by rubbing it hard, often with a brush: *to scrub the floor/walls* **2** [T] **scrub sth (off)** to remove sth by scrubbing: *to scrub the dirt off the walls* **3** [T] (*informal*) to cancel a plan, project, etc.: *They were forced to scrub their vacation plans.* —**scrub** *noun* [sing.]

scruff·y /'skrʌfi/ *adj.* (**scruff·i·er**; **scruff·i·est**) dirty and messy: *a group of scruffy teenagers*

scru·ples /'skruplz/ *noun* [plural] moral beliefs that stop you from doing sth that you think is wrong: *If you had any scruples, you'd return the money.*

scru·pu·lous /'skrupyələs/ *adj.* **1** very careful or paying great attention to detail: *a scrupulous investigation into the causes of the disaster* **2** careful to do what is right or honest: *Even the most scrupulous businessman might have been tempted.* ☞ The opposite is **unscrupulous**. —**scru·pu·lous·ly** *adv.*: *scrupulously honest*

scru·ti·nize /'skrutn·aɪz/ *verb* [T] to look at or examine sth carefully

scru·ti·ny /'skrutn·i/ *noun* [U] careful exam-

ination or study of sb/sth: *The police kept all the suspects under close scrutiny.*

scu·ba div·ing /'skubə ˌdaɪvɪŋ/ *noun* [U] swimming under water, using special equipment for breathing

scuf·fle /'skʌfl/ *noun* [C] a fight in which people try to push each other roughly: *There were scuffles between police and demonstrators.*

sculp·tor /'skʌlptər/ *noun* [C] a person who makes figures or objects from stone, wood, clay, etc.

sculp·ture /'skʌlptʃər/ *noun* **1** [U] the art of making figures or objects from stone, wood, clay, etc. **2** [C,U] a work or works of art that were made from stone, wood, clay, etc.: *a modern sculpture in bronze*

scum /skʌm/ *noun* [U] **1** a covering of a dirty or unpleasant substance on the surface of a liquid **2** (*informal*) a person or people who you think should not be respected

scur·ry /'skəri/ *verb* [I] (*pres. part.* **scur·ry·ing**; *3rd pers. sing. pres.* **scur·ries**; *p.t., p.p.* **scur·ried**) to run quickly with short steps; to hurry: *The mice scurried across the floor.*

SE *abbr.* southeast; southeastern

☆ **sea** /si/ *noun* **1** [C] often **Sea** a particular large area of salt water. A sea is smaller than an ocean and may be surrounded by land: *the Mediterranean Sea* ○ *the Black Sea* **2** [C,U] (used especially in stories) the ocean: *a stormy sea* ○ *The pieces of wood floated out to sea.*
IDM **a sea of sth** a large amount or number of sth: *The stadium was just a sea of people.* ○ *a sea of green at the St. Patrick's Day parade*
at sea sailing in a ship: *They spent about three weeks at sea.*

☆ **sea·food** /'sifud/ *noun* [U] fish and other animals from the ocean that can be eaten as food

'**sea gull** *noun* [C] = GULL

seal[1] /sil/ *noun* [C] **1** a gray animal with short fur that lives in and near the ocean and that eats fish. Seals have no legs and swim with the help of short flat limbs (**flippers**). **2** a special mark that you put on an important piece of paper or letter to show that it is genuine or that it has not been opened: *the Presidential seal* **3** something that stops air or liquid from getting in or out of something: *The plane lost pressure because of a faulty seal.* **4** a small piece of paper, metal, plastic, etc. on a package, bottle, etc. that you must break before you can open it

seal[2] /sil/ *verb* [T] **1** to close or fasten an envelope, a package, etc.: *Courtney sealed the package with tape.* ○ *a sealed envelope* **2** **seal sth (up)** to fill a hole or cover sth so that air or liquid does not get in or out **3** to make sth definite: *to seal an agreement* ○ *Another goal at the end of the game sealed their victory.*
PHRV **seal sth off** to stop any person or thing from entering or leaving an area or building: *The building was sealed off by the police.*

tʃ	dʒ	v	θ	ð	s	z	ʃ
chin	June	van	thin	then	so	zoo	she

☆ **'sea ˌlevel** *noun* [U] the level of the ocean when it is halfway between high tide and low tide (used for measuring the height of things on land): *200 feet above/below sea level*

'sea ˌlion *noun* [C] a type of gray animal with short fur and no legs, that lives in and near the ocean and eats fish ☞ A sea lion is a type of seal¹(1).

seam /sim/ *noun* [C] the line where two pieces of cloth are sewn together

☆ **search¹** /sərtʃ/ *verb* [I,T] **search (sb/sth) (for sb/sth)**; **search (through sth)(for sth)** to examine sb/sth carefully because you are looking for something; to look for sth that is missing: *to search sb for drugs* ○ *The police searched the area for clues.* ○ *They are still searching for the missing child.* ○ *She searched through the papers on the desk, looking for the letter.*

☆ **search²** /sərtʃ/ *noun* [C] an act of searching: *the search for the missing boy*

IDM in search of sb/sth looking for sb/sth: *The early explorers went in search of gold.*

search·ing /'sərtʃɪŋ/ *adj.* (used about a look, question, etc.) trying to find out the truth: *The customs officers asked a lot of searching questions about our trip.*

'search ˌparty *noun* [C] (*pl.* **search parties**) a group of people who look for sb who is lost or missing: *to send out a search party*

'search ˌwarrant *noun* [C] an official piece of paper that gives the police the right to search a building, etc.

sea·shell /'siʃɛl/ *noun* [C] the empty shell of a small animal that lives in the ocean

sea·shore /'siʃɔr/ *noun* [U] the part of the land that is next to the ocean, especially where people go on vacation

sea·sick /'sisɪk/ *adj.* feeling sick because of the movement of a boat or ship: *to feel/get seasick* —**sea·sick·ness** *noun* [U]

sea·side /'sisaɪd/ *adj.* (only *before* a noun) on the coast: *a seaside resort, community, hotel, etc.*

☆ **sea·son¹** /'sizn/ *noun* [C] **1** one of the four periods into which the year is divided (spring, summer, fall and winter) **2** the period of the year when sth is common or popular or when sth usually happens or is done: *The football season is from September to January.* ○ *the dry/rainy season* ○ *the holiday season* (= late December and early January)

IDM in season (used about fresh foods) available in large quantities: *Tomatoes are cheapest when they are in season.*

out of season (used about wild animals or fish) not able to be hunted or caught legally because it is the wrong time of year: *He was arrested for shooting ducks out of season.*

season's greetings (used to wish sb a nice Christmas, Hanukkah, New Year, etc.)

sea·son² /'sizn/ *verb* [T] to add salt, pepper, spices, etc. to food in order to make it taste better

sea·son·al /'sizənl/ *adj.* happening or existing at a particular time of the year: *We hire several seasonal employees each summer.*

sea·soned /'siznd/ *adj.* (only *before* a noun) having a lot of experience of sth: *a seasoned traveler*

sea·son·ing /'sizn·ɪŋ/ *noun* [C,U] salt, pepper, spices, etc. that you add to food to make it taste better

ˌseason 'ticket *noun* [C] a ticket that allows you to go to sports games, concerts, etc. as often as you want during a particular period of time

☆ **seat¹** /sit/ *noun* [C] **1** something that you sit on: *Please take a seat* (= please sit down). ○ *the back seat of a car* ○ *We're in row 26, seats A and B.* ○ *I'd like a window seat* (= next to a window). **2** the part of a chair, bicycle, etc. that you sit on **3** (*old-fashioned*) the part of the body that you sit on **4** the part of a piece of clothing that covers your seat (3) **5** a position in the government of a country, state, city, etc. that you win in an election: *to win/lose a seat* ○ *She's running for a seat on the school board.*

seat² /sit/ *verb* [T] **1** (often passive) (*formal*) to sit down: *Please be seated.* **2** to find a place for sb to sit, e.g. in a restaurant: *Please wait here – the hostess will seat you.* **3** to have seats or chairs for a particular number of people: *The hall can seat about 500 people.*

☆ **'seat belt** (*also* **'safety belt**) *noun* [C] a belt that you wear in a car or an airplane to protect you from injury if there is an accident: *Please fasten your seat belts during takeoff and landing.*

seat·ing /'sitɪŋ/ *noun* [U] the seats or chairs in a place, or the way that they are arranged: *The seating will need to be changed.* ○ *a seating plan*

sea·weed /'siwid/ *noun* [U] a plant that grows in the ocean

sec /sɛk/ *noun* [C] (*informal*) = SECOND³(2)

Sec. *abbr.* = SECRETARY(3)

se·cede /sə'sid/ *verb* [I] **secede (from sth)** (used about a state, a region, etc.) to officially stop being part of a country: *South Carolina was the first state to secede from the Union in 1860.* —**se·ces·sion** /sə'sɛʃn/ *noun* [U]

se·clud·ed /sə'kludəd/ *adj.* far away from other people, roads, etc.; very quiet: *secluded sandy beaches* ○ *a secluded area* —**se·clu·sion** /sə'kluʒn/ *noun* [U]

☆ **sec·ond¹** /'sɛkənd/ *pron., det., adv.* 2nd; next after first: *We are going on vacation the second week in July.* ○ *She poured herself a second glass of wine.* ○ *students who speak English as a second language* ○ *Our team finished second in the contest.* ○ *New York is the second most populous state, after California.* ☞ For more information, look at Appendix 2.

i	ɪ	ɛ	æ	ɑ	ɔ	ʌ	ʊ	u
see	sit	ten	cat	hot	saw	cup	put	too

IDM **have second thoughts (about sb/sth)** to have doubts or not to be sure if you have made the right decision about sb/sth: *I'm having second thoughts about accepting their offer.*
next/second/third to last ➪ LAST¹
on second thought (used to say that you have changed your opinion about sth): *Let's do it tomorrow. Wait – on second thought, let's do it today.*

☆ **sec·ond²** /'sɛkənd/ *noun, pron.* (*also* **the second**) [sing.] a person or thing that comes next after the first: *January second* (= the 2nd day in January) ○ *the second of January* ○ *Terry was the second to arrive.*

☆ **sec·ond³** /'sɛkənd/ *noun* **1** [C] one of the 60 parts into which a minute is divided: *the second hand on a watch* **2** [C] (*also informal* **sec**) a short time: *Just a second – I'm coming!* **3** [C, usually pl.] a product that has a small fault and that is sold cheaply: *The clothes are all seconds.* **4 seconds** [plural] another amount of food that you take after you have eaten your first amount of that food: *There's plenty of spaghetti left – who wants seconds?*
IDM **wait a minute/second** ➪ WAIT¹

sec·ond⁴ /'sɛkənd/ *verb* [T] to support sb's proposal or idea at a meeting so that it can then be discussed and voted on

sec·ond- /'sɛkənd/ (used with a superlative) next in rank after the one that is best, largest, fastest, etc.: *the city's second-largest bank* ○ *the second-highest mountain in the world*

☆ **sec·ond·ar·y** /'sɛkən,dɛri/ *adj.* **1** of less importance than sth else: *These are secondary issues which can be discussed later.* **2** caused by or developing from sth else: *She developed a secondary infection following a bad cold.*

'secondary school *noun* [C] (*formal*) a school for children who are about twelve to eighteen years old ☛ Look at **elementary school, middle school** and **high school**.

second-'class *adj.* of little importance: *Old people should not be treated as second-class citizens.*

sec·ond·hand /,sɛkənd'hænd/ *adj., adv.* **1** already used or owned by sb else: *a secondhand car* ○ *I bought this camera secondhand.* **2** (used about news or information) that you heard from sb else and did not see or experience yourself

secondhand 'smoke *noun* [U] smoke in the air that you breathe in from a cigarette, etc. that sb else is smoking

sec·ond·ly /'sɛkəndli/ *adv.* (used when you are giving your second reason or opinion) also: *Anyway, I think it's too expensive, and secondly, we don't really need it.*

second 'nature *noun* [U] something that has become a habit or that you can do easily because you have done it so many times: *With practice, typing becomes second nature.*

second-'rate *adj.* of poor quality: *a second-rate poet*

se·cre·cy /'sikrəsi/ *noun* [U] the state of being or keeping sth secret: *The negotiations took place in total secrecy.* ○ *To ensure secrecy, no visitors are allowed in the research center*

☆ **se·cret¹** /'sikrət/ *adj.* **1** secret (from sb) that is not or must not be known to other people: *The file was marked "Top Secret."* ○ *a secret address* ○ *secret talks between the two governments* ○ *a secret love affair* **2** doing sth that you do not tell anyone else about: *a secret drinker* ○ *She has a secret admirer.* —**se·cret·ly** *adv.*: *They had been secretly engaged for several years.*

☆ **se·cret²** /'sikrət/ *noun* **1** [C] something that is not or must not be known by other people: *to keep a secret* ○ *to tell sb a secret* ○ *I can't tell you where we're going – it's a secret.* ○ *It's no secret that they don't like each other* (= everybody knows). **2** [sing.] the only way or the best way of doing or achieving sth: *What is the secret of your success* (= how did you become so successful)?
IDM **in secret** without other people knowing: *to meet in secret*

secret 'agent *noun* = AGENT(3)

sec·re·tar·i·al /,sɛkrə'tɛriəl/ *adj.* connected with the work that a secretary (1) does: *secretarial skills*

☆ **sec·re·tar·y** /'sɛkrə,tɛri/ *noun* [C] (*pl.* **sec·re·tar·ies**) **1** a person who works in an office. A secretary types letters, answers the telephone, makes appointments, etc. **2** a person in a club or other organization whose duty is to write down records of meetings, etc. **3** often **Secretary** (*abbr.* **Sec.**) a person who is the head of a large department in the U.S. government: *the Secretary of Agriculture/the Agriculture Secretary*

Secretary of 'State *noun* [C] (*pl.* **Secretaries of State**) the official in the U.S. government who is responsible for dealing with foreign countries

se·crete /sɪ'krit/ *verb* [T] (used about a part of a plant, animal or person) to produce a liquid: *a hormone secreted by the female of the species* —**se·cre·tion** /sɪ'kriʃn/ *noun* [C,U] (*formal*)

se·cre·tive /'sikrətɪv/ *adj.* liking to keep things secret from other people: *Wendy is very secretive about her private life.* —**se·cre·tive·ly** *adv.*

sect /sɛkt/ *noun* [C] a group of people who have a particular set of religious or political beliefs. A sect has often broken away from a larger group.

☆ **sec·tion** /'sɛkʃn/ *noun* [C] **1** one of the parts into which something can be or has been divided: *I'd like to sit in the nonsmoking section.* ○ *the string section of an orchestra* ○ *the financial section of a newspaper* ○ *The library has an*

S

ə	y	w	t̬	eɪ	aɪ	ɔɪ	aʊ	oʊ
about	yes	woman	butter	say	five	boy	now	go

excellent reference section. **2** a view or drawing of sth as if it were cut from the top to the bottom and seen from the side

sec·tor /ˈsɛktər/ *noun* [C] **1** a part of the business activity of a country: *The manufacturing sector has declined in recent years.* ○ *the public/ private sector* **2** a part of an area that has been divided for military or government purposes: *Shots were fired near the central sector of the border.*

sec·u·lar /ˈsɛkyələr/ *adj.* not concerned with religion

☆ **se·cure¹** /səˈkyʊr/ *adj.* **1** free from worry or doubt; confident: *to feel secure about the future* ○ *Children need to feel secure.* ○ *to be financially secure* ☞ The opposite is **insecure**. **2** not likely to be lost; safe: *Business is good, so his job is secure.* ○ *a secure investment* **3** not likely to fall or be broken; firmly fastened: *That ladder doesn't look very secure.* **4 secure (against/ from sth)** well locked or protected: *This hospital is not secure enough to hold violent patients.* ○ *a country with secure borders* —**se·cure·ly** *adv.*: *All doors and windows must be securely fastened.*

se·cure² /səˈkyʊr/ *verb* [T] **1** to fasten or lock sth firmly: *The load was secured with ropes.* ○ *Secure the rope to a tree or a rock.* **2** to get sth, especially after using a lot of effort: *to secure a victory in the election*

☆ **se·cu·ri·ty** /səˈkyʊrəṭi/ *noun* [U] **1** the state of feeling safe and being free from worry: *Children need the security of a stable home environment.* ○ *financial security* (= having enough money for your present and future needs) ☞ The opposite is **insecurity**. Look also at **Social Security**. **2** things that you do to protect sb/sth from thieves, attack, war, etc.: *Security was tightened at the airport before the President arrived.* ○ *a maximum-security prison* (= for dangerous criminals) ○ *a security guard* **3** the department of a company, a college, etc. that is responsible for protecting its buildings and people: *If you see something suspicious, call security immediately.*

se·dan /səˈdæn/ *noun* [C] a car with a hard roof, usually four doors and a separate area (**trunk**) for luggage ☞ picture at **car**.

se·date¹ /səˈdeɪt/ *adj.* quiet, calm or formal

se·date² /səˈdeɪt/ *verb* [T] to give sb a drug or medicine to make him/her calm or sleepy —**se·da·tion** /səˈdeɪʃn/ *noun* [U]: *The doctor put her under sedation.*

sed·a·tive /ˈsɛdəṭɪv/ *noun* [C] a drug or medicine that makes you calm or sleepy ☞ Look at **tranquilizer**.

sed·en·tar·y /ˈsɛdn̩ˌtɛri/ *adj.* that involves a lot of time sitting down: *a sedentary lifestyle*

sed·i·ment /ˈsɛdəmənt/ *noun* [C,U] a solid substance that forms at the bottom of a liquid

se·duce /səˈdus/ *verb* [T] **1** to persuade sb to have sex with you, especially sb young and

without much experience **2** to persuade sb to do sth that he/she would not usually agree to do: *stores attempting to seduce customers into parting with their money* —**se·duc·tion** /səˈdʌkʃn/ *noun* [C,U]

se·duc·tive /səˈdʌktɪv/ *adj.* **1** sexually attractive, especially referring to a woman: *a seductive smile* **2** very attractive or appealing: *the seductive climate of southern California* ○ *a seductive argument/opinion* (= one which you are tempted to agree with)

☆ **see** /si/ *verb* (*p.t.* **saw** /sɔ/; *p.p.* **seen** /sin/) **1** [I,T] to become aware of sth, using your eyes: *It was so dark that we couldn't see.* ○ *I can't see that car's license number without my glasses.* ○ *I just saw a rat!* ○ *He looked for her but couldn't see her in the crowd.* ☞ Look at the note at **look¹**. **2** [T] to look at or watch a movie, play, television program, etc.: *Did you see that program on alligators on TV last night?* ○ *Have you seen Spielberg's new movie yet?* **3** [T] to get information: *Go and see if the mailman has come yet.* ○ *I saw in the paper that they're going to build a new stadium.* **4** [T] to meet or visit sb: *I saw Marie this weekend; we had dinner together.* ○ *You should see a doctor about that cough.* ○ *I've been seeing a lot of Paul these days* (= meeting him often). **5** [I,T] to understand sth; to realize sth: *Do you see what I mean?* ○ *"You have to press the return key first." "Oh, I see."* ○ *She doesn't see the point in spending so much money on a car.* ○ *I thought he was a nice guy, but now I see I was wrong.* ○ *I always saw my dad as a good role model.* **6** [T] to imagine: *I can't see her changing her mind now.* **7** [T] to do what is necessary in a situation; to make sure that sb does sth: *I'll see that he gets the letter.* ○ *Please see that the kids brush their teeth.* **8** [T] (*formal*) to go with or accompany sb: *He asked me if he could see me home, but I said no.*

IDM **as far as I can see/tell** ⇨ FAR²

I'll see; We'll see I'll think about what you have asked me and give you my decision later: *"Can we go swimming today, Dad?" "I'll see."*

let me see; let's see ⇨ LET

see if... to try: *I'll see if I can find time to do it.*

see you (around/later) (*informal*) (used for saying goodbye to sb)

wait and see ⇨ WAIT¹

you see (used for giving a reason): *She's very unhappy. You see, he was her first real boyfriend.*

PHRV **see about sth/doing sth** to deal with sth: *I've got to go to the bank to see about my traveler's checks.*

see sb off to say goodbye to sb who is leaving a place, especially at an airport, a bus station, etc.

see through sb/sth to be able to see that sb/sth is not what he/she/it appears: *The police immediately saw through his story.*

ər	ɪr	ɛr	ɑr	ɔr	ʊr	ʒ	h	ŋ
bird	near	hair	car	north	tour	vision	hat	sing

see to it that... to make sure that sth happens: *Please see to it that there are enough chairs for everyone.*

☆**seed** /sid/ *noun* [C,U] the small hard part of a plant from which a new plant of the same kind can grow: *a packet of sunflower seeds* ○ *Grass seed should be sown in the spring.*

seed·less /'sidləs/ *adj.* having no seeds: *seedless grapes*

seed·ling /'sidlɪŋ/ *noun* [C] a very young plant that has grown from a seed

seed·y /'sidi/ *adj.* (**seed·i·er; seed·i·est**) looking messy, dirty, or in bad condition; not respectable: *a seedy nightclub, hotel, etc.*

See·ing Eye dog /ˌsiŋ 'aɪ dɔg/ *noun* [C] (*trademark*) a dog that has been trained to guide a person who is unable to see

☆**seek** /sik/ *verb* [T] (*p.t., p.p.* **sought** /sɔt/) (*formal*) **1** to try to find or get sth: *Politicians are still seeking a peaceful solution.* ○ *The mayor plans to seek a second term in office.* **2 seek sth (from sb)** to ask sb for sth: *You should seek advice from a lawyer about what to do next.* ○ *to seek help* **3 seek (to do sth)** to try to do sth: *The new law seeks to protect the rights of single parents.*

☆**seem** /sim/ *verb* [I] **seem (to sb) (to be) sth; seem like sth** (not in the continuous tenses) to give the impression of being or doing sth; to appear: *Shelly seems like a very nice girl.* ○ *Shelly seems to be a very nice girl.* ○ *It seems to me that we have no choice.* ○ *Keith seems very interested in a career in medicine.* ○ *It doesn't seem as if/though they will find a solution to the problem.* ○ *It seems like we've been waiting for hours.* —**seem·ing·ly** *adv.*: *a seemingly endless list of complaints*

seem·ing /'simɪŋ/ *adj.* (*formal*) (only *before a noun*) appearing to be sth: *Despite her seeming enthusiasm, Sandra didn't really help much.*

seen *p.p.* of SEE

seep /sip/ *verb* [I] (used about a liquid) to flow very slowly through sth: *Water started seeping in through small cracks.*

see·saw /'siso/ (*also* **teeter-totter**) *noun* [C] an outdoor toy for children that consists of a long piece of wood, etc. that is balanced in the middle. One child sits on each end of the seesaw, and one goes up while the other is down.

seethe /sið/ *verb* [I] **1** to be very angry: *I was just seething at what he had said.* **2** to be very crowded: *The streets were seething with people.* ○ *a seething mass of people* (= a lot of people crowded together)

☆**seg·ment** /'sɛgmənt/ *noun* [C] **1** a section or part of sth: *a segment of a circle* ○ *a segment of the population* **2** one of the parts into which an orange can be divided

seg·re·gate /'sɛgrəgeɪt/ *verb* [T] **segregate sb/sth (from sb/sth)** to separate one group of people from the rest, especially because of

race or religion, or to separate people in a particular place: *the effects of segregating African-American children in schools* ☞ Look at **desegregate** and **integrate.** —**seg·re·ga·tion** /ˌsɛgrə'geɪʃn/ *noun* [U]: *racial segregation* (= separating people of different races)

☆**seize** /siz/ *verb* [T] **1** to take hold of sth suddenly and firmly: *The thief seized her purse and ran off with it.* ○ *to seize sb by the arm* ○ (*figurative*) *Mark was seized by a strong desire to laugh.* **2** to take control or possession of sb/sth: *The police seized 50 pounds of illegal drugs.* ○ *to seize power* ○ *Rebel forces seized the capital early this morning.*

IDM seize/take the initiative ⇨ INITIATIVE

PHRV seize (on/upon) sth to recognize an opportunity and to use it eagerly: *The President's opponents seized upon any opportunity to embarrass him.*

sei·zure /'siʒər/ *noun* **1** [U] seizing or being seized: *the seizure of 30 pounds of heroin by the Coast Guard* **2** [C] a sudden loss of consciousness with movements that are not controlled and sometimes violent: *an epileptic seizure*

☆**sel·dom** /'sɛldəm/ *adv.* not often: *It seldom snows here in March.* ○ *We very seldom go to the theater.*

☆**se·lect¹** /sə'lɛkt/ *verb* [T] to choose sb/sth from a number of similar things: *You can select whatever you want from the prizes on display.* ○ *The best candidates will be selected for interview.*

☞ **Select** is more formal than **choose** and suggests that a great deal of care is taken when making the decision.

se·lect² /sə'lɛkt/ *adj.* consisting of or available to only a small group of special people: *a select audience of business executives*

☆**se·lec·tion** /sə'lɛkʃn/ *noun* **1** [U] the act of choosing or being chosen: *All candidates must go through a rigorous selection procedure.* ○ *the selection of athletes for the Olympics* **2** [C] a number of people or things that have been chosen: *a selection of hits from the fifties and sixties* **3** [C,U] a collection of products in a store that are for sale: *They have a wide selection of toys at the mall.* ○ *Selection is as important as price to shoppers.*

se·lec·tive /sə'lɛktɪv/ *adj.* **1** careful when choosing: *She's very selective about who she invites to her parties.* ○ *a college with a highly selective admissions policy* **2** of or concerning only some people or things; not general: *selective enforcement of a law* —**se·lec·tive·ly** *adv.*

self /sɛlf/ *noun* [C] (*pl.* **selves** /sɛlvz/) a person's own nature or qualities: *It's good to see you back to your old self again* (= said to sb who has been sick, sad, worried, etc.). ○ *Her mean remark revealed her true self.*

self-ad·dressed ˌstamped ˈenvelope** *noun* [C] (*abbr.* **SASE**) an empty envelope

tʃ	dʒ	v	θ	ð	s	z	ʃ
chin	June	van	thin	then	so	zoo	she

with your own address and a stamp on it, that you send to a company in order to receive sth back from them

self-a'ssured *adj.* believing that you can do sth or succeed at sth —**self-assurance** /-ə'ʃʊrəns/ *noun* [U]

self-'centered *adj.* thinking only about yourself and not about other people ☞ Look at selfish.

self-'confident *adj.* feeling sure about your own value and abilities —**self-confidence** *noun* [U]: *Some women still lack the self-confidence to apply for executive jobs.*

self-'conscious *adj.* too worried about what other people think about you: *Men are often very self-conscious about losing their hair.* —**self-consciously** *adv.* —**self-consciousness** *noun* [U]

self-con'trol *noun* [U] the ability to control your emotions and appear calm even when you are angry, afraid, excited, etc.: *to lose/keep your self-control*

self-de'fense *noun* [U] the use of force to protect yourself or your property: *Lee is learning karate for self-defense.* ○ *to shoot sb in self-defense* (= because he/she is about to attack you)

self-'discipline *noun* [U] the ability to control yourself and do the things that you must do, especially in order to improve your life

self-em'ployed *adj.* working for yourself and earning money from your own business

self-es'teem *noun* [U] the feeling of pride that you have about yourself: *Many teenagers suffer from low self-esteem.*

self-'help *noun* [U] using your own efforts to do sth or deal with your problems, instead of relying on other people: *a self-help book*

self-in'dulgent *adj.* allowing yourself to have or do things you enjoy (sometimes when it would be better to control yourself): *a self-indulgent morning spent relaxing in the bathtub* —**self-indulgence** *noun* [C,U]

self-in'flicted *adj.* (used about an injury) that you have done to yourself: *He died of a self-inflicted gunshot wound to the head.*

self-'interest *noun* [U] concern for what is best for yourself rather than for other people

☆ **self·ish** /'sɛlfɪʃ/ *adj.* thinking only about your own needs or wishes and not about other people's needs or wishes: *a selfish attitude* ○ *I'm sick of your selfish behavior!* ☞ The opposite is unselfish. —**self·ish·ly** *adv.* —**self·ish·ness** *noun* [U]

self·less /'sɛlfləs/ *adj.* (*formal*) thinking about other people's needs or wishes rather than your own: *his years of selfless devotion to his sick wife*

self-'made *adj.* having become rich or successful by your own efforts: *a self-made multimillionaire*

self-'pity *noun* [U] the state of thinking too much about your own problems or troubles and feeling how unlucky you are

self-'portrait *noun* [C] a picture that you drew or painted of yourself

self-re'liant *adj.* not depending on help from sb/sth else —**self-reliance** *noun* [U]

self-re'spect *noun* [U] the feeling of pride in yourself: *Old people need to keep their dignity and self-respect.* —**self-respecting** *adj.* (in negative sentences): *No self-respecting Elvis Presley fan* (= nobody who is proud to be a fan of Elvis Presley) *should be without this book.*

self-'righteous *adj.* believing that you are always right and other people are wrong; thinking that you are better than other people —**self-righteousness** *noun* [U]

self-'service (*also* **self-'serve**) *adj.* (only before a noun) (used about a store, a gas station, etc.) where you serve yourself and then pay a person who works there (**cashier**)

self-suf'ficient *adj.* able to produce or provide everything that you need without help from sb or having to buy from others

☆ **sell** /sɛl/ *verb* (*p.t., p.p.* **sold** /soʊld/) **1** [I,T] **sell (sb) (sth); sell (sth) (to sb)** to give sth to sb who pays for it and is then the owner of it: *We are going to sell our car.* ○ *I sold my guitar for $200.* ○ *Would you sell me your ticket?* ○ *I was too late – the car had already been sold.* ○ *I offered them a lot of money, but they wouldn't sell.* ○ *He sold his business at an enormous profit.* **2** [T] to offer for sale: *Excuse me, do you sell greeting cards?* **3** [I] **sell (for/at sth)** to be sold or available for sale at a particular price: *These watches sell for $1,000 each in the retail stores, but you can have this one for $500.* **4** [I] to be sold to or bought by many people; to attract buyers: *Her books sell well in Europe.* **5** [T] to be sold in a particular quantity: *This newspaper sells over a million copies a day.* **6** [T] to cause people to want to buy sth; to help sth to attract buyers: *They rely on advertising to sell their products.* ☞ The noun for 1 - 6 is sale. **7** [T] **sell sth to sb; sell sb on sth** to persuade sb to accept sth: *to sell an idea to sb* ○ *She's completely sold on the idea of moving to Florida* (= she thinks it's a very good idea and wants to do it).

IDM **be sold out (of sth)** (used about a concert, an event, a store, etc.) to have had all the tickets or goods bought so that no more are available: *The concert was sold out weeks ago.* ○ *We're sold out of the book, but we could order a copy for you.*

PHRV **sell sth off** to sell a number of things, often at a low price, in order to get rid of them or to get money quickly: *They had to sell off several antiques in order to pay their tax bill.*

sell out to be sold completely, so that no more are available for sale: *By the time I got to the store, all the newspapers had sold out.*

i	ɪ	ɛ	æ	ɑ	ɔ	ʌ	ʊ	u
see	sit	ten	cat	hot	saw	cup	put	too

☆ **sell·er** /ˈsɛlər/ *noun* [C] **1** a person or business that sells sth: *a flower seller* ○ *The real estate market has many sellers but few buyers right now.* **2** something that is sold (especially in the amount described): *This magazine is a big seller in the 25-40 age group.* ☞ Look at **bestseller**.

sell·out /ˈsɛlaʊt/ *noun* [C] a concert, sports event, etc. for which all the tickets are sold: *The concert was a sellout.* ○ *The Orioles won 5 – 2 before a sellout crowd of 46,444.*

selves *pl.* of SELF

sem·blance /ˈsɛmbləns/ *noun* [sing., U] (*formal*) **(a) semblance of sth** the appearance of being sth or of having a certain quality: *After the earthquake, life slowly returned to some semblance of normality.*

se·men /ˈsimən/ *noun* [U] the liquid containing sperm that is produced by the male sex organs

☆ **se·mes·ter** /səˈmɛstər/ *noun* [C] one of two periods of time into which a school, college or university year is divided: *I'm taking an art history course second semester.*

sem·i·cir·cle /ˈsɛmiˌsərkl/ *noun* [C] one half of a circle; something that is arranged in this shape: *I want you all to sit in a semicircle.*

sem·i·co·lon /ˈsɛmiˌkoʊlən/ *noun* [C] a mark (;) used in writing or printing for separating parts of a sentence or items in a list

sem·i·fi·nal /ˈsɛmifaɪnl; ˈsɛmaɪ-; ˌsɛmiˈfaml/ *noun* [C] one of the two games in a sports competition whose winners play in the final

sem·i·fi·nal·ist /ˌsɛmiˈfaml·ɪst; ˌsɛmaɪ-/ *noun* [C] a player or team that plays in a semifinal; a person who has reached the last stage of a competition before the final

☆ **sem·i·nar** /ˈsɛmənar/ *noun* [C] **1** a short course or meeting in which a certain subject is taught or discussed: *a seminar on health and nutrition* **2** a class at a college etc. in which a small group of students discuss or study a subject with a teacher

☆ **Sen·ate** /ˈsɛnət/ *noun* [C] often **the Senate** the upper body of government in the U.S. and some other countries or in many U.S. states: *the Senate Foreign Affairs Committee*

☞ Look at **Congress** and **House of Representatives**.

☆ **sen·a·tor** /ˈsɛnətər/ *noun* [C] (*abbr.* **Sen.**) a member of a Senate: *She's a former senator from Maryland.* ○ *Senator Kennedy* —**sen·a·to·ri·al** /ˌsɛnəˈtɔriəl/ *adj.*: *a senatorial committee*

☆ **send** /sɛnd/ *verb* [T] (*p.t., p.p.* **sent** /sɛnt/) **1 send sth/sb (to sb/sth); send (sb) sth** to cause sth/sb to go or be taken somewhere without going there yourself: *to send a letter/ an e-mail* ○ *to send a message to sb* ○ *Don't forget to send me a postcard.* ○ *We sent out the invitations two months before the wedding.* ○ *She sent the children to bed early.* ○ *My com-*
pany is sending me on a business trip next month.* ○ *to send sb to prison* **2** to cause sb/sth to move in a particular direction, often quickly or as a reaction that cannot be prevented: *The news sent stock prices soaring yesterday.*

PHRV **send sth in** to send sth to a place where it will be officially dealt with: *I sent my application in three weeks ago, but I still haven't had a reply.*

send sth off to mail sth: *I'll send the information off today.*

se·nile /ˈsinaɪl/ *adj.* confused, unable to remember things or to take care of yourself (because of old age) —**se·nil·i·ty** /səˈnɪləti/ *noun* [U]

☆ **sen·ior¹** /ˈsinyər/ *adj.* **1 senior (to sb)** having a high or higher rank in a company, an organization, etc.: *a senior managerial position* ○ *He's senior to me.* ○ *a meeting of senior government officials* **2 Senior** (*abbr.* **Sr.**) (used to show that a man is the father of sb with the same name): *John Brown Sr.* ☞ Look at **junior**. **3** connected with the final year of high school or college: *the senior class*

☆ **sen·ior²** /ˈsinyər/ *noun* [C] **1** a student in the final year of high school or college: *He's a senior at Yale.* ☞ Look at **freshman**, **sophomore** and **junior**. **2** = SENIOR CITIZEN: *Tickets are $7 for adults and $5 for seniors and students.* **3** somebody who is older or of higher rank (than one or more other people): *My oldest sister is ten years my senior.*

☆ ˌ**senior ˈcitizen** (*also* **senior**) *noun* [C] a person who is 65 years old or older

ˌ**senior ˈhigh school** *noun* [C] a school that is usually for students in grades 10, 11 and 12 ☞ Look at **high school** and **junior high school**.

sen·ior·i·ty /ˌsinˈyɔrəti; -ˈyɑr-/ *noun* [U] the rank or importance that a person has in a company, organization, etc. in relation to others, often related to how long he/she has worked there: *Decisions about employee layoffs are based on seniority.*

sen·sa·tion /sɛnˈseɪʃn/ *noun* **1** [C] a feeling that is caused by sth affecting the body or part of the body: *a pleasant/an unpleasant sensation* ○ *I felt a burning sensation on my skin.* **2** [U] the ability to feel when touching or being touched: *For some time after the accident, he had no sensation in his legs.* **3** [C] a feeling or impression in the mind or body that is not caused by anything definite and may be false: *I had the peculiar sensation that I was floating in the air.* **4** [C] a feeling of great excitement, surprise or interest among a group of people or people in general; sb/sth that causes this: *The young Canadian caused a sensation by beating the top seed.* ○ *The band was an overnight sensation* (= became famous and popular immediately).

sen·sa·tion·al /sɛnˈseɪʃn·l/ *adj.* **1** causing, or

S

trying to cause, a feeling of great excitement or shock among people, especially in a way that you do not approve of: *sensational events* ○ *the most sensational murder trial this century* ○ *This magazine specializes in sensational stories about the rich and famous.* **2** extremely good; beautiful; very exciting: *You look sensational!* —**sen·sa·tion·al·ly** *adv.*

☆**sense¹** /sɛns/ *noun* **1** [C] one of the five natural physical powers that make it possible for a person or animal to get information about the world around: *I have a cold and I've lost my sense of smell.* **2** [U, sing.] the ability to understand or appreciate sth; the ability to recognize what sth is: *She seems to have lost all sense of reality.* ○ *I like him – he's got a great sense of humor.* ○ *I'm always getting lost. I have absolutely no sense of direction.* **3** [U, sing.] a natural ability to do or produce sth well: *Good business sense made her a millionaire.* **4** [U, sing.] a feeling or consciousness of sth: *I felt a tremendous sense of relief when all of my final exams were over.* ○ *She only visits her family out of a sense of duty.* **5** [U] the ability to think or act in a reasonable or sensible way; practical intelligence: *At least he had enough sense to stop when he realized he was making a mistake.* ○ *I think there's a lot of sense in what you're saying.* ☞ Look at **common sense**. **6** [U] good reason; use or point: *There's no sense in going any further – we're obviously lost.* ○ *What's the sense in making things more difficult for yourself?* **7** [C] (used about a word, phrase, etc.) a meaning or possible meaning: *This word has two senses.* ○ *It was awesome in the traditional sense of the word.*

IDM **in a sense** in one particular way but not in other ways; partly: *In a sense you're right, but there's more to the matter than that.*

make sense 1 to be possible to understand; to have a clear meaning: *What does this sentence mean? It doesn't make sense to me.* **2** (used about an action) to be sensible or logical: *I think it would make sense to wait for a while before making a decision.*

make sense of sth to be able to understand sth that is not clear or is difficult to understand: *I can't make sense of these instructions.*

sense² /sɛns/ *verb* [T] to realize or become aware of sth; to get the feeling that sth is the case: *I sensed that something was wrong.*

sense·less /'sɛnsləs/ *adj.* **1** having no meaning or purpose: *The police described the murder as "a senseless act of violence."* **2** unconscious

sen·si·ble /'sɛnsəbl/ *adj.* having or showing the ability to think or act in a reasonable way; having or showing good judgment: *a sensible man* ○ *It was a realistic and sensible plan.* —**sen·si·bly** /-əbli/ *adv.*: *Melissa tries to eat sensibly and exercise every day.*

☞ Compare **sensible** and **sensitive**. **Sensible** is connected with common sense, reasonable action and good judgment. **Sensitive** is connected with feelings and emotions and with the five senses.

☆**sen·si·tive** /'sɛnsətɪv/ *adj.* **1** sensitive (to sth) showing that you are aware of and understand people's feelings, problems, etc.: *to be sensitive to sb's feelings/wishes* ☞ The opposite for this sense is **insensitive**. **2** sensitive (about/to sth) easily upset, offended or annoyed, perhaps because of having strong feelings about a particular matter: *Don't be so sensitive! I was only joking.* ○ *She's still sensitive about her divorce.* ○ *He's very sensitive to criticism.* **3** easily hurt or damaged; painful, especially if touched: *a new soap for sensitive skin* **4** (used about a scientific instrument, a piece of equipment, etc.) able to measure very small changes **5** (used about a subject, a situation, etc.) needing to be dealt with carefully because it is likely to cause anger or trouble: *Religion is often a sensitive subject.* ○ *sensitive files/documents* ○ *This is a sensitive period in the negotiations between the two countries.* —**sen·si·tive·ly** *adv.* —**sen·si·tiv·i·ty** /ˌsɛnsə'tɪvəti/ *noun* [U]: *I think your comments showed a complete lack of sensitivity.*

sen·sor /'sɛnsər/ *noun* [C] a piece of equipment that can find certain sounds, movements, etc.

sen·su·al /'sɛnʃuəl/ *adj.* connected with physical or sexual pleasure: *the sensual rhythms of Latin music* ○ *a life devoted to sensual pleasure and luxury* —**sen·su·al·i·ty** /ˌsɛnʃu'æləti/ *noun* [U]

sen·su·ous /'sɛnʃuəs/ *adj.* giving pleasure to or affecting the mind or body through the senses: *a soft and sensuous voice*

sent *p.t., p.p.* of SEND

☆**sen·tence¹** /'sɛntns/ *noun* **1** [C] (*grammar*) a group of words containing a subject and a verb, that expresses a statement, a question, etc. When a sentence is written, it begins with a capital letter and ends with a period: *a grammatically correct sentence* ○ *You don't need to write a long letter. A couple of sentences will be enough.* ☞ Look also at **run-on sentence**. **2** [C,U] the punishment given by a judge to sb who has been found guilty of a crime: *a 25-year prison sentence* ○ *He is serving a life sentence in a maximum security prison.* ○ *the death sentence*

sen·tence² /'sɛntns/ *verb* [T] **sentence sb (to sth)** (used about a judge) to tell sb who has been found guilty of a crime what the punishment will be: *The judge sentenced her to three months in prison for shoplifting.* ○ *He was sentenced to life imprisonment for murder.*

sen·ti·ment /'sɛntəmənt/ *noun* **1** [C,U] an attitude or opinion that is often caused or influenced by emotion: *His comments expressed my*

sentiments exactly. ○ *a strong anti-war senti-ment* **2** [U] gentle feelings such as sympathy, love, happy memories, etc. that influence action or behavior (sometimes in situations where this is not suitable): *There's no room for sentiment in business.*

sen·ti·men·tal /ˌsɛntəˈmɛntl/ *adj.* **1** caused by or connected with gentle feelings such as sympathy, love, happy memories, etc.: *The jewelry had great sentimental value to me.* **2** having or showing these gentle emotions, sometimes in a silly way: *How can you be sentimental about that old car?* ○ *a sentimental love song* —**sen·ti·men·tal·i·ty** /ˌsɛntəmɛnˈtæləti/ *noun* [U]

sen·try /ˈsɛntri/ *noun* [C] (*pl.* **sen·tries**) a soldier who stands outside a building and guards it

sep·a·ra·ble /ˈsɛpərəbl/ *adj.* able to be separated ☞ The opposite is **inseparable**.

☆ **sep·a·rate¹** /ˈsɛprət/ *adj.* **1 separate (from sth/sb)** apart; not joined or together: *You should always keep your cash and credit cards separate.* **2** different; not connected: *A lot of married couples have separate bank accounts.* ○ *In a separate incident, a man was shot in Northeast Washington last night.* —**sep·a·rate·ly** *adv.*: *Accessories are sold separately.*

☆ **sep·a·rate²** /ˈsɛpəreɪt/ *verb* **1** [I,T] **separate (sb/sth) (from sb/sth)** to stop being together; to cause people or things to stop being together; to divide people or things: *I think we should separate into two groups.* ○ *I got separated from my friends in the crowd.* ○ *Separate the egg white from the yolk.* **2** [T] **separate sb/sth (from sb/sth)** to keep people or things apart, or to be between people or things with the result that they are apart: *I always try to separate business from pleasure.* ○ *When the players started fighting, the referee moved in to separate them.* ○ *The two sides of the city are separated by the river.* **3** [I] (used about a married couple, etc.) to stop living together: *His parents separated when he was still a baby.*

☆ **sep·a·rat·ed** /ˈsɛpəreɪtəd/ *adj.* (used about a married couple) not living together anymore but not divorced: *My wife and I are separated.*

☆ **sep·a·ra·tion** /ˌsɛpəˈreɪʃn/ *noun* [C,U] **1** the act of separating or being separated; a situation or period of being apart: *The soldiers are returning home after a long separation from their families.* **2** a legal agreement where a married couple lives apart (but does not get a divorce): *a trial separation*

☆ **Sep·tem·ber** /sɛpˈtɛmbər/ *noun* [C,U] (*abbr.* **Sept.**) the ninth month of the year; coming before October ☞ For examples of the use of the months in sentences, look at **January**.

se·quel /ˈsikwəl/ *noun* [C] **1** a book, movie, etc. that continues the story of the previous one **2** something that happens after, or is the result of, a previous event

☆ **se·quence** /ˈsikwəns/ *noun* **1** [C] a number of related actions, events, etc. that happen or come one after another: *Investigators are trying to determine the sequence of events that led to the accident.* **2** [U] the order in which a number of things happen or are arranged: *The photographs are arranged in sequence.*

se·quoi·a /sɪˈkwɔɪə/ *noun* [C] = REDWOOD

se·rene /səˈrin/ *adj.* calm and peaceful: *a serene smile* —**se·rene·ly** *adv.* —**se·ren·i·ty** /səˈrɛnəti/ *noun* [U]

ser·geant /ˈsɑrdʒənt/ *noun* [C] (*abbr.* **Sgt.**) an officer of low rank in the military forces or police

se·ri·al /ˈsɪriəl/ *noun* [C] a single story in a magazine or on television that is told in a number of parts over a period of time: *the first part of a six-part drama serial* ☞ Look at the note at **series**.

'serial ˌkiller *noun* [C] a person who has killed several people, one after another, using the same method

'serial ˌnumber *noun* [C] the number marked on sth to identify it and to distinguish it from other things of the same type: *the serial numbers of traveler's checks*

☆ **se·ries** /ˈsɪriz/ *noun* [C] (*pl.* **series**) **1** a number of things that come one after another and are of the same type or connected: *a series of events* ○ *a concert series* ○ *There has been a series of burglaries in the area recently.* **2** a number of programs on television or on the radio which have the same main characters and each tell a complete story

☞ Compare **series** and **serial**. In a **series**, each part is a different, complete story involving the same main characters. In a **serial**, the same story continues in each part.

3 (in sports) a number of games that are played one after another by the same two teams: *the NBA championship series between the Chicago Bulls and the Los Angeles Lakers*

☆ **se·ri·ous** /ˈsɪriəs/ *adj.* **1** (used about problems, situations, etc.) bad; important; causing worry: *a serious injury* ○ *serious consequences* ○ *Pollution is a very serious problem.* ○ *serious crime* **2** needing to be treated as important, not just for fun: *Don't laugh – it's a serious matter.* ○ *a serious discussion* ○ *She's had quite a few boyfriends, but only one serious relationship.* **3** (used about a person) not joking; thoughtful: *Are you serious about starting your own business* (= are you really going to do it)? ○ *He's extremely serious. I don't think I've ever seen him laugh.* ○ *You're looking very serious. Was it bad news?* —**se·ri·ous·ness** *noun* [U]: *We must make people aware of the seriousness of the situation.*

☆ **se·ri·ous·ly** /ˈsɪriəsli/ *adv.* **1** in a serious way: *Three people were seriously injured in the accident.* ○ *My sister is seriously considering buying*

S

a house in Maine. ○ It's time you started to think seriously about the future. **2** (used for indicating that you are not joking or that you really mean what you are saying): *Seriously, I do appreciate all your help.* ○ *Seriously, you have nothing to worry about.*

IDM take sb/sth seriously to treat sb or sth as important: *Nobody takes him seriously.* ○ *You take everything too seriously! Relax and enjoy yourself.*

ser·mon /ˈsərmən/ *noun* [C] a speech on a religious or moral matter that is given as part of a service in church or temple

ser·ra·ted /səˈreɪṭəd; ˈsɛreɪṭəd/ *adj.* having a row of points in V-shapes along the edge: *a knife with a serrated edge*

ser·vant /ˈsərvənt/ *noun* [C] (*old-fashioned*) a person who is paid to work in sb's house, doing work such as cooking, cleaning, etc. ☛ Look at **maid** and **civil servant**.

☆ **serve** /sərv/ *verb* **1** [I,T] to work for a country, a company, an organization, the army, etc.; to be useful to sb: *The role of the police is to serve the community.* ○ *She has served on a number of committees.* ○ *He served in the army during the Korean War.* ○ *During his long political career he served under six different Presidents.* **2** [T] to give food or drinks to sb during a meal; to take an order and then bring food or drinks to sb (in a restaurant, bar, etc.): *Breakfast is served from 7:30 to 9:00 a.m.* ○ *We waited for half an hour until a waiter finally served us.* **3** [T] to provide sb (especially the public) with sth necessary or useful in daily life: *The area is served by two major airports.* **4** [I,T] **serve (sb) (as sth)** to be good enough for or suitable for a particular purpose; to perform a particular function: *The smallest bedroom serves as my office.* ○ *His bad attitude only served to make him even less popular.* ○ *The program no longer serves any useful purpose.* **5** [T] to spend a period of time in prison as a punishment: *He is currently serving a ten-year sentence for fraud.* **6** [T] (used about an amount of food) to be enough for a certain number of people: *According to the recipe, this dish serves four.* **7** [I,T] (in tennis and similar sports) to start play by hitting the ball

IDM serve sb right (used when sth bad happens to sb and you have no sympathy) to be deserved by sb: *"I feel sick." "It serves you right for eating so much."*

serv·er /ˈsərvər/ *noun* [C] **1** a computer that controls information which can be shared by a group of connected computers **2** a person whose job is to take orders and bring people food and drinks in a restaurant

☆ **serv·ice¹** /ˈsərvəs/ *noun* **1** [U] working for a country, a company, an organization, the army, etc.: *The congressman was thanked for his years of service to the party.* ○ *He was accused of trying to avoid military service dur-*

ing the Vietnam War. ○ *He left the police force after thirty years' service.* **2** [C] a system or an organization that provides the public with sth necessary or useful in daily life; the job that an organization does: *a personal shopping service* ○ *an Internet service provider* ○ *The delivery company is starting a new overnight service.* ○ *We offer a number of financial services.* **3** [C, usually sing.] one of certain government departments or public institutions: *the foreign service* **4 the service** [sing.] the military forces: *Our daughter was in the sevice for five years.* **5** [U] the work or the quality of work done by sb when serving a customer: *I enjoyed the food, but the service was terrible.* ○ *If you have any problem with the computer, call our customer service department.* **6** [C] a religious ceremony, usually including prayers, singing, etc.: *a funeral service* **7** [C] (in tennis and similar sports) the act of hitting the ball at the start of play; a player's turn to serve

serv·ice² /ˈsərvəs/ *verb* [T] to examine and, if necessary, repair a car, machine, etc.: *My car hasn't been serviced since last year.*

ˈservice charge *noun* [C] the amount of money that is added to the cost of sth for special extra services: *There is a $2 service charge for each ticket ordered by phone.*

ˈservice ˌstation *noun* [C] = GAS STATION

serv·ing /ˈsərvɪŋ/ *noun* [C] an amount of food for one person: *This cake has 450 calories per serving!*

ses·sion /ˈsɛʃn/ *noun* [C] **1** a meeting or series of meetings of an official body (a court, Congress, etc.) **2** a period of doing a particular activity: *The whole tape was recorded in one session.* ○ *a weekly session with a therapist*

IDM in session (used about an official committee, a court, etc.) holding a meeting; doing its official work; not closed for vacation: *This court is now in session.*

☆ **set¹** /sɛt/ *noun* **1** [C] **set (of sth)** a number of things that belong together: *a set of dishes* ○ *a 4-piece towel set* ○ *a set of rules* **2** [C] a piece of equipment for receiving television signals: *a TV set* **3** [C] the scenery for a play or movie: *a musical with spectacular sets* **4** [C] (in tennis) a group of games forming part of a match: *She won the match in three straight sets.*

☆ **set²** /sɛt/ *verb* (*pres. part.* **set·ting**; *p.t., p.p.* **set**) **1** [T] to put sb/sth in a particular position; to place sth somewhere: *He set a large bowl of soup in front of me.* ○ *The hotel is set in a beautiful area.* **2** [T] (often passive) to place the action of a book, play, movie, etc. in a particular time, situation, etc.: *The movie is set in 16th-century Spain.* **3** [T] to cause a particular state or event; to start sth happening: *The new governor set the prisoners free.* ○ *The rioters set a number of cars on fire.* ○ *Her comment set him thinking.* **4** [T] to prepare or arrange sth for a particular purpose: *I set my*

alarm for 6:30. ○ *to set the table* (= put the plates, knives, forks, etc. on it) ○ *Did you set the VCR to record that movie?* **5** [T] to establish sth or make sth definite: *Try to set a good example for the younger kids.* ○ *Can we set a limit of $100 on the cost of materials?* ○ *They haven't set a date for their wedding yet.* ○ *He has set a new world record.* **6** [I] to become firm or hard: *Put the dessert in the refrigerator for two hours to set.* **7** [T] to fasten a precious stone, etc. in a piece of jewelry: *The pin had three diamonds set in gold.* **8** [I] (used about the sun, etc.) to go down below the horizon ☞ The opposite is **rise**. **9** [T] to put a broken bone in its correct position and often to put it in a special hard case (**cast**) so that it can heal: *The doctor set her broken leg.* **10** [T] (*old-fashioned*) to arrange sb's hair while it is wet so that it becomes curly, wavy, etc.: *She went to the salon to have her hair set.*

☞ For idioms containing **set**, look at the entries for the nouns, adjectives, etc.; e.g. **set sail** is at **sail**.

PHRV **set sb/sth apart (from sb/sth)** to make sb/sth different from or better than others: *Her terrific sense of humor really sets her apart from the other candidates.*

set sth aside 1 to leave or save sth for a particular purpose: *Roll out the pie crust, then set it aside while you prepare the filling.* ○ *Part of the hall has been set aside for an exhibit of students' artwork.* **2** to agree to pay no attention to sth for a period of time because other things are more important: *We decided to set aside our differences for the sake of the kids.*

set sb/sth back to delay sb/sth: *The bad weather has set our plans back by six weeks.*

set in to arrive and remain for a period of time: *It looks like some dark clouds are beginning to set in.*

set off to leave on a trip: *We set off at 3 o'clock this morning.*

set sth off to do sth which starts a reaction: *When this door is opened, it sets off an alarm.*

set out to leave on a trip: *They set out at dawn.*

set out to do sth to decide to achieve sth: *She set out to become America's first woman President.*

set (sth) up to start; to establish a business, etc.: *The company has set up a new branch in Atlanta.* ○ *After she finished law school, she set up in a practice in her hometown.*

☆ **set³** /sɛt/ *adj.* **1** definite and not changing; firm: *There are no set hours in my job.* ○ *He's getting more and more set in his ways* (= with fixed habits and routines which he is unwilling to change) *as he gets older.* ☞ She has very set ideas about what's right and what's wrong. **2** **set (for sth); set (to do sth)** ready, prepared or likely to do sth: *Okay, I'm all set – let's go!* ○ *I was all set to leave when the phone*

rang. ○ *The Chicago Bulls look set for another victory.*

IDM **be set against sth/against doing sth** to be opposed to sth: *She's dead* (= extremely) *set against moving to the country.*

be set on sth/on doing sth to be determined to do sth: *She's set on a career in acting.* ○ *My heart was set on that house* (= I really wanted it).

set·back /'sɛtbæk/ *noun* [C] a difficulty or problem that stops you from making progress as fast as you want to

☆ **set·ting** /'sɛtɪŋ/ *noun* [C] **1** surroundings; the place where sth happens: *The resort is in a beautiful setting in the woods.* ○ *They decided that a rural church would be the perfect setting for their wedding.* **2** one of the positions of the controls of a machine: *Use the iron's lowest setting for this delicate fabric.*

☆ **set·tle** /'sɛtl/ *verb* **1** [I,T] to go and live permanently in a new country, an area, a town, etc.: *the pioneers who settled the Wild West* ○ *He served in the Army for eight years before settling in New Haven.* **2** [I,T] to reach an agreement about sth; to end an argument; to find a solution to a disagreement: *They settled the lawsuit without going to court.* ○ *They were willing to settle out of court.* **3** [T] to decide or arrange sth finally (e.g. a plan, an action, etc.): *Everything's settled. We leave on the nine o'clock flight on Friday.* **4** [I] to get into or put sb into a comfortable position: *I settled back in front of the TV for the evening.* **5** [I,T] to become or to make sth (e.g. your stomach or nerves) calm or relaxed: *Have a drink. It might settle your nerves.* **6** [T] to pay sth (a bill, a debt, etc.): *to settle a bill* ○ *The insurance company settled the claim very quickly.* **7** [I] to come to rest in a certain position; to land: *Snow settled on some parts of the Midwest for the first time this season.* **8** [I] (used about a liquid) to become clear or still

PHRV **settle down 1** to become calm and quiet: *Settle down! It's time to start class.* **2** to get into a comfortable position, sitting or lying: *I made a cup of tea and settled down with a good book.* **3** to start having a quieter way of life, especially by staying in the same place or getting married, etc.: *She had a number of part-time jobs before she eventually settled down.*

settle for sth to accept sth that is not as good as you hoped it would be: *You'll have to settle for something cheaper.*

settle in; settle into sth to get used to or start feeling comfortable in a new home, job, etc.: *How are the kids settling in at their new school?* ○ *to settle into a routine*

settle on sth to choose sth after considering many different things; to decide on sth

set·tled /'sɛtld/ *adj.* feeling comfortable, calm

and not likely to change (in a home, a job, a way of life, etc.): *We feel very settled here.*

☆**set·tle·ment** /ˈsɛtlmənt/ *noun* **1** [C,U] an agreement, usually official, that ends an argument; the act of reaching this kind of agreement: *The strike lasted for several weeks until a settlement was reached.* ○ *the settlement of a dispute* **2** [C] an amount of money that is officially given to sb to end an argument: *The judge awarded a $4 million settlement to the accident victim.* **3** [C] a place that a group of people have built and live in, where few or no people lived before: *a settlement in the jungle*

☆**set·tler** /ˈsɛtlər; ˈsɛtl̩·ər/ *noun* [C] a person who goes to live permanently in a new country, particularly an undeveloped one or one with a small population: *early settlers in Virginia*

☆**sev·en** /ˈsɛvən/ *number* 7; one more than 6 ☞ For examples of how to use numbers in sentences, look at **six**. Look also at Appendix 2.

sev·en- /ˈsɛvən/ (in compounds) having seven of the thing mentioned: *a seven-headed monster*

☆**sev·en·teen** /ˌsɛvənˈtin/ *number* 17; one more than sixteen ☞ For examples of how to use numbers in sentences, look at **six**. Look also at Appendix 2. —**sev·en·teenth** /ˌsɛvənˈtinθ/ *pron., det., adv.* ☞ Look at the examples at **sixth**.

☆**sev·enth¹** /ˈsɛvənθ/ *pron., det., adv.* 7th, next after sixth ☞ Look at the examples at **sixth**. For more information on numbers, look at Appendix 2.

☆**sev·enth²** /ˈsɛvənθ/ *noun* [C] the fraction 1/7; one of seven equal parts of sth ☞ Look at the examples at **sixth**. For more information on numbers, look at Appendix 2.

☆**sev·en·ty** /ˈsɛvənti/ *number* 70; one more than sixty-nine ☞ For examples of how to use numbers in sentences, look at **sixty**. Look also at Appendix 2. —**sev·en·ti·eth** /ˈsɛvəntiəθ/ *pron., det., adv.* ☞ Look at the examples at **sixth**.

sev·er /ˈsɛvər/ *verb* [T] **1** to break, separate or divide by cutting: *The construction workers accidentally severed a power line.* **2** to end sth (a relationship, etc.): *He has severed all ties with his former friends.*

☆**sev·er·al** /ˈsɛvrəl/ *pron., det.* more than two but not very many; some: *It took her several days to recover from the shock.* ○ *There were lots of applications for the job – several of them from very well-qualified people.* ○ *I've asked him several times for the money.*

☆**se·vere** /səˈvɪr/ *adj.* **1** very bad; causing bad results or feelings: *The company is in severe financial difficulty.* ○ *a severe cold, headache, illness, pain, etc.* ○ *a severe winter* (= a very cold one) **2** not kind or gentle: *I think your criticism of her work was too severe.* ○ *a severe punishment* —**se·vere·ly** *adv.*: *The roof*

was severely damaged in the storm. ○ *The report severely criticizes the mayor.* —**se·ver·i·ty** /səˈvɛrəti/ *noun* [U]: *I don't think you realize the severity of the problem.*

☆**sew** /soʊ/ *verb* (*p.t.* **sewed**; *p.p.* **sewn** /soʊn/ or **sewed**) [I,T] to join pieces of cloth, or to join sth to cloth, using a needle and thread or a machine and forming stitches: *I can't sew.* ○ *to sew a new button onto a shirt* ○ *I'll have to sew the pocket by hand.*

sew
needle
stitches
thread

PHRV **sew sth up 1** to join two things by sewing; to repair sth by sewing two things together: *to sew up a hole* ○ *The surgeon sewed up the wound.* **2** (usually passive) to arrange or organize sth so that it is certain to happen or be successful: *I think we have the deal all sewn up.* —**sew·ing** *noun* [U]

sew·age /ˈsuɪdʒ/ *noun* [U] the waste material from people's bodies and dirty water that are carried away from their homes in water in large underground pipes (**sewers**)

sew·er /ˈsuər/ *noun* [C] an underground pipe that carries used water and waste to a place where it can be cleaned and made safe with special chemicals

ˈ**sew·ing ma·chine** *noun* [C] a machine that is used for sewing

sewn *p.p.* of SEW

☆**sex** /sɛks/ *noun* **1**(also *formal* **intercourse**; **sexual intercourse**) [U] the physical act in which the sexual organs of two people touch and which can result in a woman having a baby: *to have sex with somebody* ○ *It's against their religion to have sex before marriage.* ☞ Look also at **safe sex**. **2** [U] activities or matters connected with the act of sex (1): *There's too much sex and violence on TV.* **3** [U] the state of being either male or female: *We do not discriminate on the basis of race, sex, religion or disability.* ○ *Do you mind what sex your baby is?* ☞ **Gender** has the same meaning. **4** [C] one of the two groups consisting of all male people or all female people: *the male/female sex* ○ *He's always found it difficult to get along with members of the opposite sex* (= women).

sex·ism /ˈsɛksɪzəm/ *noun* [U] treating a person unfairly, or thinking that they are inferior, because of their sex, e.g. thinking that only men can do certain jobs, such as being a firefighter

sex·ist /ˈsɛksɪst/ *adj.* connected with or showing sexism: *a sexist attitude toward women* ○ *sexist jokes* —**sex·ist** *noun* [C]

☆**sex·u·al** /ˈsɛkʃuəl/ *adj.* connected with sex: *sexual problems* ○ *the sexual organs* ○ *sexual harassment* —**sex·u·al·ly** /-əli/ *adv.*: *to be sexu-*

ally attracted to sb ∘ *a sexually transmitted disease*

ˌsexual ˈintercourse *noun* [U] (*formal*) = SEX(1)

sex·u·al·i·ty /ˌsɛkʃuˈæləṭi/ *noun* [U] the nature of sb's sexual activities or desires: *He found it difficult to come to terms with his sexuality.*

☆ **sex·y** /ˈsɛksi/ *adj.* (**sex·i·er**; **sex·i·est**) (*informal*) sexually attractive: *a sexy man* ∘ *a sexy dress* ☞ Look at **sexual**.

Sgt. *abbr.* = SERGEANT

sh /ʃ/ *interj.* be quiet!: *Sh! People are trying to sleep in here.*

shab·by /ˈʃæbi/ *adj.* (**shab·bi·er**; **shab·bi·est**) **1** in bad condition because of having been used or worn too much: *a shabby suit* **2** (used about the way that sb is treated) unfair; not generous —**shab·bi·ly** /ˈʃæbəli/ *adv.*: *shabbily dressed*

shack /ʃæk/ *noun* [C] a small, roughly built house or building

shade/shadow

a shadow

They're sitting in the **shade**.

☆ **shade¹** /ʃeɪd/ *noun* **1** [U] an area that is out of direct sunlight and is darker and cooler than areas in the sun: *It was so hot that I had to go and sit in the shade.*

☞ **Shade** [U] is an area or part of a place that is protected from the heat of the sun. A **shadow** [C] is a dark shape made by light shining on a person or object. **Shadow** [U] is an area of darkness in which it is difficult to distinguish things easily.

2 [C] something that keeps out light or makes it less bright, especially a covering that you can pull down in front of a window: *Pull* (= close) *the shades – the sun is too bright.* ∘ *to open/close a shade* ☞ picture at **curtain**. Look also at **lampshade**. **3 shades** [plural] (*informal*) = SUNGLASSES **4** [C] **a shade (of sth)** a type of a particular color: *a shade of green* ∘ *I'd rather have a darker shade if you have one.* ∘ *a pale shade of gray* **5** [C] a small difference or variation in the form or quality of sth: *a word with various shades of meaning* **6** [sing.] a lit-

tle bit: *Current prices are just a shade higher than last year.*

shade² /ʃeɪd/ *verb* [T] to protect sth from direct light; to give shade ¹(1) to sth: *The sun was so bright that I had to shade my eyes.*

☆ **shad·ow¹** /ˈʃædoʊ/ *noun* **1** [C] a dark shape on a surface that is caused by sth being between light and that surface: *The dog was chasing its own shadow.* ∘ *The shadows lengthened as the sun went down.* ∘ (*figurative*) *He has always lived in the shadow of his older brother.* ∘ (*figurative*) *News of the tragedy cast a shadow over the day.* ☞ Look also at **eye shadow**. **2** [U] an area that is dark because sth prevents direct light from reaching it: *His face was in shadow.* ☞ Look at the note at **shade**.

IDM **beyond/without a shadow of doubt** with no doubt at all: *His guilt has been proven beyond a shadow of doubt.*

shad·ow² /ˈʃædoʊ/ *verb* [T] to follow and watch the actions of sb, often secretly: *The police shadowed the suspect for three days.*

shad·ow·y /ˈʃædoʊi/ *adj.* **1** having many shadows; dark: *a shadowy forest* **2** difficult to see or identify clearly: *a shadowy figure coming toward me* **3** mysterious; difficult to know much about: *the shadowy world of organized crime*

shad·y /ˈʃeɪdi/ *adj.* (**shad·i·er**; **shad·i·est**) **1** giving shade; giving shelter from the sun: *We ate our picnic in a shady spot.* **2** (*informal*) not completely honest or legal: *She's made a lot of money from some pretty shady deals.*

shaft /ʃæft/ *noun* [C] **1** a long, narrow hole in which sth can go up and down or enter or leave: *an elevator shaft* ∘ *a mine shaft* **2** a bar that connects parts of a machine

shag·gy /ˈʃægi/ *adj.* (**shag·gi·er**; **shag·gi·est**) **1** (used about hair, material, etc.) long, thick and messy **2** covered with long, thick, messy hair: *a shaggy dog*

shake hands

shaking hands

☆ **shake¹** /ʃeɪk/ *verb* (*p.t.* **shook** /ʃʊk/; *p.p.* **shak·en** /ˈʃeɪkən/) **1** [I,T] to move from side to side or up and down with short, quick movements: *I was so nervous that I was shaking.* ∘ *The whole building shakes when big trucks go past.* ∘ (*figurative*) *His voice shook with emotion as he described the tragedy.* ∘ *Shake the bottle before you pour the medicine out.* ∘ *She shook him to wake him up.* **2** [T] to disturb or upset

S

sb/sth: *The scandal has shaken the whole country.* **3** [T] to cause sth to be less certain; to cause doubt about sth: *Nothing seems to shake her belief that she was right.*

IDM **shake sb's hand/shake hands (with sb)** to take sb's hand and move it up and down (as a greeting, to show that you have agreed on sth, etc.)

shake your head to move your head from side to side, as a way of expressing that you mean "No"

PHRV **shake sb/sth off** to escape from sb/sth; to remove by shaking: *I don't want to be able to shake off this cold.* ○ *Shake the crumbs off the tablecloth.*

shake² /ʃeɪk/ *noun* [C] **1** the act of shaking or being shaken physically: *a shake of the head* ○ *You'll have to give the bottle a few shakes.* **2** = MILKSHAKE

shake·up /ˈʃeɪkʌp/ *noun* [C] a complete change in the structure or organization of sth: *a dramatic government shake-up*

shak·y /ˈʃeɪki/ *adj.* (**shak·i·er**; **shak·i·est**) **1** shaking or feeling weak because you are frightened or ill **2** not firm; weak or not very good: *The table's a little shaky, so don't put anything heavy on it.* ○ *They had a shaky start to the season, losing their first two games.* —**shak·i·ly** /-əli/ *adv.*

☆ **shall** /ʃəl; *strong form* ʃæl/ *modal verb* (*negative* **shall not**) **1** I shall I/we ... (used in questions in order to offer to do sth or to make a suggestion): *Shall I give you a ride home?* ○ *Shall we go out to eat tonight?* ☞ **Should** is also used with this meaning, especially in informal speech. **2** (*formal*) (used for saying that sth must or will happen or that sb must/must not do sth): *These arrangements shall remain in effect until further notice.*

☞ This sense of **shall** is very formal and is used mainly in official situations, e.g. in a court of law. **Will** is more common and less formal.

☆ **shal·low** /ˈʃæloʊ/ *adj.* **1** not deep; with not much distance between top and bottom: *The lake is very shallow here.* ○ *Put in a shallow dish and bake for 20 minutes.* **2** not having or showing serious or deep thought: *rather a shallow young man* —**shal·low·ness** *noun* [U]

sham /ʃæm/ *noun* [C] a thing or a plan that is not really what sb pretends that it is: *Detectives quickly realized that the business was a sham.*

☆ **shame¹** /ʃeɪm/ *noun* **1** [U] the guilty feeling that you have when you think that you have done sth morally wrong, sth that causes other people to have a bad opinion of you, or sth extremely embarrassing: *She was filled with shame at the thought of how she had lied to her mother.* ☞ The adjective that describes this feeling is **ashamed**. **2** [U] the ability to have

shame (1): *He doesn't care how he behaves in public. He has no shame!* **3** [U] loss of respect from others; loss of honor: *There's no shame in finishing second.* ○ *His actions have brought shame on his whole family.* **4 a shame** [sing.] a fact or situation that makes you feel disappointed: *It's a shame you can't come. I was looking forward to seeing you.* ○ *"I failed my test." "Oh, that's such a shame."* ○ *What a shame you have to leave so soon!*

IDM **Shame on you!** (*informal*) (used to tell sb that he/she should feel ashamed): *Shame on you for behaving like that in front of our guests!*

shame² /ʃeɪm/ *verb* [T] to make sb feel ashamed

shame·ful /ˈʃeɪmfl/ *adj.* that sb should be ashamed of: *a shameful waste of taxpayers' money* —**shame·ful·ly** *adv.*: *I think you behaved shamefully.*

shame·less /ˈʃeɪmləs/ *adj.* not having or showing the feeling of shame that people would expect you to have in a particular situation: *a shameless display of greed and bad manners* —**shame·less·ly** *adv.*

☆ **sham·poo¹** /ʃæmˈpu/ *noun* (*pl.* **sham·poos**) **1** [C,U] a liquid that you use to wash your hair: *a shampoo for oily hair* **2** [C] the act of washing sth with shampoo

sham·poo² /ʃæmˈpu/ *verb* [T] (*pres. part.* **sham·poo·ing**; *3rd pers. sing. pres.* **sham·poos**; *p.t., p.p.* **sham·pooed**) to wash with shampoo

sham·rock /ˈʃæmrɑk/ *noun* [C,U] a plant with three leaves on each stem, which is the national symbol of Ireland

shan·ty·town /ˈʃæntitaʊn/ *noun* [C] a small town or part of a city where poor people live in bad conditions in small badly built houses, etc.

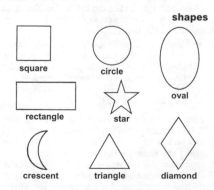

shapes

square circle oval
rectangle star
crescent triangle diamond

☆ **shape¹** /ʃeɪp/ *noun* **1** [C,U] the physical outline or outer form of sth: *a round/square/oblong shape* ○ *a card in the shape of a heart* ○ *clothes to fit women of all shapes and sizes* **2** [C] something that has a particular outline

or outer form: *Squares, circles and triangles are all different shapes.* **3** [U] the condition of sb or sth; the good or bad state of sb or sth: *The house is old, but it's still in pretty good shape.* ○ *She was in such bad shape* (= so sick) *that she had to be taken to the hospital.* **4** [sing.] **the shape of sth** the organization, form or structure of sth: *Recent developments have changed the shape of the company.*

IDM **be/get bent out of shape** ⇨ BENT²

in shape healthy and physically fit: *Regular exercise will keep your body in shape.*

out of shape not physically fit: *You're out of shape. You should get more exercise.*

take shape to start to develop well: *Plans to expand the company are beginning to take shape.*

☆ **shape²** /ʃeɪp/ *verb* [T] **1** **shape sth (into sth)** to make sth into a particular form: *Shape the dough into small balls.* **2** to influence the way in which sth develops; to cause sth to have a particular form or nature: *His political ideas were shaped by his upbringing.*

-shaped /ʃeɪpt/ (in compounds) having a certain shape; having the shape of the thing mentioned: *an L-shaped room*

☆ **share¹** /ʃɛr/ *noun* **1** [sing.] **share (of sth)** a part or an amount of sth that has been divided between several people: *We each pay a share of the household bills.* ○ *I'm willing to take my share of the blame.* **2** [C] **share (in/of sth)** one of the equal parts into which the ownership of a company is divided. Shares in a company can be bought and sold: *She holds 100 shares of Kellogg stock.*

IDM **have (more than) your (fair) share of sth** to have (more than) the usual or expected amount of sth: *We've had more than our fair share of trouble today.*

share² /ʃɛr/ *verb* **1** [I,T] **share (sth) (with sb)** to have, use, do or pay sth together with another person or other people; to have sth that sb else also has: *I share an apartment with four other people.* ○ *There's only one room available, so we'll have to share.* ○ *We share the same interests.* **2** [I,T] **share (sth) (with sb)** to let sb else have or use sth that you have: *I shared my sandwich with Kim at lunch.* **3** [T] **share sth (with sb)** to tell sb about sth; to allow sb to know sth: *Sometimes it helps to share your problems.*

share·hold·er /ˈʃɛrhoʊldər/ *noun* [C] an owner of shares¹(2) in a company

shark

shark /ʃɑrk/ *noun* [C,U] a large, often dangerous, ocean fish that has many sharp teeth

☆ **sharp¹** /ʃɑrp/ *adj.* **1** having a fine edge or point; that can cut or make a hole in sth easily: *a sharp knife* ○ *sharp teeth* ☞ The opposite is **blunt**. **2** clear; allowing details to be seen clearly: *the sharp outline of the hills* ○ *a sharp contrast between the lives of the rich and the poor* **3** able to think, act, understand, see or hear quickly: *a sharp mind* ○ *sharp eyesight* **4** (used about a change of direction) very great and sudden: *a sharp rise/fall in inflation* ○ *Take a sharp right at the next intersection.* **5** (used about actions or movements) quick and sudden: *One sharp blow was enough to end the fight.* **6** (used about words, remarks, etc.) angry or severe; intended to upset or be critical: *During the debate, there was a sharp exchange of views between the two candidates.* **7** (used about pain) very strong and sudden: *a sharp pain in the chest* ☞ The opposite is **dull**. **8** (used about sth that affects the senses) not mild or gentle, often causing a bad feeling: *sharp cheese* ○ *a sharp wind* **9** (*informal*) fashionable and attractive: *a sharp suit* **10** (*symbol* ♯) (in music) half a tone higher than the stated note: *in the key of C sharp minor* ☞ Look at **flat¹**(5). **11** (in music) higher than the correct note: *That last note was sharp. Can you sing it again?* ☞ Look at **flat¹**(6). —**sharp·ly** *adv.*: *The road bends sharply to the left.* ○ *"Mind your own business!" she said sharply.* ○ *Stock prices fell very sharply this morning.* —**sharp·ness** *noun* [U]

sharp² /ʃɑrp/ *adv.* **1** (used about a time) exactly: *Be here at three o'clock sharp.* **2** (in music) slightly higher than the correct note ☞ Look at **flat²**(2).

sharp³ /ʃɑrp/ *noun* [C] (*symbol* ♯) (in music) a note that is half a step higher than the note with the same letter ☞ Look at **flat³**.

☆ **sharp·en** /ˈʃɑrpən/ *verb* [I,T] to become, or to make sth, sharp or sharper: *to sharpen a knife* ○ *The campaign sharpened public awareness of the problem.*

sharp·en·er /ˈʃɑrpənər/ *noun* [C] an object or tool that is used for making sth sharp

shat·ter /ˈʃætər/ *verb* **1** [I,T] (of glass, etc.) to break into very small pieces: *I dropped the glass and it shattered on the floor.* ○ *The force of the explosion shattered the windows.* **2** [T] to destroy completely: *Her hopes were shattered by the news.*

☆ **shave¹** /ʃeɪv/ *verb* [I,T] **shave (sth) (off)** to remove hair from the face or another part of the body with a razor: *He's too young to shave.* ○ *I was shaving when the doorbell rang.* ○ *to shave your legs* ○ *When did you shave off your mustache?* ☞ Look also at **clean-shaven**.

PHRV **shave sth off (sth)** to cut very thin pieces from a surface (in order to make it

smooth or to make it fit sth): *We'll have to shave a little off the door to make it close.*

shave² /ʃeɪv/ *noun* [C, usually sing.] the act of shaving: *He hadn't had a shave yet.*

IDM a close call/shave ➪ CLOSE¹

shav·er /'ʃeɪvər/ (*also* **electric razor**) *noun* [C] an electric tool that is used for shaving hair

shawl /ʃɔl/ *noun* [C] a large piece of cloth, made of wool, etc. that is worn by a woman around the shoulders or that is wrapped around a baby

☆ **she** /ʃi/ *pron.* (the subject of a verb) the female person or animal who has already been mentioned: *"What does your sister do?" "She's a dentist."* ∘ *I asked her a question, but she didn't answer.*

shear /ʃɪr/ *verb* [T] (*p.t.* **sheared**; *p.p.* **sheared** or **shorn**) to cut the wool off a sheep

shears /ʃɪrz/ *noun* [plural] a tool that is like a very large pair of scissors and that is used for cutting things, often outdoors

shed¹ /ʃed/ *noun* [C] a small building where things are stored: *Put the lawnmower back in the shed.* ∘ *a tool shed*

shed² /ʃed/ *verb* (*pres. part.* **shed·ding**; *p.t., p.p.* **shed**) **1** [I,T] to lose sth, such as hair or skin, because it falls off: *This snake sheds its skin every year.* ∘ *The cat shed all over my new jacket!* ∘ *Fall is coming and the trees are beginning to shed their leaves.* **2** [T] to get rid of or remove sth that is not wanted: *The town hopes to shed its image as a dull place.* ∘ *Companies in the area have shed thousands of jobs in the past year.*

IDM shed blood (*formal*) (usually passive) to kill or injure people: *A great deal of blood was shed during the war.*

shed light on sth to make sth clear and easy to understand

shed tears (*formal*) to cry: *It was a sad occasion and many tears were shed.*

she'd /ʃid/ *short for* SHE HAD, SHE WOULD

sheep

horn
fleece

ram lamb ewe

☆ **sheep** /ʃip/ *noun* [C] (*pl.* **sheep**) an animal with a coat of wool that is kept on farms and used for its wool or meat

☞ A male sheep is a **ram**, a female sheep is a **ewe** and a young sheep is a **lamb**. The noise that sheep make is written as **baa**. The meat from sheep is called **mutton**. Look at the note at **meat**.

sheep·ish /'ʃipɪʃ/ *adj.* feeling ashamed or em-

barrassed because you have done sth silly: *a sheepish grin* —**sheep·ish·ly** *adv.*

sheer /ʃɪr/ *adj.* **1** (only *before* a noun) complete, absolute; involving nothing else except: *It's sheer stupidity to drink and drive.* ∘ *Her success is due to sheer hard work.* ∘ *The first thing you notice is the sheer size of the building.* **2** very steep; almost vertical: *Don't walk near the edge. It's a sheer drop to the ocean.*

☆ **sheet** /ʃit/ *noun* [C] **1** a large piece of material used on a bed. Sheets are used in pairs and you sleep between the top and bottom sheet. ☞ picture at **bed**. **2** a piece of paper: *a sheet of notebook paper* ∘ *Write each answer on a separate sheet.* ☞ Look at **balance sheet**. **3** a flat, thin piece of any material, especially glass or metal

sheik /ʃik; ʃeɪk/ *noun* [C] an Arab ruler

☆ **shelf** /ʃelf/ *noun* [C] (*pl.* **shelves** /ʃelvz/) a long flat piece of wood, glass, etc. that is fastened to a wall or in a cupboard, that you can stand things on: *I put up a shelf in the kitchen.* ∘ *a bookshelf*

☆ **shell¹** /ʃel/ *noun* **1** [C,U] a hard covering that protects eggs, nuts and some animals: *a collection of seashells* ∘ *an empty shell* ∘ *a turtle's shell* **2** [C] a metal container filled with explosives that is fired by a large gun

shell² /ʃel/ *verb* [T] **1** to take the shell¹(1) off sth that can be eaten: *to shell peanuts* **2** to fire shells¹(2) at a place

PHRV shell sth out (*informal*) to pay more money for sth than you want to: *The bus didn't come, so I had to shell out $10 for a cab ride home.*

she'll /ʃil/ *short for* SHE WILL

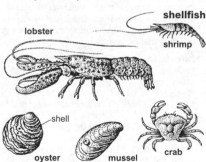

shellfish
lobster
shrimp
shell
oyster mussel crab

shell·fish /'ʃelfɪʃ/ *noun* (*pl.* **shellfish**) [C,U] a type of animal that lives in water and has a shell, or these animals eaten as food

☆ **shel·ter¹** /'ʃeltər/ *noun* **1** [U] **shelter (from sth)** protection from danger or bad weather: *to give somebody food and shelter* ∘ *I took shelter under his umbrella.* **2** [C] a building or a structure that gives protection or cover, e.g. from danger, bad weather or attack: *a shelter for the homeless* ∘ *a picnic shelter* ∘ *a bomb shelter*

shel·ter² /'ʃeltər/ *verb* **1** [I] **shelter (from sth)**

ər	ɪr	ɛr	ɑr	ɔr	ʊr	ʒ	h	ŋ
bird	near	hair	car	north	tour	vision	hat	sing

to find protection or shelter1 : *They sheltered from the rain under a tree.* ○ *There are 100 refugees sheltering in foreign embassies.* **2** [T] **shelter sb/sth (from sb/sth)** to protect sb/sth; to give sb/sth shelter1 : *The trees shelter the house from the wind.* ○ *The embassy is now sheltering nearly 100 refugees.*

shel·tered /ˈʃɛltərd/ *adj.* **1** (used about a place) protected from bad weather: *The campers found a sheltered spot for their tent.* **2** protected from bad things in your life: *a sheltered childhood in the country*

shelve /ʃɛlv/ *verb* [T] to decide not to continue with a plan, etc.: *Plans for a new stadium have been shelved.*

shelves /ʃɛlvz/ *pl.* of SHELF

shelv·ing /ˈʃɛlvɪŋ/ *noun* [U] a set of shelves

shep·herd /ˈʃɛpərd/ *noun* [C] (especially in the past) a person who takes care of sheep ☞ Look also at **German shepherd**.

sher·bet /ˈʃərbət/ *noun* [U] a frozen sweet food, similar to ice cream, made from water, sugar, fruit juice and sometimes milk

☆ **sher·iff** /ˈʃɛrəf/ *noun* [C] the law officer who is elected to the highest position in the police force of a county

☞ The **police** work in towns and cities; the **sheriff** and the sheriff's **deputies** are in charge of the areas of a county outside towns and cities, e.g. on farms.

sher·ry /ˈʃɛri/ *noun* [C,U] (*pl.* **sher·ries**) a type of strong Spanish wine; a glass of this wine: *sweet/dry sherry*

she's /ʃiz/ *short for* SHE IS, SHE HAS

shield[1] /ʃild/ *noun* [C] **1** a large piece of metal or wood that soldiers used to carry to protect themselves. Now certain police officers carry shields: *riot shields* **2** a person or thing that is used for protection: *The metal door acted as a shield against the explosion.*

shield[2] /ʃild/ *verb* [T] **shield sb/sth (against/ from sb/sth)** to protect sb/sth from danger or damage: *I shielded my eyes from the bright light with my hand.*

shift[1] /ʃɪft/ *verb* **1** [T] to move sb/sth from one position to another: *This plan will shift more responsibility onto individual citizens.* **2** [I] to change position or direction: *The media's attention has shifted to the possible cause of the accident.* **3** [I,T] to change the position of the gears in a car: *She shifted into first and quickly drove off.*

shift[2] /ʃɪft/ *noun* **1** [C] **a shift (in sth)** a change in the position or nature of sth: *There has been a shift in public opinion away from war.* ○ *a shift in policy/a policy shift* **2** [C] (in a factory, etc.) a division of the working day; the people who work during this period: *an eight-hour shift* ○ *to work the day/night shift* **3** [U] (*also* **ˈshift key**) [C] the key on a com-

puter keyboard, etc. that you press in order to type capital letters

shim·mer /ˈʃɪmər/ *verb* [I] to shine with a soft light that seems to be moving: *The tears shimmered in her eyes.* ○ *moonlight shimmering on the lake*

shin /ʃɪn/ *noun* [C] the front part of your leg above your ankle and below your knee ☞ picture on page A24.

☆ **shine[1]** /ʃaɪn/ *verb* (*p.t., p.p.* **shone** /ʃoʊn/) **1** [I] to give out or to reflect light: *moonlight shining on the lake* ○ *The lake shone in the light of the moon.* ○ (*figurative*) *The child's eyes shone with happiness.* **2** [T] to point the light of a flashlight, etc. at sb/sth: *The police officer shone a flashlight on the man's face.* **3** [I] **shine (at/in sth)** to do a school subject, a sport, etc. very well: *She has always shone at languages.*

☆ **shine[2]** /ʃaɪn/ *verb* [T] (*p.t., p.p.* **shined**) to polish sth so that it reflects light: *to shine your shoes*

shine[3] /ʃaɪn/ *noun* [sing., U] brightness, caused by light reflecting, because sth has been polished: *There's a beautiful shine on that table.*

shin·gle /ˈʃɪŋɡl/ *noun* [C] one of many flat pieces of wood or other material which are put one on top of another to make the roof of a house ☞ picture at **overlap.**

☆ **shin·y** /ˈʃaɪni/ *adj.* (**shin·i·er; shin·i·est**) bright; reflecting light: *The shampoo leaves your hair soft and shiny.* ○ *a shiny new car*

☆ **ship[1]** /ʃɪp/ *noun* [C] a large boat used for carrying passengers or cargo by sea: *to travel by ship* ○ *a cruise ship* ○ *The captain went on board ship.* ○ *The ship sails at noon.* ○ *The ship sank.* ☞ picture at **boat.** A **boat** is smaller than a ship. We use **vessel** in formal English for ship.

☆ **ship[2]** /ʃɪp/ *verb* [T] (**ship·ping; shipped**) to send or carry sth from one place to another, especially in large quantities: *The pineapples are shipped by air* (= in airplanes) *to ensure freshness.*

☆ **ship·ment** /ˈʃɪpmənt/ *noun* **1** [C] a quantity of goods sent from one place to another: *a shipment of grain* **2** [U] the transportation of goods from one place to another: *cargo ready for shipment*

☆ **ship·ping** /ˈʃɪpɪŋ/ *noun* [U] the transportation of goods from one place to another: *The price of the book is $17.95, plus $2.00 for shipping and handling.*

ship·wreck /ˈʃɪprɛk/ *noun* [C] **1** an accident at sea in which a ship is destroyed by a storm, rocks, etc. ☞ A person or a ship that has suffered such an accident has been **shipwrecked. 2** a ship that has been damaged or destroyed in an accident or by a storm, etc.

ship·yard /ˈʃɪpyɑrd/ *noun* [C] a place where ships are repaired or built

shirk /ʃərk/ *verb* [I,T] (*formal*) to avoid doing

S

tʃ	dʒ	v	θ	ð	s	z	ʃ
chin	**J**une	**v**an	**th**in	**th**en	**s**o	**z**oo	**sh**e

sth that is difficult or unpleasant: *to shirk your responsibilities*

☆ **shirt** /ʃərt/ *noun* [C] a piece of clothing made of cotton, etc., worn (especially by men) on the upper part of the body: *He wears a shirt and tie for work.*

☞ picture on page A26. A shirt usually has a **collar** at the neck, long or short **sleeves**, and **buttons** on the front.

shiv·er /ˈʃɪvər/ *verb* [I] to shake slightly, especially because you are cold or frightened: *shivering with cold/fright* —**shiv·er** *noun* [C]: *The thought sent a shiver down my spine.*

☆ **shock¹** /ʃak/ *noun* **1** [C,U] the feeling that is caused by sth unpleasant happening suddenly; the situation that causes this feeling: *The sudden noise gave him a real shock.* ○ *The bad news came as a huge shock to her.* ○ *I'm still suffering from shock at the news.* **2** [C] = ELECTRIC SHOCK: *Don't touch that wire – you'll get a shock.* **3** [C] a violent hit or shaking (from a crash, an explosion, etc.): *the shock of the earthquake* ☞ Look also at **aftershock**. **4** [U] (in medicine) a condition of extreme weakness caused by damage to the body: *He was in/went into shock after the accident.*

☆ **shock²** /ʃak/ *verb* [T] **1** to cause an unpleasant feeling of surprise in sb: *We were shocked by his death.* ○ *The employees were shocked at the news that the store was going to close.* **2** to make sb feel disgust and anger: *The pictures of the starving children shocked the world.*

☆ **shock·ing** /ˈʃakɪŋ/ *adj.* making you feel worried, upset or angry: *a shocking act of violence*

shod·dy /ˈʃadi/ *adj.* (**shod·di·er**; **shod·di·est**) made carelessly or with poor quality materials: *shoddy goods* —**shod·di·ly** /-əli/ *adv.*

shoes

lace — shoe — sole
heel — pump
sneaker (*also* tennis shoe)
sandal
slipper
moccasin
boot cowboy boot

☆ **shoe** /ʃu/ *noun* [C] a type of covering for the foot, usually made of leather or plastic: *a pair of shoes* ○ *running shoes* ○ *What size shoes do you wear?* ○ *I tried on a nice pair of shoes, but they didn't fit.* ○ *Wait for me – I just have to tie my shoes.* ☞ Look also at **horseshoe** and **tennis shoe**.

IDM **in sb's shoes** in the situation that sb else is in: *Put yourself in my shoes – how would you feel?* ○ *I would hate to be in his shoes right now.*

shoe·lace /ˈʃuleɪs/ *noun* [C] = SHOESTRING

shoe·string /ˈʃustrɪŋ/ *noun* [C] (*also* **shoelace**) a long piece of string or leather that is used to fasten a shoe: *to tie/untie your shoestrings*

IDM **on a shoestring** using very little money: *My mother brought up five children on a shoestring.*

shone *p.t., p.p.* of SHINE¹

shoo¹ /ʃu/ *interj.* (usually said to animals or small children) Go away!

shoo² /ʃu/ *verb p.t., p.p.* **shooed**
PHRV **shoo sb/sth away, off, out, etc.** to make sb/sth go away by saying "shoo" and waving your hands: *I shooed the birds away from the garden.*

shook *p.t.* of SHAKE¹

shook up /ˌʃʊk ˈʌp/ *adj.* (*informal*) (not before a noun) feeling upset or shocked

☆ **shoot¹** /ʃut/ *verb* (*p.t., p.p.* **shot** /ʃat/) **1** [I,T] **shoot (sth) (at sb/sth)** to fire a gun, etc.: *Don't shoot!* ○ *She shot an arrow at the target but missed it.* **2** [T] to injure or kill sb/sth with a gun: *The police officer was shot in the arm.* ○ *The soldier was shot to death.* **3** [I,T] to move quickly and suddenly in one direction; to make sth move in this way: *The car shot past me at 100 miles per hour.* ○ *She shot her boyfriend an angry look* (= looked at him very quickly and angrily). **4** [I] **shoot (down, up, etc. sth)** (of pain) to go very suddenly along part of your body: *The pain shot up my leg.* **5** [I,T] (in basketball, etc.) to try to kick or hit the ball into the net: *Let's go out and shoot some baskets* (= throw the ball through the basket). **6** [I,T] to make a movie or photograph of sth: *They shot the scene ten times.*

PHRV **shoot sb down** to kill sb with a gun
shoot sth down to make an airplane, etc. crash to the ground by shooting it: *The helicopter was shot down by a missile.*
shoot up 1 to increase very quickly: *Prices have shot up in the past year.* **2** (*slang*) to put illegal drugs into your body, using a special type of needle

shoot² /ʃut/ *noun* [C] **1** an occasion when a professional photographer or director takes photographs or makes a movie: *a video shoot* **2** a new part of a plant or tree

shoot³ /ʃut/ *interj.* (*informal*) (used to show that you are annoyed, disappointed, or surprised): *Oh, shoot – I just missed the bus.*

S

☆ **shoot·ing** /'ʃutɪŋ/ *noun* [C,U] an act of firing a gun at sb/sth: *Two people were injured in a gang-related shooting Friday night.* ○ *They hid inside until the shooting stopped.*

☆ **shop** /ʃɑp/ *noun* **1** [C] a small store which usually sells only one type of product: *a gift shop* ☛ **Store** is more common than **shop**. **2** [C] = WORKSHOP(1): *Our car is still in the shop.* **3** [U] = INDUSTRIAL ARTS

IDM **talk shop** ⇨ TALK¹

☆ **shop²** /ʃɑp/ *verb* [I] (**shop·ping**; **shopped**) to go to a store or stores in order to buy things: *I prefer to shop on my own.* ○ *He's shopping for some new clothes.*

☛ **Go shopping** is more common than **shop**: *We go shopping every Saturday.* ○ *to go Christmas shopping*

PHRV **shop around (for sth)** to look at the price and quality of an item in different shops before you decide where to buy it: *We shopped around for the best deal on a new car.* —**shop·per** *noun* [C] —**shop·ping** *noun* [U]: *She did the grocery shopping.* ○ *a shopping list*

shop·keep·er /'ʃɑpkipər/ (*also* **storekeeper**) *noun* [C] a person who owns or manages a small store

☆ **shop·lift** /'ʃɑplɪft/ *verb* [I,T] to steal sth from a store while pretending to be a customer —**shop·lift·er** *noun* [C]: *Shoplifters will be prosecuted.* ☛ Look at the note at **thief.** —**shop·lift·ing** *noun* [U]: *He was arrested for shoplifting.*

'shopping bag *noun* [C] a large bag, usually made of heavy paper with a flat bottom and two handles, that you can put things into after you have bought them

'shopping cart *noun* [C] a large basket on wheels that you push around in a store and put things in when you are shopping ☛ picture at **cart.**

'shopping ,center *noun* [C] a place where there are many stores, either outside or in a covered building

'shopping mall *noun* [C] = MALL

☆ **shore** /ʃɔr/ *noun* [C,U] the land along the edge of an ocean or a lake: *The swimmer kept close to the shore.* ○ *The sailors went on shore (= on land).* ☛ **Ashore** has the same meaning as "on shore."

shorn *p.p.* of SHEAR

☆ **short¹** /ʃɔrt/ *adj.* **1** not measuring much from one end to the other: *a short line* ○ *a short distance* ○ *This essay is pretty short.* ○ *short hair* ☛ The opposite is **long. 2** less than the average height: *a short, fat man* ☛ The opposite is **tall. 3** not lasting a long time: *a short visit* ○ *She left a short time ago.* ○ *to have a short memory* (= to only remember things that happened recently) **4** **short (of/on sth)** not having enough of what is needed: *Because of illness, the team is two players short.* ○ *Good secretaries*

are in short supply (= there are not enough of them). ○ *We're a little short of money right now.*

IDM **be short for sth** to be used as a shorter way of saying sth: *"Bill" is short for "William."*

for short as a short form: *Her name is Diana, but we call her "Di" for short.*

get the short end of the stick (*informal*) to be treated unfairly, or to be forced to do sth that nobody else wants to do

in the long/short term ⇨ TERM¹

short² /ʃɔrt/ *adv.* suddenly: *She stopped short when she saw the accident.*

IDM **fall short (of sth)** not to be enough; not to reach sth: *The raise fell short of the union's demands.*

run short (of sth) to have used up most of sth so there is not much left: *We're running short of coffee.*

short of sth except for: *He's tried to make money by every means, short of stealing it.*

stop short of sth/doing sth ⇨ STOP¹

short³ /ʃɔrt/ *noun* [C] (*informal*) = SHORT CIRCUIT

IDM **in short** in a few words; briefly: *Einstein had one of the greatest minds the world has ever known: in short, he was a genius.* ☛ Look also at **shorts.**

☆ **short·age** /'ʃɔrtɪdʒ/ *noun* [C] a situation where there is not enough of sth: *a food, housing, water, etc. shortage* ○ *a shortage of science teachers*

short 'circuit (*also informal* **short**) *noun* [C] a bad electrical connection that causes a machine to stop working

short-'circuit *verb* [I,T] to have a short circuit or to cause a machine to have one: *The lights short-circuited.*

short·com·ing /'ʃɔrtkʌmɪŋ/ *noun* [C, usually pl.] a fault or weakness: *As a leader, she had many shortcomings.*

short·cut /'ʃɔrtkʌt/ *noun* [C] a quicker, easier or more direct way to get somewhere or to do sth: *He took a shortcut to school through the park.*

☆ **short·en** /'ʃɔrtn/ *verb* [I,T] to become shorter or to make sth shorter: *I'll have to shorten these pants – they're way too long.*

short·en·ing /'ʃɔrtn·ɪŋ/ *noun* [U] a type of white fat made from vegetable oil that is used in making cookies, etc.

short·hand /'ʃɔrthænd/ *noun* [U] a method of writing quickly that uses signs or short forms of words

short-lived /,ʃɔrt'lɪvd; -'laɪvd/ *adj.* lasting only for a short time

☆ **short·ly** /'ʃɔrtli/ *adv.* soon; in a short time: *The manager will see you shortly.*

☆ **shorts** /ʃɔrts/ *noun* [plural] **1** a type of short pants ending above the knee that you wear in hot weather, while playing sports, etc.

☞ picture on page A27. **2** men's underpants: *boxer shorts*

☞ Notice that, because **shorts** is a plural word, we cannot say, for example, "a new short." The following are possible: *I need to get some new shorts.* ○ *I need to get a new pair of shorts.*

short·sight·ed /ˌʃɔrtˈsaɪtəd/ *adj.* not considering what will probably happen in the future: *a short-sighted attitude* ☞ Look also at **nearsighted**.

,**short 'story** *noun* [C] (*pl.* ,**short 'stories**) a piece of writing that is shorter than a novel: *a collection of short stories by O. Henry.*

'**short-term** *adj.* (only *before* a noun) lasting for a short period of time from the present: *short-term plans*

☆ **shot¹** /ʃɑt/ *noun* [C] **1** an act of firing a gun, etc., or the noise that this makes: *to take a shot at the target* ○ *The police officer fired a warning shot into the air.* **2 a shot (at sth/at doing sth)** (*informal*) an attempt to do sth: *Let me have a shot at it* (= let me try to do it). **3** (in sports) an act of kicking or throwing a ball: *He took a shot from near the foul line.* **4** a photograph or a picture in a movie: *I got some good shots of the runners as they crossed the line.* **5** an injection of a drug, especially in order to prevent a disease: *a shot of penicillin* ○ *a flu shot* **6** a small drink of strong alcohol

shot² *p.t., p.p.* of SHOOT¹

☆ **shot·gun** /ˈʃɑtɡʌn/ *noun* [C] a gun used for shooting small animals and birds that fires small metal balls ☞ Look at the note at **gun**.

the 'shot put *noun* [sing.] a sport in which people try to throw a heavy metal ball as far as possible

☆ **should** /ʃəd; *strong form* ʃʊd/ *modal verb* (*negative* **should not**; *short form* **should·n't** /ˈʃʊdnt/) **1** (used for giving your opinion or asking for advice): *You should try that new restaurant.* ○ *The police should do something about it.* ○ *He really shouldn't work so hard.* ○ *Should I try again?* **2** (used with "have" to say that sb did the wrong thing): *I'm tired. I shouldn't have gone to bed so late/I should have gone to bed earlier.* **3** (used for saying that you expect sth is true or will happen): *It's 4:30. They should be in New York by now.* ○ *The party should be a lot of fun.* **4** (*formal*) (used after "if" or with the same meaning as "if," when you think that sth is not likely to happen): *If you should decide to accept, please phone us.* ○ *Should you decide to accept…* **5** (used after certain adjectives, in phrases beginning with "that"): *It's not right that something like this should happen.* ○ *It's funny that you should mention that…*

☆ **shoul·der¹** /ˈʃoʊldər/ *noun* [C] **1** the part of the body between the neck and the top of the arm: *He hurt his shoulder.* ○ *He carried his*

little girl on his shoulders. ○ *to shrug your shoulders* (= to raise your shoulders, especially as a way of showing that you do not know an answer or that you are not interested) ☞ picture on page A24. **2** a part of a dress, coat, etc. that covers this part of the body **3** a narrow part along the side of a road where cars can stop in an emergency

IDM **have a chip on your shoulder** ⇨ CHIP¹
rub elbows/shoulders with sb ⇨ RUB

shoul·der² /ˈʃoʊldər/ *verb* [T] **1** to accept the responsibility for sth: *She shouldered all the blame for the accident.* **2** to push sb/sth with your shoulder¹(1) : *He shouldered everybody aside and disappeared through the door.*

'**shoulder bag** *noun* [C] a type of bag that you carry over one shoulder with a long strap

'**shoulder blade** *noun* [C] one of the two large flat bones on each side of your back, below your shoulders¹(1)

shouldn't *short for* SHOULD NOT

☆ **shout** /ʃaʊt/ *verb* **1** [I] **shout (at/to sb); shout (out)** to speak or cry out in a very loud voice: *There's no need to shout – I can hear you.* ○ *The teacher shouted angrily at the boys.* ○ *to shout out in pain, excitement, etc.* **2** [T] **shout sth (at/to sb); shout sth out** to say sth in a loud voice: *"Look out!" she shouted.* ○ *The captain shouted out instructions to his team.*

PHRV **shout sb down** to prevent sb from being heard by shouting at him/her (often in a public meeting): *to shout down a speaker* —**shout** *noun* [C]

shove /ʃʌv/ *verb* [I,T] to push with a sudden, rough movement: *They pushed and shoved to the front of the line.* ○ *The police officer shoved the suspect into a cell.* ○ (*informal*) *"What should I do with this box?" "Oh, just shove it in the closet."* —**shove** *noun* [C, usually sing.]: *She gave the door a shove with her elbow.*

☆ **shov·el¹** /ˈʃʌvl/ *noun* [C] a tool with a long handle that is used for moving dirt, snow, sand, etc.: *a snow shovel* ☞ picture at **dig**.

☆ **shov·el²** /ˈʃʌvl/ *verb* [I,T] to move sth or clean sth with a shovel: *to shovel dirt into a hole* ○ *to shovel the sidewalk* (= to clear snow off it)

☆ **show¹** /ʃoʊ/ *noun* **1** [C] a program on television or on the radio: *There's a show I want to see tonight.* ○ *my favorite TV show* **2** [C] a play in a theater: *a Broadway show* **3** [C] a collection of things for people to look at, often in a special large building: *a dog show* ○ *the Detroit auto show* (= where new types of cars are displayed) **4** [C,U] the outward expression of an emotion that is not what you really feel or that does not have much meaning: *Although she hated him, she put on a show of politeness.* ○ *His bravery is all show* (= he is not as brave as he pretends to be). **5** [sing.] a sign of sth: *The military conducted exercises as a show of strength in the region.*

IDM **for show** intended to impress people; not to be used: *Those dishes are only for show – nobody ever uses them.*

be on show to be located in a place where people can see it: *The collection is on show at the Museum of Modern Art.*

☆ **show²** /ʃoʊ/ *verb* (*p.t.* **showed**; *p.p.* **shown** /ʃoʊn/ or **showed**) **1** [T] **show sb/sth (to sb)** to make it possible for other people to see sb/sth: *I showed the letter to him.* ○ *I showed him the letter.* ○ *She showed me what she had bought.* ○ *They're showing his latest movie at the theater at the mall.* **2** [T] to lead or guide sb to a place: *Let me show you to your room.* ○ *A guide showed us around the museum.* **3** [T] to help sb to do sth by doing it yourself; to explain sth: *Can you show me how to put the disk in the computer?* **4** [T] to make sth clear; to give information about sth: *Research shows that most people get too little exercise.* ○ *The picture showed the effects of the storm.* **5** [I] to be able to be seen; to appear: *Her anger showed in her eyes.* ○ *There's a hole in my sock, but it doesn't show.* **6** [T] to allow sth to be seen: *This gray carpet doesn't show the dirt.* **7** [T] to cause people to notice a particular quality: *She was the only one who ever showed him any kindness.* ○ *He didn't want to show what he was really thinking.* ○ *She was showing signs of stress.*

PHRV **show (sth) off** (*informal*) to try to impress people by showing them how good you are at sth or by showing them sth that you are proud of. *He's always showing off in front of his friends.* ○ *She wanted to show off her new bike.*

show up 1 (*informal*) to arrive, especially when sb is expecting you: *I thought you'd never show up.* **2** to be able to be seen: *The fracture showed up clearly on the X-ray.*

'**show** ˌ**business** (also *informal* **show·biz** /ˈʃoʊbɪz/) *noun* [U] the business of entertaining people, in the theater, in movies, on television, etc.

show·down /ˈʃoʊdaʊn/ *noun* [C] a final argument at the end of a long disagreement

☆ **show·er¹** /ˈʃaʊər/ *noun* [C] **1** a way of washing your body by standing under running water: *He took a shower after the football practice.* **2** a place in a bathroom where you can stand under running water to wash your whole body: *She's in the shower.* **3** a short period of rain **4** a lot of very small objects that fall together: *a shower of debris* **5** a party at which people give presents to a woman who is about to get married or have a baby: *a bridal shower*

show·er² /ˈʃaʊər/ *verb* **1** [T] **shower sb/sth with sth** to cause a great number of very small objects to fall on sb/sth: *to be showered with debris, broken glass, confetti, etc.* ○ (*figura-*

tive) *He was showered with praise for his excellent work.* **2** [I] to take a shower¹(1)

show·ing /ˈʃoʊɪŋ/ *noun* **1** [C] an act of showing a movie, etc.: *The second showing of the movie begins at 8 o'clock.* **2** [sing.] how sb/sth behaves; how successful sb/sth is in a competition, etc.: *After a strong showing in the primaries, he should win the party's nomination.*

shown *p.p.* of SHOW²

show·off /ˈʃoʊɔf; -ɑf/ *noun* [C] a person who tries to impress others by showing them how good he/she is at sth: *She's such a showoff.* ☞ This word is used when we are criticizing somebody.

show·room /ˈʃoʊrum/ *noun* [C] a type of store where products such as cars or furniture are displayed

shrank *p.t.* of SHRINK

shrap·nel /ˈʃræpnəl/ *noun* [U] small pieces of metal that are thrown in various directions from an exploding bomb or bullet

shred¹ /ʃrɛd/ *noun* **1** [C, usually pl.] a small thin piece that has been cut or torn from sth: *He tore the letter to shreds.* ○ *After the storm, the boat's sails were in shreds.* **2 a shred of sth** [sing.] (in negative sentences) a very small amount of sth: *There wasn't a shred of evidence against her.*

shred² /ʃrɛd/ *verb* [T] (**shred·ding**; **shred-ded**) to tear or cut sth into shreds¹(1)

shrewd /ʃrud/ *adj.* using or showing good judgment, especially in order to achieve success: *a shrewd politician* ○ *a shrewd investment* —**shrewd·ly** *adv.*

shriek /ʃrik/ *verb* **1** [I] to give a sudden scream in a high voice: *He shrieked in fright.* ○ *The girls were shrieking with laughter.* **2** [T] to scream sth in a high voice: *"Stop it!" he shrieked.* —**shriek** *noun* [C]: *She gave a loud shriek of pain.*

shrill /ʃrɪl/ *adj.* (used about a sound) high and unpleasant: *a shrill whistle*

shrimp /ʃrɪmp/ *noun* [C] (*pl.* **shrimp** or **shrimps**) a small sea creature with a shell that turns pink when you cook it

shrine /ʃram/ *noun* [C] a place that is holy for members of a religion, or that people want to visit because it is associated with a special person or thing

shrink /ʃrɪŋk/ *verb* (*p.t.* **shrank** /ʃræŋk/ or **shrunk** /ʃrʌŋk/; *p.p.* **shrunk** or **shrunk·en**) [I,T] to become smaller, often after being washed; to make sth smaller: *Oh no! My T-shirt shrank!* ○ *I shrank my T-shirt. The water must have been too hot.* ○ *The rate of inflation has shrunk to 4%.* ☞ picture on p.618
PHRV **shrink from sth/doing sth** to be unwilling to do sth because you find it unpleasant

shriv·el /ˈʃrɪvl/ *verb* [I,T] **shrivel (sth) (up)** to dry up and become smaller and full of lines, usually in hot or dry conditions; to make sth do this: *The drought is killing animals and*

S

shrink

"Oh, no! My T-shirt **shrank** in the dryer!"

shriveling crops. ○ (*figurative*) *Profits shriveled up during the recession.*

shroud¹ /ʃraʊd/ *noun* [C] **1** a cloth or sheet that is used in some countries to wrap a dead body before it is buried **2** something that covers or hides sth: *a shroud of secrecy*

shroud² /ʃraʊd/ *verb* [T] (usually passive) to cover or hide sth with sth: *The tops of the mountains were shrouded in mist.* ○ *His past is shrouded in mystery.*

shrub /ʃrʌb/ *noun* [C] a small bush

shrub·ber·y /ˈʃrʌbəri/ *noun* [U] an area planted with shrubs

shrug /ʃrʌg/ *verb* [I,T] (**shrug·ging**; **shrugged**) to raise your shoulders as a way of showing that you do not know or do not care about sth: *"Who knows?" he said and shrugged.* ○ *"It doesn't matter to me," he said, shrugging his shoulders.*

PHRV shrug sth off to treat sth as if it is not important to you —**shrug** *noun* [C, usually sing.]: *He answered his mother with a shrug.*

shrunk, shrunken ⇨ SHRINK

shud·der /ˈʃʌdər/ *verb* [I] to shake with fear, etc.: *Just thinking about the accident makes me shudder.* ○ *I shudder to think how much this dinner is going to cost.* —**shud·der** *noun* [C]

shuf·fle¹ /ˈʃʌfl/ *verb* **1** [I] to walk by sliding your feet along instead of lifting them off the ground: *A little girl shuffled past, wearing her mother's shoes.* **2** [T] **shuffle sb/sth (around)** to move things or people around so that they are in a different order or position: *My job is so boring – all I do is shuffle papers.* **3** [I,T] to mix a deck of playing cards before a game: *It's your turn to shuffle.* ○ *He shuffled the cards carefully.*

shuf·fle² /ˈʃʌfl/ *noun* [C, usually sing.] **1** a shuffling¹(1) way of walking **2** an act of moving things or people around so that they are in a different order or position: *a major shuffle of senior management* **3** an act of shuffling¹(3) cards

shun /ʃʌn/ *verb* [T] (**shun·ning**; **shunned**) to avoid sb/sth; to keep away from sb/sth: *The aging actress shunned publicity.*

☆ **shut¹** /ʃʌt/ *verb* [I,T] (*pres. part.* **shut·ting**; *p.t., p.p.* **shut**) **1** [T] to change the position of sth so that it covers a hole, etc.; to fold sth together; to close: *Could you shut the door?* ○ *I can't shut my suitcase.* ○ *He shut his eyes and tried to go to sleep.* **2** [I] to move or be moved into a closed position: *This window won't shut all the way.* **3** [T] to prevent sb/sth from leaving or moving; to trap sth: *She shut herself in her room and refused to come out.* ○ *Tony shut his fingers in the door of the car.*

PHRV shut (sth) down (used about a factory, etc.) to be closed for a long time or forever; to close sth (a factory, etc.) for a long time or forever: *Financial problems forced the business to shut down.* ○ *They shut down the factory for safety reasons.*

shut sb/sth off (from sth) to keep sb/sth apart from sth: *He shuts himself off from the rest of the world.*

shut sth off to turn off a supply of electricity, water, gas, etc.: *The utility company shut off gas to the building after the fire was reported.*

shut sb/sth out 1 to keep sb/sth out: *Anna was shut out of the decision-making process.* ○ *He tried to shut out all thoughts of the accident.* **2** to win a game without letting the other team score any points: *Pittsburgh shut out Atlanta 5–0.*

shut up (*informal*) to stop talking; to be quiet: *Tell her to shut up and get back to work.* ○ *Shut up! I'm trying to work.*

☞ It is not polite to tell somebody to shut up.

shut sb up (*informal*) to make sb stop talking: *Nothing can shut him up once he gets started.*

shut² /ʃʌt/ *adj.* (not before a noun) in a closed position: *Make sure the door is shut before you leave.*

☞ Remember that we can use **closed** before a noun: *a closed door*, but not **shut**.

shut·down /ˈʃʌtdaʊn/ *noun* [C] the closing of a company or the stopping of a machine: *Even a temporary shutdown could cost the airline millions of dollars.*

shut·ter /ˈʃʌtər/ *noun* [C] **1** one of a pair of wooden or metal covers that is attached to a window and that can be opened or closed **2** the part at the front of a camera that opens for a very short time to let light in so that a photograph can be taken

shutter

shutter

shut·tle /ˈʃʌtl/ *noun* [C] **1** an airplane or a bus that travels regularly between two places: *I'm*

catching the seven o'clock shuttle to Washington. **2** = SPACE SHUTTLE

☆ **shy¹** /ʃaɪ/ adj. (**shy·er**; **shy·est**) nervous and uncomfortable with other people. Shy people do not usually say very much to people they do not know: *She's very shy around strangers.* ○ *a shy smile* ○ *He isn't shy about expressing his opinions.* —**shy·ly** adv.: *Meg smiled shyly at the camera.* —**shy·ness** noun [U]: *He didn't overcome his shyness until he was in his twenties.*

shy² /ʃaɪ/ verb pres. part. **shy·ing**; 3rd pers. sing. pres. **shies**; p.t., p.p. **shied**
PHRV **shy (away) from sth/from doing sth** to avoid doing sth because you are afraid: *He shied away from telling her the truth.*

sib·ling /'sɪblɪŋ/ noun [C] (formal) a brother or a sister: *Jealousy between siblings is very common.*

☞ In ordinary language we use **brother(s)** and **sister(s)**: *Do you have any brothers and sisters?*

☆ **sick** /sɪk/ adj. **1** not in good health; not well; ill: *a sick child* ○ *You're more likely to get sick when you haven't had enough sleep.* ○ *I was sick last week and missed three days of school.* ☞ Look at the note at **ill**. **2** (not before a noun) (also **sick to your stomach**) having a bad feeling in your stomach so that any food in it may be thrown up through your mouth: *I feel sick – I think it was that fish I ate.* **3** (informal) cruel or in bad taste: *a sick joke about blind people* **4 the sick** noun [plural] people who are not in good health: *The sick and injured were carried away from the battlefield.*
IDM **be sick** to throw up food from the stomach through your mouth: *I think I'm going to be sick.*
be sick (and tired) of sb/sth; **be sick to death of sb/sth** to feel tired of or annoyed by sb/sth: *I'm sick and tired of his attitude.*
make sb sick to make sb very angry: *Oh, quit complaining. You make me sick!*

sick·en /'sɪkən/ verb [T] to make sb feel disgusted: *Even the smell of the place sickens me.*

sick·en·ing /'sɪkənɪŋ/ adj. disgusting; very unpleasant: *It was a sickening sight.*

'**sick leave** noun [U] a period of time spent away from work, etc. because of illness: *Joe has been on sick leave for two weeks.*

☆ **sick·ness** /'sɪknəs/ noun **1** [U] the state of being sick: *A lot of workers are absent because of sickness.* **2** [C,U] a particular type of illness: *motion sickness*

☆ **side¹** /saɪd/ noun [C] **1** any of the flat outer surfaces of an object: *A cube has six sides.* ○ *this side up* (= an instruction on a box, etc. that tells you which way to store it) **2** [C] any of the flat outer surfaces of an object except the top or the bottom: *A box has a top, a bottom and four sides.* **3** any of the surfaces of sth except the top, bottom, front or back: *I*

went around to the side of the building. ○ *The side of the car was damaged.* **4** the edge of sth; the area near this: *A triangle has three sides.* ○ *He waited at the side of the road.* **5** either of the two flat surfaces of sth thin: *Write on both sides of the paper.* **6** the right or the left part of your body, especially from under your arm to the top of your leg: *She lay on her side.* **7** either of the two parts of a place or object, separated by a real or an imaginary line: *She was arrested for driving on the wrong side of the road.* ○ *He moved to the other side of the room.* ○ *on the other side of the wall* ○ (figurative) *We don't often see her generous side.* **8** = SIDE ORDER **9** either of two teams or groups of people who play or fight against each other: *Whose side are you on?* (= Who do you support?) ○ *The two sides agreed to stop fighting.* **10** the position, opinion or attitude of a person or group of people that is different from that held by another person or group of people: *Do you believe his side of the story?* **11** your mother's or your father's family: *There is no history of cancer on his mother's side.*
IDM **from side to side** moving continuously from right to left and back again: *The boat rocked from side to side.*
get on the right/wrong side of sb to please/annoy sb : *He tried to get on the right side of his new boss.*
on/from all sides in/from all directions; generally: *There was agreement on all sides.*
on the big, small, high, etc. side (informal) slightly too big, small, high, etc.
on the safe side ⇨ SAFE¹
on the side 1 in addition to your main job: *He's a waiter on the side.* **2** served separately: *a salad with dressing on the side*
right side up ⇨ RIGHT¹
side by side next to each other; close together: *They walked side by side along the road.*
take sides (with sb) to show that you support one person rather than another: *Parents should never take sides when their children are fighting.*

side² /saɪd/ verb
PHRV **side with sb (against sb)** to support sb in an argument: *She always sides with her son against her husband.*

side³ /saɪd/ adj. (only before a noun) at the side¹(3) of a building: *The thief entered the house by breaking a side window.*

side·burns /'saɪdbɚnz/ noun [plural] hair that grows down a man's face in front of and below his ears

-sided /'saɪdəd/ (in compounds) having a certain number or type of sides: *A cube is a six-sided figure.*

'**side dish** noun [C] = SIDE ORDER

'**side ef,fect** noun [C] an unpleasant effect that sth may have in addition to the effects it

S

is supposed to have: *Side effects of the drug may include headaches or diarrhea.*

side·kick /ˈsaɪdkɪk/ *noun* [C] (*informal*) a person who helps and spends a lot of time with sb who is more important: *the Lone Ranger and his sidekick, Tonto*

side·line /ˈsaɪdlaɪn/ *noun* **1 the sidelines** [plural] the lines that mark the two long sides of a sports field or tennis court; the area behind this outside the playing area: *The team's coach was giving orders from the sidelines.* ◦ (*figurative*) *It was a controversial issue, so she decided to remain on the sidelines.* **2** [C] something that you do in addition to your regular job, usually to earn extra money: *He's an engineer, but he makes furniture as a sideline.*

ˈside ˌorder (*also* **side dish**, *informal* **side**) *noun* [C] an item of food that you order in a restaurant to have with your main meal: *a side order of potato salad*

ˈside street *noun* [C] a narrow or less important street that usually joins a main street

side·track /ˈsaɪdtræk/ *verb* [T] (often passive) to make sb forget what he/she is supposed to be doing or talking about and start doing or talking about sth less important

☆ **side·walk** /ˈsaɪdwɔk/ *noun* [C] a slightly raised narrow surface at the side of a street, for people to walk on: *The kids rode their bikes on the sidewalk.* ☛ picture on page A28.

☆ **side·ways** /ˈsaɪdweɪz/ *adj., adv.* **1** to, toward or from one side: *The truck slid sideways and hit a barrier.* ◦ *a sideways glance* **2** with one of the sides at the top: *We'll have to turn the table sideways to get it through the door.*

sid·ing /ˈsaɪdɪŋ/ *noun* [C] horizontal boards that cover the outside walls of a house ☛ picture on page A28.

si·dle /ˈsaɪdl/ *verb* [I] **sidle up/over (to sb/sth)** to move toward sb/sth in a nervous way, as if you do not want anybody to notice you

siege /sidʒ/ *noun* [C,U] **1** the situation in which an army surrounds a town in order to capture it. When there is a siege, nobody is allowed into or out of the town.: *the siege of Sarajevo* **2** a situation in which a building containing a criminal is surrounded by police for a long period of time: *The house was under siege for several hours, until the man released the hostages.*

si·es·ta /siˈɛstə/ *noun* [C] a short rest that people take after lunch, especially in hot countries: *to have/take a siesta*

sieve /sɪv/ *noun* [C] a type of kitchen tool that has a metal or plastic net, used for separating solids from liquids or very small pieces of food from large pieces —**sieve** *verb* [T]

sift /sɪft/ *verb* **1** [T] to pass flour, sugar, etc. through a sieve **2** [I,T] **sift (through) sth** to examine sth very carefully: *It took weeks to sift through all the evidence.*

☆ **sigh** /saɪ/ *verb* **1** [I] to let out a long, deep breath that shows you are tired, sad, relieved, etc.: *She sighed with disappointment at the news.* **2** [T] to say sth with a sigh (1): *"I'm so tired," he sighed.* —**sigh** *noun* [C]: *"Well, that's over," she said, with a sigh of relief.*

☆ **sight¹** /saɪt/ *noun* **1** [U] the ability to see: *He lost his sight in the war* (= he became blind). **2** [sing.] **sight of sb/sth** the act of seeing sb/sth: *We flew over Paris and had our first sight of the Eiffel Tower.* ◦ *Throw that dress away. I can't stand the sight of it anymore.* **3** [U] a position where sb/sth can be seen: *When the finish line was within sight, the Kenyan runner accelerated.* ◦ *She didn't let her nephew out of her sight.* **4** [C] something that you see: *the familiar sights and sounds of home* **5 sights** [plural] places of interest that are often visited by tourists: *When you come to New York, I'll show you the sights.*

IDM **at first glance/sight** ➭ FIRST¹
catch sight/a glimpse of sb/sth ➭ CATCH¹
in sight likely to happen or come soon: *A peace settlement is in sight.*
lose sight of sb/sth ➭ LOSE
on sight as soon as sb/sth is seen: *The soldiers were ordered to shoot the enemy on sight.*
set your sights on sth to decide that sth is your goal and try hard to achieve it: *Josh set his sights on an acting career.*

sight² /saɪt/ *verb* [T] to see sb/sth, especially after looking out for him/her/it: *The wanted man has been sighted in Miami.*

sight·ing /ˈsaɪtɪŋ/ *noun* [C] an occasion when sb/sth is seen: *the first sighting of a new star*

☆ **sight·see·ing** /ˈsaɪtsiɪŋ/ *noun* [U] visiting the sights of a city, etc. as a tourist: *We did some sightseeing in Rome.*

sight·se·er /ˈsaɪtsiər/ *noun* [C] a person who visits the sights of a city ☛ Look at **tourist**.

☆ **sign¹** /saɪn/ *noun* [C] **1** a board, notice, etc. that gives you a piece of information, an instruction or a warning: *What does that sign say?* ◦ *a road sign* ◦ *Follow the signs to Route 66.* **2 sign (of sth)** something that shows that sb/sth is present or exists or may happen: *The patient was showing some signs of improvement.* ◦ *The first sign of trouble was last week.* ◦ *As we drove down Main Street, there was no sign of life anywhere* (= we couldn't see anyone). **3** a movement that you make with your head, hands or arms that has a particular meaning: *I made a sign for him to follow me.* ◦ *He gave the thumbs-up sign to his crew.* **4** a type of shape, mark or symbol that has a particular meaning: *a plus sign* ◦ *the dollar sign* **5** (*also* **ˌsign of the ˈzodiac**) one of the twelve divisions or symbols of the zodiac: *I'm a Leo. What's your sign?*

☆ **sign²** /saɪn/ *verb* **1** [I,T] to write your name on a letter, document, etc. to show that you have written it or that you agree with what it says.

When you sign your name you always write it in the same way.: *"Could you sign here, please?"* ○ *I forgot to sign the check.* ○ *The two presidents signed the treaty.* **2** [T] (in sports, entertainment, etc.) to employ sb by having him/her sign²(1) an official statement: *The Baltimore Orioles signed Fernandez to a one-year contract.* **3** [I,T] to communicate by using sign language

PHRV **sign in/out** to write your name to show you have arrived at or left a building, etc.

sign up (for sth) to agree formally to do sth: *I signed up for driving lessons.*

☆ **sig·nal¹** /ˈsɪgnəl/ *noun* [C] **1** a sign, action or sound that sends a particular message: *The army waited for the signal to attack.* ○ *The flag went down as a signal for the race to begin.* **2** a set of lights used to tell drivers when they should stop and go: *a traffic signal* ☛ Look also at **turn signal**. **3** a series of radio waves, etc. that are sent out or received: *a signal from a satellite*

sig·nal² /ˈsɪgnəl/ *verb* [I,T] to make a signal; to send a particular message using a signal: *She was signaling wildly that something was wrong.* ○ *He signaled his disapproval by leaving the room.* ○ *The police officer signaled to the driver to stop.*

☆ **sig·na·ture** /ˈsɪgnətʃər/ *noun* [C] a person's name, written by himself/herself and always written in the same way: *I couldn't read his signature.*

sig·nif·i·cance /sɪgˈnɪfəkəns/ *noun* [U] the importance or meaning of sth: *Few people realized the significance of the discovery.*

☆ **sig·nif·i·cant** /sɪgˈnɪfəkənt/ *adj.* **1** important: *Police said that the time of the murder was extremely significant.* **2** so large that you notice it: *There has been a significant increase in the number of crimes reported this year.* **3** having a particular meaning: *She gave me a significant smile.*

sig·nif·i·cant·ly /sɪgˈnɪfəkəntli/ *adv.* **1** in a noticeable way: *Attitudes have changed significantly since the 1960s.* **2** in a way that shows a particular meaning: *He thanked almost everybody but, significantly, he did not mention Terry.*

sig·ni·fy /ˈsɪgnəfaɪ/ *verb* [T] (*pres. part.* **sig·ni·fy·ing**; *3rd pers. sing. pres.* **sig·ni·fies**; *p.t., p.p.* **sig·ni·fied**) (*formal*) to be a sign of sth; to mean: *What do those lights signify?*

ˈ**sign ˌlanguage** *noun* [U] a language used especially by people who cannot hear or speak using hand movements instead of spoken words

Sikh /sik/ *noun* [C] a member of one of the religions of India (**Sikhism**) that developed from Hinduism but teaches that there is only one god —**Sikh·ism** /ˈsikɪzm/ *noun* [U]

☆ **si·lence¹** /ˈsaɪləns/ *noun* [C,U] **1** [U] complete quiet; no sound: *A loud crash broke the silence.*

○ *There must be absolute silence during the exam.* **2** [C] a period when nobody speaks or makes a noise: *His response was a stony silence.* **3** [U] not making any comments on sth: *I can't understand his silence on the matter.*

IDM **in silence** without talking or making a noise

si·lence² /ˈsaɪləns/ *verb* [T] to make sb/sth be silent or quiet: *She silenced the crowd by raising her hand.* ○ *He was determined to silence his critics* (= to make them stop criticizing him).

si·lenc·er /ˈsaɪlənsər/ *noun* [C] a part that can be attached to the end of a gun to reduce the noise when it is fired

☆ **si·lent** /ˈsaɪlənt/ *adj.* **1** making no noise; very quiet: *The house was empty and silent.* **2** not speaking; not using spoken words: *The police officer told her she had the right to remain silent.* ○ *a silent prayer* (= one that is not said out loud) ○ *So far, she has remained silent about her future plans.* **3** (of a letter) not pronounced: *The "b" in "comb" is silent.* —**si·lent·ly** *adv.*

sil·hou·ette /ˌsɪluˈɛt/ *noun* [C] the dark outline or black shape of sth seen against a light background

sil·i·con /ˈsɪlɪkən; -kən/ *noun* [U] (*symbol* **Si**) a chemical substance that is used for making computer parts (**chips**), glass, etc.

silk /sɪlk/ *noun* [U] the soft smooth cloth that is made from threads produced by an insect: *a silk blouse*

silk·y /ˈsɪlki/ *adj.* (**silk·i·er**; **silk·i·est**) smooth, soft and shiny; like silk: *silky hair*

sill /sɪl/ *noun* [C] a long thin piece of wood that is at the bottom of a window

☆ **sil·ly** /ˈsɪli/ *adj.* (**sil·li·er**; **sil·li·est**) **1** not showing thought or understanding; foolish: *a silly question* ○ *Stop being so silly!* **2** appearing ridiculous so that people will laugh: *I'm not wearing that costume – I'd look too silly in it.* —**sil·li·ness** *noun* [U]

si·lo /ˈsaɪloʊ/ *noun* [C] (*pl.* **si·los**) a tall round building on a farm, used for storing grain ☛ picture at **barn**.

silt /sɪlt/ *noun* [U] sand, soil or mud that is carried along by a river and then left somewhere when the river flows more slowly

☆ **sil·ver¹** /ˈsɪlvər/ *noun* [U] **1** a valuable gray-white metal that is used for making jewelry, ornaments, coins, etc.: *That's a nice ring. Is it silver?* **2** objects that are made of silver, e.g. cups, dishes, etc.: *The thieves stole some jewelry and some valuable silver.*

☆ **sil·ver²** /ˈsɪlvər/ *adj.* made of silver¹(1) or having the color of silver: *a silver spoon* ○ *a silver sports car*

ˌ**silver ˌanniˈversary** *noun* [C] the 25th anniversary of a wedding ☛ Look at **golden anniversary**.

ˌ**silver ˈmedal** *noun* [C] a small flat round piece of silver that is given to the person or

tʃ	dʒ	v	θ	ð	s	z	ʃ
chin	June	van	thin	then	so	zoo	she

team that comes second in a sports competition: *to win a silver medal at the Olympic Games* ☞ Look at **gold medal** and **bronze medal**.

‚silver ¹medalist *noun* [C] a person who wins a silver medal

☆ **sil·ver·ware** /ˈsɪlvərwer/ *noun* [U] knives, forks, spoons, etc. that are made of silver or some other metal

☆ **sim·i·lar** /ˈsɪmələr/ *adj.* **similar (to sb/sth)** the same in a way or in some ways but not completely the same: *All the books he writes are very similar.* ○ *Your handwriting is very similar to mine.*

☆ **sim·i·lar·i·ty** /ˌsɪməˈlærəṭi/ *noun* (*pl.* **sim·i·lar·i·ties**) **1** [U] the quality of being similar: *I noticed the similarity in the way the two sisters thought and spoke.* **2** [C] a way in which people or things are similar: *Although there are some similarities between the two towns, there are a lot of differences too.*

sim·i·lar·ly /ˈsɪmələrli/ *adv.* (*formal*) also; in a similar way: *The plural of "shelf" is "shelves." Similarly, the plural of "wolf" is "wolves."*

sim·il·e /ˈsɪməli/ *noun* [C,U] a way of describing sth by comparing it to sth else which has the same qualities, using the words "like" or "as." For example, if you say that sb has hair like gold, it means that he/she has very shiny blond hair. ☞ Look also at **metaphor**.

sim·mer /ˈsɪmər/ *verb* [I,T] to cook gently in a liquid that is just below the boiling point: *Let the vegetables simmer for a few more minutes.*

PHR V simmer down (*informal*) to become more calm and less angry, excited, etc.

☆ **sim·ple** /ˈsɪmpl/ *adj.* **1** easy to understand, do or use; not difficult or complicated: *This dictionary is written in simple English.* ○ *a simple task* ○ *I can't just quit my job. It's not as simple as that.* **2** without decoration or unnecessary extra things; plain: *a simple black dress* ○ *The food is simple but perfectly cooked.* **3** (used about a person or a way of life) natural and uncomplicated: *a simple life in the country* **4** (used for saying that the thing you are talking about is the only thing that is important or true): *I'm not going to buy it for the simple reason that I don't have enough money.* **5** (*old-fashioned*) unintelligent; slow to understand

the ‚simple ¹past *noun* [sing.] = PAST TENSE

the ‚simple ¹present *noun* [sing.] = PRESENT TENSE

sim·plic·i·ty /sɪmˈplɪsəṭi/ *noun* [U] **1** the quality of being uncomplicated and easy to understand, do or use: *We all admired the simplicity of the plan.* **2** the quality of having no decoration or unnecessary extra things: *I like the simplicity of her paintings.*

sim·pli·fy /ˈsɪmpləfaɪ/ *verb* [T] (*pres. part.* **sim·pli·fy·ing**; *3rd pers. sing. pres.* **sim·pli·fies**; *p.t., p.p.* **sim·pli·fied**) to make sth easier to do or understand; to make sth less complicated:

The process of registering to vote has been simplified. —**sim·pli·fi·ca·tion** /ˌsɪmpləfəˈkeɪʃn/ *noun* [C,U]

sim·plis·tic /sɪmˈplɪstɪk/ *adj.* making sth that is complicated seem simpler than it really is

☆ **sim·ply** /ˈsɪmpli/ *adv.* **1** in a way that makes sth easy to understand: *Could you explain it more simply?* **2** in a plain way; without decoration or unnecessary extra things: *They live simply, with very few luxuries.* **3** (used for emphasis) absolutely; completely: *This is simply the best book ever written on the subject.* **4** only; just: *Don't get mad. The whole problem is simply a misunderstanding.*

sim·u·late /ˈsɪmyəleɪt/ *verb* [T] to create the effect or appearance of sth else: *The astronauts trained in a machine that simulates conditions in space.*

sim·u·la·tion /ˌsɪmyəˈleɪʃn/ *noun* [C,U] the act of simulating or a simulated form of a real situation, event, etc.: *a computer simulation of a trip in the space shuttle*

si·mul·ta·ne·ous /ˌsaɪmlˈteɪniəs/ *adj.* happening at exactly the same time: *simultaneous broadcasts of the President's speech on all major TV networks* —**si·mul·ta·ne·ous·ly** *adv.*

sin¹ /sɪn/ *noun* [C,U] an act or way of behaving that breaks a religious law: *He believes it is a sin for two people to live together without being married.* ○ *They confess their sins to the priest every week.*

sin² /sɪn/ *verb* [I] (**sin·ning**; **sinned**) to do sth that breaks a religious law

☆ **since¹** /sɪns/ *prep.* from a particular time in the past until a later time in the past or until now: *It was the first time they'd won since 1984.* ○ *I haven't seen him since last Tuesday.* ○ *Where have you been? I've been waiting for you since 5:30.* ○ *She has had a number of jobs since college.*

☞ We use both **since** and **for** to talk about how long something has been happening. We use **since** when we are talking about the *beginning* of the period of time, and **for** when we are talking about the *length* of the period of time: *I've known her since 1993.* ○ *I've known her for five years.*

☆ **since²** /sɪns/ *conj.* **1** from the time when sth happened until a later time in the past or until now: *He hasn't written to us since he moved to Britain.* ○ *I've been working in a bank ever since I finished high school.* ○ *It was strange to see my old house again because I hadn't been there since I was a child.* **2** because; as: *Since they obviously forgot to call me, I'll have to call them.*

☆ **since³** /sɪns/ *adv.* **1** from a particular time in the past until a later time in the past or until now: *He had come to see us a few weeks earlier, but he hadn't been back since.* ○ *We went out for dinner together about six months ago, but I*

i	ɪ	ɛ	æ	ɑ	ɔ	ʌ	ʊ	u
see	sit	ten	cat	hot	saw	cup	put	too

haven't seen her since. ○ *My parents bought this house in 1985, and we've lived here ever since.* **2** at a time after a particular time in the past: *We got divorced two years ago and she has since married someone else.* ○ *He had dropped out of school at the age of 16 and had since found a job in a restaurant.*

☆ **sin·cere** /sɪnˈsɪr/ *adj.* **1** (used about a person) really meaning or believing what you say; honest; not pretending: *Do you think she was being sincere when she said she admired me?* **2** (used about sth that a person says or feels) true; that is really meant: *Please accept our sincere apologies.* ☞ The opposite is **insincere.** —**sin·cere·ly** *adv.*: *I am sincerely grateful to you for all your help.* ○ *Sincerely,...* (at the end of a formal letter)

sin·cer·i·ty /sɪnˈsɛrəti/ *noun* [U] the quality of being sincere; honesty: *Nobody doubts the sincerity of her political views.* ☞ The opposite is **insincerity.**

sin·ful /ˈsɪnfl/ *adj.* breaking a religious law; morally wrong

☆ **sing** /sɪŋ/ *verb* [I,T] (*p.t.* **sang** /sæŋ/; *p.p.* **sung** /sʌŋ/) to make musical sounds with the voice: *He always sings when he's in the shower.* ○ *The birds were singing outside my window.* ○ *She sang all her most popular songs at the concert.* —**sing·ing** *noun* [U]: *singing lessons*

singe /sɪndʒ/ *verb* [I,T] (*pres. part.* **singe·ing**) to burn or to make sth burn slightly on the edge or tip: *The bear's fur was singed in the forest fire.*

☆ **sing·er** /ˈsɪŋər/ *noun* [C] a person who sings, especially in public

☆ **sin·gle¹** /ˈsɪŋgl/ *adj.* **1** (only *before* a noun) only one: *He gave her a single red rose.* ○ *I managed to finish the whole job in a single afternoon.* **2** (only *before* a noun) (used for emphasis when you are thinking about an individual thing, especially when it forms part of a group): *You answered every single question right. Good job!* ○ *the single most important issue facing the country today* **3** not married: *Are you married, single or divorced?* ○ *a single mother* **4** (only *before* a noun) for the use of only one person: *a single bed* ☞ Look at **double.**

IDM **(in) single file** in a line, one behind the other: *You'll have to walk (in) single file – the path is very narrow.*

sin·gle² /ˈsɪŋgl/ *noun* **1** [C] a small record that has only one song on each side: *the new single from the Fugees* ☞ Look at **LP** and **album.** **2 singles** [plural] people who are not married: *Thursday is singles night at Bill's Bar.* **3 sin·gles** [plural] a game of tennis, etc. in which one player plays against one other player: *the final of the women's singles* ☞ Look at **doubles.**

sin·gle³ /ˈsɪŋgl/ *verb*

PHRV **single sb/sth out (for sth)** to give special attention or treatment to one person or thing from a group: *He singled Sue Taylor out for praise.*

single-'digit *adj.* (only *before* a noun) connected with a number from 1 to 9: *single-digit inflation*

single-'family *adj.* (only *before* a noun) (used about a house) built to be used by one family: *sales of single-family homes*

single-'handedly *adv.* done by one person; done without help from anybody else

single-'minded *adj.* having one clear aim or purpose: *I admired her single-minded determination to win.*

single 'parent *noun* [C] a parent who takes care of his/her child or children alone: *a single-parent family*

single-'sex *adj.* (used about a school, education, etc.) only for boys or only for girls ☞ Look at **coeducational.**

sin·gly /ˈsɪŋgli/ *adv.* one by one; individually: *You can buy the tapes either singly or in packages of three.*

sin·gu·lar¹ /ˈsɪŋgyələr/ *adj.* (*grammar*) in the form that is used for talking about one person or thing only: *"Table" is a singular noun; "tables" is a plural noun.*

sin·gu·lar² /ˈsɪŋgyələr/ *noun* [sing.] (*grammar*) the form that is used for talking about one person or thing only: *The word "clothes" has no singular.* ○ *What's the singular of "people"?*

sin·is·ter /ˈsɪnəstər/ *adj.* making you feel that sth bad will happen; frightening: *a sinister atmosphere* ○ *There's something sinister about him. He frightens me.*

☆ **sink¹** /sɪŋk/ *verb* (*p.t.* **sank** /sæŋk/ or **sunk** /sʌŋk/; *p.p.* **sunk**) **1** [I,T] to go down or make sth go down under the surface or to the bottom of water, etc.: *If you throw a stone into water, it sinks.* ○ *The boat sank to the bottom of the ocean.* ○ *Three ships were sunk by enemy planes.* ○ *My feet sank into the mud.* ☞ picture at **float.** **2** [I] to get lower; to fall to a lower position or level: *After a few days, the flood water began to sink.* ○ *We watched the sun sink slowly below the horizon.* **3** [I] (used about a person) to move or fall to a lower position, usually because you are tired or weak: *I came home very tired and sank into a chair.* **4** [I] to decrease in value, number, amount, strength, etc.: *The price of the stock has sunk from over $2 to 65¢ per share.*

IDM **your heart sinks** ⇨ HEART

PHRV **sink in** (used about information, an event, an experience, etc.) to be completely understood; to become clear in the mind: *It took a long time for the shocking news to sink in.*

☆ **sink²** /sɪŋk/ *noun* [C] a large bowl in a kitchen or bathroom that is connected to the water

ə	y	w	t̬	eɪ	aɪ	ɔɪ	aʊ	oʊ
about	yes	woman	butter	say	five	boy	now	go

supply with pipes and faucets. You wash things such as dishes, vegetables, etc. or your hands or face in a sink.

sin·ner /ˈsɪnər/ *noun* [C] a person who breaks a religious law or behaves in a way that is morally wrong

si·nus /ˈsaɪnəs/ *noun* [C] (often plural) one of the spaces in the bones of the face that are connected to the nose: *I have a terrible cold and all my sinuses are blocked.*

sip /sɪp/ *verb* [I,T] (**sip·ping**; **sipped**) to drink, taking only a very small amount of liquid into your mouth at a time: *We sat in the sun, sipping lemonade.* —**sip** *noun* [C]: *to take a sip of water*

si·phon /ˈsaɪfn/ *verb* [T] **siphon sth into/out of sth**; **siphon sth off/out** to remove a liquid from a container (or to transfer it from one container to another) through a tube

☆ **sir** /sər/ *noun* (used as a polite way of speaking to a man, especially one of higher social or military rank than you, or one whose name you do not know): *Good morning, sir.* ○ *Excuse me, sir – is this your briefcase?* ○ *Dear Sir/Dear Madam:...* (= used at the beginning of a formal letter to a person that you do not know) ☞ Look also at **ma'am**.

si·ren /ˈsaɪrən/ *noun* [C] a machine that makes a long, loud sound in order to warn people about sth, e.g. on an ambulance, a fire-engine or a police car: *a police siren*

sir·loin /ˈsərlɔɪn/ *noun* [C,U] (a piece of) good quality beef that comes from the back of a cow: *a sirloin steak*

☆ **sis·ter** /ˈsɪstər/ *noun* [C] **1** a girl or woman who has the same parents as another person: *I have one brother and two sisters.* ○ *We're sisters.* ○ *Keisha is my sister.* ☞ Look at **half-sister** and **stepsister**. In English there is no common word that means "both brothers and sisters": *Do you have any brothers or sisters?* The word **sibling** is very formal. **2 Sister** a member of certain female religious groups; a nun: *Sister Mary Louise* **3** (*informal*) a girl or woman who is your friend or who is from the same social class, race, etc. as you **4** a company, an organization or a ship, etc. that belongs to the same group: *We have a sister company in France.*

ˌsister ˈcity *noun* [C] (*pl.* **sister cities**) one of two towns or cities in different countries that have a special relationship: *Okayama is San Jose's sister city in Japan.*

ˈsister-in-law *noun* [C] (*pl.* **sisters-in-law**) **1** the sister of your husband or wife **2** the wife of your brother

☆ **sit** /sɪt/ *verb* (*pres. part.* **sit·ting**; *p.t., p.p.* **sat** /sæt/) **1** [I] to be in a position on a chair, etc. in which the upper part of your body is upright and your weight is supported at the bottom of your back: *We sat in the back yard all afternoon.* ○ *She was sitting on the sofa,*

talking to her mother. ○ *Just sit still and behave yourself!* **2** [I] **sit (down)** to lower the body into the position of sitting: *Come and sit next to me. I want to talk to you.* **3** [T] **sit sb (down)** to put sb into a sitting position; to make sb sit down: *He picked up his daughter and sat her down on a chair.* ○ *She sat me down and offered me a cup of coffee.* **4** [I] to be in a particular place or position: *The letter sat on the table for several days before anybody opened it.* **5** [I] (*formal*) (used about an official group of people) to have a meeting or series of meetings: *The Supreme Court is sitting this week.*

PHR V **sit around** (*informal*) to sit and do nothing active for a period of time: *people sitting around, visiting about the weather*

sit back to relax and not take an active part in what other people are doing: *Sit back and relax for a while – Bobby will mow the lawn.*

sit in on sth to go to a meeting, class, etc. as a visitor, but without taking part in it actively: *We sat in on a history seminar at the college.*

sit sth out to not take part in an activity, e.g. a game, a dance etc.: *I've played enough cards tonight; I think I'll sit this one out.*

sit through sth to stay in your seat until sth has finished (especially if it is boring): *I don't think I can sit through another hour of this movie.*

sit up 1 to move into a sitting position when you have been lying down or leaning back: *Sit up straight or you'll hurt your back!* **2** to not go to bed although it is very late: *We sat up all night talking.*

sit·com /ˈsɪtkɑm/ *noun* [C] a funny program on television that shows the same characters in a different situation each week

☆ **site** /saɪt/ *noun* [C] **1** a piece of land that is used or will be used for building on or for another special purpose: *a construction site* (= a place where a building is being constructed) ○ *The company is looking for a site for its new offices.* **2** a place where sth happened or existed in the past: *the site of a Civil War battle* **3** = WEB SITE

sit·ter /ˈsɪtər/ *noun* [C] = BABYSITTER

sit·u·at·ed /ˈsɪtʃueɪtəd/ *adj.*

IDM **be situated (at, in, on, etc.)** (*formal*) to be in a particular place or position: *The hotel is conveniently situated close to the beach.* ☞ **Be located** is more common than **be situated**.

☆ **sit·u·a·tion** /ˌsɪtʃuˈeɪʃn/ *noun* [C] the things that are happening in a particular place or at a particular time: *The situation in the Middle East is extremely serious.* ○ *Tim is in a difficult situation right now.* ○ *the economic situation*

ˈsit-up *noun* [C] a physical exercise in which you lie on your back and use the muscles in your stomach to raise the upper part of your body to a sitting position: *Kristi does 25 sit-ups every morning.*

ər	ɪr	ɛr	ɑr	ɔr	ʊr	ʒ	h	ŋ
bird	near	hair	car	north	tour	vision	hat	sing

☆ **six** /sɪks/ *number* 6; one more than five: *The answers are on page six.* ○ *She invited twenty people, but only six came.* ○ *Six (of the students) are absent today.* ○ *They have six cats.* ○ *My son is six (years old) next month.* ○ *The class is in room 6.* ○ *a birthday card with a big six on it* ○ *We're having dinner at six (o'clock).* ☞ For more information on numbers, look at Appendix 2.

six- /sɪks/ (in compounds) having 6 of the thing mentioned: *a six-day week*

ˈ**six-pack** *noun* [C] a group of six cans or bottles that are sold together: *a six-pack of soda*

☆ **six·teen** /sɪkˈstin/ *number* 16; one more than fifteen ☞ For examples of how to use numbers in sentences, look at **six.** Look also at Appendix 2. —**six·teenth** /sɪkˈstinθ/ *pron., det., adv.* ☞ Look at the examples at **sixth.**

☆ **sixth**[1] /sɪksθ/ *pron., det., adv.* 6th; next after fifth: *I've had five cups of coffee already, so this is my sixth.* ○ *This is the sixth time I've tried to call him.* ○ *Mahler's Sixth Symphony* ○ *King George VI* (= King George the Sixth) *of England* ☞ For more information about numbers in dates, measurements, prices, etc., look at Appendix 2.

☆ **sixth**[2] /sɪksθ/ *noun* [C] the fraction 1/6th; one of six equal parts of sth ☞ For more information on numbers, look at Appendix 2.

☆ **six·ty** /ˈsɪksti/ *number* **1** 60; one more than fifty-nine: *Sixty people went to the meeting.* ○ *There are sixty pages in the book.* ○ *He retired at age sixty/when he was sixty.* ☞ For more information on numbers, look at Appendix 2. **2 the sixties** [plural] the numbers, years or temperatures between 60 and 69: *I don't know the exact number of members, but it's in the sixties.* ○ *The Beatles were the most famous band of the sixties.* ○ *The temperature tomorrow will be in the high sixties.*

IDM in your sixties between the age of 60 and 69: *I'm not sure how old she is, but I should think she's in her sixties.* ○ *in your early/mid/late sixties* —**six·ti·eth** /ˈsɪkstiəθ/ *pron., det., adv.* ☞ Look at the examples at **sixth.**

siz·a·ble (*also* **size·a·ble**) /ˈsaɪzəbl/ *adj.* fairly large: *a sizable chunk of our income*

☆ **size**[1] /saɪz/ *noun* **1** [U] the amount by which sth is big or small: *I was surprised at the size of the hotel. It was enormous!* ○ *Canadian quarters are about the same size as American ones.* ○ *The planet Uranus is about four times the size of Earth.*

☞ When we ask about the size of something, we usually say, "How big...?": *How big is your house?* We say, "What size...?" when we ask about the size of something that is produced in a number of fixed measurements: *What size shoes do you wear?*

2 [C] one of a number of fixed measurements in which sth is made: *Do you have this dress in a larger size?* ○ *What size pizza do you want: medium or large?* ○ *I wear size 9 shoes.*

size[2] /saɪz/ *verb*

PHRV size sb/sth up to think carefully about sb/sth in order to form an opinion: *The team members sized up their opponents as they went out onto the field.*

-sized /saɪzd/ (*also* **-size**) (in compounds) of the size that is mentioned: *a medium-sized apartment*

siz·zle /ˈsɪzl/ *verb* [I] to make the sound of food frying in hot fat: *I could hear the bacon sizzling in the kitchen.*

Rollerblade (*also* **in-line skate**) **rollerskate**

skateboard **ice skate**

skate[1] /skeɪt/ *noun* [C] **1** = ICE SKATE[1] **2** = ROLLER SKATE ☞ Look also at **in-line skate.**

skate[2] /skeɪt/ *verb* [I] **1** = ICE SKATE[2]: *They skated across the frozen lake.* **2** = ROLLER SKATE —**skat·er** *noun* [C]

skate·board /ˈskeɪtbɔrd/ *noun* [C] a narrow board with wheels attached to it that you can stand on and ride —**skate·board·er** *noun* [C] —**skate·board·ing** *noun* [U]

☆ **skel·e·ton**[1] /ˈskɛlətn/ *noun* [C] the structure formed by all the bones in a human or animal body: *a dinosaur skeleton in the Science Museum* ○ *the human skeleton*

skel·e·ton[2] /ˈskɛlətn/ *adj.* (only *before* a noun) (used about an organization, a service, etc.) having the smallest number of people that is necessary for it to operate: *On Sundays, the office is kept open by a skeleton staff.*

skep·tic /ˈskɛptɪk/ *noun* [C] a person who doubts that sth is true, right, etc. —**skep·ti·cal** /-kl/ *adj.* **skeptical (of/about sth)** —**skep·ti·cal·ly** /-kli/ *adv.*

sketch[1] /skɛtʃ/ *noun* [C] **1** a simple, quick drawing without many details: *He drew a rough sketch of the new building on the back of an envelope.* **2** a short comedy scene, usually part of a television program **3** a short description without any details: *a sketch of life in Paris in the 1920s*

sketch[2] /skɛtʃ/ *verb* [I,T] to draw a sketch1: *I sat on the grass and sketched the lake.*

sketch·y /ˈskɛtʃi/ *adj.* (**sketch·i·er; sketch·i·est**) not having many or enough details: *He only gave me a sketchy account of the accident.*

tʃ	dʒ	v	θ	ð	s	z	ʃ
chin	**J**une	**v**an	**th**in	**th**en	**s**o	**z**oo	**sh**e

ski

binding
boot
ski
pole
ski

downhill skiing **cross-country skiing**

ski¹ /ski/ *noun* [C] one of a pair of long, flat, narrow pieces of wood, metal or plastic that are fastened to boots and used for moving over snow: *a pair of skis*

ski² /ski/ *verb* [I] (*pres. part.* **ski·ing**; *p.t.*, *p.p.* **skied**) to move over snow on skis: *When did you learn to ski?*

☞ **Go skiing** is a common way of talking about skiing for pleasure: *They go skiing in Colorado every year.*

—**ski·er** /ˈskiər/ *noun* [C]: *a good skier* —**ski·ing** *noun* [U]: *downhill/cross-country skiing*

skid /skɪd/ *verb* [I] (**skid·ding**; **skid·ded**) (used about a vehicle) to be out of control and move or slide sideways on the road: *I skidded on a patch of ice.* —**skid** *noun* [C]

☆ **skill** /skɪl/ *noun* **1** [U] the ability to do sth well, especially because of training, practice, etc.: *It takes great skill to make such beautiful jewelry.* ○ *This is an easy game to play. No skill is required.* **2** [C] an ability that is required in order to do a job, an activity, etc. well: *The course will help you to develop your reading and listening skills.* ○ *management skills* ○ *Typing is a skill I have never mastered.*

☆ **skilled** /skɪld/ *adj.* **1** (used about a person) having skill; skillful: *a skilled worker* **2** (used about work, a job etc.) requiring skill or skills; done by people who have been trained: *a highly skilled job* ○ *Skilled work is difficult to find in this area.* ☞ The opposite is **unskilled**.

skil·let /ˈskɪlət/ *noun* [C] = FRYING PAN

☆ **skill·ful** /ˈskɪlfl/ *adj.* **1** (used about a person) very good at doing sth: *a skillful painter, politician, etc.* ○ *He's very skillful with his hands.* **2** done very well: *skillful guitar playing* —**skill·ful·ly** *adv.*: *The play was skillfully directed by a young student.*

skim /skɪm/ *verb* (**skim·ming**; **skimmed**) **1** [T] to remove sth from the surface of a liquid: *to skim the fat off the gravy* **2** [I,T] **skim (through/over) sth** to read sth quickly in order to get the main idea, without paying attention to the details and without reading every word: *I usually just skim through the newspaper in the morning.* **3** [I,T] to move quickly over a surface, near it but without touching it, or without touching it very often: *The plane flew very low, skimming the tops of* the buildings. ○ *I watched a big bird skim across the water.*

skim ˈmilk *noun* [U] milk from which all the cream has been removed

skimp·y /ˈskɪmpi/ *adj.* (**skimp·i·er**; **skimp·i·est**) using or having less than is necessary: *a skimpy meal* ○ *a skimpy swimsuit* (= not covering much of the body)

☆ **skin¹** /skɪn/ *noun* [C,U] **1** the natural outer covering of a human or animal body: *to have light, dark, sensitive, etc. skin* ○ *skin cancer* **2** (often in compounds) the skin of an animal that has been removed from its body and that is often used for making things: *a sheepskin jacket* **3** the natural outer covering of some fruits or vegetables; the outer covering of a sausage: *Remove the skins from the tomatoes.* ☞ Look at the note at **rind**. **4** the thin solid surface that can form on a liquid: *Don't leave the paint can open, or the paint will get a skin on it.*

IDM **by the skin of your teeth** (*informal*) (used about a successful action) just; with very little time, space etc. extra: *It was a real struggle, but we got through it by the skin of our teeth.*

have a thick skin ⇨ THICK¹

skin² /skɪn/ *verb* [T] (**skin·ning**; **skinned**) to remove the skin ¹ from sth

skin·head /ˈskɪnhɛd/ *noun* [C] a young white person with shaved or extremely short hair. Skinheads are often associated with violent behavior against people of other races.

skin·ny /ˈskɪni/ *adj.* (**skin·ni·er**; **skin·ni·est**) (*informal*) (used about a person) too thin ☞ Look at the note at **thin**.

skin·tight /ˌskɪnˈtaɪt/ *adj.* (used about a piece of clothing) fitting very tightly and showing the shape of the body

skip /skɪp/ *verb* (**skip·ping**; **skipped**) **1** [I] to move along quickly and lightly in a way that is similar to dancing, with little jumps and steps, from one foot to the other: *A little girl came skipping along the street.* **2** [T] to not go to sth that you should go to; to not have sth that you should have: *I got up late, so I skipped breakfast.* **3** [I,T] **skip (over) sth** (used about part of a book, story, etc.) to leave sth out; to not read or talk about sth and move to the next part: *I think I'll skip the next chapter. It looks really boring.*

IDM **cut/skip class** ⇨ CLASS

skip·per /ˈskɪpər/ *noun* [C] the captain of a boat or ship

skir·mish /ˈskərmɪʃ/ *noun* [C] a small fight or battle

☆ **skirt¹** /skərt/ *noun* [C] a piece of clothing that is worn by women and girls and that hangs down from the waist: *a short skirt* ☞ picture on page A26.

skirt² /skərt/ *verb* **1** to go around the edge of sth: *a road that skirts the western edge of the*

S

metro area **2** to avoid talking about sth directly: *The boss has been skirting the issue of our raise.*

skit /skɪt/ *noun* [C] a short, funny play or scene

skull /skʌl/ *noun* [C] the bone structure of a human or animal head: *a fractured skull*

skunk /skʌŋk/ *noun* [C] a small wild animal with black and white fur and a thick tail. Skunks spray a liquid with a very strong, bad smell from their bodies when they are in danger or frightened.

skunk

☆ **sky** /skaɪ/ *noun* [C,U] (*pl.* **skies**) the space that you can see when you look up from the earth, and where you can see the sun, moon and stars: *a clear blue sky* ○ *I saw a little bit of blue sky between the clouds.*

☞ We usually talk about **the sky**: *I saw a plane high up in the sky.* ○ *The sky looks very dark. I think it's going to rain.* However, when **sky** follows an adjective, we usually use **a / an**: *a cloudless sky* or sometimes the plural form **skies**: *cloudless skies.*

sky-'high *adj., adv.* very high

sky·light /'skaɪlaɪt/ *noun* [C] a window in the roof of a house or other building ☞ picture on page A28.

sky·line /'skaɪlaɪn/ *noun* [C] the shape that is made by tall buildings, etc. against the sky: *the Manhattan skyline*

sky·rock·et /'skaɪrɑkət/ *verb* [I] to increase or rise very quickly: *skyrocketing prices*

sky·scrap·er /'skaɪskreɪpər/ *noun* [C] a very tall building

slab /slæb/ *noun* [C] a thick, flat piece of sth: *huge concrete slabs*

slack[1] /slæk/ *adj.* **1** loose; not tightly stretched: *Leave the rope slack.* **2** (used about a period of business) not busy; not having many customers or much activity: *Prices remained low because of slack demand for the products.*

slack[2] /slæk/ *noun* [U] a part of a rope, etc. that is loose or not tightly stretched ☞ Look also at **slacks**.

IDM **cut/give sb some slack** (*informal*) to be less critical of sb and not get angry if he/she makes mistakes

pick/take up the slack to do some extra work because the person, group, etc. who usually does it is not there: *If those government benefits are cut, charities and volunteer organizations will have to take up the slack.*

slack·en /'slækən/ *verb* [I,T] **1** to become or make sth slower or less active: *Industrial production has slackened in recent months.* ○ *His pace slackened toward the end of the race.* **2** to

become or make sth less tight: *The rope slackened and he pulled his hand free.* ○ *After a while she slackened her grip on my arm.*

slack·er /'slækər/ *noun* [C] (*slang*) a person who does not work hard and wastes a lot of time

slacks /slæks/ *noun* [plural] (*old-fashioned*) pants: *a pair of slacks*

slain *p.p.* of SLAY

sla·lom /'slɑləm/ *noun* [C] (in skiing) a race along a course on which people have to move from side to side between poles

slam /slæm/ *verb* (**slam·ming**; **slammed**) **1** [I,T] to close or make sth close very loudly and with great force: *I heard the front door slam.* ○ *She slammed her book shut and rushed out of the room.* **2** [T] to put sth somewhere very quickly and with great force: *He slammed my letter on the table and stormed out.* ☞ Look at **grand slam**. **3** [T] to criticize sb/sth very strongly: *Citizens' groups slammed the proposal to increase the state sales tax.*

slam-'dunk (*also* **slam dunk**) *noun* [C] (in basketball) an act of jumping very high and pushing the ball through the basket with great force from above —**slam-dunk** *verb* [I,T]

slan·der /'slændər/ *noun* [C,U] an untrue spoken statement about sb that is intended to damage the good opinion that other people have of him/her; the crime of making this kind of statement ☞ Look at **libel**. —**slan·der** *verb* [T]

☆ **slang** /slæŋ/ *noun* [U] very informal words and expressions that are more common in spoken language. Slang is sometimes used only by a particular group of people (e.g. children, soldiers) and often stays in fashion for a short time. Some slang is not polite: *"Barf" is slang for "vomit."*

slant[1] /slænt/ *verb* **1** [I,T] to lean or make sth lean in a particular direction; to be not straight: *My handwriting slants backwards.* **2** [T] (*usually passive*) to describe information, events, etc. in a way that supports a particular group or opinion: *All the political articles in that newspaper are slanted toward the administration.*

slant[2] /slænt/ *noun* **1** [sing.] a position that leans or slopes in a particular direction **2** [C] an attitude or a way of thinking about sth, especially one that supports a particular group or opinion: *This new information puts a completely different slant on the discussion.*

slap[1] /slæp/ *verb* [T] (**slap·ping**; **slapped**) **1** to hit sb/sth with the inside of your hand: *She slapped him across the face.* ○ *to slap sb on the back* (= to congratulate him/her) **2** to put sth onto a surface quickly and carelessly: *to slap some paint onto a wall*

slap[2] /slæp/ *noun* [C] an act of hitting sb/sth with the inside of your hand: *I gave him a slap across the face.*

S

IDM a slap on the wrist a punishment that is not severe, or that sb thinks is not severe enough: *a drug dealer who only got a slap on the wrist from the judge*

slap·stick /'slæpstɪk/ *noun* [U] a type of comedy that is based on simple jokes, e.g. people falling over or hitting each other

slash /slæʃ/ *verb* **1** [I,T] to make a long cut in sth with a violent action: *Several cars have had their tires slashed in that parking lot.* **2** [T] to reduce an amount of money, etc. very much: *The price of coffee has been slashed by about 20%.*

slat /slæt/ *noun* [C] one of the long narrow pieces of wood, metal or plastic in a cupboard door, a covering for a window, etc.

slate¹ /sleɪt/ *noun* [U] a type of dark gray rock that can easily be split into thin flat pieces

slate² /sleɪt/ *verb*
IDM be slated to do sth; be slated for sth to be planned to do sth or to happen at a particular time: *The new store is slated to open in April.* ○ *an empty lot that has been slated for development*

slaugh·ter /'slɔtər/ *verb* [T] **1** to kill an animal, usually for food **2** to kill a large number of people at one time, especially in a cruel way or when they cannot defend themselves: *Men, women and children were slaughtered and whole villages destroyed.* ☞ Look at the note at **kill.** —**slaugh·ter** *noun* [U]: *the slaughter of innocent people during the war*

slaugh·ter·house /'slɔtərhaʊs/ *noun* [C] a place where animals are killed for food

☆**slave¹** /sleɪv/ *noun* [C] a person who is owned by another person and has to work for that person

slave² /sleɪv/ *verb* [I] **slave (away)** to work very hard: *I slaved over a hot stove for hours to cook this meal!*

☆**slav·er·y** /'sleɪvəri/ *noun* [U] **1** the system of having slaves: *the abolition of slavery after the Civil War* **2** the situation of being a slave: *The two boys were captured and sold into slavery.*

slay /sleɪ/ *verb* [T] (*p.t.* **slew** /slu/; *p.p.* **slain** /sleɪn/) to kill violently; to murder: *Many young soldiers were slain in the battle.* —**slay·ing** /'sleɪŋ/ *noun* [C,U]

slea·zy /'slizi/ *adj.* (**slea·zi·er; slea·zi·est**) (often used about a place) dirty, in bad condition and having an immoral or criminal atmosphere: *a sleazy nightclub*

sled /slɛd/ *noun* [C] a vehicle without wheels that is used for traveling on snow. You can slide down a hill on a small sled. Large sleds are often pulled by dogs. ☞ Look at **sleigh** and **toboggan.**

sled

sleek /slik/ *adj.* (used about a vehicle) having an elegant, smooth shape: *a sleek new sports car*

☆**sleep¹** /slip/ *noun* **1** [U] the natural condition of rest when your eyes are closed and your mind and body are not active or conscious: *Most people need about eight hours' sleep every night.* ○ *I didn't get much sleep last night.* ○ *Do you ever talk in your sleep?* **2** [sing.] a period of sleep (1): *I haven't had a decent night's sleep in months.*
IDM get to sleep to succeed in sleeping: *I couldn't get to sleep last night.*
go to sleep 1 to start sleeping; to enter the state of sleep: *He got into bed and went to sleep quickly.* ○ *Go to sleep. Everything will seem better in the morning.* **2** (used about an arm, a leg, etc.) to lose the sense of feeling in it
put (an animal) to sleep to kill an animal that is sick or injured because you want to stop it from suffering

☆**sleep²** /slip/ *verb* (*p.t., p.p.* **slept** /slɛpt/) **1** [I] to be in a state of sleep ¹(1) for a period of time: *Did you sleep well last night?* ○ *I only slept for a couple of hours last night.*

☞ We use **to sleep** for talking about sleeping in general, but we use **to be asleep** to talk about being in the state of sleep when something else happens: *I was asleep when the telephone rang.* We use **to go to sleep** to talk about starting to sleep. (NOT: *I slept at ten o'clock last night* but: *I went to sleep at ten o'clock last night.*)

2 [T] (used about a place) to have enough beds for a particular number of people: *a camper that sleeps four people*
PHRV sleep in to sleep until later than usual in the morning because you do not have to get up
sleep over to sleep at sb else's house
sleep together; sleep with sb to have sex with sb (usually when you are not married to or living with that person): *Do you think she's slept with him?*

sleep·er /'slipər/ *noun* [C] (with an adjective) a person who sleeps in a particular way. If you are a light sleeper you wake up easily: *a light/heavy sleeper*

'sleeping bag *noun* [C] a large soft bag that you sleep in when you go camping, etc.

'sleeping pill *noun* [C] a pill that helps you to sleep

sleep·less /'sliplǝs/ *adj.* (used about a period, usually the night) without sleep —**sleep·less·ness** *noun* [U] ☞ Look at **insomnia.**

sleep·walk /'slipwɔk/ *verb* [I] to walk around while you are asleep

☆**sleep·y** /'slipi/ *adj.* (**sleep·i·er; sleep·i·est**) **1** tired and ready to go to sleep: *These pills might make you feel a little sleepy.* **2** (used about a place) very quiet and not having much

activity: *a sleepy rural town* —**sleep·i·ly** /-əli/ *adv.*

sleet /slit/ *noun* [U] a mixture of rain and snow ☛ Look at the note at **weather**. —**sleet** *verb* [I]

sleeve

sleeve

☆ **sleeve** /sliv/ *noun* [C] one of the two parts of a piece of clothing that cover the arms or part of the arms: *a blouse with long sleeves*

-sleeved /slivd/ (*also* **-sleeve**) (in compounds) with sleeves of a particular kind: *a short-sleeved shirt* ○ *a long-sleeved dress*

sleeve·less /'slivləs/ *adj.* without sleeves

sleigh /sleɪ/ *noun* [C] a vehicle that is used for traveling on snow and that is usually pulled by horses ☛ Look at **sled** and at the note at **Santa Claus**.

slen·der /'slɛndər/ *adj.* **1** (used about a person or part of sb's body) thin in an attractive way: *long slender fingers* **2** smaller in amount or size than you would like: *a slender margin of victory*

slept *p.t., p.p.* of SLEEP[2]

slew¹ /slu/ *noun* [sing.] (*informal*) **a slew of sth** a large number or amount of sth

slew² *p.t.* of SLAY

☆ **slice¹** /slaɪs/ *noun* [C] **1** a flat piece of food that is cut from a larger piece: *a thick/thin slice of bread* ○ *a slice of pizza* ☛ picture at **bread**. **2** a part of sth: *The owners had taken a large slice of the profits.*

☆ **slice²** /slaɪs/ *verb* **1** [T] to cut into slices ¹(1) : *Peel and slice the apples.* ○ *thinly sliced ham* **2** [I,T] to cut through or into sth: *He sliced through the rope with a knife.*

slick¹ /slɪk/ *adj.* **1** done smoothly and well, and seeming to be done without any effort: *The actors gave a slick, highly professional performance.* **2** skillful at persuading people but perhaps not completely honest: *slick advertising* **3** (used about a surface) smooth and slippery: *The truck's wheels were spinning on the slick, icy road.*

slick² /slɪk/ *noun* [C] = OIL SLICK

☆ **slide¹** /slaɪd/ *verb* (p.t., p.p. **slid** /slɪd/) **1** [I,T] to move or make sth move smoothly along a surface: *She slid on the ice and fell down.* ○ *A large drop of rain slid down the window.* ○ *"Here you are," he said, sliding the keys across the table.* ○ *a sliding door* (= one that you open by sliding it to one side) **2** [I,T] to move or make sth move quietly without being noticed: *I slid out of the room when nobody was looking.* ○ *She slid her hand into her bag and took out a gun.* **3** [I] (used about prices, values, etc.) to go

down slowly and continuously: *The pound is sliding against the dollar.*

☆ **slide²** /slaɪd/ *noun* [C] **1** a small piece of photographic film in a plastic or cardboard frame

☛ If you shine light through a slide using a **projector**, you can make the photograph appear on a **screen**.

2 a small piece of glass that you put sth on when you want to examine it under a microscope **3** a long piece of metal, etc. that children can slide down (e.g. in a playground) **4** a continuous slow movement down (e.g. of prices, values, levels, etc.): *a slide in the value of the dollar* **5** (usually in compounds) a sudden fall of rocks, earth, etc. down a slope: *a mudslide*

☆ **slight** /slaɪt/ *adj.* **1** very small; not important or serious: *I've got a slight problem, but it's nothing to get worried about.* ○ *a slight change, difference, increase, improvement, etc.* ○ *I don't have the slightest idea* (= no idea at all) *what you're talking about.* **2** (used about a person's body) thin and delicate: *his slight figure*

☆ **slight·ly** /'slaɪtli/ *adv.* a little: *I'm slightly older than she is.*

☆ **slim** /slɪm/ *adj.* (**slim·mer**; **slim·mest**) **1** thin in an attractive way: *a tall, slim woman* ☛ Look at the note at **thin**. **2** not as big as you would like: *Her chances of success are very slim.*

slime /slaɪm/ *noun* [U] a thick unpleasant sticky liquid: *The pond was covered with green slime and smelled terrible.*

slim·y /'slaɪmi/ *adj.* (**slim·i·er**; **slim·i·est**) **1** covered with slime **2** (*informal*) (used about a person) very friendly, but in a way that you do not trust or like

sling¹ /slɪŋ/ *noun* [C] a piece of cloth that you put under your arm and tie around your neck to support a broken arm, wrist, etc. ☛ picture at **Band-Aid**.

sling² /slɪŋ/ *verb* [T] (*p.t., p.p.* **slung**) **1** to put or throw sth somewhere in a rough or careless way: *He slung his bat to the side of the field in anger.* **2** to put sth into a position where it hangs loosely: *She was carrying her bag slung over her shoulder.*

sling·shot /'slɪŋʃɑt/ *noun* [C] a Y-shaped stick with a band of rubber attached to each side, that is used by children for shooting stones

slingshot

☆ **slip¹** /slɪp/ *verb* (**slip·ping**; **slipped**) **1** [I] slip **(on sth)** to slide accidentally, lose your balance and fall or nearly fall: *Don't slip on that floor. I just mopped it.* ○ *His foot slipped on the step and he fell down.* **2** [I] to slide accidentally out of the correct position or out of sb's hand: *This hat's too big. It keeps slipping down over*

tʃ	dʒ	v	θ	ð	s	z	ʃ
chin	**June**	**van**	**thin**	**then**	**so**	**zoo**	**she**

my eyes. ○ *The glass slipped out of my hand and smashed on the floor.* ○ *(figurative) I didn't intend to tell them. It just slipped out.* **3** [I] to move or go somewhere quietly, quickly, and often without being noticed: *While everyone was dancing, we slipped away and went home.* **4** [T] **slip sth (to sb); slip (sb) sth** to put sth somewhere or give sth quietly and often without being noticed: *She picked up the money and slipped it into her pocket.* **5** [I,T] **slip into/out of sth; slip sth on/off** to put on or take off a piece of clothing quickly and easily: *I'm just going to slip into something cooler.* ○ *I slipped off my shoes.* **6** [I] to fall a little (in value, level, etc.): *Sales have been slipping slightly over the last few months.*

IDM **fall/slip through the cracks** ⇨ CRACK¹

let sth slip to tell a secret, some information, etc. without intending to: *He let slip that he had been in prison.*

slip your mind to be forgotten: *I'm sorry – the meeting completely slipped my mind.*

PHRV **slip up** *(informal)* to make a mistake: *It looks like somebody slipped up. Your name isn't on the list.*

slip² /slɪp/ *noun* [C] **1** an act of slipping¹(1): *Be careful when you go up onto the roof. One slip and you could fall off.* **2** a slight fall in value, level, etc.: *a slip in the governor's popularity* **3** a small mistake: *to make a slip of the tongue* (= to say sth wrong, without intending to) **4** a small piece of paper: *I made a note of her name on a slip of paper.* ○ *a bank deposit slip* **5** a piece of clothing that is worn by a woman under a dress or skirt ☞ picture on page A26.

IDM **give sb the slip** *(informal)* to escape from sb who is following or chasing you

slipped disk *noun* [C] an injury that happens when one of the soft parts between the bones in sb's back has moved out of its correct position, causing pain

slip·per /ˈslɪpər/ *noun* [C] a light soft shoe that is worn in the house: *a pair of slippers* ☞ picture at **shoe**.

slip·per·y /ˈslɪpəri/ *adj.* (used about a surface or an object) difficult to move over or hold because it is smooth, wet, greasy, etc.: *a slippery floor* ○ *The fish was cold and slippery.*

slit¹ /slɪt/ *noun* [C] a long narrow cut or opening: *We could see into the room through a slit in the curtains.*

slit² /slɪt/ *verb* [T] (**slit·ting**; *p.t., p.p.* **slit**) to make a long narrow cut in sth: *She slit the envelope open with a knife.* ○ *He slit his wrists in a suicide attempt.*

slith·er /ˈslɪðər/ *verb* [I] to slide along in an unsteady or twisting way: *I saw a snake slithering down a rock.*

slob /slɑb/ *noun* [C] *(informal)* (used as an insult) a very lazy or messy person

slo·gan /ˈsloʊɡən/ *noun* [C] a short phrase that is easy to remember and that is used in politics or advertising: *Anti-war slogans had been painted all over the walls.* ○ *"Faster than light" is the advertising slogan for the new car.*

slop /slɑp/ *verb* (**slop·ping**; **slopped**) *(informal)* [I,T] (used about a liquid) to spill over the edge of its container, or to cause a liquid to do this: *He filled his glass too full, and some of the beer slopped onto the table.*

☆**slope¹** /sloʊp/ *noun* **1** [C] a piece of land that goes up or down: *We walked down a slope and came to the river.* ○ *a steep/gentle slope* ○ *ski slopes* **2** [sing.] the amount that a surface is not level; the fact of not being level: *a slope of 20 degrees* ○ *The slope of the field makes it really difficult to play on.*

☆**slope²** /sloʊp/ *verb* [I] to not be level or upright; to have a slope (2): *The road slopes down to the river.* ○ *a sloping roof*

slop·py /ˈslɑpi/ *adj.* (**slop·pi·er**; **slop·pi·est**) **1** (used about a piece of work, etc.) not done carefully, neatly or thoroughly **2** (used about a person) careless or messy: *a sloppy worker*

slosh /slɑʃ/ *verb* *(informal)* **1** [I] (used about a liquid) to move around noisily inside a container: *The water sloshed around in the bucket.* **2** [T] to put liquid somewhere in a careless and messy way: *Careful! You're sloshing water all over the floor!*

☆**slot¹** /slɑt/ *noun* [C] **1** a long straight narrow opening in a machine, etc.: *Put your money into the slot and take the ticket.* **2** a place in a schedule, a system, etc.: *The network has moved the program to a later time slot.*

slot² /slɑt/ *verb* [I,T] (**slot·ting**; **slot·ted**) to fit into a particular space: *These two metal pieces slot into the frame here.*

slot ma·chine *noun* [C] a machine on which you can play games and win money. You work it by putting money into a slot and then pushing a button or pulling a handle.

slouch¹ /slaʊtʃ/ *verb* [I] to sit, stand or walk in a lazy way, with your head and shoulders hanging down

slouch² /slaʊtʃ/ *noun*

IDM **be no slouch (at sth/at doing sth)** *(informal)* to be very good at doing sth: *Ashley's a very good tennis player, and she's no slouch at golf, either.*

☆**slow¹** /sloʊ/ *adj.* **1** moving, doing sth or happening without much speed; not fast: *The traffic is always very slow downtown.* ○ *Aren't you finished with your homework yet? You're always so slow!* ○ *a slow improvement in his condition* **2** **slow to do sth; slow (in/about) doing sth** not doing sth immediately: *Jane was slow to react to the news.* ○ *They've been very slow in answering my letter.* **3** not busy, lively or exciting: *Business is pretty slow these days.* **4** not quick to learn or understand: *I'm sorry, but I don't understand what you mean. I must be a little slow.* ○ *a slow learner* **5** showing a time that is earlier than the real time:

That clock is five minutes slow (= e.g. it says it is 8:55 when the correct time is 9:00). —**slowness** *noun* [U]

slow² /sloʊ/ *adv.* at a slow speed; slowly

☞ It is possible to use **slow** as an adverb, but **slowly** is much more common, especially in more formal writing. However, **slow** is often used in compounds: *slow-moving traffic*. The comparative forms **slower** and **more slowly** are both common: *Could you speak a little slower/more slowly, please?*

☆ **slow³** /sloʊ/ *verb* [I,T] to start to move, do sth or happen at a slower speed; to cause sth to do this: *Jane ran along the path for a few minutes and then slowed to a walk.*

PHRV **slow (sb/sth) down/up** to start to move, do sth or happen at a slower speed; to cause sth to do this: *Can't you slow down a little bit? You're driving way too fast.* ○ *These problems have slowed up the whole process.*

☆ **slow·ly** /'sloʊli/ *adv.* at a slow speed; not quickly: *He walked slowly along the street.* ○ *The economy is slowly improving.* ☞ Look at the note at **slow²**.

slow 'motion *noun* [U] (in a movie or on television) a method of making action appear much slower than in real life: *They showed the winning touchdown again, this time in slow motion.*

sludge /slʌdʒ/ *noun* [U] thick, soft mud or waste

slug /slʌg/ *noun* [C] a small animal with a long wet body, that moves slowly along the ground and eats plants. ☞ picture at **snail**.

slug·gish /'slʌgɪʃ/ *adj.* slow-moving; not lively: *This hot weather is making me feel very sluggish.* ○ *sluggish economic growth*

☆ **slum** /slʌm/ *noun* [C] (*also* **the slums** [plural]) an area of a city where living conditions are extremely bad, and where the buildings are dirty and have not been repaired for a long time

slum·ber /'slʌmbər/ *noun* [C] (*old-fashioned*) sleep: *The princess fell into a deep slumber.* —**slum·ber** *verb* [I]

slump¹ /slʌmp/ *verb* [I] **1** to fall or sit down suddenly when your body feels heavy and weak, usually because you are tired or sick: *Her face turned very white, and then suddenly she slumped over the table.* **2** (used about trade, prices, the value of sth, etc.) to fall suddenly and by a large amount: *Shares in the company slumped 33¢ to $1.81 yesterday.*

slump² /slʌmp/ *noun* [C] **1** a sudden large fall in business, the value of sth, etc.: *a slump in house prices* **2** a period when a country's economy is doing very badly and there is a lot of unemployment

slung *p.t., p.p.* of SLING²

slur¹ /slər/ *noun* [C] **a slur (against/on sb/sth)** a false statement or an insult that is

unfair and is intended to harm sb/sth: *Two white students were banned from campus for making racial slurs against a black student.*

slur² /slər/ *verb* [T] (**slur·ring; slurred**) to speak words in a way that is not clear, often because you are drunk

slurp /slərp/ *verb* [I,T] (*informal*) to drink noisily: *I hate the way he slurps when he drinks coffee.* —**slurp** *noun* [C]

slush /slʌʃ/ *noun* **1** [U] snow that has partly melted and that is often very wet and dirty **2** [C,U] a drink that is made from crushed ice with a fruit flavor —**slush·y** *adj.*

slut /slʌt/ *noun* [C] a sexually immoral woman ☞ This word is used as a very strong insult.

sly /slaɪ/ *adj.* **1** (used about a person) good at deceiving people or doing things in secret **2** (used about an action) suggesting that you know sth secret: *a sly smile* —**sly·ly** *adv.*

smack¹ /smæk/ *verb* [T] to hit sb/sth with the inside flat part of your hand: *She smacked him right on the head.*

PHRV **smack of sth** to make you think that sb/sth has an unpleasant attitude or quality: *This change in the admissions policy smacks of racism.* —**smack** *noun* [C]

smack² /smæk/ (*also* **smack-'dab**) *adv.* (*informal*) exactly; right; directly: *He ran right smack into the wall.*

☆ **small** /smɔl/ *adj.* **1** not large in size, number, amount, etc.: *a small car, apartment, town, etc.* ○ *a small group of people* ○ *a small amount of money* **2** young: *He has a wife and three small children.* **3** not important or serious; slight: *Don't worry. It's only a small problem.*

☞ **Small** is the most usual opposite of **big** or **large**. **Little** is often used with another adjective to express an emotion, as well as the idea of smallness: *a sweet little girl* ○ *a nice little house*. The comparative and superlative forms **smaller** and **smallest** are common, and small is often used with words like "fairly," "pretty" and "very": *My room is smaller than yours.* ○ *The town is pretty small.* ○ *a very small car*. **Little** does not usually have a comparative or superlative form in more formal written English.

IDM **in a big/small way** ⇨ WAY¹ —**small** *adv.*: *She painted the picture way too small.*

small 'change *noun* [U] coins that have a low value

small 'claims court *noun* [C,U] a court that deals with cases involving small amounts of money, where people do not need lawyers to speak for them

small·pox /'smɔlpɑks/ *noun* [U] a serious infectious disease that causes a high fever and leaves marks on the skin. In the past, many people died from smallpox.

small-'scale (usually *before* a noun) *adj.* (used about an organization or activity) not

large; limited in what it does: *a small-scale business*

'small talk *noun* [U] polite conversation, e.g. at a party, about unimportant things

☆ **smart¹** /smɑrt/ *adj.* **1** intelligent; able to learn and think quickly: *He's not smart enough to be a politician.* **2** showing good judgment or resulting from quick thinking: *smart investments* ○ *a smart decision* ☛ The opposite for both senses is **dumb**.

smart² /smɑrt/ *verb* [I] to feel a stinging pain in your body: *The smoke made her eyes smart.* ○ *(figurative) He was still smarting from her insult.*

smarts /smɑrts/ *noun* [U] *(informal)* intelligence; the ability to think quickly and in a practical way: *He doesn't have enough smarts to run his own business.*

smash¹ /smæʃ/ *verb* **1** [I,T] **smash sth (up)**; **smash sth open** to break violently into many pieces: *The glass smashed into a thousand pieces.* ○ *The police had to smash the door open.* **2 smash (sth) against, into, through, etc.** [I,T] to move with great force in a particular direction: *The car smashed into a tree.* ○ *He smashed his hand through the window.*

smash /smæʃ/ *noun* [C] *(also* **smash 'hit)** *(informal)* a song, play, movie, etc. that is very successful

smear¹ /smɪr/ *verb* [T] **1 smear sth on/over sth/sb**; **smear sth/sb with sth** to spread a sticky substance across sth/sb: *The little boy had smeared chocolate all over his clothes.* ○ *Her face was smeared with grease.* **2** to say unfavorable and untrue things about an important person in order to damage his/her reputation

smear² /smɪr/ *noun* [C] **1** a mark made by smearing: *a smear of paint on her dress* ☛ Look also at **Pap smear.** **2** something unfavorable and untrue that is said in a newspaper, etc. about an important person

☆ **smell¹** /smɛl/ *verb* **1** [T] to notice, identify or examine sb/sth by using your nose: *He could smell something burning.* ○ *Can you smell gas?* **2** [I] to be able to smell (1): *I can't smell very well because I have a cold.* **3** [I] **smell (like sth)** to have a particular smell: *Dinner smells good!* ○ *This perfume smells like roses.* **4** [I] to have a bad smell: *Your feet smell.*

☛ We do not use **smell** or other verbs of the senses (e.g. **taste, see, hear**) in the continuous tense. Instead we often use **can**, e.g.: *I can smell smoke.* ○ *Do you hear somebody outside?*

☆ **smell²** /smɛl/ *noun* **1** [U] the ability to smell¹(1) : *Dogs have a very good sense of smell.* **2** [C,U] the impression that you get of sth by using your nose; the thing that is smelled: *the great smell of steaks cooking on the grill*

○ *a strong smell* **3** [C] an unpleasant smell (2): *What's that smell?*

☆ **smell·y** /'smɛli/ *adj.* **(smell·i·er; smell·i·est)** *(informal)* having a bad smell: *smelly feet*

☆ **smile** /smaɪl/ *noun* [C] an expression on your face in which the corners of your mouth turn up, showing happiness, pleasure, etc.: *to have a smile on your face* ○ *"It's nice to see you," he said with a smile.* —**smile** *verb* [I]: *She smiled at the camera.* ○ *He was smiling with happiness.*

smirk /smɜrk/ *noun* [C] a silly or unpleasant smile which you have when you are pleased with yourself or think sb/sth is stupid —**smirk** *verb* [I]

smock /smɑk/ *noun* [C] a type of long loose shirt that you wear over your clothes to protect them while you are working, painting, etc.

☆ **smog** /smɑg; smɔg/ *noun* [U] a mixture of fog and smoke, caused by pollution, that is in the air over some cities

☆ **smoke¹** /smoʊk/ *noun* **1** [U] the gas that you can see in the air when something is burning: *Thick smoke poured from the chimney.* ○ *a room full of cigarette smoke* **2** [C, usually sing.] *(informal)* an act of smoking a cigarette, etc.: *He went outside for a quick smoke.*

☆ **smoke²** /smoʊk/ *verb* **1** [I,T] to breathe in smoke through a cigarette, etc. and let it out again; to have the habit of doing this regularly: *Is it all right if I smoke?* ○ *I used to smoke a pack of cigarettes a day.* **2** [I] to give out smoke: *The factory chimneys were smoking.* —**smok·ing** /'smoʊkɪŋ/ *noun* [U]: *She's trying to quit smoking.* —**smok·ing** *adj.*: *I'd like a table in the smoking section.*

smoked /smoʊkt/ *adj.* (used of certain types of food) preserved and given a special taste by being hung in smoke: *smoked salmon*

,**smoke-'free** *adj.* (used about a place) where people are not allowed to smoke cigarettes, etc.: *smoke-free offices*

☆ **smok·er** /'smoʊkər/ *noun* [C] a person who smokes cigarettes, etc.: *She's a chain smoker* (= she finishes one cigarette and then immediately lights another). ☛ The opposite is **nonsmoker.**

smok·y /'smoʊki/ *adj.* **(smok·i·er; smok·i·est)** **1** full of smoke; producing a lot of smoke: *a smoky hallway* ○ *a smoky fire* **2** with the smell, taste or appearance of smoke: *This bacon has a smoky flavor.*

smol·der /'smoʊldər/ *verb* [I] to burn slowly without a flame: *a cigarette smoldering in the ashtray* ○ *(figurative) Her eyes were smoldering with rage.*

☆ **smooth¹** /smuð/ *adj.* **1** having a flat surface with no lumps or holes: *smooth skin* ○ *a smooth piece of wood* **2** (of a liquid mixture) without lumps: *Stir the sauce until it is smooth.* **3** (of a trip in a car, etc.) with an even, comfortable

ər	ɪr	ɛr	ɑr	ɔr	ʊr	ʒ	h	ŋ
bird	near	hair	car	north	tour	vision	hat	sing

movement: *The flight was very smooth.* **4** without difficulties: *The transition from the old method to the new one has been very smooth.* **5** too pleasant or polite to be trusted ☞ We use this word in a critical way, usually about a man or his actions. —**smooth·ness** *noun* [U]

smooth² /smuð/ *verb* [T] **smooth sth (back, down, out, etc.)** to move your hands in the direction mentioned over the surface of sth to make it smooth: *I smoothed the tablecloth out.* ∘ (*figurative*) *They are trying to smooth out the problems in the manufacturing process.*

smooth·ly /'smuðli/ *adv.* without any difficulty: *My work has been going really smoothly.*

smoth·er /'smʌðər/ *verb* [T] **1** to kill sb by not allowing him/her to breathe: *She was smothered with a pillow.* **2** to cover sth (with too much of a substance): *He smothered his toast with jelly.* **3** to stop sth from burning by covering it: *to smother the flames with a blanket*

smudge¹ /smʌdʒ/ *noun* [C] a dirty or messy mark: *His homework was covered in ink smudges.*

smudge² /smʌdʒ/ *verb* **1** [T] to make sth dirty or messy by touching it: *Leave your painting to dry or you'll smudge it.* **2** [I] to become messy, without a clean line around it: *Her lipstick smudged when she kissed him.*

smug /smʌg/ *adj.* (**smugger**; **smuggest**) too pleased with yourself: *Don't look so smug.* ☞ We use this word in a critical way. —**smug·ly** *adv.* —**smug·ness** *noun* [U]

smug·gle /'smʌgl/ *verb* [T] to take things into or out of a country in a way which is against the law; to take a person into or out of a place in secret: *The drugs had been smuggled through customs.* ∘ *The illegal immigrants were smuggled across the border.* —**smug·gler** /'smʌglər/ *noun* [C]: *a drug smuggler* —**smug·gling** /'smʌglɪŋ/ *noun* [U]

☆ **snack¹** /snæk/ *noun* [C] a small amount of food, e.g. cookies or candy, that you eat quickly between main meals: *I had a snack at the mall.*

snack² /snæk/ *verb* [I] to eat a snack instead of a meal or between meals: *Encourage your children to snack on healthy things instead of junk food.*

'**snack bar** *noun* [C] a type of small restaurant where you can buy a snack

snag¹ /snæg/ *noun* [C] a small difficulty or disadvantage that is often unexpected or hidden: *Plans to build the prison hit a snag when local residents started to protest.*

snag² /snæg/ *verb* [T] (**snag·ging**; **snagged**) **1** to catch a piece of clothing, etc. on sth sharp and tear it **2** (*informal*) to succeed in getting sth before other people have a chance to get it: *Quick – let's snag those seats in the front row!*

shell
snail

slug

snail /sneɪl/ *noun* [C] a type of animal with a soft body without legs that is covered by a shell. Snails move very slowly.

'**snail mail** *noun* [U] (*slang*) letters, messages, etc. that are written and sent on paper and not from one computer to another ☞ Look at e-mail.

☆ **snake¹** /sneɪk/ *noun* [C] a type of long thin animal without legs that slides along the ground by moving its body from side to side: *a poisonous snake* ∘ *Todd got bitten by a snake.* ☞ Look also at **rattlesnake**.

snake² /sneɪk/ *verb* [I] (*also* **snake its way**) to move like a snake: *The road snakes its way through the mountains.*

☆ **snap¹** /snæp/ *verb* (**snap·ping**; **snapped**) **1** [I,T] to break suddenly with a sharp noise: *The branch snapped.* ∘ *The weight of the snow snapped the branch in two.* ∘ (*figurative*) *Suddenly, something just snapped and I lost my temper with him.* **2** [I,T] to close quickly with a sharp noise: *The lid of the box snapped shut.* **3** [I,T] to speak or say sth in a quick angry way: *"Do it now!" she snapped.* **4** [I] to try to bite sb/sth: *The dog snapped at the child's hand.* **5** [T] (*informal*) to take a quick photograph of sb/sth

IDM **snap your fingers** to make a sharp noise by moving your middle finger quickly against your thumb

PHRV **snap sth up** to buy or take sth quickly, especially because it is very cheap

snap² /snæp/ *noun* [C] **1** an act or the sound of snapping: *The piece of wood broke with a snap.* **2** a small round metal object with two parts that you press together in order to fasten a piece of clothing ☞ picture at **zipper**.

snap³ /snæp/ *adj.* (*informal*) (only *before* a noun) done quickly and suddenly, often without much careful thought: *a snap decision*

snap·py /'snæpi/ *adj.* (**snap·pi·er**; **snap·pi·est**) (*informal*) quick and lively: *a snappy ad slogan* ∘ *Bring me another cup of coffee – and make it snappy* (= do it quickly)!

snap·shot /'snæpʃɑt/ *noun* [C] a photograph that is taken quickly and informally

snare /snɛr/ *noun* [C] a trap used to catch birds or small animals —**snare** *verb* [T] (*figurative*): *The killer was snared by undercover police.*

snarl¹ /snɑrl/ *verb* [I,T] (used about an animal) to make an angry sound while showing the teeth: *The dog snarled at the stranger.* ∘ (*figurative*) *"Get out of here!" he snarled.*

snarl² /snɑrl/ *noun* [C] **1** an angry sound or remark **2** a mass of hair, threads, etc. that are

S

tʃ	dʒ	v	θ	ð	s	z	ʃ
chin	**June**	**van**	**thin**	**then**	**so**	**zoo**	**she**

twisted together and messy: *Her hair was full of snarls.* ○ *(figurative) traffic snarls*

snatch¹ /snætʃ/ *verb* [T] **1** to (try to) take or pull sth/sb away quickly: *He snatched the gun from her hand.* ○ *My bag was snatched* (= stolen). ☞ Look at **grab**. It is similar in meaning. **2** to take or get sth quickly when you have just enough time to do so: *Kidnappers snatched the newborn baby from the hospital's maternity ward.*

snatch² /snætʃ/ *noun* **1** [sing.] an act of snatching sth: *I made a snatch at the ball.* **2** [C, usually pl.] a short part or period of something: *I heard snatches of conversation from the next room.*

sneak /snik/ *verb* (*p.t., p.p.* **sneaked** or **snuck** /snʌk/) **1** [I] **sneak into, out of, past, etc. sth; sneak in, out, away, etc.** to go very quietly in the direction mentioned, so that no one can see or hear you: *Instead of working, he sneaked out to go shopping.* ○ *The prisoner sneaked past the guards.* **2** [T] (*informal*) to take sth secretly or without permission: *She snuck a piece of candy when no one was looking.*

☞ Many people do not like the use of **snuck**, especially in formal writing. However, it is very common in informal speech.

PHRV **sneak up (on sb/sth)** to approach sb very quietly, especially so that you can surprise him/her

☆**sneak·er** /ˈsnikər/ (*also* **tennis shoe**) *noun* [C] a type of comfortable shoe that you wear to play sports or with informal clothes: *a pair of sneakers* ☞ picture at **shoe**.

sneak·ing /ˈsnikɪŋ/ *adj.* (only *before* a noun) (of feelings, etc.) not expressed; secret: *I have a sneaking suspicion that he's lying.*

sneer /snɪr/ *verb* [I] **sneer (at sb/sth)** to behave or speak as if sth is not good enough for you: *She sneered at his attempts to speak French.* —**sneer** *noun* [C]

coughing

cough/sneeze
handkerchief
sneezing

☆**sneeze** /sniz/ *noun* [C] a sudden burst of air coming out through your nose and mouth that happens, for example, when you have a cold —**sneeze** *verb* [I]: *Dust makes me sneeze.*

snick·er /ˈsnɪkər/ *verb* [I] **snicker (at sb/sth)** to laugh quietly to yourself in an unkind way: *They snickered at his old clothes.* —**snick·er** *noun* [C]

sniff /snɪf/ *verb* **1** [I] to breathe air in through the nose in a way that makes a sound, especially because you have a cold or you are

crying: *Quit sniffing and blow your nose.* **2** [I,T] **sniff (at) sth** to smell sth by sniffing: *"I smell gas," he said, sniffing the air.* ○ *The dog sniffed at the bone.* —**sniff** *noun* [C]

snif·fle /ˈsnɪfl/ *verb* [I] to sniff continuously, especially because you have a cold or you are crying

snip /snɪp/ *verb* [I,T] (**snip·ping; snipped**) to cut using scissors, with a short quick action —**snip** *noun* [C]

snob /snɑb/ *noun* [C] a person who thinks he/ she is better than sb of a lower social class and who admires people who have a high social position: *Don't be such a snob!* —**snob·bish** /ˈsnɑbɪʃ/ (*also* **snobby** /ˈsnɑbi/) *adj.*: *She had a snobbish attitude toward her husband's family.*

snob·ber·y /ˈsnɑbəri/ *noun* [U] behavior or attitudes that are typical of a snob

snoop /snup/ *verb* [I] to look around secretly and without permission in order to find out information, etc.: *If I catch you snooping around here again, I'll call the police!*

snooze /snuz/ *verb* [I] (*informal*) to sleep for a short period of time, especially during the day —**snooze** *noun* [C, usually sing.]: *I had a little snooze on the couch.* ☞ Look at **nap**.

snore /snɔr/ *verb* [I] to breathe noisily through your nose and mouth while you are asleep: *She heard her father snoring in the next room.* —**snore** *noun* [C]

snor·kel /ˈsnɔrkl/ *noun* [C] a short tube that a swimmer who is just below the surface of the water can use to breathe through

snort /snɔrt/ *verb* [I] **1** (used about animals) to make a noise by blowing air through the nose: *The horse snorted in fear.* **2** (used about people) to make a noise through your nose as a way of showing that you do not like sth, or that you are impatient —**snort** *noun* [C]

snot /snɑt/ *noun* [U] (*informal*) the liquid produced by the nose

snout /snaʊt/ *noun* [C] the long nose of certain animals: *a pig's snout*

☆**snow¹** /snoʊ/ *noun* [U] small, soft, white pieces of frozen water that fall from the sky in cold weather: *Three inches of snow fell during the night.* ○ *Most of the snow had melted by early March.* ○ *Greg shoveled the snow off the front steps.* ☞ Look at the note at **weather**.

☆**snow²** /snoʊ/ *verb* [I] (used with the subject *it*) (used of snow) to fall from the sky: *It snowed all night.*

IDM **be snowed in** to be unable to leave home or travel because the snow is too deep

be snowed under to have more work, etc. than you can deal with

☆**snow·ball¹** /ˈsnoʊbɔl/ *noun* [C] a lump of snow that is pressed into the shape of a ball and that children play with and throw

snow·ball² /ˈsnoʊbɔl/ *verb* [I] to quickly grow bigger and bigger or more and more serious,

etc.: *After Ted lost his job, our debts just seemed to snowball until we went bankrupt.*

snow·board
/'snoʊbɔrd/ *noun* [C] a type of wide board that you fasten to both your feet and use for moving down hills or mountains that are covered with snow —**snow·board·ing** *noun* [U]

snowboard
snowboard

snow·drift
/'snoʊdrɪft/ (*also* **drift**) *noun* [C] a deep pile of snow that has been made by the wind

snow·fall /'snoʊfɔl/ *noun* **1** [C] the snow that falls on one occasion: *heavy snowfalls* **2** [U] the amount of snow that falls in a particular place: *What is the average annual snowfall in Ohio?*

☆ **snow·flake** /'snoʊfleɪk/ *noun* [C] one of the small, soft, white pieces of frozen water that fall together as snow

snow·man /'snoʊmæn/ *noun* [C] (*pl.* **snow-men**) /-mɛn/ the figure of a person made out of snow, usually by children

snow·mo·bile
/'snoʊmoʊbil/ *noun* [C] a small vehicle with two parts like skis in the front and special wheels in the back for moving over snow and ice

snowmobile

snow·plow /'snoʊplaʊ/ *noun* [C] a type of vehicle that is used to clear snow away from roads

snow·storm /'snoʊstɔrm/ *noun* [C] a winter storm in which a lot of snow falls, often with strong winds ☞ Look at **blizzard**. It is similar in meaning.

snow·y /'snoʊi/ *adj.* (**snow·i·er**; **snow·i·est**) with a lot of snow: *snowy weather* ○ *a snowy scene*

snub /snʌb/ *verb* (**snub·bing**; **snubbed**) [T] to treat sb rudely, e.g. by refusing to look at or speak to him/her: *His latest movie was snubbed by the awards committee* (= they did not give it an award). —**snub** *noun* [C]: *When they weren't invited to the party, they considered it a snub.*

snuck *p.t., p.p.* of SNEAK

snug /snʌg/ *adj.* **1** warm and comfortable: *The children were snug in bed.* **2** fairly tight: *Make sure your seat belt is snug across your lap.* —**snug·ly** *adv.*

snug·gle /'snʌgl/ *verb* [I] **snuggle (up to sb)**; **snuggle (up)** to get into a position that makes you feel safe, warm and comfortable, usually next to another person: *She snuggled up to her mother.* ○ *I snuggled under the blanket to get warm.*

☆ **so¹** /soʊ/ *adv.* **1** (used to emphasize an adjective or adverb, especially when there is a particular result) to the extent (that); to a great degree: *She's so sick (that) she can't get out of bed.* ○ *He was driving so fast that he couldn't stop.* ○ *I haven't enjoyed myself so much in years.* ○ *So many people came to the concert that some couldn't get in.* ☞ Look at the note at **such**. **2** (*informal*) very: *You've been so nice. How can I thank you?* ○ *Rob is so cute!* ○ *That is so disgusting!* ○ *Thanks so much!* **3** (used in place of something that has been said already, to avoid repeating it): *Are you flying in? If so* (= if you are flying), *I can meet you at the airport.* ○ *"I failed, didn't I?" "I'm afraid so, Susan."*

☞ In formal language, you can refer to actions that somebody has mentioned using **do** with **so**: *If you have not yet paid your bill, please do so* (= pay your bill) *immediately.*

4 (not with verbs in the negative) also, too: *He's a teacher and so is his wife.* ○ *"I've been to New York." "So have I."* ○ *I like singing and so does Helen.* ☞ For negative sentences, look at **neither**. **5** (used to show that you agree that sth is true, especially when you are surprised): *"It's getting late." "So it is. We'd better go."*

IDM **and so on (and so forth)** (used at the end of a list to show that it continues in the same way): *They sell pens, pencils, paper and so on.*

I told you so (used to tell sb that he/she should have listened to your advice): *"I missed the bus." "I told you so. I said you needed to leave earlier."*

it (just) so happens (used to introduce a surprising fact) by chance: *It just so happened that we were going the same way, so he gave me a ride.*

or so (used to show that a number, time, etc. is not exact): *A hundred or so people came to the meeting.*

so as to do sth (*formal*) with the intention of doing sth; in order to do sth: *We must change the law so as to improve its effectiveness.* ○ *They moved silently so as not to scare the animals.*

so long (*informal*) goodbye: *So long! See you next week!*

so much for sth (used for expressing that sth is finished or not helpful): *So much for that diet! I didn't lose any weight at all.*

☆ **so²** /soʊ/ *conj.* **1** with the result that; therefore: *She felt very tired, so she went to bed early.* **2 so (that)** with the purpose that; in order that: *She wore dark glasses so that nobody would recognize her.* **3** (used to introduce a new topic into a conversation): *So, Jason, how's it going in school?* **4** (used to show how one part of a story follows another): *So that's how I first met your mother.*

IDM **so what?; so?** (*informal*) (showing that you think sth is not important) Why should I

care?: *"It's late." "So what? We don't have to go to school tomorrow."*

so³ /soʊ/ *adj.* (not before a noun)
be so to be true: *"Ms. Smith, you claim you were at home on June 14. Is that so?" "Yes, that is so."* ○ *Oh, no! Say it isn't so!*
just so ⇨ JUST²

So. *abbr.* south

soak /soʊk/ *verb* **1** [I,T] to become or make sth completely wet: *Leave the dishes to soak for a while.* ○ *I'm going to soak these pants in hot water to get the stain out.* **2** [I] **soak into/ through sth; soak in** (used about a liquid) to pass into or through sth: *Blood had soaked through the bandage.*
PHRV **soak sth up** to draw sth in (especially a liquid): *I soaked the water up with a cloth.* ○ (*figurative*) *She loves to lie on a beach, soaking up the sunshine.*

soaked /soʊkt/ *adj.* (not before a noun) extremely wet: *I got soaked waiting for my bus in the rain.*

soak·ing /'soʊkɪŋ/ (*also* ˌsoaking 'wet) *adj.* extremely wet

'so-and-so *noun* [C] (*pl.* **so-and-sos**) (*informal*) **1** a person who is not named: *If somebody calls and says, "This is So-and-so and I'm selling storm windows," just hang up.* **2** a person that you do not like (used to avoid saying a swear word): *He's a mean old so-and-so.*

☆**soap** /soʊp/ *noun* **1** [U] a substance that you use for washing and cleaning: *He washed his hands with soap.* ○ *a bar of soap* **2** [C] (*informal*) = SOAP OPERA

'soap ˌopera (also *informal* **soap**) *noun* [C] a story about the lives and problems of a group of people which continues every day or several times a week on television or radio

soap·y /'soʊpi/ *adj.* full of soap: *Wash in plenty of warm soapy water.*

soar /sɔr/ *verb* [I] **1** to fly high in the air: *There were eagles soaring overhead.* **2** to rise very fast: *The plane soared into the air.* ○ *Prices are soaring because of inflation.* **3** to be very high or tall: *The ceiling soars 65 feet above the main hall.*

sob /sɑb/ *verb* [I] (**sob·bing**; **sobbed**) to cry loudly while taking in sudden, sharp breaths; to speak while you are crying: *"He doesn't love me anymore!" she sobbed.* —**sob** *noun* [C]

so·ber¹ /'soʊbər/ *adj.* **1** (of a person) not under the influence of alcohol **2** (of a person or an attitude) serious or thoughtful: *a sober expression* ○ *a sober reminder of just how dangerous drugs can be* **3** (of a color) not bright or likely to be noticed: *a sober gray suit*

so·ber² /'soʊbər/ *verb*
PHRV **sober (sb) up** to become, or to make sb, sober¹(1): *I need a cup of black coffee to sober me up.*

so·ber·ing /'soʊbərɪŋ/ *adj.* making you feel serious: *sobering news*

'so-called *adj.* (only *before* a noun) (used to show that the words you use to describe sb/sth are not correct): *Her so-called friends only wanted her money* (= they are not really her friends).

☆**soc·cer** /'sɑkər/ *noun* [U] a game that is played by two teams of eleven players who try to kick a round ball into a goal: *a soccer game*

so·cia·ble /'soʊʃəbl/ *adj.* enjoying the company of other people; friendly

☆**so·cial** /'soʊʃl/ *adj.* **1** concerning the relations between people or groups of people; relating to the organization of society: *a period of rapid social change* ○ *social problems* **2** concerning the rank of people in society: *We share the same social background.* **3** connected with meeting people and enjoying yourself: *a social club* ○ *She has a busy social life.* **4** (used about

soccer

light
stands
center circle
referee
referee's assistant
forwards (*also* strikers)
sweeper
midfielders
defenders
field
goal
goalkeeper (*also* goalie)
penalty area goal line

animals) living and looking for food together: *Lions are social animals.* —**so·cial·ly** /-ʃəli/ *adv.*: *We work together, but I don't know him socially.*

so·cial·ism /'souʃl·ɪzəm/ *noun* [C] the political theory and practice that is based on the belief that all people are equal, that wealth should be equally divided and that most large businesses and industries should be owned by the government ☞ Look at **capitalism** and **communism.** —**so·cial·ist** /'souʃl·ɪst/ *noun* [C, *adj.*]

so·cial·ize /'souʃl·aɪz/ *verb* **1** [I] **socialize (with sb)** to spend time with people in a friendly way, e.g. at parties, etc. **2** [T] (usually passive) to take control of a business, an industry, etc. away from its private owners and give control to the government: *a socialized economy*

social 'science *noun* [C,U] (*also* **'social studies** [plural]) the study of people in society, including economics, politics and sociology

Social Se'curity *noun* [U] a type of insurance system that is run by the U.S. government, which pays money regularly to people who are old or unable to work: *old people living on Social Security* ∘ *to receive your Social Security check*

Social Se'curity ,number *noun* [C] a number that the U.S. government uses to identify you, and that you use when you fill out official forms, apply for a job, etc.

'social work *noun* [U] work that involves giving help to people with problems because they are poor, unable to work, etc. —**'social worker** *noun* [C]

☆**so·ci·e·ty** /sə'saɪəti/ *noun* (*pl.* **so·ci·e·ties**) **1** [C,U] the people in a country or area, thought of as a group, who have shared customs and laws: *a civilized society* ∘ *in Western society* ∘ *The aim is to create a less violent society.* ∘ *Society's attitude toward women has changed considerably during the last century.* **2** [C] (used especially in names) an organization of people who share a particular interest or purpose: *the Oregon Historical Society*

so·ci·ol·o·gist /ˌsousi'alədʒɪst/ *noun* [C] an expert in sociology

so·ci·ol·o·gy /ˌsousi'alədʒi/ *noun* [U] the study of human societies and social behavior —**so·ci·o·log·i·cal** /ˌsousiə'ladʒɪkl/ *adj.*

☆**sock** /sak/ *noun* [C] a piece of clothing that you wear on your foot and lower leg, inside your shoe: *a pair of socks* ☞ picture on page A26.

IDM knock your socks off ⇨ KNOCK²

sock·et /'sakət/ *noun* [C] **1** = OUTLET(1) **2** a hollow place where sth fits: *your eye socket*

☆**so·da** /'soudə/ *noun* **1** [C,U] (*also* **pop**; **'soda pop**) a sweet drink with bubbles in it that does not contain alcohol **2** [U] (*also* **soda**

water) water that has bubbles in it and is often mixed with alcohol: *a Scotch and soda*

☆**so·fa** /'soufə/ *noun* [C] = COUCH: *a sofa bed* (= a sofa that you can pull out to make a bed)

☆**soft** /sɔft/ *adj.* **1** not hard or firm: *a soft bed* ∘ *The ground is very soft after all that rain.* **2** smooth and nice to touch; not rough: *soft skin, hands, etc.* ∘ *a soft towel* **3** (used about sounds, voices, words, etc.) quiet or gentle; not loud or angry: *She spoke in a soft whisper.* ∘ *soft music in the background* **4** (used about light, colors etc.) gentle and pleasant; not bright: *The room was decorated in soft pinks and greens.* **5** (used about people and animals) (too) kind and gentle; not hard or strict: *They criticized the mayor for being soft on crime.*

IDM have a soft spot for sb/sth (*informal*) to be especially fond of sb/sth: *I've got a soft spot for my old math teacher.* —**soft·ness** *noun* [U]

soft·ball /'sɔfbɔl/ *noun* **1** [U] a team game that is similar to baseball, but played with a slightly larger ball on a slightly smaller field **2** [C] the ball that is used in this game

soft-'boiled *adj.* (used about an egg) boiled inside its shell for a short time so that the yellow part (**the yolk**) is still soft

☆**'soft drink** *noun* [C] a cold drink that contains no alcohol

☆**soft·en** /'sɔfn/ *verb* **1** [I,T] to become softer or gentler; to make sb/sth softer or gentler: *Add one cup softened butter or margarine.* ∘ *The teacher's expression softened as I explained why I was late.* **2** [T] to make sth seem less severe: *to try to soften the effect of bad news*

☆**soft·ly** /'sɔfli/ *adv.* gently or quietly: *"Don't wake the kids up," she whispered softly.*

soft-'spoken *adj.* having a gentle, quiet voice: *He was a kind, soft-spoken man.*

☆**soft·ware** /'sɔftwɛr/ *noun* [U] programs that you use to operate a computer: *There's a lot of educational software available now.* ☞ Look at **hardware.**

sog·gy /'sagi/ *adj.* (**sog·gi·er**; **sog·gi·est**) very wet; having too much liquid in it

☆**soil¹** /sɔɪl/ *noun* **1** [C,U] the substance that plants, trees, etc. grow in; earth: *poor soil* ☞ Look at the note at **ground¹.** **2** [U] the land that is part of a country: *to set foot on American soil* (= to arrive in the U.S.)

soil² /sɔɪl/ *verb* [T] (*formal*) to make sth dirty

so·lar /'soulər/ *adj.* **1** of or relating to the sun: *solar energy* **2** using the sun's energy: *solar heating*

the 'solar ,system *noun* [sing.] the sun and the planets that move around it

sold *p.t., p.p.* of SELL

☆**sol·dier** /'souldʒər/ *noun* [C] a member of an army: *The soldiers marched past.*

'sold-out *adj.* (only *before* a noun) (used about a concert, performance, etc.) for which all the available tickets have been sold

tʃ	dʒ	v	θ	ð	s	z	ʃ
chin	June	van	thin	then	so	zoo	she

☆ **sole¹** /soʊl/ *adj.* (only *before* a noun) **1** only; single: *His sole interest is football.* **2** belonging to one person only; not shared: *My ex-wife has sole custody of our kids.* —**sole·ly** /ˈsoʊlli/ *adv.* *(formal)*: *I agreed to come solely on account of your mother.*

sole² /soʊl/ *noun* **1** [C] the flat part of your foot that you walk on ☞ picture on page A24. **2** [C] the part of a shoe or sock that covers the bottom surface of your foot: *These shoes have leather uppers and synthetic soles.* ☞ picture at **shoe. 3** [C,U] (*pl.* **sole**) a small flat sea fish that can be eaten as food

sol·emn /ˈsɑləm/ *adj.* **1** very serious: *Her solemn face told them that the news was bad.* **2** sincere; done or said in a formal way: *to make a solemn promise* ∘ *a solemn warning* —**so·lem·ni·ty** /səˈlɛmnəti/ *noun* [U] —**sol·emn·ly** *adv.*: *"I have something very important to tell you," she began solemnly.*

so·lic·it /səˈlɪsət/ *verb* *(formal)* **1** [T] to ask sb for money, help, support, etc.: *They tried to solicit support for the proposal.* **2** [I,T] to approach sb, especially in a public place, and offer sex in return for money **3** [I,T] to try to sell sth to sb

so·lic·i·tor /səˈlɪsətər/ *noun* [C] **1** a person who tries to sell things to people: *telephone solicitors* (who call people and try to sell them sth over the telephone) **2** a lawyer who works for the government of the U.S. or of a particular city or state **3** (*BrE*) a lawyer in Britain who gives legal advice to people and prepares legal documents

☆ **sol·id¹** /ˈsɑləd/ *adj.* **1** hard and firm; not in the form of liquid or gas: *It was so cold that the pond was frozen solid.* ∘ *Is the baby eating solid food yet?* **2** having no holes or spaces inside; not hollow: *a solid mass of rock* ∘ *The briefcase was packed solid with $50 bills.* **3** (only *before* a noun) made of the same substance inside and outside: *a solid gold necklace* **4** strong, firm and therefore reliable: *a solid little car* **5** reliable; of sufficient quality and amount: *He was arrested by the police with no solid evidence against him.* **6** without a break or pause: *I slept for twelve solid hours/twelve hours solid.* —**so·lid·i·ty** /səˈlɪdəti/ *noun* [U]

sol·id² /ˈsɑləd/ *noun* [C] **1** a substance or object that is hard; not a liquid or gas: *Liquids become solids when frozen.* **2** an object that has length, width and height, not a flat object: *A cube is a solid.*

sol·i·dar·i·ty /ˌsɑləˈdærəti/ *noun* [U] the support of one group of people for another, because they agree with their aims: *Many local people expressed solidarity with the strikers.*

so·lid·i·fy /səˈlɪdəfaɪ/ *verb* [I,T] (*pres. part.* **so·lid·i·fy·ing**; *3rd pers. sing. pres.* **so·lid·i·fies**; *p.t., p.p.* **so·lid·i·fied**) to become or make sth hard or solid

sol·id·ly /ˈsɑlɪdli/ *adv.* **1** strongly: *a solidly built house* **2** continuously: *It rained solidly all day.*

sol·i·taire /ˌsɑləˈtɛr/ *noun* [U] a card game for one player

sol·i·tar·y /ˈsɑləˌtɛri/ *adj.* **1** alone; without other people: *She lives a solitary life in a remote part of Montana.* **2** (only *before* a noun) one on its own with no others around: *a solitary figure walking up the hillside* **3** (only *before* a noun) only one; single: *I can't think of a solitary example* (= not even one).

ˌ**solitary conˈfinement** (also *informal* **solitary**) *noun* [U] a punishment in which a person in prison is kept completely alone: *to be kept in solitary confinement*

sol·i·tude /ˈsɑlətud/ *noun* [U] the state of being alone: *to live in solitude*

so·lo¹ /ˈsoʊloʊ/ *noun* [C] (*pl.* **so·los**) a piece of music for only one person to play or sing: *a piano solo* ∘ *to sing/play a solo* ☞ Look at **duet**.

so·lo² /ˈsoʊloʊ/ *adj., adv.* (done) alone; by yourself: *a solo flight* ∘ *to fly solo*

so·lo·ist /ˈsoʊloʊɪst/ *noun* [C] a person who plays or sings a piece of music alone

sol·u·ble /ˈsɑlyəbl/ *adj.* that will dissolve in liquid: *These tablets are soluble in water.* ☞ The opposite is **insoluble**.

☆ **so·lu·tion** /səˈluʃn/ *noun* **1** [C] **a solution (to sth)** a way of solving a problem, dealing with a difficult situation, etc.: *a solution to the conflict in the Middle East* **2** [C] **a solution (to sth)** the answer (to a puzzle, etc.): *The solution to the crossword will be published next week.* **3** [C,U] (a) liquid in which sth solid has been dissolved

☆ **solve** /sɑlv/ *verb* [T] to find an answer to or a way of dealing with a problem, question, difficulty, etc.: *The government is trying to solve the problem of inflation.* ∘ *The police have not managed to solve the crime.* ∘ *to solve a puzzle, mystery, etc.* ☞ The noun is **solution**.

sol·vent /ˈsɑlvənt/ *noun* [C,U] a liquid that can dissolve another substance

som·ber /ˈsɑmbər/ *adj.* sad and serious: *a somber mood* —**som·ber·ly** *adv.*

☆ **some** /səm; *strong form* sʌm/ *det., pron.* **1** a certain amount or number: *We need some butter and some potatoes.* ∘ *I don't need any more money – I've still got some.*

☞ In negative sentences and in questions we use **any** instead of **some**: *Do we need any butter?* ∘ *I need some more money. I don't have any.* But look at **2** for examples of questions where **some** is used.

2 (used in questions when you expect or want the answer "yes"): *Would you like some more cake?* ∘ *Can I take some of this paper?* **3** (used when you are referring to certain members of a group or certain types of a thing and not all of them): *Some students enjoy this kind of*

i	ɪ	ɛ	æ	ɑ	ɔ	ʌ	ʊ	u
see	sit	ten	cat	hot	saw	cup	put	too

work; some don't. ○ Some of his books are very exciting. **4** (also **some...or other**) (used for talking about a person or thing whose name you do not know): There's some woman at the door. ○ I read about it in some newspaper or other.

☆ **some·bod·y** /ˈsʌmbʌdi; -bɑdi/ (also **someone** /ˈsʌmwʌn/) pron. a person (not known or not mentioned by name): How are you? Somebody said that you were sick. ○ She's getting married to someone she met at work. ○ There's somebody at the door. ○ I think you should talk to someone else (= another person) about this problem.

☞ **Somebody**, **anybody** and **everybody** are used with a singular verb but are sometimes followed by a plural pronoun (except in formal language): Somebody is coming. ○ Somebody left their coat behind. ○ Does everybody have something to eat? ○ I'll see everybody at work and tell them the news. The difference between **somebody** and **anybody** is the same as the difference between **some** and **any**. Look at the note at **some**.

☆ **some·day** /ˈsʌmdeɪ/ adv. (also **some day**) at some time in the future: I hope you'll come and visit me someday.

☆ **some·how** /ˈsʌmhaʊ/ adv. **1** in a way that is not known or certain: The car's in the shop, but I'll get to work somehow. ○ Somehow we had gotten completely lost. **2** for a reason you do not know or understand: I somehow get the feeling that I've been here before.

☆ **some·one** /ˈsʌmwʌn/ pron. = SOMEBODY

some·place /ˈsʌmpleɪs/ adv. = SOMEWHERE

som·er·sault /ˈsʌmərsɔlt/ noun [C] a movement in which you roll all the way over with your feet going over your head: to do a forward/backward somersault

☆ **some·thing** /ˈsʌmθɪŋ/ pron. **1** a thing that is not known or not named: I've got something in my eye. ○ Wait a minute – I forgot something. ○ Would you like something else (= another thing) to drink? ○ Let's get something to eat. ○ I have something important to tell you.

☞ The difference between **something** and **anything** is the same as the difference between **some** and **any**. Look at the note at **some**.

2 a thing that is helpful, useful or worth considering: There's something in what your mother says.

IDM **have something to do with** to be connected or concerned with: The program has something to do with the environment.

or something (informal) (used for showing that you are not sure about what you have just said): "What's his job?" "I think he's a plumber or something."

something like similar to: A blackberry is something like a raspberry.

☆ **some·time** /ˈsʌmtaɪm/ adv. at a time that you do not know exactly or have not yet decided: I'll call you sometime this evening. ○ I should go and see her sometime.

☆ **some·times** /ˈsʌmtaɪmz/ adv. on some occasions; now and then: Sometimes I drive to work and sometimes I take the bus. ○ I sometimes watch TV in the evenings.

☆ **some·what** /ˈsʌmwʌt/ adv. a little: Somewhat to my surprise, he apologized. ○ The newspaper got somewhat wet in the rain, but we could still read it.

☆ **some·where** /ˈsʌmwɛr/ (also **someplace**) adv. **1** at, in, or to a place that you do not know or name exactly: I saw your glasses somewhere downstairs. ○ "Did they go to the lake?" "No, I think they went somewhere else (= to another place) this year."

☞ The difference between **somewhere** and **anywhere** is the same as the difference between **some** and **any**. Look at the note at **some**.

2 (used when you do not know the exact time, number, etc.): Your ideal weight should probably be somewhere around 140 pounds.

☆ **son** /sʌn/ noun [C] a male child ☞ Look at **daughter**.

☆ **song** /sɔŋ/ noun **1** [C] a piece of music with words that you sing: a folk song **2** [U] the act of singing: to burst into song **3** [C,U] the musical sounds that a bird makes

song·writ·er /ˈsɔŋraɪtər/ noun [C] a person whose job is to write songs

son·ic /ˈsɑnɪk/ adj. connected with sound waves

ˈson-in-law noun [C] (pl. **sons-in-law**) your daughter's husband

☆ **soon** /sun/ adv. **1** not long after the present time or the time mentioned: It will soon be dark. ○ He left soon after me. ○ We should arrive at your house soon after twelve. **2** early; quickly: Don't leave so soon. Stay for dinner. ○ How soon can you get here?

IDM **as soon as** at the moment (that); when: Call me as soon as you hear some news. ○ I'd like your reply as soon as possible (= at the earliest possible moment).

no sooner did/had...than... immediately when or after: No sooner had I shut the door than I realized I'd left my keys inside.

sooner or later at some time in the future; one day: I suppose I'll hear from her sooner or later.

would just as soon do sth ⇨ JUST¹

soot /sʊt/ noun [U] black powder that comes from burning things and collects in chimneys

soothe /suð/ verb [T] **1** to make sb calmer or less upset; to comfort sb: to soothe a crying child **2** to make aches or pains less severe: The doctor gave me some skin cream to soothe

the irritation. —**sooth·ing** *adj.: soothing music* ○ *a soothing massage* —**sooth·ing·ly** *adv.*

so·phis·ti·cat·ed /səˈfɪstəkeɪtəd/ *adj.* **1** having or showing a lot of experience of the world and social situations; knowing about things such as fashion, new ideas, etc.: *She's a very sophisticated young woman.* **2** able to understand difficult or complicated things: *Voters are much more sophisticated these days.* **3** (used about machines, systems, etc.) advanced and complicated: *sophisticated computer equipment* ☞ The opposite is **unsophisticated.** —**so·phis·ti·ca·tion** /səˌfɪstəˈkeɪʃn/ *noun* [U]

☆ **soph·o·more** /ˈsɑfmɔr/ *noun* [C] a student who is in the tenth grade in high school or the second year of college ☞ Look at **freshman**, **junior** and **senior**.

so·pran·o /səˈprænoʊ/ *noun* [C] (*pl.* **so·pran·os** /-noʊz/) the highest singing voice; a woman, girl, or boy with this voice

sor·did /ˈsɔrdəd/ *adj.* unpleasant; not honest or moral: *We discovered the truth about his sordid past.*

☆ **sore¹** /sɔr/ *adj.* painful: *to have a sore throat* ○ *I feel all right after the operation, but my stomach is still very sore.*

IDM a sore point a subject that is likely to make sb upset or angry when mentioned —**sore·ness** *noun* [U]: *You might get some soreness of the skin.*

sore² /sɔr/ *noun* [C] a painful place on the body where the skin is infected

sore·ly /ˈsɔrli/ *adv.* (*formal*) very greatly; very much: *You'll be sorely missed when you leave.*

so·ror·i·ty /səˈrɔrəti; -ˈrɑr-/ *noun* [C] (*pl.* **so·ror·i·ties**) a social organization for female students at some colleges and universities ☞ Look also at **fraternity** (1).

sor·row /ˈsɑroʊ; ˈsɔ-/ *noun* (*formal*) **1** [U] great sadness: *I'd like to express my sorrow at the death of your father.* **2** [C] an event, etc. that causes great sadness: *the joys and sorrows of our relationship* —**sor·row·ful** /-fl/ *adj.* —**sor·row·ful·ly** *adv.*

☆ **sor·ry¹** /ˈsɑri; ˈsɔri/ *adj.* (**sor·ri·er**; **sor·ri·est**) **1** (not before a noun) **sorry (for/about sth)**; **sorry (to do sth/that ...)** (used for apologizing for sth that you have done): *I'm sorry I kept you all waiting.* ○ *I'm really sorry for spilling that wine.* ○ *I'm sorry about not telling you the news earlier.* ○ *I'm sorry to be so late.* ○ *I'm so sorry that I interrupted your meal. I'll call you back later.* ☞ Look at the note at **excuse²**. **2** (not before a noun) **sorry (to do sth/that)**; **sorry (for/about sth)** sad or disappointed: *I was sorry to miss you on Saturday.* ○ *I was sorry not to get the job.* ○ *"Simon's mother died last week." "Oh, I'm sorry."* **3** (used for politely saying "no" to sth, disagreeing with sth or introducing bad news): *"Would you like to come to supper on Friday?" "I'm sorry, I'm*

busy that evening." ○ *I'm sorry, I don't agree with you. I think we should accept the offer.* ○ *We are sorry to inform you that your application has been unsuccessful.* **4** (only *before* a noun) very bad: *the sorry state of education in this school district*

IDM be/feel sorry for sb to feel sympathy or pity for sb: *I feel very sorry for the families of the victims.* ○ *Stop feeling sorry for yourself!*

☆ **sor·ry²** /ˈsɑri; ˈsɔri/ *interj.* **1** (used for apologizing, making excuses, etc.): *Sorry, I didn't see you standing behind me.* ○ *Sorry I'm late – the bus didn't come on time.* ☞ Look at the note at **excuse²**. **2** (used for asking sb to repeat sth you did not hear properly): *"My name's Maggie Wiseman." "Sorry? Maggie who?"*

☆ **sort¹** /sɔrt/ *noun* [C] a type or kind: *What sort of music do you like?* ○ *That's the sort of car I'd like to have.* ○ *different sorts of people* ○ *Every student received an award of some sort.*

IDM a sort of sth; **sort of a sth** (*informal*) a type of sth; sth similar to sth: *Can you hear a sort of ticking noise?*

sort of (*informal*) fairly; in a way: *I feel sort of sick.* ○ *I'd sort of like to go, but I'm not sure.*

☆ **sort²** /sɔrt/ *verb* [T] to put things into different groups or places so that they are organized correctly: *I'm just sorting these papers into the right files.* ○ *The computer will sort the words into alphabetical order.*

PHRV sort sth out 1 to organize sth or make sth clean and neat: *It will take time to sort out all this information.* **2** to find an answer to a problem: *I haven't found an apartment yet, but I hope to sort something out soon.*

sort through sth to go through a number of things, in order to organize them or find sth that you are looking for

SOS /ˌɛs oʊ ˈɛs/ *noun* [sing.] a call or signal from sb/sth that needs help, especially a ship or plane

'so-,so *adj., adv.* (*informal*) all right, but not really good/well: *"How are you?" "So-so."*

sought *p.t., p.p.* of SEEK

'sought-,after *adj.* (usually *before* a noun) that people want very much, because it is of high quality or rare

☆ **soul** /soʊl/ *noun* **1** [C] the part of a person that is believed to continue to exist after the body is dead: *Christians believe that their souls go to heaven when they die.* **2** [C,U] deep feeling and thought: *The music was performed perfectly, but it lacked soul.* **3** [C] (used with adjectives expressing affection or pity) person: *She's a kind old soul.* **4** [sing.] (in negative statements) a person: *There wasn't a soul in sight* (= there was nobody). **5** [U] (*also* **'soul music**) a type of popular African-American music which expresses deep feelings: *a soul singer*

soul·ful /ˈsoʊlfl/ *adj.* having or showing deep feeling: *a soulful expression*

☆ **sound¹** /saʊnd/ *verb* **1** [I] to give a particular impression when heard or heard about; to seem: *That sounds like a child crying.* ○ *She sounded upset and angry on the phone.* ○ *The rain sounds heavy.* ○ *You sound like my mother!* ○ *He sounds like a very nice person from his letter.* ○ *It doesn't sound as if he's very reliable.* ○ *Your idea sounds pretty good – let's give it a try.* **2** [T] to cause sth to make a sound: *to sound the horn of your car*

IDM **raise/sound the alarm** ⇨ ALARM¹

PHRV **sound sb out** to ask sb questions in order to find out what he/she thinks or intends: *I'm going to sound out the boss about my proposal.*

☆ **sound²** /saʊnd/ *noun* **1** [C] something that you hear or that can be heard: *the sound of voices* ○ *She opened the door without a sound.* **2** [U] what you hear; impressions received by hearing: *Light travels faster than sound.* ○ *sound waves* **3** **the sound** [sing.] the loudness on a television, radio, etc.: *Can you turn the sound up/down?* **4** [C] a long, fairly wide area of water that connects two large bodies of water

IDM **the sound of sth** the impression that you have of sth when you hear or read about it: *She must be an interesting person, by the sound of it.* ○ *I don't like the sound of these new regulations.*

☆ **sound³** /saʊnd/ *adj.* **1** healthy and strong; in good condition: *a sound state of health* ○ *The structure of the bridge is basically sound.* **2** sensible; that you can rely on: *sound advice*

IDM **safe and sound** ⇨ SAFE¹ —**sound·ness** *noun* [U]

sound⁴ /saʊnd/ *adv.*

IDM **be sound asleep** to be deeply asleep

ˈsound bite *noun* [C] a part of speech by a politician, etc. which is broadcast on television and radio and is short enough for people to remember

ˈsound ef·fects *noun* [plural] sounds other than speech or music that are used in a play, movie, computer game, etc. to create the required effect

sound·ly /ˈsaʊndli/ *adv.* thoroughly or deeply: *Our team was soundly beaten this afternoon.* ○ *The children were sleeping soundly.*

sound·proof /ˈsaʊndpruf/ *adj.* made so that no sound can get in or out

sound·track /ˈsaʊndtræk/ *noun* [C] the recorded sound and music from a movie or computer game

☆ **soup** /sup/ *noun* [U] liquid food made by cooking meat, vegetables, etc. in water: *chicken soup* ○ *a can of soup*

ˈsoup kitchen *noun* [C] a place where very poor people can go to get meals for free or for a very low cost

☆ **sour** /ˈsaʊər/ *adj.* **1** having a sharp taste like that of a lemon: *sour pickles* **2** (used especially about milk) tasting or smelling bad because it is no longer fresh **3** having or showing a bad temper; unpleasant: *a sour expression*

IDM **go/turn sour** to become unpleasant or unsatisfactory: *Their relationship turned sour after a few months.*

sour ˈgrapes pretending to dislike or not to want sth when you secretly want it but cannot have it: *She said she didn't want to come to the party anyway, but I think that was just sour grapes.* —**sour·ly** *adv.* —**sour·ness** *noun* [U]

☆ **source** /sɔrs/ *noun* [C] **1** a place, person or thing where sth comes or starts from or where sth is obtained: *Sales tax is an important source of income for the state.* ○ *the source of the Nile* (= the place where the river starts) **2** a person, book, etc. that supplies information: *Police have refused to reveal the source of their information.*

ˌsour ˈcream *noun* [U] a type of thick cream with a sour taste, used in cooking and as a sauce on foods

☆ **south** /saʊθ/ *noun* [sing.] (*abbr.* **S.**; **So.**) **1** (*also* **the south**) one of the four main points of the compass; the direction that is on your right when you face the sunrise: *warm winds from the south* ○ *Which way is south?* ☞ picture at **north**. **2** **the south** the part of any country, city, etc. that lies farther toward the south than other parts: *Temperatures will be lower across the whole state, with some snow in the south.* **3** **the South** the southeastern states of the U.S., especially the states that fought against the northern states in the Civil War ☞ Look also at **Deep South**.

☆ **south²** /saʊθ/ *adj.* in or toward the south, or from the south: *the south coast of the island* ○ *The new offices will be on the city's south side.* ○ *a south wind*

☆ **south³** /saʊθ/ *adv.* to or toward the south: *If you keep going south, you will soon reach the freeway.* ○ *We live just south of Chicago.* ○ *The house faces south.*

IDM **down south** in or to the states in the southeastern U.S.: *We all headed down south for our spring vacation.*

south·bound /ˈsaʊθbaʊnd/ *adj.* traveling or leading toward the south: *the southbound lanes of I-95*

☆ **south·east¹** /ˌsaʊθˈist/ *noun* [sing.] (*abbr.* **SE**) **1** (*also* **the southeast**) the direction or point of the compass that is between south and east ☞ picture at **north**. **2** (*also* **the southeast**) a region that is toward the southeast: *the southeast of the country*

☆ **south·east²** /ˌsaʊθˈist/ *adj., adv.* in, from or to the southeast of a place or country: *the coast of southeast Florida* ○ *Continue southeast for about ten miles.*

south·east·er·ly /ˌsaʊθˈistərli/ *adj.* **1** toward

S

the southeast: *in a southeasterly direction*
2 (used about a wind) coming from the southeast

south·east·ern /ˌsaʊθˈistərn/ *adj.* in or from the southeast of a place or country

south·east·ward /ˌsaʊθˈistwərd/ *adv.* toward the southeast: *Follow the highway southeastward.*

south·er·ly /ˈsʌðərli/ *adj.* **1** to, toward or in the south: *Keep going in a southerly direction.* **2** (used about winds) coming from the south: *a southerly wind*

☆**south·ern** (*also* **Southern**) /ˈsʌðərn/ *adj.* of, in or from the south of a place: *Los Angeles is in southern California.* ○ *She speaks with a southern accent.*

south·ern·er (*also* **Southerner**) /ˈsʌðərnər/ *noun* [C] a person who was born in or lives in the southern part of a country, especially the southeastern U.S.

the ˌSouth ˈPole *noun* [sing.] the point on the surface of the Earth which is farthest south ☞ picture at **earth**.

south·ward /ˈsaʊθwərd/ *adj., adv.* toward the south: *in a southward direction*

south·west[1] /ˌsaʊθˈwɛst/ *noun* [sing.] (*abbr.* **SW**) **1** (*also* **the southwest**) the direction or point of the compass that is between south and west ☞ picture at **north**. **2** (*also* **the southwest; the Southwest**) a region that is toward the southwest of a place or country. In the U.S., this includes Arizona, New Mexico and southern California: *paintings that show scenes of the old Southwest*

☆**south·west**[2] /ˌsaʊθˈwɛst/ *adj., adv.* in, from or to the southwest of a place or country: *the southwest coast of France* ○ *If you look southwest, you can see the ocean.*

south·west·er·ly /ˌsaʊθˈwɛstərli/ *adj.* **1** toward the southwest: *in a southwesterly direction* **2** (used about a wind) coming from the southwest

south·west·ern /ˌsaʊθˈwɛstərn/ *adj.* in or from the southwest of a place or country: *southwestern Italy*

south·west·ward /ˌsaʊθˈwɛstwərd/ *adv.* toward the southwest: *Follow the road southwestward.*

☆**sou·ve·nir** /ˌsuvəˈnɪr; ˈsuvənɪr/ *noun* [C] something that you buy and keep to remind you of a place where you have been on vacation or of a special event

sov·er·eign[1] /ˈsavərən; ˈsavrən/ *adj.* (usually *before* a noun) (used about a country) not controlled by any other country; independent

sov·er·eign[2] /ˈsavərən; ˈsavrən/ *noun* [C] a king or queen

sov·er·eign·ty /ˈsavrənti/ *noun* [U] the power that a country has to control its own government

the Soviet Union /ˌsoʊviət ˈyunyən; -viət-/ *noun* [sing.] a large country that formerly

existed in eastern Europe and northern Asia, including what is now Russia, Ukraine, Kazakhstan and several other countries. The Soviet Union had a Communist government. —**Soviet** *noun* [C], *adj.*

sow[1] /saʊ/ *noun* [C] an adult female pig ☞ Look at the note at **pig**.

sow[2] /soʊ/ *verb* [T] (*p.t.* **sowed**; *p.p.* **sown** /soʊn/ or **sowed**) **sow A (in B); sow B (with A)** to plant seeds in the ground: *to sow seeds in the garden* ○ *to sow a field with wheat*

soy·bean /ˈsɔɪbin/ *noun* [C] a type of bean that can be used to make food products such as artificial meat and milk

ˈsoy sauce *noun* [U] a dark brown sauce that is made from soybeans and that you add to food, especially Chinese or Japanese food

spa /spa/ *noun* [C] (*pl.* **spas**) a place where people go to relax, exercise, eat healthy foods and have health and beauty treatments, especially as a vacation

☆**space**[1] /speɪs/ *noun* **1** [C,U] an area that is empty or not used: *Is there enough space for me to park the car there?* ○ *a parking space* ○ *We're a little short of space.* ○ *There's a space here for you to write your name.* ○ *wide open spaces* (= empty areas of countryside) ☞ Look at **room** and the note at **place**[1]. **2** [U] (*also* ˌ**outer ˈspace**) the area which surrounds the Earth and all the other planets and stars: *Sally Ride was the first American woman to go into space.* ○ *space travel* **3** [C, usually sing.] a period of time: *Mandy has been sick three times in the space of four months.*

space[2] /speɪs/ *verb* **1** [T] **space sth (apart/ out)** to arrange things so that there are spaces between them **2** [I] **space (out)** (*slang*) to stop paying close attention and start thinking about nothing in particular

☆**space·craft** /ˈspeɪskræft/ *noun* [C] (*pl.* **spacecraft**) a vehicle that travels in space

space·ship /ˈspeɪsʃɪp/ *noun* [C] a vehicle in which people can travel into space

ˈspace ˌshuttle (*also* **shuttle**) *noun* [C] a vehicle in which people can travel into space, that can be used more than once

spa·cious /ˈspeɪʃəs/ *adj.* having a lot of space or room; large in size —**spa·cious·ness** *noun* [U]

☆**spade** /speɪd/ *noun* **1** [C] a tool that you use for digging. A spade has a long wooden handle and a flat, often pointed, piece of metal (**a blade**) at one end. ☞ Look at **shovel**. **2 spades** [plural] the group (**suit**) of playing cards with pointed black leaves on them: *the king of spades* ☞ picture and note at **card**. **3** [C] one of the cards from this suit: *Do you have a spade?*

☆**spa·ghet·ti** /spəˈgɛti/ *noun* [U] a type of Italian food (**pasta**) made from flour and water, that looks like long strings: *I'll cook some spaghetti.* ○ *spaghetti sauce*

i	ɪ	ɛ	æ	a	ɔ	ʌ	ʊ	u
see	sit	ten	cat	hot	saw	cup	put	too

span¹ /spæn/ *noun* [C] **1** the length of sth from one end to the other: *the span of a bridge* **2** the length of time that sth lasts or continues: *Young children have a short attention span.*

span² /spæn/ *verb* [T] (**span·ning; spanned**) **1** to form a bridge over sth: *The river is spanned by a concrete bridge.* **2** to last or continue for a particular period of time: *Her career in politics spanned more than fifty years.*

spank /spæŋk/ *verb* [T] to hit a child on his/ her buttocks with an open hand as a punishment

☆ **spare¹** /spɛr/ *adj.* (only *before* a noun) **1** extra; kept available for use in case it is needed: *The spare tire is kept in the trunk.* ○ *a spare room* **2** not used for work: *What do you do in your spare time?*

spare² /spɛr/ *noun* [C] an extra thing of the same kind that you can use: *I blew a fuse. Where do you keep your spares?*

☆ **spare³** /spɛr/ *verb* [T] **1** to be able to give sb/sth to sb: *Can you spare any change?* ○ *I am very grateful that you could spare the time to see me.* **2** to not hurt or damage sb/sth: *to spare sb's life* **3** to use as little as possible of sth: *No expense was spared at the wedding.* **4** to stop sb from having a bad experience: *I told him what happened, but spared him all the details.*

IDM **to spare** more than is needed: *There's no time to spare. We need to leave right away.*

ˌ**spare** ˈ**part** *noun* [C] a part for a machine, engine, etc. that you can use to replace an old part which is damaged or broken

spar·ing·ly /ˈspɛrɪŋli/ *adv.* (*formal*) using only a little of sth; carefully: *to use sth sparingly*

spark¹ /spɑrk/ *noun* [C] **1** a small bright piece of burning material **2** a flash of light that is caused by electricity: (*figurative*) *a spark of anger*

spark² /spɑrk/ *verb* [T] to cause sth: *Eric's comments sparked a tremendous argument.*

spar·kle /ˈspɑrkl/ *verb* [I] to shine with many small points of light: *The river sparkled in the sunlight.* ○ (*figurative*) *Patty's eyes sparkled with excitement.* —**spar·kle** *noun* [C,U]

spar·kling /ˈspɑrklɪŋ/ *adj.* **1** that sparkles: *sparkling blue eyes* **2** (used about wine or water) with bubbles in it: *sparkling white wine* **3** very clean: *sparkling floors and counters*

spark·plug /ˈspɑrkplʌg/ *noun* [C] the small piece of equipment that produces sparks in an engine

spar·row /ˈspæroʊ/ *noun* [C] a small brown bird that is very common

sparse /spɑrs/ *adj.* small in quantity or amount: *a sparse crowd* —**sparse·ly** *adv.*: *a sparsely populated area* —**sparse·ness** *noun* [U]

Spar·tan (*also* **spartan**) /ˈspɑrtn/ *adj.* (*formal*)

very simple and not comfortable: *Spartan living conditions*

spasm /ˈspæzəm/ *noun* [C,U] a sudden tightening of a muscle that you cannot control: *painful muscular spasms in the leg*

spat *p.t., p.p.* of SPIT¹

spate /speɪt/ *noun* [sing.] a sudden large number or amount of sth: *a spate of robberies in town*

spa·tial /ˈspeɪʃl/ *adj.* (*formal*) connected with the size or position of sth

spat·u·la /ˈspætʃələ/ *noun* [C] (*pl.* **spat·u·las**) a kitchen tool with a wide flat blade and a long handle, that is used for turning or lifting food

☆ **speak** /spik/ *verb* (*p.t.* **spoke** /spoʊk/; *p.p.* **spoken** /ˈspoʊkən/) **1 speak (to sb) (about sb/sth)** [I] to talk or say things: *I'd like to speak to the manager, please.* ○ *Could you speak more slowly?* ○ *I was so angry I could hardly speak.*

☞ **Speak** and **talk** have almost the same meaning, although **speak** is slightly more formal. In addition, **talk** is more likely to be used about a conversation, while **speak** is often used when only one person is saying something: *Speaking personally, I'm all in favor of the idea.* ○ *We talked all night.* ○ *I ought to speak to Ben's parents about his bad behavior.*

2 [T] to know and be able to use a language: *Does anyone here speak German?* ○ *a French-speaking guide* **3** [I] **speak (on/about sth)** to make a speech to a group of people: *Professor Hurst has been invited to speak on British foreign policy.* **4** [I] **speak (to sb)** (*informal*) (usually in negative sentences) to be friendly with sb: *They had an argument and now they're not speaking to each other.*

IDM **be on speaking terms (with sb)** to be friendly with sb (after an argument): *Thankfully, they are back on speaking terms again.*

so to speak (used when you are describing sth in an unusual way or in a way which is not strictly true): *She lost her head, so to speak, when the fire alarm rang.*

speak for itself to be very clear so that no other explanation is needed: *The statistics speak for themselves.*

speak your mind to say exactly what you think, even though you might offend sb

PHRV **speak for sb** to express the thoughts or opinions of sb else: *I cannot speak for my colleagues.*

speak out (against sth) to say clearly and publicly that you think sth is bad or wrong

speak up to speak louder

☆ **speak·er** /ˈspikər/ *noun* [C] **1** a person who makes a speech to a group of people: *Tonight's speaker is a well-known writer.* **2** (*also formal*

S

loudspeaker) the part of a radio, stereo system, etc. from which the sound comes out **3** a person who speaks a particular language: *a native Russian speaker*

spear /spɪr/ *noun* [C] a long pole with a sharp point at one end, used for hunting or fighting

spear·head /ˈspɪrhɛd/ *verb* [T] to lead an attack, etc.: *The Environmental Agency is spearheading the campaign.*

spear·mint /ˈspɪrmɪnt/ *noun* [U] a type of leaf with a fresh taste that is used in candy, etc.: *spearmint chewing gum* ☞ Look at **peppermint**.

☆ **spe·cial**[1] /ˈspɛʃl/ *adj.* **1** not usual or ordinary; important for some particular reason: *He shouldn't get special treatment just because he's famous.* ○ *a special occasion* ○ *Are you doing anything special tonight?* **2** (only *before* a noun) for a particular purpose: *special education for children with learning difficulties* ○ *There's a special tool for doing that.*

spe·cial[2] /ˈspɛʃl/ *noun* [C] **1** something, such as a television program, that is not usual or ordinary but is made or done for a particular occasion: *a prime-time news special on TV* **2** something, such as a meal in a restaurant, or a product in a store that is available for only a short time or at a lower price than usual: *Today's special is roast beef and mashed potatoes.*

☆ **spe·cial·ist** /ˈspɛʃl·ɪst/ *noun* [C] a person with special or deep knowledge of a particular subject: *My doctor sent me to see a heart specialist.*

spe·cial·ize /ˈspɛʃl·aɪz/ *verb* [I] **specialize (in sth)** to give most of your attention to one subject, type of product, etc.: *This store specializes in clothes for big and tall men.* ○ *a lawyer who specializes in divorce cases* —**spe·cial·i·za·tion** /ˌspɛʃl·əˈzeɪʃn/ *noun* [U]

spe·cial·ized /ˈspɛʃl·aɪzd/ *adj.* to be used for a particular purpose: *a specialized system* ○ *specialized training*

☆ **spe·cial·ly** /ˈspɛʃl·i/ *adv.* (usually before a past participle) for a particular purpose or reason: *These dogs have been specially trained to find smuggled drugs.* ○ *a specially designed chair for people with back problems*

spe·cial·ty /ˈspɛʃl·ti/ *noun* [C] (*pl.* **specialties**) **1** an area of study or a subject that you know a lot about **2** something made by a person, place, business, etc. that is very good and that they are famous for: *The chef's specialty is baked salmon in a cream sauce.*

☆ **spe·cies** /ˈspiʃiz; -siz/ *noun* [C] (*pl.* **species**) a group of plants or animals that are very similar to each other and that can breed together: *an endangered species*

☆ **spe·cif·ic** /spəˈsɪfɪk/ *adj.* **1** detailed or exact: *You need to give the class specific instructions on what they should do.* **2** particular; not general: *Everyone was given a specific job to do.*

—**spe·cif·i·cal·ly** /-kli/ *adv.*: *paper manufactured specifically for laser printers* ○ *I specifically told you not to do that.*

spec·i·fi·ca·tion /ˌspɛsəfəˈkeɪʃn/ *noun* [C, usually pl.] detailed information about how sth has been or must be built or made: *The parts that were supplied do not meet our technical specifications.*

spec·i·fy /ˈspɛsəfaɪ/ *verb* [T] (*pres. part.* **specifying**; *3rd pers. sing. pres.* **specifies**; *p.t., p.p.* **specified**) to say or name sth clearly or in detail: *Please specify any dates when you are not available.* ○ *The regulations specify the maximum number of people the building can hold.*

spec·i·men /ˈspɛsəmən/ *noun* [C] **1** an example of a particular type of thing, often studied by experts or scientists: *There is a fine specimen of that type of tree in Yosemite National Park.* **2** a small amount of sth that is tested for medical or scientific purposes: *Specimens of the patient's blood were tested in the hospital laboratory.*

speck /spɛk/ *noun* [C] a very small spot or mark: *a speck of dust* ○ *The car was just a tiny speck on the horizon.*

spec·ta·cle /ˈspɛktəkl/ *noun* [C,U] something that is impressive, interesting or unusual to look at: *the thrilling spectacle of the New Year's Day parade*

spec·ta·cles /ˈspɛktəklz/ *noun* [plural] (*old-fashioned, formal*) = GLASSES

spec·tac·u·lar /spɛkˈtækyələr/ *adj.* very impressive, interesting or attractive: *The view from the top of the hill is really spectacular.* ○ *a spectacular display of fireworks* —**spec·tac·u·lar·ly** *adv.*

☆ **spec·ta·tor** /ˈspɛkteɪtər/ *noun* [C] a person who watches a show, sports game, etc.

spec·ter /ˈspɛktər/ *noun* [C, usually sing.] **the specter (of sth)** an idea that frightens you because of sth bad that might happen in the future: *the specter of unemployment*

spec·trum /ˈspɛktrəm/ *noun* [C, usually sing.] (*pl.* **spectra** /ˈspɛktrə/ or **spectrums**) **1** the set of seven colors into which white light can be separated: *You can see the colors of the spectrum in a rainbow.* **2** a full or wide range of sth: *speakers representing the whole spectrum of political opinions*

spec·u·late /ˈspɛkyəleɪt/ *verb* **1** [I,T] **speculate (about/on sth)** to think about sth without having all the facts or information: *to speculate about the outcome of the next election* **2** [I] to buy and sell with the aim of making money but with the risk of losing it: *to speculate on the stock market* —**spec·u·la·tor** /-leɪtər/ *noun* [C] —**spec·u·la·tion** /ˌspɛkyəˈleɪʃn/ *noun* [C,U]: *The report prompted speculation that the company would have to close one of its factories.* ○ *stock market speculation*

sped *p.t., p.p.* of SPEED[2]

ər	ɪr	ɛr	ɑr	ɔr	ʊr	ʒ	h	ŋ
bird	near	hair	car	north	tour	vision	hat	sing

☆ **speech** /spitʃ/ *noun* **1** [U] the act of speaking or the state of being able to speak: *to lose the power of speech* ○ *freedom of speech* (= to say your opinions openly) **2** [U] the particular way of speaking of a person or group of people: *She's writing a paper on children's speech patterns.* **3** [C] a formal talk that you give to a group of people: *The mayor is going to make a speech to city businesspeople.* ○ *to give a speech*

speech·less /'spitʃləs/ *adj.* not able to speak, e.g. because you are shocked, very angry, etc.: *His remark left the group totally speechless.*

☆ **speed¹** /spid/ *noun* **1** [U] fast movement: *to gather/pick up speed* ○ *With a final burst of speed, Jackson won the race.* **2** [C,U] the rate at which sb/sth moves or travels: *The car was traveling at a speed of 40 miles an hour.* ○ *to travel at high speed*

speed² /spid/ *verb* [I] (*p.t., p.p.* **sped** /spɛd/ or **speed·ed**) **1** to go or move very quickly: *He sped around the corner on his bicycle.* ○ *The fire engine sped past us.* **2** (only used in the continuous tenses) to drive a car, etc. faster than the legal speed limit: *The police said she had been speeding.*

PHRV **speed (sth) up** (to cause sth) to go faster: *plans to speed up mail delivery* ○ *The traffic sped up once it reached the expressway.*

speed·boat /'spidbout/ *noun* [C] a small fast boat with an engine

speed·ing /'spidɪŋ/ *noun* [U] the act of driving a car, etc. faster than the legal speed limit: *Maria got a speeding ticket on I 90 yesterday.*

☆ **speed ,limit** *noun* [C, usually sing.] the highest speed that you may drive without breaking the law on a particular piece of road

speed·om·e·ter /spɪ'dɑmətər/ *noun* [C] a piece of equipment in a car, etc. that tells you how fast you are traveling

speed·way /'spidweɪ/ *noun* [C] a type of track that is specially built for car or motorcycle racing

speed·y /'spidi/ *adj.* (**speed·i·er**; **speed·i·est**) fast; quick: *to make a speedy recovery from an illness* —**speed·i·ly** *adv.*

☆ **spell¹** /spɛl/ *verb* (*p.t., p.p.* **spelled** /spɛld/ or **spelt** /spɛlt/) **1** [I,T] to write or say the letters of a word in the correct order: *I never learned to spell very well in school.* ○ *How do you spell your last name?* ○ *His name is spelled P-H-I-L-I-P.* **2** [T] (used about a set of letters) to form a particular word: *A-I-S-L-E spells "aisle."* **3** [T] to mean; to have sth as a result: *Another poor harvest would spell disaster for the region.*

PHRV **spell sth out 1** to write or say the letters of a word or name in the correct order **2** to explain sth in detail or in a very clear way

spell² /spɛl/ *noun* **1** [C] a short period of time: *the recent cold spell* **2** [usually sing.] (in stories, etc.) a state or condition that was caused by magic, or the special words that sb says in order to use magic: *The evil witch cast a spell on the prince.* ○ (*figurative*) *He's completely under her spell.*

☆ **spell·ing** /'spɛlɪŋ/ *noun* **1** [C,U] the way that a word is spelled: *My grandfather changed the spelling of his name when he came to America.* **2** [U] the act of using letters to form words, or the ability to spell words correctly: *Roger is very good at spelling.*

'spelling bee *noun* [C] a competition in which children take turns spelling words out loud. The child who can spell the most words correctly is the winner.

☆ **spend** /spɛnd/ *verb* (*p.t., p.p.* **spent** /spɛnt/) **1** [I,T] **spend (sth) (for/on sth)** to give or pay money for sth: *How much do you spend on food each week?* ○ *You can't keep on spending like that if you want to retire early.* **2** [T] to pass time: *I spent a whole evening writing letters.* ○ *I'm spending the weekend at my parents' house.* ○ *He spent two years in Rome.*

☆ **spend·ing** /'spɛndɪŋ/ *noun* [U] the giving of large amounts of money by an organization to pay for services such as education: *The government wants to increase spending on health care.*

sperm /spərm/ *noun* **1** [C] (*pl.* **sperm** or **sperms**) a very small cell that is produced by a male animal and that can join with a female egg to create a new life **2** [U] the liquid that contains sperm

sphere /sfɪr/ *noun* [C] **1** any round object shaped like a ball ☞ picture at **cube**. **2** an area of interest or activity: *Many countries are having difficulties in the economic sphere.* —**spher·i·cal** /'sfɪrɪkl; 'sfɛr-/ *adj.*

☆ **spice¹** /spaɪs/ *noun* **1** [C,U] a substance (especially a powder) that is made from part of a plant and used to give flavor to food: *I use a lot of herbs and spices in my cooking.* ○ *Pepper and paprika are two common spices.* **2** [U] excitement and interest: *to add spice to a drama*

spice² /spaɪs/ *verb* [T] **1 spice sth (with sth)** to add spice¹(1) to food **2 spice sth (up) (with sth)** to add excitement to sth

☆ **spic·y** /'spaɪsi/ *adj.* (**spic·i·er**; **spic·i·est**) containing spice: *Mexican food is very spicy.*

spider

spider

web

spi·der /'spaɪdər/ *noun* [C] a type of small animal (like an insect) with eight legs. Spiders make (**spin**) special nets (**webs**) to catch insects for food.

tʃ	dʒ	v	θ	ð	s	z	ʃ
chin	June	van	thin	then	so	zoo	she

spike /spaɪk/ *noun* [C] a piece of metal, wood, etc. that has a sharp point at one end: *an iron fence with spikes on the top*

spill

He **spilled** his milk.

☆ **spill¹** /spɪl/ *verb* [I,T] (to cause a liquid) to pour out from sth by accident: *I spilled some wine on the carpet.* ○ *(figurative) There were so many people that the party spilled over into the neighbors' yard.*

IDM **spill the beans** (*informal*) to tell a person sth when you are supposed to be keeping it secret

spill² /spɪl/ *noun* [C] an act of spilling (a large amount of) sth; the amount that is spilled: *an oil spill* ○ *Clean up any spills immediately.*

☆ **spin¹** /spɪn/ *verb* (**spin·ning**; *p.t., p.p.* **spun** /spʌn/) **1** [I,T] **spin (sth) (around)** (to cause sth) to turn around quickly: *Mary spun around when she heard someone call her name.* ○ *(figurative) After three glasses of whiskey, my head was spinning.* **2** [I,T] to make thread from a mass of wool, cotton, etc.

spin² /spɪn/ *noun* **1** [C] an act of spinning (1): *The car skidded on the ice and went into a spin.* **2** [U] fast turning motion: *to put some spin on a ball* (= in sports like pool, tennis, etc.) **3** [sing., U] a way of reporting about a person or an event that is intended to influence the public's opinion of him/her/it: *White House aides attempted to put a positive spin on the reports of budget cuts.* ☞ Look also at **spin doctor**.

spin·ach /'spɪnɪtʃ/ *noun* [U] a plant with large green leaves that can be cooked and eaten as a vegetable

spi·nal /'spaɪnl/ *adj.* connected with the bones of the back (**the spine**)

'spin ,doctor *noun* [C] a person who works for sb else, e.g. for a politician, and tries to give the public a favorable impression of that person and his/her actions

spine /spaɪn/ *noun* [C] **1** the bones of the back of a person or animal **2** one of the sharp points on some plants and animals **3** the narrow part of a book that you can see when it is on a shelf

spin·off (*also* **spin-off**) /'spɪnɔf; -ɑf/ *noun* [C] **1** a useful result that you did not expect **2** a television program whose main characters were originally less important characters on another, earlier program

spin·ster /'spɪnstər/ *noun* [C] (*old-fashioned*) a woman who has never been married ☞ **Bachelor** can be used about a man of any

age, but you usually use **spinster** when you are talking about an older woman.

spi·ral¹ /'spaɪrəl/ *noun* [C] a long curve that goes around and around a central point —**spi·ral** *adj.*: *a spiral staircase*

spi·ral² /'spaɪrəl/ *verb* [I] to move upward or downward in a spiral, especially very quickly: *Food prices are spiraling out of control.*

spire /'spaɪər/ *noun* [C] a tall pointed tower on the top of a church, etc.

☆ **spir·it** /'spɪrɪt/ *noun* **1** [C] the part of a person that many people believe still exists after his/her body is dead: *the spirits of the dead* **2** [C] a ghost or being that exists but that does not have a body: *the Holy Spirit* **3** [U] energy, strength of mind or courage: *The constant setbacks finally broke his spirit.* **4** [C,U] the mood or attitude of mind of sb/sth: *the spirit of goodwill in the holiday season* ○ *to be in high/low spirits* (= in a happy/sad mood) ○ *Everyone got into the spirit of the party* (= joined in with enthusiasm). ○ *the American spirit of enterprise and innovation* **5** [U] a strong feeling of loyalty toward a group, an organization, etc. and of wanting to help it: *fun activities to build school spirit* ○ *community spirit* **6** [U] the real and intended meaning of a rule, agreement, etc.: *Judges should consider the spirit as well as the letter of the law.* **7** **spirits** [plural] = LIQUOR

spir·it·ed /'spɪrɪtəd/ *adj.* lively and full of energy: *The President gave a spirited defense of his policies.* ○ *a spirited debate*

☆ **spir·i·tu·al¹** /'spɪrɪtʃuəl; -tʃəl/ *adj.* **1** concerning your deep thoughts, feelings or emotions: *to fulfill your spiritual needs* ☞ Look at **material**. **2** concerning a church or religion: *Tibet's exiled spiritual leader, the Dalai Lama* —**spir·i·tu·al·ly** *adv.*

spir·i·tu·al² /'spɪrɪtʃuəl; -tʃəl/ *noun* [C] a religious song, often expressing deep feelings, that was first sung by African-Americans when they were slaves in the southern U.S.

☆ **spit¹** /spɪt/ *verb* [I,T] (**spit·ting**; *p.t., p.p.* **spat** /spæt/ *or* **spit**) **spit (sth) (out)** to send liquid, food, etc. out from your mouth: *No spitting allowed!* ○ *You're not allowed to chew gum in class – spit it out.*

spit² /spɪt/ *noun* [U] (*informal*) the liquid in your mouth ☞ Look at **saliva**.

☆ **spite** /spaɪt/ *noun* [U] the desire to hurt or annoy sb: *He stole her letters out of* (= because of) *spite.*

IDM **in spite of sth** (used to show that sth did not have the result or effect that you would have expected): *The game was played in spite of the bad weather.* ○ *In spite of all her hard work, Sue failed the test.*

☆ **splash¹** /splæʃ/ *verb* [I,T] (to cause a liquid) to fly in drops and make sb/sth wet: *The girls were splashing each other with water.* ○ *They were splashing around in the pool.* ○ *Be careful not to splash paint onto the floor.*

☆ **splash²** /splæʃ/ *noun* [C] **1** an act or sound of splashing: *Paul jumped into the pool with a big splash.* **2** a mark or spot that was made by sth splashing: *splashes of oil on the stove* **3** a bright area of color: *Flowers add a splash of color to a room.*

splat·ter /'splætər/ *verb* [I,T] (used about a liquid) to splash and make sb/sth wet or dirty; to make a liquid do this: *The paint was splattered all over the floor.*

splen·did /'splɛndəd/ *adj.* **1** very good; excellent: *a splendid example of early American art* **2** of impressive or grand appearance: *a splendid Gothic cathedral* —**splen·did·ly** *adv.*

splen·dor /'splɛndər/ *noun* [U] beauty that is grand and that impresses people: *They spent $10 million to restore the hotel to its former splendor.*

splint /splint/ *noun* [C] a piece of wood or metal that is used to keep a broken bone in the right position

splin·ter¹ /'splintər/ *noun* [C] a small thin sharp piece of wood, metal or glass that has broken off a larger piece: *I have a splinter in my finger.* ○ (*figurative*) *a radical splinter group* (= that has separated from the main group)

splin·ter² /'splintər/ *verb* [I,T] to break into small thin sharp pieces

☆ **split¹** /split/ *verb* (*pres. part.* **split·ting**; *p.t., p.p.* **split**) **1** [I,T] **split (sb) (up) (into sth)** (to cause people) to divide into different groups: *Let's split into two groups.* ○ *The students have been split into five groups according to their ability.* ○ *Voters are split over the issue of gun control.* **2** [T] to divide or share sth: *We split the cost of the meal between us.* **3** [I,T] **split (sth) (into sth)** to break into two or more parts, usually from end to end, making a long line: *My grocery bag split open.*

PHRV split up (with sb) to end a marriage or relationship: *He split up with his girlfriend.*

split² /split/ *noun* [C] **1** a division in a group: *Disagreement about foreign policy led to a split within the Republican party.* **2** a long cut or hole in sth

‚**split 'second** *noun* [C] a very short period of time: *It only took me a split second to decide.*

splurge /splərdʒ/ *verb* [I] **splurge (on sth)** (*informal*) to spend a lot of money on sth that you do not really need: *We splurged on lunch at the Ritz.*

☆ **spoil** /spɔɪl/ *verb* **1** [T] to make sth useless or unsuccessful, or not as good as before: *The new apartment building will spoil the view.* ○ *Our vacation was spoiled by bad weather.* ○ *Eating between meals will spoil your appetite.* **2** [T] to do too much for sb, especially a child, so that you have a bad effect on his/her character: *Her son is such a spoiled brat!* **3** [I] (used about food) to begin to decay and therefore not be good to eat or drink: *These vegetables have*

spoiled. **4** [T] to treat sb/yourself very well for a certain period of time in order to make this person/yourself happy: *Sometimes I spoil my wife and take her breakfast in bed.*

spoils /spɔɪlz/ *noun* [plural] things that have been stolen, or taken in a war or battle

spoke¹ /spouk/ *noun* [C] one of the thin pieces of metal that connect the center of a wheel to the outside edge ☞ picture at **bicycle**.

spoke² *p.t.* of SPEAK

spoken *p.p.* of SPEAK

☆ **spokes·man** /'spouksmən/ *noun* [C] (*pl.* **spokes·men** /-mən/) a person who is chosen to speak for a group or organization

☞ A woman is called a **spokeswoman**. **Spokesperson** is now often preferred because it can be used for a man or a woman.

☆ **sponge** /spʌndʒ/ *noun* [C,U] a piece of rubber or plastic (or of a natural substance also called "sponge"). Sponges have many small holes, soak up water and are used for cleaning things or for washing yourself.

☆ **spon·sor¹** /'spɑnsər/ *noun* [C] **1** a person or an organization that helps to pay for a special sports event, etc. or pays for an event or program to be broadcast on television (usually so that it can advertise its products) **2** a person who agrees to pay money to a charity if sb else completes a particular activity: *I need sponsors for a marathon in aid of cancer research.* **3** a person who suggests or supports a proposal for a new law: *She is a chief sponsor of the new anti-drug legislation.* —**spon·sor** *verb* [T]: *A large soft drink company is sponsoring the next basketball tournament.* ○ *a bill sponsored by Senator Nancy Kassebaum* —**spon·sor·ship** *noun* [U]: *Corporate sponsorship has brought millions of dollars into tennis.*

spon·ta·ne·ous /spɑn'teɪniəs/ *adj.* done or happening naturally; not planned: *a spontaneous burst of applause* —**spon·ta·ne·ous·ly** *adv.* **spon·ta·ne·i·ty** /ˌspɑntə'neɪəti; ˌspɑntn-eɪ-/ *noun* [U]

spook·y /'spuki/ *adj.* (**spook·i·er**; **spook·i·est**) (*informal*) frightening: *The house is dark and spooky.*

spool /spul/ *noun* [C] a round object that thread, film, wire, etc. are wound around when you buy them ☞ Look at **reel**.

☆ **spoon¹** /spun/ *noun* [C] an object with a round end and a long handle that you use for eating, stirring or serving food: *Give each person a knife, fork and spoon.* ○ *a wooden spoon for cooking*

spoon² /spun/ *verb* [T] to lift or serve sth with a spoon: *Spoon the mixture into a pan.*

spoon·ful /'spunfʊl/ *noun* [C] the amount that one spoon can hold: *a spoonful of sugar*

spo·rad·ic /spə'rædɪk/ *adj.* not done or happening regularly: *There have been sporadic*

outbursts of gunfire during the night. —**spo·rad·i·cal·ly** /-ˈkli/ *adv.*

☆ **sport¹** /spɔrt/ *noun* [C, U] a physical game or activity that you do for exercise or because you enjoy it: *Soccer is my favorite sport.* ○ *John played a lot of sports when he was in high school.* ○ *an Olympic sport* ○ *amateur/ professional sports* ○ *the sports section of the newspaper*

IDM **a good sport** a person who reacts in a good way when things do not go well for him/ her

sport² /spɔrt/ *verb* [T] to wear or have sth in order to impress other people: *She showed up sporting her new baseball cap.*

sport·ing /ˈspɔrtɪŋ/ *adj.* (only *before* a noun) connected with sports: *a sporting event* ○ *sporting goods*

sports car *noun* [C] a low, fast car, often with a roof that you can open

sports·man /ˈspɔrtsmən/ *noun* [C] (*pl.* **sports·men** /-mən/) a man who enjoys hunting wild animals and fishing

sports·man·ship /ˈspɔrtsmənʃɪp/ *noun* [U] good behavior and fair play in sports

☆ **spot¹** /spɑt/ *noun* [C] **1** a particular place or area: *The Grand Canyon is a popular vacation spot.* **2** a small round mark of a different color on sth: *Leopards have dark spots.* **3** a small dirty mark on sth: *You have a spot of gravy on your shirt.* **4** a short item of entertainment or an advertisement on television or the radio: *a thirty-second TV spot*

IDM **have a soft spot for sb/sth** ⇨ SOFT

on the spot at the same time and place as sth else that is happening or that just happened: *Paul was caught stealing money and was fired on the spot.*

put sb on the spot to make sb answer a difficult question or make a difficult decision without having much time to think

spot² /spɑt/ *verb* [T] (**spot·ting; spot·ted**) to see or notice sb/sth: *The suspect was spotted at Miami International Airport.*

spot check *noun* [C] a test on one of a group of people or things which is not planned or expected

spot·less /ˈspɑtləs/ *adj.* having no spots¹(3) or marks; very clean: *Her house is always spotless.* ○ (*figurative*) *She has a spotless record of public service.*

spot·light /ˈspɑtlaɪt/ *noun* **1** [C] a lamp that can send a strong beam of light onto a small area. Spotlights are often used in theaters. ☞ picture at **light. 2 the spotlight** [sing.] the center of public attention or interest: *to be in the spotlight*

spouse /spaʊs/ *noun* [C] your husband or wife

☞ **Spouse** is a formal or official word, used on forms, documents, etc.

spout¹ /spaʊt/ *noun* [C] a tube or pipe through which liquid comes out

spout² /spaʊt/ *verb* [I,T] **1** (used about a liquid) to come out from sth with force; to make a liquid do this: *The broken pipe spouted several gallons of water per minute.* **2** (*informal*) to say sth, using a lot of words, in a way that is not interesting: *He spouted racist remarks all through dinner.*

sprain /spreɪn/ *verb* [T] to injure part of your body by bending or turning it suddenly: *to sprain your ankle* —**sprain** *noun* [C]: *Your wrist isn't broken. It's just a bad sprain.*

sprang *p.t.* of SPRING²

sprawl /sprɔl/ *verb* [I] **1** to sit or lie with your arms and legs spread out: *kids sprawling on the couch, watching TV* **2** to cover a large area of land (in a way that is not planned): *The city sprawls across 40 square miles.* —**sprawl** *noun* [U]: *suburban sprawl* —**sprawled** /sprɔld/ *adj.* (not before a noun): *They were all sprawled on the floor when I came in.* —**sprawl·ing** *adj.*: *the sprawling suburbs*

☆ **spray¹** /spreɪ/ *noun* **1** [U] liquid in very small drops that is blown through the air: *the spray of a fountain* **2** [C,U] liquid in a special can that is forced out under pressure when you push a button: *hair spray* ○ *spray paint*

spray

spray

can

☆ **spray²** /spreɪ/ *verb* [I,T] (used about a liquid) to be sent out in very small drops with great force; to send a liquid out in this way: *The water sprayed out from the hole in the pipe.* ○ *Somebody sprayed paint on my door!* ○ *Somebody sprayed my door with paint.*

☆ **spread¹** /sprɛd/ *verb* (*p.t., p.p.* **spread**) **1** [T] **spread sth (out) (on/over sth)** to open or arrange sth so that you can see all of it: *Jenny's homework was spread out on the kitchen table.* **2** [T] **spread A on B; spread B with A** to cover a surface with a soft substance: *to spread butter on bread* ○ *to spread bread with butter* **3** [I,T] to affect a larger area or a bigger group of people; to make sth do this: *Violence has spread throughout the region.* ○ *Rats and flies spread disease.* **4** [I] to continue for a great distance: *The swamp spreads for several miles along the coast.* **5** [T] **spread sth (over sth)** to divide sth so that it continues for a longer period of time: *You can spread your payments over a period of three years.*

PHRV **spread (sb/yourself) out** to move away from the others in a group of people: *The police spread out to search the whole area.*

spread² /sprɛd/ *noun* **1** [U] the act of spreading sth or being spread: *Dirty drinking water encourages the spread of disease.* **2** [C,U] soft food that you eat on bread: *Don't eat butter.*

ər	ɪr	ɛr	ɑr	ɔr	ʊr	ʒ	h	ŋ
bird	near	hair	car	north	tour	vision	hat	sing

Use a low-fat spread. **3** [C] a newspaper or magazine article that covers one or more pages: *a four-page spread* **4** [C] a large farm or open area of land: *My grandfather owns a 1500-acre spread in New Mexico.*

spread·sheet /'sprɛdʃit/ *noun* [C] a computer program for working with rows of numbers, used especially for calculating business profits, sales, payments, etc.

spree /spri/ *noun* [C] (*informal*) a time when you go out and do a lot of sth that you enjoy: *a shopping spree*

sprig /sprɪg/ *noun* [C] a small piece of a plant with leaves on it

spring

☆ **spring¹** /sprɪŋ/ *noun* **1** [C,U] the season of the year which follows winter and comes before summer. In spring the weather gets warmer and plants begin to grow: *a cold, wet spring* ○ *in the spring of 1998* ○ *There's a feeling of spring in the air.* **2** [C] a place where water comes up naturally from under the ground: *a hot spring* **3** [C] a long piece of thin metal or wire that is bent around and around. After you push or pull a spring it goes back to its original shape and size: *bed springs* **4** [C] an act of jumping up or moving quickly: *With one spring, the cat landed on the table.*

☆ **spring²** /sprɪŋ/ *verb* (*p.t.* **sprang** /spræŋ/; *p.p.* **sprung** /sprʌŋ/) [I] **1** to jump or move quickly: *When the alarm went off, Ray sprang out of bed.* ○ *to spring to your feet* ○ (*figurative*) *Everyone sprang to her defense when the boss started criticizing her.* **2 spring from sth** to be the result of: *Her behavior springs from fear.*

PHRV spring sth on sb (*informal*) to tell sb sth that is a surprise or not expected: *I hate to spring this on you, but can you get me that data by tomorrow?*

spring up to appear or develop quickly or suddenly: *Internet cafes are springing up everywhere.*

spring·board /'sprɪŋbɔrd/ *noun* [C] a low board that you jump on before jumping into water, over sth, etc. It helps you jump higher.

‚spring 'break *noun* [C,U] a vacation for high school or college students in the spring

☆ **spring·time** /'sprɪŋtaɪm/ *noun* [U] the period of spring

sprin·kle /'sprɪŋkl/ *verb* [T] **1 sprinkle A (on/onto/over B); sprinkle B (with A)** to throw drops of water or small pieces of sth over a surface: *to sprinkle sugar on cereal* ○ *to sprinkle cereal with sugar* **2** [I] to rain lightly

sprin·kler /'sprɪŋklər/ *noun* [C] a piece of equipment that sends out water in small drops. Sprinklers are used on grass and for putting out fires in buildings: *a sprinkler system*

sprint¹ /sprɪnt/ *verb* [I,T] to run a short distance as fast as you can

sprint² /sprɪnt/ *noun* [C] a short run or a short fast race

sprout¹ /spraʊt/ *verb* [I,T] (used about a plant) to begin to grow or to produce new leaves: *The seeds are sprouting.*

sprout² /spraʊt/ *noun* [C] **1** a new part that has grown on a plant **2** a young plant that is used as a vegetable: *bean sprouts* ☞ Look also at **Brussels sprout.**

spruce¹ /sprus/ *noun* [C,U] a type of tree with thin sharp leaves

spruce² /sprus/ *verb*

PHRV spruce (sb/sth/yourself) up to make sb/sth/yourself clean or attractive

sprung *p.p.* of SPRING²

spun *p.p.* of SPIN¹

spunk·y /'spʌŋki/ *adj.* (*informal*) having a lot of energy or courage: *a spunky cheerleader*

spur¹ /spər/ *noun* [C] **1** a sharp piece of metal that a rider wears on the back of his/her boots to help control a horse and to make it go faster **2** something that encourages you or that makes sth happen more quickly

IDM on the spur of the moment without planning; suddenly: *I decided to go on the spur of the moment.*

spur² /spər/ *verb* [T] (**spur·ring; spurred**) to encourage sb to do sth; to make sth increase more quickly: *new policies designed to spur economic growth*

spurn /spərn/ *verb* [T] (*formal*) to refuse sth that sb has offered to you: *to spurn an offer of friendship*

spurt¹ /spərt/ *verb* [I,T] (used about a liquid) to come out with great force; to make a liquid do this: *Blood spurted from the wound.*

spurt² /spərt/ *noun* [C] **1** a stream of liquid that comes out suddenly and with great force **2** a sudden increase in speed or effort: *a growth spurt*

sput·ter /'spʌtər/ *verb* **1** [I] to make a series of sounds like a person spitting or coughing: *He fell into the pool and came up coughing and sputtering.* ○ *The engine suddenly sputtered and stopped.* **2** [I,T] to speak with difficulty e.g. because you are very angry or excited: *"How dare you!" she sputtered.*

spy¹ /spaɪ/ *noun* [C] (*pl.* **spies**) a person who tries to get secret information about another country, person or organization

spy² /spaɪ/ *verb* (*pres. part.* **spy·ing**; *3rd pers. sing. pres.* **spies**; *p.t., p.p.* **spied**) **1** [I] **spy (on sb/sth)** to try to get (secret) information about sb/sth ☞ Look at **espionage.** **2** [T] (*formal*) to see: *They spied a campfire in the distance.*

sq. *abbr.* square

squab·ble /'skwɑbl/ *verb* [I] to argue in a

tʃ	dʒ	v	θ	ð	s	z	ʃ
chin	June	van	thin	then	so	zoo	she

noisy way about sth that is not very important
—**squab·ble** *noun* [C]

squad /skwɑd/ *noun* [C] a group of people who work as a team: *the rescue squad*

'squad car *noun* [C] a police car

squad·ron /ˈskwɑdrən/ *noun* [C] a group of soldiers, military ships or airplanes, etc.

squal·id /ˈskwɑləd/ *adj.* very dirty, messy and unpleasant: *squalid housing conditions*

squall /skwɔl/ *noun* [C] a sudden storm with strong winds

squal·or /ˈskwɑlər/ *noun* [U] the state of being very dirty, messy or unpleasant: *to live in squalor*

squan·der /ˈskwɑndər/ *verb* [T] to waste time, money, etc.: *Karen squandered everything she earned on clothes and music.*

☆ **square¹** /skwɛr/ *adj.* **1** having four straight sides of the same length: *a square table* **2** shaped like a square: *a square face* ○ *a dress with a square neck* **3** (*abbr.* **sq.**) (used for talking about the area of sth): *If a room is 12 feet long and 10 feet wide, its area is 120 square feet.* **4** (used about sth that is square (1) in shape) having sides of a particular length: *The picture is eight inches square* (= each side is eight inches long). **5** not owing any money: *Here is the $10 I owe you. Now we're square.* **6** (*informal*) (used about a person) unfashionable and uncomfortable in social situations
IDM **a square meal** a good meal that makes you feel full

☆ **square²** /skwɛr/ *noun* [C] **1** a shape that has four sides of the same length and four angles of 90 degrees (**right angles**): *There are 64 squares on a chess board.* ☞ picture at **shape**. **2** (*also* **Square**) (*abbr.* **sq.; Sq.**) an open space in a town or city that has buildings all around it: *Times Square in New York City* ○ *the market square* **3** the number that you get when you multiply another number by itself: *Sixteen is the square of four.* ☞ Look at **square root**.

square³ /skwɛr/ *verb* **1** [I,T] **square (sth) with sth** to agree, or make sth agree, with sth else: *Your conclusion doesn't really square with the facts.* **2** [T] to multiply a number by itself

square⁴ /skwɛr/ *adv.* (*informal*) directly: *to look sb square in the eye*
IDM **fair and square** ⇨ FAIR²

'square dance *noun* [C] a traditional American country dance for four couples who face each other, forming a square

square·ly /ˈskwɛrli/ *adv.* directly: *I think the blame falls squarely on her.*

,square 'root *noun* [C] a number that produces another particular number when it is multiplied by itself: *The square root of sixteen is four.* ☞ Look at **square²(3)**.

squash¹ /skwɑʃ; skwɔʃ/ *verb* **1** [T] to damage or crush sth by pressing it hard so that it becomes flat: *Carlos squashed a cockroach with his shoe.* **2** [I,T] to go into a place, or

move sb/sth to a place, where there is not much space: *We all squashed into the back of the car.*

squash² /skwɑʃ; skwɔʃ/ *noun* [C,U] a type of large heavy fruit with thick skin that is cooked and eaten as a vegetable

squat¹ /skwɑt/ *verb* [I] (**squat·ting; squat·ted**) **1** to sit down with your feet on the ground and your knees bent and your buttocks just above the ground **2** to go and live in an empty building without permission from the owner

squat² /skwɑt/ *adj.* (**squat·ter; squat·test**) short and fat or thick: *an ugly, squat building*

squat·ter /ˈskwɑtər/ *noun* [C] a person who squats(2) in a building

squawk /skwɔk/ *verb* [I] (used especially about a bird) to make a loud unpleasant noise
—**squawk** *noun* [C]

squeak /skwik/ *verb* [I,T] to make a short high noise that is not very loud: *Dave's new shoes squeaked as he walked.* ○ *I heard a mouse squeaking.* —**squeak** *noun* [C] —**squeak·y** *adj.*: *squeaky brakes* ○ *a squeaky voice*

squeal /skwil/ *verb* [I,T] to make a loud high noise that is a sign of pain, fear or enjoyment: *The baby squealed with delight at the new toy.* —**squeal** *noun* [C]: *The car stopped with a squeal of tires.* ☞ A **squeal** is louder and longer than a **squeak**, but it is not as loud as a **scream**.

squea·mish /ˈskwimɪʃ/ *adj.* (used about a person) easily upset by sth unpleasant, e.g. the sight of blood

☆ **squeeze¹** /skwiz/ *verb* **1** [T] **squeeze sth (out); squeeze sth (from/out of sth)** to press sth hard for a particular purpose: *She squeezed his hand and wished him luck.* ○ *to squeeze a tube of toothpaste* ○ *to squeeze an orange/a lemon* (= to get the juice) ○ *to squeeze juice from an orange* **2** [I,T] **squeeze (sb/sth) into, through, etc. sth; squeeze (sb/sth) through, in, past, etc. sth**, to go or move sb/sth into, through, etc. a place where there is not much space: *Excuse me. Can I squeeze past?* ○ *We can squeeze another person into the back of the car.* ○ (*figurative*) *Do you think you can squeeze in another appointment this afternoon?*

squeeze

squeezing

squeeze² /skwiz/ *noun* **1** [C] an act of squeezing (1) sb/sth, e.g. as a sign of love or affection: *Doug gave my shoulder a squeeze.* ☞ Look at **hug**. **2** [sing.] a situation where there is not much space: *It was a tight squeeze to get everybody in the car.* **3** [C] the amount of liquid that you get from squeezing an orange, a lemon, etc.: *a squeeze of lemon* **4** [C, usually sing.] a difficult situation in which there is not enough money, time, etc.: *A budget squeeze forced Congress to reduce spending.*

squelch /skwɛltʃ/ *verb* [T] to stop sth, e.g. an idea, from continuing: *to squelch a rumor*

squid /skwɪd/ *noun* [C] (*pl.* **squids** or **squid**) a sea animal with a long, soft body and ten long arms (**tentacles**)

squint /skwɪnt/ *verb* [I] to look at sth with your eyes almost closed: *to squint in bright sunlight*

squirm /skwɜrm/ *verb* [I] to move your body in a way which shows you are uncomfortable, bored or embarrassed

squir·rel /ˈskwɜrəl/ *noun* [C] a small brown-ish-gray animal with a long thick tail that lives in trees and eats nuts

squirt /skwɜrt/ *verb* [I,T] (used about a liquid) to be forced out from sth in a thin fast stream; to make a liquid move in this way; to hit sb/sth with a liquid in this way: *I squeezed the bottle and mustard squirted out.* ○ *He squirted water at me from a hose.* ○ *He squirted me with water.*

St. *abbr.* **1** Saint: *St. Peter* **2** Street: *220 Jefferson St.*

☆ **stab¹** /stæb/ *verb* [T] (**stab·bing**; **stabbed**) to push a knife or other pointed object into sb/sth: *The man was stabbed fourteen times.*

stab² /stæb/ *noun* [C] **1** an injury that was caused by a knife, etc.: *a stab wound* **2** a sudden sharp pain: *a stab of pain* ○ (*figurative*) *a stab of guilt*

IDM take a stab at sth/doing sth (*informal*) to try to do sth: *I'll take a stab at painting your portrait.*

stab·bing /ˈstæbɪŋ/ *noun* [C] an occasion when sb stabs sb else: *There have been two stabbings in the neighborhood this week.*

sta·bi·lize /ˈsteɪbl·aɪz/ *verb* [I,T] to become or to make sth unlikely to move, change or end: *The patient's condition has stabilized.* ○ *The government has tried to stabilize prices.* ☞ The opposite is **destabilize**.

☆ **sta·ble¹** /ˈsteɪbl/ *adj.* not likely to move, change or end: *This ladder doesn't seem very stable.* ○ *The patient is in stable condition.* ○ *a stable relationship* ☞ The opposite is **unstable**. —**sta·bil·i·ty** /stəˈbɪləti/ *noun* [U]: *After so much change, we now need a period of stability.*

sta·ble² /ˈsteɪbl/ *noun* [C] a building where horses are kept

☆ **stack¹** /stæk/ *noun* [C] **1** a neat pile of sth: *a stack of plates, books, etc.* **2 the stacks** [plural] the area of a library with many shelves where most of the books are kept

stack² /stæk/ *verb* [T] **stack sth (up)** to put sth into a pile: *Could you stack those chairs for me?*

☆ **sta·di·um** /ˈsteɪdiəm/ *noun* [C] (*pl.* **sta·di·ums** or (*formal*) **sta·di·a** /-diə/) a large sports ground with rows of seats around it: *a football stadium*

☆ **staff** /stæf/ *noun* [C, usually sing.] **1** the group of people who work for a particular organization: *the hospital's administrative staff*

☞ **Staff** is usually used in the singular. We say **a staff member** (NOT **a staff**) to talk about one person who works for an organization.

2 the people who work at a school, college, or university, but do not teach students (e.g. secretaries, library employees, etc.): *faculty, staff and administrators* —**staff** *verb* [T] (usually passive): *The service department is staffed by trained professionals.*

stag /stæg/ *noun* [C] = BUCK¹(2)

☆ **stage¹** /steɪdʒ/ *noun* **1** [C] one part of the progress or development of sth: *The first stage of the project lasts for three weeks.* ○ *the early stages of the game* ○ *At this stage, it's too early to say what will happen.* **2** [C] a raised floor in a theater or concert hall, etc. on which actors, musicians, etc. perform: *to go on stage* **3** [sing., U] the world of theater; the profession of acting in front of people in a theater: *a star of stage and screen*

☆ **stage²** /steɪdʒ/ *verb* [T] **1** to organize a performance of a play, concert, etc. for the public **2** to organize an event: *to stage a protest march*

stage·coach /ˈsteɪdʒkoʊtʃ/ *noun* [C] a type of vehicle, pulled by horses, that was used in past times to carry passengers over a fixed route, often over long distances

stag·ger /ˈstægər/ *verb* **1** [I] to walk in an unsteady way, as if you are going to fall down, e.g. because you are sick, drunk or carrying sth heavy **2** [T] to arrange a number of events so that they do not all happen at the same time

stag·ger·ing /ˈstægərɪŋ/ *adj.* that you find difficult to believe: *a staggering $2 billion profit* —**stag·ger·ing·ly** *adv.*

stag·nant /ˈstægnənt/ *adj.* **1** (used about water) not flowing and therefore dirty and having a bad smell **2** (used about business, etc.) not active; not developing: *a stagnant economy*

stag·nate /ˈstægneɪt/ *verb* [I] to not be active; not to develop or change: *a stagnating economy* —**stag·na·tion** /stægˈneɪʃn/ *noun* [U]

☆ **stain** /steɪn/ *verb* [I,T] to leave a colored mark that is difficult to remove: *Don't spill any of that red wine. It'll stain the carpet.* —**stain** *noun* [C]: *The blood left a stain on his shirt.*

stained glass *noun* [U] pieces of colored glass that are used in church windows, etc.: *a stained-glass window*

stain·less steel /ˌsteɪnləs ˈstil/ *noun* [U] steel that does not stain or rust: *a stainless steel pan*

☆ **stair** /stɛr/ *noun* **1 stairs** [plural] a series of steps that lead from one level of a building to another: *The elevator wasn't working, so I had*

S

ə	y	w	t̬	eɪ	aɪ	ɔɪ	aʊ	oʊ
about	yes	woman	butter	say	five	boy	now	go

to use the stairs. ○ at the bottom/top of the stairs ○ two flights (= sets) of stairs ○ I heard somebody coming down the stairs. ○ She ran up the stairs. ☞ Look at **downstairs** and **upstairs**.

☞ Compare **stair** and **step**. **Stairs** or **flights of stairs** are usually inside buildings. **Steps** are usually outside buildings and made of stone or concrete.

2 [C] one of the steps in a series of stairs (1): She sat down on the bottom stair to read the letter.

☆ **stair·case** /ˈstɛrkeɪs/ (also **stair·way** /ˈstɛrweɪ/) noun [C] a set of stairs, usually with bars (**rails**) on each side that you can hold onto ☞ Look at **escalator**.

☆ **stake¹** /steɪk/ noun **1** [C] a wooden or metal pole with a point at one end that you push into the ground, e.g. to support a tent **2** stakes [plural] the things that you might win or lose in a game or in a particular situation: We play cards for money, but never for very high stakes. **3** [C] a part of a company, etc. that you own, usually because you have invested money in it: Foreign investors now have a 20% stake in the company.

IDM **at stake** in danger of being lost; at risk: He thought very carefully about the decision because he knew his future was at stake.

stake² /steɪk/ verb [T] **stake sth (on sth)** to put your future, etc. in danger by doing sth, because you hope that it will bring you a good result: She is staking her political reputation on this issue.

IDM **stake a/your claim (to/on sth)** to say that you have a right to have sth: Both towns have staked their claim to the title of "The Hot Dog Capital of America."

PHRV **stake sth out 1** (used especially about the police, etc.) to watch a place secretly, over a period of time: Police staked out the airport after a bomb threat was made. **2** to say publicly that sth belongs to you or that you have a right to it: The Vice President has staked out a tough position on crime.

☆ **stale** /steɪl/ adj. **1** (used about food or air) old and not fresh anymore: The bread is stale. ○ stale cigarette smoke **2** not interesting or exciting anymore: She says her marriage has gone stale.

stale·mate /ˈsteɪlmeɪt/ noun [sing., U] a situation in an argument in which neither side can win or make any progress

☆ **stalk¹** /stɔk/ noun [C] one of the long thin parts of a plant which the flowers, leaves or fruit grow on

stalk² /stɔk/ verb **1** [T] to follow an animal or a person quietly and secretly in order to get close and possibly hurt or kill him/her/it: a lion stalking its prey ○ He was arrested for stalking a Hollywood actress. **2** [I] to walk stiff-

ly in an angry or arrogant way: He got up and stalked out of the room. —**stalk·er** noun [C] —**stalk·ing** noun [U]

stall¹ /stɔl/ noun [C] **1** a small area with walls around it and a toilet or a shower in it: There were only two stalls in the women's restroom. ○ a shower stall **2** a small enclosed area inside a building (**a barn**) for one animal, especially a horse

stall² /stɔl/ verb [I,T] **1** (used about a vehicle) to stop suddenly because the engine fails; to make a vehicle do this accidentally: The bus stalled in the middle of the street. **2** to avoid doing sth or to try to stop sth from happening until a later time: I've asked them several times for the money, but they keep stalling.

stal·lion /ˈstælyən/ noun [C] an adult male horse ☞ Look at the note at **horse**.

stal·wart /ˈstɔlwərt/ adj. loyal and hard-working: a stalwart member of the Democratic Party —**stal·wart** noun [C]: a committee of party stalwarts

stam·i·na /ˈstæmənə/ noun [U] the ability to do sth that requires a lot of physical or mental effort for a long time: It takes a lot of stamina to run a marathon.

☆ **stamp¹** /stæmp/ noun [C] **1** (also **postage stamp**) a small piece of paper that you stick onto a letter or package to show that you have paid for it to be mailed: I need three 32-cent stamps. ☞ Look also at **food stamp**. **2** a small object that prints some words, a design, the date, etc. when you press it onto a surface: a rubber stamp **3** the mark made by a stamp (2): a stamp in my passport

☆ **stamp²** /stæmp/ verb [T] **stamp A (on B)**; **stamp B (with A)** to print some words, a design, the date, etc. by pressing a small object (**a stamp**) onto a surface: to stamp a passport ○ The date is stamped on the receipt. ☞ Look also at **self-addressed stamped envelope**.

IDM **stamp your feet** to put your feet down very heavily on the ground, one at a time, again and again

PHRV **stamp sth out** to put an end to sth completely: The police are trying to stamp out this kind of crime.

stam·pede /stæmˈpid/ verb [T] (used about a group of animals or people) to rush in a particular direction in a wild and uncontrolled way —**stam·pede** noun [C]: a stampede toward the exits

stance /stæns/ noun [C, usually sing.] **1** stance (on sth) an attitude (especially moral or political) toward sth: the President's stance on foreign affairs **2** the position in which sb stands (especially in sports when you are preparing to hit the ball)

☆ **stand¹** /stænd/ verb [I,T] (p.t., p.p. stood /stʊd/) **1** [I] to be on your feet; to be upright:

ər	ɪr	ɛr	ɑr	ɔr	ʊr	ʒ	h	ŋ
bird	near	hair	car	north	tour	vision	hat	sing

He was standing near the window. **2** [I] **stand (up)** to rise to your feet from another position: *He stood up when I entered the room.* **3** [T] to put sb/sth in a particular place or in an upright position: *She stood the vaccum cleaner in the closet.* **4** [I] to be or to remain in a particular position or situation: *The lighthouse stands on a hill.* ○ *The house has stood empty for ten years.* ○ *He is very critical of the law as it stands* (= as it is now). **5** [I] (used about an offer, a decision, etc.) to be or to remain unchanged: *Does your decision still stand?* **6** [I] to be of a particular height, level, amount, etc.: *The world record stands at 6 feet, 10 inches.* **7** [I] to have an opinion or view (about sth): *I don't know where I stand on immigration.* **8** [I] **stand to do sth** to be in a situation where you are likely to do sth: *If he has to sell the company, he stands to lose a lot of money.* **9** [T] (in negative sentences and questions, with *can/could*) to be able to bear or tolerate sb/sth: *I can't stand that obnoxious guy on the local radio.* ○ *How can you stand it when she practices her trumpet?*

IDM **stand in line** to wait in a line of people: *We stood in line for two hours to buy tickets.*

PHRV **stand aside** to move to one side: *People stood aside to let the police past.*

stand back to move back: *The police officer told everybody to stand back.*

stand by 1 to be present, but do nothing in a situation: *How can you stand by and let them treat their animals like that?* **2** to be ready to act: *The ambulance is standing by in case anyone gets injured.*

stand by sb to continue to support sb in a difficult situation: *Phil stood by his wife when she was accused of murder.*

stand by sth to not change a decision, a belief, an idea, etc.: *School officials stood by their plan despite heavy criticism from parents.*

stand for sth 1 to be a short form of sth: *What does NAACP stand for?* **2** to support sth (e.g. an idea or opinion): *I hate everything that the party stands for.*

stand out to be easily seen or noticed

stand sb up (*informal*) not keep an appointment with sb: *Ed's date stood him up, so he went to the movie alone.*

stand up for sb/sth to say or do sth which shows that you support sb/sth: *I admire her. She really stands up for what she believes in.*

stand up to sb/sth to defend yourself against sb who is stronger or more powerful

☆ **stand²** /stænd/ *noun* **1** [C] a table or small store on the sidewalk or in a large public building from which you can buy things or get information: *a popcorn stand* ○ *a company stand at a trade show* **2** [C] a piece of furniture that you can put things on or in: *a music stand* **3** **stands** [plural] a large area with rows of seats at the side of a sports field where people

sit to watch the sports game ☞ picture at **football**. **4** [C, usually sing.] = WITNESS STAND

IDM **make a stand (against sb/sth)** to defend yourself, your opinion, etc. strongly against sb/sth

take a stand (on sth) to say publicly what you think and intend to do about sth

☆ **stan·dard¹** /ˈstændərd/ *noun* [C] **1** a level of quality: *a high standard of teaching* ○ *We need to improve educational standards in this state.* ○ *This work is not up to your usual standard.* ☞ Look also at **standard of living**. **2** a level of quality that you compare sth else with: *By my mother's standards, this house is extremely messy.* ○ *He is an excellent player by any standard.* **3** [usually pl.] a level of behavior that is morally acceptable: *Many people are worried about falling standards in modern society.*

☆ **stan·dard²** /ˈstændərd/ *adj.* **1** of the normal type; without anything special or extra: *This is the standard model. The deluxe version costs more.* **2** part of the normal situation; not unusual in any way: *It is standard practice to ask students to fill out this form when they arrive.* **3** (used about language) that people generally accept as normal and correct: *standard English*

stan·dard·ize /ˈstændərdaɪz/ *verb* [T] (often passive) to make things of a certain type the same as each other: *students' scores on standardized tests* —**stan·dard·i·za·tion** /ˌstændərdəˈzeɪʃn/ *noun* [U]

standard of ˈliving *noun* [C] (*pl.* **standards of living**) the level of wealth and comfort that a person, group or country has in everyday life: *Most people enjoy a high standard of living in this country.*

stand·by /ˈstændbaɪ/ *noun* [C] (*pl.* **stand·bys**) a person or thing that is ready to be used if necessary: *I have a computer now, but I still keep my old typewriter as a standby.* ○ *a standby ticket* (= a cheap ticket, e.g. for a flight, that you can get at the last moment if a seat is available)

IDM **on standby** ready; waiting to do sth: *When the fighting began, all local hospitals were put on standby.*

stand·ing¹ /ˈstændɪŋ/ *noun* [C,U] the opinion that other people have of sb: *The consequences for America's international standing could be extremely serious.*

stand·ing² /ˈstændɪŋ/ *adj.* (only *before* a noun) continuing to exist; permanent: *I have a standing invitation to go and stay with them whenever I want to.*

stand·off /ˈstændɔf; -ɑf/ *noun* [C] a situation in an argument, a battle, etc. in which no one can gain an advantage or no progress can be made

stand·point /ˈstændpɔɪnt/ *noun* [C] a particular way of thinking about sth: *The program*

S

tʃ	dʒ	v	θ	ð	s	z	ʃ
chin	June	van	thin	then	so	zoo	she

looked at the problems of education from the standpoint of the teacher.

stand·still /'stænstɪl/ noun [sing.] a situation of no movement, progress or activity: *The traffic came to a complete standstill.*

stank *p.t.* of STINK

sta·ple¹ /'steɪpl/ noun [C] **1** a small thin piece of bent wire that you push through pieces of paper in order to fasten them together using a special tool (**stapler**) **2** a basic or main part of sth: *Rice is a staple of the Japanese diet.* ◦ *game shows and soap operas, the traditional daytime TV staples*

sta·ple² /'steɪpl/ verb [T] to fasten sth to sth else using a staple¹(1): *Staple the letter to the application form.* —**sta·pler** /'steɪplər/ noun [C]

☆ **star¹** /stɑr/ noun [C] **1** a large ball of burning gas in outer space that you see as a small point of light in the sky at night: *It was a clear night and the stars were shining brightly.* **2** a shape with a number of points sticking out in a regular pattern: *The children decorated the classroom with paper stars.* ☞ picture at **shape**. **3** a printed shape like a star (2) that is used for indicating a level of quality: *a five-star hotel* **4** a famous person in acting, music or sports: *a movie star* **5** a person who does sth extremely well: *She's one of the star players on the team.*

star² /stɑr/ verb (**star·ring**; **starred**) **1** [I] **star (in sth)** to be one of the main actors in a play, movie, etc.: *Michelle Pfeiffer is set to star in an exciting new adventure movie.* **2** [T] to have sb as a main actor: *The movie stars Sandra Bullock as a computer programmer.*

starch /stɑrtʃ/ noun [C,U] **1** a white substance with no taste in foods such as potatoes, rice and bread **2** a substance that is used for making cloth stiff

star·dom /'stɑrdəm/ noun [U] the position of being a famous person in acting, music or sports

☆ **stare** /stɛr/ verb [I] **stare (at sb/sth)** to look at sb or sth continuously for a long time because you are interested, surprised, etc.: *Everybody stared at his hat.* ◦ *I stared at her in disbelief.* ◦ *He didn't reply; he just stared into the distance.*

stark¹ /stɑrk/ adj. **1** very bare and plain and therefore not attractive: *a stark landscape* **2** clearly unpleasant: *the stark realities of a life of poverty* **3** very clear: *a stark contrast between the inner city and the suburbs*

stark² /stɑrk/ adv.
IDM **stark naked** completely naked

the ˌStars and ˈStripes noun [sing.] the national flag of the U.S.

☆ **start¹** /stɑrt/ verb **1** [I,T] **start (sth/to do sth/doing sth)** to begin doing sth: *Turn over your test papers and start now.* ◦ *We'll have to start* (= leave) *early if we want to be in Chicago by 10.* ◦ *Prices start at $5.* ◦ *What time do you have*

to start work in the morning? ◦ *After waiting for an hour, the customers started to complain.* ◦ *She started playing the piano when she was six.* **2** [I,T] to begin to happen or to make sth begin to happen: *What time does the concert start?* ◦ *I'd like to start the meeting now.* ◦ *The fight started when the boys were leaving the club.* ◦ *The police think a young woman may have started the fire.* ☞ Look at the note at **begin**. **3** [I] to have a beginning or a first part: *Her last name starts with "W," not "V."* ◦ *Our property starts by the fence over there.* **4** [I,T] **start (sth) (up)** to create a company, an organization, etc.; to be created: *They've decided to start their own business.* ◦ *There are a lot of new companies starting up in that area now.* **5** [I,T] **start (sth) (up)** (used about a machine, a car, etc.) to begin to work; to make a machine, a car, etc. begin to work: *The car won't start.* ◦ *We heard an engine starting up in the street.* ◦ *Start up the computer and enter your password.* ◦ *He got onto his motorcycle, started the engine and rode away.*

IDM **to start (off) with 1** in the beginning; at first: *Everything was fine to start with, but then there were problems.* **2** (used for giving your first reason for sth): *"Why are you so mad?" "Well, to start off with, you're late, and secondly you lied to me."*

get/start the ball rolling ⇨ BALL

PHRV **start (sth) off** to begin (sth) in a particular way: *I'd like to start off the conference by welcoming you all to New York.*

start on sth to begin doing sth that needs to be done: *I suppose we should get started on those dirty dishes.*

start out to begin your life, career, etc. in a particular way: *She started out as a teacher in Ohio.*

start over to begin again: *I've made a lot of mistakes – I'd better start over.*

☆ **start²** /stɑrt/ noun **1** [C, usually sing.] the beginning or first part of sth: *The chairman made a short speech at the start of the meeting.* ◦ *I told you it was a bad idea from the start.* **2** [C, usually sing.] an act of starting: *We've got a long way to drive today, so let's get an early start.* ◦ *to make a fresh start in life* ☞ Look also at **head start**. **3** [C, usually sing.] a sudden quick movement that your body makes because you are surprised or afraid

IDM **get off to a good, bad, etc. start** to start well, badly, etc.: *My day got off to a good start – I got a check in the mail this morning.*

start·er /'stɑrtər/ noun [C] a player on a sports team who plays when the game begins

IDM **for starters** (*informal*) (used for giving your first reason for sth): *"Why can't we go on vacation?" "Well, for starters, we can't afford it..."*

star·tle /'stɑrtl/ verb [T] to make sb/sth suddenly surprised or frightened —**star·tled** adj.:

He had a startled look on his face. —**star·tling** adj.: I have some startling news for you!

star·va·tion /stɑr'veɪʃn/ noun [U] suffering or death because there is not enough food: to die of starvation

☆ **starve** /stɑrv/ verb [I,T] to suffer very badly or die from hunger; to make sb/sth suffer or die in this way: Millions of people are starving in the poorer countries of the world. ○ That winter many animals starved to death. ○ You need to eat more – you're starving yourself.

IDM **be starved for/of sth** to suffer because you are not getting enough of sth that you need: The children had been starved of love for years.

be starving; be starved (informal) to be extremely hungry: When will dinner be ready? I'm starving!

stat /stæt/ noun [C, usually pl.] = STATISTIC

☆ **state¹** /steɪt/ noun 1 [C] the condition that sb/sth is in at a particular time: the state of the economy ○ a state of shock 2 [C] a part of a country, especially the U.S., that has its own government and can make some of its own laws: state and federal laws ○ the former governor of the state of Ohio ○ Fill in your city, state and Zip code on the last line. ○ Iowa State University (= the public university that is supported by money from the state of Iowa) 3 [C] (formal) a country, especially outside the U.S.: Pakistan has been an independent state since 1947. ☞ Look at the note at **country**. 4 [U, sing.] the government of a country: the relationship between church and state ○ heads of state (= government leaders) ☞ Look also at **Secretary of State**. 5 [U] very formal events and behavior connected with governments and the leaders of countries: President Nixon's state visit to China

IDM **state of affairs** a situation: This state of affairs cannot be allowed to continue.

state of mind mental condition: How would you describe her state of mind at that time?

☆ **state²** /steɪt/ verb [T] to say or write sth, often formally: Your letter states that you sent the package on March 31, but we never received it. ○ As I stated earlier, I do not believe that this information is accurate.

the ¹State De¡partment noun [sing.] the U.S. government department that is in charge of dealing with foreign countries ☞ Look at **Secretary of State**.

state·ly /'steɪtli/ adj. (**state·li·er; state·li·est**) formal and dignified: a stately old building

☆ **state·ment** /'steɪtmənt/ noun [C] 1 something that you say or write, often formally: The Vice President will make a statement about the defense cuts today. ○ After the accident I had to go to the police station to give a statement. 2 a printed list of all the money going into or coming out of a bank account during a certain period of time

¡state-of-the-¹art adj. (usually before a noun) using the most modern knowledge or technology that is available: a state-of-the-art sound system

states·man /'steɪtsmən/ noun [C] (pl. **states·men** /-mən/) an important and experienced politician who has earned public respect

☆ **state·wide** /¡steɪt'waɪd/ adj., adv. across a whole state: a statewide poll

stat·ic¹ /'stætɪk/ adj. not moving or changing: House prices are static.

stat·ic² /'stætɪk/ noun [U] 1 (also ¡static elec'tricity) electricity that collects on a surface 2 sudden loud noises on a radio or television, caused by electricity in the atmosphere

☆ **sta·tion¹** /'steɪʃn/ noun [C] 1 a building or structure along a road, railroad track, etc. where buses, trains, etc. stop so that passengers can get on and off: a railroad/train station ○ a bus station ○ a subway station 2 a building where a particular service or activity is based: a fire station (= where the fire department is based) ○ a gas station ○ a police station 4 a company that broadcasts programs on the radio or on television: a local radio station ☞ Look at **channel**.

sta·tion² /'steɪʃn/ verb [T] (often passive) to send soldiers, etc. to a particular place: During his time in the army, he was stationed in South Korea.

sta·tion·ar·y /'steɪʃn·¡ɛri/ adj. not moving: He crashed into the back of a stationary vehicle.

sta·tion·er·y /'steɪʃn·¡ɛri/ noun [U] paper and envelopes for writing letters

¹station ¡wagon (also informal **wagon**) noun [C] a car with a door at the back and a large area for luggage inside, behind the back seat ☞ picture at **car**.

☆ **sta·tis·tic** /stə'tɪstɪk/ noun 1 [C] (also informal **stat**) a number that shows a fact or provides information about sth: the grim statistic that crime increased by 12% last year 2 **statistics** [plural] numbers that have been collected in order to provide information about sth: Statistics indicate that more than 95% of American homes have a television. ○ crime statistics 3 **statistics** [U] the science of collecting and analyzing numbers that provide information about sth —**sta·tis·ti·cal** /stə'tɪstɪkl/ adj.: statistical information, evidence, etc. —**sta·tis·ti·cal·ly** /-kli/ adv.

☆ **stat·ue** /'stætʃu/ noun [C] a figure of a person or animal, that is made of stone or metal and usually put in a public place: the Statue of Liberty

stat·ure /'stætʃər/ noun [U] (formal) 1 the height of a person: He's fairly small in stature. 2 the importance that sb has because people have a high opinion of his/her skill or achievement: Her research has given her considerable stature in the scientific world.

ə	y	w	t̬	eɪ	aɪ	ɔɪ	aʊ	oʊ
about	yes	woman	butter	say	five	boy	now	go

S

☆ **sta·tus** /ˈstætəs; ˈsteɪtəs/ *noun* **1** [sing.] your social or professional position in relation to other people: *Teachers don't have a very high status in this country.* **2** [U] a high social position: *The new job gave him much more status.* **3** [U] your legal position: *Please indicate your name, age and marital status* (= whether you are married, single, or divorced).

the status quo /ˌstætəs ˈkwoʊ; ˌsteɪtəs-/ *noun* [sing.] the situation that exists at a particular time

ˈstatus ˌsymbol *noun* [C] something that a person owns that shows that he/she is rich or has a high position in society

stat·ute /ˈstætʃut/ *noun* [C] a rule or law

stat·u·to·ry /ˈstætʃəˌtɔri/ *adj.* decided or controlled by law: *a statutory right*

staunch /stɔntʃ/ *adj.* believing in sth or supporting sb/sth very strongly; loyal: *a staunch supporter of the Democratic Party*

stave /steɪv/ *verb*

PHRV stave sth off to stop sth bad from happening now, although it may happen at a later time: *to stave off a financial crisis*

☆ **stay¹** /steɪ/ *verb* [I] **1** to continue to be somewhere and not go away: *Sara stayed in bed until 11 o'clock.* ○ *I can't stay long.* ○ *Stay on this road until you get to Wells Street.* **2** to continue to be in a particular state or situation without change: *I can't stay awake any longer.*

☞ **Remain** and **stay** are similar in meaning but **remain** is more formal.

3 to be somewhere as a visitor or guest: *We stayed with friends in Boston.* ○ *to stay at a hotel* ○ *Can you stay for lunch?*

IDM stay put (*informal*) to remain in one place: *We like this apartment, so we'll probably stay put for a few years.*

PHRV stay behind to remain in a place after other people have gone

stay in to remain at home: *I'm going to stay in and watch TV.*

stay on to remain at a place or in a position longer than necessary or normal, or after other people have left: *He decided to stay on as the financial manager after the business had been sold.*

stay out to remain out, especially late at night

stay up to not go to bed: *I'm going to stay up to watch the late movie.*

stay² /steɪ/ *noun* [C] a period of time that you stay somewhere: *Did you enjoy your stay in Texas?*

☆ **stead·y¹** /ˈstɛdi/ *adj.* (**stead·i·er; stead·i·est**) **1** not moving or shaking: *You need a steady hand to take good pictures.* ☞ The opposite is **unsteady**. **2** developing or happening at a regular rate: *a steady increase in exports* **3** staying the same; not changing over a period of time: *If you drive at a steady 55 miles*

an hour, you will use less gas. ○ *He hasn't been able to find a steady job.* —**stead·i·ly** /ˈstɛdəli/ *adv.*: *Unemployment has fallen steadily since 1995.*

stead·y² /ˈstɛdi/ *verb* [I,T] (*pres. part.* **stead·y·ing**; *3rd pers. sing. pres.* **stead·ies**; *p.t., p.p.* **stead·ied**) to make sth steady or to become steady: *She thought she was going to fall, so she put out a hand to steady herself.*

☆ **steak** /steɪk/ *noun* [C,U] a thick, flat piece of meat (especially from a cow) or fish: *a piece of steak* ○ *a salmon steak* ☞ Look at **chop²**.

☆ **steal** /stil/ *verb* (*p.t.* **stole** /stoʊl/; *p.p.* **stolen** /ˈstoʊlən/) **1** [I,T] **steal (sth) (from sb/sth)** to take sth that belongs to another person secretly and without permission: *The terrorists were driving a stolen car.*

☞ You **steal** things, but you **rob** people (of things): *My camera was stolen!* ○ *I've been robbed!* ○ *They robbed me of all my money!* ○ *He was arrested for robbing a bank.* Look also at **burglarize** and at the note at **thief**.

2 [I] **steal away, in, out, etc.** (*formal*) to move somewhere secretly and quietly

stealth /stɛlθ/ *noun* [U] (*formal*) behavior that is secret or quiet: *The terrorists operate by stealth.* —**stealth·y** *adj.* —**stealth·i·ly** *adv.*

☆ **steam¹** /stim/ *noun* [U] **1** the hot gas that water changes into when it boils: *Steam was rising from the coffee.* **2** the power that can be produced from steam (1): *a steam engine*

IDM blow/let off steam (*informal*) to release energy or express strong feeling by behaving in a noisy or uncontrolled way

run out of steam (*informal*) to have no more energy

steam² /stim/ *verb* **1** [I] to send out steam: *steaming hot soup* **2** [T] to cook sth in steam: *steamed vegetables*

IDM be/get steamed (up) (*informal*) to be/become very angry or worried about sth

PHRV steam (sth) up to cover sth or become covered with steam: *My glasses steam up when I come in from the cold.*

steam·boat /ˈstimboʊt/ *noun* [C] a large boat that is driven by steam, especially on rivers

steam·rol·ler /ˈstimroʊlər/ *noun* [C] a big heavy vehicle with wide wheels that is used for making the surface of a road flat

☆ **steel¹** /stil/ *noun* [U] a very strong metal that is made from iron mixed with carbon. Steel is used for making knives, tools, machines, etc. ☞ Look also at **stainless steel**.

steel² /stil/ *verb* [T] **steel yourself** to prepare yourself for sth difficult or unpleasant: *Steel yourself for a shock.*

☆ **steep** /stip/ *adj.* **1** (used about a hill, mountain, street, etc.) rising or falling quickly: *I don't think I can ride my bike up that hill. It's too steep.* **2** (used about an increase in sth)

ər	ɪr	ɛr	ɑr	ɔr	ʊr	ʒ	h	ŋ
bird	near	hair	car	north	tour	vision	hat	sing

very big and sudden **3** (*informal*) very expensive —**steep·ly** *adv.*: *House prices have risen steeply this year.* —**steep·ness** *noun* [U]

steeped /stipt/ *adj.* **be steeped in sth** having a lot of sth; full of sth: *The city of Boston is steeped in history.*

stee·ple /'stipl/ *noun* [C] a church tower that has a pointed top

☆ **steer¹** /stɪr/ *verb* [I,T] to control the direction that a vehicle is going in, by using a wheel, etc.: *Can you push the car while I steer?* ○ *to steer a boat, ship, bicycle, motorcycle, etc.* ○ (*figurative*) *She tried to steer the conversation away from the subject of money.*

☞ **Steer** means to control the direction of a vehicle. If you **drive** a car or truck, **ride** a bicycle/motorcycle or **sail** a boat, you steer it and you are also in control of everything else.

steer² /stɪr/ *noun* [C] a young male cow that has had part of its sexual organs removed and is usually raised for its meat

steer·ing /'stɪrɪŋ/ *noun* [U] the mechanical parts that control the direction that a vehicle is going in .

☆ **'steering wheel** (*also* **wheel**) *noun* [C] the wheel in a car, etc. that you use to steer it

☆ **stem¹** /stɛm/ *noun* [C] **1** one of the long thin parts of a plant which the leaves or flowers grow on **2** the main part of a word onto which other parts are added: *"Writ-" is the stem of the words "write," "writing," "written" and "writer."*

stem² /stɛm/ *verb* **stem·ming; stemmed**
PHRV **stem from sth** to be caused by sth; to have sth as an origin: *His interest in Egypt stems from the time he spent there when he was a child.*

stench /stɛntʃ/ *noun* [C, usually sing.] a very bad smell

☆ **step¹** /stɛp/ *verb* [I] (**step·ping; stepped**) to lift one foot and put it down in a different place when you are walking: *Be careful! Don't step in the mud.* ○ *to step forward/back* ○ *Ouch! You stepped on my foot!*

PHRV **step down** to give up a position of authority: *Anne is stepping down as chairperson at the end of the year.*

step in to become involved in a difficult situation, usually in order to help

step out to leave a place for a short period of time: *Sorry, Mrs. Brown just stepped out. Can I take a message?*

step sth up to increase sth: *The army has decided to step up its recruiting efforts.*

☆ **step²** /stɛp/ *noun* [C] **1** the act of lifting one foot and putting it down in a different place: *Nick took two steps forward and then stopped.* ○ *I heard steps outside the window.* **2** one action in a series of actions that you take in order to achieve sth: *the first step toward peace* **3** one of the surfaces on which you put your foot when

you are going up or down stairs, a ladder, etc.: *the top/bottom step* ○ *a flight* (= a set) *of steps* ☞ Look at the note at **stair**.

IDM **in step (with sb/sth); out of step (with sb/sth)** moving/not moving your feet at the same time as other people when you are marching, dancing, etc.: (*figurative*) *politicians who are totally out of step with young people today*

take steps to do sth to take action in order the achieve sth: *to take steps to reduce unemployment*

watch your step ⇨ WATCH²

step·brother /'stɛpbrʌðər/ *noun* [C] the son of your stepmother or stepfather from an earlier marriage or relationship

step-by-'step *adj.* (only *before* a noun) moving slowly and gradually from one action or stage to the next: *clear step-by-step instructions*

step·child /'stɛptʃaɪld/ *noun* [C] (*pl.* **step·child·ren** /-tʃɪldrən/) the child of your husband or wife from an earlier marriage or relationship

step·daughter /'stɛpdɔtər/ *noun* [C] the daughter of your husband or wife from an earlier marriage or relationship

step·father /'stɛpfaðər/ *noun* [C] the man who has married your mother after the death or divorce of your father

step·lad·der /'stɛplædər/ *noun* [C] a short ladder with two parts that can stand on its own. You can fold it up when you are not using it. ☞ picture at **ladder**.

step·mother /'stɛpmʌðər/ *noun* [C] the woman who has married your father after the death or divorce of your mother

step·son /'stɛpsʌn/ *noun* [C] the son of your husband or wife from an earlier marriage or relationship

☆ **ster·e·o** /'stɛrioʊ/ *noun* **1** [U] the system for playing recorded music, speech etc. in which the sound is directed through two channels: *This program is in stereo.* **2** [C] (*also* **'stereo system**) a piece of equipment for playing recorded music, etc. that has two speakers: *a car stereo* —**ster·e·o** *adj.*: *a stereo broadcast*

☆ **ster·e·o·type¹** /'stɛriətaɪp/ *noun* [C] a common idea about a type of person or thing, which is often not true in reality: *the stereotype of the loud, obnoxious New Yorker* —**ster·e·o·typ·i·cal** /ˌstɛriə'tɪpɪkl/ *adj.*

ster·e·o·type² /'stɛriətaɪp/ *verb* [T] to have or show a common, fixed idea about a type of person or thing, which is often not true in reality: *Women are often stereotyped as housewives in TV commercials.*

ster·ile /'stɛrəl/ *adj.* **1** not able to produce young animals or babies **2** completely clean and free from tiny living things that can cause disease (**bacteria**): *sterile medical instruments* **3** with no interest or creative ideas: *a sterile discussion* —**ste·ril·i·ty** /stə'rɪləti/ *noun* [U]

S

tʃ	dʒ	v	θ	ð	s	z	ʃ
chin	**June**	**van**	**thin**	**then**	**so**	**zoo**	**she**

S

ster·il·ize /ˈstɛrəlaɪz/ *verb* [T] **1** to make sb/sth completely clean and free from tiny living things that can cause disease (**bacteria**) **2** (usually passive) to perform an operation on a person or an animal so that he/she/it cannot have babies —**ster·il·i·za·tion** /ˌstɛrələˈzeɪʃn/ *noun* [U]

ster·ling /ˈstɜrlɪŋ/ *adj.* of very high quality: *a sterling performance* ○ *sterling silver* (= that is 92.5% pure silver)

stern¹ /stɜrn/ *adj.* very serious and severe; not smiling: *a stern expression* ○ *a stern warning* —**stern·ly** *adv.*

stern² /stɜrn/ *noun* [C] the back end of a ship or boat ☞ Look at **bow²**(2).

ster·oid /ˈstɛrɔɪd; ˈstɪr-/ *noun* [C, usually pl.] a type of drug that can be used to treat illnesses or injuries, but that some people take illegally in order to make their muscles bigger or to improve their performance in sports

steth·o·scope /ˈstɛθəskoʊp/ *noun* [C] a piece of equipment that a doctor uses in order to listen to your heart and breathing

stew /stu/ *noun* [C,U] a type of food that you make by cooking meat and vegetables in liquid for a long time

stew·ard /ˈstuərd/ *noun* [C] (*old-fashioned*) a man who serves the passengers on an airplane ☛ **Flight attendant** is more common nowadays.

stew·ard·ess /ˈstuərdəs/ *noun* [C] (*old-fashioned*) a woman who serves the passengers on an airplane ☛ **Flight attendant** is more common nowadays.

☆ **stick¹** /stɪk/ *noun* **1** [C] a small thin piece of wood from a tree **2** [C] a long thin piece of wood that you use in some sports: *a hockey stick* ☛ Look at **bat²**, **club²**(2) and **racket¹**. **3** [C] a long thin piece of sth: *a stick of dynamite* **4 the sticks** [U] (*informal*) an area that is far away from big cities and does not have interesting cultural activities

IDM **the short end of the stick** ⇨ SHORT¹

☆ **stick²** /stɪk/ *verb* (*p.t., p.p.* **stuck** /stʌk/) **1** [I,T] **stick (sth) in/into (sth)** to push a pointed object into sth; to be pushed into sth: *Stick a fork into the meat to see if it's done.* ○ *I can't move. There's a piece of wire sticking in my leg.* **2** [I,T] to attach sth to sth else or to become attached to sth else by using glue, etc.: *to stick a stamp on an envelope* ○ *Jelly sticks to your fingers.* **3** [I] **stick (in sth)** (used about sth that can usually be moved) to become firmly attached in one position so that it cannot be moved: *The car was stuck in the mud.* **4** [T] (*informal*) to put sth somewhere: *Just stick your umbrella in the closet.*

IDM **poke/stick your nose into sth** ⇨ NOSE¹

PHRV **stick around** (*informal*) to stay or wait somewhere

stick by sb (*informal*) to continue to give sb help and support even in difficult times

stick by sth to refuse to change a decision, belief, etc.: *Despite this news, analysts are sticking by their earlier economic forecasts.*

stick out (*informal*) to be very noticeable: *The new apartment building really sticks out from the older buildings around it.*

stick (sth) out to be further out than sth else or to push sth further out than sth else: *The boy's head was sticking out of the window.* ○ *Don't stick your tongue out.*

stick it/sth out (*informal*) to stay in a difficult or unpleasant situation until the end

stick to sth to continue with sth and not change to anything else: *You need to plan a sensible budget and then stick to it.*

stick together (*informal*) (used about two or more people) to stay friendly and loyal to each other

stick up to point upward: *You look funny. Your hair's sticking up!*

stick up for sb/yourself/sth to support or defend sb/yourself/sth: *Don't worry. I'll stick up for you if there's any trouble.*

☆ **stick·er** /ˈstɪkər/ *noun* [C] a piece of paper with writing or a picture on one side that you can stick onto a car window, book, wall, etc.

'**stick shift** *noun* [C] a system of gears in a car that the driver must move (**shift**) by hand, or a car with this system of gears

☆ **stick·y** /ˈstɪki/ *adj.* (**stick·i·er; stick·i·est**) **1** (used for describing a substance that can stick to sth else, or sth that is covered with this kind of substance): *This candy is very sticky.* ○ *I have sticky fingers after eating that ice cream.* **2** (*informal*) (used about a situation) difficult or unpleasant

☆ **stiff¹** /stɪf/ *adj.* **1** (used about material, paper, etc.) fairly hard and not easy to bend: *My new shoes feel a little stiff.* **2** (used about parts of the body) not easy to move: *My arm feels really stiff after playing tennis yesterday.* **3** (used about a liquid) very thick; almost solid: *Beat the egg whites until they are stiff.* **4** difficult or strong: *We face some stiff competition from the Bloomington High team.* ○ *stiff opposition to the plan* **5** (used about sb's behavior) not relaxed or friendly; formal: *She's often a little stiff around strangers.* **6** (used about a wind) fairly strong and steady: *a stiff breeze* **7** (used about an alcoholic drink) strong: *a stiff whiskey* —**stiff·ly** *adv.*: *He smiled stiffly.* —**stiff·ness** *noun* [U]

stiff² /stɪf/ *adv.* (used *after* a past participle) extremely: *to be bored, frozen, scared, etc. stiff*

stiff·en /ˈstɪfn/ *verb* **1** [I] (used about a person) to suddenly become very still, usually because you are afraid or angry: *Alison stiffened as she heard a noise outside the door.* **2** [I,T] to make sth stronger or more severe: *Congress voted to stiffen penalties for convicted drug dealers.*

sti·fle /ˈstaɪfl/ *verb* **1** [T] to stop sth from happening, developing or continuing: *Her strict*

education had stifled her natural creativity. ○ to stifle a yawn **2** [I,T] to be or to make sb unable to breathe easily: *Richard was almost stifled by the smoke.* —**sti·fling** *adj.*: *The heat was stifling.*

stig·ma /ˈstɪgmə/ *noun* [C,U] a bad reputation that sth has because a lot of people have a set idea that it is wrong, often unfairly: *There is still a lot of stigma attached to being unemployed.* —**stig·ma·tize** /ˈstɪgmətaɪz/ *verb* [T]

☆ **still¹** /stɪl/ *adv.* **1** (used for talking about sth that started at an earlier time) continuing until now or until the time you are talking about: *Do you still live in Miami?* ○ *It's still raining.* ○ *In 1994, Rob was still a student.* **2** in addition; more: *There are still ten days to go until my vacation.* **3** (used before or after a comparative adjective or adverb, to make it stronger): *It was very cold yesterday, but today it's colder still.* ○ *The state's biggest shopping mall will soon be surrounded by still more stores and restaurants.* **4** (used for talking about an action or opinion that you do not expect, because sth else makes it surprising) even so: *He had a bad headache, but he still went to the party.*

☆ **still²** /stɪl/ *adj., adv.* **1** without moving: *Stand still! I want to take your picture!* **2** quiet or calm: *The water was perfectly still.* —**still·ness** *noun* [U]: *the stillness of the air on a cold winter night*

still³ /stɪl/ *noun* [C] a single photograph that is taken from a scene in a movie

still·born /ˈstɪlbɔrn/ *adj.* (used about a baby) dead when it is born

stilt /stɪlt/ *noun* [C, usually pl.] **1** one of two long pieces of wood, with places to rest your feet on, on which you can walk above the ground: *a pair of stilts* **2** one of a set of poles that support a building above the ground or water

stilt·ed /ˈstɪltəd/ *adj.* (used about a way of speaking or writing) unnatural and very formal

stim·u·lant /ˈstɪmyələnt/ *noun* [C] a drug or medicine that makes you feel more active: *Caffeine is a mild stimulant.*

stim·u·late /ˈstɪmyəleɪt/ *verb* [T] **1** to make sth active or more active: *Exercise stimulates the blood circulation.* ○ *The President has decided to cut taxes in order to stimulate the economy.* **2** to make sb feel interested and excited about sth: *School doesn't really stimulate him.* —**stim·u·la·tion** /ˌstɪmyəˈleɪʃn/ *noun* [U]

stim·u·lat·ing /ˈstɪmyəleɪtɪŋ/ *adj.* interesting and exciting: *a stimulating discussion*

stim·u·lus /ˈstɪmyələs/ *noun* [C,U] (*pl.* **stim·u·li** /-laɪ/) something that causes activity, development or interest: *The President recommended using tax cuts as an economic stimulus.*

☆ **sting¹** /stɪŋ/ *verb* [I,T] (*p.t., p.p.* **stung** /stʌŋ/) **1** (used about an insect, a plant, etc.) to make

sb/sth feel a sudden pain by pushing sth sharp into their skin and injecting poison into them: *Ow! I just got stung by a wasp!* ○ *Be careful. Those plants sting.* **2** to make sb/sth feel a sudden, sharp pain: *Soap stings if it gets in your eyes.* **3** to make sb feel very hurt and upset because of sth you say: *Kate was stung by her father's criticism.*

☆ **sting²** /stɪŋ/ *noun* [C] **1** an injury that is caused by an insect pushing a sharp pointed part of its body into you: *a bee sting on the leg* **2** a sharp pain that feels like a sting²(1) : *the sting of soap in your eyes* **3** a complicated investigation in which the police use a trick in order to catch sb while he/she is doing sth illegal

stin·gy /ˈstɪndʒi/ *adj.* (**stin·gi·er; stin·gi·est**) not willing to give or share sth (especially money); not generous: *Don't be so stingy with the gravy.*

stink /stɪŋk/ *verb* [I] (*p.t.* **stank** /stæŋk/ or **stunk** /stʌŋk/; *p.p.* **stunk**) **1** to have a very strong and unpleasant smell: *Yuck! Something stinks in here!* **2** (*informal*) to seem to be very bad or unpleasant: *This job really stinks!* —**stink** *noun* [C]

stint /stɪnt/ *noun* [C] a fixed period of time that you spend doing sth: *Her employment experience includes a two-year stint in the navy.*

stip·u·late /ˈstɪpyəleɪt/ *verb* [T] (*formal*) to say exactly and officially what must be done: *The law stipulates that all schools provide special education for children who require it.* —**stip·u·la·tion** /ˌstɪpyəˈleɪʃn/ *noun* [C,U] (*formal*): *One of the stipulations in his will prohibits the sale of the paintings to private collectors.*

☆ **stir¹** /stər/ *verb* (**stir·ring; stirred**) **1** [T] to move a liquid, etc. around and around, using a spoon, etc.: *She stirred her coffee with a teaspoon.* **2** [I,T] to move or make sb/sth move gently: *The boy stirred in his sleep.* ○ *A sudden wind stirred the leaves.* **3** [T] to make sb feel a strong emotion: *The story stirred Carol's imagination.* ○ *a stirring speech*

PHRV **stir sth up** to cause a strong feeling in other people: *The manager accused him of stirring up trouble.*

stir² /stər/ *noun* **1** [C] the action of stirring: *Give the soup a stir.* **2** [sing.] general excitement or shock: *Short skirts caused quite a stir when they first appeared in the 1960s.*

stir-fry *verb* [T] (*pres. purt.* **stir-fry·ing**; *3rd pers. sing. pres.* **stir-fries**; *p.t., p.p.* **stir-fried**) to cook vegetables, meat, etc. by frying them for a short time in very hot oil while stirring them —**stir-fry** *noun* [C,U] (*pl.* **stir-fries**)

stir·rup /ˈstərəp/ *noun* [C] one of the two metal objects that you put your feet in when you are riding a horse ☞ picture at **horse**.

☆ **stitch¹** /stɪtʃ/ *noun* [C] **1** one of the small lines of thread that you can see on a piece of material after it has been sewn ☞ picture at **sew**.

ə	y	w	ṭ	eɪ	aɪ	ɔɪ	aʊ	oʊ
about	yes	woman	butter	say	five	boy	now	go

S

2 [usually pl.] one of the small pieces of thread that a doctor uses to sew your skin together if you cut yourself very badly, or after an operation **3** one of the small circles of yarn that you put around a needle when you are knitting ☛ picture at **knit**. **4** [usually sing.] a sudden pain that you get in the side of your body, e.g. after you have been running

IDM **in stitches** (*informal*) laughing so much that you cannot stop

stitch² /stɪtʃ/ *verb* [I,T] to sew or fasten sth together using stitches¹: *Can you stitch my bag back together?*

☆ **stock¹** /stɑk/ *noun* **1** [C,U] a supply of things that are available to be sold or used: *The new store has a large stock of records, tapes and CDs.* ∘ *We'll have to order extra stock if we sell a lot more this week.* ∘ *farmers' stocks of grain and hay for the winter* **2** [C,U] a share in a company that people can buy and sell; the value of the shares in a company that have been sold to people (**investors**): *to invest in stocks and bonds* ∘ *They own over $1 million worth of stock in a major oil company.* **3** [C,U] a liquid that you use to make soups, sauces, etc.. It is made by boiling meat, bones, vegetables, etc. in water.

IDM **in stock/out of stock** in/not in the supply of things that a store, etc. has available for sale

take stock (of sth) to think about sth very carefully before deciding what to do next: *Let's see how things go for a week or so and then take stock of the situation.*

stock² /stɑk/ *verb* [T] **1** (usually used about a store) to have a supply of sth: *They stock foods from all over the world.* **2** to provide sth with a supply of sth: *a well-stocked bookstore*

PHRV **stock up (on sth)** to collect a large supply of sth for future use: *to stock up with food for the winter*

stock³ /stɑk/ *adj.* (only *before* a noun) (used for describing sth that sb says) used so often that it does not have much meaning: *She just uses the same stock phrases over and over.*

stock·bro·ker /ˈstɑkbroʊkər/ (*also* **broker**) *noun* [C] a person whose job is to buy and sell stocks¹(2) for other people

ˈ**stock ex·change** *noun* [C] **1** a place where stocks¹(2) are bought and sold: *the New York Stock Exchange* **2** (*also* ˈ**stock market**) the business or activity of buying and selling stocks¹(2)

stock·ing /ˈstɑkɪŋ/ *noun* [C] one of a pair of thin pieces of clothing that fit tightly over a woman's foot and leg: *a pair of stockings* ☛ picture on page A26. Look also at **panty·hose** and **tights**.

ˈ**stocking cap** *noun* [C] a type of warm, soft knitted hat ☛ picture at **cap**.

☆ ˈ**stock ·market** *noun* [C] **1** = STOCK EXCHANGE (2) **2** the prices of stocks that are bought and

sold in general: *Low interest rates and a rising stock market could lead to more takeovers of companies.*

stock·pile /ˈstɑkpaɪl/ *noun* [C] a large amount or number of sth that is kept available for use in the future: *the nation's stockpile of nuclear weapons* —**stock·pile** *verb* [T]

stock·y /ˈstɑki/ *adj.* (used about a person's body) short but strong and heavy

stole *p.t.* of STEAL

sto·len *p.p.* of STEAL

☆ **stom·ach¹** /ˈstʌmək/ *noun* [C] **1** the part of your body where food is digested after you have eaten it **2** the front part of your body below your chest and above your legs: *a fat stomach* ∘ *She turned over onto her stomach.* ☛ picture on page A24. Look also at **belly** and **tummy**.

stom·ach² /ˈstʌmək/ *verb* [T] (usually in negative sentences and questions) to be able to watch, listen to, accept, etc. sth that you think is unpleasant: *I can't stomach too much violence in movies.*

☆ **stom·ach·ache** /ˈstʌmɪkeɪk/ *noun* [C] a pain in your stomach: *I have a terrible stomach-ache.* ☛ Look at the note at **ache**.

stomp /stɑmp/ *verb* [I] **1** [I,T] **stomp (on sth)** to put your foot down very heavily on the ground or on sth else: *She stomped on the spider and squashed it.* **2** to walk with heavy steps, especially because you are angry: *He stomped up the stairs to his room and slammed the door.*

☆ **stone¹** /stoʊn/ *noun* **1** [U] a hard solid substance that is found in the ground: *The house was made of gray stone.* ∘ *a stone wall* **2** [C] a small piece of rock: *The boy picked up a stone and threw it into the river.* **3** [C] = PRECIOUS STONE

stone² /stoʊn/ *verb* [T] to throw stones¹(2) at sb/sth, e.g. as a punishment: *The two women were stoned to death.*

stoned /stoʊnd/ *adj.* (*slang*) under the influence of illegal drugs, especially marijuana

ston·y /ˈstoʊni/ *adj.* (**ston·i·er**; **ston·i·est**) **1** (used about the ground) having a lot of stones in it, or covered with stones **2** not friendly: *There was a stony silence as he walked into the room.*

stood *p.t., p.p.* of STAND¹

☆ **stool** /stul/ *noun* **1** [C] a seat that does not have a back or arms: *a bar stool* **2** [C,U] (*formal*) a piece of solid waste from the body

stool

stoop¹ /stup/ *verb* [I] to bend your head and shoulders forward and downward: *Cathy had to stoop to get through the low doorway.*

PHR V **stoop to sth/to doing sth** to do sth bad or wrong (that you would normally not do): *I would never stoop to cheating.*

stoop² /stup/ *noun* **1** [C] a small set of steps that lead to the door of a house, with a flat area at the top: *neighbors sitting on the front stoop* **2** [sing.] a way of holding your body, bending your head and shoulders forward and downward: *to walk with a stoop*

☆ **stop¹** /stɑp/ *verb* (**stop·ping**; **stopped**) **1** [I] to finish moving, happening or operating: *He walked along the road for a while, and then stopped.* ○ *I need to stop at the store to get some milk.* ○ *I think the rain's stopped.* ○ *Oh no! My watch stopped.* **2** [T] to make sb/sth finish moving, happening or operating: *I stopped someone on the street to ask the way to the post office.* ○ *Stop the car – I need to get out!* **3** [T] to end or finish an activity: *Stop making that noise!* ○ *We stopped work for half an hour to have a cup of coffee.* ○ *It's stopped raining now.*

☞ If you **stop to do** something, you stop in order to do it: *On the way into the office, I stopped to smoke a cigarette.* If you **stop doing** something, you do not do it anymore: *I'm trying to stop smoking.*

4 [T] **stop sb/sth from doing sth** to make sb/sth end or finish an activity; to prevent sb/sth from doing sth: *Can't you stop the car from making that noise?* ○ *Nothing will stop me from loving you.* **5** [T] to prevent money, especially a check, from being paid: *The bank stopped the check because there was no money in his account.*

IDM **stop at nothing** to do anything in order to get what you want, even if it is wrong or dangerous

stop short of sth/doing sth to almost do sth, but then decide not to do it at the last minute: *They made several indirect comments, but they stopped short of calling her a thief.*

PHR V **stop by (sth)** to visit sb/sth for a short time, especially before going to another place: *You'll have to stop by our house if you're ever in Washington.*

stop off (at/in…) to stop during a trip to do sth: *We stopped off in Oakland to see some friends before coming home.*

☆ **stop²** /stɑp/ *noun* [C] **1** an act of stopping or a state of being stopped: *Be sure your seat belt is fastened in case we have to make a sudden stop.* ○ *The elevator came to a stop on the third floor.* **2** the place where a bus, train, etc. stops so that people can get on and off: *a bus stop* **3** a place where sb stops during a trip, or the time he/she spends there: *Our first stop on the tour will be the Museum of Modern Art.*

IDM **to put a stop to sth** to prevent sth bad or unpleasant from continuing

stop·light /'stɑplaɪt/ *noun* [C] = TRAFFIC LIGHT

stop·o·ver /'stɑpoʊvər/ *noun* [C] a short stop

in a long trip, especially by plane: *a stopover in Chicago on the way to Washington*

stop·per /'stɑpər/ *noun* [C] an object that you put into the top of a bottle in order to close it. A stopper can be made of glass, plastic or cork.

stop·watch /'stɑpwɑtʃ/ *noun* [C] a watch which can be started and stopped by pressing a button so that you can measure exactly how long sth takes

☆ **stor·age** /'stɔrɪdʒ/ *noun* [U] the keeping of things until they are needed; the place where they are kept: *storage space* ○ *I'm going to keep my stuff in storage on campus this summer.*

☆ **store¹** /stɔr/ *noun* [C] **1** a building or part of a building where things are bought and sold: *a furniture store* ○ *Can you go to the store and pick up some bread and milk?* ☞ Look at **convenience store**, **department store** and **grocery store**. **2** a supply of sth that you keep for future use

IDM **in store (for sb/sth)** going to happen in the future: *There's a surprise in store for you when you get home!*

☆ **store²** /stɔr/ *verb* [T] to keep sth or a supply of sth for future use: *to store information in a computer* ○ *All the documents are stored in a safe.*

store·keep·er /'stɔrkipər/ *noun* [C] = SHOP-KEEPER

store·room /'stɔrrum/ *noun* [C] a room where things are kept until they are needed

stork /stɔrk/ *noun* [C] a large white bird with a long beak, neck and legs. Storks often live near water.

☆ **storm¹** /stɔrm/ *noun* [C] very bad weather, with heavy rain, strong winds, etc.: *Look at those black clouds. I think there's going to be a storm.* ○ *a thunderstorm, snowstorm, etc.* ○ *(figurative) The proposed tax increase caused a storm of protest.*

☞ **Storm** is the general word for very bad weather. A very strong wind is a **gale**. A very bad snowstorm is a **blizzard**. A storm with a very strong circular wind is called a **cyclone**, **hurricane** or **tornado**.

storm² /stɔrm/ *verb* **1** [I] to enter or leave somewhere in a very angry and noisy way: *She grabbed her books and stormed out of the room.* **2** [T] to attack a building, town, etc. suddenly and violently in order to take control of it: *Heavily armed police stormed the building and freed the hostages inside.*

storm·y /'stɔrmi/ *adj.* (**storm·i·er**; **storm·i·est**) **1** (used for talking about very bad weather, with strong winds, heavy rain, etc.): *a stormy night* **2** involving a lot of angry arguments and strong feeling: *a stormy debate in Congress* ○ *a stormy relationship*

☆ **sto·ry** /'stɔri/ *noun* [C] (*pl.* **sto·ries**) **1** a description of people and events that are not

S

real: *He always reads the children a bedtime story.* ○ *a detective, ghost, love, etc. story* ○ *She told us a story about an old woman who lived in a shoe.* **2** a description of true events that happened in the past: *the story of the American Revolution* ○ *his life story* **3** an article or report in a newspaper or magazine: *The plane crash was the front-page story in most newspapers.* **4** one floor or level of a building: *The building will be ten stories high.* ○ *a two-story house*

☆**stove** /stoʊv/ *noun* [C] **1** (*also* **range**) a piece of equipment in a kitchen that uses electricity or natural gas to heat and cook food. A stove has an oven for baking things and a flat top for cooking food in

stove
—burner
—oven

pots and pans. **2** a type of heater. A stove is a closed metal box in which you burn wood, coal, etc.: *a wood-burning stove*

stow /stoʊ/ *verb* [T] **stow sth (away)** to put sth away in a particular place until it is needed

stow·a·way /'stoʊəweɪ/ *noun* [C] a person who hides in a ship or an airplane so that he/she can travel without paying

strad·dle /'strædl/ *verb* [T] **1** (used about a person) to sit or stand with one leg on each side of sth: *to straddle a chair* **2** (used about a building, bridge, etc.) to be on both sides of sth: *The park straddles the border between the two states.*

strag·gle /'strægl/ *verb* [I] to walk, etc. slowly and in a disorganized way, not together with the rest of a group: *By 5:00, most of the tour group had straggled back to the bus.*

☆**straight¹** /streɪt/ *adj.* **1** not bent or curved: *a straight line* ○ *straight hair* (= not curly) ○ *straight teeth* (= in even rows) ○ *Keep your back straight!* ☞ picture at **hair** and **line**. **2** (not before a noun) in a level or upright position: *That picture isn't straight.* **3** honest, truthful and direct: *Politicians never give straight answers.* ○ *Are you being straight with me?* **4** (*also formal* **heterosexual**) sexually attracted to people of the other sex (= a man to a woman or a woman to a man) ☞ Look also at **gay**. **5** (used between a number and a noun) happening or coming one after another; in a row: *The Sharks celebrated four straight wins on the road last night.* ○ *Inflation has fallen for the fifth straight month.* **6** (used about an alcoholic drink) on its own, without ice, water or any other liquid: *a straight Scotch*

IDM **earn/get straight A's** to receive the grade "A" (= the best grade) in all of your classes

get sth straight to make sure that you understand sth completely: *Let's get this straight.*

You're sure that you've never seen this man before?

keep a straight face to stop yourself from smiling or laughing

set the record straight ➭ RECORD¹

☆**straight²** /streɪt/ *adv.* **1** in a straight line: *Go straight for about two miles until you come to some traffic lights.* ○ *He was looking straight ahead.* ○ *to sit up straight* (= with a straight back) **2** without any delay; directly: *I want you to come straight home after school.* ○ *to walk straight past sb/sth* **3** happening or coming one after another, without stopping: *Jody slept for twelve hours straight last night.* **4** (informal) in an honest and direct way: *Tell me straight, Doctor – how bad is the cancer?*

☆**straight·en** /'streɪtn/ *verb* **1** [I,T] **straighten (sth) (up/out)** to become straight or to make sth straight: *The road straightens at the bottom of the hill.* ○ *to straighten your tie* **2** [T] **straighten sth (up)** to make sth, e.g. a room or a desk, clean and neat: *to straighten up the living room*

PHRV **straighten sth out** to remove the confusion or difficulties from a situation

straighten up to stand up straight and tall

straight·for·ward /,streɪt'fɔrwərd/ *adj.* **1** easy to do or understand; simple: *straightforward instructions* **2** honest and open: *a straightforward person*

☆**strain¹** /streɪn/ *noun* **1** [C,U] the condition of being pulled or stretched too tightly: *The rope finally broke under the strain.* ○ (figurative) *The war has put a great strain on the country's economy.* **2** [C,U] a state of worry and tension, or something that causes this: *to be under a lot of strain at work* ○ *Mom's illness put a strain on the whole family.* ○ *the strain of being a manager* **3** [C,U] an injury to part of your body that is caused by using it too much: *a back strain* **4** [C] one type of plant, animal etc. which has particular characteristics: *a new strain of the bacteria which is resistant to medication*

strain² /streɪn/ *verb* **1** [I,T] to make a great effort to do sth: *I had to strain to hear what they were saying.* **2** [T] to injure a part of your body by using it too much: *Don't read in the dark. You'll strain your eyes.* ○ *to strain a muscle* **3** [T] to put a lot of pressure on sth: *Money problems have strained their relationship.* **4** [T] to separate a solid and a liquid by pouring them into a special container with small holes in it

strained /streɪnd/ *adj.* not natural or friendly: *Relations between the two countries are strained.*

strait /streɪt/ *noun* [C] a narrow area of water that joins two larger seas or oceans: *the Bering Strait*

strait·jack·et /'streɪtdʒækət/ *noun* [C] a type of strong jacket that is used to stop mental

patients, etc. from moving their arms so that they cannot hurt themselves or other people

strand /strænd/ *noun* [C] a single piece of cotton, wool, hair, etc.

strand·ed /'strændəd/ *adj.* left in a place that you cannot get away from, e.g. because you have no money or transportation

☆ **strange** /streɪndʒ/ *adj.* **1** unusual or unexpected: *A very strange thing happened to me on the way home.* ○ *a strange noise* ○ *She usually wears jeans. It's really strange to see her in a skirt.* **2** that you have not seen, visited, met, etc. before: *a strange town* ○ *My mother told me not to talk to strange men.*

☞ We do not use **strange** to talk about a person or thing that comes from a different country. Look at **foreign**.

—**strange·ly** *adv.*: *The streets were strangely quiet.* ○ *Tim's been acting strangely these days.*
—**strange·ness** *noun* [U]

☆ **strang·er** /'streɪndʒər/ *noun* [C] **1** a person that you do not know: *I had to ask a complete stranger to help me with my suitcase.*

☞ We do not use **stranger** to talk about a person who comes from a different country. Look at **foreigner**.

2 a person who is in a place that he/she does not know: *I'm a stranger to this part of the country.*

stran·gle /'stræŋgl/ *verb* [T] **1** to kill sb by squeezing his/her neck or throat with your hands, a rope, etc. **2** to prevent sth from developing

☆ **strap¹** /stræp/ *noun* [C] a long narrow piece of leather, cloth, plastic, etc. that you use for carrying sth or for keeping sth in position: *a dress with thin shoulder straps*

strap² /stræp/ *verb* [T] (**strapped; strap·ping**) to keep sb/sth in position by using a strap or straps: *The fighter pilot was securely strapped into the cockpit.*

strapped /stræpt/ *adj.* having very little money: *The local school system is strapped for cash.* ○ *financially strapped state governments*

stra·te·gic /strə'tidʒɪk/ *adj.* **1** helping you to achieve a plan; giving you an advantage **2** connected with a country's plans to achieve success in a war or in its defense system: *strategic planning* **3** (used about bombs and other weapons) intended to hit places of military or economic importance in an enemy country —**stra·te·gi·cal·ly** /-kli/ *adv.*: *The island is strategically important.*

☆ **strat·e·gy** /'stræṭədʒi/ *noun* (*pl.* **strat·e·gies**) **1** [C] a plan that you use in order to achieve sth: *a strategy to reduce inflation* **2** [U] the act of planning how to do or achieve sth: *military strategy*

☆ **straw** /strɔ/ *noun* **1** [U] the long stems of plants (e.g. wheat) that are dried and then

used for animals to sleep on or for making baskets, mats, etc.: *a straw hat* **2** [C] one piece of straw (1) **3** [C] a long plastic or paper tube that you can drink through

IDM **draw straws** ⇨ DRAW¹
the last/final straw an extra problem that is added to a difficult or unpleasant situation, and which makes you think you cannot tolerate the situation any longer

☆ **straw·ber·ry** /'strɔ-ˌbɛri/ *noun* [C] (*pl.* **straw·ber·ries**) a small soft red fruit with small yellow seeds on the outside: *fresh strawberries* ○ *strawberry jam*

 strawberry

stray¹ /streɪ/ *verb* [I] **1** to go away from the place where you should be for no particular reason: *The children had strayed from their mother in the grocery store.* **2** not keeping to the subject you should be thinking about or discussing: *The discussion strayed from the official agenda.*

stray² /streɪ/ *adj.* (only *before* a noun) accidentally lost or separated, or going in the wrong direction: *a stray dog* ○ *She was killed by a stray bullet.*

stray³ /streɪ/ *noun* [C] (*pl.* **strays**) an animal that is lost from home

streak /strik/ *noun* [C] **1 streak (of sth)** a thin line or mark: *The cat had brown fur with streaks of white in it.* **2** a part of a person's character that sometimes shows in the way he/she behaves: *a selfish streak* **3** a continuous period of good or bad luck in a sports game: *a winning/losing streak*

streak² /strik/ *verb* [I] to run or move very fast

☆ **stream¹** /strim/ *noun* [C] **1** a small river **2** the constant movement of a liquid or gas: *a stream of cool air coming from the vent* **3** a constant movement of people or things: *a stream of traffic* **4** a large number of things which happen one after another: *a stream of letters, telephone calls, questions, etc.*

stream² /strim/ *verb* [I] **1** (used about a liquid, gas or light) to flow in large amounts: *Blood was streaming from the cut on his forehead* ○ *Sunlight was streaming in through the windows.* **2** (used about people or things) to move somewhere in a continuous flow: *People were streaming out of the stadium.*

stream·er /'strimər/ *noun* [C] a long piece of colored paper that you use for decorating a room before a party, etc.

stream·line /'strimlaɪn/ *verb* [T] **1** to give a vehicle, etc. a long smooth shape so that it will move easily through air or water **2** to make an organization, process, etc. work better by making it simpler and more efficient: *The company has decided to streamline its production processes.*

ə	y	w	ṭ	eɪ	aɪ	ɔɪ	aʊ	oʊ
about	yes	woman	butter	say	five	boy	now	go

S

☆**street** /strit/ *noun* [C] **1** a road in a town or city that has stores, houses, etc. on one or both sides: *to walk along/down the street* ○ *to cross the street* ○ *Don't stand in the street – you'll get hit by a car!* ○ *a narrow/wide street* ○ *a street map* ☞ Look at the notes at **avenue** and **road**. **2 Street** (*abbr.* **St.**) [sing.] (used in names of streets): *to go shopping on Main Street* ○ *264 Chestnut St.*

IDM **on the street(s)** **1** in public; among most people: *additional government funding to put more police on the streets* ○ *the most common opinion on the street* **2** without a home or job: *teenagers living on the streets*

street·car /'stritkɑr/ (*also* **trolley**) *noun* [C] a type of city bus that uses electricity and runs on metal tracks in the street

☆**strength** /strɛŋkθ/ *noun* **1** [U] the quality of being physically strong; the amount of this quality that you have: *a woman of great physical strength* ○ *He pulled with all his strength, but the rock would not move.* **2** [U] the ability of an object to hold heavy weights or not to break or be damaged easily: *All our suitcases are tested for strength before they leave the factory.* **3** [U] the quality of being powerful: *America's economic strength* ○ *extra-strength pain relief capsules* **4** [U] how strong a feeling or opinion is: *I didn't realize the strength of her hatred of politics.* **5** [C,U] the good qualities and abilities of a person or thing: *His greatest strength is his ability to communicate with people.* ○ *the strengths and weaknesses of a plan*

IDM **on the strength of sth** as a result of information, advice, etc.: *Many people voted for him on the strength of his performance in the debates.*

☆**streng·then** /'strɛŋkθən/ *verb* [I,T] to become stronger or to make sth stronger: *exercises to strengthen your muscles* ○ *Support for the President seems to be strengthening.*

stren·u·ous /'strɛnyuəs/ *adj.* needing or using a lot of effort or energy: *You should avoid strenuous physical exercise for a while.* —**stren·u·ous·ly** *adv.*

☆**stress¹** /strɛs/ *noun* **1** [C,U] a state of worry and tension that is caused by difficulties in your life, having too much work, etc.: *He's been under a lot of stress since his wife went into the hospital.* ○ *The doctor told her that she was suffering from stress.* ○ *the stresses and strains of life in a big city* **2** [U] **stress (on sth)** the special force or emphasis that you give to sth because you think it is important: *There should be more stress on learning foreign languages in schools.* **3** [U] the force or emphasis that you put on a word or part of a word when you say it: *In the word "dictionary," the main stress is on the first syllable.* **4** [C,U] **stress (on sth)** a physical force that may cause sth to bend or break

stress² /strɛs/ *verb* **1** [T] to give sth special force or emphasis because you think it is important: *The senator stressed the need for a peaceful solution.* **2** [I,T] **stress (sb) (out)** (*informal*) to feel or cause sb to feel worried and unable to relax: *Ben's really stressing over his biology exam.*

stressed /strɛst/ (*also* ,**stressed** '**out**) *adj.* (*informal*) feeling worried and unable to relax: *I'm totally stressed about my final exam.*

☆**stress·ful** /'strɛsfl/ *adj.* causing stress¹(1) : *a stressful job*

☆**stretch¹** /strɛtʃ/ *verb* **1** [I,T] to pull sth so that it becomes longer or wider; to become longer or wider in this way: *The artist stretched the canvas tightly over the frame.* ○ *My T-shirt stretched out of shape when I washed it.* **2** [I,T] to push out your arms, legs, etc. as far as possible: *He got out of bed and stretched before going into the bathroom.* ○ *She stretched out her arm to take the book.* **3** [I] (used about a piece of land or water, etc.) to cover a large area: *The long white beaches stretch for miles along the coast.* **4** [I,T] to last or make sth last a long time: *The heat wave stretched into early September.* ○ *We'll have to think of a way to stretch our food budget.*

IDM **stretch your legs** to go for a walk after sitting down for a long time

PHRV **stretch out** to relax by lying down with all your body flat: *to stretch out in front of the fire*

stretch² /strɛtʃ/ *noun* **1** [C] **stretch (of sth)** an area of land or water: *a beautiful stretch of countryside* **2** [C, usually sing.] the act of stretching ¹(2)

IDM **at a stretch** without stopping: *six hours at a stretch*

the home stretch ⇨ HOME²

stretch·er /'strɛtʃər/ *noun* [C] a piece of cloth supported by two poles that is used for carrying a person who has been injured in an accident, etc.

☆**strict** /strɪkt/ *adj.* **1** not allowing people to break rules or behave badly: *Tom's always very strict with his children.* ○ *a strict teacher* ○ *I went to a very strict school.* **2** that must be obeyed completely: *I gave her strict instructions to be home before 9:00.* **3** exactly correct; precise: *a strict interpretation of the law*

☆**strict·ly** /'strɪkli/ *adv.* **1** in a strict way: *Speed limits are strictly enforced in this county.* **2 strictly for sb/sth** only for sb/sth, and nobody/nothing else: *Mom's cellular phone is strictly for business calls.*

IDM **strictly speaking** to be exactly correct or precise: *Strictly speaking, the tomato is not a vegetable. It's a fruit.*

stride¹ /straɪd/ *verb* [I] (*p.t.* **strode** /stroʊd/; *p.p.* **strid·den** /'strɪdn/) to walk with long steps, often because you are feeling very confi-

ər	ɪr	ɛr	ɑr	ɔr	ʊr	ʒ	h	ŋ
bird	near	hair	car	north	tour	vision	hat	sing

dent or determined: *He strode up to the house and knocked on the door.*

stride² /straɪd/ *noun* [C] a long step

IDM **make great strides** to make very quick progress

take sth in stride to deal with a new or difficult situation easily and without worrying

☆ **strike¹** /straɪk/ *noun* [C] **1** a period of time when people refuse to go to work, usually because they want more money or better working conditions: *a one-day strike* ○ *to go on strike for better working conditions* ○ *The workers have been on strike for two weeks now.* **2** a sudden military attack, especially by aircraft **3** (in baseball) an act of trying but failing to hit a ball that was thrown, or a ball that was thrown correctly but not hit ☞ Look at the note at **baseball. 4 a strike against sb/sth** an unfavorable quality or a disadvantage that sb/sth has: *These kids already have two strikes against them: they live in a dangerous neighborhood, and their parents aren't home enough.*

☆ **strike²** /straɪk/ *verb* (*p.t., p.p.* **struck** /strʌk/) **1** [T] (*formal*) to hit: *The stone struck me on my face.* ○ *to strike sb with your hand* ○ *The boat struck a rock and began to sink.*

☞ In these three examples it is more common to use the word **hit**: *The stone hit me on my face,* but if you are talking about lightning you must use **strike**: *The building had been struck by lightning.*

2 [I,T] to attack sb/sth suddenly: *The enemy aircraft struck just after 2 a.m.* ○ *The earthquake struck Northridge in 1994.* **3** [T] **strike sb (as sth)** to give sb a particular impression, often a strong one: *Does anything here strike you as unusual?* **4** [T] (used about a thought or an idea) to come suddenly into sb's mind: *It suddenly struck me that she would be the ideal person for the job.* **5** [I,T] (used about a clock) to ring a bell so that people know what time it is: *The church clock struck three.* **6** [T] to discover gold, oil, etc. **7** [I] to go on strike¹(1) : *The workers voted to strike for more money.*

IDM **strike a balance (between A and B)** to find a middle way between two extremes

strike a deal (with sb) to make an agreement with sb

strike a chord (with sb) to say or do sth that makes other people feel sympathy, excitement, etc.

PHRV **strike back** to attack sb/sth that has attacked you: *The President threatened to strike back if the rebels attacked the military base.*

strike out (*informal*) to be unsuccessful at sth that you are trying to do: *The company struck out with its first attempt to produce a laptop computer, but its latest product looks like a winner.*

strike (sb) out (in baseball) to try to hit the

ball unsuccessfully three times so that you are not allowed to try any longer, or to cause sb to do this

strike up sth (with sb) to start a conversation or friendship with sb

strik·er /ˈstraɪkər/ *noun* [C] a person who is on strike¹(1)

strik·ing /ˈstraɪkɪŋ/ *adj.* very noticeable; making a strong impression: *There was a striking similarity between the two men.* —**strik·ing·ly** *adv.*: *strikingly attractive*

☆ **string¹** /strɪŋ/ *noun* **1** [C,U] the thin cord that you use for tying things, etc.; a piece of this: *I need some string to tie around this box.* ○ *a ball of string* ○ *a balloon on the end of a string* ☞ picture at **knot. 2** [C] a piece of thin wire, etc. on a musical instrument: *A guitar has six strings.* **3 the strings** [plural] the musical instruments in an orchestra, etc. that have strings (2) **4** [C] **a string of sth** a line of things that are joined together on the same piece of thread: *a string of pearls* **5** [C] **a string of sth** a series of people, things or events that follow one after another: *a string of visitors* ○ *a string of complaints*

IDM **(with) no strings attached** with no special conditions: *We will send you a free copy of the magazine, with no strings attached.*

pull strings ⇨ PULL¹

string² /strɪŋ/ *verb* [T] (*p.t., p.p.* **strung** /strʌŋ/) **string sth (up)** to hang up a line of things with a piece of string, etc.: *Colored lights were strung up along the front of the hotel.*

PHRV **string sb/sth out** to make people or things form a line with spaces between each person or thing

string sth together to put words or phrases together to make a sentence, speech, etc.

ˈstring bean (*also* **green bean**) *noun* [C] as long, thin green vegetable that is cooked and eaten when the seeds inside are still small

strin·gent /ˈstrɪndʒənt/ *adj.* (used about a law, rule, etc.) very severe and strict

☆ **strip¹** /strɪp/ *noun* [C] a long narrow piece of sth: *a strip of paper* ○ *a strip of sandy beach*

strip² /strɪp/ *verb* (**strip·ping; stripped**) **1** [I,T] to take off your clothes; to take off sb else's clothes: *The doctor asked him to strip to the waist* (= above his waist). ○ *I was stripped and searched at the airport by two customs officers.* **2** [T] **strip sb/sth (of sth)** to take sth away from sb/sth: *They stripped the house of all its furniture.* ○ *The President had been stripped of most of his power.* **3** [T] **strip sth (off)** to remove sth that is covering a surface: *to strip the paint off a door*

☆ **stripe** /straɪp/ *noun* [C] a long narrow band of color: *Zebras have black and white stripes.* ☞ picture at **pattern.** Look also at **Stars and Stripes.**

striped /straɪpt; ˈstraɪpəd/ *adj.* having stripes:

tʃ	dʒ	v	θ	ð	s	z	ʃ
chin	**June**	**van**	**thin**	**then**	**so**	**zoo**	**she**

S

a red-and-white striped dress ☞ picture at **pat-tern**.

strip·per /'strɪpər/ *noun* [C] a person whose job is to take off his/her clothes in order to entertain people

strip·tease /'strɪptiz/ *noun* [C,U] entertainment in which sb takes off his/her clothes, usually to music

strive /straɪv/ *verb* [I] (*p.t.* **strove** /stroʊv/; *p.p.* **striv·en** /'strɪvn/) (*formal*) **strive (for sth)** to try very hard to do or get sth: *The company always strives to satisfy its customers.*

strode *p.t.* of STRIDE[1]

stroke[1] /stroʊk/ *verb* [T] to move your hand gently over sb/sth, in a loving way: *She stroked his hair affectionately.*

☆ **stroke**[2] /stroʊk/ *noun* **1** [C] one of the movements that you make when you are writing or painting: *a brush stroke* **2** [C] a sudden illness which attacks the brain and can leave a person unable to move part of their body, speak clearly, etc.: *to have/suffer a stroke* **3** [C] one of the movements that you make when you are swimming, rowing, playing tennis, etc.: *a forehand stroke* (= in tennis, etc.) **4** [C,U] one of the styles of swimming: *backstroke* ☞ Look at **crawl**.

IDM **a stroke of luck** something lucky that happens unexpectedly

stroll /stroʊl/ *verb* [I] to take a slow walk for pleasure: *to stroll along the beach* —**stroll** *noun* [C]: *to take a stroll through the park*

stroller baby carriage

stroll·er /'stroʊlər/ *noun* [C] a type of chair with four wheels that you can push a small child in as you walk along

☆ **strong**[1] /strɔŋ/ *adj.* **1** (used about a person) physically powerful; able to lift or carry heavy things: *I need someone strong to help me move this bookcase.* ○ *to have strong arms, muscles, etc.* **2** (used about an object) able to hold heavy weights; not easily broken or damaged: *That chair isn't strong enough for you to stand on.* ○ *a strong piece of rope* **3** intense; felt deeply: *There was strong opposition to the idea.* ○ *strong support for the governor's plan* ○ *He has strong views on the subject* (= he will not change them easily). ○ *strong feelings* **4** powerful and likely to succeed: *She's a strong candidate for the job.* **5** (used about a smell, taste, etc.) powerful and intense: *a strong smell of garlic* ○ *strong coffee* ○ *a strong drink* (= with a lot of alcohol in it) **6** powerful and moving

quickly: *strong winds* ☞ In **1** - **6**, the related noun is **strength**. **7** (used after a noun) having a particular number of people: *The army was 50,000 strong.*

strong[2] /strɔŋ/ *adv.*

IDM **be going strong** (*informal*) to be continuing, even after a long time: *The company was formed in 1851 and is still going strong.*

☆ **strong·ly** /'strɔŋli/ *adv.* very much; to a great degree: *The directors are strongly opposed to the idea.* ○ *to feel very strongly about sth*

strove *p.t.* of STRIVE

struck *p.t.*, *p.p.* of STRIKE[2]

☆ **struc·ture**[1] /'strʌktʃər/ *noun* **1** [C,U] the way that the parts of sth are put together or organized: *the structure of the brain* ○ *the political and social structure of a country* **2** [C] a building or sth that has been built or made from a number of parts: *a two-story wooden structure* —**struc·tur·al** /'strʌktʃərəl/ *adj.*: *Several windows were broken in the explosion but there was no structural damage* (= no damage to the walls, floors, etc.).

struc·ture[2] /'strʌktʃər/ *verb* [T] to arrange sth in an organized way: *a carefully structured English course*

☆ **strug·gle**[1] /'strʌgl/ *verb* [I] **1** to try very hard to do sth although it is difficult: *Maria was struggling with her English homework.* ○ *We struggled up the hill with our heavy suitcases.* **2** to make violent movements when you are trying to escape from sb/sth: *He shouted and struggled, but he couldn't get free.*

strug·gle[2] /'strʌgl/ *noun* [C] **1** a fight: *All countries should join together in the struggle against terrorism.* **2** [usually sing.] a great effort: *After a long struggle, she finally managed to graduate.*

strum /strʌm/ *verb* [I,T] (**strum·ming**; **strummed**) to play a guitar by moving your hand up and down over the strings

strung *p.t.*, *p.p.* of STRING[2]

strut /strʌt/ *verb* [I] (**strut·ting**; **strut·ted**) to walk in a proud way

stub /stʌb/ *noun* [C] **1** a short piece of sth, such as a pencil, that remains after the rest of it has been used **2** the part of a ticket, check, etc. that you can keep as a record of payment

☆ **stub·born** /'stʌbərn/ *adj.* not wanting to do what other people want you to do; refusing to change your plans or decisions: *She's too stubborn to apologize.* ○ *a stubborn refusal* —**stub·born·ly** *adv.* —**stub·born·ness** *noun* [U]

stuck[1] *p.t.*, *p.p.* of STICK[2]

☆ **stuck**[2] /stʌk/ *adj.* (not before a noun) **1** not able to move: *This drawer's stuck. I can't open it at all.* **2** not able to continue with an exercise, etc. because it is too difficult: *If you get stuck, ask your teacher for help.*

stud /stʌd/ *noun* [C] **1** [C] a small round piece of metal on the surface of sth: *a black leather jacket with studs all over it* **2** [C] (*slang*) a man

i	ɪ	ɛ	æ	ɑ	ɔ	ʌ	ʊ	u
see	sit	ten	cat	hot	saw	cup	put	too

who is thought to be sexually attractive and who has many relationships **3** a small round earring that you wear through a hole in your ear **4** [C,U] a horse or a number of horses or other animals that are kept for breeding young animals (of high quality): *a stud farm*

stud·ded /ˈstʌdəd/ *adj.* **studded with sth** covered or decorated with studs (1) or other small objects: *The crown is studded with diamonds.*

☆ **stu·dent** /ˈstudnt/ *noun* [C] a person who is studying at a school, college or university: *Julia is a medical student at Harvard.* ○ *a part-time college student* ○ *Ashley wasn't a very good student in high school.* ○ *a student teacher* (= a person who is learning to be a teacher) ☞ Look at **graduate** and **undergraduate**.

ˌ**student ˈbody** *noun* [C] (*pl.* **student bodies**) all the students at a school, college or university

☆ **stu·di·o** /ˈstudioʊ/ *noun* [C] (*pl.* **stu·di·os**) **1** a room where an artist or photographer works **2** a room or building where television or radio programs, movies, or records are made **3** (*also* ˌ**studio aˈpartment**) an apartment with only one main room which is used as a living room and bedroom

stu·di·ous /ˈstudiəs/ *adj.* (*formal*) (used about a person) spending a lot of time studying

☆ **stud·y¹** /ˈstʌdi/ *verb* (*pres. part.* **stud·y·ing**; *3rd pers. sing. pres.* **stud·ies**; *p.t., p.p.* **studied**) **1** [I,T] to spend time learning about sth: *Lawrence has been studying hard for his final exams.* ○ *to study French in college* **2** [T] to look at sth very carefully: *to study a map*

☆ **stud·y²** /ˈstʌdi/ *noun* (*pl.* **studies**) **1** [C] scientific research into a particular subject and a book or article that a person writes after studying it: *a scientific study of the causes of heart disease* **2 studies** [plural] a group of several related subjects that sb studies at a college or university: *She's majoring in media studies.* **3** [U] the act of learning about sth: *One hour every afternoon is left free for quiet study.* **4** [C] a room in a house where you go to read, write or study

ˈ**study hall** *noun* [U] a period of time during the school day when a student is supposed to study and do work for his/her other classes

☆ **stuff¹** /stʌf/ *noun* [U] (*informal*) a substance or a group of things or activities (used instead of the name of the thing that you are talking about): *What's that green stuff at the bottom of the bottle?* ○ *You can just put your stuff on the chair over there.* ○ *The hotel was great – there was a swimming pool and a game room and stuff.* ○ *I have a whole bunch of stuff to do this weekend.*

stuff² /stʌf/ *verb* **1** [T] **stuff sth (with sth)** to fill sth with sth: *The pillow was stuffed with feathers.* **2** [T] **stuff sth into sth** to put sth into sth quickly or carelessly: *He quickly stuffed a*

few clothes into a suitcase. **3** [T] **stuff yourself (with sth)** to eat a lot: *The kids have been stuffing themselves with candy and ice cream all afternoon.* **4** [T] **stuff sth (with sth)** to put a mixture of small pieces of food (**stuffing**) into a chicken, vegetable, etc. before you cook it: *stuffed green peppers* **5** [T] to fill the body of a dead bird or animal with special material so that it continues to look as if it is alive

IDM **be stuffed** (*informal*) to have eaten so much food that you cannot eat any more: *I can't eat another bite – I'm stuffed!*

ˌ**stuffed ˈanimal** *noun* [C] a toy in the shape of an animal, that is made of soft fabric and is filled with soft material

stuff·ing /ˈstʌfɪŋ/ *noun* [U] **1** (*also* **dressing**) a mixture of small pieces of food that you put inside a chicken, vegetable, etc. before you cook it **2** the material that you put inside pillows, etc.: *Oh, no! My teddy bear's stuffing is coming out!*

stuff·y /ˈstʌfi/ *adj.* (**stuff·i·er**; **stuff·i·est**) **1** (used about a room, etc.) having air that is not fresh **2** (*informal*) (used of a person, of behavior, etc.) formal and old-fashioned

stum·ble /ˈstʌmbl/ *verb* [I] **1** to hit your foot against sth when you are walking or running and almost fall down: *I stumbled as I was getting out of the boat.* **2 stumble (over sth)** to make a mistake when you are speaking, playing music, etc.: *The news anchor stumbled over the name of the Russian tennis player.*

PHRV **stumble across/on/upon sb/sth** to meet or find sb/sth by chance

ˈ**stum·bling block** *noun* [C] something that causes trouble or a difficulty, so that you cannot get what you want

stump¹ /stʌmp/ *noun* [C] the part that is left after sth has been cut down, broken off, etc.: *a tree stump*

stump² /stʌmp/ *verb* **1** [T] (*informal*) to cause sb to be unable to answer a question or find a solution for a problem: *I was completely stumped by question 14.* **2** [I] **stump (for sb)** to give speeches in order to persuade people to vote for a particular person in an election

stun /stʌn/ *verb* [T] (**stun·ning**; **stunned**) **1** to make a person or animal unconscious or confused by hitting him/her/it on the head **2** to make a person very surprised by giving him/her some unexpected news: *His sudden death stunned his friends and colleagues.* —**stunned** *adj.*: *There was a stunned silence after Margaret announced her resignation.*

stung *p.t., p.p.* of STING¹

stunk *p.p.* of STINK

stun·ning /ˈstʌnɪŋ/ *adj.* (*informal*) very attractive or impressive: *a stunning woman* ○ *a stunning success*

stunt¹ /stʌnt/ *noun* [C] **1** something that you do to get people's attention: *a publicity stunt* **2** a very difficult or dangerous thing that sb

S

does to entertain people: *His latest stunt was jumping over ten cars on his motorcycle.*

stunt² /stʌnt/ *verb* [T] to stop sb/sth from growing or developing properly: *A bad diet can stunt a child's growth.*

stunt·man /ˈstʌntmæn/ (*also* **stunt·wom·an** /ˈstʌntwʊmən/) *noun* [C] (*pl.* **stunt·men**; **stunt·wom·en**) a person who does a stunt¹(2) in a movie in the place of an actor

stu·pen·dous /stuˈpɛndəs/ *adj.* very large, grand or impressive: *a stupendous achievement*

☆ **stu·pid** /ˈstupəd/ *adj.* **1** not intelligent; foolish: *Don't be so stupid – of course I'll help you!* ○ *It was stupid of him to trust her.* ○ *He was stupid to trust her.* **2** (only *before* a noun) (*informal*) (a word that shows that you do not like sb/sth): *I'm tired of hearing about his stupid car.* —**stu·pid·i·ty** /stuˈpɪdəti/ *noun* [U] —**stu·pid·ly** *adv.*

stur·dy /ˈstərdi/ *adj.* (**stur·di·er**; **stur·di·est**) strong; that will not break easily: *a sturdy chair* —**stur·di·ness** *noun* [U]

stut·ter /ˈstʌtər/ *verb* [I,T] to have difficulty when you speak, so that you keep repeating the first sound of a word —**stut·ter** *noun* [C]: *to speak with a stutter*

☆ **style¹** /staɪl/ *noun* **1** [C,U] the way that sth is done, built, etc.: *a new style of architecture* ○ *a Japanese-style noodle restaurant* **2** [C,U] the way that sb usually writes, behaves, etc.: *Hemingway's style is very clear and simple.* ○ *Going to nightclubs just isn't my style.* **3** [U] the state of being of very good quality in appearance or behavior: *a dress with real style* ○ *They don't have many parties but when they do, they do it in style.* **4** [C,U] the fashion, shape or design of sth: *We stock all the newest styles.* ○ *a hairstyle*

IDM **in style/out of style** fashionable/unfashionable: *This simple gray jacket will never go out of style.*

style² /staɪl/ *verb* [T] to arrange sb's hair in an attractive way

styl·ish /ˈstaɪlɪʃ/ *adj.* fashionable and attractive

Sty·ro·foam /ˈstaɪrəfoʊm/ *noun* [U] (*trademark*) a light, firm plastic substance that is used to stop heat from escaping or to pack things so that they do not get broken: *a Styrofoam coffee cup*

suave /swɑv/ *adj.* (usually used about a man) very polite, charming, and well behaved (sometimes too much so)

sub¹ /sʌb/ *noun* [C] (*informal*) **1** = SUBMARINE **2** = SUBSTITUTE¹(2)

sub² /sʌb/ *verb* [I] (**sub·bing**; **subbed**) (*informal*) = SUBSTITUTE²(2)

sub·con·scious /ˌsʌbˈkɑnʃəs/ *noun* [sing.] the hidden part of your mind that can affect the way that you behave, even though you do not know it exists —**sub·con·scious** *adj.*: *the subconscious mind* —**sub·con·scious·ly** *adv.*

sub·di·vide /ˌsʌbdəvaɪd; ˌsʌbdəˈvaɪd/ *verb* [I,T] to divide or be divided into smaller parts

sub·di·vi·sion /ˈsʌbdəvɪʒn/ *noun* [C] an area with a lot of houses that were built at the same time, often in a similar style

sub·due /səbˈdu/ *verb* [T] to defeat or bring sb/sth under control: *to subdue a rebel army* ○ *She tried hard to subdue her emotions.*

sub·dued /səbˈdud/ *adj.* **1** not very loud or bright: *subdued lighting* **2** (used about a person) sad or quiet

☆ **sub·ject¹** /ˈsʌbdʒɛkt; -dʒɪkt/ *noun* [C] **1** a person or thing that is being considered, shown or talked about: *the subject of a paper* ○ *What are your views on this subject?* ○ *to change the subject* (= start talking about sth else) ○ *I tried several times to bring up the subject of money.* ○ *the novel's controversial subject matter* **2** an area of knowledge that you study in school, college, etc.: *She's taking four subjects this semester: French, English, psychology and history.* **3** (*grammar*) the person or thing that performs the action described by the verb in a sentence: *In the sentence "The cat sat on the mat," "the cat" is the subject.*

sub·ject² /səbˈdʒɛkt/ *verb*
PHRV **subject sb/sth to sth** to cause sb/sth to experience sth bad

sub·ject³ /ˈsʌbdʒɛkt; -dʒɪkt/ *adj.* **subject to sth 1** controlled or affected by sth: *Restaurants are subject to strict health regulations.* ○ *All times listed are approximate and subject to change.* **2** depending on sth as a condition: *Construction will begin in May, subject to approval by the city council.*

sub·jec·tive /səbˈdʒɛktɪv/ *adj.* influenced by your own feelings and opinions instead of by facts alone: *a subjective interpretation of events* ☞ The opposite is **objective**. —**sub·jec·tive·ly** *adv.*

the sub·junc·tive /səbˈdʒʌŋktɪv/ *noun* [sing.] (*grammar*) the form of a verb that expresses doubt, possibility, a wish, etc. in certain languages. For example, in the sentence, "I recommend that she see a doctor," "see" is in the subjunctive. —**sub·junc·tive** *adj.*

sub·let /ˈsʌblɛt/ *verb* [T] to rent to sb else a room, an apartment, etc. that you are renting from sb else, usually for a short period of time —**sub·let** *noun* [C]: *a list of summer sublets available near campus*

sub·lime /səˈblaɪm/ *adj.* wonderful; having a quality that makes you admire it very much

sub·ma·rine /ˈsʌbmərin; ˌsʌbməˈrin/ *noun* [C] **1** a type of boat that can travel under the water as well as on the surface **2** (*also* **sub·marine 'sandwich**) a type of sandwich in a large, long bread roll, filled with different kinds of meats and cheese, lettuce, tomatoes, etc.

sub·merged /səbˈmərdʒd/ *adj.* under water: *submerged rocks just below the surface*

ər	ɪr	ɛr	ɑr	ɔr	ʊr	ʒ	h	ŋ
bird	near	hair	car	north	tour	vision	hat	sing

sub·mis·sion /səbˈmɪʃn/ *noun* **1** [C,U] the act of sending a plan or statement to an official organization so that it can be discussed or considered; the plan or statement that you send: *Send us your submission of no more than 300 words by noon Friday.* **2** [U] the state of accepting sb else's power or control

sub·mit /səbˈmɪt/ *verb* (**sub·mit·ting**; **sub·mit·ted**) **1** [T] **submit sth (to sb/sth)** to give or propose sth to sb/sth so that it can be discussed or considered: *Applications must be submitted by March 31.* **2** [I] **submit (to sb/sth)** to accept sb/sth's power or control: *After a bitter struggle, the rebels were forced to submit.*

sub·or·di·nate¹ /səˈbɔrdn·ət/ *adj.* (*formal*) **subordinate (to sth)** less important than sth else

sub·or·di·nate² /səˈbɔrdn·ət/ *noun* [C] a person who is of lower rank or position

sub·poe·na /səˈpinə/ *noun* [C] an official legal document that orders sb to go and give evidence (**testify**) in a court of law —**sub·poe·na** *verb* [T]: *She was subpoenaed to testify for the defense.*

sub·scribe /səbˈskraɪb/ *verb* [I] **1 subscribe (to sth)** to pay for a newspaper or magazine to be sent to you regularly, or for a special computer or television service: *Do you subscribe to a daily paper?* **2 subscribe to sth** (*formal*) to agree with an idea, belief, etc.: *I don't subscribe to the view that all war is wrong.*

sub·scrib·er /səbˈskraɪbər/ *noun* [C] a person who pays to receive a newspaper or magazine regularly, or to use a special computer or television service: *cable TV subscribers*

☆ **sub·scrip·tion** /səbˈskrɪpʃn/ *noun* [C] an amount of money that you pay to receive a newspaper or magazine regularly or to use a special computer or television service

sub·se·quent /ˈsʌbsəkwənt/ *adj.* (only *before* a noun) (*formal*) coming after or later: *Many homes were damaged by the heavy rains and subsequent flooding.* —**sub·se·quent·ly** *adv.*: *The suspect was arrested and subsequently charged with first-degree murder.*

sub·side /səbˈsaɪd/ *verb* [I] to become less strong: *The storm seems to be subsiding.*

sub·sid·i·ar·y /səbˈsɪdiˌɛri/ *noun* [C] (*pl.* **sub·sid·i·ar·ies**) a business that belongs to a larger company

sub·si·dize /ˈsʌbsədaɪz/ *verb* [T] (used about a government, etc.) to pay money in order to keep prices or the cost of a service low: *The state government subsidizes school lunch programs.*

sub·si·dized /ˈsʌbsədaɪzd/ *adj.* that is partly paid for by the government: *subsidized housing for low-income families*

sub·si·dy /ˈsʌbsədi/ *noun* [C] (*pl.* **sub·si·dies**) money that the government, etc. pays to help an organization or a group of people or to help keep the cost of sth low: *agricultural subsidies*

sub·sist /səbˈsɪst/ *verb* [I] (*formal*) to manage to live with very little food or money —**sub·sis·tence** /-təns/ *noun* [U]: *The soil is only good enough for subsistence farming.*

☆ **sub·stance** /ˈsʌbstəns/ *noun* **1** [C] a solid or liquid material: *poisonous substances* ○ *The cloth is coated in a new waterproof substance.* **2** [U] the most important points or ideas of sth: *Don't repeat everything. Just tell me the substance of what they said.* **3** [U] importance, value or truth: *The novel has little substance, but it's very entertaining.*

ˈsubstance aˌbuse *noun* [U] the habit of taking too many illegal drugs and/or drinking too much alcohol

sub·stan·dard /ˌsʌbˈstændərd/ *adj.* of poor quality; not as good as usual or as it should be

☆ **sub·stan·tial** /səbˈstænʃl/ *adj.* **1** large in amount: *The storms caused substantial damage.* ○ *a substantial sum of money* **2** large or strong: *The furniture was cheap and not very substantial.*

sub·stan·tial·ly /səbˈstænʃl·i/ *adv.* **1** by a large amount: *Real estate prices have risen substantially.* **2** (*formal*) generally; in most points: *Our policy has remained substantially unchanged.*

☆ **sub·sti·tute¹** /ˈsʌbstətut/ *noun* [C] **1 substitute (for sb/sth)** something that is used or done in place of sth else: *Margarine is an inexpensive substitute for butter.* **2** (also *informal* **sub**) a person who takes the place of sb/sth else, e.g. at work: *a substitute teacher*

sub·sti·tute² /ˈsʌbstətut/ *verb* **1** [T] **substitute sb/sth (for sb/sth)** to put a person or thing in the place of sb/sth else: *You can substitute milk for the cream in the recipe.* **2** [I] (also *informal* **sub**) **substitute (for sb/sth)** to do sth or be used instead of sb/sth: *I'm too sick to work tonight – can you sub for me?* **sub·sti·tu·tion** /ˌsʌbstəˈtuʃn/ *noun* [C,U]

sub·ti·tles /ˈsʌbtaɪtlz/ *noun* [plural] the words at the bottom of the picture on television or in a movie. The subtitles translate the words of a foreign movie or program.

sub·tle /ˈsʌtl/ *adj.* **1** not very noticeable; not very strong or bright: *subtle colors* ○ *I noticed a subtle difference in her.* **2** very skillful, e.g. at deceiving or persuading people: *Advertisements persuade us to buy things in very subtle ways.* —**sub·tle·ty** /ˈsʌtlti/ *noun* [C,U] (*pl.* **sub·tle·ties**) —**sub·tly** /ˈsʌtli/ *adv.*

☆ **sub·tract** /səbˈtrækt/ *verb* [T] **subtract sth (from sth)** to take one number or quantity away from another: *If you subtract five from nine, you get four.* —**sub·trac·tion** /səbˈtrækʃn/ *noun* [C,U]

☆ **sub·urb** /ˈsʌbərb/ *noun* [C] an area where people live that is outside the central part of a city: *people who commute from the suburbs to their jobs downtown* ○ *a residential suburb of*

S

tʃ	dʒ	v	θ	ð	s	z	ʃ
chin	June	van	thin	then	so	zoo	she

St. Louis —**sub·ur·ban** /sə'bərbən/ *adj.*: *suburban school districts* ○ *suburban Chicago* (= the suburbs around Chicago)

sub·ur·bi·a /sə'bərbiə/ *noun* [U] the suburbs of cities, considered as a whole

sub·ver·sive /səb'vərsɪv/ *adj.* trying to weaken or destroy a government, religion, etc. or to challenge accepted ideas —**sub·ver·sive** *noun* [C]

☆ **sub·way** /'sʌbweɪ/ *noun* [C] an underground train system in a city: *Kristi rides the subway to work every day.*

☆ **suc·ceed** /sək'sid/ *verb* 1 [I] **succeed (in sth/ in doing sth)** to manage to achieve what you want; to do well: *Our plan succeeded.* ○ *If you keep on trying, you will eventually succeed.* ○ *A good education will help you succeed in life.* ○ *to succeed in gaining admission to college* ☛ The opposite is **fail.** 2 [I,T] to have a job or important position after sb else: *Bill Clinton succeeded George Bush as President in 1993.*

☆ **suc·cess** /sək'sɛs/ *noun* 1 [U] achieving what you want; doing well: *Hard work is the key to success.* ○ *Her first novel achieved great commercial success.* 2 [C] something or somebody that achieves what he/she/it wants to, or becomes very popular: *You should try to make a success of your marriage.* ○ *The school carnival was a huge success.* ○ *I'm sure she'll be a success, no matter what career she chooses.* ☛ The opposite is **failure.**

☆ **suc·cess·ful** /sək'sɛsfl/ *adj.* having achieved what was wanted; having become popular: *a successful attempt to climb Mount Everest* ○ *a successful actor* —**suc·cess·ful·ly** *adv.*

suc·ces·sion /sək'sɛʃn/ *noun* [C] a number of people or things that follow one after another: *We've had a succession of hot, dry summers recently.*

IDM **in succession** following one after another: *There have been three deaths in the family in rapid succession.*

suc·ces·sive /sək'sɛsɪv/ *adj.* (only *before* a noun) following one after another: *He came to work late on three successive days.* —**suc·ces·sive·ly** *adv.*

suc·ces·sor /sək'sɛsər/ *noun* [C] a person who has a job or an important position after sb else ☛ Look at **predecessor.**

suc·cinct /sək'sɪŋkt/ *adj.* said clearly, in a few words —**suc·cinct·ly** *adv.*

suc·cu·lent /'sʌkyələnt/ *adj.* (used about food) very good to eat because it is not dry

suc·cumb /sə'kʌm/ *verb* [I] **succumb (to sth)** (*formal*) to stop fighting against sth: *He succumbed to temptation and started taking drugs again.* ○ *to succumb to an illness* (= to die)

☆ **such**[1] /sʌtʃ/ *det.* 1 (used for referring to sb/sth that you are talking about or that you mentioned earlier) of this or that type: *"Can I talk to Mr. Wallis?" "Sorry, there's no such person here."* ○ *I don't believe in ghosts. There's*

no such thing. 2 (used for emphasizing the degree of sth): *It was such a boring movie that I fell asleep.* ○ *Let's have lunch on the patio. It's such a nice day.* ○ *It seems like such a long time since the last time we met.*

☛ You use **such** before a noun or before a noun that has an adjective in front of it: *Tommy is such a jerk!* ○ *Susan is such a good athlete.* You use **so** before an adjective that is used without a noun: *Don't be so dumb.* ○ *It was so cold we stayed at home.* Compare: *It was such a cold night that we stayed at home.*

3 (used for talking about the result of sth): *The statement was worded in such a way that it did not upset anyone.*

☆ **such**[2] /sʌtʃ/ *pron.* (*formal*) (used for referring to sb/sth that you are talking about or that you mentioned earlier) this or that type of person or thing: *The economic situation is such that we all have less money to spend.*

IDM **as such** (*formal*) 1 in the exact meaning of the word: *I don't believe in capital punishment as such, but I do believe that the punishment should fit the crime.* 2 without anything else; alone: *Poverty as such does not mean unhappiness, but it can make life very uncomfortable.*

such as for example: *Fatty foods such as French fries are bad for you.*

suck /sʌk/ *verb* 1 [I,T] to pull a liquid into your mouth, by making your lips into a round shape and pulling your cheeks in: *to suck milk through a straw* ☛ picture at **blow.** 2 [T] to pull sth in a particular direction, using force: *This vacuum cleaner really sucks up the dirt.* 3 [I,T] to have sth in your mouth and keep touching it with your lips and tongue: *All my kids sucked their thumbs.* 4 [I] (*slang*) to be very bad or unpleasant: *"How was school today?" "It sucked."* ○ *It totally sucks having to work on a Friday night.* ☛ The opposite for this meaning is **rule.**

suck·er /'sʌkər/ *noun* [C] 1 (*informal*) a person who believes everything that you tell him/her and who is easy to cheat 2 = **LOLLIPOP**

suc·tion /'sʌkʃn/ *noun* [U] 1 the act of removing air from a space so that another substance is pulled in: *A vacuum cleaner works by suction.* 2 the act of making two surfaces stick together by removing the air between them: *The hook is attached to the wall by a suction cup.*

☆ **sud·den** /'sʌdn/ *adj.* done or happening quickly, or when you do not expect it: *a sudden decision* ○ *a sudden loud noise*

IDM **all of a sudden** suddenly; unexpectedly: *All of a sudden, a rabbit ran in front of the car.* —**sud·den·ly** *adv.*: *Suddenly, everybody started shouting.* —**sud·den·ness** *noun* [U]

suds /sʌdz/ *noun* [plural] the bubbles that you get when you mix soap and water

i	ɪ	ɛ	æ	ɑ	ɔ	ʌ	ʊ	u
see	sit	ten	cat	hot	saw	cup	put	too

☆ **sue** /su/ verb [I,T] **sue (sb) (for sth)** to go to a court of law and ask for money from sb because he/she has done sth bad to you, or said sth bad about you: *She sued the business' owners for $5 million.* ○ *to sue sb for* (= because of) *racial discrimination*

suede /sweɪd/ noun [U] a type of soft leather which does not have a smooth surface and feels somewhat like cloth

☆ **suf·fer** /'sʌfər/ verb **1** [I,T] to experience sth bad, e.g. pain, sadness, difficulty, etc.: *Mary often suffers from severe headaches.* ○ *Our troops suffered heavy losses.* ○ *In a recession, it's the poor who suffer most.* **2** [I] to become worse in quality: *If you have problems at home, your work will suffer.* —**suf·fer·er** /'sʌfərər/ noun [C]: *cancer sufferers* —**suf·fer·ing** /'sʌfərɪŋ/ noun [C,U]: *The famine caused great hardship and suffering.*

☆ **suf·fi·cient** /sə'fɪʃnt/ adj. (formal) as much as is necessary; enough: *We have sufficient oil reserves to last for three months.* ☛ The opposite is **insufficient**. —**suf·fi·cient·ly** adv.

suf·fix /'sʌfɪks/ noun [C] a letter or group of letters that you add at the end of a word, and that change its meaning or the way it is used: *To form the noun from the adjective "sad," add the suffix "-ness."* ☛ Look at **prefix**.

suf·fo·cate /'sʌfəkeɪt/ verb [I,T] to die because there is no air to breathe; to kill sb in this way —**suf·fo·cat·ing** /-keɪtɪŋ/ adj.: *the suffocating summer heat* —**suf·fo·ca·tion** /ˌsʌfə'keɪʃn/ noun [U]

☆ **sug·ar** /'ʃʊɡər/ noun a sweet substance that you get from certain plants: *coffee with cream and sugar* —**sug·ar·y** /'ʃʊɡəri/ adj.

☆ **sug·gest** /səg'dʒɛst; sə'dʒ-/ verb [T] **1 suggest sth (to sb)** to propose a plan or idea for sb to discuss or consider: *Can anybody suggest ways of raising more money?* ○ *Tony suggested going out for a walk.* ○ *Tony suggested that we go out for a walk.* ○ *Tony suggested a walk.* ○ *How do you suggest we get out of this mess?*

☛ Note that we cannot use an indirect object immediately after **suggest**. So we CANNOT say e.g.: *Can you suggest me a good hotel?* We must say instead: *Can you suggest a good hotel?* Look also at the note at **recommend** (2).

2 to say that a person or thing is suitable, especially a person or thing that you know about from your own experience: *Can you suggest someone for the job?* **3** to say or show sth in an indirect way: *Are you suggesting the accident was my fault?* ○ *Forecasts suggest that inflation will fall by the end of next year.*

☆ **sug·ges·tion** /səg'dʒɛstʃən; sə'dʒ-/ noun **1** [C] a plan or idea that sb proposes or suggests: *Can I make a suggestion?* ○ *The board rejected the suggestion that they give themselves smaller bonuses.* ☛ Look at the note at **recommend**

(2). **2** [U] putting an idea into a person's mind; giving advice about what to do: *the power of suggestion in advertising* **3** [sing.] a small amount or sign of sth: *Investigations found no suggestion of illegal activities.*

sug·ges·tive /səg'dʒɛstɪv; sə'dʒ-/ adj. **1** making you think of sth: *music that was suggestive of Asia* **2** making you think about sex: *a suggestive dance* —**sug·ges·tive·ly** adv.

su·i·cid·al /ˌsuə'saɪdl/ adj. **1** (used about a person) wanting to kill himself/herself: *to feel suicidal* **2** that will probably result in your being killed: *a suicidal risk*

☆ **su·i·cide** /'suəsaɪd/ noun [C,U] the act of killing yourself: *Ben has tried to commit suicide several times.* ○ *an increase in the number of suicides*

☆ **suit¹** /sut/ noun [C] **1** a set of clothes that are made of the same material and that are fairly formal. A man's suit usually consists of a jacket and pants, and a woman's suit of a jacket and a skirt or pants. **2** a piece of clothing or set of clothes that you wear for a particular activity: *a spacesuit* ○ *a swimsuit* ○ *a suit of armor* **3** one of the four sets of thirteen playing cards (= hearts, clubs, diamonds and spades) ☛ Look at the note at **card**. **4** = LAWSUIT

IDM **file suit (against sb)** ➪ FILE²
follow suit ➪ FOLLOW

suit² /sut/ verb [T] to be convenient or suitable for sb/sth: *How would Thursday at 9:30 suit you?* ○ *It was hard to find a house that would suit our needs.*

IDM **be suited for/to sb/sth** to be suitable or right for sb/sth: *She and her husband are very well suited to each other.*

☆ **suit·a·ble** /'sutəbl/ adj. **suitable (for sb/sth)** right or convenient for sb/sth: *The movie isn't suitable for children.* ○ *Is this a suitable time to have a meeting?* ☛ The opposite is **unsuitable**. —**suit·a·bil·i·ty** /ˌsutə'bɪləti/ noun [U] —**suit·a·bly** /-əbli/ adv.: *to be suitably dressed for the party*

☆ **suit·case** /'sutkeɪs/ noun [C] a flat box with a handle that you use to carry your clothes, etc. in when you are traveling ☛ picture at **luggage**.

suite /swit/ noun [C] a set of connected rooms in a hotel

suit·or /'sutər/ noun [C] (old-fashioned) a man who wants to marry a particular woman

sul·fur /'sʌlfər/ noun [U] (symbol **S**) a yellow substance with a strong, bad smell

sulk /sʌlk/ verb [I] to be very quiet or to look unhappy because you are angry with sb about sth —**sulk·y** adj.

sul·len /'sʌlən/ adj. looking bad-tempered and not speaking to people: *a sullen teenager* —**sul·len·ly** adv.

sul·tan /'sʌltn/ noun [C] the ruler in some Muslim countries: *the Sultan of Brunei*

ə	y	w	t̬	eɪ	aɪ	ɔɪ	aʊ	oʊ
about	yes	woman	butter	say	five	boy	now	go

sul·try /ˈsʌltri/ *adj.* **1** (used about the weather) hot and damp **2** (used about a woman) very sexually attractive

☆**sum¹** /sʌm/ *noun* [C] **1** an amount of money: *The industry has spent huge sums of money to update its equipment.* ☞ Look at **lump sum**. **2** [usually sing.] the amount that you get when you add two or more numbers together: *The sum of two and five is seven.*

sum² /sʌm/ *verb* **sum·ming; summed**
PHRV **sum (sth) up** to describe in a few words the main ideas of what sb has said or written: *to sum up the main points of an argument*

☆**sum·ma·ry** /ˈsʌməri/ *noun* [C] (*pl.* **sum·ma·ries**) a short description of the main ideas or events of sth: *A brief summary of the experiment is given at the beginning of the report.* ○ *a news summary* —**sum·ma·rize** /ˈsʌməraɪz/ *verb* [T]: *Could you summarize the story so far?*

☆**sum·mer** /ˈsʌmər/ *noun* [C,U] the hottest season of the year, after spring and before fall: *Are you going away this summer?* ○ *a summer job* ○ *summer vacation* —**sum·mer·y** /ˈsʌməri/ *adj.*: *summery weather* ○ *a summery dress*

ˈsummer school *noun* [C,U] classes held during the summer at a high school or college, especially for students who need extra help

☆**sum·mer·time** /ˈsʌmərtaɪm/ *noun* [U] the season of summer: *It's busy here in the summertime.*

☆**sum·mit** /ˈsʌmət/ *noun* [C] **1** the top of a mountain **2** an important meeting between the leaders of two or more countries: *an economic summit in China*

sum·mon /ˈsʌmən/ *verb* [T] **1** (*formal*) to order a person to come to a place: *Several employees were summoned to the manager's office.* ○ *to summon help* **2** **summon sth (up)** to find strength, courage or some other quality that you need, even though it is difficult for you to do so: *She couldn't summon up the courage to leave him.*

sum·mons /ˈsʌmənz/ *noun* [C] (*pl.* **sum·mons·es**) an official order to go somewhere, especially to a court of law

☆**sun¹** /sʌn/ *noun* **1 the sun** [sing.] the star that shines in the sky during the day and that gives the earth heat and light: *The sun rises in the east and sets in the west.* ○ *the sun's rays* **2** [sing., U] light and heat from the sun (1): *Don't sit in the sun too long.* ○ *Too much sun can be harmful.*

sun² /sʌn/ *verb* [T] (**sun·ning; sunned**) **sun yourself** sit or lie in the sun in order to enjoy the heat: *a snake sunning itself on a rock*

Sun. *abbr.* Sunday

sun·bathe /ˈsʌnbeɪð/ *verb* [I] to sit or lie in the sun in order to make your skin turn brown

ˈsun block (*also* **sunscreen**) *noun* [U] a cream that you put on your skin to protect it from the sun

☆**sun·burn** /ˈsʌnbərn/ *noun* [U] red painful skin that you get after being in strong sunlight for too long —**sun·burned** /ˈsʌnbərnd/ (*also* **sun·burnt** /ˈsʌnbərnt/) *adj.*

sun·dae /ˈsʌndeɪ; -di/ *noun* [C] a type of food that consists of ice cream with fruit, nuts, sweet sauce, etc. on the top

☆**Sun·day** /ˈsʌndeɪ; -di/ *noun* [C,U] (*abbr.* **Sun.**) the first day of the week, coming before Monday ☞ For examples of the use of the days of the week in sentences, look at **Monday**.

ˈSunday school *noun* [C,U] a class held in a church on Sundays to teach children about their religion

sun·down /ˈsʌndaʊn/ *noun* [U] (*old-fashioned*) = SUNSET

sun·flow·er /ˈsʌnflaʊər/ *noun* [C] a tall plant that has a very large yellow flower with a black center. The seeds of the plant can be eaten or used to make cooking oil.

sung *p.p.* of SING

☆**sun·glass·es** /ˈsʌnglæsəs/ (*also informal* **shades**) *noun* [plural] dark glasses that protect your eyes from bright sunlight

sunk *p.p.* of SINK¹

sunk·en /ˈsʌŋkən/ *adj.* **1** below the water: *a sunken ship* **2** (used about cheeks or eyes) curving in and making you look sick **3** at a lower level than the surrounding area: *a luxury bathroom with a sunken bathtub*

☆**sun·light** /ˈsʌnlaɪt/ *noun* [U] the light from the sun

☆**sun·ny** /ˈsʌni/ *adj.* (**sun·ni·er; sun·ni·est**) having a lot of light from the sun: *a sunny day* ○ *Tomorrow will be mostly sunny, hot and humid.*

ˌsunny-side ˈup *adj.* (used about eggs) fried on one side only

☆**sun·rise** /ˈsʌnraɪz/ *noun* [U] the time when the sun comes up and the day begins: *to get up at sunrise* ☞ Look at **dawn**.

sun·screen /ˈsʌnskrin/ *noun* [U] = SUN BLOCK

☆**sun·set** /ˈsʌnsɛt/ *noun* [C,U] (*also informal* **sundown**) [U] the time when the sun goes down and night begins; the appearance of the sky when this happens: *The park closes at sunset.* ○ *a beautiful sunset*

☆**sun·shine** /ˈsʌnʃaɪn/ *noun* [U] heat and light from the sun: *warm spring sunshine*

sun·tan /ˈsʌntæn/ *noun* [C] = TAN¹(1): *suntan lotion*

☆**su·per¹** /ˈsupər/ *adj.* (*informal*) very good; wonderful: *You did a super job.*

su·per² /ˈsupər/ *adv.* (*informal*) extremely: *We're super busy this week.* ○ *a super hot day*

su·per³ /ˈsupər/ *noun* [C] (*informal*) = SUPERINTENDENT(2)

su·perb /suˈpərb/ *adj.* very good, excellent —**su·perb·ly** *adv.*

su·per·fi·cial /ˌsupərˈfɪʃl/ *adj.* **1** (used about people) not caring about serious or important things **2** only on the surface; not deep: *Don't*

worry. *It's only a superficial wound.* **3** not deep, complete or thorough: *a superficial knowledge of the subject* —**su·per·fi·cial·ly** /-ʃəli/ *adv.*

su·per·flu·ous /suˈpərfluəs/ *adj.* (*formal*) more than is wanted; not needed: *Any further explanation is superfluous.*

su·per·hu·man /ˌsupərˈhyumən/ *adj.* greater than is usual for human beings: *superhuman strength*

su·per·in·ten·dent /ˌsupərmˈtɛndənt/ *noun* [C] **1** a person in a position of high rank and with a lot of authority, especially sb who is in charge of all the schools in a particular area **2** (also *informal* **super**) a person who is in charge of a building and makes small repairs, etc. to it

☆ **su·pe·ri·or**[1] /səˈpɪriər/ *adj.* **1** better than usual or than sb/sth else: *He is clearly superior to all the other candidates.* ☛ The opposite is **inferior**. **2** higher in rank: *a superior officer* **3** thinking that you are better than other people: *I don't like that superior attitude of hers.* —**su·pe·ri·or·i·ty** /səˌpɪriˈɔrəti; -ˈɑr-/ *noun* [U]: *the superiority of the new method*

su·pe·ri·or[2] /səˈpɪriər/ *noun* [C] a person of higher rank or position

su·per·la·tive /səˈpərlətɪv/ *noun* [C] (*grammar*) the form of an adjective or adverb that expresses its highest degree: *"Most beautiful," "best" and "fastest" are all superlatives.*

☆ **su·per·mar·ket** /ˈsupərmarkət/ *noun* [C] a large store that sells food, drinks, things for cleaning your house, etc.. You choose what you want from the shelves in a supermarket and pay for everything when you leave. ☛ **Grocery store** is more common, especially in informal speech.

the su·per·nat·u·ral /ˌsupərˈnætʃərəl/ *noun* [sing.] things that cannot be explained by the laws of science: *I don't believe in the supernatural.* —**supernatural** *adj.*: *a creature with supernatural powers*

su·per·pow·er /ˈsupərpaʊər/ *noun* [C] a country that has a very large amount of military, political and economic power

su·per·son·ic /ˌsupərˈsɑnɪk/ *adj.* faster than the speed of sound

su·per·star /ˈsupərstar/ *noun* [C] (*informal*) a singer, sports player, etc. who is very famous and popular

su·per·sti·tion /ˌsupərˈstɪʃn/ *noun* [C,U] a belief that cannot be explained by reason or science: *the superstition that black cats are unlucky* —**su·per·sti·tious** /-ˈstɪʃəs/ *adj.*: *I never do anything important on Friday the 13th – I'm superstitious.*

☆ **su·per·vise** /ˈsupərvaɪz/ *verb* [I,T] to watch sb/sth to make sure that work, etc. is being done correctly or that behavior is appropriate: *Her job is to supervise the construction work.*

—**su·per·vi·sion** /ˌsupərˈvɪʒn/ *noun* [U]: *Children should not play here without supervision.* —**su·per·vi·sor** /-ˈvaɪzər/ *noun* [C]: *He reported the incident to his supervisor.*

☆ **sup·per** /ˈsʌpər/ *noun* [C,U] a meal that people eat in the evening ☛ Look at the note at **dinner**.

sup·ple /ˈsʌpl/ *adj.* that bends or moves easily; not stiff

sup·ple·ment[1] /ˈsʌpləmənt/ *noun* [C] **a supplement (to sth)** something that is added to sth else: *a nutritional supplement*

sup·ple·ment[2] /ˈsʌpləmənt/ *verb* [T] **supplement sth (with sth)** to improve sth by adding sth else to it: *to supplement your diet with vitamins*

sup·ple·men·tal /ˌsʌpləˈmɛntl/ (*also* **supplementary** /ˌsʌpləˈmɛntəri; -tri/) *adj.* added to sth else; extra: *supplemental income*

☆ **sup·ply**[1] /səˈplaɪ/ *verb* [T] (*pres. part.* **sup·ply·ing**; *3rd pers. sing. pres.* **sup·plies**; *p.t., p.p.* **sup·plied**) **supply sth (to sb); supply sb (with sth)** to give or provide sth: *The lake supplies water to the surrounding towns.* ○ *The lake supplies the surrounding towns with water.* ○ *The car matched the description supplied by the witness.* —**sup·pli·er** /səˈplaɪər/ *noun* [C]: *The computer company is one of our biggest suppliers.*

☆ **sup·ply**[2] /səˈplaɪ/ *noun* (*pl.* **supplies**) **1** [C] something that is given or provided: *The water supply was contaminated.* **2** the amount of sth that is available: *They only had a week's supply of medicine left.* ○ *In many parts of the country, water is in short supply* (= there is not much of it). **3 supplies** [plural] things that people need to use in their daily lives: *Food and medical supplies were dropped by helicopter.*

☆ **sup·port**[1] /səˈpɔrt/ *verb* [T] **1** to carry the weight of sb/sth: *Large columns support the roof.* **2** to agree with the aims of sb/sth or with an idea, a plan, etc., and to give him/her/it help, money, etc.: *I'll support you as much as I can.* ○ *a candidate who supports tougher drug laws* **3** to show that sth is true or correct: *What evidence do you have to support what you say?* **4** to give or provide sb with the money he/she needs for food, clothes, etc.: *Jim has to support two children from his previous marriage.*

☆ **sup·port**[2] /səˈpɔrt/ *noun* **1** [U] **support (for sth)** help that you give to a person or thing (often sth that is encouraging in a difficult situation): *public support for the campaign* ○ *The software manual includes a free number to call for technical support.* ○ *Thank you for your support at this difficult time.* **2** [C,U] something that carries the weight of sb/sth: *bridge supports* **3** [U] money to buy food, clothes, etc.: *She has no job, no home and no means of support.* ☛ Look at **child support**.

tʃ	dʒ	v	θ	ð	s	z	ʃ
chin	June	van	thin	then	so	zoo	she

S

S

IDM **in support of sb/sth** supporting or agreeing with sb/sth: *Steve spoke in support of the proposal.*

☆ **sup·port·er** /səˈpɔrtər/ *noun* [C] a person who supports a political candidate, a plan, etc.: *The candidate's supporters gave thousands of dollars to his campaign.*

sup·por·tive /səˈpɔrtɪv/ *adj.* giving help or sympathy

☆ **sup·pose** /səˈpouz/ *verb* [T] **1** to think, believe or consider that sth is probable: *I suppose he seems unfriendly because he is shy.* ○ *What effect do you suppose the drought is having?* **2** to pretend that sth will happen or is true: *Suppose you won a million dollars. What would you do?*

be supposed to be sth to be considered or thought to be sth: *I haven't seen it, but it's supposed to be a good play.* ○ *This is supposed to be the best Mexican restaurant in town.*

be supposed to do sth to be expected to do sth or to have to do sth: *The plane was supposed to arrive 45 minutes ago.* ○ *I'm not supposed to talk about what happened at the meeting.*

IDM **I suppose 1** (used to show that you are not certain about sth): *It's about ten years old, I suppose.* **2** (used when you agree with sth, but are not very happy about it): *"Can I have another cookie?" "I suppose so, but only one."*

sup·pos·ed·ly /səˈpouzədli/ *adv.* as people believe or suppose: *George Washington supposedly spent the night here once.*

sup·pos·ing /səˈpouzɪŋ/ *conj.* (*informal*) if sth happens or is true: *Supposing the plan goes wrong – what are we going to do then?*

sup·press /səˈprɛs/ *verb* [T] **1** to stop sth by using force: *The army suppressed the rebellion.* **2** to stop sth from being seen or known: *to suppress the truth* **3** to stop yourself from expressing your feelings, etc.: *to suppress a yawn* ○ *suppressed anger* —**sup·pres·sion** /səˈprɛʃn/ *noun* [U]

su·prem·a·cy /səˈprɛməsi/ *noun* [U] **supremacy (over sb/sth)** the state of being most powerful: *the military supremacy of the United States*

☆ **su·preme** /səˈprim/ *adj.* **1** highest in rank or position: *a supreme commander* **2** greatest or most important: *a matter of supreme importance*

the Su·preme Court *noun* [sing.] the court of law with the highest authority in the U.S. or in a particular state: *the Chief Justice of the U.S. Supreme Court*

su·preme·ly /səˈprimli/ *adv.* (*formal*) very: *to be supremely confident*

sur·charge /ˈsɜrtʃɑrdʒ/ *noun* [C] an extra amount of money that you have to pay for sth: *Most banks impose a surcharge on customers who use other banks' cash machines.*

☆ **sure¹** /ʃʊr/ *adj.* **1** (not before a noun) having no doubt about sth; certain: *I'm not sure what to do next.* ○ *Craig was sure that he'd made the right decision.* ○ *I think I had my bag when I got off the bus, but I'm not sure.*

☞ **Sure** and **certain** are very similar in meaning. **Sure**, however, cannot be used in the phrase "It is...that..." **Certain** can be used in this phrase: *It is certain that there will be a strike soon.* With **sure** we must say: *There is sure to be a strike soon.* **Sure** is less formal and more common than **certain**.

2 (not before a noun) **sure of sth** certain to get sth: *If you go and see them, you can be sure of a warm welcome.* **3** **sure to do sth** (not before a noun) certain to happen or do sth: *If you study hard, you are sure to get a good grade.* **4** that you can trust: *A noise like that is a sure sign of engine trouble.*

IDM **Be sure and/to do sth** Don't forget to do sth: *Be sure to write and tell me what happens.* ○ *Be sure and take your keys.*

make sure 1 to find out whether sth is in a certain state or has been done: *I'll go back and make sure I closed the window.* **2** to take the action that is necessary to make sth happen: *Make sure you are back home by 11 o'clock.*

sure of yourself confident about your opinions, or about what you can do

sure² /ʃʊr/ *adv.* (*informal*) **1** (used as an answer to a question) yes; of course: *"Can I borrow this book?" "Sure."* **2** without doubt; definitely: *It sure is hot today.* ○ *"Do you like ice cream?" "I sure do!"*

IDM **sure enough** as you/sb had expected: *I expected him to be early, and sure enough, he arrived five minutes before the others.*

☆ **sure·ly** /ˈʃʊrli/ *adv.* **1** without doubt: *This will surely cause problems.* **2** (used for expressing surprise at sb else's opinions, plans, actions, etc.): *Surely you're not going to walk home in the dark?*

surf¹ /sɜrf/ *verb* **1** [I] to stand or lie on a special board (**a surfboard**) in the ocean and ride on a wave toward the shore

☞ **Go surfing** is a common way of talking about surfing for pleasure.

2 [I,T] (*informal*) to search for information on an international computer information system (**the Internet**): *I spent two hours last night surfing the Net.* —**surf·er** *noun* [C]

surf² /sɜrf/ *noun* [U] the white part on the top of waves in the ocean

☆ **sur·face¹** /ˈsɜrfəs/ *noun* **1** [C] the outside part of sth: *the earth's surface* ○ *a special paint for metal surfaces* **2** [C, usually sing.] the top part of an area of water: *The submarine slowly rose to the surface.* **3** [sing.] the qualities of sb/sth that you see or notice, that are not hidden: *Everybody seems very friendly, but there is a lot of tension beneath the surface.*

i	ɪ	ɛ	æ	ɑ	ɔ	ʌ	ʊ	u
see	sit	ten	cat	hot	saw	cup	put	too

sur·face² /'sərfəs/ verb **1** [T] to cover the surface¹(1) of sth: to surface a road with asphalt **2** [I] to come to the surface of a liquid: The submarine surfaced quickly. **3** [I] (informal) to appear or become known: New evidence surfaced last night.

surge¹ /sərdʒ/ verb [I] **1** to move forward with great strength: The crowd surged toward the stage. **2** to increase quickly: Stock prices surged late yesterday.

surge² /sərdʒ/ noun [C, usually sing.] **a surge (of/in sth) 1** a sudden increase in sth: a surge in health care costs **2** a sudden strong feeling: a surge of pity

sur·geon /'sərdʒən/ noun [C] a doctor who performs medical operations (**surgery**): a brain surgeon

☆ **sur·ger·y** /'sərdʒəri/ noun [U] medical treatment in which your body is cut open so that part of it can be removed or repaired: to undergo emergency surgery ☛ Look at **plastic surgery**.

sur·gi·cal /'sərdʒɪkl/ adj. used in surgery or connected with surgery: surgical instruments ◦ surgical procedures —**sur·gi·cal·ly** /-kli/ adv.: Her tooth had to be surgically removed.

sur·ly /'sərli/ adj. (**sur·li·er; sur·li·est**) unfriendly and rude: a surly expression

sur·pass /sər'pæs/ verb [T] (formal) do sth better than sb/sth else or better than expected

sur·plus /'sərpləs/ noun [C,U] an amount that is extra or more than you need: a trade surplus of $10 billion —**sur·plus** adj. (only before a noun): surplus food

☆ **sur·prise¹** /sə'praɪz; 'sər-/ noun **1** [U] the feeling that you have when sth happens that you do not expect: They looked up in surprise when she walked in. ◦ To my surprise, the boss agreed. **2** [C] something that you did not expect: What a nice surprise to see you again! ◦ a surprise visit, attack, etc. ◦ "What's my present?" "It's a surprise."

IDM **take sb by surprise** to happen or do sth when sb is not expecting it: His remarks took me by surprise.

☆ **sur·prise²** /sə'praɪz; 'sər-/ verb [T] **1** to cause sb to feel surprise¹(1) : It wouldn't surprise me if you got the job. **2** to attack or find sb suddenly and unexpectedly: We surprised the burglars just as they were leaving our house.

☆ **sur·prised** /sə'praɪzd; 'sər-/ adj. feeling or showing surprise¹(1) : I was very surprised to see Carol there. I thought she was still on vacation.

☆ **sur·pris·ing** /sə'praɪzɪŋ; 'sər-/ adj. that causes surprise¹(1) : It's surprising how many adults can't read or write. —**sur·pris·ing·ly** adv.

sur·re·al /sə'ril/ (also **sur·re·al·is·tic** /səˌriə'lɪstɪk/) adj. very strange, like a dream

sur·ren·der /sə'rɛndər/ verb **1** [I,T] **surrender (to sb)** to stop fighting and admit that you have lost **2** [T] **surrender sb/sth (to sb)** (for-

mal) to give sb/sth to sb else: The police ordered them to surrender their weapons. —**sur·ren·der** noun [C,U]

sur·ro·gate /'sərəgət; -geɪt/ noun [C, adj. (a person or thing) that takes the place of sb/sth else: a surrogate mother (= a woman who has a baby for another woman who cannot have children)

☆ **sur·round** /sə'raʊnd/ verb [T] **surround sb/sth (by/with sth)** to be or go all around sb/sth: The yard is surrounded by a fence. ◦ The police have surrounded his house. ◦ (figurative) He is surrounded by friends.

sur·round·ing /sə'raʊndɪŋ/ adj. (only before a noun) that is near or around sth: Boston and the surrounding area

☆ **sur·round·ings** /sə'raʊndɪŋz/ noun [plural] everything that is near or around you; the place where you live: to live in pleasant surroundings ◦ animals living in their natural surroundings (= not in zoos) ☛ Look at **environment**.

sur·veil·lance /sər'veɪləns/ noun [U] a careful watch on sb who may have done sth wrong: The suspect was under police surveillance.

☆ **sur·vey¹** /sər'veɪ/ verb [T] **1** to ask people questions about their habits, opinions, etc. for a study of sth: Seventy percent of those surveyed said they liked cheese. **2** to look at the whole of sth; to examine or study sth as a whole: They surveyed the damage after the earthquake. ◦ Her new book surveys the problems of developing countries in today's world. **3** to measure an area of land in order to make a map of it

☆ **sur·vey²** /'sərveɪ/ noun [C] **1** a set of questions about people's habits, opinions, etc, for a study of sth: Surveys have shown that more and more people are getting into debt. ◦ According to a recent survey, 75% of smokers would like to quit. **2** an act of examining an area of land and making a map of it

☆ **sur·viv·al** /sər'vaɪvl/ noun [U] the state of continuing to live or exist: Small companies have to struggle for survival in today's economy. ◦ The survival rate for this type of cancer is very low.

☆ **sur·vive** /sər'vaɪv/ verb [I,T] to continue to live or exist, in or after a difficult or dangerous situation: More than a hundred people were killed in the crash and only five passengers survived. ◦ to survive a plane crash ◦ The old man survived all his children (= lived longer than them). ◦ (figurative) She has managed to survive two divorces (= to deal with them well and to continue with her life). —**sur·vi·vor** noun [C]: There were five survivors of the crash.

sus·cep·ti·ble /sə'sɛptəbl/ adj. (not before a noun) **susceptible to sth** easily damaged, affected or influenced by sb/sth: Officials worry that that air base could be susceptible to an

ə	y	w	t̬	eɪ	aɪ	ɔɪ	aʊ	oʊ
about	yes	woman	butter	say	five	boy	now	go

attack. ○ *Small babies are highy susceptible to infection.*

☆ **sus·pect¹** /səˈspɛkt/ *verb* [T] **1** to believe that sth may happen or be true: *The situation is worse than we first suspected.* ○ *She strongly suspected that he was lying.* **2** to have doubts about whether you can trust sb or believe sth: *I suspect his motives for offering to help.* **3 suspect sb (of sth)** to believe that sb is guilty of sth: *I suspected Laura of taking the money.* ☞ Look at **suspicion**.

☆ **sus·pect²** /ˈsʌspɛkt/ *noun* [C] a person who is thought to be guilty of a crime

sus·pect³ /ˈsʌspɛkt/ *adj.* possibly not true or to be trusted: *to have suspect motives* ○ *His methods are suspect.*

sus·pend /səˈspɛnd/ *verb* [T] **1 suspend sth (from sth)** to hang sth: *to suspend a decoration from the ceiling* **2** to stop or delay sth for a time: *The woman was given a suspended sentence* (= she will not go to prison unless she commits another crime). **3 suspend sb (from sth)** to send sb away from his/her school, job, position, etc. for a period of time, usually as a punishment for doing sth bad: *Gary was suspended for fighting in school.* ☞ The noun is **suspension**.

sus·pend·ers /səˈspɛndərz/ *noun* [plural] a pair of straps that hold your pants up. You put the suspenders over your shoulders and attach them to the top of your pants at the front and back.

sus·pense /səˈspɛns/ *noun* [U] the feeling that you have when you are waiting for news or for sth exciting or important to happen: *We wanted to know where we were going, but he kept us in suspense.* ○ *a movie full of action and suspense*

sus·pen·sion /səˈspɛnʃn/ *noun* **1** [C,U] delaying sth for a period of time: *The judge announced a suspension of the trial.* **2** [C,U] not being allowed to do your job or go to school for a period of time, as a punishment: *Possession of a weapon on school property will result in immediate suspension.* **3** [U] the parts that are attached to the wheels of a car, etc. that make it more comfortable to ride in

☆ **sus·pi·cion** /səˈspɪʃn/ *noun* **1** [C,U] a feeling or belief that sth is wrong or that sb has done sth wrong: *He always treats new situations with suspicion.* ○ *She was arrested on suspicion of murder.* **2** [C] a feeling that sth may happen or be true: *We had a suspicion that they would show up late.*

IDM under suspicion (used about a person) believed to have done sth wrong

☆ **sus·pi·cious** /səˈspɪʃəs/ *adj.* **1** that makes you feel or believe that sth is wrong or that sb has done sth wrong: *The old man died under suspicious circumstances.* ○ *It's very suspicious that she was not at home on the night of the murder.* ○ *a suspicious-looking person* **2 suspi-**

cious (of/about sb/sth) not trusting sb/sth: *His strange behavior made the police suspicious.* —**sus·pi·cious·ly** *adv.*: *The house was suspiciously quiet* (= as if something were wrong). ○ *to behave suspiciously*

sus·tain /səˈsteɪn/ *verb* [T] **1** to cause sth to continue for a long period of time: *to sustain economic growth* **2** to keep sb/sth alive or healthy: *His faith in God sustained him after the death of his son.* **3** (*formal*) to suffer an injury, etc.: *The victim sustained minor injuries.* ○ *The buildings sustained heavy damage in the earthquake.*

SW *abbr.* southwest; southwestern

swag·ger /ˈswægər/ *verb* [I] to walk with a swinging movement that shows that you are too confident or proud of yourself —**swag·ger** *noun* [sing.]

☆ **swal·low¹** /ˈswɑloʊ/ *verb* **1** [T] to make food, drink, etc. pass from your mouth down your throat: *It's easier to swallow pills if you take them with water.* ○ (*figurative*) *The rent swallows up most of our monthly income.* ☞ picture at **lick**. **2** [I] to make a movement in your throat, often because you are afraid or surprised, etc.: *She swallowed hard and tried to speak, but nothing came out.* **3** [T] to accept or believe sth, often too easily: *You shouldn't swallow everything they tell you!* **4** [T] to accept an insult, etc. without protest: *I find her criticisms very hard to swallow.*

swal·low² /ˈswɑloʊ/ *noun* [C] **1** an act of swallowing ¹(1, 2) **2** a common small bird

swam *p.t.* of SWIM

swamp¹ /swɑmp/ *noun* [C,U] (an area of) soft wet land

swamp² /swɑmp/ *verb* [T] **1** to cover or fill sth with water: *The boat was swamped by enormous waves.* **2** (usually passive) **swamp sb/sth (with sth)** to give sb so much of sth that they cannot deal with it: *We've been swamped with applications for the job.*

swan /swɑn/ *noun* [C] a large, usually white, bird with a very long neck that lives on lakes and rivers

swan

swap /swɑp/ *verb* [T] (**swap·ping; swapped**) (*informal*) to give sth for sth else; to exchange: *They sat by the fire, swapping stories from their days in school.* —**swap** *noun* [C]

swarm¹ /swɔrm/ *noun* [C] **1** a large group of insects, especially bees, moving around together **2** a large number of people together

swarm² /swɔrm/ *verb* [I] to fly or move in large numbers: *When the gates opened, the fans swarmed into the stadium.*

PHRV swarm with sb/sth to be too crowded or full: *The beaches are swarming with tourists at this time of year.*

ər	ɪr	ɛr	ɑr	ɔr	ʊr	ʒ	h	ŋ
bird	near	hair	car	north	tour	vision	hat	sing

swat /swɑt/ *verb* [T] (**swat·ting; swat·ted**) to hit sth, especially an insect, with sth flat

sway /sweɪ/ *verb* **1** [I,T] to move or swing slowly from side to side **2** [T] to influence: *Many people were swayed by his convincing arguments.*

☆**swear** /swɛr/ *verb* (*p.t.* **swore** /swɔr/; *p.p.* **sworn** /swɔn/) **1** [I] **swear (at sb/sth)** to use bad or offensive language: *He hit his thumb with the hammer and swore loudly.* ○ *There's no point in swearing at the car just because it won't start!* **2** [I,T] to make a serious promise: *When you testify in court, you have to swear to tell the truth.* ○ *Will you swear not to tell anyone?* ○ *I could have sworn* (= I was sure) *I heard a knock at the door.*

PHRV swear by sb/sth to believe completely in the value of sth

swear sb in (usually passive) to make sb declare that he/she will accept the responsibility of a new position: *The President will be sworn in next week.*

'**swear word** *noun* [C] a word that is considered bad and that may offend people

☆**sweat¹** /swɛt/ *noun* **1** [U] the liquid that comes out of your skin when you are hot, ill or afraid: *He stopped digging and wiped the sweat from his forehead.* ☞ Look at **perspiration**. **2 sweats** [plural] (*also* **sweat suit**) a two-piece set of clothes made of thick soft cotton fabric, usually worn for exercising or relaxing ☞ picture on page A26.

IDM no sweat (*informal*) (used to say that sth is very easy to do): *"Can you reach that shelf up there?" "Sure, no sweat."*

sweat² /swɛt/ *verb* [I] **1** to produce sweat through your skin **2 sweat (over sth)** to work hard: *I've been sweating over that problem all day.*

IDM don't sweat it (*slang*) (used to tell sb not to worry about sth): *Hey, don't sweat it. Everything's going to be OK.*

☆**sweat·er** /'swɛtər/ *noun* [C] a warm piece of clothing with long sleeves, often made of wool or cotton yarn: *a pullover sweater* ○ *a cardigan sweater* (=with buttons down the front) ☞ picture on page A27.

sweat·pants /'swɛtpænts/ *noun* [plural] a type of comfortable pants made from thick cotton cloth, often worn for exercising or relaxing ☞ picture on page A26.

☆**sweat·shirt** /'swɛt-ʃərt/ *noun* [C] a piece of clothing like a sweater made from thick cotton cloth, often with a part (**hood**) to cover your head ☞ picture on page A26.

sweat·shop /'swɛt-ʃɑp/ *noun* [C] a factory where people are forced to work very hard in poor conditions for very little money, often illegally

'**sweat suit** *noun* [C] = SWEAT¹(2)

sweat·y /'swɛti/ *adj.* (**sweat·i·er; sweat·i·est**) **1** wet with sweat: *I was hot and sweaty after*

the game and needed a shower. **2** causing you to sweat: *a hot, sweaty day*

☆**sweep¹** /swip/ *verb* (*p.t., p.p.* **swept** /swɛpt/) **1** [I,T] to clean by moving dust, dirt, etc. away with a broom: *Could you sweep under the table too?* ○ *Take your shoes off! I just swept the floor.* ○ *I'm going to sweep the leaves off the sidewalk.* ☞ Look at the note at **clean²**. **2** [T] to push, move or remove sb/sth quickly and smoothly: *He swept the money into his pocket and went out.* ○ *The huge waves swept her overboard.* **3** [I,T] to move quickly and smoothly over the area or in the direction mentioned: *Fire swept through the building.* ○ *The epidemic swept the country within weeks.* **4** [I] to move in a proud or impressive way: *Five black limousines swept past us.* ○ *She swept angrily out of the room.*

PHRV sweep (sth) up to remove dirt, dust, leaves, etc. using a broom

sweep² /swip/ *noun* [C] a long, curving shape or movement: *a bay with a broad sweep of golden sand* ○ *"Some day, all this will be yours," she said with a sweep of her hand.*

IDM a clean sweep ⇨ CLEAN¹

sweep·er /'swipər/ *noun* [C] a person or thing that sweeps¹(1) : *street sweepers*

sweep·ing /'swipɪŋ/ *adj.* **1** (used about statements, etc.) too general and possibly not accurate: *a sweeping generalization* **2** having a great and important effect: *sweeping reforms*

☆**sweet¹** /swit/ *adj.* **1** tasting like sugar; not sour or salty: *This frosting's too sweet.* **2** (used about a person) kind and thoughtful: *It's very sweet of you to remember my birthday!* **3** (used about a smell or a sound) pleasant: *The garden was full of the sweet smells of summer.* ○ *the sweet sound of children singing* **4** making you feel happy and satisfied: *an especially sweet victory*

IDM have a sweet tooth to like eating sweet things —**sweet·ness** *noun* [U]

sweet² /swit/ *noun* **1 sweets** [plural] foods that are sweet, such as candy, cookies, cake, etc.: *His dentist told him to avoid sweets between meals.* **2** [C] (*BrE*) = CANDY

sweet·en /'switn/ *verb* [T] to make sth sweet by adding sugar, honey, etc.

sweet·en·er /'switn·ər/ *noun* [C,U] a substance used instead of sugar for sweetening food or drink: *artificial sweeteners*

sweet·heart /'swithɑrt/ *noun* [C] (*old-fashioned*) a boyfriend or girlfriend: *They were childhood sweethearts.*

sweet·ie /'switi/ *noun* [C] (*informal*) a person who is loved

sweet·ly /'switli/ *adv.* in an attractive, kind or pleasant way: *She smiled sweetly.* ○ *sweetly-scented flowers*

'**sweet po·ta·to** *noun* [C,U] (*pl.* **sweet potatoes**) a yellowish-orange root that looks like a potato with pointed ends, that is cooked and eaten as a vegetable ☞ Look also at **yam**.

S

tʃ	dʒ	v	θ	ð	s	z	ʃ
chin	June	van	thin	then	so	zoo	she

☆ **swell¹** /swɛl/ *verb* (*p.t.* **swelled** /swɛld/; *p.p.* **swol·len** /'swoʊlən/ *or* **swelled**) **1** [I,T] **swell (up)** to become or to make sth bigger, fuller or thicker: *After she fell down, her ankle began to swell up.* ○ *His eyes swelled with tears.* ○ *Heavy rain had swollen the rivers.* **2** [I,T] to increase: *The crowd swelled to 600 by the end of the evening.* **3** [I] (*formal*) (used about feelings or sound) to become stronger or louder suddenly: *Hatred swelled inside him.*

swell² /swɛl/ *adj.* (*old-fashioned*) very good; wonderful

☆ **swell·ing** /'swɛlɪŋ/ *noun* **1** [C] a place on the body that is bigger or fatter than usual because of an injury or illness: *a swelling on my knee* **2** [U] the condition of being swollen: *Try to rest your ankle until the swelling goes down.*

swel·ter·ing /'swɛltərɪŋ/ *adj.* (*informal*) much too hot: *It was sweltering downtown today.*

swept *p.t., p.p.* of SWEEP¹

swerve /swərv/ *verb* [I] to change direction suddenly: *The car swerved to avoid the child.*

swift /swɪft/ *adj.* quick or fast; happening without delay: *a swift runner* ○ *a swift reaction* —**swift·ly** *adv.*

☆ **swim** /swɪm/ *verb* (*pres. part.* **swim·ming**; *p.t.* **swam** /swæm/; *p.p.* **swum** /swʌm/) **1** [I] to move your body through water: *How far can you swim?* ○ *Hundreds of tiny fish swam past.*

☞ **Go swimming** is a common way of talking about swimming for pleasure: *We go swimming every Saturday.* ○ *They went swimming before breakfast.* We can also say **go for a swim** when we are talking about one particular occasion: *I went for a swim this morning.*

2 [T] to cover or cross a distance, etc. by swimming: *I swam 25 lengths of the pool.* **3** [I] to seem to be moving or turning: *The floor began to swim before my eyes and I fainted.* **4** [I] (used about your head) to feel unclear or confused: *My head was swimming with so much new information.* —**swim** *noun* [sing.]: *Would you like to take a swim in the lake?* —**swim·mer** *noun* [C]: *a strong swimmer*

☆ **'swimming pool** (*also* **pool**) *noun* [C] a pool that is built especially for people to swim in: *an indoor/outdoor swimming pool*

'swimming trunks (*also* **trunks**) *noun* [plural] a piece of clothing like shorts that a man or boy wears to go swimming: *a pair of swimming trunks*

☆ **swim·suit** /'swɪmsut/ (*also* **bathing suit**) *noun* [C] a piece of clothing that a woman or girl wears to go swimming ☞ Look at **bikini**.

swin·dle /'swɪndl/ *verb* [T] **swindle sb/sth (out of sth)** (*formal*) to cheat sb (in order to get money, etc.): *He swindled his sister out of her inheritance.* —**swin·dle** *noun* [C]: *a tax swindle* —**swin·dler** /'swɪndlər/ *noun* [C]

swine /swaɪn/ *noun* **1** [plural] pigs **2** [C] (*informal*) a very unpleasant person: *Her husband's a complete swine.*

swing

☆ **swing¹** /swɪŋ/ *verb* (*p.t., p.p.* **swung** /swʌŋ/) **1** [I,T] to move backward and forward or from side to side, while hanging from sth; to make sb/sth move in this way: *The rope was swinging from a branch.* ○ *She sat on the wall, swinging her legs.* **2** [I,T] to move in a curve or to make sb/sth move in this way: *The door swung open and the whole class rushed out.* ○ *He swung the child up onto his shoulders.* **3** [I] to turn quickly: *She swung around when she heard the door open.* ○ (*figurative*) *His moods swing from one extreme to the other.* **4** [I,T] **swing (at sb/sth)** to try to hit sb/sth: *He swung violently at the other man but missed.*

☆ **swing²** /swɪŋ/ *noun* **1** [sing.] a swinging movement or action: *He took a swing at the ball.* **2** [C] a seat that you can swing backward and forward on, e.g. in a children's playground **3** [C] a change (in public opinion, etc.): *Opinion polls indicate a significant swing toward the right.*

IDM in full swing ➪ FULL¹

swipe¹ /swaɪp/ *verb* [T] **1** (*informal*) to steal sth **2** to pass a special plastic card through a piece of equipment that can read the information that the card contains

PHRV swipe at sth (*informal*) to (try to) hit sb/sth in an uncontrolled way: *He swiped at the wasp with a newspaper but missed.*

swipe² /swaɪp/ *noun* [C] **1** an act of hitting sb/sth or trying to hit sb/sth in an uncontrolled way **2** **a swipe (at sb/sth)** an act of criticizing or making an unfair comment about sb/sth: *During the debate, she took several swipes at her opponent's record in Congress.*

swirl /swərl/ *verb* [I,T] to move around and around quickly; to make sth do this: *Her long skirt swirled around her legs as she danced.* —**swirl** *noun* [C]

☆ **switch¹** /swɪtʃ/ *noun* [C] **1** a small button or sth similar that you press up or down in order to turn on electricity: *a light switch* **2** a sudden change: *a switch in policy*

☆ **switch²** /swɪtʃ/ *verb* **1** [I,T] **switch (sth) (over) (to sth)** to change or be changed from one thing to another: *We've switched from eating fried foods to more fresh fruit and vegetables.* ○ *The game has been switched from Saturday to Sunday.* **2** [I,T] **switch (sth) (with sb/sth); switch (sth) (around/over)** to ex-

change positions, activities, etc.: *This week you can have the car and I'll drive the pickup, and next week we'll switch.* ○ *Someone switched the signs around and everyone went the wrong way.*

PHRV **switch (sth) off/on** to press a switch in order to connect/disconnect electric power: *Don't forget to switch off the lights downstairs.*

switch·board /'swɪtʃbɔrd/ *noun* [C] the place in a large office, etc. where all the telephone calls are connected

swiv·el /'swɪvl/ *verb* [I,T] **swivel (sth) (around)** to turn around a central point; to make sth do this: *She swiveled around to face me.* ○ *He swiveled his chair toward the door.*

swol·len¹ *p.p.* of SWELL¹

swol·len² /'swoʊlən/ *adj.* thicker or wider than usual: *Her leg was badly swollen after the accident.*

swoop /swup/ *verb* [I] to fly or move down suddenly: *The bird swooped down on its prey.*

☆ **sword** /sɔrd/ *noun* [C] a weapon with a handle and a long thin metal blade

swore *p.t.* of SWEAR

sworn *p.p.* of SWEAR

swum *p.p.* of SWIM

swung *p.t., p.p.* of SWING¹

syc·a·more /'sɪkəmɔr/ *noun* [C] a type of large tree with broad leaves

syl·la·ble /'sɪləbl/ *noun* [C] a word or part of a word which contains one vowel sound: *"Mat" has one syllable and "mattress" has two syllables.*

syl·la·bus /'sɪləbəs/ *noun* [C] (*pl.* **syl·la·bus·es** or **syl·la·bi** /'sɪləbaɪ/) a list of subjects, etc. that are included in a course: *Required texts are listed on the syllabus and available in the campus bookstore.*

☆ **sym·bol** /'sɪmbl/ *noun* [C] **1 a symbol (of sth)** a sign, object, etc which represents an idea or an aspect of life: *The cross is the symbol of Christianity.* ○ *Some people think a fast car is a symbol of power and strength.* **2 symbol (for sth)** a letter, number or sign that has a particular meaning: *O is the symbol for oxygen.*

sym·bol·ic /sɪm'bɑlɪk/ *adj.* used or seen as a symbol: *The violent sea is symbolic of the character's emotions.* —**sym·bol·i·cal·ly** /-kli/ *adv.*

sym·bol·ism /'sɪmbəlɪzəm/ *noun* [U] the use of symbols to represent things, especially in art and literature

sym·bol·ize /'sɪmbəlaɪz/ *verb* [T] to be a symbol of sth: *The deepest notes in music often symbolize danger or despair.*

sym·met·ri·cal /sɪ'mɛtrɪk/ *adj.* having two halves that are exactly the same in size and shape —**sym·met·ri·cal·ly** /-kli/ *adv.*

sym·me·try /'sɪmətri/ *noun* [U] the state of having two halves that match each other exactly in size, shape, etc.

☆ **sym·pa·thet·ic** /ˌsɪmpə'θɛtɪk/ *adj.* **1** showing that you understand other people's feelings, especially their problems: *When Sandra's father died, everyone was very sympathetic.* ○ *I felt very sympathetic toward him.* ○ *He gave me a sympathetic smile.*

☞ In English, **sympathetic** does not mean "friendly and pleasant." If you want to express this meaning, you say a person is **nice**: *I met Alex's sister yesterday. She's very nice.*

2 sympathetic (to sb/sth) being in agreement with or willing to support sb/sth: *I explained our ideas, but she wasn't sympathetic to them.* ☞ The opposite is **unsympathetic**. —**sym·pa·thet·i·cal·ly** /-kli/ *adv.*

sym·pa·thize /'sɪmpəθaɪz/ *verb* [I] **sympathize (with sb/sth) 1** to understand and share sb's feelings: *I sympathize with her, but I don't know what I can do to help.* **2** to be in agreement with sb/sth: *I find it difficult to sympathize with his opinions.*

sym·pa·thiz·er /'sɪmpəθaɪzər/ *noun* [C] a person who agrees with and supports an idea or aim: *a Communist sympathizer* ☞ This word shows disapproval.

☆ **sym·pa·thy** /'sɪmpəθi/ *noun* (*pl.* **sym·pa·thies**) **1** [U] **sympathy (for/toward sb)** an understanding of other people's feelings, especially their problems: *Everyone feels great sympathy for the victims of the bombing.* ○ *I don't expect any sympathy from you.* ○ *When his wife died, he received dozens of letters of sympathy.* **2 sympathies** [plural] feelings of support or agreement: *Some members of the party have sympathies with terrorist groups.*

IDM **in sympathy (with sb/sth)** in agreement, showing that you support or approve of sb/sth: *Several union members demonstrated sympathy with the striking auto workers.*

sym·pho·ny /'sɪmfəni/ *noun* [C] (*pl.* **sym·pho·nies**) a long piece of music written for a large orchestra

☆ **symp·tom** /'sɪmptəm/ *noun* [C] **1** a change in your body that is a sign of illness: *What are the symptoms of the flu?* **2** a sign (that sth bad is happening or exists): *The riots are a symptom of a deeper problem.*

syn·a·gogue /'sɪnəgɑg/ (*also* **temple**) *noun* [C] a building where Jewish people go to pray or to study their religion

☞ Notice that when you are talking about going to a ceremony (a service) in a synagogue, you say "at synagogue/temple" or "to synagogue/temple" without "a" or "the": *I saw Mrs. Brown at temple today.*

sync /sɪŋk/ *noun*

IDM **be in sync/out of sync (with sb/sth)** (*informal*) **1** to be happening/not to be happening at the same time or speed: *The movie's soundtrack wasn't in sync with the picture.* **2** to be suitable/unsuitable for a particular situation, time etc.: *Are politicians out of sync with the concerns of young people?*

syn·chro·nize /ˈsɪŋkrənaɪz/ *verb* [T] to make sth happen or work at the same time or speed

syn·di·cat·ed /ˈsɪndəkeɪtəd/ *adj.* (used about a television series, a regular newspaper column, etc.) sold to and appearing on, many television stations or in many newspapers: *a nationally syndicated comic strip*

syn·drome /ˈsɪndroʊm/ *noun* [C] **1** a group of signs or changes in the body that are typical of an illness: *Down's syndrome* ○ *Acquired Immune Deficiency Syndrome (AIDS)* **2** a group of events, actions attitudes, etc. that are typical of a particular state or condition

syn·o·nym /ˈsɪnənɪm/ *noun* [C] a word or phrase that has the same meaning as another word or phrase in the same language: *"Big" and "large" are synonyms.* —**syn·on·y·mous** /səˈnɑnəməs/ *adj.* **synonymous (with sth)** *(figurative)*: *Wealth is not always synonymous with happiness.*

syn·tax /ˈsɪntæks/ *noun* [U] the system of rules for the structure of a sentence

syn·the·siz·er /ˈsɪnθəsaɪzər/ *noun* [C] an electronic musical instrument that can produce a wide range of different sounds

syn·thet·ic /sɪnˈθɛtɪk/ *adj.* made by a chemical process; not natural: *synthetic fabrics* —**syn·thet·i·cal·ly** /-kli/ *adv.*

syph·i·lis /ˈsɪfələs/ *noun* [U] a serious disease that passes from one person to another by sexual contact

sy·ringe /səˈrɪndʒ/ *noun* [C] an instrument that consists of a tube and a needle. It is used for taking a small amount of blood out of the body or for giving injections of drugs or medicine.

☆ **syr·up** /ˈsɪrəp/ *noun* [U] **1** a type of thick, sweet sauce that is made by boiling sugar with water or fruit juice: *pancakes with maple syrup* **2** liquid medicine that you swallow: *cough syrup*

☆ **sys·tem** /ˈsɪstəm/ *noun* **1** [C] a set of ideas or rules for organizing sth: *What kind of filing system do you have for your papers?* ○ *the metric system* **2** [C] a group of things or parts that work together: *The whole computer system crashed.* ○ *The mayor is planning to reform the school system.* **3** [C] the body of a person or animal; parts of the body that work together: *We have to get him to the hospital before the poison gets into his system.* ○ *the central nervous system* **4 the system** [sing.] the traditional methods and rules of a society: *Bob claims that he knows how to beat the system and avoid paying income taxes.*

IDM get sth out of your system *(informal)* to free yourself of a strong feeling

sys·tem·at·ic /ˌsɪstəˈmætɪk/ *adj.* done using a fixed plan or method: *a systematic search* —**sys·tem·at·i·cal·ly** /-kli/ *adv.*

Tt

T, t /ti/ *noun* [C] (*pl.* **T's; t's**) the twentieth letter of the English alphabet: *"Table" begins with (a) "T."*

t. *abbr.* = TEASPOON(2)

T. *abbr.* = TABLESPOON(2)

TA /ˌti ˈeɪ/ *abbr.* = TEACHING ASSISTANT

tab /tæb/ *noun* [C] **1** a small piece of cloth, metal or paper that is fastened to sth to help you open, hold or identify it: *You open the can by pulling the metal tab.* **2** [usually sing.] *(informal)* a bill, especially for meals or drinks in a bar or restaurant: *The office picks up the tab* (= pays the bill) *when I eat out on business trips.* ○ *I don't have any cash right now – can you put it on my tab?*

IDM keep tabs on sb/sth *(informal)* to watch sb/sth carefully; to check sth

☆ **ta·ble** /ˈteɪbl/ *noun* [C] **1** a piece of furniture with a flat top on one or more legs: *a kitchen table* ○ *a coffee table* ○ *Could you set the table for lunch?* (= put the knives, forks, plates, etc. on

it) ○ *Don't read the newspaper at the table* (= during the meal). ○ *table manners* (the way that you behave when you are eating)

☞ We put things **on the table**, but we sit **at the table** (= around the table).

2 a list of facts or figures, usually arranged in rows down a page: *a table of contents* ○ *Table 3 shows the results.*

IDM wait tables ⇨ WAIT¹

ta·ble·cloth /ˈteɪblklɔθ; -klɑθ/ *noun* [C] a piece of cloth that you put over a table, especially when having a meal

☆ **ta·ble·spoon** /ˈteɪblspun/ *noun* [C] **1** a large spoon used for serving or measuring food **2** (*also* **tablespoonful**) (*abbr.* **T.; tbsp.**) the amount that a tablespoon holds: *Add two tablespoons of sugar.*

tab·let /ˈtæblət/ *noun* [C] a small amount of medicine in solid form, that you swallow: *Take two tablets every four hours.*

ər	ɪr	ɛr	ɑr	ɔr	ʊr	ʒ	h	ŋ
bird	near	hair	car	north	tour	vision	hat	sing

'table ˌtennis (*also* **Ping-Pong**) *noun* [U] a game with rules like tennis in which you hit a light plastic ball across a table with a small flat, round wooden object (**paddle**)

tab·loid /'tæblɔɪd/ *noun* [C] a newspaper with small pages, a lot of pictures and short simple articles

ta·boo /tə'bu; tæ-/ *noun* [C] (*pl.* **ta·boos**) a religious or social custom that forbids certain actions or words —**ta·boo** *adj.*: *a taboo subject*

tack¹ /tæk/ *noun* **1** [C] = THUMBTACK **2** [C] a small nail with a broad head **3** [sing.] a way of achieving sth: *If people won't listen, we'll have to try a different tack.*

tack² /tæk/ *verb* [T] to fasten sth with tacks¹(1, 2)

PHRV **tack sth on (to sth)** to put sth extra on the end of sth: *Restaurants sometimes tack a service charge onto the bill.*

☆**tack·le¹** /'tækl/ *verb* **1** [T] to deal boldly with sth difficult: *The government must tackle the problem of rising unemployment.* ○ *Firefighters were brought in to tackle the blaze.* **2** [T] (in football) to stop another player by pulling him down **3** [I,T] (in soccer) to try to take the ball from sb on the other team

tack·le² /'tækl/ *noun* **1** [C] the act of tackling¹ (2,3): *a powerful tackle by Walker* **2** [U] the equipment you use for fishing: *bait and tackle*

tack·y /'tæki/ *adj.* (**tack·i·er**; **tack·i·est**) **1** (*informal*) cheap and of poor quality: *tacky souvenirs* **2** (used about paint, glue, etc.) not quite dry; sticky

ta·co /'takoʊ/ *noun* [C] (*pl.* **ta·cos**) a Mexican food that consists of a thin, crisp shell made of ground corn, that is filled with meat or beans and cheese, tomatoes, etc.

tact /tækt/ *noun* [U] the ability to deal with people without offending or upsetting them: *a situation that reqires patience and tact*

tact·ful /'tæktfl/ *adj.* careful not to say or do things that could offend people: *Talking about his ex-wife like that wasn't very tactful!* —**tact·ful·ly** *adv.*

☆**tac·tic** /'tæktɪk/ *noun* **1** [C, usually pl.] a way of achieving sth: *We need to decide what our tactics are going to be at the next meeting.* ○ *I don't think this tactic will work.* **2 tactics** [plural] the skillful arrangement and use of military forces in order to win a battle

tac·ti·cal /'tæktɪkl/ *adj.* **1** connected with tactics (2): *a tactical error* **2** designed to bring a future advantage: *a tactical decision* —**tac·ti·cal·ly** /-kli/ *adv.*

tad /tæd/ *noun* [sing.] (*informal*) **a tad** a small amount; a little: *The meat was just a tad over-cooked.*

tad·pole /'tædpoʊl/ *noun* [C] a young form of a frog, when it has a large black head and a long tail

☆**tag¹** /tæg/ *noun* **1** [C] a small piece of card, material, etc. fastened to sth to give informa-tion about it; a label: *a name tag* ○ *How much is this dress? There's no price tag on it.* **2** [U] a children's game in which one child runs around after the other children and tries to touch them: *to play tag*

tag² /tæg/ *verb* [T] (**tag·ging**; **tagged**) to fasten a tag¹(1) to sth

PHRV **tag along** to follow or go with sb: *The little boy tagged along with the older kids when they went to the mall.*

'tag ˌquestion *noun* [C] (*grammar*) a short phrase at the end of a sentence that changes it into a question. For example, in the sentence "It's really expensive, isn't it?" the use of the tag question means that the speaker is asking the listener to agree.

☆**tail¹** /teɪl/ *noun* **1** [C] the long thin part at the end of the body of an animal, bird, fish, etc.: *The dog barked and wagged its tail.* ☞ picture at **cat**. **2** [C] a thing like an animal's tail in its shape or position: *the tail of an airplane* **3 tails** [plural] the side of a coin that does not have the head of a person on it: *"We'll toss a coin to decide," said my father. "Heads or tails?"* ☞ Look at **heads**. **4 tails** [plural] a man's coat, short at the front but with a long, divided piece at the back. It is worn on very formal occasions, such as weddings.

tail² /teɪl/ *verb* [T] to follow sb closely, especially to watch where he/she goes, etc.

PHRV **tail off** to become less, smaller, quieter, etc.: *His voice tailed off into a whisper.*

tail·gate /'teɪlgeɪt/ *verb* [I,T] to drive too close-ly behind another vehicle

tai·lor¹ /'teɪlər/ *noun* [C] a person whose job is to make clothes, especially for men

tai·lor² /'teɪlər/ *verb* [T] (usually passive) **1** to make clothes: *a well-tailored coat* **2** to make or design sth for a special purpose: *We specialize in bank accounts tailored to meet your individual needs.*

ˌtailor-'made *adj.* **tailor-made (for sb/sth)** very suitable; perfect

taint /teɪnt/ *verb* [T] (usually passive) to have a bad effect on sth; to spoil sth so that it is no longer pure, fresh, etc.: *Dozens of people became sick after eating the tainted meat.*

☆**take** /teɪk/ *verb* [T] (*p.t.* **took** /tʊk/; *p.p.* **tak·en** /'teɪkən/) **1** to carry sb/sth or to go with sb from one place to another: *Take your coat with you – it's cold.* ○ *Could you take this letter home to your parents?* ○ *The ambulance took him to the hospital.* ○ *I'm taking the kids swimming this afternoon.* ☞ picture at **bring**. **2** to put your hand around sth and hold it (and move it toward you): *She held out the keys, and I took them.* ○ *He took a sweater out of the drawer.* ○ *She took my hand/me by the hand.* **3** to remove sth without permission: *Who took my pen?* **4** to accept or receive sth: *Will you take $2,000 for the car?* ○ *Do you take traveler's checks?* ○ *I'm not taking the blame for the accident.* ○ *She's*

tʃ	dʒ	v	θ	ð	s	z	ʃ
chin	**J**une	**v**an	**th**in	**th**en	**s**o	**z**oo	**sh**e

not going to take the job. **5** to choose sth to buy: *I'll take the blue one.* **6** to need or require sth: *It takes about an hour to drive to my office from here.* ○ *I took two years to graduate from law school.* ○ *It took a lot of courage to say that.* **7** to have enough space for sth: *How many passengers can this bus take?* **8** to use a form of transportation; to go by a particular road: *I always take the train to work.* ○ *Which road do you take to get to Madison?* **9** to swallow or put a medicine or drug into your body: *Take two tablets four times a day.* ○ *teenagers who take illegal drugs* **10** to write or record sth: *She took notes during the lecture.* **11** to write the answers to an examination: *to take a test* **12** to have lessons or go to a course in a particular subject: *Liz is taking biology next semester.* **13** to measure sth: *I took his temperature and it was almost 103°.* **14** (used with nouns to say that sb is performing an action): *Take a look at this article* (= look at it). ○ *She took a deep breath* (= breathed deeply). **15** to photograph sth: *I took a lot of pictures at the wedding.* **16** to have a particular feeling or opinion: *He takes great pleasure in visiting his grandchildren.* ○ *I wish you would take things more seriously.* **17** to understand sth in a particular way: *She took what he said as a compliment.* **18** to be able to bear sth: *I find his criticism a little hard to take.* **19** to capture a place by force: *The allied forces took the enemy's capital last night.*

IDM **be taken with sb/sth** to find sb/sth attractive or interesting

I take it (that...) I suppose: *I take it that you're not coming?*

take it from me believe me: *Take it from me – she's going to resign.*

take a lot out of sb to make sb very tired

take some doing to require a lot of work or effort

☞ For other idioms containing **take**, look at the entries for the nouns, adjectives, etc., e.g. **take place** is at **place**¹.

PHRV **take after sb** to look or behave like an older member of your family

take sth apart to separate sth into the different parts it is made of

take sth away to cause a feeling, etc. to disappear: *This asprin will take the pain away.*

take sb/sth away (from sb) to remove sb/sth: *She took the scissors away from the child.*

take sth back 1 to return sth to the place that you got it from **2** to admit that sth you said was wrong

take sth down 1 to remove a structure by separating it into the pieces it is made of: *They took the fence down and put up a brick wall.* **2** to write down sth that is said

take sb in 1 to deceive sb: *I was completely taken in by her story.*

take sth in to understand what you see, hear

or read: *There was too much in the museum to take in at one time.*

take off 1 (used about an airplane, etc.) to leave the ground and start flying **2** to become successful or popular

take sth off 1 to remove sth, especially clothes: *Come in and take your coat off.* **2** to have the period of time mentioned as a vacation: *I'm going to take a week off.*

take sth on to accept or decide to do sth: *He's taken on a lot of extra work.*

take sb out to go somewhere with sb (for a social occasion): *I'm taking Sarah out to dinner tonight.*

take sth out 1 to remove sth from inside sth else: *He took out a notebook and began to write.* **2** to arrange officially to have sth, especially from a bank or a court of law: *to take out insurance, a bank loan, a court order, etc.*

take it out on sb to behave badly toward sb because you are angry or upset about sth, even though it is not this person's fault: *I know you've been having problems, but don't take it out on me!*

take (sth) over to get control of sth or responsibility for sth: *The business is being taken over by a large corporation.* ○ *Who's going to take over as assistant when Tim leaves?*

take to sb/sth to feel a liking for sb/sth: *I took to his parents immediately.*

take to sth/doing sth to begin doing sth regularly: *Many people have taken to eating healthier foods.*

take up sth to use or fill an amount of time or space: *All her time is taken up with the new baby.*

take sth up to start doing sth regularly (e.g. as a hobby): *I recently took up yoga.*

take sb up on sth to accept an offer, etc. that sb has made: *"Come and stay with us sometime." "We'll take you up on that!"*

take sth up with sb to ask or complain about sth: *I'll take the matter up with my lawyer.*

take·off /ˈteɪkɔf; -ɑf/ *noun* [C,U] the time when an airplane leaves the ground: *The plane crashed on takeoff.*

take·out (*also* **take-out**) /ˈteɪkaʊt/ *adj.* **1** (used about food) that you buy already cooked from a restaurant to eat somewhere else: *a takeout dinner* **2** (used about a restaurant) that sells cooked food that you can eat somewhere else —**take-out** (*also* **carryout**) *noun* [C,U]

take·o·ver /ˈteɪkoʊvər/ *noun* [C] the act of taking control of sth: *the takeover of a company* ○ *a military takeover* (= in a country)

tale /teɪl/ *noun* [C] **1** a story about events that are not real: *fairy tales* **2** a report or description of sb/sth that is not necessarily true : *I've heard a lot of tales about the people who live in that house.*

i	ɪ	ɛ	æ	ɑ	ɔ	ʌ	ʊ	u
see	sit	ten	cat	hot	saw	cup	put	too

☆ **tal·ent** /ˈtælənt/ *noun* [C,U] **talent (for sth)** a natural skill or ability: *She has a talent for painting.* ○ *His work shows great talent.* —**tal·ent·ed** *adj.*: *a talented musician*

☆ **talk¹** /tɔk/ *verb* **1** [I] **talk (to/with sb); talk (about sb/sth)** to say things; to speak: *I could hear them talking downstairs.* ○ *Their little boy is just learning to talk.* ○ *Can I talk to you for a minute?* ○ *Anne is not an easy person to talk to.* ○ *We need to talk about the plans for the weekend.* ○ *I didn't understand what she was talking about.* ☞ Look at the note at **speak**. **2** [I] to discuss people's personal affairs: *His strange lifestyle started the local people talking.* **3** [T] to discuss sth: *Could we talk business after dinner?* **4** [I] **talk on/about sth** to give a lecture or speech to a group of people about a certain subject: *Mrs. Phipps will be talking about early American art.* **5** [I] to give information: *"He hasn't talked yet," said the detective, "but he will."*

IDM **know what you are talking about** ⇨ KNOW

talk shop to talk about work with colleagues outside working hours

PHRV **talk back (to sb)** to speak rudely to sb who is older or who has a higher rank than you

talk down to sb to talk to sb as if he/she is less intelligent, important, etc. than you

talk sb into/out of doing sth to persuade sb to do/not to do sth: *I didn't really want to go with them, but they talked me into it.*

talk sth over to discuss sth thoroughly, especialy to reach an agreement or a decision

☆ **talk²** /tɔk/ *noun* **1** [C] a conversation or discussion: *Tim and I had a long talk about the problem.* **2 talks** [plural] formal discussions: *The leaders of the two countries will meet for talks next week.* **3** [U] talking, especially without action, results or the right information: *You don't believe all that talk about layoffs at work, do you?* ☞ Look also at **small talk**. **4** [C] a lecture or speech: *He's giving a talk on the importance of computers in education.*

talk·a·tive /ˈtɔkətɪv/ *adj.* liking or tending to talk a lot

'talk show *noun* [C] a television program on which people talk about their lives and answer questions, often from the audience

☆ **tall** /tɔl/ *adj.* **1** (used about people or things) of more than average height; not short: *a tall young man* ○ *a tall tree, tower, chimney, etc.* ○ *Nick is taller than his brother.* **2** (used about people) of a particular height: *Claire is only five feet tall.* ○ *How tall are you?*

☞ **Tall** and **high** have similar meanings. We use **tall** to describe the height of people (*He is six feet three inches tall.*), of trees (*A tall oak tree stood in the front yard.*) and also sometimes to talk about narrow objects (*the tall skyscrapers of Manhattan*).

tam·bou·rine /ˌtæmbəˈrin/ *noun* [C] a small round musical instrument with metal discs around the edge. You can hit it or shake it.

☆ **tame¹** /teɪm/ *adj.* **1** (used about animals or birds) not wild or afraid of people: *The birds are so tame they will eat from your hand.* **2** boring; not interesting or exciting: *After the big city, you must find country life very tame.*

tame² /teɪm/ *verb* [T] to bring sth wild under your control

tamp·er /ˈtæmpər/ *verb* [I] **tamper with sth** to use, touch, change, etc. sth when you should not: *Don't eat the candy if the packaging has been tampered with.*

tam·pon /ˈtæmpɑn/ *noun* [C] a tightly-rolled piece of cotton that a woman puts inside her body to collect blood during her period (3)

☆ **tan¹** /tæn/ *noun* **1** [C] (*also* **suntan**) a darker color that your skin has after you spend time in the sun: *to get a tan* **2** [U] a pale color between yellow and brown

☆ **tan²** /tæn/ *adj.* **1** having a pale color between yellow and brown: *tan shoes* **2** having darker skin than usual because of spending time in the sun: *You look very tan – have you been on vacation?*

tan³ /tæn/ *verb* [I,T] (**tan·ning; tanned**) to become or to let sth, especially your skin, become brown with the effect of the sun: *Do you tan easily?* ○ *I'm trying to tan my legs.*

tan·ger·ine /ˌtændʒəˈrin/ *noun* [C] a fruit like a small sweet orange with a skin that is easy to take off

tan·gi·ble /ˈtændʒəbl/ *adj.* (*formal*) clear and definite: *There are tangible benefits in the new system.*

tan·gle /ˈtæŋgl/ *noun* [C] a confused mass, especially of threads, hair, branches, etc. that cannot easily be separated from each other: *My hair's full of tangles.* —**tan·gled** *adj.*: *The yarn was all tangled up.*

☆ **tank** /tæŋk/ *noun* [C] **1** a container for holding liquids or gas: *How many gallons does the gas tank hold?* ○ *a water tank* **2** a large, heavy military vehicle covered with steel and armed with guns, that moves on special wheels: *Hundreds of tanks have crossed the border and are ready to attack.*

tank·er /ˈtæŋkər/ *noun* [C] a ship for carrying gasoline, etc. in large amounts: *an oil tanker*

tan·ta·liz·ing /ˈtæntlˌaɪzɪŋ/ *adj.* (used about sth that you cannot have) attractive or tempting: *A tantalizing smell of cooking was coming from the kitchen.* —**tan·ta·liz·ing·ly** *adv.*: *tantalizingly close*

tan·trum /ˈtæntrəm/ *noun* [C] a sudden burst of anger, especially in a child

☆ **tap¹** /tæp/ *verb* (**tap·ping; tapped**) **1** [I,T] **tap (at/on sth); tap sb/sth (on/with sth)** to touch or hit sb/sth quickly and gently: *Their feet were tapping in time to the music.* ○ *They won't*

hear if you only tap on the door – knock harder! ○ *She tapped me on the shoulder and said, "Excuse me, I think you dropped this notebook."* **2** to make use of sth from a supply or reserve: *to tap the skills of young people* **3** to attach a piece of equipment to sb's telephone wires so that you can listen to telephone conversations on that line

tap² /tæp/ *noun* [C] **1** a quick gentle hit or the sound it makes: *a tap on the shoulder* **2** = FAUCET ☞ Look also at **tap water**.

IDM on tap 1 (used especially about beer) served directly from a large container (**barrel**), not in a bottle or can **2** (*informal*) ready and available for use: *information on tap via the Internet*

'tap dance *noun* [C] a dance in which you tap the rhythm with your feet, wearing special shoes with metal pieces on the bottoms to make noise —**'tap-dance** *verb* [I]

☆ **tape¹** /teɪp/ *noun* **1** [U] a long, narrow piece of plastic or paper that is sticky on one side and is used for wrapping packages, fastening pieces of paper together, etc.: *a roll of tape* ○ *electrical tape* ☞ Look also at **Scotch tape**. **2** [U] magnetic material used for recording sound, pictures or information: *I have the whole concert on tape* (= recorded). **3** [C] a cassette with magnetic material wound around it, which is used for recording or playing music, videos, etc.: *a blank tape* ○ *I have a new Tom Waits tape. Do you want to hear it?* ○ *to rewind a tape* ☞ Look at **cassette**, **CD** and **record¹** (2).

☆ **tape²** /teɪp/ *verb* [T] **1** to fasten sth with tape¹ (1): *to tape an envelope shut* **2** to record sound, music, television programs, etc. using a cassette: *There's a movie on TV tonight that I want to tape.*

'tape deck *noun* [C] the part of a stereo system on which you play tapes¹(3)

'tape ˌmeasure *noun* [C] a long thin piece of plastic or cloth with inches or centimeters marked on it. It is used for measuring things.

'tape player *noun* [C] a machine that is used for playing recordings of music or other sounds on tape¹(2)

'tape reˌcorder *noun* [C] a machine that is used for recording or playing back music or other sounds on tape¹(2)

tap·es·try /'tæpəstri/ *noun* [C,U] (*pl.* **tap·es·tries**) a piece of heavy cloth with pictures or designs sewn on it in colored thread

'tap ˌwater *noun* [U] water that comes out of taps, not water sold in bottles

tar /tɑr/ *noun* [U] **1** a thick black sticky liquid that becomes hard when it is cold. It is used for making roads, etc. **2** a harmful solid substance that is formed by burning tobacco: *low-tar cigarettes*

tar·dy /'tɑrdi/ *adj.* (*formal*) late —**tar·di·ness** *noun* [U]

☆ **tar·get¹** /'tɑrgət/ *noun* [C] **1** a person or thing that you aim at when shooting or attacking: *Attacks have been launched on military targets such as army bases.* ○ *The bomb missed its target and fell into the ocean.* ○ *The embassy was a likely target for terrorist attacks.* **2** an object, often a round board with circles on it, that you aim at in shooting practice: *I hit the target twice but missed it once.* **3** a person or thing that people blame, criticize, laugh at, etc.: *The educational system has been the target of heavy criticism.* **4** a result that you are aiming at: *Our target is to raise $10,000 for the Red Cross.* ○ *So far, we're right on target* (= making the progress we expected).

☆ **tar·get²** /'tɑrgət/ *verb* [T] **1 target sth (at/to sb/sth)** to aim or direct sth at sb/sth: *He targeted most of his criticism at the secretaries.* **2** to try to have an effect on sb/sth: *an ad campaign that targets young professional women*

tar·iff /'tærɪf/ *noun* [C] a tax that has to be paid on goods brought into a country

tar·mac /'tɑrmæk/ *noun* [U] an area at an airport with a hard surface where planes can stand or drive across: *The plane waited for two hours on the tarmac.*

tar·nish /'tɑrnɪʃ/ *verb* **1** [I,T] (used about a mirror, metal, etc.) to become less bright; to make less bright **2** [T] (used about a reputation) to spoil: *His reputation was tarnished by the scandal.*

tarp /tɑrp/ (also *formal* **tar·pau·lin** /tɑr'pɔlən/) *noun* [C] a large piece of strong, waterproof material that is used for covering things

tart¹ /tɑrt/ *adj.* having a sharp, sour taste: *a tart apple*

tart² /tɑrt/ *noun* [C,U] a small pie with a sweet filling, such as fruit or jam

☆ **task** /tæsk/ *noun* [C] a piece of work that has to be done, especially an unpleasant or difficult one: *Your first task will be to type these letters.* ○ *I found learning Arabic an almost impossible task.* ○ *They assigned me the task of organizing the class trip.*

'task force *noun* [C] a group of people who have been brought together to deal with a particular problem

☆ **taste¹** /teɪst/ *noun* **1** [U] the ability to recognize the flavor of food or drink: *Taste is one of the five senses.* **2** [sing.] the flavor of food or drink: *I don't like the taste of this coffee.* **3** [C, usually sing.] **a taste (of sth)** a small amount of sth to eat or drink: *Have a taste of this cheese to see if you like it.* ○ (*figurative*) *I had my first taste of work when I was about fifteen.* **4** [U] the ability to make good choices about whether things are suitable, of good quality, etc.: *He has excellent taste in music.* **5** [sing.] **a taste (for sth)** a liking for sth: *She has developed a taste for modern art.*

ər	ɪr	ɛr	ɑr	ɔr	ʊr	ʒ	h	ŋ
bird	near	hair	car	north	tour	vision	hat	sing

IDM **(be) in bad taste** (used about sb's behavior) (to be) unsuitable and unkind: *Some of his comments were in very bad taste.*

☆ **taste²** /teɪst/ *verb* (not in the *-ing* forms) **1** [T] to be aware of or recognize the flavor of food or drink: *Can you taste the garlic in this soup?* **2** [T] to try a small amount of food and drink; to test: *Can I taste a piece of that cheese to see what it's like?* **3** [I] **taste (like sth)** to have a particular flavor: *Some people say that frog legs taste like chicken.* ○ *to taste sour, sweet, delicious, etc.*

taste·ful /'teɪstfl/ *adj.* attractive and well-chosen: *The furniture was very tasteful.* —**taste·ful·ly** *adv.*

taste·less /'teɪstləs/ *adj.* **1** likely to offend sb: *His joke about the funeral was very tasteless.* **2** having little or no flavor: *We had some tasteless cheese sandwiches for lunch.* **3** unattractive; not well-chosen: *She was wearing a lot of tasteless jewelry.*

tast·y /'teɪsti/ *adj.* (**tast·i·er**; **tast·i·est**) having a good, strong flavor: *spaghetti with a tasty mushroom sauce*

tat·tered /'tætərd/ *adj.* old and torn: *a tattered coat*

tat·ters /'tætərz/ *noun*
 IDM **in tatters** badly torn or damaged: *Her dress was in tatters.* ○ (*figurative*) *After the divorce, my life seemed to be in tatters.*

tat·too /tæ'tu/ *noun* [C] (*pl.* **tat·toos**) a picture or pattern on sb's body that is made by sticking a needle into his/her skin and filling the holes with colored liquid —**tat·too** *verb* [T]: *She had the word "love" tattooed on her left hand.*

tattoo

taught *p.t., p.p.* of TEACH

taunt /tɔnt; tant/ *verb* [T] to try to make sb angry or unhappy by saying unkind or cruel things: *They taunted him with cries of "Big nose!"* —**taunt** *noun* [C]

Tau·rus /'tɔrəs/ *noun* [C,U] the second sign of the zodiac, the Bull; a person who was born under this sign ☞ picture at **zodiac**.

taut /tɔt/ *adj.* (used about rope, wire, etc.) stretched very tight; not loose

tav·ern /'tævərn/ *noun* [C] a bar that serves mainly beer and wine

☆ **tax¹** /tæks/ *noun* [C,U] the money that you have to pay to the government so that it can provide public services: *to pay your state and federal income taxes* ○ *to file a tax return* ○ *How much tax is there on a pack of cigarettes?* ○ *tax cuts* ☞ Look also at **sales tax**.

tax² /tæks/ *verb* [T] (often *passive*) **1** to take a tax from a sum of money, or to add it to the price of goods and services: *Lottery winnings are heavily taxed.* ○ *diesel fuel is taxed at 24.3*

cents a gallon. **2** to make a person or an organization pay tax: *A government should tax its citizens fairly*

tax·a·ble /'tæksəbl/ *adj.* on which you have to pay tax: *taxable income*

tax·a·tion /tæk'seɪʃn/ *noun* [U] **1** the system by which a government takes money from people so that it can pay for public services: *direct/indirect taxation* **2** the amount of money that people have to pay in taxes: *to increase/reduce taxation* ○ *high/low taxation*

tax-de'ductible *adj.* that can be taken off your total income before you calculate how much income tax you must pay

tax-ex'empt *adj.* (usually *before* a noun) free from having to pay taxes, or on which you do not have to pay taxes: *a tax-exempt organization* ○ *tax-exempt savings bonds*

☆ **tax·i¹** /'tæksi/ (*pl.* **tax·is**) (*also* '**tax·i·cab** /'tæksikæb/ **cab**) *noun* [C] a car with a driver, whose job is to take you somewhere in exchange for money: *Do you want to drive there or take a taxi?*

☞ The amount of money that you have to pay (your **fare**) is shown on a **meter**. People often give the taxi driver a **tip** (= a small extra amount of money that is not included in the fare).

tax·i² /'tæksi/ *verb* [I] (*pres. part.* **tax·i·ing**; *3rd pers. sing. pres.* **tax·is**; *p.t., p.p.* **tax·ied**) (used about an aircraft) to move slowly along the ground before or after flying

tax·ing /'tæksɪŋ/ *adj.* difficult; needing a lot of effort: *a taxing problem*

tax·pay·er /'tækspeɪər/ *noun* [C] a person who pays taxes

TB /ˌti 'bi/ *abbr.* = TUBERCULOSIS(2)

tbsp. *abbr.* = TABLESPOON(2)

☆ **tea** /ti/ *noun* **1** [U] a hot brown drink that you make by pouring boiling water onto the dried leaves of a bush grown in hot countries such as India and China: *a cup/pot of tea* ○ *I'll make some tea.* ○ *weak/strong tea* **2** [C,U] the dried leaves that are used for making tea (1), or a particular type of these leaves **3** [U] a drink that you make by pouring hot water onto the dried leaves of other plants: *herbal tea*
 IDM **(not) sb's cup of tea** ⇨ CUP¹

'**tea bag** *noun* [C] a small paper bag with tea leaves in it, that you use for making tea

☆ **teach** /titʃ/ *verb* (*p.t., p.p.* **taught** /tɔt/) **1** [I,T] to give sb lessons or instructions so that he/she knows how to do sth: *Colin is teaching us how to use the computer.* ○ *My mother taught me to play the piano.* ○ *He teaches English to international students.* **2** [T] to make sb believe sth or behave in a certain way: *The story teaches us that history often repeats itself.* ○ *My parents taught me always to tell the truth.*

☆ **teach·er** /ˈtitʃər/ *noun* [C] a person whose job is to teach, especially in a school: *Mrs. Wilson was my science teacher in eighth grade.* ○ *a piano teacher*

> ☞ In English-speaking countries, we do not use the word **teacher** when we speak to a teacher. The most common way to address a teacher is to use a title, e.g. **Mr.**, **Mrs.**, or **Ms.** with the teacher's last name: *Good morning, Mrs. Brown.* If the teacher is a professor at a college or university, we usually use the title **Professor** or **Doctor** with the person's last name: *Excuse me, Dr. Willis – I have a question.* In language schools and informal lessons, most teachers allow students to call them by their first names: *Can you repeat that, Jim?*

ˌteacher's ˈpet *noun* [C] (*informal*) a student who makes an effort to become a teacher's favorite student, and who is often disliked by other students because of this

teach·ing /ˈtitʃɪŋ/ *noun* **1** [U] the work or profession of a teacher: *My son went into teaching and my daughter became a doctor.* ○ *part-time teaching* ○ *teaching methods* **2** [U, plural] ideas and beliefs that are taught by sb/sth: *the teachings of Gandhi*

ˈteaching asˌsistant *noun* [C] (*abbr.* **TA**) a more advanced student who teaches or helps to teach some classes for other students at a university, while he/she is studying for a more advanced degree

tea·cup /ˈtikʌp/ *noun* [C] a cup that you drink tea from

tea·ket·tle /ˈtikɛt̬l/ (*also* **kettle**) *noun* [C] a metal container with a lid, handle and a place to pour water out of (**a spout**). It is used for boiling water.

☆ **team¹** /tim/ *noun* [C] **1** a group of people who play a sport or game together against another group: *a football team* ○ *Are you on the team?* **2** a group of people who work together: *a team of medical workers*

team² /tim/ *verb*
PHRV **team up (with sb)** to join sb in order to do sth together

team·work /ˈtimwərk/ *noun* [U] the ability of people to work together: *Good teamwork between nurses and doctors is very important.*

tea·pot /ˈtipɑt/ *noun* [C] a container that you make tea in and use to pour tea into cups. It has a lid, a handle and a small thin tube (**a spout**) that the tea is poured out of.

☆ **tear¹** /tɪr/ *noun* [C, usually pl.] a drop of water that comes from your eye when you are crying, etc.: *She wiped away his tears.* ○ *I was in tears* (= crying) *at the end of the movie.* ○ *The little girl burst into tears* (= suddenly started to cry).

"Oh, no! I just **tore** my shirt!"

She **tore** the letter in half.

☆ **tear²** /tɛr/ *verb* (*p.t.* **tore** /tɔr/; *p.p.* **torn** /tɔrn/) **1** [T] to pull paper, cloth, etc. so that it comes apart or gets a hole in it: *I tore my shirt on that nail.* ○ *He tore a hole in his favorite jacket.* ○ *Tear the paper along the dotted line.* ○ *She tore the letter in half.* ○ *I tore a page out of my notebook.* **2** [I] to become damaged by pulling: *This material doesn't tear easily.* **3** [T] to remove sth by pulling it violently and quickly: *Paul tore the poster down from the wall.* **4** [I] to move very quickly in a particular direction, often in a careless way: *Katy went tearing through the kitchen and out the door.*

PHRV **tear sth apart 1** to pull sth violently into pieces: *The bird was torn apart by the two dogs.* **2** to cause serious problems in a place, an organization, etc.: *Drugs are tearing our communities apart.*

tear yourself away (from sb/sth) to make yourself leave sb/sth or stop doing sth: *Tim can't tear himself away from that computer game.*

be torn between A and B to find it difficult to choose between two things or people

tear sth down to destroy a building: *They tore down the old houses and built a shopping mall.*

tear sth up to pull sth (usually sth made of paper) into pieces: *"I hate this picture," she said, tearing it up.*

tear³ /tɛr/ *noun* [C] a hole in paper, cloth, etc that is caused by tearing

IDM **wear and tear** ⇨ WEAR²

tear·ful /ˈtɪrfl/ *adj.* crying or very sad: *a tearful farewell*

tear·gas /ˈtɪrgæs/ *noun* [U] a type of gas that makes people's eyes fill with tears¹. It is used by the police, etc. to control large groups of people.

tease /tiz/ *verb* [I,T] to say unkind or personal things to sb because you think it is funny: *Don't pay any attention to those boys. They're only teasing.* ○ *They teased her about being fat.*

☆ **tea·spoon** /ˈtispun/ *noun* [C] **1** a small spoon that is used for stirring tea, eating, etc. **2** (*also* **teaspoonful** /-fʊl/) (*abbr.* **t.; tsp.**) the amount that a teaspoon (1) can hold

☆ **tech·ni·cal** /ˈtɛknɪkl/ *adj.* **1** involving detailed knowledge of the machines, materials, systems, etc. that are used in industry or science: *They don't have the technical knowledge to develop nuclear weapons.* **2** (used about sb's practical ability in a particular activity): *The pianist performed with great technical skill but*

i	ɪ	ɛ	æ	ɑ	ɔ	ʌ	ʊ	u
see	sit	ten	cat	hot	saw	cup	put	too

without much feeling. **3** (only *before* a noun) relating to a particular subject: *the technical terms connected with computers*

tech·ni·cal·i·ty /ˌtɛknɪˈkæləti/ *noun* [C] (*pl.* **tech·ni·cal·i·ties**) one of the details of a particular subject or activity: *The jury's verdict was thrown out on a legal technicality.*

☆ **tech·ni·cal·ly** /ˈtɛknɪkli/ *adv.* **1** following a very exact interpretation of facts or laws: *Technically, you should pay by May 1st, but it doesn't matter if it's a few days late.* **2** in a way that involves detailed knowledge of the machines, etc. that are used in industry or science: *The country is not very advanced technically.* **3** (used about sb's practical ability in a particular activity): *a technically outstanding performance*

tech·ni·cian /tɛkˈnɪʃn/ *noun* [C] a person whose work involves practical skills, especially in industry or science: *a laboratory technician*

☆ **tech·nique** /tɛkˈnik/ *noun* **1** [C] a particular way of doing sth: *new techniques for teaching languages* **2** [U] your practical ability in sth

tech·nol·o·gist /tɛkˈnɑlədʒɪst/ *noun* [C] a person who is an expert in technology

☆ **tech·nol·o·gy** /tɛkˈnɑlədʒi/ *noun* (*pl.* **tech·nol·o·gies**) **1** [U] the study and use of science for practical purposes in industry, etc. **2** [C,U] the scientific knowledge that is needed for a particular industry, etc.: *developments in computer technology* —**tech·no·log·i·cal** /ˌtɛknəˈlɑdʒɪkl/ *adj.*: *technological developments*

ted·dy bear /ˈtɛdi bɛr/ *noun* [C] a toy for children that looks like a bear

teddy bear

te·di·ous /ˈtidiəs/ *adj.* boring and lasting for a long time: *a tedious lecture*

teem /tim/ *verb* [I] **teem with sth** (usually in the *-ing* forms) (used about a place) having a lot of people or things moving around in it: *The streets were teeming with people.*

teen /tin/ *adj., noun* [C] teenage; teenager: *unmarried teen mothers*

☆ **teen·age** (*also* **teen-age**) /ˈtineɪdʒ/ (*also* **teenaged**; **teen-aged** /ˈtineɪdʒd/) *adj.* (only *before* a noun) **1** between 13 and 19 years old: *teenage children* **2** typical of or suitable for people between 13 and 19 years old: *teenage fashion*

☆ **teen·ag·er** (*also* **teen-ager**) /ˈtineɪdʒər/ *noun* [C] a person who is between 13 and 19 years old: *Her music is very popular with teenagers.*

teens /tinz/ *noun* [plural] the period of a person's life between the ages of 13 and 19: *to be in your late/early teens*

tee·pee = TEPEE

tee·ter-tot·ter /ˈtitərˌtatər/ *noun* [C] = SEE-SAW

teeth *pl.* of TOOTH

teethe /tið/ *verb* [I] (usually in the *-ing* forms) (used about a baby) to start growing its first teeth

tee·to·ta·ler /ˈtitoʊtl̩·ər/ *noun* [C] a person who never drinks alcohol

Tef·lon /ˈtɛflɑn/ *noun* [U] (*trademark*) a special smooth substance that is often used on the inside surfaces or pans to prevent food from sticking

tel·e·com·mu·ni·ca·tions /ˌtɛləkəˌmyunəˈkeɪʃnz/ *noun* [plural] the process of communicating over long distances by using electronic equipment, e.g. by radio or telephone, or the business of providing equipment and services to communicate in this way

tel·e·com·mut·ing /ˈtɛləkəmyutɪŋ/ *noun* [U] working at home, using a computer that is connected with the computers in your company's office through telephone lines —**tel·e·com·mut·er** *noun* [C]

tel·e·gram /ˈtɛləgræm/ *noun* [C] a type of short message that is sent through wires over a long distance using electrical signals and is delivered to sb on a printed form. Telegrams were more common in the past.

tel·e·graph /ˈtɛləgræf/ *noun* [C,U] a system or a piece of equipment for sending telegrams

☆ **tel·e·phone¹** /ˈtɛləfoʊn/ (*also* **phone**) *noun* **1** [U] an electrical system for talking to sb in another house, town, country, etc. by speaking into a special piece of equipment: *Can I contact you by telephone?* ○ *to make a telephone call* ○ *a telephone number*

telephone (*also* **phone**)
buttons
receiver

☞ It is more common to use **phone** rather than **telephone**, especially when you are speaking. When you make a telephone call, you first **pick up the receiver** and **dial** the number. The telephone **rings** and the person at the other end **answers** it. If he/she is already using the telephone, it is **busy**. When you finish speaking, you **hang up**.

2 [C] the piece of equipment that you use when you talk to sb by telephone (1): *Could I use your telephone?* ☞ Look also at **cellular phone** and **pay phone**.

IDM **on the phone/telephone** ➪ PHONE¹

tel·e·phone² /ˈtɛləfoʊn/ (*also* **phone**) *verb* [I,T] (*formal*) to use a telephone in order to speak to sb: *The president telephoned the astronauts to congratulate them on their success.* ☞ **Call** is more common than **telephone** or **phone**.

☆ **telephone book** (*also* **phone book**, *formal* **telephone directory**) *noun* [C] a book that

ə	y	w	t̬	eɪ	aɪ	ɔɪ	aʊ	oʊ
about	yes	woman	butter	say	five	boy	now	go

gives a list of the names, addresses and telephone numbers of the people and businesses in a particular area

tel·e·scope /ˈtɛləskoʊp/ noun [C] an instrument in the shape of a tube with special glass inside it. You look through it to make distant things, especially in outer space, appear bigger and nearer. ☞ picture at **binoculars**. Look also at **microscope**.

tel·e·vise /ˈtɛləvaɪz/ verb [T] to show sth on television: *a televised concert*

☆ **tel·e·vi·sion** /ˈtɛləvɪʒn/ (also **TV**) noun **1** [C] (also **ˈtelevision set**; ˌ**T'V set**) a piece of electrical equipment in the shape of a box. It has a glass screen which shows programs with moving pictures and sounds: *to turn the television on/off* **2** [U] the electrical system and business of sending out programs so that people can watch them on their television sets: *in the days before television* ○ *cable/satellite television* ○ *the major TV networks* ○ *She works in television.* ☞ Look also at **public television**. **3** [U] the programs that are shown on a television set: *Paul's watching television.*

IDM on television being shown by television: *What's on television tonight?*

☆ **tell** /tɛl/ verb (p.t., p.p. **told** /toʊld/) **1** [T] **tell sb (sth); tell sth (to sb)** to give information to sb by speaking or writing: *She told me her address, but I forgot it.* ○ *He wrote to tell me that his mother died.* ○ *Tell us about your vacation.* ○ *Tell me what you did yesterday.* ○ *to tell the truth/a lie* ○ *to tell a story* ○ *Excuse me, can you tell me where the post office is?* ☞ Look at the note at **say**. **2** [T] **tell sb (to do sth)** to order or advise sb to do sth: *The police officer told us to get out of the car.* ○ *Dad told me not to worry about my final exams.* ○ *Please tell me what to do.* ○ *You'll be all right if you do as you're told.* **3** [I,T] to know, see or judge (sth) correctly: *"What do you think Jenny will do next?" "It's hard to tell."* ○ *I could tell that he enjoyed the evening.* ○ *I can't tell which coat is mine. They look exactly the same.* **4** [T] (used about a thing) to give information to sb: *This book will tell you all you need to know.* **5** [I] **tell (on sb)** (*informal*) to inform a person in authority that sb has done sth wrong: *If you do that again, I'm going to tell on you!*

IDM as far as I can see/tell = FAR²

I told you (so) (*informal*) I warned you that this would happen

tell A and B apart ➪ APART

tell time to read the time from a clock or watch

to tell (you) the truth (used to emphasize that you are being honest about sth): *Well, to tell you the truth, I never even considered the cost.*

PHRV tell sb off (for sth/for doing sth) to speak to sb angrily because he/she has done sth wrong

tell·er /ˈtɛlər/ noun [C] a person who works in a bank and whose job is to receive and pay out money ☞ Look also at **ATM**.

tell·ing /ˈtɛlɪŋ/ adj. (usually *before* a noun) **1** showing your real feelings or thoughts: *a telling remark* **2** having a great effect: *the most telling evidence in the case*

tell·tale /ˈtɛlteɪl/ adj. giving information about sth secret or private: *the telltale signs of child abuse*

temp /tɛmp/ noun [C] a temporary employee, especially a secretary, who works somewhere for a short period of time when sb else is sick or on vacation, or when a business needs extra help for a short time —**temp** verb [I]: *Julie's temping at an insurance company this summer.*

☆ **tem·per** /ˈtɛmpər/ noun [C,U] a tendency to become angry and impatient easily, and to be unable to control your behavior: *Be careful of Paul. He has a violent temper.* ○ *You need to learn to control your temper.*

IDM keep/lose your temper to stay calm/to become angry

tem·per·a·ment /ˈtɛmprəmənt/ noun [C,U] a person's character, especially as it affects the way he/she behaves and feels: *to have a calm temperament*

tem·per·a·men·tal /ˌtɛmprəˈmɛntl/ adj. often and suddenly changing the way you behave

tem·per·ate /ˈtɛmpərət/ adj. (used about a climate) not very hot and not very cold

☆ **tem·per·a·ture** /ˈtɛmprətʃər/ noun **1** [C,U] how hot or cold sth is: *Heat the oven to a temperature of 450°F.* ○ *Temperatures in some parts of Michigan will fall below freezing tomorrow.* ○ *a high/low temperature* **2** [C] how hot or cold a person's body is

IDM have a temperature to have a temperature of the body that is higher than normal (when you are sick)

take sb's temperature to measure the temperature of sb's body with a special instrument (**thermometer**)

☆ **tem·ple** /ˈtɛmpl/ noun [C] **1** a building where people pray and worship in some religions: *a Buddhist temple* **2** = SYNAGOGUE **3** one of the flat parts on each side of your forehead

tem·po /ˈtɛmpoʊ/ noun (pl. **tem·pos** /ˈtɛmpoʊz/) **1** [C,U] the speed of a piece of music **2** [sing., U] the speed of an activity or event

☆ **tem·po·rar·y** /ˈtɛmpəˌrɛri/ adj. lasting for a short time; not permanent: *a temporary job* ○ *This arrangement is only temporary.* —**tem·po·rar·i·ly** /ˌtɛmpəˈrɛrəli/ adv.

☆ **tempt** /tɛmpt/ verb [T] to try to persuade or attract sb to do sth, especially sth that is wrong or silly: *His dream of riches had tempted him into a life of crime.* ○ *She was tempted to stay in bed all morning.* ○ *I'm very tempted by the idea of working in another country.*

temp·ta·tion /tɛmpˈteɪʃn/ noun **1** [U] a feel-

ing that you want to do sth, although you know that it is wrong or silly: *I resisted the temptation to have another glass of wine.* **2** [C] a thing that attracts you to do sth wrong or silly: *All that money is certainly a big temptation.*

tempt·ing /ˈtɛmptɪŋ/ *adj.* attractive and making you want to do sth: *a tempting offer* ○ *That chocolate cake looks very tempting!*

☆ **ten** /tɛn/ *number* 10; one more than nine ☞ For examples of how to use numbers in sentences, look at **six**. Look also at Appendix 2.

te·na·cious /təˈneɪʃəs/ *adj.* very determined about sth; not likely to give up or accept defeat: *a tenacious defender of human rights* —**te·nac·i·ty** /təˈnæsəti/ *noun* [U]

☆ **ten·ant** /ˈtɛnənt/ *noun* [C] a person who pays money (**rent**) to the owner of an apartment, building or a piece of land so that he/she can live in it or use it: *The previous tenants of the apartment were college students.* ☞ The owner is called a **landlord** or **landlady**.

☆ **tend** /tɛnd/ *verb* **1** [I] **tend to do sth** to often or normally do or be sth: *Women tend to live longer than men.* ○ *There tends to be a lot of traffic on that road.* ○ *My brother tends to talk a lot when he's nervous.* **2** [I,T] **tend (to) sb/sth** (*formal*) to take care of sb/sth: *He lovingly tended the roses in his garden.*

☆ **ten·den·cy** /ˈtɛndənsi/ *noun* [C] (*pl.* **ten·den·cies**) something that a person or thing does; a way of behaving: *He has a tendency to be late for appointments.* ○ *a patient with suicidal tendencies* ○ *There's a growing tendency for people to work at home.*

ten·der¹ /ˈtɛndər/ *adj.* **1** kind and loving: *She whispered a few tender words in his ear.* **2** (used about meat) soft and easy to cut or bite; not tough **3** (used about a part of the body) painful when you touch it **4** young and without much experience of life: *She went to live in London at the tender age of 15.* —**ten·der·ly** *adv.* —**ten·der·ness** *noun* [U]

ten·der² /ˈtɛndər/ *verb* [T] (*formal*) to offer or give sth formally: *After the scandal, the Senator was forced to tender her resignation.*

ten·don /ˈtɛndən/ *noun* [C] a strong cord in your body that connects a muscle to a bone

ten·e·ment /ˈtɛnəmənt/ *noun* [C] a large, old building that is divided into small apartments, especially in a poor area of a city

☆ **ten·nis** /ˈtɛnəs/ *noun* [U] a game for two or four players who hit a ball to each other over nets with rackets: *Let's play tennis.* ○ *a tennis match*

☞ In tennis you can play **singles** (a game between two people) or **doubles** (a game between two teams of two people).

¹**tennis shoe** *noun* [C] = SNEAKER

ten·or /ˈtɛnər/ *noun* [C] **1** the highest normal

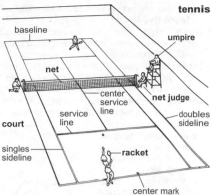

tennis

singing voice for a man; a man with this voice: *a beautiful tenor voice* ○ *Pavarotti is a famous Italian tenor.* **2** a musical instrument with the same range as a tenor voice: *a tenor saxophone*

☆ **tense¹** /tɛns/ *adj.* **1** (used about a person) not able to relax because you are worried or nervous: *She looked pale and tense.* **2** (used about a person's body) having stiff muscles because you are not relaxed **3** (used about a situation) making people feel worried and not relaxed: *Reporters described the atmosphere in the capital as "very tense."*

tense² /tɛns/ *verb* [I,T] to become tense¹(2) or to make your body tense

☆ **tense³** /tɛns/ *noun* [C,U] (*grammar*) a form of a verb that shows whether sth happens in the past, present or future

☆ **ten·sion** /ˈtɛnʃn/ *noun* **1** [C,U] the condition of not being able to relax that is caused by worry or nervousness: *I could hear the tension in her voice as she spoke.* **2** [C,U] a condition of bad feeling and lack of trust between people, countries, etc.: *There are signs of growing tensions between the two countries.* **3** [U] (used about a rope, wire, etc.) how tightly it is stretched

tent

☆ **tent** /tɛnt/ *noun* [C] a shelter made of cloth that is held up by poles and ropes. You can sleep in a tent when you go camping.

ten·ta·tive /ˈtɛntɪtɪv/ *adj.* **1** (used about plans, etc.) uncertain; not definite: *tentative arrangements for the meeting* **2** (used about a person or a person's behavior) not confident about

tʃ	dʒ	v	θ	ð	s	z	ʃ
chin	**J**une	**v**an	**th**in	**th**en	**s**o	**z**oo	**sh**e

what you are saying or doing: *a tentative smile*
—**ten·ta·tive·ly** *adv.*

☆**tenth¹** /tɛnθ/ *pron., det., adv.* 10th; next after
ninth ☞ For more information on numbers,
look at Appendix 2.

☆**tenth²** /tɛnθ/ *noun* [C] the fraction 1/10; one of
ten equal parts ☞ Look at the examples at
sixth. Look also at Appendix 2.

ten·ure /'tɛnyər/ *noun* [U] the right to stay in
a teaching job permanently at a school, college
or university

te·pee (*also* **teepee,**
tipi) /'tipi/ *noun* [C] a
type of tent made of
animal skins or the
outer covering (**bark**)
of trees, with a round
base and a pointed
top, that some Native Americans traditionally
lived in ☞ Look also at **wigwam**.

tepee

tep·id /'tɛpəd/ *adj.* (used about liquids) only
slightly warm

te·qui·la /tə'kilə/ *noun* [U] a strong alcoholic
drink that is made from a Mexican plant

☆**term¹** /tɜrm/ *noun* **1** [C] a word or group of
words, especially one that is used in connec-
tion with a particular subject: *What exactly do
you mean by the term "racist?"* ○ *a technical
term* **2 terms** [plural] **in…terms**; **in terms
of…** (used for indicating which particular
way you are thinking about sth or from which
point of view): *We ought to think about this in
financial terms.* ○ *The apartment would be
ideal in terms of size, but it's very expensive.*
3 terms [plural] the conditions of an agree-
ment: *Under the terms of the contract, you must
finish the project by January 31.* ○ *peace terms*
4 [C] one of the periods of time into which the
academic year is divided at some colleges and
universities ☞ Look at **semester**. **5** [C] a
period of time for which sth lasts: *The
President is now in his second term of office.*
IDM on equal terms (with sb) ⇨ EQUAL¹
be on good, friendly etc. terms (with sb) to
have a friendly relationship with sb
come to terms with sth to accept sth bad or
difficult
in the long/short term over a long/short
period of time in the future: *We're aiming at
an increase of 20% in the long term.* ☞ Look
also at **long-term** and **short-term**.

term² /tɜrm/ *verb* [T] to describe sb/sth by
using a particular word or expression: *the
period of history that is often termed the "Dark
Ages"*

☆**ter·mi·nal¹** /'tɜrmənl/ *adj.* (used about an ill-
ness) slowly causing death: *terminal cancer*
—**ter·mi·nal·ly** *adv.*: *a terminally ill patient*

☆**ter·mi·nal²** /'tɜrmənl/ *noun* **1** [C] a large
building where airplanes, buses, ships, or
trains begin or end their trips: *the bus termi-
nal* ○ *United Airlines flights depart from Termi-*

nal 1 at O'Hare Airport. **2** a piece of computer
equipment (usually a keyboard and screen)
that you use for getting information from a
central computer or for putting information
into it

ter·mi·nate /'tɜrməneɪt/ *verb* [I,T] (*formal*) to
end or to make sth end: *to terminate a contract*
—**ter·mi·na·tion** /,tɜrmə'neɪʃn/ *noun* [U] (*for-
mal*)

ter·mi·nol·o·gy /,tɜrmə'nɑlədʒi/ *noun* [C,U]
(*pl.* **ter·mi·nol·o·gies**) the special words and
expressions that are used in a particular pro-
fession, subject or activity: *computer termi-
nology*

ter·mite /'tɜrmaɪt/ *noun* [C] an insect that
lives mainly in warm regions and eats wood,
often causing damage to buildings

'term ,paper *noun* [C] a long piece of writing
that a student does as his/her most important
work for a course, often including research
from books in the library, etc.: *to write a term
paper on the causes of the American Revolution*

ter·race /'tɛrəs/ *noun* **1** [C] a flat area of stone
next to a house, restaurant, etc. where people
can eat, sit in the sun, etc.: *lunch on the terrace*
☞ Look at **patio**. **2** [usually pl.] one of a series
of steps that are cut into the side of a hill so
that crops can be grown there **4 Terrace**
(*abbr.* **Terr.**) [sing.] (used in names of some
streets in towns and cities, especially on hills):
133 Stanton Terrace

ter·rain /tə'reɪn/ *noun* [U] a type of land:
rough terrain

☆**ter·ri·ble** /'tɛrəbl/ *adj.* **1** very bad or serious: *a
terrible accident* ○ *That was a terrible thing to
do!* **2** sick or very upset: *I feel terrible. I think
I'm going to throw up!* ○ *You look terrible. Are
you all right?* ○ *He felt terrible when he realized
what he had done.* **3** very bad; of low quality:
The hotel was terrible. **4** (only *before* a noun)
very big or great: *You are making a terrible
mistake!*

☆**ter·ri·bly** /'tɛrəbli/ *adv.* **1** very: *I'm terribly
sorry.* **2** very badly: *I played terribly.*

ter·ri·er /'tɛriər/ *noun* [C] a type of small dog

☆**ter·ri·fic** /tə'rɪfɪk/ *adj.* **1** (*informal*) extremely
nice or good; excellent: *You're doing a terrific
job!* **2** (only *before* a noun) very great or big:
We were under a terrific amount of pressure.

ter·ri·fied /'tɛrəfaɪd/ *adj.* **terrified (of sb/sth)**
very afraid: *to be terrified of spiders* ○ *a terri-
fied face*

ter·ri·fy /'tɛrəfaɪ/ *verb* [T] (*pres. part.* **ter·ri·
fying**; *3rd pers. sing. pres.* **ter·ri·fies**; *p.t., p.p.*
ter·ri·fied) to frighten sb very much

ter·ri·to·ri·al /,tɛrə'tɔriəl/ *adj.* (only *before* a
noun) connected with the land or area of
ocean that belongs to a country or ruler: *terri-
torial waters*

☆**ter·ri·to·ry** /'tɛrə,tɔri/ *noun* (*pl.* **ter·ri·to·ries**)
[C,U] **1** an area of land that belongs to one
country or ruler: *U.S. territories in the Pacific* ○

i	$ɪ$	$ɛ$	$æ$	$ɑ$	$ɔ$	$ʌ$	$ʊ$	u
see	sit	ten	cat	hot	saw	cup	put	too

to fly over enemy territory **2** an area that sb is responsible for, e.g. in business: *Each sales rep's territory covers several counties.* **3** an area that an animal has as its own

☆**ter·ror** /'tɛrər/ *noun* **1** [U] very great fear: *He screamed in terror as the rats came toward him.* **2** [C] a person or thing that makes you feel afraid: *the terrors of the night* **3** [U] violent action (e.g. bombing, killing) for political purposes: *a terror campaign*

☆**ter·ror·ism** /'tɛrərɪzəm/ *noun* [U] the use of violent action (e.g. bombing, killing) for political purposes: *an act of terrorism*

☆**ter·ror·ist** /'tɛrərɪst/ *noun* [C] a person who is involved in the use of violent action (e.g. bombing, killing) for political purposes —**ter·ror·ist** *adj.*

☆**ter·ror·ize** /'tɛrəraɪz/ *verb* [T] to make sb feel frightened by using or threatening to use violence against him/her

terse /tərs/ *adj.* said in only a few words and in a not very friendly way: *a terse reply*

☆**test¹** /tɛst/ *noun* [C] **1** a group of questions, usually written, to measure sb's knowledge or skill in sth: *a spelling test*

☞ When you **take** a test, you can either **pass** it (which is good) or **fail** it (which is bad).

2 a short medical examination of a part of your body: *to have an eye test* ∘ *The doctor took a blood test.* **3** an experiment to find out whether sth works or to find out more information about it: *Tests show that the new drug is safe and effective.* **4** a situation or event that shows how good, strong, effective, etc. sb/sth is: *The congressional elections will be a good test of the President's popularity.*

☆**test²** /tɛst/ *verb* [T] **1** test sb (on sth) to examine sb's knowledge or skill in sth: *Are we going to be tested on this stuff?* **2** to examine a part of the body to find out if it is healthy: *to have your eyes tested* **3** test sb/sth (for sth); test sth (on sb/sth) to try, use or examine sth carefully to find out if it is working properly or what it is like: *These cars have all been tested for safety.* ∘ *Do you think medications should be tested on animals?*

tes·ta·ment /'tɛstəmənt/ *noun* [C] **1** Testament one of the two main parts into which the Christian Bible is divided: *the Old Testament* (– that describes events before the birth of Jesus Christ) ∘ *the New Testament* (= that describes events since the birth of Jesus Christ) **2** [usually sing.] (*formal*) **a testament (to sth)** something that shows that sth else exists or is true: *Spielberg's new movie is a testament to his talent and experience.*

tes·ti·cle /'tɛstɪkl/ *noun* [C] one of the two male sex organs that produce sperm

tes·ti·fy /'tɛstəfaɪ/ *verb* (*pres. part.* **tes·ti·fy·ing**; *3rd pers. sing. pres.* **tes·ti·fies**; *p.t., p.p.* **tes·ti·fied**) [I,T] to make a formal statement

that sth is true, especially as a witness in a court of law

tes·ti·mo·ny /'tɛstəmoʊni/ *noun* (*pl.* **tes·ti·mo·nies**) **1** [U] a formal statement that sth is true, especially one that is made in a court of law **2** [U, sing.] (*formal*) something that shows that sth else exists or is true: *The design was testimony to her architectural skill.*

¹**test tube** *noun* [C] a thin glass tube that is used in chemical experiments

tet·a·nus /'tɛtn·əs/ *noun* [U] a serious disease that makes your muscles, especially the muscles of your face, become stiff. It is caused by bacteria that enter the body when a cut becomes infected.

☆**text** /tɛkst/ *noun* **1** [U] the main written part of a book, newspaper, etc. (not the pictures, notes, index, etc.) **2** [C] the written form of a speech, interview, article, etc.: *The newspaper printed the complete text of the interview.* **3** = TEXTBOOK

☆**text·book** /'tɛksbʊk/ (*also* **text**) *noun* [C] a book that teaches a particular subject

tex·tile /'tɛkstaɪl/ *noun* [C] (in industry) a material that is made by weaving or knitting: *cotton textiles*

☆**tex·ture** /'tɛkstʃər/ *noun* [C,U] the way that sth feels when you touch it: *material with a silky texture*

☆**than** /ðən; ðɛn; *strong form* ðæn/ *conj., prep.* **1** (used when you are comparing two things): *He's taller than you.* ∘ *He's taller than you are.* ∘ *New York is more expensive than Cleveland.* ∘ *You speak French a lot better than she does.* **2** (used with "more" and "less" before numbers, expressions of time, distance, etc.): *He earns more than $50,000 a year.* **3** (used after "would rather" to say that you prefer one thing to another): *I'd rather go to Florida than to California.*

☆**thank** /θæŋk/ *verb* [T] **thank sb (for sth/for doing sth)** to tell sb that you are grateful: *I'm writing to thank you for the present you sent me.* ∘ *I'll go and thank him for offering to help.*

☞ Thank you and thanks are both used for telling somebody that you are grateful for something. Thanks is more informal: *Thank you very much for your letter.* ∘ *"How are you, Rachel?" "A lot better – thanks."* You can also use thank you and thanks to accept something that somebody has offered to you: *"Have a piece of cake." "Thank you. It looks delicious."* When you want to refuse something you can say no, thank you or no, thanks: *"Would you like another cup of coffee?" "No, thanks."*

IDM thank God/goodness/heaven (used for expressing relief): *Thank goodness it stopped raining!* ☞ Look at the note at **God** (2).

☆**thank·ful** /'θæŋkfl/ *adj.* (not before a noun) pleased and grateful: *We were thankful that no*

one was was seriously hurt in the fire. ○ *They were thankful for all the help they received.*

thank·ful·ly /ˈθæŋkfəli/ *adv.* fortunately: *Thankfully, no one was injured.*

thank·less /ˈθæŋkləs/ *adj.* involving hard work that other people do not notice or thank you for: *Being a housewife can sometimes be a thankless task.*

☆**thanks¹** /θæŋks/ *noun* [plural] words which show that you are grateful: *I'd like to express my thanks to all of you for coming here today.* ☞ Look at the note at **thank**.

IDM thanks to sb/sth because of sb/sth: *We missed the bus, thanks to you!*

☆**thanks²** /θæŋks/ *interj.* (*informal*) thank you: *Thanks a lot!*

☆**Thanks·giv·ing** /ˌθæŋksˈgɪvɪŋ/ *noun* [U] a holiday on the fourth Thursday in November

☞ Thanksgiving was first celebrated in 1621 by the **Pilgrims** who came from England to what is now Massachusetts. They wanted to thank God and the Native Americans for their health and the harvest. Nowadays people celebrate Thanksgiving by getting together with their families for a big meal and by thinking about what they are thankful for, e.g. their families, homes and food. Some foods that are traditionally eaten at Thanksgiving are **turkey**, **cranberry sauce** and **pumpkin pie**.

ˈ**thank-you** *noun* [C] an expression of thanks: *We sent them some flowers as a thank-you for their help.*

☆**that¹** /ðæt/ *det., pron.* (*pl.* **those** /ðoʊz/) **1** (used for describing a person or thing, especially when it is not near the person speaking): *I like that house over there.* ○ *What's that on the road?* ○ *"Can you hand me the book?" "This one?" "No, that one over there."* **2** (used for talking about a person or thing already known or mentioned): *That was the year we went to Spain, wasn't it?* ○ *Can you give me back that money I loaned you last week?*

IDM that is, ... (used when you are giving more information about sb/sth): *The meeting will be on the 26th – that is, two weeks from today.*

that's that there is nothing more to say or do: *I'm not going and that's that.*

☆**that²** /ðət; *strong form* ðæt/ *pron.* (used for introducing a relative clause) the person or thing already mentioned: *I'm reading the book that won the Pulitzer prize.* ○ *The people that live next door are French.*

☞ When **that** is the object of the verb in the relative clause, it is often left out: *I want to see the doctor (that) I saw last week.* ○ *I wore the dress (that) I bought on sale.*

☆**that³** /ðət; *strong form* ðæt/ *conj.* (used after certain verbs, nouns and adjectives to introduce a new part of the sentence): *She told me* that she was leaving. ○ *I hope that you feel better soon.* ○ *I'm sure that he will come.* ○ *It's funny that you should say that.*

☞ **That** is often left out in this type of sentence, especially in informal speech: *I thought (that) you would like it.*

☆**that⁴** /ðæt/ *adv.* (used with adjectives, adverbs) to that degree or extent: *30 miles? I can't walk that far.* ○ *She can't play the piano that well.*

thaw /θɔ/ *verb* [I,T] **thaw (sth) (out)** to become or to make sth become soft or liquid again after freezing: *Is the snow thawing?* ○ *It's starting to thaw* (= the weather is getting warmer). ○ *Always thaw chicken thoroughly before you cook it.* ☞ Look at **melt**. —**thaw** *noun* [C, usually sing.]

☆**the** /ðə; *before a vowel* ði; *strong form* ði/ *definite article* **1** (used for talking about a person or thing that is already known or that has already been mentioned): *I took the kids to the dentist.* ○ *The Johnsons are on vacation.* ○ *We met the man who bought your house.* ○ *The milk is in the refrigerator.* **2** (used when there is only one or only one group): *The sun is very strong today.* ○ *Who won the state championship?* **3** (used with numbers and dates): *This is the third piece of cake I've eaten.* ○ *I grew up in the sixties.* **4** (used with adjectives to name a group of people): *the French* ○ *the poor* **5** (used with a singular noun when you are talking generally about sth): *The dolphin is an intelligent animal.* **6** (with units of measurement, meaning "every"): *The car gets twenty miles to the gallon.* **7** (with musical instruments): *Do you play the piano?* **8** best known or most important: *You don't mean you met the Tom Cruise?* ☞ "The" is pronounced /ði/ in this sense. **9** the ...the ... (used for saying that two things change to the same extent): *The more you eat, the fatter you get.*

☆**the·a·ter** /ˈθiətər/ *noun* **1** [C] a building where you go to see plays, etc.: *I'm going to the theater* (= to see a play). **2** [C] (*also* **movie theater**) a building where you go to see movies **3** [sing., U] the work of acting in or producing plays: *He's worked in the theater for thirty years.*

the·at·ri·cal /θiˈætrɪkl/ *adj.* **1** (only *before* a noun) connected with the theater **(3)** **2** (used about behavior) unnatural and dramatic because you want people to notice it: *a theatrical gesture*

theft /θɛft/ *noun* [C,U] the crime of taking sth that belongs to another person secretly and without permission: *There have been a lot of thefts in this area recently.* ○ *She was arrested for theft.* ☞ Look at the note at **thief**.

☆**their** /ðɛr/ *det.* belonging to them: *What color is their car?* ○ *The students picked up their books and walked to the door.*

ər	ɪr	ɛr	ɑr	ɔr	ʊr	ʒ	h	ŋ
bird	near	hair	car	north	tour	vision	hat	sing

☆ **theirs** /ðɛrz/ *pron.* of or belonging to them: *Our house isn't as big as theirs.*

☆ **them** /ðəm; *strong form* ðɛm/ *pron.* (the object of a verb or preposition) **1** the people, animals or things mentioned earlier: *I'll call them now.* ○ *"I have the keys here." "Oh, good. Give them to me."* ○ *We have students from several countries, but most of them are Mexican.* ○ *"Did you mail those letters?" "Oh no – I forgot about them."* **2** (*informal*) him or her: *If anybody calls, tell them I'm busy.*

theme /θim/ *noun* [C] **1** a subject of a talk, a piece of writing, etc.: *The theme of today's discussion will be "Our Changing Cities."* ○ *the Republicans' campaign theme* **2** an idea that is developed or repeated in the work of a writer or artist: *The themes of heaven and hell were very common in paintings of this period.* **3** (*also* 'theme song; 'theme tune) a song that is always played at the beginning of a television or radio program

'**theme park** *noun* [C] a place with a lot of things to do, see, ride on, etc., which are all based on a single idea

☆ **them·selves** /ðəm'sɛlvz/ *pron.* **1** (used as the object of a verb or preposition when the people or animals who do an action are affected by it): *Helen and Sarah seem to be enjoying themselves.* ○ *People often talk to themselves when they are worried.* **2** (used for emphasis): *They themselves say that the situation cannot continue.* ○ *Did they paint the house themselves?* (= or did sb else do it for them?)

IDM (**all**) **by themselves 1** alone: *The boys are too young to go shopping by themselves.* ☞ Look at the note at **alone. 2** without help: *The kids cooked dinner all by themselves.*

☆ **then** /ðɛn/ *adv.* **1** (at) that time: *In 1990? I was in college then.* ○ *I'll be on vacation then.* ○ *I haven't seen him since then.* ○ *I'm going tomorrow. Can you wait until then?* **2** next; after that: *We're going hiking in the mountains for a week and then to the beach.* ○ *There was silence for a minute. Then he replied.* **3** in that case; therefore: *"I don't feel very well." "Then why don't you go to the doctor?"* **4** (used for emphasis after words like *now, okay, well,* etc.): *Now then, are we all ready to go?* ○ *Well then, I'll see you tomorrow.*

IDM **but then** (**again**); **then again** (used for introducing a new and different piece of information): *The weather forecast says it'll rain, but then again it's often wrong.*

(**right**) **then and there** immediately; at that time and place: *They agreed to buy the house right then and there, without even looking upstairs.*

the·ol·o·gy /θi'ɑlədʒi/ *noun* [U] the study of religion —**the·o·log·i·cal** /ˌθiə'lɑdʒɪkl/ *adj.*: *a theological college*

the·o·ret·i·cal /ˌθiə'rɛtɪkl/ *adj.* **1** based on ideas and principles, not on practical experi-

ence: *Your paper is too theoretical – you need to give more concrete examples.* **2** based on ideas about sth which may not be true in reality: *a theoretical possibility* (= which will probably never happen) —**the·o·ret·i·cal·ly** /-kli/ *adv.*: *Theoretically, we could still win, but I don't think we will.*

☆ **the·o·ry** /'θiri; 'θiəri/ *noun* (*pl.* **the·o·ries**) **1** [C] an idea or set of ideas that try to explain sth: *the theory about how life on earth began* **2** [U] the general idea or principles of a particular subject: *political theory*

IDM **in theory** as a general idea which may not be true in reality: *Your plan sounds fine in theory, but I don't know if it'll work in practice.*

ther·a·peu·tic /ˌθɛrə'pyutɪk/ *adj.* **1** helping you to relax and feel better: *I find listening to music very therapeutic.* **2** helping you to recover from an illness: *therapeutic treatment*

☆ **ther·a·py** /'θɛrəpi/ *noun* [U] treatment to help or cure an illness, injury or a mental problem, usually without drugs or medical operations: *speech therapy* ○ *He was in therapy for two weeks after his wife left him.* ☞ Look also at **physical therapy.** —**ther·a·pist** /'θɛrəpɪst/ *noun* [C]: *a speech therapist* ○ *I have an appointment with my therapist today.*

☆ **there¹** /ðɛr/ *adv.* **1** in, at or to that place: *Put the table right there in the corner.* ○ *I like Boston. My husband and I met there.* ○ *"Have you been to the new mall?" "We're going there next week."* ○ *Did you look under there?* **2** at that point (in a conversation, story, etc.): *Can I interrupt you there for a minute?* **3** available: *Her parents are always there if she needs help.*

IDM (**right**) **then and there** ⇨ THEN

there (**you are/go**) **1** (used when you give sth to sb): *There you are. Would you like any ketchup with that?* **2** (used when you are explaining sth to sb): *There – just press the switch and it starts.* **3** (used for saying that you are not surprised): *"My new tape player is already broken." "Well, there you go – that's what happens when you buy cheap stuff."*

☆ **there²** /ðər; *strong form* ðɛr/ *pron.* **1** (used as the subject of "be," "seem," "appear," etc. to say that sth exists): *Is there a god?* ○ *There's a man at the door.* ○ *There wasn't much to eat.* ○ *There's somebody singing outside.* ○ *There seems to be a mistake here.* **2** (used for calling attention to sth): *Oh look, there's Kate!*

there·af·ter /ˌðɛr'æftər/ *adv.* (*formal*) after that: *She suffered a heart attack and died shortly thereafter.*

there·by /ˌðɛr'baɪ/ *adv.* (*formal*) in that way: *We started our trip early, thereby avoiding most of the traffic.*

☆ **there·fore** /'ðɛrfɔr/ *adv.* for that reason: *The new cars have more efficient engines and therefore consume less gas.*

ther·mal /'θərml/ *adj.* **1** connected with heat: *thermal energy* **2** (used about clothes) made to

T

tʃ	dʒ	v	θ	ð	s	z	ʃ
chin	June	van	thin	then	so	zoo	she

keep you warm in cold weather: *thermal underwear*

☆ **ther·mom·e·ter** /θərˈmɑmətər/ *noun* [C] an instrument for measuring the temperature of sb's body or of a room (= how hot or cold it is)

Ther·mos /ˈθərməs/ *noun* [C] (*pl.* **Ther·mos·es**) (*also* ˈ**Thermos** ˌ**bottle**) (*trademark*) a type of container that is used for keeping a liquid or food hot or cold

ther·mo·stat /ˈθərməstæt/ *noun* [C] a device that controls the level of heat in a house or machine by switching it on and off as necessary

the·sau·rus /θɪˈsɔrəs/ *noun* [C] (*pl.* **the·sau·rus·es**) a book that contains lists of words and phrases with similar meanings

these *pl.* of THIS¹

the·sis /ˈθisəs/ *noun* [C] (*pl.* **the·ses** /ˈθisiz/) a long piece of writing on a particular subject that you do as part of a university degree

☆ **they** /ðeɪ/ *pron.* (the subject of a verb) **1** the people, animals or things that have been mentioned: *We have two children. They're both boys.* ◦ *"Have you seen my keys?" "Yes, they're on the table."* **2** people in general, or people whose identity is not known or stated: *They say it's going to be a hard winter.* **3** (used informally instead of *"he"* or *"she"*): *Somebody called for you, but they didn't leave their name.*

they'd /ðeɪd/ *short for* THEY HAD, THEY WOULD

they'll /ðeɪl/ *short for* THEY WILL

they're /ðɛr/ *short for* THEY ARE

they've /ðeɪv/ *short for* THEY HAVE

☆ **thick¹** /θɪk/ *adj.* **1** (used about sth solid) having a large distance between its opposite sides; not thin: *a thick black line* ◦ *These walls are very thick.* **2** (used for saying what the distance is between the two opposite sides of something): *The ice was six inches thick.* **3** having a lot of things close together: *a thick forest* ◦ *thick hair* **4** (used about a liquid) stiff; that does not flow easily: *a thick sauce* ◦ *This paint is too thick.* ☞ The opposite for 1 to 4 is **thin**. **5** (used about fog, smoke, etc.) difficult to see through **6** (used about sb's accent) very strong

IDM **have (a) thick skin** to be not easily upset or worried by what people say about you —**thick** *adv.*: *snow lying thick on the ground* —**thick·ly** *adv.*: *Spread the butter thickly.* ◦ *a thickly wooded area*

thick² /θɪk/ *noun*

IDM **in the thick of sth** in the most active or crowded part of sth; very involved in sth: *She always likes to be in the thick of things.*

through thick and thin through difficult times and situations: *He promised to stay with her through thick and thin.*

☆ **thick·en** /ˈθɪkən/ *verb* [I,T] to become thicker or to make sth thicker: *Tonight, the fog will thicken and then more rain will move in from the southwest.* ◦ *Add flour to thicken the sauce.*

☆ **thick·ness** /ˈθɪknəs/ *noun* [U, sing.] the quality of being thick, or how thick sth is: *Broil the steaks for 6-8 minutes, depending on the thickness of the meat.*

☆ **thief** /θif/ *noun* [C] (*pl.* **thieves** /θivz/) a person who steals things from another person

☞ A **thief** is a general word for a person who steals things, usually secretly and without violence. The name of the crime is **theft**. A **robber** steals from a bank, store, etc. and often uses violence or threats. A **burglar** steals things by breaking into a house, store, etc., usually at night, and a **shoplifter** goes into a store when it is open and takes things without paying. Look also at the note at **steal**.

thigh /θaɪ/ *noun* [C] the top part of the leg, above the knee ☞ picture on page A24.

thim·ble /ˈθɪmbl/ *noun* [C] a small object made of metal or plastic that you wear on the end of your finger to protect it when you are sewing

☆ **thin¹** /θɪn/ *adj.* (**thin·ner**; **thin·nest**) **1** (used about sth solid) having a small distance between the opposite sides; not thick: *a thin brown book* ◦ *a thin cotton shirt* ◦ *a thin slice of meat* **2** having very little flesh on the body; not fat: *You need to eat more. You're too thin!*

☞ **Thin**, **skinny**, **slim** and **underweight** all have a similar meaning. **Thin** is the most general word for describing people who have very little flesh on their bodies. **Slim** is used to describe people who are thin in an attractive way: *You're so slim! How do you do it?* If you say sb is **skinny**, you mean that he/she is too thin and not attractive. **Underweight** is a much more formal word, and is often used for describing people who are too thin in a medical sense: *The doctor says I'm underweight.*

3 (used about a liquid) that flows easily; not stiff or thick: *a thin sauce* **4** (used about mist, smoke, etc.) not difficult to see through **5** having only a few people or things with a lot of space between them: *a thin covering of trees*

IDM **through thick and thin** ⇨ THICK²

disappear, vanish, etc. into thin air to disappear completely

wear thin ⇨ WEAR¹ —**thin** *adv.* (*informal*): *Don't spread the frosting too thin.* —**thin·ly** *adv.*: *thinly sliced bread* ◦ *thinly populated areas*

thin² /θɪn/ *verb* [I,T] (**thin·ning**; **thinned**) **thin (sth) (out)** to become thinner or fewer in number; to make sth thinner: *The trees thin out toward the edge of the woods.* ◦ *Thin the sauce by adding milk.*

☆ **thing** /θɪŋ/ *noun* **1** [C] an object that is not named: *What's that red thing on the table?* ◦ *A*

i	ɪ	ɛ	æ	ɑ	ɔ	ʌ	ʊ	u
see	sit	ten	cat	hot	saw	cup	put	too

pen is a thing you write with. ○ *I need to get a few things at the grocery store.* **2** [C] a quality or state: *There's no such thing as evil* (= it doesn't exist). ○ *The best thing about my job is the way it changes all the time.* **3** [C] an action, event or statement: *When I get home, the first thing I do is turn on the TV.* ○ *A strange thing happened to me yesterday.* ○ *What a nice thing to say!* **4** [C] a fact, subject, etc.: *He told me a few things that I didn't know before.* **5 things** [plural] your clothes or personal possessions: *I'll go and pack my things.* **6 things** [plural] the circumstances or conditions of your life: *Things seem to be going very well for him right now.* **7** [C] (used for expressing your feelings about a person or animal): *Look how thin that cat is! Poor little thing!*

IDM **be a good thing (that)** to be lucky that: *It's a good thing you remembered your umbrella.*

do your own thing (*informal*) to do what you want to do, without worrying about what other people think

first thing ⇨ FIRST¹

for one thing (used for introducing a reason for something): *I think we should go by bus. For one thing, it's cheaper.*

make matters/things worse ⇨ WORSE¹

not a thing nothing; not anything: *"Do you need anything else?" "No, not a thing."* ○ *There wasn't a thing we could do about it.*

take it/things easy ⇨ EASY²

the thing is… (*informal*) (used for giving a reason for sth or explaining a problem, especially when you are trying not to hurt sb's feelings): *It sounds like a fun party, but the thing is, my parents are coming to visit then – so I can't go.*

☆**think** /θɪŋk/ *verb* (*p.t., p.p.* **thought** /θɔt/) **1** [I] **think (about sth)** to use your mind to consider sth or to form connected ideas: *Think before you speak.* ○ *What are you thinking about?* ○ *He had to think hard* (= a lot) *about the question.* **2** [T] to consider or believe; to have as an opinion: *"Do you think it's going to snow?" "No, I don't think so."* ○ *"Sue's coming tomorrow, isn't she?" "Yes, I think so."* ○ *I think that they moved to New York, but I'm not sure.* ○ *What did you think of the movie?* ○ *I don't think they are very good musicians.* **3** [I] **think of/about doing sth** to intend or plan to do sth: *We're thinking of buying a new house.* **4** [I] **think about/of sb** to consider the feelings of sb else: *She never thinks about anyone but herself.* **5** [T] to expect sth: *The job took longer than we thought.*

IDM **think better of (doing) sth** to decide not to do sth; to change your mind

think highly, a lot, not much, etc. of sb/sth to have a good, bad, etc. opinion of sb/sth

think the world of sb to love and admire sb very much

think twice (about sth/before doing sth) to

consider a plan very carefully, because it may not be a good idea

PHRV **think of sth** to create an idea in your imagination: *Who first thought of the plan?*

think sth over to consider sth carefully: *I'll think over your offer and let you know tomorrow.*

think sth through to consider carefully all the details of a plan, idea, etc: *Let's think this thing through – it's a big decision.*

think sth up to create sth in your mind; to invent: *to think up a new advertising slogan*

think·er /ˈθɪŋkər/ *noun* [C] a person who thinks about serious and important subjects

☆**think·ing¹** /ˈθɪŋkɪŋ/ *adj.* intelligent and using your mind to think about important subjects: *a newspaper for thinking people*

think·ing² /ˈθɪŋkɪŋ/ *noun* [U] **1** the act of using your mind to think about sth: *clear thinking* **2** an opinion: *This accident will make them change their thinking on safety matters.*

IDM **wishful thinking** = WISHFUL

☆**third¹** /θərd/ *pron., det., adv.* 3rd; next after second ☞ Look at the examples at **sixth**. For more information on numbers, look at Appendix 2.

IDM **next/second/third to last** = LAST¹

☆**third²** /θərd/ *noun* [C] the fraction 1/3; one of three equal parts of sth ☞ Look at the examples at **sixth**. For more information on numbers, look at Appendix 2.

,**third ˈparty** *noun* [C] (*pl.* **third parties**) a person who is not one of the two main people or groups involved in sth

the ˌThird ˈWorld *noun* [sing.] (*old-fashioned*) the poorer countries of Asia, Africa and South America

☞ This expression is often considered offensive nowadays. Many people prefer to call these countries **the developing world**.

☆**thirst** /θərst/ *noun* **1** [U, sing.] the feeling that you have when you want or need to drink: *Iced tea really quenches your thirst.* ○ *to die of thirst* **2** [sing.] **a thirst for sth** a strong desire for sth

☆**thirst·y** /ˈθərsti/ *adj.* (**thirst·i·er; thirst·i·est**) wanting or needing a drink: *I'm thirsty. Can I have a drink of water?*

☆**thir·teen** /ˌθərˈtin/ *number* 13; one more than twelve ☞ For examples of how to use numbers in sentences, look at **six**. —**thir·teenth** /ˌθərˈtinθ/ *pron., det., adv.* ☞ Look at the examples at **sixth**.

☆**thir·ty** /ˈθərti/ *number* 30; one more than twenty-nine ☞ For examples of how to use numbers in sentences, look at **sixty**. Look also at Appendix 2. —**thir·ti·eth** /ˈθərtiəθ/ *pron., det., adv.* ☞ Look at the examples at **sixth**.

☆**this¹** /ðɪs/ *det., pron.* (*pl.* **these** /ðiz/) **1** (used for talking about sb/sth that is close to you in time or space): *Take a look at this picture.* ○

ə	y	w	ţ	eɪ	aɪ	ɔɪ	aʊ	oʊ
about	yes	woman	butter	say	five	boy	now	go

These boots are really comfortable. My old ones weren't. ○ *Is this the book you asked for?* ○ *These are the letters to be filed, not those over there.* **2** (used for talking about sth that was mentioned or talked about before): *Where did you hear about this?* **3** (used for introducing sb or showing sb sth): *Chuck, this is my wife, Claudia, and these are our kids, David and Vicky.* ○ *Hello, this is Maria Diaz* (= on the telephone). **4** (used with days of the week or periods of time) of today or the present week, year, etc.: *Are you busy this afternoon?* ○ *this Friday* (= the Friday of this week) **5** (*informal*) (used when you are telling a story) a certain: *Then this woman said…*

IDM **this and that** various things: *We talked about this and that.*

☆**this²** /ðɪs/ *adv.* (used when you are describing sth) so; as much as this: *The road is not usually this busy.*

this·tle /ˈθɪsl/ *noun* [C] a wild plant with purple flowers and sharp points (**thorns**) on its leaves

thorn /θɔrn/ *noun* [C] one of the hard sharp points on the stem of some plants and bushes, e.g. on rose bushes

thorn·y /ˈθɔrni/ *adj.* (**thorn·i·er**; **thorn·i·est**) **1** (used about a problem, etc.) difficult **2** having thorns

☆**thor·ough** /ˈθɜroʊ/ *adj.* **1** careful and complete: *The police made a thorough search of the house.* **2** doing things in a very careful way, making sure that you look at every detail: *Pam is slow, but she is very thorough.* —**thorough·ness** *noun* [U]

thor·ough·ly /ˈθɜrəli/ *-roʊ-/ adv.* **1** in a thorough way: *to study a subject thoroughly* **2** completely; very; very much: *We thoroughly enjoyed our vacation.*

those *pl.* of THAT¹

☆**though¹** /ðoʊ/ *conj.* **1** in spite of the fact that; although: *Though he had very little money, Alex always managed to dress well.* ○ *She still loved him even though he had treated her so badly.* **2** but: *I'll come as soon as I can, though I can't promise to be on time.*

IDM **as if/though** ⇨ AS

☆**though²** /ðoʊ/ *adv.* (*informal*) however: *I really like Jonathan. I don't like his wife, though.*
☛ Look at the note at **although**.

thought¹ *p.t., p.p.* of THINK

☆**thought²** /θɔt/ *noun* **1** [C,U] the act of thinking: *Kim sat, lost in thought, looking at the old photographs.* **2** [U] particular ideas or a particular way of thinking: *a change in medical thought on the subject* **3** [sing., U] an act of being kind to or paying attention to sb/sth: *He didn't give any thought to the rest of his family.* **4** [C] an idea or opinion: *What are your thoughts on this subject?* ○ *The thought of living alone filled her with fear.*

IDM **have second thoughts (about sb/sth)** ⇨ SECOND¹

on second thought ⇨ SECOND¹

a school of thought ⇨ SCHOOL

☆**thought·ful** /ˈθɔtfl/ *adj.* **1** thinking deeply: *a thoughtful expression* **2** thinking about what other people want or need: *It was very thoughtful of you to send Mrs. Brown some flowers.* —**thought·ful·ly** *adv.* —**thought·ful·ness** *noun* [U]

thought·less /ˈθɔtləs/ *adj.* not thinking about what other people want or need or what the result of your actions will be —**thought·less·ly** *adv.* —**thought·less·ness** *noun* [U]

☆**thou·sand** /ˈθaʊznd/ *number* 1,000; one more than nine hundred ninety-nine

☛ Notice that you use **thousand** in the singular when you are talking about a number. You use **thousands** when you mean "a lot": *She earns twenty-five thousand dollars a year.* ○ *Thousands of people attended the meeting.* For more information about numbers, look at Appendix 2.

thou·sandth¹ /ˈθaʊznθ/ *det.* 1,000th; next after nine hundred ninety-ninth

thou·sandth² /ˈθaʊznθ/ *noun* [C] the fraction 1/1000; one of a thousand equal parts of sth

thrash /θræʃ/ *verb* **1** [T] to hit sb/sth many times with a stick, whip, etc. **2** [I] **thrash (about/around)** to move your arms, legs, etc. in an uncontrolled way, e.g. because you are in pain

PHRV **thrash sth out** to talk about sth until you reach an agreement

☆**thread¹** /θrɛd/ *noun* **1** [C,U] a long thin piece of cotton, etc. that you use for sewing, etc.: *a needle and thread* ☛ picture at sew. **2** [C] the connection between ideas, the parts of a story, etc.: *a common thread linking all the accidents*

thread² /θrɛd/ *verb* [T] **1** to put thread¹(1) through the hole in a needle: *to thread a needle* **2** to link things together by putting them onto a string, etc. **3** to pass sth narrow through a space and into a particular position: *He threaded the belt through the loops on his pants.*

IDM **thread your way through sth** to pass through sth with difficulty, moving around things or people that are in your way

thread·bare /ˈθrɛdbɛr/ *adj.* (used about material or clothes) old and very thin

☆**threat** /θrɛt/ *noun* **1** [C,U] a warning that sb may hurt, kill or punish you if you do not do what he/she wants: *Under threat of death, he did as they asked.* ○ *to make a threat against sb* ○ *to carry out a threat* **2** [C, usually sing.] a person or thing that may damage sth or hurt sb; something that indicates future danger: *a serious threat to national security*

☆**threat·en** /ˈθrɛtn/ *verb* **1** [T] **threaten sb (with sth)**; **threaten (to do sth)** to warn that

ər	ɪr	ɛr	ɑr	ɔr	ʊr	ʒ	h	ŋ
bird	near	hair	car	north	tour	vision	hat	sing

you may hurt, kill or punish sb if he/she does not do what you want: *to threaten sb with a knife* ○ *She was threatened with dismissal.* ○ *The man threatened to kill her if she didn't tell him where the money was.* **2** [I,T] to seem likely to do sth bad: *The oil slick is threatening the coastline with pollution.* —**threat·en·ing** *adj.* —**threat·en·ing·ly** *adv.*

☆**three** /θri/ *number* 3; one more than two ☞ Look at **third.** For examples of how to use numbers in sentences, look at **six.** Look also at Appendix 2.

three- /θri/ (in compounds) having three of the thing mentioned: *a three-bedroom apartment*

three-di·men·sion·al /ˌθri dəˈmɛnʃn·l/ (*also* 3-D /ˌθri ˈdi/) *adj.* having length, width and height: *a three-dimensional model*

thresh·old /ˈθrɛʃhoʊld; -ʃoʊld/ *noun* [C] **1** the bottom part of the opening for a door; the entrance to a room or building: *She stood on the threshold* (= in the entrance). **2** the time when you are just about to start sth or find sth: *on the threshold of a scientific breakthrough* **3** [usually sing.] the point at which sth begins to have an effect: *people who have a low pain threshold*

threw *p.t.* of THROW[1]

thrift·y /ˈθrɪfti/ *adj.* (**thrift·i·er; thrift·i·est**) (*old-fashioned*) careful not to spend too much money

thrill[1] /θrɪl/ *noun* [C] a sudden strong feeling of pleasure or excitement

thrill[2] /θrɪl/ *verb* [T] to make sb feel a thrill[1]: *His singing thrilled the audience.*

thrilled /θrɪld/ *adj.* (usually not before a noun) very pleased or excited: *I was just thrilled with your present.*

thrill·er /ˈθrɪlər/ *noun* [C] a movie, book, etc. with a very exciting story, often about a crime

thrill·ing /ˈθrɪlɪŋ/ *adj.* very exciting: *a thrilling victory*

thrive /θraɪv/ *verb* [I] to grow or develop well —**thriv·ing** *adj.*: *a thriving industry*

☆**throat** /θroʊt/ *noun* [C] **1** the front part of your neck: *The attacker grabbed the man by the throat.* ☞ picture on page A24. **2** the back part of your mouth and the passage down your neck through which air and food pass: *She got a piece of candy stuck in her throat.* ○ *I have a really sore throat.*

IDM clear your throat ⇨ CLEAR[3]

throb /θrɑb/ *verb* [I] (**throb·bing; throbbed**) to make strong regular movements or noises; to beat strongly: *His heart was throbbing.* ○ *Her finger throbbed with pain.* —**throb** *noun* [U]: *the throb of the ship's engines*

throne /θroʊn/ *noun* **1** [C] the special chair where a king or queen sits **2 the throne** [sing.] the position of being king or queen: *The prince is second in line to the British throne.*

throng /θrɔŋ; θrɑŋ/ *noun* [C] (*formal*) a large crowd of people

throt·tle /ˈθrɑtl/ *verb* [T] to hold sb tightly by the throat and stop him/her from breathing

☆**through**[1] /θru/ *prep.* **1** from one end or side of sth to the other: *We drove through the center of town.* ○ *She could see the outline of a tree through the mist.* ○ *to look through a telescope* ○ *James cut through the rope.* ○ *to push through a crowd of people* **2** from the beginning to the end of sth: *Food supplies will not last through the winter.* ○ *We're halfway through the book.* **3** until, and including: *The museum is open from Monday through Saturday.* **4** because of; with the help of: *Errors were made through bad organization.* ○ *David got the job through his uncle.*

☆**through**[2] /θru/ *adv.* **1** from one end or side to the other: *The gate was opened and they ran through.* **2** from the beginning to the end of sth: *He read the letter through and handed it back.*

PHRV be through (with sb/sth) to be finished with sb/sth

☆**through·out** /θruˈaʊt/ *prep., adv.* **1** in every part of sth: *The game will be shown live on television throughout the world.* **2** from the beginning to the end of sth: *We didn't enjoy the vacation because it rained throughout.* ○ *Food was scarce throughout the war.*

☆**throw**[1] /θroʊ/ *verb* (*p.t.* **threw** /θru/; *p.p.* **thrown** /θroʊn/) **1** [I,T] to send sth through the air by pushing it out of your hand: *How far can you throw?* ○ *Throw the ball to Wayne.* ○ *Throw Wayne the ball.* ○ *Protesters threw rocks at the police.* **2** [T] to put sth somewhere quickly or carelessly: *He threw his bag down in a corner.* **3** [T] to move your body or part of it quickly or suddenly: *Jenny threw herself onto the bed and sobbed.* ○ *Lee threw back his head and roared with laughter.* **4** [T] to cause sb to fall down: *The bus braked and we were thrown to the floor.* **5** [T] (*informal*) to make sb feel upset, confused or surprised: *The question really threw me – I had no idea how to answer it.* **6** [T] to put sb in a particular (usually bad) situation: *Many people were thrown out of work during the recession.* **7** [T] to send light or shade onto sth: *The house threw a shadow across the lawn.*

PHRV throw sth away 1 (*also* **throw sth out**) to get rid of sth that you do not want, e.g. by putting it in a garbage can: *That's garbage. You can throw it away.* **2** to waste or not use sth useful: *to throw away a good opportunity*

throw sth in (*informal*) to include sth else without increasing the price

throw sb out to force sb to leave

throw sth out 1 to refuse to accept sb's idea or suggestion **2** = THROW STH AWAY

throw up to send out the food in your stomach through your mouth

tʃ	dʒ	v	θ	ð	s	z	ʃ
chin	June	van	thin	then	so	zoo	she

throw² /θroʊ/ *noun* [C] **1** an act of throwing **2** the distance that sb throws sth: *a record throw of 75 meters*

thru /θru/ (used especially on signs) through ☞ Look also at **drive-thru**.

thrust¹ /θrʌst/ *verb* [I,T] (*p.t., p.p.* **thrust**) **1** to push sb/sth/yourself suddenly and with force: *The man thrust her out of the way and ran off.* **2** to make a sudden forward movement with a knife, etc.
PHRV **thrust sb/sth upon sb** to force sb to accept sb/sth

thrust² /θrʌst/ *noun* **1** [C] a strong push **2** [U] the main part or ideas of sth: *The main thrust of our research is to find ways of preventing cancer.*

thud /θʌd/ *noun* [C] the low sound that is made when sth heavy falls down —**thud** *verb* [I] (**thud·ding**; **thud·ded**): *A snowball thudded against the window.*

thug /θʌg/ *noun* [C] a violent person who may hurt other people

☆**thumb¹** /θʌm/ *noun* [C] **1** the short thick finger at the side of each hand ☞ picture on page A24. **2** the part of a glove, etc. that covers your thumb (1)
IDM **have a green thumb** ⇨ GREEN¹
thumbs up/down a sign or an expression that shows approval/disapproval: *This show got a big thumbs up from all the critics.*

thumb² /θʌm/ *verb*
PHRV **thumb through sth** to turn the pages of a book, etc. quickly

thumb·tack /ˈθʌmtæk/ (*also* **tack**) *noun* [C] a short pin with a flat top, used for fastening paper, etc. to a board or wall

thump /θʌmp/ *verb* **1** [T] to hit sb/sth with sth heavy, usually your fist **2** [I] to make a loud sound by hitting or beating heavily: *His heart was thumping with excitement.* —**thump** *noun* [C]

thun·der¹ /ˈθʌndər/ *noun* [U] the loud noise that comes after lightning when there is a storm

thun·der² /ˈθʌndər/ *verb* **1** [I] (used with *it*) to make the sound of thunder¹: *The rain poured down and it started to thunder.* **2** [I,T] to make a loud noise like thunder¹: *Traffic thundered across the bridge.* ○ *"Get back to class!" the principal thundered.*

☆**thun·der·storm** /ˈθʌndərstɔrm/ *noun* [C] a storm with thunder and lightning

☆**Thurs·day** /ˈθərzdeɪ; -di/ *noun* [C,U] (*abbr.* **Thur.; Thurs.**) the day of the week after Wednesday and before Friday ☞ For examples of the use of the days of the week, look at **Monday**.

thus /ðʌs/ *adv.* (*formal*) **1** because of or as a result of this: *Documents can be sent electronically, thus saving paper.* **2** like this; in this way: *Thus began the series of incidents which changed her life.*

thwart /θwɔrt/ *verb* [T] to stop sb doing what he/she planned to do; to prevent sth from happening

tick¹ /tɪk/ *verb* [I] (used about a clock or watch) to make regular short sounds: *I could hear the clock ticking all night.*
PHRV **tick away/by** (used about time) to pass: *The minutes ticked by, but there was still no sign of Teri.*

tick² /tɪk/ *noun* [C] **1** the regular short sound that a watch or clock makes when it is working **2** a very small animal with eight legs, like an insect, that attaches itself to the skin of animals or people in order to suck their blood **3** (*BrE*) = CHECK MARK

☆**tick·et** /ˈtɪkət/ *noun* [C] **1** a piece of paper or card that shows you have paid to travel on public transportation, or to enter a place of entertainment, etc: *a one way/round trip ticket* ○ *two tickets for the concert* ☞ Look at **season ticket. 2** an official piece of paper that you get when you have parked in the wrong place, driven too fast, etc.: *a parking ticket* **3** a list of candidates in an election who are supported by a particular political party: *to join the Republican ticket*

tick·le /ˈtɪkl/ *verb* **1** [T] to touch sb lightly with your fingers or with sth soft so that he/she laughs: *She tickled the baby's toes.* **2** [I,T] to feel or to cause the sensation of sth touching you lightly: *My nose tickles/is tickling.* ○ *The wool scarf tickled her neck.* **3** [T] (*informal*) to amuse or please sb: *We were just tickled when the governor visited our store.* —**tick·le** *noun* [C]: *I have a tickle in my throat.*

tick·lish /ˈtɪklɪʃ/ *adj.* (used about a person) sensitive and laughing a lot when sb tickles him/her

tic-tac-toe (*also* **tick-tack-toe**) /ˌtɪktækˈtoʊ/ *noun* [U] a game for two players that is played with a pencil and paper. Each person tries to win by writing three O's or three X's in a line in a frame of nine squares.

tic-tac-toe

tid·al /ˈtaɪdl/ *adj.* connected with the tides in the ocean

'tidal wave *noun* [C] a very large wave in the ocean, often caused by a storm

tid·bit /ˈtɪdbɪt/ *noun* [C] **1** a small but very good piece of food **2** an interesting piece of information

☆**tide¹** /taɪd/ *noun* [C,U] the regular change in the level of the ocean. At high tide the ocean is closer to the shore; at low tide it is farther away.: *The tide is coming in/going out.* ○ (*figurative*) *The tide* (= of public opinion) *seems to have turned in the President's favor.*

tide² /taɪd/ *verb*

PHRV **tide sb over** to help sb get through a difficult time

ti·dy /'taɪdi/ *adj.* (**ti·di·er**; **ti·di·est**) (*formal*) arranged in good order; neat: *If you keep your room tidy, it is easier to find things.* ☞ **Neat** is more common than **tidy**.

☆ **tie**[1] /taɪ/ *noun* [C] **1** (*also* **necktie**) a long thin piece of cloth that you wear around your neck with a shirt ☞ picture on page A27. Look also at **bow tie**. **2** [usually pl.] something that connects you with a particular group of people: *Police believe he has ties to the Mafia.* ○ *family ties* **3** something that limits your freedom: *He never got married because he didn't want any ties.* **4** a game or competition in which two or more teams or players get the same score: *There was a tie for first place.*

☆ **tie**[2] /taɪ/ *verb* (*pres. part.* **ty·ing**; *3rd pers. sing. pres.* **ties**; *p.t., p.p.* **tied**) **1** [T] to fasten sb/sth or fix sb/sth in position with rope, string, etc.: *The prisoner was tied to a chair.* ○ *Kay tied her hair back with a ribbon.* ○ *to tie sth in a knot* ○ *to tie your shoelaces* **2** [I,T] **tie (sth) (with sb) (for sth)** to have the same score as another player or team in a game or competition: *Wallace's touchdown tied the score at 13 in the third quarter.* ○ *Jenny tied with Sara for third place.*

PHRV **tie sb/yourself down** (often passive) to limit your freedom: *She felt too tied down at home with the kids.*

tie in (with sth) to agree with other facts or information that you have

tie sb/sth up 1 to keep sb/sth in position with rope, string, etc.: *The dog was tied up in the back yard.* **2** (usually passive) to occupy or keep sb busy: *Mr. Jones is tied up in a meeting.*

tier /tɪr/ *noun* [C] one of a number of levels: *a stadium with two tiers of seats*

ti·ger /'taɪgər/ *noun* [C] a large wild cat that has yellow fur with black stripes. Tigers live in Asia.

☞ picture at **lion**. A baby tiger is called a **cub**.

☆ **tight**[1] /taɪt/ *adj.* **1** firm and difficult to move: *a tight knot* ○ *Keep a tight hold on this rope.* **2** fitting very closely: *These shoes hurt. They're too tight.* ☞ The opposite is **loose**. **3** (in compounds) not allowing sth to get in or out: *an airtight container* **4** not having much spare time, space or money: *My schedule this week is very tight.* **5** stretched or pulled hard: *A tennis net must be kept tight.* **6** controlled very strictly: *Security is very tight at the airport.* —**tight·ness** *noun* [U]

☆ **tight**[2] /taɪt/ *adv.* firmly; closely: *Hold tight – there's a bump in the road ahead.*

☞ **Tightly**, not **tight**, is used before a past participle: *The van was packed tight with boxes.* ○ *The van was tightly packed with boxes.*

☆ **tight·en** /'taɪtn/ *verb* [I,T] **1 tighten (sth) (up)** to become tighter; to make sth tighter: *His grip on her arm tightened.* ○ *He tightened the screws as far as they would go.* **2 tighten sth (up)**; **tighten up (on sth)** to become more strict or to cause sth to become more strict: *to tighten up the law on the sale of alcohol to minors*

IDM **tighten your belt** (*informal*) to start making more careful choices about spending your money

☆ **tight·ly** /'taɪtli/ *adv.* firmly; closely: *Screw the lid on tightly.* ○ *She kept her eyes tightly closed.* ☞ Look at the note at **tight**[2].

tight·rope /'taɪtroʊp/ *noun* [C] a rope stretched high above the ground on which people walk, e.g. in a circus

tights /taɪts/ *noun* [plural] a piece of thin clothing, usually worn by women and girls, that fits tightly from the waist over the legs and feet: *a pair of tights* ☞ **Pantyhose/nylons** are thinner than **tights**.

'til /tɪl/ *prep.* (*informal*) = UNTIL

☆ **tile** /taɪl/ *noun* [C] one of the flat, square objects that are arranged in rows to cover floors, bathroom walls, etc. —**tile** *verb* [T]: *to tile the bathroom*

till /tɪl/ *prep.* (*informal*) = UNTIL

tilt /tɪlt/ *verb* [I,T] to have one end or side higher than the other; to put sth in this position: *The front seats of the car tilt forward.* ○ *She tilted her head to one side.* —**tilt** *noun* [sing.]

tim·ber /'tɪmbər/ *noun* **1** [U] trees that are used as a source of wood for building houses, etc. **2** [C] a large piece of wood: *a ship's timbers*

☆ **time**[1] /taɪm/ *noun* **1** [C] a particular point in the day or night: *What time is it?* ○ *Can you tell me the new time for the meeting?* ○ *It's time to go home.* ○ *By the time I get home, Alex will have dinner ready.* **2** [U] the passing of minutes, hours, days, etc.: *As time passed and there was still no news, we got more worried.* **3** [C,U] an amount of minutes, hours, days, etc.: *You're wasting time – get back to work!* ○ *I'll fax this letter to save time.* ○ *free time* ○ *We don't have time to stop now.* ○ *It takes a long time to learn a language.* ☞ Look also at **full-time** and **part-time**. **4** [C] a period in the past: *Did you enjoy your time in Spain?* ○ *In Shakespeare's times, few people could read.* **5** [C,U] an occasion when sb does sth or sth happens: *I called them three times.* ○ *This is the first time I've ever done this.* ○ *I'll do it better next time.* ○ *The last time I saw him, he looked sick.* **6** [C,U] a period or an occasion when sth special happens or that is suitable for sth: *harvest time* ○ *May is strawberry-picking time.* **7** [sing.] a system for measuring time in a particular part of the world: *Eastern Standard Time* ○ *We arrive*

ə	y	w	t	eɪ	aɪ	ɔɪ	aʊ	oʊ
about	yes	woman	butter	say	five	boy	now	go

in Atlanta at 11:00 local time. **8** [C,U] the number of minutes, etc. taken to complete sth, especially a race: *What was his time in the hundred meters?* **9 times** [plural] (used with a number, for comparing things): *A decent apartment is three times as expensive in New York as it is in Iowa* (= e.g. if it cost $500 in Iowa, it costs $1,500 in New York).

IDM all the time during the time that sb was doing sth or that sth was happening: *I looked everywhere for my keys and they were in my pocket all the time.*

at the same time ⇨ SAME¹

at a time on each occasion: *The elevator can hold six people at a time.*

at one time in the past; previously: *At one time, this land was covered with trees.*

at the time at a particular moment or period in the past: *I agreed at the time but later changed my mind.*

at times sometimes: *At times I wish we'd never had children.*

beat time (to sth) ⇨ BEAT¹

before your time before you were born

behind the times not modern or fashionable

for the time being just for now; not for long

from time to time sometimes; not often

give sb a hard time ⇨ HARD¹

have a bad, rotten, etc. time to not enjoy yourself: *I had a lousy time at summer camp.*

have a good, great, etc. time to enjoy yourself: *We had a wonderful time at the party.*

have a hard/rough/tough time to have problems or difficulties

have no time for sb/sth to not like sb/sth: *I have no time for people who aren't prepared to work.*

in the nick of time ⇨ NICK¹

in time (for sth/to do sth) not late; with enough time remaining for sth: *Don't worry. We'll get to the airport in time to catch your flight.*

kill time ⇨ KILL¹

once upon a time ⇨ ONCE¹

on time not late or early: *Our flight arrived right on time.*

take your time to do sth without hurrying

tell time ⇨ TELL

time after time; time and (time) again again and again; many times

time² /taɪm/ *verb* [T] **1** to choose or arrange the time that sth happens: *They timed their trip to avoid rush hour.* **2** to measure how long sb/sth takes

time clock *noun* [C] a special type of clock that prints out the time on a card that you put into it, e.g. to show when you start and finish work each day

time-con,suming *adj.* that takes or needs a lot of time

time-less /ˈtaɪmləs/ *adj.* (*formal*) that does not seem to be changed by time

time ˌlimit *noun* [C] a time during which sth must be done

time-ly /ˈtaɪmli/ *adj.* happening at just the right time: *The accident was a timely reminder of the dangers of driving on icy roads.*

tim-er /ˈtaɪmər/ *noun* [C] a machine or part of a machine that measures time

times /taɪmz/ *prep.* (used when you are multiplying one number by another): *Three times four is twelve.* ☛ Look also at **time¹**(9).

time-ta-ble /ˈtaɪmteɪbl/ *noun* [C] a plan that shows the times when a series of events are supposed to happen: *a timetable for the removal of the troops from the region*

time zone *noun* [C] one of the areas that the world is divided into, each with its own time: *Chicago is in the Central time zone.*

tim-id /ˈtɪməd/ *adj.* easily frightened; shy —**ti-mid-i-ty** /tɪˈmɪdəti/ *noun* [U] —**tim-id-ly** *adv.*

tim-ing /ˈtaɪmɪŋ/ *noun* [U] **1** the act of choosing or arranging when sth will happen: *Good timing is important when you introduce a new product.* **2** your skill at choosing or arranging the best time for sth

tin /tɪn/ *noun* (*symbol* **Sn**) [U] a soft white-colored metal that is often mixed with other metals

tinge /tɪndʒ/ *noun* [usually sing.] a small amount of a color or a feeling: *a tinge of anxiety* —**tinged** *adj.* **tinged with sth**: *Her joy at leaving was tinged with regret.*

tin-gle /ˈtɪŋgl/ *verb* [I] to have a slight stinging or prickling feeling in the skin: *His cheeks tingled as he came in from the cold.* —**tin-gle** *noun* [usually sing.]: *a tingle of excitement*

tin-ker /ˈtɪŋkər/ *verb* [I] **tinker (with sth)** to try to repair or improve sth without having enough skill or knowledge: *So many people have tinkered with the copier that it doesn't work at all anymore.*

tin-kle /ˈtɪŋkl/ *verb* [I] to make a light, ringing sound, like that of a small bell —**tin-kle** *noun* [C, usually sing.]

tin-sel /ˈtɪnsl/ *noun* [U] strings covered with little pieces of shiny paper, used as a Christmas decoration

tint¹ /tɪnt/ *noun* [C] a type or shade of a color: *white paint with a pinkish tint*

tint² /tɪnt/ *verb* [T] to add a little color to sth: *tinted glass*

☆ **ti-ny** /ˈtaɪni/ *adj.* (**ti-ni-er; ti-ni-est**) very small: *the baby's tiny fingers*

☆ **tip¹** /tɪp/ *noun* [C] **1** the thin or pointed end of sth: *the tips of your toes, fingers, etc.* ○ *the southern tip of South America* **2** a piece of useful advice: *Thanks for the tip!* **3** an extra amount of money that you give to a waiter/waitress, taxi driver, etc. to thank him/her for good service

IDM (have sth) on the tip of your tongue to be about to remember or say sth that you have forgotten for a short time: *Their name is on the*

tip of my tongue. It'll come back to me in a minute.

the tip of the iceberg a small part of a problem that is much larger

☆**tip²** /tɪp/ verb [I,T] (**tip·ping; tipped**) **1** to move so that one side is higher than the other; to make sth move in this way: *Tip the table so you can fit it through the doorway.* **2 tip (sth) (over)** to fall or turn over; to make sth turn over: *The tractor turned the corner too fast and the trailer tipped over.* ○ *The baby leaned out of his stroller and tipped it over.* **3** to give a waiter/waitress, taxi driver, etc. an extra amount of money (**a tip**) to thank him/her for good service: *You should tip the waitress about 15% of the bill.*

PHRV tip sb off to give sb secret information: *The police had been tipped off and were waiting when the burglars broke in.*

ti·pi = TEPEE

tip-off noun: *Acting on a tip-off, the police searched the house for drugs.*

tip·toe¹ /'tɪptoʊ/ noun
IDM on tiptoe standing or walking on the ends of your toes with your heels off the ground

tip·toe² /'tɪptoʊ/ verb [I] (pres. part. **tip·toe·ing**; 3rd pers. sing. pres. **tip·toes**; p.t., p.p **tip·toed**) to walk quietly and carefully on tiptoe ¹

☆**tire¹** /'taɪər/ noun [C] the thick rubber ring that fits around the outside of a wheel: *a flat tire* ○ *Remember to check your tire pressure.* ☞ picture at **bicycle**.

☆**tire²** /'taɪər/ verb **1** [I,T] **tire (sb) (out)** to feel that you need to rest or sleep; to make sb feel like this: *However hard he works, he never seems to tire.* ○ *The long walk tired us all out.* **2** [I] **tire of sth/of doing sth** (formal) to become bored or not interested in sth/doing sth: *I never tire of this view.* ☞ **Get tired of sth/of doing sth** is less formal and more common.

☆**tired** /'taɪərd/ adj. feeling that you need to rest or sleep: *She was tired after a hard day's work.* ○ *Older people get tired easily.*
IDM be sick and tired of sb/sth ⇨ SICK
be tired of sb/sth/doing sth to be impatient with or annoyed by sb/sth/doing sth: *I'm tired of this game. Let's play something else.* ○ *I'm tired of listening to the same thing over and over.*
tired out very tired —**tired·ness** noun [U]

tire·less /'taɪərləs/ adj. (formal) not getting tired: *a tireless campaigner for human rights*

tire·some /'taɪərsəm/ adj. (formal) that makes you bored or annoyed

tir·ing /'taɪərɪŋ/ adj. making you tired: *a long and tiring trip*

tis·sue /'tɪʃu/ noun **1** [C,U] the material that the bodies of animals and plants are made of: *brain tissue* ○ *Radiation can destroy the body's tissues.* **2** [C] = KLEENEX

tissue paper noun [U] thin, soft paper that you use for wrapping things that may break

☆**ti·tle** /'taɪtl/ noun **1** [C] the name of a book, play, movie, picture, etc. ☞ Look also at **subtitles**. **2** [C] a word that shows a person's rank or profession: *"Doctor," "Reverend," "Mrs." and "General" are all titles.* **3** [C] the position of champion in a sport: *Sue is playing this match to defend her title* (= to stay champion). **4** [C,U] **title (to sth)** a legal right to own sth, e.g. a car or a house, or an official piece of paper that says that sb owns sth

title role noun [C] the part in a play or movie that is used as the title of it

☆**to¹** /tə; before vowels tʊ; strong form tu/ prep. **1** in the direction of; as far as: *She's going to Cleveland.* ○ *This road goes to Denver.* ○ *Evanston is to the north of Chicago.* ○ *He went to school.* **2** (used before the person or thing that receives, sees, etc. sth): *Give that to me.* ○ *We should be kind to animals.* **3** (almost) touching sth: *He put his hands to his ears.* ○ *They sat back to back.* **4** (used to show that sth is part of sth else or fits together with sth else): *the key to the back door* ○ *Where's the lid to this pan?* ○ *the answer to my question* **5** (used about time) before: *It's two minutes to three.* **6** (used before the upper limit of a range): *a game suitable for children who are 8 to 12 years old* ○ *from beginning to end* ○ *They sell everything from matches to washing machines there.* **7** (used for expressing a reaction to sth): *To my surprise, I saw two strangers coming out of my house.* **8** (used when comparing things): *I prefer coffee to tea.* ○ *The final score was 13 to 10.* **9** (used for expressing quantity) for each unit of money, measurement, etc.: *There are 2.54 centimeters to the inch.*

☆**to²** /tə; before vowels tʊ; strong form tu/ (used with verbs to form the infinitive): *I want to go home now.* ○ *Don't forget to write.* ○ *She's learning English in order to get a better job.* ○ *Do you know which button to press?* ○ *I didn't know what to do.* ○ *He asked me to go, but I didn't want to.*

to³ /tu/ adv.
IDM to and fro backward and forward

toad /toʊd/ noun [C] a small cold-blooded animal that looks similar to a frog but that is bigger, has rough skin and lives mainly on land ☞ picture at **frog**.

toad·stool /'toʊdstul/ noun [C] a type of poisonous fungus that looks like a mushroom

☆**toast¹** /toʊst/ **1** noun [U] a thin piece of bread that is heated to make it brown: *a piece/slice of toast* ○ *buttered toast* **2** [C] an occasion at a party or a formal meal when you hold up your glass and wish sb success, happiness, etc. before you drink: *I'd like to propose a toast to the bride and groom.*
IDM be toast (slang) to be in very serious trouble: *If Dad finds out about this, we're toast!*

tʃ	dʒ	v	θ	ð	s	z	ʃ
chin	June	van	thin	then	so	zoo	she

toast² /toʊst/ *verb* [T] **1** to heat bread in order to make it brown **2** to hold up your glass and wish sb success, happiness, etc. before you drink at a party or a formal meal: *Everyone stood up and toasted the bride and groom.*

toast·er /ˈtoʊstər/ *noun* [C] an electrical machine that makes bread into toast

☆**to·bac·co** /təˈbækoʊ/ *noun* [U] the dried leaves of a plant that people smoke in cigarettes and pipes, or the plant that produces these leaves

to·bog·gan /təˈbɑgən/ *noun* [C] a type of flat board that curves up at the front and that you can sit on and ride down hills covered in snow for fun

☆**to·day** /təˈdeɪ/ *noun* [U, *adv.*] **1** (on) this day: *Today is Monday.* ○ *What should we do today?* ○ *School ends a week from today* (= on this day next week). ○ *Where is today's paper?* **2** (in) the present age: *Young people have more spending money today than in the past.* ○ *Today's computers are much smaller than the early models.*

tod·dler /ˈtɑdlər/ *noun* [C] a child who has just learned to walk

☆**toe** /toʊ/ *noun* [C] **1** one of the five small parts like fingers at the end of each foot **2** the part of a sock, shoe, etc. that covers your toes (1)

TOEFL /ˈtoʊfl/ *noun* [sing.] (*trademark*) Test of English as a Foreign Language; a test that measures your ability to read and understand English if it is not your first language. Most U.S. colleges and universities require foreign students to take the TOEFL before they can study there: *to take the TOEFL* ○ *What was your TOEFL score?*

toe·nail /ˈtoʊneɪl/ *noun* [C] one of the hard pieces that cover the end of your toes

to·fu /ˈtoʊfu/ *noun* [U] a white food made from a type of bean (**soybeans**), that is eaten in salads or in cooked foods, often instead of meat

☆**to·geth·er¹** /təˈgɛðər/ *adv.* **1** with each other; in or into the same place as or near to sb/sth else: *Can we have lunch together?* ○ *They walked home together.* ○ *I'll get all my stuff together tonight because I want to leave early.* ○ *Stand with your feet together.* **2** so that two or more things are mixed with, joined to or added to each other: *Mix the butter and sugar together.* ○ *Tie the two ends together.* ○ *Add these numbers together to find the total.* **3** at the same time: *We'll sing the next song together.*
IDM **get your act together** ⇨ ACT²
together with in addition to; as well as: *I enclose my order together with a check for $15.*

to·geth·er² /təˈgɛðər/ *adj.* (*informal*) (usually not before a noun) (used about a person) organized, capable

to·geth·er·ness /təˈgɛðərnəs/ *noun* [U] a feeling of friendship

toil /tɔɪl/ *verb* [I] (*formal*) to work very hard or for a long time at sth —**toil** *noun* [U] (*formal*)

☆**toi·let** /ˈtɔɪlət/ *noun* [C] a large bowl with a seat, attached to a drain, that you use when you need to get rid of waste material or water from your body: *to flush the toilet* ○ *Who left the toilet seat up?*

☞ We do not use **toilet** to talk about a room that has a toilet in it. A **bathroom** is any room that has a toilet, in a house or a public building.: *Scott got caught smoking in the boys' bathroom at school.* We can also use **restroom, ladies' room, women's room** or **men's room** to talk about a room with toilets in a public building: *Can you tell me where the restrooms are?* **Go to the bathroom** is a polite expression for what we do on the toilet.

☆**'toilet ,paper** *noun* [U] paper that you use to clean your body after using the toilet

toi·let·ries /ˈtɔɪlətriz/ *noun* [plural] things such as soap, toothpaste, etc. that you use when you are washing yourself, doing your hair, etc.

to·ken¹ /ˈtoʊkən/ *noun* [C] **1** something that represents or is a sign of sth else: *Please accept this gift as a token of our gratitude.* **2** a piece of metal, plastic, etc. that you use for a particular purpose, often instead of a coin: *a subway token*
IDM **by the same token** ⇨ SAME¹

to·ken² /ˈtoʊkən/ *adj.* (only *before* a noun) **1** done, chosen, etc. to give the impression that you are interested in sth when you do not mean it sincerely: *There is a token woman on the board.* ○ *They only made a token effort to fix the problem.* **2** small, but done or given as a sign that sth larger or more serious could follow: *a token payment*

told *p.t., p.p.* of TELL

tol·er·a·ble /ˈtɑlərəbl/ *adj.* of a level that you can tolerate: *Medication can reduce the pain to a tolerable level.*

tol·er·ance /ˈtɑlərəns/ *noun* [U] the ability or willingness to allow or accept sth that is bad or that you do not like or agree with: *religious tolerance* ☞ The opposite is **intolerance**. —**tol·er·ant** /-rənt/ *adj.* **tolerant (of/toward sb/sth)** ☞ The opposite is **intolerant**.

tol·er·ate /ˈtɑləreɪt/ *verb* [T] **1** to allow or accept sth that you do not like or agree with: *In a democracy, we have to be willing to tolerate opinions that are different from our own.* **2** to accept or stand sb/sth bad without complaining: *The noise was more than she could tolerate.*

toll /toʊl/ *noun* [C] **1** money that you pay to use a road, bridge, etc. **2** [usually sing.] the amount of damage done or the number of people who were killed or injured by sth: *At least 150 people died in the earthquake, though some reports say the toll was much higher.* ☞ Look also at **death toll**.

i	ɪ	ɛ	æ	ɑ	ɔ	ʌ	ʊ	u
see	sit	ten	cat	hot	saw	cup	put	too

IDM **take a heavy toll/take its toll (on sth)** to cause loss, damage, suffering, etc.

toll-'free adj. (used about a telephone number or call) that does not cost anything

☞ Toll-free telephone numbers in the U.S. and Canada have **800** or **888** as their area codes.

—**toll-free** adv.

☆**to·ma·to** /təˈmeɪṭoʊ/ noun [C] (pl. **to·ma·toes**) a soft red fruit that is often eaten raw in salads or cooked as a vegetable: *tomato juice* ☞ picture at **salad**.

tomb /tum/ noun [C] a place where a body is buried, often one with a large decorated stone above it

tom·boy /ˈtɑmbɔɪ/ noun [C] a young girl who likes to play rough games

tomb·stone /ˈtumstoʊn/ noun [C] a stone over a grave that shows the name of the person who is buried there

tom·cat /ˈtɑmkæt/ noun [C] a male cat

☆**to·mor·row** /təˈmɑroʊ; -ˈmɔr-/ noun [U, adv.] **1** (on) the day after today: *Today is Friday, so tomorrow is Saturday. ○ The ad will appear in tomorrow's paper. ○ See you tomorrow. ○ I'm going to bed. I have to get up early tomorrow morning. ○ Tomorrow night's concert has been canceled. ○ a week from tomorrow*

☞ Notice that we say "tomorrow morning," "tomorrow afternoon," etc. and NOT "tomorrow in the morning," etc. Look also at the note at **morning**.

2 the future: *The children of today are tomorrow's leaders.*
IDM **the day after tomorrow** ⇨ DAY

☆**ton** /tʌn/ noun **1** [C] a measure of weight; 2,000 pounds **2 a ton (of sth); tons (of sth)** (informal) a lot: *tons of homework ○ What's in this box? It weighs a ton!*

☆**tone¹** /toʊn/ noun **1** [C,U] the quality of a sound, especially of the human voice: *"Do you know each other?" she asked in a casual tone of voice. ○ His tone suddenly changed when Amy entered the room.* **2** [sing.] the general quality or style of sb/sth: *The tone of the meeting was optimistic.* **3** [C] one of the shades of a color: *warm tones of red and orange* **4** [C] a sound that you hear on the telephone: *the dial tone* **5** [U] how firm and strong your skin or muscles are: *exercises to improve your muscle tone*

tone² /toʊn/ verb
PHRV **tone sth down** to change sth that you have said, written, etc., to make it seem less strong

tone-deaf adj. not able to sing or hear the difference between notes in music

tongs /tɑnz; tɔnz/ noun [plural] a tool that looks like a pair of scissors but that you use to hold or pick things up

☆**tongue** /tʌn/ noun **1** [C] the soft part inside your mouth that you can move. You use your tongue for speaking, tasting things, etc. **2** [C] (formal) a language: *your mother tongue* (= the language you learned as a child)
IDM **on the tip of your tongue** ⇨ TIP¹
stick your tongue out to put your tongue outside your mouth, both for the doctor to examine or to be rude to sb

tongue-in-'cheek adj. (usually before a noun) done or said as a joke; not meant seriously

tongue ˌtwister noun [C] a phrase or sentence that is difficult to say correctly when you are speaking quickly

ton·ic /ˈtɑnɪk/ noun [C,U] something that makes you feel stronger, healthier, happier, etc.: *a vitamin tonic*

tonic ˌwater (also **tonic**) noun [U] a type of water with bubbles in it and a bitter taste, that is often added to alcoholic drinks: *a gin and tonic*

☆**to·night** /təˈnaɪt/ noun [U, adv.] (in) the evening or night of today: *Tonight is the last night of our vacation. ○ tonight's weather forecast ○ What's on TV tonight? ○ We are staying with friends tonight and traveling home tomorrow.*

ton·sil /ˈtɑnsl/ noun [C] one of the two soft lumps in your throat on each side of the back of your tongue

ton·sil·li·tis /ˌtɑnsəˈlaɪṭəs/ noun [U] an illness in which the tonsils become very sore

too/enough

Tom's sweater is **not big enough**. Kevin's sweater is **too big**.

☆**too** /tu/ adv. **1** in addition; also: *Red is my favorite color, but I like blue too. ○ Phil thinks you're right and I do too.*

☞ Notice that you say "There were lions and tigers at the zoo. There were elephants, **too**," but "There were no zebras and there were no giraffes, **either**." Look at the note at **also**.

2 (used for expressing surprise or disappointment): *Her purse was stolen. And on her birthday, too.* **3** (used before adjectives and adverbs) more than is good, allowed, possible, etc.: *These boots are too small. ○ It's too cold to go out without a coat. ○ It's too long a trip for you to go alone.*

☞ Notice that you cannot say "It's a too long trip."

4 (used in negative sentences) very: *Darla didn't do too well on her test – she only got a C.* **IDM too bad** (*informal*) **1** (used to express sympathy or to say that you are sorry about sth): *"My dog died yesterday." "Gee, that's too bad."* **2** (used to express a lack of sympathy): *"I don't like liver." "Well, too bad – that's all there is for supper."*

took *p.t.* of TAKE

hammer

tools

nail

wrench

mallet

chisel

screwdriver

pliers

drill

screw

saw

☆ **tool** /tul/ *noun* [C] a piece of equipment that you use to help you do a particular type of job: *garden tools* ○ *A cellular phone is an indispensable tool for a journalist.*

☞ A tool is usually something you can hold in your hand, e.g. a wrench or hammer. An **implement** is often used outside, e.g. for farming or gardening. A **machine** has moving parts and works with electricity, with an engine, etc. An **instrument** is often used for technical or delicate work: *a dentist's instruments* ○ *precision instruments.* A **device** is a more general word for a piece of equipment that you consider to be useful: *The machine has a safety device which switches the power off if there is a problem.*

tool·bar /'tulbɑr/ *noun* [C] (*computing*) a row of symbols at the top of a computer screen that represent certain functions which the computer can perform ☞ picture on page A29.

toot /tut/ *noun* [C] the short sound that a whistle, horn, etc. makes —**toot** *verb* [I,T]

☆ **tooth** /tuθ/ *noun* [C] (*pl.* **teeth** /tiθ/) **1** one of the hard white parts in your mouth that you use for biting and chewing: *to have a tooth pulled* ○ *The old man took out his false teeth.* ○ *wisdom teeth*

☞ You **brush** your teeth to remove pieces of food. If a tooth is **decayed** or has a **cavity** in it, the dentist may **fill** it or **extract** it/**pull out.** If your teeth are **crooked,** you can have **braces** put on them to make them **straight.** If you have had all your teeth out, you can have **false teeth** or **dentures.**

2 one of the long pointed parts of a comb, saw, etc.
IDM by the skin of your teeth ➪ SKIN[1]
grit your teeth ➪ GRIT[2]
have a sweet tooth ➪ SWEET[1]

tooth·ache /'tuθeɪk/ *noun* [C] a pain in your tooth or teeth ☞ Look at the note at **ache.**

☆ **tooth·brush** /'tuθeɪk/ *noun* [C] a small brush with a handle that you use for brushing your teeth ☞ picture at **brush.**

☆ **tooth·paste** /'tuθpeɪst/ *noun* [U] a substance that you put on your toothbrush and use for cleaning your teeth

tooth·pick /'tuθpɪk/ *noun* [C] a short pointed piece of wood that you use for getting pieces of food out from between your teeth

☆ **top¹** /tɑp/ *noun* **1** [C] the highest part of sth: *The apartment is at the top of the building.* ○ *the top of the stairs* ○ *Start reading at the top of the page.* **2** [C] the upper surface of sth: *a desktop* **3** [sing.] **the top (of sth)** the highest or most important rank or position: *to be at the top of your profession* **4** [C] the cover that you put onto sth in order to close it: *Put the tops back on the felt-tip pens or they will dry out.*

☞ A **top** or a **cap** is often small and round. You take it off by turning or screwing: *a bottle top* ○ *Unscrew cap to open.* A **lid** may be larger. You can lift it off: *a garbage can lid* ○ *Put the lid back on the box.*

5 [C] a piece of clothing, especially for women or girls, that you wear on the top part of your body: *I need a top to match my new skirt.* **6** [C] a child's toy that spins around quickly, balancing on a point
IDM at the top of your voice as loudly as possible

off the top of your head (*informal*) without preparing or thinking about sth before you speak

on top 1 on or onto the highest point: *There's a pile of books on the desk. Just put this one on top.* **2** stronger or better: *Throughout the game, the Bulls were on top.*

on top of sb/sth 1 on or onto sb/sth else: *Several demonstrators stood on top of the tank, waving flags and shouting.* **2** in addition to sb/sth else: *On top of all our other problems, the car broke down.*

☆ **top²** /tɑp/ *adj.* (only *before* a noun) highest in position, rank or degree: *one of the country's top business executives* ○ *at top speed* ○ *the top floor of the building*

top³ /tɑp/ *verb* [T] (**top·ping**; **topped**) **1** to be or form a top for sth: *cauliflower topped with cheese sauce* **2** to be higher or greater than sth: *Inflation has topped the 10% mark.*

IDM **to top it (all) off** as a final piece of bad luck: *What a rotten vacation! The flight was delayed, the airline lost our baggage and to top it all off, Rob broke his leg skiing.*

'**top hat** *noun* [C] a tall black or gray hat that a man wears on formal occasions

'**top-,heavy** *adj.* heavier at the top than the bottom and likely to fall over

☆ **top·ic** /'tɑpɪk/ *noun* [C] a subject that you talk, write or learn about

top·i·cal /'tɑpɪkl/ *adj.* connected with sth that is happening now; that people are interested in now

,**topic 'sentence** *noun* [C] a sentence, usually at the beginning of a paragraph, that gives the main idea of that paragraph

top·less /'tɑpləs/ *adj., adv.* with the breasts not covered: *a topless dancer* ○ *to sunbathe topless*

top·ping /'tɑpɪŋ/ *noun* [C,U] something that is put on the top of food to decorate it or make it taste better: *What toppings do you want on the pizza?*

top·ple /'tɑpl/ *verb* **1** [I,T] **topple (sth) (over)** to become unsteady and fall down, or to cause sth to do this: *High winds toppled several trees in the area.* **2** [T] to cause a government or leader of a country to lose power: *The country's leader was toppled by a military coup.*

,**top-'secret** *adj.* that must be kept very secret

torch¹ /tɔrtʃ/ *noun* [C] **1** a long piece of wood with burning material at the end that you carry to give light **2** (*BrE*) = FLASHLIGHT

torch² /tɔrtʃ/ *verb* [T] (*informal*) to burn sth, especially a building, on purpose in order to destroy it

tore *p.t.* of TEAR²

tor·ment¹ /tɔr'mɛnt/ *verb* [T] to cause sb great pain or unhappiness: *She was tormented by nightmares.*

tor·ment² /'tɔrmɛnt/ *noun* [C, usually pl., U] great pain in your mind or body; sth that causes this pain: *to be in torment*

torn *p.p.* of TEAR²

tor·na·do /tɔr'neɪdoʊ/ *noun* [C] (*pl.* **tor·na·does**)(also *informal* **twister**) a violent storm with a very strong wind that blows in a circle ☞ Look at the note at **storm**.

tor·pe·do /tɔr'pidoʊ/ *noun* [C] (*pl.* **tor·pe·does**) a bomb, shaped like a tube, that is fired under water from one ship toward another

tor·rent /'tɔrənt; 'tɑr-/ *noun* [C] a strong fast stream of sth, especially water: *The heavy rain turned the creek into a savage torrent.* ○ (*figurative*) *She poured out a torrent of abuse at him.*

tor·ren·tial /tə'rɛnʃl/ *adj.* (used about rain) very heavy

tor·so /'tɔrsoʊ/ *noun* [C] (*pl.* **tor·sos**) the main part of the body, not the head, arms and legs

tor·til·la /tɔr'tiyə/ *noun* [C] a type of very thin, round Mexican bread made of ground corn or wheat flour

tor·toise /'tɔrtəs/ *noun* [C] = TURTLE ☞ Look at the note at **turtle**.

tor·tu·ous /'tɔrtʃuəs/ *adj.* **1** (used about a road, etc.) with many bends: *a tortuous route through the mountains* **2** complicated, not clear and simple: *a tortuous explanation*

tor·ture /'tɔrtʃər/ *noun* [C,U] the act of causing very great pain to a person, as a punishment or to make him/her give some information: *The rebel army has been accused of rape, torture and murder.* **tor·ture** *verb* [T]: *Most of the prisoners were tortured into making a confession.* ○ (*figurative*): *She was tortured by the thought that the accident was her fault.* —**tor·tur·er** /'tɔrtʃərər/ *noun* [C]

toss /tɔs/ *verb* **1** [T] to throw sth lightly, not using all your strength: *We tossed a ball around for an hour after school.* **2** [T] **toss sth (out)** to get rid of sth that you do not need anymore, especially by putting it into the garbage: *You can just toss those magazines – I'm finished with them.* **3** [T] to mix food, e.g. salad, together in a bowl **4** [I,T] to keep moving up and down or from side to side; to make sb/sth do this: *He lay tossing and turning in bed, unable to sleep.* ○ *The rough seas tossed the ship for hours.* —**toss** *noun* [C]

toss·up /'tɔsʌp/ *noun*

IDM **sth is a tossup** (*informal*) (used to say that two things have an equal chance of happening, or that you cannot choose between two things or people): *It's a tossup whether mortgage rates will increase next year.*

tot /tɑt/ *noun* [C] a small child

☆ **to·tal**¹ /'toʊtl/ *adj.* (usually *before* a noun) **1** counting everything; complete: *What was the total number of people killed?* ○ *a total failure* ○ *They ate in total silence.* **2** (*slang*) (used to emphasize how good or bad sb/sth is): *Brad is such a total jerk!*

☆ **to·tal**² /'toʊtl/ *noun* [C] the number that you get when you add two or more numbers or amounts together

IDM **In total** when you add two or more numbers or amounts together: *The campaign raised $4 million in total.*

to·tal³ /'toʊtl/ *verb* [T] **1** to add up to a certain amount or number; to make a total of: *His debts totaled more than $10,000.* **2** (*informal*) to destroy a car completely so that it cannot be repaired

☆ **to·tal·ly** /'toʊtl·i/ *adv.* **1** completely: *Their lives were totally changed.* ○ *The situation is totally different now.* **2** (*slang*) (used to agree with sth that sb has just said): *"This class is so boring." "Yeah, totally!"*

tot·ter /'tɑtər/ *verb* [I] to stand or move in an

tʃ	dʒ	v	θ	ð	s	z	ʃ
chin	**June**	**van**	**thin**	**then**	**so**	**zoo**	**she**

touch

unsteady way as if you are going to fall
☞ Look also at **teeter-totter**.

☆**touch¹** /tʌtʃ/ *verb* **1** [I,T] (used about two or
more things, surfaces, etc.) to be or go so close
together that there is no space between them:
*They were sitting so close that their heads
touched.* ○ *This bicycle is too big. My feet don't
touch the ground.* **2** [T] to put a part of your
body, usually your hand or fingers, onto
sb/sth: *He touched her gently on the cheek.* ○
The police asked us not to touch anything. ○
(figurative) June never touches alcohol (= she
never drinks it). **3** [T] to make sb feel sadness,
sympathy, thanks, etc.: *a sad story that
touched our hearts* ☞ Look at **touched**. **4** [T]
(usually in negative sentences) to deal with a
problem or become involved in a situation:
*There were rumors of illegal activities at the
bank, but no newspaper would touch the story.*
5 [T] (in negative sentences) to be as good as
sb/sth: *He's a much better player than all the
others. No one else can touch him.*

IDM **touch base (with sb)** (*informal*) to con-
tact sb and speak with him/her for a short
time in order to exchange information

PHRV **touch down** (used about an airplane) to
land

touch on/upon sth to talk or write about sth
for only a short time

touch sth up to improve sth by making small
changes or repairs: *Use a small paintbrush to
touch up any scratches.*

☆**touch²** /tʌtʃ/ *noun* **1** [C, usually sing.] an act
of touching ¹(2) sb/sth: *I felt the touch of her
hand on my arm.* **2** [U] one of the five senses:
the ability to feel: *The sense of touch is very
important to blind people.* **3** [U] the way sth
feels when you touch it: *Marble is cold to the
touch.* **4** [C] a small detail: *The flowers on our
table were a nice touch.* **5** [sing.] **a touch (of
sth)** a small amount of sth: *He's not very sick.
It's just a touch of the flu.*

IDM **in touch/out of touch (with sb)** being/
not being in contact with sb by speaking or
writing to him/her: *During the year she was in
prison, they kept in touch by mail.*

in touch/out of touch with sth having/not
having recent information about sth: *We're
out of touch with what's going on in the rest of
the world.*

lose touch ⇨ **LOSE**

lose your touch ⇨ **LOSE**

touch·down /'tʌtʃdaʊn/ *noun* [C] (in football)
an act of carrying the ball into the area at the
end of the field (**end zone**) or of catching the
ball there. A touchdown is worth six points: *to
score a touchdown* ☞ Look at the note at **foot-
ball**.

touched /tʌtʃt/ *adj.* (not before a noun) made
to feel sadness, sympathy, thanks, etc.: *We
were touched by your thoughtful gift.*

touch·ing /'tʌtʃɪŋ/ *adj.* that makes you feel

sadness, sympathy, thanks, etc.: *The play is a
touching story of young love.*

touch·y /'tʌtʃi/ *adj.* **1** easily upset or made
angry: *Don't ask about her first marriage.
She's very touchy about it.* **2** (used about a
subject, situation, etc.) that may easily upset
people or make them angry

☆**tough** /tʌf/ *adj.* **1** not easily broken or cut;
very strong: *tough boots* ○ *tough plastic* **2** not
easily weakened by pain or difficulty; very
strong: *You need to be tough to go camping in
the winter.* **3** difficult to cut and eat: *This meat
is tough.* **4** strict; firm: *The government is
introducing tough new laws against drinking
and driving.* **5** difficult: *It will be a tough deci-
sion to make.* ○ *He's been having a very tough
time recently.*

IDM **tough (luck)!** (*informal*) (used to express
a lack of sympathy): *"I left my wallet at home."
"Well, tough – I'm not going to loan you any
money."* —**tough·ness** *noun* [U]

tough·en /'tʌfn/ *verb* [I,T] **toughen (sb/sth)
(up)** to become tough; to make sb/sth tough

tou·pee /tuˈpeɪ/ (*also* **hairpiece**, *slang* **rug**)
noun [C] a piece of artificial hair that some
men wear because they do not want people to
see that they have lost some of their own hair

☆**tour¹** /tʊr/ *noun* **1** [C] a short visit around a
city, building, etc., usually in a group with sb
who explains the things in it: *to take a guided
tour through the White House* ○ *Sandy gave us
a tour of their new house.* ☞ Look at the note
at **travel**. **2** [C] a trip that you make for pleas-
ure during which you visit many places: *to go
on a tour of the Caribbean islands* **3** [C,U] a
series of visits to different places to play
sports, give concerts, etc.: *Jon Bon Jovi is on
tour this summer.*

tour² /tʊr/ *verb* [I,T] to go on a tour¹ of a place:
*We toured a candy factory and learned how
chocolate is made.*

☆**tour·ism** /'tʊrɪzəm/ *noun* [U] the business of
providing and arranging vacations and ser-
vices for people who are visiting a place: *the
state's tourism industry*

☆**tour·ist** /'tʊrɪst/ *noun* [C] a person who visits
a place for pleasure: *a foreign tourist*

☆**tour·na·ment** /'tɜrnəmənt; 'tʊr-/ *noun* [C] a
competition in which many players or teams
play games against each other

tow¹ /toʊ/ *verb* [T] to pull a car, etc. along by a
rope or chain: *Unauthorized vehicles will be
towed away* (on a sign).

tow² /toʊ/ *noun*

IDM **in tow** (*informal*) following behind: *He
arrived with his wife and five children in tow.*

☆**to·ward** /tɔrd; təˈwɔrd/ (*also* **towards** /tɔrdz;
təˈwɔrdz/) *prep.* **1** in the direction of sb/sth: *I
saw Ken walking toward the bus stop.* ○ *She
had her back toward me.* ○ *a first step toward
world peace* **2** (used when you are talking
about your feelings about sb/sth) in relation

T

i	ɪ	ɛ	æ	ɑ	ɔ	ʌ	ʊ	u
see	sit	ten	cat	hot	saw	cup	put	too

to: *Pat felt very protective toward her younger brother.* ○ *What is your attitude toward private education?* **3** as part of the payment for sth: *The money will go toward the cost of a new school bus.* **4** near a time, date or place: *It gets cool toward evening.* ○ *The accident happened out toward the Hansons' farm.*

☆ **tow·el** /ˈtaʊəl/ *noun* [C] a piece of cloth or paper that you use for drying sb/sth/yourself: *a bath towel* ○ *paper towels*

☆ **tow·er** /ˈtaʊər/ *noun* [C] a tall narrow building or part of a building: *the Eiffel Tower* ○ *an observation tower*

☆ **town** /taʊn/ *noun* **1** [C] a place with many streets and buildings. A town is smaller than a city: *She grew up in a small town in Idaho.* ○ *I have to go into town this afternoon.* ☞ Look also at **hometown**. **2** [sing.] all the people who live in a town (1): *The whole town was on the streets, waving flags and shouting.*

IDM **go to town (on sth)** (*informal*) to do sth, especially eating, with a lot of energy and enthusiasm: *Boy, the kids sure went to town on those cookies* (= ate them eagerly)*!*

in town in the same town or city as the person who is speaking or writing: *The governor was in town yesterday to view the flood damage.*

a night on the town ⇨ NIGHT

out of town not in the same town or city as the person who is speaking or writing: *Mrs. Perez is out of town on business.* ○ *Wendy's new boyfriend is from out of town.*

ˌtown ˈhall *noun* [C] a building that contains the offices of a town's local government

town·ship /ˈtaʊnʃɪp/ *noun* [C] a part of a county in some states that has its own local government

tox·ic /ˈtɑksɪk/ *adj.* poisonous: *Toxic chemicals had leaked into the water.*

☆ **toy¹** /tɔɪ/ *noun* [C] an object for a child to play with: *Here are some toys to keep the kids occupied.* ○ *toy cars* ○ *a toy soldier* ○ *a toy store*

toy² /tɔɪ/ *verb*

PHRV **toy with sth 1** to think about doing sth, perhaps not very seriously: *She's toying with the idea of taking a year off from college.* **2** to move sth around without thinking about what you are doing: *He toyed with his food but hardly ate any of it.*

☆ **trace¹** /treɪs/ *noun* **1** [C,U] a mark or sign that shows that sb/sth existed or happened: *traces of a prehistoric village* ○ *The man disappeared without trace.* **2** [C] a very small amount of sth: *Traces of blood were found under her fingernails.*

☆ **trace²** /treɪs/ *verb* [T] **1** to find out where sb/sth is by following marks, signs or other information: *The wanted man was traced to an address in Tacoma.* **2** to find out or describe the development of sth: *She traced her family tree back to the 19th century.* **3** to make a copy

of sth by placing a piece of transparent paper over it and drawing over the lines

☆ **track¹** /træk/ *noun* **1** [C, usually pl.] a line or series of marks that are left behind by a car, person, animal, etc.: *The hunter followed the tracks of a deer.* ○ *tire tracks* ☞ Look at **footprint**. **2** [C, usually pl.] the two metal rails on which a train runs: *It's dangerous to play on the railroad tracks.* **3** [C] a special path, often in a round shape, where people, animals or cars race **4** [U] = TRACK AND FIELD: *the track team* **5** [C] one song or piece of music on a cassette, CD or record **6** [C] a group of school students who are in the same class because they have similar abilities

IDM **keep/lose track of sb/sth** to know/not know what is happening somewhere or to sb/sth: *I can't keep track of all my kids' activities and practice sessions.*

off the beaten path/track ⇨ BEAT¹

on the right/wrong track having the right/wrong kind of ideas about sth: *That's not the answer, but you're on the right track.*

on/off track happening or developing in a way that will lead to success/failure: *She tried to get the discussion back on track.*

track² /træk/ *verb* [T] **1 track sb/sth (to sth)** to follow tracks or signs in order to find sb/sth: *to track enemy planes on a radar screen* **2** to carry dirt, etc. on your shoes and leave it on the ground when you walk: *Don't track mud on the carpet!*

PHRV **track sb/sth down** to find sb/sth after searching for him/her/it

ˌtrack and ˈfield (*also* **track**) *noun* [U] sports events such as running, jumping and throwing

ˈtrack meet *noun* [C] a sports competition that includes running, jumping and throwing events

ˈtrack ˌrecord *noun* [C] what a person or organization has achieved that other people know about

tractor

☆ **trac·tor** /ˈtræktər/ *noun* [C] a large vehicle that is used on farms for pulling heavy pieces of machinery, especially in fields

ˌtractor-ˈtrailer *noun* [C] a very large truck that consists of two connected parts, which can carry a large quantity of things over a long distance ☞ picture at **truck**.

☆ **trade¹** /treɪd/ *noun* **1** [U] the buying or selling of goods or services; business: *an international trade agreement* ○ *the nation's trade deficit* ○ *Many resort towns depend on the tourist trade.*

2 [C] an act of exchanging sth for sth else: *to make a trade* **3** [C,U] a job for which you need special skill, especially with your hands: *to learn a trade* ☞ Look at the note at **work**.

☆**trade²** /treɪd/ *verb* **1** [I] **trade (in sth) (with sb)** to buy or sell goods or services: *More and more countries are trading with China.* ○ *to trade in arms* **2** [T] **trade (sb) sth (for sth)** to exchange sth for sth else: *I'll trade you my sandwich for yours.*

IDM **change/trade places (with sb)** ⇨ PLACE¹
PHRV **trade sth in (for sth)** to give sth old in part payment for sth new or newer: *Jeff traded in his station wagon for a flashy sports car.*

☆**trade·mark** /'treɪdmɑrk/ *noun* [C] (*abbr.* **TM**) a special mark or name that a company can put on its products and that cannot be used by any other company

trad·er /'treɪdər/ *noun* [C] a person who buys and sells things: *Wall Street bond traders*

☆**tra·di·tion** /trə'dɪʃn/ *noun* [C,U] a custom or belief that has continued from the past to the present: *It's a tradition to play tricks on people on April 1st.* ○ *New Orleans has a great musical tradition.* ○ *By tradition, the bride's family pays the costs of the wedding.*

☆**tra·di·tion·al** /trə'dɪʃn·l/ *adj.* **1** connected with customs or beliefs that have continued from the past to the present: *It is traditional to eat turkey on Thanksgiving.* ○ *traditional holiday decorations* **2** following or using ideas or ways of doing things that have existed for a long time; old-fashioned: *women's traditional roles as housewives and mothers* —**tra·di·tion·al·ly** *adv.*

☆**traf·fic¹** /'træfɪk/ *noun* [U] **1** the cars, etc. that are on a road: *heavy/light traffic* ○ *The traffic is at a standstill.* **2** the movement of ships, airplanes, etc.: *air traffic controllers* **3** **traffic (in sth)** the illegal buying and selling of sth: *the traffic in arms*

traf·fic² /'træfɪk/ *verb* [I] (*pres. part.* **traf·fick·ing**; *p.t., p.p.* **traf·ficked**) **traffic (in sth)** to buy and sell sth illegally: *drug trafficking*

☆**'traffic jam** *noun* [C] a long line of cars, etc. that cannot move or that can only move very slowly

☆**'traffic light** (*also* **stoplight**; **traffic signal**) *noun* [C] a sign with three colored lights (red, yellow and green) that is used for controlling the traffic where two or more streets meet

☆**trag·e·dy** /'trædʒədi/ *noun* (*pl.* **trag·e·dies**) **1** [C,U] an event or situation that causes great sadness: *A class trip to the coast ended in tragedy when the school bus was involved in a serious accident.* ○ *It's a tragedy that there are so many homeless people on the streets.* **2** [C] a serious play that has a sad ending ☞ Look at **comedy**.

trag·ic /'trædʒɪk/ *adj.* **1** that causes great sadness: *It's tragic that he died so young.* ○ *a tragic accident* **2** (only *before* a noun) with a sad

ending or in the style of tragedy (2): *a tragic novel* —**trag·i·cal·ly** /-kli/ *adv.*

☆**trail¹** /treɪl/ *noun* [C] **1** a series of marks in a long line that a person or thing leaves behind: *a trail of muddy footprints* ○ *The storm left behind a trail of destruction.* **2** a path through the countryside: *a nature trail in the woods* **3** the tracks or smell that you follow when you are hunting sb/sth: (*figurative*) *The thieves took off in a stolen car with the police on their trail.*

trail² /treɪl/ *verb* **1** [I,T] to be pulled or dragged along behind you; to make sth do this: *The bride's long dress trailed behind her as she walked down the aisle.* **2** [I] **trail behind (sb/sth)** to move or walk slowly behind sb/sth else, usually because you are tired **3** [I,T] **trail (behind) (sb)** to have a lower score than the other player or team during a game or competition: *At halftime, Cleveland was trailing seven to ten.*

☆**trail·er** /'treɪlər/ *noun* [C] **1** a vehicle with no engine that is pulled by a car, truck, etc. **2** a large vehicle in which you can sleep, cook, etc. when traveling on vacation. It can be pulled by a car or small truck. ☞ Look at **camper** (2). **3** = MOBILE HOME

'trailer park *noun* [C] an area of land where there are many houses that are built in factories (**mobile homes**)

☆**train¹** /treɪn/ *noun* [C] **1** a number of wagons that are pulled by an engine along railroad tracks: *a commuter/passenger/freight train* ○ *to catch/take a train* ○ *to get on/off a train* ○ *Hurry up or we'll miss the train.* ○ *The train pulled into/out of the station.* ☞ Note that we travel **by** train. We can also say **on the** train. **2** [usually sing.] a series of thoughts or events that are connected: *A knock at the door interrupted my train of thought.*

☆**train²** /treɪn/ *verb* **1** [T] **train sb/sth (as sth/to do sth)** to teach a person or an animal to do sth which is difficult or which needs practice: *The organization trains guide dogs for the blind.* ○ *There is a shortage of trained teachers.* **2** **train (as sth/to do sth)** [I] to learn how to do a job: *She's training as a chef.* **3** [I,T] to prepare for a race or an event by exercising; to help a person or an animal to do this: *I'm training for the Boston Marathon.* ○ *to train racehorses*

train·ee /treɪ'ni/ *noun* [C] a person who is being trained²(1,2) : *management trainees*

train·er /'treɪnər/ *noun* [C] a person who trains²(1, 3) animals or members of sports teams

☆**train·ing** /'treɪnɪŋ/ *noun* [U] preparation for a sport or job, or learning new skills: *computer training* ○ *to be in training for the Olympics*

trait /treɪt/ *noun* [C] a quality; part of sb's character

trai·tor /'treɪtər/ *noun* [C] a person who is not

ər	ɪr	ɛr	ɑr	ɔr	ʊr	ʒ	h	ŋ
bird	near	hair	car	north	tour	vision	hat	sing

loyal to his/her country, friends, etc. and harms them ☞ Look at **betray** and at **treason**.

tramp /træmp/ *noun* [C] (*old-fashioned*) a person who has no home or job and who moves from place to place

tram·ple /'træmpl/ *verb* [I,T] **trample (on) sb/sth** to walk on sb/sth and damage or hurt him/her/it: *The cows trampled the corn.* ○ *The child was trampled to death by the crowd.*

tram·po·line /,træmpə'lin/ *noun* [C] a piece of equipment that you can jump up and down on, made of a piece of strong material attached to a metal frame with springs

trance /træns/ *noun* [C] a condition of the mind in which you do not notice what is going on around you or in which you move and speak as if you were being controlled by another person or force: *to be in a trance*

tran·quil /'træŋkwəl/ *adj.* (*formal*) calm and quiet

tran·qui·li·zer /'træŋkwəlaɪzər/ *noun* [C] a drug that is used to make people sleepy or more calm

trans·ac·tion /træn'zækʃn/ *noun* [C] a piece of business: *financial transactions*

trans·at·lan·tic /,trænzət'læntɪk/ *adj.* to or from the other side of the Atlantic Ocean; across the Atlantic Ocean: *a transatlantic flight*

tran·scend /træn'sɛnd/ *verb* [T] (*formal*) to be greater or more important than sb/sth; to go beyond the limits of sth: *Environmental issues transcend national boundaries.*

trans·con·ti·nen·tal /,trænzkɑntn·'ɛntl; ,træns-/ *adj.* going across a continent

tran·script /'trænskrɪpt/ *noun* [C] **1** a written copy of what sb said **2** an official list of all the classes that sb took in high school or college and the grades that he/she received

☆**trans·fer¹** /'trænsfər; træns'fər/ *verb* (**trans-fer·ring; trans·ferred**) **1** [I,T] **transfer (sb/sth) (from...) (to...)** to move, or to make sb/sth move, from one place to another: *He has been transferred to our Tokyo branch.* ○ *I want to transfer $1,000 from my savings to my checking account.* ○ *Transfer the data onto a floppy disk.* ○ *I transferred to this school after my freshman year.* **2** [T] (*formal*) to change the ownership of sth from one person to another —**trans·fer·a·ble** /-fərəbl/ *adj.*: *This ticket is not transferable.*

☆**trans·fer²** /'trænsfər/ *noun* **1** [C,U] moving or being moved from one place, job, school or condition to another: *Paul is not happy here and has asked for a transfer.* ○ *the transfer of power from a military to a civilian government* ○ *a transfer student* **2** [C] a ticket that allows you to travel on two or more buses, etc. during one trip

☆**trans·form** /træns'fɔrm/ *verb* [T] **transform sb/sth (from sth) (into sth)** to change sb/sth

completely: *The arrival of electricity transformed people's lives.* —**trans·for·ma·tion** /,trænsfər'meɪʃn/ *noun* [C,U]

trans·fu·sion /træns'fyuʒn/ *noun* [C] the act of putting one person's blood into another person's body: *a blood transfusion*

tran·sis·tor /træn'zɪstər/ *noun* [C] a small piece of electrical equipment that is used in radios and televisions

tran·sit /'trænzət; -sət/ *noun* [U] the act of moving or being taken from one place to another: *The cartons had been damaged in transit.* ☞ Look also at **rapid transit**.

☆**tran·si·tion** /træn'zɪʃn/ *noun* [C,U] **transition (from sth) (to sth)** a change from one condition or form to another: *the transition from childhood to adolescence* —**tran·si·tion·al** /-ʃn·l/ *adj.*: *We're still in a transitional stage.*

tran·si·tive /'trænsətɪv; -zə-/ *adj.* (*grammar*) (used about a verb) that has a direct object: *In this dictionary, transitive verbs are marked "[T]."* ☞ The opposite is **intransitive**.

☆**trans·late** /'trænsleɪt; 'trænz-; træns'leɪt; trænz-/ *verb* [I,T] **translate (sth) (from sth) (into sth)** to change sth from one language to another: *This book has been translated from Czech into English.* ☞ Look at **interpret**. —**trans·la·tion** /-'leɪʃn/ *noun* [C,U]: *a word-for-word translation* ○ *to read foreign literature in translation*

trans·la·tor /'trænsleɪtər; 'trænz-/ *noun* [C] a person who translates sth that has been written ☞ Look at **interpreter**.

trans·mis·sion /træns'mɪʃn; trænz-/ *noun* **1** [U] sending sth out or passing sth on: *the transmission of television pictures by satellite* ○ *the transmission of disease* **2** [C,U] the set of parts of a car, etc. that take power from the engine to the wheels: *automatic transmission* ○ *5-speed manual transmission* **3** [C] (*formal*) a TV or radio program

☆**trans·mit** /træns'mɪt; trænz-/ *verb* [T] (**trans-mit·ting; trans·mit·ted**) **1** to send out television or radio programs, electronic signals, etc.: *The concert was transmitted live all over the world.* **2** to send or pass sth from one person or place to another: *a sexually transmitted disease*

trans·mit·ter /træns'mɪtər; trænz-/ *noun* [C] a piece of equipment that sends out television or radio programs, electronic signals, etc.

trans·par·en·cy /træns'pærənsi/ *noun* [C] (*pl.* **trans·par·en·cies**) a type of photograph that is printed on transparent plastic, or a piece of plastic on which you can write or draw. You look at a transparency by putting it in a special machine (**projector**) and shining light through it: *a transparency for the overhead projector* ☞ Look at **slide**.

☆**trans·par·ent** /træns'pærənt/ *adj.* that you can see through: *Glass is transparent.*

trans·plant¹ /træns'plænt; 'trænsplænt/ *verb*

T

[T] 1 to take a plant out of the soil and plant it in another place **2** to take out an organ or other part of sb's body and put it into another person's body

trans·plant² /ˈtrænsplænt/ *noun* [C] an operation in which an organ, etc. is transplanted: *a heart transplant*

☆**trans·port** /trænˈsport; ˈtrænsport/ *verb* [T] to move sb/sth from one place to another in a vehicle

☆**trans·por·ta·tion** /ˌtrænspərˈteɪʃn/ *noun* [U] **1** (*also* **transport**) moving sb/sth from one place to another by vehicle **2** vehicles that you travel in: *The city is providing free transportation to the stadium from downtown.* ☞ Look also at **public transportation**.

trans·ves·tite /trænsˈvɛstaɪt; trænz-/ *noun* [C] a person who likes to wear the clothes of sb of the opposite sex

☆**trap¹** /træp/ *noun* [C] **1** a piece of equipment that you use for catching animals: *a mouse-trap* ○ *The rabbit's leg was caught in the trap.* **2** [usually sing.] an unpleasant situation that is difficult to escape from: *the trap of credit card debt* **3** something that tricks or deceives you: *He thought he was going to meet a dealer, but it was a trap – the police were waiting for him.*

☆**trap²** /træp/ *verb* [T] (**trap·ping; trapped**) **1** to catch an animal, etc. in a trap **2** to keep sb in a place from which he/she cannot move or escape: *They were trapped in the room by the flames in the hallway.* **3** to catch and keep or store sth: *Special glass panels trap heat from the sun.* **4 trap sb (into sth/into doing sth)** to make sb do sth by tricking or deceiving him/her

IDM be trapped (in sth) to be unable to escape from an unpleasant situation: *Many people are trapped in low-paying jobs.*

ˌtrap ˈdoor *noun* [C] a door in a floor or ceiling

tra·peze /træˈpiz/ *noun* [C] a bar hanging from two ropes high above the ground, used as a swing especially by people who perform in a circus

trap·pings /ˈtræpɪŋz/ *noun* [plural] **the trappings (of sth)** clothes, possessions, etc. which are signs of a particular rank or position: *a big car, expensive clothes and all the other trappings of success*

☆**trash¹** /træʃ/ *noun* [U] **1** = GARBAGE(1,2,3) **2** (*slang*) people that you do not respect because they are poor, not well educated, and often do not behave morally ☞ Look also at **white trash**.

trash² /træʃ/ *verb* [T] (*informal*) **1** to damage or destroy sth, especially because you are angry: *Somebody broke into our house, stole our TV and trashed the living room.* **2** to criticize sb/sth very strongly: *My history professor trashed my paper and gave me a "D."*

ˈtrash can *noun* [C] = GARBAGE CAN

trash·y /ˈtræʃi/ *adj.* of poor quality, and often having low moral values: *trashy novels*

trau·ma /ˈtrɔmə; ˈtraʊmə/ *noun* [C,U] (an event that causes) a state of great unhappiness or shock ☞ Look at **stress¹**(1). —**trau·mat·ic** /trəˈmætɪk; trɔ-/ *adj.*: *Getting divorced can be a traumatic experience.*

☆**trav·el¹** /ˈtrævl/ *verb* **1** [I] to make a trip: *John travels a lot on business.* ○ *to travel by bus/air* ○ *They traveled through New England last fall.* ○ (*figurative*) *News travels fast in our office.* **2** [T] to make a trip of a particular distance or at a particular speed: *They traveled 200 miles to come and see us.* ○ *Their car was traveling at 70 miles an hour when it hit a tree.*

☆**trav·el²** /ˈtrævl/ *noun* **1** [U] the act of traveling: *Air travel has made the world seem a lot smaller.* ○ *a travel book*

☞ This sense of **travel** is uncountable and you can only use it to talk about the general activity of moving from place to place: *Foreign travel is very popular these days.* When you talk about going from one particular place to another, you use **trip**. A trip may be short: *a day trip*, or longer: *a trip around the world*, and can be for business or pleasure: *He's on a trip to New York to meet a client.* ○ *How about a trip to the lake this weekend?* A **tour** is a trip or walk during which you visit several places. You may go on a tour of a country, city, place of interest, etc.: *a guided tour of the campus.* A **journey** is a long, often difficult trip. **Journey** is often used in stories: *the pioneers' journey across America.*

2 travels [plural] trips, especially to places that are far away: *You must have seen lots of interesting places on your travels.*

ˈtravel ˌagency *noun* [C] (*pl.* **travel agencies**) a company that makes travel arrangements for people (reserving plane tickets and hotel rooms, etc.)

ˈtravel ˌagent *noun* [C] a person who works in a travel agency

☆**trav·el·er** /ˈtrævl·ər/ *noun* [C] a person who is traveling or who travels often

ˈtraveler's check *noun* [C] a check that you can change into foreign money when you are traveling in other countries, or that you can use instead of cash to pay for things in the U.S.: *to cash a traveler's check*

☆**tray** /treɪ/ *noun* [C] a flat piece of wood, plastic, metal, etc. with raised edges that you can carry food, drinks, etc. on: *When she was sick in bed, he took her meals to her on a tray.*

treach·er·ous /ˈtrɛtʃərəs/ *adj.* **1** that you cannot trust **2** full of hidden danger: *The roads are treacherous after yesterday's blizzard.*

treach·er·y /ˈtrɛtʃəri/ *noun* [U] the act of causing harm to sb/sth that trusts you

tread¹ /trɛd/ *verb* (*p.t.* **trod** /trɑd/; *p.p.* **trod-**

i	ɪ	ɛ	æ	ɑ	ɔ	ʌ	ʊ	u
see	sit	ten	cat	hot	saw	cup	put	too

den /'trɑdn/) [I] **tread (in/on sth)** (*old-fashioned, formal*) to step or put your foot down in or on sth

IDM **tread carefully/cautiously/lightly/softly** to act very carefully in a difficult situation: *Most of the candidates are treading very carefully on the issue of capital punishment.*

tread² /trɛd/ *noun* [C,U] the raised pattern on the outside surface of a tire

trea·son /'trizn/ *noun* [U] the act of causing harm to your country, e.g. by helping its enemies ☞ Look at **traitor**.

☆ **treas·ure¹** /'trɛʒər/ *noun* **1** [C,U] a collection of very valuable objects, e.g. made of gold, silver, etc.: *to find buried treasure* **2** [C] something that is very valuable: *the museum's art treasures*

treas·ure² /'trɛʒər/ *verb* [T] to consider sb/sth to be very special or valuable: *I will treasure those memories forever.*

☆ **treas·ur·er** /'trɛʒərər/ *noun* [C] the person who is in charge of the money that belongs to a government, a club, an organization, etc.: *the Idaho state treasurer*

☆ **treas·ur·y** /'trɛʒəri/ *noun* [C, usually sing.] **1** the money that belongs to a club, an organization, etc. **2** often **Treasury** the government department that controls public money

☆ **treat¹** /trit/ *verb* [T] **1** to act or behave towards sb/sth in a particular way: *Teenagers hate being treated like children.* ○ *You should treat older people with respect.* ○ *to treat sb badly, fairly, etc.* **2 treat sth as sth** to consider sth in a particular way: *The bomb threat was not taken seriously. It was treated as a hoax.* **3** to deal with or discuss: *This book treats the subject in great detail.* **4** to use medicine or medical care to try to make a sick or injured person well again: *a new drug to treat cancer* ○ *The boy was treated for burns at the hospital.* **5 treat sth (with sth)** to put a substance onto sth or to put sth throught a special process in order to protect it from damage, or to make it safe to use: *Most vegetables are treated with insecticide.* ○ *to treat waste water* **6 treat sb/yourself (to sth)** to give sb/ yourself sth that is very special or enjoyable: *Claire treated the kids to ice cream cones* (= she paid for them).

treat² /trit/ *noun* [C] something that is very special or enjoyable: *I brought some donuts as a treat for dessert.* ○ *It's a real treat for me to stay in bed late.*

IDM **trick or treat** ⇨ TRICK¹

☆ **treat·ment** /'tritmənt/ *noun* **1** [U] the way that you behave toward sb or deal with sth: *I don't see why girls should get any special treatment.* **2** [C,U] the use of medicine or medical care to try to make a sick or injured person well again: *a new treatment for HIV infection* ○ *emergency medical treatment* **3** [U] the use of special substances or processes in order to

protect sth or make sth safe to use: *a sewage treatment plant* (= that takes sewage out of water)

☆ **trea·ty** /'triti/ *noun* [C] (*pl.* **trea·ties**) a written agreement between two or more countries: *to sign a peace treaty*

treb·le /'trɛbl/ *noun* [C] (in music) the highest voice, instrument, or range

tree

leaf

twig

branch — trunk

☆ **tree** /tri/ *noun* [C] a tall plant with a thick wooden stem from which branches grow: *an oak tree* ○ *short/tall trees* ○ *to climb a tree* ○ *to plant/cut down a tree*

☞ The stem of a tree is called a **trunk**. The outer surface of this is **bark**. The **branches** grow out from the trunk. A tree may have **leaves** or **needles**. Look at **Christmas tree** and **family tree**.

trek /trɛk/ *noun* [C] a long hard journey, often on foot —**trek** *verb* [I] (**trek·king**; **trekked**)

☆ **trem·ble** /'trɛmbl/ *verb* [I] to shake, e.g. because you are cold, frightened, weak, etc.: *She was pale and trembling with shock.* ○ *His hand was trembling as he picked up his pen to sign.* ○ *Sue's voice trembled with excitement.* —**tremble** *noun* [C]: *There was a tremble in his voice as he told them the sad news.*

tre·men·dous /trɪ'mɛndəs/ *adj.* **1** very large or great: *a tremendous amount of work* ○ *a tremendous difference* ○ *a tremendous explosion* **2** (*informal*) very good: *You were tremendous!*

tre·men·dous·ly /trɪ'mɛndəsli/ *adv.* very; very much: *tremendously exciting* ○ *Prices vary tremendously from one store to another.*

trem·or /'trɛmər/ *noun* [C] a slight shaking or trembling: *a tremor in his voice* ○ *Some residents felt a few tremors several hours before the earthquake struck.*

trench /trɛntʃ/ *noun* [C] a long narrow hole in the ground: *to dig a trench for a pipeline*

☆ **trend** /trɛnd/ *noun* [C] a general movement or change in society or in a situation: *The current trend is towards smaller families.* ○ *a general trend for women to get married later* ○ *to follow the latest fashion trends*

IDM **set a/the trend** to start a new style or fashion

trend·y /'trɛndi/ *adj.* (**trend·i·er**; **trend·i·est**) (*informal*) fashionable

tres·pass /'trɛspæs/ *verb* [I] to go onto sb's

ə	y	w	ţ	eɪ	aɪ	ɔɪ	aʊ	oʊ
about	yes	woman	butter	say	five	boy	now	go

land without permission —**trespasser** *noun* [C]: *Trespassers will be prosecuted.*

☆**tri·al** /'traɪəl/ *noun* **1** [C,U] the process in a court of law where lawyers present evidence in order for the court to decide whether sb is guilty of a crime or not: *a fair trial* ○ *He was on trial for murder.* ○ *trial by jury* **2** [C,U] an act of testing sb/sth: *New drugs must go through extensive trials.* ○ *a trial period of three months* **IDM** **trial and error** trying different ways of doing sth until you find the best one

ˌ**trial ˈrun** (also *informal* **dry run**) *noun* [C] an occasion when you practice doing sth in order to make sure you can do it correctly later on

☆**tri·an·gle** /'traɪæŋgl/ *noun* [C] **1** a shape that has three straight sides and three angles: *a right triangle* (= with one angle of 90°) ☞ picture at **shape**. **2** a metal musical instrument in the shape of a triangle (1) that you play by hitting it with a metal stick

tri·an·gu·lar /traɪ'æŋgyələr/ *adj.* shaped like a triangle (1)

☆**tribe** /traɪb/ *noun* [C] a group of people that have the same language and customs and that are ruled by a chief or chiefs: *Native American tribes* —**trib·al** /'traɪbl/ *adj.*: *tribal dances*

tri·bu·nal /traɪ'byunl; trɪ-/ *noun* [C] a court or group of officials who have the authority to decide who is right in particular types of disagreements, especially in cases involving international law: *a military tribunal*

trib·u·tar·y /'trɪbyə,tɛri/ *noun* [C] (*pl.* **trib·u·tar·ies**) a river or stream that flows into a larger river

trib·ute /'trɪbyut/ *noun* **1** [C,U] something that you say or do to show that you respect or admire sb/sth: *A special concert was held as a tribute to the composer on his 80th birthday.* **2** [sing.] **a tribute (to sth)** a sign of how good sb/sth is: *The success of the festival is a tribute to the organizers.* **IDM** **pay tribute to sb/sth** ⇨ PAY²

☆**trick¹** /trɪk/ *noun* [C] **1** something that you do to deceive sb, in order to make him/her look stupid or to cheat him/her: *The children played a trick on the teacher.* **2** a clever or the best way of doing sth: *I can't get the top off this jar. Is there a trick to it?* **3** an act that uses special skills to make people believe sth which is not true: *The magician performed a trick in which he made a rabbit disappear.* **IDM** **do the job/trick** ⇨ JOB

trick or treat (said by children on Halloween to ask people to give them candy. If sb does not give a child any candy, then the child might do sth bad to him/her.)

☞ We use the phrase **go trick-or-treating** to talk about what children do on Halloween. Look at the note at **Halloween**.

☆**trick²** /trɪk/ *verb* [T] to deceive sb in order to make him/her do or believe sth: *He tricked me*

into lending him money. ○ *Stella was tricked out of her share of the money.*

trick·er·y /'trɪkəri/ *noun* [U] the use of a trick¹ (1) in order to deceive sb

trick·le /'trɪkl/ *verb* [I] (used about a liquid) to flow in a thin stream: *Tears trickled down his cheek.* ○ (*figurative*) *At first no one came, but then people began to trickle in.* —**trick·le** *noun* [C, usually sing.]: *The stream was only a trickle.* ○ (*figurative*) *The flood of refugees had been reduced to a trickle.*

trick·y /'trɪki/ *adj.* (**trick·i·er; trick·i·est**) difficult to do or deal with: *a tricky situation*

tri·cy·cle /'traɪsɪkl/(also *informal* **trike**) *noun* [C] a small vehicle, like a bicycle, that has one wheel at the front and two at the back

tri·fle /'traɪfl/ *noun* (*formal*) [C] something that is of little value or importance **IDM** **a trifle** a little: *It's a trifle odd that they didn't call.*

trig·ger¹ /'trɪgər/ *noun* [C] the piece of metal that you press to fire a gun: *to pull the trigger*

trig·ger² /'trɪgər/ *verb* [T] to cause sth to start or happen: *The smoke from her cigarette triggered the fire alarm.*

trike /traɪk/ *noun* [C] (*informal*) = TRICYCLE

tril·lion /'trɪlyən/ *number* the number 1,000,000,000,000 ☞ For more information about numbers, look at Appendix 2.

tril·o·gy /'trɪlədʒi/ *noun* [C] (*pl.* **tril·o·gies**) a group of three books, plays, etc. that form one set

☆**trim¹** /trɪm/ *verb* [T] (**trim·ming; trimmed**) **1** to cut a little bit off sth so that it is neat and attractive: *to trim a beard* **2 trim sth (off sth/ off)** to cut sth off because you do not need it: *Trim the fat off the meat.* **3 trim sth (with sth)** to decorate the edge of sth with sth: *a skirt trimmed with lace*

trim² /trɪm/ *adj.* not fat: *She still looks slim and trim.*

trim³ /trɪm/ *noun* **1** [C, usually sing.] an act of cutting a little bit off sth in order to make it neat and attractive: *My hair needs a trim.* **2** [U] material that you use for decorating sth

trim·mings /'trɪmɪŋz/ *noun* [plural] extra things which you add to sth to improve its appearance, taste, etc.: *turkey with all the trimmings*

trin·i·ty /'trɪnəti/ *noun* [sing.] **the Trinity** (in the Christian religion) the three forms of God: the Father, Jesus the Son and the Holy Spirit

tri·o /'trioʊ/ *noun* (*pl.* **tri·os**) [C] **1** a group of three people who play music or sing together **2** a piece of music for three people to play or sing

☆**trip** /trɪp/ *verb* (**trip·ping; tripped**) **1** [I] to knock your foot against sth when you are walking and fall or nearly fall down: *Don't leave your bag on the floor. Someone might trip over it.* ○ *She caught her foot in the root of a tree and tripped.* **2** [T] to cause sb to fall or nearly

fall down: *Lee stuck out his foot and tripped John.*

PHRV **trip (sb) up** to make a mistake; to make sb say sth that he/she did not want to say: *The journalist asked a difficult question to try to trip the Congressman up.*

☆**trip²** /trɪp/ *noun* [C] **1** an occasion during which you visit a place and return: *to take a trip to the mountains* ○ *to go on a business trip to Europe* ○ *We had to make three trips to the car to bring all the groceries in.* ☞ Look at the note at **travel**. **2** (*slang*) an experience that sb has after he/she takes illegal drugs

☆**tri·ple¹** /ˈtrɪpl/ *adj.* **1** made up of three parts: *the triple jump* **2** happening three times or containing three times as much as usual: *a triple world champion* (= one who has won three times) ○ *a triple whiskey*

☆**tri·ple²** /ˈtrɪpl/ *verb* [I,T] to make sth, or to become, three times greater

trip·let /ˈtrɪplət/ *noun* [C] one of three children or animals that are born to one mother at the same time ☞ Look at **twin**.

tri·pod /ˈtraɪpɑd/ *noun* [C] a piece of equipment with three legs that you can put a camera, etc. on

☆**tri·umph¹** /ˈtraɪʌmf/ *noun* [C,U] success, especially in a competition or battle; the feeling of joy that you have because of this: *The soldiers returned home in triumph.* ○ *The fans gave a shout of triumph.* ○ *Putting people on the moon was one of the triumphs of the twentieth century.*

tri·umph² /ˈtraɪʌmf/ *verb* [I] **triumph (over sb/sth)** to achieve success; to defeat sb/sth: *Chicago triumphed over Utah in the championships.* ○ *Although he was blind, he triumphed over his disability to become a college professor.*

tri·um·phant /traɪˈʌmfənt/ *adj.* feeling or showing great happiness because you have won or succeeded at sth: *a triumphant cheer* —**tri·um·phant·ly** *adv.*

triv·i·a /ˈtrɪviə/ *noun* [plural] detailed pieces of information that are often considered unimportant: *a trivia quiz*

triv·i·al /ˈtrɪviəl/ *adj.* of little importance

triv·i·al·ize /ˈtrɪviəlaɪz/ *verb* [T] to make sth seem less important than it is

trod *p.t.* of TREAD¹

trod·den *p.p.* of TREAD¹

trol·ley /ˈtrɑli/ *noun* [C] (*pl.* **trol·leys**) = STREETCAR

trom·bone /trɑmˈboʊn/ *noun* [C] a large brass musical instrument that you play by blowing into it and moving a long tube backward and forward

☆**troop¹** /trup/ *noun* **1** [C] a large group of people or animals **2 troops** [plural] soldiers

troop² /trup/ *verb* [I] **troop in, out, over, etc.** to move in a large group: *All the students trooped into the auditorium.*

troop·er /ˈtrupər/ *noun* [C] a member of a state police force, whose duties include making sure that people obey traffic laws

☆**tro·phy** /ˈtroʊfi/ *noun* [C] (*pl.* **tro·phies**) a silver cup, etc. that you get for winning a competition or race

☆**trop·ic** /ˈtrɑpɪk/ *noun* **1** [C, usually sing.] one of the two lines of latitude that are 23° 27′ north and south of the equator: *the tropic of Cancer* ○ *the tropic of Capricorn* ☞ picture at **earth**. **2 the tropics** [plural] the part of the world that is between these two lines, where the climate is hot

☆**trop·i·cal** /ˈtrɑpɪkl/ *adj.* coming from or connected with the hottest, wettest parts of the world: *tropical fruit* ○ *tropical rain forests*

trot /trɑt/ *verb* (**trot·ting**; **trot·ted**) [I] (used about a horse) to move fairly quickly, lifting the feet high off the ground: (*figurative*) *The boy trotted along behind his father.*

PHRV **trot sb/sth out** (*informal*) to show sb/sth to other people, even though they find him/her/it boring: *Phil always trots out his high school yearbooks when he has dinner guests.* —**trot** *noun* [sing.]

☆**trou·ble¹** /ˈtrʌbl/ *noun* **1** [C,U] (a situation that causes) problems, difficulty, worry, etc.: *If I don't get home by 11 o'clock, I'll be in trouble.* ○ *I'm having trouble getting the car started.* ○ *financial troubles* ○ *It's a very good school. The only trouble is, it's a little too far away.* **2** [sing., U] extra work or effort: *Let's eat out tonight. It will save you the trouble of cooking.* ○ *Why don't you stay overnight with us? It's no trouble.* ○ *I'm sorry to cause you so much trouble.* **3** [C,U] a situation where people are fighting or arguing with each other: *There's usually trouble in town on Saturday night after the bars close.* **4** [U] illness or pain: *I have back trouble again.*

IDM **ask for trouble** ⇨ ASK

get into trouble to get into a situation which is dangerous or in which you may be punished

go to a lot of trouble (to do sth) to put a lot of work or effort into sth: *They went to a lot of trouble to make us feel welcome.*

take the trouble to do sth to do sth even though it means extra work or effort: *He took the trouble to write and thank everyone for his presents.*

trou·ble² /ˈtrʌbl/ *verb* [T] **1** to cause sb worry, problems, etc. **2 trouble sb (for sth)** (*formal*) (used when you are asking sb extremely politely for sth or to do sth): *I hate to trouble you, but could I use your phone?* ○ *Could I trouble you for some change?*

trou·ble·mak·er /ˈtrʌblmeɪkər/ *noun* [C] a person who often causes trouble¹(1,3)

trou·ble·shoot·er /ˈtrʌblʃutər/ *noun* [C] a person whose job is to find and fix problems in machines, etc. —**trou·ble·shoot·ing** *noun* [U]

tʃ	dʒ	v	θ	ð	s	z	ʃ
chin	June	van	thin	then	so	zoo	she

trou·ble·some /'trʌblsəm/ *adj.* that causes trouble¹(1)

trough /trɔf/ *noun* [C] a long narrow container from which farm animals eat or drink

trou·sers /'traʊzərz/ *noun* (*formal* or *BrE*) = PANTS

trout /traʊt/ *noun* [C,U] (*pl.* **trout**) a type of fish that lives in rivers and that is eaten as food

tru·ant /'truənt/ *noun* [C] a student who stays away from school without permission —**truant** *adj.* —**tru·an·cy** /-ənsɪ/ *noun* [U]

truce /trus/ *noun* [C] an agreement to stop fighting for a period of time ☞ Look at cease-fire.

tractor-trailer

truck

van

pickup truck

☆ **truck¹** /trʌk/ *noun* [C] a large strong motor vehicle that is used for carrying things by road ☞ Look also at **pickup** (1).

truck² /trʌk/ *verb* [T] to transport sth by truck¹: *The city's garbage is trucked to a landfill west of town.*

☆ **truck·er** /'trʌkər/ *noun* [C] a person whose job is driving a truck, especially over long distances

truck·ing /'trʌkɪŋ/ *noun* [U] the business of transporting things by truck

truck·load /'trʌkloʊd/ *noun* [C] an amount of sth that a truck can carry at one time: *a truckload of fruit* ○ *They were selling furniture by the truckload.*

'truck stop *noun* [C] a place near a main road where you can buy gasoline, and with a cheap restaurant especially for truckers

trudge /trʌdʒ/ *verb* [I] to walk with slow, heavy steps, e.g. because you are very tired

☆ **true** /tru/ *adj.* **1** that really happened: *The novel was based on a true story.* **2** right or correct; agreeing with fact: *Is it true that Adam is leaving?* ○ *Read the statements and decide if they are true or false.* ○ *I didn't think the movie was very true to life* (= it didn't show life as it really is). **3** real or genuine: *How do you know when you have found true love?* ○ *the true value of the house* **4 true (to sth)** behaving as expected or as promised: *to be true to*

your word (= to do what you promised) ☞ The noun is **truth**.

IDM **come true** to happen in the way you hoped or dreamed: *My dream finally came true!*

ring true ⇨ RING²

tru·ly /'truli/ *adv.* **1** really: *We are truly grateful to you for your help.* **2** completely: *Now that she was a U.S. citizen, she felt truly American.* **3** expressing the truth: *I cannot truly say that I was surprised at the news.* ☞ **Yours truly** is often used at the end of a letter.

trump /trʌmp/ *noun* [C] (in some card games) a card of the suit that has a higher value than the other three suits during a particular game: *Spades are trumps.*

trum·pet /'trʌmpət/ *noun* [C] a brass musical instrument that you play by blowing into it. There are three buttons on it which you can press to make different notes.

trumpet

trun·dle /'trʌndl/ *verb* **1** [I] to move slowly: *The army trundled down the hill.* **2** [T] to push or pull sth along slowly on wheels

☆ **trunk** /trʌŋk/ *noun* **1** [C] the thick main stem of a tree ☞ picture at **tree**. **2** [C] the main part of your body (not including your head, arms and legs) **3** [C] the part at the back of a car where you put luggage, etc. **4** [C] a large box, like a large suitcase, that you use for storing or transporting things ☞ picture at **luggage**. **5** [C] an elephant's long nose ☞ picture at **elephant**. **6 trunks** [plural] = SWIMMING TRUNKS

☆ **trust¹** /trʌst/ *noun* **1** [U] **trust (in sb/sth)** the feeling that you have when you know that you can rely on sb/sth to do what he/she/it is supposed to do: *Our marriage is based on love and trust.* ○ *I put my trust in him, but he failed me.* **2** [U] responsibility: *As a teacher, you are in a position of trust.* **3** [C,U] an arrangement by which a person or an organization manages money and property for sb else: *The money was put into a trust fund for the children.*

IDM **on trust** without having proof; without checking: *I can't prove it. You must take it on trust.*

☆ **trust²** /trʌst/ *verb* **1** [T] to believe that you can rely on sb/sth to do what he/she/it is supposed to do; to believe that sb/sth will not harm you: *He said the car was safe, but I just don't trust him.* ○ *Can I trust you to behave while I am out?* ○ *You can't trust her with money.* ○ *She is not to be trusted with money.* ○ *I don't trust that dog. It looks dangerous.* **2** [I,T] **trust (in) sb/sth** to depend on sb/sth or have faith in sb/sth: *to trust in God* ○ *I'll trust your judgment.*

715 tug of war

trus·tee /trʌˈsti/ *noun* [C] a person who manages money or property for sb else

trust·ing /ˈtrʌstɪŋ/ *adj.* having or showing trust, often in situations where it is not wise to do this

trust·wor·thy /ˈtrʌstwɜrði/ *adj.* that you can trust

☆ **truth** /truθ/ *noun* (*pl.* **truths** /truðz/) **1** [U] the state or quality of being true: *There's a lot of truth in what she says.* **2** [sing.] what is true: *Please tell me the truth.* ○ *the whole truth* **3** [C] a fact or idea that is true: *scientific truths*

truth·ful /ˈtruθfl/ *adj.* **1** true or correct: *a truthful account* **2** (used about a person) who tells the truth; honest —**truth·ful·ly** *adv.*

☆ **try¹** /traɪ/ *verb* (*pres. part.* **try·ing**; *3rd pers. sing. pres.* **tries**; *p.t., p.p.* **tried**) **1** [I] to make an effort to do sth: *I tried to call you, but I couldn't get through.* ○ *She was trying hard not to laugh.* ○ *to try your best/hardest* ○ *I'm sure you can do it if you try.*

☞ **Try and** is more informal than **try to**. **Try and** cannot be used in the past tense: *I'll try to get there on time.* ○ (*informal*) *I'll try and get there on time.* ○ *I tried to get there on time, but I was too late.*

2 [T] to do, use or test sth in order to see how good or successful it is: *"I've tried everything but I can't get the baby to sleep." "Did you try taking her out in the stroller?"* ○ *Have you ever tried raw fish?* ○ *We tried the door, but it was locked.* ○ *He tried several bookstores, but none of them had the books he wanted.* **3** [T] to examine sb in a court of law in order to decide if he/she is guilty of a crime or not: *He was tried for murder.*

PHRV try sth on to put on a piece of clothing to see if it fits you properly: *Can I try these jeans on?*

try sb/sth out to test sh/sth by using him/her/it

try out for sth to try to become a member of a sports team or an actor in a play by having your skills tested: *Dave tried out for the wrestling team.*

☆ **try²** /traɪ/ *noun* [C] (*pl.* **tries**) an occasion when you make an effort to do sth; an attempt: *I don't know if I can move it by myself, but I'll give it a try.*

try·ing /ˈtraɪɪŋ/ *adj.* that makes you tired or angry: *a trying day at work*

try·out /ˈtraɪaʊt/ *noun* [C] a competition in which people's skills are tested in order to see whether they are suitable to be members of a team, actors in a play, etc.: *Tryouts for the cheerleading squad will be held next week.*

☆ **T-shirt** /ˈtiʃərt/ *noun* [C] a shirt with short sleeves, a round opening for your head to go through and no buttons ☞ picture on page A26.

tsp. *abbr.* = TEASPOON

tub /tʌb/ *noun* [C] **1** = BATHTUB: *Julie can't come to the phone – she's in the tub.* **2** a large round container with a flat bottom and no lid **3** a small plastic container with a lid, that is used for holding food: *a tub of margarine*

tu·ba /ˈtubə/ *noun* [C] a large brass musical instrument that makes a low sound

☆ **tube** /tub/ *noun* **1** [C] a long hollow pipe made of glass, metal, rubber, etc.: *Blood flowed along the tube into the bottle.* ○ *the inner tube of a bicycle tire* ○ *a laboratory test tube* **2** [C] a long thin soft container with a cap at one end made of plastic or metal. Tubes are used for holding soft substances, and you squeeze them to get the substance out: *a tube of toothpaste* ☞ picture at **container**. **3 the tube** [sing.] (*informal*) television: *What's on the tube tonight?*

tu·ber·cu·lo·sis /tʊˌbərkyəˈloʊsəs/ *noun* [U] (*abbr.* **TB**) a serious disease that especially affects the lungs

tub·ing /ˈtubɪŋ/ *noun* [U] a long piece of metal, rubber, etc. in the shape of a tube (1), or a system of tubes

tuck /tʌk/ *verb* [T] **1** to put or fold the ends or edges of sth into or around sth else so that it looks neat: *Tuck your shirt in – it looks messy like that.* ○ *He tucked the blanket around the old man's knees.* **2** to put sth away neatly or in a safe or hidden place: *He tucked his wallet away in his inside pocket.* ○ *The letter was tucked behind a pile of books.*

PHRV tuck sth away (*informal*) **1** to store sth: *They have a lot of money tucked away.* **2** to hide sth: *Their house is tucked away behind those trees.*

tuck sb in to put blankets, sheets, etc. tightly around sb, especially a child, in bed to make him/her feel comfortable and safe

☆ **Tues·day** /ˈtuzdeɪ; -di/ *noun* [C,U] (*abbr.* **Tue.**; **Tues.**) the day of the week after Monday and before Wednesday ☞ For examples of the use of the days of the week in sentences, look at **Monday**.

tuft /tʌft/ *noun* [C] a small bunch of hair, grass, etc.

tug¹ /tʌg/ *verb* [I,T] (**tug·ging**; **tugged**) to pull sth hard and quickly

tug² /tʌg/ *noun* [C] **1** a sudden hard pull: *She gave the rope a tug.* **2** (*also* **tug·boat** /ˈtʌgboʊt/) a small, strong boat that is used for pulling larger ships into a harbor

tug of war (*also* **tug-of-war**) *noun* [C] (*pl.* **tugs of war**) a game in which two people or teams pull on the ends of a rope in opposite directions. The winner is the person or team who pulls the other one over a line in the middle. : (*figurative*) *Kara was caught in an emotional tug of war between her parents when they got divorced.*

ə	y	w	t̬	eɪ	aɪ	ɔɪ	aʊ	oʊ
about	yes	woman	butter	say	five	boy	now	go

☆ **tu·i·tion** /tuˈɪʃn/ *noun* [U] the money that a student must pay in order to take classes at a college, university, or private school

tu·lip /ˈtuləp/ *noun* [C] a brightly-colored flower, shaped like a small cup, that grows from a large round root (**bulb**) in the spring

tum·ble /ˈtʌmbl/ *verb* [I] **1** to fall suddenly in a heavy way, without control: *He tripped, and tumbled all the way down the steps.* **2** (used about prices, etc.) to become lower: *The price of gas has tumbled.* **3** to move in a particular direction in a clumsy way: *I got undressed and tumbled into bed.* ○ *She opened her suitcase and all her things tumbled out of it.*

PHRV **tumble down** to fall down; to collapse: *The walls of the old house were tumbling down.* —**tum·ble** *noun* [C]

tum·bler /ˈtʌmblər/ *noun* [C] a drinking glass with straight sides that has no handle or stem

tum·my /ˈtʌmi/ *noun* [C] (*pl.* **tum·mies**) (*informal*) (used by and to small children) stomach

tu·mor /ˈtumər/ *noun* [C] a group of diseased cells that are growing abnormally in the body: *a brain tumor*

tu·mul·tu·ous /tʊˈmʌltʃuəs/ *adj.* very noisy or confused, because people are excited: *a tumultuous welcome*

☆ **tu·na** /ˈtunə/ *noun* (*pl.* **tuna**) **1** [C] a large fish that lives in the ocean **2** [U] (*also* **tuna fish**) the flesh of the fish, which is often sold in cans

☆ **tune¹** /tun/ *noun* [C,U] a series of musical notes that are arranged in a pleasant pattern: *Tina played a tune on the piano.* ○ *I can't remember the tune to that song.*

IDM **change your tune** ⇨ CHANGE¹

in tune/out of tune 1 at/not at the correct musical level (**pitch**): *You're singing out of tune.* **2** in/not in agreement with sb/sth: *The President doesn't seem to be in tune with what ordinary people are thinking.*

tune² /tun/ *verb* [T] **1** to adjust a musical instrument so that it is at the correct musical level (**pitch**) **2** to adjust an engine so that it runs well

IDM **tuned (in) to sth** listening to a particular radio station: *Stay tuned to this station for the latest news.*

PHRV **tune in (to sth)** to move the controls of a radio or television so that you can listen to or watch a particular station

tune sb/sth out (*informal*) to stop listening to sb or ignore him/her/it: *When she is nagging me like that, I just tune her out.*

tu·nic /ˈtunɪk/ *noun* [C] a piece of loose clothing that is like a long shirt

☆ **tun·nel¹** /ˈtʌnl/ *noun* [C] a passage under the ground or a river, etc. for cars, trucks and/or trains to drive through: *The train disappeared into a tunnel.* ○ *the Lincoln Tunnel*

tun·nel² /ˈtʌnl/ *verb* [I,T] to dig a tunnel¹

tur·ban /ˈtərbən/ *noun* [C] a covering for the head that is made by wrapping a long piece of cloth around the head

tur·bu·lent /ˈtərbyələnt/ *adj.* **1** in a state of disorder and confusion when things are changing fast **2** (used about water or air) moving in a violent way —**tur·bu·lence** /-ləns/ *noun* [U]

turf /tərf/ *noun* [U] **1** short thick grass and the layer of soil underneath it: *a stadium with artificial turf* **2** (*informal*) (an area that sb considers as his/her own and does not want to share with other people): *Two people were shot when they entered a rival gang's turf.*

☆ **tur·key** /ˈtərki/ *noun* (*pl.* **tur·keys**) **1** [C,U] a large bird, somewhat like a very large chicken, or its meat. Turkey is a traditional part of Thanksgiving dinner. **2** [C] (*informal*) something, especially a movie, that is unsuccessful and of very bad quality

IDM **cold turkey** ⇨ COLD¹

tur·moil /ˈtərmɔɪl/ *noun* [C, usually sing., U] a state of great excitement, noise or confusion

☆ **turn¹** /tərn/ *verb* **1** [I] to move or go around a fixed point: *The wheels turned faster and faster.* **2** [T] to hold and move sth around a central point; to make sth go around: *She turned the doorknob.* ○ *Turn the steering wheel to the right.* **3** [I] to change your position so that you are facing in a different direction: *He turned around when he heard my voice.* **4** [T] to change the position of sth: *I turned the box upside down.* ○ *She turned the page and started the next chapter.* **5** [I,T] to change direction when you are moving: *Go straight ahead and turn left by the church.* ○ *The car turned the corner.* ○ *He turned the van into the driveway.* **6** [I,T] **turn (sb/sth) (into/to sth)** (to cause) to become: *He turned very red when I asked him about the money.* ○ *How did you feel when you turned 30?* ○ *Everything the king touched turned into gold.*

☞ For expressions with **turn**, look at the noun and adjective entries, e.g. for **turn a blind eye**, look at **blind**.

PHRV **turn away** to stop looking at sb/sth: *She turned away in horror at the sight of the blood.*

turn sb away to refuse to allow a person to go into a place

turn back to go back in the same direction as you came

turn sb/sth down to refuse an offer, etc. or the person who makes it: *Why did you turn that job down?* ○ *He asked her to marry him, but she turned him down.*

turn sth down to reduce the sound or heat that sth produces: *Turn the TV down!*

turn sb in to inform the police where a criminal is

turn sth in to give sth to a person in authority: *All essays must be turned in by Friday at*

ər	ɪr	ɛr	ɑr	ɔr	ʊr	ʒ	h	ŋ
bird	near	hair	car	north	tour	vision	hat	sing

5:00. ○ *I was relieved to hear that somebody had turned my keys in to the security guard.*

turn off (sth) to leave one road and go on another: *We turn off the freeway at exit 10.*

turn sth off to move the switch, etc. on a machine, etc. to stop it from working: *He turned the TV off.*

turn sth on to move the switch, etc. on of machine, etc. to start it working: *Turn the lights on!*

turn out (for sth) to be present or appear for sth: *Thousands of people turned out to welcome the team home.*

turn out (to be sth) to be sth in the end: *The weather turned out fine.* ○ *The house that they had promised us turned out to be a tiny apartment.*

turn sth out to move the switch, etc. on a light so that it is no longer shining: *Turn the lights out before you go to bed.*

turn to sb to go to sb to get help

turn to sth to find a page in a book: *Turn to page 45.*

turn up 1 to arrive: *What time did they finally turn up?* **2** to be found: *I lost my glasses a week ago and they still haven't turned up.*

turn sth up to increase the sound or heat that sth produces: *Turn the heat up – it's freezing!*

☆ **turn²** /tərn/ *noun* [C] **1** an act of turning sb/sth around: *Give the screw another couple of turns to make sure it is really tight.* **2** a change of direction: *to make a left/right turn* ○ *a U-turn* (= when you turn around and go back in the opposite direction) **3** a bend or corner in a road, river, etc.: *Take the next turn on the left.* **4** [usually sing.] the time when you must or may do sth: *Please wait in line until it is your turn.* **5** a change: *The patient's condition has taken a turn for the worse.*

IDM **in turn** one after the other: *I spoke to each of the children in turn.*

take turns (doing sth) to do sth one after the other: *You can't both play on the computer at the same time. You'll have to take turns.*

wait your turn ⇨ WAIT¹

turning point *noun* [C] a time when an important change happens

tur·nip /'tərnəp/ *noun* [C,U] a round white vegetable that grows under the ground

turn·out /'tərnaʊt/ *noun* [C, usually sing.] the number of people who attend a sports or entertainment event, vote in an election, etc.

turn·o·ver /'tərnoʊvər/ *noun* **1** [sing.] the rate at which workers leave a company and are replaced by new ones: *a high turnover of personnel* **2** a small pie made of pastry that is folded over and filled with fruit

turn·pike /'tərnpaɪk/ *noun* [C] a type of road that you have to pay money to (**a toll**) to drive on

turn signal *noun* [C] the flashing light on a

car, etc. that shows that it is going to turn right or left

turn·stile /'tərnstaɪl/ *noun* [C] a gate that goes around and allows one person at a time to enter a place

tur·pen·tine /'tərpəntaɪn/ *noun* [U] a clear liquid with a strong smell that you use for removing paint or for making paint thinner

tur·quoise /'tərkwɔɪz/ *adj., noun* [U] (of) a greenish-blue color

☆ **tur·tle** /'tərtl/ (*also* **tortoise**) *noun* [C] an animal that has a hard shell and moves very slowly. A turtle can pull its head and legs into its shell to protect them.

turtle

☞ In scientific language, **tortoise** is used for the animals that live on land, and **turtle** is used only for the animals that live mainly in water. However, most people usually use **turtle** for both types of animals.

tur·tle·neck /'tərtlnɛk/ *noun* [C] a sweater or shirt with a high collar that covers most of your neck ☞ picture on page A27.

tusk /tʌsk/ *noun* [C] one of the two very long pointed teeth of an elephant, etc. ☞ picture at **elephant**. Elephants' tusks are made of **ivory**.

tus·sle /'tʌsl/ *noun* [C] (*informal*) a rough fight, e.g. between two or more people who want to have the same thing

tu·tor¹ /'tutər/ *noun* [C] a private teacher who teaches one person or a very small group, especially to give extra help in a particular subject

tu·tor² /'tutər/ *verb* [T] to give one person or a group extra help in a particular subject —**tu·tor·ing** *noun* [U]

tux·e·do /tʌk'sidoʊ/ *noun* [C] (*pl.* **tux·e·dos** /-doʊz/)(also *informal* **tux**) a black or white jacket and pants that a man wears on formal occasions. A tuxedo is normally worn with a bow tie.

☆ **TV** /,ti'vi/ *noun* [C,U] (*pl.* **TVs** or **TV's**) television: *Turn the TV on.* ○ *What's on TV tonight?*

TV dinner *noun* [C] a meal that has been prepared and frozen in a factory, and that you can buy in a store and heat up in the oven at home

twang /twæŋ/ *noun* [C] a tone that sb's voice makes when the sound comes from his/her nose and mouth together, especially if he/she speaks with a southern U.S. accent

tweed /twid/ *noun* [U] thick wool cloth with a rough surface

tweez·ers /'twizərz/ *noun* [plural] a small tool consisting of two pieces of metal that are joined at one end. You use tweezers for picking up or pulling out very small things: *a pair of tweezers*

T

tʃ	dʒ	v	θ	ð	s	z	ʃ
chin	**June**	**van**	**thin**	**then**	**so**	**zoo**	**she**

☆**twelve** /twɛlv/ *number* 12; one more than eleven ☞ Look at **dozen**. For examples of how to use numbers in sentences, look at **six**. Look also at Appendix 2. —**twelfth** /twɛlfθ/ *pron., det., adv.* ☞ Look at the examples at **sixth**. For more information on numbers, look at Appendix 2.

☆**twen·ty** /'twɛnti/ *number* 20; one more than nineteen ☞ For examples of how to use numbers in sentences, look at **sixty**. —**twen·ti·eth** /'twɛntiəθ/ *pron., det., adv.* ☞ Look at the examples at **sixth**.

☆**twice** /twaɪs/ *adv.* two times: *I've been to Mexico twice – once last year and once in 1984.* ○ *The movie will be shown twice daily.* ○ *Take the medicine twice a day.* ○ *Prices have risen twice as fast in this country as in Japan.*
IDM think twice (about sth/before doing sth) ⇨ THINK

twig /twɪg/ *noun* [C] a small thin branch on a tree or bush ☞ picture at **tree**.

twi·light /'twaɪlaɪt/ *noun* [U] the time after the sun has set and before it gets completely dark

☆**twin¹** /twɪn/ *noun* [C] one of two children or animals that are born to the same mother at the same time: *They look very much alike. Are they twins?* ○ *a twin brother/sister* ○ *identical twins*

twin² /twɪn/ *adj.* (only *before* a noun) **1** that is the same as, or very similar to, another thing: *the twin towers of the World Trade Center* **2** (*also* **'twin-size**) (used about a bed or a blanket, etc. for a bed) big enough for one person ☞ Look at the note at **bed¹**.

twinge /twɪndʒ/ *noun* [C] **a twinge (of sth)** **1** a sudden thought or feeling: *a twinge of fear* **2** a sudden short pain

twin·kle /'twɪŋkl/ *verb* [I] **1** to shine with a light that seems to be moving: *Stars twinkled in the night sky.* **2** (used about your eyes) to look bright because you are happy —**twin·kle** *noun* [sing.]: *From the twinkle in her eyes, we knew she was joking.*

twirl /twɜrl/ *verb* **1** [I] to spin or turn around, e.g. when you are dancing **2** [T] to twist or turn sth

☆**twist¹** /twɪst/ *verb* **1** [I,T] to turn yourself or a part of your body: *She twisted around to reach the switch behind her.* ○ *He kept twisting his head from side to side.* **2** [I,T] to turn or make sth turn into a shape or position that is not normal: *The metal twisted into strange shapes.* ○ *He twisted his knee while he was playing basketball.* **3** [T] to turn sth in a particular direction: *Twist the knob as far as it will go.* **4** [I] (used about a road, etc.) to change direction often: *a narrow, twisting driveway* **5** [T] to wind sth around and around an object: *I twisted the bandage around her knee.* **6** [T] to change the meaning of what sb said: *She claimed that the reporter had twisted her words.*

IDM twist sb's arm (*informal*) to force or persuade sb to do sth

twist² /twɪst/ *noun* [C] **1** an act of twisting sth: *She killed the chicken with one twist of its neck.* **2** a place where sth has become twisted: *Straighten out the cord so that there are no twists in it.* **3** a place where a road, river, etc. bends or changes direction: *the twists and turns of the river* **4** a change or development (especially one that you do not expect): *an unexpected twist at the end of the book*

twist·er /'twɪstər/ *noun* [C] (*informal*) = TOR-NADO

twitch /twɪtʃ/ *verb* [I,T] to make a sudden movement; to cause sth to make a sudden movement: *The rabbit twitched and then lay still.* —**twitch** *noun* [C]

☆**two** /tu/ *number* 2; one more than one ☞ Look at **second¹**. For examples of how to use numbers in sentences, look at **six**. Look also at Appendix 2.
IDM in two in or into two pieces: *The plate fell on the floor and broke in two.*

two- /tu/ (in compounds) having two of the thing mentioned: *a two-week vacation*

ty·coon /taɪ'kun/ *noun* [C] a person who is very successful in business and who is rich and powerful

Ty·le·nol /'taɪlənɑl/ *noun* [U] (*trademark*) a common type of medicine, similar to aspirin, that reduces pain and fever

☆**type¹** /taɪp/ *noun* **1** [C] **a type (of sth)** a group of people or things that share certain qualities and that are part of a larger group; a kind or sort: *Which type of paint should you use on metal?* ○ *There are several different types of apartments to choose from.* ○ *That's just the type of situation that you should avoid.* ○ *You meet all types of people in this job.* ○ *the first building of its type in the world* **2** [C] a person of a particular kind: *He's the careful type.* ☞ If you say somebody is not **your type**, you mean that they are not the sort of person that you would be friendly with. Look at **typical**. **3** [U] the letters that you use when you are typing or printing: *The type is too small to read.*

☆**type²** /taɪp/ *verb* [I,T] to write sth using a computer, typewriter, etc.: *Can you type?* ○ *to type a letter* —**typ·ing** *noun* [U]

☆**type·writ·er** /'taɪpraɪtər/ *noun* [C] a machine that you use for writing in print

type·writ·ten /'taɪprɪtn/ *adj.* written using a typewriter

ty·phoid /'taɪfɔɪd/ *noun* [U] a serious disease that can cause death. People get typhoid from bad food or water.

ty·phoon /taɪ'fun/ *noun* [C] a violent tropical storm in the Pacific or Indian Ocean with very strong winds ☞ Look at the note at **storm**.

☆**typ·i·cal** /'tɪpɪkl/ *adj.* **typical (of sb/sth)** having or showing the usual qualities of a particular person, thing or type: *a typical small*

i	ɪ	ɛ	æ	ɑ	ɔ	ʌ	ʊ	u
see	sit	ten	cat	hot	saw	cup	put	too

town ○ *There's no such thing as a typical American* (= they are all different). ○ *Such detailed descriptions are typical of her writing.*

☞ Compare **common**, **traditional** and **typical**. Something that is **common** is found often or in many places: *The robin is a common bird in America.* Something that is **traditional** has strong links with the past: *At the festival, we saw some Native Americans dressed in traditional* (NOT "typical") *costumes.* Something or someone that is **typical** is a good example of a category of people or things: *How much would a typical house cost in this neighborhood?*

☆ **typ·i·cal·ly** /ˈtɪpɪkli/ *adv.* **1** in a usual or normal case: *New employees typically earn around* $6 an hour. **2** in the normal or usual way: *Her comments were typically direct.*

typ·i·fy /ˈtɪpəfaɪ/ *verb* [T] (*pres. part.* **typ·i·fy·ing**; *3rd pers. sing. pres.* **typ·i·fies**; *p.t., p.p.* **typ·i·fied**) to be a typical example of sb/sth: *Larry's answer typified the attitudes of most students.*

ty·po /ˈtaɪpoʊ/ *noun* [C] (*pl.* **ty·pos**) a small mistake in sth that has been typed on a computer or typewriter

tyr·an·ny /ˈtɪrəni/ *noun* [U] the cruel and unfair use of power by a person or small group to govern a country or state —**ty·ran·ni·cal** /tɪˈrænɪkl/ *adj.: a tyrannical ruler*

ty·rant /ˈtaɪrənt/ *noun* [C] a cruel ruler who has complete power over the people in his/her country ☞ Look at **dictator**.

tyre /ˈtaɪər/ *noun* [C] (*BrE*) = TIRE[1]

Uu

U,u /yu/ *noun* [C] (*pl.* **U's**; **u's** /yuz/) the twenty-first letter of the English alphabet: *"Ulcer" begins with (a) "U."*

ud·der /ˈʌdər/ *noun* [C] the part of a female cow, goat, etc. that hangs like a bag between its back legs and produces milk

UFO /ˌyu ɛf ˈoʊ/ *noun* [C] (*pl.* **UFO's** or **UFOs**) unidentified flying object; a mysterious object that some people say they have seen in the sky, and that they believe may be a spacecraft from another planet: *Have you ever seen a UFO?*

ugh /ʌg; ʌh/ *interj.* (used in writing to express the sound that you make when you think sth is very unpleasant)

☆ **ug·ly** /ˈʌgli/ *adj.* (**ug·li·er**; **ug·li·est**) **1** unpleasant to look at or listen to; unattractive: *an ugly scar on her face* ○ *an ugly modern office building* **2** (used about a situation) dangerous or threatening: *The situation turned ugly when people started throwing stones.* —**ug·li·ness** *noun* [U]

uh /ʌ/ (*also* **um**) *interj.* (used in writing to show that sb cannot decide what to say next): *Well, uh, I guess it's, uh, about five miles away.*

uh-huh /ʌˈhʌ/ *interj.* (used in informal speech to say "yes" or to show that you understand or agree with sth): *"Do you see what I mean?" "Uh-huh."* ☞ Look at the note at **yes**.

uh-oh /ˈʌ oʊ/ *interj.* (used when you make a mistake or when you notice that there has been a small accident): *Uh-oh. I don't think this ink stain is going to come out.*

uh-uh /ˈʌ ʌ; ˈm m/ *interj.* (used in informal speech to say "no" or to show that you disagree with sth): *"Do you want any more chicken?" "Uh-uh. I'm full."*

ul·cer /ˈʌlsər/ *noun* [C] a painful area on your skin or inside your body. Ulcers may produce a poisonous substance and sometimes bleed: *a stomach ulcer*

ul·te·ri·or /ʌlˈtɪriər/ *adj.*

▨ **an ulterior motive** a hidden or secret reason for doing sth: *Why is he suddenly being so nice to me? He must have an ulterior motive.*

ul·ti·mate[1] /ˈʌltəmət/ *adj.* (only *before* a noun) **1** being or happening at the end; last or final: *Our ultimate goal is complete independence.* **2** the **ultimate** the greatest, best or worst: *For me, the ultimate luxury is to stay in bed until noon on a Sunday.*

ul·ti·mate[2] /ˈʌltəmət/ *noun* [sing.] **the ultimate (in sth)** (*informal*) the greatest or best: *This new car is the ultimate in comfort.*

ul·ti·mate·ly /ˈʌltəmətli/ *adv.* **1** in the end: *Whatever decision we ultimately make will be in the best interests of the school.* **2** at the most basic level: *Ultimately, this discussion is not about quality but about money.*

ul·ti·ma·tum /ˌʌltəˈmeɪtəm/ *noun* [C] (*pl.* **ul·ti·ma·tums**) a warning to a person or country that, if they do not do what you ask, you will use force or take action against them: *to issue an ultimatum to sb*

ultra- /ˈʌltrə/ (in compounds) extremely: *ultraconservative*

ul·tra·vi·o·let /ˌʌltrəˈvaɪələt/ *adj.* of a type of

ə	y	w	t̬	eɪ	aɪ	ɔɪ	aʊ	oʊ
about	yes	woman	butter	say	five	boy	now	go

light that causes your skin to turn darker and that can be dangerous in large amounts

um /ʌm; m/ *interj.* = UH

um·bil·i·cal cord /ʌmˈbɪlɪkl kɔrd/ *noun* [C] (*medical*) the tube that connects a baby to its mother before it is born

☆ **um·brel·la** /ʌmˈbrɛlə/ *noun* [C] an object that you carry to keep you dry when it is raining. An umbrella consists of a piece of cloth on a frame and a long handle. You can fold an umbrella up when you are not using it: *to open/close an umbrella*

um·pire /ˈʌmpaɪər/ *noun* [C] a person who watches a game such as baseball or tennis to make sure that the players obey the rules ☛ picture at **tennis**. Look also at **referee**. —**um·pire** *verb* [I,T]

ump·teen /ˈʌmptin/ *pron., det.* (*informal*) very many; a lot: *I've told you umpteen times to call me if you're going to be late.* —**ump·teenth** /ˈʌmptinθ/ *pron., det.*: *For the umpteenth time – call if you're going to be late!*

UN /ˌyu ˈɛn/ *abbr.* = UNITED NATIONS

☆ **un·a·ble** /ʌnˈeɪbl/ *adj.* (not before a noun) **unable to do sth** not having the time, knowledge, skill, etc to do sth; not able to do sth: *Thank you for the invitation. Unfortunately, I will be unable to attend.* ☛ The noun is **inability**.

un·ac·cept·a·ble /ˌʌnəkˈsɛptəbl/ *adj.* that you cannot accept or allow —**un·ac·cept·a·bly** /-bli/ *adv.*

un·ac·com·pa·nied /ˌʌnəˈkʌmpənid/ *adj.* alone; without sb/sth else going too: *unaccompanied children*

un·af·fect·ed /ˌʌnəˈfɛktəd/ *adj.* **unaffected (by sth)** not changed by sth: *Our department will be unaffected by the decision.*

un·aid·ed /ˌʌnˈeɪdəd/ *adv.* without any help

un·A·mer·i·can /ˌʌnəˈmɛrɪkən/ *adj.* (used about behavior, ideas, etc.) not supporting beliefs or ways of doing things that are considered typically American, e.g. freedom, honesty, a free economic system, etc.: *He says it's just un-American to restrict gun ownership.*

u·nan·i·mous /yuˈnænəməs/ *adj.* **1** (used about a group of people) all agreeing about sth: *The members of the jury were unanimous in their decision.* **2** (used about a decision, etc.) agreed on by everybody —**u·nan·i·mous·ly** *adv.*

un·armed /ˌʌnˈɑrmd/ *adj.* having no guns, knives, etc.; not armed

un·as·sum·ing /ˌʌnəˈsumɪŋ/ *adj.* not wishing to be noticed by other people

un·at·tached /ˌʌnəˈtætʃt/ *adj.* **1** not connected to sb/sth else: *This group is unattached to any political party.* **2** not married or in a serious romantic relationship

un·at·tend·ed /ˌʌnəˈtɛndəd/ *adj.* not watched; alone: *Baggage should not be left unattended at the airport.*

un·at·trac·tive /ˌʌnəˈtræktɪv/ *adj.* **1** ugly; not beautiful **2** not favorable; that does not interest you: *an unattractive business offer*

un·au·thor·ized /ˌʌnˈɔθəraɪzd/ *adj.* done without permission

un·a·vail·a·ble /ˌʌnəˈveɪləbl/ *adj.* not available: *The replacement parts are unavailable until June.* ○ *The Senator was unavailable for comment yesterday.*

un·a·void·a·ble /ˌʌnəˈvɔɪdəbl/ *adj.* that cannot be avoided or prevented —**un·a·void·a·bly** /-əbli/ *adv.*: *We were unavoidably delayed.*

un·a·ware /ˌʌnəˈwɛr/ *adj.* (not before a noun) **unaware (of sb/sth)** not knowing about or not noticing sb/sth: *She seemed unaware of all the trouble she had caused.*

un·bal·anced /ˌʌnˈbælənst/ *adj.* **1** (used about a person) somewhat crazy **2** not fair to all ideas or sides of an argument: *an unbalanced newspaper report*

un·bear·a·ble /ˌʌnˈbɛrəbl/ *adj.* too bad, painful, etc. for you to accept —**un·bear·a·bly** /-əbli/ *adv.*: *It was unbearably hot.*

un·beat·a·ble /ˌʌnˈbitəbl/ *adj.* that cannot be defeated or improved on: *The Chicago Bulls seemed unbeatable in the championship tournament.* ○ *We offer you top quality at unbeatable prices!*

un·beat·en /ˌʌnˈbitn/ *adj.* that has not been beaten or improved on: *Her world record remains unbeaten.*

☆ **un·be·liev·a·ble** /ˌʌnbɪˈlivəbl/ *adj.* very surprising; difficult to believe ☛ Look at **incredible**. —**un·be·liev·a·bly** /-bli/ *adj.*: *unbelievably bad*

un·born /ˌʌnˈbɔrn/ *adj.* not yet born: *Smoking can damage your unborn child.*

un·bro·ken /ˌʌnˈbroʊkən/ *adj.* **1** continuous; not interrupted: *a period of unbroken silence* **2** that has not been beaten: *His record for the most home runs in a season remains unbroken.*

un·but·ton /ˌʌnˈbʌtn/ *verb* [T] to open a piece of clothing that had been fastened with buttons

un·called-for /ʌnˈkɔld fɔr/ *adj.* not necessary or right: *That comment was totally uncalled-for.*

un·can·ny /ʌnˈkæni/ *adj.* strange and mysterious; that you cannot easily explain

☆ **un·cer·tain** /ʌnˈsərtn/ *adj.* **1 uncertain (about/of sth)** not sure; not able to decide: *She was still uncertain of his true feelings for her.* ○ *Chris seemed uncertain about what to do next.* **2** not known exactly or not decided: *He lost his job and his future seems very uncertain.* —**un·cer·tain·ly** *adv.*: *Kate stood uncertainly, waiting for someone to talk to her.* —**un·cer·tain·ty** /ʌnˈsərtnti/ *noun* [C,U] (*pl.* **un·cer·tain·ties**): *Today's decision will put an end to all the uncertainty.*

un·changed /ʌnˈtʃeɪndʒd/ *adj.* staying the

U

same; not changed: *The house has remained almost unchanged since the nineteenth century.*

un·char·ac·ter·is·tic /ˌʌnˌkærəktəˈrɪstɪk/ *adj.* not typical or usual —**un·char·ac·ter·is·tic·al·ly** /-kli/ *adv.*

☆ **un·cle** /ˈʌŋkl/ *noun* [C] **1** the brother of your father or mother: *my Uncle Steven* **2** the husband of your aunt ☞ Look at **aunt.**

☆ **un·clear** /ˌʌnˈklɪr/ *adj.* not easy to see, hear, know or understand: *It is unclear how the local economy will be affected by this decision.*

Uncle Sam /ˌʌŋkl ˈsæm/ *noun* [U] the U.S. government, often represented by a picture of an old man who wears a tall hat and a red, white and blue suit: *Jessica owes Uncle Sam $500 in income taxes.*

☆ **un·com·fort·a·ble** /ʌnˈkʌmftəbl; ʌnˈkʌmfərṭəbl/ *adj.* **1** not pleasant to wear, sit in, lie on, etc.: *The chairs are hard and very uncomfortable.* **2** not able to sit, lie, etc. in a position that is pleasant: *I was very uncomfortable for most of the trip.* **3** feeling or causing worry or embarrassment: *I felt very uncomfortable when they started arguing in front of me.* —**un·com·fort·a·bly** /-əbli/ *adv.*

☆ **un·com·mon** /ʌnˈkamən/ *adj.* unusual: *Snowstorms are not uncommon* (= they are fairly common) *in this part of the country.*

com·pro·mis·ing /ʌnˈkamprəmaɪzɪŋ/ *adj.* not willing to discuss sth or change a decision

un·con·cerned /ˌʌnkənˈsərnd/ *adj.* not interested in sth or not worried about it

un·con·di·tion·al /ˌʌnkənˈdɪʃənl/ *adj.* without limits or conditions: *an unconditional surrender* —**un·con·di·tion·al·ly** /-ʃənəli/ *adv.*

un·con·firmed /ˌʌnkənˈfərmd/ *adj.* not official; that may not be true or correct: *There have been unconfirmed reports of a tornado in Brown County.*

☆ **un·con·scious** /ʌnˈkanʃəs/ *adj.* **1** in a state that is like sleep. You may be unconscious after an accident if you hit your head: *She was found lying unconscious on the kitchen floor.* **2 unconscious of sb/sth** not knowing or aware of sb/sth: *He seemed unconscious of everything that was going on around him.* —**un·con·scious·ly** *adv.* —**un·con·scious·ness** *noun* [U]

un·con·sti·tu·tion·al /ˌʌnkanstəˈtuʃnl/ *adj.* not in agreement with or allowed by the basic laws (**Constitution**) of a country or state: *The Supreme Court declared the law unconstitutional.*

un·con·trol·la·ble /ˌʌnkənˈtroʊləbl/ *adj.* that you cannot control: *an uncontrollable urge to giggle* —**un·con·trol·la·bly** /-əbli/ *adv.*

un·count·a·ble noun /ˌʌnˌkaʊntəbl ˈnaʊn/ *(also* **noncount noun**) *noun* [C] *(grammar)* a noun that cannot be counted and so does not have a plural form in English, e.g. "air," "water" or "information." Uncountable nouns are marked "[U]" in this dictionary.

un·cov·er /ʌnˈkʌvər/ *verb* [T] **1** to remove the cover from sth **2** to find out or discover sth

un·de·cid·ed /ˌʌndɪˈsaɪdəd/ *adj.* **1** not having made a decision: *10% of voters were still undecided about the candidates for governor.* **2** without any result or decision; not decided: *The future of our jobs is still undecided.*

un·de·ni·a·ble /ˌʌndɪˈnaɪəbl/ *adj.* clear, true or certain: *an undeniable link between smoking and cancer* —**un·de·ni·a·bly** /-əbli/ *adv.*

under/below

a cat asleep **under** a table a letter **under** a book

a T-shirt **under** his sweater a shelf **below** a clock

☆ **un·der¹** /ˈʌndər/ *prep.* **1** in or to a position that is below or beneath sth: *Put the suitcase under the bed.* ○ *to hide under the table* ○ *The dog crawled under the fence and ran into the street.*

☞ Compare **under, below, beneath** and **underneath.** You use **under** to say that one thing is directly under another thing. There may be a space between the two things: *The cat is asleep under the table.* or one thing may be touching or covered by the other thing: *I think your letter is under that book.* You can use **below** to say that one thing is in a lower position than another thing when they are both in the same building, on the same part of the body, etc.: *They live on the floor below us.* ○ *It hurts here – just below my knee.* ○ *The phone book is on the shelf below the cookbooks.* You use **under** (not **below**) to talk about movement from one side of something to the other side: *We swam under the bridge.* You can use **beneath** to say that one thing is directly under another thing, but **under** is more common. **Beneath** is a more formal word. You can use **underneath** in place of **under** when you want to emphasize that something is being covered or hidden by another thing: *Did you look underneath the sofa as well as behind it?*

2 below the surface of sth; covered by sth: *Most of an iceberg is under the water.* ○ *Are you wearing a T-shirt under your sweater?* **3** younger than: *Nobody under twenty-one is allowed to buy alcohol.* **4** less than: *People*

tʃ	dʒ	v	θ	ð	s	z	ʃ
chin	**June**	**van**	**thin**	**then**	**so**	**zoo**	**she**

U

earning under $20,000 a year are eligible for financial assistance. **5** working for or in the control of sb: *This hotel is under new management.* **6** ruled or governed by sb/sth: *The country is now under martial law.* **7** according to a law, agreement, system, etc.: *Under our judicial system, you are considered innocent until you are proven guilty.* **8** in a particular state or condition: *under the influence of alcohol* ○ *a building under construction* ○ *I was under the impression that Bill was not very happy here.* **9** found in a particular part of a book, list, etc: *You'll find some information on Budapest under "Hungary."*

☆ **un·der²** /ˈʌndər/ *adv.* **1** below the surface of water: *I saw him struggling for a while before his head went under.* **2** less; younger: *The prices quoted are for children age 12 and under.*

un·der·class·man /ˌʌndərˈklæsmən/ *noun* [C] (*pl.* **un·der·class·men** /-mən/) a student who is in his/her first or second year in high school or college ☞ Look at **upperclassman**.

un·der·cov·er /ˌʌndərˈkʌvər/ *adj.* working or happening secretly: *an undercover agent* (= a spy)

un·der·cut /ˌʌndərˈkʌt/ *verb* [T] (*pres. part.* **un·der·cut·ting**; *p.t., p.p.* **un·der·cut**) **1** to sell at a lower price than other stores, etc.: *Big discounts chains can undercut smaller stores.* **2** to weaken sb's authority or make sth less effective: *efforts to undercut the President's welfare reform plan* ☞ Look at **undermine**. It has a similar meaning.

un·der·dog /ˈʌndərdɔg/ *noun* [C] a person who is in a weak position and is expected to lose a competition

un·der·es·ti·mate /ˌʌndərˈɛstəmeɪt/ *verb* [T] **1** to guess that the amount, etc. of sth will be less than it really is: *We underestimated the amount of food we would need.* **2** to think that sb/sth is not as strong, etc. as he/she/it really is: *Don't underestimate your opponent. She's a really good player.* ☞ The opposite is **overestimate**.

un·der·go /ˌʌndərˈgoʊ/ *verb* [T] (*p.t.* **un·der·went** /-ˈwɛnt/; *p.p.* **un·der·gone** /-ˈgɔn; -ˈgɑn/) to have a difficult or bad experience: *She underwent a five-hour operation.*

☆ **un·der·grad·u·ate** /ˌʌndərˈgrædʒuət/ (also *informal* **un·der·grad** /ˈʌndərgræd/) *noun* [C] a college or university student who has not yet earned his/her first (**bachelor's**) degree ☞ Look at **graduate**.

☆ **un·der·ground¹** /ˈʌndərgraʊnd/ *adj.* **1** under the surface of the ground: *an underground parking garage* **2** secret or illegal: *an underground radio station that supports the militia movement*

☆ **un·der·ground²** /ˌʌndərˈgraʊnd/ *adv.* **1** under the surface of the ground: *The cables all run underground.* **2** into a secret place: *She went underground to escape from the police.*

un·der·ground³ /ˈʌndərgraʊnd/ *noun* [C] (*BrE*) = SUBWAY

un·der·growth /ˈʌndərgroʊθ/ *noun* [U] bushes and plants that grow around and under trees

un·der·handed /ˈʌndərhændəd/ *adj.* secret or not honest

☆ **un·der·line** /ˈʌndərlaɪn/ *verb* [T] **1** to draw a line under a word, etc.: *Underline the subject of each sentence.* **2** to show clearly or to emphasize sth: *This accident underlines the need for more safety inspections.*

un·der·ly·ing /ˈʌndərlaɪɪŋ/ *adj.* (only *before* a noun) important but hidden: *the underlying causes of the disaster*

un·der·mine /ˈʌndərmaɪn; ˌʌndərˈmaɪn/ *verb* [T] to make sth weaker: *The public's trust in the police has been undermined.*

☆ **un·der·neath** /ˌʌndərˈniθ/ *prep., adv.* under or below: *The coin rolled underneath the chair.* ○ *This sweater's not very warm, but I have a T-shirt on underneath.* ☞ Look at the note at **under**.

un·der·paid /ˌʌndərˈpeɪd/ *adj.* paid too little

☆ **un·der·pants** /ˈʌndərpænts/ *noun* [plural] a piece of clothing that you wear under your pants or skirt ☞ picture on page A26. Look also at **panties** and **shorts** (2).

un·der·pass /ˈʌndərpæs/ *noun* [C] a road or path that goes under another road, etc.

un·der·priv·i·leged /ˌʌndərˈprɪvəlɪdʒd/ *adj.* having less money and fewer rights, opportunities, etc. than other people in society

un·der·rated /ˌʌndəˈreɪtəd/ *adj.* that people think is less intelligent, important, good, etc. than he/she/it really is

☆ **un·der·shirt** /ˈʌndərʃərt/ *noun* [C] a piece of clothing that you wear on the top part of your body, under your other clothes ☞ picture on page A26.

☆ **un·der·stand** /ˌʌndərˈstænd/ *verb* (*p.t., p.p.* **un·der·stood** /-ˈstʊd/) **1** [I,T] to get the meaning of sb/sth: *I'm not sure that I really understand.* ○ *I didn't understand the instructions.* ○ *Please speak more slowly. I can't understand you.* ○ *He can understand Italian, but he can't speak it.* **2** [T] to know how or why sth happens: *I can't understand why the engine won't start.* **3** [T] to know why sb behaves in a particular way and to feel sympathy: *It's easy to understand why she felt so mad.* ○ *His parents don't understand him.* **4** [T] (*formal*) to have heard or been told sth: *I understand that you have decided to leave.* **5** [T] to judge a situation, etc.: *As far as I understand it, the changes won't affect us.*

IDM **make yourself understood** to make your meaning clear: *I can just about make myself understood in Russian.*

un·der·stand·a·ble /ˌʌndərˈstændəbl/ *adj.* that you can understand —**un·der·stand·a·bly**

U

/-əbli/ *adv.*: *She was understandably angry about the decision.*

☆ **un·der·stand·ing¹** /ˌʌndərˈstændɪŋ/ *noun*
1 [U] the ability to think or learn about sth: *The book is beyond the understanding of most ten-year-olds.* **2** [U, sing.] knowledge of a subject, how sth works, etc.: *A basic understanding of physics is necessary for this course.* **3** [U, sing.] the ability to feel sympathy and trust for sb: *understanding between nations* **4** [U] the way in which you think sth is meant: *My understanding of the arrangement is that he will only call if there is a problem.* **5** [C, usually sing.] an informal agreement: *We came to an understanding about the money I owed him.*

☆ **un·der·stand·ing²** /ˌʌndərˈstændɪŋ/ *adj.* kind; showing sympathy toward sb

un·der·state /ˌʌndərˈsteɪt/ *verb* [T] to say that sth is smaller or less important than it really is

un·der·stat·ed /ˌʌndərˈsteɪt̮əd/ *adj.* done in a very controlled way that seems appropriate and shows good taste: *the understated elegance of the furniture in their home*

un·der·state·ment /ˈʌndərsteɪtmənt/ *noun* [C] a statement that does not show how big, important, etc. sth really is: *"Is she pleased?" "That's an understatement. She's delighted."*

un·der·stood *p.t., p.p.* of UNDERSTAND

un·der·stud·y /ˈʌndərstʌdi/ *noun* [C] (*pl.* **un·der·stud·ies**) an actor who learns the role of another actor and replaces him/her if he/she is sick

un·der·take /ˌʌndərˈteɪk/ *verb* [T] (*p.t.* **un·der·took** /-ˈtʊk/; *p.p.* **un·der·tak·en** /-ˈteɪkən/) to carry out: *The state is undertaking a major welfare reform plan.*

un·der·tak·er /ˈʌndərteɪkər/ *noun* [C] = FUNERAL DIRECTOR

un·der·tak·ing /ˈʌndərteɪkɪŋ/ *noun* [C, usually sing.] a piece of work or business: *a risky undertaking*

un·der·tone /ˈʌndərtoʊn/ *noun* [C] a feeling or attitude that is not directly expressed

un·der·wa·ter /ˌʌndərˈwɔt̮ər, -ˈwɑ-/ *adj., adv.* existing, happening or used below the surface of water: *underwater exploration* ○ *an underwater camera* ○ *Can you swim underwater?*

☆ **un·der·wear** /ˈʌndərwɛr/ *noun* [U] clothing that is worn next to the skin under other clothes

un·der·weight /ˌʌndərˈweɪt/ *adj.* weighing less than is normal or correct ☞ Look at the note at **thin**.

un·der·world /ˈʌndərwərld/ *noun* [sing.] usually **the underworld** people who are involved in crime

un·de·sir·a·ble /ˌʌndɪˈzaɪrəbl/ *adj.* unwanted or unpleasant; likely to cause problems

un·did *p.t.* of UNDO

un·dis·closed /ˌʌndɪsˈkloʊzd/ *adj.* (only before a noun) that is not known by the public: *Negotiations are taking place at an undisclosed location.*

un·di·vid·ed /ˌʌndɪˈvaɪdəd/ *adj.*
IDM **get/have sb's undivided attention** to receive sb's full attention

☆ **un·do** /ʌnˈdu/ *verb* [T] (*3rd pers. sing. pres.* **un·does**; *p.t.* **un·did**; *p.p.* **un·done**) **1** to open sth that was tied or fastened: *to undo a knot* **2** to destroy the effect of sth that has already happened: *The damage cannot be undone.*

un·done /ʌnˈdʌn/ *adj.* **1** open; not fastened or tied: *His necktie was partially undone.* **2** not done: *I left the housework undone.*

un·doubt·ed·ly /ʌnˈdaʊt̮ədli/ *adv.* definitely; without doubt: *It was undoubtedly one of her finest performances.*

☆ **un·dress** /ʌnˈdrɛs/ *verb* **1** [I] (*formal*) to take off your clothes: *I undressed and the doctor examined me.*

☞ **Get undressed** is more commonly used than **undress**: *He got undressed and took a shower.*

2 [T] to take off sb's clothes: *She undressed the child and put her into bed.* —**un·dressed** *adj.*: *He came to the door partially undressed.*

un·due /ˌʌnˈdu/ *adj.* (*formal*) (only *before* a noun) more than is necessary or reasonable: *regulations that place an undue burden on small businesses* —**un·du·ly** *adv.*: *She didn't seem unduly worried by their unexpected arrival.*

un·earth /ʌnˈərθ/ *verb* [T] to dig sth up out of the ground; to discover sth that was hidden: *Archaeologists have unearthed a Native American burial site.* ○ (*figurative*) *A journalist unearthed the real story behind the case.*

un·eas·y /ʌnˈizi/ *adj.* **1** worried; not feeling relaxed or comfortable **2** not settled; unlikely to last: *an uneasy compromise* —**un·eas·i·ness** (*also* **un·ease** /ʌnˈiz/) *noun* [U] —**un·eas·i·ly** /ʌnˈizəli/ *adv.*

☆ **un·em·ployed** /ˌʌnɪmˈplɔɪd/ *adj.* **1** not having a job; out of work: *She lost her job six months ago and has been unemployed ever since.* **2 the unemployed** *noun* [plural] the people who do not have a job: *a new training program for the unemployed*

☆ **un·em·ploy·ment** /ˌʌnɪmˈplɔɪmənt/ *noun* [U] **1** the situation of being unemployed: *If the plant closes, many local people will face unemployment.* **2** the number of people who are unemployed: *The unemployment rate rose 0.2% last month.* ○ *cities with high unemployment* **3** (*also formal* **unemployment compensation**) money that the government pays to unemployed people for a certain length of time after they lose their jobs: *people living on unemployment*

un·end·ing /ʌnˈɛndɪŋ/ *adj.* having or seeming to have no end

ə	y	w	t̮	eɪ	aɪ	ɔɪ	aʊ	oʊ
about	yes	woman	butter	say	five	boy	now	go

☆ **un·e·qual** /ˌʌnˈikwəl/ *adj.* **1** different in size, amount, level, etc. **2** not fair or balanced: *It was an unequal contest because he's a much better player than I am.* —**un·e·qual·ly** *adv.*

☆ **un·e·ven** /ˌʌnˈivən/ *adj.* **1** not completely smooth, level or regular: *The sign was painted in uneven letters.* **2** not always of the same level or quality —**un·e·ven·ly** *adv.*: *The country's wealth is unevenly distributed.*

☆ **un·ex·pect·ed** /ˌʌnɪkˈspɛktəd/ *adj.* not expected and therefore causing surprise: *an unexpected development in the case* —**un·ex·pect·ed·ly** *adv.*: *an unexpectedly large increase in the number of people with the disease*

☆ **un·fair** /ˌʌnˈfɛr/ *adj.* **unfair (to sb)** not dealing with people as they deserve; not treating each person equally: *This law is unfair to women.* ○ *It was unfair to blame her for something that was not her fault.* —**un·fair·ly** *adv.* —**un·fair·ness** *noun* [U]

un·faith·ful /ˌʌnˈfeɪθfl/ *adj.* **unfaithful (to sb/sth)** having a sexual relationship with sb who is not your husband, wife or partner: *Have you ever been unfaithful to your husband?*

un·fa·mil·iar /ˌʌnfəˈmɪlyər/ *adj.* **1** unfamiliar (to sb) not well-known to sb: *This part of town is unfamiliar to me.* **2** unfamiliar (with sth) not having knowledge or experience of sth

un·fash·ion·a·ble /ˌʌnˈfæʃn·əbl/ *adj.* not popular: *unfashionable ideas* ☞ Look at **old-fashioned**.

un·fit /ˌʌnˈfɪt/ *adj.* **unfit (for sth/to do sth)** unsuitable or not good enough for sth: *Inspectors said the meat was unfit for human consumption.* ○ *Newspaper reports called her an unfit mother.*

☆ **un·fold** /ʌnˈfoʊld/ *verb* [I,T] **1** to open out and become flat; to open out sth that was folded: *I unfolded the letter and read it.* **2** to become known, or to allow sth to become known a little at a time: *As the story unfolded, more and more surprising things were revealed.*

un·fore·seen /ˌʌnfərˈsin; -fɔr-/ *adj.* (usually *before* a noun) not expected: *an unforeseen problem*

☆ **un·for·get·ta·ble** /ˌʌnfərˈgɛt̮əbl/ *adj.* making such a strong impression that you cannot forget it

☆ **un·for·tu·nate** /ʌnˈfɔrtʃənət/ *adj.* **1** having bad luck: *The unfortunate people who lived near the river lost their homes in the flood.* **2** causing or caused by bad luck: *an unfortunate accident* **3** that you are sorry or embarrassed about: *I would like to apologize for this unfortunate mistake.*

☆ **un·for·tu·nate·ly** /ʌnˈfɔrtʃənətli/ *adv.* unluckily; it is too bad that…: *Unfortunately, there was nothing we could do to help.*

un·found·ed /ˌʌnˈfaʊndəd/ *adj.* not based on or supported by facts: *He said that the rumor was completely unfounded.*

un·friend·ly /ˌʌnˈfrɛndl/ *adj.* unkind or not polite to sb; not friendly

un·grate·ful /ˌʌnˈɡreɪtfl/ *adj.* not feeling or showing thanks (to sb) —**un·grate·ful·ly** *adv.*

☆ **un·hap·py** /ʌnˈhæpi/ *adj.* (**un·hap·pi·er; un·hap·pi·est**) **1** unhappy (about sth) sad or miserable; not happy: *She's very unhappy about losing her job.* ○ *an unhappy childhood* **2** unhappy (about/with sth) not satisfied or pleased; worried: *I'm still unhappy about the way this dress looks.* —**un·hap·pi·ly** /-əli/ *adv.* —**un·hap·pi·ness** *noun* [U]

un·health·y /ʌnˈhɛlθi/ *adj.* (**un·health·i·er; un·health·i·est**) **1** not having or showing good health: *He looks pale and unhealthy.* **2** likely to cause illness or poor health: *unhealthy conditions* **3** not natural: *an unhealthy interest in torture*

un·heard-of /ʌnˈhərdəv/ *adj.* not known; never having happened before: *Years ago, it was unheard-of for women to do jobs like that.*

u·ni·corn /ˈyunəkɔrn/ *noun* [C] an imaginary animal that looks like a white horse and has one horn growing out of its forehead

un·i·den·ti·fied /ˌʌnaɪˈdɛntəfaɪd/ *adj.* whose identity is not known: *An unidentified body has been found in the river.* ☞ Look also at **UFO**.

u·ni·form[1] /ˈyunəfɔrm/ *adj.* not changing; the same in all cases or at all times: *uniform safety standards in all 50 states* —**u·ni·for·mi·ty** /ˌyunəˈfɔrmət̮i/ *noun* [U]

☆ **u·ni·form**[2] /ˈyunəfɔrm/ *noun* [C,U] the set of clothes worn at work by the members of certain organizations or groups and by some students: *Did you have to wear a school uniform?* ○ *I didn't know he was a police officer because he wasn't in uniform.* —**u·ni·formed** *adj.*: *uniformed police officers*

u·ni·fy /ˈyunəfaɪ/ *verb* [T] (*pres. part.* **u·ni·fy·ing**; *3rd pers. sing. pres.* **u·ni·fies**; *p.t., p.p.* **u·ni·fied**) to join or link separate parts together to make one unit, or to make them similar to each other —**u·ni·fi·ca·tion** /ˌyunəfəˈkeɪʃn/ *noun* [U]

un·in·hab·it·a·ble /ˌʌnɪnˈhæbət̮əbl/ *adj.* not possible to live in

un·in·hib·it·ed /ˌʌnɪnˈhɪbət̮əd/ *adj.* behaving in a free and natural way, showing what you feel without worrying what other people think of you

un·in·sured /ˌʌnɪnˈʃʊrd/ *adj.* not having or covered by insurance: *the cost of medical treatment for uninsured patients*

un·in·tel·li·gi·ble /ˌʌnɪnˈtɛlədʒəbl/ *adj.* impossible to understand

un·in·ter·est·ed /ʌnˈɪntrəstəd; ʌnˈɪntɛrɛstəd/ *adj.* **uninterested (in sb/sth)** having or showing no interest in sb/sth: *She seemed uninterested in anything I had to say.* ☞ Look at **disinterested**. It has a different meaning.

ər	ɪr	ɛr	ɑr	ɔr	ʊr	ʒ	h	ŋ
bird	near	hair	car	north	tour	vision	hat	sing

☆ **un·ion** /'yunyən/ *noun* **1** [U, sing.] the act of joining or the situation of being joined: *the union of the separate groups into one organization* **2** [C] a group of people, organizations, countries, etc. that have been joined together to form one larger organization: *the European Union* **3** [C] (*also* **labor union**) an organization for people who do the same type of work. Unions try to get better pay and working conditions for their members.

☆ **u·nique** /yu'nik/ *adj.* **1** unlike anything else; being the only one of its type: *Shakespeare made a unique contribution to the world of literature.* **2** **unique to sb/sth** connected with only one place, person or thing: *This dance is unique to this region.* **3** very unusual: *There's nothing unique about that type of crime.*

u·ni·sex /'yunəsɛks/ *adj.* designed for and used by both men and women: *unisex fashions*

u·ni·son /'yunəsn/ *noun*
IDM **in unison** saying, singing or doing the same thing at the same time as sb else: *"No, thank you," they said in unison.*

☆ **u·nit** /'yunɪt/ *noun* [C] **1** a single thing which is complete in itself and is also part of sth larger: *The book is divided into ten units.* **2** a fixed amount or number that is used as a standard of measurement: *a unit of currency* **3** a group of people who perform a certain special function in a larger organization: *the intensive care unit of a hospital* **4** a small machine that performs a particular task or that is part of a larger machine: *The heart of a computer is the central processing unit.* **5** an apartment in a large building: *There are four two-bedroom units on each floor.* **6** a piece of furniture that can be connected to other pieces of furniture and has a particular use: *metal shelving units*

☆ **u·nite** /yu'naɪt/ *verb* **1** [I,T] to join together and act in agreement; to make this happen: *Unless we unite, our enemies will defeat us.* ○ *The President united his party behind him.* **2** [I] **unite (in sth/in doing sth)** to join together for a particular purpose: *We should all unite in seeking a solution to this terrible problem.*

☆ **u·nit·ed** /yu'naɪṭəd/ *adj.* joined together by a common feeling or aim: *Throughout the crisis, the whole country remained united.*

the U·nited Kingdom *noun* (*abbr.* **U.K.**) England, Scotland, Wales and Northern Ireland

☞ The **UK** includes England, Scotland, Wales and Northern Ireland, but *not* the Republic of Ireland, which is a separate country. **Great Britain** is England, Scotland and Wales only. **The British Isles** include England, Scotland, Wales, Northern Ireland and the Republic of Ireland.

☆ **the U·nited Nations** *noun* [sing.] (*abbr.* **UN**) the organization formed to encourage peace in the world and to deal with problems between nations

☆ **the U·nited States** (also *formal* **the U·nited States of A·merica**) *noun* [sing.] (*abbr.* **U.S.**; **US; USA**) a large country in North America made up of 50 states and the District of Columbia

☆ **u·ni·ty** /'yunəṭi/ *noun* [U] the situation in which people are united or in agreement

☆ **u·ni·ver·sal** /,yunə'vərsl/ *adj.* connected with, done by or affecting everybody in the world or everybody in a particular group: *The environment is a universal concern.* ○ *There was universal agreement that the festival was a success.* —**u·ni·ver·sal·ly** *adv.*

☆ **u·ni·verse** /'yunəvərs/ *noun* [sing.] **the universe** everything that exists, including the planets, stars, space, etc.

☆ **u·ni·ver·si·ty** /,yunə'vərsəṭi/ *noun* [C] (*pl.* **u·ni·ver·si·ties**) the highest level of educational institution, where students study for degrees and where people do academic research

☞ Compare **college** and **university**. In general, **colleges** offer courses for students who are studying for their first (*bachelor's*) degrees, while **universities** also offer courses for people who are studying for more advanced degrees. Note that we use **college**, not **university**, in many expressions even when the place we are talking about has the word "University" in its name: *a college student* ○ *"Where did you go to college?" "At Ohio State University."*

un·just /,ʌn'dʒʌst/ *adj.* not fair, right or reasonable: *an unjust legal system* ☞ The noun is **injustice**.

☆ **un·kind** /,ʌn'kaɪnd/ *adj.* not friendly or thoughtful; cruel: *That was an unkind thing to say.* —**un·kind·ly** *adv.* —**un·kind·ness** *noun* [C,U]

☆ **un·known¹** /,ʌn'noʊn/ *adj.* **1** unknown (to sb) not known (by sb): *She left the job for unknown reasons.* **2** not famous or familiar to other people: *an unknown actress*

un·known² /,ʌn'noʊn/ *noun* **1** usually **the unknown** [sing.] a place or thing that you know nothing about: *a fear of the unknown* **2** [C] a person who is not well-known by the public: *A complete unknown won the tournament.*

un·law·ful /,ʌn'lɔfl/ *adj.* (*formal*) against the law; illegal: *He was charged with unlawful possession of a handgun.*

un·lead·ed /,ʌn'lɛdəd/ *adj.* (used about gasoline) not containing the harmful substance, lead

☆ **un·less** /ən'lɛs/ *conj.* if…not; except if: *Unless something unexpected happens, I'll see you next week.* ○ *I was told that unless my work improved, I would lose the job.* ○ *Unless anyone*

tʃ	dʒ	v	θ	ð	s	z	ʃ
chin	June	van	thin	then	so	zoo	she

has anything else to say, the meeting is finished. ○ *Don't use the oven unless I'm here.* ○ *That's what I've decided to do – unless there are any objections.*

☆ **un·like** /ˌʌnˈlaɪk/ *prep.* **1** in contrast to; being different from: *Unlike all the others, I wasn't very interested in the idea.* ○ *He's extremely ambitious, unlike me.* ○ *She's unlike anyone else I've ever met.* **2** not typical of; unusual for: *It's unlike him to be late – he's usually right on time.*

☆ **un·like·ly** /ˌʌnˈlaɪkli/ *adj.* (**un·like·li·er; un·like·li·est**) **1** not likely to happen; not expected; not probable: *He is seriously ill and unlikely to recover.* ○ *In the unlikely event of a fire, use the emergency exits.* ○ *It's unlikely that I'll have any free time next week.* **2** difficult to believe: *an unlikely excuse*

un·lim·it·ed /ˌʌnˈlɪmətəd/ *adj.* without limit; as much or as great as you want

un·list·ed /ˌʌnˈlɪstəd/ *adj.* (used about a telephone number) not included in the list of telephone numbers in the telephone book so that it is not known by the public

☆ **un·load** /ˌʌnˈloʊd/ *verb* **1** [I,T] **unload (sth) (from/off sth)** to take things that have been transported off or out of a vehicle: *to unload freight off a truck* ○ *I unloaded the car when I got home from the mall.* **2** [I,T] (used about a vehicle) to have the things removed that have been transported: *Parking here is restricted to vehicles that are loading or unloading.* **3** [T] **unload sb/sth (on/onto sb)** (*informal*) to get rid of sth you do not want or to pass it to sb else

☆ **un·lock** /ˌʌnˈlɑk/ *verb* [T] to open the lock on sth using a key

☆ **un·luck·y** /ˌʌnˈlʌki/ *adj.* (**un·luck·i·er; un·luck·i·est**) having or causing bad luck; not lucky: *They were unlucky to lose because they played so well.* ○ *Thirteen is often thought to be an unlucky number.*

un·mar·ried /ˌʌnˈmærid/ *adj.* not married; single: *unmarried mothers*

un·mis·tak·a·ble /ˌʌnmɪˈsteɪkəbl/ *adj.* clear and obvious; easy to recognize —**un·mis·tak·a·bly** /-əbli/ *adv.*

un·moved /ˌʌnˈmuvd/ *adj.* not affected emotionally; feeling no sympathy, pity, sadness etc.

un·nat·u·ral /ʌnˈnætʃərəl/ *adj.* different from what is normal or expected; not natural, often in a way that seems morally wrong —**un·nat·u·ral·ly** *adv.*: *unnaturally quiet*

☆ **un·nec·es·sar·y** /ʌnˈnɛsəˌsɛri/ *adj.* not necessary; more than is needed or acceptable: *It was unnecessary to ask because I already knew the answer.* ○ *unnecessary expense* —**un·nec·es·sar·i·ly** /ʌnˌnɛsəˈsɛrəli/ *adv.*: *unnecessarily expensive*

un·no·ticed /ˌʌnˈnoʊṭəst/ *adj.* not noticed or

seen: *All my hard work went completely unnoticed.*

☆ **un·of·fi·cial** /ˌʌnəˈfɪʃl/ *adj.* **1** not accepted or approved by a person or people in authority: *an unofficial strike* **2** not known by the public: *The news of his resignation is still unofficial.* —**un·of·fi·cial·ly** *adv.*

un·or·tho·dox /ˌʌnˈɔrθədɑks/ *adj.* different from what is generally accepted, usual or traditional: *unorthodox medical treatments*

un·pack /ˌʌnˈpæk/ *verb* [I,T] to take out the things that were in a bag, suitcase, etc.: *When we got to the hotel, we unpacked and went straight to the beach.* ○ *to unpack a suitcase*

un·paid /ˌʌnˈpeɪd/ *adj.* **1** not yet paid: *an unpaid bill* **2** not receiving money for work done: *an unpaid assistant* **3** (used about work) done without payment: *unpaid overtime*

☆ **un·pleas·ant** /ʌnˈplɛznt/ *adj.* (*formal*) **1** causing you to have a bad feeling; not pleasant: *unpleasant memories* **2** not friendly; not polite: *unpleasant coworkers*

un·plug /ˌʌnˈplʌg/ *verb* [T] (**un·plug·ging; un·plugged**) to disconnect a piece of electrical equipment by removing the plug from the socket: *Be sure to unplug the iron when you're done with it.*

☆ **un·pop·u·lar** /ˌʌnˈpɑpyələr/ *adj.* **unpopular (with sb)** not popular; not liked by many people: *an unpopular politician* ○ *a product that was unpopular with consumers* —**un·pop·u·lar·i·ty** /ˌʌnˌpɑpyəˈlærəṭi/ *noun* [U]

un·prec·e·dent·ed /ˌʌnˈprɛsədɛntəd/ *adj.* never having happened or existed before, or greater than anything that has happened or existed before: *an unprecedented number of visitors to the fair*

un·pre·dict·a·ble /ˌʌnprɪˈdɪktəbl/ *adj.* changing often so that you do not know what to expect: *unpredictable behavior*

un·pro·tec·ted /ˌʌnprəˈtɛktəd/ *adj.* not safe; that could be harmed or that could harm sb/sth

IDM unprotected sex sex that could cause a sexual disease such as AIDS to be passed from one person to another, e.g. because of not using a condom

un·pro·voked /ˌʌnprəˈvoʊkt/ *adj.* not caused by an earlier action: *an unprovoked attack*

un·qual·i·fied /ʌnˈkwɑləfaɪd/ *adj.* **1** not having the qualifications or knowledge for sth: *unqualified job applicants* ○ *Most applicants were unqualified for the job.* ○ *I'm unqualified to offer an opinion on this matter.* **2** (only before a noun) (*formal*) complete; absolute: *an unqualified success*

un·ques·tion·a·ble /ʌnˈkwɛstʃənəbl/ *adj.* certain; that cannot be doubted —**un·ques·tion·a·bly** /-əbli/ *adv.*: *She is unquestionably the richest woman in the world.*

un·rav·el /ʌnˈrævəl/ *verb* [I,T] **1** (used about threads or fabric) to start to come apart: *The*

i	ɪ	ɛ	æ	ɑ	ɔ	ʌ	ʊ	u
see	sit	ten	cat	hot	saw	cup	put	too

sleeve of my sweater started to unravel. **2** (used about a complicated story, etc.) to become or to make sth become clear: *detectives trying to unravel the mystery of her disappearance*

un·real /ˌʌnˈril/ *adj.* **1** (usually not before a noun) very strange and seeming to be imagined: *The whole situation was really weird – it just seemed so unreal.* **2** not real; imagined: *His theory only works under unreal conditions.*

un·re·al·is·tic /ˌʌnriəˈlɪstɪk/ *adj.* not based on facts or accepting a situation as it really is: *unrealistic expectations*

un·rea·son·a·ble /ʌnˈriznəbl/ *adj.* **1** not willing to listen to other people; acting without good reasons: *I think she is being totally unreasonable.* **2** too great; expecting too much: *He makes unreasonable demands on his employees.* —**un·rea·son·a·bly** /-əbli/ *adv.*

un·re·li·a·ble /ˌʌnrɪˈlaɪəbl/ *adj.* that you cannot trust or depend on: *an unreliable source of information*

un·rest /ˌʌnˈrɛst/ *noun* [U] a situation in which people are angry or dissatisfied and likely to protest or fight: *social unrest*

un·ri·valed /ʌnˈraɪvld/ *adj.* better than any other of the same type; having no rival: *The hotel offers guests an unrivaled view of the coastline.*

un·roll /ˌʌnˈroʊl/ *verb* [I,T] to open from a rolled position: *He unrolled the poster and put it up on the wall.*

un·ru·ly /ʌnˈruli/ *adj.* difficult to control; without discipline: *an unruly crowd* —**un·ru·li·ness** *noun* [U]

☆ **un·safe** /ʌnˈseɪf/ *adj.* **1** dangerous; that could cause harm or damage: *That ladder looks very unsafe.* **2** in danger: *He felt very unsafe walking through the streets alone.*

☆ **un·sat·is·fac·to·ry** /ˌʌnsætəsˈfæktəri/ *adj.* not good enough: *Some students have been making unsatisfactory progress this semester.*

un·sa·vor·y /ˌʌnˈseɪvəri/ *adj.* unpleasant; that you do not trust: *an unsavory individual*

un·scathed /ˌʌnˈskeɪðd/ *adj.* not hurt; without injury: *He came out of the fight unscathed.*

un·screw /ˌʌnˈskru/ *verb* [T] **1** to remove the screws from sth **2** to open sth by turning it: *Could you unscrew the top of this bottle for me?*

un·scru·pu·lous /ʌnˈskrupyələs/ *adj.* willing to be dishonest, cruel or unfair in order to get what you want

un·sight·ly /ʌnˈsaɪtli/ *adj.* (*formal*) very unpleasant to look at; ugly: *an unsightly stain*

un·skilled /ˌʌnˈskɪld/ *adj.* not having or requiring special skill or training: *an unskilled job*

un·so·lic·it·ed /ˌʌnsəˈlɪsətəd/ *adj.* not asked for: *unsolicited advice*

un·sound /ˌʌnˈsaʊnd/ **1** in poor condition; weak: *The building is structurally unsound.* **2** based on wrong ideas and therefore mistaken

un·spec·i·fied /ʌnˈspɛsəfaɪd/ *adj.* (only *before* a noun) that has not been mentioned specifically: *The man is being held under guard at an unspecified location.*

un·spo·ken /ʌnˈspoʊkən/ *adj.* that has not been said, but is understood by everyone involved: *the unspoken message behind the governor's comments*

un·sta·ble /ˌʌnˈsteɪbl/ *adj.* **1** likely to fall down or move; not firmly fastened **2** likely to change or fail: *a period of unstable government* **3** (used about a person's moods or behavior) likely to change suddenly or frequently: *an unstable personality*

☆ **un·suc·cess·ful** /ˌʌnsəkˈsɛsfl/ *adj.* not having or resulting in success: *an unsuccessful politician* ○ *an unsuccessful attempt to climb the mountain* —**un·suc·cess·ful·ly** *adv.*

un·suit·a·ble /ʌnˈsutəbl/ *adj.* **unsuitable (for sb/sth)** not right or suitable: *material on the Internet that is unsuitable for children*

☆ **un·sure** /ˌʌnˈʃʊr/ *adj.* **1 unsure (about/of sth)** not certain; having doubts: *I didn't argue because I was unsure of the facts.* **2 unsure (of yourself)** not feeling confident about yourself: *He's young and still feels unsure of himself.*

un·sus·pect·ing /ˌʌnsəˈspɛktɪŋ/ *adj.* (only *before* a noun) not aware of danger: *He came up quietly behind his unsuspecting victim.*

un·tan·gle /ˌʌnˈtæŋgl/ *verb* [T] to separate threads, etc. which have become tied together in a confused way: *The wires got mixed up, and it took me a long time to untangle them.*

un·think·a·ble /ˌʌnˈθɪŋkəbl/ *adj.* (used of an event, etc.) impossible to imagine or consider, especially because it is too painful or difficult

un·think·ing /ˌʌnˈθɪŋkɪŋ/ *adj.* done, said, etc. without thinking carefully —**un·think·ing·ly** *adv.*

un·tie /ˌʌnˈtaɪ/ *verb* [T] (*pres. part.* **un·ty·ing**; *3rd pers. sing. pres.* **un·ties**; *p.t., p.p.* **un·tied**) to undo a knot; to free sb by undoing a rope, etc.: *I can't get this knot untied.*

☆ **un·til**[1] /ənˈtɪl/ (also *informal* **'til; till**) *conj.* up to the time when: *She waited until he was finished.* ○ *You have to stay in school until you're 16.* ○ *We won't leave until the police get here* (= we won't leave before they come). ☞ Look at the note at **until**[2].

☆ **un·til**[2] /ənˈtɪl/ (also *informal* **'til; till**) *prep.* up to the time or the event mentioned: *The restaurant is open until midnight.* ○ *Until that moment, she had been happy.* ○ *We can't leave until 10 o'clock* (= we can leave at 10 but not before).

☞ We can use **until** in both formal and informal English. **Till/'til** are more common in informal English and are not usually used at the beginning of a sentence. Make sure that you only use **till/until** to talk about a time. We use **as far as** to talk about distance: *I walked as far as the river.* We use **up to** to

ə	y	w	t̬	eɪ	aɪ	ɔɪ	aʊ	oʊ
about	yes	woman	butter	say	five	boy	now	go

talk about a number: *You can spend up to $20 on each person's present.*

un·told /ˌʌnˈtoʊld/ *adj.* (*formal*) (only *before* a noun) very great; so big, etc. that you cannot count it: *untold suffering* ○ *untold wealth*

un·used¹ /ˌʌnˈyuzd/ *adj.* that has not been used: *an unused stamp*

un·used² /ˌʌnˈyust/ *adj.* **unused to sth** not having any experience of sth; not accustomed to sth: *She was unused to so much attention.*

☆ **un·u·su·al** /ʌnˈyuʒuəl; -ˈyuʒl/ *adj.* **1** not expected or usual: *It's unusual for Joe to be late.* **2** interesting because it is different: *What an unusual hat!*

☆ **un·u·su·al·ly** /ʌnˈyuʒuəli; -ˈyuʒl·i/ *adv.* (usually before an adjective or adverb) **1** more than is common; extremely: *an unusually hot summer* **2** in a way that is not normal or typical of sb/sth: *She remained unusually quiet during the meeting.*

un·veil /ˌʌnˈveɪl/ *verb* [T] to remove a type of cloth or curtain in order to show a new painting, etc. to the public: *The governor unveiled a plaque and opened the new technology center.* ○ (*figurative*) *The President unveiled his new plan today to create more jobs.*

un·want·ed /ˌʌnˈwɑntəd/ *adj.* not wanted: *an unwanted pregnancy* ○ *a cream to remove unwanted hair*

un·war·rant·ed /ʌnˈwɔrəntəd; -ˈwɑr-/ *adj.* that is not deserved or for which there is no good reason

un·wel·come /ʌnˈwɛlkəm/ *adj.* not wanted or welcome, especially because it is unpleasant: *They received some unwelcome news yesterday.*

un·wield·y /ʌnˈwildi/ *adj.* difficult to move or carry because it is too big, heavy, etc.: *an unwieldy box*

un·will·ing /ʌnˈwɪlɪŋ/ *adj.* not wanting to do sth

un·wind /ˌʌnˈwaɪnd/ *verb* (*p.t., p.p.* **un·wound** /-ˈwaʊnd/) **1** [I,T] (used of sth that is wound around sth else) to become undone or to be pulled out: *The cord had unwound.* **2** [I] to relax, especially after working hard: *After a hard day at the office, it takes me a couple of hours to unwind.*

un·wit·ting /ʌnˈwɪtɪŋ/ *adj.* not realizing sth; not intending to do sth: *experiments that were performed on unwitting subjects* —**un·wit·ting·ly** *adv.*: *The company may have unwittingly broken the law.*

un·writ·ten /ʌnˈrɪtn/ *adj.* not existing in written form, but known and accepted by the people involved: *an unwritten agreement*

un·zip /ˌʌnˈzɪp/ *verb* [T] (**unzip·ping; un·zipped**) to open sth that had been closed or fastened with a zipper

☆ **up¹** /ʌp/ *prep., adv.* ☞ For special uses with many verbs e.g. **pick sth up**, look at the verb entries. **1** to a high or higher level or position:

The monkey climbed up the tree. ○ *I carried her suitcase up to the third floor.* ○ *I walked up the hill.* **2** into an upright position: *Everybody stood up when the judge entered the courtroom.* ○ *I had to get up early.* **3** (used for showing that an action continues until it is completed): *Eat up – it's a long time until supper.* **4** (used with verbs of closing): *Zip up your coat. It's cold.* ○ *She tied the package up with string.* **5** very close to a person or thing: *She ran up to her mother and kissed her.* **6** further along: *I live just up the street.* **7** in a particular direction, usually north: *We're going up to Minnesota tomorrow.* **8** into pieces: *We chopped the old boards up and used them for firewood.* **9** (used for showing that sth is increasing): *Prices have gone up.* ○ *Turn the volume up.*

IDM **be up to sb** to be sb's responsibility: *I can't make the decision. It's not up to me.*

be up to your ears/eyes/neck in sth (*informal*) to have more of sth than you can easily do or manage: *I can't go out tonight – I'm up to my eyes in work.*

up and down 1 rising and falling: *We knew she was still alive – her chest was moving up and down.* ○ *The kids were jumping up and down with excitement.* **2** backward and forward: *He was running up and down the block, screaming with pain.*

up to sth 1 as much/many as: *We're expecting up to 100 people at the meeting.* **2** until a particular point in time: *Up to now, things have been easy.* **3** capable of sth: *I don't feel up to cooking this evening. I'm too tired.* **4** doing sth secret and perhaps forbidden: *What are the kids up to? Go and see.*

☆ **up²** /ʌp/ *adj.* (not before a noun) **be up 1** at a higher level or position than before: *Sales are up for the third year in a row.* **2** awake and not in bed: *Aren't you up yet?* **3** (used about a period of time) finished: *Stop writing. Your time's up.* **4** (used about computers) working; in operation: *Are the computers back up yet?*

IDM **be up and running** (used about sth new) to be working well: *The new system is already up and running.*

what's up? (*informal*) what's happening?

up³ /ʌp/ *noun*

IDM **ups and downs** both good and bad luck: *Our marriage is happy, but we've had our ups and downs.*

up·bring·ing /ˈʌpbrɪŋɪŋ/ *noun* [sing.] the way a child is treated and taught how to behave by his/her parents: *a religious upbringing*

up·com·ing /ˈʌpkʌmɪŋ/ *adj.* (only *before* a noun) going to happen soon: *a schedule of upcoming events*

up·date /ˈʌpdeɪt; ˌʌpˈdeɪt/ *verb* [T] **1** to make sth more modern **2** to put the latest information into sth; to give sb the latest information: *Our database of addresses is updated regularly.* ○ *Let me update you on what happened at the*

meeting. —**up·date** /ˈʌpdeɪt/ *noun* [C]: *an up-date on a news story* (= the latest information)

up·grade /ˈʌpgreɪd; ˌʌpˈgreɪd/ *verb* [T] to change sth so that it is of a higher standard —**up·grade** /ˈʌpgreɪd/ *noun* [C]: *an upgrade of the computer system*

up·heav·al /ʌpˈhivl/ *noun* [C,U] a sudden big change, especially one that causes a lot of trouble

up·hill /ˌʌpˈhɪl/ *adj.* **1** going up a slope, toward the top of a hill ☞ The opposite is **downhill**. **2** (only *before* a noun) needing a lot of effort: *It was an uphill struggle to find a job.* —**up·hill** *adv.*: *a long walk uphill*

up·hold /ˌʌpˈhoʊld/ *verb* [T] (*p.t., p.p.* **up·held** /-ˈhɛld/) to support sth (a decision, etc.) especially when other people are against it: *The Supreme Court upheld the state court's decision.*

up·hol·stered /əˈpoʊlstərd/ *adj.* (used about a chair, etc.) covered with cloth, with a layer of soft material underneath

up·hol·ster·y /əˈpoʊlstəri/ *noun* [U] the thick soft materials used to cover chairs, car seats, etc.

up·keep /ˈʌpkip/ *noun* [U] the cost or process of keeping sth in a good condition: *The landlord pays for the upkeep of the building.*

up·lift·ing /ˌʌpˈlɪftɪŋ/ *adj.* producing a feeling of hope and happiness: *an uplifting speech*

up·on /əˈpɑn/ *prep.* (*formal*) on: *a story based upon real events* ○ *The governor was surrounded by reporters upon arrival at the airport.*

IDM once upon a time ⇨ ONCE[1]

☆ **up·per** /ˈʌpər/ *adj.* in a higher position than sth else; situated above sth: *the upper floors of a building* ○ *the upper lip* ☞ The opposite is **lower**.

IDM gain/get/have the upper hand to get into a stronger position than another person; to gain or have control over sb

up·per·case /ˌʌpərˈkeɪs/ *adj., noun* [U] (in) letters that are written or printed in a large form; (in) capital letters: *"FBI" is always written in uppercase letters.* ☞ The opposite is **lowercase**.

ˌ**upper** ˈ**class** *adj., noun* [C] (of) the highest social and economic class; people with a lot of money which may have been passed down to them by older members of their family

up·per·class·man /ˌʌpərˈklæsmən/ *noun* [C] (*pl.* **up·per·class·men** /-mən/) a student who is in his/her third or fourth year in high school or college ☞ Look at **underclassman**.

up·per·most /ˈʌpərmoʊst/ *adj.* in the highest or most important position: *Concern for her family was uppermost in her mind.*

☆ **up·right[1]** /ˈʌpraɪt/ *adj.* **1** with a straight back; standing vertically: *Please put the back of your seat in an upright position.* **2** honest and responsible: *an upright citizen*

☆ **upright[2]** /ˌʌpˈraɪt/ *adv.* **1** with a straight back: *to stand upright* **2** in or into a vertical position: *to hold sth upright*

up·ris·ing /ˈʌpraɪzɪŋ/ *noun* [C] a situation in which a group of people start to fight against the people in power in their country: *an armed uprising*

up·roar /ˈʌprɔr/ *noun* [sing., U] a loud noise of excitement, confusion, anger, etc.; an angry discussion about sth: *The meeting ended in uproar.*

up·root /ˌʌpˈrut/ *verb* [T] **1** to tear up a plant by the roots: *Strong winds had uprooted the tree.* **2** to force sb to leave his/her home and move to a new place

up·scale /ˈʌpskeɪl/ *adj.* for or connected with people from a high social and economic class: *an upscale hotel*

☆ **up·set[1]** /ʌpˈsɛt/ *verb* [T] (*pres. part.* **up·set·ting**; *p.t., p.p.* **up·set**) **1** to make sb worry or feel unhappy: *The pictures of starving children upset her.* **2** to make sth go wrong: *to upset someone's plans* **3** to make sb sick in the stomach: *Rich food usually upsets my stomach.* **4** to defeat sb in a competition, sports game, etc. when you were expected to lose: *The Bears upset the Cowboys 17-10.*

☆ **up·set[2]** /ˌʌpˈsɛt/ *adj.* **1** worried and unhappy: *She looked very upset about something.* **2** slightly sick: *I've got an upset stomach.* ☞ Note that the adjective is pronounced /ˈʌpsɛt/ when it comes before a noun and /ˌʌpˈsɛt/ in other positions in the sentence.

up·set[3] /ˈʌpsɛt/ *noun* **1** [C,U] the act of upsetting[1](1,2) or being upset: *recent economic upsets* **2** [C] a slight illness in your stomach: *a stomach upset* **3** [C] an unexpected victory in a competition, sports game, etc.: *Williams' stunning upset of the world champion*

upside down

The painting is **upside down**.

☆ **up·side down** /ˌʌpsaɪd ˈdaʊn/ *adj., adv.* with the top part turned to the bottom: *You're holding the picture upside down.* ○ *She was hanging upside down.* ☞ The opposite is **right side up**.

IDM turn sth upside down (*informal*) to make sth very messy: *He turned the house upside down looking for his keys.*

☆ **up·stairs[1]** /ˌʌpˈstɛrz/ *adv.* to or on the upper floor of a building: *to go upstairs* ○ *She's sleeping upstairs.* —**up·stairs** /ˈʌpstɛrz/ *adj.: an upstairs window*

U

upstairs² /ˌʌpˈstɛrz/ *noun* [sing.] (*informal*) **the upstairs** the upper floor of a house: *We're going to paint the upstairs.*

up·state /ˈʌpsteɪt/ *adj.* (only *before* a noun) in the northern part of a state: *a town in upstate New York* —**up·state** /ʌpˈsteɪt/ *adv.*

up·stream /ˌʌpˈstrim/ *adv.* moving against the direction that a river flows: *He swam slowly upstream.*

up·surge /ˈʌpsərdʒ/ *noun* [C, usually sing.] **an upsurge (in sth)** a sudden increase of sth: *an upsurge in violent crime*

up·tight /ˌʌpˈtaɪt/ *adj.* **1** nervous; unable to relax: *He always gets uptight before a test.* **2** angry: *Don't get so uptight – it's only a game.*

☆ **up-to-date** /ˌʌptəˈdeɪt/ *adj.* (only *before* a noun) **1** modern: *up-to-date equipment* **2** having the most recent information: *an up-to-date dictionary* ☞ Look also at the expression *up to date* at **date¹**.

up-to-the-minute /ˌʌptəðəˈmɪnɪt/ (only *before* a noun) *adj.* having the most recent information possible: *an up-to-the-minute news report*

up·town /ˌʌpˈtaʊn/ *adj., adv.* in or to the northern part of a city, or the part where the streets have larger numbers in their names ☞ Look also at **downtown**.

up·turn /ˈʌptərn/ *noun* [C] **an upturn (in sth)** an improvement or gain in sth: *an upturn in support for the candidate*

☆ **up·ward¹** /ˈʌpwərd/ *adj.* moving or directed toward a higher place or level: *an upward glance* ○ *an upward trend in exports* (= an increase)

☆ **up·ward²** /ˈʌpwərd/ (*also* **upwards** /-wərdz/) *adv.* moving toward, or in the direction of, a higher place or level: *I looked upwards.*

u·ra·ni·um /yʊˈreɪniəm/ *noun* [U] (*symbol* **U**) a radioactive metal that can be used to produce nuclear energy

U·ra·nus /yʊˈreɪməs; ˈyʊrənəs/ *noun* [sing.] the planet that is seventh in order from the sun

☆ **ur·ban** /ˈərbən/ *adj.* of a large city: *urban neighborhoods*

☆ **urge¹** /ərdʒ/ *verb* [T] **1** to try hard to persuade sb to do sth: *I urged him to fight the decision.* **2** to advise strongly, especially that sth is necessary: *Motorists are urged to drive carefully on icy roads.*
PHRV urge sb on to encourage sb: *The coach urged his team on.*

urge² /ərdʒ/ *noun* [C] a strong need or desire: *sexual urges* ○ *She felt a strong urge to stand up and scream.*

☆ **ur·gent** /ˈərdʒənt/ *adj.* needing immediate attention: *an urgent message* ○ *It's not urgent; I'll tell you about it later.* —**ur·gen·cy** /-dʒənsi/ *noun* [U]: *a matter of the greatest urgency* —**ur·gent·ly** *adv.*: *Mr. Wheeler needs to see you urgently.*

u·ri·nate /ˈyʊrəneɪt/ *verb* [I] (*formal*) to pass waste water (**urine**) from the body ☞ Go to **the bathroom** for a polite, less formal expression with the same meaning.

u·rine /ˈyʊrɪn/ *noun* [U] the yellow liquid that is passed from your body when you use the toilet

urn /ərn/ *noun* [C] a type of vase, especially one in which the ashes of a dead person are kept

☆ **us** /əs; *strong form* ʌs/ *pron.* (used as the object of a verb, or after *be*) me and another person or other people; me and you: *Come with us.* ○ *Leave us alone.* ○ *Will you write to us?* ○ *Hello, it's us again!*

☆ **U.S.** (*also* **US**) /ˌyu ˈɛs/ (*also* **U.S.A.**; **USA**) /ˌyu ɛs ˈeɪ/ *abbr.* = THE UNITED STATES: *the smallest state in the U.S.*

us·age /ˈyusɪdʒ/ *noun* **1** [U] the way that sth is used; the amount that sth is used: *With normal usage, the machine should last for years.* **2** [C,U] the way that words are normally used in a language: *a guide to English grammar and usage*

☆ **use¹** /yuz/ *verb* [T] (*pres. part.* **us·ing**; *p.t., p.p.* **used** /yuzd/) **1** when you use sth, you do sth with it for a purpose: *Could I use your phone?* ○ *We used the money to buy a house.* ○ *The building was used as a shelter for homeless people.* ○ *This information cannot be used for commercial purposes* ○ *Use your imagination!* ○ *That's a word I never use.* **2** to need or to take sth: *Don't use all the milk.* **3** to treat sb/sth in a selfish or unkind way: *He just used me to get what he wanted and then forgot about me.*
PHRV use sth up to use sth until no more is left

☆ **use²** /yus/ *noun* **1** [U] using or being used: *The use of cellular phones is now widespread.* ○ *She kept the money for use in an emergency.* ○ *Turn off the coffee maker when it is not in use.* **2** [C,U] the purpose for which sth is used: *This gadget has many uses.* **3** [U] the ability or permission to use sth: *He lost the use of his hand after the accident.* ○ *She offered them the use of her car.* **4** [U] the advantage of sth; how useful sth is: *It's no use studying for a test at the last minute.* ○ *What's the use of trying?*
IDM come into/go out of use to start/stop being used
make use of sth/sb to use sth/sb in a way that will give you an advantage

☆ **used¹** /yuzd/ *adj.* that has had an owner before: *I bought a used car.* ☞ Another word with the same meaning is **secondhand**.

☆ **used²** /yust/ *adj.*
IDM be/get used to sth/to doing sth to be or become familiar with sth or accustomed to sth: *He's used to the heat.* ○ *I'll never get used to getting up at five.*

☆ **used to** /ˈyustə; *before a vowel and in final position* ˈyustu/ *modal verb* (for talking about sth that happened often or continuously in the

U

past or about a situation which existed in the past): *She used to live with her parents* (= but she doesn't now). ○ *You used to live in Chicago, didn't you?* ○ *Did you use to smoke?* ○ *He didn't use to speak to me.*

☞ **1** We usually use **did** to form negatives and questions with **used to**: *I didn't use to like jazz.* ○ *Did she use to be in your class?* **2** Be careful not to confuse **used to** + infinitive, which only refers to the past, with **to be used to (doing) sth**, which can refer to the past, present or future. Compare: *I used to live on my own* (= but now I don't). ○ *I'm used to living on my own* (= I am accustomed to it).

☆ **use·ful** /'yusfl/ *adj.* having some practical use; helpful: *a useful tool* ○ *useful advice* —**use·ful·ly** *adv.*: *Make sure your time is spent usefully.* —**use·ful·ness** *noun* [U]

☆ **use·less** /'yusləs/ *adj.* that does not work well, or is of no use: *This new machine is useless.* ○ *It's useless to complain; you won't get your money back.* —**use·less·ly** *adv.* —**use·less·ness** *noun* [U]

☆ **us·er** /'yuzər/ *noun* [C] **1** (often in compounds) a person that uses a service, machine, place, etc.: *users of public transportation* **2** (*slang*) a person who takes illegal drugs

user-friendly /,yuzər'frɛndli/ *adj.* (used of computers, books, machines, etc.) easy or not too complicated to use

ush·er¹ /'ʌʃər/ *noun* [C] a person who shows people to their seats in a theater, church, etc.

ush·er² /'ʌʃər/ *verb* [T] to lead sb carefully in the direction mentioned: *I was ushered to my seat.*

PHRV **usher sth in** to mark the beginning of sth: *The agreement ushered in a new period of peace for the two countries.*

☆ **u·su·al** /'yuʒuəl; 'yuʒəl/ *adj.* happening or used most often: *It's usual for her to work on weekends.* ○ *He got home later than usual.* ○ *I sat in my usual seat.*

IDM **as usual** in the way that has often happened: *Here's Derek, late as usual!*

☆ **u·su·al·ly** /'yuʒuəli; 'yuʒəli/ *adv.* in the way that is usual; most often: *She's usually home by six.* ○ *Usually, we go out on Saturdays.*

u·ten·sil /yu'tɛnsl/ *noun* [C] a type of tool or object used in the home: *cooking utensils*

u·ter·us /'yutərəs/ *noun* [C] (*pl.* **u·ter·us·es** or, in scientific use, **u·ter·i** /-raɪ/) (also *old-fashioned* **womb**) the part of a woman's body where a baby grows

u·til·i·ty /yu'tɪləti/ *noun* (*pl.* **u·til·i·ties**) **1** [C] a useful public service such as the supplying of water or electricity: *Your share of the rent will be $250 a month, plus one-third of the utility bills.* ☞ Look also at **public utility**. **2** [U] (*formal*) the usefulness (of a machine, etc.)

u'tility room *noun* [C] a small room in a house, often next to the kitchen, where people sometimes have a washing machine, etc.

u·til·ize /'yutl-aɪz/ *verb* [T] (*formal*) to use sth in an effective and practical way: *to utilize computer technology in the classroom*

ut·most¹ /'ʌtmoʊst/ *adj.* (only *before* a noun) (*formal*) greatest: *a message of the utmost importance*

ut·most² /'ʌtmoʊst/ *noun* [sing.] the greatest extent, amount, degree, etc. that is possible: *I did my utmost to help.*

U·to·pi·a /yu'toʊpiə/ *noun* [C,U] an imaginary society or place where everything is perfect —**U·to·pi·an** /-piən/ *adj.*

ut·ter¹ /'ʌtər/ *adj.* (only *before* a noun) complete; total: *That's utter nonsense!* ○ *He felt like an utter fool.* —**ut·ter·ly** *adv.*: *It's utterly impossible.*

ut·ter² /'ʌtər/ *verb* [T] to speak or make a sound with your mouth: *She left without uttering a word.*

ut·ter·ance /'ʌtərəns/ *noun* [C] (*formal*) something that is said

U-turn /'yutərn/ *noun* [C] **1** a type of movement where a car, etc. turns around so that it goes back in the direction it came: *to make a U-turn* **2** a sudden change from one plan to a completely different one

V

Vv

V, v /vi/ *noun* [C] (*pl.* **V's; v's**) **1** the twenty-second letter of the English alphabet: *"Van" begins with (a) "V."* **2** the shape of a V: *The birds were flying in a V.*

V *abbr.* = VOLT, VOLTS

va·can·cy /'veɪkənsi/ *noun* [C] (*pl.* **va·can·cies**) **1** a room in a hotel, etc. that is not being used: *The sign outside the motel said "No Vacancies."* **2** a job that has not been filled: *There are two vacancies on the school board this year.*

☆ **va·cant** /'veɪkənt/ *adj.* **1** (of a house, room, seat, etc.) not being used **2** (of a job, etc.) not filled: *The position of Marketing Director is*

ə	y	w	t̬	eɪ	aɪ	ɔɪ	aʊ	oʊ
about	yes	woman	butter	say	five	boy	now	go

currently vacant. **3** showing no sign of intelligence or understanding: *a vacant expression* —**va·cant·ly** *adv.*: *She stared vacantly out of the window.*

☆ **va·ca·tion** /veɪˈkeɪʃn; və-/ *noun* [C,U] a period of rest from work or school (often when you go and stay away from home): *The boss is on vacation.* ○ *The job includes two weeks' paid vacation a year.* ○ *Summer vacation starts next Friday!* ○ *He took his vacation during the first week in July.*

va·ca·tion·er /veɪˈkeɪʃnər; və-/ *noun* [C] a person who is away from home on vacation

vac·ci·nate /ˈvæksn·eɪt/ *verb* [T] to give a person or animal a substance, often using a special needle, to prevent him/her/it from getting a particular disease: *Were you vaccinated against measles as a child?* —**vac·ci·na·tion** /ˌvæksn·ˈeɪʃn/ *noun* [C,U]

vac·cine /vækˈsin/ *noun* [C] a substance that is given to people, often using a special needle, to protect them against a particular disease: *the search for an AIDS vaccine/a vaccine against AIDS*

vac·u·um[1] /ˈvækyum/ *noun* [C] **1** a space that contains no substance and no air or gas: (*figurative*) *a vacuum in her life* (= a feeling of emptiness) **2** = VACUUM CLEANER

vac·u·um[2] /ˈvækum/ *verb* [I,T] to clean sth using a vacuum cleaner

☆ **ˈvacuum ˌcleaner** (*also* **vacuum**) *noun* [C] an electric machine that cleans carpets, etc. by sucking up dirt

vacuum cleaner

va·gi·na /vəˈdʒaɪnə/ *noun* [C] the passage in the body of a woman or female animal that connects the outer sex organs to the part where a baby grows (**uterus**) —**vag·i·nal** /ˈvædʒənl/ *adj.*

vague /veɪg/ *adj.* **1** not clear or definite: *vague memories of my childhood home* **2** not clearly seen: *a vague shape in the distance*

vague·ly /ˈveɪgli/ *adv.* **1** in a way that is not clear; slightly: *Her name is vaguely familiar.* **2** without thinking about what is happening: *He smiled vaguely and walked away.* —**vague·ness** *noun* [U]

vain /veɪn/ *adj.* **1** (*formal*) (used about a person) too proud of your appearance, or of what you can do, etc. ☞ The noun is **vanity**. **2** useless; without any hope of success: *a vain attempt* **IDM** **in vain** without success: *The firefighters tried in vain to put out the fire.* —**vain·ly** *adv.*

val·e·dic·to·ri·an /ˌvælədɪkˈtɔriən/ *noun* [C] the student who received higher grades than all the other students in his/her class in high school or college, and who gives a speech at the graduation ceremony

val·en·tine /ˈvæləntaɪn/ *noun* [C] **1** a card that you send, sometimes secretly, to someone you love or like in a romantic way ☞ It is traditional to send these cards on **Valentine's Day** (February 14). **2** the person you send a card to on Valentine's Day: *Be my valentine* (= written on a card).

val·et /væˈleɪ/ *noun* [C] a person whose job is to perform personal services for people, especially parking their cars at a hotel or restaurant

val·iant /ˈvæliənt/ *adj.* (*formal*) very brave —**val·iant·ly** *adv.*

☆ **val·id** /ˈvæləd/ *adj.* **1** that can be used or accepted legally at a certain time: *This ticket is valid for Sunday's game only.* **2** acceptable in a court of law: *a valid contract* **3** (used about a reason, etc.) strong enough to convince sb; acceptable: *I could think of no valid objections to the plan.* ☞ The opposite is **invalid**. —**va·lid·i·ty** /vəˈlɪdəti/ *noun* [U]: *the validity of an argument* ○ *the validity of a law*

☆ **val·ley** /ˈvæli/ *noun* [C] the flat land that lies between two lines of mountains or areas of higher ground, and which often has a river flowing through it

val·or /ˈvælər/ *noun* [U] great bravery, especially in war: *the soldiers' valor in battle*
☞ This word is used in old, formal or poetic writing.

☆ **val·u·a·ble** /ˈvælyəbl; -yuəbl/ *adj.* **1** worth a lot of money: *Is this ring valuable?* **2** very useful: *a valuable piece of information* ☞ The opposite is **worthless**, not **invaluable**.

val·u·a·bles /ˈvælyəblz; -yuəblz/ *noun* [plural] the small things that you own that are worth a lot of money, such as jewelry, etc.: *Please put your valuables in the hotel safe.*

☆ **val·ue**[1] /ˈvælyu/ *noun* **1** [U] the usefulness or importance of sth: *the value of education* ○ *of great/little value* **2** [C,U] the amount of money that sth is worth: *The thieves stole goods with a total value of $10,000.* ○ *Shares of IBM have increased in value this month.* ○ *to go up/down in value* ☞ Look at **face value**. **3** [C,U] the worth of sth compared with its price, or something that is worth a lot compared with it's price: *The hotel offers good value at $5 a night.* ○ *Some used equipment can be an excellent value.* **4** **values** [plural] a set of beliefs about the way people should behave; moral principles: *the traditional values of American society* ☞ Look also at **family values**.

☆ **val·ue**[2] /ˈvælyu/ *verb* [T] (*pres. part.* **val·u·ing**) **1** **value sth (at sth)** to decide the amount of money that sth is worth: *The house was valued at $70,000.* **2** to think sb/sth is very important and worth a lot: *Laura has always valued her independence.*

valve /vælv/ *noun* [C] a mechanical device which controls the flow of air, liquid or gas in

a pipe or tube: *a radiator valve* ∘ *to open/close a valve*

vam·pire /'væmpaɪər/ *noun* [C] (in horror stories) a dead person who comes out of his/her grave at night and sucks the blood of living people

☆ **van** /væn/ *noun* [C] a type of vehicle like a very large car or small covered truck, that is used for transporting people or things ☛ picture at **truck**.

van·dal /'vændl/ *noun* [C] a person who damages property (e.g. cars, store windows) on purpose —**van·dal·ism** /-dl·ɪzəm/ *noun* [U]: *The police are worried about the recent increase in vandalism.*

van·dal·ize /'vændl·aɪz/ *verb* [T] (often passive) to damage property on purpose

va·nil·la /və'nɪlə/ *noun* [U] a substance from a plant that is used for giving flavor to sweet food: *Strawberry, chocolate or vanilla ice cream?*

☆ **van·ish** /'vænɪʃ/ *verb* [I] **1** to disappear suddenly and completely: *When he turned around, the two men had vanished.* ∘ *His fear vanished when he heard his sister's voice outside the door.* **2** (used about types of things) to disappear little by little over a period of time: *This species of plant is vanishing from New England.*

van·i·ty /'vænəti/ *noun* [U] the quality of being too proud of your appearance or abilities ☛ The adjective is **vain**.

¹**vanity plate** *noun* [C, usually pl.] a metal sign (**license plate**) for a car with a special combination of letters and/or numbers that were chosen by the car's owner, e.g. to spell his/her name or an amusing word

va·por /'veɪpər/ *noun* [C,U] a substance made of very small drops of liquid which hang together in the air like a cloud: *water vapor*

var·i·a·ble¹ /'vɛriəbl; 'vær-/ *adj.* not staying the same; likely to change —**var·i·a·bil·i·ty** /ˌvɛriə'bɪləti; 'vær-/ *noun* [U]

var·i·a·ble² /'vɛriəbl; 'vær-/ *noun* [C] something that is likely to change from one situation to another

var·i·ant /'vɛriənt; 'vær-/ *noun* [C] a different form of sth

☆ **var·i·a·tion** /ˌvɛri'eɪʃn; 'vær-/ *noun* **1** [C,U] **variation (in sth)** a difference in quality or quantity between a number of things: *There was a lot of variation in the test scores* (= the scores were very different from each other). ∘ *a slight variation in color from one piece to another* **2** [C] **variation (on/of sth)** something that is almost the same as another thing but has some small differences: *All their songs are just variations on a basic theme.*

var·ied /'vɛrid; 'vær-/ *adj.* having many different kinds of things or activities: *a varied diet* ∘ *The work of an English teacher is interesting and varied.*

☆ **va·ri·e·ty** /və'raɪəti/ *noun* (*pl.* **va·ri·e·ties**) **1** [C] **a variety (of sth)** a number of different kinds of things: *You can take evening classes in a variety of subjects including photography, Spanish and computers.* **2** [U] the quality of not being the same: *There's so much variety in my new job. I do something different every day!* **3** [C] **a variety (of sth)** a type of sth: *a new variety of apple called "Perfection"*

☆ **var·i·ous** /'vɛriəs; 'vær-/ *adj.* (used for describing things that are different from each other) more than one; several: *These chairs are available in various colors.* ∘ *I decided to leave Washington for various reasons.*

var·nish /'vɑrnɪʃ/ *noun* [U] a clear liquid that you paint onto wood or other hard surfaces to protect them and make them shine —**var·nish** *verb* [T]

var·si·ty /'vɑrsəti/ *adj.* (only *before* a noun) (used about a sports team) that is the main team that represents a school or college in games against teams from other schools or colleges: *the girls' varsity basketball team*

☆ **var·y** /'vɛri; 'vær-/ *verb* (*pres. part.* **var·y·ing**; *3rd pers. sing. pres.* **var·ies**; *p.t., p.p.* **var·ied**) **1** [I] (used about a number of things) to be different from each other: *The fruits vary greatly in size and quality – be careful when you choose.* **2** [I] to become different; to change: *The price of the vacation package varies from $1,500 to $3,200, depending on the time of year.* **3** [T] to make sth different by changing it often in some way: *I try to vary my work as much as possible so I don't get bored.*

☆ **vase** /veɪs; vɑz/ *noun* [C] a container used for holding cut flowers

va·sec·to·my /və'sɛktəmi/ *noun* [C] (*pl.* **va·sec·to·mies**) a small medical operation that prevents a man from having children, by cutting the tube that carries sperm

☆ **vast** /væst/ *adj.* extremely big: *a vast sum of money* ∘ *a vast country* ∘ *The vast majority of* (almost all) *local residents support the proposal.* —**vast·ly** *adv.*: *vastly different attitudes toward the problem*

vault¹ /vɔlt/ *noun* [C] **1** a strong underground room in a bank, etc. used for keeping money and other valuable things safe **2** a room where dead people are buried

vault² /vɔlt/ *verb* [I,T] **vault (over sth)** to jump over or onto sth in one movement, using your hands or a pole to help you: *The boy vaulted over the wall.*

☆ **VCR** /ˌvi si 'ɑr/ *noun* [C] (*pl.* **VCR's**) videocassette recorder; a machine that is connected to a television, on which you can record or play television programs or movies

veal /vil/ *noun* [U] the meat from a young cow (**calf**) ☛ Look at the note at **meat**.

veer /vɪr/ *verb* [I] (used about vehicles) to change direction suddenly: *The car veered across the road and hit a tree.*

tʃ	dʒ	v	θ	ð	s	z	ʃ
chin	**J**une	**v**an	**th**in	**th**en	**s**o	**z**oo	**sh**e

veg·an /ˈvigən/ *noun* [C] a person who does not eat or use any animal products at all ☞ Look at **vegetarian**.

☆ **veg·e·ta·ble** /ˈvɛdʒtəbl/ *noun* [C] a plant which you eat as food, e.g. potatoes, carrots, onions: *fresh fruit and vegetables* ○ *vegetable soup* ○ *a vegetable garden*

veg·e·tar·i·an /ˌvɛdʒəˈtɛriən/ *noun* [C] a person who does not eat meat or fish —**veg·e·tari·an** *adj.*: *a vegetarian diet*

veg·e·ta·tion /ˌvɛdʒəˈteɪʃn/ *noun* [U] (*formal*) plant life in general; all the plants that are found in a particular place: *tropical vegetation*

veg·gie /ˈvɛdʒi/ *noun* [C, usually pl.] (*informal*) a vegetable

ve·he·ment /ˈviəmənt/ *adj.* showing strong (often negative) feeling: *a vehement attack on the candidate*

☆ **ve·hi·cle** /ˈviɪkl/ *noun* [C] (*formal*) **1** something which transports people or things from place to place, especially on land, e.g. cars, bicycles, trucks and buses: *a motor vehicle* (a vehicle with an engine) **2 a vehicle (for sth)** something which is used for communicating particular ideas or opinions: *This magazine has become a vehicle for conservative opinion.*

veil /veɪl/ *noun* [C] a piece of thin material for covering a woman's head and face

vein /veɪn/ *noun* **1** [C] one of the tubes which carry blood from all parts of the body to the heart ☞ Look at **artery**. **2** [sing., U] a particular style or quality: *After a humorous beginning, the program continued in a more serious vein.*

Vel·cro /ˈvɛlkroʊ/ *noun* [U] (*trademark*) a material that is used for fastening parts of clothes together. Velcro is used in small strips, one rough and one smooth, that stick together and make a noise when they are pulled apart.

ve·loc·i·ty /vəˈlɑsəti/ *noun* [U] (*technical*) the speed at which sth moves

vel·vet /ˈvɛlvət/ *noun* [U] a kind of material with a soft, thick surface on one side only

ven·det·ta /vɛnˈdɛtə/ *noun* [C] a serious argument that lasts for a long time (especially between an individual and an organization or between families)

vend·ing ma·chine /ˈvɛndɪŋ məˌʃin/ *noun* [C] a machine in a public place into which you put money to buy candy, drinks in cans etc.

ven·dor /ˈvɛndər/ *noun* [C] (*formal*) a person who sells sth: *a hot dog vendor at the stadium*

ve·neer /vəˈnɪr/ *noun* [C,U] **1** a thin layer of wood or plastic which you stick onto sth made of cheaper material to give it a better appearance **2 a veneer (of sth)** (*formal*) a part of sb's behavior or of a situation which hides what it is really like: *a thin veneer of politeness*

Ve·ne·tian blind /vəˌniʃn ˈblaɪnd/ *noun* [C] a covering for a window that is made of horizontal strips of plastic or metal. You can change the position of the strips in order to let more or less light into the room.

ven·geance /ˈvɛndʒəns/ *noun* (*formal*) [U] the act of hurting sb because he/she has hurt you in some way that you think is wrong: *The man wanted vengeance for the death of his wife.* ☞ Look at **revenge**.

with a vengeance with more force and determination than before or than you expected: *After a week of good weather, winter returned with a vengeance today.*

ven·i·son /ˈvɛnɪsn/ *noun* [U] the meat from a deer ☞ Look at the note at **meat**.

ven·om /ˈvɛnəm/ *noun* [U] **1** the poisonous liquid that snakes, etc. put into your body when they bite you **2** extreme anger or hatred that you show when you speak —**ven·om·ous** /ˈvɛnəməs/ *adj.*

vent /vɛnt/ *noun* [C] a hole in the wall of a room or machine which allows air to come in, and allows smoke, steam or smells to go out: *an air vent*

ven·ti·late /ˈvɛntəleɪt/ *verb* [T] to allow air to move freely in and out of a room or building: *The office is poorly ventilated.* —**ven·ti·la·tion** /ˌvɛntəˈleɪʃn/ *noun* [U]: *There was no ventilation in the room except for one tiny window.*

ven·ture[1] /ˈvɛntʃər/ *noun* [C] a project which is new and often involves a risk, because you cannot be sure that it will succeed: *I wish you luck in your new business venture.* ☞ Look also at **joint venture**.

ven·ture[2] /ˈvɛntʃər/ *verb* [I] to do sth or go somewhere new and perhaps dangerous, when you are not sure what will happen: *The company has decided to venture into Internet sales and marketing.* ○ *He ventured out into the storm in a heavy coat, hat and scarf.*

ven·ue /ˈvɛnyu/ *noun* [C] the place where a concert, sports game, conference, etc. happens: *a change of venue*

Ve·nus /ˈvinəs/ *noun* [sing.] the planet that is second in order from the sun and nearest to the earth

ve·ran·da (*also* **verandah**) /vəˈrændə/ *noun* [C] a platform attached to the side of a house, with a roof and floor but no outside wall: *to sit on the veranda* ☞ Look at **deck**, **patio** and **porch**.

☆ **verb** /vərb/ *noun* [C] a word or group of words that is used to indicate an action or state, e.g. *bring, happen,* or *be*

ver·bal /ˈvərbl/ *adj.* (*formal*) **1** spoken, not written: *a verbal warning* ☞ Look at **oral**. **2** connected with words, or the use of words: *verbal skill* —**ver·bal·ly** *adv.*

☆ **ver·dict** /ˈvərdɪkt/ *noun* [C] **1** the decision in a court of law about whether a person is guilty or not guilty, or about the facts of a legal case: *The jury returned a verdict of "not guilty."* **2** your opinion or decision about sth, which

i	ɪ	ɛ	æ	ɑ	ɔ	ʌ	ʊ	u
see	sit	ten	cat	hot	saw	cup	put	too

you tell to other people: *The general verdict was that the restaurant was too expensive.*

verge¹ /vɜrdʒ/ *noun* [C]
on the verge of sth/doing sth very near to doing sth, or to sth happening: *scientists on the verge of an exciting new discovery* ○ *The company was on the verge of going bankrupt.*

verge² /vɜrdʒ/ *verb*
PHRV **verge on sth** to be almost the same as sth; to be close to sth: *What they are doing verges on theft.*

ver·i·fy /ˈvɛrəfaɪ/ *verb* [T] (*pres. part.* **ver·i·fy·ing**; *3rd pers. sing. pres.* **ver·i·fies**; *p.t., p.p.* **ver·i·fied**) (*formal*) to check or state that sth is true: *to verify a statement* —**ver·i·fi·ca·tion** /ˌvɛrəfəˈkeɪʃn/ *noun* [C,U]

ver·min /ˈvɜrmən/ *noun* [plural] small wild animals (e.g. rats) that carry disease and destroy plants and food

ver·sa·tile /ˈvɜrsətl/ *adj.* **1** (used about an object) having many different uses: *a versatile tool that drills, cuts and polishes* **2** (used about a person) having many different skills or abilities: *a versatile performer*

☆ **verse** /vɜrs/ *noun* **1** [U] writing arranged in lines which have a definite beat and which often have the same sounds at the end: *He wrote his message of love to her in verse.* ☞ Look at **prose. 2** [C] a group of lines which form one part of a song or poem: *This song has five verses.*

☆ **ver·sion** /ˈvɜrʒn/ *noun* [C] **1** a thing which is based on sth else but which has some details that are different: *The car is available in two- and four-door versions.* ○ *the movie version of a classic novel* **2** a person's description of sth that has happened: *The two drivers gave very different versions of the accident.*

ver·sus /ˈvɜrsəs/ *prep.* **1** (*abbr.* **vs.**) (used in sports or in a court of law for showing that two teams or people are competing against each other): *the United States versus Canada* ○ *the case of Brown vs. the Board of Education* **2** (used for showing that two ideas or things are in opposition to each other, especially when you are trying to choose one of them): *It's a question of quality versus price.*

vertical horizontal diagonal

☆ **ver·ti·cal** /ˈvɜrtɪkl/ *adj.* going straight up at an angle of 90° from the ground: *a vertical line* ○ *The cliff was almost vertical.* —**ver·ti·cal·ly** /-kli/ *adv.*

☆ **ver·y¹** /ˈvɛri/ *adv.* (used with an adjective or adverb to make it stronger): *very small* ○ *very slowly* ○ *very much* ○ *"Are you hungry?" "Not very."*

☞ We use **very** with superlative adjectives: *very best, youngest, etc.* but with comparative adjectives we use **much** or **very much** (or in informal English, **a lot**): *much/very much better; much/very much younger* (more informal): *a lot better; a lot younger*

ver·y² /ˈvɛri/ *adj.* (used with a noun for emphasis): *We climbed to the very top of the mountain* (= all the way to the top). ○ *You're the very person I wanted to talk to* (= exactly the right person).

ves·sel /ˈvɛsl/ *noun* [C] (*formal*) a ship or large boat ☞ Look also at **blood vessel.**

☆ **vest** /vɛst/ *noun* [C] a piece of clothing with no sleeves, that is often worn over a shirt or blouse ☞ picture on page A27.

ves·tige /ˈvɛstɪdʒ/ *noun* [C, usually pl.] **vestiges of sth** a small part of sth that remains after the rest of it is gone: *the vestiges of Communism in Eastern Europe*

vet /vɛt/ *noun* [C] (*informal*) **1** = VETERAN(1): *Vietnam vets* (= who fought in the Vietnam War) **2** = VETERINARIAN

vet·er·an /ˈvɛtərən/ *noun* [C] **1**(also *informal* **vet**) a person who has served in the military forces, especially during a war **2** a person who has very long experience of a particular job or activity: *a veteran journalist*

☆ **vet·er·i·nar·i·an** /ˌvɛtərəˈnɛriən; ˌvɛtrə-; ˌvɛtnˈɛriən/ *noun* [C] (also *informal* **vet**) a person whose job is to give medical help to sick or injured animals; a doctor for animals —**vet·er·i·nar·y** /ˈvɛtərəˌnɛri; ˈvɛtrə-/ *adj.*: *a veterinary hospital*

ve·to¹ /ˈvitoʊ/ *verb* [T] (*pres. part.* **ve·to·ing**; *3rd pers. sing. pres.* **ve·toes**; *p.t., p.p.* **ve·toed**) to refuse to give official permission for an action or plan, when other people have agreed to it: *The President vetoed the bill after it had been passed by the Senate.*

ve·to² /ˈvitoʊ/ *noun* (*pl.* **ve·toes**) [C,U] the official power to refuse permission for an action or plan, or an act of refusing permission: *Congress is likely to override the President's veto of the tax bill.*

vi·a /ˈviə; ˈvaɪə/ *prep.* **1** going through a place: *We flew from Los Angeles to Boston via Chicago.* **2** by means of; using: *These pictures come to you via our satellite link.*

vi·a·ble /ˈvaɪəbl/ *adj.* that will be successful: *Your idea is just not commercially viable.* —**vi·a·bil·i·ty** /ˌvaɪəˈbɪləti/ *noun* [U]

vi·brant /ˈvaɪbrənt/ *adj.* **1** full of life and energy; exciting: *a vibrant city, atmosphere, personality, etc.* **2** (used about colors) bright and strong

vi·brate /ˈvaɪbreɪt/ *verb* [I] to move continuously and very quickly from side to side: *When a guitar string vibrates, it makes a sound.* —**vi·bra·tion** /vaɪˈbreɪʃn/ *noun* [C,U]:

Even at full speed, the engine causes very little vibration.

vic·ar /ˈvɪkər/ *noun* [C] (*BrE*) a priest in the official church of England

vice /vaɪs/ *noun* **1** [U] illegal actions that are evil or immoral: *the police vice squad* (=the part of the police that deals with illegal drugs, prostitutes, etc.) **2** [C] a moral weakness or bad habit: *Greed and envy are terrible vices.* ○ *My only vice is eating too much chocolate.* ☞ Look at **virtue**.

vice- /vaɪs/ (in compounds) next in importance to the rank mentioned: *the vice-chair-man*

☆ ˌvice ˈpresident *noun* [C] **1** the person with the second-highest rank in the government of some countries **2** a person in a large organization who controls a large department or group of departments: *the company's vice president of sales and marketing*

vice ver·sa /ˌvaɪs ˈvərsə; ˌvaɪsə-/ *adv.* in the opposite way to what has just been said: *All of the French documents were translated into English and vice versa* (= the English documents were translated into French).

vi·cin·i·ty /vəˈsɪnəti/ *noun*
IDM **in the vicinity (of sth)** (*formal*) in the surrounding area: *There's no bank in the immediate vicinity.*

vi·cious /ˈvɪʃəs/ *adj.* **1** cruel; done in order to hurt sb/sth: *a vicious attack* **2** (used about an animal) dangerous
IDM **a vicious circle/cycle** a situation in which one problem leads to another and the new problem makes the first problem worse —**vi·cious·ly** *adv.*

☆ **vic·tim** /ˈvɪktəm/ *noun* [C] a person or animal that is injured, killed or hurt by sb/sth: *a murder victim* ○ *The children are often the innocent victims of a divorce.*

vic·tim·ize /ˈvɪktəmaɪz/ *verb* [T] to punish or make sb suffer unfairly —**vic·tim·i·za·tion** /ˌvɪktəməˈzeɪʃn/ *noun* [U]

vic·tor /ˈvɪktər/ *noun* [C] (*formal*) the person who wins a game, competition, battle, etc.

☆ **vic·to·ry** /ˈvɪktəri/ *noun* [C,U] (*pl.* **vic·to·ries**) success in winning a battle, game, competition, etc.: *the American colonists' victory over the British troops* ○ *Sue Jenkins won a decisive victory in the school board election.* ○ *Jordan led his team to victory in the championships.* —**vic·to·ri·ous** /vɪkˈtɔriəs/ *adj.*: *the victorious team* (= the one that won)

☆ **vid·e·o** /ˈvɪdioʊ/ *noun* (*pl.* **vid·e·os**) **1** [U] the system of recording moving pictures and sound by using a camera, and showing them by using a recorder and a television: *The movie is coming out on video in May.* ○ *a video camera* **2** [C] a tape or cassette on which a movie or television program has been recorded: *We watched a video in English class today.* ○ *a video rental store* **3** [C] a short movie that is

made to be shown on television along with a popular song instead of speech: *the band's latest music video*

vid·e·o·cas·sette /ˌvɪdioʊkəˈsɛt/ *noun* [C] a cassette that contains tape on which you can record moving pictures and sound or television programs
ˌvideocasˈsette reˌcorder *noun* [C] = VCR
ˈvideo game *noun* [C] a game that you play on a special machine connected to a television, or on a special machine with a screen in a public place

vid·e·o·tape¹ /ˈvɪdioʊteɪp/ *noun* [C,U] tape used for recording moving pictures and sound or television programs

vid·e·o·tape² /ˈvɪdioʊteɪp/ *verb* [T] to record moving pictures and sound or a movie or television program onto a videotape ¹

☆ **view¹** /vyu/ *noun* **1** [U] the ability to be seen from a particular place: *The garden was hidden from view behind a high wall.* ○ *to come into/disappear from view* **2** [C] what you can see from a particular place. A view usually means sth pleasant to look at, e.g. a beautiful area of land: *There are breathtaking views from the top of the mountain.* ○ *a room with an ocean view* ☞ Look at the note at **scenery**. **3** [sing.] the ability to see sth from a particular place: *A large truck was blocking her view of the road.* **4** [C] **a view (about/on sth)** an opinion or idea about sth: *He expressed the view that standards were falling.* ○ *In my view, she has done nothing wrong.* ○ *strong views on the subject*
IDM **in full view (of sb/sth)** ⇨ FULL¹
in view of sth because of sth; as a result of sth: *In view of her apology, we decided to take no further action.*
point of view ⇨ POINT¹
with a view to/toward sth/ doing sth (*formal*) with the aim or intention of doing sth

☆ **view²** /vyu/ *verb* [T] (*formal*) **1** **view sth (as sth)** to consider or think about sth: *She viewed vacations as a waste of time.* ○ *He views these changes with suspicion.* **2** to watch or look at sth: *Viewed from this angle, the building looks much taller than it really is.*

view·er /ˈvyuər/ *noun* [C] a person who watches sth, especially television

view·point /ˈvyupɔɪnt/ *noun* [C] a way of looking at a situation; an opinion

vig·il /ˈvɪdʒəl/ *noun* [C,U] a period when you stay awake all night for a special purpose: *to hold a candlelight vigil for peace* ○ *All night she kept vigil over the sick child.*

vig·i·lant /ˈvɪdʒələnt/ *adj.* (*formal*) careful and looking out for danger —**vig·i·lance** /-əns/ *noun* [U]

vig·i·lan·te /ˌvɪdʒəˈlænti/ *noun* [C] a person (not a member of the police) who tries to prevent crime in a particular area, or to pun-

ish sb that he/she thinks has committed a crime

vig·or /'vɪgər/ noun [U] strength or energy: *After the break, we started work again with renewed vigor.* —**vig·or·ous** /'vɪgərəs/ adj.: *vigorous exercise* —**vig·or·ous·ly** adv.: *Citizens have protested vigorously against the plans to create a new waste dump.*

vile /vaɪl/ adj. very bad or unpleasant: *She's in a vile mood.* ○ *a vile smell*

vil·la /'vɪlə/ noun [C] a pleasant house in the country, usually in a warm region. A villa is often used as a vacation home.

vil·lage /'vɪlɪdʒ/ noun **1** [C] a very small town: *a small fishing village*

☞ We do not use **village** to talk about small towns in the United States. **Village** is used for places in other countries that seem more old-fashioned than American towns: *a quaint English village*

2 [sing.] all the people who live in a village (1): *The whole village is taking part in the festival.*

vil·lain /'vɪlən/ noun [C] an evil person, especially in a book or play: *In old westerns, the villains usually wear black hats.* ☞ Look at **hero**.

vine /vaɪn/ noun [C] a plant that climbs up a surface, e.g. a wall, as it grows

vin·e·gar /'vɪnɪgər/ noun [U] a liquid with a strong sharp taste that is made from wine, etc. Vinegar is often mixed with oil and put onto salads.

vine·yard /'vɪnyərd/ noun [C] a piece of land where grapes are grown for making wine

vin·tage /'vɪntɪdʒ/ adj. (only *before* a noun) **1** (used about wine) that was produced in a particular year and district: *a bottle of vintage champagne* **2** of very high quality and showing typical characateristics of sb/sth: *a vintage performance by Dustin Hoffman* **3** very old, and often valuable: *vintage clothing*

vi·nyl /'vaɪml/ noun [C,U] a type of strong plastic that is used for making floor coverings, covers for some chairs and car seats, etc.

vi·o·la /vi'oʊlə/ noun [C] a musical instrument with strings that looks like a violin but is slightly larger ☞ Note that we play **the** viola.

vi·o·late /'vaɪəleɪt/ verb [T] **1** to break sth (e.g. a rule or agreement): *to violate a peace treaty* **2** to disturb sth; not to respect sth: *to violate sb's privacy, rights, etc.* —**vi·o·la·tion** /ˌvaɪə-'leɪʃn/ noun [C,U]: *violation of human rights* ○ *a ticket for a parking violation*

☆ **vi·o·lence** /'vaɪələns/ noun [U] **1** violent behavior: *They threatened to use violence if we didn't give them the money.* ○ *Is there too much violence on TV?* ○ *an act of violence* **2** great force or energy: *the hurricane's violence*

☆ **vi·o·lent** /'vaɪələnt/ adj. **1** using physical strength, often in an uncontrolled way, to hurt or kill sb; caused by this behavior: *a violent man who abused his children* ○ *The demonstration started peacefully but later turned violent.* ○ *a violent death* **2** very strong; uncontrolled: *He has a violent temper.* ○ *a violent storm* —**vi·o·lent·ly** adv.

vi·o·let /'vaɪələt/ noun **1** [C] a small plant that grows wild or in gardens and has purple or white flowers and a pleasant smell **2** [U] a color similar to purple, between blue and red —**vi·o·let** adj.

☆ **vi·o·lin** /ˌvaɪə'lɪn/ noun [C] a musical instrument with strings, that you hold under your chin and play by moving a special stick (**a bow**) across the strings ☞ Note that we play **the** violin. Look also at **fiddle¹**.

violin
bow

VIP /ˌvi aɪ 'pi/ noun [C] (*pl.* **VIPs**) (*informal*) very important person; a person who gets or deserves special treatment and attention: *the VIP lounge at the airport*

vir·gin¹ /'vərdʒən/ noun [C] a person who has never had sex —**vir·gin·i·ty** /vər'dʒɪnəti/ noun [U]: *to lose your virginity* (= to have sex for the first time)

vir·gin² /'vərdʒən/ adj. (only *before* a noun) that has not yet been used, touched, damaged, etc.: *virgin forest*

Vir·go /'vərgoʊ/ noun (*pl.* **Vir·gos**) [C,U] the sixth sign of the zodiac, the Virgin; a person who was born under this sign ☞ picture at **zodiac.**

vir·ile /'vɪrəl/ adj. (used about a man) strong and having great sexual energy —**vi·ril·i·ty** /və'rɪləti/ noun [U]

vir·tu·al /'vərtʃuəl/ adj. (only *before* a noun) being almost or nearly sth: *Traffic came to a virtual standstill on the highways during yesterday's storm.* —**vir·tu·al·ly** /'vərtʃuəli; -tʃəli/ adv.: *The building is virtually finished.*

virtual re·al·i·ty noun [U] pictures and often also sounds, that are produced by a computer and are intended to seem almost like a real place or situation

☆ **vir·tue** /'vərtʃu/ noun **1** [U] behavior which shows high moral standards; goodness: *to lead a life of virtue* **2** [C] a good quality or habit: *Patience is a great virtue.* ☞ Look at **vice** (2). **3** [C,U] **the virtue (of sth/of doing sth)** an advantage or a useful quality of sth: *This new material has the virtue of being strong as well as very light.*

IDM **by virtue of** (*formal*) because of: *She got the job by virtue of her friendship with the company's owner*

vir·tu·ous /'vərtʃuəs/ adj. behaving in a moral or good way

vir·u·lent /'vɪrələnt; 'vɪryə-/ adj. (*formal*) **1** (used about a poison or a disease) very strong and dangerous: *a particularly virulent*

form of the flu **2** very strong and full of anger: *a virulent attack on the resident*

☆ **vi·rus** /ˈvaɪrəs/ *noun* [C] (*pl.* **vi·rus·es**) **1** a living thing, too small to be seen with the eye, that causes disease in people, animals and plants: *HIV, the virus that causes AIDS* ☞ Look at **bacteria** and **germ**. **2** (*computing*) instructions that are put into a computer program in order to cause errors and destroy information

vi·sa /ˈvizə/ *noun* [C] an official mark in your passport that shows you are allowed to enter, leave or travel through a country: *She applied for an extension when her visa expired.* ◦ *a tourist visa*

vise /vaɪs/ *noun* [C] a tool that you use to hold a piece of wood, metal, etc. firmly while you are working on it

vis·i·bil·i·ty /ˌvɪzəˈbɪləti/ *noun* [U] the distance that you can see in particular light or weather conditions: *In the fog, visibility was down to 100 feet.* ◦ *poor/good visibility*

☆ **vis·i·ble** /ˈvɪzəbl/ *adj.* that can be seen or noticed: *The stain was visible, even though he had washed his shirt twice.* ◦ *a visible improvement* ☞ The opposite is **invisible**.

vis·i·bly /-əbli/ *adv.* clearly; in a way that is easy to notice: *Tom was visibly upset.*

☆ **vi·sion** /ˈvɪʒn/ *noun* **1** [U] the ability to see; sight: *to have good, poor, normal, perfect, etc. vision* **2** [U] the ability to make great plans for the future: *a statesman of great vision* **3** [C] a picture in your imagination: *They have a vision of a world without weapons.* ◦ *I had visions of being left behind, but in fact the others had waited for me.* **4** [C] a dreamlike state often connected with a religious experience: *God appeared to Paul in a vision.*

☆ **vis·it¹** /ˈvɪzət/ *verb* **1** [I,T] to come or go to see a person or place and to spend a short time there: *I don't live here. I'm just visiting.* ◦ *We often visit relatives on weekends.* ◦ *She's going to visit her son in the hospital.* ◦ *When you go to New York City, you have to visit the Statue of Liberty.* **2** [I] **visit (with sb)** (*informal*) to talk in a friendly, informal way: *I was just visiting with Lynn in the backyard.*

☆ **vis·it²** /ˈvɪzət/ *noun* [C] a short stay with sb or in a particular place: *The President is on an official visit to Japan.* ◦ *We had a visit from Richard on Sunday.*

☆ **vis·i·tor** /ˈvɪzətər/ *noun* [C] a person who visits sb/sth: *We're not free on Sunday. We're having visitors.* ◦ *foreign visitors to California*

vi·sor /ˈvaɪzər/ *noun* [C] **1** the part of a hard hat (**a helmet**) that you can pull down to protect your eyes or face **2** a piece of plastic, cloth, etc. on a hat or in a car, which keeps the sun out of your eyes

☆ **vi·su·al** /ˈvɪʒuəl/ *adj.* connected with seeing: *the visual arts* (= painting, sculpture, movies,

etc.) —**vi·su·al·ly** *adv.*: *to be visually impaired* (= to be partly or completely blind)

visual aid *noun* [C] a picture, movie, map, etc. that helps students to learn sth

vi·su·al·ize /ˈvɪʒuəlaɪz/ *verb* [T] to imagine or have a picture in your mind of sb/sth: *It's hard to visualize what this place looked like before the factory was built.* ◦ *I can't visualize Liz as a mother.*

☆ **vi·tal** /ˈvaɪtl/ *adj.* very important or necessary: *Practice is vital if you want to speak a language well.* ◦ *vital information* —**vi·tal·ly** *adv.*: *vitally important*

vi·tal·i·ty /vaɪˈtæləti/ *noun* [U] the state of being lively or full of energy

☆ **vi·ta·min** /ˈvaɪtəmən/ *noun* [C] one of several substances that are found in certain types of food and that are very important for growth and good health: *Oranges are rich in vitamin C.* ◦ *a vitamin deficiency*

vi·va·cious /vɪˈveɪʃəs; vaɪ-/ *adj.* (used about a person, usually a woman) full of energy; lively and cheerful

viv·id /ˈvɪvəd/ *adj.* **1** (used about light or a color) strong and bright: *the vivid reds and yellows of the flowers* **2** having or producing a strong, clear picture in your mind: *a vivid description of his time in the army* ◦ *a vivid dream* —**viv·id·ly** *adv.*

☆ **vo·cab·u·lar·y** /voʊˈkæbyəˌlɛri; və-/ *noun* (*pl.* **vo·cab·u·lar·ies**) **1** [sing.] all the words in a language: *New words are always coming into the vocabulary.* **2** [C,U] all the words that sb knows or that are used in a particular book, subject, etc.: *He has a large vocabulary for such a small child.* ◦ *There are many ways to increase your English vocabulary.*

vo·cal /ˈvoʊkl/ *adj.* **1** connected with the voice: *vocal music* **2** expressing your ideas or opinions loudly or freely: *a small but vocal group of protesters*

vo·cal·ist /ˈvoʊklɪst/ *noun* [C] a singer, especially one who sings popular or jazz music

vo·ca·tion /voʊˈkeɪʃn/ *noun* [C,U] (*formal*) the feeling that you are especially suited for a particular kind of work, often one which involves helping other people; the ability to do this kind of work: *Peter followed his vocation to become a priest.*

vo·ca·tion·al /voʊˈkeɪʃnl/ *adj.* connected with the skills or qualifications that you need to do a particular job, especially a job that involves working with tools: *vocational training* ◦ *a vocational school.* (= that teaches students to do jobs that involve working with tools)

vod·ka /ˈvɑdkə/ *noun* [U] a strong clear alcoholic drink originally from Russia

☆ **voice¹** /vɔɪs/ *noun* **1** [C] the sounds that you make when you speak or sing; the ability to make these sounds: *I heard voices near the house and went out to see who it was.* ◦ *She has*

i	ɪ	ɛ	æ	ɑ	ɔ	ʌ	ʊ	u
see	sit	ten	cat	hot	saw	cup	put	too

a beautiful voice (= she can sing beautifully). ∘ He had a bad cold and lost his voice. ∘ to speak in a loud, soft, low, hoarse, etc. voice ∘ Shh! Keep your voice down! ∘ to raise/lower your voice (= to make it louder/quieter) ∘ Alan is 13 and his voice is beginning to break (= to become deep and low like a man's). **2** [U, sing.] **voice (in sth)** (the right to express) your ideas or opinions: The office employees have no voice in the running of the company. **3** [sing.] (grammar) the form of a verb that shows the relationship between the subject and the verb in a sentence: "Frost wrote this poem" is in the active voice. ∘ "This poem was written by Frost" is in the passive voice.

IDM **at the top of your voice** ➪ TOP¹

voice² /vɔɪs/ verb [T] to express your opinions or feelings: Congress voiced its objections to the President's plans.

'voice mail noun [U] an electronic system that lets you record telephone messages for sb when he/she is not available to answer the telephone ☞ Look at **answering machine**.

void¹ /vɔɪd/ noun [C, usually sing.] (formal) an empty space: (figurative) Her death left a void in their lives.

void² /vɔɪd/ adj. (formal) **void (of sth)** empty; without sth

vol. abbr. = VOLUME

vol·a·tile /'vɑlətl/ adj. **1** that can change suddenly: The situation in the Middle East is still very volatile. ∘ a volatile personality **2** (technical) (used about a liquid) that can easily change into a gas —**vol·a·til·i·ty** /ˌvɑlə'tɪləti/ noun [U]

☆ **vol·ca·no** /vɑl'keɪnoʊ/ noun [C] (pl. **vol·ca·noes**) a mountain with a hole (**crater**) at the top through which steam, hot liquid rock (**lava**), fire, etc. sometimes come out: an active/a dormant/an extinct volcano ∘ When did the volcano last erupt? —**vol·can·ic** /vɑl'kænɪk/ adj.

vol·ley /'vɑli/ noun [C] (pl. **vol·leys**) **1** a number of stones, bullets, etc. that are thrown, shot, etc. at the same time: The soldiers fired a volley over the heads of the crowd. ∘ (figurative) a volley of abuse **2** (in tennis, etc.) an act of hitting the ball before it touches the ground

vol·ley·ball /'vɑlibɔl/ noun [U] a game in which two teams try to hit a ball over a high net with their hands and not let it touch the ground

volt /voʊlt/ noun [C] (abbr. **V**) a unit for measuring electrical force

volt·age /'voʊltɪdʒ/ noun [C,U] the electrical force that is measured in volts: Danger! High voltage (on a sign near electrical equipment)

☆ **vol·ume** /'vɑlyəm; -jum/ noun (abbr. **vol.**) **1** [C] a book, especially one of a set or series: The library has over 100,000 volumes. ∘ The dictionary comes in three volumes. **2** [C,U] the amount of space that sth contains or occupies:

What is the volume of this sphere? ∘ A pound of feathers is greater in volume than a pound of gold. ☞ Look at **area**. **3** [U] the quantity or amount of sth: the volume of traffic on the roads **4** [U] the strength or degree of sound that sth makes: to turn the volume on a radio up/down

vol·un·tar·y /'vɑlən,tɛri/ adj. done or given willingly, not because you have to do it: voluntary guidelines to control advertising on the Internet ☞ Something that you must do is **mandatory**. —**vol·un·tar·i·ly** /ˌvɑlən'tɛrəli/ adv.: She left the job voluntarily – she wasn't fired.

☆ **vol·un·teer¹** /ˌvɑlən'tɪr/ noun [C] a person who offers or agrees to do sth without being forced or paid to do it: He does a lot of volunteer work at the hospital. ∘ volunteer firefighters ∘ Are there any volunteers who want to write their answers on the board?

vol·un·teer² /ˌvɑlən'tɪr/ verb **1** [I,T] **volunteer (sth); volunteer (for sth); volunteer (to do sth)** to offer sth or to do sth which you do not have to do or for which you will not be paid: They volunteered their services free of charge. ∘ She volunteered for the school's social committee. ∘ One of my friends volunteered to take us all in his car. **2** [T] to give information, etc. or make a comment or suggestion without being asked to: I volunteered a few helpful suggestions.

vom·it /'vɑmət/ verb [I,T] (formal) to bring food, etc. up from the stomach and out of the mouth ☞ It is more common to say **throw up**: I ate too much last night and threw up. —**vom·it** noun [U]: the smell of vomit

☆ **vote¹** /voʊt/ noun **1** [C] a method of deciding sth by asking people to express their choice and finding out what the majority want: Let's take a vote. All those in favor, raise your hands. **2** [C] **a vote (for/against sb/sth)** an expression of your choice in an election, etc., which you show by raising your hand or writing on a piece of paper: The votes are still being counted. ∘ There were nearly 20,000 votes for Mr. Wells. **3 the vote** [sing.] the votes given or received by a certain group in an election: The Democratic candidate received 42% of the vote.

☆ **vote²** /voʊt/ verb **1** [I,T] **vote (for/against sb/sth); vote (on sth)** to show a choice of opinion with a vote: Who did you vote for in the last election? ∘ Very few senators voted against the new law. ∘ Now that we've heard everybody's opinion, I think it's time to vote on it. ∘ They voted to ban smoking in the building. ∘ I voted Democrat. **2** [T] to choose sb for a particular position or honor: He was voted best actor.

☆ **vot·er** /'voʊtər/ noun [C] a person who votes or has the right to vote in a political election

vouch /vaʊtʃ/ verb

PHRV **vouch for sb/sth** to state that a person is honest or good or that sth is true or genuine

vouch·er /'vaʊtʃər/ *noun* [C] an official piece of paper that you can exchange for certain goods or services, instead of using money

vow¹ /vaʊ/ *noun* [C] a formal promise (especially in a religious ceremony): *marriage vows* ∘ *a vow of silence*

vow² /vaʊ/ *verb* [T] to make a serious promise: *We vowed never to discuss the subject again.*

☆ **vow·el** /'vaʊəl/ *noun* [C] a sound that you make with your lips and teeth open; one of the sounds represented in English by the letters "a," "e," "i," "o," or "u," and sometimes "y" ☞ Look at **consonant**.

voy·age /'vɔɪɪdʒ/ *noun* [C] a long trip by ship or in space: *Magellan's voyages of discovery* ∘ *a spacecraft on a voyage to Jupiter* —**voy·ag·er** /'vɔɪɪdʒər/ *noun* [C]

vs. *abbr.* = VERSUS

vul·gar /'vʌlgər/ *adj.* rude or likely to offend people, especially because it is about sex: *a vulgar joke* ∘ *a vulgar gesture* —**vul·gar·i·ty** /vʌl'gærəti; -'gɛr-/ *noun* [U] (*pl.* **vul·gar·i·ties**)

vul·ner·a·ble /'vʌlnərəbl/ *adj.* **vulnerable (to sth/sb)** easy to attack, hurt or defeat; open to danger: *Poor organization left the troops vulnerable to enemy attack.* ∘ *She felt lonely and vulnerable, living on her own in the city.* ☞ The opposite is **invulnerable.** —**vul·ner·a·bil·i·ty** /ˌvʌlnərə'bɪləti/ *noun* [U]

vul·ture /'vʌltʃər/ *noun* [C] a large bird that has no feathers on its head or neck and that eats the flesh of dead animals

Ww

W, w /'dʌblyu; 'dʌbəyu; -yə/ *noun* [C] (*pl.* **W's; w's**) the twenty-third letter of the English alphabet: *"Water" begins with (a) "W."*

W *abbr.* **1** = WATT **2** (*also* **W.**) = WEST, WESTERN¹

wack·y /'wæki/ *adj.* (**wack·i·er; wack·i·est**) (*informal*) exciting, new and crazy: *a wacky comedian*

wad /wɑd/ *noun* [C] **1** a lump or ball of soft material that is used for blocking sth, keeping sth in place, etc.: *The nurse used a wad of cotton to stop the bleeding.* **2** a large number of papers or money in a pile or rolled together

wad·dle /'wɑdl/ *verb* [I] to walk with short steps, leaning to one side and then to the other, like a duck: *A small, fat person waddled past.*

wade /weɪd/ *verb* [I] **1** to walk with bare feet in shallow water **2** to walk with difficulty through fairly deep mud, etc.: (*figurative*) *She had to wade through three thick books before she could write the essay.*

wa·fer /'weɪfər/ *noun* [C] a very thin, crisp cookie

waf·fle¹ /'wɑfl/ *noun* [C] a small, crisp cake, made of flour, eggs and milk, that has a pattern of squares on it and is eaten warm with a sweet sauce (**syrup**)

waft /wɑft; wæft/ *verb* [I,T] to move lightly through the air; to make sth move in this way: *The smell of her perfume wafted through the room.*

wag /wæg/ *verb* [I,T] (**wag·ging; wagged**) to shake up and down or move from side to side: *The dog is wagging his tail.*

☆ **wage¹** /weɪdʒ/ *noun* **1** [sing.] the amount of money paid for a certain amount of work, usually one hour: *What's the average wage in this area?* **2 wages** [plural] the pay that you receive, usually based on the number of hours that you have worked: *Any money missing from the cash register will be taken out of your wages.* ☞ Look at **salary** and at the note at **pay¹**.

wage² /weɪdʒ/ *verb* [T] **wage sth (against/on sb/sth)** to begin and continue sth, especially a war: *to wage war* ∘ *The police are waging a campaign against illegal drugs.*

☆ **wag·on** /'wægən/ *noun* [C] **1** a vehicle with four wheels that is pulled by horses, etc. and used for transporting things **2** a children's toy like an open box on wheels, with a long handle for pulling it **3** (*informal*) = STATION WAGON

wail /weɪl/ *verb* **1** [I,T] to cry or complain in a loud, high voice: *the sound of children wailing* ∘ *"Won't somebody help me?" she wailed.* **2** [I] to make a sound like this: *sirens wailing in the streets outside* —**wail** *noun* [C]: *the wail of sirens*

☆ **waist** /weɪst/ *noun* [C, usually sing.] **1** the part around the middle of the body between the stomach and the hips (and often narrower than them): *What's your waist measurement?* ∘ *a 26-inch waist* ∘ *She put her arms around his waist.* ☞ picture on page A24. **2** the part of a piece of clothing that goes around the waist

waist·line /'weɪstlaɪn/ *noun* [C, usually sing.] **1** the measurement or size of the body around the waist: *a slim waistline* **2** the part of a piece

of clothing that fits around or close to the waist: *a skirt with a high waistline*

☆**wait¹** /weɪt/ *verb* [I] **1 wait (for sb/sth) (to do sth)** to remain in a particular place, and not do anything until sb/sth arrives or until sth happens: *Wait here. I'll be back in a few minutes.* ○ *Have you been waiting long?* ○ *If I'm a little late, can you wait for me?* ○ *I wrote to them a few weeks ago and I'm still waiting for a reply.* ○ *I'm waiting to see the doctor.* ○ *He's waiting for them to tell him whether he got the job or not.* ○ *I can't wait* (= I am very eager) *to find out what happens at the end.*

☞ Compare **wait** and **expect**: *I was expecting him to be there at 7:30, but at 8 I was still waiting.* ○ *I'm waiting for my report card, but I'm not expecting to get any A's.* If you **wait**, you pass the time often doing little else, until sth happens: *I waited outside the theater until they arrived.* If you **expect** sth, you believe that sth will happen: *I'm expecting a reply from them soon, because it's been a month since I wrote.*

2 to be left or delayed until a later time; not to be done or dealt with immediately: *Is this matter urgent or can it wait?*

IDM **keep sb waiting** to make sb wait: *I'm sorry if I kept you waiting.*

wait a minute/second (*informal*) **1** (used to tell sb to stop doing sth and wait for a short time): *Wait a minute – Jeff has to tie his shoes.* **2** (used to interrupt sb because you have just noticed sth): *Hey, wait a minute – this is sugar, not salt.*

wait and see to wait and find out what will happen (perhaps before deciding to do sth)

wait tables to work in a restaurant, taking people's orders and bringing them food and drinks

wait your turn to wait until the time when you are allowed to do sth

PHRV **wait around** to stay in a place doing nothing because sb or sth is late

wait behind to stay in a place after others have left it

wait on sb to bring food, drinks, etc. to sb, usually in a restaurant

wait up (for sb) to not go to bed because you are waiting for sb to come home: *I won't be back until very late, so don't wait up.*

☆**wait²** /weɪt/ *noun* [C, usually sing.] **a wait (for sth/sb)** a period of time when you wait: *a short/long wait*

☆**wait·er** /ˈweɪtər/ *noun* [C] a man whose job is to take orders from customers and bring food and drinks to them in a restaurant ☞ **Server** is a word that can be used for a man or a woman who works in a restaurant.

'**waiting list** *noun* [C] a list of people who are waiting for sth that will be available in the future: *to put sb's name on the waiting list*

'**waiting room** *noun* [C] a room at a doctor's office, etc. where people can sit and wait

☆**wait·ress** /ˈweɪtrəs/ *noun* [C] a woman whose job is to take orders from customers and bring food and drinks to them in a restaurant ☞ **Server** is a word that can be used for a man or a woman who works in a restaurant.

waive /weɪv/ *verb* [T] (*formal*) to state that a rule, etc. does not have to be obeyed; to give up a right to sth: *The coach waived the age requirement so that Amy could play on the senior high team.* ○ *He waived his right to a trial by jury.*

waiv·er /ˈweɪvər/ *noun* [C] an official document that says that a rule, etc. does not have to be obeyed

☆**wake¹** /weɪk/ *verb* (*p.t.* **woke** /woʊk/; *p.p.* **wo·ken** /ˈwoʊkən/) **1** [I] **wake (up)** to stop being asleep: *I woke early in the morning and got right out of bed.* ○ *Wake up! It's almost 8 o'clock!* ☞ **Wake** is more formal than **wake up**. **2** [T] **wake sb (up)** to make sb stop sleeping: *Could you wake me up at 7:30 tomorrow morning?* **3** [T] **wake sb/sth up** to make sb/sth become more lively or active: *She always has some coffee to wake her up when she gets to work.*

PHRV **wake up** (*informal*) to begin to pay attention: *Hey, wake up, Rob! It's your turn next.*

wake up to sth to become aware of sth: *By the time he had woken up to the danger, it was too late.*

wake² /weɪk/ *noun* [C] **1** the track that a moving ship or boat leaves behind on the surface of the water **2** an event before a funeral when friends and family members of the dead person meet to talk together and remember him/her

IDM **in the wake of sth** (*also* **in sth's wake**) following or happening after sth, often as a result of it: *The floods left a great deal of destruction in their wake.*

☆**walk¹** /wɔk/ *verb* **1** [I] to move along on foot at a fairly slow speed: *Our little girl is just learning to walk.* ○ *"Did you drive here?" "No, I walked."* ○ *He walked with a limp.* ○ *Is the grocery store within walking distance?* (= is it close enough to walk to?) **2** [I] to move on foot for exercise or pleasure: *We walked through the park at sunset.* ☞ Look also at **hike**. **3** [T] to go on foot with sb/sth; to guide or help sb to walk: *I'll walk you home if you don't want to go on your own.* ○ *people walking their dogs in the park* **4** [T] to go along or through sth on foot: *He walked the streets all night.*

IDM **walk all over sb** (*informal*) **1** to defeat sb completely: *Rachel played fantastically and walked all over her opponent.* **2** to deal with sb as if he/she is not important: *I don't know why she lets her husband walk all over her like that.*

W

PHRV **walk away (from sb/sth)** to leave a person or a situation, without caring about what will happen to him/her/it

walk away with sth to win sth easily: *She walked away with all the prizes.*

walk off with sth to steal sth; to take sth that does not belong to you by mistake: *When I got home, I realized that I had walked off with her pen.*

walk out (of sth) to leave suddenly and angrily: *She walked out of the meeting in disgust.*

walk out (on sb) (*informal*) to leave sb forever: *He walked out on his wife and children after 15 years of marriage.*

walk up (to sb/sth) to approach (sb/sth): *He walked up to her and asked her if she wanted to dance.*

☆ **walk²** /wɔk/ *noun* **1** [C] a trip on foot for pleasure, exercise, etc.: *We went for a walk in the park.* ○ *I'm going to take the dog for a walk.* ☞ We use **go for a walk** when we are talking about a short walk that we take for pleasure. **2** [sing.] the time taken to go somewhere on foot; the distance to a place on foot: *The hotel is five minutes' walk from the beach.* **3** [sing.] a way or style of walking: *He has a funny walk.* **4** [sing.] the speed of walking: *She slowed to a walk.* **5** [C, usually sing.] a sidewalk that leads to a building, house, etc.: *She saw the mailman coming up the front walk.* ☞ picture on page A28. **6** [C] a route that you can walk along for pleasure: *This map shows a scenic walk through the woods.*

IDM **a walk of life** position in society: *She has friends from many different walks of life.*

walk·er /ˈwɔkər/ *noun* [C] **1** a person who walks: *a fast walker* ○ *This area is very popular with walkers.* **2** a metal frame that old or sick people push in front of themselves as they walk so that they do not fall down

walk·ie-talk·ie /ˌwɔki ˈtɔki/ *noun* [C] (*informal*) a small radio that you can carry with you and use to talk and listen to sb

ˈ**walk-in** *adj.* (only *before* a noun) **1** that is big enough for a person to walk into: *a walk-in closet* **2** (used about a business that offers services to the public) that you can go to without making an appointment earlier: *a walk-in health center*

ˈ**walking stick** *noun* [C] a stick that you use to lean on when you go for a walk in the country, mountains, etc.

Walk·man /ˈwɔkmən/ *noun* [C] (*pl.* **Walkmans**) (*trademark*) a small cassette player with headphones that you can carry around with you

walk·out (*also* **walk-out**) /ˈwɔkaʊt/ *noun* [C] an occasion when people leave a place or refuse to work, as a protest against sth: *Personnel staged a 24-hour walkout to protest against unsafe conditions.*

☆ **wall** /wɔl/ *noun* [C] **1** one of the sides of a room or building that join the ceiling and the floor: *You could hear people talking in the next room because the wall was so thin.* ○ *He put the poster up on the wall.* **2** a solid, upright structure made of stone, brick, etc. that is built around an area of land to protect it or to show a boundary: *There is a high wall all around the prison.* ☞ picture at **fence.**

IDM **off the wall** (*informal*) very unusual; crazy: *Some of her jokes are totally off the wall.*

drive sb up the wall ⇨ DRIVE¹

☆ **wal·let** /ˈwɔlət; ˈwɔ-/ (*also* **billfold**) *noun* [C] a small, flat, folding case in which you keep paper money, credit cards, etc.

wal·low /ˈwɔloʊ/ *verb* [I] **wallow (in sth) 1** to lie and roll around in water, etc.: *I spent an hour wallowing in a hot bath.* **2** to take great pleasure in sth (a feeling, situation, etc.): *He seems to wallow in self-pity.*

wall·pa·per /ˈwɔlˌpeɪpər/ *noun* [U] paper with a pattern on it that you stick to the walls of a room —**wall·pa·per** *verb* [T]: *We spent the weekend wallpapering the bedroom.*

ˈ**Wall Street** *noun* [U] **1** a street in New York City where many important banks and companies that exchange shares in other businesses (**stock exchanges**) are located **2** all the important companies and banks that control the financial situation in the U.S.

ˈ**wall-to-ˌwall** *adj.* (only *before* a noun) (used especially about a carpet) covering the whole floor of a room

☆ **wal·nut** /ˈwɔlnʌt/ *noun* **1** [C] a nut that you can eat, with a hard brown shell that is in two halves ☞ picture at **nut. 2** [C] (*also* ˈ**walnut tree**) the tree on which walnuts (1) grow **3** [U] the wood from the walnut tree

wal·rus /ˈwɔlrəs; ˈwɑl-/ *noun* [C] a large sea animal that lives in Arctic regions. It has two long teeth (**tusks**) coming out of its face.

waltz¹ /wɔlts; wɑls/ *noun* [C] a dance that you do with a partner, to music which has a rhythm of three beats; the music for this dance

waltz² /wɔlts; wɑls/ *verb* [I] **1** to dance a waltz¹: *They waltzed around the floor.* **2** **waltz around, in, over, up etc.** (*informal*) to move easily, carelessly or confidently: *You can't just waltz in and expect your meal to be ready for you.*

wan /wɑn/ *adj.* very pale and looking sick or tired

wand /wɑnd/ *noun* [C] a thin stick that magicians, etc. hold when they are doing magic: *I wish I could wave a magic wand and make everything better.*

☆ **wan·der** /ˈwɑndər/ *verb* **1** [I,T] to move slowly around a place or to go from place to place with no particular purpose: *We spent the afternoon wandering around the town.* ○ *He was found in a confused state, wandering the*

W

streets. **2** [I] **wander (away/off)**; **wander (from/off sth)** to leave a place or the path that you were on: *This is a dangerous area, so I don't want anybody to wander off.* ○ *(figurative) I seem to have wandered off the subject – what was I talking about?* **3** [I] (used about sb's mind, thoughts, etc.) to stop paying attention; to be unable to stay on one subject: *My attention started to wander during the lecture.* ○ *The old man's mind is wandering. He doesn't know where he is anymore.*

wane /weɪn/ *verb* [I] **1** to become less powerful, less important, smaller or weaker: *Britain's influence on world events has been waning for years.* **2** (used about the moon) to appear to become smaller

wan·na /ˈwɒnə; ˈwɒnə; ˈwʌnə/ *(informal)* (a way of writing "want to" or "want a" to show that sb is speaking in an informal way): *I wanna go home now.* ☞ Look at the note at **gonna**.

☆ **want¹** /wɒnt; wɔnt/ *verb* [T] to desire; to wish for: *He wants a new bike.* ○ *Do you want anything else?* ○ *What do they want for breakfast?* ○ *Is there anything you want to watch on TV?* ○ *I don't want to discuss it now.* ○ *I want you to call me when you get there.* ○ *The boss wants this letter typed.* ○ *I don't want Katie going out on her own at night.*

☞ **Want** and **would like** are similar in meaning, but "would like" is more polite and is used in formal situations: *"I want a drink!" screamed the child.* ○ *"Would you like some more coffee, Mrs. Sternwood?"* Look also at **wanted**.

IDM **want in/out** *(informal)* **1** to want to enter/leave a place: *I think the dog wants out.* **2** to want to be involved/not involved in a plan or situation

☆ **want²** /wɒnt; wɔnt/ *noun* [C] desire or need for sth; sth you desire or need: *All our wants were satisfied.*

IDM **for want of sth** *(formal)* because of a lack of sth: *I took the job for want of a better offer.*

'**want ad** *noun* [C] *(informal)* = CLASSIFIED ADVERTISEMENT

want·ed /ˈwɒntəd; ˈwɔn-/ *adj.* (used about a person) that the police are trying to find, because they think that he/she committed a crime: *He is wanted for arson.*

wan·ton /ˈwɒntən; ˈwɔn-/ *adj.* (usually *before* a noun) (used about an action) done in order to hurt sb or damage sth for no good reason

☆ **war** /wɔr/ *noun* **1** [U] a state of fighting between different countries or groups within countries, using armies and weapons: *war and peace* ○ *The two countries have been at war for six months.* ○ *to declare war* (= announce that a war has started) ○ *When war broke out, thousands of men were drafted into the army.* ☞ Look also at **civil war**. **2** [C] a period of

military fighting: *the Second World War* (= from 1939-1945) ○ *He was killed in the war.* ○ *to fight a war* **3** [C,U] a struggle; very strong competition between groups of people: *a price war among gas stations* **4** [sing.] **a war (against/on sb/sth)** efforts to end sth: *the war against organized crime*

war·ble /ˈwɔrbl/ *verb* [I] (usually used about a bird) to sing gently, changing the notes up and down very quickly

'**war crime** *noun* [C] an extremely cruel act that is committed during a war and is against international law —'**war criminal** *noun* [C]

ward¹ /wɔrd/ *noun* [C] **1** a separate part of a hospital, often for a particular group of patients: *the children's ward* **2** one of the sections into which a town is divided for elections **3** *(formal)* a child who is under the protection of a court of law or another adult (**guardian**), especially because his/her parents are dead

ward² /wɔrd/ *verb*

PHRV **ward sb/sth off** to keep away sb/sth that is dangerous or bad: *They lit a fire to ward off wild animals.*

war·den /ˈwɔrdn/ *noun* [C] an official who is in charge of a prison

ward·robe /ˈwɔrdroʊb/ *noun* [C] a person's collection of clothes: *I need a whole new wardrobe.*

ware /wɛr/ *noun* **1** [U] (in compounds) made from a particular type of material or suitable for a particular use: *stainless steel cookware* ☞ Look also at **hardware**, **software** and **silverware**. **2 wares** [plural] *(old-fashioned)* things that are for sale

☆ **ware·house** /ˈwɛrhaʊs/ *noun* [C] a building where large quantities of products are kept before being sent to stores

war·fare /ˈwɔrfɛr/ *noun* [U] methods of fighting a war; types of war: *guerrilla warfare* ○ *nuclear warfare*

war·head /ˈwɔrhɛd/ *noun* [C] the explosive part at the front of a bomb that can fly through the air (**a missile**)

war·i·ly ⇨ WARY

☆ **warm¹** /wɔrm/ *adj.* **1** having a temperature that is fairly high, between cool and hot: *Are you warm enough, or should I turn the heat on?* ○ *It's nice and warm in the sunshine.* ○ *I jumped up and down to keep my feet warm.* ☞ Look at the note at **hot** (1). **2** (used about clothing) preventing you from getting cold: *Take plenty of warm clothes.* **3** friendly; kind and pleasant; sincere: *I was given a very warm welcome.* **4** creating a pleasant, comfortable feeling: *warm colors* ☞ The noun from **warm** is **warmth**. —**warm·ly** *adv.*: *warmly dressed* ○ *She thanked him warmly for his help.*

☆ **warm²** /wɔrm/ *verb* [I,T] **warm (sb/sth) (up)** to become or to make sb/sth become warm or warmer: *It was cold earlier, but it's starting to*

W

warm up now. ○ I sat in front of the fire to warm up. ○ We'll just warm up some soup for lunch.

PHRV **warm to/toward sb** to begin to like sb **warm to sth** to become more interested in sth **warm up** to prepare for sth by practicing gently: *The team warmed up before the match.*

,warm-'**blooded** *adj.* having a blood temperature that does not change along with the temperature of the surroundings *Look at* **cold-blooded.**

,warm-'**hearted** *adj.* kind and friendly

☆ **warmth** /wɔrmθ/ *noun* [U] **1** a fairly high temperature or an effect created by this, especially when it is pleasant: *She felt the warmth of the sun on her face.* **2** friendliness or kindness: *I was touched by the warmth of their welcome.*

'**warm-up** (*also* **warm·up**) *noun* [C] a gentle exercise that you do to prepare yourself for some activity, e.g. a sports game

☆ **warn** /wɔrn/ *verb* **1** [I,T] **warn (sb) (of sth); warn (sb) about/against sb/sth; warn (sb) against doing sth** to tell sb to be careful or aware of sth, often bad or dangerous, that exists or might happen: *When I saw the car coming, I tried to warn him, but it was too late.* ○ *She warned me that he was not an easy man to work for.* ○ *The government is warning (the public) of possible terrorist attacks.* ○ *The radio warned people about delays on the roads this morning.* ○ *Most parents warn their kids against experimenting with drugs.* **2** [T] to advise sb (not) to do sth: *I warned you not to trust him.*

☆ **warn·ing** /wɔrnɪŋ/ *noun* [C,U] something that tells you to be careful or tells you about sth before it happens: *They ignored the warnings posted outside and entered the military base.* ○ *The computer just shut down without warning.* ○ *He gave me no warning of his arrival.*

warp /wɔrp/ *verb* [I,T] to become bent and out of shape (because of hot or damp conditions); to make sth become like this: (*figurative*) *His view of life had been warped by his unhappy experiences.* —**warped** *adj.*: *the killer's warped* (= abnormal) *mind*

war·path /wɔrpæθ/ *noun*

IDM (**be/go**) **on the warpath** (*informal*) to be very angry and ready to argue or fight

war·rant¹ /wɔrənt; 'wɑr-/ *noun* [C] a written statement that gives sb the authority to do sth: *a search warrant* (= a document that allows the police to search a house)

☆ **war·rant²** /wɔrənt; 'wɑr-/ *verb* [T] (*formal*) to make sth seem right or necessary; to deserve: *I don't think her behavior warrants such criticism.*

☆ **war·ran·ty** /wɔrənti; 'wɑr-/ *noun* [C,U] (*pl.* **war·ran·ties**) a written statement that you get when you buy sth, which promises to repair or replace it if it breaks or stops working

within a certain period of time *Look at* **guarantee.**

war·ri·or /wɔriər; 'wɑr-/ *noun* [C] (*old-fashioned, formal*) a person who fights in battle; a soldier

war·ship /wɔrʃɪp/ *noun* [C] a ship for use in war

wart /wɔrt/ *noun* [C] a small hard dry lump that sometimes grows on the face or body

war·time /wɔrtaɪm/ *noun* [U] a period of time during which there is a war

war·y /wɛri/ *adj.* (**war·i·er; war·i·est**) **wary (of sb/sth)** careful because you are uncertain or afraid of sb/sth: *He was wary of accepting the suggestion in case it meant more work for him.* —**war·i·ly** /-rəli/ *adv.*

was /wʌz; wɑz/ ⇨ BE¹,²

☆ **wash¹** /wɑʃ; wɔʃ/ *verb* **1** [I,T] to clean sb/sth/ yourself with water and often soap: *You'll have to wash this blouse by hand.* ○ *Go wash your hands before dinner.* ○ *I'll wash, you dry* (= the dishes). *Look at the note at* **clean².** **2** [I] (used about water) to flow in the direction mentioned: *I let the waves wash over my feet.* **3** [T] to carry sth by the movement of water: *The tide washed the ball out to sea.* **4** [I] to be able to be washed without being damaged: *Does this material wash well, or does the color come out?*

IDM **wash your hands of sb/sth** to refuse to be responsible for sb/sth any longer

PHRV **wash sb/sth away** (used about water) to carry sb/sth away: *The floods had washed the path away.*

wash (sth) off to (make sth) disappear from sth by washing: *Go and wash that makeup off!* **wash out** to be removed from a material by washing: *These grease marks won't wash out.* **wash up** to wash your face and hands: *Go and wash up and put on some clean clothes.*

wash sth up (often passive) (used about water) to carry sth to land and leave it there: *Police found the girl's body washed up on the beach.*

☆ **wash²** /wɑʃ; wɔʃ/ *noun* **1** [U] clothes that need to be washed or are being washed: *"Where's my red T-shirt?" "It's in the wash."* ○ *He hung the wash out on the clothesline.* **2** [C, usually sing.] an act of cleaning or being cleaned with water: *The car needs a good wash this weekend.*

IDM **do the wash** to wash clothes: *You should learn to do your own wash before you go to college.*

wash·a·ble /wɑʃəbl; 'wɔʃ-/ *adj.* that can be washed without being damaged

wash·cloth /wɑʃklɔθ; 'wɔʃ-/ *noun* [C] a small square towel that is used for washing your face, hands, etc.

wash·er /wɑʃər; 'wɔʃ-/ *noun* [C] **1** = WASHING MACHINE: *a washer and dryer* **2** a small metal

W

or rubber ring that is put between two parts of a machine to make them fit together better

☆ ¹**washing ma,chine** (*also* **washer**) *noun* [C] an electric machine that washes clothes

wash·room /'waʃrum; 'wɔʃ-/ *noun* [C] (*old-fashioned*) a room in a public building with a toilet ☞ Look at the note at **toilet**.

was·n't /'wʌznt; 'waznt/ *short for* WAS NOT

wasp /wasp; wɔsp/ *noun* [C] a black and yellow flying insect that can sting ☞ picture at **insect**.

☆ **waste¹** /weɪst/ *verb* [T] **waste sth (on sb/sth)** to use or spend sth in a careless way or for sth that is not necessary: *She wastes a lot of money on cigarettes.* ○ *Don't waste water – turn off the faucet while you brush your teeth.* ○ *He wasted his time at university because he didn't work hard.*

IDM **be wasted on sb/sth** to be too good, intelligent, etc. for sb/sth: *Expensive wine is wasted on me. I don't know anything about it.*

☆ **waste²** /weɪst/ *noun* **1 a waste (of sth)** [sing., U] an action that involves not using sth carefully or using it in an unnecessary way: *If he gives up acting, it will be a waste of great talent.* ○ *The class was a waste of time – I'd heard it all before.* **2** [U] material, food, etc. that is not needed and is therefore thrown away: *nuclear waste.* ○ *A lot of household waste can be recycled and reused.* ☞ Look at **garbage** and **trash**.

IDM **go to waste** to not be used; to be thrown away and wasted: *I can't bear to see good food going to waste!*

waste³ /weɪst/ *adj.* (only *before* a noun) no longer useful; to be thrown away: *waste material*

☆ **waste·bas·ket** /'weɪstˌbæskət/ *noun* [C] a basket or other container in which you put paper, etc. which is to be thrown away ☞ picture at **garbage can**.

wast·ed /'weɪstəd/ *adj.* **1** not necessary or successful: *a wasted trip* **2** (*slang*) under the influence of a lot of alcohol or illegal drugs: *Doug got completely wasted at Tanya's party!*

waste·ful /'weɪstfl/ *adj.* using more of sth than necessary; causing waste: *a costly and wasteful advertising campaign*

waste·land /'weɪstlænd/ *noun* [C,U] an ugly area of land that is not used or not suitable for use

☆ **watch¹** /watʃ; wɔtʃ/ *noun* **1** [C] a small instrument that shows you what time it is. You wear it around your wrist: *a digital watch* ○ *to wind/set your watch* ○ *My watch is a little bit fast/slow* (= shows a time that is later/earlier than the correct time). ○ *a watch band/strap* ☞ picture at **clock**. **2** [sing.] an act of guarding and protecting a place or a person, or the person or people who do this: *The police put a watch on the suspect's house.* ○ *a neighborhood watch patrol*

IDM **keep a close eye/watch on sb/sth** ⇨ EYE¹

keep watch to guard or to look out for danger

☆ **watch²** /watʃ; wɔtʃ/ *verb* **1** [I,T] to look carefully at sb/sth: *"Do you want to play too?" "No thanks. I'll just watch."* ○ *I watched in horror as the car swerved and crashed.* ○ *I'm watching to see how you do it.* ○ *We watch TV most evenings.* ○ *Watch what she does next.* ○ *I watched him open the door and walk away.* ○ *Detectives are watching the suspect day and night.* **2** [I,T] **watch (for sth)** to pay very careful attention to a situation; to observe: *Doctors are watching for further signs of the disease.* **3** [T] to take care of sb/sth for a short time: *Could you watch the kids while I go to the store?* **4** [T] to be careful about sb/sth in order to do the right thing or keep control: *You'd better watch what you say to her. She gets upset very easily.* ○ *No dessert for me – I'm watching my weight.*

IDM **watch it!** (*informal*) (used to warn sb to be more careful): *Hey, watch it, buddy! You almost hit my car!*

watch your step 1 to be careful about where you are walking **2** to be careful about how you behave

PHRV **watch out** to be careful because of possible danger or trouble: *Watch out! There's a car coming.* ○ *If you don't watch out, you'll lose your job.*

watch out for sb/sth to look carefully and be ready for sb/sth: *Watch out for snakes if you walk through the fields.*

watch over sb/sth to take care of or protect sb/sth: *For two weeks, she watched over the sick child.*

watch·dog /'watʃdɔg; 'wɔtʃ-/ *noun* [C] **1** a dog that has been trained to guard people, buildings, or land **2** a person or group whose job is to protect people's rights, especially in relation to large companies: *an independent watchdog group*

☆ **wa·ter¹** /'wɔtər; 'wa-/ *noun* **1** [U] the clear liquid that falls as rain and is in rivers, seas and lakes: *a glass of water* ○ *They lived in a shack with no running water.* ○ *After the heavy rain, several fields were under water.* ○ *clean drinking water* ○ *tap water* (= that comes out of a faucet) ○ *mineral water* ○ *Don't go too near the edge, or you'll fall in the water!*

☞ When water is **heated** to 212° Fahrenheit (100° C), it **boils** and becomes **steam**. When steam touches a cold surface, it **condenses** and becomes water again. When water is **cooled** below 32° Fahrenheit (0° C), it **freezes** and becomes ice. If the temperature increases, the ice **melts**. Frozen food **thaws** or **defrosts** when we take it out of the freezer.

2 waters [plural] the ocean near a particular country: *The ship was still in U.S. waters.* ○ *international waters*

tʃ	dʒ	v	θ	ð	s	z	ʃ
chin	**June**	**van**	**thin**	**then**	**so**	**zoo**	**she**

W

IDM **pass water** ⇨ PASS²

☆ **wa·ter²** /ˈwɔtər; ˈwɑ-/ *verb* **1** [T] to give water to plants **2** [I] (used about the eyes or mouth) to fill with water: *The smoke in the room made my eyes water.* ◦ *The food smelled so good that it made my mouth water.*

PHRV **water sth down 1** to add water to a liquid in order to make it weaker **2** to change a statement, report, etc. so that it is weaker

wa·ter·col·or /ˈwɔtərkʌlər; ˈwɑ-/ *noun* **1 watercolors** [plural] paints that are mixed with water, not oil **2** [C] a picture that has been painted with watercolors

☆ **wa·ter·fall** /ˈwɔtərfɔl; ˈwɑ-/ *noun* [C] a stream of water that falls down from a mountain, a high rock, etc.

ˈ**water ˌfountain** *noun* [C] = DRINKING FOUNTAIN

wa·ter·logged /ˈwɔtərlɔgd; -lɑgd; ˈwɔtər-/ *adj.* **1** very wet: *Our boots sank into the waterlogged ground.* **2** (used about a boat) full of water and likely to sink

wa·ter·mel·on /ˈwɔtərˌmɛlən; ˈwɑ-/ *noun* [C] a large, round fruit with thick, green skin. It is pink or red inside with a lot of black seeds.

wa·ter·proof /ˈwɔtərpruf; ˈwɑ-/ *adj.* that does not let water go through: *a waterproof jacket*

wa·ter·shed /ˈwɔtərʃɛd; ˈwɑ-/ *noun* [C, usually sing.] an event or point which is important because it marks the beginning of sth new

ˈ**water-ski** *verb* [I] to move across the surface of water while standing on narrow boards (**water skis**) and being pulled by a boat

wa·ter·tight /ˈwɔtərtaɪt; ˈwɑ-/ *adj.* made so that water cannot get in or out

ˈ**water ˌtower** *noun* [C] a tall structure with a very large tank of water at the top which is used to keep the water supplied to a town, etc. at a steady pressure

wa·ter·way /ˈwɔtərweɪ; ˈwɑ-/ *noun* [C] a canal, river, etc. along which boats or ships can travel

wa·ter·y /ˈwɔtəri; ˈwɑ-/ *adj.* (used especially about food or drink) containing too much water; thin and weak

watt /wɑt/ *noun* [C] (*abbr.* **W**) a unit of electrical power: *a 60-watt light bulb*

☆ **wave¹** /weɪv/ *verb* **1** [I,T] **wave (your hand) (at/to sb)** to move your hand from side to side in the air, usually to attract sb's attention or as you meet or leave sb: *She waved to me as the car drove off.* ◦ *Who are you waving at?* **2** [T] **wave sth (at sb); wave sth (around)** to hold sth in the air and move it from side to side: *The crowd was waving flags as the President rode past.* ◦ *She was talking excitedly and waving her arms around.* **3** [T] **wave sth (to sb)** to give a greeting (to sb) by waving your hand: *Wave goodbye to Grandma, Tim.* **4** [I] to move gently up and down or from side to side: *The branches of the trees waved gently in the breeze.*

PHRV **wave sth aside** to decide not to pay attention to a comment, etc. because you think it is not important

wave sb/sth away, on, etc. to move your hand in a particular direction to show sb/sth which way to go: *There was a police officer in the middle of the road, waving us on.*

☆ **wave²** /weɪv/ *noun* [C] **1** a raised line of water moving on the surface of water, especially the ocean: *boats bobbing up and down on the waves* ◦ *A huge wave swept me off my feet.* ◦ *We watched the waves roll in and break on the shore.* ◦ (*figurative*) *a wave of tourists* ☞ picture at **beach**. **2** a sudden increase or spread of a feeling or type of behavior: *There has been a wave of public sympathy for the victims.* ◦ *the recent wave of burglaries* ☞ Look at **heat wave**. **3** a form in which some types of energy move, shaped like a wave in the ocean: *sound waves* ◦ *shock waves from the earthquake* **4** a gentle curve in hair: *natural waves* ☞ Look at **perm**. **5** a movement of sth, especially your hand, from side to side in the air: *With a wave of his hand, he said goodbye and left.*

wave·length /ˈweɪvlɛŋkθ; -lɛŋθ/ *noun* [C] the distance between two sound waves

IDM **on the same wavelength** ⇨ SAME¹

wav·er /ˈweɪvər/ *verb* [I] **1** to become weak or uncertain: *He never wavered in his support for her.* **2 waver (between A and B)** to hesitate, especially when making a decision or choice

☆ **wav·y** /ˈweɪvi/ *adj.* having curves: *wavy hair* ◦ *a wavy line* ☞ picture at **hair** and **line**.

☆ **wax** /wæks/ *noun* [U] **1** a substance made from fat or oil that melts easily and is used for making candles, polish, etc. **2** (*also* **earwax**) a yellow substance like wax (1) that is found in your ears

☆ **way¹** /weɪ/ *noun* **1** [C, usually sing.] the route you take to reach somewhere: *Can you tell me the way to Elm Street?* ◦ *She lost her way and had to turn back.* ◦ *We stopped for a snack on the way home.* **2** [sing.] the route along which you move or would move if there were space: *There was a van parked in the alley, blocking our way.* ◦ *Get out of my way!* **3** [sing.] a direction or position: *Look this way!* ◦ *Shouldn't you be wearing that hat the other way around?* (= facing in the other direction) ◦ *He thought I was older than my sister, but in fact it's the other way around* (= the opposite of what he thought). **4** (*also informal* **ways**) [sing.] a distance in space or time: *It's a long way from Houston to Amarillo.* ◦ *Summer is still a long way off.* **5** [C] a method, style or manner of doing sth; a habit: *What is the best way to learn a language?* ◦ *I've discovered a terrific way of losing weight!* ◦ *There are various ways in which we can help.* ◦ *They'll have to find the money one way or another.* ◦ *He always does things his way.* **6** [C] a particular point or part

of sth: *In some ways, the meeting was very useful.* ○ *In a way, I sort of like him.* ○ *Can I help you in any way?*

IDM **be set in your ways** to be unable to change your habits, attitudes, etc.

by the way ⇨ BY²

get/have your own way to get or do what you want, although others may want sth else

give way to break or fall down: *The tree branch suddenly gave way and came crashing down.*

give way (to sb/sth) 1 to stop or to allow sb/sth else to happen, develop, etc. instead: *Old-fashioned methods have given way to new technology.* **2** to allow sb to have what he/she wants although you did not at first agree with it: *We will not give way to the terrorists' demands.*

go out of your way (to do sth) to make a special effort to do sth

in a big/small way (used for expressing the size or importance of an activity)

in the way 1 blocking the road or path: *I can't get past. There's a big truck in the way.* **2** not needed or wanted: *I felt like I was in the way at my daughter's party.*

no way 1 (*informal*) definitely not: *"Can we have a party here?" "No way! You'll wreck the house!"* **2** (*slang*) (used to show surprise, when you find sth difficult to believe): *"Vaughn got fired yesterday." "No way!"*

under way having started and making progress: *Discussions between the two sides are now under way.*

a/sb's way of life the behavior and customs that are typical of a person or group of people

way² /weɪ/ *adv.* **1** (*informal*) very far: *His name was way down at the bottom of the list.* **2** (*slang*) (used before a comparative) very much: *Paul ate way more than anybody else.* ○ *This is way better than the old one.*

☆**we** /wi/ *pron.* (the subject of a verb; used for talking about the speaker and one or more other people): *We're going to the movies.* ○ *We are both thrilled with the house.* ○ *We all left together.*

☆**weak** /wik/ *adj.* **1** (used about the body) having little strength or energy; not strong: *The child was weak with hunger.* ○ *Her legs felt weak.* ○ (*figurative*) *a weak economy* **2** likely to break: *That bridge is too weak for trucks to drive on.* **3** (used about a person's character) easy to influence; not firm: *He is too weak to be a good leader.* **4** (used about an argument, excuse, etc.) that does not convince you or seem right; not strong: *a weak argument against the proposal* **5** not easy to see or hear; not definite or strong: *I heard a weak voice whispering for help.* ○ *She gave a weak smile.* **6** (used about liquids) containing a lot of water; not strong in taste: *weak tea* **7** **weak (at/in/on sth)** not able to achieve a high standard in sth: *He's*

weak at math. ○ *His math skills are weak.* —**weak·ly** *adv.*: *The little kitten struggled weakly to its feet.*

☆**weak·en** /ˈwikən/ *verb* [I,T] **1** to become less strong; to make sb/sth less strong: *The storm weakened as it approached the coast.* ○ *The building had been weakened by the earthquake.* **2** to become less certain about sth: *Their mother was weakening. "Oh, all right," she said. "You can go."*

☆**weak·ness** /ˈwiknəs/ *noun* **1** [U] the state of being weak: *They were relying on the enemy's weakness in the air.* **2** [C] a fault or lack of strength, especially in a person's character: *It's important to know your own strengths and weaknesses.* **3** [C, usually sing.] **a weakness for sth/sb** a special and often foolish liking for sth/sb: *I have a weakness for chocolate.*

☆**wealth** /wɛlθ/ *noun* **1** [U] (owning) a lot of money, property, etc.: *They were a family of enormous wealth.* **2** [sing.] **a wealth of sth** a large number or amount of sth: *He has a wealth of experience in this area.*

☆**wealth·y** /ˈwɛlθi/ *adj.* (**wealth·i·er; wealth·i·est**) having a lot of money, etc.; rich

wean /win/ *verb* [T] **wean sb (from/off sth)** to start feeding a baby or young animal with other food as well as its mother's milk: (*figurative*) *to wean yourself off cigarettes*

☆**weap·on** /ˈwɛpən/ *noun* [C] an object which is used for fighting or for killing people, such as a gun, knife, bomb, etc.

☆**wear¹** /wɛr/ *verb* (*p.t.* **wore** /wɔr/; *p.p.* **worn** /wɔrn/) **1** [T] to have clothes, jewelry, etc. on your body: *He was wearing a suit and tie.* ○ *I wear glasses for reading.* ○ *Would you like to wear my necklace?* ○ *to wear your hair short* **2** [T] to have a certain look on your face: *He was wearing an expression of delight.* **3** [I] to become thinner or damaged because of being used or rubbed a lot **4** [T] to make a hole, path, etc. in sth by rubbing, walking, etc.: *Cut your toenails or you'll wear a hole in your socks!* **5** [I] to last for a long time without becoming thinner or damaged: *This material wears well.*

IDM **wear thin** to have less effect because of being used too much: *We've heard that story so often that it's beginning to wear thin.*

PHRV **wear (sth) away** to damage sth or to make it disappear over a period of time, by using, touching, etc. a lot; to disappear or become damaged in this way: *The shiny finish on the floor had worn away over the years.* ○ *The motion of the waves had worn a lot of the rocks away.*

wear (sth) down to become or to make sth smaller or shorter

wear sb/sth down to make sb/sth weaker by attacking, persuading, etc.: *They wore him down with constant arguments until he changed his mind.*

W

wear off to become less strong or to disappear completely: *The effects of the drug wore off after a few hours.*

wear on (used about time) to pass slowly: *They got to know each other better as the summer wore on.*

wear (sth) out to become too thin or damaged to use anymore; to cause sth to do this: *Children's shoes wear out very quickly.* ○ *You've worn out two pairs of jeans in the last six months!*

wear sb out to make sb very tired: *She wore herself out walking home with the heavy bags.* ☞ Look at **worn out.**

wear² /wɛr/ *noun* [U] **1** wearing or being worn; use as clothing: *This sweater would be good for everyday wear.* **2** (usually in compounds) things that you wear; clothes: *sportswear* ○ *underwear* **3** long use which damages the quality or appearance of sth

IDM **wear and tear** the damage caused by ordinary use

the worse for wear ⇨ WORSE¹

wea·ry /'wɪri/ *adj.* (**wea·ri·er**; **wea·ri·est**) tired: *He gave a weary smile.* —**wea·ri·ly** /-əli/ *adv.* —**wea·ri·ness** *noun* [U]

☆ **weath·er¹** /'wɛðər/ *noun* [U] the climate at a certain place and time, how much wind, rain, sunshine, etc. there is and how hot or cold it is: *What was the weather like in Hawaii?* ○ *We'll go to the beach if the weather stays nice.* ○ *They say that the weather won't change for the next few days.* ○ *The weather forecast is on after the news.*

☞ **Rain** is drops of water that fall from the clouds. **Snow** is frozen rain. It is soft and white and often settles on the ground. **Sleet** is rain that is not completely frozen. **Hail** is rain that is frozen so hard that it feels and sounds like small stones falling. When it is only raining very slightly, it is **drizzling**. When it is raining very hard, it is **pouring**. **Fog** is like a cloud at ground level. It makes it difficult to see very far ahead. **Mist** is a very thin type of fog. Look also at **storm**.

IDM **under the weather** (*informal*) not very healthy

weath·er² /'wɛðər/ *verb* **1** [T] (used about a ship or a person) to pass safely through a storm or a difficult time **2** [I,T] to change in appearance (because of the effect of the sun, air or wind)

weave /wiv/ *verb* [I,T] (*p.t.* **wove** /woʊv/ or in sense 2 **weaved**; *p.p.* **wo·ven** /'woʊvən/ or in sense 2 **weaved**) **1** to make cloth, etc. by passing threads under and over a set of threads that is attached to a frame (**loom**): *woven cloth* **2** to change direction often when you are moving so that you are not stopped by anything: *He weaved in and out through the traffic.*

web /wɛb/ *noun* **1** [C] a type of fine net that a spider makes in order to catch small insects: *A spider spins webs.* ☞ picture at **spider.** Look also at **cobweb.** **2 the Web** [sing.] = WORLD WIDE WEB

'**Web site** (*also* **Web page; site**) *noun* [C] a document or a group of documents, often with pictures, that you can look at on a computer which is connected to an international system of computers (**the Internet**)

wed /wɛd/ *verb* [I,T] (**wed·ding; wed·ded**) (*formal* or *old-fashioned*) to get married

Wed. *abbr.* = WEDNESDAY

we'd /wid/ *short for* WE HAD, WE WOULD

☆ **wed·ding** /'wɛdɪŋ/ *noun* [C] a marriage ceremony and often the meal or party that follows it (**the reception**): *I've been invited to his sister's wedding.* ○ *a wedding dress, guest, present, etc.* ○ *a wedding ring* (= one that is placed on the third finger of the left hand during a marriage ceremony and worn to show that a person is married) ○ *a wedding anniversary*

☞ **Marriage** is the word for the state of being married to somebody. It can also be used for the ceremony, with the same meaning as **wedding**. The man who is getting married is the **groom**; the woman is the **bride**. Other important people at the ceremony are the **best man**, the **maid of honor** and the **bridesmaids**. A wedding can take place in church or other religious building, or people may get married at home, in a park, a hotel, etc.

wedge¹ /wɛdʒ/ *noun* [C] a piece of wood, etc. with one thick and one narrow end that you can push into a space, in order, for example, to keep things apart: *The door was propped open with a wedge.*

wedge² /wɛdʒ/ *verb* [T] **1** to force sth apart or to prevent sth from moving by using a wedge¹: *to wedge a door open* **2** to force sth/sb to fit into a space: *The chair was wedged between the table and the door.*

wed·lock /'wɛdlɑk/ *noun* [U] (*formal*) marriage: *children born out of wedlock* (= to parents who are not married)

☆ **Wednes·day** /'wɛnzder; -di/ *noun* [C,U] (*abbr.* **Wed.**) the day of the week after Tuesday and before Thursday ☞ For examples of the use of the days of the week in sentences, look at **Monday.**

wee /wi/ *adj.*

IDM **the wee hours** the very early morning hours, soon after midnight

☆ **weed¹** /wid/ *noun* **1** [C] a wild plant that is not wanted in a garden because it prevents other plants from growing well: *Our garden is full of weeds.* ☞ Look also at **seaweed. 2** [U] (*slang*) the illegal drug marijuana

weed² /wid/ *verb* [I,T] to remove weeds¹(1) from a piece of ground, etc.

ər	ɪr	ɛr	ɑr	ɔr	ʊr	ʒ	h	ŋ
bird	near	hair	car	north	tour	vision	hat	sing

PHRV **weed sth/sb out** to remove the things or people that you do not think are good enough: *He weeded out all the letters with spelling mistakes in them.*

☆**week** /wik/ *noun* [C] **1** a period of seven days (usually beginning on Sunday and ending on Saturday: *last week/this week/next week* ○ *He left two weeks ago.* ○ *I haven't seen her for a whole week.* ○ *I play tennis twice a week.* ○ *They'll be back in a week.* ○ *I was on vacation the week before last.* ○ *My course ends the week after next.* **2** the part of the week(1) when people go to work, etc., usually from Monday through Friday: *She works hard during the week.* ○ *I work a 40-hour week.*
IDM **week in, week out** every week without a rest or change

☆**week·day** /'wikdeɪ/ *noun* [C] any day except Saturday and Sunday: *I only work (on) weekdays.*

☆**week·end** /'wikɛnd/ *noun* [C] Saturday and Sunday: *We're going camping this weekend* (= the weekend that is coming). ○ *What did you do over the weekend?* ○ *The bank is closed on the weekends.* ○ *a long weekend* (= Saturday and Sunday, plus Friday and/or Monday)

☆**week·ly** /'wikli/ *adj., adv.* happening or appearing once a week or every week: *We are paid weekly.* ○ *a weekly report*

☆**weep** /wip/ *verb* [I,T] (*p.t., p.p.* **wept** /wɛpt/) (*formal*) to let tears fall because of strong emotion; to cry: *She wept at the news of his death.* ○ *to weep for joy* ○ *to weep tears of pity*

☆**weigh** /weɪ/ *verb* **1** [T] to measure how heavy sth is, especially by using a machine (**scale**): *I weigh myself every day.* ○ *Can you weigh this package for me?* **2** [T] to have or show a certain weight: *I weigh 156 pounds.* **3** [T] **weigh sth (against sb/sth)** to consider sth carefully, especially to see whether one thing is better, more important, etc. than sth else: *We need to weigh the advantages of the plan against the risks.*
PHRV **weigh against sb/sth** to be considered important when sb/sth is being judged: *She didn't get the job because her lack of experience weighed against her.*
weigh sb down to make sb feel worried and sad: *weighed down by responsibilities*
weigh sb/sth down to make it difficult for sb/sth to move (by being heavy): *I was weighed down by my heavy backpack.*
weigh in to join a discussion or an argument by saying sth important or expressing a strong opinion: *to weigh in with your opinion* ○ *Mr. Goldman weighed in on the issue of teachers' salaries.*
weigh on sb/sth to make sb worry ☞ We also say **weigh on sb's mind**: *That problem has been weighing on my mind for a long time.*
weigh sb up to try and find out what a person is like so that you can form an opinion

☆**weight¹** /weɪt/ *noun* **1** [U] (*abbr.* **wt.**) the heaviness of sth or the amount that it weighs, especially as measured in pounds, etc.: *In two months, her weight has increased to 145 pounds.* ○ *I need to lose weight* (= become thinner and less heavy) *before I go on vacation.* ○ *He's put on weight* (= got fatter). ○ *The weight of the snow broke the branch.* **2** [C] a piece of metal with a certain heaviness that can be used to weigh an amount, especially using a scale. Weights are also used by athletes when they are practicing or in the sport of weightlifting: *a 50 pound weight* **3** [C] a heavy object: *My doctor told me not to lift heavy weights.* **4** [sing.] the worry that is caused by a problem: *Telling her the truth took a weight off his mind.*
IDM **carry weight** ➪ CARRY
pull your weight ➪ PULL¹

weight² /weɪt/ *verb* [T] **1** **weight sth (down) (with sth)** to hold sth down with a heavy object or objects: *to weight down a fishing net* **2** (usually passive) to organize sth so that a particular person or group has an advantage or a disadvantage: *The system is weighted in favor of people with a college degree.*

weight·less /'weɪtləs/ *adj.* having no weight, especially when traveling in space —**weight·less·ness** *noun* [U]

weight·lift·ing /'weɪtˌlɪftɪŋ/ *noun* [U] a sport in which people lift heavy metal objects

weight·y /'weɪti/ *adj.* (**weight·i·er; weight·i·est**) serious and important: *a weighty question*

☆**weird** /wɪrd/ *adj.* **1** strange and frightening: *a weird noise* **2** (*informal*) not normal: *weird clothes, ideas, etc.*

weird·o /'wɪrdoʊ/ *noun* [C] (*pl.* **weird·os**) (*informal*) a person who behaves in a way that is not normal and/or wears strange clothes

☆**wel·come¹** /'wɛlkəm/ *adj.* **1** received with pleasure; giving pleasure: *You're always welcome here.* ○ *welcome news* **2** **welcome to sth/ to do sth** allowed to do sth: *You're welcome to use our swimming pool.*
IDM **sb is welcome to sth** (used to say that sb can have sth because you do not want it yourself): *Take the car if you want. You're welcome to it — it's always breaking down.*
you're welcome (used as a polite reply to sb who has just thanked you): *"Thank you for your help." "You're very welcome."*

☆**wel·come²** /'wɛlkəm/ *interj.* (an expression used for greeting a person who is arriving at a place): *Welcome to America!* ○ *Welcome home!*

☆**wel·come³** /'wɛlkəm/ *noun* [C] a greeting to sb who has arrived: *Let's give a warm welcome to our next guest.*

☆**wel·come⁴** /'wɛlkəm/ *verb* [T] **1** to greet sb when he/she arrives: *The kids rushed to the door to welcome their father home.* **2** to be pleased about sth and support it: *When I told*

W

tʃ	dʒ	v	θ	ð	s	z	ʃ
chin	June	van	thin	then	so	zoo	she

my parents I wanted to work in the family business, they welcomed the idea.

weld /wɛld/ *verb* [I,T] to join pieces of metal by heating them and pressing them together

☆**wel·fare** /'wɛlfɛr/ *noun* [U] **1** money that the government pays regularly to people who are poor and have no job: *families on welfare* (= receiving welfare) ∘ *to cash your welfare check* **2** the good health and happiness of a person or group of people: *The doctor is concerned about the child's welfare.*

☆**well¹** /wɛl/ *adv.* (**bet·ter** /'bɛtər/, **best** /bɛst/) **1** in a good or satisfactory way: *You speak English very well.* ∘ *I hope your work is going well.* ∘ *Did they treat you well?* ∘ *The car sounds a lot better since it was fixed.* **2** thoroughly, completely or carefully: *Shake the bottle well before opening.* **3** (used with *can, could, may* or *might* to show that sth is probably true): *He might well be right.* **4** very much: *They got home well past midnight.* ∘ *This book is well worth reading.*

IDM **as well (as sb/sth)** in addition (to sb/sth): *The book is available on CD-ROM as well.* ∘ *He has lived in Texas as well as in Washington.* ☞ Look at the note at **also.**

bode well/ill (for sb/sth) ⇨ BODE

do well 1 to be successful: *Their daughter has done very well in college.* **2** to be getting better (after an illness): *Mr. Brown is doing well after his operation.*

may/might (just) as well (used for saying that sth can or should happen, especially when you have no choice): *I might as well tell you the truth – you'll find out anyway.*

mean well ⇨ MEAN¹

well/badly off ⇨ OFF¹

☆**well²** /wɛl/ *adj.* (**bet·ter** /'bɛtər/, **best** /bɛst/) (not before a noun) **1** (looking or feeling) healthy: *This medicine will make you feel better.* ∘ *Get well soon* (= written on a card that you send to somebody who is sick). **2** in a satisfactory state: *I hope all is well with you.*

IDM **be all very well (for sb)** (*informal*) (used for showing that you are not happy or do not agree with sth): *It's all very well for her to criticize* (= it's easy for her to criticize), *but it doesn't help the situation.*

it is just as well (that) ⇨ JUST¹

☆**well³** /wɛl/ *interj.* **1** (used when you begin the next part of a story or when you are thinking about what to say next): *Well, the next thing that happened was…* ∘ *Well now, let me see…* **2** (used for expressing doubt, hesitation, etc.): *"Do you like it?" "Well, I'm not really sure."* ∘ *Her new boyfriend seems, well, a little strange.* **3** (used for showing surprise): *Well, look who's here!* **4** (*also* **oh, well**) (used for showing that there is nothing you can do to change a situation): *Oh, well, there's nothing we can do about it.*

well⁴ /wɛl/ *noun* [C] **1** a deep hole in the ground from which water is taken: *to dig a new well* **2** = OIL WELL

well⁵ /wɛl/ *verb* [I] **well (up)** (used about a liquid) to come to the surface: *Tears welled up in her eyes*

we'll /wil; wɪl/ *short for* WE SHALL, WE WILL

well-be'haved *adj.* behaving in a way that most people think is correct

well-'being *noun* [U] a feeling of being healthy and happy

well-'done *adj.* (used about meat, etc.) cooked for a long time ☞ Look at the note at **rare.**

well-'dressed *adj.* wearing attractive and fashionable clothes

well-'heeled *adj.* wealthy; having a lot of money

well-in'formed *adj.* knowing a lot about one or several subjects

☆**well-'known** *adj.* known by a lot of people; famous

well-'meaning *adj.* (used about a person) wanting to be kind or helpful, but often not having this effect

well-'off *adj.* = WELL-TO-DO

well-read /ˌwɛl'rɛd/ *adj.* having read many books, and so knowing a lot about many subjects

well-'rounded *adj.* (usually *before* a noun) **1** (used about a person) with experiece and abilities in many different subjects **2** (used about an education, etc.) including many different subjects

well-to-'do (*also* **well-off**) *adj.* wealthy; with a lot of money

'well-,wisher *noun* [C] a person who hopes that sb/sth will be successful

Welsh /wɛlʃ/ *adj.* of Wales, its people or their language: *the Welsh coast* ∘ *He's Welsh. He was born in Cardiff.*

went *p.t.* of GO¹

wept *p.t., p.p.* of WEEP

were /wər/ ⇨ BE¹,²

we're /wɪr/ *short for* WE ARE

☆**west¹** /wɛst/ *noun* [sing.] (*abbr.* **W**) **1** (*also* **the west**) one of the four main points of the compass; the direction you look toward in order to see the sun set: *Which way is west?* ∘ *Rain is spreading from the west.* ∘ *There's a gas station to the west of here.* ☞ picture at **north. 2 the west; the West** the part of any country, city, etc. that lies further toward the west than other parts: *I live in the west of Montana.* ∘ *The climate in the west is generally drier than in the east.* **3 the West** the countries of North America and Western Europe

☆**west²** (*also* **West**) /wɛst/ *adj.* in or toward the west, or from the west: *the West Coast* (= next to the Pacific Ocean) ∘ *West St. Paul* ∘ *a west wind*

i	ɪ	ɛ	æ	ɑ	ɔ	ʌ	ʊ	u
see	sit	ten	cat	hot	saw	cup	put	too

☆**west³** /wɛst/ adv. to or toward the west: *The island is five miles west of here.* ○ *to travel west*

west·bound /ˈwɛstbaʊnd/ adj. traveling or leading toward the west: *The westbound lanes of the freeway are closed.*

west·er·ly /ˈwɛstərli/ adj. **1** to, toward or in the west: *in a westerly direction* **2** (used about winds) coming from the west

☆**west·ern¹** /ˈwɛstərn/ adj. **1** in or of the west: *the western United States* **2** (also **Western**) from or connected with countries of North America and western Europe: *Western literature*

west·ern² (also **Western**) /ˈwɛstərn/ noun [C] a movie or book about life in the past in the west of the United States

west·ern·er /ˈwɛstərnər/ noun [C] **1** a person who was born in or who lives in North America or western Europe **2** (also **Westerner**) a person who was born in or who lives in the western U.S.

west·ern·ize /ˈwɛstərnaɪz/ verb [T] to make a country or people more like North America or Western Europe, e.g. in the way people dress and behave: *The Japanese diet has become more westernized in recent years.*

west·ward /ˈwɛstwərd/ adj. toward the west: *in a westward direction* —**west·ward** (also **westwards**) adv.: *to fly westwards*

☆**wet¹** /wɛt/ adj. (**wet·ter**; **wet·test**) **1** covered in a liquid, especially water: *wet clothes* ○ *Don't get your feet wet.*

☞ **Moist** means slightly wet. **Damp** is used to describe things that are slightly wet and may feel unpleasant because of it: *Don't sit on the grass. It's damp.*

2 (used about the weather, etc.) with a lot of rain: *a wet day* **3** (used about paint, etc.) not yet dry or hard: *The ink is still wet.*

IDM a wet blanket (informal) a person who spoils other people's fun, especially because he/she will not join in

☆**wet²** /wɛt/ verb (pres. part. **wet·ting**; p.t., p.p. **wet** or **wet·ted**) [T] **1** to make sth wet **2** (used especially about young children) to make yourself or your bed, clothes, etc. wet by passing waste water (**urine**) out of the body: *Joe wet his pants this morning.*

ˈwet suit noun [C] a rubber suit that covers the whole body, used by people who swim under water or play sports in the water

we've /wiv/ short for WE HAVE

whack¹ /wæk/ verb [T] (informal) to hit sb/sth hard

whack² /wæk/ noun [C] (informal) an act of hitting sb/sth hard

IDM out of whack (informal) not functioning correctly: *The whole system is completely out of whack.*

whale

whale /weɪl/ noun [C] a very large animal that lives in the ocean and looks like a huge fish (but is, in fact, a mammal)

wharf /wɔrf/ noun [C] (pl. **wharves** /wɔrvz/) a platform made of stone or wood at the edge of the ocean, etc. where ships and boats can be tied up

☆**what** /wʌt; wɑt; weak form wət/ det., pron. **1** (used for asking for information about sb/sth): *What time is it?* ○ *What kind of music do you like?* ○ *She asked him what he was doing.* ○ *What's their phone number?* ☞ Look at the note at **which**. **2** the things (that); all the...: *What she says is true.* ○ *I believe what she said.* ○ *Is it true what she said?* ○ *I don't have much, but you can borrow what money I have.* **3** (used for showing surprise, pleasure, etc.): *What a beautiful day!*

☞ **What** can also be used alone, to express surprise: *"I just spent a thousand dollars." "What?!"* It can also be used as a reply to sb who is trying to get your attention or when you did not hear sth correctly, though this usage is not very polite: *"Jerry?" "What?" "Come here a minute."*

IDM how/what about...? ⇨ ABOUT²

how, what, where, who, etc. in the world ⇨ WORLD

... or what? (informal) (used to ask about another possibility, especially when you are annoyed): *Are you guys coming along, or what?*

what for for what purpose; why: *What's this little switch for?* ○ *What did you say that for?* ○ *"Can you come here?" "What for?"*

what if...? what would happen if...?: *What if the car broke down?*

☆**what·ev·er¹** /wʌtˈɛvər; wɑt-/ adj., pron. **1** any or every; anything or everything: *You can say whatever you want.* ○ *He took whatever help he could get.* **2** no matter what: *I still love you, whatever you may think.* ○ *Whatever she says, she doesn't really mean it.*

IDM or whatever (informal) or any other or others of a similar kind: *You don't need to wear anything fancy – jeans and a sweater or whatever.*

what·ev·er² /wʌtˈɛvər; wɑt-/ (also **what·so·ev·er** /ˌwʌtsoʊˈɛvər; ˌwɑt-/) adv. at all: *I have no reason whatever to doubt him.* ○ *"Any questions?" "None whatsoever."*

ə	y	w	t̬	eɪ	aɪ	ɔɪ	aʊ	oʊ
about	yes	woman	butter	say	five	boy	now	go

what·ev·er³ /wətˈɛvər/ *interj.* (*informal*) (used as a reply to tell sb that you do not care what happens, or that you are not interested in what he/she is talking about): *"We need to fix the back door." "Yeah, whatever."*

☆**wheat** /wit/ *noun* [U] **1** a type of grain which can be made into flour **2** the plant which produces this grain: *a field of wheat*

☆**wheel¹** /wil/ *noun* **1** [C] a round object that turns around a long stick (**axle**) that is attached to its center. Wheels are used to make a car, bicycle, etc. move or to make a machine work **2** [usually sing.] = STEERING WHEEL **3 wheels** [plural] (*informal*) a car: *Dave's been without wheels ever since his accident in June.* **IDM** **at/behind the wheel** driving a car: *Jon was behind the wheel when the accident happened.*

wheel² /wil/ *verb* **1** [T] to push along an object that has wheels; to move sb around in/on a vehicle with wheels: *He wheeled his bike up the hill.* ○ *She was wheeled back to her bed after the operation.* **2** [I] to turn around suddenly: *The man wheeled around and fired several shots at the guards.*

wheel·bar·row /ˈwilˌbæroʊ/ *noun* [C] a type of small cart with one wheel, two legs and two handles used for carrying small loads, especially outdoors

☆**wheel·chair**
/ˈwiltʃɛr/ *noun* [C] a chair with large wheels that a person who cannot walk can move around or be pushed in

wheelchair

wheeze /wiz/ *verb* [I] to make noises when you breathe, especially if you have an illness in your chest

☆**when¹** /wɛn; *weak form* wən/ *adv.* **1** at what time: *When did she get here?* ○ *I don't know when she got here.* **2** (used for talking about the time at which sth happens or happened): *Sunday is the day when I can relax.* ○ *I saw her in May when she was in town.*

☆**when²** /wɛn; *weak form* wən/ *conj.* **1** at or during the time that: *He jumped up when the phone rang.* ○ *When we were walking home, we saw an accident.*

☞ Notice that we use the present tense after "when" if we are talking about a future time: *I'll call you when I'm ready.*

2 since; as; considering that: *Why do you want more money when you've got enough already?*

☞ **When** is used for talking about something that you think will happen, but **if** is used for something you are not sure will happen. Compare: *I'll ask her when she comes* (= you

are sure that she will come). ○ *I'll ask her if she comes* (= you are not sure whether she will come or not).

☆**when·ev·er** /wɛnˈɛvər; wən-/ *conj.* at any time; no matter when: *You can borrow my car whenever you want.* ○ *Don't worry. You can give it back the next time you see me, or whenever.*

☆**where** /wɛr; *weak form* wər/ *adv., conj.* **1** at, in or to what place or position: *Where can I buy a paper?* ○ *I asked him where he lived.* ○ *Where are you going?* **2** at, in or to a place or a situation: *the town where you were born* ○ *She ran to where they were standing.* ○ *I know where we need to go.* ○ *Where possible, you should travel by bus, not car.* **3** at which place: *We came to a town where we stopped for lunch.*

where·a·bouts /ˈwɛrəbaʊts/ *noun* [U, with sing. or pl. verb] the place where sb/sth is: *The whereabouts of the stolen painting is/are unknown.*

where·as /wɛrˈæz; ˈwɛrəz/ *conj.* (used for showing a fact that is different): *He eats meat, whereas she's a vegetarian.*

where·by /wɛrˈbaɪ; ˈwɛrbaɪ/ *adv.* (*formal*) by which: *The company has a system whereby employees can get regular training.*

where·up·on /ˌwɛrəˈpɑn; -ˈpɔn; ˈwɛrəpɑn/ *conj.* (*formal*) after which: *He fell asleep, whereupon she walked quietly from the room.*

☆**wher·ev·er** /wɛrˈɛvər; wər-/ *conj.* **1** in or to any place: *You can sit wherever you want.* ○ *She comes from Bahia, wherever that is* (= I don't know where it is). **2** everywhere, in all places that: *Wherever I go, he goes.*

whet /wɛt/ *verb* **whet·ting**; **whet·ted** **IDM** **whet sb's appetite** to make sb want more of sth: *The orchestra concert whetted my appetite for classical music.*

☆**wheth·er** /ˈwɛðər/ *conj.* **1** (used after verbs like "ask", "doubt", "know", etc.) if: *He asked me whether we would be coming to the party.* **2** (used for expressing a choice or doubt between two or more possibilities): *I can't make up my mind whether to go or not.* ○ *There was some doubt as to whether she should go.*

☞ **Whether** and **if** can both be used in sense 1. Only **whether** can be used before "to" + verb: *Have you decided whether to accept the offer yet?* Only **whether** can be used after a preposition: *the problem of whether to accept the offer.*

IDM **whether or not** (used to say that sth will be true in either of the situations that are mentioned): *We will play on Saturday whether it rains or not.* ○ *Whether or not it rains, we will play on Saturday.*

whew /hwyu; hwu; fyu/ *interj.* (used to show the sound which expresses tiredness, surprise, relief, shock, etc.): *Whew! It's hot in here!*

☆ **which** /wɪtʃ/ *det., pron.* **1** (used in questions when there are a number of people or things to choose from): *Which piece of cake do you want? ○ Which hand do you write with? ○ Which is your bag? ○ She asked me which color I liked better. ○ I can't remember which of the boys is older.*

☞ **Which** or **what**? We use **which** when there is only a limited group to choose from: *Which car is yours? The Ford or the Buick?* We use **what** when the group is not limited: *What car would you choose, if you could have any one you wanted?*

2 (used for saying what thing or things you are talking about): *This is an important book which contains some valuable information. ○ (formal) The situation in which he found himself was very difficult.*

☞ In less formal English we would write: *The situation which he found himself in was very difficult.* Often the "which" is left out: *The situation he found himself in ...*

3 (used for giving more information about a thing or animal): *His best film, which won several awards, was about the Nazi concentration camps.* ☞ Note that there is a comma before "which" and at the end of the part of the sentence which it introduces. **4** (used for making a comment on what has just been said): *We had to wait 16 hours for our plane, which was really annoying.* ☞ Note that there is a comma before "which."

☆ **which·ev·er** /wɪtʃˈɛvər/ *det., pron.* any person or thing : *You can choose whichever book you want.*

whiff /wɪf/ *noun*
IDM catch/get a whiff of sth to smell sth for just a short time: *I caught a whiff of his aftershave as he leaned toward me.*

☆ **while¹** /waɪl/ *conj.* **1** during the time that; when: *He always calls while we're eating lunch.* **2** at the same time as: *She usually listens to the radio while she's driving to work.* **3** (*formal*) (used when you are contrasting two ideas): *Some countries are rich, while others are extremely poor. ○ While I understand your point, I simply do not agree with you.*

☆ **while²** /waɪl/ *noun* [sing.] a period of time (usually short): *Let's sit down here for a while.*
IDM once in a while ➪ ONCE¹
worth sb's while ➪ WORTH¹

whim /wɪm/ *noun* [C] a sudden idea or desire to do sth (often sth that is not sensible)

whim·per /ˈwɪmpər/ *verb* [I] to cry softly, especially with fear or pain —**whim·per** *noun* [C]

whine /waɪn/ *verb* **1** [I] to make a long high unpleasant sound: *The dog is whining to go out.* **2** [I,T] to complain about sth in an annoying way: *Quit whining about the food and eat your vegetables!* —**whine** *noun* [C]

whip¹ /wɪp/ *noun* [C] **1** a long thin piece of leather, etc. with a handle, that is used for making animals go faster and for hitting people as a punishment **2** a member of Congress who encourages the other members of his/her political party to vote the same way on important decisions in Congress

whip² /wɪp/ *verb* (**whip·ping**; **whipped**) **1** [T] to hit a person or animal with a whip **2** [T] to mix the white part of an egg or cream, etc. until it is light and stiff: *whipped cream* **3** [T] (*informal*) to defeat sb easily in a sports game, competition, etc.: *We really whipped the Braves last night!* **4** [I,T] to move or hit sth quickly or violently: *The wind whipped through the trees.*
PHRV whip sth out (*informal*) to take sth out quickly or suddenly: *He whipped out a pen and made a note of the number.*
whip sth up 1 to cause a strong emotion: *to whip up excitement* **2** (*informal*) to prepare food quickly: *to whip up a quick snack*

whir /wər/ *verb* [I] (**whir·ring**; **whirred**) to make a continuous low sound: *The noise of the fan whirring kept me awake.* —**whir** *noun* [C, usually sing.]

whirl¹ /wərl/ *verb* [I,T] to move around very quickly; to make sb/sth move in this way: *The dancers whirled around the room. ○ The wind whirled the leaves around and around.*

whirl² /wərl/ *noun* [sing.] the act or sound of whirling: *the whirl of the helicopter's blades*
IDM be in a whirl to be in a state of confusion: *My head's in a whirl – I'm so excited.*
give sth a whirl to try sth

whirl·pool /ˈwərlpul/ *noun* [C] a place in a river or the ocean where the water moves around and around very quickly

whirl·wind¹ /ˈwərlwɪnd/ *noun* [C] a very strong wind that forms a tall column of air moving around and around in a circle as it travels across land or water

whirl·wind² /ˈwərlwɪnd/ *adj.* (only *before* a noun) happening very quickly, often in an exciting way: *a whirlwind tour of Europe ○ a whirlwind romance*

whisk¹ /wɪsk/ *noun* [C] a tool that you use for beating the white part of an egg, cream, etc.

whisk² /wɪsk/ *verb* [T] **1** to move sb/sth quickly: *The President was whisked away in a black limousine.* **2** to beat eggs, cream, etc. very quickly with a whisk

whisk·er /ˈwɪskər/ *noun* **1 whiskers** [plural] the hair that is growing on a man's face **2** [C] one of the long hairs that grow near the mouth of a mouse, cat, etc. ☞ picture at **cat.**

whis·key /ˈwɪski/ *noun* (*pl.* **whis·keys**) [C,U] a strong alcoholic drink that is made from grain, or a glass of this drink

☆ **whis·per** /ˈwɪspər/ *verb* [I,T] to speak very quietly to sb, so that other people cannot hear what you are saying —**whis·per** *noun* [C]: *to speak in a whisper*

W

tʃ	dʒ	v	θ	ð	s	z	ʃ
chin	June	van	thin	then	so	zoo	she

☆ **whis·tle¹** /ˈwɪsl/ *noun* [C] **1** the long high sound that you make when you force air out between your lips **2** a simple musical instrument that produces a long high sound: *The referee blew his whistle to stop the game.*

whis·tle² /ˈwɪsl/ *verb* **1** [I,T] to make sounds by forcing air out between your lips or through a whistle¹(2) : *The girl was whistling as she walked down the street.* ○ *He whistled a tune to himself.* ○ *The referee whistled and the game was over.* **2** [I] to make a sound like a whistle¹(1) : *A bullet whistled past his head* (= moved quickly, with the sound of a whistle).

☆ **white¹** /waɪt/ *adj.* **1** of the very light color of snow or milk: *an old lady with white hair* ○ *white bread* **2** belonging to a race of people with pale skin, originally from Europe

IDM **black and white** ⇨ BLACK¹

☆ **white²** /waɪt/ *noun* **1** [U] white color, paint, etc.: *She was dressed in white.* **2** [C] a person who belongs to a race of people with pale skin, originally from Europe **3** [C,U] the part of an egg that turns white when it is cooked

☞ picture at **egg**. The yellow part of an egg is the **yolk**.

4 [C] the white part of the eye

IDM **in black and white** ⇨ BLACK²

white-ˈcollar *adj.* (only *before* a noun) connected with people who work in offices, not in factories: *white-collar workers* ○ *white-collar jobs* ☞ Look at **blue-collar**.

☆ **the ˈWhite House** *noun* [sing.] **1** the large house in Washington, D.C., where the U.S. President lives and works **2** the U.S. President and the branch of the U.S. government that includes the people who advise the President

☞ Some nouns are always used with **the**: *the White House* ○ *the FBI* ○ *the Internet* These nouns refer to things that are the only ones of their kind. However, we do not use **the** when we use these words in front of other words to describe them: *White House aides have denied the rumor.* ○ *The house was surrounded by FBI agents.* ○ *Visit our Internet site.*

white ˈlie *noun* [C] a lie that is not very harmful or serious

whit·en /ˈwaɪtn/ *verb* [T] to make sth white or paler in color

white ˈtrash *noun* [U] (*slang*) poor white people who are often not respected because they are not well educated and often do not behave morally

white·wash¹ /ˈwaɪtwɑʃ; -wɔʃ/ *noun* [U] a white liquid that you use for painting houses or fences

white·wash² /ˈwaɪtwɑʃ; -wɔʃ/ *verb* [T] **1** to paint a wall or fence with whitewash¹ **2** to try to hide sth bad or wrong that you have done

white·wa·ter (*also* **white water**) /ˈwaɪt̬wɔt̬ər; -ˌwɑt̬ər/ *noun* [U] water that moves very fast

through a narrow or rocky part of a river: *to go whitewater rafting*

white ˈwine *noun* [U] wine made from green grapes, that is clear or of a very pale yellow color ☞ Look at **red wine** and **rosé**.

whit·tle /ˈwɪt̬l/ *verb*

PHRV **whittle sth away**; **whittle away at sth** to remove or decrease sth gradually: *Real estate development is whittling away at the birds' natural habitat.*

whittle sth down to reduce the size or number of sth gradually: *We have whittled down the list of candidates to two finalists*

whiz¹ (*also* **whizz**) /wɪz/ *verb* [I] (**whiz·zing**; **whizzed**) (*informal*) to move very quickly, often making a high continuous sound: *Somebody went whizzing past on a motorcycle.*

whiz² /wɪz/ *noun* [C] (*pl.* **whiz·zes**) (*informal*) a person who is very intelligent or is very skillful at a particular activity: *a math whiz*

☆ **who** /hu/ *pron.* **1** (used in questions to ask sb's name, etc.): *Who did this?* ○ (*informal*) *Who did you meet at the party?* ○ (*informal*) *Who did you go with?* **2** (used in reported questions and after certain verbs): *She wondered who he was.* ○ *I can't remember who I asked to do this.* **3** (used for saying which person or what kind of person you are talking about): *I like people who say what they think.* ○ *That's the man who I met at Ann's party.* ○ *The woman who I work for is very nice.*

☞ In the last two examples (= when "who" is the object, or when it is used with a preposition) "who" can be left out: *That's the man I met at Ann's party.* ○ *The woman I work for is very nice.*

4 used for giving extra information about sb: *My mother, who's over 80, still drives a car.* ☞ Look at the note at **whom**.

IDM **how, why, where, who, etc. in the world** ⇨ WORLD

who'd /hud/ *short for* WHO HAD, WHO WOULD

☆ **who·ev·er** /huˈɛvər/ *pron.* **1** the person who (used when you do not know that person's identity): *Whoever is responsible will have to pay for the damage.* ○ *I want to speak to whoever is in charge.* **2** it does not matter who: *I don't want to see anybody – whoever it is.*

☆ **whole¹** /hoʊl/ *adj.* **1** complete; full: *He ate a whole chicken!* ○ *Hooray! We have two whole weeks off from school!* ○ *I'm just fed up with the whole thing* (= the entire situation). **2** not broken or cut: *Snakes swallow their prey whole* (= in one piece).

☆ **whole²** /hoʊl/ *noun* [sing.] **1** the whole of sth all that there is of sth: *I spent the whole of the morning cooking.* **2** a thing that is complete or full: *Two halves make a whole.*

IDM **as a whole** as one complete thing or unit: *This is true not just in New York, but also in America as a whole.*

i	ɪ	ɛ	æ	ɑ	ɔ	ʌ	ʊ	u
see	sit	ten	cat	hot	saw	cup	put	too

on the whole generally, but not true in every case: *On the whole, I think it's a very good idea.*

whole·heart·ed /ˌhoʊlˈhɑrtəd/ *adj.* complete and without doubt: *to give sb your wholehearted support* —**whole·heart·ed·ly** *adv.*: *We wholeheartedly agree with you.*

whole·sale /ˈhoʊlseɪl/ *adj.* (only *before* a noun) **1** connected with buying and selling goods in large quantities: *The wholesale price was less than half the retail price in the store.* **2** (usually about sth bad) very great; on a very large scale: *the wholesale destruction of the rainforests* —**whole·sale** *adv.*

whole·some /ˈhoʊlsəm/ *adj.* **1** good for your health: *simple wholesome food* **2** (used about a person) looking clean and attractive **3** having a moral effect that is good: *wholesome family entertainment*

who'll /hul/ *short for* WHO WILL

whol·ly /ˈhoʊli/ *adv.* completely; fully: *The government is not wholly to blame for the situation.*

☆ **whom** /hum/ *pron.* (*formal*) **1** (used in questions as the object form of "who" to ask sb's name, etc.): *Whom did you meet there?* ○ *To whom did you give the money?* **2** (used as the object form of "who" in reported questions and after certain verbs): *He asked me whom I had met.* ○ *I realized to whom I had been speaking.* **3** (used for saying which person or what kind of person the object of a verb or preposition is): *A man whom I had never met sat down beside me.* **4** (used for giving extra information about the object of a verb or preposition): *This is my wife, to whom I owe everything.*

☞ The use of **whom** instead of **who** as the object pronoun or the pronoun after prepositions is used in more formal English and in writing. We usually express a sentence such as: "*He asked me with whom I had discussed it.*" as "*He asked me who I had discussed it with.*" (Note the position of the preposition at the end.)

whoop·ing cough /ˈhupɪŋ kɔf/ *noun* [U] a serious disease, especially of children, in which they have a bad cough and make a loud noise when they breathe in after coughing

whoops /wʊps; wups/ *interj.* (*informal*) = OOPS

whoosh /wʊʃ; wuʃ/ *verb* [I] to move very fast, with the sound of air rushing —**whoosh** *noun* [C,U]

whore /hɔr/ *noun* [C] (*old-fashioned*) = PROSTITUTE

who're /ˈhuər/ *short for* WHO ARE

who's /huz/ *short for* WHO IS, WHO HAS

☆ **whose** /huz/ *det., pron.* **1** (used in questions when you are asking who sth belongs to) of whom?: *Whose car is that?* ○ *That's a nice coat – I wonder whose it is.* **2** of whom; of which: *That's the boy whose mother has just died.* ○ *a company whose most famous product is chocolate*

who've /huv/ *short for* WHO HAVE

☆ **why** /waɪ/ *adv.* for what reason: *Why was she so late?* ○ *I wonder why they went.* ○ *"I'm not staying any longer." "Why not?"* ○ *Can you tell me the reason why you are so unhappy?*
IDM **how, why, where, who, etc. in the world** ⇨ WORLD
why not... (used for making or agreeing to a suggestion): *Why not order a pizza tonight?*

wick /wɪk/ *noun* [C] the piece of string in the middle of a candle ☞ picture at **candle**.

wick·ed¹ /ˈwɪkəd/ *adj.* **1** morally bad; evil: *The wicked witch turned the prince into a frog.* ☞ Look at the note at **evil**. **2** liking to annoy other people in a way that is not serious: *a wicked sense of humor* **3** (*slang*) very good: *Rob hit a wicked home run today.* —**wick·ed·ly** *adv.* —**wick·ed·ness** *noun* [U]

wicked² /ˈwɪkəd/ *adv.* (*slang*) (used for emphasizing an adjective): *Man, it's wicked hot out there!* ○ *wicked good*

☆ **wide** /waɪd/ *adj.* **1** measuring a large amount from one side or edge to the other: *The bridge was not wide enough for two cars to go over.* ○ *a wide river* ☞ The noun is **width**. The opposite is **narrow**. Look at the note at **broad**. **2** measuring a particular amount from one side or edge to the other: *The box was only 5 inches wide.* ○ *How wide is the river?* **3** covering a large area or range, or a large number of people: *You're the nicest person in the whole wide world!* ○ *This store carries a wide range of sizes.* ○ *wide support for the proposal* **4** fully open: *The children's eyes were wide with excitement.*

☆ **wide²** /waɪd/ *adv.* as far or as much as possible; completely: *Open your mouth wide.* ○ *wide awake* ○ *a wide-open door*

☆ **wide·ly** /ˈwaɪdli/ *adv.* **1** to a large degree; a lot: *Their opinions differ widely.* **2** over a large area or range: *Steve traveled widely during his college years.*

wid·en /ˈwaɪdn/ *verb* [I,T] to become wider; to make sth wider: *The gap between rich and poor people is widening.*

wide-ranging *adj.* covering a large area or many subjects: *a wide-ranging discussion*

wide·spread /ˌwaɪdˈsprɛd; ˈwaɪdsprɛd/ *adj.* found or happening over a large area; affecting a large number of people: *The storm caused widespread damage.*

☆ **wid·ow** /ˈwɪdoʊ/ *noun* [C] a woman whose husband has died and who has not married again

wid·owed /ˈwɪdoʊd/ *adj.* being a widow or widower: *She's been widowed for ten years now.*

☆ **wid·ow·er** /ˈwɪdoʊər/ *noun* [C] a man whose wife has died and who has not married again

W

ə	y	w	t̬	eɪ	aɪ	ɔɪ	aʊ	oʊ
about	yes	woman	butter	say	five	boy	now	go

☆ **width** /wɪdθ; wɪtθ/ *noun* [C,U] the amount that sth measures from one side or edge to the other: *The room is twelve feet in width.* ○ *The carpet is available in two different widths.* ☛ picture at **length**.

wield /wild/ *verb* [T] to hold and use sth as a weapon: *Some of the men were wielding knives.* ○ *to wield a great deal of power*

wie·ner /ˈwinər/ *noun* [C] = FRANKFURTER

☆ **wife** /waɪf/ *noun* [C] (*pl.* **wives** /waɪvz/) the woman to whom a man is married

☆ **wig** /wɪg/ *noun* [C] a covering made of real or artificial hair that you wear on your head, because you do not have any hair or because you want to cover up your own hair ☛ Look at **toupee**.

wig·gle /ˈwɪgl/ *verb* [I,T] (*informal*) to move from side to side with small quick movements; to make sth do this: *Can you wiggle your ears?* —**wig·gle** *noun* [C] (*informal*)

wig·wam /ˈwɪgwɑm/ *noun* [C] a type of tent that was used by some Native Americans in the past

☆ **wild¹** /waɪld/ *adj.* **1** living or growing in natural conditions, not controlled by people: *wild animals* ○ *wild flowers* **2** (used about an area of land) not lived on, farmed, etc.: *the wild scenery of Alaska* **3** (used about a person or his/her behavior or emotions) not controlled; somewhat crazy: *The crowd went wild with excitement.* ○ *He had a wild look in his eyes.* **4 wild (about sb/sth)** (*informal*) liking sb/sth very much: *I'm not wild about their new house.* **5** not carefully done, planned or thought about: *Even if you don't know the answer, take a wild guess.* **6** (*informal*) exciting and interesting, especially because it is unusual: *a totally wild outfit* —**wild·ly** *adv.*: *to wave your arms around wildly*

wild² /waɪld/ *noun* **the wild** [sing.] natural areas (= not on farms, in zoos, etc.): *the thrill of seeing elephants in the wild*

☆ **wil·der·ness** /ˈwɪldərnəs/ *noun* [C, usually sing.] **1** an area of land with very few signs of human life: *The Antarctic is the last great wilderness.* **2** a place where plants are growing in an uncontrolled way

☆ **wild·life** /ˈwaɪldlaɪf/ *noun* [U] wild birds, plants, animals, etc.

☆ **will¹** /wəl; əl; l; *strong form* wɪl/ *modal verb* (*short form* **'ll**; *negative* **will not**; *short form* **won't** /woʊnt/) **1** (used in forming the future tenses): *He will be here soon.* ○ *I'm sure you'll pass your test.* ○ *I'll be sitting on the beach this time next week.* ○ *Next Sunday, she will have been in America for a year.* **2** (used for showing that sb is willing to do sth, or that sth is able to do sth): *"We need some more milk."* *"OK, I'll get some."* ○ *Why won't you tell me where you were last night?* ○ *I'll carry your bag for you.* ○ *My car won't start.* **3** (used for asking sb to do sth): *Will you please sit down?* ○ *Just*

wait a minute, will you? **4** (used for talking about sth that generally happens or is true): *People will stop and help if you ask politely.*

☆ **will²** /wɪl/ *verb* [T] to use the power of your mind to do sth or to make sth happen: *He willed himself to keep going to the end of the race.*

☆ **will³** /wɪl/ *noun* **1** [C,U] the power of the mind to choose what actions to take: *Both her children have very strong wills.* ○ *My father seems to have lost the will to live.* **2** [sing.] what sb wants or desires: *She was put into a nursing home against her will.* **3** [C] a legal document in which you write down who should have your money and property after your death: *Have you made a will?* ○ *Grandma left us some money in her will.*

IDM **at will** wherever and whenever you want: *The cat can go in and out of the house at will through the pet door.*

of your own free will ⇨ FREE¹

-willed /wɪld/ (in compounds) having a will³ (1) of a particular type: *strong-willed*

will·ful /ˈwɪlfl/ *adj.* **1** done on purpose, e.g. to hurt or damage sb/sth: *willful damage* **2** doing exactly what you want, no matter what other people think or say —**will·ful·ly** *adv.*

☆ **will·ing** /ˈwɪlɪŋ/ *adj.* **1** (not before a noun) **be willing to do sth** prepared to do sth; having no objection to doing sth: *Are you willing to help us?* ○ *I'm not willing to take any risks.* **2** ready or eager: *a willing helper* —**will·ing·ly** *adv.* —**will·ing·ness** *noun* [U, sing.]

wil·low /ˈwɪloʊ/ (*also* **ˈwillow tree**) *noun* [C] a tree with thin branches and long thin leaves, that grows near water

will·pow·er /ˈwɪlˌpaʊər/ *noun* [U] strength of mind; the ability to keep trying to succeed, even when sth is difficult: *It takes a lot of willpower to give up smoking.*

wilt /wɪlt/ *verb* [I] (used about a plant or flower) to bend and start to die, because of heat or lack of water

wimp¹ /wɪmp/ *noun* [C] (*informal*) a person who is weak or lacks courage —**wimp·y** *adj.*

wimp² /wɪmp/ *verb*

PHRV **wimp out** (*slang*) to lose your courage to do sth: *"Did you both go on the roller coaster?" "No, Doug wimped out at the last minute."*

☆ **win¹** /wɪn/ *verb* (*pres. part.* **win·ning**; *p.t., p.p.* **won** /wʌn/) **1** [I,T] to be the best, first or strongest in a race, game, competition, battle, an election, etc.: *to win a game, race, etc.* ○ *Murphy won and Lewis was second.* ○ *I never win at card games.* ○ *Who do you think will win the next election?* **2** [T] to get sth as a result of success in a competition, race, etc.: *How much did you win?* ○ *Who won the gold medal?*

☛ Note that we **earn** (not **win**) money at our job: *I earn $25,000 a year.*

3 [T] to get sth by hard work, great effort, etc.:

Her outstanding performance won her a great deal of praise. ○ *to win support for a plan*
PHRV win sb over (to sth) to persuade sb to support or agree with you

win² /wɪn/ *noun* [C] an act of winning a competition, game, race, etc.: *We have had two wins and three losses so far this season.*

wince /wɪns/ *verb* [I] to make a sudden quick movement (usually twisting the muscles of the face) because of a sharp pain or sth bad

winch /wɪntʃ/ *noun* [C] a machine that lifts or pulls heavy objects by using a thick chain, etc. that winds around and around a central part —**winch** *verb* [T]: *The injured climber was winched up into a helicopter.*

☆**wind¹** /wɪnd/ *noun* **1** [C,U] (*also* **the wind**) air that is moving across the surface of the earth: *There was a strong wind blowing.* ○ *A gust of wind blew his hat off.* ○ *high winds* ○ *a cold north wind* **2** [U] the breath that you need for doing exercise or playing a musical instrument: *She stopped running to get her wind back.*
IDM get wind of sth to hear about sth that is secret

☆**wind²** /waɪnd/ *verb* (*p.t., p.p.* **wound** /waʊnd/) **1** [T] to wrap sth long around sth else several times: *Wind the string around your finger or the balloon will fly away.* **2** [T] **wind sth (up)** to make sth work or move by turning a key, handle, etc.: *to wind a watch* ○ *to wind up a mechanical toy* **3** [I] (used about a road, path, etc.) to have a lot of bends or curves in it: *The path winds through the woods.*
PHRV wind down to gradually come to an end: *The meeting started to wind down about 5:30.* ☞ Look at **unwind**.
wind up to be in a place at the end of a trip or in a particular situation after other things have happened: *We wound up in a bad part of town after taking a wrong turn.* ○ *You'll wind up failing your math class if you go on like this.*

wind·fall /ˈwɪndfɔl/ *noun* [C] an unexpected gift or piece of good luck

wind·ing /ˈwaɪndɪŋ/ *adj.* with bends or curves in it: *a winding road through the hills*

wind in·stru·ment /ˈwɪnd ˌɪnstrəmənt/ *noun* [C] a musical instrument that you play by blowing through it

wind·mill /ˈwɪndmɪl/ *noun* [C] a tall building with long arms (**sails**) that stick out from it and turn in the wind. Windmills are used for pumping water, producing electricity, etc.

windmill

sail

☆**win·dow** /ˈwɪndoʊ/ *noun* [C] **1** the opening in a building, car, etc. that you can see through and that lets light in. A window usually has

glass in it: *Open the window. It's hot in here.* ○ *a store window* **2** the glass in a window (1): *to break a window* ○ *to clean the windows* **3** an area on a computer screen that has a particular type of information in it ☞ picture on page A29.

win·dow·pane /ˈwɪndoʊpeɪn/ *noun* [C] one piece of glass in a window

'window ˌshopping *noun* [U] looking at things in store windows without buying anything

win·dow·sill /ˈwɪndoʊsɪl/ *noun* [C] the shelf at the bottom of a window in a building, either inside or outside ☞ picture at **curtain**.

wind·pipe /ˈwɪndpaɪp/ *noun* [C] the tube that takes air from the throat to the lungs

☆**wind·shield** /ˈwɪndʃild/ *noun* [C] the window in the front of a car, truck, etc.

'windshield ˌwiper (*also* **wiper**) *noun* [C] one of the two moving arms (**blades**) that remove water, snow, etc. from the windshield

wind·surf /ˈwɪndsərf/ *verb* [I] to move through water standing on a special board with a sail ☞ We usually say **go windsurfing**: *Have you ever gone windsurfing?* —**wind·surf·ing** *noun* [U]

windsurfing

sail

sailboard

wind·swept /ˈwɪndswɛpt/ *adj.* **1** (used about a place) that often has strong winds: *a windswept coastline* **2** looking messy because you have been in a strong wind: *windswept hair*

☆**wind·y** /ˈwɪndi/ *adj.* (**wind·i·er; wind·i·est**) with a lot of wind: *a windy day*

☆**wine** /waɪn/ *noun* [C,U] an alcoholic drink that is made from grapes (or sometimes other fruit): *red/white/rosé wine* ○ *sweet/dry wine* ○ *French wines*

☆**wing¹** /wɪŋ/ *noun* **1** [C] one of the body parts that a bird, an insect, etc. uses for flying ☞ picture at **bird**. **2** [C] one of the two long parts that stick out from the side of an airplane and support it in the air **3** [C] a part of a building that sticks out from the main part or that was added on to the main part: *the maternity wing of the hospital* **4** [C, usually sing.] a group of people in a political party that have particular beliefs or opinions: *the right wing of the Republican party* ☞ Look at **left-wing** and **right-wing**. **5 the wings** [plural] (in a theater) the area at the sides of the stage where you cannot be seen by the audience

wing² /wɪŋ/ *verb*
IDM wing it (*slang*) to do sth, such as giving a speech, without planning or practicing

wink /wɪŋk/ *verb* [I] **wink (at sb)** to close and open one eye very quickly, usually as a private signal to sb ☞ Look at **blink**. —**wink**

W

noun [C]: *to give sb a wink* ∘ *I didn't sleep a wink* (= not at all).

☆ **win·ner** /'wɪnər/ [C] **1** a person, team or an animal that wins a competition, game, race, etc. **2** (*informal*) a person or thing that is successful or likely to be successful: *Their new design looks like a real winner!*

win·ning /'wɪnɪŋ/ *adj.* (only *before* a noun) **1** that is successful or wins a competition, game, race, etc.: *The winning ticket is number 65.* **2** attractive and showing confidence: *She flashed us her winning smile.*

win·nings /'wɪnɪŋz/ *noun* [plural] something, especially money, that you have won in a game or competition

☆ **win·ter** /'wɪntər/ *noun* [C,U] the coldest season of the year between fall and spring: *It snows a lot here in the winter.* ∘ *a cold winter day* ∘ *We went skiing in Colorado last winter.* —**win·try** /'wɪntri/ *adj.*: *wintry weather* ∘ *a wintry wind*

☆ **win·ter·time** /'wɪntərtaɪm/ *noun* [U] the period or season of winter

☆ **wipe** /waɪp/ *verb* [T] **1 wipe sth (off)** to clean or dry sth by rubbing it with a cloth, piece of paper, etc.: *Wipe your hands on the towel.* ∘ *to wipe your nose on a handkerchief* ∘ *Could you wipe off the counter?* ☞ Look at the note at **clean²**. **2 wipe sth from/off sth; wipe sth away/off/up** to remove sth by wiping (1): *Wipe the dirt off your shoes.* ∘ *He wiped the sweat from his forehead.* ∘ *Wipe up the milk you spilled.*

PHRV **wipe sth out** to destroy sth completely: *Whole towns were wiped out in the bombing raids.*

wip·er /'waɪpər/ *noun* [C] = WINDSHIELD WIPER

☆ **wire¹** /'waɪər/ *noun* [C,U] **1** a long thin piece of metal like strong string that is used for fastening things or in fences, cages, etc.: *a piece of wire* ∘ *barbed wire* ∘ *a wire fence* **2** a piece of wire (1) that is used to carry electricity

wire² /'waɪər/ *verb* [T] **1** to fasten or connect two things together using wire ¹(1) **2 wire sth (up)** to connect sth to a supply of electricity by using wires¹(2)

wir·ing /'waɪərɪŋ/ *noun* [U] the system of wires that supplies electricity to rooms in a building

wir·y /'waɪəri/ *adj.* (used about a person) small and thin but strong

☆ **wis·dom** /'wɪzdəm/ *noun* [U] the quality of being wise; the ability to make sensible decisions and judgments because of your knowledge or experience

wisdom tooth *noun* [C] (*pl.* **wisdom teeth**) one of the four teeth at the back of your mouth that appear when you are about 20 years old

☆ **wise** /waɪz/ *adj.* having or showing the knowledge or experience to make good or sensible decisions or judgments: *a wise choice* ∘ *It*

would be wiser to wait for a few days. ∘ *a wise old man* —**wise·ly** *adv.*

☆ **wish¹** /wɪʃ/ *verb* **1** [T] **wish (that)** (often with a verb in the past tense) to want sth that cannot now happen or that probably will not happen: *I wish (that) I had listened more carefully.* ∘ *I wish (that) I knew what was going to happen.* ∘ *My father wishes (that) he had gone to college.* ∘ *I wish I could help you.*

☞ Note that in more formal, correct English we use **were** instead of **was** with "I" or "he/she": *I wish I were rich.* ∘ *She wishes she were in a different job.*

2 [I] **wish (for sth)** to say to yourself that you want sth that can only happen by good luck or magic: *She closed her eyes and wished for her mother to get better.* **3** [T] **wish (to do sth)** (*formal*) to want to do sth: *I wish to make a complaint about the service here.* **4** [T] to say that you hope sb will have sth; to say sth as a greeting: *I called him up to wish him a happy birthday.* ∘ *We wish you all the best for your future career.*

☆ **wish²** /wɪʃ/ *noun* **1** [C] a feeling that you want sth: *a wish for peace* ∘ *I have no wish to see her ever again.* ∘ *Doctors should respect the patient's wishes.* **2** [C] an act of saying to yourself secretly that you want to have sth or that you want sth to happen: *to make a wish* ∘ *My wish came true* (= I got what I asked for). **3 wishes** [plural] a hope that sb will be happy or have good luck: *Best Wishes* (= at the end of a letter)

wish·ful /'wɪʃfl/ *adj.*

IDM **wishful thinking** ideas that are based on what you would like, not on facts

wisp /wɪsp/ *noun* [C] **1** a small thin bunch of hair, grass, etc. **2** a small amount of smoke

wist·ful /'wɪstfl/ *adj.* feeling or showing sadness because you cannot have what you want: *a wistful sigh* —**wist·ful·ly** *adv.*

wit /wɪt/ *noun* **1** [U] the ability to use words in a clever and amusing way **2** (*also* **wits** [plural]) intelligence; the ability to think quickly: *The game of chess is essentially a battle of wits.*

IDM **keep your wits about you** to be ready to act in a difficult situation

witch /wɪtʃ/ *noun* [C] (in former times and in stories) a woman who is thought to have magic powers that she uses to do bad things. Pictures of witches in stories show them wearing a long black coat and a tall pointed hat. ☞ Look at **wizard**.

witch·craft /'wɪtʃkræft/ *noun* [U] the use of magic powers to make things happen

☆ **with** /wɪð; wɪθ/ *prep.* **1** in the company or presence of sb/sth: *I live with my parents.* ∘ *Are you coming with us?* ∘ *I talked about the problem with my teacher.* ∘ *Does this tie go with this shirt?* ∘ *Could you put this book with the others?* **2** in the care of sb: *We left the keys with*

the neighbors. **3** having or carrying sth: *a girl with red hair* ○ *a house with a double garage* ○ *the man with a suitcase* **4** using sth: *Cut it with a knife.* ○ *I did it with his help.* **5** (used for expressing what fills, covers, etc. sth): *Fill the bowl with water.* **6** against: *He's always fighting with his brother.* ○ *I usually play tennis with my sister.* **7** agreeing with or supporting: *We've got everybody with us on this issue.* **8** because of or as a result of sth: *We were shivering with cold.* **9** (used for expressing how sth happens or is done): *Open this package with care.* ○ *to greet sb with a smile* **10** toward, concerning or compared with sb/sth: *Is he angry with us?* ○ *There's a problem with my phone bill.* ○ *Compared with New England, Virginia has mild winters.* **11** including: *With sales tax, the TV cost $275.* **12** at the same time as: *I can't concentrate with you watching me all the time.* **13** because of: *With all the problems we've got, we're not going to finish on time.*

IDM **be with sb** to be able to follow what sb is saying: *I'm sorry, I'm not quite with you. Say it again.*

☆ **with·draw** /wɪð'drɔ; wɪθ-/ *verb* (*p.t.* **with·drew** /-'dru/; *p.p.* **with·drawn** /-'drɔn/) **1** [I,T] **withdraw (sb/sth) (from sth)** (to cause sb/sth) to move back or away: *The troops withdrew from the town.* **2** [T] to take money out of a bank account: *I'd like to withdraw a hundred dollars from my savings account* ☞ Look at **deposit.** **3** [T] to remove sth or take sth away: *to withdraw an offer, a statement, etc.* **4** [I] to decide not to take part in sth: *Jackson withdrew from the race at the last minute.*

with·draw·al /wɪð'drɔəl; wɪθ-/ *noun* **1** [C,U] moving sth back or away: *the withdrawal of troops from the war zone* **2** [C] an act of taking an amount of money out of your bank account: *to make a withdrawal* **3** [U] the act of stopping doing sth, especially taking a drug: *When he quit drinking, he suffered severe withdrawal symptoms.*

with·drawn /wɪð'drɔn; wɪθ-/ *adj.* (used about a person) very quiet and not wanting to talk to other people

with·er /'wɪðər/ *verb* [I,T] **wither (away)** **1** (used about plants) to become dry and die; to make a plant do this: *The plants withered in the hot sun.* **2** to become weaker, until it disappears: *Our hopes gradually withered away.*

with·hold /wɪθ'hould; wɪð-/ *verb* [T] (*p.t., p.p.* **with·held** /-'hɛld/) (*formal*) **withhold sth (from sb/sth)** to refuse to give sth: *to withhold information from the police*

☆ **with·in** /wɪ'ðɪn; wɪ'θɪn/ *prep.* **1** in a period not longer than a particular length of time: *I'll be back within an hour.* **2** within sth **(of sth)** not further than a particular distance from sth: *The house is within three blocks of the high school.* **3** not outside the limits or range of sb/sth: *Each department must keep within its*

budget. **4** (*formal*) inside sb/sth: *The anger was still there deep within him.*

☆ **with·out** /wɪ'ðaut; wɪ'θaut/ *prep.* **1** not having, showing or being with sb/sth: *Don't go out without a coat on.* ○ *Pam drinks her coffee without milk or cream.* ○ *After three days without sleep, he was exhausted.* ○ *He spoke without much enthusiasm.* ○ *Don't leave without me.* **2** (used with a verb in the *-ing* form to mean "not"): *She left without saying goodbye.*

with·stand /wɪθ'stænd; wɪð-/ *verb* [T] (*p.t., p.p.* **with·stood** /-'stud/) (*formal*) to be strong enough not to break, give up, be damaged, etc.: *The troops were too weak to withstand another attack.*

☆ **wit·ness¹** /'wɪtnəs/ *noun* [C] **1** (*also* **eyewitness**) a person who sees sth happen and who can tell other people about it later: *There were two witnesses to the accident.* **2** a person who appears in a court of law to say what he/she has seen or what he/she knows about sb/sth: *Each witness was cross-examined.* ○ *a witness for the defense/prosecution* **3** a person who sees sb sign an official document and who then signs it himself/herself

☆ **wit·ness²** /'wɪtnəs/ *verb* [T] **1** to see sth happen and to be able to tell other people about it later: *to witness a murder* **2** to see sb sign an official document and then sign it yourself: *to witness a will*

'witness stand (*also* **stand**) *noun* [C] the place in a court of law where a witness sits when he/she is giving evidence (**testifying**)

-wit·ted /'wɪtəd/ (in compounds) having a particular type of intelligence: *quick-witted*

wit·ty /'wɪti/ *adj.* (**wit·ti·er; wit·ti·est**) intelligent and amusing; using words in a clever way: *a very witty speech*

wives *pl.* of WIFE

wiz·ard /'wɪzərd/ *noun* [C] (in stories) a man who is believed to have magic powers ☞ Look at **witch.**

wk. *abbr.* = WEEK

wob·ble /'wɑbl/ *verb* [T] to move from side to side in an unsteady way: *Put something under the leg of the table. It's wobbling.* —**wob·bly** /'wɑbli/ *adj.* (*informal*): *a wobbly table*

wok /wɑk/ *noun* [C] a large pan that is shaped like a bowl and used for cooking Chinese food ☞ picture at **pan.**

woke *p.t.* of WAKE¹

wok·en *p.p.* of WAKE¹

wolf /wulf/ *noun* [C] (*pl.* **wolves** /wulvz/) a wild animal that looks like a dog and that lives and hunts in a group (**pack**)

☆ **wom·an** /'wumən/ *noun* [C] (*pl.* **wom·en** /'wɪmən/) an adult female person: *men, women and children* ○ *a single/married/divorced woman*

-woman /'wumən/ (*pl.* **-women** /'wɪmən/) (in compounds) a woman who does a particular activity: *a businesswoman*

W

womb /wum/ *noun* [C] (*old-fashioned*) = UTERUS

'women's room *noun* [C] a room with toilets in it for women in a public building ☞ Look at **restroom** and at the note at **toilet**.

won *p.t., p.p.* of WIN[1]

☆ **won·der**[1] /'wʌndər/ *verb* **1** [I,T] to want to know sth; to ask yourself questions about sth: *I wonder what the new teacher will be like.* ○ *He started to wonder if she was all right.* ○ *I wonder who that woman over there is.* ○ *It was something that she had been wondering about for a long time.* ○ *Sometimes I wonder how they manage to live on the amount he earns.* **2** [T] **wonder (if…)** (used when you are asking sb politely to do sth): *I wonder if you could help me.* ○ *I was wondering if you could help me.*

won·der[2] /'wʌndər/ *noun* **1** [U] a feeling of surprise and admiration: *They could do nothing but stand in wonder at the sight.* **2** [C] something that causes you to feel surprise or admiration: *the wonders of modern medicine* **IDM** **it's a wonder (that)…** it's surprising that…: *It's a wonder we managed to get here on time, with all the traffic.*

no wonder it is not surprising: *You've been out every night this week. No wonder you're tired.*

☆ **won·der·ful** /'wʌndərfl/ *adj.* very good; giving great pleasure: *What wonderful weather!* ○ *It's a wonderful opportunity.* ○ *It's wonderful to see you again.* —**won·der·ful·ly** /-fli/ *adv.*

won't /woʊnt/ *short for* WILL NOT

☆ **wood** /wʊd/ *noun* **1** [U] the hard material that the trunk and branches of trees are made of: *He chopped some wood for the fire.* ○ *Most furniture is made of wood.* **2** [C] a type of wood(1): *Pine is a soft wood.* **3 the woods** [plural] an area of land that is covered with trees, smaller than a forest: *a walk in the woods* **IDM** **knock on wood** ⇨ KNOCK[2]

wood·chuck /'wʊdtʃʌk/ (*also* **groundhog**) *noun* [C] a small animal with brown fur that lives in a hole in the ground

woodchuck (*also* **groundhog**)

wood·ed /'wʊdəd/ *adj.* (used about an area of land) having a lot of trees growing on it: *a heavily wooded valley*

☆ **wood·en** /'wʊdn/ *adj.* made of wood: *wooden toys*

wood·wind /'wʊdwɪnd/ *noun* [C, usually pl.] the set of musical instruments that are made of wood and that you play by blowing into them —**wood·wind** *adj.*: *woodwind instruments*

wood·work /'wʊdwərk/ *noun* [U] the parts of a building that are made of wood (e.g. the doors, stairs, etc.)

woof /wʊf/ *noun* [C] (*informal*) (used for describing the sound (**a bark**) that a dog makes)

☆ **wool** /wʊl/ *noun* [U] **1** the soft thick hair of sheep, goats, etc. **2** thick cloth that is made from wool(1): *The sweater is 50% wool and 50% acrylic.* —**wool** *adj.*: *warm wool socks*

wool·en /'wʊlən/ *adj.* (*formal*) made of wool: *a warm woolen sweater*

wool·y /'wʊli/ *adj.* of or like wool: *The dog had a thick wooly coat.*

☆ **word**[1] /wərd/ *noun* **1** [C] a sound or letter or group of sounds or letters that expresses a particular meaning: *What's the Greek word for "computer?"* ○ *Several words are spelled wrong.* ○ *There are five letters in the word "apple."* **2** [C] a short statement or conversation: *Could I have a word with you in private?* ○ *a few words of thanks* ○ *Don't say a word about this to anyone.* **3** [sing.] a promise: *I give you my word that I won't let you down.* **IDM** **a dirty word** ⇨ DIRTY[1]

get a word in edgewise to interrupt when sb else is talking so that you can say sth yourself

have, etc. the last word ⇨ LAST[1]

in other words ⇨ OTHER

put in a (good) word for sb to say sth good about sb to sb else: *If you could put in a good word for me, I might stand a better chance of getting the job.*

take sb's word for it to believe what sb says without any proof

word for word 1 repeating sth exactly: *Sharon repeated word for word what he had told her.* **2** (in a translation) dealing with each word separately, not looking at the general meaning: *a word-for-word translation*

word[2] /wərd/ *verb* [T] (often passive) to choose carefully the words that you use to express sth: *The statement was carefully worded so that nobody would be offended by it.*

word·ing /'wərdɪŋ/ *noun* [sing.] the words that you use to express sth: *The wording of the contract was very vague.*

'word ˌprocessor *noun* [C] a type of small computer or a computer program that you can use for writing letters, reports, etc. You can correct or change what you have written before you print it out. —**word processing** *noun* [U]

wore *p.t.* of WEAR[1]

☆ **work**[1] /wərk/ *noun* **1** [U] something that requires physical or mental effort. You usually do work because you feel you have to, not for pleasure: *Her success is due to sheer hard work.* ○ *There is still a lot of work to be done.* ○ *Quit talking and get back to work!* **2** [U] what you do to earn money; the place where you go to earn money: *It is very difficult to find work in this city.* ○ *out of work* (= without a job) ○ *When do you start work?* ○ *I go to work at 8 o'clock.* ○ *The people at work gave me some flowers for my birthday.*

ər	ɪr	ɛr	ɑr	ɔr	ʊr	ʒ	h	ŋ
bird	near	hair	car	north	tour	vision	hat	sing

☞ **Work** is an uncountable noun. In some contexts we must use **job**: *I've found work at the hospital.* ○ *I have a new job at the hospital.* **Employment** is the state of having a paid job and is more formal and official than **work** or **job**. It is an uncountable noun: *Many married women are in part-time employment.* **Occupation** is the word used on forms to ask what you are or what job you do: *Occupation: student.* ○ *Occupation: bus driver.* A **profession** is a job that requires special training and higher education: *the medical profession.* A **trade** is a job that you do with your hands and that requires special skill: *He's a carpenter by trade.*

3 [U] something that you are working on or have produced: *a piece of written work* ○ *The teacher graded their work.* ○ *Is this all your own work?* ○ *an exhibit of the work of two young photographers* **4** [C] a book, painting, piece of music, etc.: *a work of art* ○ *an early work by Picasso* ○ *the complete works of Shakespeare* **5 the works** [plural] (*informal*) everything: *This car is equipped with air conditioning, a CD player, cruise control – the works!* **6 works** [plural] the act of building or repairing sth: *The Department of Public Works* **7 works** [C, with sing. or pl. verb] (often in compounds) a factory or similar building: *The city waterworks*
IDM **get/go to work (on sth)** to begin; to make a start (on sth)
have your work cut out for you to have a difficult task that you must do
in the works being prepared or developed: *A new movie about her life is currently in the works.*

☆ **work²** /wərk/ *verb* **1** [I,T] to do sth which needs physical or mental effort; to do a job, especially in order to earn money: *I won't pass math class unless I work harder.* ○ *I've been working in the yard all day.* ○ *She works for a computer company in Washington.* ○ *I'd like to work as a newspaper reporter.* ○ *Doctors often work extremely long hours.* **2** [I] (used about a machine, etc.) to do what it is meant to do, correctly; to function: *Our phone hasn't been working for several days.* ○ *Can you show me how the copy machine works?* **3** [I] to have the result or effect that you want; to be successful: *Your idea sounds good, but I don't think it will really work.* **4** [T] to make yourself/sb/sth work; to use or operate: *He works all his employees very hard.* ○ *Do you know how to work the fax machine?* **5** [I,T] to produce a particular effect; to help sth to happen: *His good reputation had obviously worked in his favor.* **6** [I,T] to move to a new position or condition: *The hinges on the door have worked loose.* ○ *We worked our way from one end of the mall to the other.*

PHRV **work on sth** to make an effort to build, repair, finish, etc. sth: *I need to work on my history paper tonight.* ○ *Dan works on old cars in his spare time.* ○ *"Do you have that data for me?" "No, but I'm working on it!"*
work out 1 to develop or progress, especially in a good way: *I hope things work out for you.* **2** to do physical exercises in order to keep your body healthy and strong: *Linda works out twice a week at the health club.*
work out (to sth) to come to a particular result or total after everything has been calculated: *The price of dinner worked out to around $30 each.*
work sb out to understand sb: *I've never been able to work her out.*
work sth out 1 to find the answer to sth; to solve sth: *I can't work out how to do this.* **2** to calculate sth: *I worked out the total cost.* **3** to plan sth: *She asked her lawyer to work out the business deal.*
work up to sth to develop or progress to sth: *Start with 15 minutes' exercise and gradually work up to 30.*
work sb/yourself up (into sth) to make sb/yourself become angry, excited, upset, etc.: *He had worked himself up into a state of anxiety about his interview.* ☞ Look also at **worked up**.

work·a·ble /'wərkəbl/ *adj.* that can be used or that can operate in an efficient way ☞ The opposite is **unworkable**.
work·a·hol·ic /,wərkə'halɪk/ *noun* [C] a person who works a lot and feels that he/she needs to work all the time
☆ **work·book** /'wərkbʊk/ *noun* [C] a book with questions and exercises in it that you use when you are studying sth
,**worked 'up** *adj.* (*informal*) (not before a noun) **worked up (about/over sth)** very nervous, excited or upset about sth: *There's no need to get all worked up about it!*
☆ **work·er** /'wərkər/ *noun* [C] **1** (often in compounds) a person who works, especially one who does a particular type of job or belongs to a certain group of people: *factory workers* ○ *an office worker* ○ *migrant workers* ☞ Look also at **coworker**. **2** a person who does physical work: *manual workers* **3** a person who works in a particular way: *a slow worker*
,**workers' compen'sation** (also *old-fashioned* **workmen's compensation**) *noun* [U] money that must be paid to a worker by his/her company if he/she is injured or becomes sick as a result of his/her work
work·fare /'wərkfɛr/ *noun* [U] a system in which poor people must do some work which is given to them by the government before they receive a regular payment from the government ☞ Look also at **welfare**.
work·force /'wərkfɔrs/ *noun* [C] **1** the total number of people who work in a company,

W

factory, etc. **2** the total number of people in a country who are able to work: *Ten percent of the workforce is unemployed.*

☆**work·ing** /'wɜrkɪŋ/ *adj.* (only *before* a noun) **1** employed; having a job: *the problems of childcare for working parents* **2** connected with your job: *He stayed with the same company for the whole of his working life.* ∘ *The company offers excellent working conditions.* **3** good enough to be used, although it could be improved: *I have a working knowledge of French.*

IDM in working order ⇨ ORDER¹

the ¹working class *noun* [sing.] the group of people in a society who usually do physical work, especially in industry: *unemployment among the working class* ∘ *a working-class area* ∘ *a working-class family*

work·ings /'wɜrkɪŋz/ *noun* [plural] the way in which a machine, an organization, etc. operates: *It's very difficult to understand the workings of the legal system.*

work·load /'wɜrkloʊd/ *noun* [C] the amount of work that you have to do

work·man /'wɜrkmən/ *noun* [C] (*pl.* **workmen**) a man who works with his hands, especially building or making things

work·man·ship /'wɜrkmənʃɪp/ *noun* [U] the quality of sth that has been made or built

¹workmen's compen¹sation *noun* [U] (*old-fashioned*) = WORKERS' COMPENSATION

work·out /'wɜrkaʊt/ *noun* [C] a period of physical exercise, e.g. when you are practicing for a sport or staying healthy

☆**work·sheet** /'wɜrkʃit/ *noun* [C] a piece of paper with questions or exercises on it that you use when you are studying sth

☆**work·shop** /'wɜrkʃap/ *noun* [C] **1** (*also* **shop**) a place where things are made or repaired **2** a time when a group of people meet and discuss or learn more about a particular subject

work·sta·tion /'wɜrk,steɪʃn/ *noun* [C] an area in an office for one person, with a desk and a computer that is connected to a large computer system

¹work-¹study *noun* [U] work that a student does in order to gain experience and earn money to pay for his/her education: *a campus work-study program*

☆**world** /wɜrld/ *noun* **1 the world** [sing.] the Earth with all its countries and people: *an explorer who sailed around the world* ∘ *a map of the world* ∘ *changes in the world's climate* ∘ *the most beautiful place in the world* ∘ *English is a world language* (= used all over the world). **2** [sing.] a particular part of the earth: *the western world* ∘ *the English-speaking world* **3** [sing.] the life and activities of people on earth; their experience: *It is hard to imagine what the world of our grandchildren will be like.* ∘ *It's time you learned something about the real world!* ∘ *the modern world* **4** [C] (often in

compounds) a particular area of activity or group of people or things: *the world of sports* ∘ *the medical world* ∘ *the animal world* **5** [C] a planet with life on it: *Do you believe there are other worlds out there?* **6** [sing.] everybody: *The whole world seemed to know the news before me!*

IDM how, why, where, who, etc. in the world (*informal*) (used for emphasizing sth or expressing surprise: *Where in the world have you been?*

the outside world people, places, activities, etc. that are beyond the area where you live and your everyday experience

the real world ⇨ REAL¹

think the world of sb/sth ⇨ THINK

do sb a world of good (*informal*) to be very good or helpful for sb: *The vacation has done her a world of good.*

¹world-¹famous *adj.* known all over the world: *a world-famous writer*

world·ly /'wɜrldli/ *adj.* **1** connected with ordinary life, not with the spirit: *He left all his worldly possessions to his nephew.* **2** having a lot of experience and knowledge of life and people: *a sophisticated and worldly teenager*

¹world ¹war *noun* [C] a war that involves a lot of important countries: *the Second World War* (=from 1939-1945)

☆**world·wide** /,wɜrld'waɪd/ *adj., adv.* (happening) in the whole world: *The situation has caused worldwide concern.* ∘ *The product will be marketed worldwide.*

the ¹World Wide ¹Web (*also informal* **the Web**) *noun* [sing.] (*abbr.* **WWW**) the international system of computers that makes it possible for you to see information from around the world on your computer ☞ Look at **Internet**.

worm

☆**worm¹** /wɜrm/ *noun* [C] **1** a small animal with a long thin body and no bones or legs: *an earthworm* **2 worms** [plural] worms (1) that live inside a person or an animal and may cause disease: *Our dog has worms.*

worm² /wɜrm/ *verb*

PHRV worm your way/yourself along, through, etc. to move slowly or with difficulty in the direction mentioned, e.g. by moving in between a lot of people or things: *I managed to worm my way through the crowd.*

worn *p.p.* of WEAR¹

¹worn-¹out (*also* **worn out**) *adj.* **1** too old or damaged to use any more: *a worn-out sweater* **2** extremely tired: *I'm all worn out. I think I'll go to bed early.*

W

☆ **wor·ried** /ˈwərid/ *adj.* **worried (about sb/sth)**; **worried (that…)** anxious or unhappy: *Don't look so worried. Everything will be all right.* ◦ *I'm worried about Jane.*

☆ **wor·ry¹** /ˈwəri/ *verb* (*pres. part.* **wor·rying**; *3rd pers. sing. pres.* **wor·ries**; *p.t., p.p.* **wor·ried**) **1** [I] **worry (about sb/sth)** to be anxious (about sb, a problem, an event, etc.): *"Don't worry, Mom," said Peter, "I won't stay out late." ◦ There's nothing to worry about. ◦ He worries if I don't call every weekend.* **2** [T] **worry sb/yourself (about sb/sth)** to make sb/yourself anxious (about sb/sth): *You look depressed. What's worrying you? ◦ She worried herself sick when he was away.*

wor·ry² /ˈwəri/ *noun* (*pl.* **wor·ries**) **1** [U] an anxious state or feeling: *His son has caused him a lot of worry recently.* **2** [C] something that makes you worry; a problem: *financial worries*

wor·ry·ing /ˈwəriŋ/ *adj.* that makes you worry: *a worrying situation*

☆ **worse¹** /wərs/ *adj.* (the comparative of *bad*) **1** not as good as sth else: *The weather in March was worse than in February. ◦ My English is getting worse and worse.* **2** (not before a noun) more sick; less well: *The doctors say that he's getting worse.*

IDM **make matters/things worse** to make a situation, problem, etc. even more difficult or dangerous than before

the worse for wear (*informal*) damaged; not in good condition: *This suitcase looks somewhat the worse for wear.*

☆ **worse²** /wərs/ *adv.* (the comparative of *badly*) **1** less well: *She speaks German even worse than I do.* **2** more severely or to a greater degree: *He was hurt worse than we had originally thought.*

☆ **worse³** /wərs/ *noun* [U] something that is worse¹ than sth else: *The situation was already bad, but there was worse to come.*

☆ **wors·en** /ˈwərsn/ *verb* [I,T] to become worse or to make sth worse: *Relations between the two countries have worsened.*

☆ **wor·ship¹** /ˈwərʃəp/ *noun* [U] praying to and showing respect for God or a god: *Different religions have different forms of worship.*

☆ **wor·ship²** /ˈwərʃəp/ *verb* (**wor·ship·ing**; **wor·shiped** or **wor·ship·ping**; **wor·shipped**) **1** [I,T] to pray to and show respect for God or a god: *In primitive societies, people worshiped the sun.* **2** [T] to love or admire sb/sth very much: *She worshiped her husband.* **—wor·ship·er** *noun* [C]

☆ **worst¹** /wərst/ *adj.* (the superlative of *bad*) the least pleasant or suitable: *It's been the worst winter that I can remember.*

☆ **worst²** /wərst/ *adv.* (the superlative of *badly*) **1** least well: *A lot of the kids were naughty, but my son behaved worst of all!* **2** the most severely or to the greatest degree: *All the rooms need*

to be painted, but the kitchen needs it worst of all.

☆ **worst³** /wərst/ *noun* [sing.] **the worst** something that is the least satisfactory or desirable: *My parents always expect the worst if I'm late.*

IDM **at (the) worst** if the worst happens or if you consider sb/sth in the worst way: *The problem doesn't look too serious. At worst we'll have to make a few small changes.*

if (the) worst comes to (the) worst if the worst possible situation develops

☆ **worth¹** /wərθ/ *adj.* **1** having a particular value (in money): *"How much is that house worth?" "It must be worth at least $200,000."* **2 worth doing, etc.** (used as a way of recommending or advising): *That museum's really worth visiting if you have time. ◦ It's already nine o'clock. It's not worth going shopping now.*

☞ We can say either: *It isn't worth repairing the car.* OR: *The car isn't worth repairing.*

IDM **get your money's worth** ⇨ MONEY

worth it enjoyable or useful to do or have, even if it means extra cost, effort, etc.: *Don't bother cooking a big meal. It isn't worth it – we're not hungry.*

worth sb's while helpful, useful or interesting to sb

☆ **worth²** /wərθ/ *noun* [U] **1** value or usefulness: *She has proved her worth as a member of the team.* **2** the amount of sth that the money mentioned will buy: *ten dollars' worth of gasoline* **3** the amount of sth that will last for the time mentioned: *two days' worth of food*

☆ **worth·less** /ˈwərθləs/ *adj.* **1** having no value or use: *It's worthless – it's only a piece of plastic!* **2** (used about a person) having bad qualities

worth·while /wərθˈwaɪl/ *adj.* enjoyable, useful or satisfying enough to be worth the cost or effort: *Working for so little money just isn't worthwhile. ◦ Medicine is a very worthwhile career.*

☆ **wor·thy** /ˈwərði/ *adj.* (**wor·thi·er**; **wor·thi·est**) **1 worthy of sth/to do sth** good enough for sth, or deserving sth: *The program is worthy of our support. ◦ He felt he was not worthy to accept such responsibility.* **2** (usually *before* a noun) deserving respect or consideration: *a worthy leader ◦ a worthy cause*

☆ **would** /wəd; əd; d/ strong form /wʊd/ *modal verb* (short form **'d**; negative **would not**; short form **wouldn't** /ˈwʊdnt/) **1** (used when talking about the result of an event that you imagine): *He would be delighted if you went to see him. ◦ She'd be stupid not to accept. ◦ I would have done more if I'd had the time.* **2** (used as the past form of "will" when you report what sb says or thinks): *They said that they would help us. ◦ She didn't think he would do a thing like that.* **3** (used for asking sb politely to do sth):

W

Would you come this way, please? **4** (used with "like" or "love" as a way of asking or saying what sb wants): *Would you like to come with us?* ○ *I'd love a piece of cake.* **5** to be willing to do sth: *She just wouldn't do what I asked her.* **6** (used after "wish"): *I wish the sun would come out.* **7** (used for talking about things that often happened in the past): *When he was young, he would often walk in these woods.* **8** (used for commenting on behavior that is typical): *You would say that. You always support him.* **9** (used when you are giving your opinion): *I'd say she's about 40.*

☆ **wound¹** /wund/ *noun* [C] an injury to part of your body, especially a cut, often received in fighting: *Wash and bandage the wound.* ○ *a bullet wound* ○ *The wound is healing well.*

☆ **wound²** /wund/ *verb* [T] (usually passive) **1** to injure sb's body with a weapon: *He was wounded in the leg during the war.* ☞ Look at the note at **hurt**. **2** (*formal*) to hurt sb's feelings deeply: *I was wounded by his criticism.* —**the wounded** *noun* [plural]: *the sick and the wounded*

wound³ *p.t., p.p.* of WIND³

wove *p.t.* of WEAVE

wov·en *p.p.* of WEAVE

☆ **wow** /waʊ/ *interj.* (*informal*) (used for expressing how much you admire or are pleasantly surprised by sth): *Wow! What a great car!*

☆ **wrap** /ræp/ *verb* [T] (**wrap·ping**; **wrapped**) **1 wrap sth (up) (in sth)** to put paper or cloth around sb/sth as a cover: *to wrap up a present* ○ *The baby was found wrapped in a blanket on the hospital doorstep.* **2 wrap sth around sb/sth** to tie sth such as paper or cloth around an object or a part of the body: *The man had a bandage wrapped around his head.*

IDM **be wrapped up in sth** to be deeply involved and interested in sb/sth: *They were completely wrapped up in each other. They didn't notice I was there.*

PHRV **wrap sth up** to bring sth to an end; to finish sth: *to wrap up a meeting*

wrap (sb/yourself) up to put warm clothes on (sb/yourself)

wrap·per /ˈræpər/ *noun* [C] a piece of paper or plastic which covers a piece of candy, a food package, etc.

wrap·ping /ˈræpɪŋ/ *noun* [C,U] paper or cloth that is used for covering or packing sth: *Remove the outer wrapping before heating the pie.*

ˈwrapping ˌpaper *noun* [U] paper which is used for wrapping presents: *a sheet of wrapping paper*

wrath /ræθ/ *noun* [U] (*old-fashioned, formal*) very great anger

wreak /rik/ *verb*

IDM **wreak havoc (on sth)** to cause great damage: *The earthquake wreaked havoc on the state.*

wreath /riθ/ *noun* [C] (*pl.* **wreaths** /riðz;

riθz/) a circle of flowers or leaves, especially one that is used as a decoration at Christmas

wreck¹ /rɛk/ *noun* **1** [C] a car, plane, etc. which has been badly damaged, especially in an accident: *The car was a wreck, but the truck escaped almost without damage.* **2** [U] an accident that destroys or badly damages a car, truck, ship, etc.: *the wreck of the Titanic* **3** [C] a ship that has sunk or been badly damaged in the ocean: *Divers searched the wreck.* **4** [C, usually sing.] (*informal*) a person or thing that is in a very bad condition: *a nervous wreck*

wreck² /rɛk/ *verb* [T] to destroy, damage or spoil sth completely: *Vandals had wrecked the playground.* ○ *A fishing boat was wrecked in the storms.* ○ *The airline strike wrecked all our vacation plans.*

wreck·age /ˈrɛkɪdʒ/ *noun* [U] the broken pieces of sth that has been wrecked

wrench¹ /rɛntʃ/ *noun* [C] **1** a metal tool with an end shaped so that it can be used for turning nuts (2) ☞ picture at **tool**. **2** a sudden, violent pull or turn

wrench² /rɛntʃ/ *verb* [T] **wrench sb/sth (away, off, etc.)** to pull or turn sb/sth strongly and suddenly: *He wrenched the wheel to the left and stopped the car on the grass.* ○ (*figurative*) *The movie was so exciting that I could hardly wrench myself away.*

wres·tle /ˈrɛsl/ *verb* [I] to fight by trying to get hold of your opponent's body and throw him/her to the floor. People wrestle as a sport.

PHRV **wrestle with sth** to try hard to find an answer to sth; to struggle

wres·tler /ˈrɛslər/ *noun* [C] a person who wrestles as a sport

wres·tling /ˈrɛslɪŋ/ *noun* [U] a sport in which two people fight and try to throw each other to the floor: *a wrestling match*

wretch·ed /ˈrɛtʃəd/ *adj.* very unhappy; miserable

wrig·gle /ˈrɪgl/ *verb* [I,T] **1** to move about, or to move a part of your body, with short, quick movements, especially from side to side: *She wriggled her toes in the water.* **2** to move in the direction mentioned by making quick, turning movements: *The worm wriggled back into the soil.*

PHRV **wriggle out of sth/out of doing sth** (*informal*) to avoid sth by making clever excuses: *It's your turn to do the dishes – you can't wriggle out of it this time!*

wring /rɪŋ/ *verb* [T] (*p.t., p.p.* **wrung** /rʌŋ/) **wring sth (out)** to press and squeeze sth in order to remove water from it

☆ **wrin·kle¹** /ˈrɪŋkl/ *noun* [C] a small line in sth, e.g. on the skin of your face which you get as you grow older, or in your clothes

wrin·kle² /ˈrɪŋkl/ *verb* [I,T] to form wrinkles (in sth): *She wrinkled her nose at the smell.* ○ *This skirt wrinkles easily.* —**wrin·kled** /ˈrɪŋkld/ *adj.*: *an old lady with a wrinkled face*

ər	ɪr	ɛr	ɑr	ɔr	ʊr	ʒ	h	ŋ
bird	near	hair	car	north	tour	vision	hat	sing

☆**wrist** /rɪst/ *noun* [C] the part of your body where your arm joins your hand ☞ picture on page A24.

IDM a slap on the wrist ⇨ SLAP²

☆**wrist·watch** /'rɪstwɑtʃ; -wɔtʃ/ *noun* [C] a watch on a band which you wear around your wrist

writ /rɪt/ *noun* [C] a legal order to do or not to do sth, given by a court of law or a person in authority

☆**write** /raɪt/ *verb* (*p.t.* **wrote** /roʊt/; *p.p.* **written** /'rɪtn/) **1** [I,T] to make words, letters, etc., especially on paper, using a pen, pencil, etc.: *Some children can read and write before they start school.* ∘ *I can't write with this pen.* ∘ *Write your account number on the bottom of your check.* **2** [T] to create a book, story, song, etc. and write it on paper: *He wrote his wife a poem.* ∘ *Who wrote the music for that movie?* **3** [I,T] to write and send a letter, etc. to sb: *Have you written to your mother recently?* ∘ *I'm writing to thank you for the birthday present you sent me.* ∘ *She wrote that they were all well and would be home soon.* ∘ *I wrote a letter to my son./I wrote my son a letter.* ∘ *I wrote her (= wrote a letter to her) yesterday.* **4** [T] **write sth (out) (for sb)** to fill or complete a form, check, document, etc. with the necessary information: *I wrote out a check for $10.* ∘ *The doctor quickly wrote a prescription for me.*

PHRV write back (to sb) to send a reply to sb
write sth down to write sth on paper, especially so that you can remember it
write in (to sb/sth) to write a letter to an organization, etc. to order sth, give an opinion, etc.
write off/away (to sb/sth) (for sth) to write a letter to an organization, etc. to order sth or ask for sth
write sb/sth off to accept or decide that sb/sth will not be successful or useful: *Don't write him off yet. He could still win.*
write sth off to accept that you will not get back an amount of money you have lost or spent: *to write off a debt*
write sth out to write the whole of sth on paper: *I want you to write out the exercise in your notebook.*
write sth up to write sth in a complete and final form, often using notes that you have made: *to write up your notes from a lecture*

write-in /'raɪtɪn/ *noun* [C] a vote that you give to sb who is not an official candidate in an election, by writing his/her name on the piece of paper (**ballot**) used for voting

'**write-off** /'raɪtɔf/ *noun* [C] an amount of money that you will not get back because it has been lost or because sb cannot pay a debt

☆**writ·er** /'raɪtər/ *noun* [C] a person who writes, especially one whose job is to write books, stories, etc.

writhe /raɪð/ *verb* [I] to turn and roll your body around: *She lay writhing in pain.*

☆**writ·ing** /'raɪtɪŋ/ *noun* [U] **1** words that have been written or printed; the way a person writes: *This card has no writing inside. You can put your own message in it.* ∘ *I can't read your writing – it's too small.* **2** the books, etc. that sb has written or the style in which sb writes: *Love is a common theme in his early writing.* ∘ *Her writing lacks realism.* **3** the activity or job of writing books, etc.: *It's difficult to earn much money from writing.*
IDM in writing in written form: *I'll confirm the offer in writing next week.*

☆**writ·ten** /'rɪtn/ *adj.* expressed on paper; not just spoken: *a written agreement* ∘ *a written test and an oral test*

☆**wrong¹** /rɔŋ/ *adj.* **1** not true or not correct; not right: *the wrong answer* ∘ *What you said was totally wrong.* ∘ *You have the wrong number* (= on the telephone). **2** not the best; not suitable; not right: *That's the wrong way to hold the bat.* ∘ *I think she married the wrong man.* **3** (not before a noun) **wrong (with sb/sth)** not as it should be; not working correctly: *You look upset. Is something wrong?* ∘ *What's wrong with the car this time?* ∘ *She has something wrong with her leg.* **4** **wrong (to do sth)** bad or against the law; not good or right: *The man said that he had done nothing wrong.* ∘ *I think it was wrong of us not to invite him.*
IDM get on the right/wrong side of sb ⇨ SIDE¹
on the right/wrong track ⇨ TRACK¹

☆**wrong²** /rɔŋ/ *adv.* in an incorrect way; not right: *I always pronounce that word wrong.* ☞ Look at the note at **wrongly**.
IDM get sb wrong (*informal*) to misunderstand sb: *Don't get me wrong! I don't dislike him.*
go wrong (with sth) to happen or develop in the wrong way: *I always get blamed for everything that goes wrong!* ∘ *Don't worry – nothing should go wrong with the equipment.*

☆**wrong³** /rɔŋ/ *noun* **1** [U] what is bad or against the law: *Children quickly learn the difference between right and wrong.* **2** [C] an action or situation which is not fair: *A terrible wrong has been done. Those men should never have gone to prison.*
IDM in the wrong (*formal*) responsible for sth bad that has happened

wrong⁴ /rɔŋ/ *verb* [T] (*formal*) to do sth to sb which is bad or unfair: *people who have been wronged by inaccurate reports in the media*

wrong·ful /'rɔŋfl/ *adj.* (*formal*) (only before a noun) not fair, not legal or not moral: *She sued her former employer for wrongful dismissal.* —**wrongfully** *adv.*

☆**wrong·ly** /'rɔŋli/ *adv.* in a wrong or mistaken way: *This letter was wrongly addressed.*

W

tʃ	dʒ	v	θ	ð	s	z	ʃ
chin	June	van	thin	then	so	zoo	she

☞ The adverb **wrong** is used after a verb or the object of a verb, especially in conversation: *He spelled my name wrong.* The adverb **wrongly** is especially used before a past participle or a verb: *My name was wrongly spelled.*

wrote *p.t.* of WRITE

wrung *p.t., p.p.* of WRING

wry /raɪ/ *adj.* expressing a mixture of disappointment and amusement: *"Never mind," she said with a wry grin. "At least we got one vote."* —**wry·ly** *adv.*

wt. *abbr.* = WEIGHT¹(1)

WWW *abbr.* = WORLD WIDE WEB

Xx

X, x /ɛks/ *noun* [C] (*pl.* **X's**; **x's**) the twenty-fourth letter of the English alphabet: *"Xylophone" begins with (an) "X."*

☞ **X** is used instead of the name of a person if you do not know or do not want to say the name: *Mr. and Mrs. X.*

X *adj.* (used about movies that no one under age 17 is allowed to see, especially because they are about sex)

xen·o·pho·bi·a /ˌzɛnəˈfoʊbiə; ˌzinə-/ *noun* [U] fear or hatred of people from other countries —**xen·o·pho·bic** /-ˈfoʊbɪk/ *adj.*

Xer·ox /ˈzɪrɑks/ *noun* [C] (*trademark*) **1** a machine that produces copies of documents on paper **2** a copy produced by a Xerox machine: *a Xerox of the letter* —**xer·ox** *verb* [T]

XL *abbr.* extra large

X·mas /ˈkrɪsməs; ˈɛksməs/ *noun* [U] (*informal*) (used as a short form, especially in writing) Christmas: *Merry Xmas to all our customers.*

X-rat·ed /ˈɛksreɪṭəd/ *adj.* (usually *before* a noun) not suitable for children because it is about sex or violence: *the album's X-rated lyrics*

☆ **X-ray** /ˈɛksreɪ/ *noun* [C] **1** [usually pl.] a ray of energy that makes it possible to see inside solid objects (e.g. the human body) so that they can be examined and a photograph of them can be made **2** a photograph that is made with an X-ray machine: *The X-ray showed that the bone was not broken.* —**X-ray** *verb* [T]: *She had her chest X-rayed.*

xy·lo·phone /ˈzaɪləfoʊn/ *noun* [C] a musical instrument that consists of a row of wooden or metal bars of different lengths. You play it by hitting these bars with a small hammer.

Yy

Y, y /waɪ/ *noun* [C] (*pl.* **Y's**; **y's**) the twenty-fifth letter of the English alphabet: *"Yawn" begins with (a) "Y."*

yacht /yɑt/ *noun* [C] a large boat with sails and/or a motor, used for pleasure: *a yacht race*

y'all /yɔl/ *pron.* (*informal*) (used in the southern U.S.) you; all of you: *Why don't y'all come in and have some iced tea?*

yam /yæm/ *noun* [C] an orange-colored root that looks like a potato with pointed ends, that is cooked and eaten as a vegetable ☞ Look also at **sweet potato**.

yank /yæŋk/ *verb* [I,T] (*informal*) to pull with a sudden quick movement and with great force: *She yanked at the door handle and it came off in her hand.* —**yank** *noun* [C]

Yank /yæŋk/ *noun* (*informal*) = YANKEE (2,4)

☆ **Yan·kee** /ˈyæŋki/ *noun* [C] **1** a person who comes from or lives in New England (= the northeastern states of the U.S.) **2** (also *informal* **Yank**) (used as an insult by people in the southern U.S.) a person who comes from or lives in the northern U.S. **3** a soldier who fought for the northern states in the U.S. Civil War (1861–1865) **4** (also *informal* **Yank**) (used as an insult by people outside the U.S.) an American

yap /yæp/ *verb* [I] (**yap·ping**; **yapped**) (used about dogs, especially small ones) to bark in an excited way, making short high noises

☆ **yard** /yɑrd/ *noun* [C] **1** a piece of land next to or around a house with grass, flowers, bushes,

i	ɪ	ɛ	æ	ɑ	ɔ	ʌ	ʊ	u
see	sit	ten	cat	hot	saw	cup	put	too

trees, etc. on it: *The kids were playing in the yard.* ○ *the front/back yard* ☞ picture on page A28. Look at **garden** and **lawn**. **2** an area, usually without a roof, used for a particular type of work or purpose: *a shipyard* **3** (*abbr.* **yd.**) a measure of length; 0.914 of a meter. There are three feet (or 36 inches) in a yard: *This fabric costs $5.99 a yard.* ☞ For more information on measurements, look at Appendix 2.

'yard sale *noun* [C] a sale, held outside sb's house, of used things that people do not want anymore ☞ Look also at **rummage sale**.

yard·stick /'yɑrdstɪk/ *noun* [C] a standard by which things can be compared: *Test scores should not be the only yardstick by which students are judged.*

☆**yarn** /yɑrn/ *noun* **1** [U] thick thread (usually made of wool or cotton) that is used for knitting, etc. **2** [C] (*informal*) a story that sb tells, especially one that is exaggerated

☆**yawn** /yɔn/ *verb* [I] to open your mouth wide and breathe in deeply, especially when you are tired or bored: *"I just got up," she said, yawning.* ○ *I kept yawning all through the lecture.* ○ **yawn** *noun* [C]: *"How much longer will it take?" he said with a yawn.*

yd. *abbr.* = YARD (3)

yeah /yɛə/ *interj.* (*informal*) yes ☞ Look at the note at **yes**.

☆**year** /yɪr/ *noun* (*abbr.* **yr.**) **1** [C] the time it takes the earth to go once around the sun, about 365 days **2** [C] (*also* **'calendar year**) the period from January 1 to December 31; 365 or 366 days divided into 12 months or 52 weeks: *last year/this year/next year* ○ *The population of the country will be 70 million by the year 2000.* ○ *We go on vacation at this time every year.* ○ *the year before last/the year after next* ○ *a leap year* (= one that has 366 days) **3** [C] any period of 12 months, measured from any point: *It's been several years since the last time I saw him.* ○ *She worked here for twenty years.* ○ *He quit school just over a year ago.* ○ *They've been living in New Jersey for the last few years.* **4** [C] a period of a year in connection with schools, the business world, etc.: *The school year runs from September through May.* ○ *the fiscal year* **5** [C] (used in connection with the age of sb/sth) a period of 12 months: *He's ten years old today.* ○ *a six-year-old daughter* ○ *This car is almost five years old.* ○ *The company is now in its fifth year.*

☞ Note that you say: *He's ten* or: *He's ten years old* but NOT: *He's ten years.* Look at the note at **age**.

6 years [plural] a long time: *It happened years ago.*

IDM **(all) year round** for the whole year: *Most of the resorts are open all year round.*

year after year every year for many years

year·book /'yɪrbʊk/ *noun* [C] a book that is produced each year by the students at a school or college, with pictures of students, teachers, sports teams, and events that happened during the year

☆**year·ly** /'yɪrli/ *adj., adv.* (happening) every year or once a year: *a yearly pay raise* ○ *The conference is held yearly in Santa Barbara.*

yearn /yərn/ *verb* [I] **yearn (for sb/sth)** ; **yearn (to do sth)** to want sb/sth very much, especially sth that you cannot have —**yearning** *noun* [C,U]

yeast /yist/ *noun* [U] a substance used for making bread rise and for making beer, wine, etc.

☆**yell** /yɛl/ *verb* [I,T] to shout very loudly, often because you are angry, excited or in pain: *There's no need to yell at me – I can hear you perfectly well.* —**yell** *noun* [C]

☆**yel·low¹** /'yɛloʊ/ *adj.* having the color of lemons or butter: *dark/light yellow* ○ *a bright/pale yellow dress*

yel·low² /'yɛloʊ/ *noun* [C,U] the color of lemons or butter; something that is this color: *a bright shade of yellow* ○ *the yellows and browns of the leaves in the fall*

yel·low·ish /'yɛloʊɪʃ/ *adj.* slightly yellow

☆**the 'Yellow ,Pages** *noun* [plural] (*trademark*) a telephone book (on yellow paper) that lists all the business companies, etc. in a certain area, in sections according to the products or services they provide

yelp /yɛlp/ *noun* [C] a sudden short cry, especially of pain, fear or excitement —**yelp** *verb* [I]

yen /yɛn/ *noun* [C] (*pl.* **yen**) the unit of money used in Japan

yep /yɛp/ *interj.* (*informal*) yes

☆**yes** /yɛs/ *interj.* **1** (used when answering a question to which another possible answer is "no"): *"Are you having a good time?" "Yes, I am!"* ○ *I asked him if he wanted to come, and he said yes.* **2** (used for saying that a statement is correct or for agreeing with one): *"You spend way too much money." "Yes, you're right."* **3** (used when agreeing to a request): *"Is it all right if I sit here?" "Yes, of course."* **4** (used when accepting an offer): *"More coffee?" "Yes, please."* **5** (used for showing you have heard sb or will do what they ask): *"Waiter!" "Yes, ma'am."* **6** (used when saying that a negative statement is not true): *"You don't care about anyone but yourself." "Yes, I do!"* **7** (*informal*) (used to express great pleasure or satisfaction): *Yes! Jordan scored the winning basket!*

☞ **Yes** is used mainly in writing and more formal speech. In informal speech, we usually use other words such as **yeah** or **uh-huh**.

☆**yes·ter·day** /'yɛstərdeɪ; -di/ *adv., noun* [C,U] (on) the day before today: *Did you watch that*

Y

ə	y	w	t̬	eɪ	aɪ	ɔɪ	aʊ	oʊ
about	yes	woman	butter	say	five	boy	now	go

show on TV yesterday? ○ yesterday morning/afternoon/evening ○ I mailed the letter the day before yesterday (= if I am speaking on Wednesday, I mailed it on Monday). ○ Did it really happen three weeks ago? It seems like only yesterday. ○ Do you still have yesterday's newspaper? ○ Yesterday was the best day I've had in a long time.

☆**yet¹** /yɛt/ adv. **1** (used with negative verbs or in questions for talking about sth that has not happened but that you expect to happen): We haven't had any serious problems yet. ○ Has it stopped raining yet? ○ There was a pile of work on my desk which I hadn't yet done. ○ I haven't seen that movie yet. ○ Did you do your homework yet? **2** (used with negative verbs) now; as early as this: You don't have to go yet – your flight doesn't leave until 5:00. **3** (used especially with may or might) at some time in the future: With a little bit of luck, they might win yet. **4** (used with comparatives or "another" to emphasize the size or amount of sth): This is yet another reason to cancel the project. **5** (used with superlatives) until and including now/then; so far: This is her best performance yet. **6** but; in spite of that: Their plan was simple yet successful.
IDM **as yet** until now: As yet, little is known about the disease.
yet again (used for emphasizing how often sth happens) once more: Yet again, Jim was late for class.
yet to do, etc. (if you have yet to do sth, it means that you have not done it but may possibly do it in the future): The final decision has yet to be made.

yet² /yɛt/ conj. but (when sth is surprising after the first part of the statement): He seems nice, yet there's something about him I don't like.

☆**yield¹** /yild/ verb **1** [T] to produce crops, profits or results: How much wheat does each field yield? ○ Did the experiment yield any new information? **2** [I] **yield (to sb/sth)** (formal) to stop resisting sb/sth (so that you do what sb has demanded): The government refused to yield to the hostage takers' demands. ☞ **Give in** is less formal. **3** [I] **yield (to sb/sth)** to allow other traffic to go first or to join the road in front of you: You have to yield to traffic on the highway here. **4** [T] to allow sb to have control of sth that you were controlling: The army has yielded power to the rebels. **5** [I] **yield to sth** (formal) to be replaced by sth, especially sth newer: Old-fashioned methods have yielded to new technology. ☞ **Give way** is more common. **6** [I] (formal) to bend or break: The dam finally yielded under the weight of the water. ☞ **Give way** is more common.

yield² /yild/ noun [C] the amount that is produced: Wheat yields are down 5% this year. ○ This investment has an annual yield of 12%.

yo /you/ interj. (slang) (used in very informal situations to get sb's attention, as a greeting or as a response to sb who calls your name): Yo, Mike! Over here! ○ Yo, dudes – how's it going? ○ "Rick?" "Yo!"

yo·ga /ˈyougə/ noun [U] a system of exercises that helps you control and relax both your mind and your body

☆**yo·gurt** /ˈyougərt/ noun [C,U] a slightly sour, thick liquid food made from milk

yoke /youk/ noun [C] a piece of wood fastened across the necks of two animals when they are pulling a cart, etc.: (figurative) the yoke of slavery

yolk /youk/ noun [C,U] the yellow part in the middle of an egg: He ate the yolk and left the white. ☞ picture at **egg**.

Yom Kip·pur /ˌyɑm kɪˈpʊr; ˌyɔm-/ noun [U] a Jewish religious holiday on which Jewish people do not eat, and pray that God will forgive them for the things they have done wrong

yon·der /ˈyɑndər/ adv. (used mainly in the southern U.S.) over there, at a place that is fairly far away: I thought I saw a deer way over yonder.

☆**you** /yu/ pron. **1** the person or people being spoken to or written to: You can play the guitar, can't you? ○ I've told you about this before. ○ Bring your purse with you. ○ Hey, you! Get off my lawn!
☞ Notice that we do not write **you** with a capital "Y," even when we are writing a letter to someone.
2 (used with a noun, adjective or phrase when calling sb sth): You idiot! What do you think you're doing? **3** a person (not a particular one); people in general: You don't see many tourists here at this time of year. ○ The more you earn, the more taxes you pay.
☞ **One** has the same meaning, but is much more formal: One tries to help as much as one can.
IDM **you guys**; **you all** (informal) (used when speaking to two or more people): Do you guys want to order a pizza? ☞ **You guys** and **you all** can be used when speaking to both men and women.

you'd /yəd; strong form yud/ short for YOU HAD, YOU WOULD

you'll /yəl; strong form yul/ short for YOU WILL

☆**young¹** /yʌŋ/ adj. (**young·er** /ˈyʌŋgər/. **young·est** /ˈyʌŋgəst/) not having lived or existed for very long: They have two young children. ○ young plants ○ teenagers and young adults ○ I'm a year younger than her. ○ My father was the youngest of eight children. ○ young fashions (= for young people)
IDM **young at heart** behaving or thinking like a young person, even if you are not young

☆**young²** /yʌŋ/ *noun* [plural] **1** young animals: *Swans will attack to protect their young.* **2 the young** young people when you are thinking about them as a group: *The young of today are the adults of tomorrow.*

young·ster /'yʌŋstər/ *noun* [C] (*old-fashioned*) a child or young person: *There is very little entertainment for youngsters in this town.*

☆**your** /yər; *strong form* yɔr; yʊr/ *det.* **1** belonging to or connected with the person or people being spoken to: *What's your apartment like?* ○ *Thanks for all your help.* ○ *How old are your kids now?* ○ *It would be helpful if you could all give me your addresses.* **2** belonging to or connected with people in general: *When your life is as busy as mine, you don't have much time to relax.* **3** (used for saying that sth is well-known to people in general): *So this is your typical Florida beach, is it?*

you're /yər; *strong form* yɔr; yʊr/ *short for* YOU ARE

☆**yours** /yərz; *strong form* yɔrz; yʊrz/ *pron.* **1** belonging to or connected with you: *Is this bag yours or mine?* ○ *I was talking to a friend of yours the other day.* **2 Yours** (used at the end of a letter): *Yours truly...* ○ *Yours...*

☆**your·self** /yər'sɛlf/ *pron.* (*pl.* **your·selves** /-'sɛlvz/) **1** (used as the object of a verb or preposition when you are speaking to sb and talking about this person/these people doing an action and also being affected by it): *Be careful or you'll hurt yourself.* ○ *Here's some money. Buy yourselves a present.* ○ *You're always talking about yourself!* **2** (used for emphasis): *You yourself told me there was a problem last week.* ○ *Did you fix the car yourselves?* (= or did sb else do it for you?) **3** in your normal state; healthy: *You don't look yourself today.*
IDM by yourself/yourselves 1 alone: *Do you live by yourself?* **2** without help: *You can't cook dinner for ten people by yourself. Let me help you.*

☆**youth** /yuθ/ *noun* (*pl.* **youths** /yuðz/) **1** [U] the period of your life when you are young, especially the time between being a child and an adult: *He was a very good athlete in his youth.* **2** [U] the fact or state of being young: *I think that his youth will be a disadvantage in this job.* **3** [C] (*formal* or *old-fashioned*) a young person (usually a young man, and often one that you do not have a good opinion of): *There were groups of youths standing around on the street corners.* **4** (*also* **the youth**) [plural] young people as a group: *What kind of future do the youth of this country have?*

youth·ful /'yuθfl/ *adj.* **1** having the qualities that are typical of young people: *She was almost fifty but still full of youthful enthusiasm.* **2** young or relatively young: *The movie stars a youthful Jimmy Stewart.*

youth ,hostel *noun* [C] a type of cheap and simple hotel where people (especially young people) can stay when they are traveling around on vacation

you've /yuv/ *short for* YOU HAVE

yo-yo /'youyou/ *noun* [C] (*pl.* **yo-yos**) a toy which is a round piece of wood or plastic with a string around the middle. You put the string around your finger and can make the yo-yo go up and down the string.

yr. *abbr.* (*pl.* **yrs.**) = YEAR

yuck /yʌk/ *interj.* (*informal*) (used for saying that you think sth is very bad or disgusting): *Oh, no – not cabbage! Yuck!*

yuck·y /'yʌki/ *adj.* (**yuck·i·er; yuck·i·est**) (*informal*) disgusting; very unpleasant: *What a yucky color!*

yum /yʌm/ *interj.* (*informal*) (used for saying that you think sth tastes very good): *Yum! Chocolate pudding!*

yum·my /'yʌmi/ *adj.* (**yum·mi·er; yum·mi·est**) (*informal*) tasting very good; delicious

yup·pie /'yʌpi/ *noun* [C] a successful young professional person who earns a lot of money and spends it on expensive things ☞ This word is often used in a critical way.

Z

Zz

Z, z /zi/ *noun* [C] (*pl.* **Z's; z's**) the twenty-sixth letter of the English alphabet: *"Zero" begins with (a) "Z."*

za·ny /'zeini/ *adj.* (**za·ni·er; za·ni·est**) funny in an unusual and crazy way: *a zany comedian*

zap /zæp/ *verb* [T] (**zap·ping; zapped**) (*informal*) to kill sb with a weapon, especially one that uses electricity: *The object of the game is to zap the aliens with your laser cannon.*

zeal /zil/ *noun* [U] (*formal*) great energy or enthusiasm: *religious zeal*

zeal·ous /'zɛləs/ *adj.* using great energy and enthusiasm —**zeal·ous·ly** *adv.*

tʃ	dʒ	v	θ	ð	s	z	ʃ
chin	June	van	thin	then	so	zoo	she

ze·bra /ˈzibrə/ *noun* [C] (*pl.* **zebra** or **zebras**) an African wild animal that looks like a horse, with black and white stripes all over its body

zebra

buttonhole button zipper

☆**ze·ro** /ˈzɪroʊ/ *number, pron.* **1** 0; one less than one **2** nothing at all; none at all: *My chances of passing the test are zero.*

☞ We often pronounce the number **0** as "oh" when we are saying long numbers, e.g. telephone numbers, out loud: *555-0390* (= "five five five, oh three nine oh") ○ *My Zip code is 02134* (= "oh two one three four").

zest /zɛst/ *noun* [U, sing.] **zest (for sth)** a feeling of excitement, pleasure and interest: *She is a very active person, with a great zest for life.*

zig·zag /ˈzɪgzæg/ *noun* [C] a line with left and right turns, one after the other at sharp angles: *curtains with a zigzag pattern* ☞ picture at **pattern.** —**zig·zag** *verb* [I] (**zig·zag·ging; zig·zagged**): *We took a road that zigzagged through the mountains.*

zip /zɪp/ *verb* [T] (**zip·ping; zipped**) **zip sth (up)** to fasten sth with a zipper: *There was so much in the bag that it was difficult to zip it up.*

☆**'Zip code** *noun* [C] a group of numbers that you put at the end of an address. The Zip code helps the post office to sort letters by machine.

☆**zip·per** /ˈzɪpər/ *noun* [C] a device for fastening clothes, bags, etc. which consists of two rows of metal or plastic teeth, one on each side of an opening. You can join these rows together to close the opening.

zit /zɪt/ *noun* [C] (*slang*) = PIMPLE

the zo·di·ac /ˈzoʊdiæk/ *noun* [sing.] a diagram of the positions of the planets and stars, which is divided into twelve equal parts (**signs**)

☞ The signs of the zodiac are used in **astrology** and **horoscopes** in newspapers and magazines. People often refer to the signs and to the influence that they think these have on a person's personality and future.

zone /zoʊn/ *noun* [C] an area that is different from those around it e.g. because sth special happens there: *the war zone* ○ *a no-passing zone* ☞ Look also at **time zone.**

☆**zoo** /zu/ *noun* [C] (*pl.* **zoos**) a park where many kinds of living (especially wild) animals are kept so that people can look at them: *to go to the zoo* ○ *She thinks that it's wrong to keep animals in zoos.*

zo·ol·o·gy /zoʊˈɑlədʒi/ *noun* [U] the scientific study of animals ☞ Look at **botany** and **biology.** —**zo·o·log·i·cal** /ˌzoʊəˈlɑdʒɪkl/ *adj.* —**zo·ol·o·gist** /zoʊˈɑlədʒɪst/ *noun* [C]

zoom /zum/ *verb* [I] to move very quickly and with a loud noise: *A motorcycle zoomed past.* **PHRV** **zoom in (on sb/sth)** to make an object that you are filming appear bigger by using a special lens: *The camera zoomed in on a face in the crowd.*

'zoom lens *noun* [C] a camera lens that can make an object being photographed appear gradually bigger or smaller so that it seems to be getting closer or farther away

zuc·chi·ni /zuˈkini/ *noun* [C,U] (*pl.* **zucchini** or **zucchinis**) a long vegetable with green skin, that is eaten cooked

Z

signs of the zodiac

Aries	Taurus	Gemini	Cancer	Leo	Virgo
March 21 - April 20	April 21 - May 20	May 21 - June 20	June 21 - July 20	July 21 - August 19/22	August 20/23 - September 22

 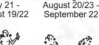

Libra	Scorpio	Sagittarius	Capricorn	Aquarius	Pisces
September 23 - October 22	October 23 - November 21	November 22 - December 20	December 21 - January 20	January 21 - February 19	February 20 - March 20

i	ɪ	ɛ	æ	ɑ	ɔ	ʌ	ʊ	u
see	sit	ten	cat	hot	saw	cup	put	too

APPENDIX 1
Irregular verbs

APPENDIX 2
Expressions using numbers

APPENDIX 3
Maps and geographical names

APPENDIX 1

Irregular Verbs

In this list you will find the infinitive form of the verb followed by the past tense and the past participle. Where two forms are given, look up the verb in the main part of the dictionary to see whether there is a difference in meaning.

Infinitive	Past Tense	Past Participle
arise	arose	arisen
awake	awoke	awoken
be	was/were	been
bear	bore	borne
beat	beat	beaten
become	became	become
befall	befell	befallen
begin	began	begun
bend	bent	bent
bet	bet	bet
bid	bid, bade	bid, bidden
bind	bound	bound
bite	bit	bitten
bleed	bled	bled
blow	blew	blown
break	broke	broken
breed	bred	bred
bring	brought	brought
broadcast	broadcast	broadcast
build	built	built
burn	burned, burnt	burned, burnt
burst	burst	burst
buy	bought	bought
cast	cast	cast
catch	caught	caught
choose	chose	chosen
cling	clung	clung
come	came	come
cost	cost	cost
creep	crept	crept
cut	cut	cut
deal	dealt	dealt
dig	dug	dug
dive	dived, dove	dived
do	did	done
draw	drew	drawn
dream	dreamed, dreamt	dreamed, dreamt

drink	drank	drunk
drive	drove	driven
dwell	dwelt, dwelled	dwelt, dwelled
eat	ate	eaten
fall	fell	fallen
feed	fed	fed
feel	felt	felt
fight	fought	fought
find	found	found
flee	fled	fled
fling	flung	flung
fly	flew	flown
forbid	forbade, forbad	forbidden
forecast	forecast, forecasted	forecast, forecasted
foresee	foresaw	foreseen
foretell	foretold	foretold
forget	forgot	forgotten
forgive	forgave	forgiven
forgo	forwent	forgone
forsake	forsook	forsaken
freeze	froze	frozen
get	got	gotten
give	gave	given
go	went	gone
grind	ground	ground
grow	grew	grown
hang	hung, hanged	hung, hanged
have	had	had
hear	heard	heard
hide	hid	hidden
hit	hit	hit
hold	held	held
hurt	hurt	hurt
input	input, inputted	input, inputted
keep	kept	kept
kneel	knelt, kneeled	knelt, kneeled
know	knew	known
lay	laid	laid
lead	led	led
leap	leaped, leapt	leaped, leapt
leave	left	left
lend	lent	lent
let	let	let
lie[3]	lay	lain
light	lit, lighted	lit, lighted
lose	lost	lost
make	made	made
mean	meant	meant
meet	met	met
mislead	misled	misled
misread	misread	misread
mistake	mistook	mistaken
misunderstand	misunderstood	misunderstood

mow	mowed	mown, mowed
offset	offset	offset
outdo	outdid	outdone
outgrow	outgrew	outgrown
overcome	overcame	overcome
overdo	overdid	overdone
overhear	overheard	overheard
override	overrode	overridden
overrun	overran	overrun
oversee	oversaw	overseen
oversleep	overslept	overslept
overtake	overtook	overtaken
overthrow	overthrew	overthrown
pay	paid	paid
prove	proved	proven, proved
put	put	put
quit	quit	quit
read	read	read
rebuild	rebuilt	rebuilt
repay	repaid	repaid
rethink	rethought	rethought
rewind	rewound	rewound
rewrite	rewrote	rewritten
rid	rid	rid
ride	rode	ridden
ring	rang	rung
rise	rose	risen
run	ran	run
saw	sawed	sawed, sawn
say	said	said
see	saw	seen
seek	sought	sought
sell	sold	sold
send	sent	sent
set	set	set
sew	sewed	sewn, sewed
shake	shook	shaken
shear	sheared	sheared, shorn
shed	shed	shed
shine	shone	shone
shoot	shot	shot
show	showed	shown, showed
shrink	shrank, shrunk	shrunk, shrunken
shut	shut	shut
sing	sang	sung
sink	sank	sunk
sit	sat	sat
slay	slew	slain
sleep	slept	slept
slide	slid	slid
sling	slung	slung
slit	slit	slit
sneak	sneaked, snuck	sneaked, snuck

sow	sowed	sown, sowed
speak	spoke	spoken
speed	sped	sped
spell	spelled, spelt	spelled, spelt
spend	spent	spent
spin	spun	spun
spit	spat, spit	spat, spit
split	split	split
spread	spread	spread
spring	sprang	sprung
stand	stood	stood
steal	stole	stolen
stick	stuck	stuck
sting	stung	stung
stink	stank, stunk	stunk
stride	strode	stridden
strike	struck	struck
string	strung	strung
strive	strove	striven
swear	swore	sworn
sweep	swept	swept
swell	swelled	swollen, swelled
swim	swam	swum
swing	swung	swung
take	took	taken
teach	taught	taught
tear	tore	torn
tell	told	told
think	thought	thought
throw	threw	thrown
thrust	thrust	thrust
tread	trod	trodden
undercut	undercut	undercut
undergo	underwent	undergone
understand	understood	understood
undertake	undertook	undertaken
undo	undid	undone
unwind	unwound	unwound
uphold	upheld	upheld
upset	upset	upset
wake	woke	woken
wear	wore	worn
weave	wove, weaved	woven, weaved
weep	wept	wept
wet	wet, wetted	wet, wetted
win	won	won
wind[2]	wound	wound
withdraw	withdrew	withdrawn
withhold	withheld	withheld
withstand	withstood	withstood
wring	wrung	wrung
write	wrote	written

APPENDIX 2

Expressions using Numbers

The Numbers

1	one	1st	first
2	two	2nd	second
3	three	3rd	third
4	four	4th	fourth
5	five	5th	fifth
6	six	6th	sixth
7	seven	7th	seventh
8	eight	8th	eighth
9	nine	9th	ninth
10	ten	10th	tenth
11	eleven	11th	eleventh
12	twelve	12th	twelfth
13	thirteen	13th	thirteenth
14	fourteen	14th	fourteenth
15	fifteen	15th	fifteenth
16	sixteen	16th	sixteenth
17	seventeen	17th	seventeenth
18	eighteen	18th	eighteenth
19	nineteen	19th	nineteenth
20	twenty	20th	twentieth
21	twenty-one	21st	twenty-first
22	twenty-two	22nd	twenty-second
30	thirty	30th	thirtieth
40	forty	40th	fortieth
50	fifty	50th	fiftieth
60	sixty	60th	sixtieth
70	seventy	70th	seventieth
80	eighty	80th	eightieth
90	ninety	90th	ninetieth
100	a/one hundred	100th	hundredth
101	a/one hundred and one	101st	hundred and first
200	two hundred	200th	two hundredth
1,000	a/one thousand	1,000th	thousandth
10,000	ten thousand	10,000th	ten thousandth
100,000	a/one hundred thousand	100,000th	hundred thousandth
1,000,000	a/one million	1,000,000th	millionth

Examples:

528: five hundred (and) twenty-eight ○ *2,976: two thousand, nine hundred (and) seventy-six* ○ *50,439: fifty thousand, four hundred (and) thirty-nine*

Note A comma is used to separate the "thousands," e.g. *25,000.* For the use of the point (.) in decimals, look at the next section. In numbers such as *100* or *1,000,* we can say "one hundred" or "a hundred," "one thousand" or "a thousand." In conversation it is more usual to say "a" unless we want to stress that it is *one* and not *two,* for example. 0 can be said as "zero," "nothing" or "o." In the following sections you will see the most usual way of saying it in each type of expression.

Fractions and decimals

½	a/one half	⅓	a/one third
¼	a quarter/one fourth	⅖	two fifths
⅛	an/one eighth	⁷⁄₁₂	seven twelfths
¹⁄₁₀	a/one tenth	1½	one and a half
¹⁄₁₆	a/one sixteenth	2⅜	two and three eighths

0.1 (zero) point one
0.25 (zero) point two five
0.33 (zero) point three three
1.75 one point seven five
3.976 three point nine seven six

Mathematical Expressions

+ plus
− minus
× times *or* multiplied by
÷ divided by
= equals
% percent

3^2 three squared

5^3 five cubed

6^{10} six to the power of ten

Examples:

6 + 9 = 15 *six plus nine equals (or is) fifteen*
5 × 6 = 30 *five times six equals thirty* or *five multiplied by six is thirty*

75% (seventy-five percent) of the class passed the test.

Weight

	1 ounce (oz.)
16 ounces	= 1 pound (lb.)
2,000 pounds	= 1 ton (t.)

Examples:

The baby weighed 7 lb. 4 oz. (seven pounds four ounces).
She weighs 122 pounds.

Length

	1 inch (in.)
12 inches	= 1 foot (ft.)
3 feet	= 1 yard (yd.)
1,760 yards	= 1 mile (mi.)

Examples:

Height: 5 ft. 9 in. (five foot nine or five feet nine)
The hotel is 30 yds. (thirty yards) from the beach.
The car was doing 50 m.p.h. (fifty miles per hour).
The room is 11' x 9'6" (eleven feet by nine feet six or eleven foot by nine foot six).

Area

	1 square inch (sq. in.)
144 square inches	= 1 square foot (sq. ft.)
9 square feet	= 1 square yard (sq. yd.)
4,840 square yards	= 1 acre
640 acres	= 1 square mile (sq. mi.)

Examples:

They have a 200-acre farm.
The fire destroyed 40 square miles of forest.

Capacity

3 teaspoons (tsp.)	= 1 tablespoon (tbs.)
16 tablespoons	= 8 ounces = 1 cup (c.)
	2 cups = 1 pint (pt.)
	2 pints = 1 quart (qt.)
	4 quarts = 1 gallon (gal.)

Examples:

I bought a quart of milk at the grocery store.
The gas tank holds ten gallons.

Time

6:00	six (o'clock)
6:05	five after/past six *or* six o five
6:10	ten after/past six *or* six ten
6:15	quarter after/past six *or* six fifteen
6:20	twenty after/past six *or* six twenty
6:30	six thirty
6:35	twenty five to/of seven *or* six thirty-five
6:40	twenty to/of seven *or* six forty
6:45	(a) quarter to/of seven *or* six forty-five
6:50	ten to/of seven *or* six fifty
6:55	five to/of seven *or* six fifty-five
10:12	twelve minutes after/past ten *or* ten twelve
1:10	ten after/past one *or* one ten
7:56	four minutes to/of eight *or* seven fifty-six

Note If we need to make it clear in conversation that we are talking about the morning instead of the evening, we can say "in the morning" or "a.m." If we are talking about the time between noon and midnight we can say "in the afternoon," "in the evening," "at night," or "p.m." a.m. and p.m. are slightly more formal. A twenty-four hour clock is used in the armed forces and for airline schedules, etc.

Examples:

Office hours are 9 a.m. to 5:30 p.m.
Something woke me up at two o'clock in the morning.
Your plane departs at 17:30 (seventeen thirty).

Dates

Dates can be written in numbers or in numbers and words:

4/15/98 April 15, 1998

and are said as:

April fifteenth, nineteen ninety-eight

Examples:

Her birthday is August 9 (August ninth).
The hotel will be closed May 3 – June 1 (from May third through June first).

Temperature

People use the Fahrenheit
scale in the United States
except in scientific contexts.

Examples:

Water freezes at 32°F and boils at 212°F.
The high temperature this afternoon will be 68°.
Overnight temperatures below zero are expected,
dropping to -10 (minus ten) before morning.
He has a temperature of 102°. I think he has the flu.

Money

Amount		Coin/Bill
1¢	one cent	a penny
5¢	five cents	a nickel
10¢	ten cents	a dime
25¢	twenty-five cents	a quarter
$1.00	a/one dollar	a dollar bill
$5.00	five dollars	a five-dollar bill
$10	ten dollars	a ten-dollar bill
$20	twenty dollars	a twenty-dollar bill
$100	a/one hundred dollars	a hundred-dollar bill

Examples:

$3.35: Three thirty-five; three dollars and thirty-five cents ○ 59¢: fifty-nine cents ○ Do you have a quarter for the phone? ○ The parking meter doesn't take pennies. ○ The apartment costs $500 (five hundred dollars) a month.

Telephone Numbers

When we talk about telephone numbers, we say each number separately. Most U.S. telephone numbers have seven numbers, which we divide into groups of three and four, with a hyphen separating them, e.g.: 656-5078:

six five six – five o seven eight.

If you are calling a number in a different state or sometimes in a different town, you have to use the *area code* before the number. It is usually three numbers and is sometimes written in parentheses.

Examples:

(301) 656-5078.
202 is the area code for Washington, DC.
If you are calling somebody in a large company, you can ask for their *extension number*.
(202) 458-2000 x 2019 (extension two o one nine)

APPENDIX 3

Maps and Geographical Names

The United States and Canada

Arctic Ocean

ALASKA
- Fairbanks
- Anchorage
- Juneau

YUKON
- Whitehorse

NORTHWEST TERRITORIES
- Yellowknife

BRITISH COLUMBIA

CANADA

ALBERTA
- Edmonton

SASKATCHEWAN
- Regina

MANITOBA
- Winnipeg

ONTARIO

QUEBEC
- Quebec

NEWFOUNDLAND
- St. John's

PRINCE EDWARD ISLAND
- Charlottetown

NOVA SCOTIA
- Halifax

NEW BRUNSWICK
- Fredericton

Lake Superior

Great

NORTH DAKOTA

MONTANA
- Helena

WASHINGTON
- Seattle
- Olympia
- Vancouver
- Victoria

OREGON
- Portland
- Salem

- international boundary
- state / provincial boundary
- national capital
- city

1000 miles

1000 km

500

500

0

0

THE STATES OF THE UNITED STATES

State	(abbreviation)	State Capital	Other Major Cities
Alabama /ˌæləˈbæmə/	AL	Montgomery /mɑntˈgʌməri, mənt-/	Birmingham /ˈbɜːmɪŋhæm/
Alaska /əˈlæskə/	AK	Juneau /ˈdʒuːnoʊ/	Anchorage /ˈæŋkərɪdʒ/
			Fairbanks /ˈfɛrbæŋks/
			Tucson /ˈtuːsɑn, tuˈsɑn/
Arizona /ˌærəˈzoʊnə/	AZ	Phoenix /ˈfiːnɪks/	
Arkansas /ˈɑrkənsɔ/	AR	Little Rock /ˈlɪtl rɑk/	Los Angeles /lɔs ˈændʒələs/
California /ˌkæləˈfɔrnyə/	CA	Sacramento /ˌsækrəˈmɛntoʊ/	San Diego /ˌsæn diˈeɪgoʊ/
			San Francisco /ˌsæn frənˈsɪskoʊ/
Colorado /ˌkɑləˈredoʊ, -ˈrɑdoʊ/	CO	Denver /ˈdɛnvər/	
Connecticut /kəˈnɛtɪkət/	CT	Hartford /ˈhɑrtfərd/	
Delaware /ˈdɛləwɛr/	DE	Dover /ˈdoʊvər/	Miami /maɪˈæmi/
Florida /ˈflɔrədə, ˈflɑr-/	FL	Tallahassee /ˌtæləˈhæsi/	Orlando /ɔrˈlændoʊ/
			Savannah /səˈvænə/
Georgia /ˈdʒɔrdʒə/	GA	Atlanta /ətˈlæntə/	
Hawaii /həˈwaɪi/	HI	Honolulu /ˌhɑnəˈluːlu/	
Idaho /ˈaɪdəhoʊ/	ID	Boise /ˈbɔɪzi, -si/	Chicago /ʃɪˈkɑgoʊ, -ˈkɔgoʊ/
Illinois /ˌɪləˈnɔɪ/	IL	Springfield /ˈsprɪŋfild/	
Indiana /ˌɪndiˈænə/	IN	Indianapolis /ˌɪndiəˈnæpələs/	
Iowa /ˈaɪəwə/	IA	Des Moines /dəˈmɔɪn/	Wichita /ˈwɪtʃətɔ/
Kansas /ˈkænzəs/	KS	Topeka /təˈpikə/	
Kentucky /kənˈtʌki/	KY	Frankfort /ˈfræŋkfərt/	New Orleans /nu ˈɔrliənz, -ˈɔrlənz, -ɔrˈlinz/
Louisiana /luˌiziˈænə/	LA	Baton Rouge /ˌbætn ˈruʒ/	Portland /ˈpɔrtlənd/
Maine /meɪn/	ME	Augusta /ɔˈgʌstə/	Baltimore /ˈbɔltəmɔr/
Maryland /ˈmɛrələnd/	MD	Annapolis /əˈnæpələs/	
Massachusetts /ˌmæsəˈtʃusɪts/	MA	Boston /ˈbɔstən/	Detroit /dɪˈtrɔɪt/
Michigan /ˈmɪʃɪgən/	MI	Lansing /ˈlænsɪŋ/	Minneapolis /ˌmɪniˈæpələs/
Minnesota /ˌmɪnəˈsoʊtə/	MN	St. Paul /ˌseɪnt ˈpɔl/	
Mississippi /ˌmɪsəˈsɪpi/	MS	Jackson /ˈdʒæksn/	St. Louis /ˌseɪnt ˈluɪs/
Missouri /məˈzʊri, -ˈzʊrə/	MO	Jefferson City /ˌdʒɛfərsn ˈsɪti/	
Montana /mɑnˈtænə/	MT	Helena /ˈhɛlənə/	
Nebraska /nəˈbræskə/	NE	Lincoln /ˈlɪŋkən/	Las Vegas /lɑs ˈveɪgəs/
Nevada /nəˈvædə, -ˈvɑdə/	NV	Carson City /ˌkɑrsn ˈsɪti/	
New Hampshire /ˌnu ˈhæmpʃər/	NH	Concord /ˈkɑŋkərd/	Newark /ˈnuərk/
New Jersey /ˌnu ˈdʒɜrzi/	NJ	Trenton /ˈtrɛntn/	Albuquerque /ˈælbəkɜrki/
New Mexico /ˌnu ˈmɛksɪkoʊ/	NM	Santa Fe /ˌsæntə ˈfeɪ/	Buffalo /ˈbʌfəloʊ/
New York /ˌnu ˈyɔrk/	NY	Albany /ˈɔlbəni/	New York /ˌnu ˈyɔrk/
			Rochester /ˈrɑtʃəstər, -tʃɛs-/
			Charlotte /ˈʃɑrlət/
North Carolina /ˌnɔrθ kærəˈlaɪnə/	NC	Raleigh /ˈrɔli, ˈrɑli/	Fargo /ˈfɑrgoʊ/
North Dakota /ˌnɔrθ dəˈkoʊtə/	ND	Bismarck /ˈbɪzmɑrk/	

785

Ohio /oʊ'haɪoʊ/

Oklahoma /ˌoʊklə'hoʊmə/
Oregon /'ɔregən, 'ɑr-, -gɑn/
Pennsylvania /ˌpensl'venyə/

Rhode Island /roʊd 'aɪlənd/
South Carolina /ˌsaʊθ kærə'laɪnə/
South Dakota /ˌsaʊθ də koʊtə/
Tennessee /ˌtenə'si/
Texas /'teksəs/

Utah /'yutɔ, 'yutɑ/
Vermont /vər'mɑnt/
Virginia /vər'dʒɪnyə/
Washington /'wɑʃɪŋtən, -wɑ-/
West Virginia /ˌwest vər'dʒɪnyə/
Wisconsin /wɪs'kɑnsn/
Wyoming /waɪ'oʊmɪŋ/

THE GREAT LAKES

Lake Erie /ˌleɪk 'ɪri/
Lake Huron /ˌleɪk 'hyʊrən, -ən/
Lake Michigan /ˌleɪk 'mɪʃɪgən/
Lake Ontario /ˌleɪk ɑn'terioʊ/
Lake Superior /ˌleɪk sə'pɪriər/

THE PROVINCES AND TERRITORIES OF CANADA

Province/territory
Alberta /æl'bɜrtə/
British Columbia /ˌbrɪtɪʃ kə'lʌmbiə/
Manitoba /ˌmænə'toʊbə/
New Brunswick /nu'brʌnzwɪk/
Newfoundland /'nufənlənd, -fənd-/
Northwest Territories /ˌnɔrθwest 'terətɔriz/
Nova Scotia /ˌnoʊvə 'skoʊʃə/
Ontario /ɑn'terioʊ/
Prince Edward Island /ˌprɪns ˌedwərd 'aɪlənd/
Quebec /kwɪ'bek/
Saskatchewan /sæ'skætʃəwɑn, -wən/
Yukon Territory /'yukɑn 'terətɔri/

Columbus /kə'lʌmbəs/ OH

Oklahoma City /ˌoʊkləhoʊmə 'sɪti/ OK
Salem /'seɪləm/ OR
Harrisburg /'hærəsbɜrg/ PA

Providence /'prɑvədəns/ RI
Columbia /kə'lʌmbiə/ SC
Pierre /pɪr/ SD
Nashville /'næʃvɪl/ TN
Austin /'ɔstən/ TX

Salt Lake City /ˌsɔlt leɪk 'sɪti/ UT
Montpelier /mɑnt'pilyər/ VT
Richmond /'rɪtʃmənd/ VA
Olympia /ə'lɪmpiə/ WA
Charleston /'tʃɑrlstən/ WV
Madison /'mædəsn/ WI
Cheyenne /ʃaɪ'æn/ WY

Provincial/territorial Capital
Edmonton /'edməntən/
Victoria /vɪk'tɔriə/
Winnipeg /'wɪnəpeg/
Fredericton /'fredrɪktən/
St. John's /seɪnt 'dʒɑnz/
Yellowknife /'yeloʊnaɪf/
Halifax /'hæləfæks/
Toronto /tə'rɑntoʊ/
Charlottetown /'ʃɑrləttaʊn/
Quebec /kwɪ'bek/
Regina /rɪ'dʒaɪnə/
Whitehorse /'waɪthɔrs/

Cleveland /'klivlənd/
Cincinnati /ˌsɪnsə'næti/
Tulsa /'tʌlsə/
Portland /'pɔrtlənd/
Philadelphia /ˌfɪlə'delfiə/
Pittsburgh /'pɪtsbɜrg/

Sioux Falls /su 'fɔlz/
Memphis /'memfəs/
Dallas /'dæləs/
Fort Worth /ˌfɔrt 'wɜrθ/
Houston /'hyustən/
San Antonio /ˌsæn æn'toʊnioʊ/

Norfolk /'nɔrfək/
Seattle /si'ætl/

Milwaukee /mɪl'wɔki/

Other Major Cities

Vancouver /væn'kuvər/

Ottawa /'ɑtəwə/

Montreal /ˌmɑntri'ɔl/

The British Isles

786

- - - - international boundary
——— national boundary
■ capital of the United Kingdom
● national capital

0 50 100 miles
0 50 100 km

Atlantic
Ocean

SCOTLAND

Edinburgh

North
Sea

NORTHERN
IRELAND

Belfast

Irish Sea

REPUBLIC
OF IRELAND

Dublin

WALES

ENGLAND

Cardiff

London

English Channel

Cities of the British Isles

Belfast /ˈbɛlfæst, ˌbɛlˈfæst/
Cardiff /ˈkɑrdɪf/
Dublin /ˈdʌblən/
Edinburgh /ˈɛdnbərə/
London /ˈlʌndən/

Australia and New Zealand

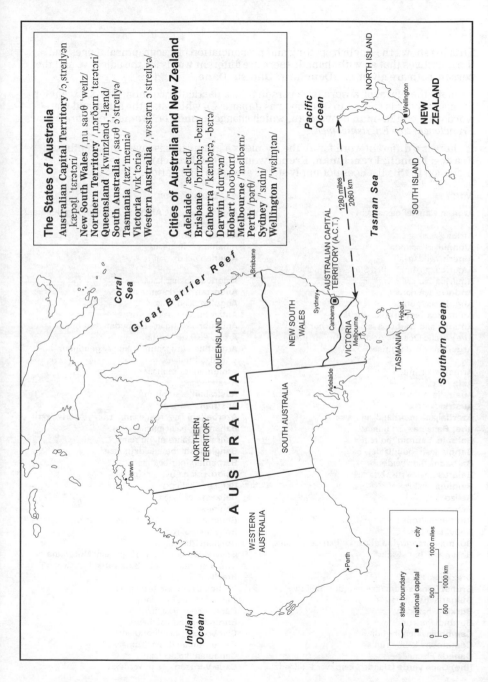

The States of Australia

Australian Capital Territory /ɔˌstreɪlyən ˌkæpətl ˈterətəri/
New South Wales /ˌnu saʊθ ˈweɪlz/
Northern Territory /ˌnɔrðərn ˈterətəri/
Queensland /ˈkwinzlənd, -lænd/
South Australia /ˌsaʊθ ɔˈstreɪlyə/
Tasmania /tæzˈmeɪniə/
Victoria /vɪkˈtɔriə/
Western Australia /ˌwestərn ɔˈstreɪlyə/

Cities of Australia and New Zealand

Adelaide /ˈædl-eɪd/
Brisbane /ˈbrɪzbən, -beɪn/
Canberra /ˈkænbərə, -berə/
Darwin /ˈdarwən/
Hobart /ˈhoʊbɑrt/
Melbourne /ˈmɛlbərn/
Perth /pərθ/
Sydney /ˈsɪdni/
Wellington /ˈwɛlɪŋtən/

Indian Ocean

Coral Sea

Great Barrier Reef

Brisbane

QUEENSLAND

NORTHERN TERRITORY

Darwin

WESTERN AUSTRALIA

SOUTH AUSTRALIA

Adelaide

Perth

A U S T R A L I A

NEW SOUTH WALES

Sydney

Canberra
AUSTRALIAN CAPITAL TERRITORY (A.C.T.)

VICTORIA
Melbourne

TASMANIA

Hobart

Southern Ocean

Tasman Sea

1280 miles
2060 km

Pacific Ocean

NORTH ISLAND

Wellington

NEW ZEALAND

SOUTH ISLAND

state boundary
national capital
city

0 500 1000 miles
0 500 1000 km

Geographical names

This list shows the English spelling and pronunciation of geographical names and the adjectives that go with them. If there are different words for the adjective and the person, both are given, e.g. **Denmark: Danish; Dane**.

To make the plural of a word for a person from a particular country, add **-s**, except for **Swiss** and words ending in **-ese** (such as **Japanese**), which stay the same, and for words that end in **-man** or **-woman**, which change to **-men** or **-women**, e.g. *three Frenchmen; two Englishwomen*.

If there is a different word for all the people as a group, this is given in parentheses: **France: French; Frenchman, Frenchwoman; (the French)**.
Inclusion in this list does not imply status as a sovereign nation.

Noun	*Adjective; Person*
Afghanistan /æfˈgænəstæn/	**Afghan** /ˈæfgæn/; **Afghani** /æfˈgæni/, **Afghanistani** /æfˌgænəˈstæni/
Africa /ˈæfrɪkə/	**African** /ˈæfrɪkən/
Albania /ælˈbeɪniə/	**Albanian** /ælˈbeɪniən/
Algeria /ælˈdʒɪriə/	**Algerian** /ælˈdʒɪriən/
America ⇨ (the) United States of America	
America /əˈmɛrɪkə/	**American** /əˈmɛrɪkən/
Andorra /ænˈdɔrə/	**Andorran** /ænˈdɔrən/
Angola /æŋˈgoʊlə/	**Angolan** /æŋˈgoʊlən/
Antarctica /æntˈɑrktɪkə,-ˈɑrtɪkə/	**Antarctic** /æntˈɑrktɪk,-ˈɑrtɪk/
Antigua and Barbuda /ænˌtigə ən bɑrˈbudə/	**Antiguan** /ænˈtigən/, **Barbudan** /bɑrˈbudn/
(the) Arctic Ocean /ˌɑrktɪk ˈoʊʃn, ˌɑrtɪk-/	**Arctic** /ˈɑrktɪk, ˈɑrtɪk/
Argentina /ˌɑrdʒənˈtinə/	**Argentine** /ˈɑrdʒəntin, -taɪn/; **Argentinian** /ˌɑrdʒənˈtɪniən/
Armenia /ɑrˈminiə/	**Armenian** /ɑrˈminiən/
Asia /ˈeɪʒə/	**Asian** /ˈeɪʒn/
Australia /ɔˈstreɪlyə/	**Australian** /ɔˈstreɪlyən/
Austria /ˈɔstriə/	**Austrian** /ˈɔstriən/
Azerbaijan /ˌæzərbaɪˈdʒan, ˌazər-/	**Azerbaijani** /ˌæzərbaɪˈdʒani, azər-/, **Azeri** /əˈzɛri/
(the) Bahamas /bəˈhaməz/	**Bahamian** /bəˈheimiən/
Bahrain, Bahrein /baˈreɪn/	**Bahraini, Bahreini** /baˈreini/
Bangladesh /baŋɡləˈdɛʃ, bæn-/	**Bangladeshi** /baŋɡləˈdɛʃɪ, bæŋ/
Barbados /bɑrˈbeɪdoʊs/	**Barbadian** /bɑrˈbeɪdiən/
Belarus /ˌbyɛləˈrus, bɪləˈrus/	**Belorussian** /ˌbyɛləˈrʌʃn, bɪlə-/
Belgium /ˈbɛldʒəm/	**Belgian** /ˈbɛldʒən/
Belize /bəˈliz/	**Belizean** /bəˈliziən/
Benin /bəˈnin/	**Beninese** /bəˌniˈniz, bɛnəˈniz/
Bhutan /buˈtɑn/	**Bhutani** /buˈtɑni/; **Bhutanese** /butnˈiz/
Bolivia /bəˈlɪviə/	**Bolivian** /bəˈlɪviən/
Bosnia-Herzegovina /ˌbazniə ˌhɛrtsəgoʊˈvinə/	**Bosnian** /ˈbazniən/
Botswana /batˈswanə/	**Boswanan** /batˈswanən/; (person: **Motswana** /matˈswanə/, people: **Batswana** /bætˈswanə/)
Brazil /brəˈzɪl/	**Brazilian** /brəˈzɪlyən/
Brunei Darussalam /bruˌnaɪ ˌdarusəˈlam/	**Brunei, Bruneian** /bruˈnaɪən/
Bulgaria /bʌlˈgɛriə/	**Bulgarian** /bʌlˈgɛriən/
Burkina /bərˈkinə/	**Burkinese** /bərkəˈniz/
Burundi /buˈrʊndi/	**Burundian** /buˈrʊndiən/
Cambodia /kæmˈboʊdiə/	**Cambodian** /kæmˈboʊdiən/
Cameroon /ˌkæməˈrun/	**Cameroonian** /kæməˈruniən/
Canada /ˈkænədə/	**Canadian** /kəˈneɪdiən/
(the) Cape Verde Islands /ˌkeɪp ˌvərd ˈaɪləndz/	**Cape Verdean** /ˌkeɪp ˈvərdiən/

(the) Caribbean Sea /ˌkærəˌbiən ˈsi, kəˌrɪbiən-/
Central African Republic /ˌsentrəl ˌæfrɪkən
 rɪˈpʌlɪk/
Chad /tʃæd/
Chile /ˈtʃɪli/
China /ˈtʃaɪnə/
Colombia /kəˈlʌmbiə/
Comoros /ˈkɑməroʊz/
Congo /ˈkɑŋgoʊ/
(the Democratic Republic of the) Congo
 /ˈkɑŋgoʊ/
Costa Rica /ˌkoʊstə ˈrikə, kɑstə-/
Côte d'Ivoire /ˌkoʊt diˈvwɑr/
Croatia /kroʊˈeɪʃə/
Cuba /ˈkyubə/
Cyprus /ˈsaɪprəs/
(the) Czech Republic /ˌtʃɛk rɪˈpʌblɪk/
Denmark /ˈdɛnmɑrk/
Djibouti /dʒɪˈbuʈi/
Dominica /dɑməˈnikə/
(the) Dominican Republic /dəˌmɪnɪkən rɪˈpʌblɪk/
Ecuador /ˈɛkwˈdɔr/
Egypt /ˈidʒɪpt/
El Salvador /ɛl ˈsælvədɔr/
England /ˈɪŋglənd/

Equatorial Guinea /ˌikwəˌtɔriəl ˈgɪni, ˌɛkwə-/
Eritrea /ˌɛrəˈtriə/
Estonia /ɛ stoʊniə/
Ethiopia /ˌiθiˈoʊpiə/
Europe /ˈyʊrəp/
Fiji /ˈfidʒi/
Finland /ˈfɪnlənd/
France /fræns/

FYROM (Former Yugoslav Republic of Macedo-
nia) /ˈfaɪrɑm/
Gabon /gæˈboʊn/
(the) Gambia /ˈgæmbiə/
Georgia /ˈdʒɔrdʒə/
Germany /ˈdʒərməni/
Ghana /ˈgɑnə/
Gibraltar /dʒɪˈbrɔltər/
Great Britain /ˌgreɪtˈbrɪtn/
Greece /griːs/
Grenada /grəˈneɪdə/
Guatemala /ˌgwɑʈəˈmɑlə/
Guinea /ˈgɪni/
Guinea-Bissau /ˌgɪni bɪˈsaʊ/
Guyana /gaɪˈænə/
Haiti /ˈheɪʈi/
Holland /ˈhɑlənd/ ➪ (the) Netherlands
Honduras /hɑnˈdʊrəs/
Hong Kong /ˌhɑŋ ˈkɑŋ/
Hungary /ˈhʌŋgəri/
Iceland /ˈaɪslənd/
India /ˈɪndiə/
Indonesia /ˌɪndəˈniʒə/
Iran /iˈrɑn/
Iraq /ɪˈrɑk, ɪˈræk/
Ireland /ˈaɪərlənd/

Israel /ˈɪzreɪl, ˈɪzriəl/

Caribbean /ˌkærəˈbiən, kəˈrɪbiən-/

Chadian /ˈtʃædiən/
Chilean /ˈtʃɪliən, tʃɪˈleɪən/
Chinese /ˌtʃaɪˈnɪz/
Colombian /kəˈlʌmbiən/
Comoran /ˈkɑmərən, kəˈmɔrən/
Congolese /ˌkɑŋgəˈlɪz/

Costa Rican /ˌkoʊstə ˈrikən, ˌkɑstə-/

Croatian /kroʊˈeɪʃn/
Cuban /ˈkyubən/
Cypriot /ˈsɪpriət/
Czech /tʃɛk /
Danish /ˈdeɪnɪʃ/; Dane /deɪn/
Djiboutian /dʒɪˈbuʈiən/
Dominican /ˌdɑməˈnikən/
Dominican /dəˈmɪnɪkən/
Ecuadorian /ˌɛkwəˈdɔriən/
Egyptian /ɪˈdʒɪpʃn/
Salvadorean /ˌsælvəˈdɔriən/
English /ˈɪŋglɪʃ/; Englishman /ˈɪŋglɪʃmən/,
 Englishwoman /ˈɪŋglɪʃˌwʊmən/, (the English)
Equatorial Guinean /ˌikwəˌtɔriəl ˈgɪniən, ˌɛkwə-/
Eritrean /ˌɛrəˈtriən/
Estonian /ɛˈstoʊniən/
Ethiopian /iθiˈoʊpiən/
European /ˌyʊrəˈpiən/
Fijian /ˈfidʒiən/
Finnish /ˈfɪnɪʃ/; Finn /fɪn/
French /frɛntʃ/; Frenchman /ˈfrɛntsmən/,
 Frenchwoman /ˈfrɛntʃˌwʊmən/, (the French)

Gabonese /ˌgæbəˈnɪz/
Gambian /ˈgæmbiən/
Georgian /ˈdʒɔrdʒən/
German /ˈdʒərmən/
Ghanian /ˈgɑniən/
Gibraltarian /dʒɪˌbrɔlˈtɛriən/
British /ˈbrɪtɪʃ/; Briton /ˈbrɪtn/, (the British)
Greek /grik/
Grenadian /grəˈneɪdiən/
Guatemalan /ˌgwɑʈəˈmɑlən/
Guinean /ˈgɪniən/

Guyanese /ˌgaɪəˈnɪz/
Haitian /ˈheɪʃn/

Honduran /hɑnˈdʊrən/

Hungarian /hʌŋˈgɛriən/
Icelandic /aɪsˈlændɪk/; Icelander /ˈaɪslændər/
Indian /ˈɪndiən/
Indonesian /ˌɪndəˈniʒn/
Iranian /ɪˈreɪniən/
Iraqi /ɪˈrɑki, ɪˈræki/
Irish /ˈaɪrɪʃ/; Irishman /ˈaɪrɪʃmən/, Irishwoman
 /ˈaɪrɪʃˌwʊmən/, (the Irish)
Israeli /ɪzreɪli/

Italy /'ɪt̬l·i/
Jamaica /dʒə'meɪkə/
Japan /dʒə'pæn/
Jordan /'dʒɔrdn/
Kazakhstan /ˌkazak'stɑn, ˌkæzæk'stæn/
Kenya /'kɛnyə/
Kirgyzstan /ˌkɪrgɪ'stɑn, -'stæn/
Kiribati /'kɪrəbæs/
Korea /kə'riə/:
 North Korea
 South Korea
Kuwait /ku'weɪt/
Laos /laʊs, laoʊs/
Latvia /'lætviə/
Lebanon /'lɛbənən, -nən/
Lesotho /lə'soʊtoʊ, lə'sutu/

Liberia /laɪ'bɪria/
Libya /'lɪbiə/
Liechtenstein /'lɪktənstaɪn/
Lithuania /lɪθu'eɪniə/
Luxembourg /'lʌksəmbərg/
Madagascar /ˌmædə'gæskər/

Malawi /mə'lawi/
Malaysia /mə'leɪʒə/
(the) Maldives /'mɔldivz, -daivz/
Mali /'mɑli/
Malta /'mɔltə/
Mauritania /ˌmɔrə'teɪniə/
Mauritius /mə'rɪʃəs/
Mexico /'mɛksɪkou/
Moldova /mal'doʊvə, mɔl-/
Monaco /'manəkoʊ, mə'nakoʊ/
Mongolia /maŋ'goʊliə/
Montserrat /ˌmantsə'ræt/
Morocco /mə'rakoʊ/
Mozambique /ˌmoʊzæm'bik/
Myanmar /'myanmar/
Namibia /nə'mɪbiə/
Nauru /nɑ'uru/
Nepal /nə'pɔl, nə'pɑl/
(the) Netherlands /'nɛðərləndz/

New Zealand /ˌnu 'ziländ/
Nicaragua /ˌnɪkə'rɑgwɑ/
Niger /'naɪdʒər, ni'ʒɛr/
Nigeria /naɪ'dʒɪriə/
Norway /'nɔrweɪ/
Oman /oʊ'man/
Pakistan /'pækəstæn/
Panama /'pænəmɑ/
Papua New Guinea /ˌpæpyuə ˌnu 'gɪni/
Paraguay /'pærəgwaɪ/
Peru /pə'ru/
(the) Philippines /'fɪləpinz, ˌfɪlə'pinz/

Poland /'poʊlənd/
Portugal /'pɔrtʃəgl/
Qatar /'katar/
Romania /rʊ'meɪnia, roʊ-/
Russia /'rʌʃə/

Italian /ɪ'tælyən/
Jamaican /dʒə'meɪkən/
Japanese /ˌdʒæpə'niz/
Jordanian /dʒɔr'deɪniən/
Kazakh /kə'zɑk, -'zæk/
Kenyan /'kɛnyən, 'kinyən/
Kirgyz /kɪr'giz/

North Korean /nɔrθ kə'riən/
South Korean /saʊθ kə'riən /
Kuwaiti /ku'weɪt̬i/
Laotian /leɪ'oʊʃn/
Latvian /'lætviən/
Lebanese /ˌlɛbə'niz/
Sotho /'soʊtoʊ, 'sutu/; (person: Mosotho
 /mə'soʊtoʊ, mə'sutu/, people: Basotho
 /bə'soʊtoʊ, bə'sutu/)

Liberian /laɪ'bɪriən/
Libyan /'lɪbiən/
Liechtenstein; Liechtensteiner /'lɪktənstaɪnər/
Lithuanian /lɪθu'eɪniən/
Luxembourg; Luxembourger /'lʌksəmbərgər/
Madagascan /mædə'gæskən/; Malagasy
 /mælə'gæsi/
Malawian /mə'lawiən/
Malaysian /mə'leɪʒn/
Maldivian /mɔl'dɪviən/
Malian /'mɑliən/
Maltese /ˌmɔl'tiz/
Mauritanian /ˌmɔrə'teɪniən/
Mauritian /mə'rɪʃn/
Mexican /'mɛksɪkən/
Moldovan /mal'doʊvn, mɔl-/
Monacan /'manəkən, mə'nakən/
Mongolian /maŋ'goʊliən/
Montserratian /ˌmantsə'reɪʃn/
Moroccan /mə'rakən/
Mozambiquean /ˌmoʊzæm'bikən/

Namibian /nə'mɪbiən/
Nauruan /nɑ'uruən/
Nepalese /ˌnɛpə'liz/
Dutch /dʌtʃ/; Dutchman /'dʌtʃmən/, Dutchwoman
 /'dʌtʃˌwʊmən/, (the Dutch)
New Zealand; New Zealander /ˌnu'ziləndər/
Nicaraguan /ˌnɪkə'rɑgwɑn/
Nigerien /naɪˌdʒɪri'ɛn, ni'ʒɛriən/
Nigerian /naɪ'dʒɪriən/
Norwegian /nɔr'widʒən/
Omani /oʊ'mani/
Pakistani /ˌpækə'stæni/
Panamanian /ˌpænə'meɪniən/
Papuan /'pæpyuən/
Paraguayan /ˌpærə'gwaɪən, -'gweɪ-/
Peruvian /pə'ruviən/
Philippine /'fɪləpin, ˌfɪlə'pin/; Filipino
 /fɪlə'pinoʊ/
Polish /'poʊlɪʃ/; Pole /poʊl/
Portuguese /ˌpɔrtʃə'gɪz, 'pɔrtʃəgiz/
Qatari /kə'tari/
Romanian /rʊ'meɪniən, roʊ-/
Russian /'rʌʃn/